MICROSOFT

Office 2000

Post Advanced Concepts and Techniques

WORD 2000 EXCEL 2000 ACCESS 2000 POWERPOINT 2000

Gary B. Shelly
Thomas J. Cashman
Misty E. Vermaat

Contributing Authors
Mary Z. Last
Philip J. Pratt
James S. Quasney
Jeffrey J. Quasney
Susan L. Sebok
Joy L. Starks

COURSE TECHNOLOGY
ONE MAIN STREET
CAMBRIDGE MA 02142
Thomson Learning™

Australia • Canada • Denmark • Japan • Mexico • New Zealand • Philippines
Puerto Rico • Singapore • South Africa • Spain • United Kingdom • United States

Printed in the United States of America

For more information, contact:

Course Technology
One Main Street
Cambridge, Massachusetts 02142, USA

or find us on the World Wide Web at: www.course.com

PHOTO CREDITS: **Microsoft Word 2000** *Project 7, pages WD 7.2-3* Man and woman researching, hand writing, Courtesy of PhotoDisc, Inc.; *Project 8, pages WD 8.2-3* Web site, clothing merchandise, Courtesy of Land's End; circuit board, Courtesy of PhotoDisc, Inc.; *Project 9, pages WD 9.2-3* Two dresses, shirt with tie, suit, Courtesy of EyeWire. **Microsoft Excel 2000** *Project 7, pages E 7.2-3* Two couples, Courtesy of PhotoDisc, Inc.; *Project 8, pages E 8.2-3* Woman in cafeteria, chef, boy with lunch tray, people in cafeteria, Courtesy of PhotoDisc, Inc.; *Project 9, pages E 9.2-3* Chester Carlson, Courtesy of Bettmann/Corbis. **Microsoft Access 2000** *Project 7, pages A 7.2-3* Alien, balloon, globe, banner, stars, ticket, clown, rabbit in the hat, Courtesy of Image Club; *Project 8, pages A 8.2-3* Web site, Courtesy of Peapod, Inc.; bag and basket of groceries, shirt, tennis balls, Courtesy of EyeWire; man, calculator, airplane, pills, hand holding disc, Courtesy of PhotoDisc, Inc.; Access software box, Courtesy of Microsoft Corporation; *Project 9, pages A 9.2-3* Women working out, FitLinxx monitor and equipment, Courtesy of FitLinxx, Inc.; legs pumping iron, man working out, Courtesy of PhotoDisc, Inc. **Microsoft PowerPoint 2000** *Project 5, pages PP 5.2-3* Workers, eye, Courtesy of PhotoDisc, Inc.; globes, Courtesy of Map Art by Cartesia Software; *Project 6, pages PP 6.2-3* Help Wanted sign, classified advertisements, hand on keyboard, two workers, Courtesy of PhotoDisc, Inc.

ISBN 0-7895-5691-X

2 3 4 5 6 7 8 9 10 BC 04 03 02 01 00

MICROSOFT

Office 2000

Post Advanced Concepts and Techniques

WORD 2000 EXCEL 2000 ACCESS 2000 POWERPOINT 2000

CONTENTS

Microsoft Word 2000

PROJECT 7

WORKING WITH A MASTER DOCUMENT, AN INDEX, AND A TABLE OF CONTENTS

PROJECT 8

CREATING AN ONLINE FORM

Microsoft Excel 2000

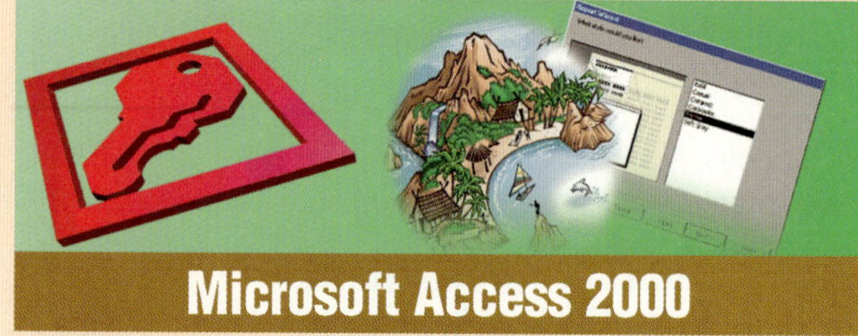

PROJECT 7

Creating a Report Using Design View

PROJECT 8

Customizing Forms Using Visual Basic for Applications (VBA), Charts, and PivotTable Objects

PROJECT 9

Administering a Database System

INTEGRATION FEATURE

USING ACCESS DATA IN OTHER APPLICATIONS

Microsoft PowerPoint 2000

PROJECT 5

CREATING A SELF-RUNNING PRESENTATION USING ANIMATION EFFECTS

Preface

The Shelly Cashman Series® offers the finest textbooks in computer education. We are proud of the fact that our *Microsoft Office 4.3*, *Microsoft Office 95*, and *Microsoft Office 97* textbooks have been the most widely used books in computer education. Each edition of our Office textbooks has included innovations, many based on comments made by the instructors and students who use our books. The *Microsoft Office 2000* books continue with the innovation, quality, and reliability that you have come to expect from the Shelly Cashman Series.

In our *Microsoft Office 2000* books, you will find an educationally sound and easy-to-follow pedagogy that combines a step-by-step approach with corresponding screens. All projects and exercises in this book are designed to take full advantage of the Office 2000 enhancements. The popular Other Ways and More About features offer in-depth knowledge of Office 2000. The project openers provide a fascinating perspective of the subject covered in the project. The project material is developed carefully to ensure that students will see the importance of learning Office 2000 applications for future course work.

Objectives of This Textbook

Microsoft Office 2000: Post-Advanced Concepts and Techniques is intended for a three-credit hour, third-semester computer applications course. This book assumes that students are quite familiar with Microsoft Word, Microsoft Excel, Microsoft Access, and Microsoft PowerPoint. The prerequisite topics are covered in the companion textbooks *Microsoft Office 2000: Introductory Concepts and Techniques* and *Microsoft Office 2000: Advanced Concepts and Techniques*. The objectives of this book are:

- To extend and solidify the students' knowledge of Microsoft Word 2000, Microsoft Excel 2000, Microsoft Access 2000, and Microsoft PowerPoint 2000.
- To help students demonstrate their proficiency in the Microsoft Office applications by preparing them to pass the Microsoft Office User Specialist Exam for Microsoft Word 2000, Microsoft Excel 2000, Microsoft Access 2000, and Microsoft PowerPoint 2000.
- To acquaint students with the proper procedures to create and manipulate sophisticated documents, workbooks, databases, and presentations suitable for course work, professional purposes, and personal use
- To develop an exercise-oriented approach that allows students to learn by example
- To encourage independent study, and help those who are working alone in a distance education environment

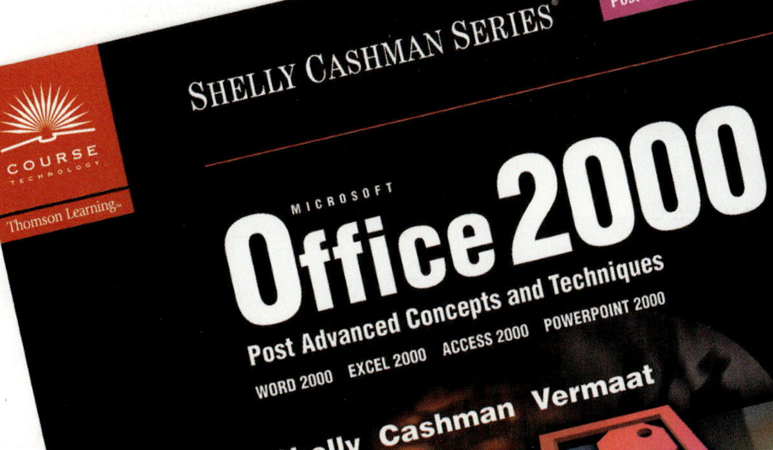

Approved by Microsoft as Courseware for the Microsoft Office User Specialist Program

This book, when used in combination with the companion textbooks *Microsoft Office 2000: Introductory Concepts and Techniques* and *Microsoft Office 2000: Advanced Concepts and Techniques* in a three-semester sequence, has been approved by Microsoft as courseware for the Microsoft Office User Specialist (MOUS) program. After completing the projects and exercises in this book and its companion books, students will be prepared to take the Expert level Microsoft Office User Specialist Exams for Microsoft Word 2000, Microsoft Excel 2000, Microsoft Access 2000 (proposed), and Microsoft PowerPoint 2000 (proposed).

By passing the certification exam for a Microsoft software application, students demonstrate their proficiency in that application to employers. This exam is offered at participating centers, participating corporations, and participating employment agencies. See Appendix D for additional information on the MOUS program and for a table that includes the Word 2000, Excel 2000, Access 2000, and PowerPoint 2000 MOUS skill sets and corresponding page numbers where a skill is discussed in the book, or visit the Web site at www.mous.net.

The Shelly Cashman Series Microsoft Office User Specialist Center Web page (Figure 1) has more than fifteen Web pages you can visit to obtain additional information on the MOUS Certification program. The Web page (www.scsite.com/off2000/cert.htm) includes links to general information on certification, choosing an application for certification, preparing for the certification exam, and taking and passing the certification exams.

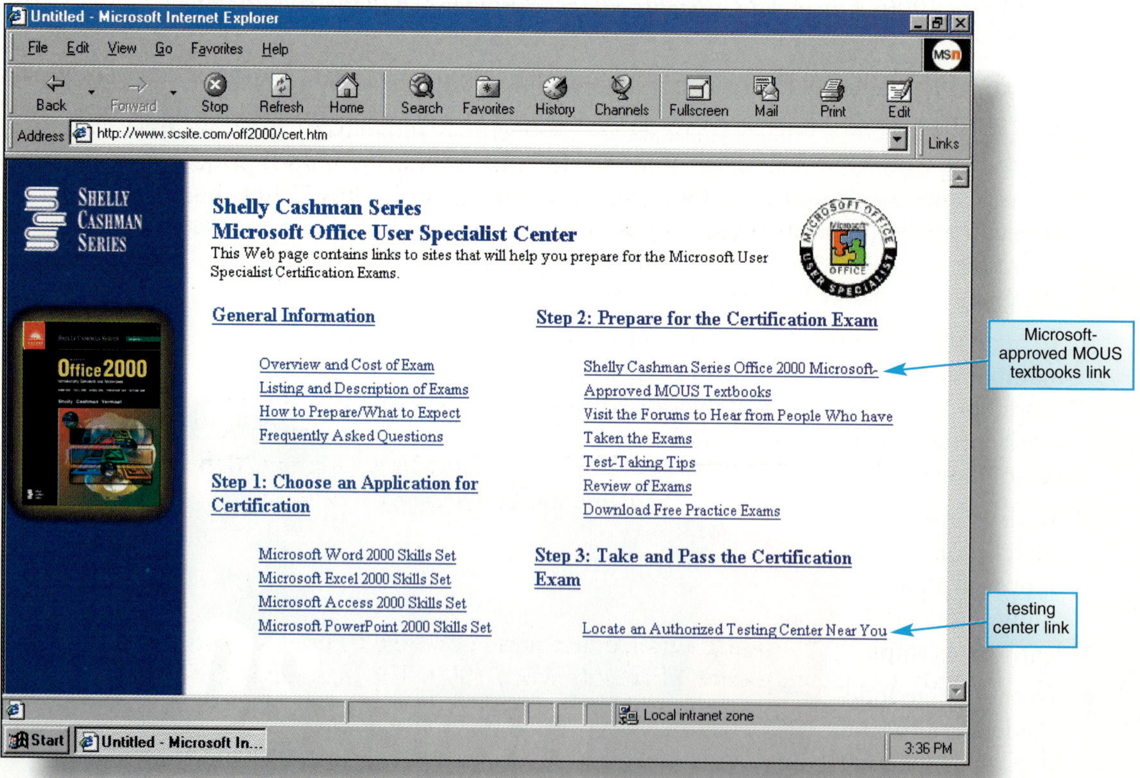

FIGURE 1

The Shelly Cashman Approach

Features of the Shelly Cashman Series *Microsoft Office 2000* books include:

- **Project Orientation:** Each project in the book presents a practical problem and complete solution in an easy-to-understand approach.
- **Step-by-Step, Screen-by-Screen Instructions:** Each of the tasks required to complete a project is shown using a step-by-step, screen-by-screen approach. The steps are accompanied by full-color screens.
- **Thoroughly Tested Projects:** Every screen in the book is correct because it is produced by the author only after performing a step, resulting in unprecedented quality.
- **Other Ways Boxes and Quick Reference Summary:** Office 2000 provides a variety of ways to carry out a given task. The Other Ways boxes displayed at the end of most of the step-by-step sequences specify the other ways to do the task completed in the steps. Thus, the steps and the Other Ways box make a comprehensive reference unit. In addition, a Quick Reference Summary, at the back of this book and also available on the Web, summarizes the ways application-specific tasks can be completed.
- **More About Feature:** These marginal annotations provide background information that complements the topics covered, adding depth and perspective to the learning process.
- **Integration of the World Wide Web:** We have integrated the World Wide Web into the students' Office 2000 learning experience in different ways. For example, we have added (1) More Abouts that send students to Web sites for up-to-date information and alternative approaches to tasks; (2) a MOUS information Web page and a MOUS map Web page so students can better prepare for the Microsoft Office Use Specialist (MOUS) Certification examinations; (3) an Office 2000 Quick Reference Summary Web page that summarizes the ways to complete tasks (mouse, menu, shortcut menu, and keyboard); and (4) project reinforcement Web pages in the form of true/false, multiple choice, and short answer questions, and other types of student activities.

Other Ways

1. Click Form Field Options button on Forms toolbar
2. Right-click form field, click Properties on shortcut menu

Digitizing

Digitizing produces some dazzling objects that add interest to presentations. Many artists have traded their paint brushes and easels for the mouse and monitor. To view some of their creations, visit the PowerPoint 2000 More About Web page (www.scsite.com/pp2000/more.htm) and click Digitizing.

Organization of This Textbook

Microsoft Office 2000: Post-Advanced Concepts and Techniques consists of three projects each on Microsoft Word 2000, Microsoft Excel 2000, and Microsoft Access 2000, two projects on Microsoft PowerPoint 2000, four short Integration or Web Features following each application, four appendices, and a Quick Reference Summary. A short description of each follows.

Microsoft Word 2000

This textbook begins by providing detailed instruction on how to use the post-advanced commands and techniques of Microsoft Word 2000. The material is divided into three projects and the Integration Feature as follows:

Project 7 – Working with a Master Document, an Index, and a Table of Contents In Project 7, students learn how to organize and work with a long document. Topics include inserting, reviewing, and deleting comments; tracking changes; accepting and rejecting tracked changes; saving multiple versions; embedding an Excel worksheet;

adding a caption; creating a cross-reference; password-protecting a document; working with a master document and subdocuments; adding an AutoShape; grouping drawing objects; creating a table of figures; marking index entries; building an index; creating a table of contents; and adding a bookmark.

Project 8 – Creating an Online Form In Project 8, students learn how to create an online form and then use Word to fill in the form. Topics include creating a document template; highlighting text; inserting a table into a form; inserting a text box into a form; inserting a drop-down list box into a form; inserting a check box into a form; formatting form fields; using the Format Painter button; adding Help text to form fields; drawing a rectangle; adding a texture fill effect to a drawing object; animating text, protecting a form; saving form data in a text file; and modifying the location of workgroup templates.

Project 9 – Using Visual Basic for Applications (VBA) with Word In Project 9, students enhance an online form by modifying its appearance, adding macros, and inserting an ActiveX control. Topics include creating a new style; filling a drawing object with a bitmap picture; adding a 3-D effect to a drawing object; recording and executing a macro; assigning a macro to a toolbar button; copying, renaming, and deleting macros; viewing a macro's VBA code; adding comments and VBA code statements to a macro; attaching a macro to the exit property of a form field; inserting, formatting, and setting properties of an ActiveX control; and writing VBA code statements for an ActiveX control.

Integration Feature – Linking an Excel Worksheet and Charting Its Data in Word In the Integration Feature, students are introduced to linking Excel data to a Word document. Topics include linking an Excel worksheet to a Word document; creating a chart; linking Excel data to the chart; and editing a linked object.

Microsoft Excel 2000

Following the three post-advanced projects and Integration Feature on Microsoft Word 2000, this textbook presents three post-advanced projects and a Web Feature on Microsoft Excel 2000. The topics presented are as follows:

Project 7 – Using Visual Basic for Applications (VBA) with Excel In Project 7, students learn how to automate tasks by incorporating VBA into their workbooks. Topics include protecting worksheets with passwords; using the macro recorder; executing macros; security; adding buttons to toolbars and commands to menus; creating a user interface by adding controls to a worksheet; setting properties; writing VBA code; using the Visual Basic Editor; validating incoming data; and using event-driven programs.

Project 8 – Auditing, Data Validation, and Solving Complex Problems In Project 8, students learn how to go about solving complex problems. Topics include using the Auditing toolbar; using data validation; goal seeking; using Solver to solve multiple problems; saving multiple scenarios with Scenario Manager; analysis of Solver answers and multiple scenarios; and workbook properties.

Project 9 – Importing External Data, Tracking and Routing Changes, and Creating Data Maps, PivotCharts, and PivotTables In Project 9, stucents learn how to import data into an Excel workbook, collaboration techniques, and advanced data analysis techniques. Topics include importing data from a text file, an Access database, and a Web page; turning Track Changes on and off; accepting and rejecting changes; serially routing a workbook to recipients; creating a data map; creating a PivotChart and PivotTable; analyzing a worksheet database using a PivotChart and PivotTable; and sharing and merging workbooks.

Web Feature – Creating a PivotTable List Web Page Using Excel In this Web Feature, students learn how to create and manipulate a PivotTable list. Topics include saving a worksheet database as a PivotTable list; viewing the PivotTable list using a browser; changing the view of the PivotTable list; adding summary totals; sorting columns of data; filtering techniques; removing fields and adding fields to a PivotTable list; and improving the appearance of a PivotTable list.

Microsoft Access 2000

Following the three post-advanced projects and Web Feature on Microsoft Excel 2000, this textbook provides detailed instruction on post-advanced topics in Microsoft Access 2000. The topics are divided into three projects and one Integration Feature as follows:

Project 7 – Creating a Report Using Design View In Project 7, students learn to use Design view to create complex reports involving data from queries that join multiple tables. Topics include relating multiple tables; creating a Lookup Wizard field that uses a separate table; changing join properties in a query; changing field properties in a query; filtering a query's Recordset; creating and running a parameter query; including a subreport in a report; adding a date and page number to a report; and creating and printing mailing labels.

Project 8 – Customizing Forms Using Visual Basic for Applications (VBA), Charts, and PivotTable Objects In Project 8, students learn ways to enhance forms to make them more useable and also how to create forms using Design view. Topics include adding command buttons to forms; modifying VBA code associated with a command button; adding a combo box that will be used for searching to a form; modify the properties of the combo box, using the combo box to search; creating a form using Design view; adding a subform control to a form; adding charts to a form; and creating and using a PivotTable form.

Project 9 – Administering a Database System In Project 9, students learn the issues and techniques involved in administering a database system. Topics include converting a database to an earlier version of Access; using the Table Analyzer, Performance Analyzer, and Documenter; creating a custom input mask; specifying referential integrity options; setting Startup options; setting a password; encrypting a database; creating a grouped data access page; creating and using a replica; synchronizing a Design Master and a replica; and creating and running SQL commands.

Integration Feature – Using Access Data in Other Applications In this Integration Feature, students learn how to prepare Access data for use in other applications. Topics include using the Export command to export database data to an Access worksheet; using drag-and-drop to export data to a Word document; and using the Export command to create a snapshot of a report.

Microsoft PowerPoint 2000

The final Microsoft Office 2000 software application covered in this textbook is Microsoft PowerPoint 2000. The material is presented in two post-advanced projects and a Web Feature as follows:

Project 5 – Creating a Self-Running Presentation Using Animation Effects In Project 5, students create a self-running presentation to view at a kiosk. Topics include inserting an animated slide from another presentation; embedding animated clip art, an Excel chart, a PowerPoint chart, and a Word table; inserting and formatting an AutoShape; removing background objects from a slide; using custom animation effects; and setting automatic slide timings.

Project 6 – Using Visual Basic for Applications (VBA) with PowerPoint In Project 6, students use VBA to develop an electronic career portfolio designed for viewing during a job interview. The slides are customized for each interview and include clip art, a photograph, and a video clip. Topics include creating a new toolbar and adding buttons; using the macro recorder to create a macro that prints handouts displaying four slides per page; and assigning the macro to a command on the File menu.

Web Feature – Distributing Presentations to Remote Audiences In the Web Feature, students learn to use the Pack and Go Wizard to condense files and include the PowerPoint Viewer. Topics include downloading a file from a Web server; setting discussion options; and subscribing to a publication.

Appendices

Appendix A presents a detailed step-by-step introduction to the Microsoft Office Help system. Students learn how to use the Office Assistant, as well as the Contents, Answer Wizard, and Index sheets in the Help window. Appendix B describes how to publish Office Web pages to a Web server. Appendix C shows students how to reset the menus and toolbars in any Office application. Appendix D introduces students to the Microsoft Office User Specialist (MOUS) Certification program and includes a MOUS map that lists a page number in the book for each of the MOUS activities.

Microsoft Office 2000 Quick Reference Summary

This book concludes with a detailed Quick Reference Summary. In the Microsoft Office 2000 applications, you can accomplish a task in a number of ways, such as using the mouse, menu, shortcut menu, and keyboard. The Quick Reference Summary provides a quick reference to each task presented in this textbook.

End-of-Project Exercises

A notable strength of the Shelly Cashman Series *Microsoft Office 2000* books is the extensive student activities at the end of each project. Well-structured student activities can make the difference between students merely participating in a class and students retaining the information they learn. The activities in the Shelly Cashman Series *Microsoft Office 2000* books include the following.

- **What You Should Know** A listing of the tasks completed within a project together with the pages where the step-by-step, screen-by-screen explanations appear. This section provides a perfect study review for students.

- **Project Reinforcement on the Web** Every project has a Web page accessible from www.scsite.com/off2000/reinforce.htm. The Web page includes true/false, multiple choice, and short answer questions, and additional project-related reinforcement activities that will help students gain confidence in their Office 2000 abilities.
- **Apply Your Knowledge** This exercise requires students to open and manipulate a file on the Data Disk for the Office 2000 books. To obtain a copy of the Data Disk, follow the instructions on the inside back cover of this textbook.
- **In the Lab** Three in-depth assignments per project require students to apply the knowledge gained in the project to solve problems on a computer.
- **Cases and Places** Up to seven unique case studies that require students to apply their knowledge to real-world situations.

Shelly Cashman Series Teaching Tools

A comprehensive set of Teaching Tools accompanies this textbook in the form of a CD-ROM. The CD-ROM includes an Instructor's Manual and teaching and testing aids. The CD-ROM (ISBN 0-7895-4636-1) is available through your Course Technology representative or by calling one of the following telephone numbers: Colleges and Universities, 1-800-648-7450; High Schools, 1-800-824-5179; Career Colleges, 1-800-477-3692; Canada, 1-800-268-2222; and Corporations and Government Agencies, 1-800-340-7450.

- **Instructor's Manual** The Instructor's Manual is made up of Microsoft Word files. The files include lecture notes, solutions to laboratory assignments, and a large test bank. The files allow you to modify the lecture notes or generate quizzes and exams from the test bank using your own word processing software. Where appropriate, solutions to laboratory assignments are embedded as icons in the files. When an icon appears, double-click it and the application will start and the solution will display on the screen. The Instructor's Manual includes the following for each project: project objectives; project overview; detailed lesson plans with page number references; teacher notes and activities; answers to the end-of-project exercises; test bank of 110 questions for every project (25 multiple-choice, 50 true/false, and 35 fill-in-the-blank) with page number references; and transparency references. The transparencies are available through the Figures in the Book. The test bank questions are numbered the same as in Course Test Manager. Thus, you can print a copy of the project test bank and use the printout to select your questions in Course Test Manager.
- **Figures in the Book** Illustrations for every screen and table in the textbook are available in JPEG format. Use this ancillary to create a slide show from the illustrations for lecture or to print transparencies for use in lecture. You also may create your own PowerPoint presentations and insert these illustrations.
- **Course Test Manager** Course Test Manager is a powerful testing and assessment package that enables instructors to create and print tests from the large test bank. Instructors with access to a networked computer lab (LAN) can administer, grade, and track tests online. Students also can take online practice tests, which generate customized study guides.
- **Course Syllabus** Any instructor who has been assigned a course at the last minute knows how difficult it is to come up with a course syllabus. For this reason, sample syllabi are included for each of the Word 2000 products that can be customized easily to a course.

- **Lecture Success System** Lecture Success System files are for use with the application software, a personal computer, and projection device to explain and illustrate the step-by-step, screen-by-screen development of a project in the textbook without entering large amounts of data.
- **Instructor's Lab Solutions** Solutions and required files for all the In the Lab assignments at the end of each project are available.
- **Lab Tests/Test Outs** Tests that parallel the In the Lab assignments are supplied for the purpose of testing students in the laboratory on the material covered in the project or testing students out of the course.
- **Project Reinforcement** True/false, multiple choice, and short answer questions, and additional project-related reinforcement activities for each project help students gain confidence in their Word 2000 abilities.
- **Student Files** All the files that are required by students to complete the Apply Your Knowledge exercises are included.
- **Interactive Labs** Eighteen hands-on interactive labs that take students from ten to fifteen minutes each to step through help solidify and reinforce mouse and keyboard usage and computer concepts. Student assessment is available.
- **WebCT Content** This ancillary includes book-related content that can be uploaded to your institution's WebCT site. The content includes a sample syllabus, practice tests, a bank of test questions, a list of book-related links, and lecture notes from the Instructor's Manual.

Acknowledgments

The Shelly Cashman Series would not be the leading computer education series without the contributions of outstanding publishing professionals. First, and foremost, among them is Becky Herrington, director of production and designer. She is the heart and soul of the Shelly Cashman Series, and it is only through her leadership, dedication, and tireless efforts that superior products are made possible. Becky created and produced the award-winning Windows series of books.

Under Becky's direction, the following individuals made significant contributions to these books: Doug Cowley, production manager; Ginny Harvey, series specialist and developmental editor; Ken Russo, senior Web designer; Mike Bodnar, associate production manager; Stephanie Nance, graphic artist and cover designer; Mark Norton, Web designer; Meena Mohtadi, production editor; Marlo Mitchem, Chris Schneider, Hector Arvizu, Kenny Tran, Kathy Mayers, and Dave Bonnewitz, graphic artists; Jeanne Black and Betty Hopkins, Quark experts; Nancy Lamm, Lyn Markowicz, Margaret Gatling, and Laurie Sullivan, copyeditors; Marilyn Martin, Kim Kosmatka, Cherilyn King, Mary Steinman, and Pat Hadden, proofreaders; Cristina Haley, indexer; Sarah Evertson of Image Quest, photo researcher; and Susan Sebok and Ginny Harvey, contributing writers.

Special thanks go to Richard Keaveny, managing editor; Jim Quasney, series consulting editor; Lora Wade, product manager; Erin Bennett, associate product manager; Francis Schurgot, Web product manager; Marc Ouellette, associate Web product manager; Scott Wiseman, online developer; Rajika Gupta, marketing manager; and Erin Runyon, editorial assistant.

Gary B. Shelly
Thomas J. Cashman
Misty E. Vermaat

Microsoft Word 2000

Working with a Master Document, an Index, and a Table of Contents

OBJECTIVES

You will have mastered the material in this project when you can:

- Insert, modify, review, and delete comments
- Track changes in a document
- Save multiple versions of a document
- Accept and reject tracked changes
- Embed an Excel worksheet into a Word document
- Add and modify a caption
- Create a cross-reference
- Mark index entries
- Keep paragraphs together
- Password-protect a document
- Work with a master document and subdocuments
- Create and modify an outline
- Add an AutoShape
- Group drawing objects
- Create a table of figures
- Build and modify an index
- Create and modify a table of contents
- Add a bookmark
- Create alternating headers
- Set a gutter margin
- Use the Document Map

Hot Topics

So Many Papers, So Many Styles

Assistive Technology for Special Education. History and Myth. Journalism Ethics. Healthcare Reform. Internet Issues. All of these topics and many more may be the subject of one of your next papers. Depending on your course of study, you are likely to encounter a variety of styles from a number of established documentation sources that will direct you in the composition of research papers, reports, and reference documents. In Project 7, you will use Word 2000 to produce a reference document titled Computer Security containing multiple pages, a table of contents, a table of figures, and an index.

After selecting a topic, the work begins: researching your subject, finding reference materials, taking notes, and outlining. Then you write a series of drafts, check language and style, and rewrite the final paper, and maybe more than once! To ensure that the reader of your paper can navigate easily, you need a table of contents and an index. It is a good habit to verify your references and make certain that all your sources are given the appropriate credit. The citation procedure may seem tedious, but it is the way your readers know how to find additional information on the subjects and the way you

table of figures

index

ethically give credit to the individuals who have researched these topics before you.

Finally, you must consider the type of binding. You do not want your hard work misplaced or lost. Although folders or other kinds of binders are a nice final addition, some instructors have certain preferences for handing in your completed work, and you always should be aware of their requirements.

In academia, three major style systems for writers of research and scientific papers generally are recognized. Scholars in the humanities fields use The Modern Language Association (MLA). The MLA style is organized in the *MLA Handbook for Writers of Research Papers*. Researchers in the social sciences use another popular style developed by the American Psychological Association (APA). The APA style is documented in the *Publication Manual of the American Psychological Association*. The third style is the number system used by the Council of Biology Editors (CBE). The CBE manual, *Scientific Style and Format*, describes the citation-sequence system and the name-year system used by writers in the applied sciences.

Writers also consult other style handbooks such as *The Chicago Manual of Style*, the *American Chemical Society Handbook for Authors*, the *Microsoft Manual of Style for Technical Writers*, and others.

Teams of instructors and scholars develop the style guidelines in each of these major publications. The *MLA Handbook*, for example, originated in 1951 for MLA members, and later was expanded to become a guide for undergraduates. Subsequent revisions are published on a regular basis. The MLA makes the guide available on the Internet, which includes up-to-date conventions for documenting sources on the World Wide Web. You can visit MLA online (www.mla.org).

Keeping up with the latest revisions can be a challenge for both the developers of the guides and the individuals who need to access them for their academic, professional, or personal use. With the vast amount of information available on the Web, however, it is easy to find a host of tips and suggestions that can provide documentation, resource directories, topics, ideas, assistance, and more. For additional information, visit the Word 2000 More About Web page (www.scsite.com/wd2000/more.htm).

Microsoft Word 2000

Microsoft Word 2000

Working with a Master Document, an Index, and a Table of Contents

CASE PERSPECTIVE

Textbooks Press is an international company that publishes college textbooks. Personnel director, Marge Bauer, strongly believes that a company's success depends on solid communications with and among employees. To this end, Marge has implemented a variety of strategies aimed at improving employee relations. One of these, a multipage reference document, called the Employee Information and Guidelines (EIG), is distributed to all employees. Employees at Textbooks Press find the EIG documents extremely valuable, ranging from topics covering employee behavior to ethical activities to technical skills. Suggestions, however, have been made that the EIG documents be more organized including items such as a table of contents and index.

Employees in the personnel department assemble these documents, often with assistance from employees in other departments. In coordinating all the comments and edits of these documents, Marge has noticed a lot of inefficiencies. As a part-time computer specialist at Textbooks Press, you have been assigned the task of redesigning the production of the EIG documents.

Introduction

During the course of your academic studies and professional endeavors, you may find it necessary to compose a document that is many pages in length or even one that is hundreds of pages. When composing a long document, you must ensure that the document is organized so that a reader easily can locate material within the document. Sometimes a document of this nature is called a **reference document**.

By placing a table of contents at the beginning of the document and an index at the end, you help a reader navigate through a long document. If a document contains several illustrations, each illustration should have a caption. Also, the illustrations could be listed in a table, called a table of figures, that identifies the location of each figure in the document. For long documents that will be viewed online, you should incorporate hyperlinks so that a user can click the link to jump from one portion of the document to another.

Project Seven — Master Document, Index, and Table of Contents

Project 7 uses Word to produce the reference document shown in Figure 7-1. The document, called the Employee Information and Guidelines (EIG) #22, is distributed to all employees at Textbooks Press. Notice that the inner margin between facing pages has extra space to allow duplicated copies of the documents to be bound – without the binding covering the words.

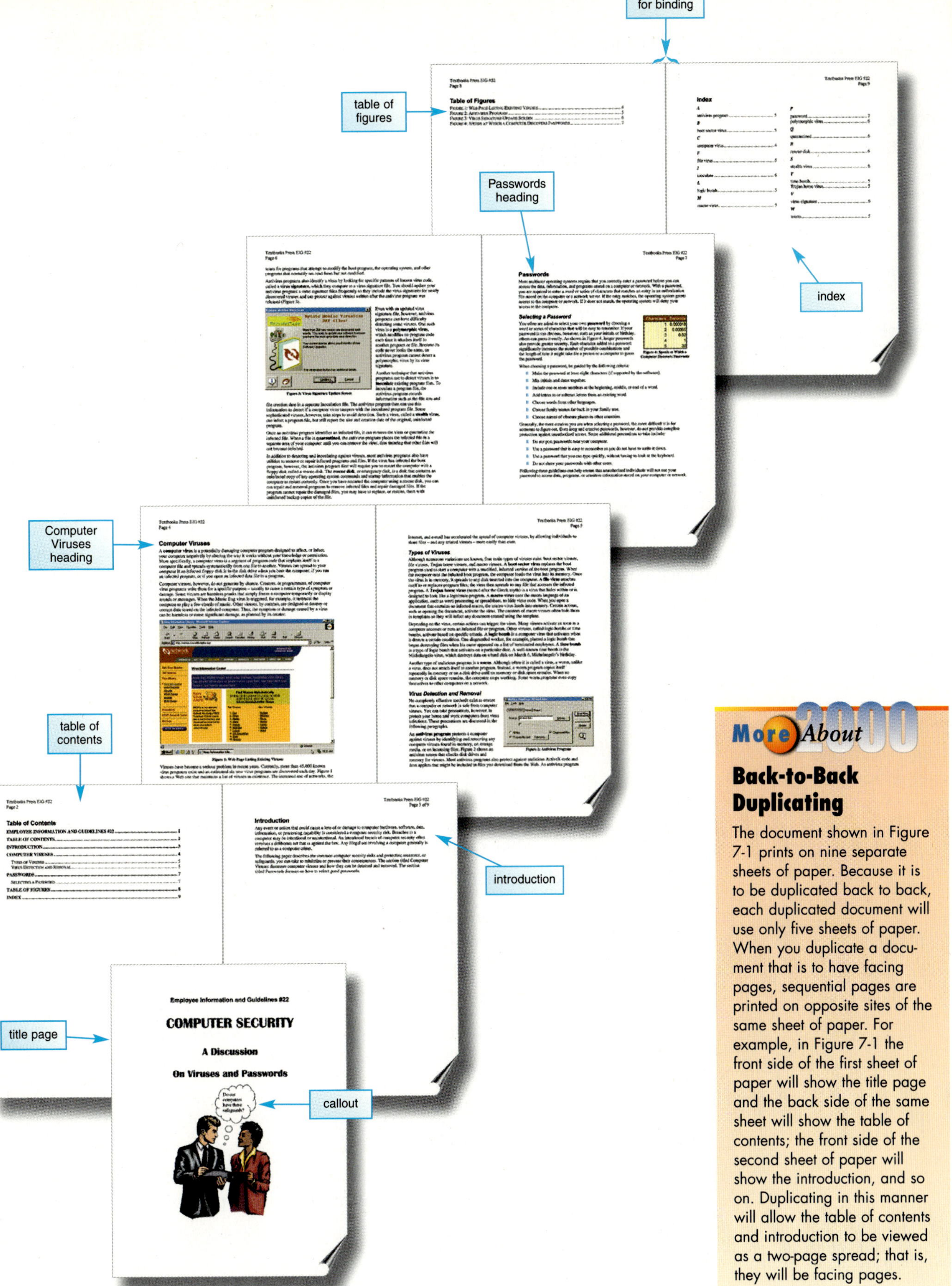

FIGURE 7-1

More About 2000

Back-to-Back Duplicating

The document shown in Figure 7-1 prints on nine separate sheets of paper. Because it is to be duplicated back to back, each duplicated document will use only five sheets of paper. When you duplicate a document that is to have facing pages, sequential pages are printed on opposite sites of the same sheet of paper. For example, in Figure 7-1 the front side of the first sheet of paper will show the title page and the back side of the same sheet will show the table of contents; the front side of the second sheet of paper will show the introduction, and so on. Duplicating in this manner will allow the table of contents and introduction to be viewed as a two-page spread; that is, they will be facing pages.

Reference Documents

For a sample reference document on the Web that contains elements commonly found in long documents, visit the Word 2000 More About Web page (www.scsite.com/wd2000/more.htm) and then click Sample Reference Document.

The EIG #22 document begins with a title page. The callout on the title page is designed to entice the receiver to open the document and read it. Next is the table of contents, followed by an introduction. The document then discusses two issues: computer viruses and passwords. At the end of the document is a table of figures and an index to assist a reader in locating information. A miniature version of the EIG #22 document is shown in Figure 7-1; for a more readable view, visit www.scsite.com/wd2000/project7.htm.

The personnel department has asked employees in the information systems department to write the content for the computer viruses and passwords sections of the document and then e-mail the files for inclusion in EIG #22. Jean, a systems analyst in the information systems department, has e-mailed the completed Computer Viruses file to the personnel department. Jeff, an IS auditor, has written a first draft of the passwords section and e-mailed it to his boss, Carlos, for review. After Jeff receives it back from Carlos, he will make any necessary adjustments to the document and then e-mail it to the personnel department.

The personnel department will incorporate the two completed files, Computer Viruses and Passwords, into a single file. They will create a title page, table of contents, introduction, table of figures, and index so the document is organized.

The following pages explain how Carlos reviews the document, how Jeff modifies it, and how the personnel department assembles the final document. For purposes of this project, certain files that are e-mailed to various people or departments are included on the Data Disk. If you did not download the Data Disk, see the inside back cover for instructions for downloading the Data Disk or see your instructor.

Starting Word

Follow these steps to start Word or ask your instructor how to start Word for your system.

TO START WORD

1. Click the Start button on the taskbar.
2. Click New Office Document on the Start menu. If necessary, click the General tab when the New Office Document dialog box displays.
3. Double-click the Blank Document icon in the General sheet.
4. If the Word window is not maximized, double-click its title bar to maximize it. Click View on the menu bar and then click Print Layout. If the Office Assistant displays, right-click it and then click Hide on the shortcut menu.

Office starts Word. After a few moments, an empty document titled Document1 displays in the Word window. Because this project uses floating graphics, you will use print layout view; thus, the Print Layout View button on the horizontal scroll bar is recessed.

Resetting Menus and Toolbars

To set the menus and toolbars so they appear exactly as shown in this book, you should reset your menus and toolbars as outlined in Appendix C or follow these steps.

TO RESET MENUS AND TOOLBARS

1. Click View on the menu bar and then point to Toolbars. Click Customize on the Toolbars submenu.
2. When the Customize dialog box displays, click the Options tab, make sure the top three check boxes have check marks and then click the Reset my usage data button. When the Microsoft Word dialog box displays, click the Yes button.
3. Click the Toolbars tab. Click Standard in the Toolbars list and then click the Reset button. When the Reset Toolbar dialog box displays, click the OK button.
4. Click Formatting in the Toolbars list and then click the Reset button. When the Reset Toolbar dialog box displays, click the OK button. Click the Close button.

Word resets the menus and toolbars.

Displaying Formatting Marks

It is helpful to display formatting marks that indicate where in the document you pressed the ENTER key, SPACEBAR, and other keys. Follow this step to display formatting marks.

TO DISPLAY FORMATTING MARKS

1. Double-click the move handle on the left side of the Standard toolbar to display the entire toolbar. If the Show/Hide ¶ button on the Standard toolbar is not recessed already, click it.

Word displays formatting marks in the document window, and the Show/Hide ¶ button on the Standard toolbar is recessed.

Reviewing a Document

Jeff, the IS auditor in the Information Systems department at Textbooks Press, has written a first draft of the section of the EIG #22 document that is to discuss passwords. He has e-mailed this draft to his supervisor, Carlos, for review. After reading through the Passwords Draft file, Carlos has some suggested changes.

Carlos could print a copy of the document and write his suggested changes using proofreader's revision marks as shown in Figure 7-2a on the next page. Instead of writing his suggestions on the printed draft copy, however, Carlos plans to use Word's **change-tracking feature** and enter his suggested changes directly into the document. Then, Jeff can choose to accept or reject each of the changes online. As a comparison, Figure 7-2b on the next page shows the final copy of the Passwords file, after Jeff reviews the changes suggested by Carlos and modifies the document accordingly. When comparing Figures 7-2a and 7-2b, you will notice that Jeff makes most of the changes suggested by Carlos.

The following pages illustrate the change-tracking feature of Word.

Proofreading Marks

For more information on marks and abbreviations used by proofreaders, visit the Word 2000 More About Web page (www.scsite.com/wd2000/more.htm) and then click Proofreading Marks.

Passwords

Most multiuser operating systems require that you correctly enter a password before you can access the data, information, and programs stored on a computer or network. With a password, you are required to enter a word or series of characters that matches an entry in an authorization file stored on the computer or a network server. If the entry matches, the operating system grants access to the computer or network. If it does not match, the operating system will deny your access to the computer.

Selecting a Password

You often are asked to select your own **password** by choosing a word or series of characters that will be easy to remember. If your password is too obvious, however, such as your initials or birthday, others can guess it easily. As shown in Figure 1, longer passwords also provide greater security. Each character added to a password significantly increases the number of possible combinations and the length of time it might take for a person or a computer to guess the password.

Characters	Seconds
1	0.000018
2	0.00065
3	0.02
4	1
5	30

Figure 1: Speeds at Which a Computer Discovers Passwords

When choosing a password, be guided by the following criteria:

- Make the password at least eight characters (if supported by the software).
- Mix initials and dates together.
- Include one or more numbers at the beginning, middle, or end of a word.
- Add letters to or subtract letters from an existing word.
- Choose words from other languages.
- Choose family names far back in your family tree.
- Choose names of obscure places in other countries.

Generally, the more creative you are when selecting a password, the more difficult it is for someone to figure out. Even long and creative passwords, however, do not provide complete ...d access. Some additional precautions to take include:

- ... near your computer.
- ... easy to remember so you do not have to write it down.
- ...u can type quickly, without having to look at the keyboard.
- ...swords with other users.

...n help ensure that unauthorized individuals will not use your ...rams, or sensitive information stored on your computer or network.

(b) Final Version of Passwords File

Passwords

Most multiuser operating systems require that you correctly enter a password before you can access the data, information, and programs stored on a computer or network. With a password, you are required to enter a word or series of characters that matches an entry in an authorization file stored on the computer or a network server. If the entry matches, the operating system grants access to the computer or network. If it does not match, the operating system will deny your access to the computer.

Selecting a Password

You often are asked to select your own password by choosing a word or series of characters that will be easy to ~~learn by heart~~ remember. If your password is too obvious, however, such as your initials or birthday, others can guess it easily. Longer passwords also provide greater security. Each character added to a password significantly increases the number of possible combinations and the length of time it might take for a person or a computer to guess the password.

insert chart here

When choosing a password, be guided by the following criteria:

- Make the password at least eight or more characters (if supported by the software).
- Mix initials and dates together.
- Include one or more numbers at the beginning, middle, or end of a word.
- Add letters to or subtract letters from an existing word.
- Choose words from other languages.
- Choose family names far back in your family tree.
- Choose names of obscure places in other countries.

Generally, the more creative you are when selecting a password, the more difficult it is for someone to figure out. Even long and creative passwords, however, do not provide complete protection against unauthorized access. Some additional precautions to take include:

- Do not post passwords near your computer.
- Use a password that is easy to remember so you do not have to write it down.
- Use a password that you can type quickly, without having to look at the keyboard.
- Do not share your passwords with other users.

Following these guidelines can help ensure that unauthorized individuals will not use your password to access data, programs, or sensitive information stored on your computer or network.

FIGURE 7-2

(a) Draft of Passwords File with Suggested Changes

Opening a Document

The first step in reviewing a document is to open it. Carlos is to review the Passwords Draft file that Jeff has completed. For purposes of this book, the Passwords Draft file that Carlos is to review is located on the Data Disk. If you did not download the Data Disk, see the inside back cover for instructions for downloading the Data Disk or see your instructor.

Open the Passwords Draft file as described in the steps below.

TO OPEN A DOCUMENT

1. If necessary, insert the Data Disk into drive A. Click the Open button on the Standard toolbar.
2. When the Open dialog box displays, if necessary, click the Look in box arrow and then click 3½ Floppy (A:). Click Passwords Draft.
3. Click the Open button in the Open dialog box.

Word opens the Passwords Draft file and displays it in the Word window.

Saving the Document with a New Name

To preserve the contents of the original Passwords Draft file, save a copy of it with a new name as described in the following steps.

TO SAVE A DOCUMENT WITH A NEW FILE NAME

1. With a floppy disk in drive A, click File on the menu bar and then click Save As.
2. Type `Passwords` in the File name text box. Do not press the ENTER key.
3. If necessary, click the Save in box arrow and then click 3½ Floppy (A:).
4. Click the Save button in the Save As dialog box.

Word saves the document on a floppy disk in drive A with the file name Passwords (see Figure 7-3 on the next page).

Zooming Text Width

When you zoom text width, Word displays text on the screen as large as possible in print layout view without extending the right margin beyond the right edge of the document window. Perform the following steps to zoom text width.

TO ZOOM TEXT WIDTH

1. Click the Zoom box arrow on the Standard toolbar.
2. Click Text Width in the Zoom list.

Word places the right margin at the right edge of the document window. Word computes the zoom percentage based on a variety of settings. Your percentage may be different.

Comments

If you have a pen-equipped computer, you can insert pen comments that become drawing objects in the document. Likewise, if your computer has a microphone and sound card, you can record voice comments that are attached to the document as recordings.

Inserting Comments

A **comment**, or annotation, is a note inserted into a document that does not affect the text of the document. Reviewers often use comments to communicate suggestions, tips, and other messages to the author of a document. For example, Carlos believes that the last sentence in the first paragraph below the Selecting a Password heading would have more impact if it referenced a table. Perform the following steps to insert a comment of this nature into the document.

Steps To Insert a Comment

1 Select the text on which you wish to comment (in this case, the last sentence of the first paragraph below the Selecting a Password heading). Click Insert on the menu bar and then point to Comment (Figure 7-3).

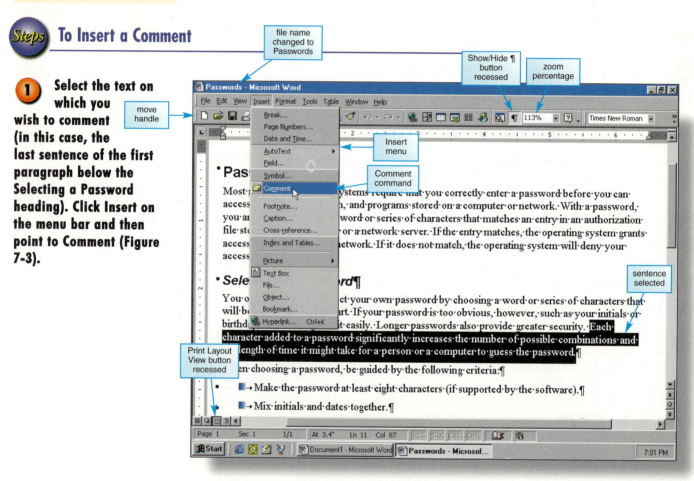

file name changed to Passwords

move handle

Show/Hide ¶ button recessed

zoom percentage

Insert menu

Comment command

sentence selected

Print Layout View button recessed

FIGURE 7-3

2 **Click Comment.**

Word opens a comment pane in the lower portion of the Word window and highlights in yellow the selected text in the document window (Figure 7-4). The insertion point is positioned in the comment pane to the right of the comment reference mark, which contains the reviewer's initials followed by the comment number. The comment reference mark also displays in the document window to the right of the selected text. Your reviewer initials will differ from this figure.

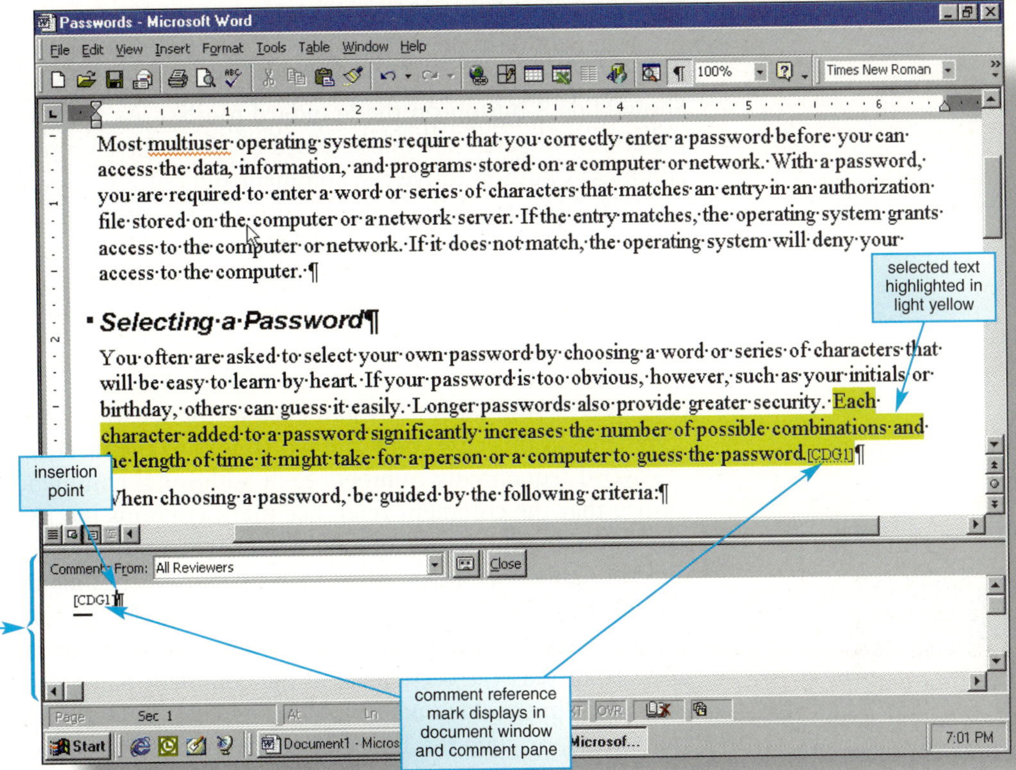

FIGURE 7-4

3 **Press the SPACEBAR. Type** `I suggest you insert a table here to emphasize the importance of this sentence.` **Point to the Close button in the comment pane (Figure 7-5).**

Click the Close button.

Word closes the comment pane.

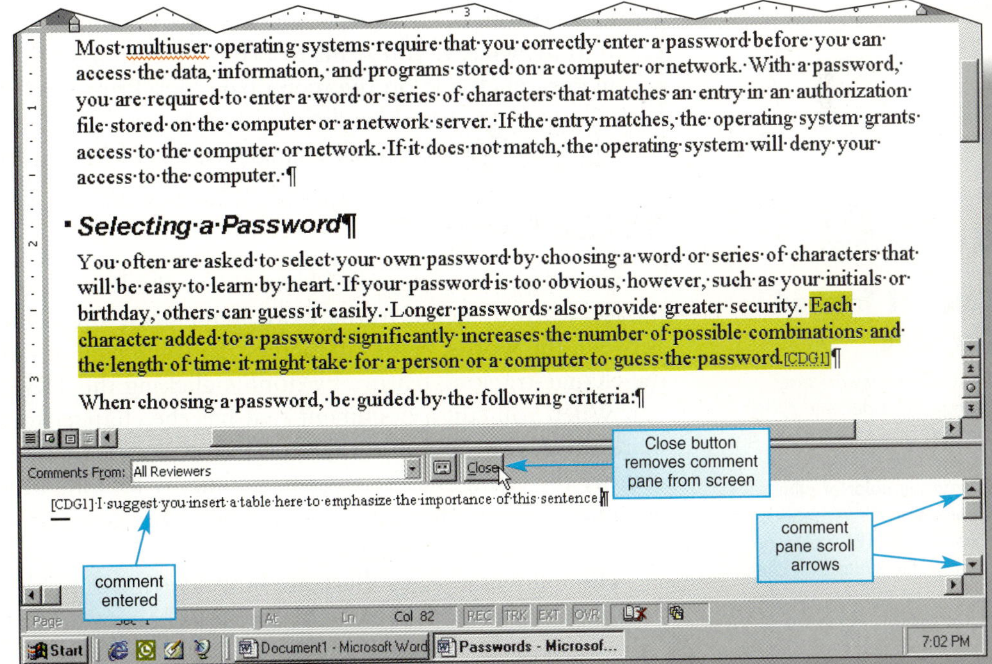

FIGURE 7-5

1. Click Insert Comment button on Reviewing toolbar

When Word closes the comment pane and returns to the document window, the comment disappears from the screen. If, when you close the comment pane, the comment reference mark does not display in the document window, click the Show/Hide ¶ button on the Standard toolbar. As with footnotes, if you point to the comment reference mark, Word displays the comment and the name of the comment's author above the comment reference mark as a ScreenTip.

Word uses predefined settings for the reviewer initials that display in the comment pane and the document window. If the initials that display are not correct, you can change them by clicking Tools on the menu bar, clicking Options, clicking the User Information tab, entering correct initials in the Initials text box, and then clicking the OK button.

Instead of selecting text on which you wish to comment (as shown in Step 1 on page WD 7.10), you simply can click at the location where you want to insert the comment. In this case, only the word next to the insertion point is highlighted.

Word sequentially numbers each additional comment you insert into a document. Notice that the comment reference mark contains the reviewer's initials. Thus, you can determine the writer of a comment when multiple reviewers insert comments into the same document. Also, each reviewer's comments are highlighted in a different color to visually help you differentiate reviewer's comments.

You modify comments using the comment pane at the bottom of the Word window. To display the comments in the comment pane, double-click the comment reference mark in the document window, or click View on the menu bar and then click Comments, or click the Edit Comment button on the Reviewing toolbar. Edit the comment as you would any Word text and then click the Close button in the comment pane.

When you print a document, comments normally do not print. If you want them to print along with the document, click File on the menu bar, click Print, click the Options button, place a check mark in the Comments check box, and then click the OK button twice. If you want to print the comments only (without printing the document), click File on the menu bar, click Print, click the Print what box arrow, click Comments, and then click the OK button.

The next step is to track changes while editing the document.

More About 2000

The Reviewing Toolbar

To display the Reviewing toolbar, click View on the menu bar, point to Toolbars, and then click Reviewing. The Reviewing toolbar contains buttons that enable you to work with comments, tracked changes, highlighting, and document versions.

Tracking Changes

Carlos has two suggested changes for the Passwords document: (1) change the phrase, learn by heart, to the word, remember, and (2) insert the words, or more, between the words, eight characters. To track changes in a document, you turn on the change-tracking feature by double-clicking the TRK status indicator on the status bar. When you edit a document that has the change-tracking feature enabled, Word marks all text or graphics that you insert, delete, or modify. Thus, an author can identify the changes a reviewer has made by looking at the revision marks in the document. The author also has the ability to accept or reject any change that a reviewer has made to a document.

The following pages illustrate how a reviewer tracks changes to a document and then how the author reviews the tracked changes made to the document.

More About 2000

Color of Tracked Changes

If multiple reviewers track changes to a document, the changes of each reviewer are marked in a different color. To change the color or other aspects of reviewer marks, right-click the TRK status indicator on the status bar, click Options on the shortcut menu, adjust settings in the Track Changes dialog box, and then click the OK button.

To Track Changes

1 Double-click the TRK status indicator on the status bar.

Word darkens the characters in the TRK status indicator on the status bar (Figure 7-6).

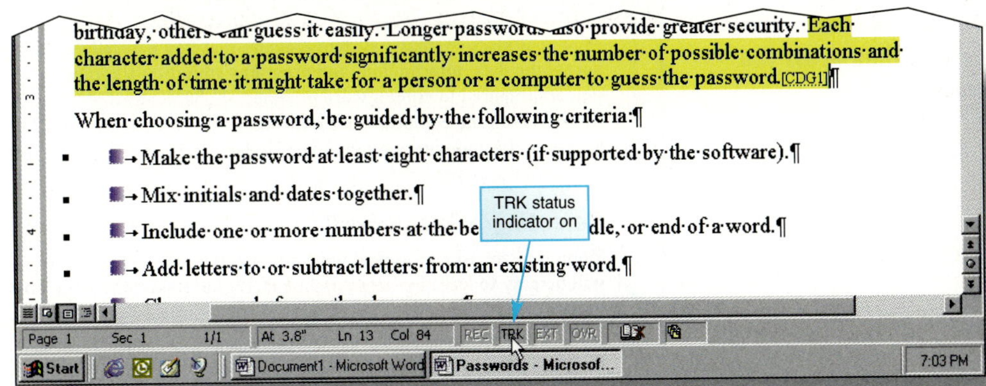

FIGURE 7-6

2 Select the text, learn by heart (Figure 7-7).

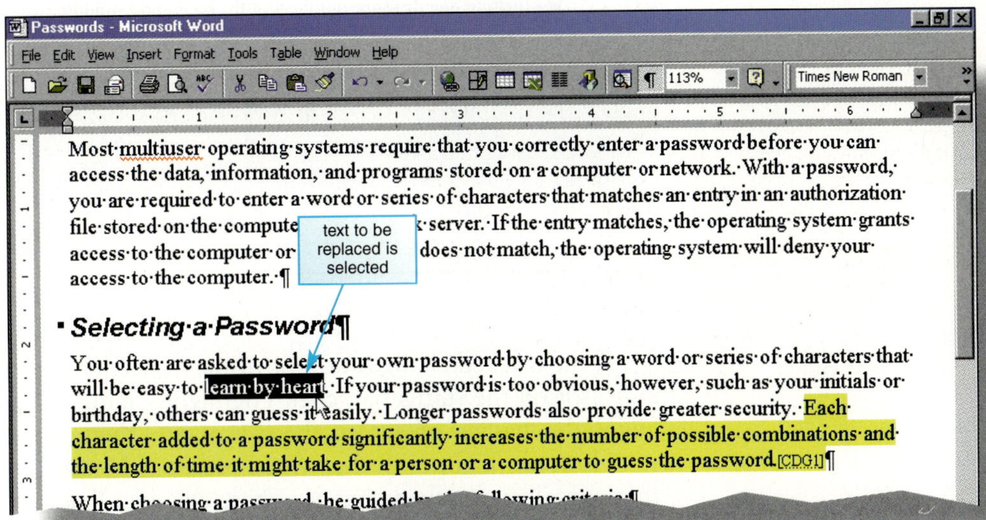

FIGURE 7-7

3 With the text still selected, type `remember` **as the replacement text.**

*Word marks the selection, learn by heart, as deleted, and marks the word, remember, as inserted (Figure 7-8). Deleted text displays in color with a horizontal line through it, called a **strikethrough**, and inserted text displays in color and underlined.*

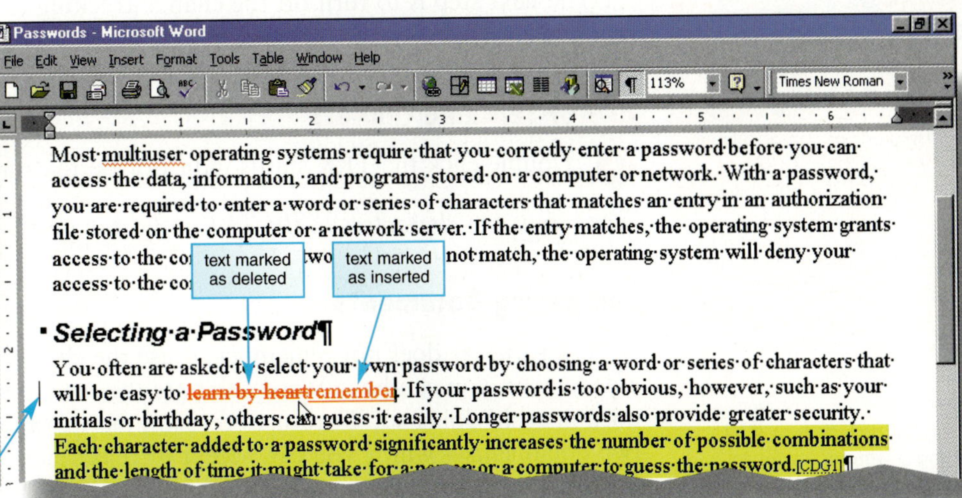

FIGURE 7-8

4 **Click to the left of the first letter c in the word, characters, in the first bulleted item. Type** or more **and then press the SPACEBAR.**

Word marks the inserted text, or more, as inserted (Figure 7-9). That is, it displays in color and underlined.

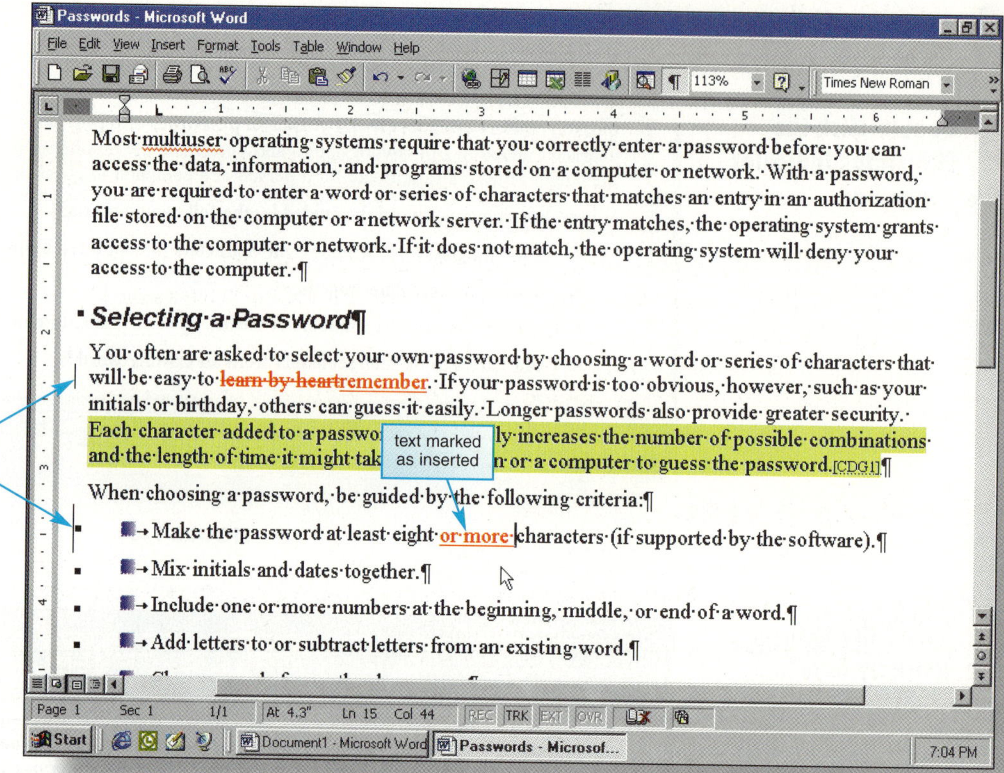

FIGURE 7-9

1. Click Track Changes button on Reviewing toolbar

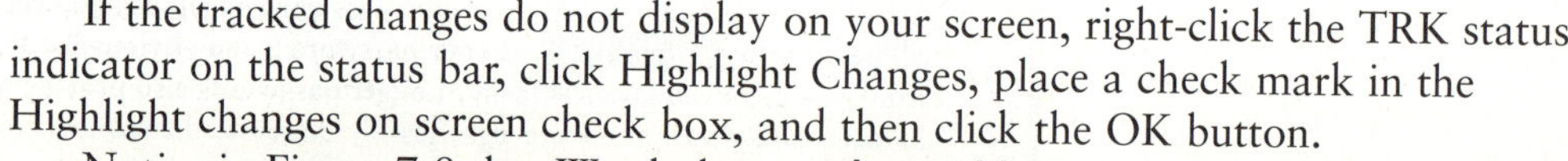

If the tracked changes do not display on your screen, right-click the TRK status indicator on the status bar, click Highlight Changes, place a check mark in the Highlight changes on screen check box, and then click the OK button.

Notice in Figure 7-9 that Word places a **changed line** at the left edge of each line that contains a tracked change. These changed lines, along with the strikethrough for deleted text and the underline for inserted text, are called **revision marks**.

As with comments, if you point to a tracked change, Word displays a ScreenTip that identifies the reviewer's name and the type of change made by that reviewer.

The next step is to turn off the change-tracking feature, as described in the following step.

Tracked Changes

To display or print a document with tracked changes showing, right-click the TRK status indicator on the status bar, click Highlight Changes on the shortcut menu, place a check mark in the appropriate check box, and then click the OK button. If you remove the check marks from the check boxes, Word displays and prints the document as if all changes were accepted.

TO STOP TRACKING CHANGES

1 Double-click the TRK status indicator on the status bar.

Word dims the characters in the TRK indicator on the status bar (see Figure 7-10).

Comparing Documents

If a reviewer does not remember to use the change-tracking feature while editing a document, you can have Word compare the reviewer's document to your original document. In doing so, Word uses revision marks to mark all differences between the two documents – which you can accept or reject later. To compare two documents, open the reviewer's document, click Tools on the menu bar, point to Track Changes, click Compare Documents, and then open your original document.

Saving Multiple Versions of a Document

When Jeff receives the reviewed document from Carlos via e-mail, he wants to preserve a copy of the document that contains the tracked changes. Instead of saving it with a new file name, he opts to save a separate version of the document. Using the version feature saves disk space because Word only saves changes among versions – as opposed to a complete copy of the file. The downside is that you cannot modify a version; you only can open and print versions.

When you save a version of a document, you insert a description of the version so you can identify it at a later time. The version represents the current state, or snapshot, of the document.

For purposes of this project, you will save a version of the Passwords document that is on your disk. Perform the following steps to save a version of a document.

Versions

To automatically save a version of a document when you close the document, click File on the menu bar, click Versions, place a check mark in the Automatically save a version on close check box, and then click the Close button.

To Save a Version of a Document

1 Click File on the menu bar and then point to Versions (Figure 7-10).

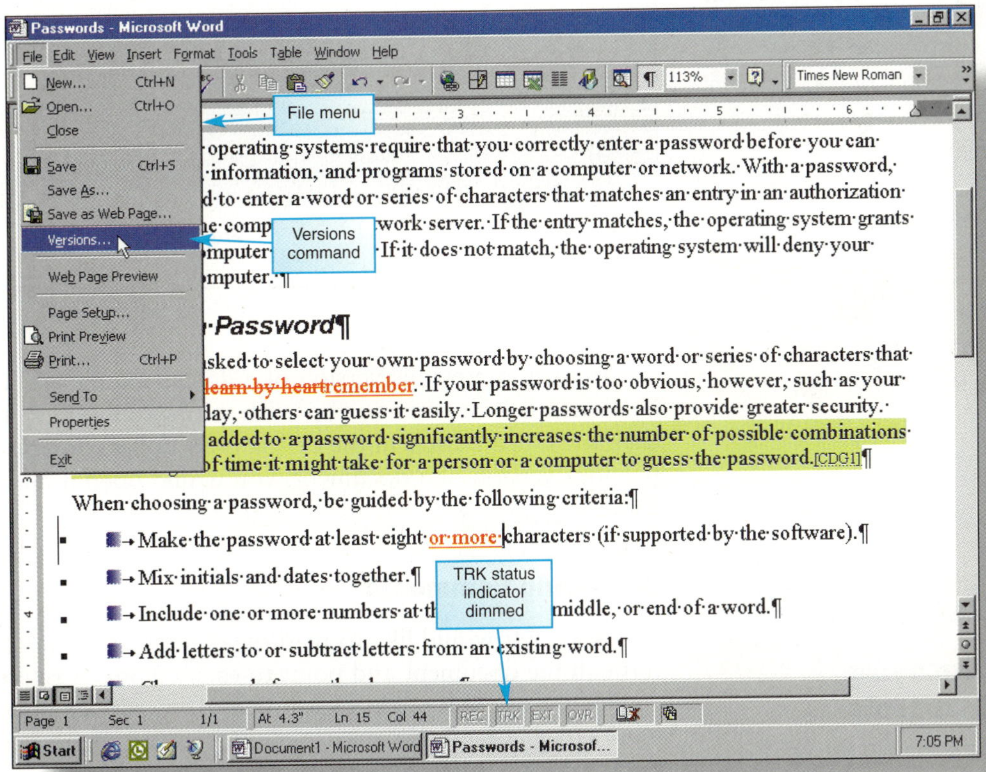

FIGURE 7-10

2 **Click Versions. When the Versions in Passwords dialog box displays, click the Save Now button. When Word displays the Save Version dialog box, type** `Contains comments and tracked changes from Carlos.` **Point to the OK button.**

Word displays the Versions in Passwords dialog box, followed by the Save Version dialog box (Figure 7-11).

Click the OK button.

Word saves the current state of the document along with the entered comment.

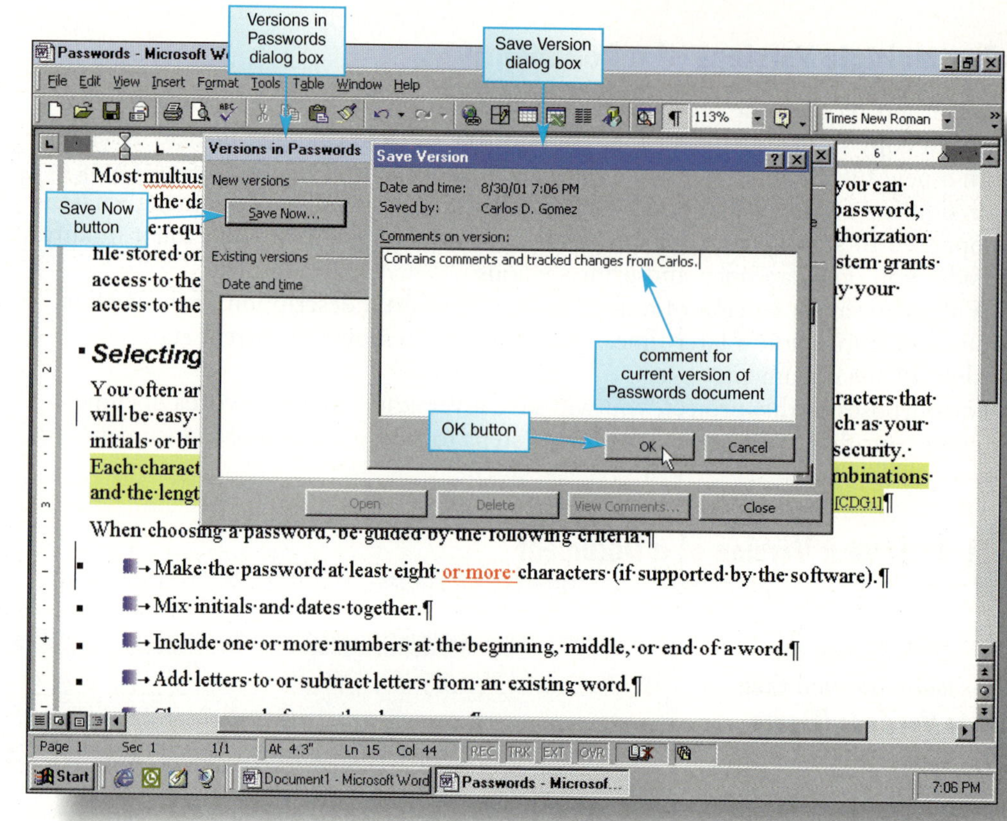

FIGURE 7-11

1. Click Save Version button on Reviewing toolbar

To open a previous version of a document, click File on the menu bar, click Versions, click the version you wish to open in the Existing versions list, and then click the Open button in the dialog box. If, for some reason, you wanted to edit a previous version of a document, you would open it and then save it with a new file name.

Displaying Comments

If a comment's text does not display in a ScreenTip when you point to the comment reference mark or if the comment is not highlighted in yellow, click Tools on the menu bar, click Options, click the View tab, place a check mark in the ScreenTips check box, and then click the OK button.

Reviewing Comments

Next, Jeff would like to read the comments from Carlos. You could scroll through the document and point to each comment reference mark to read the comments, but you might overlook one or more comments using this technique. A more efficient method is to use the Reviewing toolbar as shown in the following steps.

Steps To Review Comments

1 If the Reviewing toolbar does not display on your screen, click View on the menu bar, point to Toolbars, and then click Reviewing. Press CTRL+HOME to position the insertion point at the top of the document. Point to the Next Comment button on the Reviewing toolbar.

With the insertion point at the top of the document, the review of comments will begin at the top of the document (Figure 7-12).

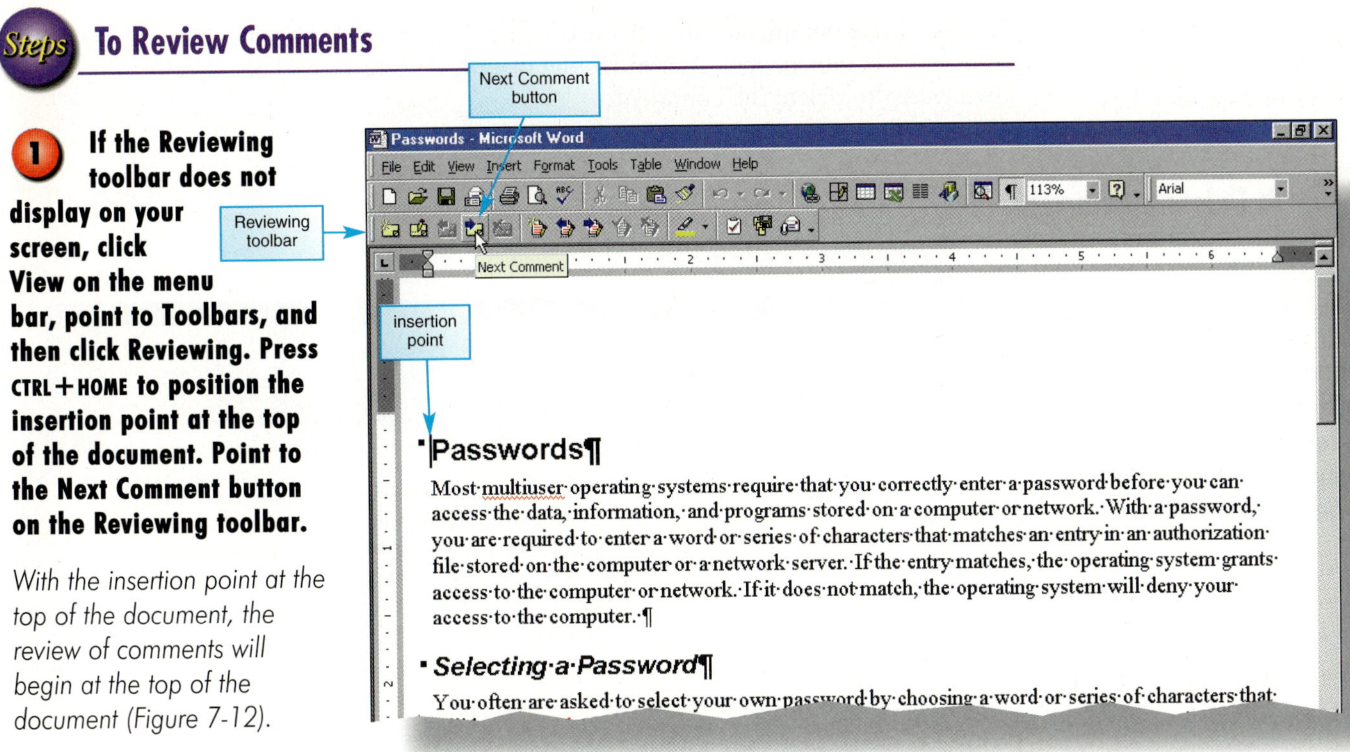

FIGURE 7-12

2 Click the Next Comment button. Point to the comment reference mark.

Word displays the first comment as a ScreenTip (Figure 7-13).

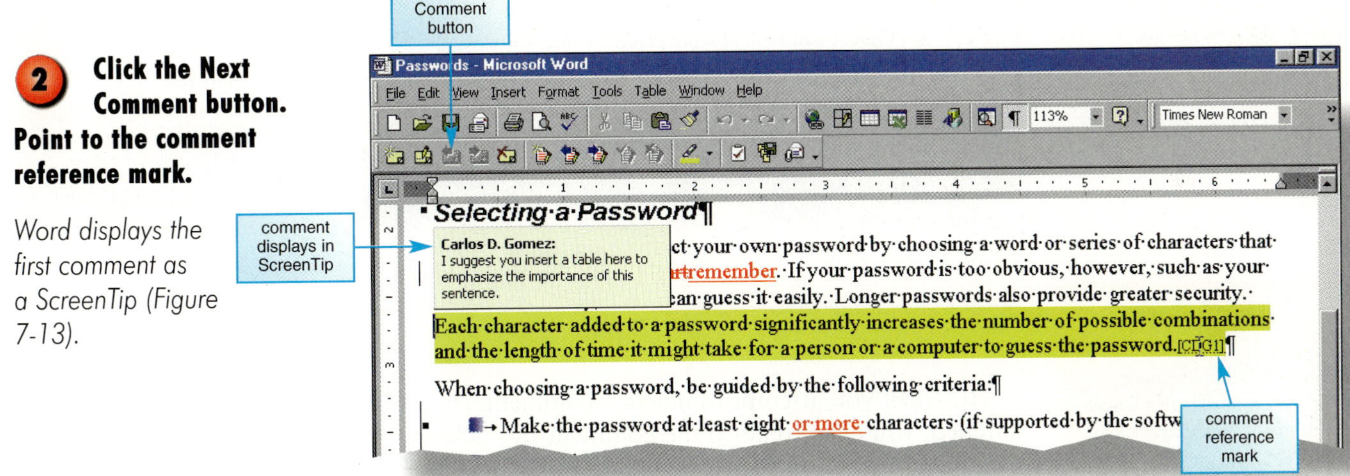

FIGURE 7-13

Other Ways

1. Scroll through document and point to comment reference mark
2. On Select Browse Object menu, click Comments
3. On File menu click Print, click Print what box arrow, click Comments, click OK button

If the document contains multiple comments, you would click the Next Comment button on the Reviewing toolbar to display each subsequent comment. You also can click the Previous Comment button to display a comment earlier in the document.

Deleting Comments

After you have finished reviewing a comment, you can remove it from the document. When you delete a comment, Word automatically renumbers all remaining comments.

You delete comments from the document window, not from the comment pane. To delete a comment, you first move the insertion point to it. Then, perform the following step to delete the comment.

Steps To Delete a Comment

1 **With the insertion point at the beginning of the yellow highlight of the comment to delete, click the Delete Comment button on the Reviewing toolbar.**

Word removes the comment from the document (Figure 7-14).

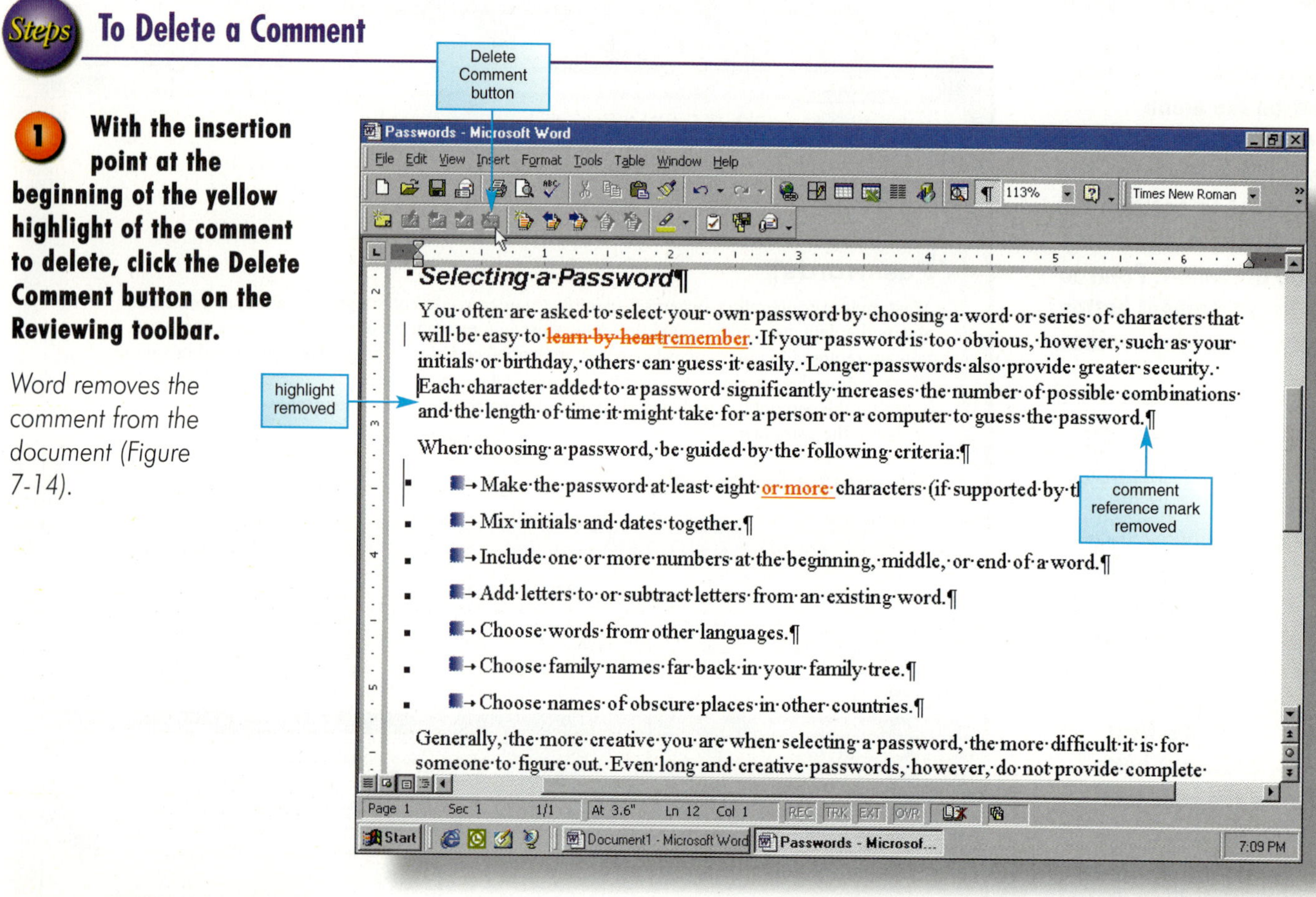

FIGURE 7-14

Other Ways

1. Right-click the comment reference mark, click Delete Comment on shortcut menu

If, when you attempt to delete a comment, the Delete Comment button is dimmed, you need to go to the comment by clicking the Next Comment or Previous Comment button on the Reviewing toolbar.

Reviewing Tracked Changes

The next step for Jeff is to review the changes made by Carlos and decide if he wants to accept or reject them. To do this, be sure the revision marks display on the screen. If they do not, right-click the TRK status indicator on the status bar, click Highlight Changes on the shortcut menu, be sure the Highlight changes on screen check box contains a check mark, and then click the OK button. With the revision marks displaying on the screen, perform the following steps to review the tracked changes.

To Review Tracked Changes

1 Press CTRL+HOME. Right-click the TRK status indicator on the status bar. Point to Accept or Reject Changes.

Word displays a tracking changes shortcut menu (Figure 7-15).

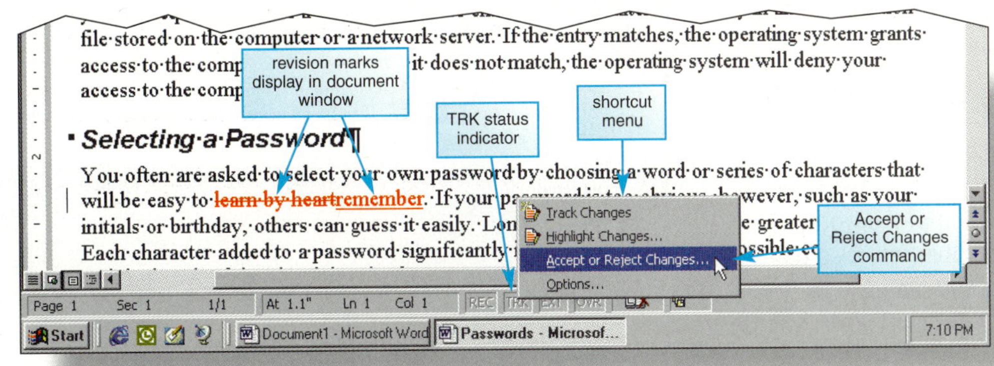

FIGURE 7-15

2 Click Accept or Reject Changes. When the Accept or Reject Changes dialog box displays, be sure Changes with highlighting is selected in the View area and then point to the Find Next button.

Word displays the Accept or Reject Changes dialog box (Figure 7-16). The Changes with highlighting option ensures that tracked changes display on the screen for your review.

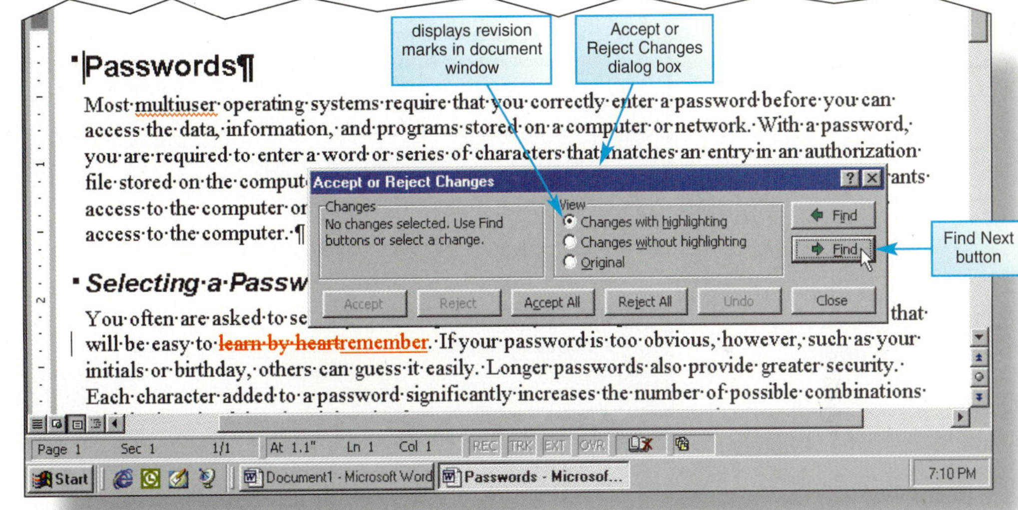

FIGURE 7-16

3 Click the Find Next button. Point to the Accept button.

Word highlights the first change in the document, which is the deletion of the phrase, learn by heart (Figure 7-17). If you look to the right of this change, you see the insertion of the word, remember. Thus, the reviewer suggests you replace the phrase, learn by heart, with the word, remember. You agree with this change and, therefore, wish to accept it.

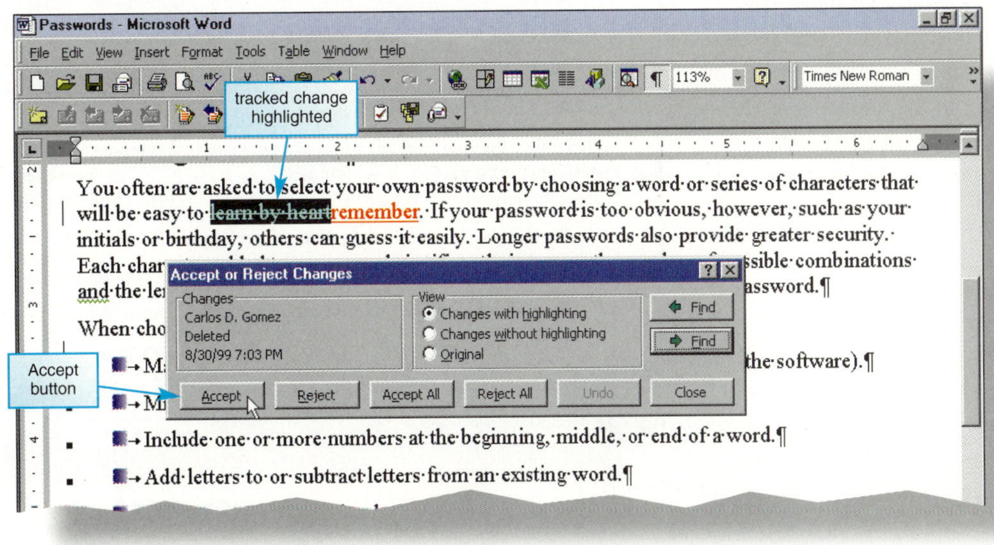

FIGURE 7-17

Click the Accept button.

Word accepts the tracked change by removing the phrase, learn by heart, from the document (Figure 7-18). The next tracked change is highlighted, which is the insertion of the word, remember. You also agree with this change.

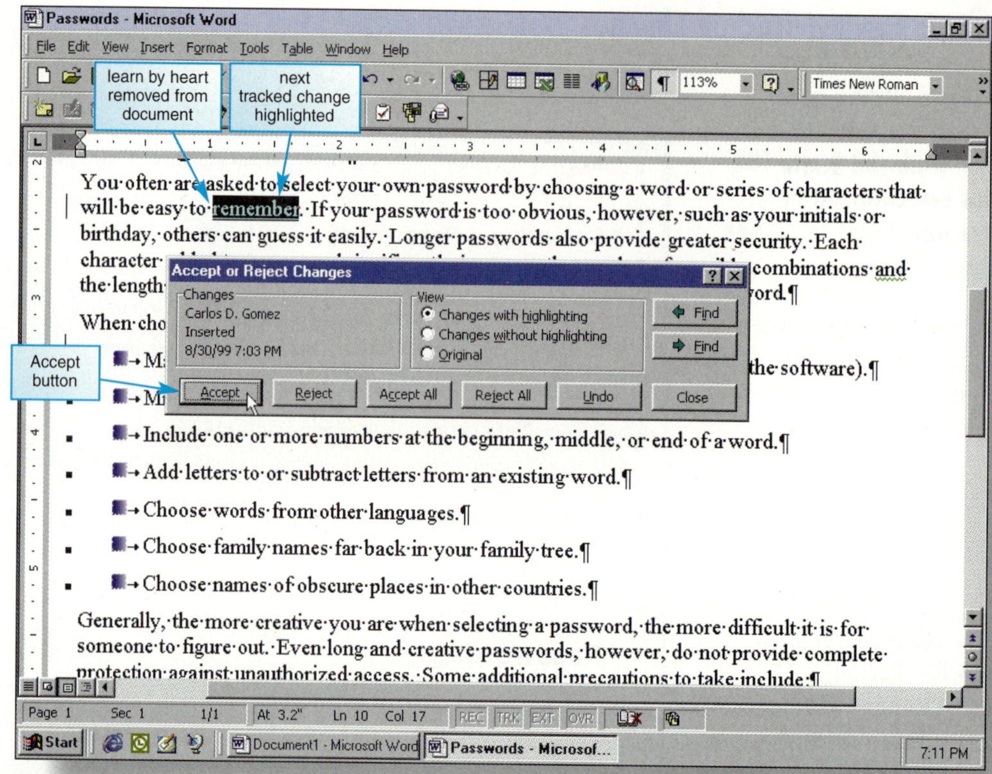

FIGURE 7-18

Click the Accept button again.

Word inserts the word, remember, into the document and removes its revision marks (Figure 7-19). The next tracked change is highlighted, which is the insertion of the words, or more. You feel this change is not necessary because of the words, at least, in the same sentence. Thus, you disagree with this change and will reject it.

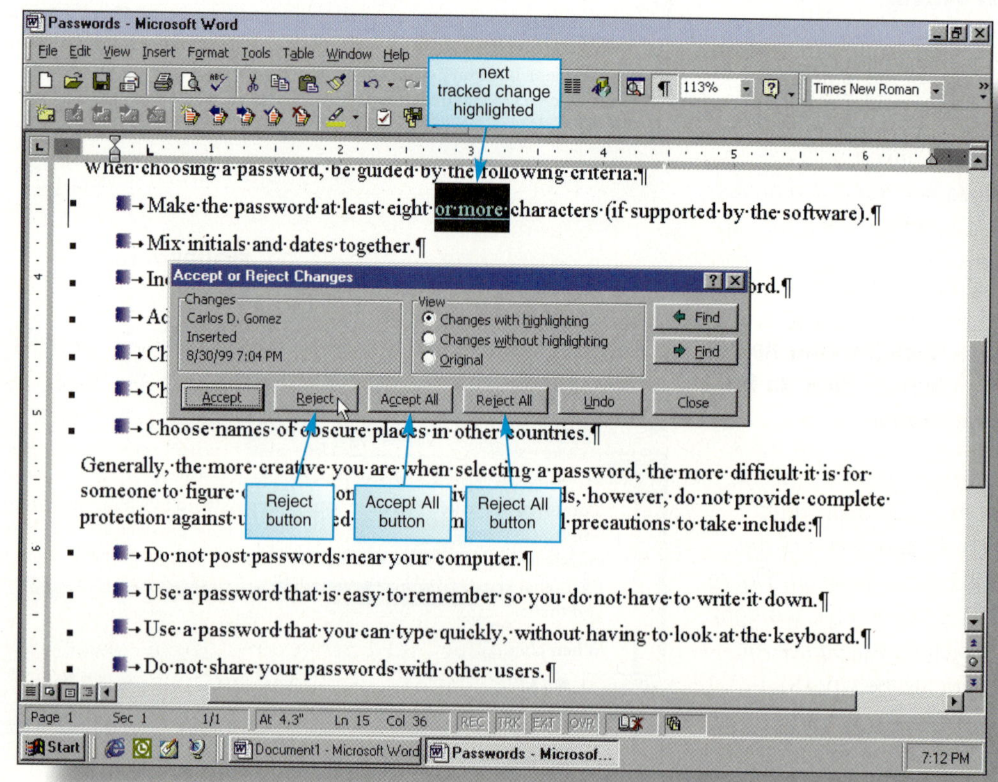

FIGURE 7-19

6 **Click the Reject button. If Word displays a dialog box asking if you wish to search from the beginning of the document, click the OK button.**

Word rejects the tracked change and does not insert the words, or more, into the document (Figure 7-20). Because this is the last tracked change in the document, Word displays a dialog box indicating no tracked changes remain.

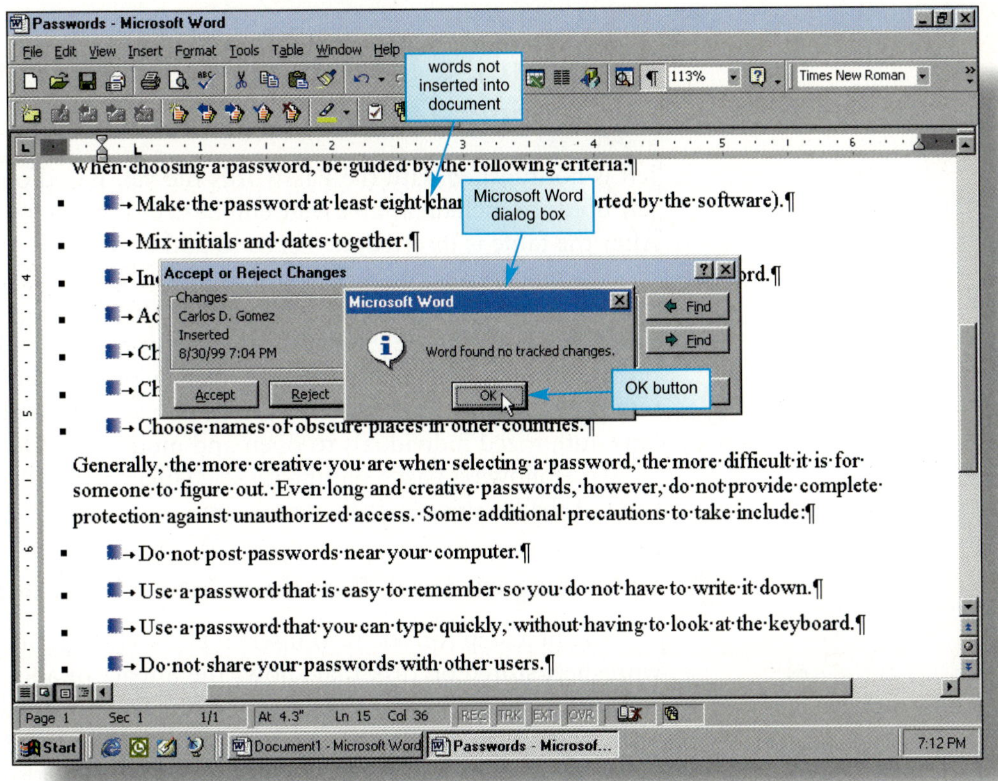

FIGURE 7-20

7 **Click the OK button. Click the Close button in the Accept or Reject Changes dialog box. Click View on the menu bar, point to Toolbars, and then click Reviewing.**

Word removes the Accept or Reject Changes dialog box and the Reviewing toolbar from the screen.

Other Ways

1. Click Next Change button on Reviewing toolbar, click Accept Change button on Reviewing toolbar to accept change or click Reject Change button on Reviewing toolbar to reject change

If you are certain you plan to accept all changes in a document containing tracked changes, you can accept all the changes at once by clicking the Accept All button in the Accept or Reject Changes dialog box (see Figure 7-19). Likewise, you can click the Reject All button in the Accept or Reject Changes dialog box to reject all the changes at once. If you click either of these buttons by mistake, you can click the Undo button on the Standard toolbar to undo the action.

You can see how a document will look if you accept all the changes, without actually accepting them, by right-clicking the TRK status indicator on the status bar, clicking Highlight Changes, removing the check mark from the Highlight changes on screen check box, and then clicking the OK button. If you want a hard copy that shows how the document will look if you accept all the changes, right-click the TRK status indicator on the status bar, click Highlight Changes, remove the check mark from the Highlight changes in printed document check box and then print the document.

Preparing a Document to be Included in a Longer Document

Jeff is not finished with the Passwords file yet. Based on the comment from Carlos, Jeff needs to include a table that emphasizes how longer passwords are more secure. After the table is inserted, he needs to add a figure caption to the table – because the EIG documents always have figure captions. Then, he will modify the text so that it references the figure. The last page of the EIG documents is an index, so Jeff will mark any words in the Passwords document that should appear in the index. As a precaution, Jeff will ensure that the items within the bulleted lists do not split across two pages. Finally, Jeff will save the document with a password, which will allow only authorized individuals to open and modify the file in the future.

The following pages outline these changes to the Passwords document. The final copy of the Passwords document is shown in Figure 7-2b on page WD 7.8.

Embedding an Excel Worksheet into a Word Document

The first step for Jeff is to insert a table as suggested by Carlos. Jeff has an Excel worksheet stored on disk that shows the impact of adding more characters to a password (see Figure 7-2b). Jeff will embed the Excel worksheet on disk into the Word document.

When you **embed** an object, such as an Excel worksheet, the object becomes part of the destination file, which is the Passwords document in this case. That is, if the contents of the object (the Excel worksheet) change, the change will not be reflected in the embedded object. If you want to change the contents of the object, you double-click it to open the application in which the object was created (Excel, in this case). Any changes you make to the source file (the Excel worksheet) in the source application (Excel) will be reflected in the destination document (the Passwords file).

By contrast, when you **link** an object and the contents of this object changes, the change is reflected automatically in the destination file. With a linked object, the destination file stores a link, or connection, to the location of the source file. Because you want to send only a single file to the personnel department for inclusion in the EIG #22 document, you will embed the Excel worksheet instead of link it.

For purposes of this project, the Excel worksheet named Passwords Table is located on the Data Disk. If you did not download the Data Disk, see the inside back cover for instructions for downloading the Data Disk or see your instructor.

Perform the following steps to embed the Passwords Table (source file) into the Passwords file (destination file).

More About 2000

Microsoft Excel 2000

For more information on features of Excel documents, visit the Word 2000 More About Web page (www.scsite.com/wd2000/more.htm) and then click Microsoft Excel 2000.

More About 2000

Embedded Objects

If you wanted to edit the embedded object (the Excel worksheet) from the destination document (the Word document), you would double-click the embedded object. This starts the source application (Excel) and displays the source file (the Excel worksheet) in the source application (Excel). When you quit the source application (Excel), any modifications made to the source document (the Excel worksheet) are reflected in the destination document (the Word file).

To Embed an Object

1 **Position the insertion point at the end of the last sentence in the first paragraph below the Selecting a Password heading. Click Insert on the menu bar and then point to Object (Figure 7-21).**

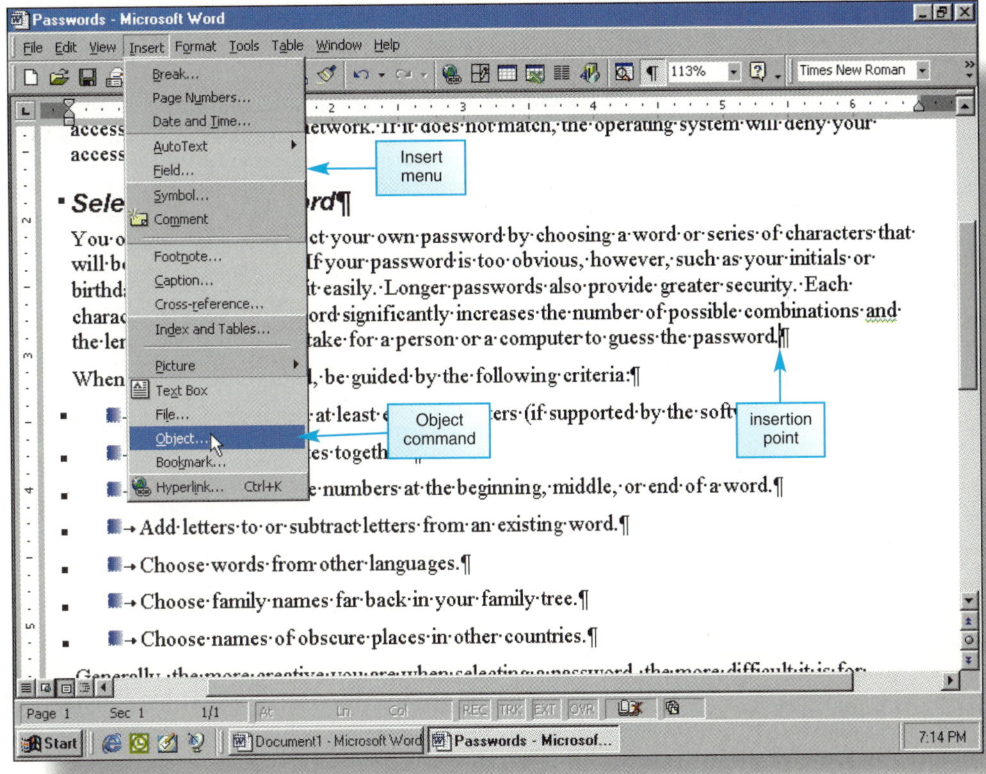

FIGURE 7-21

2 **Click Object. When the Object dialog box displays, if necessary, click the Create from File tab. With the Data Disk in drive A, click the Browse button. When the Browse dialog box displays, locate the Passwords Table file on the Data Disk. Click Passwords Table in the list and then click the Insert button in the Browse dialog box. When the Object dialog box is visible again, point to the OK button.**

Word displays the Object dialog box (Figure 7-22). The xls following the file name, Passwords Table, identifies the file as an Excel worksheet.

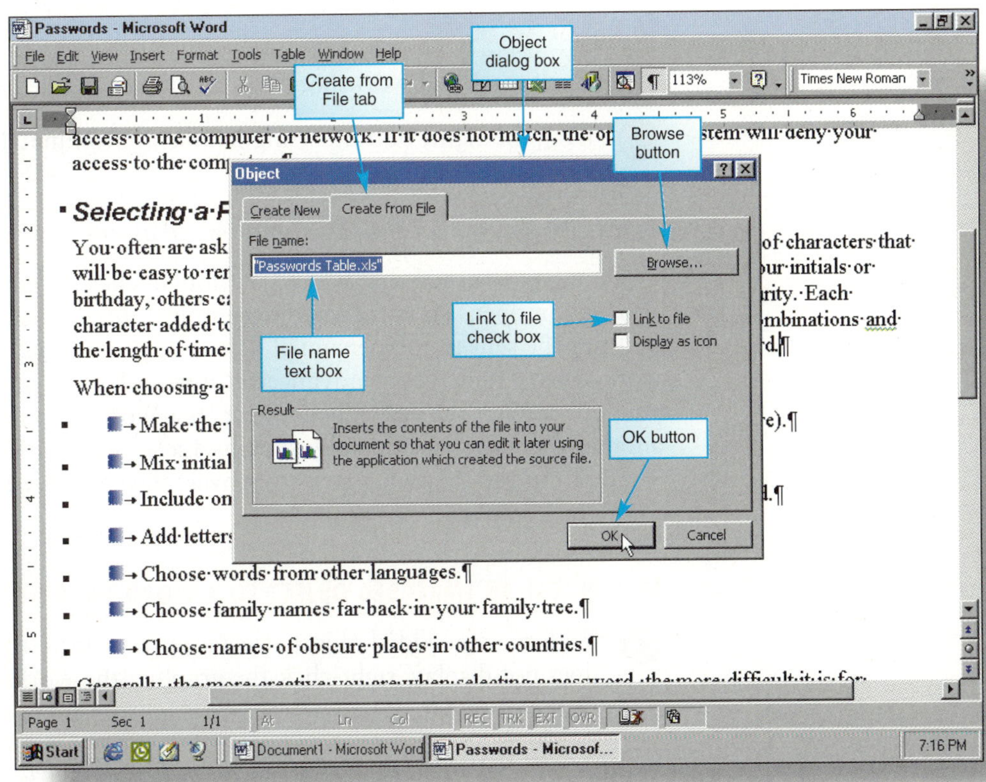

FIGURE 7-22

Click the OK button.

Word inserts the Excel worksheet as an embedded object (Figure 7-23).

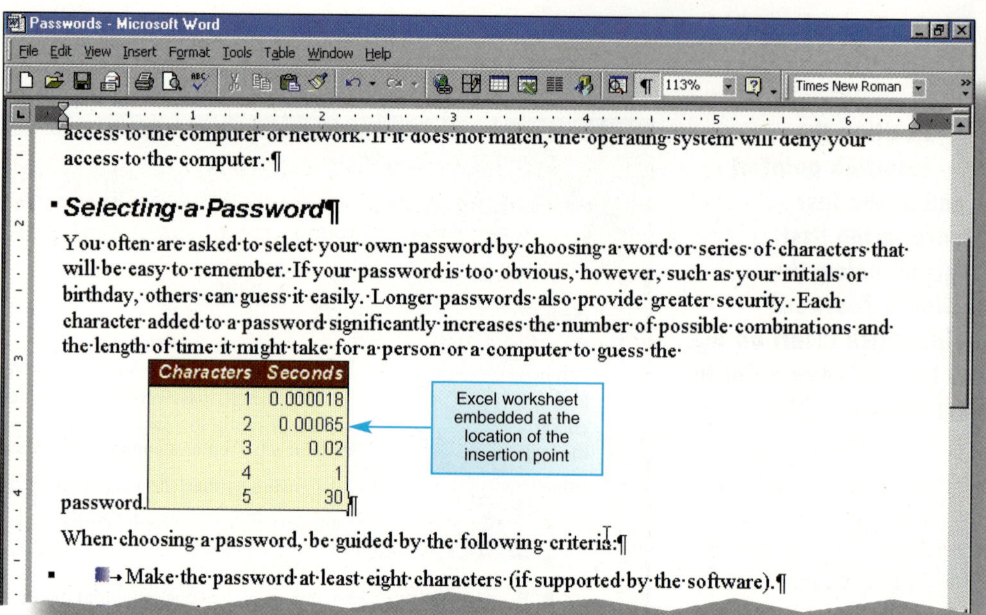

FIGURE 7-23

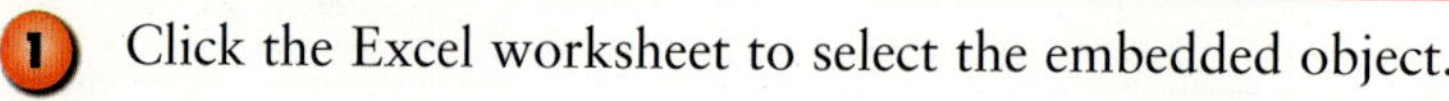

Other Ways

1. Copy object in source application to Office Clipboard; in destination application, on Edit menu click Paste Special, click Paste, click Formatted Text (RTF), click OK button

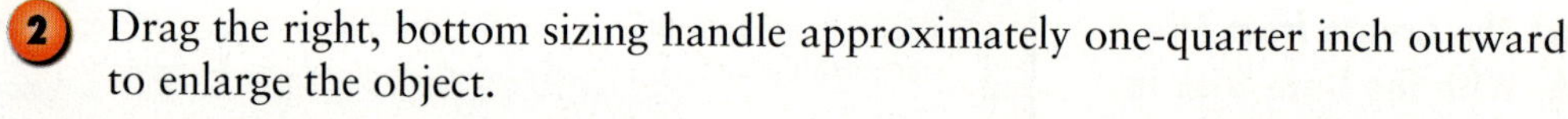

If you wanted to link the Excel worksheet instead of embed it, you would place a check mark in the Link to file check box in the Object dialog box (see Figure 7-22 on the previous page).

You want the Excel worksheet to be slightly larger in the document. Thus, perform the following steps to resize the object.

TO RESIZE AN OBJECT

1. Click the Excel worksheet to select the embedded object.
2. Drag the right, bottom sizing handle approximately one-quarter inch outward to enlarge the object.

Word enlarges the worksheet about one-quarter inch (see Figure 7-24).

You have learned that when you double-click an embedded object, the source application opens so you can edit the object. Because this document (the Passwords file) is to be sent to the personnel department and users in this department have not worked with some of the advanced features of Word and are unfamiliar with Excel, you will convert the embedded object to a Word graphic. Doing so will prevent another user from accidentally starting Excel while in Word.

Perform the following step to convert the embedded object (the Excel worksheet) to a Word graphic.

TO CONVERT AN EMBEDDED OBJECT TO A WORD GRAPHIC

1. With the embedded object selected, press CTRL+SHIFT+F9. If the Picture toolbar does not display, right-click the graphic (the worksheet) and then click Show Picture Toolbar.

Word converts the Excel worksheet from an embedded object to a Word graphic and displays the Picture toolbar (see Figure 7-24).

The worksheet no longer is an embedded object – it is a Word graphic. Thus, you cannot double-click it to edit it in Excel.

Notice in Figure 7-23 that the worksheet is inline; that is, the worksheet is part of the current paragraph. You want to position the worksheet to the right of the paragraph and have the text wrap to the left of the worksheet. Thus, the graphic needs to be a floating graphic instead of an inline graphic. To do this, you change the graphic's wrapping style to Square as shown in the following steps.

To Change an Inline Graphic to a Floating Graphic

1 With the graphic still selected, click the Text Wrapping button on the Picture toolbar and then point to Square (Figure 7-24).

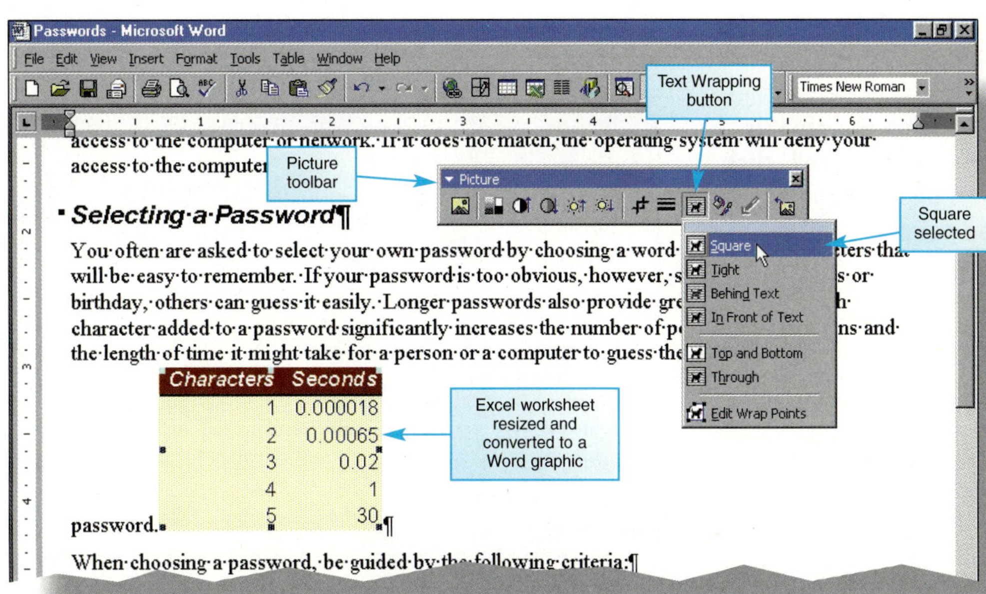

FIGURE 7-24

2 Click Square. If necessary, scroll down to display the graphic and then drag the graphic to the right of the paragraph as shown in Figure 7-25.

Word converts the graphic from inline to floating so you can position it anywhere on the page.

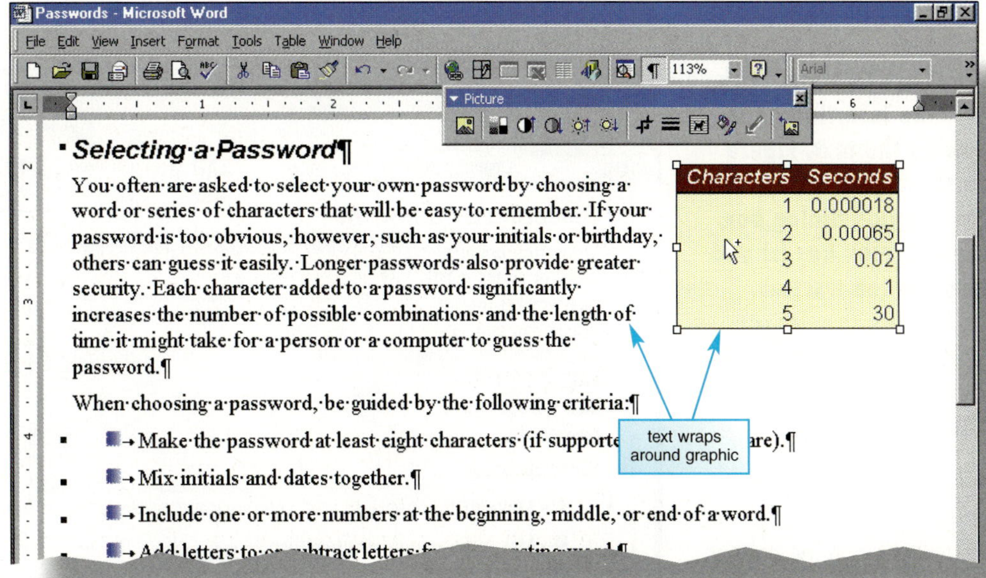

FIGURE 7-25

The next step is to add a caption to the graphic.

Adding a Caption

At the end of the EIG documents is a table of figures, which lists all figures and their corresponding page numbers. Word generates this table of figures from the captions in the document. A **caption** is a label with a number that you can add to a graphic, table, or other object. If you move, delete, or add captions in a document, Word renumbers remaining captions in the document automatically.

Perform the following steps to add a caption to the graphic.

To Add a Caption

1 With the graphic still selected, click Insert on the menu bar and then point to Caption (Figure 7-26).

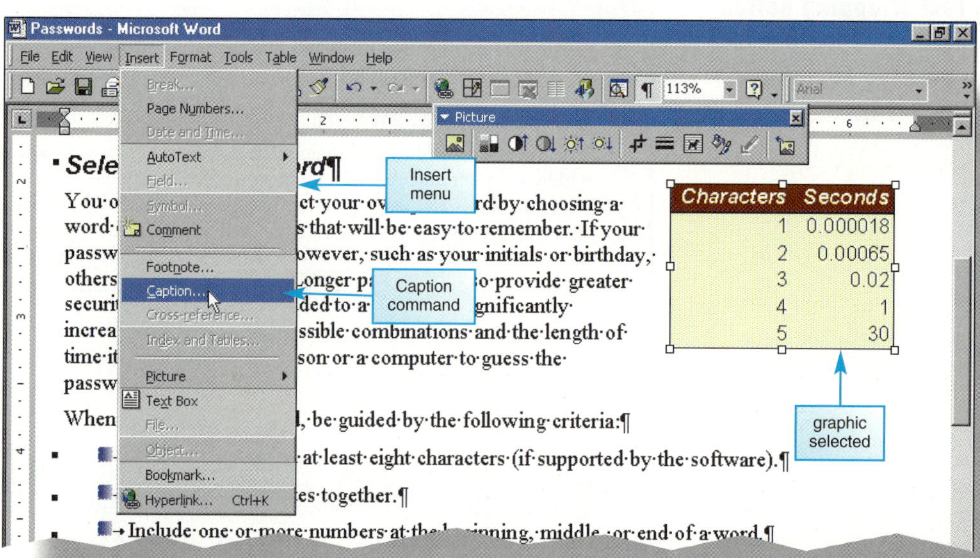

FIGURE 7-26

2 Click Caption. With the insertion point following the text, Figure 1, in the Caption text box of the Caption dialog box, press the COLON key (:) and then press the SPACEBAR. Type `Speeds at Which a Computer Discovers Passwords` **and then point to the OK button.**

Word displays the Caption dialog box (Figure 7-27). Word will position the caption for this figure below the graphic.

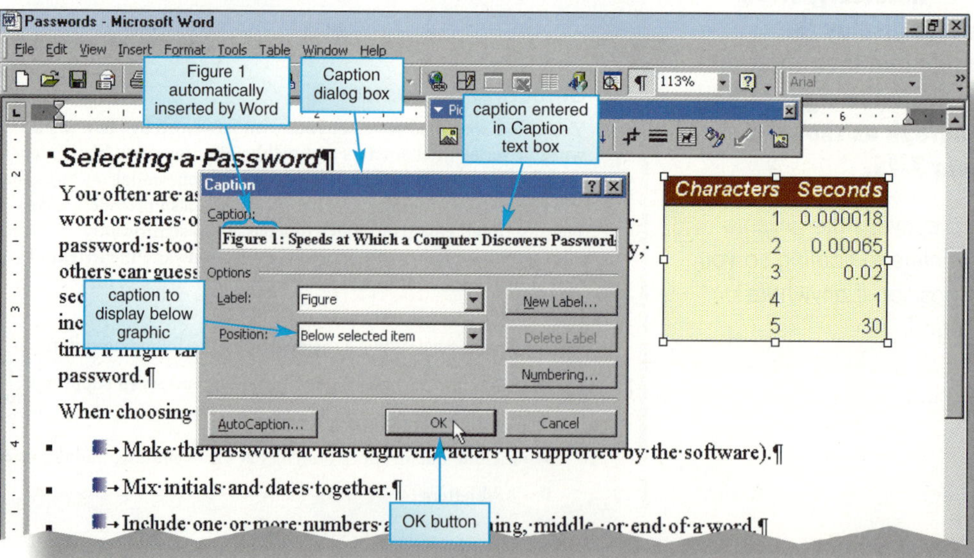

FIGURE 7-27

3 Click the OK button.

Word inserts the caption in a text box below the selected graphic (Figure 7-28). In a later step, you will resize the caption so that all of its text displays on two lines.

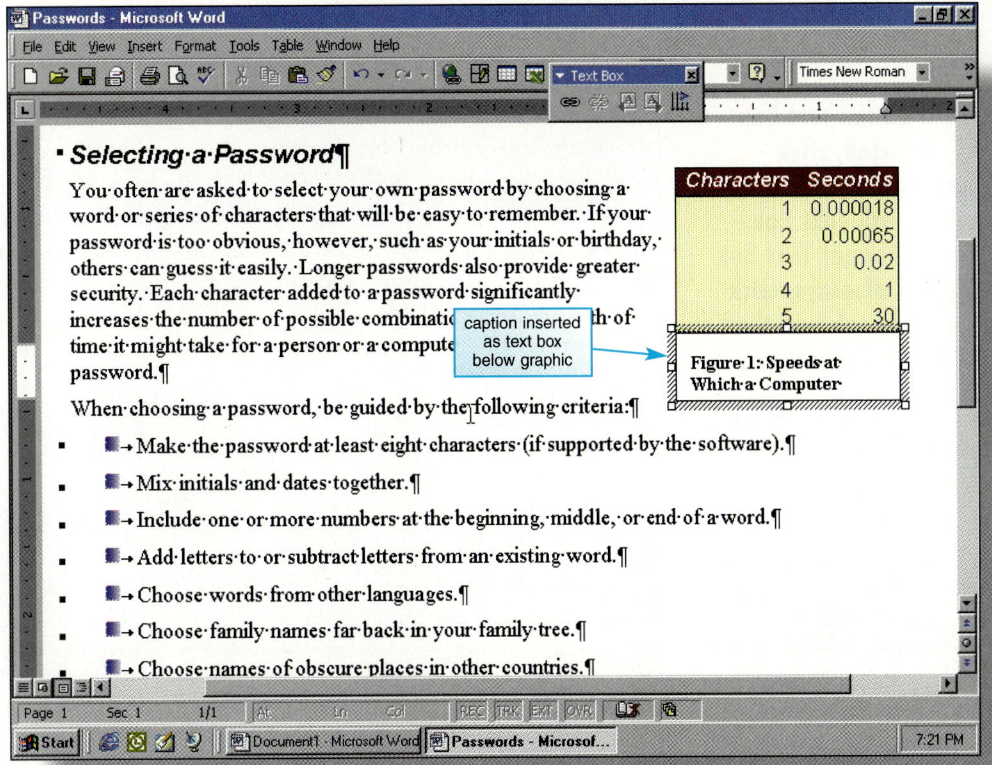

FIGURE 7-28

If, at a later time, you insert a new item with a caption or move or delete items containing captions, Word automatically updates caption numbers throughout the document. For example, this caption currently has a figure number of 1. When you insert this document into the EIG #22 document, it actually will be figure number 4. Word automatically will renumber it after you insert this document into the EIG #22 document.

A caption contains a field. In Word, a **field** is a placeholder for data that you expect might change in a document. Examples of fields you have used in previous projects are page numbers, merge fields, IF fields, Fill-in fields, and the current date.

Because the caption number is a field, you update it using the same technique used to update a field. That is, to update all caption numbers, select the entire document and then press F9 or right-click the selection and then click Update Field. When you print a document, Word updates the caption numbers automatically, whether or not the document window displays the updated caption numbers.

When you add a caption to an inline graphic, the caption is not inserted in a text box. As just illustrated, however, the caption for a floating graphic is inserted in a text box. If you plan to generate a table of figures for a document, a caption cannot be in a text box. Instead, it has to be in a frame. Perform the steps on the next page to convert the text box to a frame.

Captions

If your caption displays with extra characters inside curly braces {}, then Word is displaying field codes instead of field results. Press ALT+F9 to display the caption correctly as field results. If your caption prints field codes, click Tools on the menu bar, click Options, click the Print tab, remove the check mark from the Field codes check box, click the OK button, and then print the document again.

To Convert a Text Box to a Frame

1 **With the text box selected, click Format on the menu bar, and then click Text Box. When the Format Text Box dialog box displays, click the Text Box tab and then point to the Convert to Frame button.**

Word displays the Format Text Box dialog box (Figure 7-29).

2 **Click the Convert to Frame button. When Word displays a dialog box indicating some formatting of the frame may be lost, click the OK button. If Word displays a dialog box asking if you want a Frame command on the Insert menu, click the Cancel button.**

Word converts the text box to a frame. You did not format the text box; thus, you will not lose any formatting in the conversion from a text box to the frame.

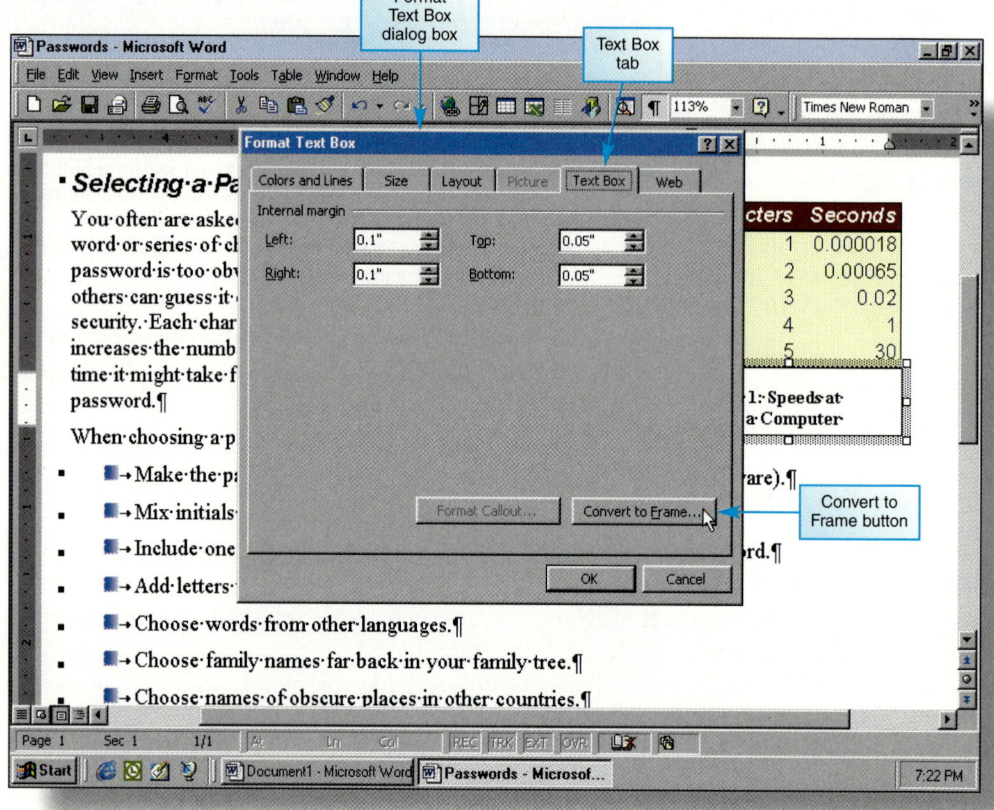

FIGURE 7-29

Notice in Figure 7-28 on the previous page that the caption has a border around it. This is because Word automatically placed a border around the caption when it was a text box. You do not want the border around the caption. You also want to center and resize the caption. Perform the following steps to modify the caption.

TO MODIFY THE CAPTION

1. Double-click the move handle on the Formatting toolbar to display the entire toolbar. With the caption frame selected, click the Border button arrow and then click No Border.
2. If necessary, drag the middle, right sizing handle until the text of the caption displays in the frame as two lines.
3. Click in the caption text and then click the Center button on the Formatting toolbar.

4 If necessary, drag the text box to center the caption below the graphic. Do not drag in the middle of the text box; you must drag the text box rectangle to move the text box.

The caption displays as shown in Figure 7-30.

The next step is to refer to the new figure in the document text.

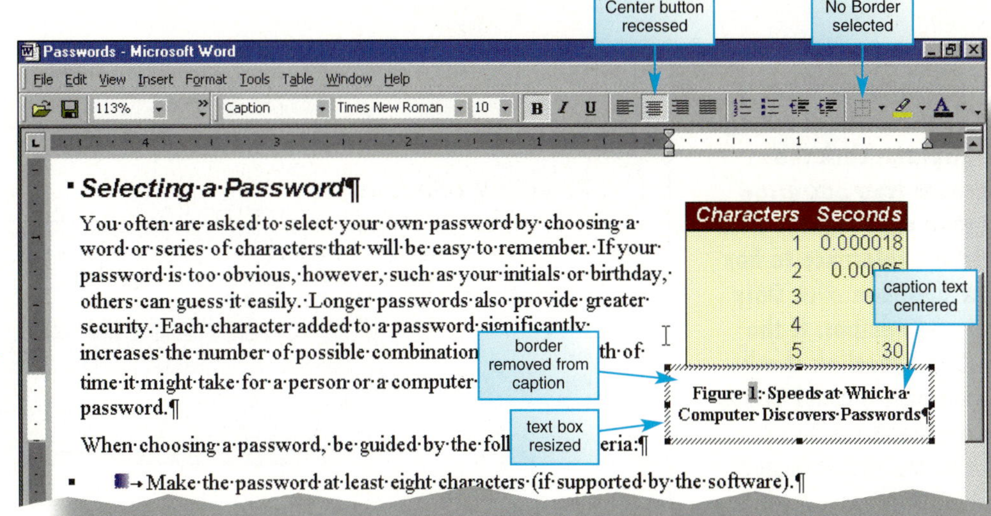

FIGURE 7-30

Creating a Cross-Reference

In the EIG documents, the text always makes reference to any figure and explains the contents of the figure. Thus, you want to enter a phrase into the document that refers to the figure. Recall that the Passwords file will be inserted into a larger file. You do not know what the figure number of the graphic will be in the new document. In Word, you can create a **cross-reference**, which is a link to an item such as a heading, caption, or footnote in a document. By creating a cross-reference to the caption, the text that mentions the figure will update whenever the caption to the figure updates.

Perform the following steps to create a cross-reference.

To Create a Cross-Reference

1 **Position the insertion point in front of the sentence beginning with the text, Longer passwords also provide. Type** `As shown in` **and then press the SPACEBAR. Click Insert on the menu bar and then point to Cross-reference (Figure 7-31).**

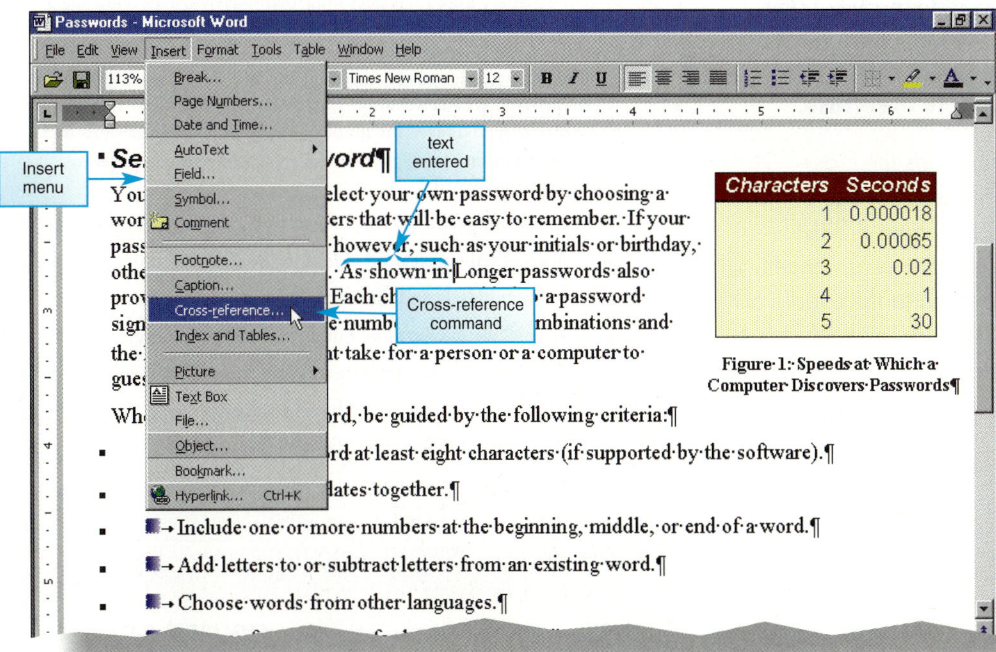

FIGURE 7-31

2 Click Cross-reference. When the Cross-reference dialog box displays, click the Reference type box arrow and then click Figure. Click the Insert reference to box arrow and then click Only label and number. If the Insert as hyperlink check box contains a check mark, remove the check mark. Point to the Insert button.

Word displays the Cross-reference dialog box (Figure 7-32). You want the text to display only the label (the word, Figure) and the label number (the figure number).

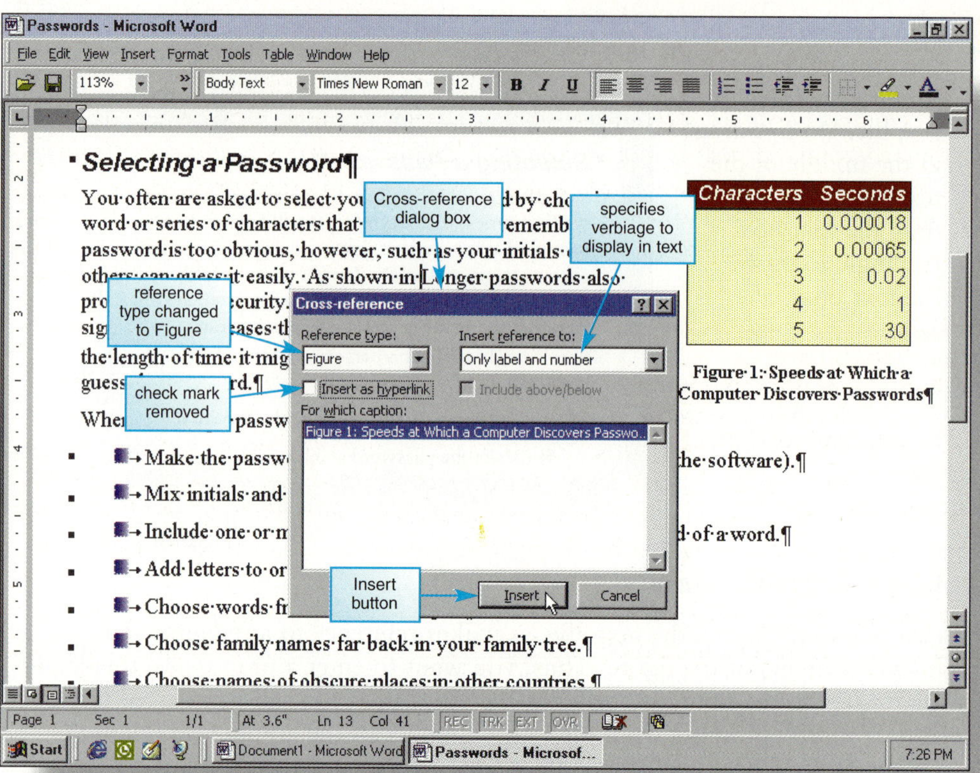

FIGURE 7-32

3 Click the Insert button. Click the Close button in the Cross-reference dialog box. Press the COMMA key (,) and then press the SPACEBAR. Press the SHIFT+F3 keys twice to change the entire word, longer, to lowercase.

Word inserts the cross-reference to the figure into the text (Figure 7-33). Because the word, longer, has moved to the middle of the sentence, it should not be capitalized.

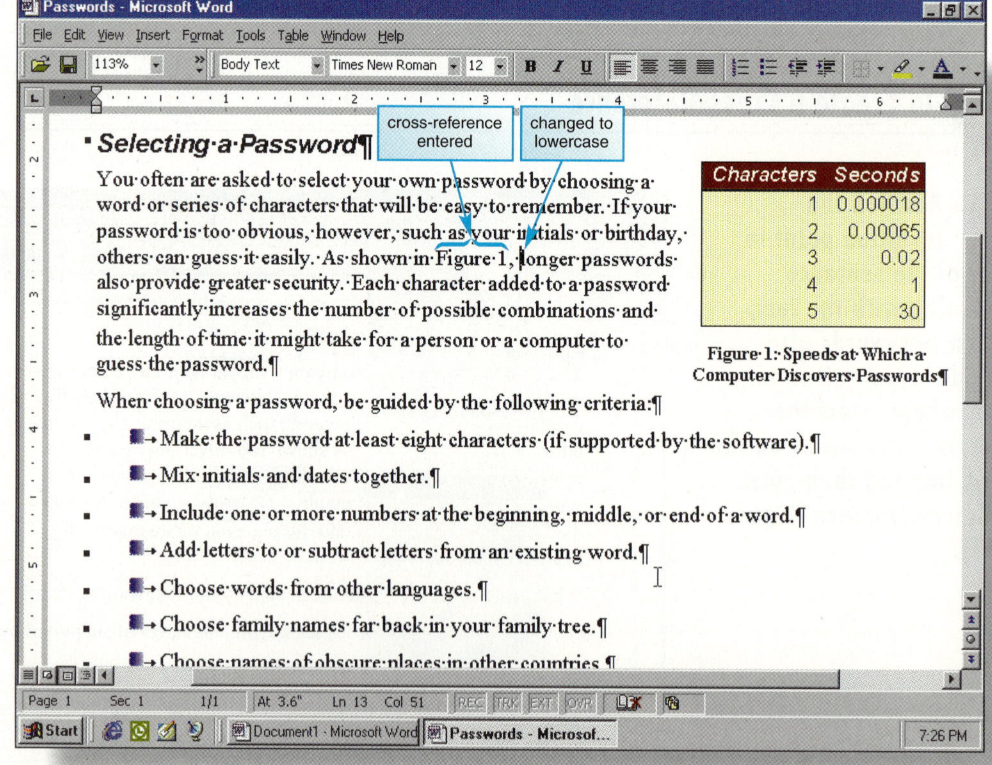

FIGURE 7-33

Each time you press the SHIFT+F3 keys, Word changes the case of the selected text or of the word containing the insertion point. That is, it cycles from initial caps (capitalizing the first letter of each word) to all uppercase to all lowercase.

Like caption numbers, a cross-reference is a field. In many cases, Word automatically updates cross-references in a document if the item it refers to changes. To manually update a cross-reference, select the cross-reference and then press F9, or right-click the selection and then click Update Field.

The next step is to mark any index entries in this document.

Cross-References

If your cross-reference displays odd characters inside curly braces {}, then Word is displaying field codes instead of field results. Press ALT+F9 to display the cross-reference correctly. If your cross-reference prints field codes, click Tools on the menu bar, click Options, click the Print tab, remove the check mark from the Field codes check box, click the OK button, and then print the document again.

Marking Index Entries

At the end of the EIG documents is an index, which lists important terms discussed in the document along with each term's corresponding page number. For Word to generate the index, you first must mark any item you wish to appear in the index. When you mark an index entry, Word creates a field that is used to build the index. The fields are hidden and display on the screen only when you are displaying formatting marks; that is, when the Show/Hide ¶ button on the Standard toolbar is recessed.

In this document, you want the word, password, in the first sentence below the Selecting a Password heading to be marked as an index entry. To alert the reader that this term is in the index, you also bold it in the document. Perform the following steps to mark this index entry.

To Mark an Index Entry

1 Select the text you wish to appear in the index (the word, password, in this case). Press ALT+SHIFT+X.

Word displays the Mark Index Entry dialog box (Figure 7-34).

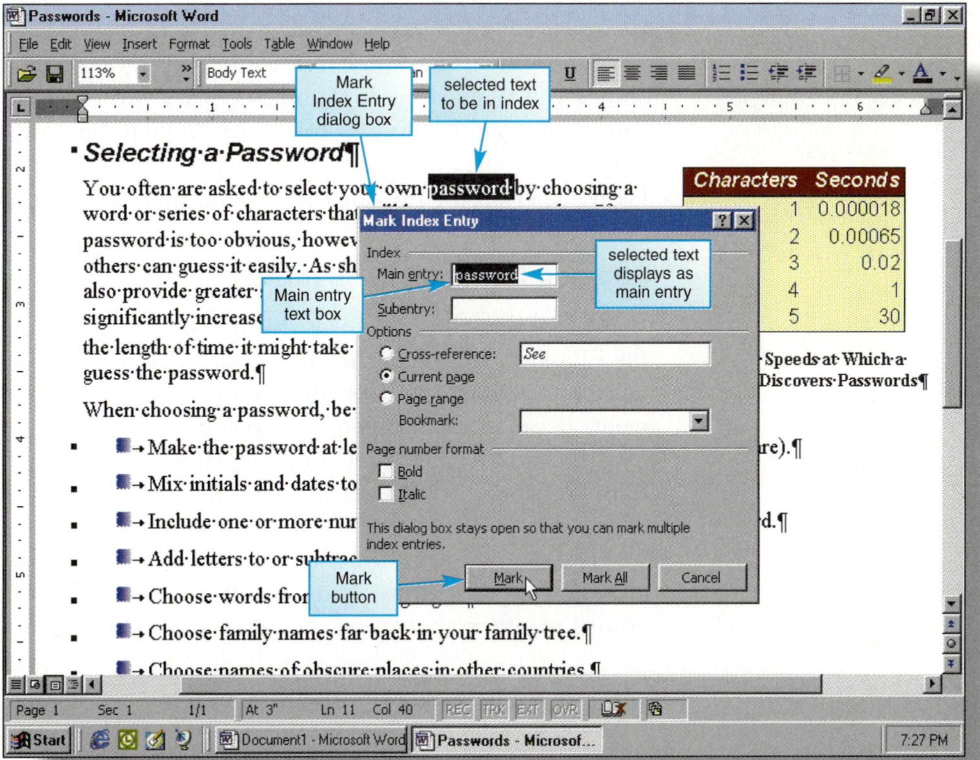

FIGURE 7-34

2 **Click the Mark button. Click the Close button in the Mark Index Entry dialog box. Select the word, password, in front of the left brace and then bold it.**

Word inserts an index entry field into the document (Figure 7-35). These fields display on the screen only when the Show/Hide ¶ button on the Standard toolbar is recessed.

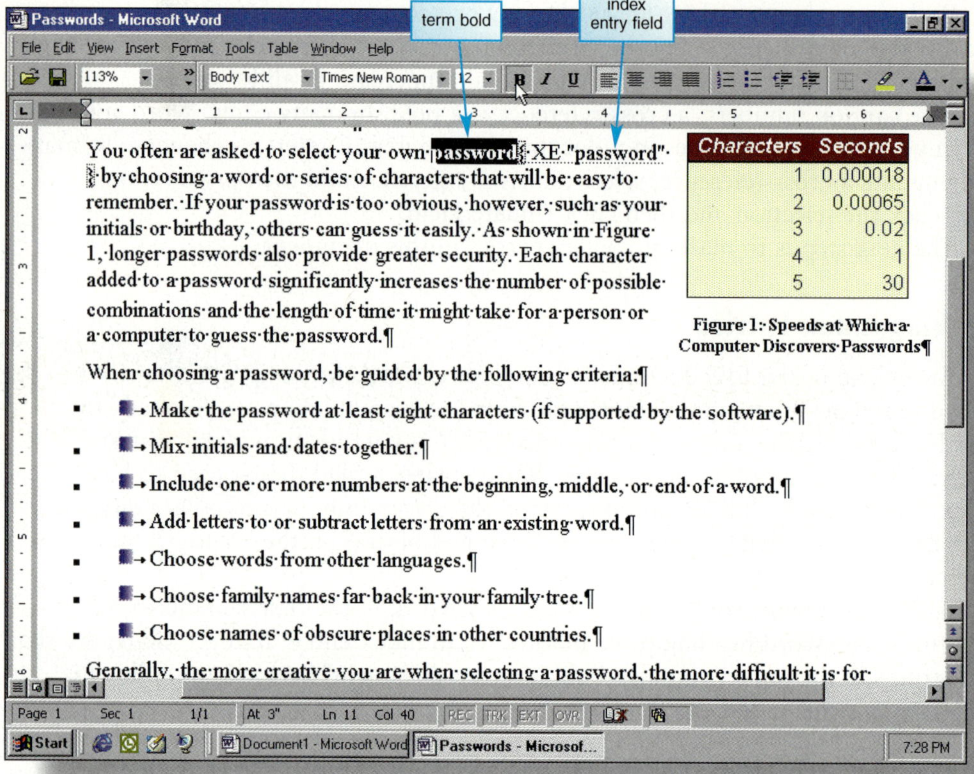

FIGURE 7-35

Other Ways

1. Select text, on Insert menu click Index and Tables, click Index tab, click Mark Entry button, click Mark button, click Close button

Word leaves the Mark Index Entry dialog box open until you close it, which allows you to mark multiple index entries without having to reopen the dialog box continually. To do this, click in the document window, scroll to and select the next index entry, click the Main entry text box in the Mark Index Entry dialog box (see Figure 7-34 on the previous page), and then click the Mark button.

Keeping Paragraphs Together

Recall that the Passwords document will be incorporated into a larger document, the EIG #22. Although the Passwords document fits on a single page now, Jeff is unsure as to how the Passwords document will be inserted into the EIG #22 document. Because it is not good practice to print part of a bulleted list at the bottom of one page and print the remaining portion of the same bulleted list at the top of the following page, Jeff will ensure that the items within the bulleted lists do not split across two pages.

The paragraph before the bulleted list and the items within the bulleted list are all separate paragraphs. Thus, you must instruct Word to print all of these paragraphs together; that is, on the same page, as shown in the following steps.

Steps To Keep Paragraphs Together

1 **Select the paragraphs to keep together (the paragraph before the bulleted list and the bulleted list). Right-click the selection and then click Paragraph on the shortcut menu. When the Paragraph dialog box displays, click the Line and Page Breaks tab and then make sure the Keep lines together check box contains a check mark. Point to the OK button.**

Word displays the Paragraph dialog box (Figure 7-36). A check mark displays in the Keep lines together check box.

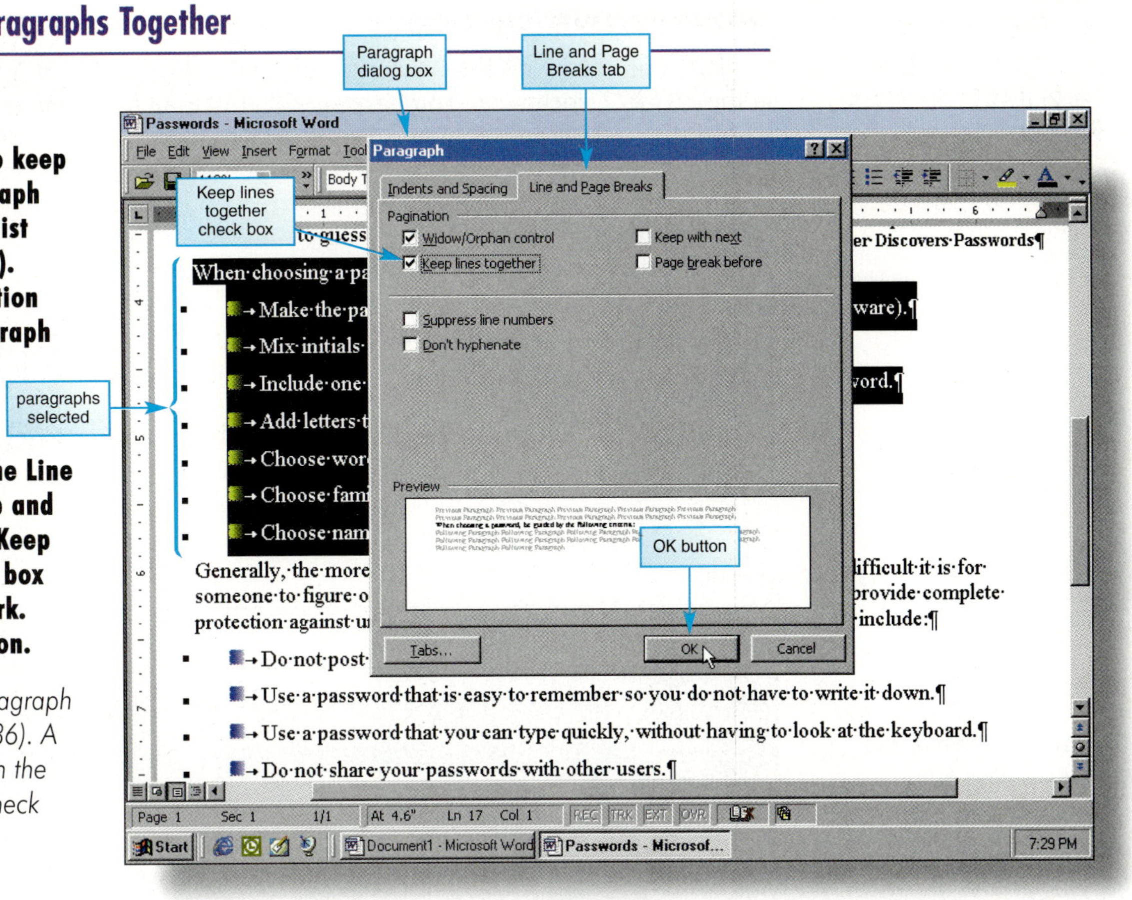

FIGURE 7-36

2 **Click the OK button.**

Word keeps the eight paragraphs that comprise the bulleted list and the paragraph preceding the list together so that they print on the same page.

3 **Repeat Steps 1 and 2 for the second bulleted list in the Passwords document. Click outside the selection to remove the highlight.**

The options in the Line and Page Breaks tab of the Paragraph dialog box (Figure 7-36) are designed to provide you with options in how paragraphs print. The Keep lines together check box that was illustrated in the previous steps also can be used to ensure that a page break does not occur within a single paragraph, by positioning the insertion point in the appropriate paragraph and then selecting the check box. If you do not want a page break to occur between two paragraphs, you would click in the appropriate paragraph and then place a check mark in the Keep with next check box. Similarly, if you want a page break to occur immediately before a paragraph, you would place a check mark in the Page break before check box.

A **widow** is created when the last line of a paragraph displays by itself at the top of a page, and an **orphan** occurs when the first line of a paragraph displays by itself at the bottom of a page. Word, by default, prevents widows and orphans from occurring in a document. If, for some reason, you wanted to allow a widow or an orphan in a document, you would position the insertion point in the appropriate paragraph, display the Line and Page Breaks sheet in the Paragraph dialog box, and then remove the check mark from the Widow/Orphan control check box.

Selecting Passwords

For more information on selecting good passwords, visit the Word 2000 More About Web page (www.scsite.com/wd2000/more.htm) and then click Selecting Passwords.

Password-Protecting a File

Jeff is finished with the Passwords file and is ready to send it to you for inclusion in the EIG #22 document. You have specified that all incoming documents be password-protected, which requires a user to enter a password if he or she wishes to open or modify the document. This procedure helps to ensure that the document inserted into the EIG #22 document is correct and has been modified by only authorized individuals.

In Word, a password may be up to 15 characters in length and can include letters, numbers, spaces, and symbols. Passwords are **case-sensitive**, which means that the password always must be entered in the same case in which it was saved. That is, if you enter a password in all capital letters, it must be entered in capital letters when the file is opened or modified.

You instruct Jeff to use the password, sunshine (in lowercase), for the file. Perform the following steps to password-protect the file.

To Password-Protect a File

1 Click File on the menu bar and then click Save As. When the Save As dialog box displays, if necessary, change the Save in location to drive A. Click the Tools button arrow and then point to General Options.

Word displays the Save As dialog box (Figure 7-37).

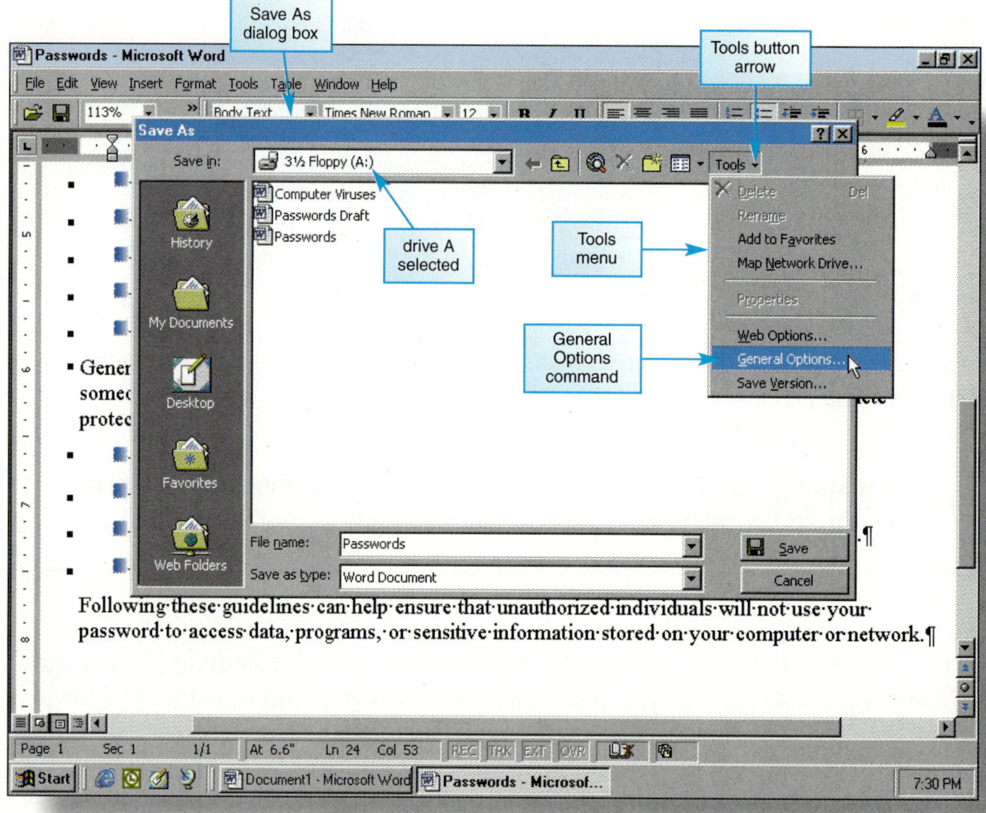

FIGURE 7-37

2 **Click General Options. When the Save dialog box displays, type** sunshine **in the Password to open text box. Point to the OK button.**

Word displays the Save dialog box (Figure 7-38). When you enter the password, sunshine, Word displays a series of asterisks (*) instead of the actual characters you type.

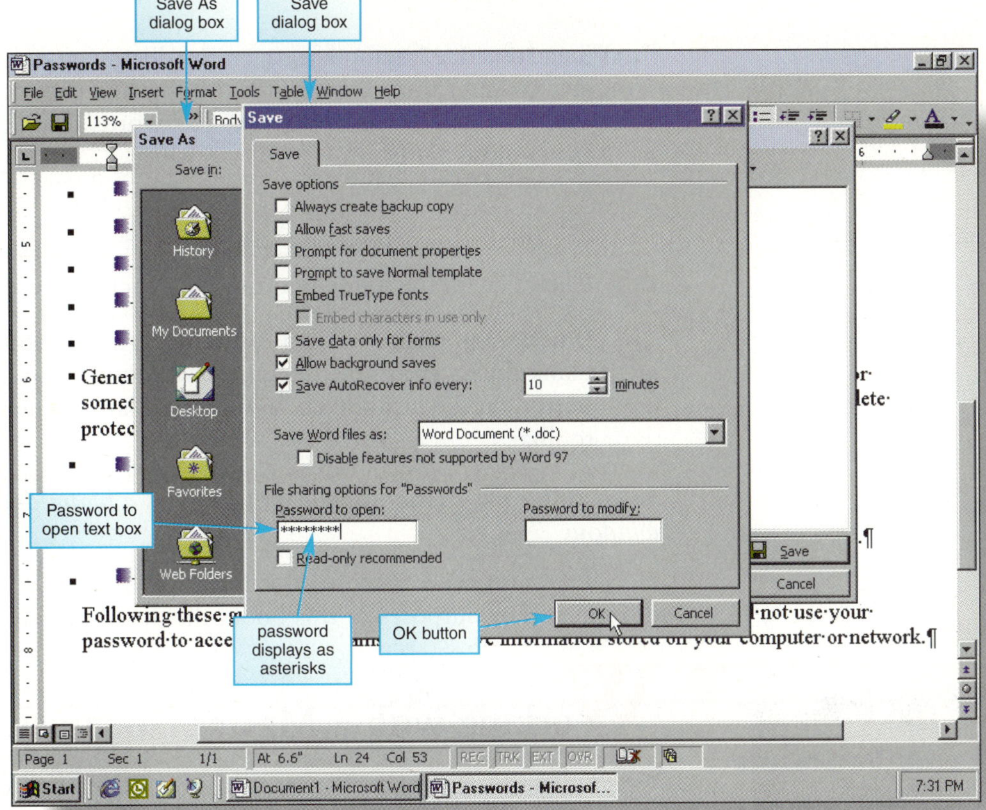

FIGURE 7-38

3 **Click the OK button. When Word displays the Confirm Password dialog box, type** sunshine **in the text box. Point to the OK button in the Confirm Password dialog box.**

Word displays the Confirm Password dialog box (Figure 7-39). Again, the password displays as a series of asterisks (*) instead of the actual characters you type.

4 **Click the OK button. When the Save As dialog box is visible again, click its Save button.**

Word saves the document with the password, sunshine.

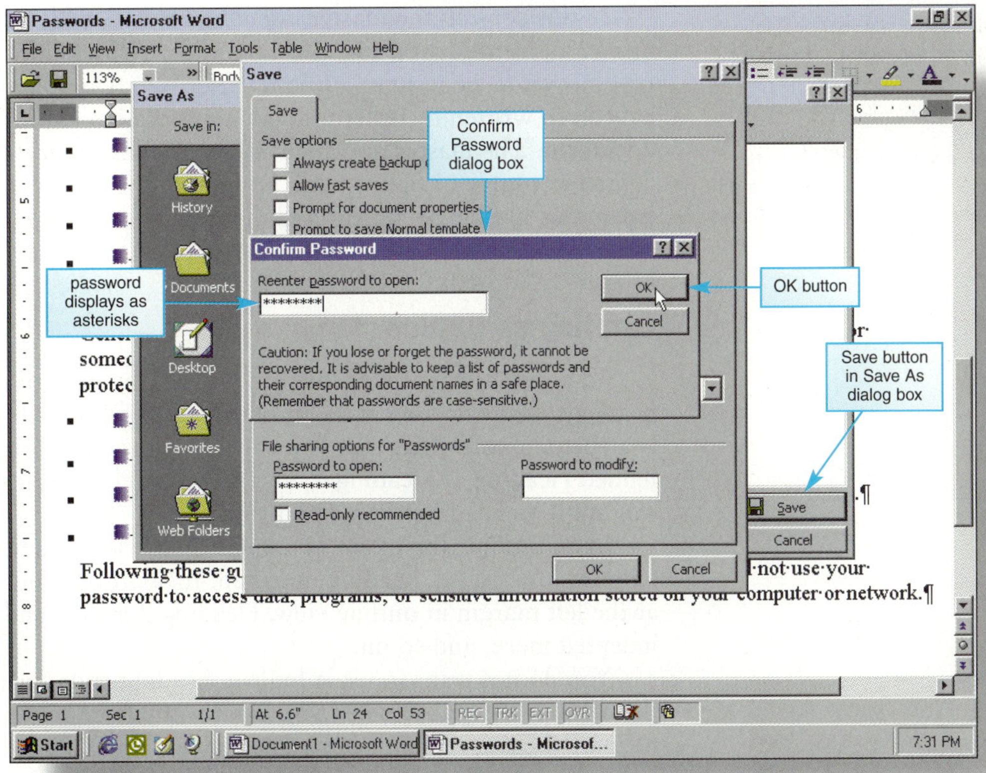

FIGURE 7-39

When someone attempts to open the document in the future, he or she will be prompted to enter the password. Recall that the password must be entered in the same case in which it was saved. The Passwords file is complete. Perform the following steps to close the file.

TO CLOSE THE DOCUMENT

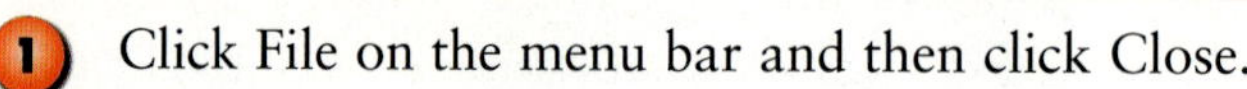

1. Click File on the menu bar and then click Close.

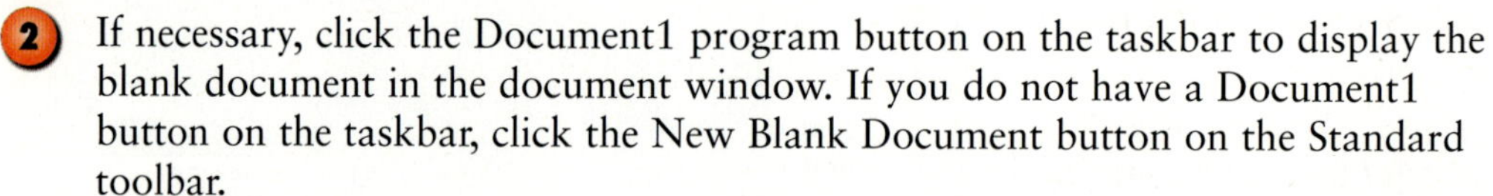

2. If necessary, click the Document1 program button on the taskbar to display the blank document in the document window. If you do not have a Document1 button on the taskbar, click the New Blank Document button on the Standard toolbar.

Word closes the Passwords file and displays a blank document in the document window.

Jeff e-mails the Passwords document to you for inclusion in the EIG #22 document. For purposes of this book, the document is on your disk.

More About 2000

Master Documents

Master documents can be used when multiple people prepare different sections of a document or when a document contains separate elements such as the chapters in a book. If multiple people in a network need to work on the same document, divide the document into subdocuments and store the master document on the network server. Then, multiple users can work on different sections of the document simultaneously.

Working with a Master Document

When you are creating a document from a series of other documents, you may want to create a master document to organize all the documents. A **master document** is simply a document that contains other documents, which are called the **subdocuments.** In addition to subdocuments, a master document can contain its own text and graphics.

In this project, the master document is EIG #22, which contains three subdocuments: an Introduction file, the Computer Viruses file, and the Passwords file. The first has yet to be written, and the latter two (Computer Viruses and Passwords) have been written by other individuals and e-mailed for inclusion in the EIG #22 document. The master document also contains other items: a title page, a table of contents, a table of figures, and an index. The following pages illustrate how to create this master document and insert the necessary elements into the document to create the EIG #22 document.

Creating an Outline

To create a master document, you must be in outline view. You then enter the headings of the document as an outline using Word's built-in heading styles. A **style** is a customized format that you can apply to text. Word has nine heading styles named Heading 1, Heading 2, and so on. Each contains different formatting that you can apply to headings in a document.

In an outline, the major heading displays at the left margin with each subordinate, or lower-level, heading indented. In Word, the built-in Heading 1 style displays at the left margin in outline view. Heading 2 style is indented, Heading 3 style is indented more, and so on.

You do not want to use a built-in heading style for the paragraphs of text within the document because when you create a table of contents, Word places all lines formatted using the built-in heading styles in the table of contents. Thus, the text below each heading is formatted using the Body Text style. By using styles for the document, all pages will be formatted similarly – even though various people create them.

The EIG #22 document contains the following seven major headings: Employee Information and Guidelines #22, Table of Contents, Introduction, Computer Viruses, Passwords, Table of Figures, and Index (see Figure 7-1 on page WD 7.5). Two of these headings (Computer Viruses and Passwords) are not entered in the outline; instead they are part of the subdocuments that you insert into the master document in the next section. You want each heading to print at the top of a new page. Because you might want to format the pages within a heading differently from those pages in other headings, you will insert next page section breaks between each heading as shown in the following steps.

Steps To Create an Outline

1 Click the Outline View button on the horizontal scroll bar. If your screen does not display the Outlining toolbar, click View on the menu bar, point to Toolbars, and then click Outlining. If the three buttons identified on the Outlining toolbar in this figure are not recessed on your screen, click the button(s).

Word switches to outline view (Figure 7-40). An ***outline symbol*** *displays to the left of each paragraph. You use outline symbols to rearrange text or display and hide text.*

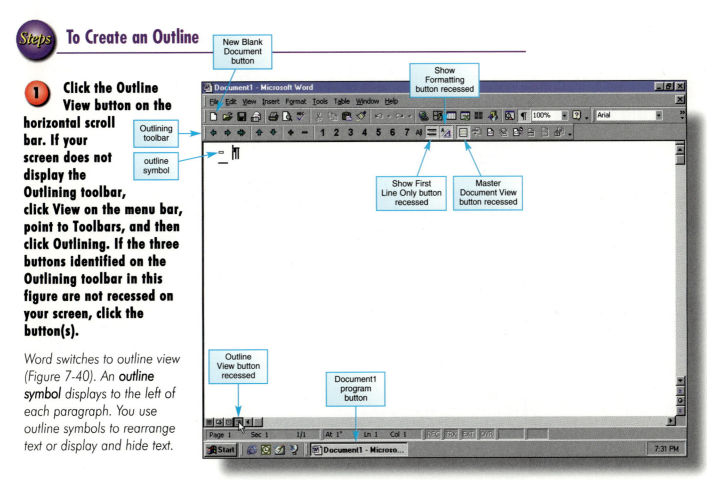

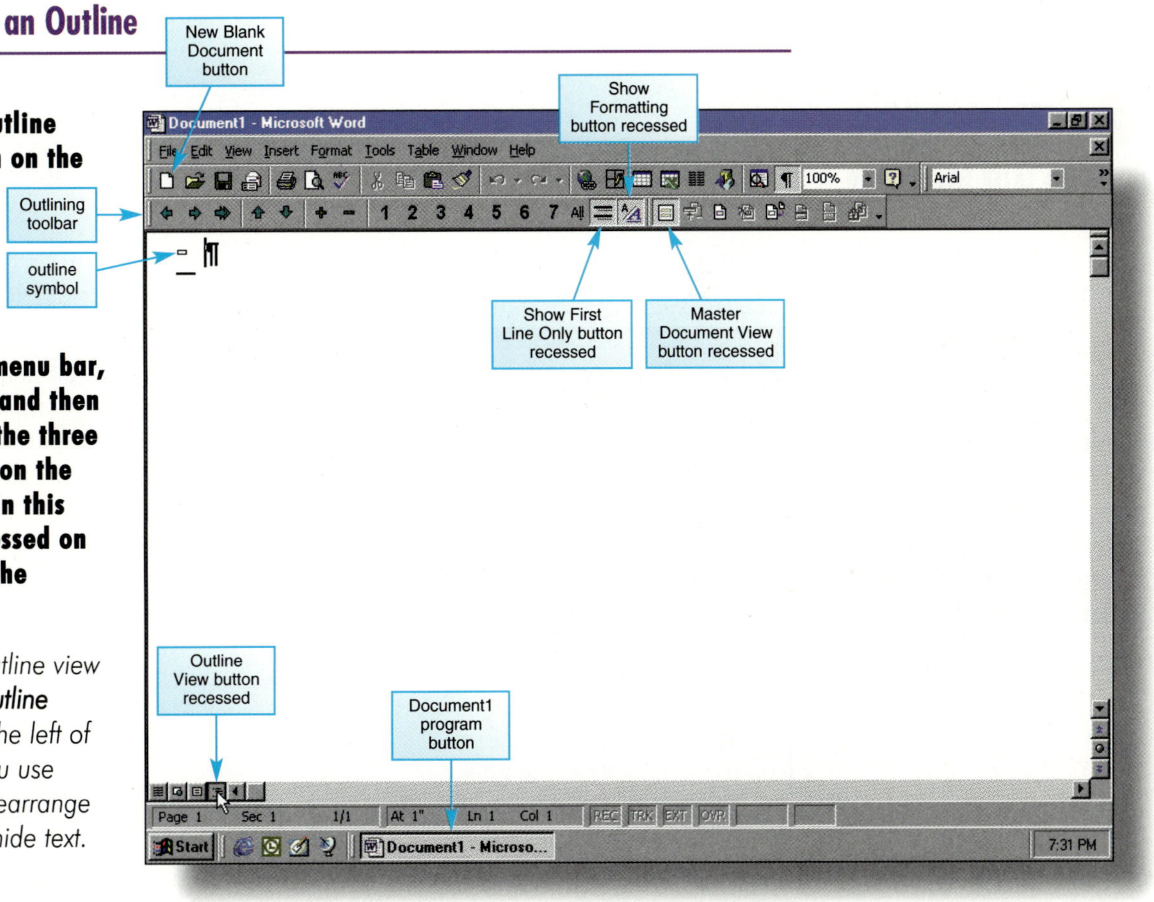

New Blank Document button

Show Formatting button recessed

Outlining toolbar

outline symbol

Show First Line Only button recessed

Master Document View button recessed

Outline View button recessed

Document1 program button

FIGURE 7-40

2 Type `Employee Information and Guidelines #22` **and then press the ENTER key.**

Word enters the first heading using the built-in Heading 1 style (Figure 7-41).

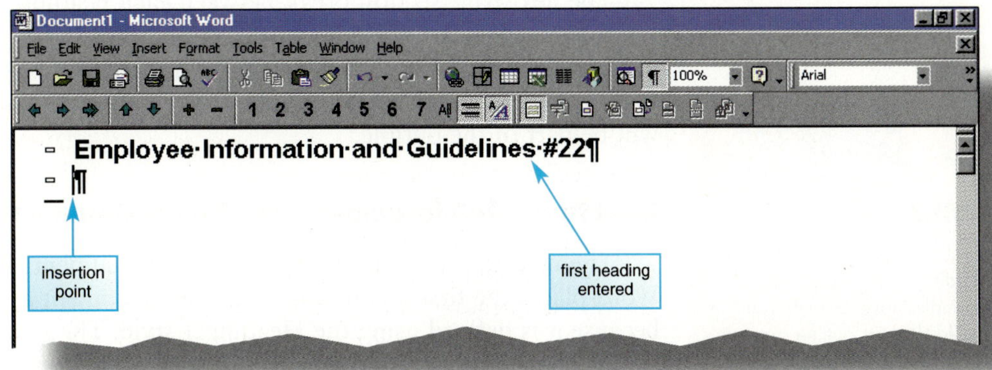

FIGURE 7-41

3 **Click Insert on the menu bar and then click Break. When the Break dialog box displays, click Next page in the Section break types area and then click the OK button.**

Word inserts a next page section break below the first heading.

4 **Type** `Table of Contents` **and then press the ENTER key (Figure 7-42).**

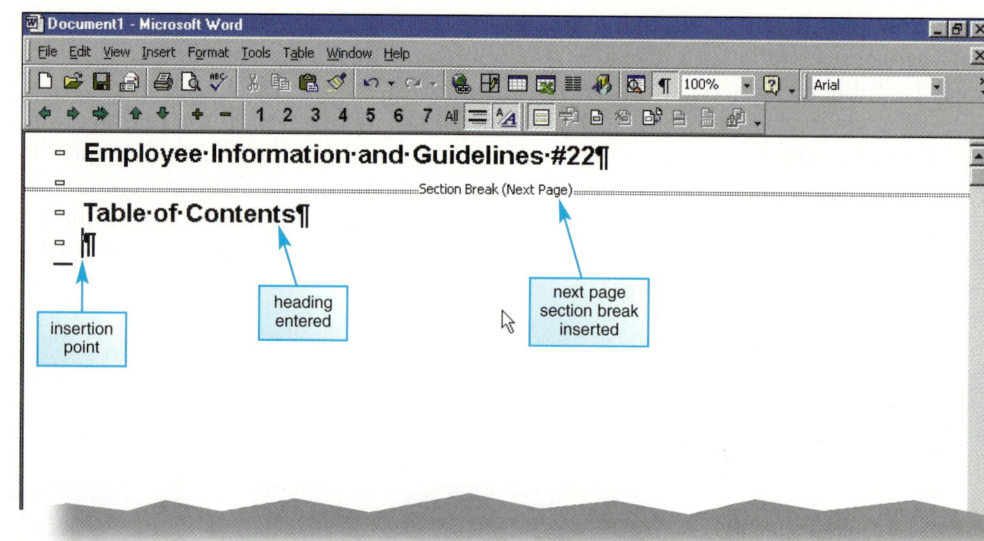

FIGURE 7-42

5 **Repeat Step 3. Type** `Introduction` **and then press the ENTER key. Repeat Step 3. Type** `Table of Figures` **and then press the ENTER key. Repeat Step 3. Type** `Index` **and then press the ENTER key (Figure 7-43).**

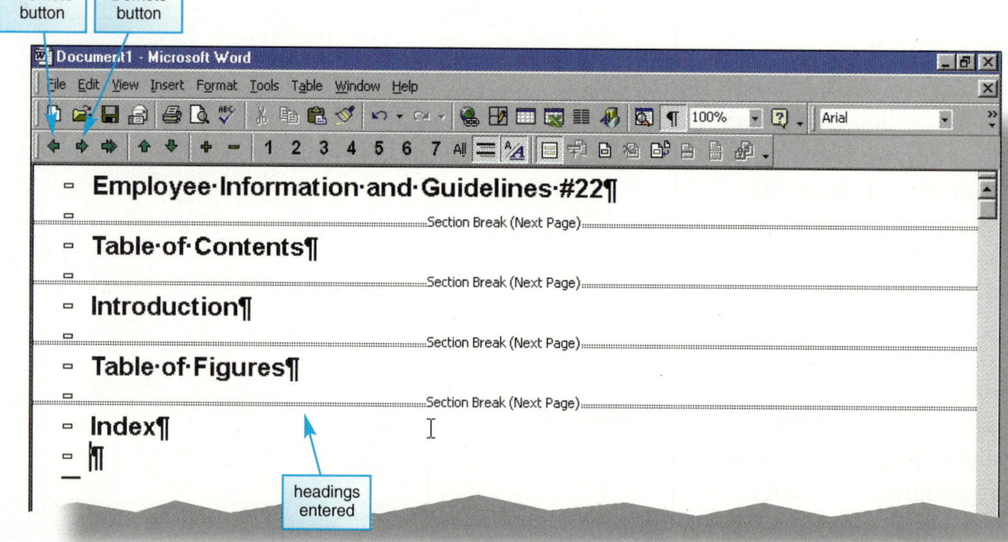

FIGURE 7-43

Other Ways

1. On View menu click Outline

More About 2000

Outlines

If you wanted to rearrange the headings in an outline, for example move one up, you would drag its outline symbol in the direction you wanted to move it.

The next page section break between each heading will cause each heading to begin at the top of a new page.

The two missing major headings (Computer Viruses and Passwords) are in the files on the Data Disk. When you insert these files as subdocuments, the headings will be part of the outline.

Inserting a Subdocument in a Master Document

The next step is to insert one of the subdocuments into the master document. Word places the first line of text in the subdocument at the first heading level because it is defined using the Heading 1 style. The remaining two headings in the subdocument use the Heading 2 style, and thus are subordinate to the first heading. Nonheading text uses the Body Text style. Figure 7-44 shows the Computer Viruses subdocument and identifies the styles used in the document.

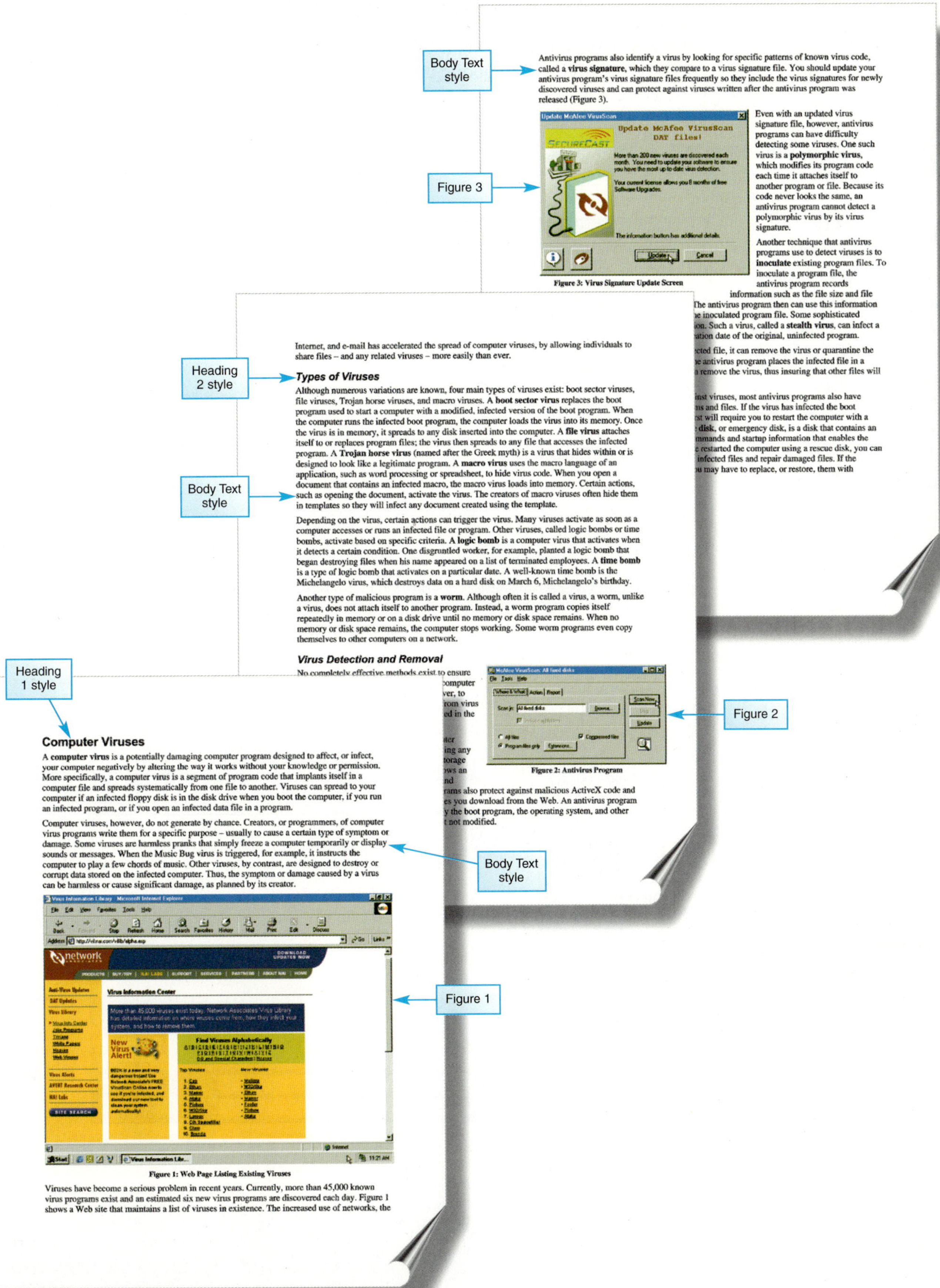
Body Text style
Figure 3
Heading 2 style
Body Text style
Heading 1 style
Figure 2
Body Text style
Figure 1
Computer Viruses
Types of Viruses
Virus Detection and Removal
Figure 1: Web Page Listing Existing Viruses
Figure 2: Antivirus Program
Figure 3: Virus Signature Update Screen

FIGURE 7-44

The subdocument to be inserted is named Computer Viruses and is located on the Data Disk. If you did not download the Data Disk, see the inside back cover for instructions for downloading the Data Disk or see your instructor. Perform the following steps to insert a subdocument.

Steps To Insert a Subdocument

1 Position the insertion point where you want to insert the subdocument (on the section break between the Introduction and Table of Figures headings). Point to the Insert Subdocument button on the Outlining toolbar (Figure 7-45).

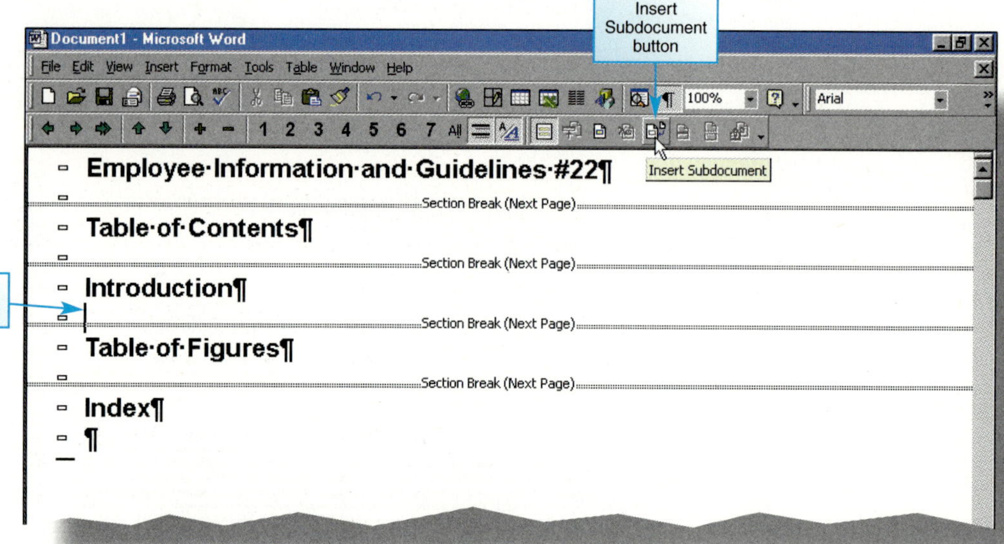

FIGURE 7-45

2 With the Data Disk in drive A, click the Insert Subdocument button. When the Insert Subdocument dialog box displays, if necessary, change the Look in location to drive A. Click Computer Viruses and then point to the Open button in the dialog box.

Word displays the Insert Subdocument dialog box (Figure 7-46). The document will be inserted at the location of the insertion point in the outline.

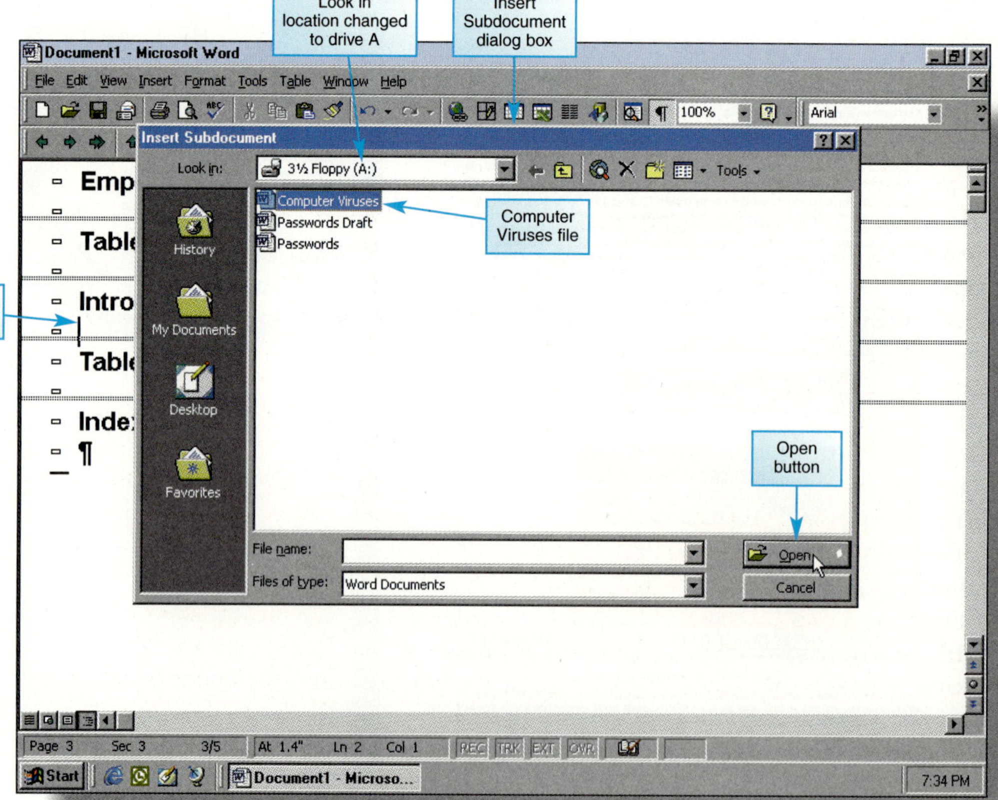

FIGURE 7-46

3 Click the Open button in the Insert Subdocument dialog box. Scroll up to display the top of the inserted subdocument.

Word inserts the Computer Viruses file into the outline (Figure 7-47). Notice the document contains marked index entries. Only the first line of each paragraph displays because the Show First Line Only button on the Outlining toolbar is recessed.

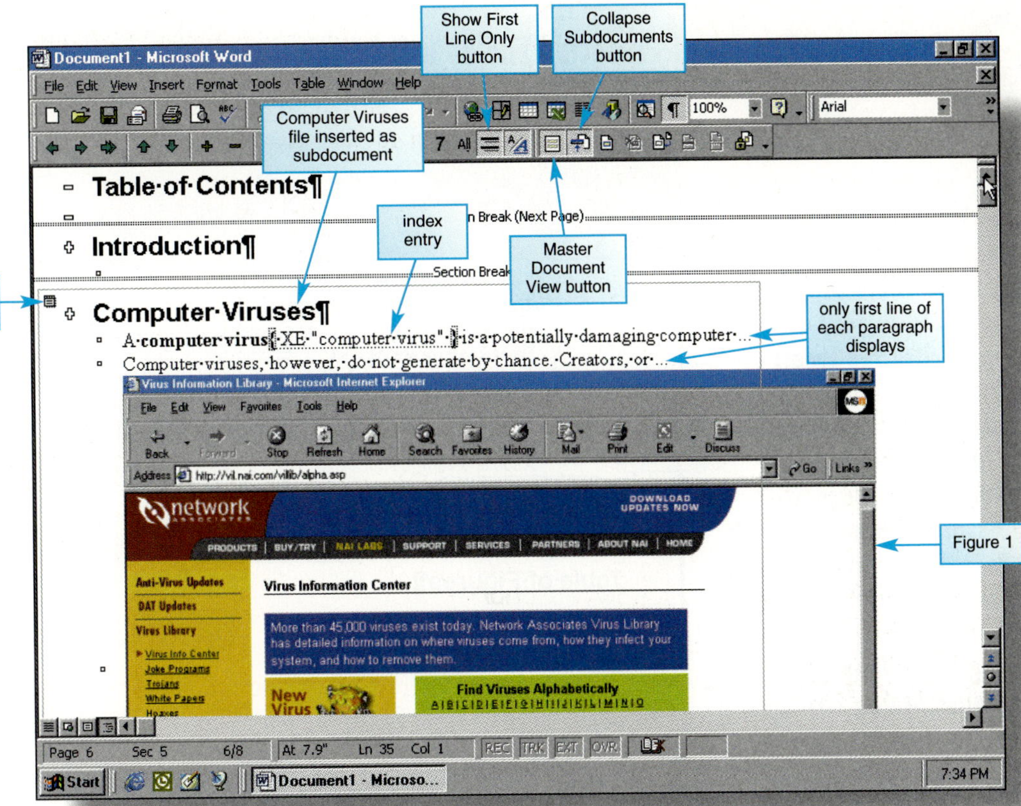

FIGURE 7-47

The inserted file shown in Figure 7-47 is the same document shown in Figure 7-44 on page WD 7.39. Notice that in Figure 7-47 only the first line of each paragraph displays. This is because the Show First Line Only button on the Outlining toolbar is recessed. If you wanted to display all lines in all paragraphs, you would click the Show First Line Only button so it is not recessed.

The master document shown in Figure 7-47 is expanded. When in outline view, an **expanded** document is one that displays the contents of its subdocuments. A **collapsed** document, by contrast, displays subdocuments as hyperlinks; that is, instead of displaying the contents of the subdocuments, Word displays the name of the subdocuments in blue and underlined. Later in this project, you work with a collapsed document.

To collapse an expanded document and display subdocuments as hyperlinks, click the Collapse Subdocuments button on the Outlining toolbar. To expand subdocuments, click the Expand Subdocuments button on the Outlining toolbar.

You can open a subdocument in a separate document window and modify it. To open a collapsed subdocument, click the hyperlink. To open an expanded subdocument, double-click the subdocument icon (see Figure 7-47) to the left of the document heading. If the subdocument icon does not display on the screen, click the Master Document View button on the Outlining toolbar. When you are finished working on a subdocument, close it and return to the master document by clicking File on the menu bar and then clicking Close.

The next step is to insert another subdocument below the Computer Viruses subdocument. The subdocument to be inserted is the Passwords file that you modified earlier in this project. Recall that you saved the document with the password, sunshine. Thus, you will enter that password when prompted by Word as shown in the steps on the next page.

The Lock Icon

If a lock icon displays next to a subdocument's name, either the master document is collapsed or the subdocument is locked. If the master document is collapsed, simply click the Expand Subdocuments button on the Outlining toolbar. If the subdocument is locked, you will be able to open the subdocument but will not be able to modify it.

To Insert a Password-Protected File as a Subdocument

1 Scroll down and position the insertion point on the next page section break above the Table of Figures heading. With your disk in drive A, click the Insert Subdocument button on the Outlining toolbar. When the Insert Subdocument dialog box displays, if necessary, change the Look in location to drive A. Click Passwords and then click the Open button in the dialog box. When the Password dialog box displays, type sunshine **as the password.**

Word displays the Password dialog box, which requests your password for the Passwords file (Figure 7-48). Asterisks display instead of the actual password.

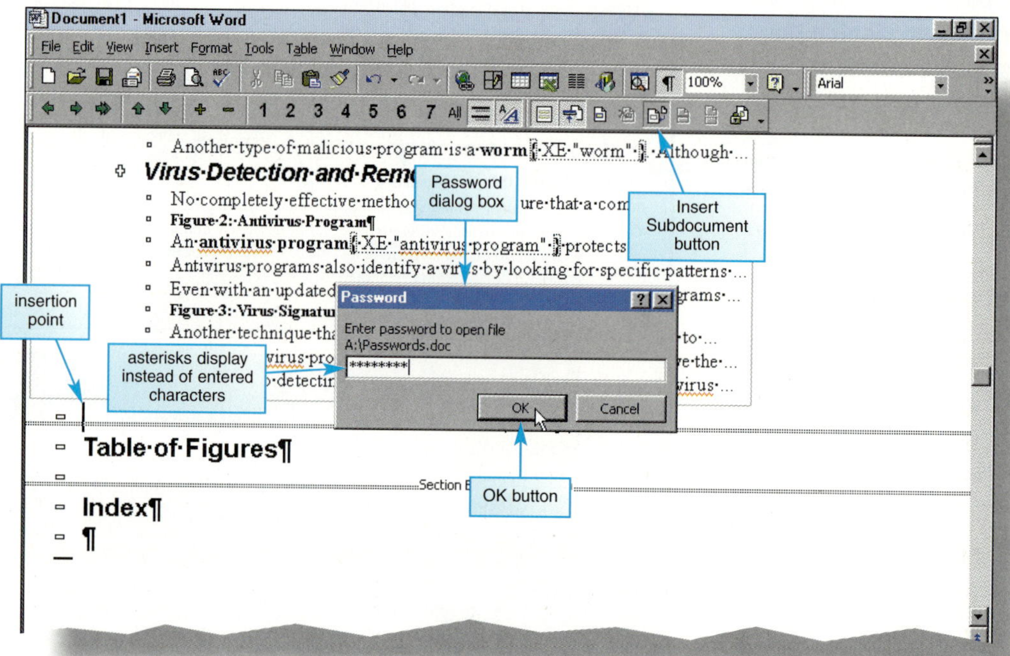

FIGURE 7-48

Click the OK button.

Word inserts the Passwords file into the document (Figure 7-49). The document shown in this figure is the same one shown in Figure 7-2b on page WD 7.8.

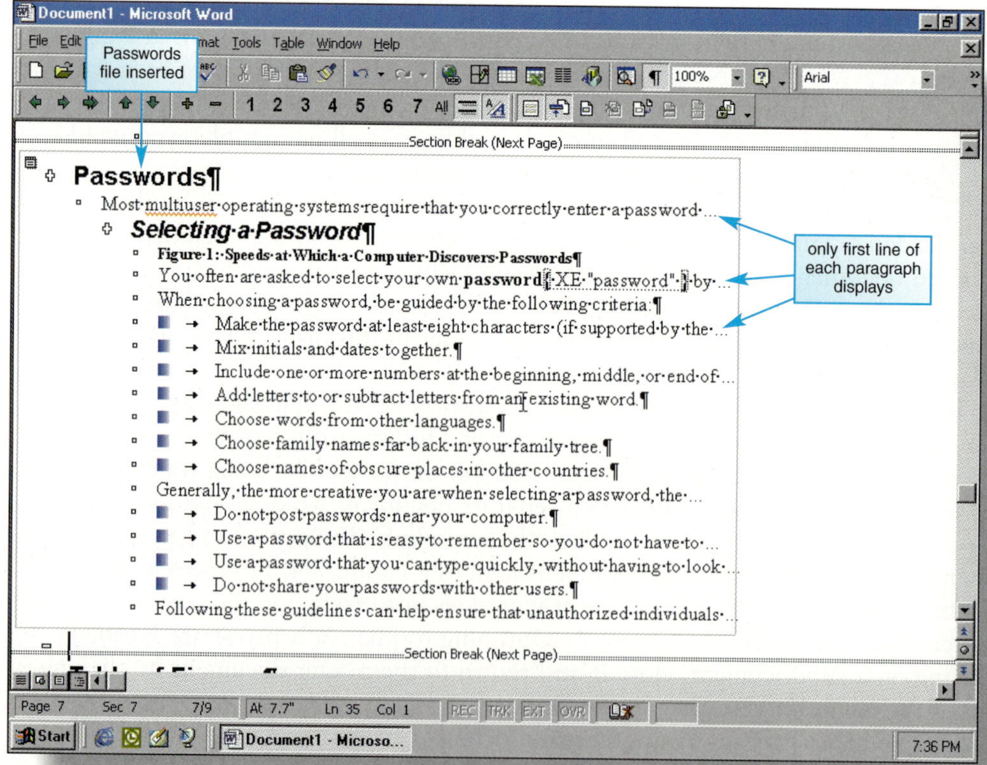

FIGURE 7-49

Because you have performed several tasks, you should save the document as described in the following steps.

TO SAVE A DOCUMENT

1. With your floppy disk in drive A, click the Save button on the Standard toolbar.
2. Type `EIG #22` in the File name text box. Do not press the ENTER key after typing the file name.
3. If necessary, change the Save in location to drive A. Click the Save button in the Save As dialog box.

Word saves the document on a floppy disk in drive A with the file name, EIG #22 (see Figure 7-50).

When you save a master document, Word also saves the subdocument files on the disk. Thus, the EIG #22 file, the Computer Viruses file, and the Passwords file all are saved when you save the EIG #22 file.

Creating Subdocuments

If the Create Subdocument button is dimmed, you need to expand subdocuments by clicking the Expand Subdocuments button on the Outlining toolbar. Then, the Create Subdocument button should be available.

Creating a Subdocument from a Master Document

The next step is to create a subdocument for the Introduction section of the EIG #22 document. Perform the following steps to create a subdocument.

To Create a Subdocument

1. **Press CTRL+HOME and then double-click the heading, Introduction, to select it. Point to the Create Subdocument button on the Outlining toolbar (Figure 7-50).**

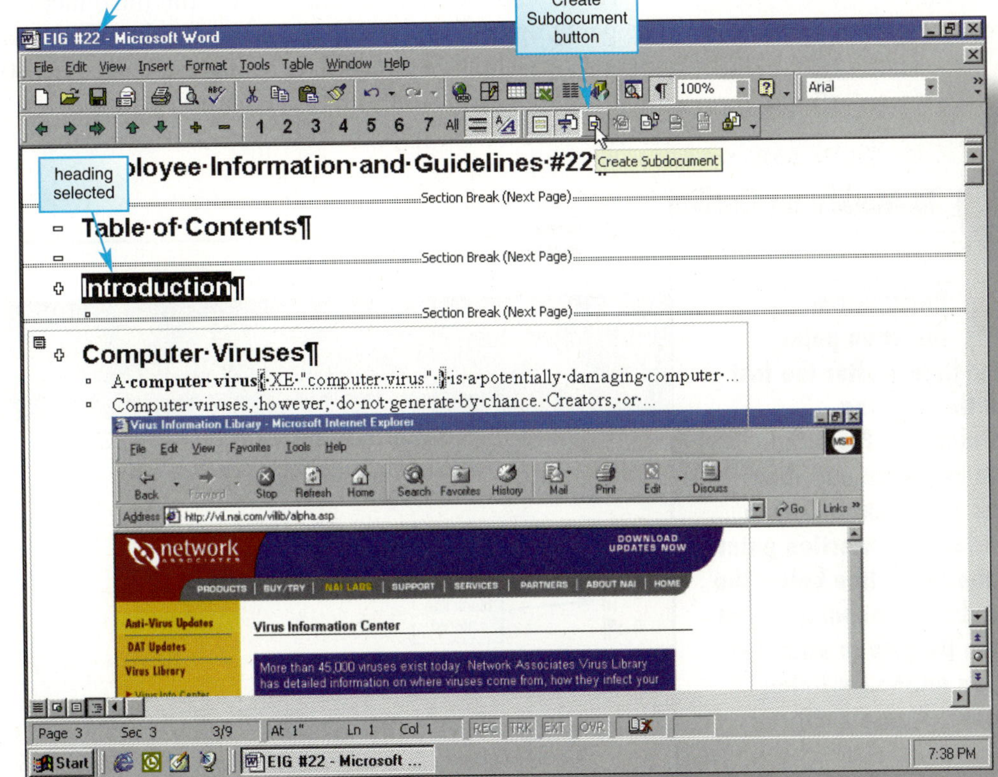

FIGURE 7-50

2 Click the Create Subdocument button.

Word creates a subdocument for the Introduction heading (Figure 7-51). Word places a continuous section break above the subdocument; do not remove this section break.

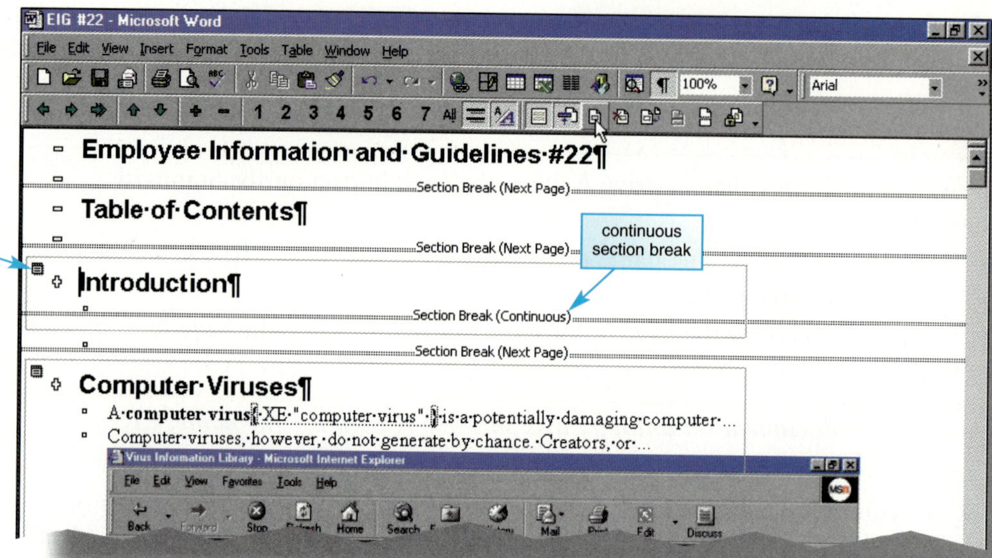

FIGURE 7-51

The next time you save the EIG #22 document, Word will create another document called Introduction on your disk.

Modifying an Outline

You would like to enter the text for the Introduction section of the document. The paragraphs of text in the Introduction should not use a built-in heading style; instead, they should be formatted using the Body Text style. You can enter the text in outline view as shown in the following steps.

Steps To Modify an Outline

1 Position the insertion point immediately after the last n in the heading, Introduction. Press the ENTER key twice and then press the UP ARROW key to position the insertion point on the blank line below the Introduction heading. Point to the Demote to Body Text button on the Outlining toolbar (Figure 7-52).

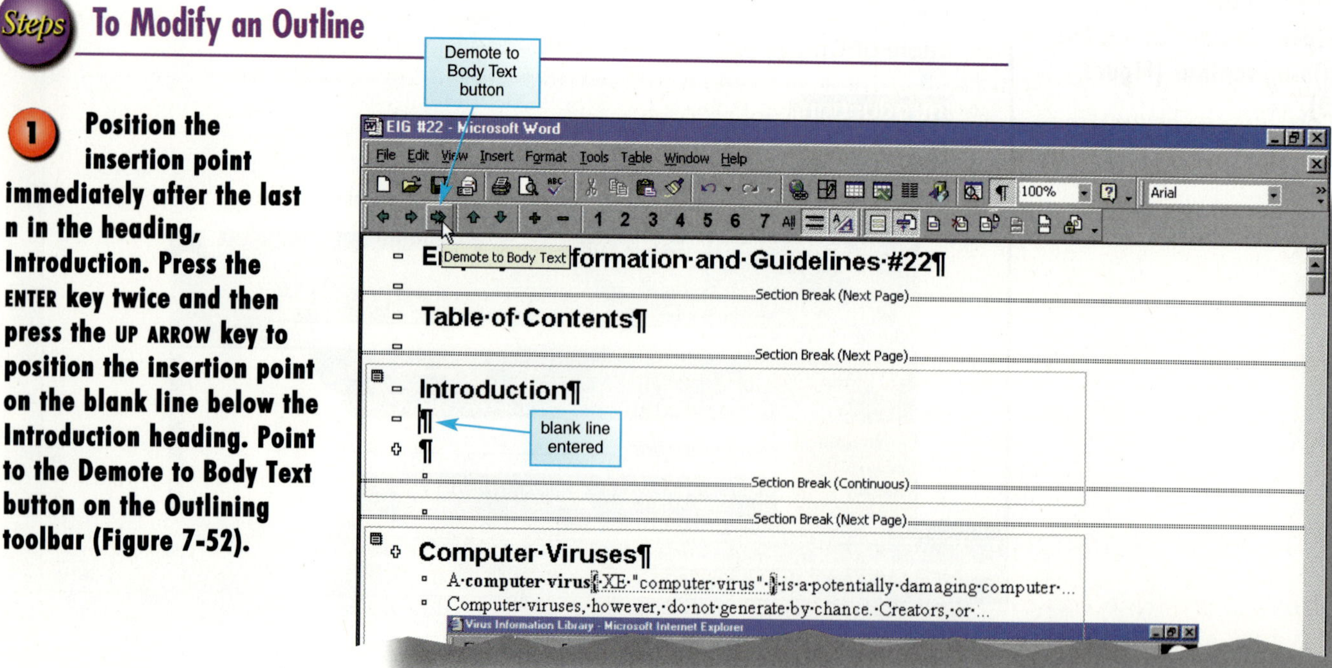

FIGURE 7-52

2 **Click the Demote to Body Text button.**

Word changes the style of the current line from Heading 1 to Body Text (Figure 7-53).

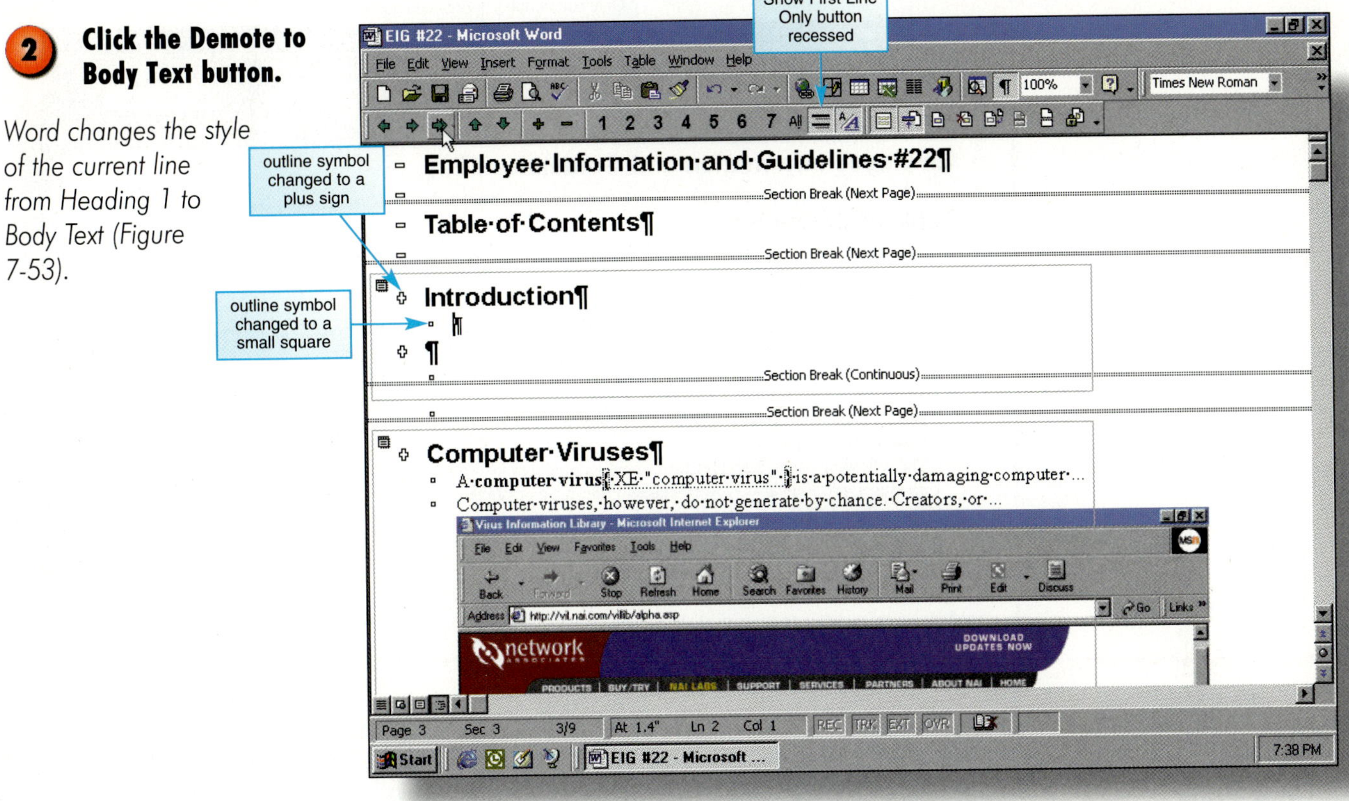

FIGURE 7-53

Notice in Figure 7-53 that the outline symbols changed. The outline symbol to the left of the Introduction heading changed from a minus sign to a plus sign, indicating the heading has subordinate text displaying on the screen. The outline symbol below the Introduction heading changed from a minus sign to a small square, indicating it is formatted using the Body Text style.

If you wanted to change a heading to a lower-level, or subordinate, heading style instead of to the Body Text style, such as for a subheading, you would press the TAB key or click the Demote button on the Outlining toolbar or drag the outline symbol to the right. Likewise, to change a heading to a higher-level heading, you would press the SHIFT+TAB keys or click the Promote button on the Outlining toolbar or drag the outline symbol to the left.

The next step is to enter the text of the introduction as described in the following steps.

TO ENTER BODY TEXT INTO AN OUTLINE

1. If the Show First Line Only button on the Outlining toolbar is recessed, click it.
2. With the insertion point on the line below the Introduction heading, type the first paragraph shown in Figure 7-54 on the next page. Press the ENTER key.
3. Type the second paragraph shown in Figure 7-54.

The Introduction section is complete (Figure 7-54).

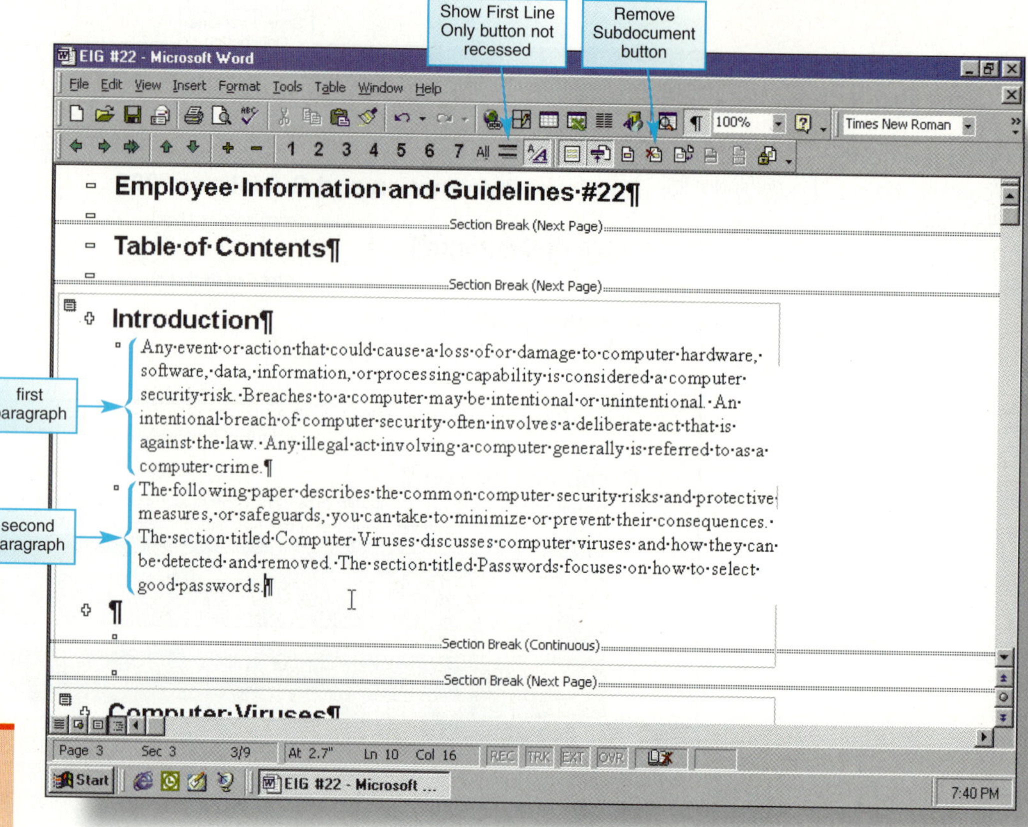

FIGURE 7-54

More About 2000

Outline View

When the Show First Line Only button on the Outline toolbar is recessed, only the first line of each paragraph displays. When the button is not recessed, all text associated with the paragraph displays.

In outline view, text does not display formatted. Instead, each subheading is intended below the previous heading. Text formatted using the Body Text style, such as that shown in Figure 7-54, also displays indented. To display text properly formatted, switch to print layout view.

If, for some reason, you wanted to remove a subdocument from a master document, you would expand the subdocuments, click the subdocument icon to the left of the subdocument's first heading, and then press the DELETE key. Although Word removes the subdocument from the master document, the subdocument file remains on disk.

You may, for some reason, want to convert a subdocument to part of the master document – breaking the connection between the text in the master document and the subdocument. To do this, expand the subdocuments, click the subdocument icon, and then click the Remove Subdocument button on the Outlining toolbar.

Entering Text and Graphics as Part of the Master Document

The next step is to create the title page for the EIG #22 document. The completed title page is shown in Figure 7-55. You decide not to create a subdocument for the title page; instead you will enter the text as part of the master document. Because the title page contains graphics, however, you will work in print layout view as opposed to outline view.

On the title page, you want only the first line of text (Employee Information and Guidelines #22) to show up in the table of contents. Thus, only the first line should be the Heading 1 style. The remaining lines will be formatted using the Body Text style. To be sure that all text below the Heading 1 style is formatted to the Body Text style, demote the blank line below the heading to body text as described in the following steps.

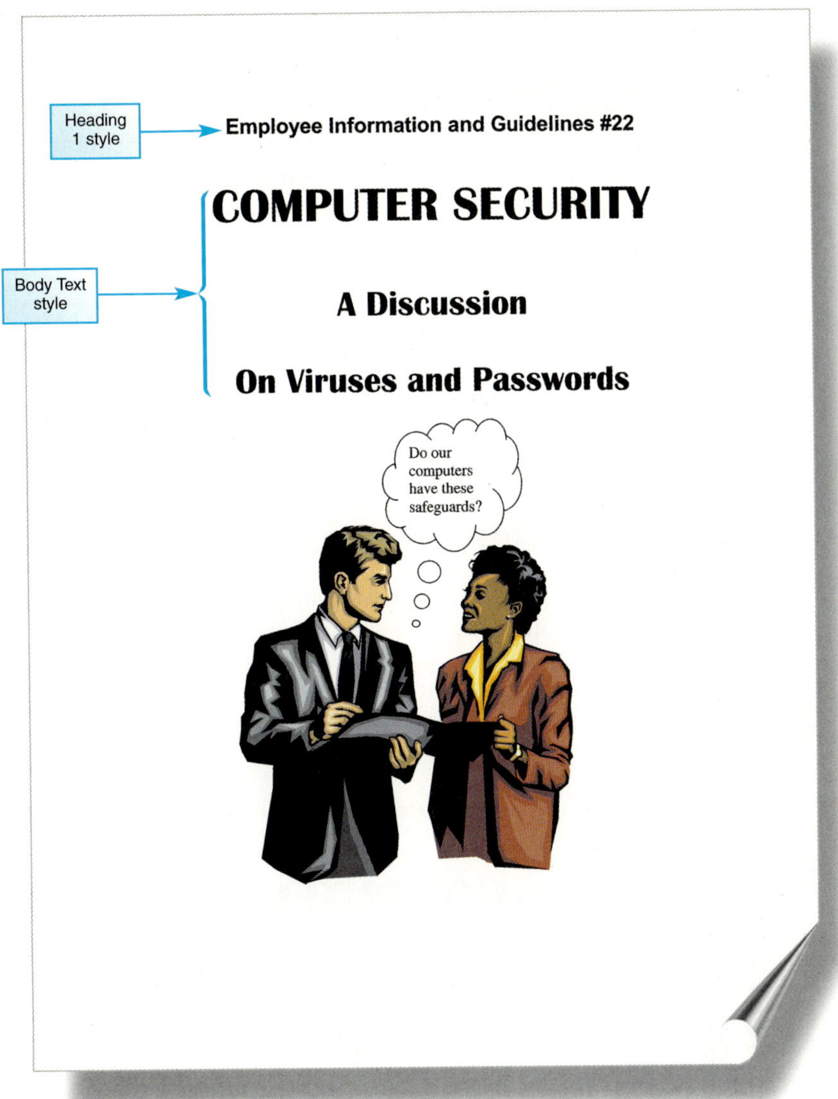

FIGURE 7-55

TO DEMOTE A LINE TO BODY TEXT

1. In outline view, position the insertion point on the section break below the Employee Information and Guidelines #22 heading.
2. Click the Demote to Body Text button on the Outlining toolbar.

Word changes the current line from Heading 1 style to Body Text style (Figure 7-56).

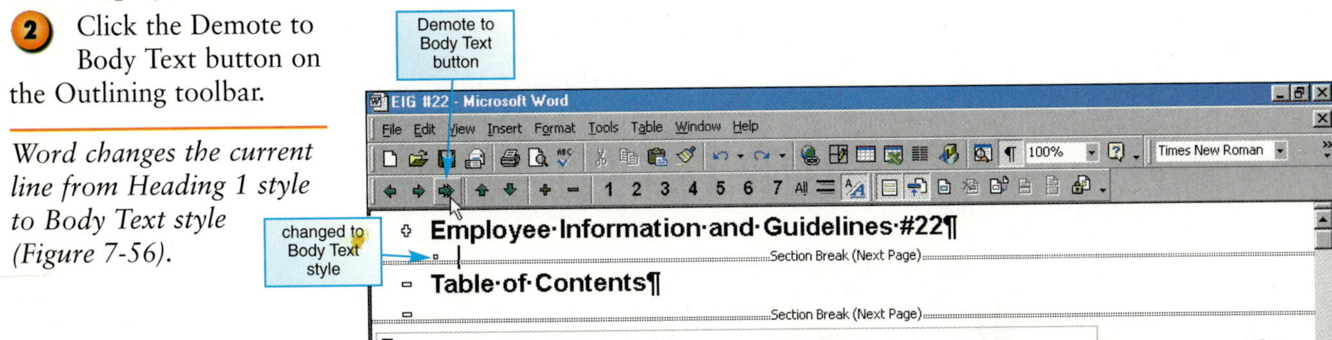

FIGURE 7-55

Enter the text for the title page as described in the following steps.

TO ENTER AND FORMAT TITLE PAGE TEXT

1. Click the Print Layout View button on the horizontal scroll bar to switch to print layout view. Click the Zoom box arrow and then click Page Width.
2. With the insertion point at the end of the first line on the title page, press the ENTER key twice. Press the UP ARROW key to position the insertion point on the blank line.
3. Press CTRL+2 to change line spacing to double. Press the ENTER key.
4. Type `COMPUTER SECURITY` and then press the ENTER key. Type `A Discussion` and then press the ENTER key. Type `On Viruses and Passwords` and then press the ENTER key two times.
5. Center all lines on the title page, including the blank lines.
6. Change the COMPUTER SECURITY line to 36-point Britannic Bold font.
7. Change the lines, A Discussion and On Viruses and Passwords, to 26-point Britannic Bold font.

The title page displays as shown in Figure 7-57.

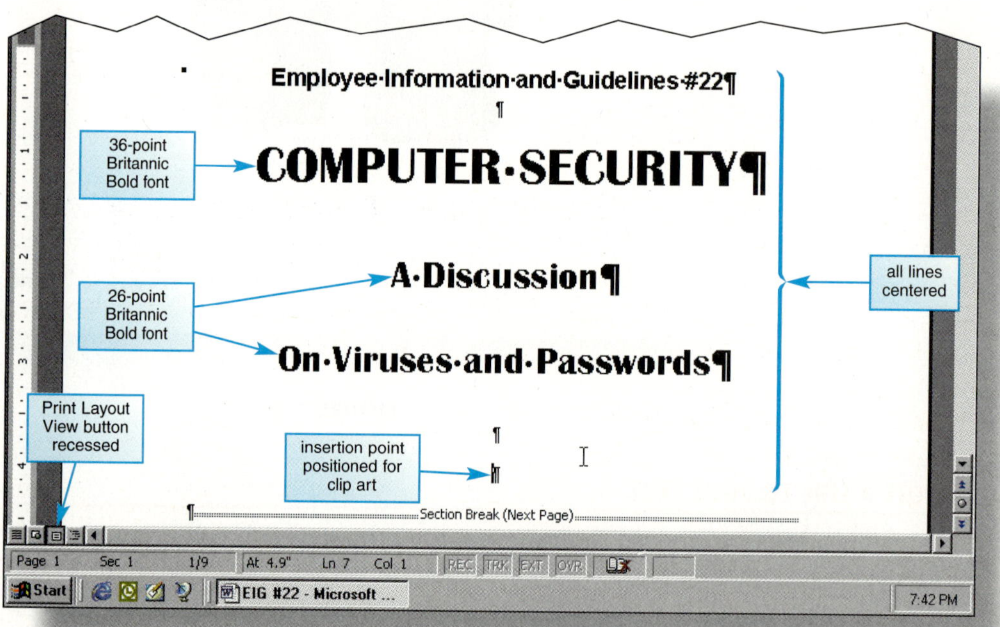

FIGURE 7-57

The next step is to insert the clip art image of a man and woman talking as described in the following steps.

TO INSERT CLIP ART

1. Click the second paragraph mark below the last line of text on the title page (see Figure 7-57). Click Insert on the menu bar, point to Picture, and then click Clip Art.
2. When the Insert ClipArt window opens, click the Search for clips text box. Type `man woman talking` and then press the ENTER key.

3. Click the clip that matches the one shown in Figure 7-58. Click the Insert clip button on the Pop-up menu.
4. Click the Close button on the Insert ClipArt window's title bar.

Word inserts the graphic of the man and woman talking at the location of the insertion point as an inline object (see Figure 7-58).

The next step is to add a callout to the title page.

Adding an AutoShape

You can insert two types of graphics into a Word document: a picture and a drawing object. A **picture** is a graphic that was created in another program. Examples of pictures are scanned images, photographs, and clip art. A **drawing object** is a graphic that you create using Word. You can modify or enhance drawing objects using the Drawing toolbar. Examples of drawing objects include AutoShapes, curves, lines, and WordArt drawing objects.

In a previous project, you created special text effects using WordArt. In this project, you add an **AutoShape**, which is a predefined shape in Word. Examples of AutoShapes include rectangles, circles, triangles, arrows, flowcharting symbols, stars, banners, and callouts. You can add text to most AutoShapes simply by clicking the shape and typing the text.

Perform the following steps to add a callout AutoShape that contains text.

AutoShapes

To fill an AutoShape with color, change the color of its borders, rotate the AutoShape, or add shadow or 3-D effects to an AutoShape, select the drawing object and then click the appropriate button on the Drawing toolbar.

To Add an AutoShape

1. **Double-click the move handle on the Standard toolbar to display the entire toolbar. If the Drawing toolbar is not displaying on your screen, click the Drawing button on the Standard toolbar. Click the AutoShapes button on the Drawing toolbar, point to Callouts, and then point to the Cloud Callout (Figure 7-58).**

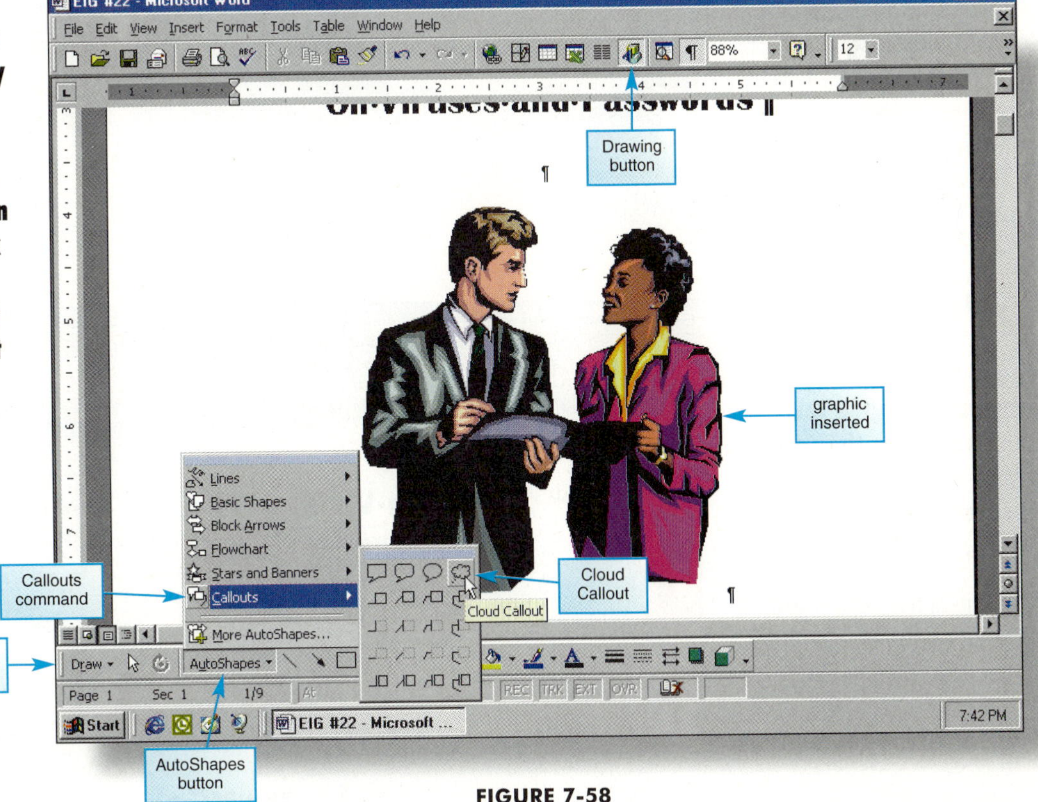

FIGURE 7-58

2 Click the Cloud Callout. Position the mouse pointer as shown in Figure 7-59.

Word displays the crosshair mouse pointer in the document window (Figure 7-59). You drag the crosshair mouse pointer to form the AutoShape.

FIGURE 7-59

3 Drag the mouse upward and rightward to form a cloud callout similar to the one shown in Figure 7-60. If, once the callout is drawn, you need to resize it, simply drag the sizing handles.

Word displays the cloud callout in the document (Figure 7-60). The insertion point blinks inside the callout. The callout may cover a portion of the graphic; if this occurs, you will move it in the next step.

FIGURE 7-60

4 Type Do our computers have these safeguards? **If necessary, drag the text box surrounding the callout upward so the callout does not cover any part of the graphic.**

Word enters the callout text and displays the callout in its new location (Figure 7-61).

FIGURE 7-61

Even though the text displays in the callout on the screen and more than likely displays properly in print preview, some printers will not print the text in the callout unless the callout is a certain width. The width requirement varies from printer to printer. You should print the title page now to determine if your callout text prints properly. If it does not, make the callout wider and try printing the title page again. Repeat this process until the text in the callout prints properly.

If, when you create an AutoShape, the insertion point is not in the shape, you can add text to an AutoShape by right-clicking the AutoShape and then clicking Add Text on the shortcut menu. To edit existing text, click in the existing text or right-click the existing text and then click Edit Text on the shortcut menu.

Rotating an Object

To rotate a drawing object or flip a drawing object 90 degrees, select the object, click the Draw button on the Drawing toolbar, point to Rotate or Flip, and then select the desired command. You also can rotate a selected object to any degree by clicking the Free Rotate button on the Drawing toolbar and then dragging a round handle on a corner of the object. When the object is in the desired position, click outside the object.

Grouping Drawing Objects

Notice in Figure 7-61 that the callout now covers a portion of the title page text. Thus, the next step is to move the callout and the graphic. If you move the callout, it moves independent of the graphic; likewise, if you move the graphic, it moves independent of the callout. You would like both objects (the callout and the graphic) to move together as a single unit. Thus, you must group the objects together.

The objects you wish to group must be floating. Recall that the graphic of the man and woman talking is inline. Perform the following steps to change the inline graphic to a floating graphic.

TO CHANGE AN INLINE GRAPHIC TO FLOATING GRAPHIC

1. Click the graphic of the man and woman talking.
2. If the Picture toolbar does not display, right-click the graphic and then click Show Picture toolbar on the shortcut menu. Click the Text Wrapping button on the Picture toolbar and then point to Square (Figure 7-62).
3. Click Square on the Picture toolbar.

Word changes the graphic from inline to floating.

FIGURE 7-62

The next step is to group the two floating objects together so they can be moved as a single unit. Perform the steps on the next page to group objects.

To Group Objects

1 If necessary, scroll down to display both graphics. With the graphic of the man and woman talking still selected, hold down the SHIFT key while clicking the cloud callout. Click the Draw button on the Drawing toolbar and then point to Group.

Word selects both objects, the graphic of the man and woman talking and the cloud callout (Figure 7-63).

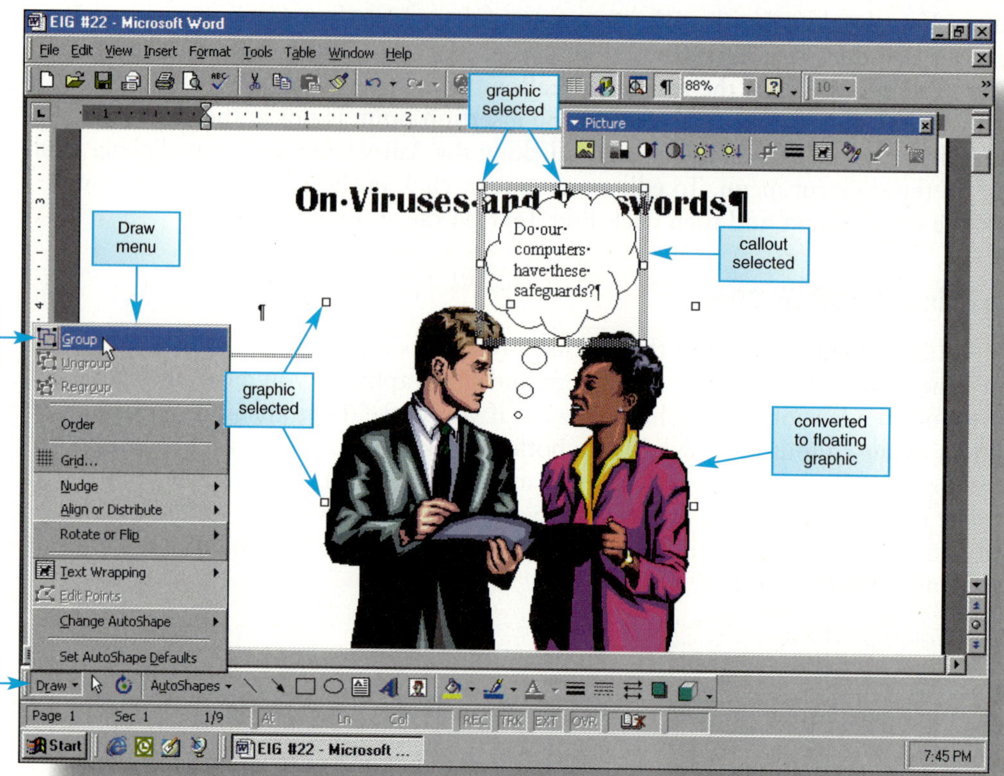

FIGURE 7-63

2 Click Group.

Word groups the two objects together into a single object (Figure 7-64). Notice the sizing handles now display surrounding both objects together.

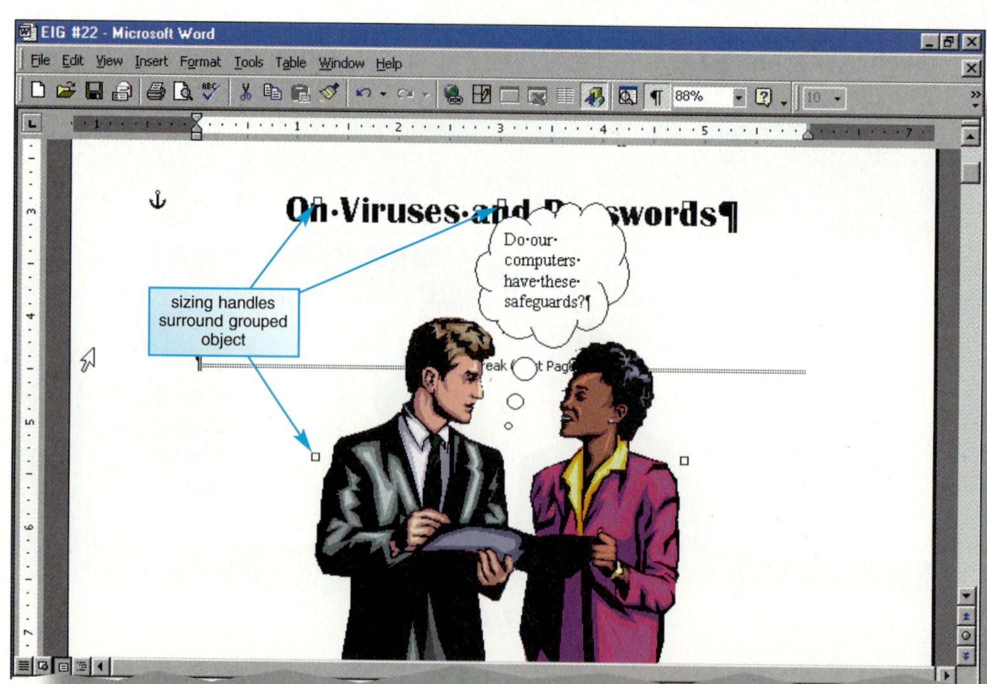

FIGURE 7-64

If, for some reason, you wanted the objects to be separated again, you could **ungroup** them by selecting the grouped object, clicking the Draw button on the Drawing toolbar and then clicking Ungroup. If the Ungroup command is dimmed, you are attempting to ungroup an image that Word cannot ungroup.

The next step is to move the grouped object down so it does not cover the text of the title page. Because the graphic is so large and you want to see the entire graphic on the page as you move it, you display the entire page in the document window before moving the graphic, as described in the following steps.

TO MOVE A GRAPHIC

1. Click the Zoom box arrow on the Standard toolbar and then click Whole Page.
2. Point to the middle of the graphic and drag the graphic to its new location; in this case, drag it down so it does not cover any words on the title page (Figure 7-65).
3. Click the Zoom box arrow on the Standard toolbar and then click Page Width.
4. Click the Drawing button on the Drawing toolbar to remove the Drawing toolbar from the screen.
5. Click the Save button on the Standard toolbar to save the document.

Word moves both objects together as a single unit.

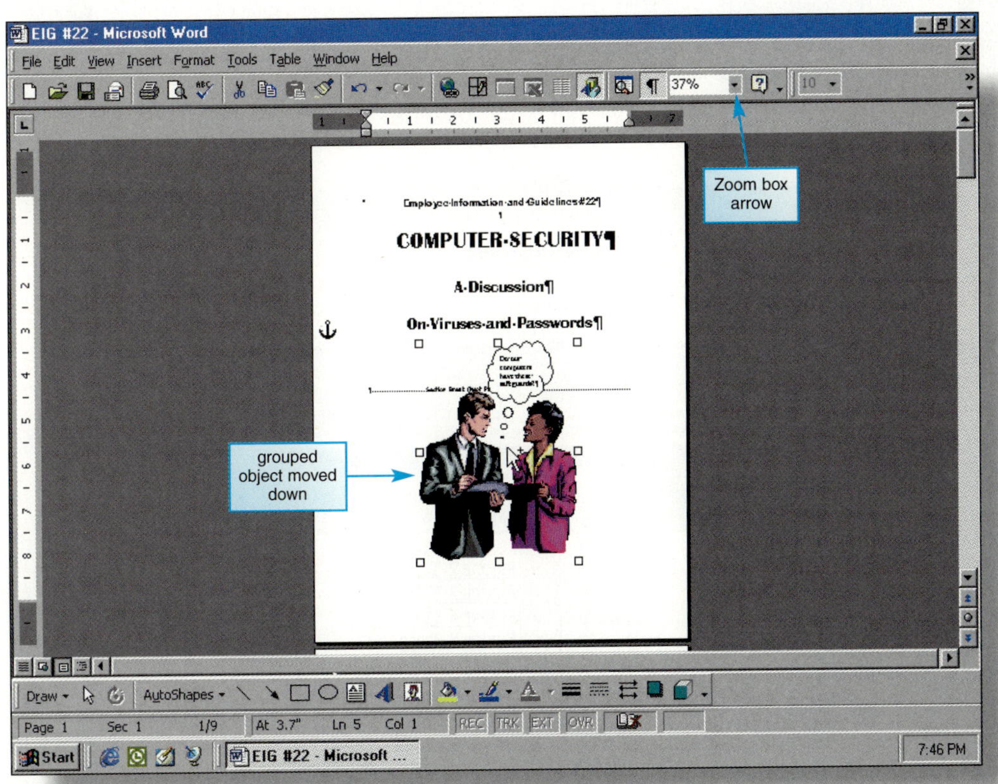

FIGURE 7-65

The title page is complete. The next step is to create the table of figures for the EIG #22 document.

Creating a Table of Figures

All EIG #22 documents have a table of figures following the text of the document. A **table of figures** is a list of all illustrations such as graphics, pictures, and tables in a document. Word creates the table of figures from the captions in the document. Perform the following steps to create a table of figures.

To Create a Table of Figures

1 Scroll down to display the Table of Figures heading. Position the insertion point at the end of the heading. Press the ENTER key. Click Insert on the menu bar and then point to Index and Tables (Figure 7-66).

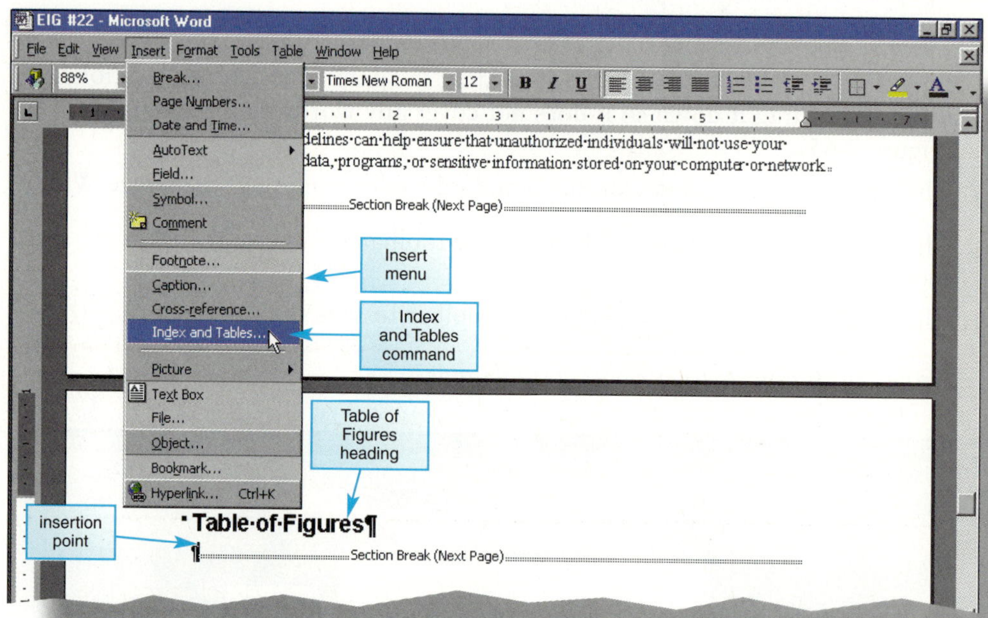

FIGURE 7-66

2 Click Index and Tables. When the Index and Tables dialog box displays, if necessary, click the Table of Figures tab. Be sure that the three check boxes in your dialog box contain check marks. Point to the OK button.

Word displays the Table of Figures sheet in the Index and Tables dialog box (Figure 7-67).

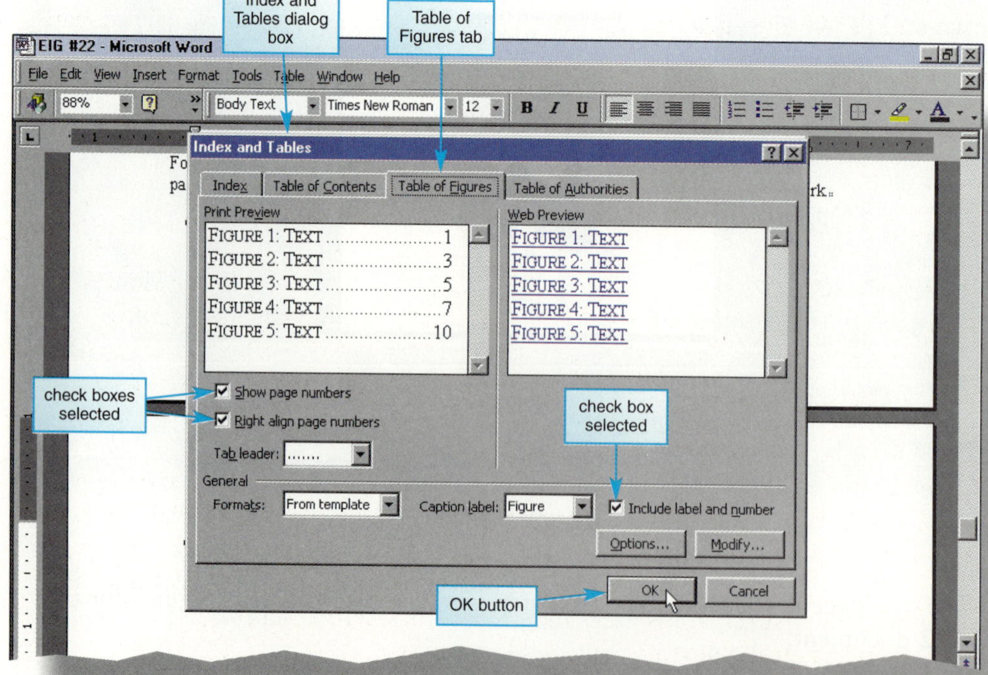

FIGURE 7-67

3 **Click the OK button.**

Word creates a table of figures at the location of the insertion point (Figure 7-68).

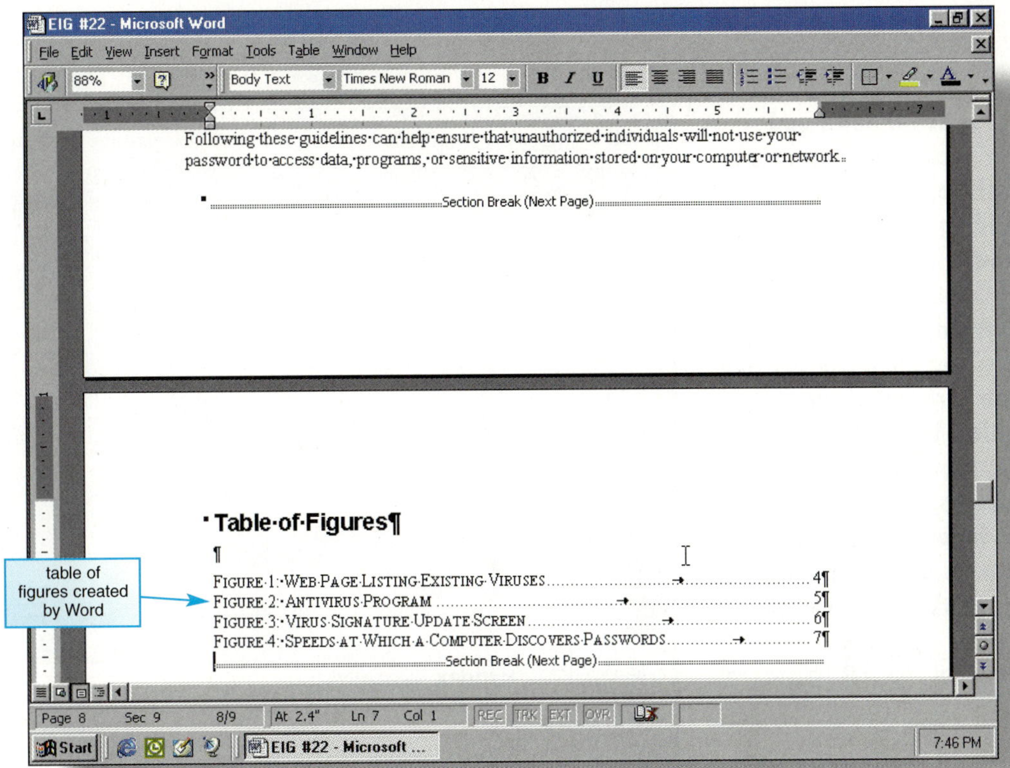

FIGURE 7-68

When you modify captions in a document or move illustrations to a different location in the document, you will have to update the table of figures. To do this, click to the left of the table and then press F9.

If you did not use captions to create labels for your illustrations in a document and would like Word to generate a table of figures, you can instruct Word to create the table using the built-in style you used for the captions. To do this, click the Options button in the Table of Figures sheet to display the Table of Figures Options dialog box.

The next step is to build an index for the document.

Building an Index

As mentioned earlier in this project, the EIG documents end with an **index**, which lists important terms discussed in the document along with each term's corresponding page number. For Word to generate the index, you first must mark any item you wish to appear in the index. Earlier in this project, you marked an entry in the Passwords file. The Computer Viruses file also already has index entries marked.

When you have marked all index entries, you can have Word build the index from the index entry fields in the document. The index entry fields display on the screen when the Show/Hide ¶ button on the Standard toolbar is recessed; that is, when you display formatting marks. Because these index entry field codes may alter the document pagination, you should hide field codes before building an index. Perform the tasks on the next page to build an index.

More About 2000

Index Entries

Instead of marking index entries in a document, you can create a concordance file, which Word uses to mark index entries automatically. The concordance file contains two columns: (1) the first column identifies the text in the document you want Word to mark as an index entry, and (2) the second column lists the index entries to be generated from the text in the first column. To mark entries in the concordance file, click the AutoMark button in the Index and Tables dialog box.

To Build an Index

1 **Scroll down and click the paragraph mark below the Index heading. If the Show/Hide ¶ button on the Standard toolbar is recessed, click it. Click Insert on the menu bar and then click Index and Tables. When the Index and Tables dialog box displays, if necessary, click the Index tab. Click the Formats box arrow. Scroll to and then click Formal.**

Word displays the Index sheet in the Index and Tables dialog box (Figure 7-69). The Formats box contains a variety of available index styles.

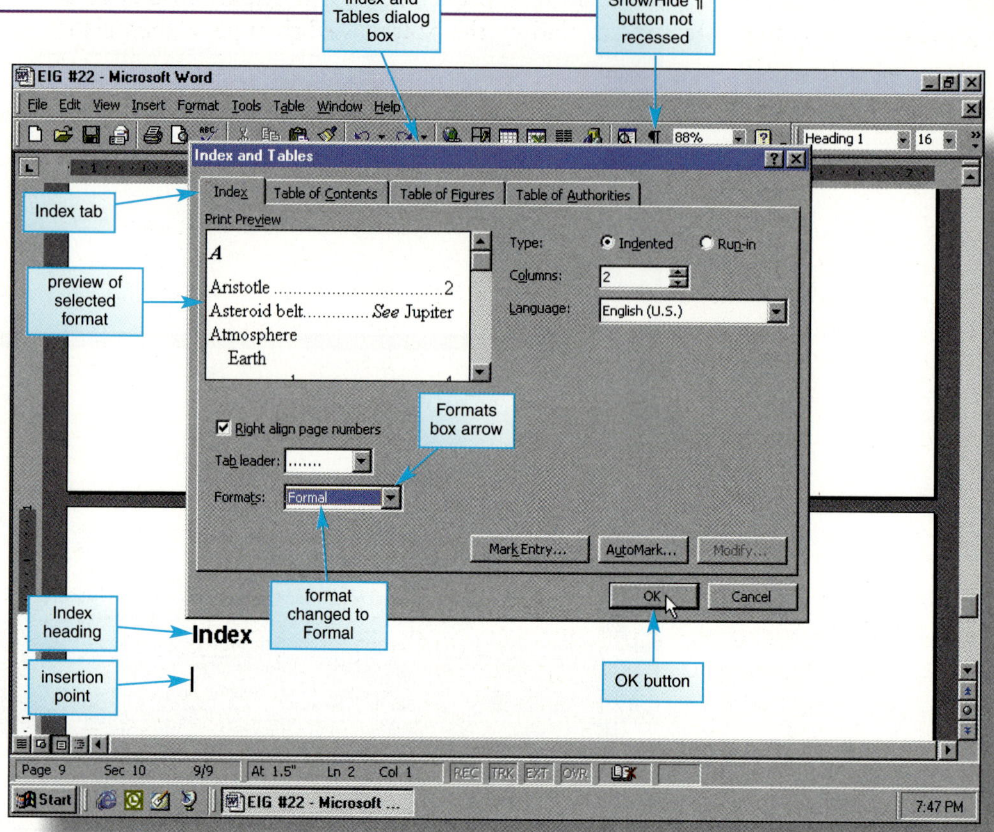

FIGURE 7-69

2 **Click the OK button. If necessary, click outside the index to remove the selection.**

Word creates a formal index at the location of the insertion point (Figure 7-70).

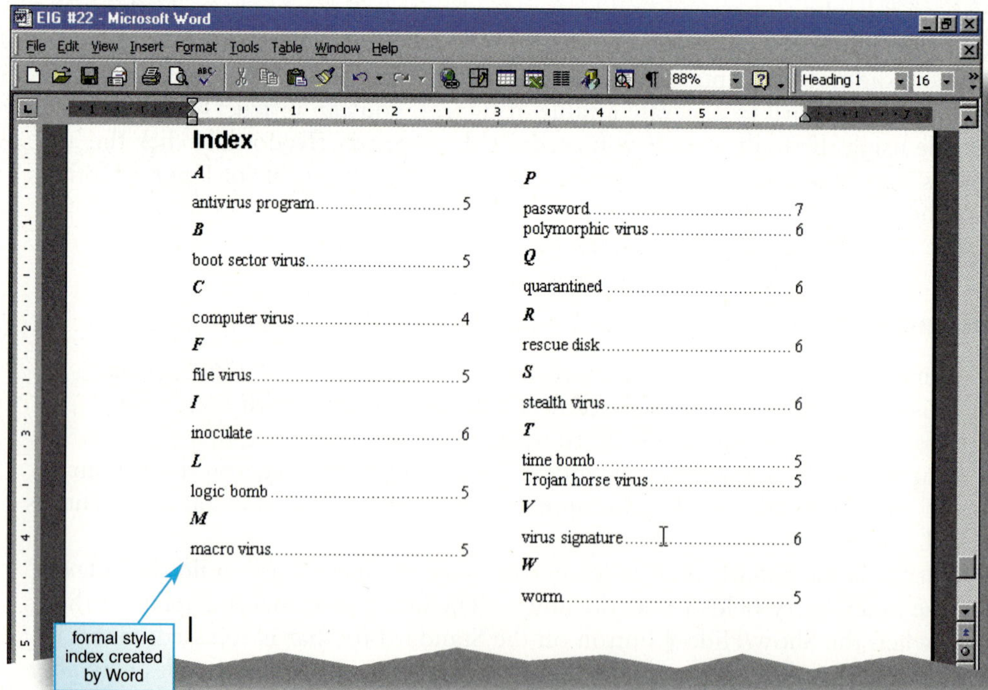

FIGURE 7-70

To update an index, click to the left of the index and then press F9. To delete an index, click to the left of the index and then press SHIFT+F9 to display field codes. Drag through the entire field code, including the braces, and then press the DELETE key.

The next step is to create the table of contents for the EIG #22 document.

Indexes and Tables

If your index, table of contents, or table of figures displays odd characters inside curly braces {}, then Word is displaying field codes instead of field results. Press ALT+F9 to display the index or table correctly. If your index or table prints field codes, click Tools on the menu bar, click Options, click the Print tab, remove the check mark from the Field codes check box, click the OK button, and then print the document again.

Creating a Table of Contents

A **table of contents** is a list of all headings in a document and their associated page numbers. When you use Word's built-in heading styles (e.g., Heading 1), you can instruct Word to create a table of contents from these headings. In the EIG #22 document, the heading of each section used the Heading 1 style and subheadings used the Heading 2 style. Thus, perform the following steps to create a table of contents from heading styles.

Steps To Create a Table of Contents

1 Scroll up and click to the right of the Table of Contents heading. Press the ENTER key. Click Insert on the menu bar and then click Index and Tables. When the Index and Tables dialog box displays, if necessary, click the Table of Contents tab. Click the Formats box arrow and then click Formal.

Word displays the Table of Contents sheet in the Index and Tables dialog box (Figure 7-71). The Formats list contains a variety of available table of contents styles.

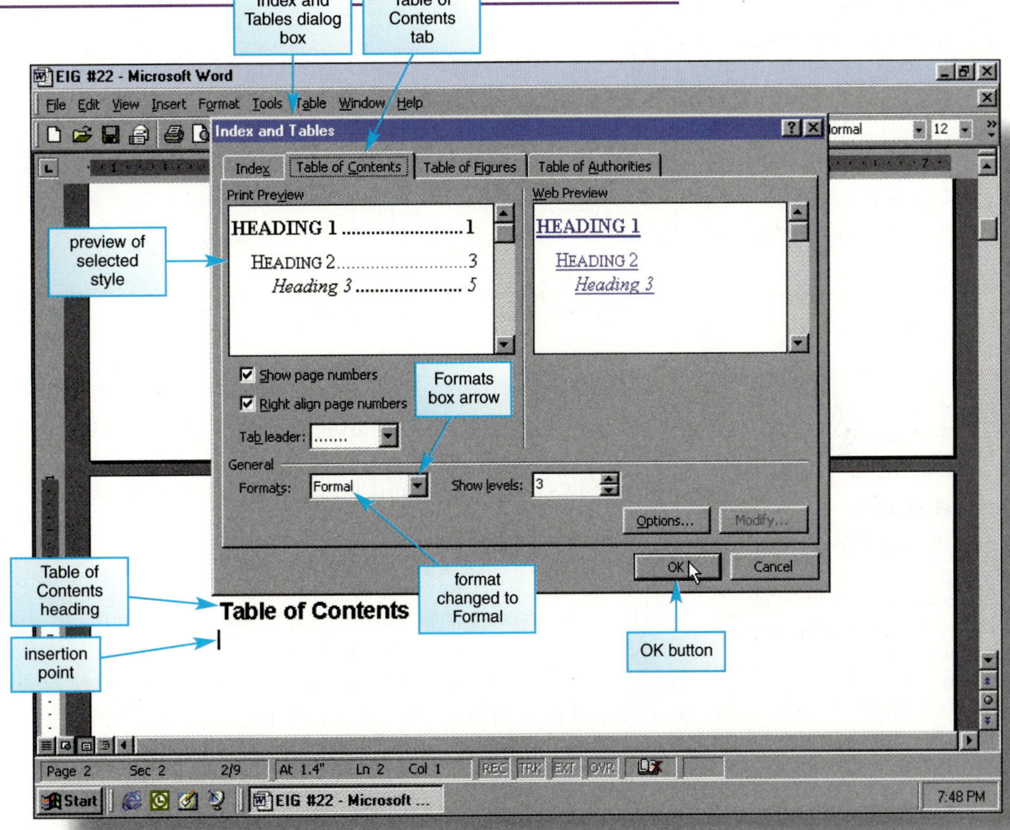

FIGURE 7-71

2 **Click the OK button. If a dialog box displays asking if you want to replace the selected table of contents, click the No button.**

Word creates a formal table of contents at the location of the insertion point (Figure 7-72).

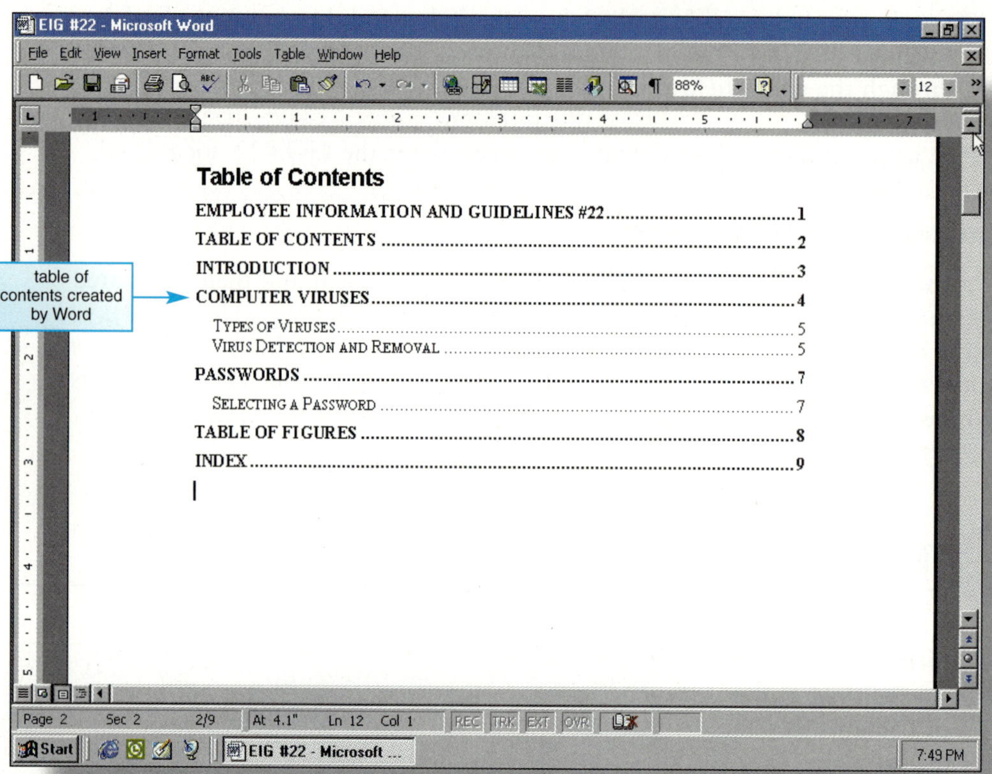

FIGURE 7-72

Modifying a Table of Contents

If the table of contents that Word generates contains a heading that you do not want, change the style applied to the heading from a built-in heading to a non-heading style. Then, update the table of contents.

When you change headings or text in a document, you should update its associated table of contents. To update a table of contents, click to the left of the table of contents and then press F9.

The next step is to add bookmarks to the document.

Adding Bookmarks

In a document that contains a table of contents or a table of figures, you can use these tables to navigate through a document. That is, you can click any of the entries in either table and Word displays the associated text or graphics in the document window. For example, if you click Figure 2 in the table of figures, Word displays the page containing Figure 2.

To further assist users in navigating through a document, you can add bookmarks. A **bookmark** is an item in a document that you name for future reference. For example, you could bookmark the two headings, Computer Viruses and Passwords, so that users easily could jump to these two areas of the document. Perform the following steps to add these bookmarks.

Bookmarks

To show bookmarks in a document, click Tools on the menu bar, click Options, click the View tab, place a check mark in the Bookmarks check box, and then click the OK button. If your bookmark displays an error message, select the entire document and then press F9 to update the fields in the document.

To Add a Bookmark

1 **Scroll to the Computer Viruses heading in the document. Drag through the heading Computer Viruses. Click Insert on the menu bar and then point to Bookmark (Figure 7-73).**

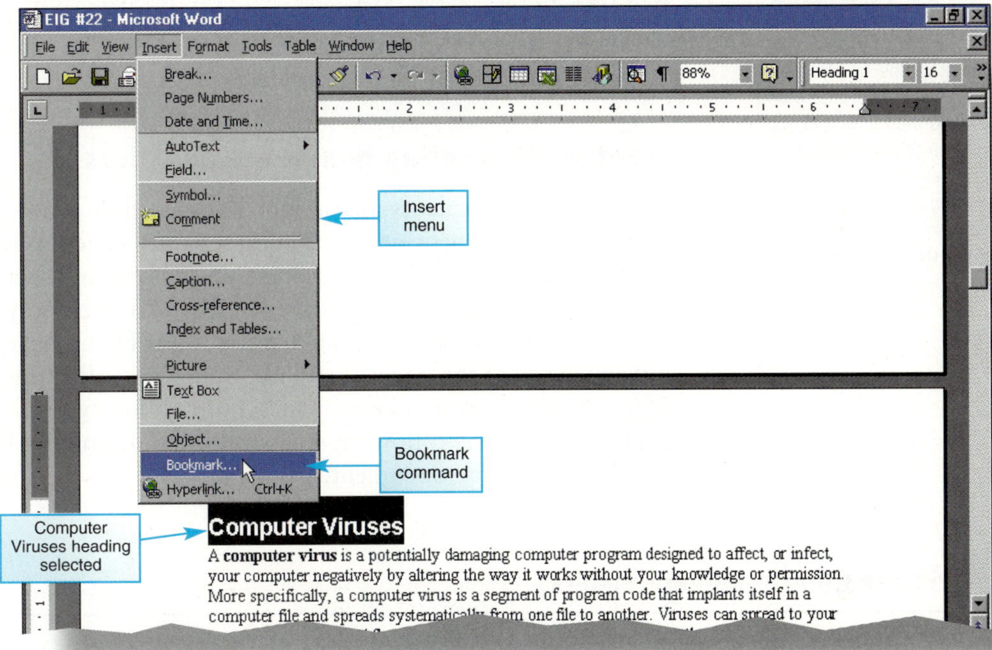

FIGURE 7-73

2 **Click Bookmark. When the Bookmark dialog box displays, type** ComputerViruses **in the Bookmark name text box and then point to the Add button.**

Word displays the Bookmark dialog box (Figure 7-74). Bookmark names can contain only letters, numbers, and the underscore character (_). Also, they must begin with a letter and contain no spaces.

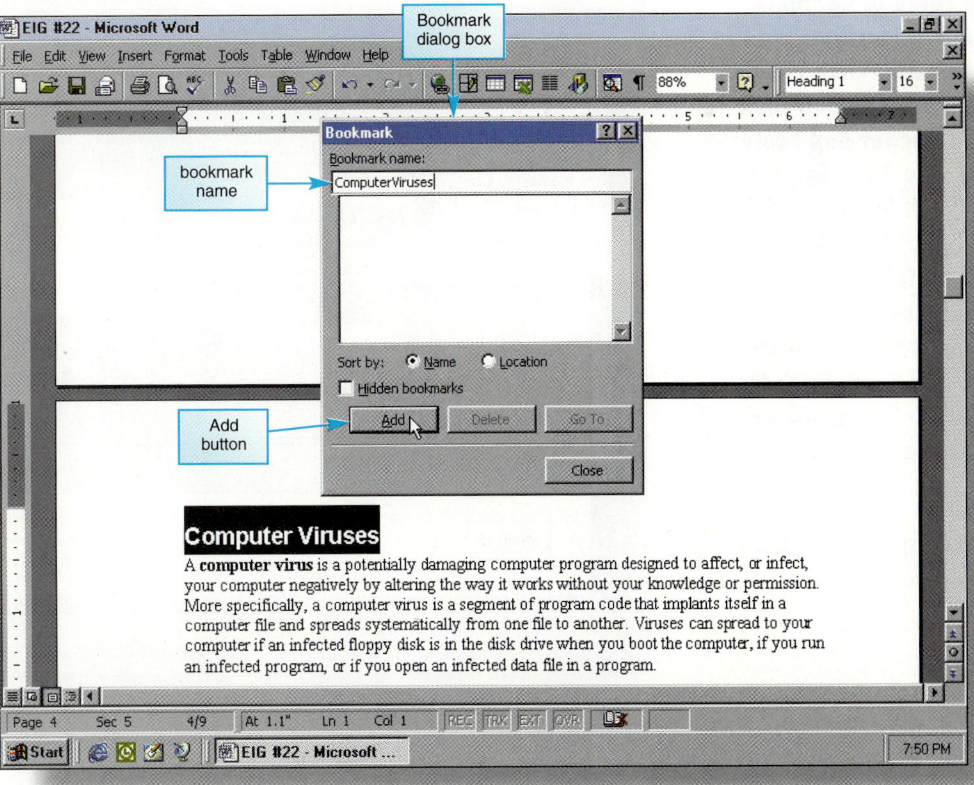

FIGURE 7-74

3 **Click the Add button.**

Word adds the bookmark name to the list of existing bookmarks for the document.

4 **Repeat Steps 1 through 3 for the Passwords heading in the document.**

The Go To Dialog Box

To display the Go To dialog box, click Edit on the menu bar and then click Go To; or click the Select Browse Object button on the vertical scroll bar and then click Go To; or double-click the Page indicator on the status bar; or press F5.

Once you have added bookmarks, you can jump to a bookmark by displaying the Bookmark dialog box, clicking the bookmark name in the list, and then clicking the Go To button; or by displaying the Go To dialog box, clicking bookmark in the list, selecting the bookmark name, and then clicking the Go To button.

The text of the document now is complete. The next step is to place a header on all pages except the title page.

Creating Alternating Headers and Footers

The EIG documents are designed so that they can be duplicated back to back. That is, the document prints on nine separate pages. When you duplicate it, however, pages one and two are printed on opposite sides of the same sheet of paper. Thus, the nine page document when printed back-to-back only uses five sheets of paper.

In many books and documents that have facing pages, the page number is on the outside edges of the pages. In Word, you accomplish this task by specifying one type of header for even-numbered pages and another type of header for odd-numbered pages. Perform the following steps to create alternating headers beginning with the second page of the document.

To Create Alternating Headers

1 Position the insertion point in the Table of Contents heading (section 2 of the document), click View on the menu bar and then click Header and Footer. Click the Page Setup button on the Header and Footer toolbar. When the Page Setup dialog box displays, if necessary, click the Layout tab. Click Different odd and even. Click the Apply to box arrow and then click This point forward.

Word displays the Page Setup dialog box (Figure 7-75).

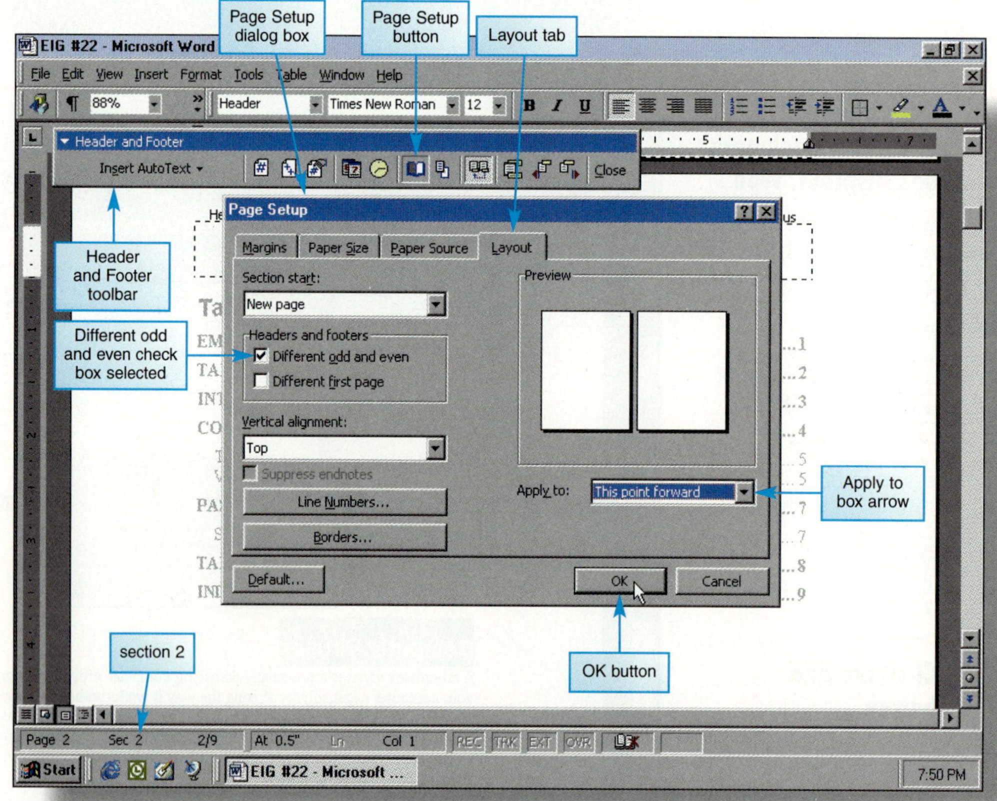

FIGURE 7-75

2 **Click the OK button. If the Same as Previous button on the Header and Footer toolbar is recessed, click it. Type** Textbooks Press EIG #22 **and then press the ENTER key. Type** Page **and then press the SPACEBAR. Click the Insert Page Number button on the Header and Footer toolbar. Press the ENTER key. Point to the Show Next button on the Header and Footer toolbar.**

Word displays the Even Page Header area (Figure 7-76). You want text on even page numbers to be left-aligned and text on odd page numbers to be right-aligned. The Show Next button will display the Odd Page Header area.

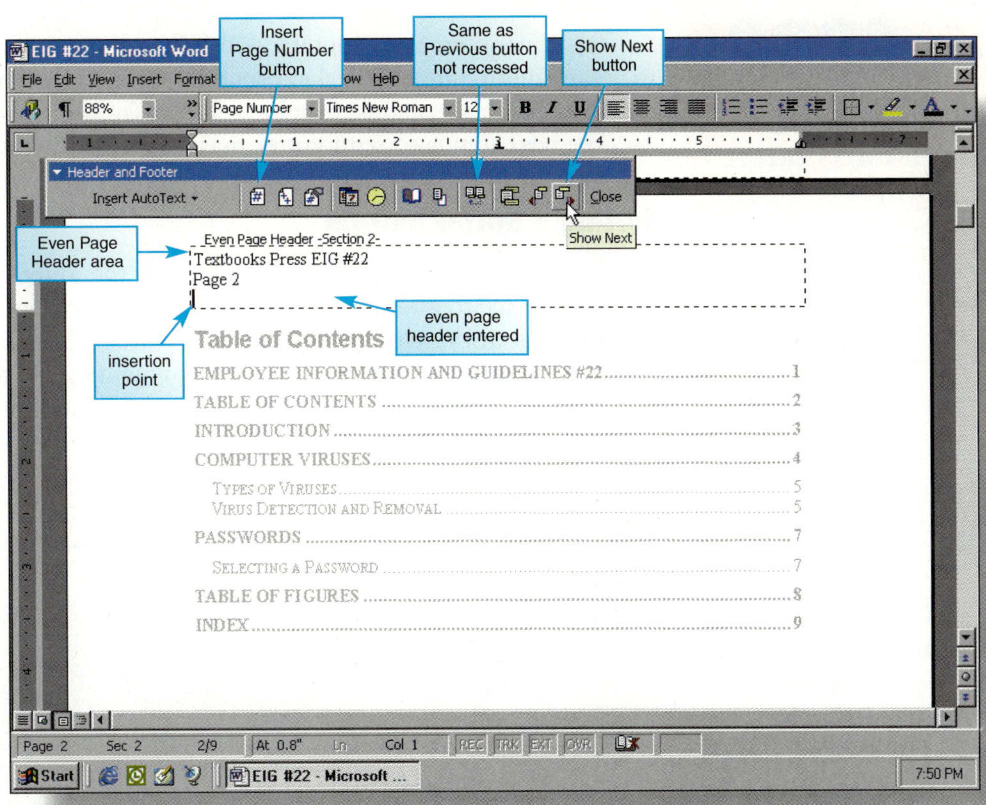

FIGURE 7-76

3 **Click the Show Next button. If the Same as Previous button on the Header and Footer toolbar is recessed, click it. Point to the right edge of the Odd Page Header area so a right-align icon displays next to the mouse pointer and then double-click. Type** Textbooks Press EIG #22 **and then press the ENTER key. Type** Page **and then press the SPACEBAR. Click the Insert Page Number button on the Header and Footer toolbar. Press the ENTER key.**

The odd page header is complete (Figure 7-77).

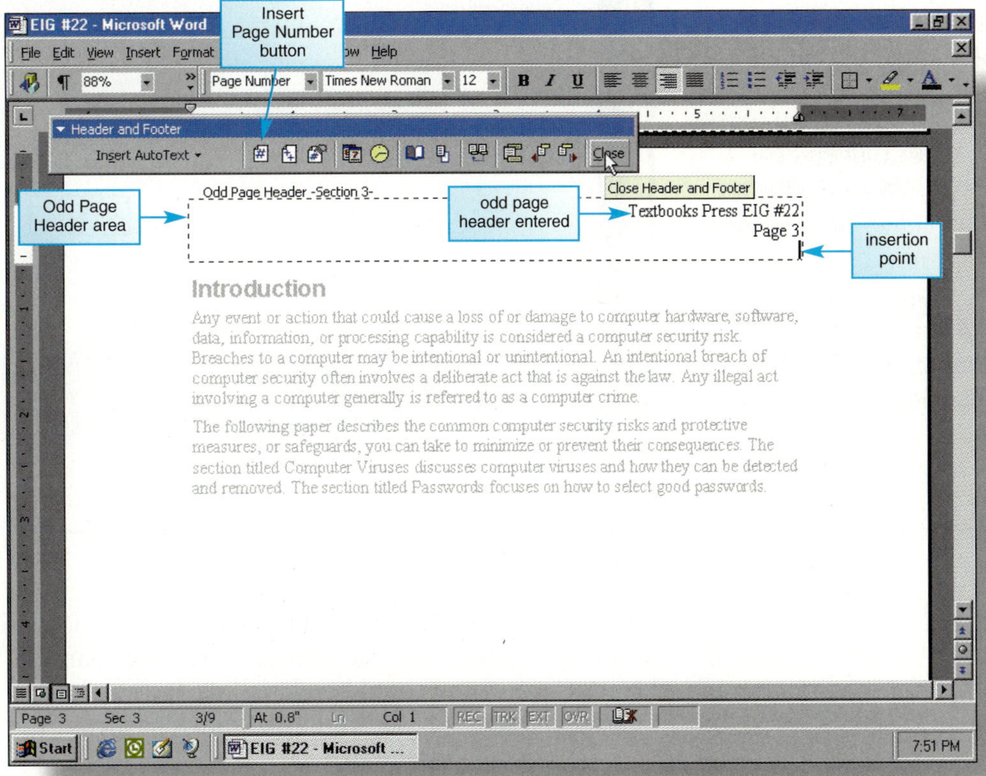

FIGURE 7-77

4 **Click the Close button on the Header and Footer toolbar.**

Publishing and Graphic Arts Terms

For more information on terms used in publishing and graphic arts, visit the Word 2000 More About Web page (www.scsite.com/wd2000/more.htm) and then click Publishing and Graphic Arts Terms.

To create alternating footers, you follow the same basic procedure as you would to create alternating headers, except you enter text in the footer area instead of the header area.

The next step is to set a gutter margin for the document.

Setting a Gutter Margin

The EIG documents are designed so that the inner margin between facing pages has extra space to allow printed versions of the documents to be bound (such as stapled) – without the binding covering the words. This extra space in the inner margin is called the **gutter margin**. Perform the following steps to set a three-quarter inch left and right margin and a one-half inch gutter margin.

To Set a Gutter Margin

1 **Click File on the menu bar and then click Page Setup. When the Page Setup dialog box displays, if necessary, click the Margins tab. Type .75 in the Left text box, .75 in the Right text box, and .5 in the Gutter text box. Click the Apply to box arrow and then click Whole document. Point to the OK button.**

Word displays the Page Setup dialog box (Figure 7-78). The Preview area illustrates the position of the gutter margin.

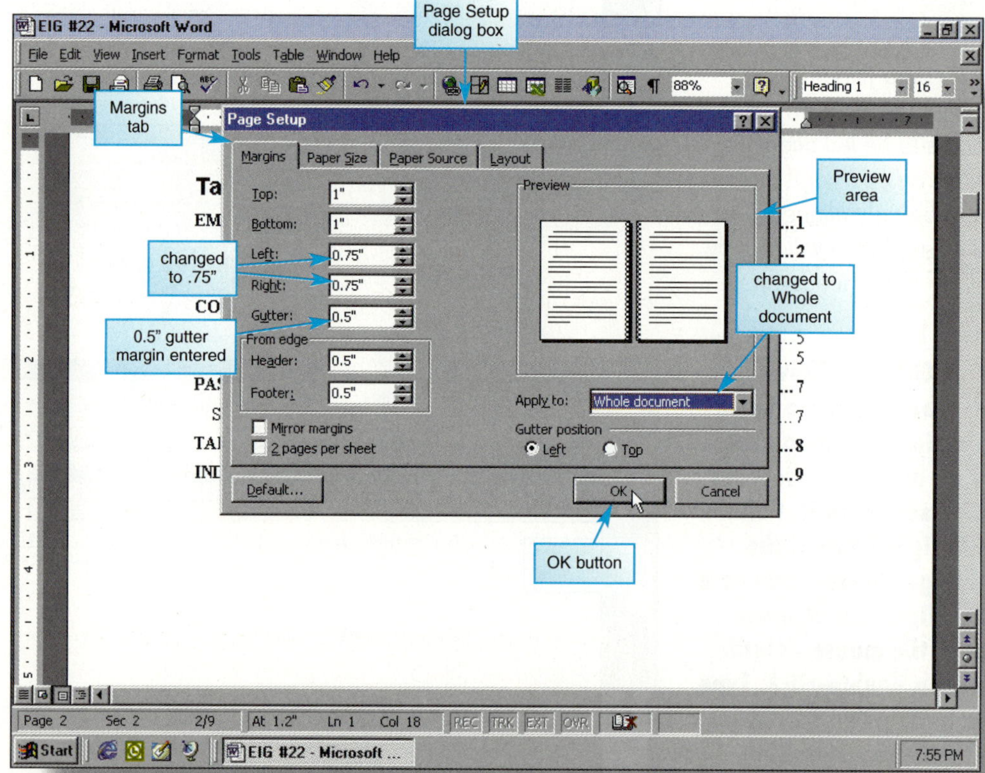

FIGURE 7-78

2 **Click the OK button.**

Word sets the gutter margin for the entire document.

Because you have changed the margins, it is possible the page numbers of the headings, figures, and index entries may have changed. Whenever you modify pages in a document, you should update the page numbers in the table of contents, table of figures, and index as shown in the following steps.

Steps To Update the Table of Contents, Table of Figures, and Index

1 **Be sure the Show/Hide ¶ button on the Standard toolbar is not recessed. Click Edit on the menu bar and then click Select All. Press F9. When the Update Table of Contents dialog box displays, if necessary, click Update page numbers only to select it. Point to the OK button.**

Word displays the Update Table of Contents dialog box (Figure 7-79). The entire document is selected.

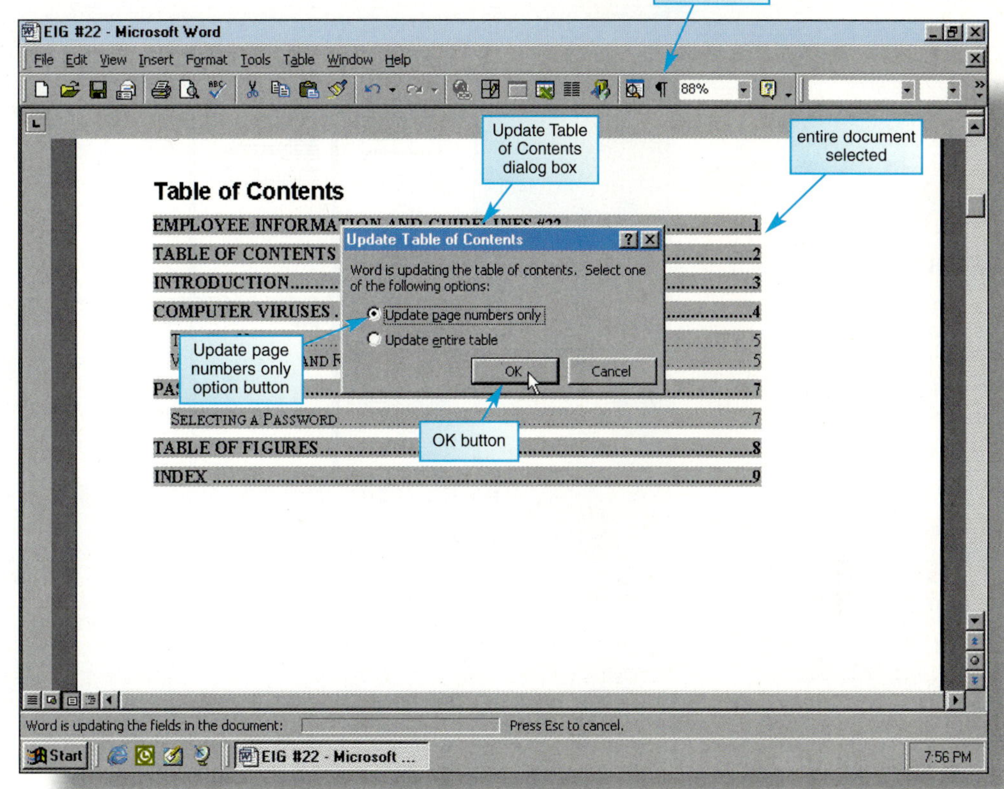

FIGURE 7-79

2 **Click the OK button. When the Update Table of Figures dialog box displays, click the OK button. Click to remove the selection.**

Word updates the page numbers in the table of figures, table of contents, and index.

To visually see the layout of all of the pages in the document, display all the pages in print preview as described in the following steps.

TO DISPLAY SEVERAL PAGES IN PRINT PREVIEW

1. Double-click the move handle on the Standard toolbar to display the entire toolbar. Click the Print Preview button on the Standard toolbar.
2. Click the Multiple Pages button on the Print Preview toolbar. Click the right-bottom icon in the grid (when the description reads 2 x 6 pages) to display the pages in the EIG document as shown in Figure 7-80 on the next page.
3. Click the Close button on the Print Preview toolbar.

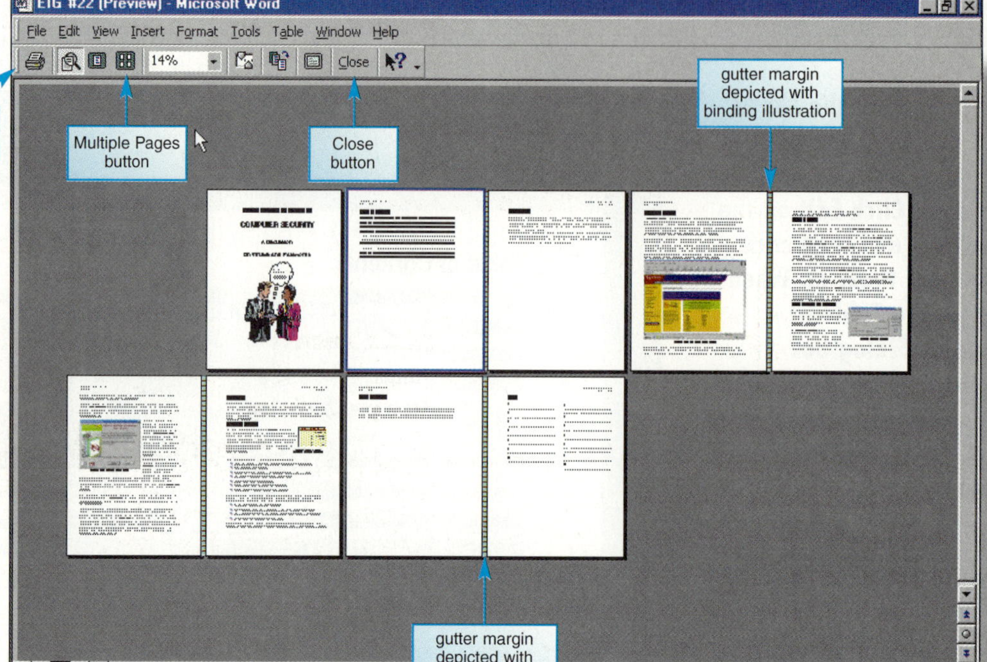

FIGURE 7-80

The reference document for this project now is complete. Perform the following steps to save it again, print it, and then close the document.

TO SAVE THE DOCUMENT AGAIN

1. Click the Save button on the Standard toolbar.

Word saves the reference document with the same file name, EIG #22.

TO PRINT THE DOCUMENT

1. Click the Print button on the Standard toolbar.

The completed reference document prints each page shown in Figure 7-1 on page WD 7.5 on a separate piece of paper.

TO CLOSE THE DOCUMENT

1. Click File on the menu bar and then click Close.

Opening a Master Document

You may wish to open a master document at a later date to edit or print its contents. When you open the master document, the subdocuments are collapsed; that is, the subdocuments display as hyperlinks. Thus, switch to outline view and expand the subdocuments as shown in the following steps.

More About 2000

Callouts

If text in a callout does not print, you need to make the callout wider. To do this, you will need to ungroup the drawing object first.

More About 2000

Printing

If you want to save ink, print faster, or minimize printer overrun errors, lower the printer resolution. Click File on the menu bar, click Print, click the Properties button in the Print dialog box, click the Graphics tab, click the Resolution box arrow, click a lower resolution than that displayed currently, click the Apply button, click the OK button, and then click the Close button.

More About 2000

Subdocuments

If you want to change the name of a subdocument, you cannot use Windows Explorer. Instead, display the document in outline view, click the Collapse Subdocuments button on the Outlining toolbar, and then click the hyperlink of the document to be renamed. When the subdocument displays in its own Word window, click File on the menu bar, click Save As, change the document name, and then click the Save button in the dialog box. Then, return to the master document by clicking File on the menu bar and then clicking Close.

Steps To Open a Master Document

1 Open the EIG #22 document. Click the Outline View button on the horizontal scroll bar. Be sure the Show All Headings button on the Outlining toolbar is recessed and the Show First Line Only button is not recessed. Scroll down to display the hyperlinks. Point to the Expand Subdocuments button on the Outlining toolbar.

Word displays the EIG #22 document in outline view (Figure 7-81).

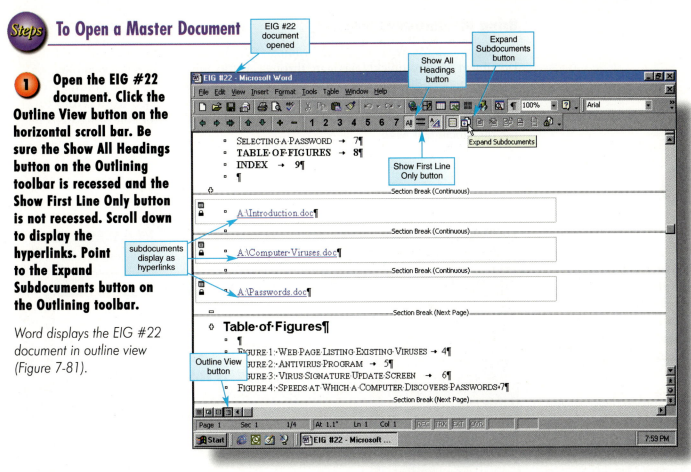

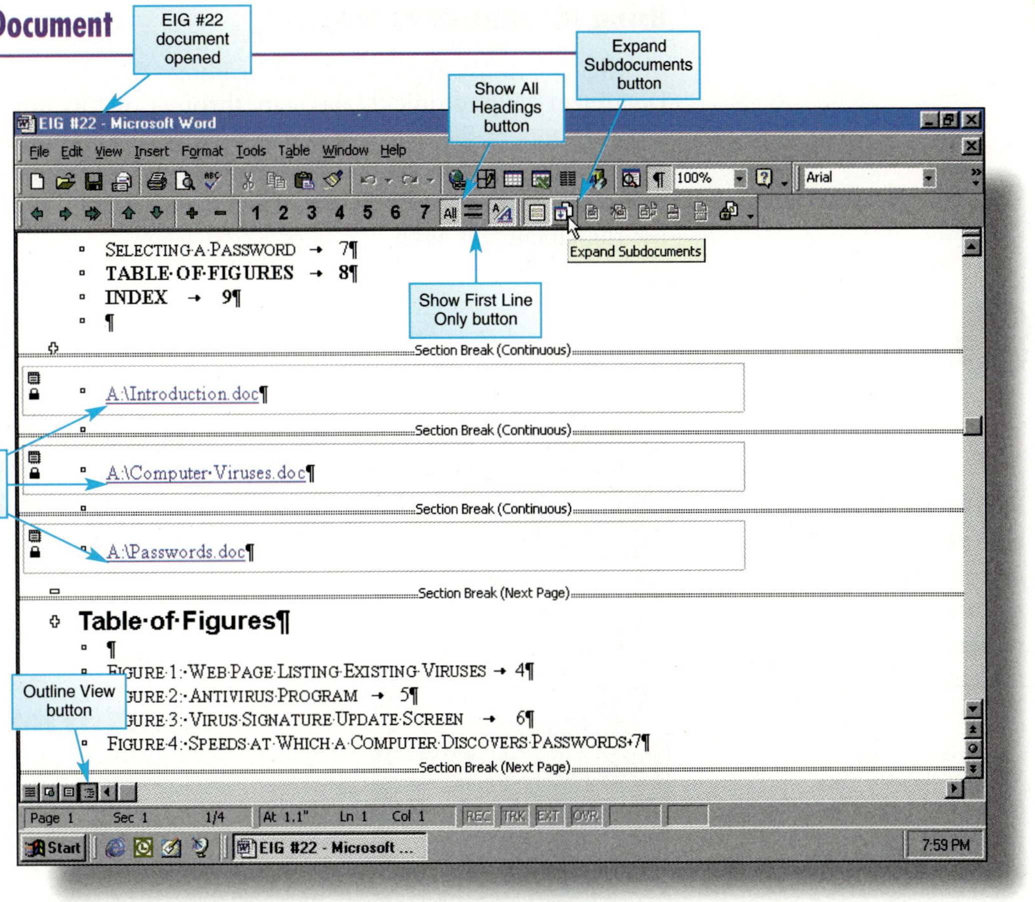

FIGURE 7-81

2 Click the Expand Subdocuments button. When the Passwords dialog box displays, type `sunshine` **and then click the OK button.**

Word displays the contents of the subdocuments in the master document (Figure 7-82).

3 Click the Print Layout View button.

The master document is ready to be printed or modified.

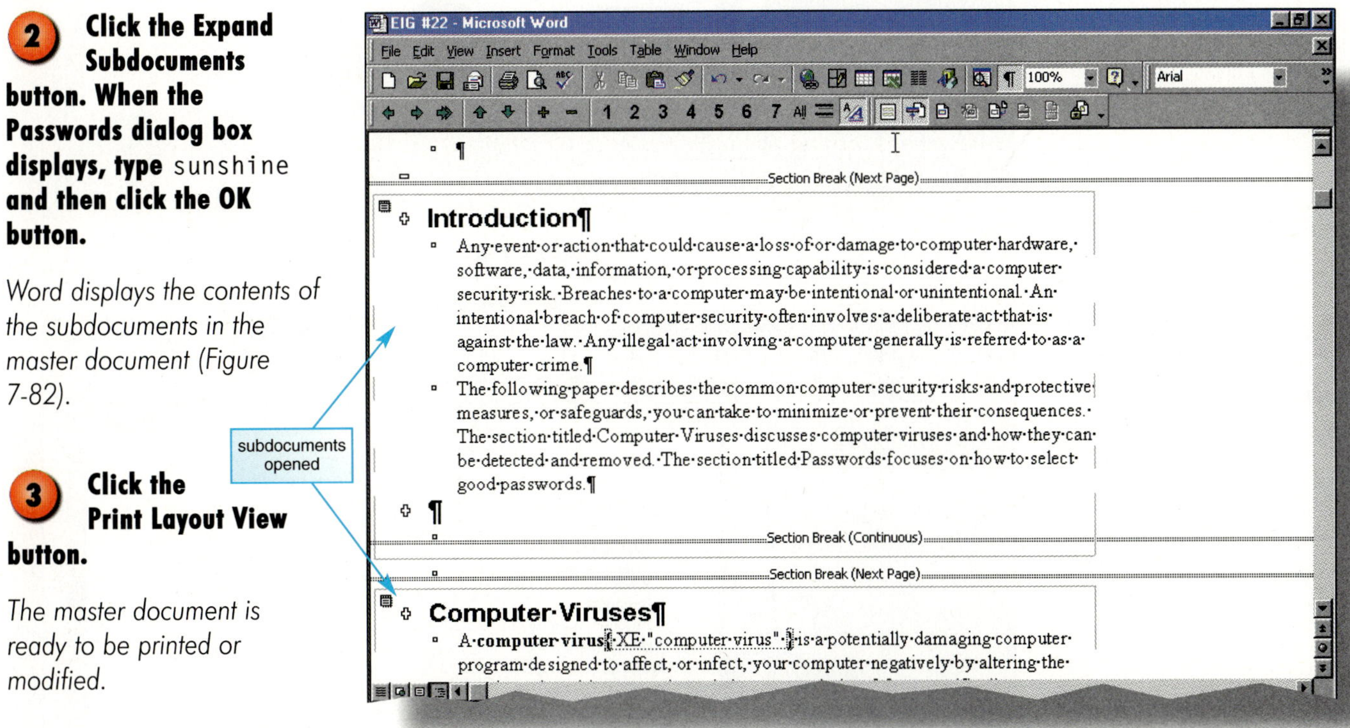

FIGURE 7-82

Using the Document Map

When you use Word's built-in heading styles in a document, you can use the Document Map to quickly navigate through the document. The **Document Map** is a separate area at the left edge of the Word window that displays these headings in an outline format. When you click a heading in the Document Map, Word scrolls to and displays that heading in the document window. Perform the following steps to use the Document Map.

To Use the Document Map

1 Click the Document Map button on the Standard toolbar. Right-click the Document Map and then click All on the shortcut menu to ensure that all headings display.

Word displays the Document Map in a separate pane at the left edge of the Word window (Figure 7-83). The Document Map lists all headings that are formatted using Word's built-in heading styles.

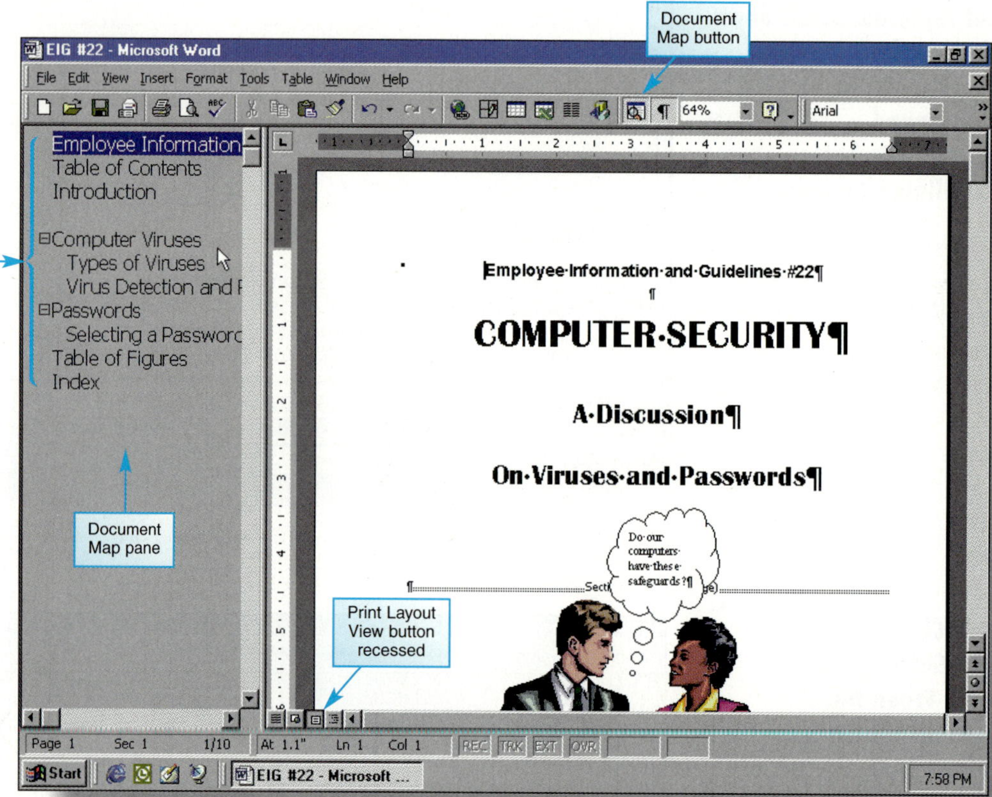

FIGURE 7-83

2 Click Table of Contents in the Document Map pane.

Word scrolls to and displays the Table of Contents heading at the top of the document window (Figure 7-84).

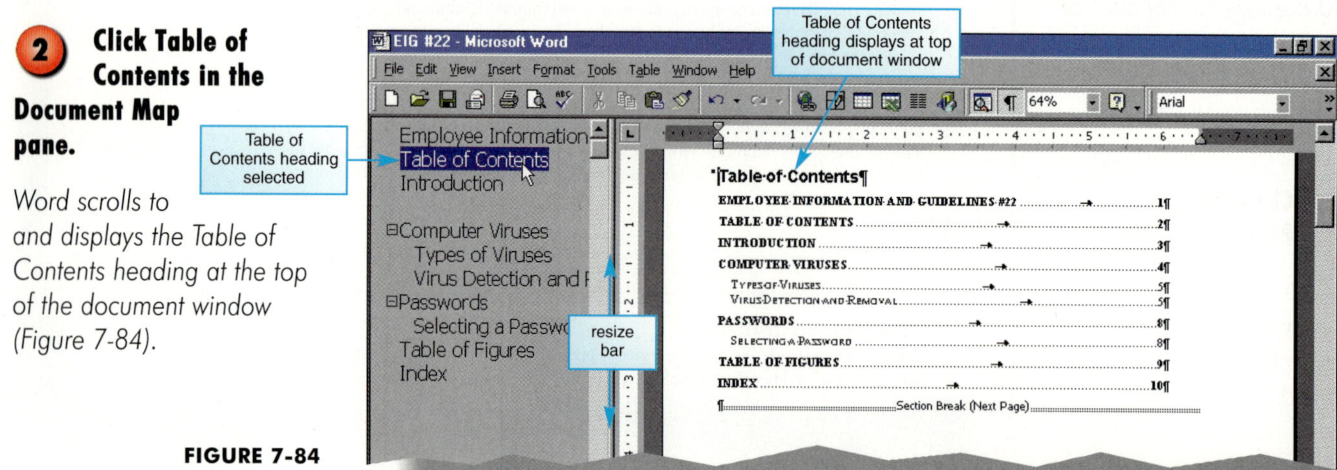

FIGURE 7-84

To display any subheadings below a heading, click the plus sign (+) to the left of the heading. Likewise, to hide any subheadings below a heading, click the minus sign (-) to the left of the heading.

If a heading is too wide for the Document Map pane, you do not need to make the Document Map pane wider – simply point to the heading to display a ScreenTip that shows the complete heading. You can, however, change the width of the Document Map pane by dragging the resize bar to the left or right.

Quick Reference

For a table that lists how to complete the tasks covered in this book using the mouse, menu, shortcut menu, and keyboard, see the Word Quick Reference Summary at the back of this book or visit the Shelly Cashman Series Office Web page (www.scsite.com/off2000/qr.htm) and then click Microsoft Word 2000.

Modifying the Table of Contents and Index

Assume you wanted to change the title of the Table of Contents to just the word, Contents. Assume also that you want to change the index entry for computer virus to just the word, virus. After making these changes to the document, you must update the table of contents and the index as shown in the following steps.

To Modify a Table of Contents and Index

1 Drag through the words, Table of, in the Table of Contents heading and then press the DELETE key. If the Show/Hide ¶ button on the Standard toolbar is not recessed, click it. Click the Computer Viruses heading in the Document Map pane. Double-click the move handle on the Formatting toolbar to display the entire toolbar. Double-click the bold word, computer, to select it and then click the Bold button to remove the bold. Double-click the word, computer, inside the braces and then press the DELETE key.

The document is modified (Figure 7-85). You display formatting marks to change the index entry fields.

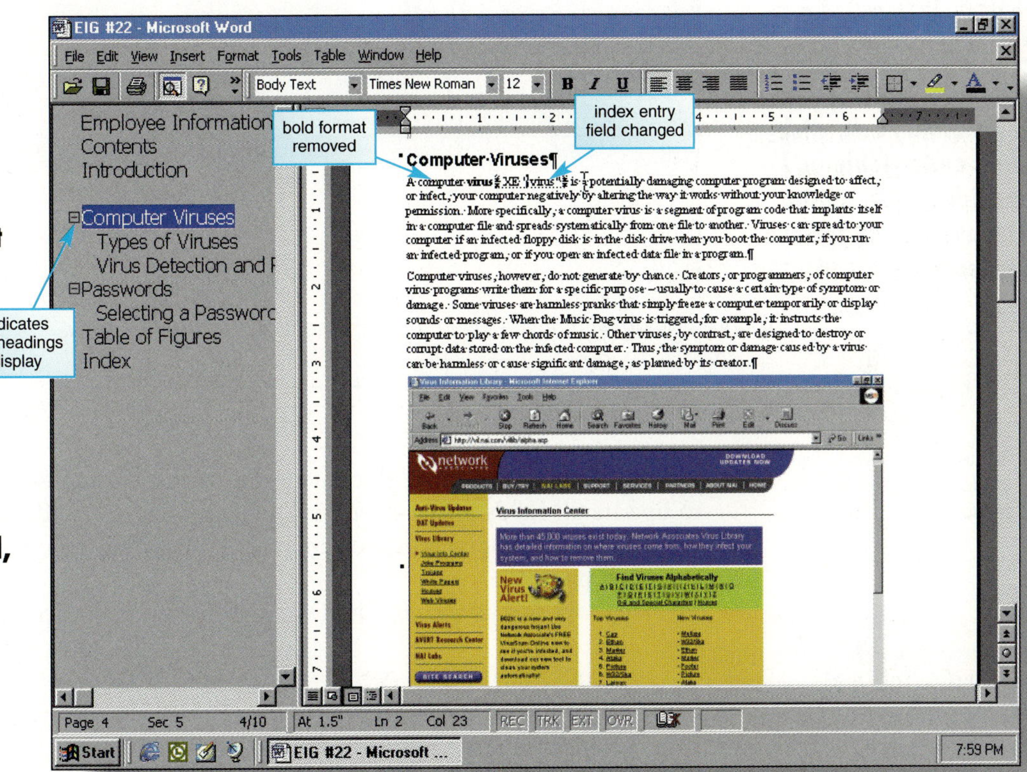

FIGURE 7-85

2 **Double-click the Standard toolbar to display the entire toolbar. Click the Show/Hide ¶ button on the Standard toolbar. Click Edit on the menu bar and then click Select All. Press F9. When the Update Table of Contents dialog box displays, click Update entire table and then point to the OK button.**

Word displays the Update Table of Contents dialog box (Figure 7-86).

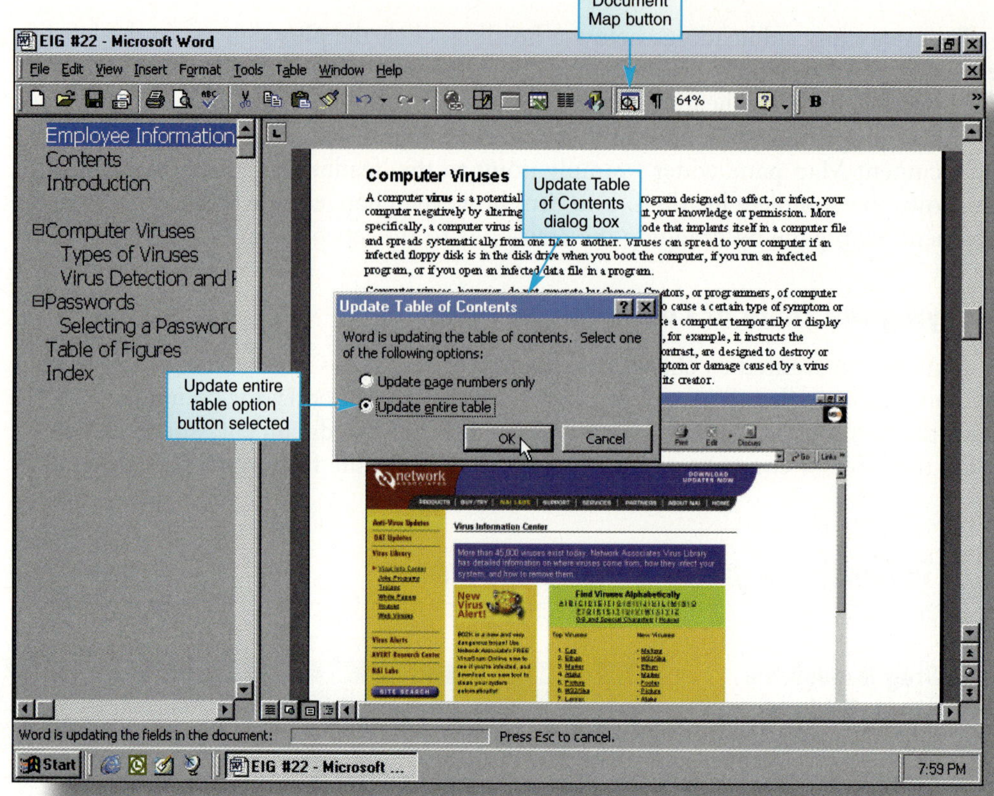

FIGURE 7-86

3 **Click the OK button. When Word displays the Update Table of Figures dialog box, click Update entire table and then click the OK button. Click anywhere to remove the selection.**

Word updates the Table of Figures, along with any fields in the document, including the index.

Other Ways

1. Right-click selection, click Update Field on shortcut menu

More About 2000

Microsoft Certification

The Microsoft Office User Specialist (MOUS) Certification program provides an opportunity for you to obtain a valuable industry credential - proof that you have the Word 2000 skills required by employers. For more information, see Appendix D or visit the Shelly Cashman Series MOUS Web page at www.scsite.com/off2000/cert.htm.

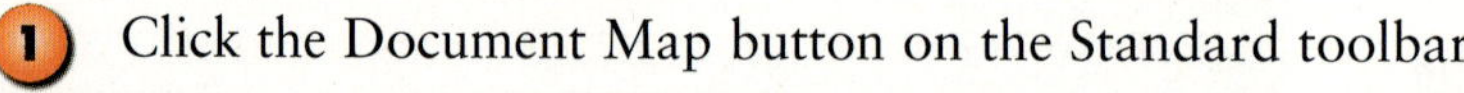

By selecting the entire document and then pressing F9, you are instructing Word to update all fields in the document, which includes fields in the table of contents, table of figures, index, and bookmarks. If you want to update a single field, select it and then press F9.

The next step is to hide the Document Map, as described in the following step.

TO HIDE THE DOCUMENT MAP

1 Click the Document Map button on the Standard toolbar.

Word removes the Document Map pane from the Word window.

You also can hide the Document Map by double-clicking the resize bar to its right. You are finished modifying the document. Perform the following step to quit Word.

TO QUIT WORD

1 Click the Close button in the Word window. When Word displays a dialog box asking if you wish to save changes, click the No button.

The Word window closes.

CASE PERSPECTIVE SUMMARY

You send the redesigned EIG #22 document to Marge for her approval. She is thrilled with the new design. The table of contents, table of figures, and index really organize the document for a reader. She gives you approval to duplicate and distribute the document.

Marge would like you to conduct training classes for company employees on the change-tracking features of Word. You send an e-mail announcing the schedule and topic of the training classes. Next, you write a set of instructions to distribute to each attendee at the training classes. Your first class is tomorrow – it sure will be nice to be on the other side of the podium!

Project Summary

Project 7 introduced you to creating a long document with a table of contents, a table of figures, and an index. You inserted, modified, reviewed, and deleted comments. You also tracked changes and accepted and rejected the tracked changes. You learned how to save multiple versions of a document, embed an Excel worksheet, add and modify a caption, create a cross-reference, mark index entries, add a bookmark, keep paragraphs together, password-protect a document, create alternating headers, set a gutter margin, add an AutoShape, and group drawing objects. You also worked with master documents and subdocuments. Finally, you used the Document Map to navigate through the document.

What You Should Know

Having completed this project, you should now be able to perform the following tasks:

- Add a Bookmark *(WD 7.59)*
- Add a Caption *(WD 7.26)*
- Add an AutoShape *(WD 7.49)*
- Build an Index *(WD 7.56)*
- Change an Inline Graphic to a Floating Graphic *(WD 7.25, WD 7.51)*
- Close the Document *(WD 7.36, WD 7.64)*
- Convert a Text Box to a Frame *(WD 7.28)*
- Convert an Embedded Object to a Word Graphic *(WD 7.24)*
- Create a Cross-Reference *(WD 7.29)*
- Create a Subdocument *(WD 7.43)*
- Create a Table of Contents *(WD 7.57)*
- Create a Table of Figures *(WD 7.54)*
- Create Alternating Headers *(WD 7.60)*
- Create an Outline *(WD 7.37)*
- Delete a Comment *(WD 7.18)*
- Demote a Line to Body Text *(WD 7.47)*
- Display Formatting Marks *(WD 7.7)*
- Display Several Pages in Print Preview *(WD 7.63)*
- Embed an Object *(WD 7.23)*
- Enter and Format Title Page Text *(WD 7.48)*
- Enter Body Text into an Outline *(WD 7.45)*
- Group Objects *(WD 7.52)*
- Hide the Document Map *(WD 7.68)*
- Insert a Comment *(WD 7.10)*
- Insert a Password-Protected File as a Subdocument *(WD 7.42)*
- Insert a Subdocument *(WD 7.40)*
- Insert Clip Art *(WD 7.48)*
- Keep Paragraphs Together *(WD 7.33)*
- Mark an Index Entry *(WD 7.31)*
- Modify a Table of Contents and Index *(WD 7.67)*
- Modify an Outline *(WD 7.44)*
- Modify the Caption *(WD 7.28)*
- Move a Graphic *(WD 7.53)*
- Open a Document *(WD 7.9)*
- Open a Master Document *(WD 7.65)*
- Password-Protect a File *(WD 7.34)*
- Print the Document *(WD 7.64)*
- Quit Word *(WD 7.68)*
- Reset Menus and Toolbars *(WD 7.7)*
- Resize an Object *(WD 7.24)*
- Review Comments *(WD 7.17)*
- Review Tracked Changes *(WD 7.19)*
- Save a Document *(WD 7.43)*
- Save a Document with a New File Name *(WD 7.9)*
- Save a Version of a Document *(WD 7.15)*
- Save the Document Again *(WD 7.64)*
- Set a Gutter Margin *(WD 7.62)*
- Start Word *(WD 7.6)*
- Stop Tracking Changes *(WD 7.14)*
- Track Changes *(WD 7.13)*
- Update the Table of Contents, Table of Figures, and Index *(WD 7.63)*
- Use the Document Map *(WD 7.66)*
- Zoom Text Width *(WD 7.9)*

1 Using Word's Change-Tracking Feature

Instructions: Start Word. Open the document, Faxes Draft, on the Data Disk. If you did not download the Data Disk, see the inside back cover for instructions for downloading the Data Disk or see your instructor.

As shown in Figure 7-87, the document contains reviewer's comments and tracked changes. You are to review and delete the comments and then accept or reject each of the tracked changes.

A facsimile (fax) machine [CDG1] is a device that transmits and receives documents over telephone lines. The documents can contain text, drawings, or photographs, or can be handwritten. When sent or received via a fax machine, these documents are known as faxes. A stand-alone fax machine ~~reads~~scans the original document, converts the image into digitized data, and transmits the digitized image. A fax machine at the ~~other~~receiving end reads the incoming data, converts the digitized data into an image, and prints or stores a copy of the original image.¶

Fax capability also can be added to your computer using a fax modem. A fax modem is a communications device that allows you to send (and sometimes receive) electronic documents as faxes. A fax modem transmits computer-prepared documents[CDG2] such as a word processing letter, or documents that have been digitized with a scanner or digital camera. A fax modem is like a regular modem except that it is designed to transmit documents to a fax machine or to another fax modem.¶

When a computer (instead of a fax machine) receives a fax document, you can view the document on the screen or print it using special fax software. The quality of the viewed or printed fax is less than that of a word processing document because the fax actually is a large image. If you have optical character recognition (OCR) software, you also can edit the document.¶

A fax modem can be an external peripheral that plugs into a port on the back of the system unit or an internal card that is inserted into an expansion slot on the motherboard. In addition, most fax modems function as ~~regular~~ modems.¶

Close Full Screen

FIGURE 7-87

Perform the following tasks:

1. Right-click the TRK status indicator on the status bar and then click Highlight Changes on the shortcut menu. Verify the bottom two check boxes in the Highlight Changes dialog box contain check marks and then click the OK button. Print the document to see how it looks with tracked changes.
2. Click File on the menu bar, click Print, click the Options button, place a check mark in the Comments check box, click the OK button, and then click the OK button to print the document with comments. Click File on the menu bar, click Print, click the Options button, remove the check mark from the Comments check box, click the OK button, and then click the Close button to prevent comments from printing.
3. Click File on the menu bar, click Print, click the Print what box arrow, click Comments, and then click the OK button to print just the comments.
4. Right-click the TRK status indicator on the status bar and then click Highlight Changes on the shortcut menu. Remove the check mark from the Highlight changes in printed document check box and then click the OK button. Print the document to see how it looks with all marked changes made.

5. Press CTRL+HOME. Display the Reviewing toolbar. Be sure the TRK status indicator on the status bar is turned off. If it is not, double-click it to dim it. Click the Next Comment button on the Reviewing toolbar. Read the comment. Click the Delete Comment button on the Reviewing toolbar to delete the comment.
6. Click the Next Comment button on the Reviewing toolbar. Read the comment. Click the Delete Comment button on the Reviewing toolbar.
7. Press CTRL+HOME. Right-click the TRK status indicator on the status bar and then click Accept or Reject Changes on the shortcut menu. Click the Find Next button.
8. Click the Accept button to accept the insertion of the phrase, (fax).
9. Click the Accept button twice to accept the replacement of the word, reads, with the word, scans.
10. Click the Accept button twice to accept the replacement of the word, other, with the word, receiving.
11. Click the Accept button to accept the insertion of the example.
12. Click the Reject button to reject the insertion of the word, document.
13. Click the Accept button to accept the insertion of the phrase, a port on.
14. Click the Accept button to accept the insertion of the phrase, an expansion slot on.
15. Click the Reject button to reject the deletion of the word, regular. Click the Yes or OK button in each dialog box that displays. Click the Close button in the Accept or Reject Changes dialog box.
16. At the end of the document, insert the following comment: <u>Tracked changes accepted and rejected.</u>
17. Save the reviewed document with the name Faxes Revised. Print the document with comments.

1 Working with an Embedded Worksheet and Index

Problem: You work part-time for the computing services department at your school. Your supervisor has asked you to prepare a Personal Computer Buyer's Guide for students at the school. The Buyer's Guide will be available in the computer laboratory, campus library, and information booth. It will also be published on the school's intranet. A miniature version of the Personal Computer Buyer's Guide is shown in Figure 7-88 on the next page; for a more readable view, visit www.scsite.com/wd2000/project7.htm.

The Personal Computer Buyer's Guide uses an Excel worksheet, which is located on the Data Disk. If you did not download the Data Disk, see the inside back cover for instructions for downloading the Data Disk or see your instructor.

Instructions:

1. Open the document Personal Computer Buyer's Guide Draft from the Data Disk. Save the document with a new name, Personal Computer Buyer's Guide.
2. Change all margins to 1" with a gutter margin of .5". Note: Because you do not have alternating headers in this document, the gutter automatically will be at the left margin for binding at the left edge of each page.

(continued)

Working with an Embedded Worksheet and Index *(continued)*

3. Insert right-aligned page numbers as a header on every page after the first.
4. Below the paragraph in item number six (Use a worksheet to compare computers, services, and other considerations), embed the Excel worksheet named Computer System Cost Comparison, which is located on the Data Disk. Resize the chart so it fits on the page (approximately 70 percent of its original size).
5. Switch to Print Layout View. Add the following captions to the figures:
   Figure 1: Some mail-order companies, such as Dell Computer Corporation, sell computers online.
   Figure 2: A worksheet is an effective tool for summarizing and comparing the prices and components of different computer vendors.
6. Indent the left margin of each caption by .25" so that they align with the left edge of the figures. (*Hint:* Click in the caption and then drag the Left Indent Marker on the ruler to the .25" mark.)
7. At the end of the paragraph above Figure 1, add the following sentence: <u>Figure 1 shows a Web page for a popular mail-order company.</u> The text, Figure 1, in the sentence should be a cross-reference.
8. In the Item #6 paragraph (above Figure 2), add the following phrase to the end of the second sentence: <u>such as the one shown in Figure 2.</u> The text, Figure 2, in the phrase should be a cross-reference.
9. Add a bookmark, named BuyerWorksheet, to the figure caption for Figure 2.

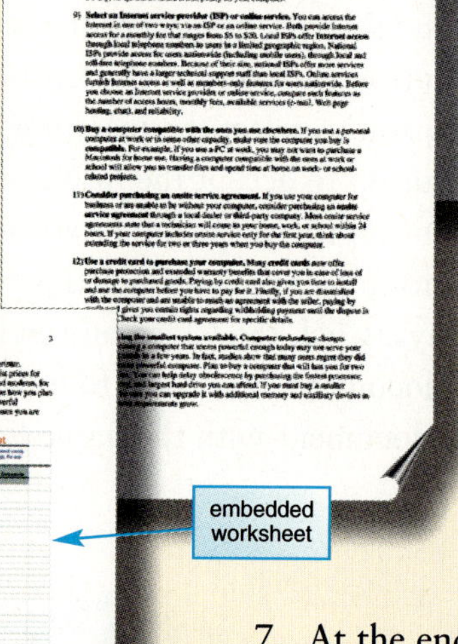

FIGURE 7-88

10. Mark the following text as index entries: software applications, research, free software, purchasing option, brand-name computers, worksheet, additional costs, best buy, Internet access, compatible, onsite service agreement, credit cards, and Computer technology. You will find each of the index entry phrases in the first paragraph of each bulleted item. After marking the entries, bold them in the text.
11. Insert a page break at the end of the document. Change the style of the first line on the new page from List Number to Heading 1. On the new page, type the heading Index using the Heading 1 style. Below the heading, build an index for the document. Use the formal format for the index. Remember to hide formatting marks prior to building the index.
12. Modify the document as follows: mark the two figure captions as index entries.
13. Update the index. Remember to hide formatting marks prior to re-building the index.
14. Go to the bookmark using the Go To dialog box.
15. Save the document again. Print the document. Staple the document along the gutter margin.

2 Working with a Master Document, Table of Contents, and Index

Problem: You are an editor for Textbooks Press, an international company that publishes college textbooks. You are to begin assembling Chapter 6 of a word processing textbook. You design chapters of the books as master documents and insert subdocuments as you receive chapter text from authors. You are responsible for inserting figure captions, creating the table of contents and index, and formatting the chapter. A miniature version of the Chapter 6 document is shown in Figure 7-89 on the next page; for a more readable view, visit www.scsite.com/wd2000/project7.htm.

You just received the first subdocument for Chapter 6. Thus, you lay out the master document for the chapter. The subdocument used in this lab is on the Data Disk. If you did not download the Data Disk, see the inside back cover for instructions for downloading the Data Disk or see your instructor.

Instructions:

1. Open the document Chapter 6 Introductory Material Draft from the Data Disk. Save the document with a new name, Chapter 6 Introductory Material.
2. If necessary, switch to print layout view. Add the following caption to the figure: The Web Club Newsletter. After it is inserted, italicize the text, The Web Club, in the caption.
3. Below the heading, Chapter Six – Newsletter, the first sentence should end with the phrase, as shown in Figure 1, with the text Figure 1 being a cross-reference. Modify the sentence accordingly.
4. Mark the phrase, desktop publishing software, in the Introduction as an index entry. Bold the phrase in the text. In the Desktop Publishing Terminology section, mark these words as index entries: nameplate, banner, issue information line, rules, ruling lines, subhead, vertical rule, wrap-around text, run-around, and pull-quote. Bold each of these words in the text.
5. Save the Chapter 6 Introductory Material file again and then close the file.

(continued)

Working with a Master Document, Table of Contents, and Index *(continued)*

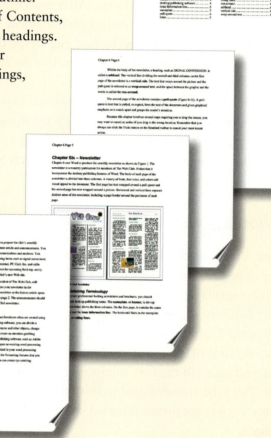

6. Start a new Word document. Switch to outline view. Enter the following Heading 1 headings on separate lines of the outline: Chapter 6 – Creating a Professional Newsletter, Table of Contents, and Index. Insert a next page section break between the headings.
7. Save the master document with the file name, Newsletter Chapter. Between the Table of Contents and Index headings, insert the Chapter 6 Introductory Material file as a subdocument.
8. If necessary, switch to print layout view. On page 1 (the title page) below the Chapter 6 – Creating a Professional Newsletter heading, enter this line double-spaced in 20-point Times New Roman: Confidential Work in Progress. Below that text, insert a clip art image of a book growing. Use the keywords, nurturing a book, to locate the graphic. Below the graphic, enter these lines double-spaced in 20-point Times New Roman: Authors: J. Riggins and H. Stein; Editor: B. Baccaro; Proofreader: L. Lopez; Date to Film: 10/22/2001; and Bound Book Date: 11/19/2001. Center all text and graphics on the title page.
9. Build an index for the document. In the Index sheet, use the formal format for the index and place a check mark in the Right align page numbers check box. Remember to hide formatting marks prior to building the index.
10. Create a table of contents for the document. Use the Formal format.

FIGURE 7-89

In the Lab

11. Beginning on the second page (the table of contents), create a header as follows: print the words, Chapter 6 Page, followed by the page number at the left margin. The title page does not have a header. Note: Because you do not want facing pages in this document, you do not create alternating headers.
12. Change all margins to 1" with a gutter margin of .5". Be sure to change the Apply to box to Whole document. Note: Because you do not have alternating headers in this document, the gutter automatically will be at the left margin for binding at the left edge of each page.
13. Verify that the following headings begin on a new page: Table of Contents, Objectives, Case Perspective, Chapter Six – Newsletter, and Index. If any do not, insert a next page section break.
14. Because you modified the margins, update the table of contents and index.
15. Save the document again. Print the document. Staple the document along the gutter margin.

3 Working with a Master Document, Index, Tables of Figures and Contents, and Callouts

Problem: You are the computer specialist at Triton Library. The head librarian mentions to you that the librarians constantly are receiving questions about using the computer. Thus, she has asked you to create a series of instructional booklets, similar to mini-user manuals, for library patrons that explain various aspects of computers. The first one you create is titled How to Use Windows Explorer. A miniature version of this document is shown in Figure 7-90 on the next page; for a more readable view, visit www.scsite.com/wd2000/project7.htm.

You design the instructional booklet as a master document. You create one subdocument and insert an existing document as the other. The existing subdocument is on the Data Disk. If you did not download the Data Disk, see the inside back cover for instructions for downloading the Data Disk or see your instructor.

Instructions:

1. Open the document How to Use Windows Explorer Draft from the Data Disk. Save the document with a new name, How to Use Windows Explorer.
2. Switch to Print Layout View. Add the following captions to the figures:
   Figure 1: Step 1 in Starting Windows Explorer
   Figure 2: Step 2 in Starting Windows Explorer
   Figure 3: Step 1 in Displaying the Contents of a Folder
   Figure 4: Step 2 in Displaying the Contents of a Folder
   Figure 5: Step 1 in Expanding a Folder
   Figure 6: Step 2 in Expanding a Folder
   Figure 7: Step 1 in Collapsing a Folder
   Figure 8: Step 2 in Collapsing a Folder
   Figure 9: Step 1 in Quitting Windows Explorer
3. Add a callout to each figure, except Figure 2, that identifies the mouse pointer in each figure. Use the Line Callout 3 style of callout with each callout containing the text, mouse pointer.
4. Insert a cross-reference for each figure. Insert the cross-reference in the parenthesis that ends each sentence immediately above each figure. Insert only the word, Figure, and the figure number as the cross-reference. For cross-references in an italicized sentence, italicize the cross-reference (after inserting the cross-reference, select it and then italicize it).

(continued)

Working with a Master Document, Index, Tables of Figures and Contents, and Callouts *(continued)*

5. In the section titled The Exploring – My Computer Window, mark these words/phrases as index entries: menu bar, hierarchy, contents, folder, minus sign, subfolders, collapsing the folder, plus sign, expanding the folder, and status bar. Also, bold each of these words/phrases in the text. Mark each of the STEPS headings as index entries.
6. Save the How to Use Windows Explorer file again and then close the file.

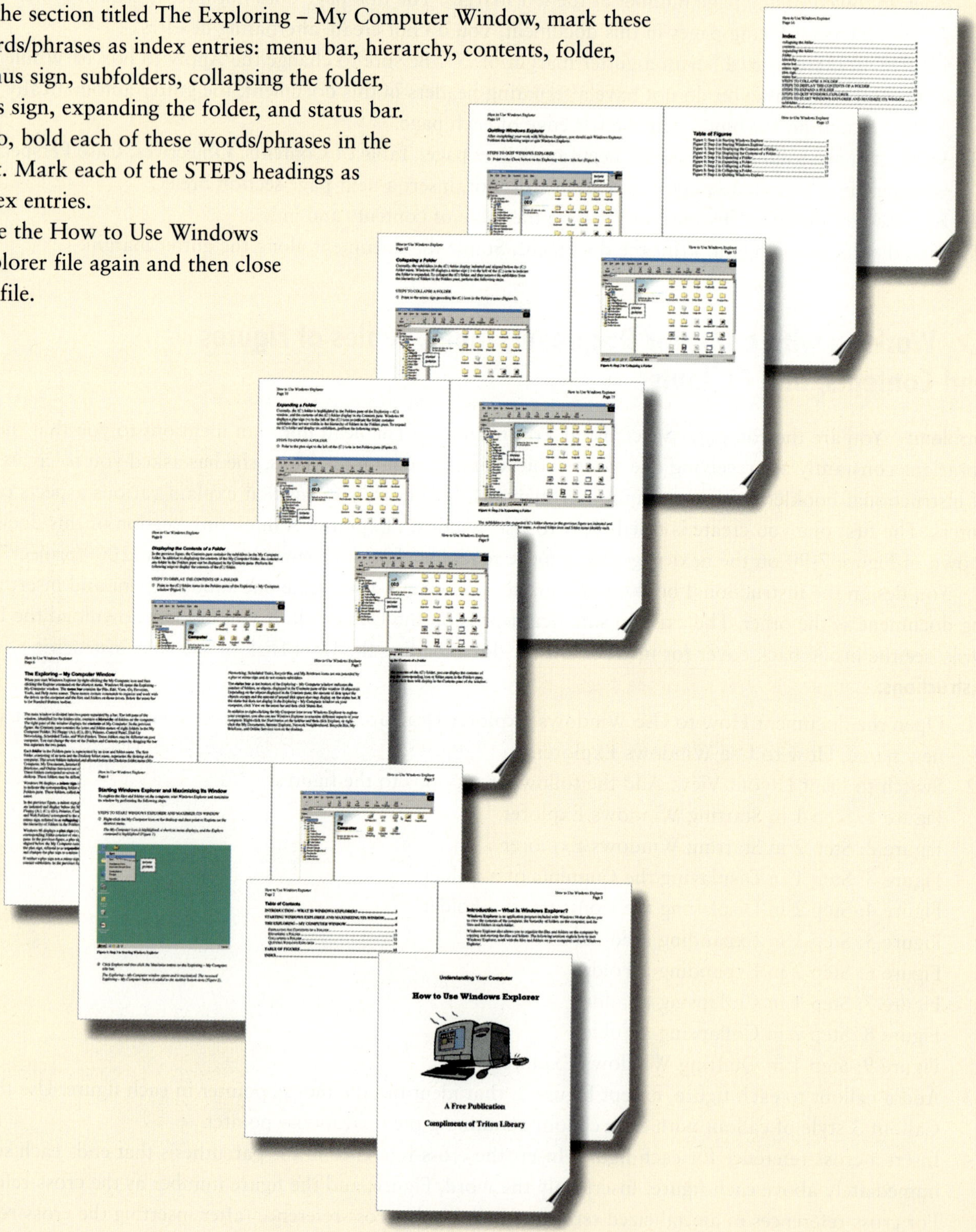

FIGURE 7-90

7. Start a new Word document. Switch to outline view. Enter the following Heading 1 headings on separate lines of the outline: Understanding Your Computer, Table of Contents, Introduction – What Is Windows Explorer?, Table of Figures, and Index. Insert a next page section break between each heading.
8. Save the master document with the file name, Understanding Your Computer. Between the Introduction and Table of Figures headings, insert the How to Use Windows Explorer file as a subdocument.
9. Create a subdocument using the Introduction – What Is Windows Explorer? heading. Using the Body Text style, enter the text for the two paragraphs shown in Figure 7-91 for the Introduction – What is Windows Explorer? section. In the Introduction, mark the phrase, Windows Explorer, as an index entry. Also, bold the phrase.

Windows Explorer is an application program included with Windows 98 that allows you to view the contents of the computer, the hierarchy of folders on the computer, and the files and folders in each folder.

Windows Explorer also allows you to organize the files and folders on the computer by copying and moving the files and folders. The following sections explain how to start Windows Explorer; work with the files and folders on your computer; and quit Windows Explorer.

FIGURE 7-91

10. On page 1 (the title page), double-spaced below the Understanding Your Computer heading, enter the following text in 28-point Rockwell bold font: How to Use Windows Explorer. Then, insert a clip art image of a computer. Use the keywords, computer cartoon, to locate the graphic. Enlarge the graphic. Below the graphic, enter these lines double-spaced in 24-point Times New Roman: A Free Publication, Compliments of the Triton Library. Center all text and graphics on the title page.
11. Build an index for the document that does not include the headings on the title page or the table of contents page. In the Index sheet, use the From template format for the index, place a check mark in the Right align page numbers check box, and change the number of columns to 1. Remember to hide formatting marks prior to building the index. *Hint:* To not include certain headings in the index, change the style of the heading to a style other than a heading style.

(continued)

Working with a Master Document, Index, Tables of Figures and Contents, and Callouts *(continued)*

12. Create a table of figures for the document. Use the From template format.
13. Create a table of contents for the document. Use the Formal format.
14. Beginning on the second page (the table of contents), create alternating headings as follows: even-numbered pages should print at the left margin the words, How to Use Windows Explorer, on the first line and Page, followed by the page number on the second line. Odd-numbered pages should print the same text at the right margin. The title page does not have a header.
15. For the entire document, set the left and right margins to 1" and set a gutter margin of .5".
16. Verify that the following headings begin on a new page: Table of Contents, Introduction – What is Windows Explorer?, Starting Windows Explorer and Maximizing Its Window, The Exploring – My Computer Window, Table of Figures, and Index. If any do not, insert a next page section break.
17. Because margins have changed, update the fields, table of contents, and index. (Select the entire document and then press F9.)
18. Save the document again. Print the document. If you have access to a copy machine, duplicate the document back-to-back.

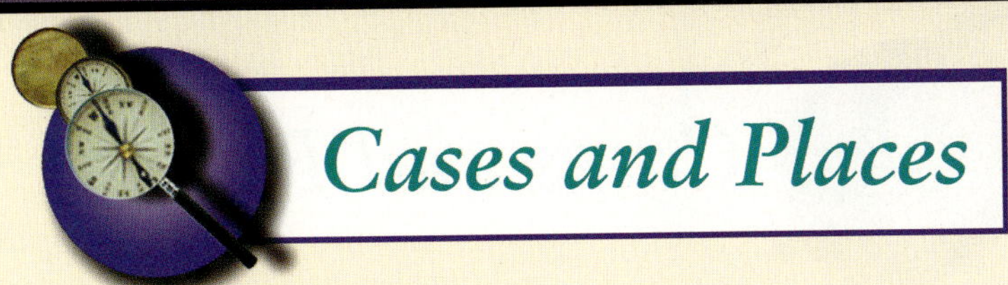

Cases and Places

The difficulty of these case studies varies:
◗ are the least difficult; ◗◗ are more difficult; and ◗◗◗ are the most difficult.

1 ◗ As editor for the school newspaper, you review all articles before they are published. One section of the newspaper spotlights a local business or organization. For the next issue, the author has prepared an article about a local hospital and sent it to you for review. The article, named Northwestern Memorial Hospital Article, is located on the Data Disk. If you did not download the Data Disk, see the inside back cover for instructions for downloading the Data Disk or see your instructor. When you review the article, you find several areas where you wish to make changes and offer suggestions. You are to use Word's change-tracking feature to insert, delete, and replace text in the article. Make at least ten changes to the article and add at least three comments. Print the article with tracked changes showing and without tracked changes showing. Also, print comments. Save the article containing the tracked changes as a version. Assume you are the author of the article and have received it back from the editor. Delete the comments and accept all the changes in the document.

2 ◗ You are an editor for Textbooks Press, an international company that publishes college textbooks. The chapter you are working on is called Project 7. You design the chapters as master documents and insert subdocuments as you receive chapter text from authors. You are responsible for creating the table of contents and index and formatting the chapter. You just received the first subdocument for Project 7. The article, named Reviewing a Document, is located on the Data Disk. If you did not download the Data Disk, see the inside back cover for instructions for downloading the Data Disk or see your instructor. Set up a master document that contains the following: title page, table of contents, reviewing a document file as a subdocument, table of figures, and index. Use the concepts and techniques presented in this project to format the document.

3 ◗◗ As your final project in CIS 210, your instructor has asked you to prepare a master document that has at least one subdocument, a title page, a table of contents, a table of figures, and an index. The subdocument is to contain the text and figures on pages 7.22 through 7.25 in this project. To capture a screen shot, display the screen on your computer and then press the PRINT SCREEN key. Then, to include the screen shot in your Word document, click the Paste button on the Standard toolbar in the Word window. Use the concepts and techniques presented in this project to format the document.

4 ▸▸ You are the computer specialist at Triton Library. The head librarian has asked you to create a series of instructional booklets, similar to mini-user manuals, for library patrons that explain the various aspects of computers. The first instructional booklet you prepared is shown in Figure 7-90 on page WD 7.76. Your assignment is to prepare the next instructional booklet for the library. Write the instructional booklet on a software application with which you are familiar and to which you have access. Use the software application's Help system, textbooks, and other instructional books for reference. The booklet is to be a how-to type of document that includes screen shots. To capture a screen shot, display the screen on your computer and then press the PRINT SCREEN key. Then, to include the screen shot in your Word document, click the Paste button on the Standard toolbar in the Word window. The figures should contain captions. The document should contain the following sections: title page, table of contents, how-to discussion, table of figures, and index. Use the concepts and techniques presented in this project to format the document.

5 ▸▸▸ You are vice president of your school's computer club. At the last meeting, several members were inquiring about MOUS (Microsoft Office User Specialist) certification. Because you also are interested in the MOUS certification, you decide to prepare a document outlining information about the exam (cost, description, how to prepare, where to take the exam, etc.). You obtain most of your information through links at the Shelly Cashman Series MOUS Web page at http://www.scsite.com/off2000/cert.htm. Because the document will be quite lengthy with many headings and subheadings, you organize it as a master document. In addition to information about MOUS, the document also contains the following: title page, table of contents, and index. Include at least one screen shot as a figure. To capture a screen shot, display the screen on your computer and then press the PRINT SCREEN key. Then, to include the screen shot in your Word document, click the Paste button on the Standard toolbar in the Word window. All figures should contain captions. Use the concepts and techniques presented in this project to format the document.

6 ▸▸▸ Your instructor in CIS 215 has distributed a worksheet that can be used to compare computers, services, and other considerations. The worksheet is an Excel document, named Computer System Cost Comparison, which is located on the Data Disk. If you did not download the Data Disk, see the inside back cover for instructions for downloading the Data Disk or see your instructor. Your assignment is to prepare a Word document that explains the type of computer you are seeking and identifies criteria important to you in purchasing a computer. The Word document should also contain the Excel worksheet as an embedded object. Edit the Excel object by double-clicking the object. Then, modify the Desired System column so that it is tailored to your specific needs. You are to obtain prices for your desired system from two local dealers and two online dealers. Again, edit the Excel worksheet from Word as you receive pricing information. When the worksheet is complete, write a paragraph below the worksheet that recommends the dealer from which you would purchase the computer along with a justification of why you selected that dealer. Use the concepts and techniques presented in this project to format the document.

Microsoft Word 2000

Creating an Online Form

OBJECTIVES

You will have mastered the material in this project when you can:

- Design an online form
- Create a document template
- Highlight text
- Insert a table into a form
- Insert a text box into a form
- Insert a drop-down list box into a form
- Insert a check box into a form
- Format form fields
- Use the Format Painter button
- Add Help text to form fields
- Draw and format a rectangle
- Animate text
- Protect a form
- Open a new document based on a template
- Fill out a form
- Save data on a form in a text file
- Modify the location of workgroup templates

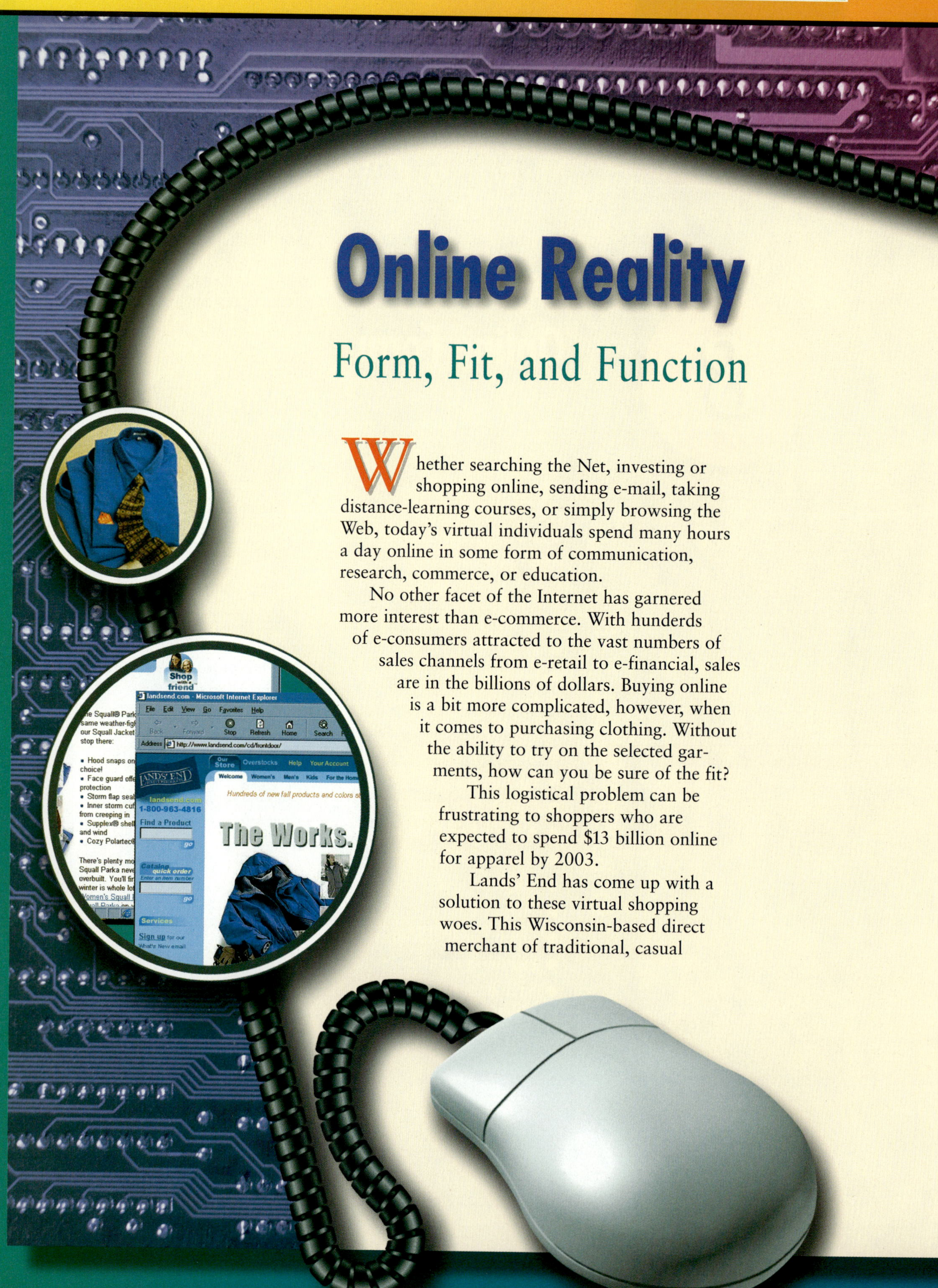

Online Reality

Form, Fit, and Function

Whether searching the Net, investing or shopping online, sending e-mail, taking distance-learning courses, or simply browsing the Web, today's virtual individuals spend many hours a day online in some form of communication, research, commerce, or education.

No other facet of the Internet has garnered more interest than e-commerce. With hundreds of e-consumers attracted to the vast numbers of sales channels from e-retail to e-financial, sales are in the billions of dollars. Buying online is a bit more complicated, however, when it comes to purchasing clothing. Without the ability to try on the selected garments, how can you be sure of the fit?

This logistical problem can be frustrating to shoppers who are expected to spend $13 billion online for apparel by 2003.

Lands' End has come up with a solution to these virtual shopping woes. This Wisconsin-based direct merchant of traditional, casual

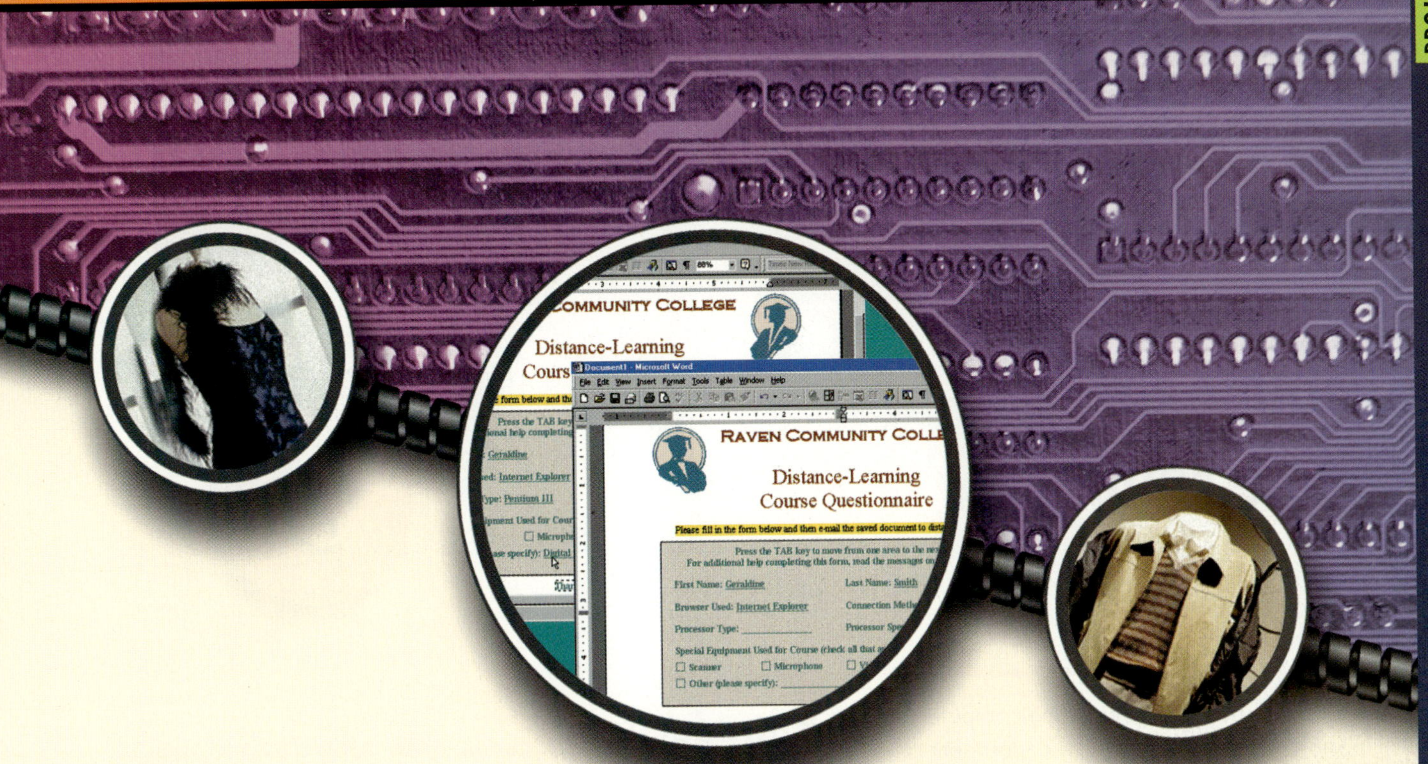

clothes has developed Your Personal Model, a personalized 3-D representation of female customers that selects the most flattering clothes for their figures, suggests specific outfits for various occasions, and provides an online dressing room to try on the garments.

Shoppers begin their Your Personal Model shopping adventure by answering several questions regarding their physical features, such as specific skin tones, face shapes, hairstyles, and hair colors. They save their profiles for future shopping sprees, and proceed to the Welcome Page.

At this point, their models appear along with custom outfits designed for their bodies and for their lifestyles. The site may make suggestions for specific occasions such as gray Chinos and a beige sweater set for a casual workplace and a simple black knit dress for an informal weekend party.

The next step is to take these garments to The Dressing Room. There, the shoppers can view the particular clothes on their models. The site gives advice on choosing the proper size and then places the items in the customers' virtual shopping carts.

Ordering is easy. If they use Your Personal Model, the contents of their shopping carts display automatically in an order form.

Gary C. Comer, an avid sailor and advertising copywriter, founded Lands' End in 1961 in Chicago to sell sailing equipment and hardware via a catalog. In the 1970s, the company's focus switched to clothing. Today, Lands' End is the second largest apparel mail-order company with sales of more than $1.37 billion to its 6.1 million customers. The Lands' End Web site (www.landsend.com) was unveiled in 1995 and receives 15 million visitors yearly.

As widespread as Internet shopping is, likewise, the emergence of the distance education environment has created a new focus for the use of forms and online communication. In Project 8, you will develop a form by creating a template in Word 2000. The form is a questionnaire for students attending distant-learning classes on the Web through Raven Community College. The form makes it possible for the college to minimize the requests about the distant-learning courses by requesting information from the students who have completed the curriculum via the online form. Students supply information about the type of equipment used in the course. This information then is provided to other students interested in the class through the school's schedule of courses.

Using Word's automated tools, the process of creating an online form is a simple task; one that will make it possible for an online reality in many aspects of your course work, professional endeavors, and personal use.

Microsoft Word 2000

Creating an Online Form

CASE PERSPECTIVE

For the past three years, the computer information systems (CIS) department at Raven Community College has offered distance-learning (DL) courses. These classes, which are conducted completely on the Web, are extremely popular among the student body because they allow students to attend class from home or at any time that fits their schedules. Consequently, students are requesting that other departments also offer courses in a DL format. In a response to student needs, the administration has requested that each academic department at the college offer one DL section of each introductory class – beginning next semester. The scheduling department has recommended that a typical computer configuration for DL courses be included as a list in the upcoming *Schedule of Courses*.

As a part-time assistant in the CIS department, you have been assigned the task of compiling this list. You decide to send an online questionnaire to all students who have completed a DL course this past semester. The questionnaire will ask for the student name, browser used, method used to connect to the Internet, type and speed of computer, and any special equipment used in the course.

Introduction

During your personal and professional life, you undoubtedly have filled out countless forms. Whether a federal tax form, a timecard, an application, an order, a deposit slip, or a questionnaire, a **form** is designed to collect information. In the past, forms were printed; that is, you received the form on a piece of paper, filled it in with a pen or pencil, and then returned it manually.

Today, people are concerned with using resources efficiently. To minimize waste of paper, save the world's trees, improve office efficiency, and improve access to data, many businesses attempt to become a paperless office. Thus, the online form has emerged. With an **online form**, you access the form using your computer, fill it out using the computer, and then return it via the computer. You may access the form at a Web site, on your company's intranet, or from your inbox if you receive it via e-mail.

Not only does an online form reduce the need for paper, it saves the time spent duplicating a form and distributing it. With more and more people owning a home computer, online forms have become a popular means of collecting personal information, as well. In Word, you easily can create an online form for distribution electronically, which then can be filled in using Word.

Project Eight — Online Form

Project 8 uses Word to create the online form shown in Figure 8-1. The form is a questionnaire e-mailed to all students that completed a distance-learning course at Raven Community College during the past semester. Upon receipt of the form, students fill it in, save it, and then e-mail it back to the college. Figure 8-1a shows how the form displays on a student's screen initially (as a blank form); Figure 8-1b shows the form partially filled in by one student; and Figure 8-1c shows how one student filled in the form.

(a) Blank Form

highlighted text

highlighted data entry item

data entry area

Help message

thank-you message

(b) Partially Filled-In Form

text box

drop-down list box arrow

check box

(c) Filled-In Form

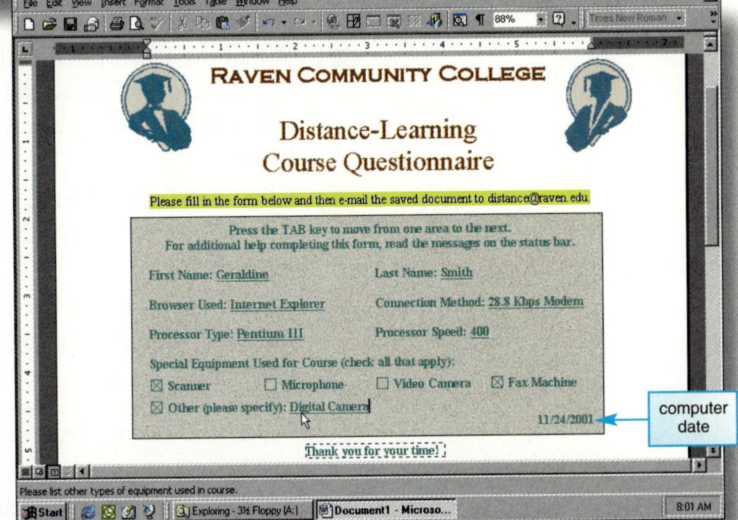

FIGURE 8-1

The form is designed so that it fits completely within the Word window – without a user having to scroll while filling in the form. The **data entry area** of the form is enclosed by a rectangle that is shaded in beige. The line above the data entry area is highlighted in yellow to draw the user's attention to the message. The thank-you message below the data entry area is surrounded by a moving rectangle.

The data entry area of the form contains four text boxes (First Name, Last Name, Processor Speed, and Other), three drop-down list boxes (Browser Used, Connection Method, and Processor Type), and five check boxes (Scanner, Microphone, Video Camera, Fax Machine, and Other). As a user presses the TAB key to move the highlight from one data entry item to the next, the status bar displays a brief Help message that is related to the location of the highlight. Note that in Word the drop-down list boxes do not display the box arrow until you TAB to the drop-down list box. The date in the lower-right corner of the data entry area is the date from the computer on which the form is being displayed.

Online Forms

For a sample online form on the Web, visit the Word 2000 More About Web page (www.scsite.com/wd2000/more.htm) and then click Sample Online Form.

Starting Word

Follow these steps to start Word or ask your instructor how to start Word for your system.

TO START WORD

1. Click the Start button on the taskbar.
2. Click New Office Document on the Start menu. If necessary, click the General tab when the New Office Document dialog box displays.
3. Double-click the Blank Document icon in the General sheet.
4. If the Word window is not maximized, double-click its title bar to maximize it. Click View on the menu bar and then click Print Layout. If the Office Assistant displays, right-click it and then click Hide on the shortcut menu.

Office starts Word. After a few moments, an empty document titled Document1 displays in the Word window. Because this project uses floating graphics, you will use print layout view; thus, the Print Layout View button on the horizontal scroll bar is recessed.

Resetting Menus and Toolbars

To set the menus and toolbars so they appear exactly as shown in this book, you should reset your menus and toolbars as outlined in Appendix C or follow these steps.

TO RESET MENUS AND TOOLBARS

1. Click View on the menu bar and then point to Toolbars. Click Customize on the Toolbars submenu.
2. When the Customize dialog box displays, click the Options tab, make sure the top three check boxes have check marks and then click the Reset my usage data button. When the Microsoft Word dialog box displays, click the Yes button.
3. Click the Toolbars tab. Click Standard in the Toolbars list and then click the Reset button. When the Reset Toolbar dialog box displays, click the OK button.
4. Click Formatting in the Toolbars list and then click the Reset button. When the Reset Toolbar dialog box displays, click the OK button. Click the Close button.

Word resets the menus and toolbars.

Displaying Formatting Marks

It is helpful to display formatting marks that indicate where in the document you pressed the ENTER key, SPACEBAR, and other keys. Follow this step to display formatting marks.

TO DISPLAY FORMATTING MARKS

1. Double-click the move handle on the left side of the Standard toolbar to display the entire toolbar. If the Show/Hide ¶ button on the Standard toolbar is not already recessed, click it.

Word displays formatting marks in the document window, and the Show/Hide ¶ button on the Standard toolbar is recessed.

Zooming Page Width

When you zoom page width, Word displays the page on the screen as large as possible in print layout view. Perform the following steps to zoom page width.

Fields

For more information about fields, visit the Word 2000 More About Web page (www.scsite.com/wd2000/more.htm) and then click Fields.

TO ZOOM PAGE WIDTH

Click the Zoom box arrow on the Standard toolbar.

Click Page Width in the Zoom list.

Word displays an entire piece of paper as large as possible in the document window. Word computes the zoom percentage based on a variety of settings. Your percentage may be different.

Designing an Online Form

To minimize the time spent creating a form on the computer, you should sketch it out on a piece of paper first. A design for the online form in this project is shown in Figure 8-2.

During the **form design**, you should create a well-thought-out draft of the form that attempts to include all essential form elements. These elements include the form's title, placement of text and graphics, instructions for users of the form, and field specifications. A **field** is a placeholder for data. A **field specification** defines characteristics of a field such as the field's type, length, format, and a list of possible values that may be entered into the field. Many users place Xs in fields where a user will be allowed to enter any type of character and 9s in fields where a user will be allowed to enter numbers only. For example, in Figure 8-2, a user can enter up to 15 of any type of character in the First Name text box and can enter up to 3 numbers in the Processor Speed text box.

With this draft of the form in hand, the next step is to create the form in Word.

RAVEN COMMUNITY COLLEGE
Distance-Learning Course Questionnaire

Please fill in the form below and then e-mail saved document to distance@ravcm.edu

Press the TAB key to move from one area to the next.
For additional help completing this form, read the messages on the status bar.

First Name: XXXXXXXXXXXXXXX Last Name: XXXXXXXXXXXXXXXXXXXXX
Browser Used: XXXXXXXXXXXXXXX Connection Method: XXXXXXXXXXXXXXXX
Processor Type: XXXXXXXXXXXXXXX Processor Speed: 999
Special Equipment Used for Course (check all that apply):
☐ Scanner ☐ Microphone ☐ Video Camera ☐ Fax Machine
☐ Other (please specify): XXXXXXXXXXXXXXXXXXXXXXXXXXXXXXXXX
MM/dd/yyyy

Thank you for your time!

possible values for Browser Used → Browser Used choices: Internet Explorer, Netscape, Other

possible values for Connection Method → Connection Method choices: 56 Kbps Modem, 33.6 Kbps Modem, 28.8 Kbps Modem, 14.4 Kbps Modem, ISDN Line, ADSL, T1 Line, Other

possible values for Processor Type → Processor Type choices: Athlon, Pentium III, Pentium II, Celeron, AMD-K6, Pentium with MMX, Pentium, Other

FIGURE 8-2

Protected Forms

If you open an existing form that has been protected, Word will not allow you to modify the form's appearance until you unprotect it. To unprotect a document, click Tools on the menu bar and then click Unprotect Document. If the form has been password-protected, you will be asked to enter a password when you invoke the Unprotect Document command.

Creating an Online Form

The process of creating an online form begins with creating a template. Next, you insert and format any text, graphics, and fields where data is to be entered on the form. Finally, before you save the form for electronic distribution, you protect it. With a protected form, users can enter data only where you have placed form fields; that is, they will not be able to modify any other items on the form. Many menu commands and toolbar buttons are dimmed, and thus unavailable, in a protected form. The steps on the following pages illustrate how to create an online form.

Creating a Template

A **template** is a file that contains the definition of the appearance of a Word document, including items such as default font, font size, margin settings, and line spacing; available styles; and even placement of text. Every Word document you create is based on a template. When you select the Blank Document icon in the New dialog box or when you click the New Blank Document button on the Standard toolbar, Word creates a document based on the Normal template. Word also provides other templates for more specific types of documents such as memos, letters, and fax cover sheets. Creating a document based on these templates can improve your productivity because Word has defined much of the document's appearance for you.

If you create and save an online form as a Word document that is based on the Normal template, users will be required to open that Word document to display the form on the screen. Next, they will fill in the form. Then, to preserve the content of the original form, they will have to save the form with a new name. If they accidentally click the Save button on the Standard toolbar, the original blank form will be replaced with a filled-in form.

If you, instead, create and save the online form as a **document template**, users will open a new document window that is based on that template. This displays the form on the screen as a brand new Word document; that is, the document does not have a file name. Thus, the user fills in the form and then simply saves it. By using a template for the form, the original form remains intact when the user clicks the Save button.

Perform the following steps to create a document template to be used for the online form and then save the template with the name Distance-Learning Questionnaire.

More About

Templates

Most documents have a file name and a three-character file extension. When a file extension displays, it is separated from the file name with a period. The extension often is assigned by an application to indicate the type of file being saved. For example, a Word document has an extension of doc and a Word template has an extension of dot. Thus, a file named July Report.doc is a Word document, and a file named Fitness Survey.dot is a Word template.

To Create a Document Template

1 Click File on the menu bar and then click New. When the New dialog box displays, if necessary, click the General tab. Click the Blank Document icon and then click Template in the Create New area. Point to the OK button.

Word displays the New dialog box (Figure 8-3). The Template option button instructs Word to create a new template, instead of a new Word document.

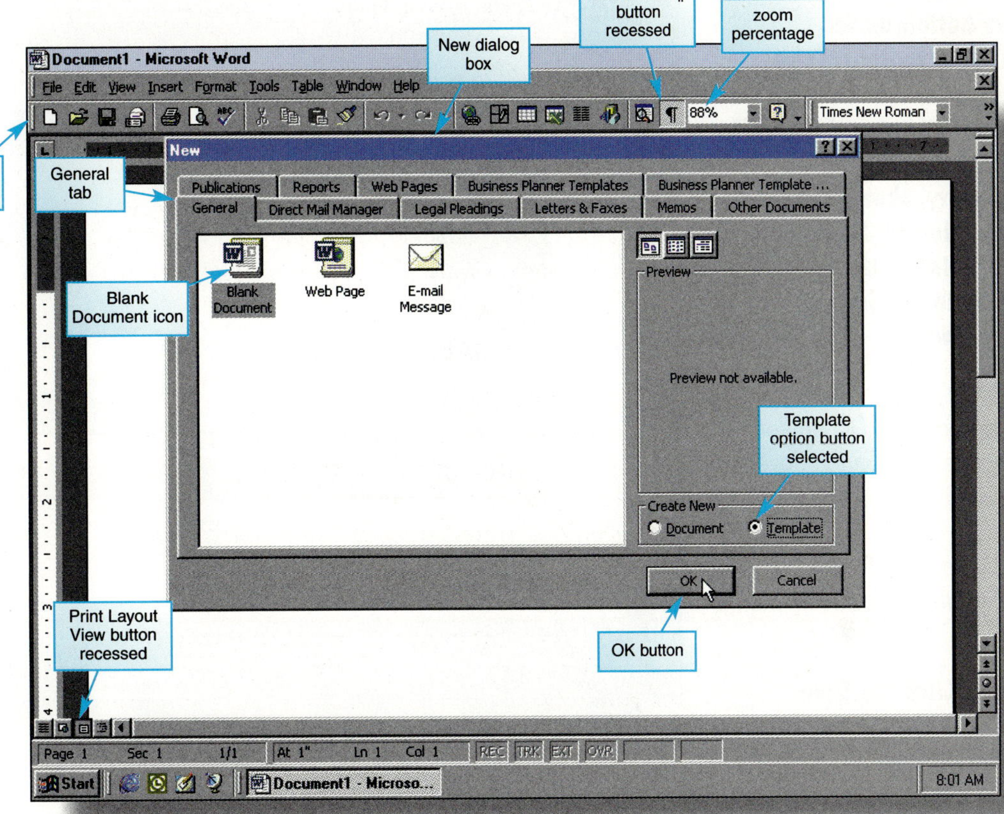

FIGURE 8-3

2 Click the OK button.

Word displays a blank template titled Template1 in the Word window (Figure 8-4).

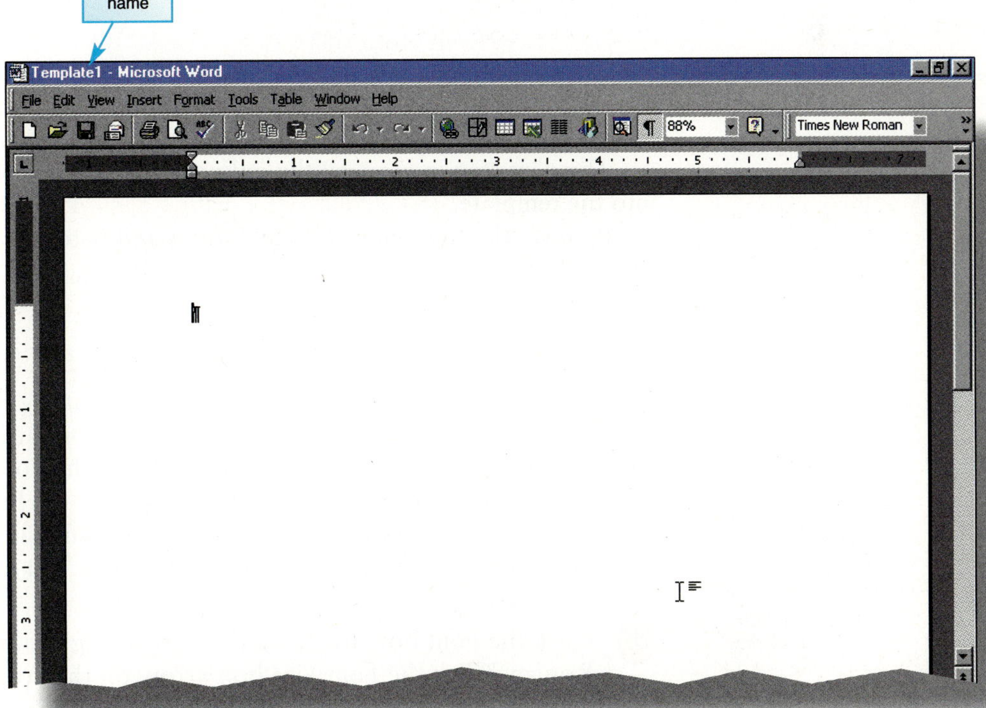

FIGURE 8-4

3 With a disk in drive A, click the Save button on the Standard toolbar. Type `Distance-Learning Questionnaire` **in the File name text box. If necessary, change the Save in location to 3½ Floppy (A:). Point to the Save button in the Save As dialog box.**

Word displays the Save As dialog box with Document Template listed in the Save as type box (Figure 8-5). Because Document Template is dimmed, you cannot change the document type.

4 Click the Save button in the Save As dialog box.

Word saves the template on the floppy disk in drive A with the file name Distance-Learning Questionnaire (see Figure 8-6).

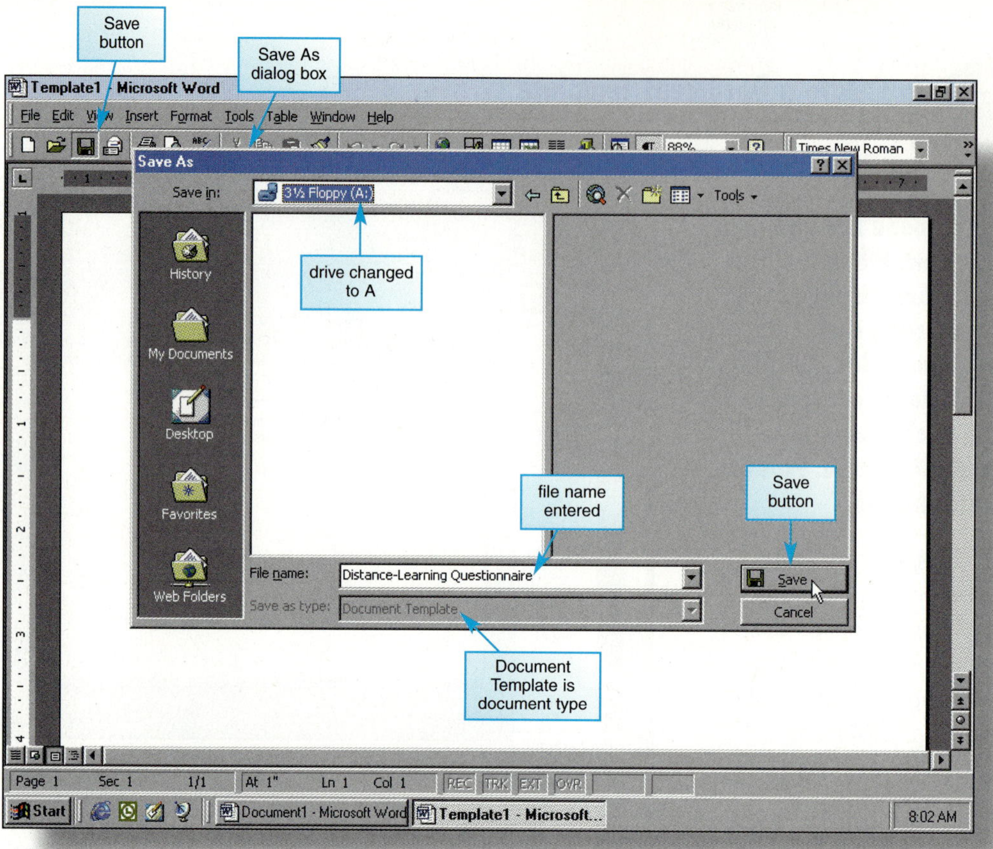

FIGURE 8-5

The next step in creating the online form is to enter the text, graphics, and fields into the template.

Perform the following steps to format and enter the college name and questionnaire title.

TO ENTER AND FORMAT TEXT

1. Double-click the move handle on the Formatting toolbar to display the entire toolbar. Click the Font box arrow on the Formatting toolbar, scroll to and then click Copperplate Gothic Bold. Click the Font Size box arrow on the Formatting toolbar and then click 22. Click the Font Color button arrow on the Formatting toolbar and then click Brown. Click the Center button on the Formatting toolbar. Type `Raven Community College` and then press the ENTER key twice.
2. Click the Font box arrow on the Formatting toolbar and then click Times New Roman. Click the Font Size box arrow on the Formatting toolbar and then click 26. Type `Distance-Learning` and then press then ENTER key. Type `Course Questionnaire` and then press the ENTER key.

The school name and questionnaire title display as shown in Figure 8-6.

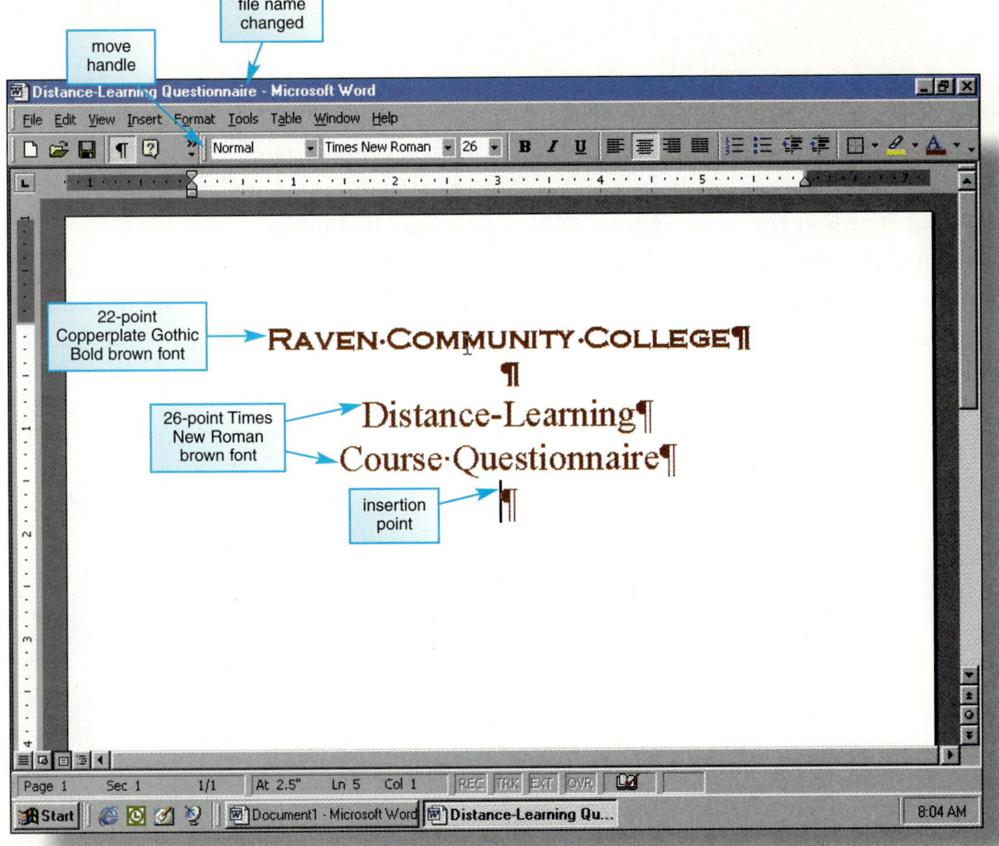

FIGURE 8-6

The next step is to insert the clip art of the male and female graduates. Word inserts clip art as inline graphics; that is, part of the current paragraph. You want to position the image of the male graduate to the left of the college name and the image of the female graduate to the right of the college name (see Figure 8-1 on page WD 8.5). Thus, the graphics need to be floating graphics instead of inline graphics. Also, the graphics are too large for this form. Thus, after you insert the graphics you will reduce their size and change their wrapping styles to Square as described in the following steps.

TO INSERT AND FORMAT CLIP ART

1. With the insertion point on line 5, click Insert on the menu bar, point to Picture, and then click Clip Art. When the Insert ClipArt window opens, click the Search for clips text box. Type `degrees caps` and then press the ENTER key.
2. Click the clip of the male graduate that matches the one shown in Figure 8-7 on the next page. Click the Insert clip button on the Pop-up menu. Click the clip of the female graduate that matches the one shown in Figure 8-7. Click the Insert clip button on the Pop-up menu. Click the Close button on the Insert ClipArt window's title bar.
3. Click the male graduate graphic to select it. If the Picture toolbar does not display, click View on the menu bar, point to Toolbars, and then click Picture. Click the Format Picture button on the Picture toolbar. When the Format Picture dialog box displays, if necessary, click the Size tab. Change the Height and Width in the Scale area to 65%. Click the OK button.
4. Click the Text Wrapping button on the Picture toolbar and then click Square. Drag the male graduate graphic to the left of the college name as shown in Figure 8-7.

5 Click the female graduate graphic to select it. If the Picture toolbar does not display, click View on the menu bar, point to Toolbars, and then click Picture. Click the Format Picture button on the Picture toolbar. When the Format Picture dialog box displays, if necessary, click the Size tab. Change the Height and Width in the Scale area to 65%. Click the OK button.

6 Click the Text Wrapping button on the Picture toolbar and then click Square. Drag the female graduate graphic to the right of the college name as shown in Figure 8-7.

7 Position the insertion point on the paragraph mark on line 5.

The graphics display on the form as shown in Figure 8-7.

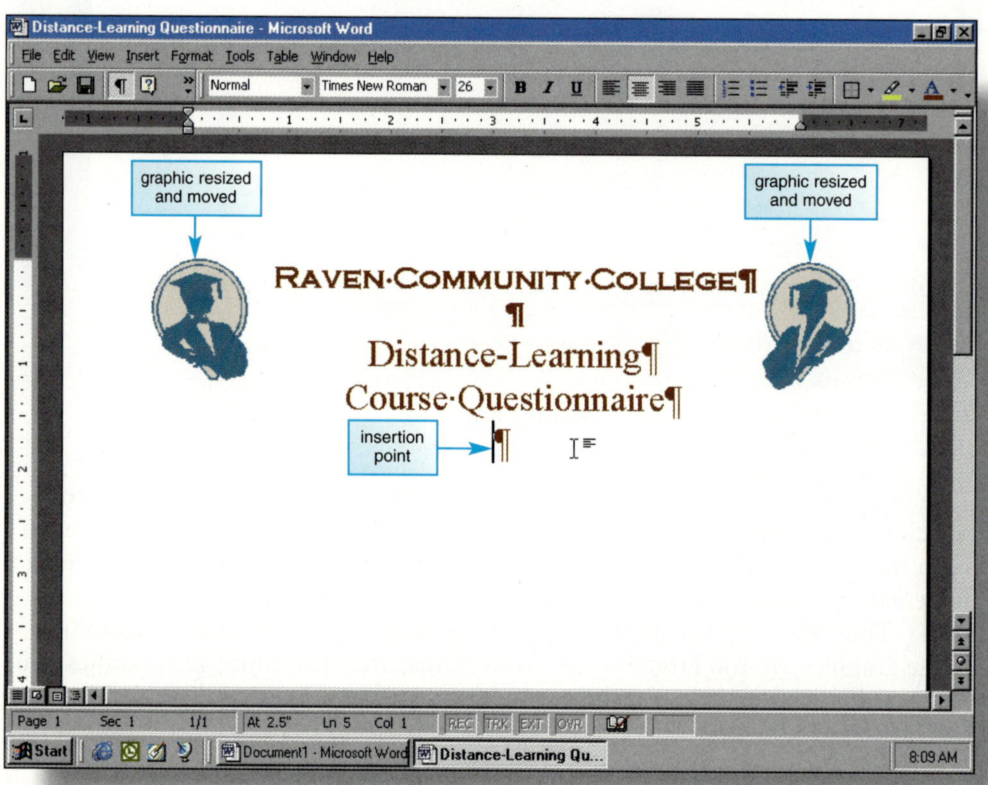

FIGURE 8-7

The next step is to enter the instructions highlighted in yellow.

Highlighting Text

You **highlight** text in an online document to alert the reader to the text's importance, much like a highlight marker does in a textbook. Because you want to draw attention to the instructions that specify where to mail the completed form, you highlight this line.

Perform the following steps to highlight text in a document.

More About 2000

Removing Highlights

To remove all highlights from a document, click Edit on the menu bar, click Select All, click the Highlight button arrow, and then click None. To remove an individual highlight, select the text from which you wish to remove the highlight, click the Highlight button arrow, and then click None.

Steps To Highlight Text

1 Click the Font Size box arrow on the Formatting toolbar and then click 12. Click the Font Color button arrow on the Formatting toolbar and then click Automatic. Press the ENTER key. Type `Please fill in the form below and then e-mail the saved document to distance@raven.edu.` **Press the ENTER key. Press CTRL+Z to undo the hyperlink format of the e-mail address. If the Highlight button on the Formatting toolbar displays yellow on its face, click the button; otherwise, click the Highlight button arrow and then click Yellow. Position the mouse pointer in the document window.**

The Highlight button is recessed and displays yellow on its face (Figure 8-8). The mouse pointer displays as an I-beam with a highlighter attached to it.

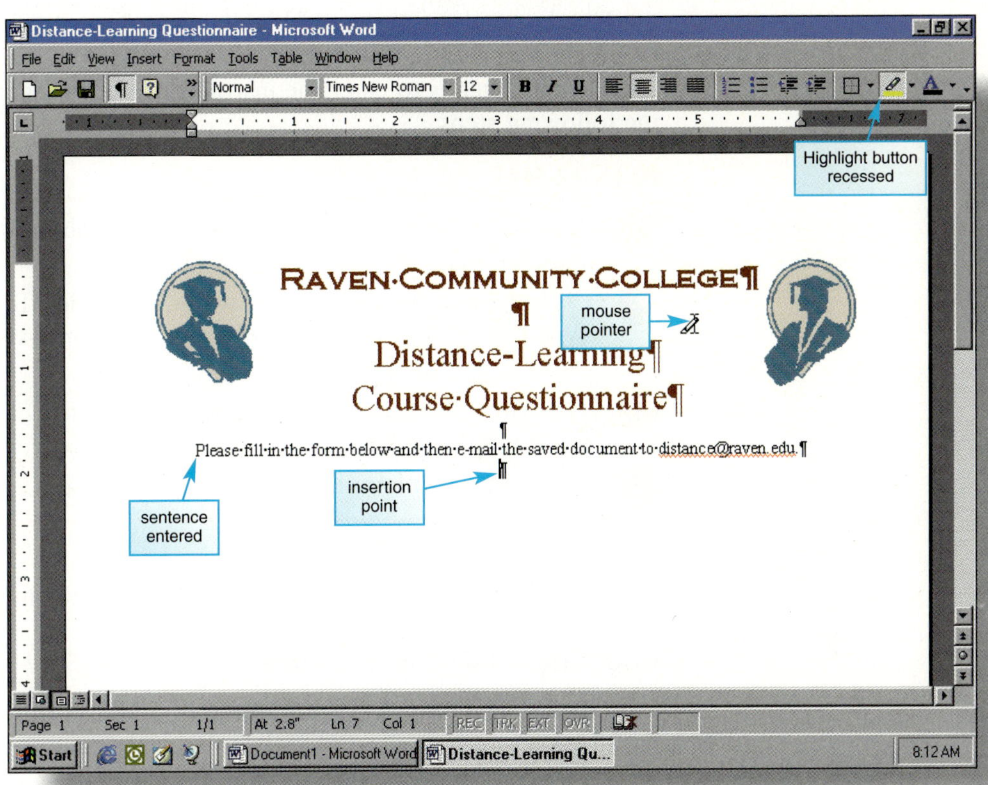

FIGURE 8-8

2 Click to the left of the sentence to highlight or drag through the sentence.

Word highlights the selected text in yellow (Figure 8-9). The Highlight button remains recessed.

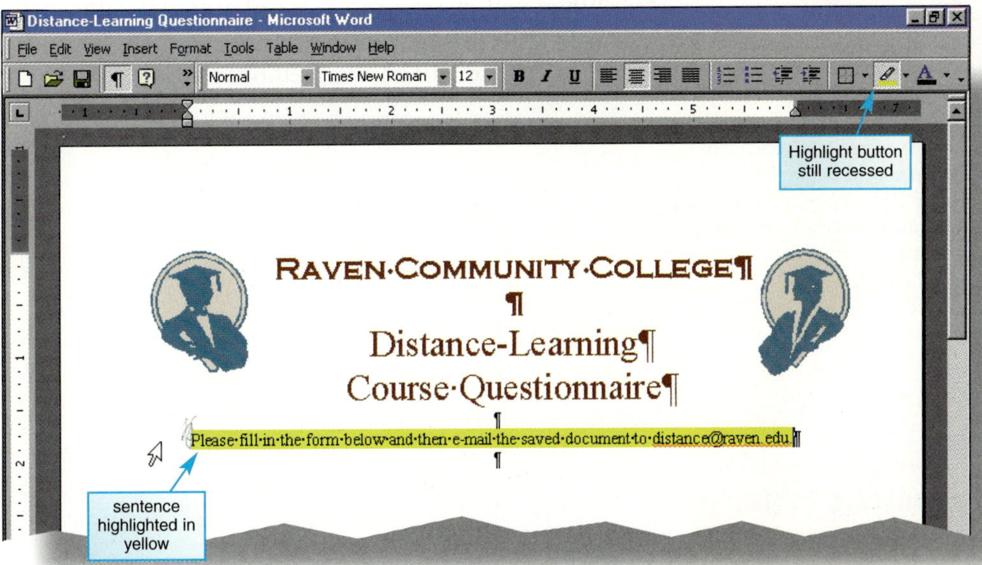

FIGURE 8-9

3 Click the Highlight button on the Formatting toolbar to turn highlighting off.

Other Ways

1. Click Highlight button on Reviewing toolbar

When the Highlight button is recessed, you can continue to select text to be highlighted. The highlighter remains active until you click the Highlight button or press the ESC key to turn it off.

Word provides a variety of highlighter colors. To change the color, click the Highlight button arrow and then click the desired color.

The next step is to enter the instructions for filling in the form as described in the following steps.

TO ENTER TEXT

1. Position the insertion point on the paragraph mark below the highlighted text and then press the ENTER key.
2. Click the Font Color box arrow and then click Teal. Click the Bold button. Type `Press the TAB key to move from one area to the next.` Press the ENTER key.
3. Type `For additional help completing this form, read the messages on the status bar.` Press the ENTER key twice.
4. Press CTRL+L to left-align the current paragraph.

The form instructions are entered.

The next step is to enter the fields into the data entry area of the form.

Inserting a Table into a Form

The first line of data entry in the form consists of the First Name text box, which begins at the left margin, and the Last Name text box, which begins at the center point. Although you could set tab stops to align the data in a form, it is easier to insert a table. For example, the first line could be a 1 x 2 table; that is, a table with one row and two columns. By inserting a 1 x 2 table, Word automatically positions the second column at the center point. Using tables in forms also keeps the data entered within the same region of the form, in case the user enters data that wraps to the next line of the screen.

When you insert a table, Word automatically surrounds it with a border. You do not want borders on tables in forms. Perform the following steps to enter a 1 x 2 table into the form and then remove its border.

Using Tables in Forms

At first glance, it might seem easier to set a tab stop wherever you would like a form field to display. Actually, it can become a complex task. Consider a row with three form fields. To space them evenly, you must calculate where each tab stop should begin. If you insert a 1 x 3 table instead, Word automatically calculates the size of three evenly spaced columns.

Formatting Tables

You can format a table in a form just as you format any other Word table. That is, you can add borders, fill cells with shading or color, change alignment of cell contents, and so on.

To Insert a Borderless Table into a Form

1 If the Forms toolbar does not display on the screen, click View on the menu bar, point to Toolbars, and then click Forms. If necessary, scroll up so that the college name is positioned at the top of the document window. With the insertion point in line 11, click the Insert Table button on the Forms toolbar. Point to the cell in the first row and second column of the grid to highlight the first two cells in the first row of the grid.

*Word displays a **grid** to define the dimension of the desired table (Figure 8-10). Word will insert the table immediately above the insertion point.*

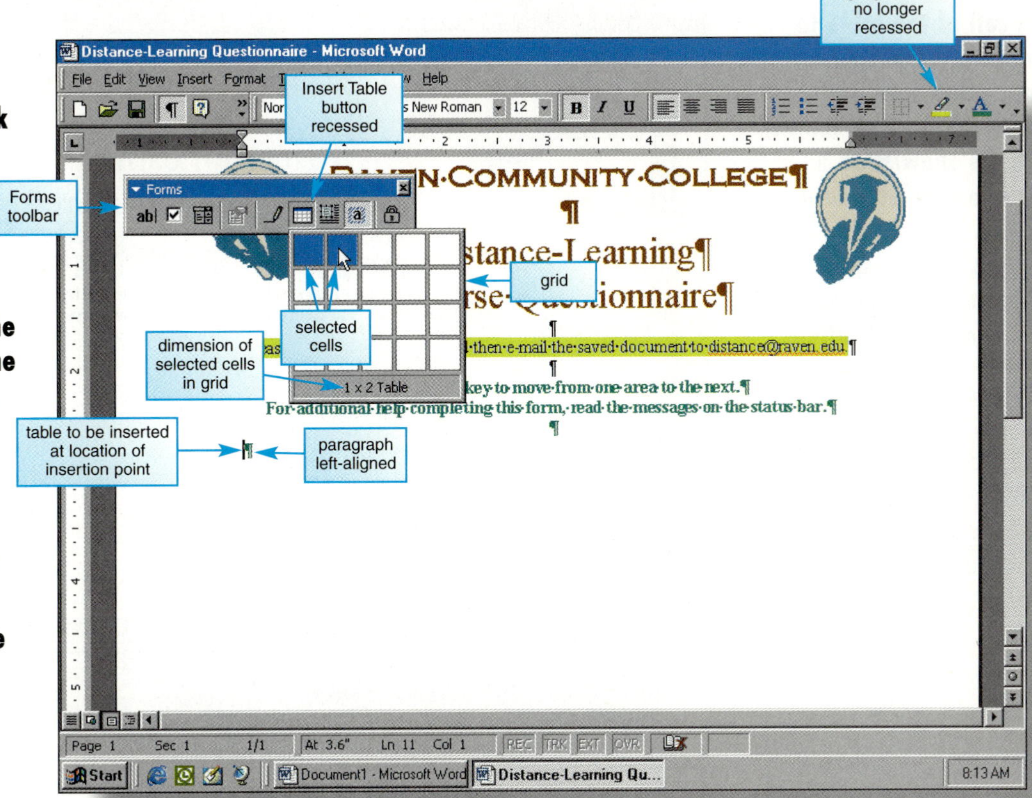

FIGURE 8-10

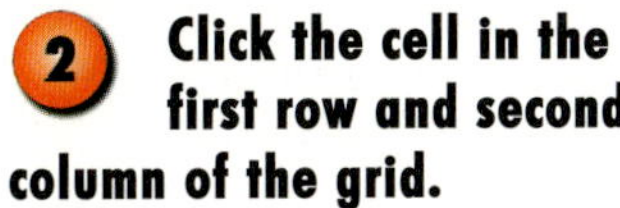

2 Click the cell in the first row and second column of the grid.

Word inserts an empty 1 x 2 table into the form. The insertion point is in the first cell (row 1 and column 1) of the table.

3 Click Table on the menu bar, point to Select, and then click Table to select the table. Click the Border button arrow on the Formatting toolbar and then point to the No Border button.

Word displays a list of border types (Figure 8-11). The table is selected in the document.

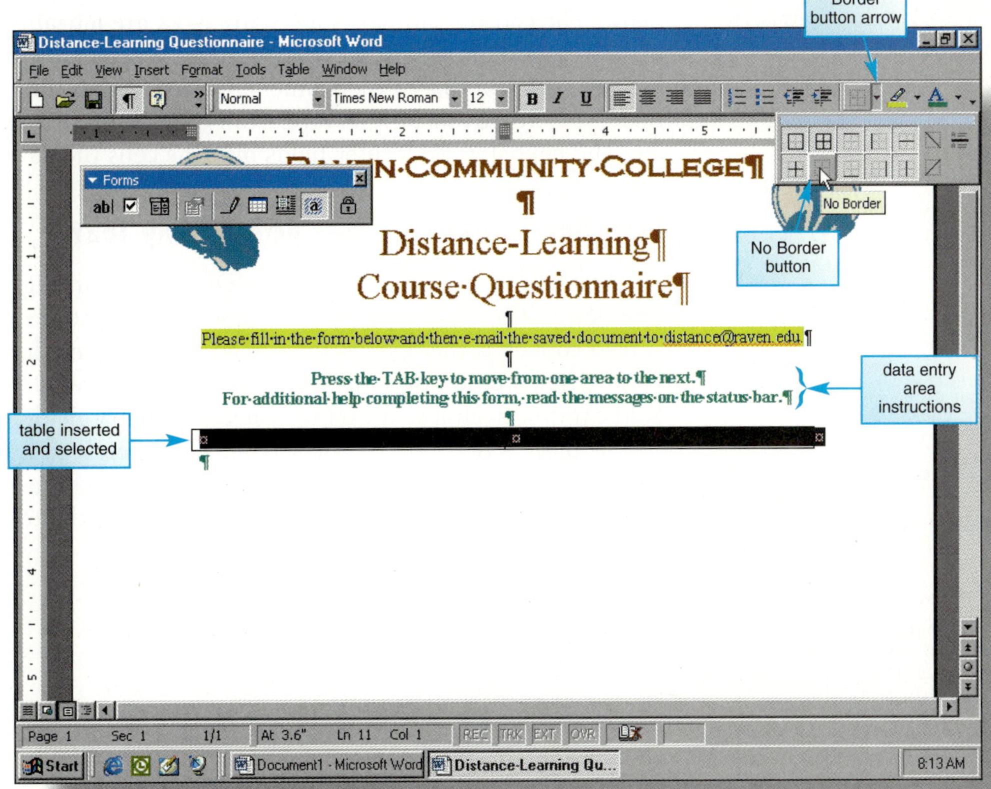

FIGURE 8-11

4 **Click the No Border button. Click in the first cell of the table to remove the highlight. If your screen does not display end-of-cell marks, click the Show/Hide ¶ button on the Standard toolbar. If your table displays gridlines, click Table on the menu bar and then click Hide Gridlines.**

Word removes the border from the cells in the table (Figure 8-12). Only the end-of-row and end-of-cell marks display in the document window to identify cells in the table.

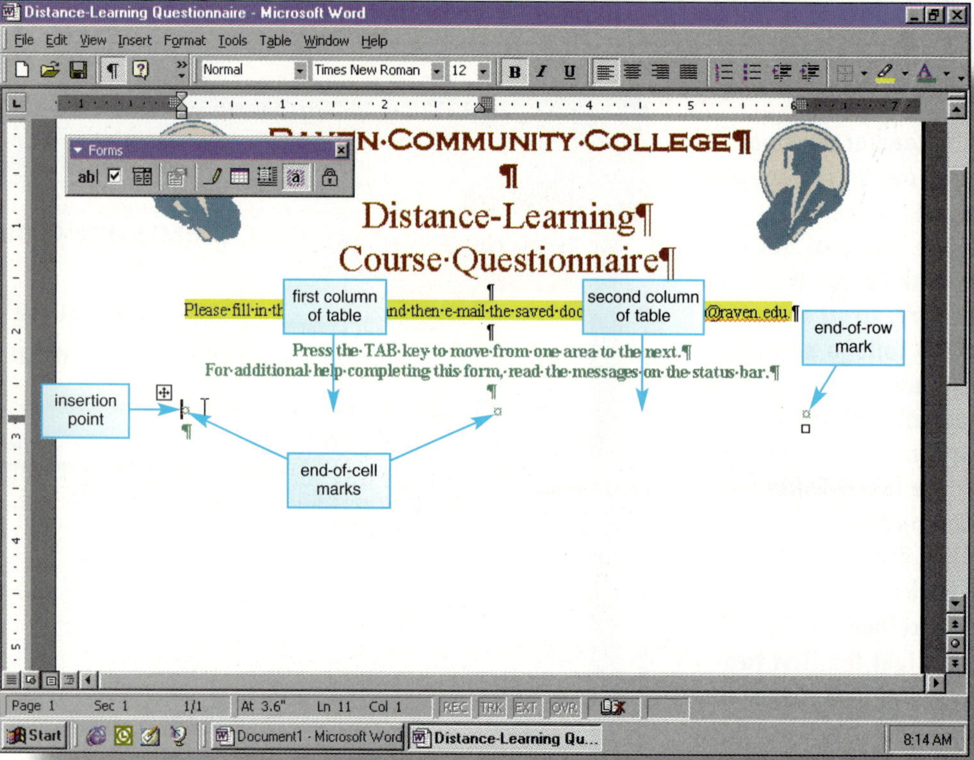

FIGURE 8-12

Other Ways

1. Click Insert Table button on Standard toolbar, click grid
2. On Table menu point to Insert, click Table, enter number of columns, enter number of rows, click OK button

Each row of a table has an end-of-row mark, and each cell has an end-of-cell mark. The end-of-cell marks in Figure 8-12 are left-aligned because the cells are formatted as left-aligned. The data you enter within a cell wordwraps just as text does between the margins of a document. To place data into a cell, you click the cell and then type. To advance rightward from one cell to the next, press the TAB key.

The next step is to enter fields into the cells of the table.

Inserting a Text Box that Accepts Any Text

The first item users enter on the Distance-Learning Course Questionnaire is their first name. The field caption text, First Name, is to display to the left of a text box. A **field caption** is the text on the screen that informs the user what to enter into the field. Often a colon or some other character follows a field caption to separate the field caption from a text box or other data entry field.

To place a text box on the screen, you insert a text form field. A **text form field** allows users to enter letters, numbers, and other characters into the field. Perform the following steps to enter the field caption and the text form field into the first cell of the table.

Gridlines

If you want to see the table gridlines while developing a form, click Table on the menu bar and then click Show Gridlines. Gridlines are formatting marks that do not print. They are designed to help users easily identify table cells, rows, and columns.

To Insert a Text Form Field

1 **With the insertion point in the first cell of the table (see Figure 8-12), type** `First Name` **and then press the COLON key (:). Press the SPACEBAR. Point to the Text Form Field button on the Forms toolbar.**

Word places the field caption into the first cell of the table (Figure 8-13).

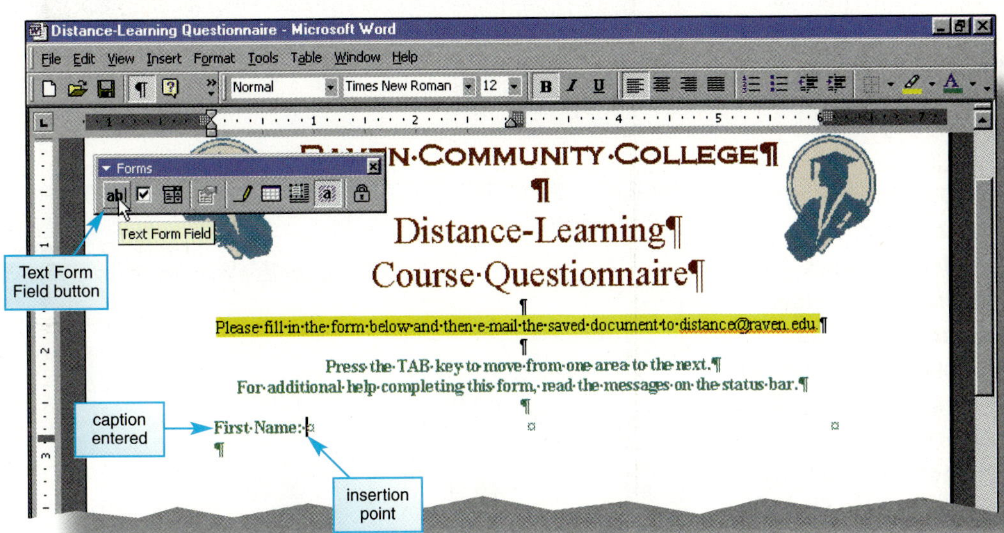

FIGURE 8-13

2 **Click the Text Form Field button. If the form field does not display shaded in gray, click the Form Field Shading button on the Forms toolbar.**

Word inserts a text form field at the location of the insertion point (Figure 8-14). The form field displays shaded in gray.

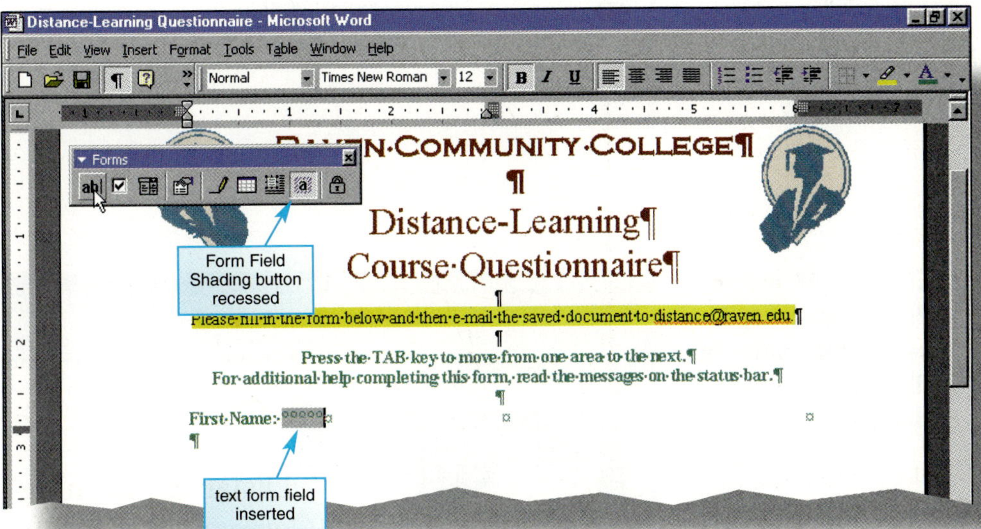

FIGURE 8-14

The text form field inserted by Word is five characters wide. You change its width, along with other characteristics of the form field, through the Text Form Field Options dialog box. You display this dialog box by double-clicking the text form field.

When this form displays on the screen initially (as a blank form), you want the text boxes and drop-down list boxes to display an underline that signifies the data entry area. The text displayed initially in a field is called the **default text**. Thus, the default text for these text boxes and drop-down list boxes on the Distance-Learning Course Questionnaire is an underline.

Because you want to limit a user's entry for the first name to 15 characters, the underline should consume 15 spaces. You also want the first letter of each word that a user enters into the First Name text box to be capitalized.

Perform the following steps to set the text form field for the first name so it displays 15 underscores as default text, limits the user's entry to 15 characters, and capitalizes the first letter of each word the user enters.

To Specify Text Form Field Options

1 Double-click the text form field. When Word displays the Text Form Field Options dialog box, press the UNDERSCORE key (_) 15 times in the Default text text box. Double-click the Maximum length box and then type 15 **as the length. Click the Text format box arrow and then click First capital. Point to the OK button.**

Word displays the Text Form Field Options dialog box (Figure 8-15).

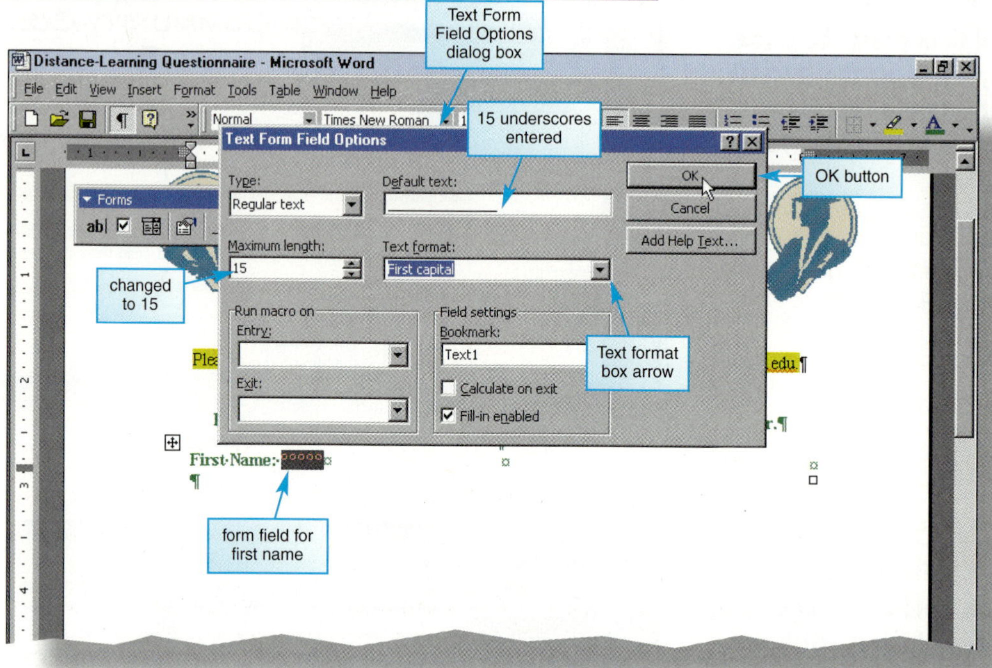

FIGURE 8-15

2 Click the OK button. Press the TAB key to move the insertion point to the beginning of the next cell in the table.

The text form field options are set (Figure 8-16).

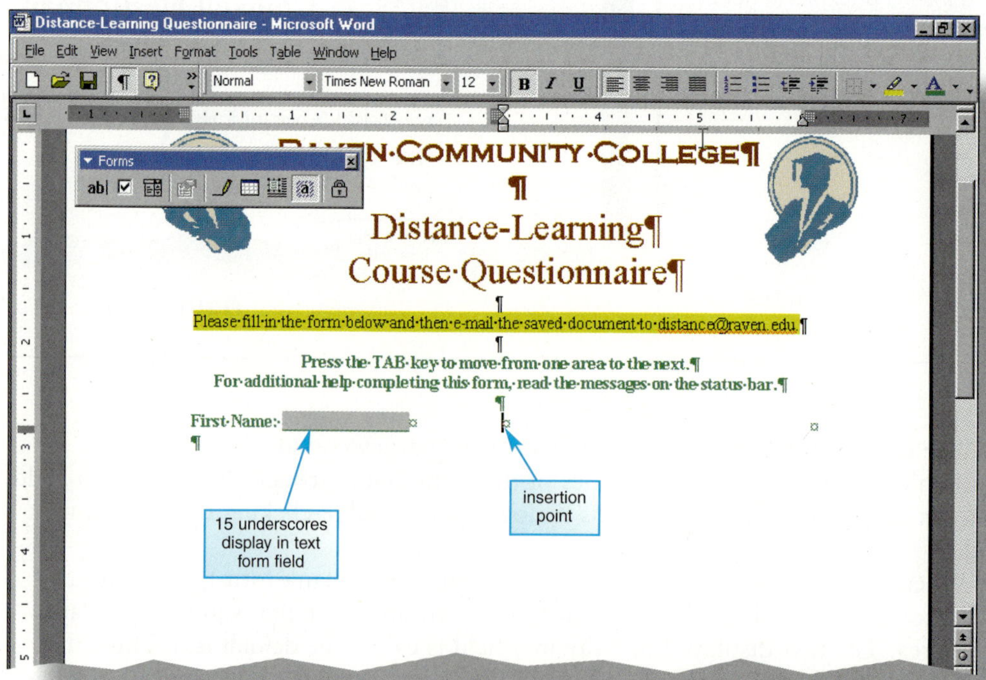

FIGURE 8-16

Other Ways

1. Click Form Field Options button on Forms toolbar
2. Right-click form field, click Properties on shortcut menu

When you click the Text format box arrow in the Text Form Field Options dialog box (see Figure 8-15), you have four choices: Uppercase, Lowercase, First capital, and Title case. If you select one of these options, Word displays a user's entry according to your selection – after the user presses the TAB key to advance out of the form field. Table 8-1 illustrates how each option displays text that a user enters into the form field.

Table 8-1 Text Formats for Text Form Fields

TEXT FORMAT	EXAMPLE
Uppercase	ALL LETTERS IN ALL WORDS ARE CAPITALIZED.
Lowercase	all letters in all words display as lowercase letters.
First capital	The first letter of the first word is capitalized.
Title case	The First Letter Of Every Word Is Capitalized.

The next form field to enter into the Distance-Learning Course Questionnaire is the last name. The only difference between the options for the form fields for the last name and first name is the last name allows up to 20 characters, instead of 15. Perform the following steps to insert and specify options for another text form field.

TO INSERT AND SPECIFY OPTIONS FOR A TEXT FORM FIELD

1. With the insertion point at the beginning of the second cell of the table, type `Last Name` and then press the COLON key. Press the SPACEBAR.
2. Click the Text Form Field button on the Forms toolbar.
3. Double-click the text form field for the last name. When Word displays the Text Form Field Options dialog box, press the UNDERSCORE key 20 times in the Default text text box. Double-click the Maximum length box and then type `20` as the length. Click the Text format box arrow and then click First capital (Figure 8-17).
4. Click the OK button.

Word displays the form field for the last name according to the settings in the Text Form Field Options dialog box.

The next step in creating the Distance-Learning Course Questionnaire is to insert a drop-down list box.

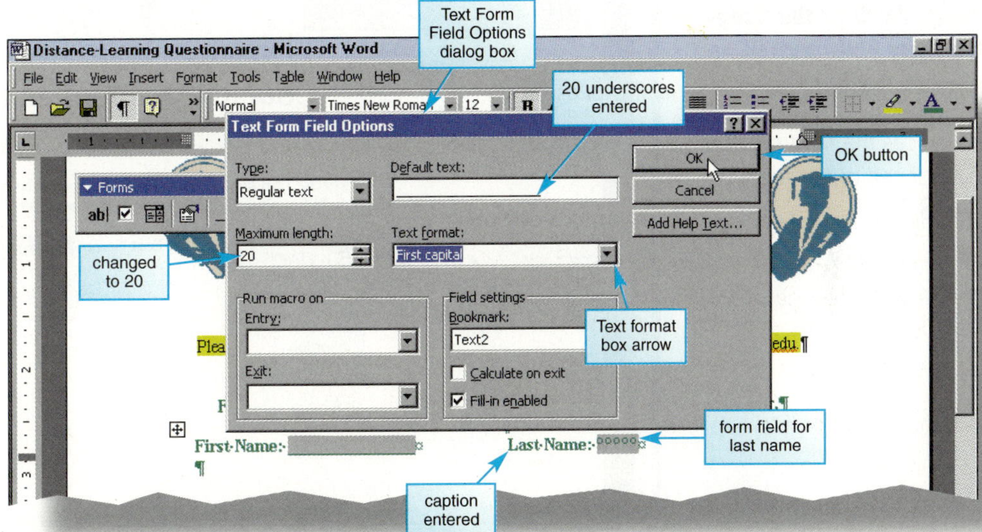

FIGURE 8-17

Inserting a Drop-Down List Box

You use a **drop-down form field** when you want to present a set of choices to a user in the form of a drop-down list box. To view the set of choices, the user clicks a box arrow that displays at the right edge of the list box (see Figure 8-1b on page WD 8.5). In this online form, the type of browser used is the first drop-down form field to be inserted. The valid choices to be presented to the user are Internet Explorer, Netscape, and Other.

Just as the first name and last name were inserted into a 1 x 2 table, the next two form fields will be inserted into a 1 x 2 table. The steps on the following pages explain how to insert the table, insert the drop-down form field, and then define the valid choices for the drop-down list.

TO INSERT A BORDERLESS TABLE INTO A FORM

1. Position the insertion point on the paragraph mark below the table containing the form field for the first name and last name. Press the ENTER key.
2. Click the Insert Table button on the Forms toolbar and then click the cell in the first row and second column of the grid.
3. Click Table on the menu bar, point to Select, and then click Table. Click the No Border button on the Formatting toolbar. Click in the first cell of the table.

Word inserts a 1 x 2 table at the location of the insertion point (see Figure 8-18). One blank line separates the two tables in the form.

Perform the following steps to insert a drop-down form field into the first cell of the table.

To Insert a Drop-Down Form Field

1 With the insertion point in the first cell of the table, type `Browser Used` **and then press the COLON key. Press the SPACEBAR. Point to the Drop-Down Form Field button on the Forms toolbar.**

Word places the field caption in the first cell of the table (Figure 8-18).

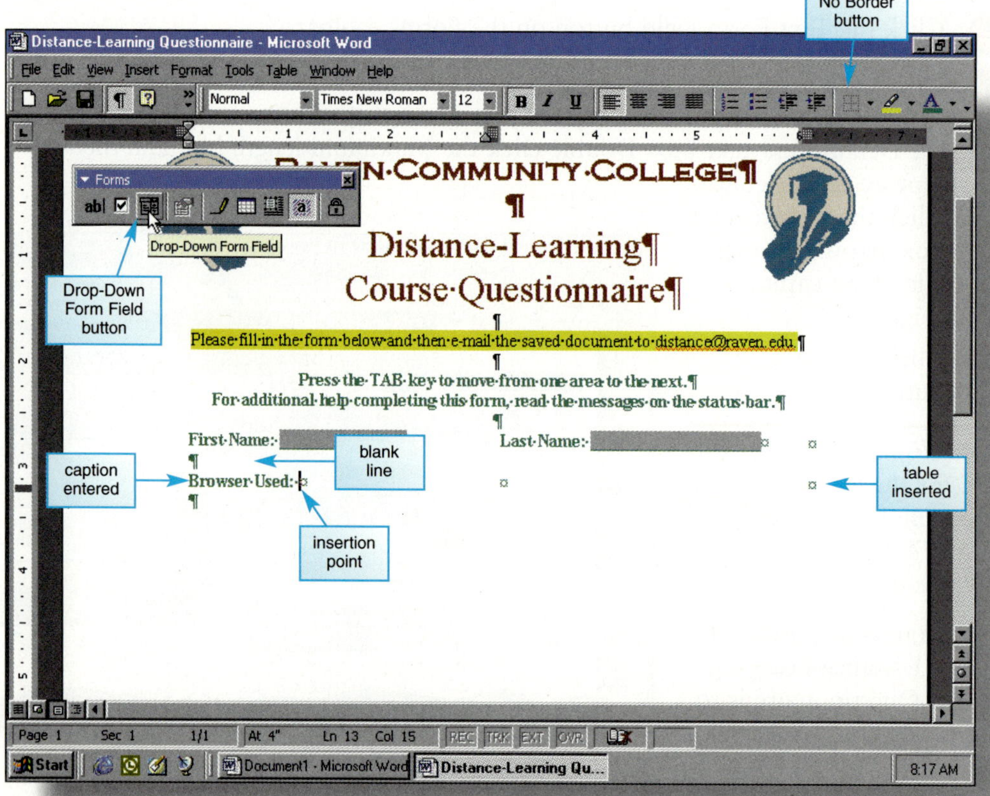

FIGURE 8-18

2 Click the Drop-Down Form Field button.

Word inserts a drop-down form field at the location of the insertion point (Figure 8-19). The form field displays shaded in gray.

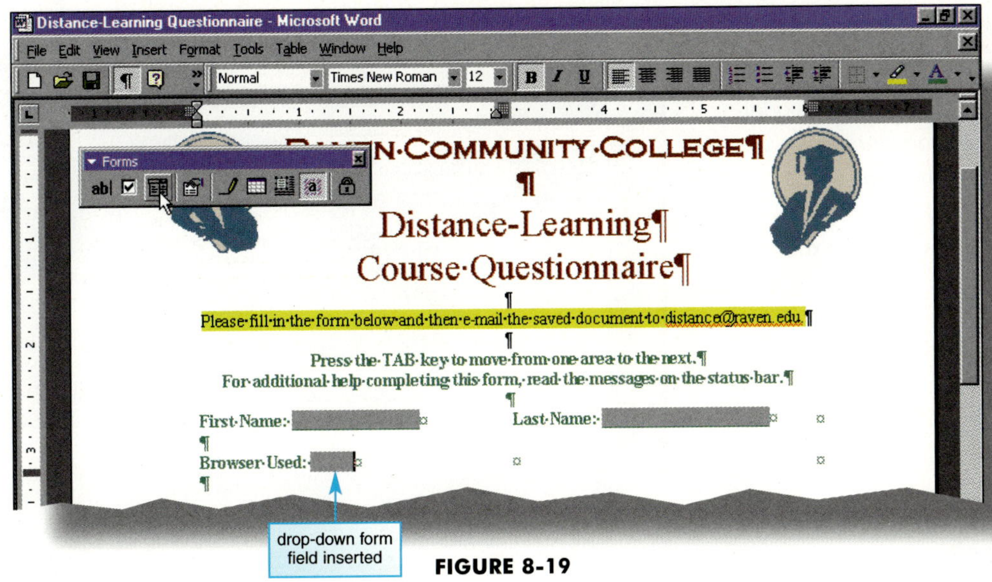

FIGURE 8-19

Recall that when the form displays on the screen initially (as a blank form), you want underscore characters to display where the text boxes and drop-down list boxes are located. This will help the user identify the data entry areas. In the text form field, you entered underscore characters as the default text. With a drop-down form field, Word displays the first item in the list on a blank form. Thus, you will enter 15 underscores as the first list item.

The drop-down form field initially is five characters wide. As you enter items into the drop-down list, Word increases the width of the form field to accommodate the item with the most number of characters. Perform the following steps to enter the items in the drop-down list, with the first item being 15 underscores.

Steps To Specify Drop-Down Form Field Options

1 Double-click the drop-down form field. When Word displays the Drop-Down Form Field Options dialog box, press the UNDERSCORE key 15 times in the Drop-down item text box and then point to the Add button.

Word displays the Drop-Down Form Field Options dialog box (Figure 8-20).

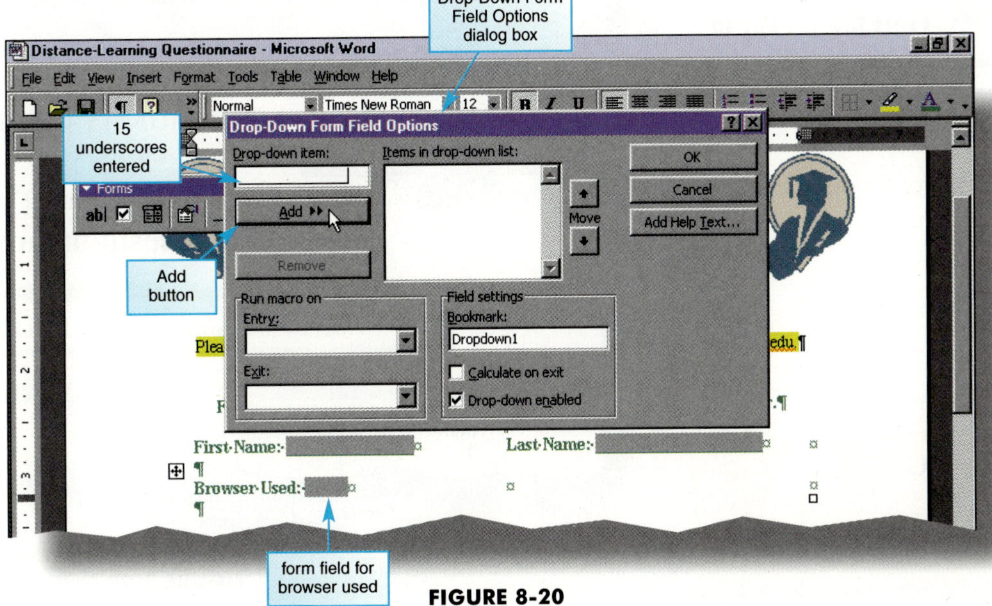

FIGURE 8-20

2 **Click the Add button.**

Word places the 15 underscore characters as the first item in the Items in drop-down list (Figure 8-21). The Drop-down item text box now is empty, waiting for your next entry.

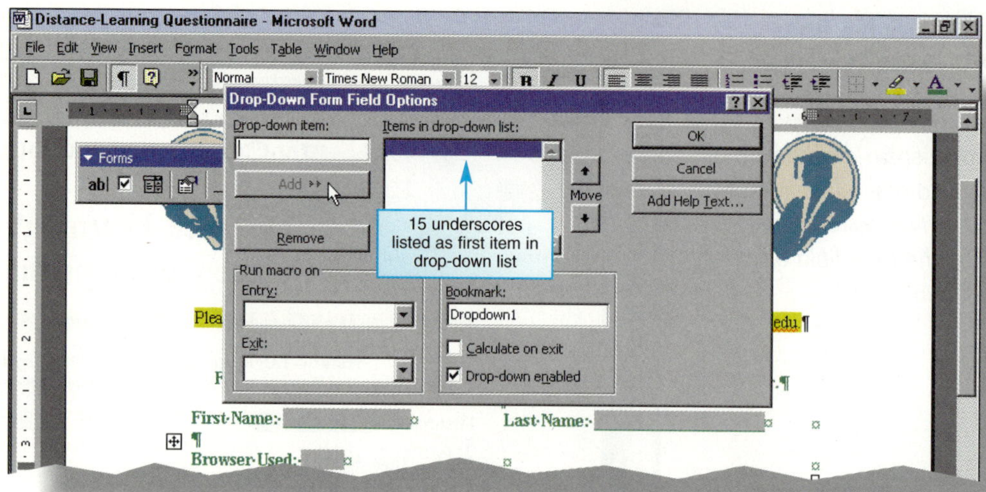

FIGURE 8-21

3 **Type** `Internet Explorer` **and then click the Add button. Type** `Netscape` **and then click the Add button. Type** `Other` **and then click the Add button. Point to the OK button.**

The items in the drop-down list are entered (Figure 8-22).

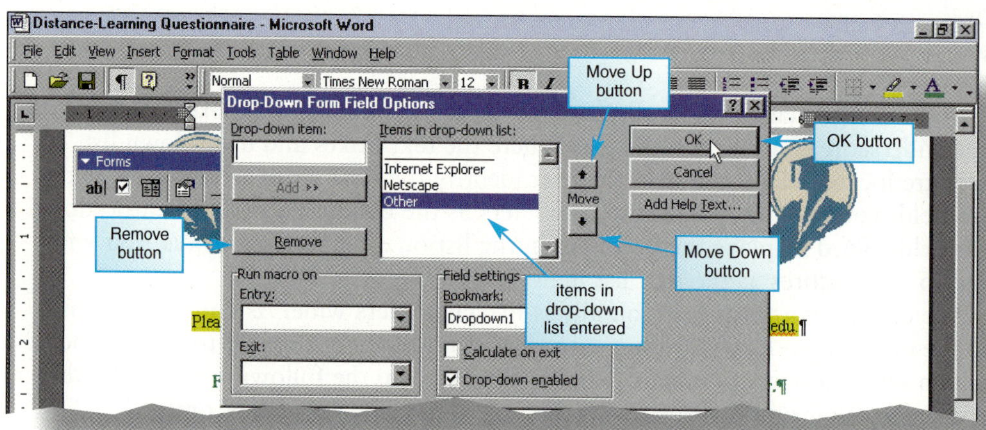

FIGURE 8-22

4 **Click the OK button. Press the TAB key to move the insertion point to the beginning of the next cell in the table.**

The list for the drop-down form field is defined (Figure 8-23).

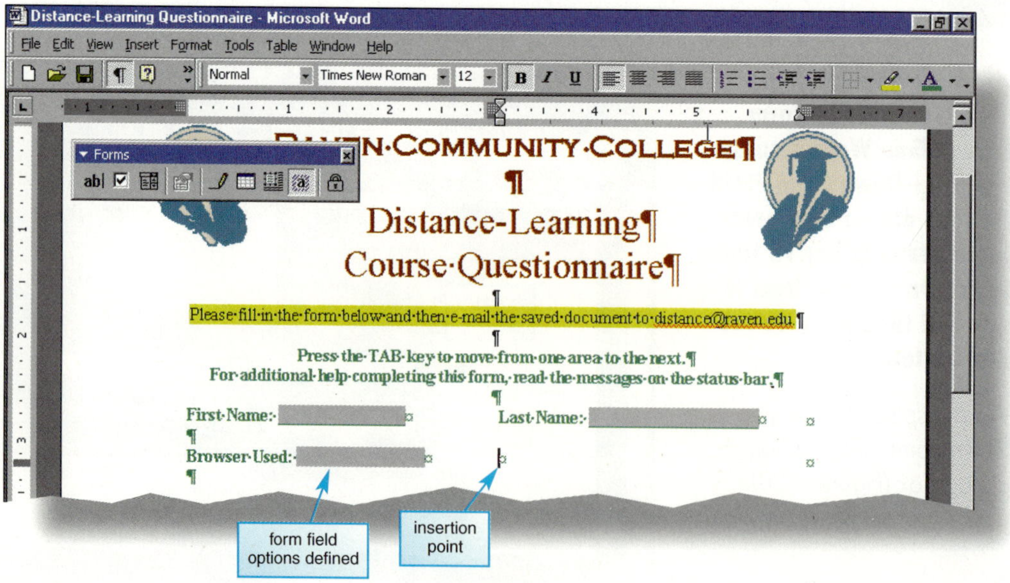

form field options defined

insertion point

FIGURE 8-23

Other Ways

1. Click Form Field Options button on Forms toolbar
2. Right-click form field, click Properties on shortcut menu

Instead of clicking the Add button (Figure 8-22) to move items from the Drop-down item text box to the Items in drop-down list, you can press the ENTER key. This alternative method will be used later in this project.

Notice in Figure 8-23 that the 15 underscores do not display on the screen yet. Word displays the first item in the drop-down list on the screen when you protect the form, which you will do later in this project.

If, after you enter items in a list box, you want to modify their order or add or delete one or more items, you would display the Drop-Down Form Field Options dialog box (Figure 8-22) by double-clicking the drop-down form field. To add more items, you simply enter the text into the Drop-down item text box and then click the OK button. To remove an item, click it in the Items in drop-down list and then click the Remove button. To reorder the list, click an item in the Items in drop-down list and then click the Move Up button or Move Down button to move the item up or down one position each time you click the appropriate button.

The Distance-Learning Course Questionnaire has two more drop-down list boxes. One requests the user's connection method and the other requests the processor type. The list for connection method is to contain these eight items: 56 Kbps Modem, 33.6 Kbps Modem, 28.8 Kbps Modem, 14.4 Kbps Modem, ISDN Line, ADSL, T1 Line, and Other. Recall that when the form displays on the screen initially (as a blank form), you want underscore characters to display where the form fields are located. To do this, you will enter 15 underscores as the first list item.

Perform the following steps to insert another drop-down form field.

TO INSERT AND SPECIFY OPTIONS FOR A DROP-DOWN FORM FIELD

1. With the insertion point in the second cell of the table, type `Connection Method` and then press the COLON key. Press the SPACEBAR.
2. Click the Drop-Down Form Field button on the Forms toolbar.
3. Double-click the drop-down form field just entered. When Word displays the Drop-Down Form Field Options dialog box, press the UNDERSCORE key 15 times in the Drop-down item text box and then press the ENTER key.
4. Type `56 Kbps Modem` and then press the ENTER key. Type `33.6 Kbps Modem` and then press the ENTER key. Type `28.8 Kbps Modem` and then press the ENTER key. Type `14.4 Kbps Modem` and then press the ENTER key. Type `ISDN Line` and then press the ENTER key. Type `ADSL` and then press the ENTER key. Type `T1 Line` and then press the ENTER key. Type `Other` and then press the ENTER key. Point to the OK button (Figure 8-24 on the next page).
5. Click the OK button.

Word defines the drop-down form field as specified in the Drop-Down Form Field Options dialog box.

Drop-Down Form Fields

Instead of clicking the Add button in the Drop-Down Form Field Options dialog box (see Figure 8-20 on page WD 8.21) to move an item from the Drop-down item text box to the Items in drop-down list, you can press the ENTER key.

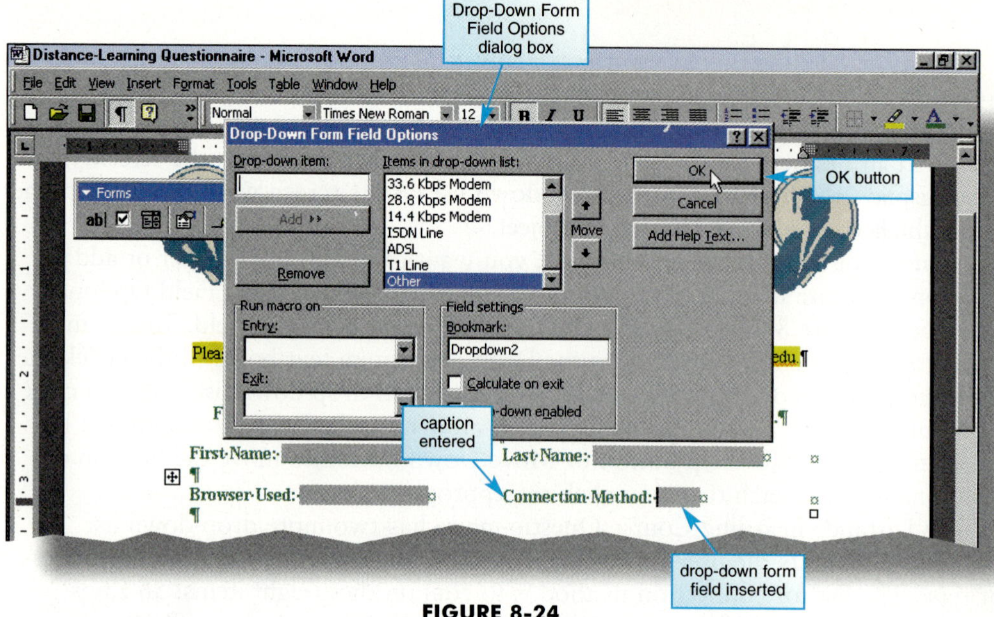

FIGURE 8-24

Just as the First Name and Last Name text boxes were inserted into a 1 x 2 table and the Browser Used and Connection Method drop-down list boxes were inserted into a 1 x 2 table, the next two form fields also will be inserted into a 1 x 2 table. Perform the following steps to insert the next 1 x 2 table.

TO INSERT A BORDERLESS TABLE INTO A FORM

1. Position the insertion point on the paragraph mark below the table containing the Browser Used and Connection Method drop-down list boxes. Press the ENTER key.
2. Click the Insert Table button on the Forms toolbar and then click the cell in the first row and second column of the grid.
3. Click Table on the menu bar, point to Select, and then click Table. Click the No Border button on the Formatting toolbar. Click in the first cell of the table.

Word inserts a 1 x 2 table two lines below the current 1 x 2 table (see Figure 8-25).

The first cell of the newly inserted table is to contain a drop-down list box that requests the processor type. The valid processor types to be in the list are Athlon, Pentium III, Pentium II, Celeron, AMD-K6, Pentium with MMX, Pentium, and Other. You also will enter 15 underscore characters as the first list item. Perform the following steps to insert another drop-down form field.

TO INSERT AND SPECIFY OPTIONS FOR A DROP-DOWN FORM FIELD

1. With the insertion point in the first cell of the table, type `Processor Type` and then press the COLON key. Press the SPACEBAR.
2. Click the Drop-Down Form Field button on the Forms toolbar.
3. Double-click the drop-down form field just inserted. When Word displays the Drop-Down Form Field Options dialog box, press the UNDERSCORE key 15 times in the Drop-down item text box and then press the ENTER key.

4. Type Athlon and then press the ENTER key. Type Pentium III and then press the ENTER key. Type Pentium II and then press the ENTER key. Type Celeron and then press the ENTER key. Type AMD-K6 and then press the ENTER key. Type Pentium with MMX and then press the ENTER key. Type Pentium and then press the ENTER key. Type Other and then press the ENTER key. Point to the OK button (Figure 8-25).

5. Click the OK button. Press the TAB key to move the insertion point to the beginning of the next cell in the table.

Word defines the drop-down form field as specified in the Drop-Down Form Field Options dialog box.

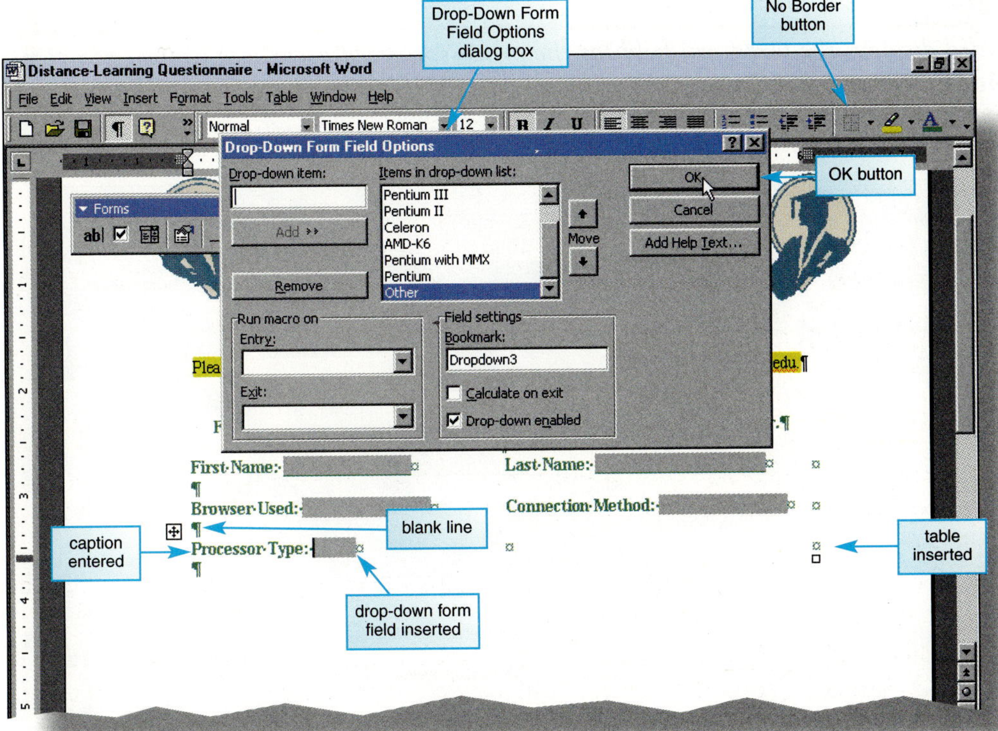

FIGURE 8-25

The next step is to insert a text form field that requires a number.

Inserting a Text Box that Requires a Number

The next form field to be entered into the Distance-Learning Course Questionnaire is for the processor speed. Processor speeds for microcomputers generally are three numbers in length such as 333, 400, or 450. You, therefore, will instruct Word to display three underscore characters when the form initially displays on the screen (as a blank form).

Valid speeds entered will vary greatly, but all speeds entered should be numeric. If you ultimately will be analyzing the data entered in a form with another type of software package such as a database, you do not want non-numeric data in fields that require numeric entries. Thus, Word can convert a non-numeric entry such as ABC to a zero.

Perform the steps on the next page to insert and format this text form field.

Text Form Field Types

When you click the Type box arrow in the Text Form Field Options dialog box (see Figure 8-26), you have six options: Regular text, Number, Date, Current date, Current time, and Calculation. Regular text accepts any keyboard character. Number requires a numeric entry. Date requires a valid date. The last three options display the date, time, or result of a calculation and do not allow a user to change this displayed value.

TO INSERT AND SPECIFY OPTIONS FOR A TEXT FORM FIELD

1. With the insertion point at the beginning of the second cell of the table, type `Processor Speed` and then press the COLON key. Press the SPACEBAR.
2. Click the Text Form Field button on the Forms toolbar.
3. Double-click the text form field for the processor speed. When Word displays the Text Form Field Options dialog box, click the Type box arrow and then click Number. Press the TAB key to position the insertion point in the Maximum length box and then type 3 as the length. Press the TAB key to position the insertion point in the Default number text box and then press the UNDERSCORE key three times. Point to the OK button (Figure 8-26).
4. Click the OK button.

Word displays the text form field for the processor speed according to the settings in the Text Form Field Options dialog box.

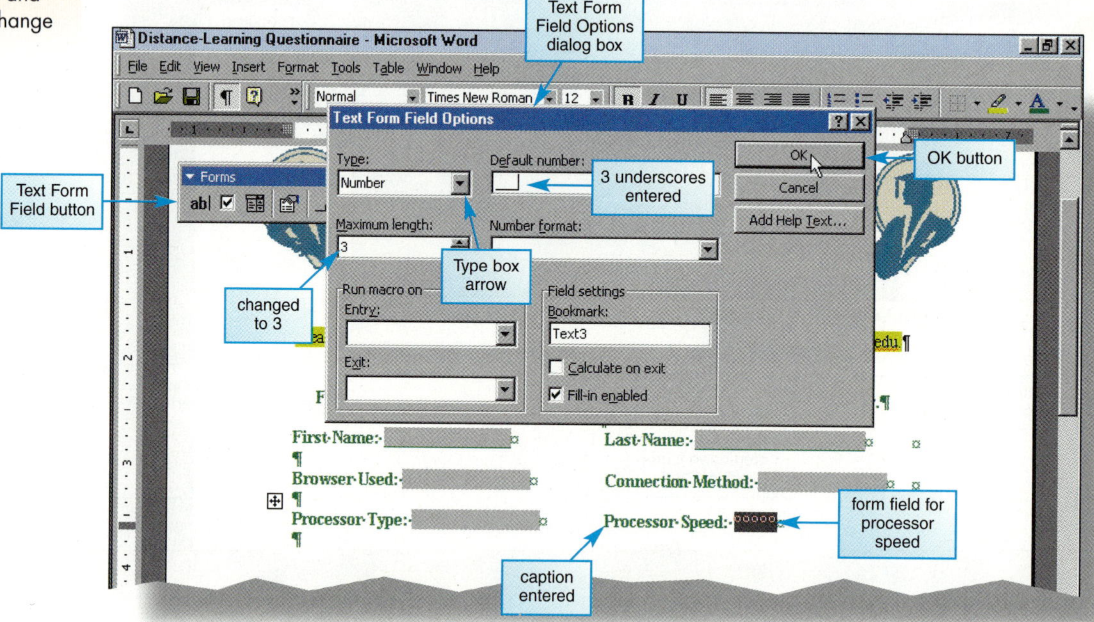

FIGURE 8-26

By changing the Type box to Number (Figure 8-26), Word will convert any non-numeric entry in this form field to a zero. Other valid text form field types are discussed later in this project.

The next step is to enter the check boxes into the Distance-Learning Course Questionnaire.

Inserting a Check Box

The bottom of the data entry area of the Distance-Learning Course Questionnaire contains five check boxes, one each for scanner, microphone, video camera, fax machine, and other. The latter (other) also has a text box to its right to allow a user to explain further. Above the check boxes is a line of instructions pertaining to the check boxes. The following pages explain how to enter this section of the form.

The first step is to enter the line of text containing instructions for the check boxes. Perform the following steps to enter this line of text.

TO ENTER TEXT

1. Position the insertion point on the paragraph mark below the table containing the fields for processor type and processor speed. Press the ENTER key.
2. Type `Special Equipment Used for Course (check all that apply)` and then press the COLON key.
3. Press CTRL+5 to change the line spacing for this and subsequent paragraphs to 1.5 lines. Press the ENTER key.

The instructions for the check boxes display as shown in Figure 8-27.

You want four check boxes to display horizontally below the check box instructions. To do this and align the check boxes evenly across the line, you insert a 1 x 4 table; that is, a table with one row and four columns. Perform the following steps to insert a 1 x 4 table into the form.

TO INSERT A BORDERLESS TABLE INTO A FORM

1. With the insertion point on the paragraph mark below the check box instructions, click the Insert Table button on the Forms toolbar and then point to the cell in the first row and fourth column of the grid (Figure 8-27).
2. Click the cell in the first row and fourth column of the grid.
3. Click Table on the menu bar, point to Select, and then click Table. Click the No Border button on the Formatting toolbar.
4. Click in the first cell of the table.

Word inserts a 1 x 4 table at the location of the insertion point (see Figure 8-28 on the next page).

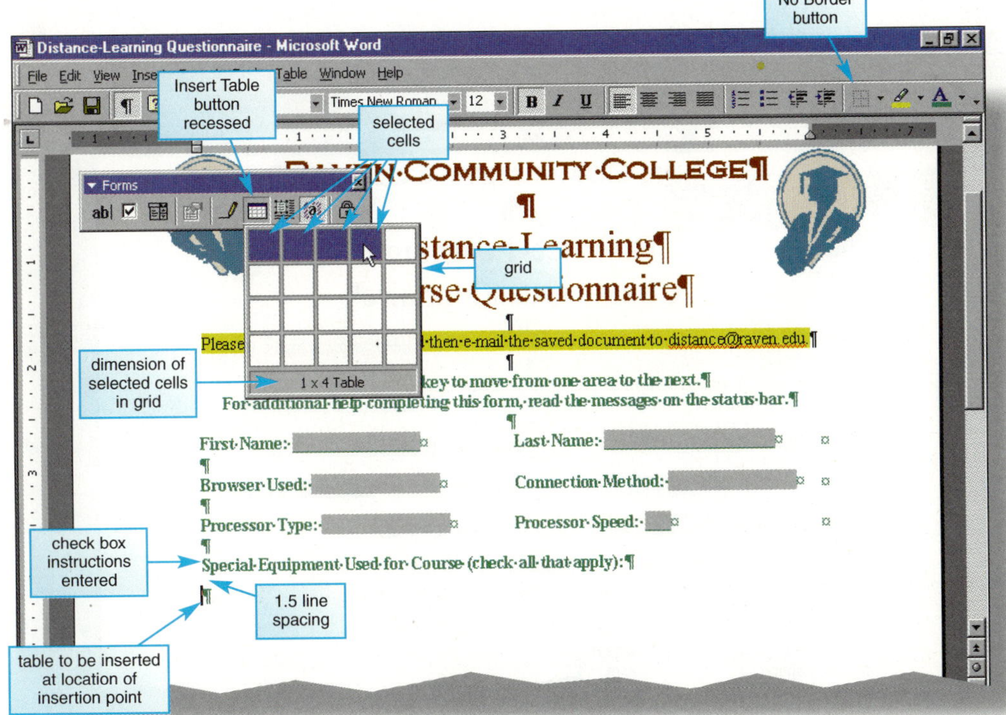

FIGURE 8-27

The next step is to insert the first check box into the first cell of the table as shown in the following steps.

To Insert a Check Box

1 **With the insertion point in the first cell of the table, point to the Check Box Form Field button on the Forms toolbar (Figure 8-28).**

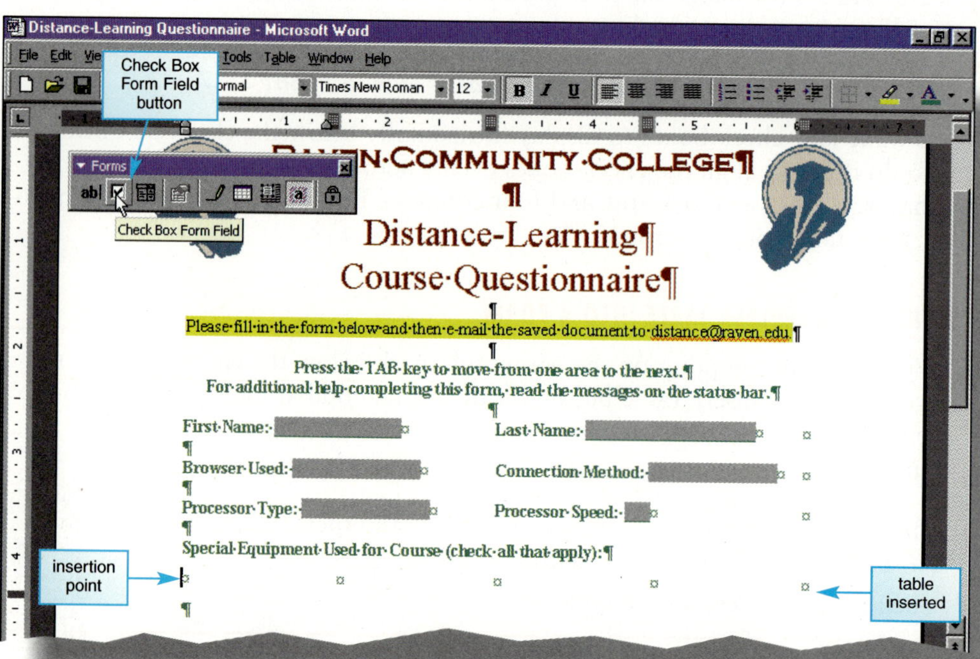

FIGURE 8-28

2 **Click the Check Box Form Field button. Press the SPACEBAR. Type** `Scanner` **and then press the TAB key.**

Word inserts a check box form field at the location of the insertion point (Figure 8-29).

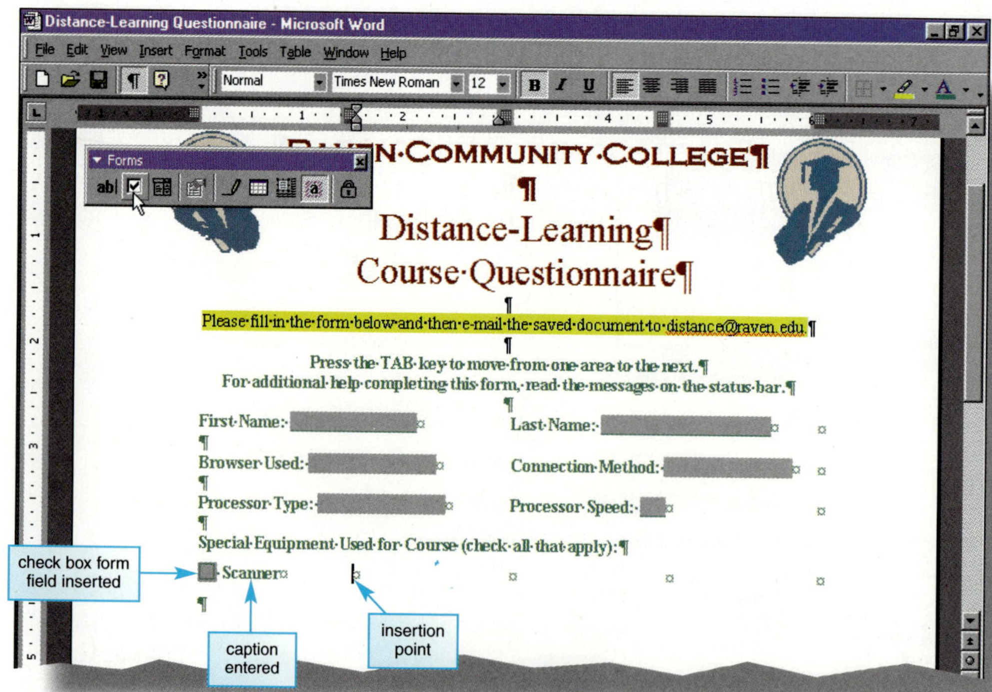

FIGURE 8-29

The next step is to enter the remaining check box fields into the form as described in the following steps.

TO ENTER ADDITIONAL CHECK BOX FORM FIELDS

1. With the insertion point in the second cell of the table, click the Check Box Form Field button on the Forms toolbar. Press the SPACEBAR. Type `Microphone` and then press the TAB key.
2. With the insertion point in the third cell of the table, click the Check Box Form Field button on the Forms toolbar. Press the SPACEBAR. Type `Video Camera` and then press the TAB key.
3. With the insertion point in the fourth cell of the table, click the Check Box Form Field button on the Forms toolbar. Press the SPACEBAR. Type `Fax Machine` and then click the paragraph mark below the 1 x 4 table.
4. With the insertion point below the 1 x 4 table, click the Check Box Form Field button on the Forms toolbar. Press the SPACEBAR. Type `Other (please specify)` and then press the COLON key. Press the SPACEBAR.

The check box form fields are inserted (Figure 8-30).

Check Boxes

If you want an X to display in a check box when the form initially displays on the screen (as a blank form), you would double-click the check box form field, click Checked in the Default value area of the Check Box Form Field Options dialog box, and then click the OK button.

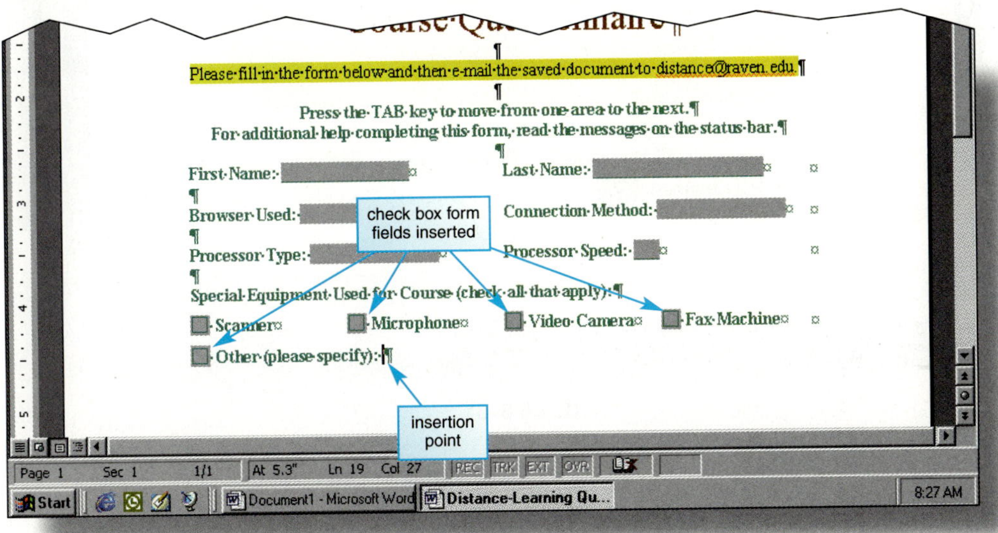

FIGURE 8-30

If users select the check box with the Other caption, you want them to explain the other type of equipment they used in the distance-learning course. To allow this, you insert a text form field as described in the following steps.

TO INSERT AND SPECIFY OPTIONS FOR A TEXT FORM FIELD

1. Click the Text Form Field button on the Forms toolbar.
2. Double-click the text form field for other (please specify). When Word displays the Text Form Field Options dialog box, press the UNDERSCORE key 30 times in the Default text text box. Point to the OK button (Figure 8-31 on the next page).
3. Click the OK button.

 Press CTRL+1 (the numeral one) to change the line spacing to single for this paragraph.

Word displays the text form field for the other types of equipment according to the settings in the Text Form Field Options dialog box. You change line spacing back to single so that the highlight on the text box consumes only one line instead of one and one-half lines.

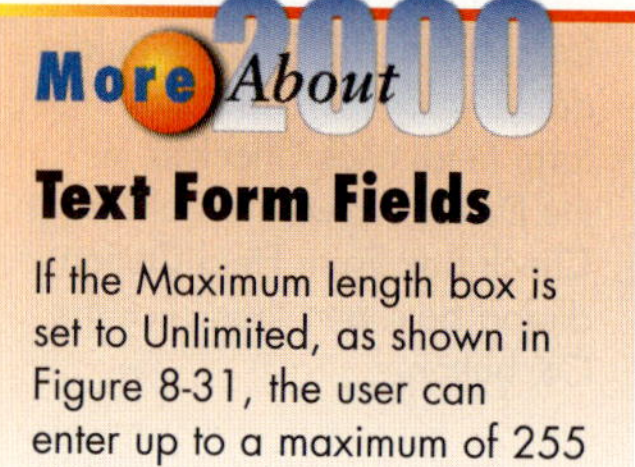

Text Form Fields

If the Maximum length box is set to Unlimited, as shown in Figure 8-31, the user can enter up to a maximum of 255 characters into the text box.

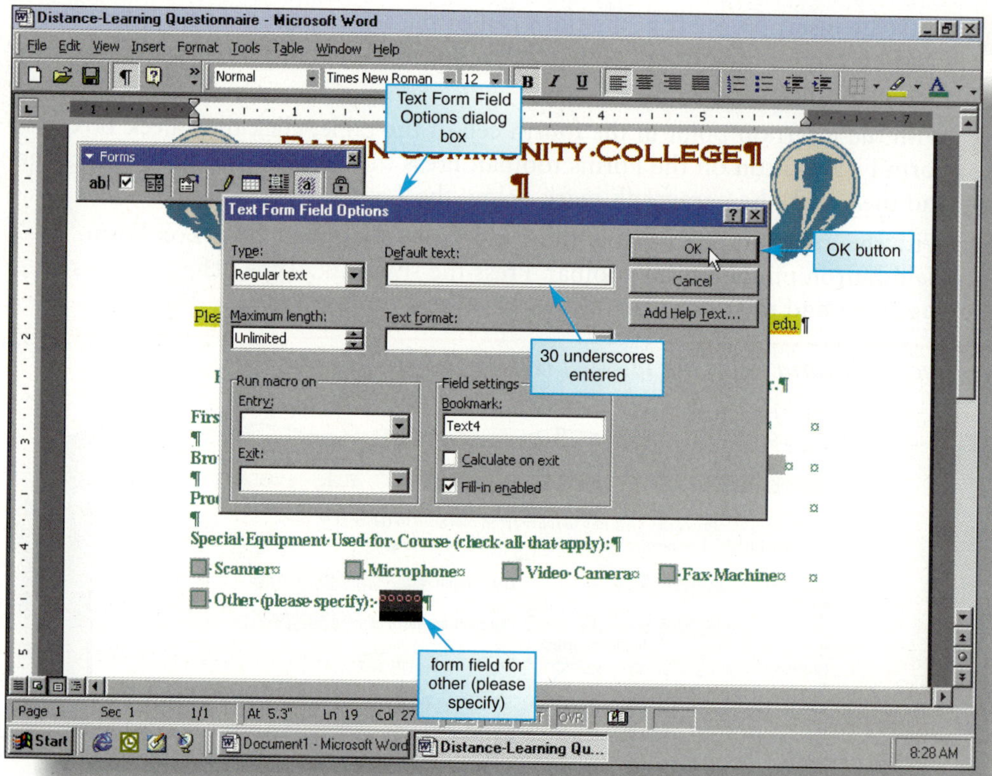

FIGURE 8-31

The next step is to display the current date on the form.

Inserting a Text Box that Displays the Current Date

The next form field to be entered into the Distance-Learning Course Questionnaire is the current date. You do not want the user to enter the date; instead, you simply want the current date to display on the form. When a user fills in and e-mails the completed form, the date the user completed the form will display.

You could insert the current date as a field by clicking Insert on the menu bar and then clicking Date and Time. If, however, you plan to analyze the data at a later time using a database or some other software and you want the current date to be part of the data saved with the form, then you must insert a text box that displays the current date. Perform the following steps to insert and specify options for this text form field as the current date.

To Insert and Specify Options for a Text Form Field as the Current Date

1 Click at the end of the last text form field entered and then press the ENTER key. Press CTRL+R to right-align the paragraph. Click the Text Form Field button on the Forms toolbar. Double-click the text form field for the current date. When Word displays the Text Form Field Options dialog box, click the Type box arrow and then click Current date. Click the Date format box arrow and then click M/d/yyyy. Point to the OK button (Figure 8-32).

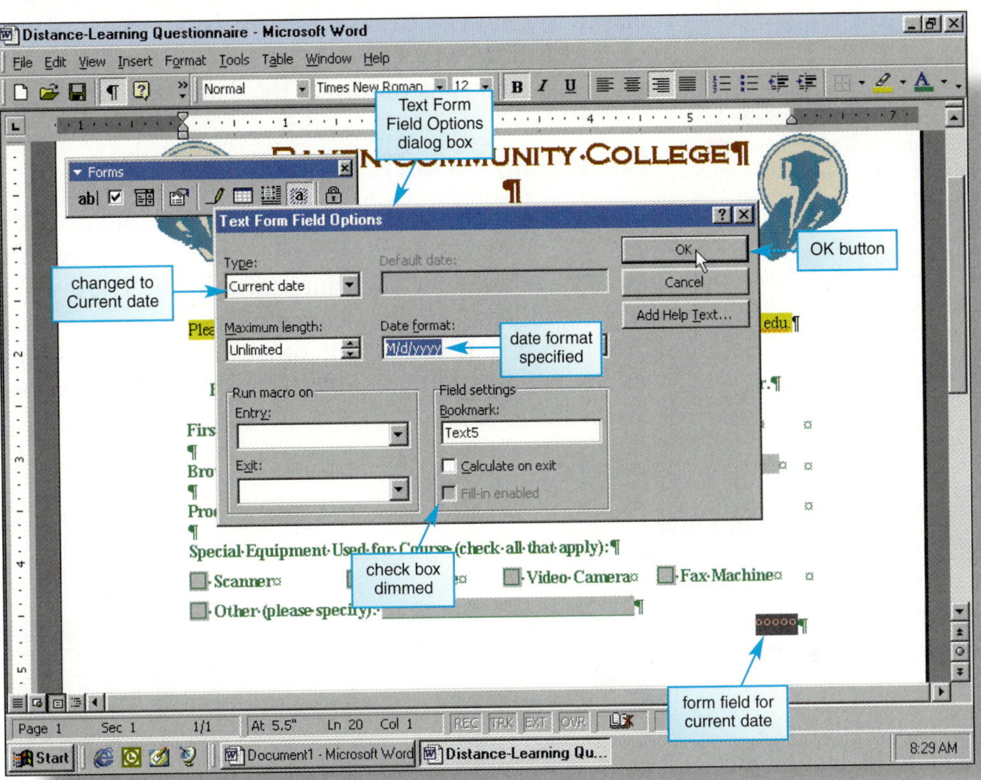

FIGURE 8-32

2 Click the OK button. Click outside the field to remove the highlight.

Word displays the current date in the form field (Figure 8-33). Your date displayed will be different.

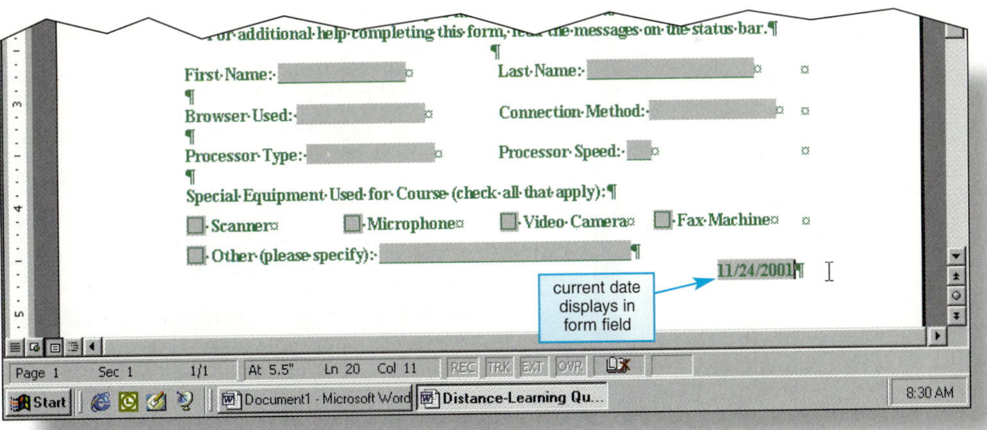

FIGURE 8-33

Notice in Figure 8-32 that the Fill-in enabled check box is dimmed in the Text Form Field Options dialog box. Word automatically dims this check box when you select Current date as the text type. When this check box is dimmed, a user is not allowed to modify the contents of the field when it displays on the screen. If you want a user to enter a date, you would select Date in the Type list instead of Current date.

Date and Time

If a text form field type has been changed to Current date (see Figure 8-32 on the previous page) or Current time and you intend to print the form, you should ensure that the date and time are current in the hard copy. Click Tools on the menu bar, click Options, click the Print tab, place a check mark in the Update fields check box, and then click the OK button.

Two other options in the Type list that also dim the Fill-in enabled check box are Current time and Calculation. That is, if you select Current time as the text type, Word displays the current time on the screen – so a user cannot change the time displayed. If you select Calculation as the text type, Word displays the result of a formula you enter.

The next step is to format the data entry fields.

Formatting Form Fields

As users enter data into the text boxes and drop-down list boxes on the form, you want the characters they type to be underlined in teal. Word prevents users from formatting data they enter into form fields. Thus, you specify any desired field formatting to fields on the form template. To format a field, you select the field and then format it as you do any other text. In this case, you use the Font dialog box to specify an underline color. Perform the following steps to underline the field for the first name in teal.

To Underline in Color

1 **Click the text form field for the first name to select it. Right-click the selection and then point to Font on the shortcut menu (Figure 8-34).**

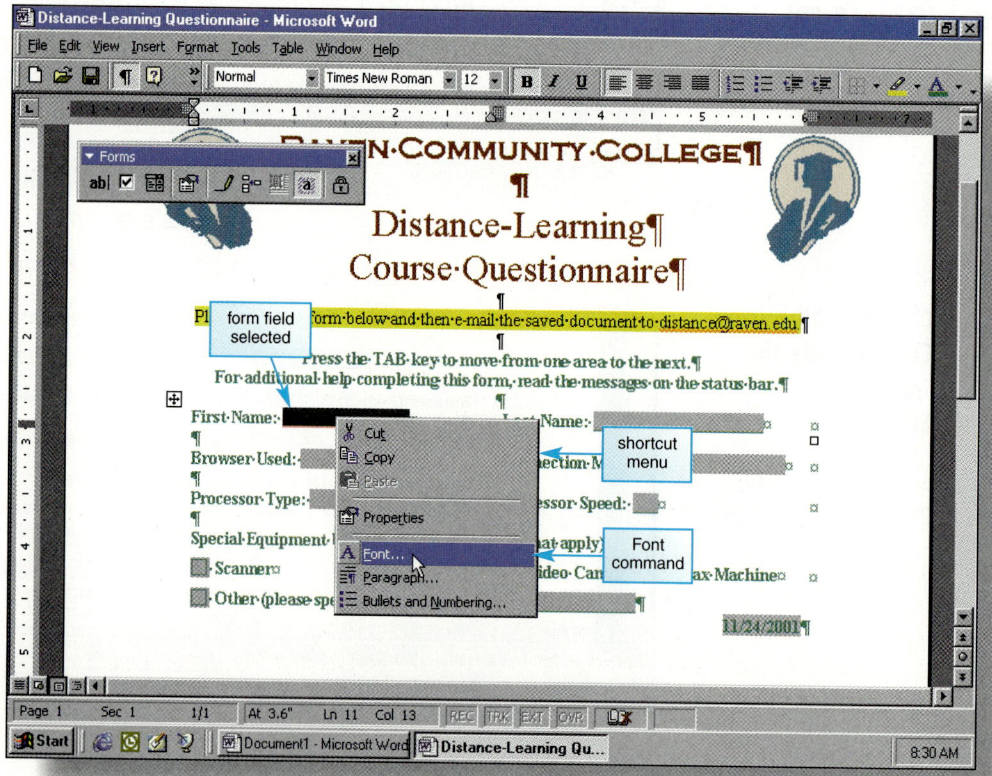

FIGURE 8-34

2 Click Font. When the Font dialog box displays, if necessary, click the Font tab. Click the Underline style box arrow and then click the first underline in the list. Click the Underline color box arrow and then click Teal. Point to the OK button.

Word displays the Font dialog box (Figure 8-35).

3 Click the OK button.

Word formats the data entry for the field to 12-point Times New Roman underlined bold teal font.

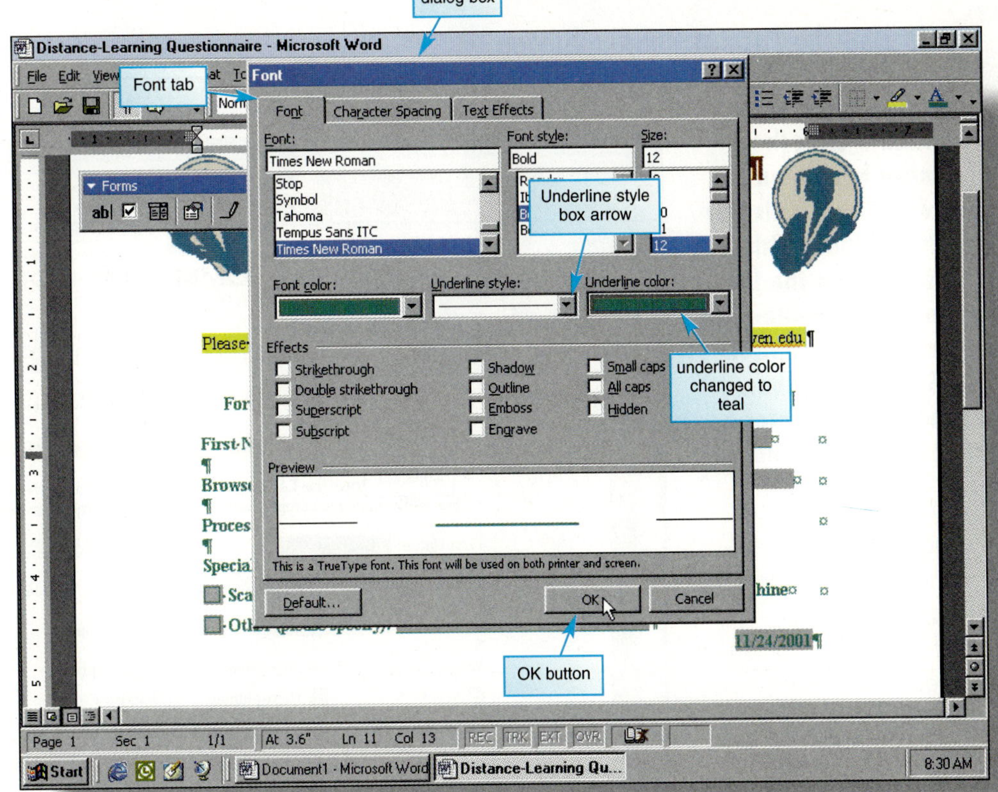

FIGURE 8-35

1. On Format menu click Font, click Font tab, select desired underline style, select desired underline color, click OK button

Because earlier you set the text form fields to display an underline when the form displays initially on the screen (as a blank form), you will not notice a change to the First Name text box after formatting it. The formatting options will take effect when you enter data into the form.

The next step is to copy this formatting to the other data entry fields on the screen.

Using the Format Painter Button

Instead of selecting each form field one at a time and then formatting it with the teal underline, you will copy the format assigned to the form field for the first name to the other text form fields and the drop-down form fields.

To copy formats from one form field to another, you select the form field from which you wish to copy formatting, click the Format Painter button to copy the selected form field's formatting specifications, and then select the form field to which you wish to copy the formatting. To select a text form field, you simply click it or drag through it. To select a drop-down form field, you drag through it.

In this project, you want to copy formats from one form field to multiple form fields. Thus, you double-click the Format Painter button so that the format painter remains active until you turn it off as shown in the steps on the next page.

Copying Formatting

If you want to copy paragraph formatting, such as alignment and line spacing, select the paragraph mark at the end of the paragraph prior to clicking the Format Painter button. If you want to copy just character formatting, such as fonts and font sizes, do not select the paragraph mark.

Steps To Use the Format Painter Button

1 **Double-click the move handle on the Standard toolbar to display the entire toolbar. With the text form field for the first name selected, double-click the Format Painter button on the Standard toolbar. Move the mouse pointer into the document window.**

Word attaches a paintbrush to the mouse pointer when the Format Painter button is recessed (Figure 8-36). The 12-point Times New Roman underlined bold teal font has been copied by the format painter.

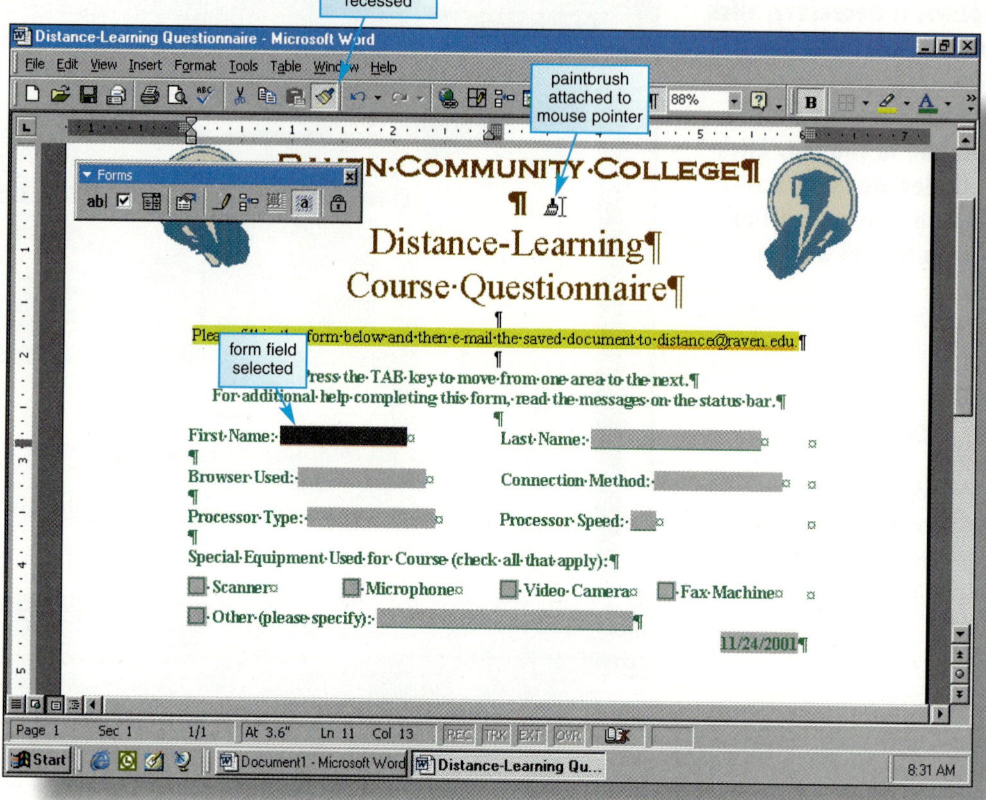

FIGURE 8-36

2 **Click the text form field for the last name.**

Word copies the 12-point Times New Roman underlined bold teal font to the text form field for the last name (Figure 8-37). The last name field is highlighted, and the format painter remains active, allowing you to select more fields to which you wish to copy the format.

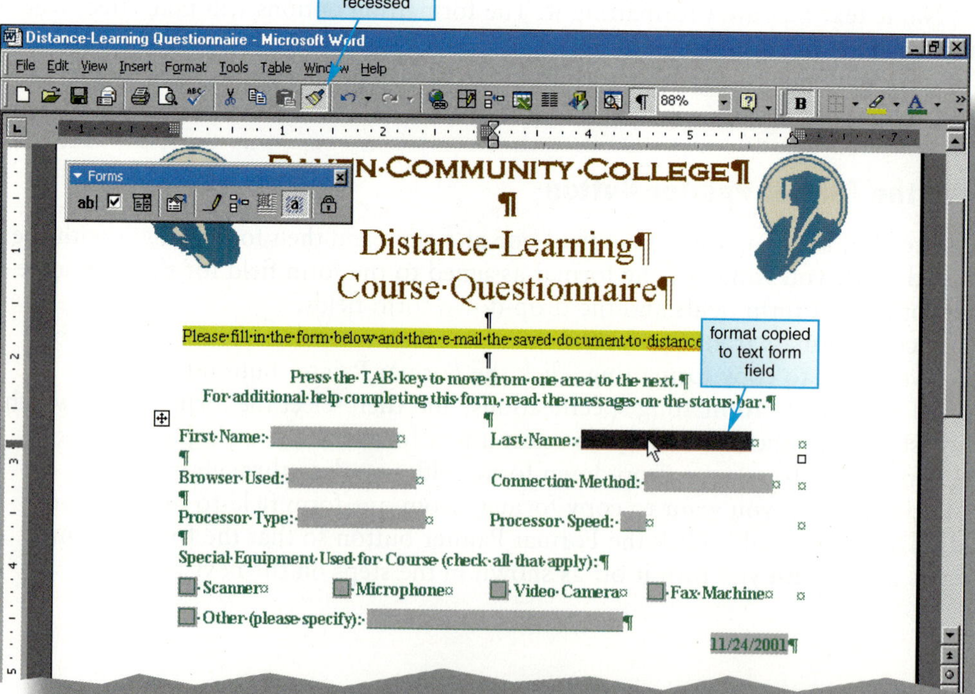

FIGURE 8-37

3 **Drag through the drop-down form field for the browser used. Drag through the drop-down form field for the connection method. Drag through the drop-down form field for the processor type. Click the text form field for processor speed. Click the text form field for other (please specify). Click the Format Painter button on the Standard toolbar.**

The format in the text form field for the first name is copied to all other text form fields and to the drop-down form fields, and the Format Painter button no longer is recessed (Figure 8-38).

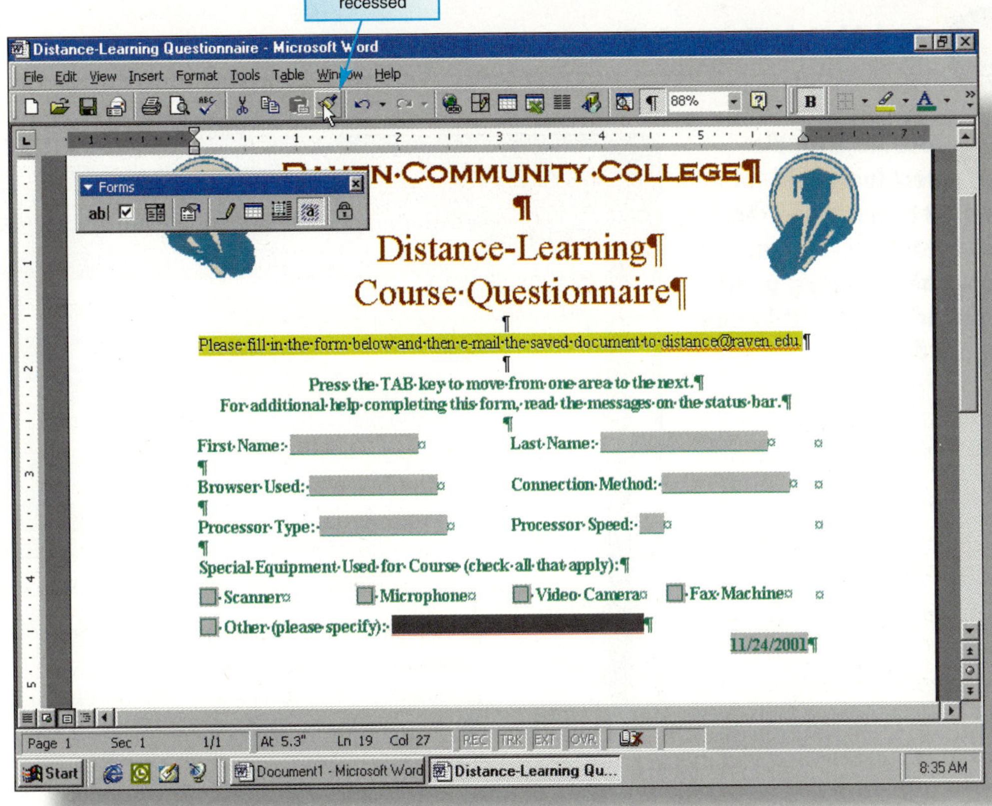

FIGURE 8-38

The next step is to add help for users to the form.

Adding Help Text to Form Fields

As users enter data into form fields, they may have a question about the purpose or function of a particular field. Thus, Word provides two Help mechanisms by which you can assist users during their data entry process. You can display a Help message on the status bar that relates to the current data entry field and/or you can display a Help dialog box when a user presses F1. In this project, you want to display brief Help messages on the status bar as a user moves from form field to form field. Perform the steps on the next page to display a Help message on the status bar when the user is entering the first name.

Help Text

When you enter Help text to display on the status bar, you are limited to 138 characters. You can create longer Help text, up to 255 characters, for those that display in a dialog box when the user presses F1. A good practice is to provide users as much help as possible; thus, you may wish to create both status bar Help text and dialog box Help text.

To Add Help Text to a Form

1 Double-click the text form field for the first name. When the Text Form Field Options dialog box displays, point to the Add Help Text button (Figure 8-39).

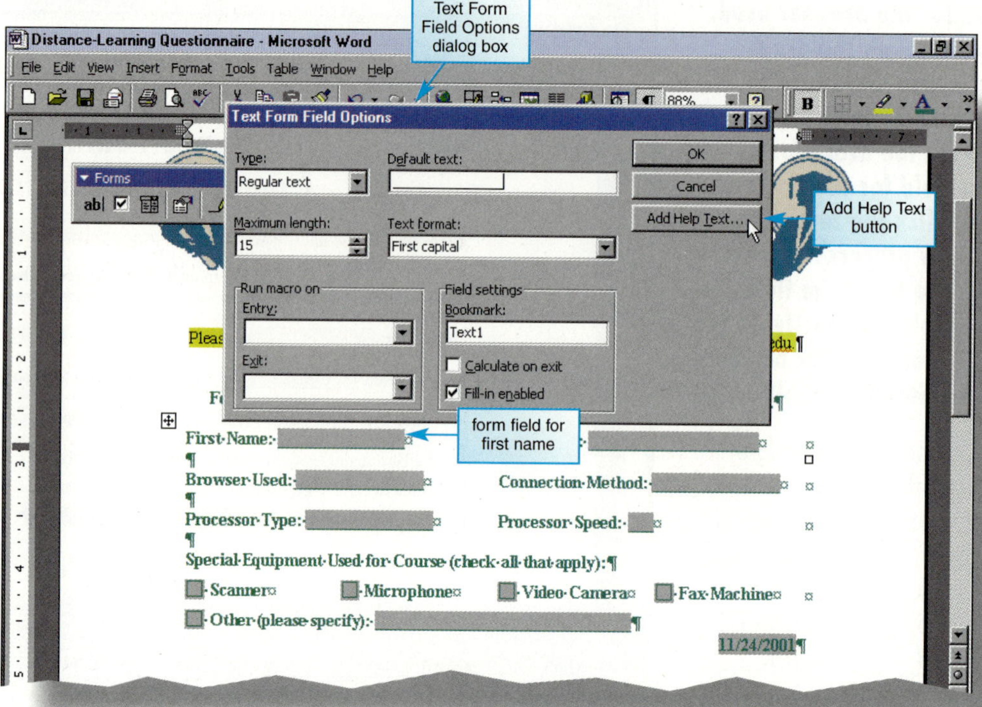

FIGURE 8-39

2 Click the Add Help Text button. When the Form Field Help Text dialog box displays, if necessary, click the Status Bar tab. Click Type your own. Type `Enter your first name.` **Point to the OK button.**

Word displays the Form Field Help Text dialog box (Figure 8-40).

3 Click the OK button. Click the OK button in the Text Form Field Options dialog box.

The Help text is entered for the text form field for the first name.

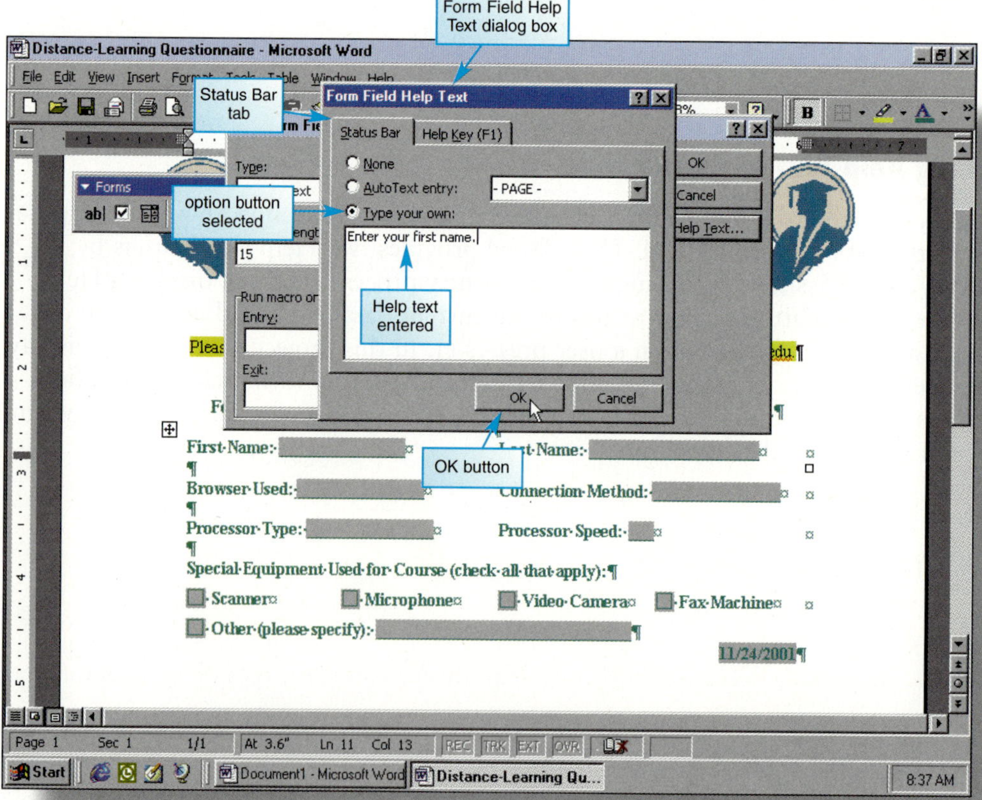

FIGURE 8-40

The Help text does not display on the status bar until you protect the form, which you will do later in this project. At that time, you will enter data into the form and see the Help text display on the status bar.

The next step is to enter the Help text for the remaining form fields in the form. You repeat the procedure in the previous steps for each data entry field on the form. The Help text for each field on the Distance-Learning Course Questionnaire is shown in Table 8-2.

F1

If you want to enter Help text in a dialog box that displays when a user presses F1, click the Help Key (F1) tab in the Form Field Help Text dialog box (see Figure 8-40). You enter Help text in the Help Key (F1) sheet in the same manner as the Status Bar sheet.

Table 8-2 Help Text for Fields on the Form

FIELD CAPTION	FIELD TYPE	HELP TEXT TO DISPLAY ON STATUS BAR
First Name	Text Form Field	Enter your first name.
Last Name	Text Form Field	Enter your last name.
Browser Used	Drop-Down Form Field	Click box arrow for list of choices.
Connection Method	Drop-Down Form Field	Click box arrow for list of choices.
Processor Type	Drop-Down Form Field	Click box arrow for list of choices.
Processor Speed	Text Form Field	Enter MHz in numbers.
Scanner	Check Box Form Field	Click check box to select or deselect.
Microphone	Check Box Form Field	Click check box to select or deselect.
Video Camera	Check Box Form Field	Click check box to select or deselect.
Fax Machine	Check Box Form Field	Click check box to select or deselect.
Other	Check Box Form Field	Click check box to select or deselect.
Other	Text Form Field	Please list other types of equipment used in course.

The following steps describe how to add the Help text shown in Table 8-2.

TO ADD MORE HELP TEXT

1. Double-click the text form field for the last name. Click the Add Help Text button in the Text Form Field Options dialog box. When the Form Field Help Text dialog box displays, if necessary, click the Status Bar tab. Click Type your own. Type `Enter your last name.` Click the OK button. Click the OK button in the Text Form Field Options dialog box.
2. Double-click the drop-down form field for the browser used.
3. Click the Add Help Text button in the Drop-Down Form Field Options dialog box. When the Form Field Help Text dialog box displays, if necessary, click the Status Bar tab. Click Type your own. Type `Click box arrow for list of choices.` Click the OK button. Click the OK button in the Text Form Field Options dialog box.
4. Double-click the drop-down form field for the connection method. Repeat Step 3.
5. Double-click the drop-down form field for the processor type. Repeat Step 3.
6. Double-click the text form field for the processor speed. Click the Add Help Text button in the Text Form Field Options dialog box. When the Form Field Help Text dialog box displays, if necessary, click the Status Bar tab. Click Type your own. Type `Enter MHz in numbers.` Click the OK button. Click the OK button in the Text Form Field Options dialog box.

7. Double-click the check box form field for scanner.
8. Click the Add Help Text button in the Check Box Form Field Options dialog box. When the Form Field Help Text dialog box displays, if necessary, click the Status Bar tab. Click Type your own. Type `Click check box to select or deselect.` Click the OK button. Click the OK button in the Text Form Field Options dialog box.
9. Double-click the check box form field for microphone. Repeat Step 8.
10. Double-click the check box form field for video camera. Repeat Step 8.
11. Double-click the check box form field for fax machine. Repeat Step 8.
12. Double-click the check box form field for other (please specify). Repeat Step 8.
13. Double-click the text form field for other (please specify). Click the Add Help Text button in the Text Form Field Options dialog box. When the Form Field Help Text dialog box displays, if necessary, click the Status Bar tab. Click Type your own. Type `Please list other types of equipment used in course.` Click the OK button. Click the OK button in the Text Form Field Options dialog box. Click outside the selection to remove the highlight.

Help text is entered for all data entry fields according to Table 8-2 on the previous page.

If you would like to change the Help text for any of the form fields, simply double-click the form field and then click the Add Help Text button in the dialog box. When the Form Field Help Text dialog box displays, if necessary, click the Status Bar tab. Make any necessary changes to the existing Help text and then click the OK button in the dialog boxes.

The next step is to remove the form field shading.

Removing Form Field Shading

The fields on the form currently are shaded (see Figure 8-41). During the design of a form, it is helpful to display field shading so that you easily can identify the fields. You, however, do not want the fields to be shaded when a user is entering data into a form. Thus, perform the following steps to remove form field shading.

Form Field Shading

If you print a form that displays form field shading, the shading will not print. To add shading to a field on a printed form, you must select the form field, click the Shading Color button arrow on the Tables and Borders toolbar, and then click the desired shading color. Likewise, if you want a border surrounding a field, select the form field, click the Border button arrow on the Tables and Borders toolbar, and then click the Outside Border button.

To Remove Form Field Shading

1 Point to the Form Field Shading button on the Forms toolbar (Figure 8-41).

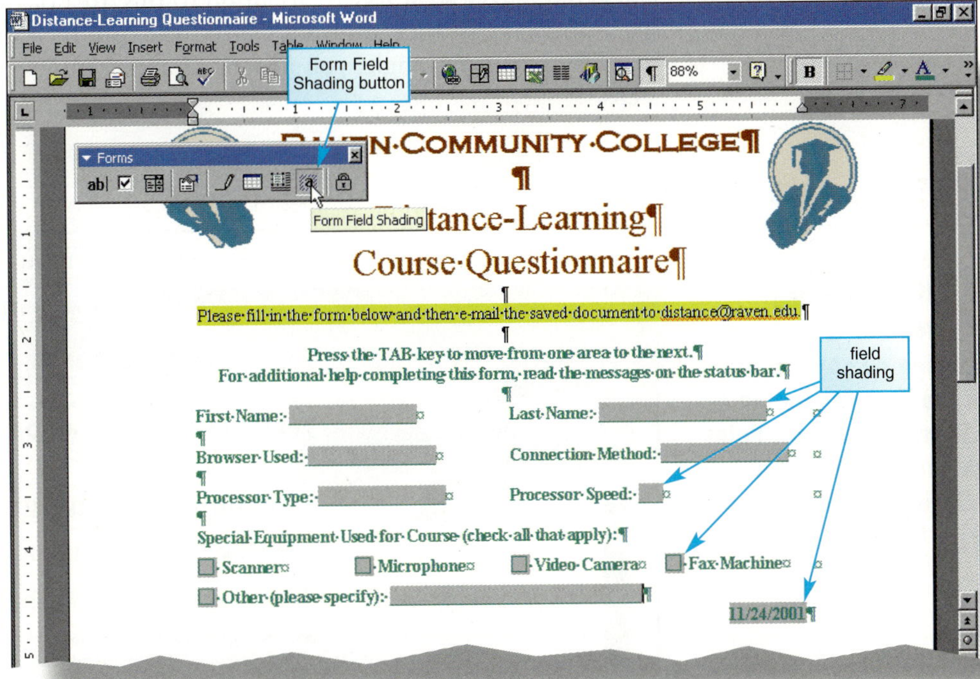

FIGURE 8-41

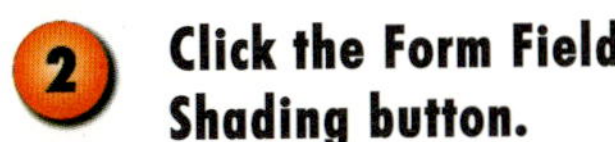

2 Click the Form Field Shading button.

Word removes the shading from the form fields (Figure 8-42).

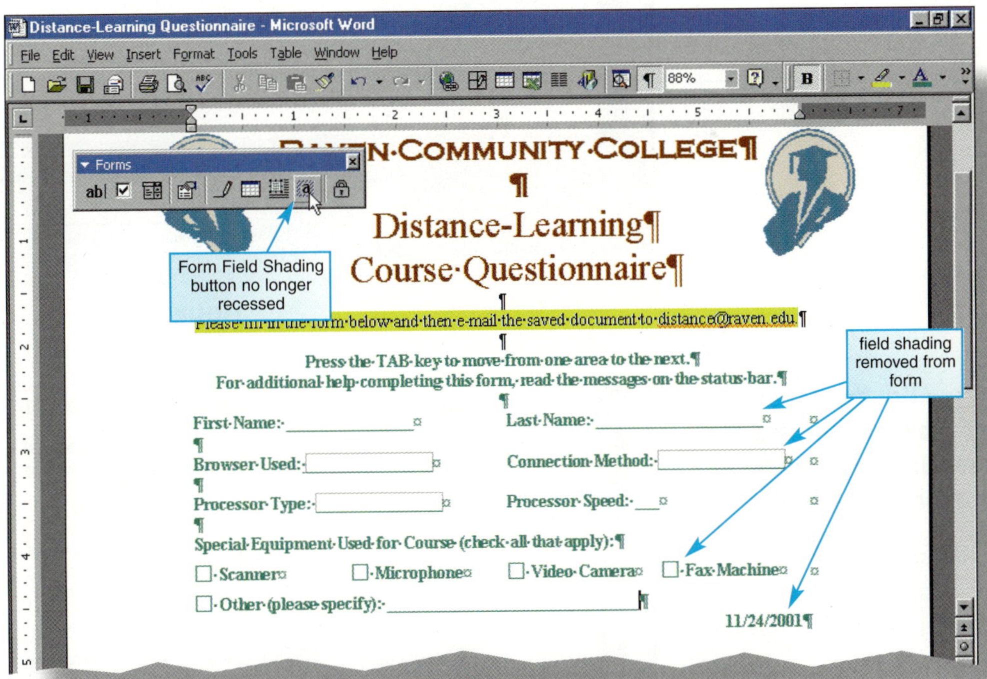

FIGURE 8-42

The next step is to emphasize the data entry area of the form.

Drawing and Formatting a Rectangle

The data entry area of the form includes all the form fields into which a user enters data. You want to call attention to this area of the form. Thus, you decide to place a rectangle around the data entry area and then fill the rectangle with a texture. To draw a rectangle, you use the Drawing toolbar as shown in the following steps.

To Draw a Rectangle

1 **If the Drawing toolbar is not displaying on your screen, click the Drawing button on the Standard toolbar. Point to the Rectangle button on the Drawing toolbar (Figure 8-43).**

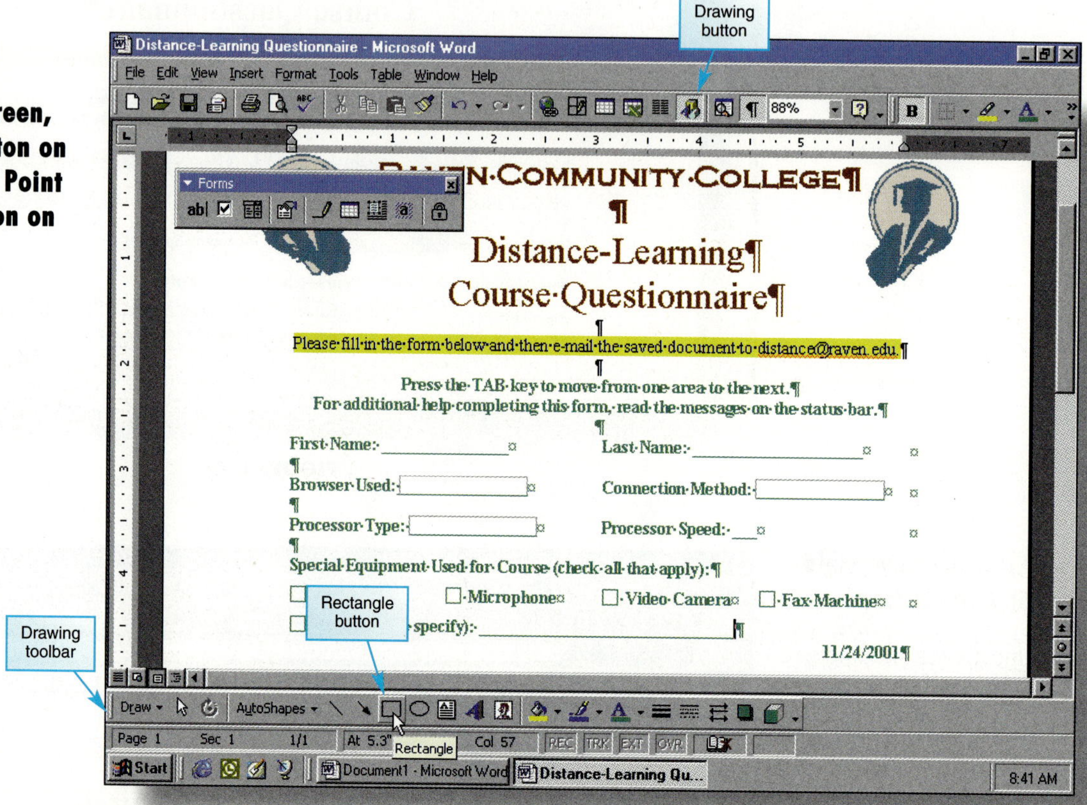

FIGURE 8-43

2 **Click the Rectangle button. Position the crosshair mouse pointer as shown in Figure 8-44.**

Word displays the mouse pointer as a crosshair, which you drag to form the size of the rectangle.

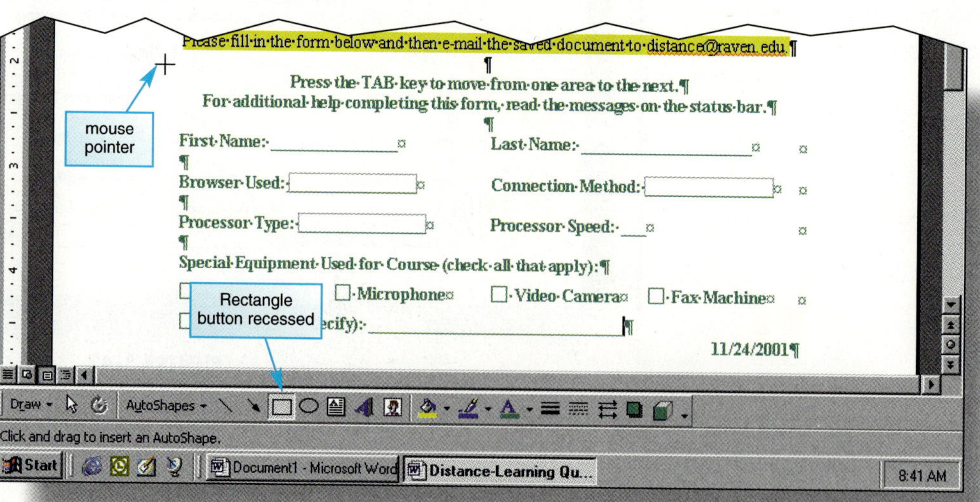

FIGURE 8-44

3 **Drag the mouse pointer downward and rightward to form a rectangle similar to the one shown in Figure 8-45.**

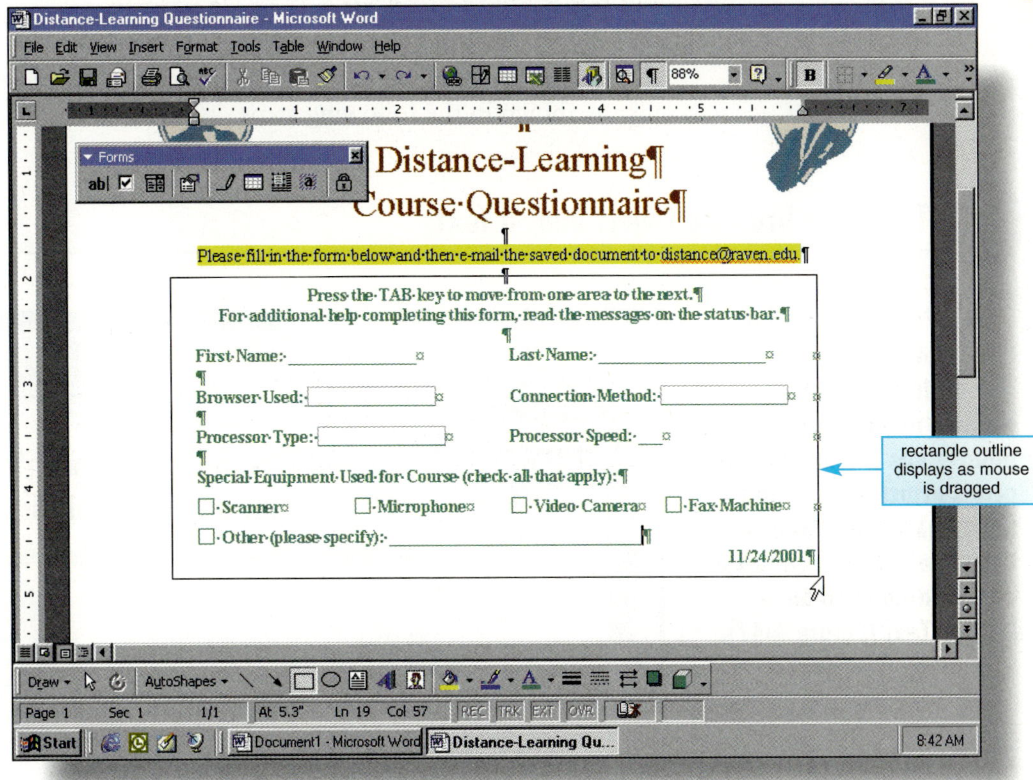

FIGURE 8-45

4 **Release the mouse button. If Word positions the text below the rectangle, click Format on the menu bar, click AutoShape, click the Layout tab, click In front of text, and then click the OK button. If, once the rectangle is drawn, you need to resize it, simply drag the sizing handles.**

When you release the mouse button, Word positions the rectangle on top of the text behind it, thus hiding the data entry area from view (Figure 8-46).

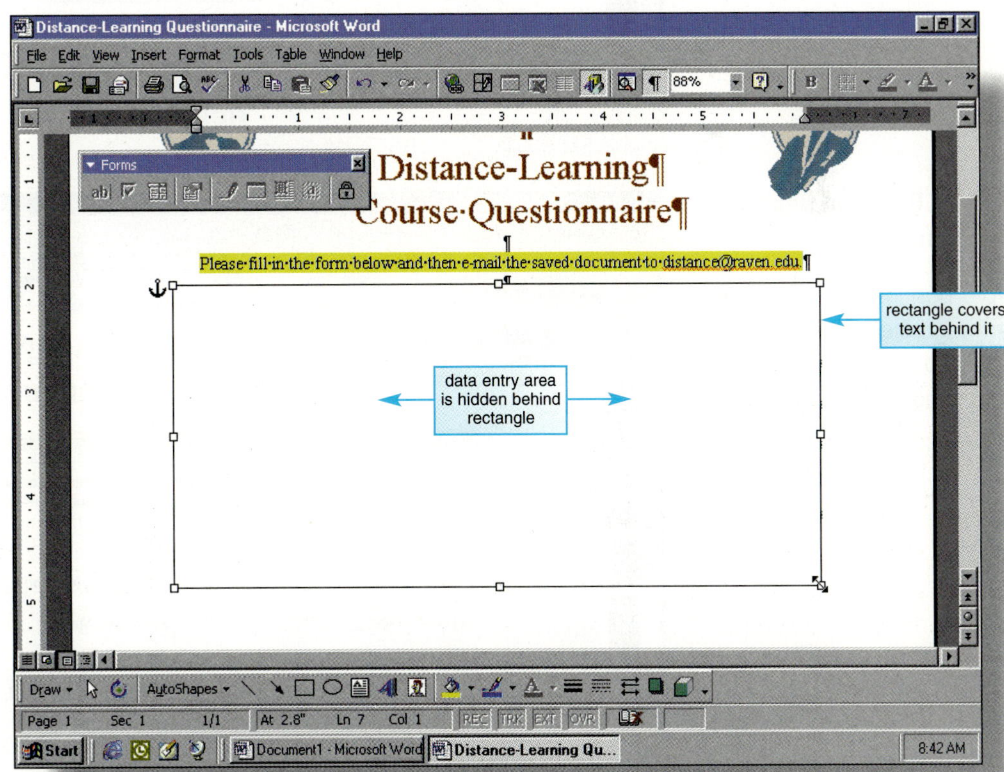

FIGURE 8-46

A rectangle is a type of drawing object. When you add a drawing object to a document, Word initially places it in front of, or on top of, any text behind it. You can change the stacking order of the drawing object so that it displays behind the text as shown in the following steps.

To Send a Drawing Object Behind Text

1 Point to the edge of the drawing object (in this case, the rectangle) until the mouse pointer has a four-headed arrow attached to it and then right-click. Point to Order on the shortcut menu and then point to Send Behind Text (Figure 8-47).

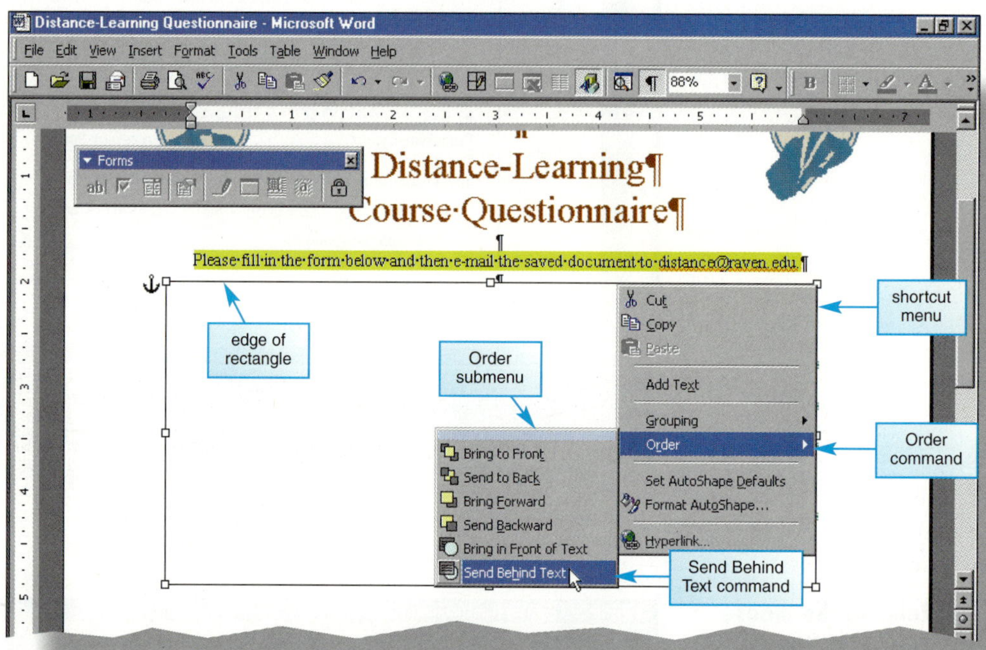

FIGURE 8-47

2 Click Send Behind Text.

Word positions the rectangle drawing object behind the text (Figure 8-48). The data entry area is visible again.

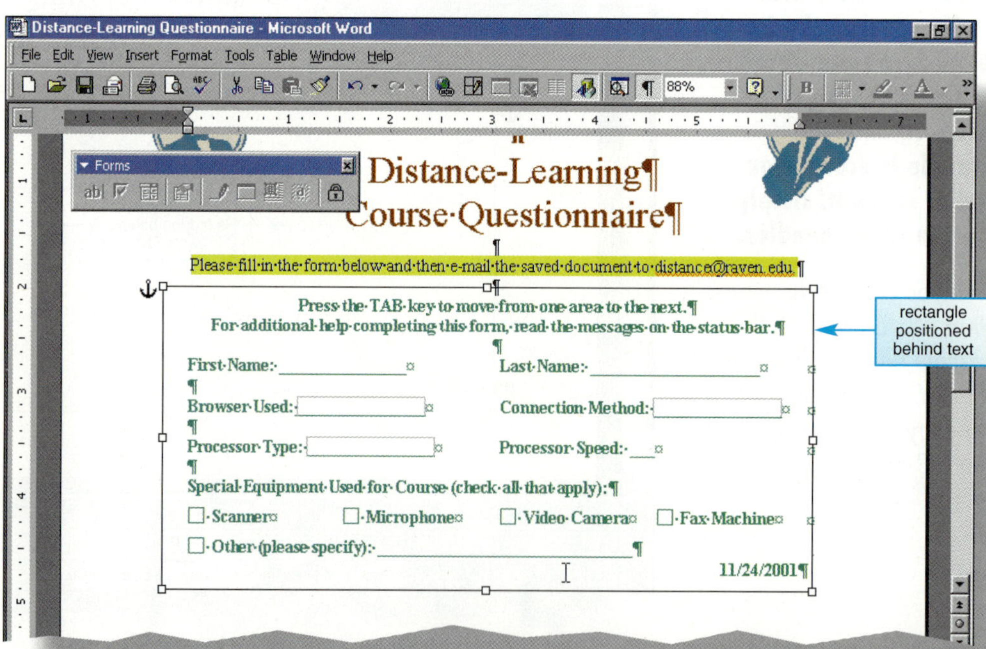

FIGURE 8-48

If you wanted to bring the drawing object on top of the text again, you would right-click one of its edges, point to Order on the shortcut menu, and then click Bring in Front of Text.

If you have multiple graphics displaying on the screen and would like them to overlap, you can change their stacking order by right-clicking the graphic to reorder, pointing to Order on the shortcut menu, and then clicking one of the first four commands on the Order submenu (see Figure 8-47). The Bring to Front command displays the selected object at the top of the stack and the Send to Back command displays the selected object at the bottom of the stack. The Bring Forward and Send Backward commands each move the drawing object forward or backward one layer in a stack.

The next step is to fill the inside of the rectangle. In Word, you can **fill**, or paint, the inside of a drawing object with a color or with an effect. **Fill effects** include gradient (two-toned) colors, textures, patterns, and pictures. Perform the following steps to format the rectangle using a texture fill effect.

Drawing Objects

To change the color of a drawing object, click the Line Color button arrow on the Drawing toolbar and then click the desired color. To add a shadow to a drawing object, click the Shadow button arrow on the Drawing toolbar and then click the desired shadow. To add a 3-D effect to a drawing object, click the 3-D button arrow on the Drawing toolbar and then click the desired effect.

To Fill a Drawing Object with a Texture

1 With the drawing object selected, click the Fill Color button arrow on the Drawing toolbar and then point to the Fill Effects button.

The available predefined fill colors display, as well as the More Colors and Fill Effects buttons (Figure 8-49).

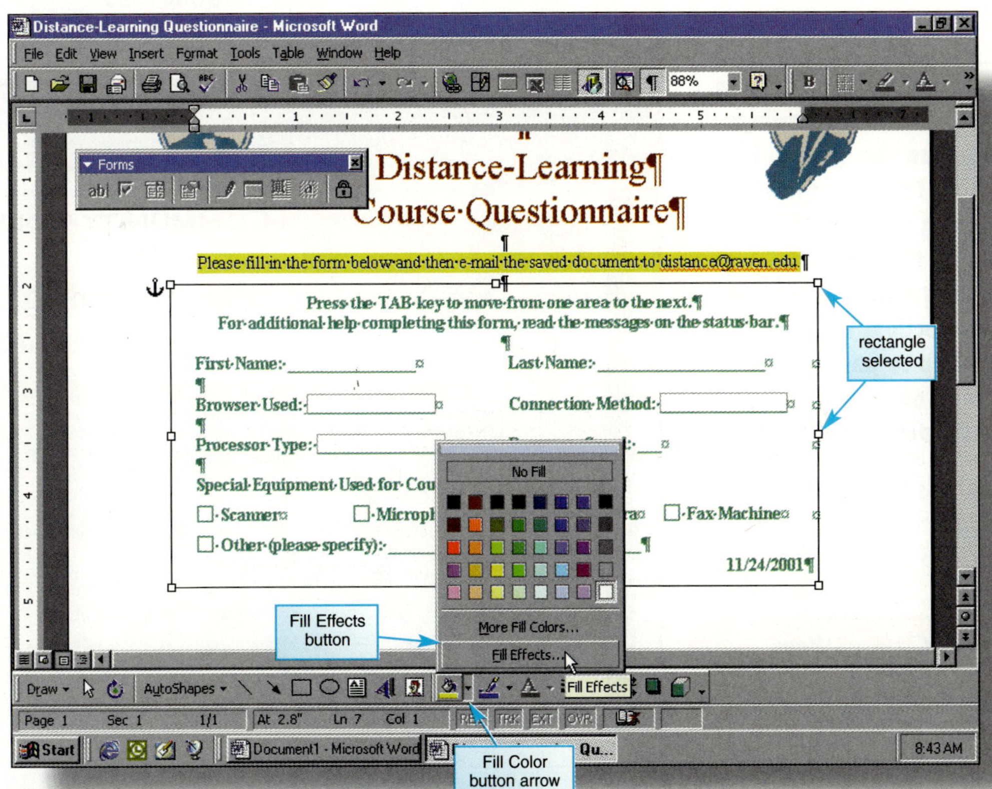

FIGURE 8-49

2 Click the Fill Effects button. When the Fill Effects dialog box displays, if necessary, click the Texture tab. Click the Recycled Paper texture in the list of textures and then point to the OK button.

Word displays the Fill Effects dialog box (Figure 8-50).

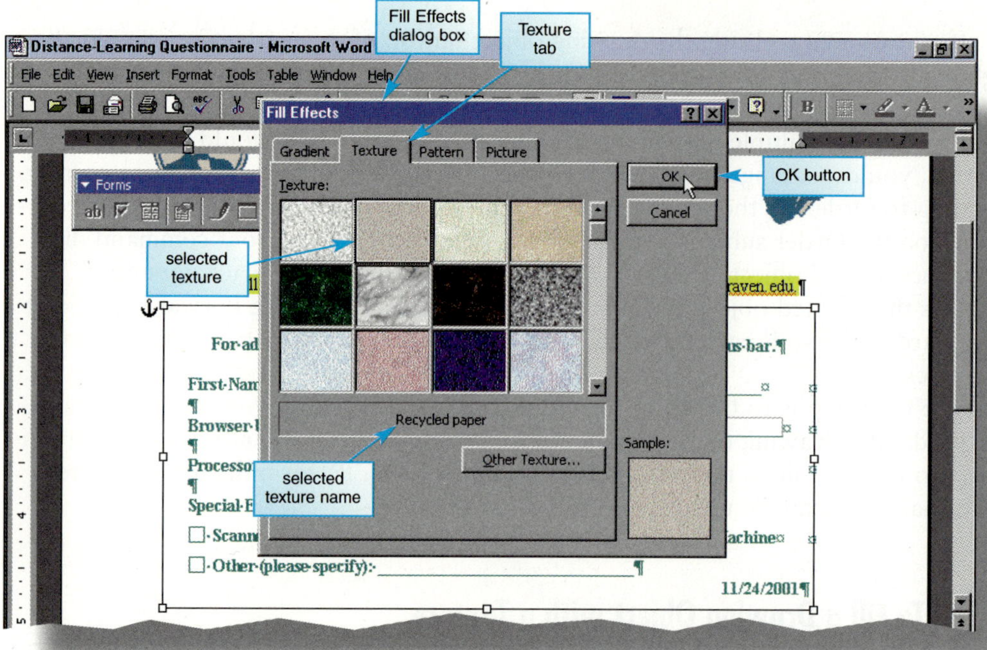

FIGURE 8-50

3 Click the OK button. Click the Drawing button on the Standard toolbar to remove the Drawing toolbar. Click outside the selected drawing object to remove the selection. If necessary, scroll up to position the college name at the top of the document window.

Word fills the rectangle with the recycled paper texture (Figure 8-51).

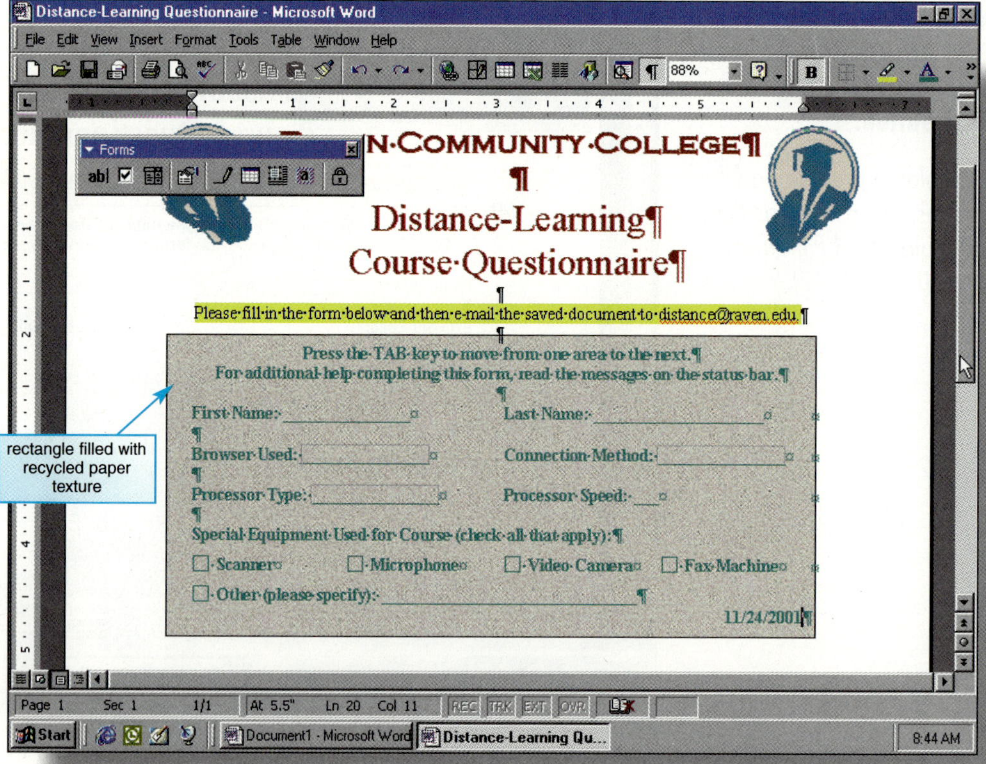

FIGURE 8-51

Other Ways

1. Right-click edge of drawing object, click Format AutoShape on shortcut menu, click Colors and Lines tab, click Fill Color button arrow, click Fill Effects button, click Texture tab, click desired texture, click OK button twice
2. Select drawing object, click AutoShape on Format menu, click Colors and Lines tab, click Fill Color button arrow, click Fill Effects button, click Texture tab, click desired texture, click OK button twice

The next step is to enter and format the thank-you message below the data entry area.

Animating Text

In an online document, you can animate text to which you wish to draw the reader's attention. When you **animate text**, it has the appearance of motion. To animate text in Word, you select it and then apply one of the predefined text effects in the Font dialog box.

For this form, you want the thank-you message below the data entry area to have a moving black rectangle around it, which is called the Marching Black Ants animation in the Font dialog box. Perform the following steps to animate the thank-you message on the online form.

Animating Text

Animated text can distract readers; thus, you should use it sparingly. If a reader wants to hide animated text, he or she should click Tools on the menu bar, click Options, click the View tab, remove the check mark from the Animated text check box, and then click the OK button.

To Animate Text

1 **Position the insertion point at the end of the current date in the data entry area and then press the ENTER key twice. Press CTRL+E to center the paragraph and then type** `Thank you for your time!`

The thank-you message is entered below the data entry area (Figure 8-52).

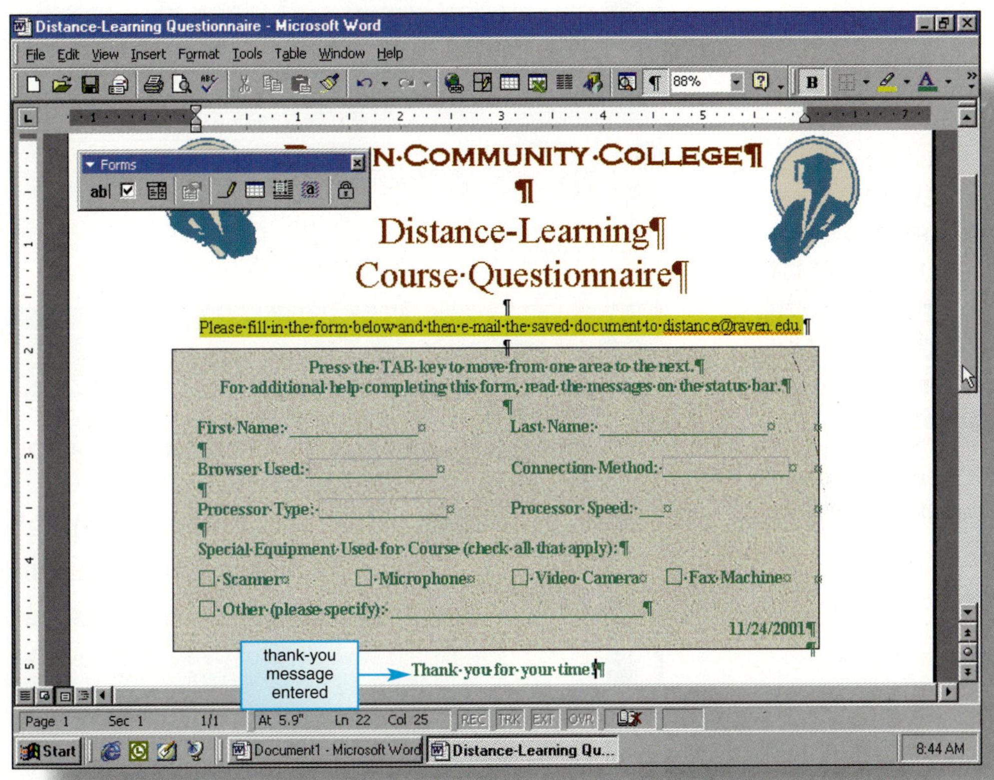

FIGURE 8-52

2 **Select the sentence just entered. Right-click the selection and then click Font on the shortcut menu. When the Font dialog box displays, if necessary, click the Text Effects tab. Click Marching Black Ants in the Animations list. Point to the OK button.**

Word displays the Font dialog box (Figure 8-53). The Preview area shows a sample of the selected animation.

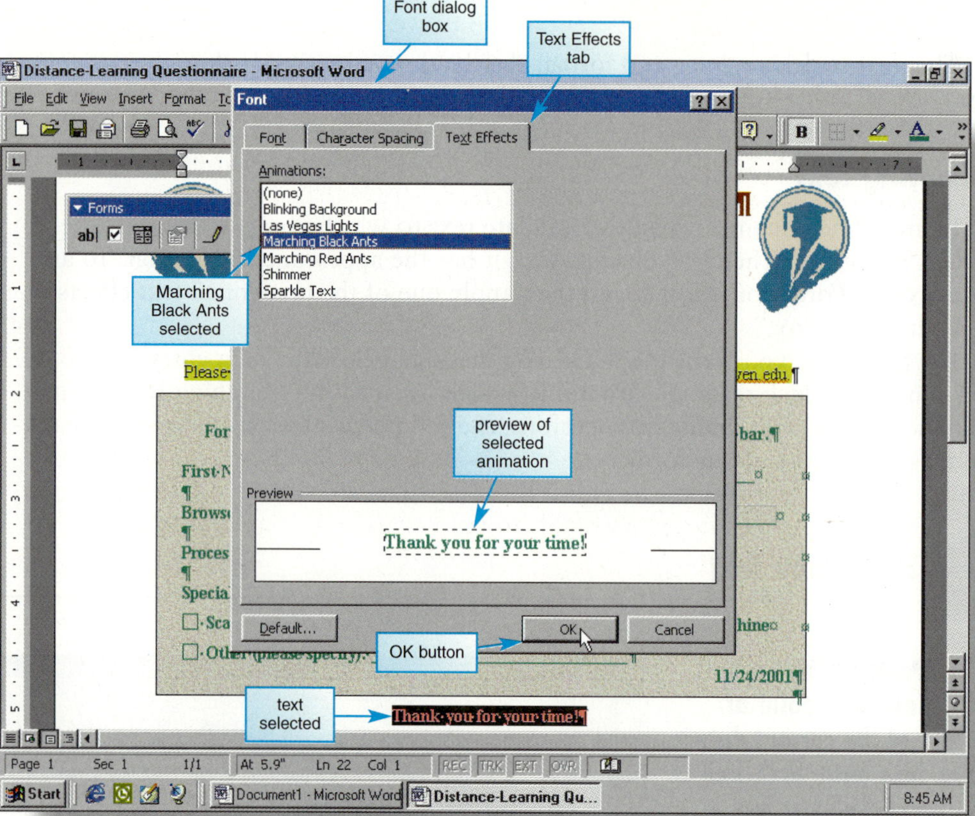

FIGURE 8-53

3 **Click the OK button. Click outside the selection to remove the highlight.**

Word applies the animation to the selected text (Figure 8-54).

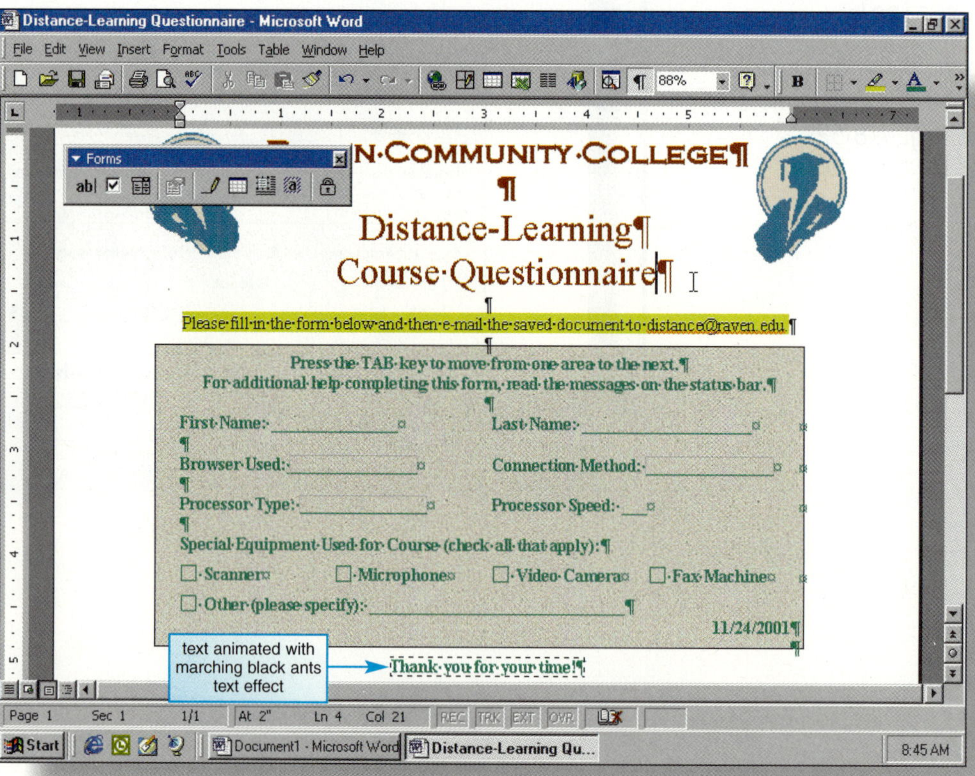

FIGURE 8-54

Other Ways

1. Select text, click Font on Format menu, click Text Effects tab, click desired animation, click OK button

If you wanted to remove an animation from text, you would select the text, right-click the selection, click Font on the shortcut menu, click the Text Effects tab, click (none) in the Animations list, and then click the OK button.

If you print a document that contains animated text, the animations do not show on the hard copy; instead, the text prints as regular text. Thus, animations are designed specifically for documents that will be viewed online.

The next step in this project is to protect the Distance-Learning Course Questionnaire.

Protecting Forms

If you want only authorized users to be able to unprotect a form, you should password-protect the form. To do this, click Tools on the menu bar, click Protect Document, click Forms in the Protect document for area, type the password in the Password (optional) text box, and then click the OK button. Then, reenter the password in the Confirm Password dialog box.

Protecting a Form

Before you allow users to work with a form you have created, you should protect it. When you **protect a form**, you are allowing users only to enter data in designated areas – specifically, the form fields that are enabled. Thus, it is crucial that you protect a form before making it available to users. Perform the following steps to protect the Distance-Learning Course Questionnaire.

To Protect a Form

1. **Point to the Protect Form button on the Forms toolbar (Figure 8-55).**

2. **Click the Protect Form button. Remove the Forms toolbar from the screen by clicking its Close button.**

Word protects the form. Word highlights the first form field on the form (see Figure 8-56 on the next page).

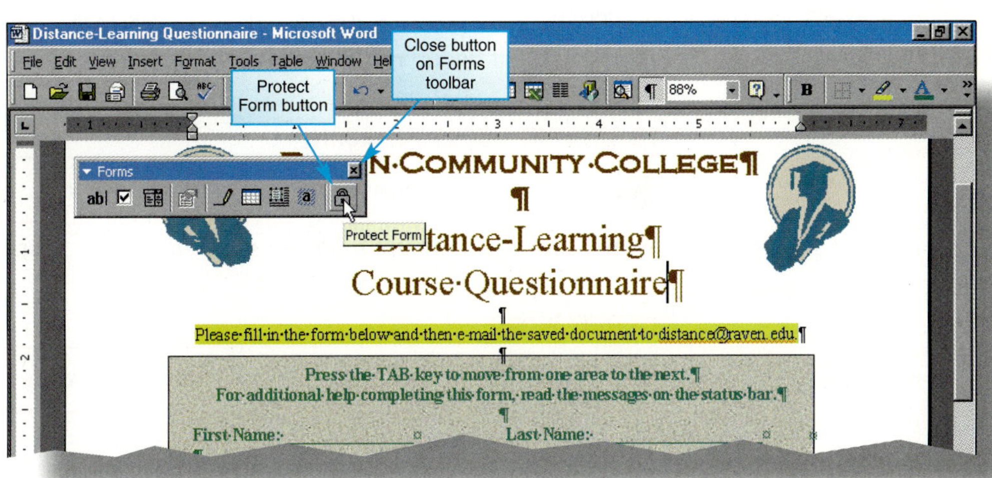

FIGURE 8-55

1. On Tools menu click Protect Document, click Forms, click the OK button

When the form is protected, a highlight displays in the first form field. To advance to the next form field, press the TAB key. To move to a previous form field, press the SHIFT+TAB keys. You will enter data into this form later in the project.

The next step is to turn off the display of formatting marks. You do not want them on the form when a user opens it. Perform the following steps to hide formatting marks.

TO HIDE FORMATTING MARKS

1. If the Show/Hide ¶ button on the Standard toolbar is recessed, click it.

Word hides the formatting marks (Figure 8-56 on the next page).

Docked Toolbars

To hide a docked toolbar, click View on the menu bar, click Toolbars, and then click the toolbar name.

Borders

If a form filled an entire page and you wanted to add a border around the perimeter of the page, you would click Format on the menu bar; click Borders and Shading; click the Page Border tab; click the desired border setting, style, color, and width; and then click the OK button. You modify the border in the same manner; that is, through the Page Border sheet in the Borders and Shading dialog box.

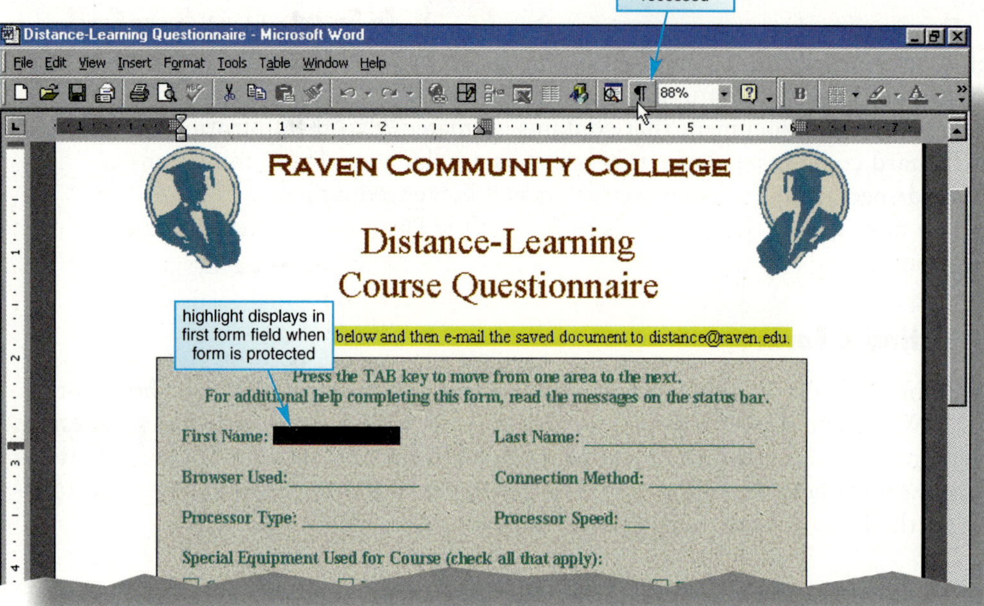

FIGURE 8-56

The online form template for this project now is complete. Perform the following steps to save it again and then quit Word.

TO SAVE THE DOCUMENT AGAIN

 Click the Save button on the Standard toolbar.

Word saves the template with the same file name, Distance-Learning Questionnaire.

TO QUIT WORD

 Click File on the menu bar and then click Exit.

The Word window closes.

Working with an Online Form

Once you have created a template, you then can make it available to users. Users do not open templates with the Open button on the Standard toolbar in Word. A developer of a template uses the Open button to open the template so it can be modified.

A user, by contrast, starts a new Word document that is based on the template. That is, when a user accesses a template, the title bar displays the default file name, Document1 (or a similar name). Instead of the Word window being blank, however, it contains text and formatting associated with the template that the user accesses. For example, Word provides a variety of templates such as those for memos, letters, fax cover sheets, and resumes. If a user accesses a memo template, Word displays the contents of a basic memo in a new document window.

When you save the template to a disk in drive A, as instructed earlier in this project, a user can access your template through the My Computer window or Windows Explorer. Perform the following steps to display a new Word document window that is based on the Distance-Learning Questionnaire template.

To Access a Template through Windows Explorer

1 Right-click the My Computer icon on the Windows desktop and then click Explore on the shortcut menu. When the Exploring window displays, click the Address text box to select it. Type a: and then press the ENTER key.

The Exploring - 3½ Floppy (A:) window displays (Figure 8-57). Notice the icon for the Distance-Learning Questionnaire template has a small yellow bar at its top.

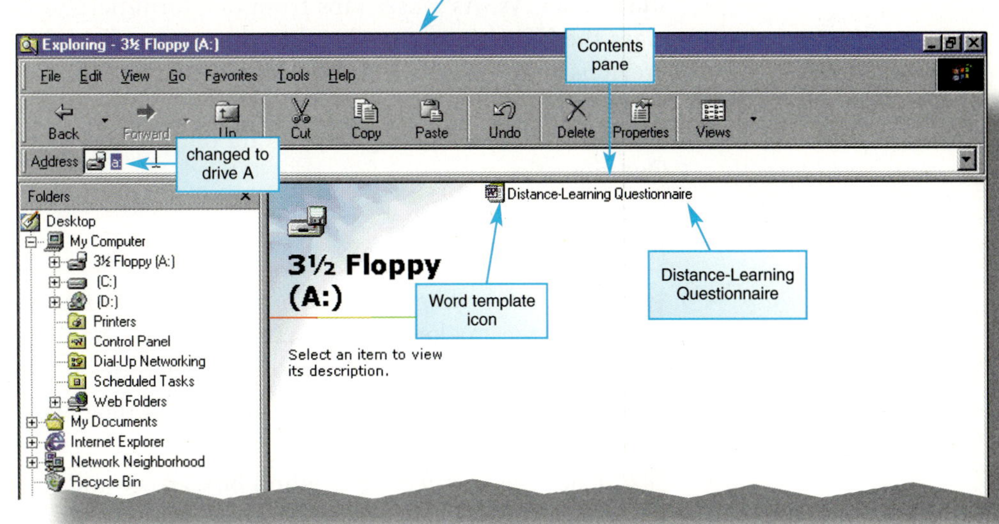

FIGURE 8-57

2 Double-click the Distance-Learning Questionnaire icon in the Contents pane. When the Word window displays, if the Show/Hide ¶ button on the Standard toolbar is recessed, click it. Click the Zoom box arrow and then click Page Width. If gridlines display, click Table on the menu bar and then click Hide Gridlines. Scroll down so the entire form displays in the Word window.

Windows starts Word and displays a new document window that is based on the contents of the Distance-Learning Questionnaire template (Figure 8-58). The highlight displays in the first form field, ready for a user's data entry.

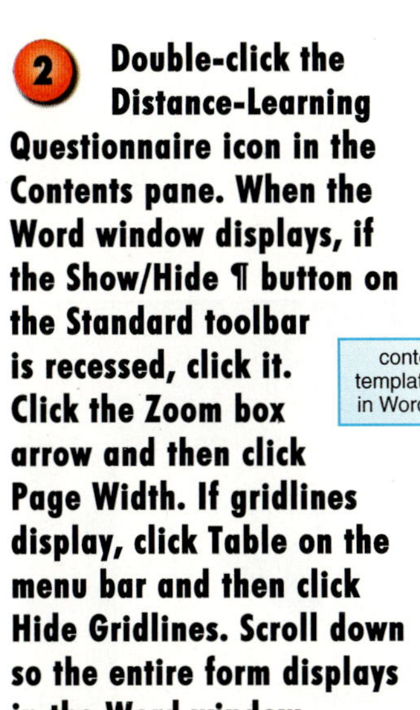

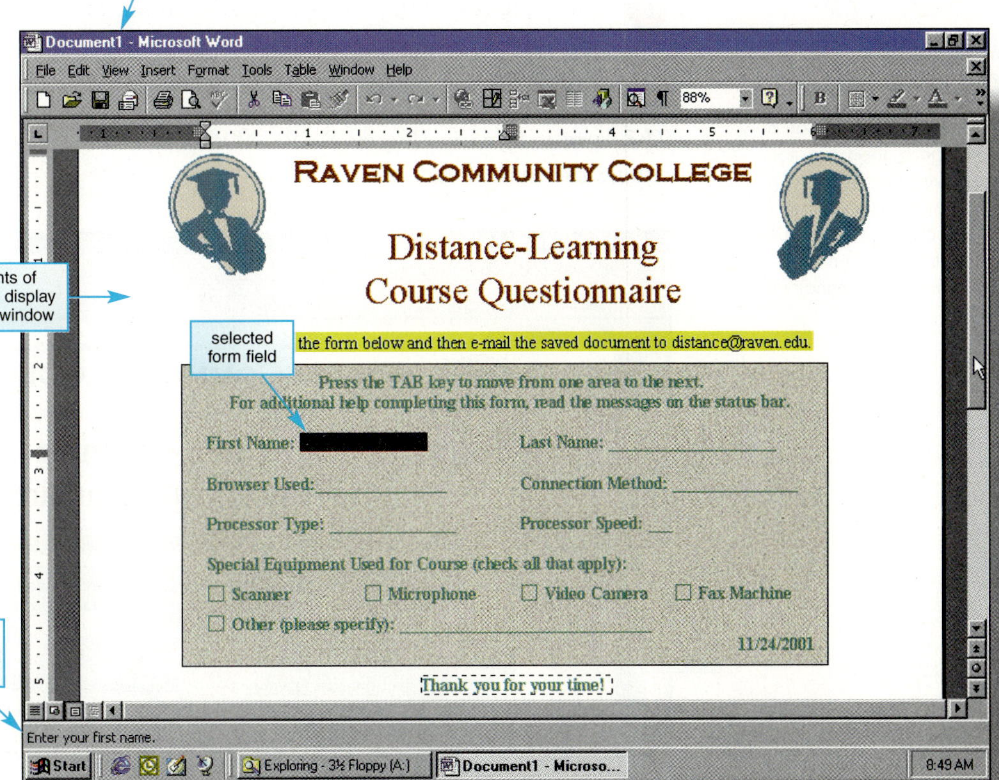

FIGURE 8-58

Other Ways

1. If the template was saved in the User Templates folder, click New on File menu, click appropriate tab, and then click icon attached to template

The next step is to enter data into the form. To advance to the next form field, a user presses the TAB key. To move to a previous form field, a user presses the SHIFT+TAB keys. As a user tabs from one form field to the next, the status bar displays the Help messages related to the current field. Notice in Figure 8-58 on the previous page that the status bar currently displays the Help message, Enter your first name.

Perform the following steps to fill out the Distance-Learning Course Questionnaire.

TO FILL OUT A FORM

1. With the highlight in the form field for the first name, type `Geraldine` and then press the TAB key. Type `Smith` in the Last Name text box. Press the TAB key to highlight the Browser Used drop-down list box and display its box arrow.
2. Click the Browser Used box arrow and then click Internet Explorer. Press the TAB key.
3. Click the Connection Method box arrow and then click 28.8 Kbps Modem. Press the TAB key.
4. Click the Processor Type box arrow and then click Pentium III. Press the TAB key.
5. Type `400` in the Processor Speed text box. Press the TAB key.
6. Click the following check boxes: Scanner, Fax Machine, and Other. Press the TAB key.
7. Type `Digital Camera` in the Other text box.

The form is filled in (Figure 8-59). Notice that the text box and drop-down list box entries are underlined in teal.

Designing Questionnaires

For more information on how to design a good questionnaire, visit the Word 2000 More About Web page (www.scsite.com/wd2000/more.htm) and then click Designing Questionnaires.

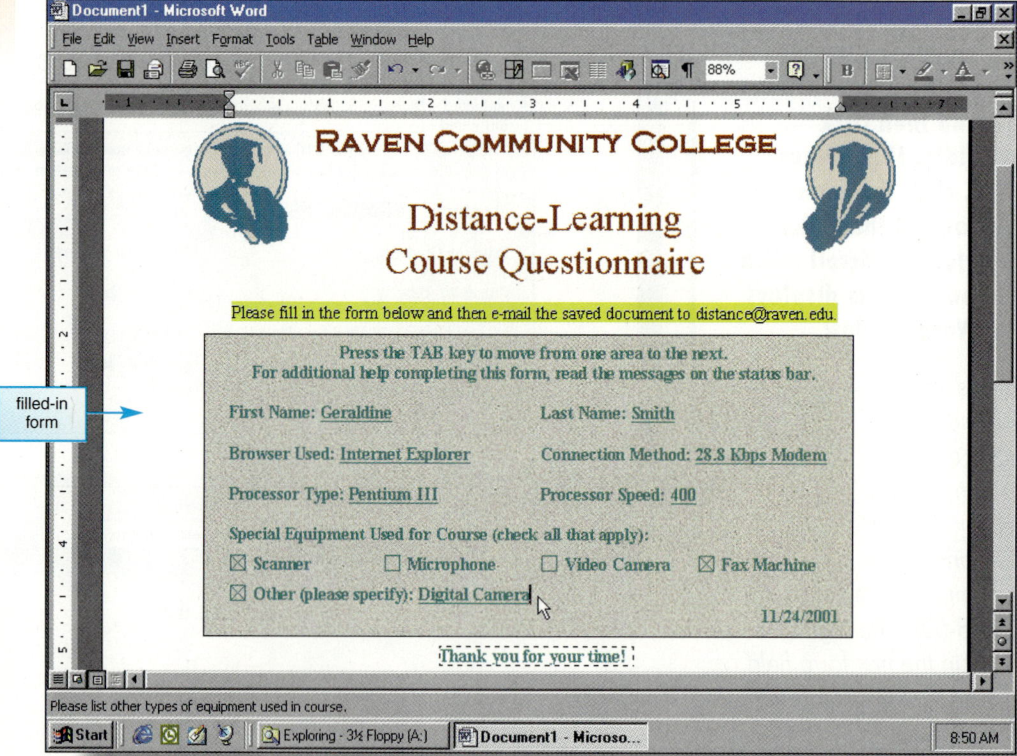

FIGURE 8-59

With the form filled in, a user can save it by clicking the Save button on the Standard toolbar. By basing the new document on a template, the blank Distance-Learning Course Questionnaire remains unchanged because users are saving a new document instead of saving a modification to the questionnaire. Perform the following steps to save the document that contains your responses.

TO SAVE A DOCUMENT

1. With a floppy disk in drive A, click the Save button on the Standard toolbar.
2. Type `Smith Form` in the File name text box.
3. If necessary, click the Save in box arrow and then click 3½ Floppy (A:).
4. Click the Save button in the Save As dialog box.

Word saves the document with the file name Smith Form on a disk in drive A (see Figure 8-61 on the next page).

You can print the document as you print any other document. Keep in mind, though, that the colors used were designed for viewing online. Thus, different color schemes would have been selected if the form had been designed for a printout. Perform the following step to print the filled-in form.

TO PRINT A FORM

1. Click the Print button on the Standard toolbar.

Word prints the form (Figure 8-60). Notice the animation on the thank-you message does not print.

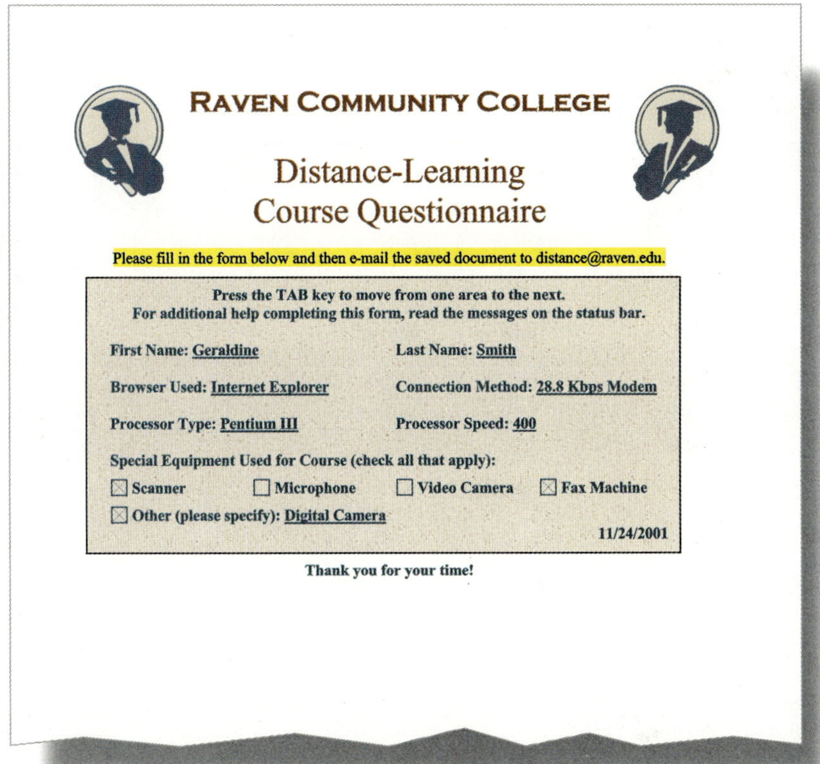
RAVEN COMMUNITY COLLEGE

Distance-Learning Course Questionnaire

Please fill in the form below and then e-mail the saved document to distance@raven.edu.

Press the TAB key to move from one area to the next.
For additional help completing this form, read the messages on the status bar.

First Name: Geraldine   Last Name: Smith

Browser Used: Internet Explorer   Connection Method: 28.8 Kbps Modem

Processor Type: Pentium III   Processor Speed: 400

Special Equipment Used for Course (check all that apply):
☒ Scanner ☐ Microphone ☐ Video Camera ☒ Fax Machine
☒ Other (please specify): Digital Camera

11/24/2001

Thank you for your time!

FIGURE 8-60

Printing

If you want to save ink, print faster, or minimize printer overrun errors, lower the printer resolution. Click File on the menu bar, click Print, click the Properties button in the Print dialog box, click the Graphics tab, click the Resolution box arrow, click a lower resolution than that displayed currently, click the Apply button, click the OK button, and then click the Close button.

Printing Data Only

If you wanted to print only data instead of the entire form, click File on the menu bar, click Print, click the Options button, place a check mark in Print data only for forms check box, click the OK button, and then click the OK button. Then, remove the check mark from the Print data only for forms check box so that future prints will print the entire form.

Microsoft Access 2000

For more information on features of Access, visit the Word 2000 More About Web page (www.scsite.com/wd2000/more.htm) and then click Microsoft Access 2000.

Saving Data on the Form

You may wish to gather the responses from the filled in questionnaires and analyze them. Depending on the number of forms completed, tabulating the data manually could be a time-consuming and monumental task. One alternative is to use database software, such as Access, to assist you in analyzing the responses. To do this, you must save the data on each questionnaire in a manner that will be recognized by the database software.

Word provides a means through the Save As dialog box to save the data in a comma-delimited text file so that it can be recognized by database software packages. A **comma-delimited text file** is a file that separates each data item with a comma and places quotation marks around text data items. See Figure 8-65 on page WD 8.55 for an example of a comma-delimited text file.

Perform the following steps to save the data from the form into a text file.

Steps To Save Form Data in a Text File

1 Click File on the menu bar and then click Save As. When the Save As dialog box displays, click the Tools button arrow and then point to General Options.

Word displays the Save As dialog box (Figure 8-61).

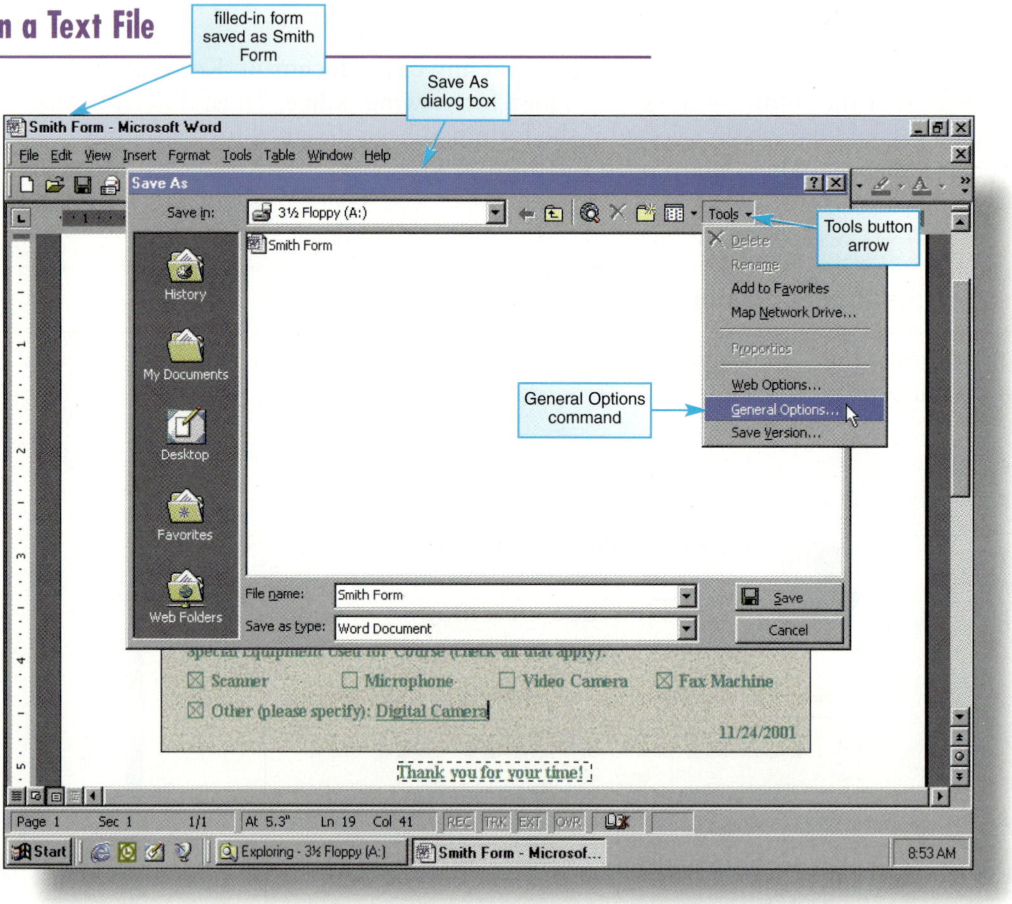

FIGURE 8-61

2 **Click General Options. When the Save dialog box displays, place a check mark in the Save data only for forms check box and then point to the OK button.**

Word displays the Save dialog box (Figure 8-62).

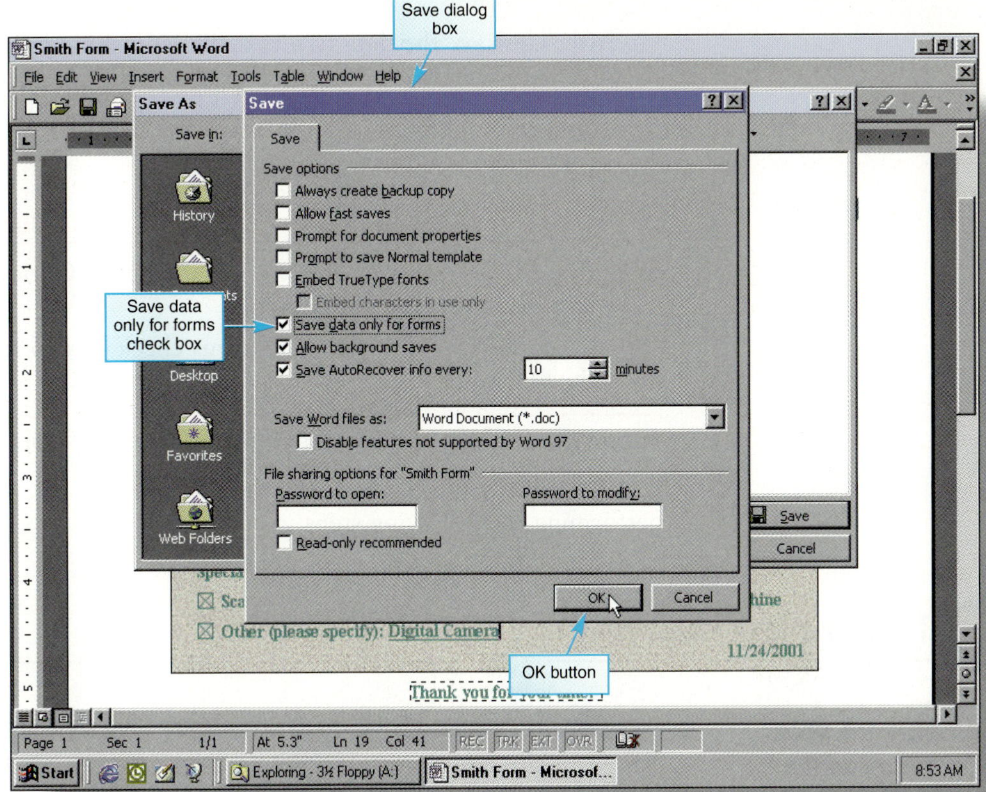

FIGURE 8-62

3 **Click the OK button. When the Save As dialog box is visible again, point to its Save button.**

Word changes the document type in the Save as type text box to Text Only (Figure 8-63).

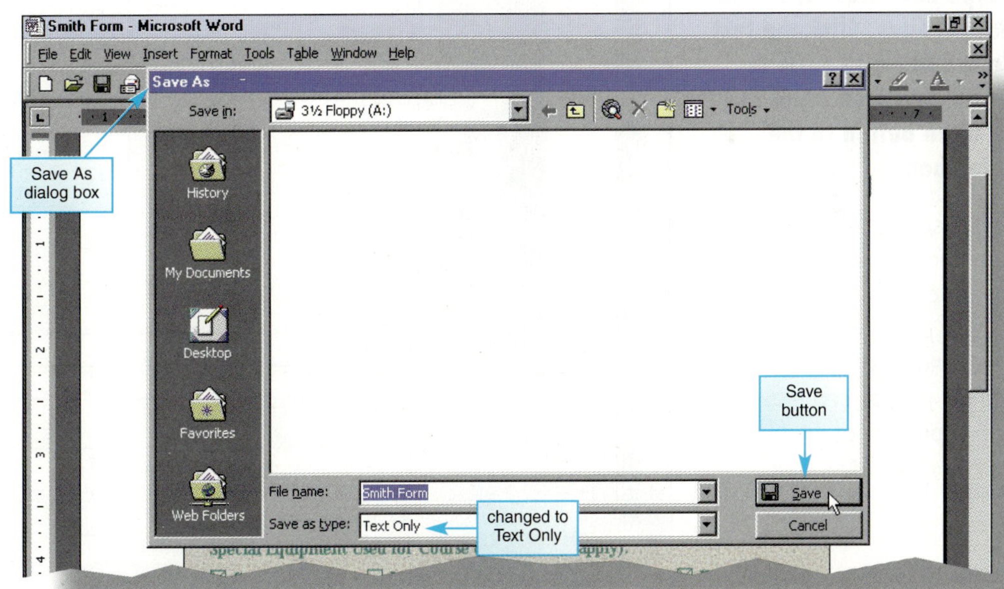

FIGURE 8-63

4 **Click the Save button in the Save As dialog box. If Word displays a dialog box indicating that some formatting may be lost, click the Yes button to continue the save because text files should not have formatting.**

Word saves the data on the form in a text file called Smith Form.

Other Ways

1. On Tools menu click Options, click Save tab, place a check mark in Save data only for forms check box, click OK button, on File menu click Save Copy As, click Save button in Save Copy As dialog box

After you save the data to a text file, you should remove the check mark from the Save data only for forms check box so that Word will save the entire form the next time you save the document. Perform the following steps to uncheck the Save data only for forms check box.

TO UNCHECK THE SAVE DATA ONLY FOR FORMS CHECK BOX

1. Click Tools on the menu bar and then click Options. When the Options dialog box displays, click the Save tab.
2. Click the Save data only for forms check box to remove the check mark. Click the OK button.

Future saves of the document will save the entire form.

If you wanted to view the contents of the text file, you could open it in Word by performing the following steps.

To Open a Text File in Word

1. **Click the Open button on the Standard toolbar. When the Open dialog box displays, if necessary, click the Files of type box arrow and then click All Files. Click the text file called Smith Form in the list and then point to the Open button in the dialog box.**

Word displays the Open dialog box (Figure 8-64). The icon for a text file looks like a piece of paper with writing on it. Depending on previous settings, your screen may not show a preview of the file.

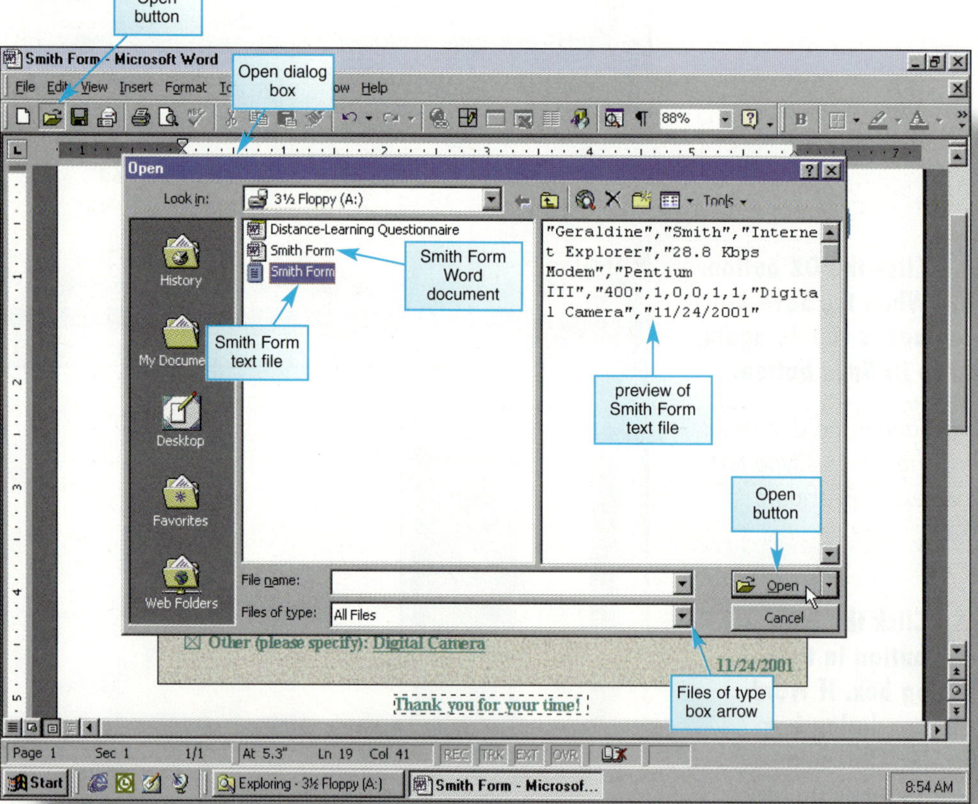

FIGURE 8-64

2 Click the Open button in the Open dialog box.

The text file displays in the Word window (Figure 8-65).

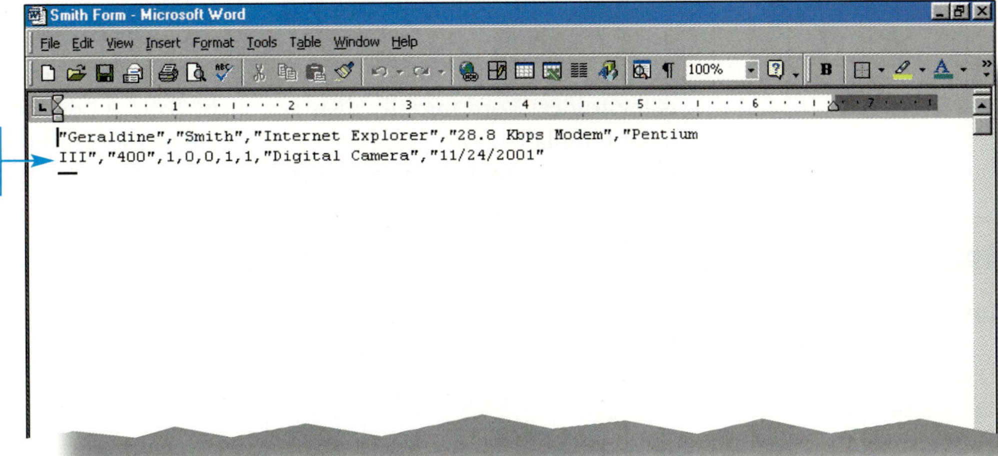

FIGURE 8-65

You also can display a text file in a text editor such as Notepad. If you wanted to print the text file, you would click the Print button on the Standard toolbar.

Notice that the text file lists all data from the form fields, separating each form field with a comma. All text box and drop-down list box entries are surrounded with quotation marks. Table 8-3 shows the form field and the corresponding entry in the text file.

For the check boxes, a value of 1 (one) indicates that the user selected the check box, and a value of 0 (zero) indicates that a user did not select the check box. The text file is ready to be imported into a database table.

Perform the following steps to close the window displaying the text file.

Table 8-3 Mapping of Form Fields to Contents of Text File

FORM FIELD CAPTION	FORM FIELD TYPE	TEXT FILE ENTRY
First Name	Text Box	"Geraldine"
Last Name	Text Box	"Smith"
Browser Used	Drop-Down List Box	"Internet Explorer"
Connection Method	Drop-Down List Box	"28.8 Kbps Modem"
Processor Type	Drop-Down List Box	"Pentium III"
Processor Speed	Text Box	"400"
Scanner	Check Box	1
Microphone	Check Box	0
Video Camera	Check Box	0
Fax Machine	Check Box	1
Other	Check Box	1
Other	Text Box	"Digital Camera"
	Date	"11/24/2001"

TO CLOSE A WINDOW

1 Click File on the menu bar and then click Close.

Word closes the window displaying the text file.

Working with Templates

If you want to modify the template, you open it by clicking the Open button on the Standard toolbar, clicking the template name, and then clicking the Open button in the dialog box. Then, you must unprotect the form by clicking the Protect Form document on the Forms toolbar or by clicking Tools on the menu bar and then clicking Unprotect Document.

When you created the template in this project, you saved it to a floppy disk in drive A. In environments other than an academic setting, you would not save the template to a floppy disk. Instead, you would save it to the Templates folder, which is the folder Word initially displays in the Save As dialog box for a file type of document template. When you save a template in the Templates folder, Word places an icon for the template in the General sheet of the New dialog box. Thus, to open a new Word document that is based on a template that has been saved in the Templates folder, you click File on the menu bar, click New, click the General tab, and then double-click the template icon. Figure 8-66 shows the template icon for the Distance-Learning Questionnaire in the General Sheet of the New dialog box.

Templates Folder

If you want a template to display in a tabbed sheet other than the General sheet, you would save the template in the appropriate subfolder of the Templates folder. If you wish to create a custom tabbed sheet, you must create a new subfolder in the Templates folder. The subfolder name will be the name of the tabbed sheet.

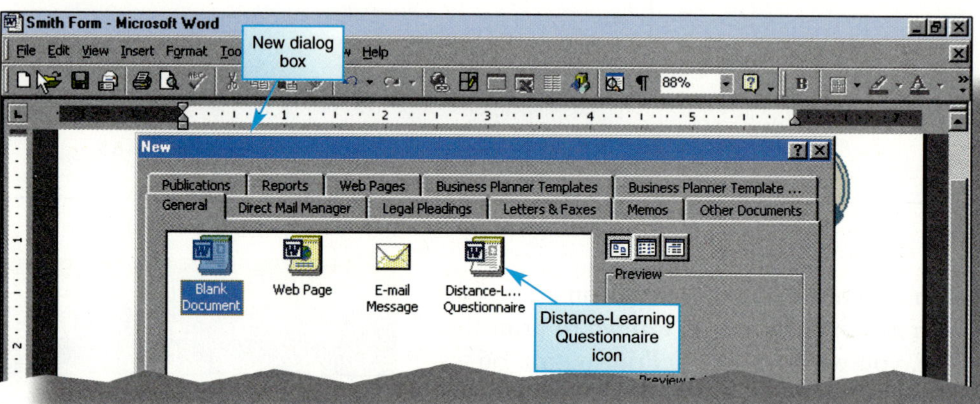

FIGURE 8-66

You also can make templates available on a network so others can share them. These templates, called **workgroup templates**, typically are stored on the network server by the network administrator as read-only files, which prevents users from inadvertently modifying them. You can change the location of workgroup templates in the Options dialog box (Figure 8-67) by clicking Tools on the menu bar, clicking Options, clicking the File Locations tab, clicking Workgroup templates in the File types list, and then clicking the Modify button. Locate the folder assigned to workgroup templates (as specified by the network administrator), and then click the OK button. With the workgroup template location specified, these templates also display in the General tab sheet in the New dialog box.

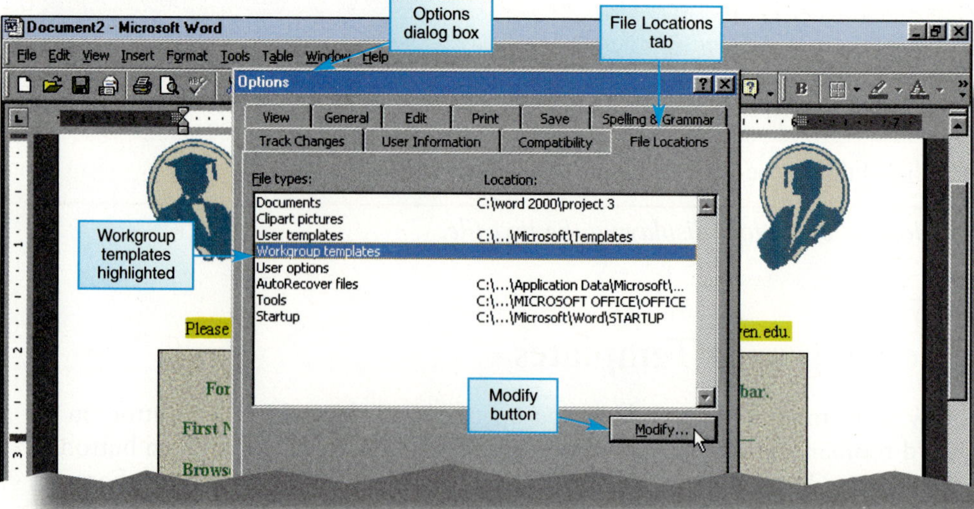

FIGURE 8-67

Notice that the Options dialog box also lists locations of other files accessed by Word. Although you can change any of these locations through the Modify button, use caution when doing so because Word may not be able to access these types of files if you move their location.

Perform the following steps to quit Word and close Windows Explorer.

TO QUIT WORD

Click File on the menu bar and then click Exit.

The Word window closes.

TO CLOSE WINDOWS EXPLORER

Click the Close button on the Exploring – 3½ Floppy (A:) window's title bar.

Windows Explorer closes.

CASE PERSPECTIVE SUMMARY

You e-mail the Distance-Learning Course Questionnaire to the 120 students that completed a distance-learning course last semester. Of the 120, you receive 77 completed forms. You decide to use Access to analyze the student responses. Thus, you save each completed form as a text file.

You create an Access database that contains a table named Distance-Learning Questionnaire Results. The table contains one field for each form field on the questionnaire. After you import the data from each text file into the table, you create a report that lists the total number of students that selected each option on the form. From this report, you create a typical computer configuration list for distance-learning courses so that it can be included in the upcoming *Schedule of Courses*.

Project Summary

Project 8 introduced you to creating an online form. You created a document template as the basis for the form. Then, you added text boxes, drop-down list boxes, and check boxes to the form. You added Help text to each of these form fields. On the form, you also highlighted text, animated text, and added a rectangle around the data entry area. After you protected the form, you opened a new document based on the template and filled out the form. You also learned how to save the data on a form in a text file and how to modify the location of workgroup templates.

Quick Reference

For a table that lists how to complete the tasks covered in this book using the mouse, menu, shortcut menu, and keyboard, see the Word Quick Reference Summary at the back of this book or visit the Shelly Cashman Series Office Web page (www.scsite.com/off2000/qr.htm) and then click Microsoft Word 2000.

What You Should Know

Having completed this project, you should now be able to perform the following tasks:

- Access a Template through Windows Explorer *(WD 8.49)*
- Add Help Text to a Form *(WD 8.36)*
- Add More Help Text *(WD 8.37)*
- Animate Text *(WD 8.45)*
- Close a Window *(WD 8.55)*
- Close Windows Explorer *(WD 8.57)*
- Create a Document Template *(WD 8.9)*
- Display Formatting Marks *(WD 8.7)*
- Draw a Rectangle *(WD 8.40)*
- Enter Additional Check Box Form Fields *(WD 8.29)*
- Enter and Format Text *(WD 8.10)*
- Enter Text *(WD 8.14, WD 8.27)*
- Fill a Drawing Object with a Texture *(WD 8.43)*
- Fill Out a Form *(WD 8.50)*
- Hide Formatting Marks *(WD 8.47)*
- Highlight Text *(WD 8.13)*
- Insert a Borderless Table into a Form *(WD 8.15, WD 8.20, WD 8.24, WD 8.27)*
- Insert a Check Box *(WD 8.28)*
- Insert a Drop-Down Form Field *(WD 8.20)*
- Insert a Text Form Field *(WD 8.17)*
- Insert and Format Clip Art *(WD 8.11)*
- Insert and Specify Options for a Drop-Down Form Field *(WD 8.23, WD 8.24)*
- Insert and Specify Options for a Text Form Field *(WD 8.19, WD 8.26, WD 8.29)*
- Insert and Specify Options for a Text Form Field as the Current Date *(WD 8.31)*
- Open a Text File in Word *(WD 8.54)*
- Print a Form *(WD 8.51)*
- Protect a Form *(WD 8.47)*
- Quit Word *(WD 8.48, WD 8.57)*
- Remove Form Field Shading *(WD 8.39)*
- Reset Menus and Toolbars *(WD 8.6)*
- Save a Document *(WD 8.51)*
- Save Form Data in a Text File *(WD 8.52)*
- Save the Document Again *(WD 8.48)*
- Send a Drawing Object Behind Text *(WD 8.42)*
- Specify Drop-Down Form Field Options *(WD 8.21)*
- Specify Text Form Field Options *(WD 8.18)*
- Start Word *(WD 8.6)*
- Uncheck the Save Data Only for Forms Check Box *(WD 8.54)*
- Underline in Color *(WD 8.32)*
- Use the Format Painter Button *(WD 8.34)*
- Zoom Page Width *(WD 8.7)*

Microsoft Certification

The Microsoft Office User Specialist (MOUS) Certification program provides an opportunity for you to obtain a valuable industry credential - proof that you have the Word 2000 skills required by employers. For more information, see Appendix D or visit the Shelly Cashman Series MOUS Web page at www.scsite.com/off2000/cert.htm.

1 Filling Out a Form

Instructions: In this assignment, you access a template through Windows Explorer. As shown in Figure 8-68, the template contains an online form. You are to fill in the form, save it, and print it. The template is located on the Data Disk. If you did not download the Data Disk, see the inside back cover for instructions for downloading the Data Disk or see your instructor. Perform the following tasks:

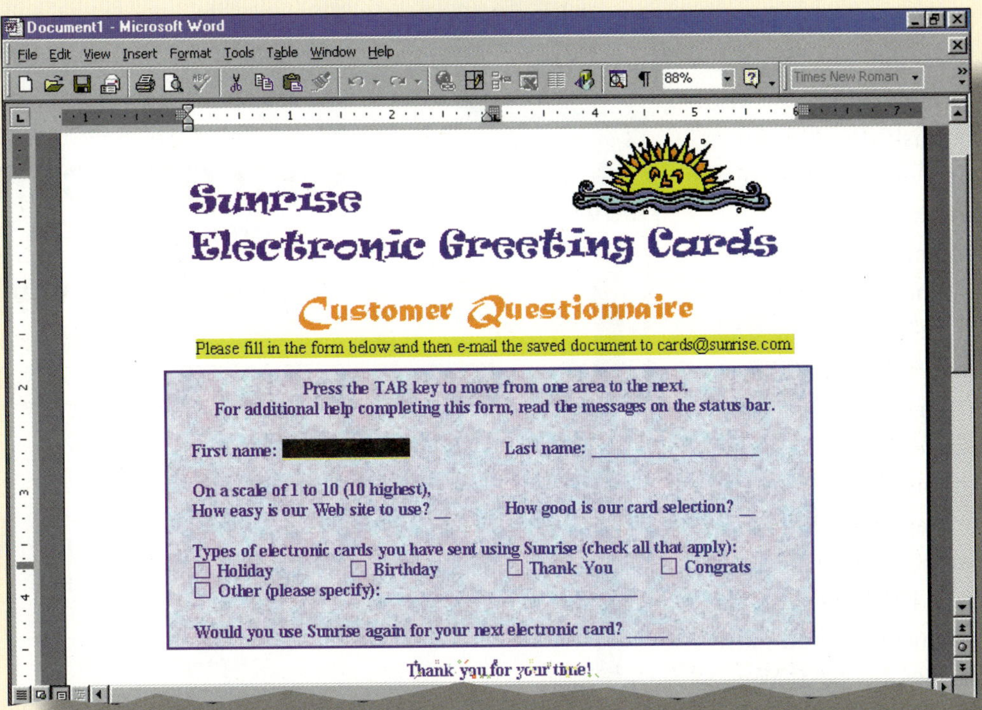

FIGURE 8-68

1. Right-click the My Computer icon on the Windows desktop and then click Explore on the shortcut menu. When the Exploring window displays, click the Address text box to select it. With the Data Disk in drive A, type `a:` and then press the ENTER key. Double-click the Sunrise Questionnaire icon in the Contents pane.
2. When Word displays a new document based on the Sunrise Questionnaire template, scroll down so the entire form fits in the Word window. If the Show/Hide ¶ button on the Standard toolbar is recessed, click it.
3. With the highlight in the First name text box, type `Julianne` and then press the TAB key.
4. With the highlight in the Last name text box, type `Robledo` and then press the TAB key.
5. Type `9` in response to How easy is our Web site to use and then press the TAB key.
6. Type `10` in response to How good is our card selection and then press the TAB key.
7. Place an X in the Birthday, Thank You, and Other check boxes by clicking them. Press the TAB key to highlight the Other (please specify) text box.
8. Type `Get Well, Good Luck` in the Other (please specify) text box and then press the TAB key.
9. With the highlight in the drop-down list box at the bottom of the form, click the box arrow and then click Yes.
10. Save the file with the name Robledo Form. Print the form.
11. Click File on the menu bar and then click Save As. When the Save As dialog box displays, click the Tools button arrow and then click General Options. When the Save dialog box displays, place a check mark in the Save data only for forms check box and then click the OK button. Click the Save button in the Save As dialog box. If Word displays a dialog box indicating that some formatting may be lost, click the Yes button.
12. Click Tools on the menu bar and then click Options. When the Options dialog box displays, click the Save tab. Click the Save data only for forms check box to remove the check mark. Click the OK button.
13. Click the Open button on the Standard toolbar. When the Open dialog box displays, click the Files of type box arrow and then click All Files. Click the text file called Robledo Form in the list and then click the Open button in the dialog box. Print the text file.

1 Creating an Online Form with a Texture Fill Effect

Problem: You work part-time for The Web Grocer. Your supervisor has asked you to prepare an online survey for customers that recently have shopped online. The survey should obtain the following information from the customer: first name, last name, time of day usually shopped, average time it takes to shop in minutes, shopping methods used, and payment method most frequently used. You prepare the online form shown in Figure 8-69.

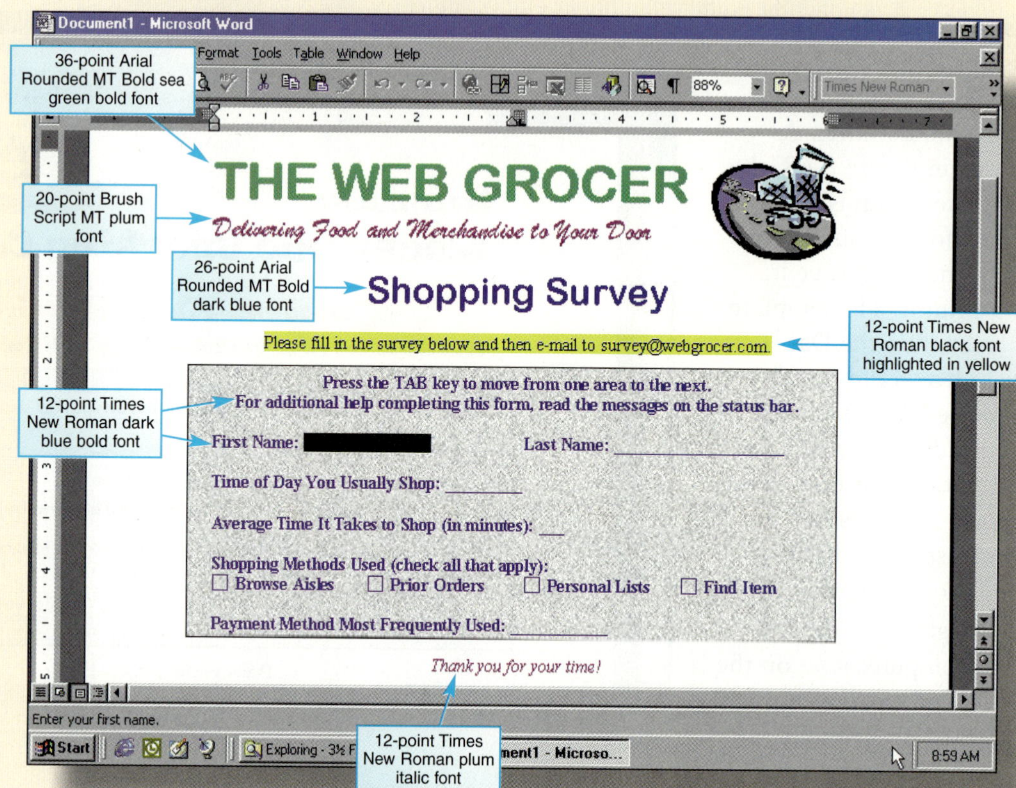

FIGURE 8-69

Instructions:

1. Create a template called Web Grocer Survey for the online form.
2. Enter and format the company name, slogan, clip art, and form title as shown in Figure 8-69.
3. Enter the form instructions and highlight them in yellow.
4. Enter the instructions in the data entry area, form field captions, and form fields as shown in Figure 8-69. First Name and Last Name are text boxes. Time of Day You Usually Shop is a drop-down list box with these choices: Morning, Afternoon, Evening, Late Night, Times Vary. The four Shopping Methods Used are check boxes. Payment Method Most Frequently Used is a drop-down list box with these choices: Personal Check, Credit Card. When the form initially displays on the screen as a blank form, the text boxes and drop-down list boxes should display underlines.
5. Enter the thank-you message as shown in Figure 8-69.
6. Draw a rectangle around the data entry area. Fill the rectangle with the newsprint texture.
7. Add Help text to all the form fields.
8. Check the spelling of the form. Protect the form. Save the form again. Print the blank form.
9. Access the template through Windows Explorer. Fill out the form. Save the filled-out form. Print the filled-out form.

2 Creating an Online Form with a Gradient Fill Effect

Problem: You work part-time for Lincoln State Bank. Your supervisor has asked you to prepare an online survey for bank customers. The survey should obtain the following information from the customer: first name, last name, method customers use to balance their bank statements, banking methods customers use, bank services customers use, and a bank service rating. You prepare the online form shown in Figure 8-70.

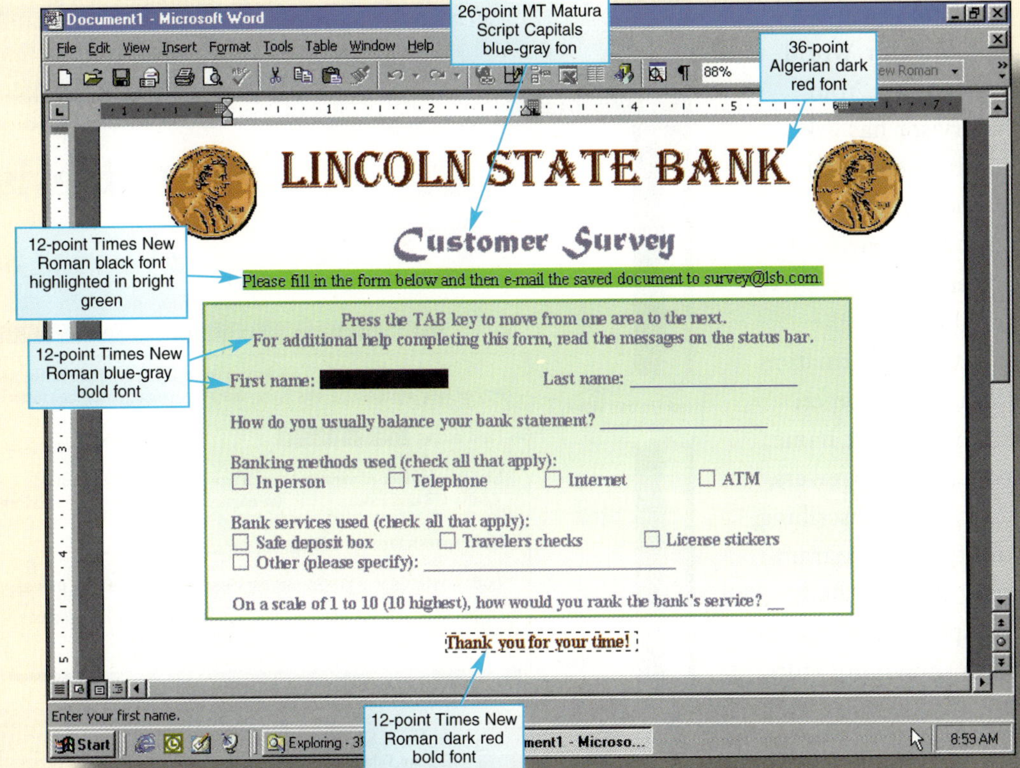

FIGURE 8-70

Instructions:

1. Create a template called Lincoln Bank Survey for the online form.
2. Enter and format the company name, clip art, and form title as shown in Figure 8-70.
3. Enter the form instructions and highlight them in bright green.
4. Enter the instructions in the data entry area, form field captions, and form fields as shown in Figure 8-70. First name and Last name are text boxes. How do you usually balance your bank statement? is a drop-down list box with these choices: Check book register, Computer software, My accountant, Other. The choices below Bank methods used and Bank services used are check boxes. The Other check box also has a text box to its right for further explanation. The bank's service rating is a text box that requires a numeric entry. When the form initially displays on the screen as a blank form, the text boxes and drop-down list boxes should display underlines.
5. Enter the thank-you message with the marching black ants animation as shown in Figure 8-70.
6. Draw a rectangle around the data entry area. Change the rectangle line color to sea green (select the rectangle and then click the Line Color box arrow on the Drawing toolbar). Fill the rectangle with a two-color gradient of light green to white (*Hint*: Click the Gradient tab in the Fill Effects dialog box).
7. Add Help text to all the form fields.
8. Check the spelling of the form. Protect the form. Save the form again. Print the blank form.
9. Access the template through Windows Explorer. Fill out the form. Save the filled-out form. Print the filled-out form.

3 Creating an Online Form with a Pattern Fill Effect

Problem: You work part-time for World Cablevision. Your supervisor has asked you to prepare an online survey requesting customer viewing preferences. The survey should obtain the following information from the customer: first name, last name, age group of viewers, reason for subscribing, and type of programming watched daily. You prepare the online form shown in Figure 8-71.

33-point Britannic Bold sea green font

25-point Times New Roman lime font

12-point Times New Roman black font highlighted in pink

12-point Times New Roman violet bold font

12-point Times New Roman plum font

FIGURE 8-71

Instructions:

1. Create a template called World Cablevision Survey for the online form.
2. Enter and format the company name, clip art, and form title as shown in Figure 8-71.
3. Enter the form instructions and highlight them in pink.
4. Enter the instructions in the data entry area, form field captions, and form fields as shown in Figure 8-71. First name and Last name are text boxes. Number of viewers in household are text boxes each requiring numeric entries. Main reason for subscribing is a drop-down list box with these choices: Better Reception, Larger Variety of Movies, Sporting Events, More Channels, Other. The five choices in the type of programming viewed daily are check boxes. The current date is a form field. When the form initially displays on the screen as a blank form, the text boxes and drop-down list boxes should display underlines.
5. Enter the thank-you message as shown in Figure 8-71.
6. Draw a rectangle around the data entry area. Change the rectangle line color to violet (select the rectangle and then click the Line Color box arrow on the Drawing toolbar). Fill the rectangle with a Wide upward diagonal pattern that has a foreground color of yellow. (*Hint*: Click the Gradient tab in the Fill Effects dialog box). Add a shadow to the rectangle (*Hint:* Use the Shadow button on the Drawing toolbar.)
7. Add Help text to all the form fields. The Help should display on the status bar, as well as when the user presses F1.
8. Check the spelling of the form. Protect the form. Save the form again. Print the blank form.
9. Access the template through Windows Explorer. Fill out the form. Save the filled-out form. Print the filled-out form.

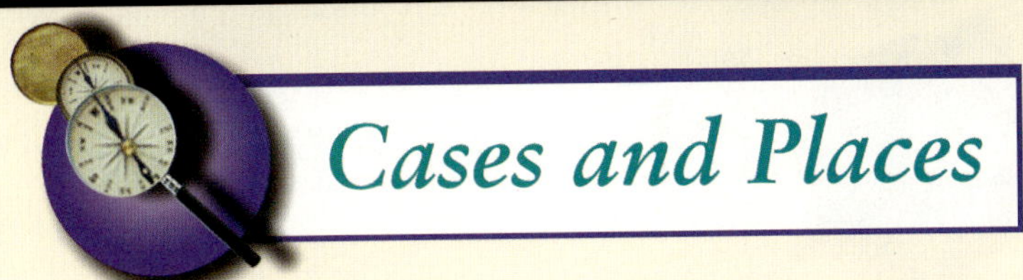

Cases and Places

The difficulty of these case studies varies:
◗ are the least difficult; ◗◗ are more difficult; and ◗◗◗ are the most difficult.

1 ◗ As a part-time assistant for Worldwide Travel, your supervisor has asked you to prepare and send an online customer preference survey to users of the online reservation system. The top of the survey should list the travel agency name, Worldwide Travel, along with the title of the survey, Customer Preference Survey. Insert an appropriate graphic of an airplane from the Clip Gallery. Immediately above the data entry area, the following sentence should be highlighted: Please fill in the form below and then e-mail the saved document to survey@wt.com. The data entry area contains the following two sentences of instructions: Press the TAB key to move from one area to the next. For help completing this form, read the messages on the status bar or press F1. The data entry area should request the customer's first name, last name, preferred ticket type (coach class, business class, first class), preferred seat type (aisle, window, no preference), number of adult passengers that usually travels with the customer, number of child passengers that usually travels with the customer, and the ticket selection criteria (lowest cost, nonstop flights, airline name, airplane type, other). If the customer selects other for the ticket selection criteria, he or she should be asked to explain further. The form should contain the current date as a form field. The data entry area should be surrounded by a rectangle filled in with an appropriate fill effect. Below the form, place an animated thank-you message. All data entry fields should have Help text that displays on the status bar, as well as when the user presses F1. Use the concepts and techniques presented in this project to create and format this online form.

2 ◗◗ As a vice president of the Student Government Association at your school, you have been asked to send a questionnaire to all students requesting feedback on the class schedules. Because each student on campus has an e-mail account, you decide to send an online form. The form should ask for student opinions and preferences on the most recent schedule of classes. Areas of interest might include satisfaction or preferences of days and times classes are offered, frequency of class meetings, class fees, and class formats (on campus, distance-learning, labs, etc.). The form should contain the current date as a form field. Include at least one text box, one drop-down list box, and three check boxes on the form. Use the concepts and techniques presented in this project to create and format the online form. Be sure to include an appropriate graphic from the Clip Gallery.

3 ◗◗ As a part-time assistant for your school's fitness center, you have been asked to send a questionnaire to all students requesting their opinion of the fitness center. Because each student on campus has an e-mail account, you decide to send an online form. The form should ask for student opinions and preferences on various aspects of the fitness center. Areas of interest might include satisfaction or preferences of hours of operation, type and availability of fitness equipment, training, fees, and facility appearance. The form should contain the current date as a form field. Include at least one text box, one drop-down list box, and three check boxes on the form. Use the concepts and techniques presented in this project to create and format the online form. Be sure to include an appropriate graphic(s) from the Clip Gallery.

Cases and Places

4 ▸▸ As a laboratory assistant for the computing center at your school, you have been asked to send a questionnaire to all students requesting feedback on the computer laboratory. Because each student on campus has an e-mail account, you decide to send an online form. The form should ask for student opinions and preferences on the computer lab facility. Areas of interest might include satisfaction or preferences of days and times the lab is open, quality and availability of personal help in the lab room, and availability and currency of equipment. The form should contain the current date as a form field. Include at least one text box, one drop-down list box, and three check boxes on the form. Use the concepts and techniques presented in this project to create and format the online form. Be sure to include an appropriate graphic from the Clip Gallery.

5 ▸▸▸ If Microsoft Access is installed on your computer, you can use it to create a database table and then use that table to analyze the data from Word forms. Your supervisor at Raven Community College would like to analyze the results of the questionnaires sent using Microsoft Access. To generate data for the database table, fill out the Project 5 Word form (Figure 8-1a on page WD 8.5) five times (acting as five separate students) and save the form data for each filled-in form in a separate text file. Start Access and then click File on the menu bar, point to Get External Data, and then click Import. When the Import dialog box displays, change the file type to Text File, locate the text file that contains one of the form's data, and then click the Import button. Use the Import Text Wizard to create a table for the form in Figure 8-1. Data in the text file is comma delimited. Use field names that match the field captions on the form. Each form field, including the current date, should have a field name. Then, import each of the remaining four text files into the existing table. After the table contains the five records, generate a report in Access that lists all the data collected from the forms.

6 ▸▸▸ If Microsoft Access is installed on your computer, you can use it to create a database table and then use that table to analyze the data from Word forms. Your supervisor at Sunrise Electronic Greeting Cards would like to analyze the results of the questionnaires sent using Microsoft Access. To generate data for the database table, fill out the Apply Your Knowledge Exercise form (Figure 8-68 on page WD 8.59) five times (acting as five separate customers) and save the form data for each filled-in form in a separate text file. Start Access and then click File on the menu bar, point to Get External Data, click Import. When the Import dialog box displays, change the file type to Text File, locate the text file that contains one of the form's data, and then click the Import button. Use the Import Text Wizard to create a table for the form in Figure 8-68. Data in the text file is comma delimited. Use field names that define the field captions on the form. Each form field should have a field name. Then, import each of the remaining four text files into the existing table. After the table contains the five records, generate a report in Access that lists all the data collected from the forms.

Microsoft Word 2000

Using Visual Basic for Applications (VBA) with Word

OBJECTIVES

You will have mastered the material in this project when you can:

- Set a security level in Word
- Unprotect a document
- Format a character as an in margin drop cap
- Create a new style
- Fill a drawing object with a bitmap picture
- Add a 3-D effect to a drawing object
- Record and execute a macro
- Assign a macro to a toolbar button
- Record an automatic macro
- View a macro's VBA code
- Add comments to a macro's VBA code
- Modify a macro's VBA code
- Add code statements to a macro's VBA code
- Insert a VBA procedure
- Plan a VBA procedure
- Enter code statements in a VBA procedure
- Run a macro when a user exits a form field
- Insert an ActiveX control
- Format and set properties for an ActiveX control
- Write a VBA procedure for an ActiveX control

WINTER DANCE PARTY

BUDDY HOLLY

JP RICHARDSON

RITCHIE VALENS

Chantilly Lace Makes Me Spend My Money

On a snowy night, Buddy Holly, Ritchie Valens, and J.P. Richardson climbed aboard a chartered plane to travel from Iowa to their next gig in North Dakota. These vocalists were part of the Winter Dance Party, a whirlwind tour of top recording artists performing nightly throughout the Midwest. That day, February 3, 1959, is what Don McLean calls, the day the music died, in his hit record, "American Pie," as the plane crashed five miles from the airport. No one aboard survived.

Chantilly Lace

J.P. Richardson

45 RPM

side 2

These performers were at the peak of their careers. J.P. Richardson, better known as the Big Bopper, had broken into Billboard's Top 100 with "Chantilly Lace." He had written that song and many others while taking breaks at his disc jockey job at a small Texas radio station.

He used "Chantilly Lace" on the flip side of a record featuring "The Purple People Eater Meets the Witch Doctor," his mix of two successful songs, "The Purple People Eater" and "Witch Doctor." Most radio stations, however, preferred to play "Chantilly Lace," and when the Big Bopper performed it on "The Dick Clark Saturday Night Beech-Nut Show," he was an overnight sensation. "Chantilly Lace" was the third most played record in 1958.

In the song, Chantilly Lace is the name of the woman with a pretty face and a ponytail hangin' down. She is named after the city in northern France famous for producing delicate lace. No doubt this big-eyed girl with a giggle in her talk would like the finer things in life, including elegant apparel and designer sportswear.

This clothing is the mainstay of The Warnaco Group, a New York-based manufacturer of women's and men's apparel and accessories. This merchandise is sold under such brand names as Warner's, Calvin Klein, and Chaps by Ralph Lauren in more than 16,000 stores throughout North America and Europe.

Warnaco CEO Linda Wachner keeps close tabs on manufacturing costs and inventory. Although she pleasantly refers to herself as Miss Linda to her business associates, her hard-hitting management style has helped name her as one of Fortune's 50 Most Powerful Women in American Business. She also is CEO of California-based Authentic Fitness, the manufacturer of Speedo® swimsuits, so she knows how consumers spend their money.

Warnaco produces approximately eight million garments per year. To keep track of the fabrics and trimmings needed to produce these garments, the company has developed a database application similar to the one you will produce in this Word 2000 project.

The database consists of thousands of records containing details about each item in the company's warehouse, such as a specific button shape, a bow size, and a lace color. The program allows employees to access, retrieve, and use this data efficiently. In only a few minutes, an employee can gather all the materials needed to fill an order.

And whether that order calls for 1,000 zippers or 5,000 yards of lace, you can bet Miss Linda says this database helps make her corporation, in the Big Bopper's words, a-what I like.

Microsoft Word 2000

Using Visual Basic for Applications (VBA) with Word

CASE PERSPECTIVE

As a part-time assistant in the CIS department, you were asked to design an online questionnaire for students who recently completed a distance-learning course. Your supervisor has several suggestions for improving the form. First, you are to change the color scheme and the graphics on the form. Second, the form should display without formatting marks showing and be positioned properly in the Word window without the user having to scroll. Third, if a user enters a letter or other nonnumeric value into the Processor Speed text box, the form should display an error message. Fourth, if a user enters text into the Other text box, the form automatically should place an X in the Other check box. Finally, you are to add a button to the Standard toolbar that instructs Word to save the data only when you save the form. Then, instead of setting options in a dialog box for each form you receive, you simply click this button, saving you many extra steps in the process of analyzing the student responses.

To complete this project, you will need the online form template created in Project 8. (If you did not create the template, see your instructor for a copy.)

Introduction

When you issue an instruction to Word by clicking a button or a command, Word must have a step-by-step description of the task to be accomplished. For example, when you click the Print button on the Standard toolbar, Word follows a precise set of steps to print your document. In Word, this precise step-by-step series of instructions is called a **procedure.** A procedure also is referred to as a **program** or **code.**

The process of writing a procedure is called **computer programming.** Every Word command on a menu and button on a toolbar has a corresponding procedure that executes when you click the command or button. **Execute** means that the computer carries out the step-by-step instructions. In a Windows environment, an event causes the instructions associated with a task to be executed. An **event** is an action such as clicking a button, clicking a command, dragging a scroll box, or right-clicking selected text.

Although Word has many toolbar buttons and menu commands, it does not include a command or button for every possible task. Thus, Microsoft has included with Word a powerful programming language called Visual Basic for Applications. The **Visual Basic for Applications (VBA)** programming language allows you to customize and extend the capabilities of Word.

Project Nine — Visual Basic for Applications (VBA)

In this project, you improve upon the online form created in Project 8 (see Figure 8-1 on page WD 8.5). Figure 9-1a shows the revised blank form, in which the fonts, font sizes, graphics, highlight color, and fill effect in the drawing object are changed. Figure 9-1b shows an error message that displays if a user makes

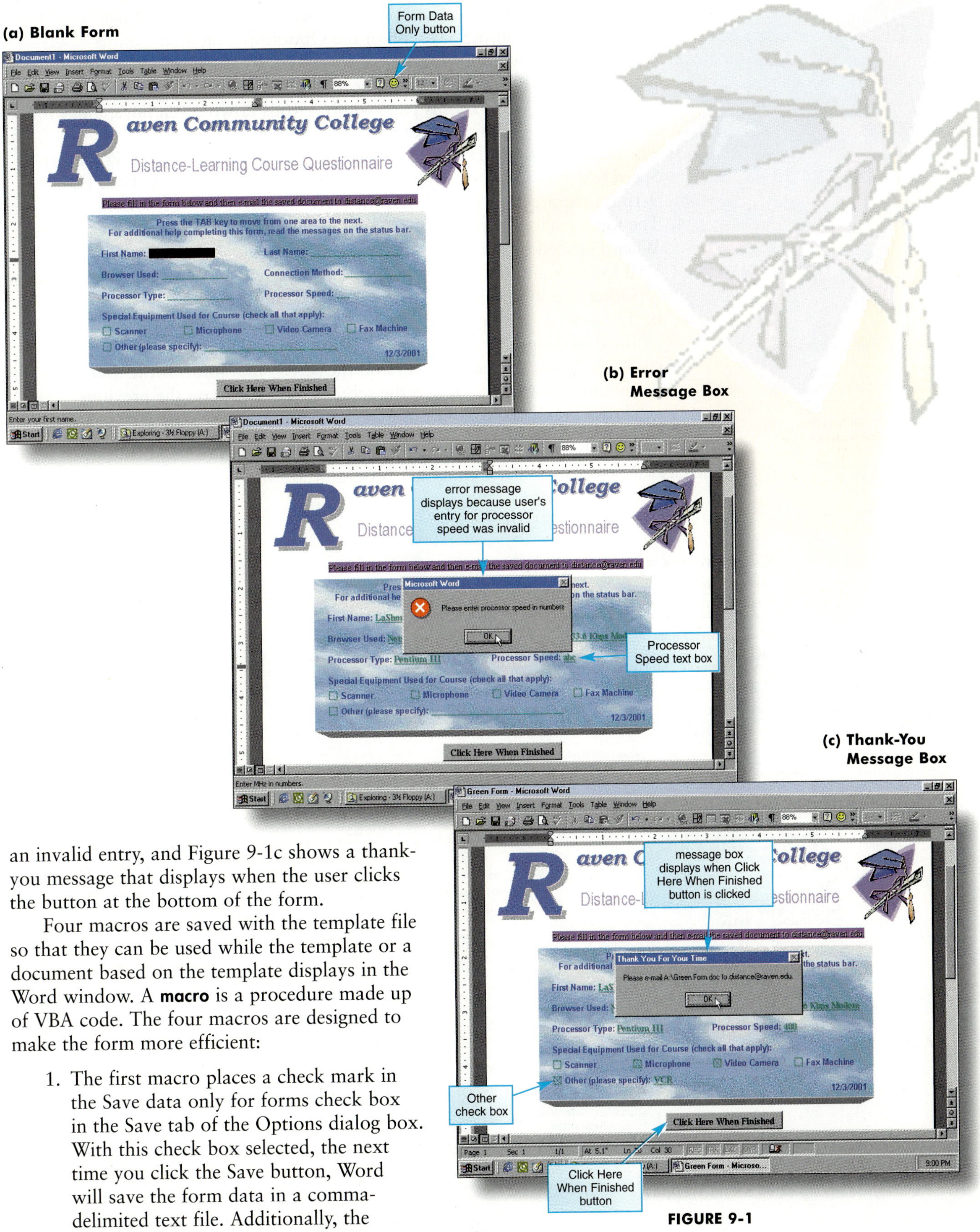

(a) Blank Form

Form Data Only button

(b) Error Message Box

error message displays because user's entry for processor speed was invalid

Processor Speed text box

(c) Thank-You Message Box

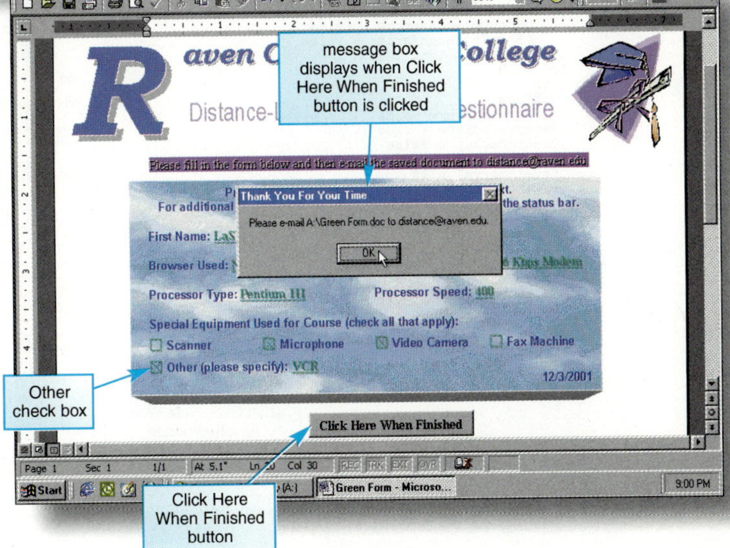

FIGURE 9-1

an invalid entry, and Figure 9-1c shows a thank-you message that displays when the user clicks the button at the bottom of the form.

Four macros are saved with the template file so that they can be used while the template or a document based on the template displays in the Word window. A **macro** is a procedure made up of VBA code. The four macros are designed to make the form more efficient:

1. The first macro places a check mark in the Save data only for forms check box in the Save tab of the Options dialog box. With this check box selected, the next time you click the Save button, Word will save the form data in a comma-delimited text file. Additionally, the Standard toolbar contains a new button called the Form Data Only button.

When you click the Form Data Only button or press ALT+D (the shortcut key assigned to the button), Word places a check mark in the Save data only for forms check box in the Save tab of the Options dialog box.

2. The second macro controls how the form initially displays on the screen (as a blank form). When a user starts a new Word document that is based on the form template, Word zooms page width, scrolls down seven lines, hides formatting marks, and hides gridlines.
3. The third macro displays an error message if the user leaves the Processor Speed text box blank or enters a nonnumeric entry in the text box. Figure 9-1b on the previous page shows the error message.
4. The fourth macro performs three actions when the user clicks the Click Here When Finished button:
   a. If the user entered text in the Other text box, then Word places an X in the Other check box (just in case the user left it blank).
   b. The Save As dialog box displays so the user can assign a file name to the filled-in form.
   c. A thank-you message displays on the screen that informs the user what file should be e-mailed back to the school. Figure 9-1c on the previous page shows the thank-you message for a filled-in form.

Figure 9-2 shows the VBA code for these macros. You have learned that code, such as this, often is called a computer program.

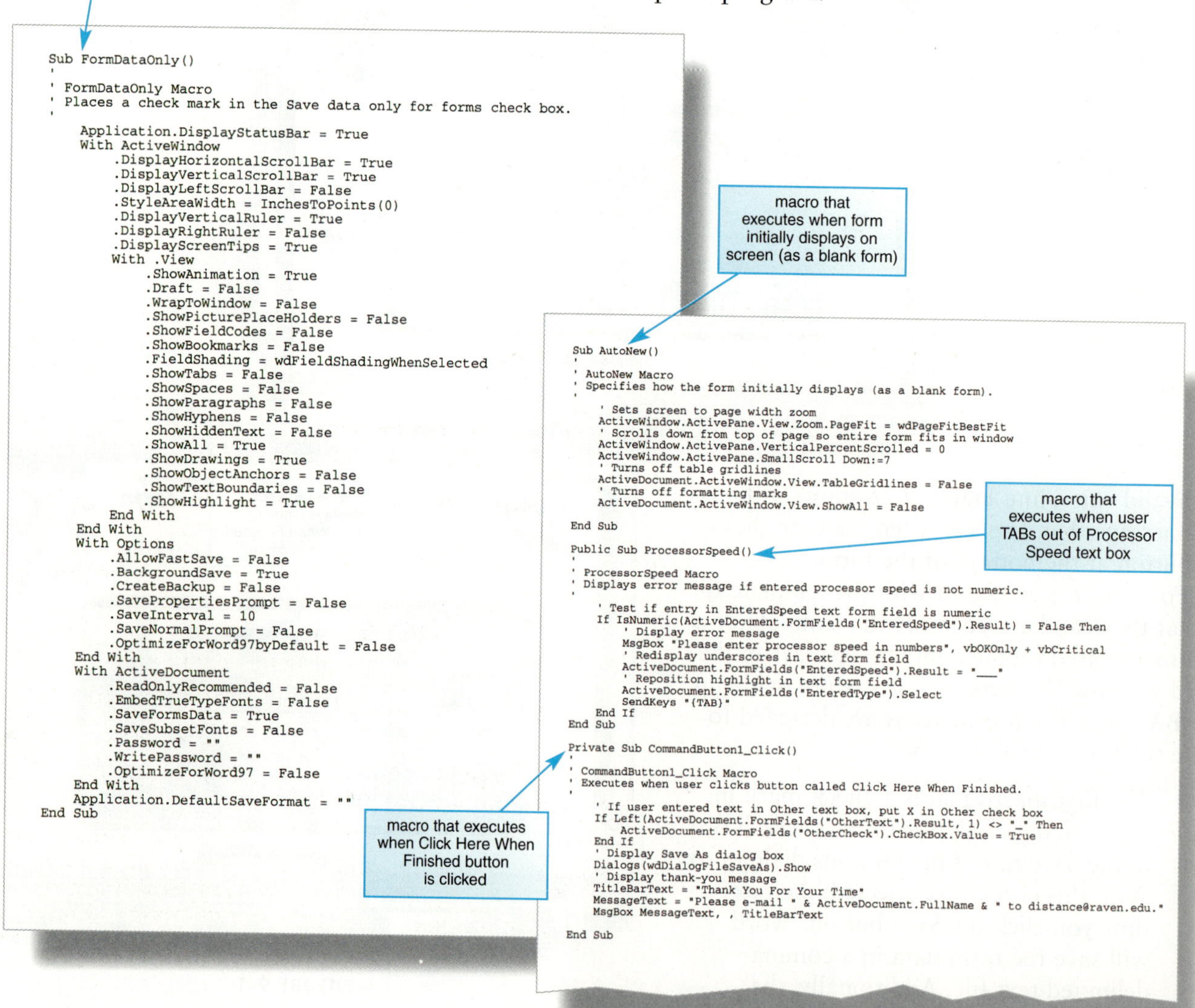


```
Sub FormDataOnly()
'
' FormDataOnly Macro
' Places a check mark in the Save data only for forms check box.
'
    Application.DisplayStatusBar = True
    With ActiveWindow
        .DisplayHorizontalScrollBar = True
        .DisplayVerticalScrollBar = True
        .DisplayLeftScrollBar = False
        .StyleAreaWidth = InchesToPoints(0)
        .DisplayVerticalRuler = True
        .DisplayRightRuler = False
        .DisplayScreenTips = True
        With .View
            .ShowAnimation = True
            .Draft = False
            .WrapToWindow = False
            .ShowPicturePlaceHolders = False
            .ShowFieldCodes = False
            .ShowBookmarks = False
            .FieldShading = wdFieldShadingWhenSelected
            .ShowTabs = False
            .ShowSpaces = False
            .ShowParagraphs = False
            .ShowHyphens = False
            .ShowHiddenText = False
            .ShowAll = True
            .ShowDrawings = True
            .ShowObjectAnchors = False
            .ShowTextBoundaries = False
            .ShowHighlight = True
        End With
    End With
    With Options
        .AllowFastSave = False
        .BackgroundSave = True
        .CreateBackup = False
        .SavePropertiesPrompt = False
        .SaveInterval = 10
        .SaveNormalPrompt = False
        .OptimizeForWord97byDefault = False
    End With
    With ActiveDocument
        .ReadOnlyRecommended = False
        .EmbedTrueTypeFonts = False
        .SaveFormsData = True
        .SaveSubsetFonts = False
        .Password = ""
        .WritePassword = ""
        .OptimizeForWord97 = False
    End With
    Application.DefaultSaveFormat = ""
End Sub
```

```
Sub AutoNew()
'
' AutoNew Macro
' Specifies how the form initially displays (as a blank form).
'
    ' Sets screen to page width zoom
    ActiveWindow.ActivePane.View.Zoom.PageFit = wdPageFitBestFit
    ' Scrolls down from top of page so entire form fits in window
    ActiveWindow.ActivePane.VerticalPercentScrolled = 0
    ActiveWindow.ActivePane.SmallScroll Down:=7
    ' Turns off table gridlines
    ActiveDocument.ActiveWindow.View.TableGridlines = False
    ' Turns off formatting marks
    ActiveDocument.ActiveWindow.View.ShowAll = False

End Sub

Public Sub ProcessorSpeed()
'
' ProcessorSpeed Macro
' Displays error message if entered processor speed is not numeric.
'
    ' Test if entry in EnteredSpeed text form field is numeric
    If IsNumeric(ActiveDocument.FormFields("EnteredSpeed").Result) = False Then
        ' Display error message
        MsgBox "Please enter processor speed in numbers", vbOKOnly + vbCritical
        ' Redisplay underscores in text form field
        ActiveDocument.FormFields("EnteredSpeed").Result = "___"
        ' Reposition highlight in text form field
        ActiveDocument.FormFields("EnteredType").Select
        SendKeys "{TAB}"
    End If
End Sub

Private Sub CommandButton1_Click()
'
' CommandButton1_Click Macro
' Executes when user clicks button called Click Here When Finished.
'
    ' If user entered text in Other text box, put X in Other check box
    If Left(ActiveDocument.FormFields("OtherText").Result, 1) <> "_" Then
        ActiveDocument.FormFields("OtherCheck").CheckBox.Value = True
    End If
    ' Display Save As dialog box
    Dialogs(wdDialogFileSaveAs).Show
    ' Display thank-you message
    TitleBarText = "Thank You For Your Time"
    MessageText = "Please e-mail " & ActiveDocument.FullName & " to distance@raven.edu."
    MsgBox MessageText, , TitleBarText

End Sub
```

FIGURE 9-2

Starting Word and Opening an Office Document

The first step in this project is to open the template for the online form that was created in Project 8 so that you can modify it. (If you did not create the template, see your instructor for a copy.) Perform the following steps to start Word and open the Distance-Learning Questionnaire file.

TO START WORD AND OPEN AN OFFICE DOCUMENT

1. With the disk containing the Distance-Learning Questionnaire file in drive A, click the Start button on the taskbar and then click Open Office Document.
2. When the Open Office Document dialog box displays, if necessary, click the Look in box arrow and then click 3½ Floppy (A:). Click the Files of type box arrow and then click All Files.
3. Double-click the file named Distance-Learning Questionnaire.
4. If the Word window is not maximized, double-click its title bar to maximize it. Click View on the menu bar and then click Print Layout. If the Office Assistant displays, right-click it and then click Hide on the shortcut menu.
5. Scroll down so the entire form displays in the Word window.

Office starts Word. After a few moments, an empty document titled Document1 displays in the Word window. Because this project uses floating graphics, you will use print layout view; thus, the Print Layout View button on the horizontal scroll bar is recessed.

Saving the Document with a New File Name

To preserve the contents of the Distance-Learning Questionnaire file created in Project 8, save a copy of it with a new file name as described in the following steps.

TO SAVE THE DOCUMENT WITH A NEW FILE NAME

1. With a floppy disk in drive A, click File on the menu bar and then click Save As.
2. Type `DL Course Questionnaire` in the File name text box. Do not press the ENTER key.
3. If necessary, click the Save in box arrow and then click 3½ Floppy (A:).
4. Click the Save button in the Save As dialog box.

Word saves the document on a floppy disk in drive A with a new file name of DL Course Questionnaire.

Unprotecting a Document

The template for the Distance-Learning Course Questionnaire online form is protected. When a document is **protected**, users cannot modify it in any manner – except for entering values into form fields placed on the form. Thus, before you can modify the online form, you must unprotect the form as shown in the steps on the next page.

Unprotecting Documents

If Word requests a password when you attempt to unprotect a document, you must enter a password in order to unprotect and then change the document. If you do not know the password, you cannot change the look of the form but you can enter data into its form fields.

To Unprotect a Document

1. **Click Tools on the menu bar and then point to Unprotect Document (Figure 9-3).**

2. **Click Unprotect Document.**

Word unprotects the DL Course Questionnaire template.

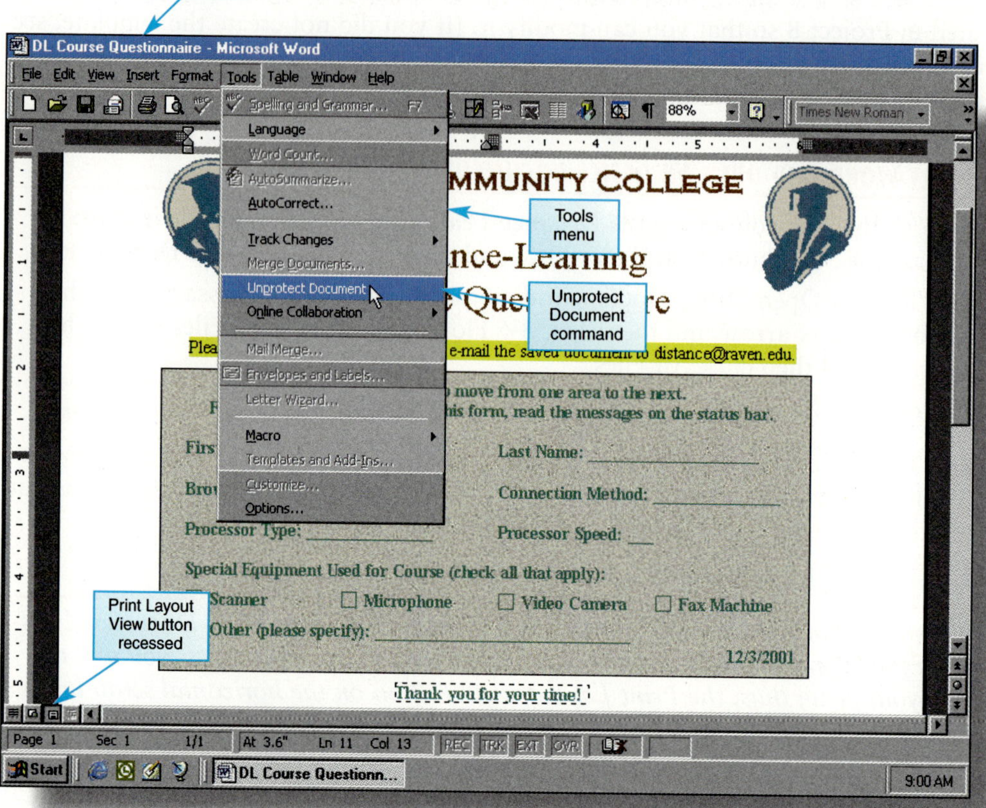

FIGURE 9-3

With the template unprotected, you can change its contents. Later in this project, after you have completed the modifications, you will protect the document again.

Resetting Menus and Toolbars

To set the menus and toolbars so they appear exactly as shown in this book, you should reset your menus and toolbars as outlined in Appendix C or follow these steps.

TO RESET MENUS AND TOOLBARS

1. Click View on the menu bar and then point to Toolbars. Click Customize on the Toolbars submenu.
2. When the Customize dialog box displays, click the Options tab, make sure the top three check boxes have check marks and then click the Reset my usage data button. When the Microsoft Word dialog box displays, click the Yes button.
3. Click the Toolbars tab. Click Standard in the Toolbars list and then click the Reset button. When the Reset Toolbar dialog box displays, click the OK button.

 Click Formatting in the Toolbars list and then click the Reset button. When the Reset Toolbar dialog box displays, click the OK button. Click the Close button.

Word resets the menus and toolbars.

Displaying Formatting Marks

It is helpful to display formatting marks that indicate where in the document you pressed the ENTER key, SPACEBAR, and other keys. Follow this step to display formatting marks.

TO DISPLAY FORMATTING MARKS

1. Double-click the move handle on the left side of the Standard toolbar to display the entire toolbar. If the Show/Hide ¶ button on the Standard toolbar is not already recessed, click it.

Word displays formatting marks in the document window, and the Show/Hide ¶ button on the Standard toolbar is recessed.

Zooming Page Width

When you zoom page width, Word displays the page on the screen as large as possible in print layout view. Perform the following steps to zoom page width.

TO ZOOM PAGE WIDTH

 Click the Zoom box arrow on the Standard toolbar.

 Click Page Width in the Zoom list.

Word displays the left and right edges of a piece of paper as large as possible in the document window. Word computes the zoom percentage based on a variety of settings. Your percentage may be different.

Setting a Security Level in Word

A **computer virus** is a potentially damaging computer program designed to affect, or infect, your computer negatively by altering the way it works without your knowledge or permission. Currently, more than 45,000 known computer viruses exist and an estimated six new viruses are discovered each day. The increased use of the networks, the Internet, and e-mail has accelerated the spread of computer viruses.

To combat this evil, most computer users run antivirus programs that search for viruses and destroy them before they ever have a chance to infect the computer. Macros are a known carrier of viruses, because of the ease with which a person can write code for a macro. For this reason, you can reduce the chance your computer will be infected with a macro virus by setting a **security level** in Word. These security levels allow you to enable or disable macros. An **enabled macro** is a macro that Word will execute, and a **disabled macro** is a macro that is unavailable to Word. Table 9-1 on the next page summarizes the three available security levels in Word.

Viruses

For more information about viruses, visit the Word 2000 More About Web page (www.scsite.com/wd2000/more.htm) and then click Viruses.

Digital Signatures

A digital signature is a digital identification code that you can attach to a macro so that a user can verify the macro's legitimacy. To attach a digital signature, you must have a digital certificate installed on your computer. For more information on digital signatures, search for help using the phrase, protecting documents from viruses.

Table 9-1 Word Security Levels

SECURITY LEVEL	CONDITION
High	Word will execute only macros that are digitally signed. All other macros are disabled when the document is opened.
Medium	Upon opening a document that contains macros from an unknown source, Word displays a dialog box asking if you wish to enable the macros.
Low	Word turns off macro virus protection. The document is opened with all macros enabled, including those from unknown sources.

If Word security is set to high and you attach a macro to a document, Word will disable that macro when you open the document. Because you will be creating macros in this project, you should ensure that your security level is set to medium. Thus, each time you open this Word document or any other document that contains a macro from an unknown source, Word displays a dialog box warning that a macro is attached and allows you to enable or disable the macros. If you are confident of the source (author) of the document and macros, you should click the Enable Macros button in the dialog box. If you are uncertain about the reliability of the source of the document and macros, then you should click the Disable Macros button.

Perform the following steps to set Word's security level to medium.

To Set a Security Level in Word

1 Click Tools on the menu bar, point to Macro, and then point to Security (Figure 9-4).

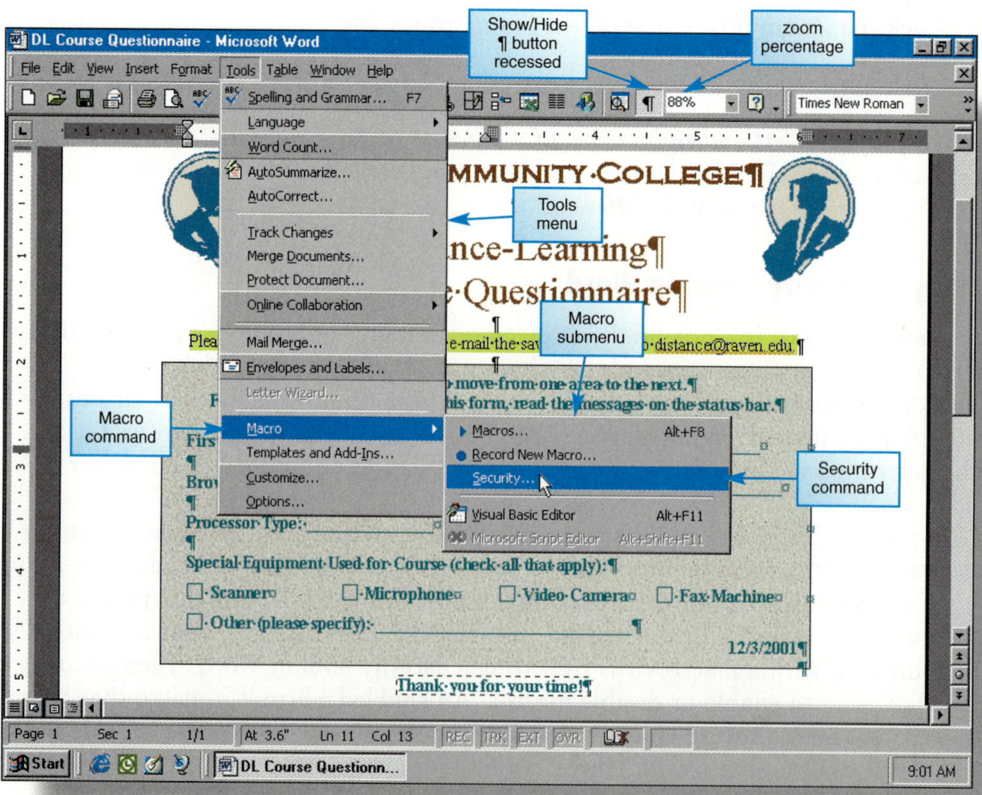

FIGURE 9-4

Click Security. When the Security dialog box displays, if necessary, click the Security Level tab. Click Medium and then point to the OK button.

Word displays the Security dialog box (Figure 9-5). The Medium option button is selected.

3 Click the OK button.

Word sets its security level to medium.

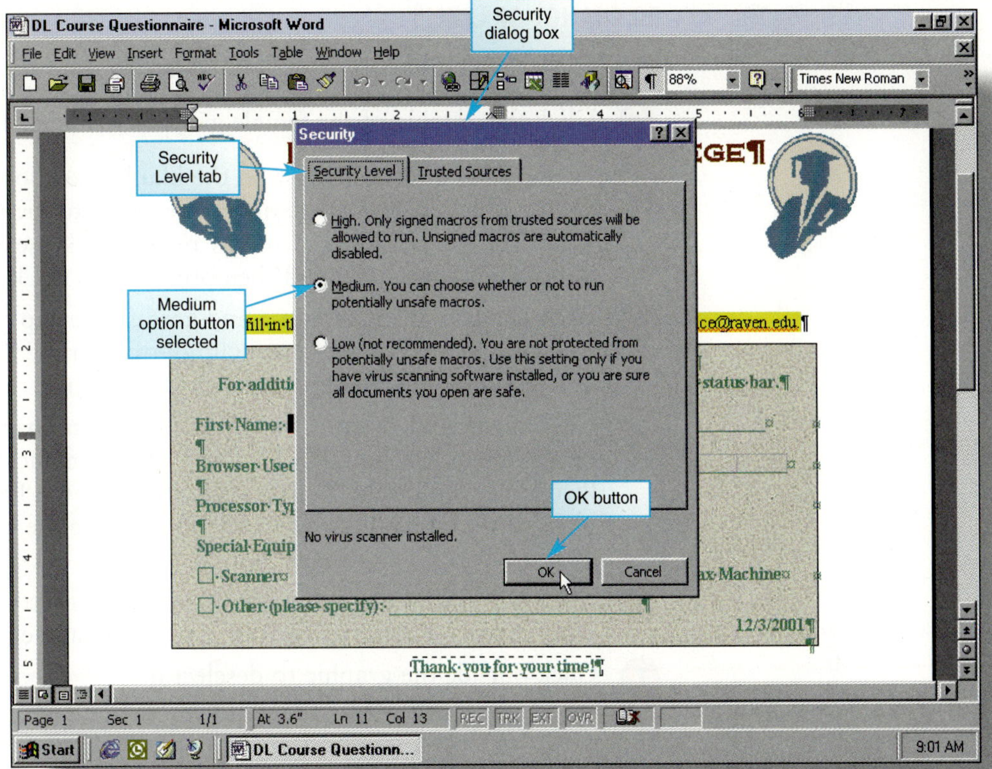

FIGURE 9-5

The next time you open a document that contains a macro from an unauthorized source, Word will ask if you wish to enable or disable them.

Modifying a Form

As requested by your supervisor, you will change the look of the Distance-Learning Course Questionnaire. You will change the graphics, the fonts, the font sizes, the highlight color, and the fill inside the rectangle drawing object. The following pages discuss how you modify the online form.

Modifying Graphics, Fonts, and Font Sizes

The first step in modifying the online form is to remove the existing graphics of the male and female graduates and insert a new graphic of a graduation cap and diploma. The new clip art image is too large for the form; thus, you will reduce it to 40 percent of its original size. Because Word inserts the clip art image as inline, you will change it to floating by clicking the Square command on the Text Wrapping menu. Then, you will move the graphic to the right of the college name and form name. Perform the steps on the next page to change the graphics on the form.

TO CHANGE GRAPHICS

1. Click the graphic of the male graduate to select it. Press the DELETE key.
2. Click the graphic of the female graduate to select it. Press the DELETE key.
3. Position the insertion point on the blank line above the text highlighted in yellow. Click Insert on the menu bar, point to Picture, and then click Clip Art. When the Insert ClipArt window opens, click the Search for clips text box. Type `graduation cap` and then press the ENTER key.
4. Click the clip of the diploma and graduation cap that matches the one shown in Figure 9-6. Click the Insert clip button on the Pop-up menu. Click the Close button on the Insert ClipArt window's title bar.
5. Click the graphic to select it. If the Picture toolbar does not display, click View on the menu bar, point to Toolbars, and then click Picture. Click the Format Picture button on the Picture toolbar. When the Format Picture dialog box displays, if necessary, click the Size tab. Change the Height and Width in the Scale area to 40%. Click the OK button.
6. Click the Text Wrapping button on the Picture toolbar and then click Square. Drag the graphic to the right of the college name as shown in Figure 9-6.
7. Click outside the graphic to deselect it.

The graphic is resized and positioned as shown in Figure 9-6.

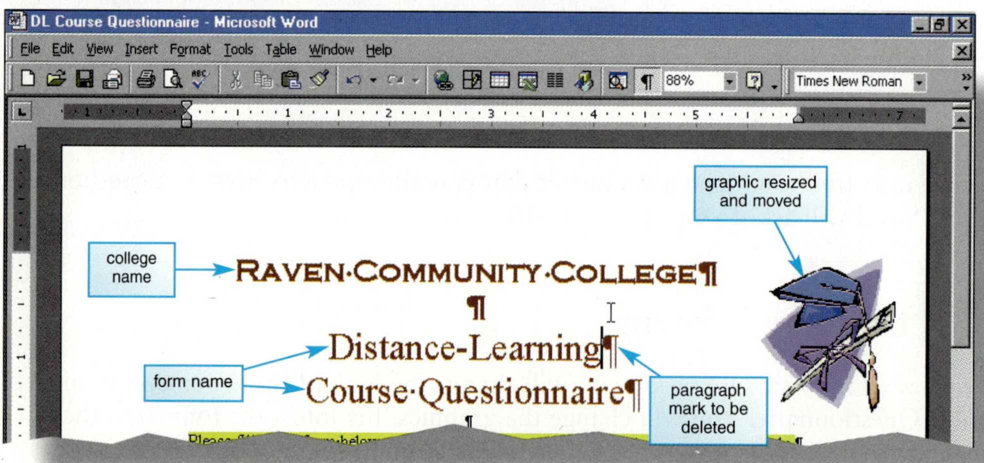

FIGURE 9-6

The next step in modifying the Distance-Learning Course Questionnaire is to change the alignment, font, font style, font size, and color of the college name and form name as described in the following steps.

TO MODIFY TEXT

1. Select the line containing the college name, Raven Community College. Right-click the selection and then click Font on the shortcut menu. When the Font dialog box displays, if necessary, click the Font tab. Scroll to and then click Bookman Old Style in the Font list. Click Bold Italic in the Font style list. Scroll to and then click 28 in the Size list. Click the Font color box arrow and then click Light Blue. Click Shadow in the Effects area. Click the OK button.

2. Double-click the move handle on the Formatting toolbar to display the entire toolbar. Click the Align Left button on the Formatting toolbar.
3. Click the paragraph mark following the word, Learning, in the form name, Distance-Learning (see Figure 9-6). Press the DELETE key to remove the paragraph mark.
4. Press the SPACEBAR. Select the two lines containing the form name, Distance-Learning Course Questionnaire. Right-click the selection and then click Font on the shortcut menu. When the Font dialog box displays, if necessary, click the Font tab. Scroll to and then click Arial Narrow in the Font list. If necessary, click Regular in the Font style list. Click 24 in the Size list. Click the Font color box arrow and then click Lavender. Click the OK button.
5. Click the paragraph mark below the selected form name. Press the ENTER key to insert another blank line between the form name and the yellow highlighted text.

The college name and form name display as shown in Figure 9-7.

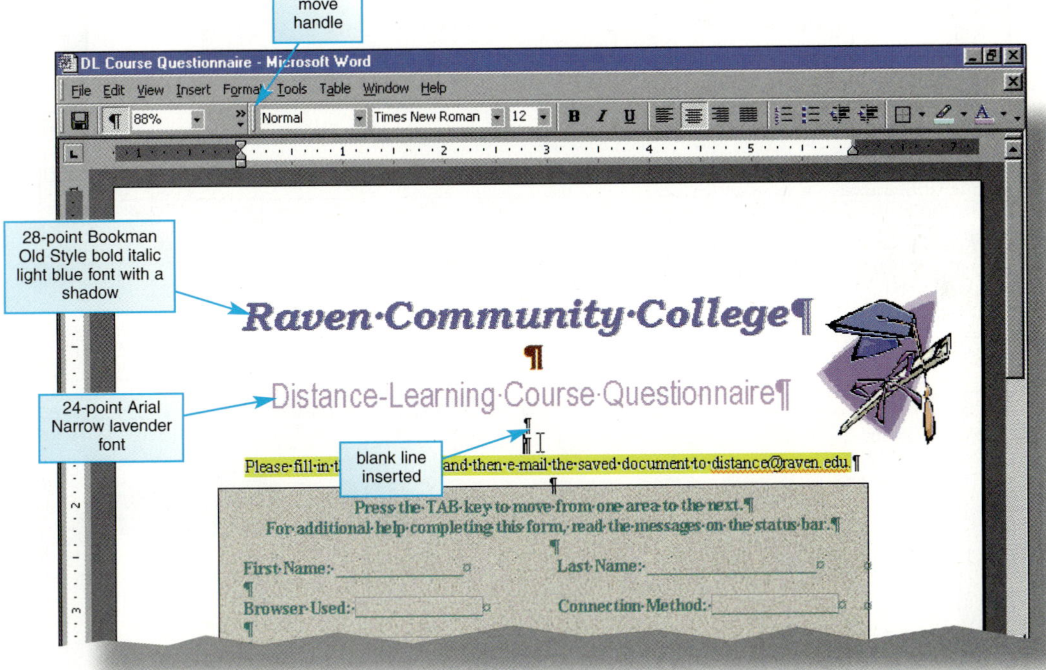

FIGURE 9-7

The next step is to format the first character of the college name as a drop cap.

Formatting a Character as an In Margin Drop Cap

You can format the first character or word to be dropped in a paragraph. A **dropped capital letter**, or **drop cap**, appears larger than the rest of the characters in the paragraph. In Word, text in the paragraph can wrap around the dropped character or the drop cap can display in the margin to the left of the paragraph text. Word refers to the latter as an in margin drop cap. Perform the steps on the next page to format a character as an in margin drop cap.

Drop Caps

In the desktop publishing field, an in margin drop cap sometimes is referred to as a stick-up cap. If you wanted text to wrap around a drop cap instead of extending it into the margin, you would click Dropped in the Drop Cap dialog box.

Steps To Format a Character as an In Margin Drop Cap

1 **Position the insertion point in the paragraph to contain the drop cap, in this case, the college name. Click Format on the menu bar and then click Drop Cap. When the Drop Cap dialog box displays, click In Margin and then point to the OK button.**

Word displays the Drop Cap dialog box (Figure 9-8).

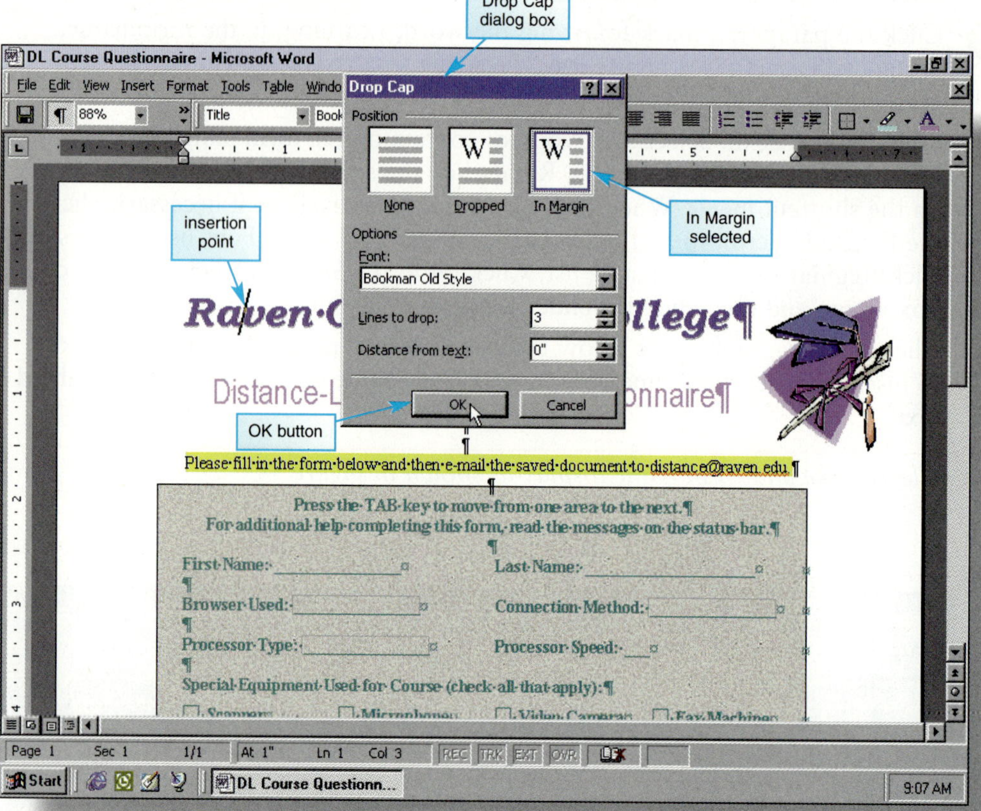

FIGURE 9-8

2 **Click the OK button.**

Word drops the letter R into the margin of the document and places a text frame around the drop cap (Figure 9-9). Notice that the right edge of the letter R is ***truncated****, or chopped off.*

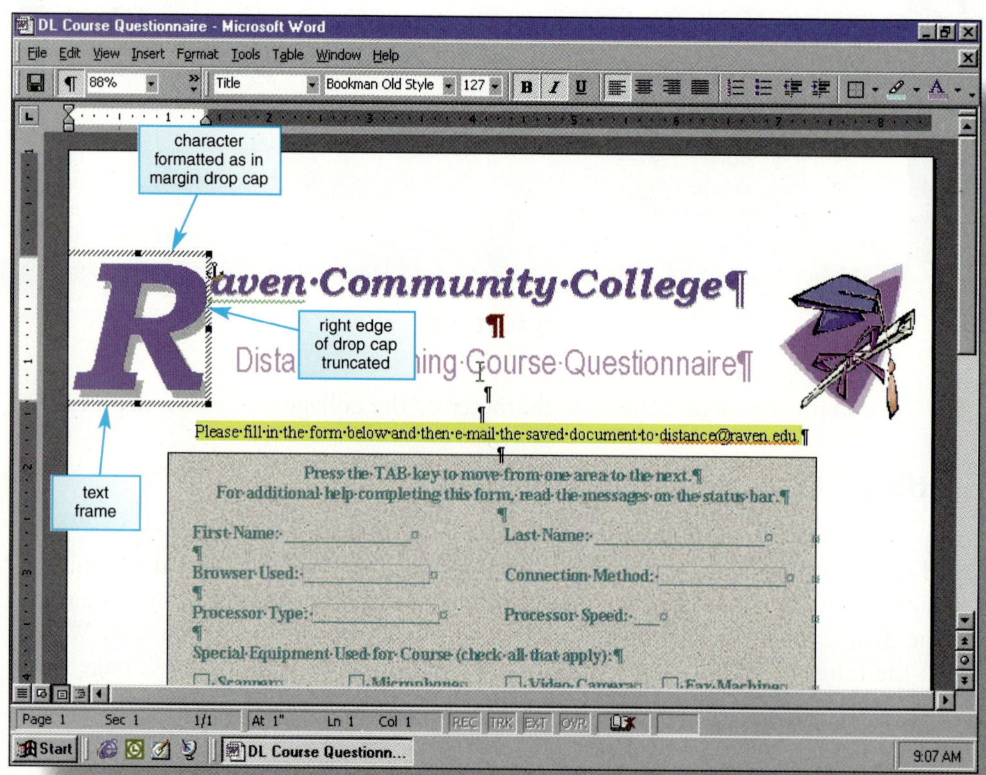

FIGURE 9-9

3 **Drag the right-middle sizing handle on the text frame rightward until the entire drop cap displays. With the text frame selected, click the Font Size box on the Formatting toolbar, type** `121` **as the new font size, and then press the ENTER key. Point to an edge of the text frame until the mouse pointer displays a four-headed arrow and then drag the drop cap rightward and align it with the college name as shown in Figure 9-10. If necessary, drag the graphic of the diploma and cap to the left so the top of the form is centered.**

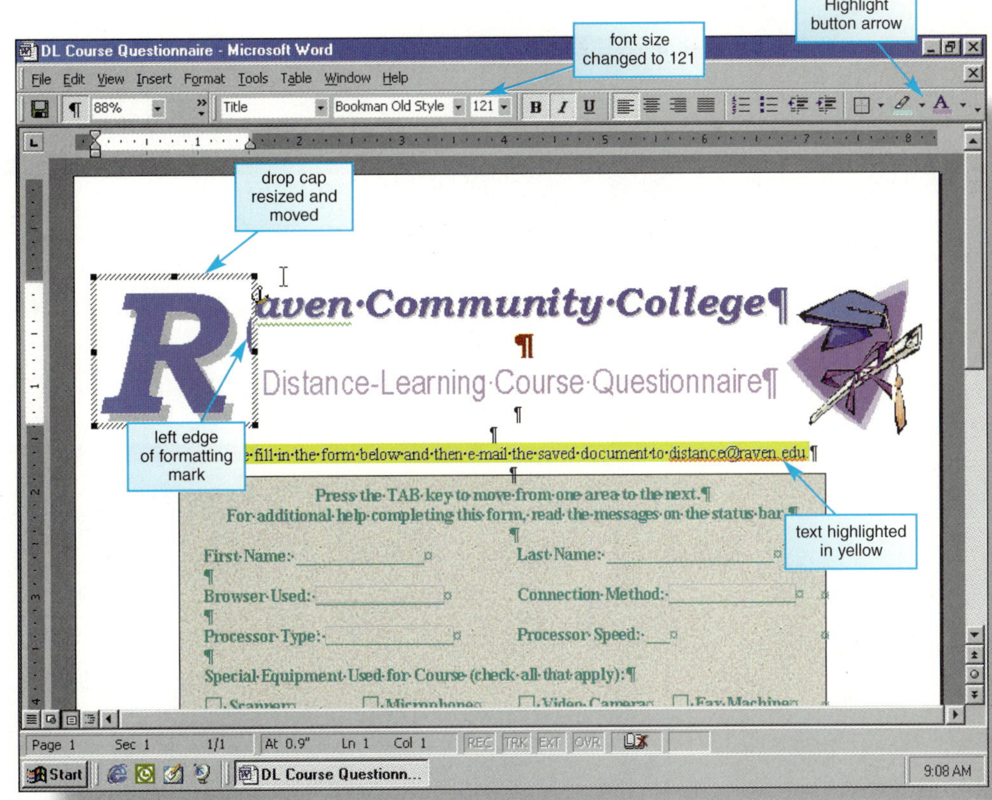

FIGURE 9-10

As shown in Figure 9-9, Word places a text frame around a drop cap. A **text frame** is a container for text that allows you to position the text anywhere on the page. The text inside the text frame is a separate paragraph and, thus, ends with a proofreaders paragraph mark. In Figure 9-10, notice that only the left edge of the paragraph mark displays. Depending on your settings, a portion of this paragraph mark may or may not display on your screen. This formatting mark will not print. Also, if you click the Show/Hide ¶ button on the Standard toolbar, the paragraph mark will disappear from the screen.

As illustrated in the previous steps, you also can resize a text frame. To remove the frame from displaying in the document window, simply click outside the frame to display the insertion point elsewhere in the document.

The next step is to change the highlight color of the format instructions from yellow to pink as described in the following steps.

TO CHANGE A HIGHLIGHT COLOR

1. Select the form instructions that currently are highlighted in yellow.
2. Click the Highlight button arrow on the Formatting toolbar and then click Pink.

Word changes the highlight on the form instructions from yellow to pink (Figure 9-11 on the next page).

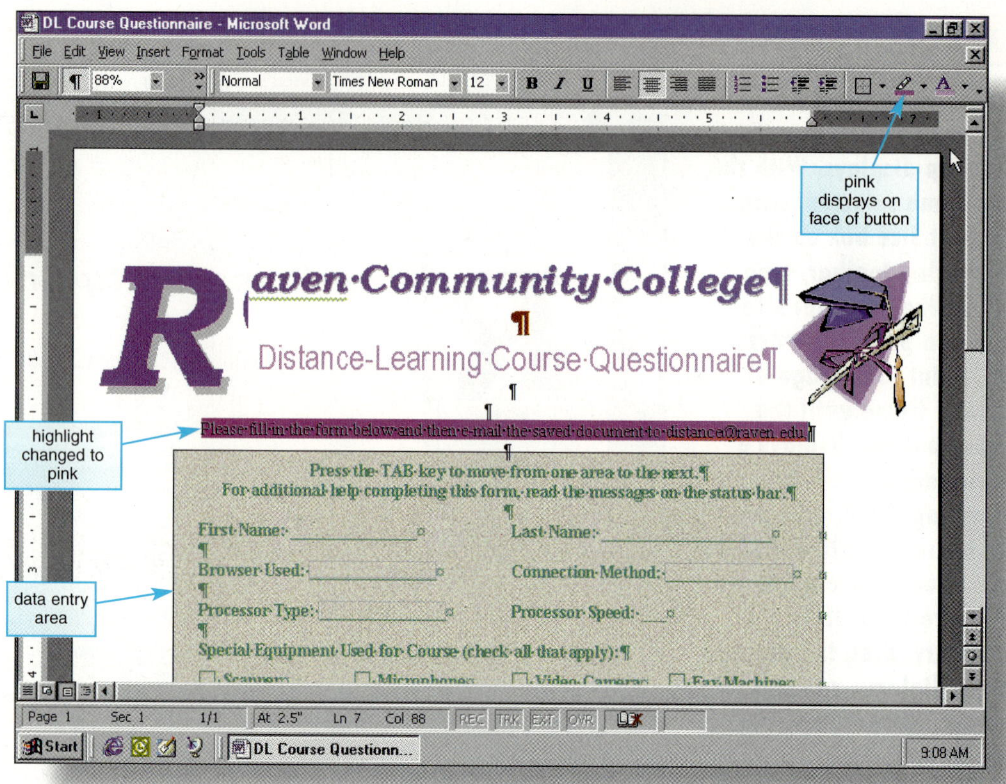

FIGURE 9-11

The next step is to change the format of the text in the data entry area.

Creating a New Style

All text in the data entry area should be formatted to 11-point Arial bold indigo font. You could select each text item in the data entry area, one at a time, and change its font to Arial, its font size to 11, its font style to bold, and its font color to indigo.

A timesaving alternative is to use a style. A **style** is a customized format that you can apply to text. Although Word has many built-in styles, none of them is an 11-point Arial bold indigo font. Thus, you can create your own new style and then apply this style to the text in the data entry area of the form.

Word has two types of styles: character and paragraph. A **character style** defines attributes for selected text such as font, font size, and font style. A **paragraph style** defines formatting for a paragraph such as line spacing, text alignment, and borders. Paragraph styles also can include a character style definition. In the data entry area of this form, you want to change text to 11-point Arial bold indigo font. Thus, you will create a character style.

Perform the following steps to create a new character style, called DataEntryArea, that formats selected text to 11-point Arial bold indigo font.

Styles

To create a character style, click the Style type box arrow in the New Style dialog box and then click Character. To create a paragraph style, click the Style type box arrow in the New Style dialog box and then click Paragraph. If you accidentally create a paragraph style for a character style, all current paragraph formatting will be applied to the selected text. In this case, for example, a paragraph style would include the centered format.

To Create a Style that has a Shortcut Key

1 Click Format on the menu bar and then click Style. When the Style dialog box displays, point to the New button.

Word displays the Style dialog box (Figure 9-12). Your list of styles may be different.

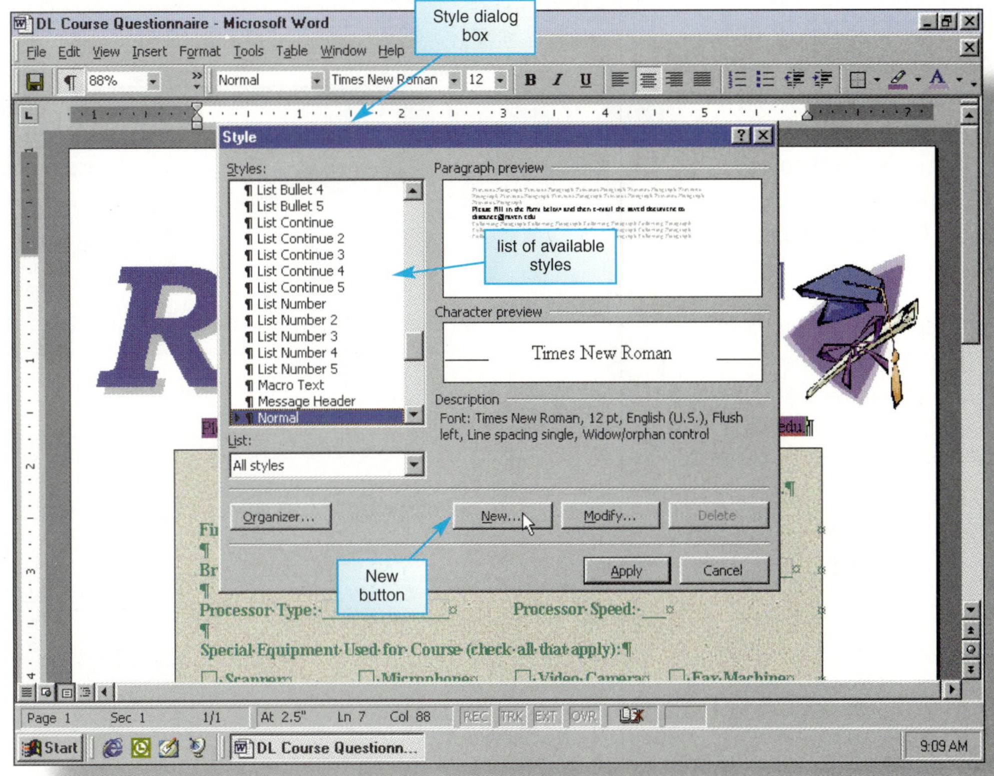

FIGURE 9-12

2 Click the New button. When the New Style dialog box displays, type `DataEntryArea` **in the Name text box. Click the Style type box arrow and then click Character. Click the Format button and then point to Font.**

Word displays the New Style dialog box (Figure 9-13). A list of available formatting commands displays above or below the Format button. Some commands are dimmed because they relate to paragraph styles.

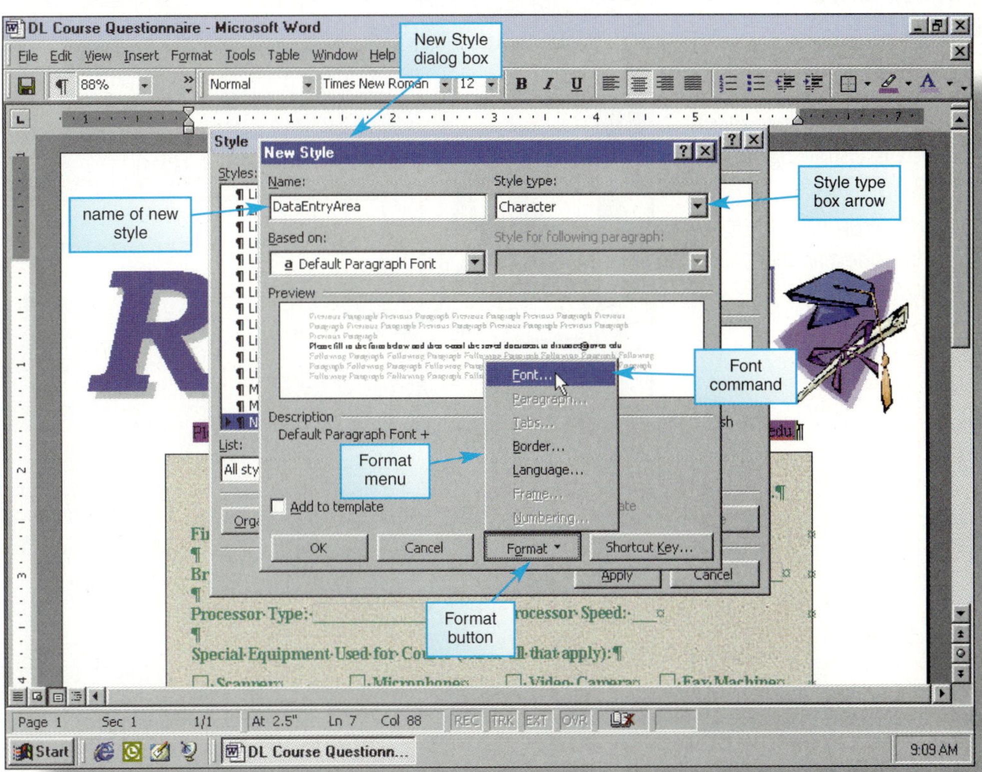

FIGURE 9-13

3 **Click Font. When the Font dialog box displays, if necessary, click the Font tab. Scroll to and click Arial in the Font list. Click Bold in the Font style list. Click 11 in the Size list. Click the Font color button arrow and then click Indigo. Point to the OK button.**

Word displays the Font dialog box (Figure 9-14). The Preview area reflects the current settings in the dialog box.

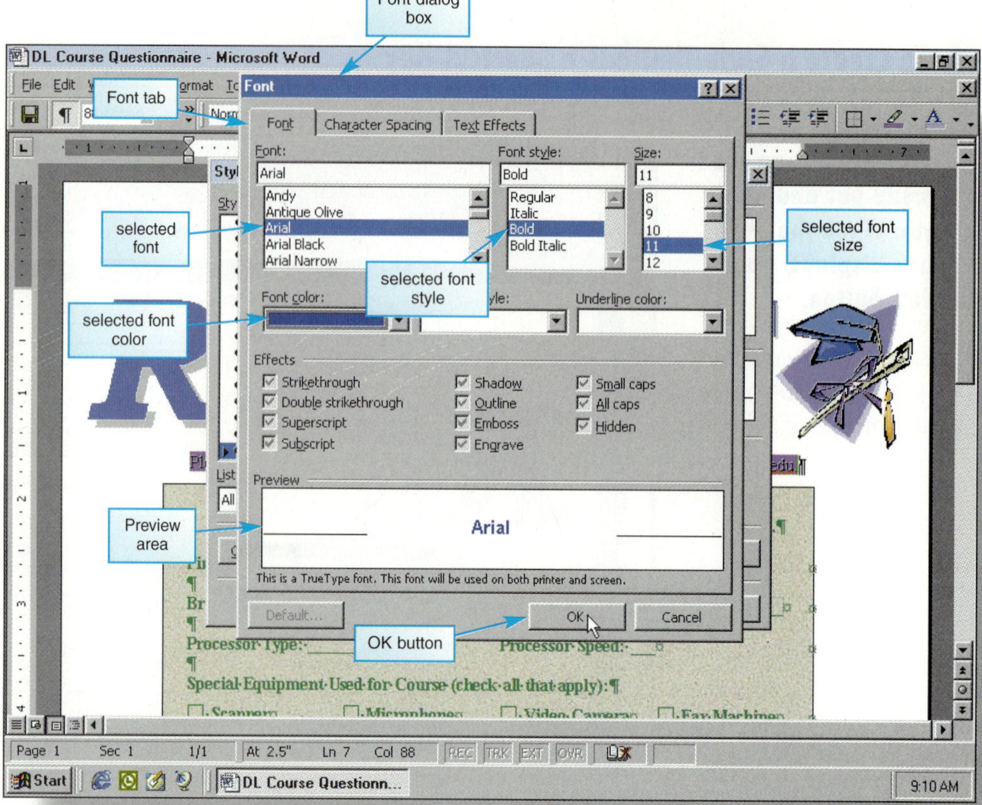

FIGURE 9-14

4 **Click the OK button. Point to the Shortcut Key button in the New Style dialog box.**

Word closes the Font dialog box and the entire New Style dialog box is visible again (Figure 9-15). The Description area lists the formatting assigned to the DataEntryArea style.

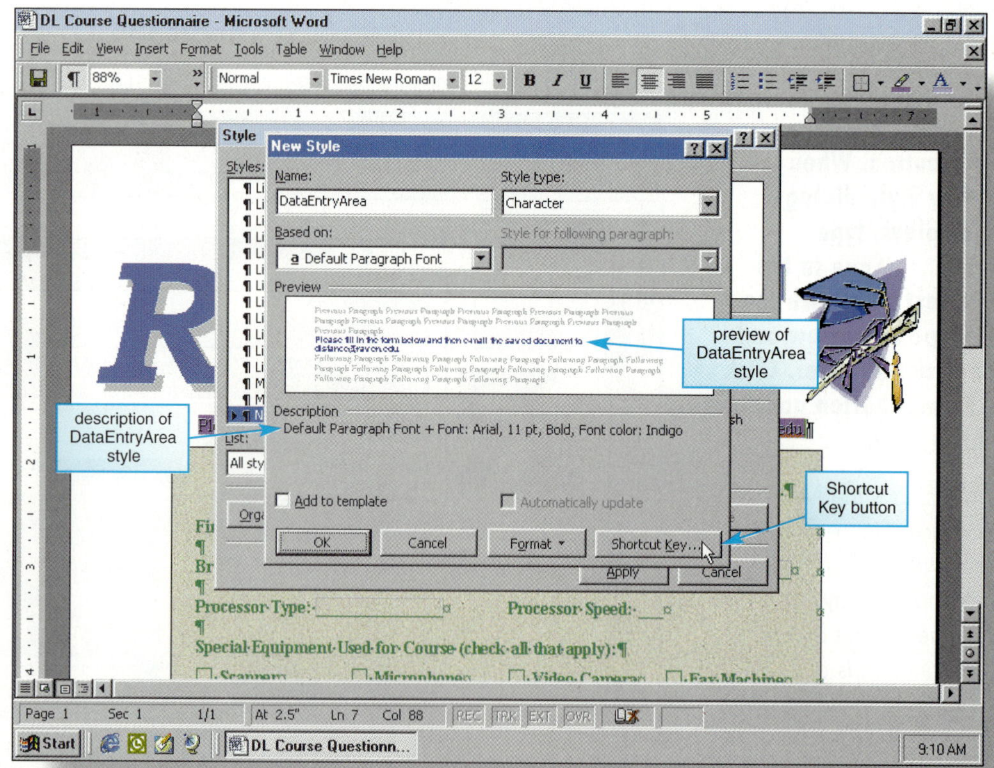

FIGURE 9-15

5 Click the Shortcut Key button. When the Customize Keyboard dialog box displays, press the ALT+C keys. Point to the Assign button.

Word displays the Customize Keyboard dialog box (Figure 9-16). The characters you pressed, ALT+C, display in the Press new shortcut key text box.

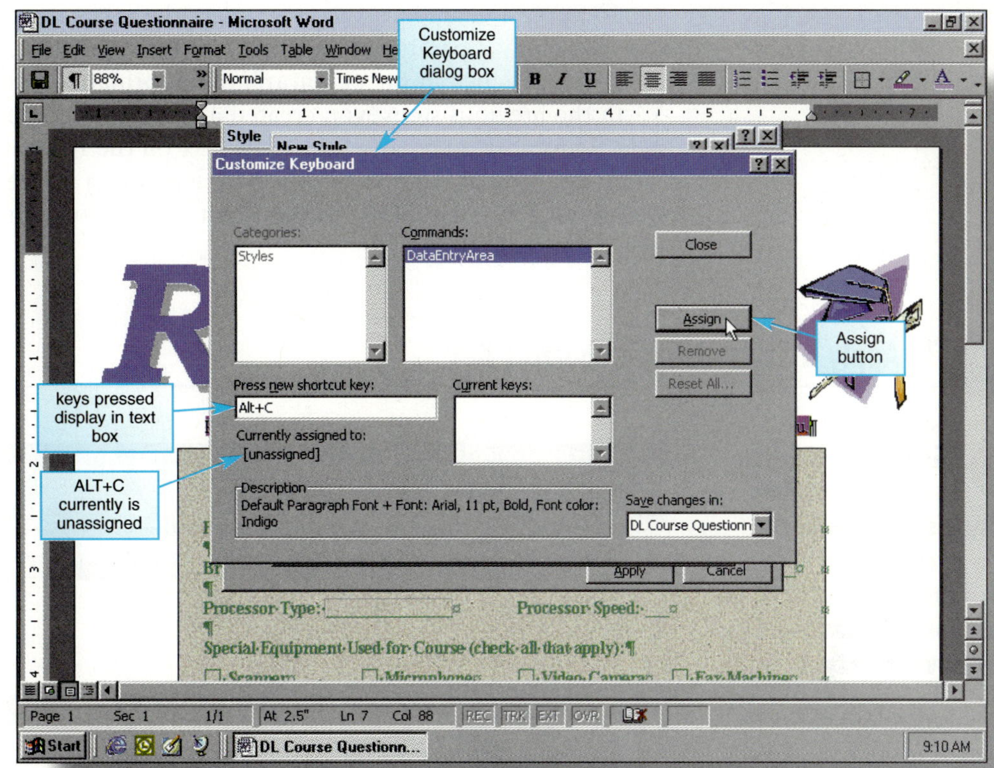

FIGURE 9-16

6 Click the Assign button. Point to the Close button.

Word assigns the shortcut key, ALT+C, to the style named DataEntryArea (Figure 9-17).

7 Click the Close button. When the entire New Style dialog box is visible again, click its OK button. When the entire Style dialog box is visible again, click its Close button.

Word creates the DataEntryArea style along with its shortcut key, ALT+C.

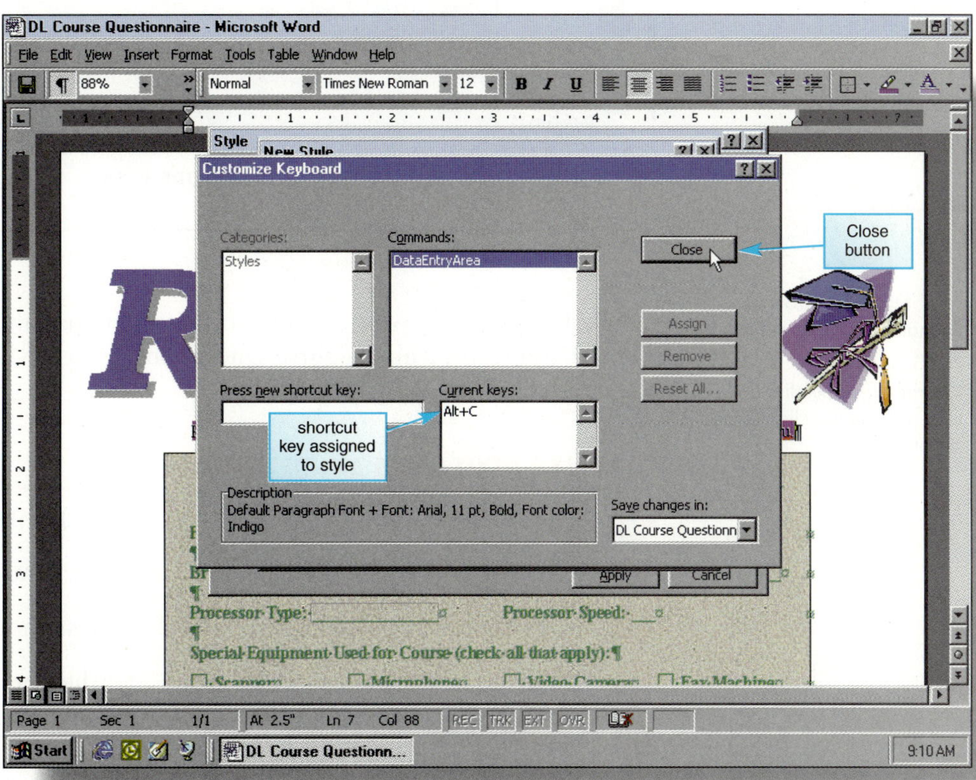

FIGURE 9-17

To apply a character style, you select the text to be formatted and then apply the style. To apply a paragraph style, you do not need to select text before applying the style – simply click in the paragraph to be formatted and then apply the style.

In the previous steps, you created a shortcut key of ALT+C for the DataEntryArea style. Thus, instead of using the Style box on the Formatting toolbar to apply the DataEntryArea style to text in the data entry area of the Distance-Learning Course Questionnaire, you will use the shortcut key. Perform the following step to apply a style using a shortcut key.

To Apply a Style Using a Shortcut Key

1 Select the first two sentences of data entry instructions in the data entry area of the form. Press the ALT+C keys. Click outside the selection to remove the highlight.

Word formats the selected text to 11-point Arial bold indigo font (Figure 9-18).

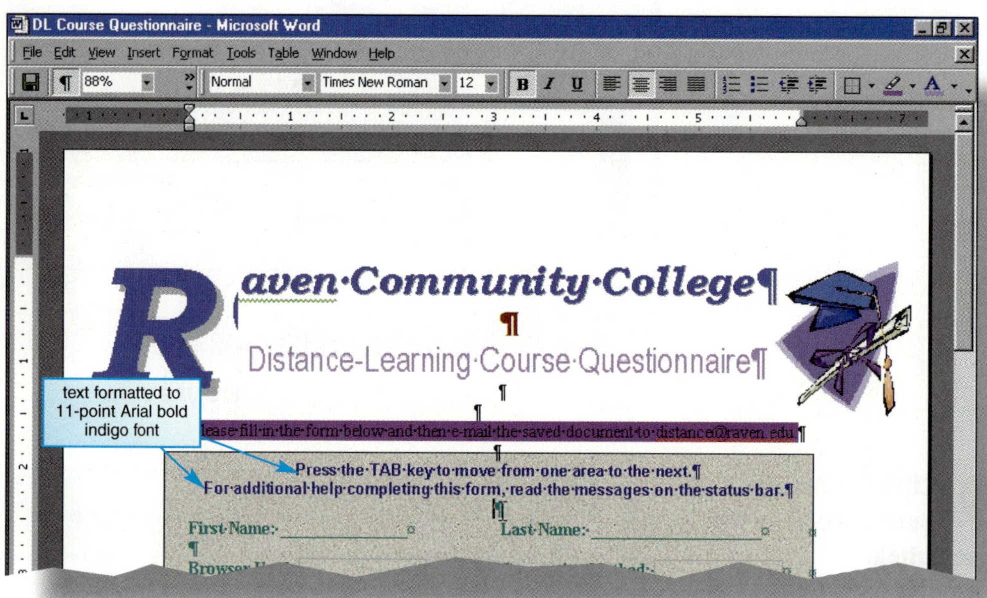

FIGURE 9-18

Other Ways

1. Click Style box arrow on Formatting toolbar, click style name
2. On Format menu click Style, click style name, click Apply button

Perform the following steps to format the remaining text in the data entry area of the Distance-Learning Course Questionnaire to the DataEntryArea style using the ALT+C keys.

TO APPLY A STYLE USING A SHORTCUT KEY

1. Select the text, First Name:, and then press the ALT+C keys.
2. Select the text, Last Name:, and then press the ALT+C keys.
3. Select the text, Browser Used:, and then press the ALT+C keys.
4. Select the text, Connection Method:, and then press the ALT+C keys.
5. Select the text, Processor Type:, and then press the ALT+C keys.
6. Select the text, Processor Speed:, and then press the ALT+C keys.
7. Select the text, Special Equipment Used for Course (check all that apply):, and then press the ALT+C keys.

8. Select the text, Scanner, and then press the ALT+C keys.
9. Select the text, Microphone, and then press the ALT+C keys.
10. Select the text, Video Camera, and then press the ALT+C keys.
11. Select the text, Fax Machine, and then press the ALT+C keys.
12. Select the text, Other (please specify):, and then press the ALT+C keys.
13. Select the date in the lower-right corner of the data entry area and then press the ALT+C keys. Click outside the selection to remove the highlight.

The text in the data entry area is formatted to 11-point Arial bold indigo font (Figure 9-19).

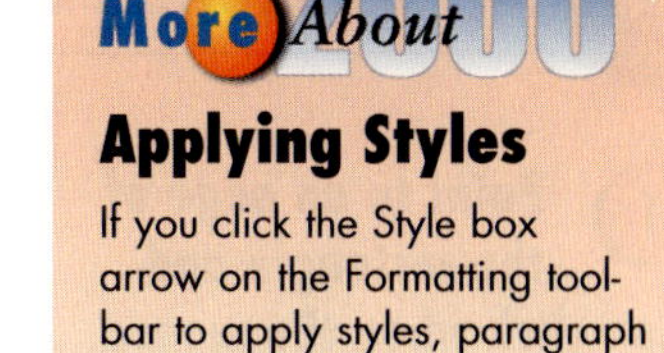

Applying Styles

If you click the Style box arrow on the Formatting toolbar to apply styles, paragraph style names display a proofreader's paragraph mark and character style names display an underlined letter a.

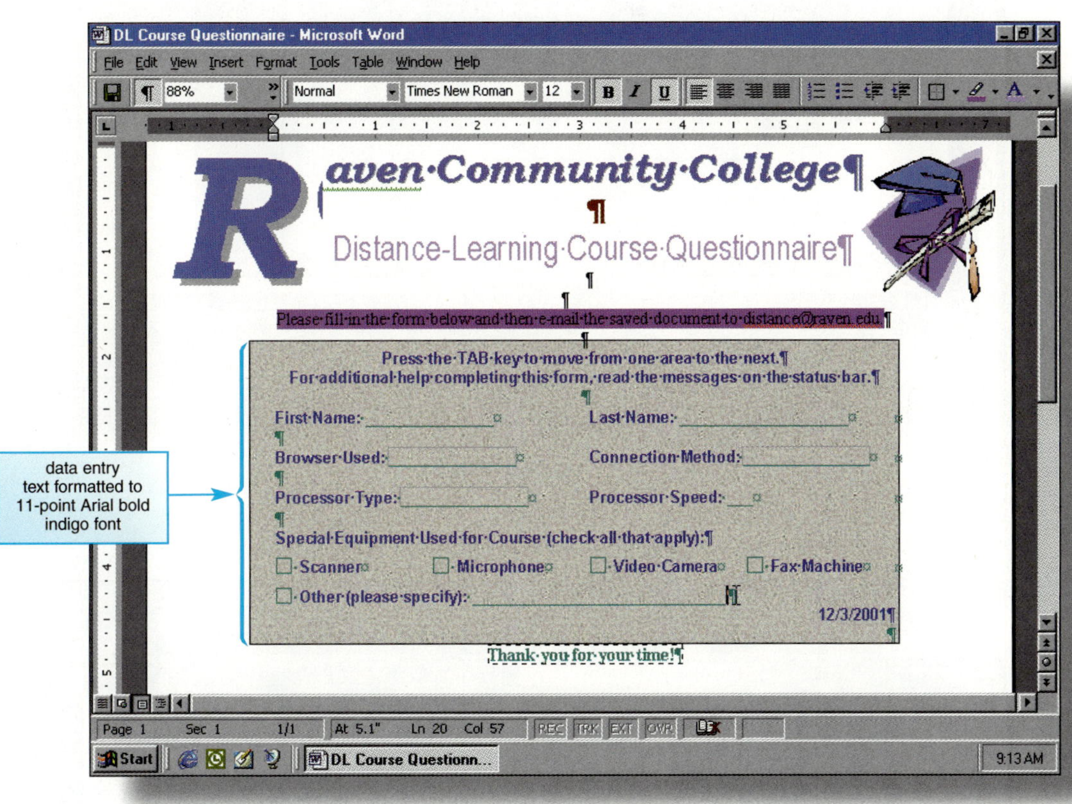

FIGURE 9-19

Filling a Drawing Object with a Bitmap Picture

The data entry area in the form is surrounded with a rectangle drawing object, which currently is filled with the recycled paper texture. Other available fill effects include gradient (two-toned) colors, patterns, and pictures. In this project, you want a bitmap picture in the rectangle drawing object. A **bitmap** is a graphic composed of rows and columns of dots that form a picture.

Windows includes several bitmap files that it uses for wallpaper. These bitmap files often are stored in the Windows folder on the hard drive or server. You will use the one called Clouds as fill in the rectangle drawing object. If you cannot locate the Clouds bitmap file, it also is on the Data Disk. If you did not download the Data Disk, see the inside back cover for instructions for downloading the Data Disk.

Perform the steps on the next page to fill the rectangle with the Clouds bitmap file.

To Fill a Drawing Object with a Bitmap Picture

1 **Point to an edge of the rectangle and then click when the mouse pointer has a four-headed arrow attached to it. Double-click the move handle on the Standard toolbar to display the entire toolbar. If the Drawing toolbar is not on the screen, click the Drawing button on the Standard toolbar. Click the Fill Color button arrow on the Drawing toolbar and then click the Fill Effects button. When the Fill Effects dialog box displays, if necessary, click the Picture tab. Point to the Select Picture button.**

Word displays the Fill Effects dialog box (Figure 9-20). The rectangle is selected.

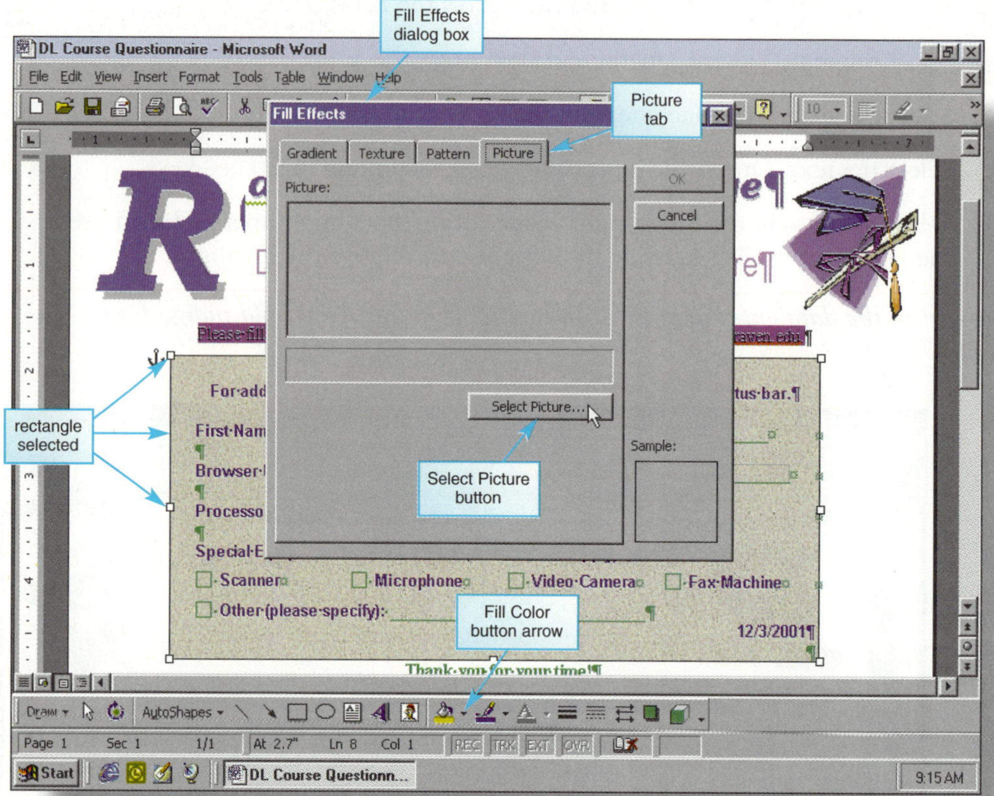

FIGURE 9-20

2 **Click the Select Picture button. Use the Look in box to locate the Clouds bitmap file on your computer or on the Data Disk. Click Clouds in the list and then point to the Insert button.**

Word displays the Select Picture dialog box (Figure 9-21). Depending on your computer settings, a sample of the Clouds bitmap file may or may not display as a preview.

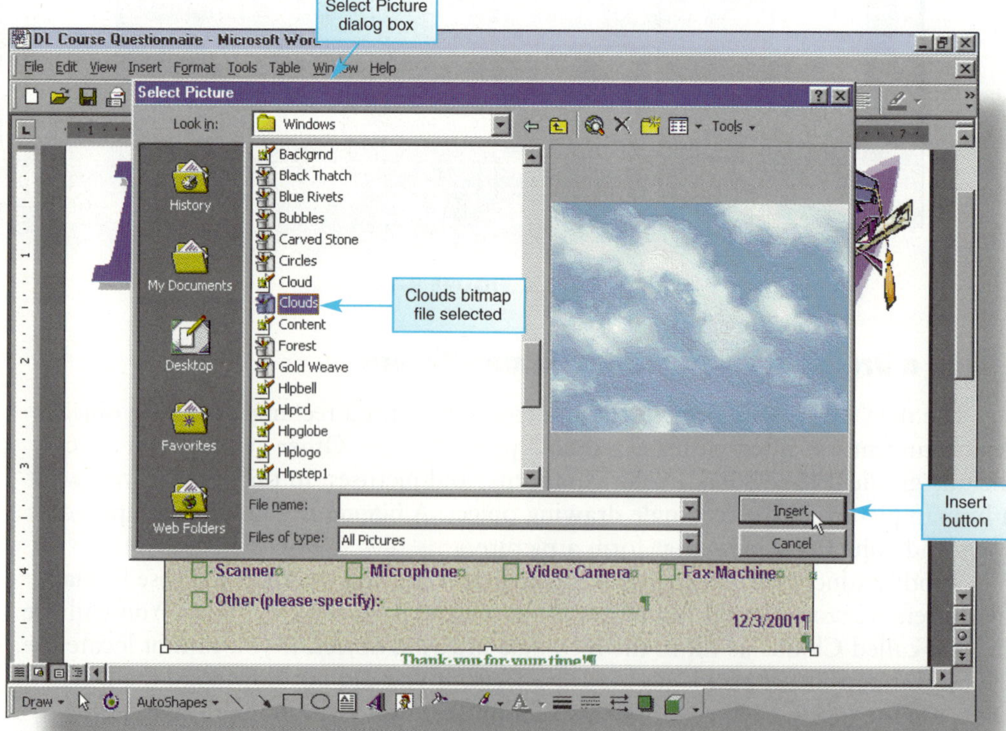

FIGURE 9-21

3 **Click the Insert button. When the entire Fill Effects dialog box is visible again, point to its OK button.**

Word displays the selected picture in the Picture area of the Fill Effects dialog box (Figure 9-22).

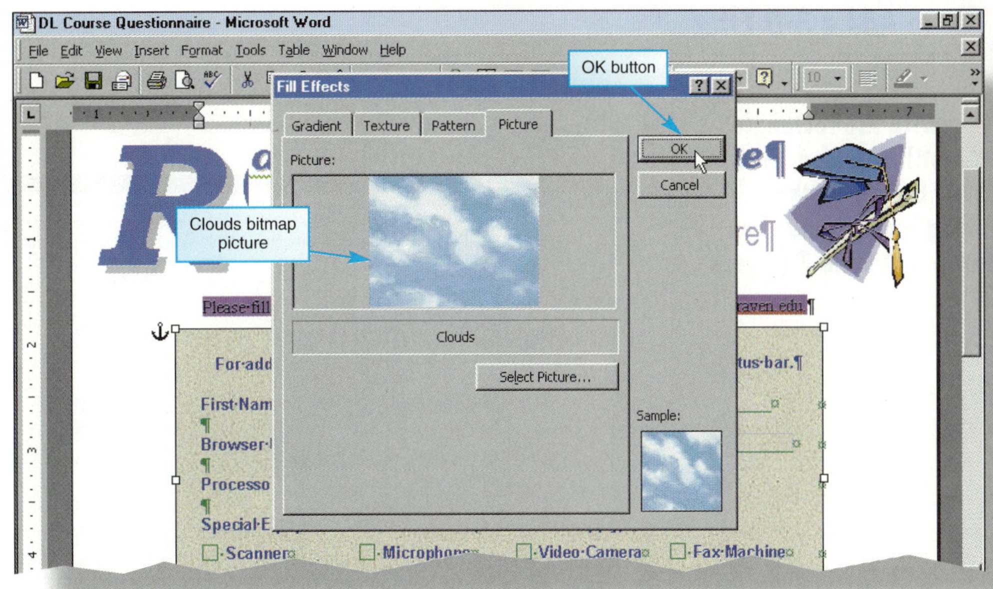

FIGURE 9-22

4 **Click the OK button.**

Word fills the rectangle with the Clouds bitmap picture (Figure 9-23).

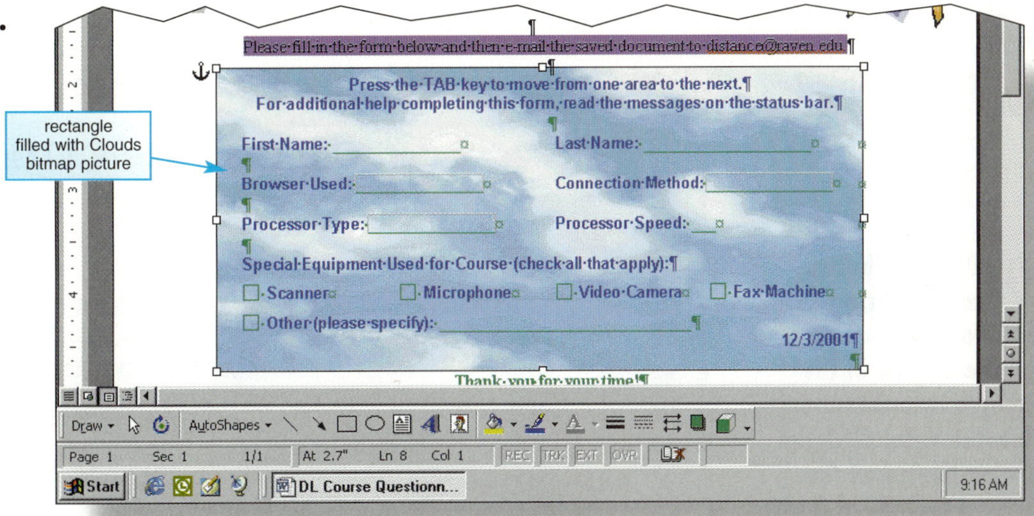

FIGURE 9-23

> ## Other Ways
> 1. Right-click edge of drawing object, click Format AutoShape on shortcut menu, click Colors and Lines tab, click Fill Color button arrow, click Fill Effects button, click Picture tab
> 2. Select drawing object, click Format AutoShape on Format menu, click Colors and Lines tab, click Fill Color button arrow, click Fill Effects button, click Picture tab

Notice in Figure 9-23 that Word stretches the picture so that it fills the entire drawing object.

The next step is to add a 3-D effect to the rectangle.

Adding a 3-D Effect to a Drawing Object

You can add a shadow or a 3-D effect to a drawing object by using the Shadow button and 3-D buttons on the Drawing toolbar, respectively. Perform the steps on the next page to add a 3-D effect to the rectangle surrounding the data entry area of the Distance-Learning Course Questionnaire.

To Add a 3-D Effect

1 **With the rectangle still selected, click the 3-D button on the Drawing toolbar and then point to 3-D Style 7 (Figure 9-24).**

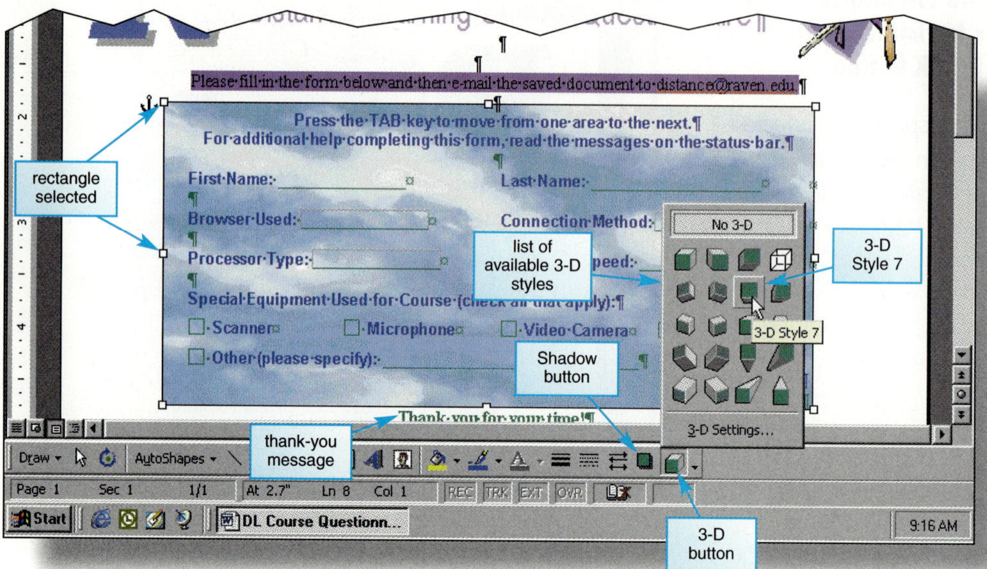

FIGURE 9-24

2 **Click 3-D Style 7.**

Word adds the 3-D Style 7 effect to the rectangle.

3 **Drag the bottom-middle sizing handle on the rectangle up until the bottom of the rectangle is immediately below the date. Click the Drawing button on the Standard toolbar to remove the Drawing toolbar. Delete the line below the data entry area that contains the thank-you message.**

The online form displays as shown in Figure 9-25.

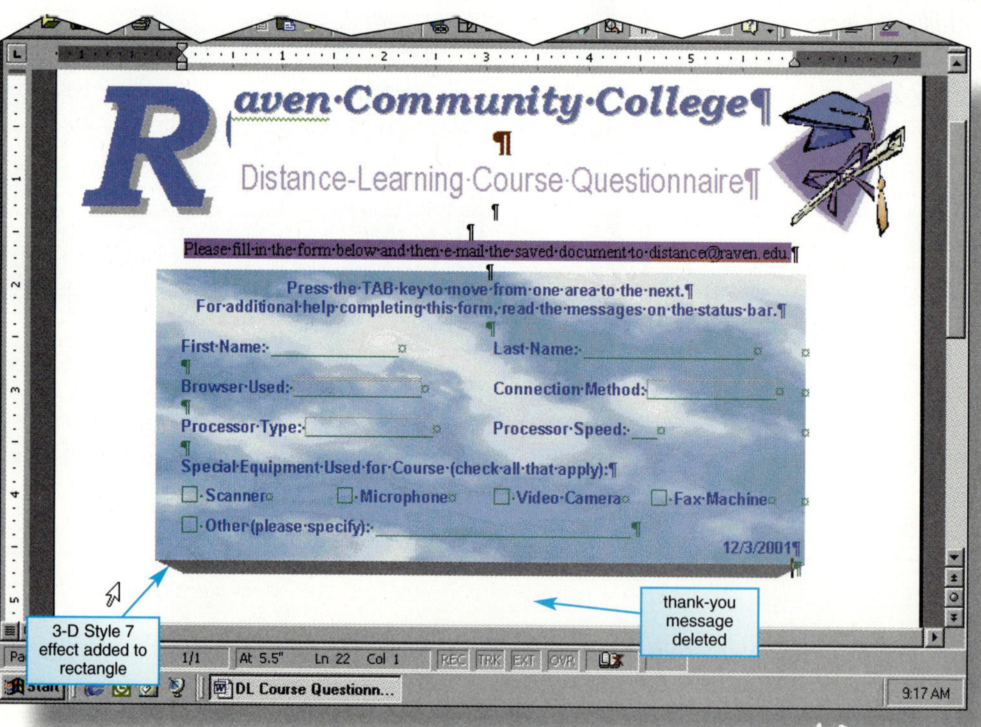

FIGURE 9-25

If you wanted to add a shadow instead of a 3-D effect, you would click the Shadow button on the Drawing toolbar (see Figure 9-24).

Because you have performed many formatting tasks thus far, perform the following step to save the form again.

TO SAVE A DOCUMENT

1. Click the Save button on the Standard toolbar.

Word saves the DL Course Questionnaire on a floppy disk in drive A.

3-D Effects

You can change the color, rotation, depth, lighting, or texture of a 3-D effect by using the 3-D Settings toolbar. To display this toolbar, click the 3-D button on the Drawing toolbar and then click the 3-D Settings button in the list.

Using a Macro to Automate a Task

As previously discussed, a macro consists of a series of Word commands or instructions that are grouped together as a single command. This single command is a convenient way to automate a difficult or lengthy task. Macros often are used for formatting or editing activities, to combine multiple commands into a single command, or to select an option in a dialog box with a single keystroke.

To create a macro, you can use the macro recorder or the Visual Basic Editor. The following pages discuss how to use the macro recorder to create a macro. Later in this project, you use the Visual Basic Editor to create a macro.

Recording and Executing a Macro

When you receive filled-in forms from users, your next step will be to analyze the data on the forms. Often, you want to use database software, such as Access, to assist you in analyzing the responses on the forms. You have learned that you must save the data on each questionnaire in a comma-delimited text file so that Access can use the data. To do this, you must place a check mark in the Save data only for forms check box in the Save sheet in the Options dialog box – prior to clicking the Save button on the Standard toolbar.

If you receive 70 completed forms, then you will be performing the following steps 70 times: click Tools on the menu bar, click Options, click the Save tab, place a check mark in the Save data only for forms check box, and then click the OK button. A timesaving alternative is to create a macro that places the check mark in the check box. Then, you simply execute the macro and click the Save button. Thus, the purpose of the first macro you create in this project is to select an option in a dialog box.

Word has a **macro recorder** that creates a macro automatically based on a series of actions you perform while it is recording. The macro recorder is similar to a video camera in that it records all actions you perform on a document over a period of time. Once you turn on the macro recorder, it records your activities; when you are finished recording activities, you turn off the macro recorder to stop the recording. After you have recorded a macro, you can **execute the macro**, or play it back, any time you want to perform that same set of actions.

To create the macro that will place a check mark in the Save data only for forms check box, you will follow this sequence of steps:

1. Start the macro recorder and specify options about the macro.
2. Place a check mark in the Save data only for forms check box in the Save sheet in the Options dialog box.
3. Stop the macro recorder.

The impressive feature of the macro recorder is that you actually step through the task as you create the macro – allowing you to see exactly what the macro will do before you use it.

When you first create the macro, you have to name it. The name for this macro is FormDataOnly. **Macro names** can be up to 255 characters long; they can contain numbers, letters, and underscores; they cannot contain spaces and other punctuation.

Earlier in this project, you assigned a shortcut key to a style. Likewise, you can assign a shortcut key to a macro, which allows you to run the macro by using its name or by pressing the shortcut key. Perform the following steps to record the macro and assign ALT+D as its shortcut key.

Steps To Record a Macro

1 Double-click the REC status indicator on the status bar. When the Record Macro dialog box displays, type `FormDataOnly` **in the Macro name text box. Click the Store macro in box arrow and then click Documents Based On DL Course Questionnaire. Select the text in the Description box and then type** `Places a check mark in the Save data only for forms check box.` **Point to the Keyboard button.**

Word displays the Record Macro dialog box (Figure 9-26).

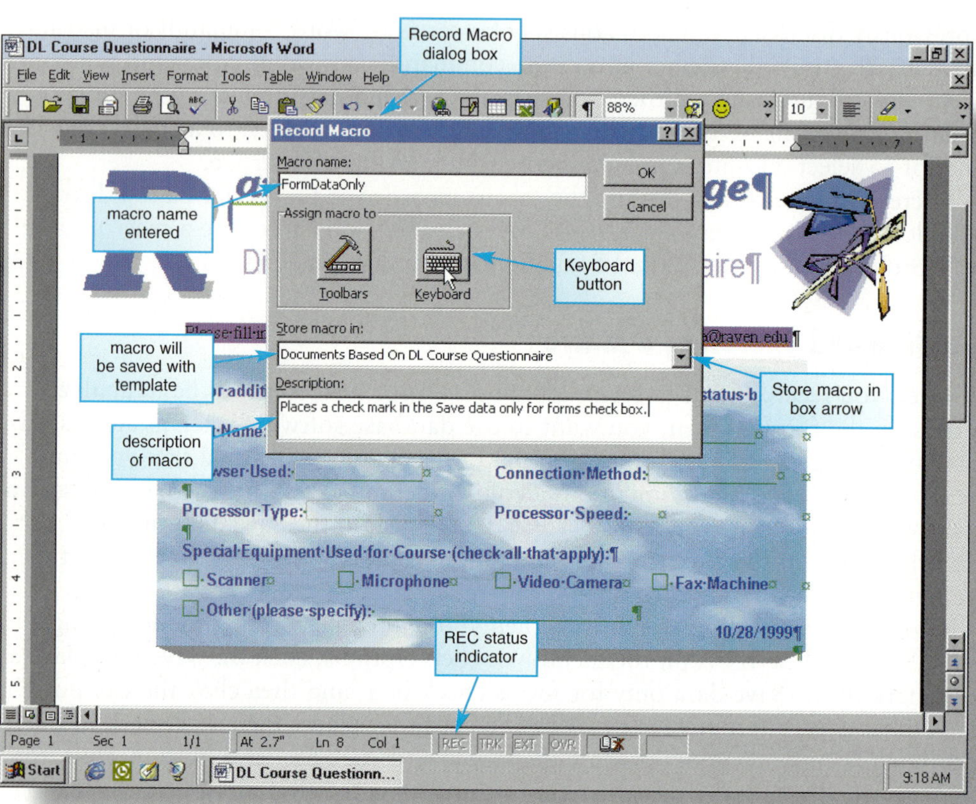

FIGURE 9-26

2 Click the Keyboard button. When the Customize Keyboard dialog box displays, press the ALT+D keys. Point to the Assign button.

Word displays the Customize Keyboard dialog box (Figure 9-27). The characters you pressed, ALT+D, display in the Press new shortcut key text box.

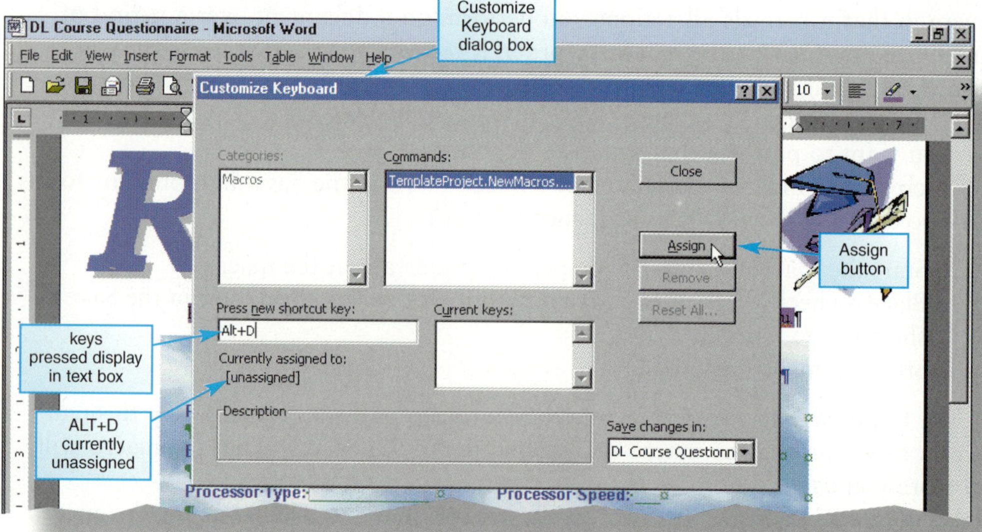

FIGURE 9-27

3 Click the Assign button. Click the Close button in the Customize Keyboard dialog box.

Word assigns the shortcut key, ALT+D, to the FormDataOnly macro, closes the Customize Keyboard and Record Macro dialog boxes, darkens the REC characters on the status bar, and then displays the Stop Recording toolbar in the document window (Figure 9-28). Any task you do will be part of the macro. When you are finished recording the macro, you will click the Stop Recording button on the Stop Recording toolbar.

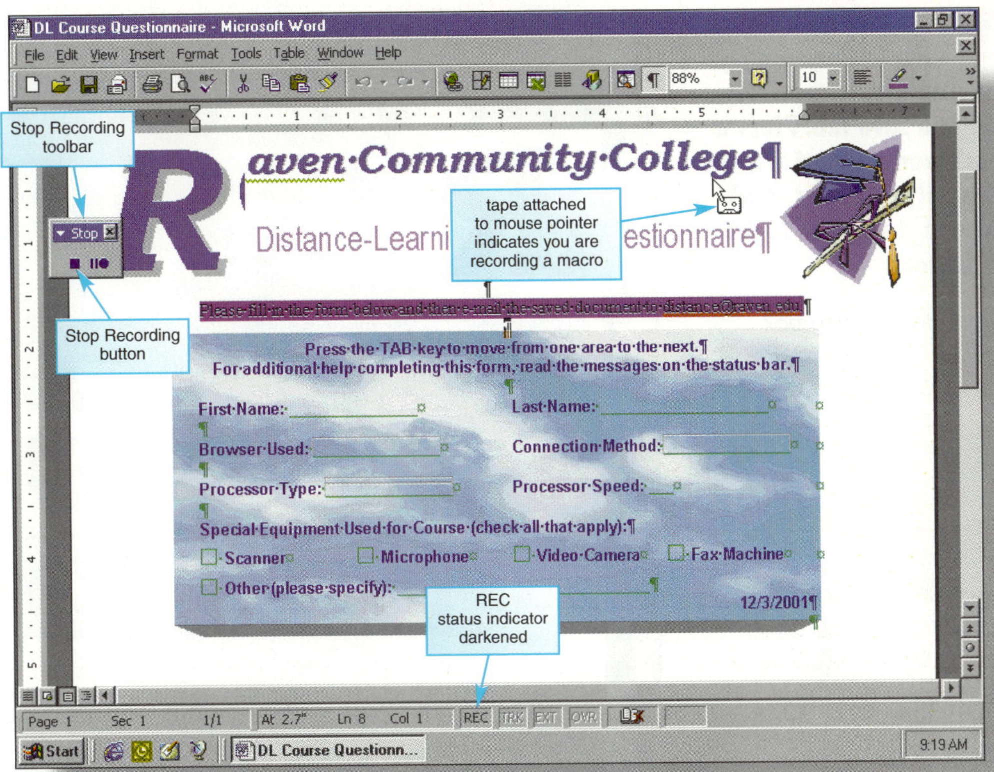

FIGURE 9-28

4 Click Tools on the menu bar and then point to Options.

When you are recording a macro and the mouse pointer is in a menu or pointing to a command button, the tape does not display next to the pointer (Figure 9-29).

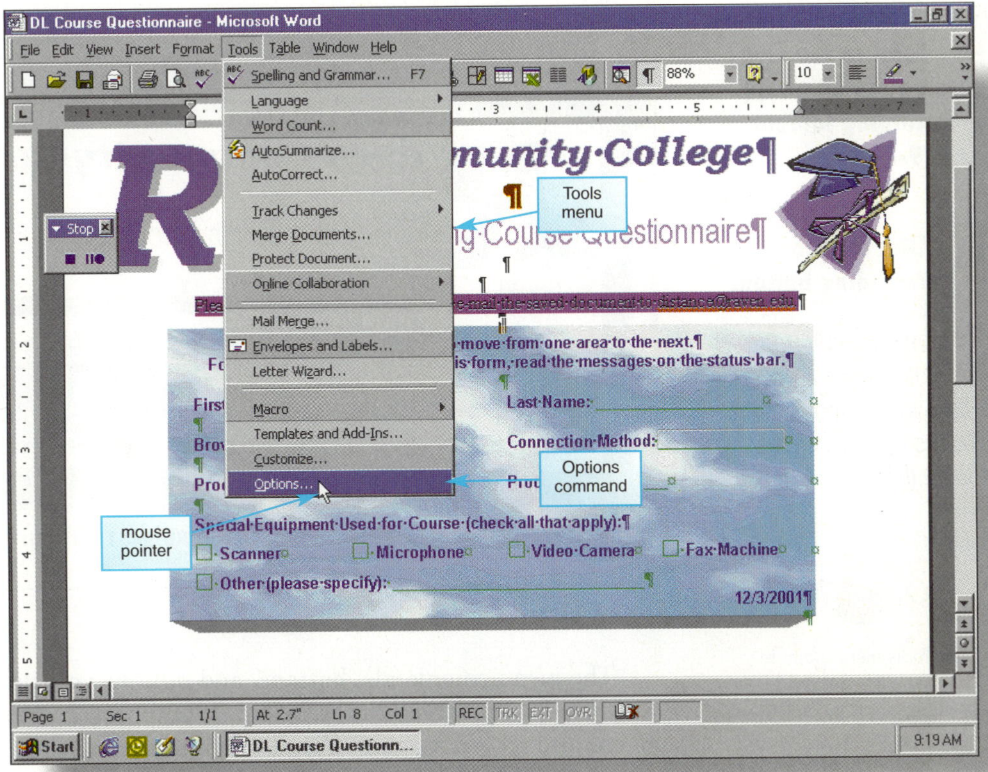

FIGURE 9-29

5 **Click Options. When the Options dialog box displays, if necessary, click the Save tab. Place a check mark in the Save data only for forms check box and then point to the OK button.**

The Options dialog box displays as shown in Figure 9-30.

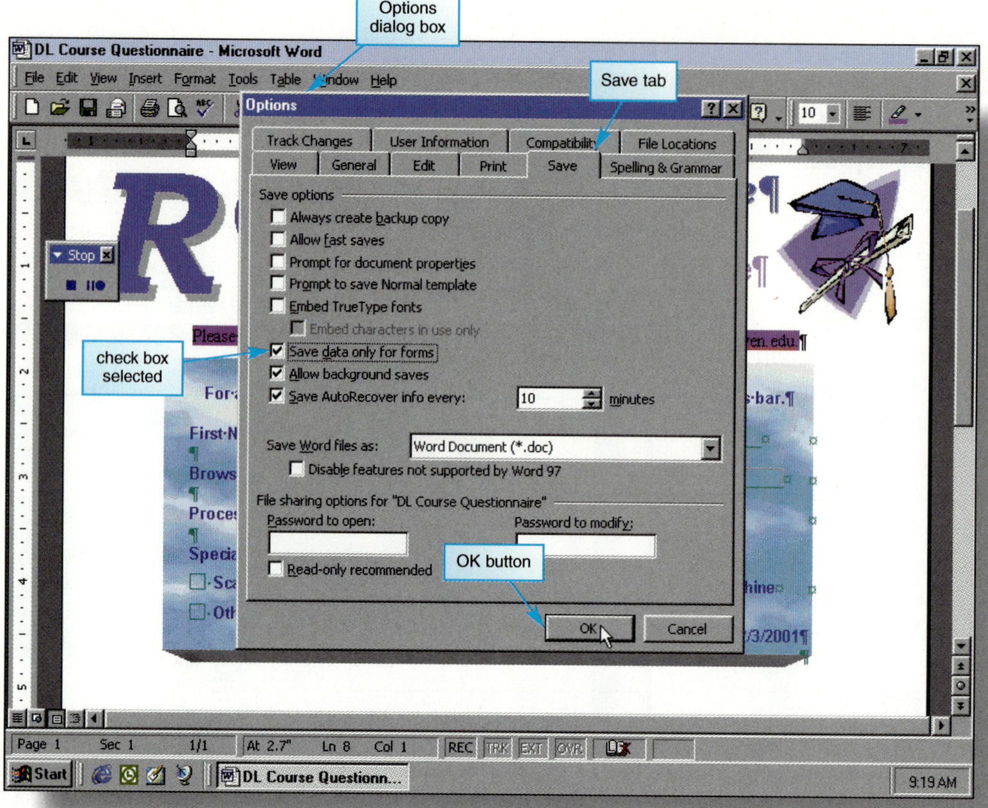

FIGURE 9-30

6 **Click the OK button. Point to the Stop Recording button on the Stop Recording toolbar (Figure 9-31).**

7 **Click the Stop Recording button.**

Word stops recording the document activities, closes the Stop Recording toolbar, and dims the REC status indicator on the status bar.

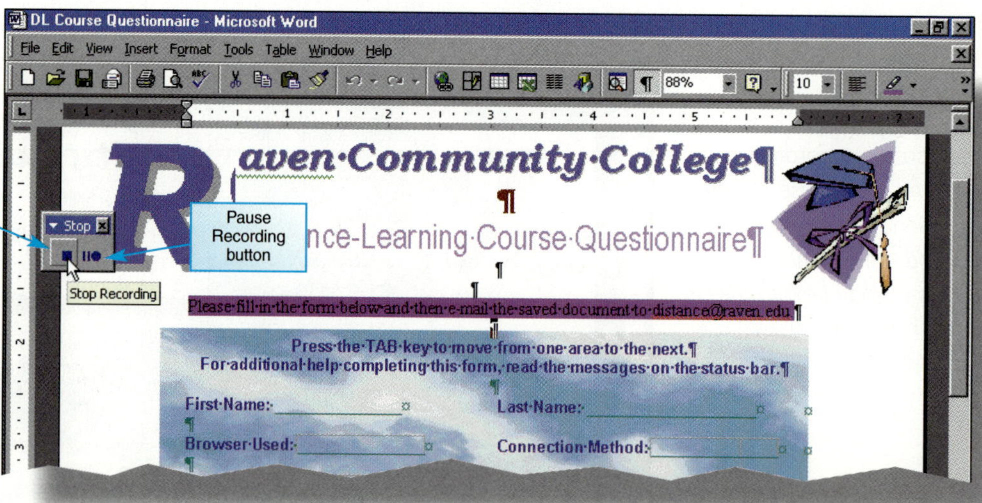

FIGURE 9-31

Other Ways

1. On Tools menu point to Macro, click Record New Macro, enter macro name, click Keyboard button, press shortcut keys, click Assign button, click Close button, record macro, click Stop Recording button on Stop Recording toolbar

The menu commands, buttons, and options you clicked while the macro recorder was running are stored in the macro. If you recorded the wrong actions, delete the macro and record it again. You delete a macro by clicking Tools on the menu bar, pointing to Macro on the Tools menu, and then clicking Macros on the Macro submenu. When the Macro dialog box displays, click the name of the macro (FormDataOnly), click the Delete button, and then click the Yes button. Finally, record the macro again.

If, while recording a macro, you want to perform some actions that should not be part of the macro, click the Pause Recording button on the Stop Recording toolbar (see Figure 9-31) to suspend the macro recorder. The Pause Recording button changes to a Resume Recorder button that you click when you want to continue recording.

In the Record Macro dialog box (Figure 9-26 on page WD 9.26), you select the location to store the macro in the Store macro in box. If you wanted a macro to be available to all documents you create that are based on the normal template, you would select All Documents (Normal.dot) in the Store macro in list. Most macros created with the macro recorder, however, are document specific, and thus are stored in the current template or document.

The next step is to execute, or run, the macro to ensure that it works. Recall that you assigned the shortcut key, ALT+D, to this macro. Perform the following steps to run the macro.

More About

The Macro Recorder

While recording a macro, you must use the keyboard to record your actions because the macro recorder does not record mouse movements. For example, to move the insertion point to the top of the document, you would press the CTRL+HOME keys instead of dragging the scroll box to the top of the scroll bar. Likewise, you would use keyboard keys to move the insertion point or to select, copy, or move items.

To Run a Macro

1 **Click Tools on the menu bar and then click Options. When the Options dialog box displays, if necessary, click the Save tab. Remove the check mark from the Save data only for forms check box and then click the OK button. Press the ALT+D keys.**

Word performs the instructions stored in the FormDataOnly macro. Verify that the macro worked properly by displaying the Options dialog box.

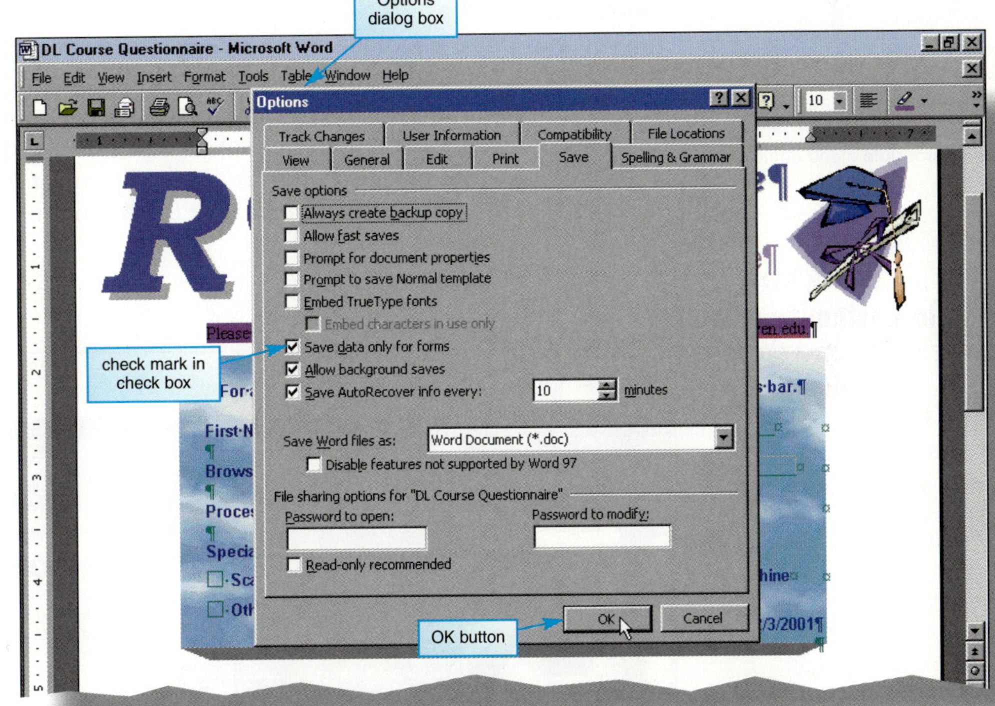

FIGURE 9-32

2 **Click Tools on the menu bar and then click Options. When the Options dialog box displays, if necessary, click the Save tab. Point to the OK button.**

A check mark displays in the Save data only for forms check box, indicating that the macro executed properly (Figure 9-32).

3 **Click the OK button.**

Other Ways

1. On Tools menu point to Macro, click Macros, click macro name in Macro name list box, click Run button
2. Press ALT+F8, click macro name in macro name list box, click Run button
3. Click Run Macro button on Standard toolbar in Visual Basic Editor

You should remove the check mark from the Save data only for forms check box so that future saves will save the entire form.

TO UNCHECK THE SAVE DATA ONLY FOR FORMS CHECK BOX

1. Click Tools on the menu bar and then click Options. When the Options dialog box displays, if necessary, click the Save tab.
2. Remove the check mark from the Save data only for forms check box. Click the OK button.

Word removes the check mark from the Save data only for forms check box.

Customizing Word

In addition to customizing toolbars and their buttons, you can customize menus using the Customize dialog box. To add a command to a menu, for example, you click Commands in the Categories list in the Commands sheet and then drag the desired command to the appropriate menu name.

Assigning a Macro to a Toolbar Button

You can customize toolbars by adding buttons, deleting buttons, and changing the function or appearance of buttons. You also can assign a macro to a button. In this project, you want to create a toolbar button for the FormDataOnly macro so that instead of pressing the shortcut keys, you can click the button to place a check mark in the Save data only for forms check box in the Save sheet in the Options dialog box.

You customize a toolbar through the Customize command on the Tools menu. The key to understanding how to customize a toolbar is to recognize that when you have the Customize dialog box open, Word's toolbars and menus are in Edit mode. **Edit mode** allows you to modify the toolbars and menus.

Perform the following steps to assign the FormDataOnly macro to a new button on the Standard toolbar and then change the button image.

To Customize a Toolbar

1. **Click Tools on the menu bar and then point to Customize (Figure 9-33).**

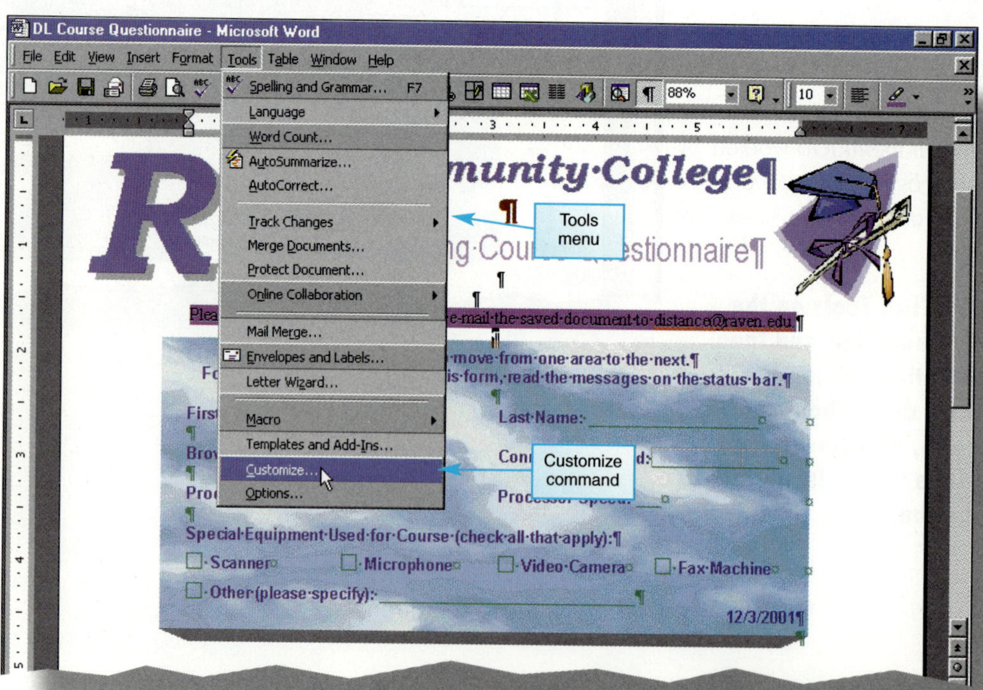

FIGURE 9-33

2 **Click Customize. When the Customize dialog box displays, if necessary, click the Commands tab. Scroll to and then click Macros in the Categories list. Click Template.Project. NewMacros.FormDataOnly in the Commands list.**

The Customize dialog box displays (Figure 9-34).

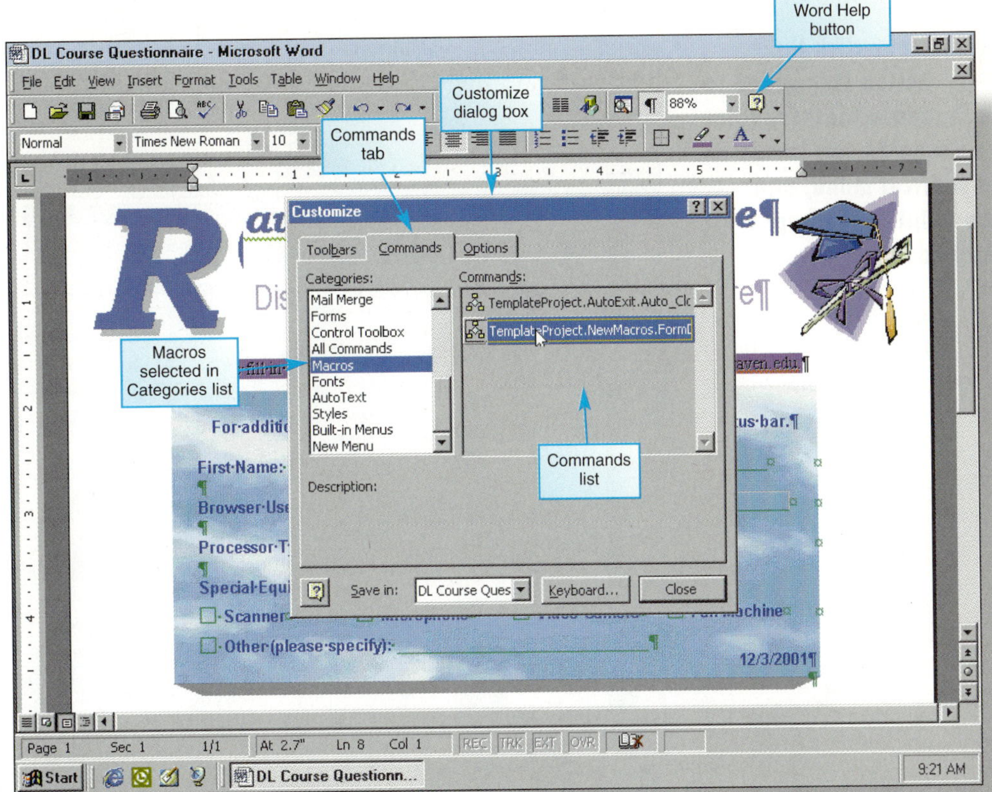

FIGURE 9-34

3 **Drag the selected command in the Commands list to the right of the Microsoft Word Help button on the Standard toolbar.**

A button containing the text, TemplateProject. NewMacros.FormDataOnly, displays next to the Microsoft Word Help button on the Standard toolbar (Figure 9-35). Because the button is so long, the toolbar may wrap to two lines. A thick border surrounds the new button indicating Word is in Edit mode.

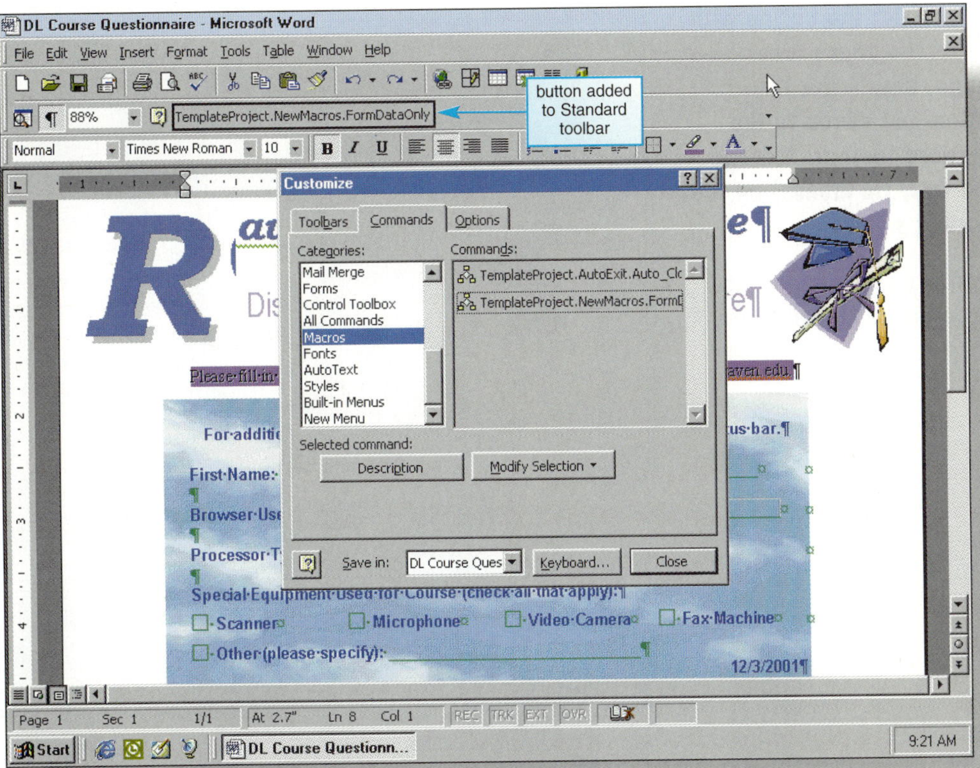

FIGURE 9-35

4 **Right-click the button just added to the Standard toolbar, point to Change Button Image on the shortcut menu, and then point to the happy face image.**

Word displays a palette of button images from which you can select (Figure 9-36).

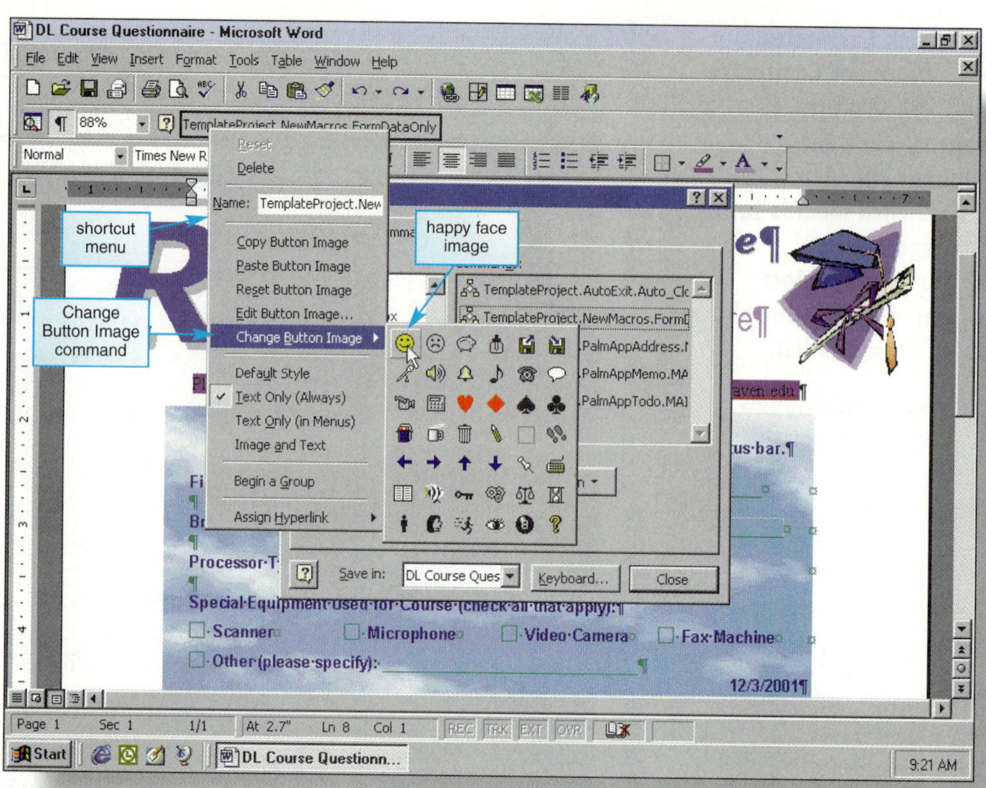

FIGURE 9-36

5 **Click the button with the happy face image. Right-click the button just added to the Standard toolbar. Point to Text Only (in Menus) on the shortcut menu.**

Word places the happy face image on the button (Figure 9-37).

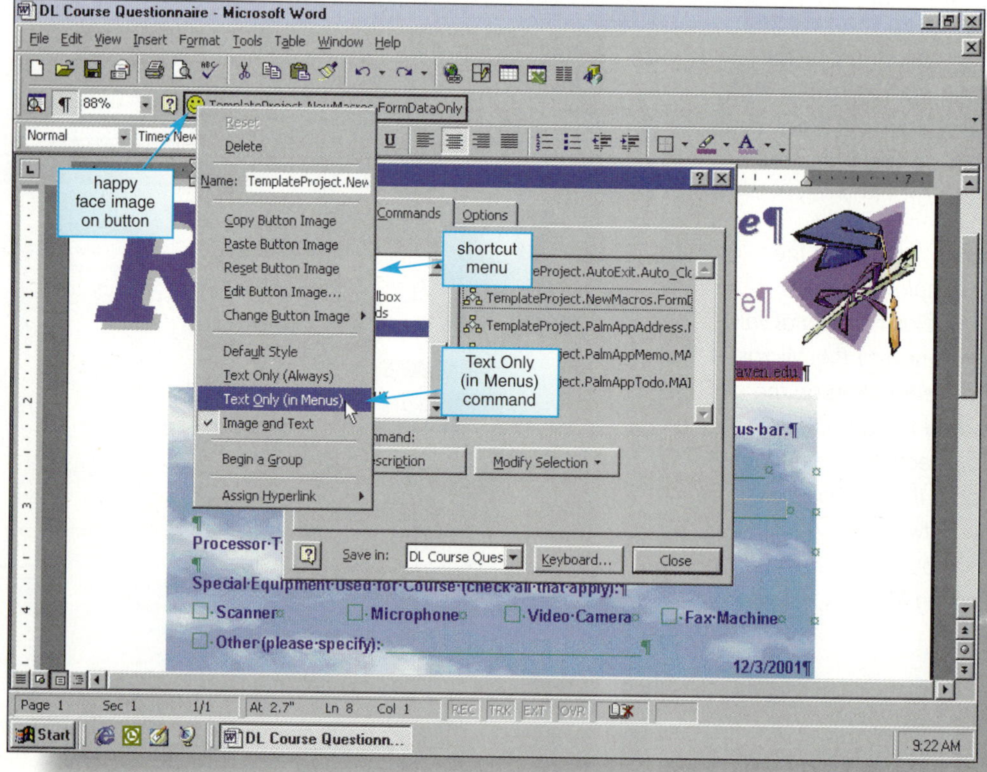

FIGURE 9-37

6 Click Text Only (in Menus). Point to the Close button in the Customize dialog box.

The text, TemplateProject.NewMacros.FormDataOnly, no longer displays on the button (Figure 9-38). If you add the macro to a menu at a later time, the text will display in the menu.

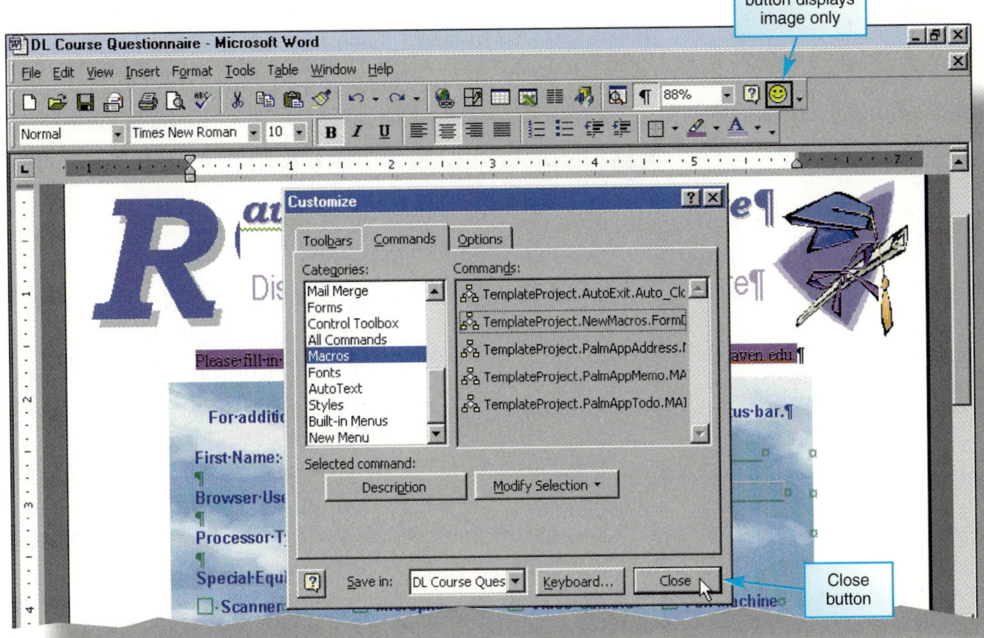

FIGURE 9-38

7 Click the Close button in the Customize dialog box. Point to the Form Data Only button on the Standard toolbar.

Word quits Edit mode. The Form Data Only button displays on the Standard toolbar with the ScreenTip, Form Data Only (Figure 9-39).

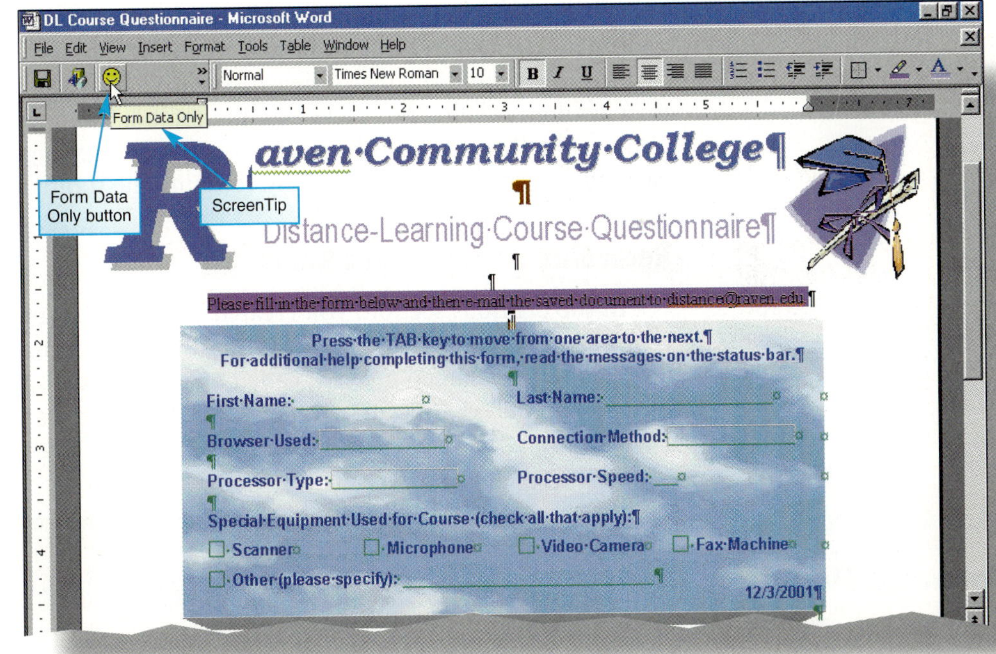

FIGURE 9-39

8 Click the Form Data Only button on the Standard toolbar.

Word places a check mark in the Save data only for forms check box in the Save sheet in the Options dialog box.

Other Ways

1. Right-click toolbar, click Customize on the shortcut menu, click Commands tab
2. Click View, click Toolbars, click Customize, click Commands tab

You can verify that the Form Data Only button worked by clicking Tools on the menu bar, clicking Options, clicking the Save tab, and then confirming that a check mark displays in the Save data only for forms check box. Because you do not want the check mark in the check box now, remove it as described in the steps on the next page.

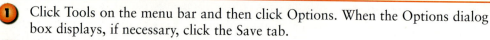

TO UNCHECK THE SAVE DATA ONLY FOR FORMS CHECK BOX

 Click Tools on the menu bar and then click Options. When the Options dialog box displays, if necessary, click the Save tab.

 Remove the check mark from the Save data only for forms check box. Click the OK button.

Word removes the check mark from the Save data only for forms check box.

If you wanted to assign a Web address to a button so that when the user clicks the button the associated Web page displays on the screen, you would right-click the button with the Customize dialog box displaying as shown in Figure 9-37 on page WD 9.32, point to the Assign Hyperlink command, click Open, enter the Web address in the Assign Hyperlink dialog box, and then click the OK button.

You can add as many buttons as you want to a toolbar. You also can change the image on any button or change an existing button's function. For example, when in Edit mode (the Customize dialog box is active), you can right-click the Save button on the Standard toolbar and assign it a macro or a hyperlink. The next time you click the Save button, Word would execute the macro or start the application associated with the hyperlink, instead of saving a document.

As you add buttons, other buttons on the toolbar will be demoted to the More Buttons list. You also can create new toolbars. To create a new toolbar, click the Toolbars tab in the Customize dialog box and then click the New button.

To remove a button from a toolbar, while in Edit mode, right-click the button and then click Delete on the shortcut menu.

You reset the toolbars to their installation default by clicking the Toolbars tab in the Customize dialog box, selecting the toolbar name in the Toolbars list, and then clicking the Reset button. Because it is so easy to change the buttons on a toolbar, each project in this book begins by resetting the toolbars.

Recording an Automatic Macro

In the previous section, you created a macro, assigned it a unique name (FormDataOnly), and then created a toolbar button that executed the macro. Word also has five prenamed macros, called **automatic macros**, that execute automatically when a certain event occurs. Table 9-2 lists the name and function of these automatic macros.

Automatic Macros

A document can contain only one AutoClose, AutoNew, and AutoOpen macro. The AutoExec and AutoExit macros, however, are not stored with the document; instead, they must be stored in the Normal template. Thus, one AutoExec and only one AutoExit macro can exist for all Word documents.

Table 9-2 Automatic Macros

MACRO NAME	RUNS
AutoClose	When you close a document containing the macro
AutoExec	When you start Word
AutoExit	When you quit Word
AutoNew	When you create a new document based on a template containing the macro
AutoOpen	When you open a document containing the macro

The name you use for an automatic macro depends on when you want certain actions to occur. In this project, when a user creates a new Word document that is based on the DL Course Questionnaire template, you want the online form to display properly in the Word window. Thus, you will create an AutoNew macro using the macro recorder.

Because the form displays properly when zoom is set to page width, you will record the steps to change the zoom to page widt. Also, you want the entire form to display in the Word window so that the user does not have to scroll to position the form. When you display the form in the Word window, the top of the form displays. Thus, you will go to the top of the page by dragging the scroll box to the top of the vertical scroll bar and then click the scroll arrow at the bottom of the vertical scroll bar several times to position the form properly.

Perform the following steps to create an AutoNew macro.

To Create an Automatic Macro

1 Double-click the REC status indicator on the status bar. When the Record Macro dialog box displays, type `AutoNew` **in the Macro name text box. Click the Store macro in box arrow and then click Documents Based On DL Course Questionnaire. In the Description text box, type** `Specifies how the form initially displays (as a blank form).` **Point to the OK button.**

Word displays the Record Macro dialog box (Figure 9-40).

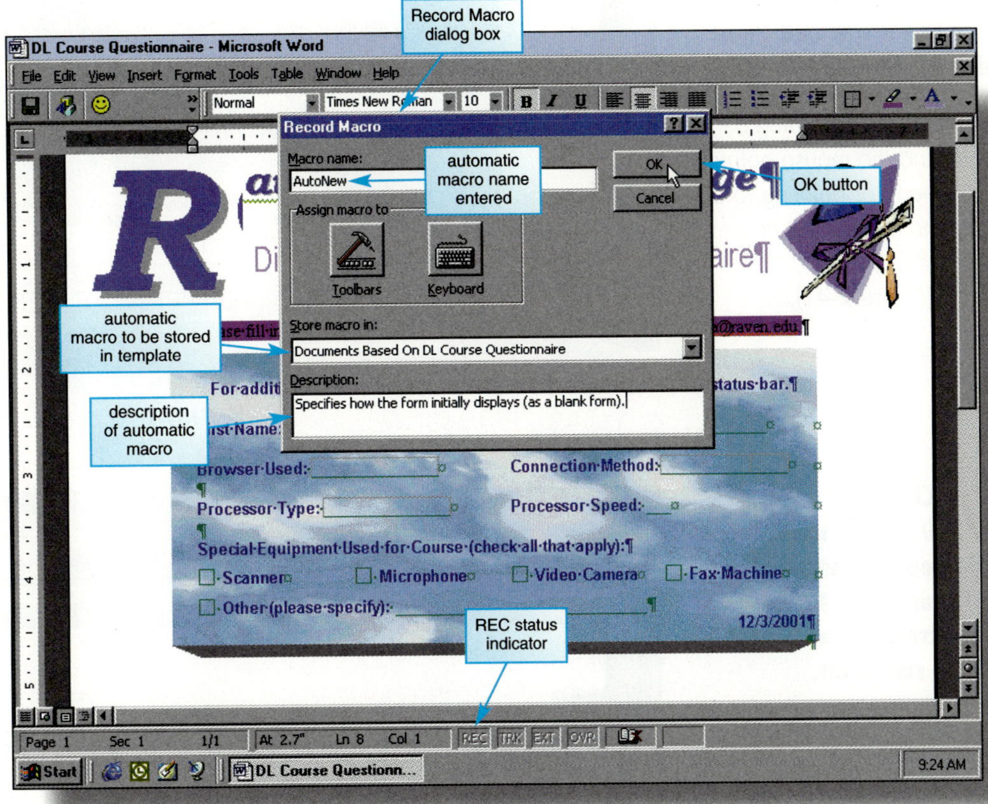

FIGURE 9-40

2 **Click the OK button.**

Word closes the Record Macro dialog box and then displays the Stop Recording toolbar in the document window.

3 **Double-click the move handle on the Standard toolbar to display the entire toolbar. Click the Zoom box arrow and then point to Page Width.**

When you are recording a macro and the mouse pointer is in a menu or pointing to a command button, the tape does not display next to the pointer (Figure 9-41).

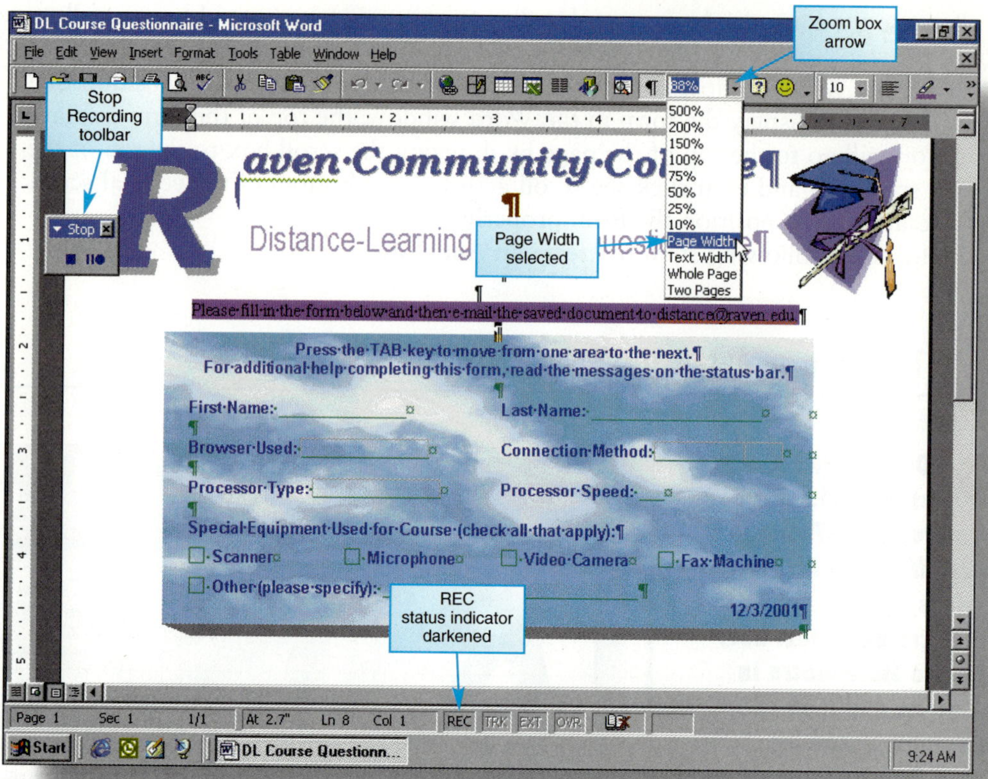

FIGURE 9-41

4 **Click Page Width. Drag the scroll box to the top of the vertical scroll bar. Point to the down scroll arrow on the vertical scroll bar.**

Word changes the zoom to page width and displays the top of the page in the document window (Figure 9-42).

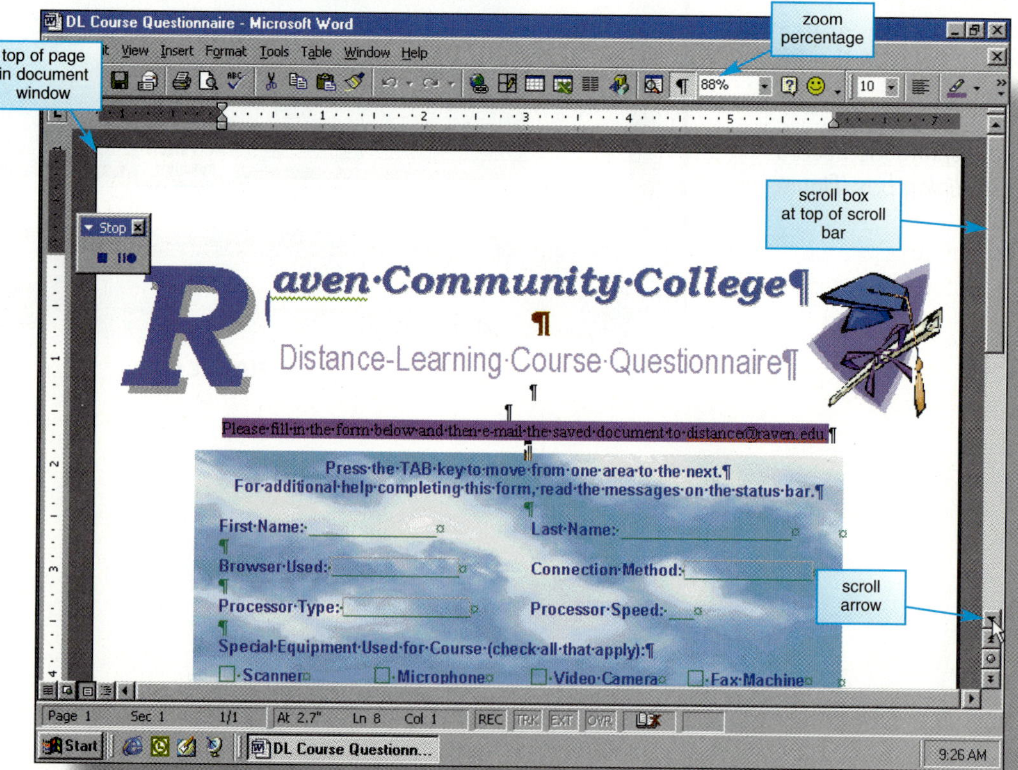

FIGURE 9-42

5 **Click the down scroll arrow on the vertical scroll bar six times. Point to the Stop Recording button on the Stop Recording toolbar.**

The online form displays as shown in Figure 9-43.

6 **Click the Stop Recording button.**

Word stops recording the document activities, closes the Stop Recording toolbar, and dims the REC status indicator on the status bar.

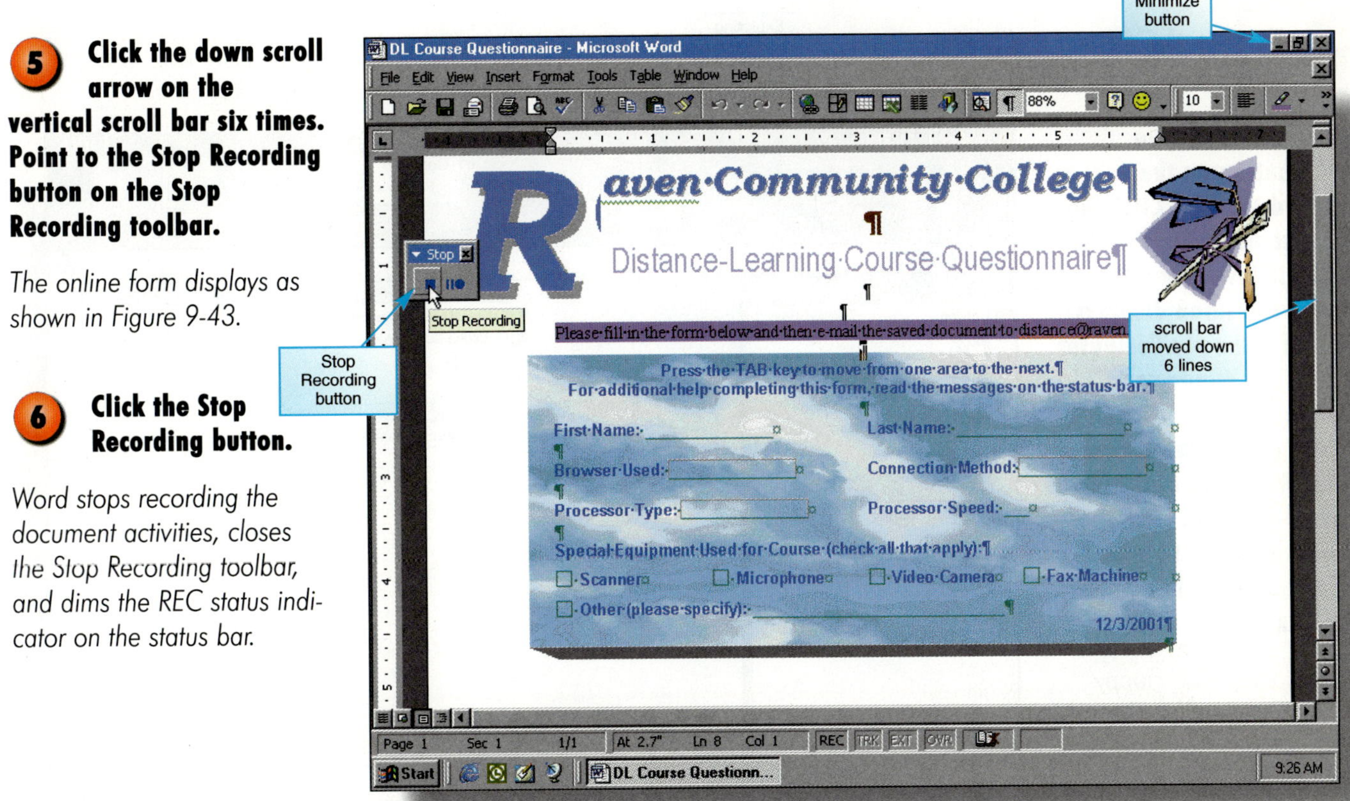

FIGURE 9-43

Other Ways

1. On Tools menu point to Macro, click Record New Macro, enter macro name, click Keyboard button, press shortcut keys, click Assign button, click Close button, record macro, click Stop Recording button on Stop Recording toolbar

To test the automatic macro, you activate the event that causes the macro to execute. For example, the AutoNew macro runs whenever you create a new Word document that is based on the template. You learned in Project 8 that when you save a template to a disk in drive A, a user can create a Word document based on a template through the My Computer window or Windows Explorer.

Perform the steps on the next page to display a new Word document window that is based on the DL Course Questionnaire template.

More About 2000

Recording and Running Macros

If Word does not allow you to record or run a macro in a document, the document probably is marked as read-only. To record or run a macro in this document, save it with a new name using the Save As dialog box and then record or run the macro in the newly named document.

To Test the AutoNew Macro

1 **Click the Save button on the Standard toolbar. Click the Minimize button in the Word window. When the Windows desktop displays, right-click the My Computer icon on the Windows desktop and then click Explore on the shortcut menu. When the Exploring window displays, click the Address text box to select it. Type a: and then press the ENTER key.**

The Exploring - 3½ Floppy (A:) window displays (Figure 9-44). Word is still running.

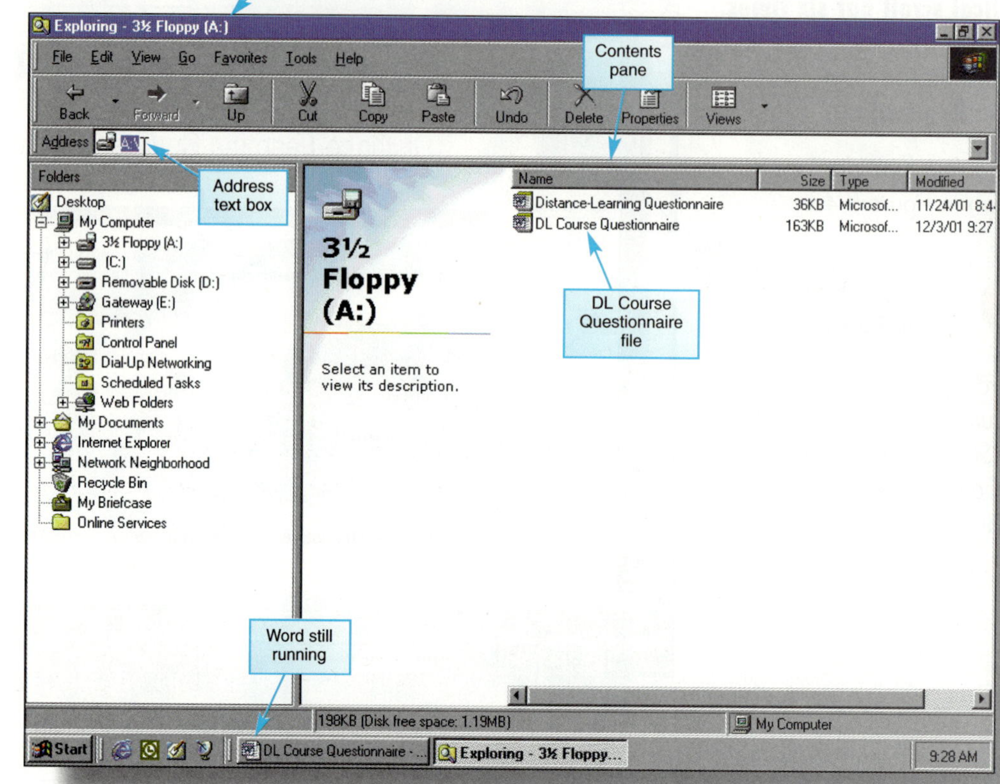

FIGURE 9-44

2 **Double-click the DL Course Questionnaire icon in the Contents pane.**

Word displays a new document window that is based on the contents of the DL Course Questionnaire (Figure 9-45). The zoom is set to page width and the screen scrolls down six lines as instructed by the AutoNew macro.

3 **Click the Close button at the right edge of the Word title bar. If necessary, click the DL Course Questionnaire - Microsoft Word program button on the taskbar.**

The new document window closes. The DL Course Questionnaire template displays on the screen.

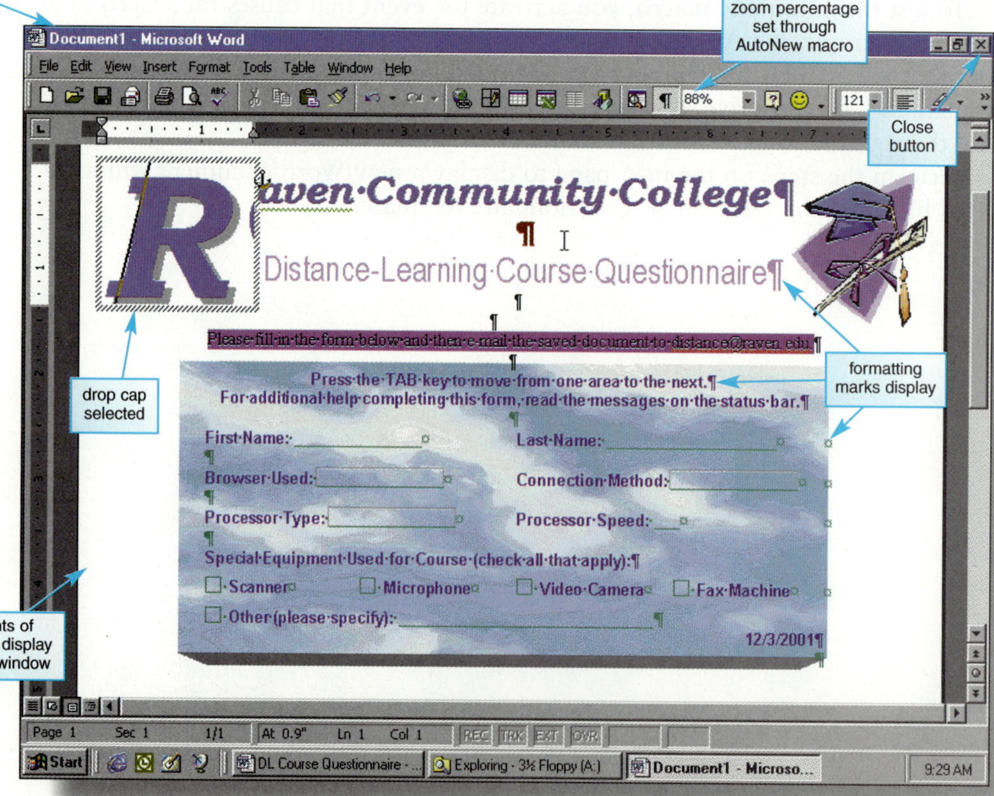

FIGURE 9-45

Notice in Figure 9-45 that the drop cap is selected. Recall that when you make a form available for users to access, you first protect the form. Protecting a form places the highlight in the first form field and allows users to access only the form fields. You did not protect the form yet because you are not finished modifying it. You simply tested the AutoNew macro to be sure it worked according to your plan.

When testing the AutoNew macro, you noticed that the formatting marks displayed on the screen (see Figure 9-45). You also noticed that the screen actually should scroll down one more line so it fits better in the Word window. Thus, you want to edit this macro. To edit a macro, you use VBA. The next section discusses VBA.

Editing a Recorded Macro

The next step in this project is to edit the AutoNew macro. Word uses VBA to store a macro's instructions. Thus, to edit a recorded macro, you use the Visual Basic Editor. All Office applications use the **Visual Basic Editor** to enter, modify, and view VBA code associated with a document. The following pages explain how to use the Visual Basic Editor to view, enter, and modify VBA code.

Using VBA

For more information about Using Visual Basic for Applications, visit the Word 2000 More About Web page (www.scsite.com/wd2000/more.htm) and then click Using VBA.

Viewing a Macro's VBA Code

As described earlier, a macro consists of VBA code, which the macro recorder automatically creates. You view the VBA code assigned to a macro through the Visual Basic Editor. Perform the following steps to view the VBA code associated AutoNew macro in the DL Course Questionnaire.

To View a Macro's VBA Code

1 Click Tools on the menu bar, point to Macro, and then point to Macros (Figure 9-46).

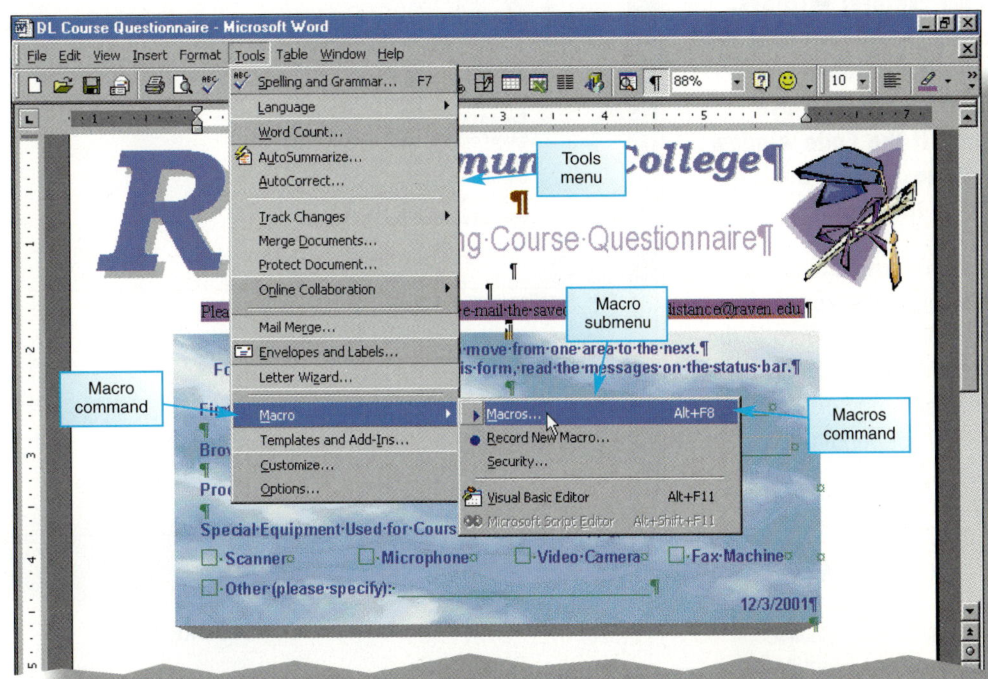

FIGURE 9-46

2 **Click Macros. When the Macros dialog box displays, click the Macros in box arrow and then click DL Course Questionnaire (template). Click AutoNew in the Macro name list and then point to the Edit button.**

The Macros dialog box displays (Figure 9-47).

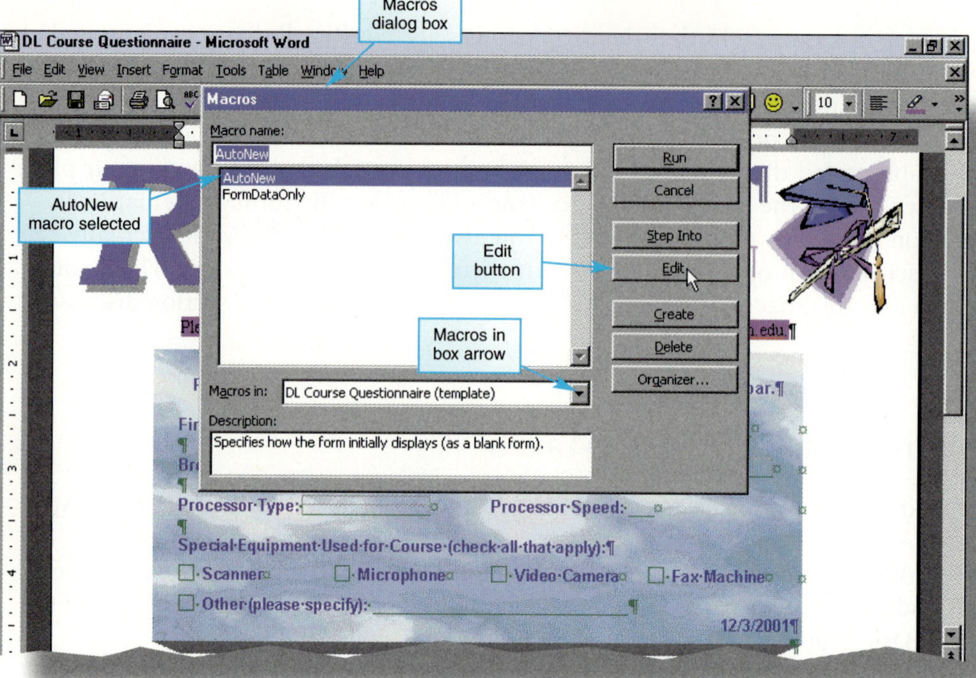

FIGURE 9-47

3 **Click the Edit button. If the Code window does not display, click View on the menu bar and then click Code. If the Project Explorer displays, click its Close button. If the Properties window displays, click its Close button. If the Code window is not maximized, double-click its title bar.**

The Visual Basic Editor starts and displays the VBA code for the AutoNew macro in the Code window (Figure 9-48). Your screen may display differently depending on previous Visual Basic Editor settings.

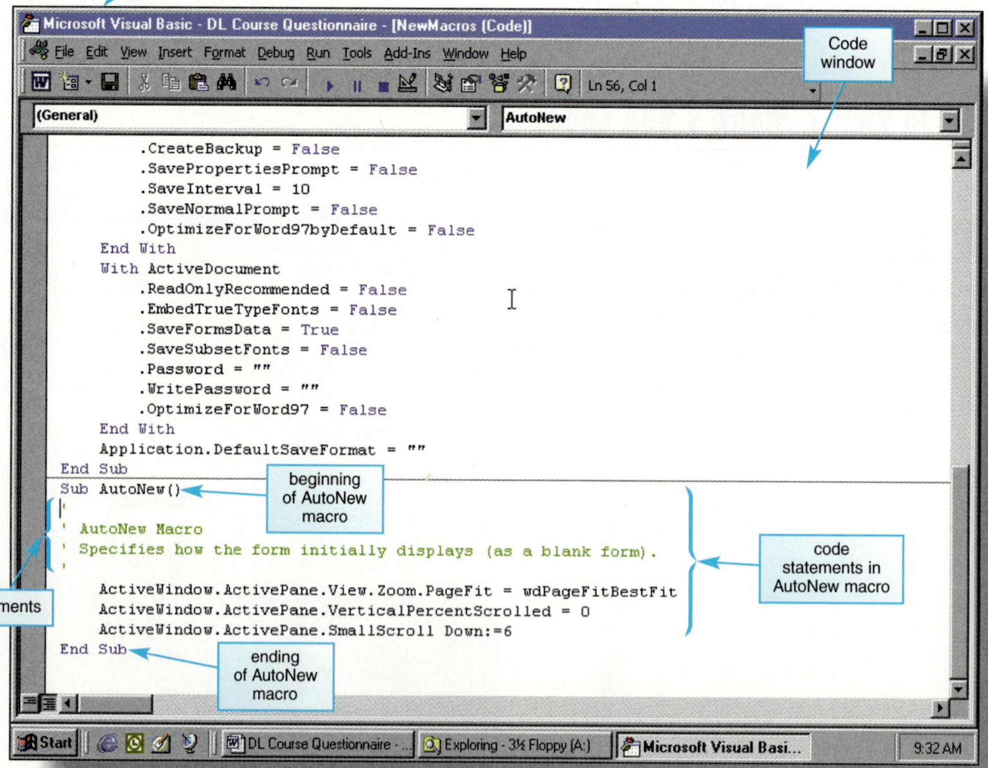

FIGURE 9-48

Other Ways

1. On Tools menu point to Macro, click Visual Basic Editor, scroll to desired procedure
2. Press ALT+F11, scroll to desired procedure

You have learned that the named set of instructions associated with a macro is called a procedure. It is this set of instructions, beginning with the words Sub AutoNew in Figure 9-48 and continuing sequentially to the line with the words End Sub, that is executed when you run the macro.

If you scroll up the Code window, you will see the code associated with the FormDataOnly macro. By scrolling through the two procedures of VBA code, you can see that the macro recorder generated many instructions.

The instructions within a procedure are called **code statements**. Each code statement can contain keywords, variables, constants, and operators. Table 9-3 explains the function of each of these elements of a code statement.

Table 9-3 Elements of a Code Statement

CODE STATEMENT ELEMENT	DEFINITION	EXAMPLES
Keyword	Recognized by Visual Basic as part of its programming language. Keywords display in blue in the Code window.	Sub End Sub
Variable	An item whose value can be modified during program execution.	ActiveWindow.Active.Pane.SmallScroll TitleBar Text
Constant	An item whose value remains unchanged during program execution.	7
Operator	A symbol that indicates a specific action.	= +

A procedure begins with a **Sub statement** and ends with an **End Sub statement**. As shown in Figure 9-48, the Sub statement is followed by the name of the procedure, which is the macro name (AutoNew). The parentheses following the macro name in the Sub statement are required. They indicate that arguments can be passed from one procedure to another. Passing arguments is beyond the scope of this project, but the parentheses still are required. The End Sub statement signifies the end of the procedure and returns control to Word. For clarity, code statement lines between the Sub statement and End Sub statement are indented four spaces.

Adding Comments to a Macro

Adding comments before and within a procedure help you remember the purpose of the macro and its code statements at a later date. **Comments** begin with the word Rem or an apostrophe (') and display in green in the Code window. In Figure 9-48, for example, the macro recorder placed four comment lines below the Sub statement. These comments display the name of the macro and its description, as entered in the Record Macro dialog box. Comments have no effect on the execution of a procedure; they simply provide information about the procedure, such as its name and description.

The macro recorder, however, does not add comments to the executable code statements in the procedures. Any code statement that is not a comment is considered an **executable code statement**. The AutoNew procedure in Figure 9-48 contains three executable code statements. The first, ActiveWindow.ActivePane.View.Zoom.PageFit = wdPageFitBestFit, changes the zoom to page width. The macro recorder generated this code statement when you clicked the Zoom box arrow on the Standard toolbar and then clicked the Page Width command.

VBA Statements

Instead of a long VBA statement on a single line, you can continue a VBA statement on the next line by placing an underscore character (_) at the end of the line to be continued and then pressing the ENTER key. To place multiple VBA statements on the same line, place a colon (:) between each statement.

The next two code statements scroll the screen downward six lines from the top of the page. The macro recorder generated these code statements when you dragged the scroll box to the top of the vertical scroll bar and then clicked the down scroll arrow on the vertical scroll bar six times.

You would like to enter comments that explain the purpose of executable code statements in the AutoNew procedure. You make changes, such as these, using the Visual Basic Editor. The Visual Basic Editor is a full-screen editor, which allows you to enter a procedure by typing lines of VBA code as if you were using word processing software. At the end of a line, you press the ENTER key or use the DOWN ARROW key to move to the next line. If you make a mistake in a code statement, you can use the arrow keys and the DELETE or BACKSPACE keys to correct it. You also can move the insertion point to previous lines to make corrections.

Perform the following steps to add comments above the executable code statements in the AutoNew procedure.

To Add Comments to a Procedure

1 Click to the left of the letter A in the first code statement beginning with the word ActiveWindow in the AutoNew procedure and then press the ENTER key to add a blank line before the code statement. Press the UP ARROW key. Type `' Sets screen to page width zoom` **and then press the DOWN ARROW key. Make sure you enter the apostrophe at the beginning of the comment.**

The first comment is entered and displays in green (Figure 9-49).

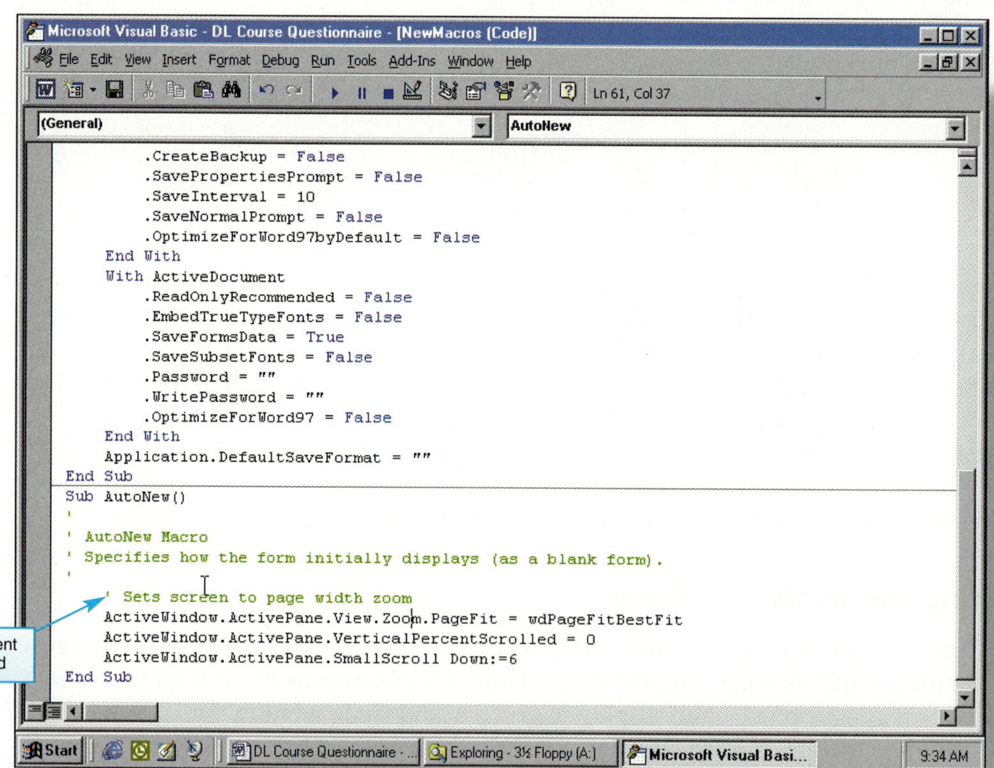

FIGURE 9-49

2 **Click to the left of the letter A in the second code statement beginning with the word ActiveWindow and then press the ENTER key to add one blank line before the code statement. Press the UP ARROW key. Type** `' Scrolls down from top of page so entire form fits in window` **and then press the DOWN ARROW key. Make sure you enter the apostrophe at the beginning of the comment.**

The second comment is entered and displays in green (Figure 9-50).

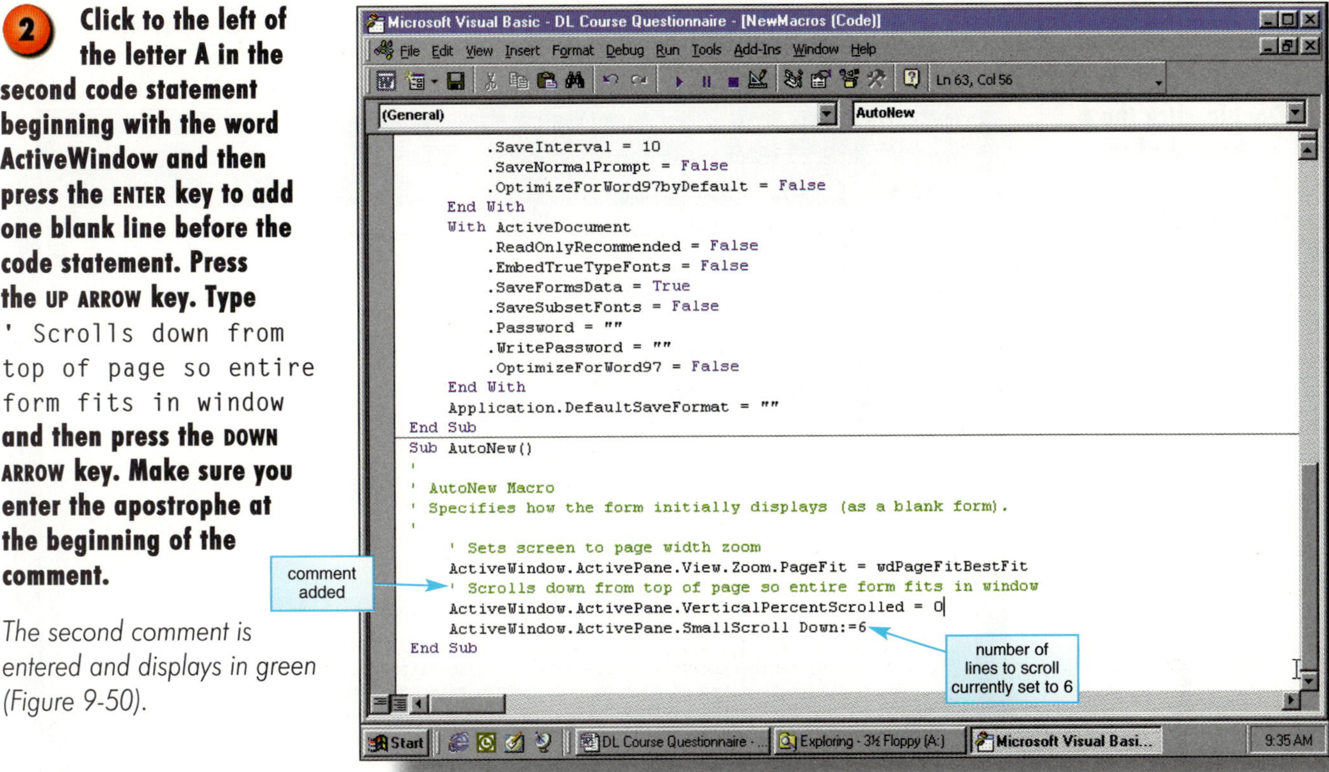

FIGURE 9-50

Modifying Existing Code in a Macro

The next step is to modify existing code in the AutoNew macro. Recall that when you tested the AutoNew macro, you noticed you should scroll down one more line so the college name displays closer to the top of the screen (see Figure 9-45 on page WD 9.38). Thus, you would like to change the 6 in the third executable code statement in the AutoNew procedure to a 7. Perform the step on the next page to change the constant in the executable code statement from a 6 to a 7.

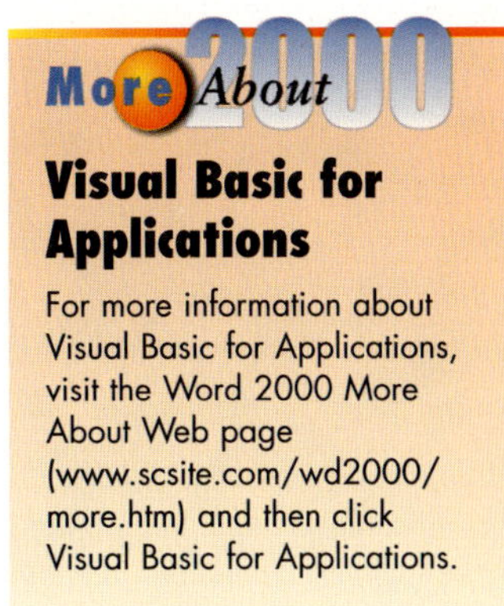

Visual Basic for Applications

For more information about Visual Basic for Applications, visit the Word 2000 More About Web page (www.scsite.com/wd2000/more.htm) and then click Visual Basic for Applications.

To Modify Existing Code

1 Double-click the 6 at the end of the executable code statement above the End Sub statement. Type 7 **as the new number of lines to scroll.**

The code statement is modified (Figure 9-51).

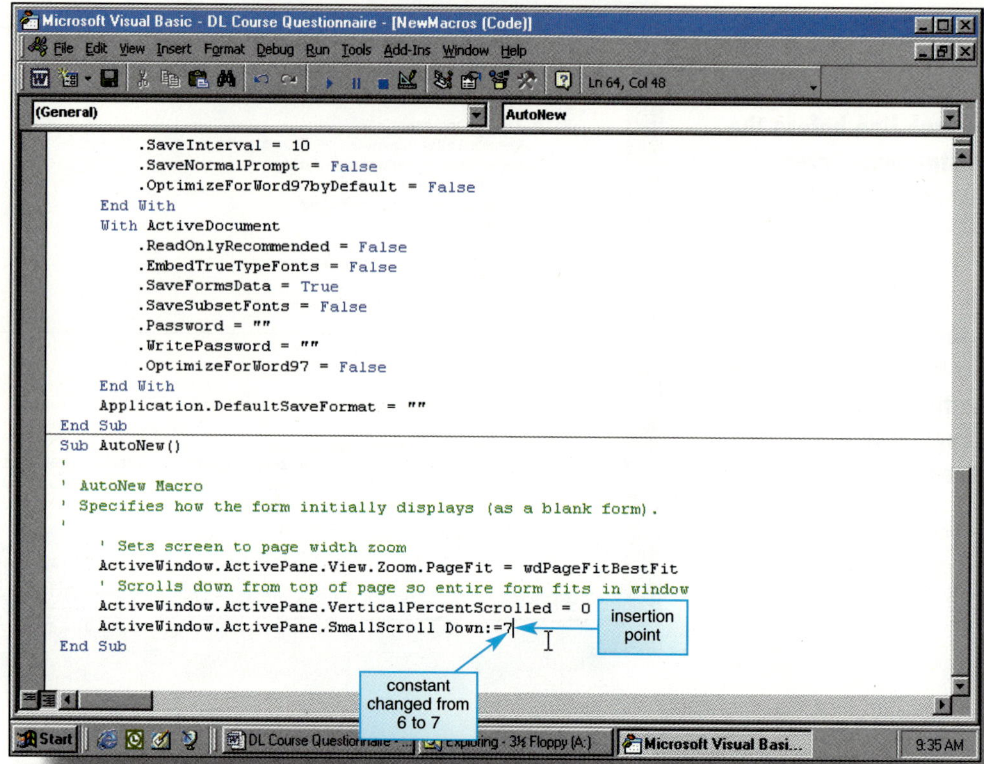

FIGURE 9-51

The next step is to add two more executable code statements to the AutoNew macro.

Entering Code Statements

In addition to changing the zoom to page width and scrolling down seven lines, you would like to hide formatting marks and gridlines when a user initially displays this form (as a blank form). Thus, you will add two executable code statements, each preceded by a comment. Table 9-4 shows the code statements to be entered.

Table 9-4 Code Statements Added to AutoNew Procedure

First new code statement	' Turns off table gridlines
Second new code statement	ActiveDocument.ActiveWindow.View.TableGridlines = False
Third new code statement	' Turns off formatting marks
Fourth new code statement	ActiveDocument.ActiveWindow.View.ShowAll = False

Perform the following step to add these code statements to the procedure.

To Add Code Statements to a Procedure

1. **With the insertion point following the 7 as shown in Figure 9-51, press the ENTER key. Type the first new code statement shown in Table 9-4. Press the ENTER key. Enter the remaining three code statements shown in Table 9-4. Make sure you enter an apostrophe at the beginning of each comment line.**

The new code statements are entered into the AutoNew procedure (Figure 9-52).

```
        .EmbedTrueTypeFonts = False
        .SaveFormsData = True
        .SaveSubsetFonts = False
        .Password = ""
        .WritePassword = ""
        .OptimizeForWord97 = False
    End With
    Application.DefaultSaveFormat = ""
End Sub
Sub AutoNew()
'
' AutoNew Macro
' Specifies how the form initially displays (as a blank form).
'
    ' Sets screen to page width zoom
    ActiveWindow.ActivePane.View.Zoom.PageFit = wdPageFitBestFit
    ' Scrolls down from top of page so entire form fits in window
    ActiveWindow.ActivePane.VerticalPercentScrolled = 0
    ActiveWindow.ActivePane.SmallScroll Down:=7
    ' Turns off table gridlines
    ActiveDocument.ActiveWindow.View.TableGridlines = False
    ' Turns off formatting marks
    ActiveDocument.ActiveWindow.View.ShowAll = False

End Sub
```

new code statements entered

Start | DL Course Questionnaire - ... | Exploring - 3½ Floppy (A:) | Microsoft Visual Basi... | 9:37 AM

FIGURE 9-52

You now are finished modifying the AutoNew macro. Thus, perform the following steps to close the Visual Basic Editor and return control to Word.

To Close the Visual Basic Editor

1. **Point to the Close button on the right edge of the Microsoft Visual Basic title bar (Figure 9-53).**

2. **Click the Close button.**

The Visual Basic Editor closes and control returns to Word.

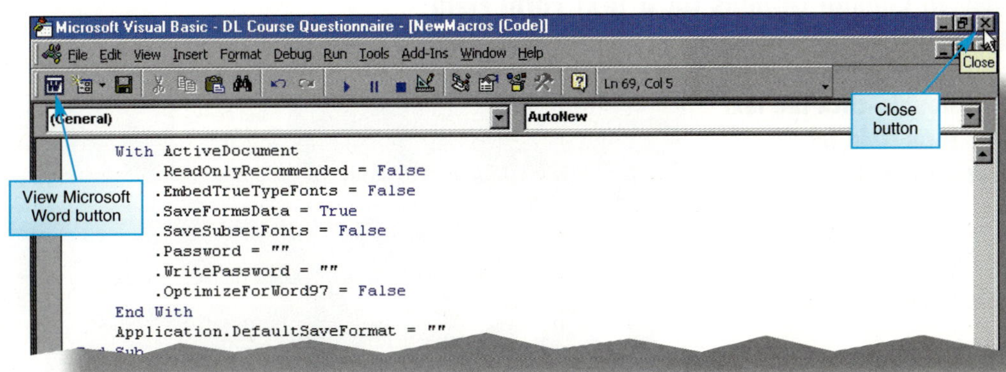

FIGURE 9-53

Other Ways

1. On File menu click Close and Return to Microsoft Word
2. Press ALT+Q

Instead of closing the Visual Basic Editor, you can click the **View Microsoft Word button** on the Visual Basic toolbar (Figure 9-53) to minimize the Visual Basic Editor and return control to Word. If you plan to switch between Word and the Visual Basic Editor, then use the View Microsoft Word button; otherwise use the Close button.

Creating a Macro from Scratch Using VBA

The next macro to be created in this project is the one that displays an error message if the user enters a nonnumeric value in the Processor Speed text box (see Figure 9-1b on page WD 9.5). The macro is to execute when the user presses the TAB key to advance out of the Processor Speed text box. The following pages explain how to create this macro and attach it to the text form field for the processor speed.

Modifying Form Field Options

The Processor Speed text box is a text form field. To modify a text form field, you double-click the text form field to display the Text Form Field Options dialog box. You have two changes to make in the dialog box: change the type and enter a bookmark.

In Project 8, you wanted only numbers to display in the text form field. Thus, you changed the text form field's type to Numeric. Doing so ensured that if a user entered a nonnumeric value in the text form field during data entry, the entry automatically was converted to a zero. In this project, you want to display an error message if the user enters a nonnumeric value. Thus, you must change the text form field's type back to Regular text so that you can display an error message if a user makes an incorrect entry.

Because you will be writing VBA code that references this text form field, you also want to change the bookmark for this text form field. You have learned that a **bookmark** is an item in a document that you name for future reference. Currently, the bookmark is Text3, which is not very descriptive. A more meaningful bookmark would be EnteredSpeed. Notice this new bookmark does not have a space between the words, Entered and Speed. This is because a bookmark cannot contain any spaces; a bookmark also must begin with a letter.

Perform the following steps to change the text form field type and change the bookmark.

Bookmark Names

Each time you create a form field, Word assigns it a sequential default bookmark name. For example, the first text form field has a bookmark name of Text1, the second text form field has a bookmark name of Text2, the third text form field has a bookmark name of Text3, and so on.

Steps To Change Options for a Text Form Field

1 Double-click the text form field for processor speed.

Word displays the Text Form Field Options dialog box (Figure 9-54).

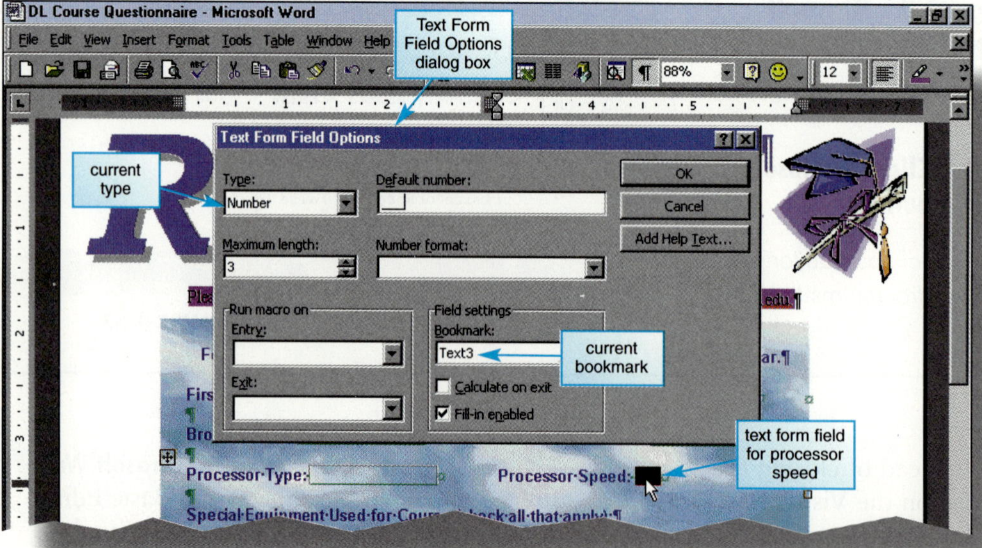

FIGURE 9-54

2 **Click the Type box arrow and then click Regular text. Double-click the text in the Bookmark text box and then type** `EnteredSpeed` **as the new bookmark. Point to the OK button.**

The form field options display as shown in figure 9-55.

3 **Click the OK button.**

Word changes the form field options as specified in the Text Form Field Options dialog box.

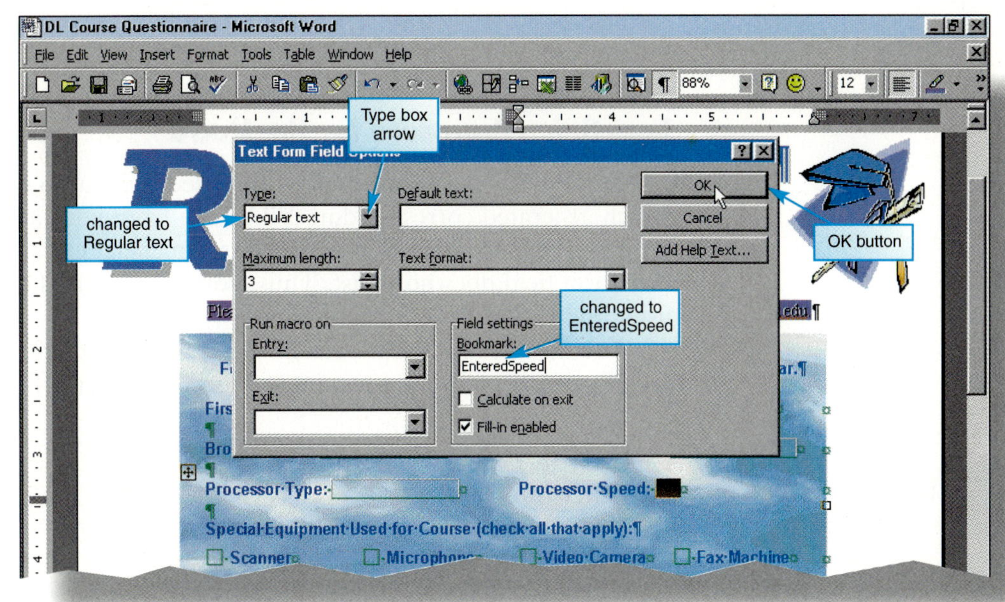

FIGURE 9-55

The next step is to change the bookmark for the drop-down list box for the processor type from Dropdown3 to a more meaningful name because this form field also will be referenced in the VBA code. Perform the following steps to change the bookmark for the drop-down form field.

TO CHANGE A BOOKMARK FOR A DROP-DOWN FORM FIELD

1. Double-click the drop-down form field for processor type.
2. When the Drop-Down Form Field Options dialog box displays, double-click the text in the Bookmark text box and then type `EnteredType` as the new bookmark. Point to the OK button (Figure 9-56).
3. Click the OK button.

Word changes the form field options as specified in the Drop-Down Form Field Options dialog box.

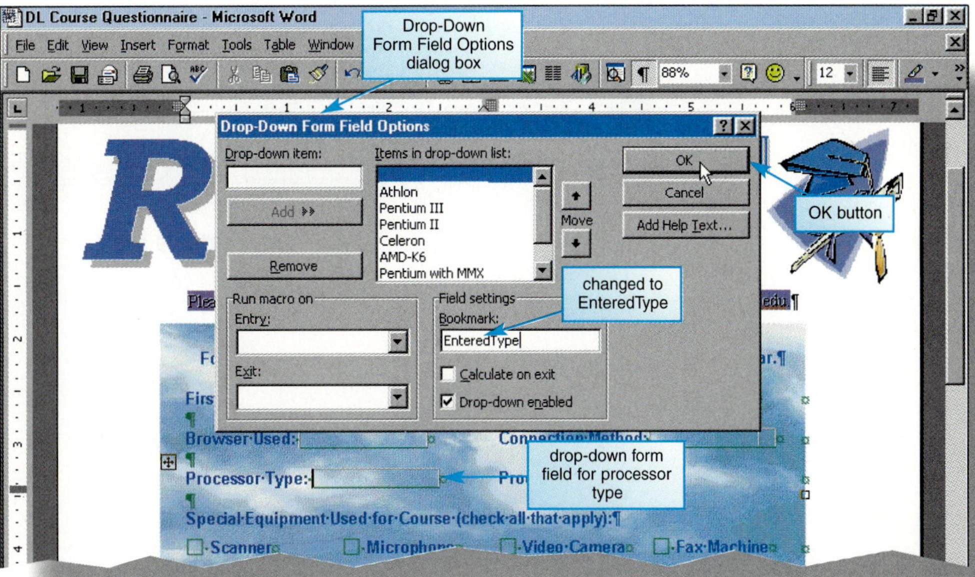

FIGURE 9-56

The next step is to insert a new procedure for the macro using the Visual Basic Editor.

Inserting a Procedure for the Macro

For the previous two macros, you used the macro recorder to create the macros, which generated corresponding VBA code from your actions. For this macro, you cannot record the displaying of the error message because an error message for this text form field does not exist. Thus, you must write the VBA code for this macro using the Visual Basic Editor.

You have learned that each macro is a procedure in Visual Basic. Perform the following steps to insert a new empty procedure named ProcessorSpeed.

Steps To Insert a Visual Basic Procedure

1 Press the ALT+F11 keys to display the Visual Basic Editor in a new window. If the Project Explorer displays, click its Close button. If the Properties window displays, click its Close button. If the Code window does not display, click View on the menu bar and then click Code. If necessary, maximize the Code window. Click the Insert UserForm button arrow and then point to Procedure.

The Visual Basic Editor displays as shown in Figure 9-57.

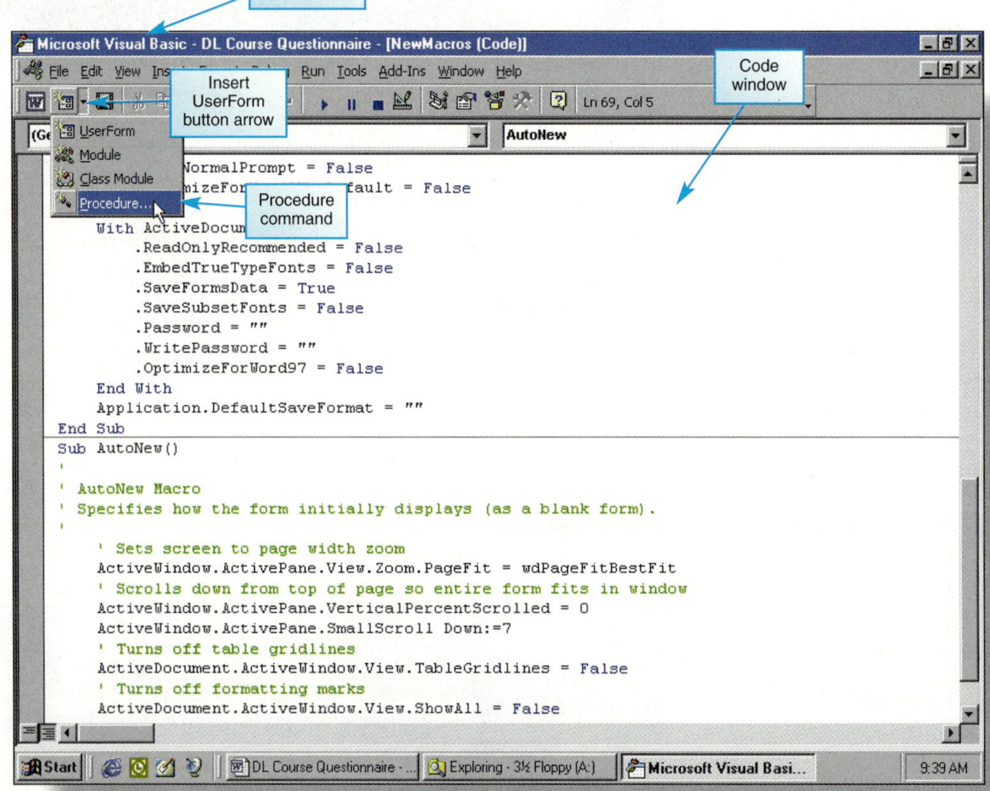

FIGURE 9-57

2 Click Procedure. When Word displays the Add Procedure dialog box, type `ProcessorSpeed` **in the Name text box and then point to the OK button.**

The Add Procedure dialog box displays (Figure 9-58).

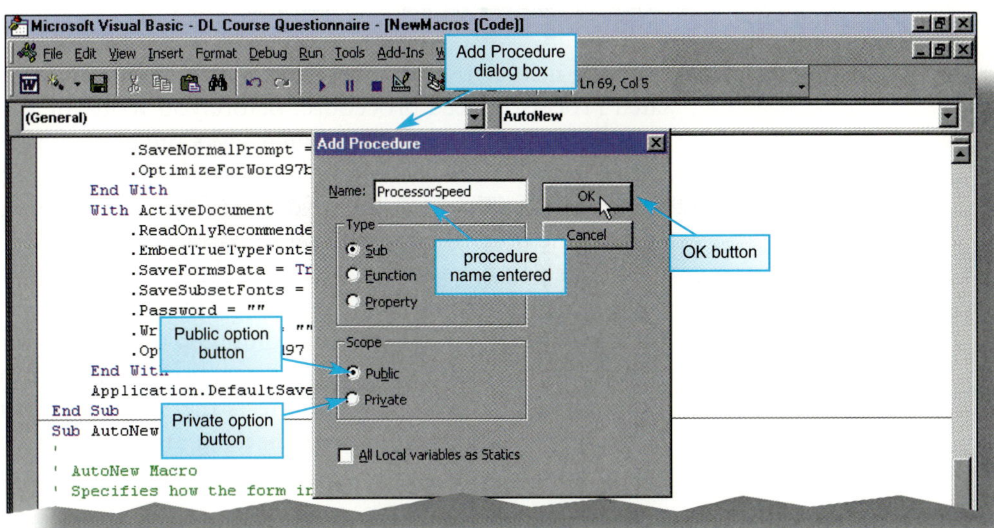

FIGURE 9-58

3 Click the OK button.

A new procedure called ProcessorSpeed displays in the Code window (Figure 9-59).

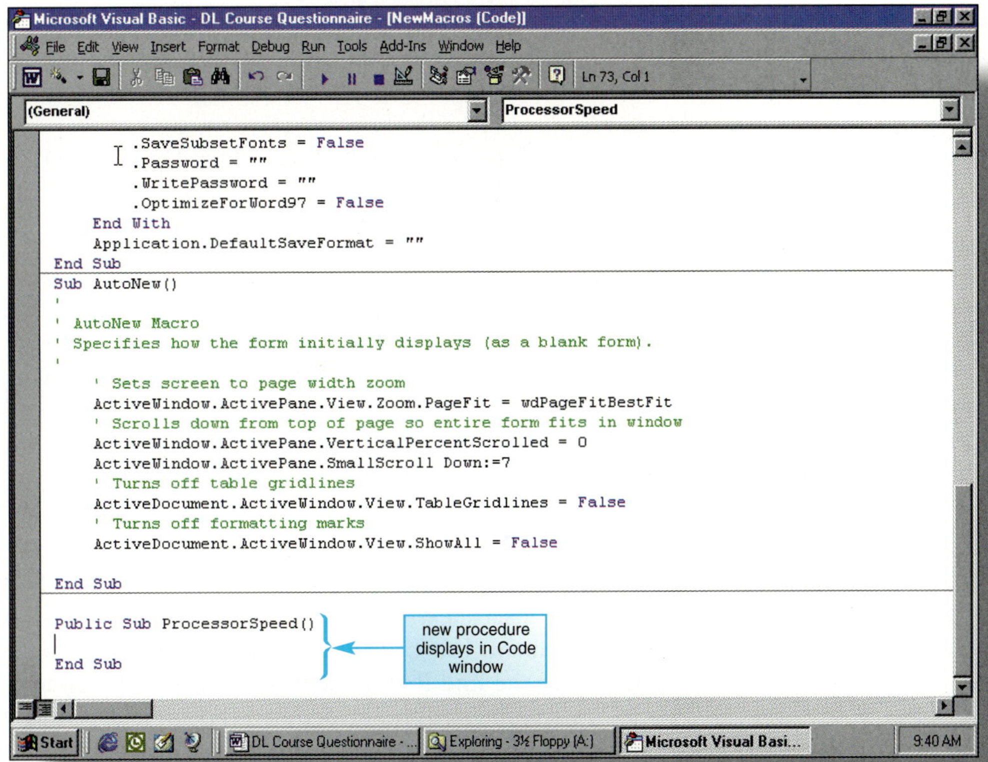

FIGURE 9-59

1. On Insert menu click Procedure, enter procedure name, click OK button

Notice in Figure 9-59 that Sub and End Sub statements automatically are inserted into the procedure. The Sub statement, however, begins with the keyword **public** which means that this procedure can be executed from other documents or programs. **Private**, by contrast, means that the procedure can be executed only from this document. If you wanted a procedure to be private, would click Private in the Scope area in the Add Procedure dialog box (see Figure 9-58).

Planning and Writing a VBA Procedure

The next step is to write and then enter the code statements for the newly created ProcessorSpeed procedure. Before you write the statements, you should plan the procedure; that is, determine what tasks the procedure is to accomplish and the order in which the tasks should be executed. Planning the procedure is an extremely important activity because the order of statements determines the sequence of execution. If the order of statements is incorrect, the procedure will not execute properly.

Once you have planned the procedure thoroughly, the next step is to write the VBA code statements on paper similar to that shown in Table 9-5. Then, before entering the procedure into the computer, test it by putting yourself in the position of Word and stepping through the instructions one at a time. As you step through the procedure, think about how it affects the Word document. Testing a procedure before entering it is called **desk checking** and is an extremely important part of the development process.

Table 9-5 Code Statements for ProcessorSpeed Procedure

LINE | *VBA CODE STATEMENT*

```
1   Public Sub ProcessorSpeed()
2   '
3   ' ProcessorSpeed Macro
4   ' Displays error message if entered processor speed is not numeric.
5   '
6       ' Test if entry in EnteredSpeed text form field is numeric
7       If IsNumeric(ActiveDocument.FormFields("EnteredSpeed").Result) = False Then
8           ' Display error message
9           MsgBox "Please enter processor speed in numbers", vbOKOnly + vbCritical
10          ' Redisplay underscores in text form field
11          ActiveDocument.FormFields("EnteredSpeed").Result = "___"
12          ' Reposition highlight in text form field
13          ActiveDocument.FormFields("EnteredType").Select
14          SendKeys "{TAB}"
15      End If
16  End Sub
```

In the code statements shown in Table 9-5, lines 2, 3, 4, 5, 6, 8, 10, and 12 are comments. Lines 1 and 16 contain the Sub and End Sub statements that automatically were inserted when you created the procedure. Line 7 is the first executable code statement. It is called an **If...Then statement** because it executes the line(s) of code up to the End If statement if the result of a condition is true. The condition in line 7 is IsNumeric(ActiveDocument.FormFields("EnteredSpeed").Result) = False. In nonprogramming terms, this condition is testing whether the user entered a number in the EnteredSpeed form field. (Recall that earlier in this project, you changed the bookmark for this form field to EnteredSpeed.) If not, then the statements up to the End If statement will be executed. If the user did enter a number, then the statements up to the End If statement are not executed and control returns back to Word.

If the user entered a nonnumeric value in the EnteredSpeed form field, then the next executable code statement is in line 9, which uses the MsgBox keyword to display a message box on the screen. The text inside the quotation marks displays inside the message box; vbOKOnly places an OK button in the message box, and vbCritical places an icon of an X in the dialog box. Table 9-6 discusses other types of icons that can display in a message box.

Table 9-6 Types of Icons for a Message Box

ICON	*VISUAL BASIC CONSTANT*
Letter X	vbCritical
Question mark	vbQuestion
Exclamation point	vbExclamation
Information symbol	vbInformation

After a user reads the message in the message box and clicks the OK button, the next executable code statement is in line 11, which replaces the users invalid entry with underscores. Then, line 13 positions the highlight in the EnteredType drop-down form field and line 14 presses the TAB key so that the highlight is positioned in the EnteredSpeed text form field – ready for the user to make another entry in the Processor Speed text box.

Having desk checked the code statements on paper, you now are ready to enter them into the Visual Basic Editor. Perform the following steps to enter the code statements into the ProcessorSpeed procedure.

InputBox

A MsgBox displays a message and one or more buttons that the user can click. If you would like the user to enter information that you can use in the VBA procedure, you should display an InputBox. An InputBox displays a message, a text box, and one or more buttons that the user can click. If the user clicks the OK button, the entered text is saved for use later in the procedure.

To Enter the ProcessorSpeed Procedure

1 **With the insertion point on the blank line between the Sub and End Sub statements in the Code window, type the code statements shown in lines 2 through 15 in Table 9-5. Make sure you enter an apostrophe at the beginning of each comment line. For clarity, indent code statements as shown in Table 9-5**

The ProcessorSpeed procedure is entered (Figure 9-60).

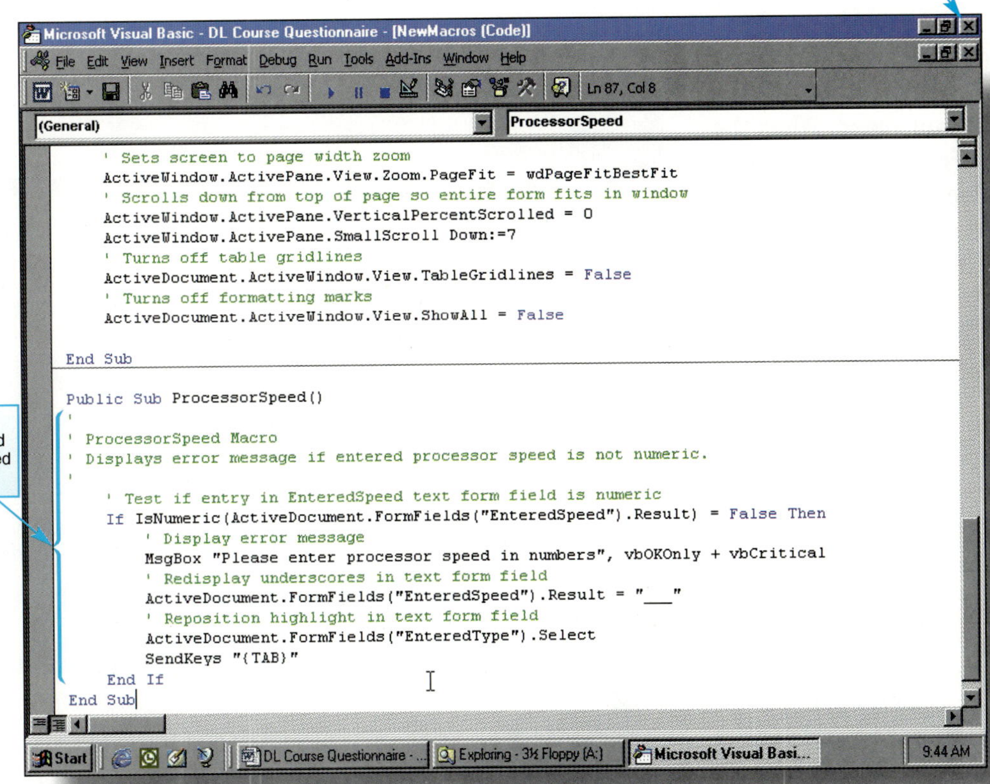

FIGURE 9-60

2 **Verify your code statements by comparing them to Figure 9-60.**

3 **Click the Close button on the right edge of the Microsoft Visual Basic title bar to return to the template.**

The Microsoft Visual Basic window closes and control returns to Word.

The next step is to attach this procedure for the macro to the text form field for the processor speed.

Running a Macro When a User Exits a Form Field

You want the ProcessorSpeed macro that you just created in the Visual Basic Editor to execute whenever a user presses the TAB key to move out of the Processor Speed text box. That is, pressing the TAB key out of the Processor Speed text box is the event that is to trigger execution of the procedure. With respect to form fields, Word allows you to execute a macro under these two circumstances: (1) when the user enters a form field and (2) when the user exits the form field. You specify when the macro should run through the Text Form Field Options dialog box. Perform the following steps to instruct Word to execute the ProcessorSpeed macro when a user exits the text form field for processor speed.

To Run a Macro When a User Exits a Form Field

1 Double-click the text form field for the processor speed. When the Text Form Field Options dialog box displays, click the Exit box arrow, scroll to and then click ProcessorSpeed. Point to the OK button.

Word displays the Text Form Field Options dialog box (Figure 9-61). The selected macro name displays in the Exit box.

2 Click the OK button.

The form field options are set as specified in the Text Form Field Options dialog box.

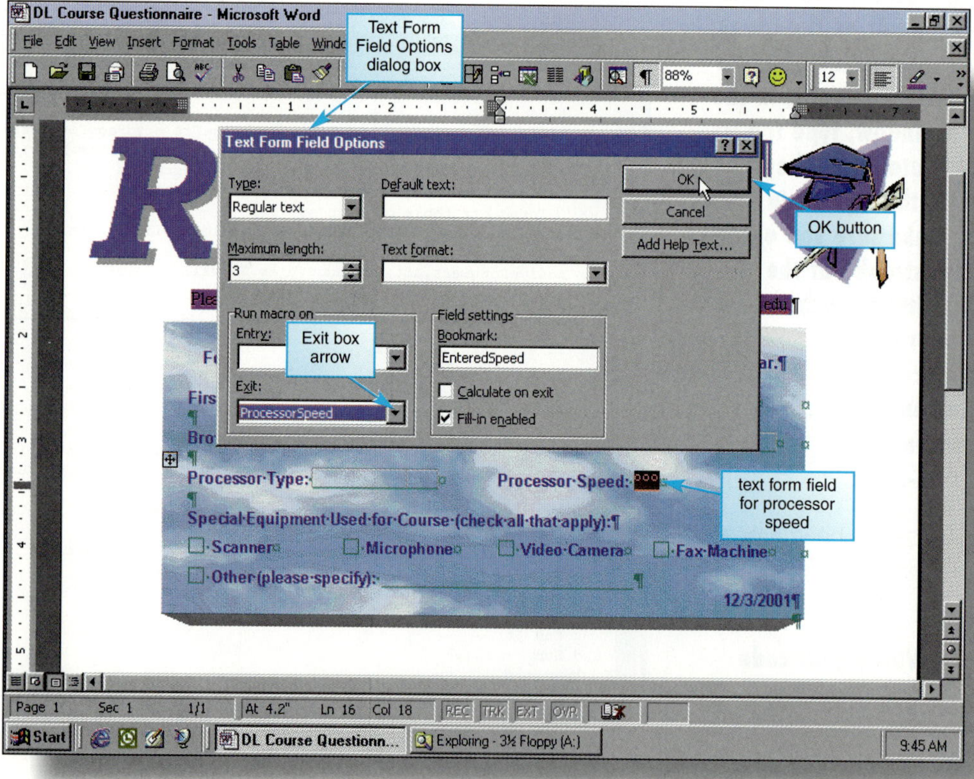

FIGURE 9-61

When you click the Entry or Exit box arrow in the Run macro on area of the Text Form Field Options dialog box, Word displays all available macros. You can select any one macro to run when the user enters or exits each form field in the form.

The ProcessorSpeed macro is complete. You will test this macro at the end of this project, after you create the next VBA procedure.

Adding an ActiveX Control to a Form

ActiveX

For more information about ActiveX, visit the Word 2000 More About Web page (www.scsite.com/wd2000/more.htm) and then click ActiveX.

In addition to the form fields available on the Forms toolbar, you can insert an ActiveX control to a Word form. An **ActiveX control** is an object, such as a button or check box, that can be included in a form to be published on the World Wide Web. The major difference between a form field and an ActiveX control is that form fields require the use of Word, whereas ActiveX controls do not. Thus, if you intend to create a Web page form, you should place ActiveX controls on the form instead of form fields.

ActiveX controls have the appearance and functionality of Windows controls. For example, the check box ActiveX control displays like any check box in any Windows dialog box. A check box form field, by contrast, has an appearance unique to Word. That is, it displays an X (instead of a check mark). Users that are familiar with Windows applications will find it easier to work with ActiveX controls than working with form fields. With form fields, a user has to TAB from one form field to another to select it. With an ActiveX control, the user can click in the form field or TAB into it.

Adding an ActiveX control to a form involves four major activities: insert the ActiveX control, format the ActiveX control, set properties of the ActiveX control, and write the macro for the ActiveX control using VBA. Word refers to the time in which you perform these four activities as **design mode**. When you run the form (fill it in) as a user does, by contrast, you are in **run mode**. The following pages explain how to add an ActiveX control to an online form.

Inserting an ActiveX Control

For this form, you would like to insert a command button that the users click when they are finished filling in the form. When they click the button, you want three actions to occur:

1. If the user entered text in the Other text box, then Word places an X in the Other check box (in case the user forgot to place an X in the check box).
2. Word displays the Save As dialog box so the user can assign a file name to the filled-in form.
3. Word displays a thank-you message on the screen.

To insert an ActiveX control, such as a command button, you use the Control Toolbox toolbar. Perform the steps on the next page to insert a command button on the online form.

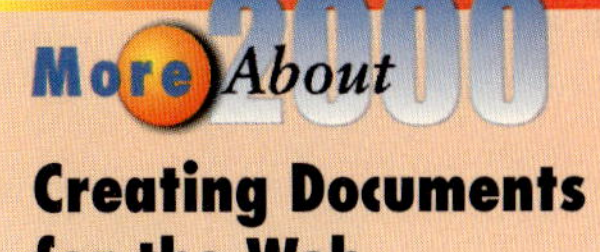

Creating Documents for the Web

For more information about how to create documents to be published on the World Wide Web, visit the Word 2000 More About Web page (www.scsite.com/wd2000/more.htm) and then click Creating Documents for the Web.

To Insert an ActiveX Control

1 If the Control Toolbox toolbar does not display on the screen already, click View on the menu bar, point to Toolbars, and then click Control Toolbox. Click the paragraph mark at the end of the data entry area and then press the ENTER key. Center the paragraph mark. Position the insertion point on the centered paragraph mark below the data entry area. Point to the Command Button button on the Control Toolbox toolbar (Figure 9-62).

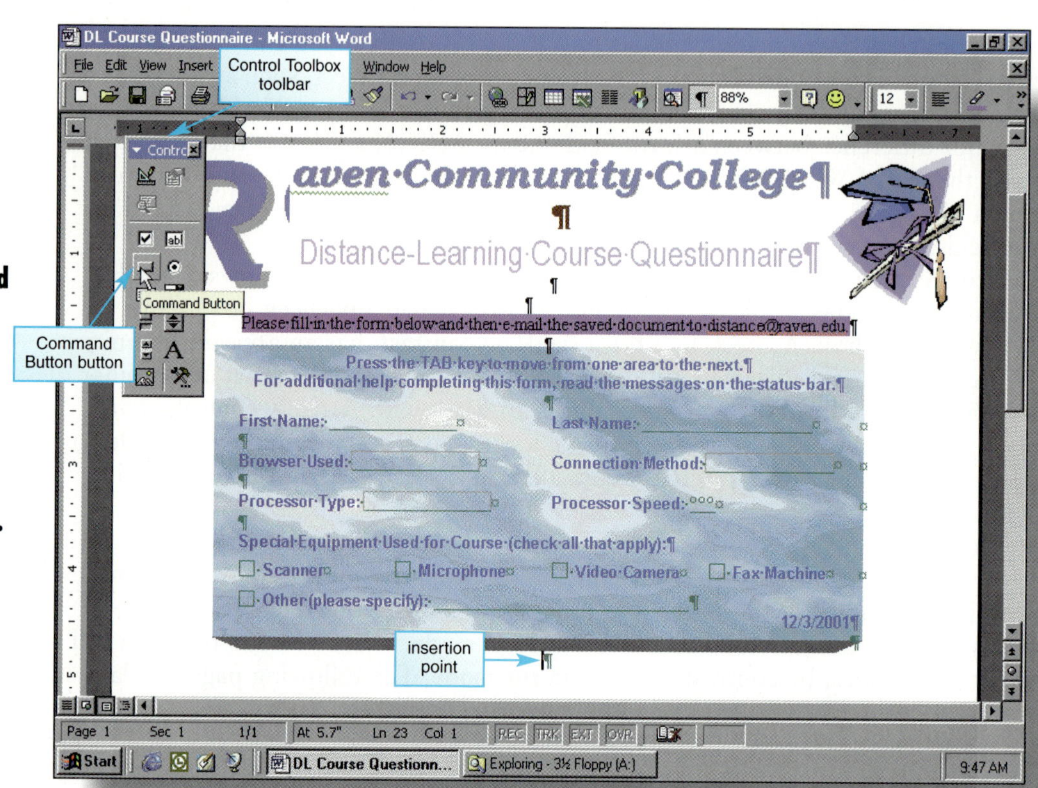

FIGURE 9-62

2 Click the Command Button button.

Word inserts a standard-sized command button at the location of the insertion point and switches to design mode (Figure 9-63). The text CommandButton1 partially displays on the face of the button. The button is selected and is surrounded by sizing handles.

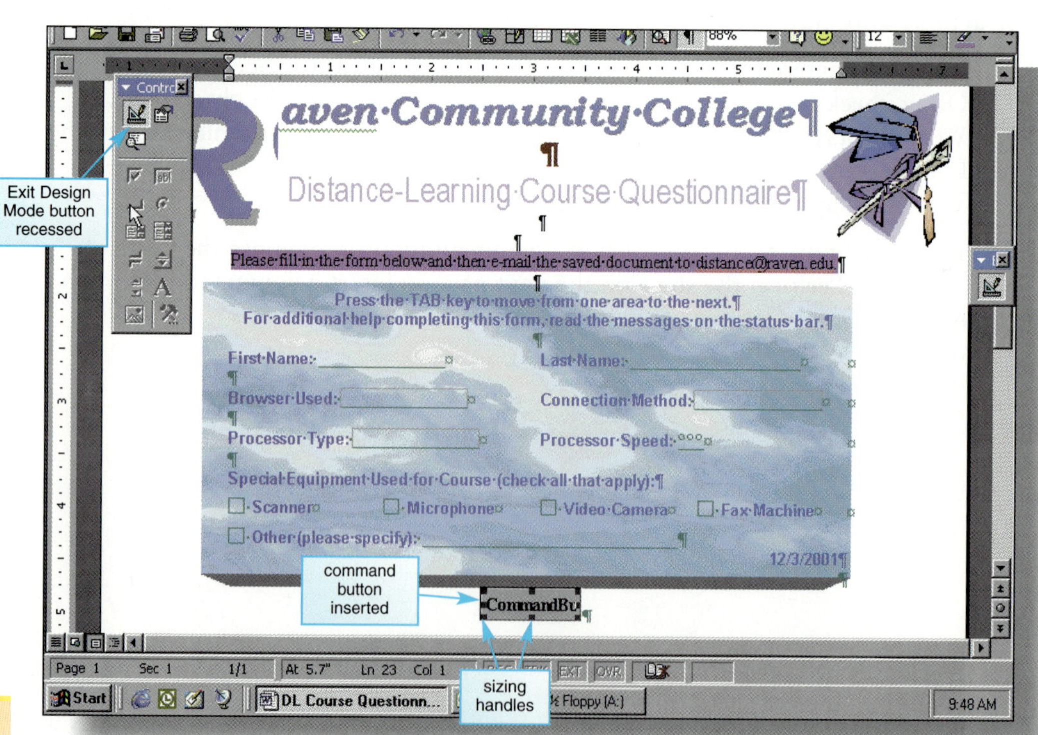

FIGURE 9-63

Other Ways

1. Click Design Mode button on Visual Basic toolbar

When you click a button on the Control Toolbox toolbar, Word automatically switches to design mode, changes the Design Mode button on the Control Toolbox toolbar to an Exit Design Mode button, and recesses the Exit Design Mode button.

The Control Toolbox toolbar buttons are summarized in Table 9-7.

Table 9-7 Summary of Buttons on the Control Toolbox Toolbar

BUTTON	NAME	FUNCTION	BUTTON	NAME	FUNCTION
	Design Mode	Changes to design mode; Design Mode button changes to Exit Design Mode button when in design mode		Combo Box	Inserts a drop-down list box
	Properties	Displays Properties window		Toggle Button	Inserts a toggle button
	View Code	Displays Code window in Visual Basic Editor		Spin Button	Inserts a spin button
	Check Box	Inserts a check box		Scroll Bar	Inserts a scroll bar
	Text Box	Inserts a text box		Label	Inserts a label
	Command Button	Inserts a command button		Image	Inserts an image
	Option Button	Inserts an option button		More Controls	Displays a list of additional controls
	List Box	Inserts a list box			

The next step is to format the ActiveX control.

Formatting the ActiveX Control

Word inserts the command button as an inline object; that is, part of the current paragraph. You want the command button to be a floating object so that you can position it anywhere on the form. Thus, perform the following steps to convert the command button from inline to floating.

To Format the ActiveX Control

1 Right-click the command button just inserted and then point to Format Control on the shortcut menu (Figure 9-64).

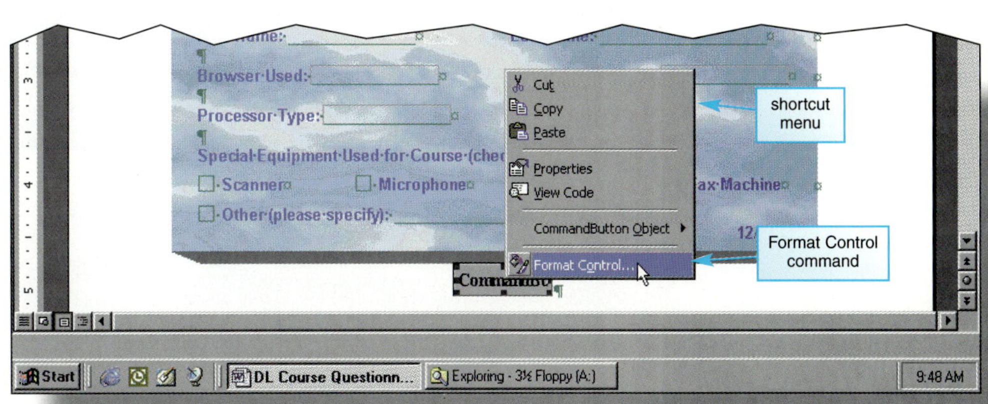

FIGURE 9-64

2 Click Format Control. When the Format Object dialog box displays, if necessary, click the Layout tab. Click Square in the Wrapping style area. Click Center in the Horizontal alignment area. Point to the OK button.

Word displays the Format Object dialog box (Figure 9-65). A square wrapping style changes an object to floating.

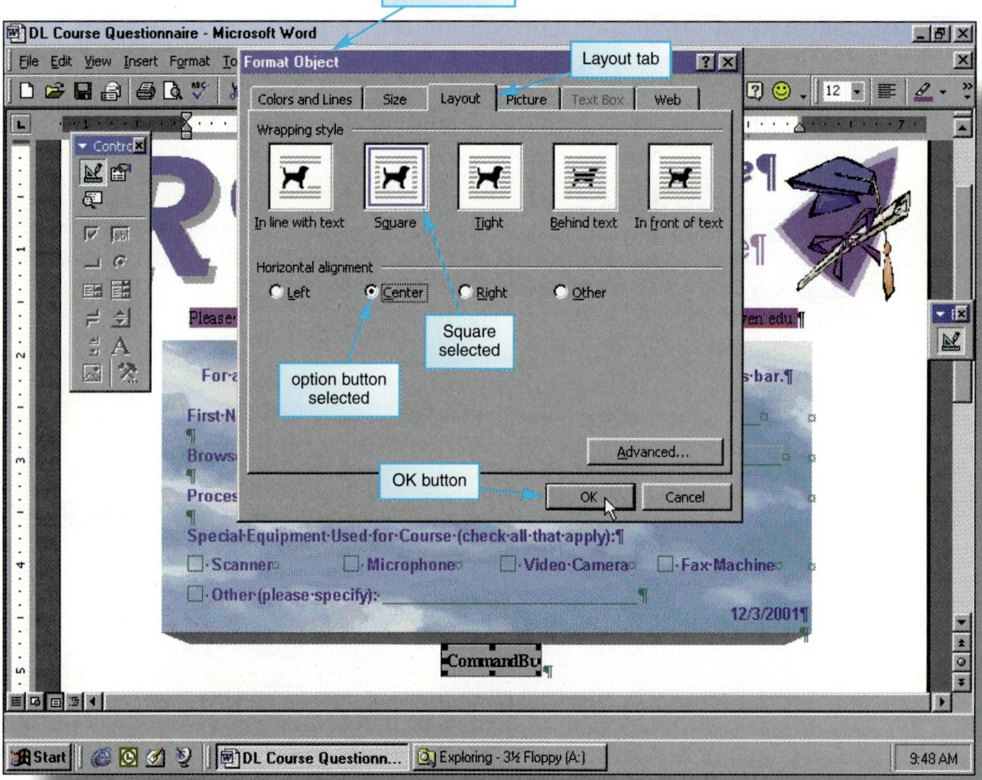

FIGURE 9-65

3 Click the OK button. Drag the control so there is about one-quarter inch between the top of the command button and the bottom of the data entry area.

The command button is positioned as shown in Figure 9-66.

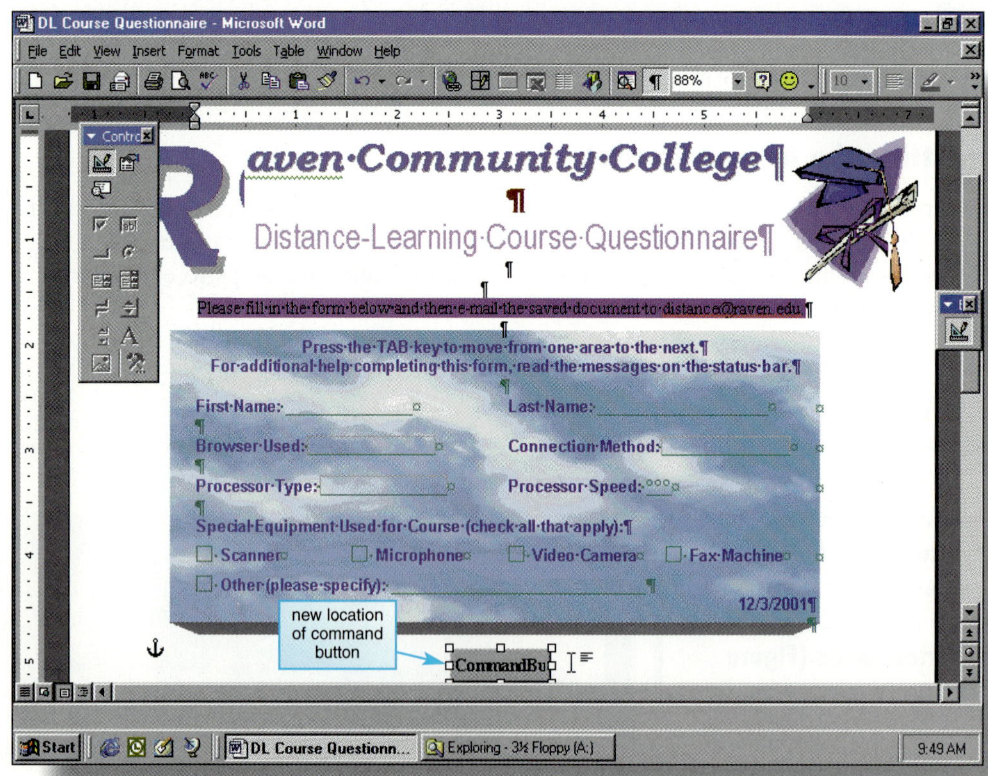

FIGURE 9-66

The next step is to set the properties of the ActiveX control.

VBA Help

For help with VBA, code statements, and properties, display the Office Assistant and then type `VBA help` in the What would you like to do? text box. Click the Search button and then click Get Help for Visual Basic for Applications in Word.

Setting Properties of an ActiveX Control

In Word, a command button ActiveX control has 20 different **properties** (see Figure 9-68 on the next page), such as caption (the words on the face of the button), background color, foreground color, height, width, font, and so on. After you insert a command button into a form, you can change any one of the 20 properties to improve its appearance and modify its function.

For this command button, you want to change its caption to the text, Click Here When Finished. Perform the following steps to change the Caption property of an ActiveX control.

To Set Properties of an ActiveX Control

1 With the command button selected and Word in design mode, point to the Properties button on the Control Toolbox toolbar (Figure 9-67).

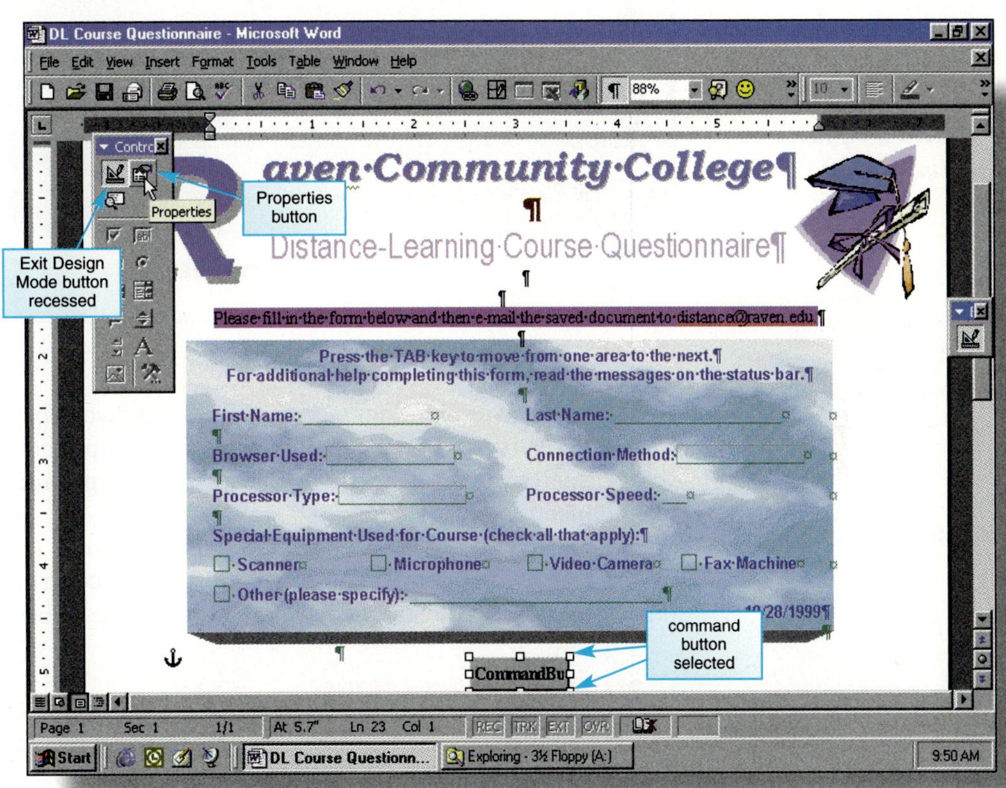

FIGURE 9-67

2 **Click the Properties button. When the Properties window displays, if necessary, click the Alphabetic tab. Click Caption in the list and then type** `Click Here When Finished` **as the new caption. Point to the Close button on the Properties window.**

Word displays the Properties window for the command button ActiveX control (Figure 9-68). The Caption property is changed.

3 **Click the Close button on the Properties window.**

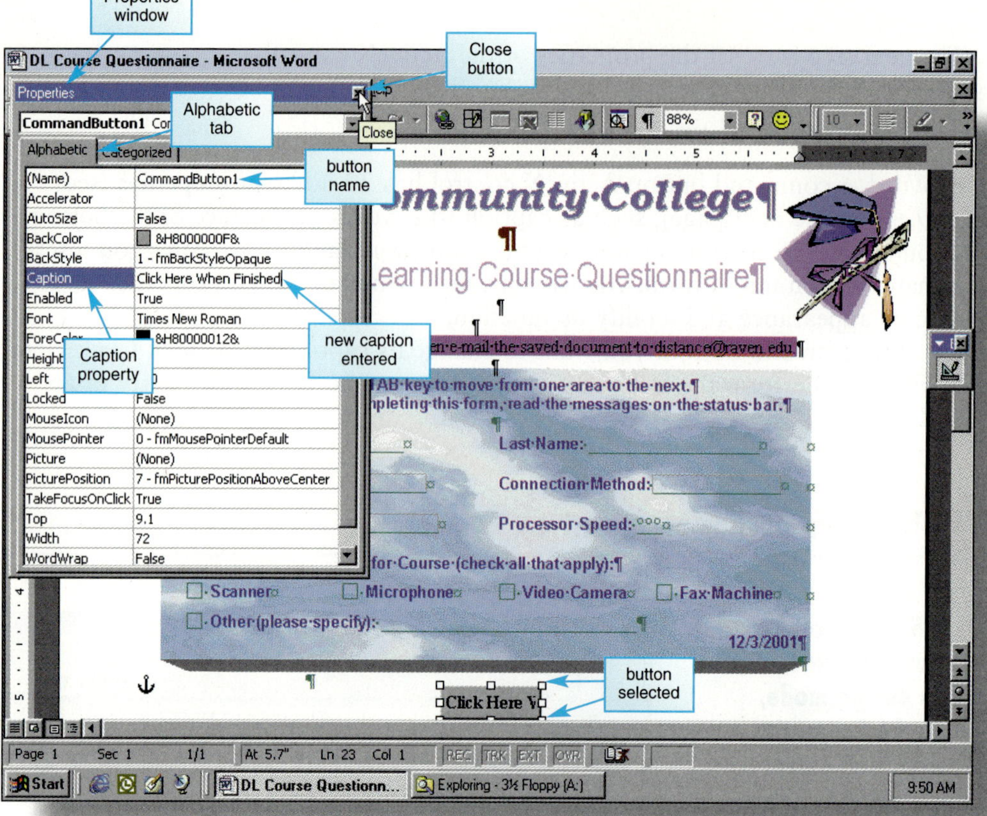

FIGURE 9-68

Other Ways

1. In design mode, right-click control, click Properties on shortcut menu
2. Click Properties Window button on toolbar when Visual Basic Editor is active

The Properties window in Figure 9-68 has two tabs, Alphabetic and Categorized. The Alphabetic sheet displays the properties in alphabetical order. The Categorized sheet displays the properties by subject, such as appearance, behavior, font, and miscellaneous.

The next step is to resize the command button so that the entire caption displays on the face of the button. You resize an ActiveX control the same way you resize any other object – by dragging its sizing handles as described in the following steps.

TO RESIZE AN ACTIVEX CONTROL

1. Drag the right middle sizing handle to the right until the entire caption displays on the face of the command button.
2. If necessary, drag the command button so it is centered on the form.

The command button displays as shown in Figure 9-69.

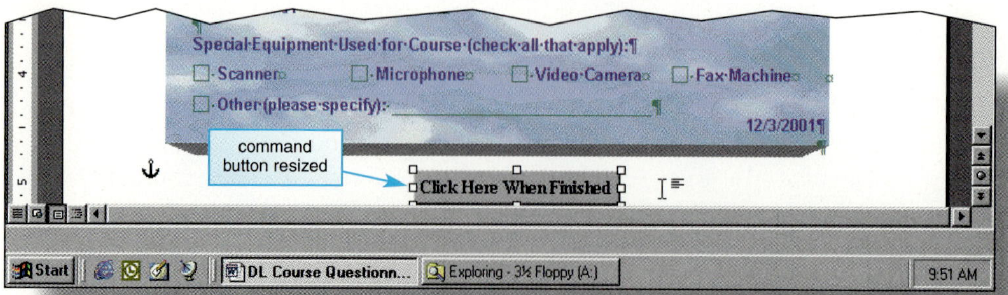

FIGURE 9-69

The next step is to enter the VBA code that will execute when a user clicks this command button.

Writing the Macro for the ActiveX Control

The next step is to write and then enter the procedure for the macro that will execute when a user clicks the Click Here When Finished button. Clicking the button is the event that triggers execution of the macro.

As mentioned earlier, you should plan a procedure by writing its VBA code on paper similar to that shown in Table 9-8. Then, before entering the procedure into the computer, you desk check it.

Table 9-8 Click Here When Finished Button Procedure

LINE	*VBA CODE STATEMENT*
1	`Private Sub CommandButton1_Click`
2	`'`
3	`' CommandButton1_Click Macro`
4	`' Executes when user clicks button called Click Here When Finished.`
5	`'`
6	`    ' If user entered text in Other text box, put X in Other check box`
7	`    If Left(ActiveDocument.FormFields("OtherText").Result, 1) <> "_" Then`
8	`        ActiveDocument.FormFields("OtherCheck").CheckBox.Value = True`
9	`    End If`
10	`    ' Display Save As dialog box`
11	`    Dialogs(wdDialogFileSaveAs).Show`
12	`    ' Display thank-you message`
13	`    TitleBarText = "Thank You For Your Time"`
14	`    MessageText = "Please e-mail " & ActiveDocument.FullName & " to distance@raven.edu."`
15	`    MsgBox MessageText, , TitleBarText`
16	`End Sub`

Notice in line 1 that the name of the procedure in the Sub statement is CommandButton1_Click, which Word determines from the name of the button (see Figure 9-68), and the event that causes the procedure to execute (Click).

The first executable code statement is an If...Then statement in line 7. This statement tests if the user entered text in the Other text box, which will have a bookmark of OtherText. If it does, then line 8 instructs Word to place an X in the Other check box, which will have a bookmark of OtherCheck; otherwise, Word skips lines 8 and proceeds to line 10.

The next executable code statement is in line 11, which displays the Save As dialog box on the screen – allowing the user to save the form. Finally, line 15 displays a message box that contains two variables. The first is for the message text, which is defined in line 14; and the second is for the title bar text, which is defined in line 13. Because the text for the title bar and message is so long, variables are used to define these elements of the message box.

As illustrated earlier in this project, you use the Visual Basic Editor to enter code statements into a procedure. With Word in design mode and the ActiveX control selected, you can click the View Code button on the Control Toolbox toolbar to display the control's procedure in the Code window of the Visual Basic Editor.

The code statements in lines 7 and 8 use bookmarks that need to be defined. You have learned that you enter a bookmark in the Form Field Options dialog box. Perform the following steps to change the default bookmarks for the Other check box form field and the Other text form field.

TO CHANGE BOOKMARKS FOR FORM FIELDS

1. Double-click the check box form field for Other.
2. When the Check Box Form Field Options dialog box displays, double-click the text in the Bookmark text box and then type `OtherCheck` as the new bookmark. Click the OK button.
3. Double-click the text box form field for Other.
4. When the Text Form Field Options dialog box displays, double-click the text in the Bookmark text box and then type `OtherText` as the new bookmark. Click the OK button.

Word changes form field options as specified in the Form Field Options dialog boxes.

Perform the following steps to enter the code statements for the procedure for the macro that will execute when a user clicks the Click Here When Finished button.

Steps To Enter the Click Here When Finished Button Procedure

1 With Word in design mode, click the Click Here When Finished button and then point to the View Code button on the Control Toolbox toolbar (Figure 9-70).

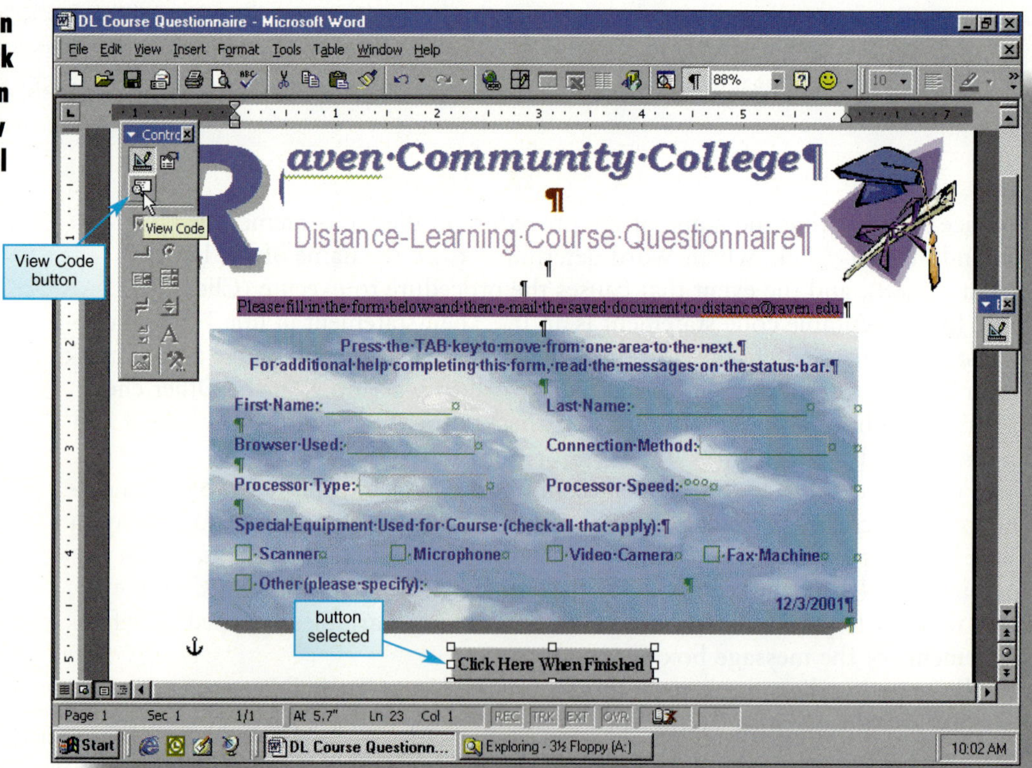

FIGURE 9-70

2 Click the View Code button. When the Visual Basic Editor displays, if the Project Explorer window displays, click its Close button. Double-click the Code window title bar to maximize the window.

Word starts the Visual Basic Editor and displays the Microsoft Visual Basic window (Figure 9-71). The Visual Basic Editor automatically inserts the Sub and End Sub statements and positions the insertion point between the two statements.

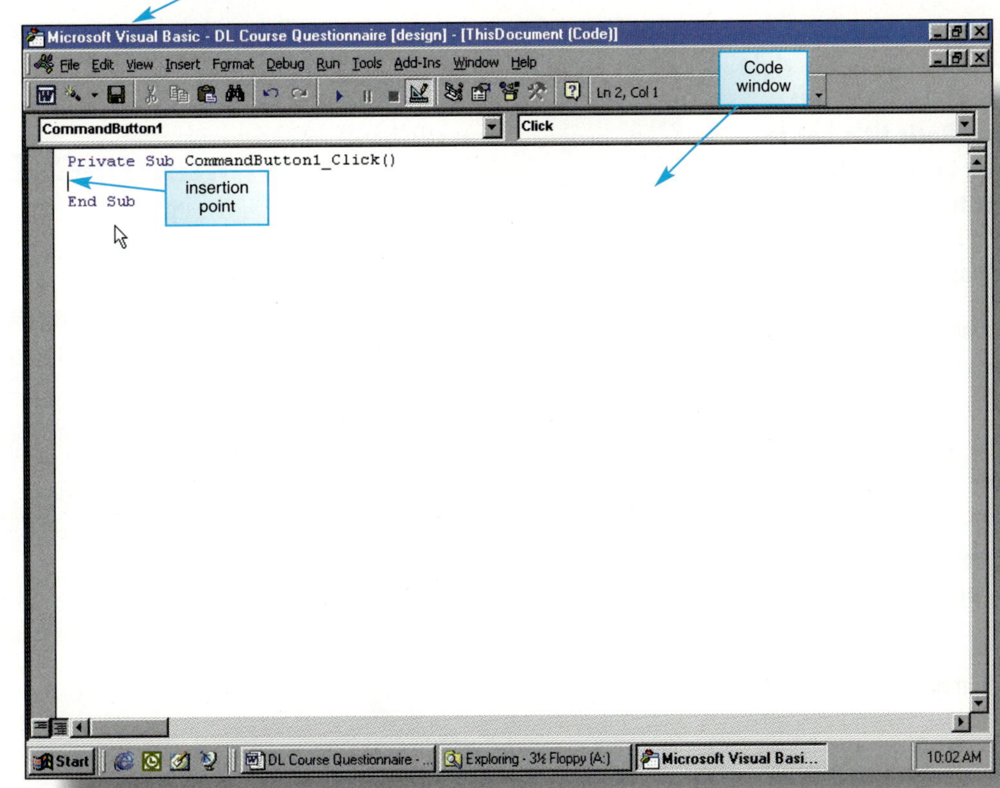

FIGURE 9-71

3 With the insertion point on the blank line between the Sub and End Sub statements in the Code window, type the code statements shown in lines 2 through 15 in Table 9-8 on page WD 9.59. Make sure you enter an apostrophe at the beginning of each comment line. For clarity, indent the code statements as shown in Table 9-8.

The command button procedure is complete (Figure 9-72).

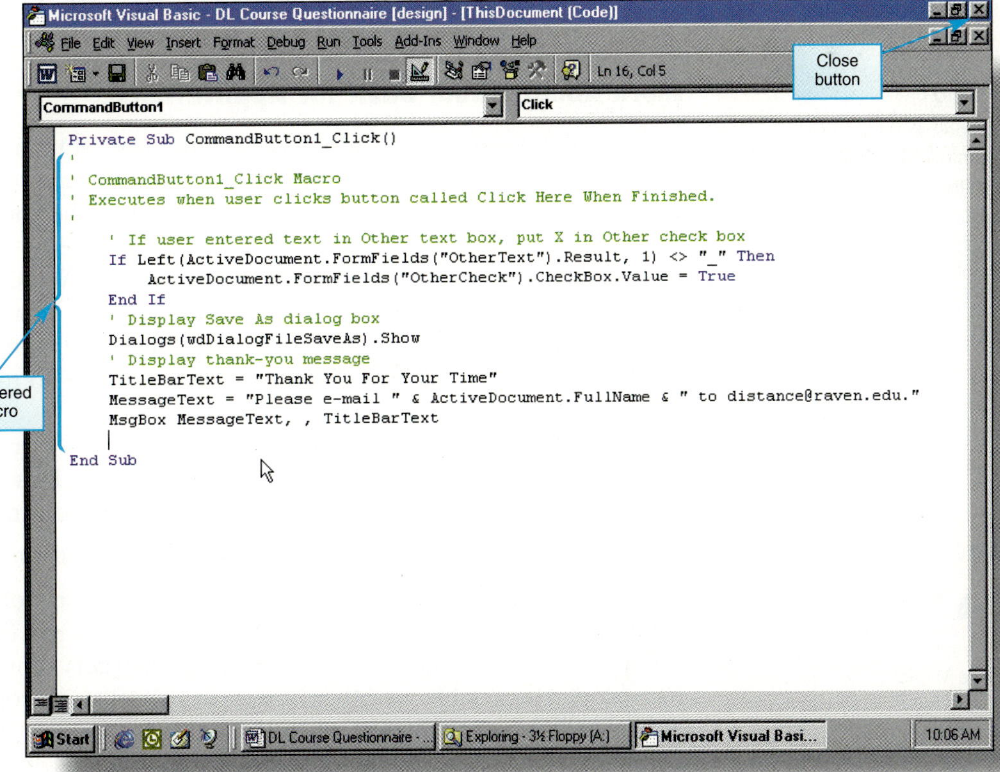

FIGURE 9-72

4 Verify your code statements by comparing them to Figure 9-72.

5 **Click the Close button on the right edge of the Microsoft Visual Basic title bar to return to the online form. Point to the Exit Design Mode button on the Control Toolbox toolbar.**

The online form displays as shown in Figure 9-73.

6 **Click the Exit Design Mode button. Click the Close button on the Control Toolbox toolbar title bar.**

Word returns to run mode, which means if you click the Click Here When Finished button, Word will execute the associated macro.

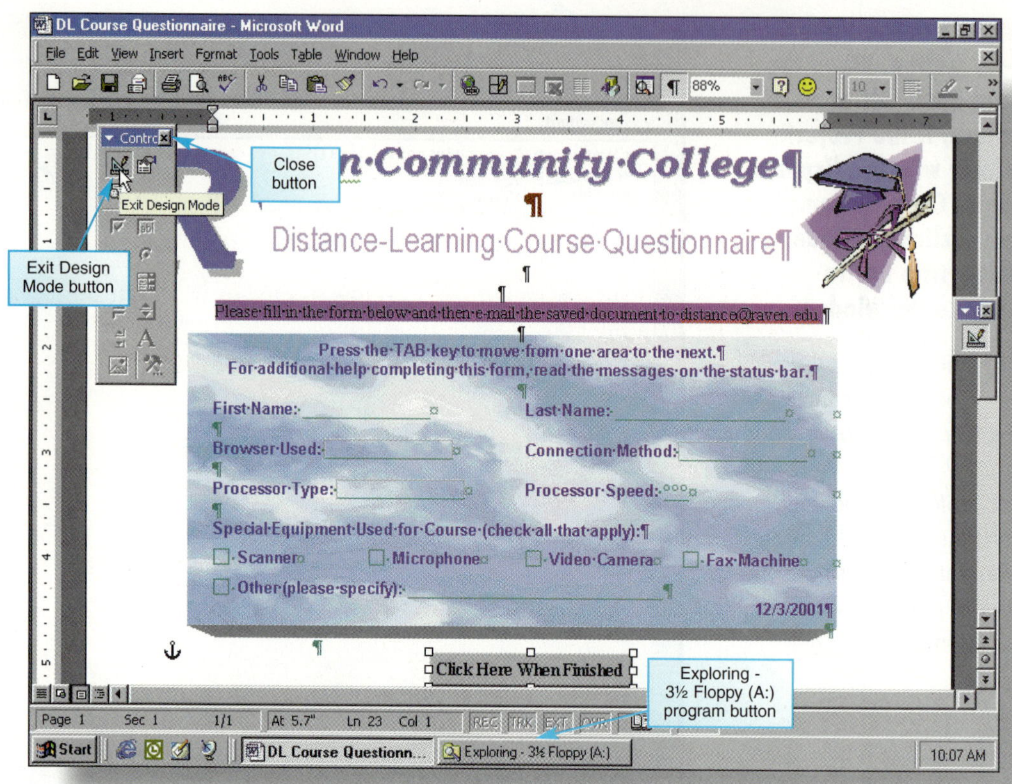

FIGURE 9-73

1. In design mode, double-click control
2. In design mode, right-click control, click View Code on shortcut menu
3. Click Visual Basic Editor button on Visual Basic toolbar

Web Forms

If you intend to publish a form on the World Wide Web, you should limit ActiveX controls to the standard HTML controls, which include the following: checkbox, dropdown box, textbox, submit, reset, password, option button, list box, text area, submit with image, and hidden.

More About Visual Basic for Applications

Visual Basic for Applications uses many more statements than those presented in this project. These statements, however, should help you understand the basic makeup of a Visual Basic statement. For example, the code statement in line 11 of Table 9-8 on page WD 9.59 that displays the Save As dialog box includes a period. The entry on the left side of the period tells Word which object you want to affect (in this case, the dialog box). An **object** can be a document, a form field, a bookmark, a dialog box, a button, or any other control on a form. The entry on the right side of the period tells Word what you want to do to the object (in this case, display it).

Earlier you were shown how to change an object's properties using the Properties window (Figure 9-68 on page WD 9.58). This code statement from the ProcessorSpeed macro changed an object's property during execution of a procedure:

```
ActiveDocument.ActiveWindow.View.TableGridlines = False
```

This statement changes the TableGridlines property of the View object in the ActiveWindow object in the ActiveDocument object to false; that is, it hides table gridlines. An equal sign in a code statement instructs Word to make an assignment to a property, variable, or other object. In the previous code statement, the TableGridlines property was set to False.

Testing the Online Form

The macros for the DL Course Questionnaire file are complete. The next step is to protect the online form, save it, and then test it.

Protecting Forms

If you want only authorized users to be able to unprotect a form, you should password-protect the form. To do this, click Tools on the menu bar, click Protect Document, click Forms in the Protect document for area, type the password in the Password (optional) text box, and then click the OK button. Then, reenter the password in the Confirm Password dialog box.

TO PROTECT THE FORM

1. Click Tools on the menu bar and then click Protect Document.
2. When the Protect Document dialog box displays, click Forms in the Protect document for area, and then click the OK button.

Word protects the form.

TO SAVE A DOCUMENT

1. Click the Save button on the Standard toolbar.

Word saves the template with the same file name, DL Course Questionnaire.

TO TEST THE FORM

1. Click the Exploring – 3½ Floppy (A:) program button on the taskbar (see Figure 9-73) to display Windows Explorer.
2. Double-click the DL Course Questionnaire icon in the Contents pane to display a new Word document based on the contents of the DL Course Questionnaire. If Word displays a dialog box, click the Enable Macros button. As instructed by the AutoNew macro, the Word document should zoom page width, scroll down seven lines, hide table gridlines, and hide formatting marks (see Figure 9-1a on page WD 9.5).
3. With the highlight in the First Name text box, type `LaShonda` and then press the TAB key. Type `Green` in the Last Name text box. Press the TAB key to highlight the Browser Used drop-down list box and display its box arrow.
4. Click the Browser Used box arrow and then click Netscape. Press the TAB key.
5. Click the Connection Method box arrow and then click 33.6 Kbps Modem. Press the TAB key.
6. Click the Processor Type box arrow and then click Pentium III. Press the TAB key.
7. Type `abc` in the Processor Speed text box. Press the TAB key. As instructed by the ProcessorSpeed macro, an error message should display (see Figure 9-1b on page WD 9.5). Click the OK button in the message box. Type `400` in the Processor Speed text box. Press the TAB key.
8. Click the following check boxes: Microphone and Video Camera.
9. Press the TAB key three times to position the highlight in the Other text box. Type `VCR` and then click the Click Here When Finished button.
10. As defined by the CommandButton1_Click procedure, Word displays the Save As dialog box. Change the Save in location to drive A. Type `Green Form` in the File name text box and then click the Save button in the dialog box. When the save is finished, the CommandButton1_Click procedure then displays a thank-you message box that indicates the name and location of the file the user should e-mail back to the college (see Figure 9-1c on page WD 9.5). Click the OK button in the message box. Notice that Word placed an X in the Other check box.

Printing

If you want to print a form and wish to save ink, print faster, or minimize printer overrun errors, lower the printer resolution. Click File on the menu bar, click Print, click the Properties button in the Print dialog box, click the Graphics tab, click the Resolution box arrow, click a lower resolution than that displayed currently, click the Apply button, click the OK button, and then click the Close button.

11. Assume you are the person tabulating the form results at the college and just received the Green Form. Click the Form Data Only button on the Standard toolbar, which instructs Word to place a check mark in the Save form data only check box in the Options dialog box. Click File on the menu bar and then click Save Copy As. Type `Green Form` in the File name text box and then click the Save button to save the document as a text file. Click the Yes button in the dialog box.

You have tested all aspects of the form. If a Word or Visual Basic error message displayed while you tested the form, you need to make necessary corrections and then retest the form. To do this, close the Word window displaying the blank form. Unprotect the template. Make the corrections. Protect the template again. Save the template again. Retest the form. Repeat this procedure until the form displays as intended.

You are finished with the form. Perform the following steps to quit Word and close Windows Explorer.

TO QUIT WORD

1. Click File on the menu bar and then click Exit.

The Word window closes.

TO CLOSE WINDOWS EXPLORER

1. Click the Close button on the Exploring - 3½ Floppy (A:) window's title bar.

Windows Explorer closes.

Copying, Renaming, and Deleting Macros

You may find it necessary to copy a macro, rename a macro, or delete a macro. Macros cannot be copied or renamed from Word; instead, you must use the Visual Basic Editor. You can, however, delete a macro from Word.

TO COPY A MACRO

1. Click Tools on the menu bar, point to Macro, and then click Macros. When the Macros dialog box displays, click the macro name to copy, and then click the Edit button to start the Visual Basic Editor and display the macro in the Code window.
2. Select all the text in the macro's VBA procedure; that is, drag from the Sub statement to the End Sub statement (including the Sub and End Sub statements).
3. Click Edit on the menu bar and then click Copy.
4. Click Edit on the menu bar and then click Paste.

You can paste a macro into the same document or a different document.

TO RENAME A MACRO

1. Click Tools on the menu bar, point to Macro, and then click Macros. When the Macros dialog box displays, click the macro name to rename, and then click the Edit button to start the Visual Basic Editor and display the macro in the Code window.
2. Select the macro name following the keyword Sub at the beginning of the macro's procedure and then type a new macro name.

The macro will be renamed in the Macros dialog box.

TO DELETE A MACRO

1. Click Tools on the menu bar, point to Macro, and then click Macros.
2. When the Macros dialog box displays, click the macro name to delete, and then click the Delete button.
3. Click the Yes button in the Microsoft Word dialog box.

CASE PERSPECTIVE SUMMARY

Before showing the modified DL Course Questionnaire to your supervisor, you decide to have two of your co-workers test it to be sure it works properly. They find one error. You unprotect the template, fix the error, protect the form again, and then test it one final time, just to be sure the error is fixed. Then, you e-mail the DL Course Questionnaire to your supervisor for her review. She is quite pleased with the results. Realizing the power of Visual Basic for Applications with Word, she asks you to train three members of her staff on how to create VBA procedures in Word.

Project Summary

Project 9 introduced you to working with macros and Visual Basic for Applications (VBA). You modified the template for the online form created in Project 8. To change its appearance, you formatted a letter as an in margin drop cap, changed the text by creating and applying a new style, filled the drawing object with a bitmap picture, and then added a 3-D effect to the drawing object. Then, you created a macro using the macro recorder and assigned the macro to a toolbar button. Next, you recorded an automatic macro. You viewed the macro's code using the Visual Basic Editor and added comments and code statements to the macro. You create another macro that executed when the user exits a form field. Finally, you inserted an ActiveX control, formatted it, set its properties, and wrote a VBA procedure for it.

More About 2000

Quick Reference

For a table that lists how to complete the tasks covered in this book using the mouse, menu, shortcut menu, and keyboard, see the Word Quick Reference Summary at the back of this book or visit the Shelly Cashman Series Office Web page (www.scsite.com/off2000/qr.htm) and then click Microsoft Word 2000.

What You Should Know

Having completed this project, you should now be able to perform the following tasks:

- Add a 3-D Effect *(WD 9.24)*
- Add Code Statements to a Procedure *(WD 9.45)*
- Add Comments to a Procedure *(WD 9.42)*
- Apply a Style Using a Shortcut Key *(WD 9.20)*
- Change a Bookmark for a Drop-Down Form Field *(WD 9.47)*
- Change a Highlight Color *(WD 9.15)*
- Change Bookmarks for Form Fields *(WD 9.60)*
- Change Graphics *(WD 9.12)*
- Change Options for a Text Form Field *(WD 9.46)*
- Close the Visual Basic Editor *(WD 9.45)*
- Close Windows Explorer *(WD 9.64)*
- Copy a Macro *(WD 9.64)*
- Create a Style that has a Shortcut Key *(WD 9.17)*
- Create an Automatic Macro *(WD 9.35)*
- Customize a Toolbar *(WD 9.30)*
- Delete a Macro *(WD 9.65)*
- Display Formatting Marks *(WD 9.9)*
- Enter the Click Here When Finished Button Procedure *(WD 9.60)*
- Enter the ProcessorSpeed Procedure *(WD 9.51)*
- Fill a Drawing Object with a Bitmap Picture *(WD 9.22)*
- Format a Character as an In Margin Drop Cap *(WD 9.14)*
- Format the ActiveX Control *(WD 9.55)*
- Insert a Visual Basic Procedure *(WD 9.48)*
- Insert an ActiveX Control *(WD 9.54)*
- Modify Existing Code *(WD 9.44)*
- Modify Text *(WD 9.12)*
- Protect the Form *(WD 9.63)*
- Quit Word *(WD 9.64)*
- Record a Macro *(WD 9.26)*
- Rename a Macro *(WD 9.65)*
- Reset Menus and Toolbars *(WD 9.8)*
- Resize an ActiveX Control *(WD 9.58)*
- Run a Macro *(WD 9.29)*
- Run a Macro When a User Exits a Form Field *(WD 9.52)*
- Save a Document *(WD 9.25, WD 9.63)*
- Save the Document with a New File Name *(WD 9.7)*
- Set a Security Level in Word *(WD 9.10)*
- Set Properties of an ActiveX Control *(WD 9.57)*
- Start Word and Open an Office Document *(WD 9.7)*
- Test the AutoNew Macro *(WD 9.38)*
- Test the Form *(WD 9.63)*
- Uncheck the Save Data Only for Forms Check Box *(WD 9.30, WD 9.34)*
- Unprotect a Document *(WD 9.8)*
- View a Macro's VBA Code *(WD 9.39)*
- Zoom Page Width *(WD 9.9)*

Microsoft Certification

The Microsoft Office User Specialist (MOUS) Certification program provides an opportunity for you to obtain a valuable industry credential – proof that you have the Word 2000 skills required by employers. For more information, see Appendix D or visit the Shelly Cashman Series MOUS Web page at www.scsite.com/off2000/cert.htm.

1 Debugging VBA Code

Instructions: In this assignment, you access a template through Windows Explorer. As shown in Figure 9-74, the template contains an online form. The form contains two macros: one that executes when you initially display the form on the screen and another that executes when you click the command button at the bottom of the screen. Each macro contains one coding error. You are to test the code by filling in the form. Then, correct the Visual Basic errors as they display on the screen.

The template is located on the Data Disk. If you did not download the Data Disk, see the inside back cover for instructions for downloading the Data Disk or see your instructor.

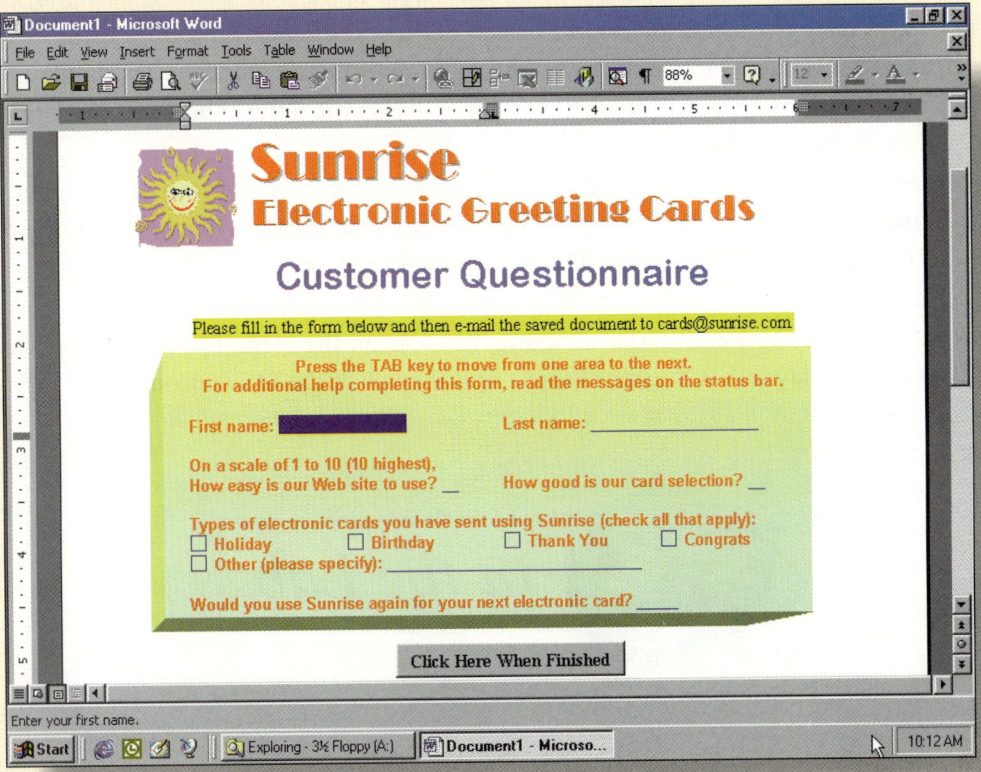

FIGURE 9-74

Perform the following tasks:

1. Right-click the My Computer icon on the Windows desktop and then click Explore on the shortcut menu. When the Exploring window displays, click the Address text box to select it. With the Data Disk in drive A, type `a:` and then press the ENTER key. Double-click the SG Questionnaire icon in the contents pane to display a new document based on the SG Questionnaire template.
2. When Word displays a dialog box about macros, click the Enable Macros button.
3. When a Visual Basic error message displays, click its OK button. If necessary, maximize the Visual Basic window. Notice the text, .TableGrdlines =, is highlighted because Visual Basic did not recognize it. The text should say, .TableGridlines = (it is missing the letter i). Click the selected text and insert the letter i between the letters r and d in Gridlines. Then, click the Continue button on the Visual Basic Standard toolbar. Close the Visual Basic window by clicking its Close button.

(continued)

Debugging VBA Code *(continued)*

4. With the highlight in the First name text box, type `Mario` and then press the TAB key.
5. With the highlight in the Last name text box, type `Hernandez` and then press the TAB key.
6. Type `10` in response to How easy is our Web site to use? Press the TAB key.
7. Type `8` in response to How good is our card selection? Press the TAB key.
8. Place an X in the Holiday and Birthday check boxes by clicking them. Press the TAB key five times.
9. With the highlight on the drop-down list box at the bottom of the form, click the box arrow and then click Yes.
10. Click the Click Here When Finished button. When the Visual Basic error message displays, click the Debug button. If necessary, click the Microsoft Visual Basic - SG Questionnaire program button on the taskbar to display the Visual Basic Editor. Notice the code statement that displays the Save As dialog box is highlighted as an error. The word Show is misspelled as Shw. Insert the letter o between the letters h and w. Click the Continue button on the Visual Basic Standard toolbar.
11. Type `Hernandez Form` in the Save As dialog box, change the Save in location to drive A, and then click the Save button in the Save As dialog box. When Word asks if you want to save changes to the template, click the No button. Click the OK button in the Thank You message box.
12. Print the filled-in form.
13. Press the ALT+F11 keys. In the Visual Basic window, click File on the menu bar and then click Print. When the Print dialog box displays, click Current Project and then click the OK button.

1 Creating an Automatic Macro for an Online Form

Problem: You created the online form shown in Figure 8-69 on page WD 8.60 for The Web Grocer. Your supervisor has asked you to change its appearance and create a macro for the form so it displays properly on the screen when a user first displays it (as a blank form). You modify the form so it looks like the one shown in Figure 9-75.

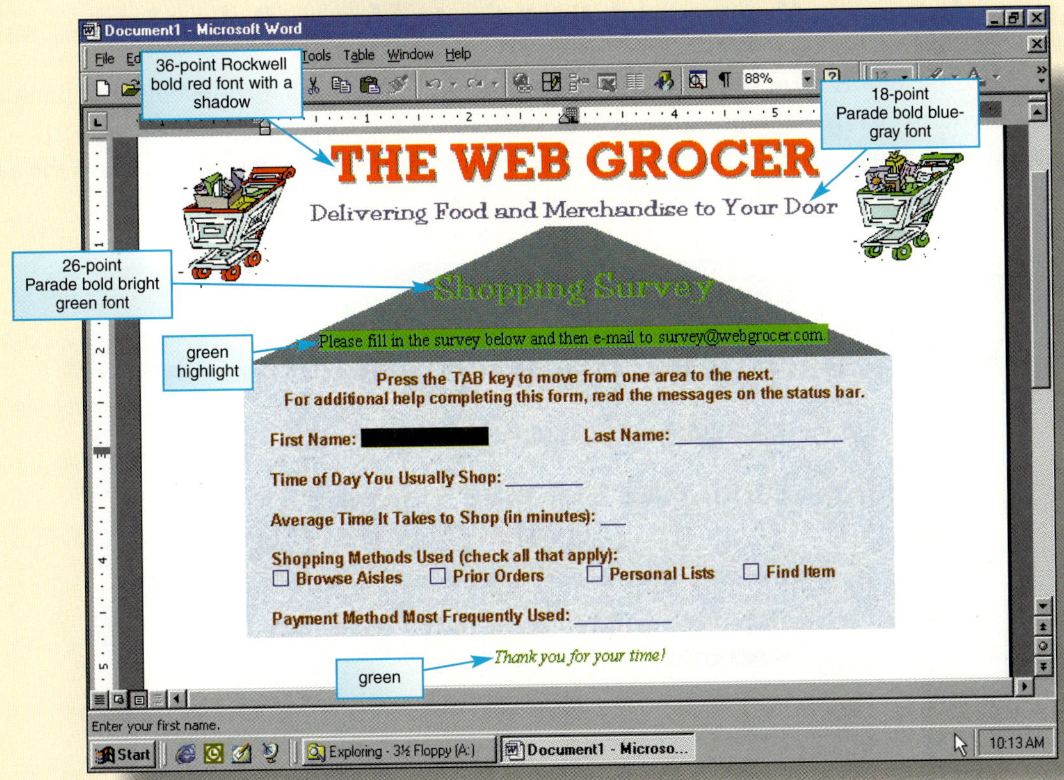

FIGURE 9-75

Instructions:

1. Open the template called Web Grocer Survey that you created in Lab 1 of Project 8 on page WD 8.60. Save the survey with a new file name of WG Survey.
2. Modify the formats of the company name, slogan, form title, form instructions, and thank-you message as shown in Figure 9-75. Remove the current clip art and insert the ones shown in Figure 9-75. Resize the clip art images to 60 percent of their original size.
3. Change the fill effect in the rectangle drawing object to the Blue tissue paper texture. Add the 3-D effect called 3-D Style 20.
4. Create a new character style called DataEntryArea that is formatted to an 11-point Arial bold brown font that has a shortcut key of ALT+D. Apply the style to all text in the data entry area.
5. Create an automatic macro called AutoNew using the macro recorder. The macro should change the zoom percentage to page width and scroll down so the entire form fits in the document window. Test the macro.
6. Modify the macro in the Visual Basic Editor so that it also hides formatting marks and table gridlines. Also, modify the number of lines it scrolls down, if necessary. Test the macro again.
7. Print the Visual Basic code for the macro (in the Visual Basic Editor, click File on the menu bar, click Print, click Current project, click the OK button).
8. Protect the form. Save the form. Print the blank form.
9. Access the template through Windows Explorer. Fill out the form. Save the filled-out form. Print the filled-out form.

2 Creating an Automatic Macro and ActiveX Control for an Online Form

Problem: You created the online form shown in Figure 8-70 on page WD 8.61 for Lincoln State Bank. Your supervisor has asked you to change its appearance, create a macro for the form so it displays properly on the screen when a user first displays it (as a blank form), and add a button that automatically displays the Save As dialog box for the user. You modify the form so it looks like the one shown in Figure 9-76.

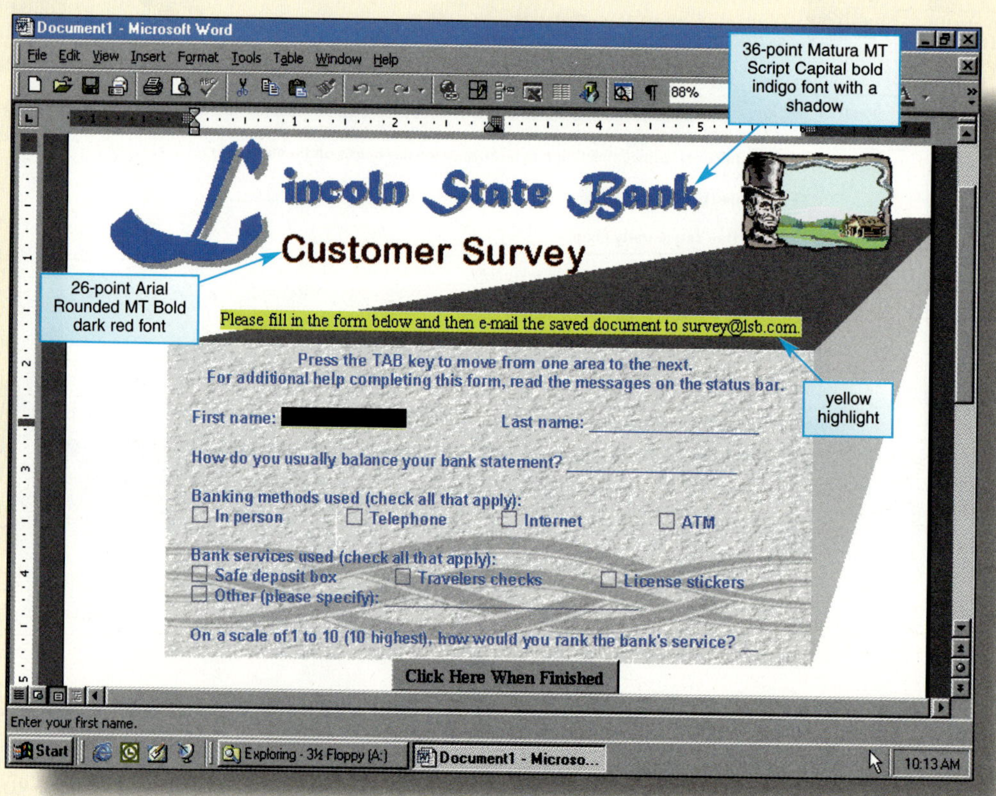

FIGURE 9-76

Instructions:

1. Open the template called Lincoln Bank Survey that you created in Lab 2 of Project 8 on page WD 8.61. Save the survey with a new file name of LB Survey.
2. Modify the formats of the company name, form title, and form instructions as shown in Figure 9-76. Remove the current clip art and insert the one shown in Figure 9-76. Resize the clip art image to 30 percent of its original size. Left-align the company name and then format the first letter of the company name as an in margin drop cap. Change its font size to 94 and reposition it if necessary.
3. Change the fill effect in the rectangle drawing object to the bitmap file called Backgrnd. It is located with the Windows wallpaper bitmap files and also is on the Data Disk. Add the 3-D effect called 3-D Style 19.
4. Create a new character style called DataEntryArea that is formatted to an 11-point Arial bold indigo font that has a shortcut key of ALT+D. Apply the style to all text in the data entry area.
5. Create an automatic macro called AutoNew using the macro recorder. The macro should change the zoom percentage to page width and scroll down so the entire form fits in the document window. Test the macro.

6. Modify the macro in the Visual Basic Editor so that it also hides formatting marks and table gridlines. Also, modify the number of lines it scrolls down, if necessary. Test the macro again.
7. Remove the thank-you message line. Insert a command button ActiveX control. Format the command button as a floating object. Change its caption property to the text, Click Here When Finished. Change its Font property to 12-point Times New Roman bold font. Resize the button so the entire caption displays. Add code to the button so that when the user clicks the button it displays the Save As dialog box and displays a thank-you message.
8. Print the Visual Basic code for the macros (in the Visual Basic Editor, click File on the menu bar, click Print, click Current project, click the OK button).
9. Protect the form. Save the form. Print the blank form.
10. Access the template through Windows Explorer. Fill out the form. Save the filled-out form. Print the filled-out form.

3 Creating an Automatic Macro, Data Entry Macros, and ActiveX Control for an Online Form

Problem: You created the online form shown in Figure 8-71 on page WD 8.62 for World Cablevision. Your supervisor has asked you to change its appearance, create a macro for the form so it displays properly on the screen when a user first displays it (as a blank form), create a macro for each of the number of viewers text form fields, add a button that automatically displays the Save As dialog box for the user, and create a macro and corresponding button on the toolbar that places a check mark in the Save form data only check box. You modify the form so it looks like the one shown in Figure 9-77.

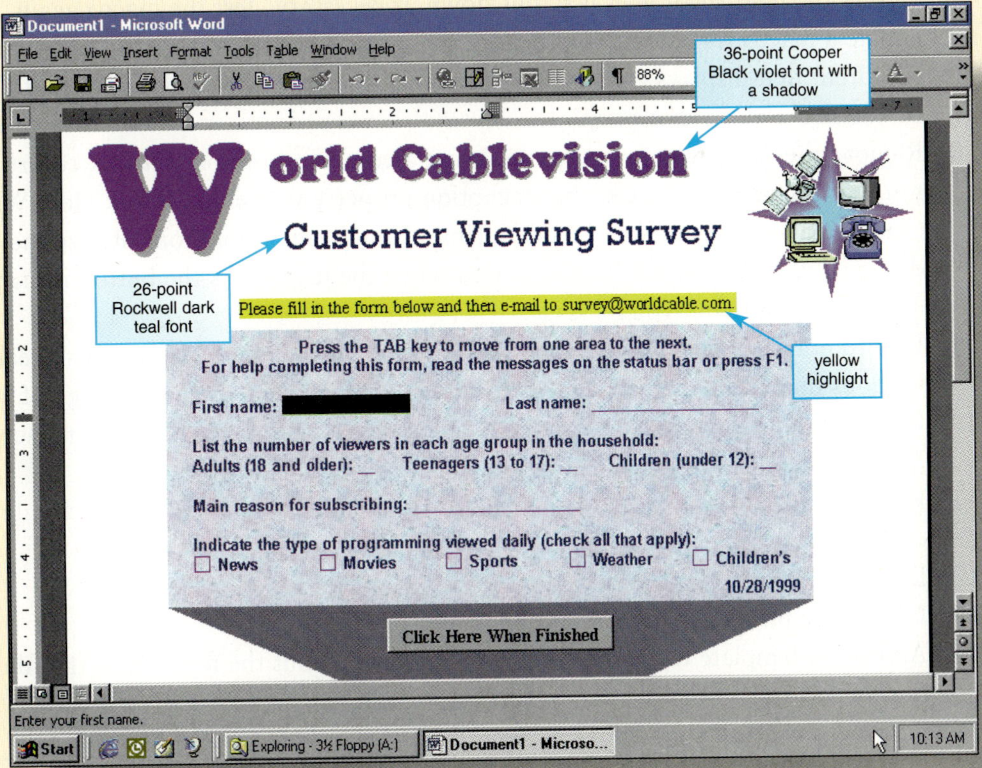

FIGURE 9-77

(continued)

Creating an Automatic Macro, Data Entry Macros, and ActiveX Control for an Online Form *(continued)*

Instructions:

1. Open the template called World Cablevision Survey that you created in Lab 3 of Project 8 on page WD 8.62. Save the survey with a new file name of WC Survey.
2. Modify the formats of the company name, form title, and form instructions as shown in Figure 9-77 on the previous page. Remove the current clip art and insert the one shown in Figure 9-77. Left-align the company name and then format the first letter of the company name as an in margin drop cap. Change its font size to 105 and reposition it if necessary.
3. Change the fill effect in the rectangle drawing object to the Bouquet texture. Add the 3-D effect called 3-D Style 15.
4. Create a new character style called DataEntryArea that is formatted to an 11-point Arial bold dark teal font that has a shortcut key of ALT+D. Apply the style to all text in the data entry area.
5. Create an automatic macro called AutoNew using the macro recorder. The macro should change the zoom percentage to page width and scroll down so the entire form fits in the document window. Test the macro.
6. Modify the macro in the Visual Basic Editor so that it also hides formatting marks and table gridlines. Also, modify the number of lines it scrolls down, if necessary. Test the macro again.
7. Create a macro for each of the three number of viewers text boxes on the screen (Adults, Teenagers, and Children) that displays an error message when the user exits each text box if the user leaves the entry blank or enters a nonnumeric entry.
8. Remove the thank-you message line. Insert a command button ActiveX control. Format the command button as a floating object. Change its caption property to the text, Click Here When Finished. If necessary, change its Font property to 12-point Times New Roman bold font. Resize the button so the entire caption displays. Add code to the button so that when the user clicks the button it displays the Save As dialog box and displays a thank-you message.
9. Record a macro that places a check mark in the Save data only for forms check box in the Save tab of the Options dialog box. Create a toolbar button for this macro; use the image of a coffee cup for the button.
10. Copy the AutoNew macro to a macro called TestMacro. Change the TestMacro name to the name MacroTest.
11. Print the Visual Basic code for the macros (in the Visual Basic Editor, click File on the menu bar, click Print, click Current project, click the OK button).
12. Delete the macro called MacroTest.
13. Protect the form. Save the form. Print the blank form.
14. Access the template through Windows Explorer. Fill out the form. Save the filled-out form. Print the filled-out form.

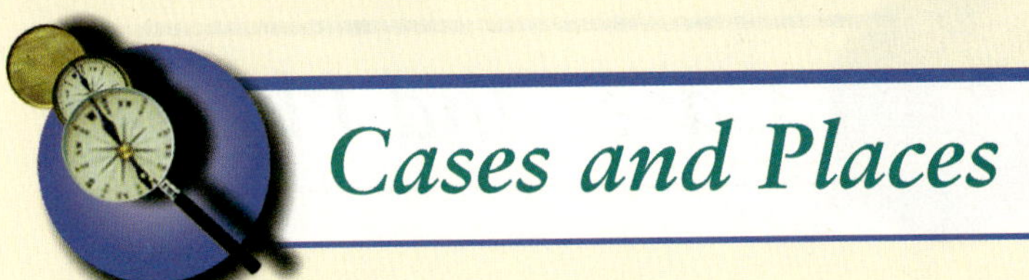

Cases and Places

The difficulty of these case studies varies:
◗ are the least difficult; ◗◗ are more difficult; and ◗◗◗ are the most difficult.

1 ◗ You created the online form for World Travel that was defined in Cases and Places Assignment 1 in Project 8 on page WD 8.63. Your supervisor has asked you to change its appearance; that is, change its fonts, font sizes, fill effects, colors, and clip art, and use a drop cap in the company name. He also asked that the form include the following:

1. When the form initially displays on the screen (as a blank document), Word zooms page width, scrolls down to display the entire form in the Word window, hides formatting marks, and hides gridlines.
2. If the user leaves the text boxes containing entries for the number of adult passengers or the number of child passengers blank or enters a nonnumeric entry, an error message should display.
3. The form should contain a Click Here When Finished button that when clicked does the following:
   a. If the user entered text in the Other text box, then Word places an X in the Other check box (just in case the user left it blank).
   b. The Save As dialog box displays so the user can assign a file name to the filled-in form.
   c. A thank-you message displays on the screen that informs the user what file should be e-mailed back to the school.

Use the concepts and techniques presented in this project to create and format this announcement.

2 ◗◗ You created the questionnaire for the Student Government Association at your school that was defined in Cases and Places Assignment 2 in Project 8 on page WD 8.63. The president of the Student Government Association has asked you to change the questionnaire's appearance (all fonts, font sizes, colors, graphics, and fill effects), create a macro for the form so it displays properly on the screen when a user first displays it (as a blank form), and add a button that when clicked automatically displays the Save As dialog box for the user and then displays a thank-you message. Use the concepts and techniques presented in this project to modify the online form. Be sure to use a different graphic from the Clip Gallery.

3 ◗◗ You created the questionnaire for your school's fitness center that was defined in Cases and Places Assignment 3 in Project 8 on page WD 8.63. The director of the fitness center has asked you to change the questionnaire's appearance (all fonts, font sizes, colors, graphics, and fill effects), create a macro for the form so it displays properly on the screen when a user first displays it (as a blank form), and add a button that when clicked automatically displays the Save As dialog box for the user and then displays a thank-you message. Use the concepts and techniques presented in this project to modify the online form. Be sure to use a different graphic from the Clip Gallery.

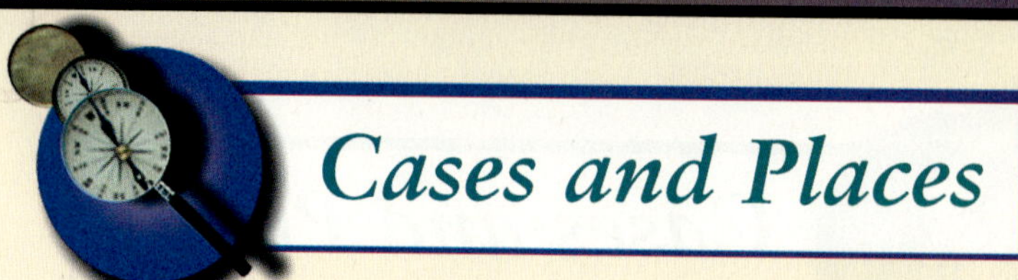

Cases and Places

4 ▶▶ You created the questionnaire for the computing center at your school that was defined in Cases and Places Assignment 4 in Project 8 on page WD 8.64. The director of the computing center has asked you to change the questionnaire's appearance (all fonts, font sizes, colors, graphics, and fill effects), create a macro for the form so it displays properly on the screen when a user first displays it (as a blank form), and add a button that when clicked automatically displays the Save As dialog box for the user and then displays a thank-you message. Use the concepts and techniques presented in this project to modify the online form. Be sure to use a different graphic from the Clip Gallery.

5 ▶▶▶ Your supervisor at Raven Community College would like to publish the Distance-Learning Course Questionnaire (Figure 9-1 on page WD 9.5) on the Web. Thus, all of the form fields must be changed to ActiveX controls; that is, you have to delete the Word form fields and insert similar ActiveX controls. Also, she would like every text box and drop-down list box to display an error message if the user leaves the entry blank, which means you will write a VBA procedure for each of the objects. Use the concepts and techniques presented in this project to modify the online form.

6 ▶▶▶ Your supervisor at Sunrise Electronic Greeting Cards would like to publish the Customer Questionnaire (Figure 9-74 on page WD 9.67) on the Web. Thus, all of the form fields must be changed to ActiveX controls; that is, you have to delete the Word form fields and insert similar ActiveX controls. Also, he would like every text box and drop-down list box to display an error message if the user leaves the entry blank, which means you will write a VBA procedure for each of the objects. Use the concepts and techniques presented in this project to modify the online form.

Microsoft Word 2000

Linking an Excel Worksheet and Charting Its Data in Word

CASE PERSPECTIVE

At a recent meeting of managers at World Link Cable, an agenda item led to a discussion about the types of new cable channels that World Link should offer. After much debate, the meeting attendees had the following question, What are the main reasons that our current customers subscribe to cable television? As marketing manager, Pauline Krause said she could obtain an answer to this question by including a survey in customer statements that asks the cable television subscribers to indicate the reasons they switched to cable television service from regular television service. The department heads compiled the following items for the survey: better reception, commercial-free channels, commercial-free movies, concerts, more channels, movie channels, sporting events, and weather.

One month later, Pauline received the completed surveys. Having tabulated the results in the form of an Excel worksheet, she would like to communicate these results to the department managers at World Link Cable. As her assistant, Pauline has asked you to create a memo that links the Excel worksheet to the memo. She also would like a chart of the Excel worksheet to portray the survey results graphically.

Introduction

With Microsoft Office 2000 products, you can insert part or all of a document, called an **object**, created in one application into a document created in another application. For example, you could insert an Excel worksheet into a Word document. In this case, the Excel worksheet (the object) is called the **source document** (inserted from) and the Word document is called the **destination document** (inserted into). You can use one of three techniques to insert objects from one application to another: copy and paste, embed, or link.

When you copy an object by clicking the Copy button on the Standard toolbar and then paste it by clicking the Paste button on the Standard toolbar, the source document becomes part of the destination document. You edit a pasted object using editing features of the destination application. For example, an Excel worksheet would become a Word table that you can edit in Word.

Similarly, an embedded object becomes part of a destination document. The difference between an embedded object and a pasted object is that you edit the contents of an embedded object using the editing features of the source application. For example, an embedded Excel worksheet remains as an Excel worksheet in the Word document. To edit the worksheet in the Word document, you double-click the worksheet to display Excel menus and toolbars in the Word window. If, however, you edit the Excel worksheet by opening the worksheet from within Excel, the embedded object will not be updated in the Word document.

A linked object, by contrast, does not become part of the destination document even though it appears to be part of it. Rather, a connection is established between the source and destination documents so that when you open the destination document, the linked object displays as part of it. When you edit a linked object, the source application starts and opens the source

Office 2000

For more information on the features of Microsoft Office 2000, visit the Word 2000 More About Web page (www.scsite.com/wd2000/more.htm) and then click Microsoft Office 2000 Features.

document that contains the linked object. For example, a linked Excel worksheet remains as an Excel worksheet. To edit the worksheet from the Word document, you double-click the worksheet to start Excel and display the worksheet in an Excel window. Unlike an embedded object, if you edit the Excel worksheet by opening it from Excel, the linked object will be updated in the Word document, too.

You would use the link method when the contents of an object are likely to change and you want to ensure that the most current version of the object displays in the source document. Another reason to link an object is if the object is large, such as a video clip or a sound clip.

As shown in Figure 1, this integration feature links an Excel worksheet to a Word document (a memo) and then links the Excel worksheet data to a Word chart. That is, the Excel worksheet is inserted into the Word document in the form of an Excel worksheet. Word also uses the data in the Excel worksheet to chart the worksheet data. Because the data is inserted into the Word document as a link, any time you open the memo in Word, the latest version of the Excel worksheet data displays in the memo. Figure 1a shows the memo draft (without any links to Excel); Figure 1b shows the Excel worksheet; and Figure 1c shows the final copy of the memo with links to the Excel worksheet and its data.

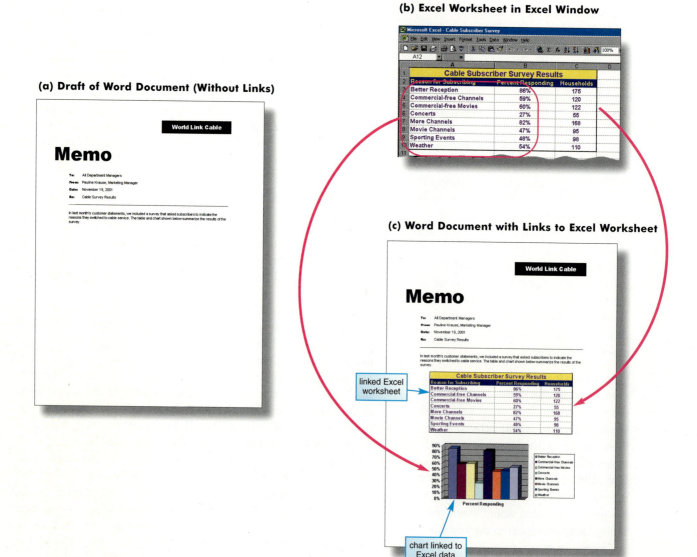

(a) Draft of Word Document (Without Links)

(b) Excel Worksheet in Excel Window

Cable Subscriber Survey Results

Reason for Subscribing	Percent Responding	Households
Better Reception	86%	175
Commercial-free Channels	59%	120
Commercial-free Movies	60%	122
Concerts	27%	55
More Channels	82%	168
Movie Channels	47%	95
Sporting Events	48%	98
Weather	54%	110

(c) Word Document with Links to Excel Worksheet

linked Excel worksheet

chart linked to Excel data

FIGURE 1

Starting Word and Opening a Document

The first step in this integration feature is to open the draft of the memo that is to include the linked worksheet data. The memo file named Cable Survey Memo Draft is located on the Data Disk. If you did not download the Data Disk, see the inside back cover for instructions for downloading the Data Disk or see your instructor. Perform the following steps to open the memo.

TO OPEN A DOCUMENT

1. If necessary, insert the Data Disk in drive A. Click the Start button on the taskbar and then click Open Office Document.
2. When the Open Office Document dialog box displays, if necessary, click the Look in box arrow and then click 3½ Floppy (A:). Double-click the file named Cable Survey Memo Draft.
3. When the Word window displays, if necessary, maximize it. Reset toolbars as described in Appendix C.
4. Click View on the menu bar and then click Print Layout. If the Show/Hide ¶ button on the Standard toolbar is not recessed, click it.

Word becomes active, opens the Cable Survey Memo Draft file, and displays it in the Word window.

Saving the Document with a New File Name

To preserve the contents of the original Cable Survey Memo Draft file, save a copy of it with a new file name as described in the following steps.

TO SAVE A DOCUMENT

1. With a floppy disk in drive A, click File on the menu bar and then click Save As.
2. Type `Cable Survey Memo` in the File name text box. Do not press the ENTER key.
3. If necessary, click the Save in box arrow and then click 3½ Floppy (A:).
4. Click the Save button in the Save As dialog box.

Word saves the document on a floppy disk in drive A with a new file name of Cable Survey Memo.

Linking an Excel Worksheet

The next step in this integration feature is to insert the Excel worksheet (source document) into the Cable Survey Memo (destination document) as a linked object. The Excel worksheet (Cable Subscriber Survey) is located on the Data Disk. Perform the steps on the next page to link the Excel worksheet to the Word document.

Excel Worksheets

To insert a blank Excel worksheet into a Word document, click the Insert Microsoft Excel Worksheet button on the Standard toolbar and then click the grid at the location that represents the number of rows and columns to be in the worksheet. The menus and toolbars change to Excel menus and toolbars. To redisplay Word menus and toolbars, click outside the Excel worksheet in the Word document.

To Link an Excel Worksheet to a Word Document

1 **Position the insertion point on the paragraph mark at the end of the memo (below the paragraph of text). Click Insert on the menu bar and then point to Object (Figure 2).**

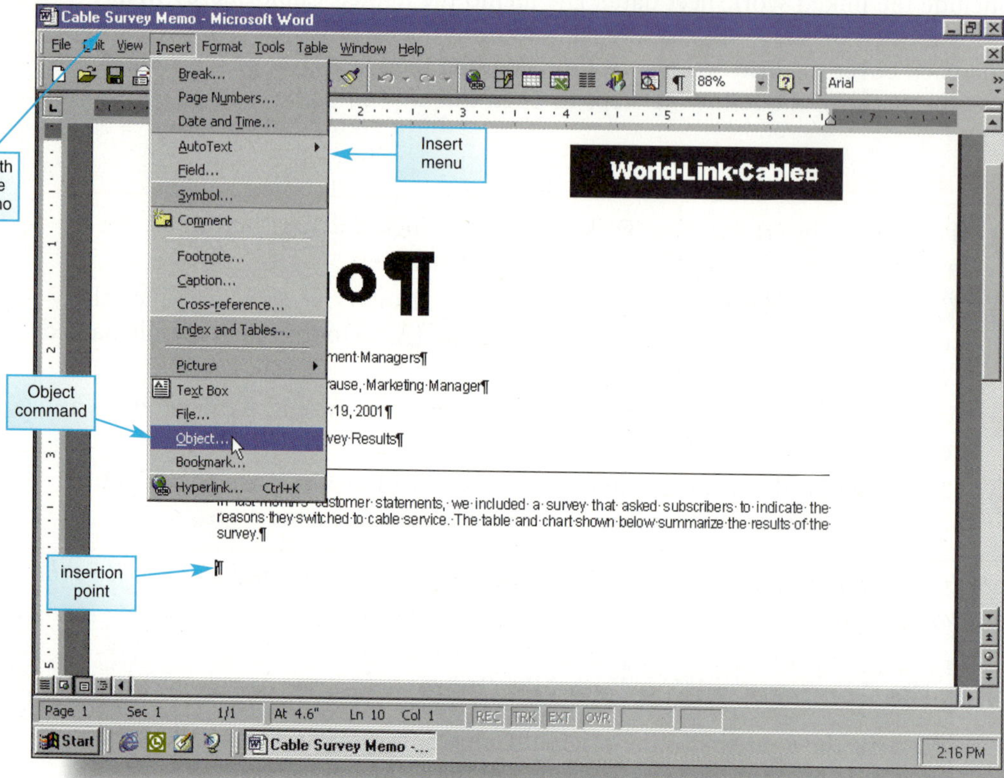

FIGURE 2

2 **Click Object. When the Object dialog box displays, if necessary, click the Create from File tab. With the Data Disk in drive A, click the Browse button. When the Browse dialog box displays, locate the Excel file called Cable Subscriber Survey on the Data Disk. Click Cable Subscriber Survey in the list and then point to the Insert button in the Browse dialog box.**

Word displays the Object dialog box and then the Browse dialog box (Figure 3).

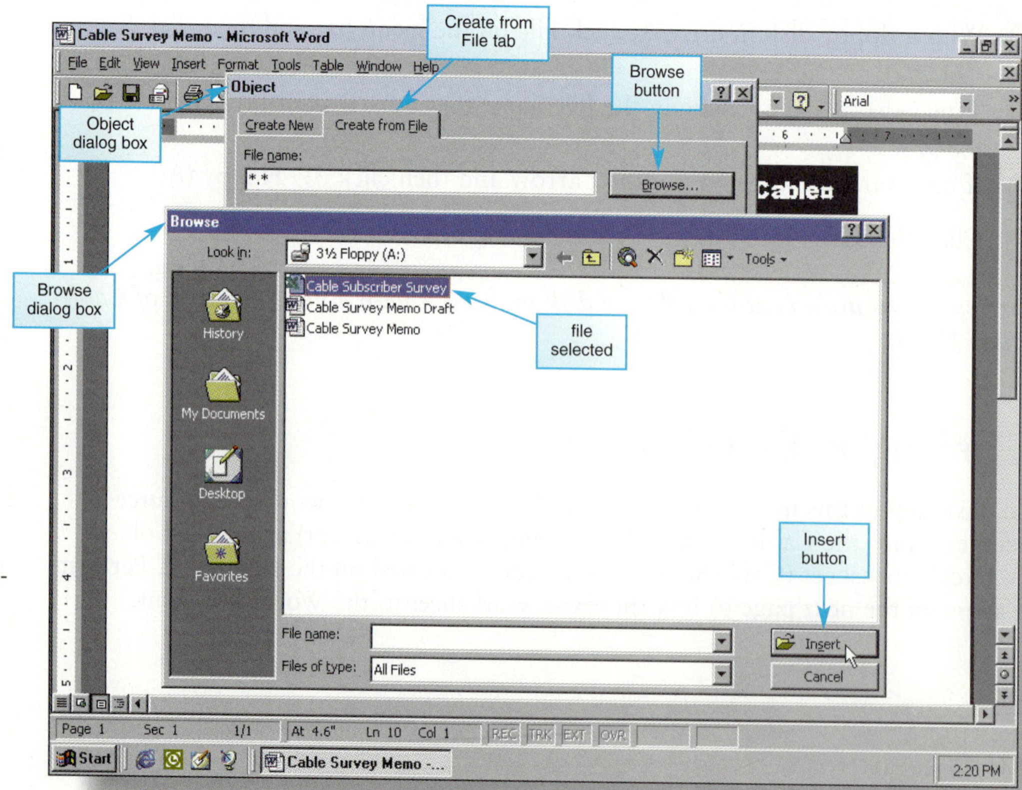

FIGURE 3

3 Click the Insert button. When the Browse dialog box closes and the entire Object dialog box is visible again, place a check mark in the Link to file check box and then point to the OK button.

The Object dialog box displays the name of the selected file in the File name text box (Figure 4). The .xls following the file name, Cable Subscriber Survey, identifies the file as an Excel worksheet.

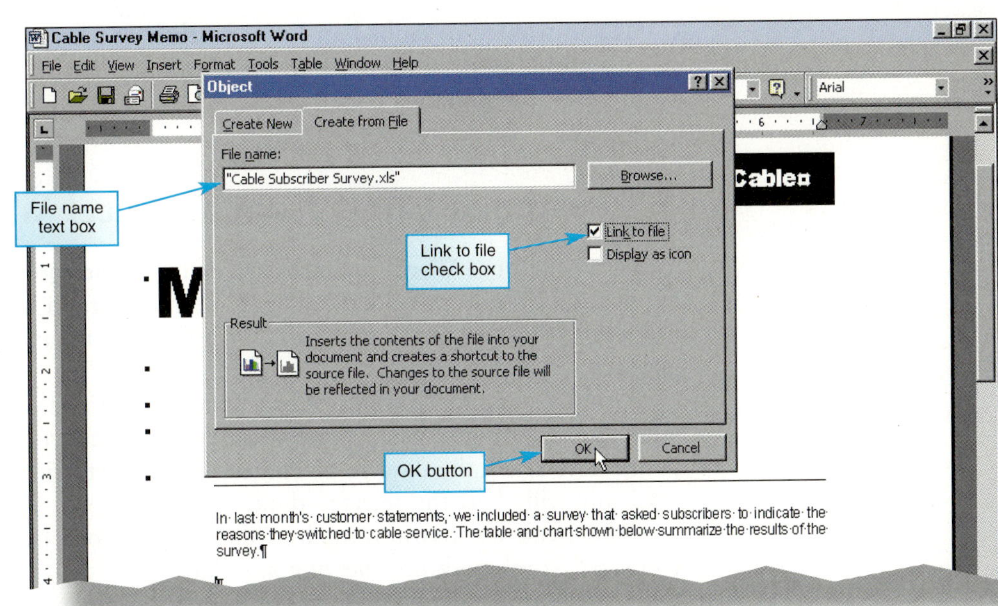

FIGURE 4

4 Click the OK button. Double-click the move handle on the Formatting toolbar to display the entire toolbar. Click the Center button on the Formatting toolbar.

Word inserts the Excel worksheet as a linked object at the location of the insertion point (Figure 5). The object is centered between the document margins.

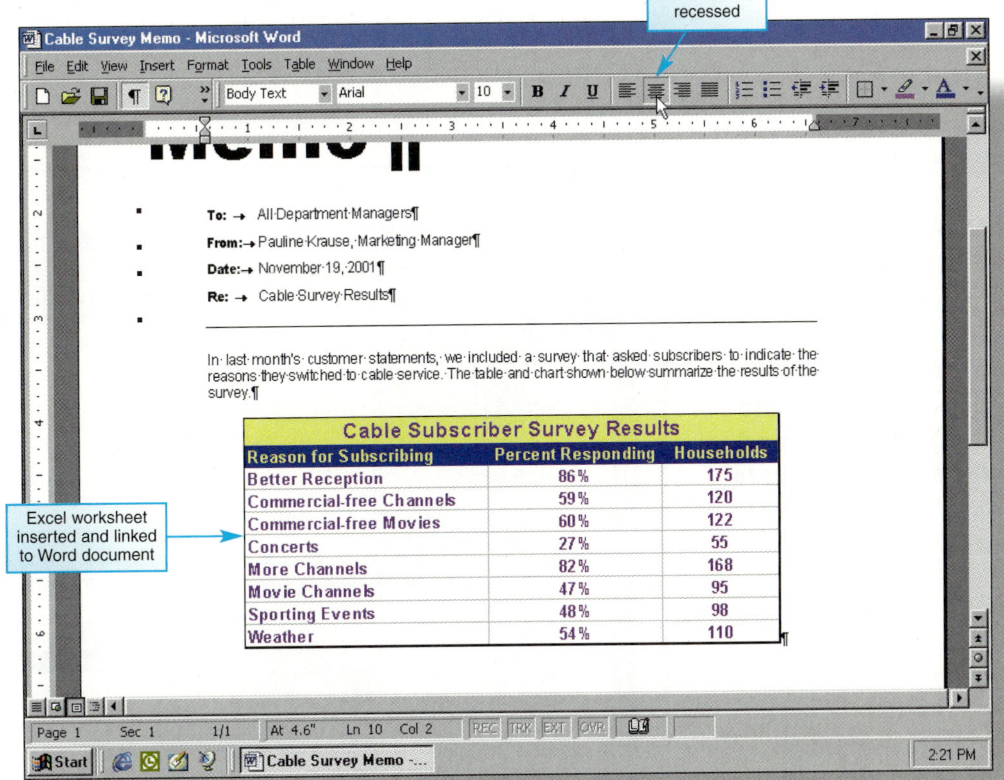

FIGURE 5

Other Ways

1. Copy object in source application to Office Clipboard; in destination application, on Edit menu click Paste Special, click Paste link, click Microsoft Excel Worksheet Object, click OK button

The Excel worksheet now is linked to the Word document. If you save the Word document and reopen it, the worksheet will display just as it does in Figure 5. If you wanted to delete the worksheet, you would select it and then press the DELETE key.

If you wanted to embed an Excel worksheet instead of link it, you would not place a check mark in the Link to file check box in the Object dialog box (see Figure 4 on the previous page).

Creating a Chart from an Excel Worksheet

You easily can use Word to chart data through **Microsoft Graph 2000**, a charting application that is embedded in Word. Because Graph is an embedded application, it has its own menus and commands. With these commands, you can modify the appearance of the chart.

Graph can chart data in a Word table or it can chart data from another Office application, such as Excel. If you want Graph to chart data that is in a Word table, you should select the data to be charted prior to starting Graph, and Graph automatically will chart the selected data.

When you want Graph to chart data from another application, such as Excel, you start Graph without selecting any data. In this case, Graph creates a sample chart with sample data. Then, you either can copy and paste or link the data from another application to the sample chart.

In this integration feature, you want to link the Excel data to the chart in the Word document. Thus, you will start Graph and it will create a sample chart. Then, you will link the Excel data to the chart. Perform the following steps to start Graph.

To Create a Chart

1 Position the insertion point on the paragraph mark to the right of the Excel worksheet in the Word document and then press the ENTER key. Click Insert on the menu bar, point to Picture, and then point to Chart (Figure 6).

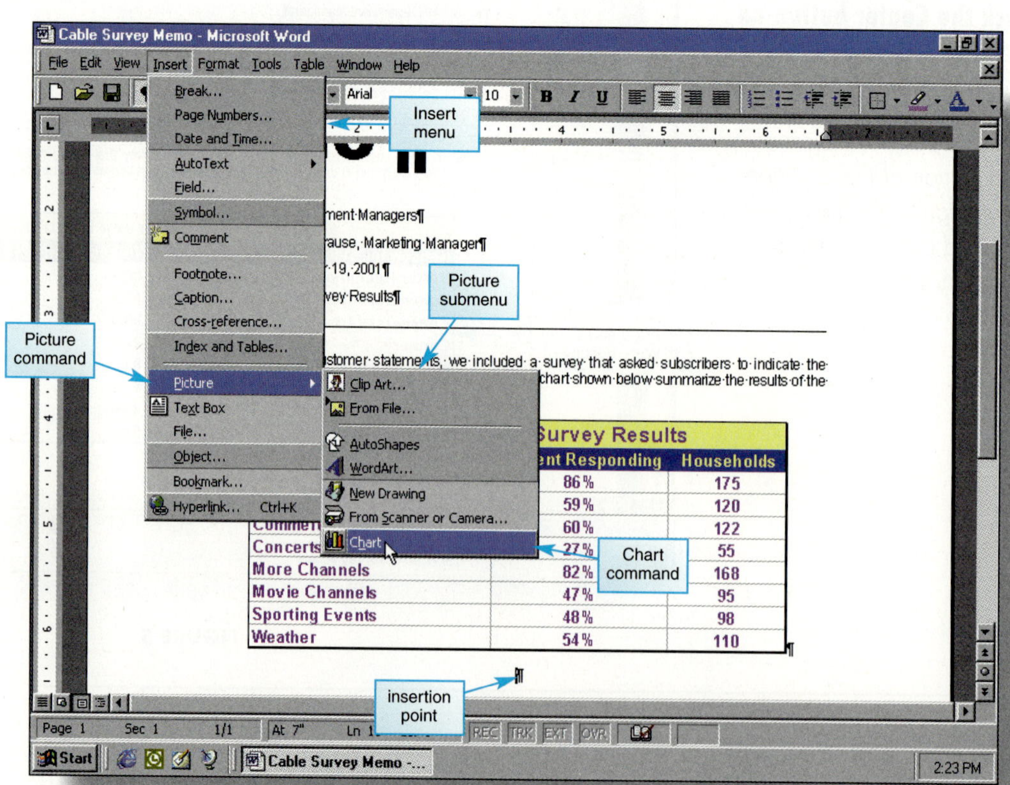

FIGURE 6

2 **Click Chart. If your screen does not display a Datasheet window, click the View Datasheet button on the Standard toolbar.**

Word starts the Microsoft Graph 2000 application (Figure 7). Graph creates a sample chart at the location of the insertion point and displays sample data in the Datasheet window.

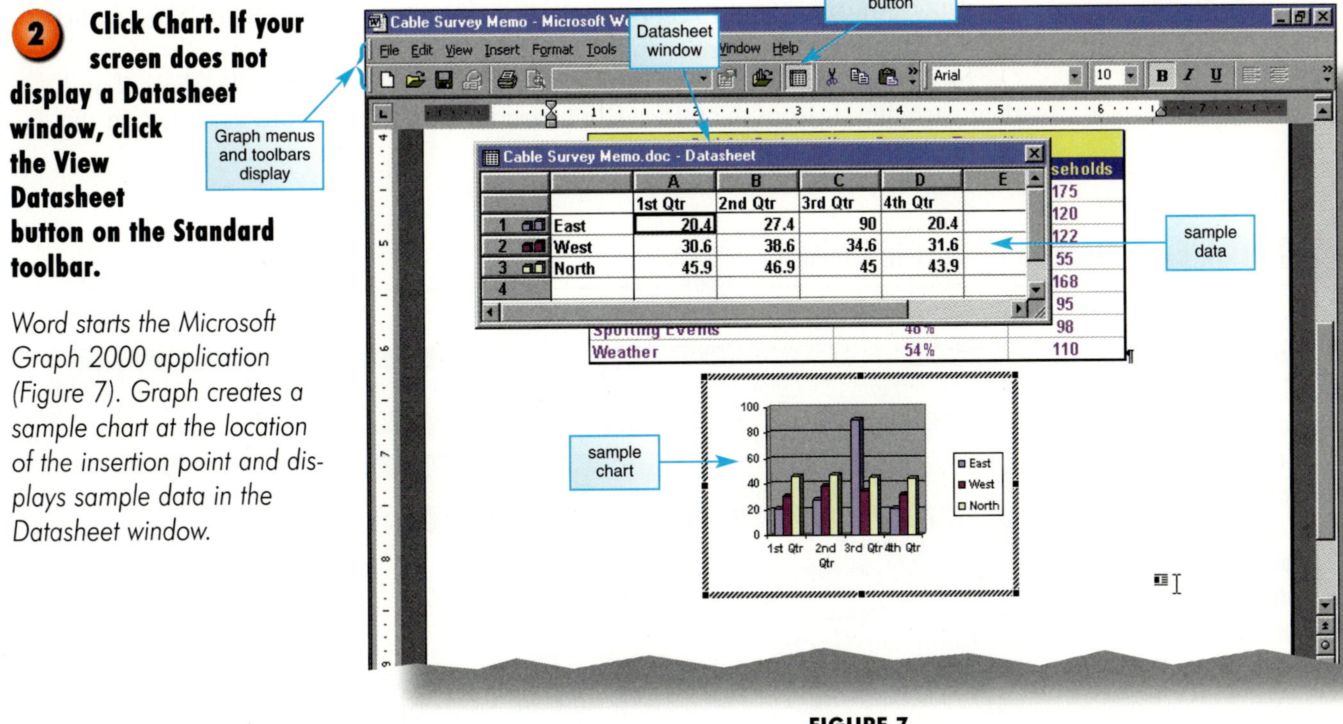

FIGURE 7

The menus on the menu bar and buttons on the toolbars change to Graph menus and toolbars. That is, the Graph program is running inside the Word program.

You can copy and paste data from an Excel worksheet into the sample chart or you can link the Excel data to the sample chart. In this integration feature, you will link the data to the chart. To link the data, you start Excel and display the workbook containing the worksheet data to be linked, copy the data in the worksheet to the Office Clipboard, and then use Word's Paste Link command to link the data on the Clipboard into the Word document.

Thus, the first step in linking the data from the Excel worksheet to the Word chart is to open the Excel workbook that contains the worksheet data to be charted. The Excel workbook that contains the data to be linked to the chart is the Cable Subscriber Survey, which is located on the Data Disk. Perform the following steps to start Excel and open this workbook.

TO START EXCEL AND OPEN AN EXCEL DOCUMENT

1. If necessary, insert the Data Disk into drive A. Click the Start button on the taskbar and then click Open Office Document.
2. When the Open Office Document dialog box displays, if necessary, click the Look in box arrow and then click 3½ Floppy (A:). Double-click the Excel file named Cable Subscriber Survey.
3. When the Excel window displays, if necessary, double-click its title bar to maximize the Excel window.
4. Reset Excel toolbars as described in Appendix C.

Excel starts and displays the Cable Subscriber Survey in the Excel window (see Figure 8 on the next page).

Starting Excel

If a Word document that displays on the screen contains a linked Excel worksheet, you also can start Excel by double-clicking the Excel worksheet in the Word document. For example, if you double-click the Cable Subscriber Survey worksheet in the Word document, Excel starts and then displays the Excel worksheet in an Excel window.

With both Word and Excel open, you can switch between the applications by clicking the appropriate program button on the taskbar.

Next, you will copy to the Office Clipboard the Excel data to be charted and then paste link it from the Office Clipboard to the chart in Word as shown in the following steps.

Steps To Link Excel Data to a Chart in Word

1 In the Excel window, drag through cells in the range of A3:B10. Double-click the move handle on the Standard toolbar to display the entire toolbar. Click the Copy button on the Standard toolbar.

The Excel window is active (Figure 8). A marquee displays around the range A3:B10, which has been copied to the Office Clipboard.

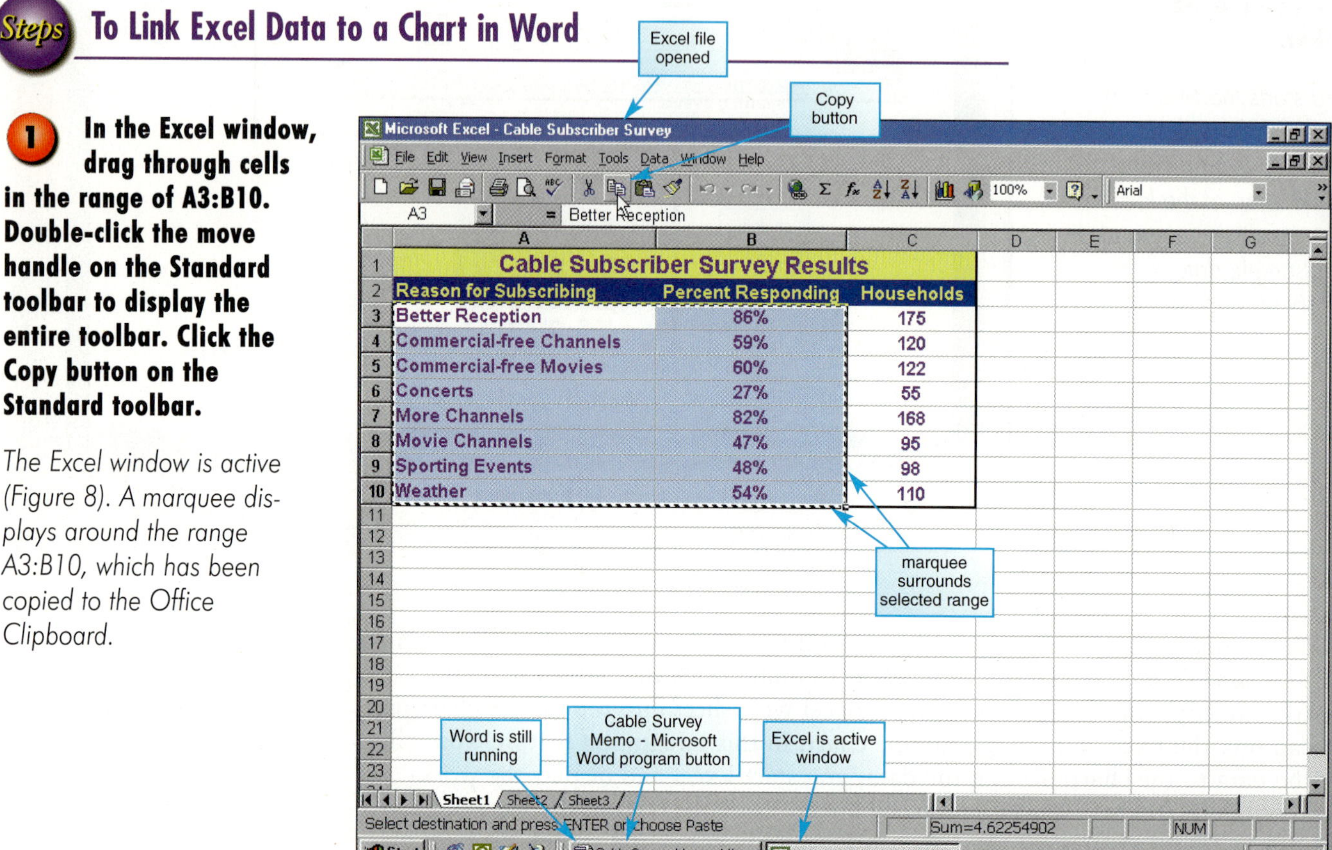

FIGURE 8

2 **Click the Cable Survey Memo - Microsoft Word program button on the taskbar. Click anywhere in the Datasheet window. Click Edit on the menu bar and then point to Paste Link.**

The Word window is active (Figure 9).

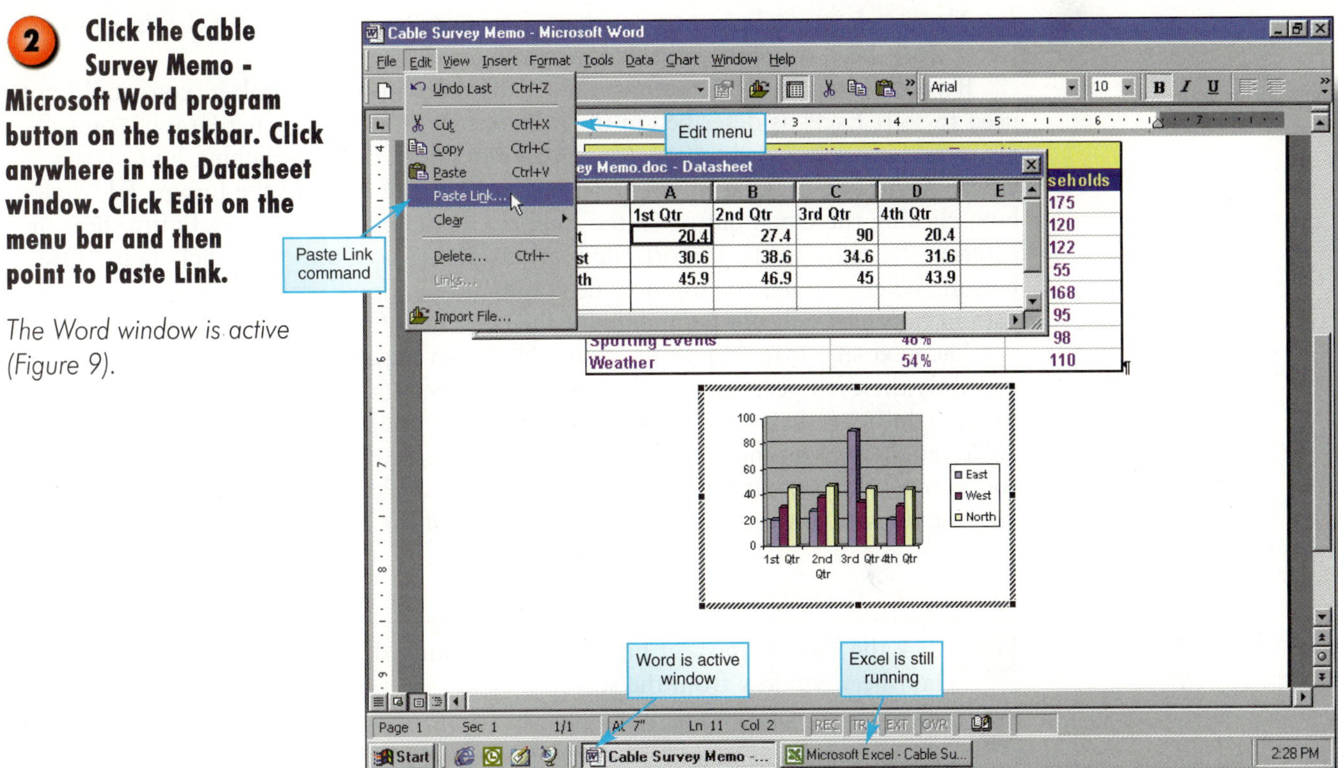

FIGURE 9

3 **Click Paste Link. When Graph displays a dialog box indicating the linked data will replace existing data, click the OK button.**

Graph copies the data from the Office Clipboard into the Datasheet window, replacing the sample data in the Datasheet window (Figure 10). Graph then charts the contents of the Datasheet window.

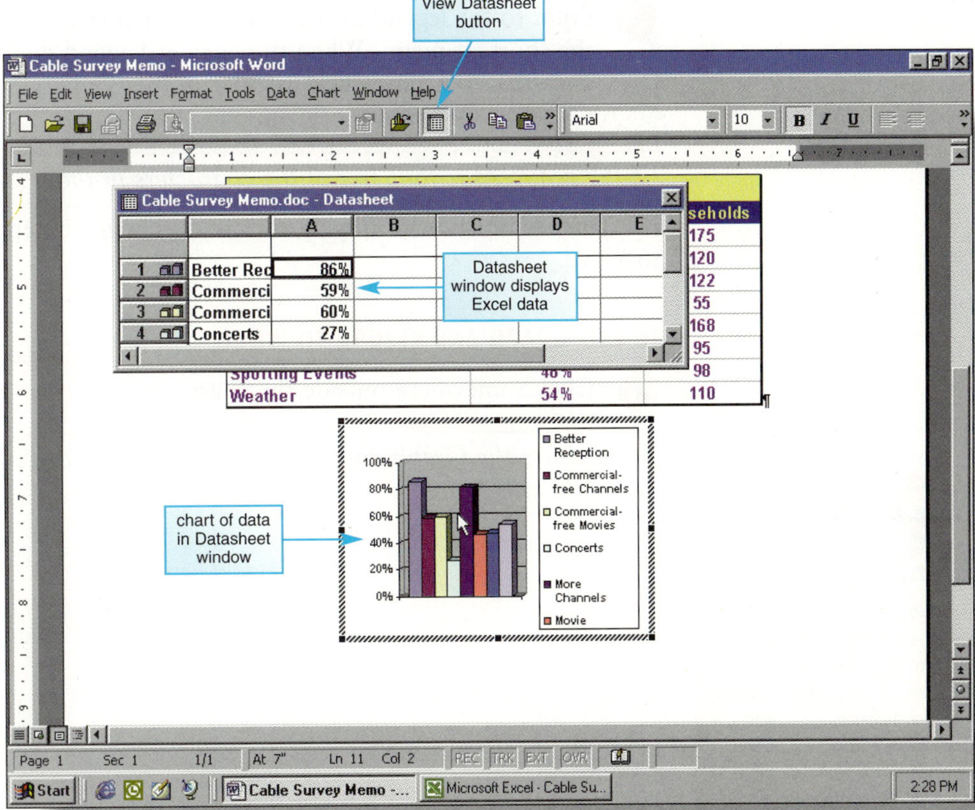

FIGURE 10

The Excel data is linked to the chart. Thus, if you change any of the data in the Excel worksheet, it will be reflected in the chart.

If you wanted to copy and paste the chart data, instead of link it, you would not need to start Excel as described in the previous steps. After starting Graph, you simply would instruct Word to copy the Excel worksheet data by clicking Edit on the Graph menu bar, clicking Import File, locating the file name in the Import File dialog box, clicking the Open button in the Import File dialog box, clicking Entire sheet or entering the range in the Import File Options dialog box, and then clicking the OK button. When you use the Import File command to copy Excel worksheet data, the data in the chart will not be updated if the contents of the Excel worksheet change.

The next step is to format the chart. Notice in Figure 10 on the previous page that only the even percentages display along the vertical axis on the chart and only six of eight items display in the legend. To display odd percentage values (such as 70% and 90%), you increase the size of the chart. To display all the legend items, you decrease the size of the characters in the legend. Perform the following steps to increase the size of the chart and reduce the size of the characters in the legend.

TO FORMAT THE CHART IN GRAPH

1. Click the View Datasheet button on the Standard toolbar to remove the Datasheet window from the screen.
2. Point to the right-middle sizing handle on the selection rectangle that surrounds the chart and legend and drag it rightward until the chart and legend are as wide as the table.
3. Point to the bottom-middle sizing handle on the selection rectangle and drag it downward approximately one inch.
4. Point to the legend in the chart and then right-click. Click Format Legend on the shortcut menu. When the Format Legend dialog box displays, if necessary, click the Font tab. Click Regular in the Font style list. Click 8 in the Size list. Click the OK button.

Graph reduces the font size of the characters in the legend and resizes the chart.

You are finished modifying the chart. The next step is to exit Graph and return to Word.

TO EXIT GRAPH AND RETURN TO WORD

1. Click somewhere outside the chart.

Word closes the Graph application (Figure 11). Word's menus and toolbars redisplay below the title bar.

Linking Excel Data

If you want to display a linked worksheet as an icon, instead of as the worksheet itself, do the following: copy the data to be linked in Excel, switch to Word, click Edit on the menu bar, click Paste Special, click Paste link, click the desired option in the As list, place a check mark in the Display as icon check box, and then click the OK button.

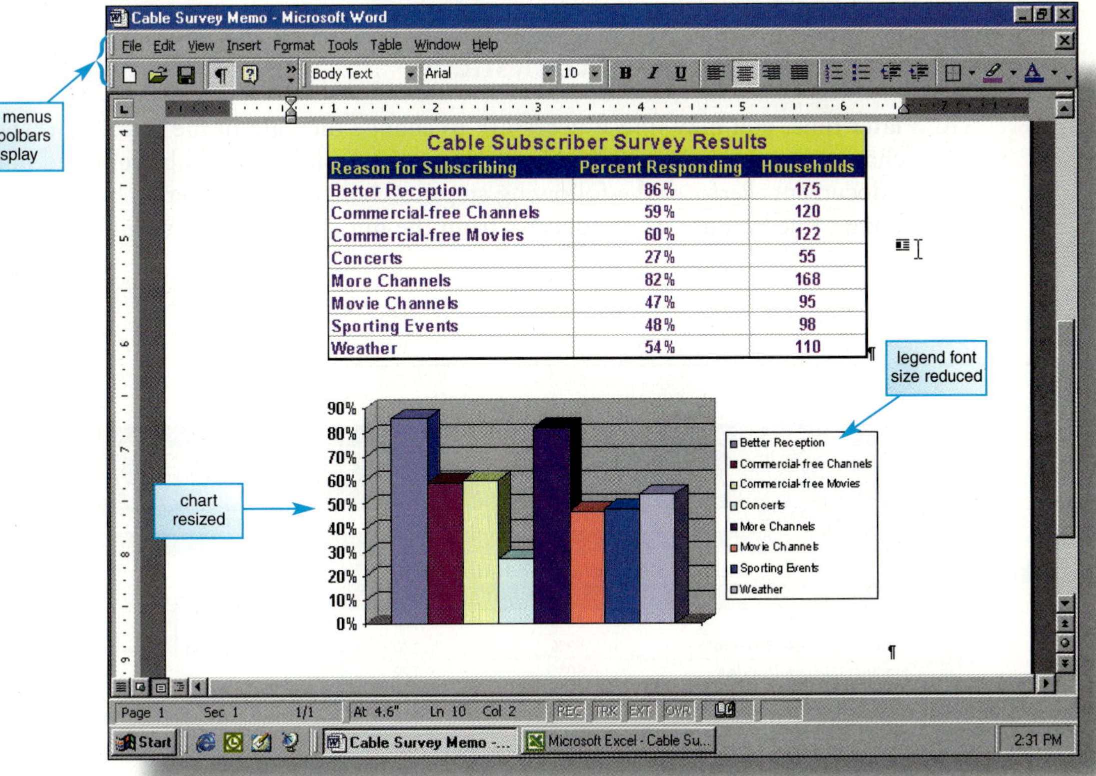

Cable Subscriber Survey Results		
Reason for Subscribing	Percent Responding	Households
Better Reception	86%	175
Commercial-free Channels	59%	120
Commercial-free Movies	60%	122
Concerts	27%	55
More Channels	82%	168
Movie Channels	47%	95
Sporting Events	48%	98
Weather	54%	110

FIGURE 11

If, for some reason, you wanted to modify an existing chart in a document, you would double-click the chart to reopen the Microsoft Graph 2000 application. Then, you can make any necessary changes to the chart. When you are finished making changes to the chart, click anywhere outside the chart to return to Word.

You are finished with the memo. Save the document again, print it, and then quit Word as described in the following steps.

TO SAVE A DOCUMENT

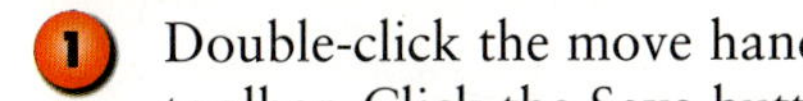

1. Double-click the move handle on the Standard toolbar to display the entire toolbar. Click the Save button on the Standard toolbar.

Word saves the document on a floppy disk in drive A.

TO PRINT A DOCUMENT

1. Click the Print button on the Standard toolbar.

Word prints the memo as shown in Figure 1c on page WDI 2.2.

TO QUIT WORD

1. Click the Close button on Word's title bar.

The Word window closes.

Editing a Linked Worksheet

At a later time, you may find it necessary to change the data in the Excel worksheet. Any changes you make to the Excel worksheet while in Excel will be reflected in the Word document. Perform the following steps to change the number of households preferring cable because of its concerts from the number 55 to the number 65.

To Edit a Linked Object

1 With the Excel worksheet displaying on the screen, click cell C6 to select it. Type 65 **and then press the ENTER key.**

The number in cell C6 changes from 55 to 65 (Figure 12). Excel recalculates all formulas in the workbook.

Microsoft Excel - Cable Subscriber Survey

Cable Subscriber Survey Results		
Reason for Subscribing	Percent Responding	Households
Better Reception	86%	175
Commercial-free Channels	59%	120
Commercial-free Movies	60%	122
Concerts	32%	65
More Channels	82%	168
Movie Channels	47%	95
Sporting Events	48%	98
Weather	54%	110

value in cell C6 changed from 55 to 65

new percentage calculated

FIGURE 12

2 Click the Save button on the Standard toolbar. Click the Close button at the right edge of Excel's title bar.

Excel saves the changes to the worksheet. The Excel window closes.

3 Start Word and then open the Cable Survey Memo document on your disk. If the chart does not display updated data, double-click the chart and then click outside the chart to exit Graph.

The Word document displays the updates to the Excel worksheet object and chart object (Figure 13).

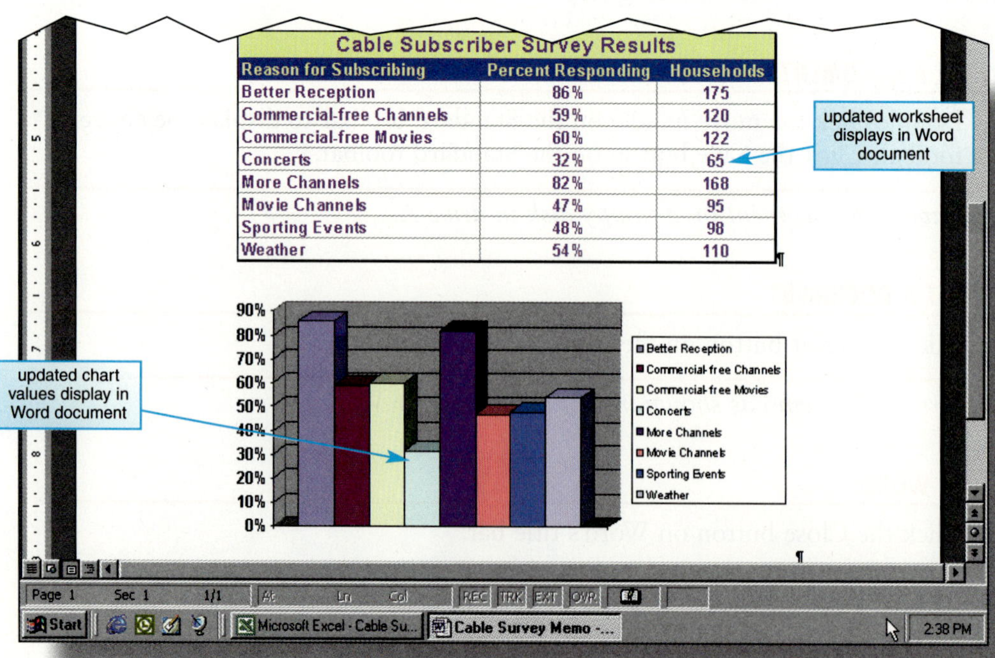

FIGURE 13

You also can edit any of the cells in the Excel worksheet (the object) while it displays as part of the Word document. To edit the worksheet, you double-click it. If Excel is running already, the system will switch to it and display the linked workbook in Excel. If Excel is not running, the system will start Excel automatically and then display the linked workbook in Excel.

Perform the following series of steps to save the Word document and then quit Word.

Quick Reference

For a table that lists how to complete the tasks covered in this book using the mouse, menu, shortcut menu, and keyboard, see the Word Quick Reference Summary at the back of this book or visit the Shelly Cashman Series Office Web page (www.scsite.com/off2000/qr.htm) and then click Microsoft Word 2000.

TO SAVE THE WORD DOCUMENT AGAIN

1. Click the Save button on the Standard toolbar.

Word saves the revised Cable Survey Memo on a floppy disk in drive A.

TO QUIT WORD

1. Click the Close button at the right edge of Word's title bar.

The Word window closes.

CASE PERSPECTIVE SUMMARY

Pauline distributes the memo to the department managers so they can review it prior to the next weekly meeting. At the meeting, they quickly conclude from the memo that the majority of current customers subscribe to their cable service for two major reasons: better reception and more channels. Thus, they decide to offer seven additional cable channels beginning in two months.

After the meeting, Jerry Cromwell asks Pauline how she included the table and chart in the memo. Pauline confesses that she actually did not compose the memo and directs Jerry to you so that you can show him how to link documents between applications.

Integration Feature Summary

This Integration Feature introduced you to linking an Excel worksheet into a Word document. You also linked Excel data to a chart using Word's embedded Microsoft Graph charting application. Then, you modified the linked worksheet to see the changes reflected in the Word document.

More About 2000

Microsoft Certification

The Microsoft Office User Specialist (MOUS) Certification program provides an opportunity for you to obtain a valuable industry credential - proof that you have the Word 2000 skills required by employers. For more information, see Appendix D or visit the Shelly Cashman Series MOUS Web page at www.scsite.com/off2000/cert.htm.

In the Lab

1 Linking an Excel Table to a Word Document

Problem: Cecilia Doranski, director of admissions at Eastern University, has created an Excel worksheet that lists the number of full-time and part-time students majoring in each department on campus. She would like you to prepare a memo that includes the Excel worksheet.

Instructions:

1. Create a memo using a memo template. Save the memo using the name Department Major Memo. The memo is to all department heads, from Cecilia Doranski, and should have a subject of Full-Time and Part-Time Student Distribution by Department. In the memo, type the following paragraph: `The table shown below lists the total number of full-time and part-time students in each department on campus. Please call me if you have any questions.`
2. Link the Excel worksheet to the Word memo file.
3. Save the Word memo file again.
4. Print the Word memo file.

2 Linking Data from an Excel Worksheet to a Word Document

Problem: Cecilia Doranski, director of admissions at Eastern University, has created an Excel worksheet that lists the number of full-time and part-time students majoring in each department on campus. She would like you to prepare a memo that includes a chart of the Excel worksheet data.

Instructions:

1. Create a memo using a memo template. Save the memo using the name Department Major Memo With Chart. The memo is to all department heads, from Cecilia Doranski, and should have a subject of Full-Time and Part-Time Student Distribution by Department. In the memo, type the following paragraph: `The chart shown below shows the total number of full-time and part-time students in each department on campus. Please call me if you have any questions.`
2. In the memo, create a chart and then link the Excel worksheet data to the Word chart.
3. Save the Word memo file again.
4. Print the Word memo file.

3 Creating an Excel Worksheet and Linking It to a Word Document

Problem: Your science instructor, Ms. Yolatnik, has requested that you collect the daily high and low temperatures for a ten-day period and create an Excel worksheet that lists the data. Then, you are to prepare a memo that links the Excel worksheet into the memo and includes a chart that links to the Excel worksheet data.

Instructions:

Create a memo to Ms. Yolatnik using a memo template. Explain the contents of the worksheet and chart in the memo. Link the Excel worksheet to the Word memo file. In the memo, create a chart and then link the Excel worksheet data to the Word chart. Save the Word memo file again. Print the Word memo file.

Microsoft Excel 2000

PROJECT 7

Using Visual Basic for Applications (VBA) with Excel

OBJECTIVES

You will have mastered the material in this project when you can:

- Use the Undo button to undo multiple changes
- Use passwords to allow an authorized user to access the protection scheme
- Use the macro recorder to create a macro
- Execute a macro
- Customize a toolbar by adding a button
- Customize a menu by adding a command
- Understand Visual Basic for Applications code
- Add controls to a worksheet, such as command buttons, scroll bars, check boxes, and spin buttons
- Assign properties to controls
- Write a procedure to automate data entry into your worksheet
- Validate incoming data
- Explain event-driven programs

Start Planning Today

Turn Your Paycheck into a Nest Egg

How many years until you retire? 40? 25? 10? 5? Not a clue? Whenever you do receive that last paycheck, you need to be prepared for the financial and emotional impact of not commuting to work daily.

Some experts recommend starting retirement savings with the very first paycheck. But how can you save for retirement when you have tuition payments, a car loan, utility bills, and rent or mortgage payments? The answer is careful planning, starting right now.

Fewer than 50 percent of Americans are saving specifically for their retirement needs, although nearly 75 percent know they should be increasing retirement dollars. Financial planners previously estimated that retirees needed 70 percent of their preretirement income to live relatively comfortably during their golden years. Today, however, some planners have bumped up their estimates to 100 percent.

Workers are retiring earlier and living longer than ever before. Considering that the average person spends 18 years in retirement, you need to plan for that time early in your career. During your retirement, you will be faced with buying new cars,

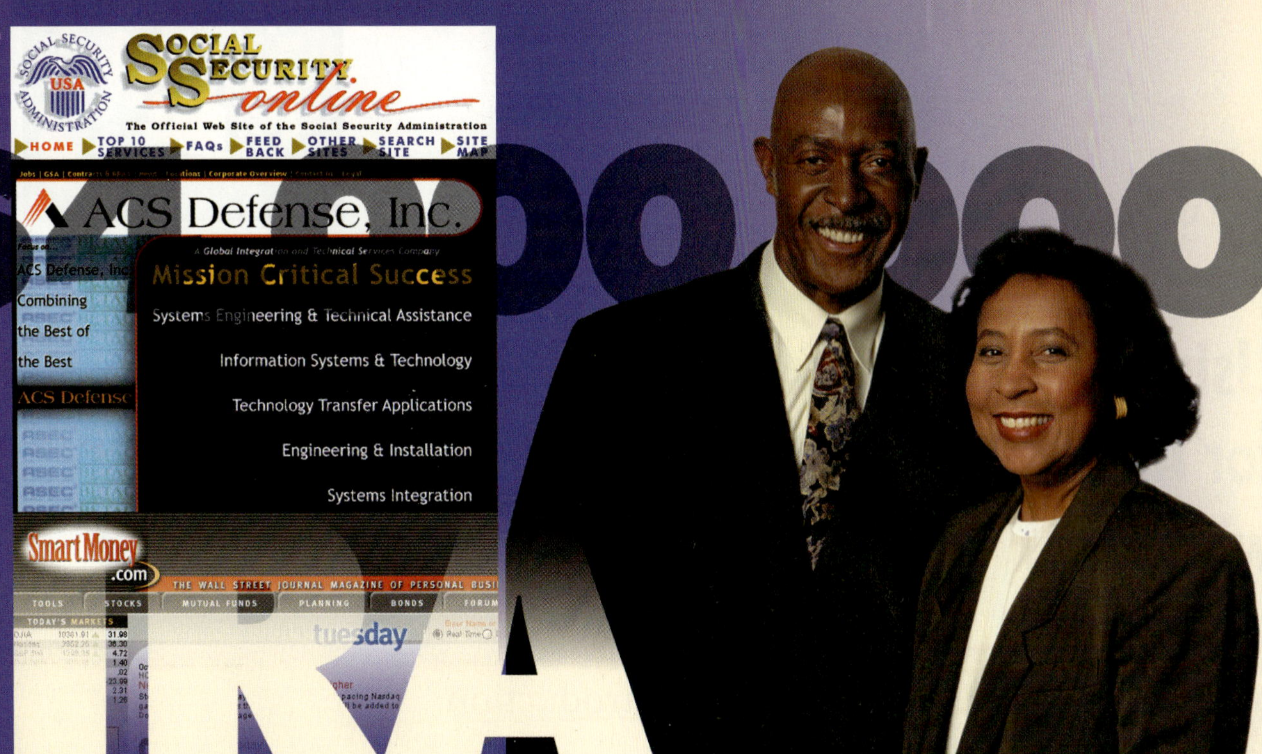

replacing your appliances, putting a new roof on your home, and needing prescription drugs and hearing aids.

Inflation is a factor in the retirement picture, too. If you spend $25,000 on living expenses the year you retire, you will need $56,000 for these same expenses 20 years later if inflation rises four percent yearly.

You have no control over some retirement plans, such as Social Security or a company pension. You have absolute control, however, over other preretirement strategies, such as IRAs and company-sponsored savings plans. One of the most appealing investment options is a 401(k) plan. This strategy allows investors to shelter their money, meaning they do not pay taxes on the funds until they retire. Many employers contribute to their employees' 401(k) plan, sometimes as much as 50 percent of the employee's contribution.

In this Excel project, you will see just how advantageous 401(k) plans can be. You will use the Visual Basic for Applications programming language to build a planning worksheet for the Golden Years.com Internet company. You then will input current salary, employee investment, employer match, rate of return, and years of service. You will see that regular contributions to this 401(k) plan for 45 years could yield more than $4 million, even without receiving salary increases.

So where do you start planning for your retirement? The Internet abounds with sites brimming with financial calculators and investment strategies. Begin with the Social Security Administration's site (www.ssa.gov) and find a link to the Social Security Benefit Estimate Program that calculates your potential Social Security payments. Other sites, such as the Administration on Aging (www.aoa.dhhs.gov/retirement), the American Savings Education Council (www.asec.org), and SmartMoney (www.smartmoney.com), have a multitude of interactive tools and worksheets.

Whatever investment strategy you choose, the sooner you start saving, the more prepared you will be to crack your nest egg and live your golden years with financial security.

Microsoft Excel 2000

Using Visual Basic for Applications (VBA) with Excel

PROJECT 7

CASE PERSPECTIVE

Nelson Portugal is vice president of personnel for Golden Years.com, a senior multi-service Internet company. Nelson's main task is to convince potential and current employees that Golden Years.com offers excellent benefits.

Golden Years.com's most lucrative benefit is a 401(k) plan. A **401(k) plan** is a retirement savings program that allows employees to invest pretax dollars through payroll deductions.

Nelson has a planning workbook. Any change to the data causes the planning workbook to recalculate all formulas instantaneously, thus showing the results of investing in the company's 401(k) plan.

Nelson wants to put the workbook on the company's intranet so potential and current employees easily can determine the financial advantages of the 401(k) plan. The problem is that without an easy-to-use interface that steps the user through the entry of data, there is too much room for error. Nelson has asked you to use Visual Basic for Applications to create a user-friendly interface for entering data into the workbook in three phases.

Introduction

Before a computer can take an action and produce a desired result, it must have a step-by-step description of the task to be accomplished. The step-by-step description is a series of precise instructions called a **procedure**. A procedure also is called a **program** or **code**. The process of writing a procedure is called **computer programming**. Every Excel command on a menu and button on a toolbar has a corresponding procedure that executes when you click the command or button. **Execute** means that the computer carries out the step-by-step instructions. In a Windows environment, the instructions associated with a task are executed when an **event** takes place, such as clicking a button, clicking a command, dragging a scroll box, or right-clicking a cell.

Because a command or button in Excel does not exist for every possible worksheet task, Microsoft has included a powerful programming language called Visual Basic for Applications. The **Visual Basic for Applications (VBA)** programming language allows you to customize and extend the capabilities of Excel.

In this project, you will learn how to create macros using a code generator called a **macro recorder**. A **macro** is a procedure made up of VBA code. It is called a macro, rather than a procedure, because it is created using the macro recorder. You also will learn how to add buttons to toolbars and commands to menus and associate these with macros. Finally, you will learn the basics of VBA including creating the interface, setting the properties, and writing the code.

Project Seven — Golden Years.Com's 401(k) Planning Worksheet

From your meeting with Nelson, you have determined the following needs and source of data.

Needs: The easy-to-use interface for the 401(k) planning workbook will be implemented in three phases:

Phase 1 – Create a macro using the macro recorder that prints the worksheet in portrait orientation using the Fit to option. Assign the macro to a button on the Standard toolbar (Figure 7-1a) and to a command on the File menu so the user can execute the macro by clicking the button or the command.

Phase 2 – Create a button on the worksheet as shown in Figure 7-1a, assign the button properties, and write an associated procedure (Figure 7-1b) that steps the user through entering the required data in the range C5:C10.

Phase 3 – Create an area on the worksheet called an Adjustment Center (Figure 7-2 on the next page) that allows the user to enter his or her name and annual salary using a button and the remaining data using scroll bars, a check box, and spin buttons. Verify that the annual salary entered is positive.

Source of Data: The workbook shown in Figure 7-1a, without the button on the worksheet and the button on the toolbar, is available to you on the Data Disk under the file name Golden Years.

(a) Worksheet

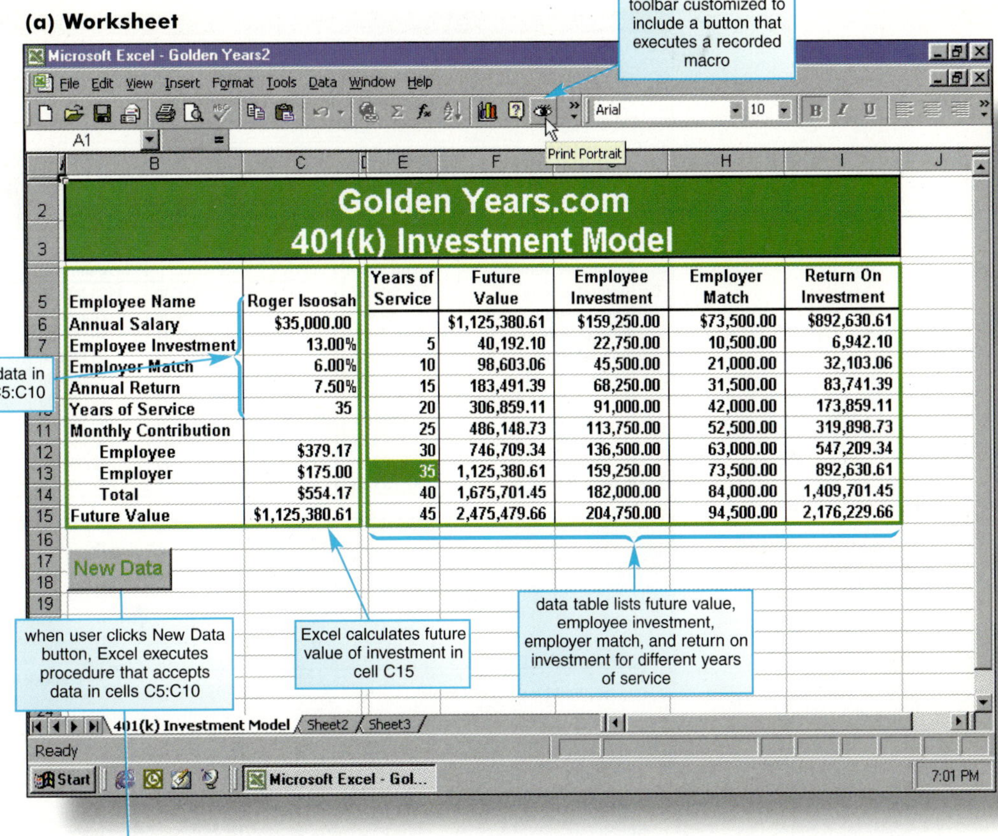

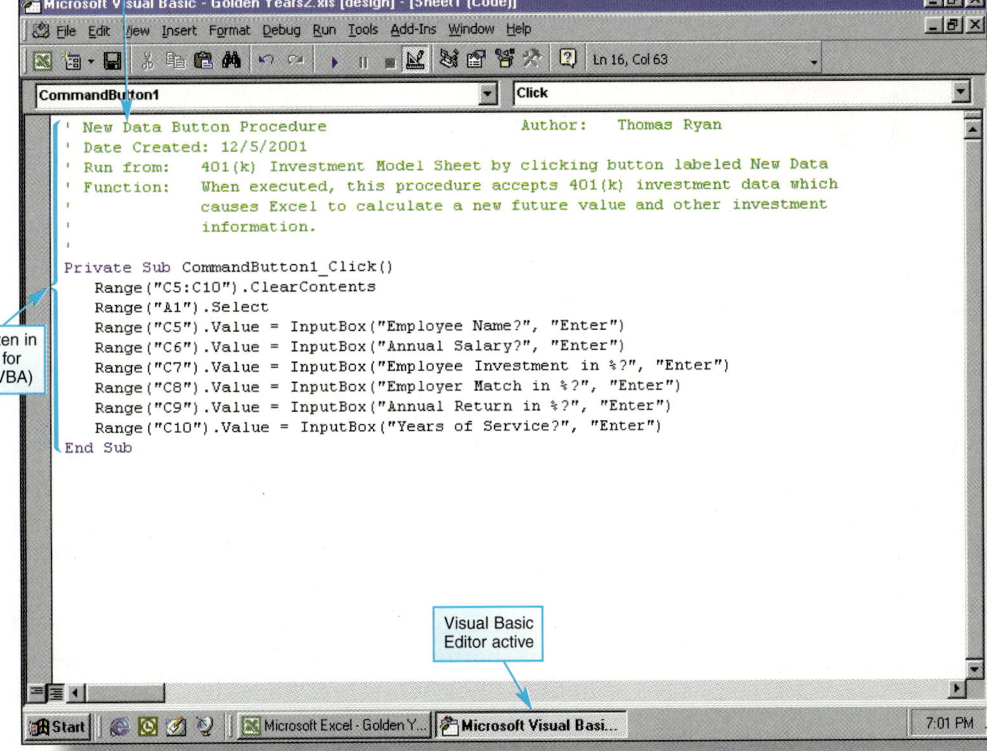

(b) Visual Basic for Applications

FIGURE 7-1

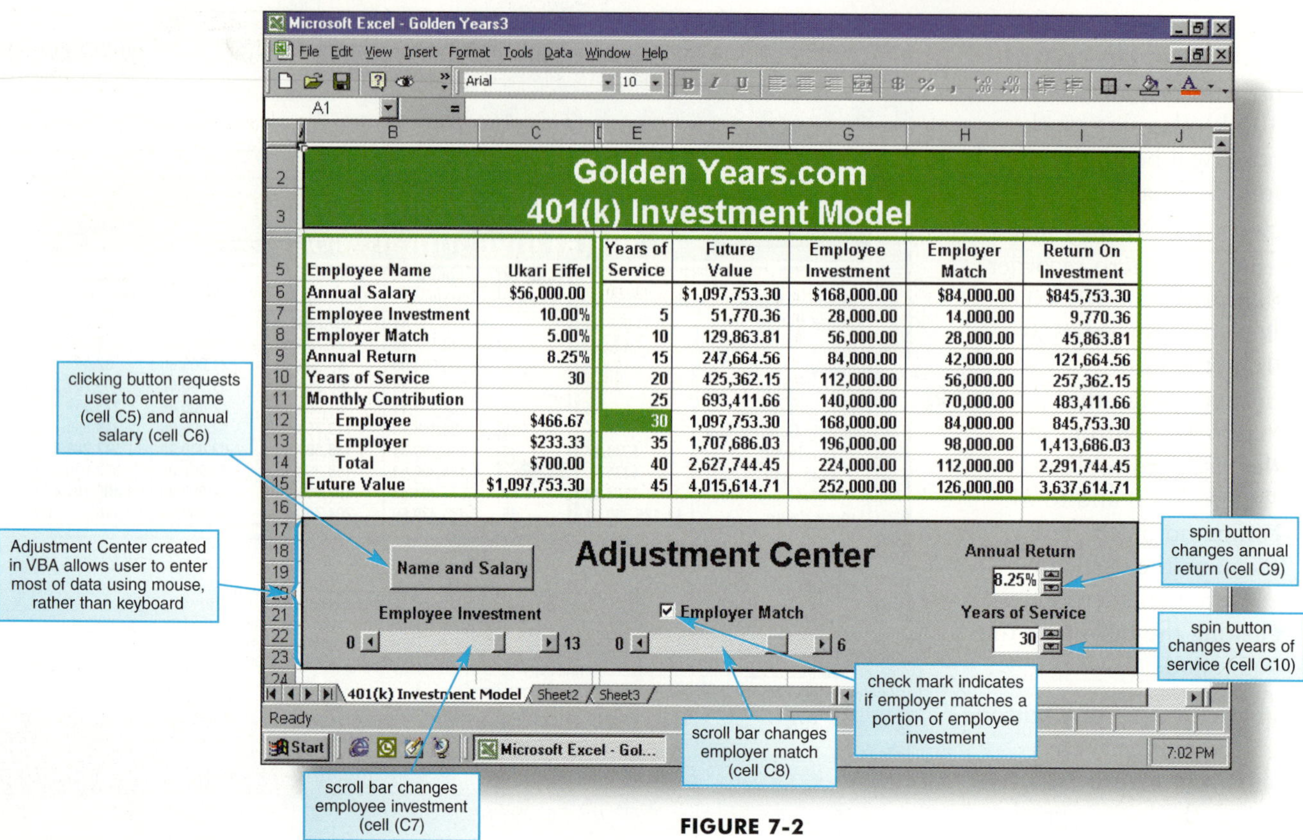

FIGURE 7-2

More About

Opening Workbooks

Macros are an easy place for malcontents to hide computer viruses. For this reason, Excel 2000 displays a dialog box whenever you open a workbook with a macro. The dialog box requires that you choose to enable or disable the attached macro before it will open the workbook. If you disable the macro and the macro contains a virus, it cannot damage your system. You should enable macros only if you trust the author who created the workbook with the macro.

Starting Excel and Opening a Workbook

Perform the following steps to start Excel, reset the toolbars, and open the workbook Golden Years from the Data Disk.

TO START EXCEL AND OPEN A WORKBOOK

1. Insert the Data Disk in drive A. See the inside back cover of this book for instructions for downloading the Data Disk.
2. Click the Start button on the taskbar and then click Open Office Document.
3. When the Open Office Document dialog box displays, click the Look in box arrow and then click 3½ Floppy (A:). Double-click Golden Years in the list.
4. When the Golden Years workbook displays, click Tools on the menu bar, and then click Customize.
5. When the Customize dialog box displays, click the Options tab, make sure the top three check boxes are selected, click the Reset my usage data button, and then click the Yes button.
6. Click the Toolbars tab. Click Standard, click the Reset button, and then click the OK button. Click Formatting, click the Reset button, and then click the OK button. Click Worksheet Menu Bar, click the Reset button, and then click the OK button. Click the Close button.

The Golden Years workbook displays in the Excel window (Figure 7-3).

The 401(k) Investment Model sheet in the Golden Years workbook is divided into two parts (Figure 7-3). The left side contains the data (range C5:C10) and the results (range C12:C15). The key cell is C15, which displays the future value of the investment.

The right side of the worksheet is a data table that varies the years of service in column E and organizes the results of four formulas in the range F7:I15 — future value (column F), employee investment (column G), employer match (column H), and return on investment (column I). In this worksheet, the return on investment is the future value less the sum of the employee and employer investment.

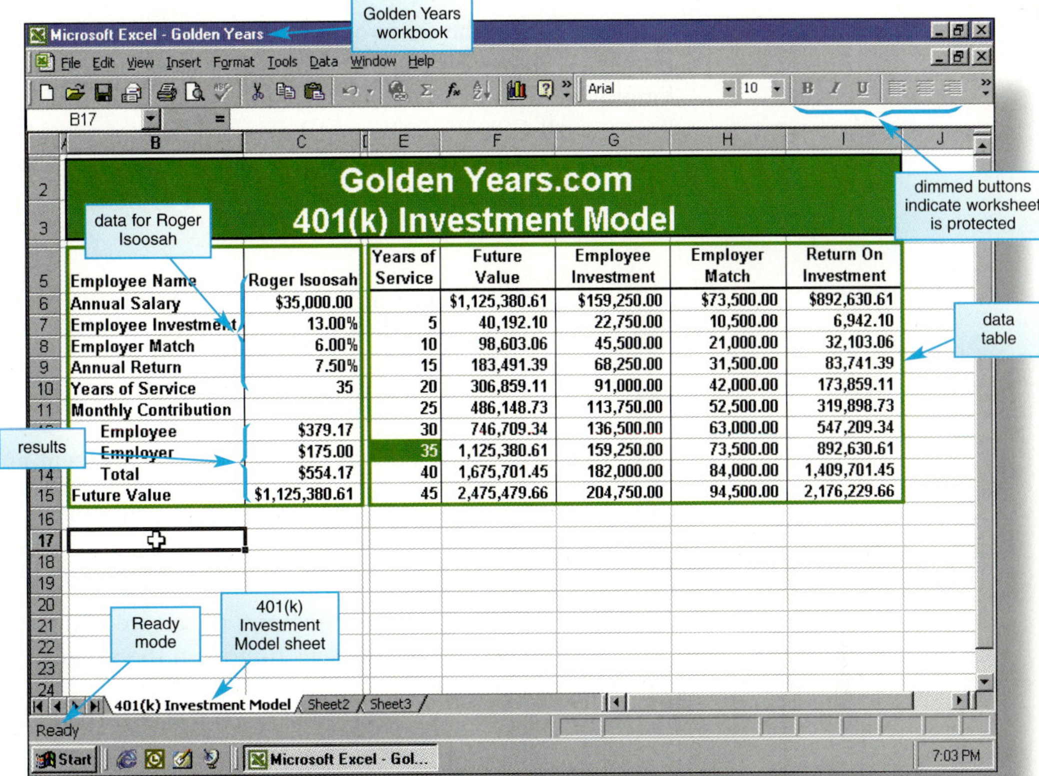

FIGURE 7-3

Many of the buttons on the toolbars are dimmed. When buttons are dimmed and Excel is in Ready mode, then the worksheet is protected. In this case, the cells in the range C5:C10 are unlocked so users can enter data, but the rest of the cells in the worksheet are protected, and therefore, cannot be changed. Later in this project, the worksheet will be unprotected so changes can be made to it.

Gaining Confidence in a Workbook

Additional ways exist to uncover details of workbooks created by someone else. For example, the File | Page Setup, File | Print Preview, Tools | Options, and Insert | Name | Define commands can tell you if the author used any peculiar settings. The Tools | Macro | Macros command will list the macros in the workbook.

Gaining Confidence in a Workbook Created by Someone Else

When you modify a workbook created by someone else, such as Golden Years, you should learn as much as you can about the workbook before you modify it. You can learn more about a workbook by doing the following:

1. Press CTRL+ LEFT QUOTATION MARK (`) to display the formulas version to gain an understanding of what formulas and functions are used in the workbook, and which cells are referenced by the formulas and functions.
2. Use Range Finder or the auditing commands to show which cells are referenced in formulas and functions. You double-click a cell with a formula or function to activate Range Finder.
3. Check which cells are locked and which cells are unlocked. Usually all cells in a workbook are locked, except for those in which you enter data. For example, on the 401(k) Investment Model worksheet in Golden Book, only the cells in the range C5:C10 are unlocked.
4. Enter sample data and verify the results.

To illustrate the entry of sample data, the following employee data will be used: Employee Name (cell C5) — Sarah Dakota; Annual Salary (cell C6) — $73,000.00; Employee Investment (cell C7) – 6.50%; Employer Match (cell C8) – 5.00%; Annual Return (cell C9) – 5.50%; and Years of Service (cell C10) – 30. Before entering the data, select the range C5:C10 so that Excel automatically makes the next cell in the range the active one when you complete a cell entry by pressing the ENTER key.

401(k) Plans

Most employers who contribute to 401(k) plans require an employee to be vested before the employer-matching contributions are assigned to the employee. Usually a company requires an employee to be employed continually for 3 to 5 years to be vested. 401(k) plans, however, can be transferred from one employer to another.

TO AUTOMATE DATA ENTRY BY SELECTING A RANGE OF CELLS

1. Click cell C5 and then select the range C5:C10. In cell C5, type `Sarah Dakota` as the employee name and then press the ENTER key.
2. In cell C6, type `73000` as the annual salary and then press the ENTER key.
3. In cell C7, type `6.5%` as the employee investment and then press the ENTER key.
4. In cell C8, type `5%` as the employer match and then press the ENTER key.
5. In cell C9, type `5.5%` as the annual return and then press the ENTER key.
6. In cell C10, type `30` as the years of service and then press the ENTER key. Click cell B17 to remove the selection from the range C5:C10.

The worksheet displays with the updated results, including a new future value of $639,147.65 in cell C15 (Figure 7-4).

As shown in Figure 7-4, if Sarah Dakota earns $73,000 a year and invests 6.5% of her income a year in the 401(k) plan, then in 30 years her investment will be worth $639,147.65. If she works an additional ten years, then cell F14 shows Sarah's investment will be worth an astonishing $1,218,002.28. These future values assume the annual return on the investment will be a conservative 5.5%. They also assume that Sarah will never get a raise, which means the investment could be worth significantly more if she does get raises, because she is investing a percentage of her income, rather than a fixed amount.

Outside of winning the lotto or a large inheritance, a 401(k) plan is the easiest way for a person on a fixed income to legally become a millionaire at some point in his or her lifetime. Once you start drawing funds from a 401(k) plan, you are required to pay taxes on what you withdraw. If you withdraw any funds before you are 59½ years old, then you must pay a 10 percent penalty on withdrawals.

	B	C	E	F	G	H	I
5	Employee Name	Sarah Dakota	Years of Service	Future Value	Employee Investment	Employer Match	Return On Investment
6	Annual Salary	$73,000.00		$639,147.65	$142,350.00	$109,500.00	$387,297.65
7	Employee Investment	6.50%	5	48,187.88	23,725.00	18,250.00	6,212.88
8	Employer Match	5.00%	10	111,588.85	47,450.00	36,500.00	27,638.85
9	Annual Return	5.50%	15	195,005.74	71,175.00	54,750.00	69,080.74
10	Years of Service	30	20	304,757.67	94,900.00	73,000.00	136,857.67
11	Monthly Contribution		25	449,158.69	118,625.00	91,250.00	239,283.69
12	Employee	$395.42	30	639,147.65	142,350.00	109,500.00	387,297.65
13	Employer	$304.17	35	889,116.85	166,075.00	127,750.00	595,291.85
14	Total	$699.58	40	1,218,002.28	189,800.00	146,000.00	882,202.28
15	Future Value	$639,147.65	45	1,650,718.06	213,525.00	164,250.00	1,272,943.06

FIGURE 7-4

As shown in the previous set of steps, when you select a range before entering data, Excel automatically advances one cell down when you press the ENTER key. If the worksheet consists of multiple columns and you enter the last value in a column, then Excel moves to the top of the next column.

Follow these steps to change the data in the range C5:C10 back to its original values.

TO UNDO A GROUP OF ENTRIES USING THE UNDO BUTTON

1. Click the Undo button arrow on the Standard toolbar (Figure 7-4).
2. When the Undo list displays, drag from the top down through Sarah Dakota and then release the left mouse button. Click cell B17.

Excel changes the range C5:C10 back to its original values and recalculates all formulas and the data table. The 401(k) Investment Model worksheet displays as shown earlier in Figure 7-3 on page E 7.7.

The Undo Button

To undo recent actions one at a time, click the Undo button on the Standard toolbar. To undo several actions, click the Undo button arrow and select from the list. Excel will undo the selected action as well as all the actions above it.

Unprotecting a Password-Protected Worksheet

The 401(k) Investment Model worksheet in the Golden Years workbook is protected. When a worksheet is protected, users cannot change data in locked cells or modify the worksheet in any manner. Thus, before modifying the worksheet in the three phases, it must be unprotected. A **password** ensures that users will not unprotect the worksheet by using the Unprotect command. The 401(k) Investment Model worksheet password is fortune.

A password, such as fortune, can contain any combination of letters, numerals, spaces, and symbols, and it can be up to 15 characters long. Passwords are case-sensitive, so if you vary the capitalization when you assign the password, you must type the same capitalization later when you unprotect the worksheet.

The following steps show how to unprotect the password-protected worksheet.

To Unprotect a Password-Protected Worksheet

1. **Click Tools on the menu bar, point to Protection, and then point to Unprotect Sheet on the Protection submenu.**

The Tools menu and Protection submenu display (Figure 7-5).

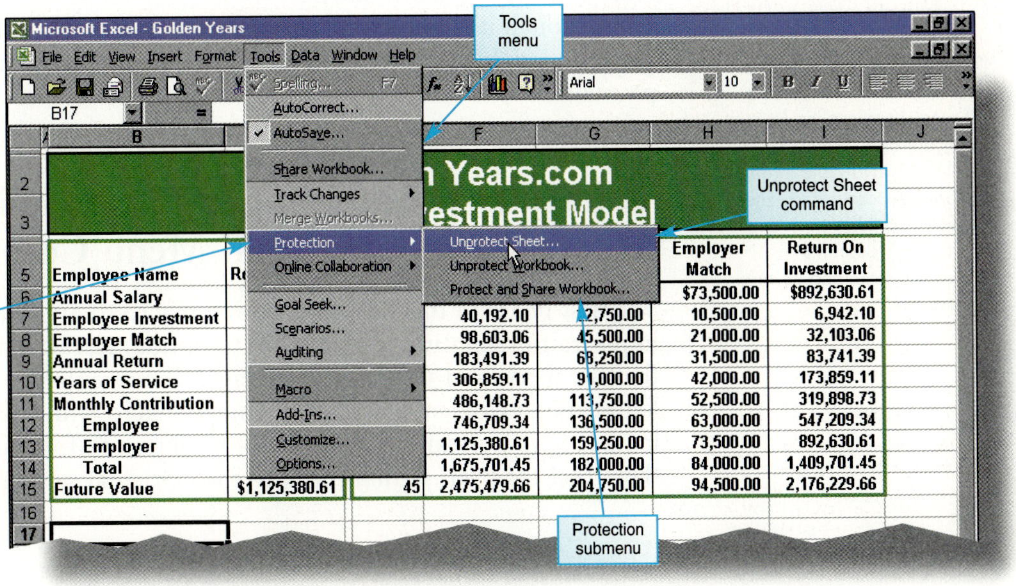

FIGURE 7-5

2 Click Unprotect Worksheet. When the Unprotect Sheet dialog box displays, type `fortune` **in the Password text box and then point to the OK button.**

The Unprotect Sheet dialog box displays (Figure 7-6). Excel displays asterisks in place of the password fortune so no one can look over your shoulder and copy the password.

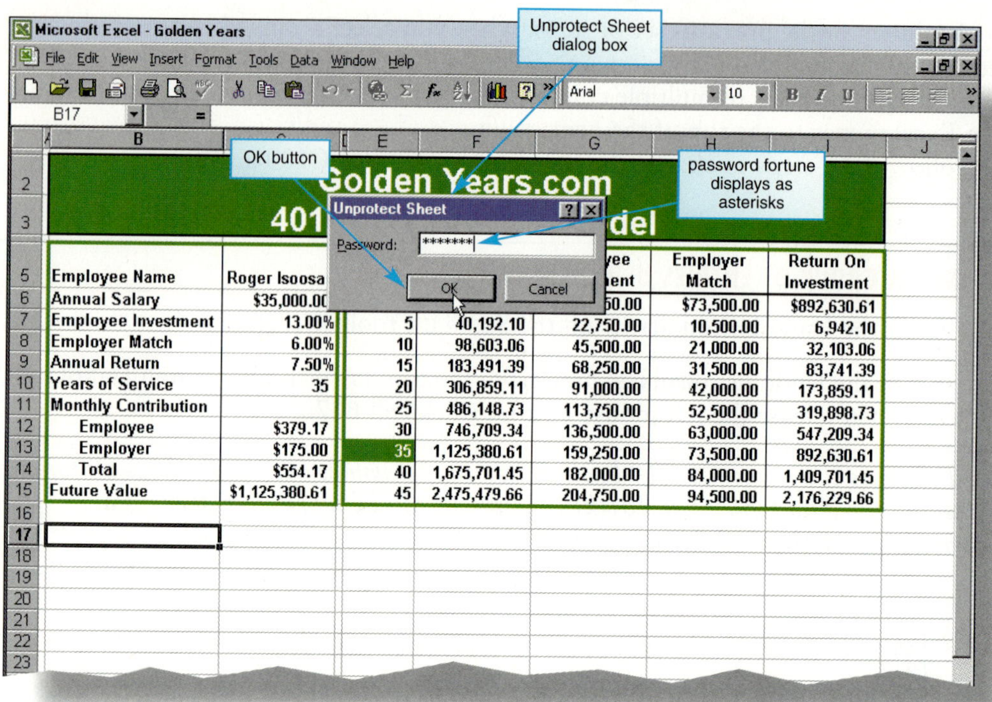

FIGURE 7-6

Click the OK button.

Excel unprotects the 401(k) Investment Model worksheet.

1. Press ALT+T, press P, press P

With the worksheet unprotected, you can modify the contents of cells regardless of whether they are locked or unlocked. If you decide to password-protect a worksheet, make sure you write down the password and keep it in a secure place. If you lose the password, you cannot open or gain access to the password-protected worksheet.

The Protection submenu shown in Figure 7-5 on the previous page also has an **Unprotect Workbook command**. The workbook protection level protects the structure and windows of the workbook, but not individual worksheets. Protecting the structure of a workbook means that users cannot add, delete, move, hide, unhide, or rename sheets. Protecting a workbook's windows means users cannot move, resize, hide, unhide, or close them.

Although it is not necessary in this project to unprotect the workbook, you can do so by invoking the Unprotect Workbook command and using fortune as the password.

Password-Protection

Excel offers three basic levels of password-protection: (1) file level when you save it on disk; (2) workbook level so the window cannot be modified; and (3) worksheet level so locked cells cannot be changed. The first level is available through the Save As command. The second and third levels are available through the Protection command on the Tools menu.

Phase 1 — Recording a Macro and Assigning It to a Toolbar Button and Menu Command

The first phase of this project creates a macro to automate printing the worksheet in portrait orientation using the Fit to option. Recall that the Fit to option ensures that the worksheet will fit on one page. The orientation for the printout was set to landscape in Golden Years. The planned macro will change the orientation from landscape to portrait and use the Fit to option to force it to fit on one page. It will then reset the print settings back to their original settings.

The purpose of this macro is to give users the option of printing the worksheet in landscape orientation by clicking the Print button on the Standard toolbar or executing the macro to print the worksheet in portrait orientation. Once the macro is created, it will be assigned to a button on the Standard toolbar and a command on the File menu.

The Macro Recorder

The macro recorder is unforgiving. Once it is turned on, Excel records every action you take. If you make a mistake, you must start over. For this reason, you need to plan carefully from start to finish what you intend to do before you turn the macro recorder on.

Recording a Macro

Excel has a **macro recorder** that creates a macro automatically based on a series of actions you perform while it is recording. As with a tape recorder, the macro recorder records everything you do to a workbook over time. The macro recorder can be turned on, during which time it records your activities, and then turned off to stop the recording. Once the macro is recorded, it can be played back, or executed, as often as you want.

It is easy to create a macro. Simply turn on the macro recorder and carry out the steps to be recorded.

1. Switch from landscape orientation to portrait orientation and from 100% normal size printing to fit to one page.
2. Print the worksheet.
3. Switch from portrait orientation to landscape orientation and from fit to one page to 100% normal size printing.
4. Stop the macro recorder.

What is impressive about the macro recorder is that you actually step through the task as you create the macro. Therefore, you see exactly what the macro will do before you use it.

When you first create the macro, you have to name it. The name then is used later to reference the macro when you want to execute it. The macro name in this project is PrintPortrait. **Macro names** can be up to 255 characters long; they can contain numbers, letters, and underscores; they cannot contain spaces and other punctuation. Perform the following steps to record the macro.

To Record a Macro to Print the Worksheet in Portrait Orientation Using the Fit to Option

1 Click Tools on the menu bar. Point to Macro and then point to Record New Macro on the Macro submenu.

The Tools menu and Macro submenu display (Figure 7-7).

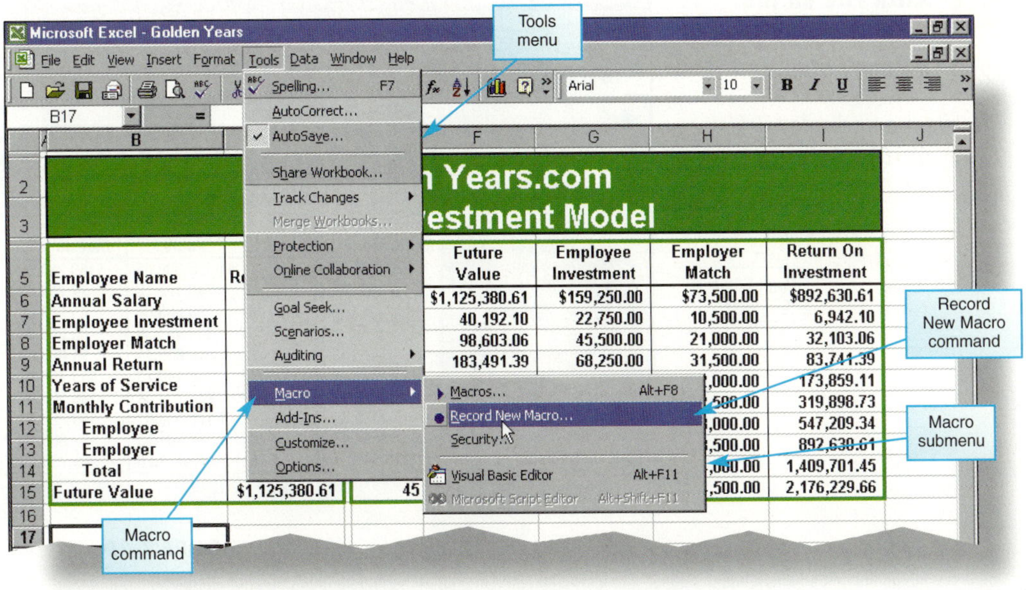

FIGURE 7-7

2 Click Record New Macro. When the Record Macro dialog box displays, type `PrintPortrait` **in the Macro name text box. Type** `r` **in the Shortcut key text box, and then type** `Macro prints worksheet in portrait orientation on one page` **in the Description text box. Make sure the Store macro in box displays This Workbook. Point to the OK button.**

The Record Macro dialog box displays as shown in Figure 7-8. The shortcut key for executing the macro is CTRL+R.

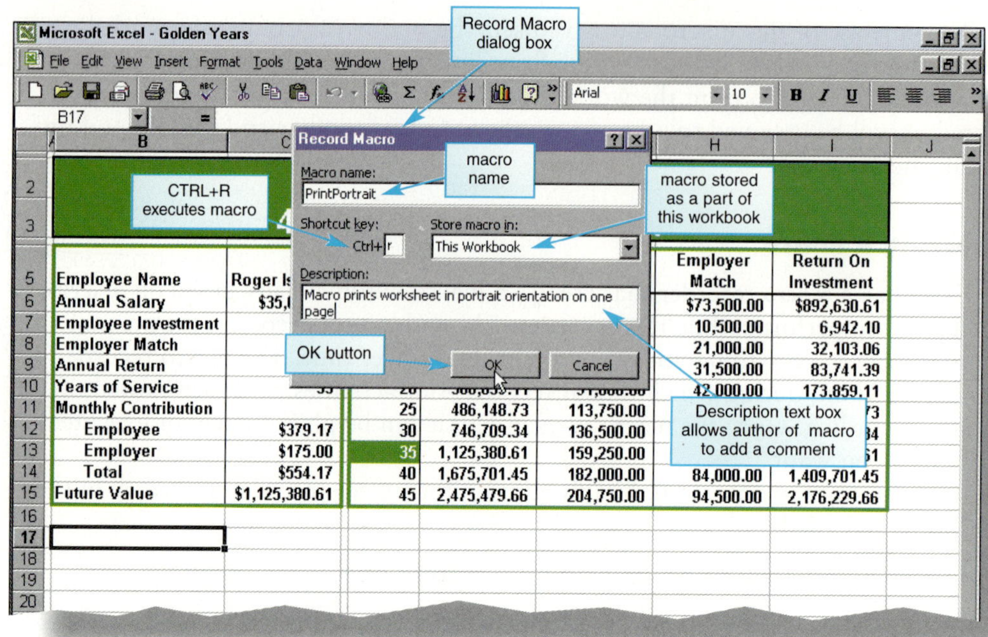

FIGURE 7-8

3 Click the OK button.

The Stop Recording toolbar displays. Any task you do will be part of the macro. When you are finished recording the macro, clicking the Stop Recording button on the Stop Recording toolbar ends the recording.

FIGURE 7-9

4 Click File on the menu bar and then point to Page Setup.

The File menu displays (Figure 7-10).

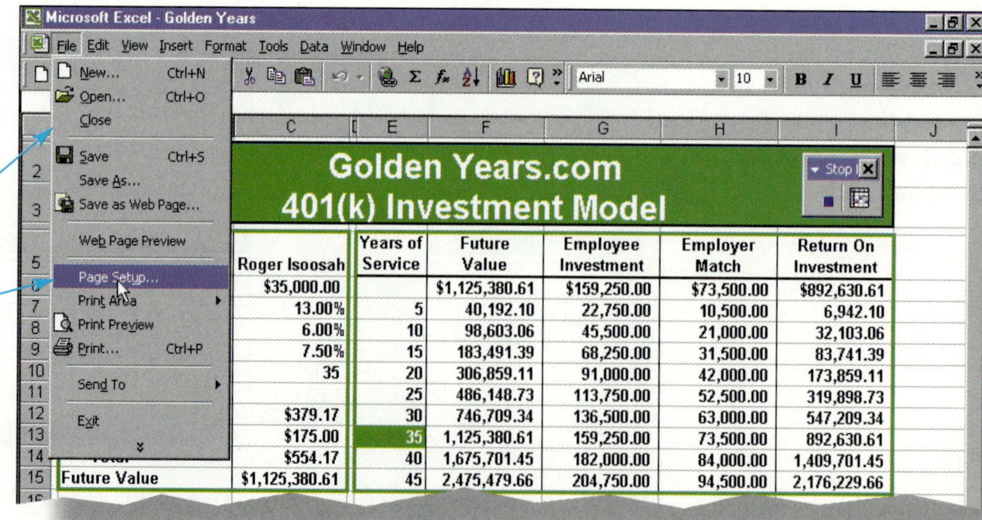

FIGURE 7-10

5 **Click Page Setup. When the Page Setup dialog box displays, click the Page tab, click Portrait in the Orientation area, click Fit to in the Scaling area, and then point to the Print button.**

The Page Setup dialog box displays as shown in Figure 7-11.

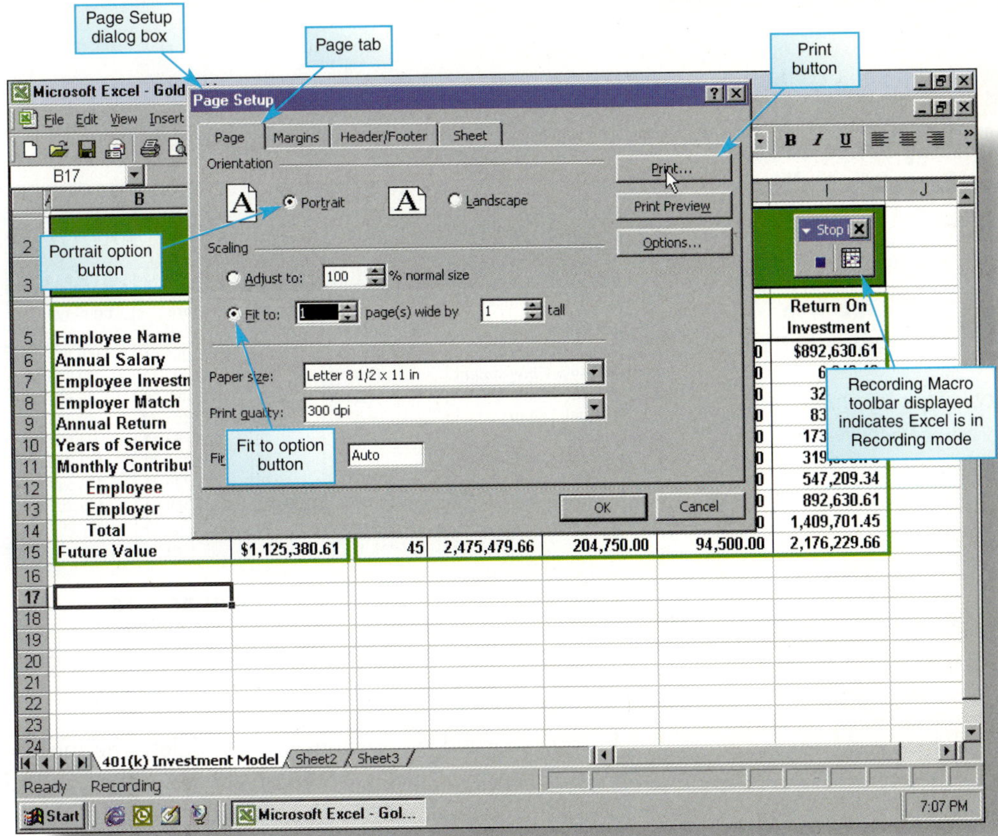

FIGURE 7-11

6 **Click the Print button. When the Print dialog box displays, click the OK button. Click File on the menu bar and then click Page Setup. When the Page Setup dialog box displays, if necessary, click the Page tab, click Landscape in the Orientation area, click Adjust to in the Scaling area, type** 100 **in the % normal size box, and then point to the OK button.**

After the worksheet prints in portrait orientation on one page, the Page Setup dialog box displays as shown in Figure 7-12.

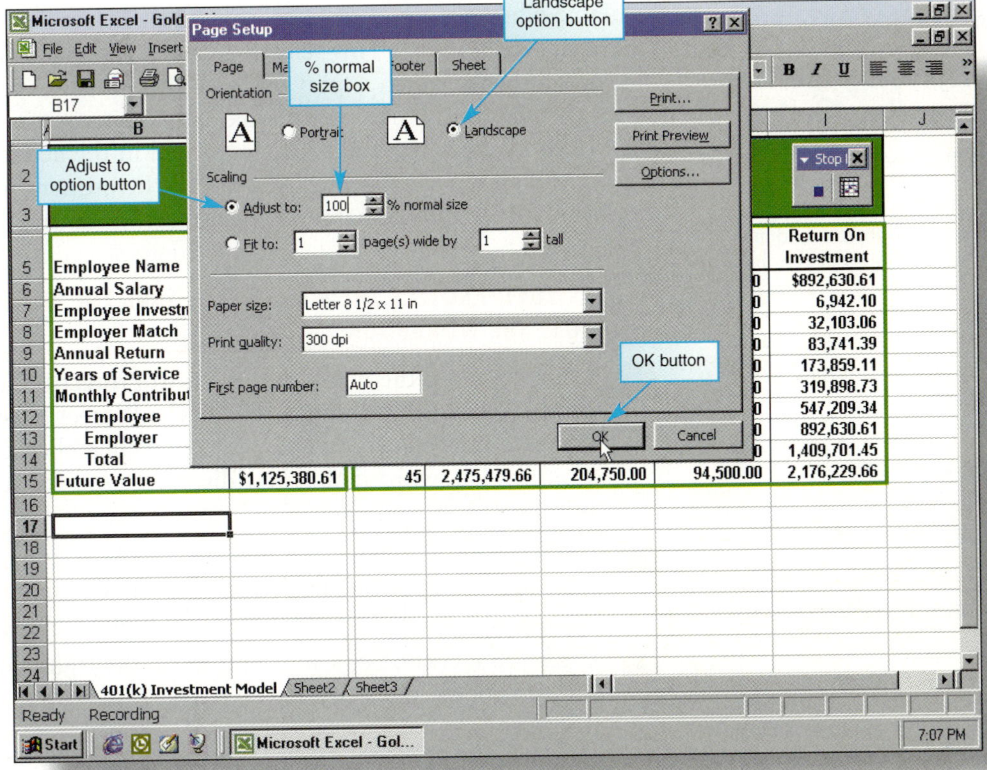

FIGURE 7-12

7 **Click the OK button. Point to the Stop Recording button on the Stop Recording toolbar (Figure 7-13).**

8 **Click the Stop Recording button.**

Excel stops recording the worksheet activities and hides the Stop Recording toolbar.

FIGURE 7-13

Other Ways

1. Click Record Macro button on Visual Basic toolbar
2. Press ALT+T, press M, press R

Displaying the Stop Recording Toolbar

If the Stop Recording toolbar does not display when you begin to record a macro, right-click a toolbar and then click Stop Recording on the shortcut menu.

More About 2000

Macros and Protected Worksheets

Excel displays an error message if you execute a macro that attempts to modify a protected worksheet. If you want to modify a protected worksheet using a macro, then have the macro unprotect the worksheet at the beginning and then have the macro protect the worksheet at the end.

If you recorded the wrong actions, delete the macro and record it again. You delete a macro by clicking Tools on the menu bar, pointing to Macro on the Tools menu, and then clicking Macros on the Macro submenu. When the Macro dialog box displays, click the name of the macro (PrintPortrait) and then click the Delete button. Finally, record the macro again.

In the Record Macro dialog box (Figure 7-8 on page E 7.12), you select the location to store the macro in the Store macro in box. If you want a macro to be available whenever you use Microsoft Excel, select Personal Macro Workbook in the Store macro in list. This selection causes the macro to be stored in the **Personal Macro Workbook**, which is part of Excel. If you click New Workbook, then Excel stores the macro in a new workbook. Most macros created with the macro recorder are workbook-specific, and thus, are stored in the active workbook.

The following steps protect the 401(k) Investment Model worksheet, save the workbook using the file name Golden Years1, and then close the workbook.

TO PASSWORD-PROTECT THE WORKSHEET, SAVE THE WORKBOOK, AND CLOSE THE WORKBOOK

1. Click Tools on the menu bar, point to Protection, and then click Protect Sheet on the Protection submenu. When the Protect Sheet dialog box displays, type `fortune` in the Password text box and then click the OK button. When the Confirm Password dialog box displays, type `fortune` and then click the OK button.
2. Click File on the menu bar and then click Save As. When the Save As dialog box displays, type `Golden Years1` in the File name text box. Make sure 3½ Floppy (A:) displays in the Save in box and then click the Save button.
3. Click the workbook's Close button on the right side of its menu bar to close the workbook and leave Excel active.

Excel protects the worksheet, saves the workbook on drive A, and then closes the Golden Years1 workbook.

Opening a Workbook with a Macro and Executing the Macro

A **computer virus** is a potentially damaging computer program designed to affect, or infect, your computer negatively by altering the way it works without your knowledge or permission. Currently, more than 13,000 known computer viruses exist and an estimated six new viruses are discovered each day. The increased use of the networks, the Internet, and e-mail has accelerated the spread of computer viruses.

To combat this evil, most computer users run antivirus programs that search for viruses and destroy them before they ever have a chance to infect the computer. Macros are a known carrier of viruses, because of the ease at which a person can add code to macros. For this reason, each time you open a workbook with a macro associated with it, Excel displays a Microsoft Excel dialog box warning that a macro is attached and that macros can contain viruses. Table 7-1 summarizes the buttons users can select from to continue the process of opening a workbook with macros.

Macro Viruses

To guard against macro viruses in workbooks created by someone else, you should purchase antivirus software that is designed to detect and repair files infected with a virus. For more information on antivirus software, visit the Excel 2000 More About Web page (www.scsite.com/ex2000/more.htm) and click Antivirus Software.

Table 7-1 Buttons in the Microsoft Excel Dialog Box When Opening a Workbook with Macros

BUTTON	DESCRIPTION
Disable Macros	Macros are unavailable to the user
Enable Macros	Macros are available to the user to execute
More Info	Opens the Microsoft Excel Help window and displays information on viruses and workbook macros

If you are confident of the source (author) of the workbook and macros, click the Enable Macros button. If you are uncertain about the reliability of the source of the workbook and macros, then click the Disable Macros button. For more information on this topic, click the More Info button.

The following steps open the Golden Years1 workbook to illustrate the Microsoft Excel dialog box that displays when a workbook contains a macro. The steps then show how to execute the recorded macro PrintPortrait by using the shortcut key CTRL+R. Recall that the shortcut key was established in Step 2 of the previous set of steps.

More About

Antivirus Software

If your antivirus software is compatible with Office 2000, then you can select the lowest level of security in the Security dialog box. You display the Security dialog box by clicking Tools on the menu bar, Macro on the Tools menu, and Security on the Macro submenu. The antivirus software will scan all incoming workbooks for viruses, regardless of the level of security you choose.

To Open a Workbook with a Macro and Execute the Macro

1 With Excel active, click File on the menu bar and then click Open. When the Open dialog box displays, click the Look in box arrow, and then click 3 ½ Floppy (A:). Double-click the file name Golden Years1.

The Microsoft Excel dialog displays (Figure 7-14).

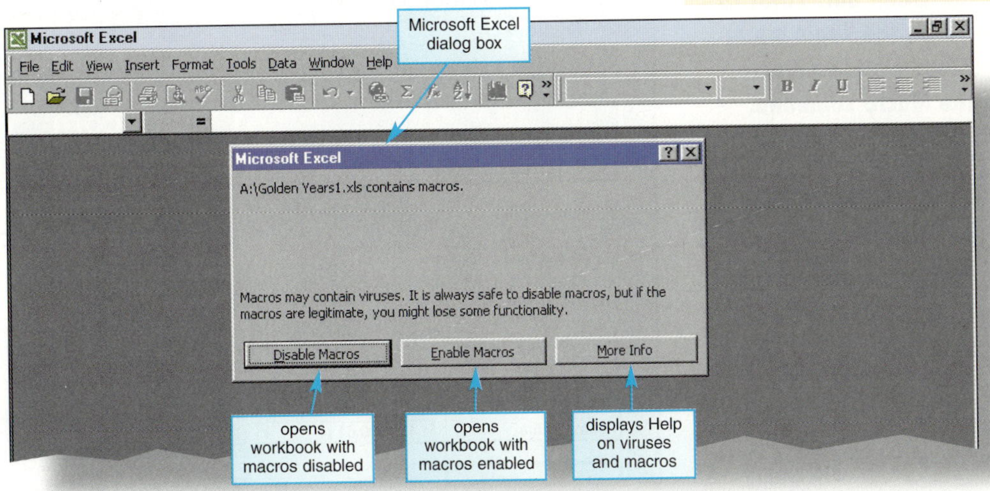

FIGURE 7-14

2 Click the Enable Macros button. When the 401(k) Investment Model worksheet in the Golden Years1 workbook displays, press CTRL+R.

Excel opens the workbook Golden Years1. The Excel window blinks for several seconds as the macro executes. The report prints as shown in Figure 7-15.

Golden Years.com
401(k) Investment Model

		Years of Service	Future Value	Employee Investment	Employer Match	Return On Investment
Employee Name	Roger Isoosah					
Annual Salary	$35,000.00		$1,125,380.61	$159,250.00	$73,500.00	$892,630.61
Employee Investment	13.00%	5	40,192.10	22,750.00	10,500.00	6,942.10
Employer Match	6.00%	10	98,603.06	45,500.00	21,000.00	32,103.06
Annual Return	7.50%	15	183,491.39	68,250.00	31,500.00	83,741.39
Years of Service	35	20	306,859.11	91,000.00	42,000.00	173,859.11
Monthly Contribution		25	486,148.73	113,750.00	52,500.00	319,898.73
Employee	$379.17	30	746,709.34	136,500.00	63,000.00	547,209.34
Employer	$175.00	35	1,125,380.61	159,250.00	73,500.00	892,630.61
Total	$554.17	40	1,675,701.45	182,000.00	84,000.00	1,409,701.45
Future Value	$1,125,380.61	45	2,475,479.66	204,750.00	94,500.00	2,176,229.66

worksheet printed in portrait orientation using Fit to option

FIGURE 7-15

Other Ways

1. On Tools menu point to Macro, click Macros, double-click macro name
2. Press ALT+F8, double-click macro name
3. Click Run Macro button on Visual Basic toolbar

If you are running antivirus software, you may want to turn off the security warning shown in Figure 7-14 on the previous page. You can turn off the security warning by clicking Tools on the menu bar, pointing to Macro, and then clicking **Security** on the Macros submenu. When the **Security dialog box** displays, click the **Low option button**. Then the next time you open a workbook with an attached macro, Excel will open the workbook immediately, rather than display the dialog box shown in Figure 7-14.

Viewing a Macro's VBA Code

As described earlier, a macro is comprised of VBA code, which is created automatically by the macro recorder. You can view the VBA code through the Visual Basic Editor. The **Visual Basic Editor** is used by all Office applications to enter, modify, and view VBA code. To view the macro's VBA code, complete the following steps.

To View a Macro's VBA Code

1 Click Tools on the menu bar. Point to Macro on the Tools menu and then point to Macros on the Macro submenu.

The Tools menu and Macro submenu display (Figure 7-16).

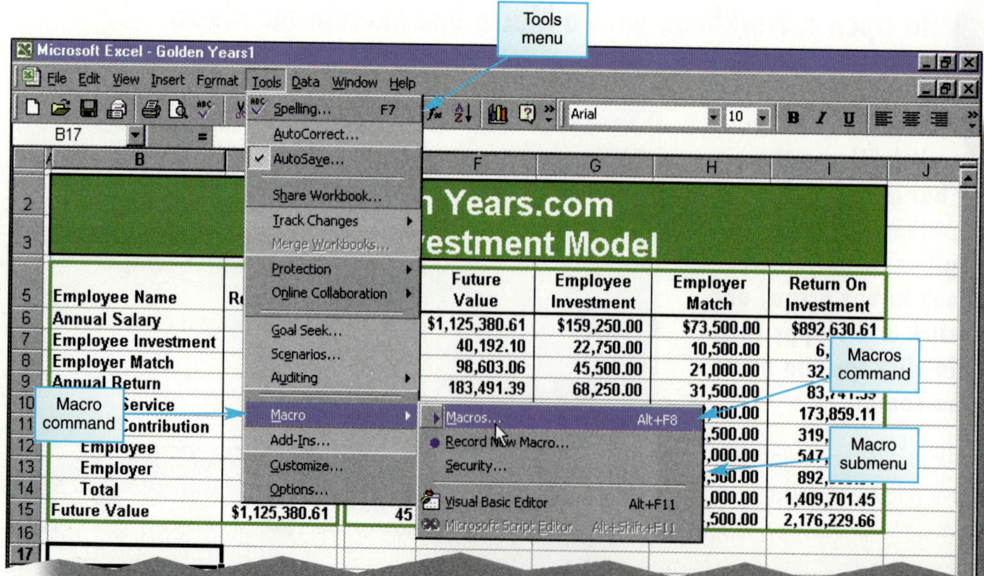

FIGURE 7-16

2 Click Macros. When the Macro dialog box displays, click PrintPortrait in the list, and then point to the Edit button.

The Macro dialog box displays as shown in Figure 7-17.

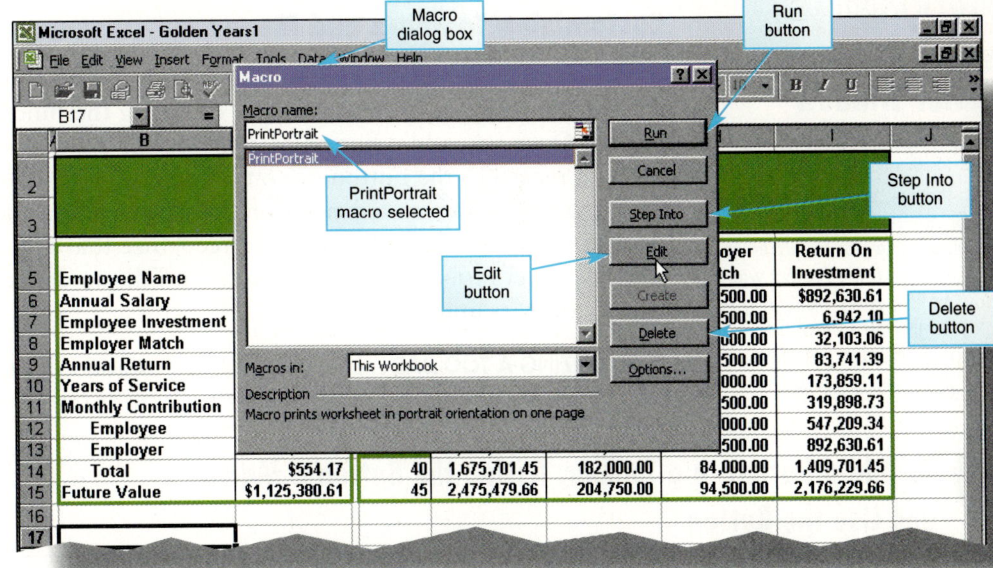

FIGURE 7-17

3 Click the Edit button.

The Visual Basic Editor starts and displays the VBA code in the macro PrintPortrait (Figure 7-18). Your screen may display differently depending on how it displayed the last time the Visual Basic Editor was activated.

4 Scroll through the VBA code. When you are finished, click the Visual Basic Editor Close button on the right side of the title bar.

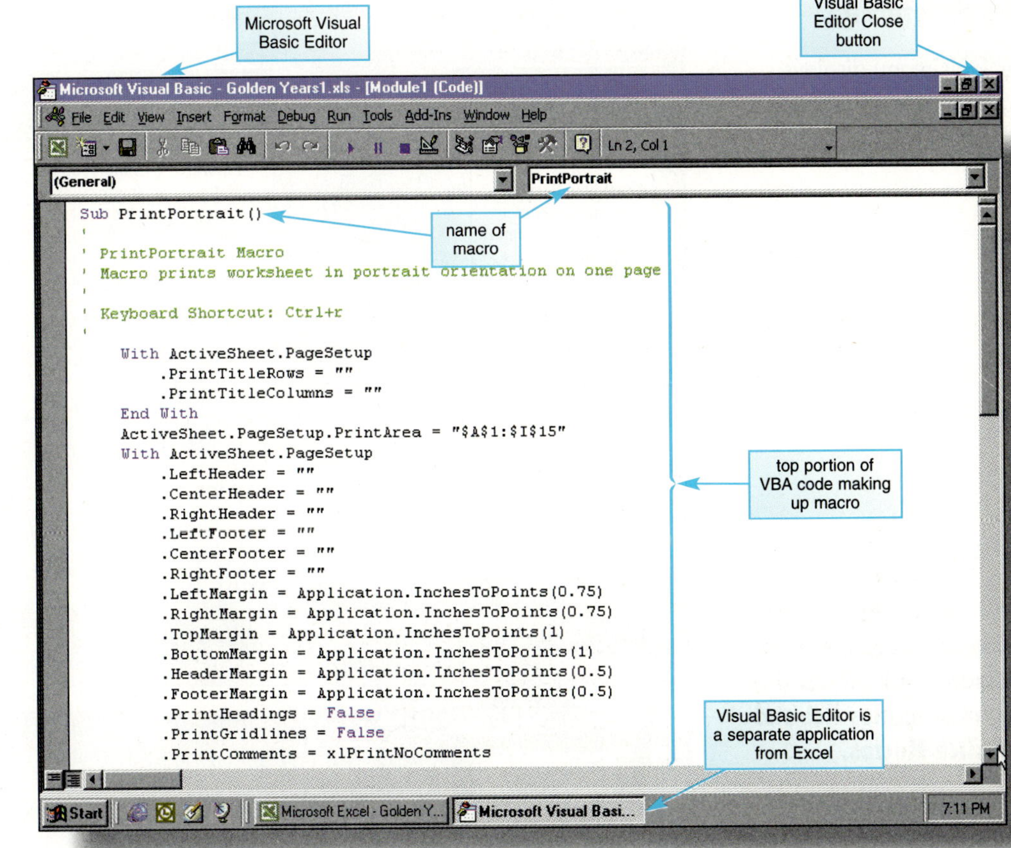

FIGURE 7-18

Other Ways

1. Click Visual Basic Editor button on Visual Basic toolbar

It is this set of instructions, beginning with line 1 in Figure 7-18 and continuing sequentially to the last line, that is executed when you invoke the macro. By scrolling through the VBA code, you can see that the macro recorder generates a lot of instructions. In this case, 75 lines of code are generated to print the worksheet in portrait orientation using the Fit to option.

The Visual Basic Editor Window

If the window displaying the VBA code displays differently than the one shown in Figure 7-18, double-click the Code window's title bar to maximize the window. If the Project window or Properties window display on the left side of the Visual Basic Editor window, then click their Close buttons.

Customizing Toolbars and Menus

You can customize toolbars and menus by adding buttons and commands, deleting buttons and commands, and changing the function of buttons and commands. Once you add a button to a toolbar or a command to a menu, you can assign a macro to the button or command. You customize a toolbar or menu by invoking the **Customize command** on the Tools menu. The key to understanding how to customize a toolbar or menu is to recognize that when the Customize dialog box is open, Excel's toolbars and menus are in Edit mode. **Edit mode** allows you to modify the toolbars and menus.

CUSTOMIZING A TOOLBAR The following steps add a button to the Standard toolbar, change the button image, and assign the PrintPortrait macro to the button.

To Add a Button to a Toolbar, Assign the Button a Macro, and Use the Button

1. **Click Tools on the menu bar and then point to Customize.**

The Tools menu displays (Figure 7-19)

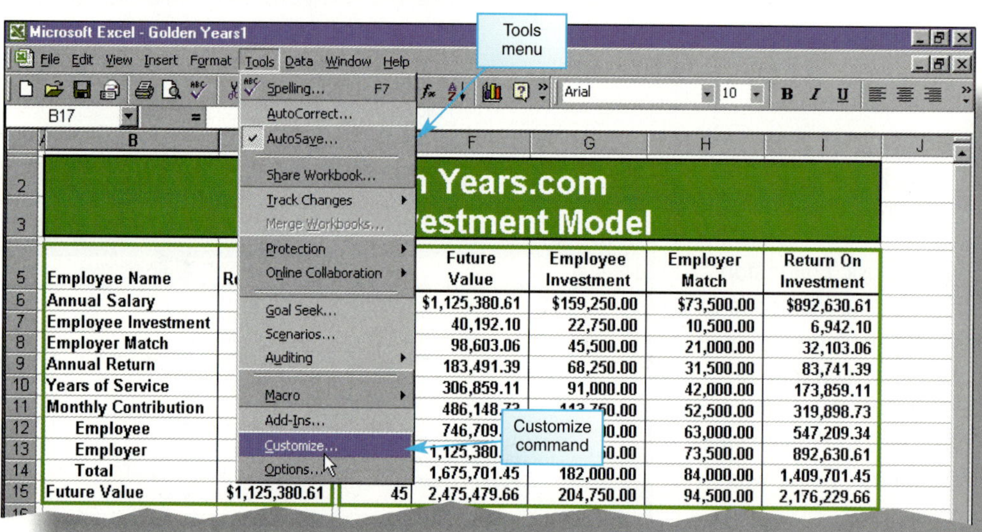

FIGURE 7-19

2. **Click Customize. When the Customize dialog box opens, click the Commands tab. Scroll down in the Categories list and then click Macros.**

The Customize dialog box displays as shown in Figure 7-20. The two items in the Commands list for the Macro category are Custom Menu Item and Custom Button.

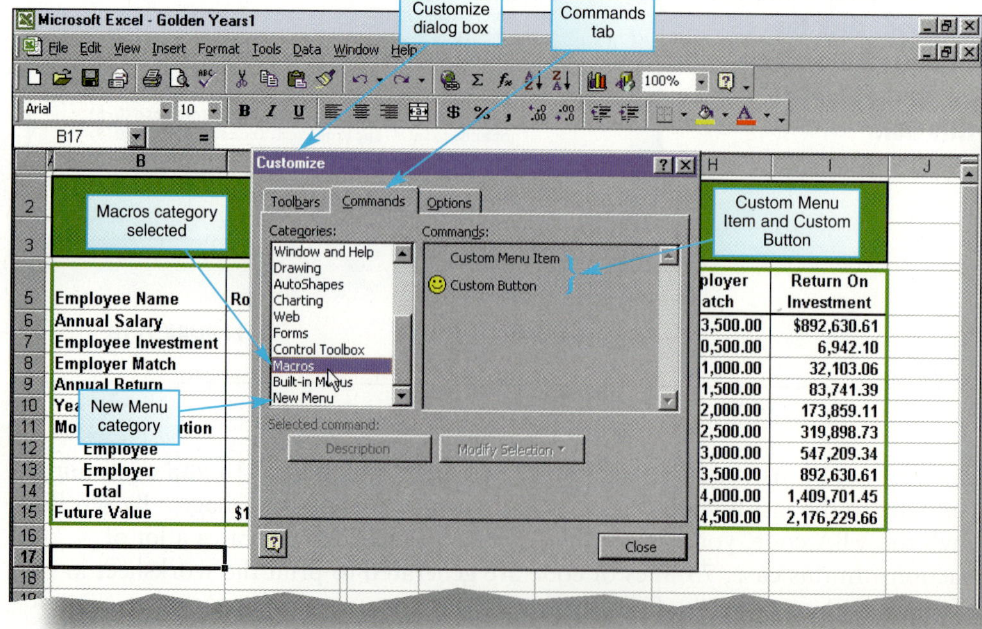

FIGURE 7-20

3 Drag the button with the smiley face image in the Commands list to the right of the Microsoft Excel Help button on the Standard toolbar.

The button with the smilly face image displays next to the Microsoft Excel Help button on the Standard toolbar (Figure 7-21). A heavy border surrounds the button with the smiley face image indicating Excel is in Edit mode.

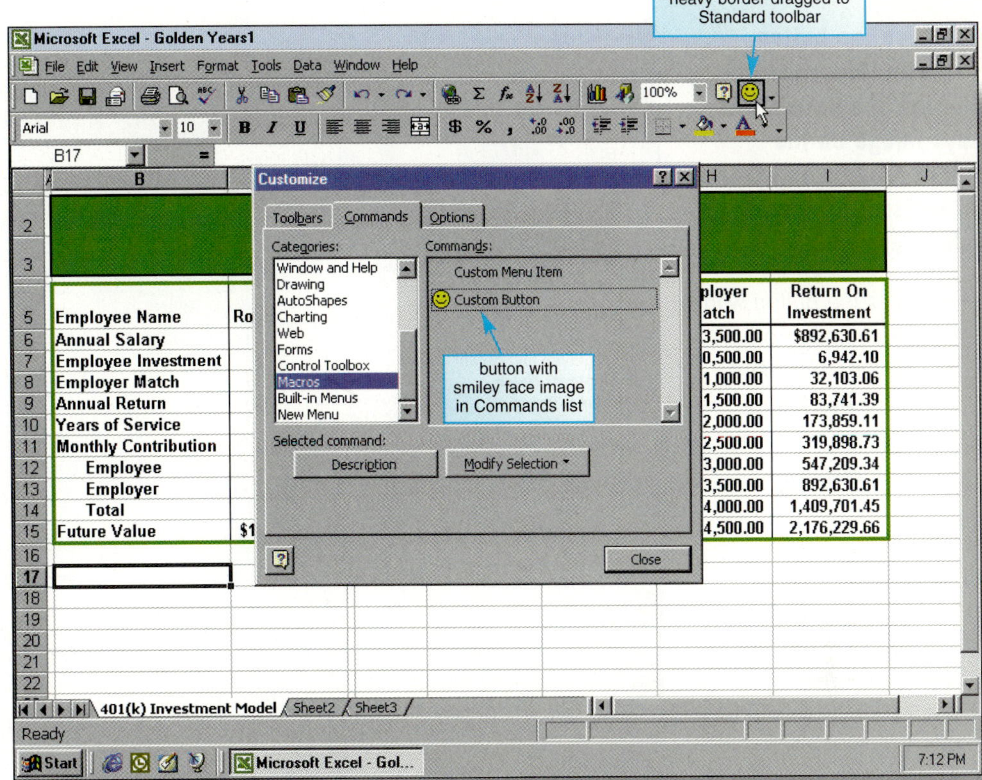

FIGURE 7-21

4 Right-click the button with the smiley face image on the Standard toolbar. When the shortcut menu displays, type `Print Portrait` **in the Name text box. Point to Change Button Image on the shortcut menu. When the Change Button Image palette displays, point to the button with the eye image.**

Excel displays a palette of button images to select from (Figure 7-22).

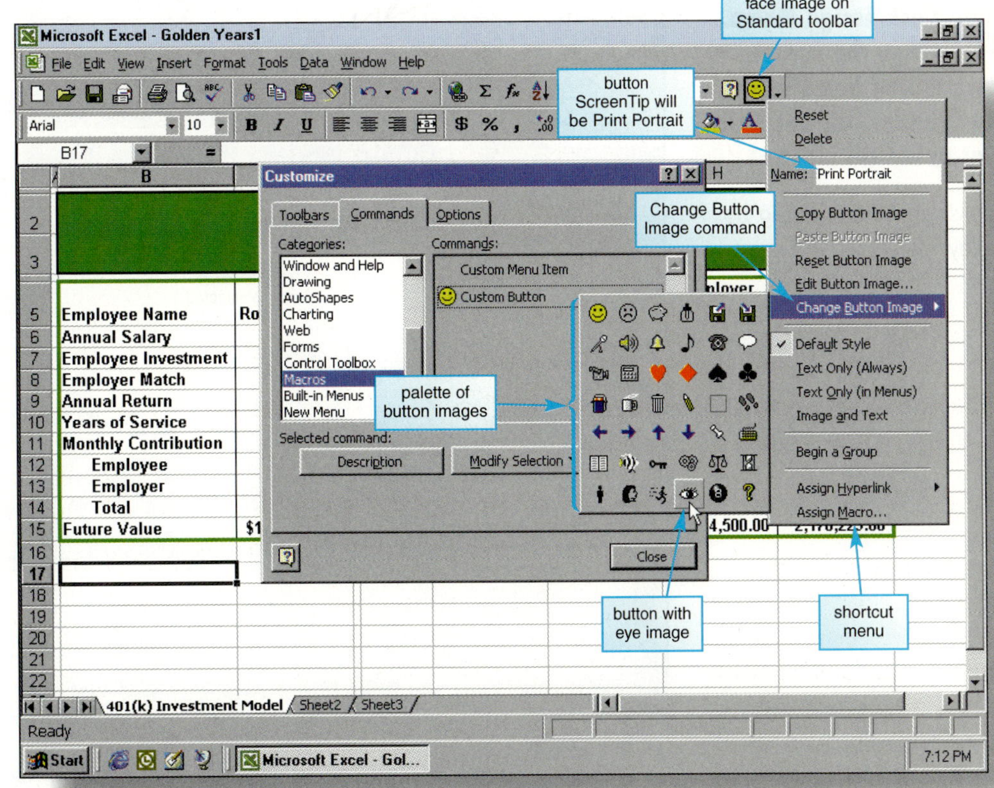

FIGURE 7-22

5 Click the button with the eye image. Right-click the button with the eye image on the Standard toolbar and then point to Assign Macro on the shortcut menu.

Excel replaces the button with the smiley face image on the Standard toolbar with the button with the eye image (Figure 7-23) and the shortcut menu displays.

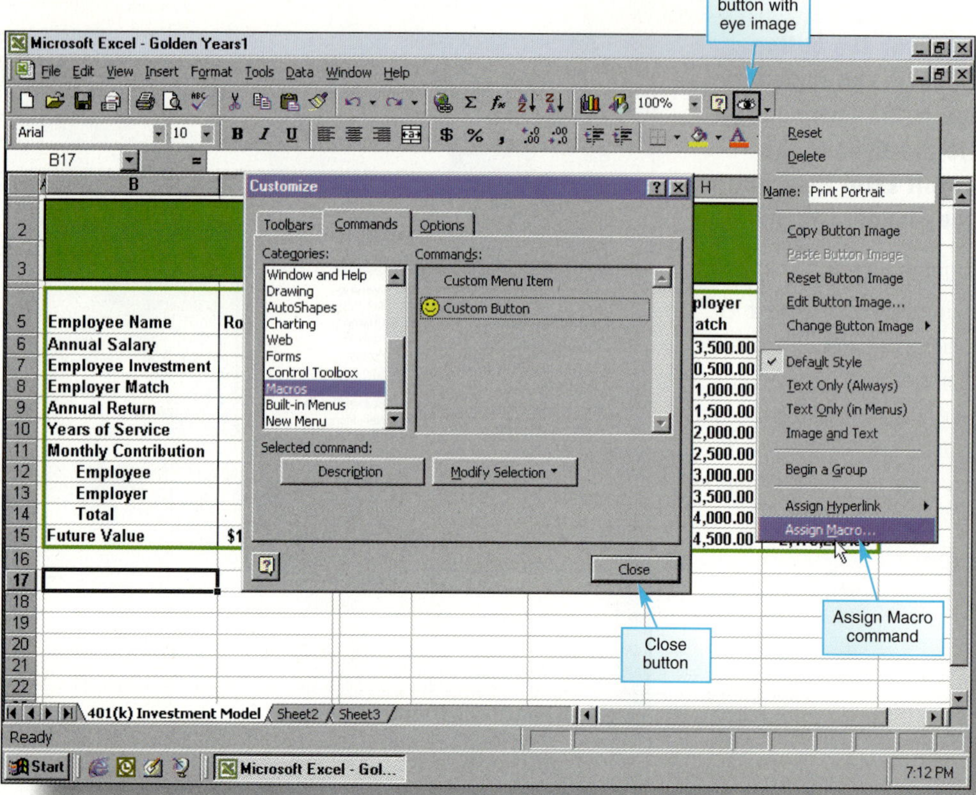

FIGURE 7-23

6 Click Assign Macro. When the Assign Macro dialog box displays, click PrintPortrait and then point to the OK button.

The Assign Macro dialog box displays as shown in Figure 7-24.

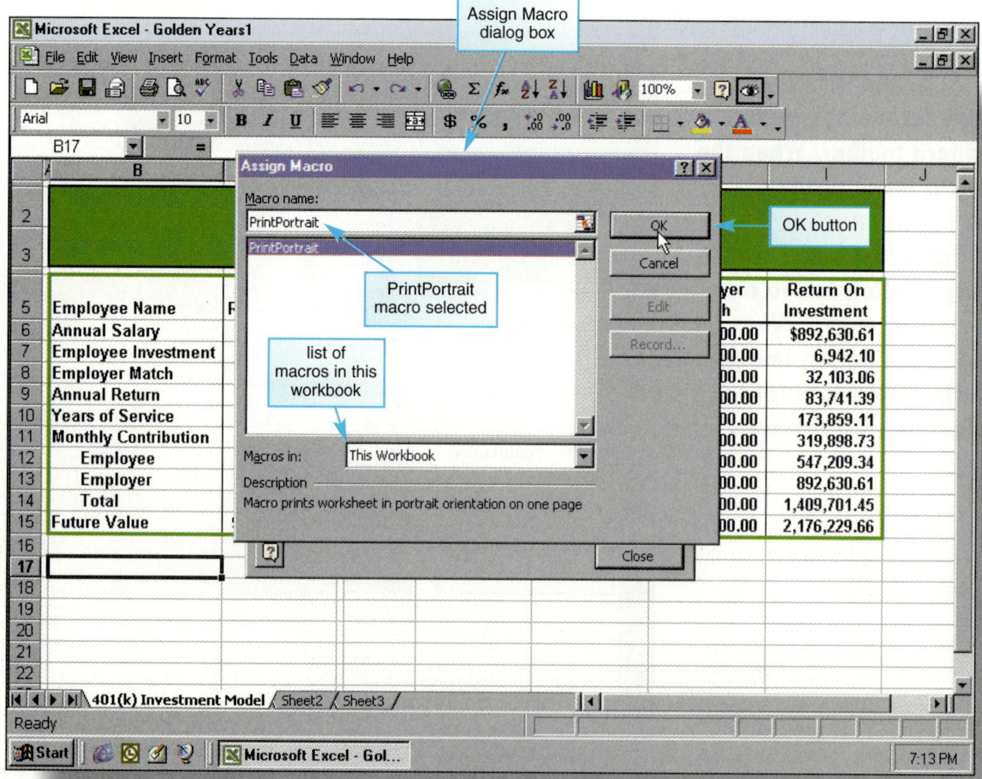

FIGURE 7-24

7 **Click the OK button. Click the Close button at the bottom of the Customize dialog box. Point to the Print Portrait button on the Standard toolbar.**

Excel quits Edit mode. The Print Portrait button displays on the Standard toolbar with the ScreenTip Print Portrait (Figure 7-25).

8 **Click the Print Portrait button on the Standard toolbar.**

After a few seconds, the worksheet prints in portrait orientation as shown in Figure 7-15 on page E 7.16.

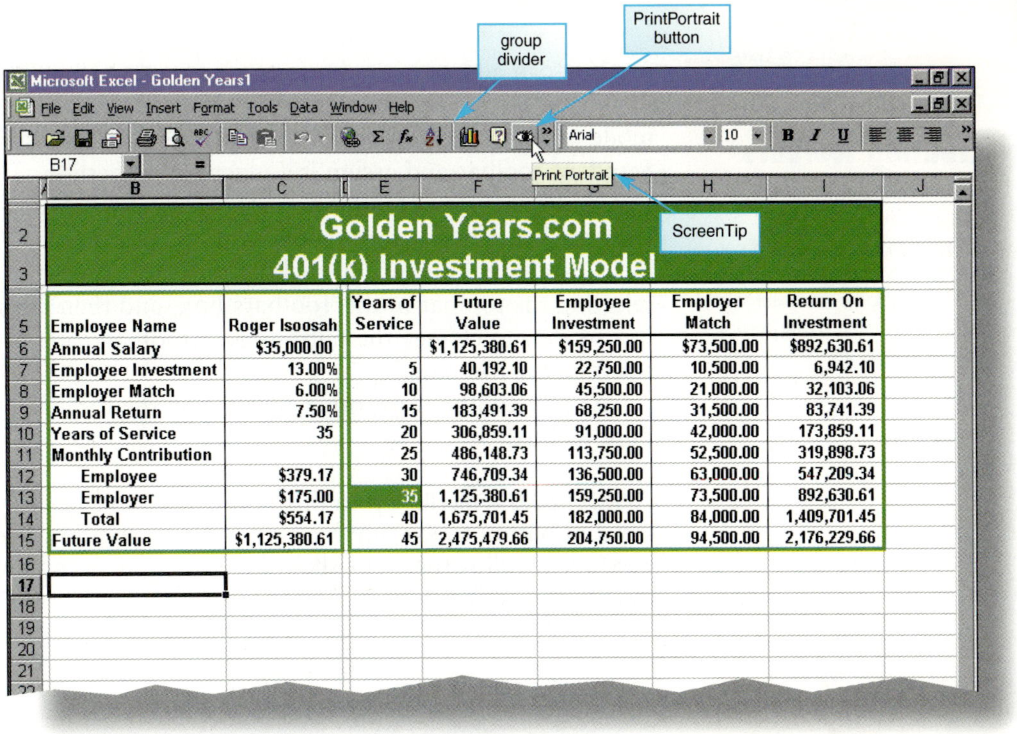

FIGURE 7-25

Other Ways

1. Right-click toolbar, click Customize on shortcut menu, click Commands tab
2. Click View, click Toolbars, click Customize, click Commands tab
3. Click Modify Selection button in Customize dialog box

The previous steps illustrate how easy it is in Excel to add a button to a toolbar and assign the button a macro.

Excel includes a complete repertoire of commands for editing buttons on a toolbar as shown on the shortcut menu in Figure 7-23. Table 7-2 briefly describes each of the commands on the shortcut menu.

Table 7-2 Summary of Commands on the Button Shortcut Menu

COMMAND	DESCRIPTION
Reset	Changes the icon on the selected button to the original icon and disassociates the macro with the button
Delete	Deletes the selected button
Name box	Changes the ScreenTip for a button and changes the command name for a command on a menu
Copy Button Image	Copies the button image to the Office Clipboard
Paste Button Image	Pastes the button image on the Office Clipboard to the selected button
Reset Button Image	Changes the button image back to the original image
Edit Button Image	Allows you to edit the button image
Change Button Image	Allows you to choose a new button image
Default Style; Text Only (Always); Text Only (in Menus); Image and Text	Allows you to choose one of the four styles to indicate how the button should look
Begin a Group	Groups buttons by drawing a vertical line (divider) on the toolbar (see the group dividing line in Figure 7-25)
Assign Hyperlink	Assigns a hyperlink to a Web page or Office document to the button
Assign Macro	Assigns a macro to the button

Creating Toolbars

You can create new toolbars and add buttons to them, rather than add buttons to current toolbars. To create a new toolbar, click the Toolbars tab in the Customize dialog box and then click the New button.

You can add as many buttons as you want to a toolbar. You also can change the image on any button or change a button's function. For example, when in Edit mode (the Customize dialog box is active) you can right-click the Save button on the Standard toolbar and assign it a macro or hyperlink. The next time you click the Save button, the macro will execute or Excel will launch the application associated with the hyperlink, rather than saving the workbook. You reset the toolbars to their installation default by clicking the Toolbars tab in the Customize dialog box, selecting the toolbar in the Toolbars box, and then clicking the Reset button. Because it is so easy to change the buttons on a toolbar, each project in this book begins by resetting the toolbars.

As you add buttons, other buttons on the toolbar will be demoted to the More Buttons box.

CUSTOMIZING A MENU Up to this point, you have been introduced to using a shortcut key and button to execute a macro. Excel also allows you to add commands to a menu. The following steps show how to add a command to the File menu to execute the PrintPortrait macro.

To Add a Command to a Menu, Assign the Command a Macro, and Invoke the Command

1 **Click Tools on the menu bar and then click Customize. When the Customize dialog box displays, if necessary, click the Commands tab. Scroll down in the Categories box and then click Macros. Click File on the menu bar to display the File menu.**

The Customize dialog box and File menu display as shown in Figure 7-26.

FIGURE 7-26

2 Drag the Custom Menu Item entry from the Commands list in the Customize dialog box immediately below the Print command on the File menu.

Excel adds Custom Menu Item to the File menu (Figure 7-27). A heavy border surrounds Custom Menu Item on the File menu indicating Excel is in the Edit mode.

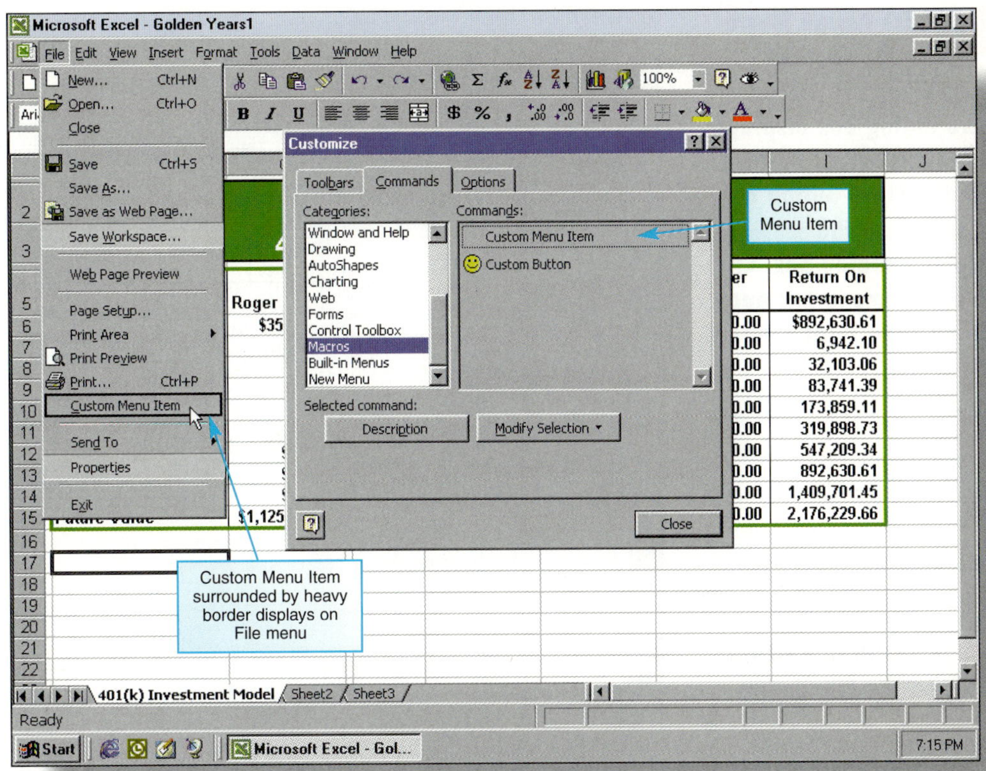

FIGURE 7-27

3 Right-click Custom Menu Item on the File menu and then click the Name text box on the shortcut menu. Type `Print Po&rtrait Ctrl+R` **as the new name of this entry on the File menu. Point to Assign Macro on the shortcut menu.**

The shortcut menu displays (Figure 7-28). The ampersand (&) preceding the letter r in Portrait instructs Excel to use the letter r as the access key. The **access key** *is the underlined letter that you can press to invoke the command when the menu displays.*

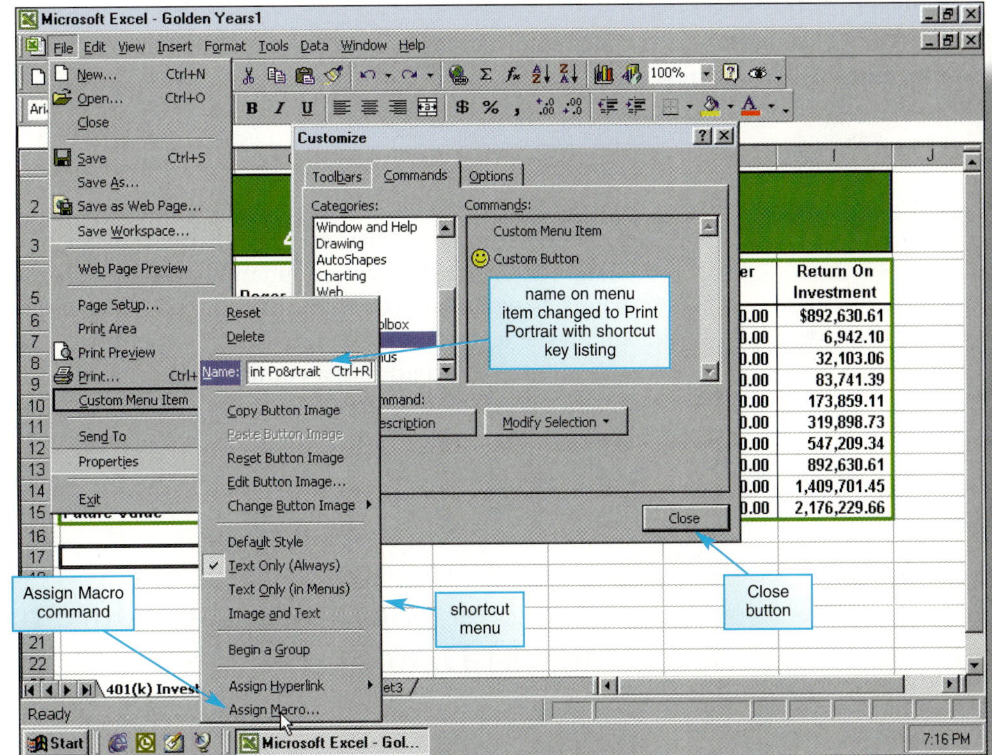

FIGURE 7-28

4 **Click Assign Macro on the shortcut menu. When the Assign Macro dialog box displays, double-click Print Portrait. Click the Close button at the bottom of the Customize dialog box. Click File on the menu bar and then point to Print Portrait.**

Excel quits the Edit mode. The File menu displays with the new command Print Portrait on the menu (Figure 7-29). The underlined letter r in Portrait is the access key.

5 **Click Print Portrait on the File menu.**

After several seconds, the worksheet prints in portrait orientation as shown in Figure 7-15 on page E 7.16.

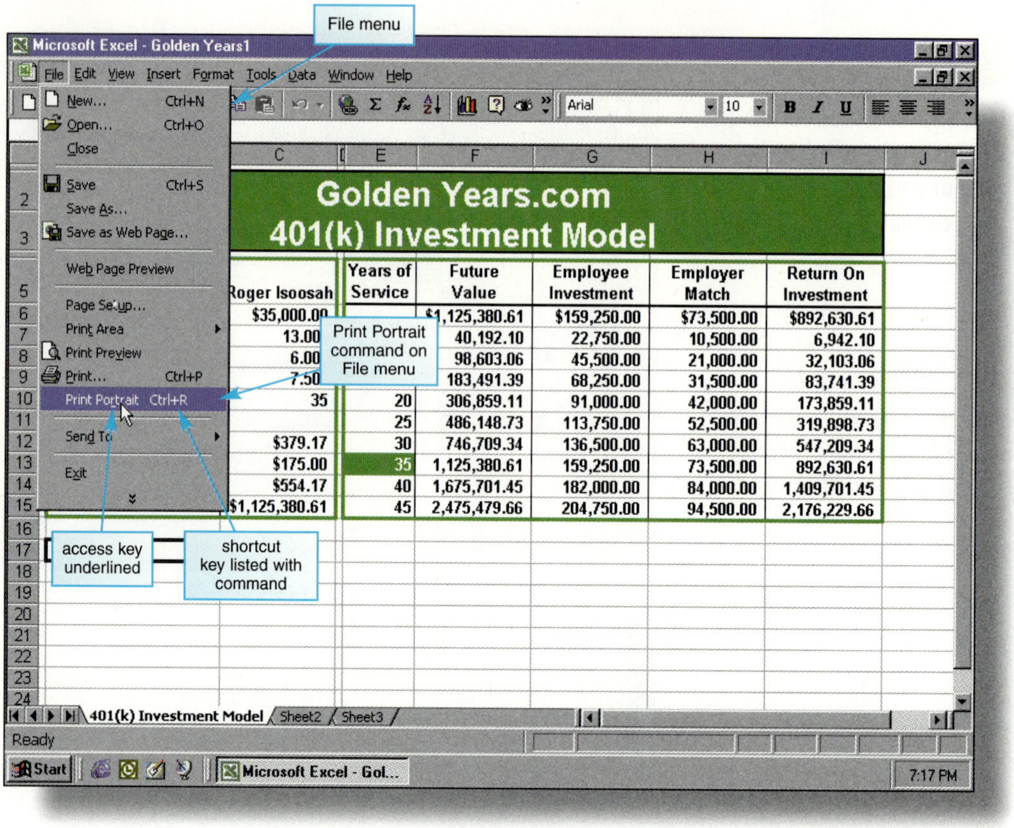

FIGURE 7-29

6 **Click the Save button on the Standard toolbar to save the workbook using the file name Golden Years1.**

Other Ways

1. Right-click toolbar, click Customize on shortcut menu, click Commands tab
2. Click View, click Toolbars, click Customize, click Commands tab

More About

Creating New Menus

You can create an entire new menu on the menu bar by dragging New Menu from the Categories box in the Customize dialog box to the menu bar. You then can add new commands to the new menu using the procedure described in the previous sequence of steps.

You have the same customization capabilities with menus as you do with toolbars. All of the shortcut commands described in Table 7-2 on page E 7.21 apply to menus as well. Any command specific to buttons pertains to editing the button image on the left side of a command on a menu.

An alternative to adding a command to a menu is to add a new menu name to the menu bar and add commands to its menu. You can add a new menu name to the menu bar by selecting New Menu in the Categories list of the Customize dialog box (Figure 7-27 on the previous page) and dragging New Menu from the Commands list to the menu bar.

Phase 2 — Creating a Procedure to Automate the 401(k) Data Entry

Earlier on page E 7.8, the data for Sarah Dakota was entered to calculate new future value information. A novice user, however, might not know what cells to select or how much 401(k) data is required to obtain the desired results. To facilitate entering the 401(k) data, Phase 2 calls for creating a Command Button control (Figure 7-30a) and an associated procedure (Figure 7-30b) that steps the user through entering the data using dialog boxes.

(a) Worksheet with Button

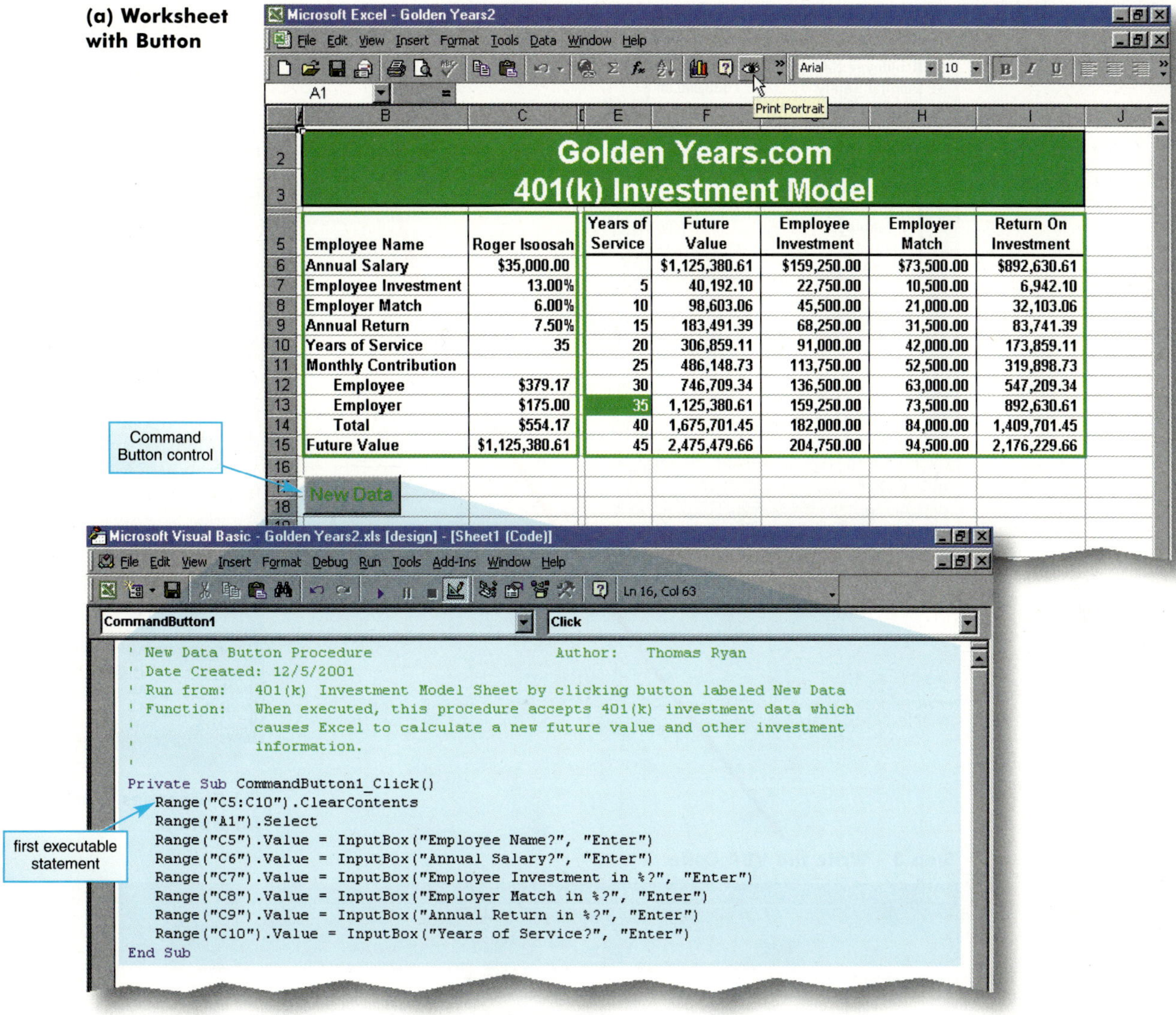

Microsoft Excel - Golden Years2

Command Button control

	Golden Years.com 401(k) Investment Model						
Employee Name	Roger Isoosah	Years of Service	Future Value	Employee Investment	Employer Match	Return On Investment
Annual Salary	$35,000.00		$1,125,380.61	$159,250.00	$73,500.00	$892,630.61
Employee Investment	13.00%	5	40,192.10	22,750.00	10,500.00	6,942.10
Employer Match	6.00%	10	98,603.06	45,500.00	21,000.00	32,103.06
Annual Return	7.50%	15	183,491.39	68,250.00	31,500.00	83,741.39
Years of Service	35	20	306,859.11	91,000.00	42,000.00	173,859.11
Monthly Contribution		25	486,148.73	113,750.00	52,500.00	319,898.73
Employee	$379.17	30	746,709.34	136,500.00	63,000.00	547,209.34
Employer	$175.00	35	1,125,380.61	159,250.00	73,500.00	892,630.61
Total	$554.17	40	1,675,701.45	182,000.00	84,000.00	1,409,701.45
Future Value	$1,125,380.61	45	2,475,479.66	204,750.00	94,500.00	2,176,229.66

New Data

Microsoft Visual Basic - Golden Years2.xls [design] - [Sheet1 (Code)]

first executable statement

```
' New Data Button Procedure                    Author:   Thomas Ryan
' Date Created: 12/5/2001
' Run from:    401(k) Investment Model Sheet by clicking button labeled New Data
' Function:    When executed, this procedure accepts 401(k) investment data which
'              causes Excel to calculate a new future value and other investment
'              information.
'
Private Sub CommandButton1_Click()
   Range("C5:C10").ClearContents
   Range("A1").Select
   Range("C5").Value = InputBox("Employee Name?", "Enter")
   Range("C6").Value = InputBox("Annual Salary?", "Enter")
   Range("C7").Value = InputBox("Employee Investment in %?", "Enter")
   Range("C8").Value = InputBox("Employer Match in %?", "Enter")
   Range("C9").Value = InputBox("Annual Return in %?", "Enter")
   Range("C10").Value = InputBox("Years of Service?", "Enter")
End Sub
```

(b) Procedure

FIGURE 7-30

A **Command Button control** is different from a toolbar button in that it is an object you draw on the worksheet. Once you trigger the event by clicking the Command Button control, the instructions in the associated procedure guide the user through entering the required 401(k) data in the range C5:C10. The Command Button control also is the user interface. The **user interface** can be as simple as a button and as complex as a series of windows that accept data and display results. The user interface, together with the procedure, is called an **application**. Thus, the name Visual Basic for Applications.

If you step through the procedure (Figure 7-30b) beginning at the line just below Private Sub CommandButton1_Click(), you can see how a procedure methodically steps the user through entering the data in the range C5:C10:

1. The first line clears the range C5:C10.
2. The second line selects cell A1.
3. Lines three through eight accept data for the cells in the range C5:C10, one cell at a time.

Applications are built using the three-step process shown in Figure 7-31 on the next page: (1) create the user interface; (2) set the properties; and (3) write the VBA code. Before you can create the user interface, the 401(k) Investment Model worksheet in the Golden Years1 workbook must be unprotected. The steps on the next page unprotect the worksheet.

Visual Basic for Applications

All of the applications in Office 2000 (Word, Excel, Access, and PowerPoint) use Visual Basic for Applications. Thus, what you learn in this project applies to the other applications as well. Today, Visual Basic is the most widely used Windows applications programming language.

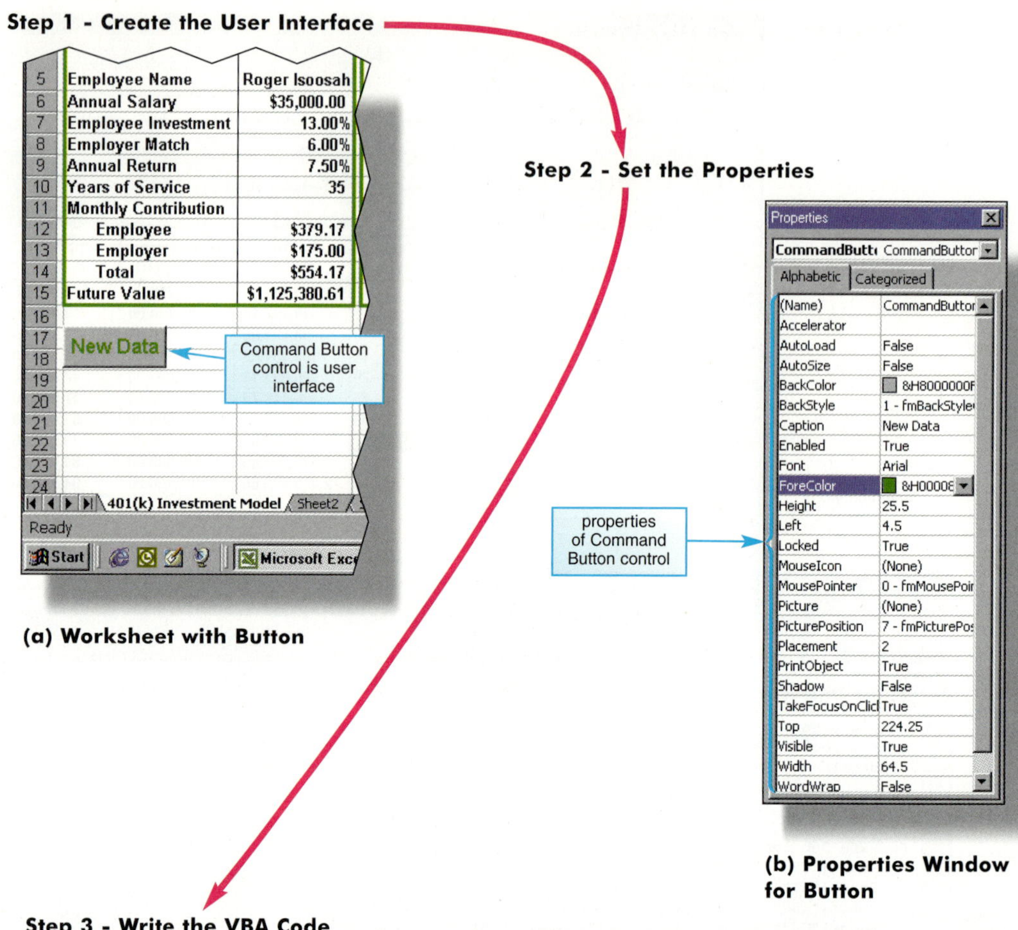

(a) Worksheet with Button

(b) Properties Window for Button

Step 3 - Write the VBA Code

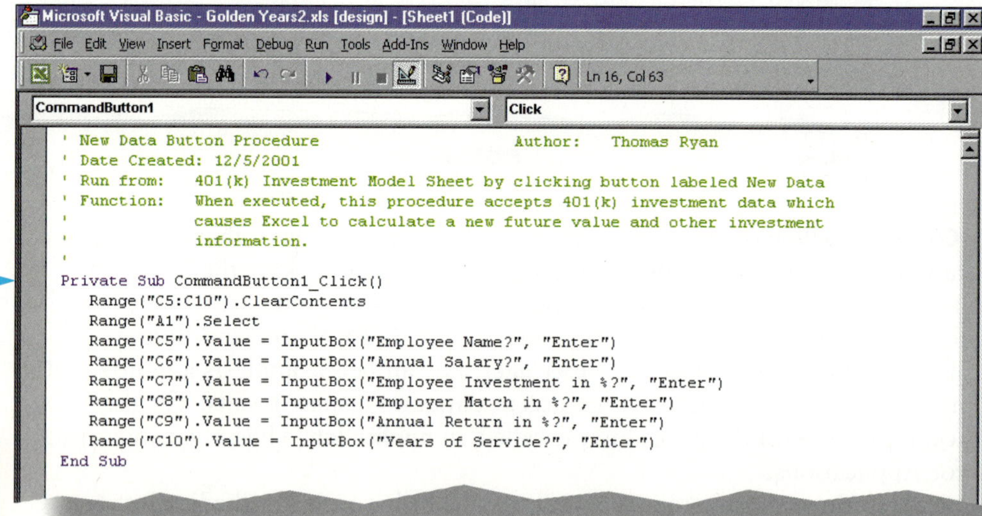


```
' New Data Button Procedure                              Author:   Thomas Ryan
' Date Created: 12/5/2001
' Run from:    401(k) Investment Model Sheet by clicking button labeled New Data
' Function:    When executed, this procedure accepts 401(k) investment data which
'              causes Excel to calculate a new future value and other investment
'              information.
'
Private Sub CommandButton1_Click()
   Range("C5:C10").ClearContents
   Range("A1").Select
   Range("C5").Value = InputBox("Employee Name?", "Enter")
   Range("C6").Value = InputBox("Annual Salary?", "Enter")
   Range("C7").Value = InputBox("Employee Investment in %?", "Enter")
   Range("C8").Value = InputBox("Employer Match in %?", "Enter")
   Range("C9").Value = InputBox("Annual Return in %?", "Enter")
   Range("C10").Value = InputBox("Years of Service?", "Enter")
End Sub
```

(c) VBA Code Associated with Button

FIGURE 7-31

TO UNPROTECT A PASSWORD-PROTECTED WORKSHEET

1. With the Golden Years1 workbook open, click Tools on the menu bar, point to Protection, and then click Unprotect Worksheet on the Protection submenu.
2. When the Protect dialog box displays, type `fortune` as the password and then click the OK button.

More About 2000

Earlier Excel Version Macros

Earlier versions of Excel use the XLM programming language rather than VBA for its macros. Excel 2000 supports both programming languages. That is, you can execute macros created using XML. Excel 2000, however, will not allow you to create macros in XLM.

Step 1 – Create the User Interface

The most common way to execute a procedure in Excel is to create a Command Button control. To create the control, click the **Command Button button** on the **Control Toolbox toolbar**. You use the mouse to locate and size the control in the same way you locate and size an embedded chart. You then assign properties and the procedure to the control while Excel is in Design mode.

With respect to Visual Basic for Applications, Excel has two modes: Design mode and Run mode. **Design mode** allows you to resize controls, assign properties to controls, and enter VBA code. **Run mode** means that all controls are active. That is, if you click a control it triggers the event and Excel executes the procedure associated with the control. The following steps add a Command Button control to the worksheet.

Design Mode

If Excel is in Run mode and you click any control button on the Control Toolbox toolbar, Excel immediately switches to Design mode.

To Add a Command Button Control to the Worksheet

1 **Right-click a toolbar at the top of the screen. When the shortcut menu displays, click Control Toolbox.**

The Control Toolbox toolbar displays.

2 **Click the Command Button button on the Control Toolbox toolbar. Move the mouse pointer (a cross hair) to the upper-left corner of cell B17. Drag the mouse pointer so the rectangle defining the button area appears as shown in Figure 7-32 and hold.**

A light border surrounds the proposed button area in the worksheet (Figure 7-32). When you click the Command Button button, Excel automatically switches to Design mode.

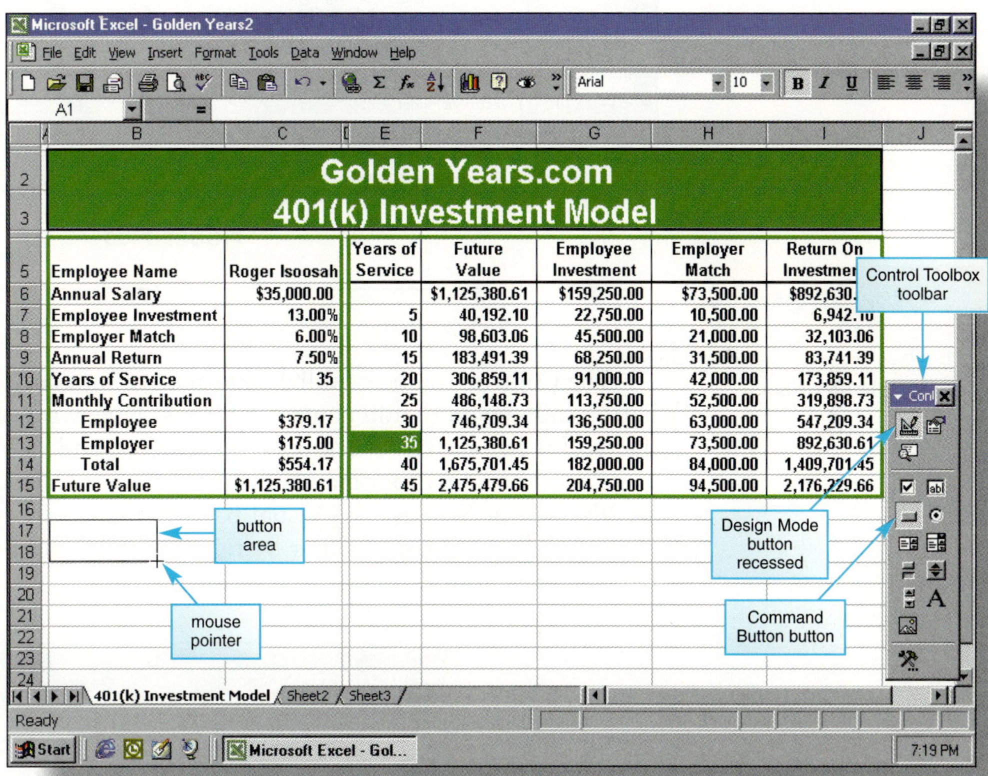

FIGURE 7-32

Release the left mouse button.

Excel displays the button with the default caption CommandButton1 (Figure 7-33). Because Excel is in design mode and the button is selected, the button is surrounded by sizing handles.

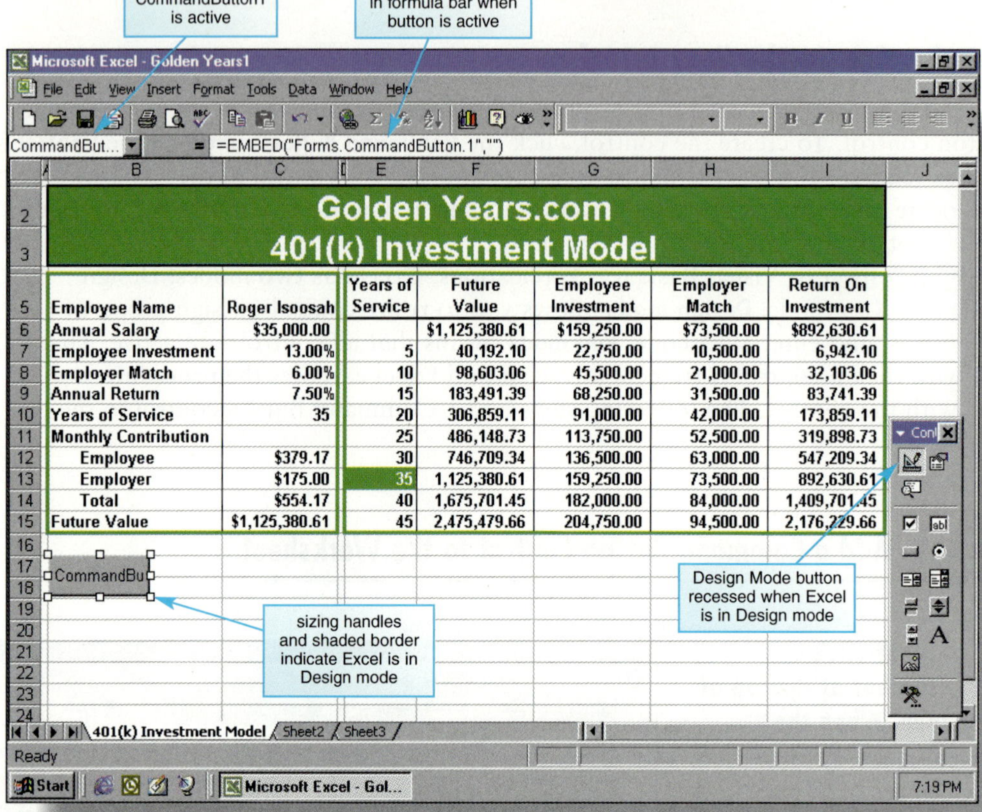

FIGURE 7-33

1. Click Design Mode button on Visual Basic toolbar

The Control Toolbox toolbar buttons are summarized in Table 7-3. Many of the buttons allow you to add controls that you have worked with previously in Excel to the worksheet, such as check boxes, list boxes, and scroll bars.

Another toolbar that may be helpful as you use Visual Basic for Applications is the **Visual Basic toolbar**. The Visual Basic toolbar is shown in Figure 7-34. You can display the Visual Basic toolbar by right-clicking a toolbar and then clicking Visual Basic on the shortcut menu.

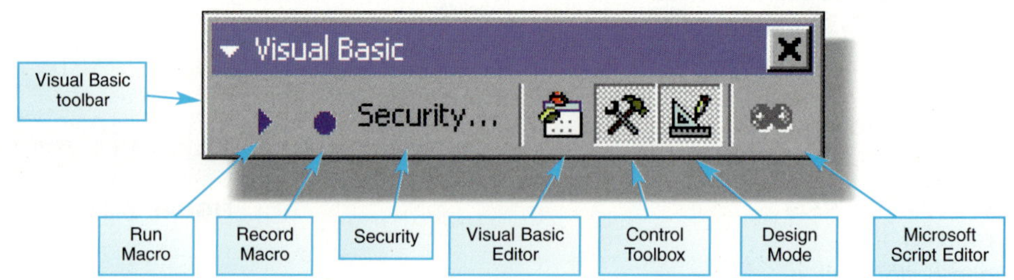

FIGURE 7-34

Table 7-3 Summary of Buttons on the Control Toolbox Toolbar

BUTTON	NAME	FUNCTION
	Design Mode	Changes to design mode; Design Mode button changes to Exit Design Mode button when in design mode
	Properties	Displays Properties window
	View Code	Displays VBA code in Visual Basic Editor
	Check Box	Adds a Check Box control
	Text Box	Adds a Text Box control
	Command Button	Adds a Command Button control
	Option Button	Adds an Option Button control
	List Box	Adds a List Box control
	Combo Box	Adds a Combo Box control
	Toggle Button	Adds a Toggle Button control
	Spin Button	Adds a Spin Button control
	Scroll Bar	Adds a Scroll Bar control
	Label	Adds a Label control
	Image	Adds an Image control
	More Controls	Displays a list of additional controls

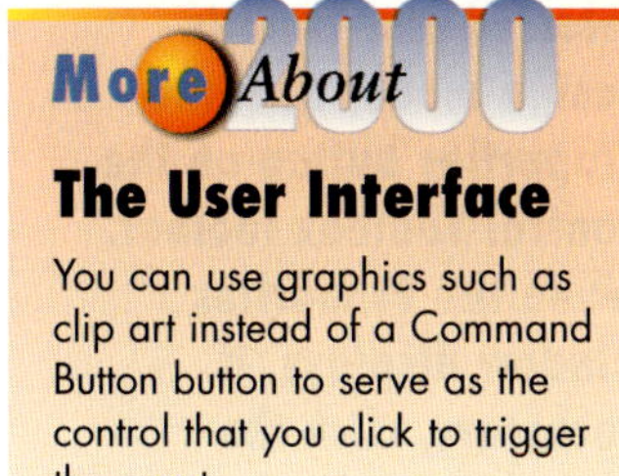

More About

The User Interface

You can use graphics such as clip art instead of a Command Button button to serve as the control that you click to trigger the event.

Step 2 – Set the Properties

A Command Button control has 25 different **properties** (Figure 7-31b on page E 7.26), such as caption (the words on the face of the button), background color, foreground color, height, width, font, and so on. Once you add a Command Button control to a worksheet, you can change any one of the 25 properties to improve its appearance and modify how it works. The steps on the next page change the button's caption, the font size of the caption, and the color of the caption.

More About

More Controls

The last button described in Table 7-3 is the More Controls button. If you click the More Controls button, nearly 200 additional controls display, similar to those in Table 7-3, that are available to incorporate in a user interface.

To Set the Command Button Control Properties

1 **With the Command Button control selected and Excel in design mode, click the Properties button on the Control Toolbox toolbar. When the Properties window displays, if necessary, click the Alphabetic tab, click Caption, and then type** `New Data` **as the caption. Click ForeColor, click the ForeColor arrow, click the Palette tab, and then point to the color green (column 5, row 5).**

Excel displays the Properties window for the Command Button control (Figure 7-35). The Caption property is New Data and the ForeColor Palette sheet displays.

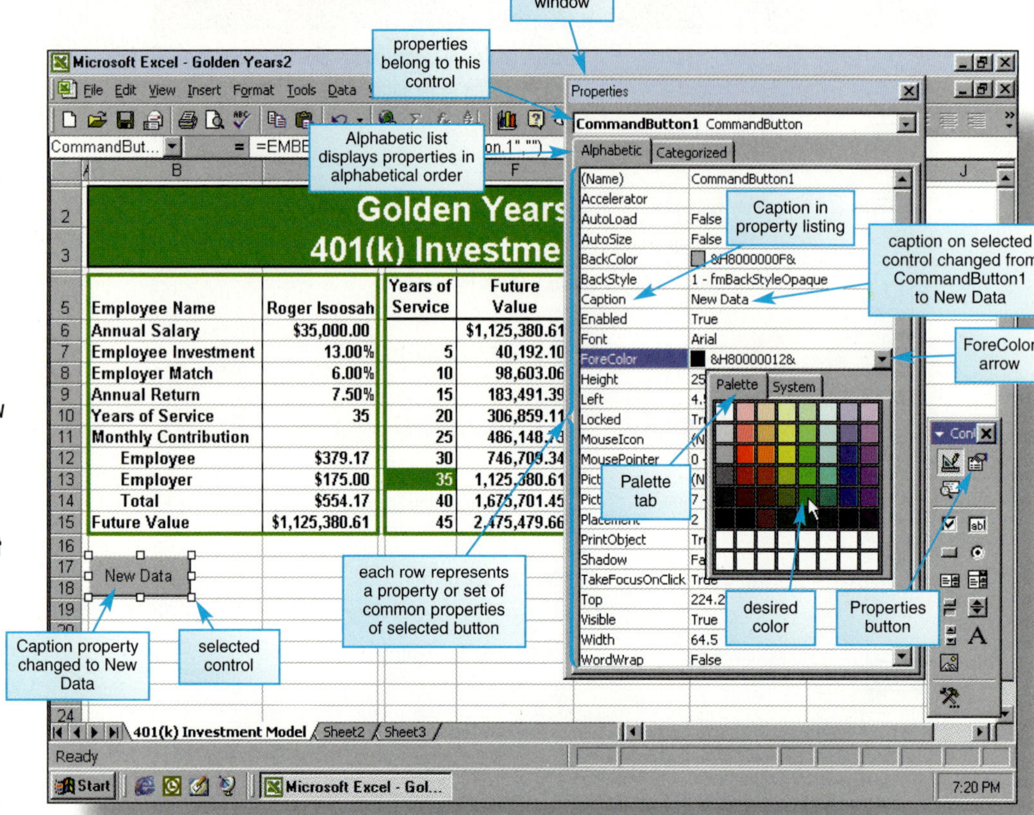

FIGURE 7-35

2 **Click the color green. Click Font in the Properties window and then click the Font button. When the Font dialog box displays, click Bold in the Font style list and 12 in the Size list. Point to the OK button.**

The Properties window and Font dialog box display as shown in Figure 7-36.

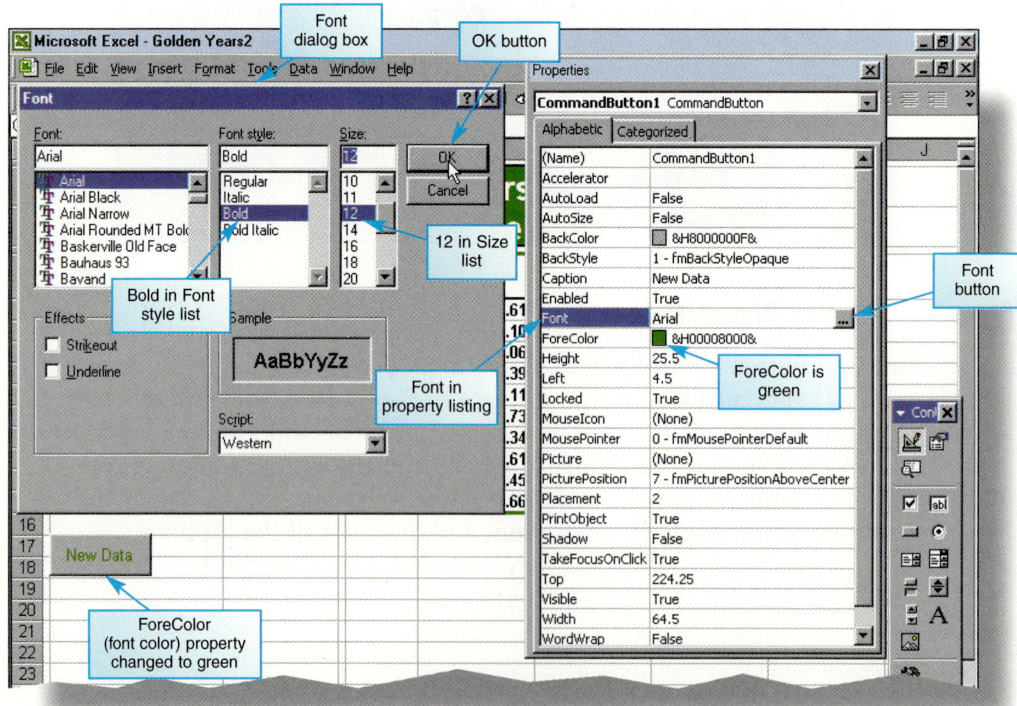

FIGURE 7-36

3 **Click the OK button.**

The Command Button control and its Properties window display as shown in Figure 7-37.

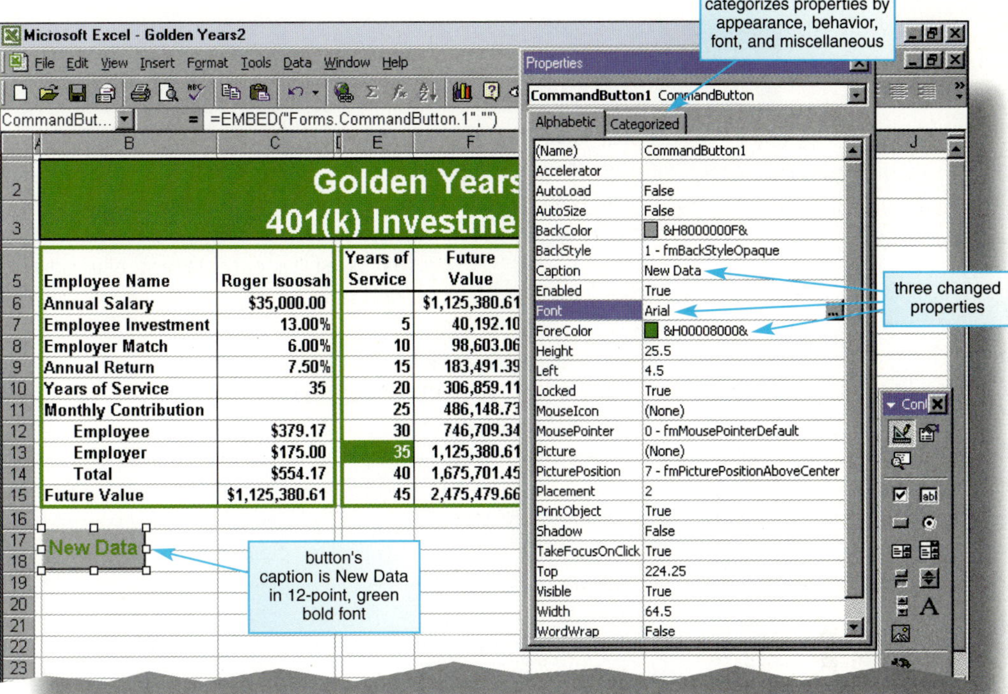

FIGURE 7-37

Other Ways

1. In Design mode, right-click control, click Properties on shortcut menu
2. Click Properties Window button on toolbar when Visual Basic Editor is active

The Properties window (Figure 7-37) has two tabs, Alphabetic and Categorized. The **Alphabetic list** displays the properties in alphabetical order. The **Categorized list** displays the properties in categories, such as appearance, behavior, font, and miscellaneous.

Depending on the application, you can modify any one of the Command Button control properties shown in Figure 7-35on page E 7.30, much like you changed the Caption and Font properties in the previous steps.

Step 3 – Write the VBA Code

The next step is to write and then enter the procedure that will execute when you click the New Data button.

PLANNING A PROCEDURE When you trigger the event that executes a procedure, Excel steps through the Visual Basic statements one at a time, beginning at the top of the procedure. Thus, when you plan a procedure, remember that the order in which you place the statements in the procedure is important because the order determines the sequence of execution.

Once you know what you want the procedure to do, write the VBA code on paper similar to Table 7-4 on the next page. Then, before entering the procedure into the computer, test it by putting yourself in the position of Excel and stepping through the instructions one at a time. As you do so, think about how it affects the worksheet. Testing a procedure before entering it is called **desk checking** and is an important part of the development process.

Adding comments before a procedure will help you remember its purpose at a later date. In Table 7-4, the first seven lines are comments. **Comments** begin with the word Rem or an apostrophe ('). These comments contain overall documentation and are placed before the procedure, above the Sub statement. Comments have no effect on the execution of a procedure; they simply provide information about the procedure, such as name, creation date, and function.

Improving Productivity

Looking for ways to improve your productivity? If you find yourself entering the same Excel steps repeatedly, you can use the macro recorder or VBA to complete the steps automatically. This can improve your productivity by eliminating routine tasks and simplifying complex tasks.

Table 7-4 New Data Button Procedure

```
LINE  VBA CODE
1     ' New Data Button Procedure                     Author:   Thomas Ryan
2     ' Date Created: 12/5/2001
3     ' Run from:       401(k) Investment Model Sheet by clicking button labeled New Data
4     ' Function:       When executed, this procedure accepts 401 (k) investment data which
5     '                 causes Excel to calculate a new future value and other investment
6     '                 information.
7     '
8     Private Sub CommandButton1_Click()
9        Range("C5:C10").ClearContents
10       Range("A1").Select
11       Range("C5").Value = InputBox("Employee Name?", "Enter")
12       Range("C6").Value = InputBox("Annual Salary?", "Enter")
13       Range("C7").Value = InputBox("Employee Investment in %?", "Enter")
14       Range("C8").Value = InputBox("Employer Match in %?", "Enter")
15       Range("C9").Value = InputBox("Annual Return in %?", "Enter")
16       Range("C10").Value = InputBox("Years of Service?", "Enter")
17    End Sub
```

A procedure begins with a **Sub statement** and ends with an **End Sub statement** (lines 8 and 17 in Table 7-4). The Sub statement includes the keyword Private or Public followed by the name of the procedure, which Excel determines from the name of the button (CommandButton1), and the event that causes the procedure to execute (Click). **Private** means that the procedure can be executed only from this workbook. **Public** means that it can be executed from other workbooks or programs. Thus, the name of the Command Button control procedure is CommandButton1_Click.

Entering VBA Comments

If a horizontal line displays between the comment and Sub statement, press the ENTER key after the last comment to begin a new line. Then, press the DELETE key to delete the horizontal line.

The parentheses following the keyword Click in the Sub statement in line 8 are required. They indicate that arguments can be passed from one procedure to another. Passing arguments is beyond the scope of this project, but the parentheses still are required. The End Sub statement signifies the end of the procedure and returns Excel to Ready mode.

The first executable statement in Table 7-4 is line 9, which clears the cells in the range C5:C10. Line 10 selects cell A1 to remove clutter from the screen. One at a time, lines 11 through 16 accept data from the user and assign the data to the cells in the range C5:C10. Each one of the six statements handles one cell each. To the right of the equal sign in lines 11 through 16 is the InputBox function. A **function** returns a value to the program. In this case, the InputBox function displays a dialog box and returns the value entered by the user. For example, in line 11 the InputBox function displays a dialog box with the message, "Employee Name?" When the user responds and enters a name, the InputBox function returns the value entered to the program and assigns it to cell C5.

To enter a procedure, you use the Visual Basic Editor. To activate the Visual Basic Editor, Excel must be in Design mode. With the control selected, you click the **View Code button** on the Control Toolbox toolbar.

The **Visual Basic Editor** is a full-screen editor, which allows you to enter a procedure by typing the lines of VBA code as if you were using word processing software. At the end of a line, you press the ENTER key or use the DOWN ARROW key to move to the next line. If you make a mistake in a statement, you can use the arrow keys and the DELETE or BACKSPACE key to correct it. You also can move the insertion point to previous lines to make corrections.

USING THE VISUAL BASIC EDITOR TO ENTER A PROCEDURE The following steps activate the Visual Basic Editor and create the procedure for the New Data button.

To Enter the New Data Button Procedure

1 With Excel in Design mode and the New Data button selected, point to the View Code button on the Control Toolbox toolbar.

The selected New Data button and Control Toolbox toolbar display as shown in Figure 7-38.

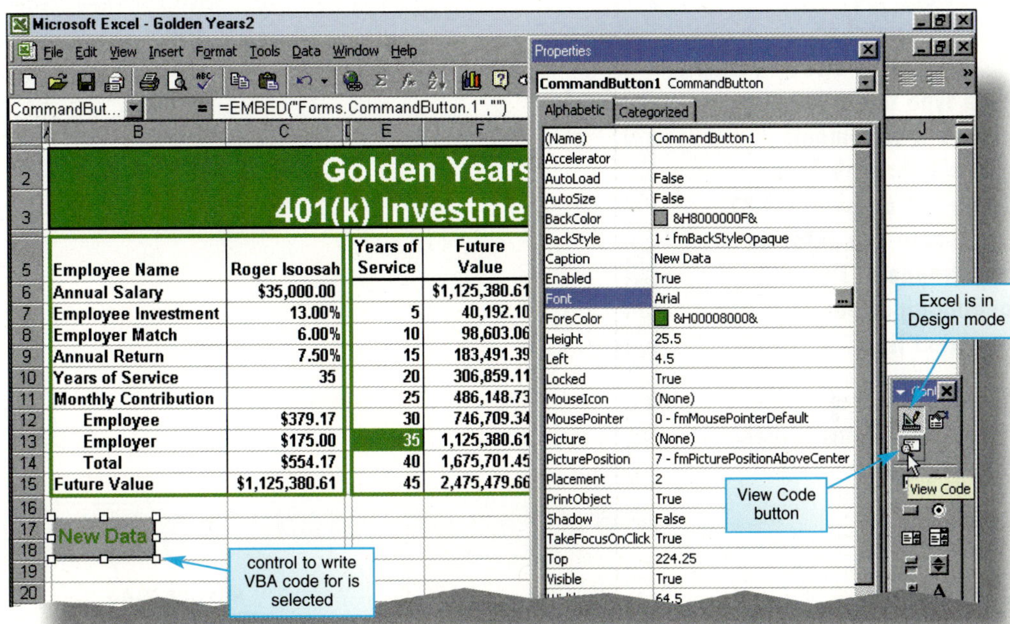

FIGURE 7-38

2 Click the View Code button. When the Visual Basic Editor displays, if the Project Explorer window displays on the left, click its Close button. Double-click the title bar to maximize the Code window on the right.

Excel starts the Visual Basic Editor and displays the Microsoft Visual Basic window (Figure 7-39). The Visual Basic Editor automatically inserts the Sub and End Sub statements and positions the insertion point between the two statements as shown.

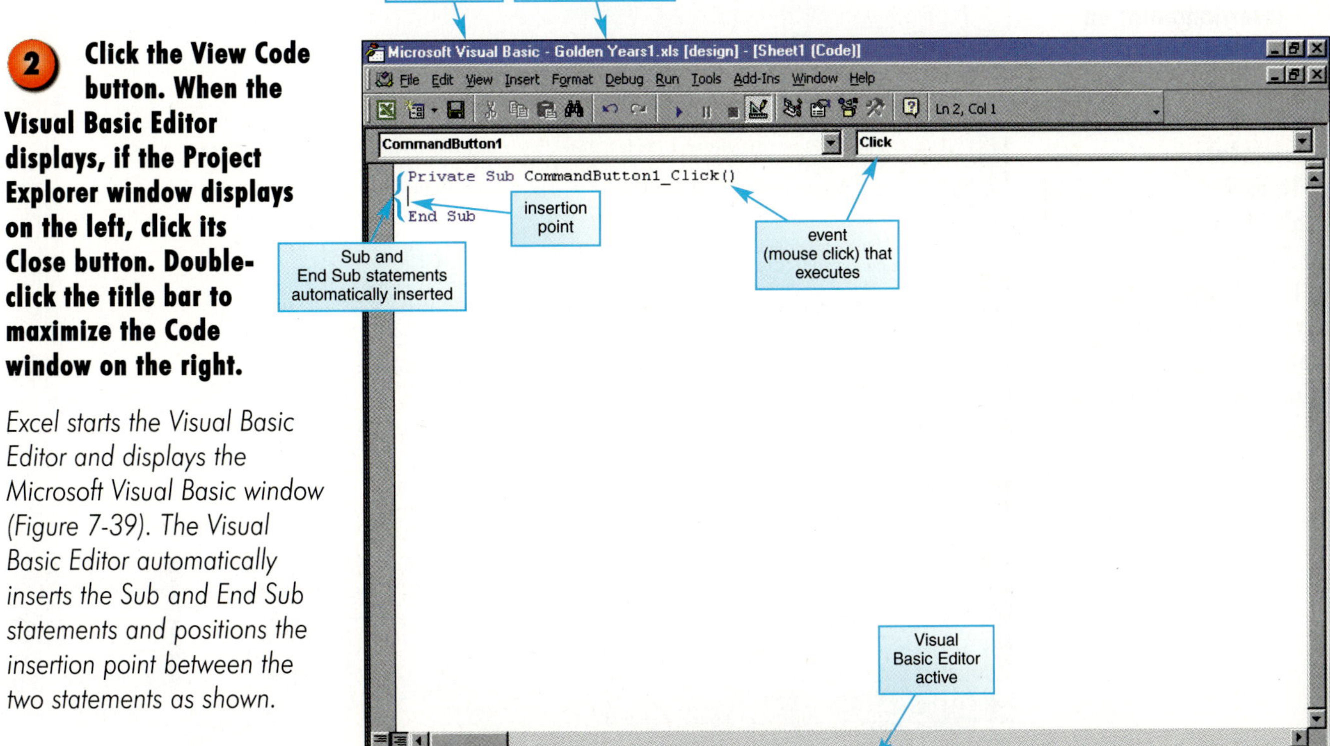

FIGURE 7-39

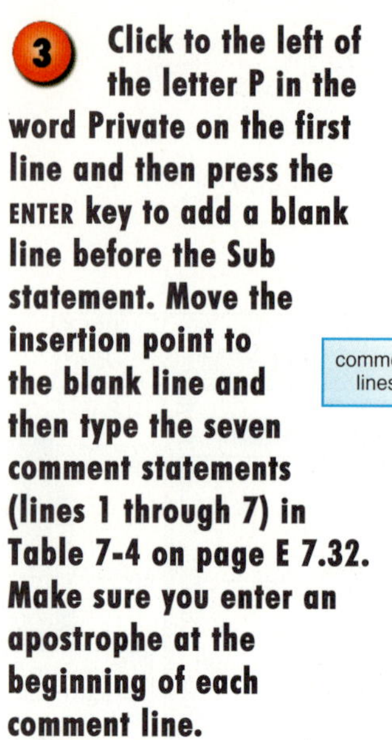

3 **Click to the left of the letter P in the word Private on the first line and then press the ENTER key to add a blank line before the Sub statement. Move the insertion point to the blank line and then type the seven comment statements (lines 1 through 7) in Table 7-4 on page E 7.32. Make sure you enter an apostrophe at the beginning of each comment line.**

Excel automatically displays the comment lines in green (Figure 7-40).

apostrophe (') begins comment line
pressing ENTER key starts new line
comment lines
comments display in green
Microsoft Visual Basic - Golden Years1 ... [Code)]
File Edit View Insert Format Debug Run Tools Add-Ins Window Help
Ln 7, Col 2
CommandButton1
Click
' New Data Button Procedure Author: Thomas Ryan
' Date Created: 12/5/2001
' Run from: 401(k) Investment Model Sheet by clicking button labeled New Data
' Function: When executed, this procedure accepts 401 (k) investment data which
' causes Excel to calculate a new future value and other investment
' information.
'
Private Sub CommandButton1_Click()
End Sub
Start
Microsoft Excel - Golden Y...
Microsoft Visual Basi...
7:22 PM

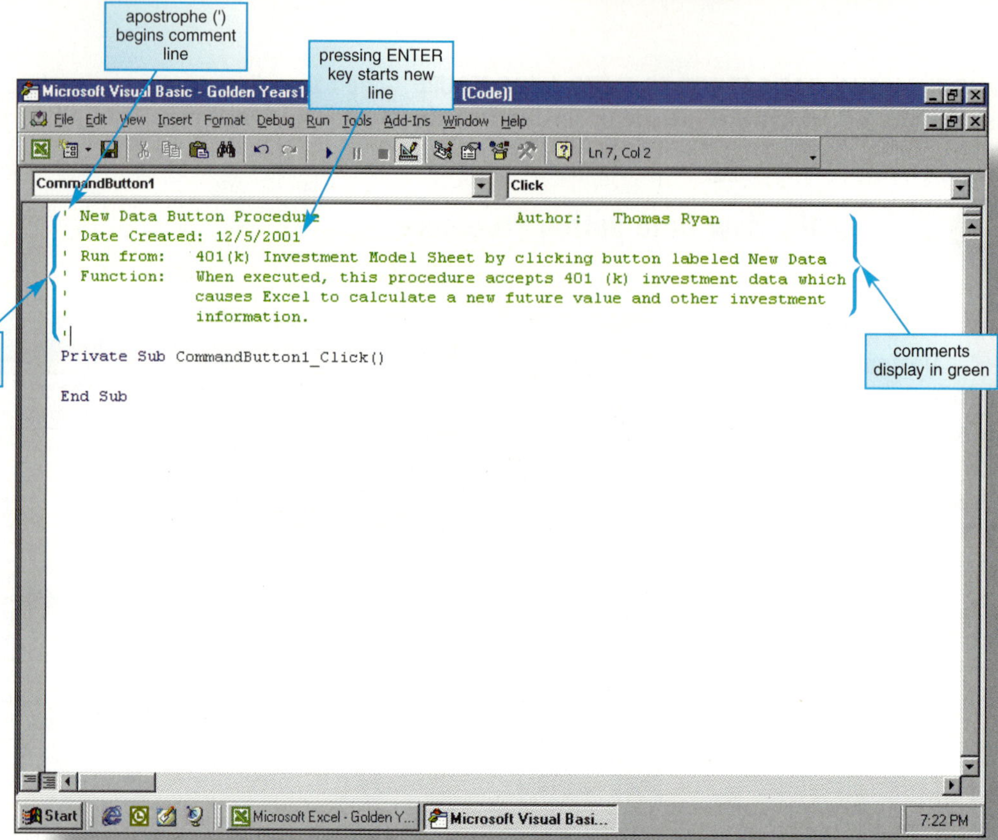

FIGURE 7-40

4 **Position the insertion point on the blank line between the Sub and End Sub statements. Enter lines 9 through 16 in Table 7-4 on page E 7.32. For clarity, indent all lines between the Sub statement and End Sub statement by three spaces.**

The Command Button control procedure is complete (Figure 7-41).

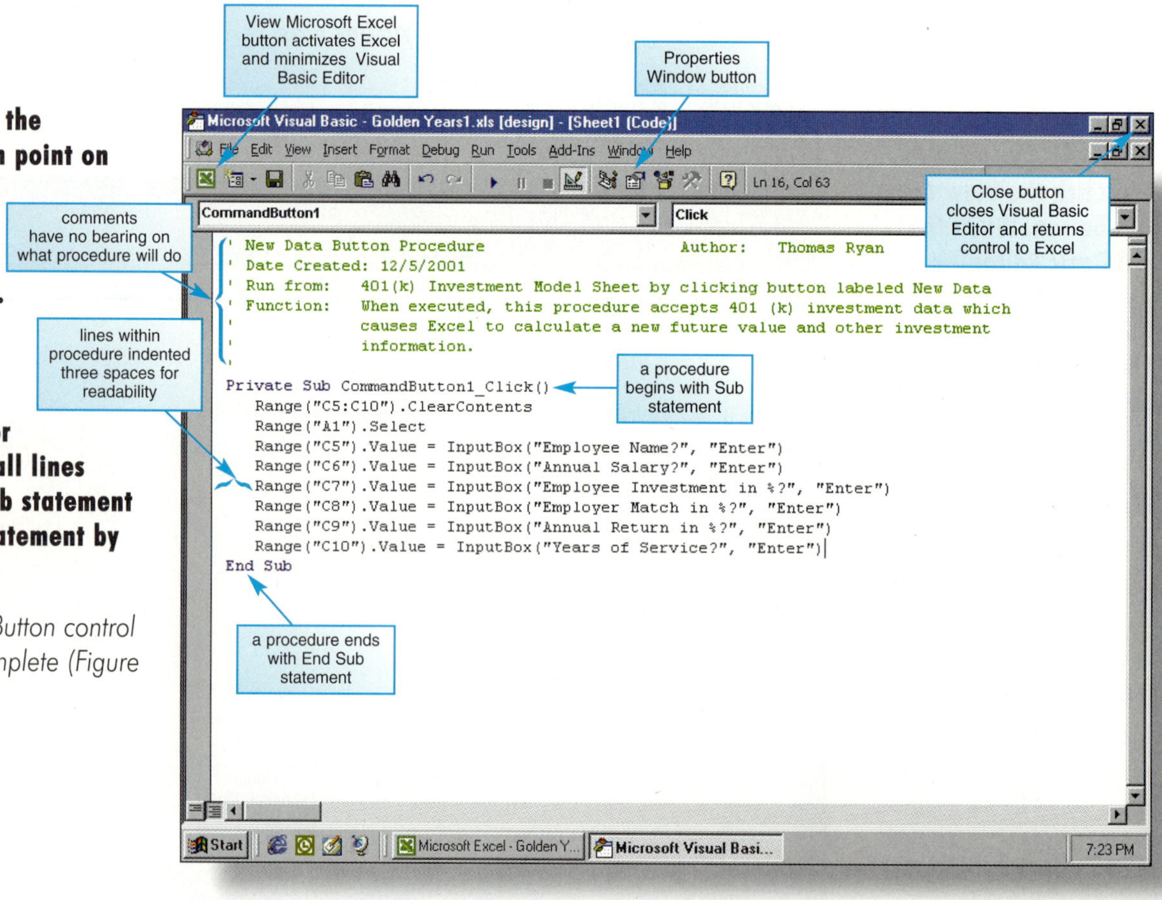

View Microsoft Excel button activates Excel and minimizes Visual Basic Editor
Properties Window button
comments have no bearing on what procedure will do
lines within procedure indented three spaces for readability
Close button closes Visual Basic Editor and returns control to Excel
a procedure begins with Sub statement
a procedure ends with End Sub statement
Microsoft Visual Basic - Golden Years1.xls [design] - [Sheet1 (Code)]
File Edit View Insert Format Debug Run Tools Add-Ins Window Help
Ln 16, Col 63
CommandButton1
Click
' New Data Button Procedure Author: Thomas Ryan
' Date Created: 12/5/2001
' Run from: 401(k) Investment Model Sheet by clicking button labeled New Data
' Function: When executed, this procedure accepts 401 (k) investment data which
' causes Excel to calculate a new future value and other investment
' information.
'
Private Sub CommandButton1_Click()
Range("C5:C10").ClearContents
Range("A1").Select
Range("C5").Value = InputBox("Employee Name?", "Enter")
Range("C6").Value = InputBox("Annual Salary?", "Enter")
Range("C7").Value = InputBox("Employee Investment in %?", "Enter")
Range("C8").Value = InputBox("Employer Match in %?", "Enter")
Range("C9").Value = InputBox("Annual Return in %?", "Enter")
Range("C10").Value = InputBox("Years of Service?", "Enter")
End Sub
Start
Microsoft Excel - Golden Y...
Microsoft Visual Basi...
7:23 PM

FIGURE 7-41

5 Click the Close button on the right side of the Microsoft Visual Basic title bar to return to the worksheet.

The worksheet displays as shown in Figure 7-42.

6 Click the Exit Design Mode button on the Control Toolbox toolbar. Click the Close button on the right side of the Control Toolbox toolbar title bar to hide it.

Excel returns to Run mode, which means if you click the New Data button, Excel will execute the associated procedure.

Microsoft Excel - Golden Years1

=EMBED("Forms.CommandButton.1","")

Golden Years.com
401(k) Investment Model

Employee Name	Roger Isoosah	Years of Service	Future Value	Employee Investment	Employer Match	Return On Investment
Annual Salary	$35,000.00		$1,125,380.61	$159,250.00	$73,500.00	$892,630.61
Employee Investment	13.00%	5	40,192.10	22,750.00	10,500.00	6,942.10
Employer Match	6.00%	10	98,603.06	45,500.00	21,000.00	32,103.06
Annual Return	7.50%	15	183,491.39	68,250.00	31,500.00	83,741.39
Years of Service	35	20	306,859.11	91,000.00	42,000.00	173,859.11
Monthly Contribution		25	486,148.73	113,750.00	52,500.00	319,898.73
Employee	$379.17	30	746,709.34	136,500.00	63,000.00	547,209.34
Employer	$175.00	35	1,125,380.61	159,250.00	73,500.00	892,630.61
Total	$554.17	40	1,675,701.45	182,000.00	84,000.00	1,409,701.45
Future Value	$1,125,380.61	45	2,475,479.66	204,750.00	94,500.00	2,176,229.66

New Data

sizing handles indicate Excel is in Design mode

Control Toolbox toolbar Close button

Exit Design Mode button

401(k) Investment Model / Sheet2 / Sheet3

Ready

Start | Microsoft Excel - Gol... | 7:24 PM

FIGURE 7-42

Other Ways

1. In Design mode, right-click control, click View Code on shortcut menu
2. Click Visual Basic Editor button on Visual Basic toolbar

Two ways exist to return control to the worksheet from the Visual Basic Editor. The Close button (Figure 7-41) closes the Visual Basic Editor and returns control to the worksheet. The **View Microsoft Excel button** on the Visual Basic toolbar (Figure 7-41), returns control to Excel, but only minimizes the Visual Basic Editor. If you plan to switch between Excel and the Visual Basic Editor, then use the View Microsoft Excel button, otherwise use the Close button.

More About Visual Basic for Applications

Visual Basic for Applications includes many more statements than those presented here. Even this simple procedure, however, should help you understand the basic makeup of a Visual Basic statement. For example, each of the statements within the procedure shown in Figure 7-41 includes a period. The entry on the left side of the period tells Excel which object you want to affect. An **object** can be a cell, a range, a chart, a worksheet, a workbook, a button, or any other control you create on a worksheet. The entry on the right side of the period tells Excel what you want to do to the object. You can place a method or property on the right side of the period. For example, the statement

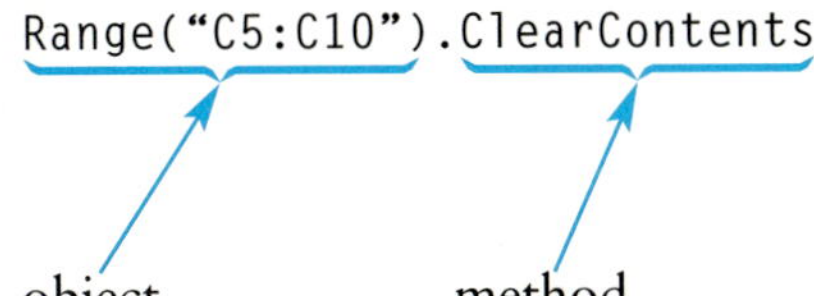

clears the range C5:C10. You use a **method**, such as ClearContents, to change an object's behavior. In this case, the method ClearContents is changing the behavior of the range by deleting its contents.

Printing VBA Code

To print the VBA code while the Visual Basic Editor is active, click File on the menu bar and then click Print.

Running Procedures

Always save a workbook before you execute a procedure in case it does something unexpected. This is especially true when testing a procedure.

Earlier you were shown how to change an object's properties using the Properties window (Figure 7-35 on page E 7.30). The following example shows that you also can change an object's property during execution of a procedure. The object in this case is a Command Button control.

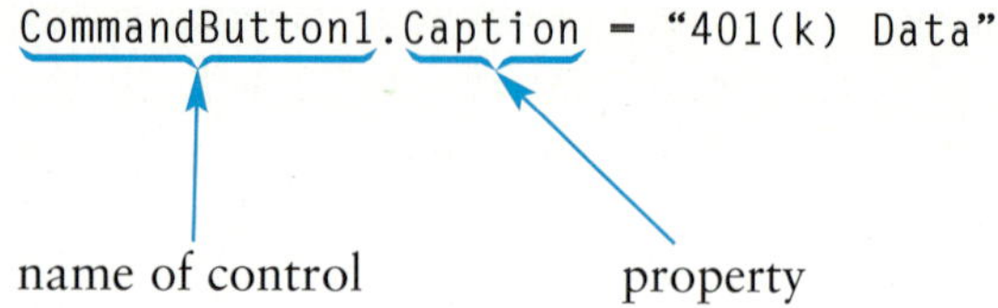

This statement changes the Caption property of the button to 401(k) Data during execution of the procedure.

The second statement in the procedure in Figure 7-41

```
Range("A1").Select
```

selects cell A1, which, in effect, hides the heavy border that surrounds the active cell. Several of the statements in the procedure also include equal signs. An **equal sign** instructs Excel to make an assignment to a cell. For example, when executed as part of the procedure

```
Range("C5").Value = InputBox("Employee Name?", "Enter")
```

instructs Excel to display a dialog box called Enter with the prompt message, Employee Name?, and then assigns cell C5 the value entered by the user in response to the dialog box. Thus, the first argument in the InputBox function is the message to the user and the second argument identifies the dialog box in its title bar.

Testing the 401(k) Data Entry Procedure

Perform the steps below to enter the following 401(k) data: Employee Name (cell C5) – Crystal Deal; Annual Salary (cell C6) - $72,500.00; Employee Investment (cell C7) – 8.50%; Employer Match (cell C8) – 3.00%; Annual Return (cell C9) – 9.50%; and Years of Service (cell C10) – 40. Before attempting to enter data using the New Data button, it is important that you exit Design mode and close the Control Toolbox toolbar as indicated in Step 6 of the previous set of steps.

To Enter 401(k) Data Using the New Data Button

1 Click the New Data button. When Excel displays the first Enter dialog box with the prompt message, Employee Name?, type `Crystal Deal` **as the employee name.**

Excel clears the range C5:C10 and then selects cell A1. Next, it displays the Enter dialog box shown in Figure 7-43.

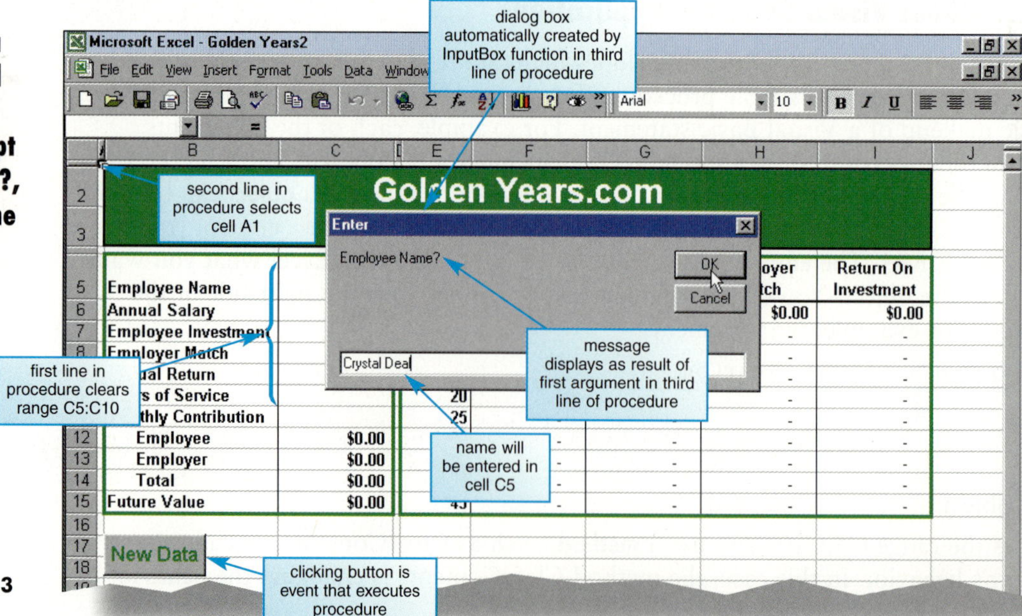

FIGURE 7-43

2 Click the OK button in the Enter dialog box or press the ENTER key. When Excel displays the next Enter dialog box with the prompt message, Annual Salary?, type 72500 **as the annual salary.**

Excel assigns the text Crystal Deal to cell C5 and displays the second Enter dialog box as shown in Figure 7-44.

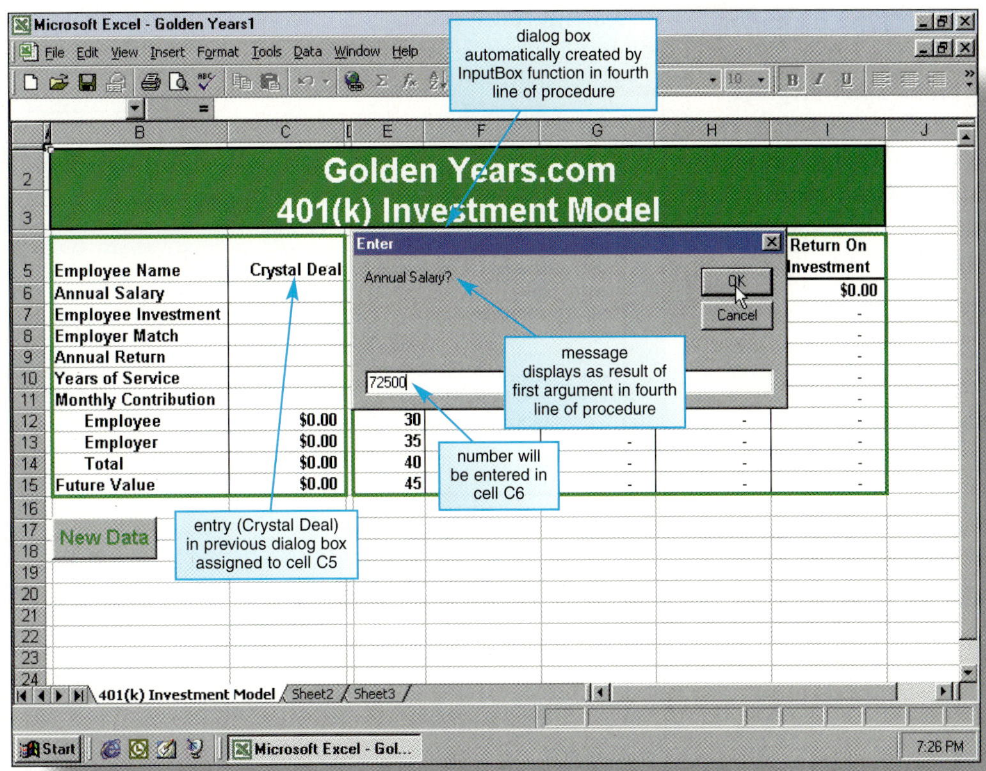

FIGURE 7-44

3 Click the OK button in the Enter dialog box. When Excel displays the next Enter dialog box with the prompt message, Employee Investment in %?, type 8.5% **as the employee investment. (Remember to type the percent (%) sign.)**

Excel assigns $72,500.00 to cell C6 and displays the third Enter dialog box as shown in Figure 7-45.

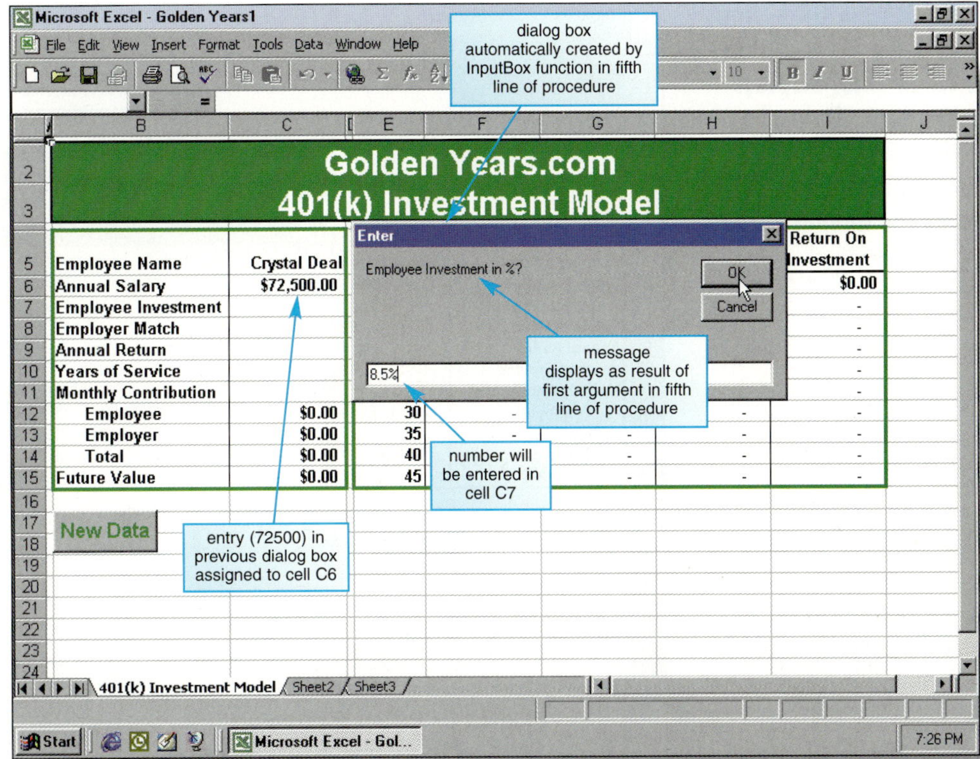

FIGURE 7-45

4 **Click the OK button in the Enter dialog box. When Excel displays the next Enter dialog box with the prompt message, Employer Match in %?, type** 3% **as the employer match.**

Excel assigns the 8.50% to cell C7 and displays the fourth Enter dialog box as shown in Figure 7-46.

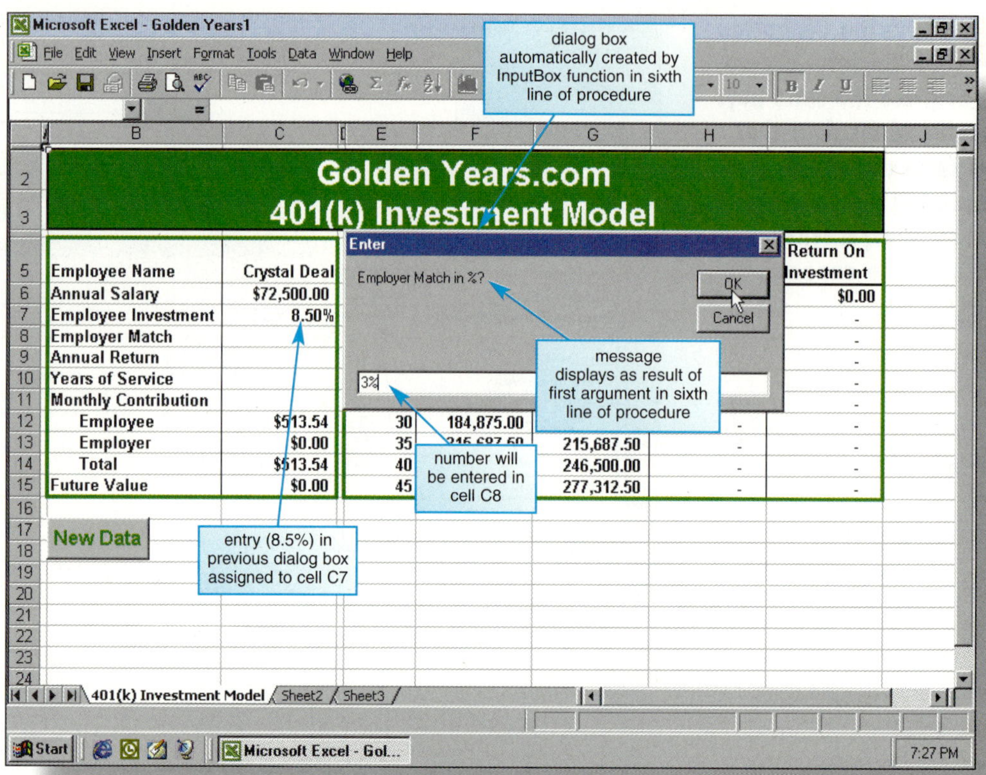

FIGURE 7-46

5 **Click the OK button in the Enter dialog box. When Excel displays the next Enter dialog box with the prompt message, Annual Return in %?, type** 9.5% **as the annual return.**

Excel assigns 3.00% to cell C8 and displays the fifth Enter dialog box as shown in Figure 7-47.

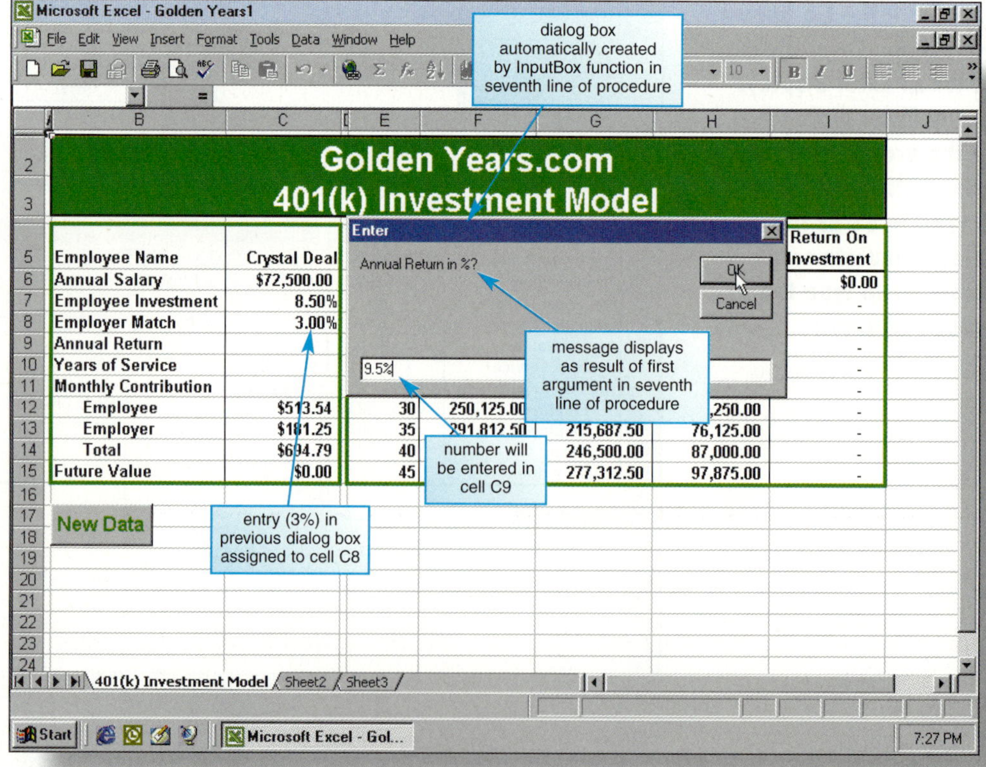

FIGURE 7-47

6 **Click the OK button in the Enter dialog box. When Excel displays the next Enter dialog box with the prompt message, Years of Service?, type** 40 **as the years of service.**

Excel assigns 9.5% to cell C9 and displays the sixth Enter dialog box as shown in Figure 7-48.

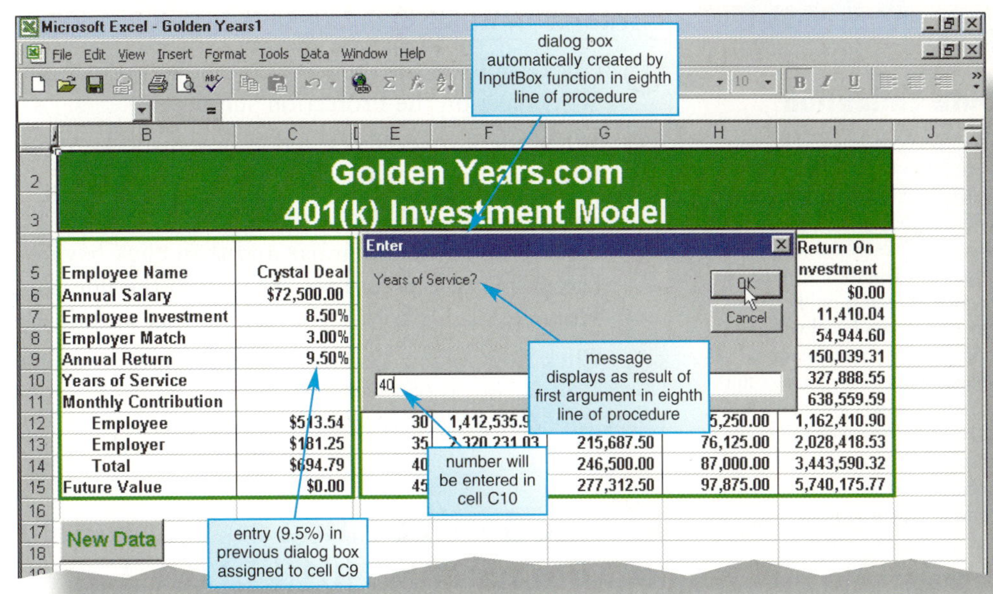

FIGURE 7-48

7 **Click the OK button in the Enter dialog box.**

Excel assigns 40 to cell C10 and displays the results for Crystal Deal in the range C12:C15 (Figure 7-49). Excel also recalculates the data table.

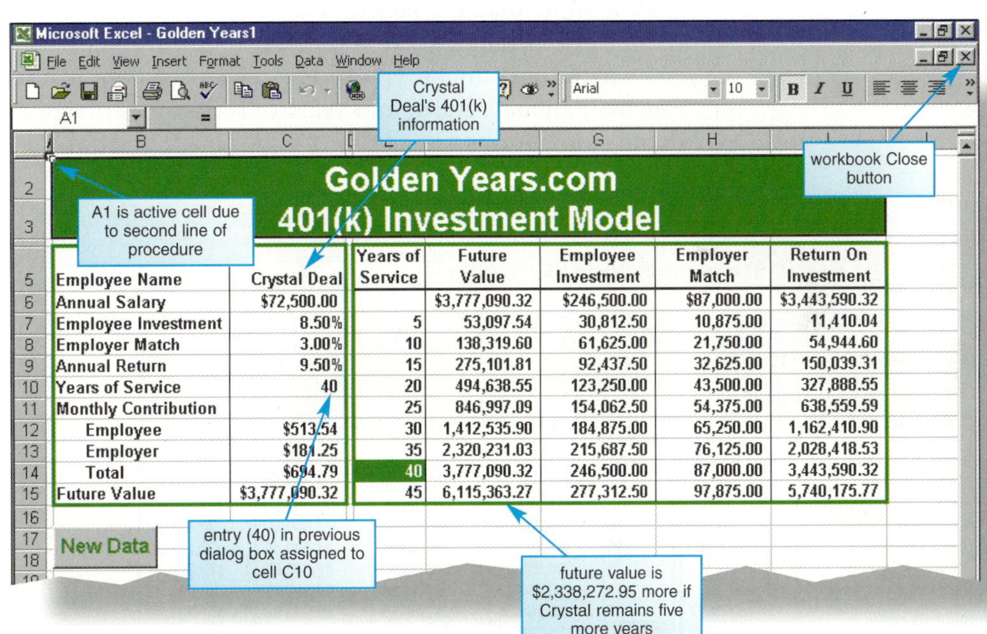

FIGURE 7-49

Figure 7-49 shows that the future value of Crystal Deal's investment of $513.54 a month (cell C12) for 40 years is an impressive $3,777,090.32 (cell F14). Crystal's total 401(k) investment is $246,500.00 (cell G14) and the total employer match is $87,000.00 (cell H14).

Based on this example, you can see the significance of using a VBA to automate the worksheet tasks, especially if the users know little about computers. In this worksheet, each time the user clicks the New Data button, the procedure guides him or her through entering the 401(k) data and placing it in the correct cells.

With Phase 2 of this project complete, the final step is to protect the worksheet and save the workbook.

Data Validation

The VBA code entered in Step 4 on page E 7.34 does not check the incoming data to be sure it is reasonable. For example, if a user enters a negative value for the Years of Service in Step 6 on the previous page, then Excel will calculate an incorrect Future Value. In the next phase of this project, you will learn how to write VBA code that will ensure that unreasonable numbers are rejected. See the VBA code in Figure 7-80 on page E 7.63 for an example.

TO PROTECT A WORKSHEET AND SAVE THE WORKBOOK

1. Click Tools on the menu bar, point to Protection, and then click Protect Worksheet on the Protection submenu.
2. When the Protect Sheet dialog box displays, type `fortune` in the Password text box and then click the OK button. When the Confirm Password dialog box displays, type `fortune` and then click the OK button.
3. Click File on the menu bar and then click Save As. When the Save As dialog box displays, type `Golden Years2` in the File name text box. Make sure 3½ Floppy (A:) displays in the Save in box and then click the Save button.
4. Click the Golden Years2 Close button on the right side of its menu bar.

Phase 2 of this project is complete.

Phase 3 — Creating an Adjustment Center to Automate the 401(k) Data Entry

The final phase of this project requires that you add additional controls to the worksheet to automate the 401(k) data entry. In Phase 2, all of the data was entered using input dialog boxes that displayed one after the other when you triggered the event by clicking the New Data button. This phase uses input dialog boxes for only the name and annual salary. The remaining data (employee investment, employer match, annual return, and years of service) is entered using scroll bars, a check box, and spin buttons.

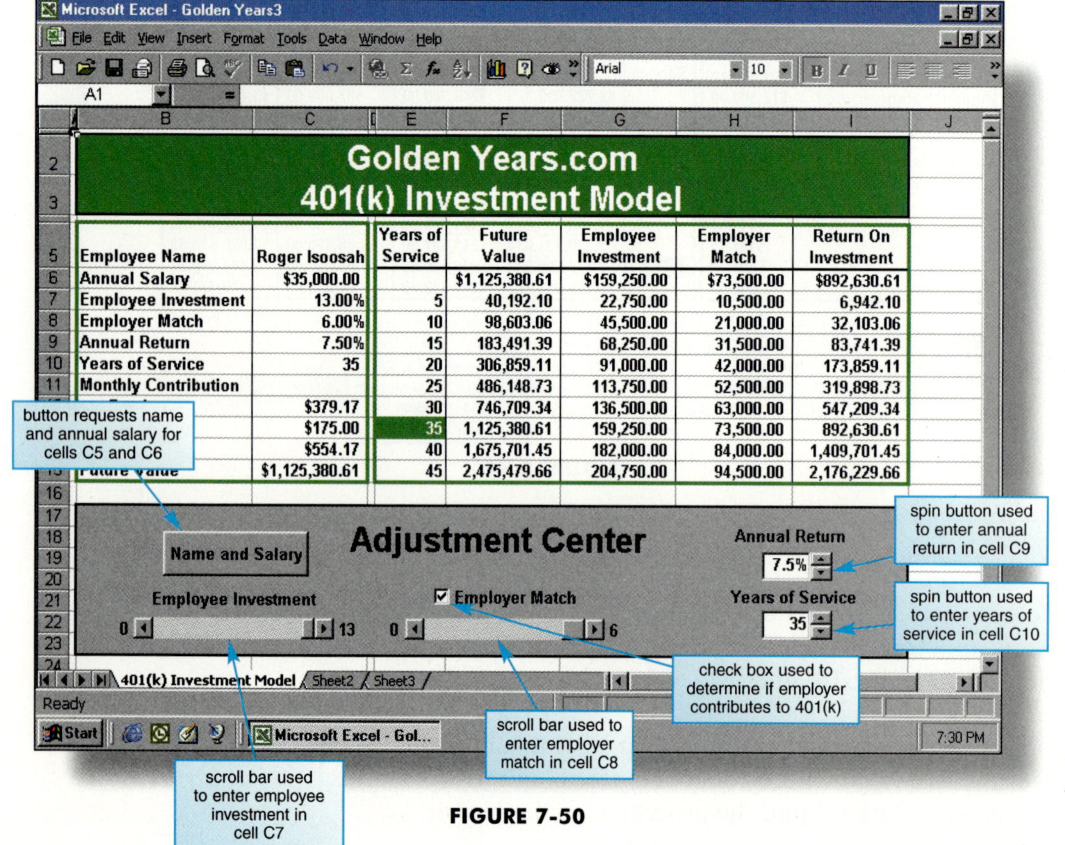

FIGURE 7-50

Consider the Adjustment Center in Figure 7-50. When you click the Name and Salary button, Excel displays input dialog boxes to accept the employee name for cell C5 and the annual salary for cell C6.

The Employee Investment scroll bar immediately below the Name and Salary button allows you to set the employee investment in cell C7. Recall that a scroll bar is made up of three separate areas you can click or drag – the **scroll arrows** on each side that you can click; the **scroll box** between the scroll buttons that you can drag; and the **scroll bar** that you can click that extends from one scroll arrow to the other.

The Employee Investment scroll bar has a minimum value of 0% and a maximum value of 13%. When you click one of its scroll arrows, the employee investment percent in cell C7 increases or decreases by 0.5%, depending on which scroll arrow you click. If you click the scroll bar on either side of the scroll box, the employee investment percent in cell C7 increases or decreases by 1%. Finally, you can drag the scroll box to the right or left to increase or decrease the employee investment percent in cell C7.

The Employer Match scroll bar (bottom center in Figure 7-50) works the same way, except that the change in the employer match is 0.25% when you click a scroll arrow, and the scroll bar runs from 0% to 6%.

The Employer Match check box in the middle of the Adjustment Center in Figure 7-50 indicates if the Employer Match scroll bar is enabled or disabled. If the check mark is present, then the scroll bar below the check box is enabled. If the check mark is removed, then cell C8 is set equal to 0% and the scroll bar is disabled.

The Annual Return spin button in the upper-right corner of the Adjustment Center increases or decreases the annual return in cell C9 by 0.25% each time you click a spin button arrow. A **spin button** has two buttons, one to increment and one to decrement the value in the cell with which it is associated. The Years of Service spin button in the lower-right corner of the Adjustment Center increases or decreases the years of service in cell C10 by one each time you click a spin button arrow.

The following steps open the workbook Golden Years1, save it using the file name Golden Years3, unprotect the 401(k) Investment Model worksheet, and display the Control Toolbox toolbar.

Visual Basic Jobs

Visual Basic is the most popular programming language used in the computer field today. If you are interested in pursuing a high-paying programmer/analyst career, visit the Excel 2000 More About Web page (www.scsite.com/ex2000/more.htm) and click Visual Basic Jobs.

TO OPEN AND SAVE A WORKBOOK, UNPROTECT A WORKSHEET, AND DISPLAY THE CONTROL TOOLBOX TOOLBAR

1. Click the Open button on the Standard toolbar. When the Open dialog box displays, click the Look in box arrow and select 3½ Floppy (A:). Double-click Golden Years1.
2. Click File on the menu bar and then click Save As. When the Save As dialog box displays, type `Golden Years3` in the File name text box and then click the Save button in the Save As dialog box.
3. Click Tools on the menu bar, point to Protection, and then click Unprotect Sheet on the Protection submenu. When the Unprotect dialog box displays, type `fortune` in the Password text box and then click the OK button.
4. Double-click the move handle on the Formatting toolbar (see Figure 7-51). Right-click a toolbar and then click Control Toolbox. Drag the Control Toolbox toolbar to the lower-right corner of the window.

Excel opens the workbook Golden Years1, saves it using the file name Golden Years3, unprotects the 401(k) Investment Model worksheet, and displays the Control Toolbox toolbar.

Visual Basic

To learn more about Visual Basic, visit the Excel 2000 More About Web page (www.scsite.com/ex2000/more.htm) and click Visual Basic Development Exchange.

Step 1 – Create the User Interface

The first step is to create the Adjustment Center user interface shown in Figure 7-50. After creating the gray background for the Adjustment Center in the range B17:I23, the following must be added to it:

1. A Command Button control
2. Two Scroll Bar controls
3. A Check Box control
4. Two Spin Button controls
5. Label controls to identify controls and display data

When you first create a user interface, you position the controls as close as you can to their final location on the screen, and then after setting the properties you finalize the locations of the controls. Therefore, the following steps make no attempt to position the controls exactly in the locations shown in Figure 7-50.

Steps To Add Controls to a User Interface

1 Select the range B17:I23. Click the Fill Color arrow on the Formatting toolbar and then click Gray – 25% (column 8, row 4) on the Fill Color palette. Click the Borders button arrow on the Formatting toolbar and then click Thick Box Border (column 4, row 3) on the Borders palette.

2 Click the Command Button button on the Control Toolbox toolbar and then drag the mouse pointer so the control displays as shown in Figure 7-51.

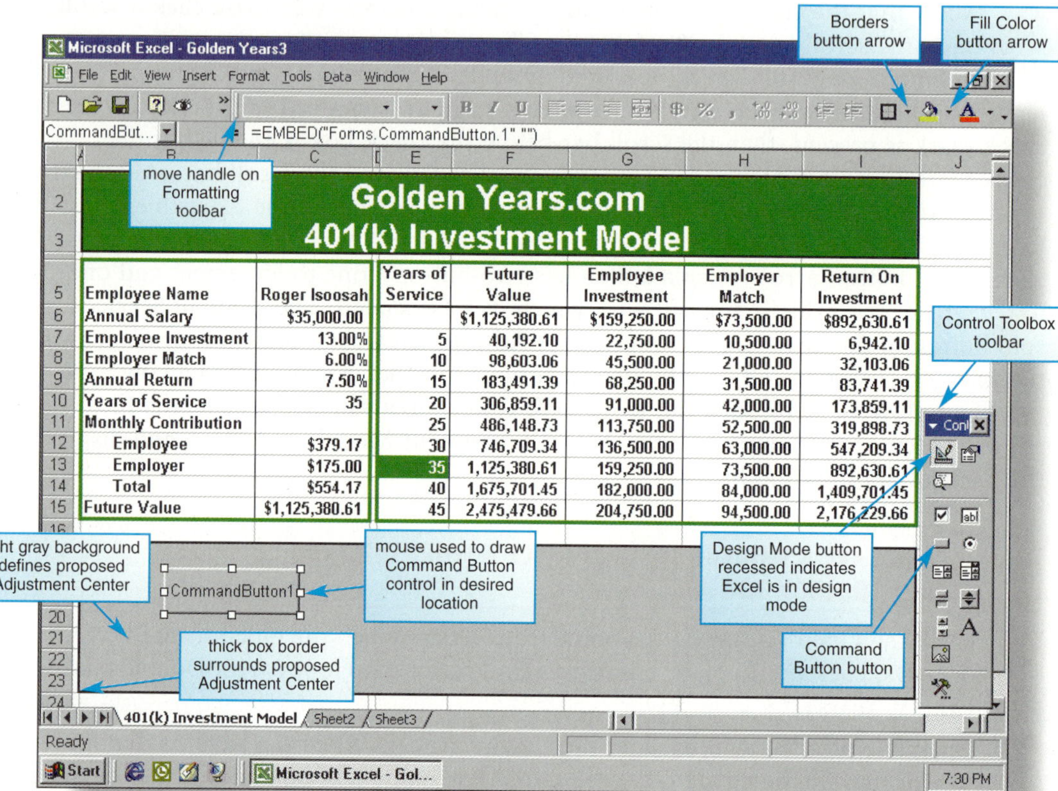

FIGURE 7-51

3 Click the Scroll Bar button on the Control Toolbox toolbar and then move the mouse pointer to approximately the center of cell B22. Drag the mouse pointer so the Scroll Bar control displays as shown in Figure 7-52.

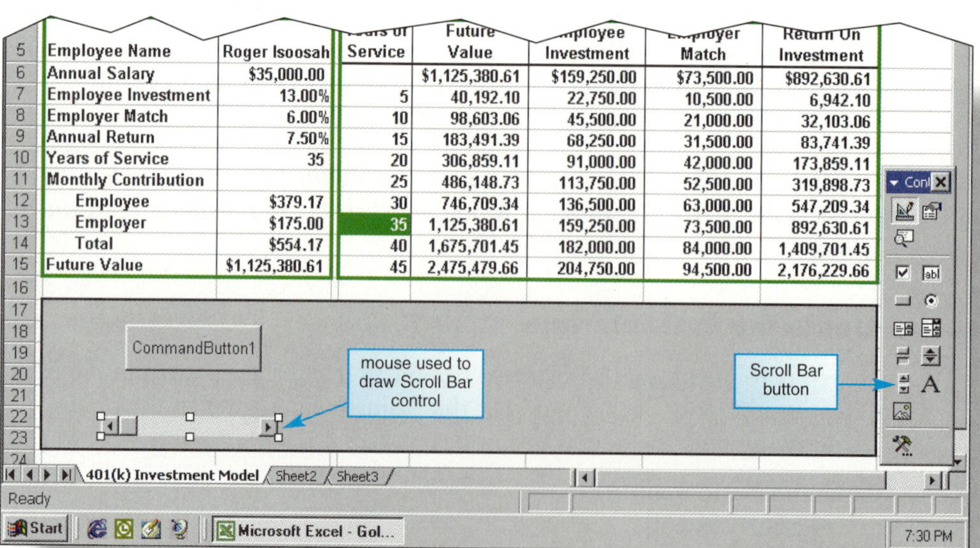

FIGURE 7-52

4 **Point to the Scroll Bar control. Hold down the CTRL key and then drag a copy of the Scroll Bar control to the location shown in Figure 7-53. It is important that you release the left mouse button before you release the CTRL key.**

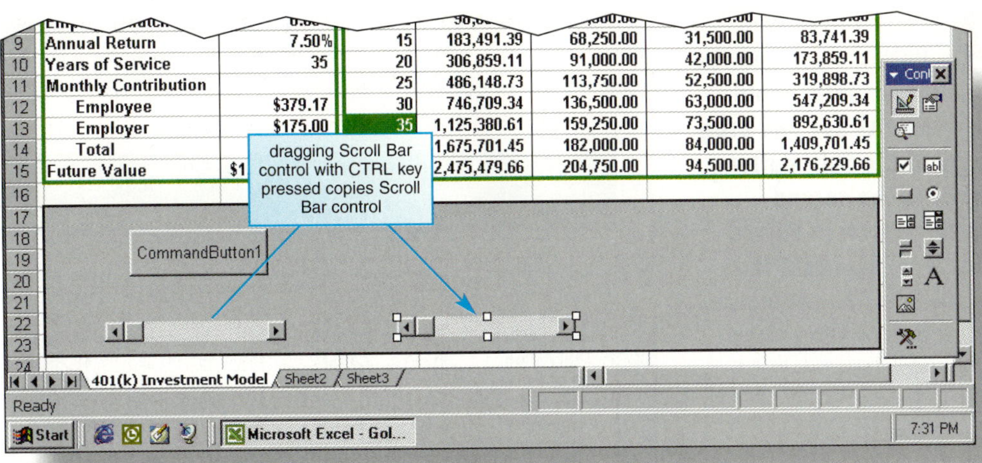

FIGURE 7-53

5 **Click the Check Box button on the Control Toolbox toolbar and then move the mouse pointer to the upper-left corner of the location of the Check Box control shown in Figure 7-54. Drag the mouse pointer so the rectangle defining the Check Box control area displays with half of the word CheckBox1 showing.**

The check box will be resized after its caption is changed later in this project.

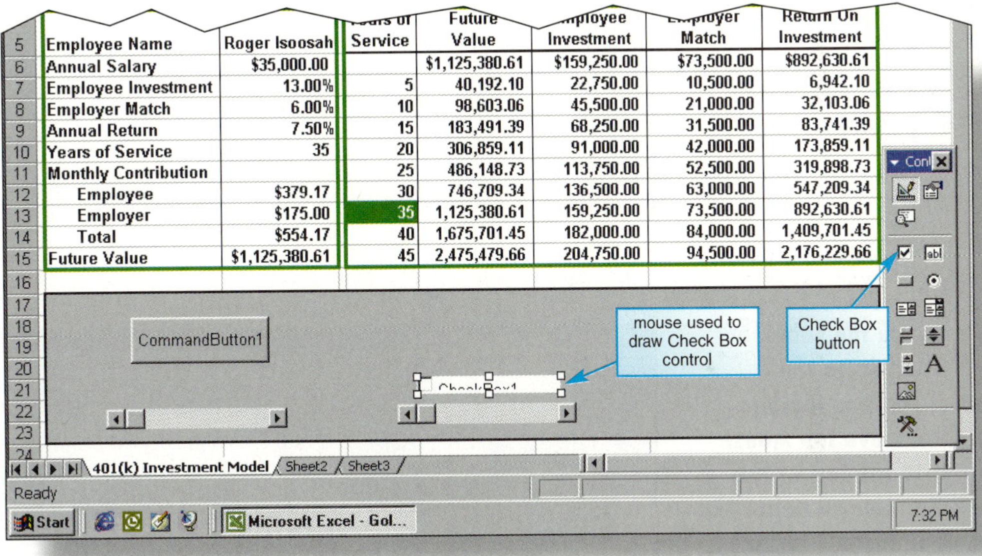

FIGURE 7-54

6 **Click the Spin Button button on the Control Toolbox toolbar and then move the mouse pointer to the upper-left corner of the location of the Spin Button control shown in Figure 7-55. Drag the mouse pointer so the rectangle defining the Spin Button control area displays as shown in Figure 7-55.**

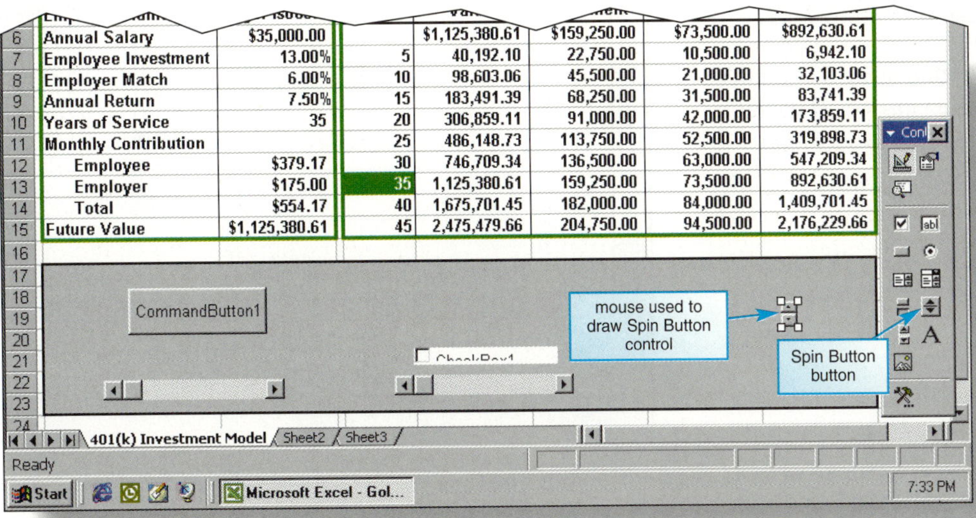

FIGURE 7-55

7 **Point to the Spin Button control in the Adjustment Center. Hold down the CTRL key and drag a copy of the Spin Button control to the second location shown in Figure 7-56. It is important that you release the left mouse button before you release the CTRL key.**

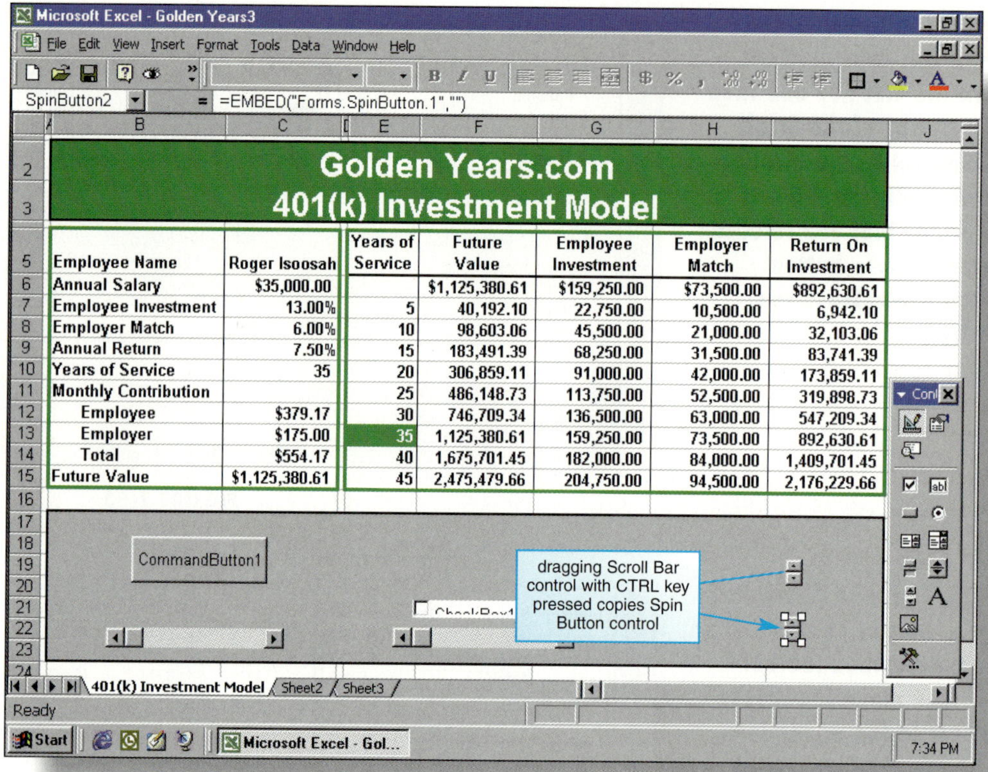

FIGURE 7-56

8 **Click the Label button on the Control Toolbox toolbar and then move the mouse pointer to the left of the Scroll Bar control below the CommandButton1 button. Drag the mouse pointer so the rectangle defining the Label control displays as shown in Figure 7-57.**

This Label control is used to indicate the lowest value (zero) on the scroll bar.

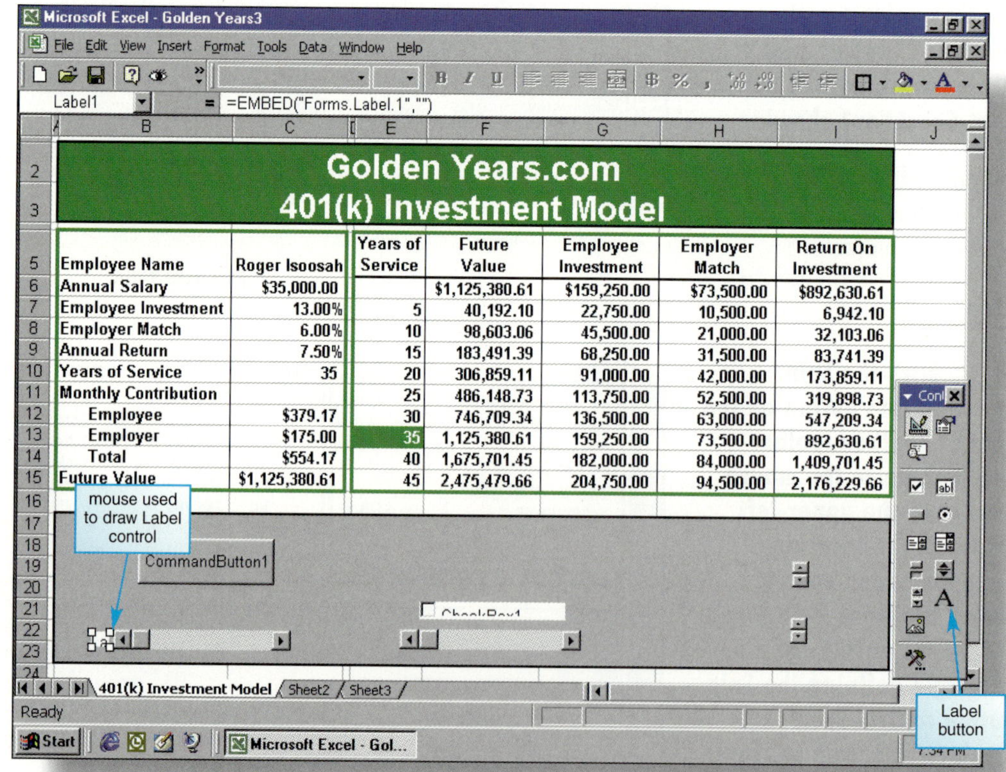

FIGURE 7-57

9 **Point to the Label control. Hold down the CTRL key and then drag a copy of the Label control created in Step 8 immediately above the left Scroll Bar control. With the CTRL key held down, drag the newly copied Label control to the next location where a Label control is required. Continue in this fashion until you have a total of ten Label controls as shown in Figure 7-58.**

All the controls needed for this application are in the Adjustment Center.

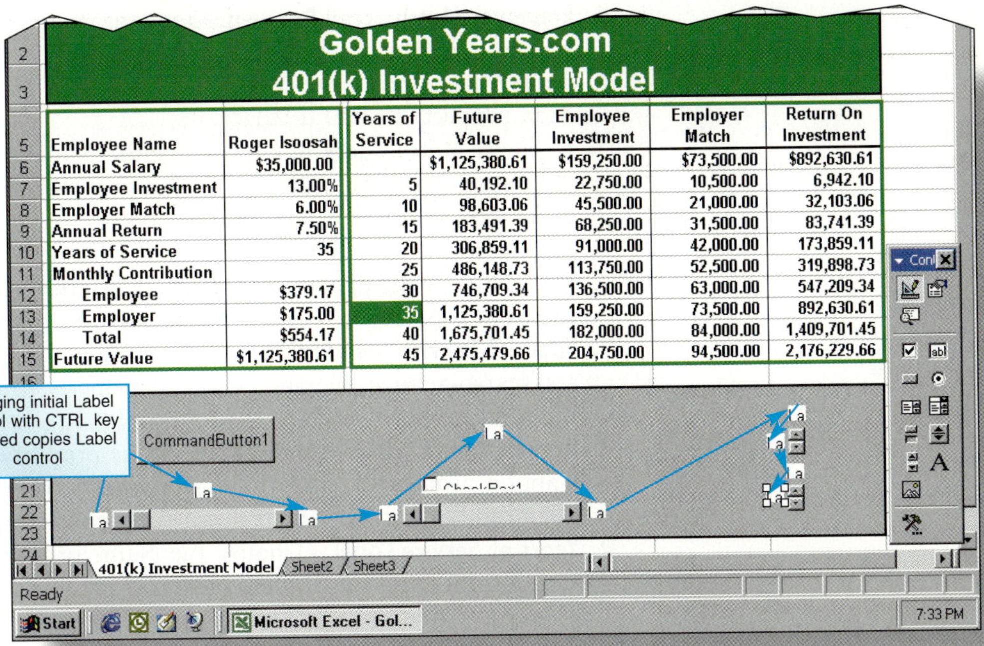

Golden Years.com
401(k) Investment Model

Employee Name	Roger Isoosah	Years of Service	Future Value	Employee Investment	Employer Match	Return On Investment
Annual Salary	$35,000.00		$1,125,380.61	$159,250.00	$73,500.00	$892,630.61
Employee Investment	13.00%	5	40,192.10	22,750.00	10,500.00	6,942.10
Employer Match	6.00%	10	98,603.06	45,500.00	21,000.00	32,103.06
Annual Return	7.50%	15	183,491.39	68,250.00	31,500.00	83,741.39
Years of Service	35	20	306,859.11	91,000.00	42,000.00	173,859.11
Monthly Contribution		25	486,148.73	113,750.00	52,500.00	319,898.73
Employee	$379.17	30	746,709.34	136,500.00	63,000.00	547,209.34
Employer	$175.00	35	1,125,380.61	159,250.00	73,500.00	892,630.61
Total	$554.17	40	1,675,701.45	182,000.00	84,000.00	1,409,701.45
Future Value	$1,125,380.61	45	2,475,479.66	204,750.00	94,500.00	2,176,229.66

dragging initial Label control with CTRL key pressed copies Label control

CommandButton1

401(k) Investment Model / Sheet2 / Sheet3

Ready

Start | Microsoft Excel - Gol... | 7:33 PM

FIGURE 7-58

Other Ways

1. Select control, click CTRL+C to copy, click CTRL+V to paste
2. Select control, click Copy button on Standard toolbar; click Paste button on Standard toolbar
3. Right-click control, click Copy on shortcut menu, click Paste on shortcut menu
4. Select control, on Edit menu click Copy, on Edit menu click Paste

When you create a Label control, a caption is associated with it. The Caption property for the first Label control is Label1. For the next Label control you create, the Caption property is Label2, and so on. Because of the size of the Label controls in Figure 7-58, you can only see a portion of the caption, such as the La.

If you compare Figure 7-58 with Figure 7-50 on page 7.41, you will notice that except for captions and some minor repositioning of the controls, the Adjustment Center user interface is complete. If you want to delete a control, select it while in Design mode and press the DELETE key. If you want to resize a control, select it while in design mode and drag its sizing handles. If you want to reposition a control, select it and drag it to its new location.

Step 2 – Set the Properties

The next step is to set the properties for the sixteen controls that make up the user interface. The sixteen controls can best be seen by referring to Figure 7-50 on page E 7.41 counting the button, labels, scroll bars, check box, and spin buttons. The properties will be set as follows:

1. **Constant Label and Check Box** — Set the BackColor property of the Label controls that identify other controls and the Check Box control to Button Face gray so it agrees with the gray background of the user interface. Set the Font property to Bold. Set the Caption property and Text Align property for each Label control that identifies another control. Increase the font size of the Adjustment Center title to size 20.
2. **Command Button** – Change the Caption property to Name and Salary and resize the button so the entire caption shows.
3. **Employee Investment Scroll Bar** – Change the Name property to scrEmployeeInvest, the SmallChange property to 50 (0.5%), the LargeChange property to 100 (1%), the Min property to 0 (0%), and the Max property to 1300 (13%).

4. **Employer Match Scroll Bar** — Change the Name property to scrEmployerMatch, the SmallChange property to 25 (0.25%), the LargeChange property to 100 (1%), the Min property to 0 (0%), and the Max property to 600 (6%).
5. **Employer Match Check Box** – Change the Name property to chkEmployerMatch and the Caption property to Employer Match. Resize the check box so the new caption displays.
6. **Annual Return Spin Button** – Change the Name property to spnAnnualReturn, the SmallChange property to 25 (0.25%), the Min property to 0 (0%), and the Max property to 10000 (100%).
7. **Years of Service Spin Button** – Change the Name property to spnYearsofService, the SmallChange property to 1, the Min property to 1, and the Max property to 75.
8. **Annual Return Label** – Change the Name property to lblAnnualReturn, the Caption property to 5%, the Font property to Bold, the TextAlign property to align right, and the SpecialEffect property to sunken.
9. **Years of Service Label** – Change the Name property to lblYearsofService, the Caption property to 10, the Font property to Bold, the TextAlign property to align right, and the SpecialEffect property to sunken.

Excel automatically assigns the first Command Button control the name CommandButton1. If you create a second Command Button control, Excel will call it CommandButton2, and so on. In the controls just listed, some will have their Name property changed as indicated, while others will not. Usually, you do not change the Name property of Label controls that identify other controls in the user interface. On the other hand, controls that are referenced in the VBA code should be given names that help you recall the control. Table 7-5 summarizes the controls whose Name property will be changed because they will be referenced in the VBA code.

Table 7-5 Referenced Controls and Their Names

CONTROL	NAME
Employee Investment Scroll Bar	scrEmployeeInvest
Employer Match Scroll Bar	scrEmployerMatch
Employer Match Check Box	chkEmployerMatch
Annual Return Spin Button	spnAnnualReturn
Years of Service Spin Button	spnYearsofService
Annual Return Label	lblAnnualReturn
Years of Service Label	lblYearsofService

The name of a control, such as scrEmployeeInvest, must begin with a letter, cannot exceed 255 characters, and cannot have a space, period, exclamation point, or the characters @, &, $, or #. You should develop a naming convention of your own and then use it consistently to name controls. In this book, the first three characters of the name identify the control. For example: scr stands for scroll bar; chk stands for check box; and spn stands for spin button. Following the three characters are words that identify what the control is controlling. In this case, scrEmployeeInvest is a scroll bar controlling the value in cell C7, the Employee Investment. You also must make sure that the names are unique in an application, because duplicate names are not allowed.

SETTING THE CONSTANT LABELS AND CHECK BOX PROPERTIES When you create a Label control, it has a white background. If the Label control identifies another control, the background color is changed so it becomes part of the user interface background. If the Label control is going to display a value that varies, the background is left white. The following steps use the SHIFT key to select all the Label controls that identify other controls and the Check Box control so that the BackColor property can be changed for all selected items at once. The Font property of the selected controls is also changed to bold. After the BackColor and Font are changed, then each Label control is selected and the properties are set.

Steps To Set Properties of the Constant Label Controls and Check Box Control

1 With Excel in Design mode, click the Label control in the lower-left corner of the user interface. Hold down the SHIFT key and then one at a time, click the Label controls that will remain constant and the Check Box control (bottom of Figure 7-59). Release the SHIFT key. Click the Properties button on the Control Toolbox toolbar. When the Properties window displays, click BackColor, click the BackColor arrow, if necessary, click the System tab, and then point to Button Face in the list.

The selected Label controls, the Check Box control, and the Properties window display as shown in Figure 7-59.

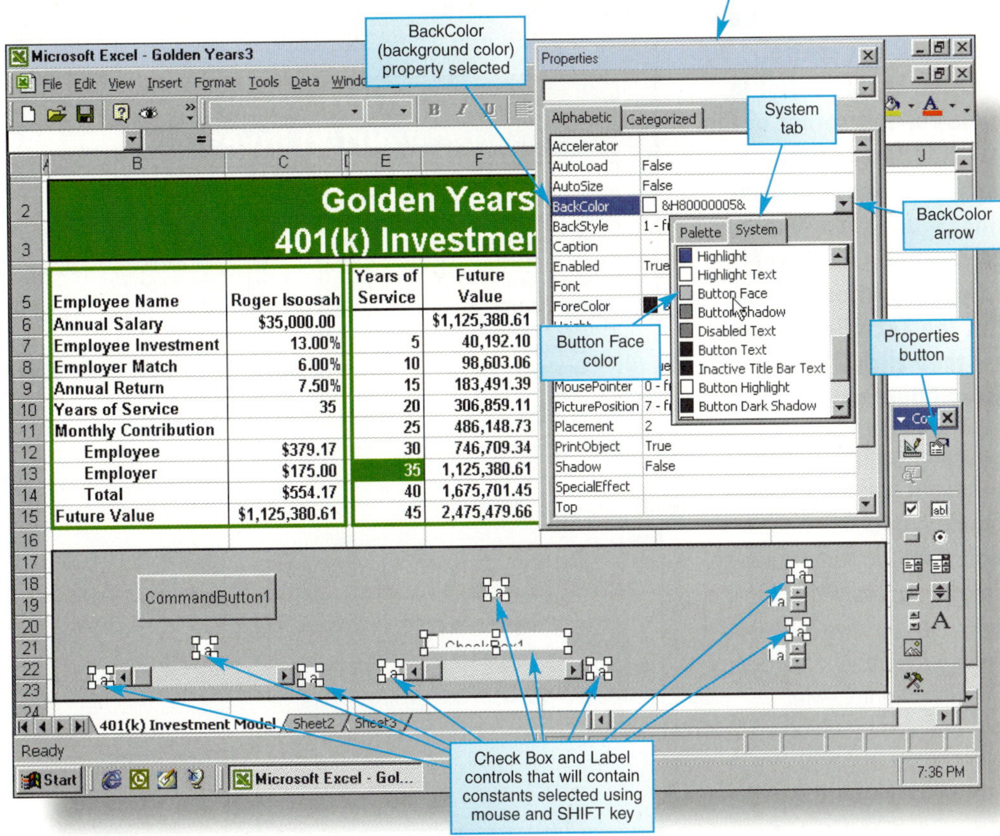

FIGURE 7-59

2 Click Button Face. Click Font in the Properties window and then click the Font button. When the Font dialog box displays, click Bold in the Font style list and then point to the OK button.

The Properties window and Font dialog box display as shown in Figure 7-60. The selected Label controls and Check Box control have a gray background.

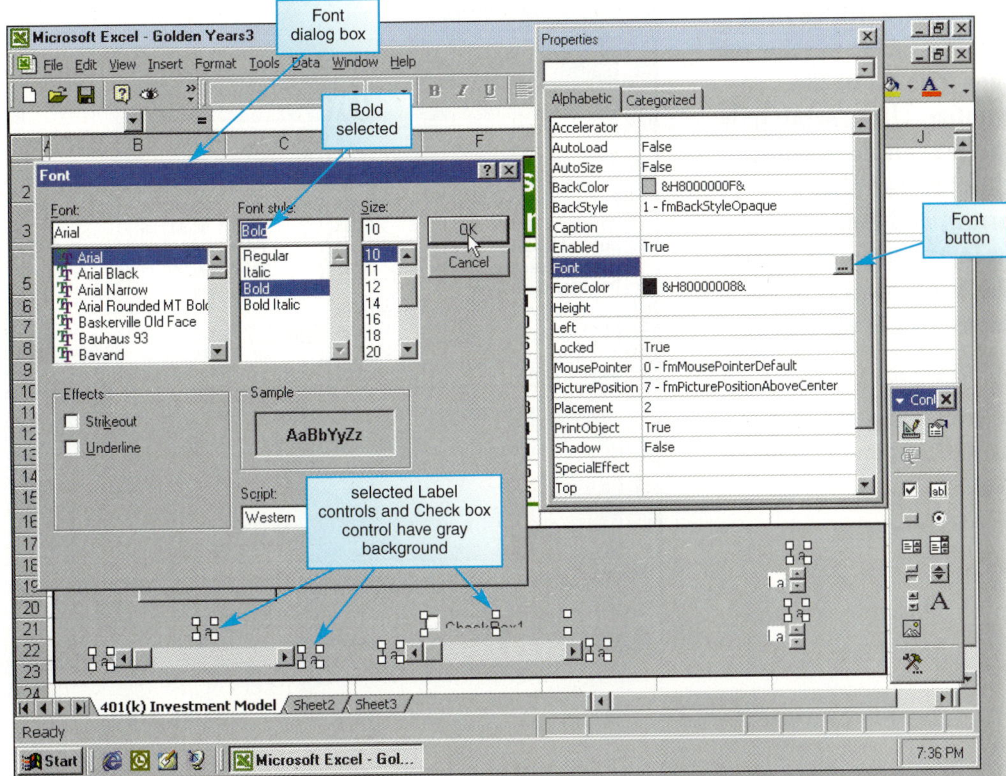

FIGURE 7-60

3 **Click the OK button. Click the ESC key to deselect the Label controls and Check Box control. Click the Label control in the lower-left corner of the user interface. Click Caption in the Properties window and then type** 0 **as the caption. Click TextAlign in the Properties window, click the TextAlign arrow, and then click 2 - fmTextAlignCenter.**

The Label control in the lower-left corner is selected and the Properties window displays its properties as shown in Figure 7-61. Only a portion of the zero (0) displays in the Label control in the Adjustment Center.

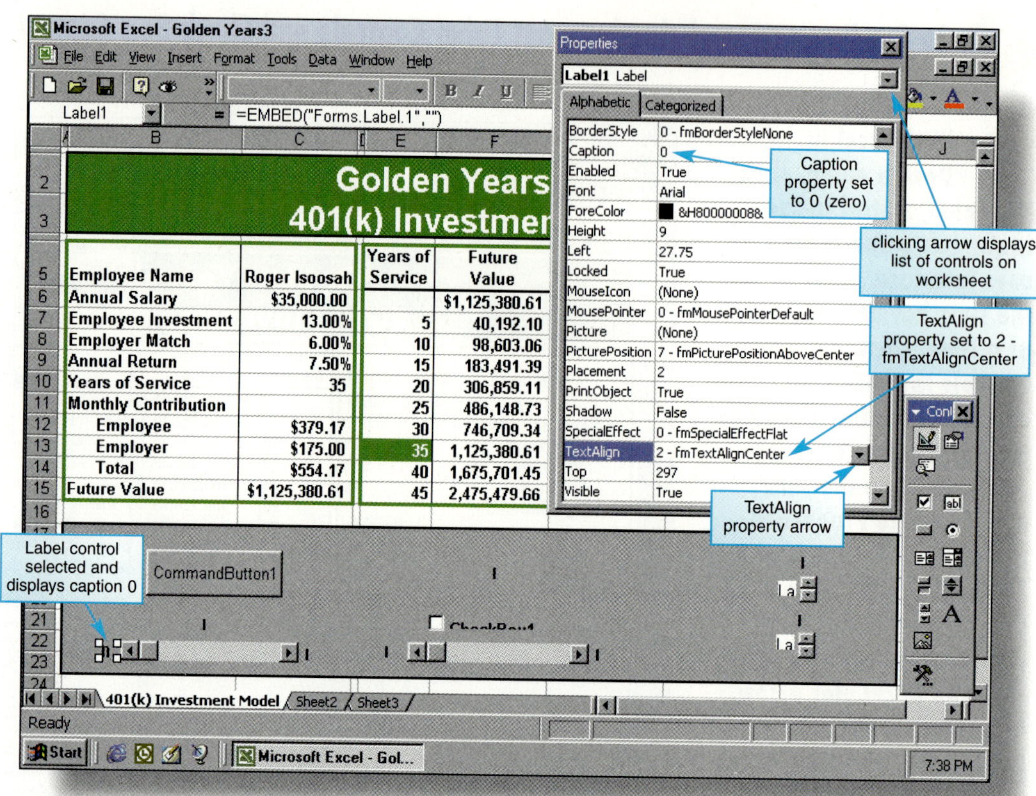

FIGURE 7-61

4 **Click the Label control to the right of the Employee Investment scroll bar. Click Caption in the Properties window and then type** 13 **as the caption. Click TextAlign in the Properties window, click the TextAlign arrow, and then click 2 - fmTextAlignCenter. Resize the Label control so the caption 13 is visible.**

The Properties window for the selected Label control displays as shown in Figure 7-62.

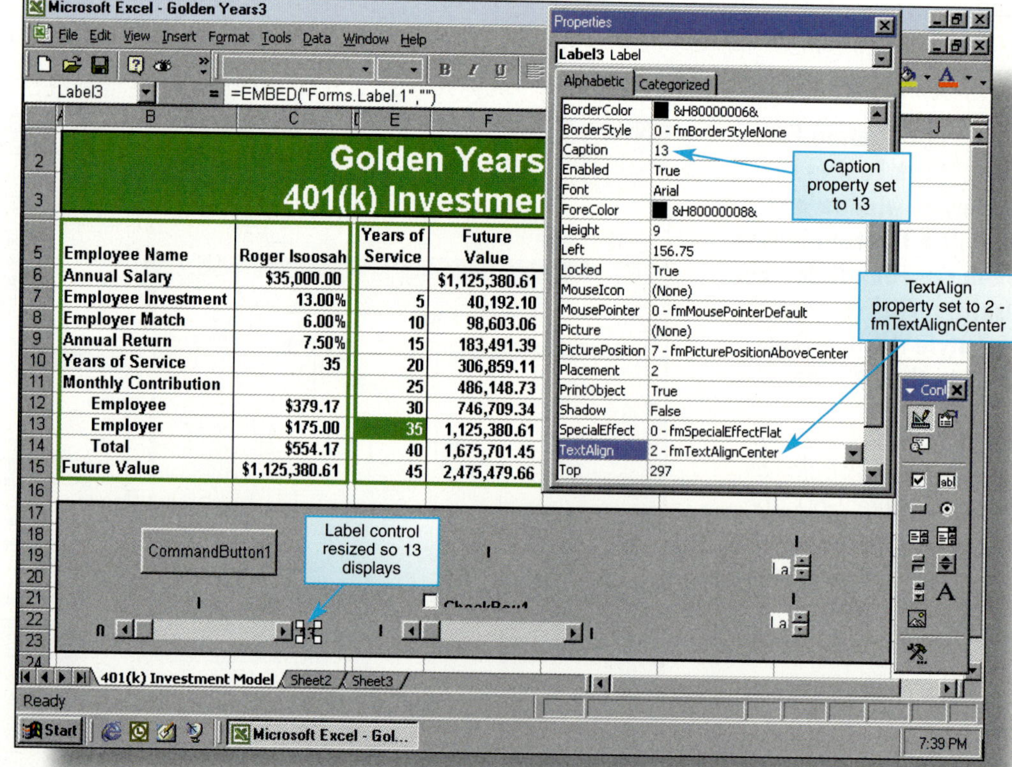

FIGURE 7-62

5 **Click the Label control on the left side between the Command Button control and the Scroll Bar control. Click Caption in the Properties window and then type** `Employee Investment` **as the caption. Click TextAlign in the Properties window. Click the TextAlign arrow and then click 2 - fmTextAlignCenter. Resize the Label control so the caption Employee Investment is visible**

The Properties window displays as shown in Figure 7-63.

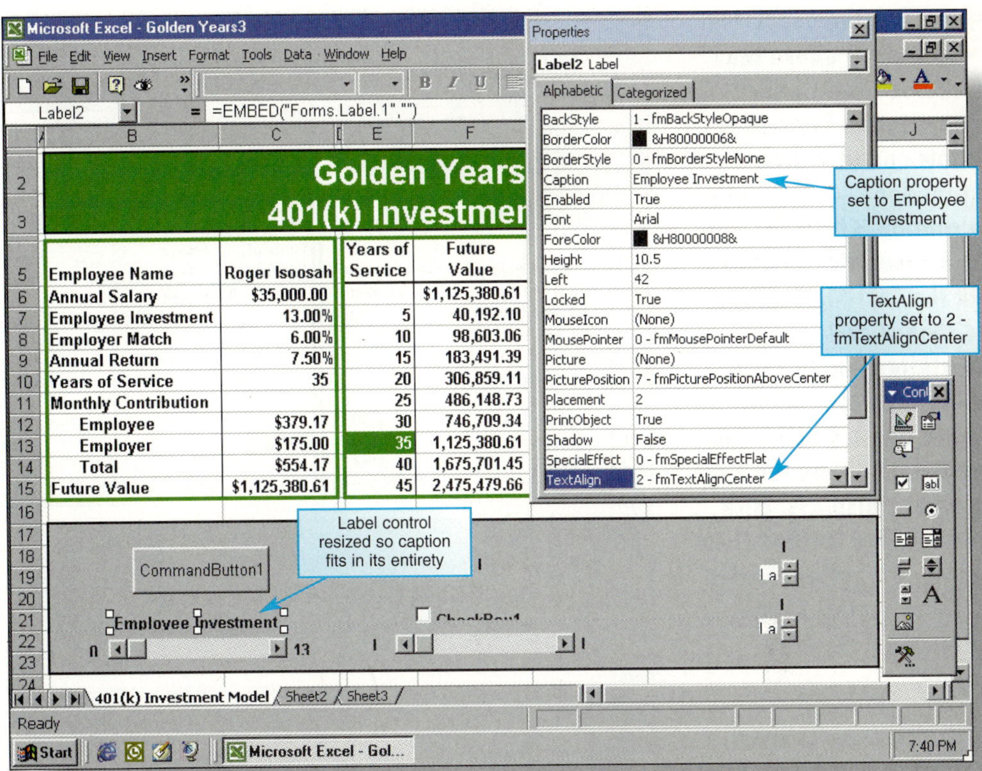

FIGURE 7-63

6 **Click the Label control to the left of the second Scroll Bar control. Click Caption in the Properties window and then type** `0` **as the caption. Click TextAlign in the Properties window, click the TextAlign arrow, and then click 2 - fmTextAlignCenter. Click the Label control on the right side of the second Scroll Bar control. Click Caption in the Properties window and then type** `6` **as the caption. Click TextAlign in the Properties window, click the TextAlign arrow, and then click 2 - fmTextAlignCenter.**

The Properties window for the selected Label control displays as shown in Figure 7-64.

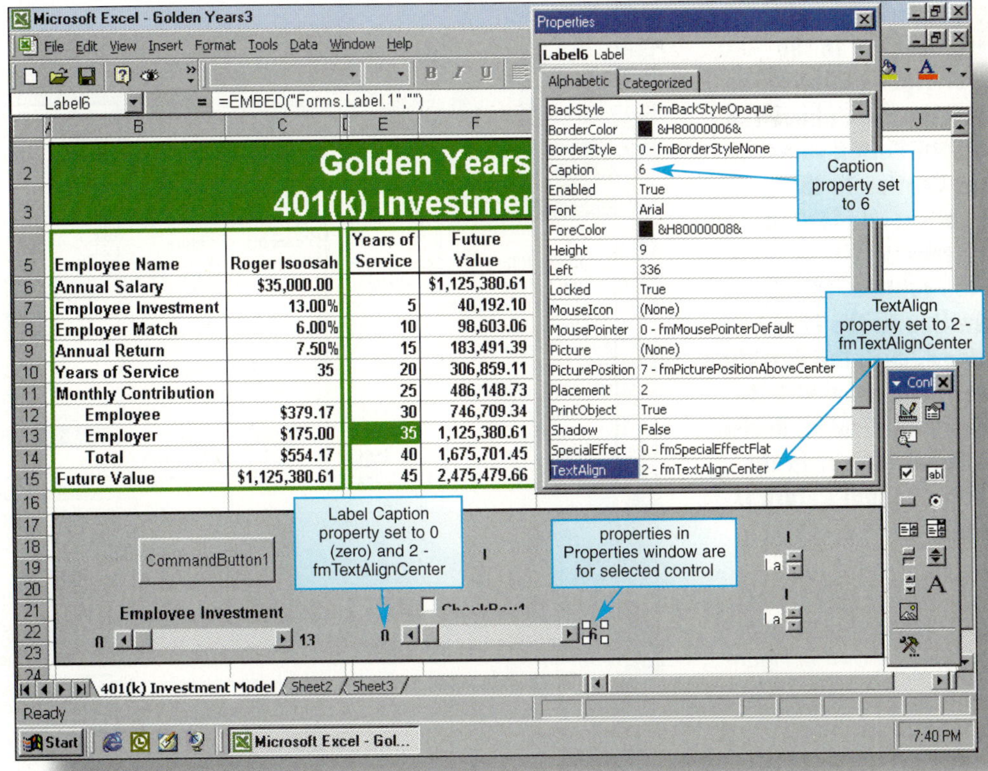

FIGURE 7-64

7 **Click the Label control above the Check Box control. Click Caption in the Properties window and then type** `Adjustment Center` **as the caption. Click TextAlign in the Properties window, click the TextAlign arrow, and then click 2 - fmTextAlignCenter. Click Font in the Properties window and then click the Font button. When the Font dialog box displays, click 20 in the Size list and then click the OK button. Resize the Label control so the caption displays in its entirety.**

The Properties window for the selected Label control displays as shown in Figure 7-65.

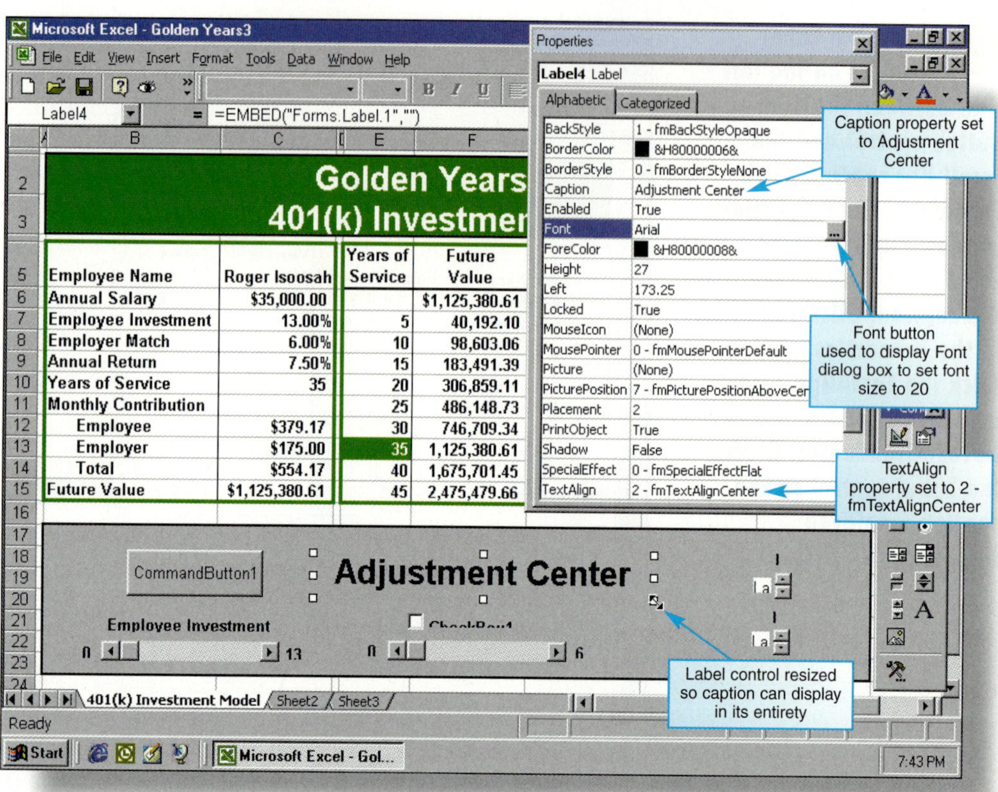

FIGURE 7-65

8 **Click the Label control in the upper-right corner of the user interface, above the top Spin Button control. Click Caption in the Properties window and then type** `Annual Return` **as the caption. Click TextAlign in the Properties window, click the TextAlign arrow, and then click 2 - fmTextAlignCenter. Resize the Label control so the caption Annual Return is visible.**

The Properties window for the selected Label control displays as shown in Figure 7-66.

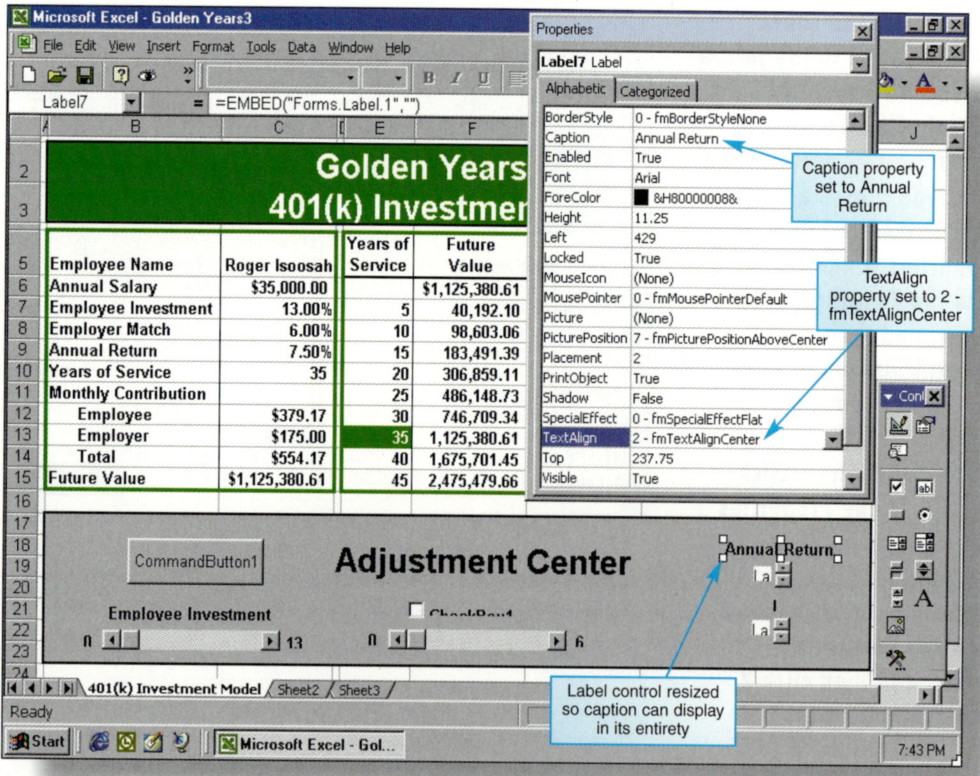

FIGURE 7-66

9 **Click the Label control above the lower Spin Button control. Click Caption in the Properties window and then type** `Years of Service` **as the caption. Click TextAlign in the Properties window, click the TextAlign arrow, and then click 2 - fmTextAlignCenter. Resize the Label control so the caption Years of Service is visible.**

The Properties window for the selected Label control displays as shown in Figure 7-67.

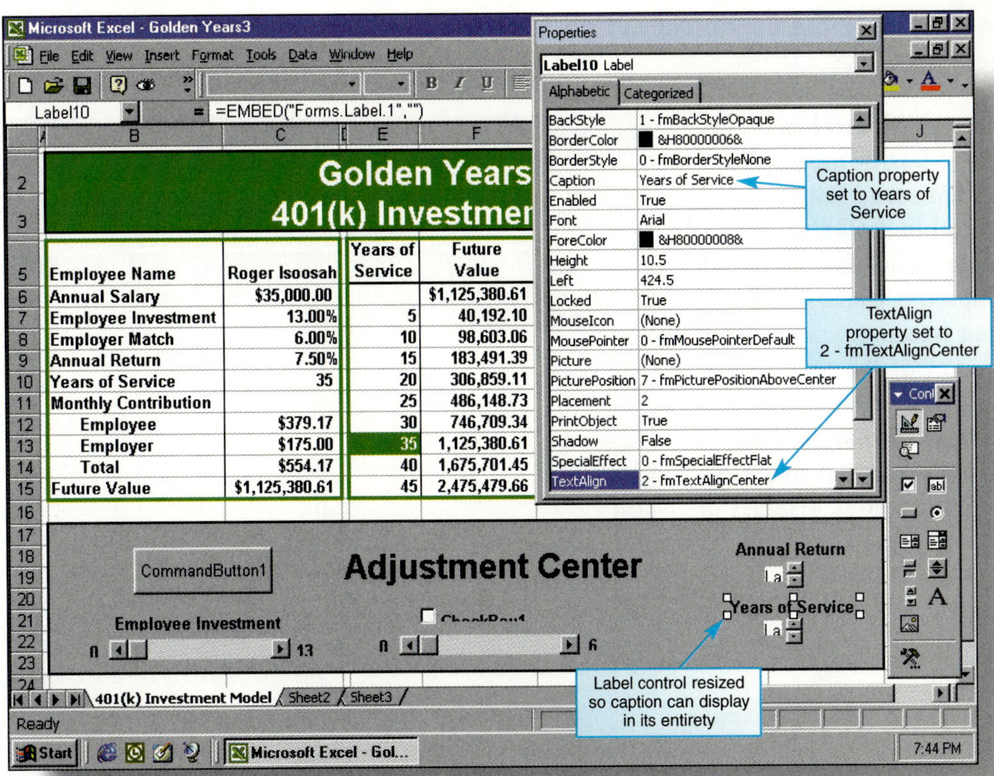

FIGURE 7-67

Every control has its own set of properties. When you select multiple controls as in Step 1 on page E 7.47, then Excel displays only those properties that are common to the controls selected.

SETTING THE COMMAND BUTTON CONTROL PROPERTIES The next step is to change the caption on the Command Button control from CommandButton1 to Name and Salary, and resize it so the caption on the button displays in its entirety.

To Set the Command Button Control Properties

1 **With Excel in Design mode, click the Command Button control in the Adjustment Center. Click Caption in the Properties window and then type** `Name and Salary` **as the caption. Drag one of the sizing handles surrounding the Command Button control so that the caption displays in its entirety.**

The button and its properties display as shown in Figure 7-68.

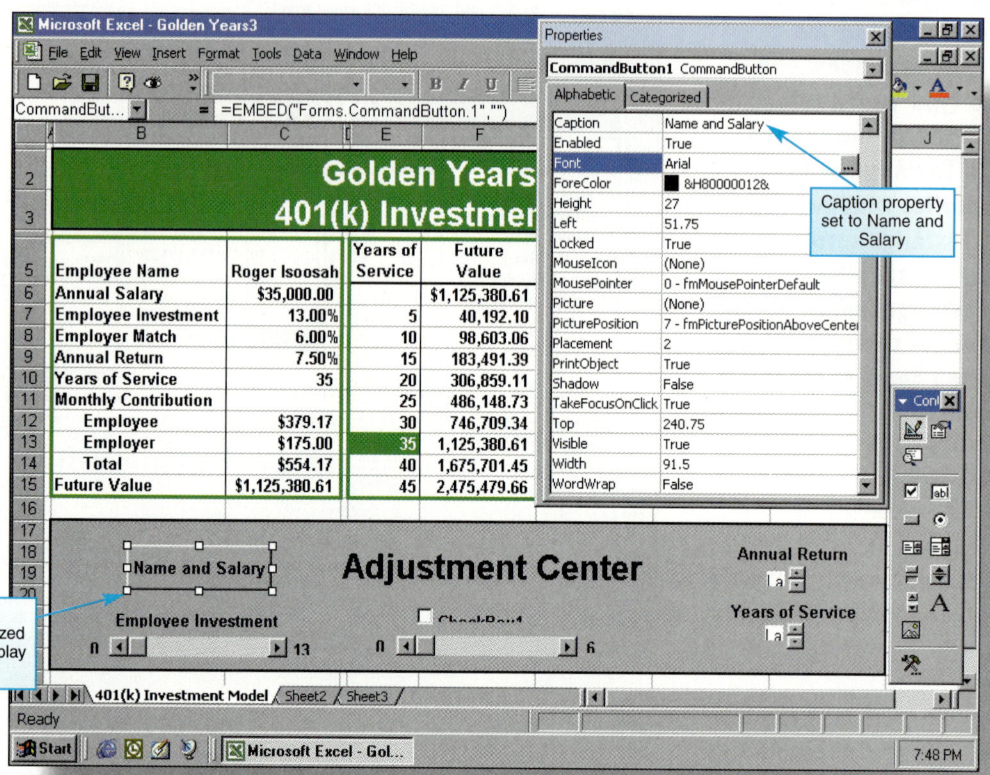

FIGURE 7-68

As you can see from the Properties window shown in Figure 7-68, a Command Button control has many different properties. One that may interest you that is not being used in this project is the MousePointer property. If you click MousePointer in the Properties window and then click the MousePointer arrow, you will see several mouse pointers listed, many that you are familiar with from your experiences in Excel. If you change the MousePointer property, the mouse pointer will change when you point to the button. You can choose from the Hour Glass, I-beam, arrow, and cross.

SETTING THE EMPLOYEE INVESTMENT SCROLL BAR PROPERTIES The next step is to set the Employee Investment Scroll Bar properties. The function of this Scroll Bar control is to assign cell C7 a value. When you use a control, such as a scroll bar, you must set the Min and Max properties. The **Min property** is the least value the control can register. The **Max property** is the maximum value the control can register. You also have to set the SmallChange and LargeChange values. The **SmallChange property** is the value the control will change by each time you click the scroll arrow. The **LargeChange** property is the value the control will change by each time you click the scroll bar.

You only can assign whole numbers for these four properties. This increases the complexity of the VBA code because the cell in question must be assigned a decimal number. Thus, to assign the cell the maximum value 0.13 (13%), you must actually set the Maximum property to 1300, and then later in the VBA code divide by 10000 to assign the cell a value of 0.13.

To Set the Employee Investment Scroll Bar Properties

1 With Excel in Design mode, click the Employee Investment scroll bar. Click Name in the Properties window and then type `scrEmployeeInvest` **as the name. Change the LargeChange property to** `100`**, the Max property to** `1300`**, the Min property to** `0`**, and the SmallChange property to** `50`**.**

The Employee Investment scroll bar Properties window displays as shown in Figure 7-69

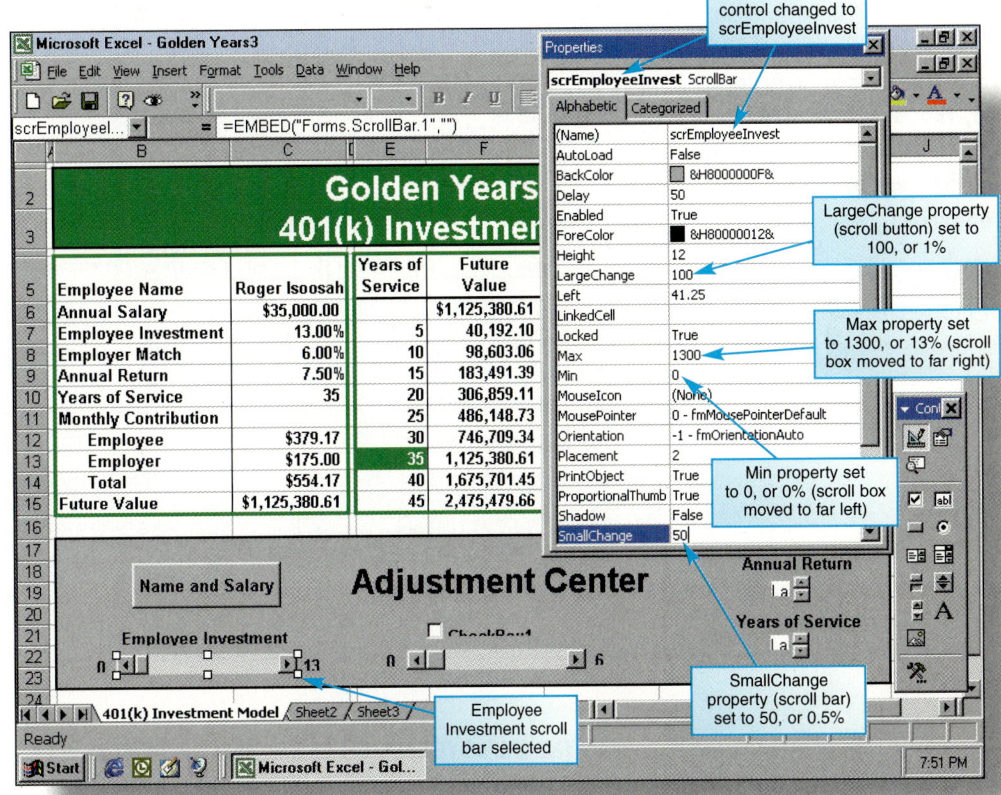

FIGURE 7-69

Excel automatically will determine how far to move the scroll button on the scroll bar when you click the scroll button (small change) and when you click the scroll boxes (large change) from the four numeric values entered in Step 1.

SETTING THE EMPLOYER MATCH SCROLL BAR PROPERTIES The step on the next page sets the Employer Match Scroll Bar properties. The property settings are similar to those assigned to the Employee Investment scroll bar. Once the VBA code is written, this scroll bar will assign a value to cell C8.

To Set the Employer Match Scroll Bar Properties

1 **With Excel in Design mode, click the Employer Match scroll bar. Click Name in the Properties window and then type** `scrEmployerMatch` **as the name. Change the LargeChange property to** 100**, the Max property to** 300**, the Min property to** 0**, and the SmallChange property to** 25**.**

The Employer Match scroll bar Properties window displays as shown in Figure 7-70

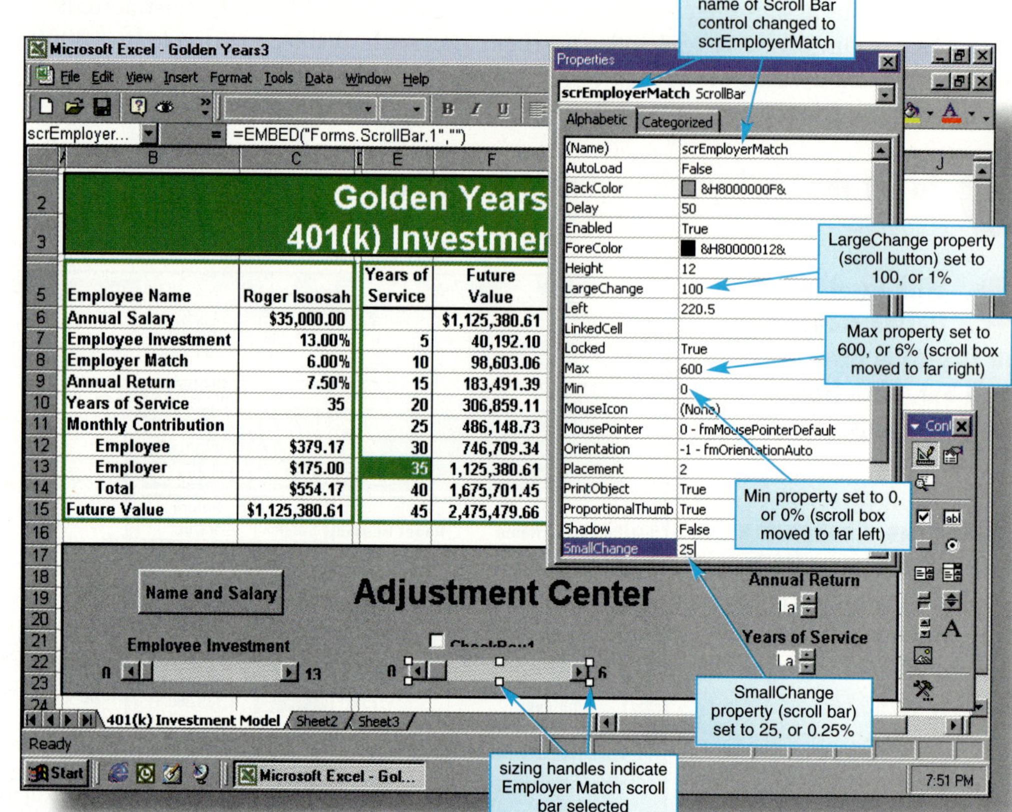

FIGURE 7-70

The Max Property

One of the more difficult concepts to understand about scroll bars is why the Max property is set to such a large number (600 in Figure 7-70), when the maximum value of the scroll bar is only 6% (.06). The two reasons are (1) the Max property can be set equal to only a whole number; and (2) the large number allows you to assign reasonable increments to the SmallChange and LargeChange properties of the scroll bar.

SETTING THE EMPLOYER MATCH CHECK BOX PROPERTIES The Employer Match check box enables or disables the Employer Match Scroll Bar control. If the Employer Match check box contains a check mark, then the Employer Match scroll bar is enabled and it can be used to change the value in cell C8. If the check box is empty, then the Employer Match scroll bar control is disabled. The VBA code will enable or disable the scroll bar based on the check box status. The following step sets the Employer Match Check Box properties.

To Set the Employer Match Check Box Properties

1 With Excel in Design mode, click the Employer Match check box. Click Name in the Properties window and then type chkEmployerMatch **as the name. Click Caption in the Properties window and then type** Employer Match **as the caption. Click Value in the Properties window and then type** True**. Resize the Check Box control so the caption Employer Match is visible.**

The Employer Match check box Properties window displays as shown in Figure 7-71.

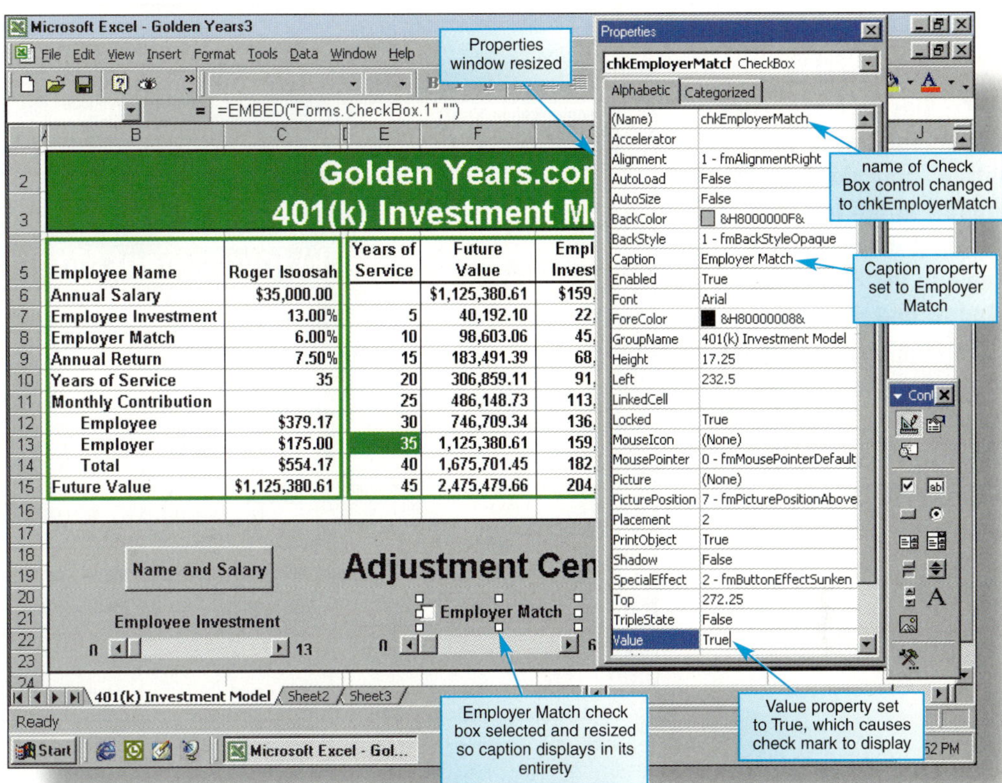

FIGURE 7-71

Setting the Value property to True inserts a check mark in the Employer Match check box. Because the insertion point is still active in the Value property, the check mark does not show in Figure 7-71. The check mark does show up in Figure 7-72 on the next page.

SETTING THE ANNUAL RETURN AND YEARS OF SERVICE SPIN BUTTON PROPERTIES The Annual Return spin button increments or decrements the value in cell C9 by 0.25%. The Years of Service spin button increments or decrements the value in cell C10 by one. With a spin button, the up arrow increases the value and the down arrow decreases the value. The Label controls to the left of the Spin Button controls (Figure 7-70) indicate the values assigned to the associated cells. The Min, Max, and SmallChange properties must be set. The SmallChange property indicates the change each time you click an arrow.

The steps on the next page set the properties for the Annual Return and Years of Service spin buttons.

More About 2000

Properties

Many properties, such as the Value property (Figure 7-71), can be only one of two states — True or False. If it is True, then the property is turned on. If it is False, then the property is turned off. For example, assigning the Value property the value True, means that the check mark will display in the Employee Match check box.

To Set Properties for the Annual Return Spin Button and Years of Service Spin Button

1 **With Excel in Design mode, click the Annual Return spin button. Drag the Properties window to the left side of the Excel window. Click Name in the Properties window and then type** `spnAnnualReturn` **as the name. Change the Max property to** `10000`**, the Min property to** `0`**, and the SmallChange property to** `25`**.**

The Annual Return spin button Properties window displays as shown in Figure 7-72.

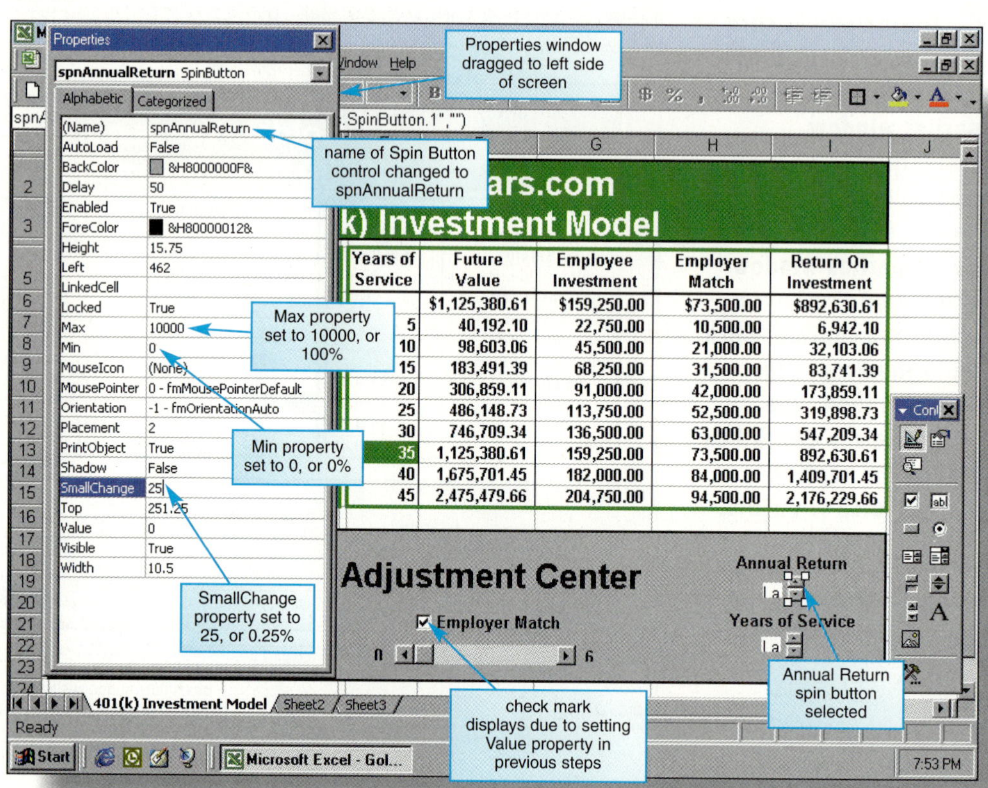

FIGURE 7-72

2 **Click the Years of Service spin button. Click Name in the Properties window and then type** `spnYearsofService` **as the name. Change the Max property to** `75`**, the Min property to** `1`**, and the SmallChange property to** `1`**.**

The Years of Service spin button Properties window displays as shown in Figure 7-73

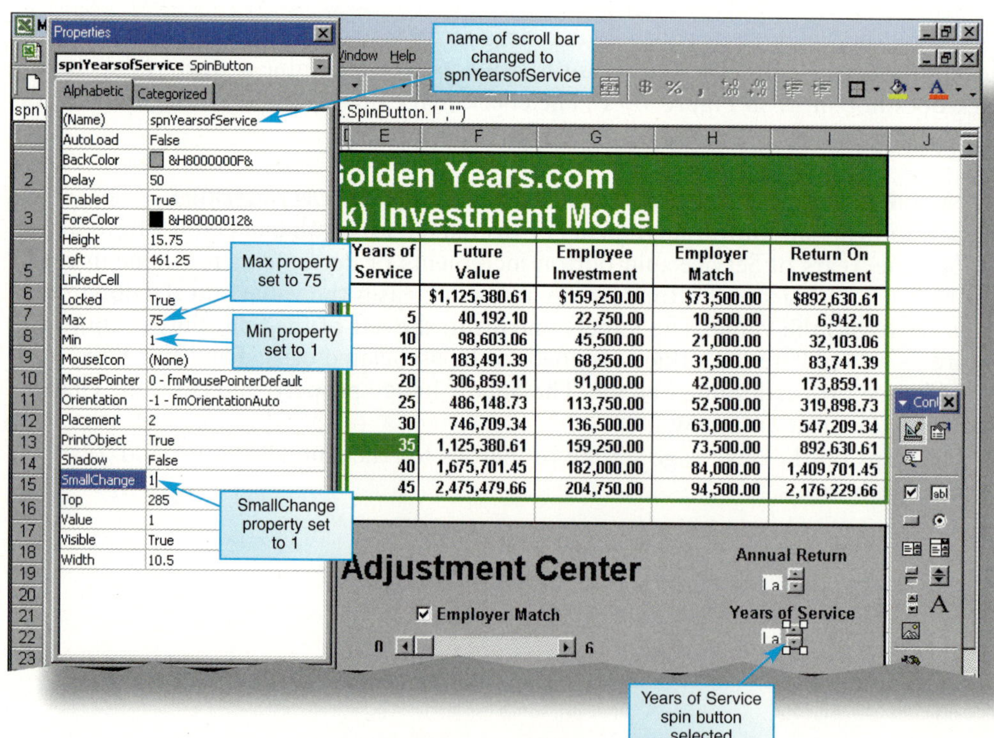

FIGURE 7-73

The least value the Annual Return spin button can be set to is 0 (0%). The greatest value is 10000 (100%). Once the VBA code is written, each time you click a button, the annual return in cell C9 will change by 0.25%. At this point in the project, no relationship exists between the Annual Return spin button and cell C9. This relationship will be established later in the VBA code. A similar relationship will be established between the Years of Service spin button and cell C10.

SETTING THE LABEL CONTROL PROPERTIES FOR THE ANNUAL RETURN AND YEARS OF SERVICE SPIN BUTTONS The Label controls to the left of the two Spin Button controls will be used to display the values of their respective spin buttons. Thus, when you click one of the Annual Return spin buttons, the new value will display in the Label control next to the spin button as well as in cell C9. The following steps set the Name property, Caption property, SpecialEffect property, and TextAlign property for the two Label controls to the left of the Spin Button controls. The SpecialEffect property option will give the two Label controls a 3-D sunken appearance.

To Set the Label Control Properties for the Annual Return and Years of Service Spin Button

1 With Excel in Design mode, click the Label control to the left of the Annual Return spin button. Click Name in the Properties window and then type `lblAnnualReturn` **as the name. Click Caption in the Properties window and then type** `5%` **as the caption. Change the Font property to bold. Change the SpecialEffect property to 2 - fmSpecialEffectSunken and the TextAlign property to 3 - fmTextAlignRight. Resize the Label control as shown in Figure 7-74.**

The Annual Return Spin Button label Properties window displays as shown in Figure 7-74.

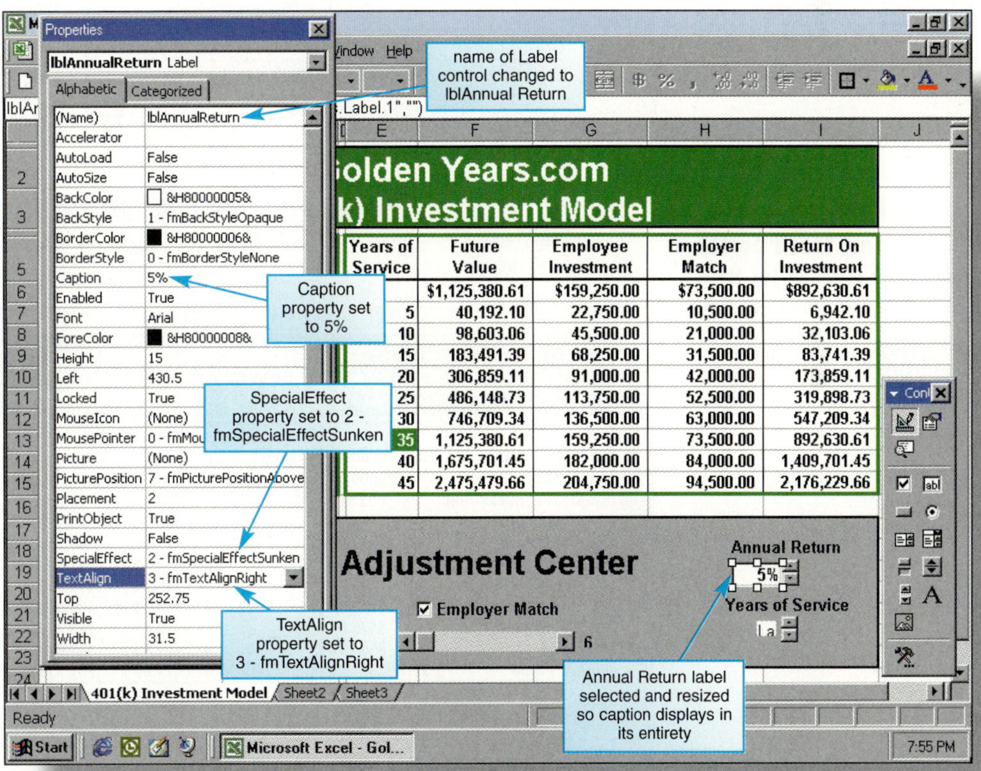

FIGURE 7-74

2 **Click the Label control to the left of the Years of Service Spin Button control. Click Name in the Properties window and then type** `lblYearsofService` **as the name. Change the Font property to bold. Click Caption in the Properties window and then type** `10` **as the caption. Change the SpecialEffect property to 2 - fmSpecialEffectSunken and the TextAlign property to 3 - fmTextAlignRight. Resize the Label control as shown in Figure 7-75.**

The Years of Service Spin Button label Properties window displays as shown in Figure 7-75

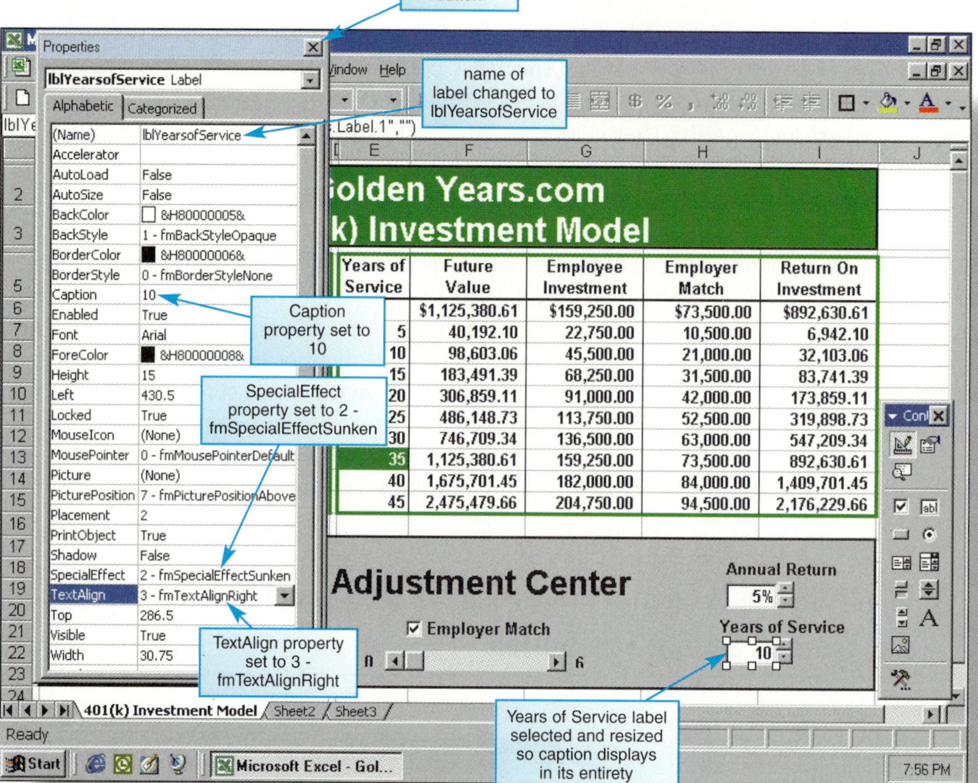

FIGURE 7-75

3 **Click the Properties window Close button on the right side of its title bar.**

The Adjustment Center displays as shown in Figure 7-76.

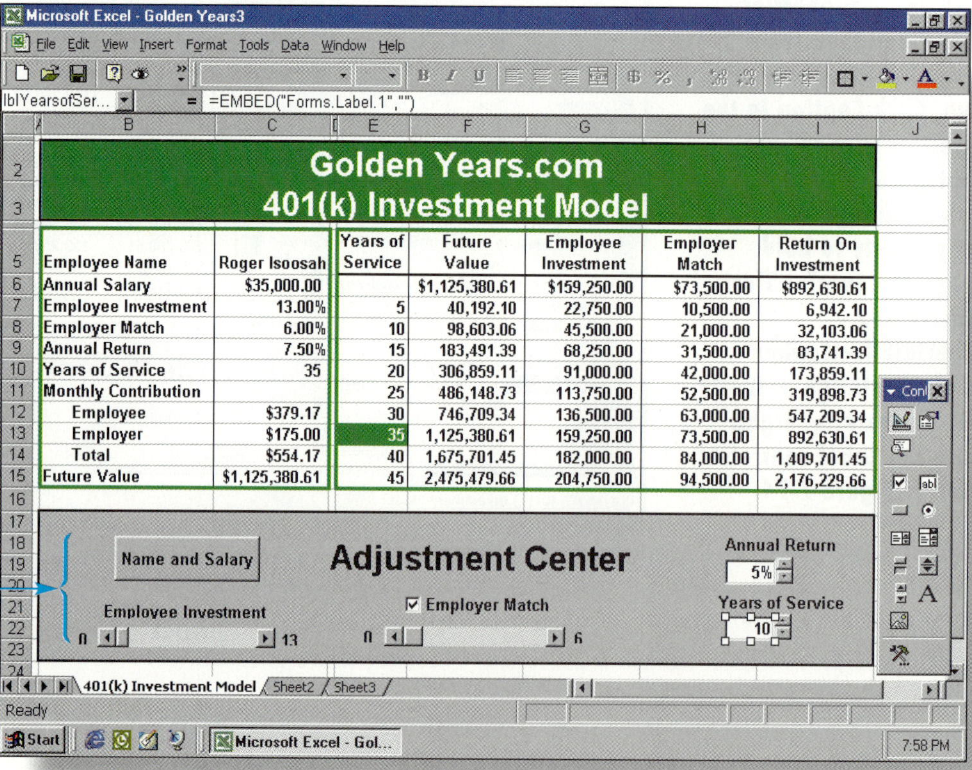

FIGURE 7-76

Later in the VBA code, the Label controls will be set equal to the corresponding Spin Button controls through the use of the names. For example, the VBA statement

```
lblAnnualReturn = spnAnnualReturn.Value / 100 & "%"
```

assigns the value of the Annual Return Spin Button control divided by 100 to the its corresponding Label control. The & "%" appends a percent sign to the number that displays in the Label control.

The Microsoft Script Editor

The Microsoft Script Editor allows you to develop complex Web pages that interact with your company's data, whether the data is in Excel or a database. The Script Editor generates what is known as Active Server Pages. These Web pages contain both HTML and program code. For more information, click Tools, point to Macro, and then click Microsoft Script Editor. When the Microsoft Script Editor displays, click Help on the menu bar, and then click Contents.

FINE-TUNING THE USER INTERFACE After setting the properties for all the controls, you can fine-tune the size and location of the controls in the Adjustment Center. With Excel in Design mode, you have three ways to reposition a control:

1. Drag the control to its new location.
2. Select the control and use the arrow keys to reposition it.
3. Select the control and set the control's Top and Left properties in the Properties window.

To use the third technique, you need to know the distance the control is from the top of row 1 (column headings) and the far left of column A (row headings) in points. Recall, that a point is equal to 1/72 of an inch. Thus, if the Top property of a control is 216, then the control is 3 inches (216 / 72) from the top of the window.

You also can resize a control in two ways:

1. Drag the sizing handles.
2. Select the control and set the control's Height and Width properties in the Properties window.

As with the Top and Left properties, the Height and Width properties are measured in points. Table 7-6 lists the exact points for the Top, Left, Height, and Width properties of each of the controls in the Adjustment Center.

Table 7-6 Exact Locations of Controls in Adjustment Center

CONTROL	TOP	LEFT	HEIGHT	WIDTH
Name and Salary Command Button	241.5	58.5	27	90.75
Employee Investment Label	276	51.75	13.5	102.75
Employee Investment Scroll Bar	293.25	40.5	12.75	124.5
Employee Investment 0 Label	294	32.25	13.5	6.75
Employee Investment 13 Label	294	168	13.5	12
Adjustment Center Label	234.75	168	22.5	200.25
Employer Match Check Box	272.25	226.5	16.5	99
Employer Match Scroll Bar	293.25	209.25	12.75	124.5
Employer Match 0 Label	294	200.25	13.5	6.75
Employer Match 6 Label	294	337.5	13.5	6.75
Annual Return Label	237	399	12	102
Annual Return Spin Button	252.75	462	17.25	13.5
Annual Return Label	252.75	432	17.25	30
Years of Service Label	273.75	401.25	12	102
Years of Service Spin Button	288	462	17.25	13.5
Years of Service Label	288	432	17.25	30

The following steps resize and reposition the controls in the Adjustment Center using the values in Table 7-6.

To Resize and Reposition the Controls in the Adjustment Center

1 Click the Properties button on the Control Toolbox toolbar. Drag the Properties window to the right side of the Excel window. Click the Name and Salary button. Change its Top, Left, Height, and Width properties to those listed in Table 7-6.

The Name and Salary Command Button control Properties window displays as shown in Figure 7-77.

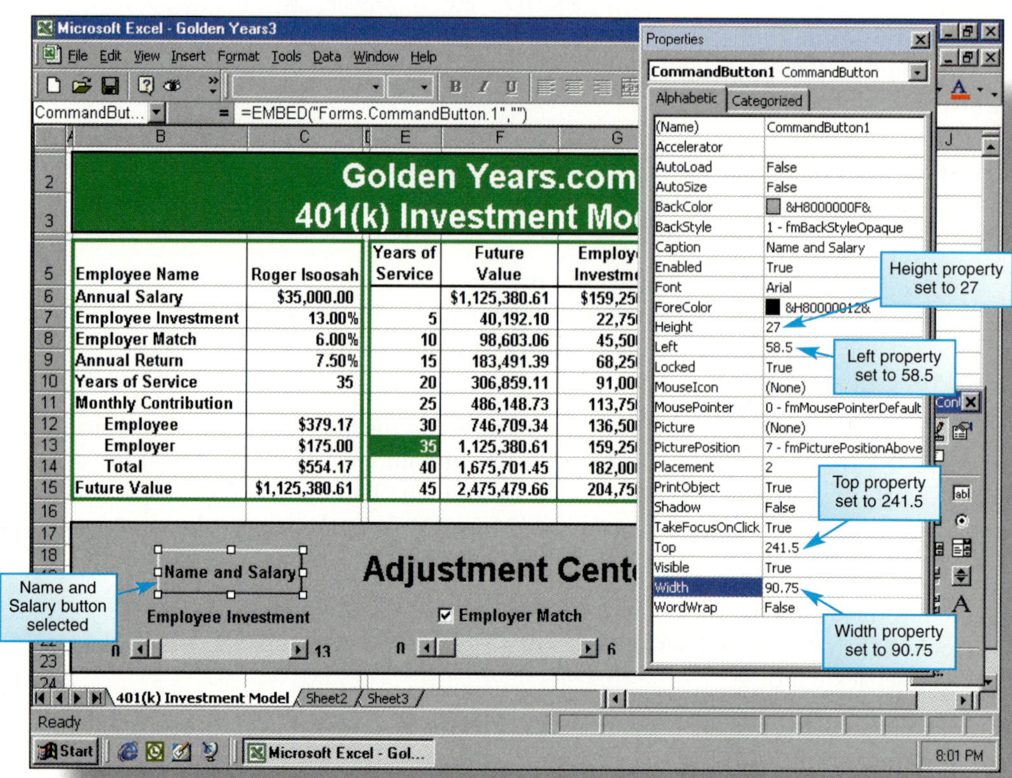

FIGURE 7-77

2 One at a time, select the controls and change their Top, Left, Height, and Width properties to those listed in Table 7-6. Close the Properties window and then deselect the Years of Service label by clicking cell A1.

The Adjustment Center displays as shown in Figure 7-78.

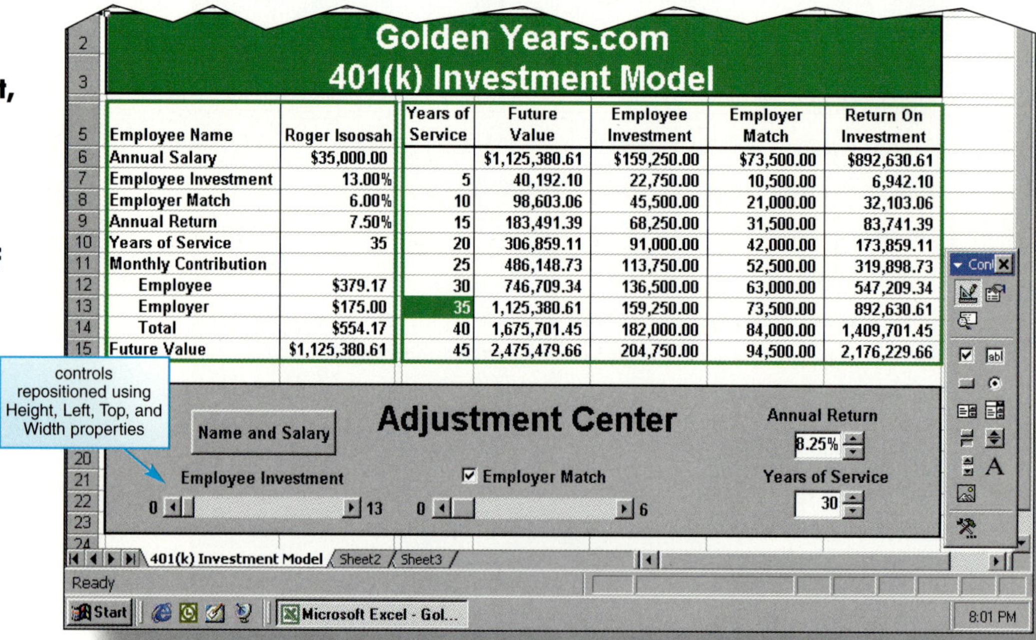

FIGURE 7-78

3 Click the Save button on the Standard toolbar.

Excel saves the workbook using the file name Golden Years3.

Step 3 – Write the Code

The next step is to write a procedure for each of the following six controls: (1) Name and Salary Button; (2) Employee Investment Scroll Bar; (3) Employer Match Check Box; (4) Employer Match Scroll Bar; (5) Annual Return Spin Button; and (6) Years of Service Spin Button.

NAME AND SALARY BUTTON PROCEDURE The function of the Name and Salary button is to accept the employee name and annual salary. It also assigns values to the names of the Scroll Bar controls and Spin Button controls, which in turn resets the values in the range C7:C10. The Name and Salary Button procedure is shown in Table 7-7.

Table 7-7 Name and Salary Button Procedure

LINE *VBA CODE*

```
1   ' Name and Salary Button Procedure                        Author:    Thomas Ryan
2   ' Date Created: 12/5/2001
3   ' Run from:      401(k) Investment Model Sheet by clicking button labeled Name and
4   '                Salary
5   ' Function:      This procedure initializes the scroll bars and spin buttons,
6   '                clears the range C5:C6, selects cell A1, accepts the employee
7   '                name (cell C5) and annual salary (cell C6), and validates the
8   '                annual salary before assigning it to cell C6.
9   '
10  Private Sub CommandButton1_Click()
11     scrEmployeeInvest = 100
12     scrEmployerMatch = 0
13     spnAnnualReturn = 500
14     spnYearsofService = 10
15     Range("C5:C6").ClearContents
16     Range("A1").Select
17     Range("C5").Value = InputBox("Employee Name?", "Enter")
18     AnnualSalary = InputBox("Annual Salary?", "Enter")
19     Do While AnnualSalary <= 0
20        AnnualSalary = InputBox("Annual salary must be >= to zero.", "Please Re-enter")
21     Loop
22     Range("C6").Value = AnnualSalary
23  End Sub
```

In Table 7-7, lines 1 through 9 are comments and have no bearing on the execution of this procedure. Comments help you remember the function of a procedure. Lines 10 and 23 identify the beginning and end of the procedure. Lines 11 through 14 initialize the Scroll Bar controls and Spin Buttons controls by assigning values to their names. Line 15 clears cells C5 and C6 in preparation to receive the employee name and annual salary. Line 16 selects cell A1 so the heavy border surrounding the active cell does not clutter the screen.

Line 17 accepts the employee name and assigns it to cell C5. Lines 18 through 22 accept and validate the annual salary to ensure it is greater than zero. The annual salary is accepted in line 18. Line 19 is called a **Do-While statement.** It tests to see if the annual salary accepted in line 18 is less than or equal to zero. If the annual salary is less than or equal to zero, line 20 displays an error message and requests that the user reenter the annual salary. The **Loop statement** in line 21 transfers control back to the corresponding Do-While statement in line 19, which tests the annual salary again.

Looping

VBA has several statements that allow looping through a series of statements. They are Do-While or Do-Until, which loops while or until a condition is True; For-Next, which uses a counter to repeat statements a specified number of times; and For Each-Next, which repeats a group of statements for each object in a collection.

The VBA code in lines 19 through 21 is called a **loop**. If the variable AnnualSalary is greater than zero, then the Do-While statement in line 19 transfers control to line 22, which assigns the value of AnnualSalary to cell C6. Line 23 halts execution of the procedure and returns Excel to Ready mode.

The variable AnnualSalary first was used in line 18. A **variable** is a location in the computer's memory whose value can change as the program executes. You create variables in VBA code as you need them. In this case, a variable is needed to hold the value accepted from the user in lines 18 and 20. Variable names follow the same rules as control names (see page E 7.46).

The following steps enter the Name and Salary Button procedure shown in Table 7-7 on the previous page.

To Enter the Name and Salary Button Procedure

1 With Excel in Design mode, click the View Code button on the Control Toolbox toolbar (see Figure 7-38 on page E 7.33). Click the Object box arrow at the top of the window and then click CommandButton1 in the alphabetical list.

The Visual Basic Editor starts. When the CommandButton1 control is selected, the Visual Basic Editor displays the Sub and End Sub statements for the procedure and positions the insertion point between the two statements (Figure 7-79).

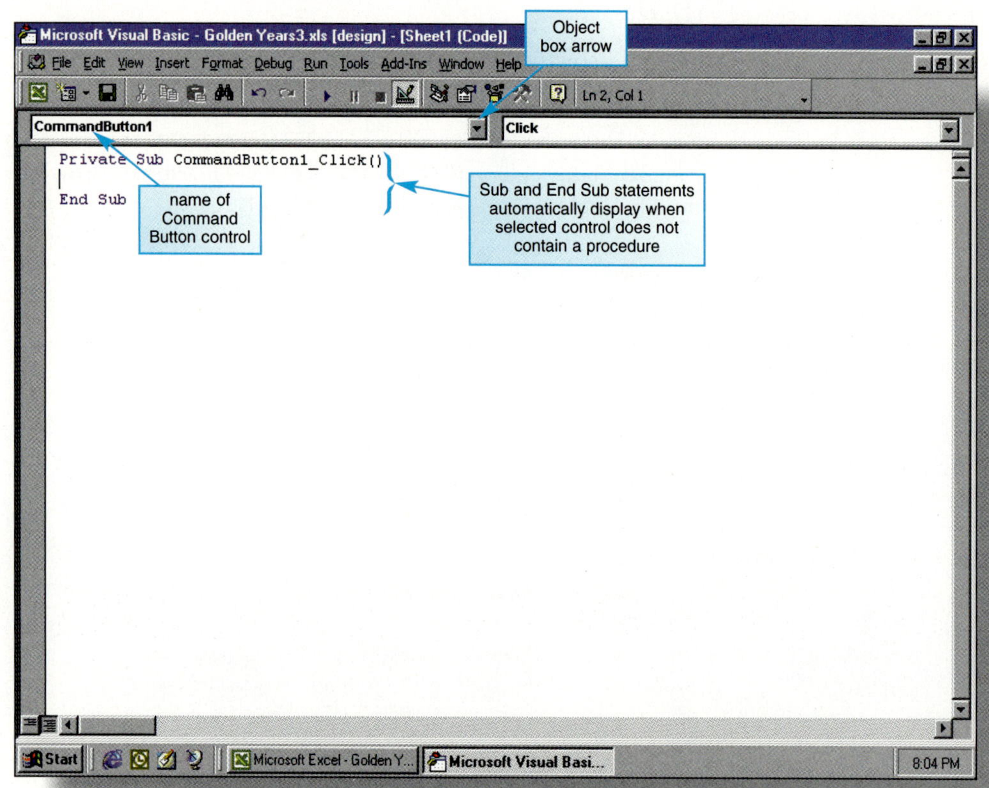

FIGURE 7-79

2 **Click before the P in Private and then press the ENTER key. Enter the lines 1 through 9 in Table 7-7 on page E 7.61. Click the blank line between the Sub and End Sub statements. Enter lines 11 through 22 in Table 7-7.**

The Name and Salary Button procedure displays as shown in Figure 7-80.

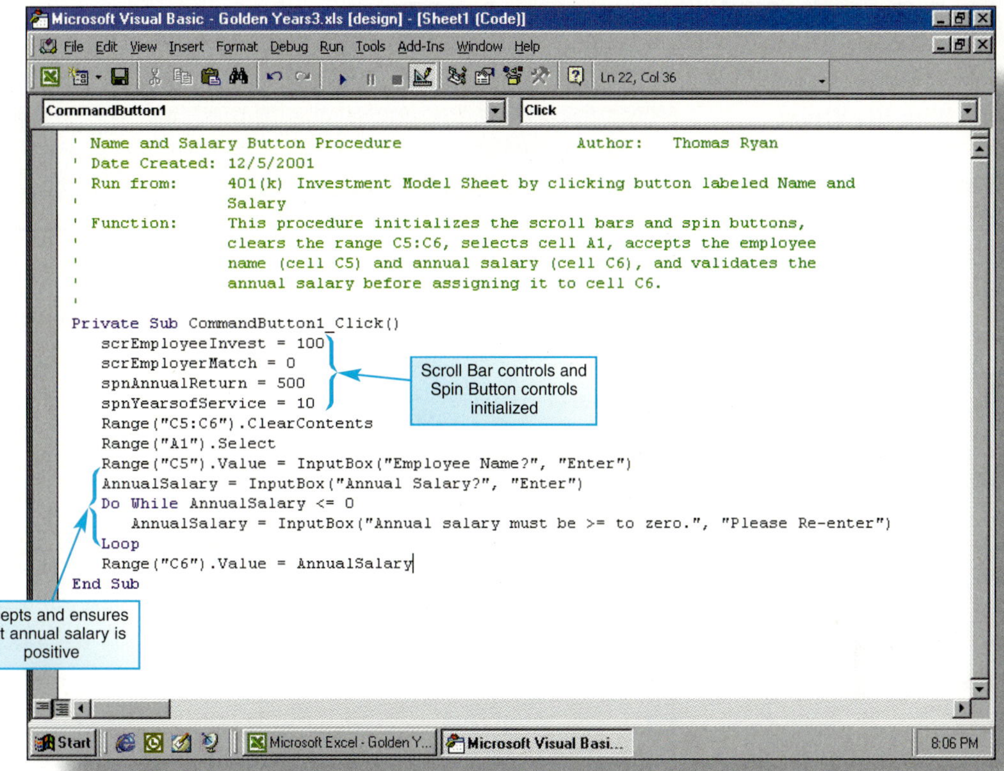

FIGURE 7-80

EMPLOYEE INVESTMENT SCROLL BAR PROCEDURE The Employee Investment Scroll Bar procedure assigns the value of the scroll bar to cell C7. The procedure is shown in Table 7-8.

Table 7-8 Employee Investment Scroll Bar Procedure

LINE	STATEMENT
1	' Employee Investment Scroll Bar Procedure Author: Thomas Ryan
2	' Date Created: 12/5/2001
3	' Run from: 401(k) Investment Model Sheet by clicking the scroll bar labeled
4	' Employee Investment
5	' Function: This procedure assigns the value of the Employee Investment scroll
6	' bar to cell C7.
7	'
8	Private Sub scrEmployeeInvest_Change()
9	Range("C7").Value = scrEmployeeInvest.Value / 10000
10	End Sub

In Table 7-8, the first seven lines are comments. Lines 8 and 10 define the beginning and end of the procedure. Line 9 assigns the value of the Scroll Bar control (scrEmployeeInvest) divided by 10000 to cell C7. Recall that the scroll bar was assigned a Max property of 1300, which is equivalent to 130,000%. Thus, the value of scrEmployeeInvest must be divided by 10000 to assign the correct percentage value to cell C7. The steps on the next page enter the Employee Investment Scroll bar procedure shown in Table 7-8.

To Enter the Employee Investment Scroll Bar Procedure

1 **With the Visual Basic Editor active, click the Object box arrow at the top of the window and then click scrEmployeeInvest.**

The Visual Basic Editor displays the Sub and End Sub statements for this procedure and positions the insertion point between the two statements.

2 **Enter the VBA code shown in Table 7-8 on the previous page.**

The Employee Investment Scroll Bar procedure displays as shown in Figure 7-81.

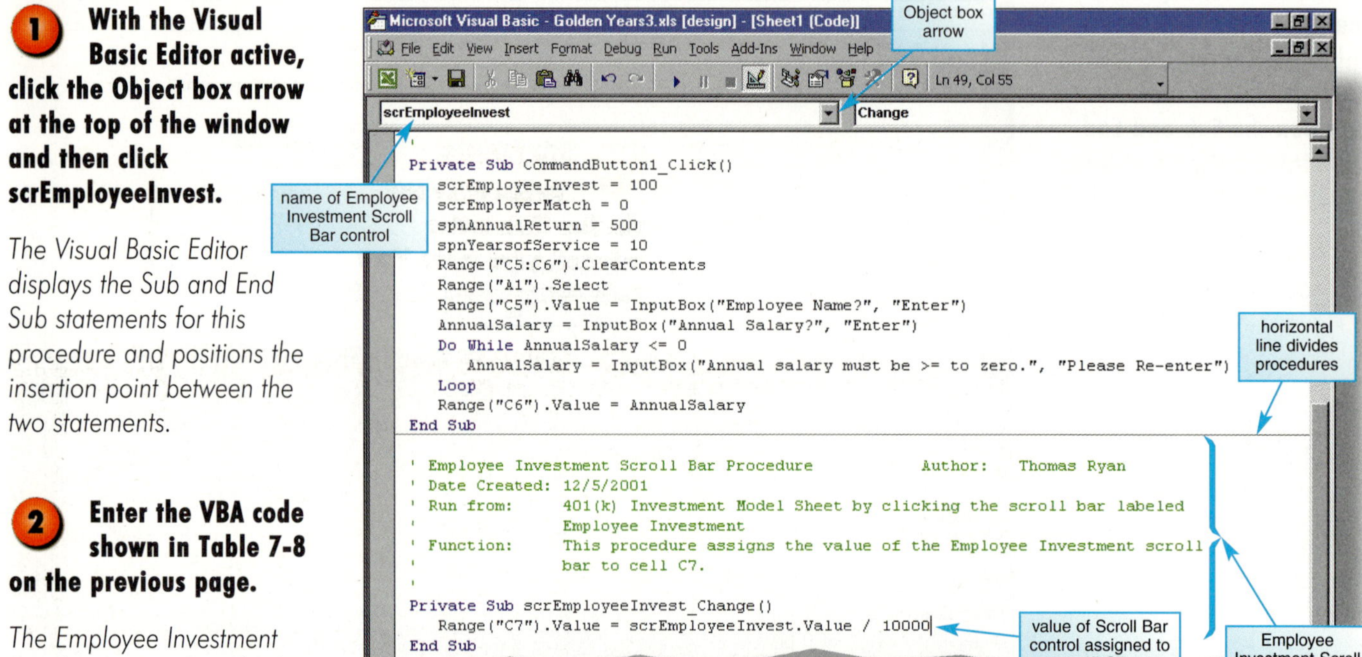
Microsoft Visual Basic - Golden Years3.xls [design] - [Sheet1 (Code)]
Object box arrow
Ln 49, Col 55
scrEmployeeInvest
Change
name of Employee Investment Scroll Bar control
Private Sub CommandButton1_Click()
scrEmployeeInvest = 100
scrEmployerMatch = 0
spnAnnualReturn = 500
spnYearsofService = 10
Range("C5:C6").ClearContents
Range("A1").Select
Range("C5").Value = InputBox("Employee Name?", "Enter")
AnnualSalary = InputBox("Annual Salary?", "Enter")
Do While AnnualSalary <= 0
AnnualSalary = InputBox("Annual salary must be >= to zero.", "Please Re-enter")
Loop
Range("C6").Value = AnnualSalary
End Sub
horizontal line divides procedures
' Employee Investment Scroll Bar Procedure Author: Thomas Ryan
' Date Created: 12/5/2001
' Run from: 401(k) Investment Model Sheet by clicking the scroll bar labeled
' Employee Investment
' Function: This procedure assigns the value of the Employee Investment scroll
' bar to cell C7.
Private Sub scrEmployeeInvest_Change()
Range("C7").Value = scrEmployeeInvest.Value / 10000
End Sub
value of Scroll Bar control assigned to cell C7
Employee Investment Scroll Bar procedure

FIGURE 7-81

EMPLOYER MATCH CHECK BOX PROCEDURE As with the other procedures, the Employer Match Check Box procedure executes only when you click the check box. If the check box is checked, then the name of the check box (chkEmployerMatch) is equal to the logical value True. If the check box is unchecked, then the name of the check box is equal to the logical value False. Adding a check mark or removing a check mark triggers the event that executes the Employee Match Check Box procedure shown in Table 7-9.

Table 7-9 Employer Match Check Box Procedure

LINE *STATEMENT*

```
' Employer Match Check Box Procedure                    Author:   Thomas Ryan
' Date Created: 12/5/2001
' Run from:     401(k) Investment Model Sheet by clicking check box labeled
'               Employer Match
' Function:     This procedure assigns the value of the Employer Match scroll bar
'               or 0 (zero) to cell C8.
'
Private Sub chkEmployerMatch_Click()
   If chkEmployerMatch.Value = True Then
      Range("C8").Value = scrEmployerMatch.Value / 10000
   Else
      scrEmployerMatch = 0
      Range("C8").Value = 0
   End If
End Sub
```

In Table 7-9, lines 1 through 7 are comments. Lines 8 and 15 define the beginning and end of the procedure. Lines 9 through 14 include an If-Then-Else statement. An **If-Then-Else statement** represents a two-way decision with action specified for each of the two alternatives. The computer never executes both the true and false alternatives. It selects one or the other.

If the logical test (chkEmployerMatch = True) is true in line 9 of Table 7-9, then line 10 is executed and cell C8 is set equal to scrEmployerMatch divided by 10000. If the logical test is false, then lines 12 and 13 are executed. Line 12 repositions the scroll box to zero percent (0%) and line 13 sets cell C8 equal to zero percent (0%). The following steps enter the code.

To Enter the Employer Match Check Box Procedure

1 With the Visual Basic Editor active, click the Object box arrow at the top of the window and then click chkEmployerMatch.

The Visual Basic Editor displays the Sub and End Sub statements for this procedure and positions the insertion point between the two statements.

2 Enter the VBA code shown in Table 7-9.

The Employer Match Check Box procedure displays as shown in Figure 7-82.

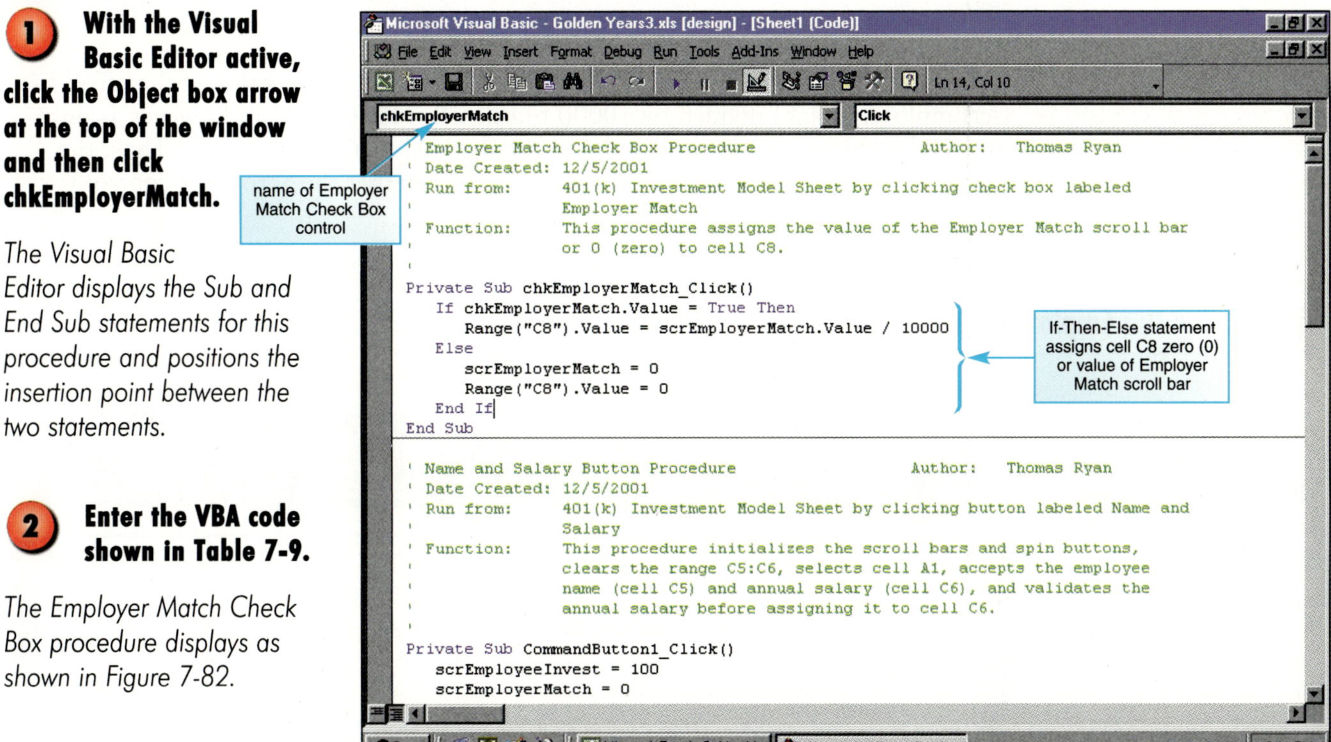

FIGURE 7-82

EMPLOYER MATCH SCROLL BAR PROCEDURE The Employer Match Scroll Bar procedure executes whenever you use the Scroll Bar control below the check box. The Scroll Bar control is active only when the Employer Match Check Box control is checked. The Scroll Bar control event assigns the value of scrEmployerMatch to cell C8. The Employer Match Scroll Bar procedure is shown in Table 7-10.

Table 7-10 Employer Match Scroll Bar Procedure

```
LINE  STATEMENT
1     ' Employer Match Scroll Bar Procedure                Author:   Thomas Ryan
2     ' Date Created: 12/5/2001
3     ' Run from:     401(k) Investment Model Sheet by clicking the scroll bar labeled
4     '               Employer Match
5     ' Function:     This procedure assigns the value of the Employer Match scroll bar
6     '               to cell C8.
7     '
8     Private Sub scrEmployerMatch_Change()
9        If chkEmployerMatch.Value = True Then
10          Range("C8").Value = scrEmployerMatch.Value / 10000
11       End If
12    End Sub
```

In Table 7-10, line 10 in the If-Then statement assigns the value of the scroll bar (scrEmployerMatch) divided by 10000 to cell C8. This statement, however, is only executed if the logical test in line 9 (chkEmployerMatch =True) is true. Thus, the Employer Match Check Box control determines whether the Scroll Bar control is active. The following steps enter the code.

To Enter the Employer Match Scroll Bar Procedure

1 **With the Visual Basic Editor active, click the Object box arrow at the top of the window and then click scrEmployerMatch.**

The Visual Basic Editor displays the Sub and End Sub statements for this procedure and positions the insertion point between the two statements.

2 **Enter the VBA code shown in Table 7-10.**

The Employer Match Scroll Bar procedure displays as shown in Figure 7-83.

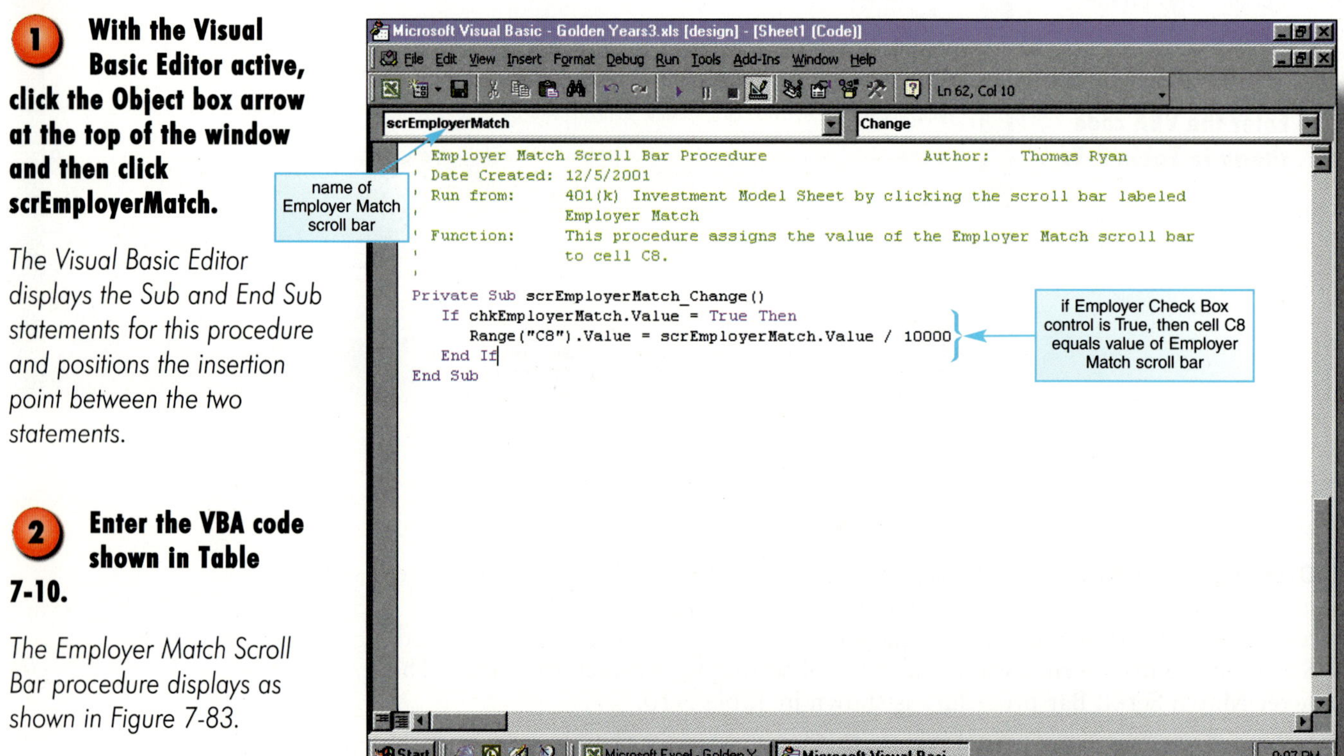

FIGURE 7-83

ANNUAL RETURN SPIN BUTTON PROCEDURE The Annual Return Spin Button procedure executes whenever you click one of it buttons. Its function is to set the percent value in cell C9 and in the corresponding Label control. Recall that you set the SmallChange property to 25, which when divided by 1000 equals 0.25%. The Annual Return Spin Button Control procedure is shown in Table 7-11.

Table 7-11 Annual Return Spin Button Procedure

LINE	STATEMENT
1	`' Annual Return Spin Button Procedure                Author:   Thomas Ryan`
2	`' Date Created: 12/5/2001`
3	`' Run from:       401(k) Investment Model Sheet by clicking the spin button`
4	`'                 labeled Annual Return`
5	`' Function:       This procedure assigns the value of the Annual Return spin button`
6	`'                 to cell C9.`
7	`'`
8	`Private Sub spnAnnualReturn_Change()`
9	`   lblAnnualReturn = spnAnnualReturn.Value / 100 & "%"`
10	`   Range("C9").Value = spnAnnualReturn.Value / 10000`
11	`End Sub`

In Table 7-11, line 9 uses the names of the two controls to assign the value of the Spin Button control to the Label control. In this case, spnAnnualReturn is divided by 100 because a percent should display as a whole number percent in the Label control. The & "%" at the end of line 9 appends a percent sign to the value. Line 10 assigns the value of spnAnnualReturn divided by 10000 to cell C9. The following steps enter the code.

To Enter the Annual Return Spin Button Procedure

1 With the Visual Basic Editor active, click the Object box arrow at the top of the window and then click spnAnnualReturn.

The Visual Basic Editor displays the Sub and End Sub statements for this procedure and positions the insertion point between the two statements.

2 Enter the VBA code shown in Table 7-11.

The Annual Return Spin Button procedure displays as shown in Figure 7-84.

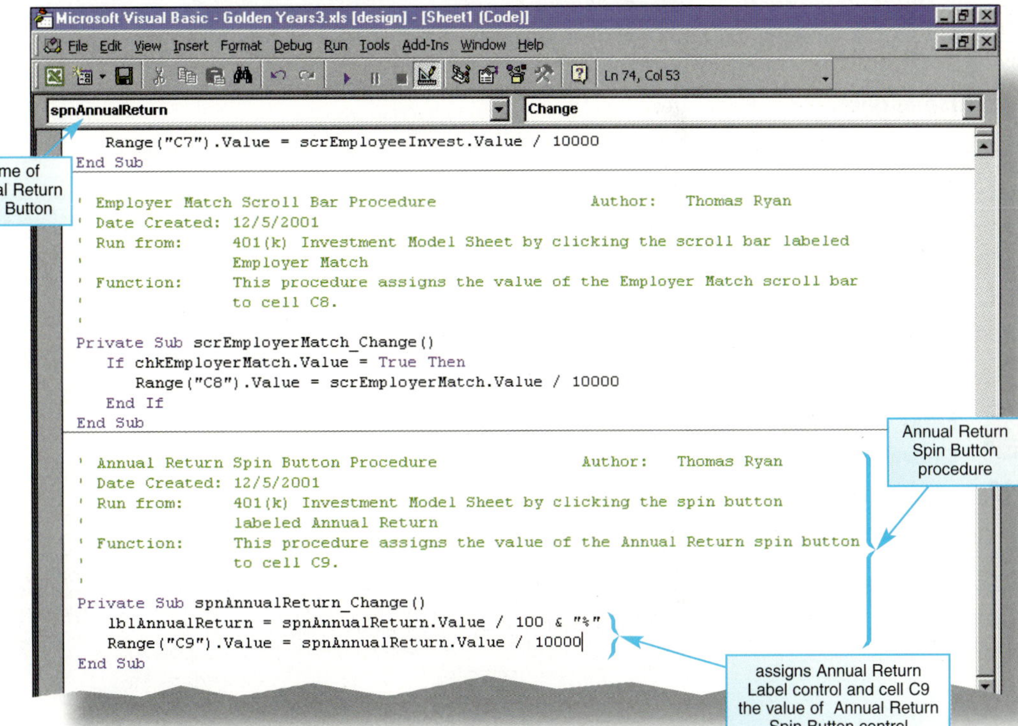

FIGURE 7-84

YEARS OF SERVICE SPIN BUTTON PROCEDURE The Years of Service Spin Button procedure determines the value assigned to cell C10 and in the corresponding Label control and is executed by Excel when the user clicks one of the buttons making up the Spin Button control. The procedure is shown in Table 7-12.

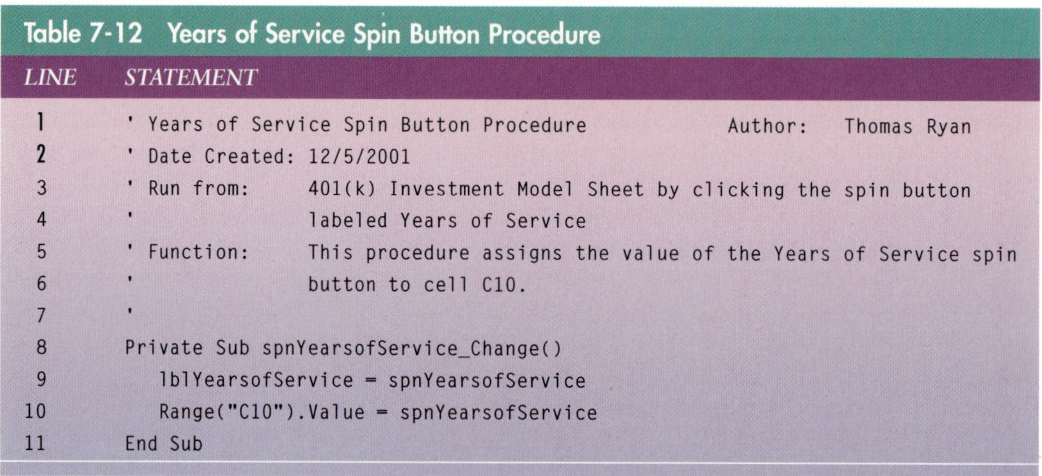

Table 7-12 Years of Service Spin Button Procedure

LINE	STATEMENT
1	' Years of Service Spin Button Procedure Author: Thomas Ryan
2	' Date Created: 12/5/2001
3	' Run from: 401(k) Investment Model Sheet by clicking the spin button
4	' labeled Years of Service
5	' Function: This procedure assigns the value of the Years of Service spin
6	' button to cell C10.
7	'
8	Private Sub spnYearsofService_Change()
9	lblYearsofService = spnYearsofService
10	Range("C10").Value = spnYearsofService
11	End Sub

In Table 7-12, line 9 assigns spnYearsofService (value of the Spin Button control) to the corresponding Label control. Line 10 assigns the value of spnYearsofService to cell C10. The following steps enter the code.

Steps To Enter the Years of Service Spin Button Procedure

1 With the Visual Basic Editor active, click the Object box arrow at the top of the window and then click spnYearsofService.

The Visual Basic Editor displays the Sub and End Sub statements for this procedure and positions the insertion point between the two statements.

2 Enter the VBA code shown in Table 7-12.

The Years of Service Spin Button procedure displays as shown in Figure 7-85.

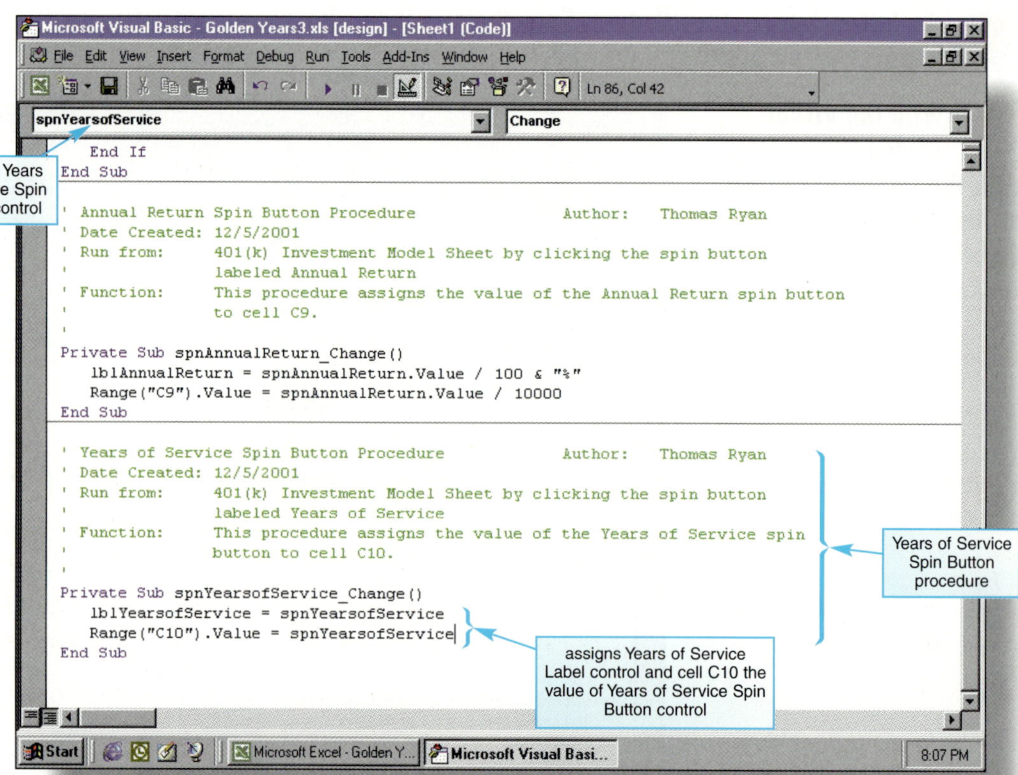

FIGURE 7-85

The VBA code is complete. The following steps close the Visual Basic Editor, quit Design mode, protect the worksheet, and save the workbook. Before closing the Visual Basic Editor, you should verify your code by comparing it with Figures 7-80 through 7-85.

TO CLOSE THE VISUAL BASIC EDITOR, PROTECT THE WORKSHEET, AND SAVE THE WORKBOOK

1. Click the Close button on the right side of the Visual Basic Editor title bar.
2. When the Excel window displays, click the Exit Design Mode button on the Control Toolbox toolbar. Close the Control Toolbox toolbar.
3. Click Tools on the menu bar, point to Protection, and then click Protect Sheet. When the Protect dialog box displays, enter `fortune` in the Password text box. Verify the password when prompted.
4. Click the Save button on the Standard toolbar to save the workbook using the file name Golden Years3.

Debugging VBA Code

The Visual Basic Editor allows you to locate the source of errors in your code using the Debug menu. You can set breakpoints in your code that will cause Excel to stop executing your code at a certain point. At that time, Excel shows the current executing code in the Editor. You can point at variables in your code to make sure they are set correctly. Alternatively, you can step through your code line by line to make sure that the code is being executed in the order that you expect it to. Click Microsoft Visual Basic Help on the Help menu in the Visual Basic Editor for more information about debugging.

Testing the Controls

The final step is to test the controls in the Adjustment Center. Use the following data: Employee Name – Ukari Eiffel; Annual Salary (cell C6) — $56,000.00; Employee Investment (cell C7) – 10%; Employer Match (cell C8) – 5%; Annual Return (cell C9) – 8.25%; and Years of Service (cell C10) – 30.

TO TEST THE CONTROLS IN THE ADJUSTMENT CENTER USER INTERFACE

1. Click the Name and Salary button in the Adjustment Center.
2. When Excel displays the Enter dialog box with the prompt message, Employee Name?, type `Ukari Eiffel` as the employee name.
3. When Excel displays the Enter dialog box with the prompt message, Annual Salary? Type the negative number `-56000` as the annual salary.
4. When Excel displays the Enter dialog box with the prompt message, Annual salary must be >= to zero. Type `56000` as the annual salary.
5. Use the Employee Investment scroll bar to change the value in cell C7 to 10%.
6. Click the Employer Match check box if it does not have a check mark.
7. Use the Employer Match scroll bar to change the value in cell C8 to 5%.
8. Click the Annual Return spin button arrows to change the value in cell C9 to 8.25%.
9. Click the Years of Service spin button arrows to change the value in cell C10 to 30.

The future value of Ukari Eiffel's 401(k) investment is $1,097,753.30 as shown in cell C15 of Figure 7-86 on the next page. If she changes her years of service to 45 years, the 401(k) investment is worth $4,015,614.71 (cell F15). Both future value amounts assume she will never get a raise.

More About 2000

The Visual Basic Editor

When you open the Visual Basic Editor, the same Visual Basic windows display that displayed when you closed it the last time.

More About

Quick Reference

For a table that lists how to complete the tasks covered in this book using the mouse, menu, shortcut menu, and keyboard, see the Excel Quick Reference Summary at the back of this book or visit the Office 2000 Web page (www.scsite.com/office 2000/qr.htm), and then click Microsoft Excel 2000.

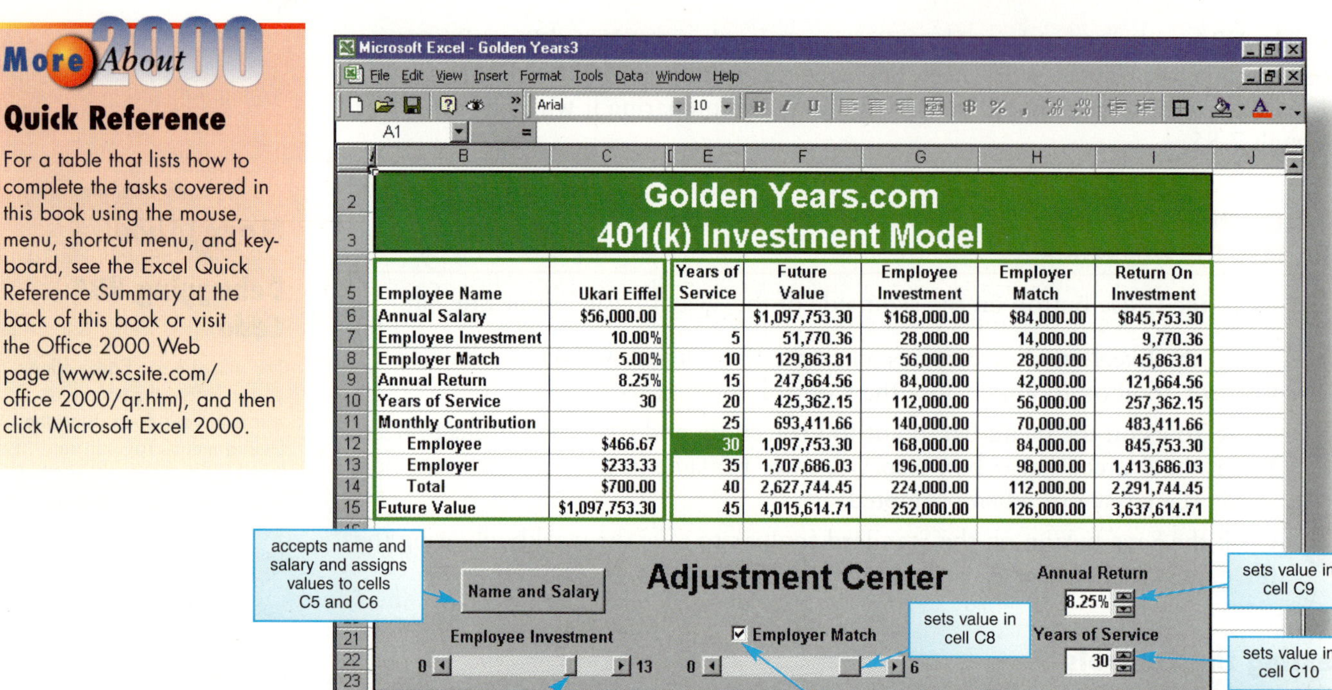

Employee Name	Ukari Eiffel	Years of Service	Future Value	Employee Investment	Employer Match	Return On Investment
Annual Salary	$56,000.00		$1,097,753.30	$168,000.00	$84,000.00	$845,753.30
Employee Investment	10.00%	5	51,770.36	28,000.00	14,000.00	9,770.36
Employer Match	5.00%	10	129,863.81	56,000.00	28,000.00	45,863.81
Annual Return	8.25%	15	247,664.56	84,000.00	42,000.00	121,664.56
Years of Service	30	20	425,362.15	112,000.00	56,000.00	257,362.15
Monthly Contribution		25	693,411.66	140,000.00	70,000.00	483,411.66
Employee	$466.67	30	1,097,753.30	168,000.00	84,000.00	845,753.30
Employer	$233.33	35	1,707,686.03	196,000.00	98,000.00	1,413,686.03
Total	$700.00	40	2,627,744.45	224,000.00	112,000.00	2,291,744.45
Future Value	$1,097,753.30	45	4,015,614.71	252,000.00	126,000.00	3,637,614.71

FIGURE 7-86

Microsoft Certification

The Microsoft Office User Specialist (MOUS) Certification program provides an opportunity for you to obtain a valuable industry credential – proof that you have the Excel 2000 skills required by employers. For more information, see Appendix D or visit the Shelly Cashman Series MOUS Web page at www.scsite.com/off2000/cert.htm.

If the controls in the Adjustment Center do not work as indicated here, then unprotect the worksheet, display the Control Toolbox toolbar, click the Design Mode button on the Control Toolbox toolbar, and check the controls' properties and VBA code.

Quitting Excel

The project is complete. To quit Excel, follow the steps below.

TO QUIT EXCEL

1. Click the Close button on the right side of the title bar.
2. If the Microsoft Excel dialog box displays, click the No button.

CASE PERSPECTIVE SUMMARY

With the three workbooks developed in this project, the vice president of personnel, Nelson Portugal, can post the new workbook to the intranet as you complete each phase. The final phase, Golden Years3, includes the easy-to-use Adjustment Center interface that allows the user to enter any reasonable 401(k) data with ease, and quickly determine the future value of the investment.

Project Summary

In this project, you learned how to unprotect and protect a worksheet and workbook using a password. In Phase 1, you learned how to record a macro and assign it to a button on a toolbar and to a command on a menu. In Phase 2, you learned how to create a Command Button control, assign it properties, and write VBA code that executes when you click the button. In Phase 3, you learned how to create a user interface made up of a Command Button control, Scroll Bar controls, a Check Box control, Label controls, and Spin Button controls. In this phase, you learned about many of the frequently used properties in Visual Basic for Applications. You also learned how to write VBA code that included looping and decision making.

What You Should Know

Having completed this project, you should be able to perform the following tasks:

- Add a Button to a Toolbar, Assign the Button a Macro, and Use the Button (*E 7.18*)
- Add a Command Button Control to the Worksheet (*E 7.27*)
- Add a Command to a Menu, Assign the Command a Macro, and Invoke the Command (*E 7.22*)
- Add Controls to a User Interface (*E 7.42*)
- Automate Data Entry by Selecting a Range of Cells (*E 7.8*)
- Close the Visual Basic Editor, Protect the Worksheet, and Save the Workbook (*E 7.69*)
- Enter 401(k) Data Using the New Data Button (*E 7.36*)
- Enter the Annual Return Spin Button Procedure (*E 7.67*)
- Enter the Employee Investment Scroll Bar Procedure (*E 7.64*)
- Enter the Employer Match Check Box Procedure (*E 7.65*)
- Enter the Employer Match Scroll Bar Procedure (*E 7.66*)
- Enter the Name and Salary Button Procedure (*E 7.62*)
- Enter the New Data Button Procedure (*E 7.33*)
- Enter the Years of Service Spin Button Procedure (*E 7.68*)
- Open a Workbook with a Macro and Execute the Macro (*E 7.15*)
- Open and Save a Workbook, Unprotect a Worksheet, and Display the Control Toolbox Toolbar (*E 7.41*)
- Protect a Worksheet and Save the Workbook (*E 7.40*)
- Password-Protect the Worksheet, Save the Workbook, and Close the Workbook (*E 7.14*)
- Quit Excel (*E 7.70*)
- Record a Macro to Print the Worksheet in Portrait Orientation Using the Fit to Option (*E 7.11*)
- Resize and Reposition the Controls in the Adjustment Center (*E 7.60*)
- Set Properties for the Annual Return Spin Button and Years of Service Spin Button (*E 7.56*)
- Set Properties of the Constant Label Controls and Check Box Control (*E 7.47*)
- Set the Command Button Control Properties (*E 7.30, E 7.52*)
- Set the Employee Investment Scroll Bar Properties (*E 7.53*)
- Set the Employer Match Check Box Properties (*E 7.55*)
- Set the Employer Match Scroll Bar Properties (*E 7.54*)
- Set the Label Control Properties for the Annual Return and Years of Service Spin Button (*E 7.57*)
- Start Excel and Open a Workbook (*E 7.6*)
- Test the Controls in the Adjustment Center User Interface (*E 7.69*)
- Undo a Group of Entries Using the Undo Button (*E 7.9*)
- Unprotect a Password-Protected Worksheet (*E 7.9*)
- View a Macro's VBA Code (*E 7.16*)

1 Creating Macros and Customizing Menus and Toolbars

Instructions: Start Excel and perform the following tasks.

1. Open the Black Hat Cabinetry payroll workbook (Figure 7-87a) from the Data Disk. If you do not have a copy of the Data Disk, then see the inside back cover of this book.
2. Reset the toolbars to their installation settings (see Step 6 on page E 7.6).
3. Unprotect the worksheet. The password is black.
4. Enter your name, course, laboratory assignment number (Apply 7-1), date, and instructor name in the range A11:A15.
5. Use the Record New Macro command to create a macro that prints the range A2:B15. Call the macro PrintNameRate, use the shortcut CTRL+N, change the name of the author in the Description box to your name, and store the macro in this workbook. When the Stop Recording toolbar displays, do the following: (a) select the range A2:B15; (b) click File on the menu bar and then click Print; (c) click the Selection option in the Print what area of the Print dialog box; (d) click the OK button; and (e) click the Stop Recording button on the Stop Recording toolbar.
6. Press ALT+F8 to display the Macro dialog box. Run the PrintNameRate macro. Press ALT+F8 to display the Macro dialog box a second time. Select the PrintNameRate macro and then click the Edit button. When the Visual Basic Editor displays the macro, click File on the menu bar and then click Print. Hand in both printouts to your instructor.
7. Add a button to the Standard toolbar (Figure 7-87a) and a command to the File menu (Figure 7-87b). Assign the button and command the PrintNameRate macro.
8. Run the macro as follows: (a) click the button you added to the Standard toolbar; (b) on the File menu, click the Print Name and Rate command; and (c) press CTRL+N. Hand in the three printouts to your instructor.
9. Protect the worksheet. Use the first six characters of your last name as the password. Save the workbook using the file name Black Hat Cabinetry1.
10. Reset the toolbars to their installation settings (see Step 6 on page E 7.6).

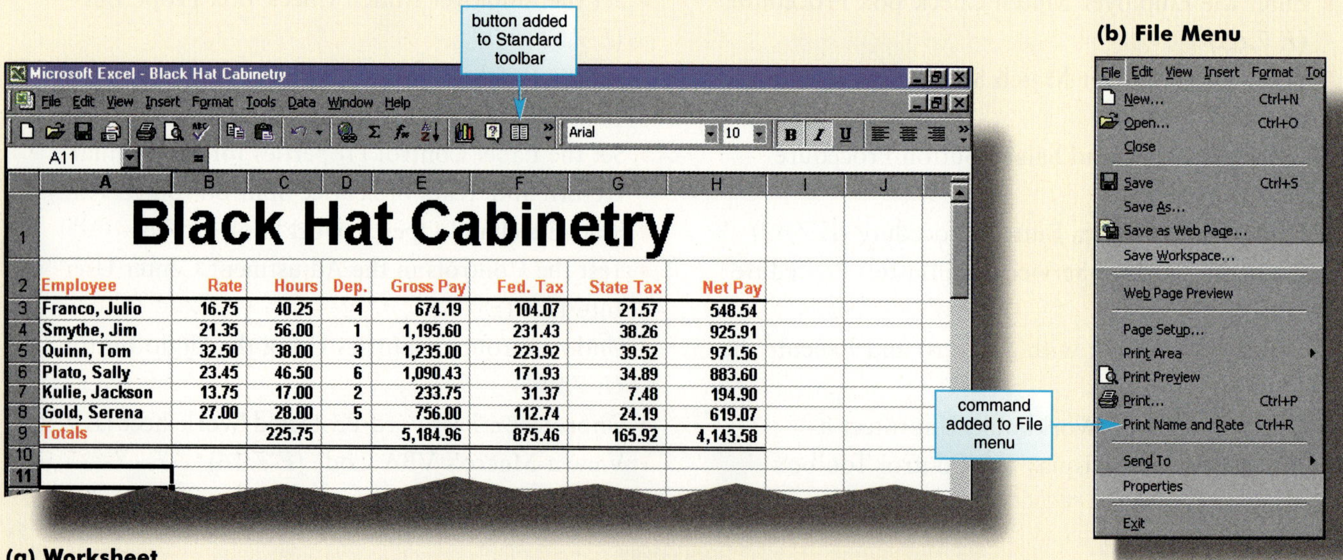

(a) Worksheet

FIGURE 7-87

1 Automating a Loan Analysis Worksheet

Problem: Your consulting firm specializes in Visual Basic for Applications. The president of Auto Loans +, Marcus Shehee, has contracted with you to automate the entry of loan data into a Loan Analysis worksheet.

Instructions Part 1: Start Excel and perform the following tasks.

1. Open the Auto Loans + workbook from the Data Disk. If you do not have a copy of the Data Disk, then see the inside back cover of this book.
2. Reset the toolbars to their installation settings (see Step 6 on page E 7.6).
3. Unprotect the Loan Analysis worksheet. The password is auto.
4. Display the Control Toolbox toolbar. Click the Command Button button on the Control Toolbox toolbar. Draw the button in the range D3:D5 as shown in Figure 7-88a on the next page.
5. With the Command Button control selected, click the Properties button on the Control Toolbox toolbar. Change the following properties: (a) Caption = Loan Data; (b) ForeColor = Purple (column 8, row 6 on the palette); and (c) PrintObject = False.
6. Click the View Code button on the Control Toolbox toolbar. Enter the procedure shown in Figure 7-88b on the next page. Check your code carefully. On the File menu, click Print to print the procedure.
7. Close the Microsoft Visual Basic Editor. Click the Exit Design Mode button on the Control Toolbox toolbar. Hide the Control Toolbox toolbar.
8. Enter your name, course, laboratory assignment number (Lab 7-1), date, and instructor name in the range B17:B21.
9. Use the newly created button to determine the monthly payment for the following loan data and print the worksheet for each data set: (a) Price = $46,500; Down Payment = $13,250; Interest Rate = 9.50%; and Years = 5; (b) Price = $29,750; Down Payment = $3,000; Interest Rate = 10.75%; and Years = 3. The Monthly Payment for (a) is $698.31 and for (b) is $872.60.
10. Protect the worksheet. Use the password auto. Save the workbook using the file name Auto Loans + Automated.

Instructions Part 2: With the workbook Auto Loans + Automated created in Part 1 open, do the following:

1. Unprotect the worksheet. The password is auto.
2. Use the Record New Macro command to create a macro that prints the formulas version of the worksheet. Call the macro PrintFormulas, use the shortcut CTRL+F, change the name of the author in the Description box to your name, and store the macro in this workbook.
3. With the Stop Recording toolbar on the screen, do the following: (a) press CTRL+SINGLE LEFT QUOTATION MARK; (b) on the File menu, click Page Setup, click Landscape option, click Fit to option, click the Print button in the Page Setup dialog box, and then click the OK button; (c) press CTRL+LEFT SINGLE QUOTATION MARK; (d) on the File menu, click Page Setup, click Portrait option, click Adjust to option, type 100 in the Adjust to box, and then click the OK button; and (e) click the Stop Recording button on the Stop Recording toolbar.
4. Press ALT+F8 to display the Macro dialog box. Run the PrintFormulas macro. Press ALT+F8 to display the Macro dialog box a second time. Select the PrintFormulas macro and then click the Edit button. When the Visual Basic Editor displays the macro, click File on the menu bar and then click Print. Hand in both printouts to your instructor.

(continued)

Automating a Loan Analysis Worksheet *(continued)*

5. Add a button to the Standard toolbar (Figure 7-88a) and a command to the File menu (Figure 7-88c). Assign the button and command the PrintFormulas macro.
6. Run the macro as follows: (a) click the button you added to the Standard toolbar; (b) on the File menu, click Print Formulas; and (c) press CTRL+F. Hand in the three printouts to your instructor. The button will not print as part of the worksheet because the PrintObject property was set to False earlier.
7. Do not protect the worksheet because the Print Formulas macro will not work with a protected worksheet. Save the workbook using the file name Auto Loans + Automated2.

(a) Worksheet

button added to Standard toolbar

Microsoft Excel - Auto Loans + Automated

Print Portrait

Auto Loans +

We Take Your Interest To Heart

Price	$32,195.00	Loan Data	Rate	8.75%
Down Payment	$6,500.00		Years	7
Loan Amount	$25,695.00		Monthly Payment	$410.16

Year	Beginning Balance	Ending Balance	Paid On Principal	Interest Paid
1	$25,695.00	$22,911.57	$2,783.43	$2,138.44
2	22,911.57	19,874.58	3,036.99	1,884.88
3	19,874.58	16,560.93	3,313.65	1,608.23
4	16,560.93	12,945.42	3,615.51	1,306.37
5	12,945.42	9,000.55	3,944.87	977.01
6	9,000.55	4,696.32	4,304.23	617.65
7	4,696.32	-	4,696.32	225.55
		Subtotal	$25,695.00	$8,758.12
		Down Payment		$6,500.00
		Total Cost		$40,953.12

(c) File Menu

File Edit View Insert Format
New... Ctrl+N
Open... Ctrl+O
Close
Save Ctrl+S
Save As...
Save as Web Page...
Web Page Preview
Page Setup...
Print Area
Print Preview
Print... Ctrl+P
Print Formulas Ctrl+F
Send To
Exit

command added to File menu

Microsoft Visual Basic - Auto Loans + Automated.xls [design] - [Sheet1 (Code)]

```
' Loan Data Button Procedure                    Author:    Jim Quasney
' Date Created: 12/12/2002
' Run from:    Loan Analysis Sheet by clicking button labeled Loan Data
' Function:    When executed, this procedure accepts loan data data which
'              causes Excel to calculate a new monthly payment.
'
Private Sub CommandButton1_Click()
   Range("C3:C4").ClearContents
   Range("F3:F4").ClearContents
   Range("A15").Select
   Range("C3").Value = InputBox("Price?", "Enter")
   Range("C4").Value = InputBox("Down Payment?", "Enter")
   Range("F3").Value = InputBox("Annual Interst Rate?", "Enter")
   Range("F4").Value = InputBox("Length of Loan in Years?", "Enter")
End Sub
```

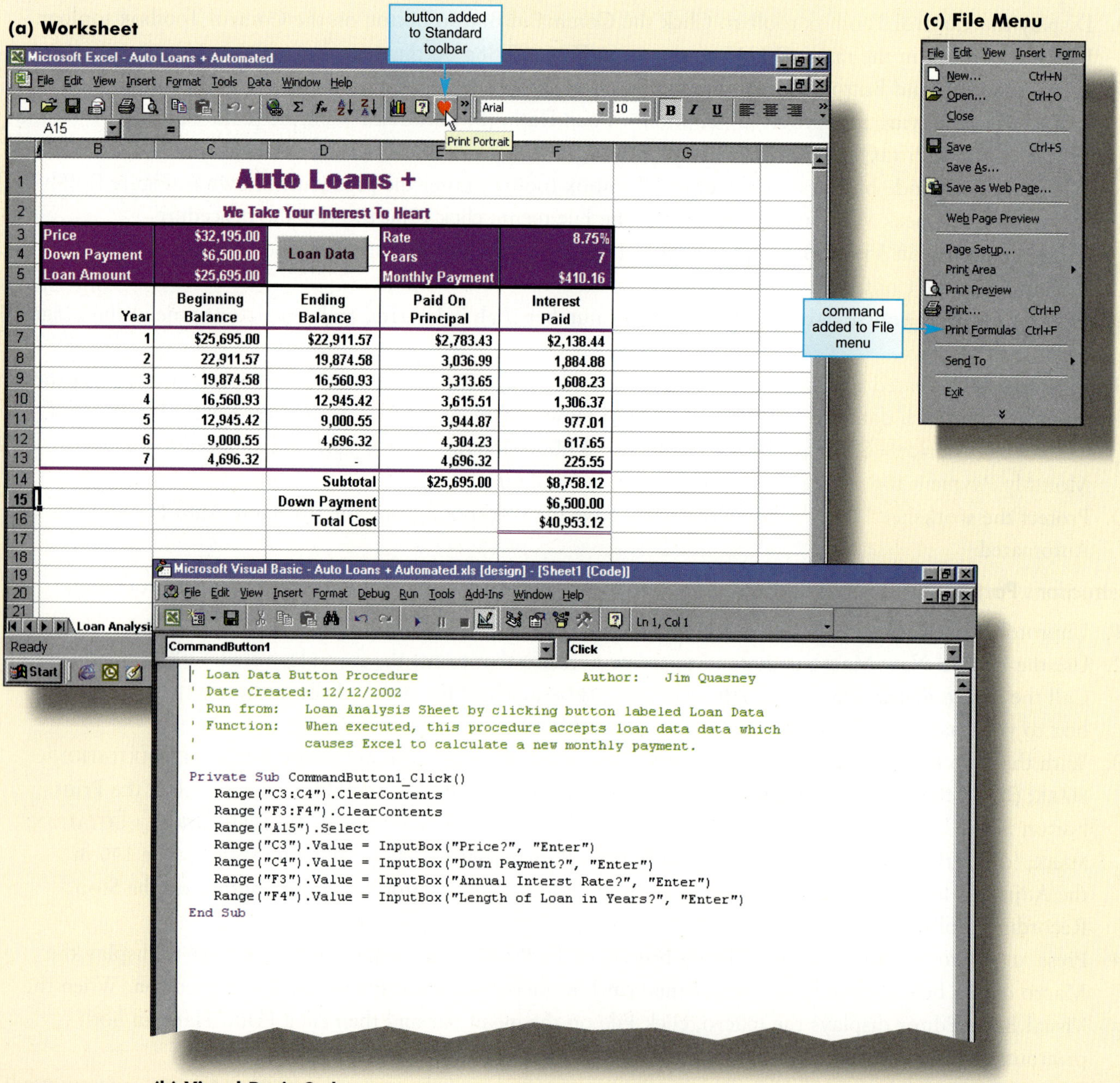

(b) Visual Basic Code

FIGURE 7-88

2 Automating a Projected Income Statement

Problem: You are in charge of the Help Desk at KT Ltd. Your primary responsibility is to help users with their computer hardware and software problems. The chief financial officer (CFO) informed your manager that she needs a workbook (Figure 7-89) automated to make it easier for her accountants to use. Because you are taking an advanced Excel course in the evening that includes Visual Basic for Applications, she has asked you to automate the data entry in cells D4 (Units Sold); D5 (Price per Unit); D14 (Material Cost per Unit); and D16 (Manufacturing Cost per Unit). All other cells in the worksheet use formulas.

Microsoft Excel - KT Ltd Automated

Row			
2	KT Ltd. Projected Income Statement		
3	Revenue		
4		Units Sold	50,000
5		Price per Unit	$20.00
6		Total Revenue	$1,000,000
7	Fixed Expenses		
8		Administrative	$125,000
9		Equipment	250,000
10		Marketing	250,000
11		Salary and Benefits	265,000
12		Total Fixed Expenses	$890,000
13	Variable Expenses		
14		Material Cost per Unit	$2.50
15		Total Material Cost	$125,000
16		Manufacturing Cost per Unit	$2.50
17		Total Manufacturing Cost	$125,000
18		Total Variable Expenses	$250,000
19	Summary		
20		Total Expenses	$1,140,000
21		Operating Income	($140,000)

Break-Even Analysis

Units	Revenue	Expenses	Income
	$1,000,000	$1,140,000	($140,000)
10,000	200,000	940,000	(740,000)
20,000	400,000	990,000	(590,000)
30,000	600,000	1,040,000	(440,000)
40,000	800,000	1,090,000	(290,000)
50,000	1,000,000	1,140,000	(140,000)
60,000	1,200,000	1,190,000	10,000
70,000	1,400,000	1,240,000	160,000
80,000	1,600,000	1,290,000	310,000
90,000	1,800,000	1,340,000	460,000
100,000	2,000,000	1,390,000	610,000

Reset — Units Sold: 0 to 100,000 — Price Per Unit $20.00 — Material Cost Per Unit $2.50 — Mfg Cost Per Unit $2.50

FIGURE 7-89

Instructions: Start Excel and complete the following tasks.

1. Open the KT Ltd workbook from the Data Disk. If you do not have a copy of the Data Disk, see the inside back cover of this book.
2. Reset the toolbars to their installation settings (see Step 6 on page E 7.6).
3. Unprotect the Projected Income Statement worksheet. The password is kt.
4. Color the background of the range F16:I21 gray (column 8, row 4 on the Fill Color palette). Draw a thick box border (column 4, row 3 on the Borders palette) around the range F16:I21.
5. Display the Control Toolbox toolbar. Use the concepts and techniques developed in this project to add the fourteen controls shown in the lower-right corner of Figure 7-89. The Units Sold scroll bar should assign a value to cell D4. The Price Per Unit spin button should assign a value to cell D5. The Material Cost Per Unit scroll button should assign a value to cell D14. The Mfg Cost Per Unit spin button should assign a value to cell D16.
6. Modify the properties of the fourteen controls as described in Table 7-13 on the next page.
7. Enter your name, course, laboratory assignment number (Lab 7-2), date, and instructor name in the range B23:B27. Save the workbook using the file name KT Ltd Automated.
8. The Reset Button procedure should set the Units Sold scroll bar (scrUnitsSold) to 50000; the Price Per Unit Spin Button (spnPrice) to 2000; the Material Cost Per Unit (spnMaterialCost) to 250; and the Mfg Cost Per Unit (spnMfgCost) to 250. It should also select cell A1.

(continued)

Automating a Projected Income Statement *(continued)*

Table 7-13 Controls and Their Properties

CONTROL	NAME	CAPTION	BACK COLOR	FONT	TEXT ALIGN	WORD WRAP	SPECIAL EFFECT	MAX	MIN	SMALL CHG	LARGE CHG
Reset Button	btnReset	Reset		8-point bold							
0 Label		0	Gray - 25%	8-point bold	Center						
Units Sold Label		Units Sold	Gray - 25%	8-point bold	Center						
100,000 Label		100,000	Gray - 25%	8-point bold	Center						
Units Sold Scroll Bar	scrUnitsSold							100000	0	100	1000
Price Per Unit Label		Price Per Unit	Gray - 25%	8-point bold	Center	True					
Price Per Unit Spin Button	spnPrice							9999	0	10	
Price Per Unit Spin Button Label		$20.00		10-point bold	Right		Sunken				
Material Cost Per Unit Label		Material Cost Per Unit	Gray - 25%	8-point bold	Center	True					
Material Cost Per Unit Spin Button	spnMaterialCost							9999	0	10	
Material Cost Per Unit Spin Button Label		$2.50		10-point bold	Right		Sunken				
Mfg Cost Per Unit Label		Mfg Cost Per Unit	Gray - 25%	8-point bold	Center	True					
Mfg Cost Per Unit Spin Button	spnMfgCost							9999	0	10	
Mfg Cost Per Unit Spin Button Label		$2.50		10-point bold	Right		Sunken				

9. The Units Sold Scroll Bar procedure should assign the value of the scroll bar (scrUnitsSold) to cell D4. For example,

```
Range("D4").Value = scrUnitsSold.Value
```

10. The Price Per Unit Spin Button procedure should assign the value of spnPrice / 100, formatted to the Currency style, to the Price Per Unit Spin Button Label control. It should also assign the value of spnPrice / 100 to cell D5. For example,

```
lblPrice = Format$(spnPrice.Value / 100, "currency")
Range("D5").Value = spnPrice.Value / 100
```

    The Format$ function in the first line formats the result that will display in the Price Per Unit Spin Button Label control to include a floating dollar sign and two decimal positions to the right of the decimal. The value assigned to cell D5 will display in the same format because the cell was formatted to the Currency style as part of the normal worksheet formatting.

11. The Material Cost Per Unit Spin Button procedure should assign the value of spnMaterialCost / 100, formatted to the Currency style, to the Material Cost Per Unit Spin Button Label control. It should also assign the value of spnMaterialCost / 100 to cell D14. For example,

```
lblMaterialCost = Format$(spnMaterialCost.Value / 100, "currency")
Range("D14").Value = spnMaterialCost.Value / 100
```

12. The Mfg Cost Per Unit Spin Button procedure should assign the value of the spnMfgCost / 100, formatted to the Currency style, to the Mfg Cost Per Unit Spin Button Label control. It should also assign the value of spnMfgCost / 100 to cell D16. For example,
```
lblMfgCost = Format$(spnMfgCost.Value / 100, "currency")
Range("D16").Value = spnMfgCost.Value / 100
```
13. Click the Microsoft Excel button on the taskbar. Click the Exit Design Mode button on the Control Toolbox toolbar. Hide the Control Toolbox toolbar. Print the worksheet.
14. Use the newly designed user interface to determine the operating income for the following projections and print the worksheet for each data set: (a) Units Sold = 72,000; Price per Unit = $22.40; Material Cost per Unit = $3.50; and Manufacturing Cost per Unit = $2.90. (b) Units Sold = 47,000; Price per Unit = $5.50; Material Cost per Unit = $1.50; and Manufacturing Cost per Unit = $0.90. The Operating Income in cell D21 for (a) is $262,000 and for (b) is ($744,300).
15. Click the Visual Basic Editor button on the taskbar. On the File menu, click Print to print the VBA code. Close the Visual Basic Editor.
16. Protect the worksheet. Use the password kt. Click the Save button on the Standard toolbar to save the workbook using the file name KT Ltd Automated.

3 Automating a Five-Year Projected Financial Statement

Problem: As the spreadsheet specialist at BroadBand.com, you have been asked to use your Visual Basic for Applications skills to automate the Five-Year Projected Financial Statement worksheet shown in Figure 7-90 on the next page. The objective is to simplify data entry for the company's financial analysts. This worksheet projects financial information for a five-year period based on the previous year's sales and additional data. The user interface on the right side of the screen accepts the assumptions in the range B21:B25. The numbers in rows 5 through 18 are based on these assumptions.

The user interface has two buttons, one spin button, and three scroll bars. The Reset Assumptions button resets the assumptions as follows: (a) cell B21 = 50,000; (b) cell B22 = $5.00; (c) cell B23 = 10%; (d) cell B24 = 5%; and (e) cell B25 = 60%. The Units Sold in 2000 button accepts and ensures the units sold in 2000 is greater than zero and then assigns it to cell B21. The Unit Cost spin button changes the unit cost in cell B22. The Annual Sales Growth scroll bar changes the annual sales growth in cell B23. The Annual Price Decrease scroll bar changes the annual price decrease in cell B24. The Margin scroll bar changes the margin in cell B25.

Instructions: Start Excel and complete the following tasks.

1. Open the BroadBand workbook from the Data Disk. If you do not have a copy of the Data Disk, see the inside back cover of this book.
2. Reset the toolbars to their installation settings (see Step 6 on page E 7.6).
3. Unprotect the Financial Statement worksheet. The password is broadband.
4. Color the background of the range H2:J18 gray (column 8, row 4 on the Fill Color palette). Draw a thick box border (column 4, row 3 on the Borders palette) around the range H2:J18.

(continued)

Automating a Five-Year Projected Financial Statement *(continued)*

5. Display the Control Toolbox toolbar. Use the concepts and techniques developed in this project to add the seventeen controls shown on the right side of Figure 7-90.
6. Modify the properties of the seventeen controls as described in Table 7-14.
7. Enter your name, course, laboratory assignment number (Lab 7-3), date, and instructor name in the range H21:H25. Save the workbook using the file name BroadBand Automated.

Microsoft Excel - BroadBand Automated

	A	B	C	D	E	F
2	BroadBand.com					
3	Five-Year Projected Financial Statement					
4		2001	2002	2003	2004	2005
5	Sales	740,260	793,549	850,675	911,913	977,559
6	Total Cost of Sales	285,000	305,516	327,510	351,086	376,360
7	Gross Income	455,260	488,033	523,165	560,826	601,199
8	Expenses					
9	Advertising	112,039	120,032	128,601	137,787	147,634
10	Rent	10,800	11,880	13,068	14,375	15,812
11	Salaries	133,247	142,839	153,121	164,144	175,961
12	Supplies	11,104	11,903	12,760	13,679	14,663
13	Other Expenses	4,800	18,000	6,000	7,200	9,600
14	Total Expenses	271,990	304,654	313,551	337,185	363,670
15						
16	Gross Profit	183,270	183,378	209,614	223,642	237,529
17	Income Taxes	36,654	36,676	41,923	44,728	47,506
18	Net Income	146,616	146,703	167,691	178,913	190,023
20	Assumptions					
21	Units Sold in 2000	50,000				
22	Unit Cost	$5.70				
23	Annual Sales Growth	12.25%				
24	Annual Price Decrease	4.50%				
25	Margin	61.50%				

Reset Assumptions

Units Sold in 2000

Unit Cost $5.70

Annual Sales Growth 0 100

Annual Price Decrease 0 100

Margin 0 100

Financial Statement / Sheet2 / Sheet3

Ready

Start | Microsoft Excel - Bro... | 9:04 PM

FIGURE 7-90

8. The Reset Assumptions Button procedure resets the assumptions as follows:

```
Range("B21").Value = 50000
spnUnitCost = 500
scrAnnualSalesGrowth = 1000
scrAnnualPriceDecrease = 500
scrMargin = 6000
Range("J25").Select
```

9. The Units Sold in 2000 Button procedure accepts and validates the units sold in 2000 in cell B21 as follows:

```
UnitsSold = InputBox("Units Sold in 2000?", "Enter")
Do While UnitsSold <= 0
   UnitsSold = InputBox("Units Sold in 2000 must be > zero.", "Please Re-enter")
Loop
Range("B21").Value = UnitsSold
```

10. The Units Cost Spin Button procedure enters the unit cost in the Unit Cost Spin Button Label control and in cell B22 as follows:

```
lblUnitCost = Format$(spnUnitCost.Value / 100, "currency")
Range("B22").Value = spnUnitCost.Value / 100
```

The Format$ function in the first line formats the result that will display in the Unit Cost Spin Button Label control to include a floating dollar sign and two decimal positions to the right of the decimal.

In the Lab

Table 7-14 Controls and Their Properties

CONTROL	NAME	CAPTION	BACK COLOR	FONT	TEXT ALIGN	WORD WRAP	SPECIAL EFFECT	MAX	MIN	SMALL CHG	LARGE CHG
Reset Assumptions Button	btnReset	Reset Assumptions		8-point bold		True					
Units Sold in 2000 Button	btnUnitsSold	Units Sold in 2000		8-point bold							
Unit Cost Label		Unit Cost	Gray - 25%	8-point bold	Center						
Unit Cost Spin Button	spnUnitCost							10000	0	10	
Unit Cost Spin Button Label		$5.00		10-point bold	Right		Sunken				
All three 0 Labels		0	Gray - 25%	8-point bold	Center						
All three 100 Labels		100	Gray - 25%	8-point bold	Center						
Annual Sales Growth Label		Annual Sales Growth	Gray - 25%	8-point bold	Center						
Annual Sales Growth Scroll Bar	scrAnnualSales Growth							10000	0	25	100
Annual Price Decrease Label		Annual Price Decrease	Gray - 25%	8-point bold	Center						
Annual Price Decrease Scroll Bar	scrAnnualPrice Decrease							10000	0	25	100
Margin Label		Margin	Gray - 25%	8-point bold	Center						
Margin Scroll Bar	scrMargin							10000	0	25	100

The value assigned to cell B22 will display in the same format because the cell was formatted to the Currency style as part of the normal worksheet formatting.

11. The Annual Sales Growth Scroll Bar procedure changes the annual sales growth in cell B23 as follows:
    `Range("B23").Value = scrAnnualSalesGrowth.Value / 10000`
12. The Annual Price Decrease Scroll Bar procedure and the Margin Scroll Bar procedure work in a fashion similarly to the Annual Sales Growth scroll bar, except that they assign values to cells B24 and B25, respectively.
13. Click the Microsoft Excel button on the taskbar. Click the Exit Design Mode button on the Control Toolbox toolbar. Hide the Control Toolbox toolbar. Print the worksheet.
14. Use the newly designed interface to determine the five-year projections based on the following assumptions and print the worksheet for each data set: (a) Units Sold in 2000 = 78,000; Unit Cost = $6.70; Annual Sales Growth = 20%; Annual Price Decrease = 7.5%; and Margin = 62.5% and (b) Units Sold in 2000 = 97,000; Unit Cost = $12.50; Annual Sales Growth = 18.5%; Annual Price Decrease = 2.5%; and Margin = 66%. The Net Income for the year 2005 in cell F18 for (a) is $452,761 and for (b) is $1,580,253.
15. Click the Visual Basic Editor button on the taskbar. On the File menu, click Print to print the VBA code. Close the Visual Basic Editor.
16. Protect the worksheet. Use the password broadband. Click the Save button on the Standard toolbar to save the workbook using the file name BroadBand Automated.

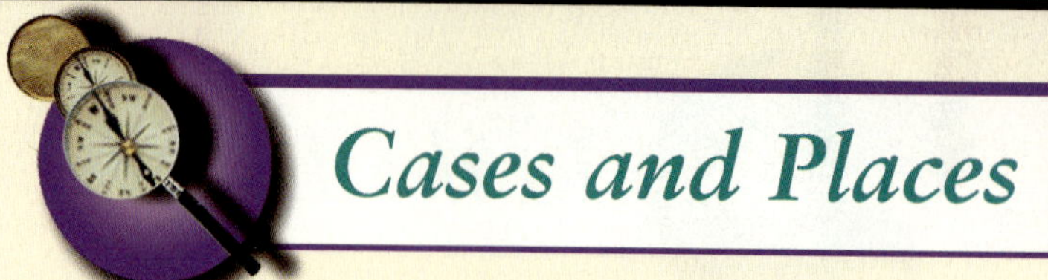

Cases and Places

The difficulty of these case studies varies:
▶ are the least difficult; ▶▶ are more difficult; and ▶▶▶ are the most difficult.

1 ▶ Open the workbook Solar Works from the Data Disk. Print the Projections worksheet. Create a macro that prints the cell formulas version of the Projections worksheet in landscape orientation using the Fit to option. Make sure the macro resets the Page Setup options before terminating. Execute the macro. Print the macro. Save the workbook with the name Solar Works1. Hand in the three printouts to your instuctor.

2 ▶ Open the workbook Solar Works from the Data Disk. Create a Command Button control to the right of the Assumptions box. Change the button's caption to Assumptions. Write a procedure for the Command Button control that accepts data for each of the five assumptions in the range B21:B25. Print the Projections worksheet. Print the Command Button control procedure. Use the Assumptions button to enter the following data sets and then print the worksheet for each data set: (a) Manufacturing = 38%; R & D = 6%; Marketing = 15%; Corporate = 16%; Commissions = 5%. (b) Manufacturing = 43%; R & D = 9%; Marketing = 10%; Corporate = 18%; Commissions = 6%. The Total Net Income in cell E18 for (a) is $1,021,151.80 and for (b) is $714,806.26. Save the workbook with the name Solar Works2. Hand in the four printouts to your instructor.

3 ▶ Using a browser search engine, such as AltaVista, type the keywords `Visual Basic for Applications`. Visit three Web pages that show VBA code solving a problem. Print each Web page. Hand in the three printouts to your instructor.

4 ▶▶ Open the workbook Solar Works from the Data Disk. Create a well-balanced user interface made up of a Reset button and five scroll bars, one for each of the cells in the range B21:B25. Have the Reset button set the five assumptions to 50%, 10%, 15%, 15%, and 5%, respectively. The scroll bars should range from 0% to 100% and increment by 0.25% (scroll arrows) and 1% (scroll bars). Use the titles in the Assumptions box in the range A21:A25 for the names of the scroll bars. Print the worksheet. Use the interface to enter the data specified in Cases and Places Exercise 2 above. Save the workbook with the name Solar Works3. Hand in the three printouts to your instructor.

5 ▶▶▶ Open the workbook Dollar Bill's Bank Loan Analysis from the Data Disk. Modify the procedure associated with the New Loan button on the worksheet so that it validates the price, down payment, interest rate, and years as follows: (a) the price must be between $0.00 and $50,000.00 inclusive; (b) the down payment must be between $0.00 and $50,000.00 inclusive; (c) the interest rate must be between 5% and 30% inclusive; and (d) the years must be between 0.25 and 15 inclusive. Print the procedure. Create and enter two sets of valid data. Print the worksheet for each set. Hand in the three printouts to your instructor.

Microsoft Excel 2000

Auditing, Data Validation, and Solving Complex Problems

OBJECTIVES

You will have mastered the material in this project when you can:

- Use the Auditing toolbar to analyze a worksheet
- Add data validation rules to cells
- Use trial and error to solve a problem on a worksheet
- Use Excel's Solver to solve a complex problem
- Password protect a workbook file
- Use Excel's Scenario Manager to record and save different sets of what-if assumptions and the corresponding results
- Create a Scenario Summary of scenarios
- Create a Scenario PivotTable
- Set and change the properties of a worksheet

Food for Thought

Worksheets Help Serve the Community

Health-conscious Americans not only are looking for ways to maintain health and fitness, but also are concerned about the needs of less-fortunate citizens. At least one person in every ten in the United States relies on food pantries and soup kitchens to avoid going hungry. Interestingly, 60 percent of these people have graduated from high school and have attended college. One in five is a child.

Although difficult to comprehend, it is estimated that 30 million Americans are in danger of going hungry. In large part, these families and individuals are helped through the efforts of America's Second Harvest, the nation's largest hunger-relief charity network of food banks. Corporate donors, local businesses, and individuals provide surplus food to the food banks, which then is distributed to more than 50,000 local agencies. A network of 189 food banks serves all 50 states and Puerto Rico, and distributes more than one billion pounds of donated food and groceries each year.

Among Second Harvest's food banks is the Greater Chicago Food Depository. The Food Depository collects donated surplus food from wholesale food manufacturers; produce growers and distributors, food store chains, and restaurants. After gathering the food, Food Depository drivers deliver the provisions to warehouses where the products are distributed later to charitable food pantries, soup kitchens, and shelters throughout the Chicago area.

With the huge distribution of food each year, employees needed a more efficient method of keeping track of these goods than using manual methods. With the ease in which Excel can be used to facilitate auditing and analyzing data, the Food Depository developed Excel worksheets, similar to the worksheet developed in this project.

In Project 8, the Union Cafeteria has a need to audit, validate data, and solve complex problems related to providing healthy meals for various sports teams on campus.

The majority of the project concentrates on working with the cafeteria's menu planning worksheet to solve complex problems that involve changing values in cells to arrive at a solution while abiding by constraints imposed by changes.

The Food Depository uses Excel worksheets to organize, tabulate, and summarize hundreds of pallets and thousands of pounds of food shipped each week to its warehouses. The worksheets are useful particularly for analyzing the food quantities to ensure that packagers receive food deliveries just when they need it. Improved quality control at processing plants also is a result, eliminating food surpluses, excess shipments, and fewer mislabeled and slightly damaged packages.

Now when drivers deliver to the warehouses, employees keep track of inventory, are able to provide instant analysis, and project storage needs. One of their Excel worksheets contains a template to enter the quantity of salvage goods; a second worksheet records items that need repacking. Workers generate reports, study the worksheets to determine their needs, prepare for the amounts of foods expected to arrive the following day, and survey how much warehouse space is needed to ensure sufficient room for the products.

The Excel worksheets have been a tremendous help in providing the Food Depository with the tools they need to efficiently feed more than 300,000 Chicagoans annually. Food for thought.

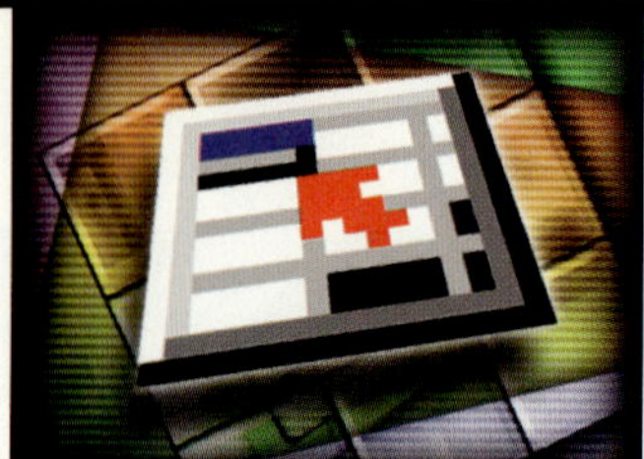

Microsoft Excel 2000

Auditing, Data Validation, and Solving Complex Problems

CASE PERSPECTIVE

College sports are very competitive and teams are looking for any advantage they can find to boost their performance. Recently, the Union Cafeteria has been receiving requests from various campus sport teams for special meal requirements. Groups, such as the volleyball and track teams, would like to have meals prepared based on certain nutritional needs. As the assistant cafeteria manager, you have been asked to prepare a worksheet that will select the correct serving portions of various foods to meet the needs of the track team. You have been given the additional task of maximizing the cafeteria's profit on each meal.

Maxine Hill, your manager, has given you a list of foods, their serving size, and their nutritional value. You also have the cost per serving of each item and the price for which each serving can be sold. Each item must be dished out in a predetermined serving size and cannot be sold in partial servings. For example, a hamburger can consist of two servings of beef, but not one and a half. Both Maxine and the track team coach also have asked for documentation that shows the nutritional requirements have been satisfied.

Introduction

This project introduces you to auditing a worksheet, data validation, and solving complex problems. Auditing allows you to check both the cells being referenced in a formula and the formulas that reference a cell. Auditing a worksheet is especially helpful when you want to learn more about a workbook created by someone else or you want to verify the formulas in a newly created workbook.

Data validation allows you to define cells in such a way that only certain values are accepted. This feature also allows you to display a prompt message when the user selects the cell and an error message if the user attempts to enter a value outside of a valid range that you define.

The majority of this project introduces you to solving complex problems that involve changing values of cells to arrive at a solution, while abiding by constraints imposed on the changing values. The worksheet in Figure 8-1a on page E 8.6 shows the details of the special meal requirements for this project as described in the Case Perspective. Columns B, C, and D each refer to one of the three dishes that can make up a meal, Beef, Potatoes, and Mixed Vegetables. The row titles in rows 4 through 8 in column A refer to the characteristics of each serving, such as Serving Price, Serving Cost, Profit per Serving, Fat Content, and Carbohydrate Content. Row 9 is where you enter the number of servings of each food category. In this case, the number of servings must be between 1 and 4. Once you enter the number of servings of each food in cells B9, C9, and D9, Excel determines the results of the suggested meal in rows 11 through 15, Total Fat in Meal, Total Carbohydrate in Meal, Total Price, Total Cost, and Total Profit. The objective here is to keep the fat content low, keep carbohydrates high, and maximize the profit.

The only way to solve some problems is to keep trying different data, in this case varying the servings of the three different types of food, until you are satisfied with the solution. This process is called trial and error. Often, you can use trial and error to solve a problem on your own. Other times, so many possible solutions exist to a problem, that the best way to solve the problem is to use a computer. Excel gives you tools to solve such problems. One of these tools is Solver. Solver allows you to specify up to 200 different cells that can be adjusted to find a solution to a problem. Solver allows you to place constraints on the variables. A constraint is a limitation on the possible values that a cell can contain. Once you define the constraints and tell Solver what to look for, it will try many possible solutions until it finds the best one.

In Figure 8-1b on the next page, the values of cells B9, C9, and D9 have been modified by Solver to find the best combination of servings for a meal where beef is the main entrée. When Solver finishes solving a problem, you can instruct it to create an Answer Report. An Answer Report (Figures 8-1c and 8-1e on page E 8.7) shows the answer that Solver found, the values that were manipulated by Solver to find the answer, and the constraints that were used to solve the problem.

Excel's Scenario Manager is a what-if analysis tool that allows you to record and save different sets of what-if assumptions used to forecast the outcome of a worksheet model. You will use Scenario Manager to manage two different sets of Solver data. Figure 8-1d on the next page shows a scenario where chicken has substituted beef as the main entrée. Scenario Manager also allows you to create reports that summarize the scenarios on your worksheet. Figure 8-1f on page E 8.7 shows a Scenario Summary and Scenario PivotTable that concisely report the differences in the two scenarios in Figures 8-1b and 8-1d.

More About 2000

Constraints

The constraints of a problem are the rules that you must follow to solve a given problem. You even may add constraints to cells that are not referenced in the formulas you are solving. Solver will modify these types of cells to meet the constraints, but they will not affect the solution. For example, you can change row or column headers, or worksheet headers to explain better to the user the results of a Solver solution.

Project Eight — Union Cafeteria Menu Planning Worksheet

After your discussion with Maxine, you determine the following needs and source of data.

Needs: The track team would like the cafeteria to come up with a meal that has no more than 25 grams of fat, and at least 40 grams of carbohydrates. Maxine would like you to determine the best meal that includes servings of a chicken dish or a beef dish, a potato dish, and a mixed vegetables dish. The meal must consist of at least one serving of each dish, and no more than four servings of each dish. When determining the amounts of each dish to include in the meal, you must maximize the profit to the cafeteria while operating within the constraints that the track team has placed on you.

More About 2000

The Solver Add-In

If you do not have Solver installed on your computer, see your instructor about obtaining the Microsoft Office 2000 CD-ROMs. To load the Solver Add-In, use the Add-Ins command on the Tools menu and then check the Solver option box and follow the instructions.

(b) Solution with Beef as Main Entrée

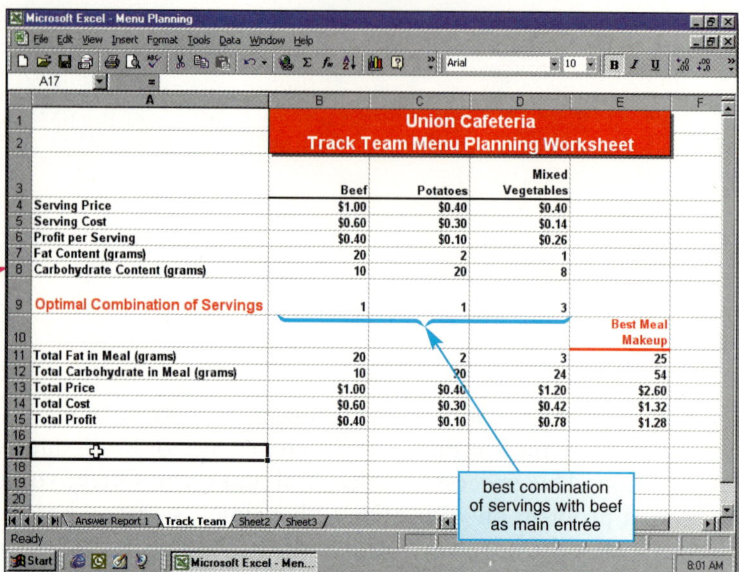

	Beef	Potatoes	Mixed Vegetables	
Serving Price	$1.00	$0.40	$0.40	
Serving Cost	$0.60	$0.30	$0.14	
Profit per Serving	$0.40	$0.10	$0.26	
Fat Content (grams)	20	2	1	
Carbohydrate Content (grams)	10	20	8	
Optimal Combination of Servings	1	1	3	
				Best Meal Makeup
Total Fat in Meal (grams)	20	2	3	25
Total Carbohydrate in Meal (grams)	10	20	24	54
Total Price	$1.00	$0.40	$1.20	$2.60
Total Cost	$0.60	$0.30	$0.42	$1.32
Total Profit	$0.40	$0.10	$0.78	$1.28

(a) Worksheet without a Solution

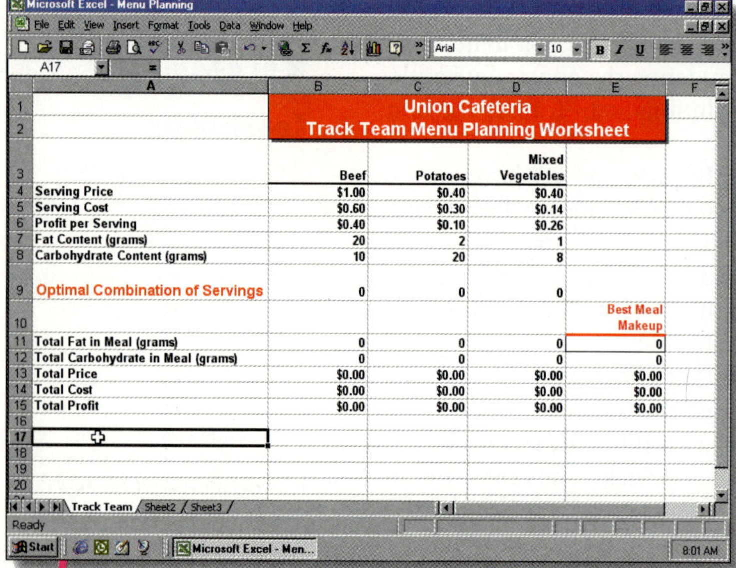

	Beef	Potatoes	Mixed Vegetables	
Serving Price	$1.00	$0.40	$0.40	
Serving Cost	$0.60	$0.30	$0.14	
Profit per Serving	$0.40	$0.10	$0.26	
Fat Content (grams)	20	2	1	
Carbohydrate Content (grams)	10	20	8	
Optimal Combination of Servings	0	0	0	
				Best Meal Makeup
Total Fat in Meal (grams)	0	0	0	0
Total Carbohydrate in Meal (grams)	0	0	0	0
Total Price	$0.00	$0.00	$0.00	$0.00
Total Cost	$0.00	$0.00	$0.00	$0.00
Total Profit	$0.00	$0.00	$0.00	$0.00

(d) Solution with Chicken as Main Entrée

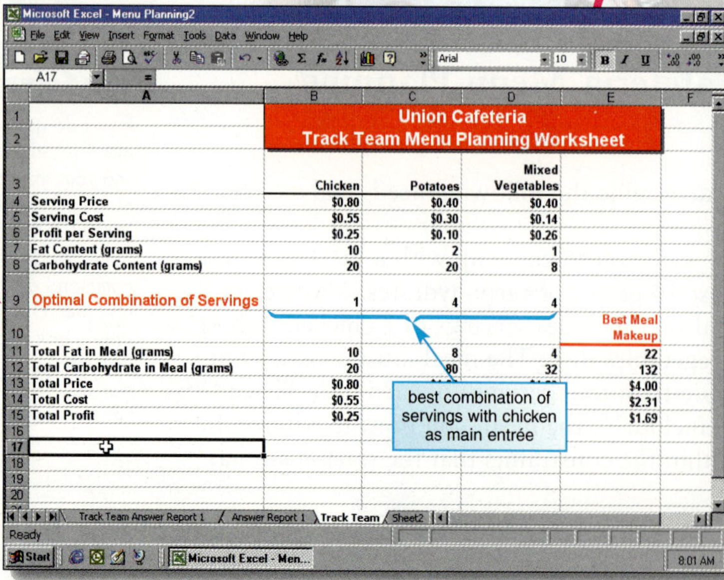

	Chicken	Potatoes	Mixed Vegetables	
Serving Price	$0.80	$0.40	$0.40	
Serving Cost	$0.55	$0.30	$0.14	
Profit per Serving	$0.25	$0.10	$0.26	
Fat Content (grams)	10	2	1	
Carbohydrate Content (grams)	20	20	8	
Optimal Combination of Servings	1	4	4	
				Best Meal Makeup
Total Fat in Meal (grams)	10	8	4	22
Total Carbohydrate in Meal (grams)	20	80	32	132
Total Price	$0.80			$4.00
Total Cost	$0.55			$2.31
Total Profit	$0.25			$1.69

FIGURE 8-1

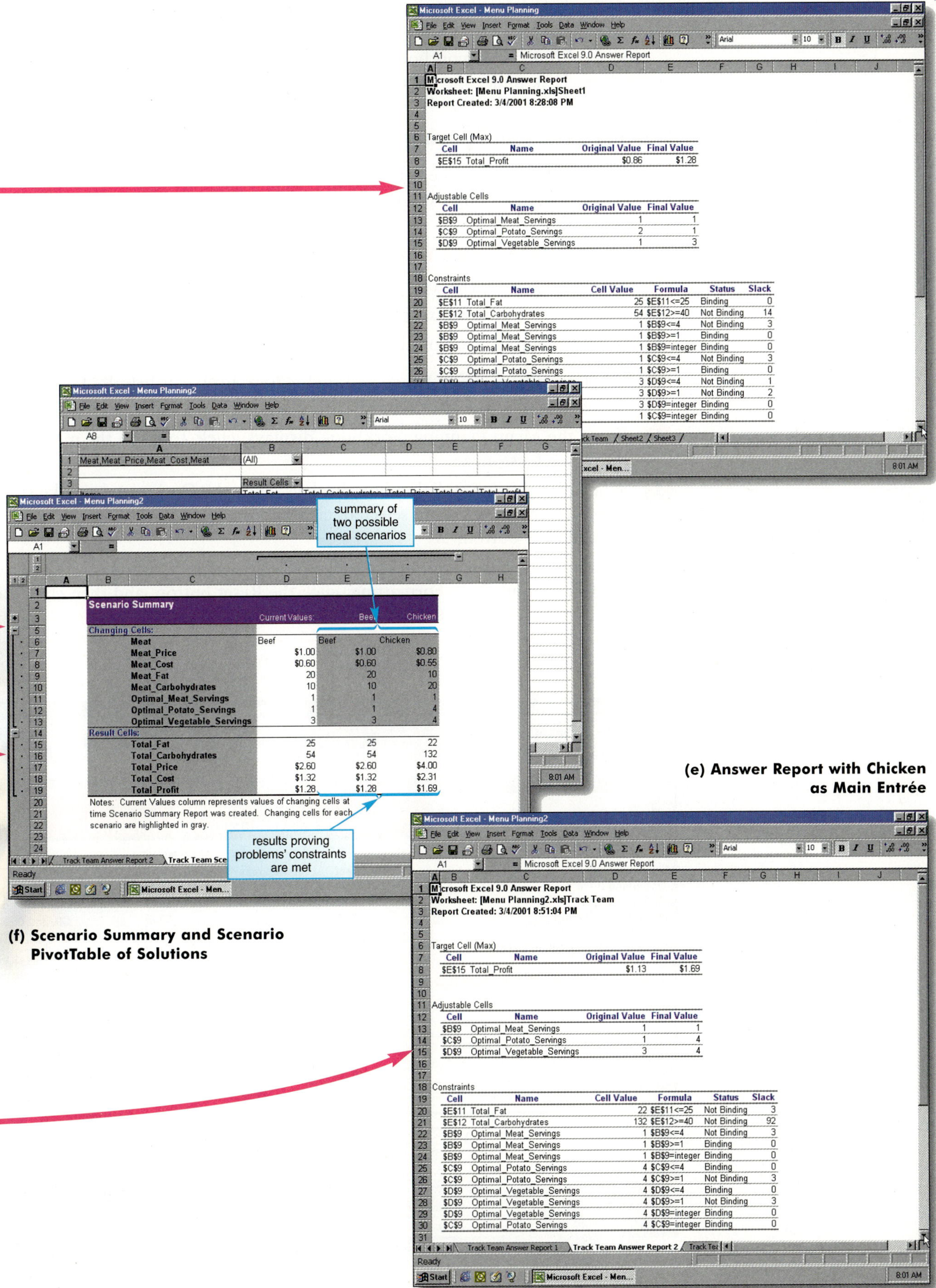

(c) Answer Report with Beef as Main Entrée

(e) Answer Report with Chicken as Main Entrée

(f) Scenario Summary and Scenario PivotTable of Solutions

Finally, reports need to be generated for the coach that indicate the nutritional needs have been met.

Source of Data: The workbook shown in Figure 8-1a on page E 8.6 is available on the Data Disk under the file name Menu Planning.

Starting Excel and Opening a Workbook

Perform the following steps to start Excel, reset the toolbars, and open the workbook Menu Planning from the Data Disk.

TO START EXCEL AND OPEN A WORKBOOK

1. Insert the Data Disk in drive A. See the inside back cover of this book for instructions for downloading the Data Disk.
2. Click the Start button on the taskbar and then click Open Office Document.
3. When the Open Office Document dialog box displays, click the Look in box arrow and then click 3½ Floppy (A:). Double-click Menu Planning in the list.
4. When the Menu Planning workbook displays, click Tools on the menu bar, and then click Customize.
5. When the Customize dialog box displays, click the Options tab, make sure the top three check boxes are selected, click the Reset my usage button, and then click the Yes button.
6. Click the Toolbars tab. Click Standard, click the Reset button, and then click the OK button. Click Formatting, click the Reset button, and then click the OK button. Click the Close button.

The Menu Planning workbook displays in the Excel window (Figure 8-2).

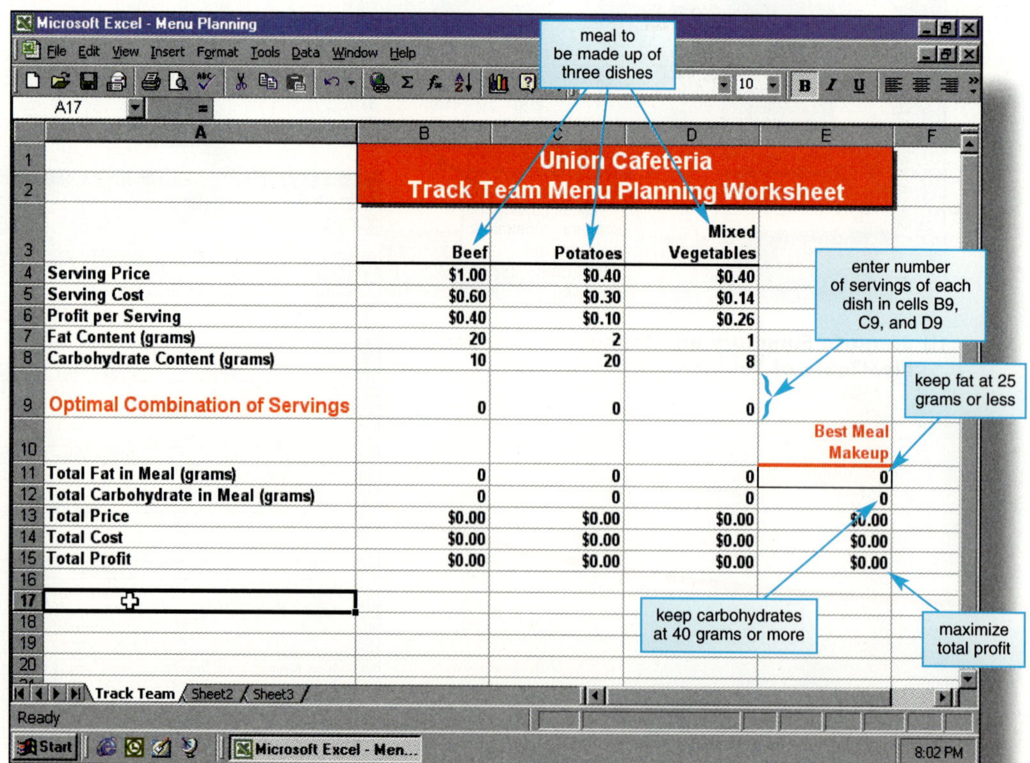

FIGURE 8-2

The Track Team sheet shown in Figure 8-2 consists of information for three types of dishes. Rows 4 through 8 show the information for one serving of each type of dish. Row 9 contains the optimal combination of servings, which is the information that needs to be determined in this project. Rows 11 through 15 show the totals for each dish based on the serving amounts entered in the range B9:D9. As cells B9, C9, and D9 change, the values in the range B11:D15 are updated. Finally, the grand totals for the entire meal are calculated in the range E11:E15. The goals are to keep the total fat in the meal (cell E11) less than or equal to 25, keep the total carbohydrates in the meal (cell E12) greater than or equal to 40, and maximize the total profit made on each meal (cell E15).

The current worksheet displays beef as one of the dishes. One of the requirements is to create meals within the constraints for both beef and chicken. Therefore, the information in column B needs to be modified later in the project to reflect the price, cost, and nutritional properties of the chicken dish.

Auditing

The term **auditing** refers to the practice of proving the correctness of a worksheet. The **Auditing toolbar** supplies several tools that you can use to analyze the formulas in a worksheet.

Auditing is useful both for analyzing a complex worksheet and for finding the source of errors that may occur in your worksheet. Excel provides visual auditing tools that display cues in the worksheet to help you understand the worksheet. These cues take the form of tracer arrows and circles around cells. **Tracer arrows** are blue arrows that point from cell to cell and let you know what cells are referenced in a formula in a particular cell. Tracer arrows become red when one of the cells referenced contains an error.

Auditing

Auditing is a very important job function in corporations and government. For more information about auditing, visit the Excel 2000 More About Web page (www.scite.com/ex2000/more.htm) and click Auditing.

Displaying the Auditing Toolbar

When you want to audit a worksheet, you can display the Auditing toolbar. The Auditing toolbar contains buttons that allow you to trace the details of a formula or locate the source of errors in a worksheet. The Auditing toolbar is accessible only through the Tools menu. To view the Auditing toolbar, complete the steps on the next page.

To Display the Auditing Toolbar

1 Click Tools on the menu bar, point to Auditing, and then point to Show Auditing Toolbar on the Auditing submenu.

The Tools menu and Auditing submenu display (Figure 8-3).

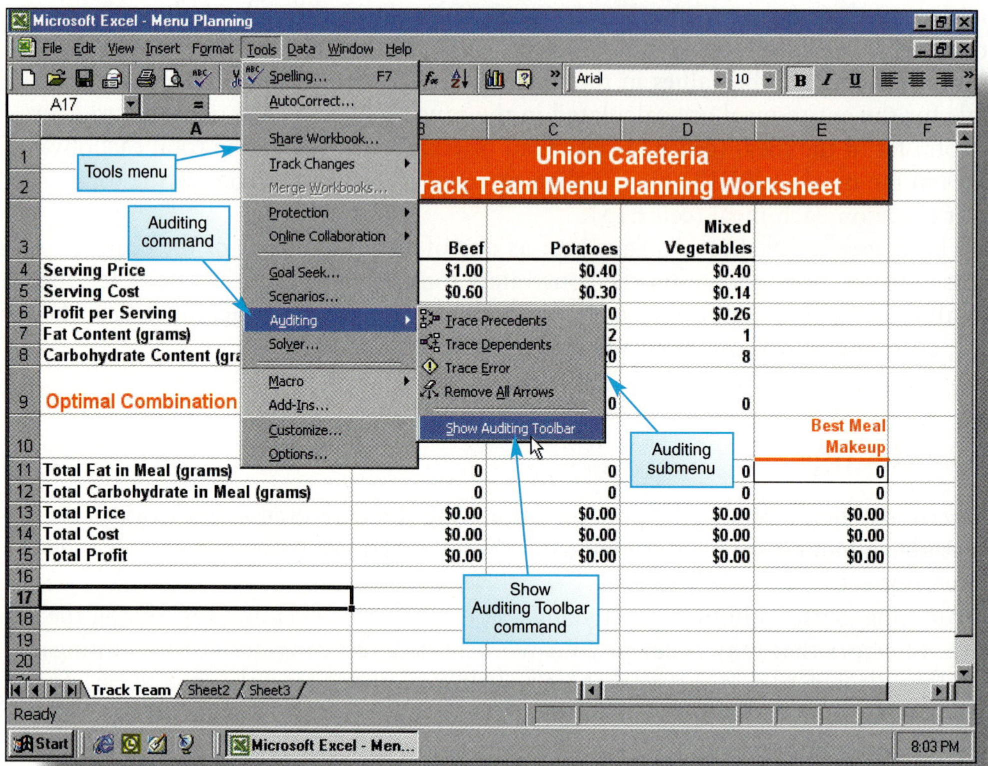

FIGURE 8-3

2 Click Show Auditing Toolbar.

The Auditing toolbar displays (Figure 8-4). Excel displays the Auditing toolbar on the screen in the same location and with the same shape as it displayed the last time it was used.

FIGURE 8-4

1. Press ALT+T, press U, press S

Tracing Precedents with the Auditing Toolbar

A formula that relies on other cells for a computation is said to have precedents. **Precedents** are cells that are referenced in a formula. For example, if you assign cell A5 the formula =A1+A2, then cells A1 and A2 are precedents of cell A5. Tracing precedent cells shows you how a particular cell is calculated. Often a precedent cell has precedents itself. For instance, in the previous example, if you assign cell A1 the formula =B1+B2, then cell A1, which is a precedent of cell A5, also has precedents. Excel allows you to trace the precedents of precedents as well. However, you can audit only one cell at a time. That is, Excel does not allow you to audit ranges. The following steps show the precedent cells for the total profit of the best meal makeup in cell E15.

To Trace Precedents

1 Click cell E15 and then click the Trace Precedents button on the Auditing toolbar.

Excel draws an arrow across the range B15:E15.

2 Click the Trace Precedents button two more times.

Excel draws arrows indicating the precedents of the cells in the range B15:D15 (Figure 8-5).

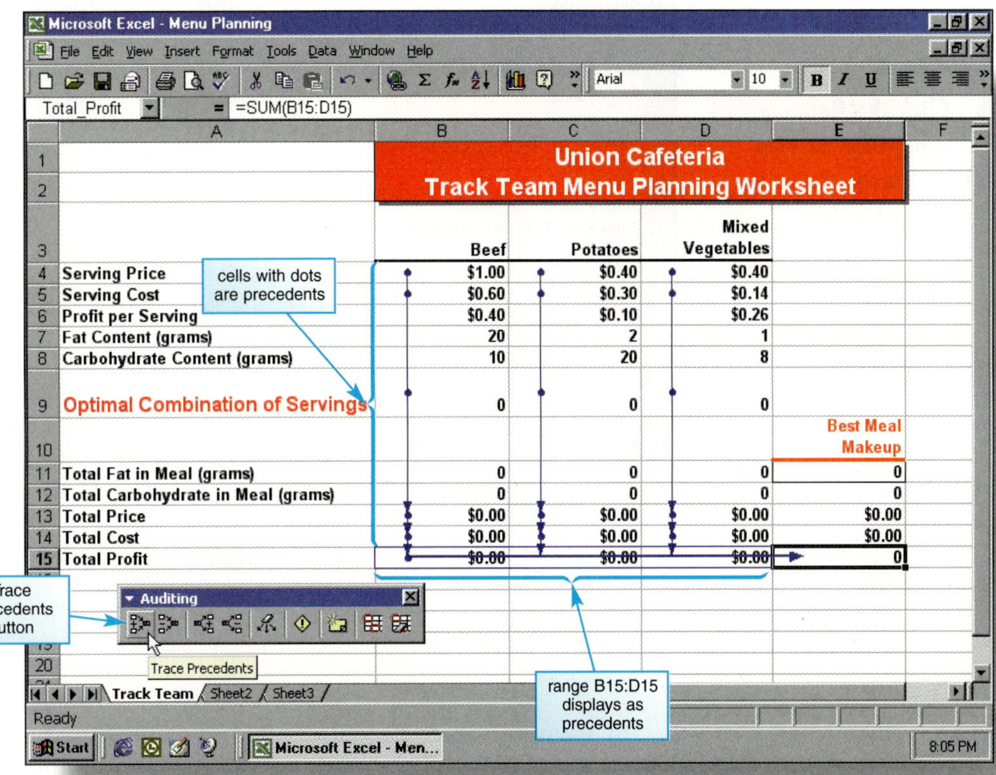

FIGURE 8-5

The arrows shown in Figure 8-5 have arrowheads on cells that are traced, and dots on cells that are direct precedents of the cells with arrowheads. For example, cell B15 is a precedent of cell E15, the total profit cell, and cell B15 has precedents above it in cells B4, B5, B9, B13, and B14. As you click the Trace Precedents button, you visually can follow the levels of precedents through the worksheet.

Other Ways

1. On Tools menu point to Auditing, click Trace Precedents
2. Press ALT+T, press U, press T

Removing Precedent Arrows with the Auditing Toolbar

After understanding the precedents of a particular cell, you can remove the precedent arrows one level at a time.

To Remove the Trace Precedent Arrows

1 Click the Remove Precedent Arrows button on the Auditing toolbar.

Excel removes the arrows across the range B4:D12, the last level of precedent arrows added.

2 Click the Remove Precedent Arrows button two more times on the Auditing toolbar.

Excel removes the remaining precedent arrows (Figure 8-6).

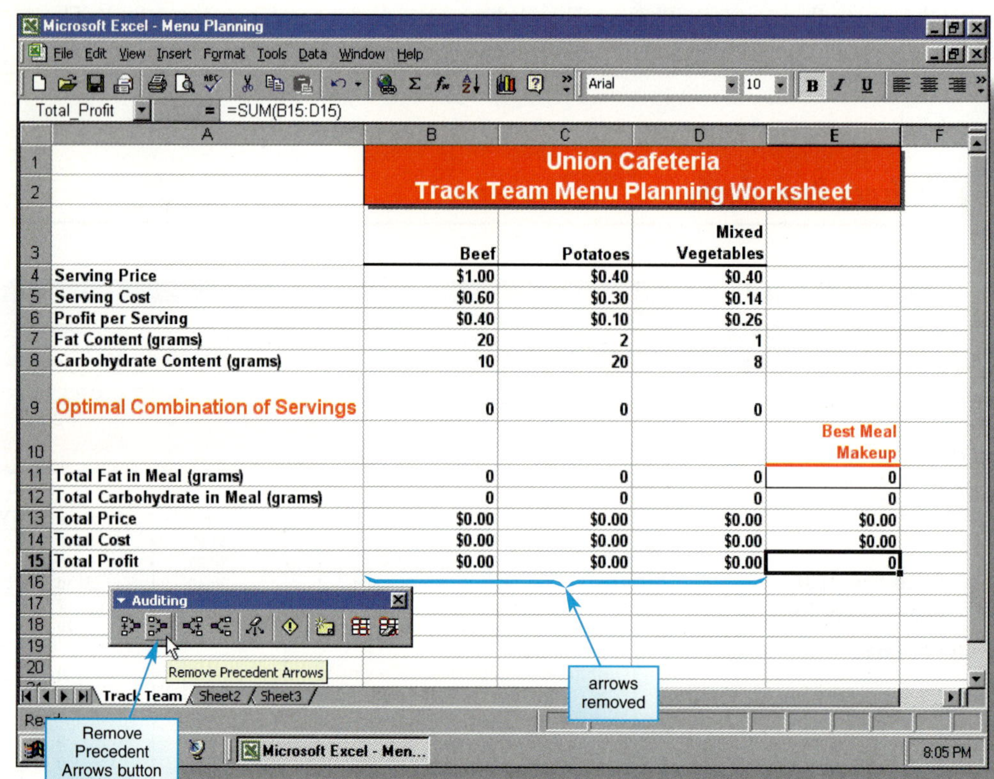

FIGURE 8-6

1. On Tools menu point to Auditing, click Remove All Arrows
2. Press ALT+T, press U, press A

More About 2000

Tracing Precedents and Dependents

When no more levels of precedents are available on the worksheet, Excel will beep if you try to trace another level. If you double-click a tracer arrow, the cell at the end of the arrow will be selected. This is useful on complex worksheets where the destination of an arrow may not be easy to follow.

By using the Trace Precedents and Remove Precedent Arrows buttons in combination, you slowly can begin to see the structure of the worksheet that is hidden in the formulas within the cells. By doing more analysis, you can assure yourself that you understand the worksheet and that no obvious errors are apparent to the casual viewer.

Tracing Dependents with the Auditing Toolbar

A cell is a **dependent** if it is referenced in a formula in another cell. Often, it is useful to find out where a cell is being used in a worksheet to perform subsequent calculations. In other words, which cells in the worksheet use the cell in question? The following steps trace the dependents of the optimal servings of beef in cell B9.

To Trace Dependents

1 Click cell B9 and then click the Trace Dependents button on the Auditing toolbar.

Excel draws arrows to cells B11, B12, B13, and B14.

2 Click the Trace Dependents button two more times.

Excel draws arrows indicating the remaining dependents of cell B9 (Figure 8-7).

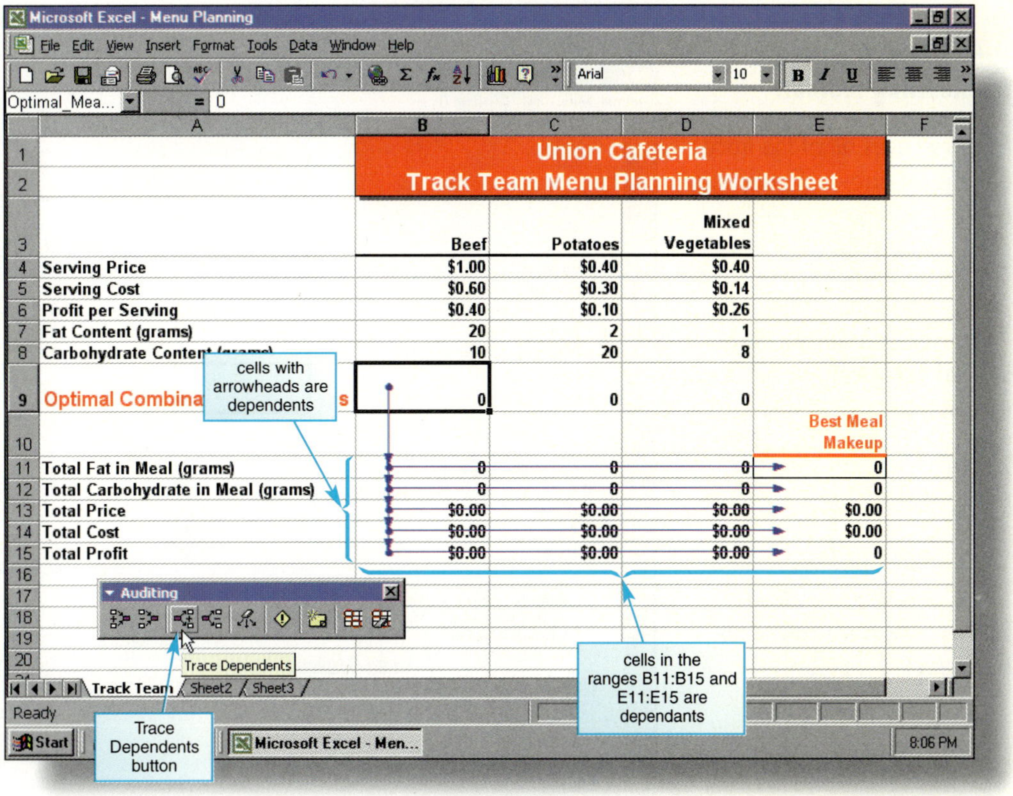

FIGURE 8-7

Other Ways

1. On Tools menu point to Auditing, click Trace Dependents
2. Press ALT+T, press U, press D

Figure 8-7 indicates that cells B11, B12, B13, and B14 depend on cell B9. Subsequently, cells B15 and the range E11:E15 depend on those cells. Clearly, before any results can be computed in cells B15 and the range E11:E15, cell B9 must have a value.

Removing All Arrows with the Auditing Toolbar

When you have finished auditing the worksheet with the Auditing toolbar, the easiest way to clear all of the trace arrows is to use the **Remove All Arrows button** on the Auditing toolbar.

To Remove the Trace Dependent Arrows

1. **Click the Remove All Arrows button on the Auditing toolbar.**

Excel removes all of the trace dependent arrows (Figure 8-8).

2. **Click the Close button on the right side of the Auditing toolbar to close it.**

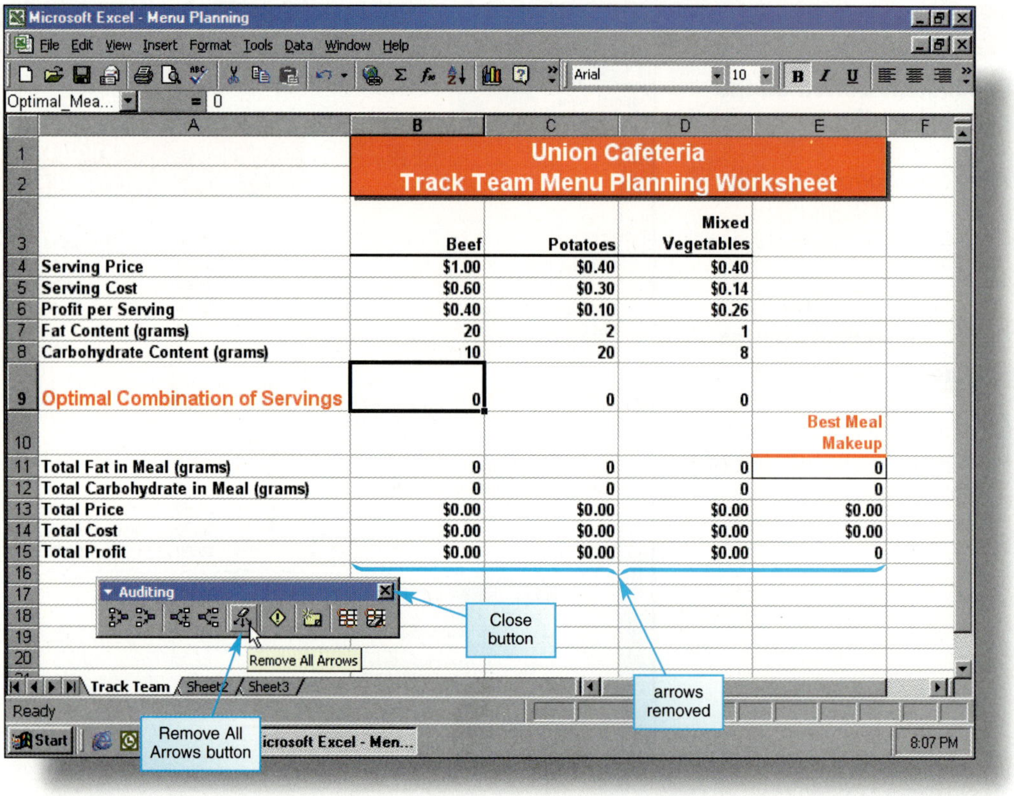

FIGURE 8-8

1. On Tools menu point to Auditing, click Remove All Arrows
2. Press ALT+T, press U, press A

Sometimes, a cell has precedents or dependents on other worksheets or in other workbooks. In this case, Excel will draw a dashed arrow to an icon of a worksheet to indicate that the precedent or dependent is outside of the current worksheet. If you click the dashed arrow and the workbook that contains the precedent or dependent is open, Excel displays the Go To dialog box that allows you to navigate to that location.

Figure 8-9 shows the buttons on the Auditing toolbar. Table 8-1 summarizes the buttons on the Auditing toolbar.

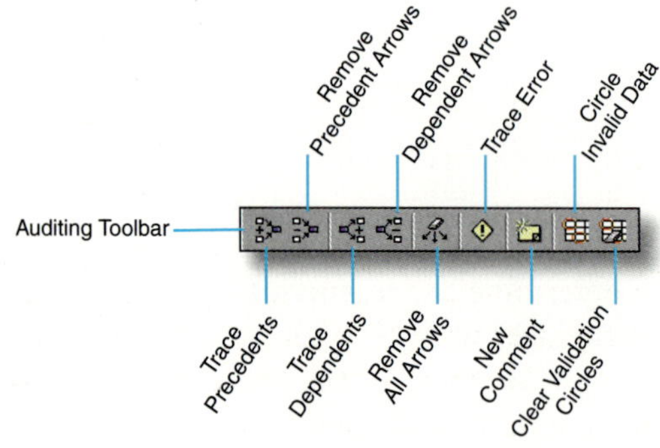

FIGURE 8-9

Table 8-1 Summary of Buttons on the Auditing Toolbar

BUTTON	NAME	FUNCTION
	Trace Precedents	Draws tracer arrows from the cells that affect the formula in the current cell.
	Remove Precedent Arrows	Removes tracer arrows from one level of precedents on the active worksheet.
	Trace Dependents	Draws tracer arrows to the cells that use the current cell in their formula.
	Remove Dependent Arrows	Removes tracer arrows from one level of dependents on the active worksheet.
	Remove All Arrows	Removes all tracer arrows drawn with the Trace Precedents and Trace Dependents buttons.
	Trace Error	If the active cell contains an error value, draws tracer arrows to the cells that may be causing the error value to appear.
	New Comment	Attaches a comment to the active cell.
	Circle Invalid Data	Draws circles around the cells that contain values outside of the limits defined by using the Validation command on the Data menu.
	Clear Validation Circles	Clears the circles drawn by the Circle Invalid Data button.

The **Trace Error button** is used when you see an error in a cell and want to trace the source of the error. If you see an error in a cell, including #DIV/0!, #NAME?, #NA, #NULL!, #NUM!, #REF!, and #VALUE!, the Trace Error button will display red tracer arrows to inform you of the precedents of the cell that contains the error. You then can inspect the precedent cells to see if you can determine the cause of the error and correct it.

The **New Comment button** allows you to place comments in cells so you can make notes to yourself or to others about questionable data in the worksheet. For example, if you are auditing someone else's worksheet and you believe that a cell should be the precedent of a particular cell, you can make a note that will display when the other user opens the worksheet. Comments are discussed further in Project 9.

The **Circle Invalid Data button** and the **Clear Validation Circles button** are used in combination with Excel's data validation capability discussed in the next section. If a cell contains data validation parameters and the current data in the cell is outside of those validation criteria, the Circle Invalid Data button draws a circle around the cell. The Clear Validation Circles button is used to clear these circles.

Validation Circles

Validation circles are red to indicate that these cells contain error values. Excel will display a maximum of 256 invalid data circles at a time.

Data Validation, Trial and Error, and Goal Seek

Often, it is necessary to limit the values that should be placed in a particular cell. Excel allows you to place limitations on the values of cells by using data validation. **Data validation** restricts the values that may be entered into a cell by the worksheet user. Excel allows you to determine the restrictions placed on data entered into a cell, set an input message that the user will see when selecting the cell, and set an error message that displays when a user violates the restrictions placed on the cell. By implementing these features, you limit the possibilities for error on a worksheet by giving the user as much information as possible about how to use the worksheet properly.

Data Validation

If you have the Office Assistant turned on, Data Validation input and error messages will be displayed as part of the Assistant. Input and error messages can be up to 255 characters in length.

One important aspect of Excel's data validation is that the rules apply only when the user enters data into the cell manually. That is, if a cell is calculated by a formula or set in a way other than direct input by the user, Excel does not check the validation rules.

Adding Data Validation to Cells

Recall from the Needs section for this project on page E 8.5, serving sizes must be whole numbers and at least one of each type of serving must be included in a meal, but no more than four of each type per meal. By examining the worksheet, you can see that cells B9, C9, and D9 must have these restrictions. Data validation is added to cells by using the **Validation command** on the Data menu.

Steps To Add Data Validation

1 Select the range B9:D9. Click Data on the menu bar and then point to Validation.

The Data menu displays (Figure 8-10).

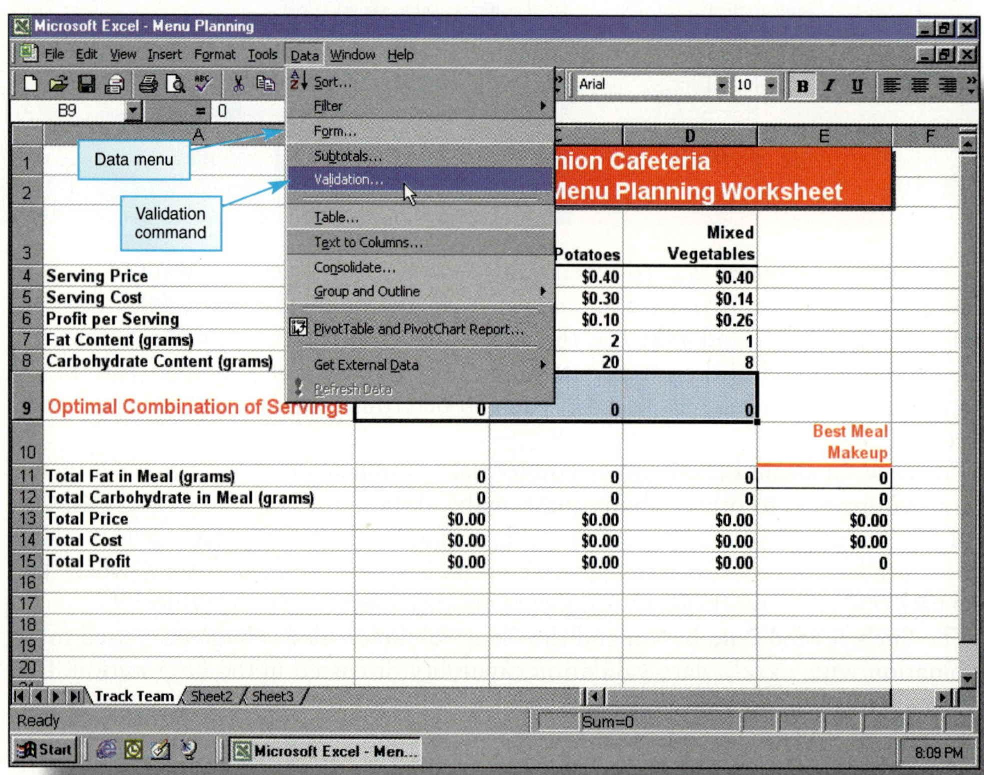

FIGURE 8-10

2

2 Click Validation. When the Data Validation dialog box displays, click the Allow box arrow and then select Whole number. Click the Data box arrow and then select between. Type 1 **in the Minimum text box and type** 4 **in the Maximum text box. Point to the Input Message tab.**

The Data Validation dialog box displays (Figure 8-11).

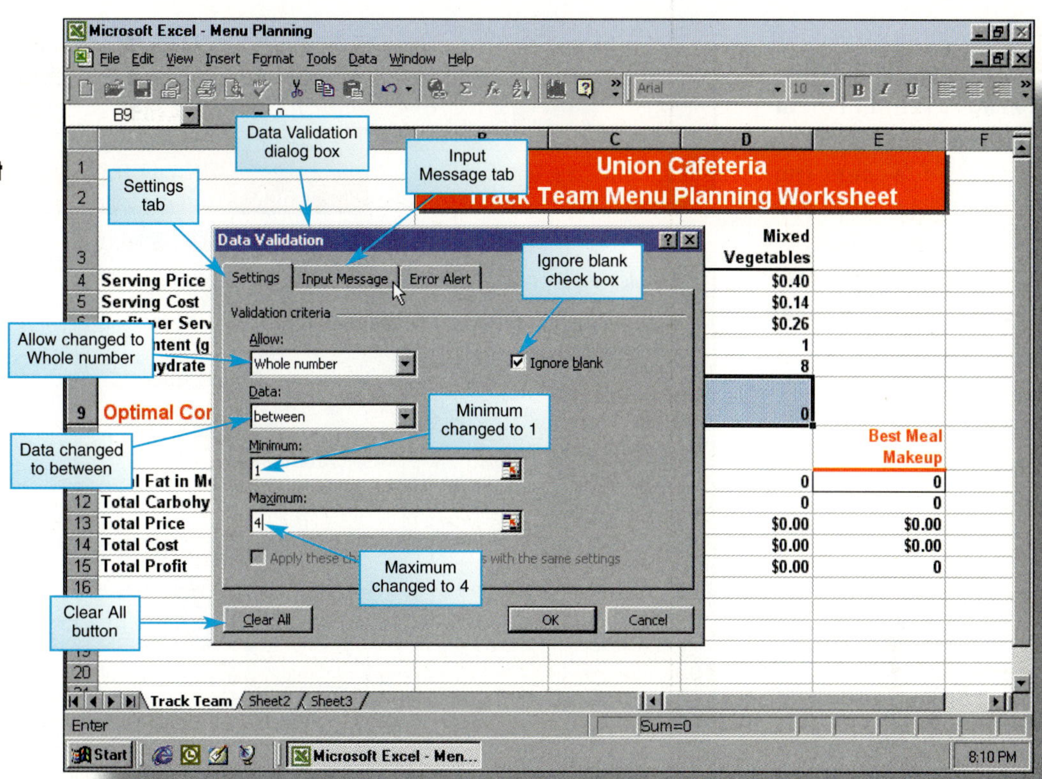

FIGURE 8-11

3 Click the Input Message tab and then type Serving Size **in the Title text box. Type** Enter a serving size that is greater than zero and less than five. **in the Input message text box. Point to the Error Alert tab.**

The Input Message tab displays (Figure 8-12).

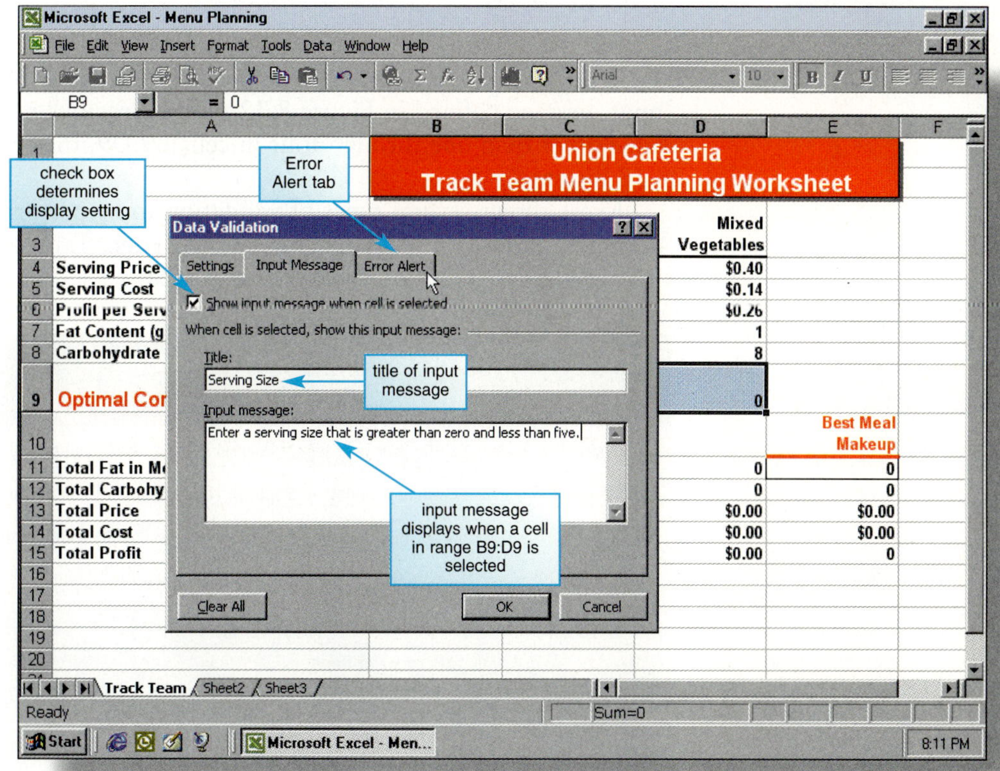

FIGURE 8-12

4 **Click the Error Alert tab and then type** `Serving Size Error` **in the Title text box. Type** `You must enter a serving size that is greater than zero and less than five.` **in the Error message text box and then point to the OK button.**

The Error Alert tab displays (Figure 8-13).

5 **Click the OK button.**

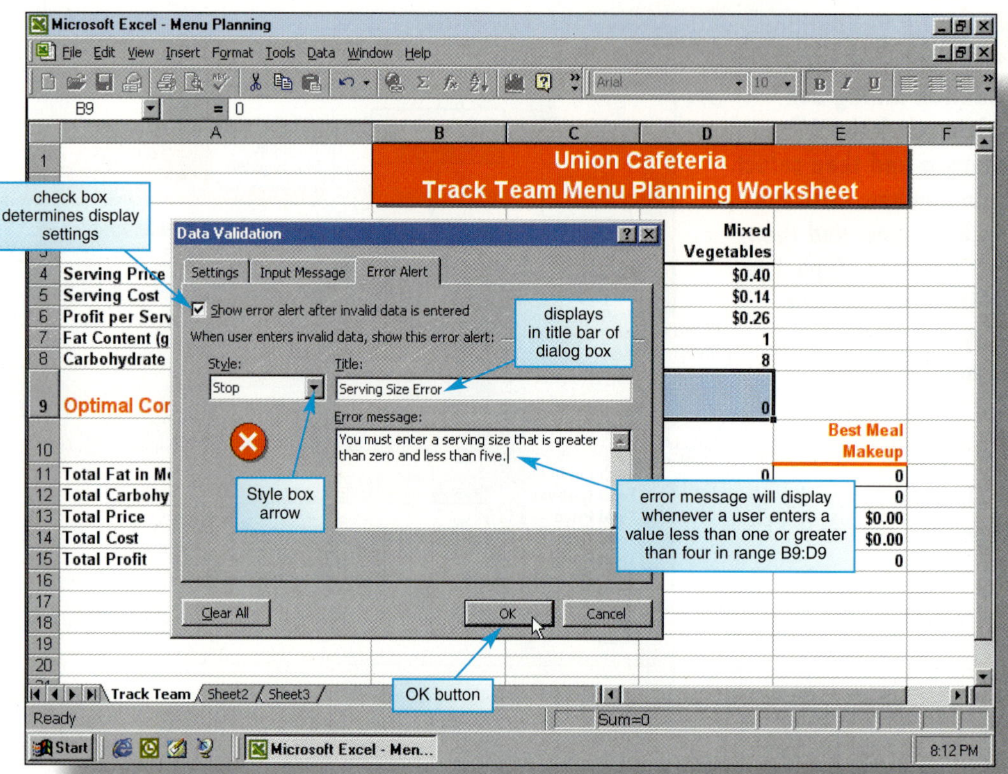

FIGURE 8-13

Other Ways

1. Press ALT+D, press L

When the user selects one of the cells in the range B9:D9, Excel displays the input message defined in Figure 8-12 on the previous page. When the user enters a value other than one through four in cells B9:D9, the error message defined in Figure 8-13 displays.

Excel allows several types of validation to be performed in the Validation criteria area shown in Figure 8-11 on the previous page. Table 8-2 shows the various criteria types available in the Validation criteria area.

Table 8-2 Types of Validation Criteria Allowed

ALLOW	MEANING
Any value	Allows the user to enter anything in the cell. Use if you simply want to display an input message.
Whole number	Allows whole numbers in a specific range. Use the Data box to specify how the validation takes place.
Decimal	Allows decimal numbers in a specific range. Use the Data box to specify how the validation takes place.
List	Specifies a range where a list of valid values can be found.
Date	Allows a range of dates.
Time	Allows a range of times.
Text length	Allows a certain length text string to be input. Use the Data box to specify how the validation takes place.
Custom	Allows user to specify a formula that will validate the data entered by the user.

More About 2000

Validation Types

When using the Custom validation type, you can use a formula that evaluates to either true or false. If the value is false, then the user may not enter data in the cell. For example, if you have a cell that contains an employee's salary, you may want to disallow the user from entering a percentage in a cell that contains the employee's raise for this year if the salary is zero, indicating that the employee is no longer with the company.

The Ignore blank check box should be cleared if you want to require that the user enter something in the cell. By leaving the Ignore blank check box selected, Excel allows the user to select the cell, and then leave the cell with no data being entered.

Using Trial and Error to Solve a Complex Problem

Trial and error refers to the practice of adjusting cells in a worksheet manually to try to find a solution to a problem. In the Track Team worksheet, you could adjust cells B9, C9, and D9 until the criteria for fat content and carbohydrate content are met. While many combinations of possible values exist, you could try keeping one or two of the values constant while adjusting the others.

Trial and error is more than just guessing. Because you understand the constraints on the problem and the goals, you use logic to make subsequent trials better than the previous. For example, if you increase the servings of potatoes by two and it causes the total fat content of the meal to exceed 25, you may try to increase the serving by one to see if that keeps the totals within the constraints.

To Use Trial and Error to Attempt to Solve a Complex Problem

1 Click cell B9 and type 5 **as the number of servings of beef and then press the ENTER key. Point to the Retry button.**

The Serving Size Error dialog box displays (Figure 8-14), because 5 is outside the limits of acceptable values for this cell. The Serving Size ScreenTip displays because cell B9 is selected.

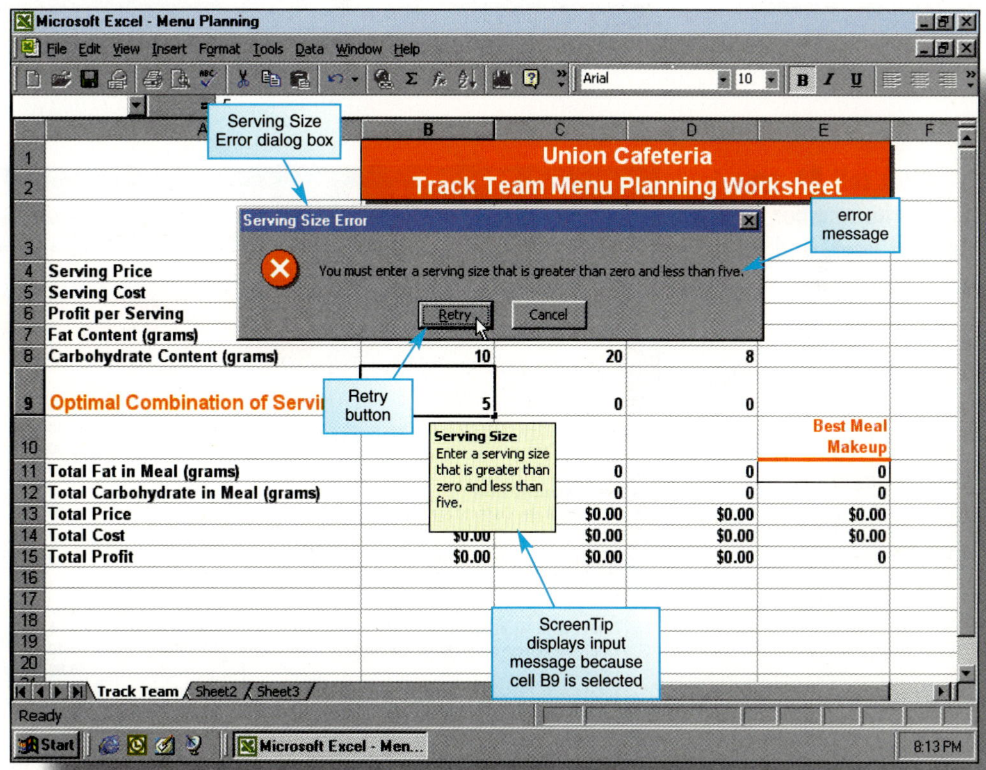

FIGURE 8-14

2 Click the Retry button. Type 2 **as the number of servings of beef in cell B9. Click cell C9 and then type** 2 **as the number of servings of potatoes. Click cell D9, type** 2 **as the number of servings of mixed vegetables, and then press the ENTER key.**

The Serving Size ScreenTip displays because cell D9 is selected. Excel displays the new values and updates the totals in the range B11:E15 as shown in Figure 8-15. The value of 46 in cell E11 indicates that the maximum allowable fat content of 25 grams has been exceeded.

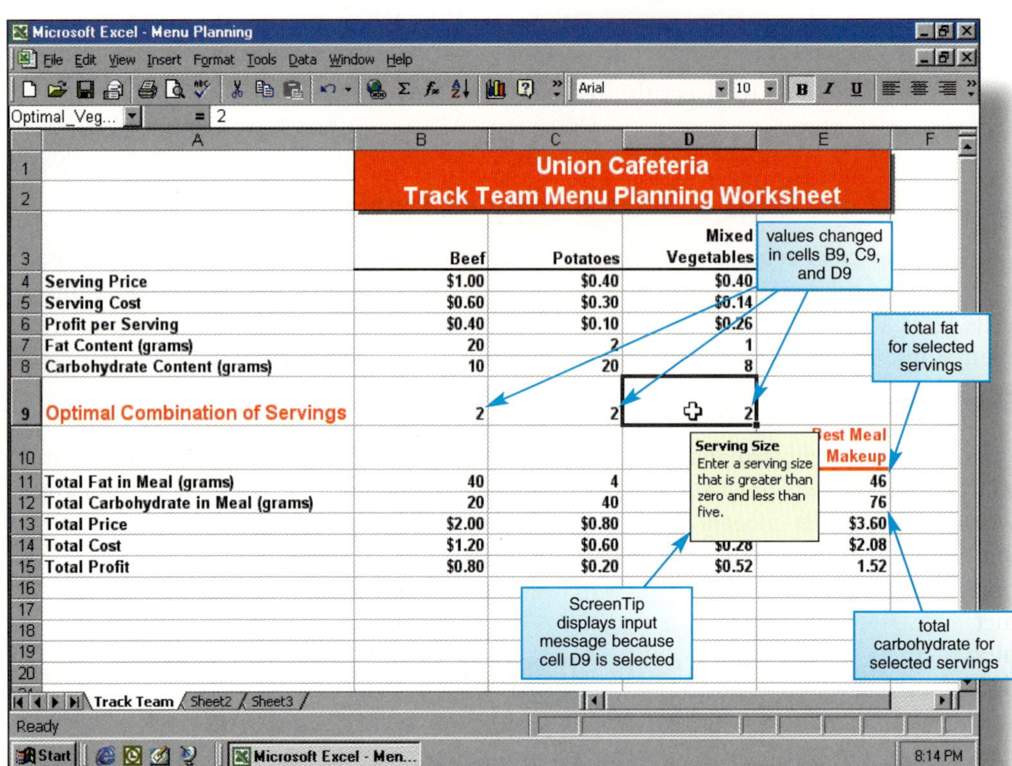

FIGURE 8-15

3 Click cell B9, type 1 **as the number of servings of beef, and then press the ENTER key.**

Excel displays the recalculated values for the worksheet (Figure 8-16). The value of 26 in cell E11 again indicates that the maximum allowable fat content of 25 grams has been exceeded.

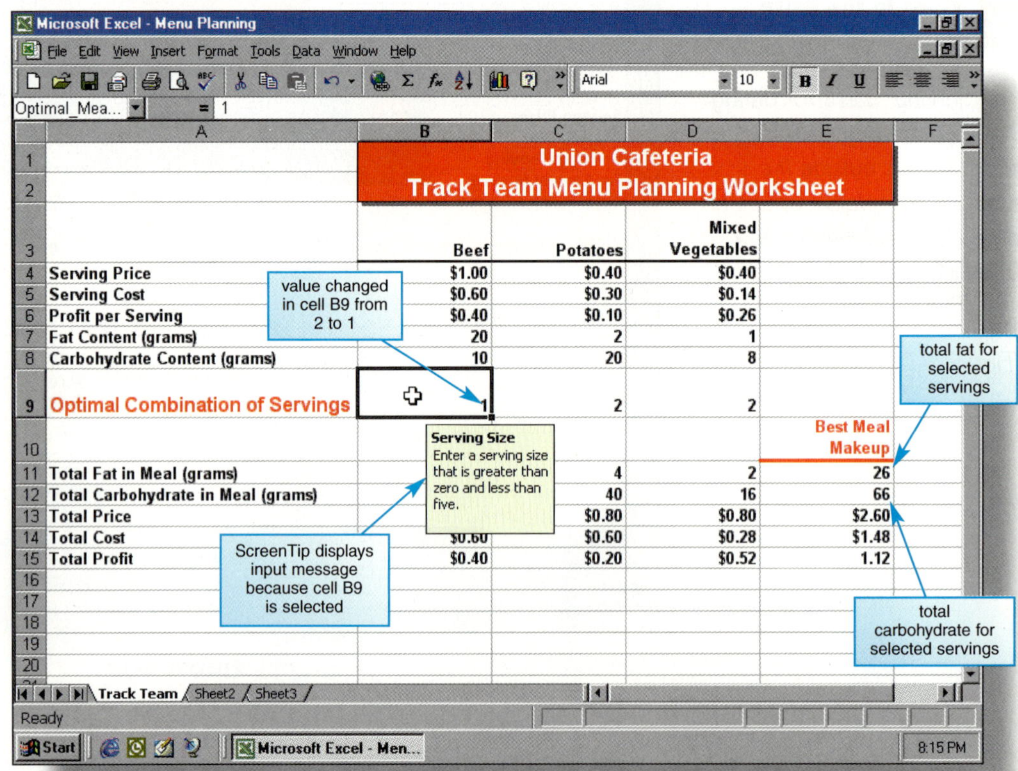

FIGURE 8-16

Trial and error can be used on simple problems in many cases. Many limitations exist to using trial and error, however. The Menu Planning worksheet has three cells (B9, C9, and D9) that can be adjusted to solve the problem. Because each cell can contain a value between 1 and 4, 64 different combinations are possible that you could try, many of which may give the proper fat and carbohydrate contents to the meal. The biggest drawback to using trial and error in this situation is that you must maximize the profit while meeting the other conditions. Rather than using trial and error to test all 64 possible meal combinations and see which one produces the most profit while meeting the nutritional constraints, Excel provides other tools to help solve problems where cells can contain a number of values.

Goal Seeking

Goal seeking is a methodology in which you know what answer you want a formula in a cell to be, but you do not know the value to place in a cell that is involved in the formula. You can goal seek by changing the value in a cell that is used indirectly in the formula.

Goal Seeking to Solve a Complex Problem

If you know the result you want a formula to produce, you can use **goal seeking** to determine the value of a cell on which a formula depends. In the Menu Planning worksheet, the total fat content for the meal is one result that can be sought by varying the number of servings of one of the meal items. Goal seeking takes trial and error one step further by automatically changing the value of a cell until a single criteria is met in another cell. In this case, suppose you suspect that by varying the number of mixed vegetable servings, you can achieve the goal of 25 grams of fat for the meal. In doing this, you hope that the other constraints of the problem also are satisfied.

The following steps show how goal seek can be used to alter the servings of mixed vegetables to keep the total fat content of the meal less than or equal to 25 grams.

To Use the Goal Seek Command to Attempt to Solve a Complex Problem

1 Click cell E11, the cell that contains the total fat content in the meal. Click Tools on the menu bar and then point to Goal Seek.

The Tools menu displays (Figure 8-17).

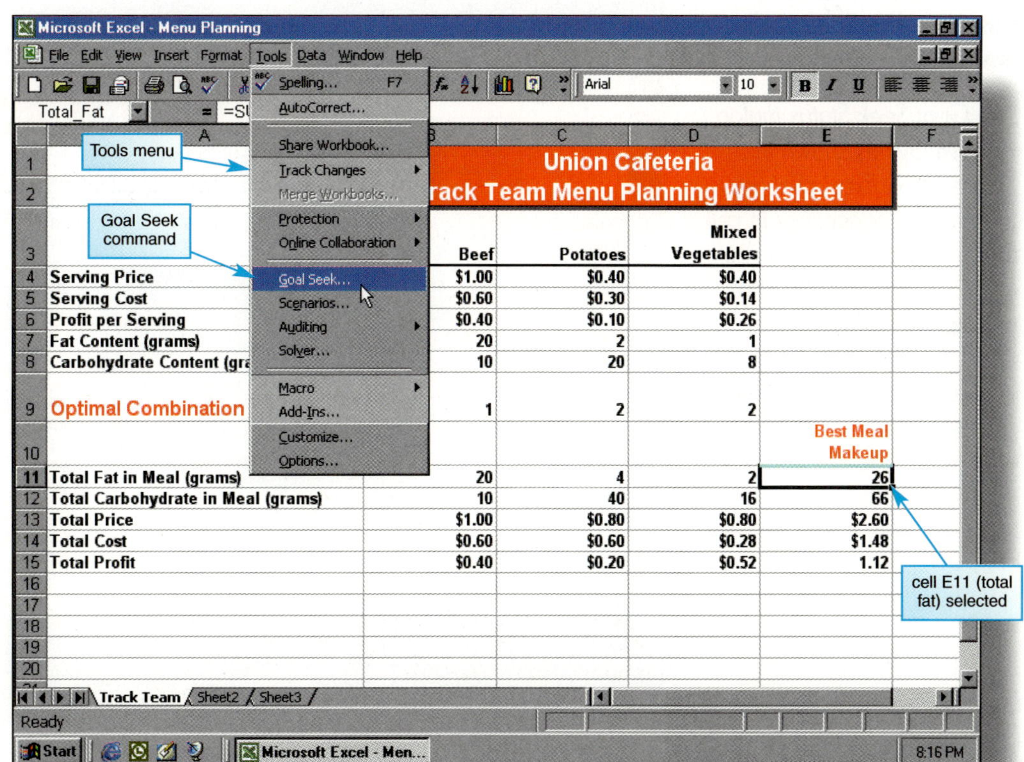

FIGURE 8-17

2 **Click Goal Seek.**

The *Goal Seek dialog box* displays. The Set cell box is assigned the cell reference of the active cell in the worksheet (cell E11) automatically.

3 **Click the To value text box. Type** 25 **and then click the By changing cell box. Click cell D9 on the worksheet. Point to the OK button.**

The Goal Seek dialog box displays as shown in Figure 8-18. A marquee displays around cell D9.

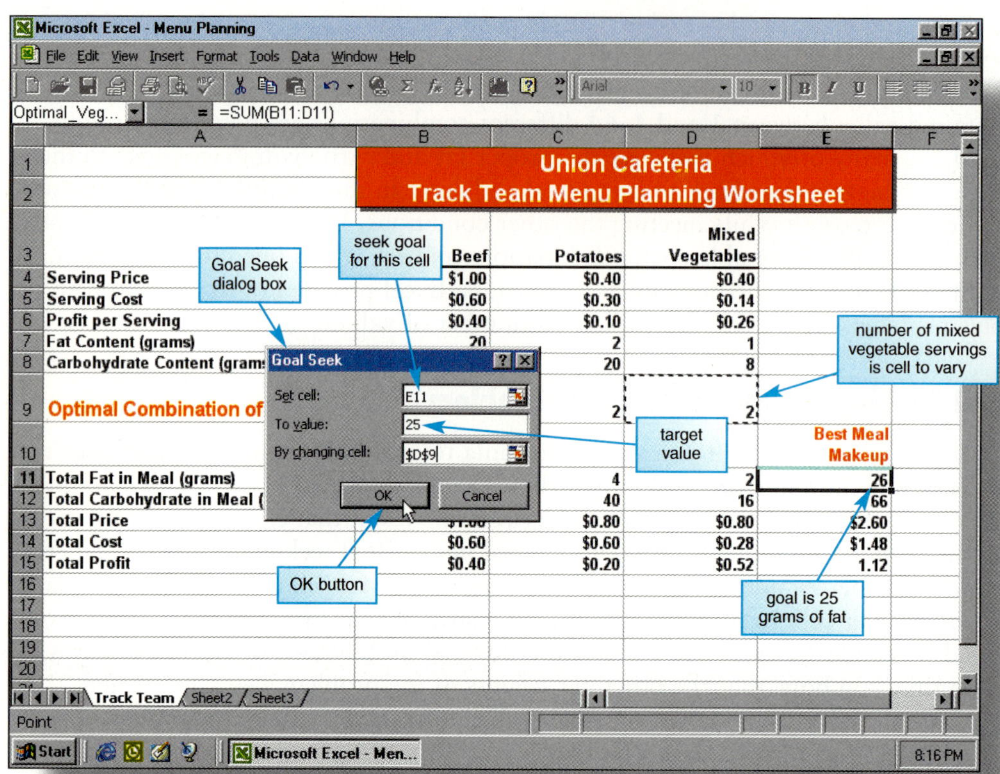

FIGURE 8-18

4 **Click the OK button. Point to the OK button in the Goal Seek Status dialog box.**

The *Goal Seek Status dialog box* displays as shown in Figure 8-19. Excel changes the number of servings in cell D9 to 1 and the value in cell E11 is updated to 25. The dialog box indicates that Excel found a solution and shows that the target value has been met.

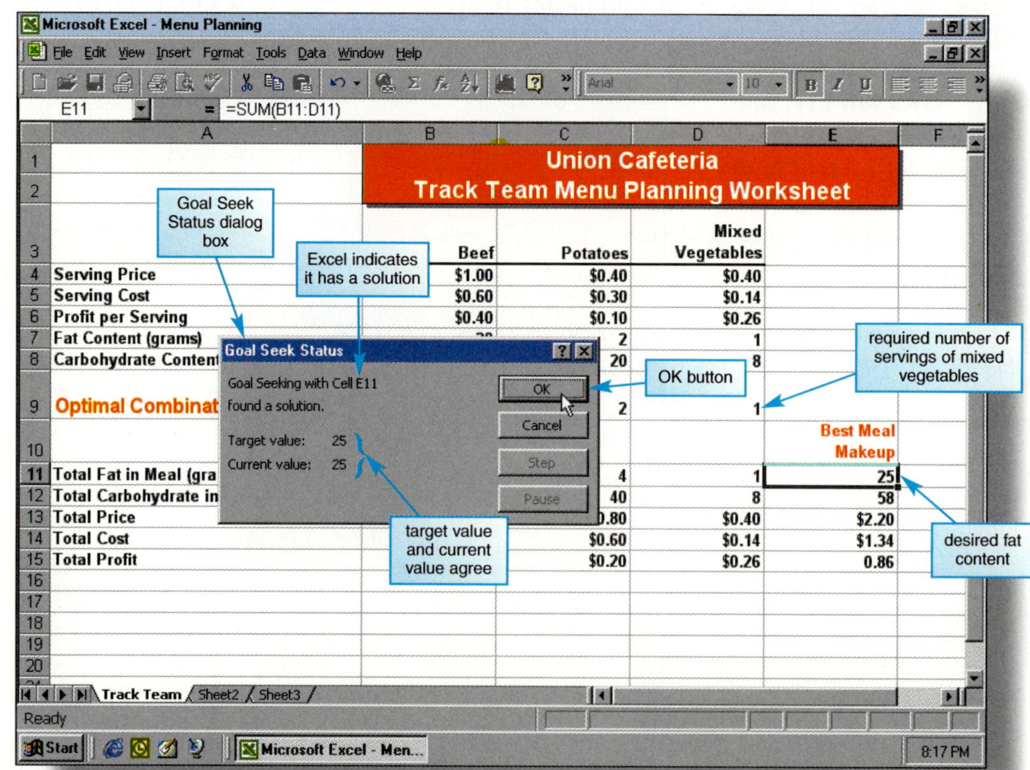

FIGURE 8-19

5 Click the OK button. Click cell A17 to deselect cell E11.

The Goal Seek Status dialog box disappears and Excel displays the updated worksheet (Figure 8-20).

Microsoft Excel - Menu Planning

	A	B	C	D	E	F
1		Union Cafeteria				
2		Track Team Menu Planning Worksheet				
3		Beef	Potatoes	Mixed Vegetables		
4	Serving Price	$1.00	$0.40	$0.40		
5	Serving Cost	$0.60	$0.30	$0.14		
6	Profit per Serving	$0.40	$0.10	$0.26		
7	Fat Content (grams)	20	2	1		
8	Carbohydrate Content (grams)	10	20	8		
9	Optimal Combination of Servings	1	2	1		
10					Best Meal Makeup	
11	Total Fat in Meal (grams)	20	4	1	25	
12	Total Carbohydrate in Meal (grams)	10	40	8	58	
13	Total Price	$1.00	$0.80	$0.40	$2.20	
14	Total Cost	$0.60	$0.60	$0.14	$1.34	
15	Total Profit	$0.40	$0.20	$0.26	$0.86	
16						
17						
18						

servings are within acceptable range

fat content meets requirement

carbohydrate content meets requirement

total profit

FIGURE 8-20

1. Press ALT+T, press G

Goal seeking assumes you can change the value of only one cell referenced directly or indirectly. In this example, to change the fat content to 25 grams per serving, the number of servings of mixed vegetables must change to 1. This assumes that no other serving sizes change.

As you learned previously, you do not have to reference directly the cell to vary in the formula or function. The total fat content is calculated as a sum of the cells in the range B11:D11. The formula does not include a direct reference to the mixed vegetable serving size in cell D9. Because the total fat in the mixed vegetable servings is dependent on the number of servings of mixed vegetables, however, Excel is able to goal seek on the total fat content by varying the number of servings of mixed vegetables.

The total fat content (cell E11) and the total carbohydrate content (cell E12) satisfy the nutritional needs of the meal. Still, you have no way of knowing whether the constraint of maximizing profit (cell E15) has been achieved. Your manager requires that total profit be maximized while satisfying the nutritional needs of the track team. Surely, other combinations of the three meal items satisfy the nutritional requirements and produce greater total profit than $0.86 per meal as shown in Figure 8-20.

Using Solver to Solve Complex Problems

Solver allows you to solve complex problems where a number of variables can be changed in a worksheet in order meet a goal in a particular cell. As just stated, goal seeking allows you to change only one cell, and trial and error requires too much uncertainty and time to solve complex problems adequately.

Solver uses a technique called linear programming to solve problems. **Linear programming** is a complex mathematical process used to solve problems that include multiple variables and the minimizing or maximizing of result values. Solver

Linear Programming

For more information about linear programming, visit the Excel 2000 More About Web page (www.scite.com/ex2000/more.htm) and click Linear Programming.

essentially tries as many possible combinations of solutions as it can. On each attempt to solve the problem, Solver checks to see if it has found a solution.

Figure 8-21a shows the results of using Solver on the Track Team worksheet. Cells B9, C9, and D9 are called the changing cells. **Changing cells** are those cells that will be modified by Solver to solve the problem. The total profit in cell E15 serves as the **target cell**, which means that Solver will attempt to meet some criteria (maximize profit) in this cell by varying the changing cells. **Constraints** are the requirements that have been placed on certain values in the problem. For example, the total fat in the meal must not exceed 25 grams, and the total carbohydrates in the meal must not be less than 40 grams.

Figure 8-21b shows a Solver Answer Report. An **Answer Report** is a worksheet that displays the results of a Solver calculation in a concise format. The report satisfies the requirement to document the results of the menu analysis.

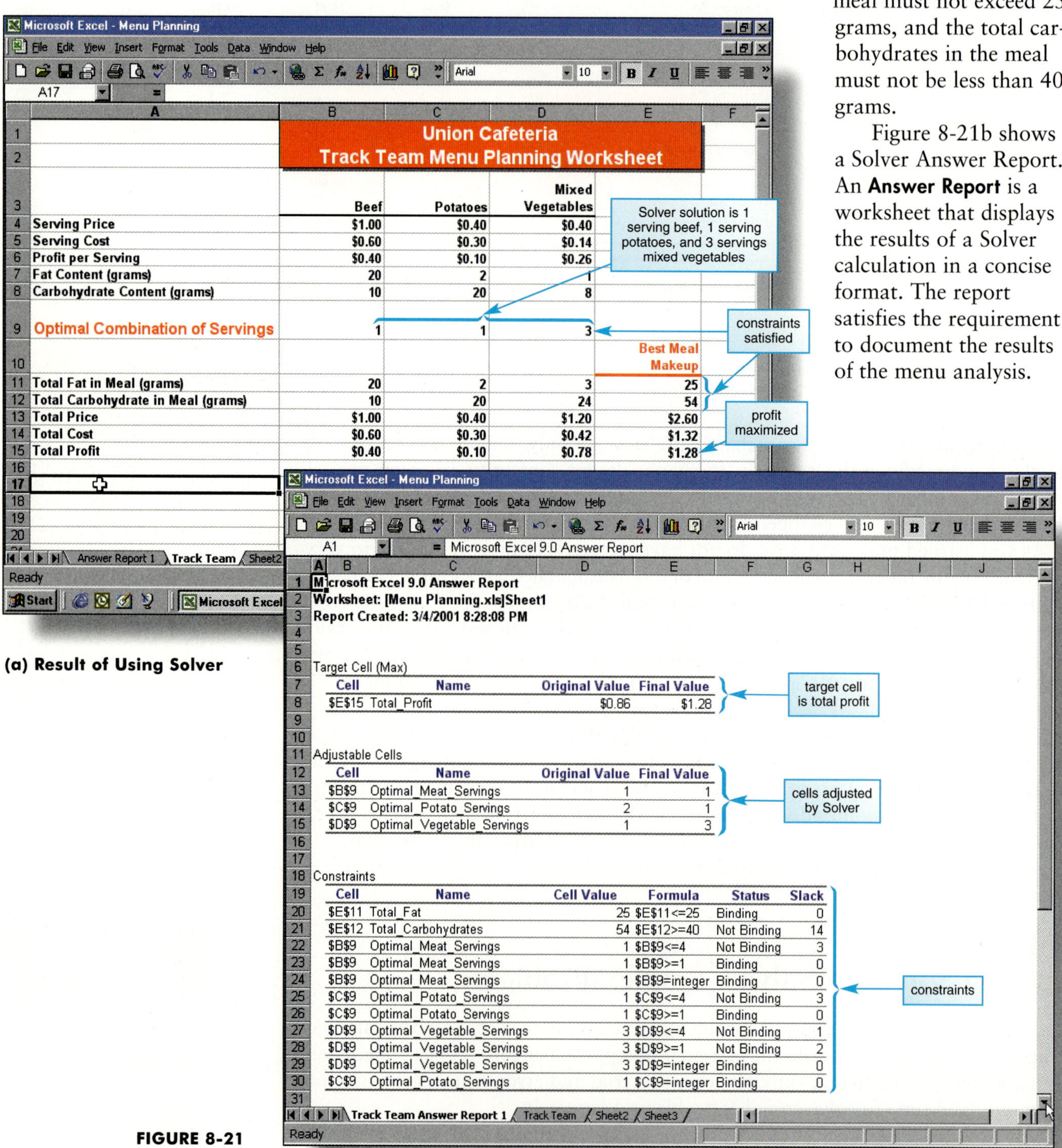

(a) Result of Using Solver

(b) Solver Answer Report

FIGURE 8-21

Using Solver to Find the Optimal Combination of Servings

The Tools menu contains the **Solver command**, which starts Solver. If the Solver command does not display on your Tools menu, then you must use the Add-Ins command on the Tools menu to add it. The cell that is the target for Solver is the total profit cell, E15. The goal is to maximize the value in that cell. The cells that can be changed by Solver to accomplish this goal are cells B9, C9, and D9, which contain the number of servings of each dish. The constraints are summarized in Table 8-3.

The following steps show how to use Solver to solve the Menu Planning worksheet within the given constraints.

Table 8-3 Additional Constraints for Solver

CELL	OPERATOR	CONSTRAINT
B9	<=	4
B9	>=	1
B9	int	
C9	<=	4
C9	>=	1
C9	int	
D9	<=	4
D9	>=	1
D9	int	
E11	<=	25
E12	>=	40

To Use Solver to Find the Optimal Combination

Click Tools on the menu bar and then point to Solver.

The Tools menu displays (Figure 8-22).

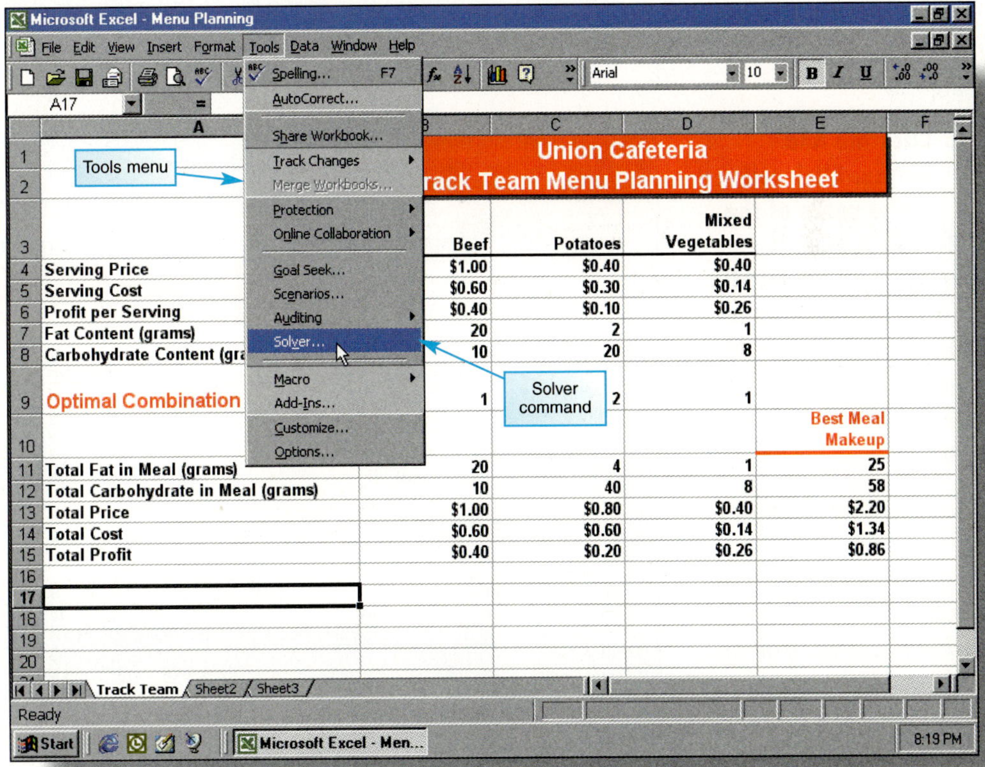

FIGURE 8-22

2 Click Solver. When the Solver Parameters dialog box displays, click cell E15 to set the target cell. Click the By Changing Cells box and then select the range B9:D9. Point to the Add button.

Excel displays the Solver Parameters dialog box as shown in Figure 8-23. The Set Target Cell displays as Total_Profit because Total_Profit is the cell name for cell E15 in the original worksheet.

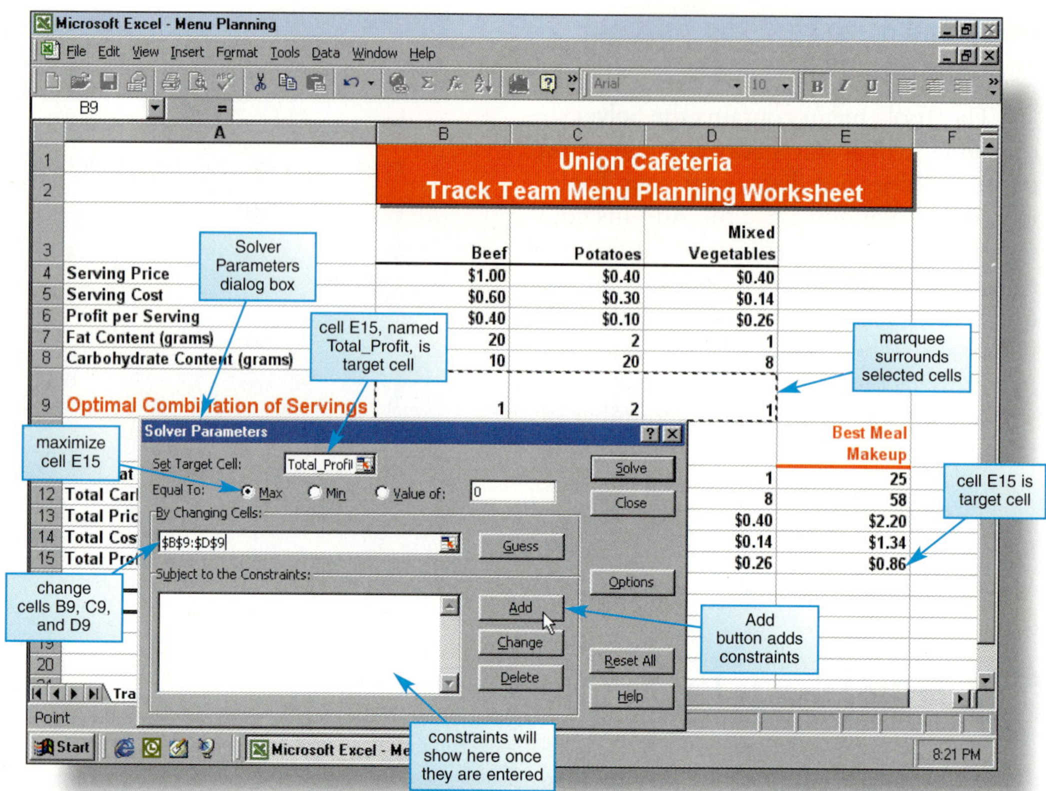

FIGURE 8-23

3 Click the Add button. Click cell B9 to set the value of the Cell Reference box. If necessary, click the middle box arrow and then select <= in the list. Type 4 in the Constraint text box and then point to the Add button.

The Add Constraint dialog box displays with the first constraint (Figure 8-24). This constraint means that cell B9 must be less than or equal to 4.

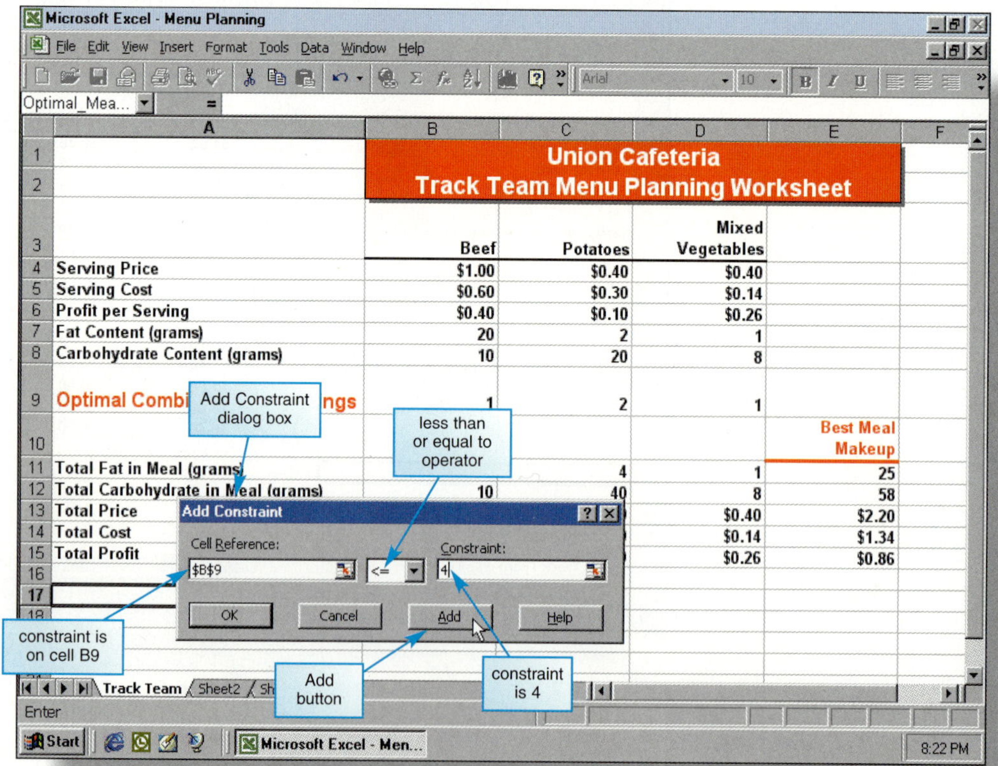

FIGURE 8-24

4 **Click the Add button. Click cell B9 to set the value of the Cell Reference box. Click the middle box arrow and then select >= in the list. Type** 1 **in the Constraint text box and then point to the Add button.**

The values for the second constraint display (Figure 8-25). This constraint means that cell B9 must be greater than or equal to 1.

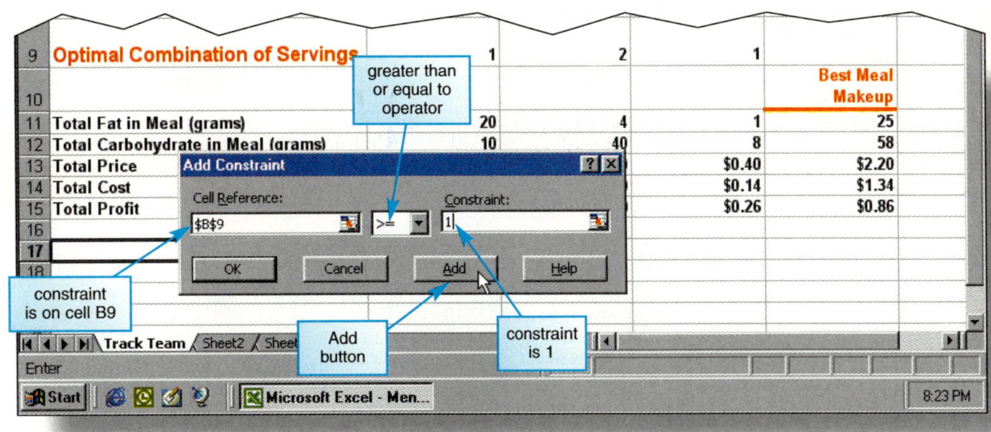

FIGURE 8-25

5 **Click the Add button. Click cell B9 to set the value of the Cell Reference box. Click the middle box arrow and then select int in the list. Point to the Add button.**

The values for the third constraint display (Figure 8-26). This constraint means that cell B9 must be assigned an integer.

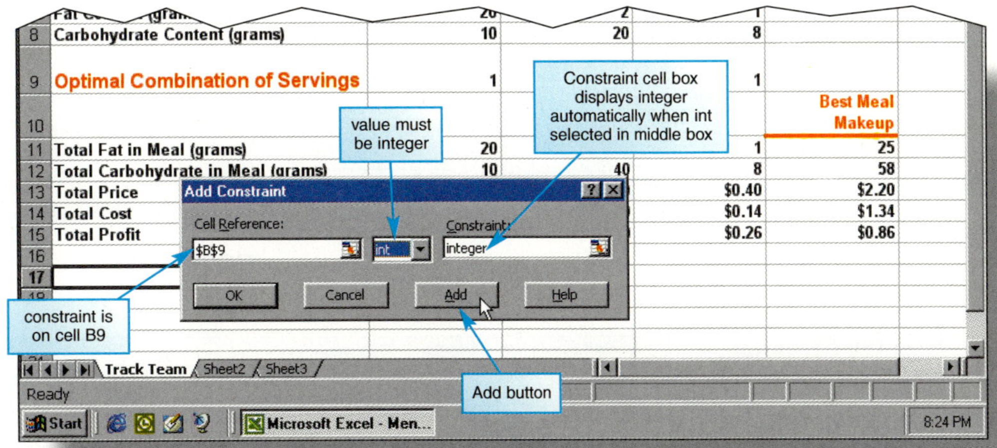

FIGURE 8-26

6 **Click the Add button. Enter the remaining constraints shown in Table 8-3 on page E 8.25, beginning with the contraints for cell C9. When finished with the final constraint, click the OK button. Point to the Options button.**

Excel displays all of the constraints in the Subject to the Constraints list box (Figure 8-27).

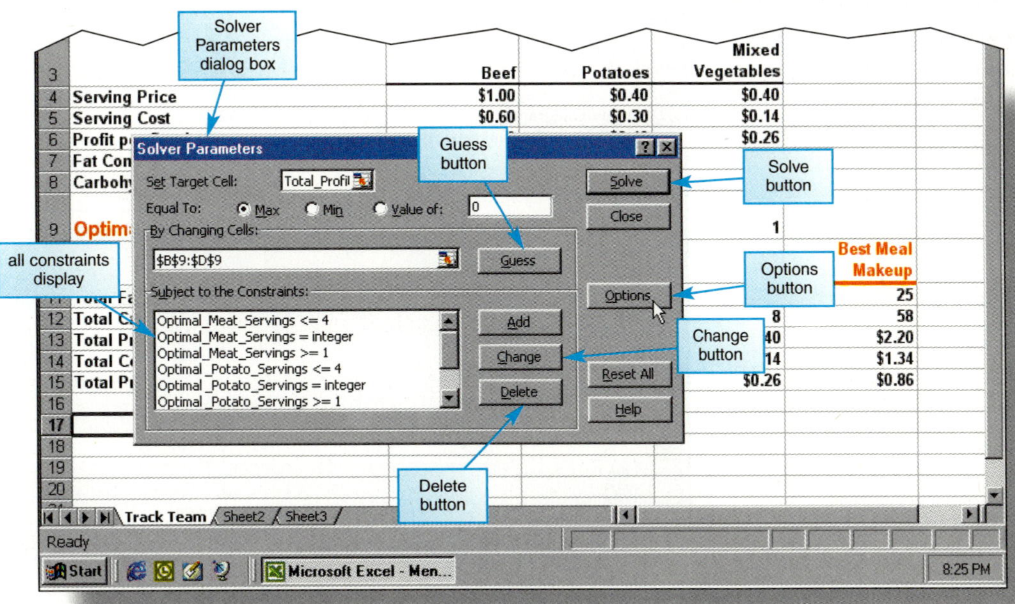

FIGURE 8-27

7 **Click the Options button. When the Solver Options dialog box displays, click Assume Linear Model. Point to the OK button.**

The Solver Options dialog box *displays (Figure 8-28).*

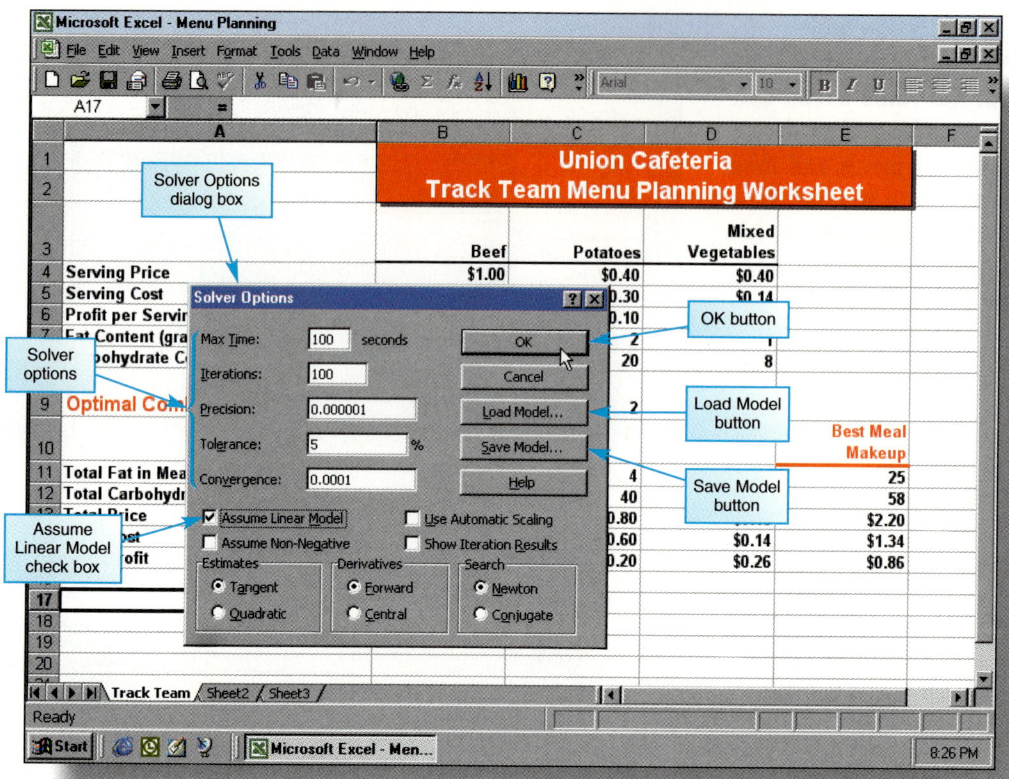

FIGURE 8-28

8 **Click the OK button. When the Solver Parameters dialog box displays again, click the Solve button.**

The Solver Results dialog box *displays. Excel indicates that it has found a solution to the problem (Figure 8-29).*

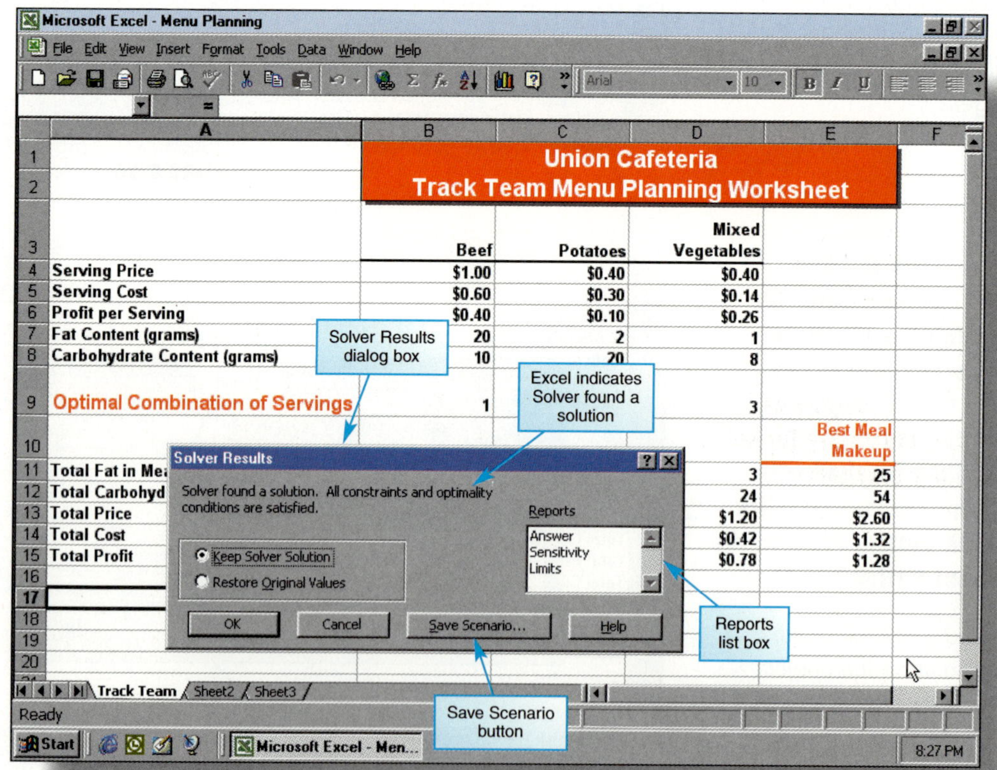

FIGURE 8-29

9 Select Answer in the Reports list and then point to the OK button.

The Solver Results dialog box displays as shown in Figure 8-30.

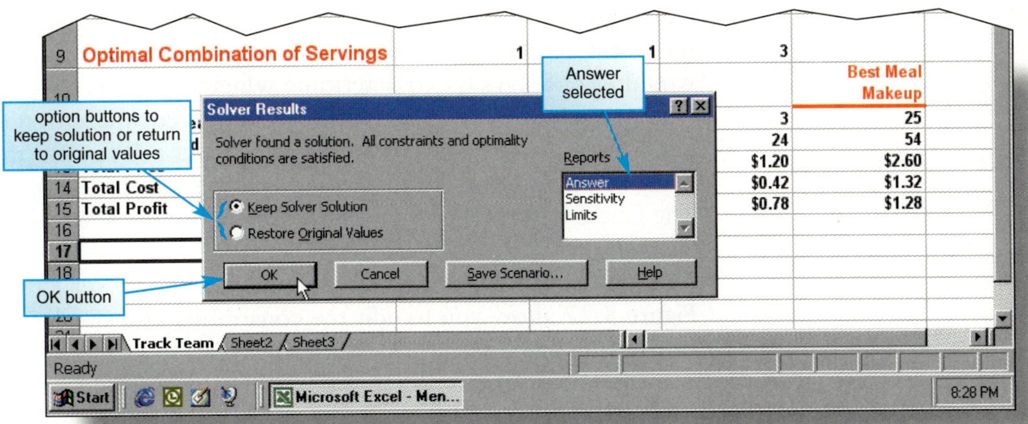

FIGURE 8-30

10 Click the OK button.

Excel displays the values found by Solver and recalculates the totals (Figure 8-31). All of the constraints of the problem have been satisfied.

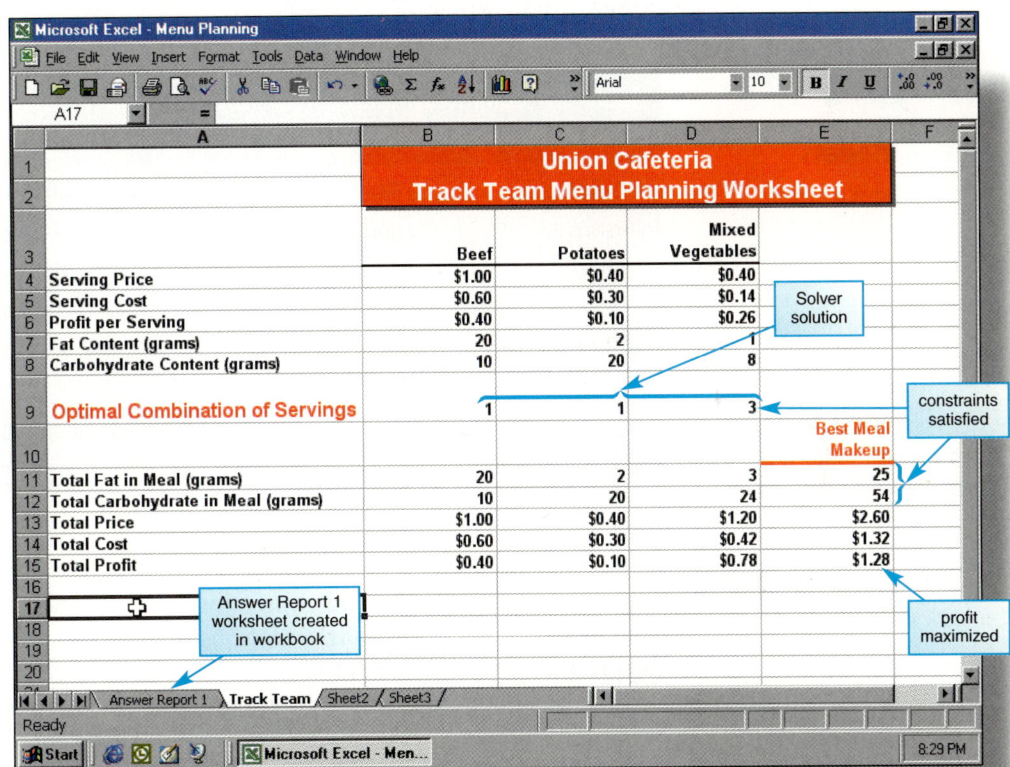

FIGURE 8-31

1. Press ALT+T, press V

Figure 8-31 shows that all of the constraints in the problem have been satisfied. The profit is $1.28 per meal, which is much better than the result of $0.86 that was calculated using the Goal Seek command in Figure 8-20 on page E 8.23.

When adding constraints, as shown in Figure 8-24 on page E 8.26, Solver allows you to enter a cell reference followed by an operator. If the operator is <=, >= or =, you enter the constraint value in the **Constraint cell box**. The constraint can be a value or a cell reference. The other valid operators are **int**, for an integer value, or **bin**, for cells that contain only one of two values, such as yes/no or true/false.

Rather than selecting the range B9:D9 as the changing cells in Step 6, clicking the **Guess button** in the Solver Parameters dialog box (Figure 8-27 on page E 8.27) would have Solver try to determine which cells affect the target cell. The button works much the same way as the Trace Precedents button does on the Auditing toolbar. Solver searches the formula in the target cell to determine which cells are precedents of the target cell and then adds these cells to the **By Changing Cells box** for you. The Guess button is not always accurate, however, which would have required a change to the cells selected by Solver.

The **Change button** and **Delete button** in the Solver Parameters dialog box in Figure 8-27 allow you to edit the constraints that display in the Subject to the Constraints list box.

The Solver Options dialog box in Figure 8-28 on page E 8.28 contains several technical parameters that allow you to configure the inner workings of Solver. Many of the other parameters are beyond the scope of this discussion. Usually, you already have the information for a problem that lets you determine which parameters you need to vary. Table 8-4 shows the meaning of some of the parameters that you may use from time to time.

Solver Parameters

Sometimes Solver will give you a message telling you that the target cell values do not converge. This means that Solver can meet all of the constraints, but the target value, such as the Total Profit in cell E15 in Figure 8-31 on the previous page, can be increased or decreased indefinitely. Usually, this means that you have not specified enough constraints.

Table 8-4 Commonly Used Solver Parameters in the Solver Options Dialog Box

PARAMETER	MEANING
Max Time	The total time that Solver should spend trying different solutions expressed in seconds.
Iterations	The number of different combinations of possible answer values that Solver should try.
Tolerance	Instructs Solver how close it must come to the target value to consider the problem to be solved. For example, if the target value is 100 and the Tolerance is 5%, then 95 is an acceptable answer.
Assume Linear Model	If selected, assumes that this problem is linear in nature. That is, the changing values have a proportional effect on the value of the target cell.
Assume Non-Negative	If selected, for all changing cells that do not have constraints on them, Solver should keep these numbers positive.

More About

Solver Models

When you save a model, which is a collection of the data in the target cell, changing cells, and constraints, Excel does not save the solution as well. The solution can be saved separately by using the Save Scenario option in the Solver Results dialog box shown in Figure 8-29 on page E 8.28. When saving a model, the data is saved in an area you select in a worksheet. You should carefully note where you save models because Excel does not label or mark the model in any way.

Excel saves the current Solver parameters automatically. Only the most recent parameters are saved. If you want to use new values in Solver and want to save the target cell, changing cell, and constraint values for Solver, the **Load Model button** and **Save Model button** in the Solver Options dialog box allow you to save the values and then re-use them in the future.

The **Save Scenario button** shown in Figure 8-29 on page E 8.28 allows you to save the results of Solver in a separate area in your workbook. Scenarios are discussed in detail later in this project.

When using Solver, two other issues must be kept in mind. First, some problems do not have solutions. The constraints may be constructed in such a way that an answer cannot be found that satisfies all of the constraints. Second, sometimes multiple answers solve the same problem. Solver does not indicate when this is the case, and you will have to use your own judgment to determine if this is the case. As long as you are confident that you have given Solver all of the constraints for a problem, however, all answers should be equally valid.

More About

Solver Scenarios

When you click the Save Scenario button in the Solver Results dialog box, Solver creates a record of the values of the changing cells that solved the problem. You can name this result and then be able to recall it in the future. It is important to note that the target cell value is not changed, just the changing cells' values.

Viewing a Solver Answer Report

The **Solver Answer Report** summarizes the problem that you have presented to Solver. It shows the original and final values of the target cell along with the original and final values of the cells that Solver adjusted to find the answer. Additionally, it lists all of the constraints that you imposed on Solver.

The Answer Report documents that a particular problem has been solved correctly. Because it lists all of the relevant information in a concise format, you use the Answer Report to make certain that you have entered all of the constraints and allowed Solver to vary all the cells necessary to solve the problem. You also can use the report to reconstruct the Solver model in the future.

Other Solver Reports

The Sensitivity Report shows how sensitive the Solver solution is to changes in the constraints and the target cell. The Limits Report shows the upper and lower values that the changing cells can have and still solve the problem given the constraints. Both of these reports are generated as separate worksheets in the current workbook, just as the Answer Report.

To View the Answer Report

1 Click the Answer Report 1 tab at the bottom of the window.

The Solver Answer Report displays (Figure 8-32).

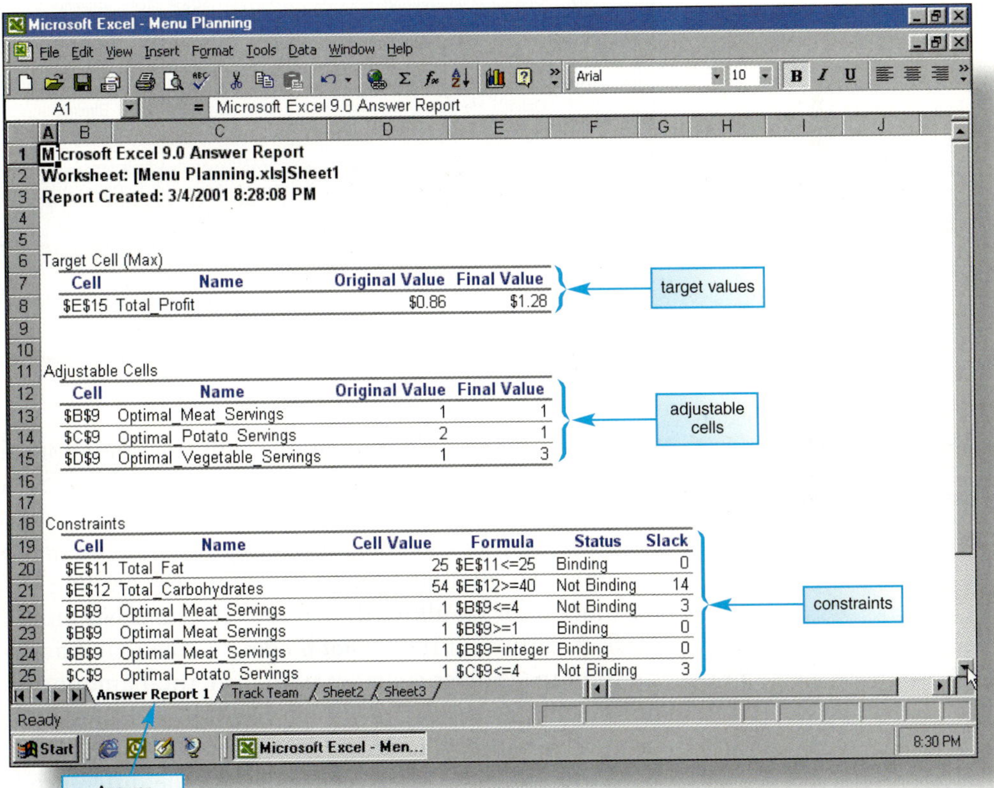

Cell	Name	Original Value	Final Value
E15	Total_Profit	$0.86	$1.28

Cell	Name	Original Value	Final Value
B9	Optimal_Meat_Servings	1	1
C9	Optimal_Potato_Servings	2	1
D9	Optimal_Vegetable_Servings	1	3

Cell	Name	Cell Value	Formula	Status	Slack
E11	Total_Fat	25	E11<=25	Binding	0
E12	Total_Carbohydrates	54	E12>=40	Not Binding	14
B9	Optimal_Meat_Servings	1	B9<=4	Not Binding	3
B9	Optimal_Meat_Servings	1	B9>=1	Binding	0
B9	Optimal_Meat_Servings	1	B9=integer	Binding	0
C9	Optimal_Potato_Servings	1	C9<=4	Not Binding	3

FIGURE 8-32

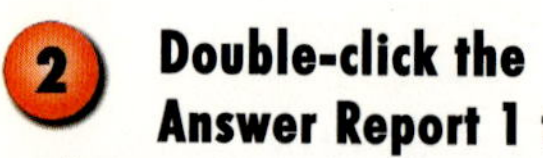

2 Double-click the Answer Report 1 tab and type `Track Team Answer Report 1` **as the worksheet name. Use the scroll bar to scroll down to view the remaining cells of the Answer Report.**

The tab shows the new worksheet name and the remainder of the Answer Report displays (Figure 8-33).

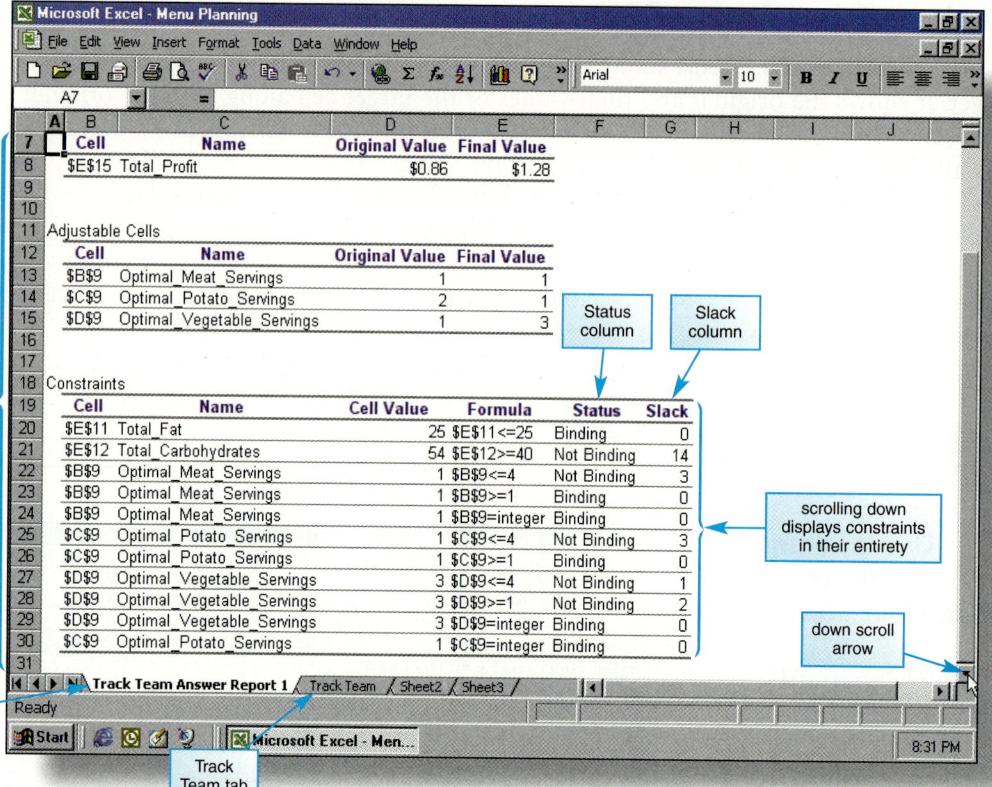

Cell	Name	Original Value	Final Value
E15	Total_Profit	$0.86	$1.28

Cell	Name	Original Value	Final Value
B9	Optimal_Meat_Servings	1	1
C9	Optimal_Potato_Servings	2	1
D9	Optimal_Vegetable_Servings	1	3

Cell	Name	Cell Value	Formula	Status	Slack
E11	Total_Fat	25	E11<=25	Binding	0
E12	Total_Carbohydrates	54	E12>=40	Not Binding	14
B9	Optimal_Meat_Servings	1	B9<=4	Not Binding	3
B9	Optimal_Meat_Servings	1	B9>=1	Binding	0
B9	Optimal_Meat_Servings	1	B9=integer	Binding	0
C9	Optimal_Potato_Servings	1	C9<=4	Not Binding	3
C9	Optimal_Potato_Servings	1	C9>=1	Binding	0
D9	Optimal_Vegetable_Servings	3	D9<=4	Not Binding	1
D9	Optimal_Vegetable_Servings	3	D9>=1	Not Binding	2
D9	Optimal_Vegetable_Servings	3	D9=integer	Binding	0
C9	Optimal_Potato_Servings	1	C9=integer	Binding	0

FIGURE 8-33

More About

Answer Reports

The slack value in the Answer Report tells you where you may have some flexibility in the answer that Solver has found. The less slack that a changing cell has, the less you can change it and still meet the constraints of the problem. Slack tells you where you still have options in the Solver answer.

Figure 8-33 displays additional information about the constraints that you placed on the problem and how the constraints were used to solve the problem. Column F, the **Status column**, indicates whether the constraint was binding or not. A constraint that is **binding** is one that limited the final solution in some way. For example, the total fat content of the meal is binding because the solution maximizes the amount of fat allowed by the track team. No more fat content is allowed in the meal. A constraint that is **not binding** is one that was not a limiting factor in the solution that Solver came up with. The total amount of carbohydrates in the meal is not binding because the solution could have included more or less carbohydrates if necessary to meet the other constraints.

Column G, the **Slack column**, shows the difference between the value in the cell in that row and the limit of the constraint. Cell G21 shows that the slack for the Total_Carbohydrates is 14. This means that the solution contains 14 more grams of carbohydrates than the minimum required in the constraints. Cells that are binding have zero slack.

More About

File Protection

Once you have protected your workbook with a password, it is important to write the password down or memorize it for future reference. No way to get around the requirement for a password exists once you have saved the file with a password.

Saving the Workbook with Passwords

Excel allows you to protect your data at the worksheet level, workbook level, and file level. At the worksheet level, you protect cells. At the workbook level, you protect the Excel window. Both of these levels of protection are available through the Protection command on the Tools menu as described in Project 7. The highest level of protection is file protection. **File protection** lets you assign a password to a workbook for users who are allowed to view the workbook and a separate password for users who are permitted to modify the workbook.

File protection is performed when Excel saves a workbook. Even though you are the workbook creator, you will be prompted for the passwords when you open the workbook later. The following steps save the workbook with passwords.

To Save the Workbook with Passwords

1 Click the Track Team tab at the bottom of the window. Click File on the menu bar and then click Save As. Type Menu Planning2 **in the File name text box and, if necessary, select 3½ Floppy (A:) in the Save in list. Click the Tools button on the Save As dialog box toolbar and then point to General Options.**

The Save As dialog box and Tools button menu display (Figure 8-34).

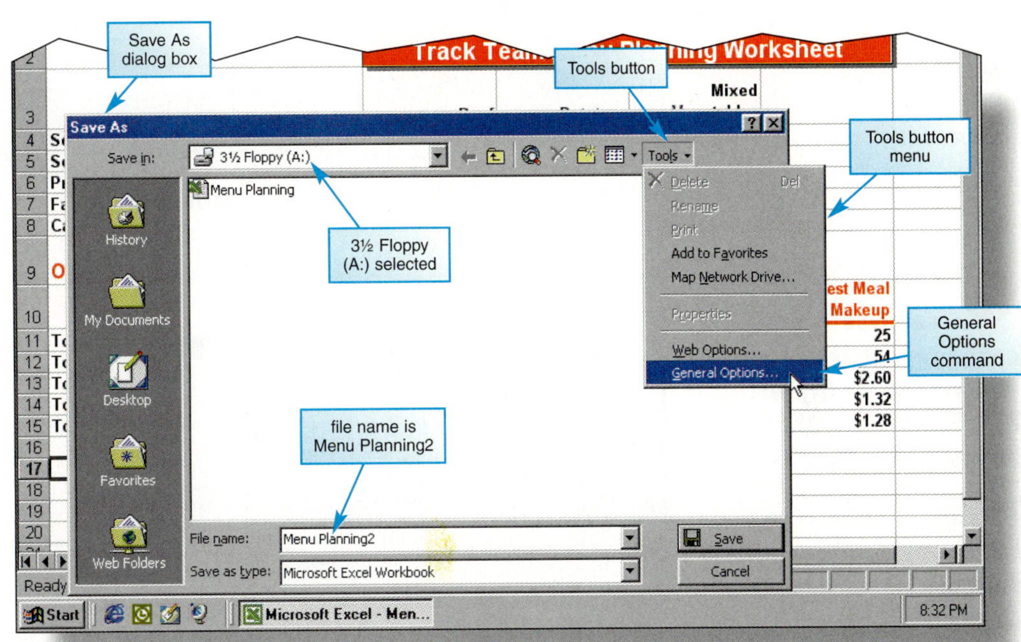

FIGURE 8-34

2 Click General Options. Type cafeteria **in the Password to open text box. Type** cafeteria **in the Password to modify text box. Point to the OK button.**

The Save Options dialog box displays. Excel displays asterisks in the place of the password cafeteria in both text boxes so no one is able to see the password you typed (Figure 8-35).

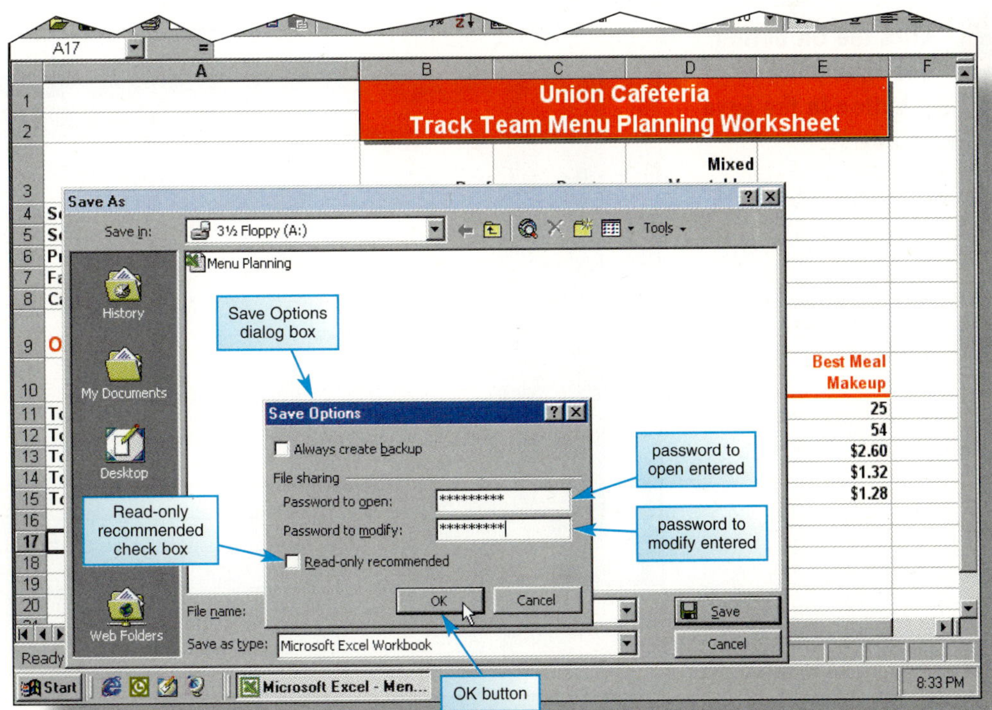

FIGURE 8-35

3 Click the OK button and then type `cafeteria` **in the Reenter password to proceed text box. Point to the OK button.**

The Confirm Password dialog box displays. Again, Excel displays asterisks in the place of the password cafeteria (Figure 8-36).

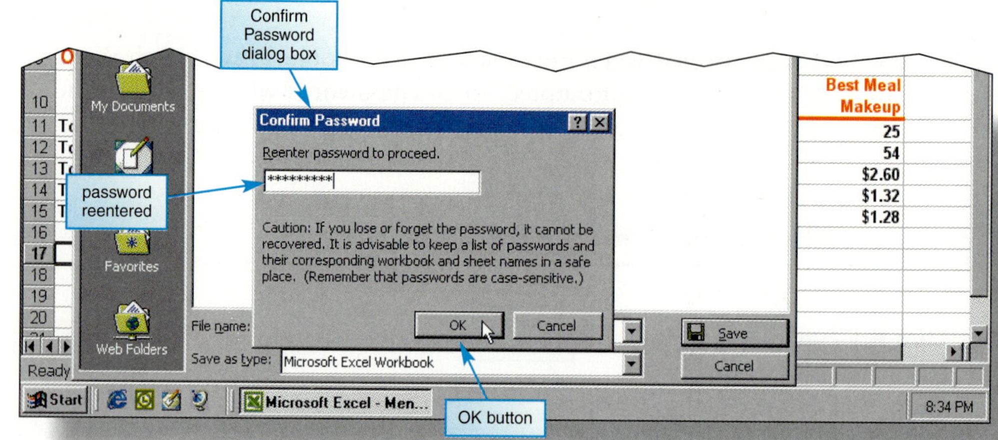

FIGURE 8-36

4 Click the OK button and type `cafeteria` **in the Reenter password to modify text box. Point to the OK button.**

The Confirm Password dialog box displays for the password to modify the workbook (Figure 8-37).

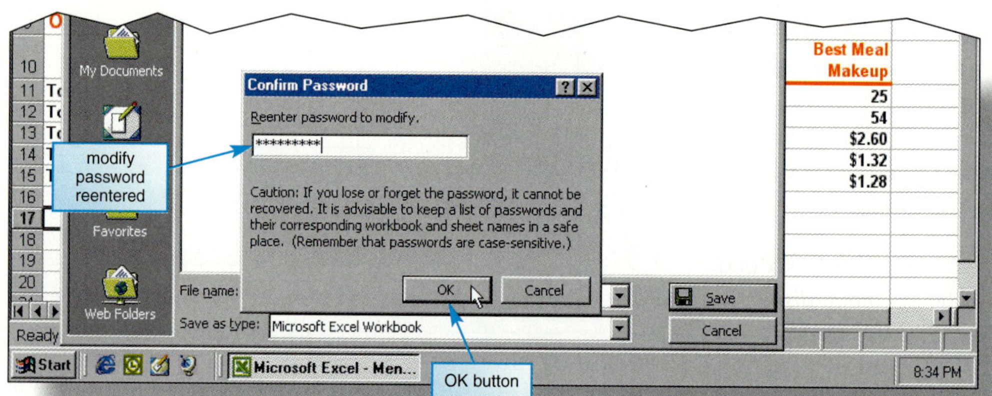

FIGURE 8-37

5 Click the OK button and then point to the Save button in the Save As dialog box.

The Save As dialog box displays (Figure 8-38).

6 Click the Save button.

Excel saves the password protected file to drive A.

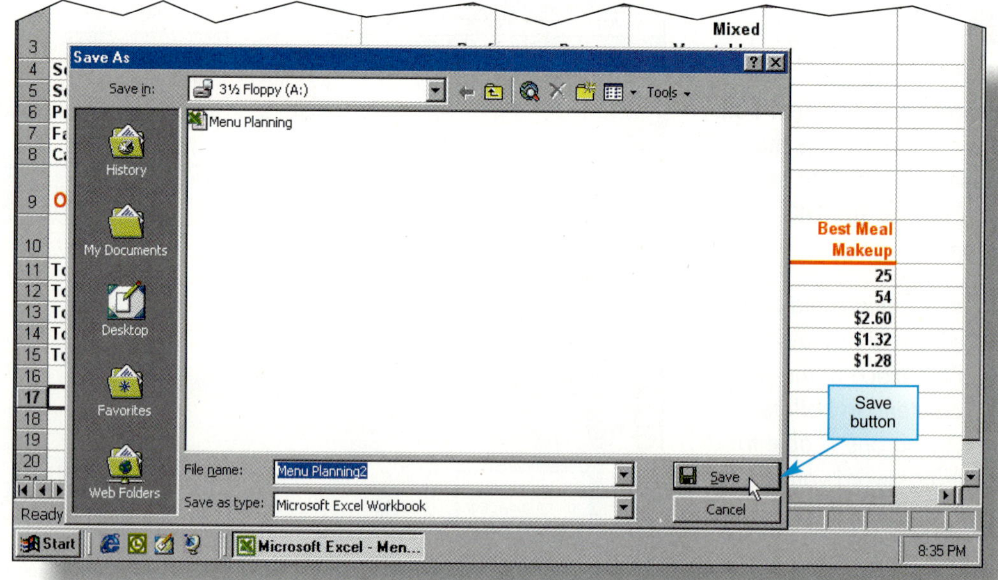

FIGURE 8-38

Other Ways

1. With Save As dialog box open, press ALT+L, press G

The workbook now is protected with a password and when a user opens the workbook, Excel will prompt for a password to view the workbook. If the user enters the correct password, Excel prompts for the password to modify the workbook. At this point, the user may choose to open the workbook as read-only, meaning that the user can only view the contents of the workbook and not modify the workbook. The **Read-only recommended check box** shown in Figure 8-35 on page E 8.33 allows you to notify users who open your workbook that it is best to open the workbook as read-only.

Read-Only Workbooks

You can save a file and recommend read-only access to others who open the worksheet. This is not a guarantee, however, that the user will follow the recommendation. To ensure that the worksheet truly is read-only, you must use a file password and keep the password to yourself.

Using Scenario Manager to Analyze Data

Excel's **Scenario Manager** allows you to record and save different sets of what-if assumptions (data values) called scenarios. For example, each different main entrée (beef and chicken) can be considered a scenario. A meal containing beef and meeting the other constraints is the first scenario. The second scenario consists of a meal that contains chicken, which has different amounts of fat and carbohydrates and different costs. Each set of values in these examples represents a what-if assumption. The primary uses of Scenario Manager are to:

1. Create different scenarios with multiple sets of changing cells
2. Build summary worksheets that contain the different scenarios
3. View the results of each scenario on your worksheet

The remainder of this project shows how to use Scenario Manager for each of the three uses listed above. Once you create the scenarios, you can instruct Excel to build the summary worksheets, including a Scenario Summary and a Scenario PivotTable.

More About

Scenario Manager

Worksheets are used primarily for what-if analysis. You enter values into cells and instantaneously the results change in the dependent cells. As you continue to change values in the key cells, you lose the previous results. If you want to go back, you have to reenter the data. Scenario Manager allows you to store the different sets of values (called scenarios) so you can redisplay them easily with a few clicks of the mouse button. Each scenario can have up to 32 sets of changing cells.

Saving the Current Data as a Scenario

The current data on the worksheet consists of the Beef scenario and contains the values that correctly solve one of the problems presented. These values can be saved as a scenario that can be accessed later or compared side by side with other scenarios. The steps on the next page create the Beef scenario using the **Scenarios command** on the Tools menu.

To Save the Current Data as a Scenario

1 Click Tools on the menu bar and point to Scenarios.

The Tools menu displays (Figure 8-39).

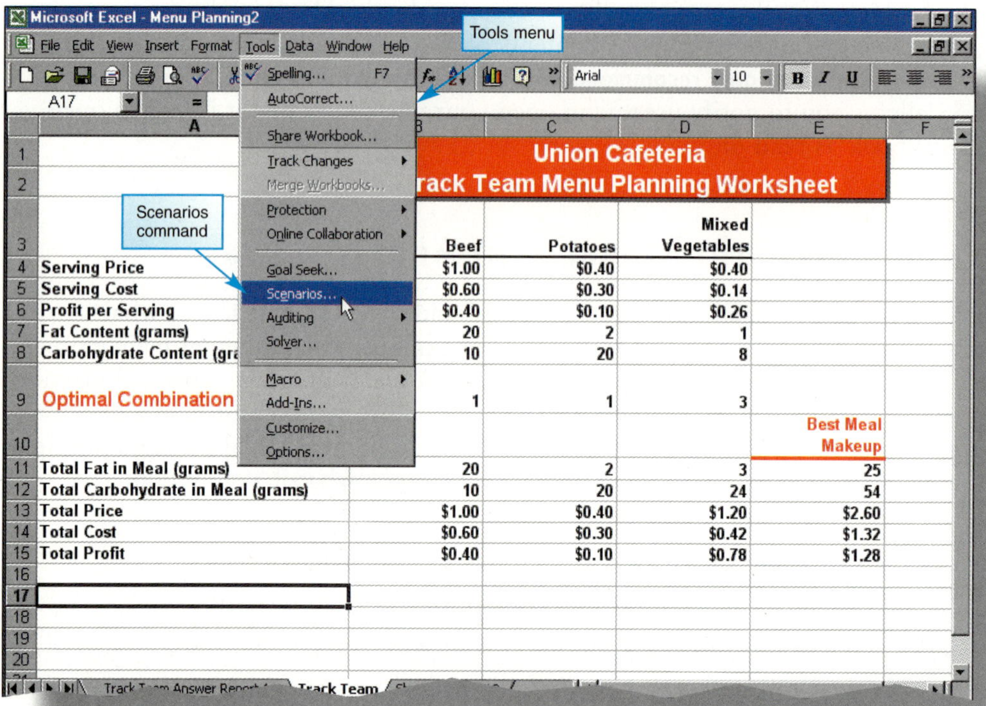

FIGURE 8-39

2 Click Scenarios. When the Scenario Manager dialog box displays, point to the Add button.

The Scenario Manager dialog box *displays indicating that no scenarios are defined (Figure 8-40). It also instructs you to choose Add to add scenarios.*

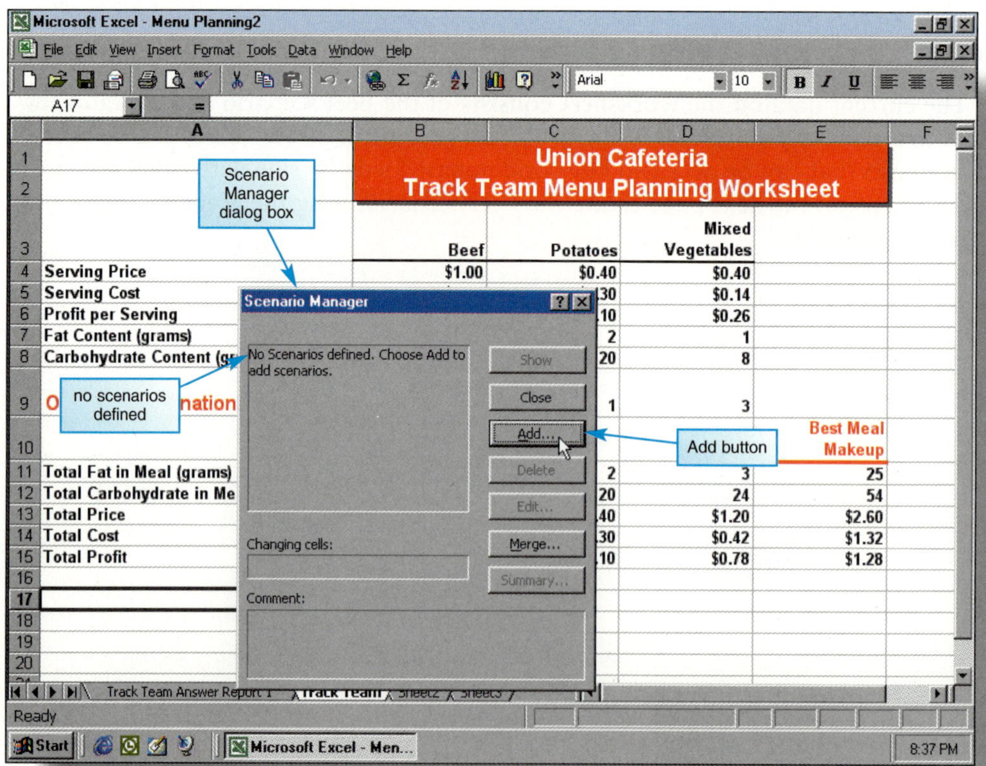

FIGURE 8-40

3 **Click the Add button. When the Add Scenario dialog box displays, type Beef in the Scenario name text box. Point to the Collapse Dialog button.**

The Add Scenario dialog box displays (Figure 8-41).

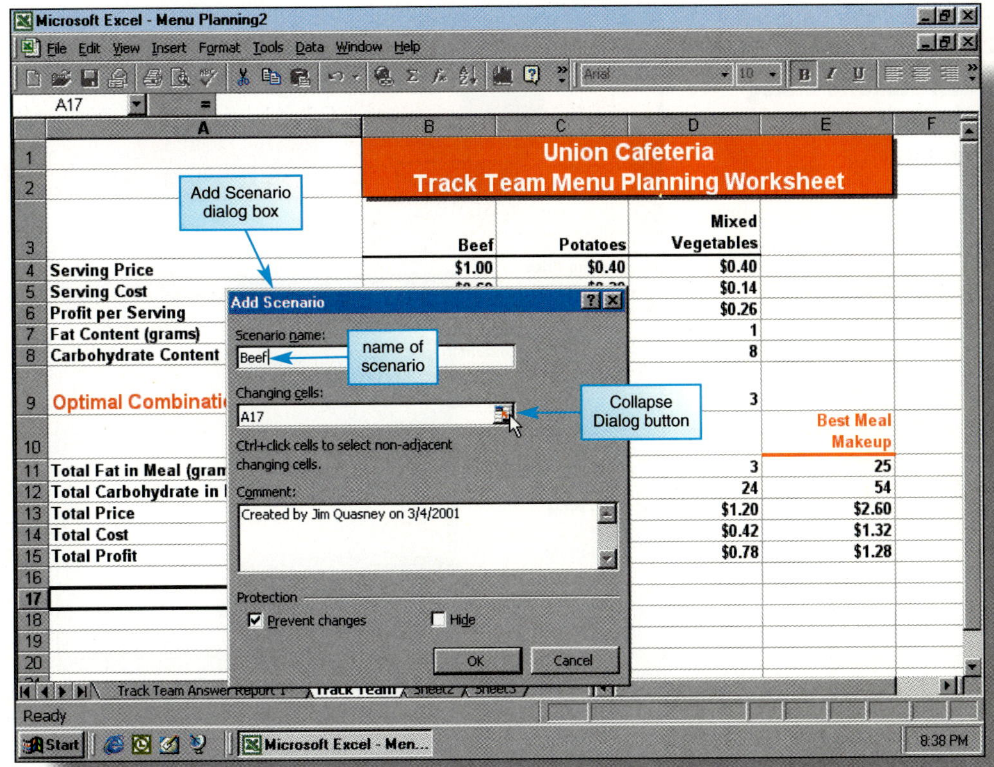

FIGURE 8-41

4 **Click the Collapse Dialog button. When the Add Scenario – Changing cells dialog box displays, click cell B3, hold down the CTRL key, and then click cells B4, B5, B7, B8, B9, C9, and D9. Release the CTRL key. Point to the Collapse Dialog button in the Add Scenario - Changing cells dialog box.**

A marquee displays around the selected cells. Excel assigns the cells to the Changing cells text box (Figure 8-42).

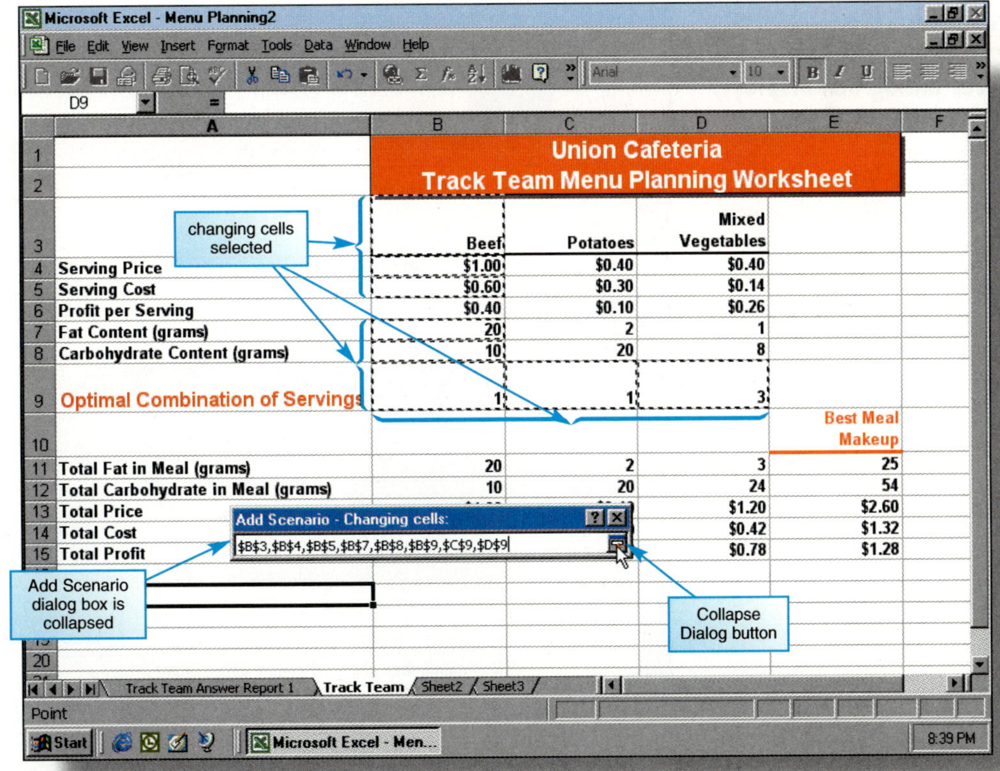

FIGURE 8-42

5 Click the Collapse Dialog button. When the Edit Scenario dialog box displays, point to the OK button.

*The Add Scenario dialog box changes to the **Edit Scenario dialog box** (Figure 8-43).*

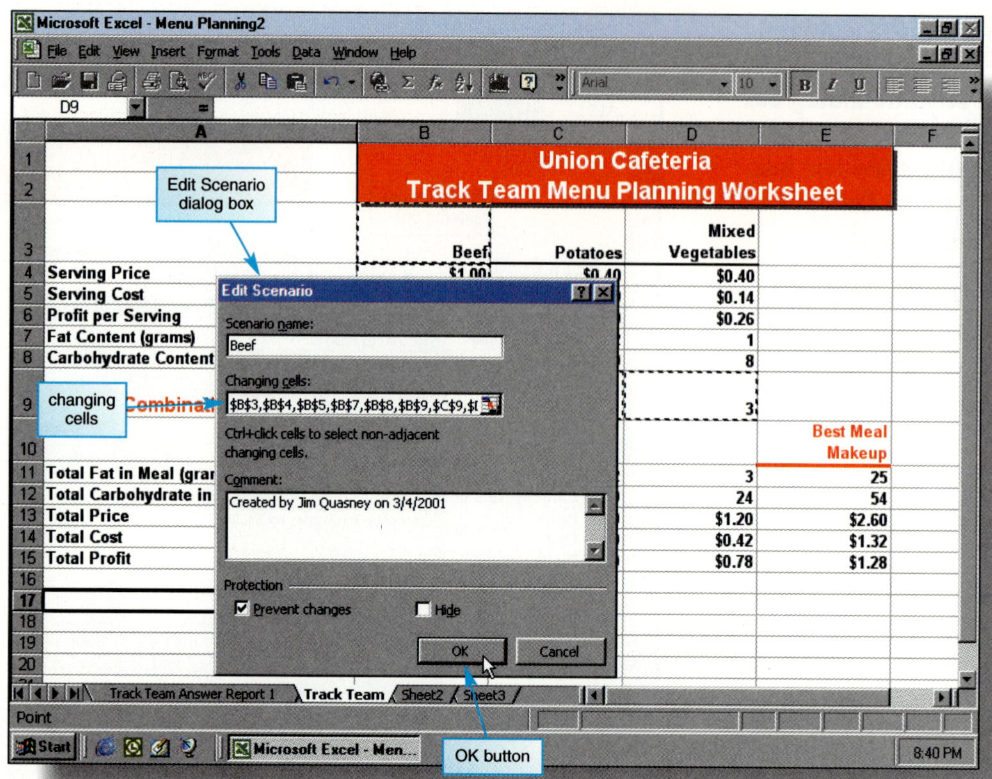

FIGURE 8-43

6 Click the OK button. When the Scenario Values dialog box displays, point to the OK button.

*The **Scenario Values dialog box** displays. The cell names selected display in a numbered list with their current values (Figure 8-44). Because names were assigned to these cells when the worksheet was created, the cell names, rather than cell references, display in the numbered list.*

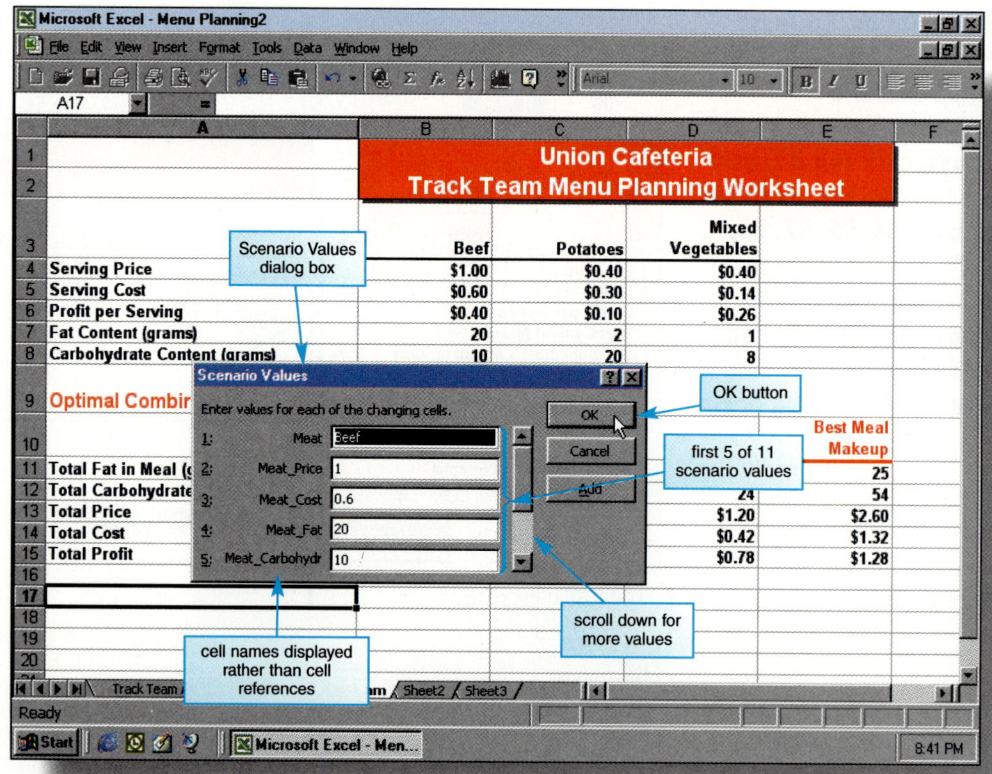

FIGURE 8-44

7 Click the OK button. When the Scenario Manager dialog box displays, point to the Close button.

The Beef scenario displays in the Scenario list (Figure 8-45). Excel displays the names of the Changing cells in the Changing cells box.

8 Click the Close button in the Scenario Manager dialog box.

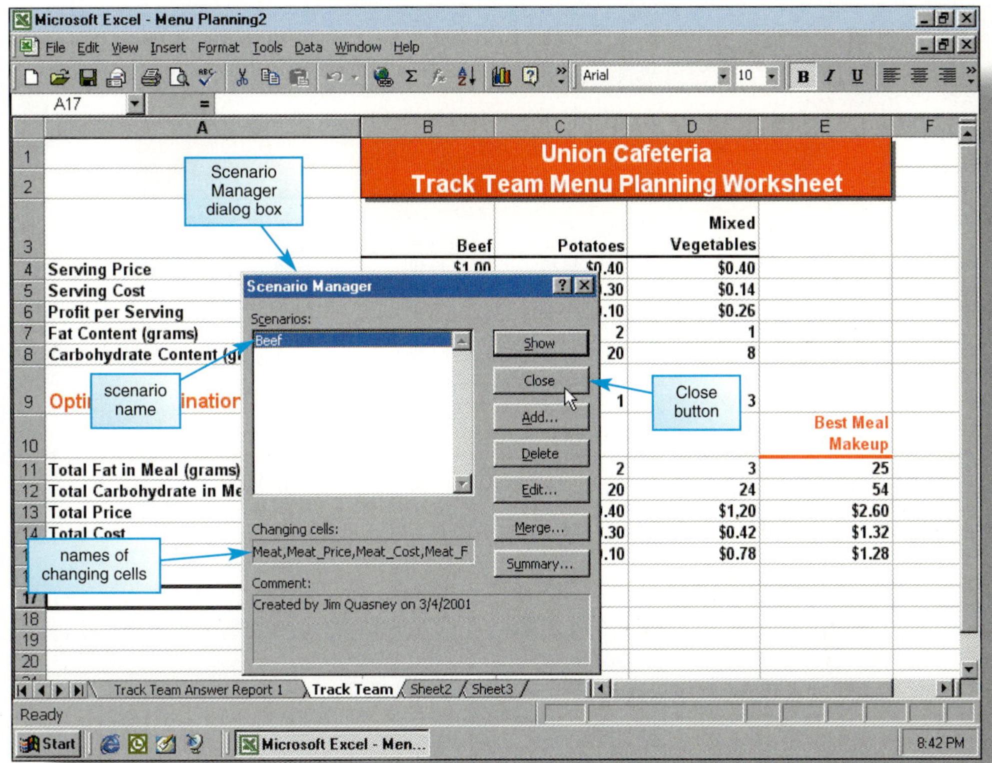

FIGURE 8-45

Other Ways

1. Press ALT+T, press E

More About 2000

New Scenarios

When beginning to create scenarios in a worksheet, the following guidelines help in organizing the data. First, create a base scenario that contains the original values of the worksheet. Second, name the cells that will be changing cells and result cells, as has been done in the worksheet in this project. Finally, if you plan to save different types of scenarios in a worksheet (that is different changing cells), use a naming convention for the scenarios that will help you remember which scenarios contain which set of changing cells.

Once the scenario has been saved, you can recall it at any time using Scenario Manager. In Figure 8-44, the values of the cells in the Scenario Values dialog box are defaulted to the current changing cells in the worksheet. By changing the text boxes next to the cell names, you can save different values in the scenario from what is shown in the worksheet.

The next step is to change the values on the worksheet to show the data when using a chicken dish as the main entrée.

Creating a New Scenario

Because the Beef scenario is saved, you can enter the data for the Chicken scenario directly in the worksheet and then use Solver to solve the Chicken scenario (Figure 8-46a on the next page) in the same way that you solved the Beef scenario. The same constraints apply for both scenarios, so Solver does not require you to reenter all of the constraints. The Answer Report (Figure 8-46b on the next page) meets the requirement that you create supporting documentation for your answer. After solving the Chicken scenario, you save the scenario in the same manner that you saved the Beef scenario.

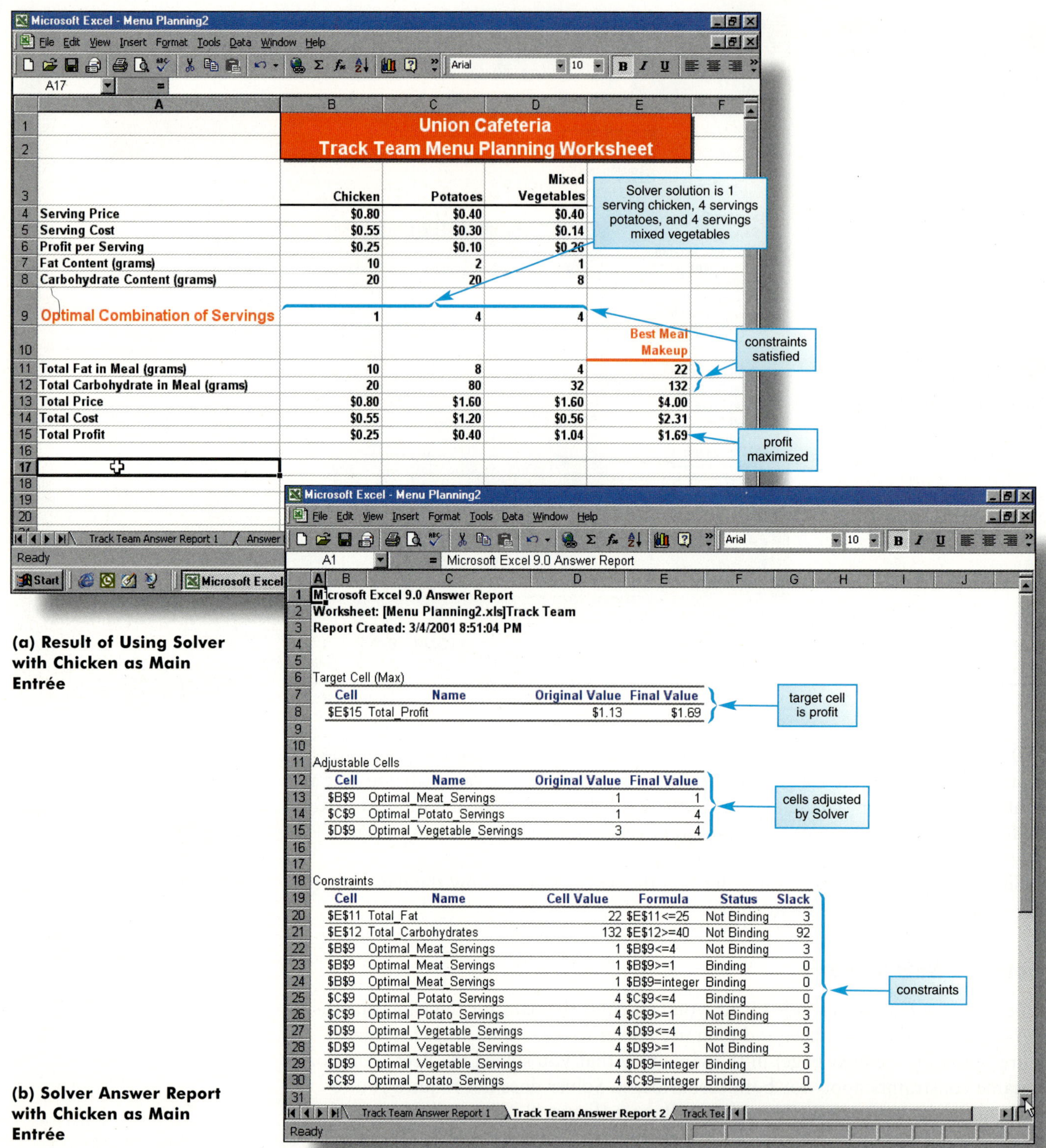

	Chicken	Potatoes	Mixed Vegetables	Best Meal Makeup
Serving Price	$0.80	$0.40	$0.40	
Serving Cost	$0.55	$0.30	$0.14	
Profit per Serving	$0.25	$0.10	$0.26	
Fat Content (grams)	10	2	1	
Carbohydrate Content (grams)	20	20	8	
Optimal Combination of Servings	1	4	4	
Total Fat in Meal (grams)	10	8	4	22
Total Carbohydrate in Meal (grams)	20	80	32	132
Total Price	$0.80	$1.60	$1.60	$4.00
Total Cost	$0.55	$1.20	$0.56	$2.31
Total Profit	$0.25	$0.40	$1.04	$1.69

Target Cell (Max)

Cell	Name	Original Value	Final Value
E15	Total_Profit	$1.13	$1.69

Adjustable Cells

Cell	Name	Original Value	Final Value
B9	Optimal_Meat_Servings	1	1
C9	Optimal_Potato_Servings	1	4
D9	Optimal_Vegetable_Servings	3	4

Constraints

Cell	Name	Cell Value	Formula	Status	Slack
E11	Total_Fat	22	E11<=25	Not Binding	3
E12	Total_Carbohydrates	132	E12>=40	Not Binding	92
B9	Optimal_Meat_Servings	1	B9<=4	Not Binding	3
B9	Optimal_Meat_Servings	1	B9>=1	Binding	0
B9	Optimal_Meat_Servings	1	B9=integer	Binding	0
C9	Optimal_Potato_Servings	4	C9<=4	Binding	0
C9	Optimal_Potato_Servings	4	C9>=1	Not Binding	3
D9	Optimal_Vegetable_Servings	4	D9<=4	Binding	0
D9	Optimal_Vegetable_Servings	4	D9>=1	Not Binding	3
D9	Optimal_Vegetable_Servings	4	D9=integer	Binding	0
C9	Optimal_Potato_Servings	4	C9=integer	Binding	0

(a) Result of Using Solver with Chicken as Main Entrée

(b) Solver Answer Report with Chicken as Main Entrée

FIGURE 8-46

The relevant information for the Chicken scenario (Figure 8-46a) is that the serving price is 80 cents per serving, the serving cost is 55 cents per serving, the fat content of one serving is 10 grams, and the carbohydrate content is 20 grams per serving. These values must be entered into the appropriate cells before you can use Solver.

To Add the Data for a New Scenario

1 **Click cell B3 and type** `Chicken` **as the column heading. Click cell B4 and type** `.80` **as the serving price. Click cell B5 and type** `.55` **as the serving cost. Click cell B7 and type** `10` **as the fat content in grams. Click cell B8, type** `20` **as the carbohydrate content in grams, and then press the ENTER key.**

The menu planning worksheet displays with the chicken entrée replacing the beef entrée (Figure 8-47).

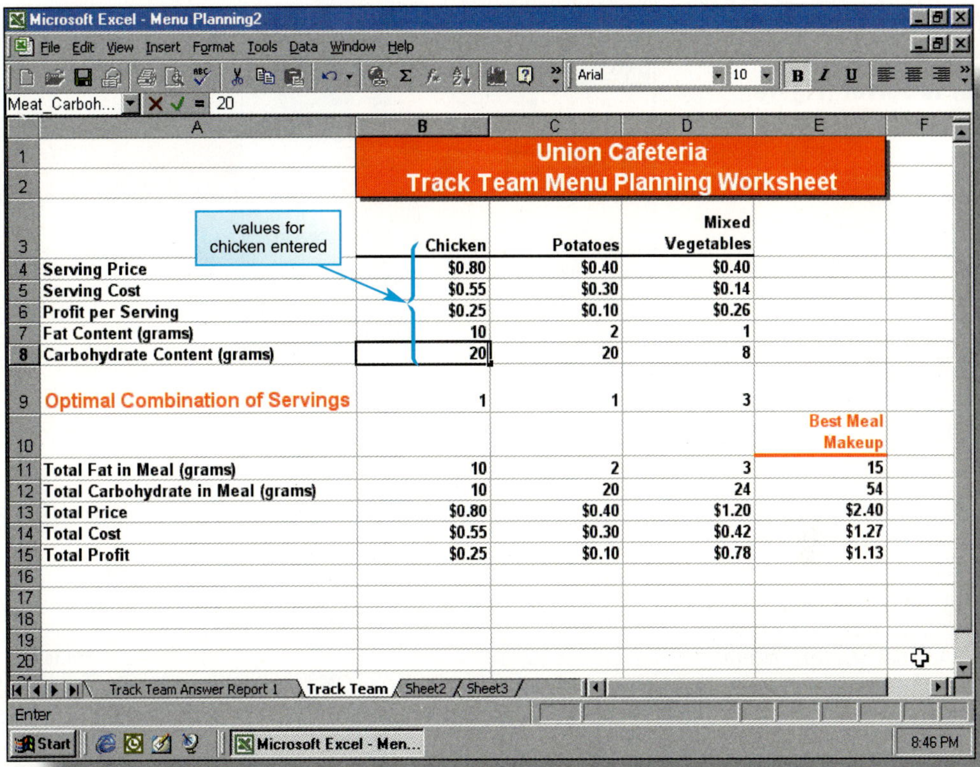

Microsoft Excel - Menu Planning2

	A	B	C	D	E
1		Union Cafeteria			
2		Track Team Menu Planning Worksheet			
3		Chicken	Potatoes	Mixed Vegetables	
4	Serving Price	$0.80	$0.40	$0.40	
5	Serving Cost	$0.55	$0.30	$0.14	
6	Profit per Serving	$0.25	$0.10	$0.26	
7	Fat Content (grams)	10	2	1	
8	Carbohydrate Content (grams)	20	20	8	
9	Optimal Combination of Servings	1	1	3	
10					Best Meal Makeup
11	Total Fat in Meal (grams)	10	2	3	15
12	Total Carbohydrate in Meal (grams)	10	20	24	54
13	Total Price	$0.80	$0.40	$1.20	$2.40
14	Total Cost	$0.55	$0.30	$0.42	$1.27
15	Total Profit	$0.25	$0.10	$0.78	$1.13

values for chicken entered

FIGURE 8-47

Next, Solver must be used to find the optimal combination of servings that satisfies the constraints and maximizes profit for the Union Cafeteria.

Using Solver to Find a New Solution

Just as with the Beef scenario, the Chicken scenario must be solved before saving it as a scenario. Figure 8-47 shows that the total fat and total carbohydrate content of the current solution satisfies the requirements of less than or equal to 25 grams of fat, and at least 40 grams of carbohydrates. It is unknown, however, whether the solution maximizes the total profit. Solver takes this requirement into consideration.

To Use Solver to Find a New Solution

1 Click Tools on the menu bar and then point to Solver (Figure 8-48).

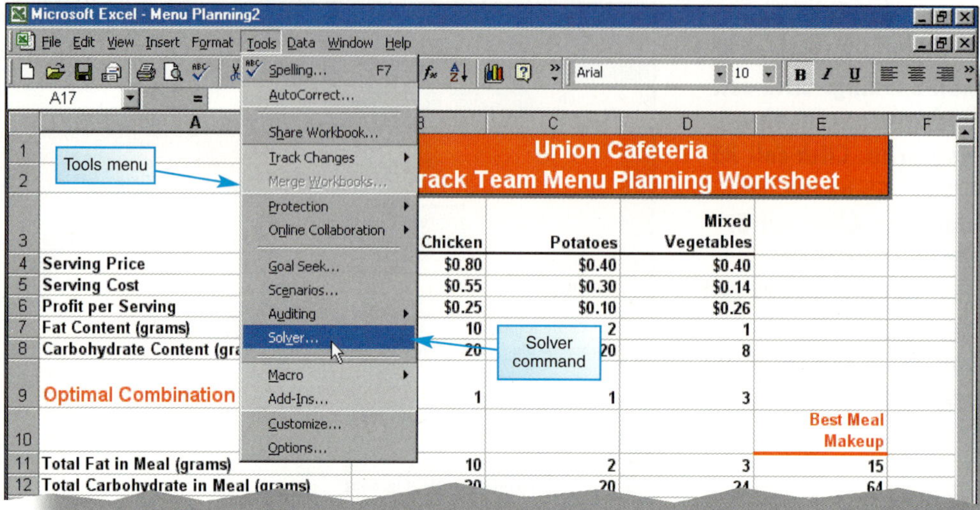

FIGURE 8-48

2 Click Solver. When the Solver Parameters dialog box displays, point to the Solve button.

The Solver Parameters dialog box displays with the previous target cell and constraints (Figure 8-49). Because the constraints remain the same for chicken as they were for beef, no additional entries are required in the Solver Parameters dialog box.

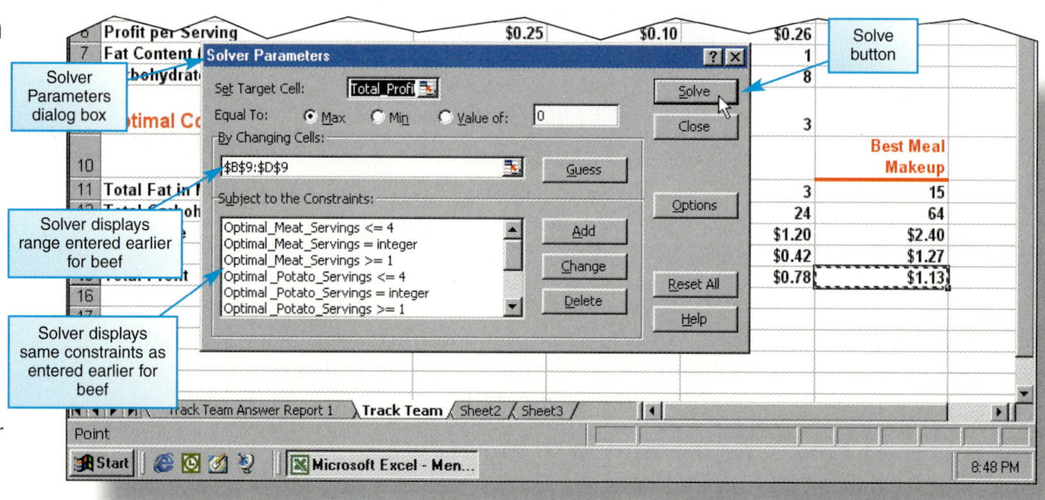

FIGURE 8-49

3 Click the Solve button. When the Solver Results dialog box displays, click Answer in the Reports list. Point to the OK button.

The Solver Results dialog box displays indicating that Solver found a solution to the problem (Figure 8-50).

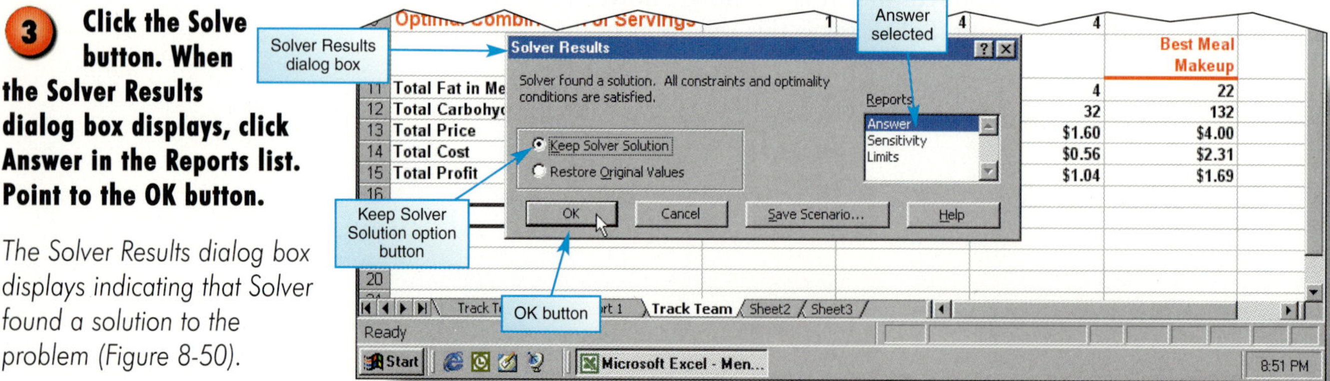

FIGURE 8-50

Click the OK button.

The solution displays in the worksheet. The constraints have been satisfied (Figure 8-51).

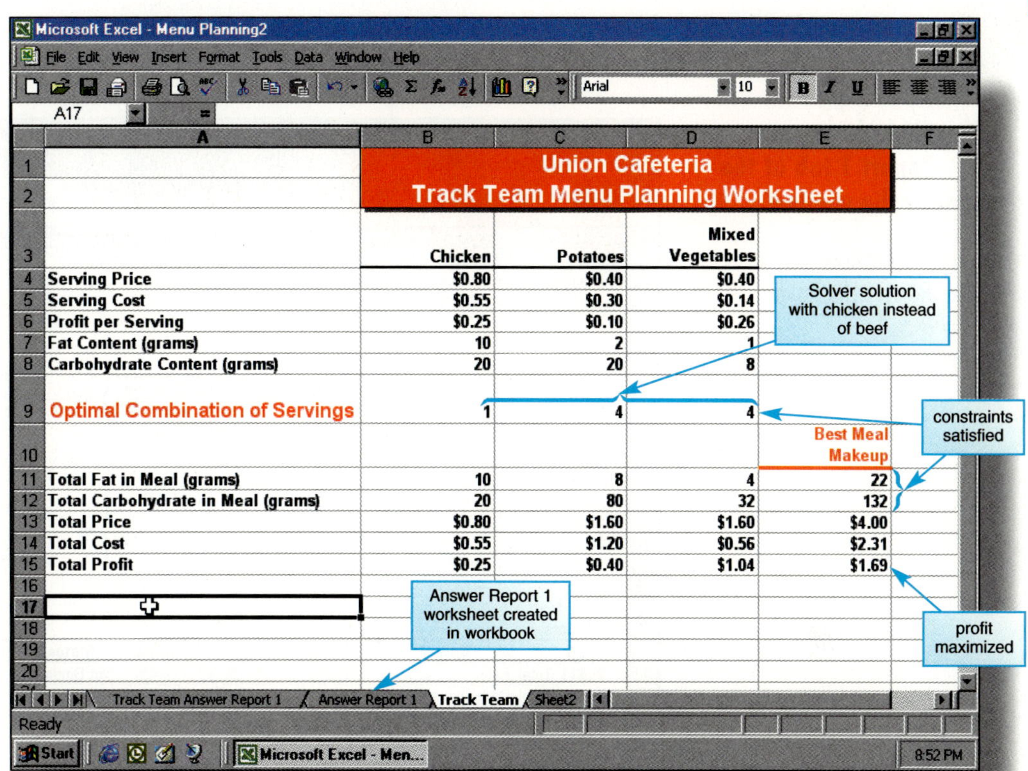

FIGURE 8-51

Other Ways

1. Press ALT+T, press V
2. Press ALT+S

As shown in Figure 8-51, Solver found a solution that satisfies all of the constraints and maximizes profit. With the beef entrée, the servings breakdown was one serving of beef, one serving of potatoes, and three servings of mixed vegetables (Figure 8-31 on page E 8.29). With the chicken entrée, the servings breakdown is one serving of chicken, four servings of potatoes, and four servings of mixed vegetables (Figure 8-51). The profit for the beef entrée was $1.28. The profit for the chicken entrée is $1.69.

The next step is to view the Answer Report for the chicken entrée solution that will be presented to the track team coach.

Quick Reference

For a table that lists how to complete the tasks covered in this book using the mouse, menu, shortcut menu, and keyboard, see the Excel Quick Reference Summary at the back of this book or visit the Office 2000 Web page (www.scsite.com/off2000/qr.htm), and then click Microsoft Excel 2000.

To View the Second Answer Report

1 **Click the Answer Report 1 tab at the bottom of the window.**

The chicken entrée Solver Answer Report displays (Figure 8-52).

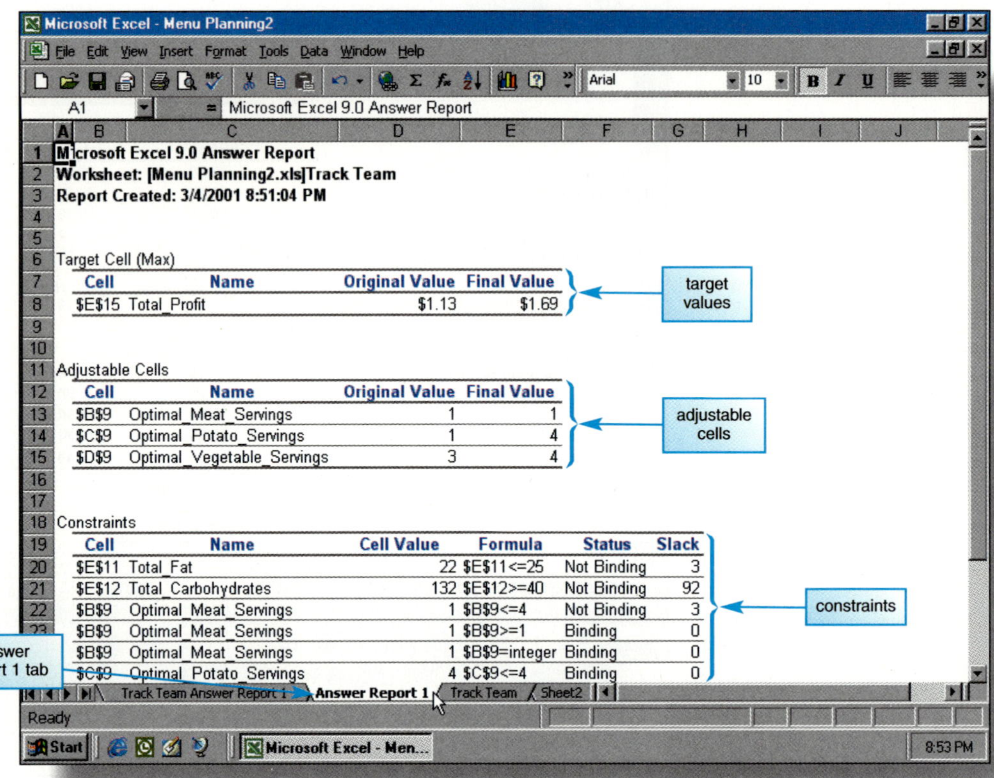

FIGURE 8-52

2 **Double-click the Answer Report 1 tab and then type** `Track Team Answer Report 2` **as the worksheet name. Use the scroll bar to scroll down to view the remaining cells of the chicken entrée Answer Report.**

The worksheet is renamed and the remainder of the Answer Report for the chicken entrée displays (Figure 8-53).

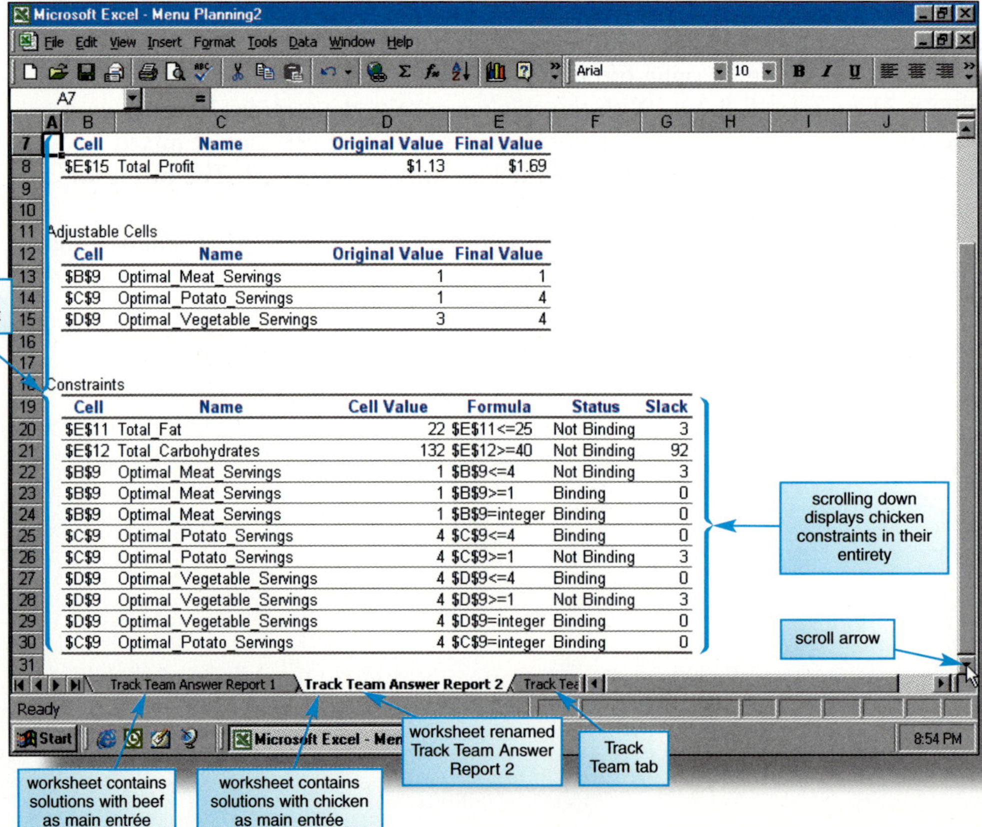

FIGURE 8-53

The Answer Report indicates that the meal has three fewer grams of fat than the maximum allowed, and 92 more grams of carbohydrates than the minimum allowed. The meal is low in fat and high in carbohydrates, which is what the track team coach wanted. Furthermore, the profit on the chicken meal is far better than that of the beef meal.

The next step is to save the chicken entrée solution as a scenario so that it can be referenced in the future.

Saving the Second Solver Solution as a Scenario

The power of Scenario Manager becomes evident when you begin adding additional scenarios to your worksheet. Multiple scenarios can be compared side by side. Using multiple scenarios on the same worksheet also saves time by recycling the work that you did to create the initial worksheet.

To Save the Second Solver Solution as a Scenario

1 **Click the Track Team tab at the bottom of the window. Click Tools on the menu bar and then point to Scenarios (Figure 8-54).**

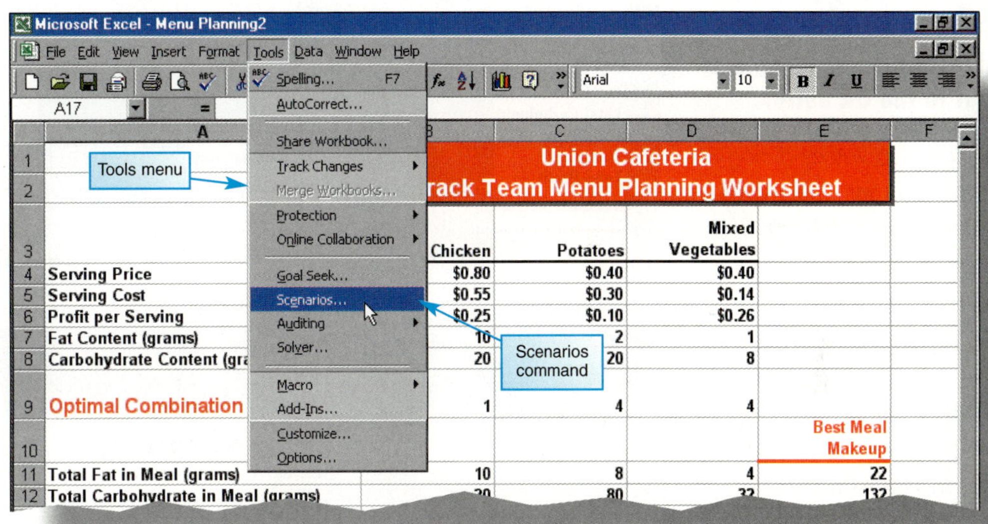

FIGURE 8-54

2 **Click Scenarios. When the Scenario Manager dialog box displays, point to the Add button (Figure 8-55).**

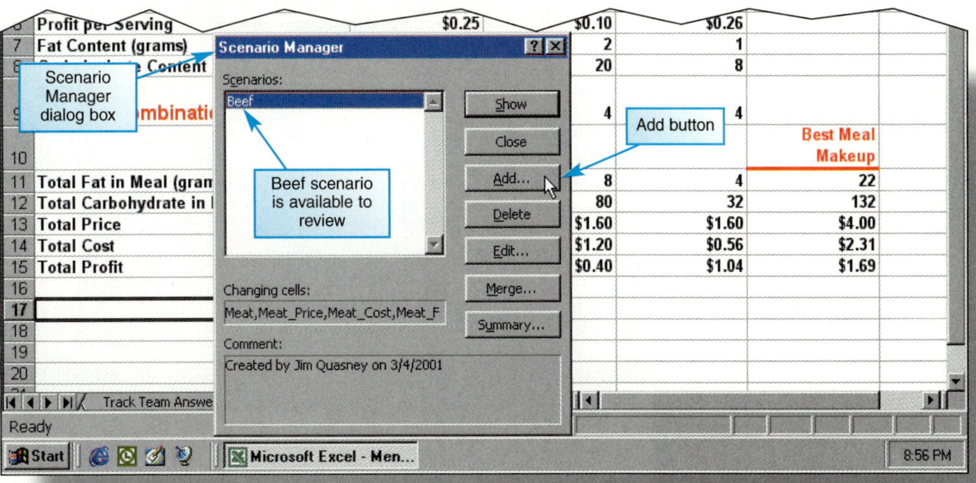

FIGURE 8-55

3 **Click the Add button. Type** `Chicken` **in the Scenario name text box and then point to the OK button.**

The Add Scenario dialog box displays. The Changing cells box defaults to the previous values used in the Beef scenario (Figure 8-56).

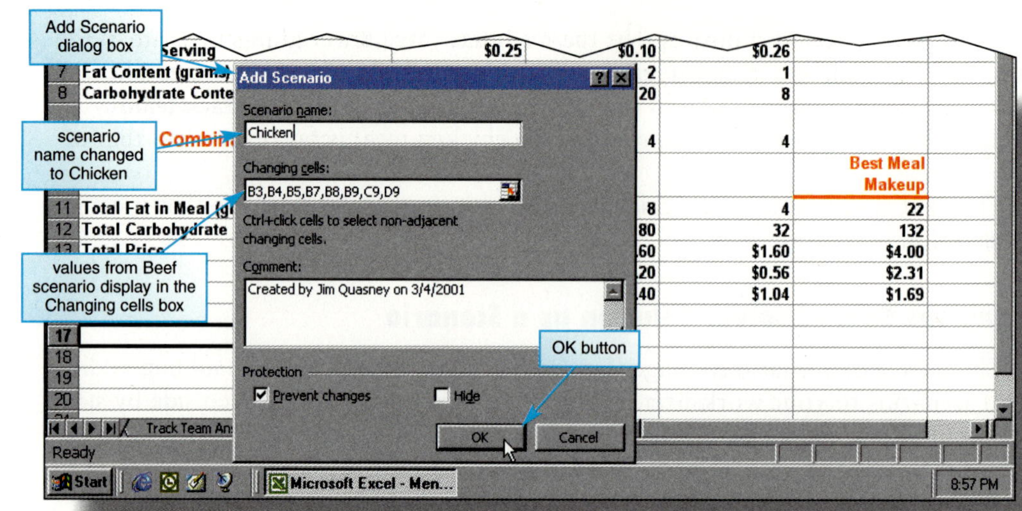

FIGURE 8-56

4 **Click the OK button. When the Scenario Values dialog box displays, point to the OK button.**

The Scenario Values dialog box displays with the values from the worksheet (Figure 8-57).

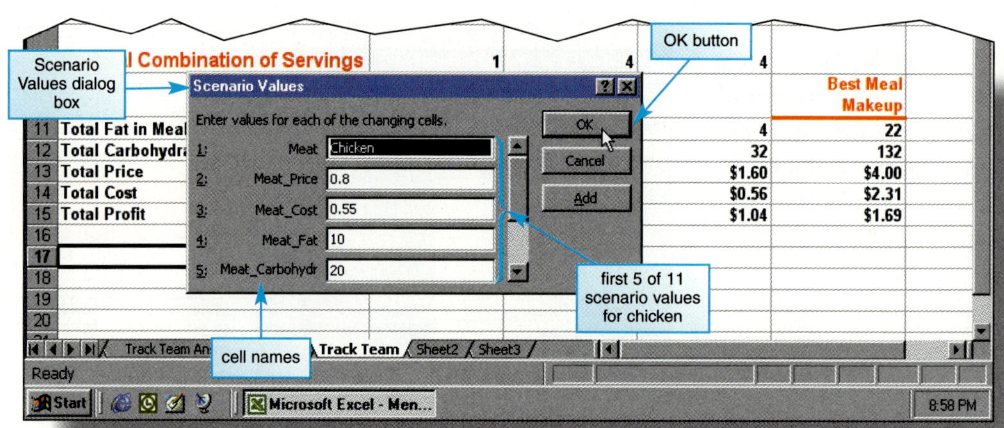

FIGURE 8-57

5 **Click the OK button. When the Scenario Manager dialog box displays, point to the Close button.**

Chicken displays along with Beef in the Scenarios list (Figure 8-58). Each name represents a different scenario.

6 **Click the Close button.**

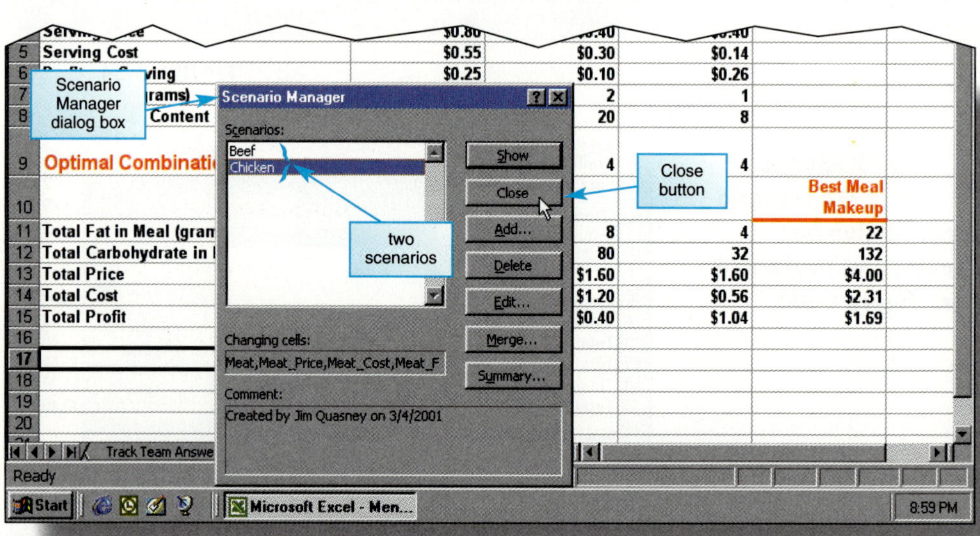

FIGURE 8-58

The Chicken scenario now can be recalled using Scenario Manager. Figure 8-57 shows the list of changing cells for the scenario. Instead of entering the data in the worksheet, you simply could enter values here for adding new scenarios. Because Solver is needed to find a solution to the scenario, however, the values were entered on the worksheet first.

The next step is to use Scenario Manager to show the Beef scenario in the worksheet.

Showing Scenarios

You can add a list of scenarios to your toolbar by using the Customize command on the Toolbars submenu of the View menu. Click the Commands tab and select Tools. Drag the Scenario command with the drop-down arrow up to the toolbar. You then can quickly switch between scenarios on the worksheet.

Showing a Scenario

Once a scenario is saved, you use the **Show button** in the Scenario Manager dialog box to display the scenario. The following steps show you how to apply the Beef scenario created earlier directly to a worksheet.

To Show a Saved Scenario

1 Click Tools on the menu bar and then point to Scenarios (Figure 8-59).

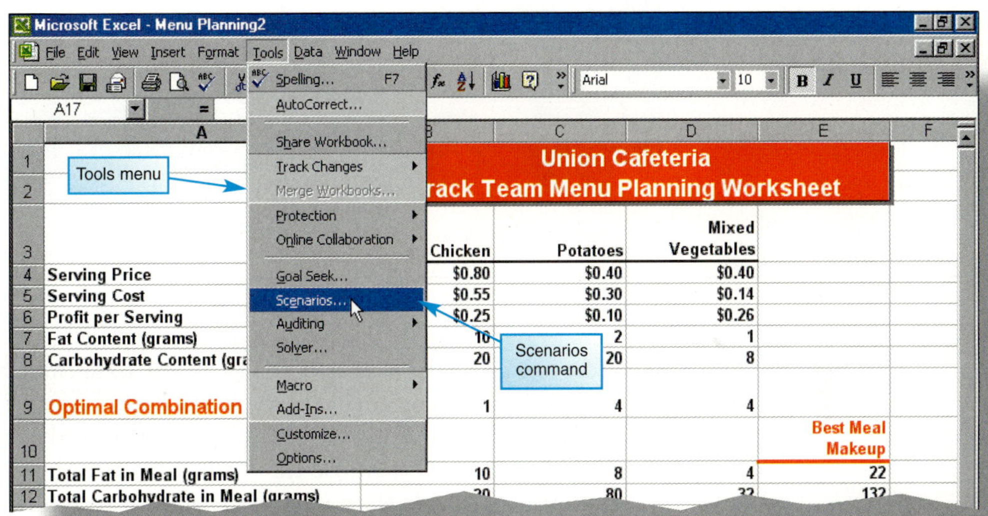

FIGURE 8-59

2 Click Scenarios. When the Scenario Manager dialog box displays, if necessary, select Beef in the Scenarios list and then point to the Show button (Figure 8-60).

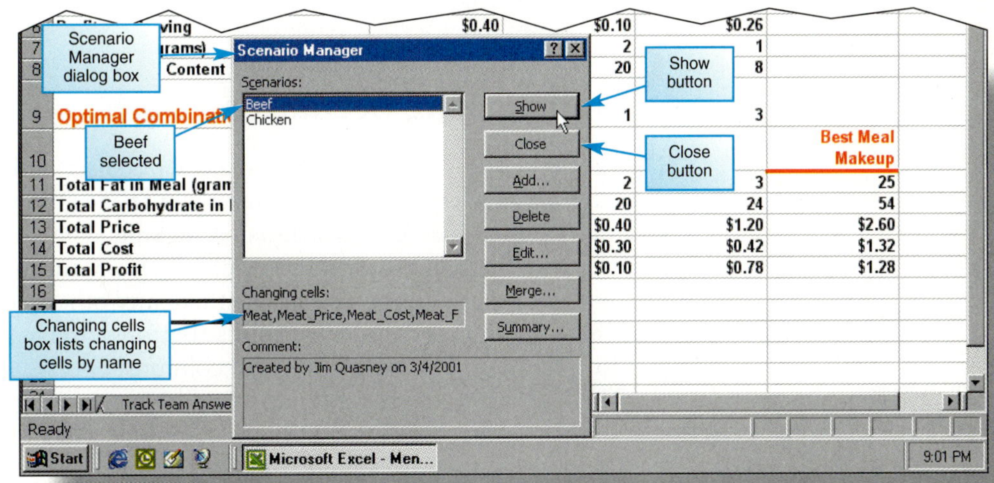

FIGURE 8-60

3 Click the Show button and then click the Close button.

Excel displays the data in the worksheet for the Beef scenario (Figure 8-61).

	A	B	C	D	E
1		Union Cafeteria			
2		Track Team Menu Planning Worksheet			
3		Beef	Potatoes	Mixed Vegetables	
4	Serving Price	$1.00	$0.40	$0.40	
5	Serving Cost	$0.60	$0.30	$0.14	
6	Profit per Serving	$0.40	$0.10	$0.26	
7	Fat Content (grams)	20	2	1	
8	Carbohydrate Content (grams)	10	20	8	
9	Optimal Combination of Servings	1	1	3	
10					Best Meal Makeup
11	Total Fat in Meal (grams)	20	2	3	25
12	Total Carbohydrate in Meal (grams)	10	20	24	54
13	Total Price	$1.00	$0.40	$1.20	$2.60
14	Total Cost	$0.60	$0.30	$0.42	$1.32
15	Total Profit	$0.40	$0.10	$0.78	$1.28

FIGURE 8-61

You can undo the scenario results by clicking the Undo button on the Standard toolbar. If desired, you then can click the Redo button on the Standard toolbar to display the scenario results again. If you had several saved scenarios, you could display each one and then use the Undo and Redo buttons to switch between them.

Scenario Manager is an important what-if tool for organizing assumptions. Using Scenario Manager, you can define different scenarios with up to 32 changing cells per scenario. Once you have entered the scenarios, you can show them one by one or you can create a Scenario Summary worksheet or a Scenario PivotTable worksheet as described in the next section.

Report Manager

Report Manager is an Add-in that allows you to print several scenarios at once. Typically, you would need to use the Show button in the Scenario Manager dialog box for each scenario you want to print and then print the worksheet. By using Report Manager, which displays on the View menu, you simply select the scenarios that you want to print and you can print them all at once.

Summarizing Scenarios

This section creates a Scenario Summary worksheet and a Scenario PivotTable worksheet. These concise reports allow you to view and manipulate several what-if situations side by side to assist decision making. The **Scenario Summary worksheet** generated by the Scenario Manager actually is an outlined worksheet (Figure 8-62a) that you can print and manipulate just like any other worksheet. An **outlined worksheet** is one that contains symbols (buttons) above and to the left, which allows you to collapse and expand rows and columns.

The **PivotTable worksheet** (Figure 8-62b) generated by the Scenario Manager also is a worksheet that you can print and manipulate like other worksheets. A **PivotTable** is a table that summarizes large amounts of information and can be manipulated to show the data from different points of view. The Scenario PivotTable compares the results of scenarios.

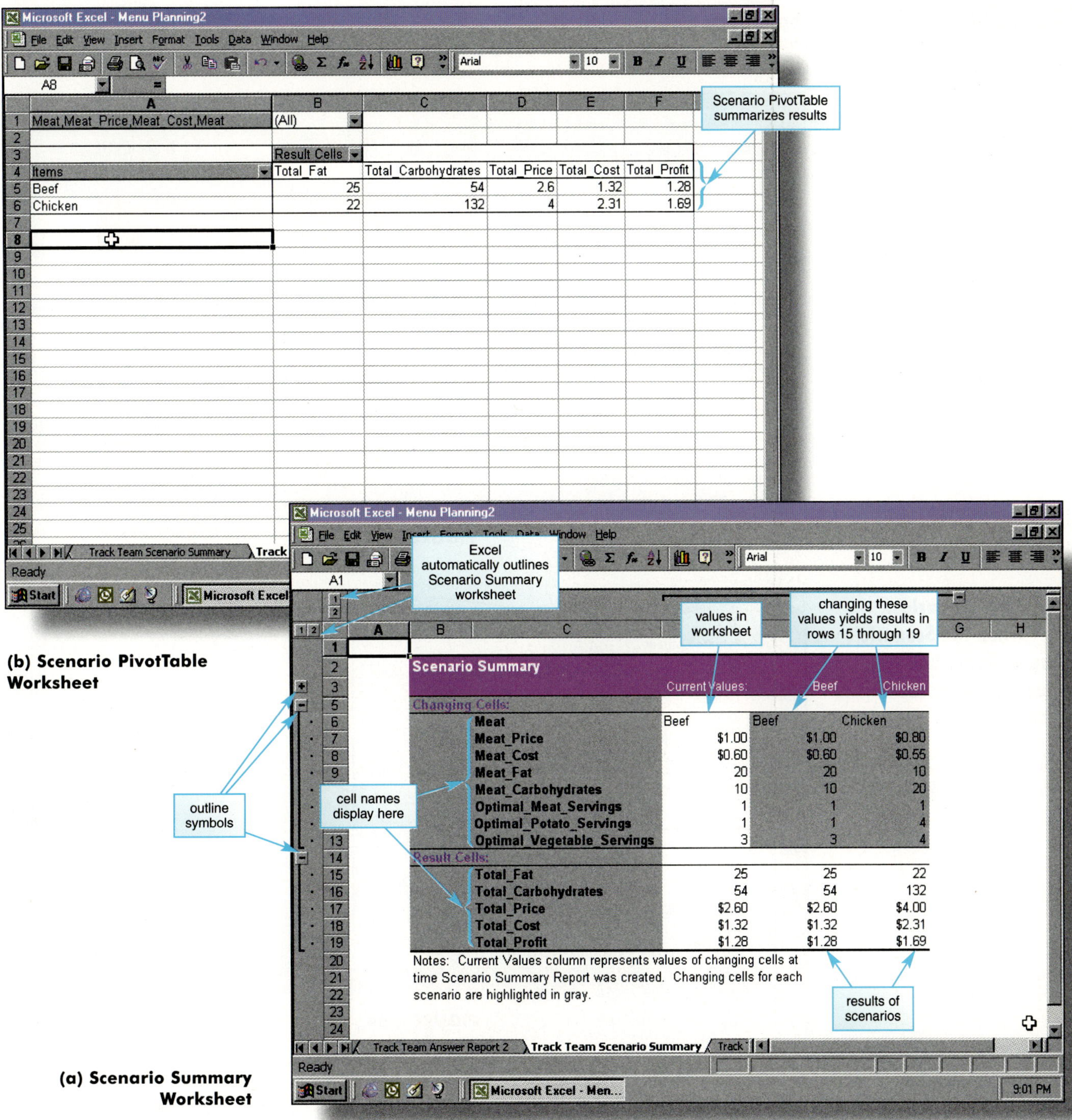

(b) Scenario PivotTable Worksheet

(a) Scenario Summary Worksheet

FIGURE 8-62

Creating a Scenario Summary Worksheet

The Scenario Summary worksheet in Figure 8-62a displays the total fat, total carbohydrates, total price, total cost, and total profit for the current worksheet values and the two scenarios. The optimal serving sizes calculated by Solver are shown for meals that include either beef or chicken as the main entrée.

To Create a Scenario Summary

1 Click Tools on the menu bar and then point to Scenarios (Figure 8-63).

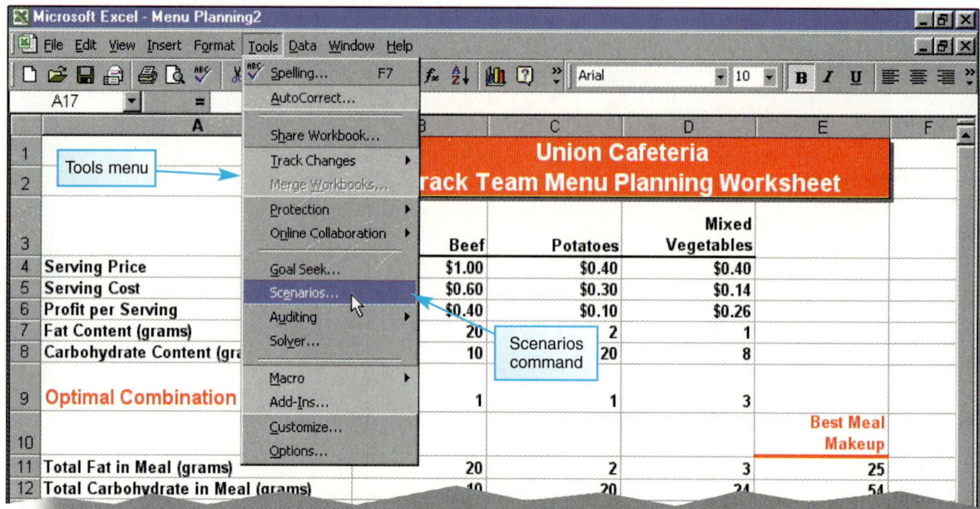

FIGURE 8-63

2 Click Scenarios. When the Scenario Manager dialog box displays, point to the Summary button.

The Scenario Manager dialog box displays (Figure 8-64).

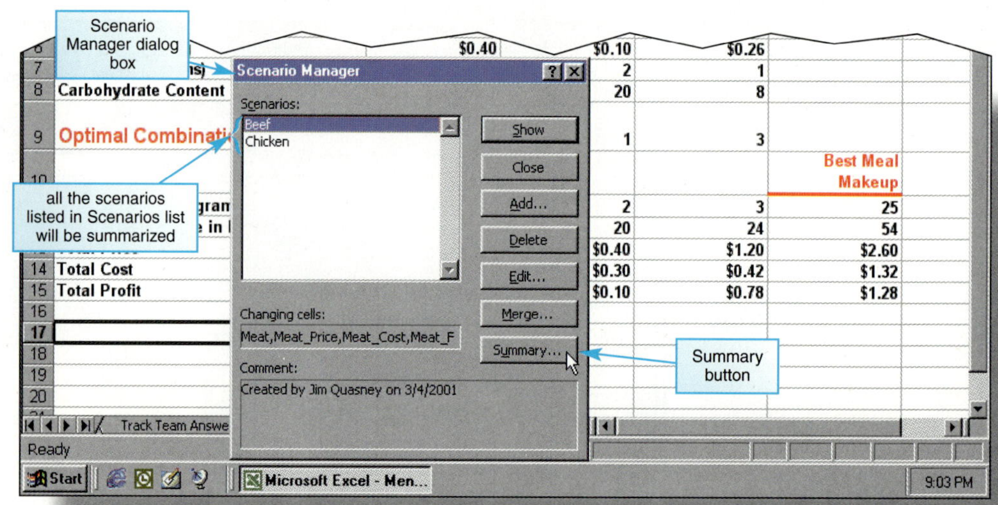

FIGURE 8-64

3 Click the Summary button. When the Scenario Summary dialog box displays, point to the OK button.

The Scenario Summary dialog box displays (Figure 8-65). The Scenario summary option button is selected in the Report type area. The dialog box offers the choice of creating a Scenario summary or a Scenario PivotTable.

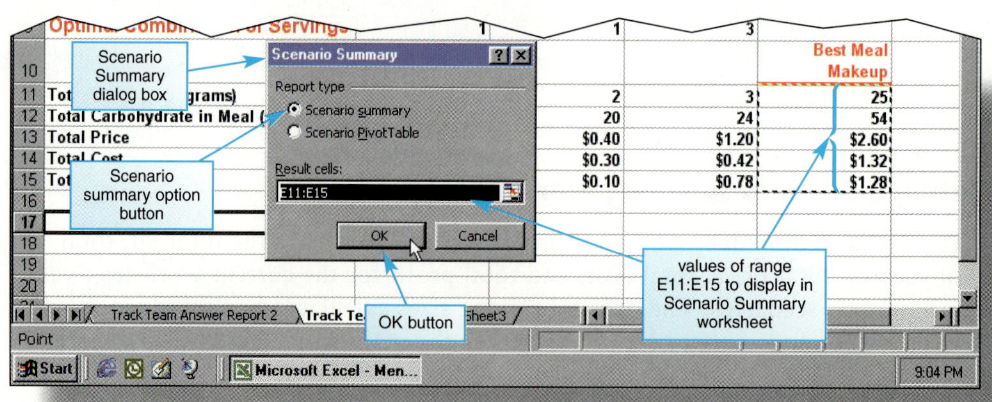

FIGURE 8-65

4 **Click the OK button. When the Scenario Summary displays, double-click the Scenario Summary tab and then type** `Track Team Scenario Summary` **as the worksheet name.**

The Scenario Summary worksheet displays as shown in Figure 8-66.

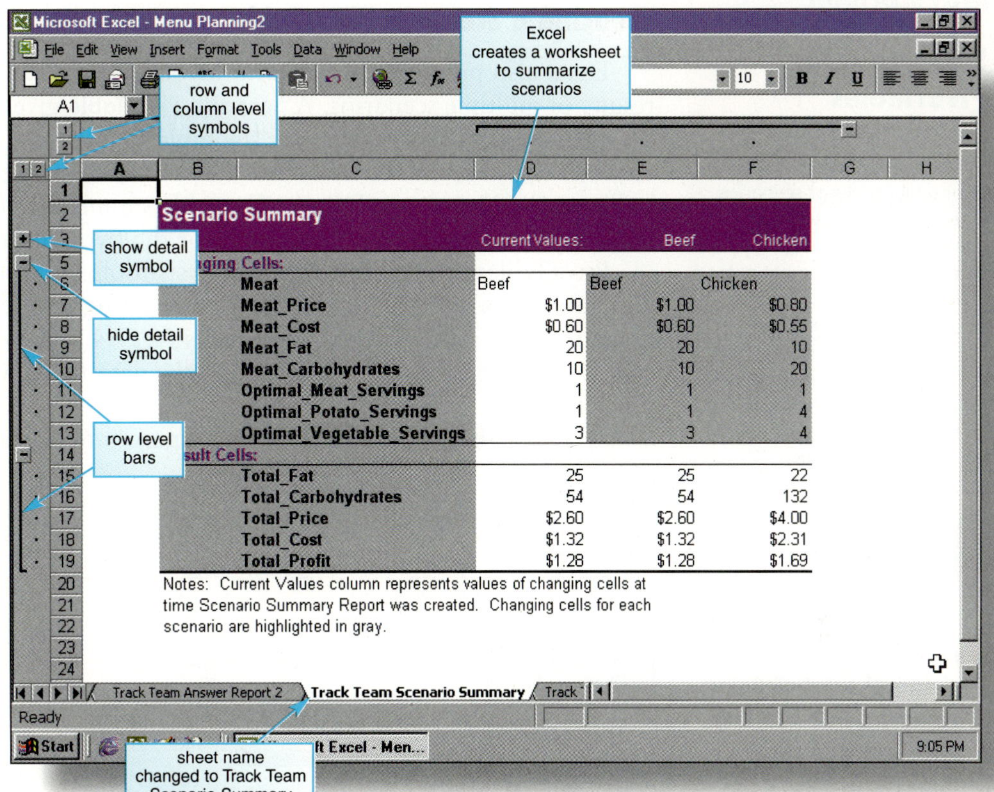

FIGURE 8-66

1. Press ALT+T, press E

Column D in the Scenario Summary worksheet in Figure 8-66 shows the results of the current values in the Menu Planning2 worksheet, which is the Beef scenario; columns E and F show the results of the two scenarios. The Scenario Summary worksheet makes it easier to compare the results of the scenarios. For example, in the Beef scenario, even though fewer portions are served, the profit is less than the Chicken scenario because the cost of one serving of beef is higher than that of chicken. Subsequently, the Union Cafeteria stands to make a better profit if the track team chooses more chicken meals than beef meals. Perhaps this indicates how the Union Cafeteria should go about marketing its meals to the track team.

In the Chicken scenario, the cost of the meal is much higher than that of the Beef scenario. Even though the price of a serving of chicken is less than that of beef, more servings of chicken are required to meet the nutritional requirements.

Working with an Outlined Worksheet

Excel automatically outlines the Scenario Summary worksheet. The outline symbols display above and to the left of the worksheet (Figure 8-66). You click the outline symbols to expand or collapse the worksheet. For example, if you click the **show detail symbol**, Excel displays additional rows or columns that are summarized on the displayed row or column. If you click a **hide detail symbol**, Excel hides any detail rows that extend through the length of the corresponding row level bar or column level bar. You also can expand or collapse a worksheet by clicking the **row level symbol** or **column level symbol** above and to the left of row title 1.

An outline is especially useful when working with large worksheets. To remove an outline, point to Group and Outline on the Data Menu and then click Clear Outline on the Group and Outline submenu.

More About 2000

Outlined Worksheets

You can outline any worksheet by clicking Auto Outline on the Group and Outline submenu. You can display the Group and Outline submenu by pointing to the Group and Outline Command on the Data menu.

Scenario PivotTables

A Scenario PivotTables is a powerful analysis tool for comparing the results of scenarios when the differences and causes of the differences among scenarios are not completely obvious. You can compare scenarios side by side, perform sorts and filters on the values of the result cells, and rotate rows and columns of the table to gain a different perspective on the results.

Creating a Scenario PivotTable

Excel also provides the Scenario PivotTable tool to help analyze and compare the results of multiple scenarios. A **Scenario PivotTable** gives you the ability to summarize the scenario data and then rotate the table's row and column titles to obtain different views of the summarized data. The PivotTable to be created in this project is shown in Figure 8-62b on page E 8.49. The table summarizes the Beef and Chicken scenarios and displays the result cells for the two scenarios for easy comparison.

PivotTables are powerful data analysis tools because they allow you to view the data in various ways by interchanging or pairing up the row and column fields by dragging the buttons located above cells A1, A4, and B3 in Figure 8-62b. The process of rotating the field values around the data fields will be discussed in the next project.

To create the PivotTable shown in Figure 8-62b, perform the following steps.

To Create a Scenario PivotTable

1. **Click the Track Team tab at the bottom of the window. Click Tools on the menu bar and then click Scenarios. When the Scenario Manager dialog box displays, point to the Summary button.**

The Scenario Manager dialog box displays (Figure 8-67).

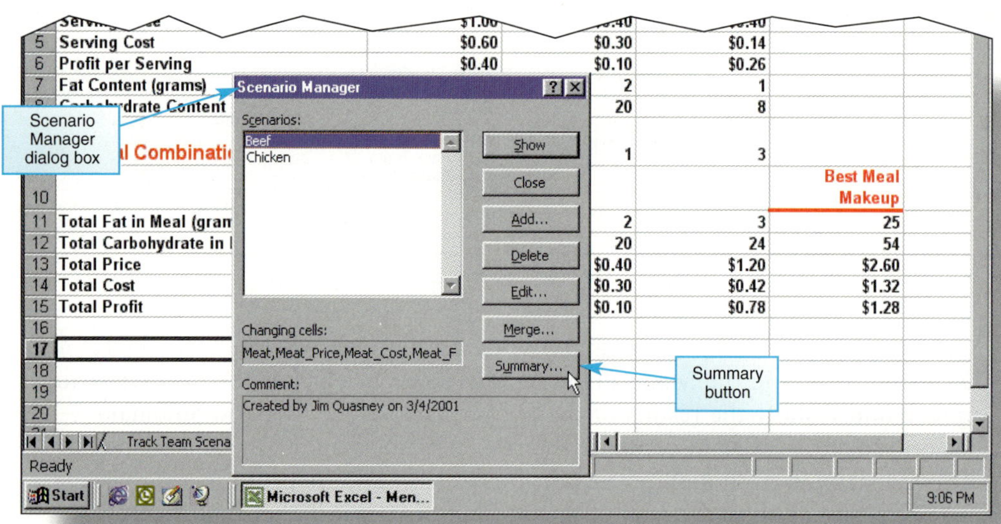

FIGURE 8-67

2. **Click the Summary button. When the Scenario Summary dialog box displays, click Scenario PivotTable. Point to the OK button.**

The Scenario Summary dialog box displays as shown in Figure 8-68. The range E11:E15 displays in the Result cells box from the previous time this dialog box displayed.

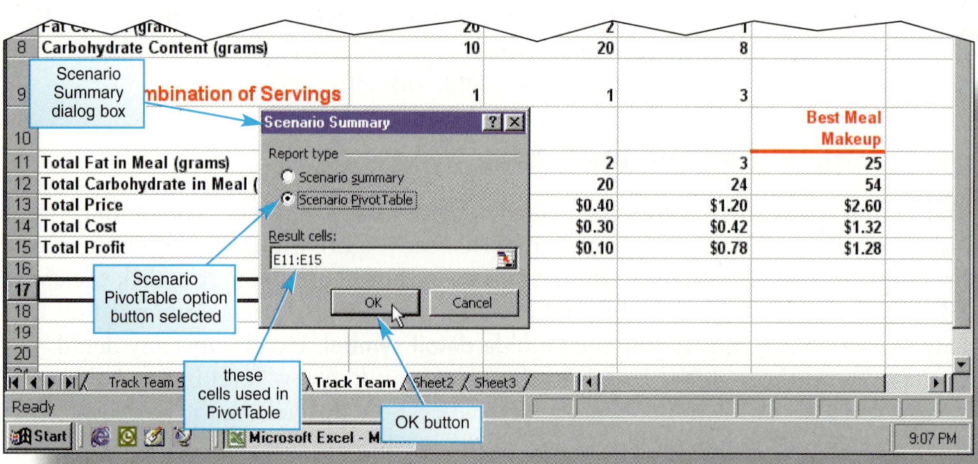

FIGURE 8-68

3 **Click the OK button.**

The Scenario PivotTable worksheet displays with the cell names of the changing values in column A (Figure 8-69). At this point the report appears useless. ***Note:*** *Your worksheet may display differently. You may not have to resize the column width in Step 4.*

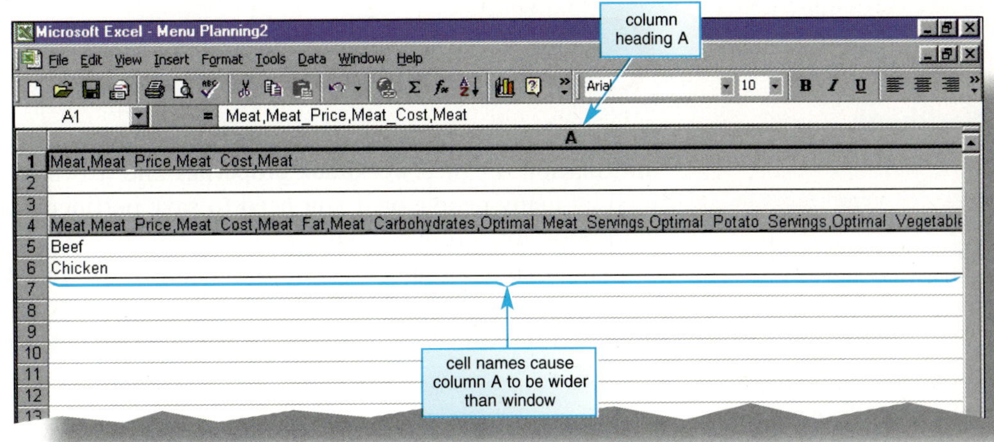

FIGURE 8-69

4 **Right-click column heading A. When the shortcut menu displays, click Column Width. When the Column Width dialog box displays, type** 35 **in the Column width text box. Click the OK button. Double-click the Scenario PivotTable tab and then type** Track Team Scenario PivotTable **as the worksheet name. Click cell A8.**

The Scenario PivotTable displays within the viewable area of the worksheet. The result cells of the two scenarios display in rows 5 and 6 as shown in Figure 8-70.

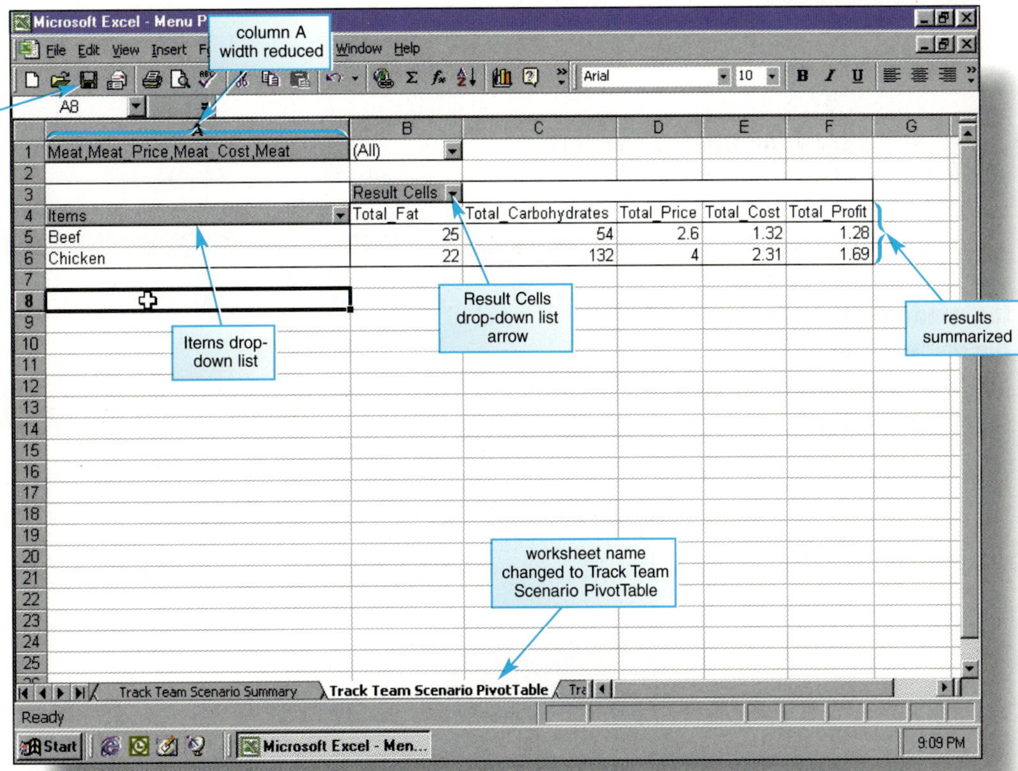

FIGURE 8-70

5 **Click the Save button on the Standard toolbar to save the workbook using the file name Menu Planning2.**

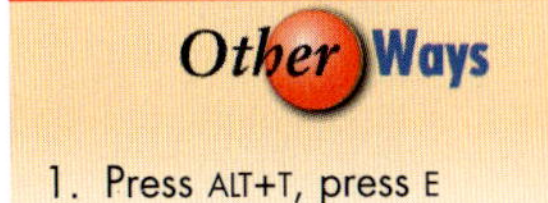

1. Press ALT+T, press E

Once the PivotTable is created, you can treat it like any other worksheet. Thus, you can print or chart a PivotTable. If you update the data in one of the scenarios, click the **Refresh Data command** on the Data menu. If you show a scenario and change values on the scenario worksheet, that is not the same as changing the scenario. If you want to change the data in a scenario, you must use Scenario Manager.

Workbook Properties

Workbook properties can be viewed from Windows Explorer by right-clicking an Excel file and then clicking Properties on the shortcut menu. This makes it easy to determine the contents and purpose of a workbook without opening it. If the user has the View as Web Page option button selected in Windows Explorer, then the user can see a preview of the workbook if the Save preview picture option button is selected in the Summary sheet.

Changing the Properties on a Workbook

Excel allows you to store a variety of information about each workbook. This information is called **workbook properties** and it is useful when workbooks will be used by many people or if you need to save pertinent data about the purpose of the workbook for future reference.

The Menu Planning workbook obviously will be very useful in the future if the track team or other teams require similar analysis for a meal. The following steps save relevant information about the Menu Planning workbook for future reference.

To Change Workbook Properties

1 Click the Track Team tab at the bottom of the window. Click File on the menu bar and then point to Properties (Figure 8-71).

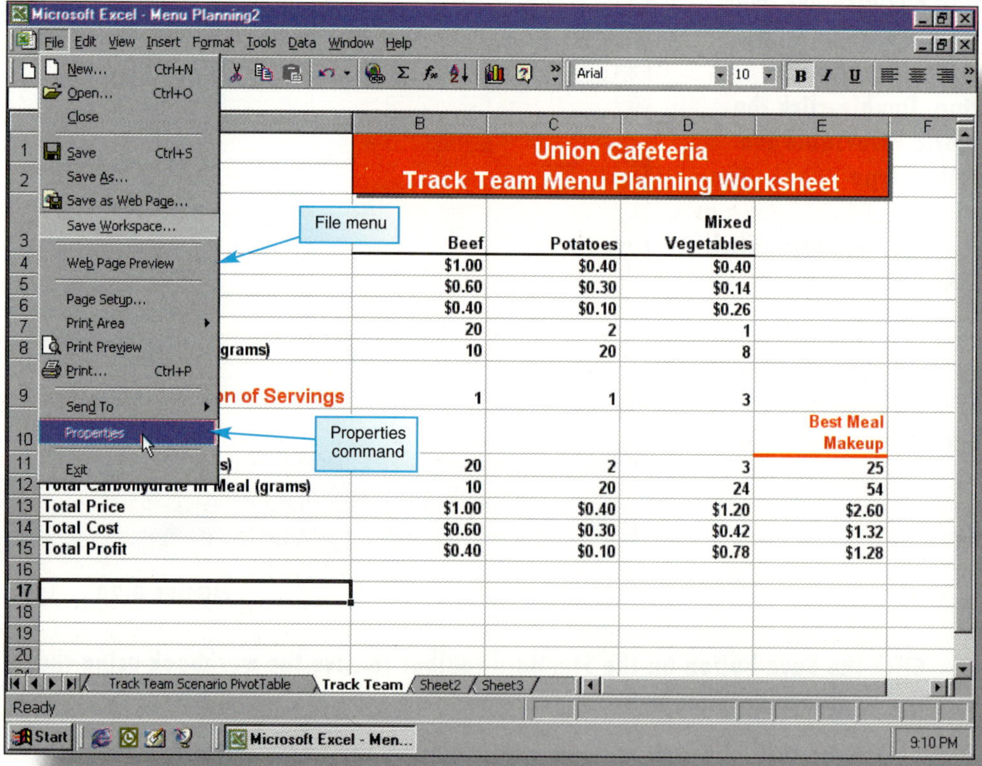

FIGURE 8-71

2

2 **Click Properties. When the Menu Planning2 Properties dialog box displays, click the Summary tab. Type** `Track Team Menu Planning` **in the Title text box. Type** `March 2001 Goals` **in the Subject text box. Type** `Maxine Hill` **in the Manager text box. In the Comments text box, type** `Planning meal for March 4, 2001. Goals met with chicken and beef.` **Point to the OK button.**

The summary fields display in the Menu Planning2 Properties dialog box as shown in Figure 8-72.

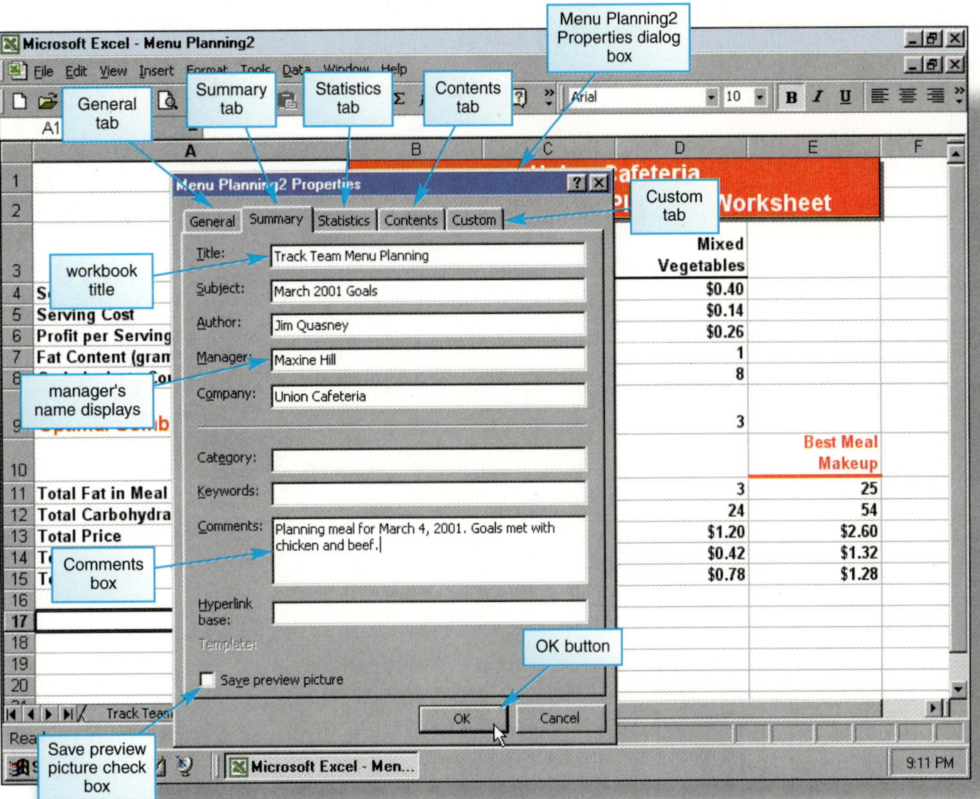

FIGURE 8-72

3 **Click the OK button.**

4 **Click the Save button on the Standard toolbar to save the workbook using the file name Menu Planning2.**

1. Press ALT+F, press I

The **Workbook Properties dialog box** contains other useful information about the workbook. Then **General tab** displays data about the workbook file, including the size of the file, creation date, date modified, and the date the file was last accessed. The **Save preview picture check box** selected on the **Summary tab** saves an image of the current worksheet that will be visible in the Open dialog box when the file is selected by the user. The **Statistics tab** displays some of the file data from the General tab in addition to a record of when the file was last opened and modified.

The **Contents tab** displays a list of all the worksheets and charts contained in the workbook. This feature allows you to search large workbooks quickly that contain many worksheets and charts when you are looking for a particular worksheet or chart.

The **Custom tab** allows you to create your own workbook properties. For example, you can add fields such as document number, editor, your telephone number, division, group, owner, or any other field you want to store with the workbook. For each item you define, you can set the data type for the value. Valid data types are Text, Date, Number, and Yes or No.

Custom Properties

You can set up custom properties that link to cells in your workbook in addition to using text fields. For example, you can have a property that contains the value in the total profit cell in the Track Team worksheet.

Quitting Excel

The project is complete. To quit Excel, follow the steps below.

TO QUIT EXCEL

1. Click the Close button on the right side of the title bar.
2. If the Microsoft Excel dialog box displays, click the No button.

CASE PERSPECTIVE SUMMARY

With the two solved scenarios developed in this project, Maxine Hill confidently can take the results to the track team to illustrate that nutritional requirements have been satisfied. She also has the confidence that the Union Cafeteria is maximizing its profit when delivering what the customer wants. The worksheet can be used in the future to develop meals for other teams.

Project Summary

In this project, you learned how to use a number of techniques to approach problem solving, including trial and error, goal seek, and Solver. You learned how to analyze a worksheet using the Auditing toolbar. You learned how to use data validation on cells and inform the user about the validation rules. Using Scenario Manager, you learned how to manage different problems on the same worksheet and then summarize the results of the scenarios with a Scenario Summary and a Scenario PivotTable. Finally, you learned how to save a workbook file with passwords and modify the properties of a workbook.

What You Should Know

Having completed this project, you now should be able to perform the following tasks:

- Add Data Validation *(E 8.16)*
- Add the Data for a New Scenario *(E 8.41)*
- Change Workbook Properties *(E 8.54)*
- Create a Scenario PivotTable *(E 8.52)*
- Create a Scenario Summary *(E 8.50)*
- Display the Auditing Toolbar *(E 8.10)*
- Quit Excel *(E 8.56)*
- Remove the Trace Dependent Arrows *(E 8.14)*
- Remove the Trace Precedent Arrows *(E 8.12)*
- Save the Second Solver Solution as a Scenario *(E 8.45)*
- Save the Current Data as a Scenario *(E 8.36)*
- Save the Workbook with Passwords *(E 8.33)*
- Show a Saved Scenario *(E 8.47)*
- Start Excel and Open a Workbook *(E 8.8)*
- Trace Dependents *(E 8.13)*
- Trace Precedents *(E 8.11)*
- Use Solver to Find the Optimal Combination *(E 8.25)*
- Use Solver to Find a New Solution *(E 8.42)*
- Use the Goal Seek Command to Attempt to Solve a Complex Problem *(E 8.21)*
- Use Trial and Error to Attempt to Solve a Complex Problem *(E 8.19)*
- View the Second Answer Report *(E 8.44)*
- View the Answer Report *(E 8.31)*

More About 2000

Microsoft Certification

The Microsoft Office User Specialist (MOUS) Certification program provides an opportunity for you to obtain a valuable industry credential - proof that you have the Excel 2000 skills required by employers. For more information, see Appendix D or visit the Shelly Cashman Series MOUS Web page at www.scsite.com/off2000/cert.htm.

1 Determining the Optimal Product Mix for a Truck Shipment

Instructions: Andreakis College Supply, Inc. ships truckloads of products to campuses for sale to local distributors. Follow the steps below to use trial and error, and then Solver to find the optimal product mix that should be shipped in a truck of 2,000 cubic feet based on the current product costs and prices. The products available for shipment include computers, stereos, and dorm-sized refrigerators. The company must ship at least 15 computers, 20 stereos, and 35 refrigerators with each shipment.

Microsoft Excel - Andreakis College Supply

	A	B	C	D	E
1	Andreakis College Supply				
2	Shipment Planning Worksheet				
3		Computers	Stereos	Dorm Sized Refrigerators	
4	Item Sales Price	1,000.00	350.00	200.00	
5	Item Cost	800.00	235.00	175.00	
6	Profit per Item	200.00	115.00	25.00	
7	Cubic Feet per Item	18	8	24	
8	Optimal Number of Items to Ship	16	109	35	
9					Shipment Totals
10	Total Cost	12,800.00	25,615.00	6,125.00	44,540.00
11	Total Profit	3,200.00	12,535.00	875.00	16,610.00
12	Total Cubic Feet	288	872	840	2000

Answer Report 1 / Shipment Planning / Sheet2 / Sheet3

FIGURE 8-73

1. Open the workbook Andreakis College Supply from the Data Disk. If you do not have a copy of the Data Disk, see the inside back cover of this book.
2. Enter your name, course, laboratory assignment number (Apply 8-1), date, and instructor name in the range A15:A19.
3. Using trial and error, enter values in cells B8, C8, and D8 to try to solve the problem.
4. Use Solver to find a solution to the problem so that the profit on the shipment is maximized. Allow Solver to change cells B8, C8, and D8. The total cubic feet of the items should not exceed 2,000 cubic feet. The results in B8, C8, and D8 should be integer values. Also, use the Assume Linear Model option in Solver.
5. Instruct Solver to create the Answer Report for your solution. Solver should find the answer as shown in Figure 8-73.
6. Go into the workbook properties and enter a title for the workbook of Andreakis College Supply Shipping Workbook. Enter your name in the Author field and your instructor's name in the Manager field.
7. Print the worksheet and the Answer Report 1 worksheet. Hand in the two printouts to your instructor.

1 Gaining Confidence in the Shocking Sound International Worksheet

Problem: You have been given the task of taking over the job of another employee who has retired. Your first task is to learn about some of the Excel workbooks for which you now are responsible.

Instructions: Start Excel and perform the following tasks.

1. Open the Shocking Sound International workbook from the Data Disk. If you do not have a copy of the Data Disk, then see the inside back cover of this book.
2. Display the Auditing toolbar. Trace two levels of precedents for cell E12. Trace one level of the precedents for cell D12. Trace one level of the dependents for cell B4. The worksheet should display as shown in Figure 8-74.

FIGURE 8-74

3. Enter your name, course, laboratory assignment number (Lab 8-1), date, and instructor's name in the range B15:B19. Print the worksheet.
4. Remove all trace arrows. Enter the value of zero in cell B6.
5. Use the Trace Error button on the Auditing toolbar to trace the error in cell E12. Use the Trace Error button to trace the error in cell E11. Print the worksheet.
6. Select the range B4:B8. Open the Data Validation dialog box. Create a validation rule that forces the user to enter a positive whole number in the cells in the selected range. Clear the Ignore blank check box.
7. Click the Error Alert tab and then create an error message with the title `Gross Sales` that contains the message `Enter a positive whole number for Gross Sales`. Click the OK button.
8. Reenter the value of zero in cell B6 and then press the ENTER key to view the error message. Select Retry and then enter 650,000 in cell B6. Print the worksheet. Hand in the three printouts to your instructor.

2 Finding the Optimal Advertising Mix

Problem: Dean and Karen's Pet Shop holds sales each month. The store's owners would like you to maximize the audience that advertisements reach in a variety of media. The owners have identified a local newspaper, a local radio station, and the local cable television station as advertising targets. Each type of media claims to be able to target a certain number of individuals in Dean and Karen's target audience with each advertisement. Each media type has a limit on how many advertisements can be placed each week and the prices vary from month to month (Figure 8-75).

Microsoft Excel - Dean and Karen

Scenario Summary	Current Values:	October campaign	November campaign
Changing Cells:			
B6	75	75	75
C6	150	100	150
D6	150	200	150
Result Cells:			
B9	7	7	7
C9	20	20	20
D9	3	3	3
E9	30	30	30
E10	163500	163500	163500
E11	3975	3125	3975

Notes: Current Values column represents values of changing cells at ...ch

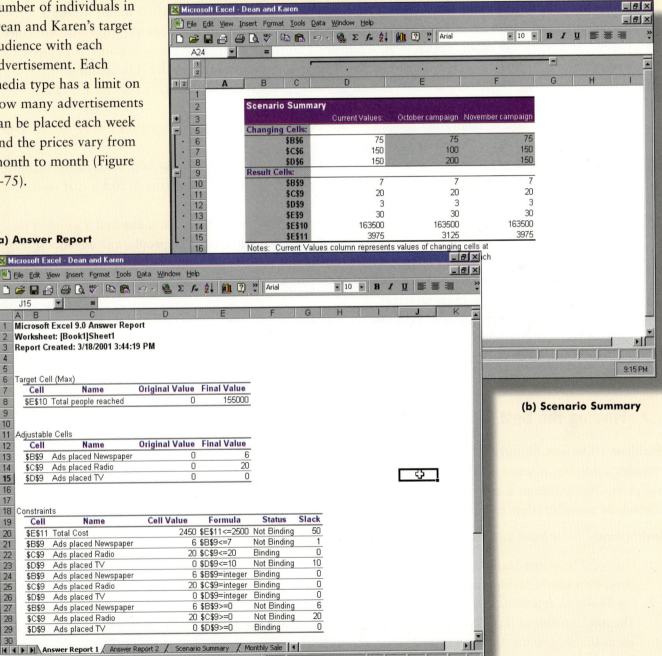

(b) Scenario Summary

Microsoft Excel - Dean and Karen

Microsoft Excel 9.0 Answer Report
Worksheet: [Book1]Sheet1
Report Created: 3/18/2001 3:44:19 PM

Target Cell (Max)

Cell	Name	Original Value	Final Value
E10	Total people reached	0	155000

Adjustable Cells

Cell	Name	Original Value	Final Value
B9	Ads placed Newspaper	0	6
C9	Ads placed Radio	0	20
D9	Ads placed TV	0	0

Constraints

Cell	Name	Cell Value	Formula	Status	Slack
E11	Total Cost	2450	E11<=2500	Not Binding	50
B9	Ads placed Newspaper	6	B9<=7	Not Binding	1
C9	Ads placed Radio	20	C9<=20	Binding	0
D9	Ads placed TV	0	D9<=10	Not Binding	10
B9	Ads placed Newspaper	6	B9=integer	Binding	0
C9	Ads placed Radio	20	C9=integer	Binding	0
D9	Ads placed TV	0	D9=integer	Binding	0
B9	Ads placed Newspaper	6	B9>=0	Not Binding	6
C9	Ads placed Radio	20	C9>=0	Not Binding	20
D9	Ads placed TV	0	D9>=0	Binding	0

(a) Answer Report

FIGURE 8-75

(continued)

Finding the Optimal Advertising Mix *(continued)*

Instructions: Start Excel and perform the following tasks.

1. Open the Dean and Karen workbook from the Data Disk.
2. Use Solver to determine the best mix of advertising for the sale in the first week of October. The advertising budget for October is $2,500. The newspaper allows a maximum of seven ads per week, the radio station allows a maximum of twenty advertisement spots per week, and the cable television station allows a maximum of ten advertisements per week. The costs for the month of October are already in the worksheet. Use the Assume Linear Model option in Solver. Instruct Solver to create an Answer Report if it can find a solution to the problem. Figure 8-75a shows the values that Solver should find for this situation.
3. Save the current worksheet as a scenario named `October campaign`. The Changing cells are the ranges B6:D6 and B9:D9.
4. Enter your name, course, laboratory assignment number (Lab 8-2), date, and instructor's name in the range B15:B19. Print the worksheet and Answer Report.
5. The sale in the week of November is much larger and is allocated a budget of $4,000. Radio advertisements will cost $150 each for that week and cable television advertisements will also cost $150 for that week. The cost of newspaper advertisements remains unchanged.
6. Use Solver to solve to the problem. Instruct Solver to create an Answer Report if it can find a solution to the problem. Solver should find that the optimal combination reaches 163,500 people, and includes seven newspaper advertisements, 20 radio advertisements, and three cable television advertisements.
7. Save the current worksheet as a scenario named `November campaign`. Print the worksheet and Answer Report (Figure 8-75a on the previous page).
8. Create a Scenario Summary (Figure 8-75b on the previous page) showing the two scenarios that you have saved in Scenario Manager. Save the workbook with the password, lab8-2, and with the file name, Dean and Karen2. Print the Scenario Summary.

3 Finding the Best Production Mix

Problem: Southern Manufacturing produces four types of file cabinets in its shop. Each type of file cabinet requires a different amount of labor input and a different amount of materials to produce a single cabinet. As the production assistant, it is your job to determine the best mix of file cabinet types to produce based on the amount of available labor and material for a given week (Figure 8-76).

Instructions: Start Excel and perform the following tasks.

1. Open the Southern Manufacturing workbook from the Data Disk. If you do not have a copy of the Data Disk, then see the inside back cover of this book.
2. Use Solver to determine the mix of products that maximizes the number of units produced in the week. The total amount of labor hours available in the first week of June is 800, and $3,000 worth of materials are available. Use the Assume Linear Model option in Solver. Instruct Solver to create an Answer Report if it can find a solution to the problem. Figure 8-76a shows the values that Solver should find.

Microsoft Excel - Southern Manufacturing

Scenario Summary

	Current Values:	June, Week 1	June, Week 2
Changing Cells:			
B5	17	17	25
C5	25	25	25
D5	9	9	20
E5	15	15	20
B6	75	75	75
C6	95	95	95
D6	45	45	45
E6	80	80	80
B8	14	14	0
C8	5	5	5
D8	15	15	15
E8	10	10	18
Result Cells:			
F8	44	44	38
F10	648	648	785
F11	3,000	3,000	2,590

(b) Scenario Summary

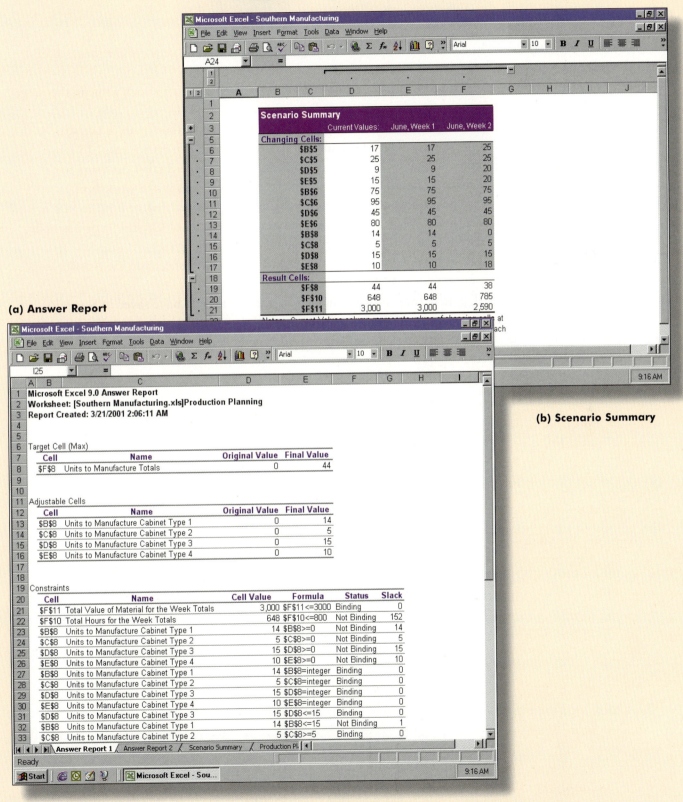

(a) Answer Report

Microsoft Excel - Southern Manufacturing

Microsoft Excel 9.0 Answer Report
Worksheet: [Southern Manufacturing.xls]Production Planning
Report Created: 3/21/2001 2:06:11 AM

Target Cell (Max)

Cell	Name	Original Value	Final Value
F8	Units to Manufacture Totals	0	44

Adjustable Cells

Cell	Name	Original Value	Final Value
B8	Units to Manufacture Cabinet Type 1	0	14
C8	Units to Manufacture Cabinet Type 2	0	5
D8	Units to Manufacture Cabinet Type 3	0	15
E8	Units to Manufacture Cabinet Type 4	0	10

Constraints

Cell	Name	Cell Value	Formula	Status	Slack
F11	Total Value of Material for the Week Totals	3,000	F11<=3000	Binding	0
F10	Total Hours for the Week Totals	648	F10<=800	Not Binding	152
B8	Units to Manufacture Cabinet Type 1	14	B8>=0	Not Binding	14
C8	Units to Manufacture Cabinet Type 2	5	C8>=0	Not Binding	5
D8	Units to Manufacture Cabinet Type 3	15	D8>=0	Not Binding	15
E8	Units to Manufacture Cabinet Type 4	10	E8>=0	Not Binding	10
B8	Units to Manufacture Cabinet Type 1	14	B8=integer	Binding	0
C8	Units to Manufacture Cabinet Type 2	5	C8=integer	Binding	0
D8	Units to Manufacture Cabinet Type 3	15	D8=integer	Binding	0
E8	Units to Manufacture Cabinet Type 4	10	E8=integer	Binding	0
D8	Units to Manufacture Cabinet Type 3	15	D8<=15	Binding	0
B8	Units to Manufacture Cabinet Type 1	14	B8<=15	Not Binding	1
C8	Units to Manufacture Cabinet Type 2	5	C8>=5	Binding	0

Answer Report 1 / Answer Report 2 / Scenario Summary / Production Pl...

FIGURE 8-76

Finding the Best Production Mix *(continued)*

3. Save the current worksheet as a scenario named `June, Week 1`. The Changing cells are the ranges B5:E6 and B8:E8.
4. Enter your name, course, laboratory assignment number (Lab 8-3), date, and instructor's name in the range B13:B17. Print the worksheet.
5. The production manager feels that perhaps the assumptions about how many labor hours it takes to produce certain products are not correct. The new assumptions are that Cabinet Type 1 takes 25 labor hours to produce, Cabinet Type 2 still takes 25 hours to produce, Cabinet Type 3 takes 20 hours to produce, and Cabinet Type 4 takes 20 hours to produce. Enter these new values in the worksheet.
6. Use Solver to find a solution to the problem. Instruct Solver to create an Answer Report if it can find a solution to the problem. Solver should report that the optimal number of units of Cabinet Type 1 is none, of Cabinet Type 2 is 5, of Cabinet Type 3 is 15, and of Cabinet Type 4 is 18.
7. Save the current worksheet as a scenario named `June, Week 2`. Print the worksheet and the Answer Report (Figure 8-76a).
8. Create a Scenario Summary (Figure 8-76b) showing the two scenarios that you have saved in Scenario Manager.
9. Save the workbook with the password, lab8-3, and with the file name, Southern Manufacturing2. Print the Scenario Summary worksheet.

Cases and Places

The difficulty of these case studies varies:
◗ are the least difficult; ◗◗ are more difficult; and ◗◗◗ are the most difficult.

1 ◗ Open the workbook Microprocessor Plus on the Data Disk. Use the Auditing toolbar to learn about the worksheet. Trace three levels of precedents for cell H12, the Total Payroll Expense. Print the worksheet with the arrows and hand it in to your instructor. Use Data Validation to limit a user's input on cell B15, the Base Salary, to a decimal value between .15 and .45. Use Data Validation to limit a user's input on cell B17, the Bonus, to a whole number between 5,000 and 25,000. Use Data Validation to allow the worksheet user to select a commission from a list that ranges from 0% to 5% in increments of .5%. Add appropriate input and error messages for the data validation as well. Save the worksheet as Microprocessor Plus2.

2 ◗ Martha Short is planning a sale in her garden shop for a few items. The store has 90 square feet of space available for the items in the sale. Table 8-5 shows the items available for sale, how much they cost Martha to purchase, how much they will be sold for, and how much space each item takes up. The amount that Martha wants to spend on purchases is $375. Martha does not think that she can sell more than 40 gardening tool sets. Create a worksheet with the necessary information and use Solver to determine the most profitable combination of items to purchase for the sale and create an Answer Report. Print the worksheet and Answer Report and hand them in to your instructor.

Table 8-5 Sale Item Information

ITEM NAME	COST	SELLING PRICE	SQUARE FEET
Garden Hose Reel	$7	$15	3
Gardening Tool Set	$6	$12	2

3 ◗ Using a browser search engine, such as AltaVista, type the keywords `Linear Programming`. Visit three Web pages that discuss how Linear Programming is used in real-world situations to solve business problems. Print each Web page. Hand in the three printouts to your instructor.

(continued)

Cases and Places

4 ▶▶ Open the workbook Microprocessor Plus on the Data Disk. Create four scenarios based on the four different compensation plans outlined in Table 8-6. Create a Scenario Summary that summarizes the result cells of H4, H7, H8, H9, H10, H11, and H12. Print the Scenario Summary worksheet. Hand in the printout to your instructor.

Table 8-6

ASSUMPTION	SCENARIO 1	SCENARIO 2	SCENARIO 3	SCENARIO 4
Base Salary	30%	25%	30%	10%
Commissions	2.5%	3.0%	2.5%	4%
Bonus	$17,750.00	$17,750.00	$15,000.00	$25,000.00
Net Sales for Bonus	$500,000.00	$500,000.00	$450,000.00	$475,000.00
Benefits	23.75%	23.75%	20.00%	25.00%
Payroll Tax	10.25%	10.25%	10.25%	10.25%

5 ▶▶▶ Your Uncle Bucks has asked for some help in picking stocks to purchase. He rates the risk level of stocks on a scale from zero to one. He wants to keep the value of each stock in his portfolio below 15 percent of the total value of his portfolio. He would like to minimize the risk level with the $50,000 he has to invest now by investing at least $45,000 of the money in certain stocks. The stocks he wants to purchase, their current price, and risk levels are shown in Table 8-7. Create the necessary worksheet and use Solver to determine the lowest risk combination of stocks in which to invest his funds.

Table 8-7 Stocks to Consider in Portfolio

STOCK	CURRENT PRICE PER SHARE	RISK FACTOR
INTC	80	.3
MSFT	91	.6
COMS	31	.22
MOT	87	.33
AOL	118	.8
YHOO	156	.75

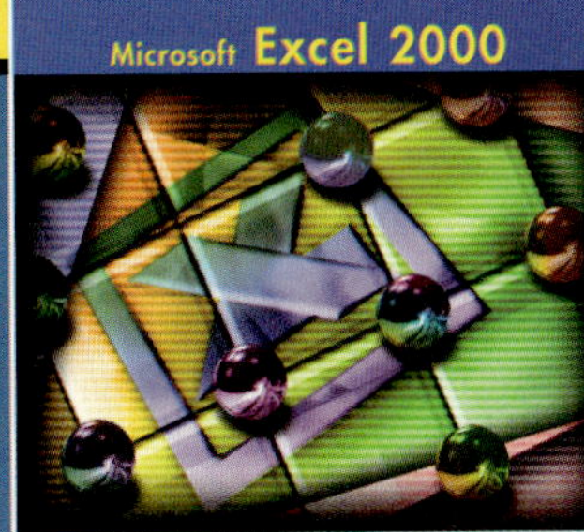

Microsoft Excel 2000

Importing External Data, Tracking and Routing Changes, and Creating Data Maps, PivotCharts, and PivotTables

OBJECTIVES

You will have mastered the material in this project when you can:

- Import data from a text file
- Import data from an Access database
- Import data from a Web page
- Insert, edit, and remove a comment
- Explain collaboration techniques
- Track changes and share a workbook
- Route a worksheet to other users
- Accept and reject tracked changes made to a workbook
- Create, edit, and format a data map
- Create a PivotChart and PivotTable
- Analyze a worksheet database using a PivotChart
- Analyze a worksheet database using a PivotTable
- Explain the concepts of sharing and merging workbooks

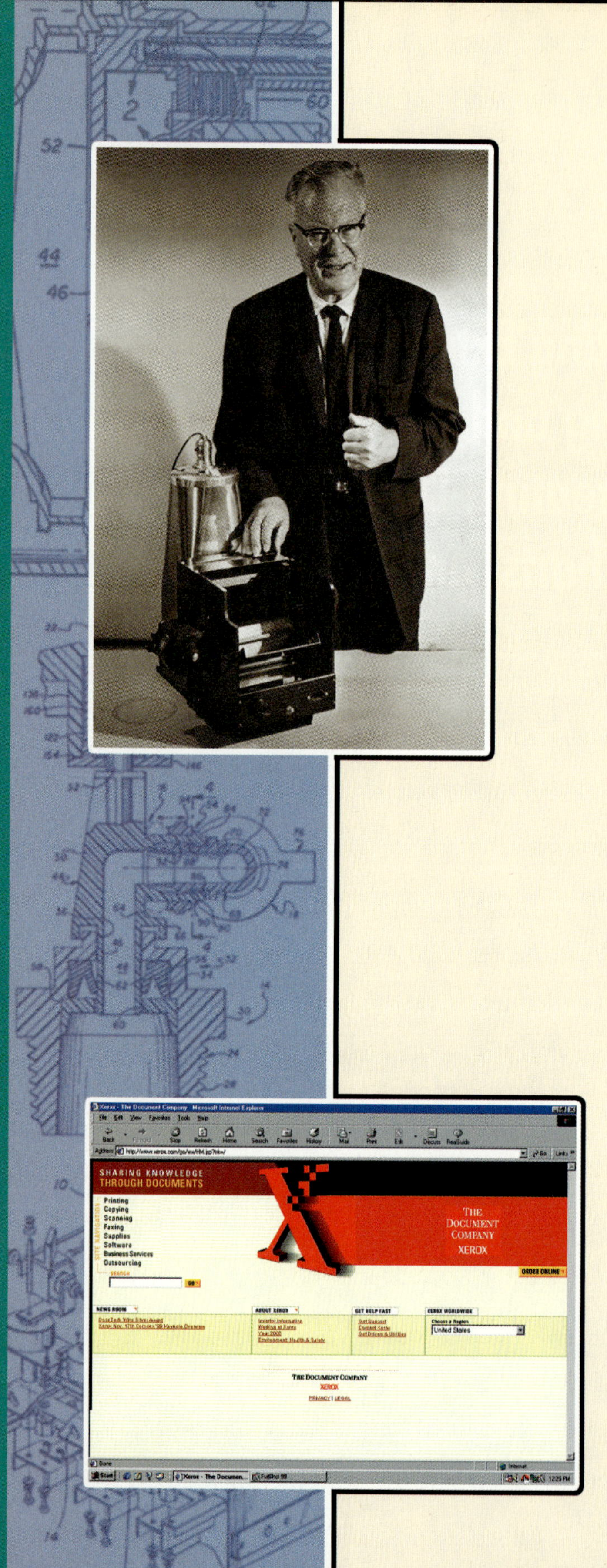

Necessity

The Mother of Invention

Necessity has been called The Mother of Invention. In an effort to find a more efficient or simplified way to perform a difficult task, many a creative project has resulted. That is how it all began for Chester Carlson, inventor of the photocopier.

In 1938, Carlson worked as a patent analyzer for an electrical component maker. In this capacity, he was required to spend numerous hours reviewing highly technical documents and drawings. Then he prepared the paperwork and applications submitted to the U.S. Patent and Trademark Office to register the company's inventions and ideas. It was during this time that Carlson developed his idea of an automated copying process. The patent office required multiple copies, which he had to duplicate manually, and redrawing the copies took hours. With his experience and technical expertise, Carlson went to work to find a better alternative.

His research led to the development of a technique based on photoconductivity, in which some materials change their electrical properties when exposed to light. He received a patent for his process, called electrophotography. In 1944, Carlson changed the name to xerography, a term derived from the Greek words for dry, and writing. He sold his right to a company that coined the word, Xerox, as the trademark for the new invention. The copier and the words, xerography (to describe the process) and Xerox (to identify the products), were introduced simultaneously in 1948. Today, Xerox, The Document Company, continues to be a major player in the document-imaging industry with innovative products.

The current light lens process when you set your original on the glass is a system of lamps, mirrors, and lenses that expose the image on a belt that has a positive electrical charge of static electricity. Digital copying uses scanner technology. To the casual observer, a digital copier looks just like the traditional light lens copier, but it provides significant advantages: not only is the image created using scanner technology, for a perfect copy, digital copiers can fully integrate with office systems for network printing, faxing, and scanning.

Most businesses utilize traditional or digital copier machines. The result of Carlson's original invention has spawned an expansive industry that markets, supplies, and services this document-imaging equipment. One such organization is Danka Office Imaging Company, Inc., providing product solutions, supplies, service, and support worldwide. The company maintains a computerized infrastructure that manages people, inventories, and marketing and product information in an extensive worksheet database from a variety of sources. Danka service field engineers are equipped with laptop computers that can access the latest data and product information on the Web for fast diagnostics and repair.

Similarly, in Project 9, you will gather information by importing data into an Excel workbook from a text file, an Access database, and a Web page. After ensuring the imported data is correct, you will analyze the data using a PivotChart and PivotTable. Excel gives you the ability to have an interactive view of worksheet data and summarize the information by rotating the table's rows and columns. Then, you will create a data map to display logistical data by geographic location.

In today's connected world, the ability to use and analyze data from a variety of sources is a necessity. As one necessity results in a related invention, the creative process continues as increasingly new demands generate better ways to perform tasks in a variety of ways.

Microsoft Excel 2000

Importing External Data, Tracking and Routing Changes, and Creating Data Maps, PivotCharts, and PivotTables

CASE PERSPECTIVE

José Velez is the marketing manager for the Burrito Land chain of fast food restaurants. The company owns restaurants in three states: New York, Texas, and Illinois. Restaurants are located on the street, in shopping malls, and in gas stations. José suspects that a shift in consumer habits has resulted in better performance for street-based restaurants.

José has requested the individual Burrito Land state offices send information regarding each store's sales along with other profile information. José has asked you, his assistant, to gather this information and produce some supporting documentation that will either confirm or reject his suspicions. José would like the data in a concise, easy-to-read format so he can present the findings to the board of directors. Each state has sent its information in different formats, because each state office operates independently of the corporate headquarters.

With your Excel background, you realize that PivotTables and PivotCharts would be helpful. Also, an Excel data map can be used to show variations in the data based on the state in which the restaurant is located.

Introduction

In today's connected world, the ability to use and analyze data from a wide variety of sources is a necessity. In this project, you will learn how to **import**, or bring, data from various external sources into an Excel worksheet and then analyze that data.

Suppose you routinely do business with a company that stores data in text format (Figure 9-1a on page E 9.6) rather than in a workbook. To make use of that data, you first input the data, and then format and manipulate it. Businesses also receive data in various database formats, such as Microsoft Access tables (Figure 9-1b), and from Web pages (Figure 9-1c).

Businesses routinely create charts to represent data visually. A **data map** (Figure 9-1f) is a type of chart that is a geographic map. It displays logistical data such as demographics, inventories, or marketing by state, region, or country. For example, Burrito Land owns restaurants in three states. To look at sales trends and current markets by geographic region, a data map can use color, symbols, and legends to represent the data and display the big picture.

Another visual way to analyze data is through the use of PivotCharts and PivotTables. A **PivotChart** (Figure 9-1g) is an interactive chart that provides the user with ways to graphically analyze data by varying the fields and categories to present different views. For example, if Burrito Land wanted to display a pie chart showing percentages for each state, a PivotChart could display that percentage using any field such as sales per state, number of mall locations per state, or locations with play areas.

Excel creates and associates a PivotTable with every PivotChart. A **PivotTable** (Figure 9-1h) is an interactive view of worksheet data that gives you the ability to summarize the database and then rotate the table's row and column titles to show different views of the summarized data. An inexperienced user with little knowledge of formulas, functions, and ranges can employ powerful what-if analyses of the data simply by clicking a field from a list of fields in a PivotChart or PivotTable.

Other techniques introduced in this project apply to issues of multiple users of the same workbook, including routing, tracking changes, and comments. If you want several people to look at a workbook and make comments, you can **route** it, or pass the workbook around, electronically. You can **track changes** to a workbook by displaying who changed what data, in which cell, and when. **Comments**, or descriptions, which do not regularly display as part of the worksheet data, can be added to the workbook itself to alert the recipients to special instructions, and later edited or deleted.

More About 2000

External Data

Imported data that maintains a refreshable link to its external source is called external data. When using external data, if a change is made to the original file, the worksheet will update as well. You can choose when to refresh the external data in the workbook.

Project Nine — Burrito Land Sales Analysis

From your meeting with José Velez, you have accumulated the following workbook specifications:

Need: Import data from the three states that have Burrito Land restaurants (Figures 9-1a, 9-1b, and 9-1c on the next page) into a worksheet containing headings and formulas, but no data (Figure 9-1d). Once the data is imported, the formulas in cells H3 and I3 must be copied to each row of data (Figure 9-1e). After the import is complete, the data in the worksheet requires verification by the state coordinators. Once the data is verified, create a data map displaying store sales and locations visually (Figure 9-1f). Finally, a PivotChart (Figure 9-1g) and its associated PivotTable (Figure 9-1h) allow interactive views of the data from the worksheet.

Source of Data: The three state coordinators for Burrito Land will submit data from their respective states via a text file (Illinois), an Access database (Texas), and a Web page (New York).

Calculations: The formulas used to calculate average sales per register in the first quarter of 2002 and 2001 are in cells H3 and I3 of the worksheet (Figure 9-1d). The formulas divide sales at the individual location by the number of registers in the store. After importing the data, the formulas need to be copied down for all rows of data.

Special Requirements: Before creating the data map, PivotChart, and PivotTable, route the workbook with the imported data (Figure 9-1e) to the three state coordinators for verification and then accept Tracked Changes.

Chart Requirements: Create a data map of the United States (Figure 9-1f) that highlights the three states. The data map also should show comparisons between the 2002 sales and the 2001 sales. Create a PivotChart (Figure 9-1g) and associated PivotTable (Figure 9-1h) that analyze sales based on any combination of states and locations.

More About 2000

Importing Data

If your system contains only a minimum installation of Excel, the first time you use one of the import features, Excel may attempt to install MSQuery. MSQuery is the supplemental application included in Microsoft Office 2000 used to retrieve data from external data sources.

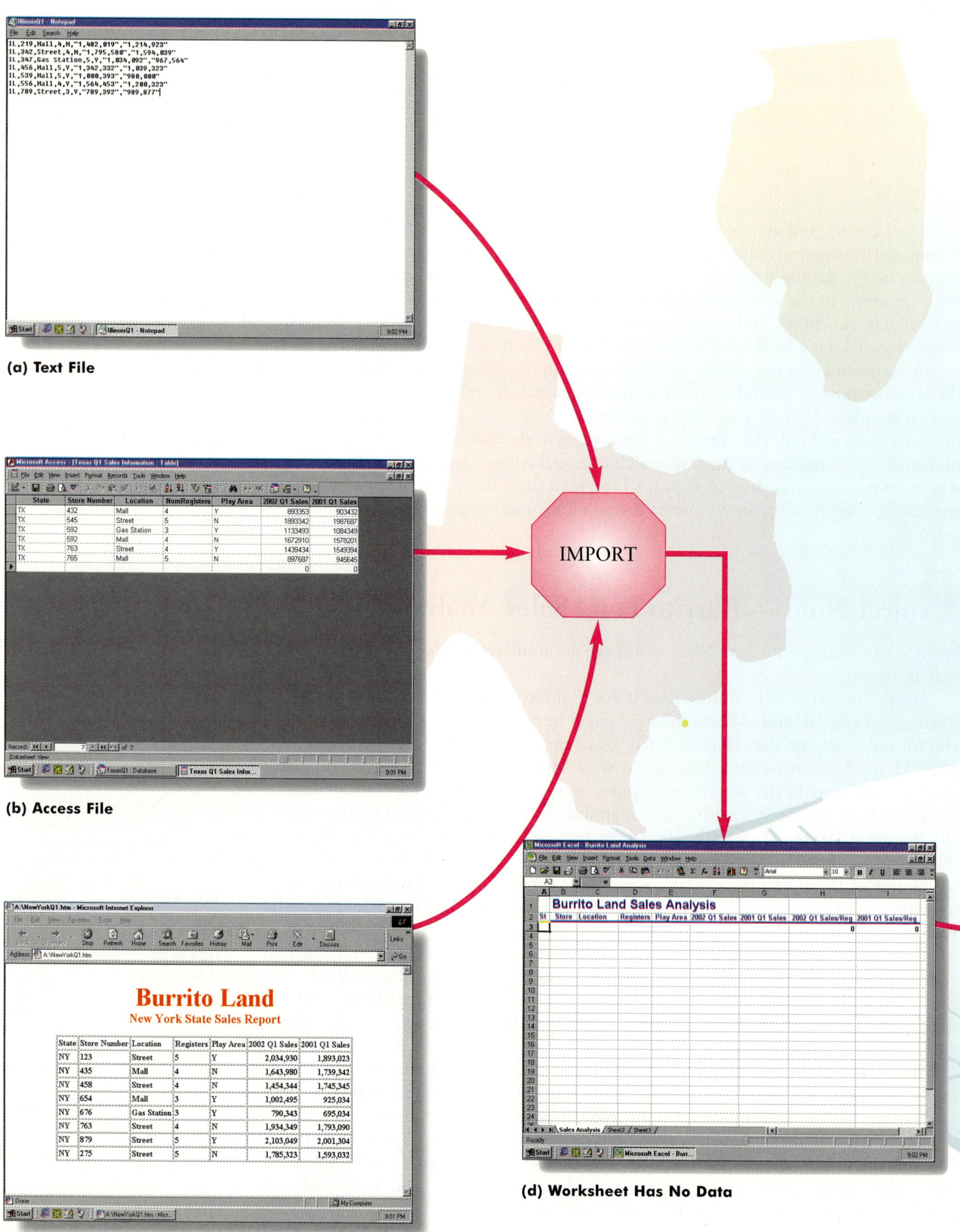

(a) Text File

(b) Access File

(c) HTML File

(d) Worksheet Has No Data

FIGURE 9-1

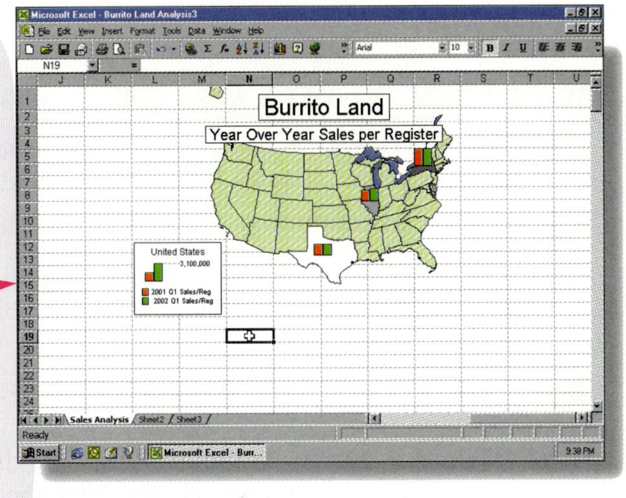

(f) Data Map

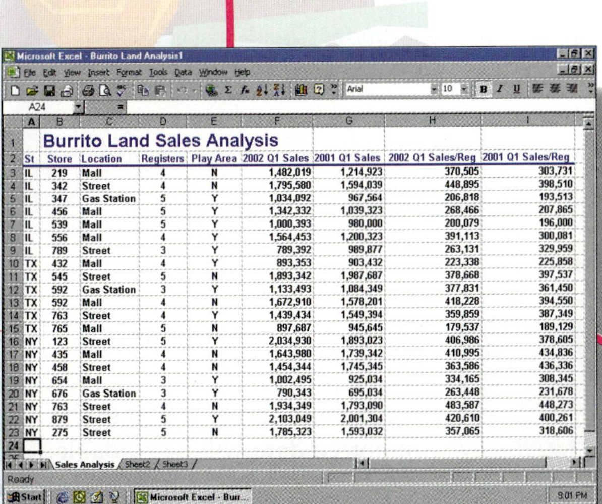

(e) Data Imported into Worksheet

(h) PivotTable

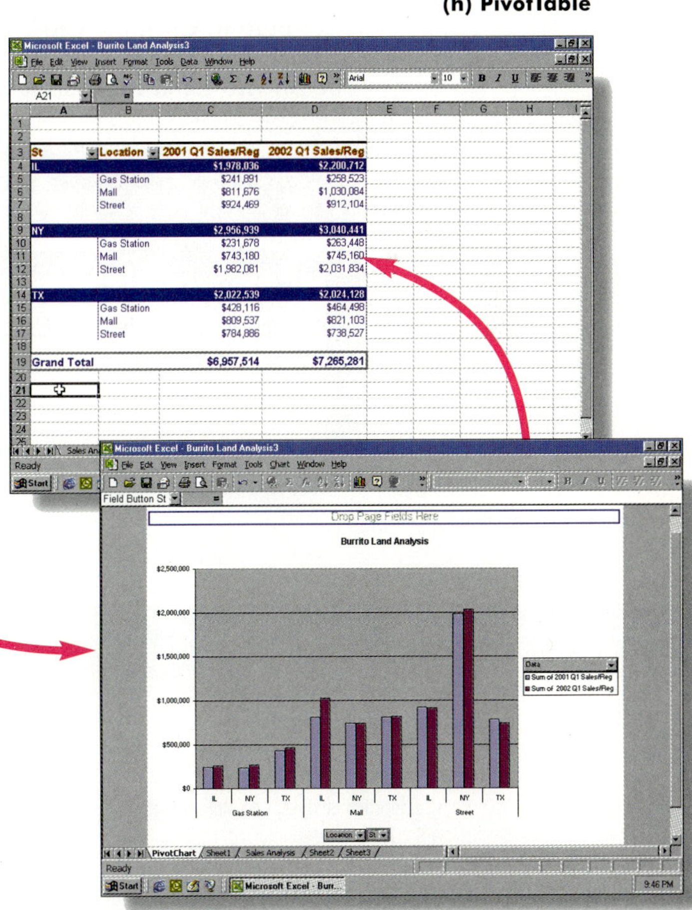

(g) PivotChart

Starting Excel and Opening a Workbook

Perform the following steps to start Excel, reset the toolbars, and open the empty workbook, Burrito Land Analysis, from the Data Disk.

TO START EXCEL AND OPEN A WORKBOOK

1. Insert the Data Disk in drive A. See the inside back cover of this book for instructions for downloading the Data Disk.
2. Click the Start button on the taskbar and then click Open Office Document.
3. When the Open Office Document dialog box displays, click the Look in box arrow and then click 3½ Floppy (A:). Double-click Burrito Land Analysis in the list.
4. When the Burrito Land Analysis workbook displays, click Tools on the menu bar, and then click Customize.
5. When the Customize dialog box displays, click the Options tab, make sure the top three check boxes are selected, click the Reset my usage data button, and then click the Yes button.
6. Click the Toolbars tab. Click Standard, click the Reset button, and then click the OK button. Click Formatting, click the Reset button, and then click the OK button. Click the Close button.

The Burrito Land Analysis workbook displays in the Excel window (Figure 9-2).

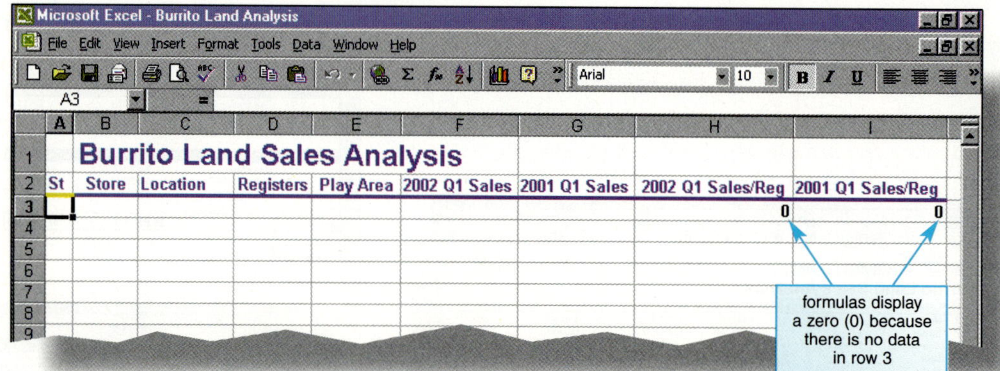

FIGURE 9-2

Table 9-1 Burrito Land Data Fields	
NAME OF FIELD	DATA DESCRIPTION
St	Standard postal abbreviation for the name of the state in which the store is located
Store	Store identification number - 3-digit number
Location	Physical location of store; i.e., Mall, Street, or Gas Station
Registers	Number of cash registers at the store - 1-digit number
Play Area	Logical Y or N field indicates whether or not the store has a play area for children
2002 Q1 Sales	First quarter sales in 2002 expressed in whole dollars
2001 Q1 Sales	First quarter sales in 2001 expressed in whole dollars
2002 Q1 Sales/Reg	Average sales per register for the first quarter of 2002 (2002 Q1 Sales / Registers)
2001 Q1 Sales/Reg	Average sales per register for the first quarter of 2001 (2001 Q1 Sales / Registers)

As shown in Figure 9-2, columns A through I have been resized and formatted so the imported data will be readable. Table 9-1 shows a summary of the column fields.

When you import data into a formatted worksheet, Excel formats the incoming data using the formats assigned to the cells as best it can.

Importing Files

Data may come to you from a variety of sources. Even though many users keep data in databases such as Microsoft Access, it is common to receive text files with fields of data separated by commas, especially from mainframe computer users. Also, with the increasing popularity of the World Wide Web, more companies are posting data on the Web. The ability to download data from the Web into an Excel worksheet is required. Importing data into Excel, rather than copying and pasting the data, also can create a refreshable link you may use to update data whenever the original file changes.

More About 2000

Opening a Text File in Excel

If you open a text file, such as IllinoisQ1.txt, in Excel, the Text Import Wizard will start automatically.

Importing Text Files

A **text file** contains electronic data created with little or no formatting. Many software applications such as Excel offer an option to import data from a text file, also called an ASCII text file. **ASCII** stands for the American Standard Code for Information Interchange.

In text files, commas, tabs, or other characters often separate the fields. Alternately, the text file may have fields of equal length in columnar format. Each record usually exists on a separate line. A **delimited file** contains a selected character, such as a comma, to separate data fields. A **fixed width file** contains data fields of equal length in the records. In the case of a fixed width file, a special character need not separate the data fields. During the import process, Excel provides a preview to help you identify the type of text file with which you are working.

The following steps import a comma delimited text file into the Burrito Land Analysis workbook using the **Text Import Wizard**. The text file on the Data Disk contains data about the first quarter sales in the state of Illinois (Figure 9-1a on page E 9.6).

More About 2000

Exporting to a Text File

In rare instances, you may want to convert your worksheet into a text file. On the File menu, the Save As command allows you to specify a text file. Some limitations exist, including the fact that you can save only one worksheet at a time, and then only the values, with no formatting, formulas, or graphics.

To Import Data from a Text File into a Worksheet

1 **With the Burrito Land Analysis worksheet active and the Data Disk in drive A, click cell A3. Click Data on the menu bar. Point to Get External Data and then point to Import Text File on the Get External Data submenu.**

The Data menu and the Get External Data submenu display (Figure 9-3).

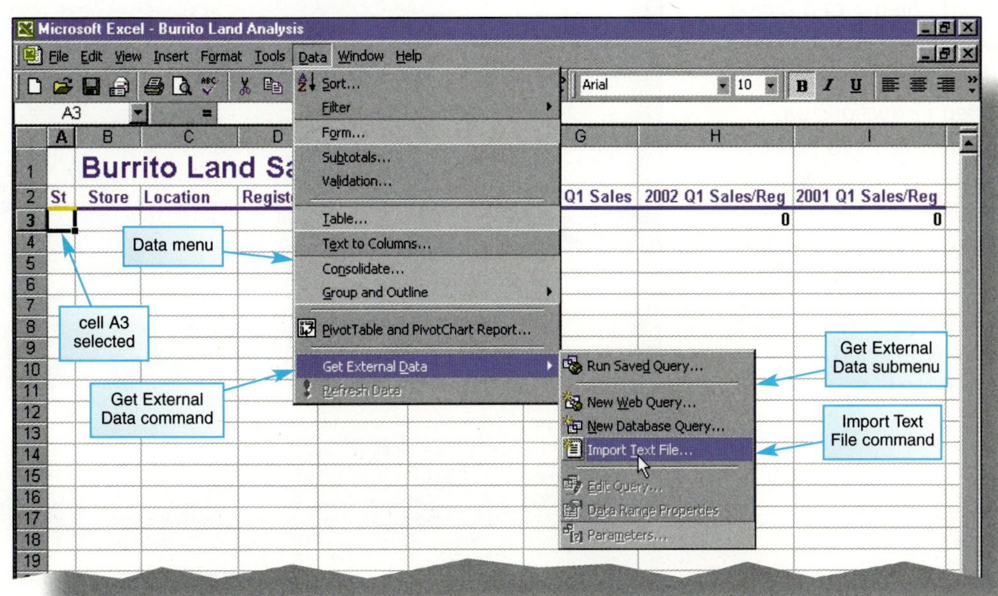

FIGURE 9-3

2 **Click Import Text File. When the Import Text File dialog box displays, click the Look in box arrow, and then click 3½ Floppy (A:). Point to IllinoisQ1.**

The text files on drive A display (Figure 9-4).

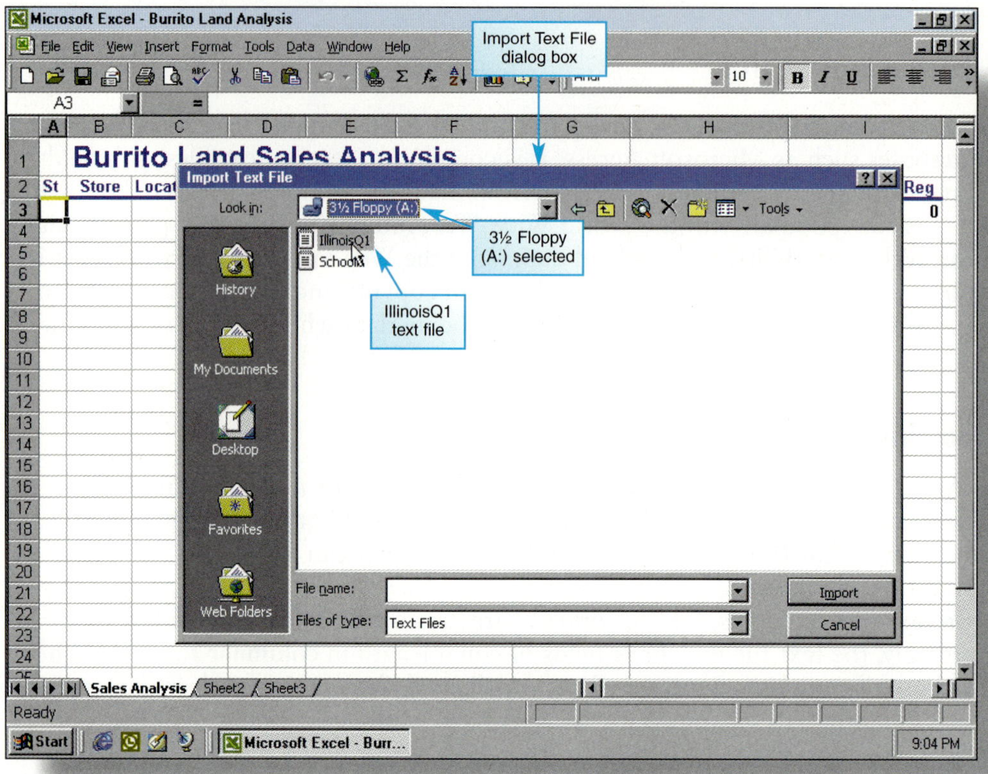

FIGURE 9-4

3 **Double-click IllinoisQ1. When the Text Import Wizard - Step 1 of 3 dialog box displays, point to the Next button.**

Excel displays the Text Import Wizard - Step 1 of 3 dialog box (Figure 9-5). The Text Import Wizard provides step-by-step instructions on importing text into Excel. The Preview box shows that the data from the file contains one record per line and the fields are separated by commas. The Delimited option button is selected in the Original data type area.

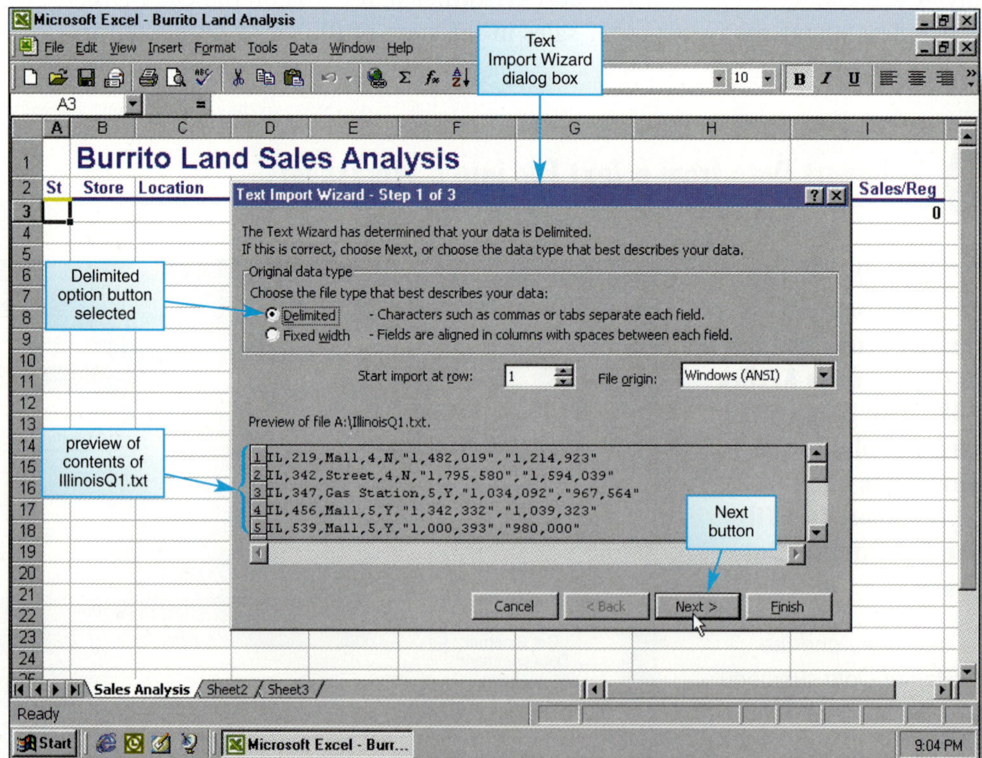

FIGURE 9-5

4 Click the Next button. When the Text Import Wizard - Step 2 of 3 dialog box displays, click Comma in the Delimiters area. Click Tab to clear the check box. Point to the Next button.

The Data preview area reflects the change (Figure 9-6). Excel correctly shows the fields of data in the Data preview area.

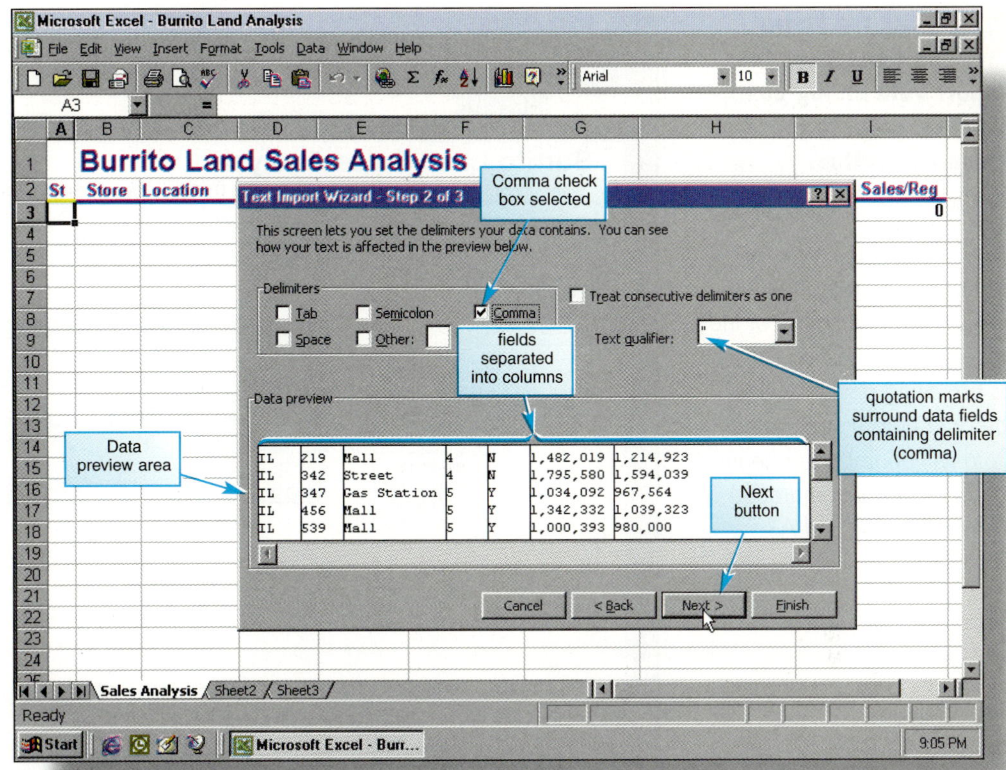

FIGURE 9-6

5 Click the Next button. When the Text Import Wizard - Step 3 of 3 dialog box displays, point to the Finish button.

The third dialog box of the Text Import Wizard displays (Figure 9-7). Step 3 allows you to select the format of each column of data. General is the default selection. The Data preview area shows the data separated based on the comma delimiter.

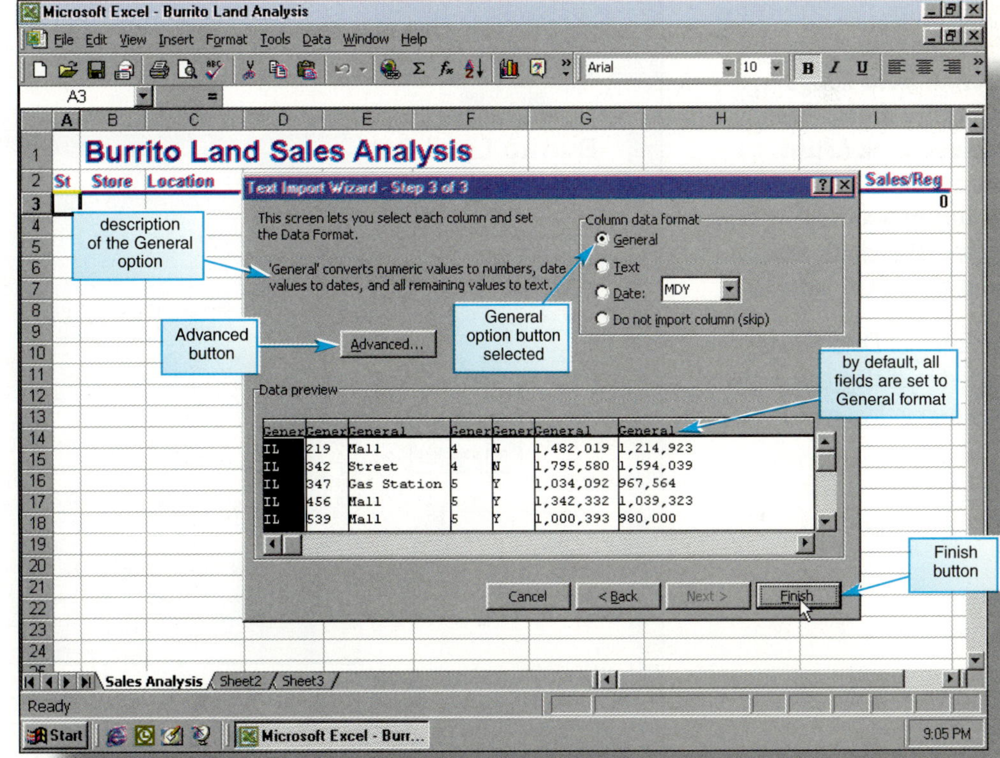

FIGURE 9-7

6 **Click the Finish button. When the Import Data dialog box displays, point to the Properties button.**

The Import Data dialog box displays (Figure 9-8). The Import Data dialog box *lets you select the location of the data in the worksheet, as well as providing a way to tailor the data before importing it. Data will be imported beginning at cell A3. A marquee displays around cell A3.*

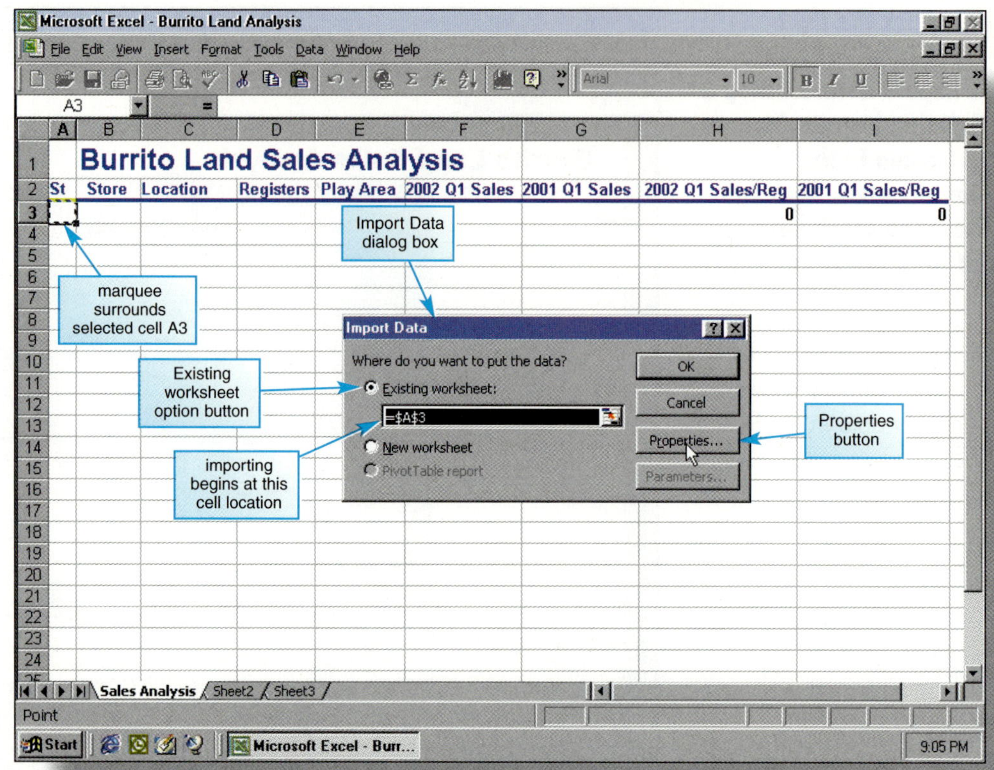

FIGURE 9-8

7 **Click the Properties button. When the External Data Range Properties dialog box displays, click Adjust column width in the Data formatting and layout area to clear the check box. Point to the OK button.**

The External Data Range Properties dialog box *displays as shown in Figure 9-9.*

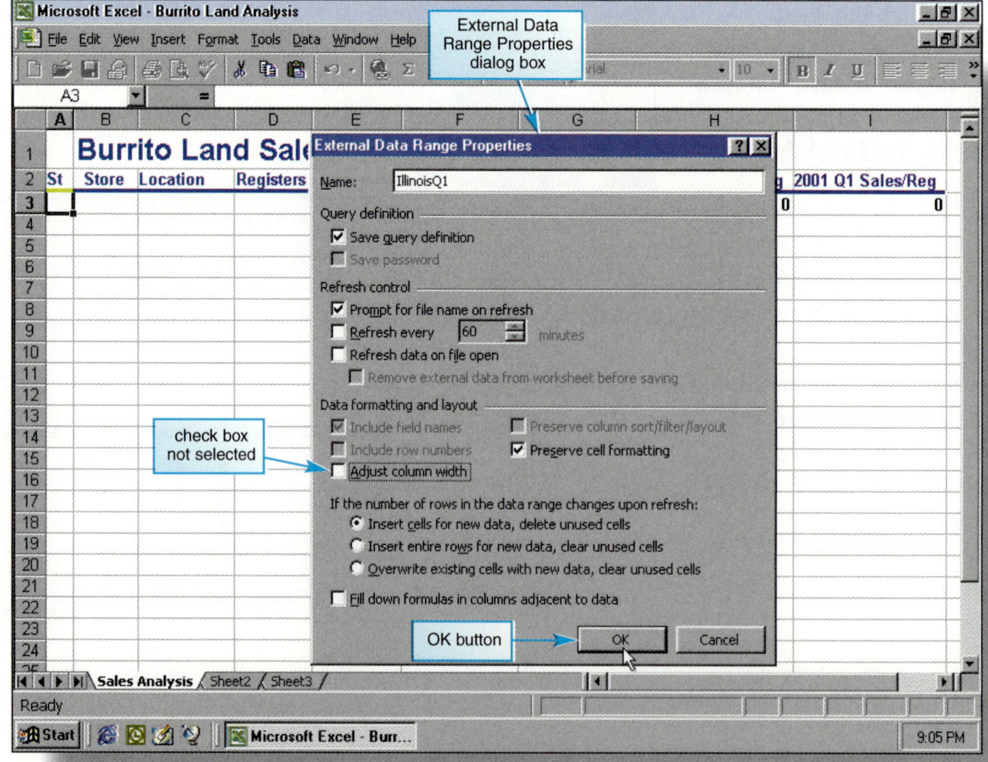

FIGURE 9-9

8 Click the OK button. When the Import Data dialog box displays, click the OK button. If the External Data toolbar displays on your screen, click its Close button.

Excel imports the data into the worksheet beginning at cell A3 (Figure 9-10).

	A	B	C	D	E	F	G	H	I
1	Burrito Land Sales Analysis								
2	St	Store	Location	Registers	Play Area	2002 Q1 Sales	2001 Q1 Sales	2002 Q1 Sales/Reg	2001 Q1 Sales/Reg
3	IL	219	Mall	4	N	1,482,019	1,214,923	370,505	303,731
4	IL	342	Street	4	N	1,795,580	1,594,039		
5	IL	347	Gas Station	5	Y	1,034,092	967,564		
6	IL	456	Mall	5	Y	1,342,332	1,039,323		
7	IL	539	Mall	5	Y	1,000,393	980,000		
8	IL	556	Mall	4	Y	1,564,453	1,200,323		
9	IL	789	Street	3	Y	789,392	989,877		

text file data imported

formulas display nonzero results because of data in row 3

FIGURE 9-10

Other Ways

1. Press ALT+D, press D, press T

More About

Dragging and Dropping a Text File

Excel allows you to drag a text file to a blank worksheet. Simply drag the file name or the icon from its location to a blank worksheet. You then can format the data easily using the Text to Columns command on the Data menu. The data does not maintain a refreshable link to the text file, however.

The commas in the last two columns of numbers in the Data preview area (Figure 9-7 on page E 9.11) are not considered to be delimiters because each of these data values was surrounded by quotation marks when the text file was created.

By default, the cell that is active when you perform the text import will become the upper-left cell of the imported range. If you want to import the data to a different location, you can specify the location in the Import Data dialog box (Figure 9-8).

By importing the text file, Excel can **refresh**, or update, the data whenever the original text file changes using the **Refresh command** on the Data menu.

Importing Access Tables

When you import data from an Access database, you start by making a query of the data. A **query** is a way to qualify the data you want to import by specifying a matching condition or asking a question of a database. You may choose to import the entire file or only a portion. For example, you can make a query to import only those records that pass a certain test, such as records containing numeric fields greater than a specific amount, or records containing text fields matching a specific value.

The steps on the next page import an entire table from an Access database using the **Database Query Wizard**. The table in the Access database on the Data Disk contains data about the first quarter sales in the state of Texas (Figure 9-1b on page E 9.6).

To Import Data from an Access Table into a Worksheet

1 Click cell A10. Click Data on the menu bar, point to Get External Data, and then point to New Database Query.

The Get External Data submenu displays (Figure 9-11).

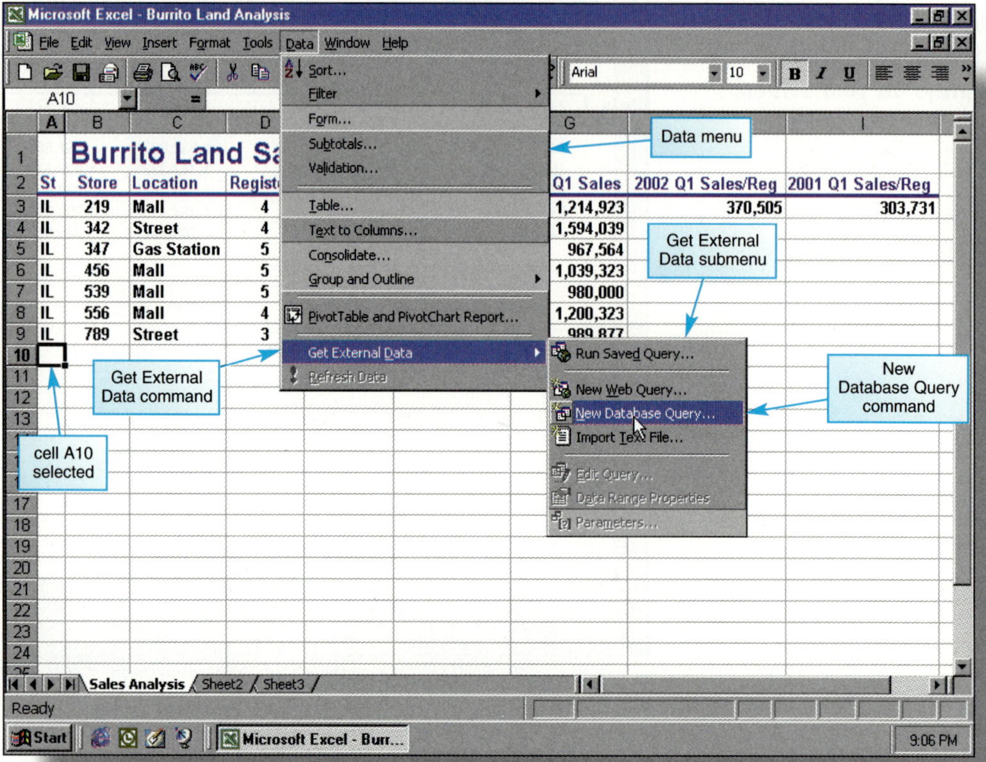

FIGURE 9-11

2 Click New Database Query. When the Choose Data Source dialog box displays, if necessary, click the Databases tab, and then click MS Access Database* in the list. Point to the OK button.

The **Choose Data Source dialog box** *displays several database application formats (Figure 9-12). This list may differ on your computer. A check mark displays in the Use the Query Wizard to create/edit queries check box.*

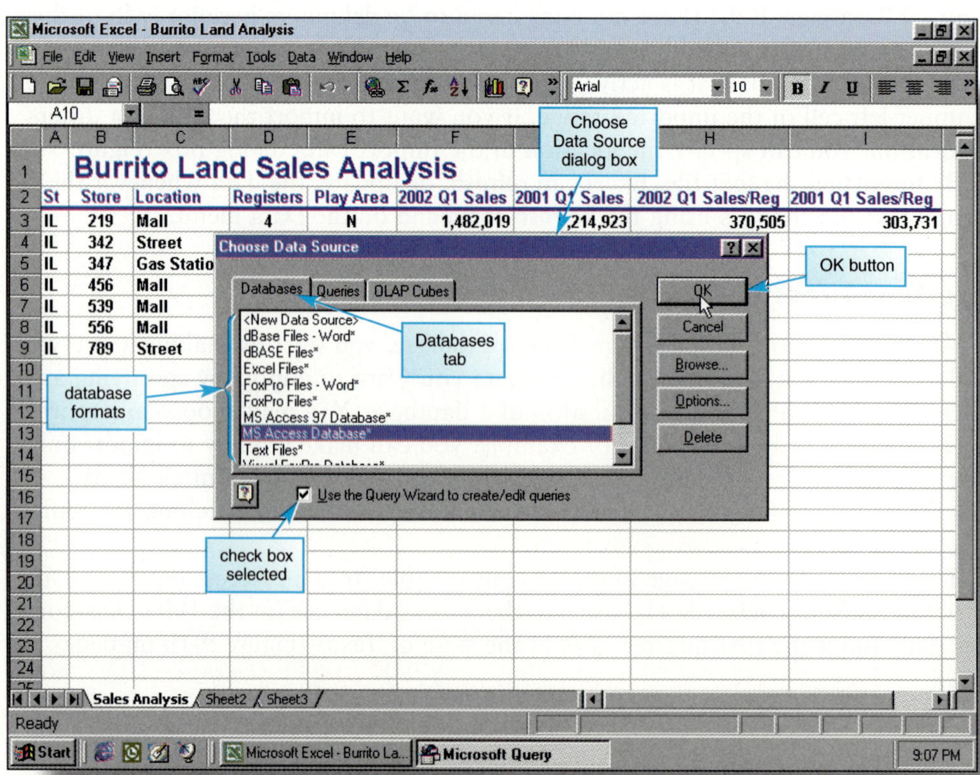

FIGURE 9-12

3 Click the OK button. When the Select Database dialog box displays, click the Drives box arrow and then click a: in the list. Point to texasq1.mdb in the Database Name list.

The Select Database dialog box displays (Figure 9-13). Your system may not display the Connecting to data source progress box.

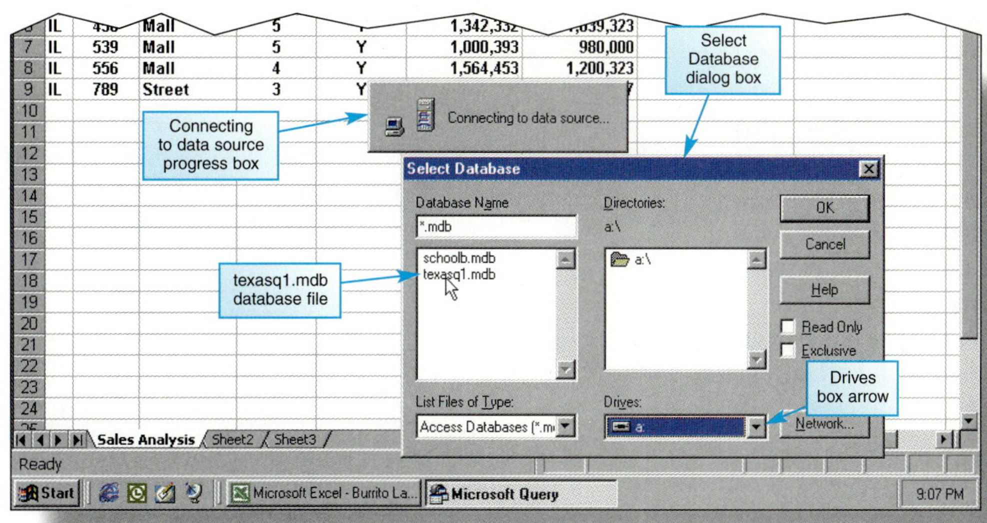

FIGURE 9-13

4 Double-click texasq1.mdb. When the Query Wizard – Choose Columns dialog box displays, select the Texas Q1 Sales Information table and then point to the Add Table button.

The database has one table to add to the query (Figure 9-14).

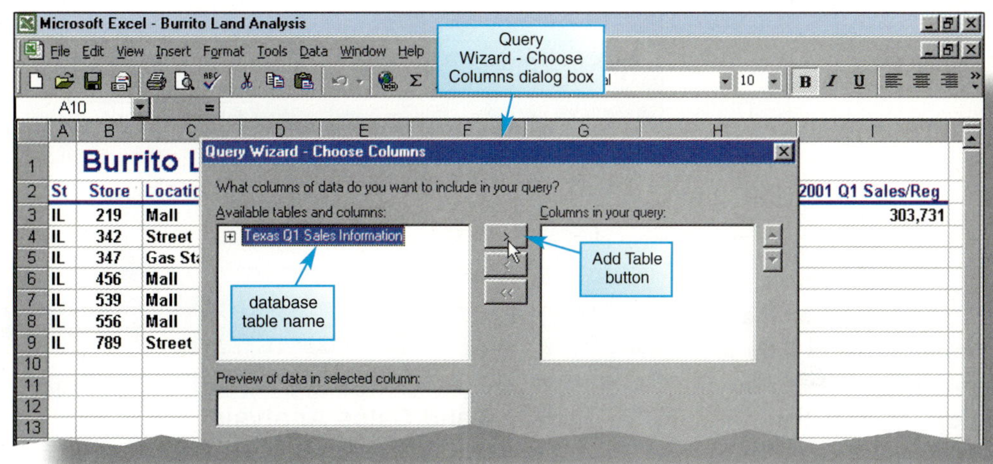

FIGURE 9-14

5 Click the Add Table button and then point to the Next button.

The fields of the Texas Q1 Sales Information table display (Figure 9-15).

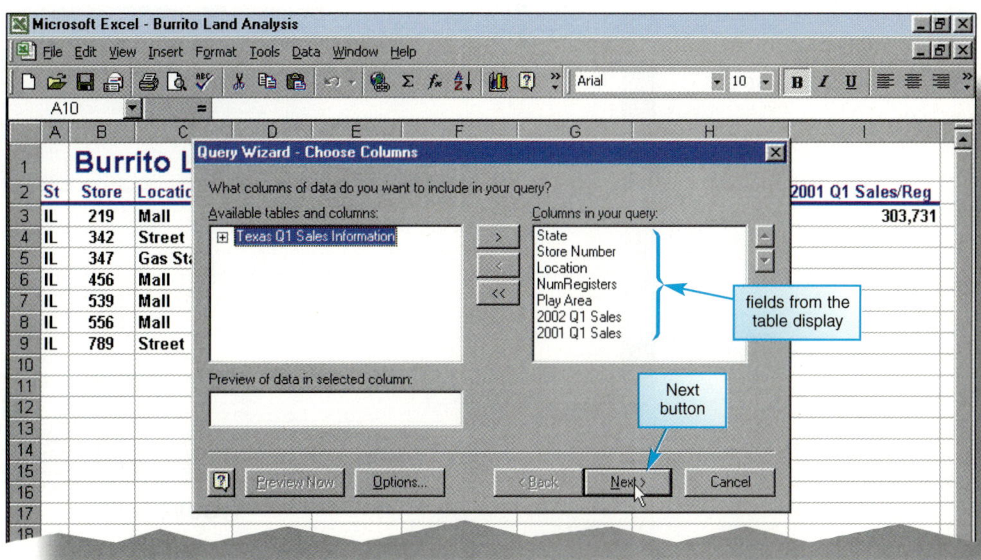

FIGURE 9-15

6 Click the Next button. When the Query Wizard - Filter Data dialog box displays, click the Next button. When the Query Wizard - Sort Order dialog box displays, click the Next button. When the Query Wizard - Finish dialog box displays, point to the Finish button (Figure 9-16).

Since the entire table is being imported without a specific query, clicking the Next button in each of the Wizard dialog boxes accepts the preset values.

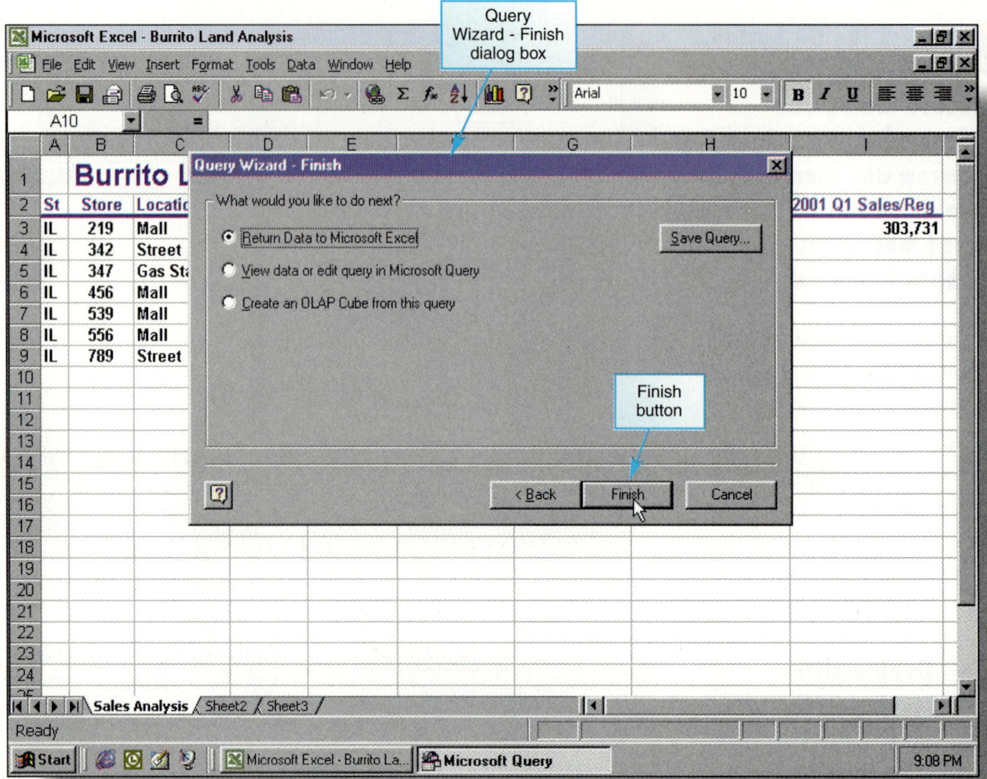

FIGURE 9-16

7 Click the Finish button. When the Returning External Data to Microsoft Excel dialog box displays, point to the Properties button.

The *Returning External Data to Microsoft Excel dialog box* displays (Figure 9-17). Data will be imported beginning at cell A10. A marquee displays around cell A10.

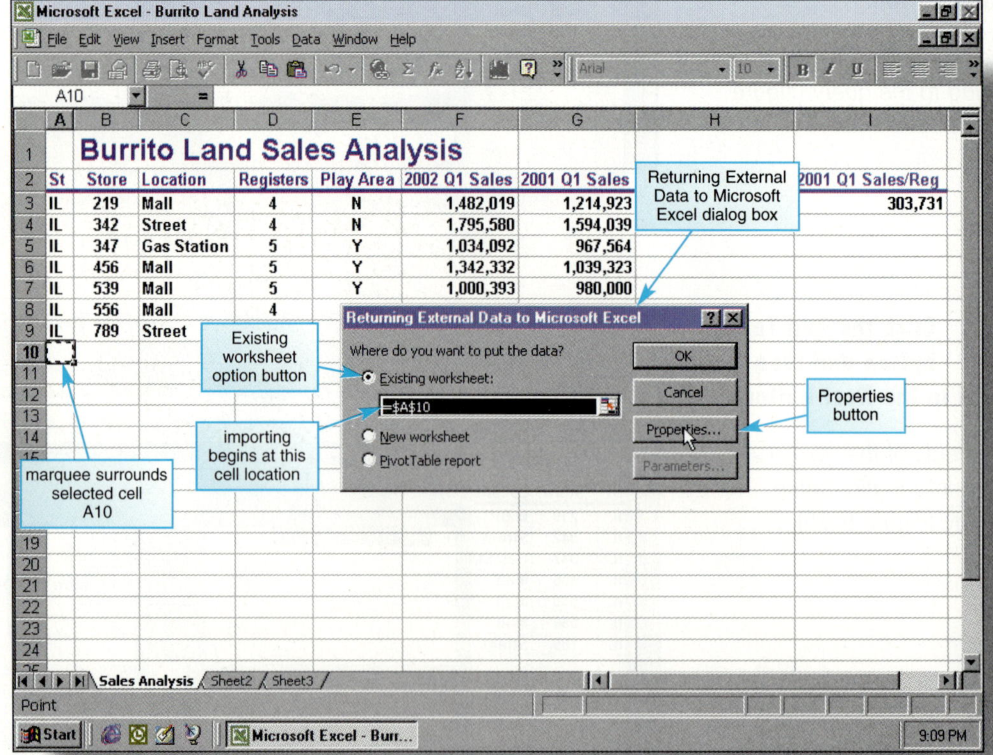

FIGURE 9-17

8 **Click the Properties button. When the External Data Range Properties dialog box displays, click Include field names and Adjust column width in the Data formatting and layout area to clear the check boxes. Point to the OK button.**

The External Data Range Properties dialog box displays (Figure 9-18). With the two check marks removed, Excel will not import the field names or adjust column widths in Excel.

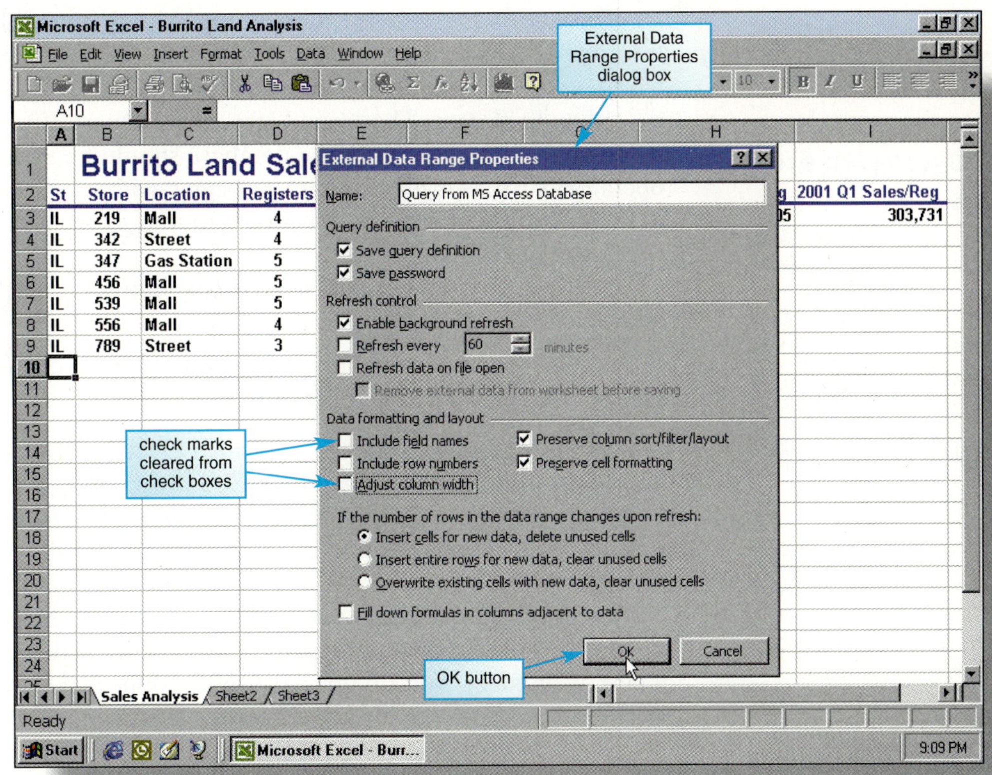

FIGURE 9-18

9 **Click the OK button. When the Returning External Data to Microsoft Excel dialog box (Figure 9-17) redisplays, click the OK button. If your system displays the External Data toolbar, click its Close button.**

The data imported from the Access database displays in the worksheet (Figure 9-19).

Microsoft Excel - Burrito Land Analysis

Burrito Land Sales Analysis

St	Store	Location	Registers	Play Area	2002 Q1 Sales	2001 Q1 Sales	2002 Q1 Sales/Reg	2001 Q1 Sales/Reg
IL	219	Mall	4	N	1,482,019	1,214,923	370,505	303,731
IL	342	Street	4	N	1,795,580	1,594,039		
IL	347	Gas Station	5	Y	1,034,092	967,564		
IL	456	Mall	5	Y	1,342,332	1,039,323		
IL	539	Mall	5	Y	1,000,393	980,000		
IL	556	Mall	4	Y	1,564,453	1,200,323		
IL	789	Street	3	Y	789,392	989,877		
TX	432	Mall	4	Y	893,353	903,432		
TX	545	Street	5	N	1,893,342	1,987,687		
TX	592	Gas Station	3	Y	1,133,493	1,084,349		
TX	592	Mall	4	N	1,672,910	1,578,201		
TX	763	Street	4	Y	1,439,434	1,549,394		
TX	765	Mall	5	N	897,687	945,645		

Access data imported

FIGURE 9-19

Other Ways
1. Press ALT+D, press D, press N

By default, the cell that is active when you perform the database query becomes the upper-left cell of the imported range. If you want to import the data to a different location, you specify the location in the Returning External Data to Microsoft Excel dialog box (Figure 9-17).

Dragging and Dropping an Access File

If you have both Excel and Access open on your desktop, you can drag and drop an entire table or query from Access to Excel. Select the table or query you want to transfer in the database window and then drag it to the location in the worksheet.

The Access file, texasq1.mdb, contains only one table, Texas Q1 Sales Information. The table contains seven fields that correspond to the columns in the worksheet. The Add Table button shown in Figure 9-14 on page E 9.15 added all the columns of data. The second step of the Query Wizard allows you to **filter**, or specify, which records from the database should be included in the result set, using operators such as is-greater-than or begins-with. For example, you can filter the data in the previous example by specifying to import records that have five or more registers.

With the data from Illinois and Texas imported, the next step is to import the New York data from a Web page.

Importing Data from a Web Page

A Web page uses a file format called HTML. **HTML** stands for **Hypertext markup language**, which is a language that Web browsers can interpret. A Web page allows you to import data into preformatted areas of the worksheet. You specify which parts of the Web page you want and how much of the HTML formatting you want to keep.

Excel creates four saved **Web queries** when you first install Excel, most of which involve investment and stock market Web pages. The next sequence of steps creates a new Web query. You do not have to be connected to the Internet to perform these steps because the Data Disk includes the Web page (Figure 9-1c on page E 9.6).

To Import Data from a Web Page into a Worksheet

1 Click cell A16. Click Data on the menu bar, point to Get External Data, and then point to New Web Query.

The Data menu and Get External Data submenu display (Figure 9-20).

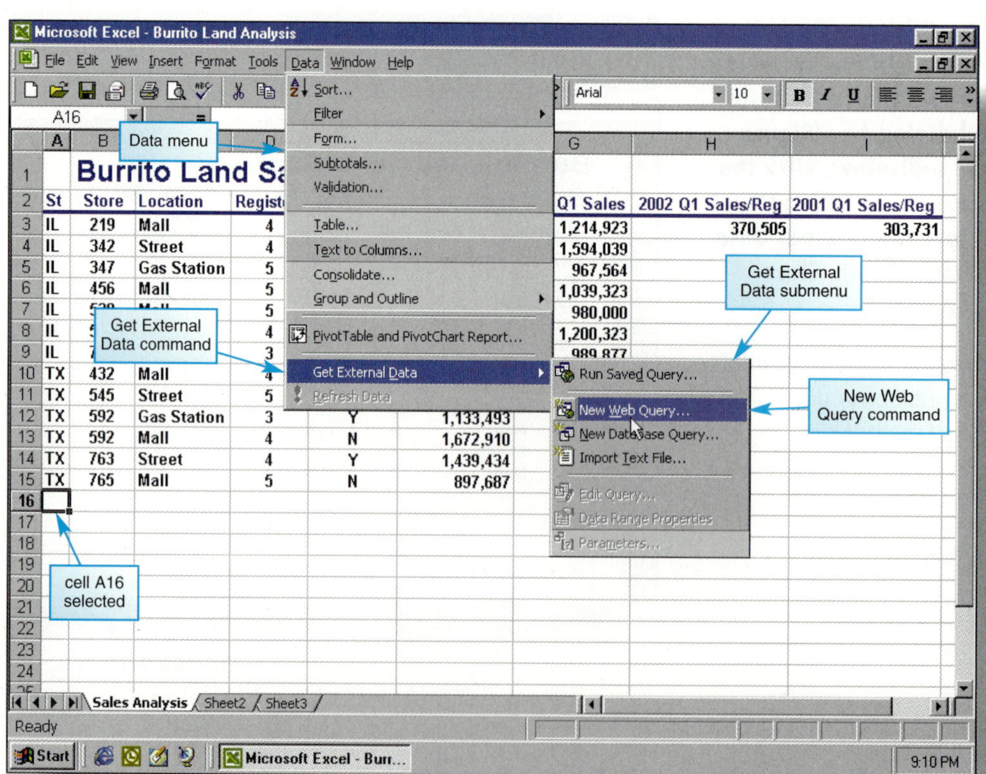

FIGURE 9-20

2 **Click New Web Query. When the New Web Query dialog box displays, type** `a:\newyorkq1.htm` **in the step 1 text box and then point to the OK button.**

The file location displays in the step 1 text box at the top of the New Web Query dialog box (Figure 9-21).

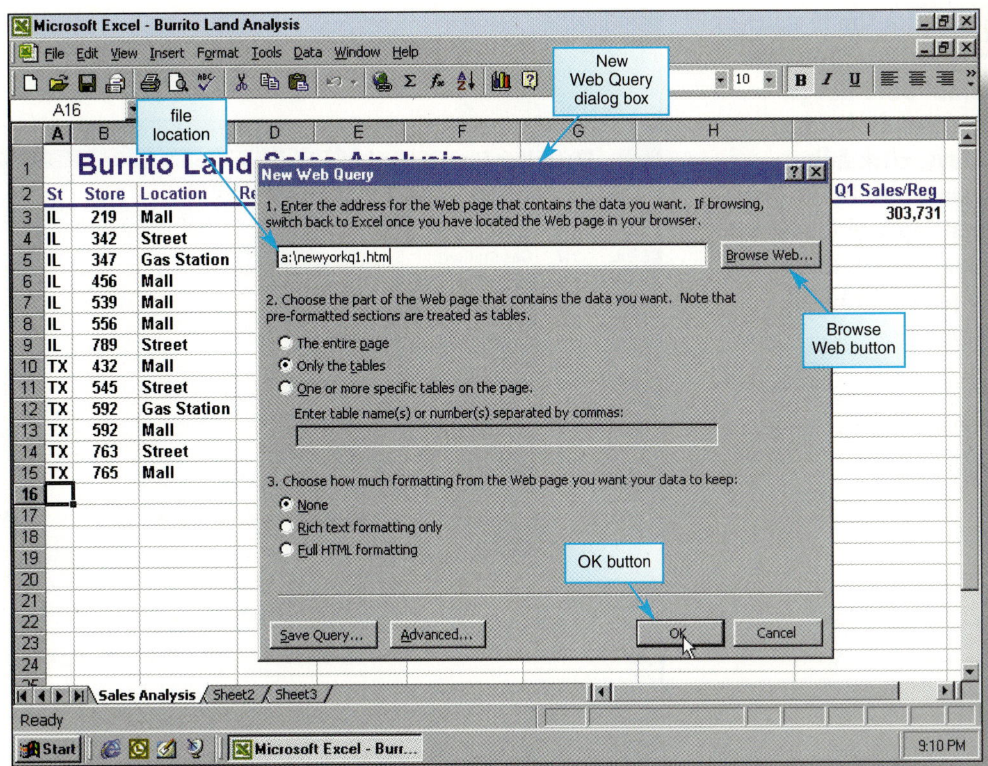

FIGURE 9-21

3 **Click the OK button. When the Returning External Data to Microsoft Excel dialog box displays, point to the Properties button.**

The Returning External Data to Microsoft Excel dialog box displays (Figure 9-22). Data will be imported beginning at cell A16. A marquee displays around cell A16.

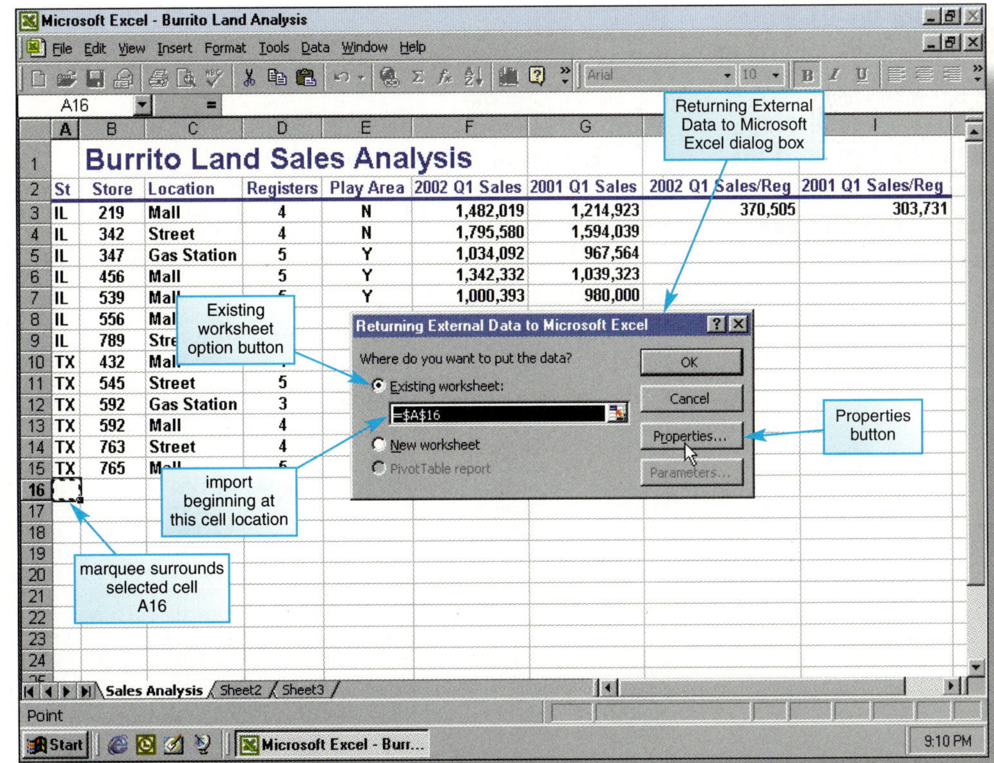

FIGURE 9-22

4 **Click the Properties button. When the External Data Range Properties dialog box displays, click Adjust column width in the Data formatting and layout area to clear the check box and then point to the OK button.**

The External Data Range Properties dialog box displays (Figure 9-23).

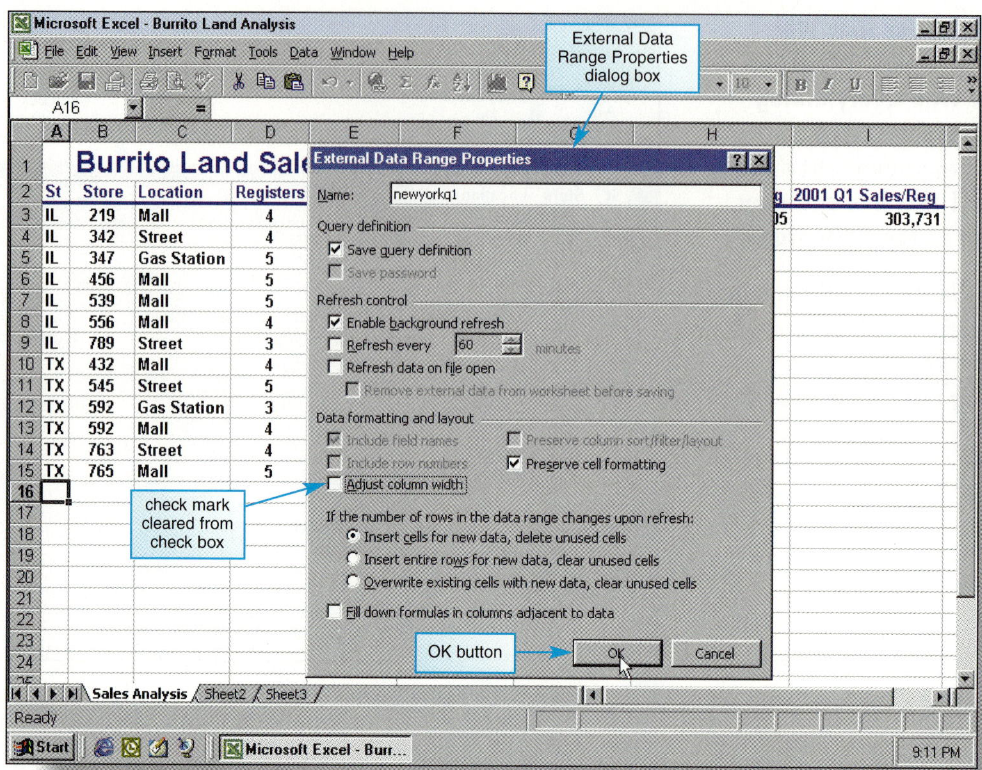

FIGURE 9-23

5 **Click the OK button. When the Returning External Data to Microsoft Excel dialog box displays, click the OK button. If the External Data toolbar displays on your screen, click its Close button.**

The data displays in the worksheet (Figure 9-24).

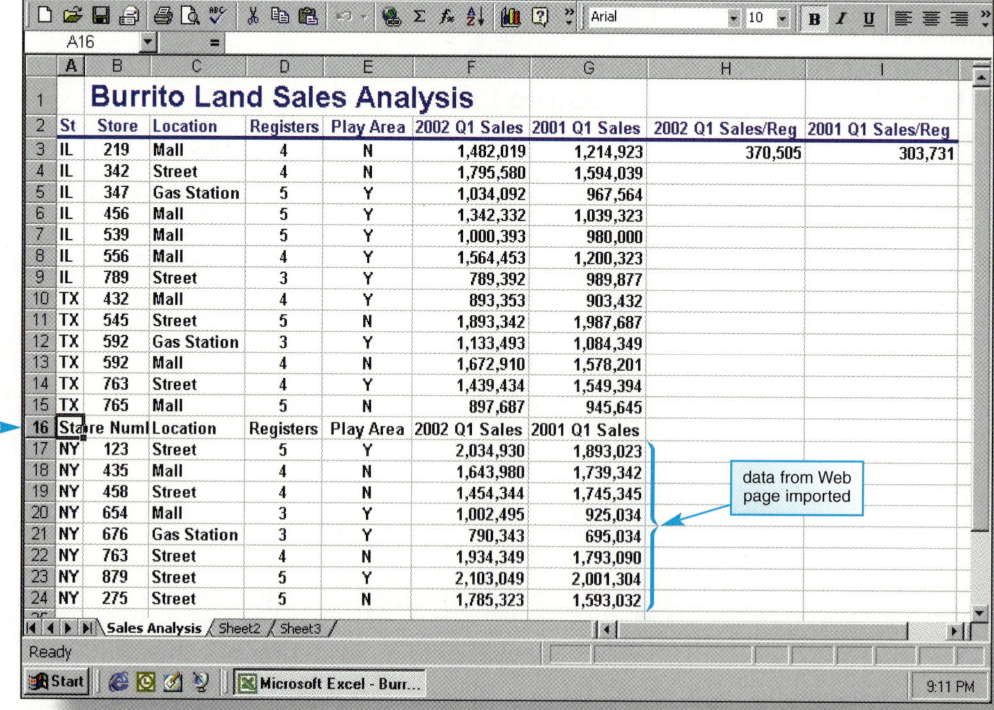

FIGURE 9-24

6 Right-click row heading 16. Point to Delete on the shortcut menu.

The shortcut menu for the selected row displays (Figure 9-25). You will delete these extra column headings from the Web page table.

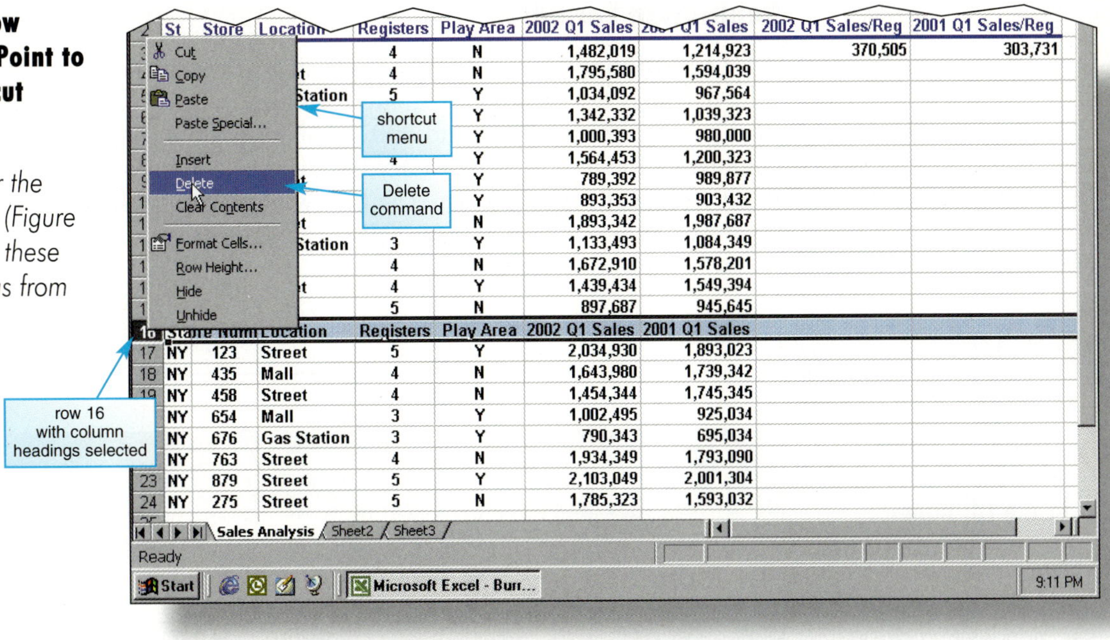

shortcut menu

Delete command

row 16 with column headings selected

FIGURE 9-25

7 Click Delete.

Excel deletes row 16, which contained the column headings from the Web page (Figure 9-26).

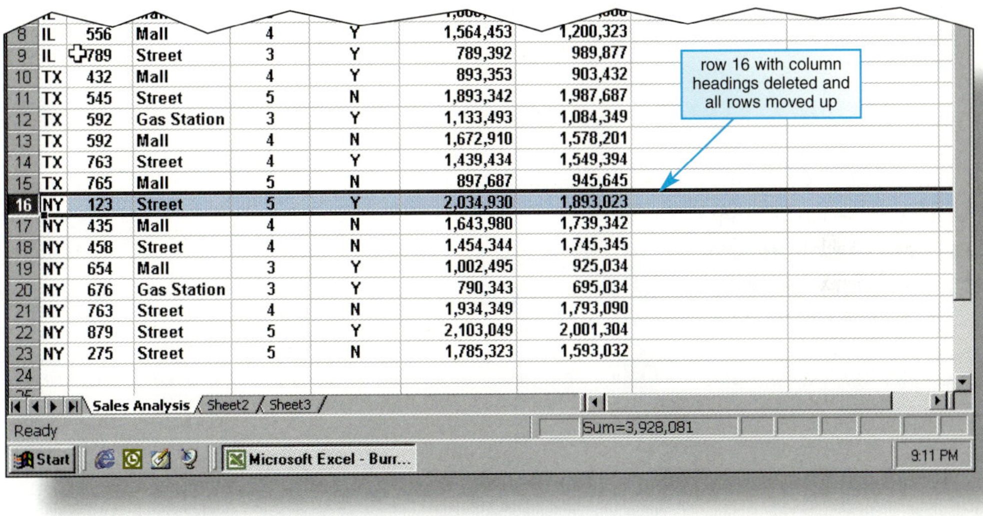

row 16 with column headings deleted and all rows moved up

FIGURE 9-26

1. Press ALT+D, press D, press S

By default, the cell that is active when you perform the Web query will become the upper-left cell of the imported range. If you want to import the data to a different location, you can specify the location in the Returning External Data to Microsoft Excel dialog box (Figure 9-22 on page E 9.19).

Using a Web query has advantages over other methods of importing data from a Web page. For example, copying data from Web pages to the Clipboard and then pasting it into Excel does not maintain the formatting. In addition, it is tedious to have to highlight just the data you want in a Web page. Finally, copying and pasting does not create a link to the Web page for future updating.

Replicating Formulas

The workbook opened at the beginning of this project contained a worksheet title, headings for each column, and formulas in cells H3 and I3 to calculate the sales per register for 2002 and 2001. This technique of copying the formulas after completing the import is necessary because the total number of records to be imported usually is unknown. The following steps use the fill handle to copy the formulas. Some spreadsheet specialists refer to copying formulas as **replication**.

To Replicate Formulas

1 Select the range H3:I3 and then point to the fill handle.

The range H3:I3 is selected (Figure 9-27). The mouse pointer changes to a cross hair when pointing to the fill handle.

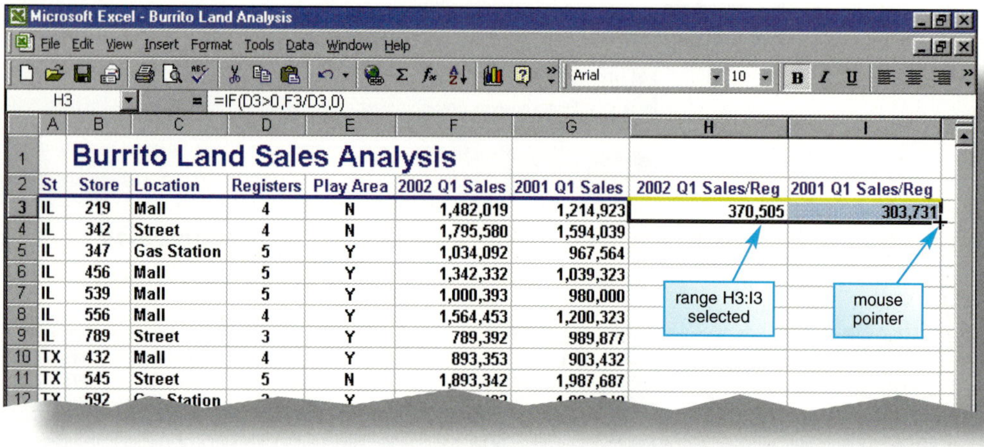

FIGURE 9-27

2 Drag the fill handle down through row 23.

Excel copies the two formulas to the range H4:I23 and displays the new values for Sales per Register (Figure 9-28).

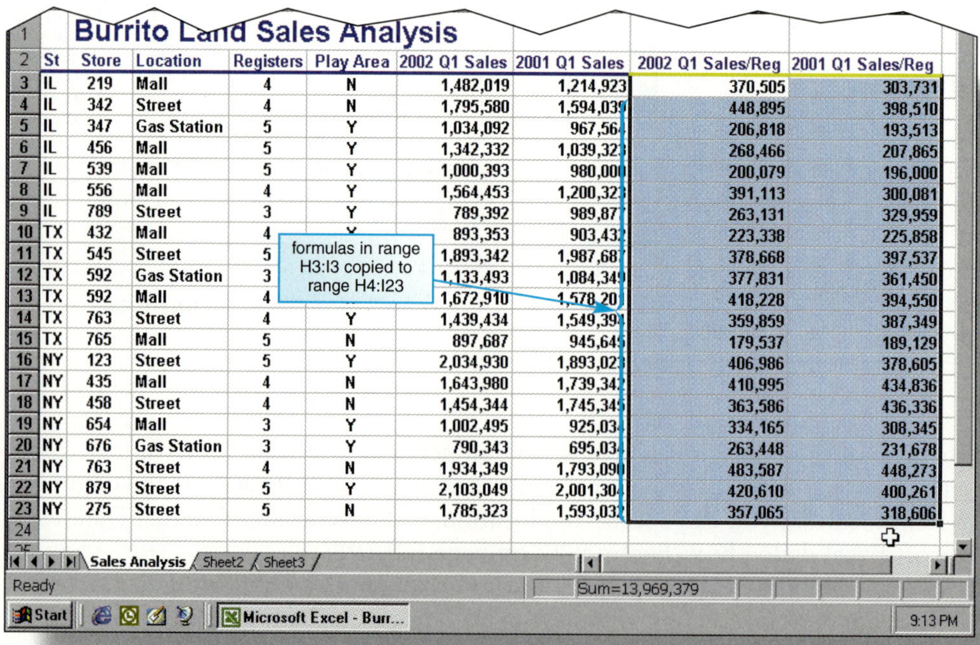

FIGURE 9-28

Other Ways

1. Click Copy button on Standard toolbar, click Paste button on Standard toolbar
2. On Edit menu click Copy, on Edit menu click Paste
3. Press CTRL+C, press CTRL+V
4. Click Copy on shortcut menu, click Paste on shortcut menu

Recall that when you copy, or replicate, a formula, Excel adjusts the cell references so the new formulas contain references corresponding to the new locations and perform calculations using the appropriate values. If you want an exact copy without replication, you must hold down the CTRL key while dragging the fill handle. Holding down the SHIFT key while dragging the fill handle inserts new cells rather than overwriting the existing data.

Saving the Workbook with a New File Name

Perform the following steps to save the workbook with the file name Burrito Land Analysis1.

TO SAVE THE WORKBOOK WITH A NEW FILE NAME

1. Click File on the menu bar and then click Save As.
2. When the Save As dialog box displays, Type `Burrito Land Analysis1` in the File name text box.
3. If necessary, click 3½ Floppy (A:) in the Save in list.
4. Click the Save button in the Save As dialog box.

Excel saves the workbook on the Data Disk in drive A using the file name Burrito Land Analysis1.

Preparing the Workbook for Routing

The next step is to add a routing comment and then verify the accuracy of the data by routing it to the state coordinators for review.

Inserting Comments

Comments are used to describe the function of a cell, a range, a sheet, or an entire workbook, or they may be used to clarify entries that might otherwise be difficult to understand. Multiple users or people reviewing the workbook often use comments to communicate suggestions, tips, and other messages. José suspects that the sales amount in cell F9 from Illinois is incorrect, and thus will add a comment to the cell before routing the workbook to the three state coordinators as shown in the steps on the next page.

More About 2000

Importing External Data

Excel assigns a name to each external data range. You can view these names by clicking the Name box arrow in the formula bar. External data ranges from text files are named with the text file name. External data ranges from databases are named with the name of the query. External data ranges from Web queries are named with the name of the Web page from which the data was retrieved.

More About 2000

Selecting External Data

If you want to view the part of your worksheet that is imported, or if you want to format or delete an external data range, click the Name box arrow in the formula bar, and then click the external data range name.

More About 2000

Saving a Workbook with External Data

Excel provides the option of saving the workbook without saving the external data so the workbook file size is reduced. Click Data Range Properties on the External Data toolbar and then click the Refresh data on file open. To save the workbook with the query definition but without the external data, click Remove external data from worksheet before saving in the Data Range Properties dialog box.

To Insert a Comment

1 Right-click cell F9. Point to Insert Comment on the shortcut menu.

The shortcut menu displays (Figure 9-29).

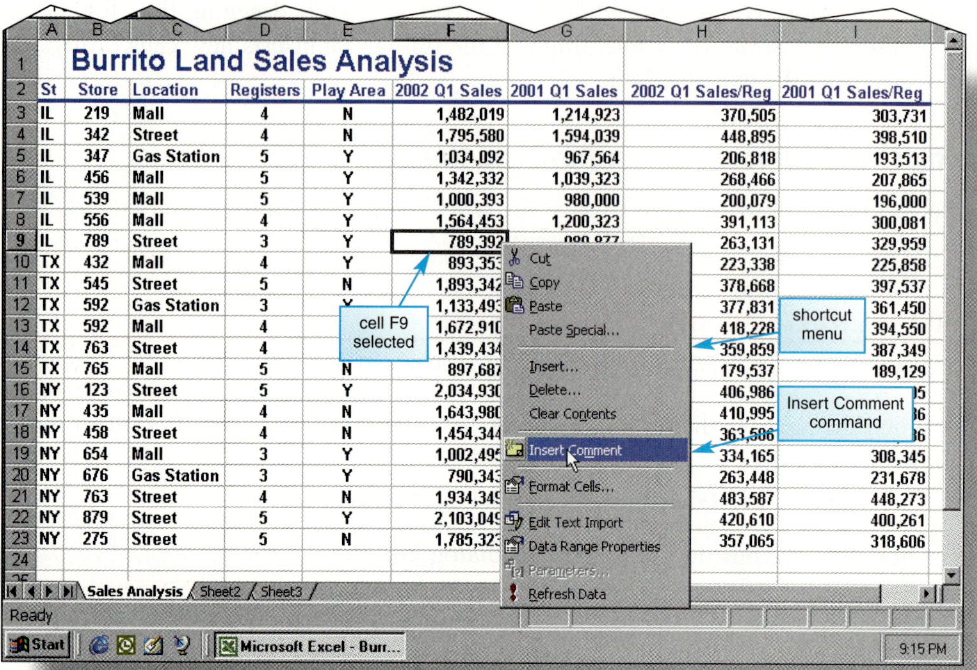

FIGURE 9-29

2 Click Insert Comment. When the comment box displays, enter the comment as shown in Figure 9-30.

Excel opens a comment box *next to the selected cell (Figure 9-30). The insertion point displays in the comment box below the system user name. Your system user name will differ from this figure. Excel adds a small red triangle, called a comment indicator, to cell F9. A small black arrow attached to the comment box points to the comment indicator.*

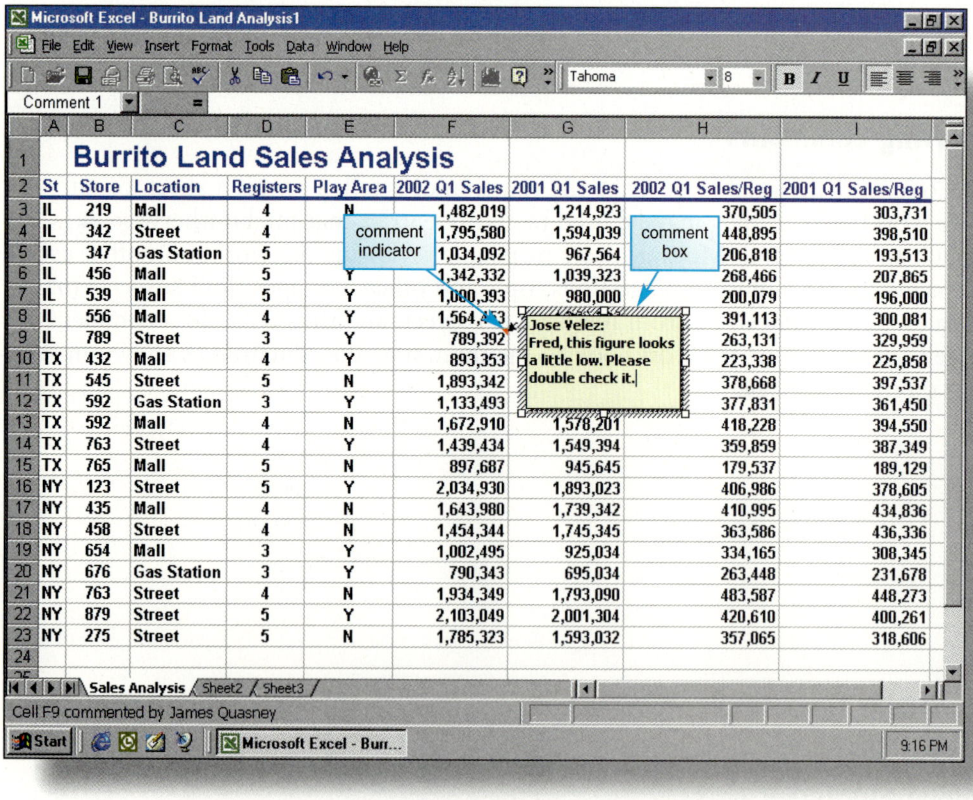

FIGURE 9-30

3 Click anywhere outside the comment box and then click the Save button on the Standard toolbar to save the workbook using the file name Burrito Land Analysis1.

Other Ways

1. On Insert menu click Comment
2. Press ALT+I, press M

When Excel closes the comment box and returns to the workbook window, the comment disappears from the screen. If you want to redisplay the comment, simply point to the cell containing the red comment indicator.

If you want to print the comments where they display on the sheet, click Comments on the View menu, move and resize the comments as necessary, and then print in the normal way. If you want to print the comments at the end of the worksheet, on the File menu, click Page Setup, and then click the Sheet tab. Click At end of sheet in the Comments box.

More About 2000

Collaboration

Another way to collaborate on workbooks is by using an Exchange folder. If you send the workbook to an Exchange folder, others working on the same project have a central location where they can go for project information. This method is preferential if many revisions need to be circulated because it saves time. Project members can look at what is relevant to them instead of going through numerous project-related e-mails.

Collaborating on Workbooks

If you plan to have others edit your workbook or suggest changes, Excel provides four ways to collaborate with others. **Collaborating** means working together in cooperation on a document with other Excel users.

First, you can **distribute** your workbook to others, physically on a disk or through e-mail using the Send To command on the File menu. With the Send To command, you may choose to embed the document as part of the e-mail message or attach the file as an e-mail attachment, which allows receivers of the e-mail message to open the file if they have the application on their system.

Second, you can **route** your workbook to a list of people who pass it along from one to another on the routing list using e-mail. The Send To command on the File menu includes a Routing Recipient command. A routing slip displays in which you can specify e-mail addresses. Excel handles creating the e-mail message with routing instructions. It even reminds people who open the document to pass it along to the next person in the routing list when they are finished.

Third, you can **collaborate** interactively with other people through discussion threads or online meetings. The integration of **NetMeeting** with Microsoft Office 2000 allows you to share and exchange files with people at different sites. When you start an online meeting from within Excel, NetMeeting automatically starts in the background and allows you to share the contents of your file.

Fourth, you can collaborate by sharing the workbook. **Sharing** means more than simply giving another user a copy of your file. Sharing implies that multiple people can work independently on the same workbook at the same time if you are in a networked environment.

With any of the collaboration choices, you should keep track of the changes that others make to your workbook.

More About 2000

Excel's Routing Capability

To e-mail or route a workbook as an attachment in Excel format, you need Excel 2000 and one of the following e-mail programs: Outlook, Outlook Express, Microsoft Exchange Client, Lotus cc:Mail or another compatible program with the Messaging Application Programming Interface (MAPI). To receive a routed workbook you need Excel 97 or later.

Tracking Changes

Tracking changes means that Excel, through the **Track Changes command** on the Tools menu, will display the edited cells with a comment indicating who made the change, when the change was made, and the original value of the cell that was changed. Tracking and sharing work together. When you turn on one, the other is enabled by default. The steps on then next page turn on Track Changes.

More About 2000

Shared Workbook Limitations

Some features of Microsoft Excel are not available when you use a shared workbook. Features such as merging cells; delete blocks of cells or worksheets; editing toolbars and menus; editing data validation restrictions and conditional formats; inserting tables, charts, pictures, or hyperlinks; drawing tools; scenarios; and editing macros are disabled temporarily while the workbook is shared. If you need to use these features, do so before you share the workbook, or remove the workbook from shared use.

To Turn on Track Changes

1 **Click Tools on the menu bar, point to Track Changes, and then point to Highlight Changes.**

The Track Changes submenu displays (Figure 9-31).

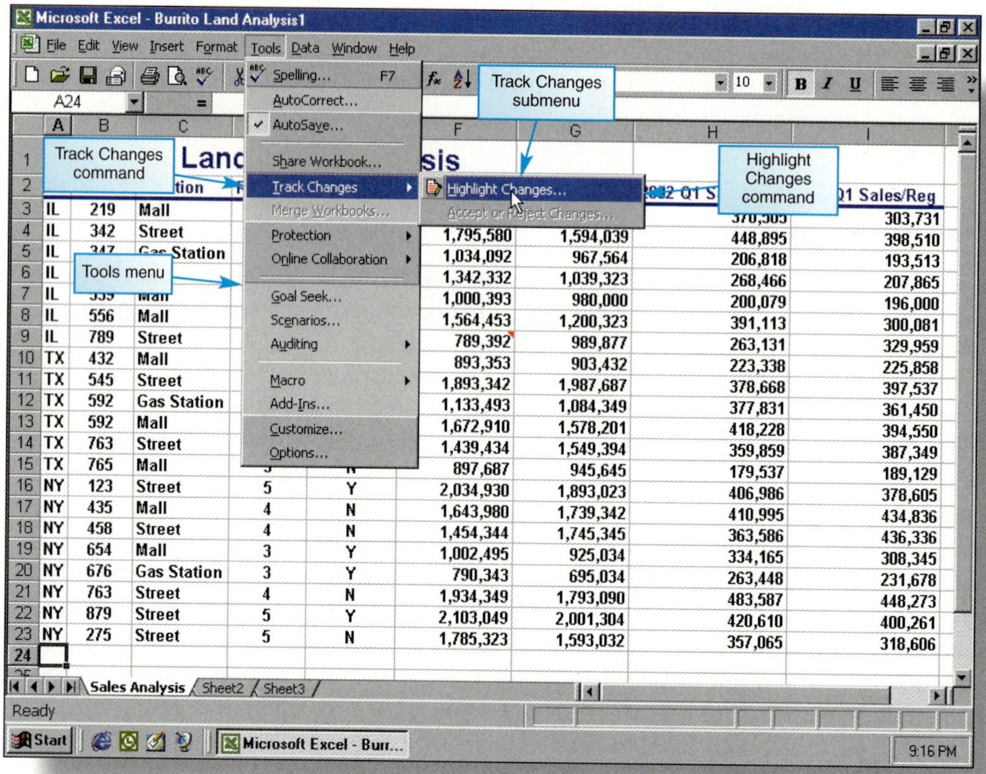

FIGURE 9-31

2 **Click Highlight Changes. When Highlight Changes dialog box displays, click Track changes while editing. If necessary, clear all of the check boxes in the Highlight which changes area. Point to the OK button.**

The Highlight Changes dialog box displays (Figure 9-32). Clicking the Track changes while editing check box also shares the workbook. The When, Who, and Where check boxes and list boxes play no role when you first enable Track Changes.

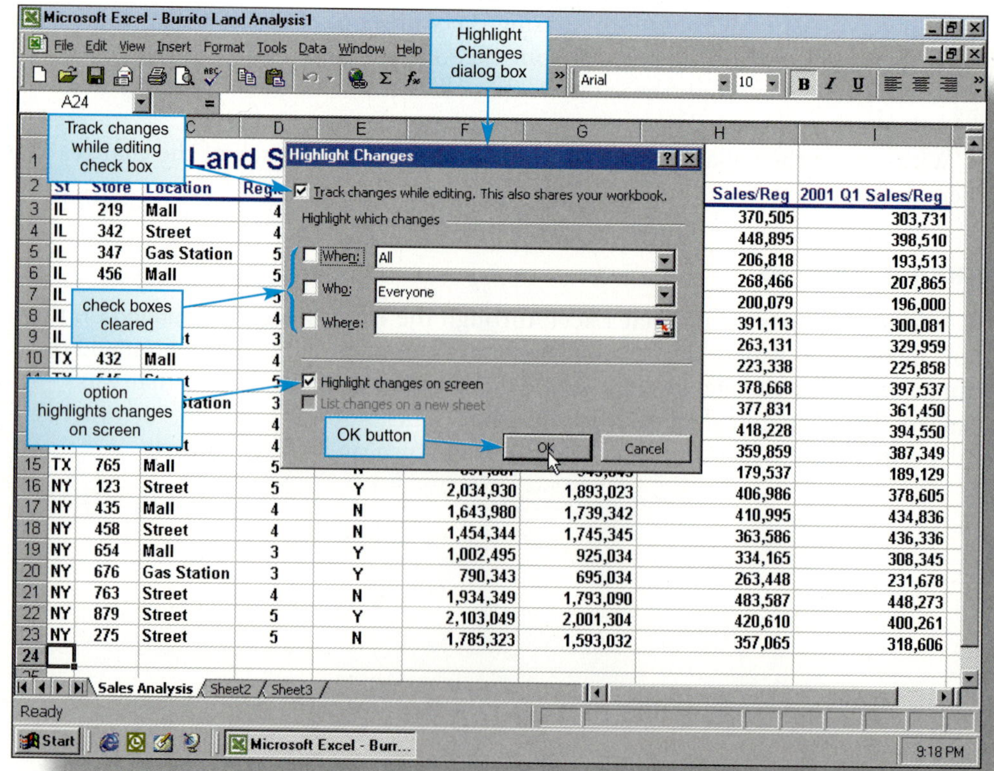

FIGURE 9-32

3 **Click the OK button. When the Microsoft Excel dialog box displays asking if you want to continue by saving, click the OK button to save the workbook.**

The title bar indicates this workbook is shared (Figure 9-33).

workbook is shared

FIGURE 9-33

1. Press ALT+T, press T, press H

Routing the Workbook

The next step is to route the workbook to the three state coordinators for Burrito Land. If you are doing this project on a PC, you will be prompted to choose the e-mail addresses of the routing recipients. If you plan actually to execute the routing, substitute the e-mail addresses shown with e-mail addresses from your address book or class. Your return e-mail contact information must be valid as well, in order to round trip the file back to you. The term **round trip** refers to sending a document to recipients and then receiving it back at some point in time.

To Route a Workbook

1 **Click File on the menu bar, point to Send To, and then point to Routing Recipient.**

The File menu and Send To submenu display (Figure 9-34).

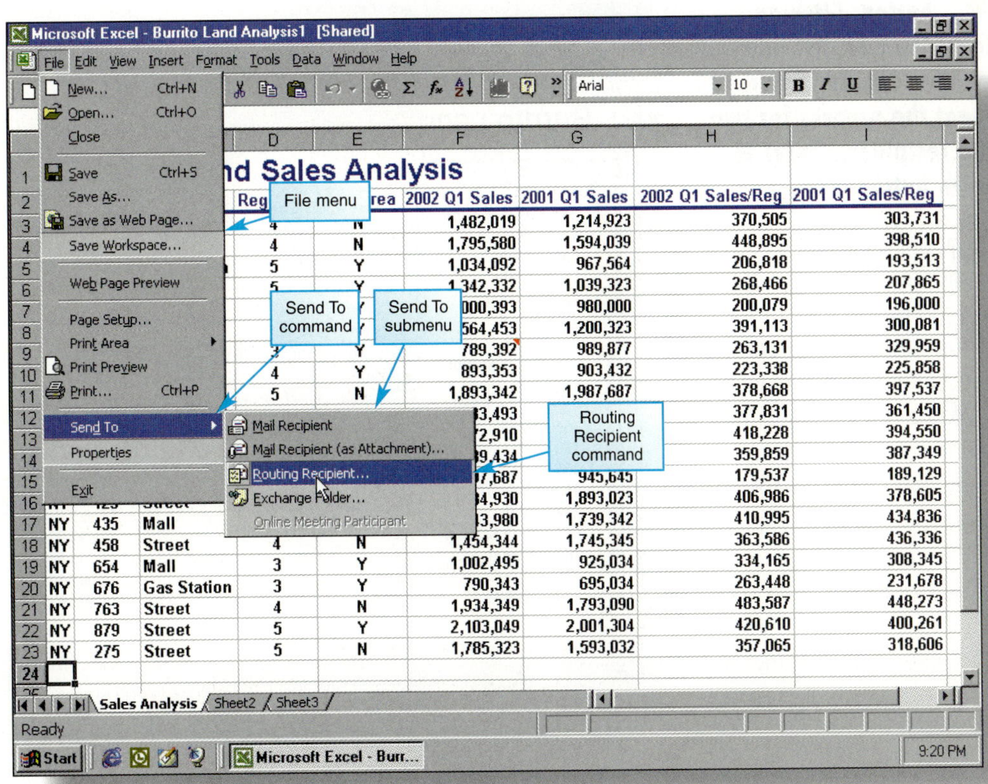

FIGURE 9-34

2 **Click Routing Recipient. If the Choose Profiles dialog box displays, choose your user profile and then click the OK button. If the Check Names dialog box displays, you may have to add your return address as a new listing to the address book. When the Routing Slip dialog box displays, point to the Address button.**

A routing slip displays that allows you to specify the recipient, subject, and message similar to an e-mail message (Figure 9-35). Your routing slip will display a different user profile name. If you are working on a networked system, see your instructor or network administrator for the correct user profile.

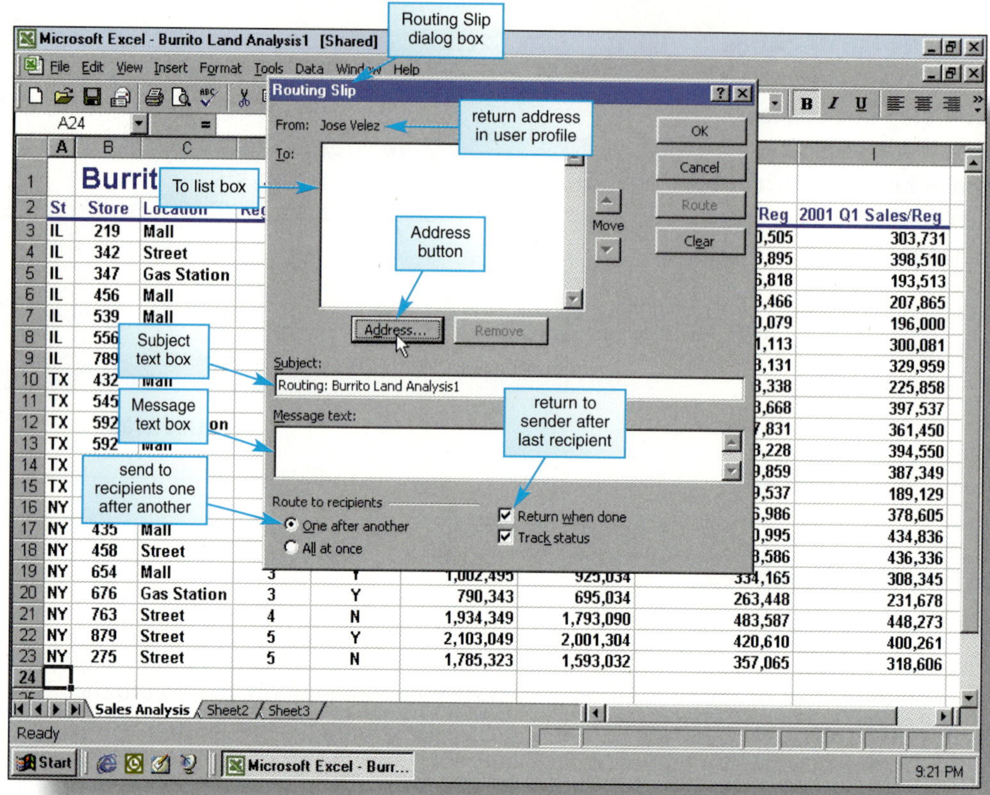

FIGURE 9-35

3 **Click the Address button. Click an address in your list and then click the To button. Repeat the process for two more recipients. Point to the OK button.**

If no addresses display in your address list, you may leave the recipients blank for the purposes of this project. To add new e-mail recipients, you would click the New button and then enter the correct information (Figure 9-36).

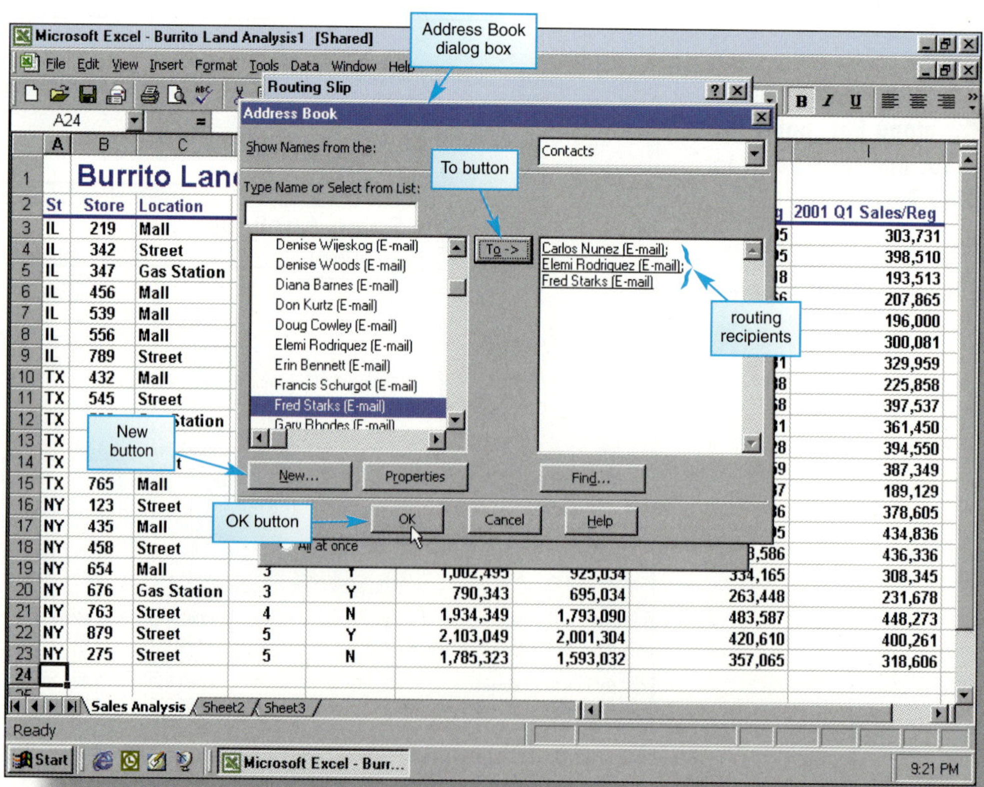

FIGURE 9-36

4 **Click the OK button. When the Routing Slip dialog box displays again, click the Message text box. Type** `Please review the attached worksheet and make changes as necessary. When you are finished reviewing, route to the next recipient. Thank you.` **Point to the Route button.**

The Routing Slip dialog box displays the addresses, subject, and message (Figure 9-37).

5 **Click the Route button.**

6 **Click the Save button on the Standard toolbar to save the workbook using the file name Burrito Land Analysis1. Click the workbook Close button on the menu bar.**

Excel saves a copy of the workbook on the floppy disk and closes the workbook.

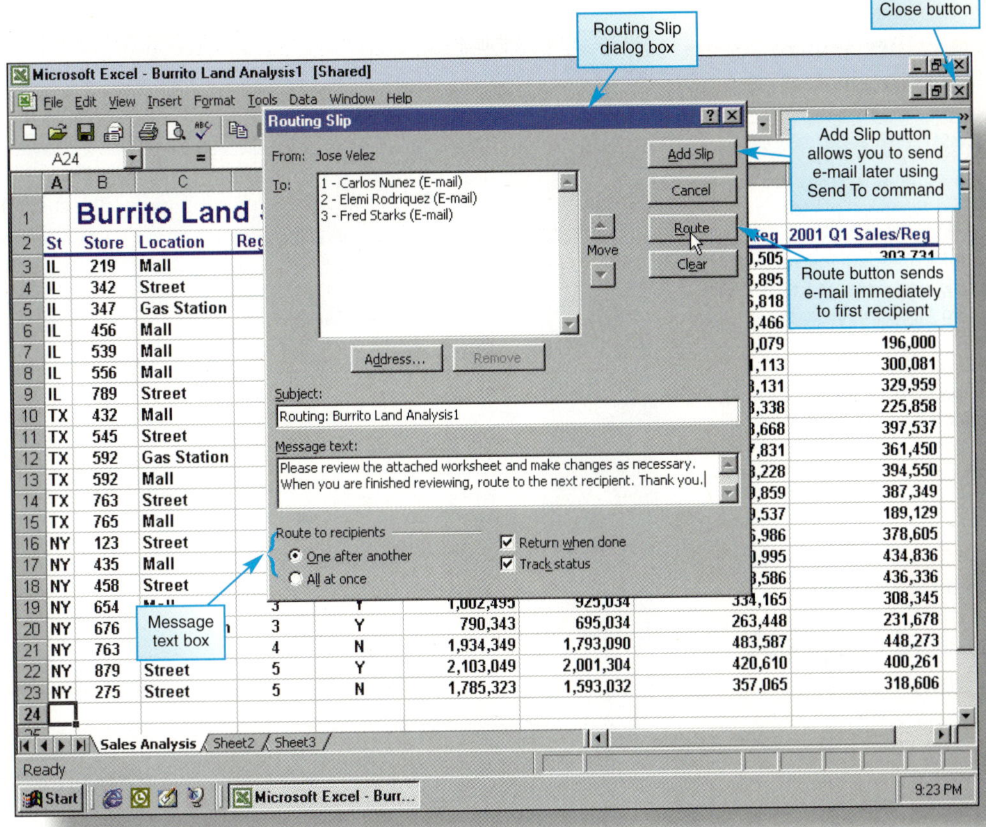

FIGURE 9-37

1. Press ALT+F, press D, press R

More About 2000

Routing Slips

Since routing workbooks among team members is an important tool for most businesses, many Web magazines have begun to publish tips and tricks for helping you perform routings tasks in Excel. To look at examples, visit the Excel 2000 More About Web page (www.scsite.com/Ex2000/more.htm) and then click Routing Tips.

In the previous sequence of steps, the e-mail to the first recipient was sent immediately when you clicked **Route button**. If you had clicked the **Add Slip button** instead of the Route button, then Excel would have asked if it should send the e-mail when the workbook was closed. Figure 9-38 on the next page illustrates the e-mail received by the first recipient, Carlos Nunez. A sample message displays and Excel automatically attaches the workbook to the message and inserts instructions to the routing recipients. As each routing recipient receives the e-mail, he or she opens the workbook and looks it over, making changes as necessary. Excel reminds each recipient to forward the workbook to the next person in the list. Excel prompts the last person to forward the workbook back to the owner.

Routing Addresses

The e-mail addresses you use in the routing slip must be valid addresses from your Contacts folder. Your own name and e-mail address must be in the Contacts folder as well, if you want to round-trip the workbook. To add an address, from the Routing Slip dialog box, click the Address button, and then click the New button.

Shared Workbook Change History

Shared workbooks usually are current, active worksheets. Excel maintains a preset change history of 30 days. If you want more time to keep track of changes, you may change the number of days. For example, when you turn on change history but are not sure exactly when the merge will take place, you can preserve the change history by setting a large number of days to maintain the change history, up to the maximum of 32,767 days.

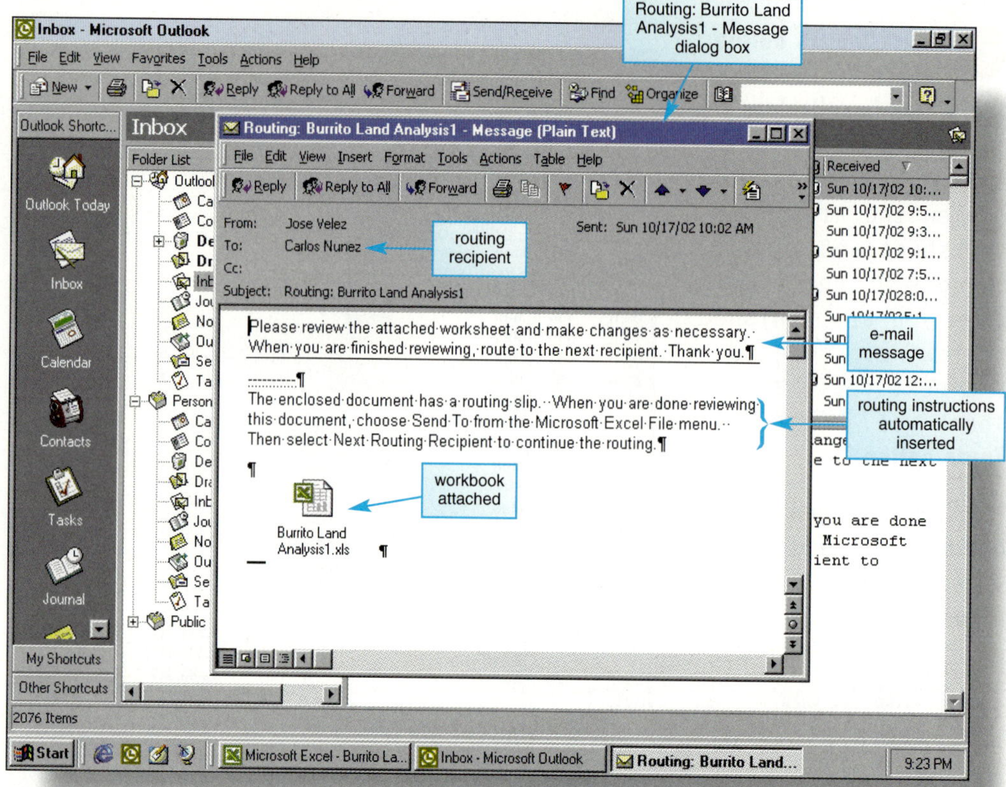

FIGURE 9-38

Excel keeps a **Change History file** with each shared workbook. In the case of a shared workbook in which you want to track the changes, Excel provides a way for users to make data entry changes, but does not allow them to modify the Change History file. Click the Tools menu and then point to Protection. In a shared workbook, the only available command is **Protect Shared Workbook**. This command displays a dialog box enabling you to protect the Change History file associated with a shared workbook, so no one can turn it off except the owner.

Reviewing Tracked Changes

Instead of writing suggestions and changes on a printed draft copy, Excel's Track Changes feature allows users to enter suggested changes directly on the workbook. The owner of the workbook then looks through each change and makes a decision about whether or not to accept it.

Reviewing the Routed Workbook

After a routed workbook has progressed through the entire routing list, it comes back to the owner. Because Highlight Changes was enabled for the Burrito Land Analysis1 workbook, the file has come back to you with each recipient's changes, corrections, and comments. As the owner, you review those changes and make decisions about whether or not to accept the changes. A tracked workbook named Burrito Land Analysis2 is stored on the Data Disk. The following steps use this workbook to illustrate reviewing the changes.

To Open a Routed Workbook and Review Tracked Changes

1 **With Excel active, click the Open button on the Standard toolbar. When the Open dialog box displays, if necessary click the Look in box arrow and then click 3½ Floppy (A:). Double-click the Burrito Land Analysis2 workbook. When the workbook displays, click Tools on the menu bar, point to Track Changes, and then point to Highlight Changes.**

The Burrito Land Analysis2 workbook displays, as does the Track Changes submenu (Figure 9-39).

FIGURE 9-39

2 **Click Highlight Changes. When the Highlight Changes dialog box displays, click When to clear the check box and then point to the OK button.**

The Highlight Changes dialog box displays (Figure 9-40). Removing the check mark from the When check box indicates you want to review all changes in the history file.

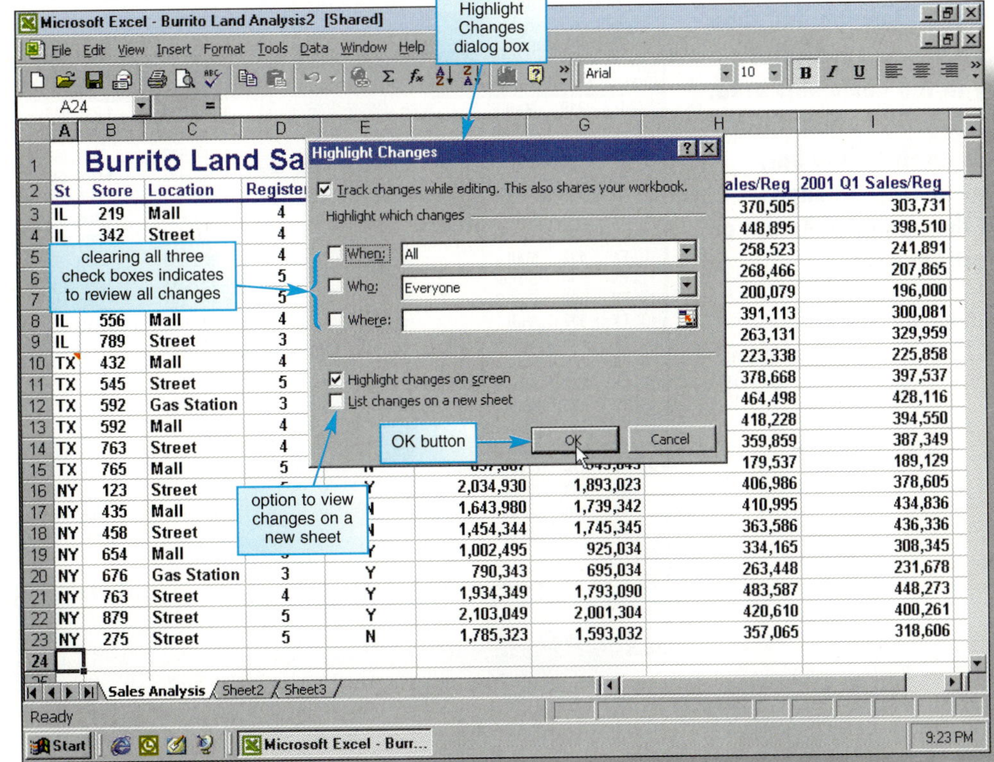

FIGURE 9-40

3 **Click the OK button. Click Tools on the menu bar and then click Options. If necessary, click the View tab and then click Comment & indicator in the Comments area. Click the OK button. Point to cell E21.**

All comments in the worksheet display. A description of the change made to cell E21 displays (Figure 9-41). Blue triangles represent a data change and red triangles represent comments.

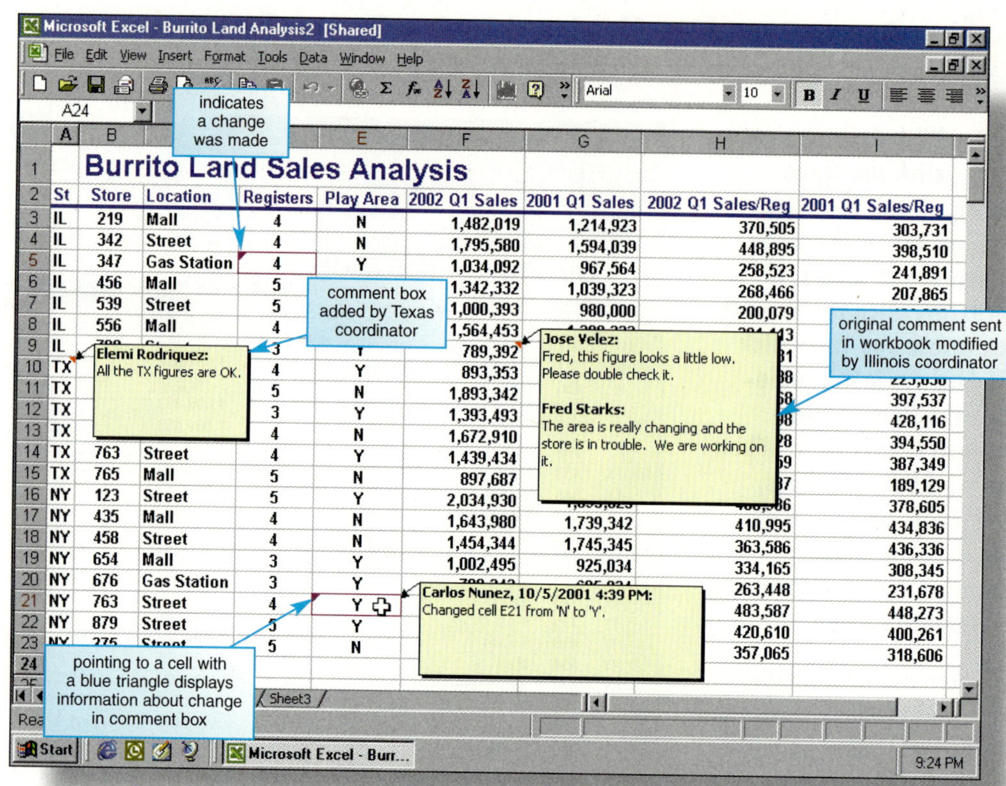

FIGURE 9-41

4 **Click Tools on the menu bar and then click Options. If necessary, click the View tab and then click Comment indicator only in the Comments area. Click the OK button. Click Tools on the menu bar, point to Track Changes, and then point to Accept or Reject Changes.**

All comments are hidden. The Track Changes submenu again displays (Figure 9-42).

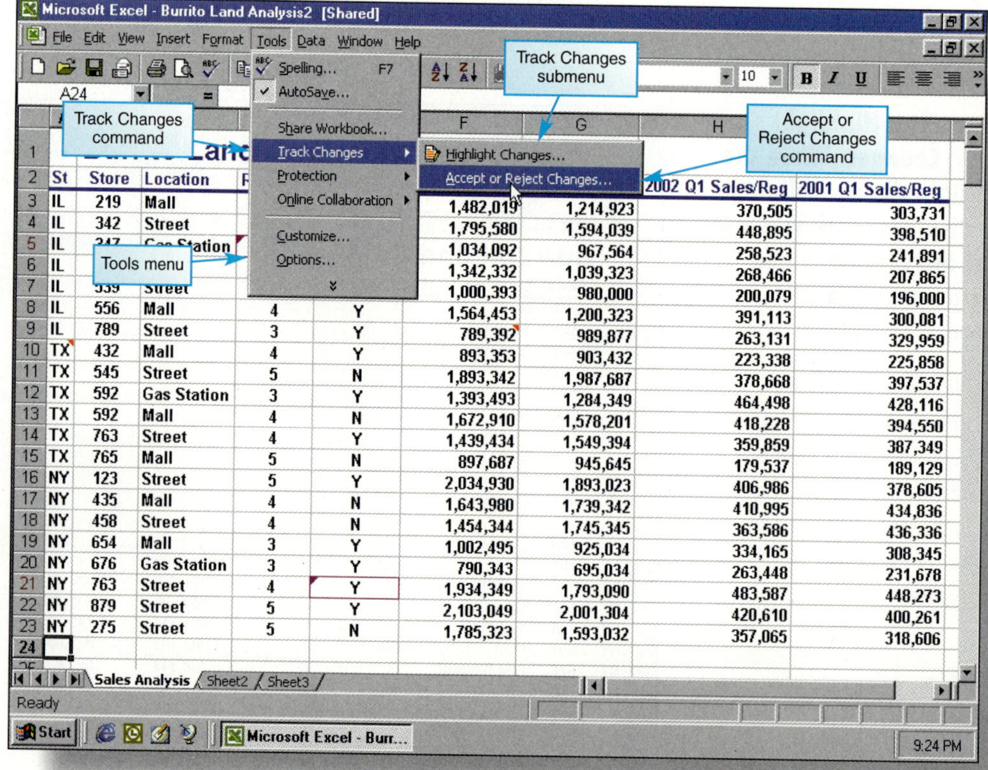

FIGURE 9-42

5 Click Accept or Reject Changes. When the Select Changes to Accept or Reject dialog box displays, if necessary, clear the check boxes and then point to the OK button.

The Select Changes to Accept or Reject dialog box allows you to specify the types of changes you want to review (Figure 9-43).

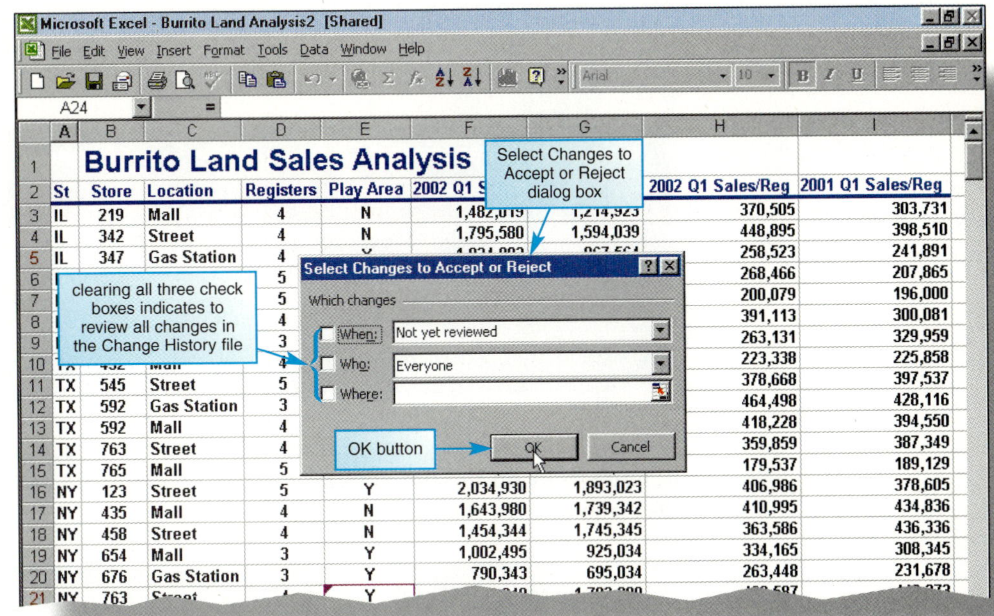

FIGURE 9-43

6 Click the OK button. When the Accept or Rejects Changes dialog box displays Change 1, point to the Accept button.

One change at a time displays in the Accept or Reject Changes dialog box (Figure 9-44). The cell with the change displays with a marquee. Excel allows you to accept or reject the changes one at a time, or all at once.

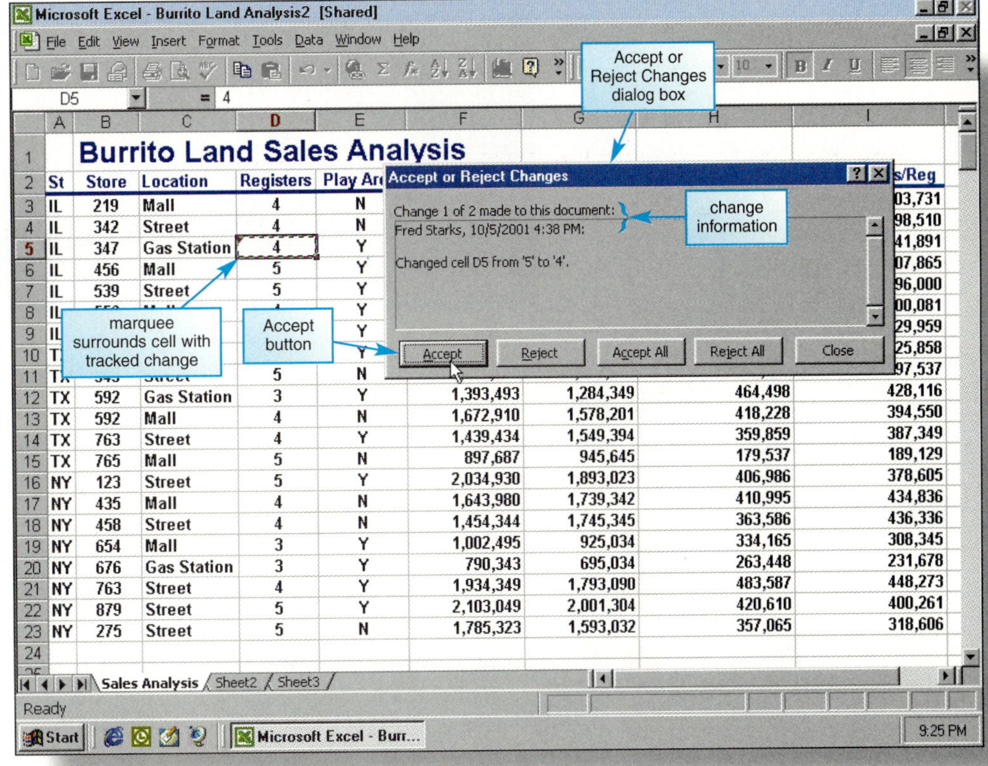

FIGURE 9-44

7 Click the Accept button. As each change displays, click the Accept button. Right-click cell A10 and then click Delete Comment on the shortcut menu. Right-click cell F9 and then click Delete Comment on the shortcut menu.

The process of reviewing and accepting the changes to the workbook is complete.

In Figure 9-43 on the previous page, you can select the category of changes in the Change History file you want to accept or reject. Table 9-2 summarizes the three check boxes.

Table 9-2 Categories of Changes in the Select Changes to Accept or Reject Dialog Box

CHECK BOX	DESCRIPTION
When	Select when you want to review changes within a time interval; the four choices are (1) Since I Last Saved; (2) All; (3) Not Yet Reviewed; and (4) Since Date
Who	View changes based on who made them
Where	View changes made to a range of cells

For each tracked change, Excel displays the Accept or Reject Changes dialog box (Figure 9-44 on the previous page) with five buttons from which to choose. Table 9-3 summarizes the five buttons.

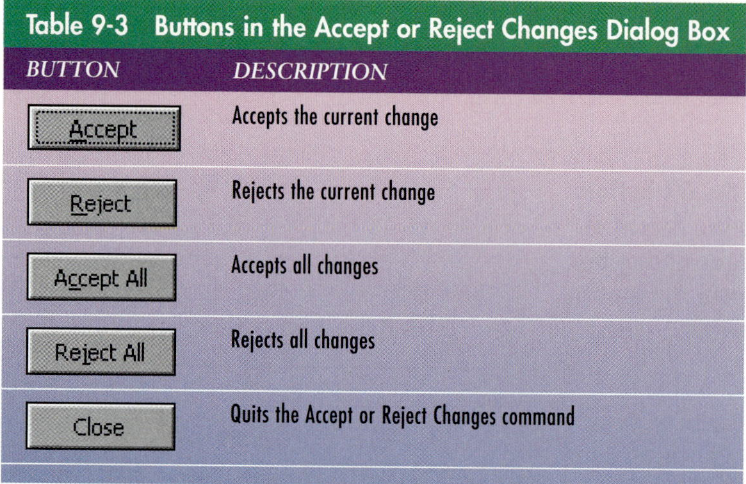

Table 9-3 Buttons in the Accept or Reject Changes Dialog Box

BUTTON	DESCRIPTION
Accept	Accepts the current change
Reject	Rejects the current change
Accept All	Accepts all changes
Reject All	Rejects all changes
Close	Quits the Accept or Reject Changes command

With the changes accepted, the following steps save the workbook using a new file name.

TO SAVE THE TRACKED CHANGES IN A WORKBOOK WITH A NEW FILE NAME

1. Click File on the menu bar and then click Save As.
2. When the Save As dialog box displays, type `Burrito Land Analysis3` in the File name text box.
3. If necessary, click 3½ Floppy (A:) in the Save in list.
4. Click the Save button in the Save As dialog box.

Excel saves the workbook on drive A, using the file name Burrito Land Analysis3.

The next step is to turn off the Track Changes feature. Excel denies access to features such as the data map and PivotChart while the workbook is shared. Perform the following steps to turn off Track Changes, which also automatically turns off sharing and saves the workbook as an exclusive one. That is, it no longer is a shared workbook.

TO TURN OFF TRACK CHANGES

1. Click Tools on the menu bar, point to Track Changes, and then click Highlight Changes.
2. When the Highlight Changes dialog box displays, click Track changes while editing to clear the check box.
3. Click the OK button in the Highlight Changes dialog box.
4. When the Microsoft Excel dialog box displays, asking you to make the workbook exclusive, click the Yes button.

The workbook displays without the word, Shared, in the title bar. Excel disables Track Changes.

When you turn off Track Changes, you turn off sharing as well. At the same time, Excel erases the change history. The workbook automatically resaves as an exclusive workbook. An **exclusive workbook** is only available to be opened by a single user.

The imports and changes complete the Burrito Land Analysis workbook. The next step is to create a data map in preparation for the Burrito Land Board of Directors' meeting.

More About 2000

Tracking Changes with Passwords

If you want to make sure others will not turn off the change history or reduce the number of days in the history, you can protect a shared workbook with a password. Click Protection on the Tools menu and then click Protect and Share Workbook on the Protection submenu. Passwords may be added only if the workbook is unshared at the time of protection.

Creating a Data Map

Microsoft Excel includes a mapping feature, called **Microsoft Map**, which you use to see the relationships between numbers and geographic regions. With a few clicks of the mouse, you can embed a data map of any location in the world in the worksheet and then format it. For example, you may add labels, text, and pins to a data map to display and analyze the sales by state. Figure 9-45 shows the data map required for this project. It is a data map of the United States, highlighting the three states where Burrito Land has stores. The Column chart on top of each of the three states compares the sales per register from the data columns 2002 Q1 Sales/Reg and 2001 Q1 Sales/Reg.

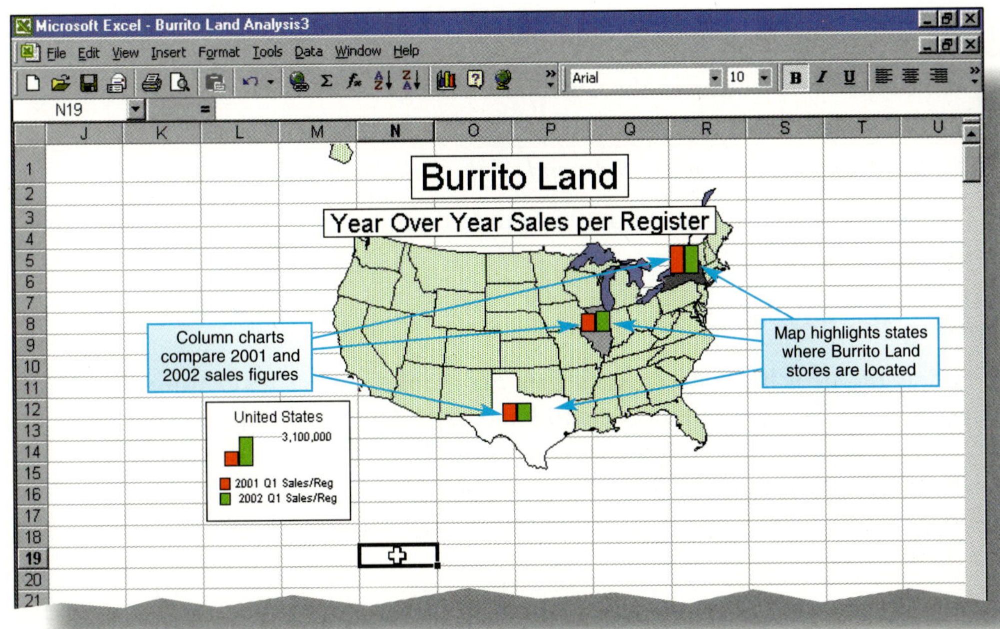

FIGURE 9-45

To use the mapping feature of Excel, you select a range of cells on your worksheet that includes geographic data, such as countries or states, and then click the **Map button** on the Standard toolbar. Once the Map button is clicked, the mouse pointer changes to a cross hair, and you can drag it to an open area on your worksheet to define the data map location and size.

The data you plan to use to create a data map must be in columnar form with standard names or abbreviations of the states (or countries) in a column. For example, the data shown in Table 9-4 can be used to create a data map because the first column contains the names of countries.

Table 9-4 Sample Data for Mapping

COUNTRY	*INTERNATIONAL OFFICES*
Venezuela	7
Colombia	5
Brazil	12
Peru	6

The state or country data does not have to be in the leftmost column. The columns need not be adjacent. You may press the CTRL key and drag to select nonadjacent multiple ranges of data, if one of the columns contains the state or country names.

If you reset the toolbars at the beginning of this project, you may not see the Map button that displays as a globe on the Standard toolbar (Figure 9-46). Clicking the More Buttons button (Figure 9-46) allows you to display the hidden buttons. If you still do not see the Map button, you need to add it using the Customize command on the Tools menu, as explained in the following steps.

Importing Data for Data Maps

Several universities and government agencies provide data on the Web related to demographics and census reports. For more information, visit the Excel 2000 More About Web page (www.scsite.com/Ex2000/more.htm) and then click Importing Data for Data Maps.

Adding the Map Button to the Standard Toolbar

Perform the following steps if your Standard toolbar does not display the Map button.

TO ADD THE MAP BUTTON TO THE STANDARD TOOLBAR

1. Double-click the move handle on the Standard toolbar to make sure the Map button is not in a demoted state.
2. If the Map button does not display when the Standard toolbar displays in its entirety, right-click a toolbar and then click Customize on the shortcut menu.
3. Click the Commands tab and then click Insert in the Categories list.
4. Click the Commands box down scroll arrow until the Map button displays.
5. Drag the Map button to the right end of the Standard toolbar.
6. Click the Close button in the Customize dialog box.

The Map button displays on the right end of the Standard toolbar (Figure 9-46).

1. On Tools menu click Customize
2. On View menu click Toolbars, click Customize

If the Map button is dimmed on the Standard toolbar, see your instructor about installing the Map feature.

Creating the Data Map

Follow the steps below to create a data map in the range L1:S17 using the data from columns A, H, and I in the Burrito Land Sales Analysis database. To draw a map, one of the columns must be made up of locations, such as the states in column A. The data map for Burrito Land will display the sum of the sales per register figures for all stores in all three states.

Steps To Create a Data Map

1 With the workbook Burrito Land Analysis3 open, select the range A2:A23. Hold down the CTRL key and then drag to select the additional range H2:I23. Point to the Map button on the Standard toolbar.

Excel highlights the selected ranges (Figure 9-46).

Microsoft Excel - Burrito Land Analysis3

Burrito Land Sales Analysis

	A	B	C	D	E	F	G	H	I
2	St	Store	Location	Registers	Play Area	2002 Q1 Sales	2001 Q1 Sales	2002 Q1 Sales/Reg	2001 Q1 Sales/Reg
3	IL	219	Mall	4	N	1,482,019	1,214,923	370,505	303,731
4	IL	342	Street	4	N	1,795,580	1,594,039	448,895	398,510
5	IL	347	Gas Station	4	Y	1,034,092	967,564	258,523	241,891
6	IL	456	Mall	5	Y	1,342,332	1,039,323	268,466	207,865
7	IL	539	Street	5	Y	1,000,393	980,000	200,079	196,000
8	IL	556	Mall	4	Y	1,564,453	1,200,323	391,113	300,081
9	IL	789	Street	3	Y	789,392	989,877	263,131	329,959
10	TX	432	Mall	4	Y	893,353	903,432	223,338	225,858
11	TX	545	Street	5	N	1,893,342	1,987,687	378,668	397,537
12	TX	592	Gas Station	3	Y	1,393,493	1,284,349	464,498	428,116
13	TX	592	Mall	4	N	1,672,910	1,578,201	418,228	394,550
14	TX	763	Street	4	Y	1,439,434	1,549,394	359,859	387,349
15	TX	765	Mall	5	N	897,687	945,645	179,537	189,129
16	NY	123	Street	5	Y	2,034,930	1,893,023	406,986	378,605
17	NY	435	Mall	4	N	1,643,980	1,739,342	410,995	434,836
18	NY	458	Street	4	N	1,454,344	1,745,345	363,586	436,336
19	NY	654	Mall	3	Y	1,002,495	925,034	334,165	308,345
20	NY	676	Gas Station	3	Y	790,343	695,034	263,448	231,678
21	NY	763	Street	4	Y	1,934,349	1,793,090	483,587	448,273
22	NY	879	Street	5	Y	2,103,049	2,001,304	420,610	400,261
23	NY	275	Street	5	N	1,785,323	1,593,032	357,065	318,606

Map button
More Buttons button
range A2:A23 selected
map ranges must include column headings
range H2:I23 selected
move handle on Standard toolbar
column A relates to map regions
Sum=$14,222,795

FIGURE 9-46

2 Click the Map button. Click the right scroll arrow at the bottom of the worksheet until cell J1 displays in the upper-left corner of the worksheet. Drag from the upper-left corner of cell L1 to the lower-right corner of cell S17 and hold.

The map location range L1:S17 is surrounded by a light border (Figure 9-47).

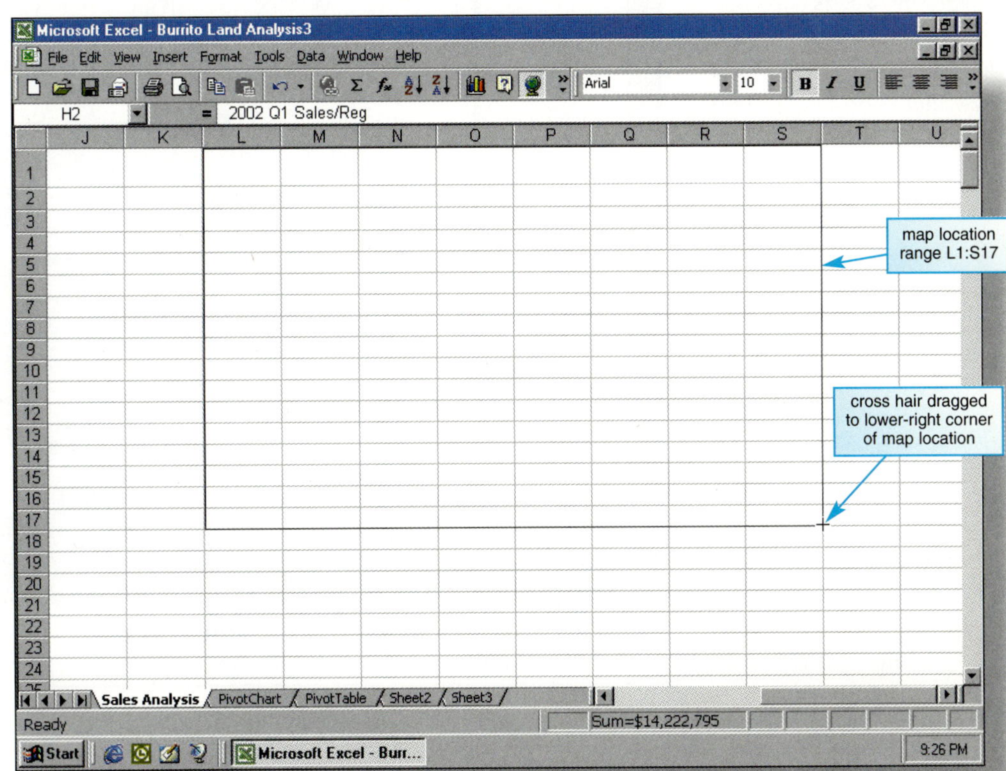

FIGURE 9-47

3 **Release the mouse button. When the Multiple Maps Available dialog box displays, click United States in North America and then point to the OK button.**

Microsoft Map's menu bar and toolbar display at the top of the screen in place of Excel's menu bar and toolbars. A heavy gray border surrounds the map location indicating it is active, and the **Multiple Maps Available dialog box** *displays (Figure 9-48).*

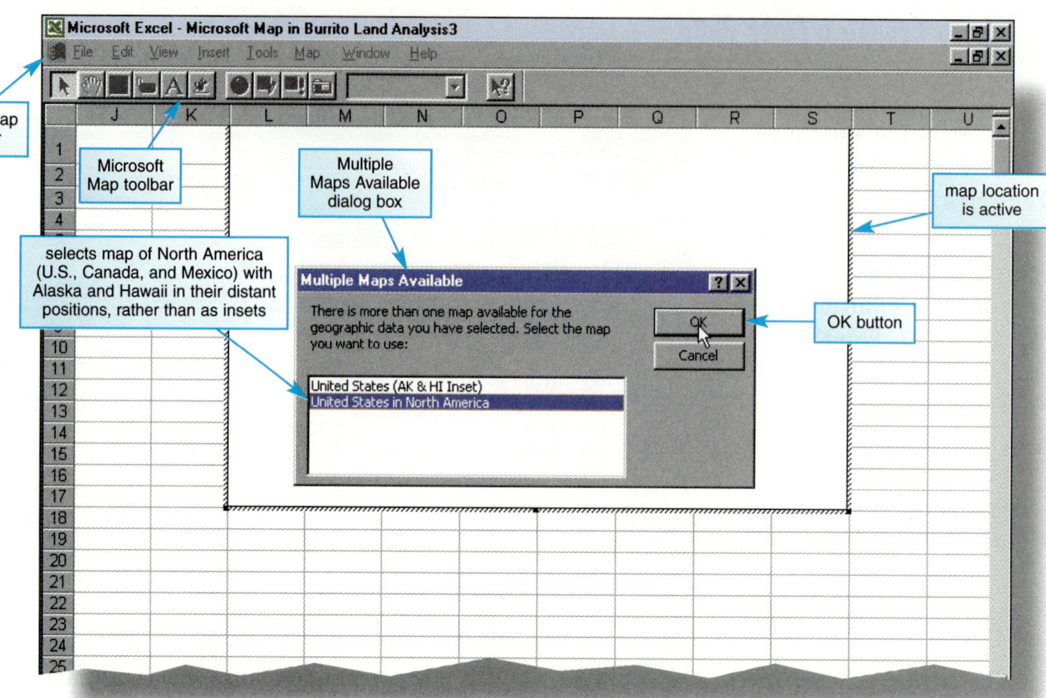

FIGURE 9-48

4 **Click the OK button.**

Microsoft Map draws a map of North America and displays the **Microsoft Map Control dialog box** *(Figure 9-49). The three states with Burrito Land stores (Illinois, Texas, and New York) display in varying shades.*

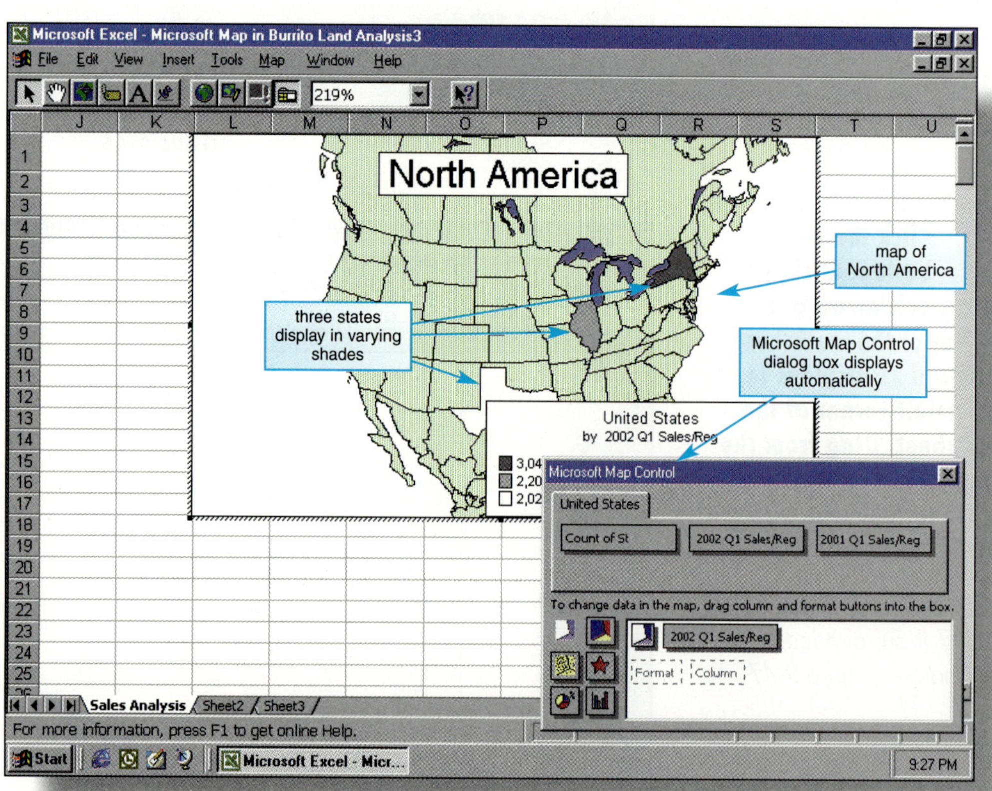

FIGURE 9-49

Other Ways

1. On Insert menu click Object, on Create New tab click Microsoft Map

The basic data map is complete. The next step is to format the data map so it displays as shown in Figure 9-45 on page E 9.35. When the data map is active (the heavy gray border indicates it is active), the menu bar and toolbar at the top of the screen can be used to manipulate the data map. Figure 9-50 describes the functions of the buttons on the **Microsoft Map toolbar**. When you first create a data map, two of the buttons on the toolbar are recessed (active) — Select Objects and Show/Hide Microsoft Map Control.

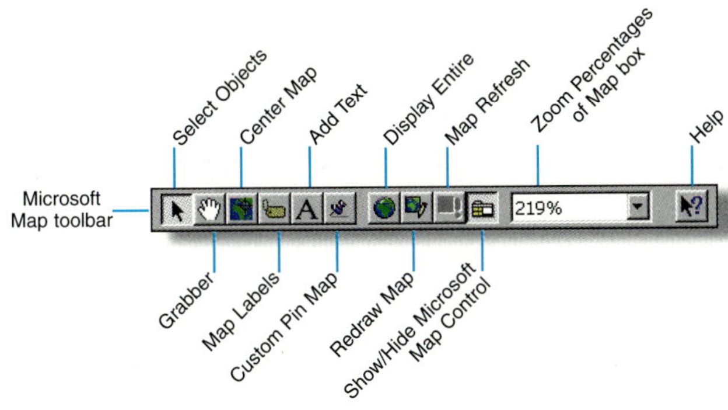

FIGURE 9-50

When the **Select Objects button** is recessed, you are able to select items within the data map location, such as legends and the data map title, and move and format them. When the **Show/Hide Microsoft Map Control button** is recessed, the Microsoft Map Control dialog box displays, which allows you to format the data map. The **Grabber button** allows you to grab the data map and move it. This button is especially useful when the data map is zoomed out and you want to see hidden parts.

Changing the Map's Features

When the data map is selected with a single click, a set of handles surrounds the data map and you can resize it, move it, or delete it. When the data map is active, by using a double-click, a heavy gray border surrounds the data map and you can change its features and format it.

The **Features command** on the shortcut menu allows you to add or delete countries from the active data map. For example, Canada or Mexico can be removed from the data map, because Burrito Land stores are located only in the United States. The steps on the next page illustrate how to change the features of a data map.

More About 2000

The Mapstats File

If you easily want to add statistical information to your data map, Microsoft Map installs a sample workbook containing demographic and geographic information. This Mapstats file includes world demographic data by Country, United States demographic data by state, Canada demographic data by province, Mexico demographic data by state, Europe demographic data by country, United Kingdom & Republic of Ireland by county, Australia demographic data by state, and South Africa and neighboring countries by region. To locate the Mapstats file, click the Start button on the taskbar and then click Find. Search for the file named Mapstats.xls.

More About 2000

Drawing the Data Map Location

Holding down the ALT key while dragging to define the data map location instructs Excel to snap the data map location to the nearest gridline on the worksheet.

More About 2000

Data Map Features

Additional characteristics can be added to a data map, such as major highways, cities, airports, lakes, or a combination of these. Right-click the data map and then click Features on the shortcut menu.

To Change the Features of a Data Map

1 **Right-click the data map and then point to Features.**

The shortcut menu displays (Figure 9-51).

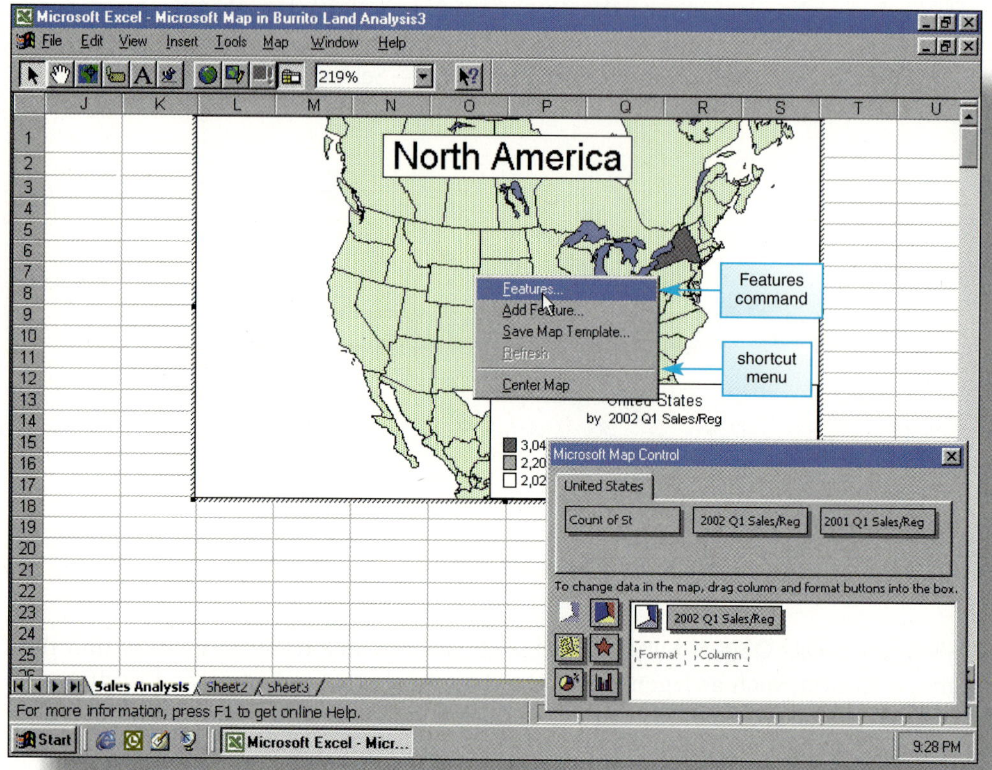

FIGURE 9-51

2 **Click Features. When the Map Features dialog box displays, click Canada, Canada Lakes, and Mexico to clear the corresponding check marks from the Visible list. Point to the OK button.**

The Map Features dialog box displays as shown in Figure 9-52. Great Lakes and United States are selected.

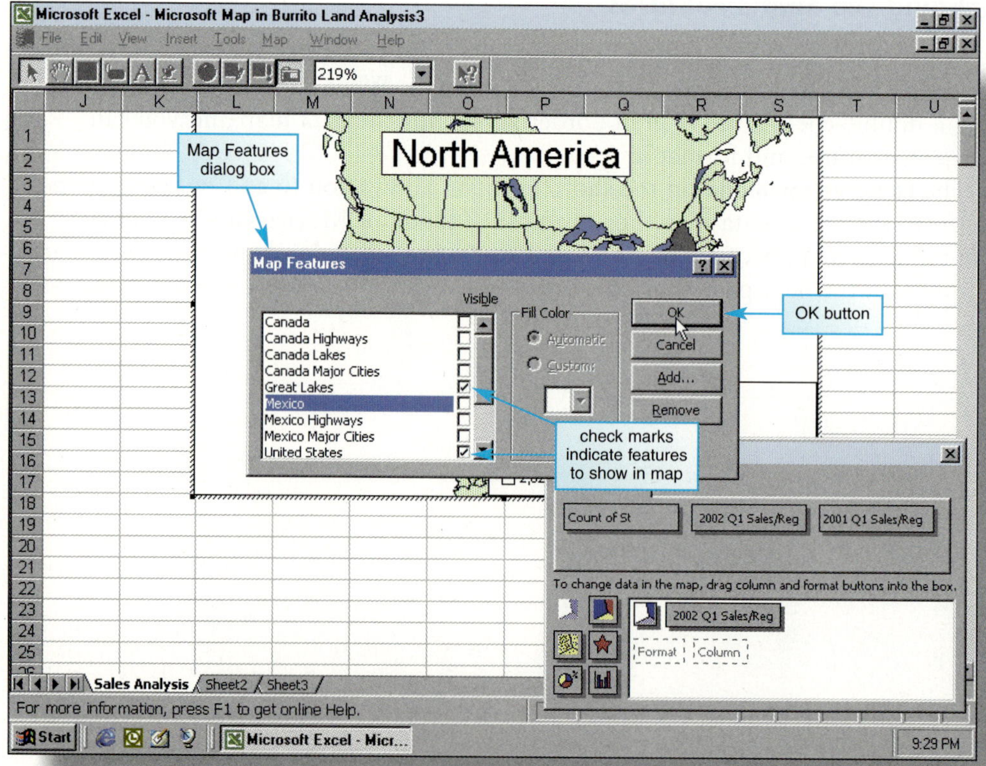

FIGURE 9-52

Click the OK button.

The data map displays without Mexico, Canada, and Canada Lakes (Figure 9-53). Only the United States and the Great Lakes display.

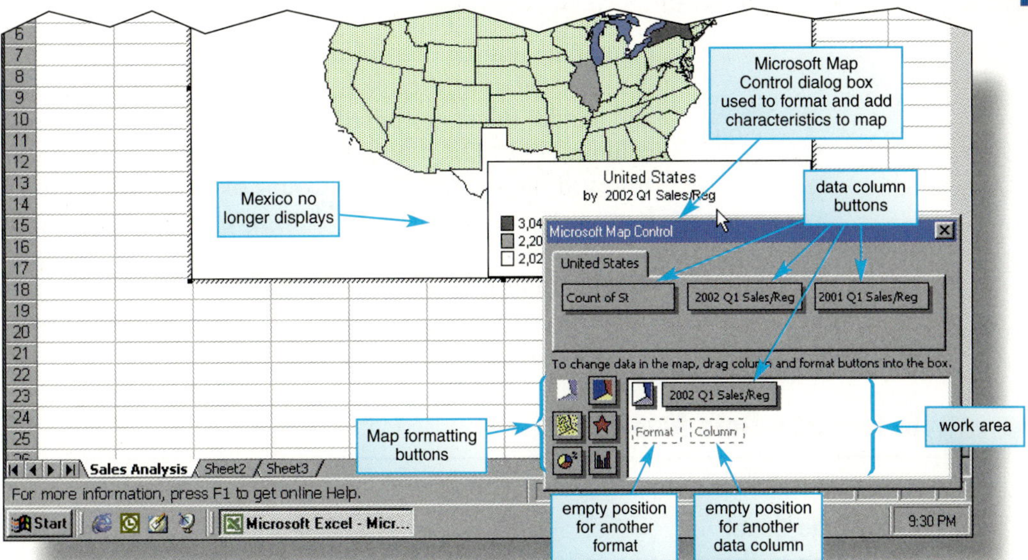

FIGURE 9-53

Other Ways

1. On Map menu click Features, click categories to remove, click OK button
2. Right-click data map, click Features on shortcut menu, click map feature in Visible box in Map Features dialog box, click Remove button, click OK button

Formatting a Data Map and Adding Column Chart Symbols

The **Microsoft Map Control dialog box** (Figure 9-53), which displays when the data map first is created, is used to format the map and add charts. The Microsoft Map Control dialog box is divided into three areas: the Data column buttons area, the Map formatting buttons area, and the work area. The **Data column buttons area** includes a button for each column heading used to create the data map. The **Map formatting buttons area** includes six formatting buttons as described in Table 9-5. The **work area** in the Microsoft Map Control dialog box is where you drag buttons from the other two areas to format the data map.

Table 9-5 Map Formatting Buttons

MAP FORMATTING BUTTON	BUTTON NAME	FUNCTION
	Value Shading	Shades each category (state) on the data map according to the value in the corresponding data column. This button is the default. Figure 9-53 shows this button in the work area; the result is the three states in different shades.
	Category Shading	Shades each category (state) on the data map differently.
	Dot Density	Displays dots within the boundaries of each category (state) on the data map. The dot density is based on the values in one column of data in the data map range.
	Graduated Symbols	Displays graduated symbols, such as varying size circles, at the center of each category (state) on the data map. The size of each symbol is based on the values in one of the columns of data in the data map range.
	Pie Chart	Displays a Pie chart for each category (state) on the data map. The slices in the Pie chart are dependent on the values of the selected column of data.
	Column Chart	Displays a column chart for each category (state) on the data map. The number of columns in the chart is dependent on the number of columns selected. The heights of the columns are dependent on the magnitude of the data for each different category (state).

As shown in Figure 9-45 on page E 9.35, the data map for this project calls for column charts for each of the three states with Burrito Land stores (IL, TX, and NY). By default, Microsoft Map activates the **Value Shading button** in the work area and shades the states based on the first numeric column in the data map range, column H (2002 Q1 Sales/Reg). To shade the three states based on the count of stores in the state, drag the Count of St button on top of the 2002 Q1 Sales/Reg button. When you drag one button on top of another in the work area, the dragged button replaces the current button. To add the column chart symbols, drag the **Column Chart button** and then the 2001 Q1 Sales/Reg and the 2002 Q1 Sales/Reg onto the work area. The following steps describe how to format the data map.

To Format a Data Map

1 Point to the Count of St button in the Data column buttons area of the Microsoft Map Control dialog box.

The mouse pointer changes to a hand grabbing a handle (Figure 9-54). A ScreenTip displays the complete name of the button when you point to it.

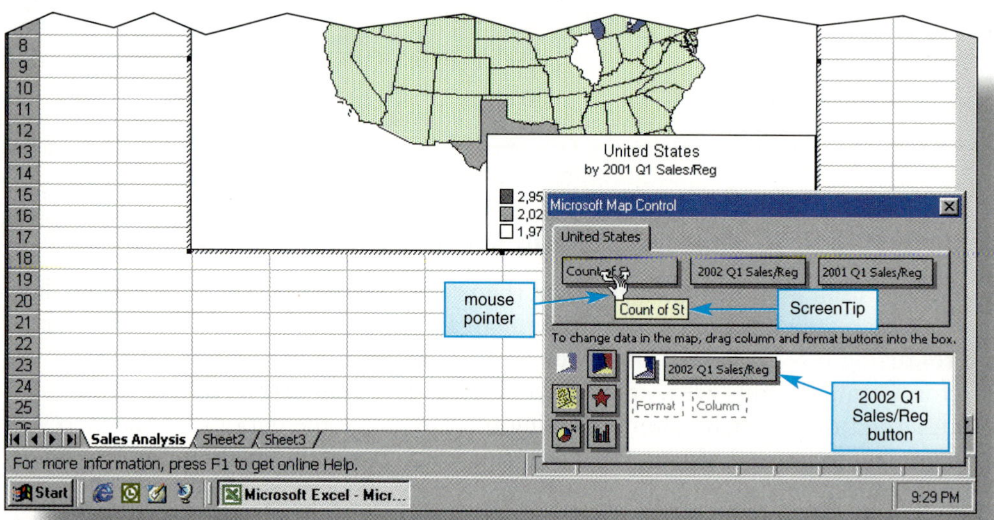

FIGURE 9-54

2 Drag the Count of St button on top of the 2002 Q! Sales/Reg button in the work area. Point to the Column Chart button in the Map formatting buttons area.

Microsoft Map changes the legend to display data about the number of stores instead of the 2002 Q1 Sales/Reg (Figure 9-55). The Grabber displays over the Column Chart button.

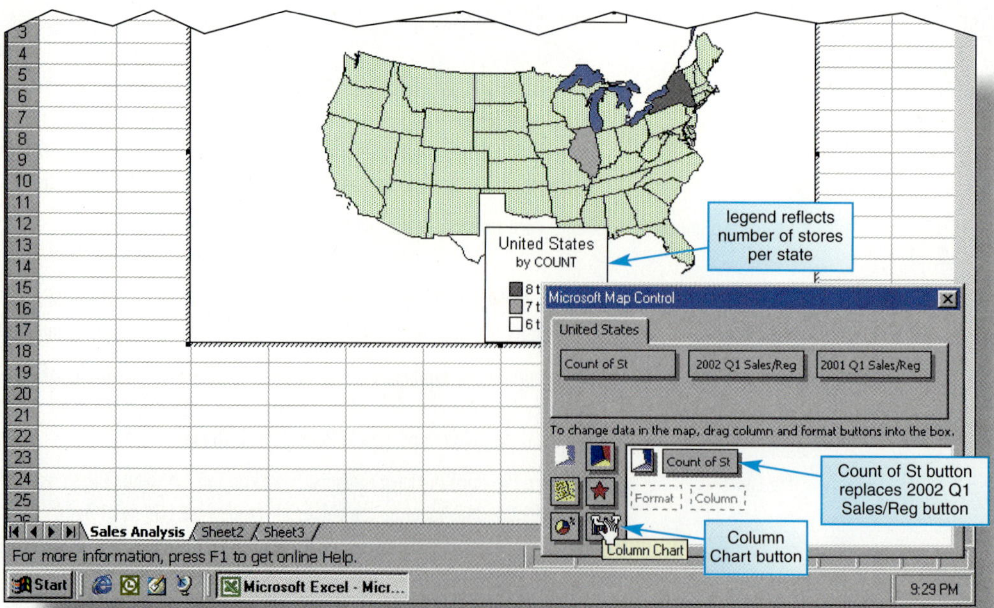

FIGURE 9-55

3 **Drag the Column Chart button onto the outlined word, Format, in the work area. One by one, drag the 2001 Q1 Sales/Reg button and the 2002 Q1 Sales/Reg button from the Data column buttons area onto the outlined word, Column, in the work area.**

The work area in the Microsoft Map Control dialog box displays as shown in Figure 9-56. Each of the three states with Burrito Land stores is assigned a Column chart on the data map. The leftmost column represents the first quarter sales per register for 2001 for a given state. The rightmost column represents the first quarter sales per register for 2002.

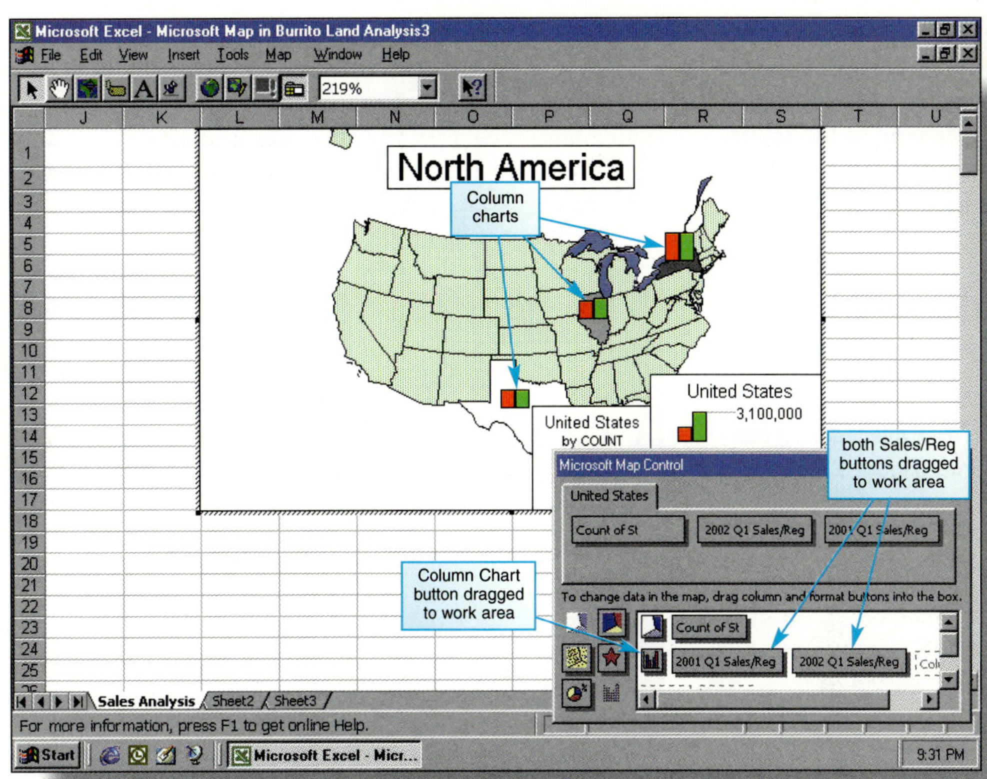

FIGURE 9-56

4 **Click the Show/Hide Microsoft Map Control button on the toolbar. Click the Shade legend in the lower-right corner of the data map location.**

The Microsoft Map Control dialog box closes and the data map displays with two legends in the lower-right corner of the data map location (Figure 9-57). The **Shade legend** *defines the shading; the* **Column chart legend** *defines the Column charts. The Shade legend is selected.*

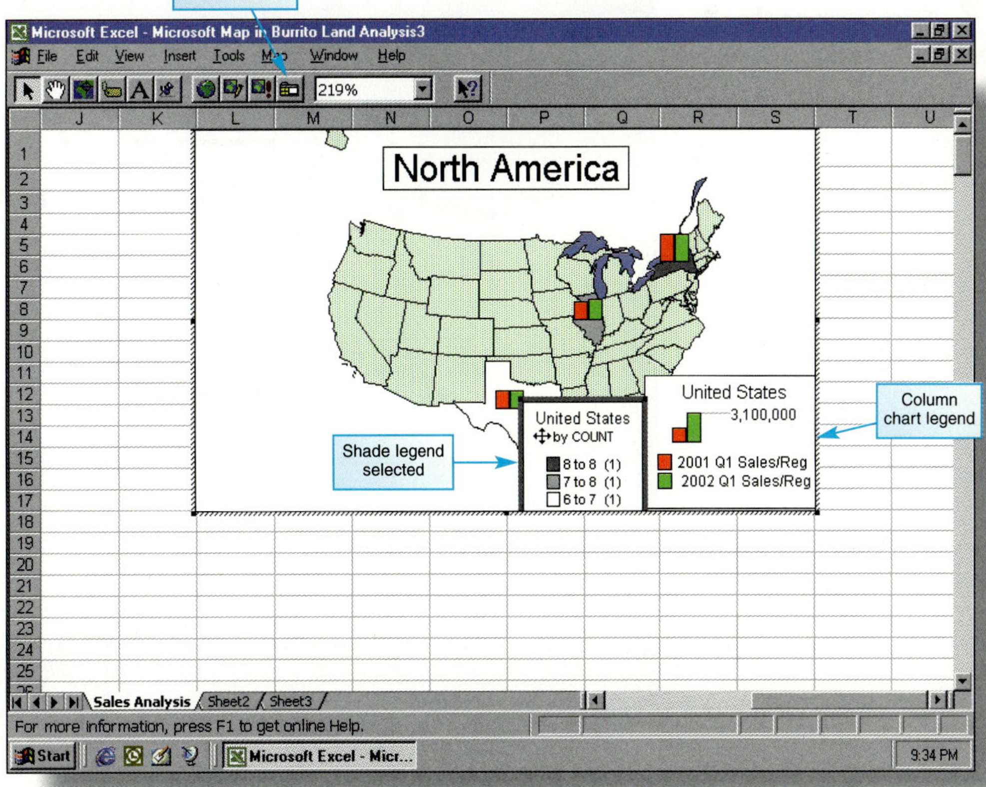

FIGURE 9-57

5 **Press the DELETE key to delete the Shade legend. Drag the Column chart legend to the lower-left corner of the data map location. Double-click the map title, North America. Type** `Burrito Land` **in the text box and then point to the OK button.**

The new title displays and the Edit Text Object dialog box displays (Figure 9-58).

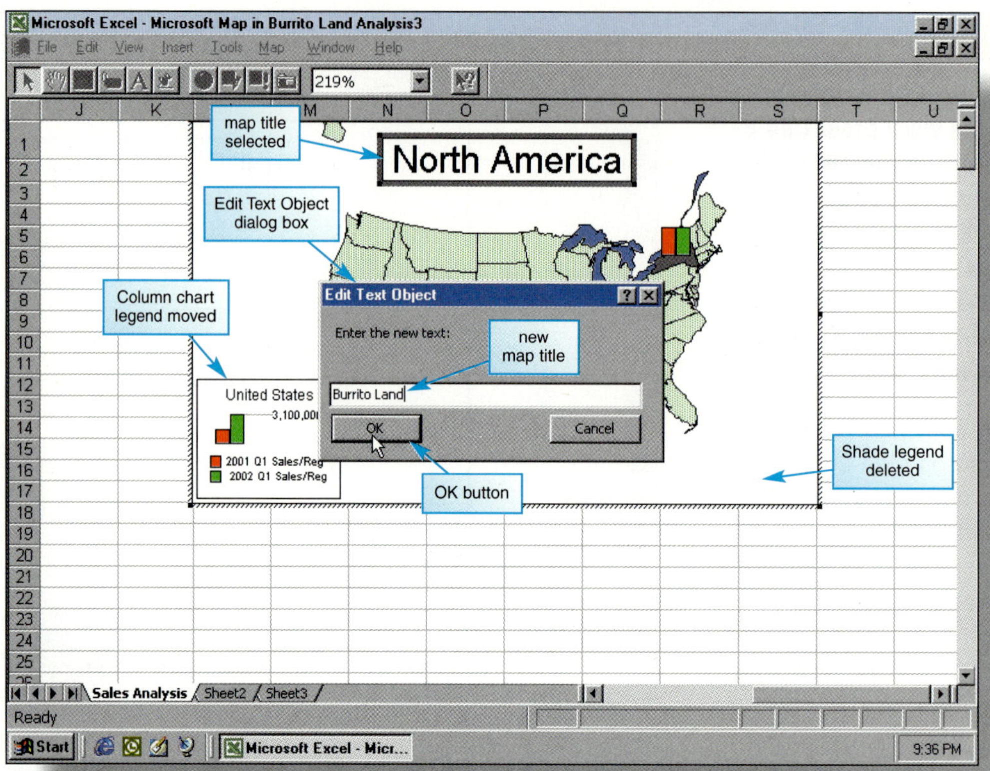

FIGURE 9-58

6 **Click the OK button. Click View on the menu bar and then point to Subtitle.**

The new title displays and the View menu displays (Figure 9-59).

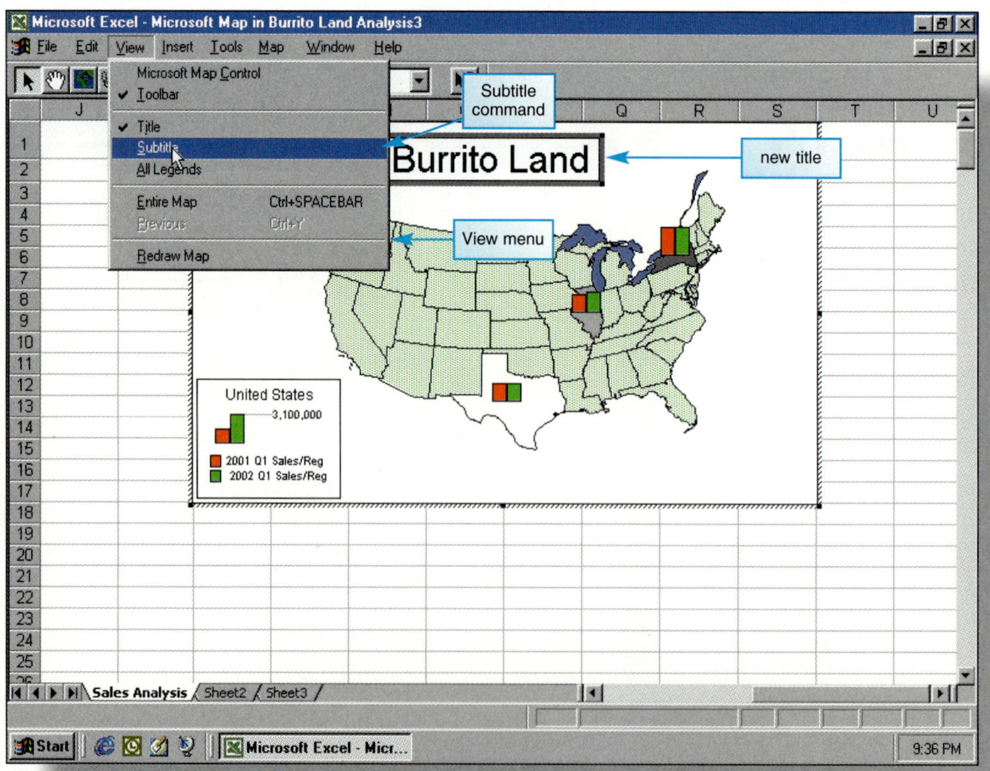

FIGURE 9-59

7 **Click Subtitle. When the Subtitle text box displays in the map, double-click it. Enter the subtitle shown in Figure 9-60. Resize and center the title and subtitle as necessary. Click cell N19 to deactivate the data map. Click the Save button on the Standard toolbar.**

The data map is complete (Figure 9-60).

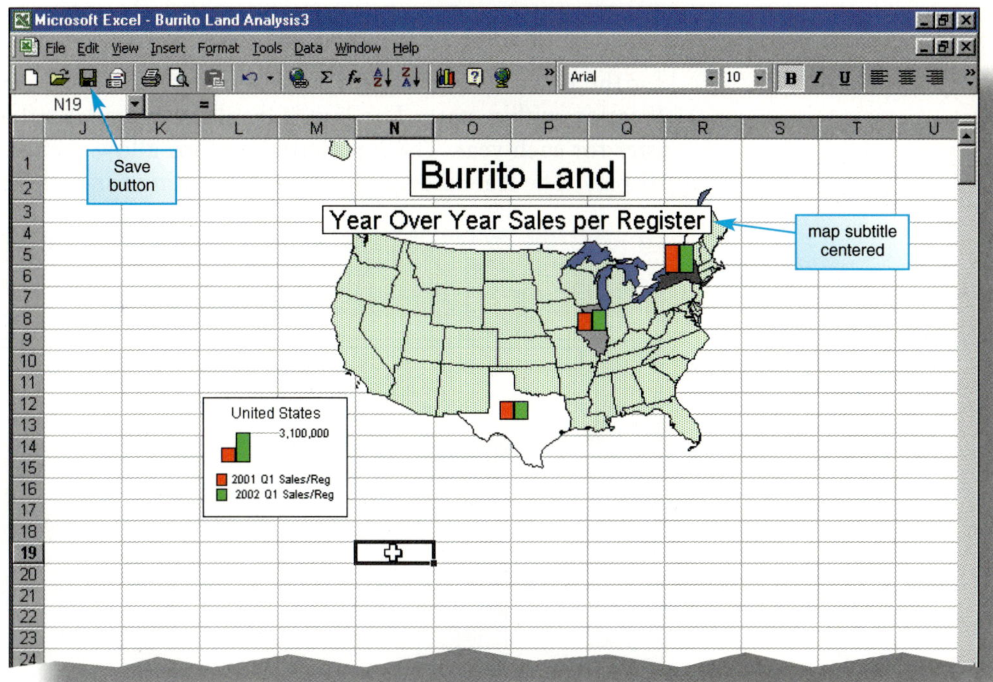

FIGURE 9-60

Formatting the Data Map Title

You can format the data map title in the same way you format chart titles. Right-click the data map title and then click Format Font on the shortcut menu.

As you can see from Figure 9-60, you can create sophisticated data maps with just a few clicks of the mouse button.

Excel's Microsoft Map feature comes with a file called Mapstats.xls. The file contains demographic data such as populations and household income. You may combine your data with the data from the Mapstats file to recognize trends and perform analysis in a map.

Creating and Formatting PivotCharts and PivotTables

A **PivotChart** is an interactive chart used to analyze data graphically by varying the fields and categories to present different views. After you create a PivotChart, you may view different levels of detail, reorganize the layout of the chart by dragging its fields, or display and hide items in drop-down lists. While you usually create a PivotChart on a separate worksheet in the same workbook containing the data you are analyzing, you can create a PivotChart on the same worksheet as the data.

When you create a PivotChart, Excel creates and associates a PivotTable automatically. A **PivotTable** is an interactive view of worksheet data that gives you the ability to summarize data in the database, and then rotate the table's row and column titles to show different views of the summarized data.

Creating a PivotChart

The **PivotChart command** on the Data menu starts the **PivotTable and PivotChart Wizard**, which guides you through creating a PivotChart. The wizard does not modify the data in any way; it simply uses the data to generate information on a new worksheet.

The required PivotChart for this project is shown in Figure 9-61. It summarizes 2001 and 2002 first quarter sales per register information by location within state for the Burrito Land Sales Analysis worksheet. The X-axis displays categories by location within state. The Y-axis displays the series values for the total sales per register for each year. The interactive buttons allow the user to choose which fields to display. The legend displays the color coding for each year.

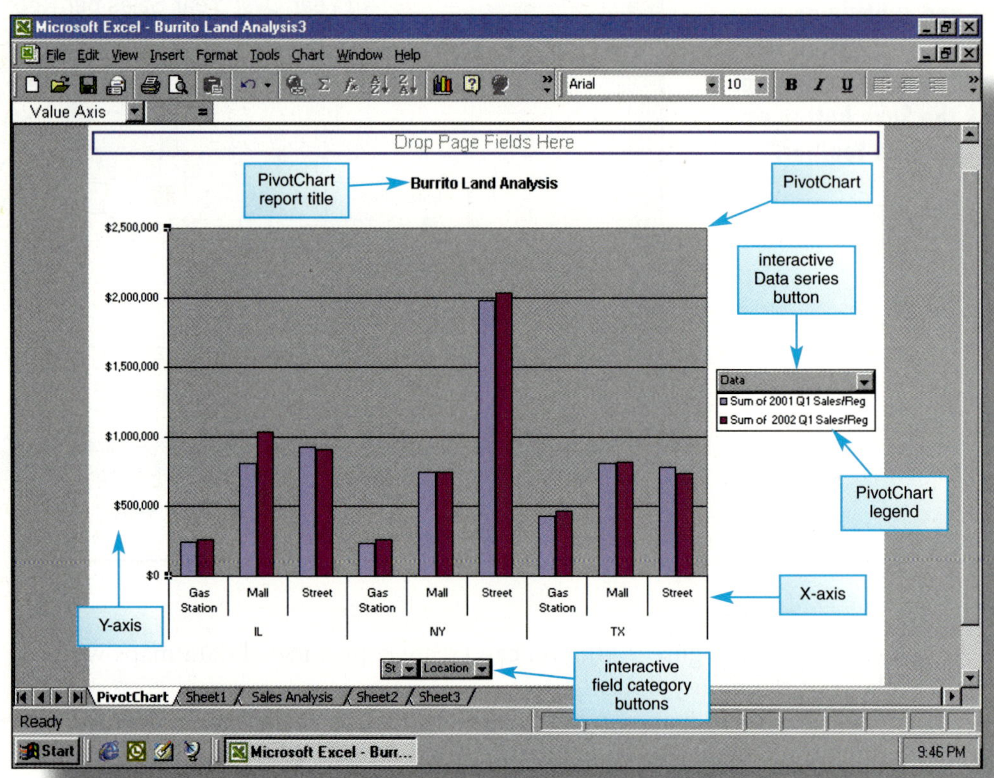

FIGURE 9-61

To create the PivotChart shown in Figure 9-61, perform the following steps.

To Create a PivotChart

1 **Scroll to cell A3 and click it. Click Data on the menu bar and then point to PivotTable and PivotChart Report (Figure 9-62).**

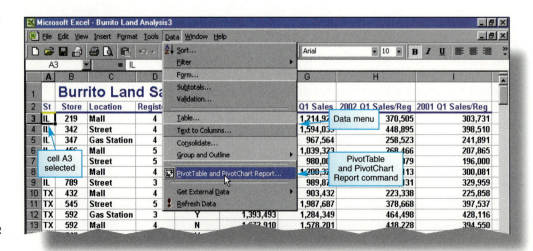

FIGURE 9-62

2 Click PivotTable and PivotChart Report. When the PivotTable and PivotChart Wizard – Step 1 of 3 dialog box displays, click PivotChart (with PivotTable). Point to the Next button.

The PivotTable and PivotChart Wizard – Step 1 of 3 dialog box *displays (Figure 9-63). The Microsoft Excel list or database and the PivotChart (with PivotTable) option buttons are selected.*

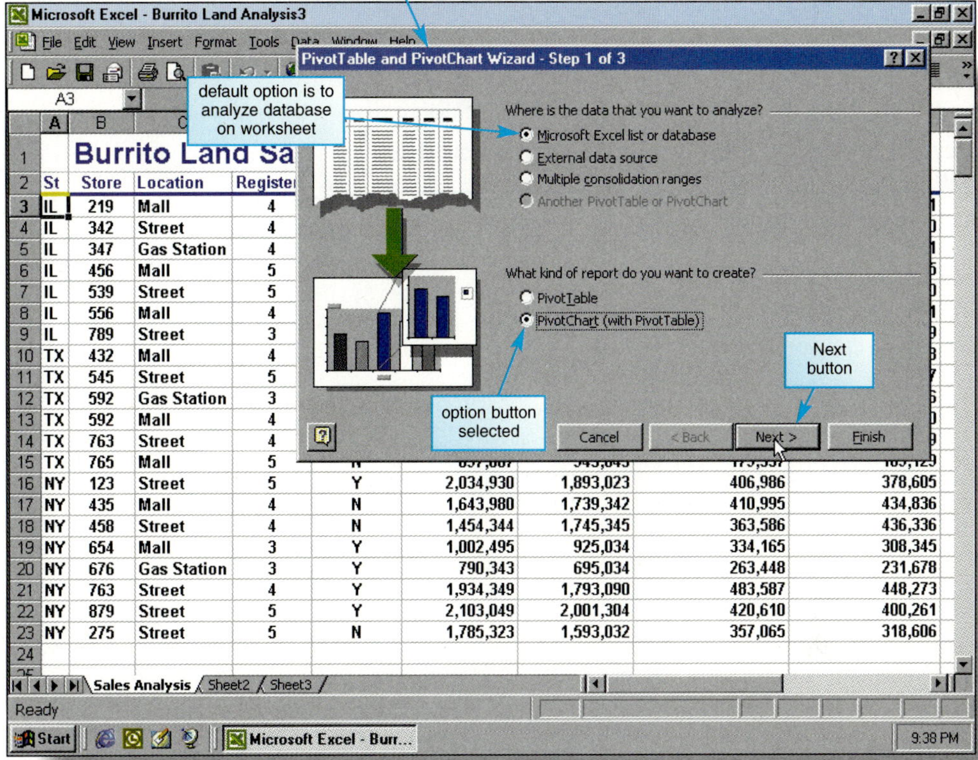

FIGURE 9-63

Click the Next button.

The PivotTable and PivotChart Wizard – Step 2 of 3 dialog box *displays. The range A2:I23 automatically is selected (Figure 9-64). A marquee surrounds the data on the worksheet.*

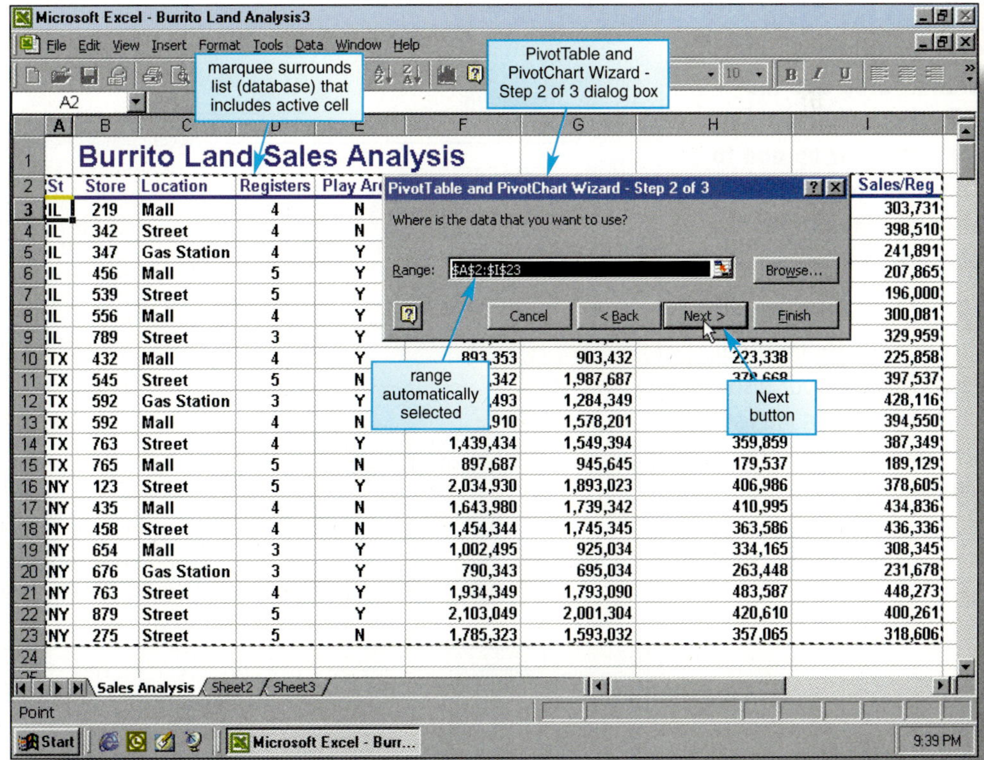

FIGURE 9-64

4 Click the Next button. When the PivotTable and PivotChart Wizard – Step 3 of 3 displays, if necessary, click New Worksheet and then point to the Finish button.

The Wizard will place the chart and table on separate worksheets in the workbook (Figure 9-65).

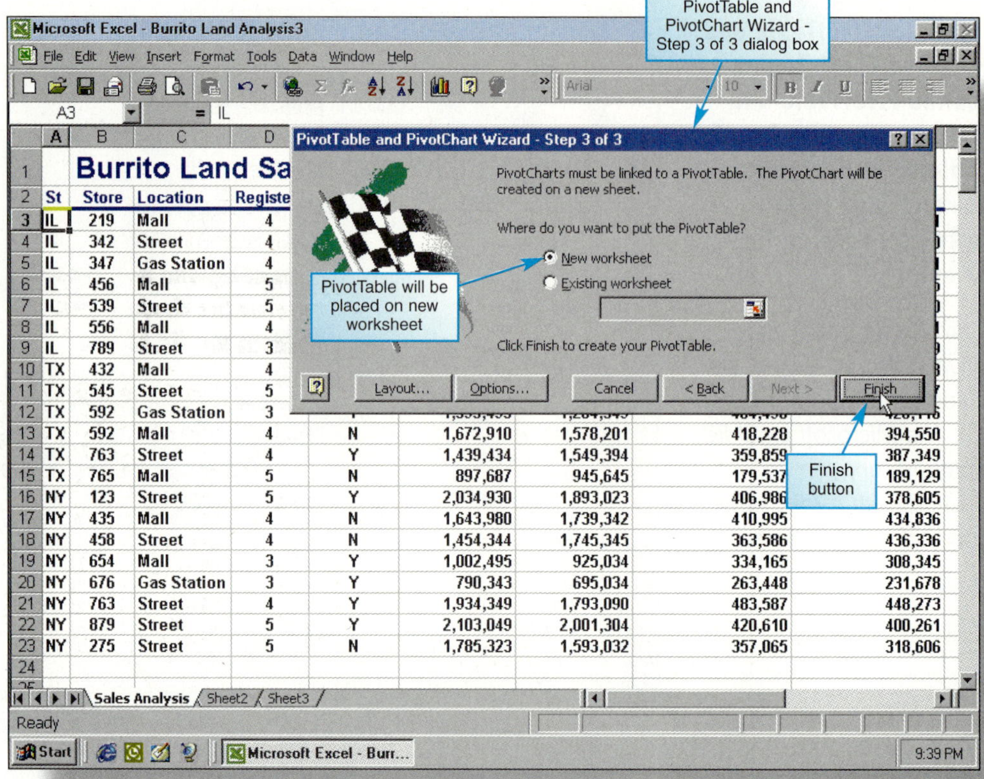

FIGURE 9-65

5 Click the Finish Button. When the PivotChart area and the PivotTable toolbar display, drag the toolbar up and to the right in order to display all areas of the PivotChart.

The PivotChart displays on a new worksheet (Figure 9-66). The PivotTable toolbar *also displays. Fields from the list of data display as buttons on the toolbar.*

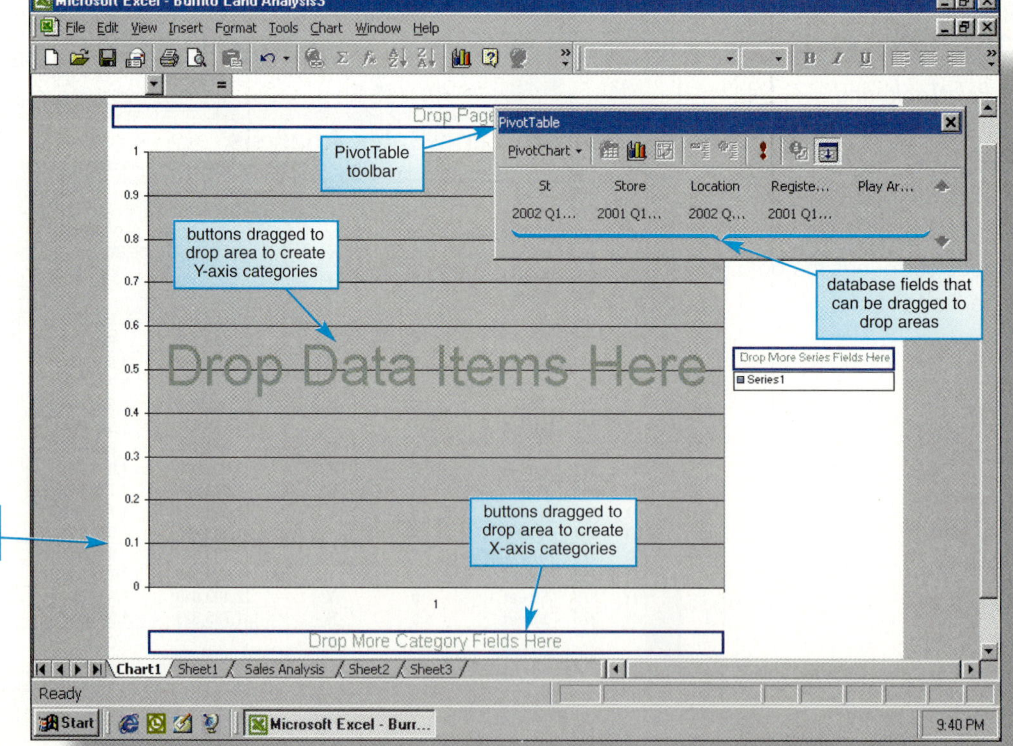

FIGURE 9-66

Other Ways

1. Press ALT+D, press P

The four main areas of a PivotChart (Figure 9-66) are described in Table 9-6.

Table 9-6 PivotChart Drop Areas

PIVOTCHART DROP AREA	DESCRIPTION OF DATA
Drop Page Fields Here	Data fields that categorize the entire chart
Drop Data Items Here	Data fields plotted on the chart, summarizing the detail of the database cells
Drop More Series Fields Here	Multiple data items plotted as a series, summarizing the detail columns of the database cells
Drop More Category Fields Here	Data fields to categorize on the X-axis

Adding Data to the PivotChart

The following steps create the PivotChart in Figure 9-61 on page E 9.46 by dropping four fields from the PivotTable toolbar onto the PivotChart area, two for the X-axis along the bottom of the chart and two for the data series in the chart. As shown in Figure 9-61, the X-axis displays location within state. The Y-axis includes the two data fields 2001 Q1 Sales/Reg and 2002 Q1 Sales/Reg.

To Add Data to the PivotChart

1 Drag the St (state) button from the PivotTable toolbar to the Drop More Category Fields Here area. Drag the Location button from the PivotTable toolbar and drop it to the right of the St (state) button. Point to the 2001 Q1 Sales/Reg button.

The State and Location field buttons display at the bottom of the PivotChart area (Figure 9-67). The sales per register buttons display to the right of the sales buttons for each year. When you point to a field button, Excel displays its full name and instructions as a ScreenTip.

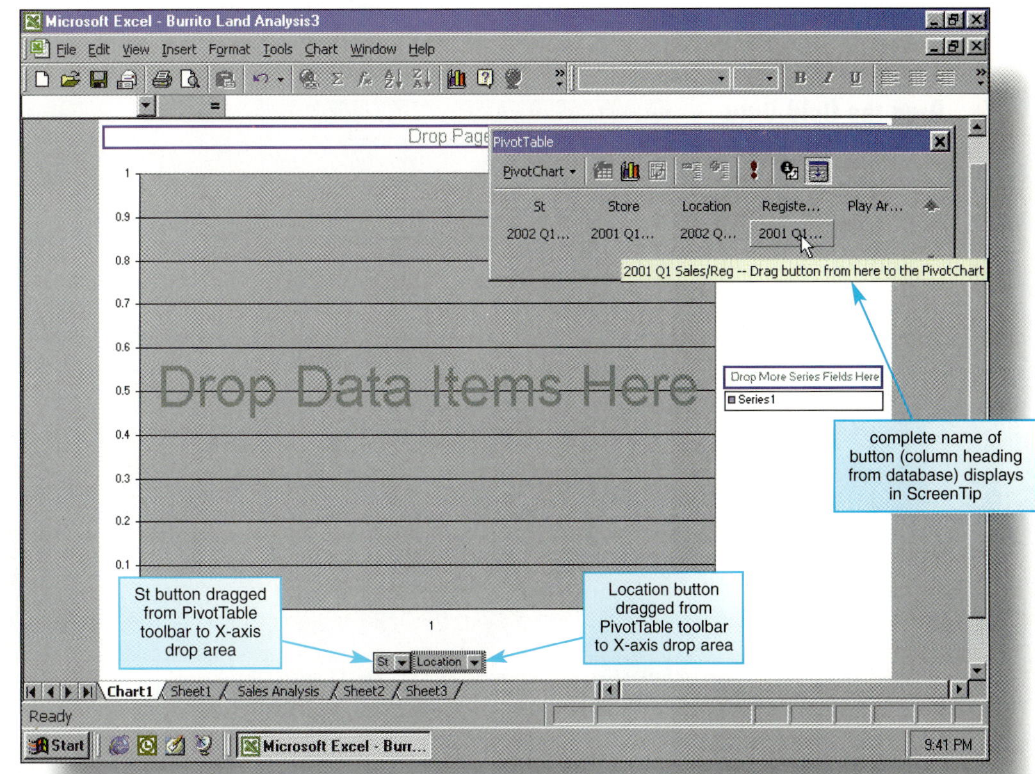

FIGURE 9-67

2 **Drag the 2001 Q1 Sales/Reg button to the Drop Data Items Here area. Drag the 2002 Q1 Sales/Reg button to the same area.**

The data fields display in the PivotChart (Figure 9-68). Because multiple fields have been added to the chart, a field Data button displays in the categories area at the bottom of the chart.

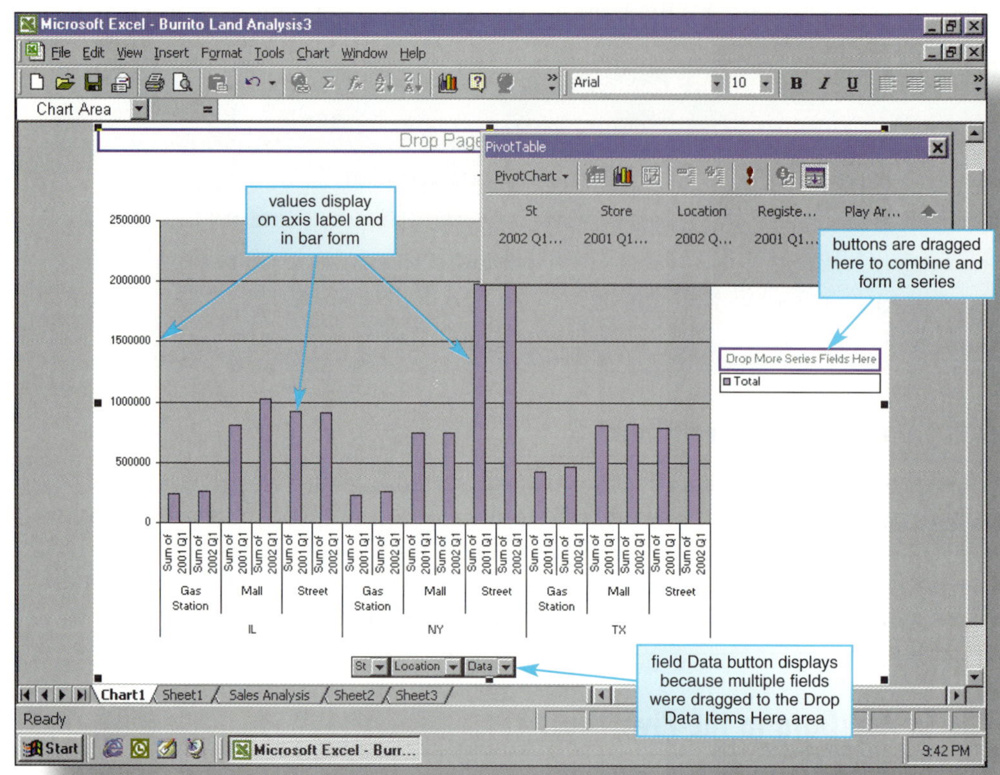

FIGURE 9-68

3 **Drag the field Data button to the Drop More Series Fields Here area.**

The two data fields display stacked (Figure 9-69).

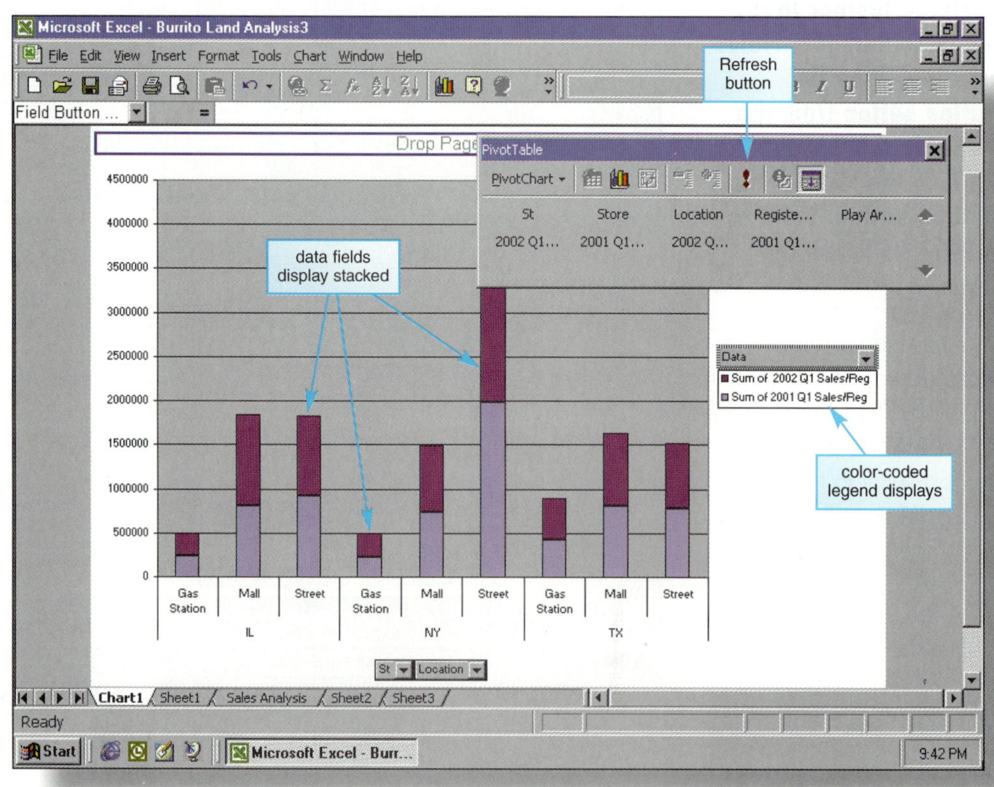

FIGURE 9-69

Other Ways

1. In PivotTable and PivotChart Wizard – Step 3 of 3 dialog box, click Layout button

Regular charts in Excel are linked directly to worksheet cells, which means that when data changes in the worksheet cell, the chart is updated automatically. PivotCharts are not linked to worksheet cells. The PivotTable toolbar contains a Refresh button (Figure 9-69) to update data when it changes on the worksheet. PivotCharts and their associated PivotTables can be based on several different types of data including Excel lists and databases, multiple data ranges that you want to consolidate, and external sources, such as Microsoft Access databases.

Formatting a PivotChart

Excel provides many ways to format PivotCharts. If you are familiar with regular charts, you will find that most formatting processes, such as choosing a chart type, displaying category or axis labels, and inserting titles, are performed the same way in PivotCharts as they are in regular charts.

The preset chart type for a PivotChart is a Stacked Column chart. PivotCharts can display any chart type except XY (Scatter), Stock, or Bubble. The following steps change the Burrito Land PivotChart from a Stacked Column chart to a Clustered Column chart that displays the two-year data side by side, adds a title, and formats the numbers along the Y-axis.

To Change the PivotChart Type and Format It

1 Click the Chart Wizard button on the PivotTable toolbar. When the Chart Wizard - Step 1 of 4 - Chart Type dialog box displays, click the Clustered Column chart in the top row of the Chart sub-type box. Point to the Next button.

The Chart Type dialog box allows you to choose the type of chart and its subtype (Figure 9-70). A preview is available with the Press and Hold to View Sample button.

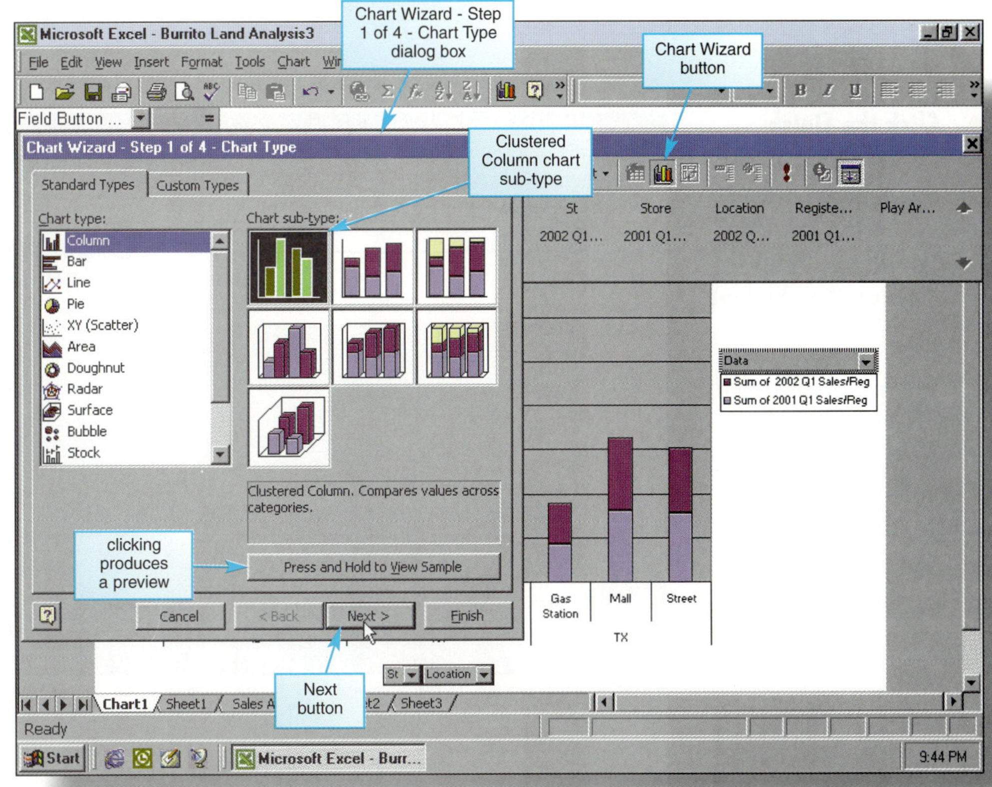

FIGURE 9-70

2 **Click the Next button. When the Chart Wizard - Step 3 of 4 - Chart Options dialog box displays, if necessary, click the Titles tab. Click the Chart title text box, type** `Burrito Land Analysis`**, and then point to the Finish button.**

The Chart Options dialog box displays as shown in Figure 9-71.

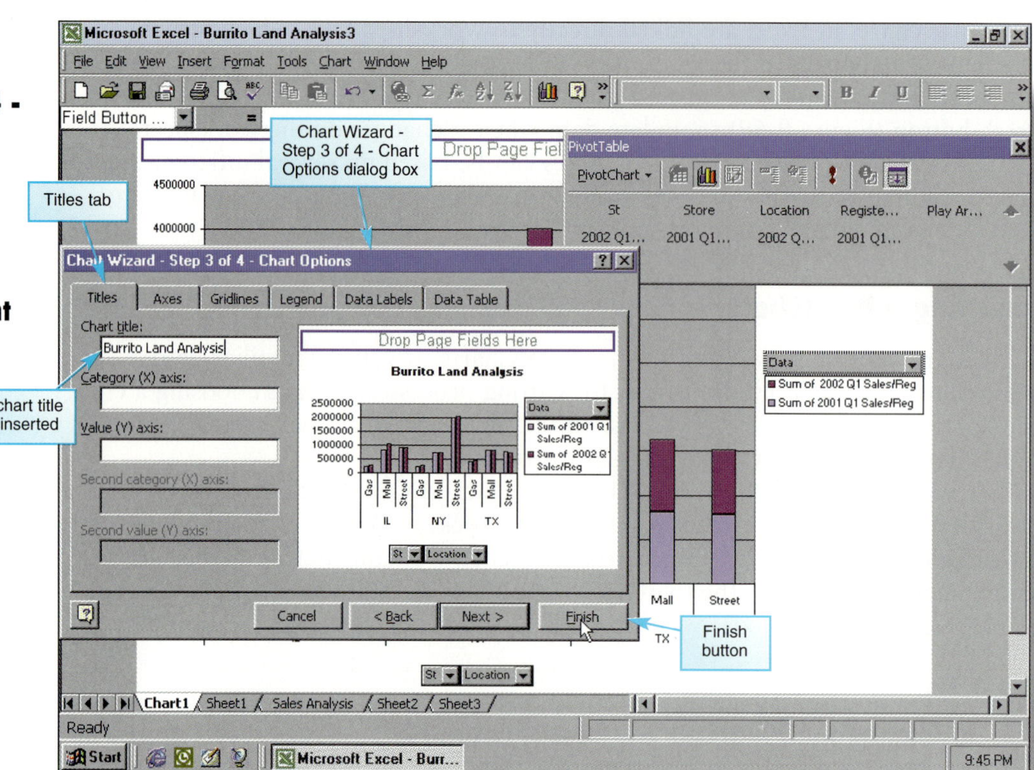

FIGURE 9-71

3 **Click the Finish button. Right-click any of the numbers along the Y-axis on the left side of the PivotChart. Point to Format Axis on the shortcut menu.**

The Chart Wizard closes and the axis shortcut menu displays (Figure 9-72). Clicking the Finish button accepted the preset values for the rest of the Chart Wizard.

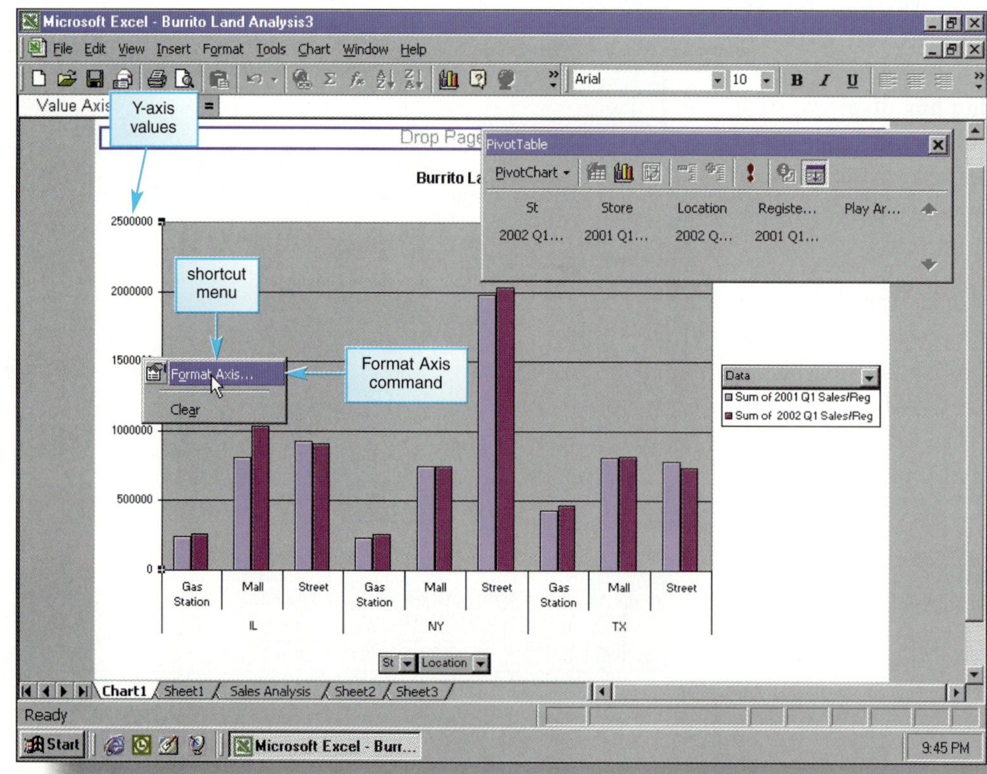

FIGURE 9-72

4 Click Format Axis. When the Format Axis dialog box displays, click the Number tab, and then click Currency in the Category box. Type 0 **in the Decimal places box. Point to the OK button.**

The Format Axis *dialog box displays as shown in Figure 9-73.*

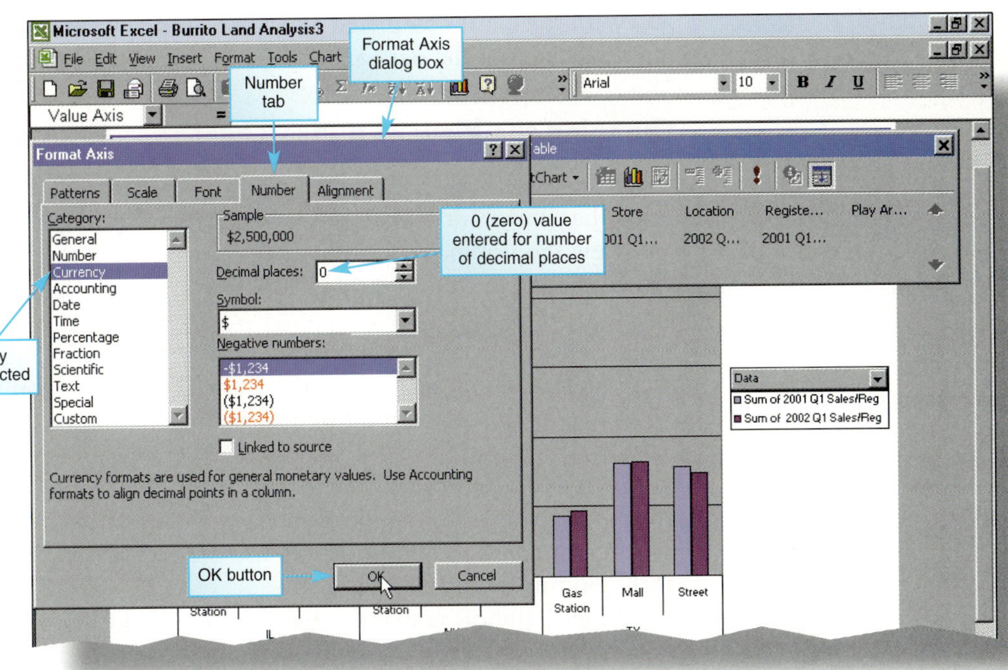

FIGURE 9-73

5 Click the OK button. Double-click the Chart1 sheet tab at the bottom of the workbook. Type PivotChart **and then press the ENTER key to rename the sheet.**

The numbers along the Y-axis display using the Currency format (Figure 9-74).

6 Click anywhere on the chart to deselect the Y-axis. Click the PivotTable toolbar Close button and then click the Save button on the Standard toolbar.

Excel saves the workbook with the PivotChart on drive A.

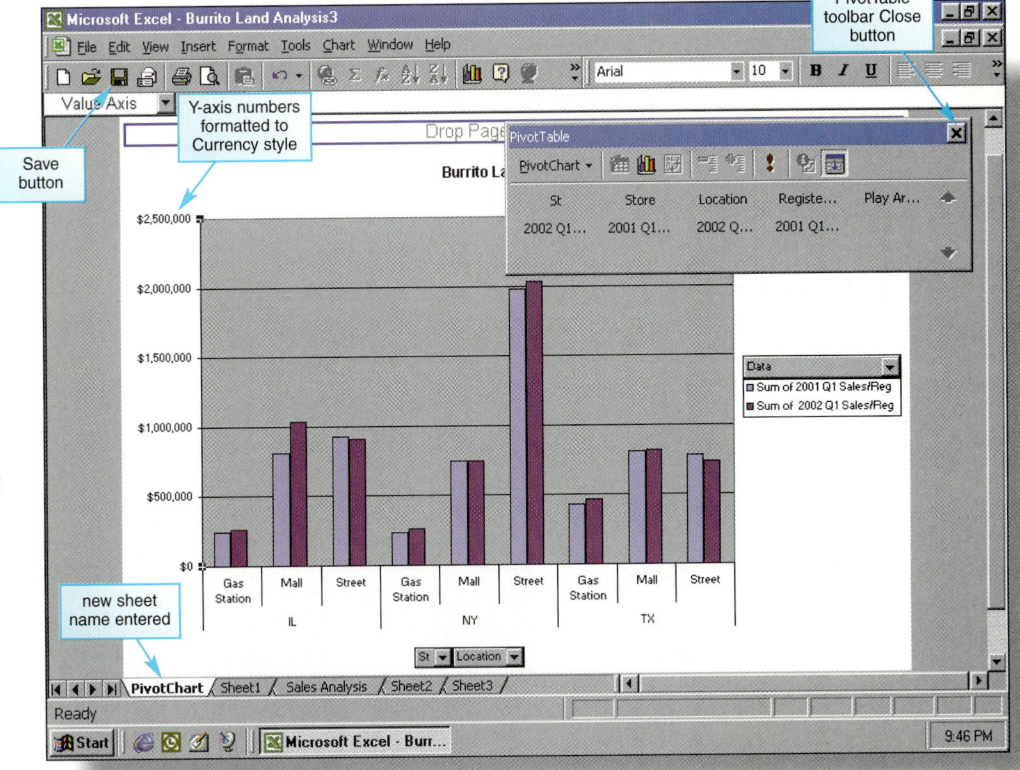

FIGURE 9-74

Other Ways

1. Click PivotChart button on PivotTable toolbar, click Options
2. Click Chart Wizard button on PivotTable toolbar, apply formatting in each step

With the chart completed and formatted appropriately, the chart can be manipulated and the data analyzed in a variety of views.

Changing the View of a PivotChart

With regular charts, you must create one chart for each view of the data summary that you want to see. With a PivotChart, you are able to create a single chart and view the summaries several ways just by using the mouse. The PivotChart provides a powerful interactive summarization of data with the visual appeal and benefits of a chart.

The Burrito Land PivotChart currently displays the sales per register data for each quarter within location within state (Figure 9-74 on the previous page).

It is easy to see common trends, such as that most locations in the three states have had increases in sales. You also can see that in general, gas station locations have a lower sum of sales per register. It might be easier to analyze that data, however, if all the gas station locations were grouped. If you want to compare the data in different combinations, you can use the interactive buttons in the categories area at the bottom of the chart.

Because Illinois and Texas have more mall locations than New York, you might want to view the data and compare only those two states rather than all three. Moving the two data ranges next to each other in the worksheet would be tedious, but in the PivotChart, you may choose which categories to display, by again using the interactive buttons at the bottom of the chart.

If you want to isolate one year versus another, for instance, you use the interactive buttons in the series area on the right of the chart.

Perform the following steps to interact with the PivotChart categories and series of data.

To Change the View of a PivotChart

1 Drag the St (state) button at the bottom of the chart to the right of the Location button.

Notice the locations are grouped together now, rather than the states (Figure 9-75).

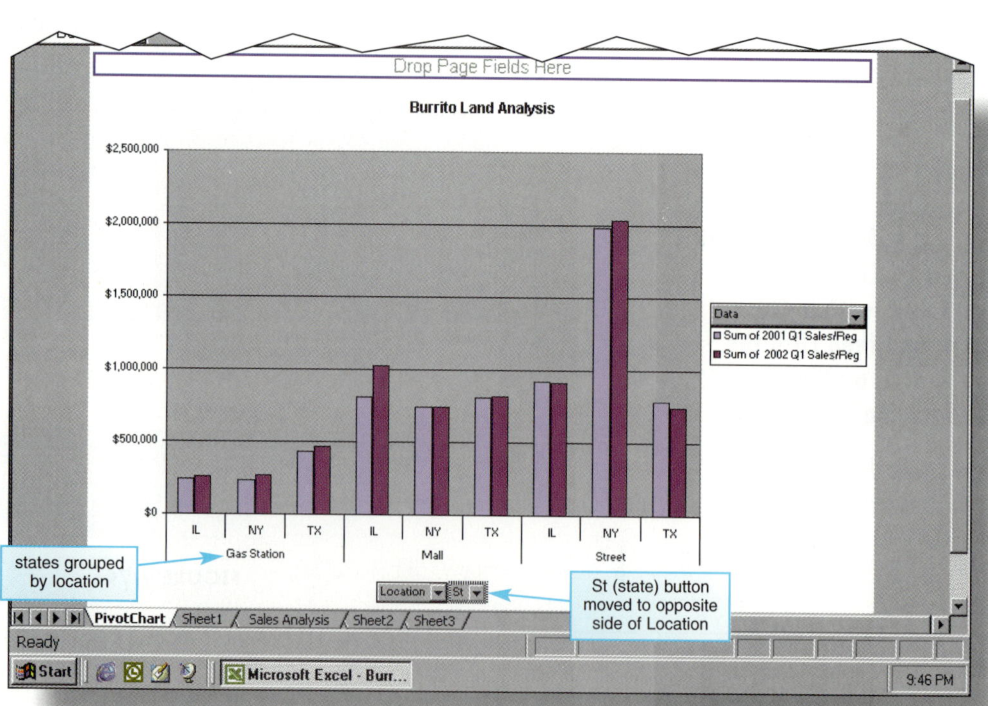

FIGURE 9-75

2 Click the Data button arrow on the right of the chart. When the list displays, click the check box next to Sum of 2001 Q1 Sales/Reg to clear the check box. Point to the OK button.

The list of data fields on the chart displays (Figure 9-76).

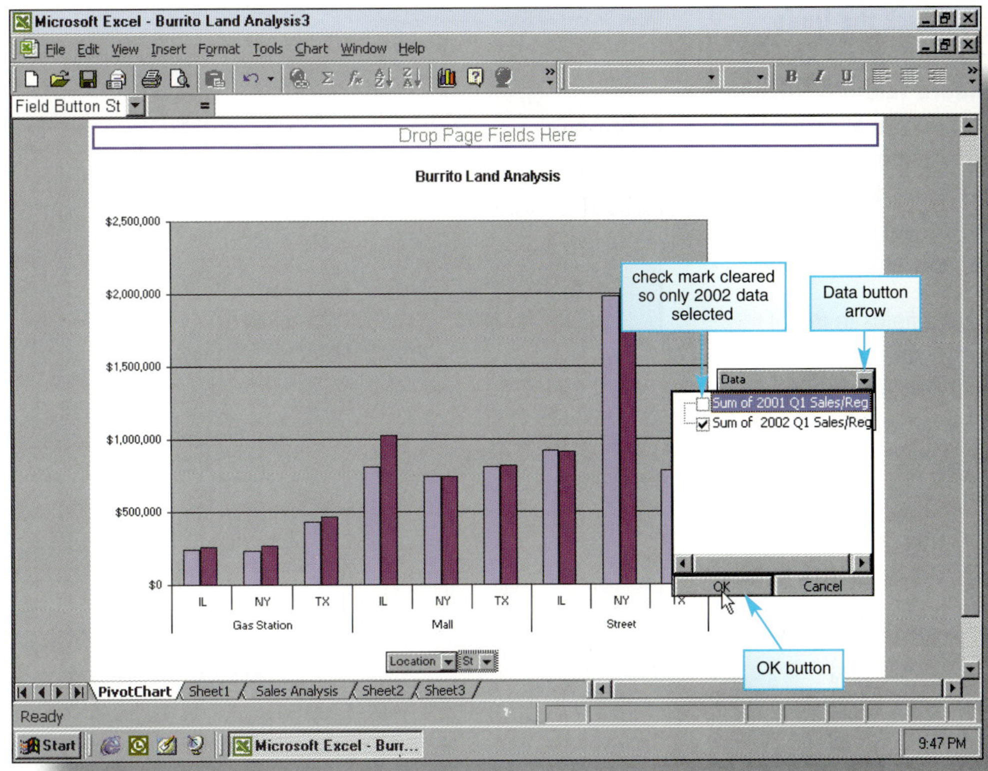

FIGURE 9-76

3 Click the OK button in the Data list box. Point to the Undo button on the Standard toolbar.

Only the data for 2002 displays (Figure 9-77). The Sum of 2002 Q1 Sales/Reg becomes a field for the entire page.

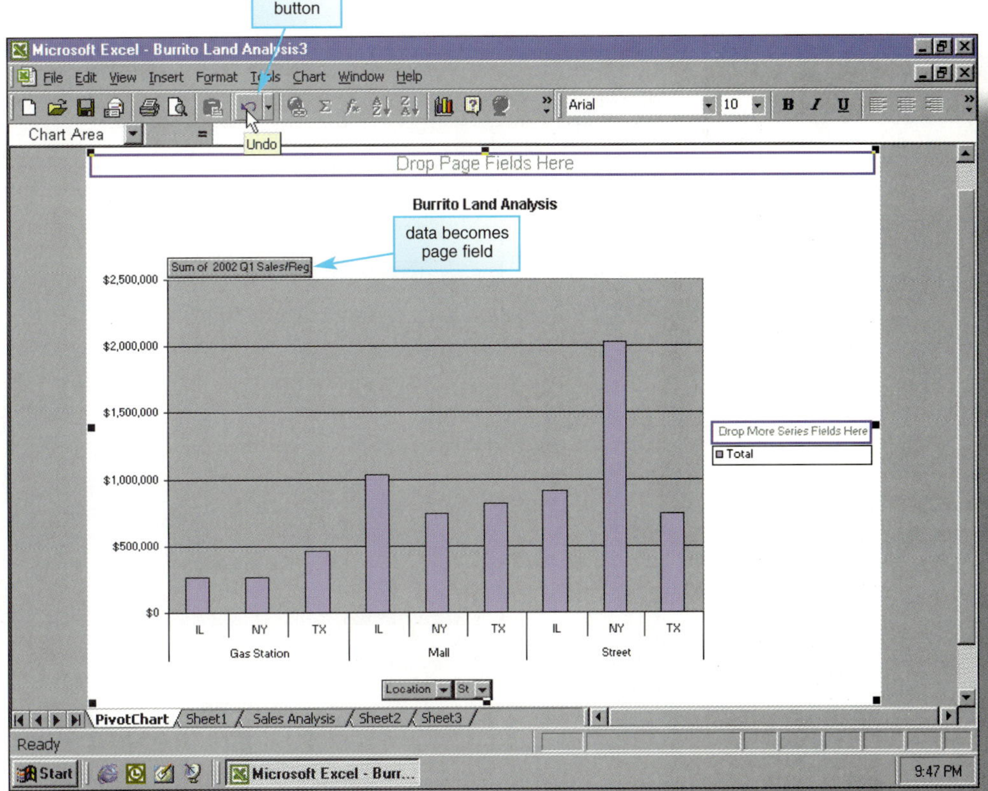

FIGURE 9-77

4 Click the Undo button on the Standard toolbar. Click the arrow on the St (state) interactive button, click the check mark for NY so it does not display, and then point to the OK button.

The data fields in the St (state) button display (Figure 9-78). The 2001 data again displays in the PivotChart.

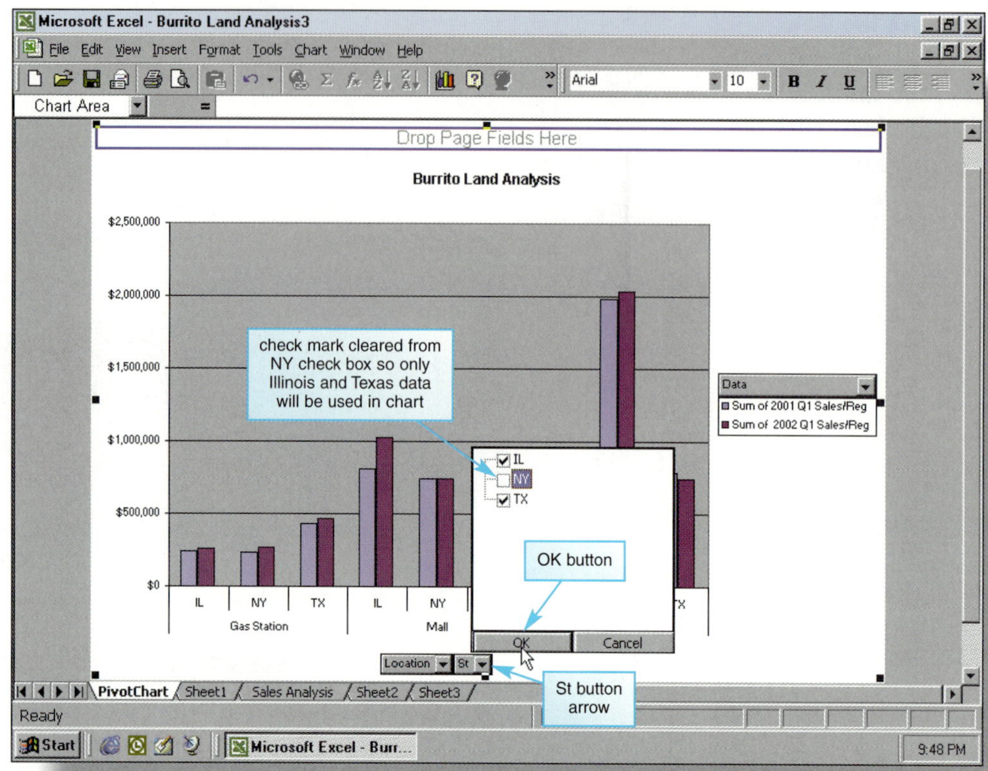

FIGURE 9-78

5 Click the OK button.

Only the data for Illinois and Texas displays (Figure 9-79).

6 Click the Undo button.

The data for all states displays (Figure 9-75 on page E 9.54).

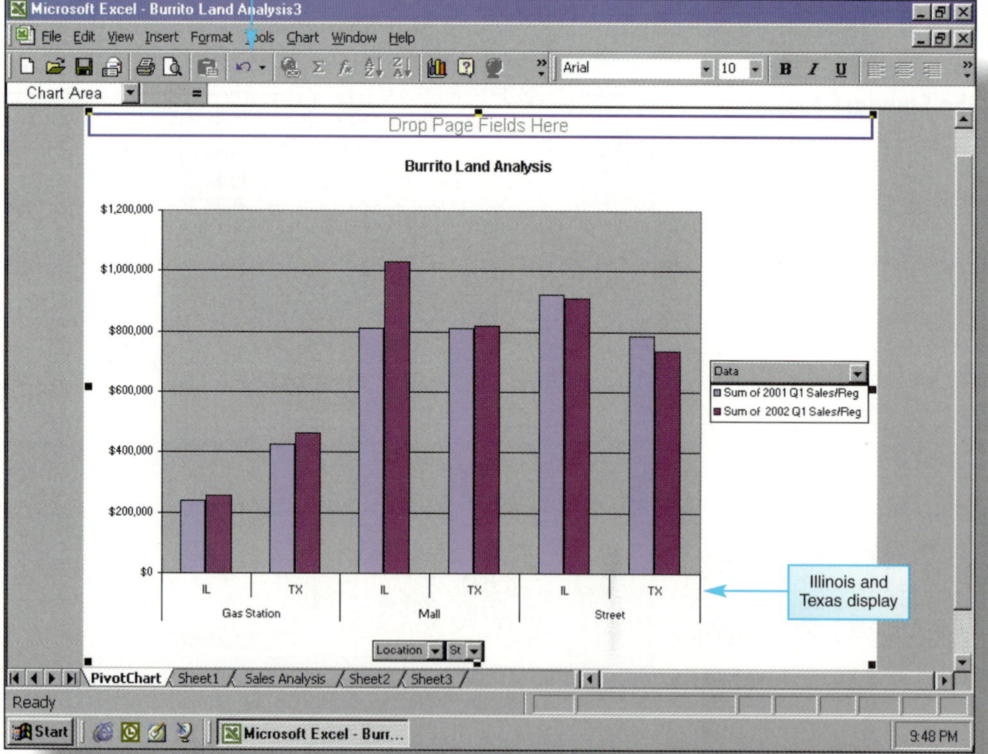

FIGURE 9-79

Other Ways

1. To remove data, drag button off chart
2. To add data, drag button from PivotChart toolbar

You can employ powerful data summarization techniques using PivotCharts. Choosing which kinds of data best represent trends and comparisons is easy with the interactive buttons on a PivotChart.

PivotTables

The PivotTable is one of the more powerful analytical tools available in Excel. PivotTables are used to show the relationships among the data in a list or a database. These tables allow you to use drag and drop to examine the data from different views.

PivotChart and PivotTable Relationships

Excel creates and associates a PivotTable on a separate sheet with every PivotChart. A PivotTable (Figure 9-80) is an interactive view of worksheet data that gives you the ability to summarize data and then rotate the table's row and column titles to show different views of the summarized data.

When you change the position of a field in a PivotChart or PivotTable, the corresponding field in the other changes automatically. **Row fields** in a PivotTable correspond to category fields in a PivotChart, while **column fields** in a PivotTable correspond to series fields in charts.

Formatting a PivotTable

When you choose to format a PivotTable, Excel displays samples in the AutoFormat dialog box with various formatting applied to the cells, borders, and numbers. You can choose from colors, patterns, alignments, fonts, and borders, which apply to the entire table. You may also apply any of the wide range of Excel's normal formats to individual cells. The following steps choose a format that contains color and borders to enhance the data.

To Format a PivotTable

1 Double-click the Sheet1 tab at the bottom of the workbook. Type `PivotTable` **and then press the ENTER key, to rename the sheet. Right-click a toolbar and click PivotTable on the shortcut menu to display the PivotTable toolbar. Point to the Format Report button on the PivotTable toolbar.**

The PivotTable, created by Excel and associated with the PivotChart, displays (Figure 9-80). If the PivotTable toolbar does not display, right-click the menu bar and click PivotTable.

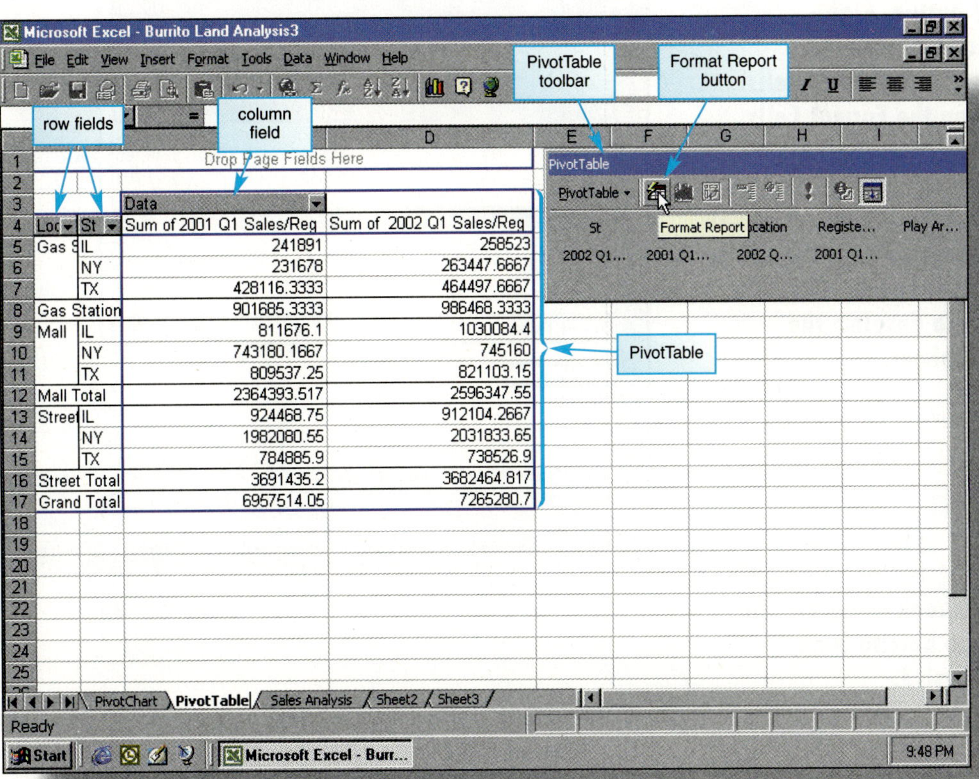

FIGURE 9-80

2 **Click the Format Report button. When the AutoFormat dialog box displays, if necessary, scroll to display Report 6. Click Report 6 and then point to the OK button.**

The AutoFormat dialog box displays report formats to add color and variety to the PivotTable (Figure 9-81).

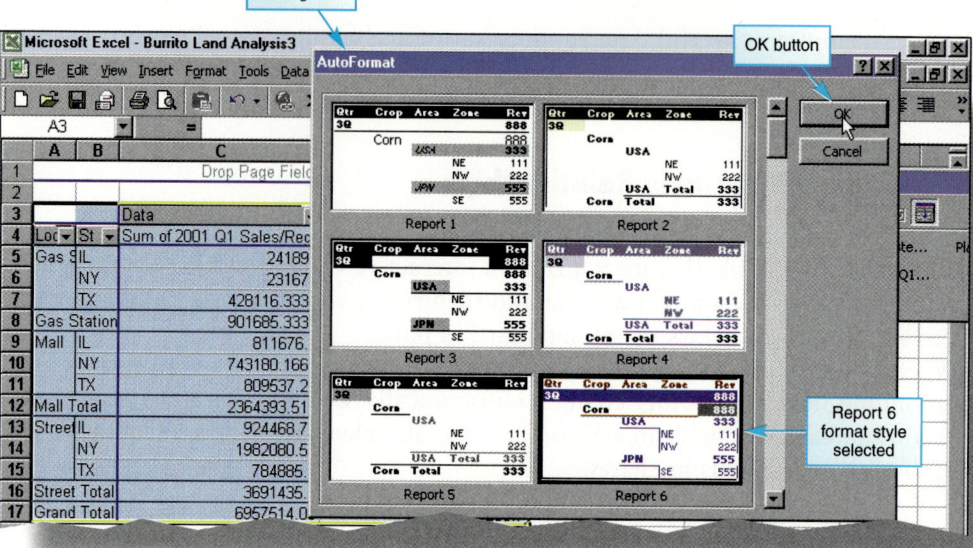

FIGURE 9-81

3 **Click the OK button. Double-click the border between column headings A and B to change column A to best fit. Click the Select All button. Right-click any cell and then click Format Cells. When the Format Cells dialog box displays, click Currency in the Category list, type 0 in the Decimal places box, and then click the OK button. Click cell A21 to deselect the worksheet.**

The PivotTable displays as shown in Figure 9-82.

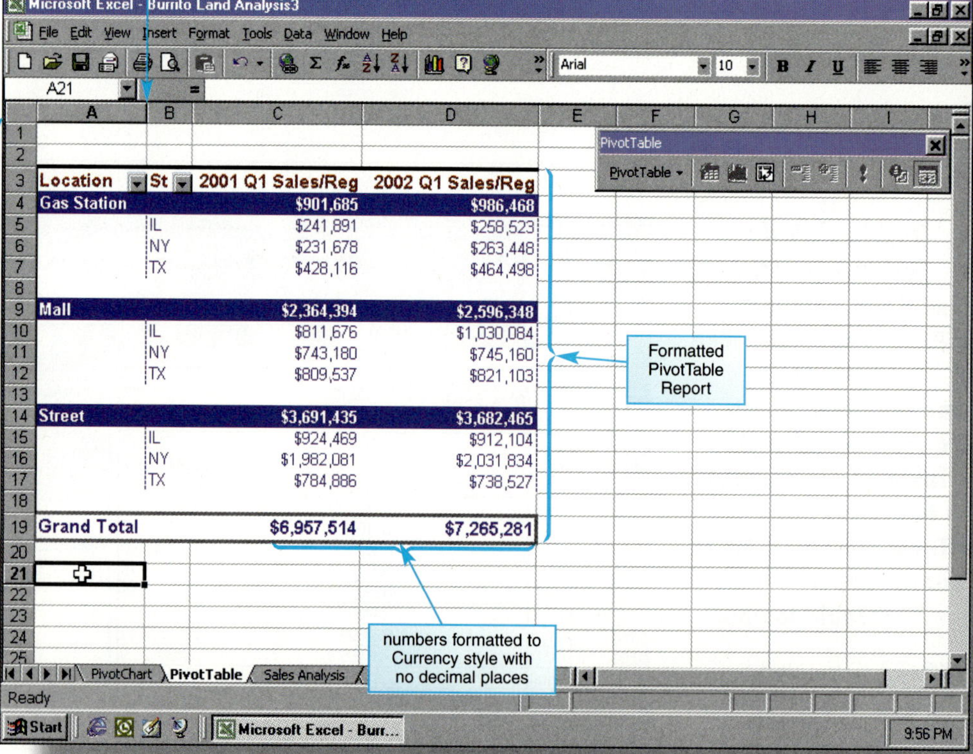

FIGURE 9-82

4 **Click the Save button to save the workbook using the file name Burrito Land Analysis3.**

Other Ways

1. Right-click table, click Format Report on shortcut menu

The AutoFormat dialog box shown in Figure 9-81 includes 12 customized formats. Use the scroll box to view the formats that do not display in the dialog box.

Each one of these customized formats offers a different look. The one you choose depends on the worksheet you are creating. If you want to remove the format on a PivotTable, you can click None in the list of formats.

Creating PivotTables

For more information about the process of creating PivotTables, visit the Excel 2000 More About Web page (www.scsite.com/Ex2000/more.htm) and then click PivotTables.

Interacting with the PivotTable

Interacting with a PivotTable is as easy as it is with the PivotChart. You can change the way the data fields are summarized, add new fields to the analysis, or you can rotate the row and column fields.

SWITCHING SUMMARY FUNCTIONS In the Burrito Land PivotChart, you may have realized that the data created in the chart summarizes the sum of the sales per register. The fact that more mall locations exist than gas station locations in any given state will make their figures higher automatically if you look at the sums. An average might be a better way to compare the locations. To change the field setting from sum to average, you simply right-click the data field in the PivotTable, click Field Settings on the shortcut menu, and then choose Average in the Summarize by list as shown in the following steps.

To Switch Summary Functions in a PivotTable

1 Right-click cell C4. Click Field Settings on the shortcut menu. When the PivotTable Field dialog box displays, click Average in the Summarize by list. Click the OK button.

The numbers in column C change from sums to averages.

2 Right-click cell D4. Click Field Settings on the shortcut menu. When the PivotTable Field dialog box displays, click Average in the Summarize by list box. Click the OK button.

The numbers in column D change from location sums to location averages (Figure 9-83).

Location	St	Average of 2001 Q1 Sales/Reg	Average of 2002 Q1 Sales/Reg
Gas Station		$300,562	$328,823
	IL	$241,891	$258,523
	NY	$231,678	$263,448
	TX	$428,116	$464,498
Mall		$295,549	$324,543
	IL	$270,559	$343,361
	NY	$371,590	$372,580
	TX	$269,846	$273,701
Street		$369,144	$368,246
	IL	$308,156	$304,035
	NY	$396,416	$406,367
	TX	$392,443	$369,263
Grand Total		$331,310	$345,966

FIGURE 9-83

3 Click the PivotTable toolbar Close button.

Table 9-7 Summary Functions for PivotTable Data Analysis

SUMMARY FUNCTION	DESCRIPTION
Sum	Sum values. This is the default function for numeric source data.
Count	The number of items.
Average	The average of the values.
Max	The largest value.
Min	The smallest value.
Product	The product of the values.
Count Nums	The number of rows that contain numeric data.
StdDev	An estimate of the standard deviation of all the data to be summarized.
StdDevp	The standard deviation of all of the data to be summarized.
Var	An estimate of the variance of all of the data to be summarized.
Varp	The variance of the data to be summarized.

Table 9-7 lists the summary functions from which you may choose through the Field Settings command on the shortcut menu to analyze your data in PivotCharts and PivotTables.

CHANGING THE VIEW OF A PIVOTTABLE You can rotate the row and column fields around the data field by dragging the buttons to different locations on the PivotTable. For example, if you drag the St (state) button to the Drop Page Fields Here area at the top of the table (above row 1 in the worksheet), you change the view of the PivotTable as shown in the following steps.

To Change the View of a PivotTable

1 Drag the St button above row 1.

Excel displays a new, different view of the PivotTable (Figure 9-84), which is easier to read than the PivotTable shown in Figure 9-83 on the previous page.

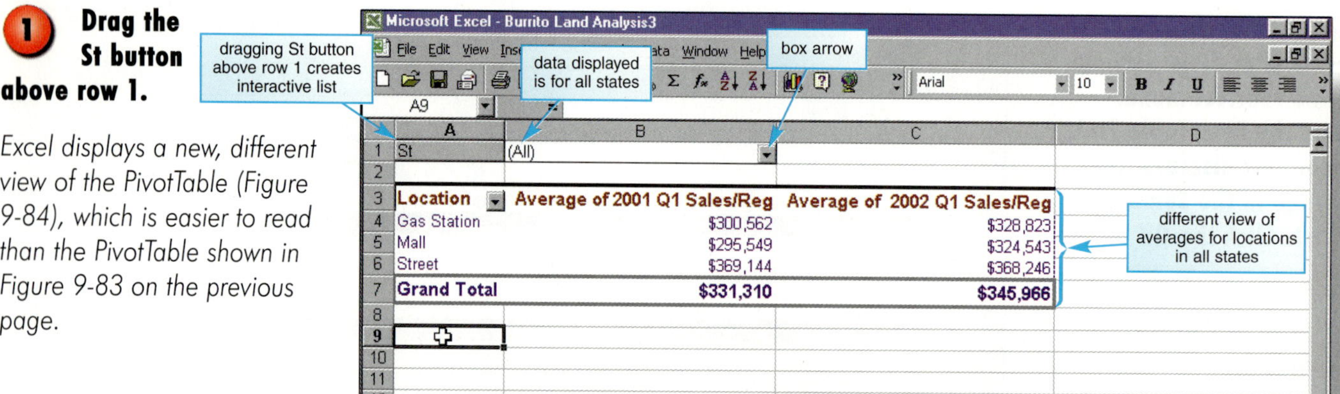

FIGURE 9-84

2 Click the St box arrow, click IL, and then click the OK button.

Excel displays the averages for each location type in the state of Illinois (Figure 9-85).

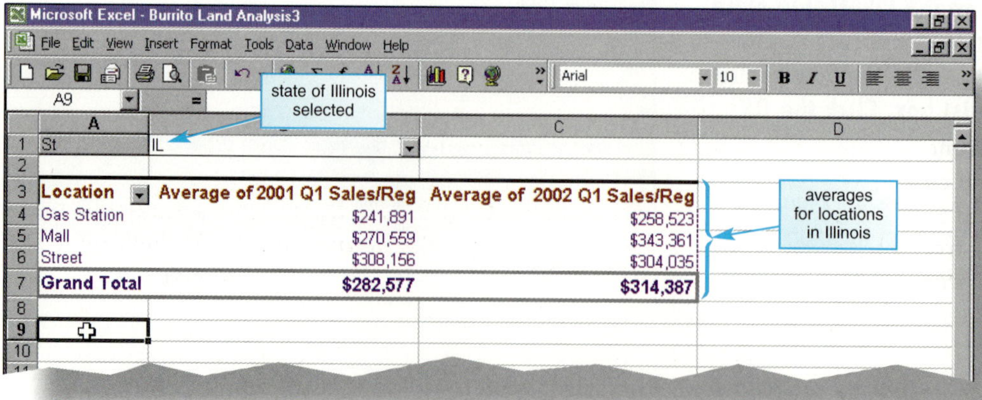

FIGURE 9-85

In Figure 9-84, the St button has a box and drop-down arrow to the right. Click the arrow to display the St list box and select the specific states whose averages you want to view.

PivotTables are powerful data analysis tools because they allow you to view the data in various ways by interchanging or pairing up the row and column fields. You can print a PivotChart or PivotTable just as you would any other worksheet. If you update the data on the Quarter 1 Sales Data sheet, click **Refresh Data** on the Data menu or click the **Refresh button** on the PivotTable toolbar to update the corresponding PivotTable and PivotChart.

Quitting Excel

The project is complete. To quit Excel, follow the steps below.

TO QUIT EXCEL

1. Click the Close button on the right side of the title bar.
2. If the Microsoft Excel dialog box displays, click the No button.

> **More About**
>
> **Changing PivotTables**
>
> At any time while the workbook containing a PivotTable is active, you can click the tab of the sheet containing the PivotTable, and then click PivotTable on the Data menu to display the PivotTable Wizard - Step 3 of 3 dialog box (Figure 9-65 on page E 9.48). Use the Layout button in this dialog box as an alternative to using drag and drop to change the view of the PivotTable.

Merging Workbooks

Instead of tracking all of the changes to a single copy of a workbook, it sometimes is necessary to merge copies of the same workbook together, because either multiple users are entering data, or new data has come in from a different source. To merge the changes from one workbook into another, both workbooks must satisfy the following requirements:

- You must make the original workbook shared, before making copies, and each workbook must be a copy of the same workbook.
- When you make copies, Track Changes or sharing must be turned on (which keeps a Change History file of the workbook).
- The Share Workbook command on the Tools menu displays a dialog box with a tab for recording the number of days to record the change history. Shared workbooks must be merged within that time period.
- If you use passwords, all workbooks involved in the merge must have the same password.
- When the copies come back, each must have a different file name.

When you have all the copies of the workbook together, you open the copy of the shared workbook into which you want to merge changes from another workbook file on disk. Then, on the Tools menu, click **Merge Workbooks**, which will display choices for you to choose a workbook or workbooks to merge. Not only is the data merged, but if comments are recorded, they display one after another in the given cell's comment box.

If Excel cannot merge the two workbooks, you still can incorporate the information from one workbook into the other, by copying and pasting the information from one workbook to another.

> **Quick Reference**
>
> For a table that lists how to complete the tasks covered in this book using the mouse, menu, shortcut menu, and keyboard, see the Excel Quick Reference Summary at the back of this book or visit the Office 2000 Web page (www.scsite.com/off2000/qr.htm), and then click Microsoft Excel 2000.

CASE PERSPECTIVE SUMMARY

With the imported data, the data map, the PivotChart, and the PivotTable developed in this project, the marketing manager for Burrito Land, José Velez, can view and analyze the sales data in a variety of ways. Links to the external data will update automatically when he refreshes his tables. During his presentation to the board of directors, he will have the ability to answer questions and clarify data by interacting with the PivotChart and PivotTable. His report will display timely, accurate, and visual data.

Project Summary

In this project, you learned how to import data in different formats into a worksheet, track changes, route workbooks, and create visual representations of the data in a worksheet. Using a preformatted worksheet, you learned how to import a text file, an Access database, and a Web table. You then learned how to Track Changes, which also shared the workbook. After routing the workbook to the coordinator from each state, you learned how to accept the changes. You then learned how to create a data map to represent data graphically according to locations. You learned how to create interactive PivotCharts and PivotTables, format them, and view them in different ways. Finally, you learned about sharing and merging workbooks.

What You Should Know

Having completed this project, you should be able to perform the following tasks:

- Add Data to the PivotChart *(E 9.49)*
- Add the Map Button to the Standard Toolbar *(E 9.36)*
- Change the Features of a Data Map *(E 9.40)*
- Change the PivotChart Type and Format It *(E 9.51)*
- Change the View of a PivotChart *(E 9.54)*
- Change the View of a PivotTable *(E 9.60)*
- Create a Data Map *(E 9.37)*
- Create a PivotChart *(E 9.46)*
- Format a Data Map *(E 9.42)*
- Format a PivotTable *(E 9.57)*
- Import Data from a Text File into a Worksheet *(E 9.9)*
- Import Data from a Web Page into a Worksheet *(E 9.18)*
- Import Data from an Access Table into a Worksheet *(E 9.14)*
- Insert a Comment *(E 9.24)*
- Open a Routed Workbook and Review Tracked Changes *(E 9.31)*
- Quit Excel *(E 9.61)*
- Replicate Formulas *(E 9.22)*
- Route a Workbook *(E 9.27)*
- Save the Workbook with a New File Name *(E 9.23)*
- Save the Tracked Changes in a Workbook with a New File Name *(E 9.34)*
- Start Excel and Open a Workbook *(E 9.8)*
- Switch Summary Functions in a PivotTable *(E 9.59)*
- Turn Off Track Changes *(E 9.35)*
- Turn On Track Changes *(E 9.26)*

Microsoft Certification

The Microsoft Office User Specialist (MOUS) Certification program provides an opportunity for you to obtain a valuable industry credential – proof that you have the Excel 2000 skills required by employers. For more information, see Appendix D or visit the Shelly Cashman Series MOUS Web page at www.scsite.com/off2000/cert.htm.

1 Creating a Data Map

Instructions: Start Excel and perform the following tasks.

1. Open the workbook, Sales Rep Database from the Data Disk. The worksheet database displays as shown in Figure 9-86a.

Microsoft Excel - Sales Rep Database

Sales Representative Database

Lname	Fname	Age	Gender	Title	St	Quota 2002	Sales 2002	Quota 2001	Sales 2001
Biagi	Linda	41	F	Manager	IL	2,073,227	2,241,750	1,983,000	2,032,575
Jacobs	Lucy	45	F	Telemarketer	NY	1,627,844	1,524,600	1,557,000	1,595,925
Groen	Jodi	35	F	Telemarketer	TX	836,451	1,536,350	800,000	820,050
Grodzieki	Fran	37	F	Sales Rep	IL	3,241,050	3,407,250	3,100,000	3,177,500
Baxter	John	35	M	Sales Rep	TX	2,456,925	2,403,750	2,350,000	2,408,750
Josef	Jeff	44	M	Manager	NY	2,875,125	3,307,500	2,750,000	2,818,750
Joseph	Albert	55	M	Manager	TX	1,568,250	1,227,500	1,500,000	1,537,500
Wade	Susan	54	F	Manager	CA	4,286,550	4,567,500	4,100,000	4,202,500
Little	Deborah	27	F	Telemarketer	IL	1,001,589	1,338,750	958,000	981,950
Russo	Lin	41	F	Sales Rep	CA	2,091,000	2,890,650	2,000,000	2,050,000
Doolittle	Jeff	34	M	Sales Rep	NY	1,306,875	1,575,000	1,250,000	1,281,250
James	Kevin	31	M	Telemarketer	CA	1,568,250	1,537,500	1,500,000	1,537,500

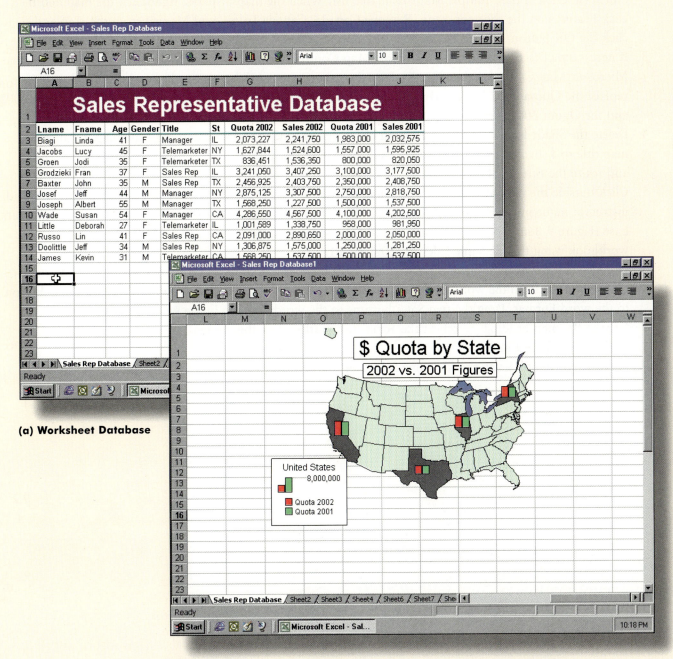

(a) Worksheet Database

Microsoft Excel - Sales Rep Database1

$ Quota by State
2002 vs. 2001 Figures

United States
8,000,000
Quota 2002
Quota 2001

(b) Data Map

FIGURE 9-86

(continued)

Creating a Data Map *(continued)*

2. Select the range, A2:J14. Click the Map button on the Standard toolbar. If your system does not display a Map button, see page E 9.36 for instructions on adding the Map button to the Standard toolbar. Scroll to view cell L1 in the upper-left corner of the screen. Drag the map from N1:U17. Choose the United States in North America in the Multiple Maps Available list. When the map displays, right-click the map and then click Features on the shortcut menu. Remove Canada, Canada Lakes, and Mexico from the map and then click the OK button.
3. If necessary, click the Show/Hide Microsoft Map Control button on the Microsoft Map toolbar. When the Microsoft Map Control dialog box displays, drag the Count of St button to the work area and drop it to replace the Quota 2002 button. Drag the Column Chart button to the word Format. Drag the Quota 2002 and the Quota 2001 buttons to the word Column.
4. Delete the Shade legend. Drag the Column chart legend to the lower-left corner of the map. Change the map title to `$ Quota by State`. Add the subtitle `2002 vs. 2001 Figures` using the View menu. Move and resize the titles as shown in Figure 9-86b.
5. Click outside the map area. Enter your name, course, computer laboratory exercise (Apply 9-1), date, and instructor name in the range A19:A23. Click the Print button on the Standard toolbar. The worksheet database (Figure 9-86a) will print on page one, the data map (Figure 9-86b) will print on page two. Save the workbook using the file name Sales Rep Database1.
6. Double-click the Map to make it active, and display the Microsoft Map Control dialog box. Drag the two Quota buttons from the work area back to the Data column buttons area. Drag the Column Chart button to the word Format. Drag the two Sales buttons to the word Column in the work area.
7. Change the map headings to reflect the actual sales rather than the quotas.
8. Print the worksheet and map.
9. Save the workbook using the file name Sales Rep Database2.

In the Lab

1 Importing Data into an Excel Worksheet

Problem: You are employed as an inventory control specialist for the local school district. You have asked each of the three grade schools to send you a list of inventory they are planning to dispose of at the end of the school year, complete with inventory number, quantity, description, location, age, purchase price, and depreciation allowance. Each school has sent the required data but in a variety of formats. School A used a mainframe computer and sent a text file with fields separated by commas. School B maintains its inventory in an Access database, and queried it, creating a table to send to you. School C posted its list on the school's intranet as a Web page.

Instructions: Perform the following tasks.

1. Open the workbook Local School District Disposables (Figure 9-87a) from the Data Disk.

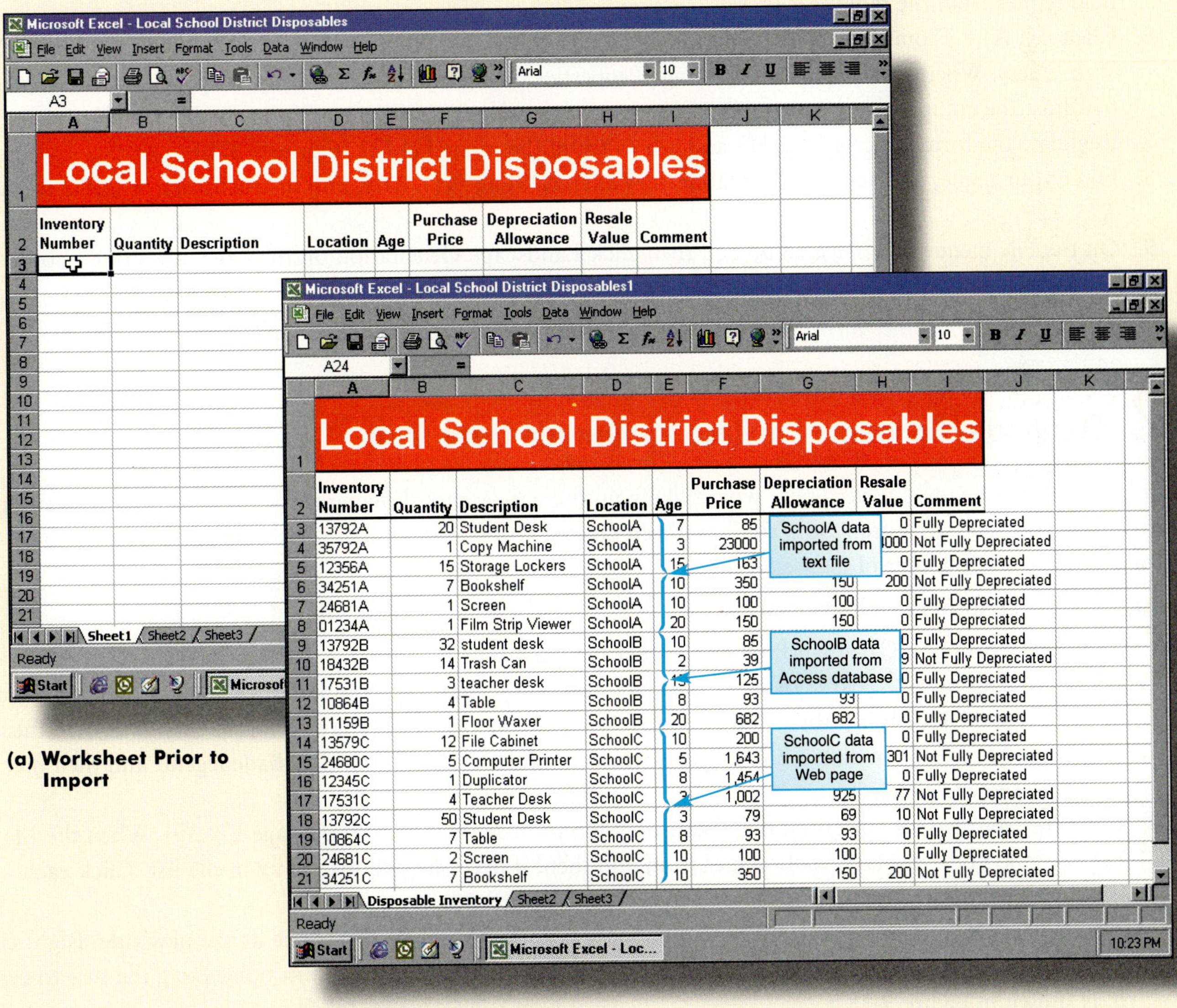

Microsoft Excel - Local School District Disposables

Local School District Disposables

Inventory Number	Quantity	Description	Location	Age	Purchase Price	Depreciation Allowance	Resale Value	Comment

(a) Worksheet Prior to Import

Microsoft Excel - Local School District Disposables1

Local School District Disposables

Inventory Number	Quantity	Description	Location	Age	Purchase Price	Depreciation Allowance	Resale Value	Comment
13792A	20	Student Desk	SchoolA	7	85		0	Fully Depreciated
35792A	1	Copy Machine	SchoolA	3	23000		000	Not Fully Depreciated
12356A	15	Storage Lockers	SchoolA	15	163		0	Fully Depreciated
34251A	7	Bookshelf	SchoolA	10	350	150	200	Not Fully Depreciated
24681A	1	Screen	SchoolA	10	100	100	0	Fully Depreciated
01234A	1	Film Strip Viewer	SchoolA	20	150	150	0	Fully Depreciated
13792B	32	student desk	SchoolB	10	85		0	Fully Depreciated
18432B	14	Trash Can	SchoolB	2	39		9	Not Fully Depreciated
17531B	3	teacher desk	SchoolB	15	125		0	Fully Depreciated
10864B	4	Table	SchoolB	8	93	93	0	Fully Depreciated
11159B	1	Floor Waxer	SchoolB	20	682	682	0	Fully Depreciated
13579C	12	File Cabinet	SchoolC	10	200		0	Fully Depreciated
24680C	5	Computer Printer	SchoolC	5	1,643		301	Not Fully Depreciated
12345C	1	Duplicator	SchoolC	8	1,454		0	Fully Depreciated
17531C	4	Teacher Desk	SchoolC	3	1,002	925	77	Not Fully Depreciated
13792C	50	Student Desk	SchoolC	3	79	69	10	Not Fully Depreciated
10864C	7	Table	SchoolC	8	93	93	0	Fully Depreciated
24681C	2	Screen	SchoolC	10	100	100	0	Fully Depreciated
34251C	7	Bookshelf	SchoolC	10	350	150	200	Not Fully Depreciated

SchoolA data imported from text file

SchoolB data imported from Access database

SchoolC data imported from Web page

(b) Worksheet After Import

FIGURE 9-87

(continued)

Importing Data into an Excel Worksheet *(continued)*

2. In cell H3, enter the formula, `=F3-G3`.
3. In cell I3, enter the formula, `=IF(H3=0,"Fully Depreciated","Not Fully Depreciated")`.
4. Click cell A3. From the Data Disk, import the text file, SchoolA. It is a comma delimited text file. In step 2 of the Text Import Wizard, click the Comma check box; otherwise accept the default settings. When the External Data Range Properties dialog box displays, click Properties, and choose not to adjust the column width.
5. Click Cell A9. From the Data Disk, import the Access database file, SchoolB. Add all the fields from the Disposable Inventory table. Accept all of the default settings. When the External Data Range Properties dialog box displays, click Properties, choose not to adjust the column width, and choose not to include the field names from the table.
6. Click cell A14. From the Data Disk, import the HTML file, SchoolC. Accept the default setting for the New Web Query. When the External Data Range Properties dialog box displays, click Properties, and choose not to adjust the column width. Manually delete the column headings imported from the HTML file.
7. Replicate the formulas from cell H3 and cell I3 to fill the range H4:I21 (Figure 9-87b).
8. Enter your name, course, computer laboratory exercise (Lab 9-1), date, and instructor name in the range A25:A29.
9. On the File menu, click Page Setup and then click Landscape Orientation on the Page tab. Print a copy of the worksheet.
10. Save the workbook using the file name Local School District Disposables1.

2 Creating a Canadian Province Population Data Map

Problem: The Canadian government would like you to create a map showing the country's 1999 population by province (right side of Figure 9-88). You have been given a worksheet database of the 1999 population by province (upper-left corner of Figure 9-88).

Instructions: Perform the following tasks:

1. Open the workbook Canadian Province Population from the Data Disk.
2. Select the data range A2:B12. Using the Map button on the Standard toolbar, draw a data map of Canada in the range C1:J23. When the Multiple Maps Available dialog box displays, choose Canada. When the Microsoft Map Control dialog box displays, click its Close button. Click the Shade legend and then press the DELETE key to delete it.
3. Click the Map Labels button on the Microsoft Map toolbar (Figure 9-50 on page E 9.39). When the Map Labels dialog box displays, click Values from and then, if necessary, choose 1999 in the list. Click each province in the data map to display its population (Figure 9-88).
4. Double-click the map title and enter `1999 Canadian Population by Province` as the new title. Right-click the new title and use the Format Font command to change the title to 14 point bold. Drag the title to center it as shown in Figure 9-88.
5. Enter your name, course, computer laboratory exercise (Lab 9-2), date, and instructor name in the range, A18:A22. Print the worksheet. Save the workbook using the file name Canadian Province Population1.

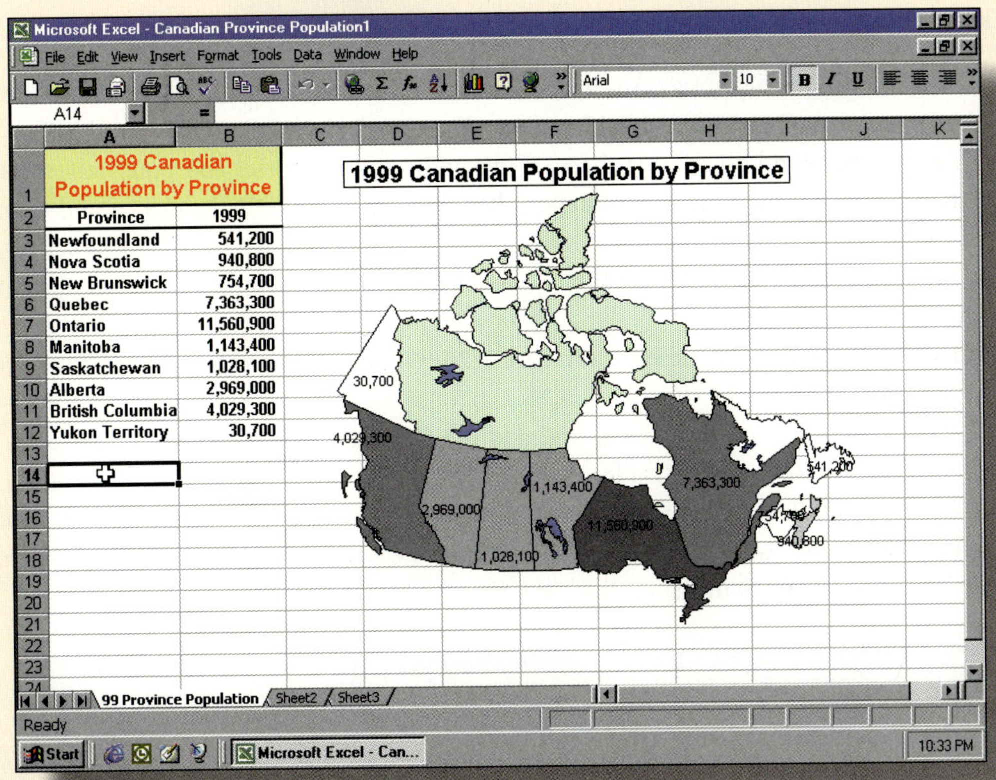

FIGURE 9-88

3 Creating a PivotChart and Associated PivotTable for an Order Entry Database

Problem: You are employed as a spreadsheet specialist in the order entry department of Bernita's Wholesale Restaurant Supply. You have been assigned the task of creating a PivotChart and PivotTable from the company's order entry worksheet database (Figure 9-89a on the next page). The PivotChart and PivotTable are shown in Figures 9-89b and 9-89c on page E 9.69.

Instructions: Perform the following tasks:

1. Open the workbook Bernita's Wholesale Restaurant Supply from the Data Disk.
2. Create the PivotChart shown in Figure 9-89b and PivotTable shown in Figure 9-89c on separate sheets. The PivotChart and PivotTable summarize dollar amount information by order number and order date. Use the PivotTable and PivotChart Wizard to create the PivotChart and associated PivotTable.
3. Add the title shown in Figure 9-89b.
4. Format the Y-axis labels to currency with no decimal places.
5. Rename the Chart1 tab PivotChart. Rename the Sheet1 tab PivotTable.

(continued)

Creating a PivotChart and Associated PivotTable for an Order Entry Database *(continued)*

6. Drag the Amount button to the Drop Data Items Here area (Y-axis). Drag the Order No and Order Date buttons to the Drop More Category Fields Here area (X-axis).
7. Select the Order Database and PivotTable sheets. Enter your name, course, computer laboratory exercise (Lab 9-3), date, and instructor name in the range A20:A24. Hold down the SHIFT key and then click the Order Database tab.
8. Print the worksheet, PivotChart, and PivotTable. Save the workbook using the file name Bernita's Wholesale Restaurant Supply1.
9. Click the Order Date box arrow to deselect the date 1/25/99. Print the PivotChart and PivotTable. Add the 1/25/99 date back in.
10. Remove the Order Number from the X-axis, and add the Description button to the right of the Order Date button. Print the PivotChart and PivotTable.
11. Close Bernita's Wholesale Restaurant Supply1 without saving changes, and then reopen it. Click the PivotTable tab. Drag the buttons to create three different views. Print the PivotTable for each view. Close the workbook without saving changes.

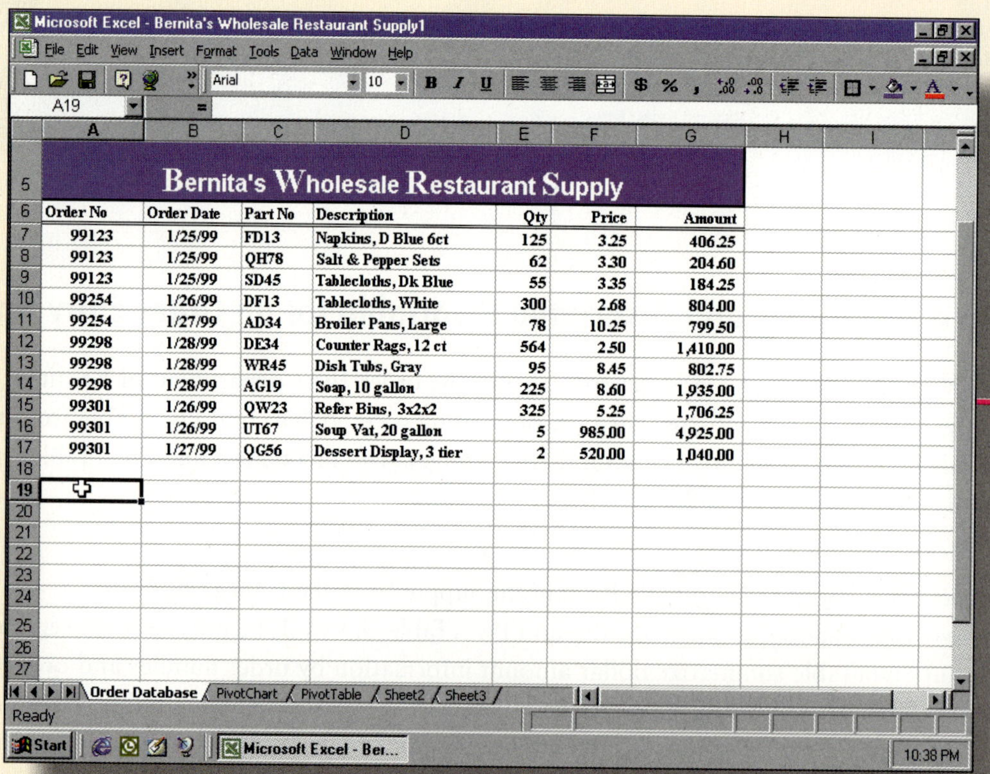

Bernita's Wholesale Restaurant Supply

Order No	Order Date	Part No	Description	Qty	Price	Amount
99123	1/25/99	FD13	Napkins, D Blue 6ct	125	3.25	406.25
99123	1/25/99	QH78	Salt & Pepper Sets	62	3.30	204.60
99123	1/25/99	SD45	Tablecloths, Dk Blue	55	3.35	184.25
99254	1/26/99	DF13	Tablecloths, White	300	2.68	804.00
99254	1/27/99	AD34	Broiler Pans, Large	78	10.25	799.50
99298	1/28/99	DE34	Counter Rags, 12 ct	564	2.50	1,410.00
99298	1/28/99	WR45	Dish Tubs, Gray	95	8.45	802.75
99298	1/28/99	AG19	Soap, 10 gallon	225	8.60	1,935.00
99301	1/26/99	QW23	Refer Bins, 3x2x2	325	5.25	1,706.25
99301	1/26/99	UT67	Soup Vat, 20 gallon	5	985.00	4,925.00
99301	1/27/99	QG56	Dessert Display, 3 tier	2	520.00	1,040.00

(a) Worksheet Database

Microsoft Excel - Bernita's Wholesale Restaurant Supply1

Drop Page Fields Here

Order Entry Information

Order No	Order Date	Sum of Amount
99123	1/25/99	
99254	1/26/99	
99254	1/27/99	
99298	1/28/99	
99301	1/26/99	
99301	1/27/99	

(b) PivotChart

Microsoft Excel - Bernita's Wholesale Restaurant Supply1

	A	B	C
3	Sum of Amount		
4	Order No	Order Date	Total
5	99123	1/25/99	795.1
6	99123 Total		795.1
7	99254	1/26/99	804
8		1/27/99	799.5
9	99254 Total		1603.5
10	99298	1/28/99	4147.75
11	99298 Total		4147.75
12	99301	1/26/99	6631.25
13		1/27/99	1040
14	99301 Total		7671.25
15	Grand Total		14217.6

(c) PivotTable

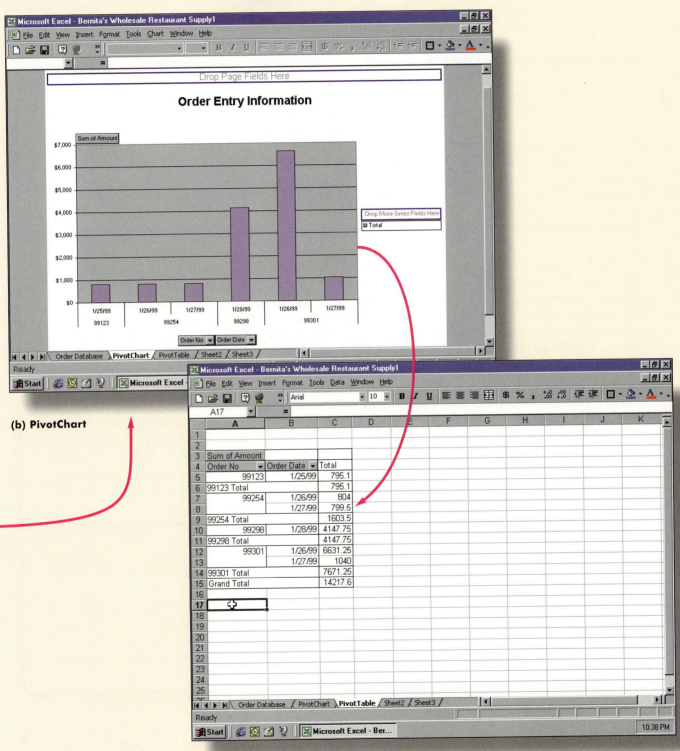

FIGURE 9-89

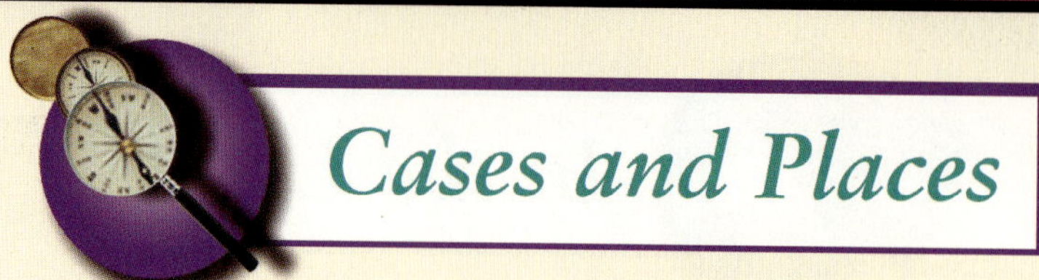

Cases and Places

The difficulty of these case studies varies:
◗ are the least difficult; ◗◗ are more difficult; and ◗◗◗ are the most difficult.

1 ◗ Open Burrito Land Analysis from the Data Disk. Import data from the table in the Access database TexasQ1 beginning in row 3. Import the text file IllinoisQ1 beginning in row 9. Copy the formulas in cell H3 and cell I3 through row 15. Enter your name, course, computer laboratory exercise (Cases and Places 9-1), date, and instructor name in the range A17:A21. Turn on Track Changes. Print the worksheet. Save the workbook using the file name Case 9-1. Route the workbook to three classmates. Tell them in the e-mail to respond within a day and make at least two changes each. When the workbook comes back to you, accept the changes. Print the worksheet. Save the workbook using the file name Case 9-1a.

2 ◗ Open the Sales Rep Database. Develop a PivotChart with the two Quota and two Sales amount fields in the Drop Data Items Here area (Y-axis) and the Gender and Age fields in the Drop More Category Fields Here (X-axis). Include a title and formatted Y-axis labels. Enter your name, course, computer laboratory exercise (Cases and Places 9-2), date, and instructor name in the range A17:A21. Save the workbook using the file name Case 9-2. Print the worksheet, PivotChart, and PivotTable. Display the PivotTable sheet. Drag the buttons to display five different views. Print the PivotTable for each.

3 ◗◗ The National Tornado Project maintains a database on the Internet about tornados in each state. The tornado data for the state of Indiana can be viewed at tornadoproject.com/alltorns/intorn.htm#top. Drag and drop three different county tables into a Word document. Remove excess spaces and insert commas between fields. Save the document as a text file. Open a new workbook in Excel, add appropriate column headings, and import the data into the workbook. Format the worksheet appropriately. Create a PivotChart and PivotTable. Print the worksheet. Print the PivotChart and PivotTable for three different views.

4 ◗◗ As an independent information specialist, World-Wide Producers has approached you for help. The company is considering building a new manufacturing center in one of five states: Illinois, Texas, Virginia, South Carolina, or Kansas. To help them decide, they want demographic data from each of the five states. Use the Find command on the Start menu to locate the MapStats.xls file, a workbook that accompanies Excel 2000. Find the most recent demographic information about the states, including Total Population, Number of Households, Total Businesses, and Total Employees, and copy it to a blank workbook. Develop a PivotChart and PivotTable to obtain different views of the data. Print five different views.

5 ◗◗◗ Using your own music recording library of CDs or tapes, create a database of the artists, musical selection title, type of music, recording medium, and year of recording. Create a PivotChart and PivotTable with year and type of music as the X-axis categories and recording medium as data (Y-axis). Print the worksheet, PivotChart, and PivotTable. Display the PivotTable sheet. Drag the buttons to display three different views. Print the PivotTable for each.

Microsoft Excel 2000

Creating a PivotTable List Web Page Using Excel

CASE PERSPECTIVE

LifeStyle Motorcycle Clothing & Apparel sells street apparel, dirt apparel, and motorcycle accessories through a nationwide sales force. The sales force is divided into districts within zones within regions. The management team consists of a sales manager for each region, an assistant manager for each zone, and a team leader for each district.

Following a year of dismal sales, Sturgis Davis was recently hired as the national sales manager. Sturgis's primary asset is his extensive cross industry and sales automation experiences. His immediate plan calls for developing an intranet-based sales reporting system that gives his management team up-to-date sales information to help make decisions.

As the spreadsheet specialist at LifeStyle Motorcycle Clothing & Apparel, Sturgis has asked you to take sales representative information supplied in a workbook and make it available to the managers and team leaders in an easy-to-use form. From your experience with Excel 2000, you know that you can create interactive Web pages. You also know that PivotTables are an ideal tool for analyzing data. You decide the best solution is to develop an interactive PivotTable list Web page.

Introduction

Excel 2000 allows you to save a workbook, a worksheet, a range of cells, or a chart as a Web page using the Save as Web Page command on the File menu. Excel also allows you to save worksheet data as a PivotTable list. A **PivotTable list** is a Web page that lets you analyze data using your Web browser, rather than Excel. Similar to a PivotTable report, a PivotTable list is an interactive table that allows you to change the view of data, filter data, and create summaries of the data. The difference between the two PivotTables is that a PivotTable report is manipulated in Excel, whereas a PivotTable list is manipulated in your Web browser.

To create a PivotTable list, you start with an Excel workbook (Figure 1a on the next page). You use the Save as Web Page command on the File menu to create the PivotTable list (Figure 1b on the next page). Once you display the PivotTable list in your Web browser, you can change the view of the data as shown in Figures 1c and 1d. Figure 1c shows the data in Figure 1b summarized by the sales representatives' education within gender. Figure 1d illustrates the filtering capabilities of a PivotTable list, showing only the rows that represent sales representatives who work in Region 1, Zone 2, District 2. The other records in the list (Figure 1b) are hidden.

For other users to interact with a PivotTable list, they must have the Office Web components installed and they must be using Microsoft Internet Explorer 4.01 or later. The Office Web components are installed automatically as part of the Office 2000 installation process.

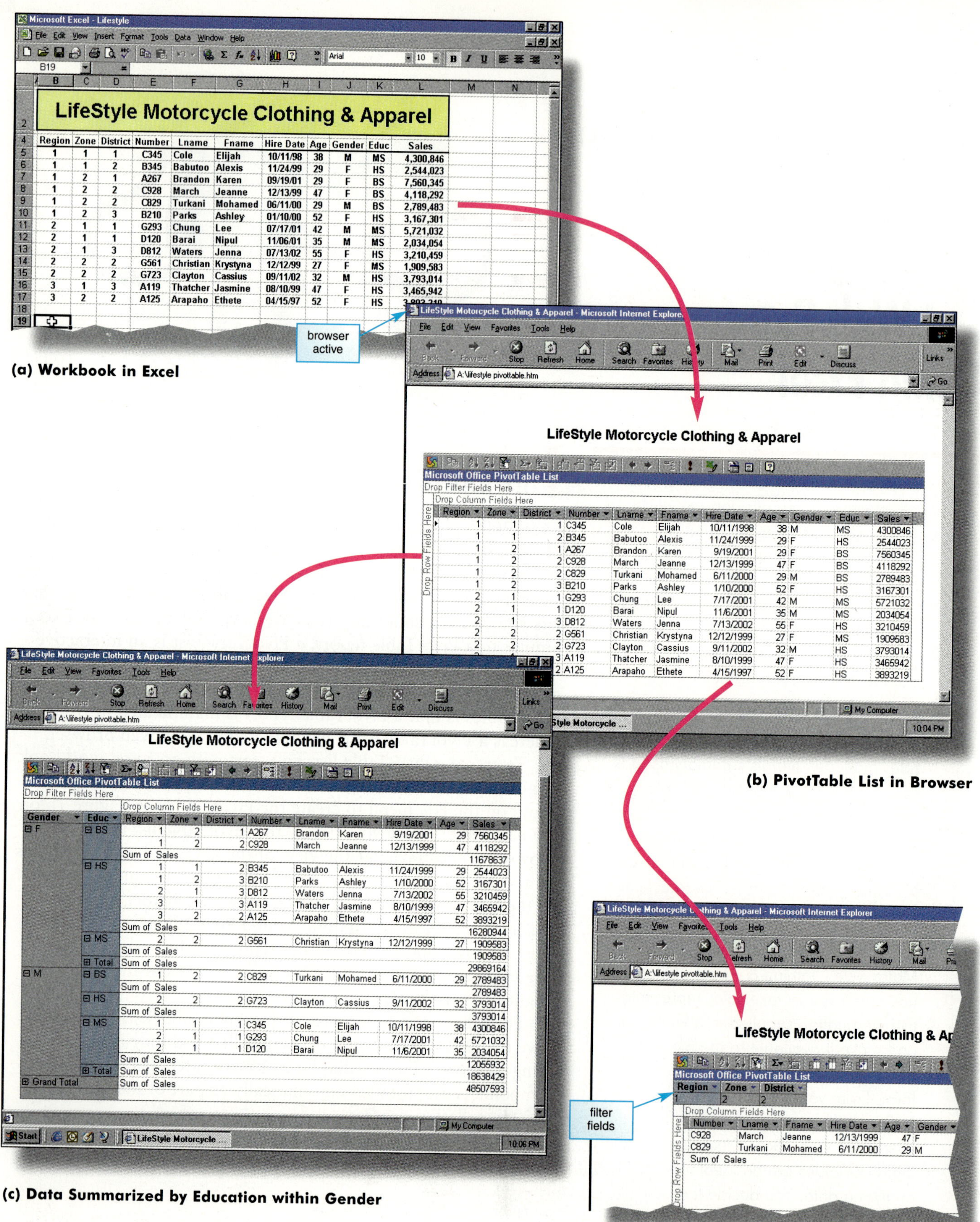
Microsoft Excel - Lifestyle
LifeStyle Motorcycle Clothing & Apparel
browser active
(a) Workbook in Excel
LifeStyle Motorcycle Clothing & Apparel - Microsoft Internet Explorer
Microsoft Office PivotTable List
Drop Filter Fields Here
Drop Column Fields Here
Drop Row Fields Here
(b) PivotTable List in Browser
(c) Data Summarized by Education within Gender
filter fields
(d) Only Region 1, Zone 2, District 2 Rows Display

FIGURE 1

PivotTables

For more information on PivotTables, visit the Excel 2000 More About Web page (www.scsite.com/ex2000/more.htm) and click PivotTables.

Saving a Worksheet Database as a PivotTable List

The first step in this project is to open the Lifestyle workbook (Figure 1a) and save the database in the range B4:L17 as a PivotTable list.

To Save a Worksheet Database as a PivotTable List

1. **Insert the Data Disk in drive A. Start Excel and then open the workbook Lifestyle on drive A. Reset your toolbars as described in Appendix C. Select the range B4:L17. Click File on the menu bar and then point to Save as Web Page.**

The File menu displays (Figure 2).

Save as Web Page command

File menu

database in range B4:L17 selected

FIGURE 2

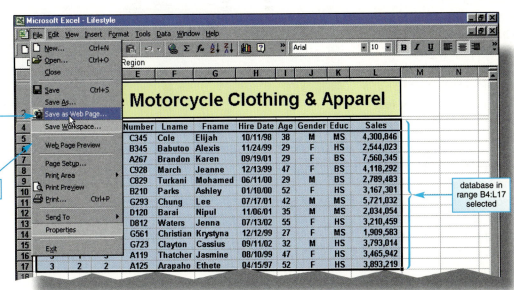

2. **Click Save as Web Page. When the Save As dialog box displays, type** `lifestyle pivottable` **in the File name text box. If necessary, click the Save in box arrow and then select 3½ Floppy (A:). Point to the Publish button.**

The Save As dialog box displays as shown in Figure 3.

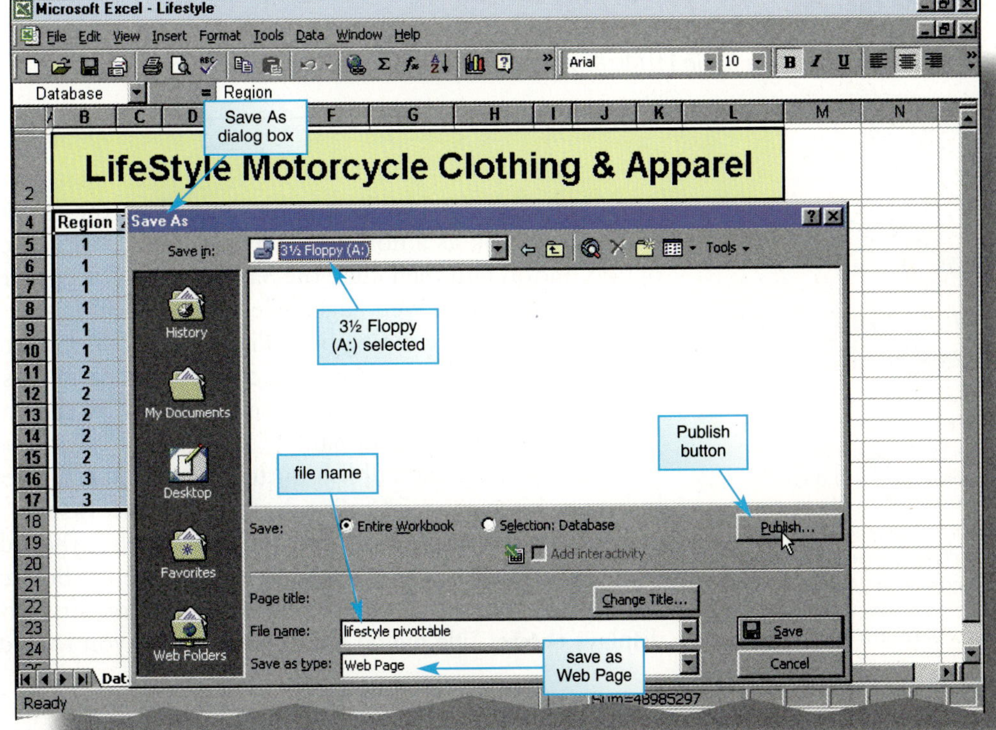

FIGURE 3

3 Click the Publish button. When the Publish as Web Page dialog box displays, click the Choose box arrow and then click Range of cells. Click Add interactivity with, click the Add interactivity with box arrow, and then click PivotTable functionality. Click the Change button. When the Set Title dialog box displays, type `LifeStyle Motorcycle Clothing & Apparel` **in the Title text box. Point to the OK button.**

The Publish as Web Page and Set Title dialog boxes display as shown in Figure 4. Selecting the Add interactivity with check box indicates that the Web page will be created with functionality.

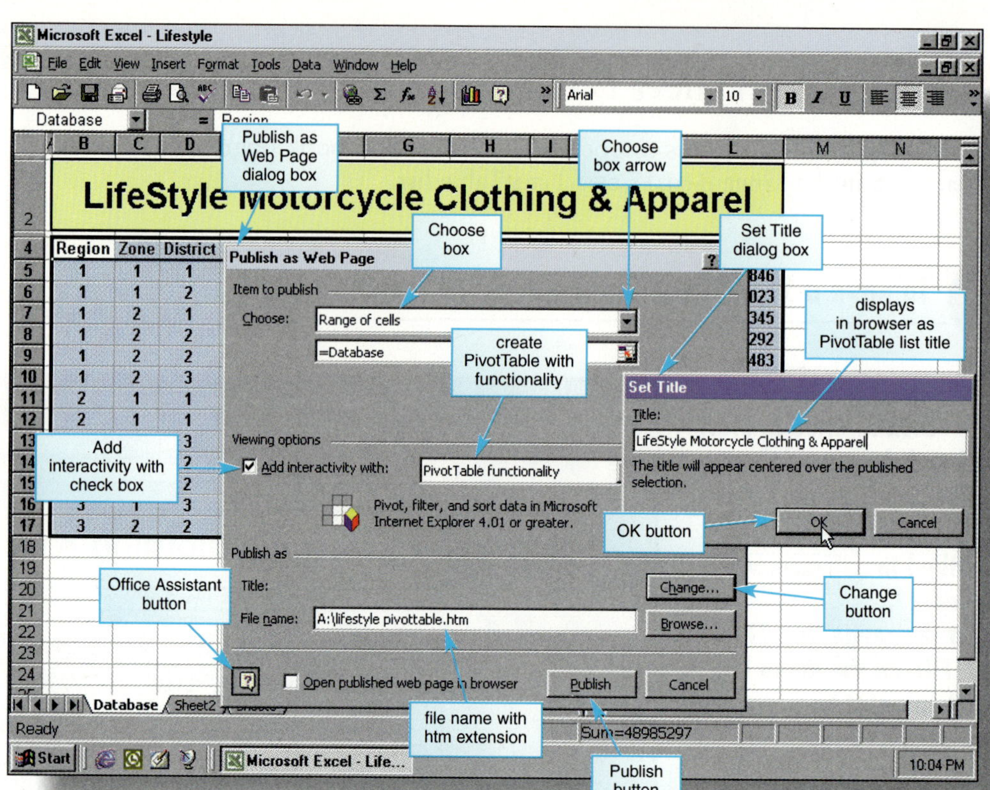

FIGURE 4

4 Click the OK button. Click the Publish button. Click the Close button on the right side of the Excel title bar. Click the Yes button in the Microsoft Excel dialog box to save the changes.

Excel saves the PivotTable list in HTML (hypertext markup language) format on drive A.

PivotTable Lists and Associated Charts

Along with a PivotTable list, you can include a chart that displays the same data graphically. If you display the PivotTable list in your browser and change the view, you will see the same changes in the chart.

If you click the Save button in Figure 3 on the previous page, Excel saves the entire workbook as a non-interactive Web page. If you click the Selection: Database option button and then click the Save button, Excel saves the selected range B4:L17 as a non-interactive Web page. Selecting the Add interactivity with check box in the Publish as Web Page dialog box (Figure 4) allows you to save the selected range as an interactive Web page. An **interactive Web page** allows you to change the values in the cells in your browser, but it does not give you the ability to rotate fields unless you add PivotTable functionality.

When you use the Publish button, you must tell Excel what you want to publish. In Figure 4, the range of cells selected on the worksheet is selected in the Choose list box. In the Viewing options area, once you select the Add interactivity with check box, the adjacent list box becomes active. The list box gives you two choices – Spreadsheet functionality or PivotTable functionality. The Change button in Figure 4 displays the **Set Title dialog box**, which allows you to add a title to the PivotTable list.

Viewing the PivotTable List Using Your Browser

With the PivotTable list saved as an HTML file, the next step is to view it using your browser as shown in the following steps.

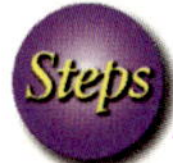

Steps To View a PivotTable List Using Your Browser

1. **Click the Launch Internet Explorer Browser button on the Quick Launch toolbar.**

2. **When the Internet Explorer window displays, type** a:\lifestyle pivottable.htm **in the Address bar, and then press the ENTER key.**

   The PivotTable list, lifestyle pivottable.htm, displays (Figure 5).

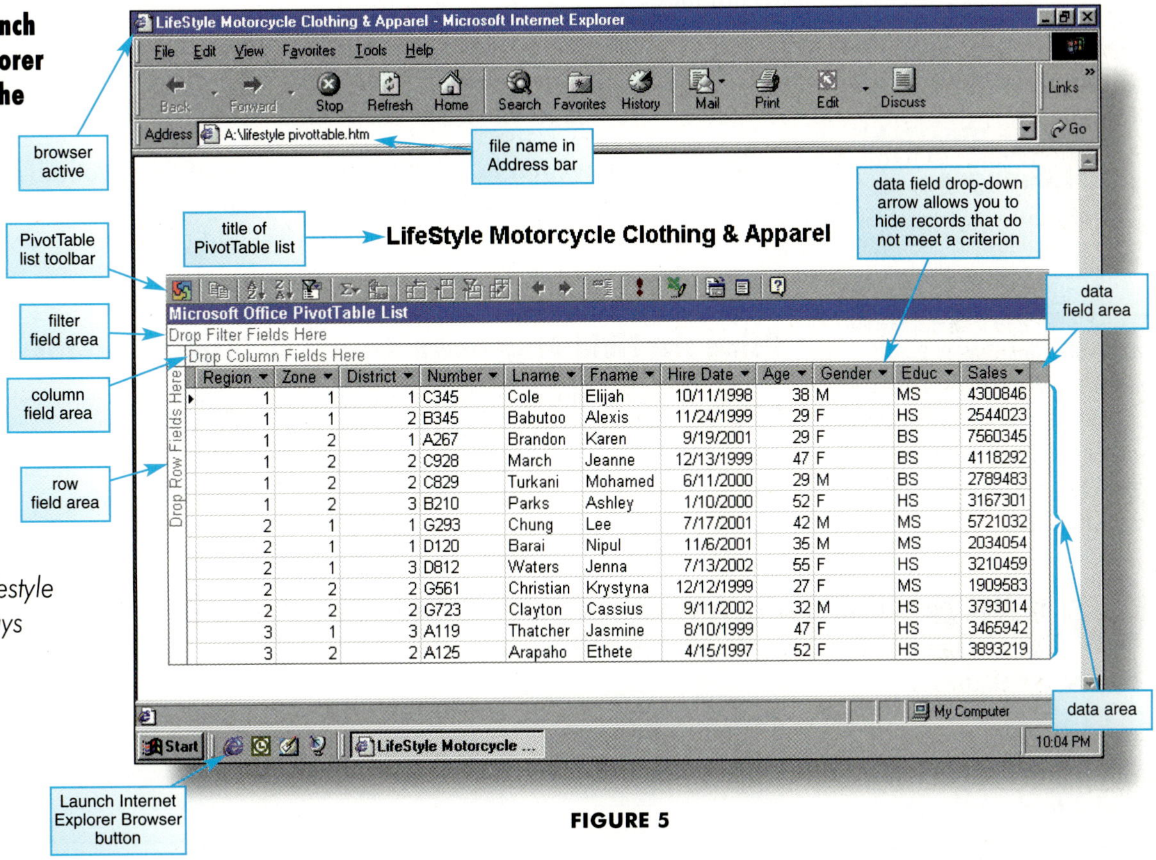

browser active
PivotTable list toolbar
filter field area
column field area
row field area
Launch Internet Explorer Browser button
file name in Address bar
title of PivotTable list
data field drop-down arrow allows you to hide records that do not meet a criterion
data field area
data area
LifeStyle Motorcycle Clothing & Apparel - Microsoft Internet Explorer
File Edit View Favorites Tools Help
Back Forward Stop Refresh Home Search Favorites History Mail Print Edit Discuss
Links
Address A:\lifestyle pivottable.htm
Go
LifeStyle Motorcycle Clothing & Apparel
Microsoft Office PivotTable List
Drop Filter Fields Here
Drop Column Fields Here
Drop Row Fields Here
Region Zone District Number Lname Fname Hire Date Age Gender Educ Sales
1 1 1 C345 Cole Elijah 10/11/1998 38 M MS 4300846
1 1 2 B345 Babutoo Alexis 11/24/1999 29 F HS 2544023
1 2 1 A267 Brandon Karen 9/19/2001 29 F BS 7560345
1 2 2 C928 March Jeanne 12/13/1999 47 F BS 4118292
1 2 2 C829 Turkani Mohamed 6/11/2000 29 M BS 2789483
1 2 3 B210 Parks Ashley 1/10/2000 52 F HS 3167301
2 1 1 G293 Chung Lee 7/17/2001 42 M MS 5721032
2 1 1 D120 Barai Nipul 11/6/2001 35 M MS 2034054
2 1 3 D812 Waters Jenna 7/13/2002 55 F HS 3210459
2 2 2 G561 Christian Krystyna 12/12/1999 27 F MS 1909583
2 2 2 G723 Clayton Cassius 9/11/2002 32 M HS 3793014
3 1 3 A119 Thatcher Jasmine 8/10/1999 47 F HS 3465942
3 2 2 A125 Arapaho Ethete 4/15/1997 52 F HS 3893219
My Computer
Start
LifeStyle Motorcycle ...
10:04 PM

FIGURE 5

The PivotTable list Web page in Figure 5 resembles an Excel worksheet with the column and row structure. The Address bar displays the URL. The title above the columns and rows is the same as the entry made in the Set Title dialog box shown in Figure 4. The toolbar immediately below the title includes buttons that allow you to complete tasks quickly, such as copy, sort, filter, calculate summaries, and move fields. Figure 6 identifies the buttons on the PivotTable list toolbar.

Office logo cube
Sort Ascending
AutoFilter
Subtotal
Move To Column Area
Move To Detail
Demote
Refresh
Property Toolbox
Help
Copy
Sort Descending
AutoCalc
Move To Row Area
Move To Filter Area
Promote
Expand or Collapse
Export to Excel
Field List

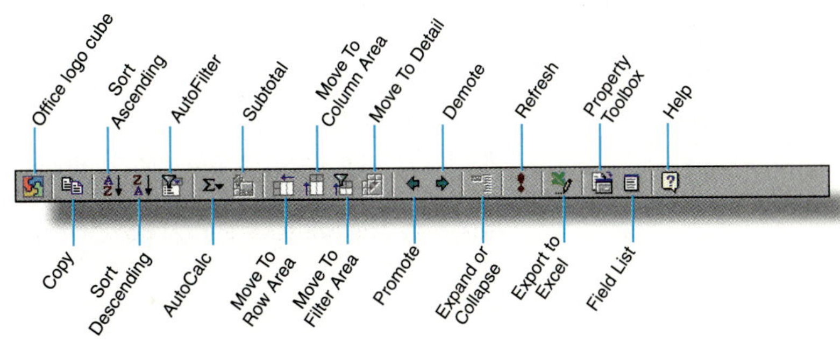

FIGURE 6

The area below the toolbar is divided into five areas as shown in Figure 5 on the previous page: (1) data area; (2) data field area; (3) row field area; (4) column field area; and (5) filter field area. The **data area** contains the data. Each entry in the data area is called an **item**. In the **data field area**, a **data field** at the top of each column identifies the data below it. For example, the Age data field identifies the ages in the same column. Each data field contains a **field drop-down arrow** that allows you to set up filters to display only records that meet a criterion. You drag data fields to the **row field area** on the left side of the PivotTable list and the **column field area** at the top of the PivotTable list to display different views of the data. You also can drag data fields to the **filter field area** to display different views of the data using filtering techniques.

More About 2000

Undoing PivotTable List Changes

If you make several changes to a PivotTable list and wish to restore it to its original view, quit your browser, launch your browser, and then display the PivotTable list again.

Changing the View of the PivotTable List

This section shows you how to change the view of the PivotTable list by (1) using the field drop-down arrows; (2) adding summary totals; (3) sorting columns of data; (4) dragging data fields to the row field area; and (5) dragging data fields to the filter field area.

Using the Field Drop-Down Arrows to Display Records That Pass a Test

You can use the field drop-down arrows at the right side of the data fields to hide rows of data that do not pass a test. This allows you to work with a subset of the data. For example, the following steps hide the rows of data representing males, leaving only the rows of data representing females displaying in the PivotTable list.

To Use Field Drop-Down Arrows to Display Records That Pass a Test

1 Click the Gender data field drop-down arrow, click M (for male) to clear the check box, and then point to the OK button.

The Gender drop-down list displays. The list of different items in the Gender column of data displays as check boxes along with a check box titled (Show All). The M check box does not have a check mark (Figure 7).

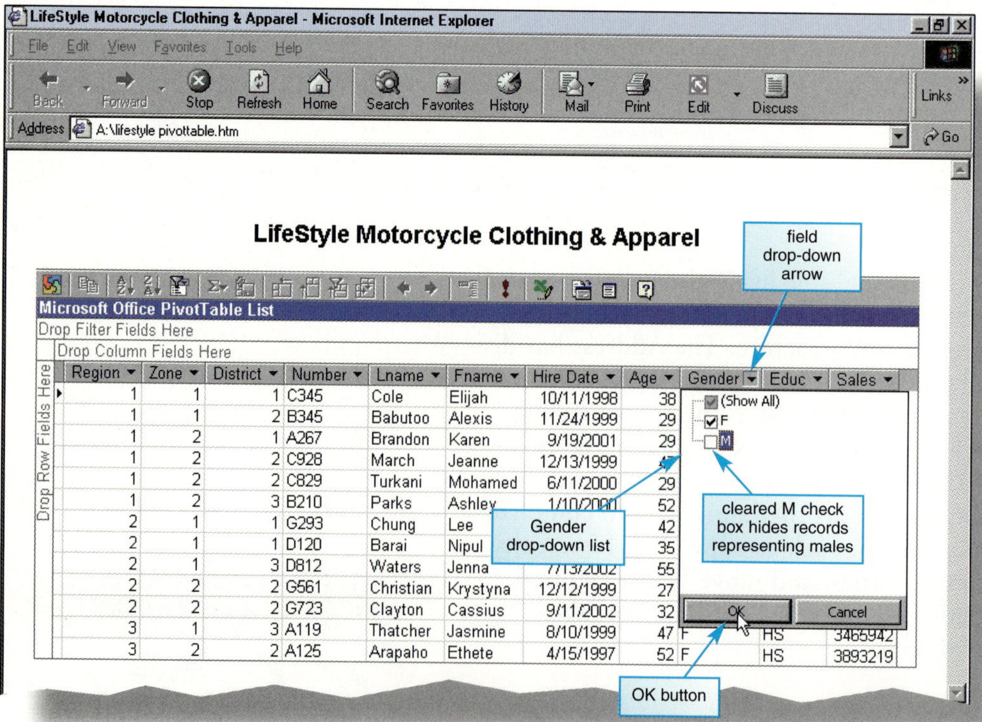

FIGURE 7

Click the OK button.

Only the rows of data representing females display (Figure 8). The rows of data representing males are hidden.

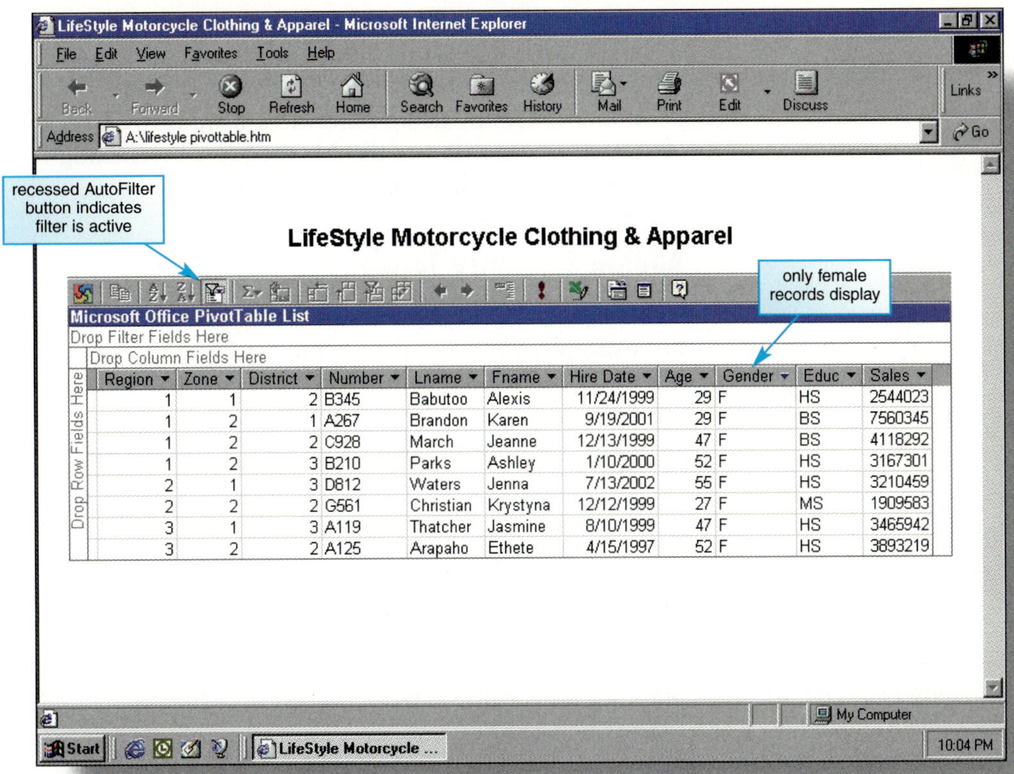

Region	Zone	District	Number	Lname	Fname	Hire Date	Age	Gender	Educ	Sales
1	1	2	B345	Babutoo	Alexis	11/24/1999	29	F	HS	2544023
1	2	1	A267	Brandon	Karen	9/19/2001	29	F	BS	7560345
1	2	2	C928	March	Jeanne	12/13/1999	47	F	BS	4118292
1	2	3	B210	Parks	Ashley	1/10/2000	52	F	HS	3167301
2	1	3	D812	Waters	Jenna	7/13/2002	55	F	HS	3210459
2	2	2	G561	Christian	Krystyna	12/12/1999	27	F	MS	1909583
3	1	3	A119	Thatcher	Jasmine	8/10/1999	47	F	HS	3465942
3	2	2	A125	Arapaho	Ethete	4/15/1997	52	F	HS	3893219

FIGURE 8

3 **Click the AutoFilter button on the toolbar.**

The filter is disabled and all rows of data display (Figure 9). The **AutoFilter button** *turns criteria on and off.*

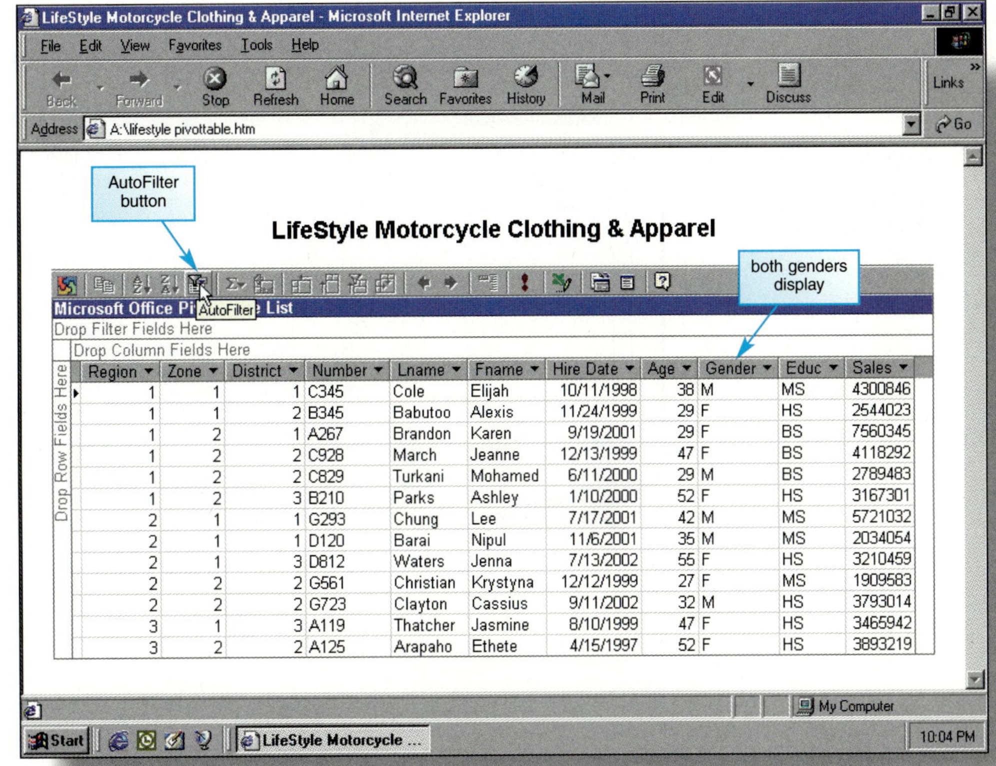

Region	Zone	District	Number	Lname	Fname	Hire Date	Age	Gender	Educ	Sales
1	1	1	C345	Cole	Elijah	10/11/1998	38	M	MS	4300846
1	1	2	B345	Babutoo	Alexis	11/24/1999	29	F	HS	2544023
1	2	1	A267	Brandon	Karen	9/19/2001	29	F	BS	7560345
1	2	2	C928	March	Jeanne	12/13/1999	47	F	BS	4118292
1	2	2	C829	Turkani	Mohamed	6/11/2000	29	M	BS	2789483
1	2	3	B210	Parks	Ashley	1/10/2000	52	F	HS	3167301
2	1	1	G293	Chung	Lee	7/17/2001	42	M	MS	5721032
2	1	1	D120	Barai	Nipul	11/6/2001	35	M	MS	2034054
2	1	3	D812	Waters	Jenna	7/13/2002	55	F	HS	3210459
2	2	2	G561	Christian	Krystyna	12/12/1999	27	F	MS	1909583
2	2	2	G723	Clayton	Cassius	9/11/2002	32	M	HS	3793014
3	1	3	A119	Thatcher	Jasmine	8/10/1999	47	F	HS	3465942
3	2	2	A125	Arapaho	Ethete	4/15/1997	52	F	HS	3893219

FIGURE 9

Summary Functions

The type of data in a field determines whether a summary function is available or not. For example, if a field contains dates, then the Sum function is not available. If a field contains text, you cannot use the Sum, Min, or Max function, but you can use Count.

When you use a field drop-down arrow to filter the data, the arrow changes to the color blue. It remains blue until you disable the filter by using the AutoFilter button or selecting the Show All check box (Figure 7 on page EW 2.6). You can add additional filters by using other field drop-down arrows. Thus, you can display a subset of a subset. If you disable the filter by clicking the AutoFilter button and then select new filters, the original disabled filter is lost.

Adding Summary Totals

A PivotTable list is more useful if you add summaries to key columns of data. For example, you can add a summary to the Sales column in Figure 9 on the previous page. Four summary functions are available through the AutoCalc button on the toolbar. The four **summary functions** are Sum, Count, Min, and Max. The following steps add the Sum summary function to the Sales column of data.

To Add a Summary Total to a Column of Data

1. **Click the Sales data field to select the entire column. Click the AutoCalc button on the toolbar and then point to Sum.**

The PivotTable list displays as shown in Figure 10.

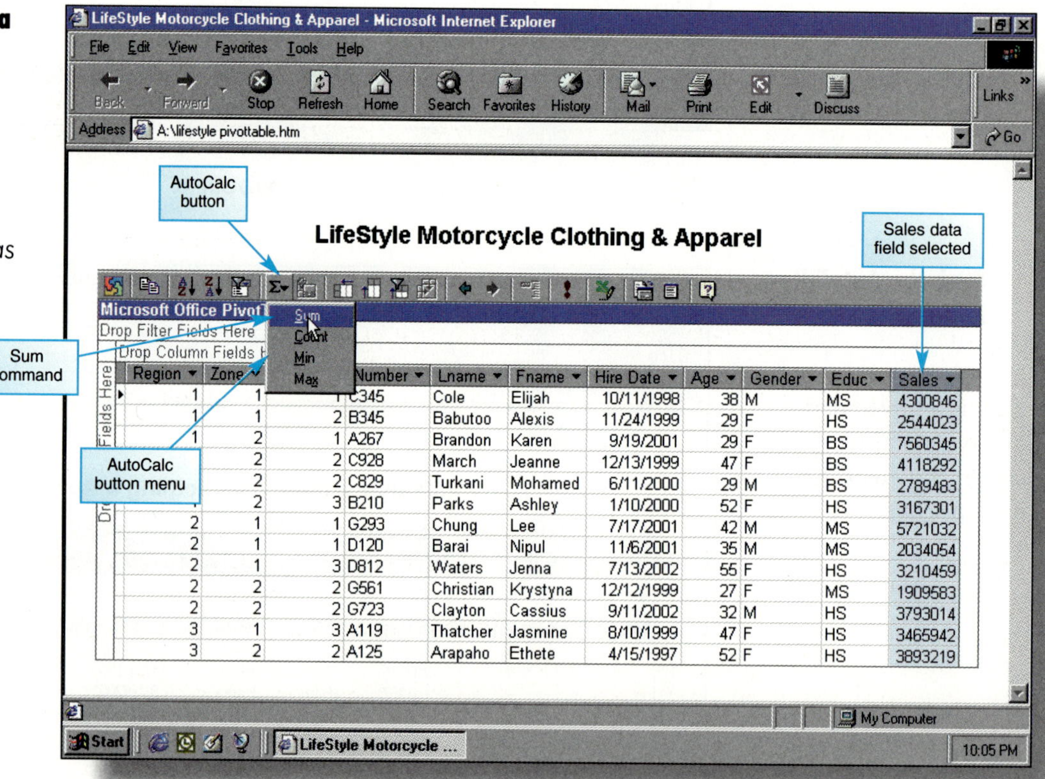

FIGURE 10

2 **Click Sum.**

A grand total displays below the Sales column of data (Figure 11).

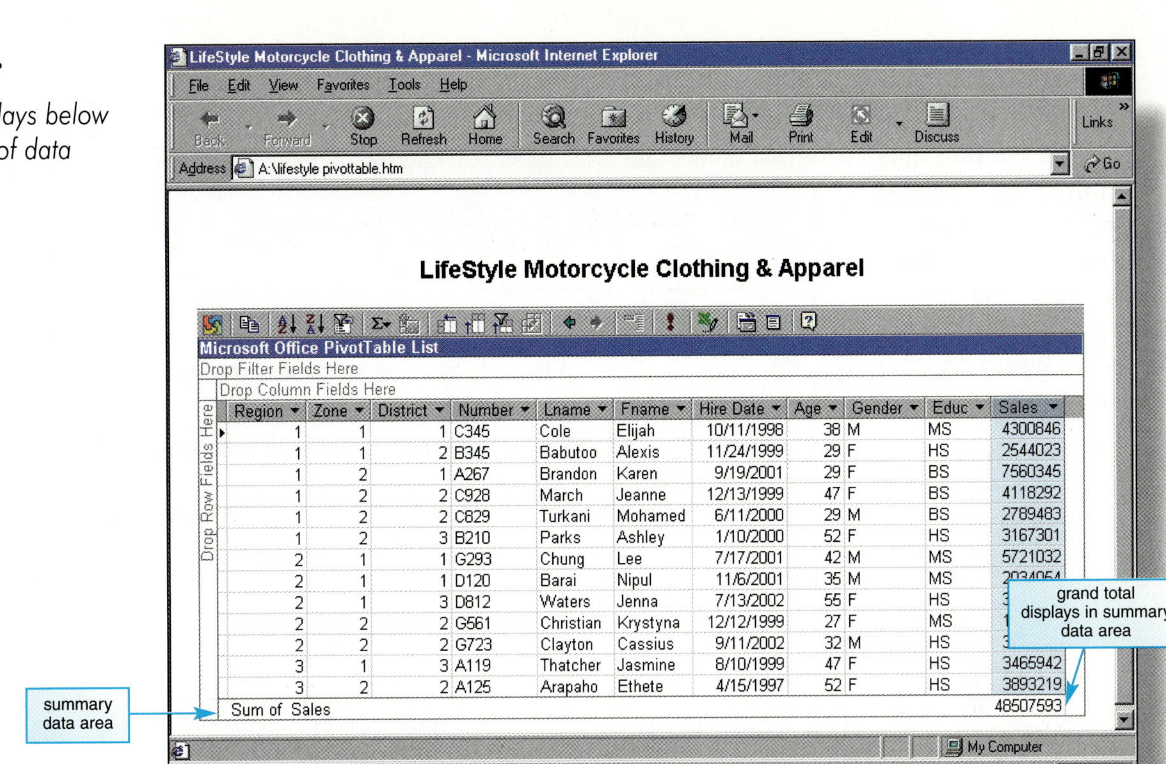

FIGURE 11

One at a time, you can select all four of the summary functions shown on the AutoCalc button menu in Figure 10. Each time you select a summary function, a new summary line is added to the summary data area.

Sorting Columns of Data

The data in a PivotTable list is easier to work with and more meaningful if you arrange the data sequentially based on one or more fields. The sort routine available with a PivotTable list is similar to Excel in that it sorts the data using the current order of the records. Thus, if you need to sort on more than one column of data, sort the minor field first on up to the major field.

The step on the next page sorts the PivotTable list in ascending sequence by education within gender.

Sort Order

The order in which numbers, text, and special characters are sorted depends on the source data and your regional settings in the Windows Control Panel.

To Sort Columns of Data

1 Click the Educ data field and then click the Sort Ascending button on the toolbar. Click the Gender data field and then click the Sort Ascending button on the toolbar.

The data in the PivotTable list is sorted by education within gender (Figure 12).

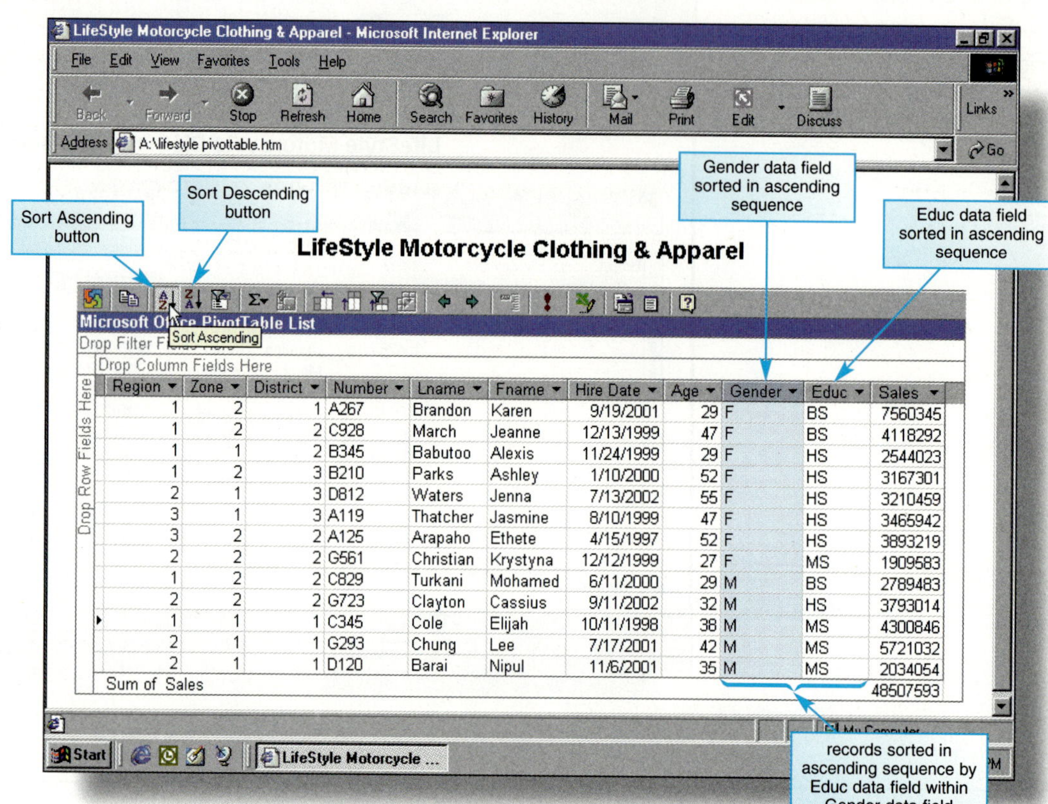

FIGURE 12

Sorting

To undo a sort and return the data to its previous order, click the recessed Sort Ascending or Sort Descending button.

With the data sorted by Educ within Gender, you now can change the view of the data by moving these data fields to the drop areas to change the view of the PivotTable list.

Dragging Data Fields to the Row Field Area

Moving data fields to the drop areas changes the view. The **drop areas** are above and to the left of the data area. Actually, you can move any data field to a drop area whether or not you first sort the column of data, but moving a data field whose column data has not been sorted to a row field or column field area often results in a useless display. The following steps drag the sorted Gender and Educ data fields to the row field area on the left side of the PivotTable list to generate a new view. The last step returns the PivotTable list to its original view.

To Drag Data Fields to the Row Field Area

1 **Drag the Gender data field to the row field area. Drag the Educ data field to the row field area and to the right of the Gender field.**

The PivotTable list changes dramatically, showing subtotals for each education category and each gender category (Figure 13).

2 **When you are finished viewing the PivotTable list, drag the Educ and Gender data fields to their original locations in the data area.**

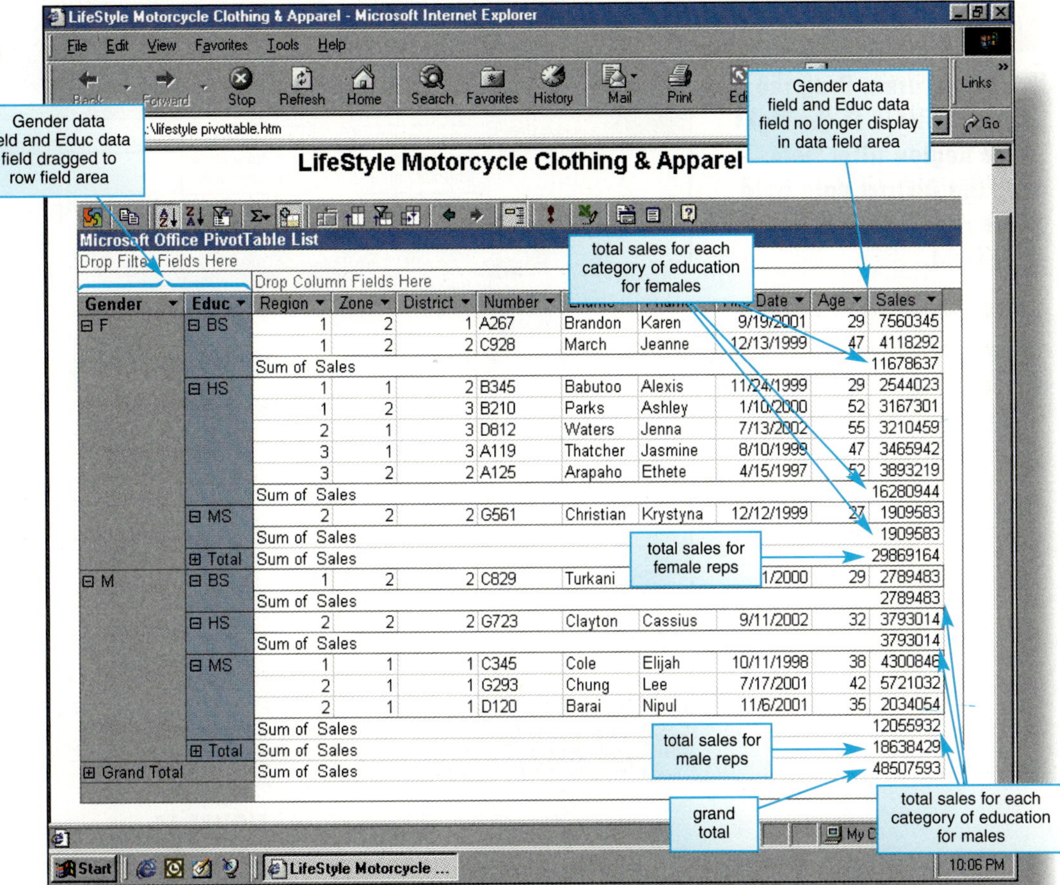

Gender	Educ	Region	Zone	District	Number	Lname	Fname	Hire Date	Age	Sales
⊟ F	⊟ BS	1	2	1	A267	Brandon	Karen	9/19/2001	29	7560345
		1	2	2	C928	March	Jeanne	12/13/1999	47	4118292
		Sum of Sales								11678637
	⊟ HS	1	1	2	B345	Babutoo	Alexis	11/24/1999	29	2544023
		1	2	3	B210	Parks	Ashley	1/10/2000	52	3167301
		2	1	3	D812	Waters	Jenna	7/13/2002	55	3210459
		3	1	3	A119	Thatcher	Jasmine	8/10/1999	47	3465942
		3	2	2	A125	Arapaho	Ethete	4/15/1997	52	3893219
		Sum of Sales								16280944
	⊟ MS	2	2	2	G561	Christian	Krystyna	12/12/1999	27	1909583
		Sum of Sales								1909583
	⊞ Total	Sum of Sales								29869164
⊟ M	⊟ BS	1	2	2	C829	Turkani		1/2000	29	2789483
		Sum of Sales								2789483
	⊟ HS	2	2	2	G723	Clayton	Cassius	9/11/2002	32	3793014
		Sum of Sales								3793014
	⊟ MS	1	1	1	C345	Cole	Elijah	10/11/1998	38	4300846
		2	1	1	G293	Chung	Lee	7/17/2001	42	5721032
		2	1	1	D120	Barai	Nipul	11/6/2001	35	2034054
		Sum of Sales								12055932
	⊞ Total	Sum of Sales								18638429
⊞ Grand Total		Sum of Sales								48507593

FIGURE 13

When you drag a data field to a drop area, the data field is moved rather than copied. Thus, in Figure 13 the data field area no longer contains the Gender and Educ data fields. They are now in the row field area. In Figure 12, only one total displayed at the bottom of the PivotTable list. In Figure 13, after dragging the two data fields, eight subtotals and one grand total display and the rows of data are divided into categories based on their respective Educ and Gender values.

Dragging Data Fields to the Filter Field Area

Another way to manipulate the view of the PivotTable list is to drag data fields to the filter field area at the top of the PivotTable list. When you drag a data field to this drop area, the data field maintains the field drop-down arrow, which allows you to apply a filter to the data. The steps on the next page drag the Region, Zone, and District data fields to the filter field area and then apply a filter.

Dragging Fields to Drop Areas

When you drag a data field to the row field area, each unique data item within the field displays down the rows of the PivotTable list. When you drag a data field to the column field area, each unique data item within the field displays across the columns of the PivotTable list.

Steps To Drag Data Fields to the Filter Field Area and Apply a Filter

1 Drag the Region data field to the filter field area. Drag the Zone data field to the right of the Region filter field. Drag the District data field to the right of the Zone filter field.

The PivotTable list displays as shown in Figure 14.

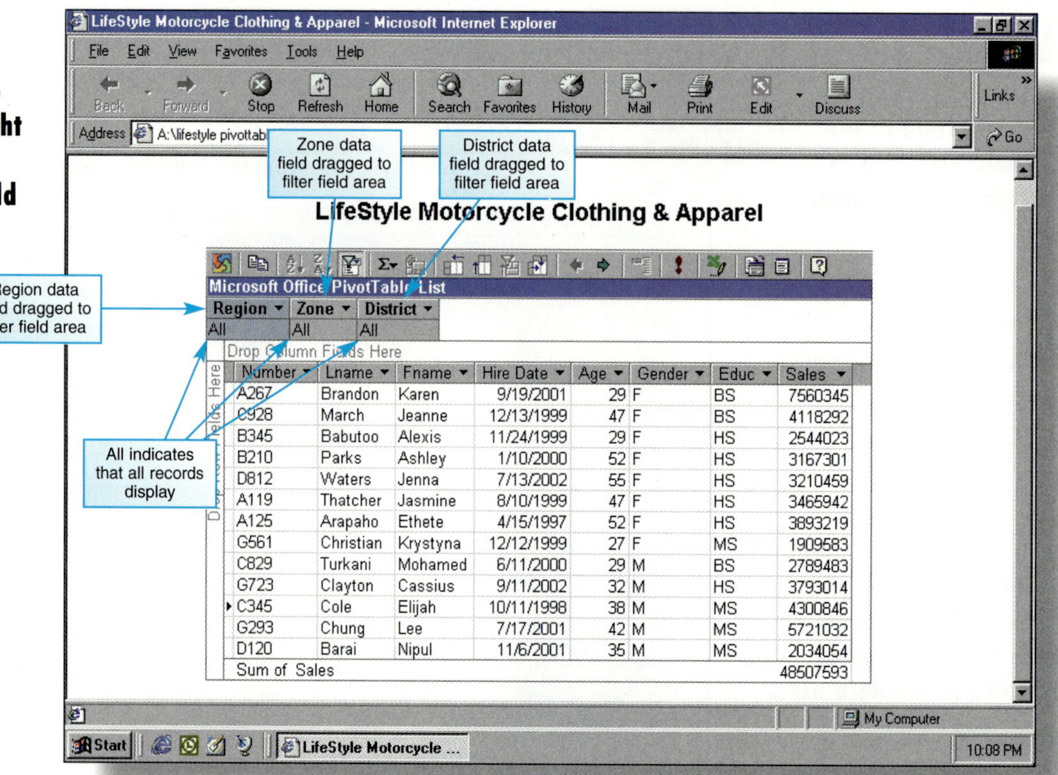

FIGURE 14

2 Click the Region data field drop-down arrow, click 1, and then click the OK button. Click the Zone data field drop-down arrow, click 2, and then click the OK button. Click the District data field drop-down arrow, click 2, and then click the OK button.

Only two rows of data display (Figure 15). The remaining rows of data failed to pass the test of belonging to Region 1, Zone 2, and District 2.

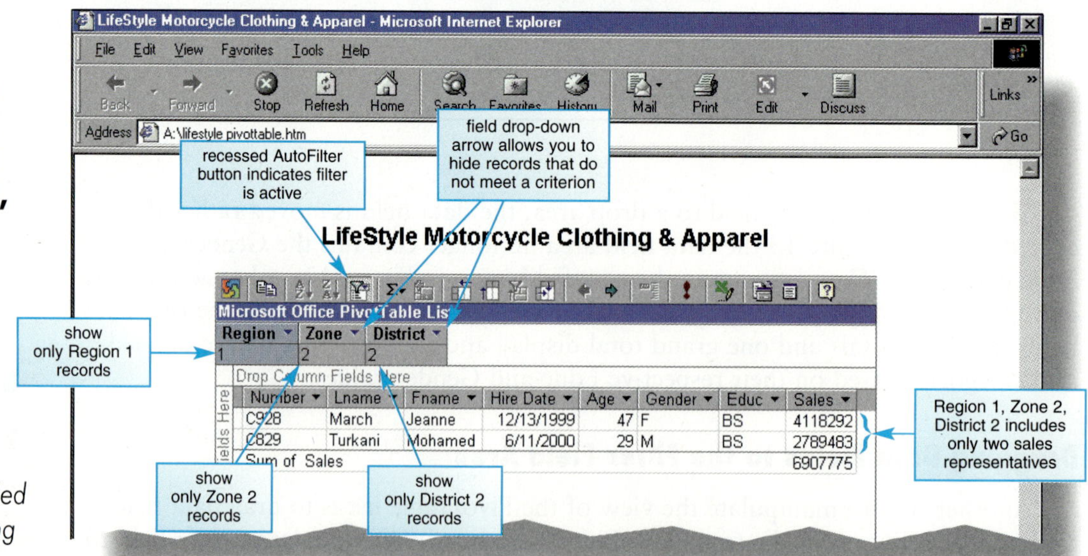

FIGURE 15

3 When you are finished viewing the PivotTable list in its current form, click the AutoFilter button on the toolbar to disable the filter. One at a time, drag the three filter fields back to their original position in the data field area.

You could have applied the filters to the data fields in the data field area, rather than dragging them to the filter field area. By dragging these fields to the filter field area, however, the rows that pass the test are cleaner and easier to read. For example, you do not have the Region, Zone, and District data fields repeating the same numbers over and over again as was the case in Figure 8 on page EW 2.7 when the filter was applied to the Gender data field.

Microsoft Certification

The Microsoft Office User Specialist (MOUS) Certification program provides an opportunity for you to obtain a valuable industry credential - proof that you have the Excel 2000 skills required by employers. For more information, see Appendix D or visit the Shelly Cashman Series MOUS Web page at www.scsite.com/off2000/cert.htm.

Removing Fields and Adding Fields to a PivotTable List

The more data fields you have in a PivotTable list, the more difficult it is to interpret the data. The following steps show how to remove the Number data field and then add the field back to the data area.

To Remove Fields from and Add Fields to a PivotTable List

1 Click the Field List button on the toolbar to display the PivotTable Field List window. Right-click the Number data field. Point to Remove Field on the shortcut menu.

The PivotTable Field List window displays a list of all the data fields in the PivotTable list (Figure 16). The Number data field and its data are selected and the shortcut menu displays. Most of the commands on the shortcut menu in Figure 16 are the same as the buttons on the toolbar.

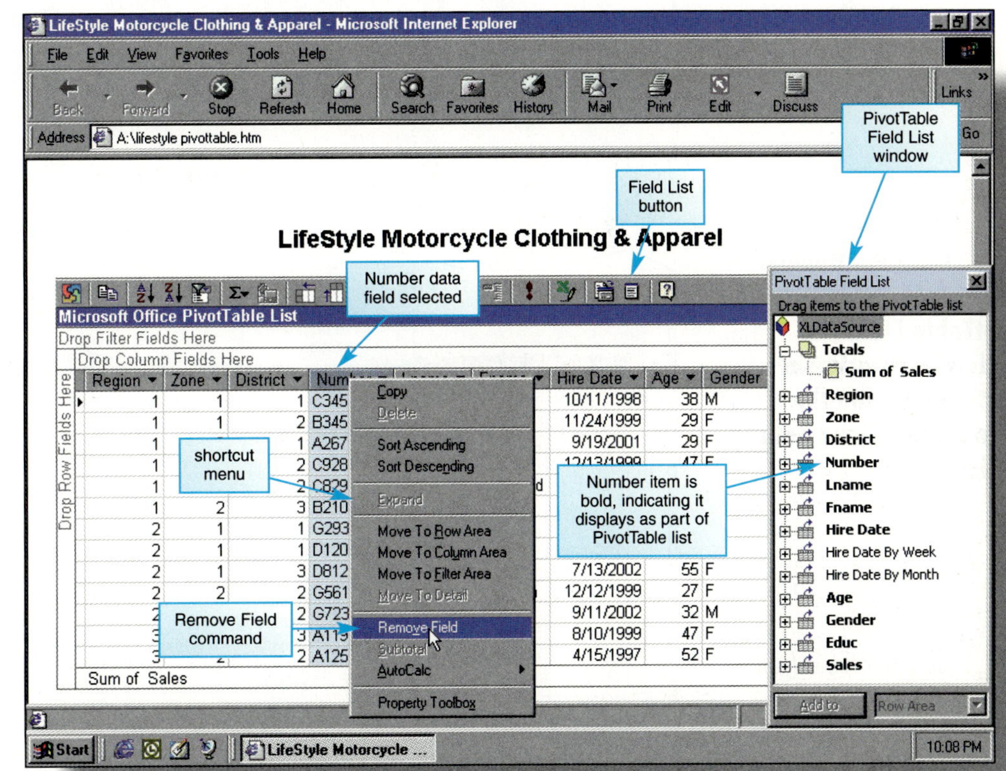

FIGURE 16

2 Click Remove Field.

The Number data field and its column of data are hidden. The word Number in the PivotTable Field List window is regular font style, whereas the active data fields are bold in the PivotTable Field List window. (Figure 17).

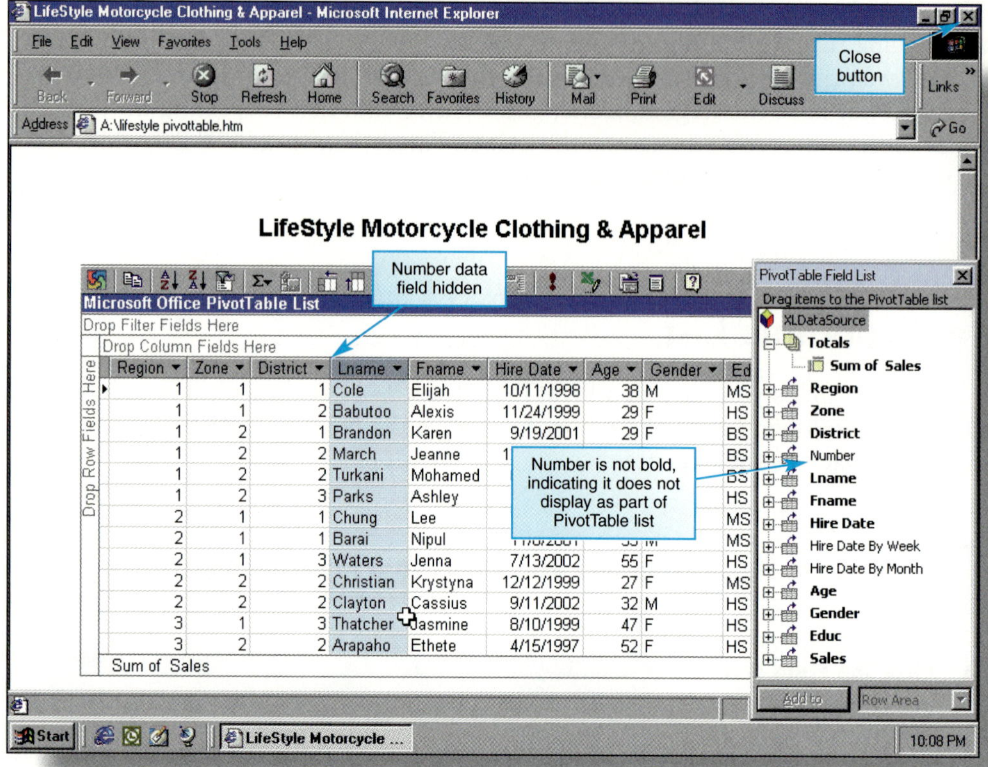

FIGURE 17

3 Drag the Number data field from the PivotTable Field List window to its original location between the District and Lname data fields.

The Number data field is added to the data area in the PivotTable list (Figure 18). The word Number is now bold in the PivotTable Field List window.

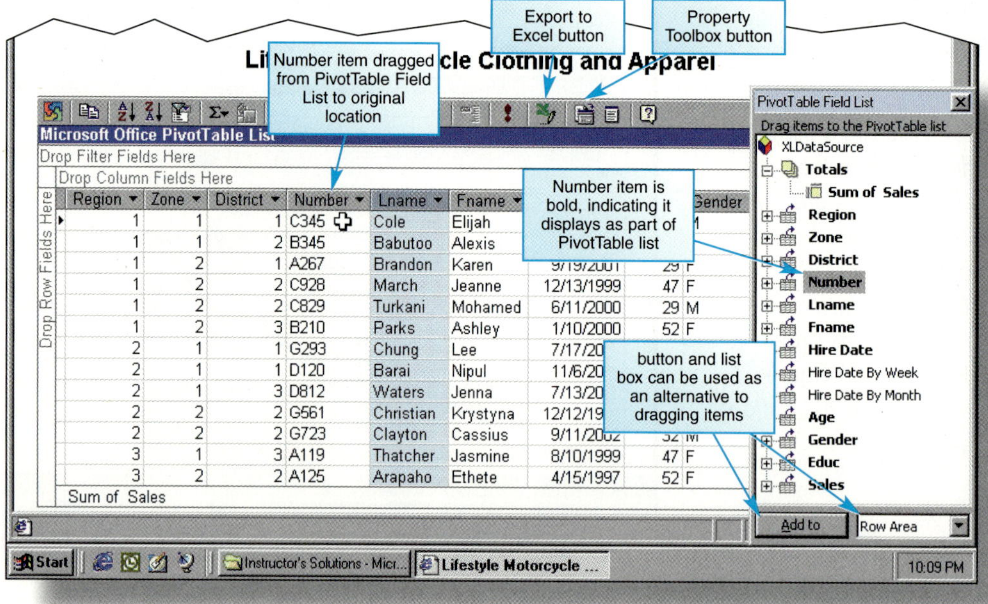

FIGURE 18

You can remove (hide) as many data fields as you want from the data area to simplify the PivotTable list. When you add data fields, you can insert them at any location. For example, you could have added the Number data field anywhere in the data area. You cannot duplicate a data field. That is, the Number data field can show up only once in the data area.

The two fields in the PivotTable Field List (Hire Date By Week and Hire Date By Month) can be used to change the view. If you click the plus signs to the left of these two fields, you can drag the date-related data fields to the drop areas and use the field drop-down arrow to establish filters.

Besides removing fields and adding fields, you can move data fields from one location in the data area to another by dragging.

Improving the Appearance of a PivotTable List

You can improve the appearance of the PivotTable list using the **Property Toolbox button** (Figure 18). For example, you can change the font, format numbers, change colors of cells, and align text. You can also increase or decrease the column width by dragging column borders as you did in Excel. Any formatting you do to the PivotTable list remains in force as long as you do not close your browser. Once you close your browser, the formats are lost.

Finally, you can export the PivotTable list to Excel by using the Export to Excel button (Figure 18). In Excel, the PivotTable list becomes a PivotTable report. You can format the PivotTable report using Excel's powerful formatting capabilities and then save it back as a PivotTable list.

The following steps close your browser.

More About 2000

Quick Reference

For a table that lists how to complete the tasks covered in this book using the mouse, menu, shortcut menu, and keyboard, see the Excel Quick Reference Summary at the back of this book or visit the Office 2000 Web page (www.scsite.com/office2000/qr.htm), and then click Microsoft Excel 2000.

TO CLOSE YOUR BROWSER

 Click the Close button on the right side of the browser's title bar.

CASE PERSPECTIVE SUMMARY

Sturgis Davis will be pleased with the PivotTable list capabilities. It will serve as the first step towards implementing his intranet-based sales reporting system. His managers and team leaders will be able to analyze the sales data by displaying different views. More importantly, they will be able to analyze the data using their browsers, rather than using Excel.

Web Feature Summary

This Web Feature introduced you to publishing an Excel worksheet as a PivotTable list Web page. You learned how to use PivotTable lists and the terms that are used to describe them. You also learned how to enhance a PivotTable list using your browser by adding summaries, filtering data so only rows that pass a test display, sorting, changing the view, and removing and adding data fields.

What You Should Know

Having completed this Web feature, you now should be able to perform the following tasks:

- Add a Summary Total to a Column of Data *(EW 2.8)*
- Close Your Browser (*EW 2.15*)
- Drag Data Fields to the Filter Field Area and Apply a Filter (*EW 2.12*)
- Drag Data Fields to the Row Field Area (*EW 2.11*)
- Remove Fields from and Add Fields to a PivotTable List (*EW 2.13*)
- Save a Worksheet Database as a PivotTable List (*EW 2.3*)
- Sort Columns of Data (*EW 2.6*)
- Use Field Drop-Down Arrows to Display Records That Pass a Test (*EW 2.6*)
- View a PivotTable List Using Your Browser (*EW 2.5*)

1 Creating the Millennium Sports Open Orders PivotTable List

Problem: You are a spreadsheet specialist for Millennium Sports, a major sports retail company with stores throughout the United States. You recently attended an Excel seminar on creating PivotTable reports and lists. You decide to use a PivotTable list to distribute information across the company's intranet that can be analyzed using a browser.

Instructions: Start Excel and open the workbook Millennium Sports Open Orders from the Data Disk. Save the range A9:G20 as a PivotTable list on drive A using the file name Millennium Sports Open Orders. Add the title `Millennium Sports Open Orders` as shown in Figure 19 before publishing the Web page. Quit Excel and open your browser. Display the PivotTable list by entering `a:\Millennium Sports Open Orders.htm` in the Address bar and then print the PivotTable list. Print the PivotTable list for each of the following:

1. Add a summary total to the Amount column. Sort the PivotTable list on Amount in ascending sequence.
2. Sort in ascending sequence by Order Date within Order No. Drag the Order No data field to the filter field area (Figure 19). Use the Order No drop-down arrow to display rows from Order 128187.

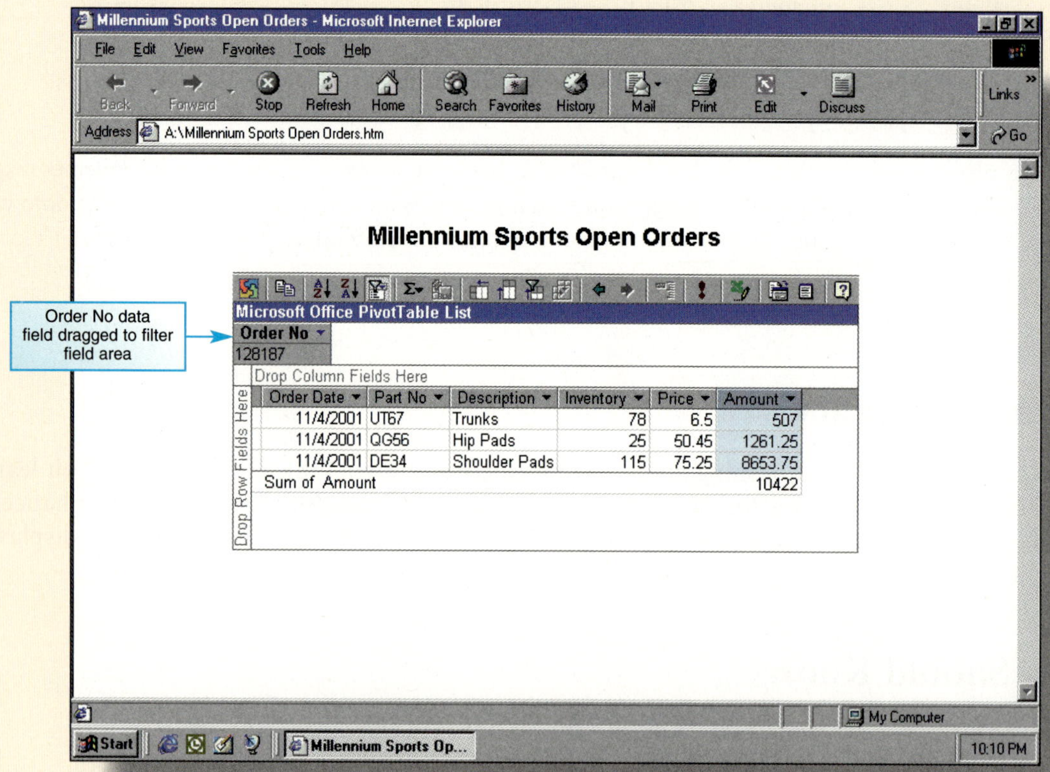

FIGURE 19

2 Creating the Match Point Tennis Club PivotTable List

Problem: You are a member of your school's Match Point Tennis Club. The members would like to access online the club's database, which includes each member's name, age, gender, class, state, major, and total credit hours. You have been asked to use your Excel skills to create a PivotTable list from the database so it can be manipulated using a browser.

Instructions: Start Excel and open the workbook Match Point Tennis Club from the Data Disk. Save the range A8:H18 as a PivotTable list on drive A using the file name Match Point Tennis Club. Add the title `Match Point Tennis Club` as shown in Figure 20 before publishing the Web page. Quit Excel and open your browser. Display the PivotTable list by entering `a:\Match Point Tennis Club.htm` in the Address bar and then print the PivotTable list. Print the PivotTable list for each of the following:

1. Add a summary total to the Credit Hrs column. Display only club members majoring in EET.
2. Sort in ascending sequence by Class within Gender. Drag the Gender and Class data fields to the row field area as shown in Figure 20.

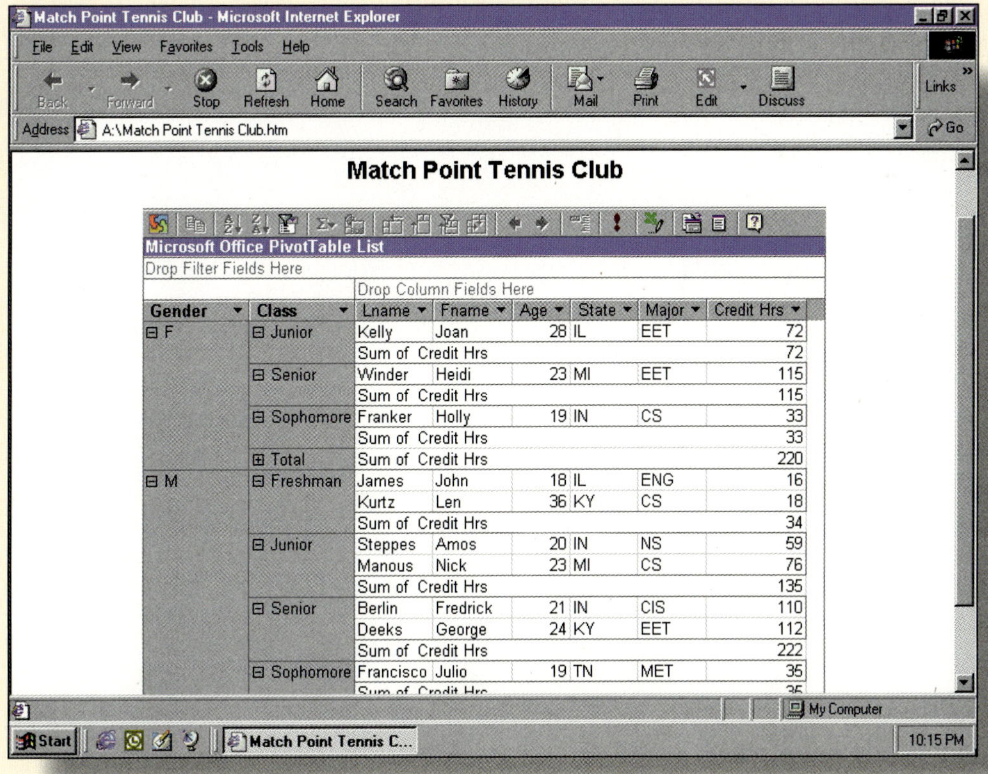

FIGURE 20

Microsoft Access 2000

Creating a Report Using Design View

OBJECTIVES

You will have mastered the material in this project when you can:

- Open a database
- Create additional tables
- Import data from an ASCII text file
- Change layout
- Relate several tables
- Create a Lookup Wizard field that uses a separate table
- Change join properties in a query
- Change field properties in a query
- Filter a query's recordset
- Create a parameter query
- Run a parameter query
- Create queries for reports
- Create a report
- Add fields to a report
- Add a subreport to a report
- Modify a subreport
- Move a subreport
- Add a date
- Add a page number
- Bold labels
- Change margins
- Create mailing labels
- Print mailing labels

Managing the Big Events

Successfully

Martians invading the earth? In 1938, Orson Welles's famous radio dramatization of the 1898 novel, *The War of the Worlds*, by H.G. Wells, caused widespread panic in the United States. Welles's version of the story had interrupted what appeared to be a live broadcast of dance music with a series of eyewitness news reports of Martian landings. Although at the time, the alarm of an entire nation was not thought to be entertaining, it was a vivid event in the memories of those who had experienced its reality.

This incident was a spoof, yet people loved hoaxes and trickery. Of note were the account of pelicans on the moon published in the *New York Sun* in 1834 and a mere few years later that century, the reporting of a bogus trans-Atlantic hot air balloon crossing, published as a news dispatch by Edgar Allen Poe, an avid practical jokester, who said, "I have great faith in fools; my friends call it self-confidence."

Into this climate of amusement and humbug strode a man who arguably was the all-time giant of American

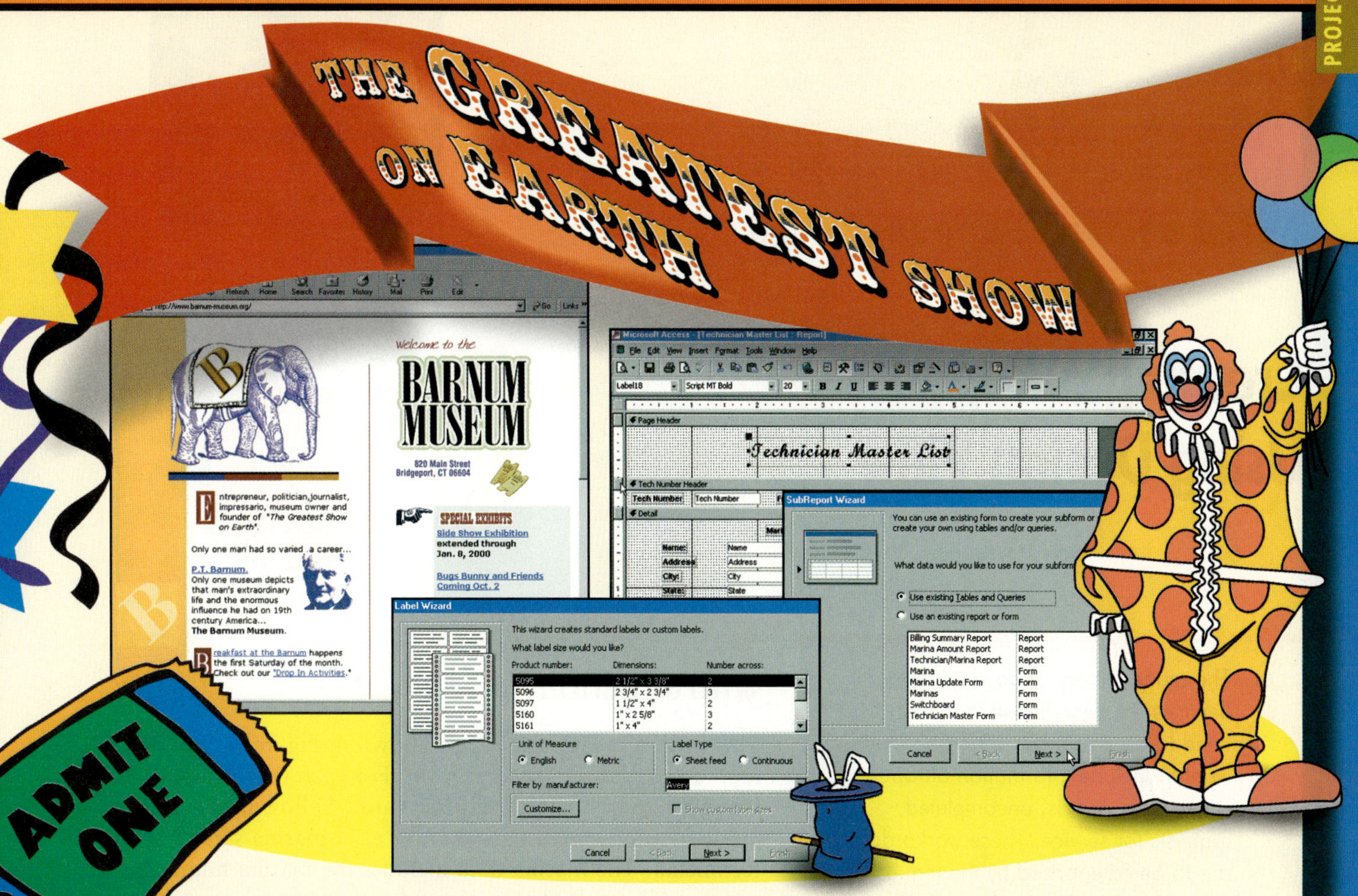

entertainment. For 60 years, Phineas Taylor Barnum reigned as The Showman to the World. Barnum launched his famous mobile circus in 1871, publicized as the The Greatest Show on Earth. The Barnum circus promoted some of the more outrageous oddities America and the world have ever seen, most of them legitimate, others born of Barnum's abundant imagination and love for the prank.

After it became known that P.T. Barnum was a master of absurdities, crowds flocked to see the infamous sideshows. The public not only expected the unusual from him, but also required it. Barnum's name became a household word. As a master presenter, Barnum preceded each new attraction with a concentrated public relations campaign. The news media ate it up, and attendance under the Big Top soared. Barnum loved the sensational, and above all, he loved people. Now, more than 100 years later, the show of shows still goes on. You can visit the Barnum Museum online (www.barnum-museum.org).

In all likelihood, you may never have the opportunity to manage an event of such magnitude as a grand-scale Barnum circus. In your professional career, however, you are likely to oversee the day-to-day operations of a business or head a large corporation that requires you to keep the organization's data centralized and maintained. With the working knowledge you have gained thus far of the powerful database management capabilities of Access 2000, you have acquired many of the skills you will need.

In this project, the more advanced concepts and techniques of Access are presented that illustrate report design from scratch using the Report Design window, inserting page numbers on a report, and creating mailing labels using the Label Wizard. If this type of application had existed in the days of P.T. Barnum, he might have used an Access database to handle the vast amounts of information required to organize the acts, maintain inventories, monitor schedules, and keep records for such a huge undertaking. In this millennium, those who take advantage of using the right tools will find themselves equipped to mange the big events successfully.

Microsoft Access 2000

Creating a Report Using Design View

CASE PERSPECTIVE

The management of Bavant Marine Services has determined that they need to expand their database. They want to include information on open workorders; that is, uncompleted requests for service. These workorders are to be categorized by the requested type of service (for example, canvas repair). Once the workorders and service categories have been added to the database, they want a query created that enables them to find open workorders for all marinas, for a single marina, or for a range of marinas (for example, marinas whose number is between EL25 and FM22). Management also wants a report that lists for each technician, each of the technician's marinas along with all open workorders for the marina. Finally, they want to be able to produce mailing labels for the technicians. Your task is to fulfill these requests.

Introduction

This project creates the report shown in Figure 7-1a. This report is organized by technician. For each technician, it lists the number, first name, and last name. Following the technician number and name, it lists data for each marina served by the technician. The marina data includes the marina number, name, address, city, state, zip code, phone number, marina type, warranty amount, and non-warranty amount. It also includes any open workorders (requests for service) for the marina. For each such workorder, the report lists the location of the boat to be serviced, the category of service (for example, engine repair), a description of the problem, and the status of the request. Additional workorder data includes the estimated hours to rectify the problem, the hours spent so far, and the date of the next scheduled service for the workorder.

The project also creates mailing labels for the technicians. These labels, which are shown in Figure 7-1b, are designed to perfectly fit the type of labels that Bavant Marine Services has purchased.

Before creating the reports and labels, you must first add two tables to the Bavant Marine Services database. These tables help Bavant track open workorders.

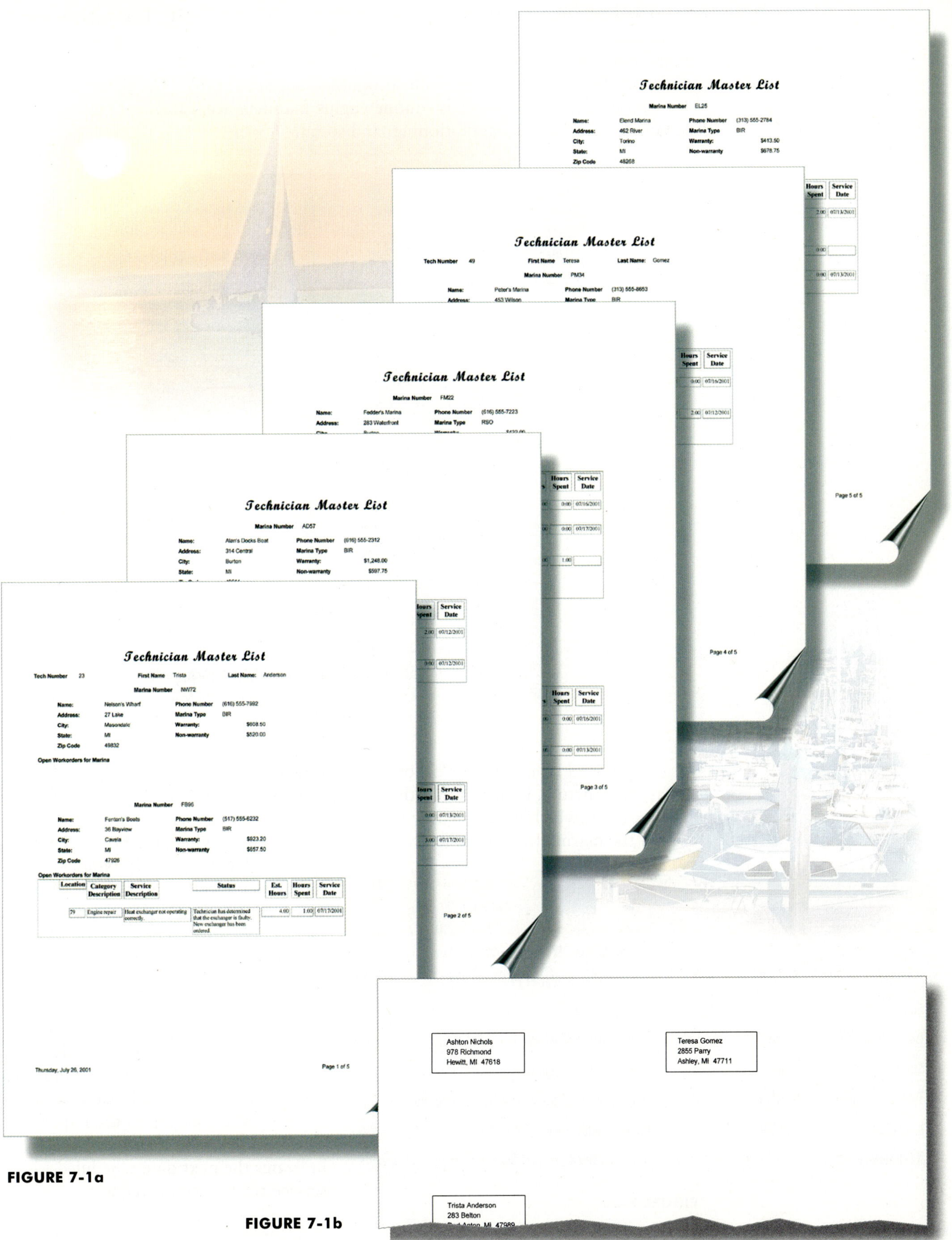

Technician Master List

Marina Number EL25

Name:	Elend Marina	Phone Number	(313) 555-2784
Address:	462 River	Marina Type	BIR
City:	Torino	Warranty:	$413.50
State:	MI	Non-warranty	$678.75
Zip Code	48268		

Page 5 of 5

Technician Master List

Tech Number 49 First Name Teresa Last Name: Gomez

Marina Number PM34

Name:	Peter's Marina	Phone Number	(313) 555-8653
Address:	453 Wilson	Marina Type	BIR

Page 4 of 5

Technician Master List

Marina Number FM22

Name:	Fedder's Marina	Phone Number	(616) 555-7223
Address:	283 Waterfront	Marina Type	RSO

Page 3 of 5

Technician Master List

Marina Number AD57

Name:	Alan's Docks Boat	Phone Number	(616) 555-2312
Address:	314 Central	Marina Type	BIR
City:	Burton	Warranty:	$1,248.00
State:	MI	Non-warranty	$597.75

Page 2 of 5

Technician Master List

Tech Number 23 First Name Trista Last Name: Anderson

Marina Number NW72

Name:	Nelson's Wharf	Phone Number	(616) 555-7992
Address:	27 Lake	Marina Type	BIR
City:	Masondale	Warranty:	$608.50
State:	MI	Non-warranty	$520.00
Zip Code	49832		

Open Workorders for Marina

Marina Number FB96

Name:	Fenton's Boats	Phone Number	(517) 555-6232
Address:	36 Bayview	Marina Type	BIR
City:	Cavela	Warranty:	$923.20
State:	MI	Non-warranty	$657.50
Zip Code	47926		

Open Workorders for Marina

Location	Category Description	Service Description	Status	Est. Hours	Hours Spent	Service Date
79	Engine repair	Heat exchanger not operating correctly.	Technician has determined that the exchanger is faulty. New exchanger has been ordered.	4.00	1.00	07/17/2001

Thursday, July 26, 2001 Page 1 of 5

FIGURE 7-1a

Ashton Nichols
978 Richmond
Hewitt, MI 47618

Teresa Gomez
2855 Parry
Ashley, MI 47711

Trista Anderson
283 Belton

FIGURE 7-1b

The first table, Category, is shown in Figures 7-2a and 7-2b. This table is used to categorize the open workorders. Figure 7-2a, which shows the structure of the table, indicates that there are two fields, Category Number (the primary key) and Category Description. Figure 7-2b shows the data in the table. The figure indicates, for example, that category 1 is routine engine maintenance, category 2 is engine repair, category 3 is air conditioning, and so on.

Category

NAME	TYPE	SIZE	DESCRIPTION
Category Number	Text	2	Category Number (Primary Key)
Category Description	Text	50	Description of Category

FIGURE 7-2a

Service Categories

CATEGORY NUMBER	CATEGORY DESCRIPTION
1	Routine engine maintenance
2	Engine repair
3	Air conditioning
4	Electrical systems
5	Fiberglass repair
6	Canvas installation
7	Canvas repair
8	Electronic systems (radar, GPS, autopilots, etc.)

FIGURE 7-2b

The second table, Open Workorders, is shown in Figures 7-3a and 7-3b. Figure 7-3a, the structure, indicates that the table contains a marina number and a location. The location, which is assigned by the marina, indicates the placement of the boat within the marina (for example, the number of the slip in which the boat is kept). The next field, Category Number, indicates the category of the service being requested. The Description field, a memo field, gives a description of the problem. The Status field, also a memo field, indicates the status of the request. The Total Hours (est) field gives an estimate of the total number of hours that will be required to satisfy the request. The Hours Spent field indicates how many hours already have been spent by a technician on the request. The final field, Next Service Date, indicates the next date scheduled for service related to this request.

Open Workorders

NAME	TYPE	SIZE	DESCRIPTION
Marina Number	Text	4	Marina Number (Portion of Primary Key)
Location	Text	6	Location (Remainder of Primary Key)
Category Number	Text	2	Category Number
Description	Memo	-	Description of Problem
Status	Memo	-	Status of Work Request
Total Hours (est)	Number	-	Estimate of Total Number of Hours Required
Hours Spent	Number	-	Hours Already Spent on Problem
Next Service Date	Date/Time	-	Date Scheduled for Next Service Related to Problem

FIGURE 7-3a

Open Workorders

MARINA	LOCATION	CATEGORY NUMBER	DESCRIPTION	STATUS	TOTAL HOURS (EST)	HOURS SPENT	NEXT SERVICE DATE
AD57	A21	3	Air conditioner periodically stops with code indicating low coolant level. Diagnose and repair.	Technician has verified the problem. Air conditioning specialist has been called.	4	2	7/12/2001
AD57	B14	4	Fuse on port motor blown on two occasions. Find cause and correct problem.	Open	2	0	7/12/2001
BL72	129	1	Oil change and general routine maintenance (check fluid levels, clean sea strainers, etc.)	Service call has been scheduled.	1	0	7/16/2001
BL72	146	2	Engine oil level has been dropping drastically. Find cause and repair.	Open	2	0	7/13/2001
EL25	11A	5	Open pockets at base of two stantions.	Technician has completed the initial filling of the open pockets. Will complete the job after the initial fill has had sufficient time to dry.	4	2	7/13/2001
EL25	15A	4	Electric-flush system will periodically not function. Find cause and repair.	Open	3	0	
EL25	43B	2	Engine overheating. Loss of coolant. Find cause and repair.	Open	2	0	7/13/2001
FB96	79	2	Heat exchanger not operating correctly.	Technician has determined that the exchanger is faulty. New exchanger has been ordered.	4	1	7/17/2001
FM22	A21	6	Canvas was severely damaged in windstorm. New canvas needs to be installed.	Open	8	0	7/16/2001
FM22	D14	8	Install new GPS and chart plotter	Scheduled	7	0	7/17/2001
FM22	D31	3	Air conditioning unit shuts down with HHH showing on the control panel.	Technician not able to repeat the problem. Air conditioning unit ran fine through multiple tests. Owner to notify technician if the problem repeats itself.	1	1	
PM34	56	8	Both speed and depth readings on data unit are significantly less than the owner thinks they should be.	Technician has scheduled appointment with owner to attempt to verify the problem.	2	0	7/16/2001
PM34	88	2	Engine seems to be making "clattering" (customer's description) noise.	Technician suspects problem with either propeller or shaft and has scheduled the boat to be pulled from the water for further investigation.	5	2	7/12/2001
TR72	B11	5	Owner had accident and left large gauge in forward portion of port side.	Technician has scheduled repair.	6	0	7/13/2001
TR72	B15	7	Canvas leaks around zippers in heavy rain. Install overlap around zippers to prevent leaks.	Overlap has been created, but still needs to be installed.	8	3	7/17/2001

FIGURE 7-3b

Microsoft Certification

The Microsoft Office User Specialist (MOUS) Certification program provides an opportunity for you to obtain a valuable industry credential — proof that you have the Access 2000 skills required by employers. For more information, see Appendix D or visit the Shelly Cashman Series MOUS Web page at www.scsite.com/off2000/cert.htm.

Figure 7-3b gives the data. For example, the first record shows that marina AD57 has requested service. The location of the boat to be serviced is slip A21. The service is in category 3 – Air Conditioning, as indicated in Figure 7-2a. The description of the problem is "Air conditioner periodically stops with code indicating low coolant level. Diagnose and repair." The status is "Technician has verified the problem. Air conditioning specialist has been called." (After verifying the problem, the technician evidently determined that the problem required a specialist.) The technician has estimated that 4 hours total will be required on the problem. So far, 2 hours of work already have been spent. The next service is scheduled for 7/12/2001.

If you examine the data in Figure 7-3b, you see that the Marina Number field cannot be the primary key. The first two records, for example, both have a marina number of AD57. Location also cannot be the primary key. The first and ninth records, for example, both have a location of A21. (Both marinas have slips numbered A21 and the boats in both slips currently require service.) Rather, the primary key is the combination of both of these fields.

It is possible for the primary key to be the combination of more than two fields. If marinas regularly placed requests to service boats that need service in more than one category, for example, Canvas Repair and Engine Repair, then the primary key would be a combination of the Marina Number, Location, and Category fields. In the Apply Your Knowledge exercise at the end of this project, you will create a table where the primary key is the combination of three fields.

Next you will create three queries. You first will create a query to join the Marina and Open Workorders tables. Then you will modify the join properties to ensure that all marinas display, even if they have no open workorders. You will modify the field properties of two of the fields and also filter the **recordset** (results) of the query. Then you will change the query to a **parameter query**, one that prompts the user for input when the query is run. Finally, you will create two queries that will be used in the report in Figure 7-1a on page A 7.5.

The report shown in Figure 7-1a contains a **subreport**, which is a report that is contained within another report. The subreport in the report in Figure 7-1a is the portion that lists the open workorders. You will create the report shown in the figure from scratch; that is, you will use Design view rather than the Report Wizard. You will create mailing labels for the technicians as shown in Figure 7-1b on page A 7.5.

You are to create the tables, queries, report, and mailing labels requested by the management of Bavant Marine Services.

Quick Reference

For a table that lists how to complete the tasks covered in this book using the mouse, menu, shortcut menu, and keyboard, visit the Office 2000 Web page (www.scsite.com/off2000/qr.htm), and then click Microsoft Access 2000.

Opening the Database

Before you complete the steps in this project, you must open the database. Perform the following steps to complete this task.

TO OPEN A DATABASE

1. Click the Start button.
2. Click Open Office Document on the Start menu and then click 3½ Floppy (A:) in the Look in box. Make sure the database called Bavant Marine Services is selected.
3. Click the Open button.

The database opens and the Bavant Marine Services : Database window displays.

Creating the Additional Tables

Before creating the queries, report, and mailing labels required by Bavant Marine Services, you need to create the two additional tables shown in Figures 7-2a, 7-2b, 7-3a, and 7-3b on pages A 7.6 and A 7.7.

Creating the New Tables

The steps to create the new tables are identical to those you have used in creating other tables. Perform the following steps to create the tables.

Steps To Create the New Tables

1 Click the Tables object. Right-click Create table in Design view and then click Open on the shortcut menu. Enter the information for the fields in the Category table as indicated in Figure 7-2a. Close the window containing the table by clicking its Close button. Click the Yes button to save the changes. Type `Category` **as the name of the table and then click the OK button.**

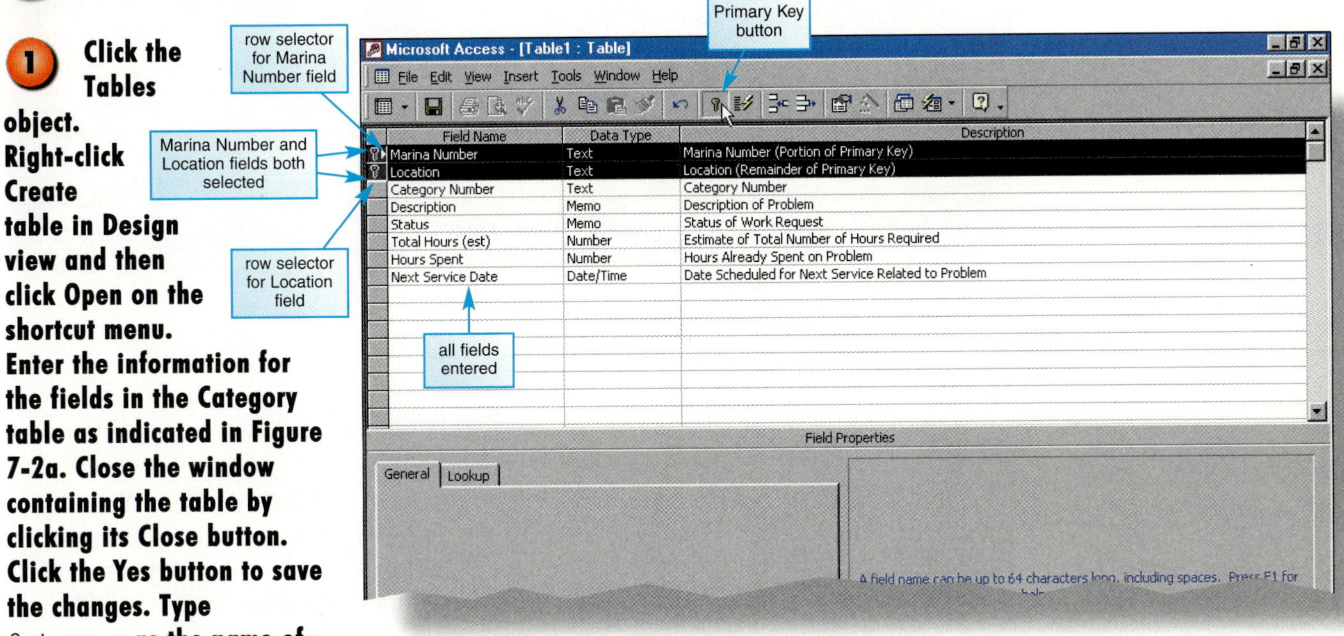

FIGURE 7-4

2 Right-click Create table in Design view and then click Open on the shortcut menu. Enter the information for the fields in the Open Workorders table as indicated in Figure 7-3a.

3 Click the row selector for the Marina Number field. Hold the SHIFT key down and click the row selector for the Location field so that both fields are selected. Click the Primary Key button on the toolbar.

The primary key consists of both the Marina Number field and the Location field (Figure 7-4).

4 **Close the window by clicking its Close button. Click the Yes button to save the table. Type** `Open Workorders` **as the name of the table and point to the OK button.**

The Save As dialog box displays (Figure 7-5).

5 **Click the OK button to save the table.**

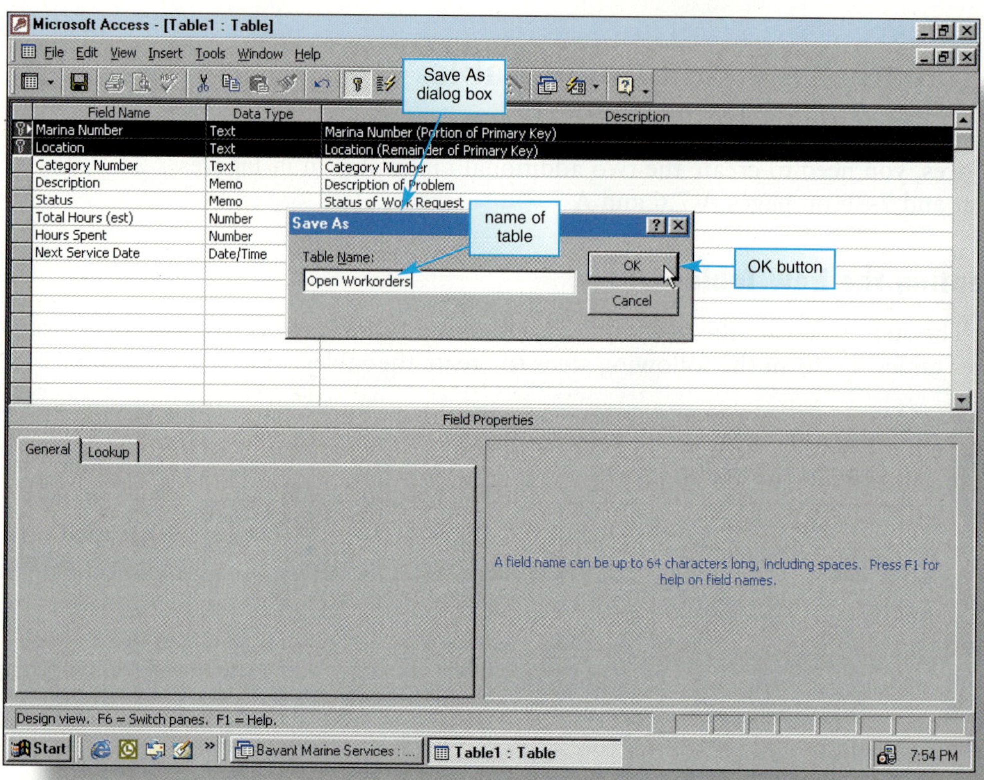

FIGURE 7-5

More About

Importing Data

When importing text files, there are several options concerning how the data in the various fields are separated. For more information about importing data, visit the Access 2000 More About page (www.scsite.com/ac2000/more.htm) and then click Import Data.

Importing the Data

Now that the tables have been created, you need to add data to them. You either could enter the data, or if the data is already in electronic form, you could import the data. The data for the Category and Open Workorders tables are on your Access Data Disk as text files. Use the following steps to import the data.

TO IMPORT THE DATA

1. With the Bavant Marine Services database open, click File on the menu bar, click Get External Data and then click Import.
2. Click the Files of type box arrow in the Import dialog box and then click Text Files. Select 3½ Floppy (A:) in the Look in list. Make sure the Category text file is selected. Click the Import button.
3. Make sure the Delimited option button is selected and click the Next button. Click First Row Contains Field Names, make sure the Tab option button is selected, and then click the Next button again.
4. Click the In an Existing Table option button and select the Category table from the list. Click the Next button, click the Finish button, and then click OK.
5. Repeat Steps 1 through 4 to import the Workorders text file.

The data for the Category and Open Workorders tables are imported.

Changing the Layout

Now that the tables contain data, you need to adjust the column sizes. Perform the following steps to change the layouts of the tables.

To Change the Layout

1. **Right-click the Category table and then click Open on the shortcut menu. Double-click the right boundary of the field selector for each field to resize the columns to best fit the data.**

2. **Close the window containing the table. When asked if you want to save the changes to the layout, click the Yes button.**

The changes to the layout for the Category table are saved.

3. **Right-click the Open Workorders table and then click Open on the shortcut menu. Drag the lower boundary of the row selector for the first record to the approximate position shown in Figure 7-6. Resize the remaining columns as shown in Figure 7-6.**

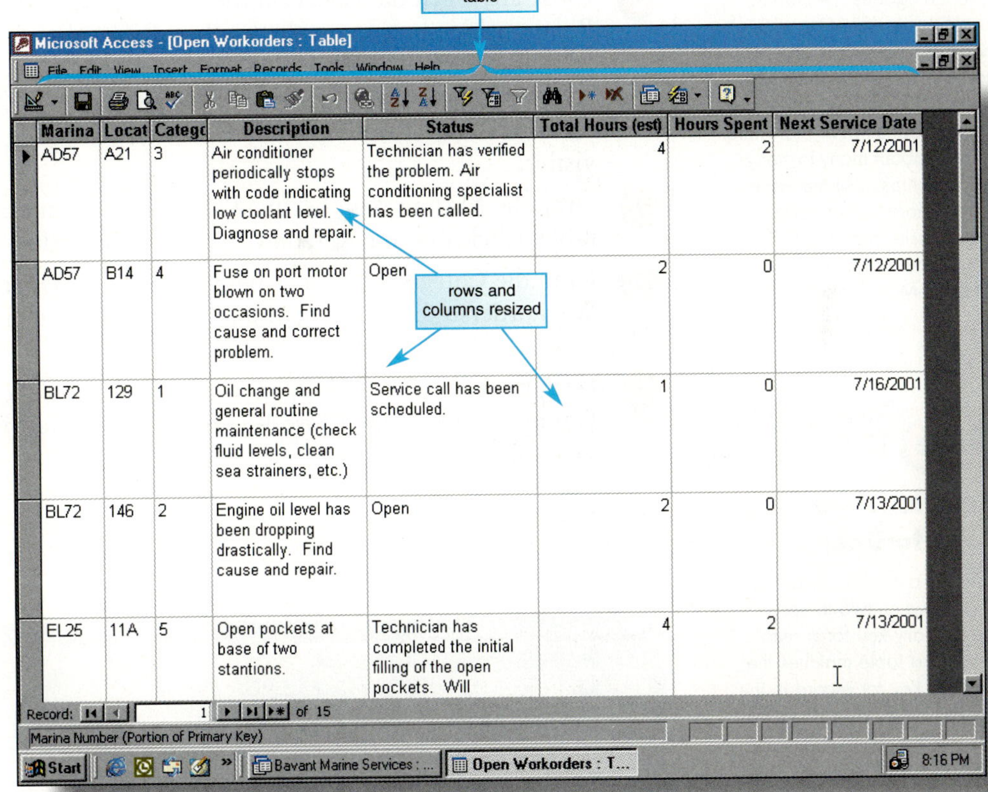

data in Open Workorders table
rows and columns resized
Microsoft Access - [Open Workorders : Table]
Marina
Locat
Categc
Description
Status
Total Hours (est)
Hours Spent
Next Service Date
AD57
A21
3
Air conditioner periodically stops with code indicating low coolant level. Diagnose and repair.
Technician has verified the problem. Air conditioning specialist has been called.
4
2
7/12/2001
AD57
B14
4
Fuse on port motor blown on two occasions. Find cause and correct problem.
Open
2
0
7/12/2001
BL72
129
1
Oil change and general routine maintenance (check fluid levels, clean sea strainers, etc.)
Service call has been scheduled.
1
0
7/16/2001
BL72
146
2
Engine oil level has been dropping drastically. Find cause and repair.
Open
2
0
7/13/2001
EL25
11A
5
Open pockets at base of two stantions.
Technician has completed the initial filling of the open pockets. Will
4
2
7/13/2001
Record: 1 of 15
Marina Number (Portion of Primary Key)
Start
Bavant Marine Services : ...
Open Workorders : T...
8:16 PM

FIGURE 7-6

4. **Close the window containing the table. When asked if you want to save the changes to the layout, click the Yes button.**

The changes to the layout for the Open Workorders table are saved.

Relationships (Many-to-Many)

If the primary key of the Open Workorders table is the combination of Marina Number, Location, and Category Code, there is a many-to-many relationship between the Marinas and Categories. (A marina can have many categories of service scheduled to be performed and a service can be scheduled to be performed at many marinas.) For more information about many-to-many relationships, visit the Access 2000 More About page (www.scsite.com/ac2000/more.htm) and then click Many-to-Many Relationships.

Relationships (One-to-One)

There is a one-to-one relationship between two tables when the primary key for a record in the first table matches the primary key for record in the second table. The Apply Your Knowledge exercise at the end of this project illustrates a one-to-one relationship. For more information about one-to-one relationships, visit the Access 2000 More About page (www.scsite.com/ac2000/more.htm) and then click One-to-One Relationships.

Relating Several Tables

Now that the tables have been created they need to be related to the existing tables. The Marina and Open Workorders tables are related through the Marina Number fields in both. The Category and Open Workorders tables are related through the Category Number fields in both. Perform the following steps to relate the tables.

TO RELATE SEVERAL TABLES

1. Close any open datasheet on the screen by clicking its Close button. Click the Relationships button on the toolbar. Right-click in the Relationships window and click Show Table on the shortcut menu. Click the Category table, click the Add button, click the Open Workorders table, click the Add button again, and then click the Close button. Resize the field boxes that display so all fields are visible.
2. Drag the Marina Number field from the Marina table to the Open Workorders table. Click Enforce Referential Integrity and then click the Create button.
3. Drag the Category Number field from the Category table to the Open Workorders table. Click Enforce Referential Integrity and then click the Create button.
4. Drag the Category and Open Workorders tables to the positions shown in Figure 7-7. Click the Close Window button and then click the Yes button to save the changes.

The relationships are created.

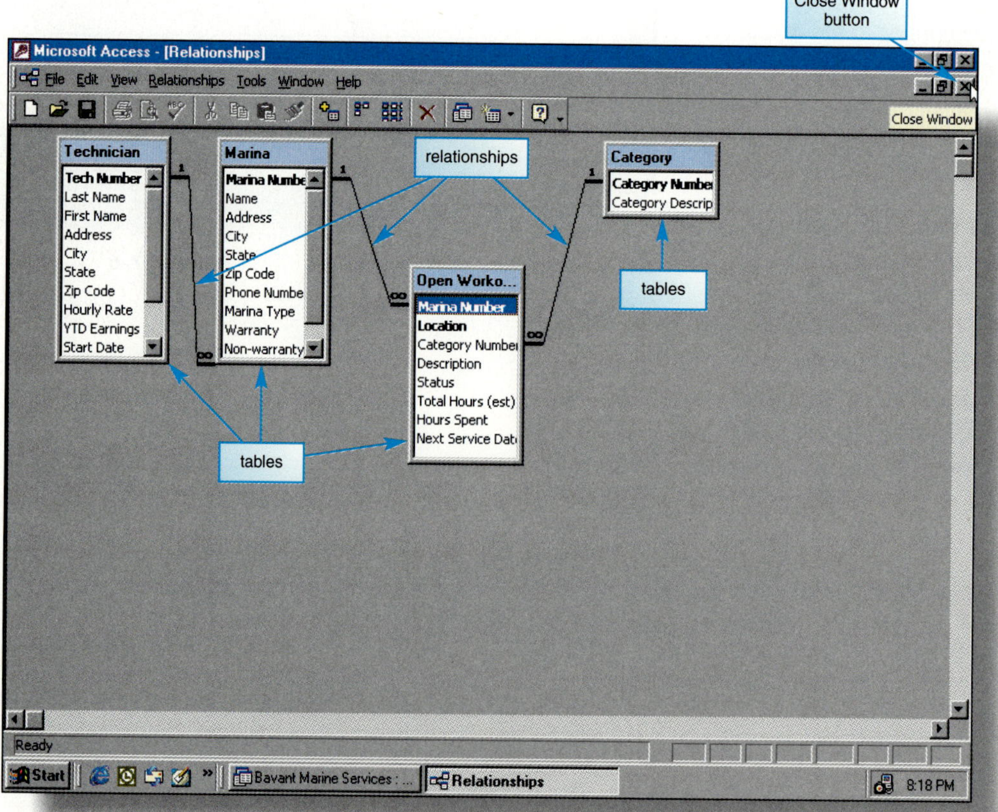

FIGURE 7-7

Creating a Lookup Wizard Field

The fact that the Open Workorders table is related to the Category table ensures that no workorder can be entered without a valid category number. It does not assist the users in knowing what category number to enter, however. To help the users who are entering data in Datasheet view, you will make the Category Number field in the Open Workorders table a Lookup Wizard field. In this case, the lookup would take place in the Category table. Perform the following steps to create a Lookup Wizard field.

To Create a Lookup Wizard Field

1 **If necessary, click the Tables object. Right-click Open Workorders, and then click Design View on the shortcut menu. Click the Data Type column for the Category Number field, click the box arrow, and then click Lookup Wizard.**

2 **If necessary, click the I want the lookup column to look up the values in a table or query button and then click the Next button. Be sure the Category table is selected and then click the Next button a second time. Click the Add All Fields button to add the Category Number and Category Description to the list of selected fields. Point to the Next button.**

The Lookup Wizard dialog box displays (Figure 7-8).

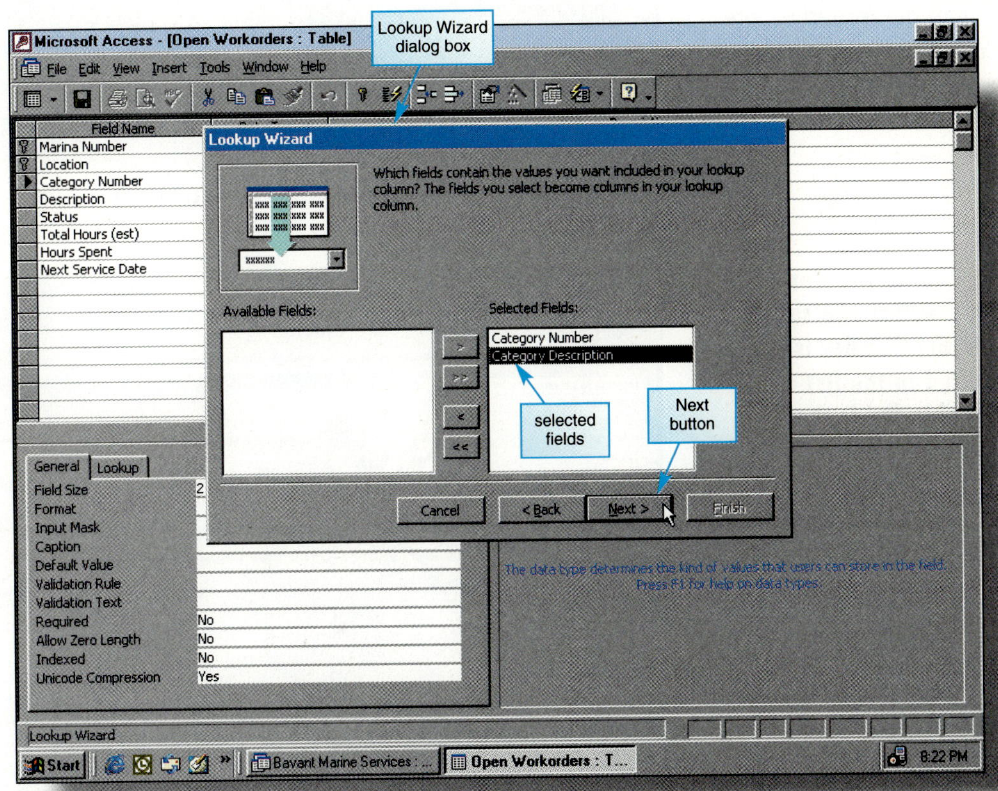

FIGURE 7-8

3 **Click the Next button, click Hide key column (recommended) to remove the check mark. Resize each column to best fit the data by double-clicking the right-hand border of the column heading. Point to the Next button.**

The Category Number column displays and the columns are resized (Figure 7-9).

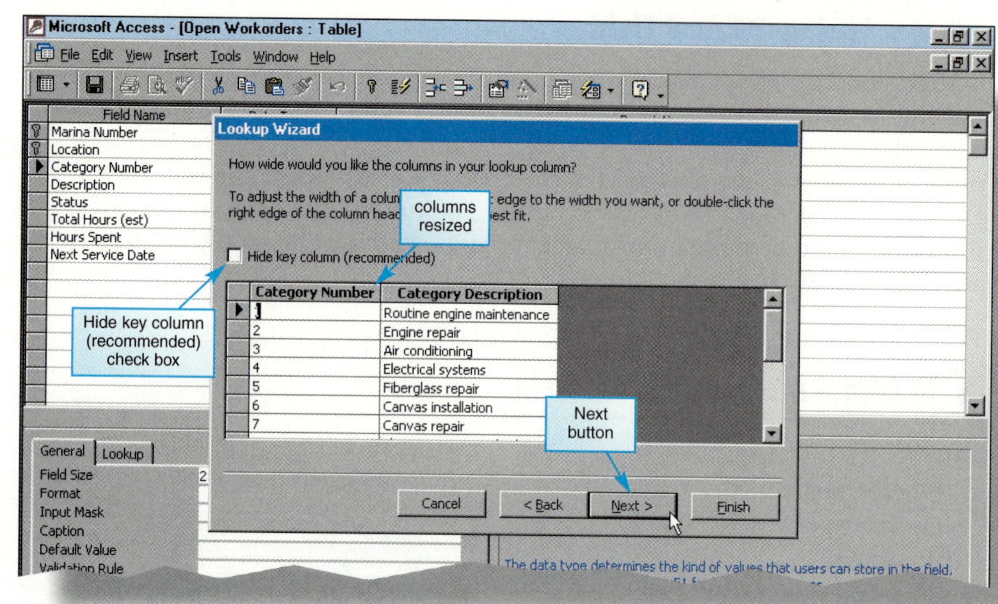

FIGURE 7-9

4 **Click the Next button, be sure Category Number is selected in the list of available fields that displays and then click the Next button a second time.**

5 **Be sure Category Number is indicated as the label for the lookup column and then point to the Finish button.**

The Lookup Wizard dialog box displays (Figure 7-10).

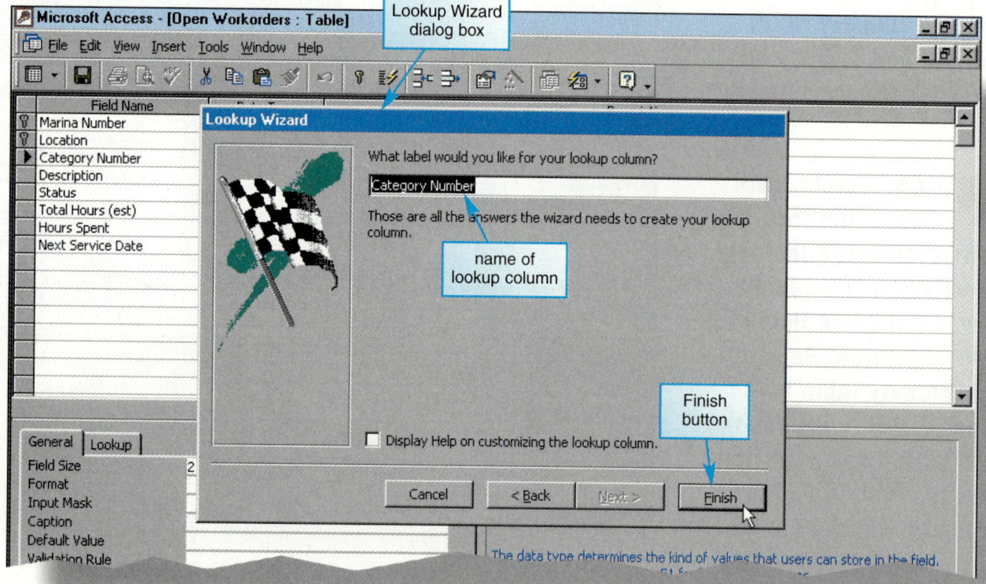

FIGURE 7-10

6 **Click the Finish button to complete the definition of the Lookup Wizard field.**

7 **Click the Yes button to save the changes to the Category Number field. Close the window by clicking the Close Window button.**

Creating Join Queries

Creating the required queries involves creating join queries. In the first query, the process also involves the modification of appropriate properties.

Creating a Query

Creating the initial query follows the same steps as in the creation of any query that joins tables. Perform the following steps to create a query that joins the Marina and Open Workorders tables.

To Create a Query

1 **If necessary, in the Database window, click Tables on the Objects bar, and then click Marina. Click the New Object: AutoForm button arrow on the Database window toolbar. Click Query. Be sure Design View is selected, and then click the OK button. If necessary, maximize the Query1 : Select Query window. Resize the upper and lower panes and the Marina field box so that all the fields in the Marina table display.**

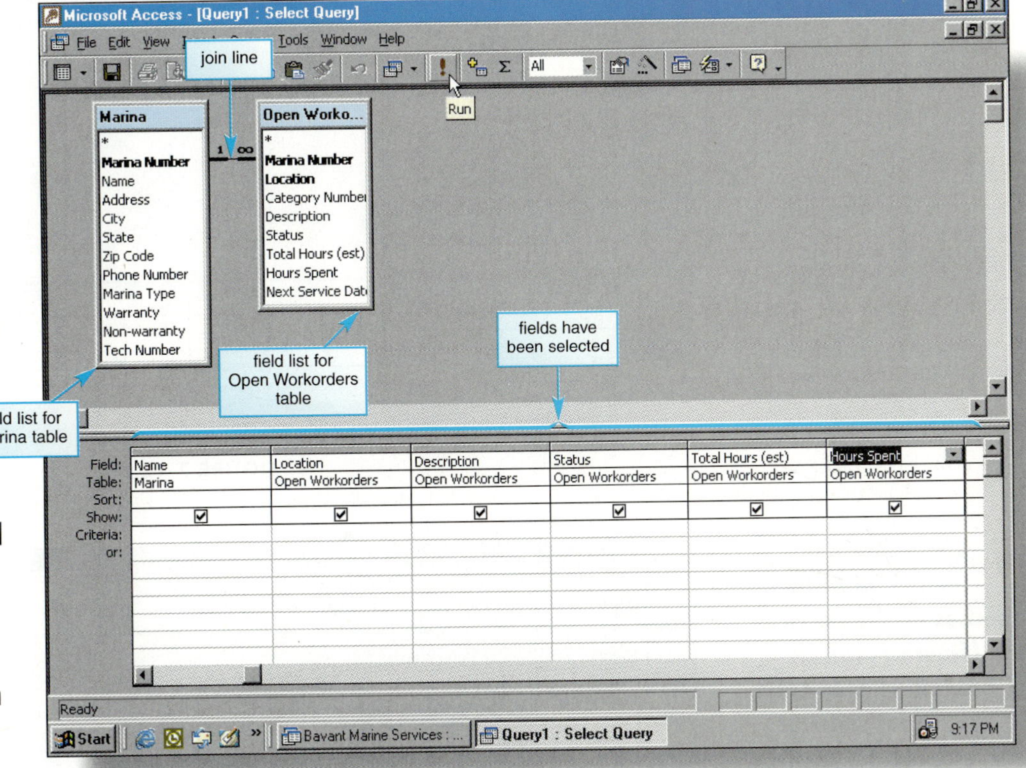

FIGURE 7-11

2 **Right-click any open area in the upper pane, click Show Table on the shortcut menu, click the Open Workorders table, click the Add button, and then click the Close button in the Show Table dialog box. Resize the Open Workorders field box so that all the fields in the Open Workorders table display. Double-click the Marina Number and Name fields from the Marina table. Double-click the Location, Description, Status, Total Hours (est), and Hours Spent fields from the Open Workorders table.**

The tables are related and the fields are selected (Figure 7-11).

Changing Join Properties

Normally records that do not match will not display in the results of a join query. A marina for which there are no workorders, for example, would not display. In order to cause such a record to display, you need to change the **join properties**, the properties that indicate which records display in a join, of the query as in the following steps.

To Change Join Properties

1 **Point to the middle portion of the join line (the portion of the line that is not bold) (Figure 7-12).**

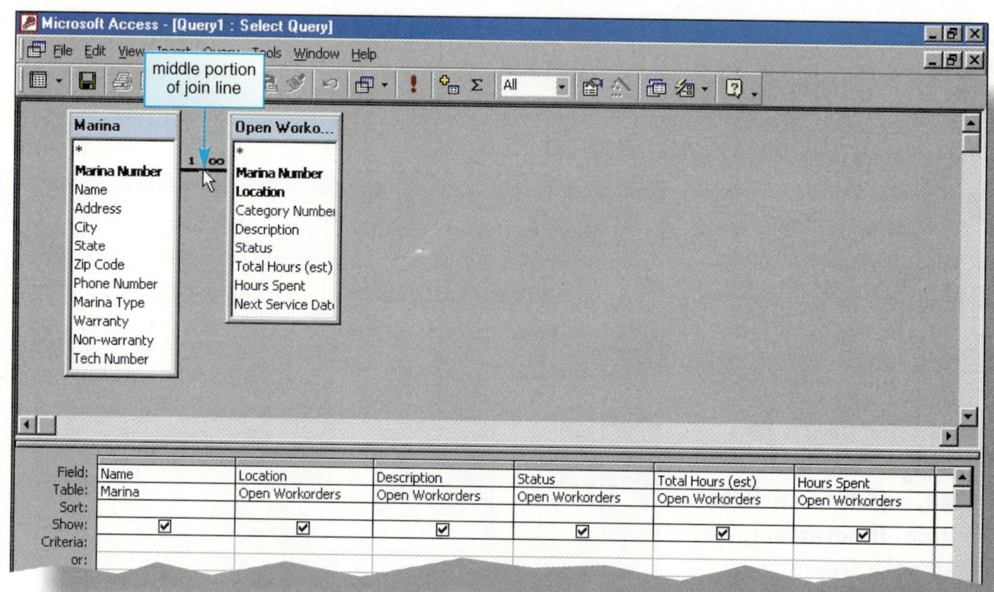

FIGURE 7-12

2 **Right-click and then point to Join Properties on the shortcut menu (Figure 7-13). (If Join Properties does not display on your shortcut menu, you did not point to the appropriate portion of the join line.)**

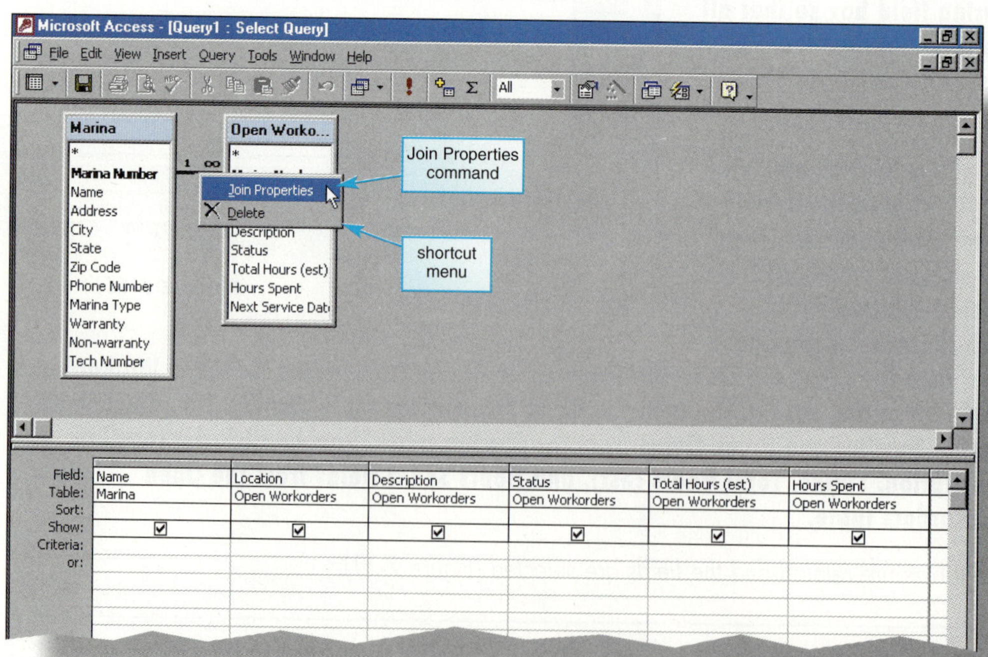

FIGURE 7-13

3 **Click Join Properties on the shortcut menu and point to option button 2.**

The Join Properties dialog box displays (Figure 7-14).

4 **Click option button 2 to include all records from the Marina table regardless of whether or not they match any open workorders. Click the OK button.**

The join properties are changed.

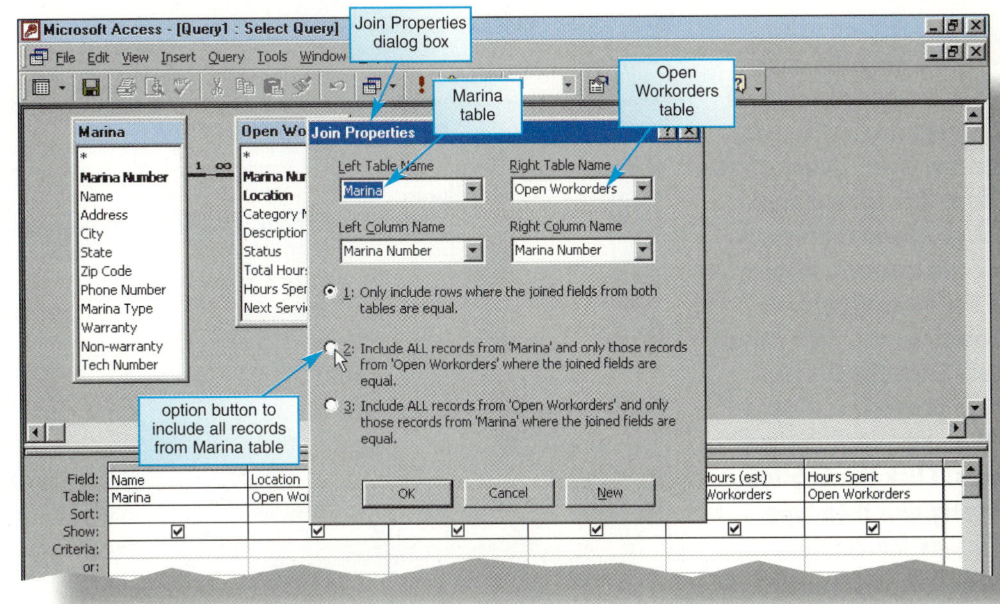

FIGURE 7-14

Changing Field Properties

You can change field properties within a query by using the Properties command and then changing the desired property in the field's property sheet. The following steps change the Format and Decimal Places properties to modify the way the contents of the Total Hours (est) and Hours Spent fields display. The steps also change the Caption properties so that the **captions** (column headings) are different from the field names.

To Change Field Properties

1 **Right-click the Total Hours (est) column and then point to Properties on the shortcut menu (Figure 7-15).**

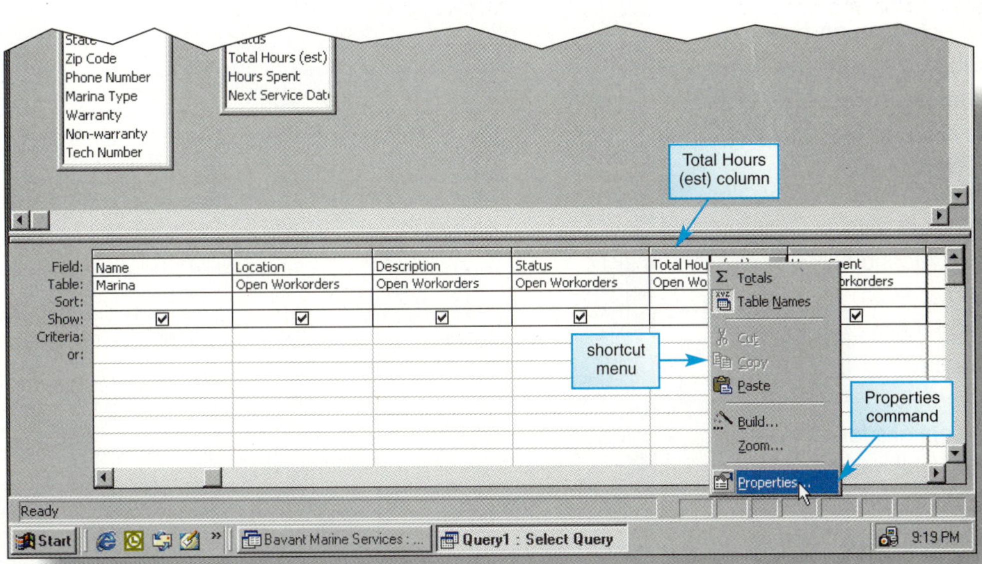

FIGURE 7-15

2 **Click Properties. Be sure the Field Properties box displays. If the Query Properties box displays, close it and right-click in the column again. Click the Format property, click the arrow to display the list of available properties, and then select Fixed. Click the Decimal Places property and type** `2` **as the number of decimal places. Click the Caption property and then type** `Est Hours` **as the caption.**

The changed properties display(Figure 7-16).

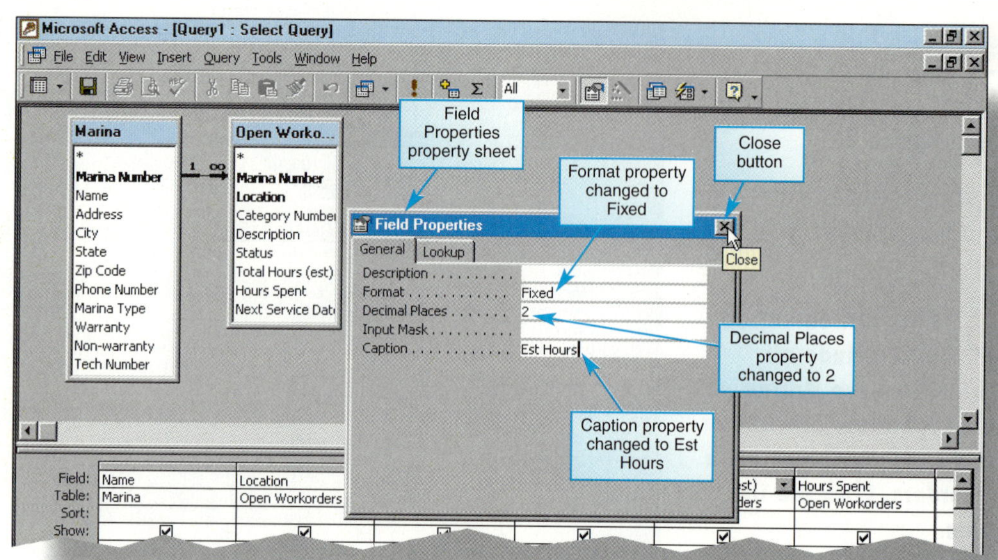

FIGURE 7-16

3 **Use the same technique to change the Format property for the Hours Spent field to Fixed, the number of decimal places to 2, and the caption to Spent Hours.**

Running the Query and Changing the Layout

Perform the following steps to run the query and change the layout.

Steps To Run the Query and Change the Layout

1 **Click the Run button on the toolbar. Point to the lower boundary of the row selector for the first record.**

The results display (Figure 7-17). Marina NW72 displays, even though it has no open workorders. The captions for the Total Hours (est) and Hours Spent fields have been changed. Both fields display with precisely two decimal places.

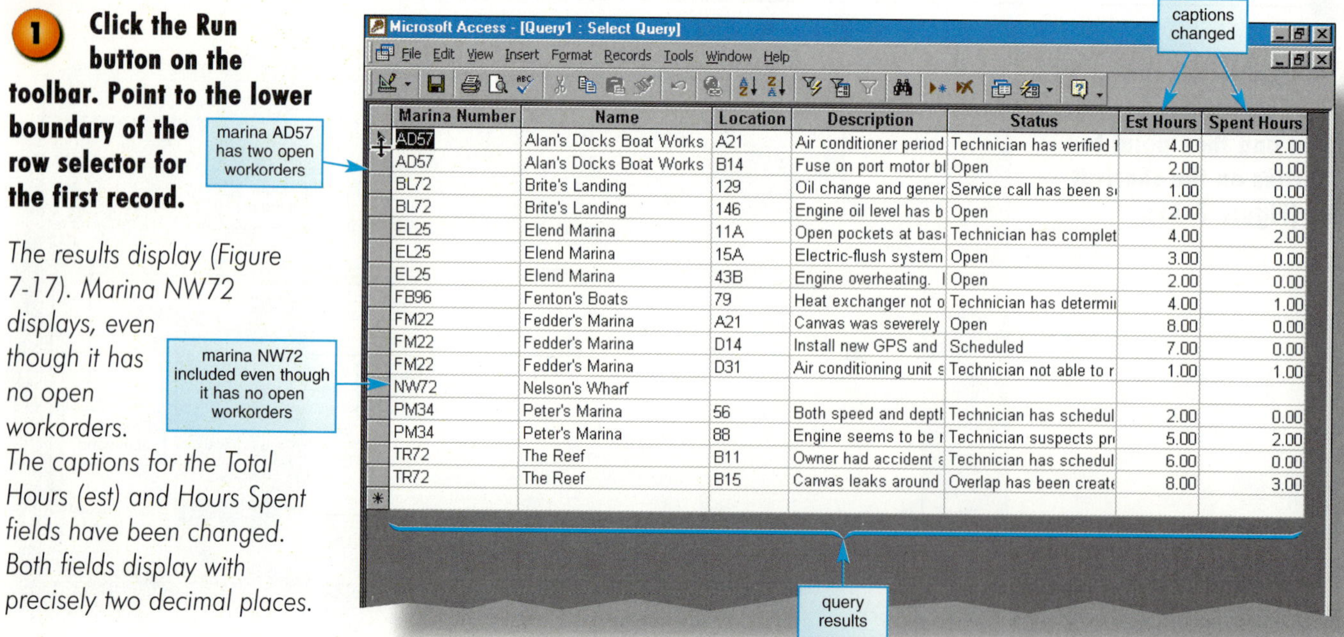

Marina Number	Name	Location	Description	Status	Est Hours	Spent Hours
AD57	Alan's Docks Boat Works	A21	Air conditioner period	Technician has verified t	4.00	2.00
AD57	Alan's Docks Boat Works	B14	Fuse on port motor bl	Open	2.00	0.00
BL72	Brite's Landing	129	Oil change and gener	Service call has been s	1.00	0.00
BL72	Brite's Landing	146	Engine oil level has b	Open	2.00	0.00
EL25	Elend Marina	11A	Open pockets at bas	Technician has complet	4.00	2.00
EL25	Elend Marina	15A	Electric-flush system	Open	3.00	0.00
EL25	Elend Marina	43B	Engine overheating.	Open	2.00	0.00
FB96	Fenton's Boats	79	Heat exchanger not o	Technician has determi	4.00	1.00
FM22	Fedder's Marina	A21	Canvas was severely	Open	8.00	0.00
FM22	Fedder's Marina	D14	Install new GPS and	Scheduled	7.00	0.00
FM22	Fedder's Marina	D31	Air conditioning unit s	Technician not able to r	1.00	1.00
NW72	Nelson's Wharf					
PM34	Peter's Marina	56	Both speed and deptl	Technician has schedul	2.00	0.00
PM34	Peter's Marina	88	Engine seems to be r	Technician suspects pr	5.00	2.00
TR72	The Reef	B11	Owner had accident a	Technician has schedul	6.00	0.00
TR72	The Reef	B15	Canvas leaks around	Overlap has been creat	8.00	3.00

FIGURE 7-17

2 **Drag the lower boundary of the row selector to the approximate position shown in Figure 7-18.**

The complete memos display.

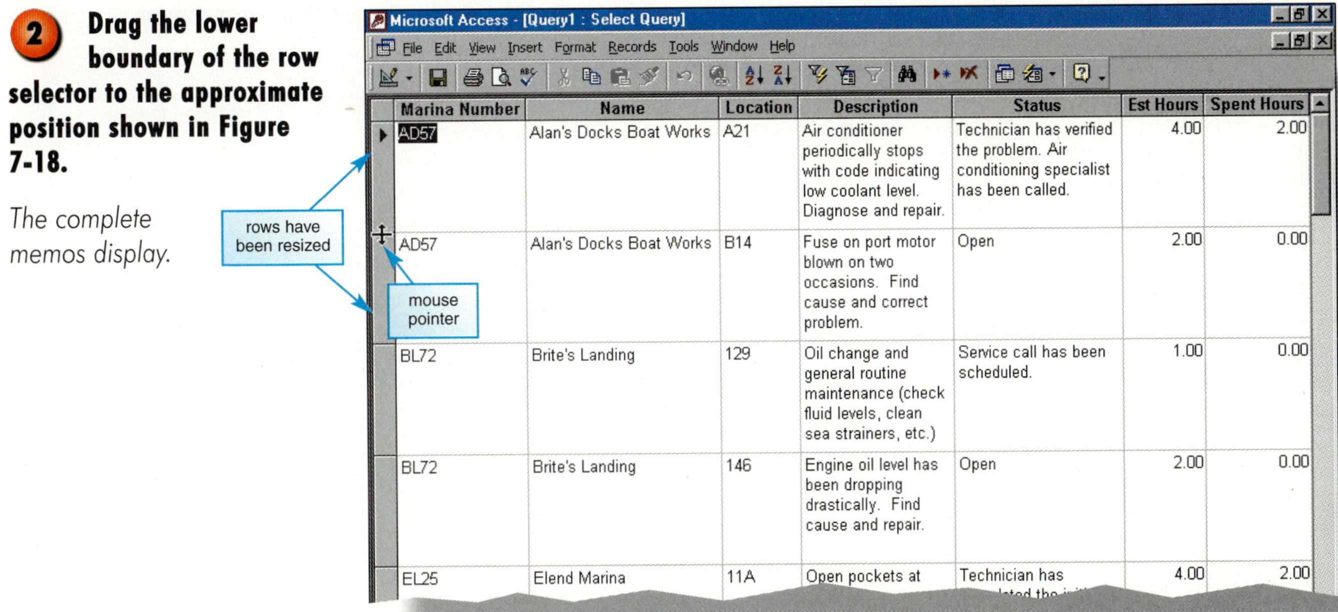

FIGURE 7-18

Filtering a Query's Recordset

Sometimes, when querying a database, there is an existing query that is similar to what you need, but is missing a single criterion. You could modify the query, adding the extra criterion. In some cases, it would be simpler, however, to run the existing query and then filter the resulting recordset, thus incorporating the additional criterion.

Filtering the Query's Recordset

You can filter the recordset (that is, the results) of a query just as you can filter a table. The following steps, for example, use Filter By Selection to restrict the records displayed to those on which the number of spent hours is 0.00.

To Filter a Query's Recordset

1 **Click the Spent Hours field on the second record to select 0.00 as the number of spent hours. Point to the Filter By Selection button (Figure 7-19).**

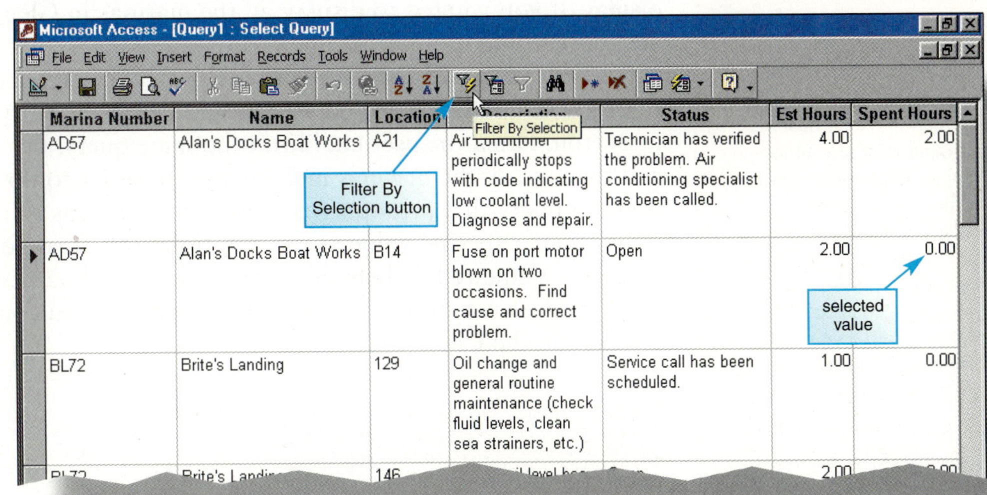

FIGURE 7-19

2 Click the Filter By Selection button. Point to the Remove Filter button.

Only those records on which the number of spent hours is 0.00 display (Figure 7-20). Nelson's Wharf, which had no open workorders, does not display because there was no value in the Spent Hours field.

3 Click the Remove Filter button so that all records once again display. Close the Query by clicking its Close Window button. Click the Yes button to save the query. Type `Work Orders by Marina` **as the name of the query and click the OK button.**

The query is saved.

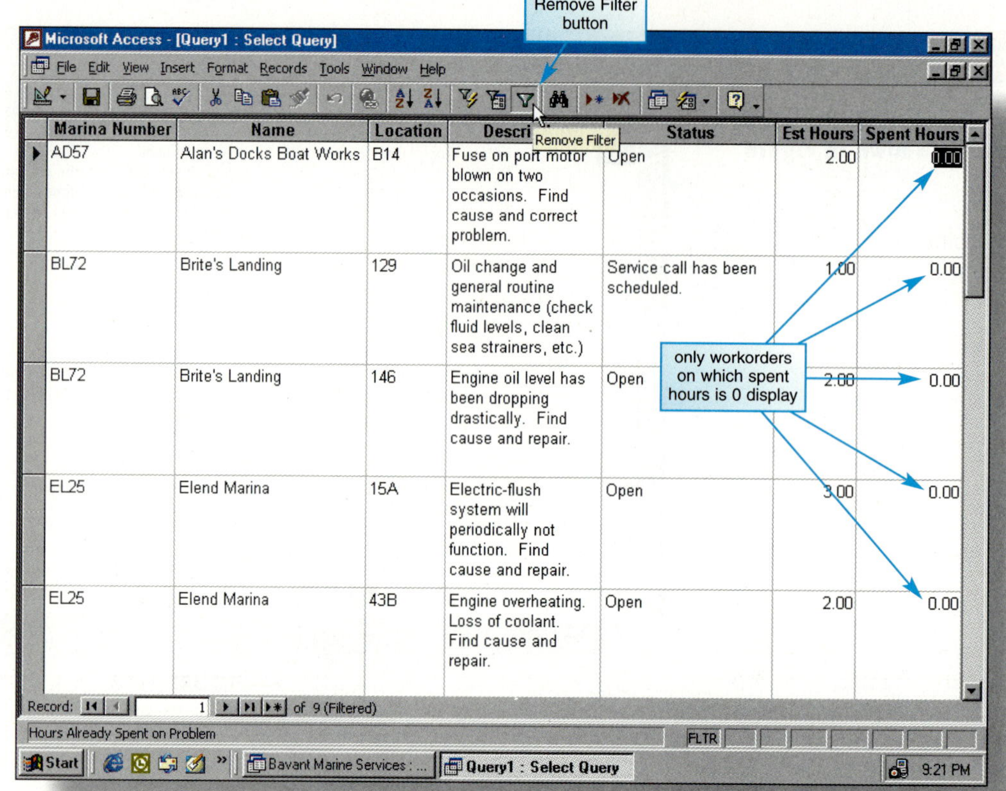

FIGURE 7-20

More About

Parameter Queries

Parameter queries are especially useful in cases where the same query is run frequently with slight changes to one or more of the query's criteria. By using parameters rather than specific values, you can enter the values for the criterion as the query is run rather than having to change the query design. For more information about parameter queries, visit the Access 2000 More About page (www.scsite.com/ac2000/more.htm) and then click Parameter Queries.

Creating a Parameter Query

Rather than giving a specific criterion when you first create the query, there are occasions where you want to be able to enter part of the criterion when you run the query and then have the appropriate results display. For example, to display all the marinas located in Burton, you could enter Burton as a criterion in the City field. From that point on, every time you ran the query, only the marinas in Burton would display. If you wanted to display all the marinas in Glenview, you would need to create another query.

A better way is to allow the user to enter the city at the time the query is run. Thus a user could run the query, enter Burton as the city and then see all the marinas in Burton. Later, the user could run the same query, but enter Glenview as the city, and then see all the marinas in Glenview. In order to do this, you create a **parameter query**, a query that prompts for input whenever it is run. You enter a parameter, rather than a specific value as the criterion. You create one by enclosing a value in a criterion in square brackets (like you enclose field names), but where the value in the brackets does not match any field. For example, you could place [Enter city] as the criterion in the City field.

You can include more than one parameter in a query. At Bavant, they want to be able to enter a beginning and ending marina number and then display all the records in the Marina table for which the marina number is between the two values entered. If the user enters AA00 and ZZ99 as the beginning and ending numbers, the display will include all marinas. If the user enters BL72 as both the beginning number and the ending number, only those workorders for marina BL72 will display. If the user enters EL25 as the beginning number and FM22 as the ending number, only those workorders on which the marina number is between EL25 and FM22 will display.

In order to allow users to enter two values, there will be two values in the criterion enclosed in square brackets, that is, two parameters, as shown in the following steps.

Queries

If you create an expression in a query in which a field name enclosed in brackets is misspelled, Access will assume that the brackets contain a parameter. When you run the query, it will ask you for a value. If this happens, notice the name specified in the dialog box, check the spelling, and then make the necessary changes.

To Create a Parameter Query

1 **In the Database window, click Queries on the Objects bar and then right-click Work Orders by Marina. Click Design View on the shortcut menu. If necessary, maximize the Work Orders by Marina : Select Query window.**

2 **Right-click the Criteria row under the Marina Number field and then point to Zoom (Figure 7-21).**

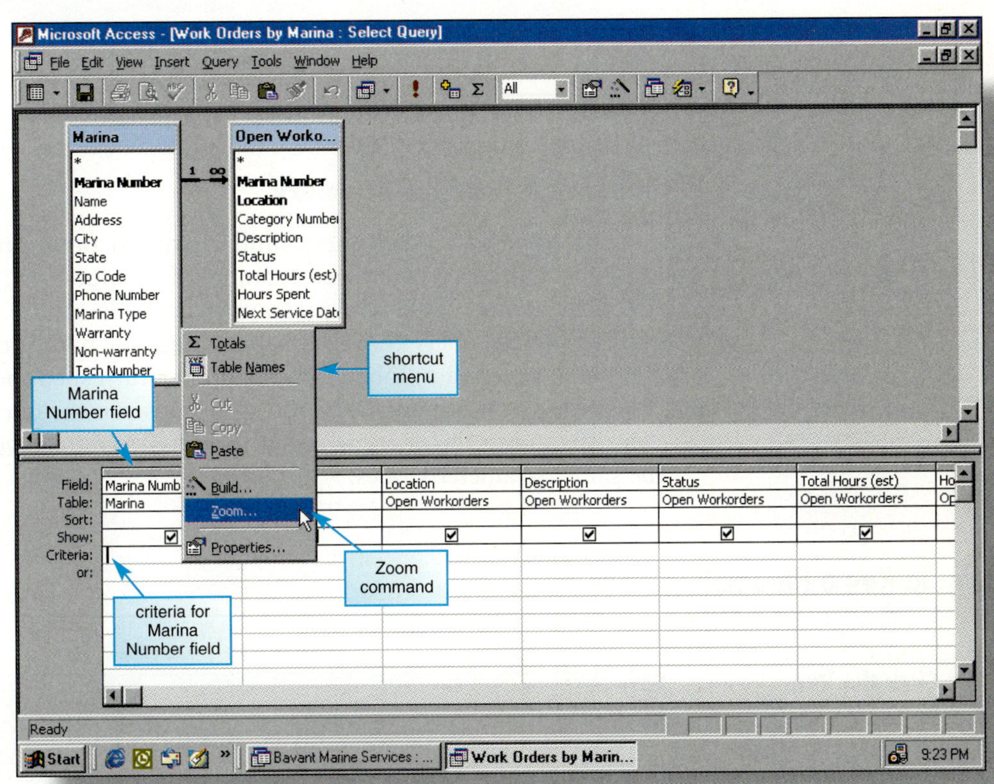

FIGURE 7-21

Click Zoom and then type `Between [Beginning marina number] and [Ending marina number]` **in the Zoom dialog box. Point to the OK button.**

The Zoom dialog box displays (Figure 7-22).

Click the OK button.

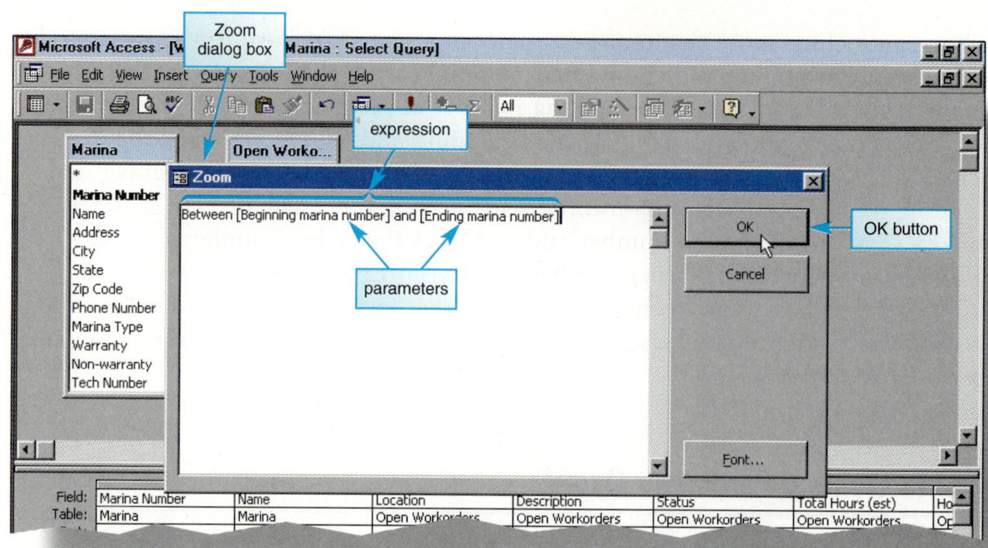

FIGURE 7-22

Running a Parameter Query

You run a parameter query similarly to any other query. The only difference is that when you do, you will be prompted for values for any parameter in the query; that is, the values for any expression enclosed in square brackets other than field names. For this query that means the values for both the beginning marina number and ending marina number. Once you have furnished these values, the appropriate results then will display. The following steps run the query from the query Design view. If you ran the query from the Database window, you would be prompted for the same parameter values.

To Run a Parameter Query

Click the Run button on the toolbar. Type `AA00` **as the beginning marina number and then click the OK button. Type** `ZZ99` **as the ending marina number (Figure 7-23). Point to the OK button.**

The Enter Parameter Value dialog box displays.

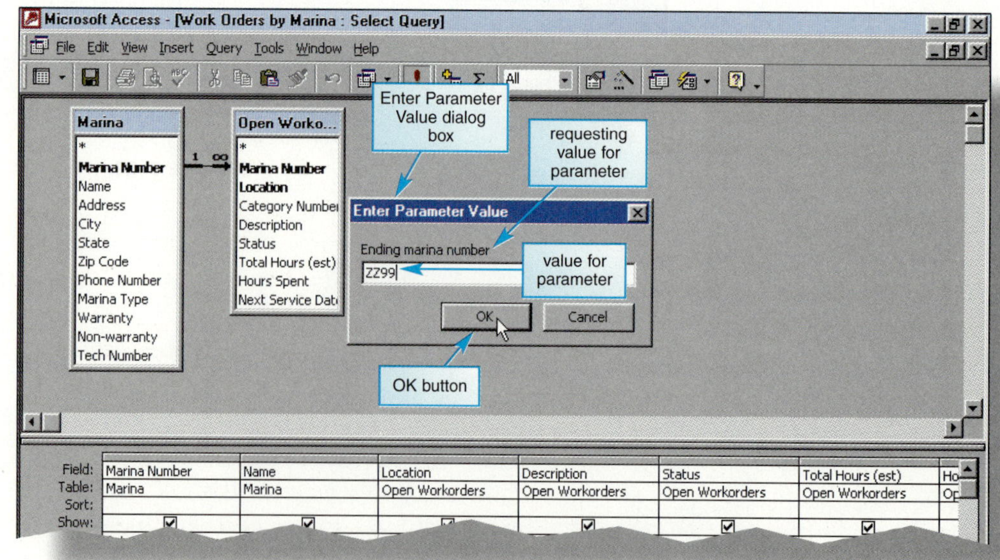

FIGURE 7-23

2 **Click the OK button.**

All records display.

3 **Click the View button to return to Design view. Click the Run button. Type** `BL72` **as the beginning marina number and then click the OK button. Type** `BL72` **as the ending marina number and then click the OK button.**

Only those workorders on which the marina number is BL72 display (Figure 7-24).

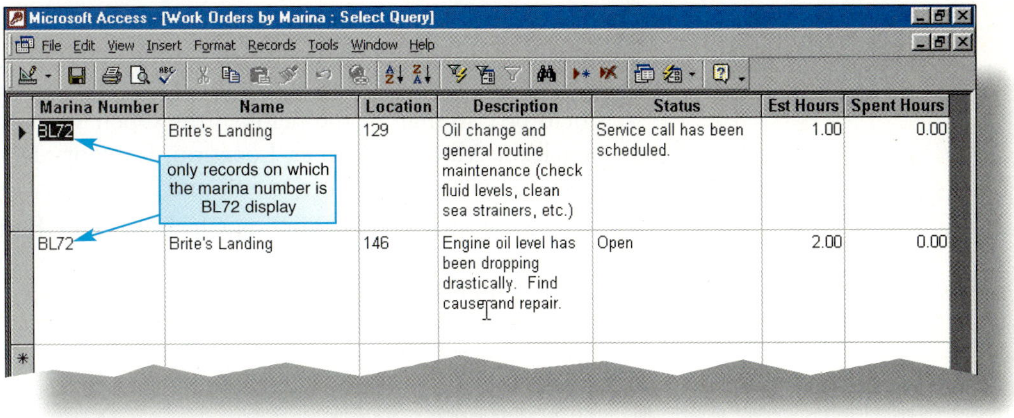

Microsoft Access - [Work Orders by Marina : Select Query]

Marina Number	Name	Location	Description	Status	Est Hours	Spent Hours
BL72	Brite's Landing	129	Oil change and general routine maintenance (check fluid levels, clean sea strainers, etc.)	Service call has been scheduled.	1.00	0.00
BL72	Brite's Landing	146	Engine oil level has been dropping drastically. Find cause and repair.	Open	2.00	0.00

only records on which the marina number is BL72 display

FIGURE 7-24

4 **Close the query by clicking its Close Window button. Click the Yes button to save the changes.**

Creating Queries for Reports

The report you will create requires two queries. The first query relates technicians and marinas and the second query relates categories and workorders. The following steps create the necessary queries.

TO CREATE THE QUERIES

1. In the Database window, click Tables on the Objects bar, if necessary, and then click Technician. Click the New Object: Query button arrow on the Database window toolbar. (Yours may read New Object: AutoForm.) Click Query. Be sure Design View is selected, and then click the OK button. If necessary, maximize the Query1 : Select Query window. Resize the upper and lower panes and the Technician field box so that all the fields in the Technician table display.
2. Right-click any open area in the upper pane, click Show Table on the shortcut menu, click the Marina table, click the Add button, and then click the Close button in the Show Table dialog box. Resize the Marina field box so that all the fields in the Marina table display. Double-click the Tech Number, First Name, and Last Name fields from the Technician table. Double-click the Marina Number, Name, Address, City, State, Zip Code, Phone Number, Marina Type, Warranty, and Non-warranty fields from the Marina table.
3. Close the query by clicking its Close Window button. Click the Yes button to save the query. Type `Technicians and Marinas` as the name of the query and then click the OK button.
4. Click Tables on the Objects bar, if necessary and then click Category. Click the New Object: Query button arrow on the Database window toolbar. Click Query. Be sure Design View is selected and then click the OK button. If necessary, maximize the Query1: Select Query window. Resize the upper and lower panes.

5. Right-click any open area in the upper pane, click Show Table on the shortcut menu, click the Open Workorders table, click the Add button and then click the Close button in the Show Table dialog box. Resize the Open Workorders field box so that all the fields in the Open Workorders table display. Double-click the Marina Number, Location, Category Description, Description, Status, Total Hours (est), Hours Spent, and Next Service Date fields.

6. Close the query by clicking its Close Window button. Click the Yes button to save the query. Type `Workorders and Categories` as the name of the query and then click the OK button.

The queries are saved.

Creating a Report

Creating the report shown in Figure 7-1a on page A 7.5 from scratch involves creating the initial report in Report Design view, adding the subreport, modifying the subreport separately from the main report, and then making the final modifications to the main report.

Creating the Initial Report

When you want to create a report from scratch, you begin with the same general procedure as when you want to use the Report Wizard to create the report. The difference is that you will select Design View rather than Report Wizard. Perform the following steps to create the initial version of the Technician Master List.

Steps To Create the Initial Report

1. **If necessary, in the Database window, click Queries on the Objects bar, and then click Technicians and Marinas. Click the New Object: Query button arrow on the Database window toolbar, and then click Report. Be sure Design View is selected and click the OK button.**

2. **Dock the toolbox at the bottom of the screen, if necessary. Be sure the field box displays. If it does not, click the Field List button on the Report Design toolbar. Point to the lower boundary of the field box.**

A blank report displays in Design view (Figure 7-25).

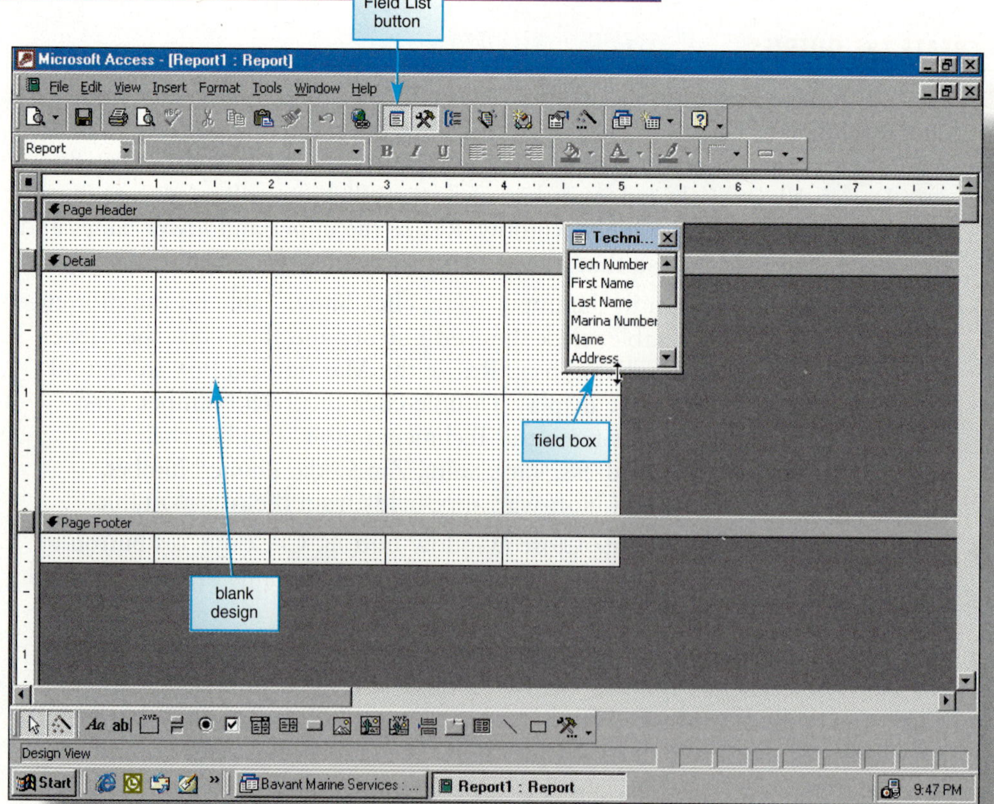

FIGURE 7-25

3 Drag the bottom boundary of the field box down so that all fields display. Move the field box to the lower-right corner of the screen by dragging its title bar. Right-click any open area of the Detail section of the report and then point to Sorting and Grouping on the shortcut menu.

The field box is moved and the shortcut menu displays (Figure 7-26).

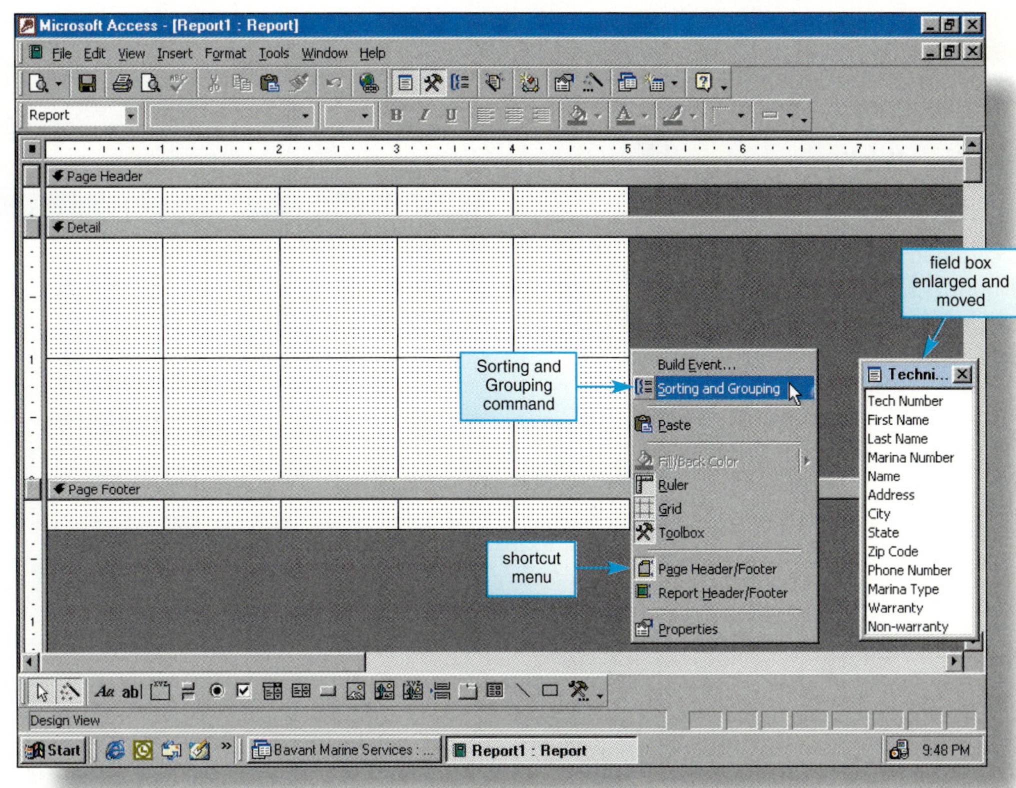

FIGURE 7-26

4 Click Sorting and Grouping, click the down arrow in the Field/Expression box, and then point to Tech Number.

The Sorting and Grouping dialog box displays (Figure 7-27). The list of available fields displays.

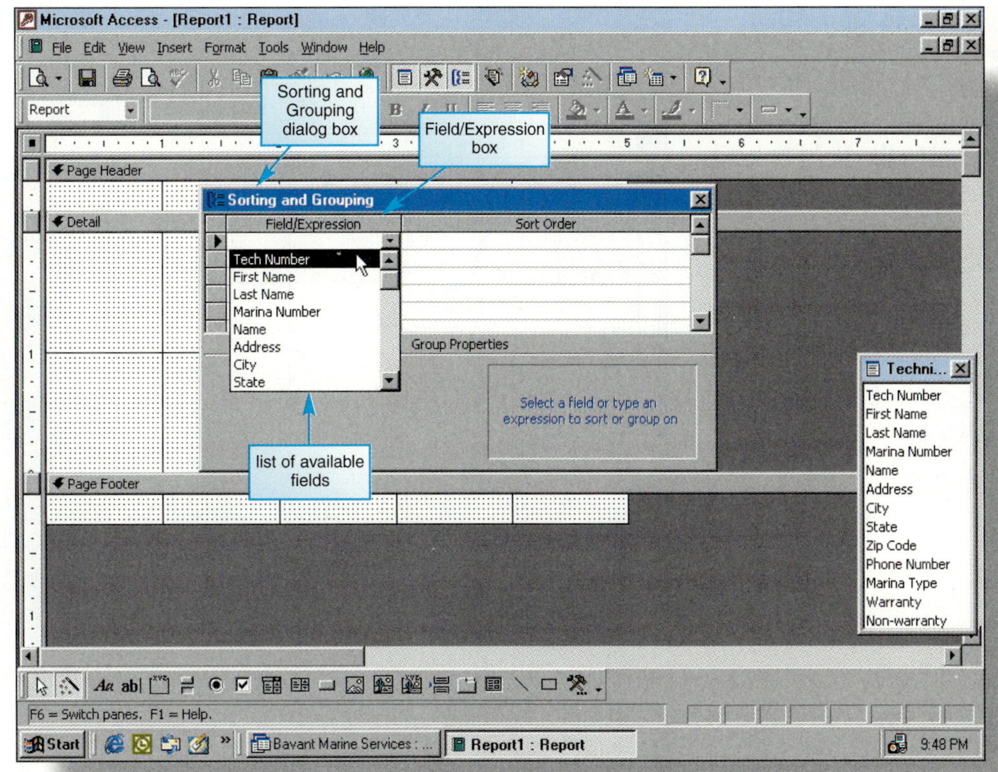

FIGURE 7-27

5 **Click Tech Number, click the Group Header property, click the Group Header box arrow, and then click Yes.**

The Group Header property is changed from No to Yes (Figure 7-28). The group header for the Tech Number field displays.

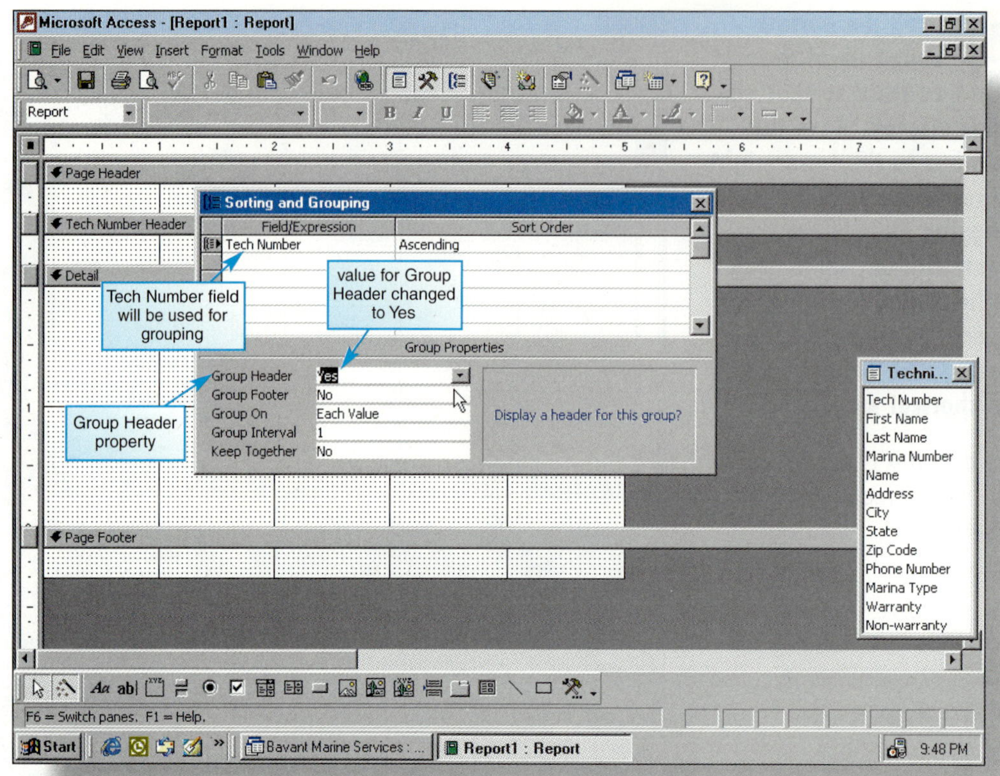

FIGURE 7-28

6 **Close the Sorting and Grouping dialog box by clicking its Close button. Point to Tech Number in the field box (Figure 7-29).**

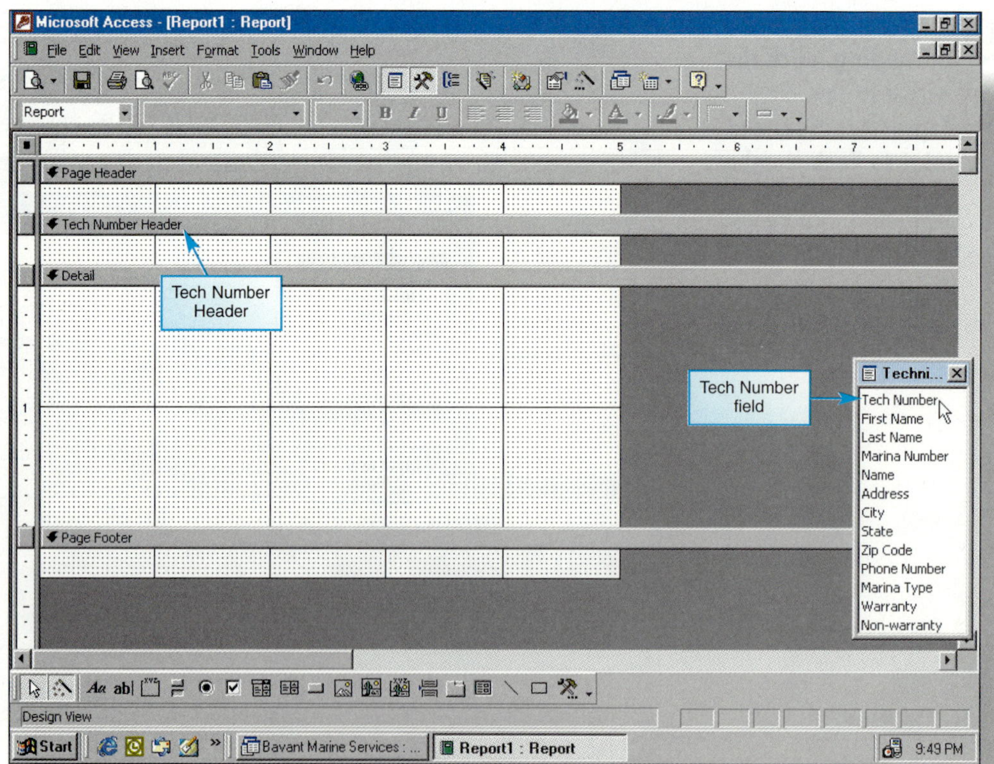

FIGURE 7-29

Adding the Fields

You can add the fields to the report by dragging them from the field list to the appropriate position on the report. The following steps add the fields to the report.

To Add the Fields

1 **Drag the Tech Number field to the approximate position shown in Figure 7-30.**

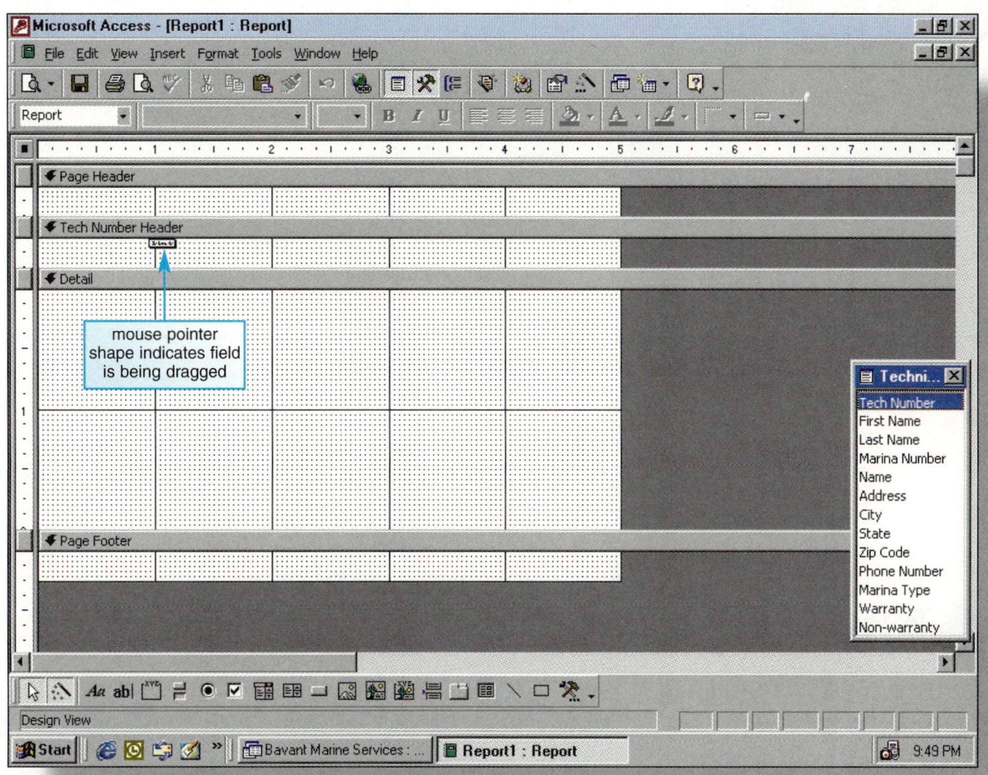

FIGURE 7-30

2 **Release the left mouse button to place the field. Use the same techniques to place the First Name and Last Name fields in the approximate positions shown in Figure 7-31. If any field is not in the correct position, drag it to its correct location. If you wish to move the control or the attached label separately, drag the large handle in the upper-left corner of the control or label.**

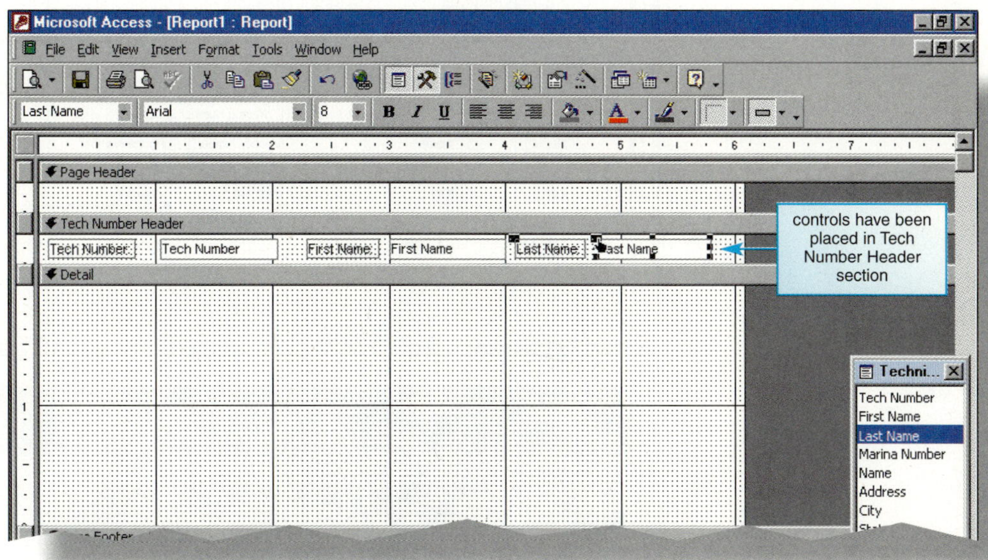

FIGURE 7-31

3 **Place the remaining fields in the positions shown in Figure 7-32 and point to the Close button in the field box.**

4 **Close the field box by clicking its Close button.**

The fields are placed. The field box no longer displays.

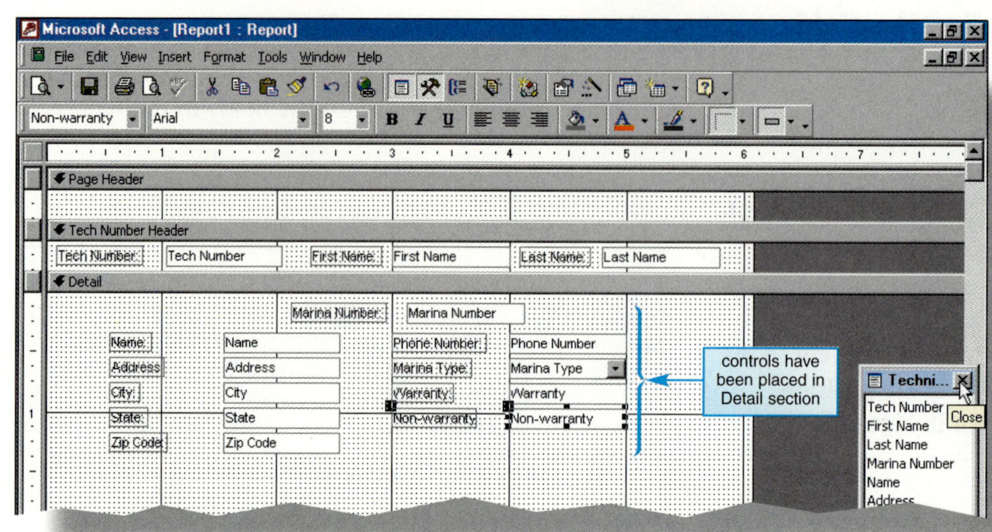

FIGURE 7-32

Saving the Report

Before proceeding with the next steps in the modification of the report, it is a good idea to save your work. Perform the following steps to save the current report.

Steps To Save the Report

1 **Point to the Save button on the Report Design toolbar (Figure 7-33).**

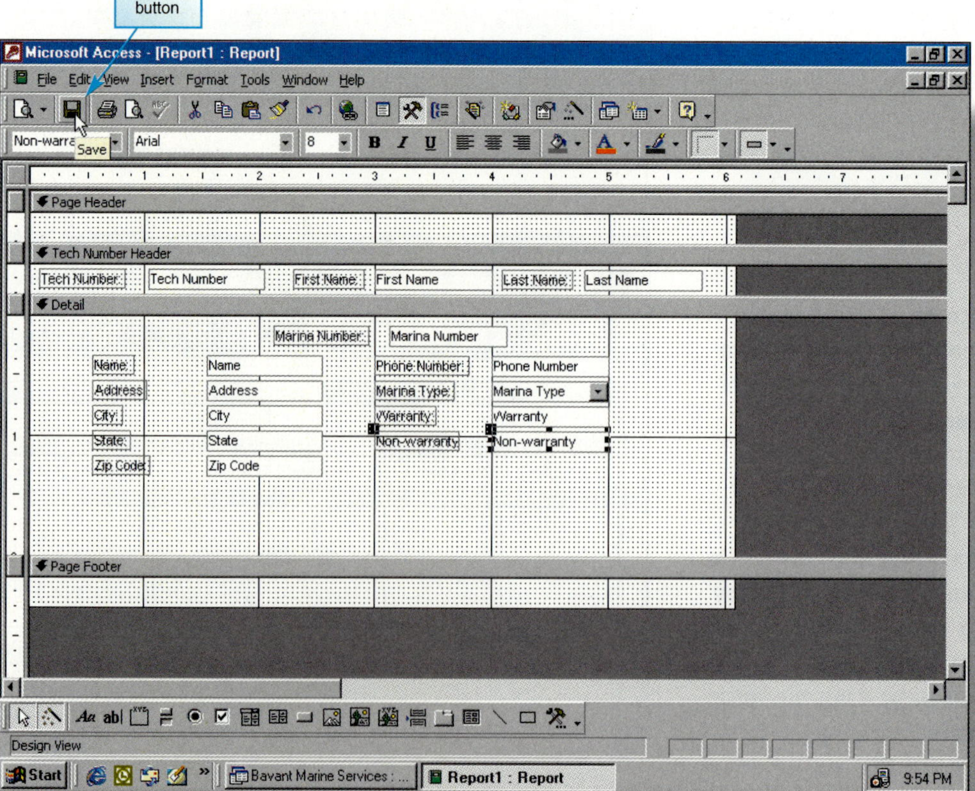

FIGURE 7-33

2 **Click the Save button and then type** `Technician Master List` **as the report name. Point to the OK button.**

The Save As dialog box displays (Figure 7-34).

3 **Click the OK button.**

The report is saved.

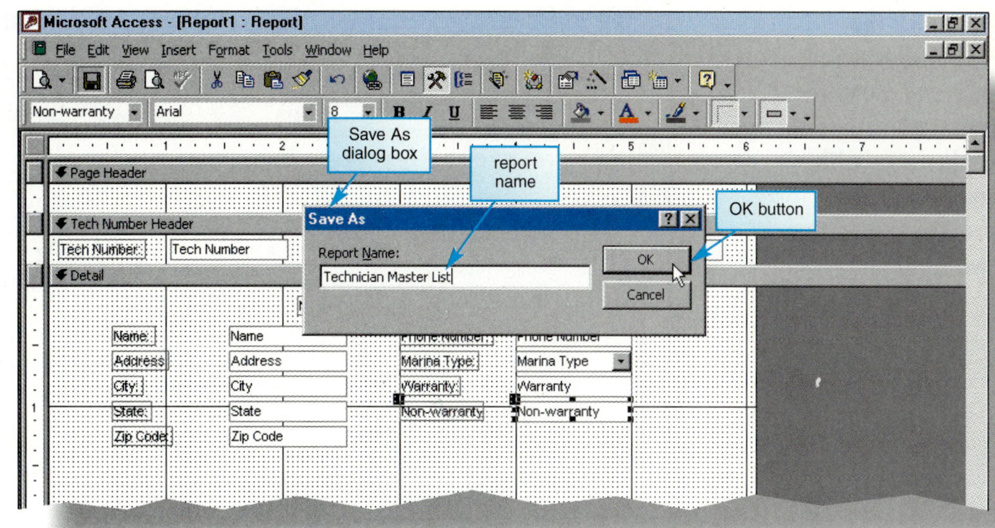

FIGURE 7-34

Adding a Subreport

To add a subreport to a report, you use the Subform/Subreport button in the toolbox. Provided the Control Wizards button is depressed, a wizard will guide you through the process of adding the subreport as in the following steps.

Subreports

A main report can contain more than one subreport. If the main report is based on a table or query, each subreport must contain information related to the information in the main report.

To Add a Subreport

1 **Be sure the Control Wizards button is depressed and point to the Subform/Subreport button in the toolbox (Figure 7-35).**

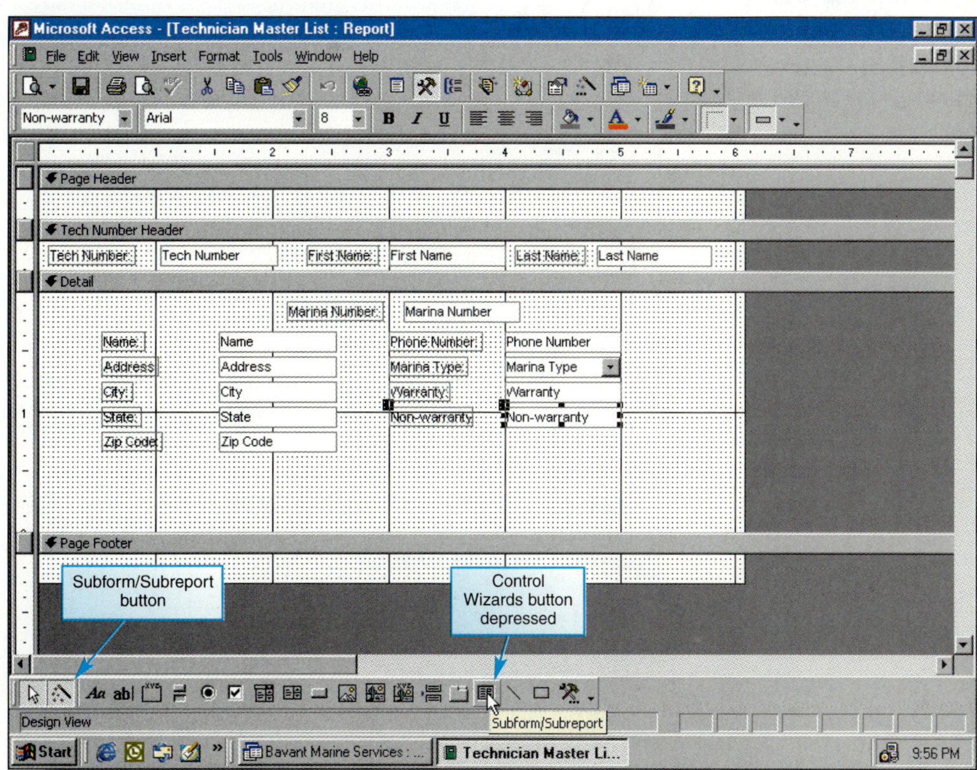

FIGURE 7-35

2 **Click the Subform/Subreport button and move the pointer, which has changed to a plus sign with a subreport, to the approximate position shown in Figure 7-36.**

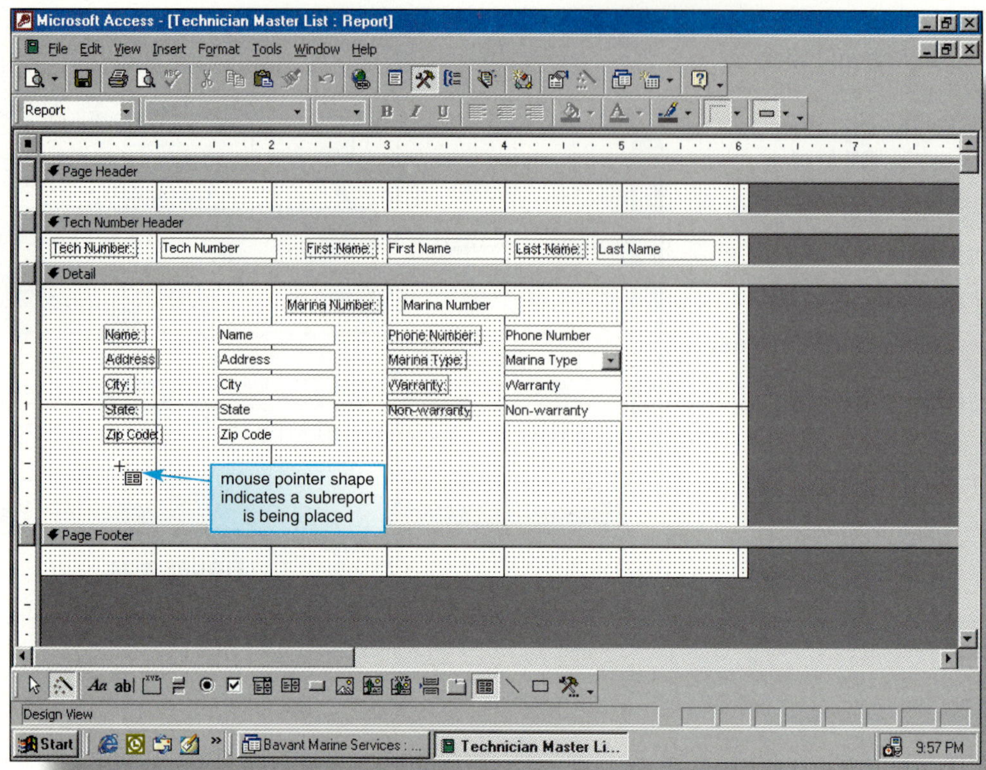

FIGURE 7-36

3 **Click the position shown in Figure 7-36. Be sure the Use existing Tables and Queries option button is selected and then point to the Next button.**

The SubReport Wizard dialog box displays (Figure 7-37).

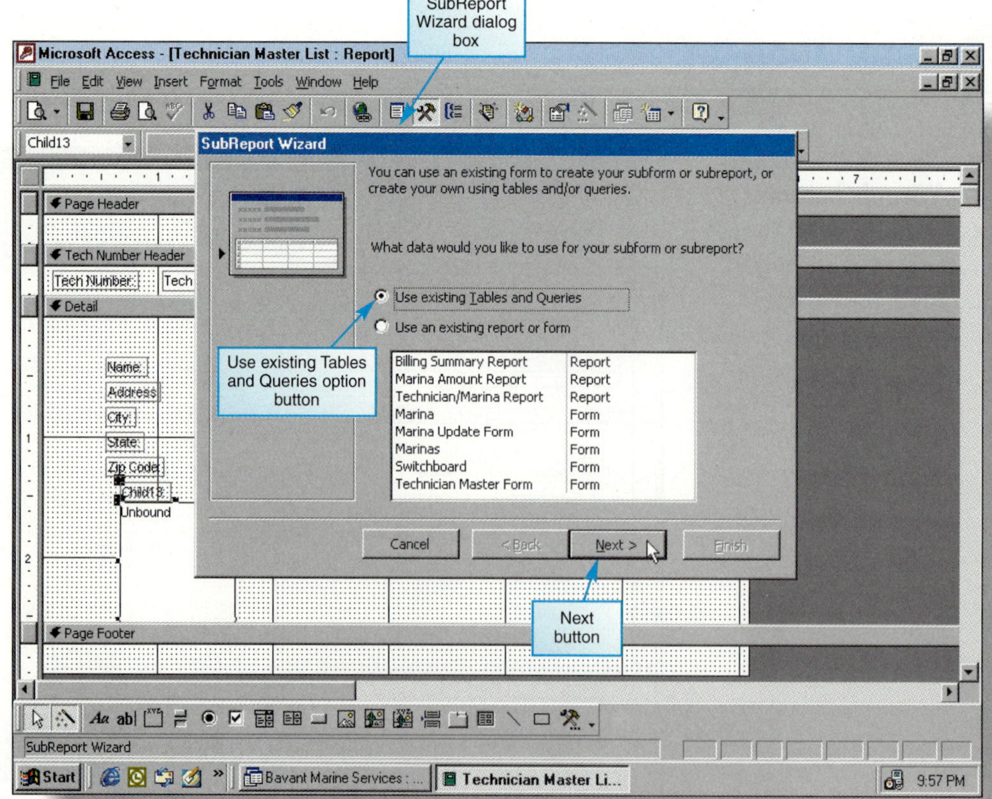

FIGURE 7-37

4 **Click the Next button. Click the Tables/Queries box arrow and then point to Query: Workorders and Categories (Figure 7-38).**

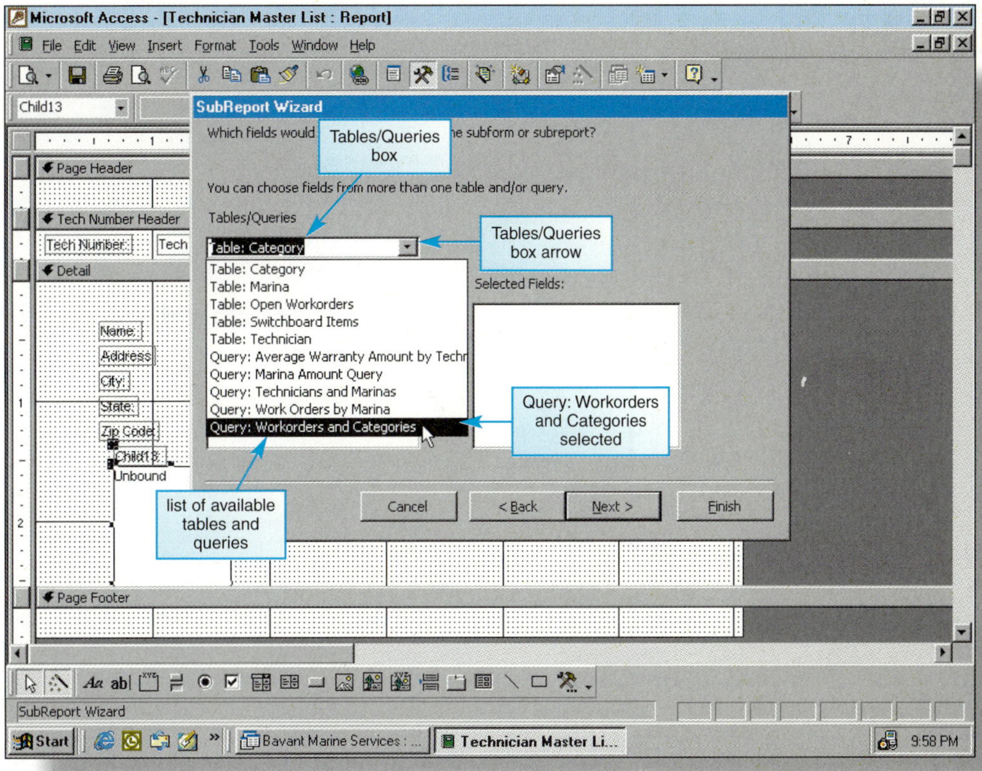

FIGURE 7-38

5 **Click Query: Workorders and Categories, click the Add All Fields button, and then point to the Next button (Figure 7-39).**

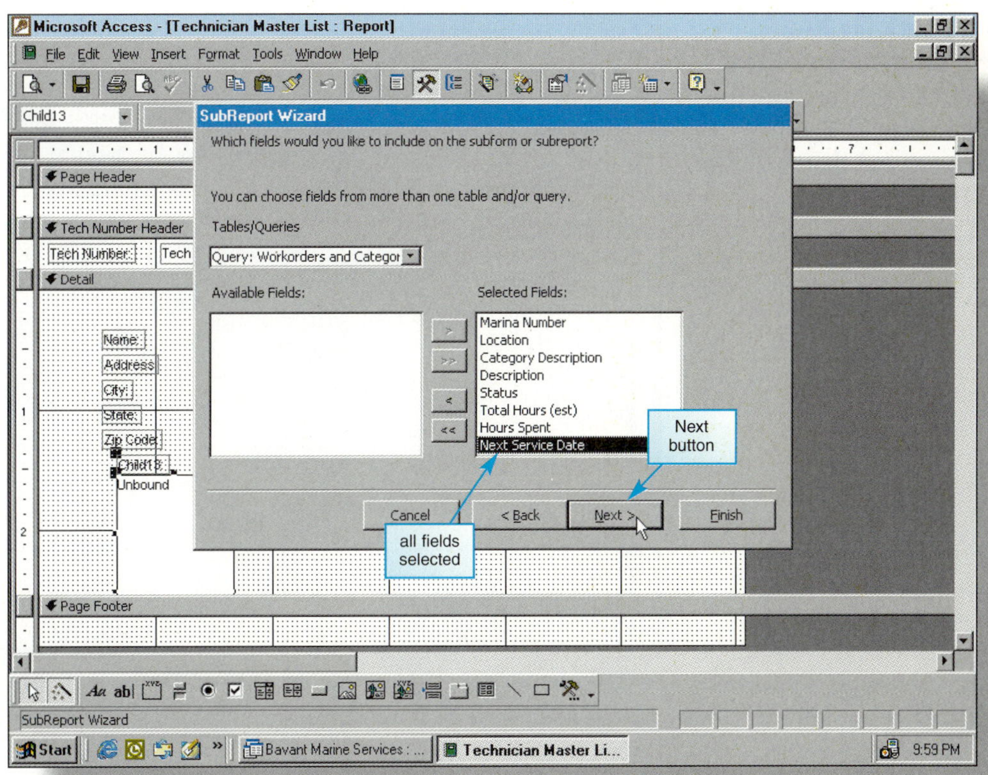

FIGURE 7-39

6 Click the Next button. Be sure the Choose from a list option button is selected and then point to the Next button.

The SubReport Wizard dialog box displays (Figure 7-40). You use this dialog box to indicate the fields that link the main report (referred to as "form" in the sentence) to the subreport (referred to as "subform"). If the fields have the same name, as they often will, you can simply select Choose from a list and then accept the selection Access already has made.

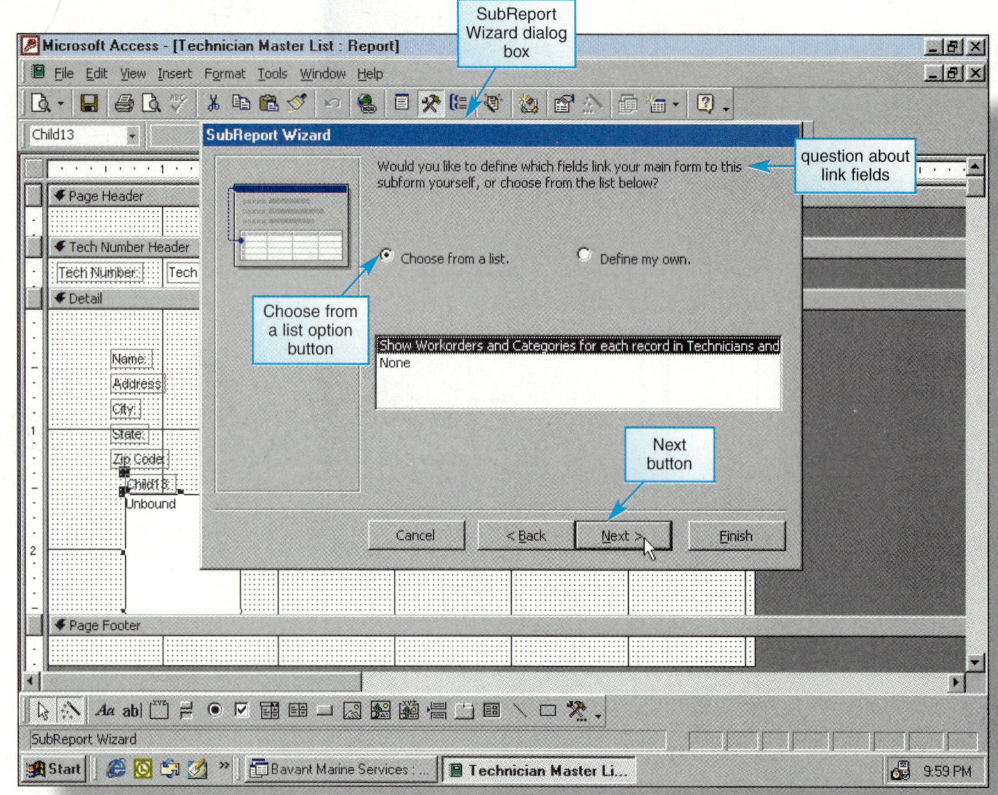

FIGURE 7-40

7 Click the Next button. Type `Open Workorders for Marina` **as the name of the subreport and then point to the Finish button (Figure 7-41).**

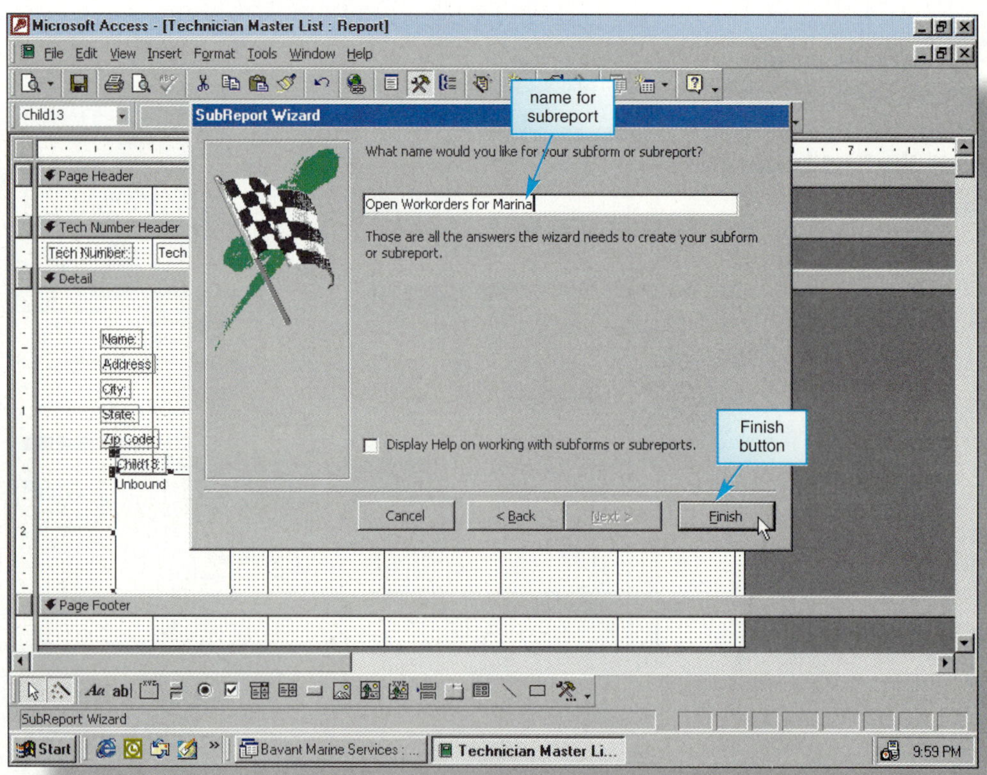

FIGURE 7-41

Click the Finish button.

The subreport is created and placed in the report design (Figure 7-42).

9 Close the report design by clicking its Close Window button. Click the Yes button to save the changes.

The report is saved. The Database window displays.

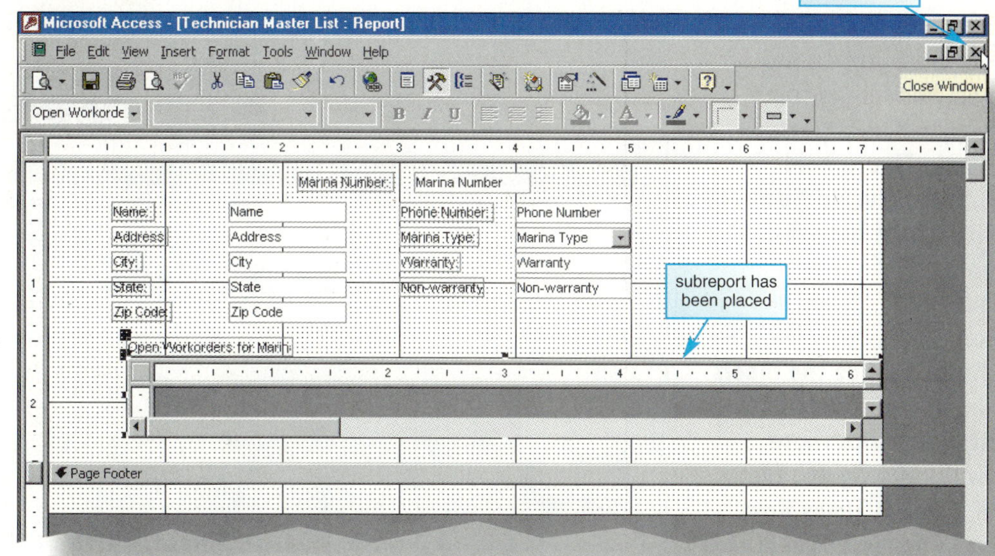

FIGURE 7-42

Modifying the Subreport

The subreport displays as a separate report in the Database window. It can be modified just like any other report. Perform the following steps to modify the subreport.

More About 2000

SubReports

A main report does not need to be based on a table or query. It can still contain one or more subreports. It simply serves as a container for the subreports, which then have no restrictions on the information they must contain.

To Modify the Subreport

1 Be sure the Reports object is selected, right-click Open Workorders for Marina, and then click Design View on the shortcut menu that displays. Point to the lower boundary of the Report Header section. The font and style of your headings may be different.

The design for the subreport displays (Figure 7-43).

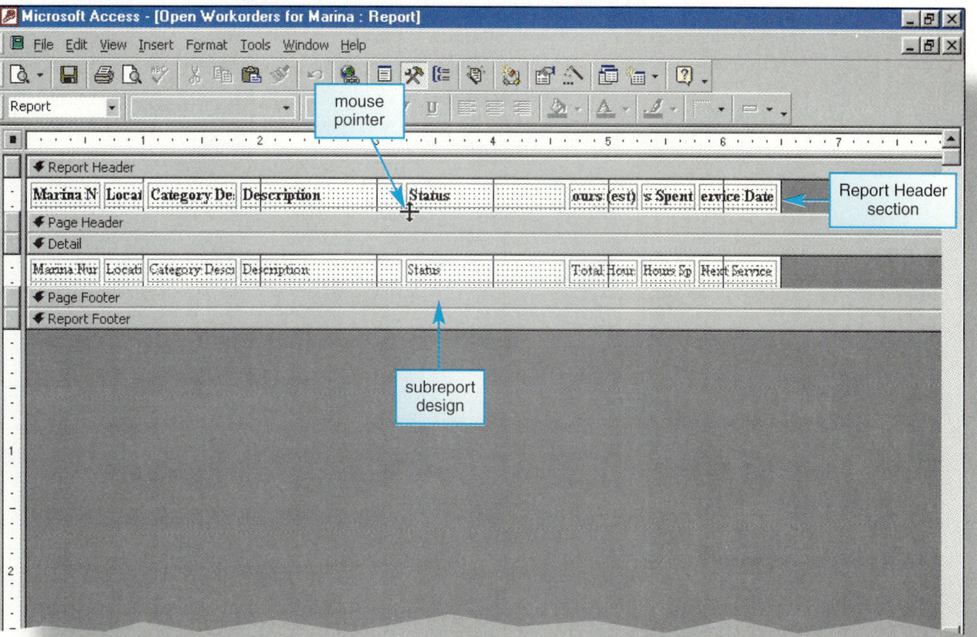

FIGURE 7-43

2 **Drag the lower boundary of the Report Header section to the approximate position shown in Figure 7-44. Delete the Marina Number controls from both the Report Header and Detail sections. Change the labels in the Report Header section to match those shown in the figure. The Font Name is Times New Roman, the Font Size is 10 and the Font Weight is Bold. (To extend a heading over two lines, press SHIFT+ENTER).**

Marina Number control deleted from Report Header section

Report Header enlarged

headings changed

Marina Number control deleted from Detail section

FIGURE 7-44

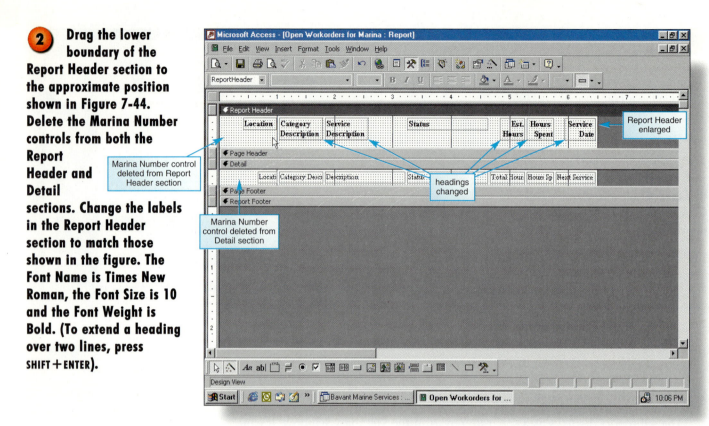

3 **Point to the ruler in the position shown in Figure 7-45.**

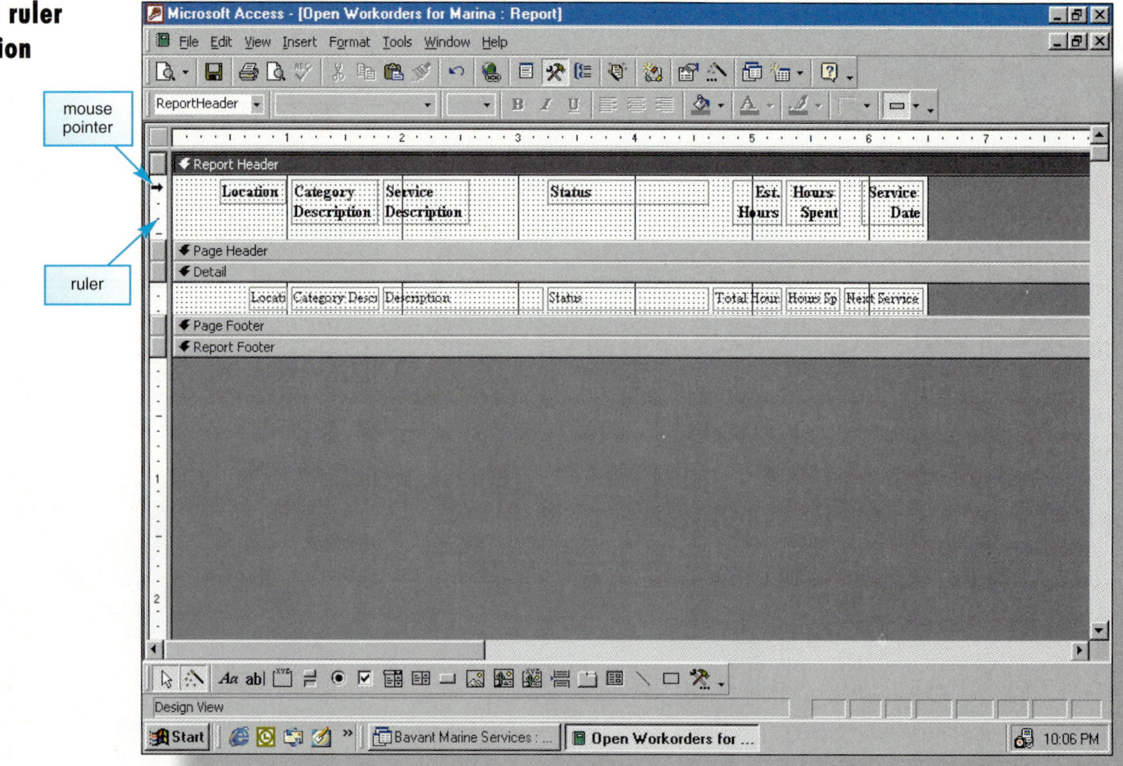

FIGURE 7-45

4 **Click the position shown in Figure 7-45.**

All the header labels are selected (Figure 7-46).

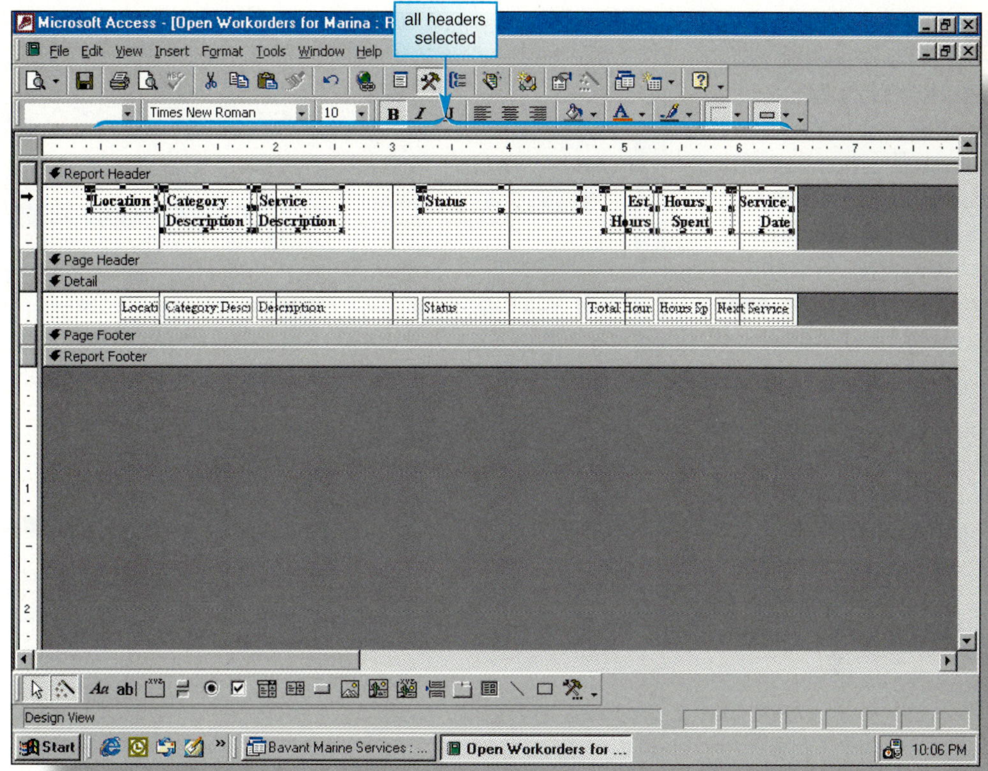

FIGURE 7-46

5 **Right-click any of the selected labels and then click Properties on the shortcut menu.**

The Multiple selection property sheet displays (Figure 7-47).

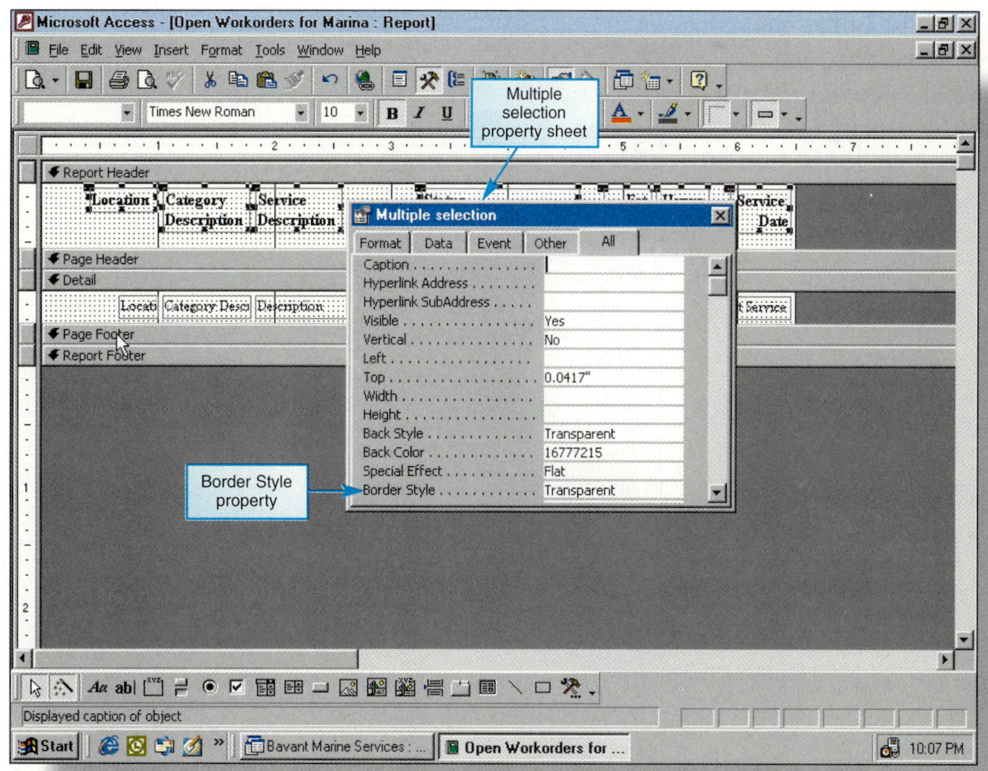

FIGURE 7-47

6 **Click the Border Style property, click the Border Style box, and then click Solid. Click the down scroll arrow so that the Text Align property displays. Click the Text Align property, click the Text Align box arrow, and then point to Center.**

The Multiple selection property sheet displays (Figure 7-48). The list of options for the Text Align property displays.

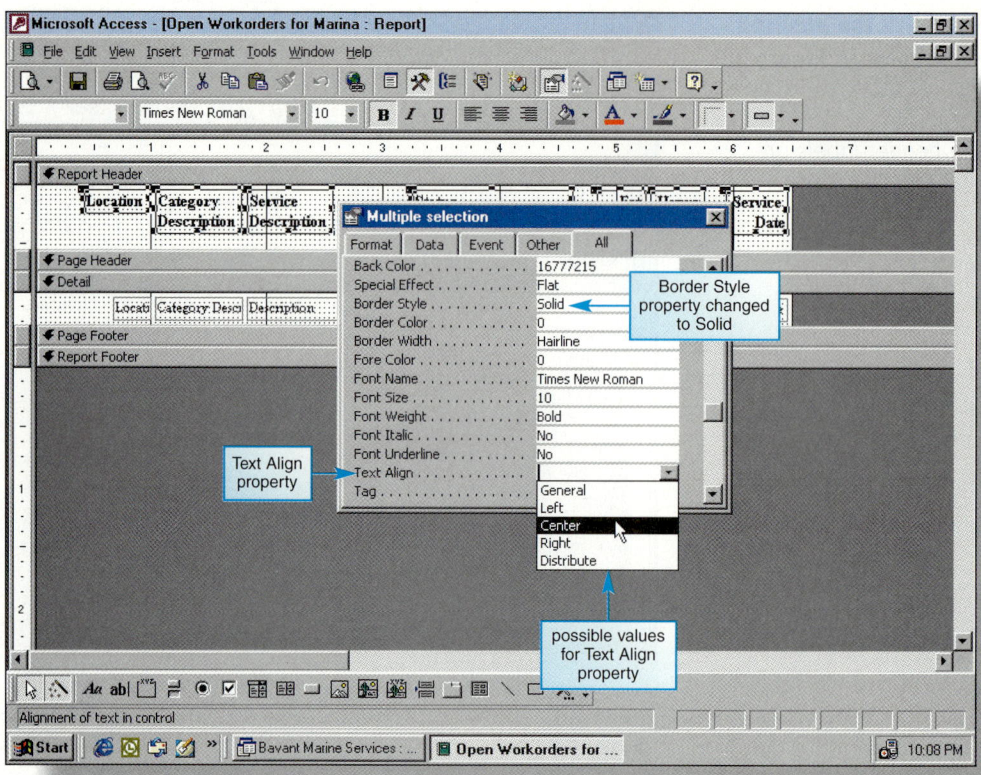

FIGURE 7-48

7 **Click Center and then close the Multiple selection property sheet by clicking its Close button. Point to the ruler in the position shown in Figure 7-49.**

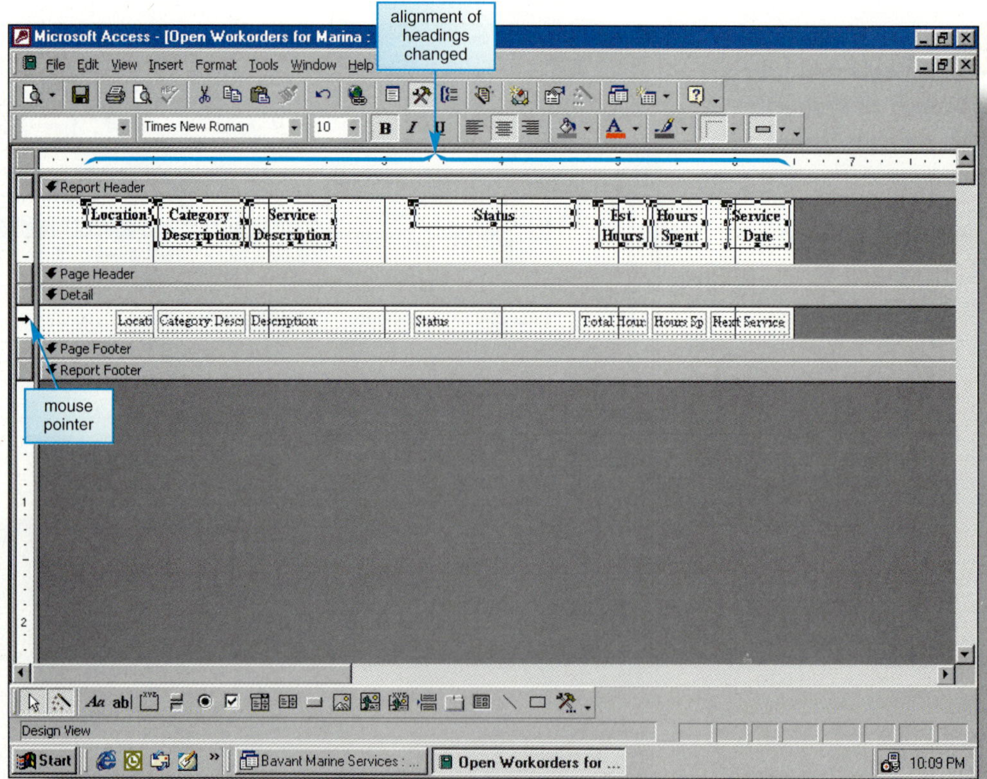

FIGURE 7-49

8 **Click the ruler in the position shown in Figure 7-49 to select all the controls in the Detail section. Right-click any of the selected controls and then click Properties on the shortcut menu. Click the Border Style property, click the Border Style box arrow, and then click Solid. Point to the Close button for the Multiple selection property sheet.**

The Border Style property is changed to Solid (Figure 7-50).

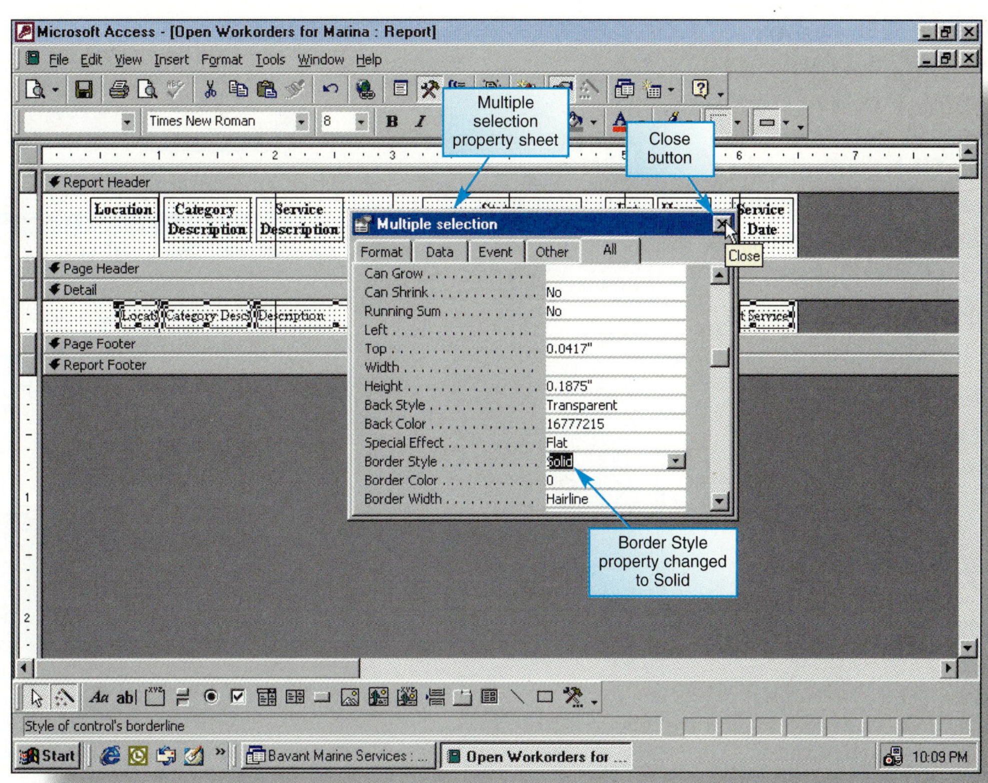

FIGURE 7-50

9 **Click the Close button. Click anywhere outside the Detail section to deselect the controls. Click the Total Hours (est) control in the Detail section. Hold down the SHIFT key and then click the Hours Spent control in the Detail section. Right-click either of the selected controls and point to Properties on the shortcut menu (Figure 7-51).**

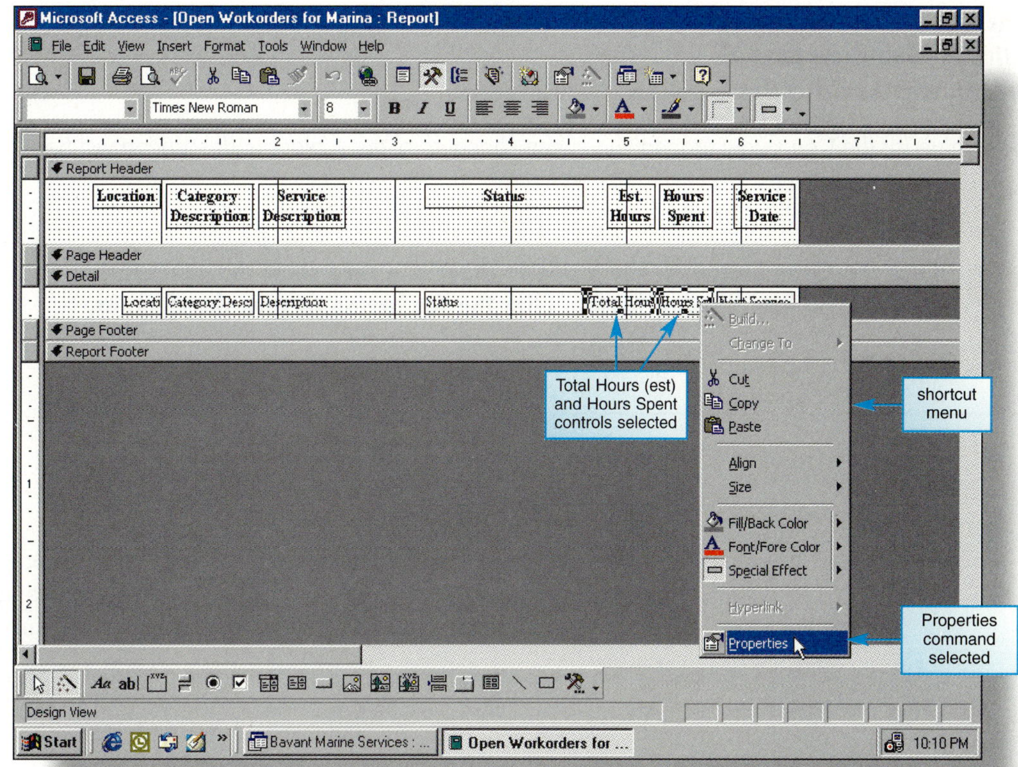

FIGURE 7-51

10 Click Properties, click the Format property, click the Format box arrow, and then click Fixed. Click the Decimal Places property, click the Decimal Places box arrow, and then click 2. Point to the Close button.

The format is changed to Fixed and the number of decimal places is changed to 2 (Figure 7-52).

11 Click the Close button for the Multiple selection property sheet.

12 Right-click the Category Description control in the Detail section and click Properties on the shortcut menu. Click the Can Grow property, click the Can Grow box arrow, and then click Yes.

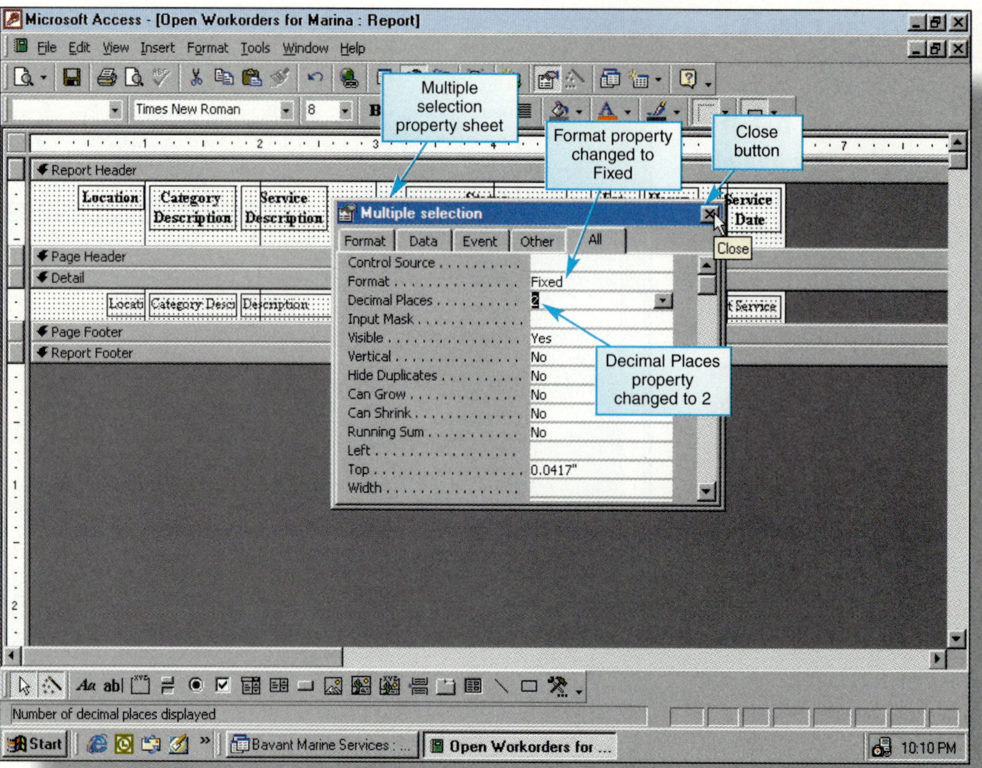

FIGURE 7-52

The value for the Can Grow property has been changed to Yes. Category description will be spread over several lines.

13 Click the Close button for the property sheet and then close the subreport by clicking its Close Window button. Click the Yes button to save the changes.

The changes are saved and the report is removed from the screen.

Moving the Subreport

To match the report shown in Figure 7-1a on page A 7.5, the subreport needs to be moved slightly to the left. The subreport can be dragged just like any other object in a report. Perform the following steps to move the subreport.

To Move the Subreport

1 **Be sure the Reports object is selected, right-click Technician Master List, and then click Design View on the shortcut menu.**

2 **Drag the subreport to the position shown in Figure 7-53.**

3 **Click anywhere outside the subreport control to deselect it.**

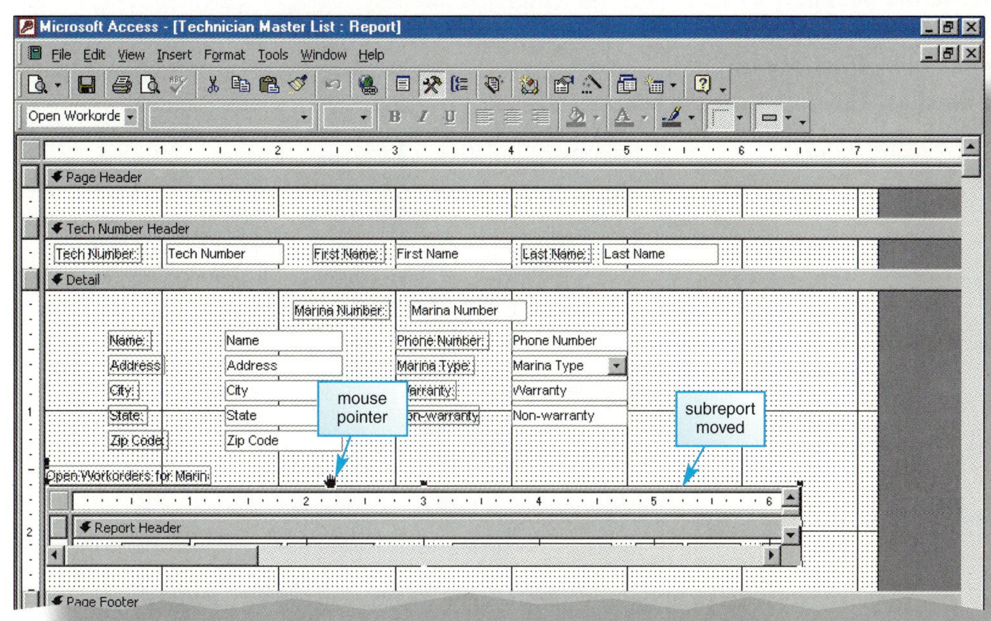

FIGURE 7-53

Adding a Date

To add a date to a report, use the Date and Time command on the Insert menu. When you do, you will be given a choice of a variety of date and time formats. After adding the date, you can drag it into the desired position. Perform the following steps to add the date.

More About

Adding a Date

After adding a date to a report, you can change the format used to display the date by right-clicking the date control and then selecting Properties on the shortcut menu. You then can select a format for the date and/or the time by changing the value for the Format property.

To Add a Date

1 **Click Insert on the menu bar and then click Date and Time on the Insert menu. Be sure that Include Date is checked and that Include Time is not checked. Be sure the date format selected is the first of the three options. Point to the OK button.**

The Date and Time dialog box displays (Figure 7-54).

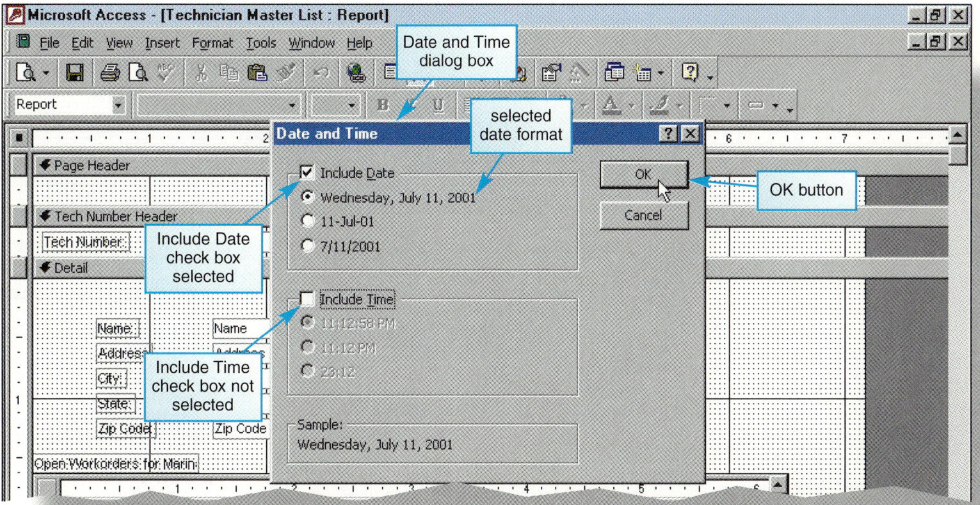

FIGURE 7-54

2 **Click the OK button to add the date. Point to the boundary of the newly-added Date control away from any of the handles. The pointer shape changes to a hand as in Figure 7-55.**

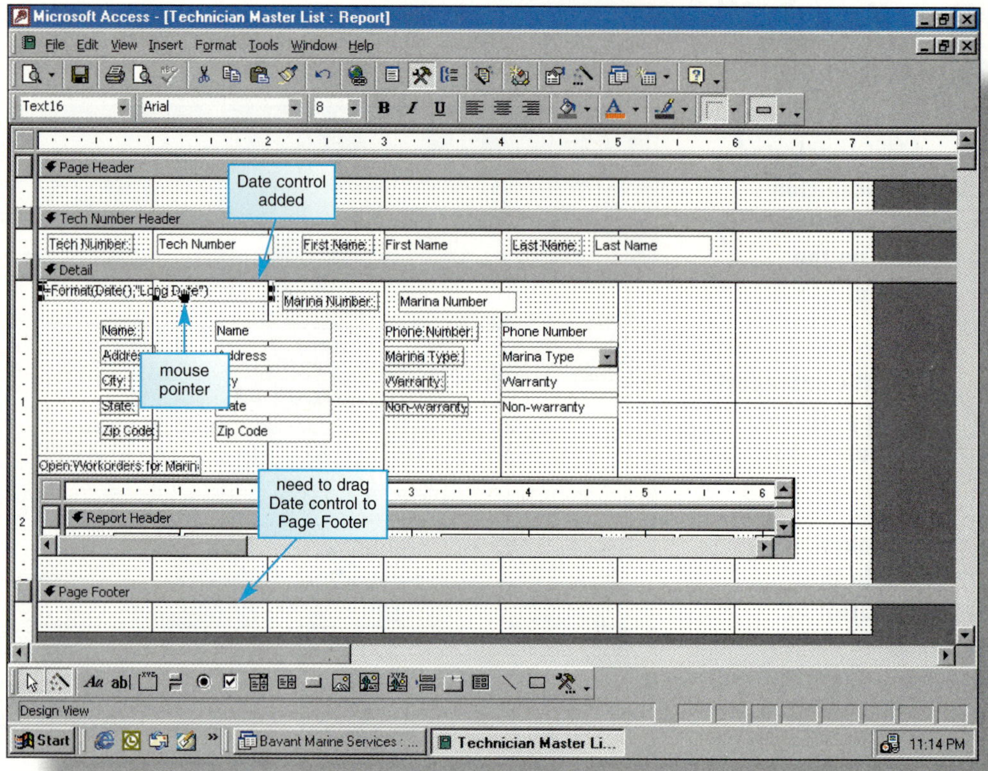

FIGURE 7-55

3 **Drag the Date control to the position shown in Figure 7-56.**

The date is added to the report.

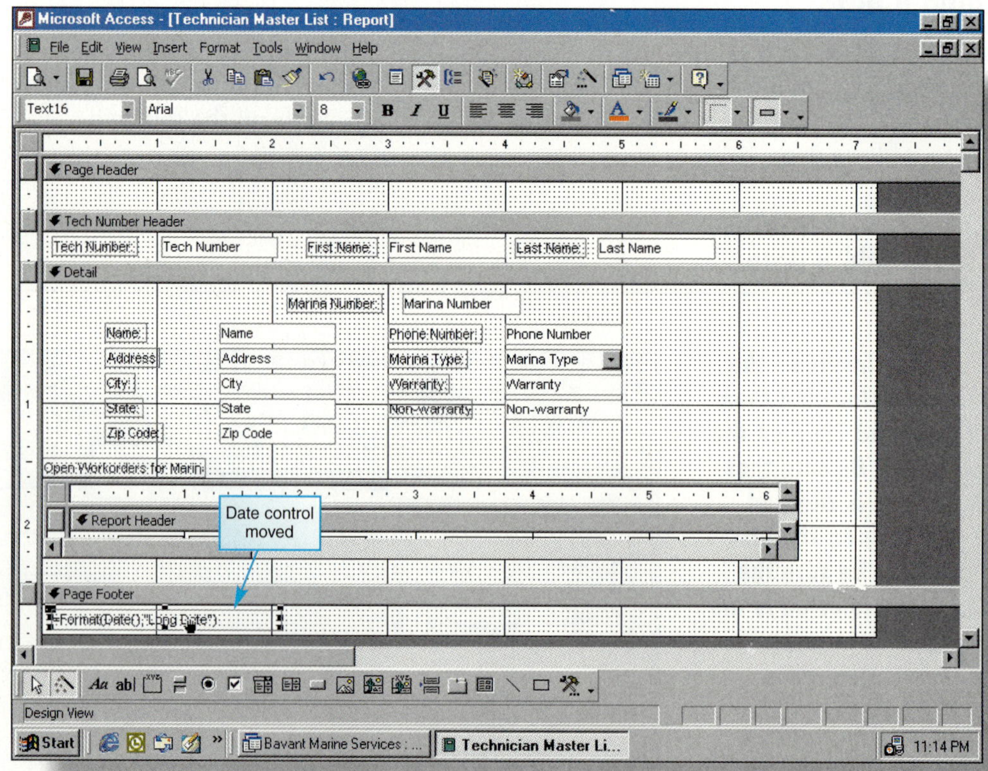

FIGURE 7-56

Adding a Page Number

To add a page number to a report, use the Page Numbers command on the Insert menu. When you do, you will be given a choice of a variety of page number formats and positions. Perform the following steps to add a page number.

More About

Adding Pages

After adding a page number to a report, you can change the format used to display the page number by right-clicking the page number control and then selecting Properties on the shortcut menu.

To Add a Page Number

1 **Click Insert on the menu bar and then click Page Numbers on the Insert menu. Be sure Page N of M, Bottom of Page [Footer], Right alignment, and Show Number on First Page are selected and then point to the OK button.**

The Page Numbers dialog box displays (Figure 7-57).

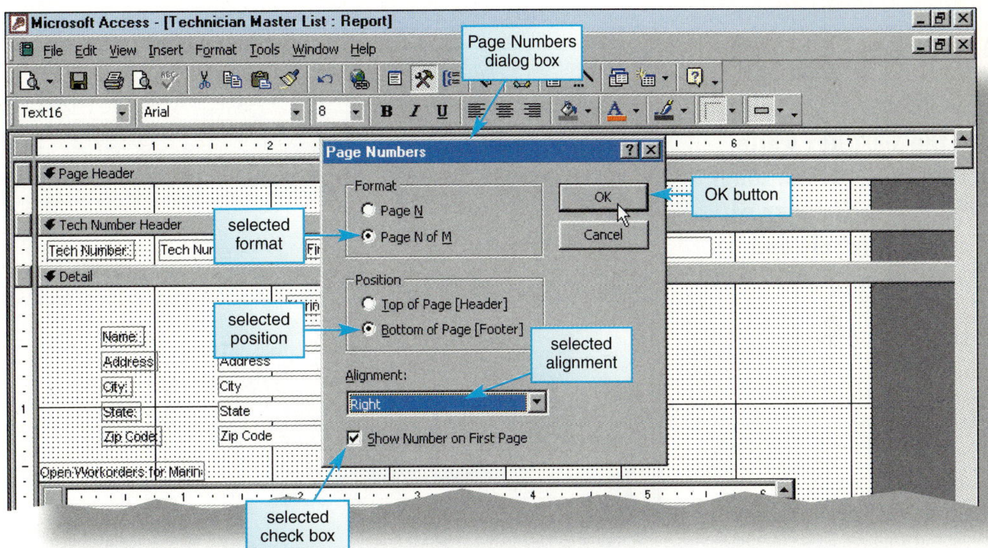

FIGURE 7-57

2 **Click the OK button to add a page number. Drag the Page Number control to the position shown in Figure 7-58.**

The page number is added.

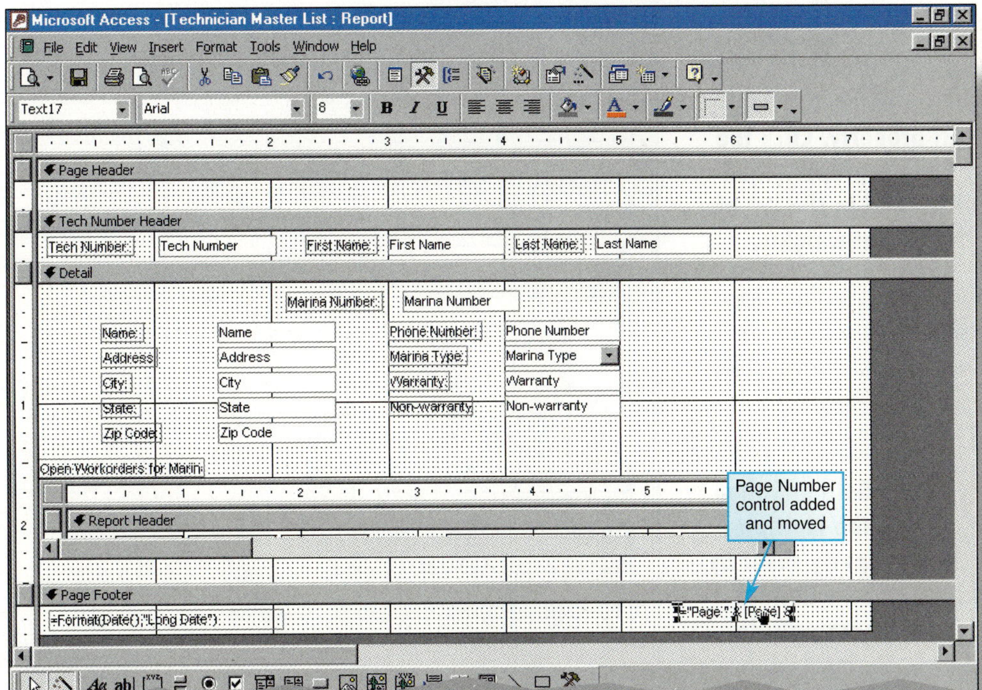

FIGURE 7-58

Bolding Labels

In the report shown in Figure 7-1a on page A 7.5, the labels are all bold. To bold the contents of one or more labels, change the Font Weight property to Bold. Perform the following steps to select all the labels and then change the Font Weight property.

To Bold Labels

1 Click the label for the Tech Number control to select it. Hold down the SHIFT key while selecting each of the other labels. Right-click any of the selected labels and point to Properties.

The shortcut menu displays (Figure 7-59).

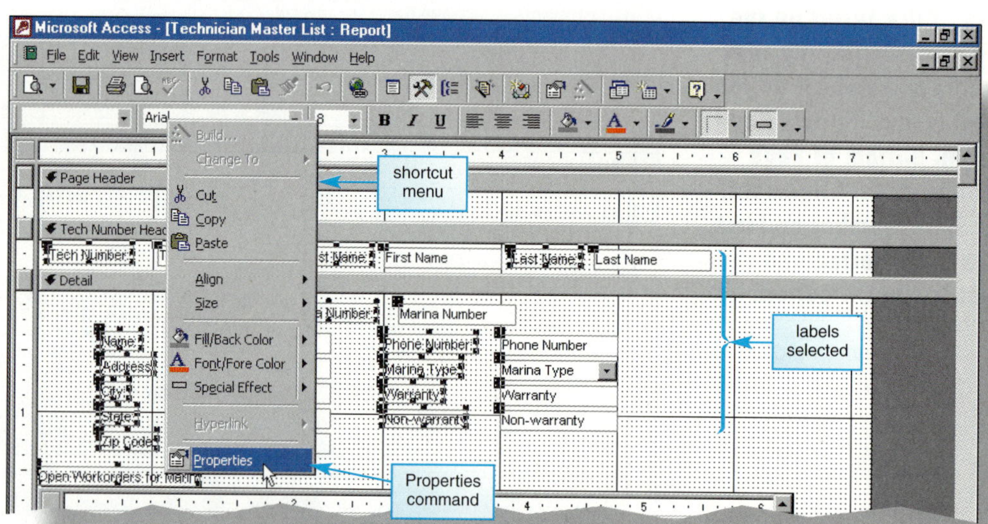

FIGURE 7-59

2 Click properties. Click the down scroll arrow to display the Font Weight property. Click the Font Weight property and point to Bold in the list of available font weights.

The Multiple selection property sheet displays (Figure 7-60) with the list of available font weights.

3 Click Bold and then close the Multiple selection property sheet by clicking its Close button. Click somewhere outside the labels to deselect the labels.

The labels are all bold.

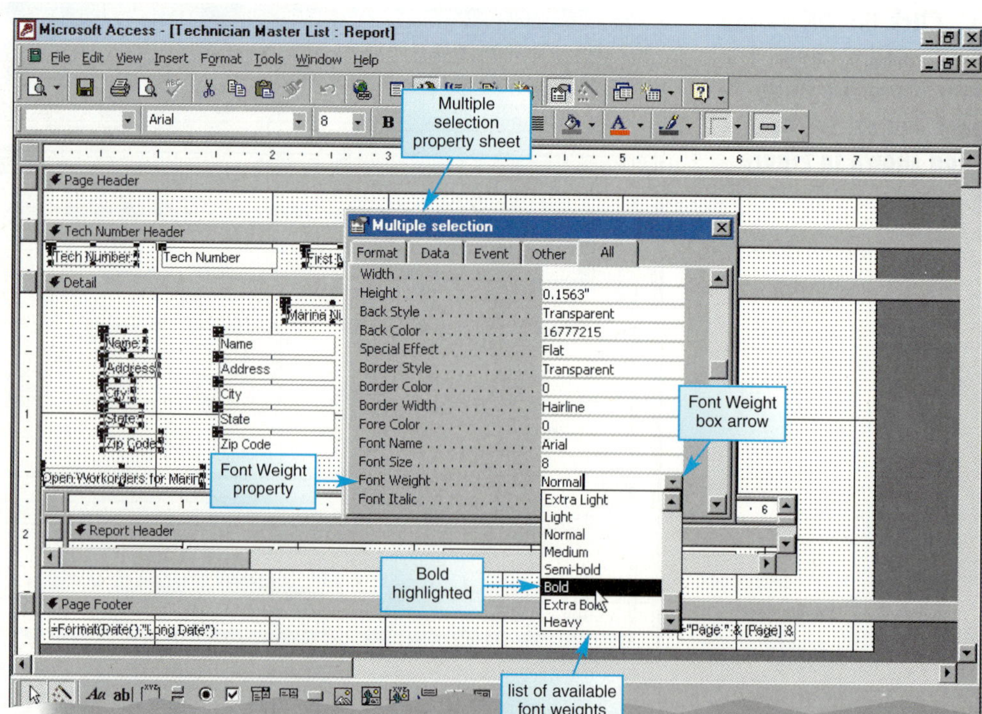

FIGURE 7-60

Adding a Title

A report title is added as a label. Assuming that the title is to display on each page, it should be added to the page header. (If it only is to display once at the beginning of the report, it instead would be added to the report header.) Perform the following steps to add a title to the page header.

To Add a Title

1 Point to the lower boundary of the page header.

The pointer changes to a double-pointing arrow (Figure 7-61).

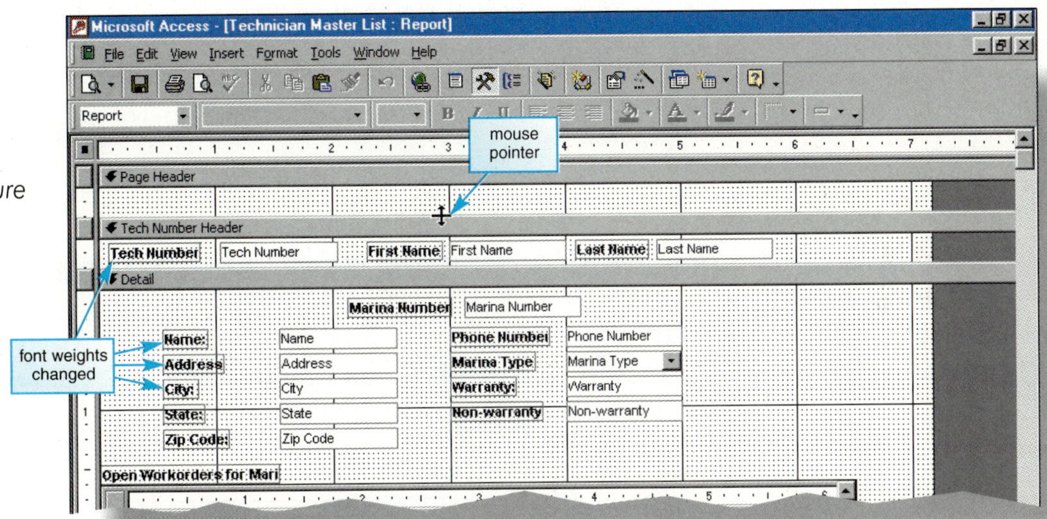

FIGURE 7-61

2 Drag the lower boundary of the page header to the approximate position shown in Figure 7-62 and point to the Label button in the toolbox.

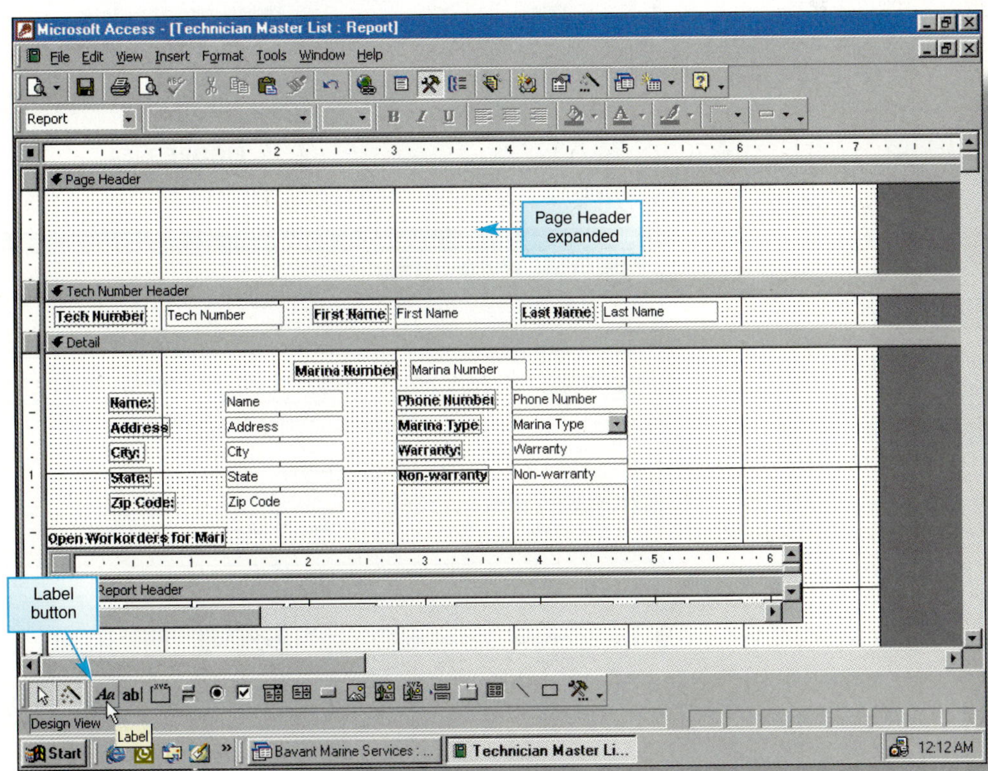

FIGURE 7-62

3 **Click the Label button and move the mouse pointer, which has changed to a plus sign with a label, to the position shown in Figure 7-63.**

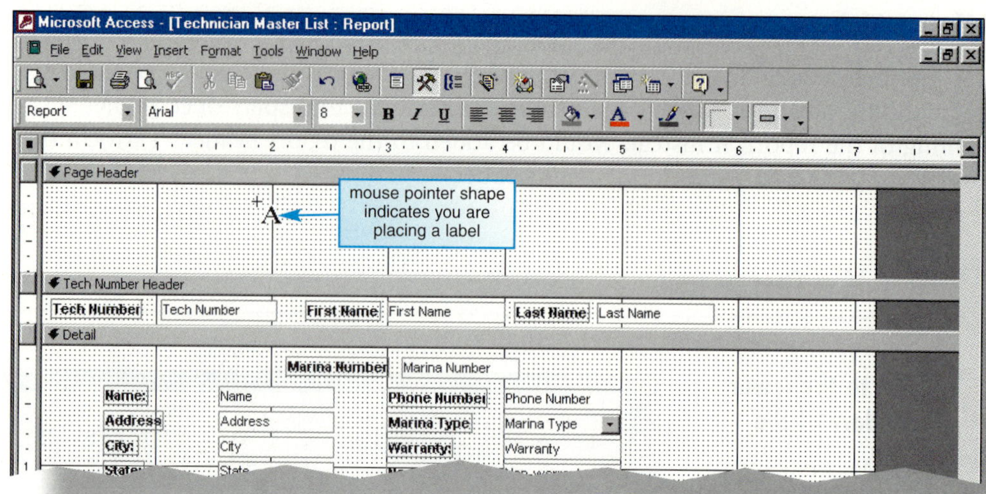

FIGURE 7-63

4 **Drag the pointer from the position shown in Figure 7-63 to the position shown in Figure 7-64.**

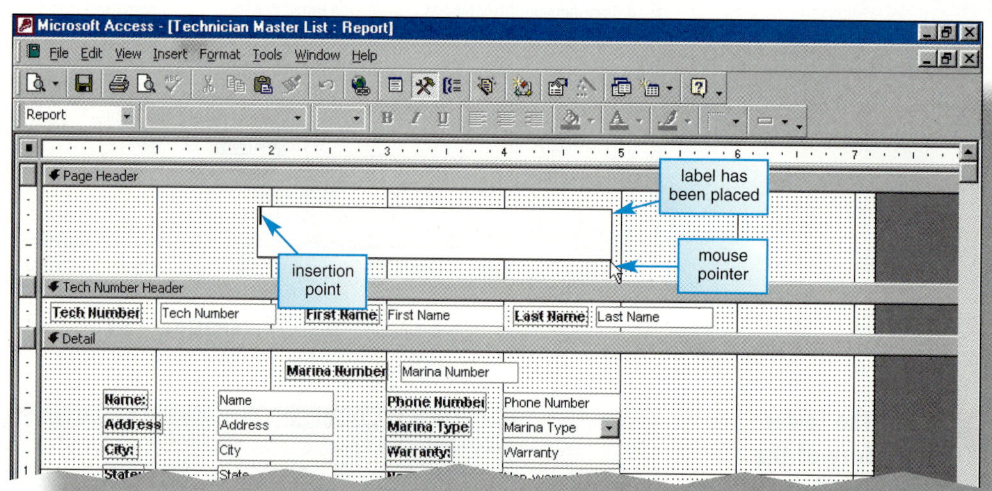

FIGURE 7-64

5 **Type** `Technician Master List` **as the title.**

The title is entered (Figure 7-65).

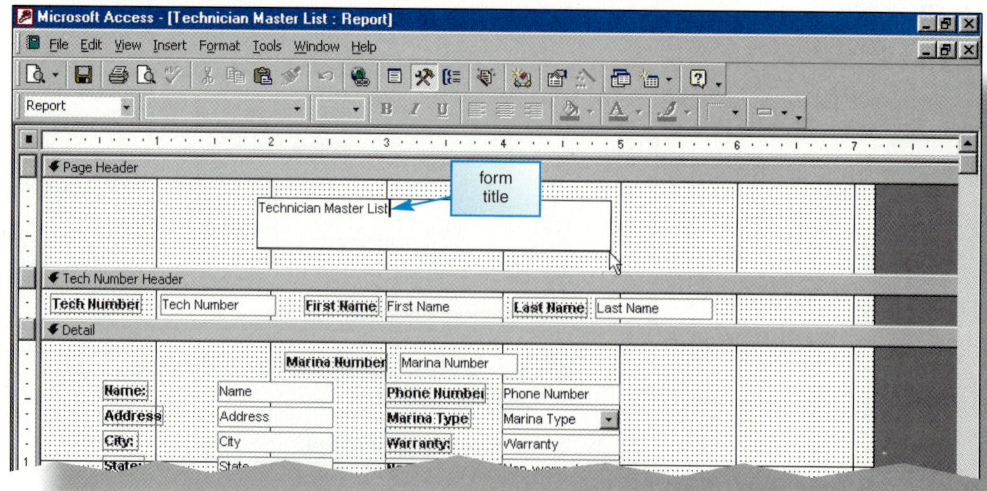

FIGURE 7-65

6 **Click somewhere outside the label containing the title to deselect the label. Next, right-click the label containing the title. Click Properties on the shortcut menu. Click the down scroll arrow so that the Font Name property displays. Click the Font Name property, click the Font Name box arrow and scroll down until Script MT Bold displays. Point to Script MT Bold. If Script MT Bold does not display in your list of fonts, pick another font.**

The Label: Label18 (your number may be different) property sheet displays (Figure 7-66) with the list of available fonts.

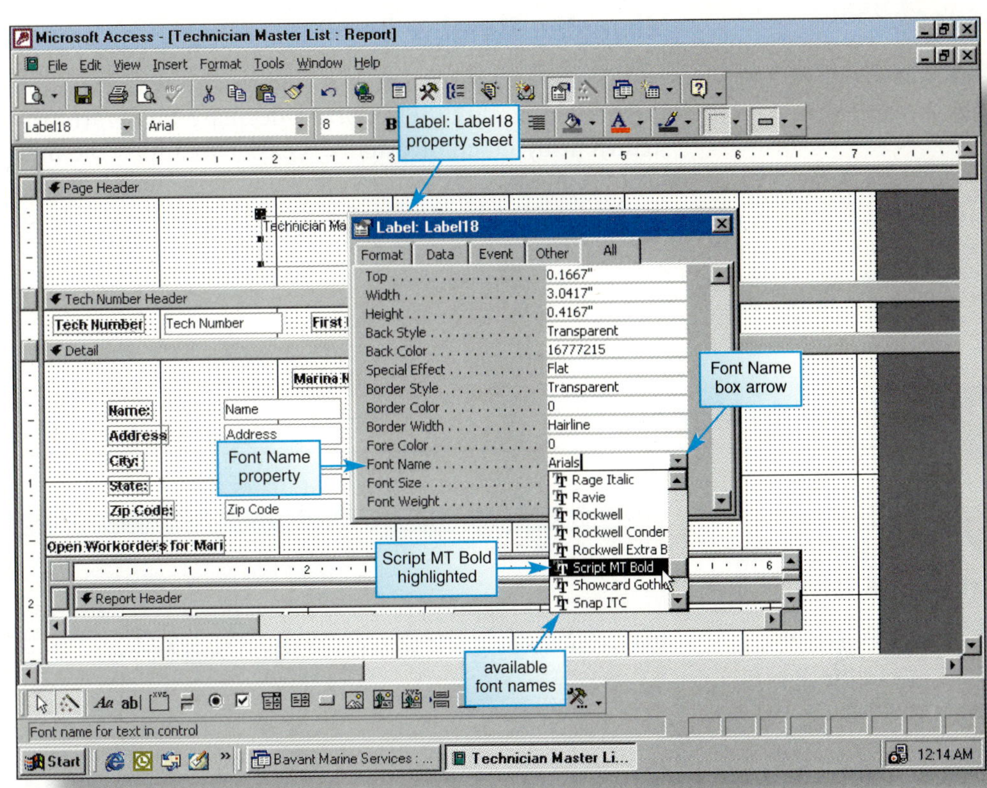

FIGURE 7-66

7 **Click Script MT Bold (or another font if Script MT Bold is not in your list.) Click the Font Size property, click the Font Size box arrow, and then click 20 as the new font size. Click the down scroll arrow so that the Text Align property displays. Click the Text Align property, click the Text Align box arrow, and then click Distribute. Close the property sheet by clicking its Close button.**

The format of the title is changed (Figure 7-67).

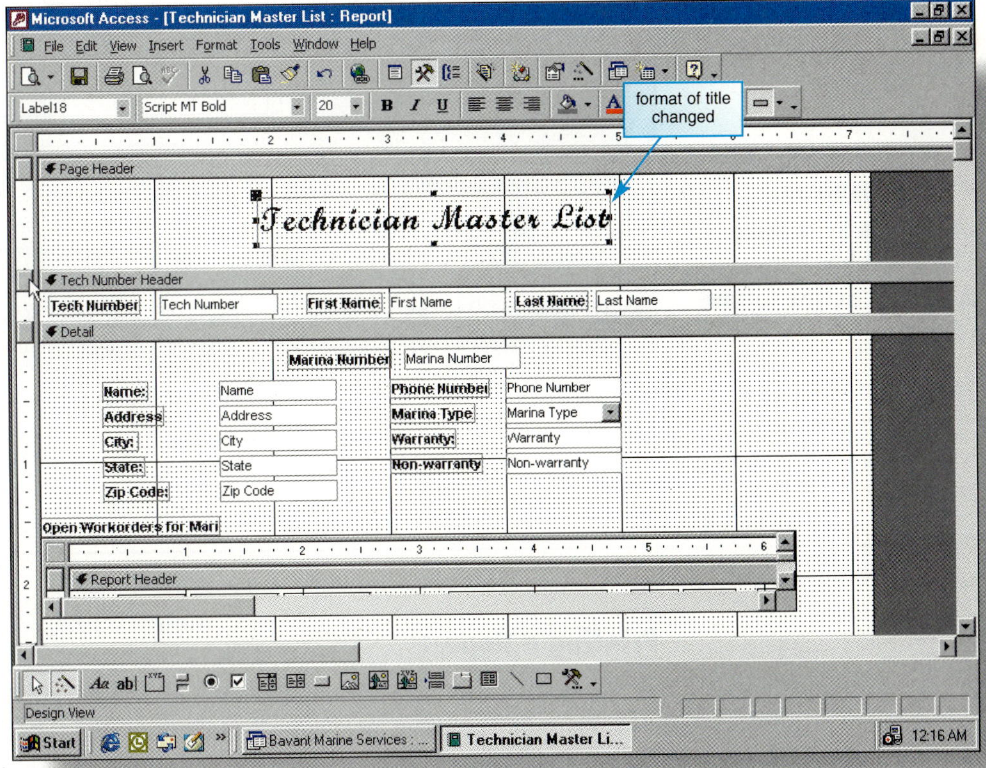

FIGURE 7-67

Margins

If you find you make the same changes to the margins on all your reports, you may wish to change the default margins. To do so, click Tools on the menu bar, click Options on the Tools menu, click the General tab, and then specify the desired margins.

Changing Margins

The report just created is slightly too wide to print across the width of the page. You could modify the report to decrease the width. If, however, you do not need to reduce it by much, it usually is easier to adjust the margins. To do so, use the Page Setup command as in the following steps, which reduces both the left and right margins to 0.5 inch.

To Change the Margins

1 Click File on the menu bar and then point to Page Setup on the File menu.

The File menu displays (Figure 7-68)

2 Click Page Setup. Be sure the Margins tab is selected. Change both the Left and Right margins to .5. Click the OK button.

The margins are changed.

3 Close the window containing the report design by clicking its Close Window button. Click the Yes button to save the changes.

The completed report displays similarly to the one shown in Figure 7-1a on page A 7.5.

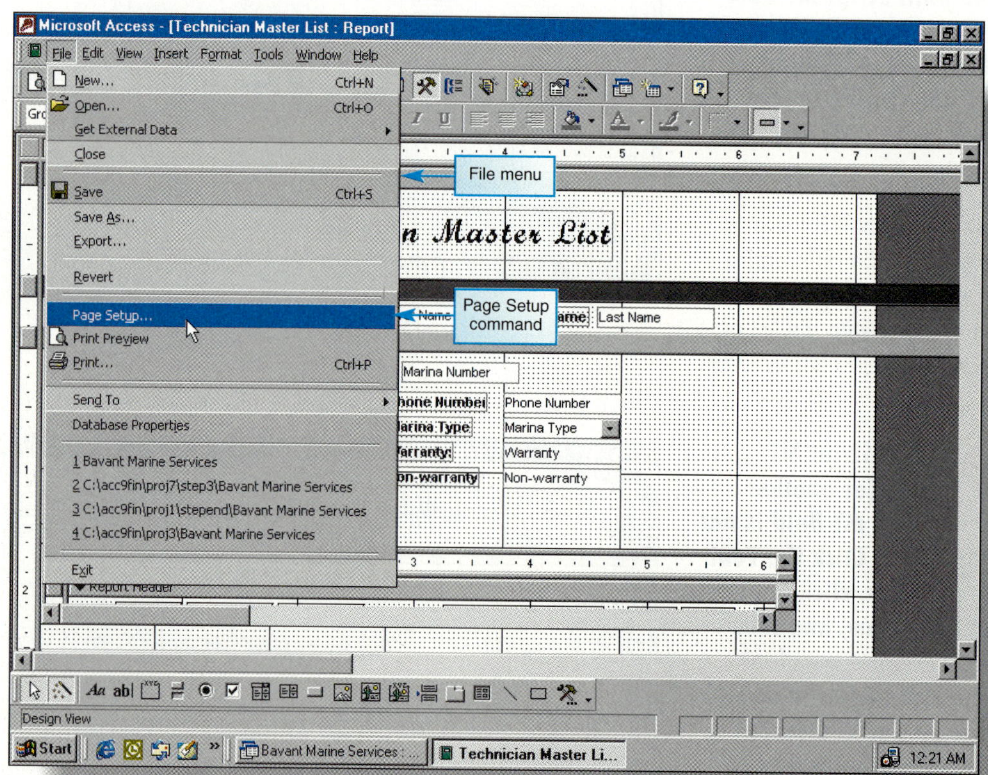

FIGURE 7-68

Printing a Report

To print a report, right-click the report in the Database window, and then click Print on the shortcut menu. Perform the steps on the next page to print the Technician Master List.

TO PRINT A REPORT

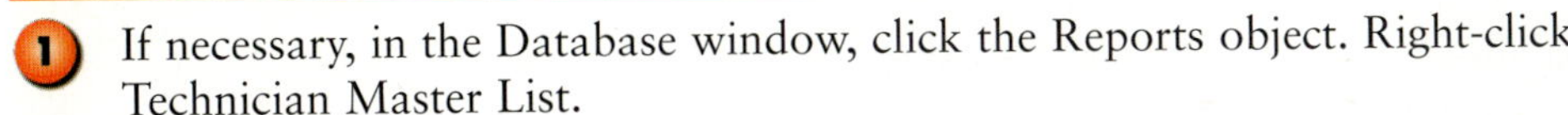

1. If necessary, in the Database window, click the Reports object. Right-click Technician Master List.
2. Click Print on the shortcut menu.

The report prints.

Mailing Labels

In order to print mailing labels, you create a special type of report. When this report prints, the data will display on the mailing labels all aligned correctly and in the order you specify.

More About

Mailing Labels

If you need to print labels that are not included in the list of available labels, you have two options. You can attempt to find labels in the list whose dimensions match your dimensions. You also can click the Customize button and specify precisely the dimensions you need.

Creating Labels

You create labels just as you create reports. There is a wizard, the Label Wizard, that assists you in the process. Using the wizard, you can specify the type and dimensions of the label, the font used for the label, and the contents of the label. Perform the following steps to create the labels.

To Create Labels

1 If necessary, in the Database window, click Tables on the Objects bar, and then click Technician. Click the New Object: Report button arrow on the Database window toolbar and then click Report. Click Label Wizard and then point to the OK button.

The New Report dialog box displays (Figure 7-69).

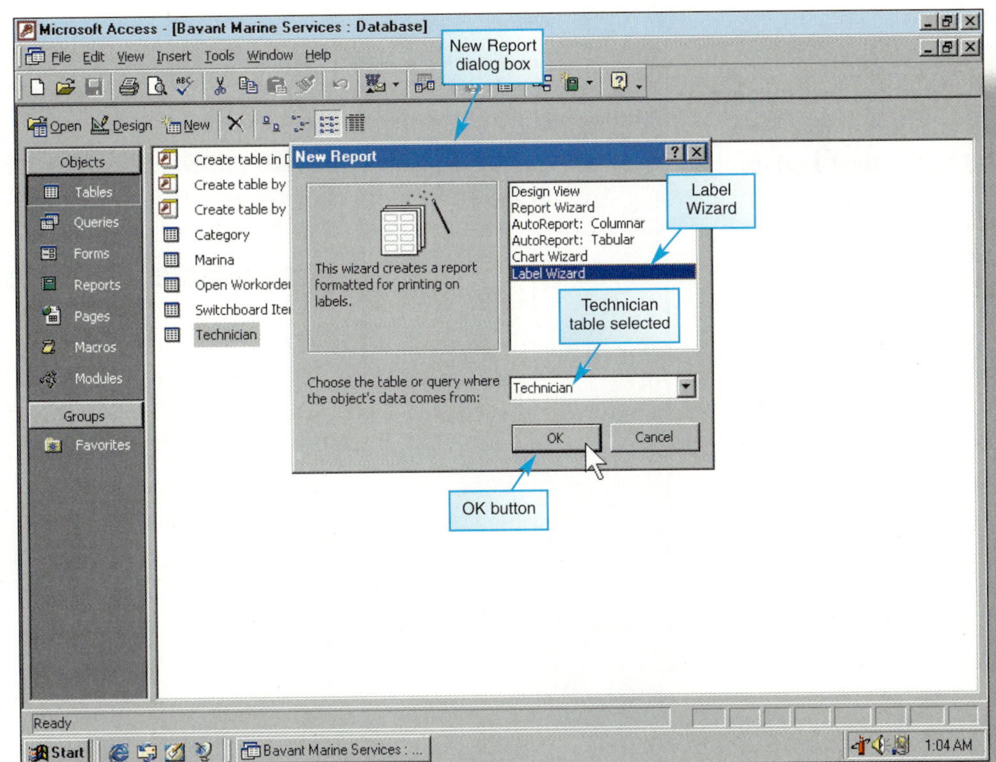

FIGURE 7-69

2 **Click the OK button. Click English as the Unit of Measure and then click the Filter by manufacturer box arrow and point to Avery.**

The Label Wizard dialog box displays (Figure 7-70) with the list of label manufacturers.

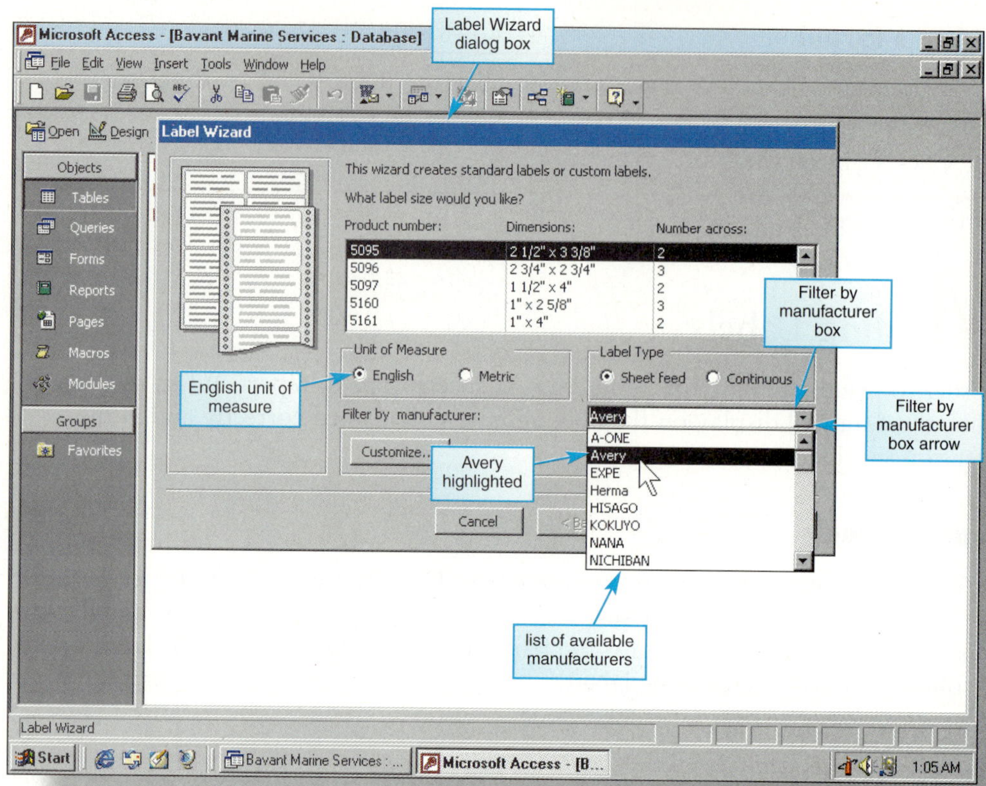

FIGURE 7-70

3 **Click Avery. Be sure product number 5095 is selected and then point to the Next button.**

The list of Avery labels displays (Figure 7-71).

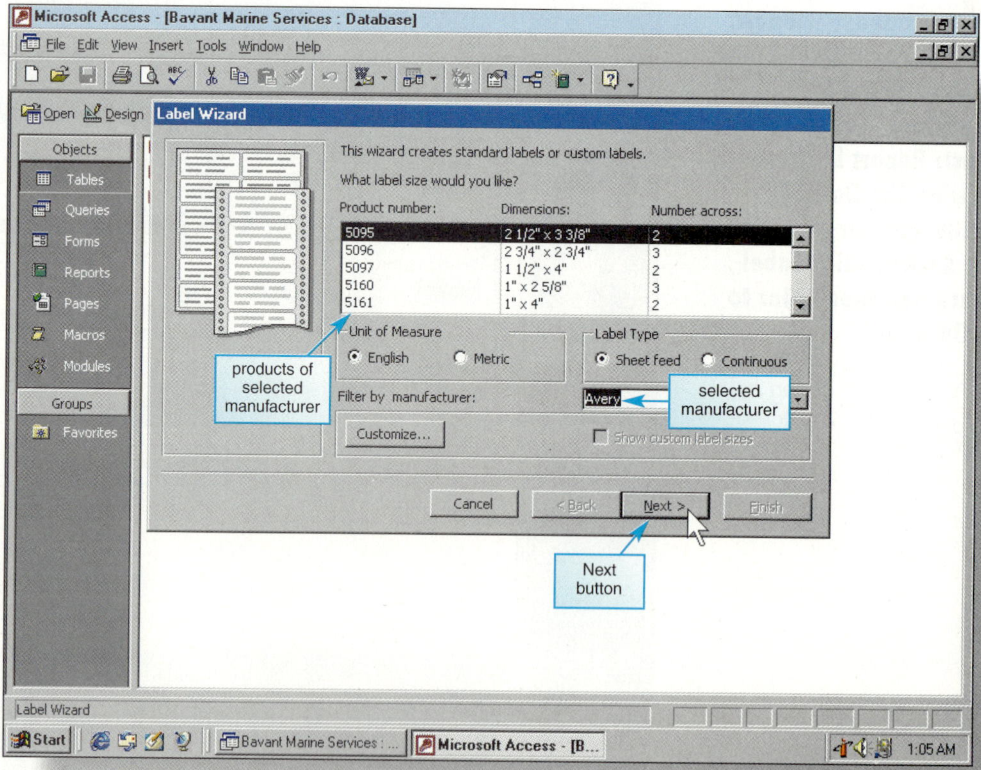

FIGURE 7-71

4 Click the Next button. Click the Next button a second time to accept the default font and color.

The Label Wizard dialog box displays asking for the contents of the mailing labels (Figure 7-72).

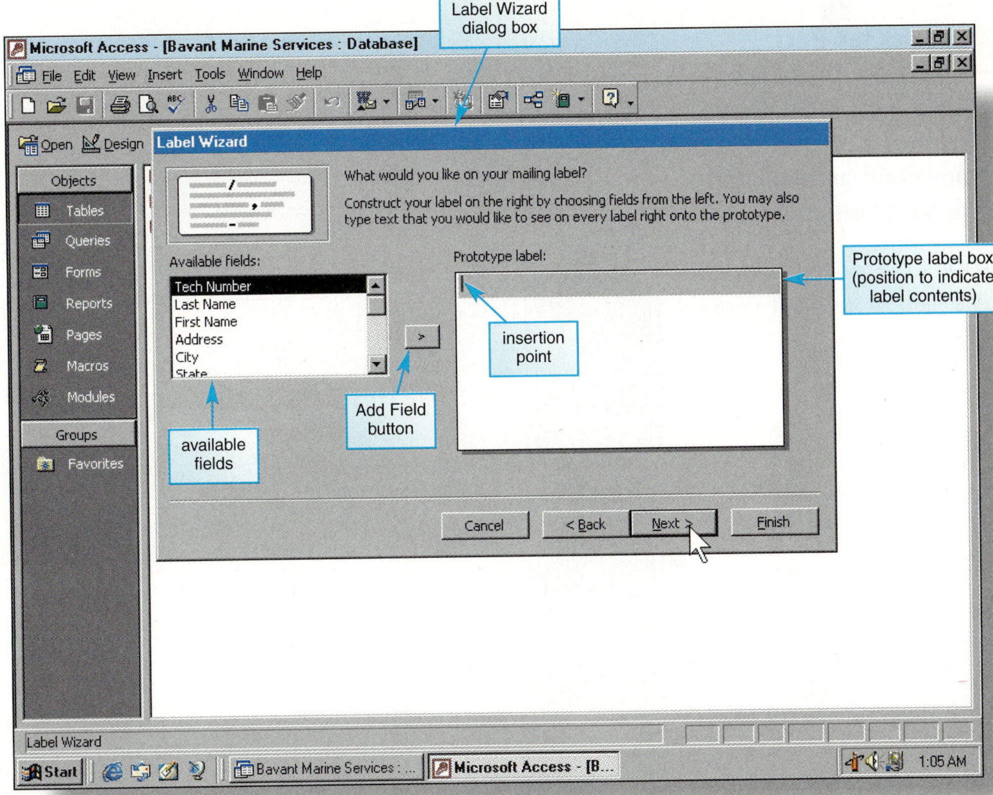

FIGURE 7-72

5 Select the First Name field, click the Add Field button, press the SPACEBAR, select the Last Name field, and then click the Add Field button. Click the second line in the label and then add the Address field. Click the third line of the label. Add the City field, type , (a comma), press the SPACEBAR, add the State field, press the SPACEBAR twice, and then add the Zip Code field. Point to the Next button.

The contents of the label are complete (Figure 7-73).

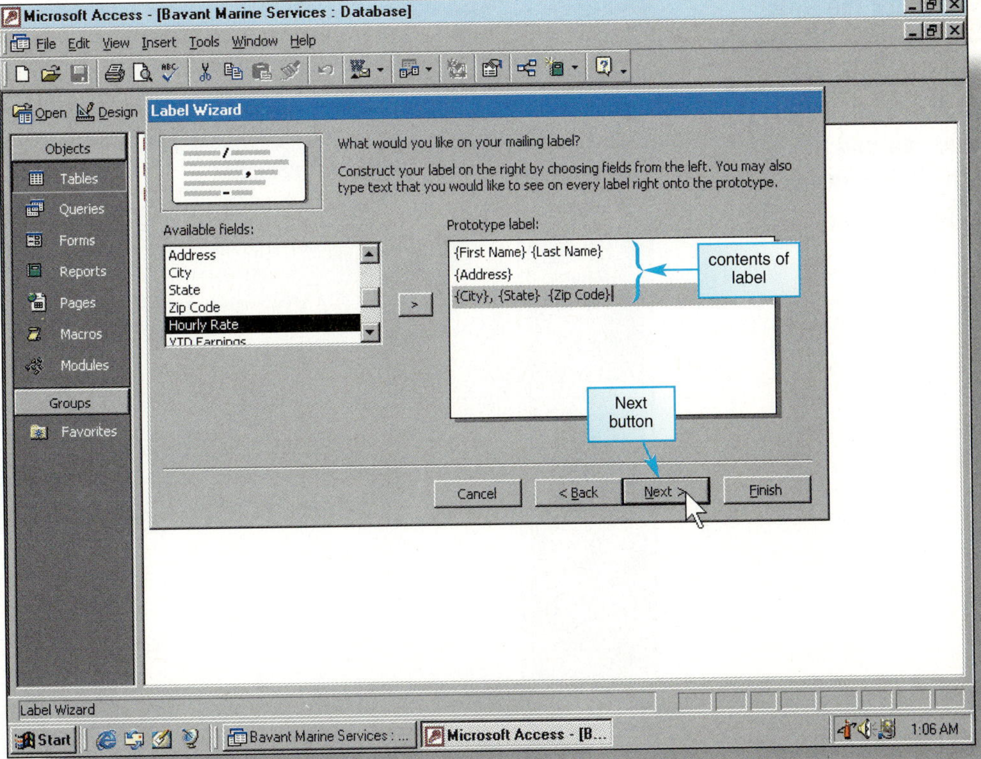

FIGURE 7-73

6 **Click the Next button. Select the Zip Code field as the field to sort by and then click the Add Field button. Point to the Next button.**

The Zip Code field is selected as the field to sort by (Figure 7-74).

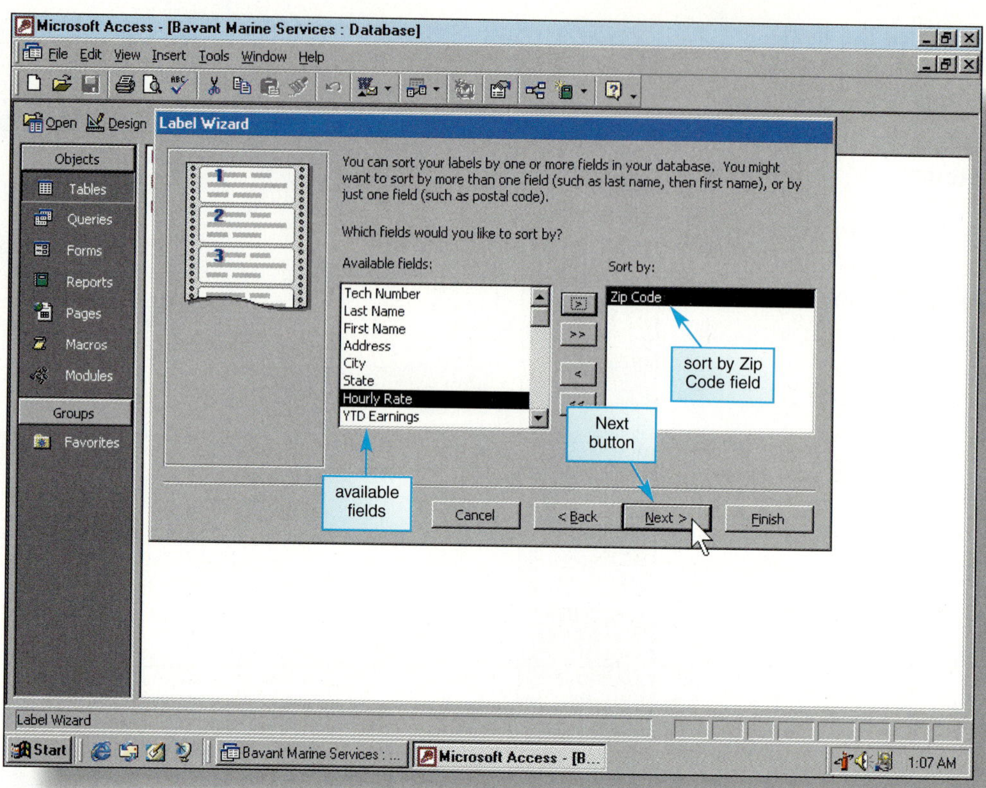

FIGURE 7-74

7 **Click the Next button. Be sure the name for the report (labels) is Labels Technician and then point to the Finish button (Figure 7-75).**

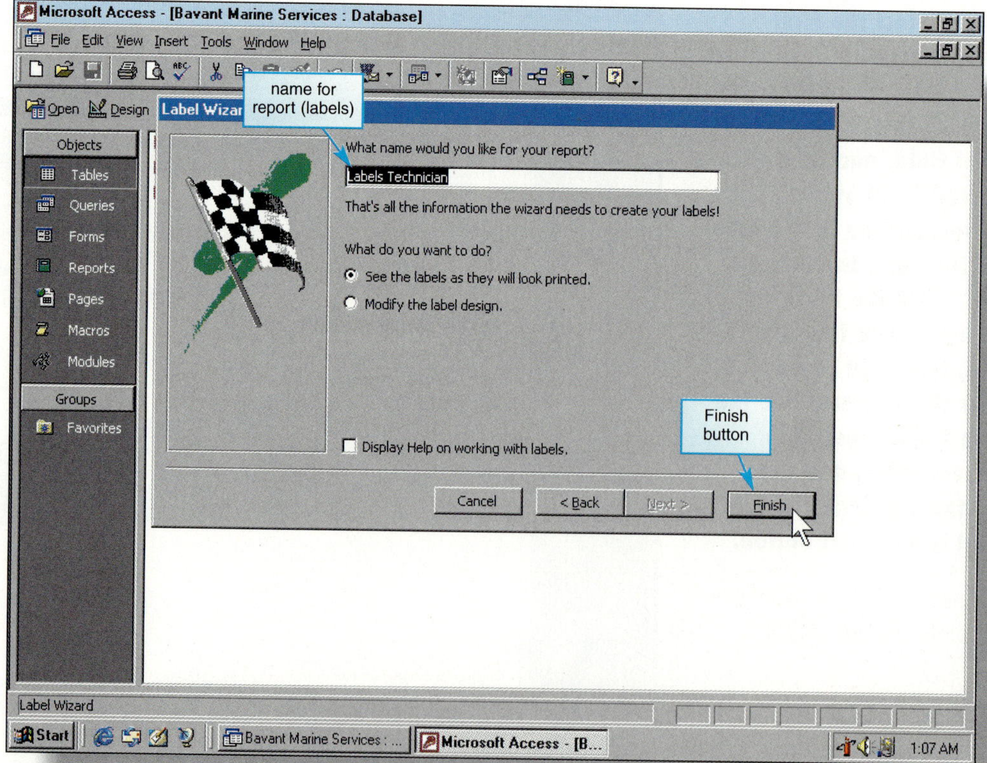

FIGURE 7-75

Click the Finish button.

The labels display (Figure 7-76) similarly to the ones in Figure 7-1b on page A 7.5.

9 Close the window containing the labels by clicking its Close button.

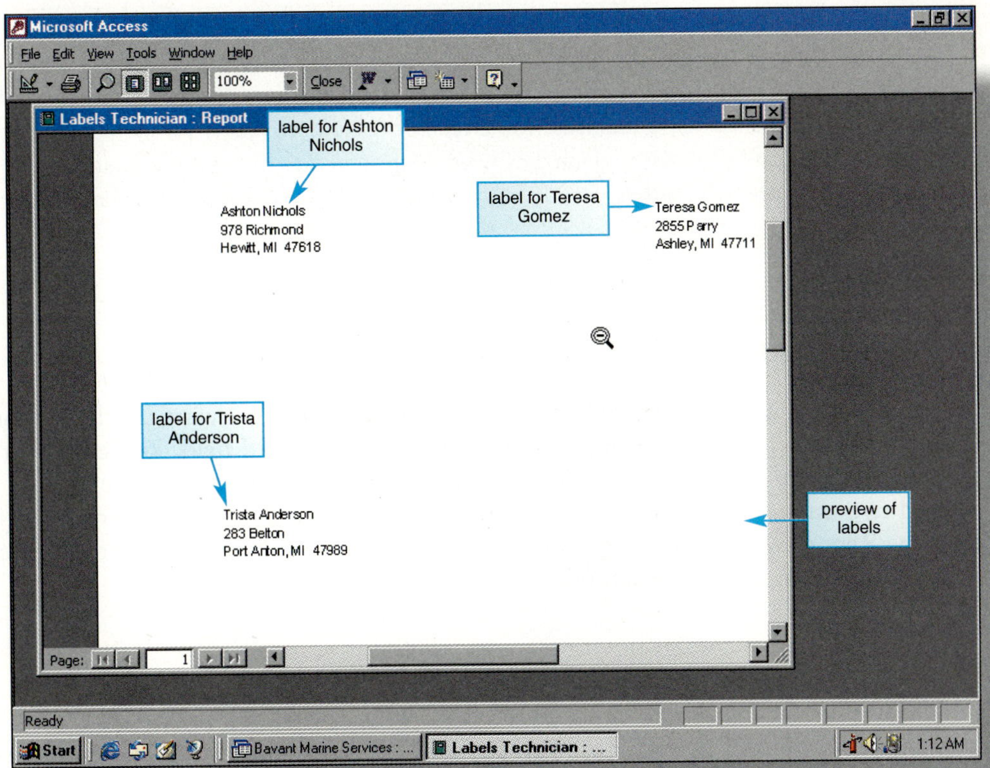

FIGURE 7-76

Printing the labels

To print the labels, right-click the label report in the Database window, and then click Print on the shortcut menu. Perform the following steps to print the labels just created.

Printing Labels

If you are printing labels on a dot-matrix or tractor-feed printer, you may have to make some changes to the page size in order to have the labels print correctly. To do so, click the Start button on the Windows desktop, click Settings, and then click Printers. Right-click your printer, click Properties, click the Paper tab, and then click the Custom icon. You can then make whatever changes might be necessary.

TO PRINT LABELS

1. If necessary, in the Database window, click the Reports object. Right-click Labels Technician.
2. Click Print on the shortcut menu. If a warning message displays, click the OK button.

The labels print.

Closing the Database

The following step closes the database by closing its Database window.

TO CLOSE A DATABASE

1. Click the Close button for the Bavant Marine Services : Database window.

CASE PERSPECTIVE SUMMARY

In Project 7, you assisted the management of Bavant Marine Services by helping them add the Category and Open Workorders tables to their databases. You created a parameter query for them so they could examine easily the open workorders for any marinas in which they were interested. You created a detailed report that lists all technicians, marinas, and open workorders. Finally, you created mailing labels for the technicians at Bavant.

Project Summary

In Project 7, you added two new tables to the Bavant Marine Services database. You then related these new tables to the existing tables. You also created a Lookup Wizard field. You created a query in which you changed the join properties as well as some field properties. You transformed the query to a paramater query. You also created two queries to be used by the report. You then created the report from scratch, using Design view rather than the Report Wizard. In the report, you used grouping and also included a subreport. Finally, you created mailing labels for the Technician table.

What You Should Know

Having completed this project, you now should be able to perform the following tasks:

Project Reinforcement at www.scsite.com/off2000/reinforce.htm

1 Adding Tables to the Sidewalk Scrapers Database

Instructions: Start Access. Open the Sidewalk Scrapers database from the Access Data Disk. See the inside back cover for instructions for downloading the Access Data Disk or see your instructor for information on accessing the files required for this book. You will create two new tables for the Sidewalk Scrapers database. The Rate table contains information on the rate that each customer pays for snow removal service. The structure and data are shown for the Rate table in Figure 7-77. There is a one-to-one relationship between the Customer table and the Rate table. The Service table contains information on when the snow removal service was performed. Because this city receives lots of snow, snow removal can be done more than once in a single day. Therefore, for each record to be unique, the primary key for the Service table must be the combination of customer number, service date, and service time. There is a one-to-many relationship between the Customer table and the Service table. The structure and data for the Service table are shown in Figure 7-78. Perform the following tasks.

1. Create the Rate table using the structure shown in Figure 7-77. Use the name Rate for the table.
2. Import the Rates worksheet to the database. The worksheet is in the Scrapers workbook on your Access Data Disk. When the Import Spreadsheet Wizard dialog box displays, be sure the Rates worksheet is selected. Be sure to check First Row Contains Column Headings. Open the table in Datasheet view and resize the columns to best fit the data. Save the changes to the layout of the table.
3. Print the Rate table.

Structure of Rate table

FIELD NAME	DATA TYPE	FIELD SIZE	PRIMARY KEY?	DESCRIPTION
Customer Number	Text	4	Yes	Customer Number (Primary Key)
Rate	Currency			Rate Charged for Snow Removal

Data for Rate table

CUSTOMER NUMBER	RATE
AL25	$13.00
AT43	$14.00
CH65	$12.00
CI05	$11.00
JB51	$15.00
LK44	$20.00
MD60	$14.00
ME02	$16.00
ST21	$12.00

FIGURE 7-77

(continued)

Adding Tables to the Sidewalk Scrapers Database *(continued)*

4. Create the Service table using the structure shown in Figure 7-78. The primary key is the combination of the Customer Number, Service Date, and Service Time fields. Use the name Service for the table.
5. Import the Services worksheet to the database. The worksheet is in the Scrapers workbook on your Access Data Disk. When the Import Spreadsheet Wizard dialog box displays, be sure the Services worksheet is selected. Be sure to check First Row Contains Column Headings. Open the table in Datasheet view and resize the columns to best fit the data. Save the changes to the layout of the table.
6. Print the Service table.
7. Click the Relationships button in the Database window, and add the Rate and Service tables to the Relationships window. Create a one-to-one relationship between the Customer table and the Rate table. Create a one-to-many relationship between the Customer table and the Service table. Print the Relationships window by making sure the Relationships window is open, clicking File on the menu bar, and then clicking Print Relationships.
8. Create a query that joins the Customer and Service tables. All records in the Customer table should display regardless of whether there is a matching record in the Service table. Display the Customer Number, Name, Service Date, and Service Time fields in the query results. Change the caption for Service Date to Snow Removal Date and the caption for Service Time to Snow Removal Time.
9. Run the query and print the results.
10. Filter the recordset to find only those customers who had snow removal performed on January 5, 2001.
11. Print the results.

Structure of Service table

FIELD NAME	DATA TYPE	FIELD SIZE	PRIMARY KEY?	DESCRIPTION
Customer Number	Text	4	Yes	Customer Number (Portion of Primary Key)
Service Date	Date/Time		Yes	Date that Snow Removal was Performed (Portion of Primary Key)
Service Time	Date/Time		Yes	Time that Snow Removal was Performed (Portion of Primary Key)

Data for Service table

CUSTOMER NUMBER	SERVICE DATE	SERVICE TIME
AT43	01/04/2001	1:30:00 PM
AT43	01/05/2001	9:00:00 PM
CH65	01/04/2001	2:30:00 PM
CH65	01/04/2001	10:00:00 PM
CI05	01/04/2001	9:00:00 AM
CI05	01/04/2001	5:00:00 PM
JB51	01/05/2001	10:00:00 AM
LK44	01/05/2001	12:00:00 PM
MD60	01/05/2001	10:00:00 AM
ME02	01/04/2001	7:30:00 AM
ME02	01/04/2001	4:00:00 PM
ST21	01/04/2001	6:00:00 AM
ST21	01/04/2001	3:30:00 PM
ST21	01/05/2001	1:00:00 AM

FIGURE 7-78

In the Lab

1 Creating Queries, a Report, and Mailing Labels for the School Connection Database

Problem: The Booster's Club wants to track items that are being reordered from the vendor. The club must know when an item was ordered and how many were ordered. The club may place an order with a vendor one day and then find that they need to order more of the same item before the original order is filled. The club also wants to be able to query the database to find out whether an item is on order. Finally, they want a report that displays vendor information as well as information about the item and its order status.

Instructions: Open the School Connection database from the Access Data Disk. See the inside back cover for instructions for downloading the Access Data Disk or see your instructor for information on accessing the files required for this book. Perform the following tasks.

1. Create a table in which to store the reorder information using the structure shown in Figure 7-79. Create an input mask for the Date Ordered field in the format MM/dd/yyyy. Use the name Reorder for the table.
2. Add the data shown in Figure 7-79 to the Reorder table.
3. Add the Reorder table to the Relationships window and establish a one-to-many relationship between the Item and Reorder tables. Print the Relationships window by making sure the Relationships window is open, clicking File on the menu bar, and then clicking Print Relationships.
4. Open the Reorder table in Design view and change the Item Id field to a Lookup Wizard field. Both the Item Id and Description fields from the Item table should display.
5. Print the table.
6. Create a query that joins the Item, Reorder, and Vendor tables. The query should display all items in the Item table whether or not they are on reorder. Display the Item Id, Description, Date Ordered, Number Ordered, Cost, and Vendor Name fields. Change the caption for Number Ordered to On Order. Run the query and print the results.

Structure of Reorder table

FIELD NAME	DATA TYPE	FIELD SIZE	PRIMARY KEY?	DESCRIPTION
Item Id	Text	4	Yes	Item Id Number (Portion of Primary Key)
Date Ordered	Date/Time		Yes	Date Item Ordered (Remainder of Primary Key)
Number Ordered	Number			Number of Items Ordered

Data for Reorder table

ITEM ID	DATE ORDERED	NUMBER ORDERED
CM12	10/05/2001	25
DM05	09/10/2001	5
DM05	10/02/2001	10
MN04	09/12/2001	2
MN04	10/04/2001	2
PL05	09/12/2001	4
WA34	09/14/2001	5
WA34	09/22/2001	4

FIGURE 7-79

(continued)

Creating Queries, a Report, and Mailing Labels for the School Connection Database *(continued)*

7. Use filter by selection to display only those records where the vendor is Trinkets 'n More. Print the results.
8. Create a parameter query for the Reorder table. The user should be able to enter a beginning and ending item id. Display all fields in the query result. Run the query to find all records where the item id is between DM05 and PL05. Print the results.
9. Run the query again to find all records where item number is WA34. Print the results.
10. Create the report shown in Figure 7-80. The report uses the Vendors and Items query as the basis for the main report and the Reorder table as the basis for the subreport. Be sure to include the current date and page numbers on the report. Use the name Vendor Master Report for the report. The report is in the same style as that demonstrated in the project. The report contains clip art in the page header. To add clip art to the report, do the following:
    a. Click the Unbound Object Frame button in the toolbox, move the mouse pointer to the page header and click.
    b. When the Insert Object dialog box displays, make sure the Create New option button is selected. Click Microsoft Clip Gallery in the Object Type box and then click OK.
    c. Click the Pictures tab, click the Academic category, and then click the first clip art item in the second row. Click Insert Clip on the shortcut menu.
    d. Resize the picture to the appropriate size for the page header.
    e. Right-click the object, click Properties on the shortcut menu, and then change the Size Mode to Zoom.
11. Print the report.
12. Create mailing labels for the Vendor table. Use Avery labels 5095 and format the label with name on the first line, address on the second line, and city, state, and zip code on the third line. There is a comma and a space after the city and 2 spaces between the state and the zip code.
13. Print the mailing labels.

In the Lab

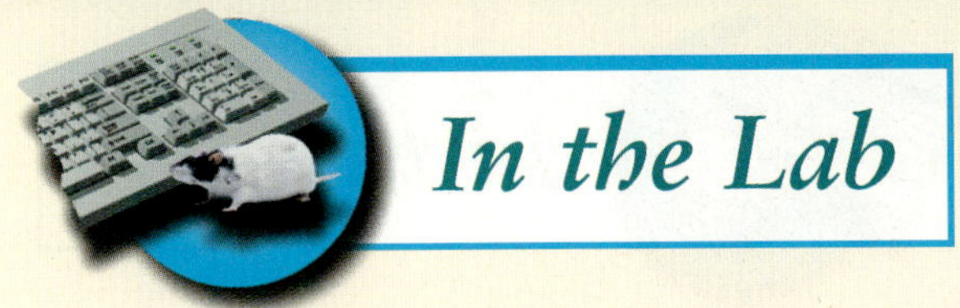

Vendor Master Report
Item Id: DM05
Description: Doormat
Cost:
$14.25
5
Vendor Master Report
Item Id: CM12
$3.75
20
Vendor Master Report
Vendor Code: GG
Name: GG Gifts
$14.00
3
$5.65
22
Page 4 of 4
$13.50
8
$16.00
12
Page 3 of 4
$2.75
25
Page 2 of 4
Vendor Master Report
Vendor Code: AL
Name: Alum Logo Inc.
Item Id: SC11
Description: Scarf
Cost:
$6.40
On Hand:
17
Reorder Status
Item Id: MN04
Description: Mouse Pad
Cost:
$9.10
On Hand:
5
Reorder Status
Date Ordered
Number Ordered
09/12/2001
2
10/4/2001
2
Item Id: BA02
Description: Baseball Cap
Cost:
$12.50
On Hand:
15
Reorder Status
Thursday, July 26, 2001
Page 1 of 4

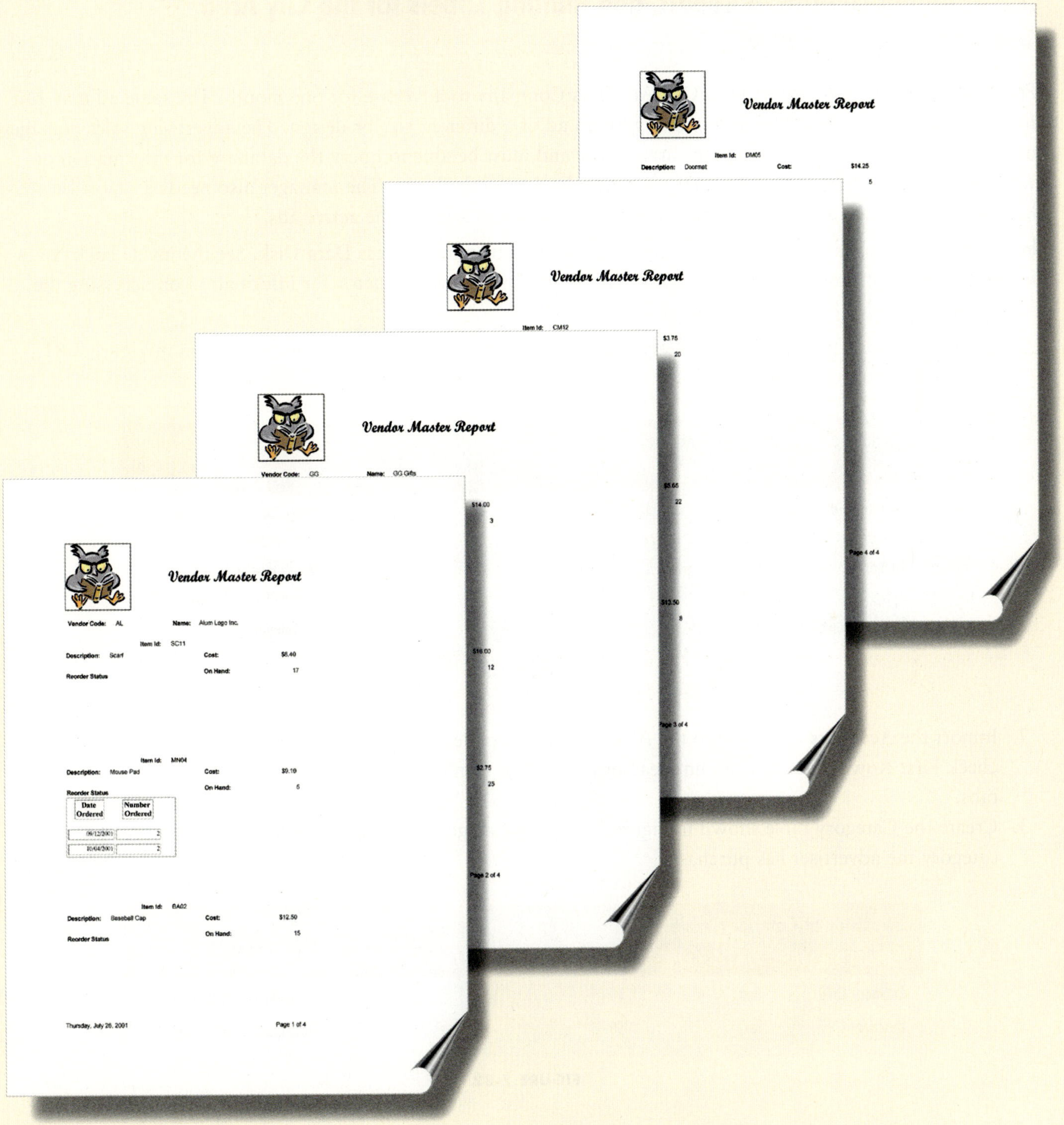

FIGURE 7-80

2 Creating Queries, a Report, and Mailing Labels for the City Area Bus Company Database

Problem: Advertisers contract with City Area Bus Company to advertise for one month. The same ad may run for several months or be replaced monthly with an ad of a different size or design. The advertising sales manager must track the active accounts for the current year and must be able to query the database for information on which advertisers currently have ads they want to display on the buses. The manager also needs a report that lists the sales rep, the accounts that the sales rep handles, and a list of the active ads.

Instructions: Open the City Area Bus Company database from the Access Data Disk. See the inside back cover for instructions for downloading the Access Data Disk or see your instructor for information on accessing the files required for this book. Perform the following tasks.

1. Create a table in which to store the active account information using the structure shown in Figure 7-81. Use the name Active Accounts for the table.

Structure of Active Accounts table

FIELD NAME	DATA TYPE	FIELD SIZE	PRIMARY KEY?	DESCRIPTION
Advertiser Id	Text	4	Yes	Advertiser Id (Portion of Primary Key)
Ad Month	Text	3	Yes	Month that Ad Is to Run (Remainder of Primary Key)
Category Code	Text	1		Ad Category

FIGURE 7-81

2. Import the Accounts text file into the Active Accounts table. The text file is on your Data Disk. Be sure to check First Row Contains Column Headings. The data is in delimited format with each field separated by tabs.
3. Create the Category table shown in Figure 7-82. The Category table contains information on the ad category the advertiser has purchased.

Structure of Category table

FIELD NAME	DATA TYPE	FIELD SIZE	PRIMARY KEY?	DESCRIPTION
Category Code	Text	1	Yes	Category Code (Primary Key)
Description	Text	50		Description of Ad Category

FIGURE 7-82

4. Import the Ad Categories text file into the Category table. The text file is on your Data Disk. Be sure to check the First Row Contains Column Headings box. The data is in delimited format with each field separated by tabs.
5. Open the Relationships window and establish a one-to-many relationship between the Advertiser table and the Active Accounts table and between the Category table and the Active Accounts table. Print the Relationships window by making sure the Relationships window is open, clicking File on the menu bar, and then clicking Print Relationships.
6. Open the Active Accounts table in Design view and change the Category Code field to a Lookup Wizard field.
7. Open the Active Accounts table in Datasheet view and resize the columns to best fit the data. Save the changes to the layout of the table.
8. Print the table.
9. Open the Category table in Datasheet view and resize the columns to best fit the data. Save the changes to the layout of the table.
10. Print the table.
11. Create a query that joins the Advertiser and the Active Accounts table. All Advertisers should display whether or not they have active accounts. Display the Advertiser Id, Name, Month, and Category Code fields. Run the query and print the results.
12. Filter the query results to find all accounts that will run ads during the month of June. Print the results.
13. Create the report shown in Figure 7-83. The report is grouped by Sales Rep Number and includes a subreport. It is in the same style as that demonstrated in the project. Be sure to include the current date and page numbers on the report. Use the name Sales Rep Master Report for the report. (Hint: Create queries for both the main report and the subreport.) Print the report.
14. Create mailing labels for the Advertiser table. Use Avery labels 5095 and format the label with name on the first line, address on the second line, and city, state, and zip code on the third line. There is a comma and a space after the city and 2 spaces between the state and the zip code. Print the mailing labels.

(continued)

Creating Queries, a Report, and Mailing Labels for the City Area Bus Company Database *(continued)*

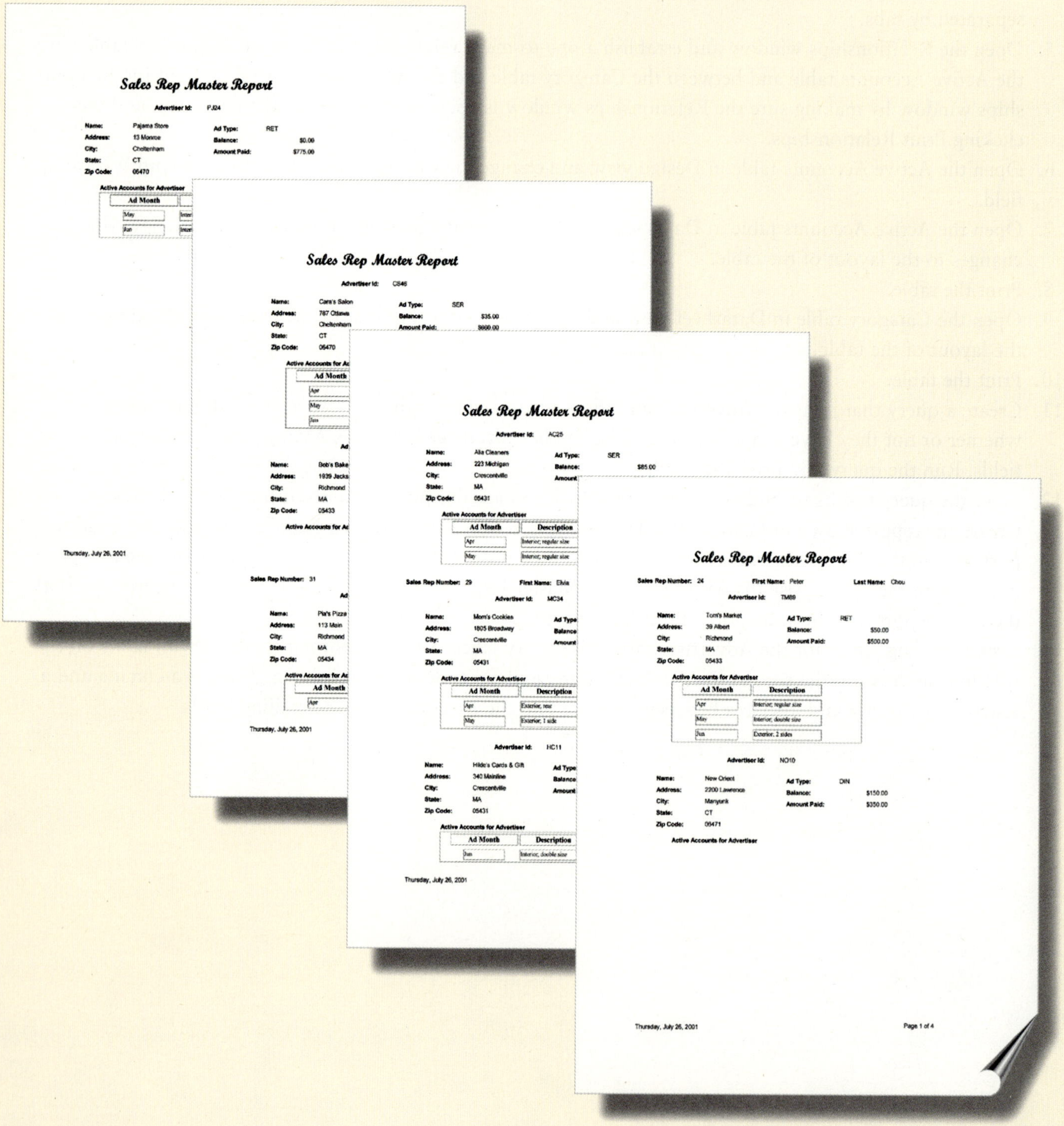

Sales Rep Master Report

Sales Rep Number: 24 **First Name:** Peter **Last Name:** Chou

Advertiser Id: TM89

Name: Tom's Market
Address: 39 Albert
City: Richmond
State: MA
Zip Code: 05433

Ad Type: RET
Balance: $50.00
Amount Paid: $500.00

Active Accounts for Advertiser

Ad Month	Description
Apr	Interior; regular size
May	Interior; double size
Jun	Exterior; 2 sides

Advertiser Id: NO10

Name: New Orient
Address: 2200 Lawrence
City: Manyunk
State: CT
Zip Code: 05471

Ad Type: DIN
Balance: $150.00
Amount Paid: $350.00

Active Accounts for Advertiser

Thursday, July 26, 2001 Page 1 of 4

FIGURE 7-83

In the Lab

3 Creating Queries, a Report, and Mailing Labels for the Resort Rentals Database

Problem: The real estate company must keep track of the units that are rented and the individuals who rented the units. Units are rented a week at a time and rentals start on Saturday. They also need to be able to query the database to determine if a particular unit is rented. Finally, they need to prepare reports for the owners that display rental information.

Instructions: Open the Resort Rentals database from the Access Data Disk. See the inside back cover for instructions for downloading the Access Data Disk or see your instructor for information on accessing the files required for this book. Perform the following tasks.

1. Create the Active Rentals table using the structure shown in Figure 7-84. Use the name Active Rentals for the table. Use an input mask for the date in the form MM/dd/yyyy.

Structure of Active Rentals table

FIELD NAME	DATA TYPE	FIELD SIZE	PRIMARY KEY?	DESCRIPTION
Rental Id	Text	3	Yes	Rental Id (Portion of Primary Key)
Start Date	Date/Time		Yes	Beginning Date of Rental (Remainder of Primary Key)
Length	Number			Length of Time in Weeks of Rental
Renter Id	Text	4		Id of Renter

FIGURE 7-84

2. Import the Rentals workbook into the Active Rentals table. The workbook is on the Access Data Disk. In the Import Spreadsheet Wizard dialog box, click the Show Named Ranges option button and select the Rentals range. Be sure to check First Row Contains Column Headings.
3. Create the Renter table using the structure shown in Figure 7-85. Use the name Renter for the table.

Structure of Renter table

FIELD NAME	DATA TYPE	FIELD SIZE	PRIMARY KEY?	DESCRIPTION
Renter Id	Text	4	Yes	Renter Id (Primary Key)
First Name	Text	10		First Name of Renter
Last Name	Text	15		Last Name of Renter
Telephone Number	Text	12		Telephone Number (999-999-9999 version)

FIGURE 7-85

(continued)

Creating Queries, a Report, and Mailing Labels for the Resort Rentals Database *(continued)*

4. Import the Rentals workbook into the Renter table. The workbook is on the Access Data Disk. In the Import Spreadsheet Wizard dialog box, click the Show Named Ranges option button and select the Renters range. Be sure to check First Row Contains Column Headings.
5. Open the Relationships window and establish a one-to-many relationship between the Renter table and the Active Rentals table. Establish a one-to-many relationship between the Rental Unit table and the Active Rentals table. Print the Relationships window by making sure the Relationships window is open, clicking File on the menu bar, and then clicking Print Relationships.
6. Open the Active Rentals table in Design view and change the Renter Id field to a Lookup Wizard field. The Renter Id, First Name, and Last Name fields should display.
7. Open the Active Rentals table in Datasheet view, resize the columns to best fit the data, save the changes, and print the table.
8. Open the Renter table in Datasheet view, resize the columns to best fit the data, save the changes, and print the table.
9. Create a join query for the Rental Unit and Active Rentals tables. All rental units should display in the result regardless of whether the unit is rented. Display the Rental Id, Address, City, Weekly Rate, Start Date, and Length fields. Change the caption for the Length field to Weeks Rented. Run the query and print the results.
10. Filter the query results to find all rental units that rent for $1,000 per week. Print the results.
11. Create a parameter query to enter a start date. The query should display the rental id, start date, length, and the first and last name of the renter. Run the query to find all records where the start date is 12/1/2001. Print the results.
12. Run the query again to find all records where the start date is 11/24/2001. Print the results.
13. Create the report shown in Figure 7-86. The report includes a subreport. Group the report by owner id. Print the report.
14. Create mailing labels for the Owner table. Use Avery labels 5095 and format the label with first and last name on the first line, address on the second line, and city, state, and zip code on the third line. There is a comma and a space after the city and 2 spaces between the state and the zip code. Print the mailing labels.

In the Lab

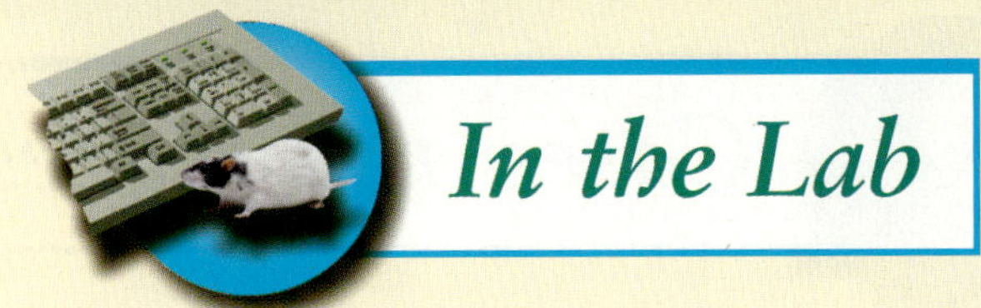

Owner Master Report
Rental Id: 144
Address: 24 Plantation
Pool
Owner Master Report
Rental Id: 101
Address: 521 Ocean
Pool
Ocean View
Owner Master Report
Rental Id: 110
Address: 523 Ocean
City: Hutchins
Pool
Ocean View
For Sale
Owner Master Report
Rental Id: 103
Address: 783 First
City: Gulf Breeze
Bedrooms: 3
Bathrooms: 3
Pool
Ocean View
For Sale
Sales Price:
Owner Master Report
Owner Id: FH15
First Name: Hilda
Last Name: Franco
Rental Id: 134
Address: 278 Second
City: Shady Beach
Bedrooms: 2
Bathrooms: 1
Sleeps: 4
Pool
Ocean View
For Sale
Sales Price: $190,000.00
Weekly Rate: $1,000.00
Active Rentals for Rental Unit
Start Date
Weeks Rented
First Name
Last Name
Telephone Number
12/22/2001
2
Thomas
Maldonad
610-555-2323
Rental Id: 121
Address: 123 Gulf
City: San Toma
Bedrooms: 3
Bathrooms: 2
Sleeps: 8
Pool
Ocean View
For Sale
Sales Price:
Weekly Rate: $1,300.00
Active Rentals for Rental Unit
Thursday, July 26, 2001
Page 1 of 5

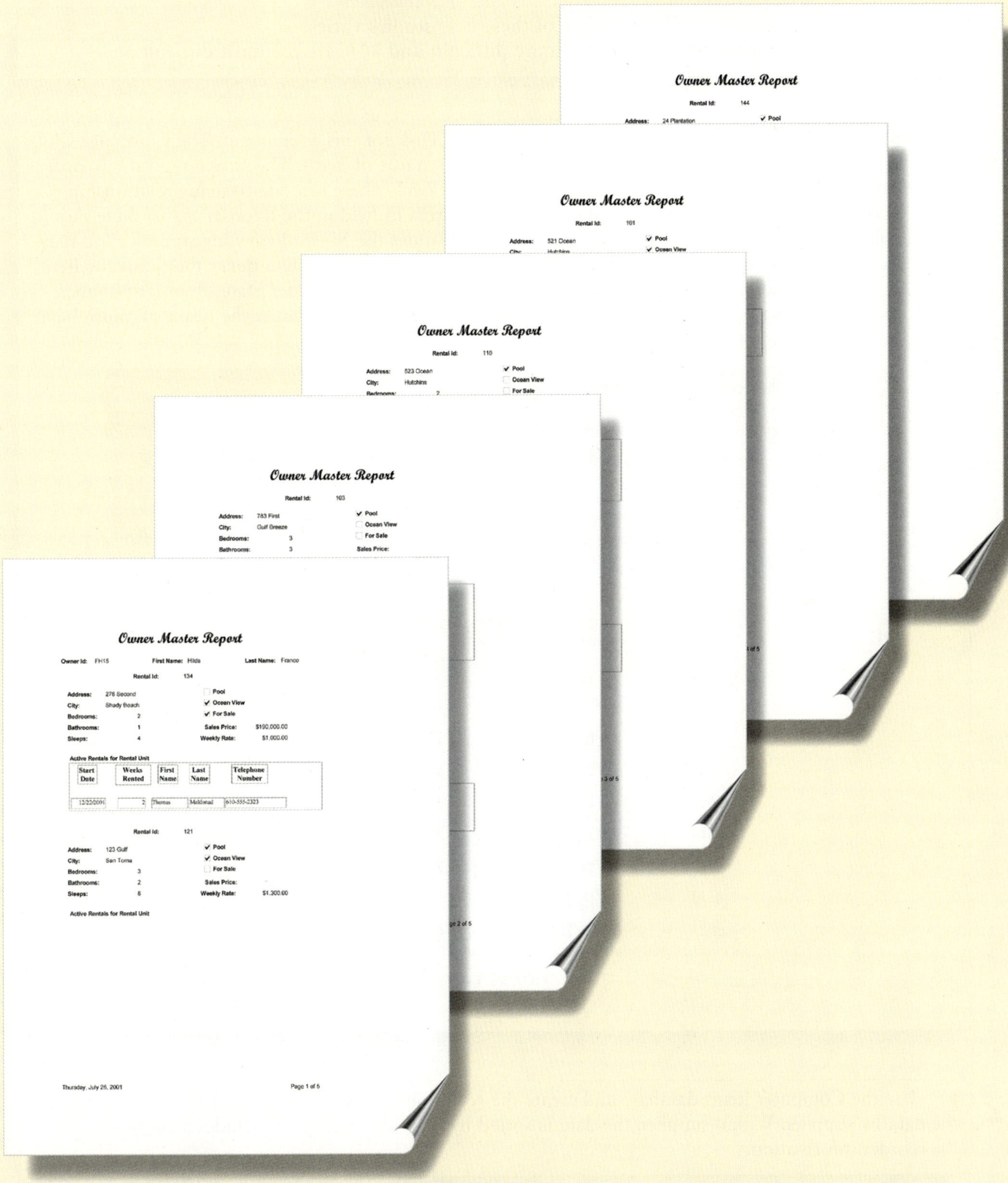

FIGURE 7-86

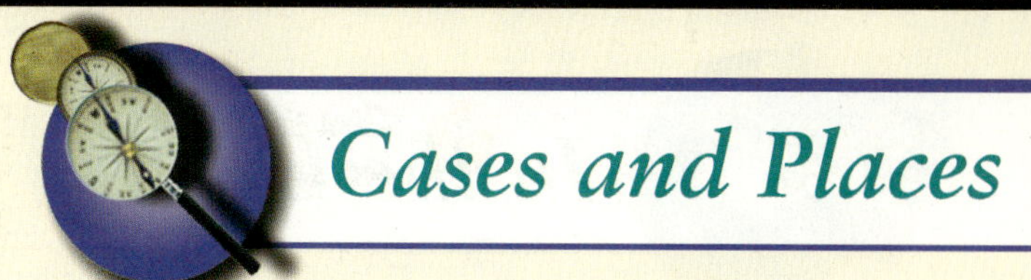

Cases and Places

The difficulty of these case studies varies:
◗ are the least difficult; ◗◗ are more difficult; and ◗◗◗ are the most difficult.

1 ◗ Use the Computer Items database on the Access Data Disk for this assignment. The Computer Club needs to add a table to the database that tracks the reorder status of items. The structure of the Reorder Status table and the data for the table are shown in Figure 7-87. There is a one-to-many relationship between the Item table and the Reorder Status table. The Item Id field in the Reorder Status table should be a Lookup Wizard field and the Reorder Date field should use the MM/dd/yyyy input mask. You may need to change the layout of the table. Print the Reorder Status table. Create a query that joins the Item, Reorder Status, and Supplier tables. Display the Item Id, Description, Reorder Date, Reorder Number, Cost, and Supplier Name fields. Include a calculated field, Reorder Cost, that is the result of multiplying Cost and Reorder Number.

Structure of Reorder Status table

FIELD NAME	DATA TYPE	FIELD SIZE	PRIMARY KEY?	DESCRIPTION
Item Id	Text	4	Yes	Item Id Number (Portion of Primary Key)
Reorder Date	Date/Time		Yes	Date Item was Reordered (Remainder of Primary Key)
Reorder Number	Number			Number of Items Ordered

Data for Reorder Status table

ITEM ID	DATE ORDERED	NUMBER ORDERED
1663	10/05/2001	10
1683	09/10/2001	12
1683	10/02/2001	5
5810	09/12/2001	4
5810	10/04/2001	2
6140	09/12/2001	2
6140	09/14/2001	5
3923	09/22/2001	4

FIGURE 7-87

2 ◗ Use the Computer Items database and create the report shown in Figure 7-88. The report groups the data by supplier. Within supplier, the data is sorted by item id. The report includes a subreport for the reorder information.

Cases and Places

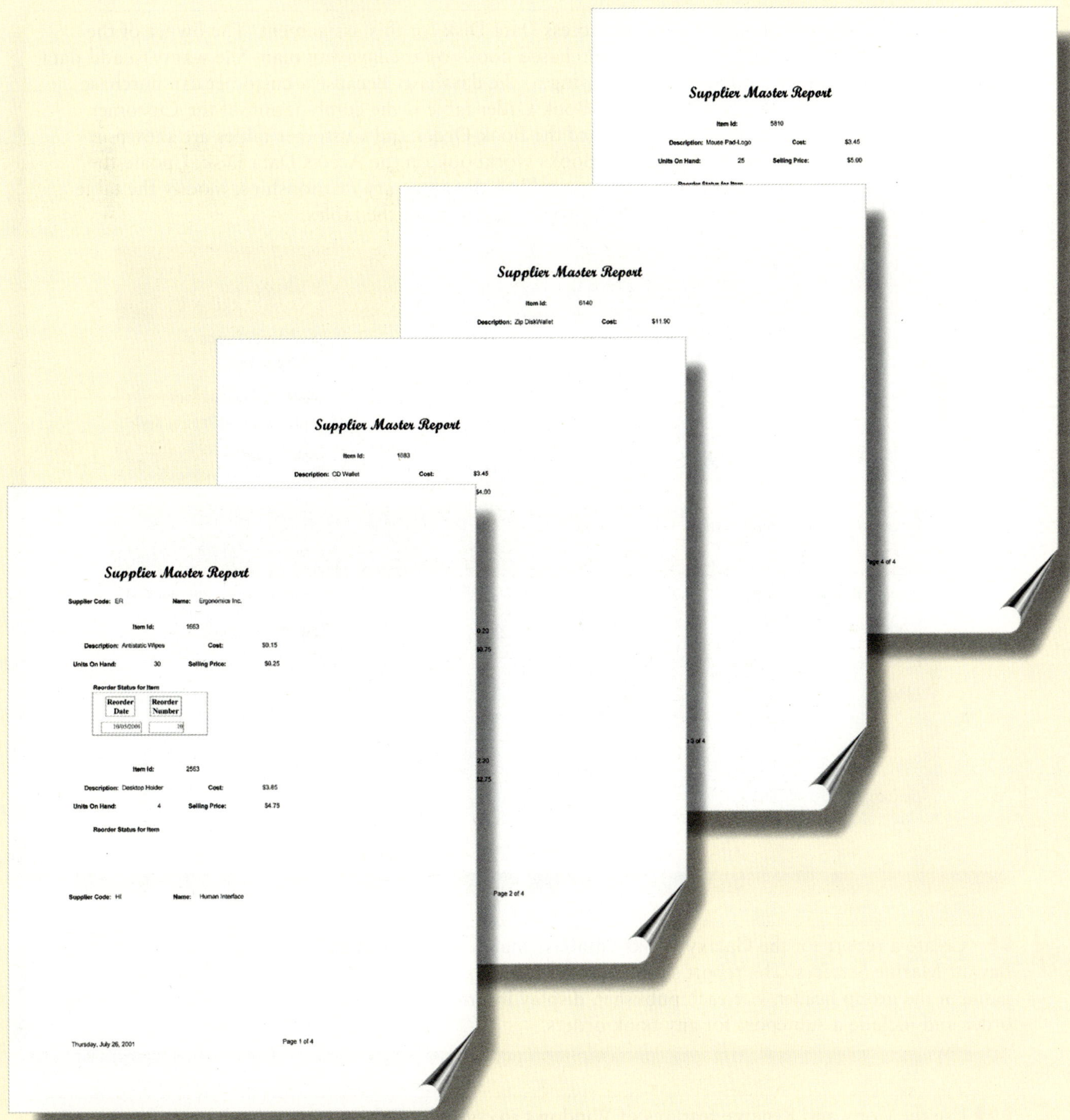

Supplier Master Report

Item Id: 5810

Description: Mouse Pad-Logo Cost: $3.45

Units On Hand: 25 Selling Price: $5.00

Page 4 of 4

Supplier Master Report

Item Id: 6140

Description: Zip Disk Wallet Cost: $11.90

Supplier Master Report

Item Id: 1683

Description: CD Wallet Cost: $3.45

$4.00

Page 2 of 4

Supplier Master Report

Supplier Code: ER Name: Ergonomics Inc.

Item Id: 1663

Description: Antistatic Wipes Cost: $0.15

Units On Hand: 30 Selling Price: $0.25

Reorder Status for Item

Reorder Date	Reorder Number
10/05/2001	20

Item Id: 2563

Description: Desktop Holder Cost: $3.85

Units On Hand: 4 Selling Price: $4.75

Reorder Status for Item

Supplier Code: HI Name: Human Interface

Thursday, July 26, 2001 Page 1 of 4

FIGURE 7-88

Cases and Places

3 ▸▸ Use the Galaxy Books database on the Access Data Disk for this assignment. The owner of the bookstore has several customers who have purchased books on the layaway plan. She wants to add data on these customers and the books they are buying to the database. Because a customer can purchase more than one book, the primary key for the Book Order table is the combination of the Customer Number and Book Code fields. The structure of the Book Order and Customer tables are shown in Figure 7-89. The data for the tables is in the Books workbook on the Access Data Disk. Update the Galaxy Books database to include these tables, establish the necessary relationships, modify the table designs to include Lookup Wizard fields, if appropriate, and print the tables.

Structure of Book Order table

FIELD NAME	DATA TYPE	FIELD SIZE	PRIMARY KEY?	DESCRIPTION
Book Code	Text	4	Yes	Book Code (Portion of Primary Key)
Customer Number	Text	3	Yes	Customer Ordering Book (Remainder of Primary Key)
Order Date	Date/Time			Date Ordered

Structure of Customer table

FIELD NAME	DATA TYPE	FIELD SIZE	PRIMARY KEY?	DESCRIPTION
Customer Number	Text	3	Yes	Customer Number (Primary Key)
Last Name	Text	15		Customer Last Name
First Name	Text	15		Customer First Name
Address	Text	15		Address
City	Text	10		City
State	Text	2		State
Zip Code	Text	5		Zip Code

FIGURE 7-89

4 ▸▸ Create a report for the Galaxy Books database that is similar in style to the report created for Bavant Marine Services. The report should group data by publisher and display the publisher code and name in the group header. For each publisher, display information about each book sorted in book code order and include a subreport for any book orders.

5 ▸▸▸ Use the Copy and Rename features of Windows to copy the Galaxy Books database and rename it as the Milky Way database. The owner of the bookstore is adding several new books that have multiple authors. For example, the authors of a new book, Asteroids and Meteors are H Brewster and G Chou. Modify the design of the Milky Way database to allow for multiple authors for a book.

Microsoft Access 2000

Customizing Forms Using Visual Basic for Applications (VBA), Charts and PivotTable Objects

OBJECTIVES

You will have mastered the material in this project when you can:

- Add command buttons to a form
- Modify VBA code associated with a command button
- Add a combo box to a form
- Use a combo box
- Modify the properties of a combo box
- Create a form using Design view
- Add a subform to a form
- Add a chart to a form
- Create a PivotTable form
- Use a PivotTable form

Smart Shopping

Happy Buyers

Consumer e-commerce spending has increased steadily over the last few years and continues to soar. Americans comprise 44 percent of the of the Web population, spending more than $111 billion in 1999. On a regular basis, popular purchases include books, software, music, travel, hardware, clothing, and electronics. Auctions, prescription sales, holiday purchases, and grocery shopping are among many more goods and services selling via the World Wide Web.

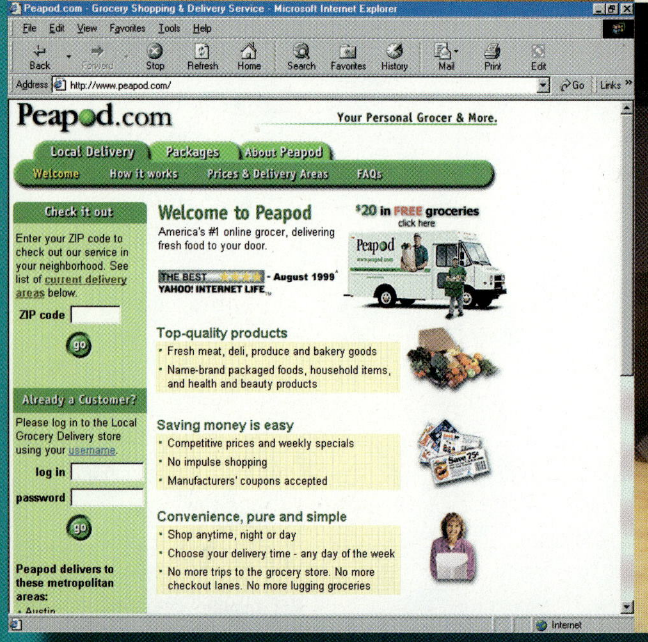

Industry experts speculate that Web surfers purchasing online could represent up to 20 percent of the grocery volume by 2003. From the convenience of their home computers, shopping in cyberspace has simplified this mundane task for many individuals in this fast-paced world. Consider that a trip to the grocery store requires 66 minutes on average. From hunting for a parking space to waiting in long checkout lines, the entire experience often is tiring and frustrating.

Using a service called Peapod, consumers in eight metropolitan areas of the United States from New York to San Francisco already are shopping regularly online. Entering data into Peapod Personal Grocer online forms, shoppers place their orders from work or home, day or night. With features such as Express Shop, you can locate all of your shopping items at once, or Personal Lists lets you organize your list into categories, making your shopping experience simple and relaxed.

Shoppers enter the store online, select, and then purchase items on their computers via forms and buttons. These forms and buttons are similar to the form and command button you will create in this Access 2000 project using advanced form techniques, the Form Design window, and an appropriate wizard. Forms allow users to place their orders, find items, create shopping lists, and then add the items to their shopping carts with a simple click of a button on the Web page.

Details such as the price and nutritional content of each item are kept in a database that is integrated with a billing system and a customer database. The products database is updated daily as prices change, new items are added to the stores' shelves, and unpopular items are removed. Produce prices change weekly.

A nutrition-conscious shopper can query the database to display a picture of the product, view its nutrition facts, and sort items by nutritional content. Selective shoppers instantly can compare prices in the database to find the best deals. Buyers can view items in their shopping carts, check subtotals any time to stay within budgets, redeem manufacturer and electronic coupons, and designate a delivery time.

Peapod delivers groceries to the customer's door. Deliveries are free for orders over $60. The driver accepts payment by check, credit card, or automatic debit from a checking account and even will return bags for recycling. Customers report top-quality products, competitive pricing, and convenience as their main reasons for using the Peapod service. The primary customer base consists of two-income families with children, individuals with disabilities, and the elderly. These groups find that the convenience of being able to order at any time and place gives them flexibility in their busy lifestyles, independence, and less stress.

Visit Peapod (www.peapod.com) on the Web to see America's #1 online grocer and how it works.

Microsoft Access 2000

Customizing Forms Using Visual Basic for Applications (VBA), Charts, and PivotTable Objects

CASE PERSPECTIVE

The management of Bavant Marine Services has three additional requests. First, they would like some improvements to the Marina Update Form. This includes placing buttons on the form for moving to the next record, moving to the previous record, adding a record, deleting a record, and closing the form. They also want users of the form to have a simple way of searching for a marina using the marina's name. They also would like an additional form, one that lists the number and name of technicians. This form should include a subform listing details concerning open workorders for each technician. It also should include two charts that graphically illustrate the number of hours spent by each technician in each of the service categories. Finally, they would like a PivotTable form that summarizes workorder data. Your task is to modify the Marina Update Form in accordance with their requests and to create the two additional forms.

Introduction

By including both command buttons and a combo box that allows users to search for marinas by name, you will enhance the Marina Update Form you created earlier (Figure 8-1). When clicked, a **command button** executes a command. For example, after creating the Next Record command button, clicking it will move to the next record.

When you add the command buttons and the combo box to the form, you will use appropriate Access wizards. The **wizards** create the button or the combo box to your specifications and place it on the form. They also create an event procedure for the button or the combo box. An **event procedure** is a series of steps that Access will carry out when an event, such as the clicking of a command button, occurs. For example, when you click the Delete Record button, the steps in the event procedure created for the Delete Record button will be executed. This procedure will cause the record to be deleted. Event procedures are written in a language called **Visual Basic for Applications**, or **VBA**, which is standard throughout Microsoft applications.

Generally, you do not need to be aware that these event procedures exist. Access creates and uses them automatically. Occasionally, you may wish to make changes to an event procedure. For example, without making changes, clicking the Add Record button clears the field contents on the form so you can enter a new record, yet, it would not produce an insertion point in the Marina Number field. You would be required to take special action, such as clicking the Marina Number field, before you could begin entering data. You can rectify this by making a change to the event procedure for the Add Record button.

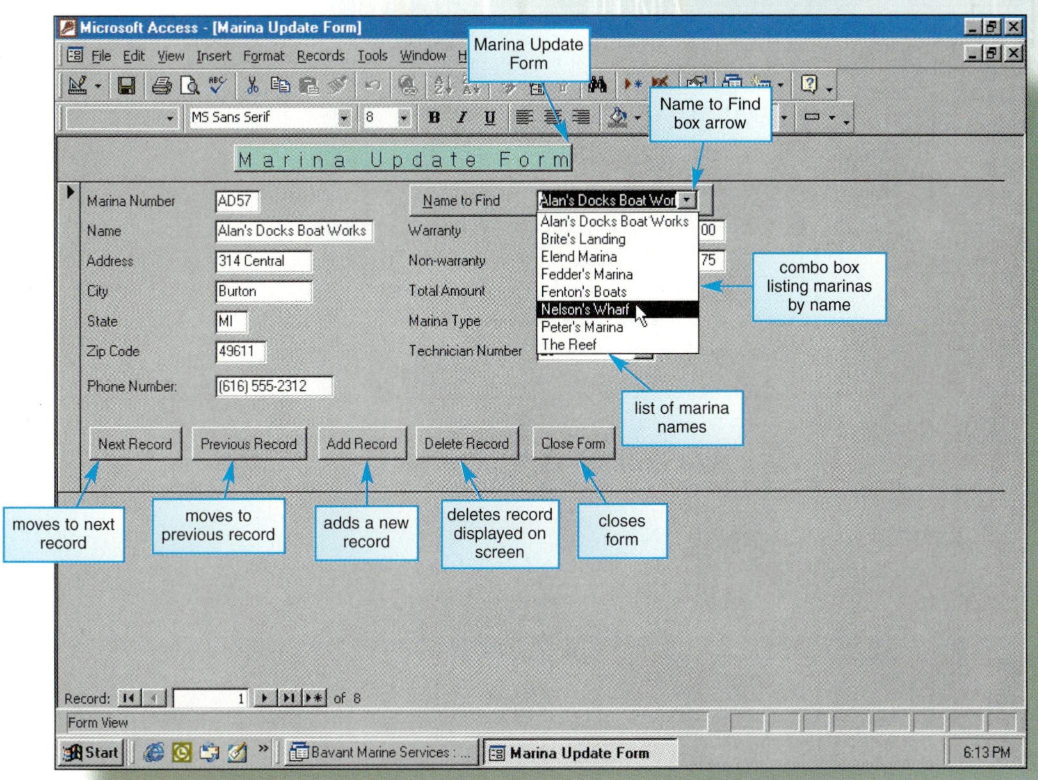

FIGURE 8-1

You also will create the form shown in Figure 8-2a on the next page and the PivotTable object in Figure 8-2b on the next page. The form in Figure 8-2a lists the Tech Number, First Name, and Last Name fields from the Technician table. It also contains a subform, which lists the Marina Number, Name, Location, Category Number, Total Hours (est), and Hours Spent for each workorder at any marina assigned to each technician. The form also contains two charts. In both charts, the bars represent the various service categories. The height of the bars in the left chart represents the total of the estimated hours. The height of the bars in the right chart represents the total of the hours spent.

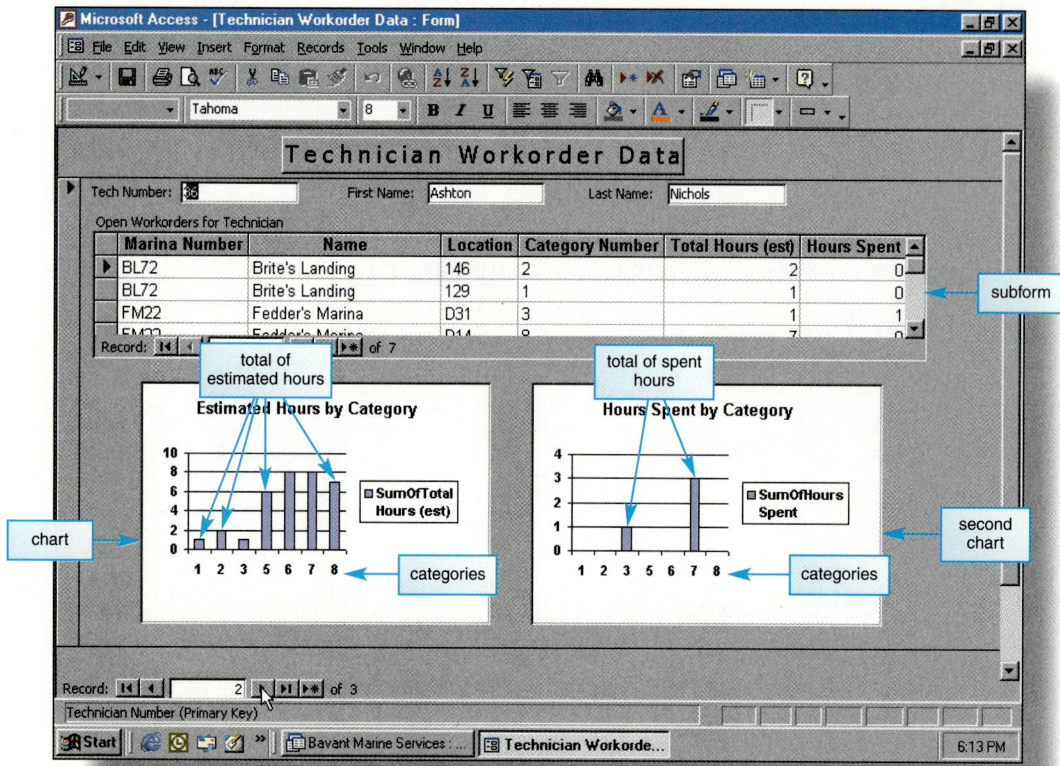

FIGURE 8-2a

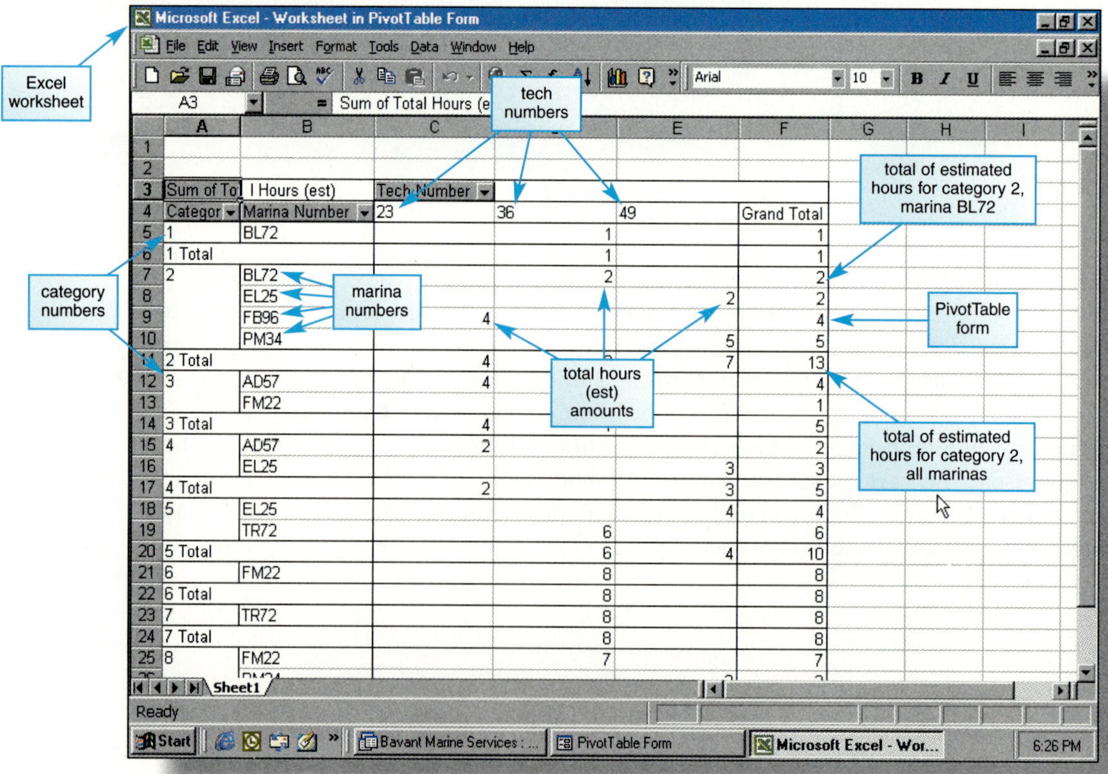

FIGURE 8-2b

The form in Figure 8-2b shows a **PivotTable** object, a special type of worksheet that allows you to summarize data in a variety of ways. To create a PivotTable form in Access, use the PivotTable Wizard. By clicking a button on this form, you can display the PivotTable object in Excel as shown in Figure 8-2b. You can then use Excel features to manipulate the PivotTable object.

The PivotTable object shown in Figure 8-2b shows the category numbers in the first column. The second column contains marina numbers. The next three columns contain the technician numbers. The final column contains totals.

Row 7 in the table, for example, indicates that for category 2 and marina BL72, technician 23 has 0 hours, technician 36 has 2 hours, and technician 49 has 0 hours, for a total of 2 hours. Row 8 indicates that for category 2 and marina EL25, technician 23 has 0 hours, technician 36 has 0 hours, and technician 49 has 2 hours, for a total of 2 hours. Row 11 indicates that for category 2, technician 23 has a total of 4 hours, technician 36 has a total of 2 hours, and technician 49 has a total of 7 hours, for a total of 13 hours.

One advantage to PivotTable forms is that they can be manipulated to change the way the data is summarized. You could interchange the Tech Number and Category Number fields so that the Tech Number field rather than the Category Number field would summarize the data as in the Figure 8-2b.

Microsoft Certification

The Microsoft Office User Specialist (MOUS) Certification program provides an opportunity for you to obtain a valuable industry credential - proof that you have the Access 2000 skills required by employers. For more information, see Appendix D or visit the Shelly Cashman Series MOUS Web page at www.scsite.com/off2000/cert.htm.

Project Eight — Using Advanced Form Techniques

You begin this project by adding the necessary command buttons to the Marina Update Form. Then, you add the combo box that allows users to find a marina using the marina's name. Next you will create a query that will be used in the form you will create. You then create the form from scratch using Design view. You will add a subform and two charts to this form. Finally, you will create a PivotTable form using Access.

Opening the Database

Before completing the tasks in this project, you must open the database. Perform the following steps to open the database.

TO OPEN A DATABASE

1. Click the Start button on the taskbar.
2. Click Open Office Document on the Start menu, and then click 3½ Floppy (A:) in the Look in box. If necessary, double-click the Access folder. Make sure the Bavant Marine Services database is selected.
3. Click the Open button.

The database opens and the Bavant Marine Services : Database window displays.

More About 2000

Quick Reference

For a table that lists how to complete the tasks covered in this book using the mouse, menu, shortcut menu, and keyboard, visit the Office 2000 Web page (www.scsite.com/off2000/qr.htm), and then click Microsoft Access 2000.

Enhancing the Form

You will enhance the form by adding command buttons and a combo box. The command buttons provide additional methods for performing common tasks. The combo box helps users to locate marinas easily.

Control Wizards

There are wizards associated with many of the controls. The wizards lead you through a series of dialog boxes that assist you in creating the control. To use the wizards, the Control Wizards button must be recessed. If not, you will need to specify all the details of the control without any assistance.

Adding Command Buttons to the Form

To add command buttons, you will use the Control Wizards button and Command Button button in the toolbox. Using the series of Command Button Wizard dialog boxes, you need to provide the action that should be taken when the button is clicked. Several categories of actions are available.

In the Record Navigation category, you will select the action Goto Next Record for one of the buttons. From the same category, you will select Goto Previous Record for another button. Other buttons will use the Add New Record and the Delete Record actions from the Record Operations category. The Close Form button will use the Close Form action from the Form Operations category.

Perform the following steps to add command buttons to move to the next record, move to the previous record, add a record, delete a record, and close the form.

To Add Command Buttons to a Form

1 **Click Forms on the Objects bar, right-click Marina Update Form, and then point to Design View on the shortcut menu.**

The shortcut menu displays (Figure 8-3).

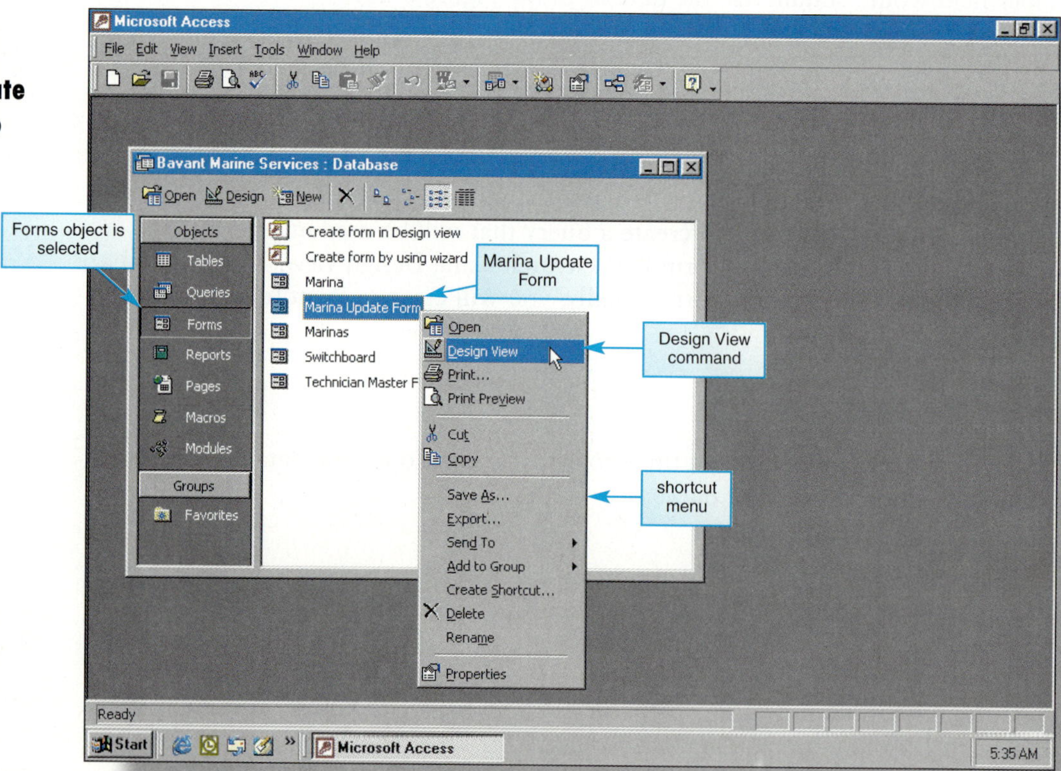

FIGURE 8-3

2 **Click Design View on the shortcut menu, and then, if necessary, maximize the window. Be sure the toolbox displays and is docked at the bottom of the screen. (If it does not display, click the Toolbox button on the Form Design toolbar. If it is not docked at the bottom of the screen, drag it to the bottom of the screen to dock it there.) If necessary, close the field box. Make sure the Control Wizards button is recessed, and then point to the Command Button button in the toolbox.**

The design of the form displays in a maximized window (Figure 8-4).

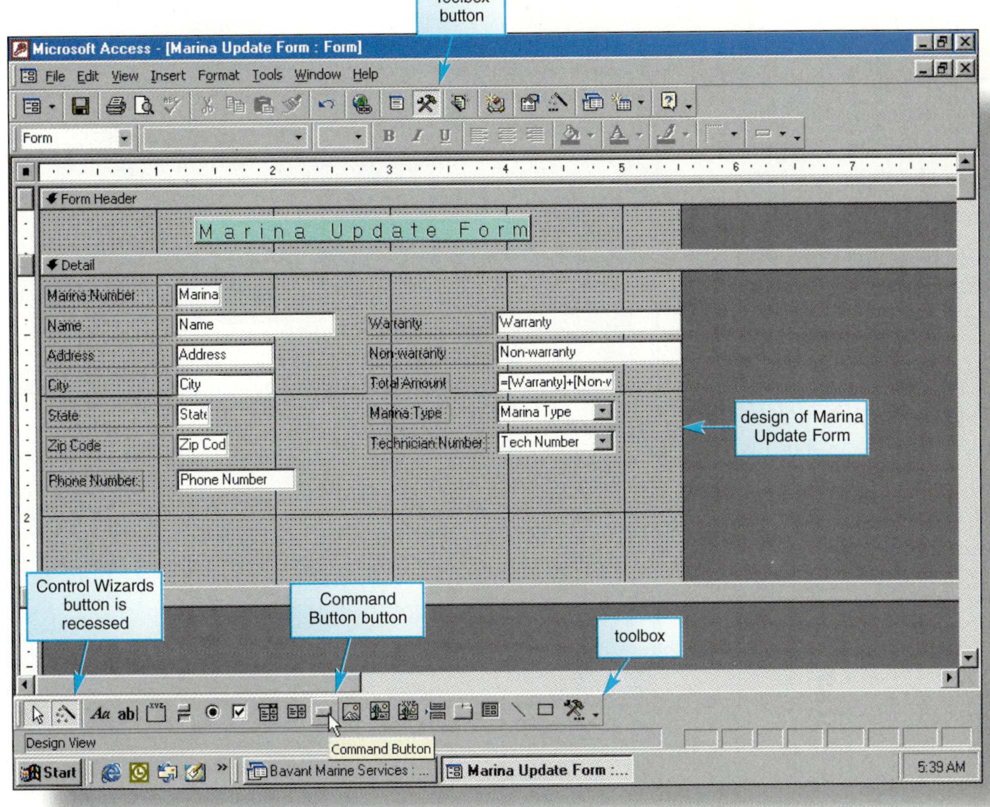

FIGURE 8-4

3 **Click the Command Button button and move the mouse pointer, whose shape has changed to a plus sign with a picture of a button, to the position shown in Figure 8-5.**

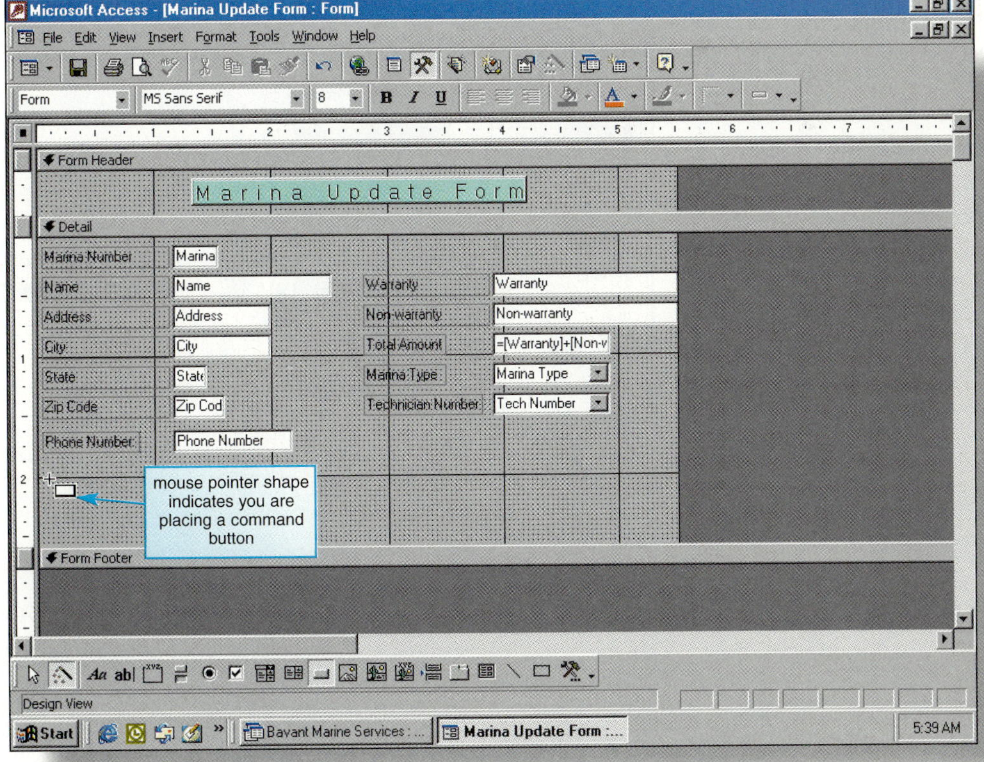

FIGURE 8-5

4 **Click the position shown in Figure 8-5. With Record Navigation selected in the Categories box in the Command Button Wizard dialog box, click Goto Next Record in the Actions box. Point to the Next button.**

The Command Button Wizard dialog box displays (Figure 8-6). Goto Next Record is selected as the action. A sample of the button displays in the Sample box.

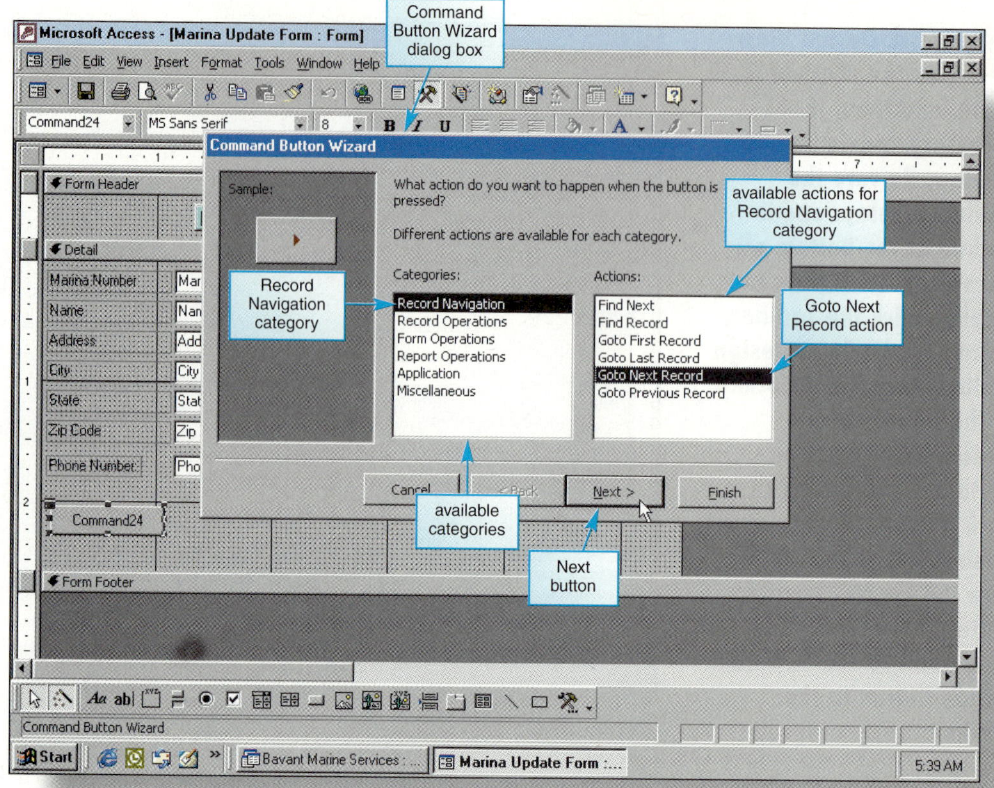

FIGURE 8-6

5 **Click the Next button. Point to the Text button.**

The next Command Button Wizard dialog box displays, asking what to display on the button (Figure 8-7). The button can contain either text or a picture.

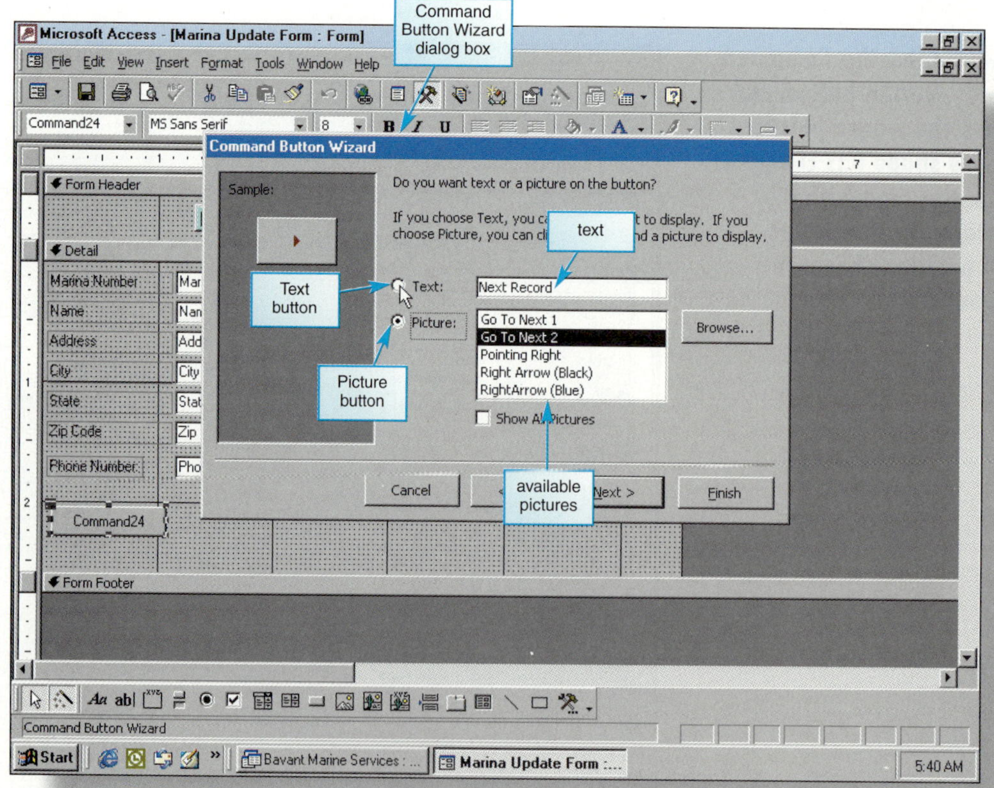

FIGURE 8-7

6 Click the Text button. Next Record is the desired text and does not need to be changed. Click the Next button, and then type `Next Record` **as the name of the button. Point to the Finish button.**

The name of the button displays in the text box (Figure 8-8).

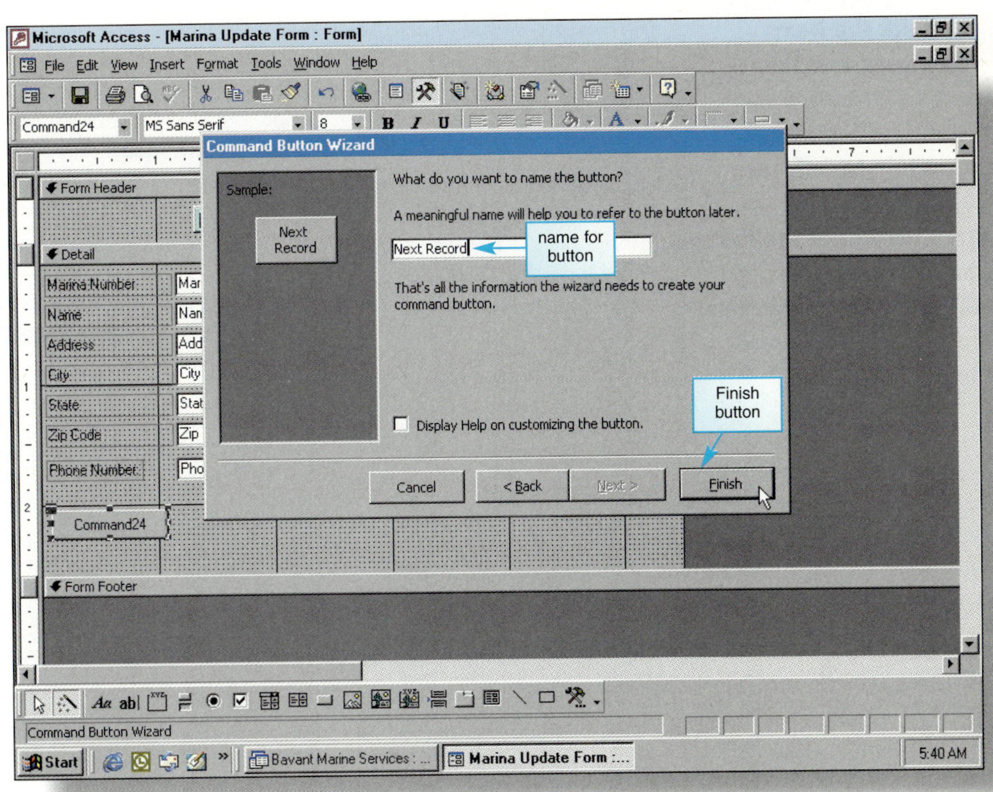

FIGURE 8-8

7 Click the Finish button.

The button displays on the form.

8 Use the techniques in Steps 3 through 7 to place the Previous Record button directly to the right of the Next Record button. Click Goto Previous Record in the Actions box. The name of the button is Previous Record.

9 Place a button directly to the right of the Previous Record button. Click Record Operations in the Categories box. Add New Record is the desired action. Point to the Next button.

The Command Button Wizard dialog box displays with the selections (Figure 8-9).

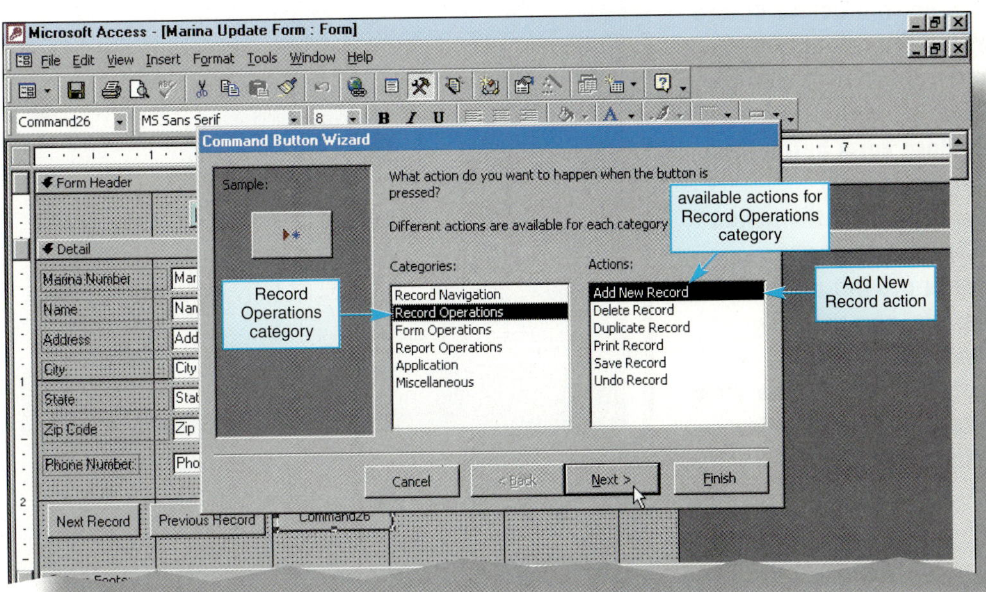

FIGURE 8-9

10 **Click the Next button and then click the Text button to indicate that the button is to contain text (Figure 8-10). Add Record is the desired text. Click the Next button, type** `Add Record` **as the name of the button, and then click the Finish button.**

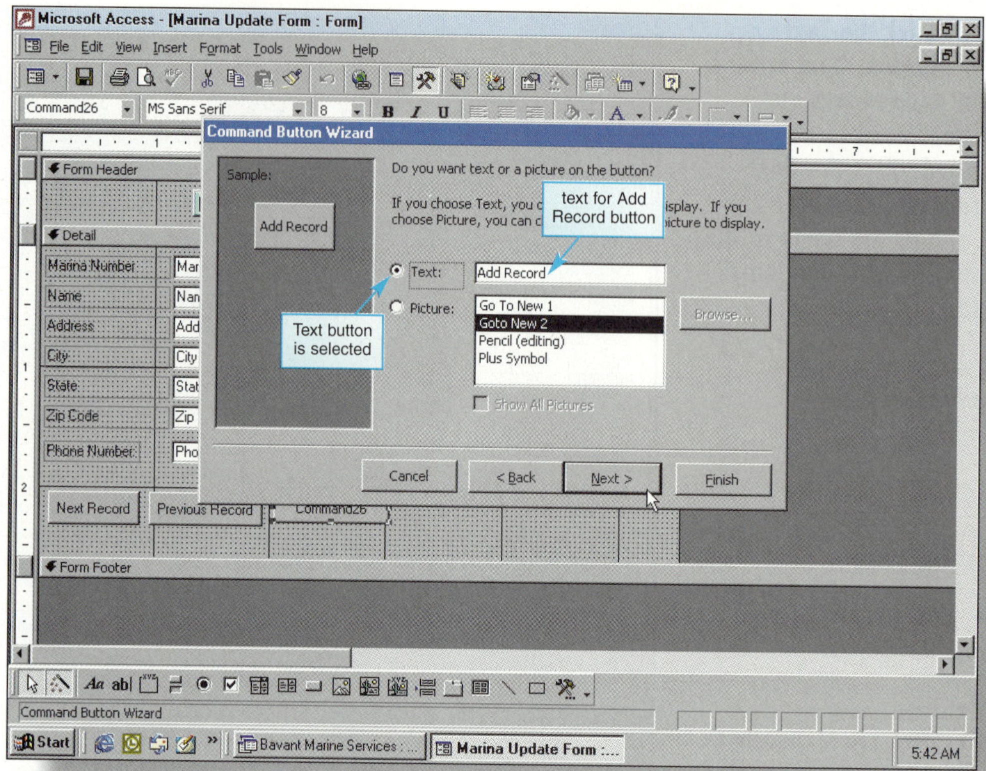

FIGURE 8-10

11 **Use the techniques in Steps 3 through 7 to place the Delete Record and Close Form buttons in the positions shown in Figure 8-11. For the Delete Record button, the category is Record Operations and the action is Delete Record. For the Close Form button, the category is Form Operations and the action is Close Form. If your buttons are not aligned properly, you can drag them to the correct positions. Point to the View button on the Form View toolbar.**

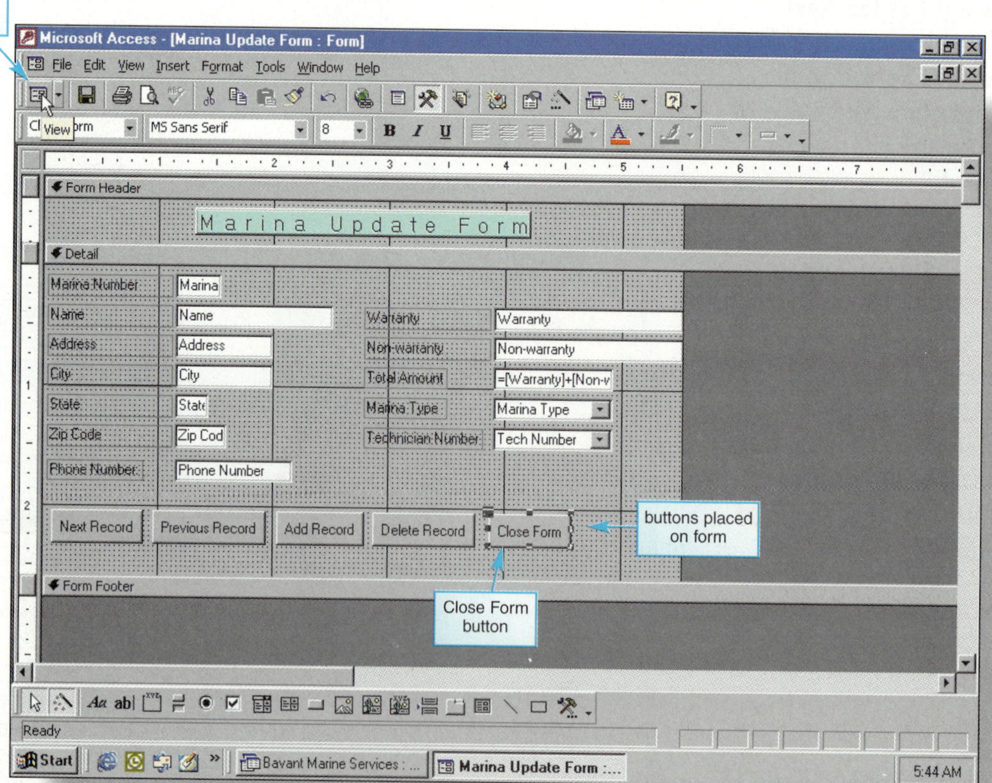

FIGURE 8-11

Click the View button.

The form displays with the added buttons (Figure 8-12).

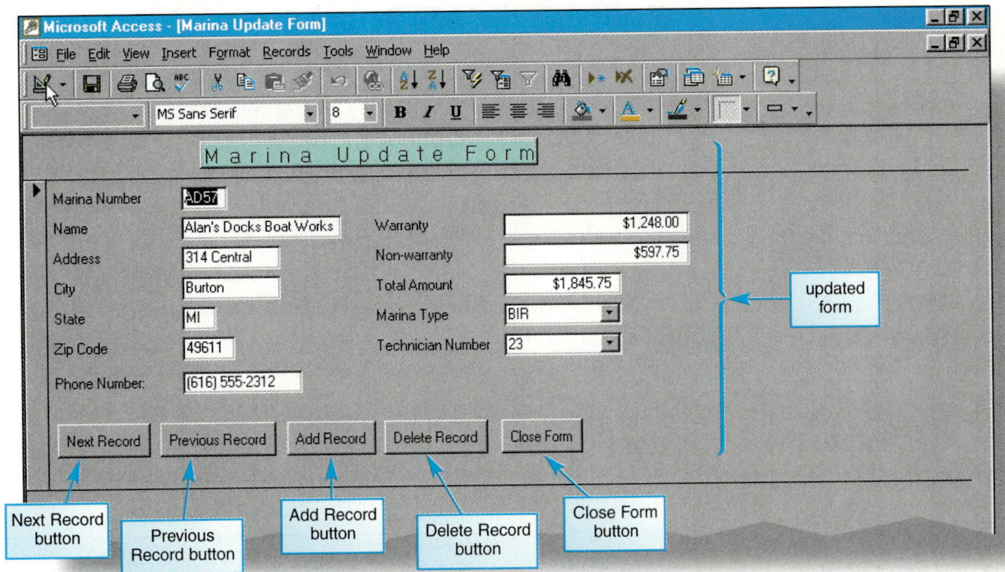

FIGURE 8-12

Using the Buttons

To move around on the form, you can use the buttons to perform the actions you specify. To move to the next record, click the Next Record button. Click the Previous Record button to move to the previous record. Clicking the Delete Record button will delete the record currently on the screen. You will get a message requesting you to verify the deletion before the record actually is deleted. Clicking the Close Form button will remove the form from the screen.

Clicking the Add Record button will clear the contents of the form so you can add a new record (Figure 8-13). Notice on the form in Figure 8-13 that an insertion point does not display. To begin entering a record, you will have to click the Marina Number field before you can start typing. To ensure that an insertion point displays in the field's text box when you click the Add Record button, you must change the focus. **Focus** is the ability to receive user input through mouse or keyboard actions. The Add Record button needs to update the focus to the Marina Number field.

More About 2000

Focus

There is a visual way to determine which object on the screen has the focus. If a field has the focus, an insertion point will display in the field. If a button has the focus, a small rectangle will appear inside the button.

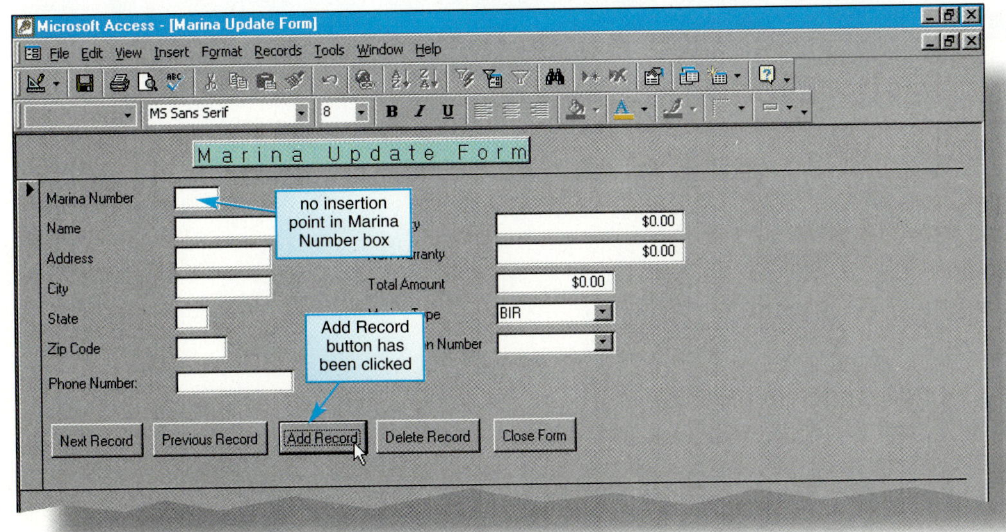

FIGURE 8-13

Modifying the Add Record Button

To display an insertion point automatically when you click the Add Record button, two steps are necessary using Visual Basic for Applications (VBA). First, you must change the name of the control for the Marina Number field to a name that does not contain spaces. Next, because Access automatically creates VBA code for the button, you must add a command to the VBA code. The added command will move the focus to the Marina Number field as soon as the button is clicked.

Perform the following steps to change the name of the Marina Number control to MarNumb and then add an additional command to the VBA code that will set the focus to MarNumb.

To Modify the Add Record Button

1 **Click the View button on the toolbar to return to the design grid. Right-click the control for the Marina Number field (the white space, not the label), and then click Properties on the shortcut menu. If necessary, click the Name property, use the DELETE or BACKSPACE key to erase the current value, and then type** `MarNumb` **as the new name.**

The name is changed (Figure 8-14).

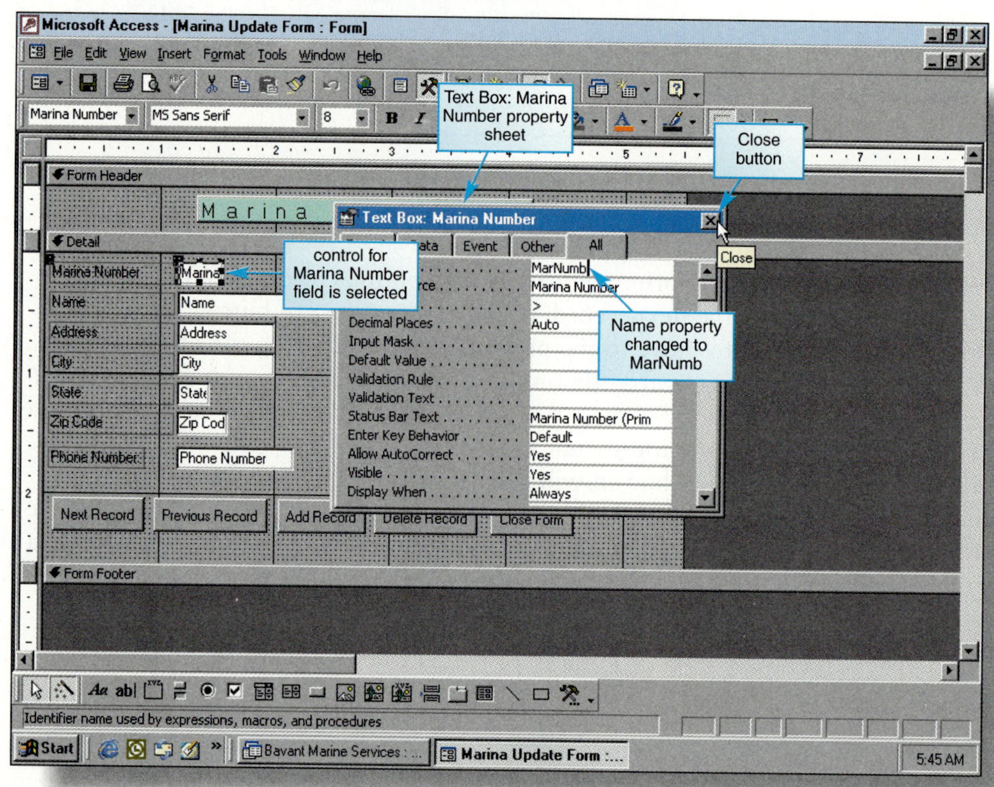

FIGURE 8-14

2 Click the Close button to close the Text Box: Marina Number property sheet. Right-click the Add Record button. Point to Build Event on the shortcut menu.

The shortcut menu displays (Figure 8-15).

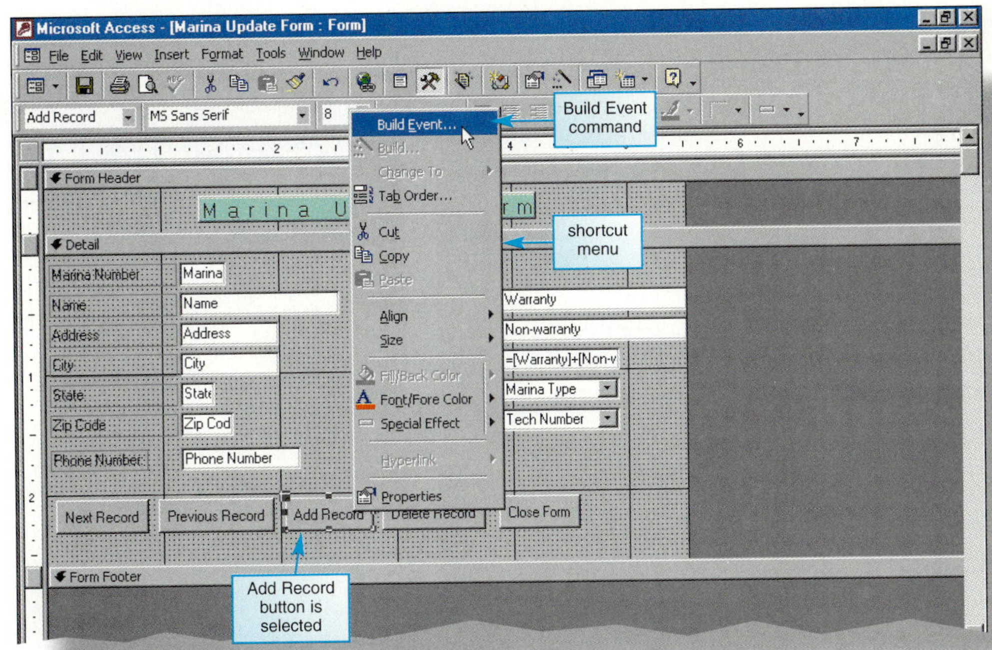

FIGURE 8-15

3 Click Build Event on the shortcut menu.

The VBA code for the Add Record button displays (Figure 8-16). The important line in this code is DoCmd, which stands for Do Command. Following DoCmd, is the command, formally called a method, that will be executed; in this case GoToRecord. Following GoToRecord are the arguments, which are items that provide information that will be used by the method. The only argument necessary in this case is acNewRec. This code indicates that Access is to move to the new record at the end of the table. This command will not set the focus to any particular field automatically, so an insertion point still will not be produced.

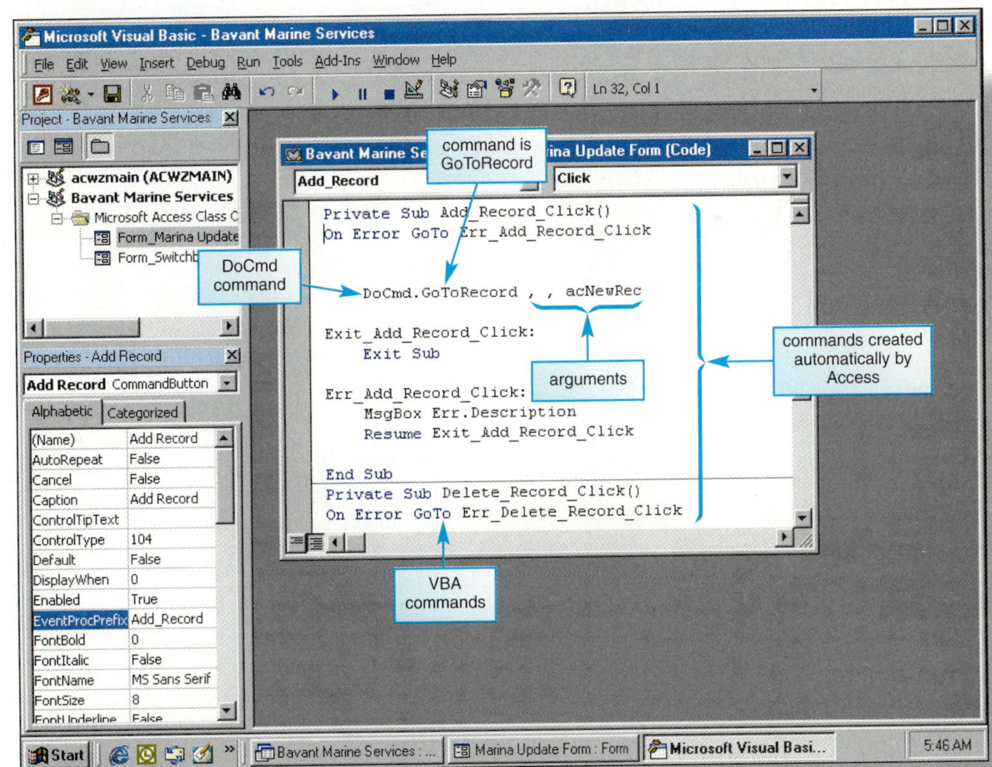

FIGURE 8-16

4 **Press the DOWN ARROW key four times, press the TAB key, and type** `MarNumb.SetFocus` **as the additional command. Press the ENTER key.**

The command is entered (Figure 8-17). While typing, a box may display indicating selections for the command. You may disregard this list. This command will set the focus in the control named MarNumb as soon as the previous command (GoToRecord) is executed.

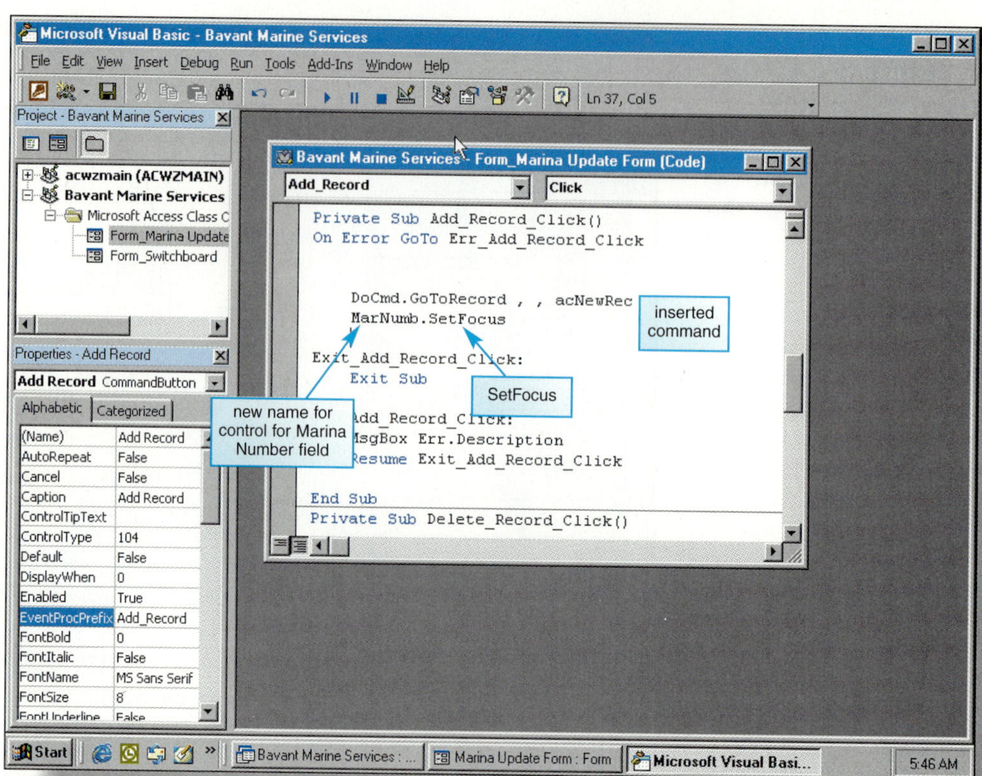

FIGURE 8-17

5 **Close the window containing the VBA code. Click the View button on the toolbar and then click the Add Record button.**

An insertion point displays in the Marina Number field (Figure 8-18).

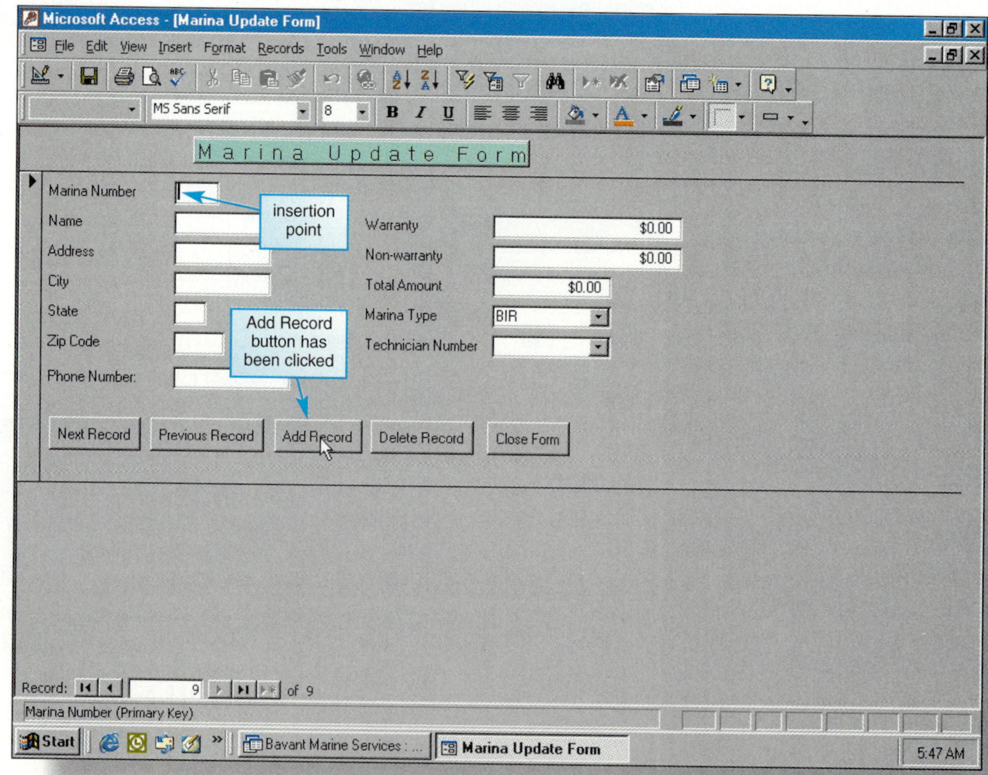

FIGURE 8-18

Creating and Using Combo Boxes

A **combo box**, such as the one shown in Figure 8-1 on page A 8.5, combines the properties of a **text box**, a box into which you can type an entry, and a **list box**, a box you can use to display a list. You could type the marina's name directly in the box or, you can click the Name to Find box arrow and Access will display a list of marina names. To select a name from the list, simply click the name.

The Add Record Button

If your spelling was not consistent, you will get an error message when you click the Add Record button. To correct the problem, return to the form design. Check to make sure the name you gave to the Marina Number control and the name in the SetFocus command are both the same (MarNumb).

Creating a Combo Box

To create a combo box, use the Combo Box button in the toolbox. The Combo Box Wizard then will guide you through the steps to create the combo box. Perform the following steps to place a combo box for marina names on the form.

To Create a Combo Box

1. **Click the View button on the toolbar to return to the design grid. Make sure the Control Wizards button is recessed, and then point to the Combo Box button in the toolbox (Figure 8-19).**

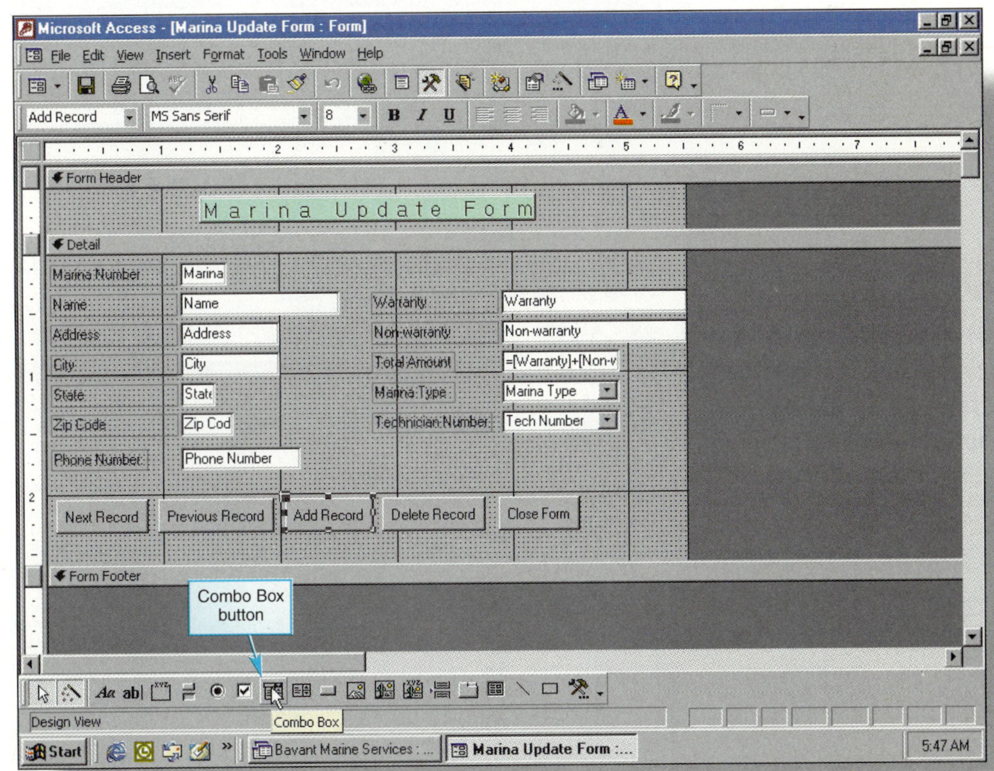

FIGURE 8-19

2 **Click the Combo Box button and then move the mouse pointer, whose shape has changed to a small plus sign with a combo box, to the position shown in Figure 8-20.**

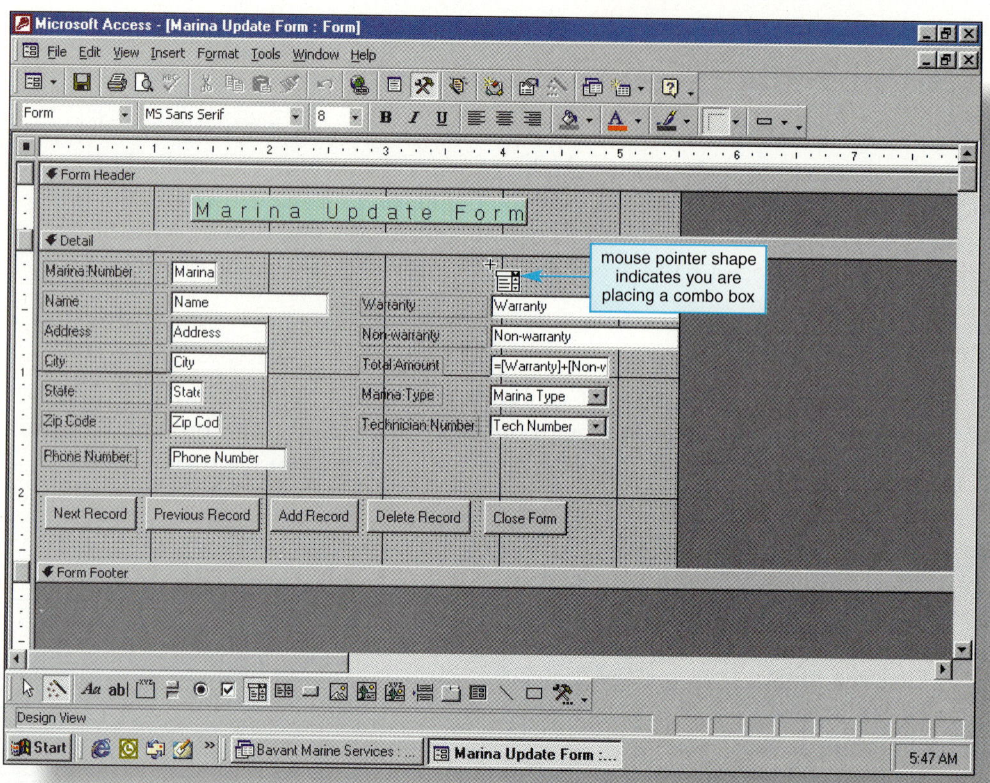

FIGURE 8-20

3 **Click the position shown in Figure 8-20 to place a combo box. Click the Find a record on my form based on the value I selected in my combo box button. Point to the Next button.**

The Combo Box Wizard dialog box displays, instructing you to indicate how the combo box is to obtain values for the list (Figure 8-21).

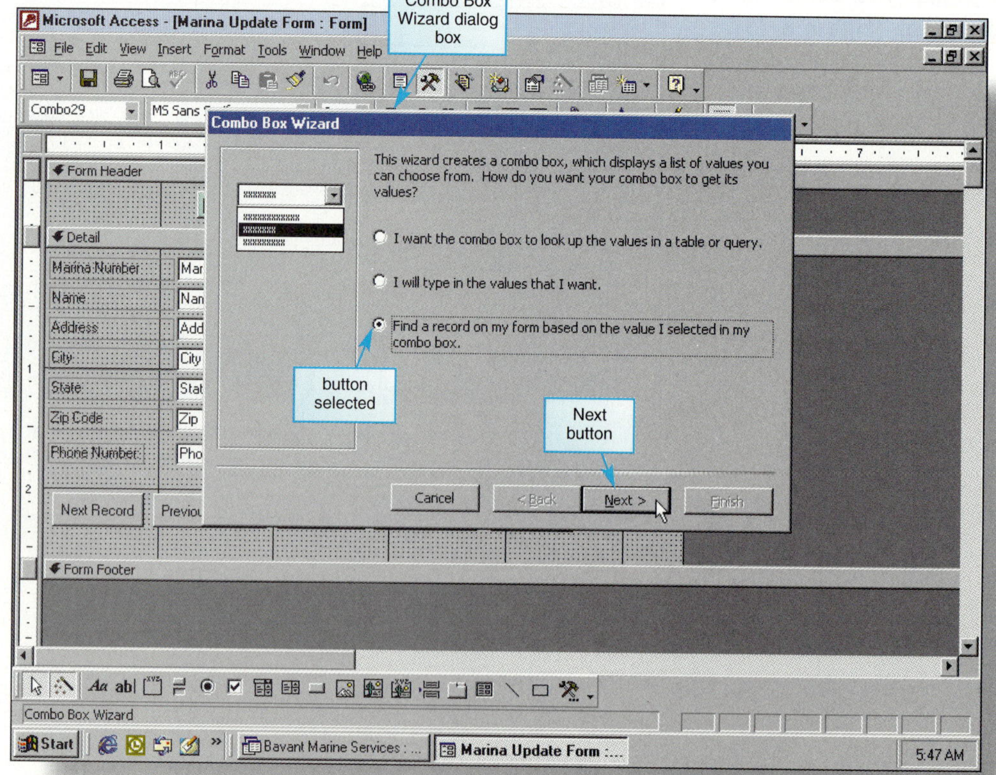

FIGURE 8-21

4 **Click the Next button, click the Name field, and then click the Add Field button to add Name as a field in the combo box. Point to the Next button.**

The Name field is added to the Selected Fields box (Figure 8-22).

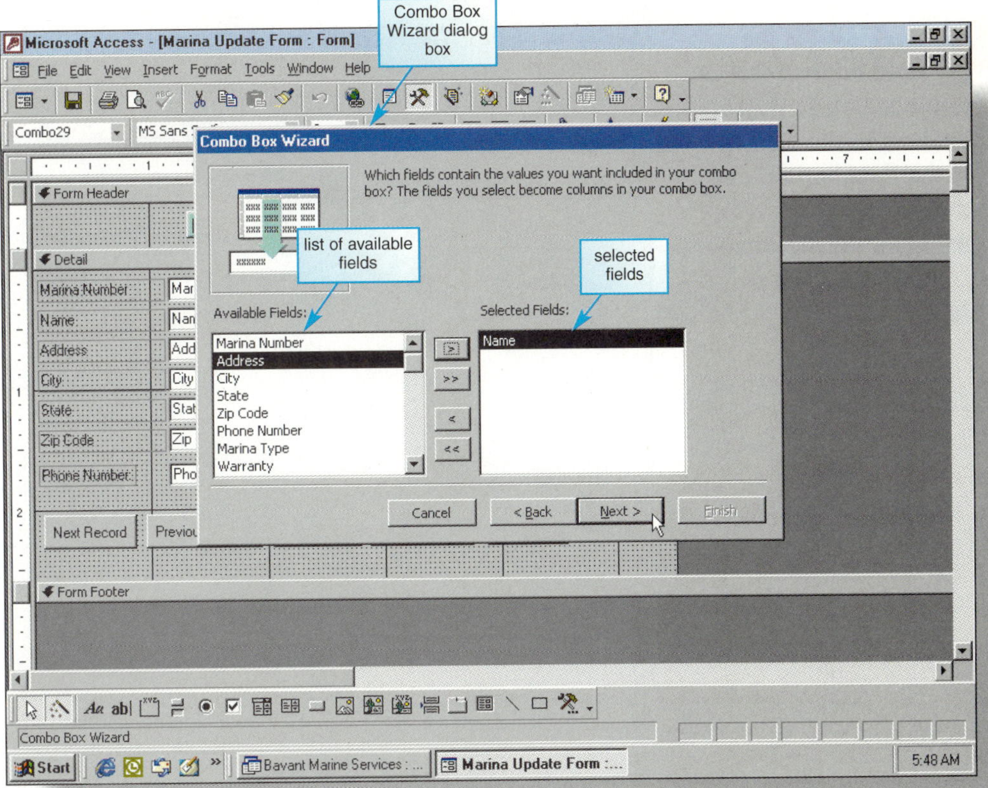

FIGURE 8-22

5 **Click the Next button. Point to the right edge of the column heading.**

The Combo Box Wizard dialog box displays (Figure 8-23), giving you an opportunity to resize the columns in the combo box.

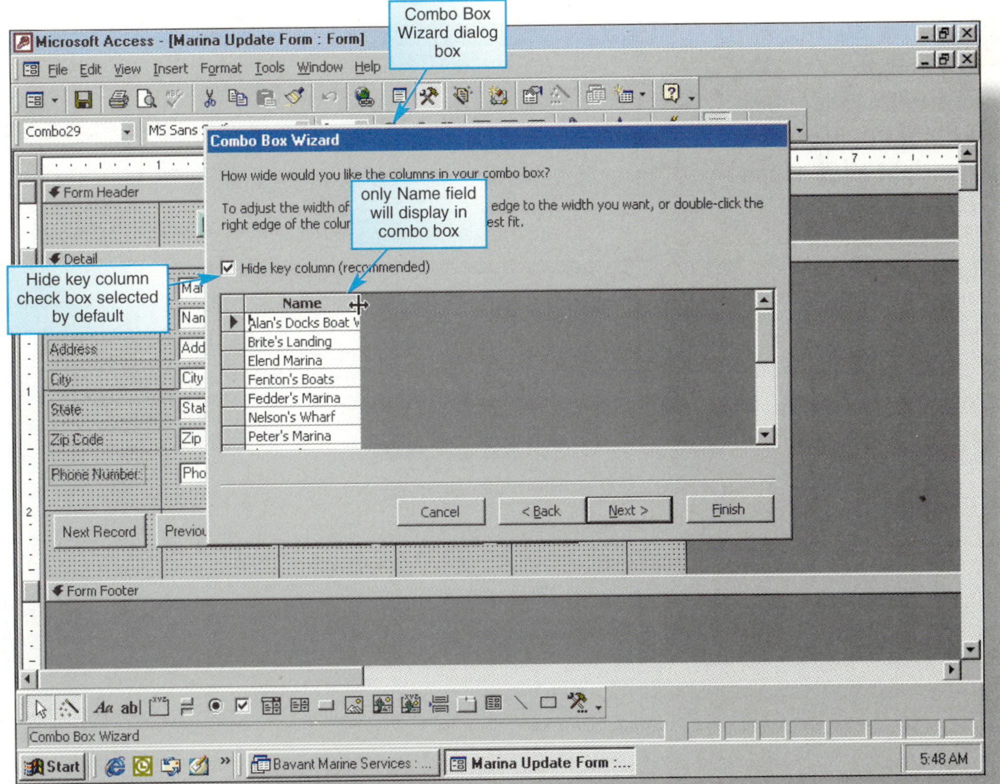

FIGURE 8-23

6 Double-click the right edge of the column heading to resize the column to the best fit. Click the Next button, and then type `&Name to Find` **as the label for the combo box. Point to the Finish button.**

The label is entered (Figure 8-24). The ampersand (&) in front of the letter N indicates that users can select the combo box by pressing the ALT+N keys.

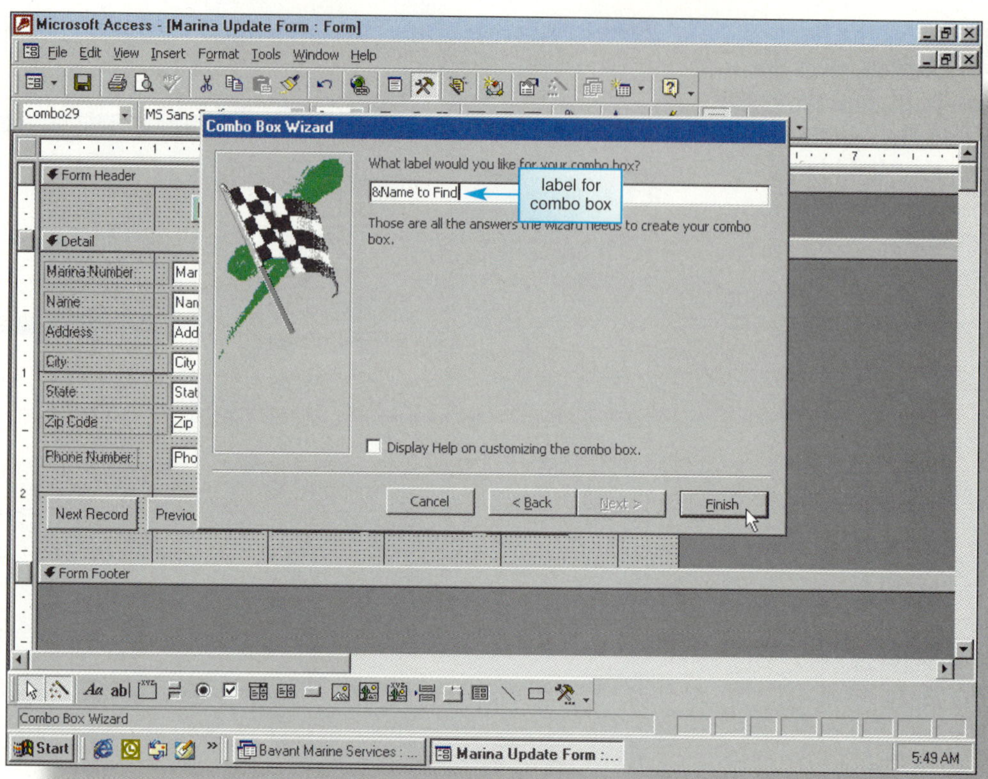

FIGURE 8-24

7 Click the Finish button. Click the label for the combo box. Point to the sizing handle on the right edge of the label.

The shape of the mouse pointer changes to a two-headed horizontal arrow, indicating that you can drag the right edge (Figure 8-25).

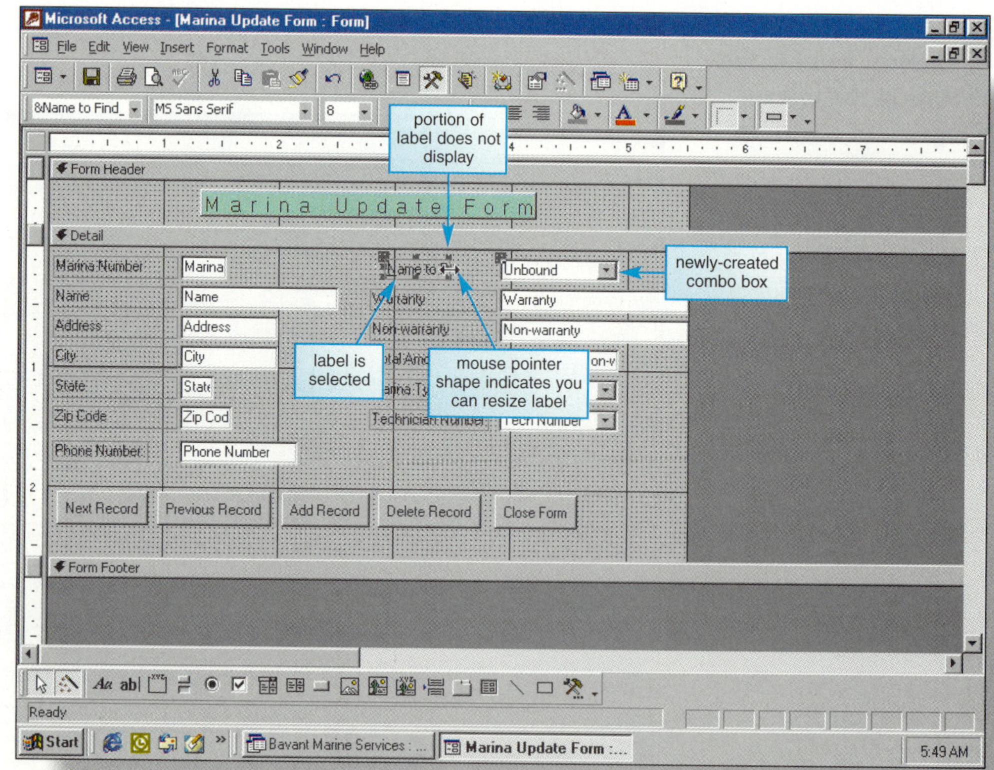

FIGURE 8-25

8 Double-click the handle so the entire label displays. Point to the View button on the toolbar.

The combo box is added and the label has been resized (Figure 8-26). The N in Name is underlined indicating that you can press the ALT+N keys to select the combo box.

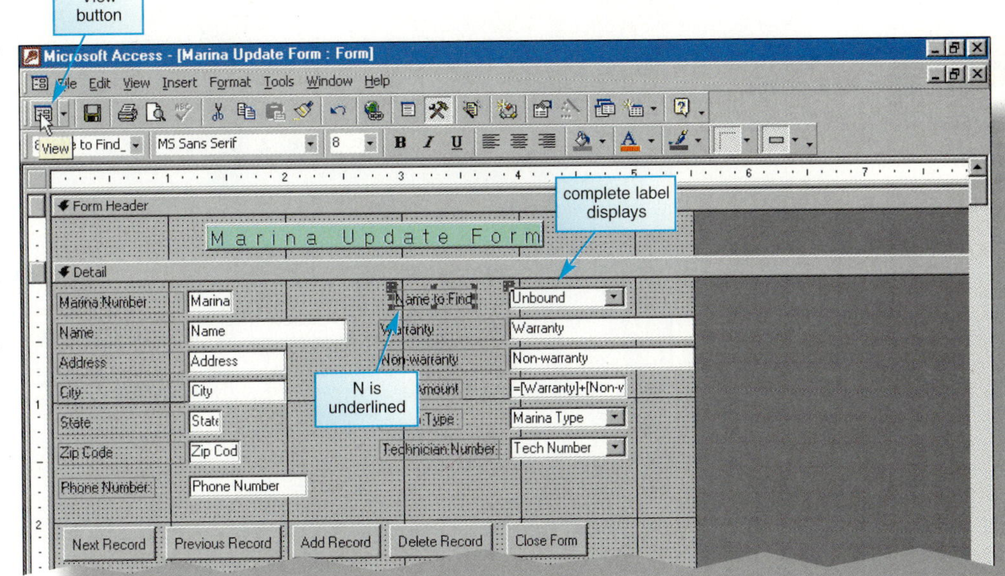

FIGURE 8-26

Using the Combo Box

Using the combo box, you can search for a marina in two ways. You either can click the combo box arrow to display a list of marina names and then select the name from the list by clicking it or, you can begin typing the name. Access will display automatically the name that begins with the letters you have typed. Once the correct name is displayed, select the name by pressing the TAB key. Regardless of the method you use, the data for the selected marina displays on the form once the selection is made.

The following steps first locate the marina whose name is Nelson's Wharf, and then use the Next Record button to move to the next marina.

To Use the Combo Box

1 Click the View button on the toolbar to display the form.

The form displays (Figure 8-27).

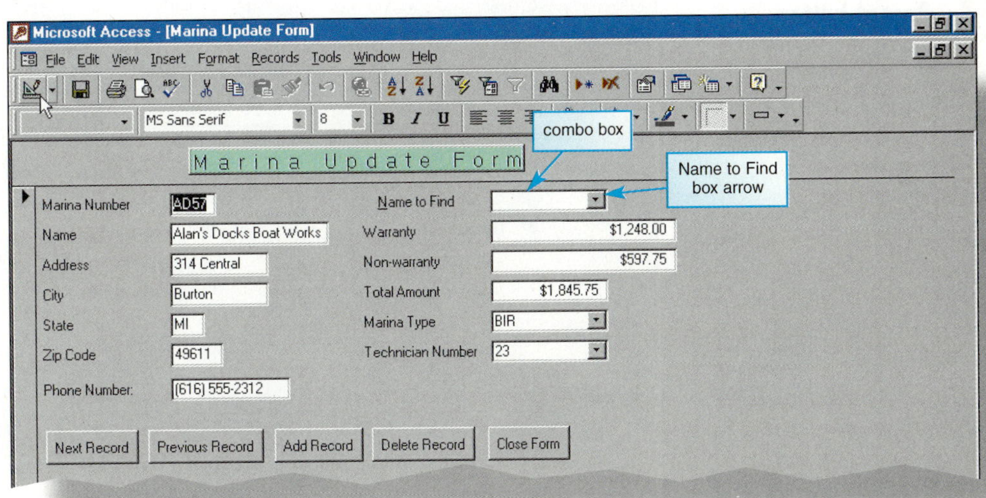

FIGURE 8-27

2 Click the Name to Find box arrow and then point to Nelson's Wharf.

The list of names displays (Figure 8-28).

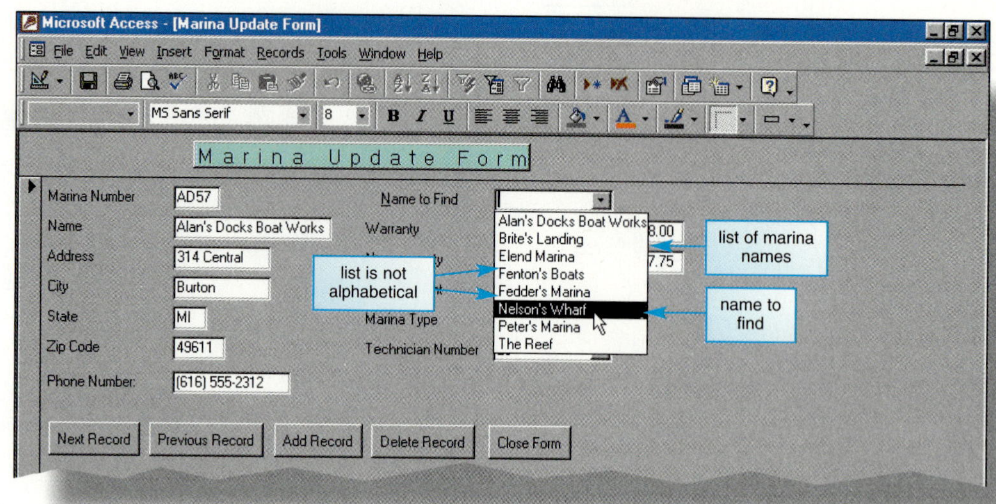

FIGURE 8-28

3 Click Nelson's Wharf.

The data for the marina whose name is Nelson's Wharf displays on the form (Figure 8-29).

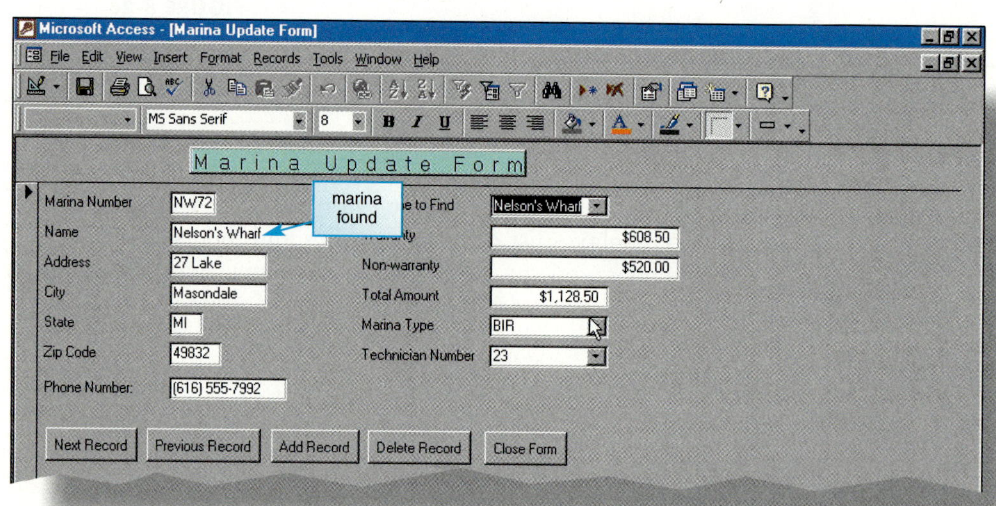

FIGURE 8-29

4 Click the Next Record button.

The data for the marina whose name is Peter's Marina displays on the form (Figure 8-30). The combo box still contains Nelson's Wharf.

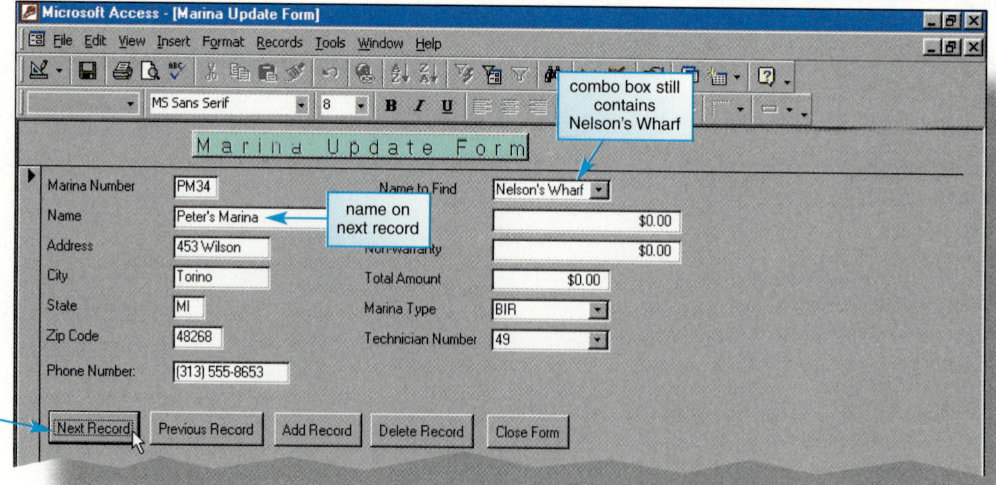

FIGURE 8-30

Issues with the Combo Box

Consider the following issues with the combo box. First, if you examine the list of names in Figure 8-28 on page A 8.22, you will see that they are not in alphabetical order (Fenton's Boats comes before Fedder's Marina). Second, when you move to a record without using the combo box, the name in the combo box does not change to reflect the name of the marina currently on the screen. Third, pressing the TAB key to move from field to field on the form should not move to the combo box.

Modifying the Combo Box

The following steps modify the query that Access has created for the combo box so the data is sorted by name. The modification to the On Current property will ensure that the combo box is kept current with the rest of the form; that is, it contains the name of the marina whose number currently displays in the Marina Number field. The final step changes the Tab Stop property for the combo box from Yes to No.

Perform the following steps to modify the combo box.

To Modify the Combo Box

1 Click the View button on the toolbar to return to the design grid. Right-click the Name to Find combo box (the white space, not the label), and then click Properties on the shortcut menu. Note the number of your combo box, which may be different from the one shown in Figure 8-31, this will be important later. Click the Row Source property, and then point to the Build button for the Row Source property.

The Combo Box: Combo29 property sheet displays (Figure 8-31). The combo box number is 29 (Combo29). The Row Source property is selected. Depending on where you clicked the Row Source property, the value may or may not be highlighted.

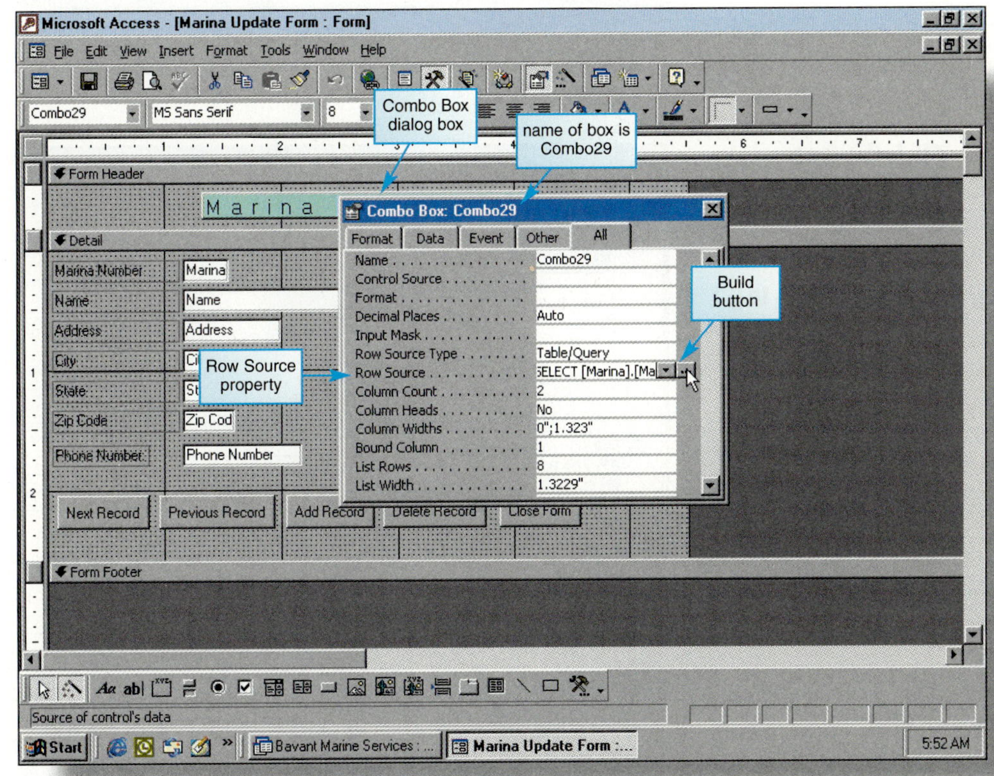

FIGURE 8-31

2 **Click the Build button. Point to the Sort row under the Name field.**

The SQL Statement : Query Builder window displays (Figure 8-32). This screen allows you to make changes just as you did when you created queries.

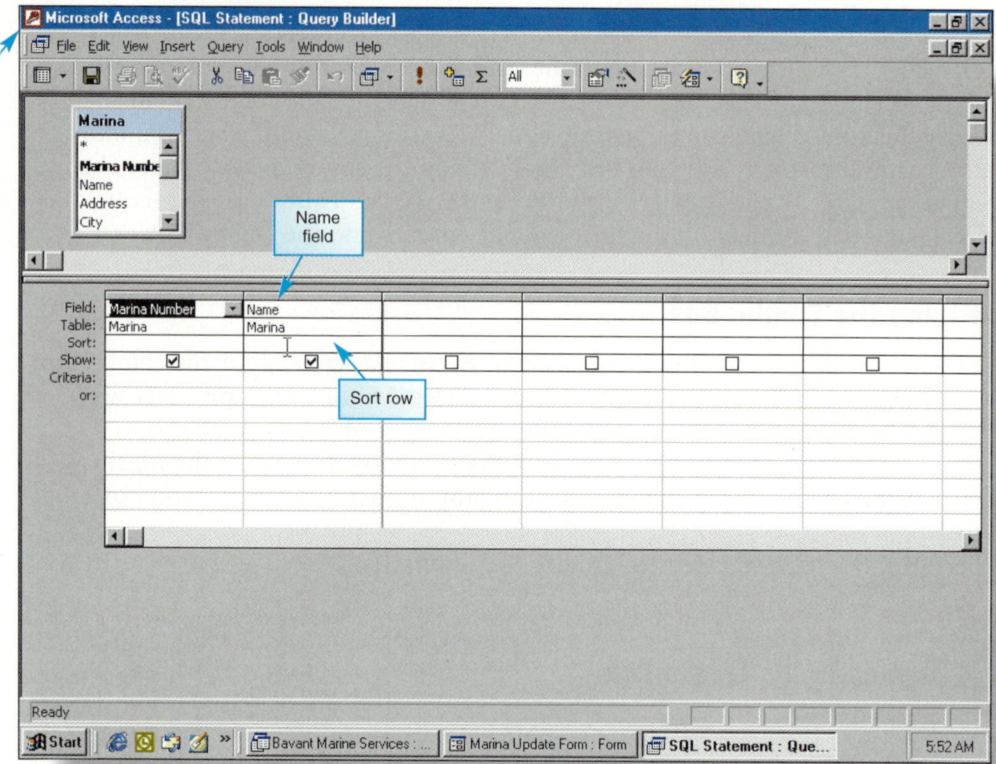

FIGURE 8-32

3 **Click the Sort row in the Name field, click the box arrow that displays, and then click Ascending. Point to the Close Window button for the SQL Statement : Query Builder window.**

The sort order is changed to Ascending (Figure 8-33).

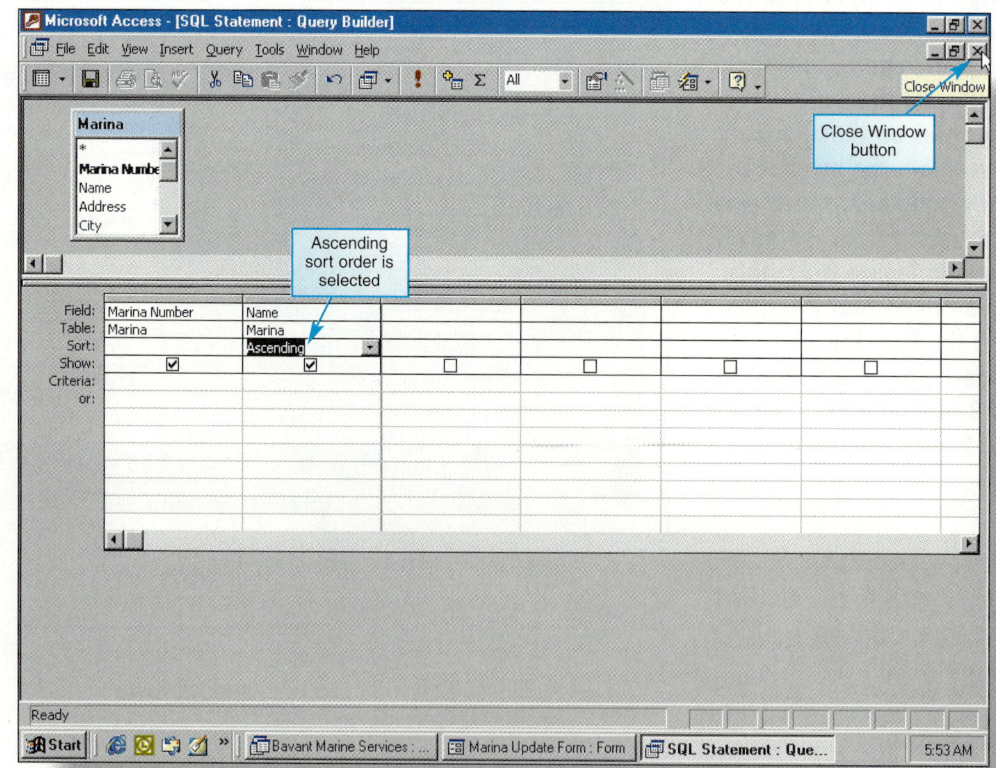

FIGURE 8-33

4 Close the SQL Statement : Query Builder window by clicking its Close Window button. Point to the Yes button in the Microsoft Access dialog box.

The Microsoft Access dialog box displays (Figure 8-34).

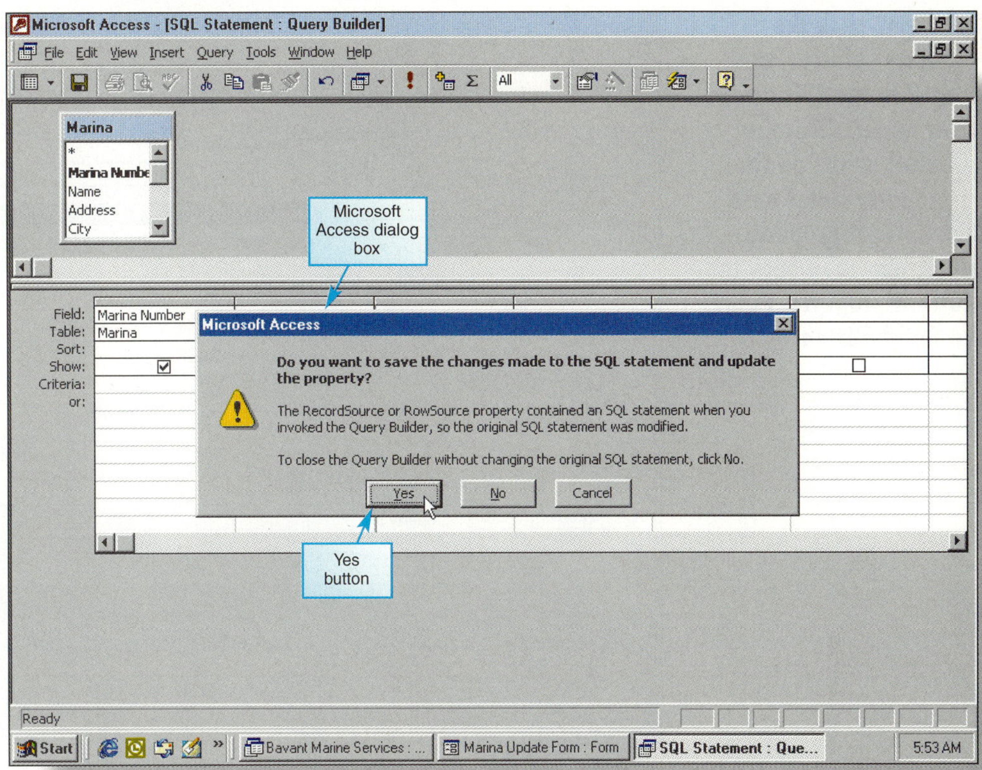

FIGURE 8-34

5 Click the Yes button to change the property, and then close the Combo Box: Combo29 property sheet. Point to the form selector, the box in the upper-left corner on the form (Figure 8-35).

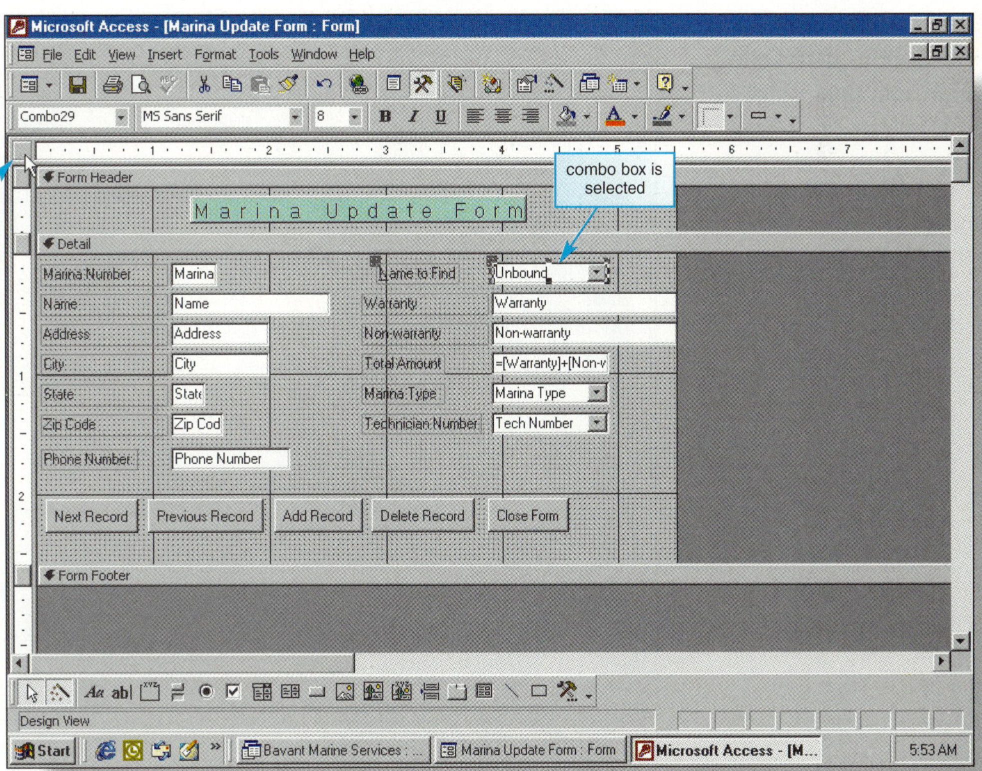

FIGURE 8-35

6 **Right-click the form selector, and then click Properties on the shortcut menu. Click the down scroll arrow on the Form property sheet until the On Current property displays, and then click the On Current property. Point to the Build button.**

The Form property sheet displays (Figure 8-36).

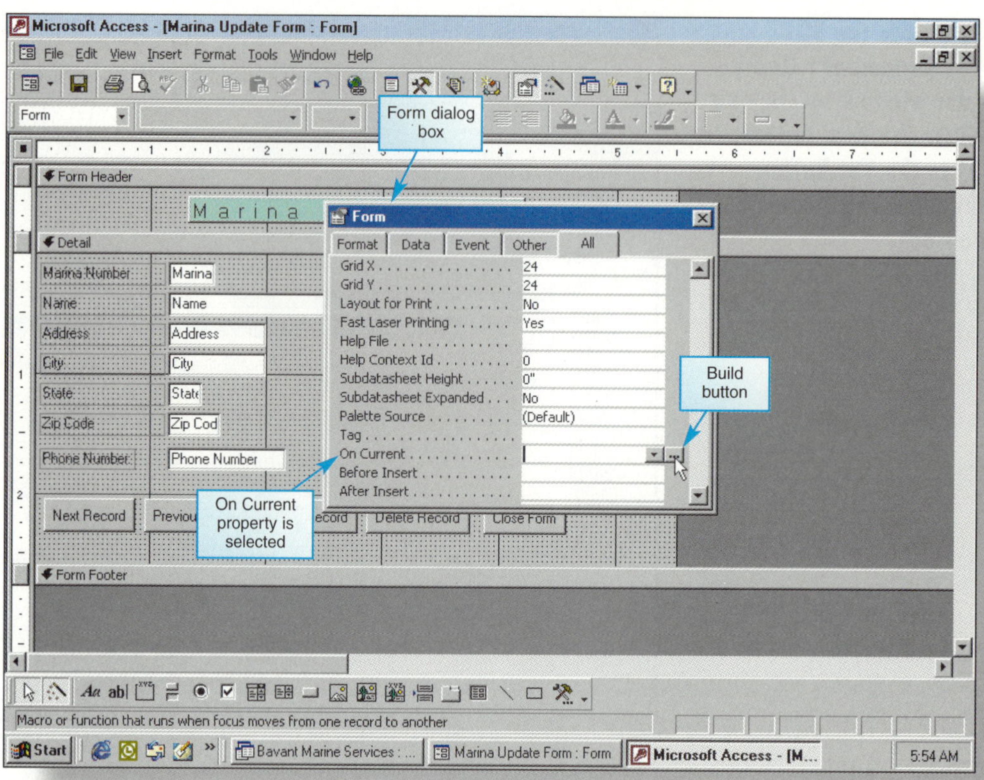

FIGURE 8-36

7 **Click the Build button, click Code Builder, and then point to the OK button.**

The Choose Builder dialog box displays (Figure 8-37). Code Builder is selected.

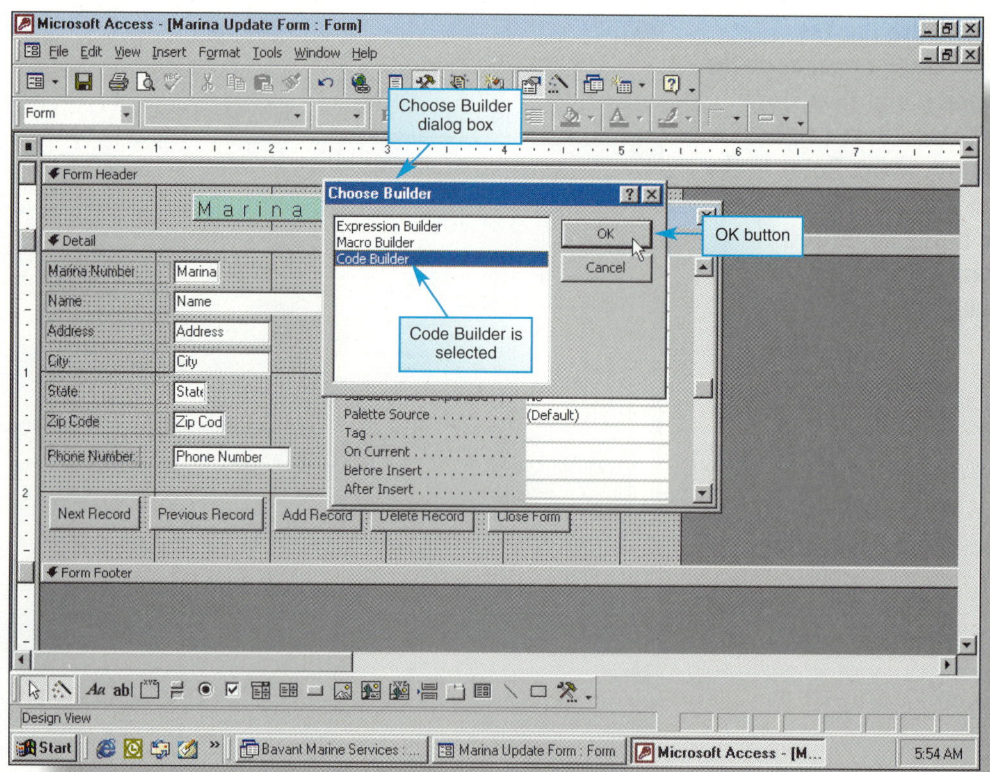

FIGURE 8-37

Click the OK button.

The code generated by Access for the form displays (Figure 8-38).

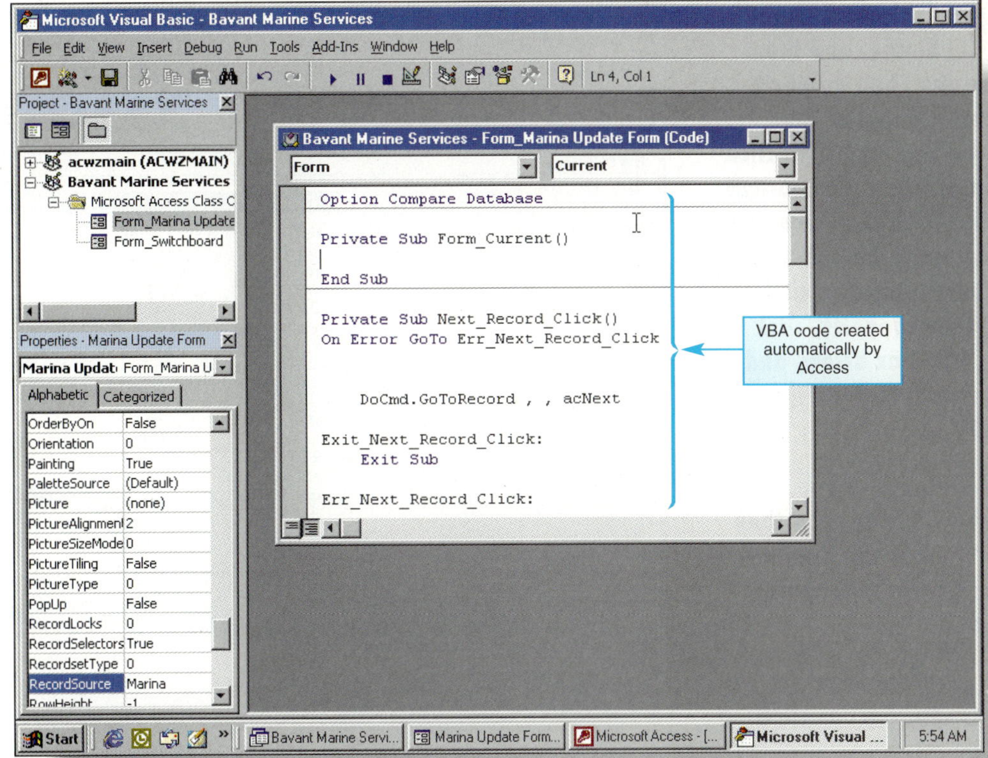

FIGURE 8-38

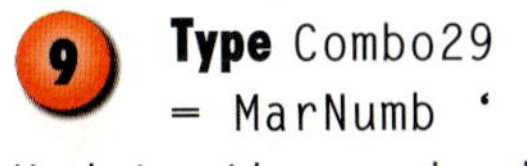

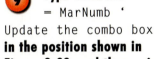

Type `Combo29 = MarNumb ' Update the combo box` **in the position shown in Figure 8-39, and then point to the Close button for the Microsoft Visual Basic – Bavant Marine Services window.**

This command assumes your combo box is Combo29. If yours has a different number, use your number in the command instead of 29. This command will update the contents of the combo box using the marina number currently in the MarNumb control. The portion of the command following the apostrophe is called a **comment***, which describes the purpose of the command.*

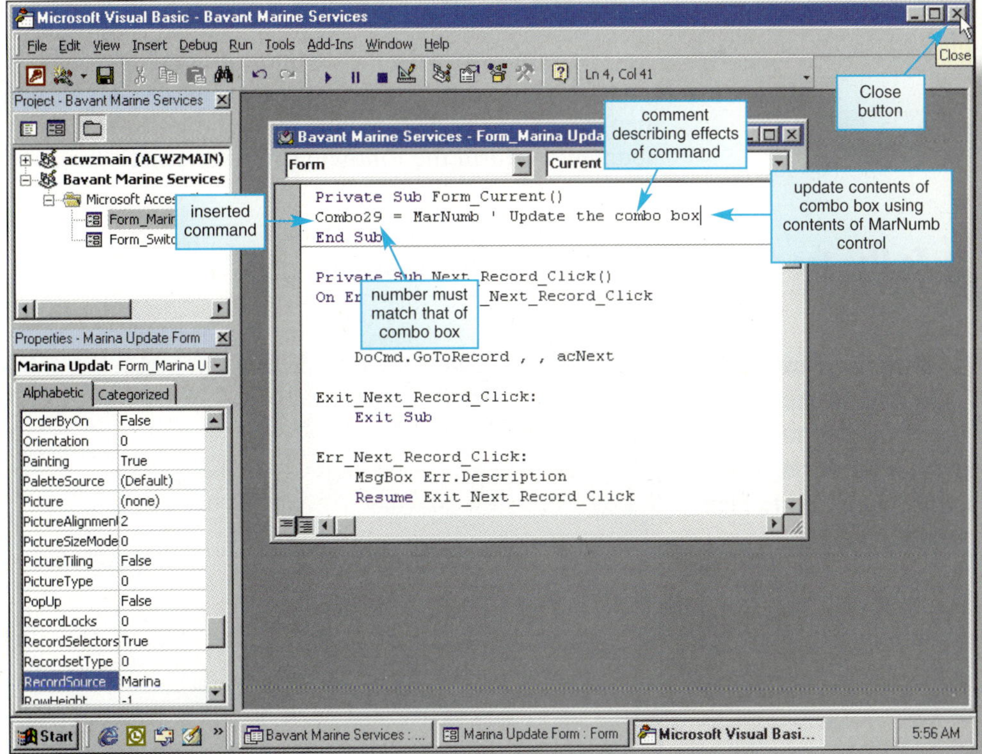

FIGURE 8-39

10 **Click the Close button, and then close the Form property sheet. Right-click the combo box, and then click Properties on the shortcut menu. Click the down scroll arrow until the Tab Stop property displays, click the Tab Stop property, click the Tab Stop box arrow, and then point to No (Figure 8-40).**

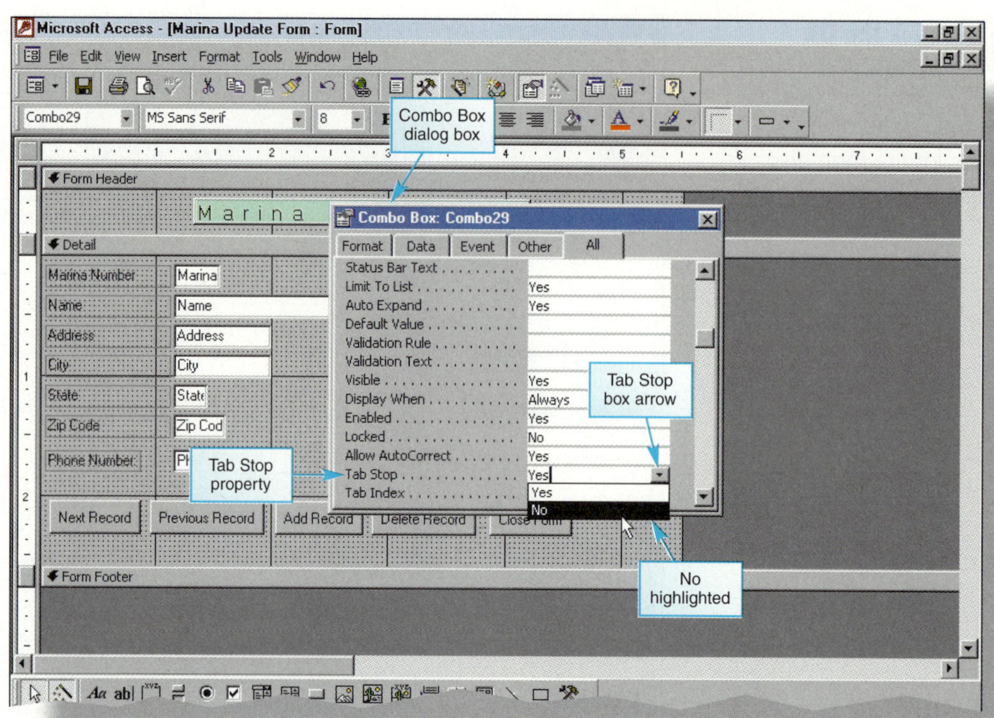

FIGURE 8-40

11 **Click No, and then close the Combo Box: Combo29 property sheet.**

The modifications to the combo box are complete.

Using the Modified Combo Box

The problems with the combo box now are corrected. The search conducted in the following steps first looks for the marina whose name is Nelson's Wharf, and then moves to the next record in the table to verify that the combo box also will be updated. Perform the following steps to search for a marina.

To Use the Combo Box to Search for a Marina

1 **Click the View button on the toolbar to display the Marina Update Form, and then click the Name to Find box arrow.**

An alphabetical list of names displays (Figure 8-41).

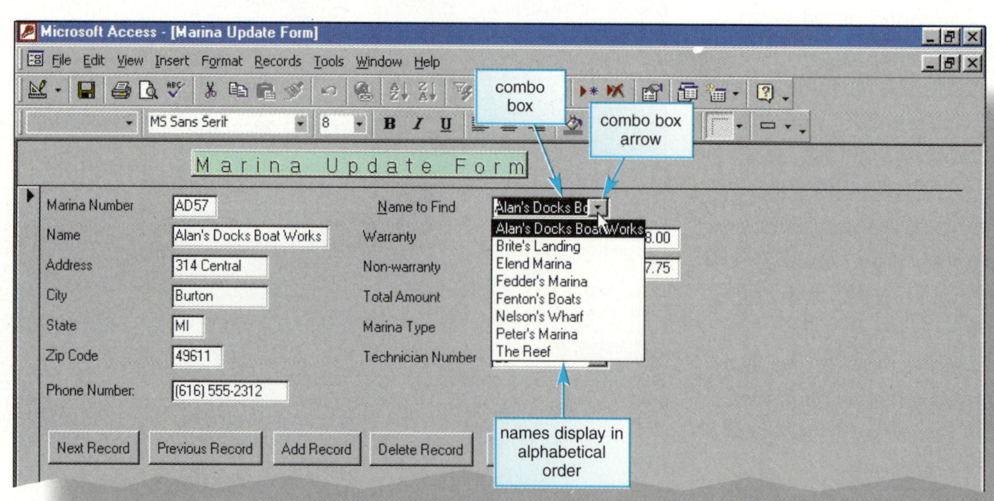

FIGURE 8-41

2 **Click Nelson's Wharf, and then point to the Next Record button.**

Marina NW72 displays on the form (Figure 8-42).

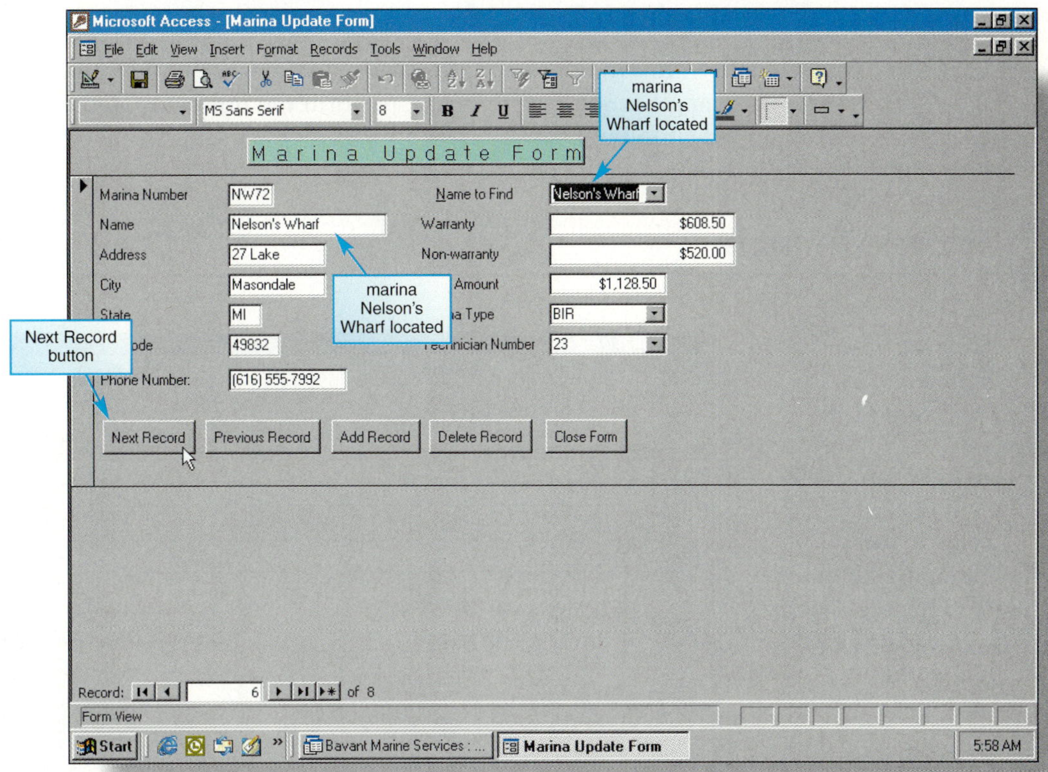

FIGURE 8-42

3 **Click the Next Record button.**

Marina PM34 displays on the form (Figure 8-43). The marina's name also displays in the combo box.

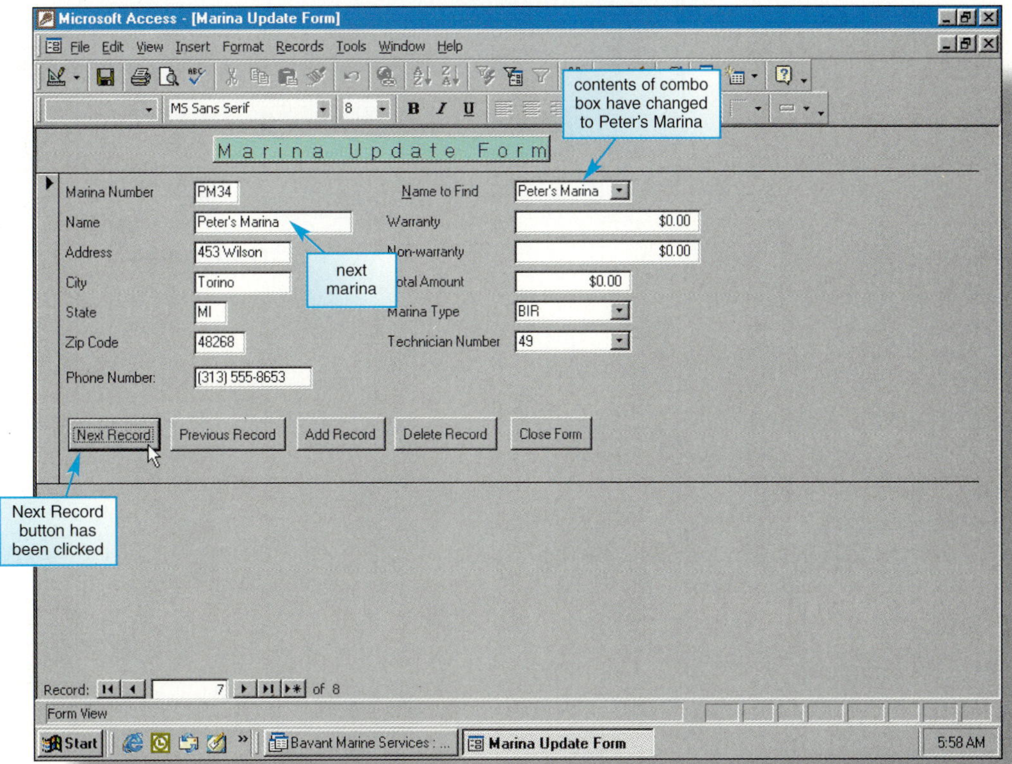

FIGURE 8-43

Placing a Rectangle

In order to emphasize the special nature of the combo box, you will place a rectangle around it. To do so, perform the following steps using the Rectangle button in the toolbox.

To Place a Rectangle

1 **Click the View button on the toolbar to return to the design grid.**

2 **Point to the Rectangle button in the toolbox (Figure 8-44). Click the View button**

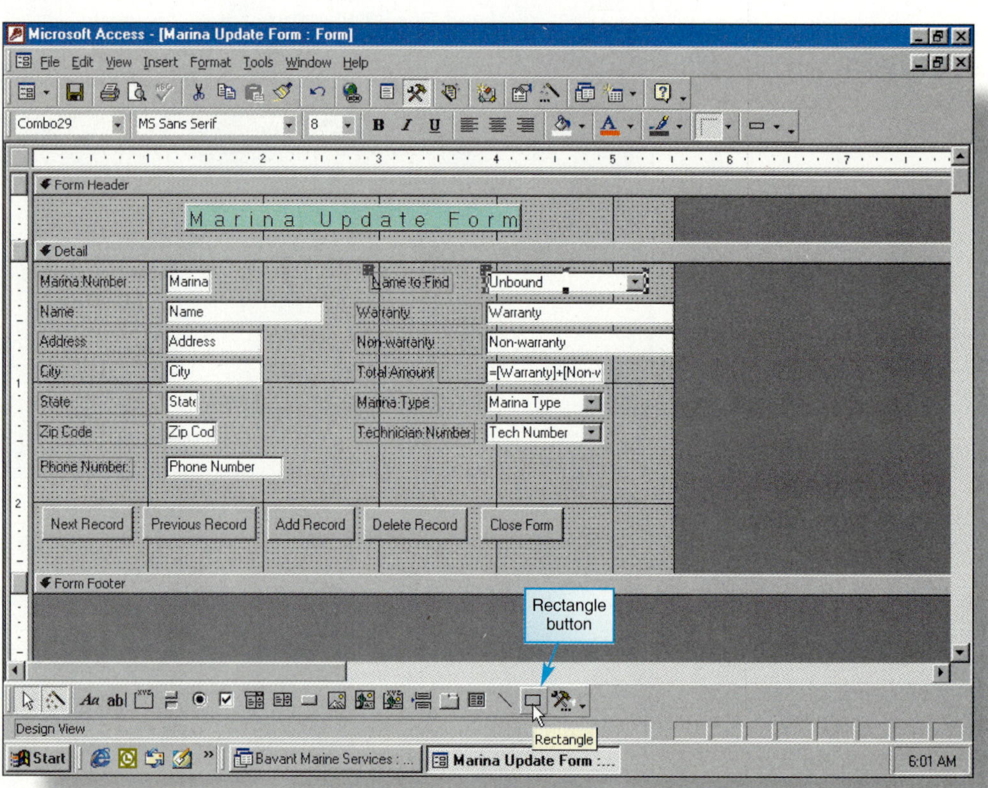

FIGURE 8-44

3 Click the Rectangle button in the toolbox and then move the pointer, whose shape has changed to a plus sign accompanied by a rectangle to the approximate position shown in Figure 8-45.

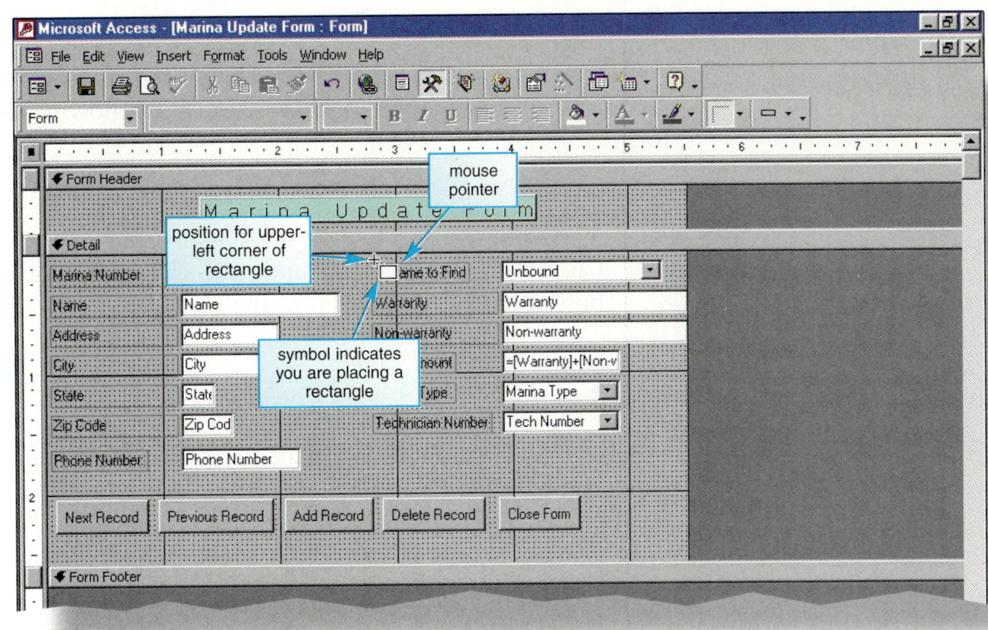

FIGURE 8-45

4 With the pointer in the position shown in Figure 8-45, press and hold the left mouse button. Drag the pointer to the approximate position shown in Figure 8-46 and then release the left mouse button.

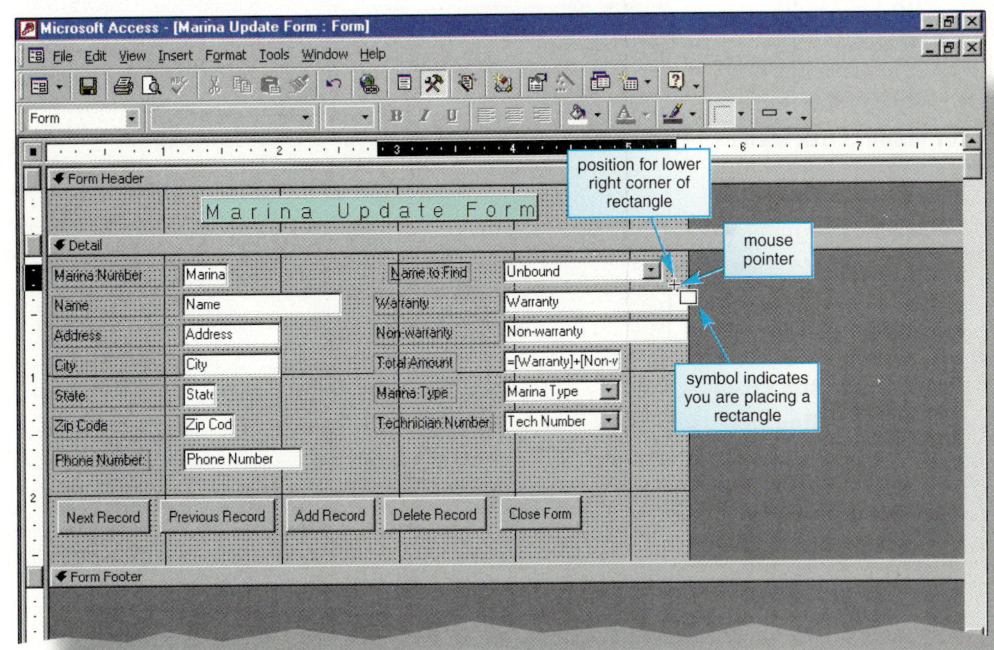

FIGURE 8-46

5 Point to the border of the newly-created rectangle, right-click, and then click Properties on the shortcut menu. Change the value of the Special Effect property to Raised. If necessary, change the value of the Back Style property to Transparent, so that the combo box will display within the rectangle. (If the Back Style property were not changed, the rectangle would completely cover the combo box and the combo box would not be visible.)

6 Close the Rectangle property sheet by clicking its Close button.

Closing and Saving a Form

To close a form, use the window's Close Window button. Then indicate whether you want to save your changes. Perform the following step to close and save the form.

TO CLOSE AND SAVE A FORM

1. Click the Close Window button to close the window, and then click the Yes button to save the design of the form.

Opening a Form

Right-click the form you want to open in the Database window, and then click Open on the shortcut menu. The form will display and can be used to examine and update data. Perform the following steps to open the Marina Update Form.

To Open a Form

1 With the Forms object selected, right-click Marina Update Form to display the shortcut menu. Click Open on the shortcut menu.

The form displays (Figure 8-47).

2 Close the form by clicking the Close Form command button.

The form no longer displays.

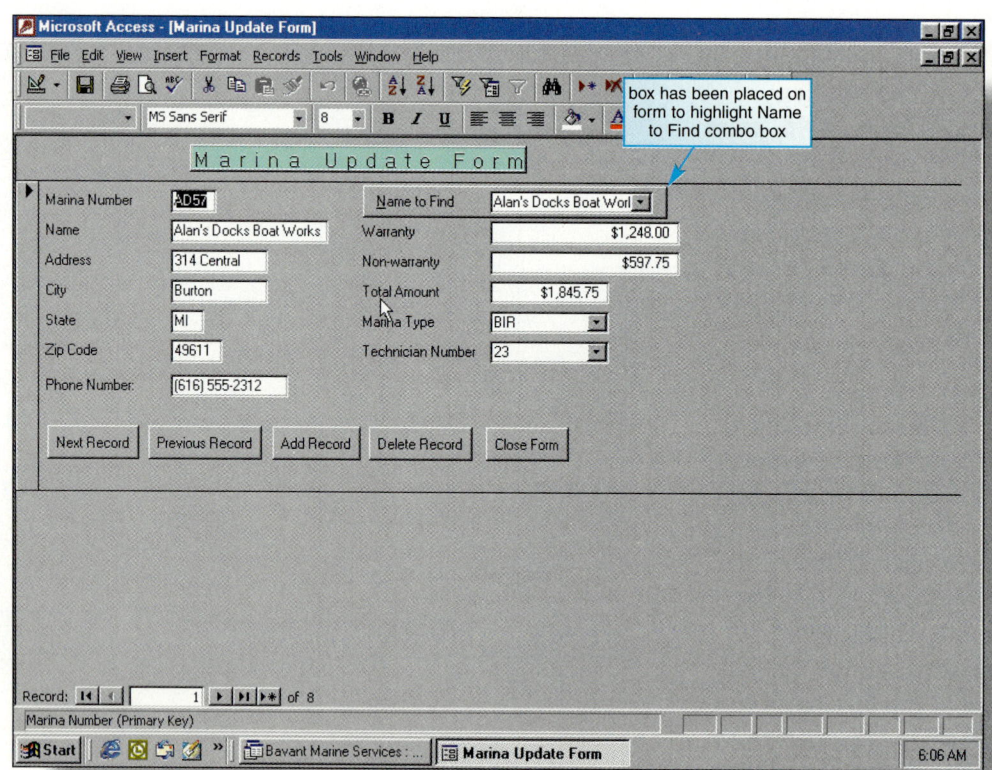

FIGURE 8-47

Creating a Form Using Design View

You have used the Form Wizard to create a variety of forms. You also can create a form without the wizard by using Design view. You will work with a blank form on which you can place all the necessary controls. In the form you create in this project, you will need to place a subform and two charts.

Creating a Query for the Subform

The subform is based on data in a query, so first you must create the query. Perform the following steps to create the query for the subform.

To Create the Query for the Subform

1 In the Database window, click Tables on the Objects bar, and then click Marina. Click the New Object: AutoForm button arrow on the Database window toolbar. Click Query. Be sure Design View is selected, and then click the OK button. Maximize the Microsoft Access – [Query1 : Select Query] window. Resize the upper and lower panes and the Marina field box so that all the fields in the Marina table display.

2 Right-click any open area in the upper pane, click Show Table on the shortcut menu, click the Open Workorders table, click the Add button, and then click the Close button for the Show Table dialog box. Resize the Open Workorders field box so that all the fields in the Open Workorders table display. Double-click the Tech Number field.

The tables are related and the Tech Number field is selected (Figure 8-48).

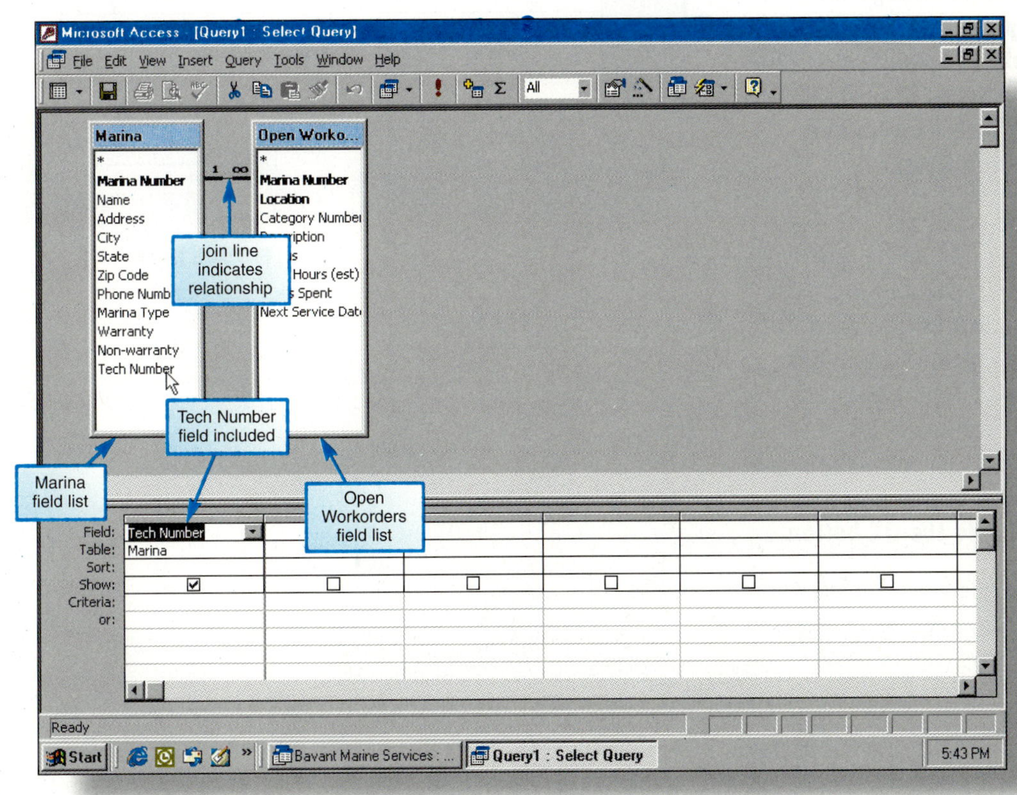

FIGURE 8-48

3 **Double-click the Marina Number and Name fields from the Marina table. Double-click the Location, Category Number, Total Hours (est), and Hours Spent fields from the Open Workorders table.**

4 **Right-click the Total Hours (est) field, click Properties, click the Caption property, and then type** `Est Hours` **as the caption. Change the caption for the Hours Spent field to Spent Hours. Click Ascending in the Sort: row for Tech Number and Marina Number.**

5 **Close the query by clicking the Close Window button. Click the Yes button to save the query. Type** `Marinas and Workorders by Technician` **as the name of the query, and then point to the OK button.**

The query is complete and the Save As dialog box displays (Figure 8-49).

6 **Click the OK button.**

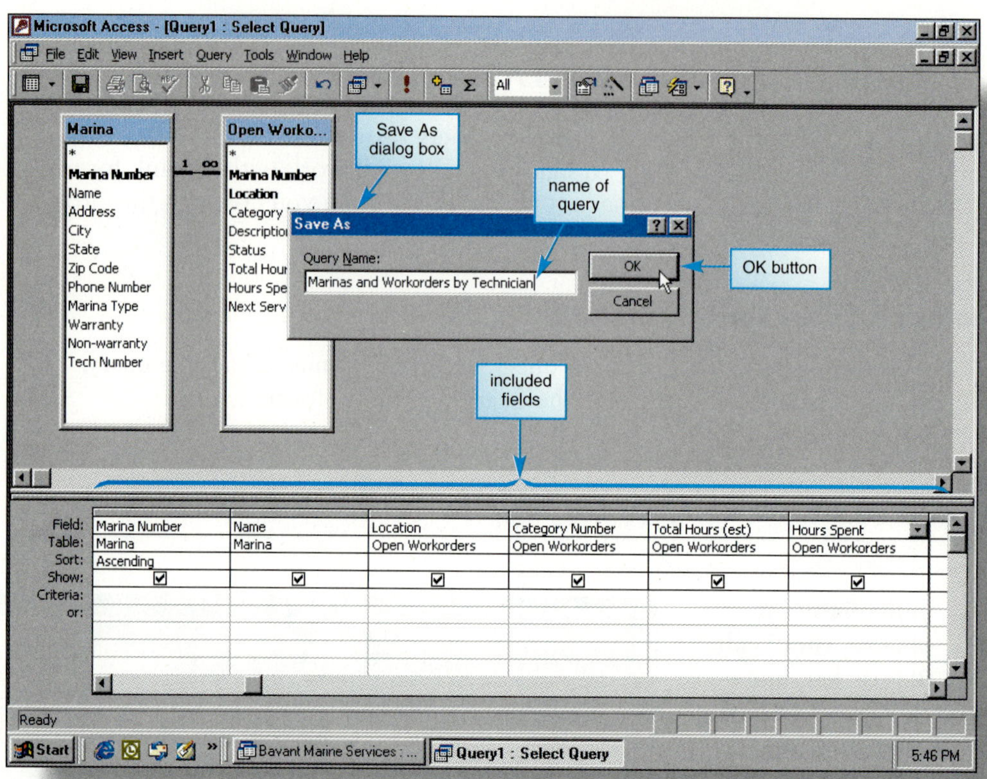

FIGURE 8-49

Creating the Form

When you want to create a form from scratch, you begin with the same general procedure as when you want to use the Form Wizard, except select Design View rather than Form Wizard. Perform the following steps to create the form.

TO CREATE THE FORM

1. If necessary, in the Database window, click Tables on the Objects bar, and then click Technician. Click the New Object: Query button arrow on the Database window toolbar. Click Form. Be sure Design View is selected, and then click the OK button.
2. Be sure the field list displays. (If it does not, click the Field List button on the toolbar.) Drag the Tech Number, First Name, and Last Name fields to the approximate positions shown in Figure 8-50. Move the attached labels for the First Name and Last Name fields to the positions shown in the figure by dragging their move handles. Point to the Close button in the field list box.
3. Close the field list box by clicking its Close button.

The field list no longer displays.

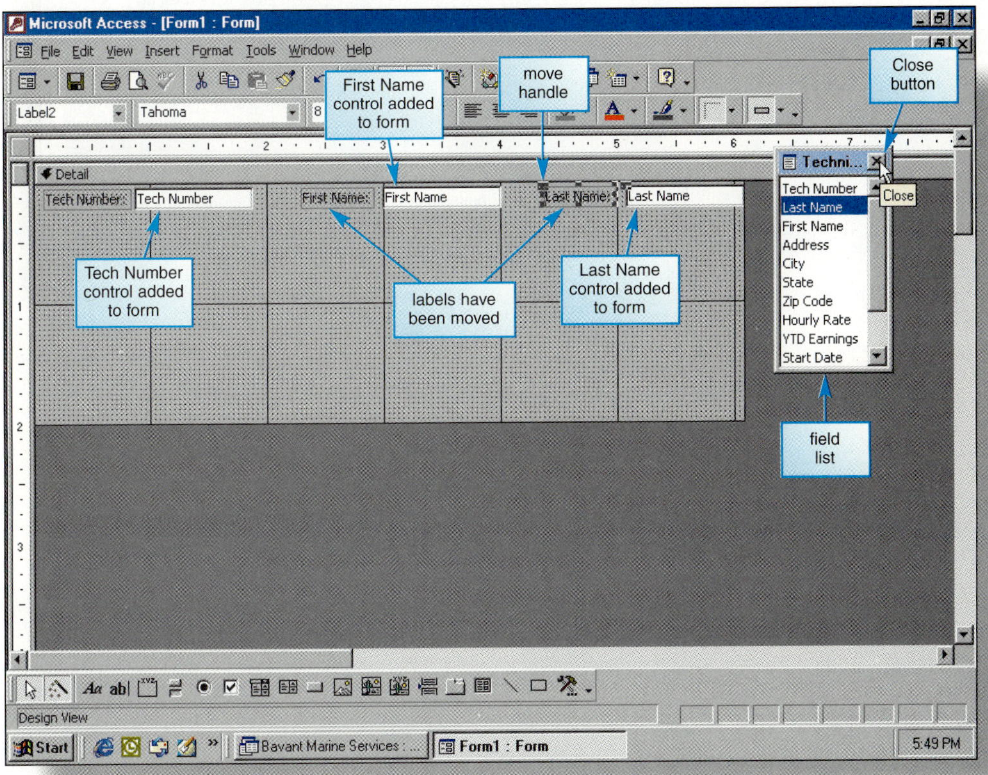

FIGURE 8-50

Placing a Subform

To place a subform on a form, you use the Subform/Subreport button in the toolbox. Provided the Control Wizards button is recessed, a wizard will guide you through the process of adding the subform as performed in the steps on the next page.

Subforms

A main form can contain more than one subform. If the main form is based on a table or query, each subform must contain information related to the information in the main form.

To Place the Subform

1. **Be sure the Control Wizards button is recessed, and then point to the Subform/Subreport button in the toolbox (Figure 8-51).**

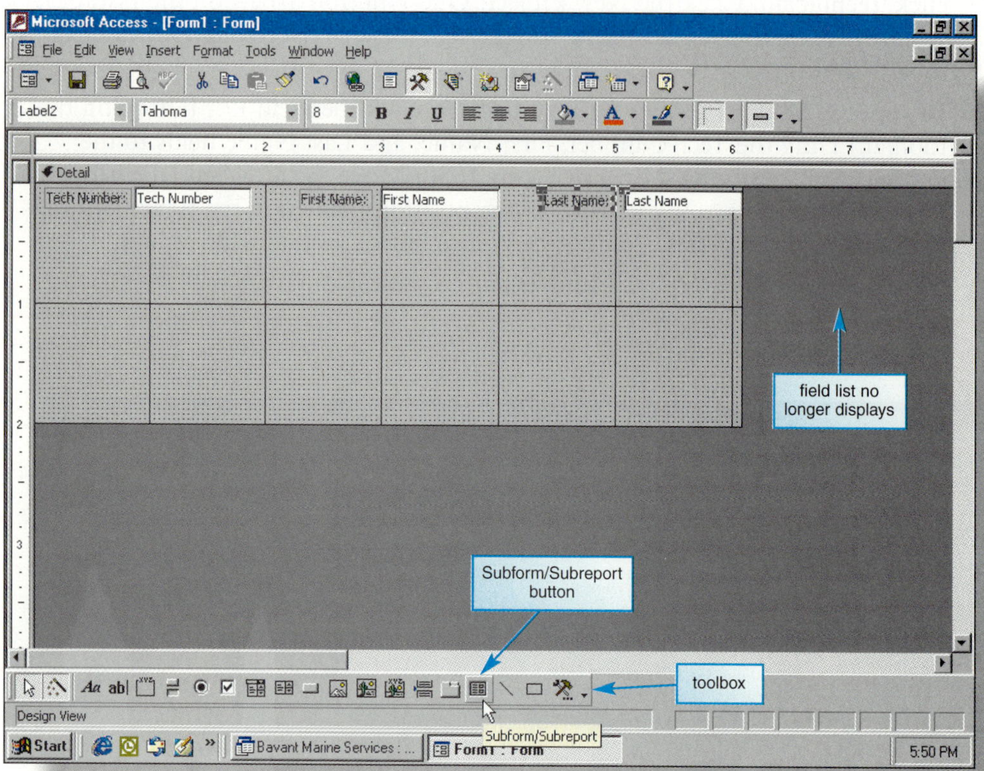

FIGURE 8-51

2. **Click the Subform/Subreport button, and then move the mouse pointer to the approximate position shown in Figure 8-52.**

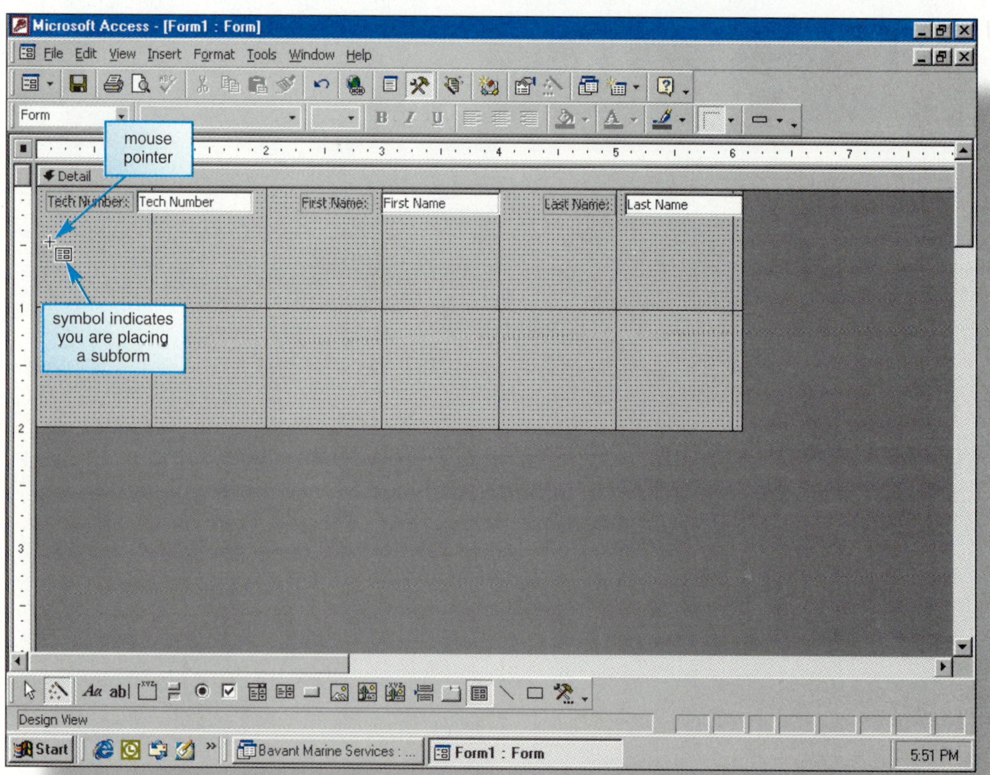

FIGURE 8-52

3 **Click the position shown in Figure 8-52. Be sure the Use existing Tables and Queries button is selected and then point to the Next button.**

The SubForm Wizard dialog box displays (Figure 8-53).

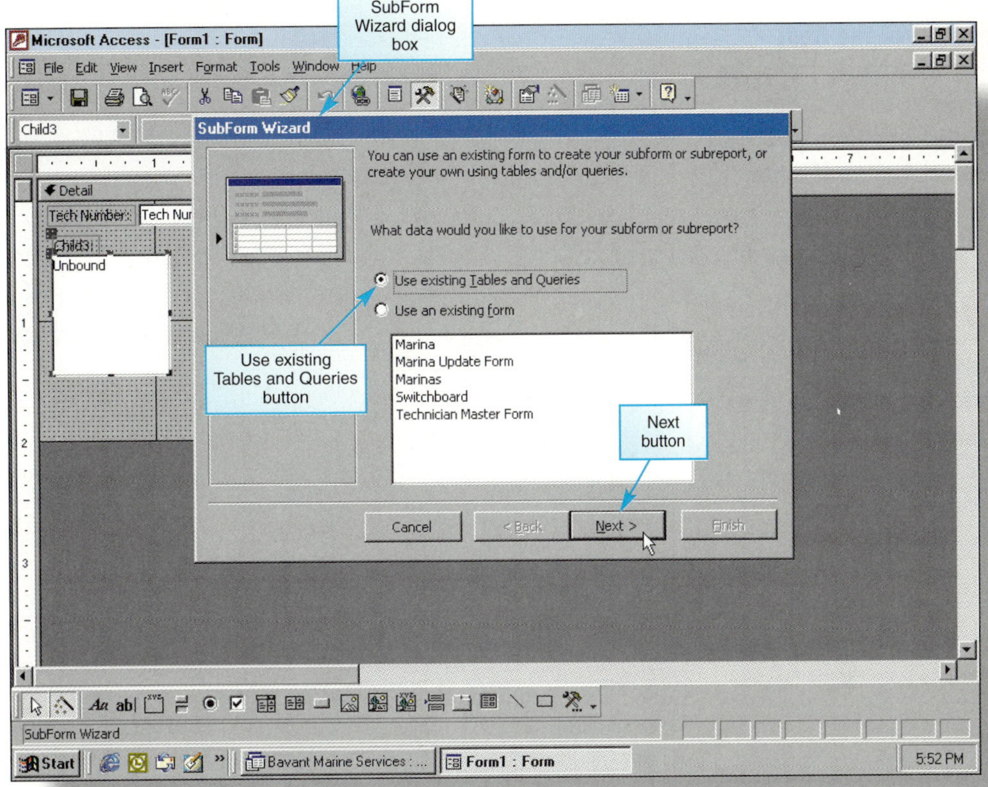

FIGURE 8-53

4 **Click the Next button. Click the Tables/Queries box arrow and then click Query: Marinas and Workorders by Technician. Click the Add All fields button and then point to the Next button.**

The Marinas and Workorders by Technician query is selected (Figure 8-54). All fields are selected.

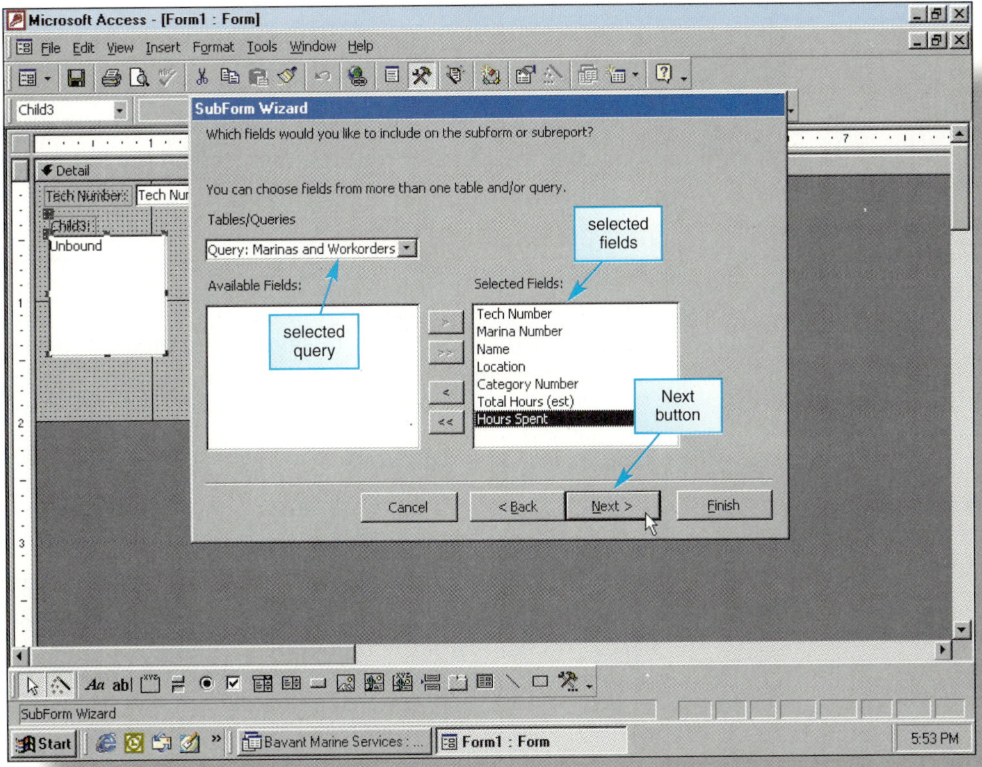

FIGURE 8-54

5 **Click the Next button. Be sure the Choose from a list button is selected and then point to the Next button (Figure 8-55).**

6 **Click the Next button. Type** `Open Workorders for Technician` **as the name of the subform and then click the Finish button.**

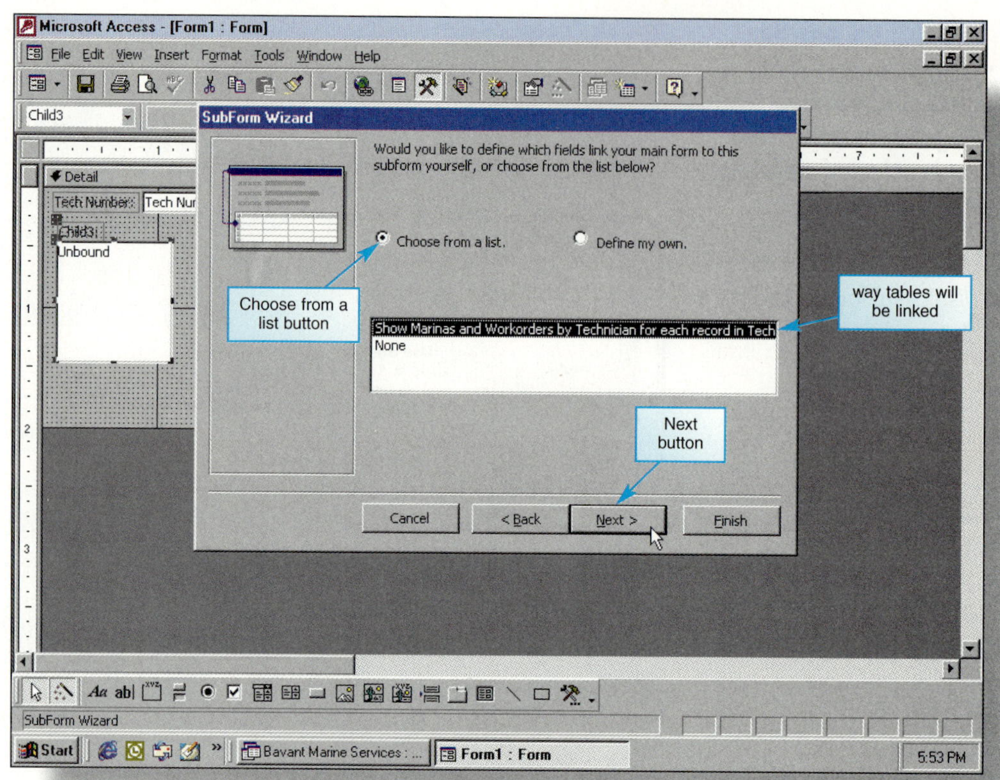

FIGURE 8-55

Closing and Saving the Form

To close a form, click the Close button. Then indicate whether you want to save your changes. Perform the following steps to close and save the form.

TO CLOSE AND SAVE A FORM

1. Close the form by clicking the Close button.
2. Click the Yes button to save the changes. Type `Technician Workorder Data` as the name of the form and then click the OK button.

Modifying the Subform

The next task is to modify the subform. The Tech Number field must be in the subform because it is used to link the data in the subform to the data in the main form, but it should not display. In addition, the remaining columns need to be resized to appropriate sizes. Perform the following steps to remove the Tech Number field and then resize the remaining columns.

Subforms

A main form does not need to be based on a table or query. If the main form is not based on a table or query, it can still contain one or more subforms. It simply serves as a container for the subforms, which then have no restrictions on the information they must contain.

To Modify the Subform

1 **In the Database window, click Forms on the Objects bar, right-click the Open Workorders for Technician form, and then click Design View on the shortcut menu.**

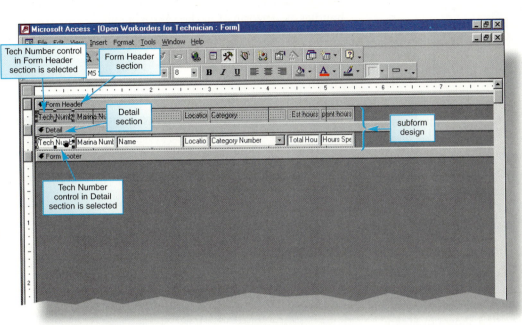

2 **Close the field box and maximize the window, if necessary. Click the Tech Number control in the Form Header section. Hold the SHIFT key down and click the Tech Number control in the Detail section.**

Both controls are selected (Figure 8-56).

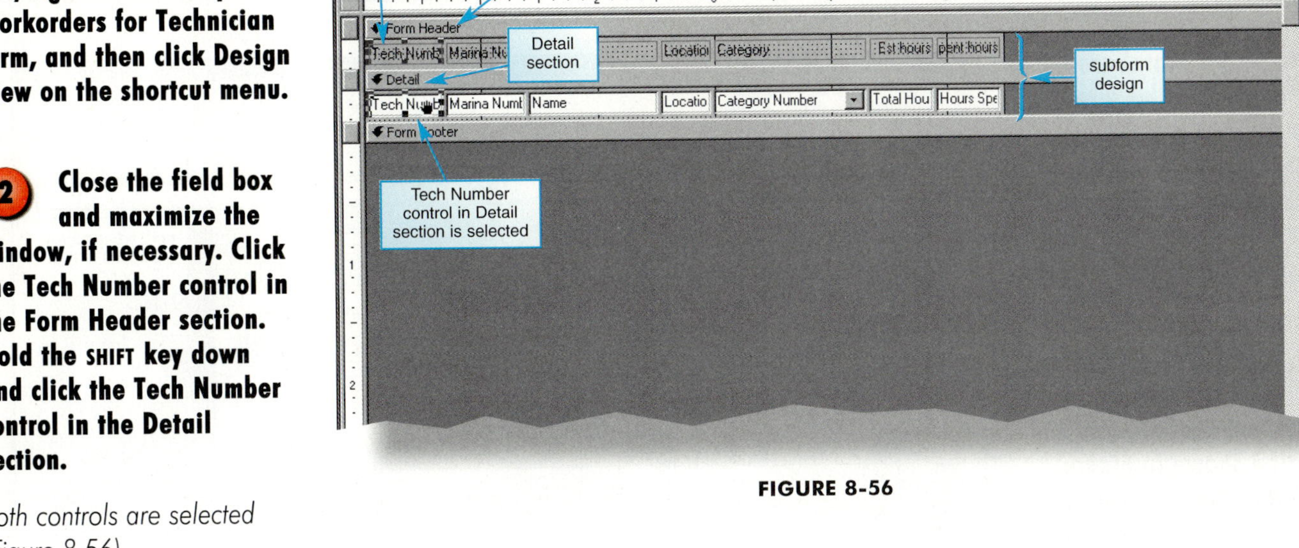

FIGURE 8-56

3 **Press DELETE to delete the two Tech Number controls from both sections. Click the View button to display the form in Datasheet view. Point to the right boundary of the field selector for the Marina Number field.**

The subform displays in Datasheet view (Figure 8-57). The Tech Number field has been removed. The mouse pointer has changed shape indicating that the Marina Number column can be resized.

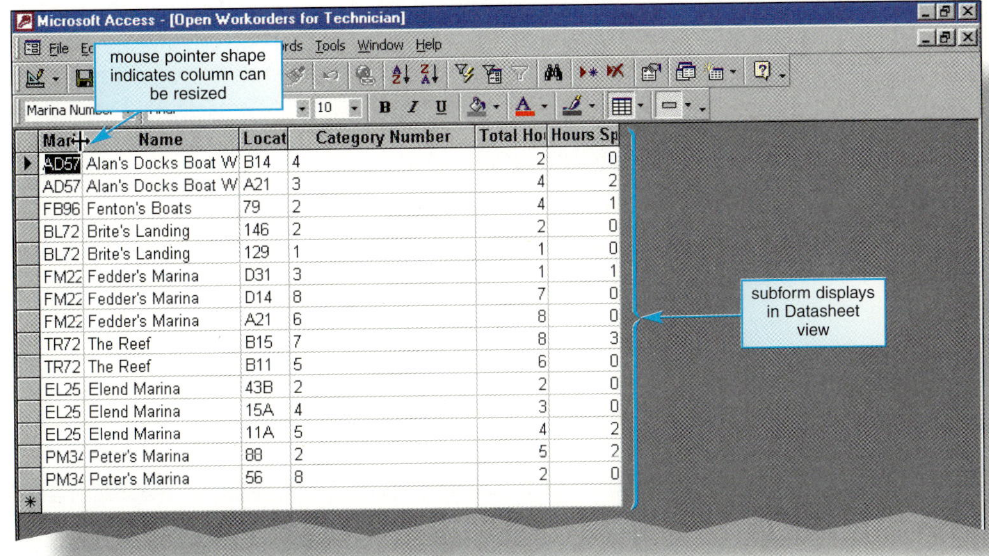

FIGURE 8-57

4 **Double-click the right boundary of each of the field selectors to resize the fields to the best size. Close the subform by clicking the Close Window button. Click the Yes button to save the changes.**

The subform has been changed.

Resizing the Subform

To resize the subform, click the subform and then drag the appropriate sizing handles as performed in the following steps.

To Resize the Subform

1 **In the Database window, be sure the Forms object is selected, right-click the Technician Workorder Data form, and then click Design View on the shortcut menu.**

2 **Click the subform to select it. Drag the right sizing handle to the position shown in Figure 8-58 and then drag the lower sizing handle to the position shown in the figure.**

The subform is resized.

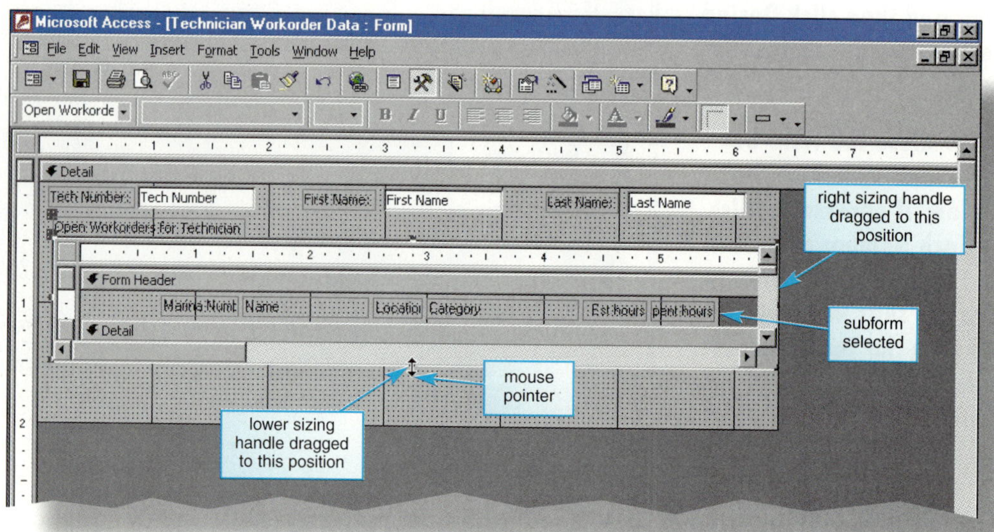

FIGURE 8-58

Inserting a Chart

To insert a chart, use the Chart command on the Insert menu. The Chart Wizard then will ask you to indicate the fields to be included on the chart and the type of chart you wish to insert. Perform the following steps to insert a chart.

To Insert a Chart

1 **Click Insert on the menu bar and then point to Chart.**

The Insert menu displays (Figure 8-59).

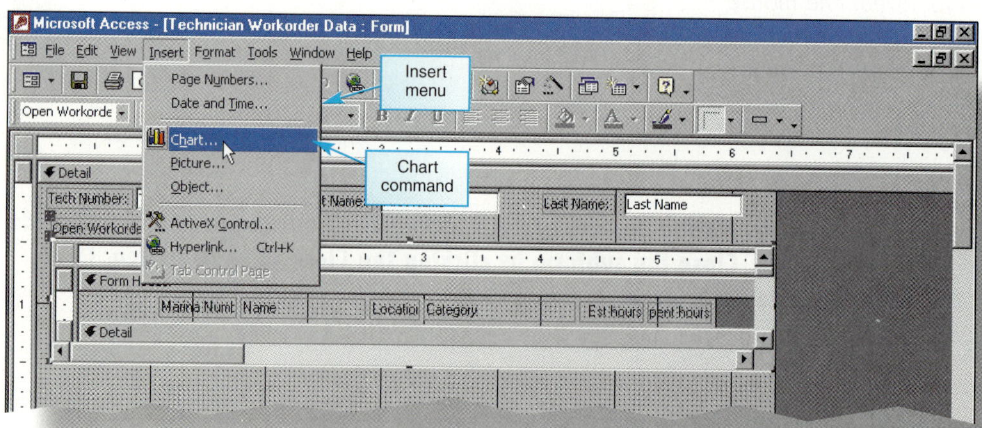

FIGURE 8-59

2 **Click Chart and then move the pointer to the approximate position shown in Figure 8-60.**

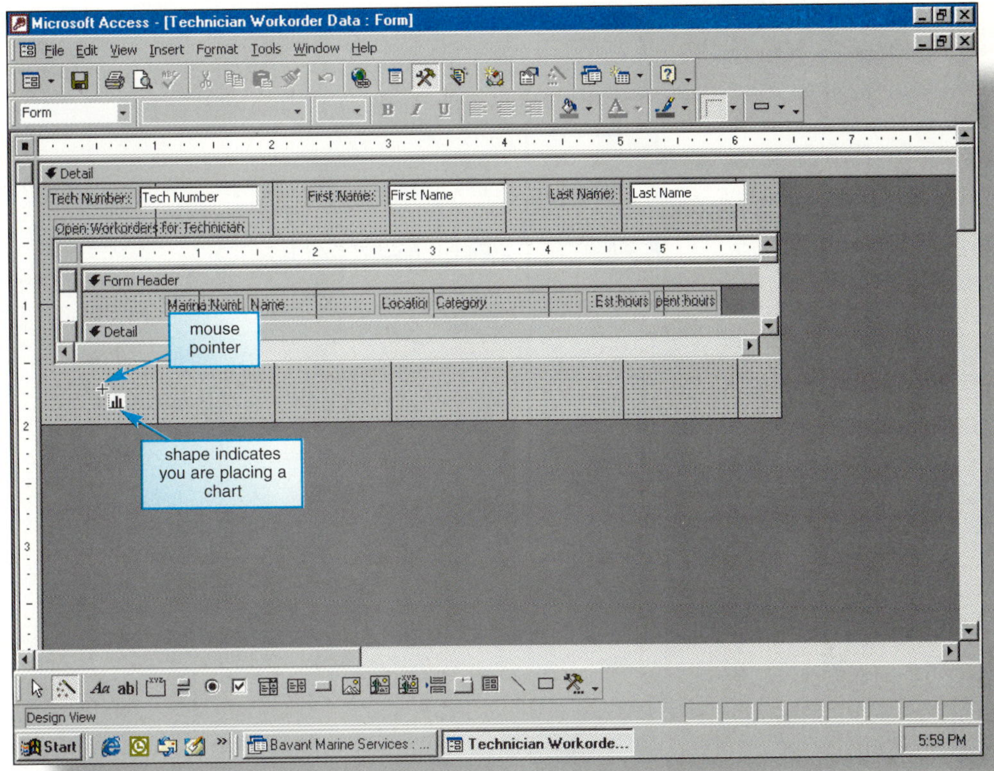

FIGURE 8-60

3 **Click the position shown in Figure 8-60. Click the Queries button in the Chart Wizard dialog box, click the Marinas and Workorders by Technician query, and then click the Next button. Select the Category Number and Total Hours (est) fields by clicking them and then clicking the Add Field button. Point to the Next button.**

The Chart Wizard dialog box displays (Figure 8-61). The fields for the chart have been selected.

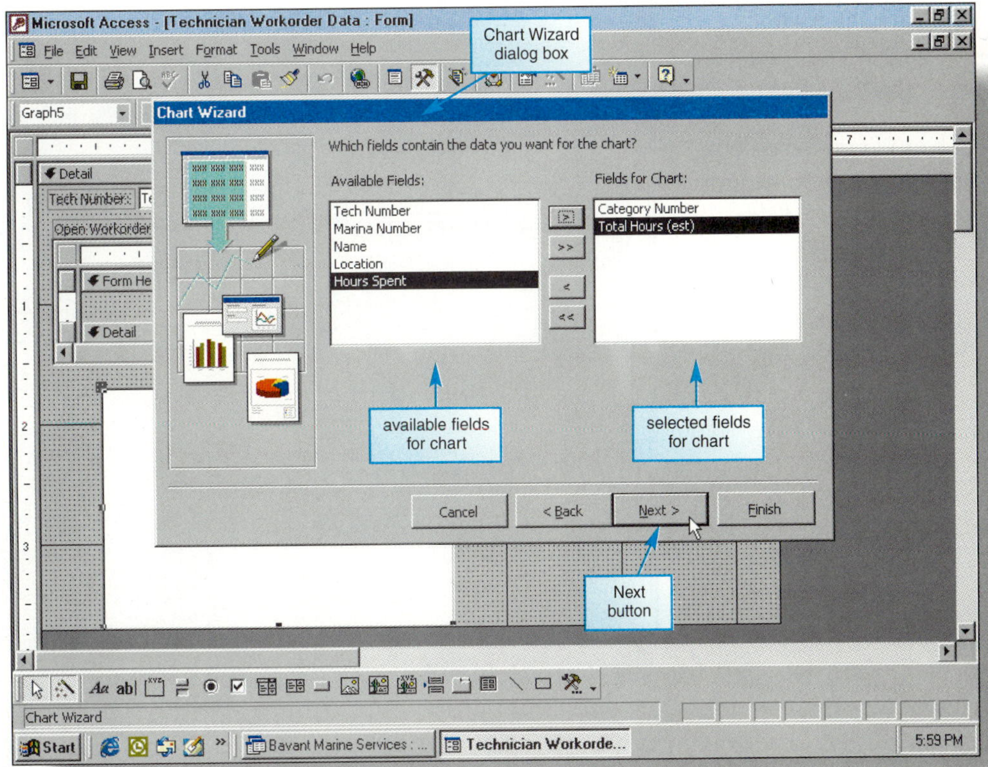

FIGURE 8-61

4 Click the Next button. Be sure the chart in the upper-left corner is selected and then point to the Next button.

The Chart Wizard dialog box displays (Figure 8-62). Use this box to select the type of chart you want to produce. A description of the selected chart type also displays in the dialog box.

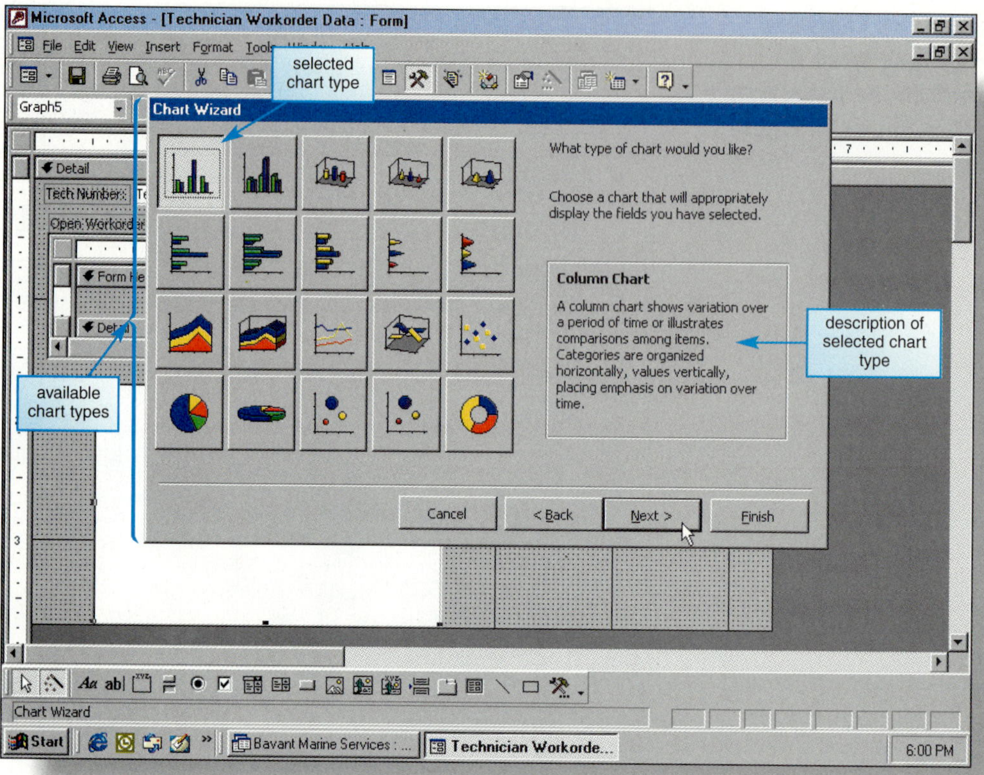

FIGURE 8-62

5 Click the Next button and then point to the Next button.

The Chart Wizard dialog box displays (Figure 8-63) indicating the x- and y-axis fields. You can click the Preview Chart button to confirm the layout of the chart.

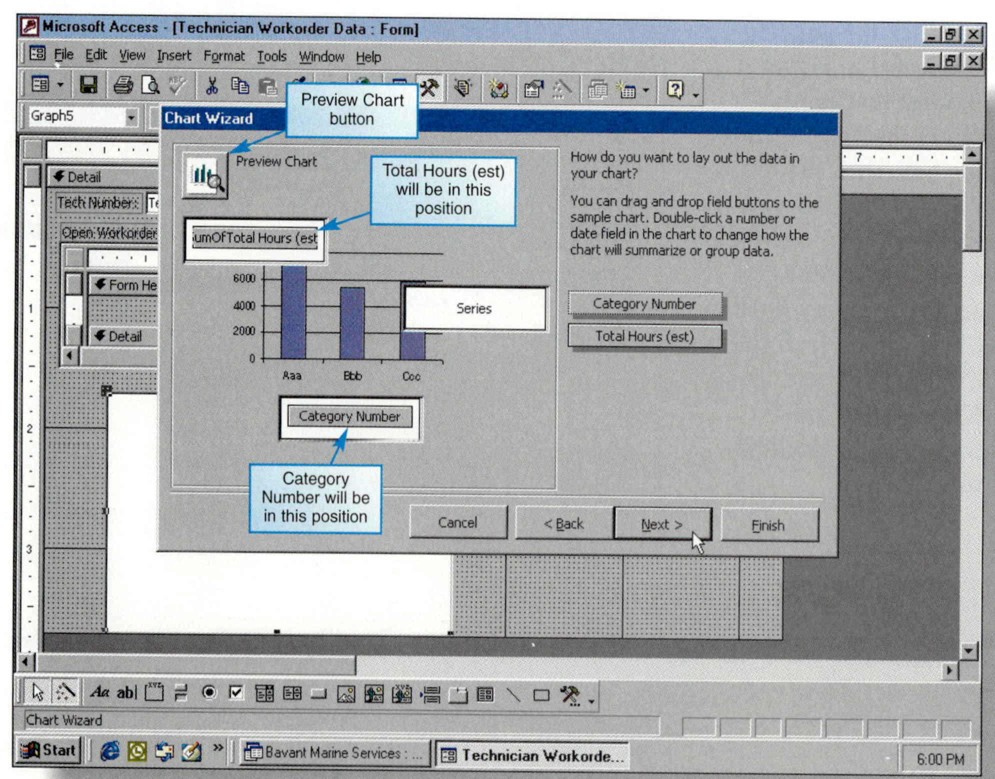

FIGURE 8-63

6 Click the Next button and then point to the Next button.

The Chart Wizard dialog box displays, indicating the fields that will be used to link the document and the chart (Figure 8-64). Linking the document and the chart ensures that the chart will accurately reflect the data for the correct technician who is currently displayed on the form.

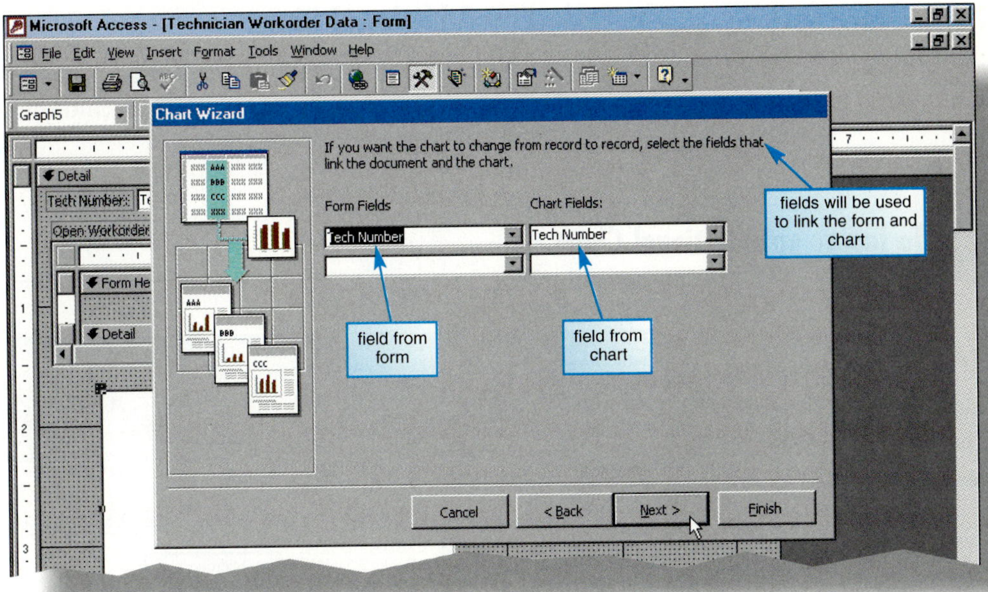

FIGURE 8-64

7 Click the Next button. Type `Estimated Hours by Category` **as the name of the chart and then click the Finish button.**

The sample chart displays on the design screen as a sample preview without using any of your data. You must display the chart in Form view to update the chart with actual data.

8 Click the View button.

The chart displays (Figure 8-65).

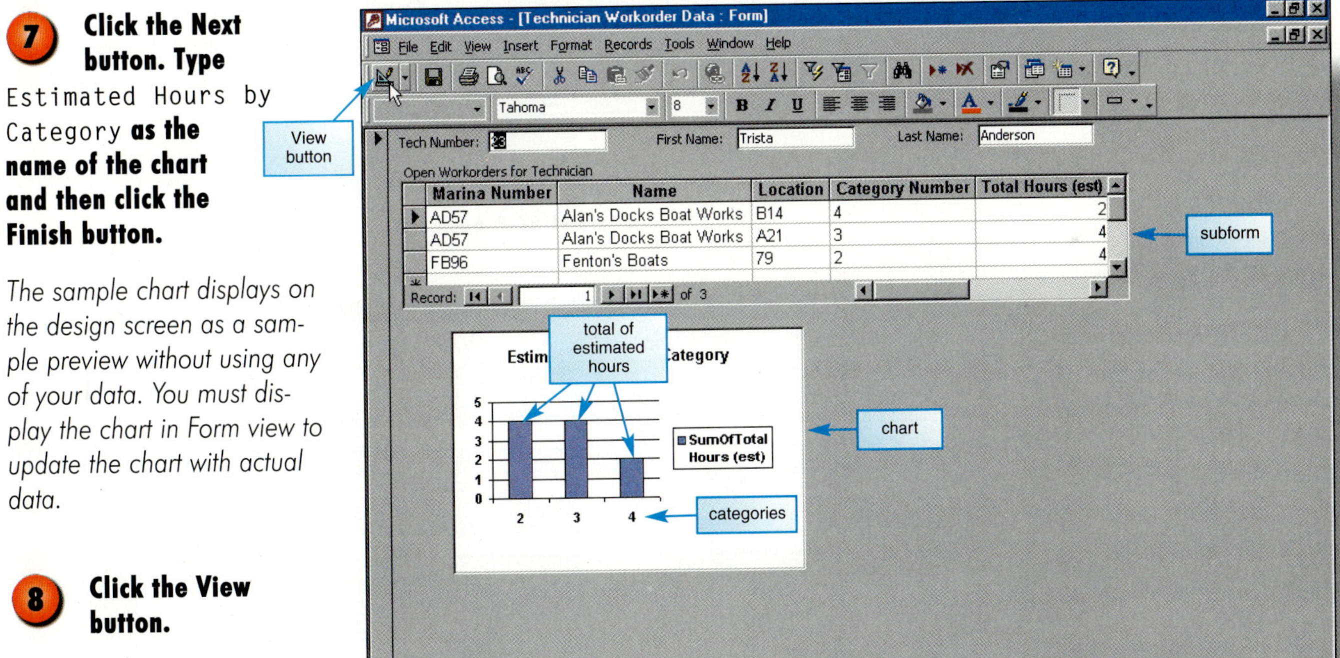

FIGURE 8-65

Across the bottom of the chart are categories (2, 3, and 4 for this technician). The height of the bars in the chart represents the total estimated hours. For category 2, for example, the bar has a height of 4 indicating the technician has a total of 4 estimated hours for services in category 2. The technician also has 4 hours in category 3 and 2 hours in category 4. None of the workorders for this technician involve any of the other categories. That is why no other categories display.

Creating a Chart

In order to create a chart using the Chart Wizard, Microsoft Graph 2000 must be installed. It is also possible to create a chart, by adding a chart that has been created previously and stored in a separate file.

Inserting an Additional Chart

Inserting the second chart requires the same steps as inserting the first chart. The only differences are in the fields to be selected and the title for the chart. Perform the following steps to insert the second chart.

To Insert an Additional Chart

1 Click the View button to return to Design view. Point to the OK button in the Microsoft Access dialog box.

The Microsoft Access dialog box displays (Figure 8-66). This message indicates that the chart is locked, that is, you cannot make any permanent changes to the data on the chart. (The chart data is calculated automatically from the current workorder data.)

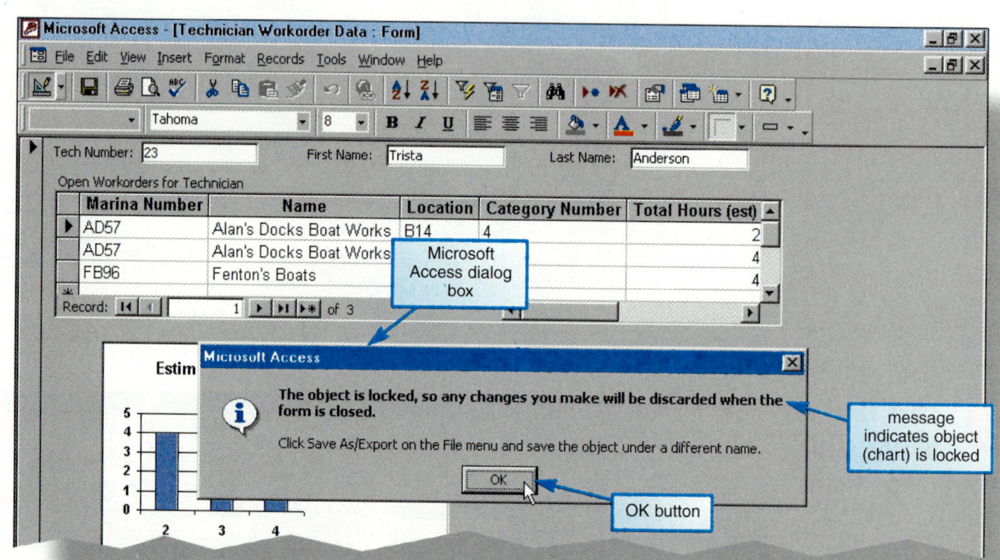

FIGURE 8-66

2 Click the OK button. Use the techniques shown in the previous section to add a second chart at the position shown in Figure 8-67. In this chart, select Hours Spent rather than Total Hours (est) and type `Hours Spent by Category` **as the name of the chart rather than Estimated Hours by Category.**

The chart is inserted.

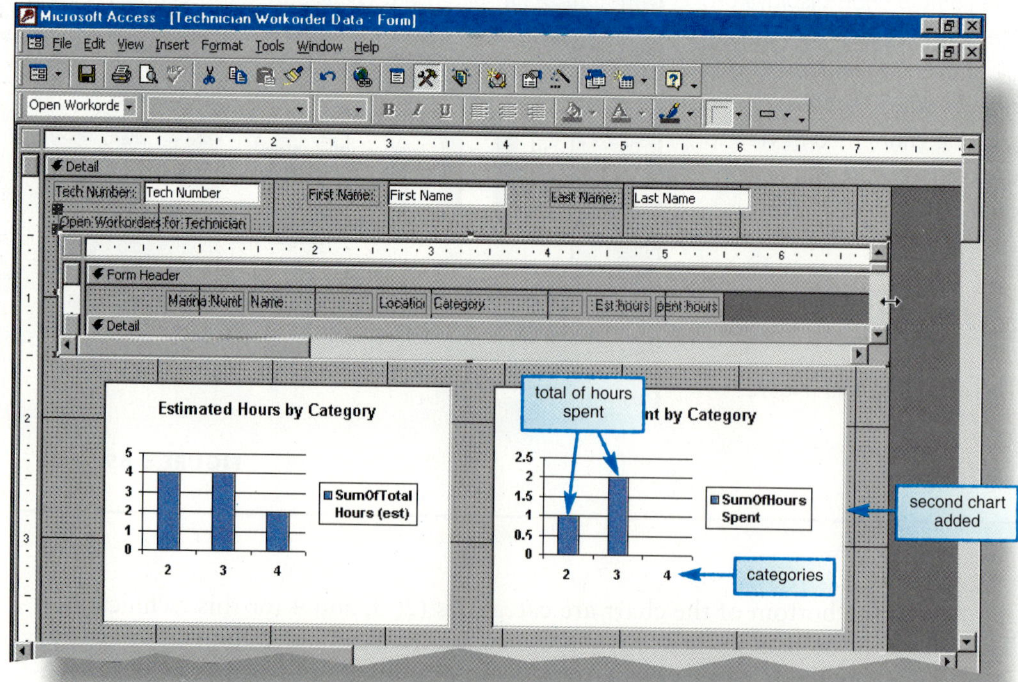

FIGURE 8-67

Adding a Title

The form in Figure 8-2a on page A 8.6 contains a title. To add a title to a form created in Design view, first click Form Header/Footer on the View menu to add a form header. Next, expand the form header to allow room for the title. You then can use the Label button in the toolbox to place the label in the form header and type the title in the label. Perform the following steps to add a title to the form.

Charts

The use of charts in Access is not restricted to forms. You can also place a chart on a report or on a data access page. The steps involved in placing such charts are the same as those for placing charts on forms. For more information about charts, visit the Access 2000 More About page (www.scsite.com/ac2000/more.htm) and then click Charts.

To Add a Title

1 Click View on the menu bar and then click Form Header/Footer on the View menu. Drag the lower boundary of the form header so that the form header is approximately the size shown in Figure 8-68. Click the Label button in the toolbox and then point to the position shown in the figure.

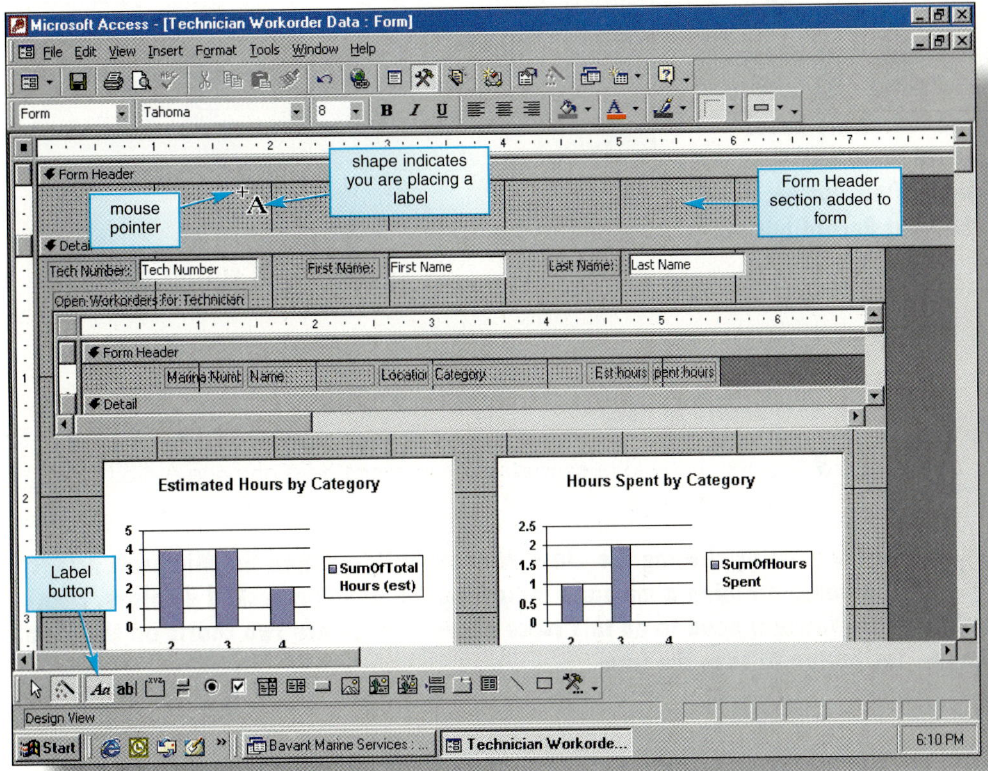

FIGURE 8-68

2 **Click the position shown in the figure and then drag the pointer so that the label has the approximate size of the one shown in Figure 8-69. Type** `Technician Workorder Data` **as the title. Click outside the label to deselect it, then right-click the label and click Properties on the shortcut menu. Change the value of the Font Size property to 14 and the value of the Text Align property to Distribute. Change the value of the Special Effect property to Raised. Close the Label property sheet and then click the View button. Point to the Next Record button.**

The completed form displays (Figure 8-69).

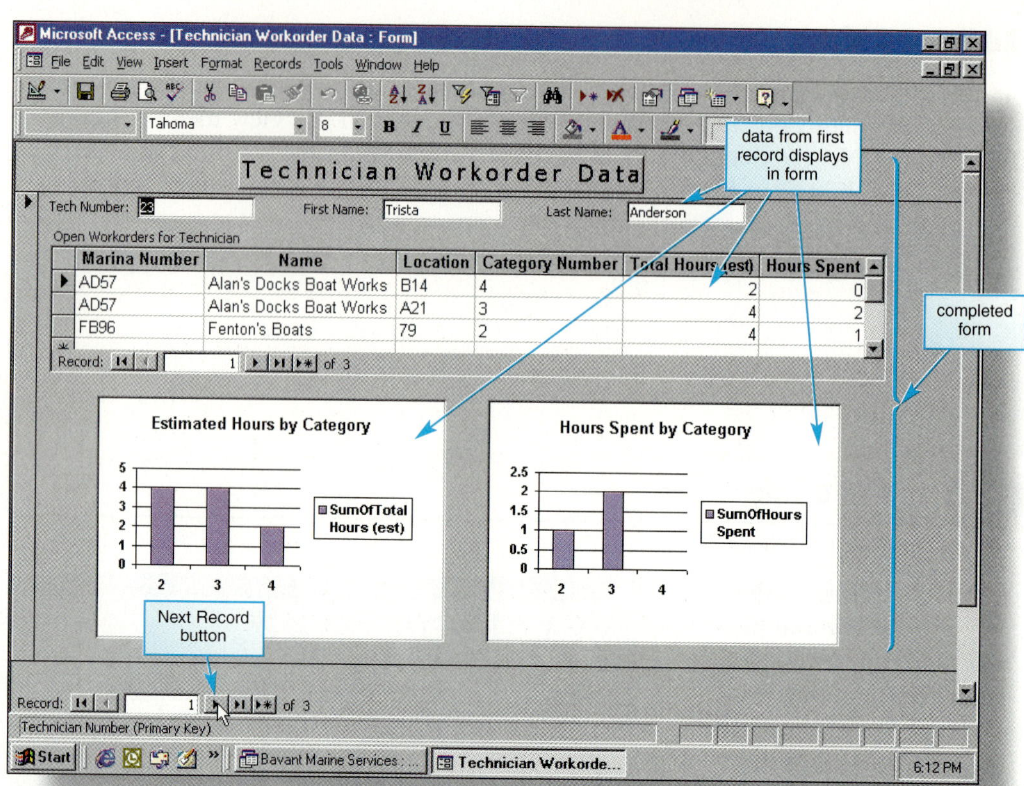

FIGURE 8-69

3 **Click the Next Record button.**

The second record displays on the form as was shown in Figure 8-2b on page A 8.6.

4 **Close the form by clicking the Close Window button. When the Microsoft Access dialog box containing a message indicating the object is locked displays, click the OK button. You will need to do this twice because there are two charts on the form. Click the Yes button to save the form.**

The form no longer displays.

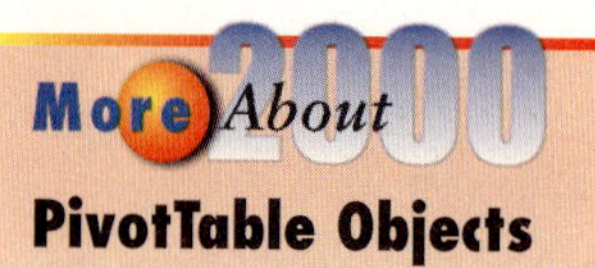

PivotTable Objects

PivotTable objects, also called PivotTable lists, represent an important and flexible way of summarizing information. For more information about PivotTable lists and their use, visit the Access 2000 More About page (www.scsite.com/ac2000/more.htm) and then click PivotTable list.

Creating and Using PivotTable Forms

To create a PivotTable form in Access, you use the PivotTable Wizard. The wizard uses Excel to create the PivotTable object and Access to create a form in which it embeds the PivotTable object. To use the PivotTable form, open the form. If you simply want to view the data in its current format, you do not need to take any additional action. If you want to use the features of Excel to manipulate the PivotTable object, however, click the Edit PivotTable Object button. Provided you have access to Excel, the PivotTable form then will display in Excel as a worksheet that you can manipulate.

Creating a PivotTable Form

Creating a PivotTable form is similar to creating any other type of form. Rather than using Design view or the Form Wizard, however, you will use the PivotTable Wizard to create a PivotTable form as performed in the following steps.

To Create a PivotTable Form

1 Click Queries on the Objects bar, click Marinas and Workorders by Technician, click the New Object: AutoForm button arrow, and then click Form.

2 Click PivotTable Wizard and then point to the OK button.

The New Form dialog box displays (Figure 8-70).

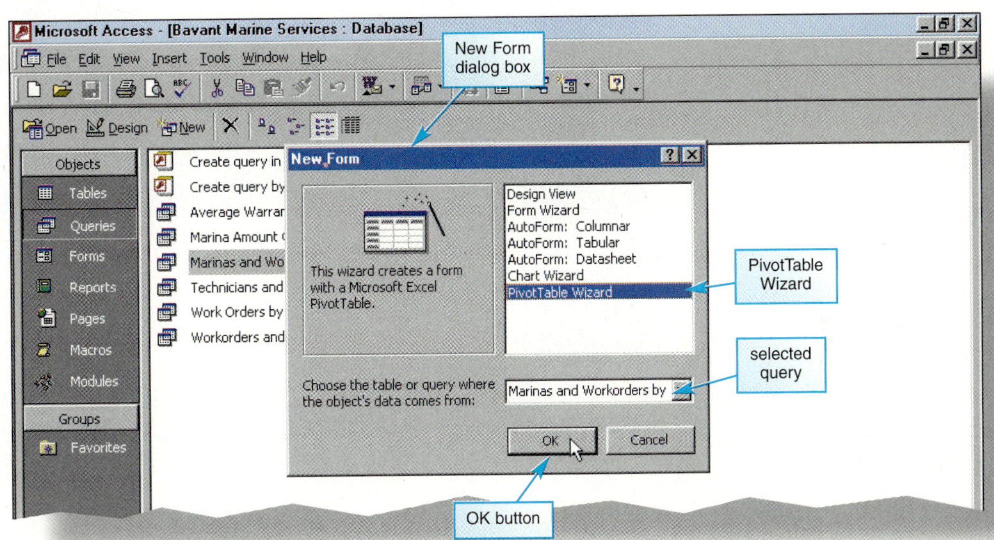

FIGURE 8-70

3 Click the OK button and then point to the Next button.

The PivotTable Wizard dialog box displays (Figure 8-71). This box contains a description of a PivotTable object and also a sample.

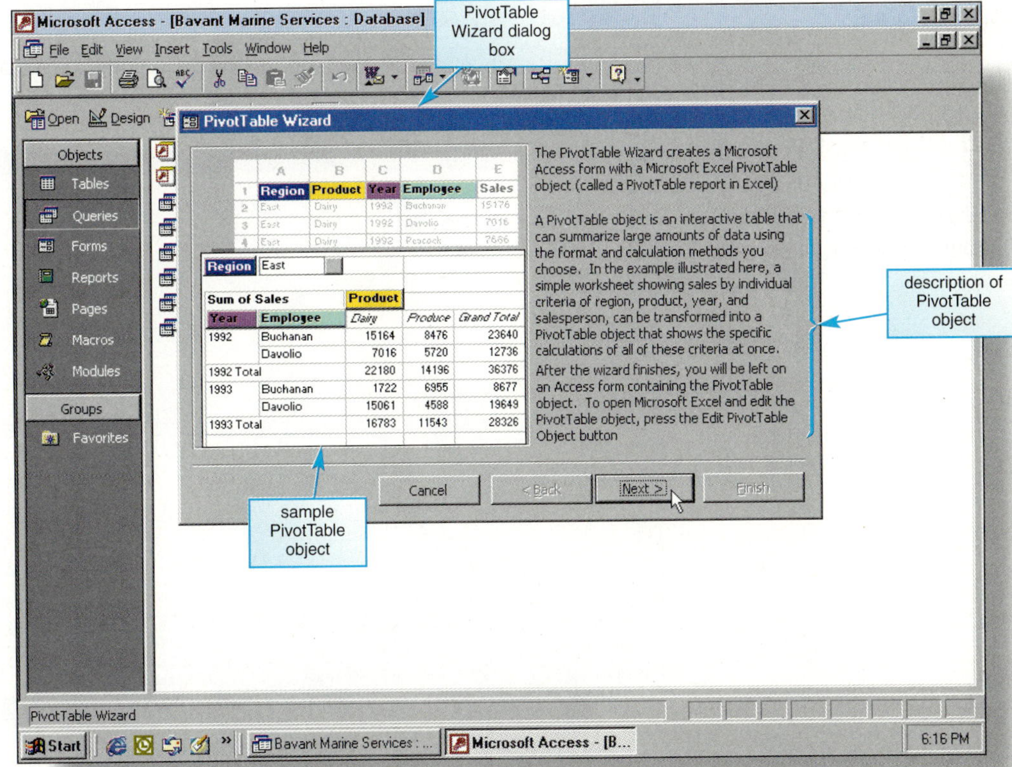

FIGURE 8-71

4 **Click the Next button. Add the Tech Number, Marina Number, Category Number, and Total Hours (est) fields to the PivotTable by selecting each one and then clicking the Add Field button. Point to the Next button.**

The PivotTable Wizard dialog box displays (Figure 8-72). The fields for the PivotTable object are selected.

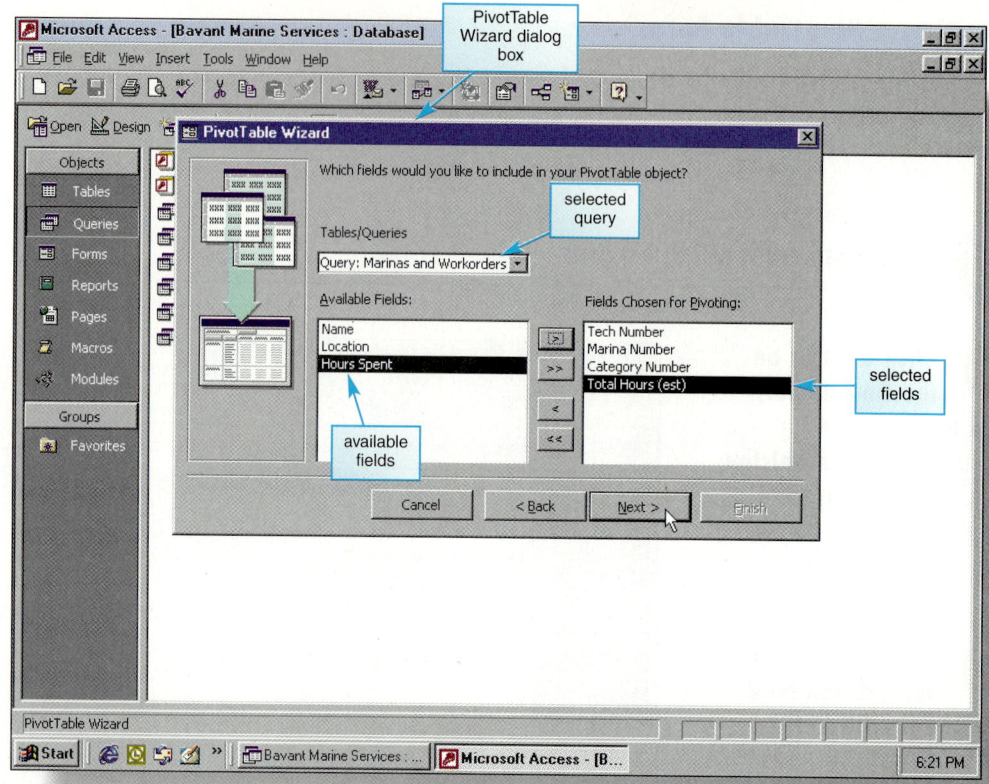

FIGURE 8-72

5 **Click the Next button. Point to the Layout button.**

The PivotTable Wizard dialog box displays (Figure 8-73). Use the Layout button to indicate the layout of the PivotTable object. Use the Options button to indicate other properties of the PivotTable object.

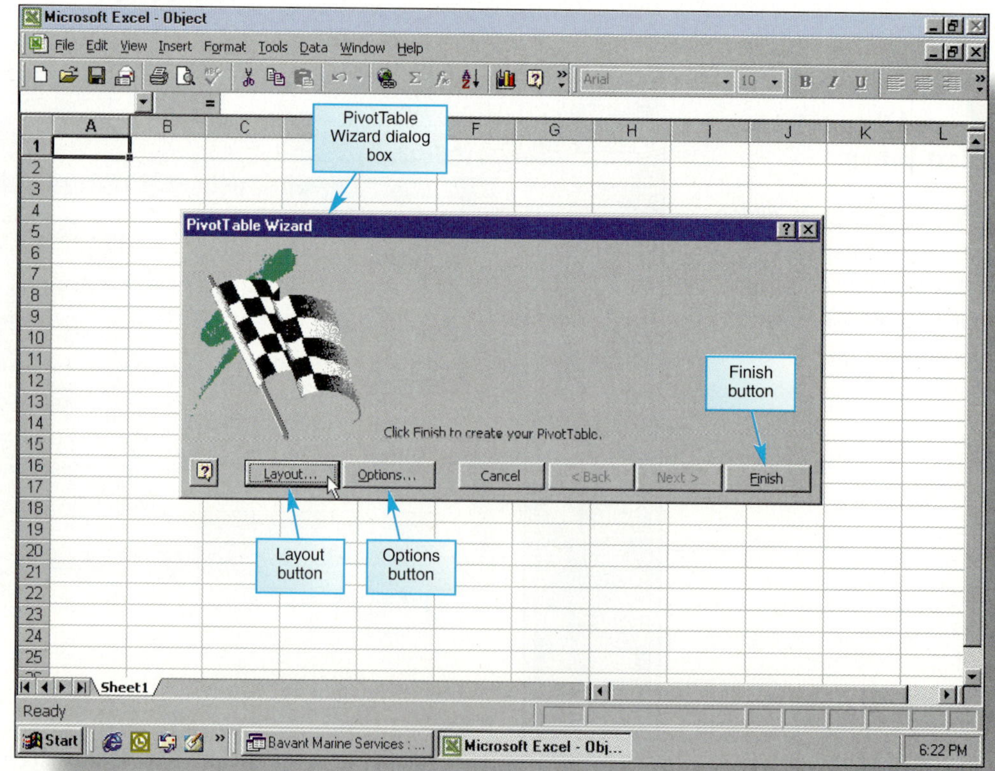

FIGURE 8-73

6 **Click the Layout button. Drag the fields from the right-hand side of the PivotTable Wizard dialog box to the positions shown in Figure 8-74. Click the OK button.**

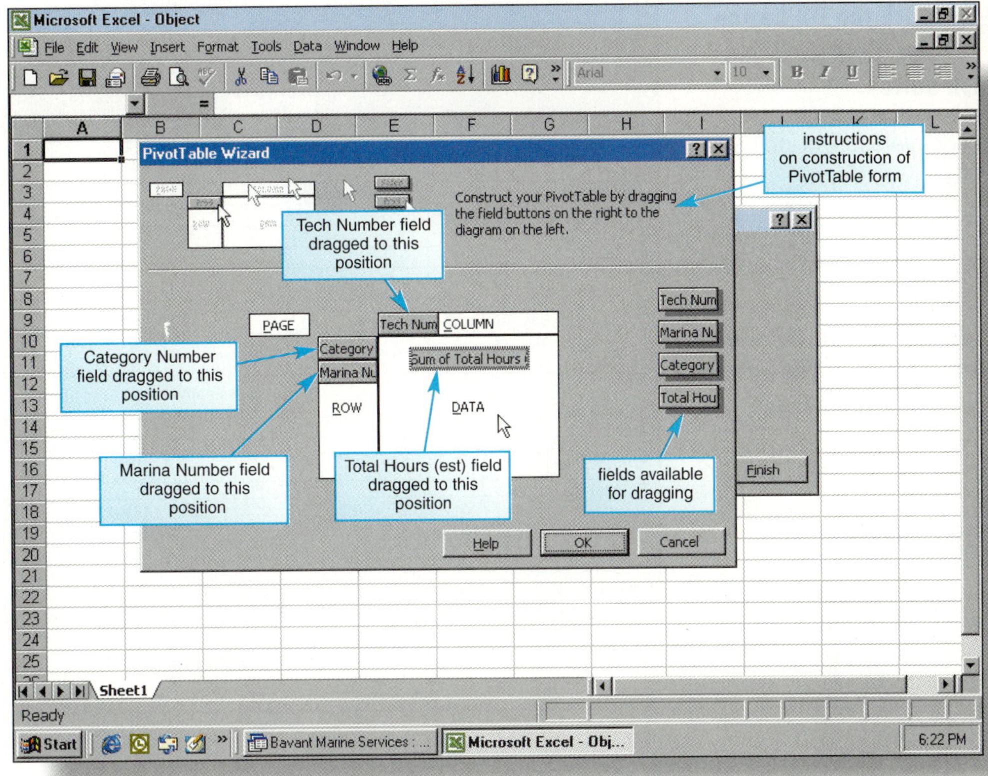

FIGURE 8-74

7 **Click the Options button. Make sure your options match those shown in Figure 8-75 and then point to the OK button.**

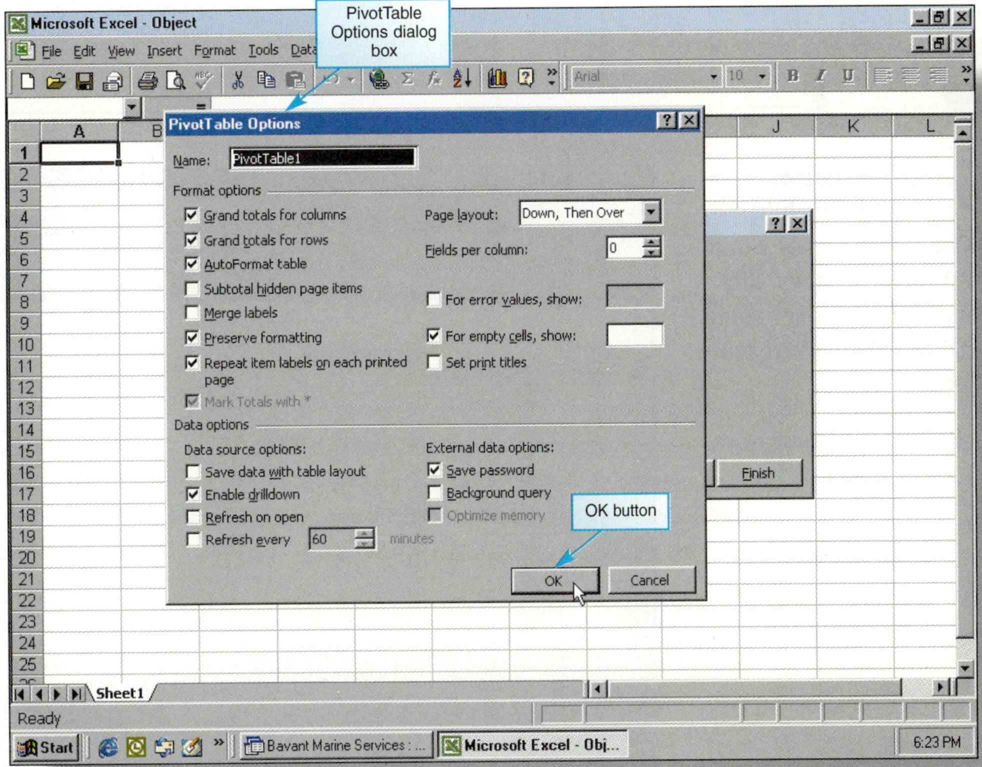

FIGURE 8-75

8 **Click the OK button and then click the Finish button.**

The completed PivotTable form displays (Figure 8-76).

9 **Close the form by clicking the Close Window button. Click the Yes button to save the form. Type** `Estimated Hours PivotTable` **as the name of the form and then click the OK button.**

The form is saved.

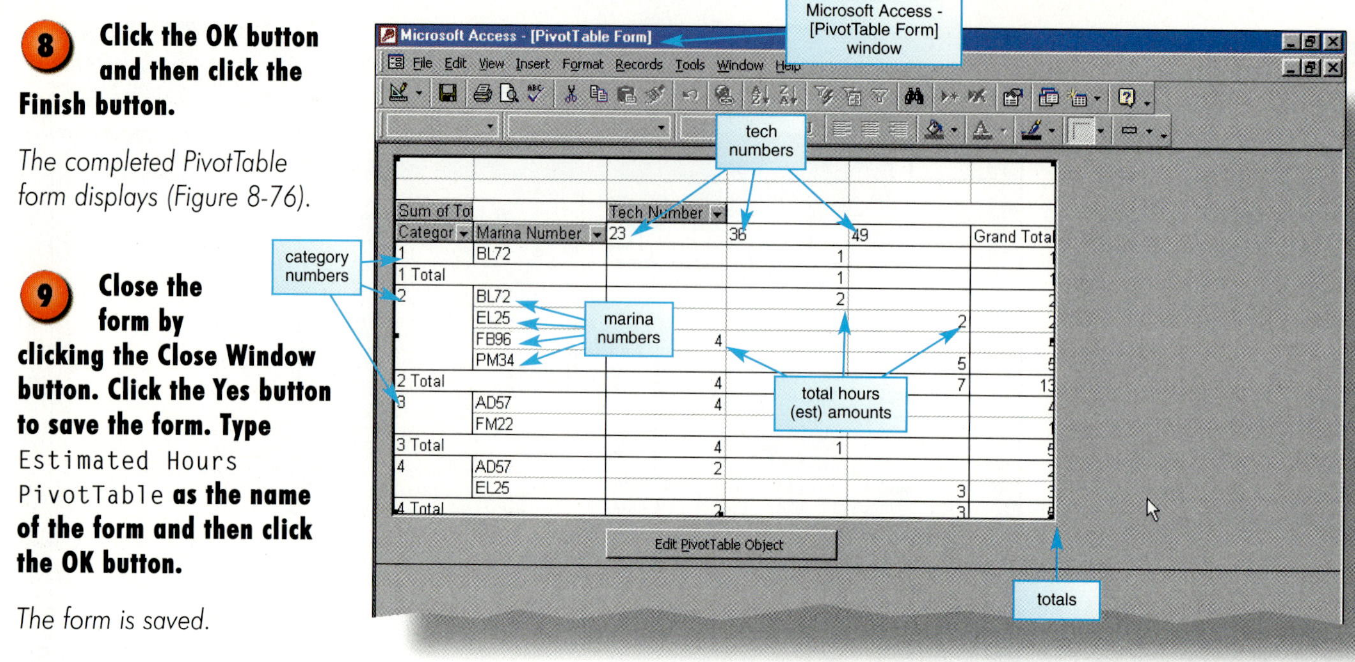

FIGURE 8-76

Using the PivotTable Form

To use the PivotTable form, perform the following steps.

To Use the PivotTable Form

1 **Click Forms on the Objects bar, right-click Estimated Hours PivotTable, and then click Open on the shortcut menu. Point to the Edit PivotTable Object button.**

The PivotTable form displays (Figure 8-77).

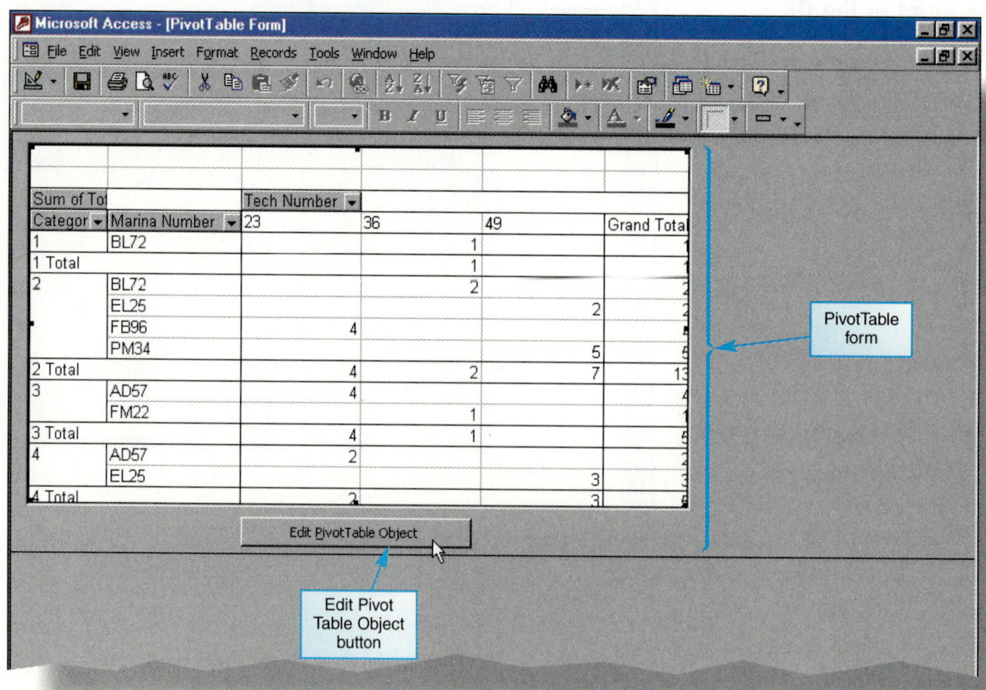

FIGURE 8-77

2 **Click the Edit PivotTable Object button. If necessary, maximize the Microsoft Excel – Worksheet in PivotTable Form window. If necessary, remove the PivotTable toolbar from the screen by clicking the Close button.**

The PivotTable form displays as an Excel worksheet (Figure 8-78). You now could use Excel to modify and analyze the PivotTable object.

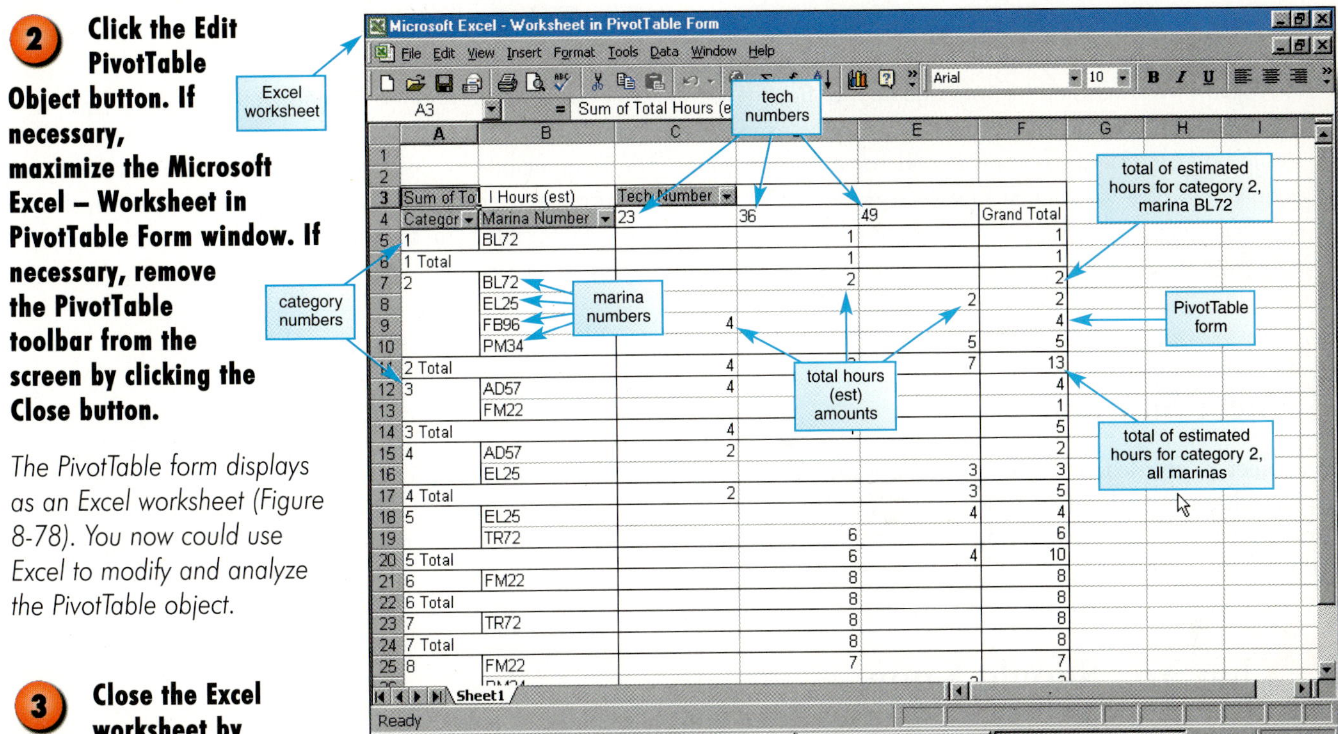

FIGURE 8-78

3 **Close the Excel worksheet by clicking the Close Window button and then close the PivotTable form in Access by clicking the Close Window button.**

The form no longer displays.

Closing the Database

The following step closes the database by closing its Database window.

TO CLOSE A DATABASE

1. Click the Close button for the Bavant Marine Services : Database window.

Pivot Table Objects

PivotTable objects can be used on data access pages, just as they can on forms. To place a PivotTable object on a data access page, use the Office PivotTable tool in the toolbox and follow the instructions.

CASE PERSPECTIVE SUMMARY

In Project 8, you assisted the management of Bavant Marine Services by modifying the Marina Update Form to include special buttons and a combo box to be used to search for a marina based on the marina's name. You also created a form listing the number and name of technicians. The form included a subform listing details concerning open workorders for each technician as well as two charts that graphically illustrate the number of hours spent by the technician in each of the service categories. Finally, you created a PivotTable form that summarized the workorder data.

Project Summary

In Project 8, you learned how to add command buttons to a form and how to create a combo box to be used for searching. You learned how to create forms from scratch using Design view. You learned how to add a subform to a form and how to add charts to a form. Finally, you learned how to create and use a form containing a PivotTable object.

What You Should Know

Having completed this project, you now should be able to perform the following tasks:

- Add a Title *(A 8.45)*
- Add Command Buttons to a Form *(A 8.8)*
- Close a Database *(A 8.51)*
- Close and Save a Form *(A 8.32, A 8.38)*
- Create a Combo Box *(A 8.17)*
- Create a PivotTable Form *(A 8.47)*
- Create the Form *(A 8.35)*
- Create the Query for a Subform *(A 8.33)*
- Insert a Chart *(A 8.40)*
- Insert an Additional Chart *(A 8.44)*
- Modify the Combo Box *(A 8.23)*
- Modify the Subform *(A 8.39)*
- Modify the Add Record Button *(A 8.14)*
- Open a Database *(A 8.7)*
- Open a Form *(A 8.32)*
- Place a Rectangle *(A 8.30)*
- Place the Subform *(A 8.36)*
- Resize the Subform *(A 8.40)*
- Use the Combo Box *(A 8.21)*
- Use the Combo Box to Search for a Marina *(A 8.28)*
- Use the PivotTable Form *(A 8.51)*

1 Modifying Forms and Creating a PivotTable Form for the Sidewalk Scrapers Database

Instructions: Start Access. Open the Sidewalk Scrapers database from the Access Data Disk. See the inside back cover for instructions for downloading the Access Data Disk or see your instructor for information on accessing the files required for this book. Perform the following tasks.

1. Modify the Customer Update Form to create the form shown in Figure 8-79. The form includes command buttons and a combo box to search for customers by name. Be sure to sort the names in ascending order and update the combo box. The user should not be able to tab to the combo box. When the Add Record button is clicked, the insertion point should be in the Customer Number field.

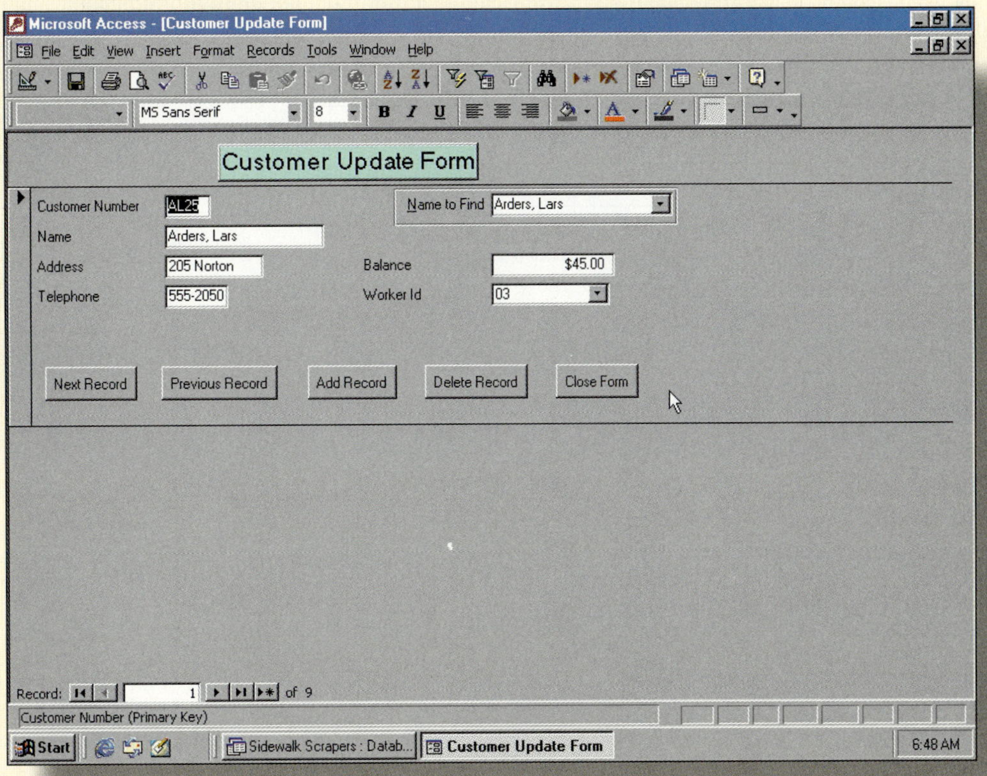

FIGURE 8-79

2. Save and print the form. To print the form, open the form, click File on the menu bar, click Print, and then click Selected Record(s) as the print range. Click the OK button.

3. Create the Balances by Worker PivotTable form shown in Figure 8-80. The table summarizes the customer balances by worker id.

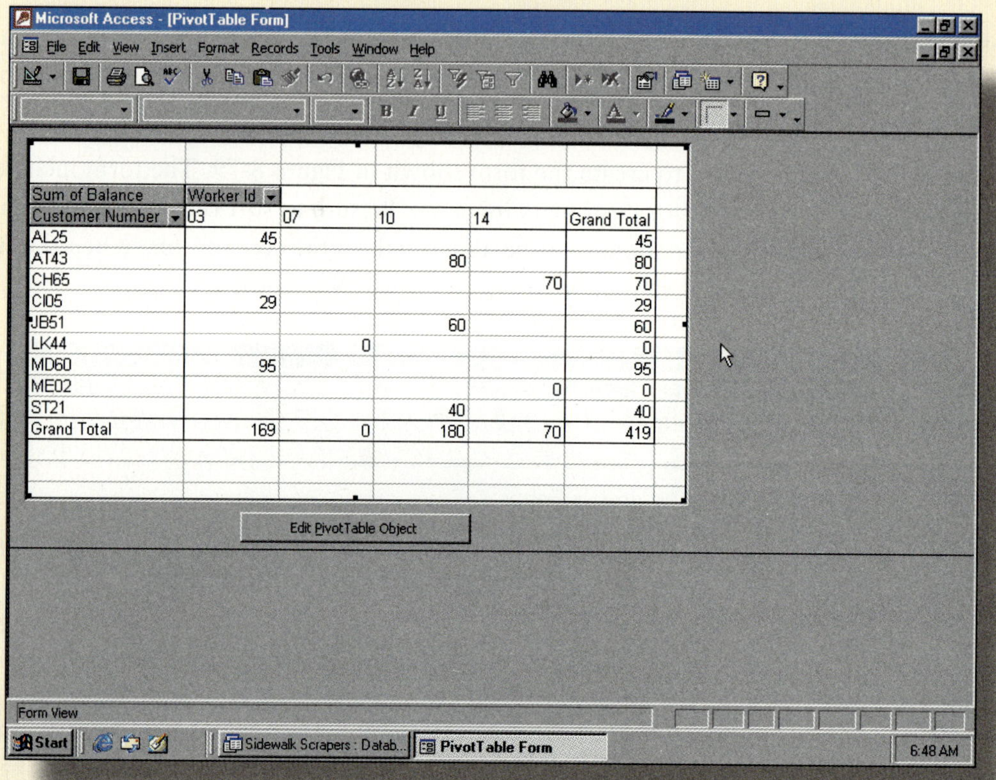

FIGURE 8-80

4. Print the Balances by Worker PivotTable form. To print the form, right-click the form in the Database window and then click Print on the shortcut menu.

1 Creating Advanced Forms and PivotTable Forms for the School Connection Database

Problem: The Booster's Club has three additional requests. First, they would like some improvements to the Item Update Form. This includes placing buttons on the form to make it easier to perform tasks such as adding a record and closing the form. They also want users of the form to have a simple way of searching for an item given its description. They also would like an additional form, one that lists the vendor code and name as well as any items that are on order with the vendor. The form should include a chart that graphically illustrates the total number ordered for each item. They also would like a PivotTable form that summarizes the reorder data.

Instructions: Start Access. Open the School Connection database from the Access Data Disk. See the inside back cover for instructions for downloading the Access Data Disk or see your instructor for information on accessing the files required for this book. Perform the following tasks.

1. Modify the Item Update Form to create the form shown in Figure 8-81. The form includes command buttons and a combo box to search for items by description. Be sure to sort the item description in ascending order and update the combo box. The user should not be able to tab to the combo box. When the Add Record button is clicked, the insertion point should be in the Item Id field.

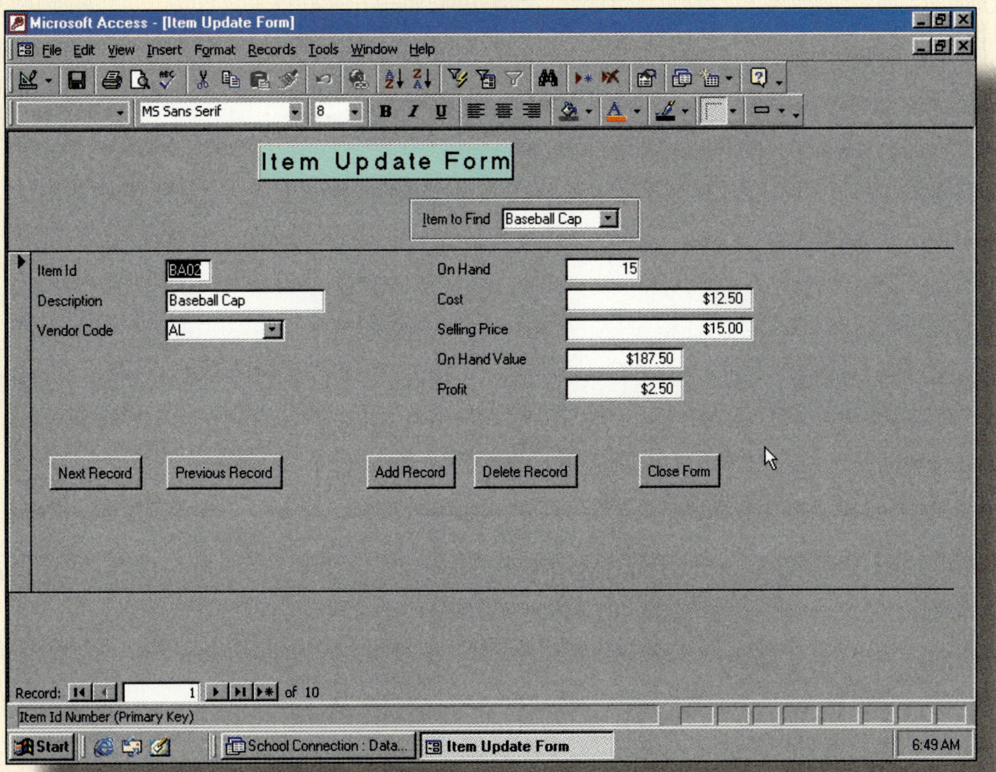

FIGURE 8-81

2. Print the form. To print the form, open the form, click File on the menu bar, click Print and then click Selected Record(s) as the print range. Click the OK button.

Creating Advanced Forms and PivotTable Forms for the School Connection Database *(continued)*

3. Create a query that joins the Item, Reorder, and Vendor tables. Display the Vendor Code, Name, Item Id, Description, Date Ordered, and Number Ordered fields. Save the query as Reorder Items by Vendor.
4. Create the Open Reorders by Vendor form shown in Figure 8-82. The subform uses the Reorder Items by Vendor query. Insert the graphic in the form header. (*Hint*: For help, see In the Lab 1 of Project 7.) The chart displays the item id on the x axis. The y axis shows the sum of the number ordered.

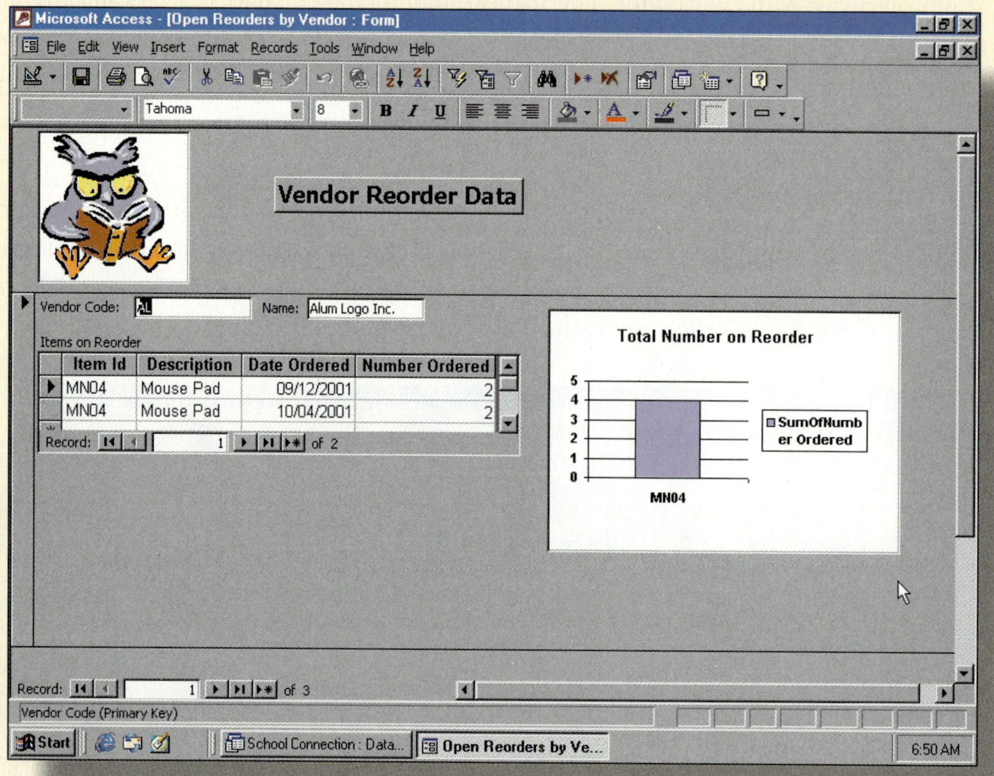

FIGURE 8-82

5. Open the Open Reorders by Vendor form and move to the record for GG Gifts. Print the form containing the data for GG Gifts. To print the form, open the form, click File on the menu bar, click Print, and then click Selected Record(s) as the print range. Click the OK button.
6. Create the Total Number Ordered PivotTable form shown in Figure 8-83. The PivotTable form summarizes the number of items on order by vendor.

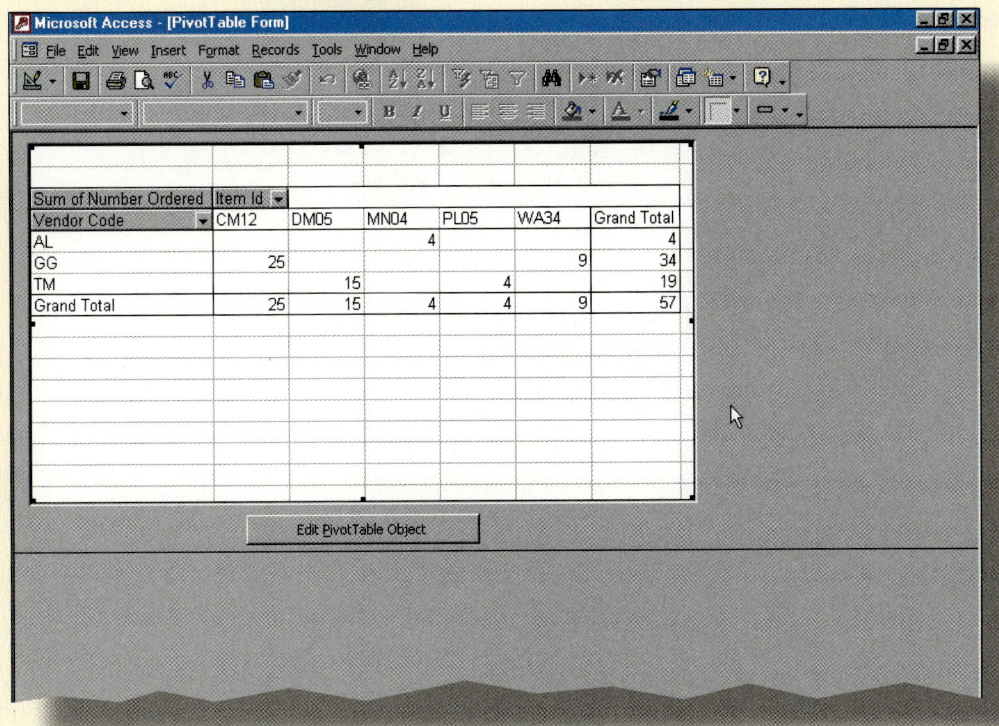

Sum of Number Ordered	Item Id					
Vendor Code	CM12	DM05	MN04	PL05	WA34	Grand Total
AL			4			4
GG	25				9	34
TM		15		4		19
Grand Total	25	15	4	4	9	57

FIGURE 8-83

7. Print the Total Number Ordered PivotTable form. To print the form, right-click the form in the Database window and then click Print on the shortcut menu.

2 Creating Advanced Forms for the City Area Bus Company Database

Problem: The City Area Bus Company has two additional requests. First, they would like some improvements to the Advertiser Update Form. This includes placing buttons on the form to make it easier to perform tasks such as adding a record and closing the form. They also want users of the form to have a simple way of searching for an advertiser given its name. They also would like an additional form, one that lists the sales rep number and name as well as active account information. The form should include two charts that graphically illustrate the totals of amounts paid and balances by advertiser.

Instructions: Open the City Area Bus Company database from the Access Data Disk. See the inside back cover for instructions for downloading the Access Data Disk or see your instructor for information on accessing the files required for this book. Perform the following tasks.

1. Modify the Advertiser Update Form to create the form shown in Figure 8-84 on the next page. The form includes command buttons and a combo box to search for advertisers by name. Be sure to sort the name in ascending order and update the combo box. The user should not be able to tab to the combo box. When the Add Record button is clicked, the insertion point should be in the Advertiser Id field.

Creating Advanced Forms for the City Area Bus Company Database *(continued)*

Microsoft Access - [Advertiser Update Form]

Advertiser Update Form

Name to Find: Alia Cleaners

Advertiser Id	AC25	Ad Type	SER
Name	Alia Cleaners	Balance	$85.00
Address	223 Michigan	Amount Paid	$585.00
City	Crescentville	Advertising Income	$670.00
State	MA	Sales Rep Number	24
Zip Code	05431		
Telephone Number	(216) 555-0987		

Next Record | Previous Record | Add Record | Delete Record | Close Form

Record: 1 of 9

Advertiser Id (Primary Key)

FIGURE 8-84

2. Print the form. To print the form, open the form, click File on the menu bar, click Print, and then click Selected Record(s) as the print range. Click the OK button.
3. Create a query that joins the Active Accounts, Advertiser, Category, and Sales Rep tables. Display the Sales Rep Number, First Name, Last Name, Advertiser Id, Name, Description and Ad Month. Save the query as Active Accounts by Sales Rep.
4. Create the Sales Rep Account Data form shown in Figure 8-85. The subform uses the Active Accounts by Sales Rep query. The charts use data from the Advertiser table.

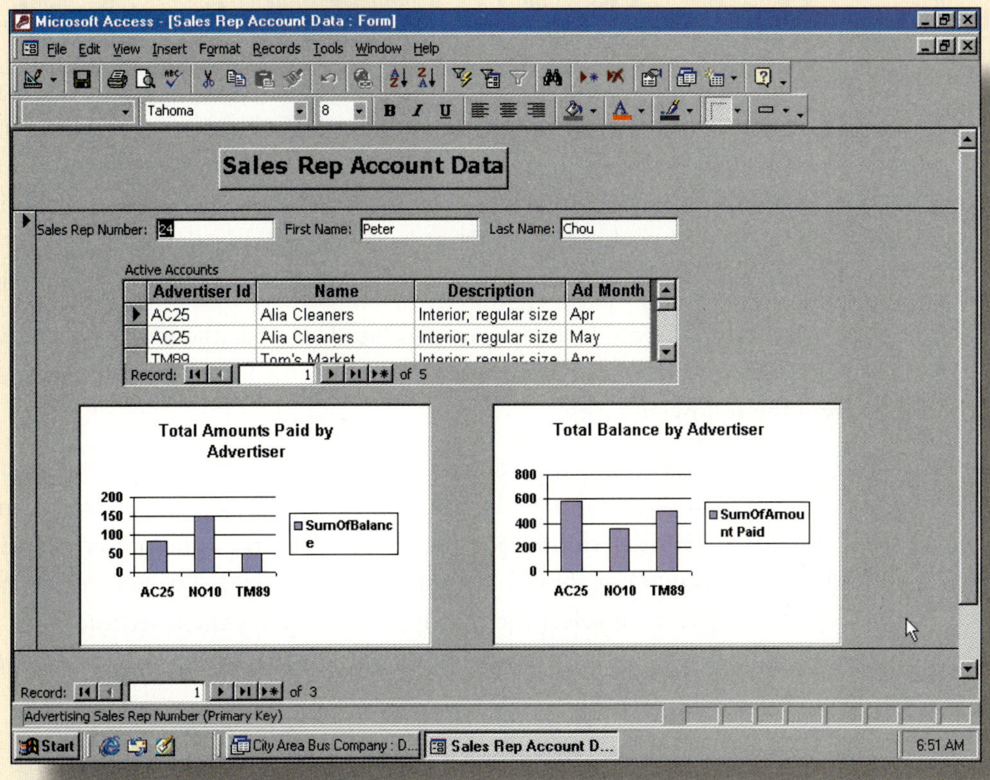

FIGURE 8-85

5. Open the Sales Rep Account Data form and move to the record for sales rep Elvia Ortiz. Print the record for Elvia Ortiz. To print the form, open the form, click File on the menu bar, click Print, and then click Selected Record(s) as the print range. Click the OK button.

3 Creating Advanced Forms and PivotTable Forms for the Resort Rentals Database

Problem: The real estate company has three additional requests. First, they would like some improvements to the Rental Update Form. This includes placing buttons on the form to make it easier to perform tasks such as adding a record, printing a record, and closing the form. They also want users of the form to have a simple way of searching for a rental unit given its address. They also would like an additional form, one that lists the owner id and name as well as any rentals. The form should include a chart that graphically illustrates the total number of weeks each unit is rented. They also would like a PivotTable form that summarizes the rental data.

Instructions: Open the Resort Rentals database from the Access Data Disk. See the inside back cover for instructions for downloading the Access Data Disk or see your instructor for information on accessing the files required for this book. Perform the following tasks.

1. Modify the Rental Update Form to create the form shown in Figure 8-86. The form includes command buttons and a combo box to search for rental units by address. Be sure to sort the addresses in ascending order and update the combo box. The user should not be able to tab to the combo box. When the Add Record button is clicked, the insertion point should be in the Rental Id field. The text for the buttons extends over two lines. To change the text, select the button, click to place the insertion point immediately after the first word, and then press SHIFT+ENTER. The First Record and Last Record buttons are Record Navigation buttons. The Print Record button is a Record Operations button.

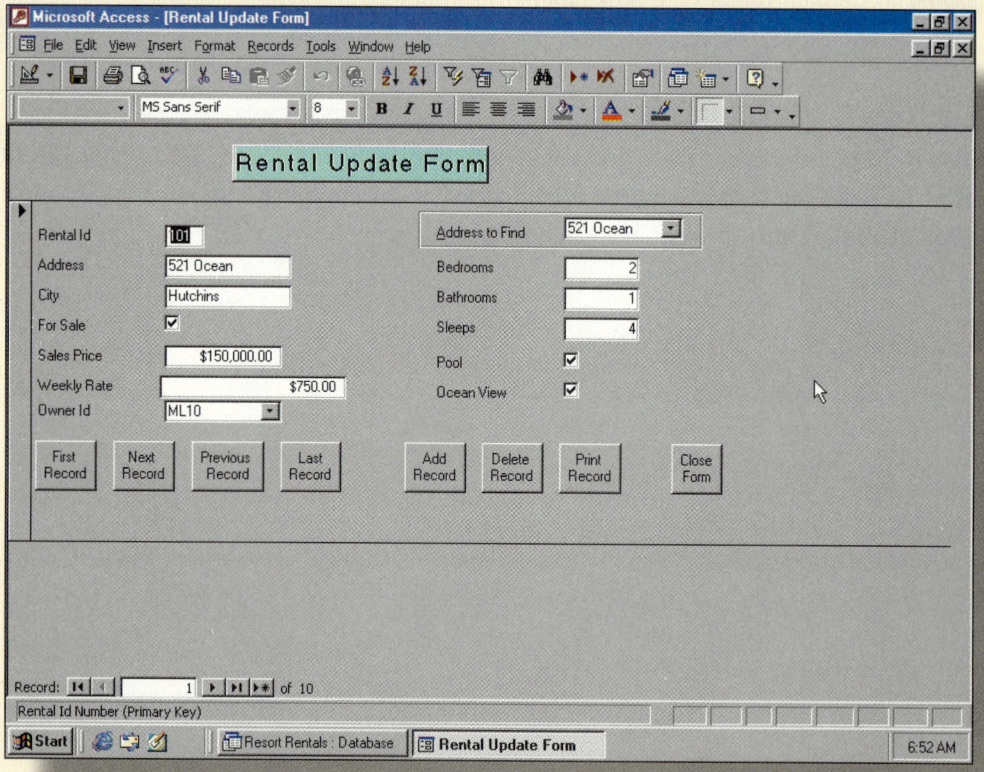

FIGURE 8-86

2. Use the Next Record button and move to record eight. Click the Print Record button to print the record.
3. Create a query that joins the Active Rentals, Owner, Rental Unit, and Renter tables. Display the following fields: Owner Id, Rental Id, Address, City, Start Date, Length, and First Name and Last Name (of the renter). Sort the results in ascending order by the Rental Id field within the Owner Id field. Save the query as Active Rentals by Owner.
4. Create the form shown in Figure 8-87. The subform uses the Active Rentals by Owner query. The chart displays the rental id on the x axis and the total number of weeks rented on the y axis. Save the form as Owner Rental Data.

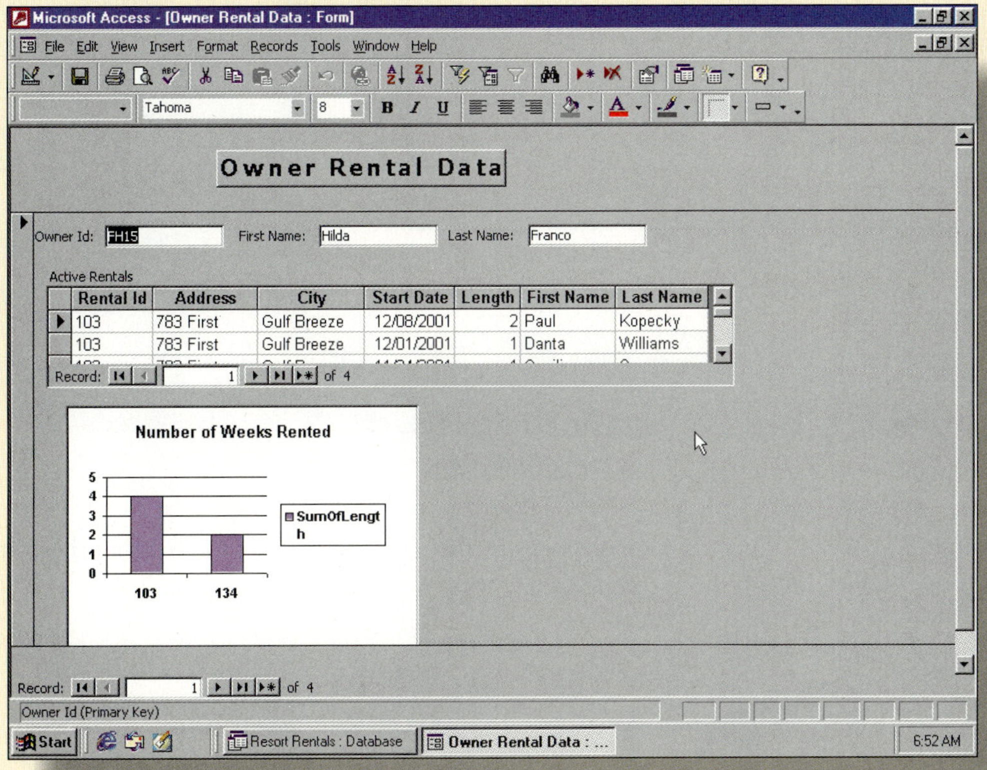

FIGURE 8-87

5. Open and print the form. To print the form, open the form, click File on the menu bar, click Print, and then click Selected Record(s) as the print range. Click the OK button.

Creating Advanced Forms and PivotTable Forms for the Resort Rentals Database *(continued)*

6. Create the Number of Weeks PivotTable form shown in Figure 8-88. The PivotTable form summarizes the number of weeks a unit is rented.

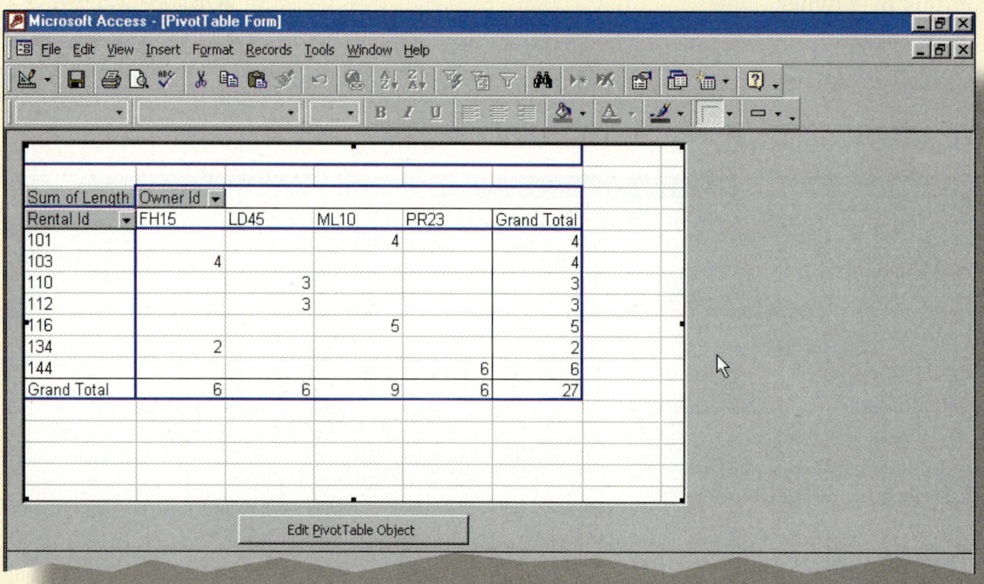

Sum of Length	Owner Id				
Rental Id	FH15	LD45	ML10	PR23	Grand Total
101			4		4
103	4				4
110		3			3
112		3			3
116			5		5
134	2				2
144				6	6
Grand Total	6	6	9	6	27

FIGURE 8-88

7. Print the Number of Weeks PivotTable form. To print the form, right-click the form in the Database window, and then click Print on the shortcut menu.

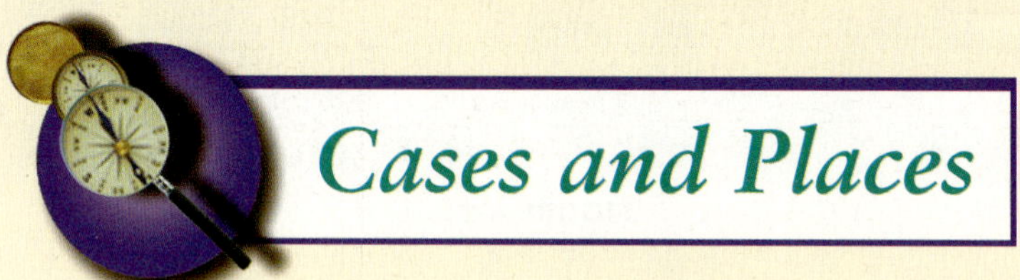

The difficulty of these case studies varies:
▸ are the least difficult; ▸▸ are more difficult; and ▸▸▸ are the most difficult.

1 ▸ Open the Computer Items database on the Access Data Disk. Modify the Item Update Form to create the form shown in Figure 8-89. The form should incorporate the combo box and button features that were illustrated in the project.

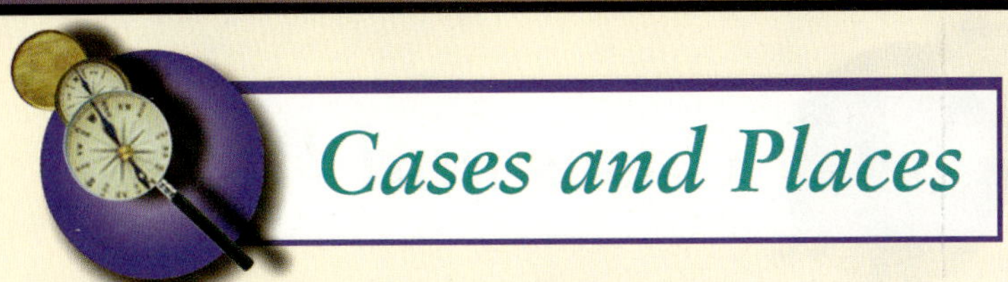

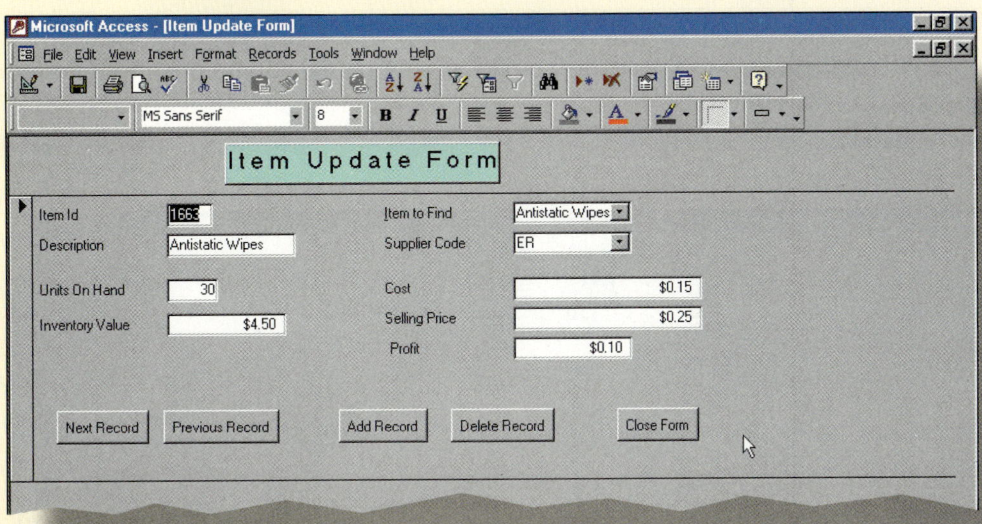

FIGURE 8-89

2 Use the Computer Items database and create the Open Reorders by Supplier form shown in Figure 8-90. The subform uses a query that joins the Item, Reorder Status, and Supplier tables. The chart graphically displays the total number of items ordered by supplier.

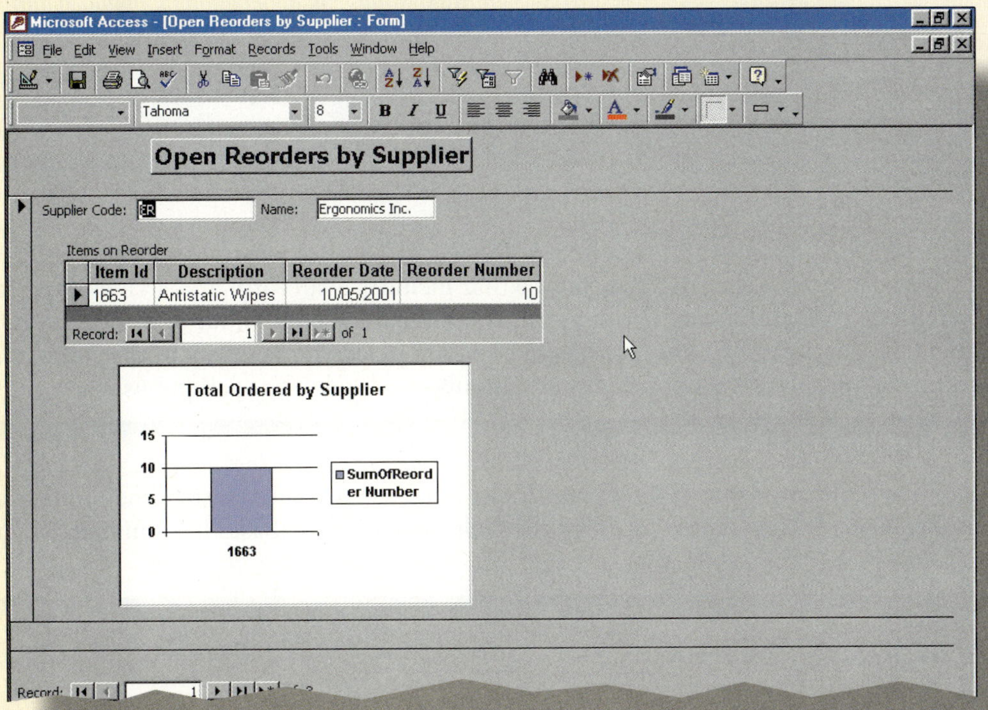

FIGURE 8-90

3 ▶▶ Open the Galaxy Books database on the Access Data Disk. Modify the Book Update Form to create the form shown in Figure 8-91. The form should incorporate the combo box and button features that were illustrated in the project.

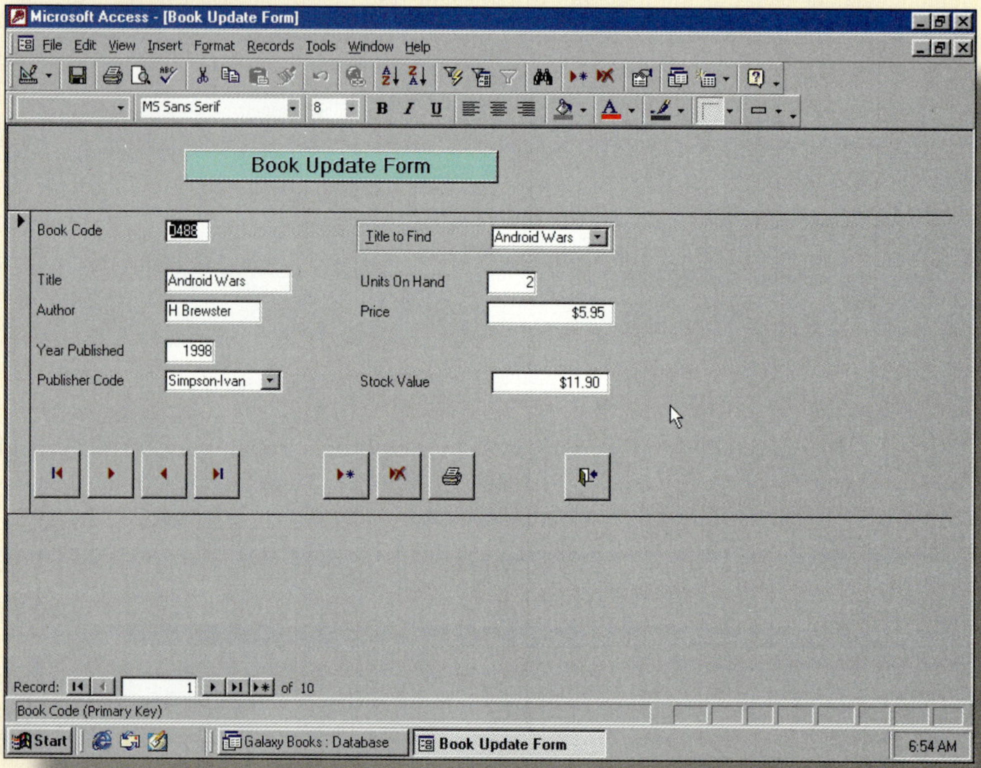

FIGURE 8-91

4 ▶▶ Create a form for the Galaxy Books database that includes a subform and a chart. The form should display the publisher code and name. The subform should include data about books on layaway. Display the book code, title, customer first and last name, and date placed on layaway in the subform. Include a chart that graphically displays the book codes and number of books for each publisher.

5 ▶▶▶ Create a PivotTable form for the Computer Items database that summarizes the number of items on order by supplier. Create a PivotTable form for the Galaxy Books database that summarizes the number of books on layaway by publisher.

Microsoft Access 2000

Administering a Database System

OBJECTIVES

You will have mastered the material in this project when you can:

- Convert a database to an earlier version of Access
- Use the Table Analyzer, Performance Analyzer, and Documenter
- Use an input mask
- Specify referential integrity options
- Set startup options
- Open a database in exclusive mode
- Set a password
- Encrypt a database
- Create a grouped data access page
- Preview a data access page
- Create and use a replica
- Synchronize a Design Master and a replica
- Create a new SQL query
- Include only certain fields
- Include all fields
- Use a criterion involving a Numeric field
- Use a criterion involving a Text field
- Use a compound criterion
- Use NOT in a criterion
- Use a computed field
- Sort the results
- Use built-in functions
- Use multiple functions in the same command
- Use grouping
- Restrict the groups that display
- Join tables
- Restrict the records in a join
- Join multiple tables

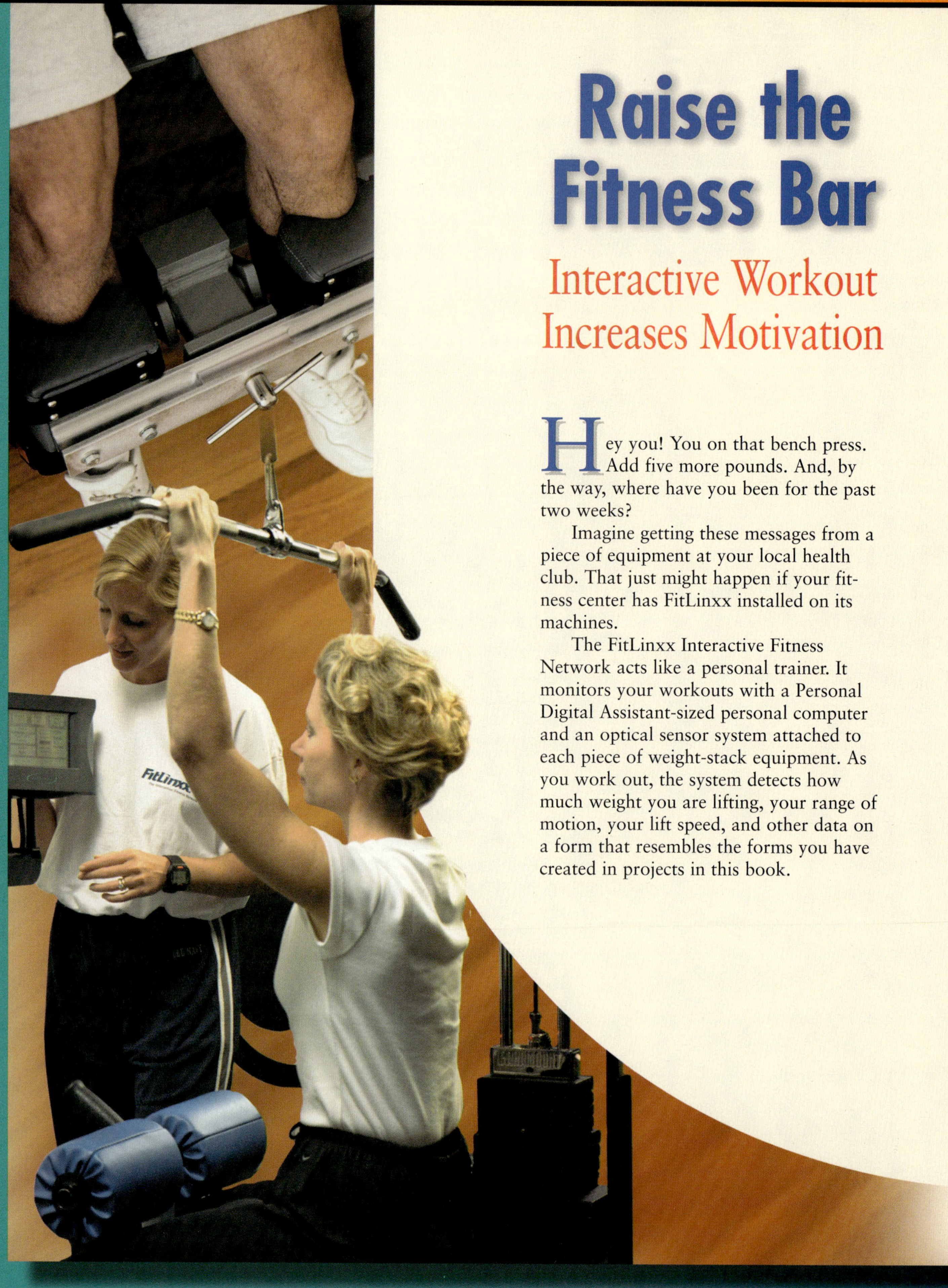

Raise the Fitness Bar

Interactive Workout Increases Motivation

Hey you! You on that bench press. Add five more pounds. And, by the way, where have you been for the past two weeks?

Imagine getting these messages from a piece of equipment at your local health club. That just might happen if your fitness center has FitLinxx installed on its machines.

The FitLinxx Interactive Fitness Network acts like a personal trainer. It monitors your workouts with a Personal Digital Assistant-sized personal computer and an optical sensor system attached to each piece of weight-stack equipment. As you work out, the system detects how much weight you are lifting, your range of motion, your lift speed, and other data on a form that resembles the forms you have created in projects in this book.

At the end of your workout, the FitLinxx network sends the data to a Microsoft Access or Microsoft SQL Server database. This database is connected to a touch-screen kiosk, so you can log in and obtain reports and graphs of your progress.

Fitness trainers traditionally use pencils and clipboards to track their clients' improvement; with FitLinxx they can log into their own computers, view a record of every workout, track trends, and create an individual's specific exercise plan. The system even tells the trainers which members have not been coming to the fitness center, and the trainers can send motivating e-mail messages to those people.

These fitness trainers perform activities related to the administration of the FitLinxx database. They help create database passwords, optimize database performance, and use add-in tools to help fitness center members optimize their exercise sessions. You will perform similar database administration actions in this project. You will replicate databases, use indexes and data type formats, set startup options, encrypt and decrypt a database, and convert an Access 2000 database to a previous version of Access.

FitLinxx is the brainchild of Keith Camhi and Andy Greenberg, who were friends at Cornell University and MIT where they studied physics, computer science, electrical engineering, and business. Camhi had joined a health club in 1991, and within six months was losing interest and thinking of quitting. He realized the value of exercise and wanted to continue the workouts, so he thought about why he was having the problem. He and Greenberg figured that software might help with the motivation factor.

They worked on a prototype system in Camhi's mother's basement beginning in 1993. A year later, they introduced a beta system in the New York Knicks basketball team's training center and a community center in Stamford, Connecticut, where FitLinxx is headquartered. Since then, they have installed their systems in more than 100 health clubs, YMCAs, and college gyms.

A subscription to the software runs about $10,000 annually, and a sensor and PDA for each piece of equipment cost about $2,000. The largest fitness centers spend from $40,000 to $250,000 to equip their entire facilities.

FitLinxx helps members achieve a safe, effective, and motivating workout. With these results, you can call the system your database workout buddy.

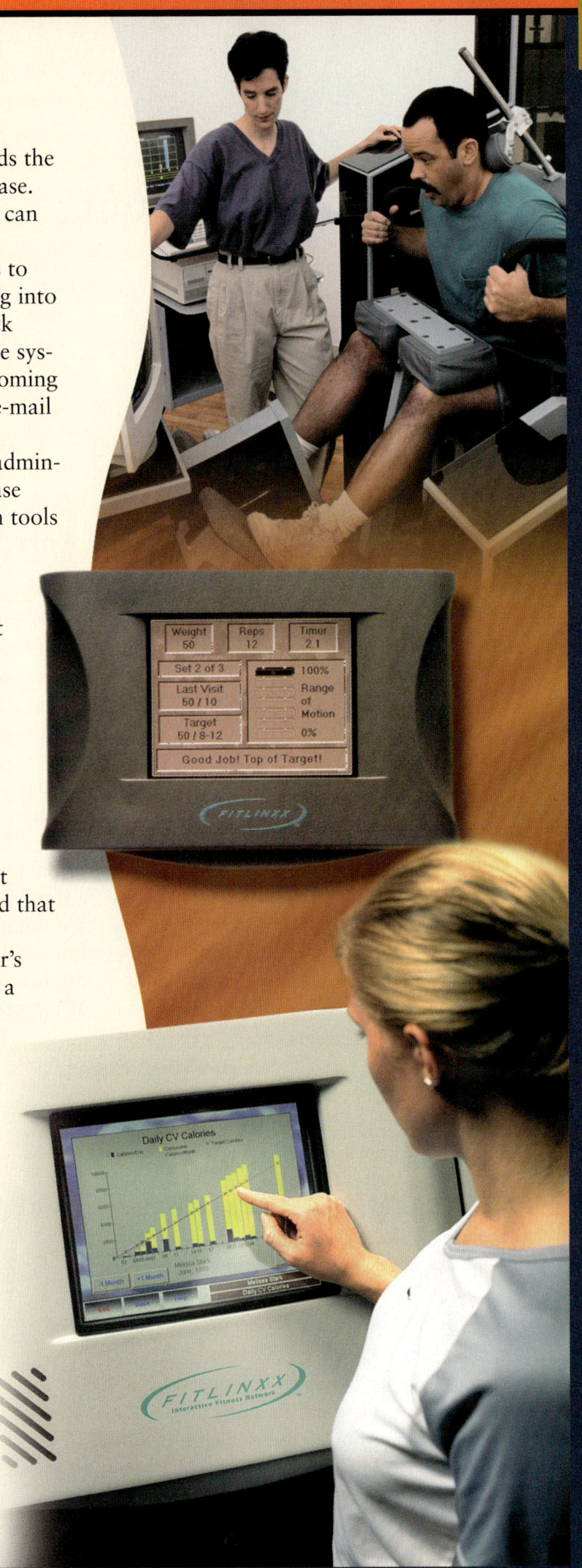

Microsoft Access 2000

Microsoft Access 2000

Administering a Database System

PROJECT 9

CASE PERSPECTIVE

The management of Bavant Marine Services is so pleased with the work you have done for them that they have decided to put you in charge of administering their database system and have asked you to determine precisely what this would entail. You found many activities that the individual in charge of administering the database must perform. These include analyzing tables for possible duplication, analyzing performance to see where improvements could be made, and producing complete system documentation. You also determined that the administrator should specify necessary integrity constraints to make sure the data is valid. Security is another issue for the administrator, who should consider the use of both passwords and encryption to protect the database from unauthorized use. Bavant wants more users to have remote access to the database, so administration would include the creation of both data access pages and replicas. You also learned how important the language called SQL has become in a database environment and determined that the administrator should be familiar with the language and how it can be used.

Introduction

Administering a database system encompasses a variety of activities (Figure 9-1). It can include conversion of a database to an earlier version. It usually includes such activities as analyzing tables for potential problems, analyzing performance to see if changes are warranted to make the system perform more efficiently, and documenting the various objects in the database. It also includes integrity issues; that is, taking steps to ensure that the data in the database is valid. These steps can include the creation of custom input masks and also the specification of referential integrity options. Securing the database through the use of passwords and encryption also is part of the administration of a database system as is the setting of startup options. Supporting remote users through data access pages and through replicas also falls in the category of administering a database. Replicas are duplicate copies of the database that could be used by individuals at remote sites and later synchronized with the actual database.

• Convert a database to an earlier version of Access
• Use the Table Analyzer
• Use the Performance Analyzer
• Use the Documenter
• Create a grouped Data Access page
• Use an Input Mask
• Specify Referential Integrity options
• Set Startup options
• Set a password
• Encrypt a database
• Create and use a replica
• Synchronize a Design Master and a replica
• Use SQL to query a database

Use the Performance Analyzer
Use the Table Analyzer
Use the Documenter
Set Startup options
Create a grouped Data Access page
Synchronize a Design Master and a replica
Set a password
Use SQL to query a database

FIGURE 9-1

SQL is an important language for querying and updating databases. It is the closest thing to a universal database language, because the vast majority of database management systems, including Access, use it in some fashion. Although many users will query and update databases through the query features of Access rather than SQL, those in charge of administering the database system should be familiar with this important language.

More About

Microsoft Certification

The Microsoft Office User Specialist (MOUS) Certification program provides an opportunity for you to obtain a valuable industry credential - proof that you have the Access 2000 skills required by employers. For more information, see Appendix D or visit the Shelly Cashman Series MOUS Web page at www.scsite.com/off2000/cert.htm.

Quick Reference

For a table that lists how to complete the tasks covered in this book using the mouse, menu, shortcut menu, and keyboard, visit the Office 2000 Web page (www.scsite.com/off2000/qr.htm), and then click Microsoft Access 2000.

Project Nine — Administering a Database System

Begin this project by creating an Access 97 version of the database for a particular user who needs it. Next use three Access tools, the Table Analyzer, the Performance Analyzer, and the Documenter. Create a custom input mask and also specify referential integrity options. Set a startup option so that the Switchboard automatically displays when the database is opened. Then secure the database by setting a password and encrypting the database. Create a grouped data access page and also create a replica for remote users of the database. Next, turn to the SQL language and write several SQL commands to query the database in a variety of ways. You will use criteria involving number and text fields, compound criteria, and criteria involving NOT. You also will use a computed field, sort query results, use built-in functions, use grouping in a query, and join tables.

Opening the Database

Before completing the tasks in this project, you must open the database. Perform the following steps to complete this task.

TO OPEN A DATABASE

1. Click the Start button on the taskbar.
2. Click Open Office Document on the Start menu, and then click 3½ Floppy (A:) in the Look in box. Make sure the Bavant Marine Services database is selected.
3. Click the Open button.

The database opens and the Bavant Marine Services : Database window displays.

Using Microsoft Access Tools

Microsoft Access has a variety of tools that are useful in administering databases. These include tools to convert a database to an earlier version of Access, to analyze table structures, to analyze performance, and to create detailed documentation.

Converting a Database to an Earlier Version

Occasionally, you might encounter someone who needs to use your database, but who has the previous version of Access. Such a user cannot access the data directly. You need to convert the database to the earlier version in order for the user to access it. Once you have done so, the user can use the converted version. To convert the database, use the Convert Database command as in the following steps.

To Convert a Database to an Earlier Version

1. **Click Tools on the menu bar, click Database Utilities on the Tools menu, click Convert Database on the Database Utilities submenu, and then point to To Prior Access Database Version (Figure 9-2).**

2. **Click To Prior Access Database Version. Select 3 ½ Floppy (A:) in the Save in box. Type** `Bavant Marine Services 97` **as the name of the file and then click the Save button.**

The Access 97 version of the database is created and available for use.

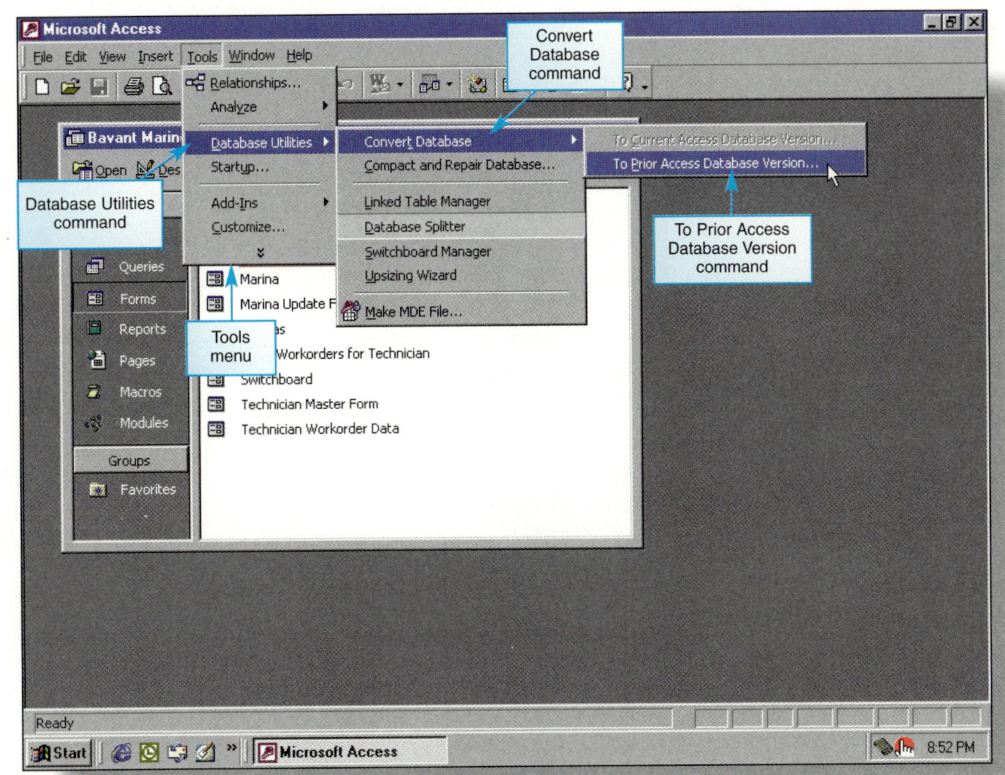

FIGURE 9-2

It is important to realize that any changes made in the converted version, will not be reflected in the original. Assuming the original version still is going to be used, the converted version should be used for retrieval purposes only. Otherwise, if you make changes they will display in one version and not the other, making your data inconsistent.

Using the Analyze Tool

Access contains an Analyze tool that performs three separate functions. It can be used to analyze tables, looking for potential redundancy (duplicated data) and to analyze performance. It will check to see if there is any way to make queries, reports, or forms more efficient and then make suggestions for possible changes. The final function of the analyzer is to produce detailed documentation of the various tables, queries, forms, reports, and other objects in the database.

Using the Table Analyzer

The Table Analyzer examines tables for **redundancy**, which is duplicated data. If found, Table Analyzer will suggest ways to split the table in order to eliminate the redundancy. Perform the steps on the next page to use the Table Analyzer.

Redundancy

There is a special technique for identifying and eliminating redundancy, called normalization. For more information about normalization, visit the Access 2000 More About page (www.scsite.com/ac2000/more.htm) and then click Normalization.

To Use the Table Analyzer

1 **Click Tools on the menu bar, click Analyze on the Tools menu, and then point to Table (Figure 9-3).**

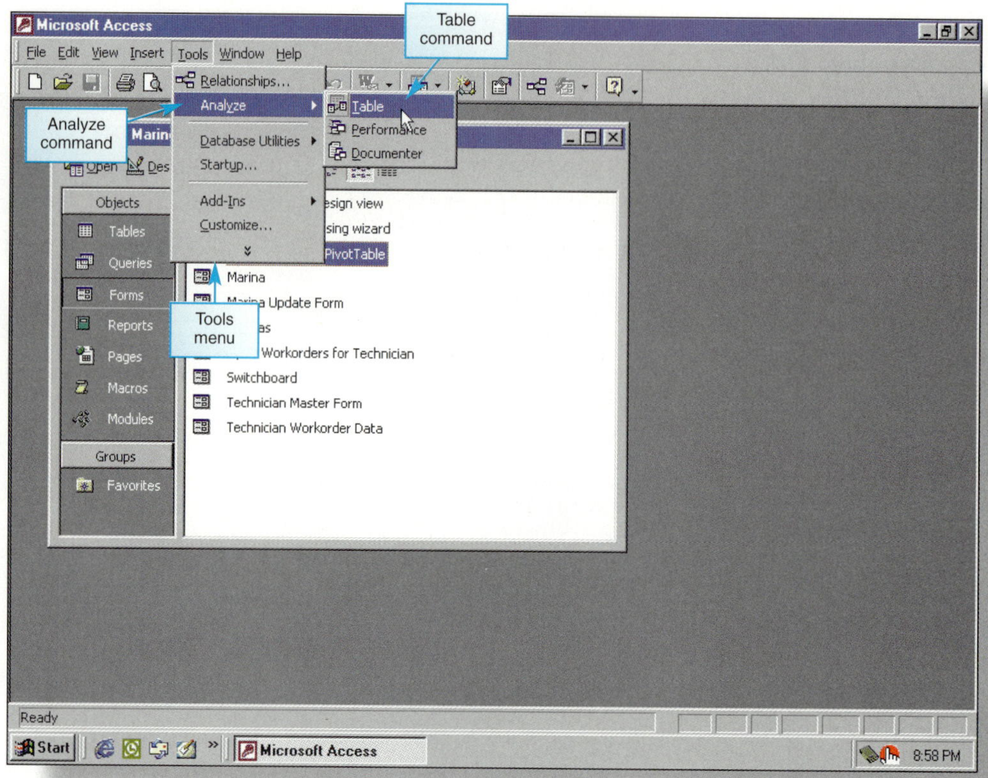

FIGURE 9-3

2 **Click Table and then point to the Next button.**

The Table Analyzer Wizard dialog box displays (Figure 9-4). The message indicates that tables may store duplicate information, which can cause problems.

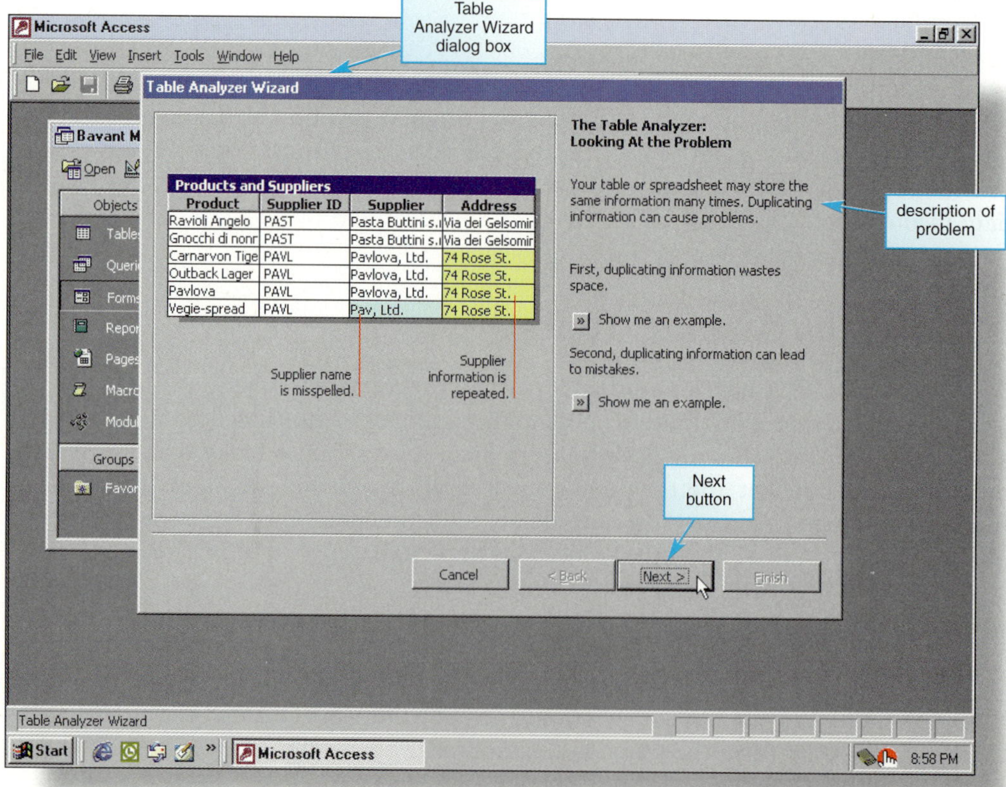

FIGURE 9-4

3 Click the Next button.

The Table Analyzer Wizard dialog box displays (Figure 9-5). The message indicates that the wizard will split the original table to remove duplicate information.

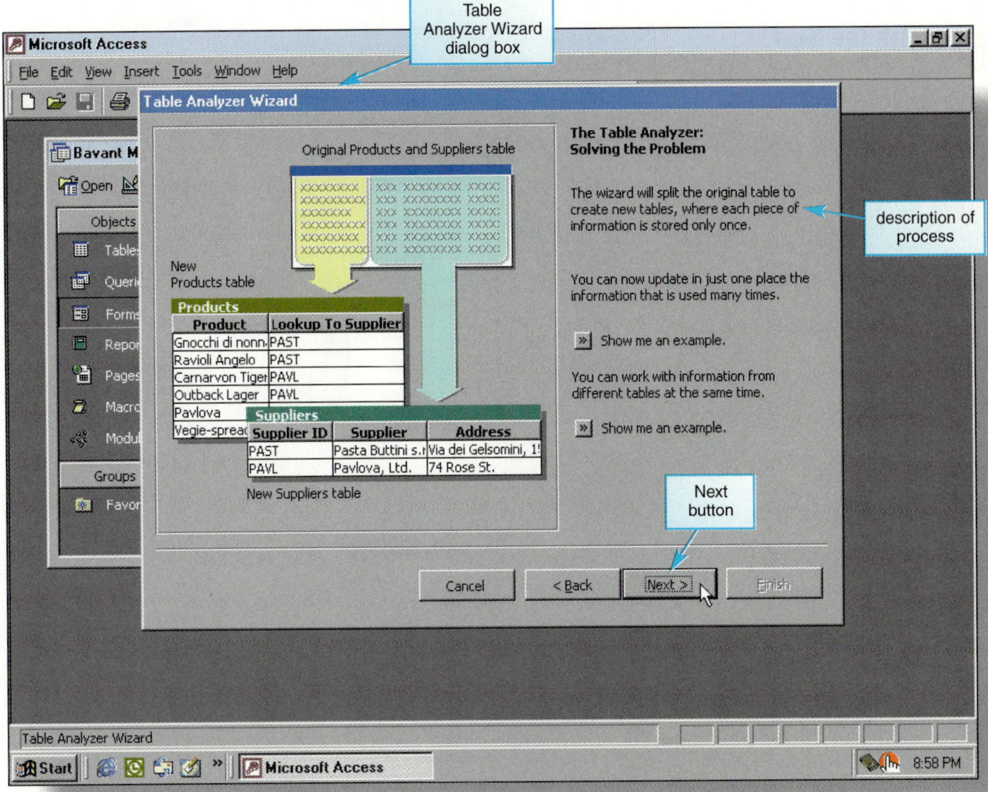

FIGURE 9-5

4 Click the Next button. Click the Marina table in the Tables box and then point to the Next button.

The Marina table is selected (Figure 9-6).

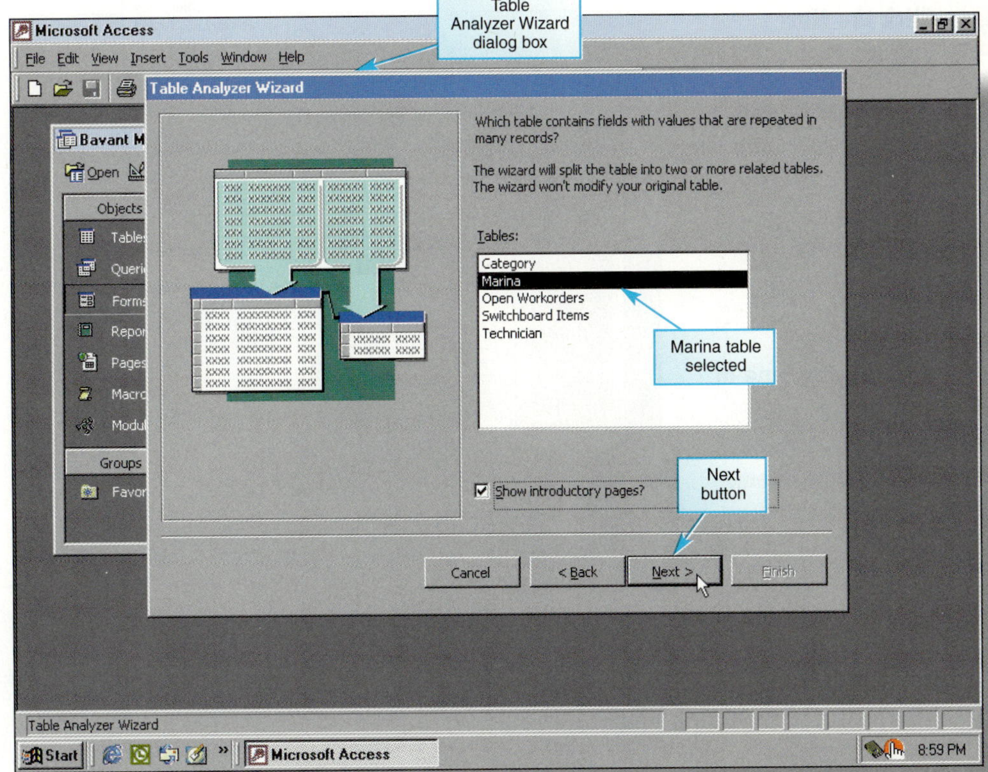

FIGURE 9-6

5 **Click the Next button. Be sure the Yes, let the wizard decide button is selected and then point to the Next button (Figure 9-7).**

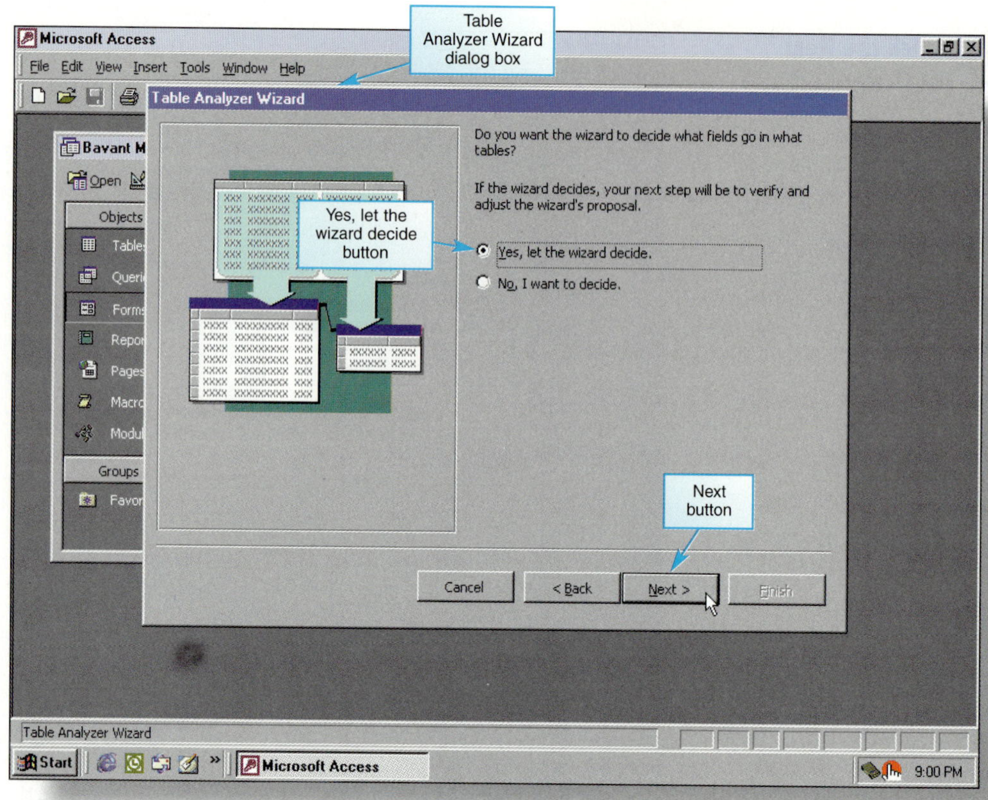

FIGURE 9-7

6 **Click the Next button.**

The Table Analyzer Wizard dialog box displays (Figure 9-8). It indicates duplicate information (for example, State, City, Zip Code). Your screen may be different.

7 **Because the type of duplication identified by the analyzer does not pose a problem, click the Cancel button.**

The structure is not changed.

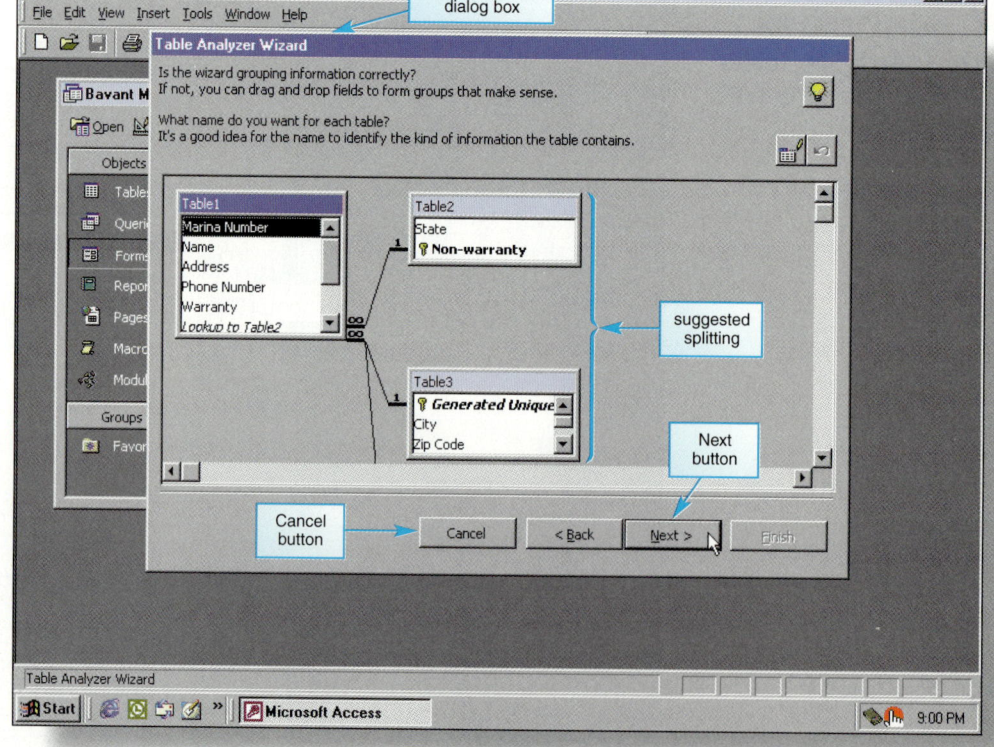

FIGURE 9-8

Other Ways

1. Click the Analyze button arrow on the Database window toolbar, click Analyze Table

Using the Performance Analyzer

The Performance Analyzer will examine the tables, queries, reports, forms, and other objects in your system, looking for changes that would improve the efficiency of your database. This could include changes to the way data is stored as well as changes to the indexes created for the system. Once it has finished, it will make recommendations concerning possible changes. Perform the following steps to use the Performance Analyzer.

To Use the Performance Analyzer

1 Click Tools on the menu bar, click Analyze on the Tools menu, and then point to Performance (Figure 9-9).

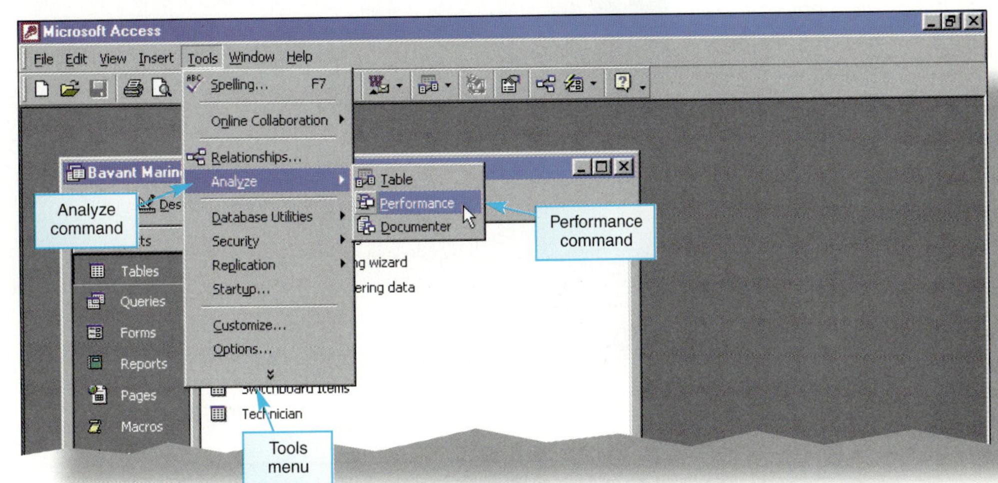

FIGURE 9-9

2 Click Performance and then click the Tables tab. Point to the Select All button.

The Performance Analyzer dialog box displays (Figure 9-10). The Tables tab is selected so that all the tables display.

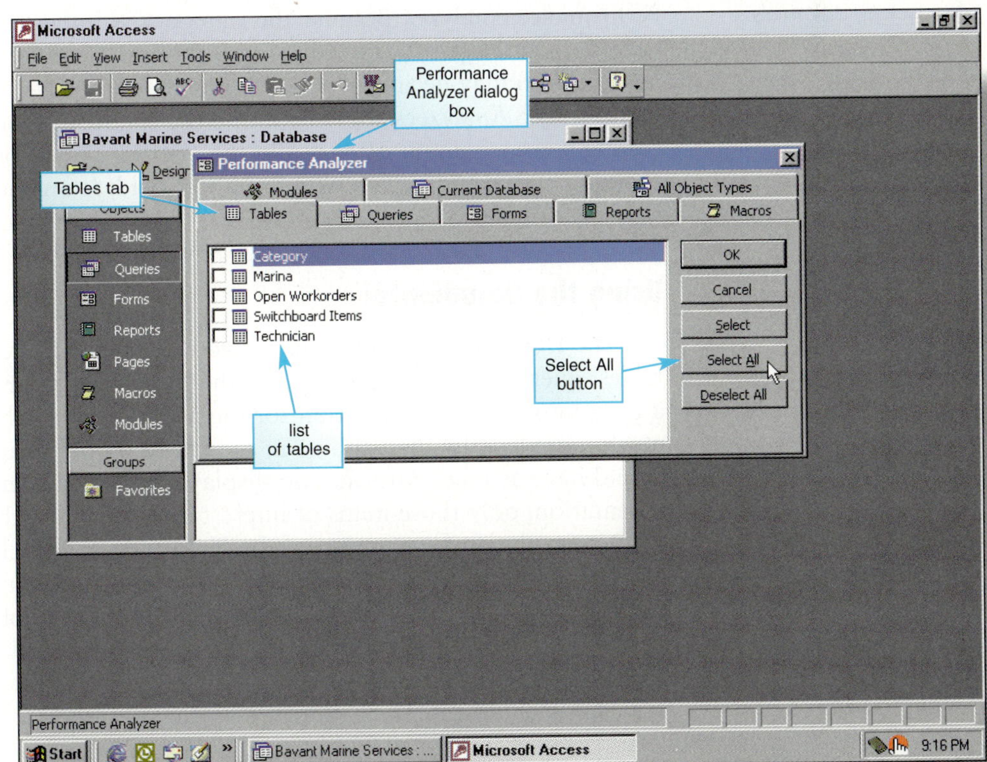

FIGURE 9-10

3 Click the Select All button to select all tables. Click the Queries tab and then click the Select All button to select all queries. Click the OK button. Point to the Close button.

The Performance Analyzer dialog box displays the results of its analysis (Figure 9-11). It indicates that you might consider changing the data type of the category number field from Text to Long Integer, which is an efficient number format, both for computations and data storage.

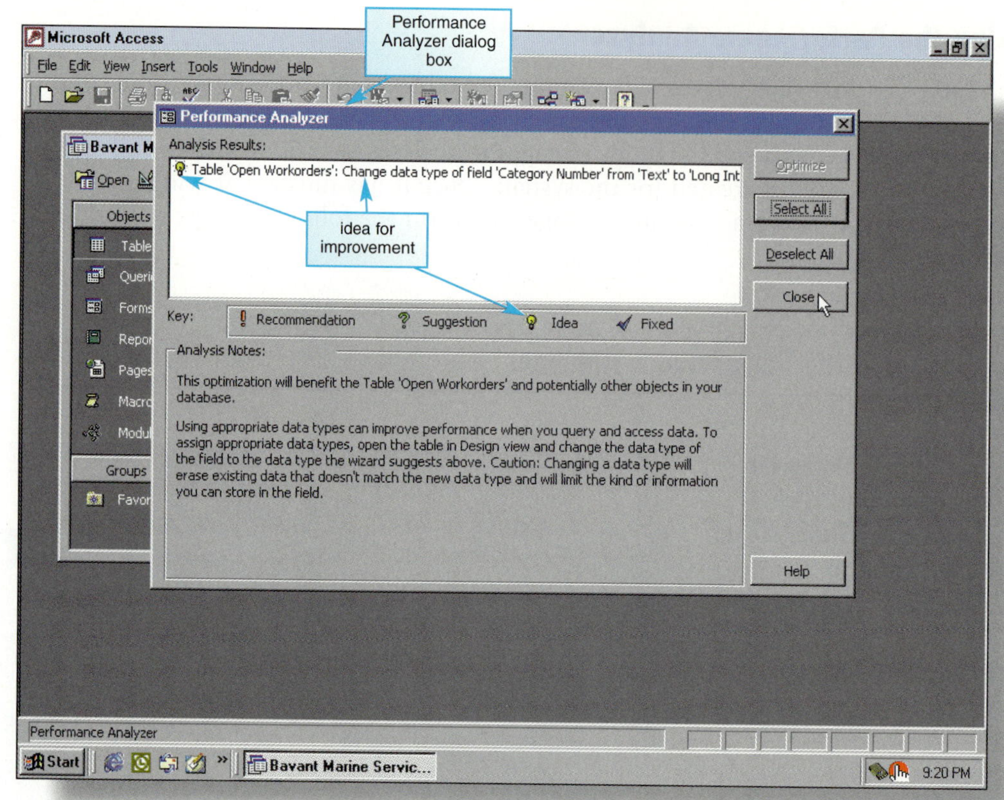

FIGURE 9-11

Click the Close button.

1. Click the Analyze button arrow on the Database window toolbar, click Analyze Performance

At this point, you can decide whether to follow the advice given by the Performance Analyzer. Because the Category Number field is used to relate tables (Category and Open Workorders), you cannot make the suggested change.

You also may decide to make a change to improve performance even though the Performance Analyzer did not indicate the change. If you have a query that is processing a large amount of data and the query is sorted on a particular field, you probably will want an index built on that field. If one does not already exist, you should create it.

Data Types

Access provides several data types. In some cases, more than one data type might be appropriate. To select the best choice for your particular circumstance, you need to know the advantages and disadvantages associated with each of the possibilities. For more information, visit the Access 2000 More About page (www.scsite.com/ac2000/more.htm) and click Data Types.

Using the Documenter

The Documenter allows you to produce detailed documentation of the various tables, queries, forms, reports, and other objects in your database. Figure 9-12 shows a portion of the documentation for the Marina table. The complete documentation is much more lengthy than shown in the figure. In the actual documentation, all fields would have as much information displayed as the Marina Number field. In this documentation, only those items of interest are shown for the other fields.

Notice the documentation of the Phone Number includes the input mask. Notice also the documentation of the Marina Type field contains the default value, the description, and the row source associated with the Lookup information for the field. The documentation for both the Marina Type and Warranty fields contain validation rules and validation text.

The following steps use the Documenter to produce documentation for the Marina table.

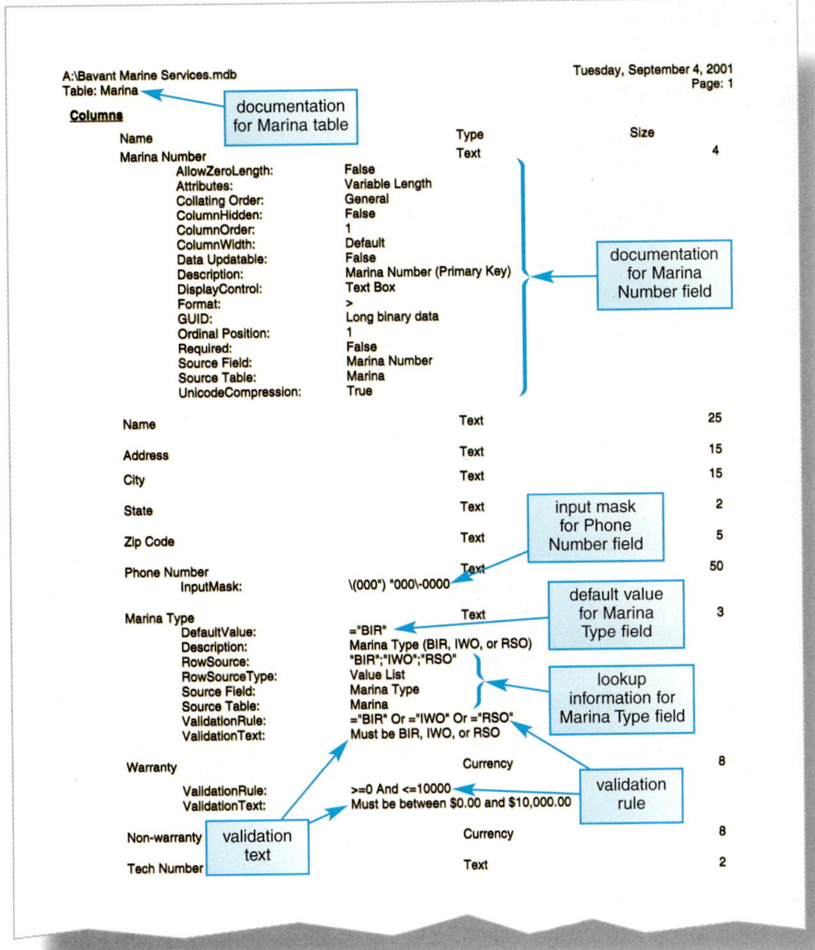

A:\Bavant Marine Services.mdb — Tuesday, September 4, 2001
Table: Marina — Page: 1

Columns

Name		Type	Size
Marina Number		Text	4
AllowZeroLength:	False		
Attributes:	Variable Length		
Collating Order:	General		
ColumnHidden:	False		
ColumnOrder:	1		
ColumnWidth:	Default		
Data Updatable:	False		
Description:	Marina Number (Primary Key)		
DisplayControl:	Text Box		
Format:	>		
GUID:	Long binary data		
Ordinal Position:	1		
Required:	False		
Source Field:	Marina Number		
Source Table:	Marina		
UnicodeCompression:	True		
Name		Text	25
Address		Text	15
City		Text	15
State		Text	2
Zip Code		Text	5
Phone Number		Text	50
InputMask:	\(000") "000\-0000		
Marina Type		Text	3
DefaultValue:	="BIR"		
Description:	Marina Type (BIR, IWO, or RSO)		
RowSource:	"BIR";"IWO";"RSO"		
RowSourceType:	Value List		
Source Field:	Marina Type		
Source Table:	Marina		
ValidationRule:	="BIR" Or ="IWO" Or ="RSO"		
ValidationText:	Must be BIR, IWO, or RSO		
Warranty		Currency	8
ValidationRule:	>=0 And <=10000		
ValidationText:	Must be between $0.00 and $10,000.00		
Non-warranty		Currency	8
Tech Number		Text	2

FIGURE 9-12

To Use the Documenter

1 Click Tools on the menu bar, click Analyze on the Tools menu, and then click Documenter. Click the Tables tab, click the Marina check box, and then point to the OK button.

The Documenter displays and the Marina table is selected (Figure 9-13).

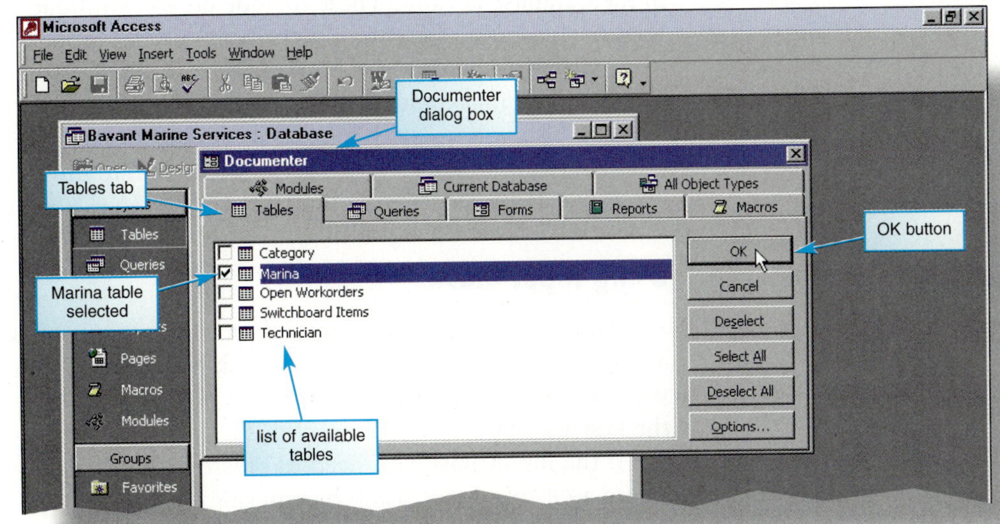

FIGURE 9-13

Click the OK button.

The documentation displays (Figure 9-14). (This may take a few minutes.) Your Object Definition window may display only a portion of the page. You can print the documentation by clicking the Print button. You also can save the documentation by using the Export command on the File menu.

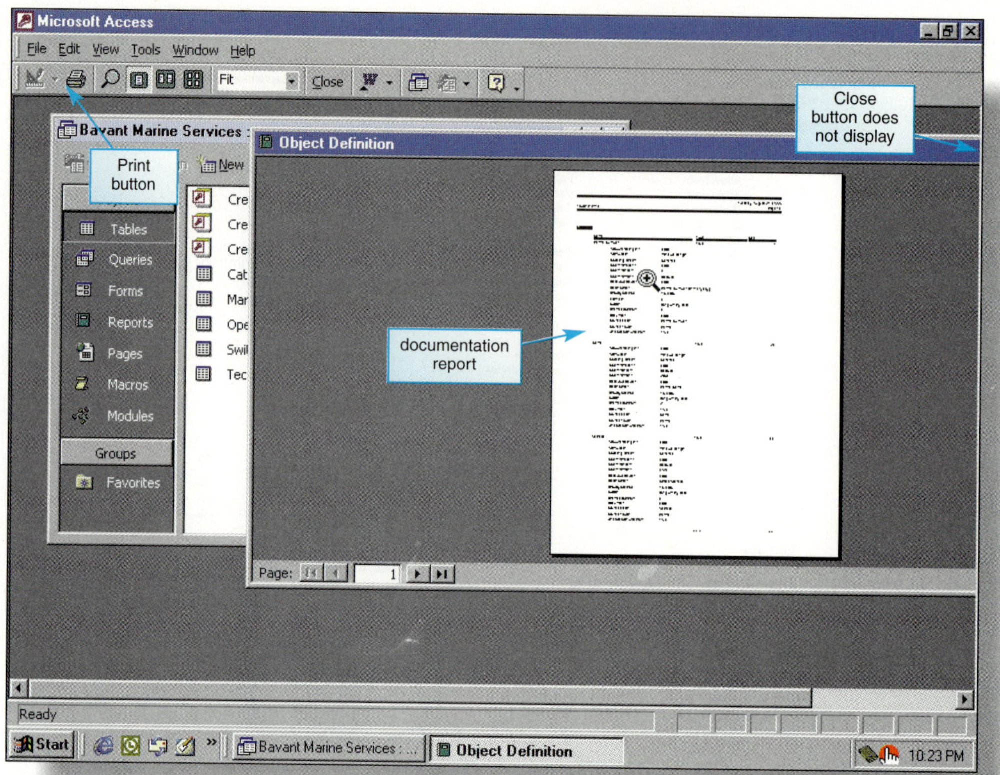

FIGURE 9-14

3 Click the Print button to print the documentation. Close the window by clicking its Close button. (If your window is in the position in Figure 9-14, drag the window to the left by dragging its Title bar. Once the Close button displays, click it.)

1. Click the Analyze button arrow on the Database window toolbar, click Documenter

Integrity and Security Features

You have used several integrity features already, that is, features to ensure the data in the database is valid. These include creating validation rules and text, specifying relationships and referential integrity, using the Input Mask Wizard to create an input mask, and creating a Lookup Wizard field. In this section, you will create a custom input mask and also specify properties associated with referential integrity.

You also will use several security features, that is features that protect the database from unauthorized use. In this section, you will set startup options, set a password, and encrypt a database.

Using Input Masks

An input mask specifies how data is to be entered and how it will display. You already may have used the Input Mask Wizard to create an input mask. Using the wizard, you can select the input mask that meets your needs from a list. This is often the best way to create the input mask.

If the input mask you need to create is not similar to any in the list, you can create a custom input mask by entering the appropriate characters as the value for the Input Mask property. Use the symbols from Table 9-1.

For example, to indicate that marina numbers must consist of two letters followed by two numbers, you would enter LL99. The Ls in the first two positions indicate that the first two positions must be letters. Using L instead of a question mark indicates that the users must enter these letters; that is, they are not optional. With the question mark, they could leave these positions blank. Using 9 rather than 0 indicates that they could leave these positions blank; that is, they are optional. Finally, to ensure that any letters entered are converted to uppercase, you would use the > symbol at the beginning of the input mask. The complete input mask would be >LL99.

Perform the following steps to enter an input mask for the Marina Number field.

Table 9-1 Input Mask Symbols

SYMBOL	TYPE OF DATA ACCEPTED	DATA ENTRY OPTIONAL
0	Digit (0 through 9) without plus (+) or minus (-) sign. Positions left blank display as zeros.	No
9	Digit or space without plus (+) or minus (-) sign. Positions left blank display as spaces.	Yes
#	Digit or space with plus (+) or minus (-) sign. Positions left blank display as spaces.	Yes
L	Letter (A through Z).	No
?	Letter (A through Z).	Yes
A	Letter or digit.	No
a	Letter or digit.	Yes
&	Any character or a space.	No
C	Any character or a space.	Yes
<	Converts any letters entered to lowercase.	Does not apply
>	Converts any letters entered to uppercase.	Does not apply
!	Characters typed in the input mask fill it from left to right.	Does not apply
\	Character following the slash is treated as a literal in the input mask.	Does not apply

To Use an Input Mask

1. **Click the Tables object, if necessary, to be sure the tables display. Right-click Marina and then click Design View on the shortcut menu. Maximize the window.**

2. **With the Marina Number field selected, click the Input Mask property and then type** >LL99 **as the value (Figure 9-15).**

3. **Close the window containing the design by clicking its Close button. When prompted to save the changes, click the Yes button.**

The changes are saved.

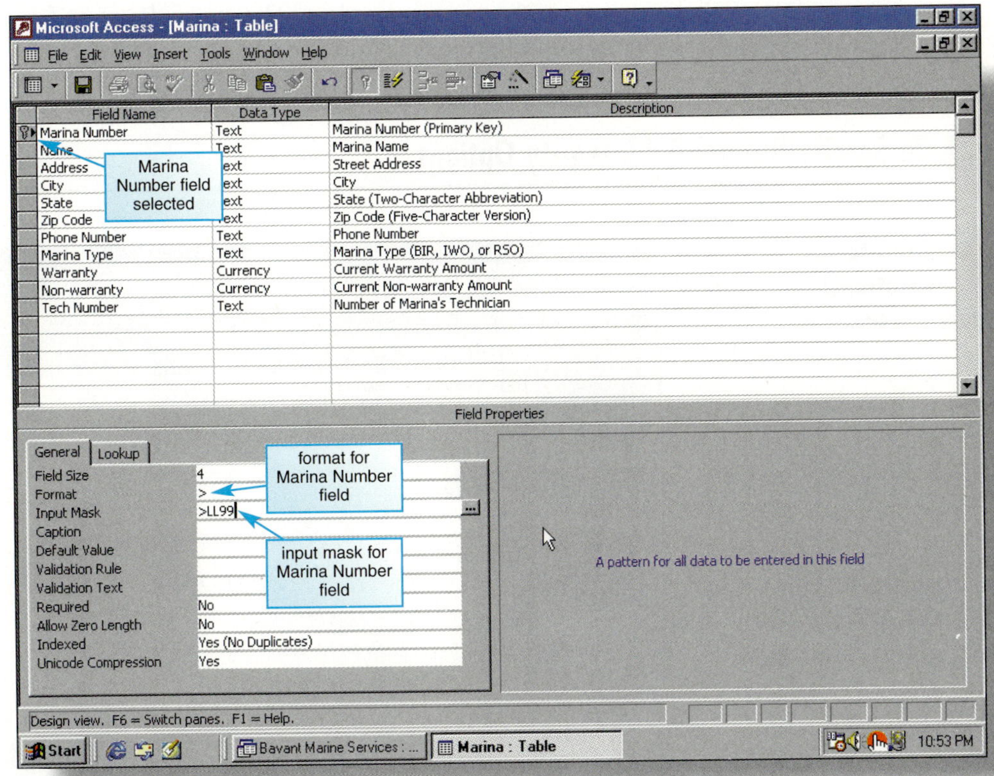

FIGURE 9-15

From this point on, anyone entering a marina number will be restricted to letters in the first two positions and numeric digits in the last two. Any letters entered in the first two positions will be converted to uppercase.

In Figure 9-15 on the previous page, the Marina Number field has both a custom input mask and a format. Technically, you do not need both. When the same field has both an input mask and a format, the format takes precedence. Because the format specified for the Marina Number field is the same as the input mask (uppercase), it will not affect the data.

More About 2000

Referential Integrity

Referential integrity is an essential property for databases, but providing support for it proved to be one of the most difficult tasks facing the developers of relational database management systems. For more information, visit the Access 2000 More About page (www.scsite.com/ac2000/more.htm) and click Referential Integrity.

Specifying Referential Integrity Options

The property that ensures that the value in a foreign key must match that of another table's primary key is called referential integrity. When specifying referential integrity, there are two ways to handle deletion. In the relationship between marinas and open workorders, deletion of a marina for which open workorders exist, such as marina EL25, would violate referential integrity. Any open workorders for marina EL25 would no longer relate to any marina in the database. The normal way to avoid this problem is to prohibit such a deletion. The other option is to **cascade the delete**, that is, have Access allow the deletion but then automatically delete any workorders related to the deleted marina.

There also are two ways to handle update of the primary key. In the relationship between categories and open workorders, changing the category number for category 1 in the Category table from 1 to 11 would cause a problem. There are open workorders on which the category number is 1. These workorders no longer would relate to any existing category. The normal way of avoiding the problem is to prohibit this type of update. The other option is to **cascade the update**; that is, have Access allow the update but then make the corresponding change on any workorder on which the category number was 1 automatically.

The following steps specify cascade the delete for the relationship between marinas and open workorders. The steps also specify cascade the update for the relationship between categories and open workorders.

To Specify Referential Integrity Options

1 **Point to the Relationships button (Figure 9-16).**

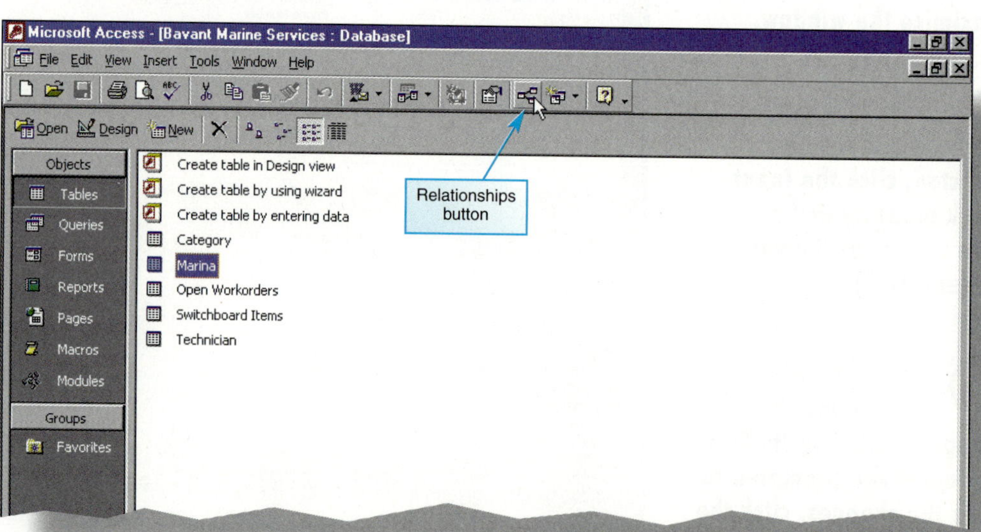

FIGURE 9-16

2 **Click the Relationships button. (If the Relationships window displays a table named Category_1, right-click the line joining Category_1 and Open Workorders and click Delete on the shortcut menu. Click Yes to permanently delete the relationship from the database. Right-click the Category_1 table and then click Hide Table on the shortcut menu). Right-click the line joining the Marina and Open Workorders tables and then point to Edit Relationship on the shortcut menu.**

The relationship between Marina and Workorders is selected (Figure 9-17).

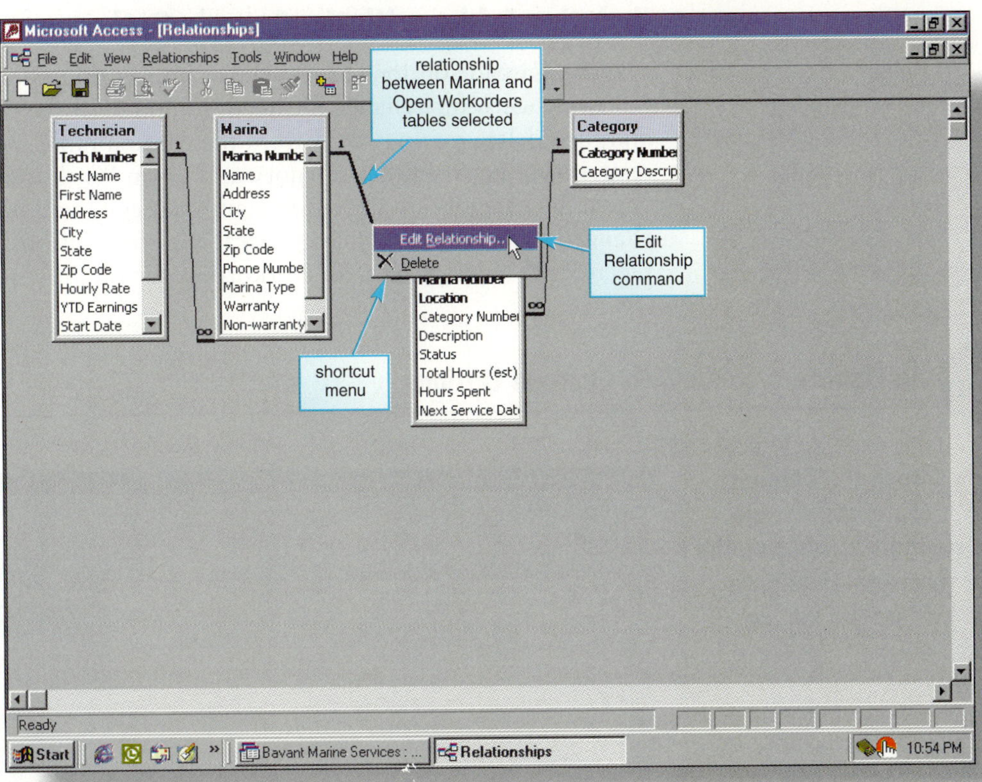

FIGURE 9-17

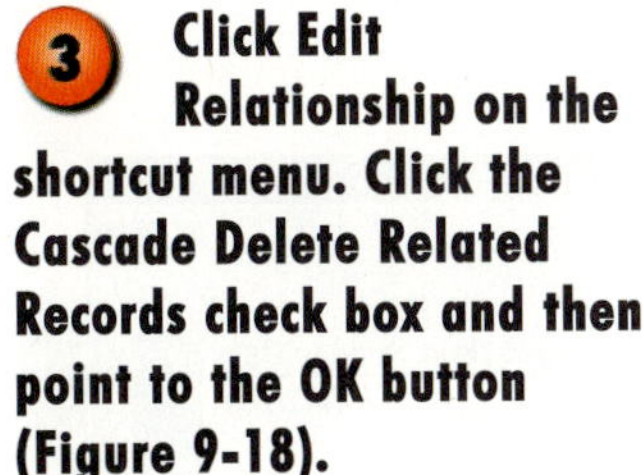

3 **Click Edit Relationship on the shortcut menu. Click the Cascade Delete Related Records check box and then point to the OK button (Figure 9-18).**

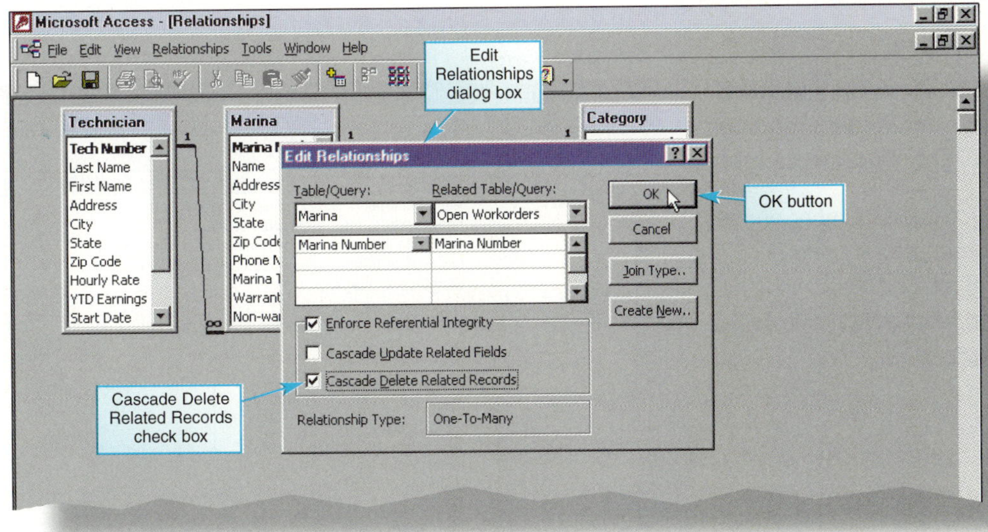

FIGURE 9-18

4 **Click the OK button.**

5 **Right-click the line joining the Category and Open Workorders tables, click Edit Relationship on the shortcut menu, click the Cascade Update Related Records check box, and then click the OK button.**

6 **Click the Close Window button for the Relationships window. Click Yes to save the changes.**

The relationships are saved.

Updating Tables with the Cascade Options

The Cascade options have a direct impact on updates to the database. The following steps first change a category number in the Category table from 1 to 11 and then delete marina EL25 from the Marina table. Because updates cascade in the relationship between the Category and Open Workorders tables, all workorders on which the category number was 1 automatically will have the category number changed to 11. Because deletes cascade in the relationship between the Marina and Open Workorders tables, all workorders for EL25 will be deleted.

To Update a Table with Cascade Options

1 Open the Category table and change the category number on the first record to 11 (Figure 9-19). Press the TAB key twice.

The change is made. Because the relationship between the Category and Open Workorders tables now allows for cascading the update, no error message displays.

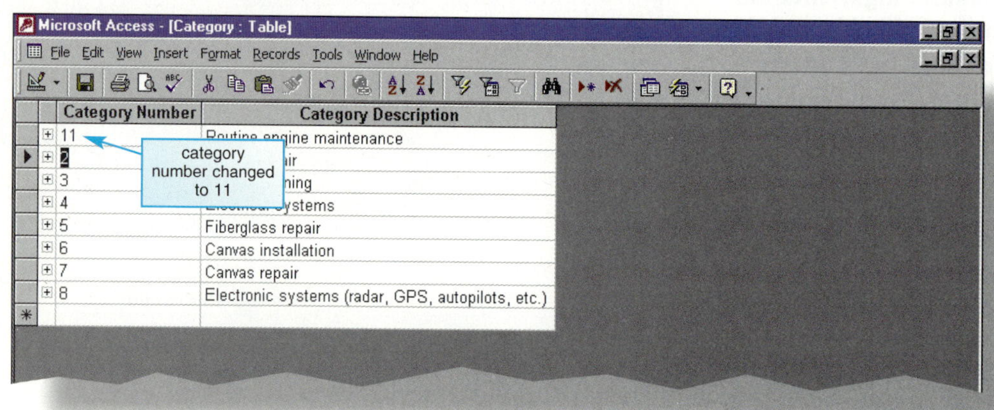

FIGURE 9-19

2 Close the Category table and then open the Open Workorders table.

The category number on the workorder for marina BL72, location 129 has been changed automatically to 11 (Figure 9-20).

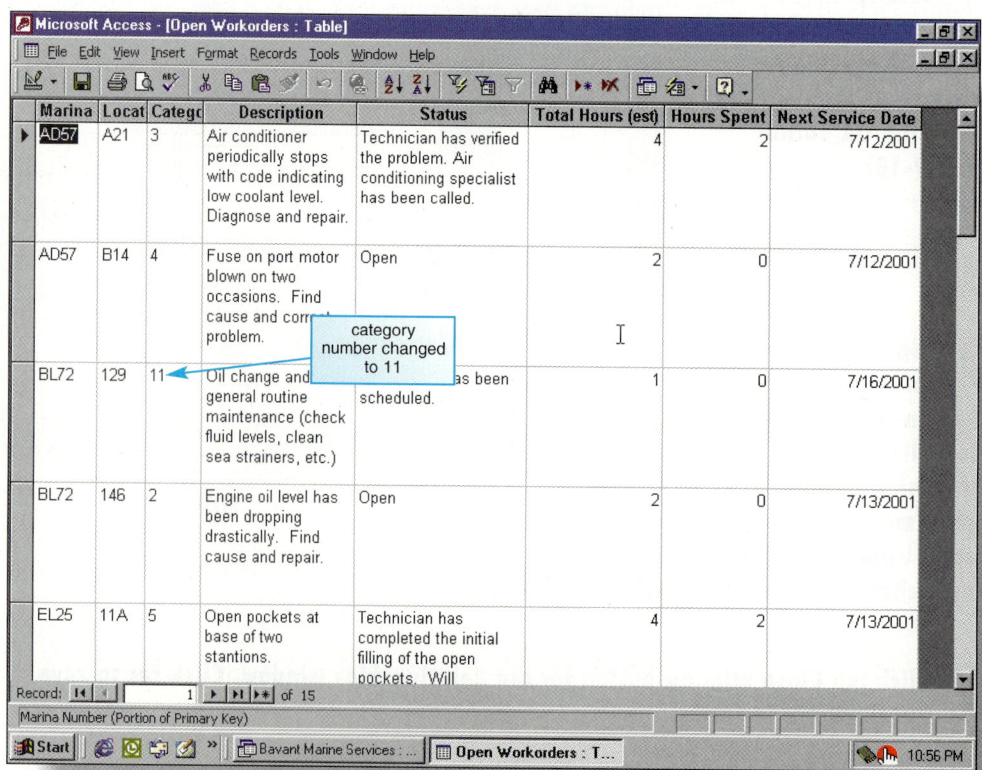

FIGURE 9-20

3 **Close the Open Workorders table. Open the Marina table and then click the record selector for marina EL25.**

Marina EL25 is selected (Figure 9-21).

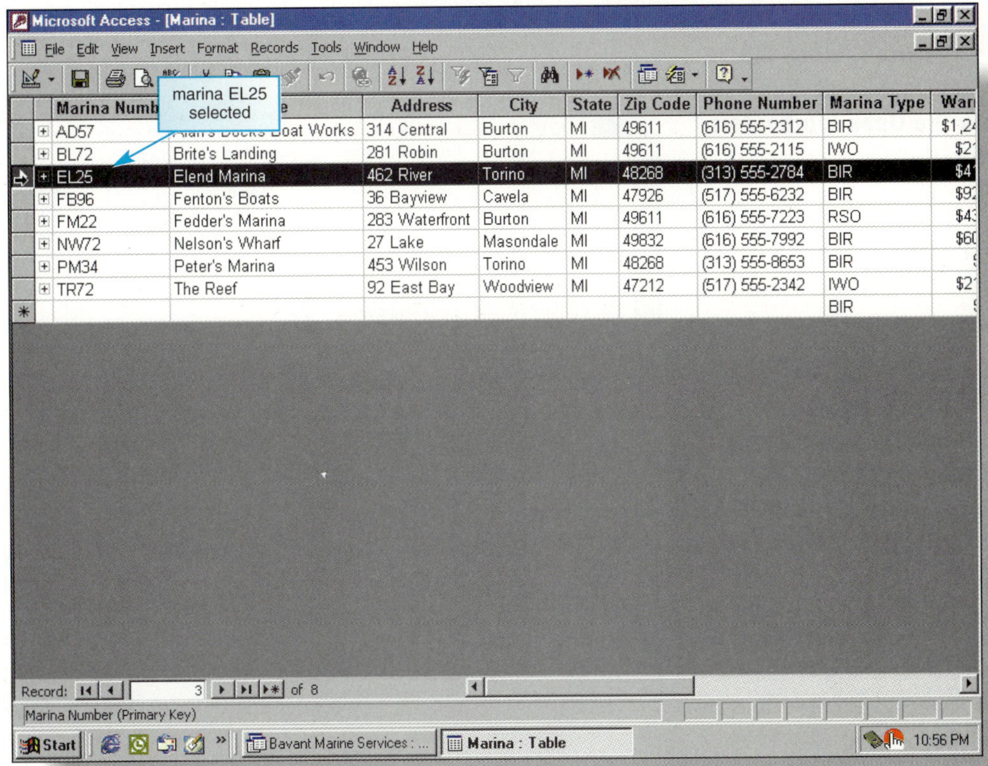

FIGURE 9-21

4 **Press the DELETE key to delete marina EL25 and then point to the Yes button.**

The Microsoft Access dialog box displays (Figure 9-22). It indicates that a record in a related table also will be deleted.

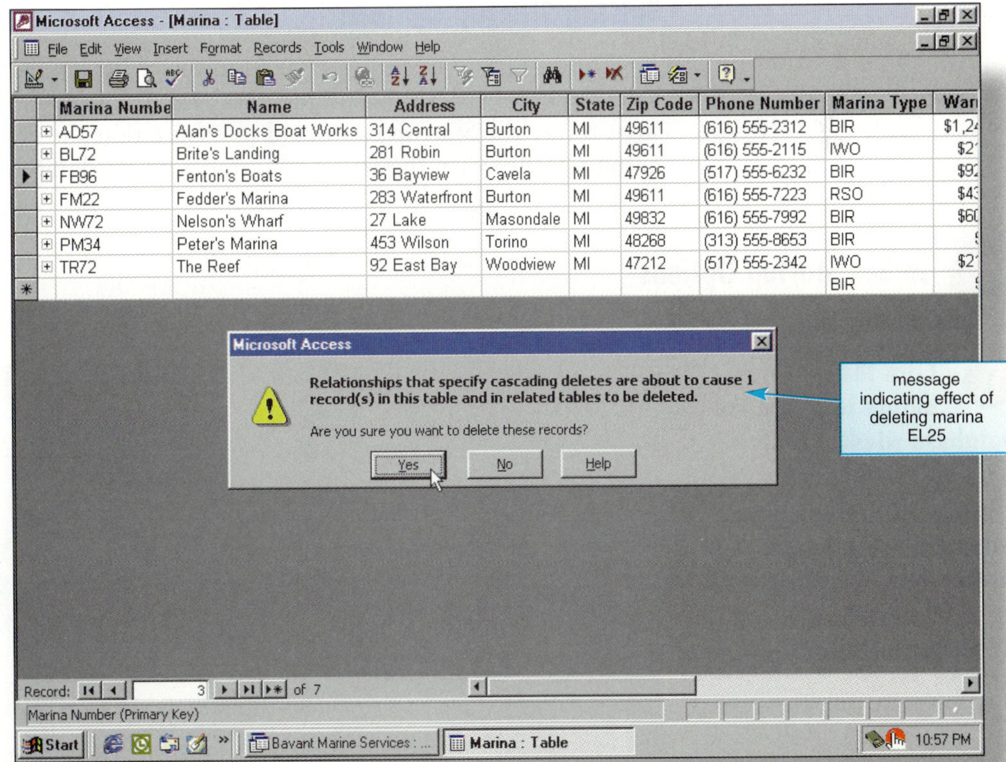

FIGURE 9-22

5 **Click the Yes button. Close the Marina table and then open the Open Workorders table.**

The workorder for marina EL25 (see Figure 9-20) has been deleted (Figure 9-23).

6 **Close the Open Workorders table by clicking the Close Window button.**

The table no longer displays.

Microsoft Access - [Open Workorders : Table]

Marina	Locat	Catego	Description	Status	Total Hours (est)	Hours Spent	Next Service Date
AD57	A21	3	Air conditioner periodically stops with code indicating low coolant level. Diagnose and repair.	Technician has verified the problem. Air conditioning specialist has been called.	4	2	7/12/2001
AD57	B14	4	Fuse on port motor blown on two occasions. Find cause and correct problem.	Open	2	0	7/12/2001
BL72	129	11	Oil change and general routine maintenance (check fluid levels, clean sea strainers, etc.)	Service call has been scheduled.	1	0	7/16/2001
BL72	146	2	Engine oil level has been dropping drastically. Find ...	Open	2	0	7/13/2001
FB96	79	2	H... operating correctly.	Technician has determined that the exchanger is faulty. New exchanger has	4	1	7/17/2001

workorder for marina EL25 deleted

FIGURE 9-23

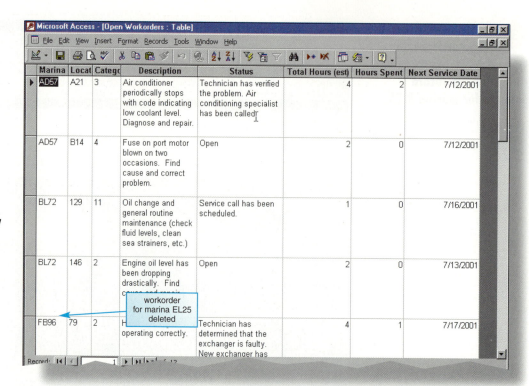

Setting Startup Options

You can use the Startup command to set **startup options**, that is, actions that will be taken automatically when the database first is opened. Perform the following steps to use the Startup command to ensure that the switchboard displays automatically when the Bavant Marine Services database is opened.

To Set Startup Options

1 **Click the Restore button to return the Database window to its original size, if necessary. Click Tools on the menu bar and then point to Startup (Figure 9-24).**

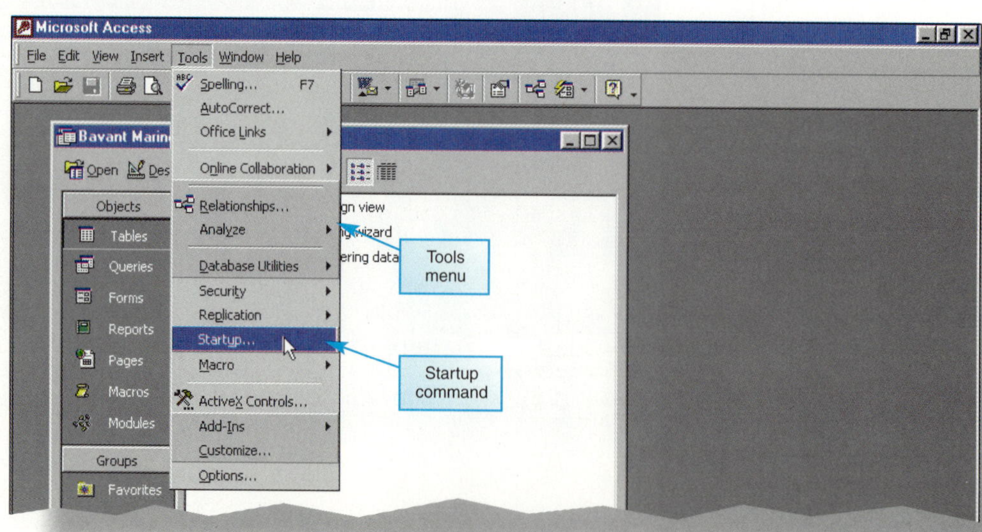

FIGURE 9-24

2 **Click Startup, click the Display Form/Page box arrow, and then point to Switchboard.**

The Startup dialog box displays (Figure 9-25). The list of available forms displays. Your list may be sorted in a different order.

3 **Click Switchboard and then click the OK button.**

The switchboard now will display whenever the database is opened.

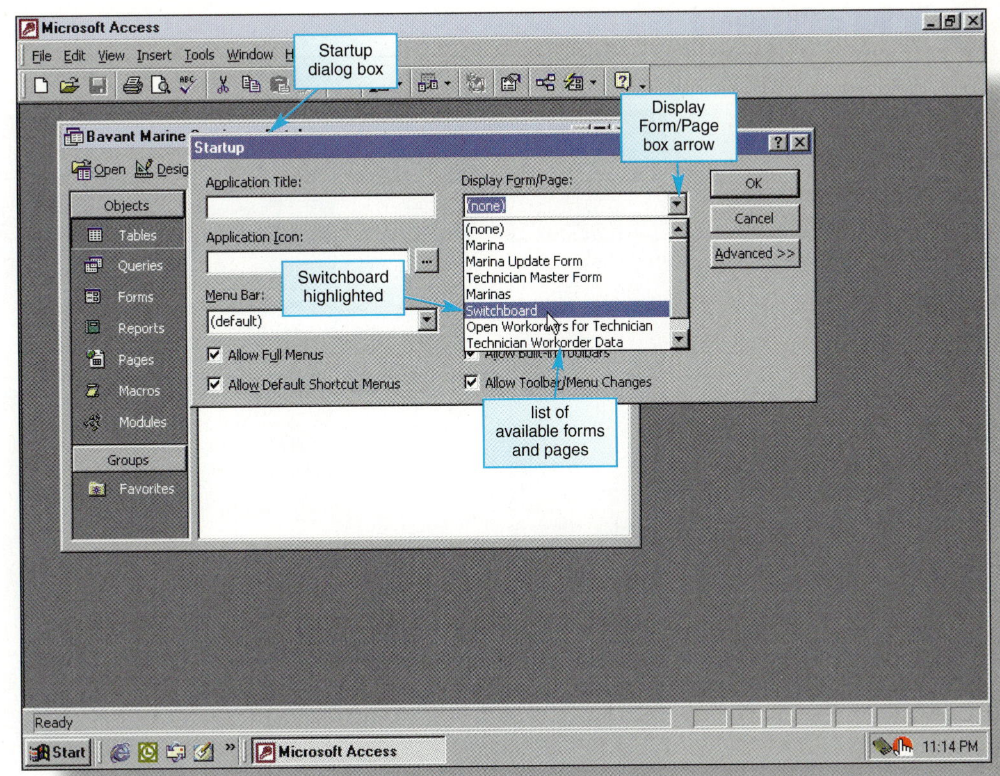

FIGURE 9-25

Setting Passwords

If you set a database password, users must enter the password before they can open the database. The password is stored as part of the database so if you lose or forget your password, you cannot open the database. Database passwords are case-sensitive.

In order to set a password, the database must be open in exclusive mode. The following steps open the Holton Clinic database in exclusive mode in preparation for setting a password.

Passwords

It is possible to set different passwords for different users. In addition, each password can be associated with a different set of privileges concerning accessing the database. For more information concerning this use of passwords, visit the Access 2000 More About page (www.scsite.com/ac2000/more.htm) and click Passwords.

TO OPEN A DATABASE IN EXCLUSIVE MODE

1. Close the Bavant Marine Services : Database window.
2. Click the Open button on the Database toolbar.
3. If necessary, click 3½ Floppy (A:) in the Look in box. Make sure the Holton Clinic database is selected.
4. Click the Open button arrow (not the button itself). Click Open Exclusive in the menu that displays.

The database opens in exclusive mode and the Holton Clinic : Database window displays.

To Set a Password

1 Click Tools on the menu bar, click Security on the Tools menu, and then point to Set Database Password (Figure 9-26).

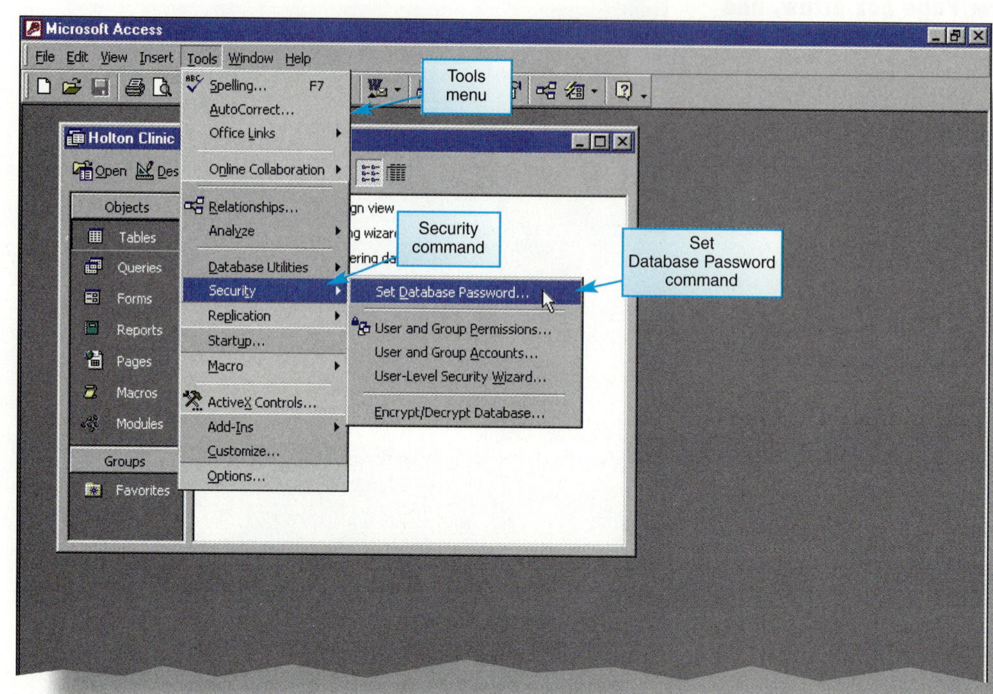

FIGURE 9-26

2 Click Set Database Password. Type your password in the Password box. Asterisks, not the actual characters, appear as you type your password. Press the TAB key and then type your password again in the Verify box. Point to the OK button.

The password is entered in both the Password box and the Verify box (Figure 9-27).

3 Click the OK button.

The password is changed.

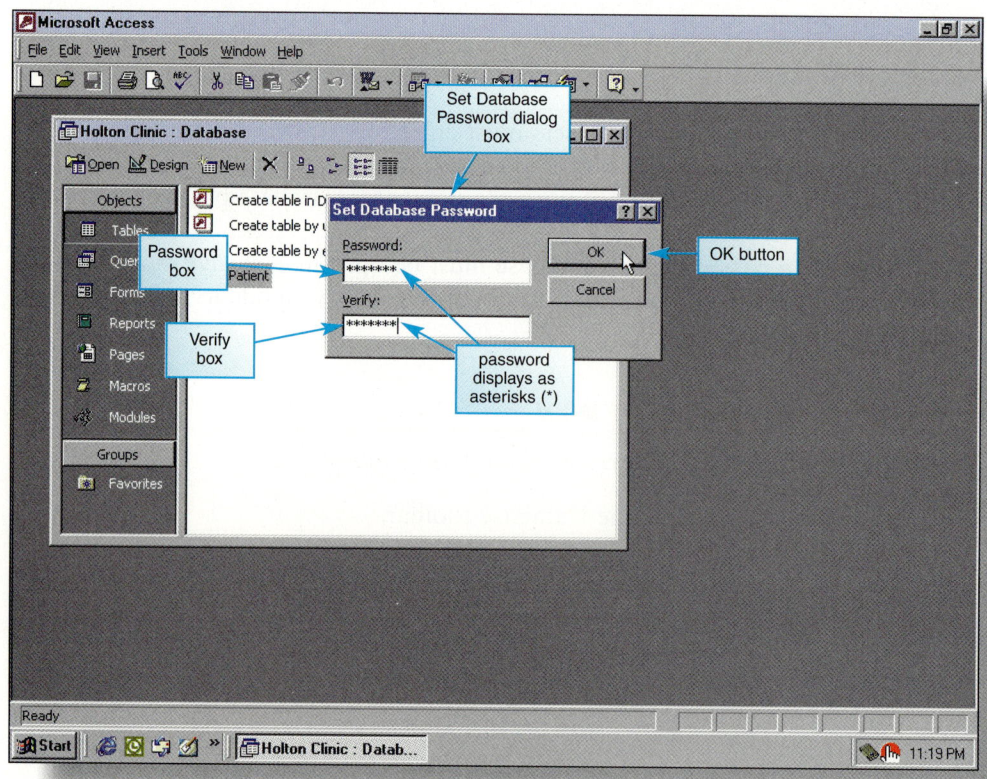

FIGURE 9-27

Now whenever a user opens the database, the user will be required to enter the password in the Password Required box (Figure 9-28).

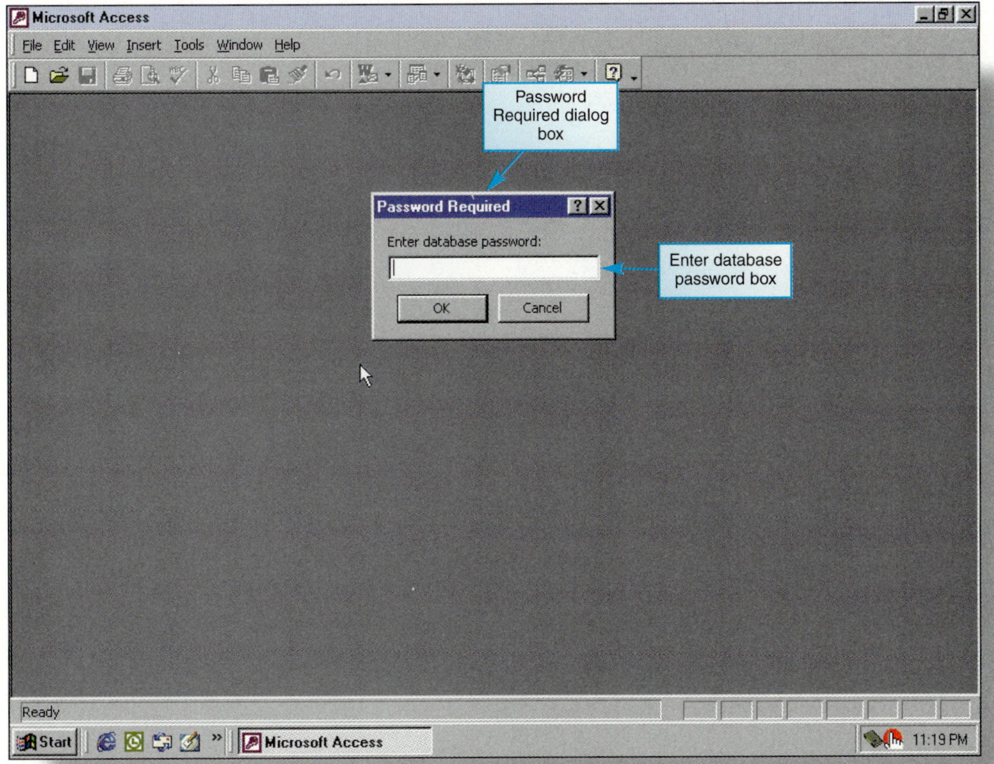

FIGURE 9-28

Encrypting a Database

Encryption refers to the storing of the data in the database in an encrypted (encoded) format. Any time a user stores or modifies data in the database, the Database Management System (DBMS) will encrypt the data before actually updating the database. Before a legitimate user retrieves the data via the DBMS, the data will be decrypted. The whole encryption process is transparent to a legitimate user, he or she is not even aware it is happening. If an unauthorized user attempts to bypass all the controls of the DBMS and get to the database through a utility program or a word processor, however, he or she will be able to see only the encrypted, and unreadable, version of the data.

In order to encrypt/decrypt a database, the database must be closed. Use the steps on the next page to encrypt a database using the Encrypt/Decrypt Database command.

Encryption

The encryption process requires Access to make an additional copy of the database, the encrypted version. Once the process is complete, the original will be deleted. During the process, however, there must be sufficient disk space available for both versions of the database. If there is not, the process will fail.

To Encrypt a Database

1 **Close the database by clicking the Holton Clinic : Database window Close button. Click Tools on the menu bar, click Security on the Tools menu, and then point to Encrypt/Decrypt Database (Figure 9-29).**

2 **Click Encrypt/ Decrypt Database. If necessary, select 3½ Floppy (A:) in the Look in box. Select the Holton Clinic database, click OK, enter your password, and then click the OK button for the Password Required dialog box. Type** `Holton Clinic Enc` **as the file name in the File name box and then click the Save button.**

The database is encrypted and called Holton Clinic Enc.

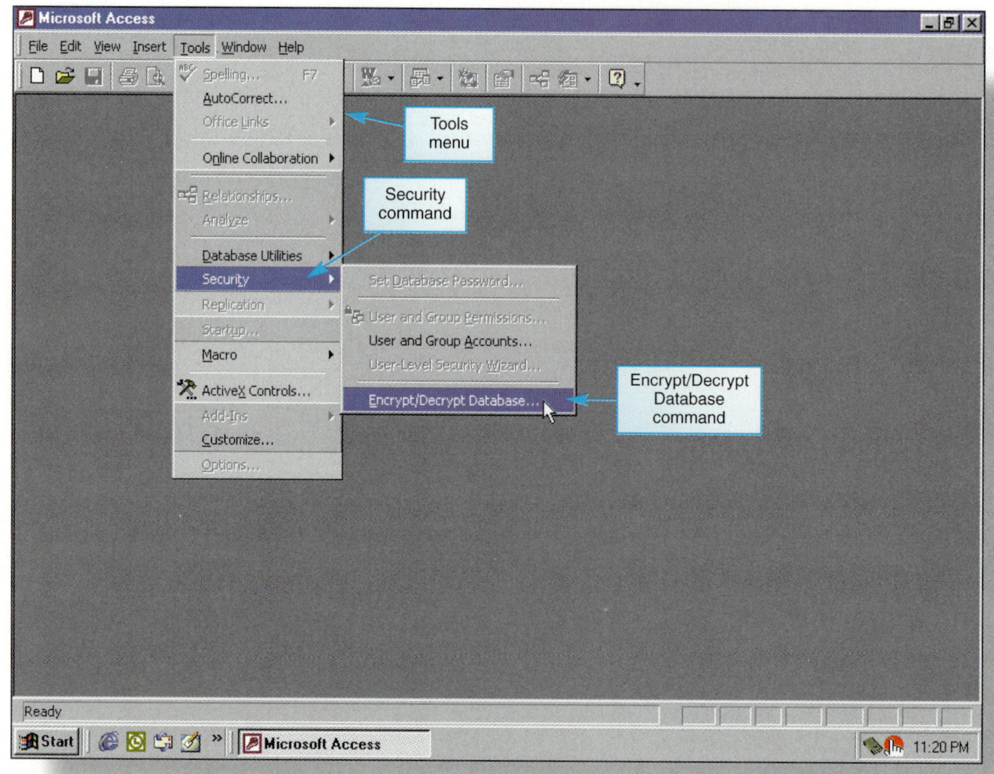

FIGURE 9-29

Removing a Password

If you no longer feel a password is necessary, you can remove it by using the Unset Database Password command as in the following steps.

To Remove a Password

1. **Open Holton Clinic in exclusive mode (see the steps on page A 9.21). Enter your password when requested.**

2. **Click Tools on the menu bar, click Security on the Tools menu, and then point to Unset Database Password (Figure 9-30).**

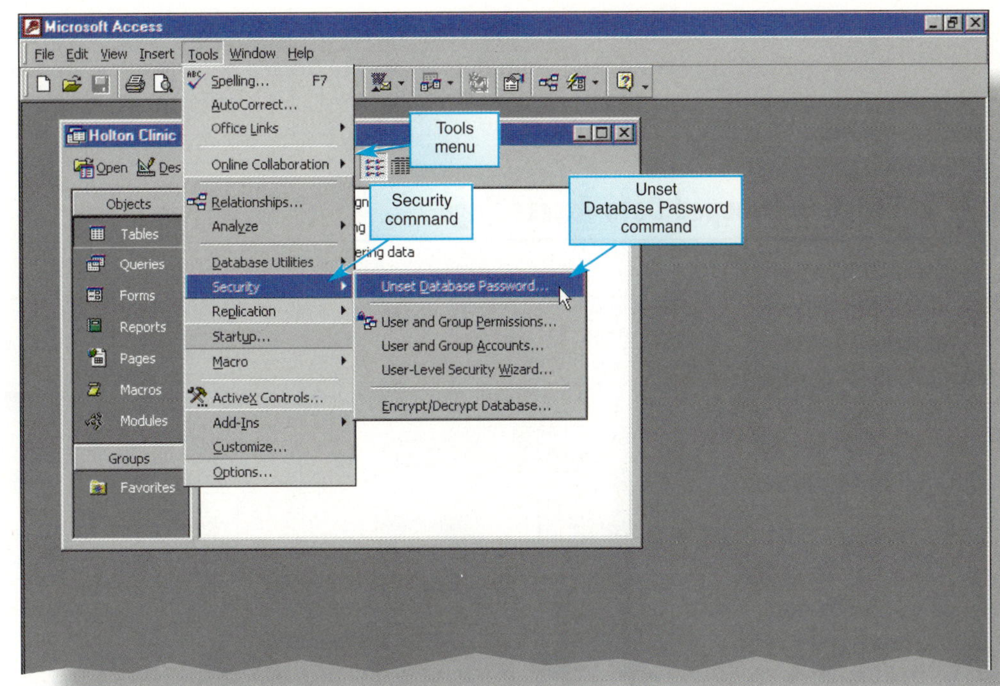

FIGURE 9-30

3. **Type the password and then point to the OK button.**

The Unset Database Password dialog box displays (Figure 9-31).

4. **Click the OK button.**

The password is removed.

5. **Close the Holton Clinic database.**

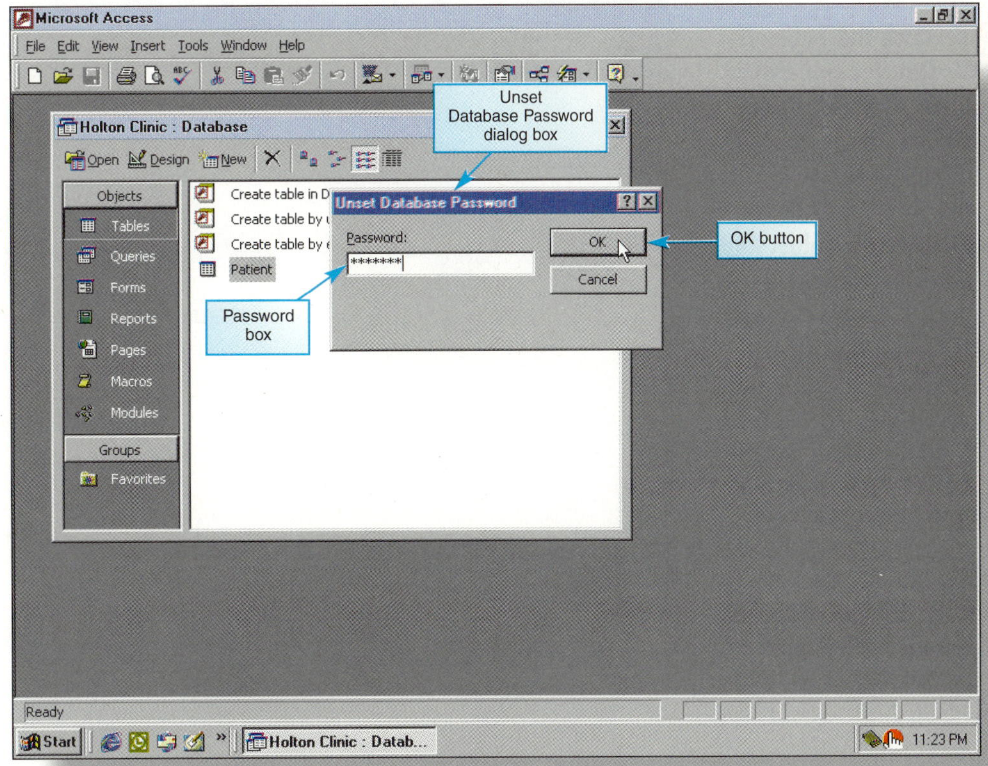

FIGURE 9-31

Creating a Grouped Data Access Page

Grouping means creating separate collections of records sharing some characteristics. You can group data in a data access page just as you can in a report. In the following steps, use the Page Wizard to identify the field to be used for grouping.

To Create a Grouped Data Access Page

1 Open the Bavant Marine Services database. When the Main Switchboard window displays, close it by clicking its Close button.

2 Click Pages on the Objects bar and maximize the Database window. Double-click Create data access page by using wizard.

3 Click the Tables/Queries box arrow and then click the Open Workorders table. Click the Add Field button to add the Marina Number field to the list of selected fields. Add the Location, Category Number, Total Hours (est), Hours Spent, and Next Service Date to the list of selected fields by clicking the field and then clicking the Add Field button. Point to the Next button.

The Marina Number, Location, Category Number, Total Hours (est), Hours Spent, and Next Service Date fields are selected (Figure 9-32).

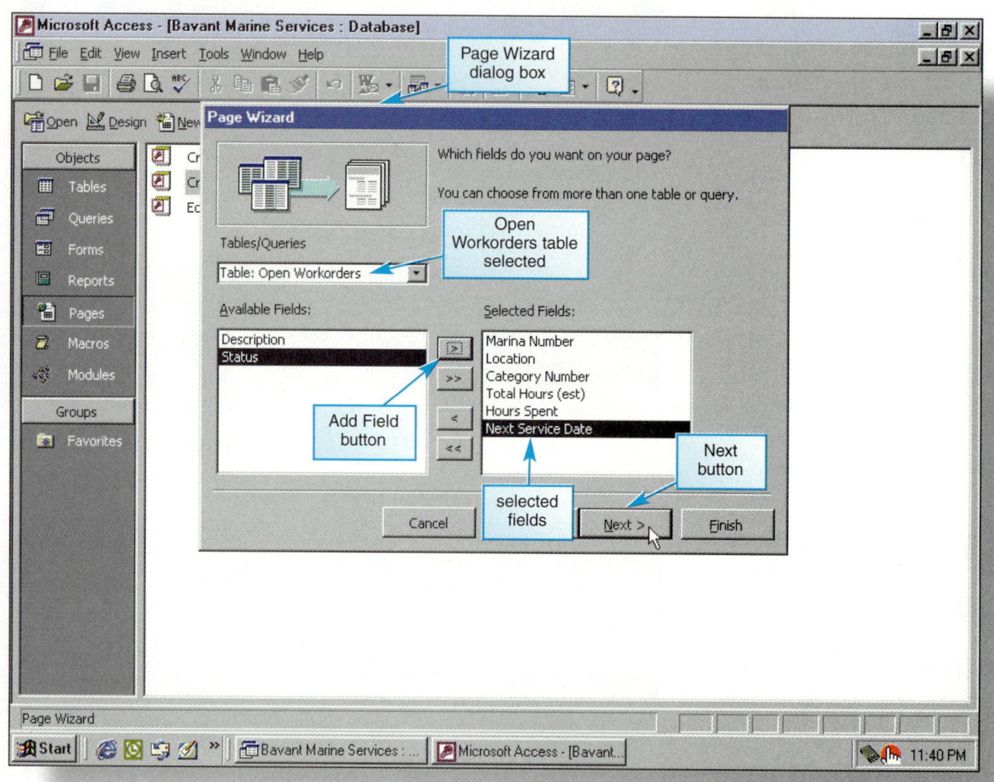

FIGURE 9-32

4 **Click the Next button and then point to the Next button.**

The Page Wizard dialog box displays, asking if you want to add grouping levels (Figure 9-33). The indicated grouping is by the Marina Number field, which is correct.

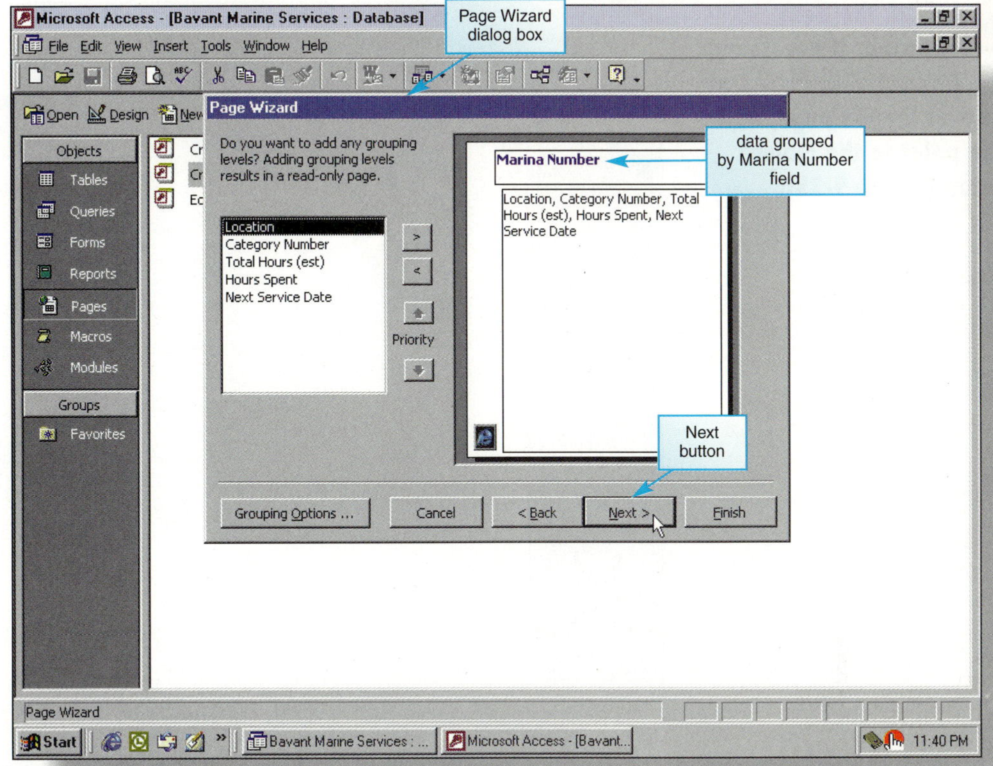

FIGURE 9-33

5 **Click the Next button. Click the 1 box arrow (the first sort box) and then select Location in the list. Point to the Next button.**

The Page Wizard dialog box displays (Figure 9-34). The Location field is selected as a sort key, meaning that the records within a group will be sorted by location.

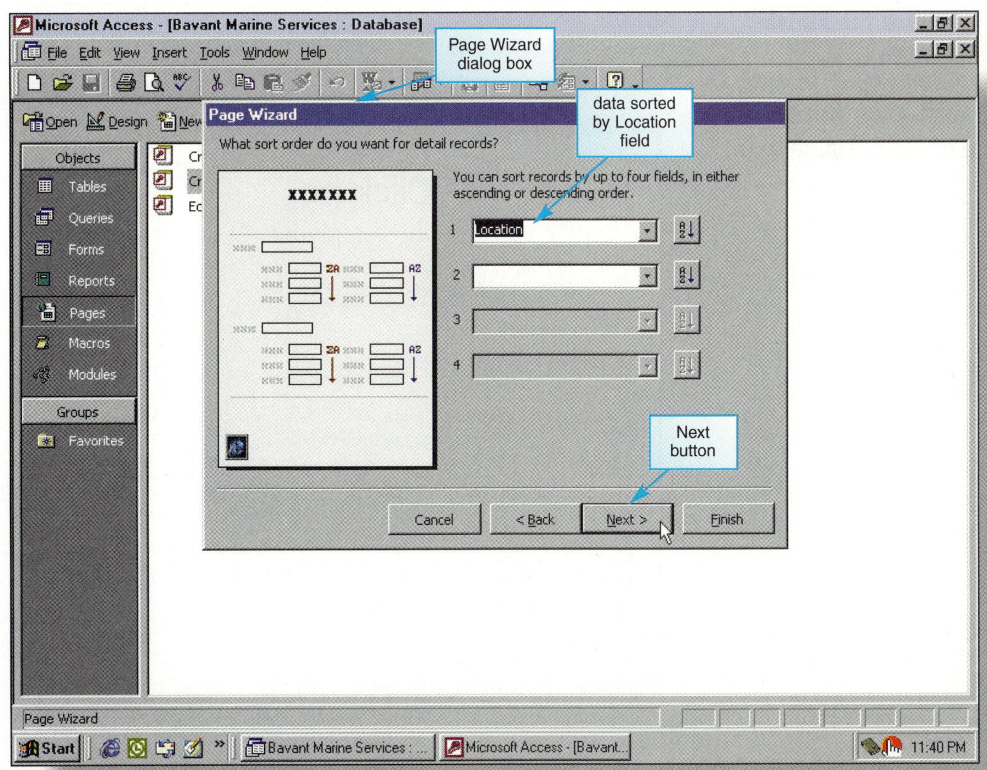

FIGURE 9-34

6 **Click the Next button. If necessary, type** `Open Workorders` **as the title for the page, and then point to the Finish button (Figure 9-35).**

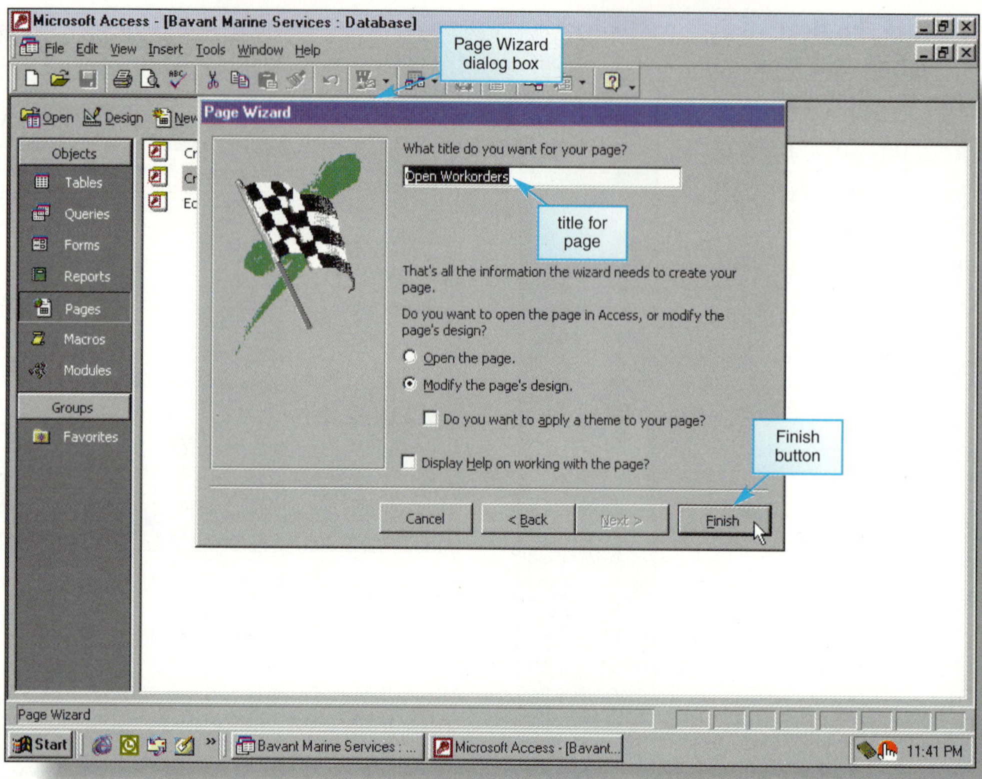

FIGURE 9-35

Click the Finish button.

The completed data access page displays (Figure 9-36).

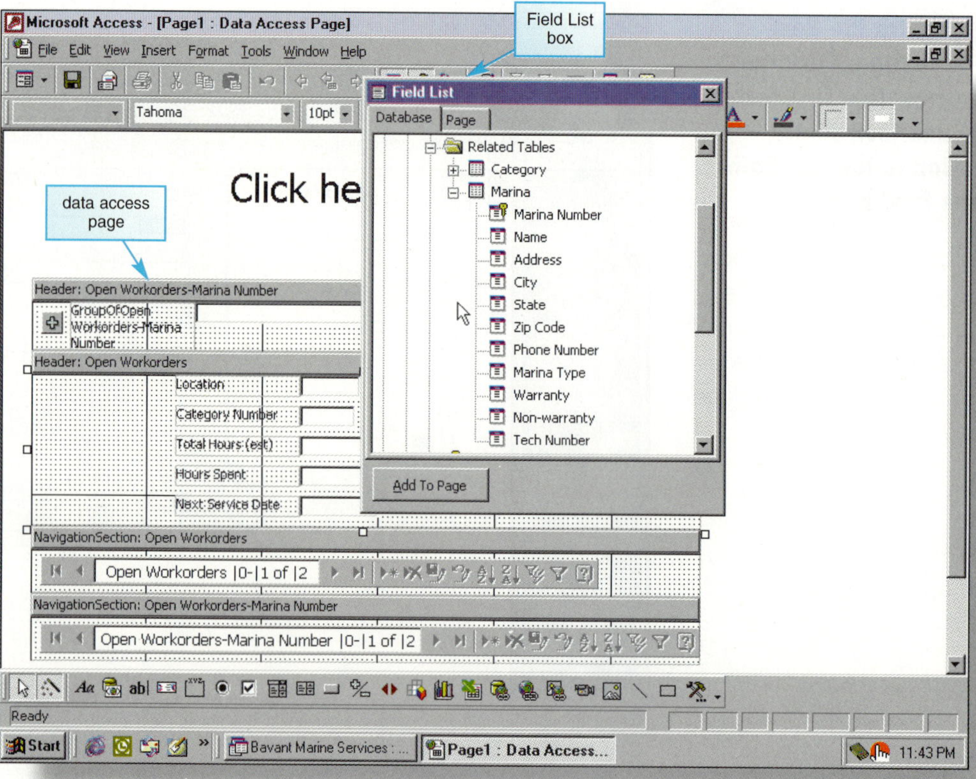

FIGURE 9-36

8 **If the Field List box displays, close it by clicking the Close button. Maximize the Page1 : Data Access Page window, if necessary. Click anywhere in the portion of the screen labeled Click here and type title text and then type** `Open Workorders by Marina` **as the title text. Point to the Close Window button.**

The title is changed (Figure 9-37).

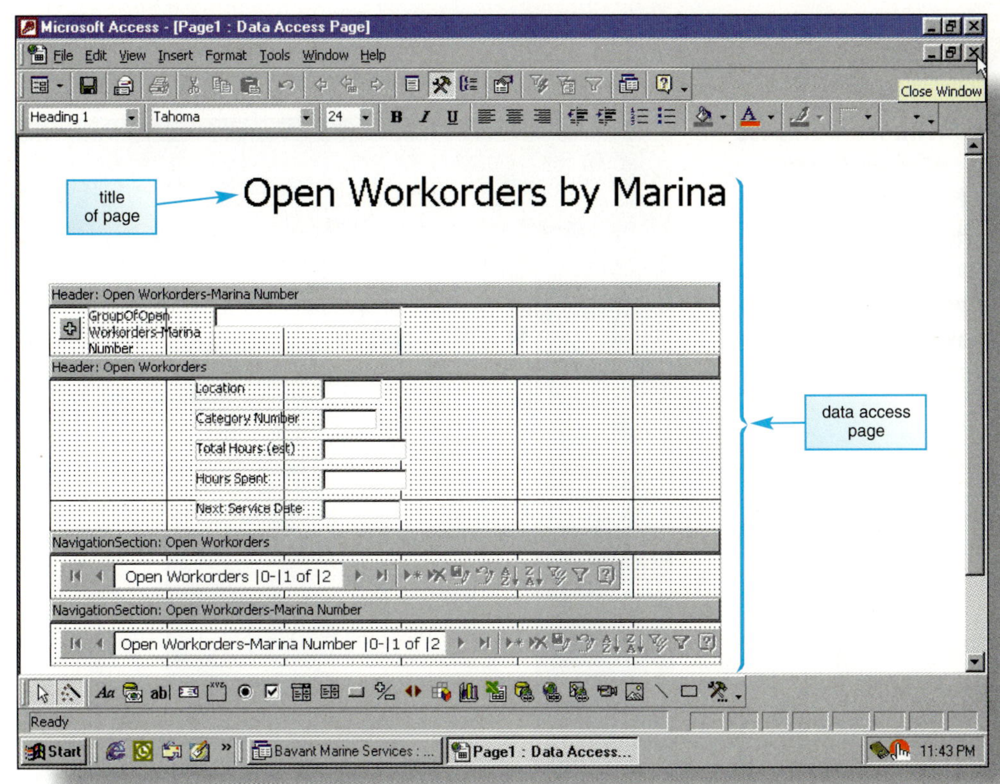

FIGURE 9-37

9 **Click the Close Window button. When asked if you want to save the changes, click the Yes button. Type** `Open Workorders by Marina` **as the name of the data access page and then click the Save button.**

The page is saved.

Other Ways

1. On Insert menu click Page
2. On Objects bar click Pages, click New

Previewing the Data Access Page

While in Access, you can preview what the page will look like in the browser by using Web Page Preview on the shortcut menu. Use the steps on the next page to preview the data access page that was just created.

To Preview the Data Access Page

1 With the Database window displaying, click Pages on the Objects bar, right-click Open Workorders by Marina, and then point to Web Page Preview on the shortcut menu (Figure 9-38).

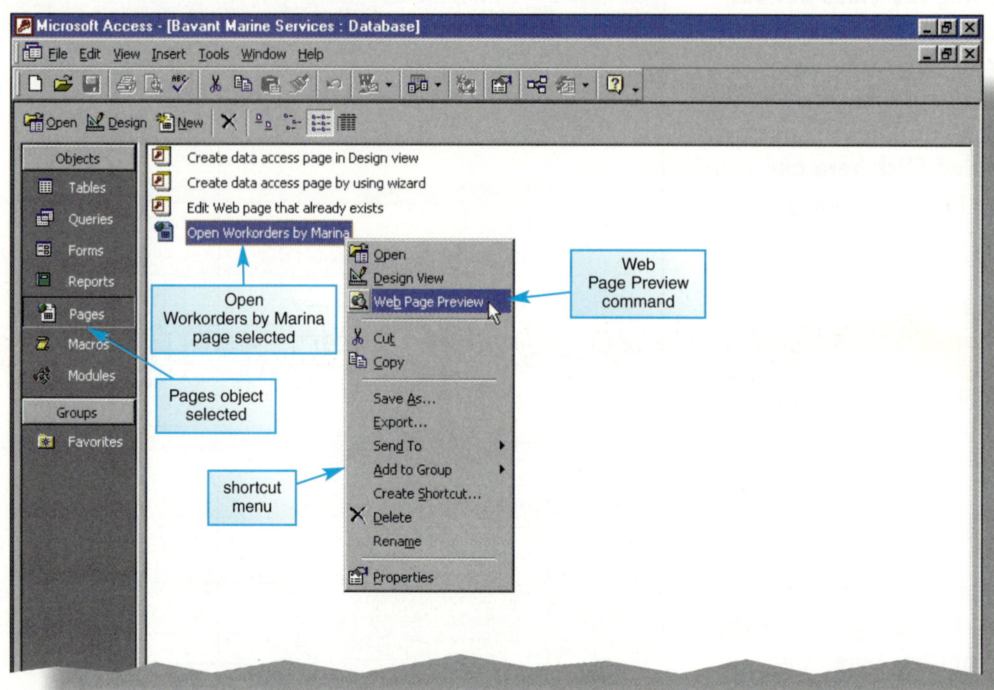

FIGURE 9-38

2 Click Web Page Preview.

The page displays within Microsoft Internet Explorer (Figure 9-39). You can click the GroupOfOpen Workorders-Marina Number button to display the workorders of marina AD57, one at a time. The plus symbol will change to a minus symbol.

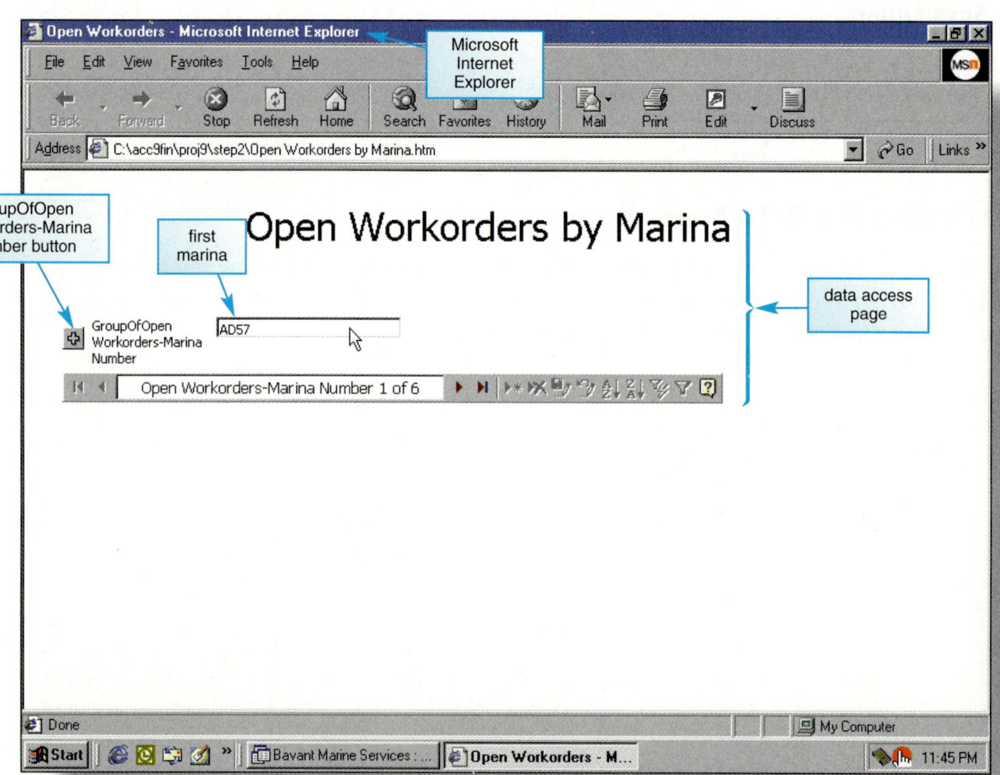

FIGURE 9-39

3 Click the GroupOfOpen Workorders-Marina Number button.

The first open workorder for marina AD57 displays (Figure 9-40). An extra navigation bar displays, indicating that this is the first of two workorders for the marina. The plus symbol changes to a minus symbol.

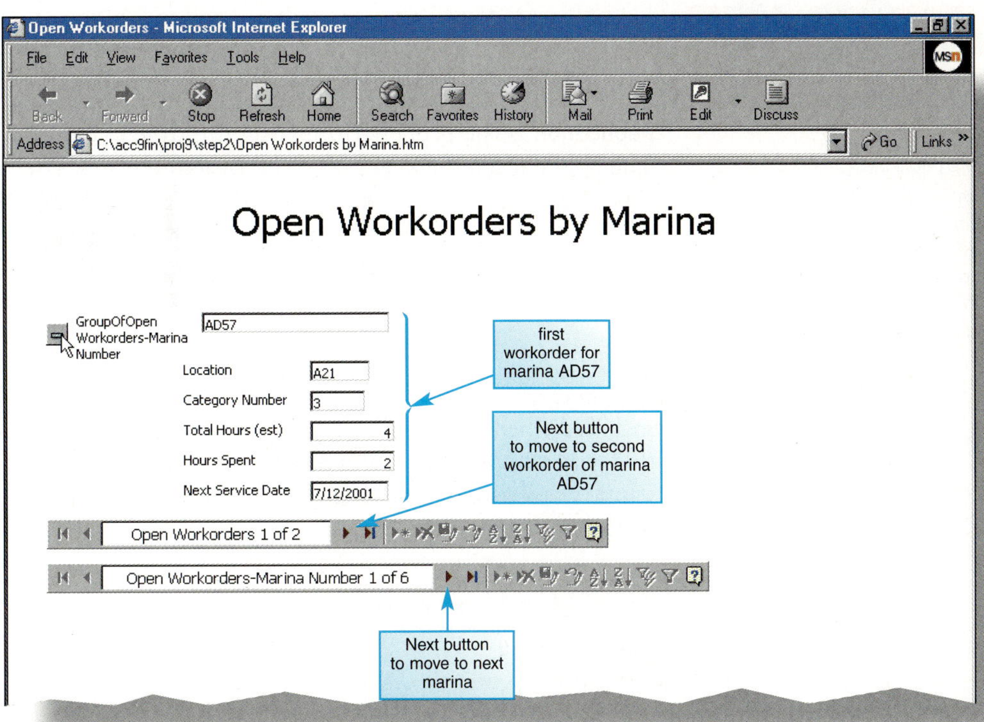

FIGURE 9-40

4 Click the Next button on the navigation bar for the workorders of the marina.

The second open workorder for marina AD57 displays (Figure 9-41).

5 Close the Open Workorders – Microsoft Internet Explorer window by clicking its Close button.

The data access page no longer displays.

6 Click the Close Window button for the Microsoft Access – [Bavant Marine Services : Database] window and then click the Close button for the Microsoft Access window.

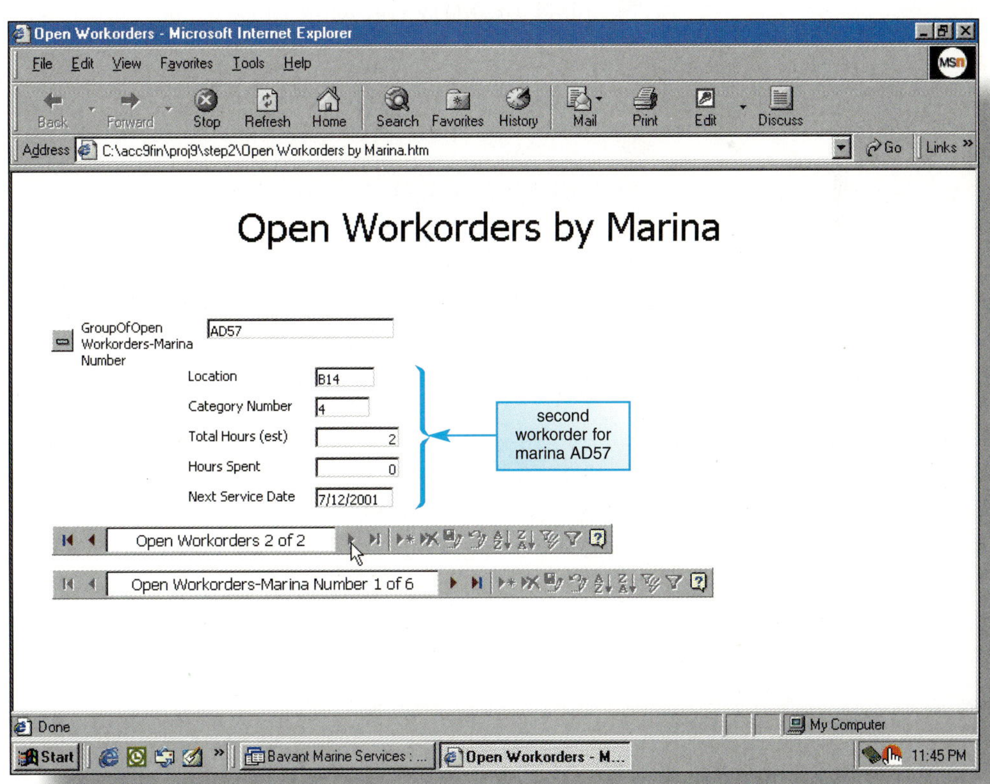

FIGURE 9-41

Replication

When many users are each using their own replicas there are potential problems in synchronizing the data. A user adding a workorder for a marina in one replica, while another user is deleting the same marina from a different replica would pose problems during synchronization. For more information concerning replication, visit the Access 2000 More About page (www.scsite.com/ac2000/more.htm) and click Replication.

Using Replication

Replication is the process of making multiple copies, called **replicas**, of a database. The original database is called the **Design Master**. The replicas then can be used at different locations. To make sure the Design Master reflects the changes made in the various replicas, the Design Master and the replicas will be **synchronized** periodically. This ensures that all databases reflect every change that has been made.

Creating a Replica

To create a replica, use the My Briefcase feature of Access. If this feature is installed, there is a My Briefcase icon on the Windows desktop. Drag the database to this icon to create a replica as in the following steps to make a replica of the Holton Clinic database. Check with your instructor to make sure the My Briefcase feature is installed before completing these steps.

TO CREATE A REPLICA

1. Use either My Computer or Windows Explorer to open a window for drive A:. Drag the Holton Clinic database from this window to the My Briefcase icon. If this is the first time you have used My Briefcase, you may see a dialog box explaining its use. Close the dialog box.
2. When the message indicating that Briefcase is making the database replica displays, asking if you want to continue, click the Yes button.
3. When the message asking if you want Briefcase to make a backup copy of your database displays, click the No button.
4. When the message asking if you want be able to make design changes in the original copy or the Briefcase copy displays, be sure that Original Copy is selected and then click the OK button.
5. Close any open windows.

The replica is created and placed in the My Briefcase folder.

Using a Replica

You can use a replica similar to any other database, except that you cannot change the structure of any of the objects in your database. Perform the following steps to add a record and change one of the names in the replica, which is stored in the My Briefcase folder.

To Use the Replica

1 Click the Start button on the taskbar, click Open Office Document on the Start menu, and then click My Briefcase in the Look in box. Make sure the Holton Clinic database is selected and then click the Open button.

2 Right-click Patient and then point to Open on the shortcut menu.

The shortcut menu displays (Figure 9-42). The symbol in front of Patient indicates that it is a replica.

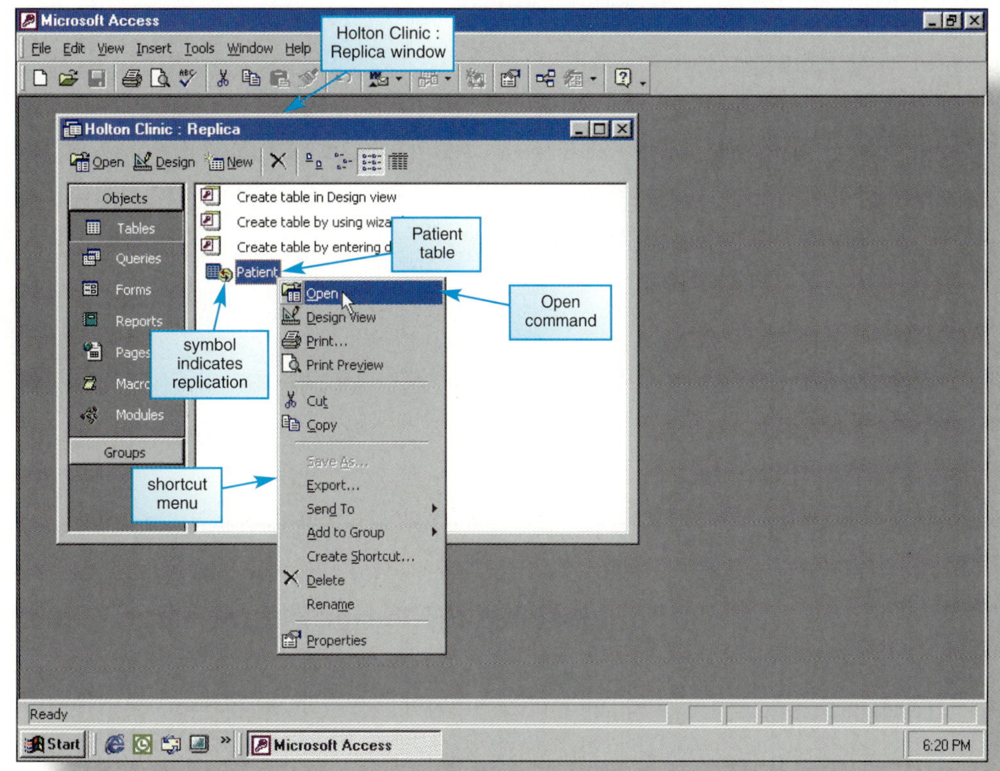

FIGURE 9-42

3 Click Open, maximize the window, and then click the New Record button. Type the final record shown in Figure 9-43.

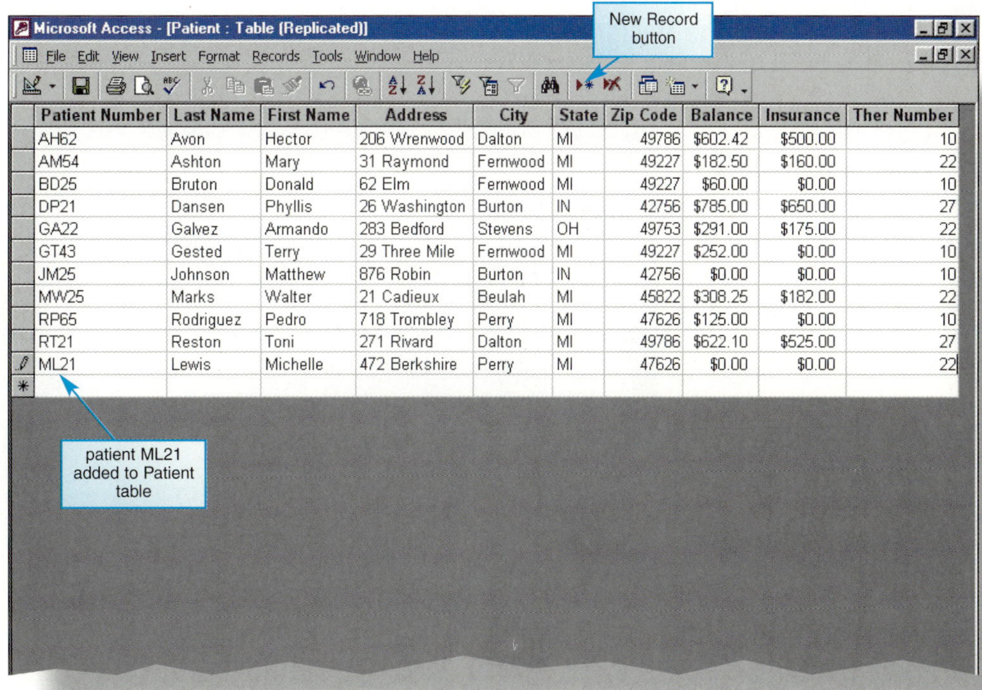

Patient Number	Last Name	First Name	Address	City	State	Zip Code	Balance	Insurance	Ther Number
AH62	Avon	Hector	206 Wrenwood	Dalton	MI	49786	$602.42	$500.00	10
AM54	Ashton	Mary	31 Raymond	Fernwood	MI	49227	$182.50	$160.00	22
BD25	Bruton	Donald	62 Elm	Fernwood	MI	49227	$60.00	$0.00	10
DP21	Dansen	Phyllis	26 Washington	Burton	IN	42756	$785.00	$650.00	27
GA22	Galvez	Armando	283 Bedford	Stevens	OH	49753	$291.00	$175.00	22
GT43	Gested	Terry	29 Three Mile	Fernwood	MI	49227	$252.00	$0.00	10
JM25	Johnson	Matthew	876 Robin	Burton	IN	42756	$0.00	$0.00	10
MW25	Marks	Walter	21 Cadieux	Beulah	MI	45822	$308.25	$182.00	22
RP65	Rodriguez	Pedro	718 Trombley	Perry	MI	47626	$125.00	$0.00	10
RT21	Reston	Toni	271 Rivard	Dalton	MI	49786	$622.10	$525.00	27
ML21	Lewis	Michelle	472 Berkshire	Perry	MI	47626	$0.00	$0.00	22

FIGURE 9-43

4 **Click the first name of patient number JM25, erase the current name, and then type** `Martin` **as the new name. Point to the Close Window button for the window containing the Patient table.**

The changes are made (Figure 9-44).

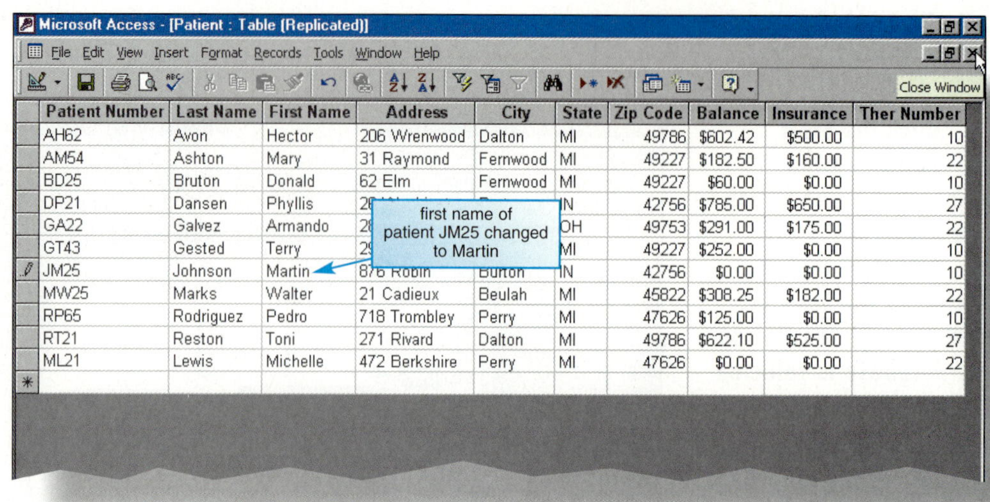

FIGURE 9-44

5 **Click the Close Window button.**

The table no longer displays.

Synchronizing the Design Master and the Replica

Now that the replica has been updated, the data in both the Design Master and the replica no longer match. In order for them to match, the updates to the replica also must be made to the Design Master. Access will make these updates automatically, using a process called synchronization. Perform the following steps to synchronize the Design Master and the replica.

Steps To Synchronize the Design Master and the Replica

1 **Close the Holton Clinic replica. Click Open on the toolbar, and then click 3½ Floppy (A:) in the Look in box. Make sure the Holton Clinic database is selected.**

2 **Click the Open button arrow (not the button itself). Click Open Exclusive in the menu that displays.**

The database opens in exclusive mode and the Holton Clinic : Database window displays.

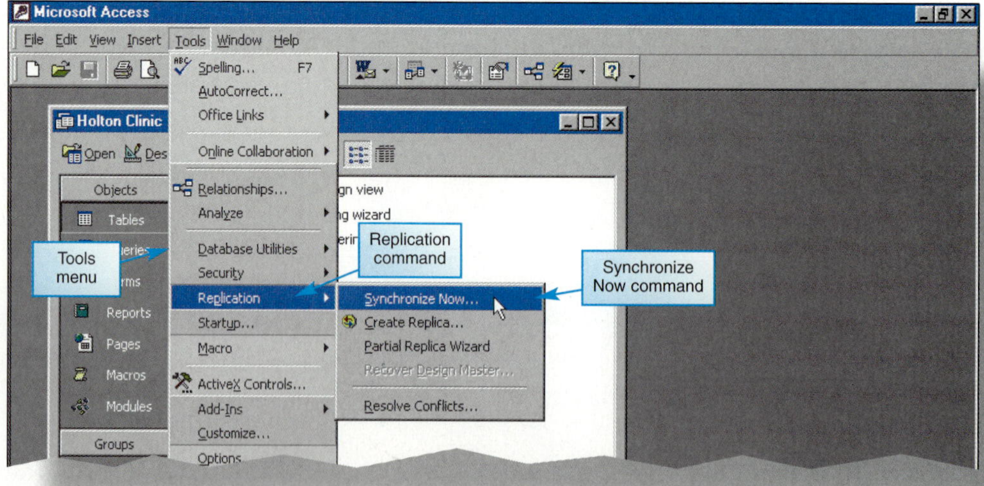

FIGURE 9-45

3 **Click Tools on the menu bar, click Replication on the Tools menu, and then point to Synchronize Now on the Replication submenu (Figure 9-45).**

4 Click Synchronize Now. Click the Directly with Replica button in the Synchronize Database 'Holton Clinic' dialog box and then click the OK button. When a message displays indicating that Access must close the database in order to perform the synchronization, click the Yes button.

The databases are synchronized. Access displays the message shown in Figure 9-46 when the process is complete.

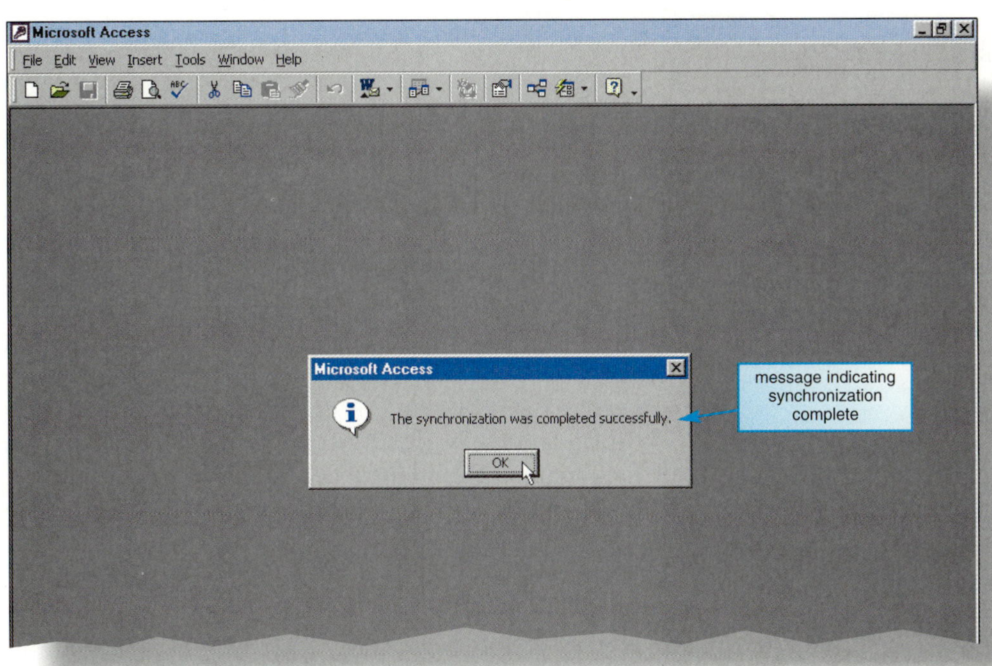

FIGURE 9-46

5 Click the OK button.

The data in the replicated database (the Design Master) now incorporates the changes made earlier to the replica, as shown in Figure 9-47.

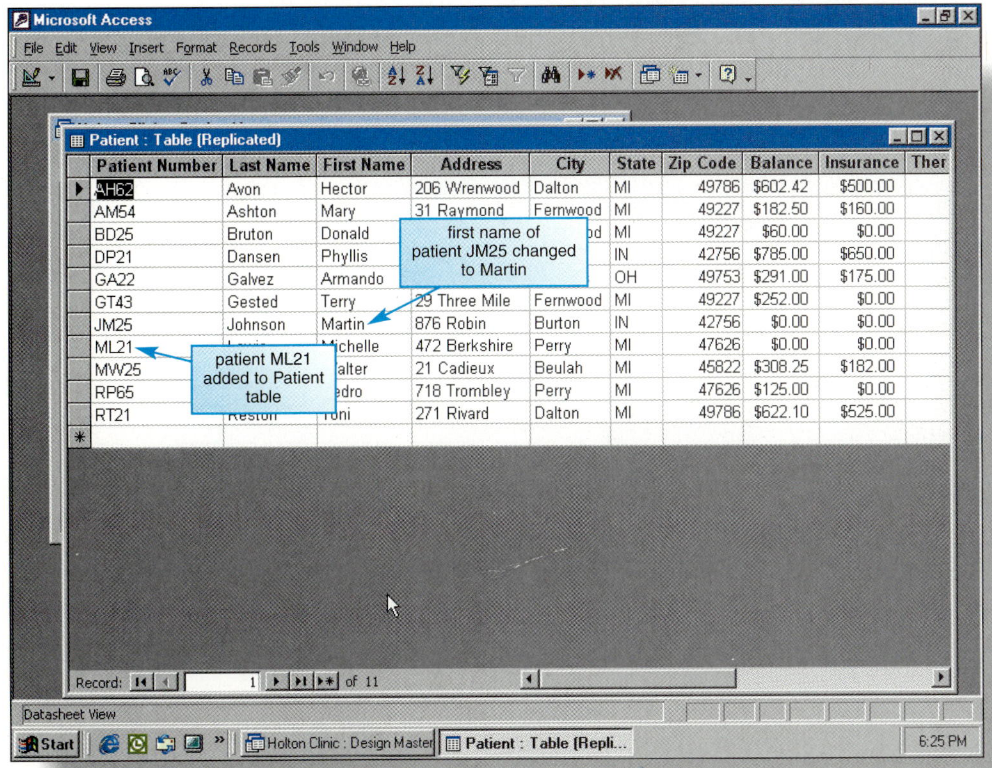

Patient Number	Last Name	First Name	Address	City	State	Zip Code	Balance	Insurance
AH62	Avon	Hector	206 Wrenwood	Dalton	MI	49786	$602.42	$500.00
AM54	Ashton	Mary	31 Raymond	Fernwood	MI	49227	$182.50	$160.00
BD25	Bruton	Donald			MI	49227	$60.00	$0.00
DP21	Dansen	Phyllis			IN	42756	$785.00	$650.00
GA22	Galvez	Armando			OH	49753	$291.00	$175.00
GT43	Gested	Terry	29 Three Mile	Fernwood	MI	49227	$252.00	$0.00
JM25	Johnson	Martin	876 Robin	Burton	IN	42756	$0.00	$0.00
ML21			472 Berkshire	Perry	MI	47626	$0.00	$0.00
MW25			21 Cadieux	Beulah	MI	45822	$308.25	$182.00
RP65			718 Trombley	Perry	MI	47626	$125.00	$0.00
RT21			271 Rivard	Dalton	MI	49786	$622.10	$525.00

FIGURE 9-47

SQL

The American National Standards Institute (ANSI) has developed standards for SQL. These standards are continually reviewed and new and improved standards are periodically proposed and accepted. For more information concerning these standards, visit the Access 2000 More About page (www.scsite.com/ac2000/more.htm) and click SQL Standards.

SQL

This section examines **Structured Query Language (SQL)**. Like creating queries in Design view, SQL furnishes users a way of querying relational databases. In SQL, you must type commands to obtain the desired resultsrather than making entries in the Design grid.

SQL was developed under the name SEQUEL at the IBM San Jose research facilities as the data manipulation language for IBM's prototype relational model DBMS, System R, in the mid-1970s. In 1980, it was renamed SQL to avoid confusion with an unrelated hardware product called SEQUEL. It is used as the data manipulation language for IBM's current production offerings in the relational DBMS arena, SQL/DS and DB2. Most relational DBMSs, including Access, use a version of SQL as a data manipulation language.

Creating a New SQL Query

Begin the creation of a new **SQL query**, which is a query expressed using the SQL language, just as you begin the creation of any other query in Access. The only difference is that you will use SQL view rather than Design view. Perform the following steps to create a new SQL query.

To Create a New SQL Query

1 **Close the Holton Clinic database, if necessary. Open the Bavant Marine Services database. When the switchboard displays, close it by clicking the Close button.**

2 **Click Queries on the Objects bar and then click the New button. Be sure Design View is selected and then click the OK button. When the Show Table dialog box displays, click its Close button. Maximize the window.**

3 **Click the View button arrow and then point to SQL View (Figure 9-48).**

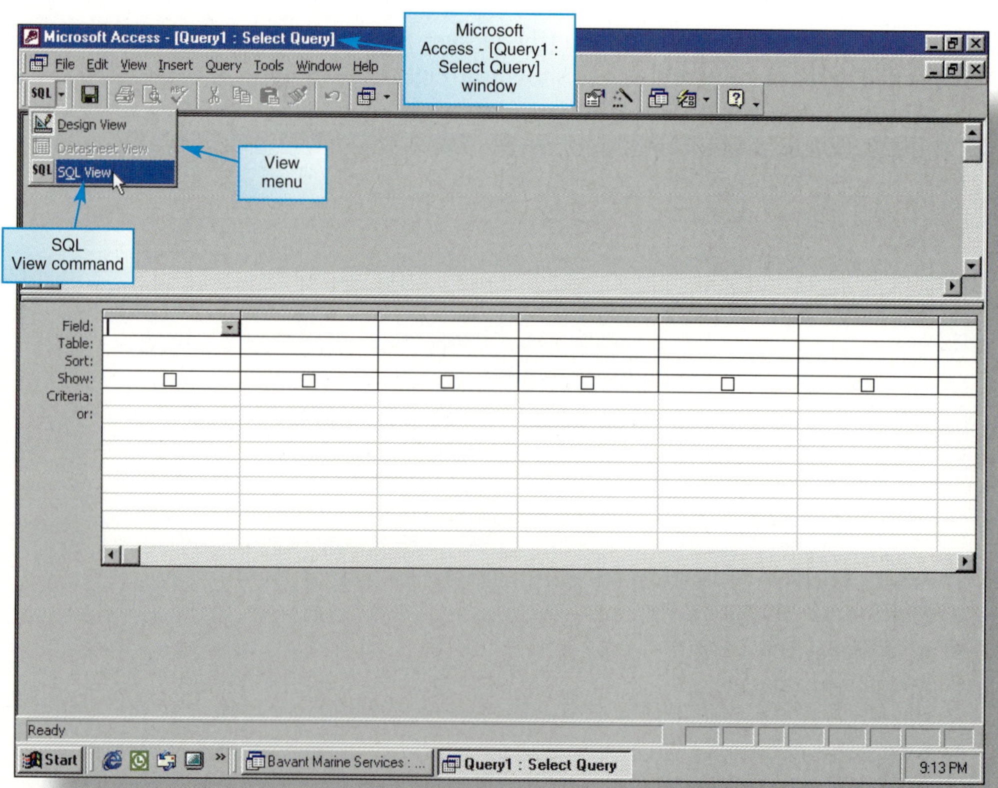

FIGURE 9-48

Click SQL View.

The Microsoft Access – [Query1 : Select Query] window displays in SQL view (Figure 9-49).

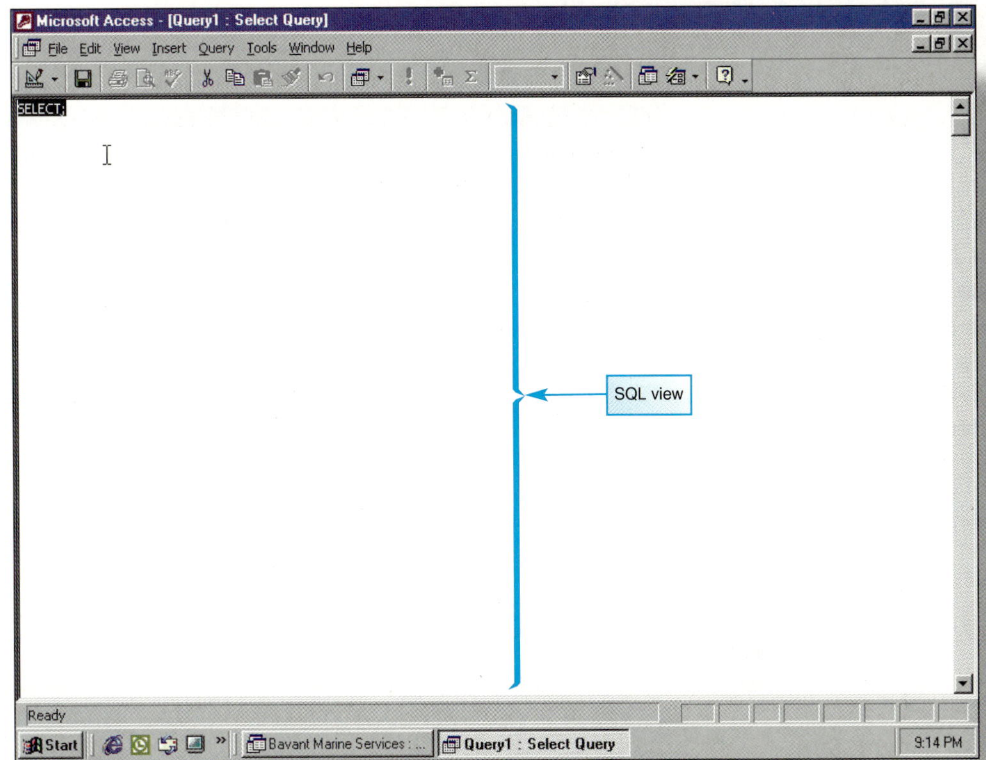

FIGURE 9-49

1. On View menu click SQL View

The basic form of an SQL expression is quite simple: SELECT-FROM-WHERE. After the SELECT, you list those fields you wish to display. The fields will display in the results in the order in which they are listed in the expression. After the FROM, you list the table or tables involved in the query. Finally, after the WHERE, you list any criteria that apply to the data you want to retrieve. The command ends with a semicolon (;).

There are no special format rules in SQL. In this text, you place the word FROM on a new line, then place the word WHERE, when it is used, on the next line. This makes the commands easier to read. Words that are part of the SQL language are entered in uppercase and others are entered in a combination of uppercase and lowercase. Because it is a common convention, and necessary in some versions of SQL, place a semicolon (;) at the end of each command.

Unlike some other versions of SQL, Access allows spaces within field names. There is a restriction, however, to the way such names are used in SQL commands. When a name containing a space displays in SQL, it must be enclosed in square brackets. For example, Marina Number must display as [Marina Number] because the name includes a space. On the other hand, City does not need to be enclosed in square brackets because its name does not include a space. In order to be consistent, all names in this text will be enclosed in square brackets. Thus, the City field would display as [City] even though the brackets are technically not required.

Including Only Certain Fields

To include only certain fields, list them after the word SELECT. If you want to list all rows in the table, you do not need to include the word WHERE. The steps on the next page list the number, name, warranty, and non-warranty amount of all marinas.

To Include Only Certain Fields

Type `SELECT [Marina Number], [Name], [Warranty], [Non-Warranty]` **as the first line of the command. Press the ENTER key and then type** `FROM [Marina];` **as the second line. Point to the Run button.**

The command is entered (Figure 9-50).

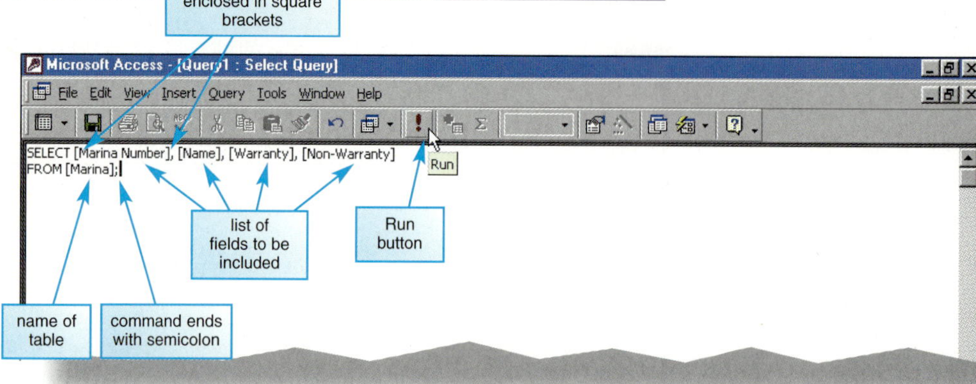

FIGURE 9-50

2 Click the Run button.

The results display (Figure 9-51). Only the fields specified are included.

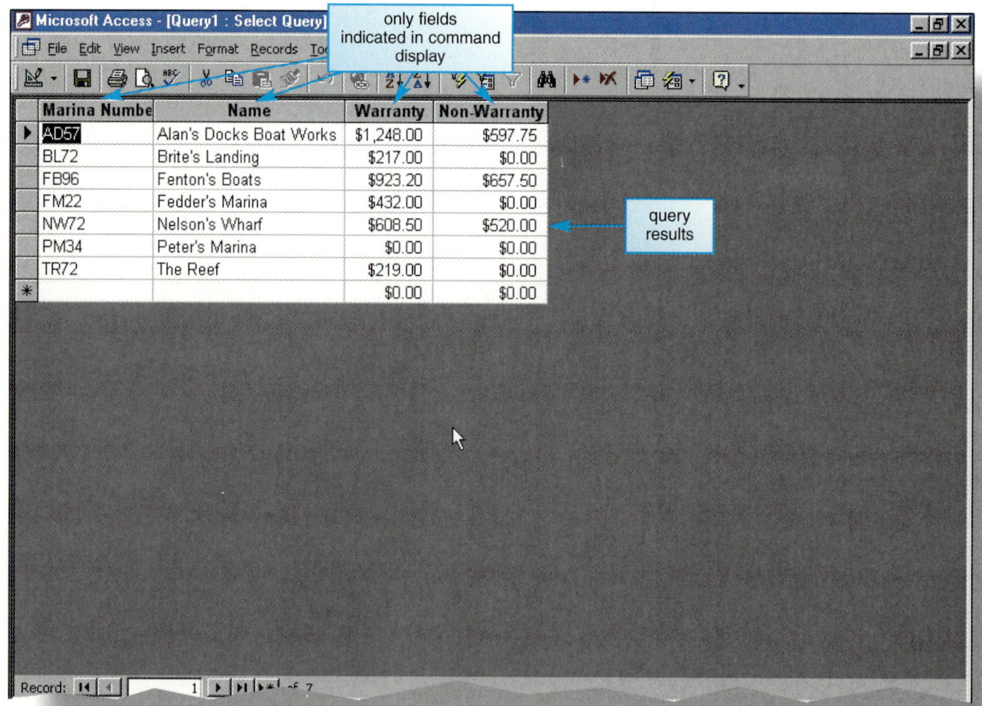

Marina Numbe	Name	Warranty	Non-Warranty
AD57	Alan's Docks Boat Works	$1,248.00	$597.75
BL72	Brite's Landing	$217.00	$0.00
FB96	Fenton's Boats	$923.20	$657.50
FM22	Fedder's Marina	$432.00	$0.00
NW72	Nelson's Wharf	$608.50	$520.00
PM34	Peter's Marina	$0.00	$0.00
TR72	The Reef	$219.00	$0.00
		$0.00	$0.00

FIGURE 9-51

Preparing to Enter a New SQL Command

To enter a new SQL command, you could close the window, click the No button when asked if you want to save your changes, and then begin the process from scratch. A quicker alternative is to use the View button and select SQL View. You then will be returned to SQL view with the current command displaying. At that point, you could erase the current command and then enter a new one. (If the next command is similar to the previous one, it may be simpler to modify the current command rather than erasing it and starting over.)

Perform the following steps to prepare to enter a new SQL command.

To Prepare to Enter a New SQL Command

1 Click the View button arrow and then point to SQL View (Figure 9-52).

2 Click SQL View.

The command once again displays in SQL view.

FIGURE 9-52

1. On View menu click SQL View

Including All Fields

To include all fields, you could use the same approach as in the previous steps; that is, list each field in the Marina table after the word SELECT. There is a short-cut, however. Instead of listing all the field names after SELECT, you can use the asterisk (*) symbol. This indicates that you want all fields listed in the order in which you described them to the system during data definition. To list all fields and all records in the Marina table, use the following steps.

To Include All Fields

1 Select and delete the current SQL command. Type `SELECT *` **as the first line of the command. Press the ENTER key and then type** `FROM [Marina];` **as the second line. Point to the Run button.**

The command is entered (Figure 9-53).

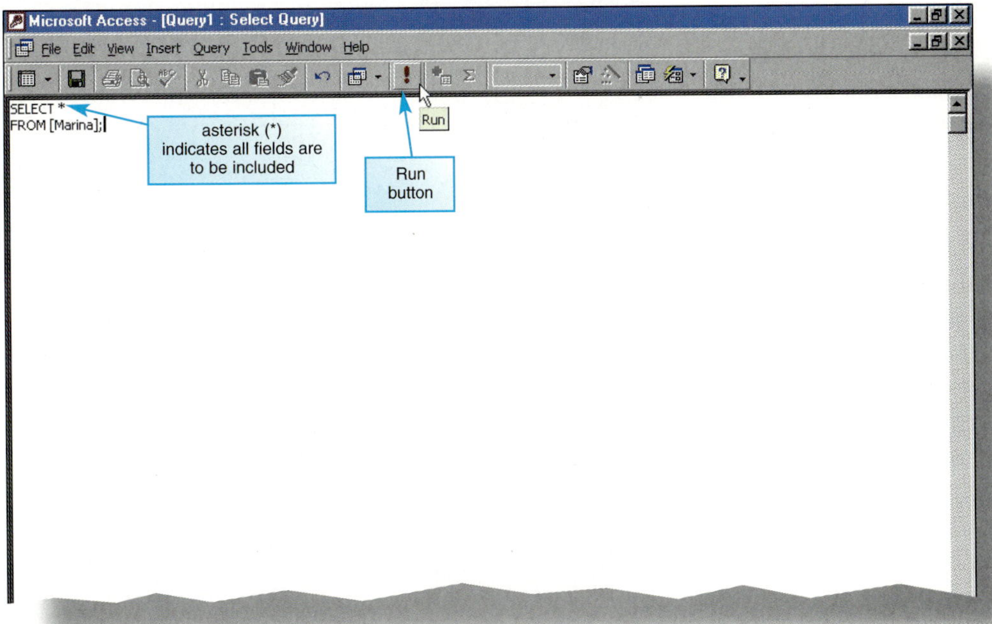

FIGURE 9-53

Click the Run button.

The results display (Figure 9-54). All fields specified are included.

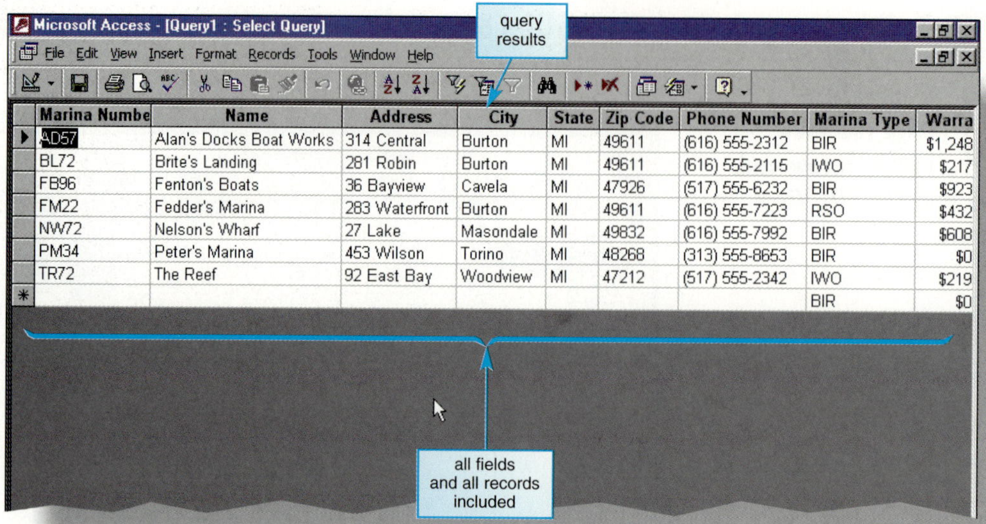

Marina Numbe	Name	Address	City	State	Zip Code	Phone Number	Marina Type	Warra
AD57	Alan's Docks Boat Works	314 Central	Burton	MI	49611	(616) 555-2312	BIR	$1,248
BL72	Brite's Landing	281 Robin	Burton	MI	49611	(616) 555-2115	IWO	$217
FB96	Fenton's Boats	36 Bayview	Cavela	MI	47926	(517) 555-6232	BIR	$923
FM22	Fedder's Marina	283 Waterfront	Burton	MI	49611	(616) 555-7223	RSO	$432
NW72	Nelson's Wharf	27 Lake	Masondale	MI	49832	(616) 555-7992	BIR	$608
PM34	Peter's Marina	453 Wilson	Torino	MI	48268	(313) 555-8653	BIR	$0
TR72	The Reef	92 East Bay	Woodview	MI	47212	(517) 555-2342	IWO	$219
*							BIR	$0

FIGURE 9-54

Using a Criterion Involving a Numeric Field

To restrict the records to be displayed, include the word WHERE followed by a criterion as part of the command. If the field involved is a Numeric field, you simply type the value. For example, to list the marina number of all marinas whose non-warranty amount is 0, you would type the condition [Non-Warranty]=0 as in the following steps.

To Use a Criterion Involving a Numeric Field

1. **Click the View button arrow, click SQL View, and then select and delete the current SQL command.**

2. **Type** `SELECT [Marina Number], [Name]` **as the first line of the command. Press the ENTER key and then type** `FROM [Marina]` **as the second line. Press the ENTER key and then type** `WHERE [Non-Warranty]=0;` **as the third line. Point to the Run button.**

The command is entered (Figure 9-55).

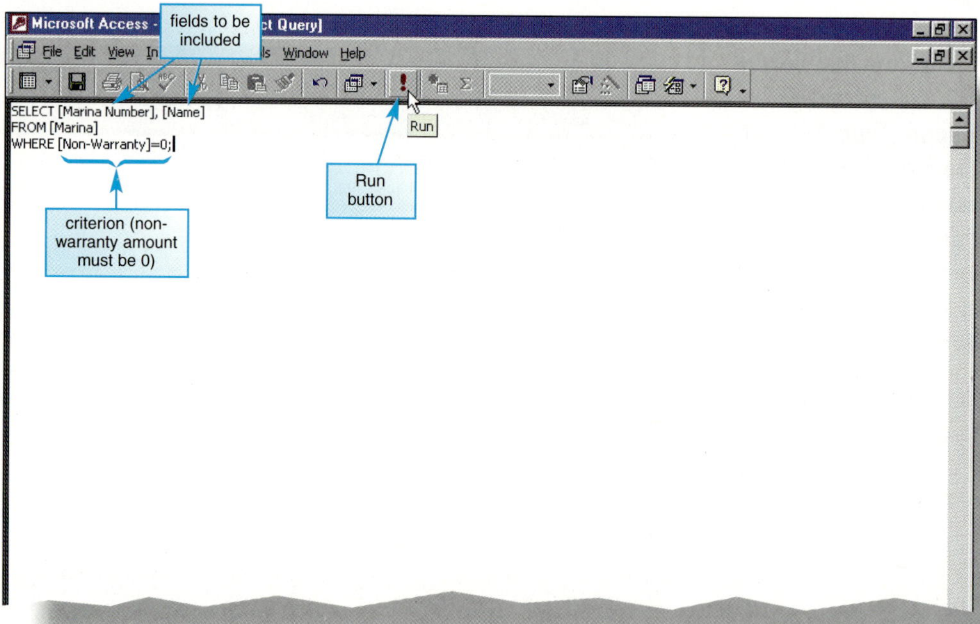

FIGURE 9-55

3 Click the Run button.

The results display (Figure 9-56). Only those marinas for which the non-warranty amount is 0 are included.

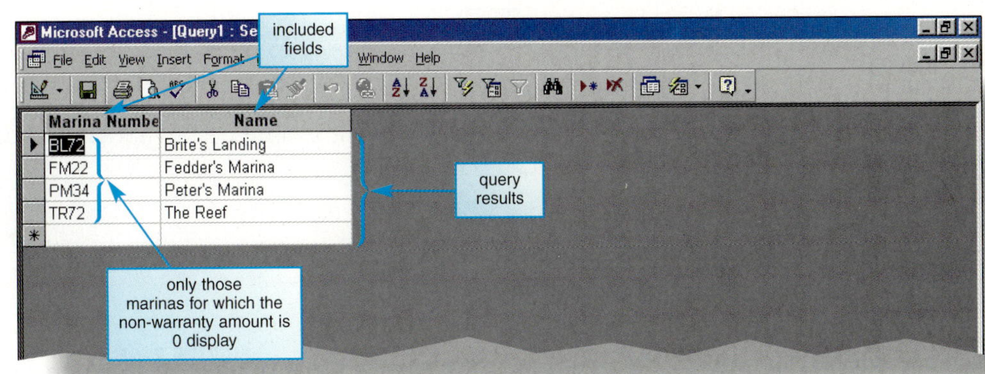

FIGURE 9-56

The criterion following the word WHERE in the preceding query is called a simple criterion. A **simple criterion** has the form: field name, comparison operator, then either another field name or a value. The possible comparison operators are shown in Table 9-2.

Table 9-2 Comparison Operators

COMPARISON OPERATOR	MEANING
=	Equal to
<	Less than
>	Greater than
<=	Less than or equal to
>=	Greater than or equal to
<>	Not equal to

Using a Criterion Involving a Text Field

If the criterion involves a Text field, the value must be enclosed in single quotation marks. In the following example, all marinas located in Burton are listed; that is, all marinas for whom the value in the City field is Burton.

Steps To Use a Criterion Involving a Text Field

1 Click the View button arrow, click SQL View, and then select and delete the current SQL command.

2 Type `SELECT [Marina Number]` **as the first line of the command. Press the ENTER key and then type** `FROM [Marina]` **as the second line. Press the ENTER key and then type** `WHERE [City]='Burton';` **as the third line. Point to the Run button.**

The command is entered (Figure 9-57).

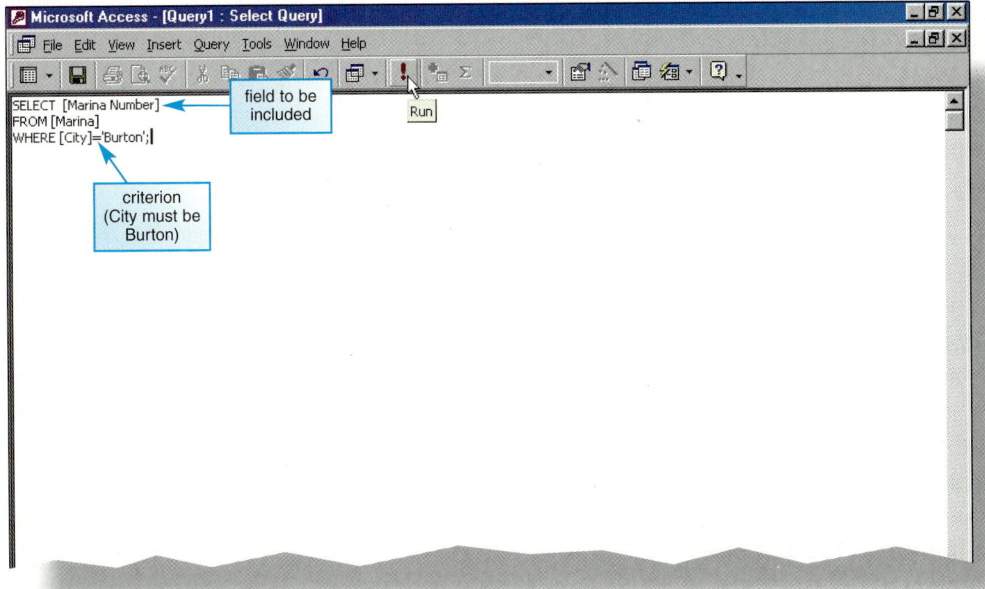

FIGURE 9-57

3 **Click the Run button.**

The results display (Figure 9-58). Only those marinas located in Burton are included.

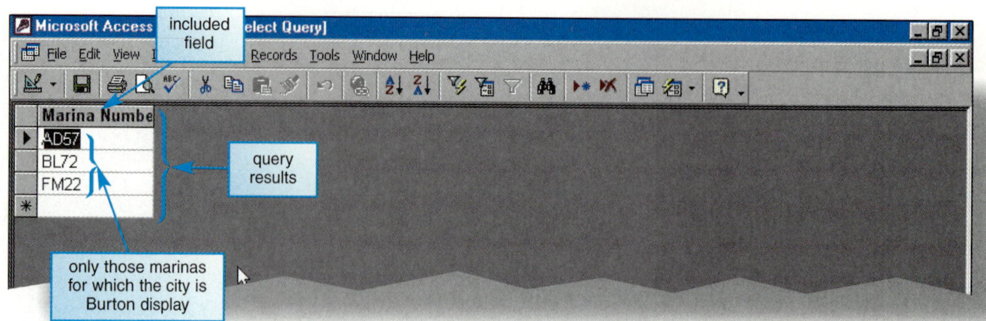

FIGURE 9-58

Using Compound Criteria

The criterion you have seen so far are called simple criterion. The next examples require compound criteria. **Compound criteria** are formed by connecting two or more simple criteria using AND, OR, and NOT. When connected by the word AND, all the simple criteria must be true in order for the compound criterion to be true. When connected by the word OR, the compound criteria will be true whenever any of the simple criterion is true. Preceding a criterion by NOT reverses the truth or falsity of the original criterion. If the original criterion is true, the new criterion will be false; if the original criterion is false, then the new one will be true.

The following steps use compound criteria to display the names of those marinas located in Burton and for whom the non-warranty amount is 0.

Steps To Use Compound Criteria

1 **Click the View button arrow, click SQL View, and then select and delete the current SQL command.**

2 **Type** `SELECT [Name]` **as the first line of the command. Press the ENTER key and then type** `FROM [Marina]` **as the second line. Press the ENTER key and then type** `WHERE [City]='Burton'` **as the third line. Press the ENTER key and then type** `AND [Non-Warranty]=0;` **as the fourth line. Point to the Run button.**

The command is entered (Figure 9-59).

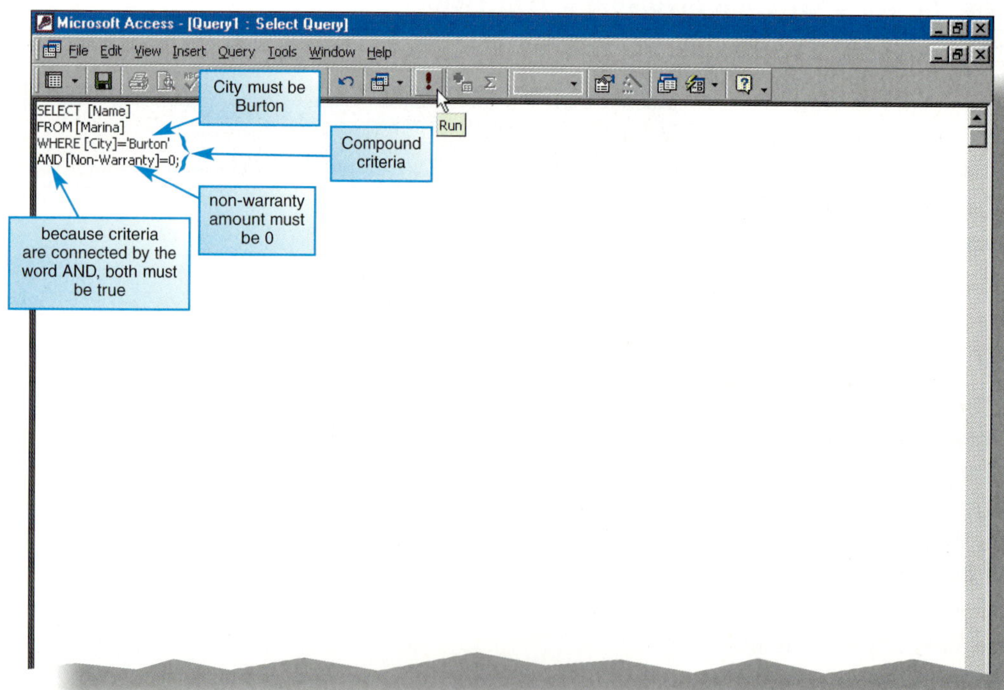

FIGURE 9-59

Click the Run button.

The results display (Figure 9-60). Only those marinas located in Burton and with a non-warranty amount of 0 are included.

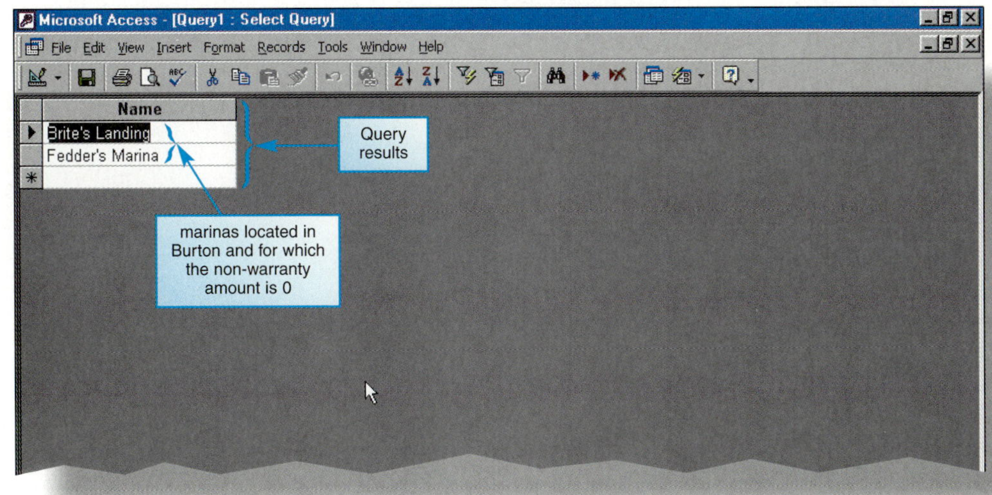

FIGURE 9-60

You use the same method to form compound criteria involving OR. Simply use the word OR instead of the word AND. In that case, the results would contain those records that satisfied either criterion.

Using NOT in a Criterion

To use NOT in a criterion, precede the criterion with the word NOT. Perform the following steps to list the names of the marinas not located in Burton.

To Use NOT in a Criterion

1. **Click the View button arrow, click SQL View, and then select and delete the current SQL command.**

2. **Type** `SELECT [Name]` **as the first line of the command. Press the ENTER key and then type** `FROM [Marina]` **as the second line. Press the ENTER key and then type** `WHERE NOT [City]='Burton';` **as the third line. Point to the Run button.**

The command is entered (Figure 9-61).

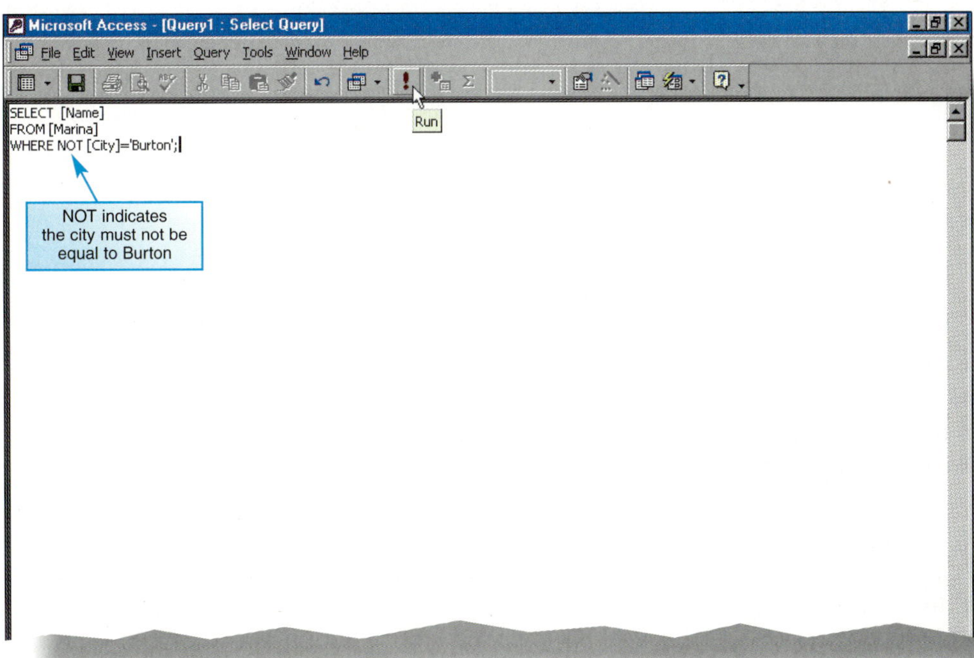

FIGURE 9-61

Click the Run button.

The results display (Figure 9-62). Only those marinas not located in Burton are included.

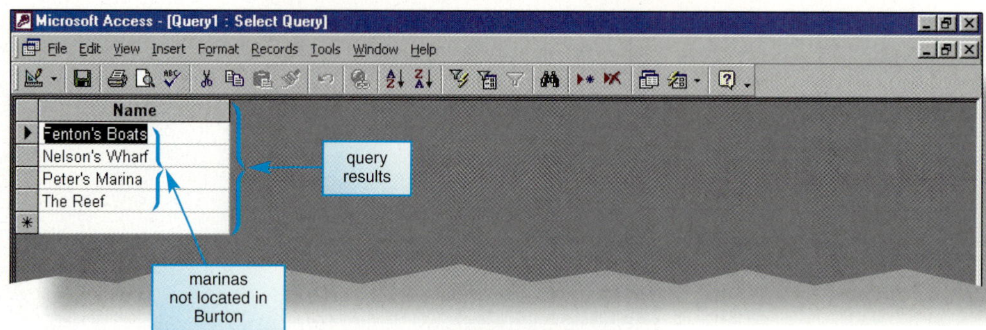

FIGURE 9-62

Using Computed Fields

Just as with queries created in Design view, you can include fields in queries that are not in the database, but that can be computed from fields that are. This type of field is called a **computed** or **calculated field**. Such computations can involve addition (+), subtraction (-), multiplication (*), or division (/). The query in the following steps includes the total amount, which is equal to the warranty amount plus the non-warranty amount.

To name the computed field, follow the computation with the word AS and then the name you wish to assign the field. The following steps assign the name Total Amount to the computed field and also list the Marina Number and Name for all marinas for which the non-warranty amount is greater than 0.

To Use a Computed Field

1. **Click the View button arrow, click SQL View, and then select and delete the current SQL command.**

2. **Type** `SELECT [Marina Number], [Name], [Warranty]+[Non-Warranty] AS [Total Amount]` **as the first line of the command. Press the ENTER key and then type** `FROM [Marina]` **as the second line. Press the ENTER key and then type** `WHERE [Non-Warranty]>0;` **as the third line. Point to the Run button.**

The command is entered (Figure 9-63).

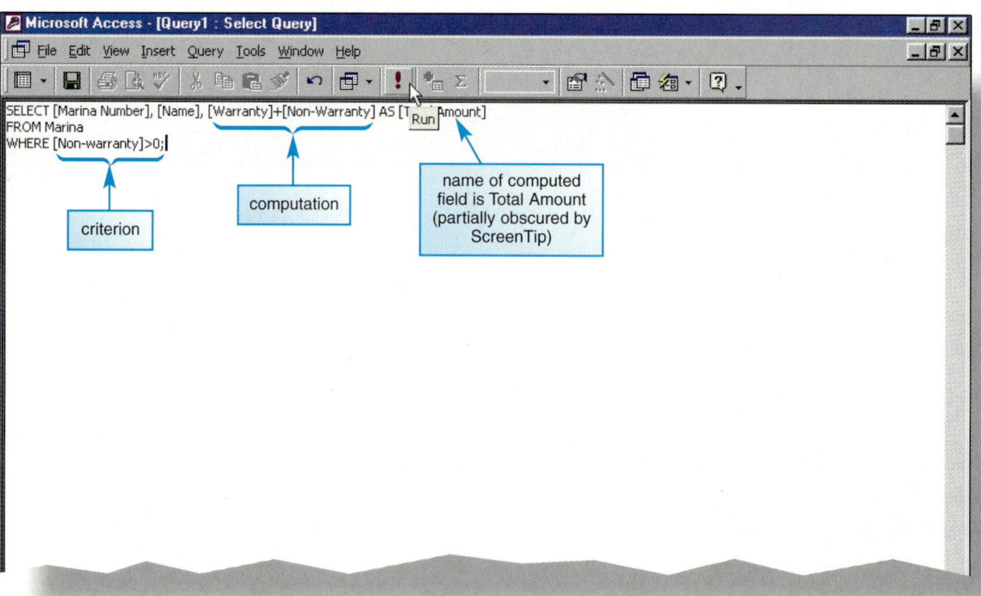

FIGURE 9-63

3 **Click the Run button.**

The results display (Figure 9-64). The total amount is calculated appropriately. Only those marinas with a non-warranty amount greater than 0 are included.

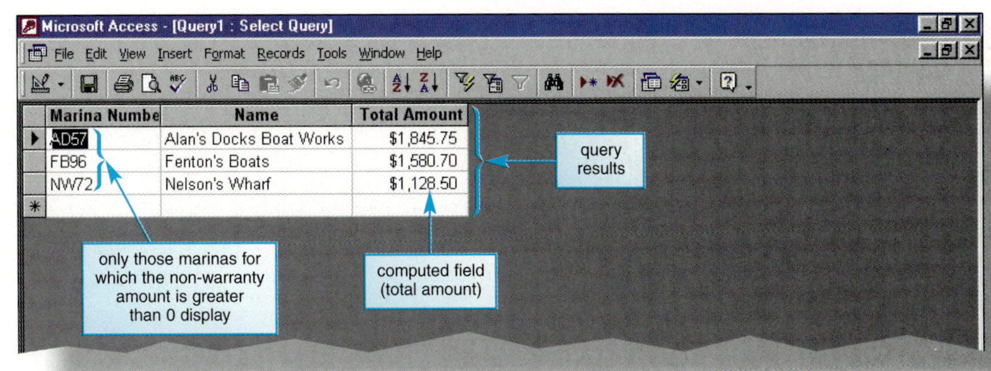

FIGURE 9-64

Sorting the Results

The field on which data is to be sorted is called a **sort key**, or simply a **key**. If the data is to be sorted on two fields, the more important key is called the **major sort key** (also referred to as the **primary sort key**) and the less important key is called the **minor sort key** (also referred to as the **secondary sort key**). To sort the output, you include the words ORDER BY, followed by the sort key. If there are two sort keys, the major sort key is listed first.

The following steps list the marina number, name, warranty amount, non-warranty amount, and technician number for all marinas. The data is to be sorted by technician number and within the marinas having the same technician number, the data is to be further sorted by warranty amount. This means that the Tech Number field is the major (primary) sort key and the Warranty field is the minor (secondary) sort key.

Sorting

In SQL, you can sort in descending order by following the sort key with DESC in the ORDER BY clause. If you have two sort keys, you could choose to sort one in descending order and the other in ascending order. For example, ORDER BY [Tech Number], [Warranty] DESC; would sort on ascending Tech Number and descending Warranty.

To Sort the Results

1 **Click the View button arrow, click SQL View, and then select and delete the current SQL command.**

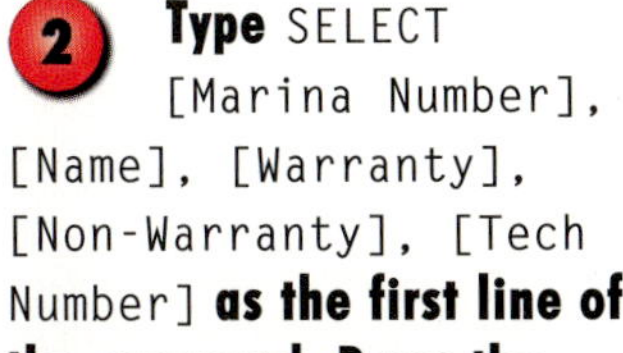

2 **Type** `SELECT [Marina Number], [Name], [Warranty], [Non-Warranty], [Tech Number]` **as the first line of the command. Press the ENTER key and then type** `FROM [Marina]` **as the second line. Press the ENTER key and then type** `ORDER BY [Tech Number], [Warranty];` **as the third line. Point to the Run button.**

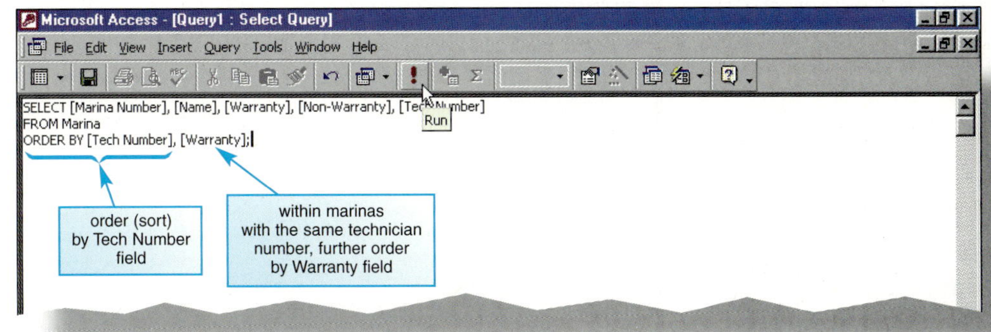

FIGURE 9-65

The command is entered (Figure 9-65). By default, the records will be sorted in ascending order.

Click the Run button.

The results display (Figure 9-66). The marinas are sorted ascending by the Tech Number field. Within the marinas of a particular technician, the results further are sorted by warranty amount.

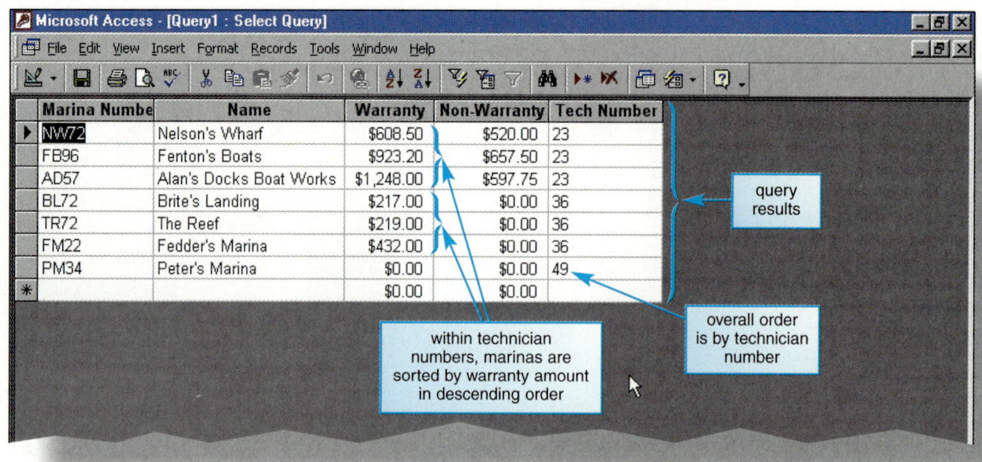

FIGURE 9-66

Using Built-In Functions

SQL has **built-in** functions (also called **aggregate** functions) to calculate the number of entries, the sum or average of all the entries in a given column, and the largest or smallest of the entries in a given column. In SQL, these functions are called COUNT, SUM, AVG, MAX, and MIN.

The following steps count the number of marinas assigned to technician 23. Perform these steps to use the COUNT function with an asterisk (*).

To Use a Built-In Function

1. **Click the View button arrow, click SQL View, and then select and delete the current SQL command.**

2. **Type** `SELECT COUNT(*)` **as the first line of the command. Press the ENTER key and then type** `FROM [Marina]` **as the second line. Press the ENTER key and then type** `WHERE [Tech Number]='23';` **as the third line. Point to the Run button.**

The command is entered (Figure 9-67).

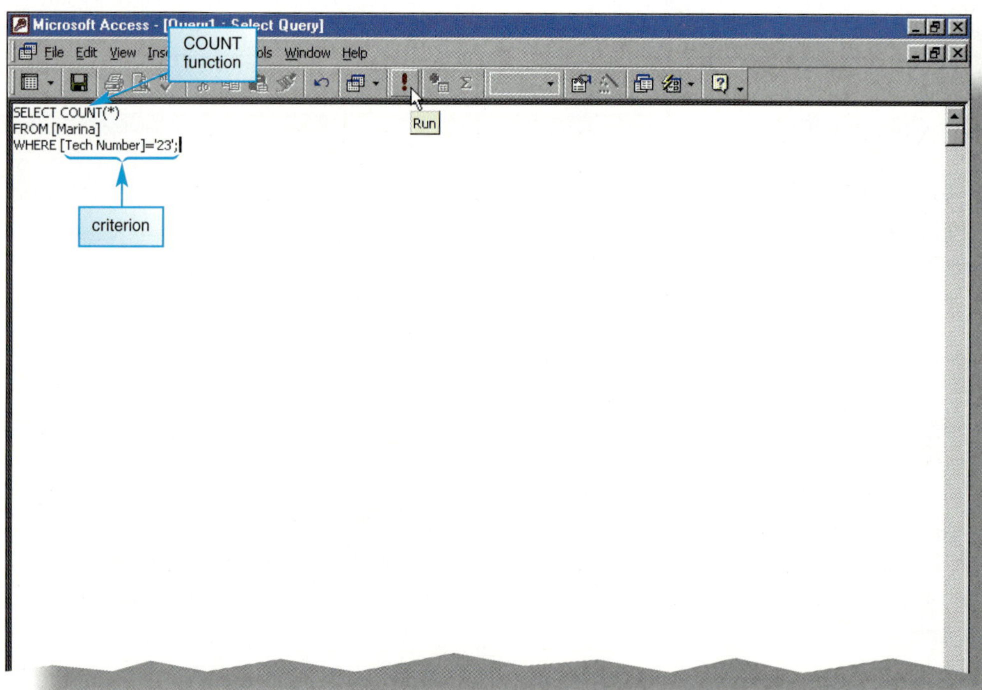

FIGURE 9-67

3 Click the Run button.

The results display (Figure 9-68). The heading Expr1000 is a default heading assigned by Access.

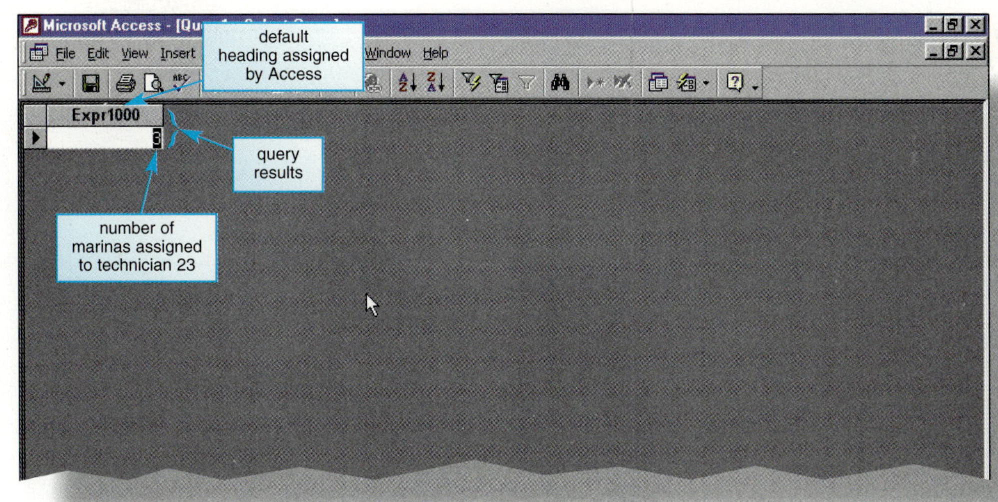

FIGURE 9-68

Using Multiple Functions in the Same Command

The only differences between COUNT and SUM, other than the obvious fact that they are computing different statistics, are that first, in the case of SUM, you must specify the field for which you want a total, rather than an asterisk (*), and second, the field must be numeric. You could not calculate a sum of names or addresses, for example. The following steps use both the COUNT and SUM functions to count the number of marinas and calculate the SUM (total) of their warranty amounts.

To Use Multiple Functions in the Same Command

1 Click the View button arrow, click SQL View, and then select and delete the current SQL command.

2 Type `SELECT COUNT(*), SUM([Warranty])` **as the first line of the command. Press the ENTER key and then type** `FROM [Marina];` **as the second line. Point to the Run button.**

The command is entered (Figure 9-69).

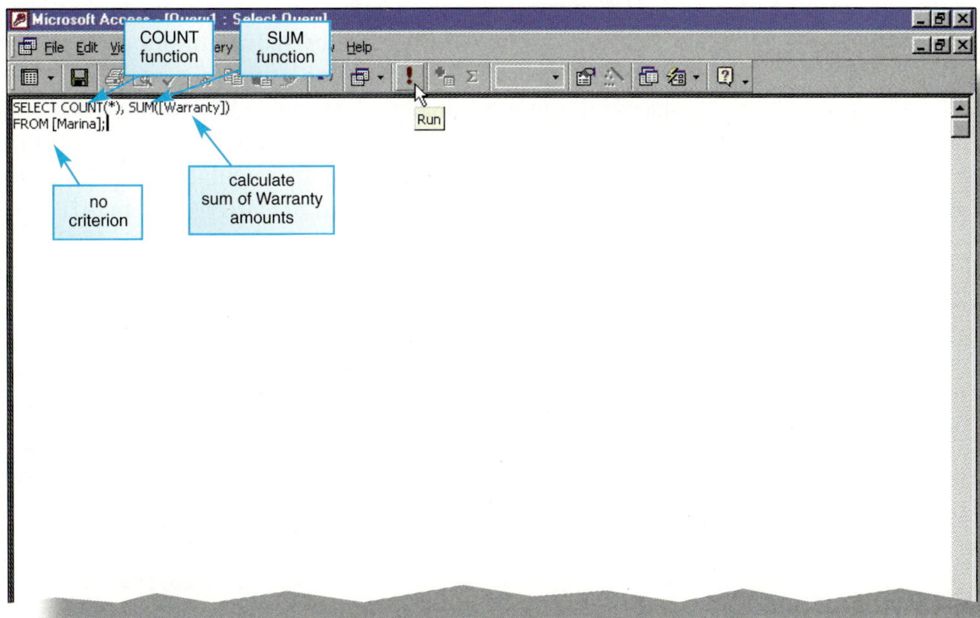

FIGURE 9-69

3 Click the Run button.

The results display (Figure 9-70). The number of marinas (7) and the total of the warranty amounts ($3,647.70) both display.

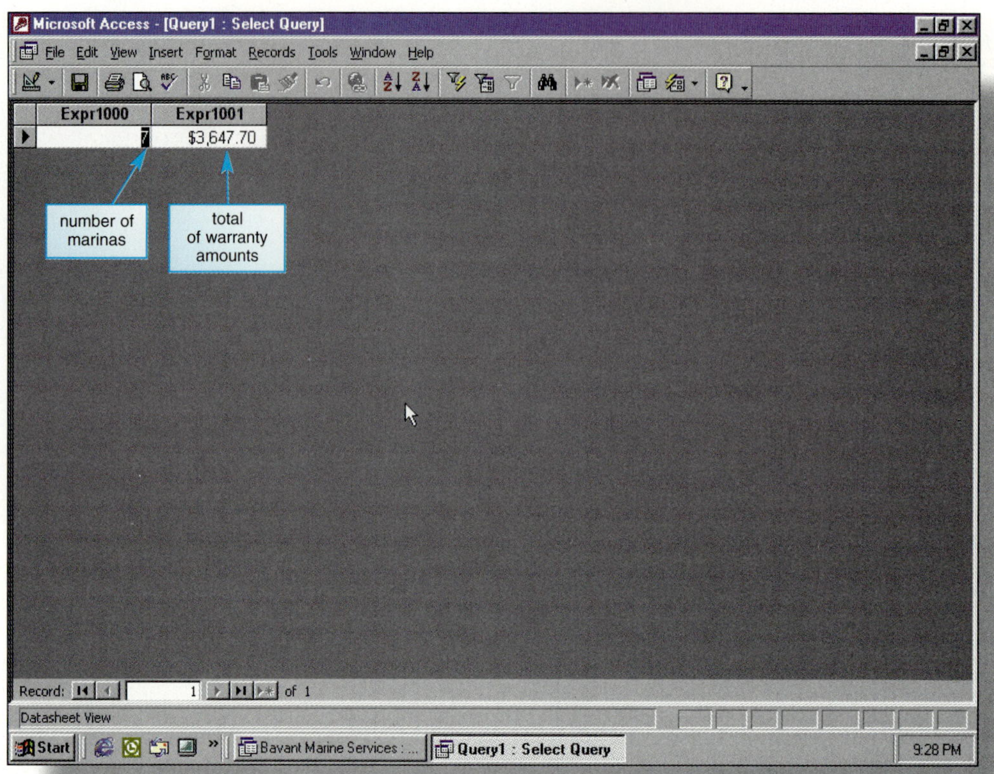

FIGURE 9-70

The use of AVG, MAX, and MIN is similar to SUM. The only difference is that a different statistic is calculated.

Using Grouping

Grouping means creating groups of records that share some common characteristic. In grouping workorders by marina number, for example, the workorders of marina AD57 would form one group, the workorders of marina BL72 would from a second, the workorders of marina FB96 would form a third, and so on.

The following steps calculate the totals of the Total Hours (est) and the Hours Spent fields for each marina. To calculate the totals, the command will include the SUM([Total Hours (est)]) and SUM([Hours Spent]). To get individual totals for each marina the command also will include the words GROUP BY followed by the field used for grouping, in this case Marina Number.

Including GROUP BY Marina Number will cause the workorders for each marina to be grouped together; that is, all workorders with the same marina number will form a group. Any statistics, such as totals, displaying after the word SELECT will be calculated for each of these groups. It is important to note that using GROUP BY does not imply that the information will be sorted. To produce the results in a particular order, you also should use ORDER BY as in the following steps.

To Use Grouping

1 Click the View button arrow, click SQL View, and then select and delete the current SQL command.

2 Type `SELECT [Marina Number], SUM([Total Hours (est)]), SUM([Hours Spent])` **as the first line of the command. Press the ENTER key and then type** `FROM [Open Workorders]` **as the second line. Press the ENTER key and then type** `GROUP BY [Marina Number]` **as the third line. Press the ENTER key and then type** `ORDER BY [Marina Number];` **as the fourth line. Point to the Run button.**

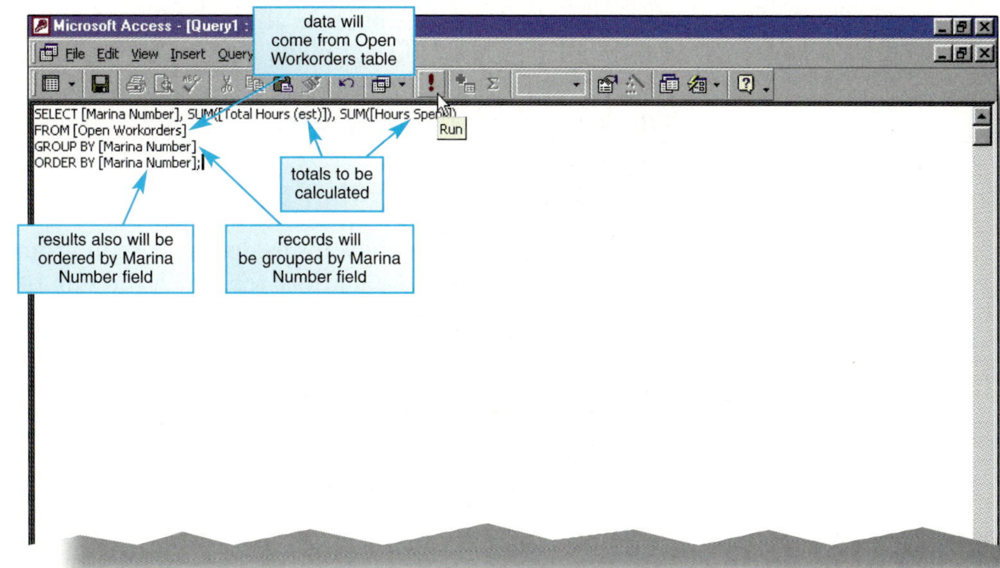

FIGURE 9-71

The command is entered (Figure 9-71).

3 Click the Run button.

The results display (Figure 9-72). The first row represents the group of workorders for marina AD57. For these workorders, the sum of the Total Hours (est) amounts is 6 and the sum of the Hours Spent amounts is 2. The second row represents the group of workorders for marina BL72. For these workorders, the sum of the Total Hours (est) amounts is 3 and the sum of the Hours Spent amounts is 0.

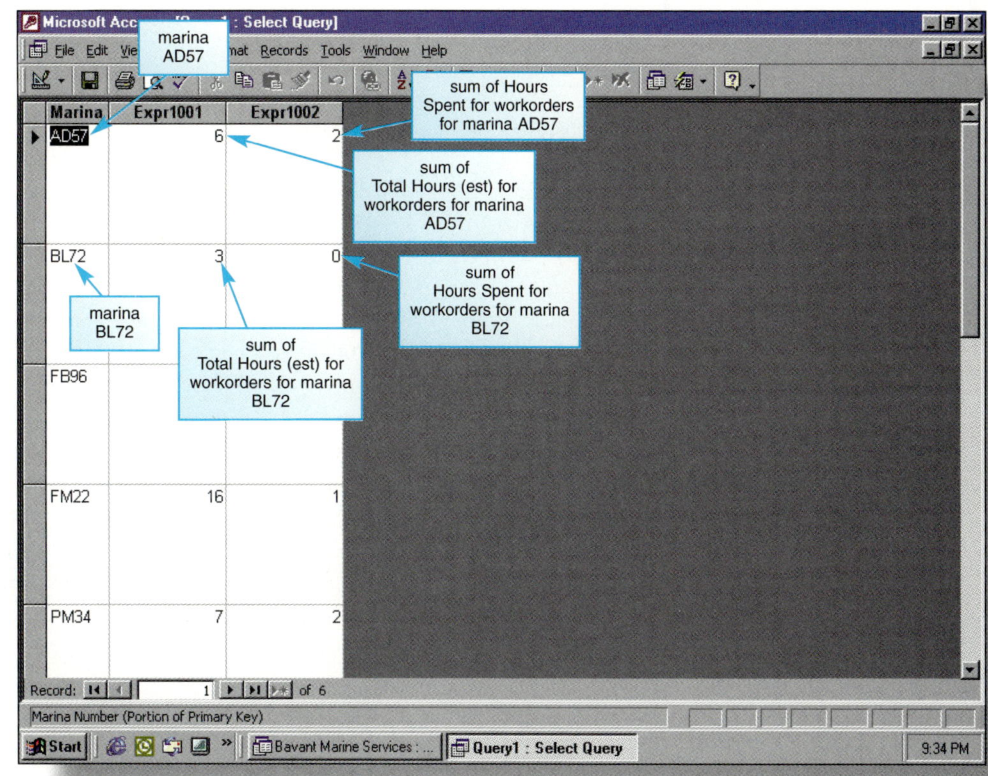

FIGURE 9-72

When rows are grouped, one line of output is produced for each group. The only things that may be displayed are statistics calculated for the group or fields whose values are the same for all rows in a group. For example, it would make sense to display the marina number, because all the workorders in the group have the same marina number. It would not make sense to display the start date, because the start date will vary from one row in a group to another. SQL could not determine which start date to display for the group.

Restricting the Groups that Display

In some cases you only want to display certain groups. For example, you may wish to display only those marinas for which the sum of Total Hours (Est) is greater than 6. This restriction does not apply to individual rows, but rather to groups. Because WHERE applies only to rows, it is not possible to accomplish the kind of selection you have here. Fortunately, the word HAVING groups in a similar way as WHERE groups rows. Use the following steps to restrict the groups that display using the word HAVING.

To Restrict the Groups that Display

1. **Click the View button arrow and then click SQL View.**

2. **Move the insertion point to the beginning of the fourth line (ORDER BY [Marina Number];) and click. Press the ENTER key, click the beginning of the new blank line and then type** `HAVING SUM([Total Hours (est)])>6` **as the fourth line. Point to the Run button.**

The command is entered (Figure 9-73).

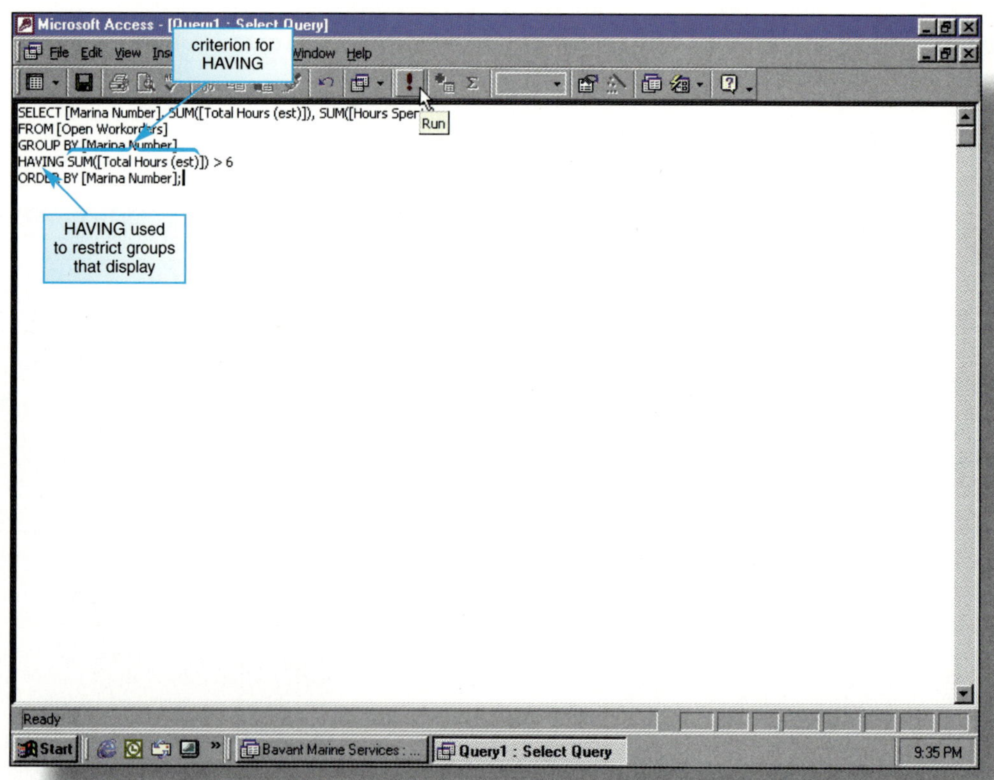

FIGURE 9-73

Click the Run button.

The results display (Figure 9-74). Only those groups for which the sum of the Total Hours (est) is greater than 6 display.

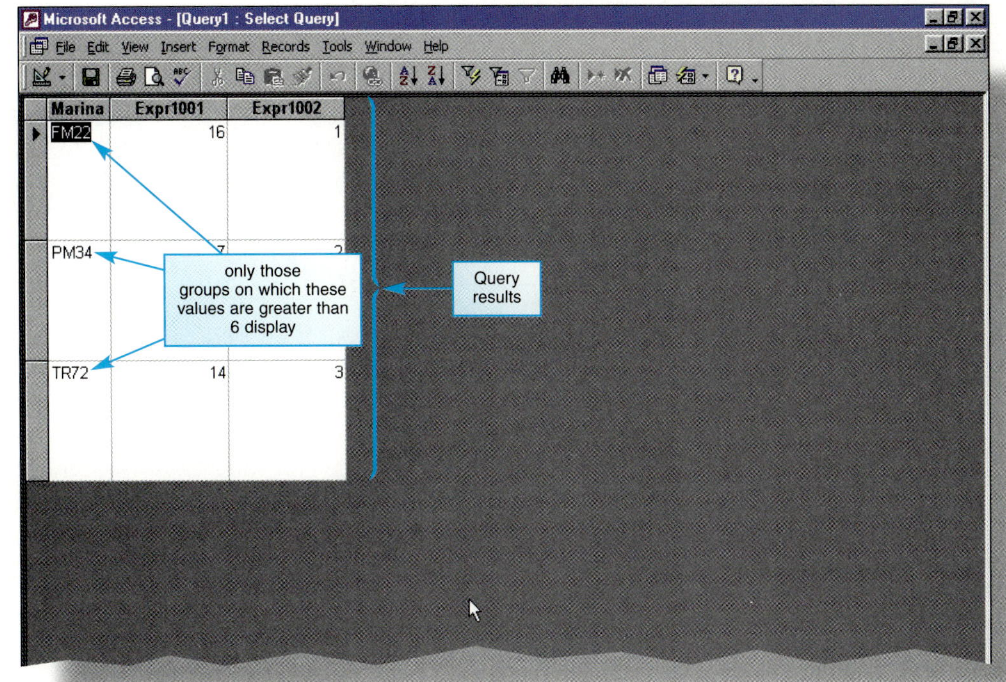

FIGURE 9-74

Joining Tables

Many queries require data from more than one table. Just as with creating queries in Design view, it is necessary to be able to **join** tables, that is, to find rows in two tables that have identical values in matching fields. In SQL this is accomplished through appropriate criteria following the word WHERE.

If you wish to list the Marina Number, Name, Location, Category Number, Total Hours (est), and Hours Spent fields for all workorders, you need data from both the Open Workorders and Marina tables. The Marina Number field is in both tables, the Name field is only in the Marina table, all other fields are only in the Open Workorders table. You need to access both tables in your SQL command, as follows:

1. After the word SELECT, you indicate all fields you want displayed.
2. After the word FROM, you list all tables involved in the query.
3. After the word WHERE, you give the criterion that will restrict the data to be retrieved to only those rows from the two tables that match.

There is a problem, however. The matching fields are both called Marina Number. There is a field in Marina called Marina Number, as well as a field in Open Workorders called Marina Number. In this case, if you only enter Marina Number, it will not be clear which table you mean. It is necessary to **qualify** Marina Number; that is, to specify which field in which table you are referring to. You do this by preceding the name of the field with the name of the table, followed by a period. The Marina Number field in the Open Workorders table is [Open Workorders].[Marina Number]. The Marina Number field in the Marina table is [Marina].[Marina Number].

Perform the steps on the next page to list the Marina Number, Name, Location, Category Number, Total Hours (est), and Hours Spent fields for all workorders.

Join

There are different types of joins that can be implemented in SQL. For example, in joining marinas and workorders in such a way that a marina will display even if it has no open workorders, you would need to perform a type of join called an outer join. For more information, visit the Access 2000 More About page (www.scsite.com/ac2000/more.htm) and click Joins in SQL.

To Join Tables

1 Click the View button arrow, click SQL View, and then select and delete the current SQL command.

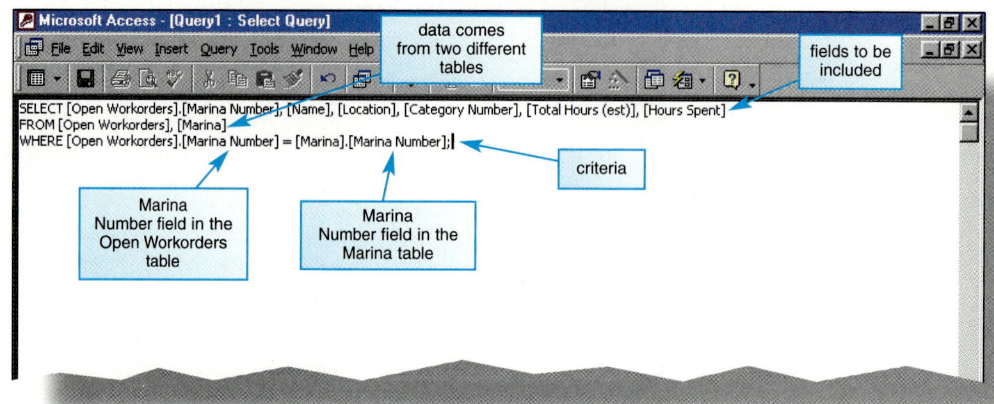

FIGURE 9-75

2 Type `SELECT [Open Workorders].[Marina Number], [Name], [Location], [Category Number], [Total Hours (est)], [Hours Spent]` **as the first line of the command. Press the ENTER key and then type** `FROM [Open Workorders], [Marina]` **as the second line. Press the ENTER key and then type** `WHERE [Open Workorders].[Marina Number]=[Marina].[Marina Number];` **as the third line.**

The command is entered (Figure 9-75).

3 Click the Run button.

The results display (Figure 9-76). They include the appropriate data from both the Open Workorders table and the Marina table.

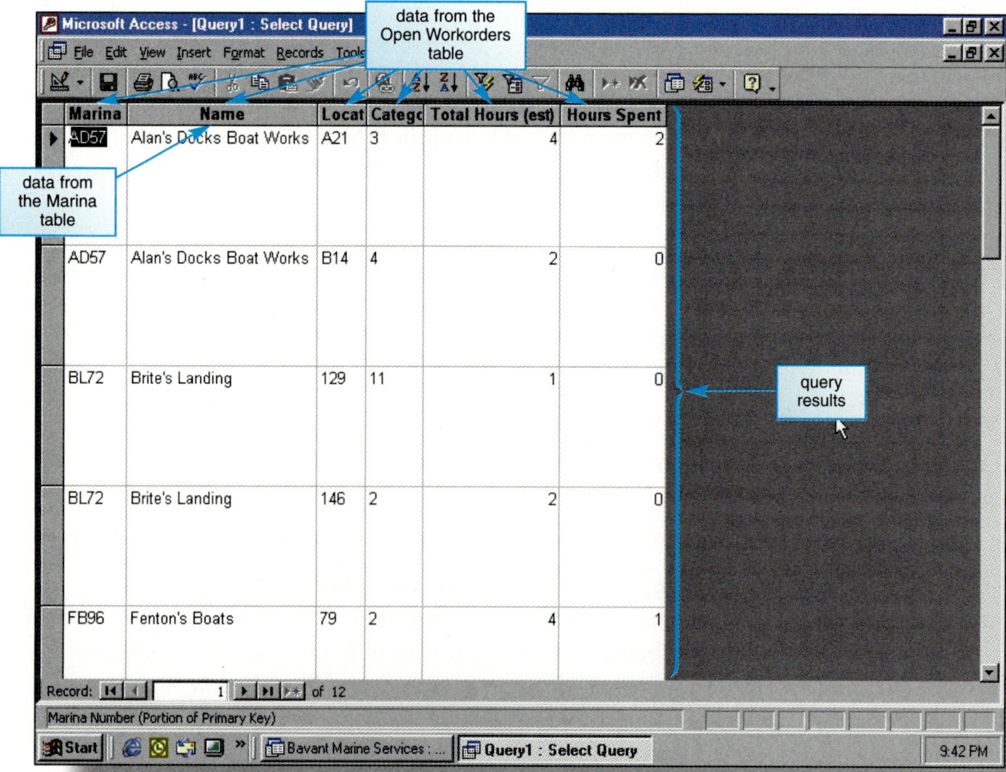

Marina	Name	Locat	Categc	Total Hours (est)	Hours Spent
AD57	Alan's Docks Boat Works	A21	3	4	2
AD57	Alan's Docks Boat Works	B14	4	2	0
BL72	Brite's Landing	129	11	1	0
BL72	Brite's Landing	146	2	2	0
FB96	Fenton's Boats	79	2	4	1

FIGURE 9-76

Note that whenever there is potential ambiguity, you must qualify the fields involved. You can qualify other fields as well, even if there is no confusion. For example, rather than [Name], you could have typed [Marina].[Name] to indicate the Name field in the Marina table. Some people prefer to qualify all fields and this is not a bad approach. In this text, you only will qualify fields when it is necessary to do so.

Restricting the Records in a Join

You can restrict the records to be included in a join by creating a compound criterion. The criterion will include the criterion necessary to join the tables along with a criterion to restrict the records. The criteria will be connected with AND. Perform the following steps to list the Marina Number, Name, Location, Category Number, Total Hours (est), and Hours Spent fields for all workorders on which the hours spent amount is greater than 0.

To Restrict the Records in a Join

1 **Click the View button arrow and then click SQL View.**

2 **Click immediately after the semicolon on the third line. Press the BACKSPACE key to delete the semicolon. Press the ENTER key and then type** `AND [Hours Spent]>0;` **as the third line.**

The command is entered (Figure 9-77).

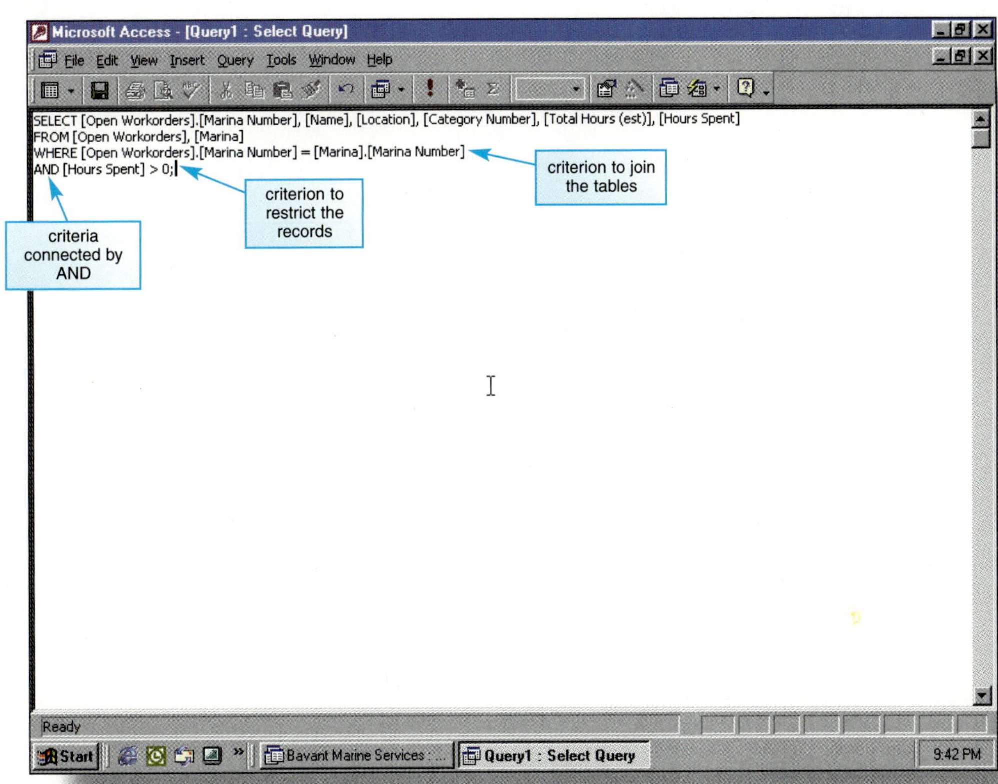

FIGURE 9-77

Click the Run button.

The results display (Figure 9-78). Only those workorders for which the hours spent amount is greater than 0 display.

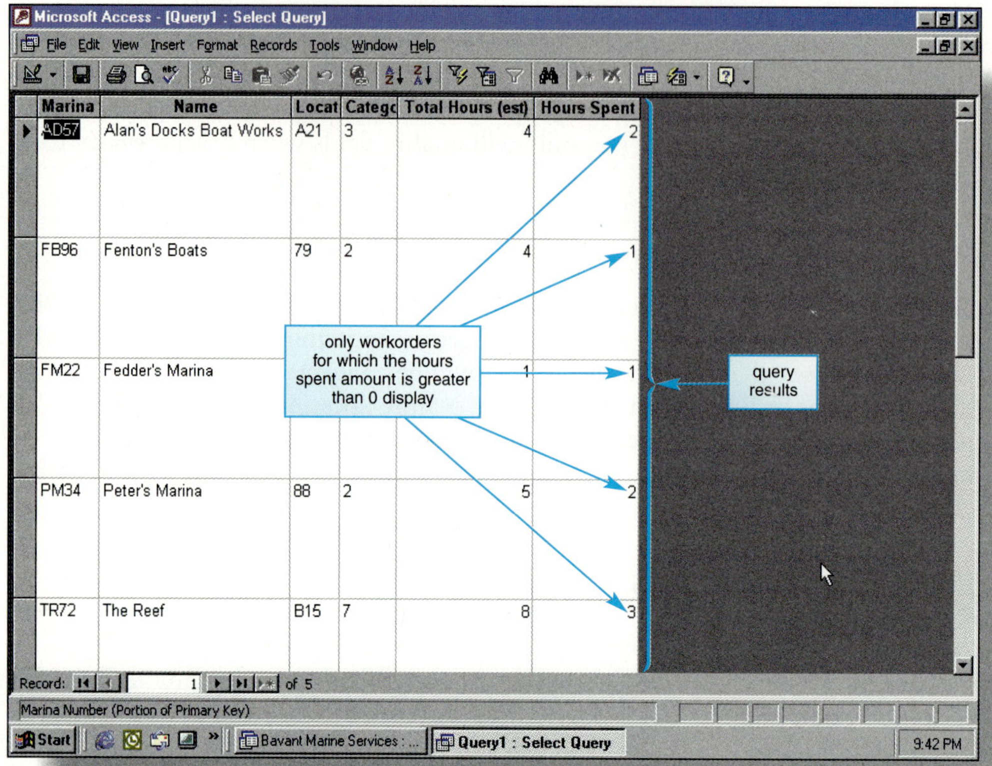

FIGURE 9-78

Joining Multiple Tables

In some cases, you will need data from more than two tables. The following steps include all the data from the previous query together with the category description, which is found in the Category table. Thus, the Category table also must be included in the query as well as a condition relating the Category and Open Workorders tables. The condition to do so is [Open Workorders].[Category Number] = [Category].[Category Number]. The following steps produce the desired results.

Steps To Join Multiple Tables

1 **Click the View button arrow, click SQL View, and then select and delete the current SQL command.**

2 **Type** `SELECT [Open Workorders].[Marina Number], [Name], [Location], [Category].[Category Number], [Category Description], [Total Hours (est)], [Hours Spent]` **as the first line of the command. Press the ENTER key and then type** `FROM [Open Workorders], [Marina], [Category]` **as the second line. Press the ENTER key and then type** `WHERE [Open Workorders].[Marina Number]=[Marina].[Marina Number]` **as the third line. Press the ENTER key and then type** `AND [Open Workorders].[Category Number]=[Category].[Category Number]` **as the fourth line. Press the ENTER key and then type** `AND [Hours Spent]>0;` **as the fifth line.**

The command is entered (Figure 9-79).

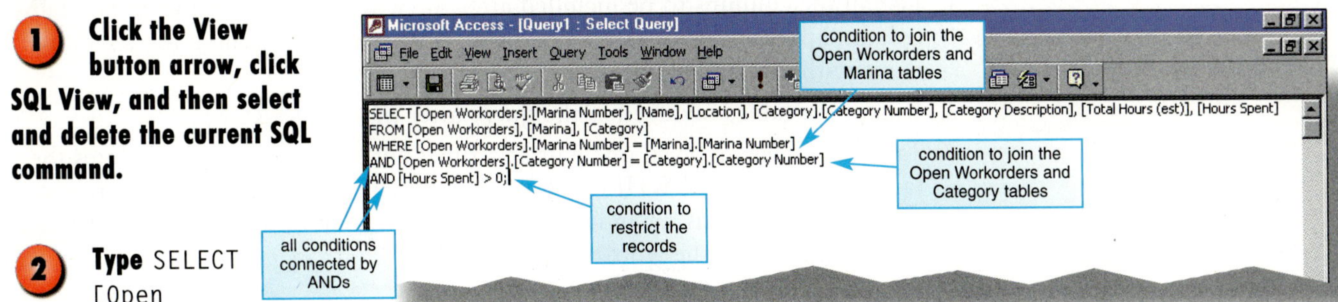

FIGURE 9-79

3 **Click the Run button. Reduce the size of the Category Description column so that all columns display.**

The results display (Figure 9-80).

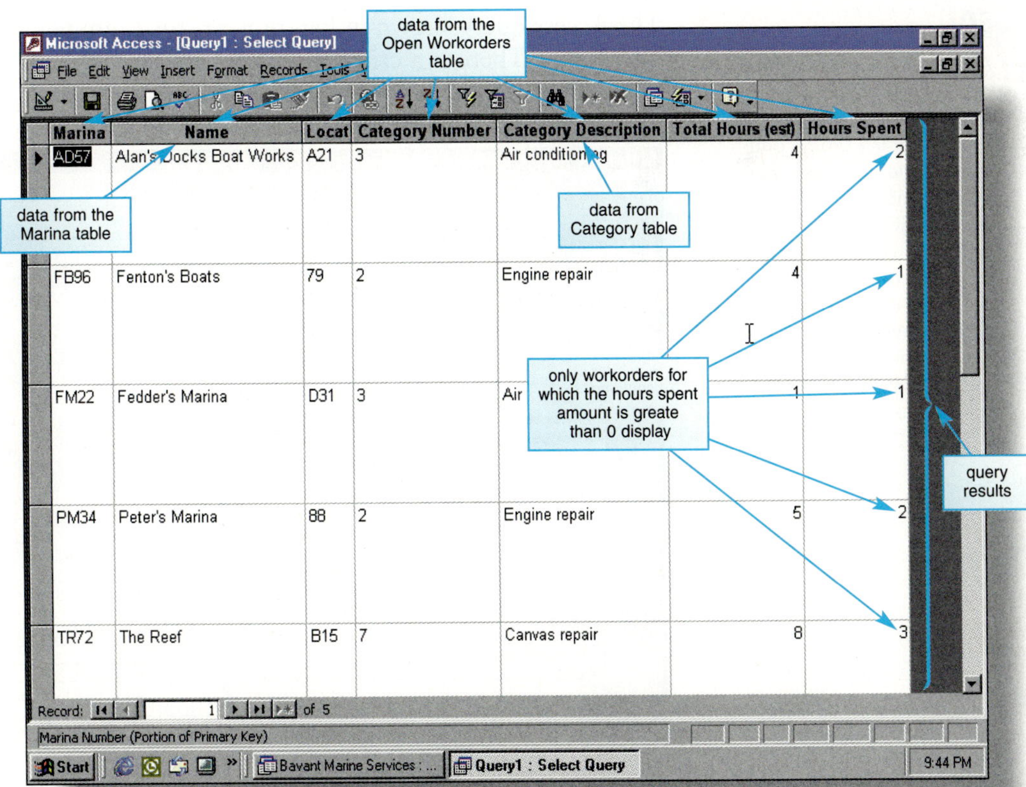

FIGURE 9-80

To create an SQL command that joins data from more than two tables, follow these steps:

1. List all the columns to be included after the word SELECT. If the name of any column appears in more than one table, qualify it by preceding the column name with the table name.
2. List all the tables involved in the query after the word FROM.
3. Take the tables involved one pair at a time, put the condition that relates the tables after the word WHERE. Join these conditions with AND. If there are any other conditions, include them after the word WHERE and connect them to the others with the word AND.

Closing The Query

The following step closes the query by closing the Query Datasheet window.

TO CLOSE A QUERY

1. Click the Close Window button for the Microsoft Access – [Query1 : Select Query] window and then click No.

> **More About**
>
> **Access-Generated SQL**
>
> After creating a SQL command, you can move to Design view. Access automatically fills in the Design grid appropriately to match your SQL command. You can then return to SQL view and once again see your command. If you make any changes in the Design grid before returning to SQL view, however, Access will reformat your command as an Access-Generated SQL command.

Comparison with Access-Generated SQL

When you create a query in Design view, Access automatically creates a corresponding SQL command that is similar to the commands you have created. The Access query shown in Figure 9-81, for example, includes the Marina Number and Name. There is a criterion in the City field (Burton), but the City field will not display in the results. The View menu displays in the figure.

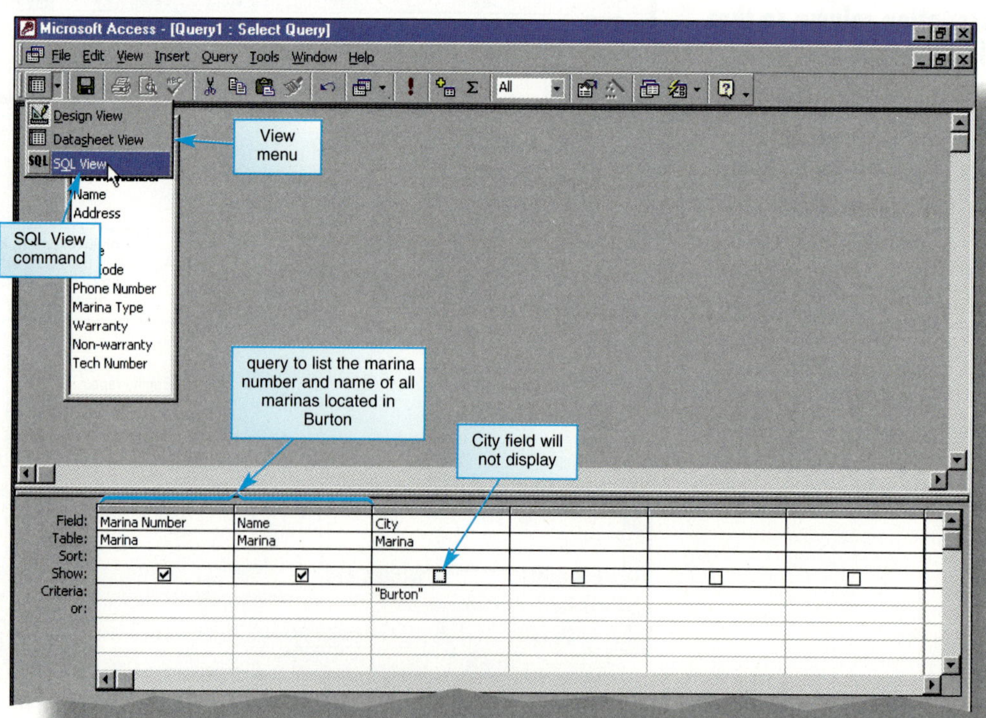

FIGURE 9-81

The corresponding SQL query is shown in Figure 9-82. It is very similar to the queries you have entered, but there are three slight differences. First, the fields are qualified (Marina.[Marina Number] and Marina.Name), even though they do not need to be. There only is one table involved in the query, so no qualification is necessary. Second, the Name field is not enclosed in square brackets. It is legitimate not to enclose it in square brackets because there are no spaces or other special characters in the field name. Finally, there are extra parentheses in the criteria around the criteria that follow the word WHERE.

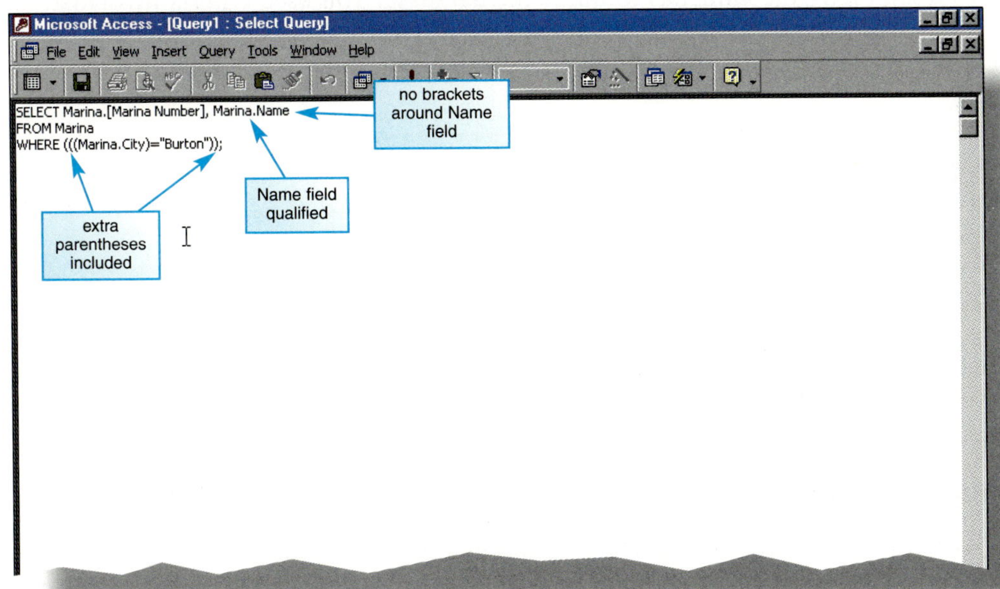

FIGURE 9-82

Both the style used by Access and the style you have been using are legitimate. The choice of style is a personal preference.

Closing the Database

The following step closes the database by closing its Database window.

TO CLOSE A DATABASE

 Click the Close button for the Bavant Marine Services : Database window.

CASE PERSPECTIVE SUMMARY

In Project 9, you assisted the management of Bavant Marine Services by becoming the administrator of their database system. You converted their database to a prior version of Access for a user who needed to query the database and did not have the current version. You analyzed both tables and performance and also produced important documentation. You also specified important integrity constraints involving an input mask and referential integrity. You made sure the database was secure by setting a password and also by encrypting the database. You created a grouped data access page for access to the data via the Internet. You also created a replica of the database for use by a remote user and then synchronized that replica with the Design Master. You also learned about the importance of SQL and used it in several queries.

Project Summary

In Project 9, you learned how to create an Access 97 version of the database. You used the Table Analyzer, the Performance Analyzer, and the Documenter. You created a custom input mask and also specified referential integrity options. You ensured that the Switchboard automatically displays when the database is opened by setting startup options. You set a password and encrypted the database. You also created a grouped data access page. You created a replica for remote users of the database, updated the replica, and synchronized the replica with the Design Master. You wrote several SQL commands to query the database. You used criteria involving both Number and Text fields, compound criteria, and criteria involving NOT. You also used a computed field, sorted query results, and used built-in functions. You used grouping in a query and also joined tables.

What You Should Know

Having completed this project, you now should be able to perform the following tasks:

- Close a Database *(A 9.57)*
- Close a Query *(A 9.56)*
- Convert a Database to an Earlier Version *(A 9.7)*
- Create a Grouped Data Access Page *(A 9.26)*
- Create a New SQL Query *(A 9.36)*
- Create a Replica *(A 9.32)*
- Encrypt a Database *(A 9.24)*
- Include All Fields *(A 9.39)*
- Include Only Certain Fields *(A 9.38)*
- Join Multiple Tables *(A 9.55)*
- Join Tables *(A 9.52)*
- Open a Database *(A 9.6)*
- Open a Database in Exclusive Mode *(A 9.21)*
- Prepare to Enter a New SQL Command *(A 9.39)*
- Preview the Data Access Page *(A 9.30)*
- Remove a Password *(A 9.25)*
- Restrict the Groups that Display *(A 9.50)*
- Restrict the Records in a Join *(A 9.53)*
- Set a Password *(A 9.22)*
- Set Startup Options *(A 9.20)*
- Sort the Results *(A 9.45)*
- Specify Referential Integrity Options *(A 9.16)*
- Synchronize the Design Master and the Replica *(A 9.34)*
- Update a Table with Cascade Options *(A 9.18)*
- Use a Built-In Function *(A 9.46)*
- Use Compound Criteria *(A 9.42)*
- Use a Computed Field *(A 9.44)*
- Use a Criterion Involving a Numeric Field *(A 9.40)*
- Use a Criterion Involving a Text Field *(A 9.41)*
- Use the Replica *(A 9.33)*
- Use an Input Mask *(A 9.15)*
- Use Grouping *(A 9.49)*
- Use Multiple Functions in the Same Command *(A 9.47)*
- Use NOT in a Criterion *(A 9.43)*
- Use the Documenter *(A 9.13)*
- Use the Performance Analyzer *(A 9.11)*
- Use the Table Analyzer *(A 9.8)*

1 Administering the Sidewalk Scrapers Database

Instructions: Start Access. Open the Sidewalk Scrapers database from the Access Data Disk. See the inside back cover for instructions for downloading the Access Data Disk or see your instructor for information on accessing the files required for this book. Perform the following tasks.

1. Use the Table Analyzer to analyze the Customer table. On your own paper, list the results of the analysis.
2. Use the Performance Analyzer to analyze all the tables and queries in the Sidewalk Scrapers database. On your own paper, list the results of the analysis.
3. Use the Documenter to produce documentation for the Rate table. Print the documentation.
4. Create a custom input mask for the Customer Number field in the Customer table. The first two characters of the customer number must be uppercase letters and the last two characters must be digits. No position may be blank. On your own paper, list the input mask that you created.
5. Open the Relationships window and edit the relationship between the Customer table and the Worker table. Cascade the update so that any changes made to the Worker Id field in the Worker table will result in a change in the Worker Id field in the Customer table. Save the changes to the layout of the Relationships window.
6. Open the Worker table in Datasheet view and change the worker id for worker 10 from 10 to 20. Close the table.
7. Print the Customer table.
8. Use SQL to create a query that joins the Customer table and the Service table. Include the Customer Number, Name, Service Date, and Service Time fields in the query results. Run the query and print the results.
9. Return to the SQL window, highlight the SQL command you used in Step 8 above and click Copy on the Query Design toolbar.
10. Start Microsoft Word, create a new document, type your name at the top of the document, and then click Paste on the Standard toolbar.
11. Print the Word document containing the SQL command.
12. Close Word and Access.

1 Administering the School Connection Database

Problem: The Booster's Club has placed you in charge of administering their database system. A database administrator must perform activities such as analyzing the performance of the DBMS, specifying integrity constraints, protecting the database from unauthorized use, creating data access pages, and using SQL.

Instructions: Start Access. Open the School Connection database from the Access Data Disk. See the inside back cover for instructions for downloading the Access Data Disk or see your instructor for information on accessing the files required for this book. Perform the following tasks.

1. Use the Performance Analyzer to analyze all the tables and queries in the School Connection database. On your own paper, list the results of the analysis.
2. Use the Documenter to print the documentation for the Reorder table.
3. Vendor Code is a field in both the Item and Vendor tables. Create an input mask for the Vendor Code field in both tables. On your own paper, list the input mask that you created.
4. Edit the relationship between the Reorder table and the Item table so that an item may be deleted from the Item table and then automatically deleted from the Reorder table.
5. Edit the relationship between the Vendor table and the Item table so that a change to the Vendor Code field in the Vendor table will result in the same change to the Vendor Code field in the Item table.
6. Open the Vendor table and change the vendor code for Trinkets 'n More to TR.
7. Print the Item table.
8. Open the Item table and delete item PL05.
9. Print the Item table and the Reorder table.
10. Create the grouped data access page for the Reorder table shown in Figure 9-83. Print the data access page for the record shown in Figure 9-83. To print the page, preview the page and then click Print on the File menu in the Microsoft Internet Explorer window.

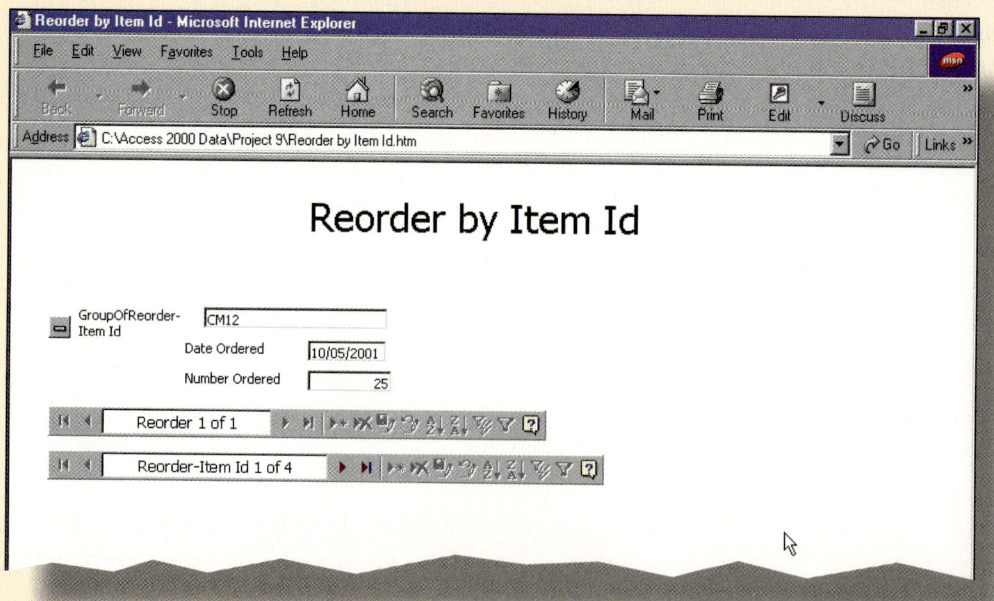

FIGURE 9-83

11. Open Microsoft Word, create a new document, and then type your name at the top. With both Access and Word open on the desktop, create the queries in Steps 12 through 15 in SQL. For each query, run the query, print the query results and copy the SQL command to the Word document. To copy the SQL command, highlight the command, click Copy on the Query Design toolbar, switch to Word, and then click Paste on the Standard toolbar.
12. Find all records in the Item table where the difference between the cost of the item and the selling price of the item is less than $2.00. Display the item id, description, cost, and selling price.
13. Join the Reorder table and the Item table. Display the item id, description, number ordered, cost, and total cost (cost * number ordered). Be sure to name the computed field, Total Cost.
14. Join the Item and Reorder tables. Display the item id, description, and number ordered for all items where the number ordered is less than 5.
15. Find the total number of reordered items for each item. Display the item id and total number reordered.
16. Print the Word document that includes the 4 SQL commands used above.

2 Administering the City Area Bus Company Database

Problem: The City Area Bus Company has placed you in charge of administering their database system. A database administrator must perform activities such as analyzing the performance of the DBMS, specifying integrity constraints, protecting the database from unauthorized use, creating data access pages, and using SQL.

Instructions: Open the City Area Bus Company database from the Access Data Disk. See the inside back cover for instructions for downloading the Access Data Disk or see your instructor for information on accessing the files required for this book. Perform the following tasks.

1. Use the Performance Analyzer to analyze all the tables and queries in the City Area Bus Company database. On your own paper, list the results of the analysis.
2. Use the Documenter to print the documentation for the Category table.
3. Sales Rep Number is a field in both the Advertiser and the Sales Rep tables. Create an input mask for the Sales Rep Number field in both tables. On your own paper, list the input mask that you created.
4. Edit the relationship between the Active Accounts and the Advertiser tables so that an advertiser may be deleted from the Advertiser table and then automatically deleted from the Active Accounts table.
5. Edit the relationship between the Sales Rep and the Advertiser tables so that a change to the Sales Rep Number field in the Sales Rep table will result in the same change to the Sales Rep Number field in the Advertiser table.
6. Open the Sales Rep table and then change the sales rep number for Pat Reed to 46.
7. Print the Advertiser table.
8. Open the Advertiser table and then delete advertiser HC11.
9. Print the Advertiser and the Active Accounts tables.
10. Create the grouped data access page for the Active Accounts table shown in Figure 9-84 on the next page. Print the data access page for the record shown in Figure 9-84. To print the page, preview the page and then click Print on the File menu in the Microsoft Internet Explorer window.

(continued)

Administering the City Area Bus Company Database *(continued)*

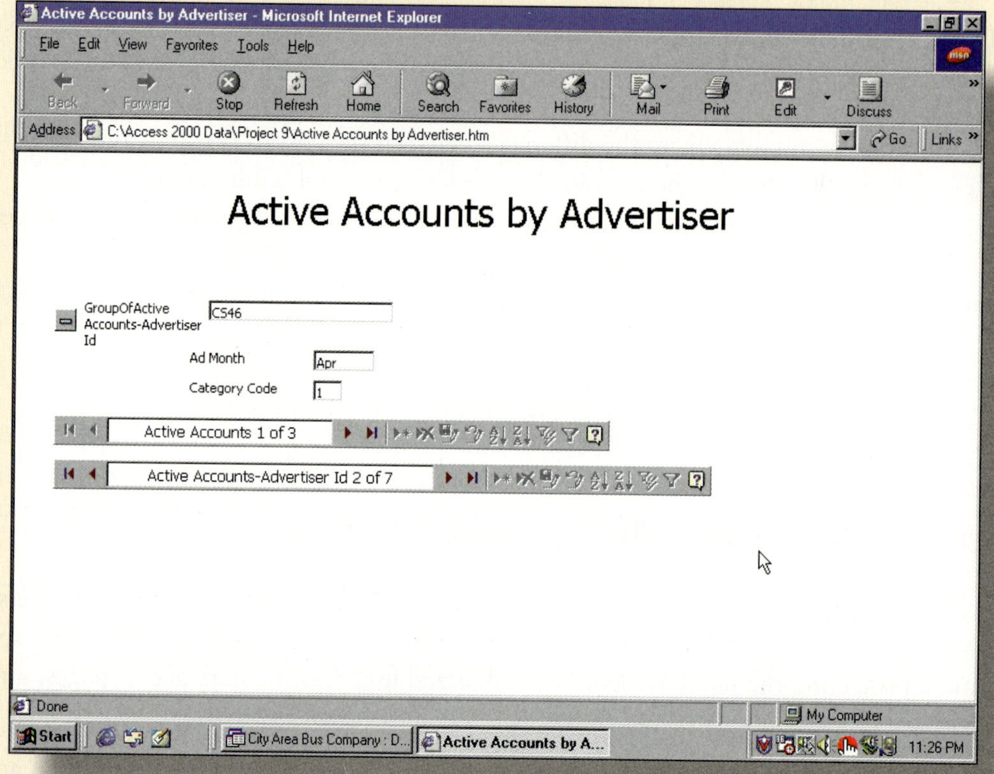

FIGURE 9-84

11. Open Microsoft Word, create a new document, and then type your name at the top. With both Access and Word open on the desktop, create the following queries in SQL. For each query, run the query, print the query results and copy the SQL command to the Word document. To copy the SQL command, highlight the command, click Copy on the Query Design toolbar, switch to Word, and then click Paste on the Standard toolbar.
12. Display the Advertiser Id, Name, City, and State fields for all advertisers. Sort the records in ascending order by city within state.
13. Display the Advertiser Id, Name, City, and Balance fields for all advertisers that are not located in the city of Crescentville. Sort the records in ascending order by city.
14. Display the sales rep's First Name and Last Name, Advertiser Id, Name, and Description fields for all active accounts that are running ads during the month of April.
15. Display the advertiser id, name, and total amount (balance + amount paid) for all records where the advertiser is located in MA.
16. Group the active accounts by advertiser id and count the number of months for which the advertiser has ads.
17. Print the Word document that includes the five SQL commands used in Steps 12 through 16.

3 Administering the Resort Rentals Database

Problem: The Resort Rentals company has placed you in charge of administering their database system. A database administrator must perform activities such as analyzing the performance of the DBMS, specifying integrity constraints, protecting the database from unauthorized use, creating data access pages, and using SQL.

Instructions: Open the Resort Rentals database from the Access Data Disk. See the inside back cover for instructions for downloading the Access Data Disk or see your instructor for information on accessing the files required for this book. Perform the following tasks.

1. Use the Performance Analyzer to analyze all the tables and queries in the Resort Rentals database. On your own paper, list the results of the analysis.
2. Use the Documenter to display the documentation for the Active Rentals table. Print page 1 of the Documenter by click Print on the File menu, and then clicking the Pages button. Enter 1 in both the From and To boxes.
3. Renter Id is a field in both the Renter and the Active Rentals tables. Create an input mask for the Renter Id field in both tables. On your own paper, list the input mask that you created.
4. Edit the relationship between the Rental Unit and the Active Rentals tables so that a rental unit may be deleted from the Rental Unit table and then automatically deleted from the Active Rentals table.
5. Edit the relationship between the Renter and the Active Rentals tables so that a change to the renter id in the Renter table will result in the same change to the renter id in the Active Rentals table.
6. Open the Renter table and then change the renter id for Stephanie Taber to R007.
7. Print the Active Rentals table.
8. Open the Rental Unit table and then delete rental id 112.
9. Print the Rental Unit and the Active Rentals tables.
10. Create the grouped data access page for the Active Rentals table shown in Figure 9-85. Print the data access page for the record shown in Figure 9-85. To print the page, preview the page and then click Print on the File menu in the Microsoft Internet Explorer window.

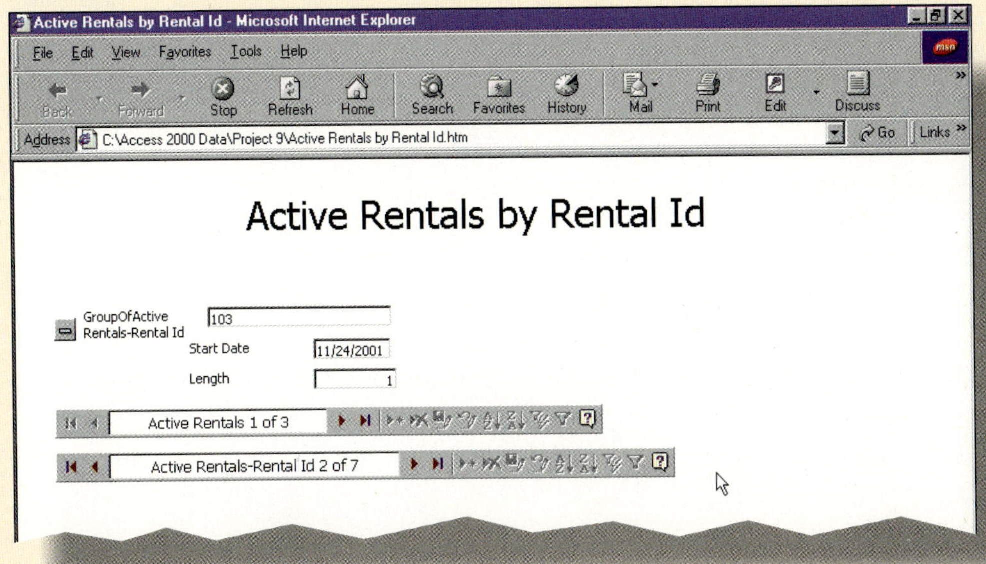

FIGURE 9-85

(continued)

Administering the Resort Rentals Database *(continued)*

11. Open Microsoft Word, create a new document, and type your name at the top. With both Access and Word open on the desktop, create the following queries in SQL. For each query, run the query, print the query results and copy the SQL command to the Word document. To copy the SQL command, highlight the command, click Copy on the Query Design toolbar, switch to Word, and then click Paste on the Standard toolbar.
12. Display and print the rental address, renter first name and last name, and total amount owed (weekly rate * length) for all active rentals.
13. Display and print the average weekly rate by city.
14. Display and print the owner's first and last name, the rental address, and the weekly rate for all rental units that have an ocean view. (*Hint*: Search Yes/No fields by using True and False as the criterion.)
15. Display and print the rental id, rental address, start date, length, and renter first and last name for all active rentals.
16. Display and print the rental data for all rental units that either are in Shady Beach or San Toma.
17. Print the Word document that includes the five SQL commands used in Steps 12 through 16.

Cases and Places

The difficulty of these case studies varies:
◗ are the least difficult; ◗◗ are more difficult; and ◗◗◗ are the most difficult.

1 ◗ Open the Computer Items database on the Access Data Disk. Perform the following database administration tasks and answer the questions about the database.

a. Run the Table Analyzer on all tables and describe the results of the analysis.
b. Run the Performance Analyzer on all tables and queries and describe the results of the analysis.
c. Set a password for the Computer Items database. Why did you choose that particular password? What will happen if you try to open the Computer Items database and cannot remember your password?
d. Create an Access 97 version of the Computer Items database.
e. Encrypt the database. What is the purpose of encryption?
f. Modify the startup options so that the switchboard opens automatically when the database is opened.

2 ◗ Use the Computer Items database and create a grouped data access page for the Reorder Status table. Print the grouped data access page. Edit the relationship between the Supplier table and the Items table to cascade the update between the two tables. Edit the relationship between the Reorder Status and the Item tables to cascade the delete between the two tables. Change the Supplier Code for Human Interface to HF. Delete the item with Item Id 1663. Print the Item, Supplier, and Reorder Status tables.

3 ◗◗ Use the Computer Items database for this assignment. Create and run the following SQL queries. Print the query results, copy the SQL commands to a Word document, and then print the Word document.

a. Find the total cost (units on hand * cost) of all items.
b. Find the average cost by supplier.
c. Display the item id, description, reorder data, reorder number, and vendor name for all items that are on reorder.
d. Display the item id, description, cost, and selling price of all items where the difference between the selling price and cost is more than $1.50.

Cases and Places

4 ▶▶ Use the Galaxy Books database on the Access Data Disk for this assignment. Create custom input masks for the Book Code and Customer Number fields. Be sure to use the input mask in all tables that include either field. Create a grouped data access page for the Book table that groups records by author. Print the grouped data access page. Edit the relationship between the Publisher table and the Book table to cascade the update between the two tables. Edit the relationship between the Book Order and the Book tables to cascade the delete between the two tables. Change the Publisher Code for Pearless Books to PR. Delete the book, No Infinity. Print the Book, Publisher, and Book Order tables. Create and run the following SQL queries. Print the query results, copy the SQL commands to a Word document, and then print the Word document.

a. Display and print all the customer data. Sort the data in ascending order by city within state.
b. Display and print the book title, price, date ordered, customer first name, and last name for all books that are on order.
c. Display and print the book code, title, price, publication year, and publisher name for all books that cost more than $6.00.
d. Display and print all the data for books that were not written by E Dearling.
e. Display and print all the data for books that are published by VanNester and cost less than $6.00.
f. Display and print the total cost of inventory and the average book price for each publisher.

5 ▶▶▶ Replicate the Galaxy Books database. Use the replica and add yourself as a customer. Select a book to purchase and add the data to the Book Order table. Synchronize the master and the replica. Use the master to print the updated tables.

Microsoft Access 2000

Using Access Data in Other Applications

CASE PERSPECTIVE

Bavant Marine Services has determined that it needs to export (copy) some of the data in its database to other formats. Bavant users proficient in Microsoft Excel want to use its powerful what-if features to analyze data concerning open workorders. Other users want the workorder data to be placed in a Microsoft Word document. They will use Word to add other items to the document, format the document in the appropriate fashion, and then print it. The results will form a key portion of an important presentation that they need to make in the near future. Bavant also wants to be able to e-mail one of the Microsoft Access reports included in the database to several users. Upon investigating the best way to accomplish this, Bavant determined they need to create a snapshot of the database. The snapshot, which is stored in a separate file, then can be sent to anyone who has the Snapshot Viewer. Your task is to help Bavant Marine Services export the data to Microsoft Excel and Microsoft Word as well as create a snapshot of the report.

Introduction

Exporting is the process of copying database objects to another database, a spreadsheet, or some other format so that another application can use the data. There are different ways to export data. The two more common ways are to use the Export command on the File menu, which you will use to export a query to a Microsoft Excel worksheet (Figure 1a on the next page), and to use drag-and-drop, which you will use to export the query to a Microsoft Word document (Figure 1b on the next page).

Microsoft Access allows you to export database objects to many different destinations including another Microsoft Access database. In addition, you can export to other databases such as dBASE and Paradox and to spreadsheet programs such as Lotus. With Access, you can export to an HTML document and to a Rich Text Format file (.rtf), which then can be opened in many word processing and desktop publishing programs.

You also can automate the process so the user can run a macro or click a button in a switchboard to export the database object to a selected format. To create such a macro, use the TransferDatabase action in the macro and then fill in the arguments appropriately. After doing so, you then could associate the running of the macro with an item on one of the pages in your switchboard.

There are occasions when you want to send a report to a user via e-mail. It would be prohibitive to send the whole database to the other user, just so the user could print or view a single report. In addition, doing so would require the other user to have Microsoft Access installed. A better way is to create a snapshot of the report. A **snapshot** is a special file that contains the report exactly as it displays when printed. You will use the Export command to create a snapshot of a report. The other user then can use the Snapshot Viewer (Figure 1c on the next page) to view or print the report.

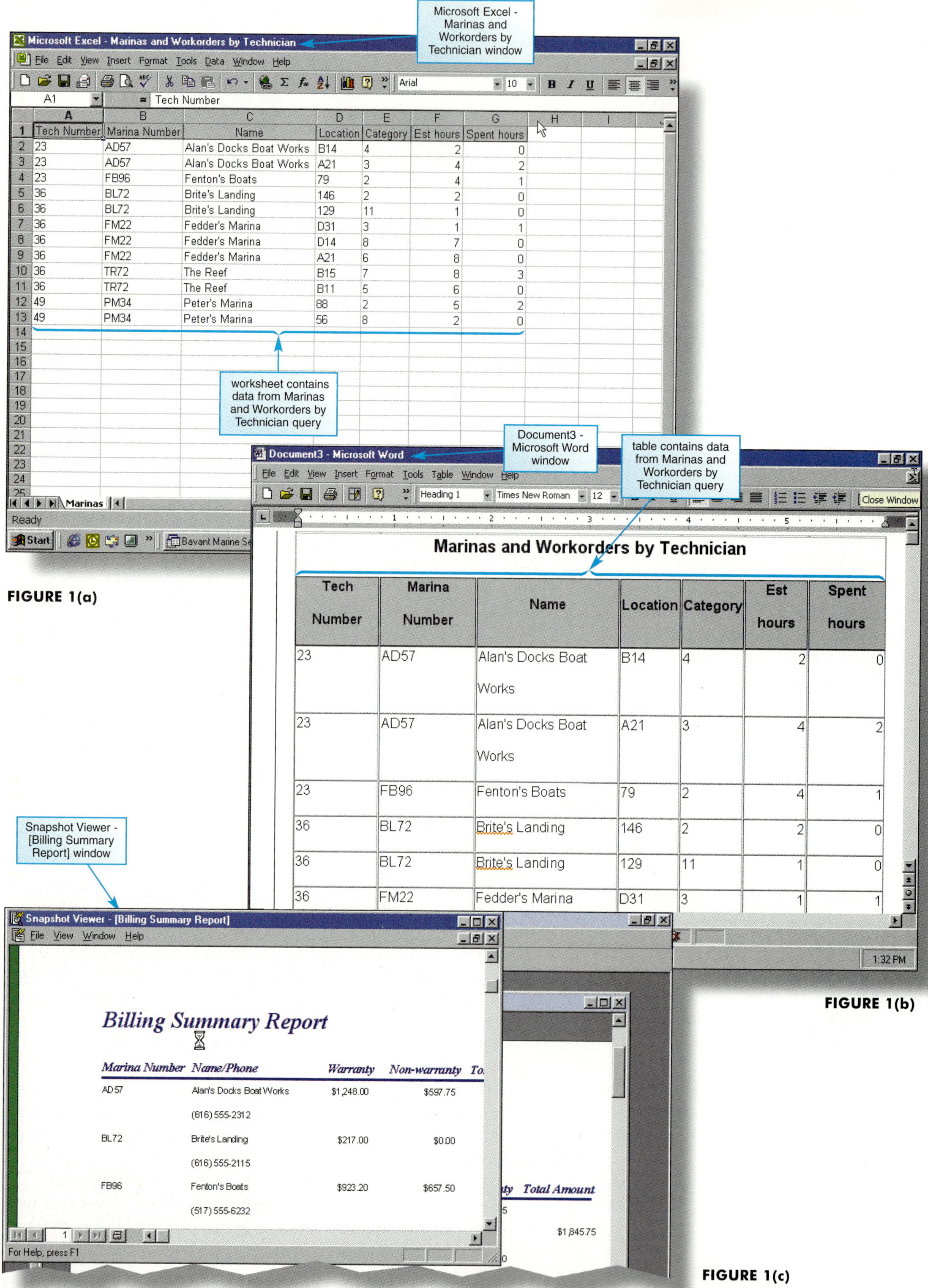

Tech Number	Marina Number	Name	Location	Category	Est hours	Spent hours
23	AD57	Alan's Docks Boat Works	B14	4	2	0
23	AD57	Alan's Docks Boat Works	A21	3	4	2
23	FB96	Fenton's Boats	79	2	4	1
36	BL72	Brite's Landing	146	2	2	0
36	BL72	Brite's Landing	129	11	1	0
36	FM22	Fedder's Marina	D31	3	1	1
36	FM22	Fedder's Marina	D14	8	7	0
36	FM22	Fedder's Marina	A21	6	8	0
36	TR72	The Reef	B15	7	8	3
36	TR72	The Reef	B11	5	6	0
49	PM34	Peter's Marina	88	2	5	2
49	PM34	Peter's Marina	56	8	2	0

FIGURE 1(a)

FIGURE 1(b)

FIGURE 1(c)

Opening the Database

Before carrying out the steps in this project, you first must open the database. To do so, perform the following steps.

TO OPEN A DATABASE

1. Click the Start button.
2. Click Open Office Document and then click 3½ Floppy (A:) in the Look in box. If necessary, click the Bavant Marine Services database name.
3. Click the Open button.
4. Close the Switchboard by clicking its Close button.

The database opens and the Bavant Marine Services : Database window displays.

Using the Export Command to Export Data to Excel

One way to export data to Excel, as well as to a variety of other formats, is to select the data to be exported and then select the Export command on the File menu. Once you have selected the command, indicate the file type, for example, Microsoft Excel 97-2000, and then click the Save button. For some of the formats, including Excel, you can select Save formatted, in which case the export process will attempt to preserve as much of the Access formatting of the data as possible. You also can select Autostart so that the application receiving the data will be started automatically once the data is exported. The resulting data then will display in the application.

Perform the following steps to use the export command to export the Marinas and Workorders by Technician query to Excel.

Exporting

The process of exporting records from a table is identical to that of exporting records from a query. Simply select the Tables object and then the table containing the records to be exported before selecting the Export command. All records and all fields from the table then will be exported.

To Use the Export Command to Export Data to Microsoft Excel

1. **If necessary, click Queries on the Objects bar, click the Marinas and Workorders by Technician query, click File on the menu bar, and then point to Export.**

The File menu displays (Figure 2).

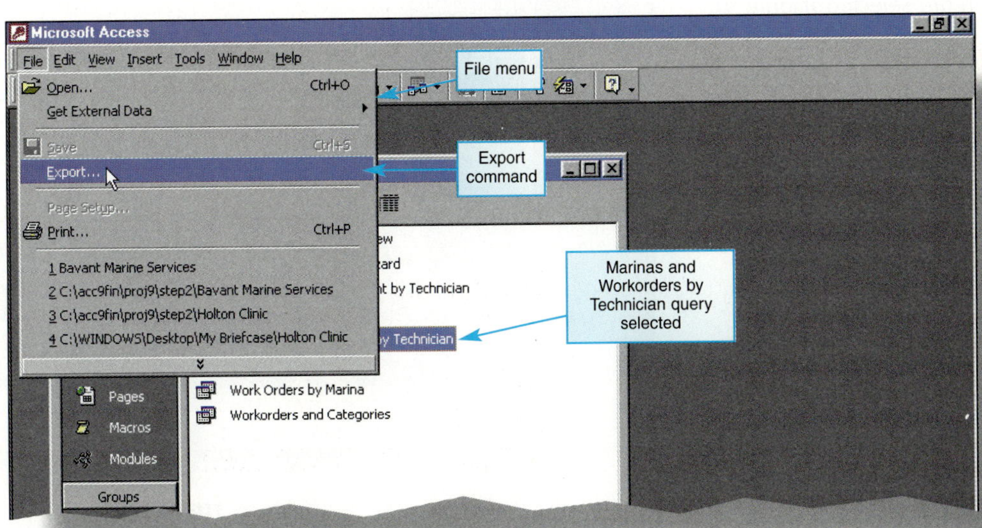

FIGURE 2

2 Click Export. Click the Save in box arrow and then click 3 ½ Floppy (A:). Click the Save as type box arrow and then point to Microsoft Excel 97-2000 in the Save as type list.

The Save as type list displays. The Save in box on your screen should display 3 ½ Floppy (A:) (Figure 3).

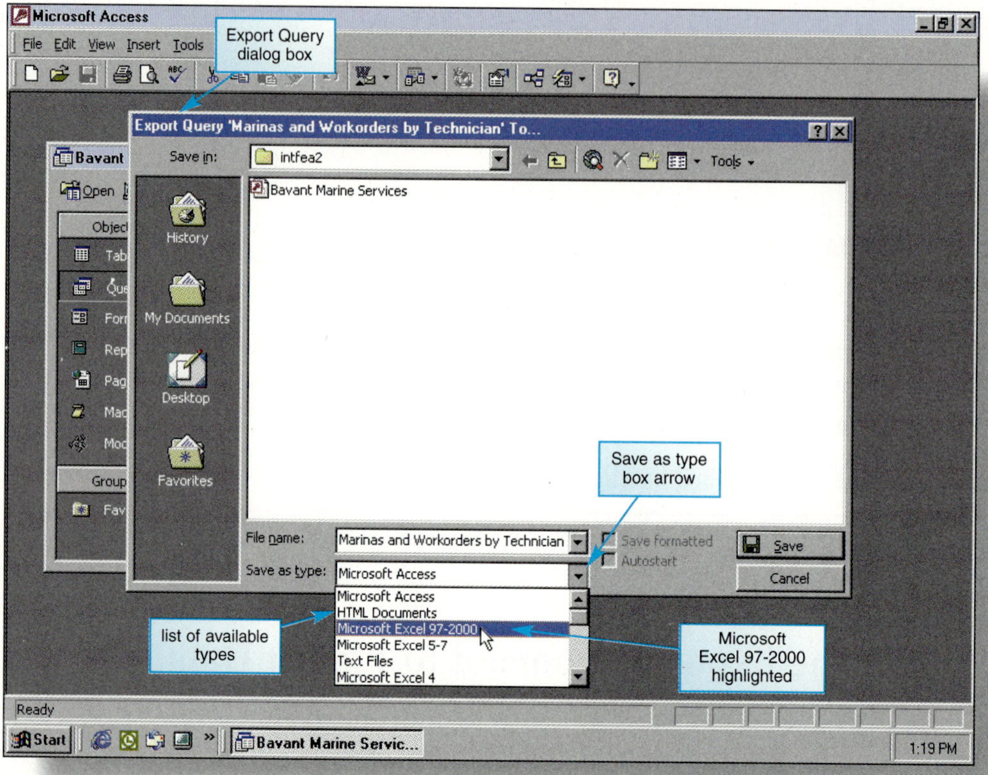

FIGURE 3

3 Click Microsoft Excel 97-2000 in the Save as type list. Click the Save formatted check box and then click the Autostart check box. Point to the Save button.

Save formatted and Autostart both are selected (Figure 4).

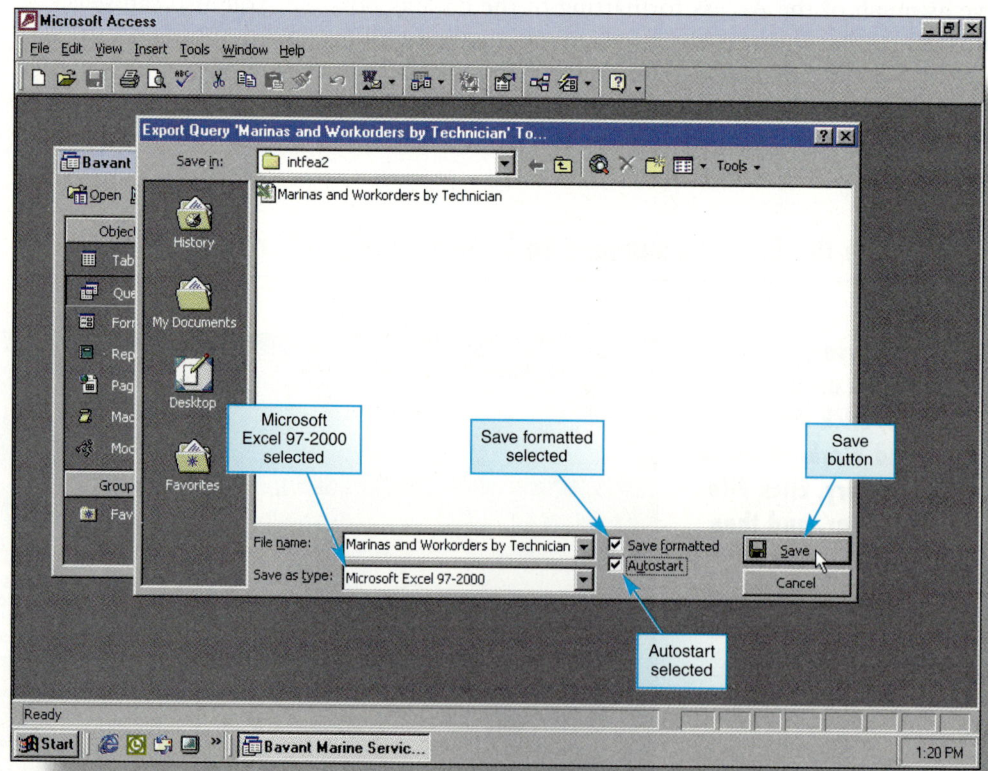

FIGURE 4

Click the Save button.

The worksheet displays (Figure 5). It contains the data from the Access query.

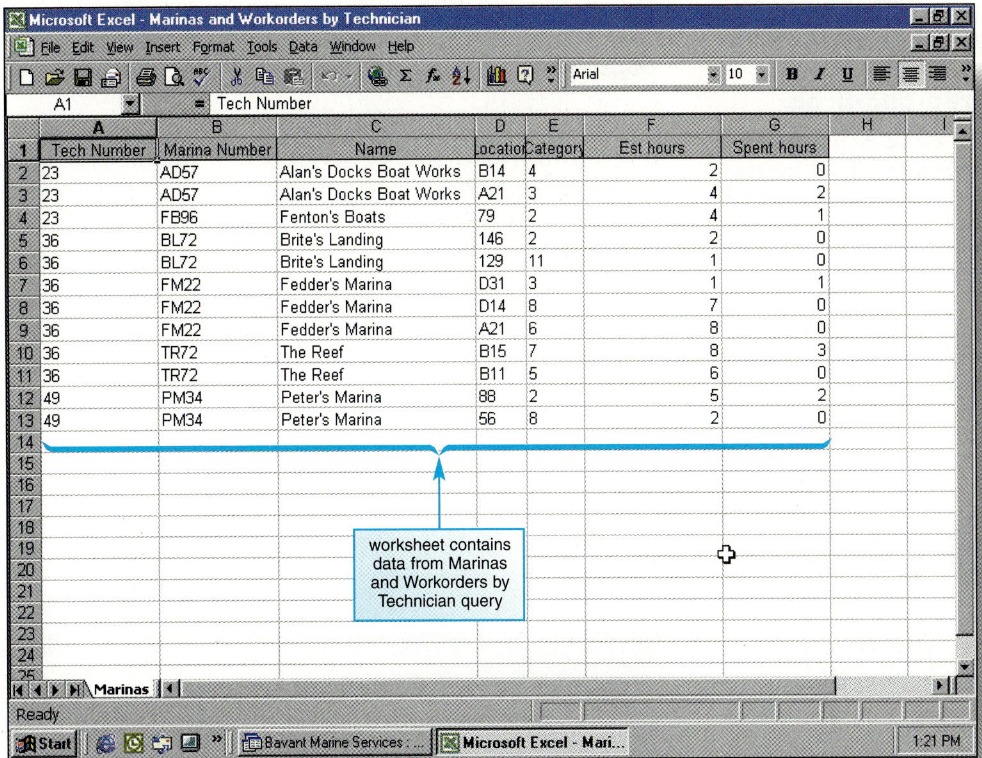

FIGURE 5

5 Resize each column to best fit the data by double-clicking the right-hand edge of the column heading.

The columns are resized (Figure 6).

6 Close the window containing the worksheet and then click the Yes button to save the changes to the column sizes. If you see a message asking if you would like to overwrite the file with the latest Excel format, click Yes. Quit Excel by clicking its Close button.

The worksheet no longer displays.

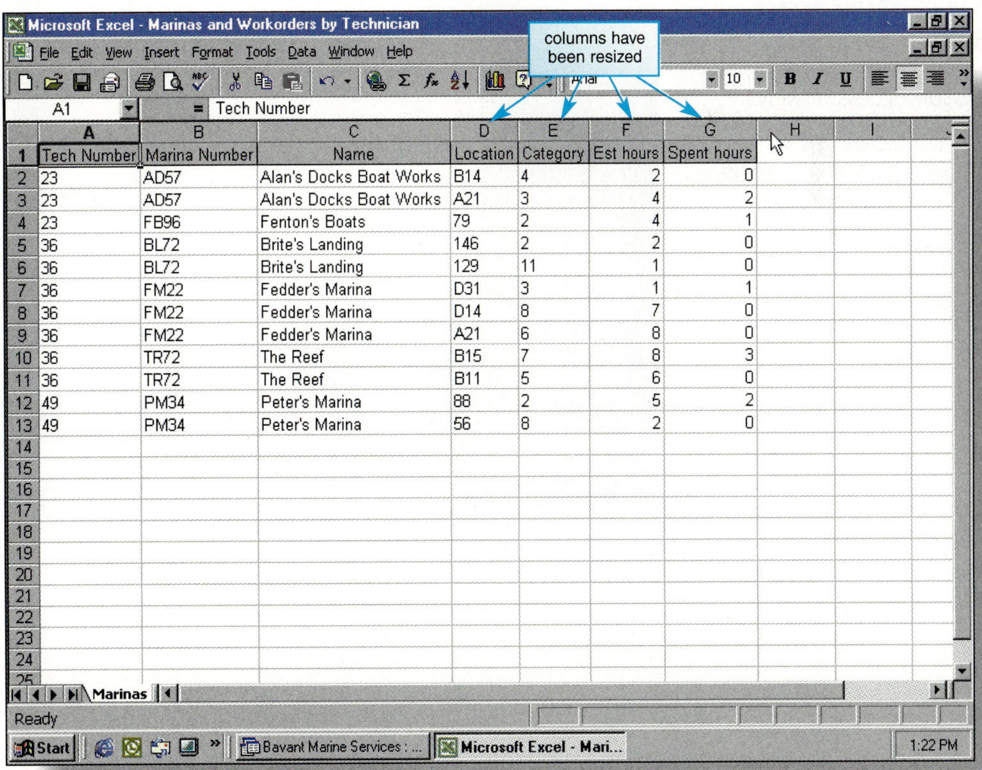

FIGURE 6

Drag-and-Drop

You can use drag-and-drop to export data to Excel just as you can to Word. Be sure Excel is running rather than Word. Drag the table or query from the database window in Access to the Excel worksheet. The records will be converted to rows in the worksheet and the fields will be converted to columns.

Using Drag-and-Drop to Export Data to Word

When using the Export command, Microsoft Word is not one of the available file types. You would need to select one of the file types that can be imported into Word, export from Access to the selected file type, and then import the file that is created into Word. A simpler way to export to Word is to use the drag-and-drop method. In this method, both Access and Word must be open simultaneously. You then drag the object to be imported from Access to the Word document. Perform the following steps to export the Marinas and Workorders by Technician query to Word using the drag-and-drop method.

To Use Drag-and-Drop to Export Data to Word

1 Click the Start button, click Programs, and then click Microsoft Word. Click the Bavant Marine Services button on the taskbar. Point to the Restore button in the Microsoft Access window.

Microsoft Access displays (Figure 7) while Microsoft Word also is running. In the figure, the Tables object is selected. Your screen may have a different object selected.

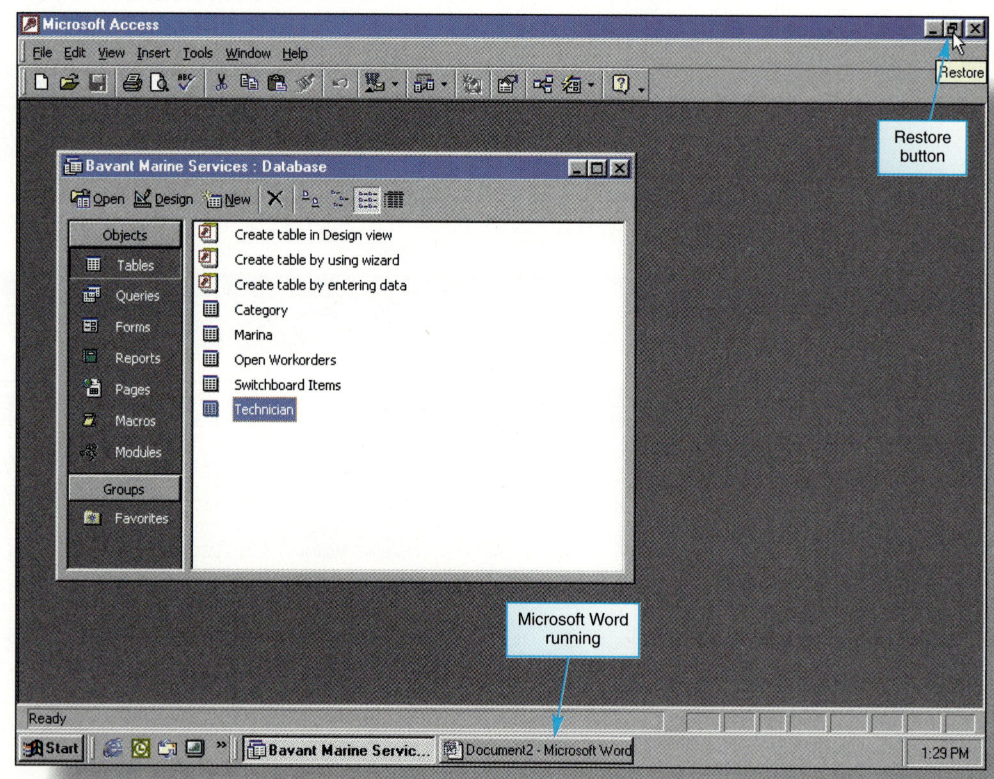

FIGURE 7

2 **Click the Restore button so that Access does not occupy the full screen. Click the Queries object, if necessary. Point to the icon for the Marinas and Workorders by Technician query.**

Both Word and Access display (Figure 8).

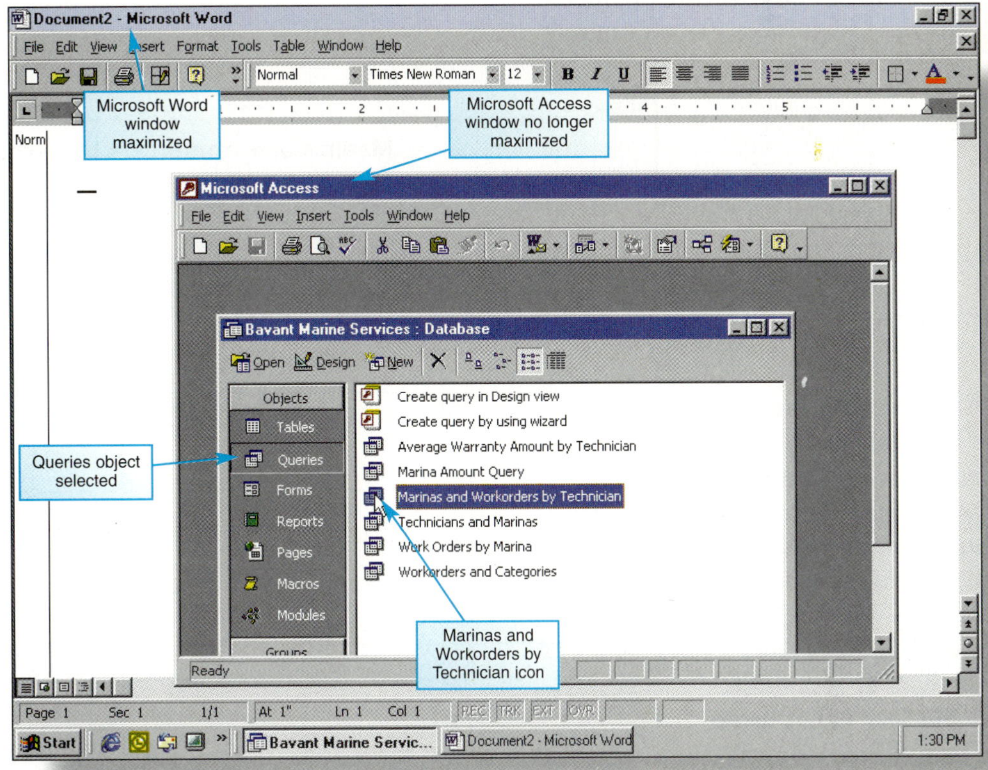

FIGURE 8

3 **Drag the query to the upper-left corner of the document (Figure 9).**

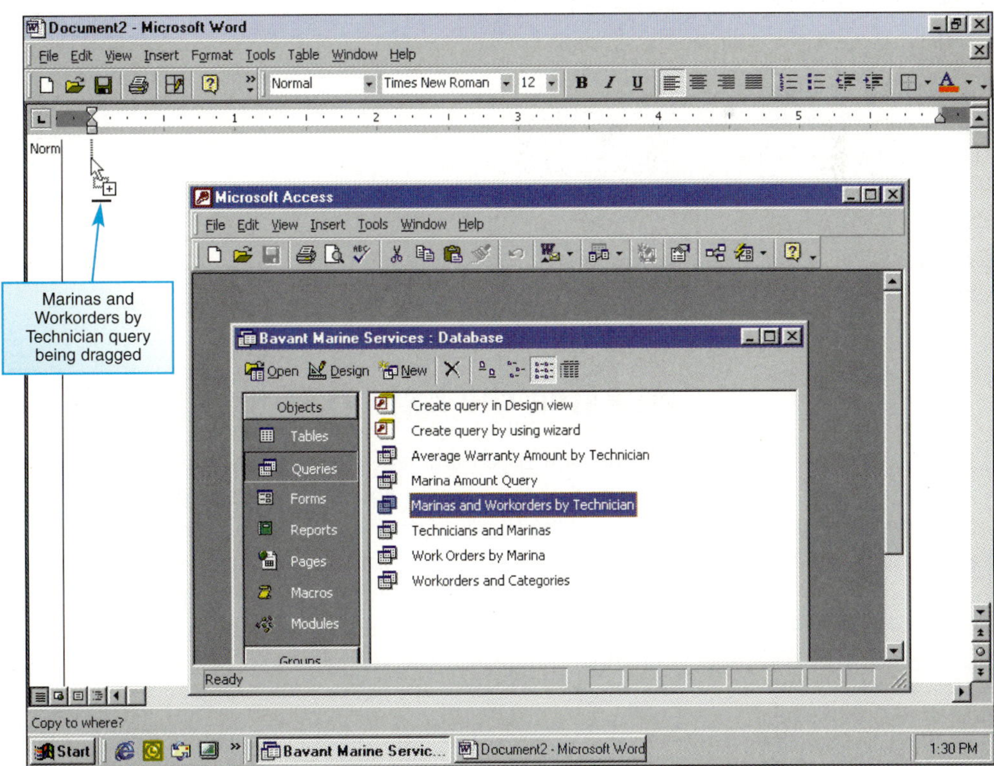

FIGURE 9

4 Release the left mouse button.

The data from the query is inserted in the Word document (Figure 10). The title of the query displays in bold font at the top of the document. The data is inserted as a Word table.

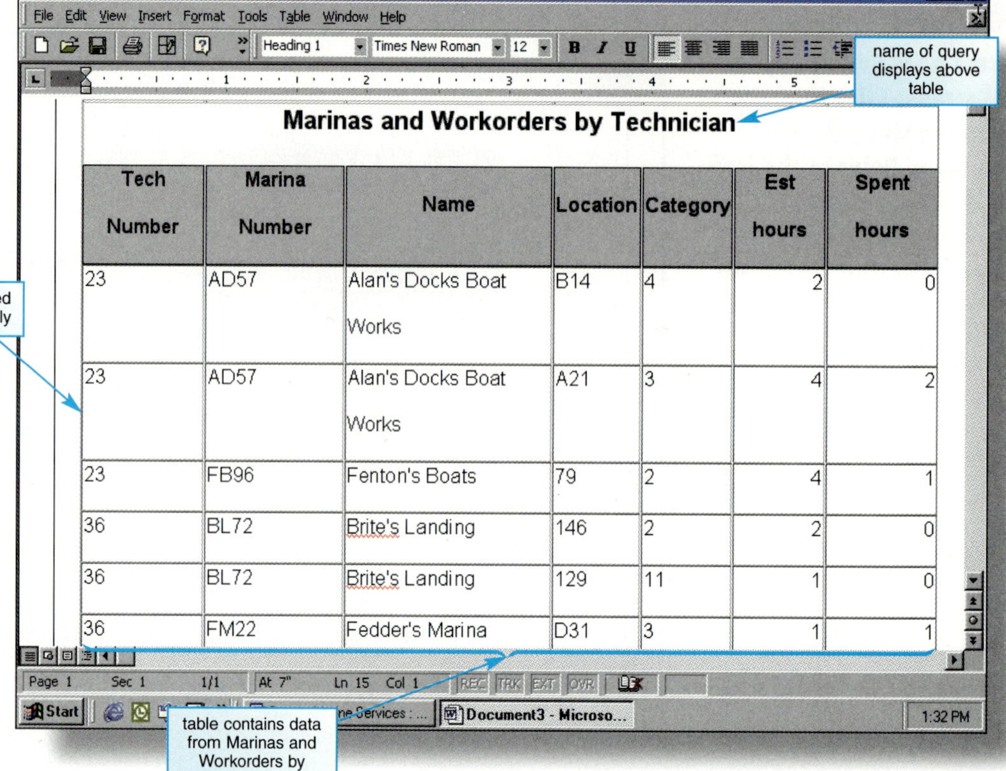

Marinas and Workorders by Technician

Tech Number	Marina Number	Name	Location	Category	Est hours	Spent hours
23	AD57	Alan's Docks Boat Works	B14	4	2	0
23	AD57	Alan's Docks Boat Works	A21	3	4	2
23	FB96	Fenton's Boats	79	2	4	1
36	BL72	Brite's Landing	146	2	2	0
36	BL72	Brite's Landing	129	11	1	0
36	FM22	Fedder's Marina	D31	3	1	1

FIGURE 10

5 Close the window containing the document by clicking its Close button. Click the Yes button when asked if you want to save the changes. Be sure the file name entered is Marinas and Workorders by Technician. Click the Save in box arrow and then click 3½ Floppy (A:). Click the Save button.

The document is saved.

6 Quit Word by clicking its Close button.

Microsoft Word no longer displays.

Using the Export Command to Create a Snapshot

If you want to send a report to someone via e-mail, the simplest way is to create a snapshot of the report. The snapshot is stored in a separate file with an extension of .snp. This file contains all the details of the report, including fonts, effects (for example, bold or italic), and graphics. In other words, the contents of the snapshot file look precisely like the report. The snapshot file can be viewed by anyone having the Snapshot Viewer; Access is not required. You can use the Snapshot Viewer to e-mail the snapshot; the recipient can use the Snapshot Viewer to view or print the snapshot.

To create a snapshot, use the Export command on the File menu as in the following steps.

More About

Quick Reference

For a table that lists how to complete the tasks covered in this book using the mouse, menu, shortcut menu, and keyboard, visit the Office 2000 Web page (www.scsite.com/off2000/qr.htm), and then click Microsoft Access 2000.

To Use the Export Command to Create a Snapshot

1 **Maximize the Microsoft Access window. Click Reports on the Objects bar, right-click the Billing Summary Report, and then click Print Preview on the shortcut menu. Click File on the menu bar and then point to Export.**

A preview of the Billing Summary Report displays (Figure 11).

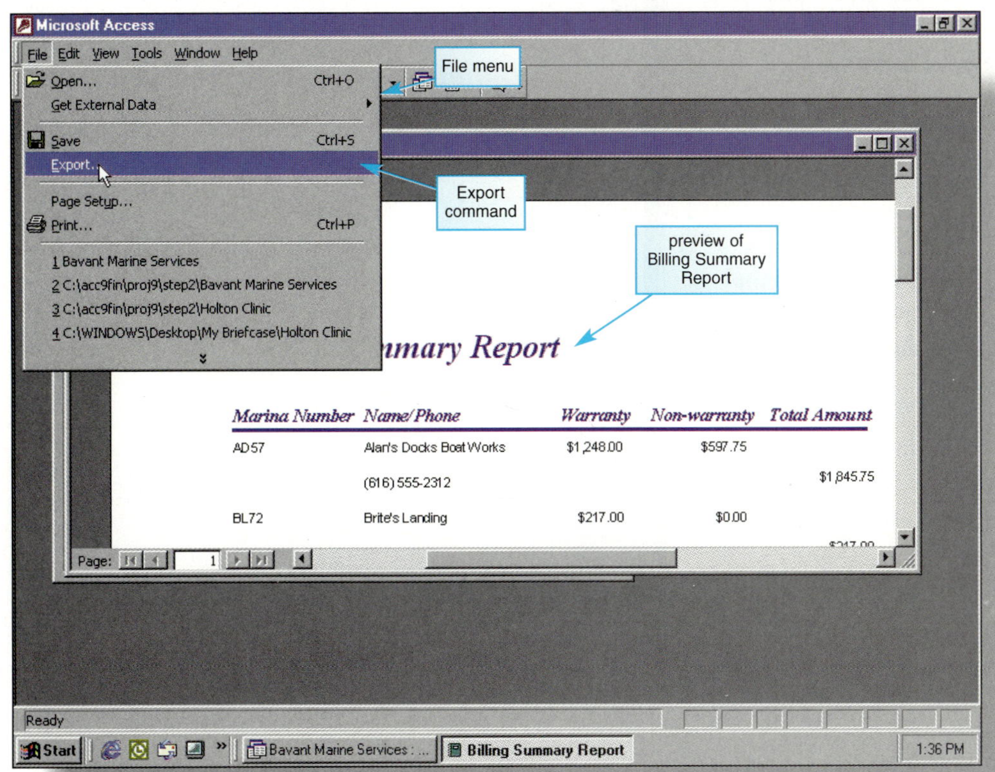

FIGURE 11

2 **Click Export and then click the Save as type box arrow. Be sure Autostart is checked. Point to Snapshot Format (Figure 12).**

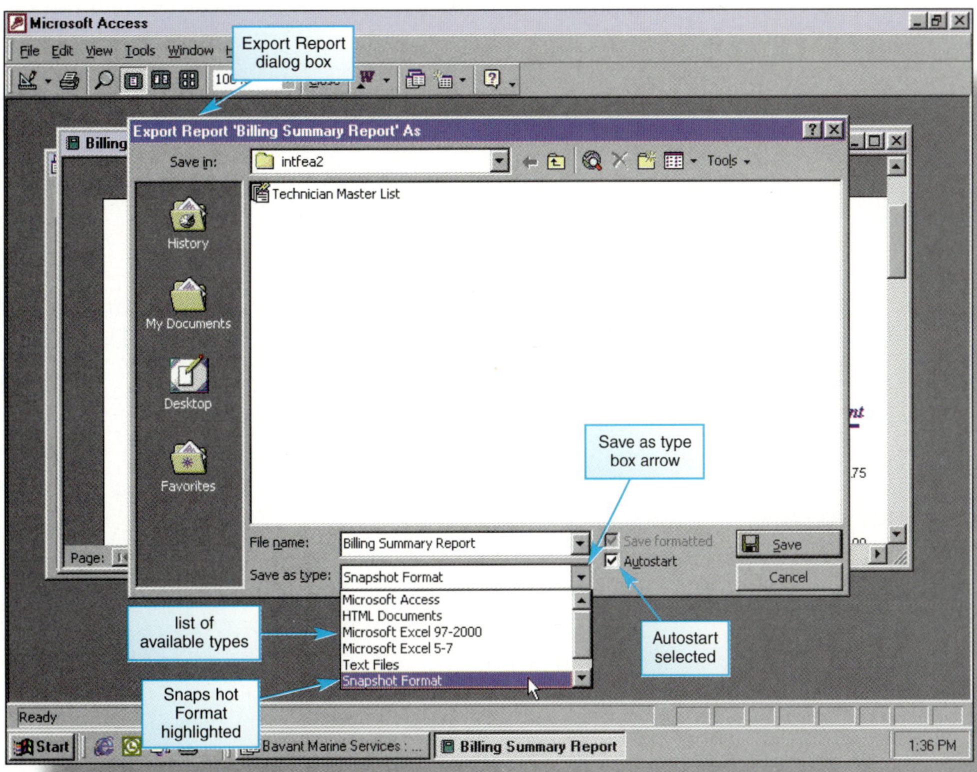

FIGURE 12

3 Click Snapshot Format. Click the Save in box arrow and then click 3 ½ Floppy (A:). Click the Save button.

The snapshot of the report displays in the Snapshot Viewer (Figure 13).

4 Close the Snapshot Viewer by clicking its Close button.

The Snapshot Viewer no longer displays.

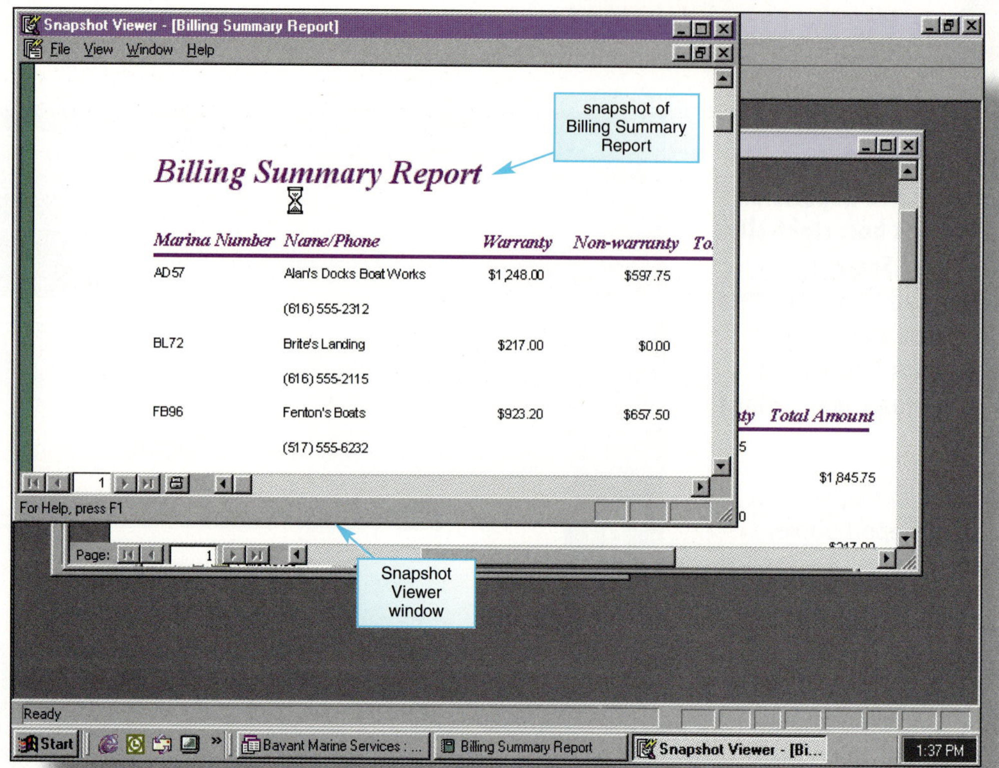

FIGURE 13

You can use the Snapshot Viewer to e-mail the snapshot to other users. The other users can use the Snapshot Viewer to view the report online or print the report.

Closing the Database

The following step closes the database by closing its Database window.

TO CLOSE A DATABASE

1. Click the Close button in the Billing Summary Report window. Click the Close button in the Bavant Marine Services : Database window.

CASE PERSPECTIVE SUMMARY

In this Integration Feature, you assisted the management of Bavant Marine Services by exporting workorder data to a Microsoft Excel worksheet and a Microsoft Word document. You also created a snapshot of the Billing Summary Report that can be viewed by anyone who has the Snapshot Viewer installed.

Integration Feature Summary

In this Integration Feature, you learned to use the Export command to export data to a Microsoft Excel worksheet. You also learned to use the drag-and-drop feature to export data to a Microsoft Word document. Finally, you learned to use the Export command to create a snapshot of a report.

What You Should Know

Having completed this Integration Feature, you now should be able to perform the following tasks:

- Close a Database *(AI 2.10)*
- Open a Database *(AI 2.3)*
- Use Drag-and-Drop to Export Data to Word *(AI 2.6)*
- Use the Export Command to Create a Snapshot *(AI 2.9)*
- Use the Export Command to Export Data to Excel *(AI 2.3)*

Microsoft Certification

The Microsoft Office User Specialist (MOUS) Certification program provides an opportunity for you to obtain a valuable industry credential - proof that you have the Access 2000 skills required by employers. For more information, see Appendix D or visit the Shelly Cashman Series MOUS Web page at www.scsite.com/off2000/cert.htm.

1 Exporting Data from the Booster's Club Database to Other Applications

Problem: The Booster's Club wants to be able to export some of the data in the Access database to other applications. Specifically, they want to export the Reorder Items by Vendor query for further processing in Excel. They also want to use the On Hand Value query in a Word document that they need to prepare.

Instructions: Start Access. Open the School Connection database from the Access Data Disk. See the inside back cover for instructions for downloading the Access Data Disk or see your instructor for information on accessing the files required for this book. Perform the following tasks.

1. Export the Reorder Items by Vendor query to Excel as shown in Figure 14. If you see the message File error, some number formats may have been lost, click OK.
2. Resize the columns to best fit the data as shown in Figure 14.
3. Print the Excel worksheet.
4. Use drag-and-drop to place the On Hand Value query in a Word document.
5. Print the Word document.

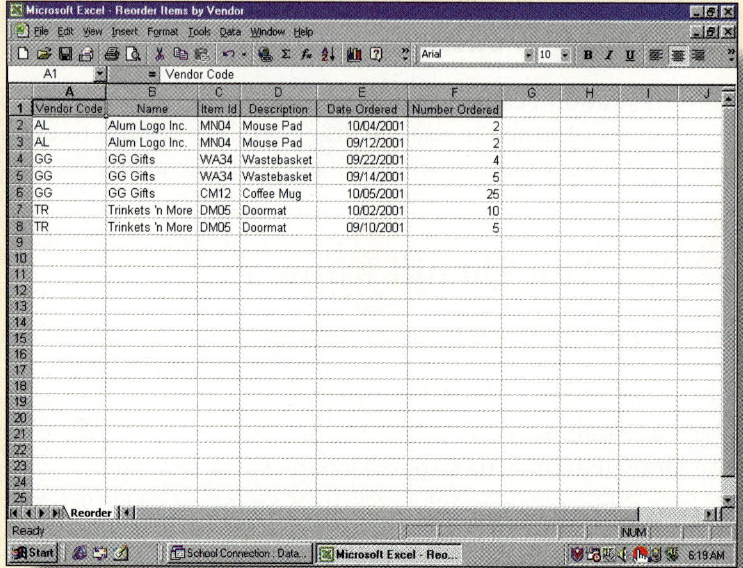

Vendor Code	Name	Item Id	Description	Date Ordered	Number Ordered
AL	Alum Logo Inc.	MN04	Mouse Pad	10/04/2001	2
AL	Alum Logo Inc.	MN04	Mouse Pad	09/12/2001	2
GG	GG Gifts	WA34	Wastebasket	09/22/2001	4
GG	GG Gifts	WA34	Wastebasket	09/14/2001	5
GG	GG Gifts	CM12	Coffee Mug	10/05/2001	25
TR	Trinkets 'n More	DM05	Doormat	10/02/2001	10
TR	Trinkets 'n More	DM05	Doormat	09/10/2001	5

FIGURE 14

Vendor/Items Report

Vendor Code	Name	Item Id	Description	Selling Price	Cost	Profit
AL	Alum Logo Inc.					
		BA02	Baseball Cap	$15.00	$12.50	$2.50
		MN04	Mouse Pad	$11.00	$9.10	$1.90
		SC11	Scarf	$12.00	$8.40	$3.60
GG	GG Gifts					
		CM12	Coffee Mug	$5.00	$3.75	$1.25
		OR01	Ornament	$4.00	$2.75	$1.25
		PP20	Pen and Pencil Set	$20.00	$16.00	$4.00
		WA34	Wastebasket	$15.00	$14.00	$1.00
TR	Trinkets'n More					
		DM05	Doormat	$17.00	$14.25	$2.75
		PN21	Pennant	$7.00	$5.65	$1.35

FIGURE 15

2 Creating a Snapshot

Problem: The Booster's Club has received several requests from people outside the school district who want to start a similar club. To help these individuals, the Booster's Club wants to be able to e-mail sample reports.

Instructions: Start Access. Open the School Connection database from the Access Data Disk. See the inside back cover for instructions for downloading the Access Data Disk or see your instructor for information on accessing the files required for this book. Perform the following tasks.

1. Preview the Vendor/Items Report shown in Figure 15 and then export the report as a snapshot.
2. Print the report that displays in the Snapshot Viewer.

Microsoft PowerPoint 2000

Creating a Self-Running Presentation Using Animation Effects

OBJECTIVES

You will have mastered the material in this project when you can:

- Add a presentation within a presentation
- Insert animated clip art
- Apply animation effects
- Insert an Excel chart
- Build a PowerPoint chart or graph
- Add a table from Word
- Insert an AutoShape
- Rotate an AutoShape
- Customize a color scheme
- Omit background graphics from the master slide
- Set automatic slide timings
- Create a self-running presentation

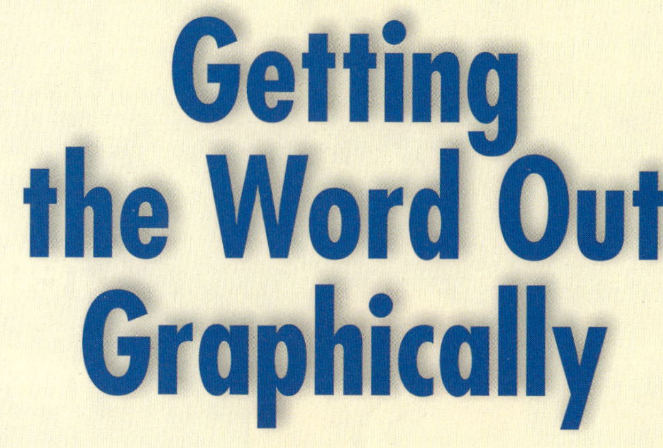

Getting the Word Out Graphically

In 1981, the modern movie, *Quest for Fire*, opened in theaters across America. Even without any dialogue, the movie conveyed a clear, compelling story about prehistoric humans who had no language to speak. Since the dawn of mankind, humans have relied on graphic images to communicate, even after the advent of spoken language. In today's global village, images play a vital role in promoting understanding between peoples of different languages.

Individuals long have used pictures, or graphics, as guides for building structures involving complex spatial relationships. Imagine trying to build the Pharaoh's pyramids without a plan drawn out on papyrus or a Boeing jet without engineering drawings.

Yet, in recent years, graphics, onscreen presentations, self-running presentations, online meetings, presentations on the Web, overhead transparencies, and 35mm slide shows have played an even greater role in the art of communication. People understand more easily when visual elements are combined. From sales presentations, to impressive slide shows in courtroom dramas, to disseminating information in kiosks, people turn to images to persuade others, to influence buying choices, or to adopt their points of view. PowerPoint is an outstanding example of the marriage of multimedia to help people present persuasive arguments or simply inform or entertain.

Information presented with images augments content. In this PowerPoint project, you will create a self-running presentation with animation effects. The presentation contains visual elements, an animated slide created in a separate PowerPoint presentation using the skills and tools you have learned previously, animated clip art, and other elements available from Excel and Word that combine so skillfully in the Office 2000 suite.

One popular method used for distributing information contained in self-running presentations is the kiosk. This freestanding, computerized information or reference center allows users to select various options to browse through or find specific material. Typical kiosks are self-service structures equipped with computer hardware and software. Kiosk manufacturers offer a variety of designs appropriate for various locations. One such manufacturer is Kiosk Information Systems (KIS). It has introduced The Stealth, with its sleek form and logical engineering. Focusing on a certain market, KIS creates a custom product to match its location. Kiosks usually are positioned where they can reach the greatest number of people and generally are placed in public places such as shopping centers, hotels, airports, stadiums, tradeshows, and conventions where customers or visitors can obtain information on available services, product information, exhibit locations, and maps.

In a world increasingly dependent on images as well as language to communicate and inform, self-running presentations are a great way to communicate information without having someone available to run the slide show. With PowerPoint, you can set up your presentation to run unattended in a booth or kiosk. A self-running presentation restarts when it is finished. With their associated multimedia devices, animation, and sound, self-running presentations and kiosks are an entertaining combination for getting the word out.

Microsoft PowerPoint 2000

Creating a Self-Running Presentation Using Animation Effects

CASE PERSPECTIVE

The quest for a healthy, toned body has reached all segments of the population. Sales of home fitness products, particularly treadmills and free weights, have surged, and health club memberships have grown to record numbers.

The Fitness Center at your school has experienced an increase in the number of students coming to exercise. When they join the Fitness Center, they express an interest in maximizing their workout time due to their busy schedules and commitments. The Fitness Center director, Tiffani Olson, wants you to develop a PowerPoint presentation to run at a kiosk near the registration counter.

You discuss holistic exercise strategies with Tiffani and decide to focus on describing how students can optimize their weekly half-hour workouts by combining aerobic exercise using a treadmill and anaerobic exercise using free weights. You will enhance the presentation with a slide from one of Tiffani's previous presentations, charts created in Microsoft Excel and in PowerPoint, a table you import from Microsoft Word, and a diagram using AutoShapes that shows the benefits of exercise. You will time the presentation so that it runs for three minutes and repeats continuously.

Introduction

People have a thirst for information. From catching the breaking news on cable television to downloading our latest e-mail messages, individuals constantly are faced with keeping up with the day's events.

One method used for disseminating information is a **kiosk**. This freestanding, self-service structure is equipped with computer hardware and software and is used to provide information or reference materials to the public. Kiosks frequently are found in public places, such as shopping centers, hotels, museums, libraries, and airport terminals, where customers or visitors may have questions about community events, local hotels, and rental cars. Many kiosks have multimedia devices for playing sound and video clips. Some have a touch screen or keyboard that serves as an input device and allows users to select various options to browse through or find specific information. Advanced kiosks allow customers to place orders, make payments, and access the Internet.

In this project, you will create a slide show for Western College's Fitness Center. This show will run continuously on a computer near the registration counter, so present and potential members can view the brief three-minute presentation that gives them information on getting the most from a half-hour workout session. The presentation slides are shown in Figures 5-1a through 5-1g.

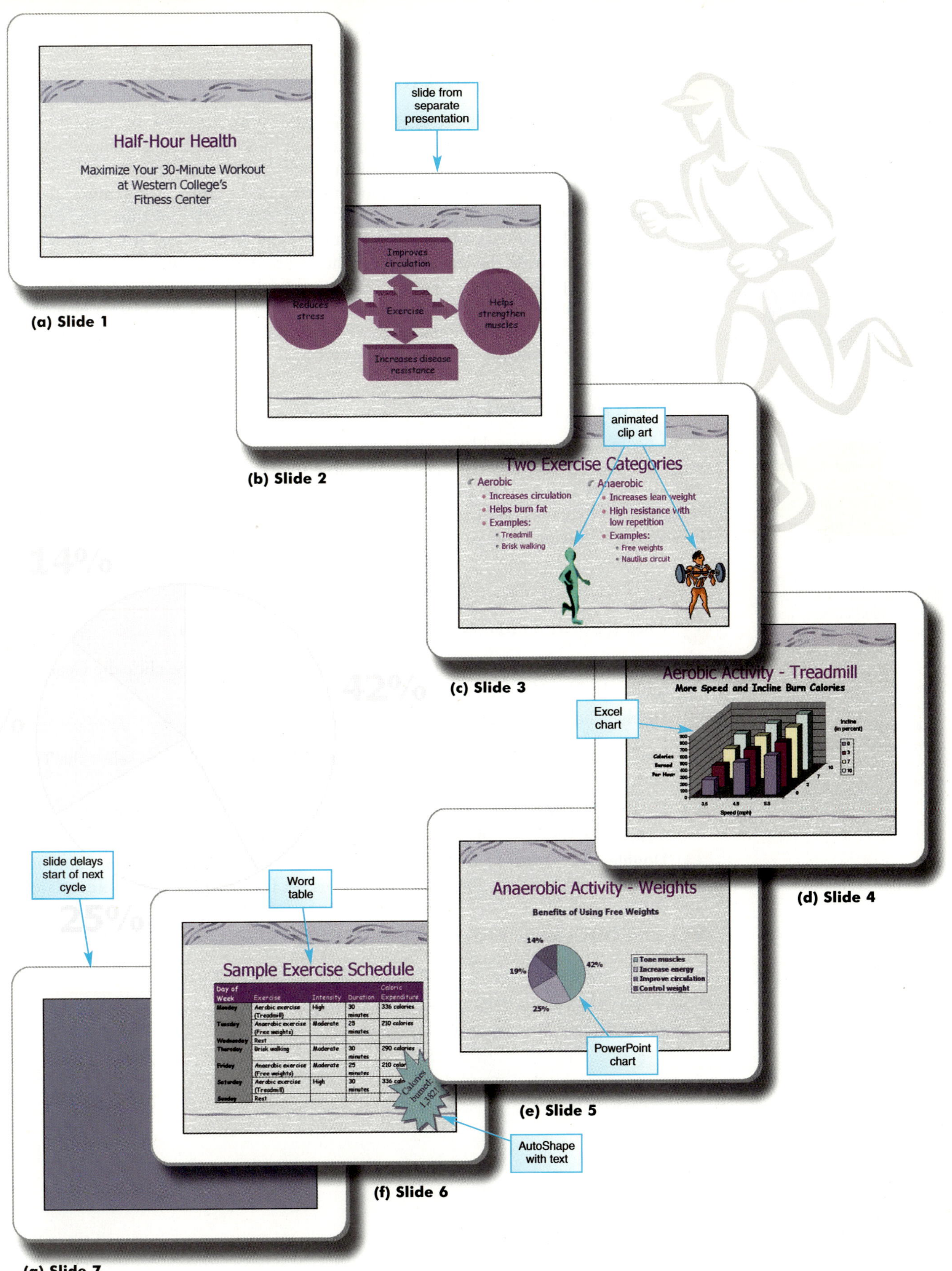

(a) Slide 1

(b) Slide 2

(c) Slide 3

(d) Slide 4

(e) Slide 5

(f) Slide 6

(g) Slide 7

FIGURE 5-1

Project Five — Half-Hour Workout

The self-running three-minute presentation created in Project 5 contains several visual elements: an animated slide created in a separate PowerPoint presentation, animated clip art, an Excel chart, a PowerPoint chart, a Word table, and an AutoShape with text. After these objects are inserted in the slides, automatic slide timings are set so that these objects display after a desired period of time. The presentation then is designated to be a self-running presentation so that it restarts when it is finished. To separate the last slide from the beginning of the presentation, a completely blank purple slide is created and set to display for a specific period of time. As with other PowerPoint presentations, the first steps are to create a new presentation, select a design template, create a title slide, and save the presentation. The following steps illustrate these procedures.

Kiosks

Microsoft donated nearly $100,000 to develop the Microsoft Internet Discovery Kiosk, an interactive exhibit used to inform and educate users about the Internet's history, technology, uses, and future. The kiosk travels to museums and libraries throughout the United States and is designed to educate and entertain. To learn more about this multimedia kiosk and to read Microsoft Chairman and CEO Bill Gates' views on this innovative project, visit the PowerPoint 2000 Project 5 More About page (www.scsite.com/pp2000/more.htm) and click Kiosk.

Starting a New Presentation

To begin, create a new, blank presentation, choose an AutoLayout, and apply a design template. The following steps review how to accomplish these tasks. The toolbars and menus also need to be reset so they display exactly as shown in this book. For a detailed explanation of resetting the toolbars and menus, see Appendix C. Perform the following steps to start a new presentation.

TO START A NEW PRESENTATION

1. Click the Start button on the taskbar.
2. Click New Office Document on the Start menu. If necessary, click the General tab in the New Office Document dialog box.
3. Double-click the Blank Presentation icon.
4. Click the OK button when the New Slide dialog box displays to select the Title Slide AutoLayout.
5. Double-click the move handle on the left side of the Standard toolbar to display the toolbar in its entirety.
6. Double-click Default Design on the status bar. Double-click the Sumi Painting design template in the Presentation Designs list in the Apply Design Template dialog box.
7. If the Office Assistant displays, right-click the Office Assistant and then click Hide on the shortcut menu.

PowerPoint displays the Title Slide AutoLayout and the Sumi Painting design template on Slide 1 in normal view (Figure 5-2).

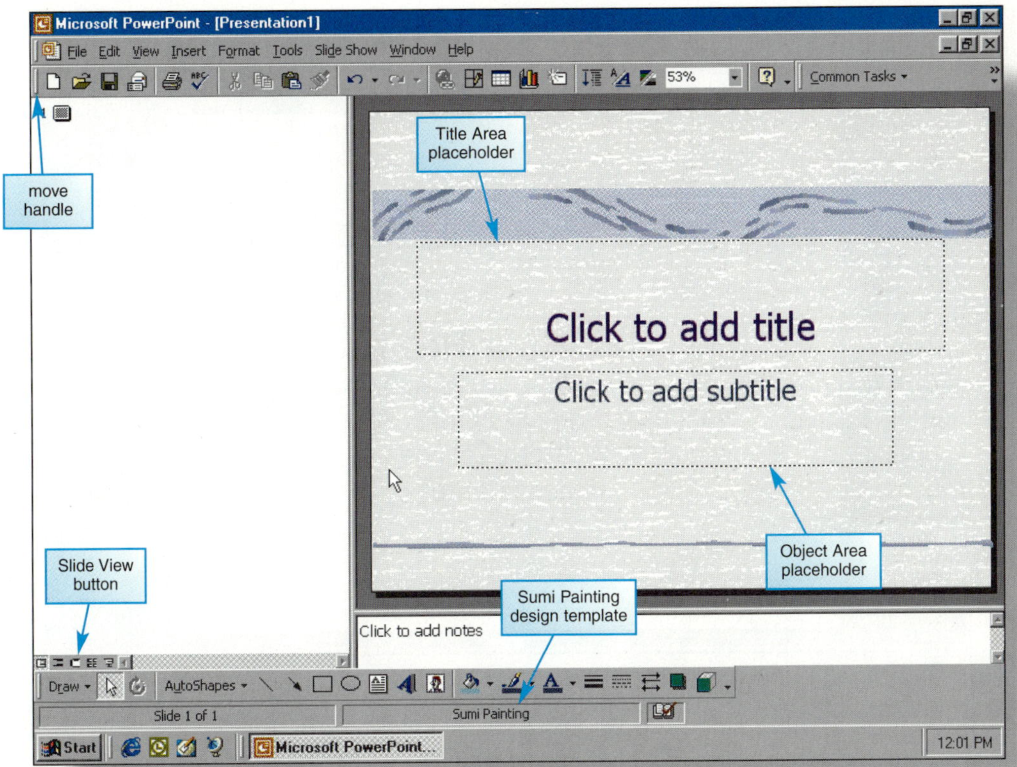

FIGURE 5-2

Creating the Title Slide in Slide View

The purpose of this presentation is to describe how students visiting Western College's Fitness Center can maximize their workout sessions. If they know the right techniques and understand how to vary their aerobic and anaerobic activities five times per week, they can obtain healthy results. The opening slide should introduce this concept. Perform the following steps to create a title slide in slide view.

Formatting Tabs

You can use tabs to align text in the placeholders. To set or clear tab stops, select the text, display the ruler, and click the tab button at the left of the horizontal ruler to display the desired type of tab. Then click the ruler where you want to set the tab. You can drag any tab marker to a new position on the ruler. The space between all default tabs changes proportionately, so that if you move a default tab to one-half inch, all default tables become spaced one-half inch apart. To clear a tab, drag the tab marker off the ruler.

TO CREATE A TITLE SLIDE IN SLIDE VIEW

1. Click the Slide View button located at the lower left of the PowerPoint window.
2. Click the Title Area placeholder to select it.
3. Type `Half-Hour Health` in the Title Area placeholder.
4. Press the CTRL+ENTER keys to move the insertion point to the Object Area placeholder.
5. Type `Maximize Your 30-Minute Workout at Western College's` and then press the SHIFT+ENTER keys.
6. Type `Fitness Center` but do not press the ENTER key.

The title text and subtitle text display in Slide 1 as shown in Figure 5-3 on the next page.

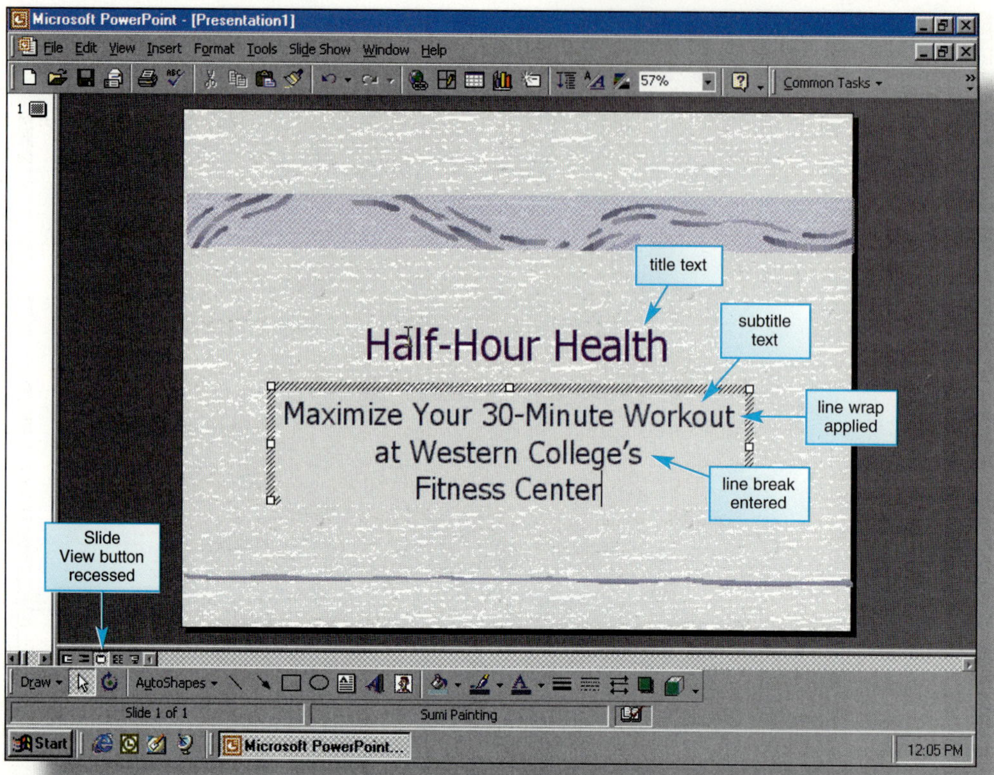

FIGURE 5-3

Using Hyperlinks

Each presentation can have only one slide master, so if you want to give various slides in your presentation entirely different looks, you can use hyperlinks to jump to other presentations that have different slide masters. To insert a hyperlink, select the text or object you want to represent the hyperlink, click the Insert Hyperlink button on the Standard toolbar, click Existing File or Web Page under Link to, locate and select the desired file, click Screen Tip and then type the explanatory text, and then click the OK button. To preview how the hyperlink will display, click the Slide Show button.

The first line of subtitle text in the Object Area placeholder uses PowerPoint's **line wrap** feature. PowerPoint line wraps text that exceeds the width of the placeholder so you can type words in a paragraph continually without pressing the ENTER key at the end of each line. PowerPoint positions the insertion point automatically at the beginning of the next line.

In this title slide, you want the words, Fitness Center, to display together on the last line of the Object Area placeholder. Sufficient space appears in the placeholder to display the word, Fitness, on the second line. You need to force that word to display on the third line, so you press the SHIFT and the ENTER keys simultaneously after you type the word, College's, to create a **line break**, which moves the insertion point to the beginning of the next line.

Although both the ENTER key and the SHIFT+ENTER keys advance the insertion point to the next line, these keystrokes produce different results. When you press the ENTER key, you create a new paragraph, which has specific attributes such as alignment and line spacing. The subtitle text in Slide 1 has the default font size of 32, line spacing of 38, and before paragraph line spacing of 8. When you press the ENTER key to insert a blank line into your slide or to create a new paragraph, you add 8 points of line spacing above this new paragraph. In contrast, when you press the SHIFT+ENTER keys, you do not create a new paragraph. The insertion point thus advances downward to a new line within the existing paragraph, and no additional line spacing is added above the new line.

Adding a Presentation within a Presentation

Tiffani has given many informative talks on campus and in the community regarding various fitness topics. She recently delivered a presentation at the local YMCA on the subject of using the computer to plug into online fitness resources. She used a PowerPoint presentation to accompany her speech, and she wants you to use one slide from that presentation in your Half-Hour Workout slide show.

The Favorites Folder

Each tab in the Insert Clip Art dialog box has a Favorites category where you can store new clips you import or commonly used clips. To add clips to the Favorites category when you are importing these files, select the Favorites category in the Clip Properties dialog box. To add existing clips to the Favorites category, click the clip, click the Add to category button on the Pop-up menu, click Favorites, and then click the Add button.

Inserting a Slide from Another Presentation

Tiffani used the PowerPoint presentation with the file name Cyberfitness for her recent presentation. It contains four slides, and the second slide, shown in Figure 5-4, displays five animated graphical shapes that depict the benefits of keeping fit. The Cyberfitness file is on your Data Disk. The steps on the next page demonstrate how to insert Slide 2 from that file into your presentation.

(a) Slide 1

desired PowerPoint slide to insert

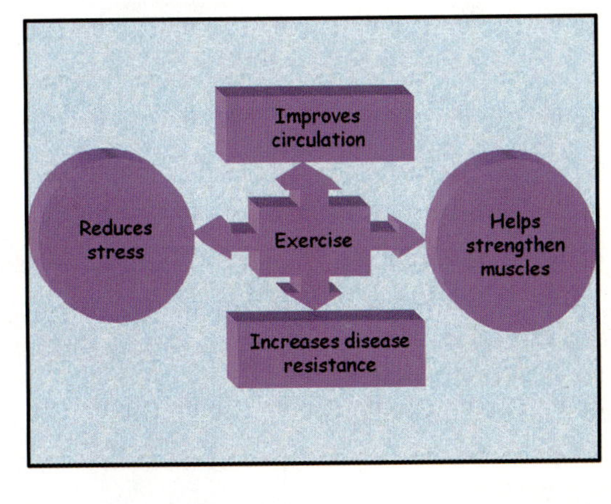

(b) Slide 2

Online Resources

- Training groups
  - Talk with virtual coaches
  - Share concerns with forum members
- Health help
  - Obtain advice from sports medicine pros
    - Orthopedic surgeons, podiatrists, and nutritionists

(c) Slide 3

Web Travel Tips

- Search for sporting events in vacation spots
  - Register online for marathons, campsites, canoeing excursions, rafting adventures
  - Buy professional sporting events tickets online
- Plan next adventure vacation
  - Find specialized tours

(d) Slide 4

FIGURE 5-4

Steps To Insert a Slide from Another Presentation

1 Insert your Data Disk into Drive A. Click Insert on the menu bar and then point to Slides from Files.

The Insert menu displays (Figure 5-5). Slides from Files is highlighted.

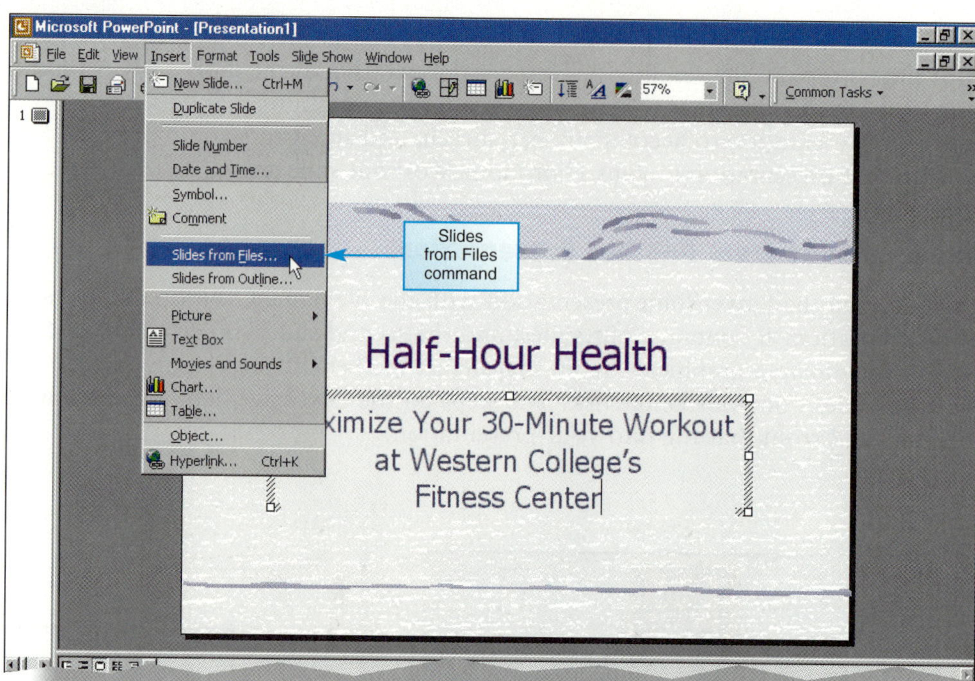

FIGURE 5-5

2 Click Slides from Files. When the Slide Finder dialog box displays, if necessary click the Find Presentation tab, and then point to the Browse button.

The Slide Finder dialog box displays (Figure 5-6). If you use several presentations on a regular basis, you can add them to your List of Favorites so you can find them easily.

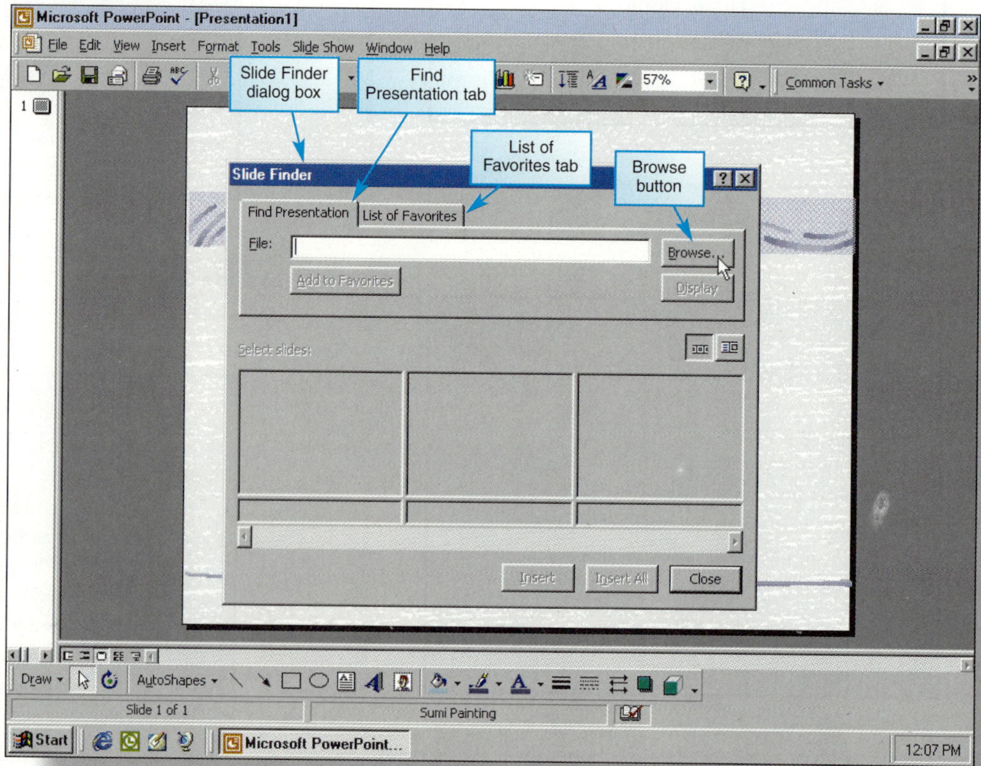

FIGURE 5-6

3 **Click the Browse button. Click the Look in box arrow and then click 3½ Floppy (A:). Click Cyberfitness in the list. Point to the Open button.**

The Browse dialog box displays (Figure 5-7). A list displays the files that PowerPoint can open. Your list may be different depending on your computer installation.

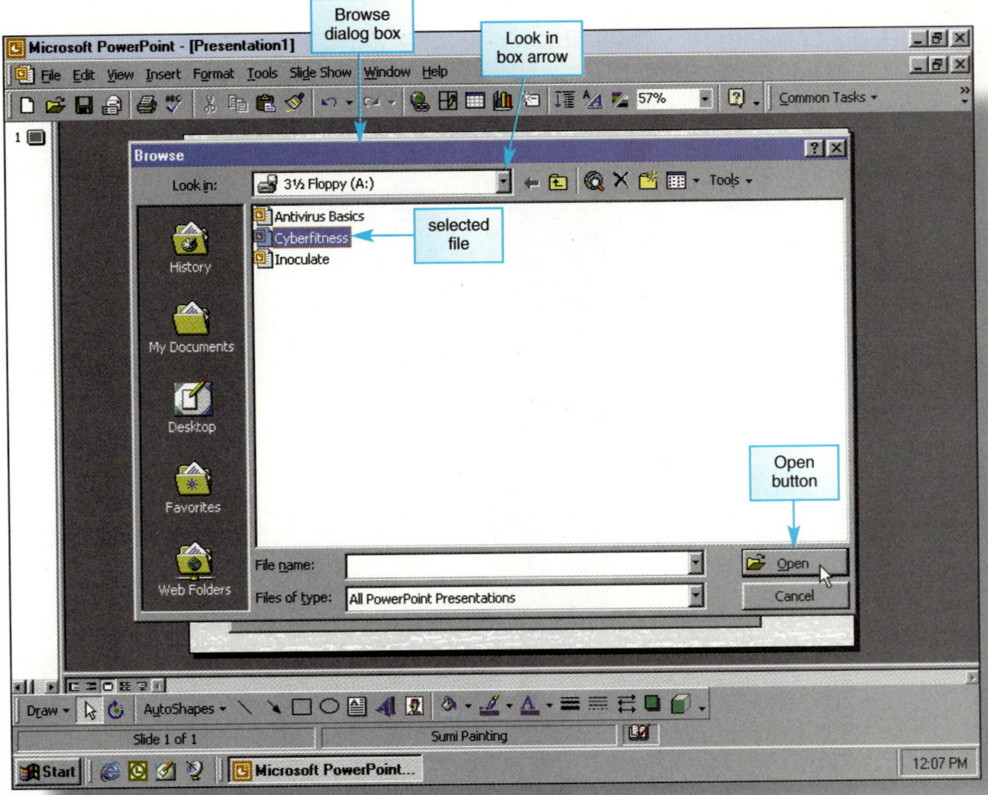

FIGURE 5-7

4 **Click the Open button. Click the Slide 2 image in the Select slides area. Point to the Insert button.**

The Slide Finder dialog box displays (Figure 5-8). The selected file, Cyberfitness, displays in the File text box. Slide 2 is the slide you want to insert in your presentation.

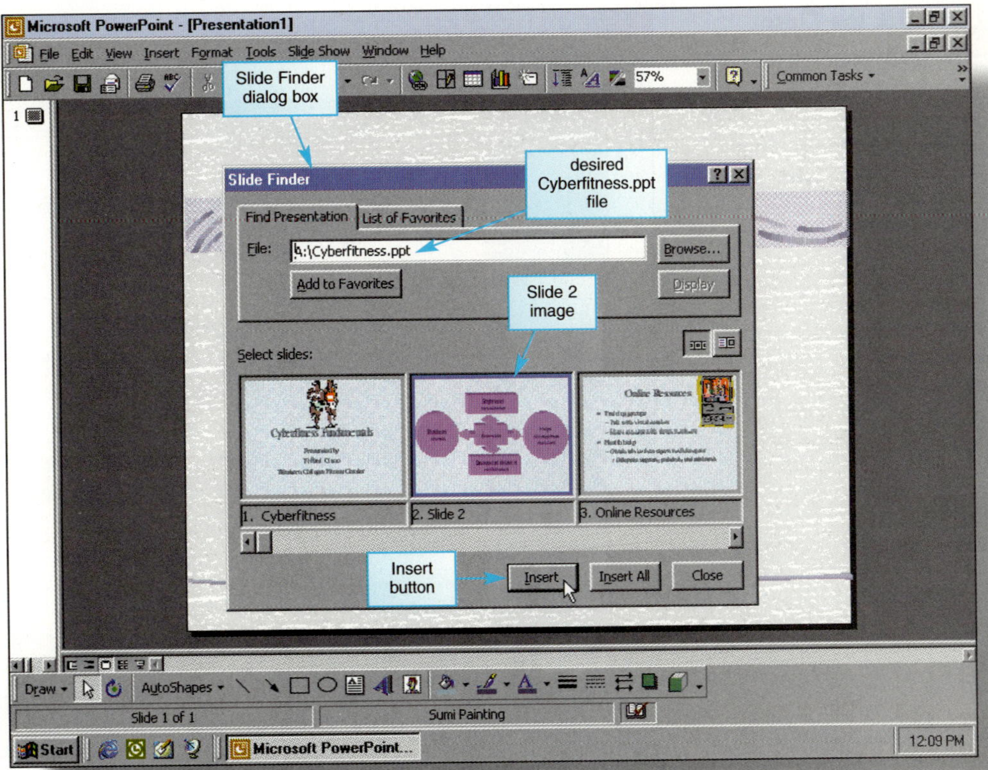

FIGURE 5-8

5 Click the Insert button. Point to the Close button.

PowerPoint inserts the Cyberfitness Slide 2 in your presentation (Figure 5-9). The Slide Finder dialog box remains open to allow you to insert additional slides.

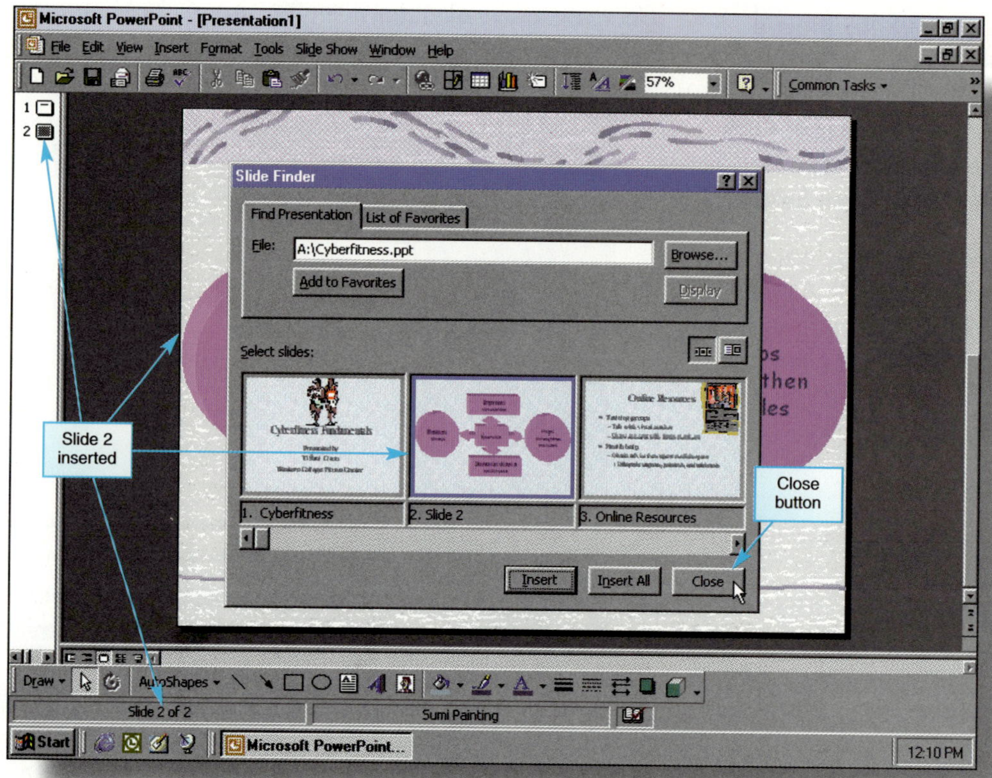

FIGURE 5-9

6 Click the Close button.

The Cyberfitness Slide 2 now is the second slide in your presentation (Figure 5-10).

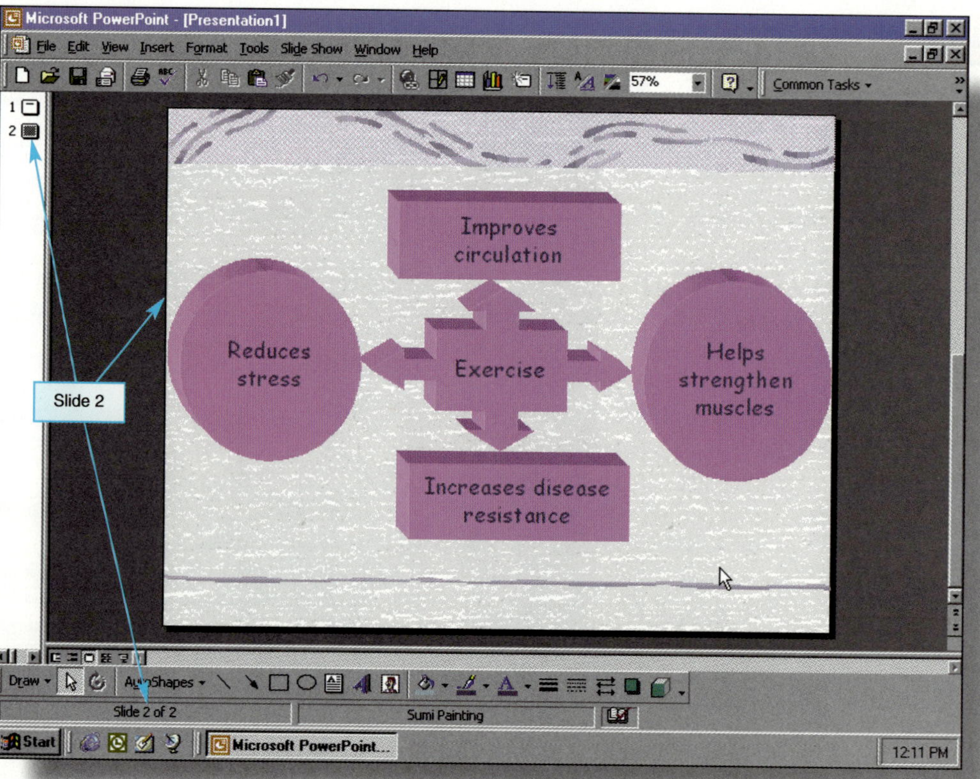

FIGURE 5-10

1. Press ALT+I, press F, press ALT+B, select desired file, press ALT+O, press ALT+S, select desired slide, press I, press ESC

If desired, you could have selected additional slides from Tiffani's Cyberfitness presentation or from other slide shows. If you believe you might want to use the Cyberfitness file at a later date, you can add that file to your Favorites folder so that it is readily accessible.

Creating a New Slide with Animated Clip Art

Your next step is to design a slide that describes the differences between aerobic and anaerobic exercise activities. The prefix, aero, means air, so an aerobic activity such as running, cycling, or brisk walking uses increased oxygen to help the circulatory system work efficiently and also to help burn fat. An anaerobic activity, in contrast, does not require additional air. Anaerobic activities like using free weights or using the Nautilus or Universal circuits increase lean weight, which helps tone the body.

Inserting a New Slide, Choosing a Layout, and Adding Text

The third slide you create will use the 2 Column Text slide layout and will have two animated clip art objects. Perform the following steps to add a new slide, choose a layout, and add text to the left Object Area placeholder.

TO ADD A SLIDE, CHOOSE A LAYOUT, AND ADD TEXT

1. Click the New Slide button on the Standard toolbar.
2. Double-click the 2 Column Text AutoLayout located in row one, column three.
3. Type `Two Exercise Categories` in the Title Area placeholder.
4. Press the CTRL+ENTER keys to move the insertion point to the left Object Area placeholder.
5. Type `Aerobic` in the left Object Area placeholder and then press the ENTER key.
6. Press the TAB key to demote the text. Type `Increases circulation` and then press the ENTER key.
7. Type `Helps burn fat` and then press the ENTER key.
8. Type `Examples:` and then press the ENTER key.
9. Press the TAB key. Type `Treadmill` and then press the ENTER key.
10. Type `Brisk walking` but do not press the ENTER key.

The text for the new slide displays in the left Object Area placeholder of the 2 Column Text AutoLayout (Figure 5-11 on the next page).

More About 2000

Custom Shows

If you want to vary the slides and the slide order in your presentation, you can select particular slides and group them together to create a custom show. To create a new custom show, click Custom Shows on the Slide Show menu and then click New. Under Slides in presentation, hold down the CTRL key, select the desired slides, and then click Add. To change the slide order, select one slide and then click an arrow to move the slide location in the list. Next, type a name for the show in the Slide show name box and then click the OK button. To preview your show, select the custom show name in the Custom Shows dialog box, and then click Show.

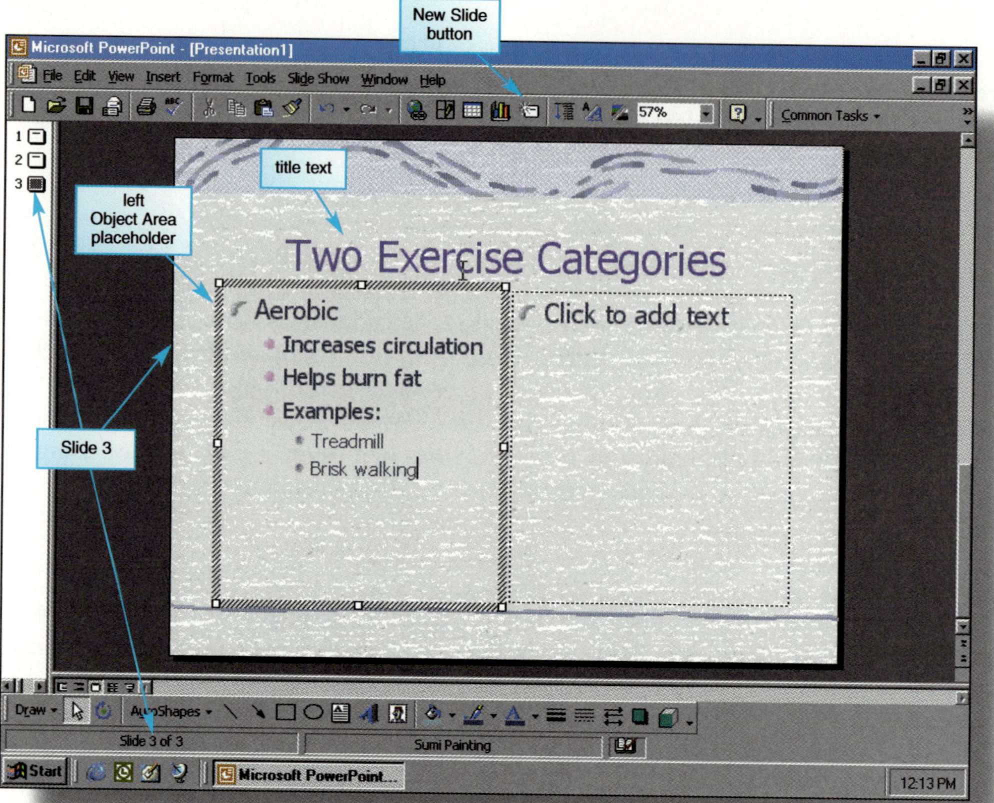

FIGURE 5-11

Now that the text is entered in the left Object Area placeholder, you need to add the text to the right Object Area placeholder. Perform the following steps to add this text.

TO ADD TEXT TO THE RIGHT PLACEHOLDER

1. Press the CTRL+ENTER keys to move the insertion point to the right Object Area placeholder.
2. Type `Anaerobic` in the right Object Area placeholder and then press the ENTER key.
3. Press the TAB key to demote the text. Type `Increases lean weight` and then press the ENTER key.
4. Type `High resistance with low repetition` and then press the ENTER key.
5. Type `Examples:` and then press the ENTER key.
6. Press the TAB key. Type `Free weights` and then press the ENTER key.
7. Type `Nautilus circuit` but do not press the ENTER key.

The text for the slide displays in the right Object Area placeholder (Figure 5-12).

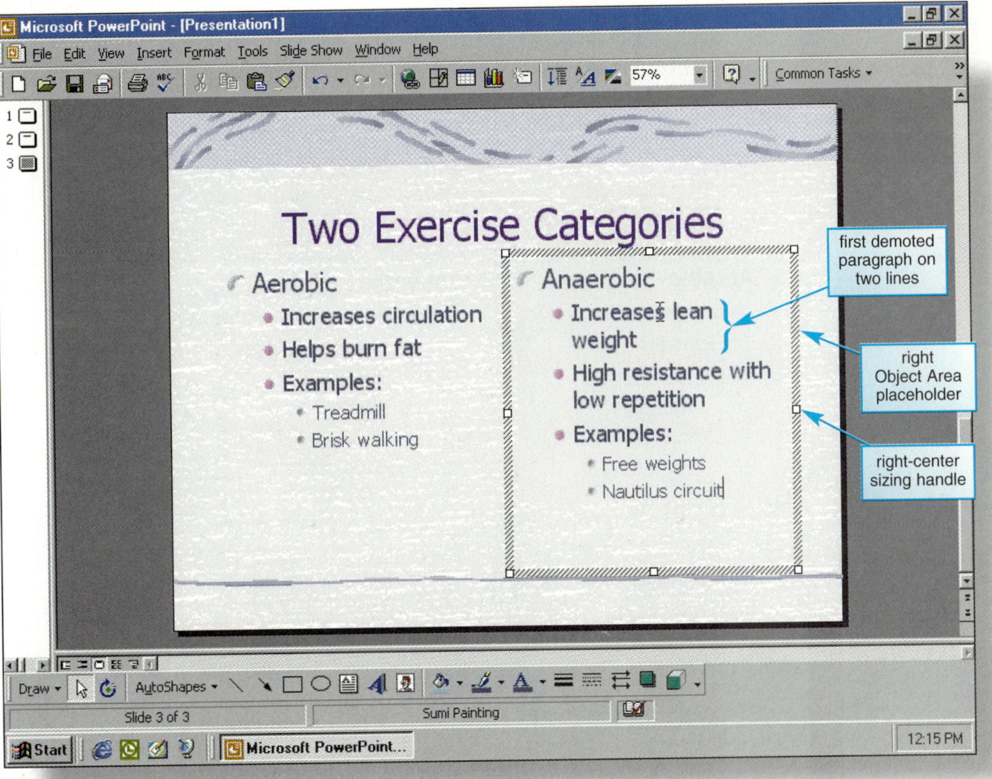

FIGURE 5-12

All text for the slide has been entered. Then next step is to add two animated clip art objects that will move when the slide show runs at the kiosk. You need sufficient space to display these objects, and you realize you can create additional space in the lower-right corner of the slide if the first demoted paragraph in the right Object Area placeholder displays on one line.

More About 2000

Locating Clip Art

The entire Clip Art Gallery may not be installed on your computer system. If not, you may need to import specific clips into the Clip Gallery. To add these clips, click the Import Clips button on the Insert ClipArt toolbar, click the Look in box arrow in the Add clip to Clip Gallery dialog box, select the desired clips, click Let Clip Gallery find this clip in its current folder or volume, click the Import button, enter clip properties, and then click OK.

Increasing the Right Object Area Placeholder Width

If you increase the width of the right placeholder, the first demoted paragraph, Increases lean weight, will display on one line. Perform the following step to increase the width of the right Object Area placeholder.

TO INCREASE THE RIGHT OBJECT AREA PLACEHOLDER WIDTH

 Drag the right-center sizing handle on the right Object Area placeholder slightly to the right.

The mouse pointer becomes a two-headed arrow. The first demoted paragraph should display on one line (Figure 5-13 on the next page). If it displays on two lines, repeat this step until you achieve the desired results.

1. Right-click right Object Area Placeholder, click Format Placeholder, click Size tab, click Width box up arrow in Size and rotate area, click OK button
2. On Format menu click Placeholder, click Size tab, click Width box up arrow in Size and rotate area, click OK button
3. Press ALT+O, press O, press RIGHT ARROW key to select Size tab, press ALT+D, type `4.25`, press ENTER

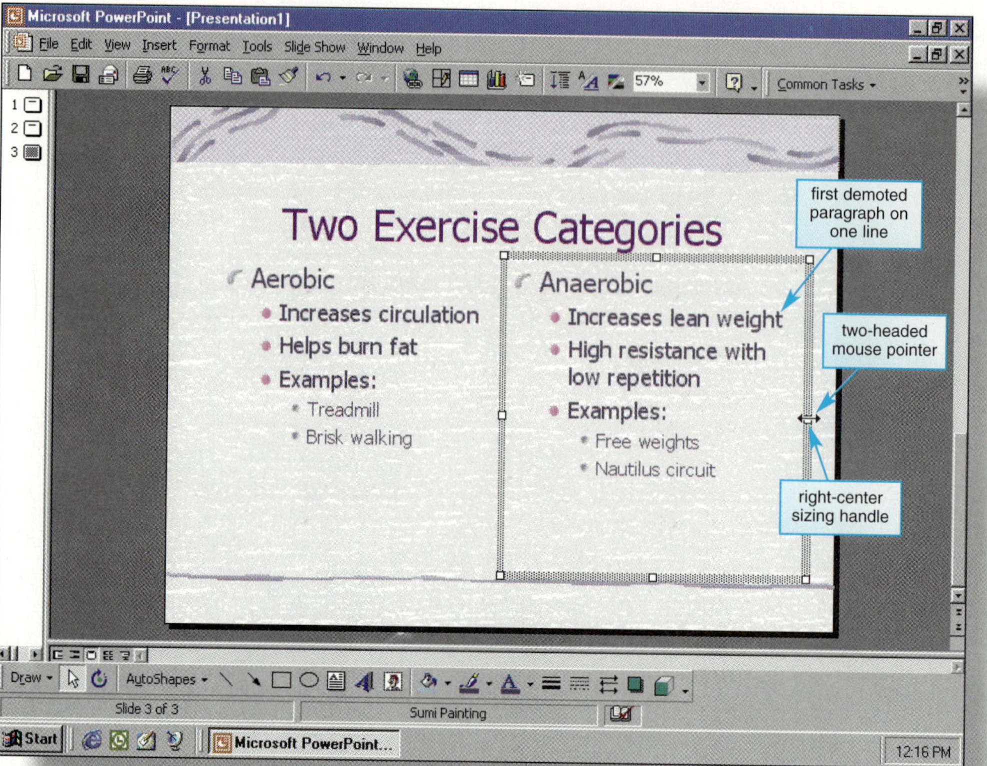

FIGURE 5-13

Additional space is added to the bottom of the slide to make room for the clip art you want to insert.

More About

GIFs

GIF files are prevalent in PowerPoint presentations and on the World Wide Web. You can create GIF files by designing images in drawing software packages such as Adobe Photoshop and then saving the file in GIF format. For instructions on creating GIF files, visit the PowerPoint 2000 Project 5 More About page (www.scsite.com/pp2000/more.htm) and click GIF.

Inserting Animated Clip Art

One of the features of Office 2000 is the animated GIF files found in the Clip Art Gallery 5.0. PowerPoint GIF files are among the numerous file formats that PowerPoint recognizes. **GIF files**, or Graphics Interchange Format files, are identified by their .gif file extension and have been compressed to reduce their file size. They often have flat, one-color backgrounds, and a maximum of 256 colors can display in the entire graphic.

The 2 Column Text AutoLayout on this slide does not have placeholders for the two clip art objects. You must, consequently, insert each file, move these objects to the desired locations on the slide, and then size them. Perform the following steps to insert the two animated files on the slide. If the two clip art object do not display in the Microsoft Clip Gallery, see your instructor for copies of these files.

TO INSERT ANIMATED CLIP ART

1. Click the Insert Clip Art button on the Drawing toolbar.
2. Click the Motion Clips tab in the Insert ClipArt window.
3. Type `people walking` in the Search for clips text box and then press the ENTER key. If necessary, scroll to display the desired clip art, a blue figure facing to the right.
4. Click the desired clip art and then click Insert clip, the top button on the shortcut menu.

5. Type `weight` in the Search for clips text box and then press the ENTER key.
6. Click the desired cartoon clip art of a muscular weightlifter and then click Insert clip on the shortcut menu.
7. Click the Close button on the Insert ClipArt title bar.

The two clip art objects display in the center of the slide (Figure 5-14).

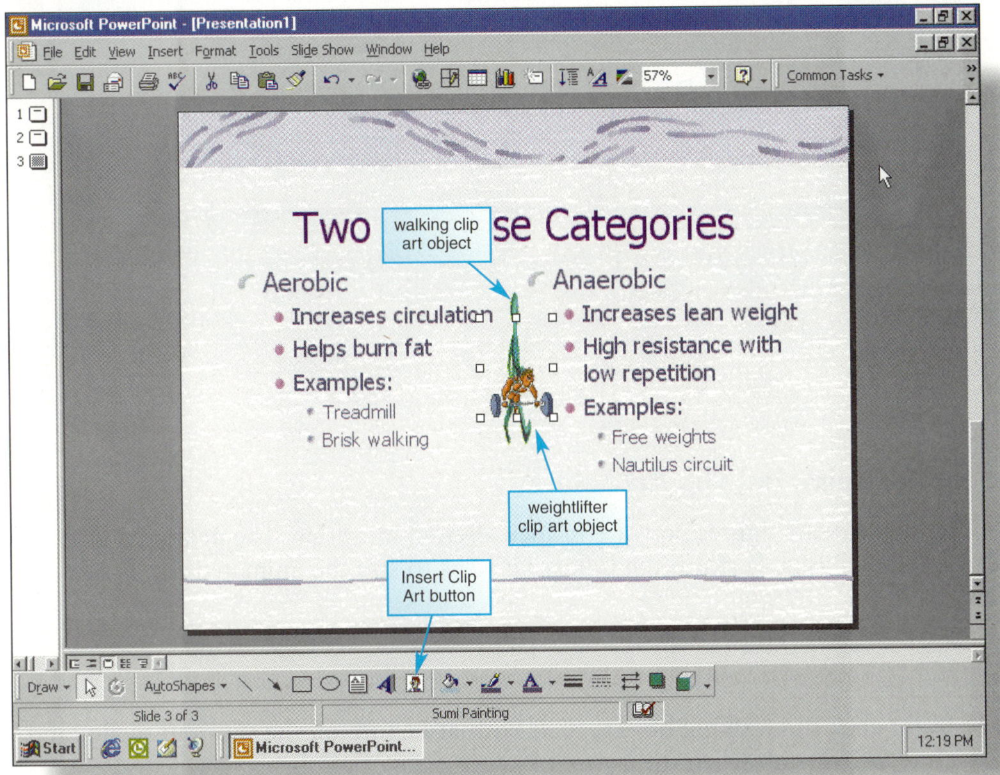

FIGURE 5-14

Moving the Animated Clip Art

Now that you have inserted the two clip art figures on the slide, you need to move these objects to new positions on the slide and then size them. The walking object should display below its present position, and the weightlifting object should display in the lower-right corner. Perform the following steps to move the animated clip art objects.

TO MOVE THE ANIMATED CLIP ART OBJECTS

1. Click the weightlifting clip art object to select it and drag it to the lower-right corner of the slide. Center the plates on the barbell on the line that extends across the bottom of the slide.
2. Click the walking clip art object and drag it downward. The figure's right big toe should just touch the line that extends across the bottom of the slide.

The two clip art objects display in their correct locations on the slide (Figure 5-15 on the next page).

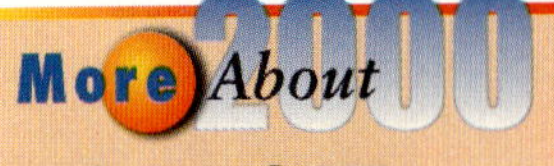

Animated GIFs

The animated clip art figures available in the Microsoft Clip Gallery or the Microsoft Clip Gallery Live site add visual interest to your slides. The World Wide Web abounds with excellent sources of additional animated GIFs. To view a collection of these files, visit the PowerPoint 2000 Project 5 More About page (www.scsite.com/pp2000/more.htm) and click Animated GIFs.

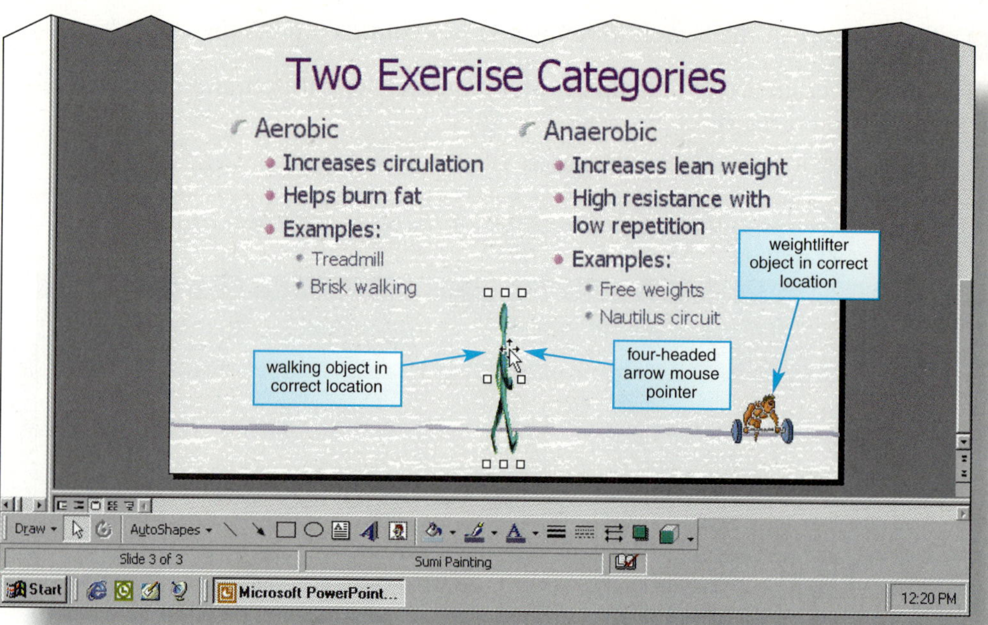

FIGURE 5-15

Sizing the Animated Clip Art

The two clip art figures now are in their desired locations. The next step is to enlarge these objects. Perform the following steps to size the animated clip art objects.

TO SIZE THE ANIMATED CLIP ART OBJECTS

1. Right-click the walking object, click Format Picture on the shortcut menu, and click the Size tab when the Format Picture dialog box displays.
2. With the Relative to original picture size check box selected, click Lock aspect ratio to remove the check. Triple-click the Width text box in the Size and rotate area and type `2.01` in the box.
3. Click the OK button.
4. Drag the walking object to re-center it in the area between the two bulleted lists.
5. Right-click the weightlifting object, click Format Picture on the shortcut menu, and click the Size tab when the Format Picture dialog box displays.
6. With the Lock aspect ratio and the Relative to original picture size check boxes selected, triple-click the Width text box in the Size and rotate area and type `1.95` in the box.
7. Click the OK button.
8. Drag the weightlifting object so that the plates on the barbell are once again centered on the line that extends across the bottom of the slide.

The two clip art objects are enlarged on the slide and restored to their correct locations (Figure 5-16). Lock aspect ratio maintains proportions, so when you deselect this check box, the walker gets wider but not taller. The Relative to original picture size check box keeps the object to scale.

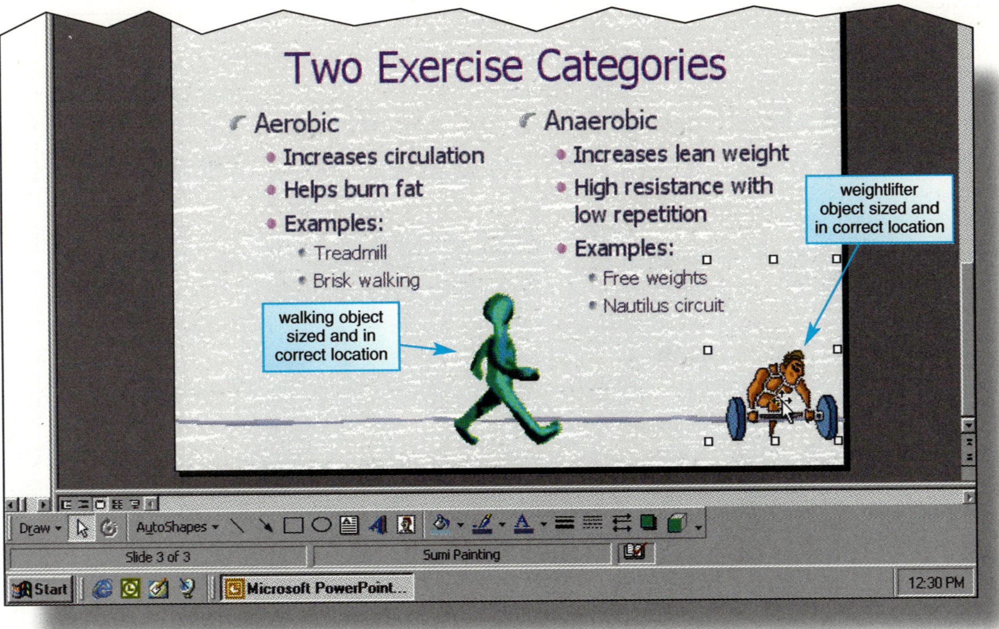

FIGURE 5-16

The third slide now is complete. The next slide will have another visual effect: an inserted chart created in Microsoft Excel.

Saving the Presentation

You now should save your presentation because you have done a substantial amount of work. The following steps summarize how to save a presentation.

TO SAVE A PRESENTATION

1. Click the Save button on the Standard toolbar.
2. Type `Half-Hour Workout` in the File name text box.
3. Click the Save in box arrow. Click 3½ Floppy (A:) in the Save in list.
4. Click the Save button in the Save As dialog box.

The presentation is saved on the floppy disk in drive A with the file name Half-Hour Workout. This file name displays on the title bar.

Inserting an Excel Chart

Aerobic activity helps strengthen the cardiovascular system and burn calories. These important benefits should be of interest to students at Western College, so you want to emphasize the aerobic qualities of a treadmill. A chart created in Microsoft Excel can depict how a treadmill's speed of 3.5, 4.5, or 5.5 miles per hour and incline ranging from 1 to 10 percent can affect the amount of calories burned. A **3-D Column chart** compares values across categories and across series. Similarly, the treadmill chart in Figure 5-17 illustrates the number of calories burned in relation to the amount of incline for the three speeds.

Previewing Animated Clip Art

If several slides in your presentation contain animated clip art, you can preview these images. Click slide sorter view, select the slides you want to preview, right-click one of the selected slides, and then click Play clip on the shortcut menu. Or you can click Animation Preview on the Slide Show menu. The transition effects and animation effects will display.

More About 2000

Changing Output Format

Slides can be printed in various sizes and orientations. For example, you can specify precise measurements and either landscape or portrait orientation. All slides in a presentation must print in the same orientation. To change the default settings, click Page Setup on the File menu, click the desired option in the Slides sized for box, click Portrait or Landscape under Slides, and click Portrait or Landscape under Notes, handouts, and outline. If you print your slides in landscape orientation, you can print your notes, handouts, and outlines in portrait orientation.

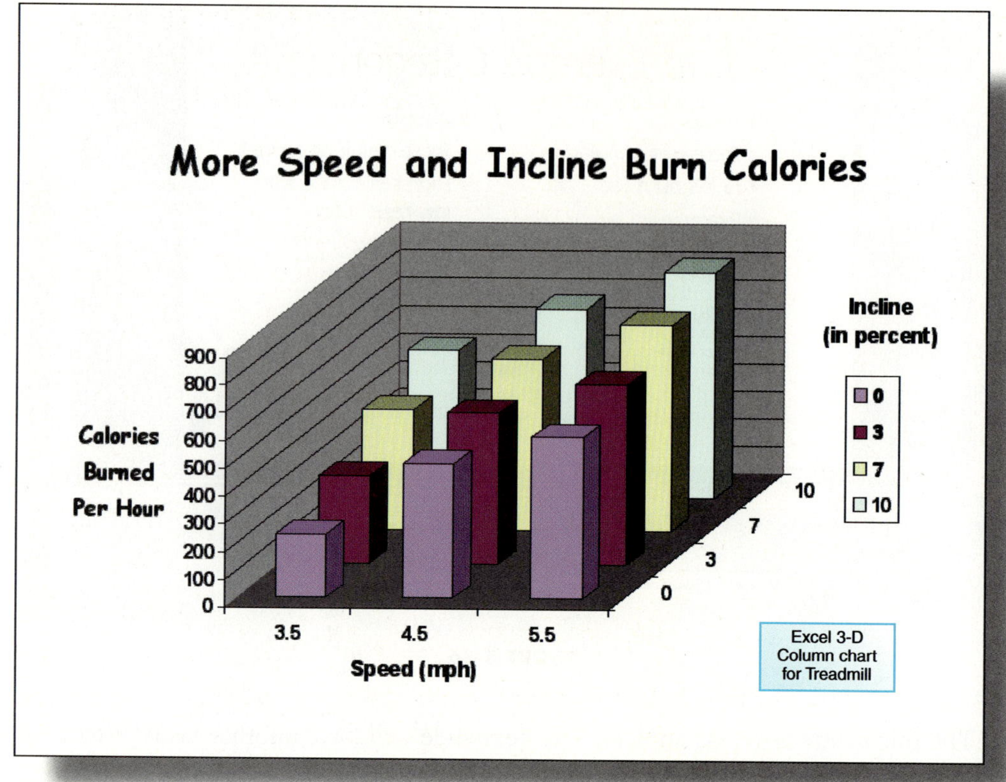

FIGURE 5-17

Copyrights

Congress passed the Online Copyright Infringement Liability Limitation Act of 1998 to address the widespread practice of online copyright infringement. This law makes it difficult for Internet Service Providers to be found liable when its users download files illegally from the Internet. To learn about the legal cases and legislative process that led to this law, visit the PowerPoint 2000 Project 5 More About page (www.scsite.com/pp2000/more.htm) and click Copyright.

PowerPoint allows you to insert, or **embed**, many types of objects into a presentation. You inserted animated clip art into Slide 3, and you will import a Microsoft Word table into Slide 6. Other objects you can embed include video clips, Microsoft PhotoDraw pictures, and Adobe Acrobat documents. Perform the following steps to insert a new slide and to insert an Excel chart from your Data Disk.

Before you insert the Excel chart, you need to create a new slide and change the slide layout to the Object layout.

TO ADD A SLIDE, CHANGE THE SLIDE LAYOUT, AND TYPE THE TITLE TEXT

1. Click the New Slide button on the Standard toolbar to display Slide 4.
2. Type the number 16 to select the Object layout from the 24 available AutoLayouts. Then, click the OK button.
3. Type `Aerobic Activity - Treadmill` as the Slide 4 title text.

Slide 4 displays the title text and the placeholder for the Excel object (Figure 5-18). When the New Slide dialog box displays, you can type a number or double-click an AutoLayout to choose a particular layout style.

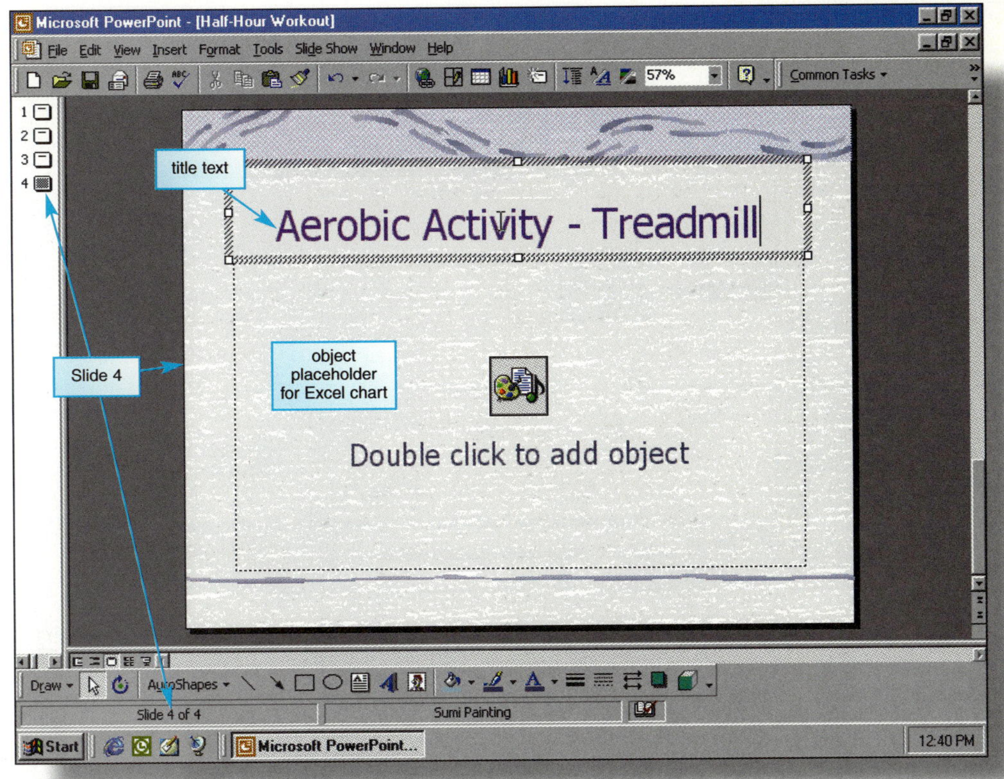

FIGURE 5-18

Other Ways

1. Move scroll bar downward to display Object layout, double-click Object layout

Slide 4 now displays the slide title and object placeholder for the Treadmill chart. The next section explains how to insert this Excel chart.

To Insert an Excel Chart

1 Double-click the object placeholder in the middle of Slide 4. Click Create from file. Point to the Browse button.

The Insert Object dialog box displays (Figure 5-19). Drive A is the current drive. The Create from file option allows you to select an object created in another application or in PowerPoint.

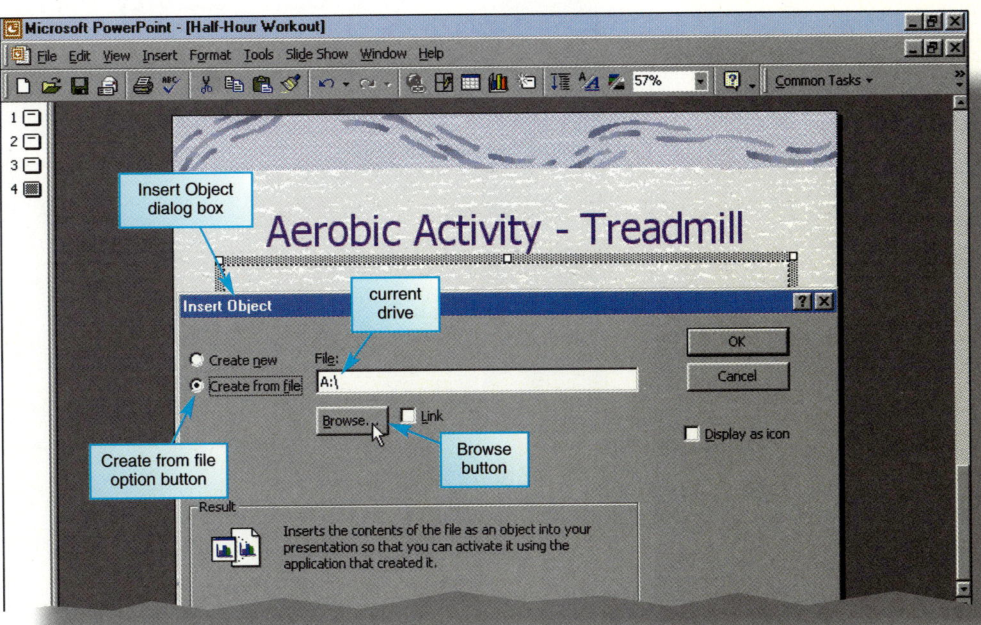

FIGURE 5-19

2 **Click the Browse button. When the Browse dialog box displays, click Treadmill. Point to the OK button.**

The Browse dialog box displays the files on the Data Disk (Figure 5-20). Treadmill is the Excel file you will insert into Slide 4.

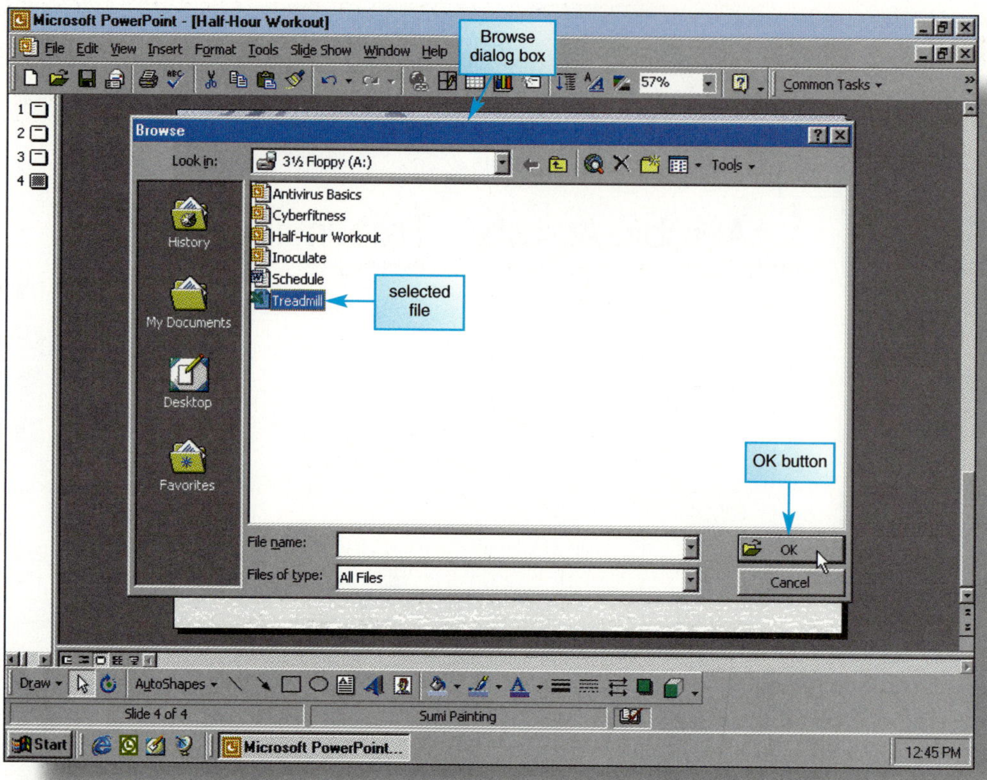

FIGURE 5-20

3 **Click the OK button. When the Insert Object dialog box displays, point to the OK button.**

The Insert Object dialog box now displays A:\Treadmill.xls in the File text box (Figure 5-21). The .xls extension indicates the file is a Microsoft Excel document.

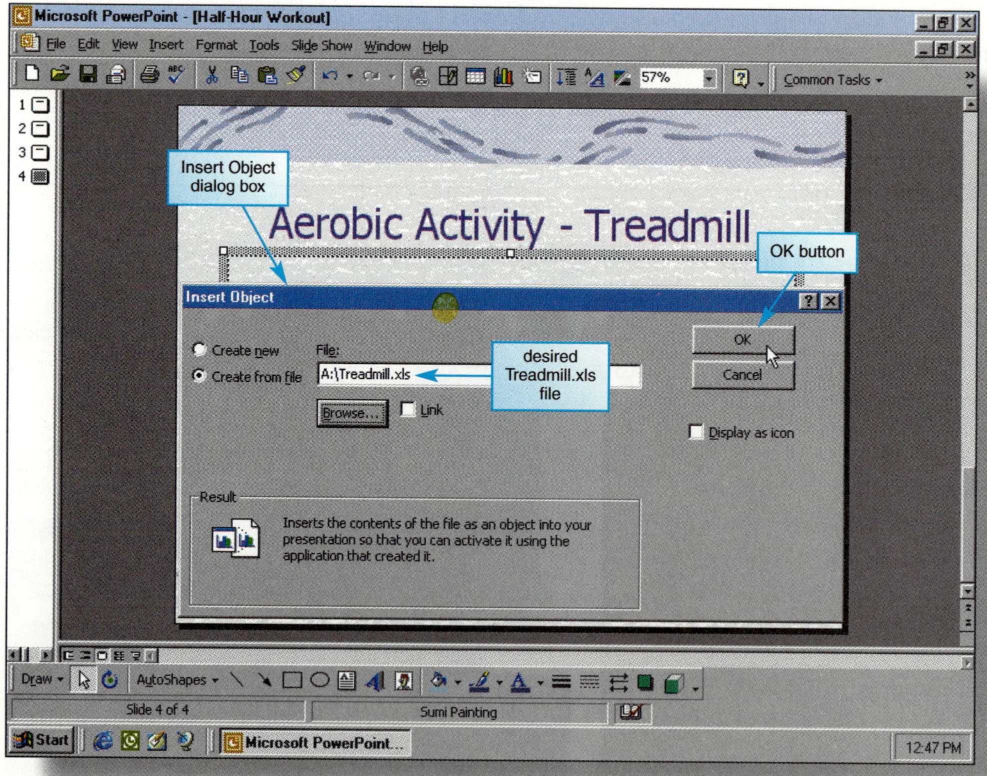

FIGURE 5-21

Click the OK button.

Slide 4 displays the Treadmill chart (Figure 5-22).

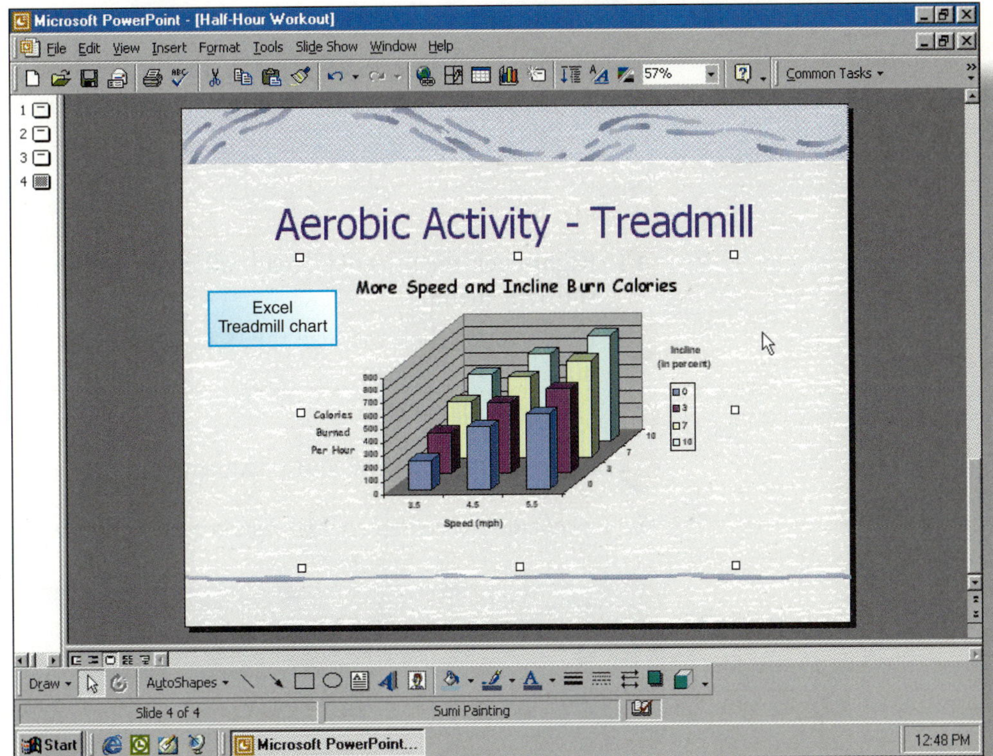

FIGURE 5-22

1. On Insert menu click Object, click Create from file, enter file name, click OK button

When you click the Create from file option button in the Insert Object dialog box, the dialog box changes. The File box replaces the Object type box. Another change to the dialog box is the addition of the **Link check box**. If the Link check box is selected, the object is inserted as a linked, instead of an embedded, object. Like an embedded object, a **linked object** also is created in another application; however, the linked object maintains a connection to its source. If the original object is changed, the linked object on the slide also changes. The linked object is stored in the **source file**, the file in which the object was created.

For example, the Excel chart you embedded into the slide is stored on the Data Disk. If you were to link rather than embed the Treadmill file, then every time the Treadmill file changed in Excel, the changes would display on the chart in Slide 4. Your PowerPoint presentation would store a representation of the original Treadmill file and information about its location. If you later moved or deleted the source file, the link would be broken, and the object would not be available. Consequently, if you make a presentation on a computer other than the one on which the presentation was created and the presentation contains a linked object, be certain to include a copy of the source files. The source files must be stored in the exact location as originally specified when you linked them to your presentation.

When you select a source file from the Browse dialog box, PowerPoint associates the file with a specific application, which is based on the file extension. For example, if you select a source file with the file extension **.doc**, PowerPoint recognizes the file as a Microsoft Word file. Additionally, if you select a source file with the file extension **.xls**, PowerPoint recognizes the file as a Microsoft Excel file.

Editing an Embedded Excel Chart

If you need to edit an Excel chart you import into your slide, double-click the chart, use the Microsoft Excel tools and menus to modify the chart, and then click outside the chart to return to PowerPoint.

Scaling an Excel Chart

The Treadmill chart on Slide 4 is sized to fit the object placeholder, but sufficient space exists on the slide to enlarge the chart. Perform the following steps to scale the chart object.

TO SCALE THE EXCEL CHART

1. Right-click the selected Treadmill chart and then click Format Object on the shortcut menu.
2. If necessary, click the Size tab. Click the Height box up arrow in the Scale area until 110% displays.
3. Click the OK button.
4. Press the LEFT ARROW and UP ARROW keys to center the chart on the slide.

The Excel chart is scaled to 110 percent of its original size (Figure 5-23).

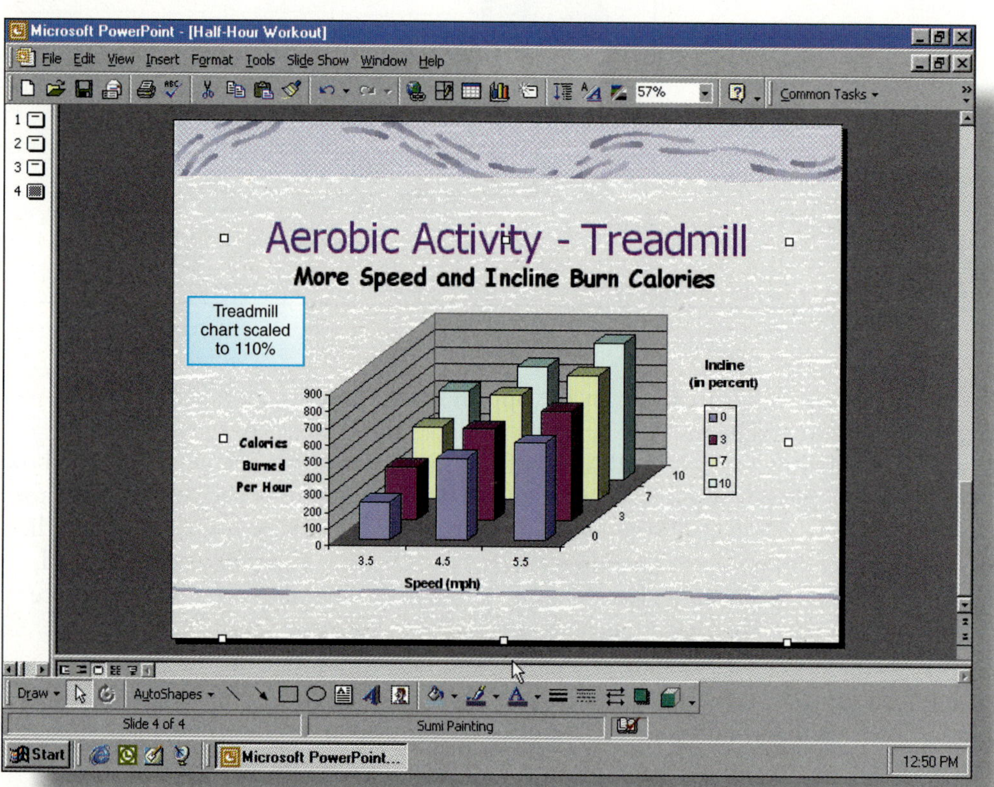

FIGURE 5-23

Slide 4 now is complete. The next slide also will have a chart; instead of importing this chart from the Data Disk, however, you will build this chart directly within your PowerPoint presentation using the supplementary application called **Microsoft Graph**.

Saving a Slide as a Graphic

Each slide can be saved in GIF format and then inserted as a picture in another program or on a Web page. To save a slide as a graphic, display the slide, click Save As on the File menu, and then click Windows Metafile or GIF Graphics Interchange Format in the Save as type box.

Building a PowerPoint Chart

The chart on Slide 4 shows the advantages of using a treadmill as a source of aerobic activity. The chart on the next slide, shown in Figure 5-24, will show four benefits of using free weights: toning muscles, increasing energy, improving circulation, and controlling weight. A **pie chart** clearly can depict the contribution of each of these four components to the total wellness benefit the students will receive by using free weights regularly. This chart type shows the relationship or proportion of parts to a whole. Each slice (or wedge) of the pie shows what percent that slice contributes to the total (100%).

More About

Applying Diagonal Borders

Borders help draw a viewer's eye toward an object on a slide. PowerPoint provides a variety of border styles and colors. To add a diagonal border, select the object, click the Line Style button on the Drawing toolbar, click More Lines, click the Colors and Lines tab in the Format Object dialog box, click the Color arrow in the Line area, click Patterned Lines, choose a diagonal border and Foreground and Background colors, click the OK button, and then change the border Style and Weight.

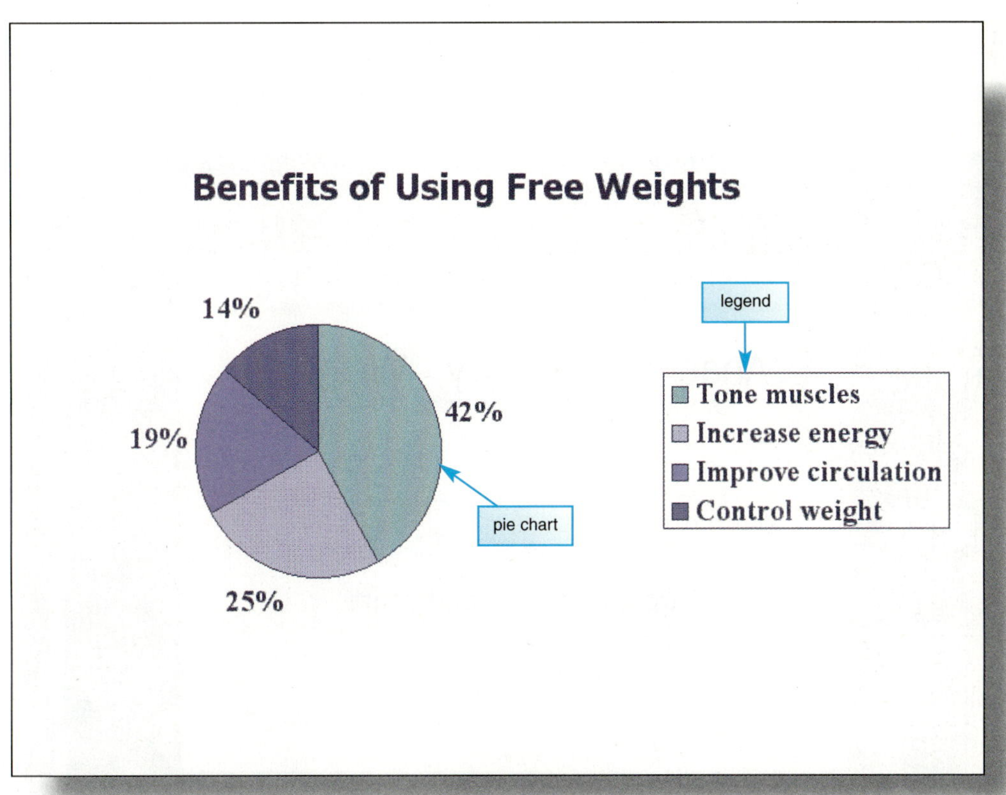

FIGURE 5-24

PowerPoint allows you to create a chart using Microsoft Graph within the application. The figures for the chart are entered in a corresponding **datasheet**, which is a rectangular grid containing columns (vertical) and rows (horizontal). Column letters display above the grid to identify particular **columns**, and row numbers display on the left side of the grid to identify particular **rows**. **Cells** are the intersections of rows and columns, and they are the locations for the chart data and text labels. For example, cell A1 is the intersection of column A and row 1. You enter numeric and text data in the **active cell**, which is the one cell surrounded by a heavy border.

Creating the chart shown in Figure 5-24 requires several steps: inserting a new slide and choosing the Chart AutoLayout, changing the chart type, replacing the sample data, and adding a chart title and data labels. The sections on the next page describe how to perform these actions.

Adding Data

In this presentation you add your own data to the datasheet. At times, however, you may want to import data from a text file, a Lotus 1-2-3 file, a Microsoft Excel worksheet or chart, or another program. This data can be a maximum of 4,000 rows by 4,000 columns, but a maximum of 255 data series can be displayed on the chart. To add this data, select the cell where you want the imported data to begin, click the Import File button on the Standard toolbar, click the data location in the Look in box, and then double-click the file you want to import. If you import a text file, the Text Import Wizard will help you arrange the data on the datasheet.

Creating a New Slide, Choosing the Chart AutoLayout, and Typing the Title Text

Before you create the anaerobic benefits pie chart, you first must insert a new slide and then change the AutoLayout and add the slide title. The following steps describe these tasks.

TO ADD A SLIDE, CHANGE THE SLIDE LAYOUT, AND TYPE THE TITLE TEXT

1. Click the New Slide button on the Standard toolbar to display Slide 5.
2. Type the number 8 to select the Chart layout from the 24 available AutoLayouts. Then, click the OK button.
3. Type `Anaerobic Activity - Weights` as the Slide 5 title text.

Slide 5 displays the title text and the placeholder for the pie chart (Figure 5-25).

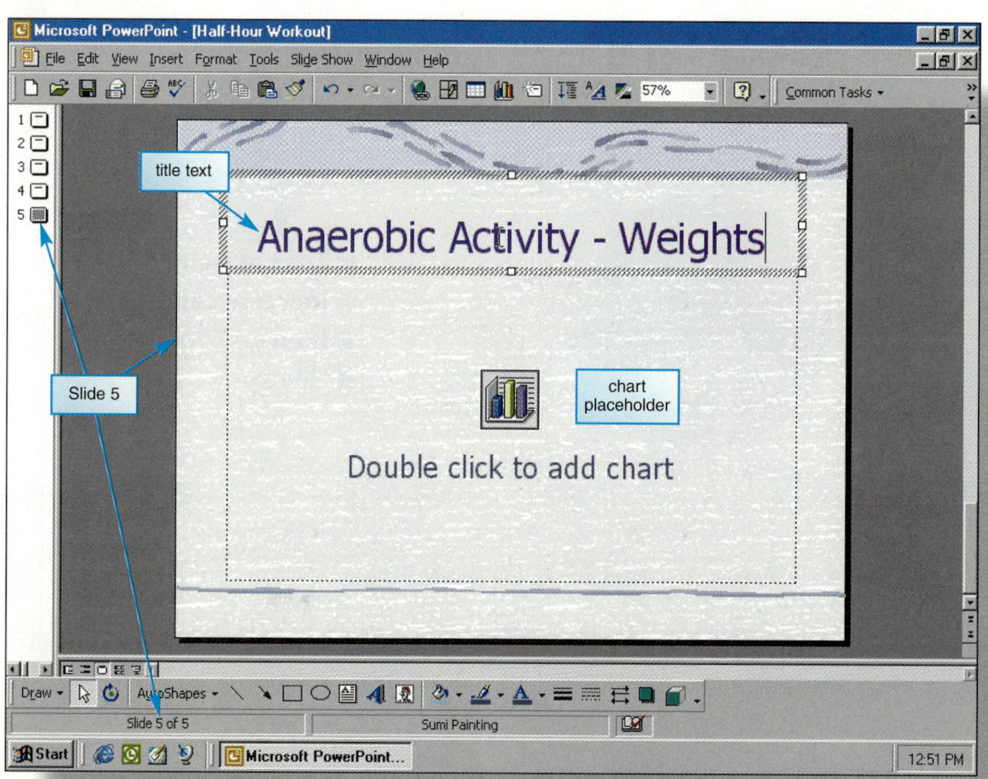

FIGURE 5-25

Other Ways

1. Move scroll bar downward to display Chart layout, double-click Chart layout

More About 2000

Chart Types

PowerPoint has a variety of 2-D, bubble, and 3-D chart types. For 2-D charts, you can change the chart type of either a group of data or the entire chart. For bubble charts, you can change only the type of the entire chart. For 3-D bar and column charts, you can change the data series to the cone, cylinder, or pyramid chart types. For most other 3-D charts, you change the entire chart when you change the chart type.

Slide 5 now displays the slide title and placeholder for the chart. The next section explains how to select a pie chart to depict the four benefits derived from using free weights.

Selecting a Different Chart Type

The default Micrograph Graph chart style is a 3-D column chart. This style is appropriate when comparing two or more items in specified intervals, such as in the Slide 4 chart depicting how various treadmill speeds and inclines affect the number of calories burned. In this free weight situation, however, you want to show how performing anaerobic activity affects the body in four ways.

A pie chart is an appropriate chart style for the free weight example. The following steps describe how to change the chart type.

To Select a Different Chart Type

1 Double-click the chart placeholder in the middle of Slide 5. Click Chart on the menu bar and then point to Chart Type.

The sample datasheet and chart display (Figure 5-26).

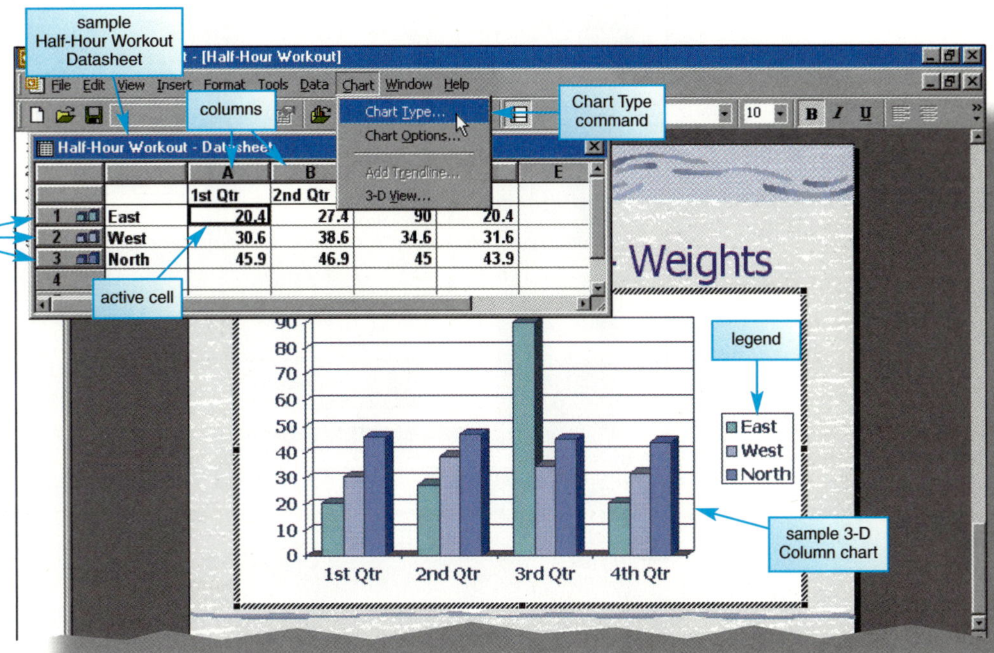

FIGURE 5-26

2 Click Chart Type. When the Chart Type dialog box displays, click Pie in the Chart type list on the Standard Types sheet. Point to the Press and Hold to View Sample button.

The Pie chart type is selected (Figure 5-27). You can view a sample of your chart before you actually change the chart type.

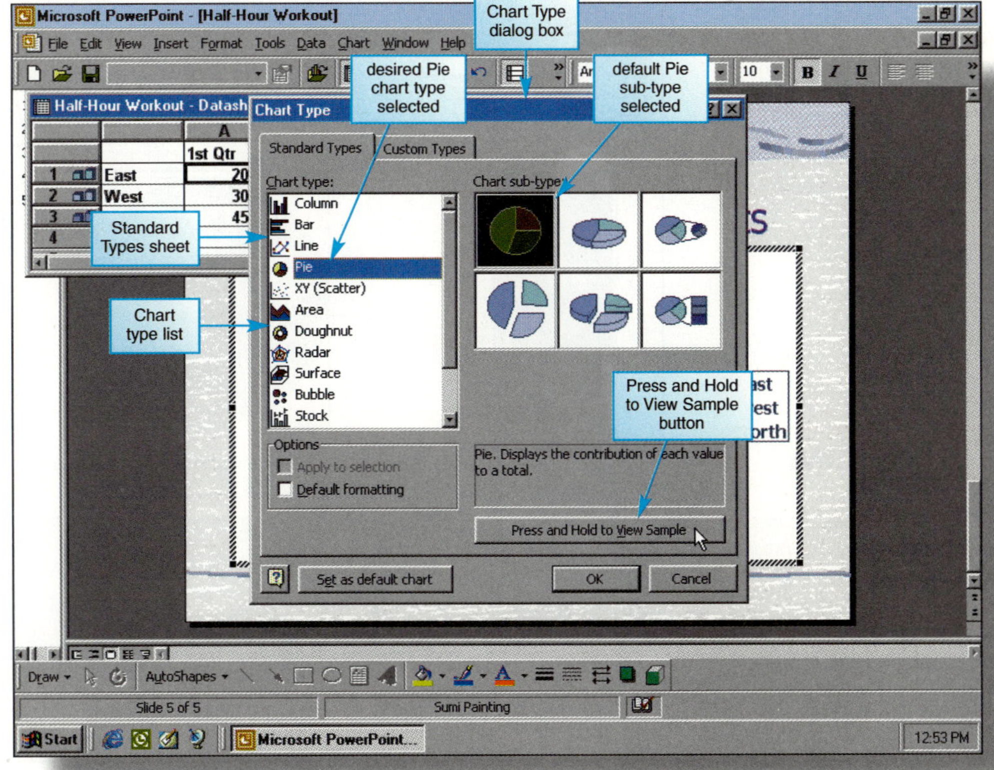

FIGURE 5-27

3 Click the Press and Hold to View Sample button.

The sample Pie chart displays (Figure 5-28).

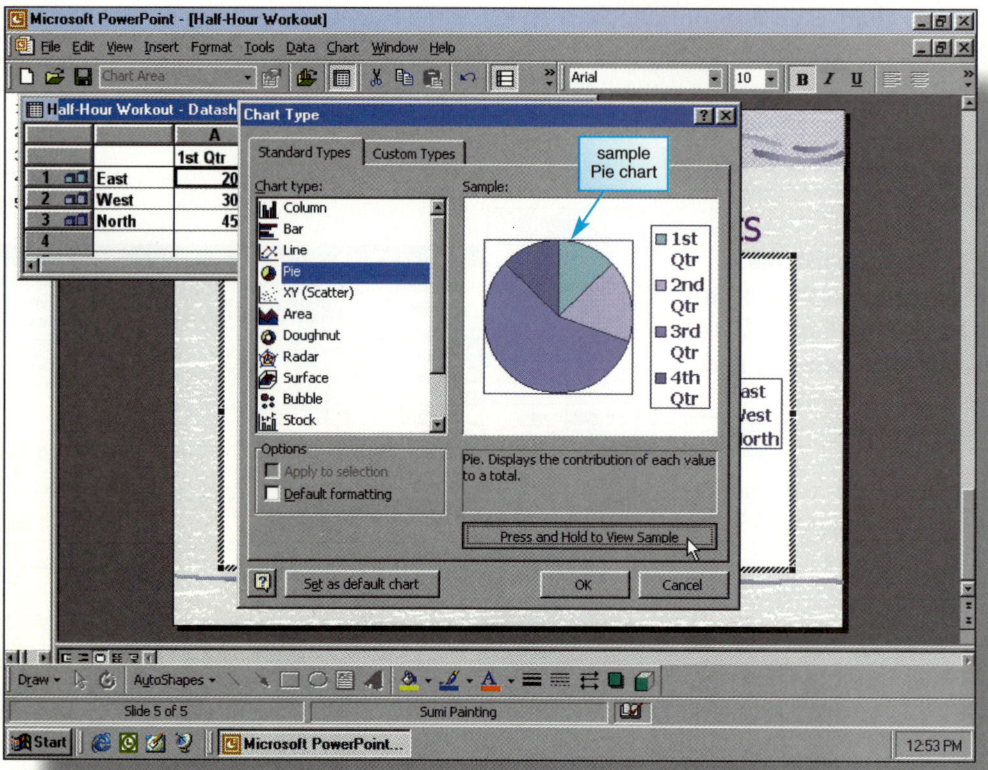

FIGURE 5-28

4 Click the OK button.

Microsoft Graph changes the chart type from a 3-D column chart to a pie chart (Figure 5-29).

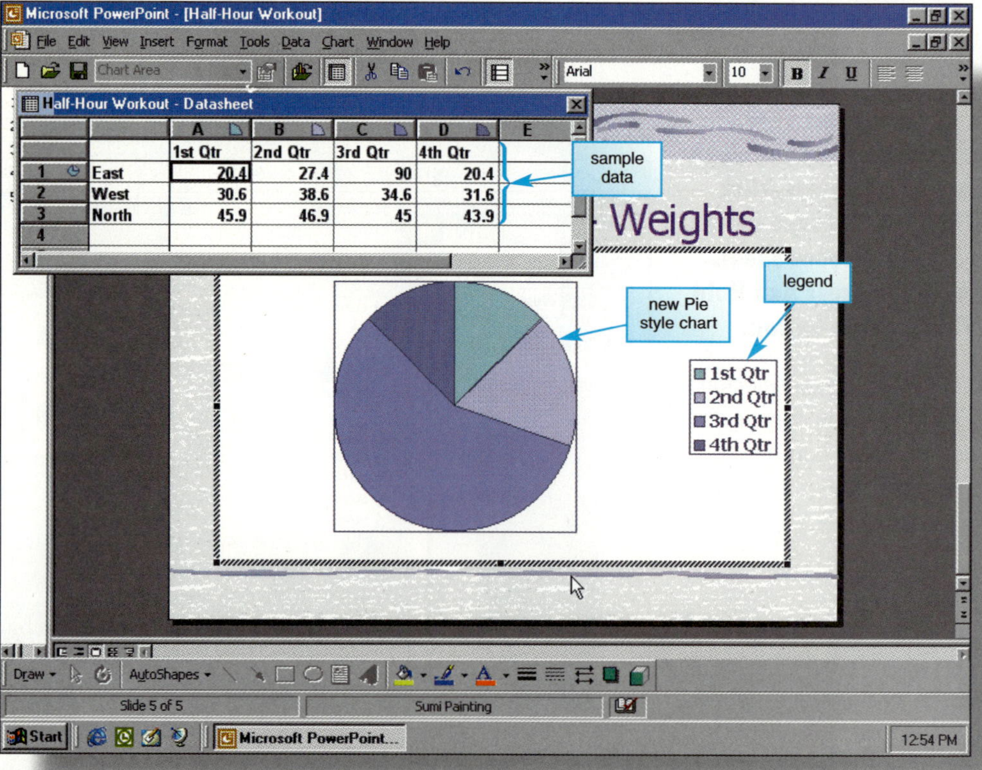

FIGURE 5-29

Other Ways

1. Double-click chart placeholder, press ALT+C, press T, press P, press V, press SPACEBAR, press TAB, press ENTER
2. Double-click chart placeholder, right-click chart, click Chart Type on shortcut menu, click Pie, click Press and Hold to View Sample button, click OK button

The sample data now is represented in a pie chart rather than the default column chart. Your next step is to replace the sample data with actual percentages.

Replacing the Sample Data

Microsoft Graph provides sample data to create the default chart. You need to change these figures to the numbers representing the amount of benefit students receive from using free weights. The following steps describe how to replace the sample data.

More About 2000

Modifying a Chart

If you work on a chart and then click Undo after returning to PowerPoint before you make any changes to the presentation, you will undo all the changes you made to your chart. In fact, you may delete the chart itself. To undo your changes, double-click the chart to activate it. Then manually undo the changes.

To Replace the Sample Data

1 **Point to cell A1, which is the intersection of column A and row 1.**

Cell A1 is selected (Figure 5-30). The mouse pointer changes to a block plus sign.

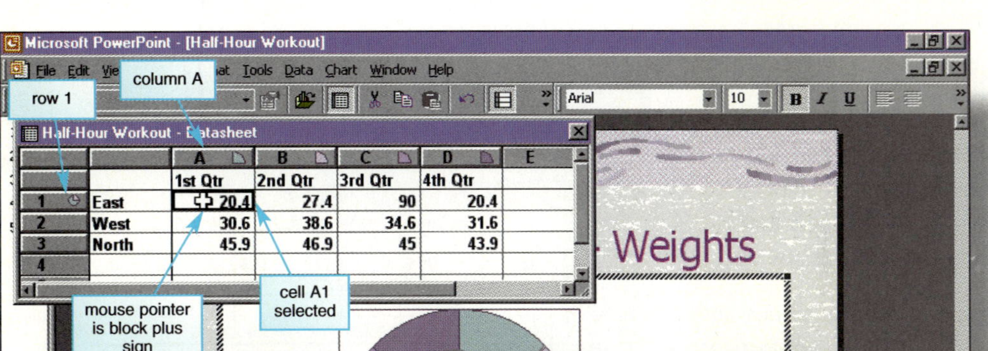

FIGURE 5-30

2 **Type** 42 **in cell A1 and press the RIGHT ARROW key. Type** 25 **in cell B1,** 19 **in cell C1, and** 14 **in cell D1. Point to the cell above cell A1 that contains the label, 1st Qtr.**

The four figures represent the percentage of benefits obtained by using free weights (Figure 5-31).

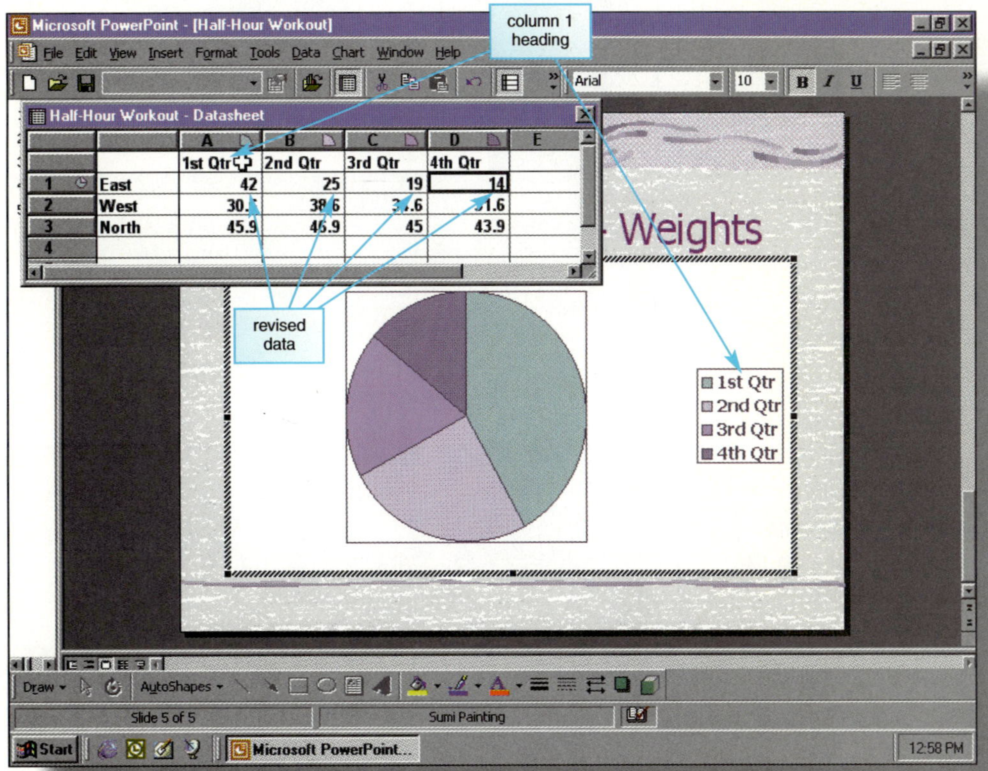

FIGURE 5-31

3 **Click the cell above cell A1 that contains the label, 1st Qtr. Type** `Tone muscles` **in this cell.**

Tone muscles is the corresponding label for the entry, 42, in cell A1 (Figure 5-32). Forty-two percent of the energy expended in using free weights goes toward toning the body.

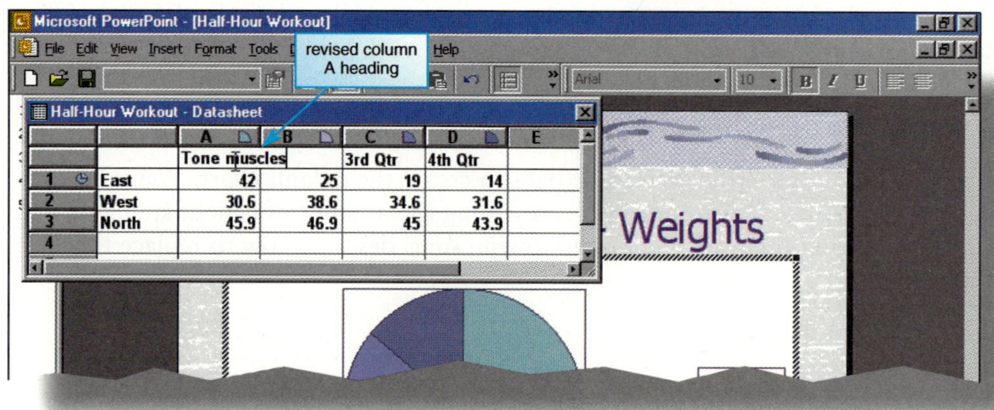

FIGURE 5-32

4 **Press the RIGHT ARROW key to advance to the cell above cell B1. Type** `Increase energy` **in this cell and press the RIGHT ARROW key.**

As you type these entries, the text displays in the datasheet and in the chart legend (Figure 5-33).

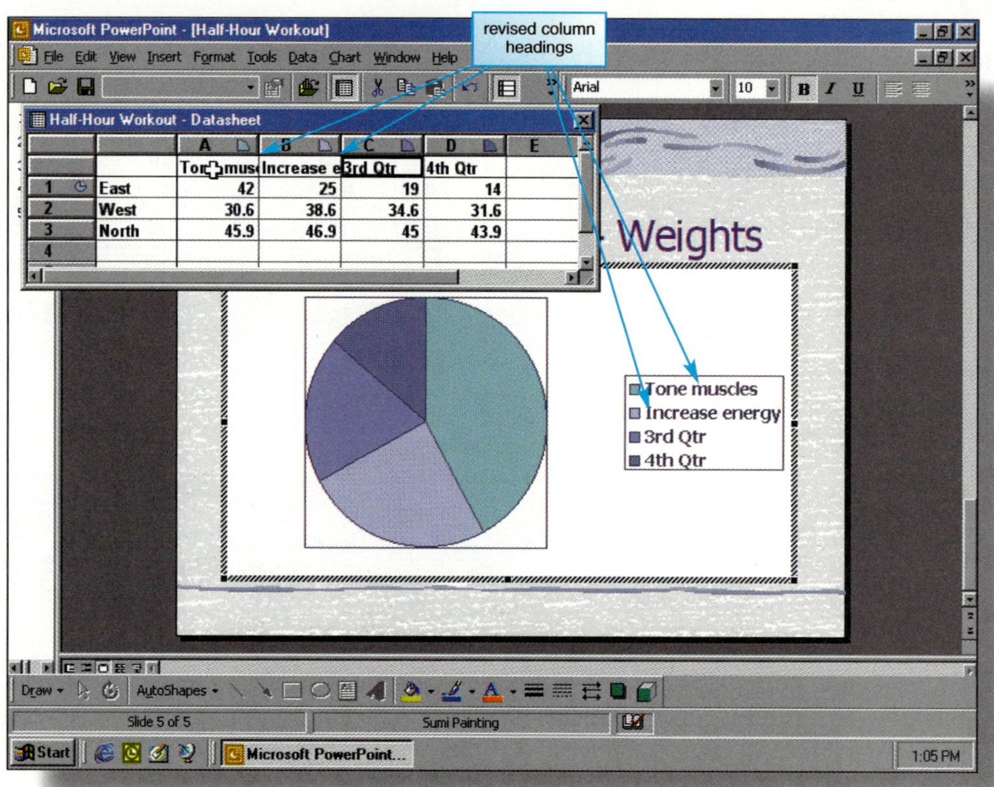

FIGURE 5-33

5 **Type** `Improve circulation` **in the cell above cell C1 and** `Control weight` **in the cell above cell D1.**

The data labels are entered, and they will display in their entirety when you modify the datasheet and chart (Figure 5-34).

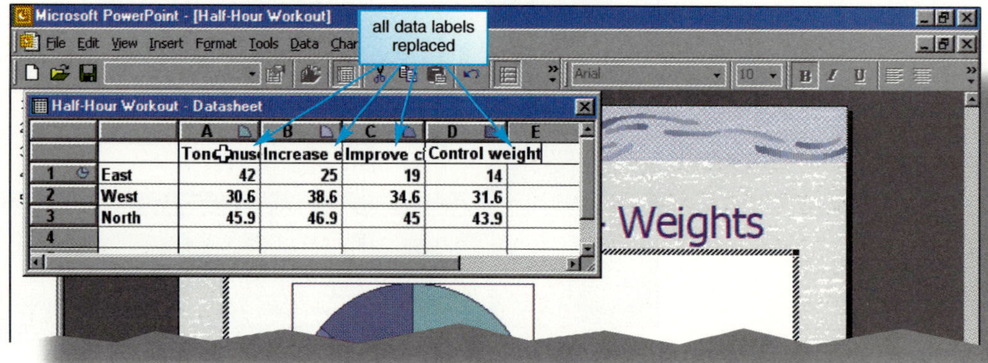

FIGURE 5-34

6 **Click the cell to the left of cell A1 that contains the label, East. Press and hold down the SHIFT key, and then click the cell to the left of cell A3 that contains the label, North.**

The three cells in the first column of the datasheet are selected (Figure 5-35).

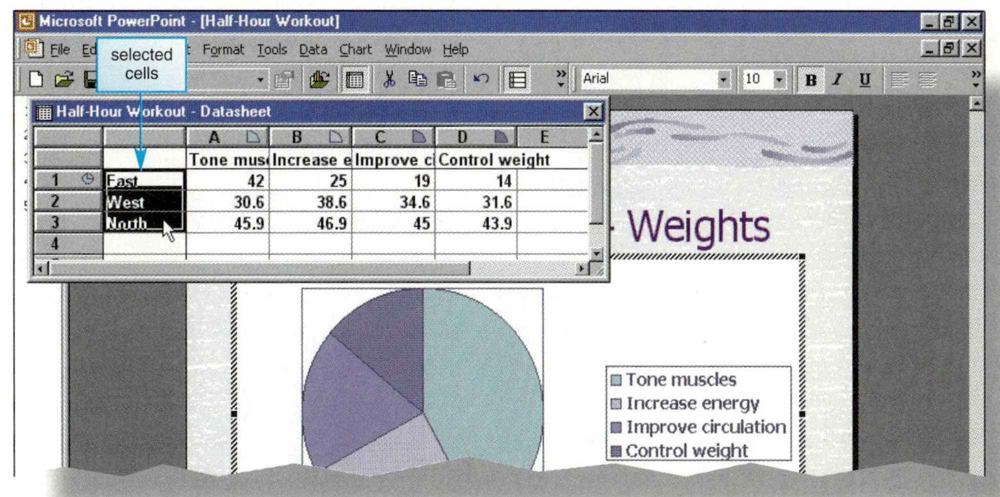

FIGURE 5-35

7 **Press the DELETE key.**

The entries in these three cells are deleted (Figure 5-36).

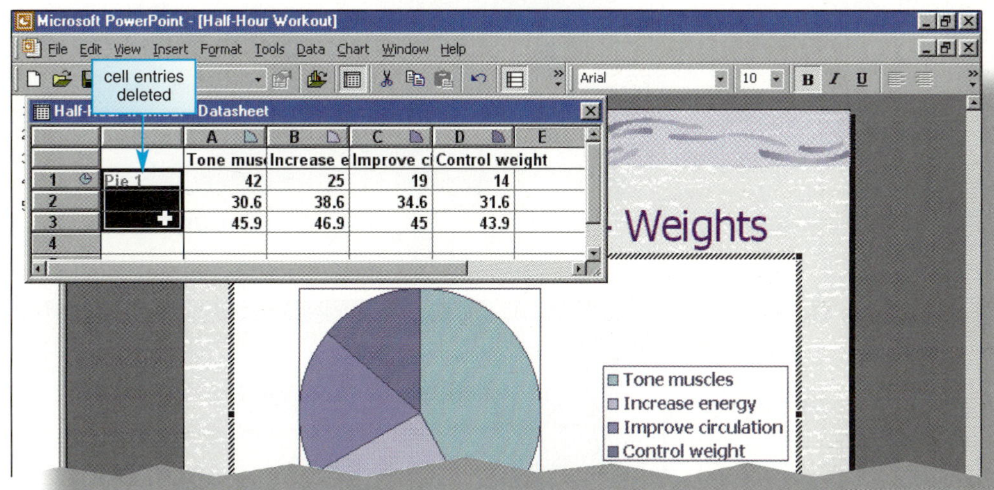

FIGURE 5-36

8 **Click cell A2. Press and hold the SHIFT key and then click cell D3.**

The eight cells in the range from A2 to D3 are selected (Figure 5-37).

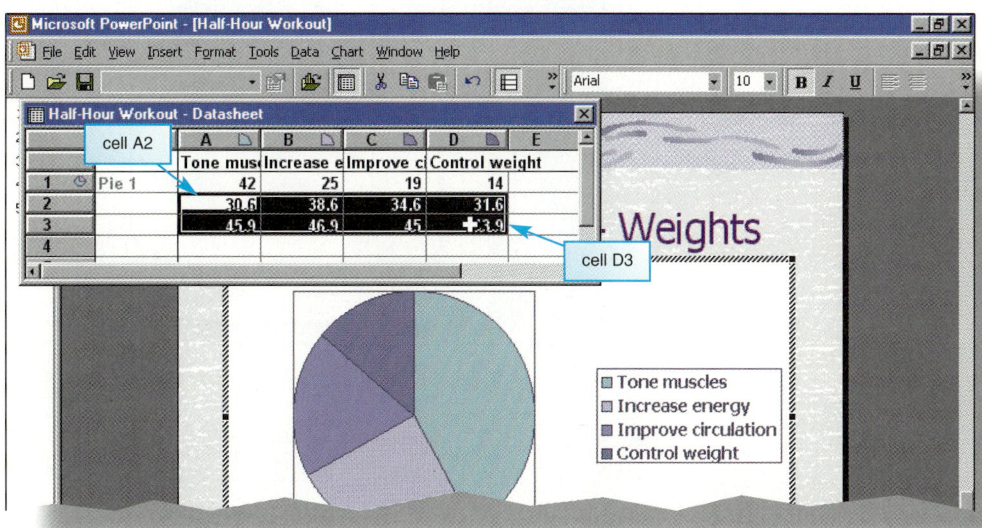

FIGURE 5-37

9 **Press the DELETE key. Point to the Close button on the datasheet.**

The entries in these eight cells are deleted (Figure 5-38).

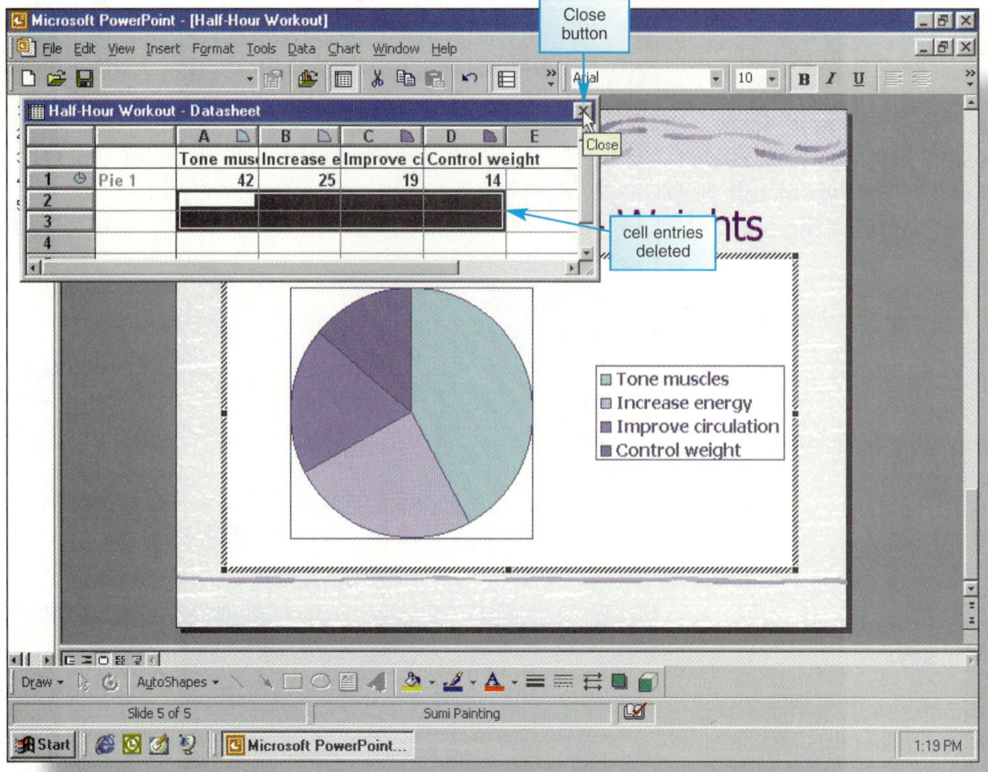

FIGURE 5-38

10 **Click the Close button.**

The datasheet closes and the revised chart and legend display (Figure 5-39).

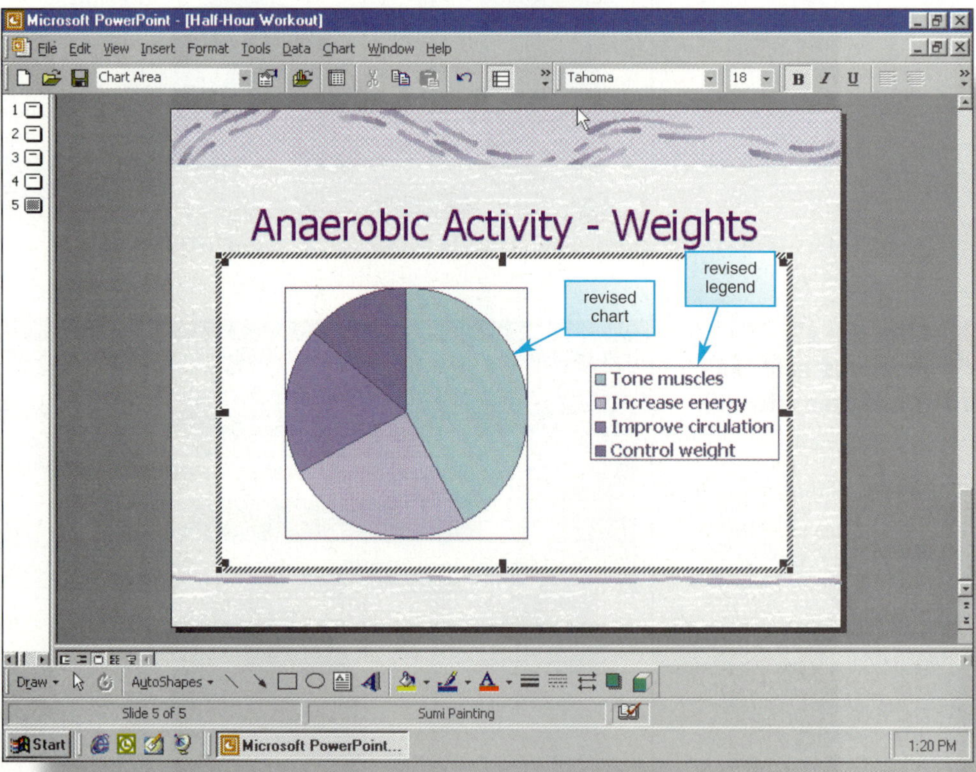

FIGURE 5-39

The free weight data has been entered in the Microsoft Graph datasheet. The four benefits – tone muscles, increase energy, improve circulation, and control weight – display in the **legend**, which identifies each slice in the chart. Microsoft Graph automatically selects the data in the first row of the datasheet as titles within the legend.

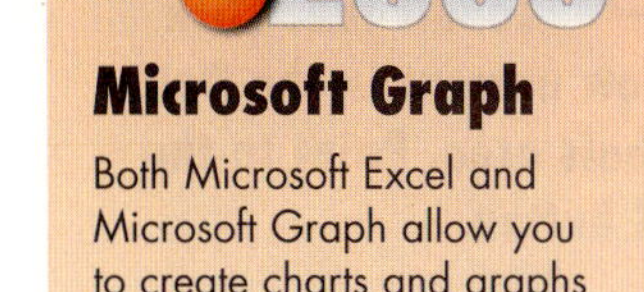

Microsoft Graph

Both Microsoft Excel and Microsoft Graph allow you to create charts and graphs for your PowerPoint presentation. To create charts or to modify charts you import, you must have these programs installed on your system. For information on installing a program or component, see your instructor.

Adding a Chart Title and Data Labels

The slices of the free weight chart now display in correct proportions. Next, you will add a title above the chart and display the benefit percentage figures. The following steps describe how to add these elements to the slide.

To Add a Chart Title and Data Labels

1 Click Chart on the menu bar and then click Chart Options.

The Chart Options dialog box displays (Figure 5-40). The three tabs – Titles, Legend, and Data Labels – allow you to display and format several chart elements.

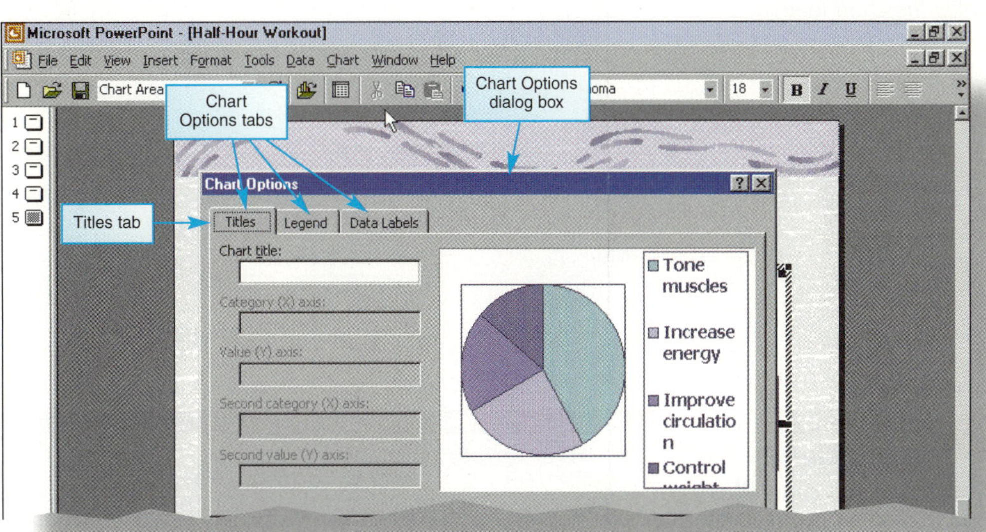

FIGURE 5-40

2 If necessary, click the Titles tab. Click the Chart title text box and then type `Benefits of Using Free Weights` **in the text box. Point to the Data Labels tab.**

The chart title displays in the chart preview box (Figure 5-41). The chart title helps viewers understand the purpose of the chart. The chart title can display on multiple lines if you press the ENTER key to start a new paragraph or the SHIFT+ENTER keys to insert a line break.

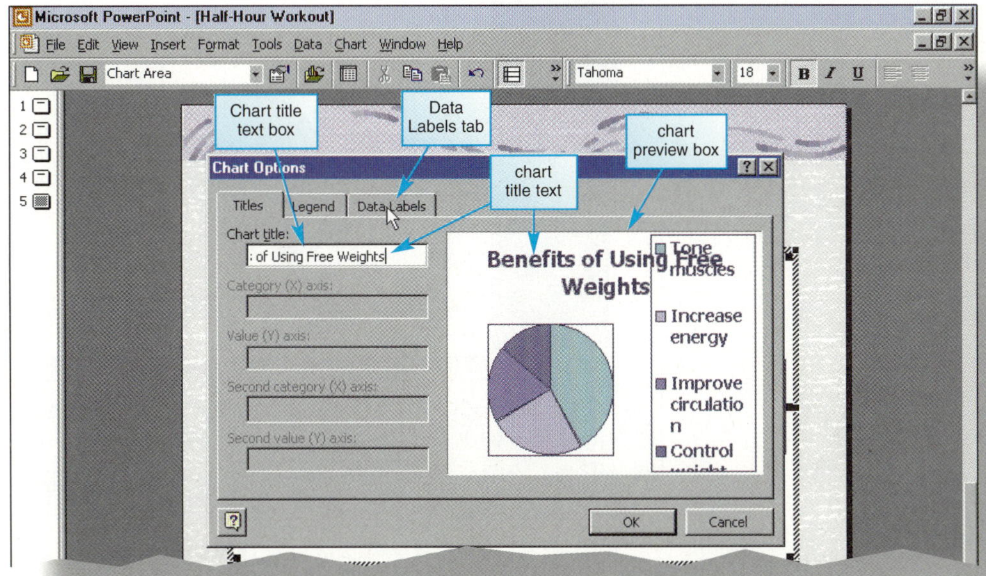

FIGURE 5-41

3 Click the Data Labels tab. Click Show percent in the Data labels area. Point to the OK button.

The benefit percentages display in the chart preview box (Figure 5-42). Various visuals can display on the chart, including the figures, the figures with a percent sign, and the data labels. You also can choose whether to display the chart legend.

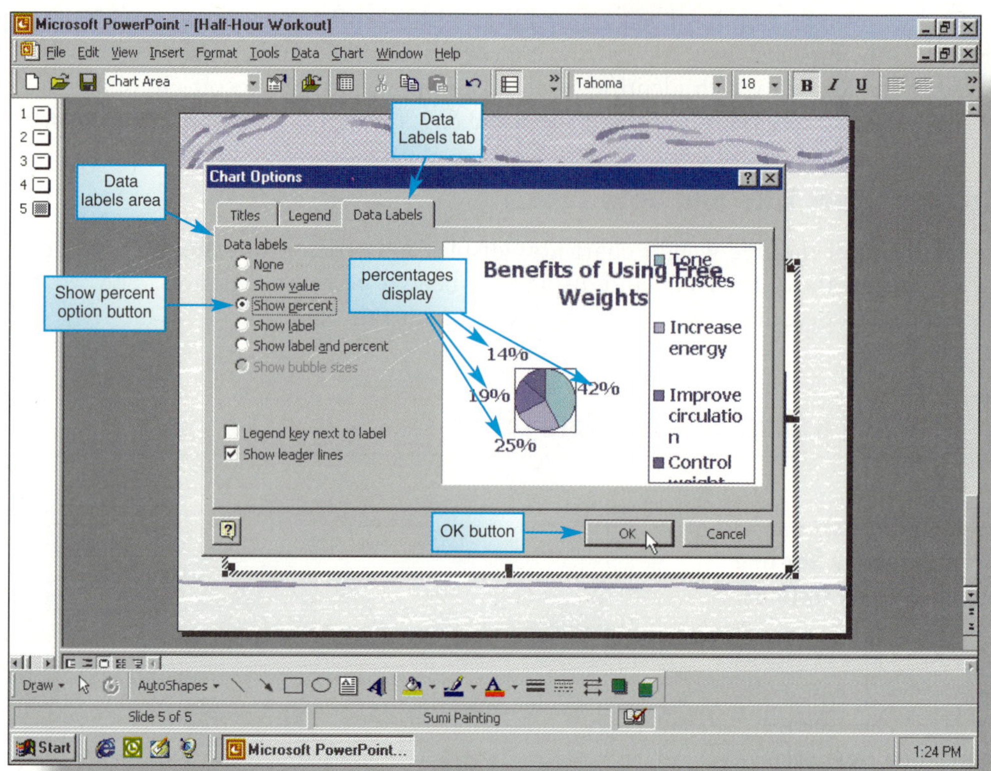

FIGURE 5-42

4 Click the OK button. Click the box surrounding the chart Plot Area.

Sizing handles display on the Plot Area box (Figure 5-43).

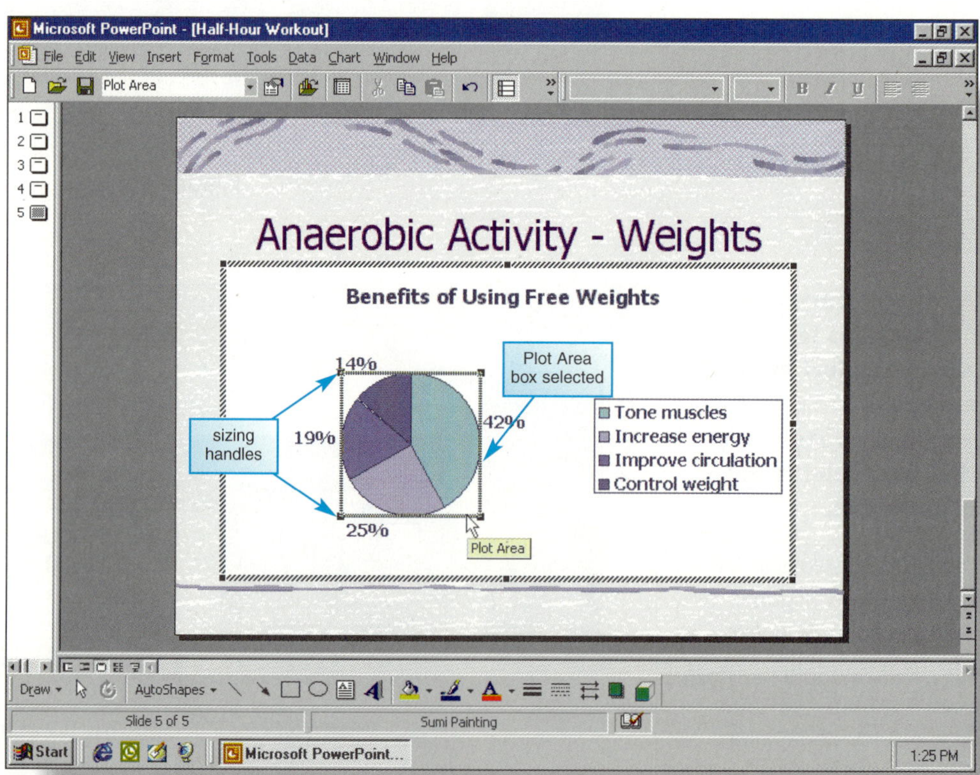

FIGURE 5-43

6 Press the DELETE key.

The Plot Area box is deleted (Figure 5-44).

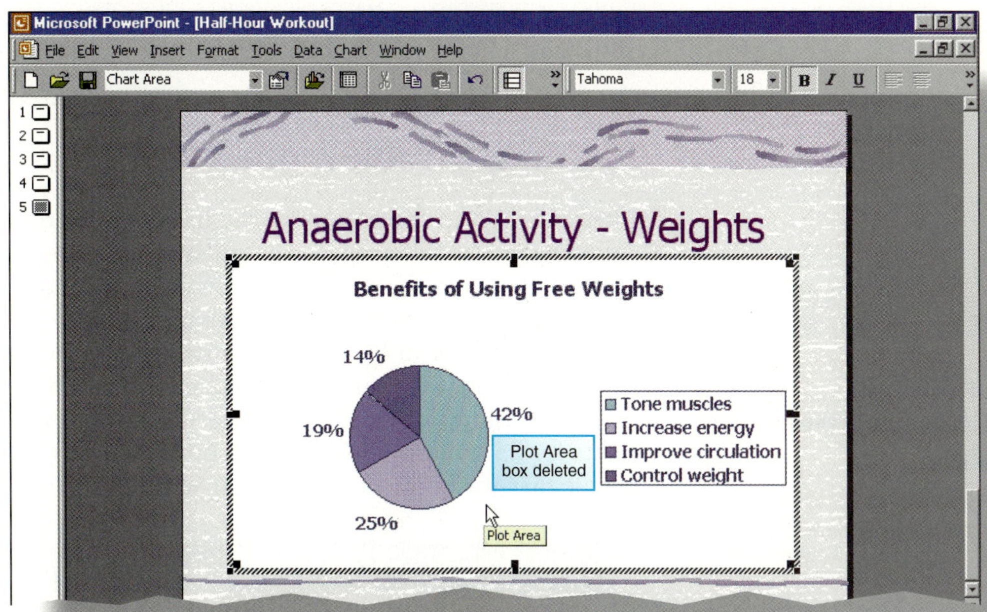

FIGURE 5-44

7 Click outside the chart placeholder to return to PowerPoint (Figure 5-45).

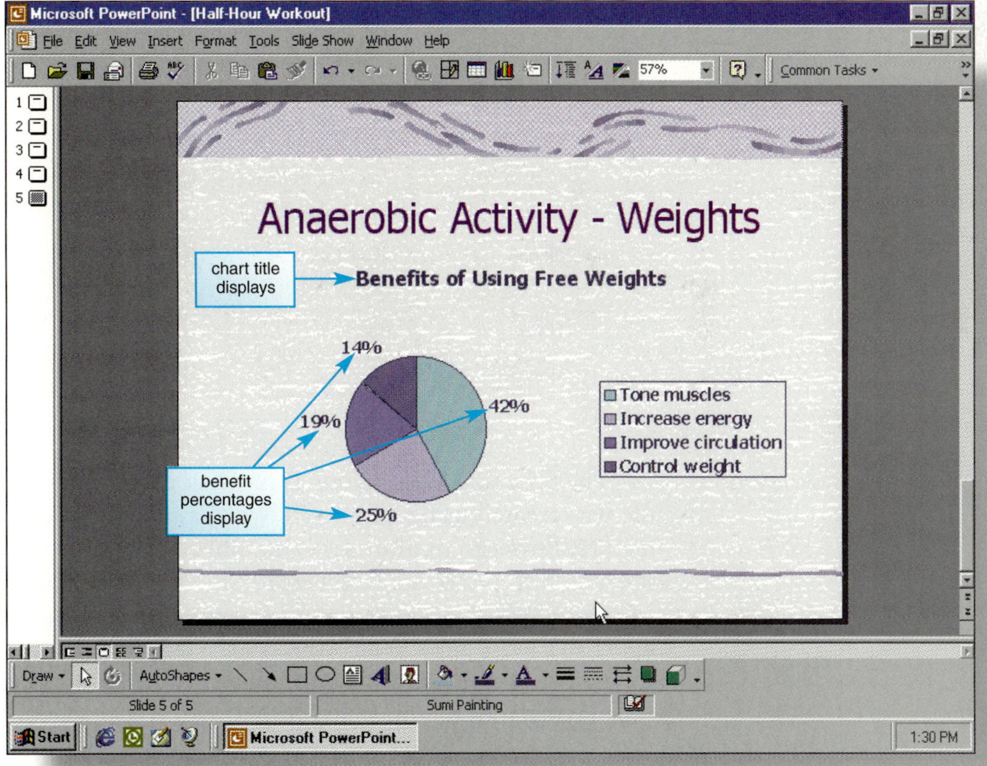

FIGURE 5-45

Other Ways

1. Select the chart placeholder, press ALT+C, press O, press TAB, type chart title text, press TAB four times, press D, press P, press ENTER

Slide 5 is complete. The next slide in the presentation describes how to vary aerobic and anaerobic workouts throughout the week.

Adding a Table from Word

Western College students now see the benefits of aerobic and anaerobic activity. Combining workouts using a treadmill and free weights should provide a good overall fitness plan. Fitness experts recommend varying aerobic and anaerobic workouts to achieve optimal results. By alternating these activities and resting two days during the week, students can benefit from a strong cardiovascular system and a toned body. In addition, they can burn 1,382 calories each week by exercising on the treadmill or by brisk walking for 30 minutes on three days and by working with free weights for 25 minutes on two days. Table 5-1 shows a sample weekly workout schedule that varies the aerobic and anaerobic activities.

More About 2000

Editing an Embedded Word Table

If you need to edit a Word chart you import into your slide, double-click the table and use the Word tools and menus to format the table. For example, to change the width of the table, click the Table Properties command on the Table menu, click the Table tab, and then change the figure in the Preferred width text box. Then click the OK button.

Table 5-1 Sample Exercise Schedule

DAY	EXERCISE	INTENSITY	WORKOUT MINUTES	CALORIES BURNED
Monday	Aerobic exercise (Treadmill)	High	30	336
Tuesday	Anaerobic exercise (Free weights)	Moderate	25	210
Wednesday	Rest			
Thursday	Brisk walking	Moderate	30	290
Friday	Anaerobic exercise (Free weights)	Moderate	25	210
Saturday	Aerobic exercise (Treadmill)	High	30	336
Sunday	Rest			
Total calories burned				1,382

The Schedule file on your Data Disk contains these elements of Table 5-1. This file was created using Microsoft Word and enhanced with Word's Table AutoFormat feature. PowerPoint allows you to embed this table into your presentation. The same steps used to insert the Excel treadmill chart into a slide are used to insert a Microsoft Word table. In the following sections, you will create a new slide and insert the Word table from your Data Disk.

Before you insert the Word table, you need to insert a new slide and change the slide layout to the Object layout.

TO ADD A SLIDE, CHANGE THE SLIDE LAYOUT, AND TYPE THE TITLE TEXT

1. Click the New Slide button on the Standard toolbar to display Slide 6.
2. Type the number 16 to select the Object layout from the 24 available AutoLayouts. Then, click the OK button.
3. Type `Sample Exercise Schedule` as the Slide 6 title text.

Slide 6 displays the title text and the placeholder for the Word object (Figure 5-46).

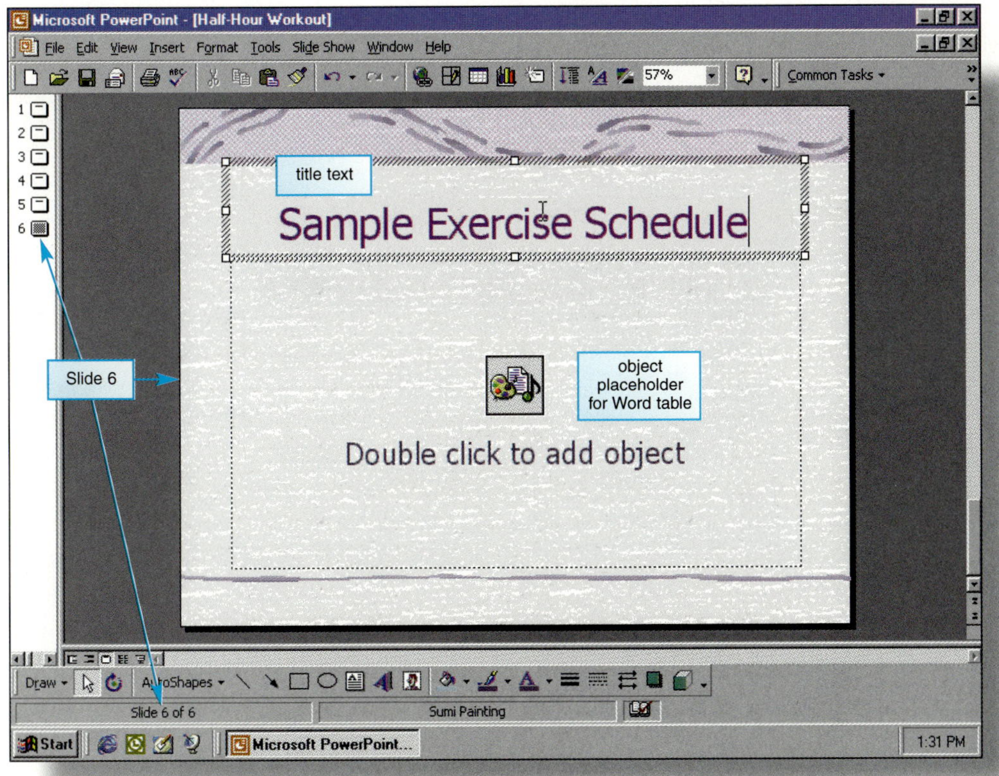

FIGURE 5-46

Other Ways

1. Move scroll bar downward to display Object layout, double-click Object layout

Slide 6 now displays the slide title and placeholder for the Schedule table. The next section explains how to insert this Word table, which has the file name Schedule.doc.

TO INSERT A WORD TABLE

1. Double-click the object placeholder in the middle of Slide 6. Click Create from file.
2. Click the Browse button. When the Browse dialog box displays, click Schedule.
3. Click the OK button. When the Insert Object dialog box displays, click the OK button.

Slide 6 displays the Schedule table (Figure 5-47 on the next page).

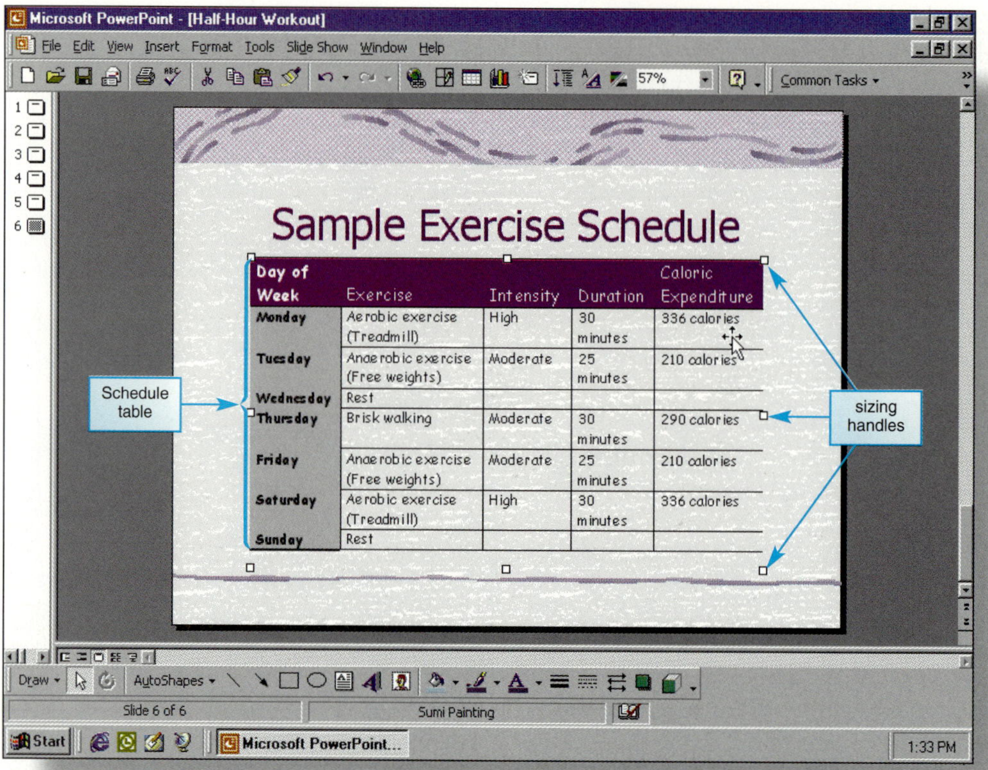

Day of Week	Exercise	Intensity	Duration	Caloric Expenditure
Monday	Aerobic exercise (Treadmill)	High	30 minutes	336 calories
Tuesday	Anaerobic exercise (Free weights)	Moderate	25 minutes	210 calories
Wednesday	Rest			
Thursday	Brisk walking	Moderate	30 minutes	290 calories
Friday	Anaerobic exercise (Free weights)	Moderate	25 minutes	210 calories
Saturday	Aerobic exercise (Treadmill)	High	30 minutes	336 calories
Sunday	Rest			

FIGURE 5-47

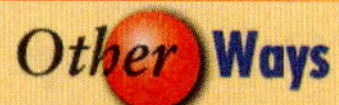

1. On Insert menu click Object, click Create from file, enter file name, click OK button

If you want to edit the Schedule table, double-click the table. This action starts Microsoft Word and opens the Schedule table as a Word document. Then make the desired changes or use the Word tools and menus to modify the table, save the table, and then click outside the table to exit Word and return to PowerPoint. These editing changes will appear in the Schedule table embedded into Slide 6. However, the source file in Word remains unchanged.

More About 2000

Creating Shapes

The geometric AutoShapes add visual interest to your slides. If you want to add a simple circle or square, click the Oval button or the Rectangle button on the Drawing toolbar and then click the document. You then can size this object, change its fill and line colors, and add a shadow. To make these changes, select the object and then use the tools on the Drawing toolbar.

Inserting and Formatting an AutoShape

As shown in Schedule table on Slide 6, the workout sessions burn calories while they improve muscle tone and cardiovascular endurance. If the Western College students exercise regularly and with high or moderate intensity, they should burn 1,382 calories weekly. You believe students would be interested in this fact, so you want to add an AutoShape that calls attention to this caloric total. An **AutoShape** is a ready-made object, such as a line, star, banner, arrow, connector, or callout. These shapes can be sized, rotated, flipped, colored, and combined to add unique qualities to a presentation. Most of the shapes contain an **adjustment handle** that allows changes to the object, such as changing the size of the point of an arrow.

You click the AutoShapes menu button on the Drawing toolbar to select a category, such as Block Arrows or Flowchart. Then you choose the desired AutoShape and click the area of the slide where you want to insert the AutoShape. You then can add text by clicking the AutoShape and typing the desired information. You also can rotate the AutoShape by clicking the **Free Rotate button** on the Drawing toolbar, positioning the mouse pointer over an AutoShape's round handle, and dragging the AutoShape.

Figure 5-48 shows the AutoShape you want to create to accompany the Schedule chart. Creating this object requires several steps. First, you must choose the desired AutoShape and insert it onto the slide. Next, you add a shadow. You then add text and resize the AutoShape to accommodate this text. Finally, you rotate the AutoShape to cover the lower-right corner of the Schedule table. The next several sections explain how to create this AutoShape.

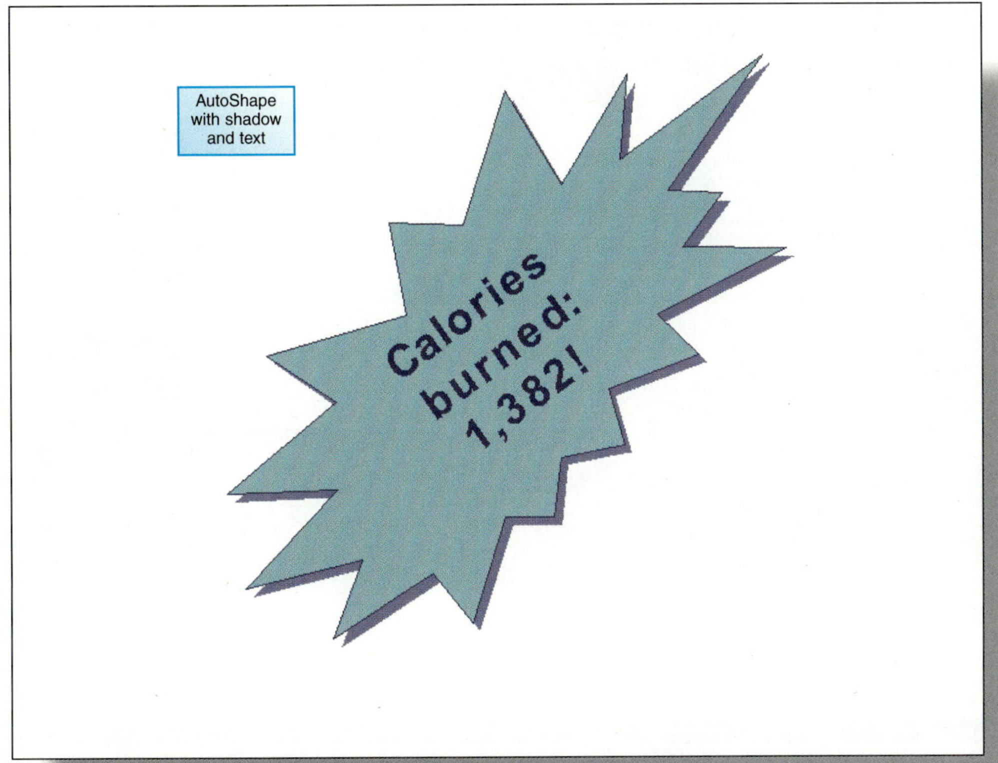

FIGURE 5-48

Inserting an AutoShape

PowerPoint has a variety of AutoShapes organized in the categories of Lines, Connectors, Basic Shapes, Block Arrows, Flowchart, Stars and Banners, Callouts, and Action Buttons. In addition, the More AutoShapes category displays AutoShapes in the Clip Gallery. The first step in creating the AutoShape object is to select the desired shape. Perform the steps on the next page to insert an AutoShape onto Slide 6.

Adding AutoShapes

Additional AutoShapes are located in the Clip Gallery. To add one of these shapes onto your slide, drag the desired AutoShape from the Clip Gallery to the desired location on your slide.

To Insert an AutoShape

1 Click the AutoShapes menu button on the Drawing toolbar, point to Stars and Banners, and then point to the Explosion 2 AutoShape (row 1, column 2).

The Stars and Banners style list displays (Figure 5-49). You may have to wait a few seconds for the full AutoShapes menu to display. The desired AutoShape, Explosion 2, is selected.

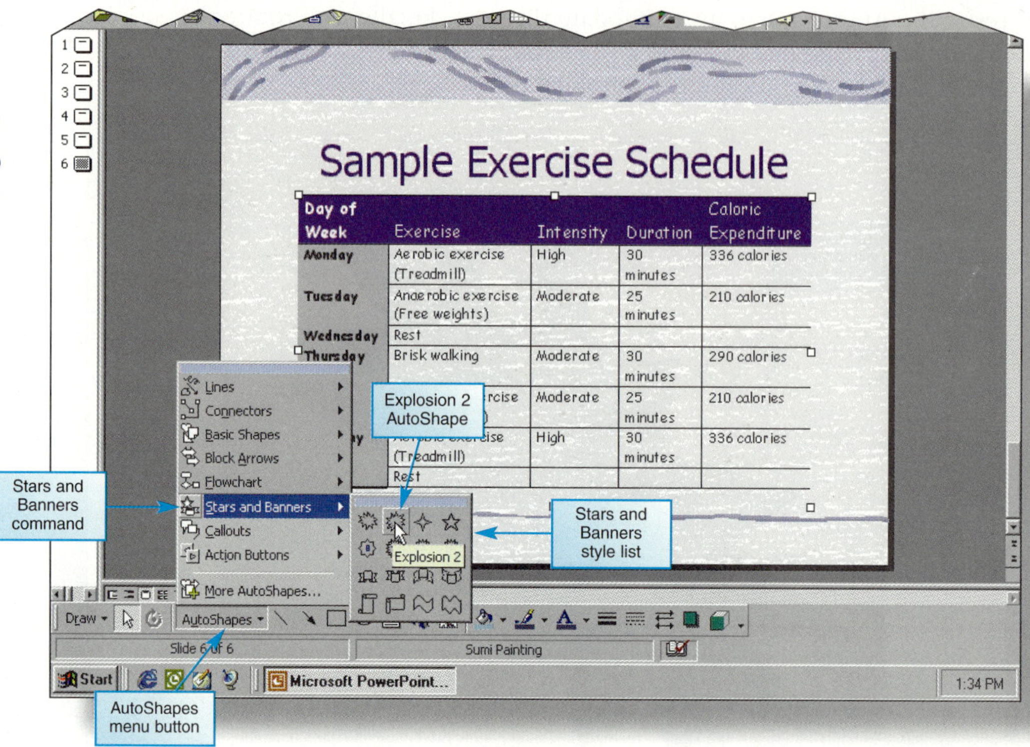

FIGURE 5-49

2 Click the Explosion 2 AutoShape. Point to the lower-right corner of the Schedule table.

The mouse pointer changes shape to a cross hair (Figure 5-50). You want the AutoShape to display at the bottom of the Caloric Expenditure column.

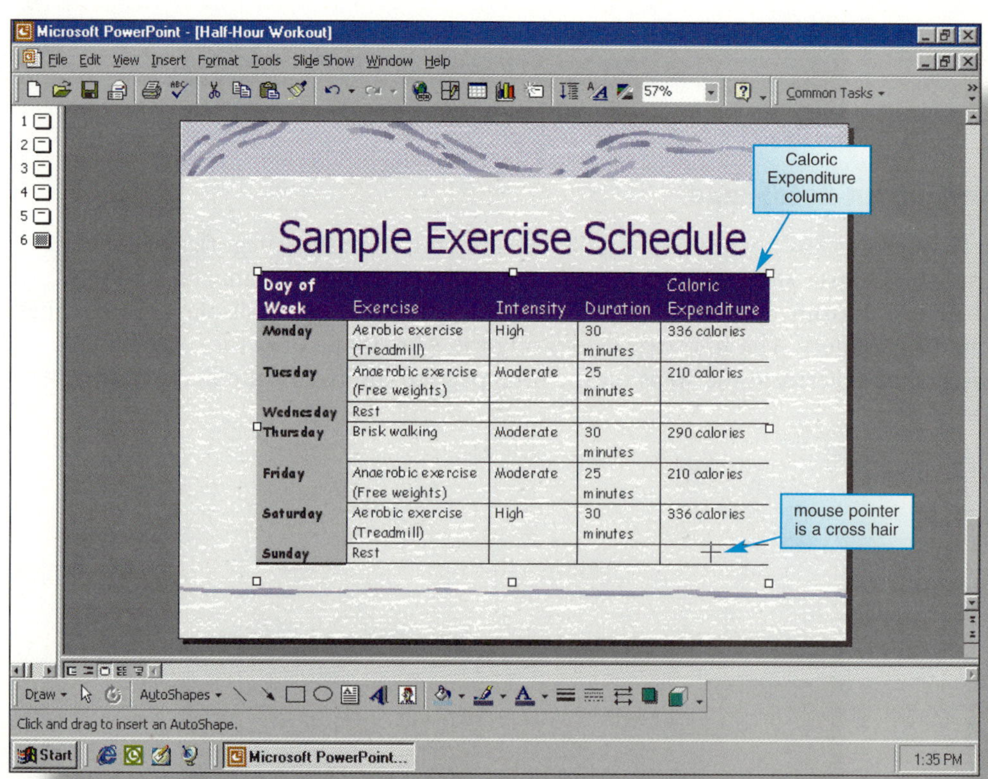

FIGURE 5-50

3 **Click the lower-right corner of the Schedule table.**

The Explosion 2 AutoShape displays at the end of the Caloric Expenditure column (Figure 5-51).

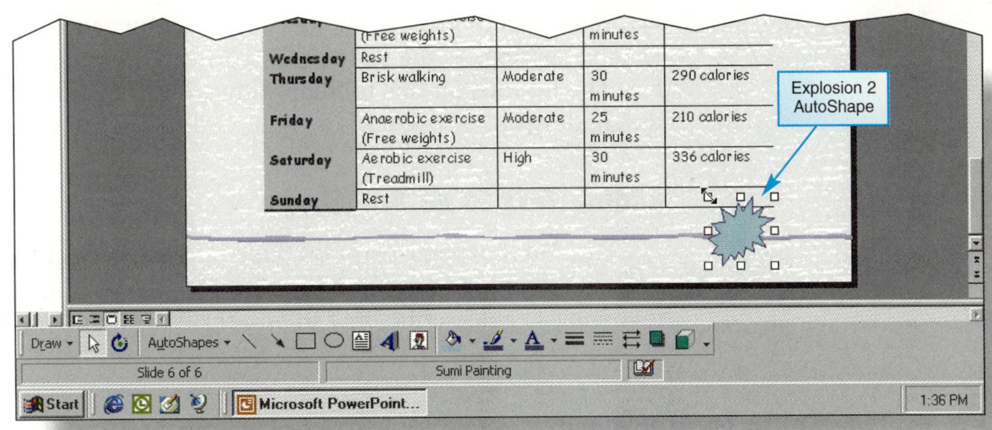

FIGURE 5-51

Now that the desired AutoShape displays on Slide 6, you want to add a shadow to give a three-dimensional appearance.

Adding a Shadow to an AutoShape

To add depth to the Explosion 2 AutoShape, you shadow it by clicking the Shadow button on the Drawing toolbar and selecting one of the 20 predefined shadow styles. Perform the following steps to add a shadow to the object.

More About

Changing AutoShapes

If you want to change the Explosion 2 AutoShape to another shape, select the AutoShape, click Draw on the Drawing toolbar, point to Change AutoShape, point to a category, and then click the desired shape.

TO ADD A SHADOW TO THE AUTOSHAPE

1. Click the Shadow button on the Drawing toolbar.
2. Click Shadow Style 6 (row 2, column 2) in the style list.

PowerPoint adds the shadow to the AutoShape (Figure 5-52).

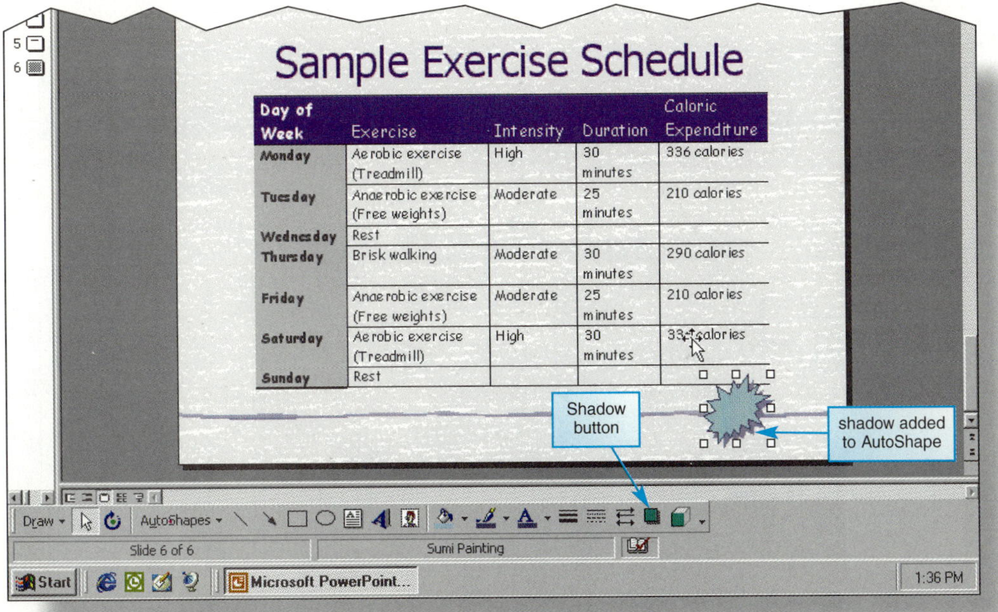

FIGURE 5-52

Once you add a shadow to an object, you can alter its appearance. If you click Shadow Settings in the Shadow list, PowerPoint displays the Shadow Settings toolbar. The buttons on this toolbar allow you to turn the shadow on or off, to nudge the shadow up, down, left, or right, and to change the shadow color.

Adding Text to an AutoShape

The AutoShape displays on Slide 6 in the correct location. The next step is to add text giving the total number of calories burned during the weekly workouts. The following steps describe how to add this information.

To Add Text to an AutoShape

1 With the AutoShape selected, type `Calories` **and then press the SHIFT+ENTER keys. On the next line, type** `burned:` **and then press the SHIFT+ENTER keys. On the third line, type** `1,382!` **as the text.**

The AutoShape text displays on three lines (Figure 5-53). You press the SHIFT+ENTER keys to create a line break, which moves the insertion point to the beginning of the next line and does not create a new paragraph.

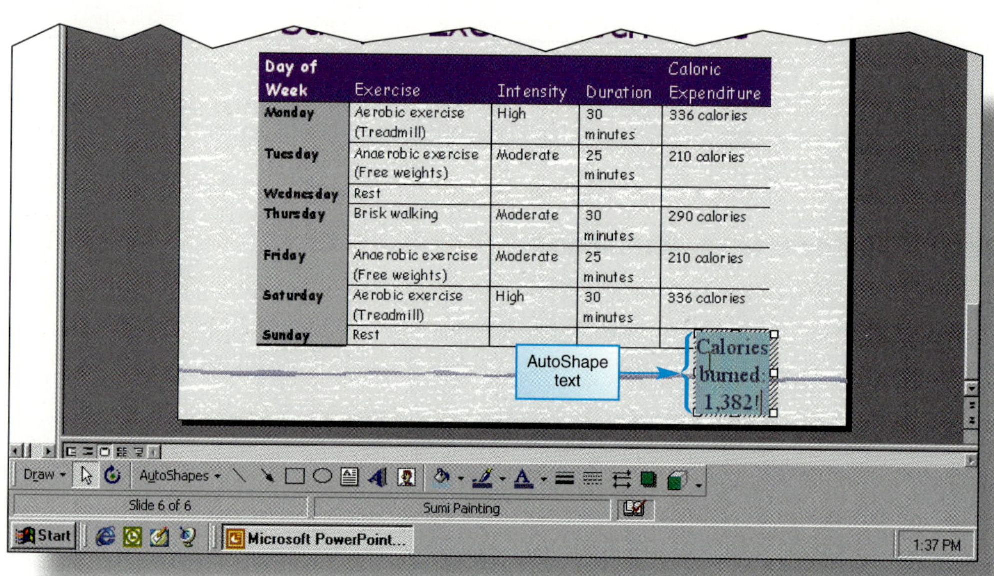

FIGURE 5-53

2 Right-click the AutoShape, click Format AutoShape on the shortcut menu, and then click the Text Box tab when the Format AutoShape dialog box displays. Point to Resize AutoShape to fit text.

The Text Box sheet in the Format AutoShape dialog box displays (Figure 5-54). The default text placement is in the center of the object, as indicated by the Text anchor point list box.

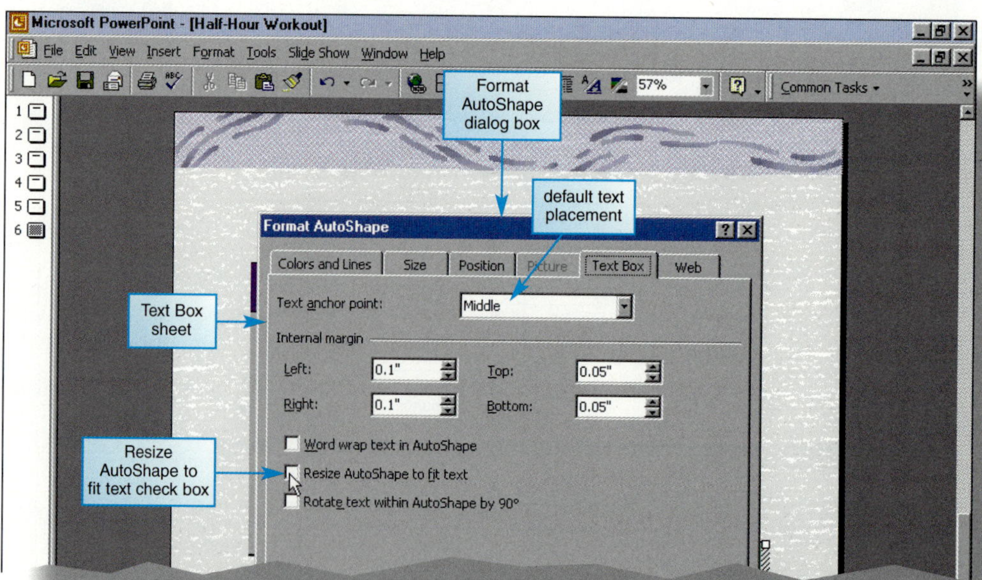

FIGURE 5-54

Click Resize AutoShape to fit text, and then point to the OK button.

PowerPoint will change the size of the AutoShape automatically based on the amount of text entered and the amount of desired internal margins (Figure 5-55). You can click the Preview button to see the resized AutoShape.

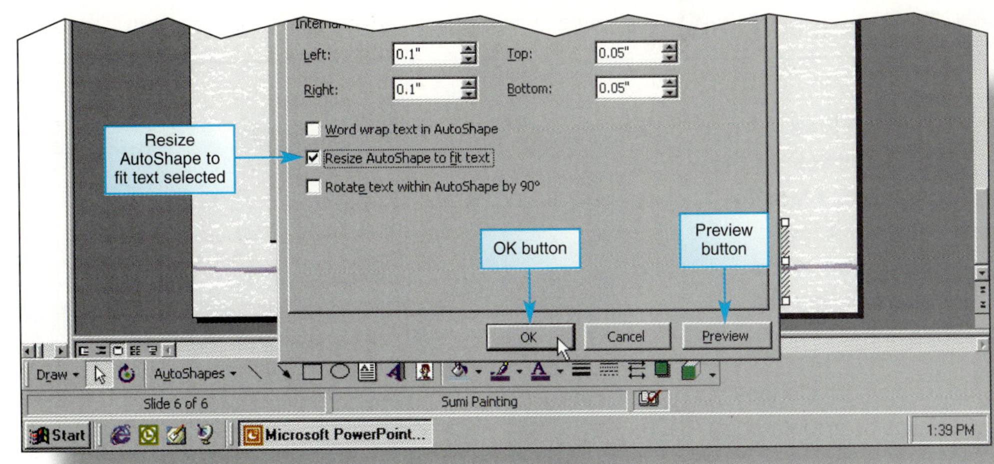

FIGURE 5-55

4 Click the OK button.

The AutoShape enlarges to accommodate the text box (Figure 5-56).

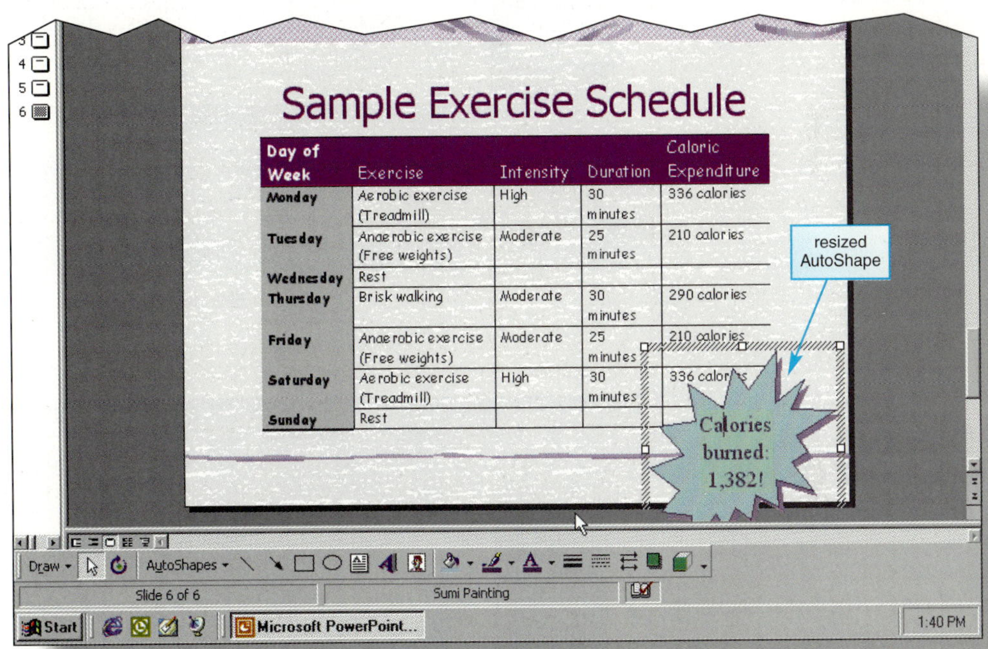

FIGURE 5-56

Text added to an AutoShape becomes part of the shape, which means that it increases font size if the AutoShape is enlarged or that it rotates or flips if the shape is rotated or flipped. If you do not want to attach text to the object, add text instead by using the Text Box tool on the Drawing toolbar and then placing the text on top of the object.

Rotating an AutoShape

The next step in creating the AutoShape is to rotate the object to add visual appeal to the slide. The **Free Rotate button** on the Drawing toolbar allows you to position the mouse pointer over one of the AutoShape's round handles and then visually turn the object to the desired degree.

Other Ways

1. Type desired text, on Format menu click AutoShape, click Text Box tab, click Resize AutoShape to fit text, click OK button
2. Type desired text, press ALT+O, press O, press CTRL+TAB to select Text Box tab, press TAB to select Resize AutoShape to fit text check box, press SPACEBAR, press ENTER
3. Click AutoShape object, drag a sizing handle until object is desired shape and size

To Rotate an AutoShape

1 **Click the Free Rotate button on the Drawing toolbar. Place the mouse pointer on the upper-right green round handles surrounding the AutoShape.**

The mouse pointer changes to a semicircular arrow when it is near one of the four green round handles (Figure 5-57).

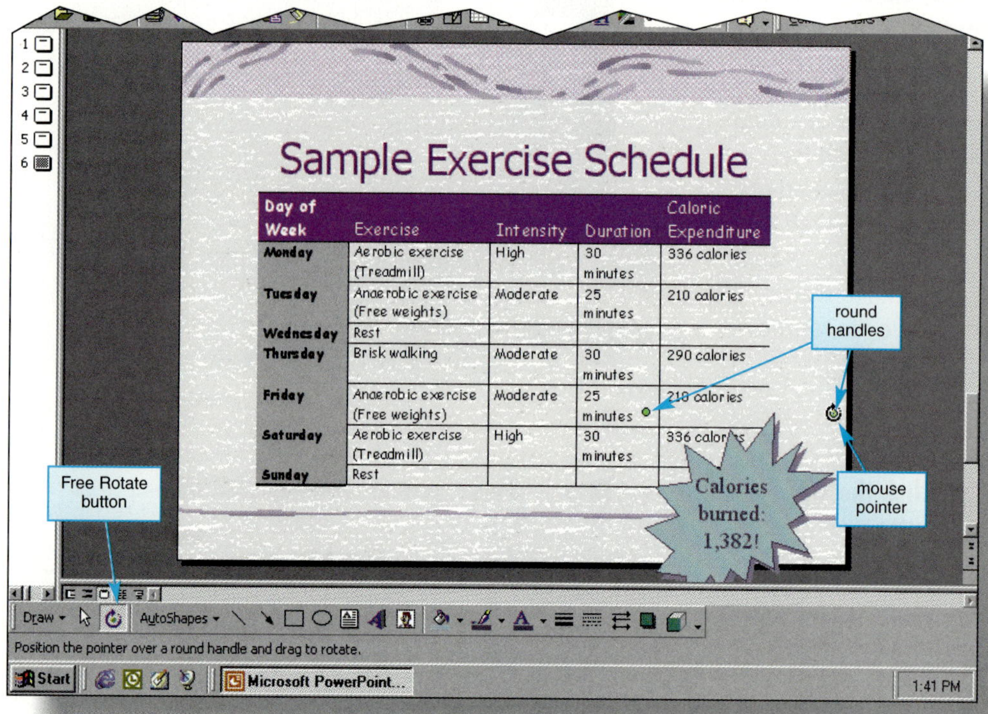

FIGURE 5-57

2 **Click the round handle and drag it to the left until it is at the top of the AutoShape.**

The mouse pointer changes to a full circle when you click the round handle (Figure 5-58). The AutoShape is rotated to the desired degree.

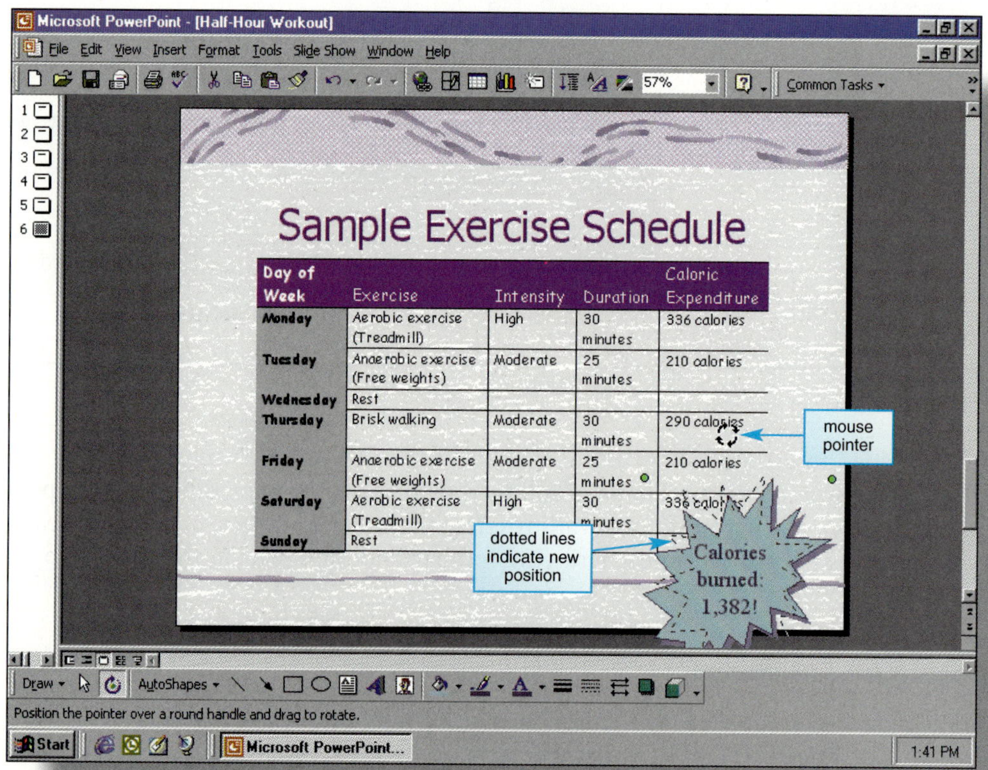

FIGURE 5-58

3 Press the ARROW keys to move the AutoShape's shadow to the edges of the slide.

The AutoShape fits nicely in the lower-right corner of the slide and emphasizes the total of the Caloric Expenditure column (Figure 5-59).

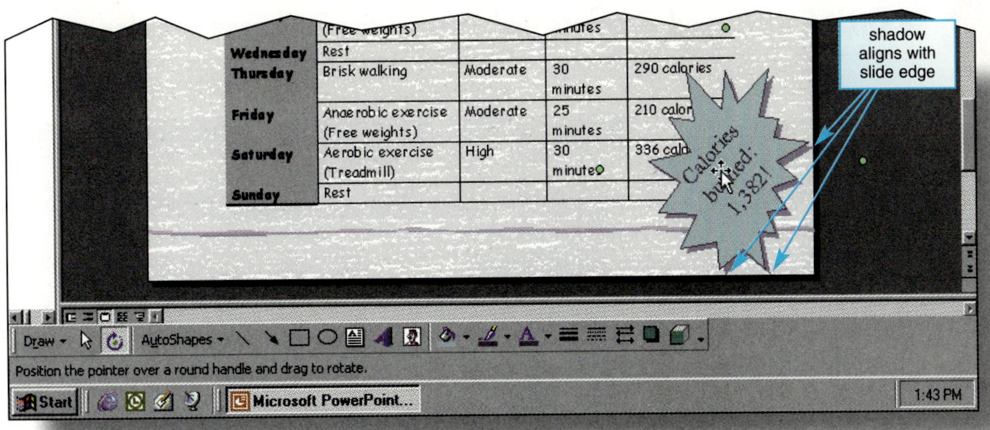

FIGURE 5-59

Other Ways

1. Click Draw button on Drawing toolbar, point to Rotate or Flip, click Free Rotate
2. On Format menu click AutoShape, click Size tab, click Rotation text box up or down arrow, click OK button
3. Press ALT+R, press P, press T
4. Press ALT+O, press O, press CTRL+TAB to select Size tab, type degrees in Rotation text box in Size and rotate area, press ENTER

The Free Rotate button allows you to visually turn the AutoShape to a desired degree. You also can apply other effects to an AutoShape object. For example, you flip a shape vertically or horizontally by clicking the Draw button on the Drawing toolbar, pointing to Rotate or Flip, and then selecting the desired effect. You also can change the font color, the fill color, and the line color and style. Indeed, these effects allow you to personalize your presentation and enhance its visual appeal.

Animating the AutoShape Object

The final step in creating Slide 6 is to animate the AutoShape object. Perform the following step to animate this object.

TO ANIMATE THE AUTOSHAPE

 Click Slide Show on the menu bar, point to Preset Animation, and then click Dissolve on the Preset Animation submenu.

PowerPoint applies the Dissolve animation effect to the AutoShape.

Slide 6 now is complete. The next step in creating the Half-Hour Health presentation is to create a completely solid slide as a final slide to separate the end of the presentation from the beginning as the slide show loops at the kiosk.

Omitting Background Graphics and Changing the Background Color

You can instruct PowerPoint to conclude a slide show gracefully with a black slide by clicking the End with black slide check box in the Options dialog box. When you run your slide show, this black slide displays with the message, End of slide show, click to exit. When the user clicks this slide, the presentation ends and the PowerPoint window returns.

The presentation in this project, however, will run continuously until a user clicks the ESC key. You will not, consequently, select the End with black slide option. An alternate method is to insert another slide and remove the background graphics. The steps on the next page describe how to create this final blank slide of your presentation and change the background color.

Rotating AutoShapes

Once you insert and format an AutoShape, you easily can rotate it 90 degrees to the left or the right. To turn the AutoShape, select the object, click Draw on the Drawing toolbar, point to Rotate or Flip, and the click Rotate Left or Rotate Right.

To Omit Background Graphics and Change the Background Color

1 **Click the New Slide button on the Standard toolbar, type** 12 **to select the Blank AutoLayout, and then click the OK button.**

Slide 7 displays (Figure 5-60).

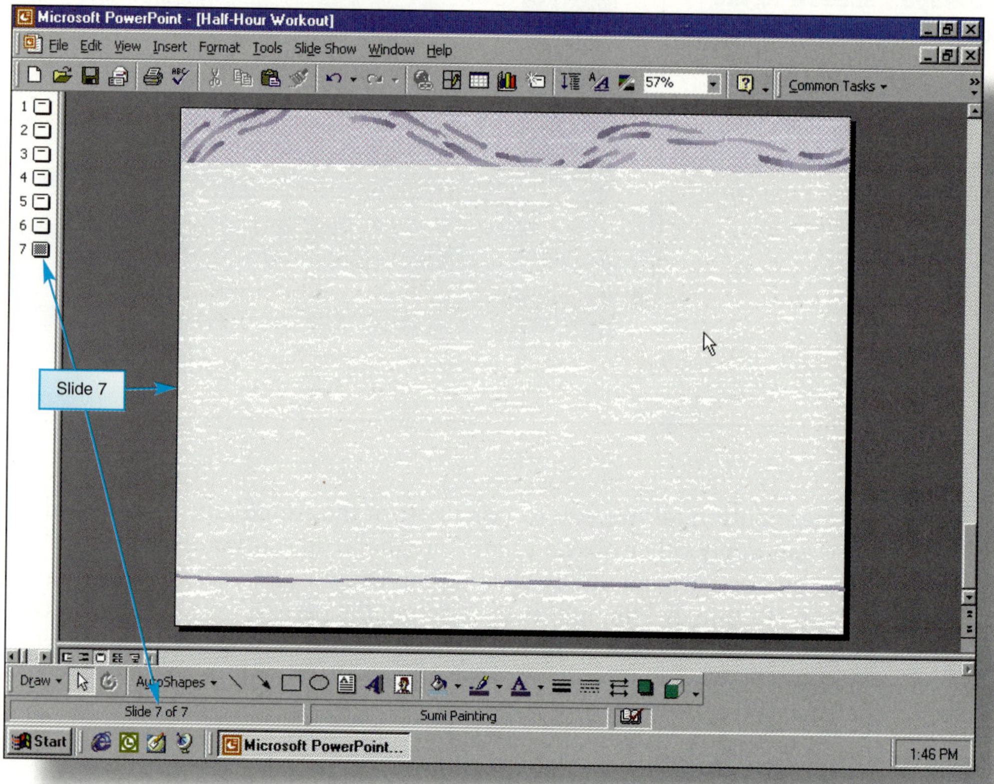

FIGURE 5-60

2 **Right-click Slide 7, click Background on the shortcut menu, and then point to Omit background graphics from master.**

The Background dialog box displays (Figure 5-61). The Sumi Painting design template has a number of background graphics, including the purple swirls at the top of the slide and the horizontal line near the bottom. You do not want these graphics to display on your last slide.

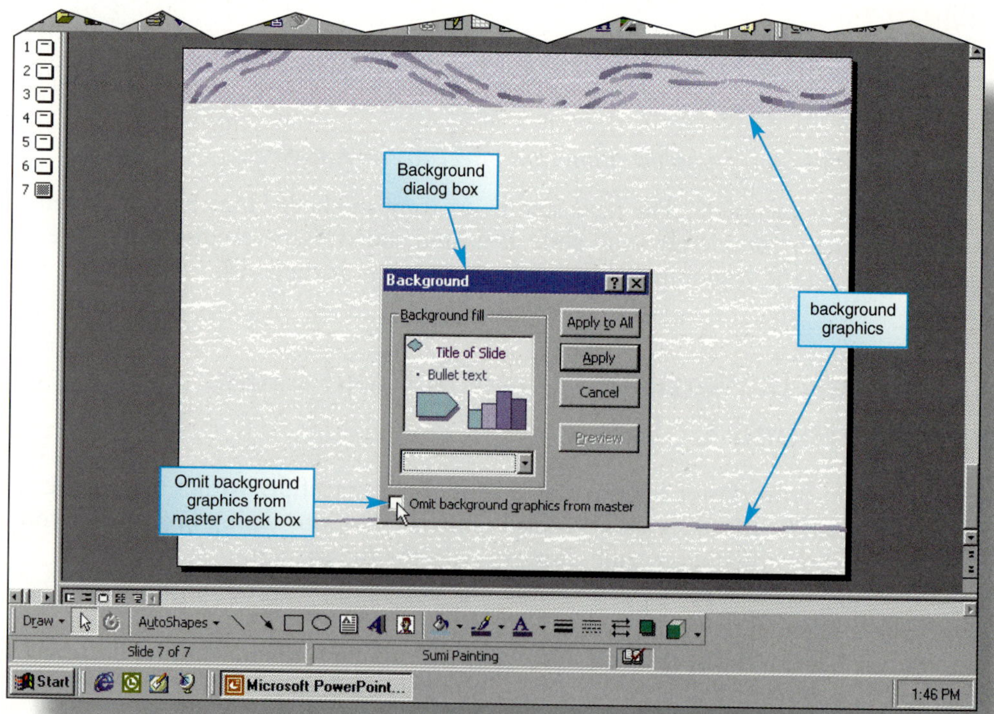

FIGURE 5-61

3 Click Omit background graphics from master. Point to the Background fill box arrow.

The background graphics will be removed from Slide 7 after you click the Apply button (Figure 5-62).

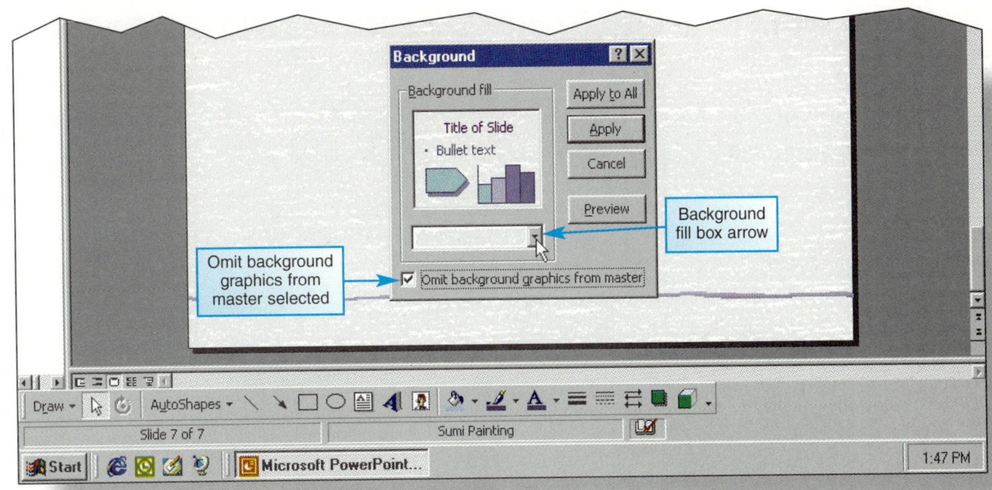

FIGURE 5-62

4 Click the Background fill box arrow. Point to the color medium purple (color 3 in the row).

The color medium purple is the default shadows color in the Sumi Painting design template color scheme (Figure 5-63).

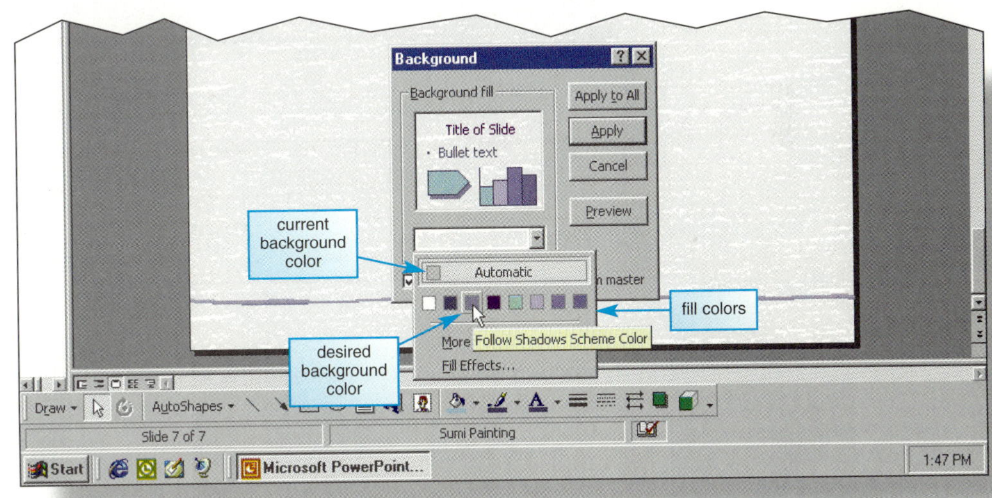

FIGURE 5-63

5 Click the color medium purple. Point to the Apply button.

The color medium purple displays in the Background Fill area (Figure 5-64). When you click the Apply button, the medium purple color is displayed on only the current slide. You would click the Apply to All button if you wanted to change the background color on all slides. You can test your color selection by clicking the Preview button.

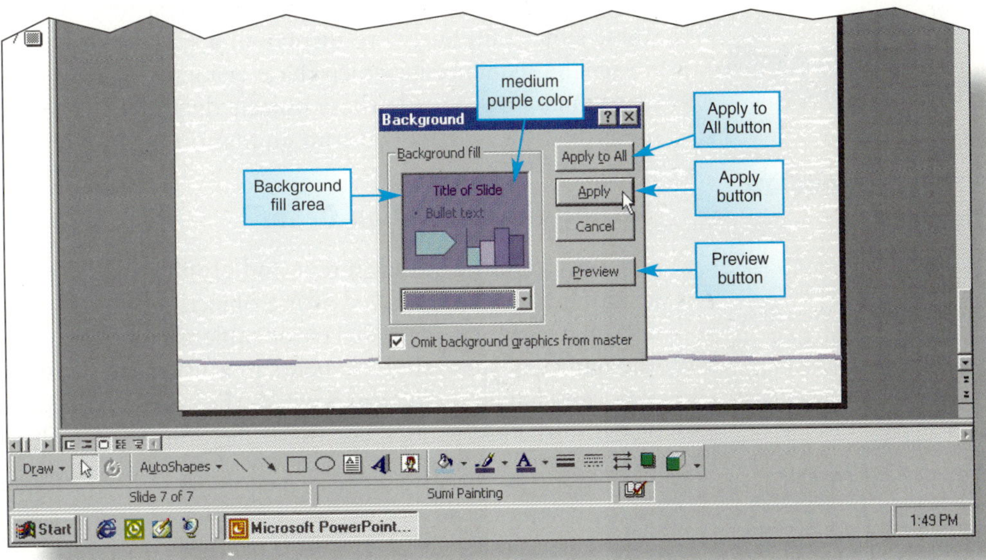

FIGURE 5-64

Click the Apply button.

Slide 7 displays with only a medium purple background (Figure 5-65).

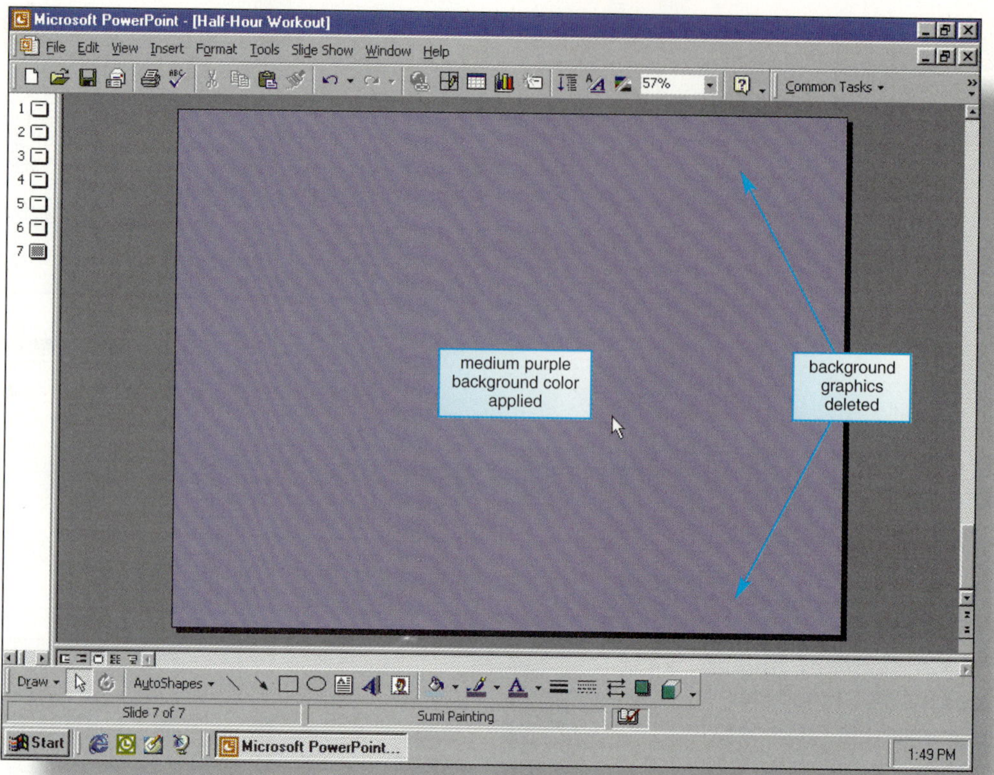

FIGURE 5-65

Other Ways

1. Press ALT+I, press N, type 12, press ENTER, press ALT+O, press K, press ALT+G, press B, press DOWN ARROW three times, press RIGHT ARROW twice, press ENTER twice

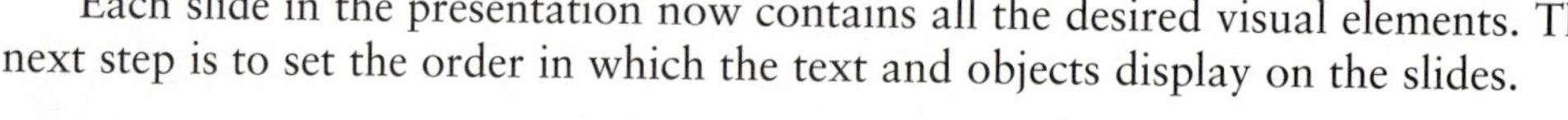

Each slide in the presentation now contains all the desired visual elements. The next step is to set the order in which the text and objects display on the slides.

Applying Custom Animation

The first six slides in the Half-Hour Workout slide show contain numerous bulleted lists and text objects. To add visual interest to your presentation, you want some of these slide components to display in a specific order. You will use custom animation to set the sequence in which these elements display on each slide. You also need to determine how quickly these objects display on the slide. The following steps describe how to apply custom animation to the presentation.

More About

Using Presentations on Demand

You can archive your PowerPoint presentation broadcasts on a Web server for on-demand playback any time. You and your collaborators can ask and reply to questions and make comments because the discussion is threaded. Colleagues can make comments directly in a document or about a document.

Setting the Animation Order

PowerPoint gives each text and graphic object on the slide a unique name. For example, title text is called a title object, a bulleted list is called a text object, clip art is called a picture, and a chart or table is called an object or a chart. You can view the names of these slide elements in a list in the Custom Animation dialog box, and you can change the order in which they display on the slide and when they display. Perform the following steps to set the animation order of the objects on Slide 3.

Steps To Set the Animation Order

1 Drag the vertical scroll box to display Slide 3. Click Slide Show on the menu bar and then click Custom Animation. When the Custom Animation dialog box displays, point to Text 2 in the Check to animate slide objects list.

The Custom Animation dialog box displays (Figure 5-66). Text 2 and Text 3 are the names of the two bulleted lists. Picture frame 4 is the name of the walking figure animated clip art object; Picture frame 5 is the name of the weightlifting animated clip art object.

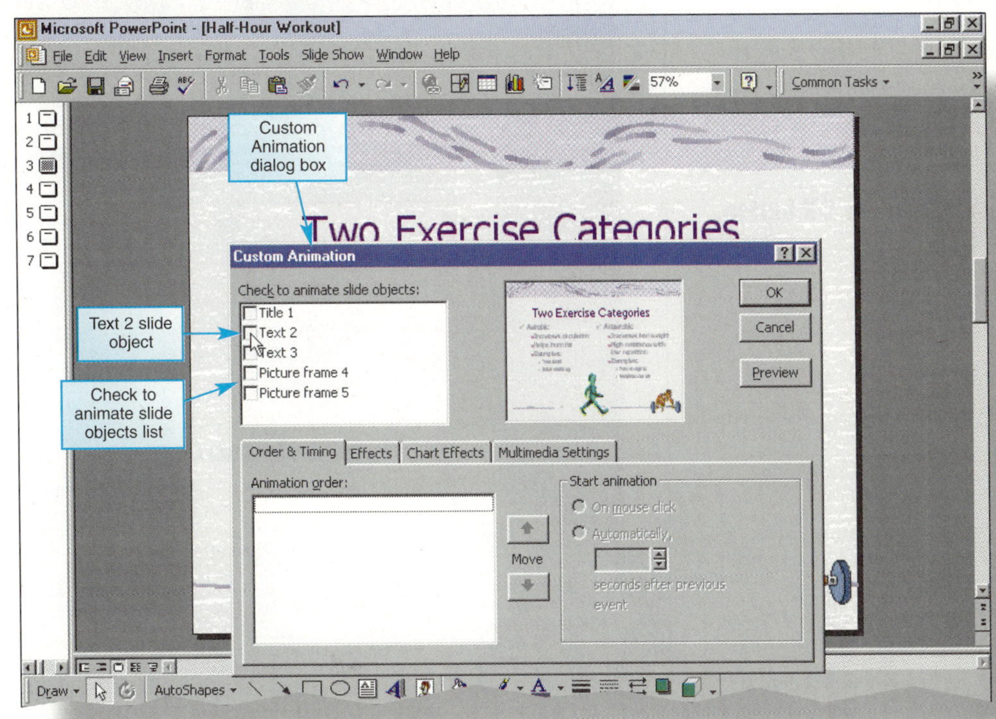

FIGURE 5-66

2 Click Text 2 in the Check to animate slide objects list. Then click Picture frame 4 in the Check to animate slide objects list, Text 3, and Picture frame 5. Point to the Preview button.

Four of the five objects on Slide 3 are animated (Figure 5-67). Their order of appearance displays in the Animation order list.

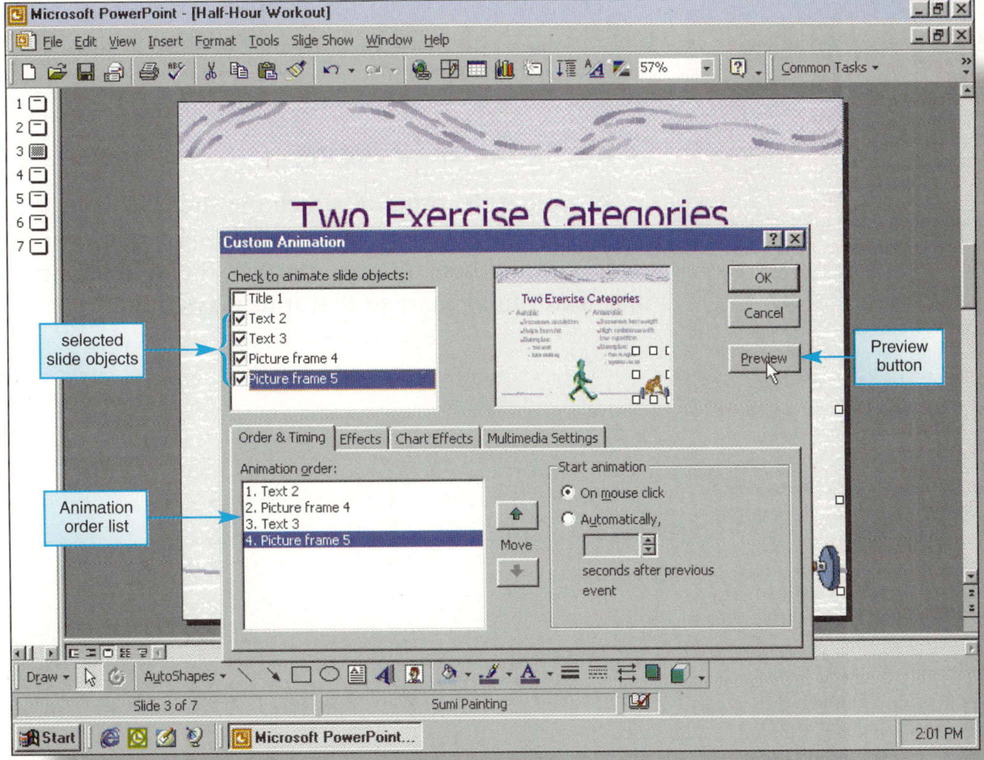

FIGURE 5-67

3 **Click the Preview button. Point to the OK button.**

Clicking the Preview button allows you to view the animation order (Figure 5-68).

Click the OK button.

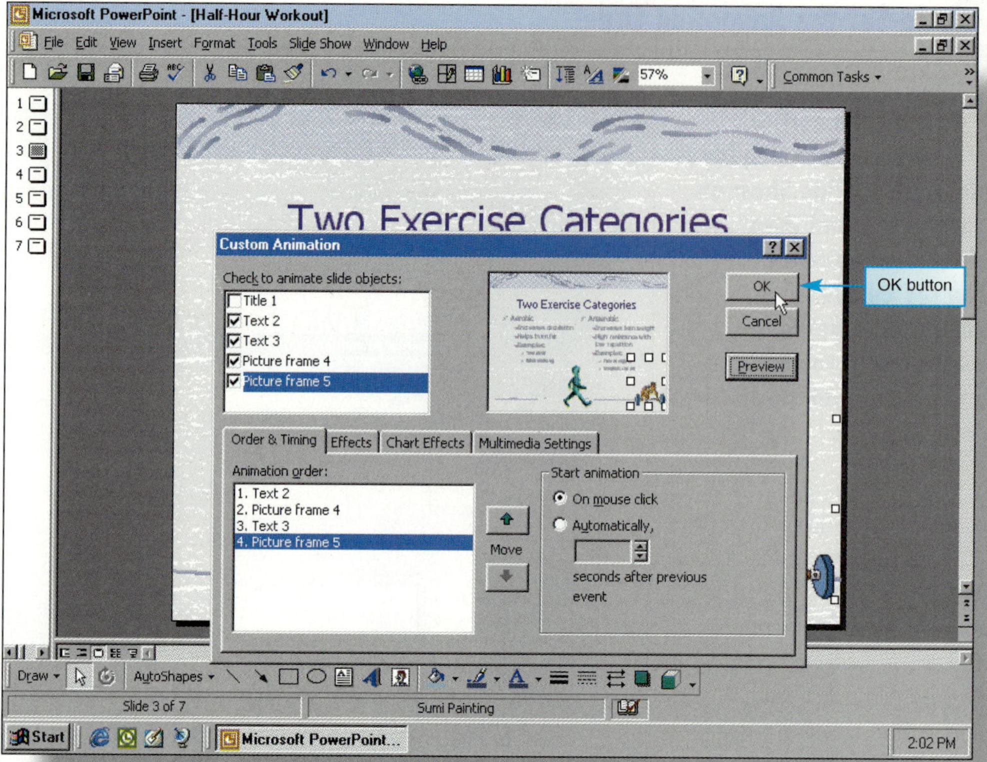

FIGURE 5-68

More About

Using NetMeeting

As you complete your presentation, you may want collaborate with and receive feedback from other people simultaneously. Microsoft has integrated its Office and NetMeeting programs so a number of people can view a presentation and share the contents of a file. You can schedule the meeting in advance by using Microsoft Outlook or start an impromptu online meeting from within your active PowerPoint presentation. If your colleagues are available and they decide to accept your invitation, the online meeting begins. They can use such tools as a whiteboard, video, and audio to present their opinions and comments. To learn more about using NetMeeting, visit the PowerPoint 2000 Project 5 More About page (www.scsite.com/pp2000/more.htm) and click NetMeeting.

The animation order for the Slide 3 objects is correct. The next custom animation changes you want to make are to determine when the two charts and the table display on the slides.

Changing the Slide Timing

Now that the order in which the slide elements display is correct, you need to determine when these elements display. The Custom Animation dialog box also is used to create these timings. Perform the following steps to set the timing for the Slide 4 treadmill chart so that it displays three seconds after the title text displays.

To Change the Slide Timing

1 Click the Next Slide button to display Slide 4. Click Slide Show on the menu bar and then click Custom Animation. When the Custom Animation dialog box displays, click Object 2 in the Check to animate slide objects list. Point to Automatically in the Start animation area.

Object 2, the treadmill chart, is selected (Figure 5-69). You can specify whether you want it to display when you click the mouse or when a particular number of seconds has elapsed.

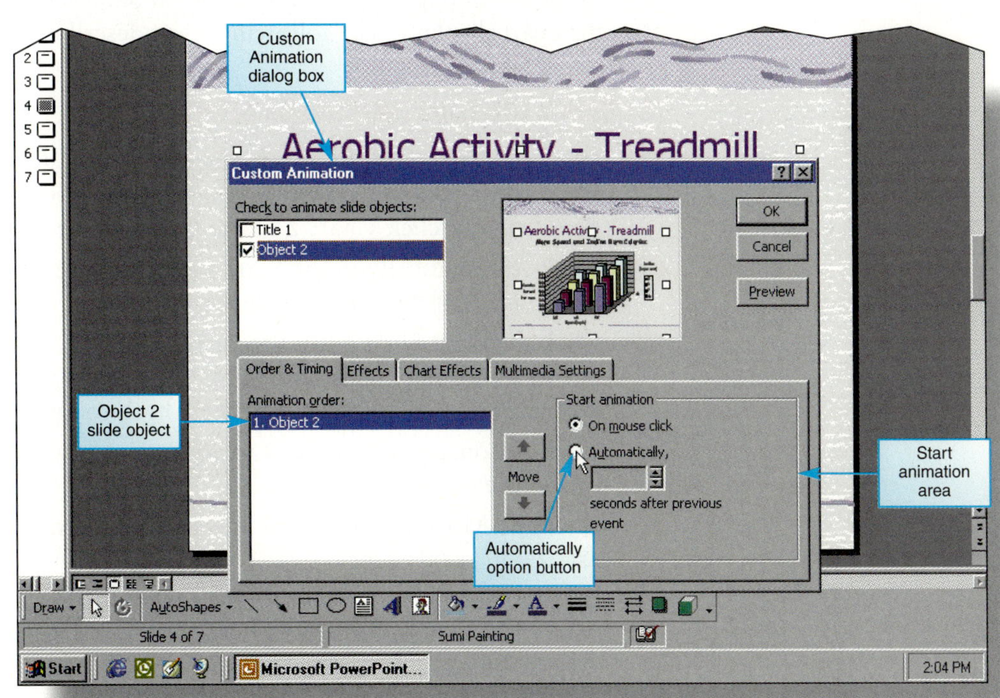

FIGURE 5-69

2 Click Automatically. Type :03 in the seconds after previous event text box. Point to the OK button.

When you run the slide show, the treadmill chart will display three seconds after the slide displays with the title text (Figure 5-70).

3 Click the OK button.

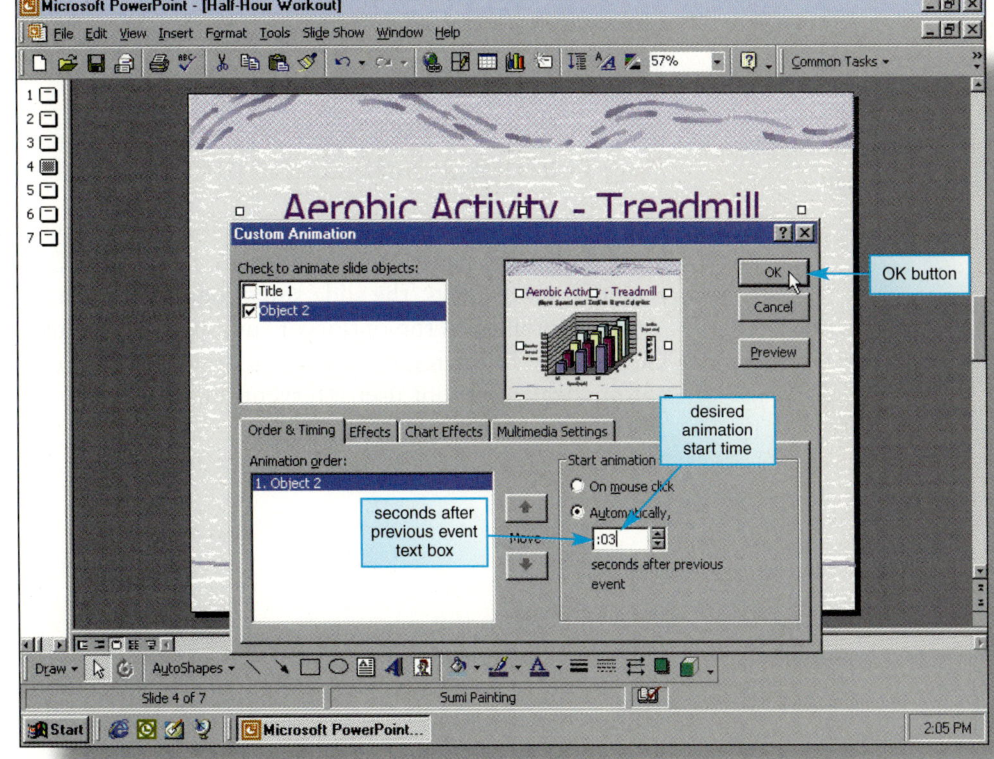

FIGURE 5-70

The Slide 4 timing is set. You need to repeat these steps to set the timings for the free weights benefits chart on Slide 5 and the schedule chart on Slide 6. You also need to set the timing for the AutoShape on Slide 6 so that it displays 10 seconds after the chart displays. The following steps describe how to add these timings.

TO CHANGE THE SLIDE TIMINGS FOR SLIDES 5 AND 6

1. Click the Next Slide button to display Slide 5. Click Slide Show on the menu bar, and then click Custom Animation. When the Custom Animation dialog box displays, click Chart 2 in the Check to animate slide objects list.
2. Click Automatically in the Start animation area. Type `:03` in the seconds after previous event text box. Click the OK button.
3. Click the Next Slide button to display Slide 6. Click Slide Show on the menu bar, and then click Custom Animation. When the Custom Animation dialog box displays, click Object 2 in the Check to animate slide objects list.
4. Click Automatically in the Start animation area. Type `:03` in the seconds after previous event text box.
5. Click the Move up button to move Object 2 to the top of the Animation order list.
6. Click Text 3 in the Animation order list. Click Automatically in the Start animation area and type `:10` in the seconds after previous event text box. Click the OK button.

The free weights benefits chart and workout schedule table will display three seconds after Slide 5 and Slide 6 display during the presentation. The AutoShape will display 10 seconds later on Slide 6.

Animation and timing have been added to the graphical objects in your slide show. You now are ready to make this slide show run automatically without user intervention.

Creating a Self-Running Presentation

The Half-Hour Workout presentation is designed to run unattended at a kiosk located near the registration counter at the Fitness Center. When the last slide in the presentation displays, the slide show **loops**, or restarts, at Slide 1.

PowerPoint has the option of running continuously until a user presses the ESC key. The following steps explain how to set the controls so the slide show runs automatically without user intervention.

Using NetShow

Instead of discussing your PowerPoint presentation using NetMeeting in real time, you may want to broadcast the file over the Internet or on an intranet. Using this method, your colleagues can view the slide show on demand at their own convenience. If you want to broadcast this presentation to more than 15 people, you will need a NetShow server. In addition, a NetShow server on a LAN or a third-party NetShow service provider is required if you will be using live video. To learn more about NetShow, visit the PowerPoint 2000 Project 5 More About page (www.scsite.com/pp2000/more.htm) and click NetShow.

To Create a Self-Running Presentation

1 Click Slide Show on the menu bar and then point to Set Up Show.

The Set Up Show options let you decide how much control, if any, you will give to your audience (Figure 5-71).

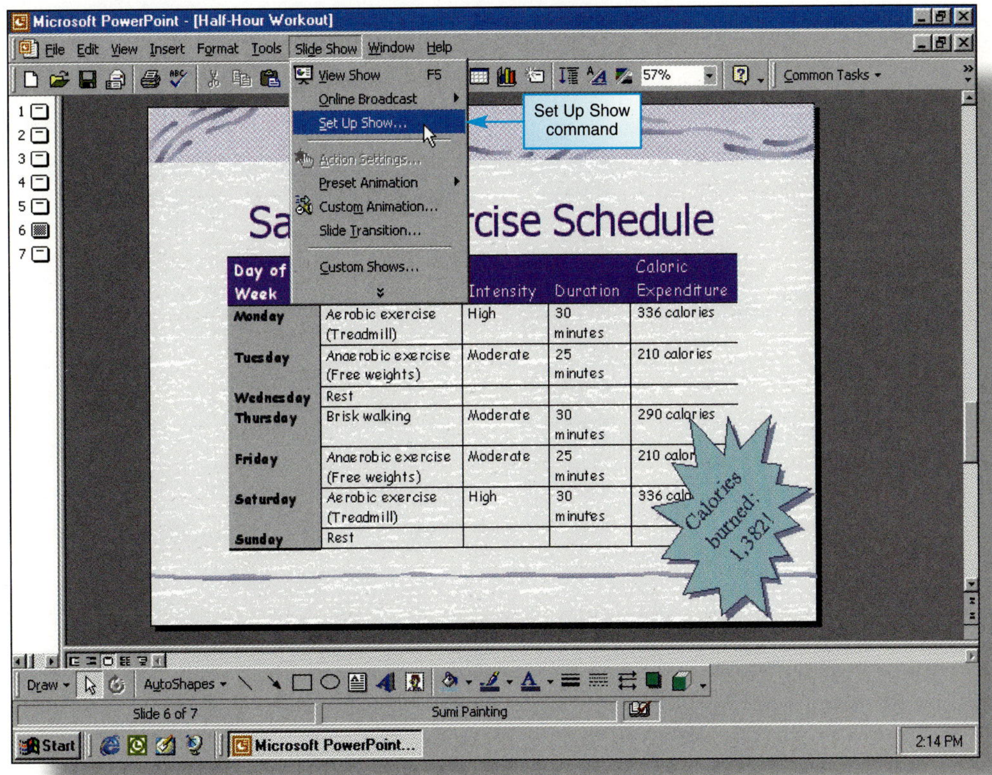

FIGURE 5-71

2 Click Set Up Show. Point to Browsed at a kiosk (full screen).

The Set Up Show dialog box displays (Figure 5-72). The default show type is Presented by a speaker (full screen). The Set Up Show dialog box is used to specify the show type, which slides to display, and how to advance slides.

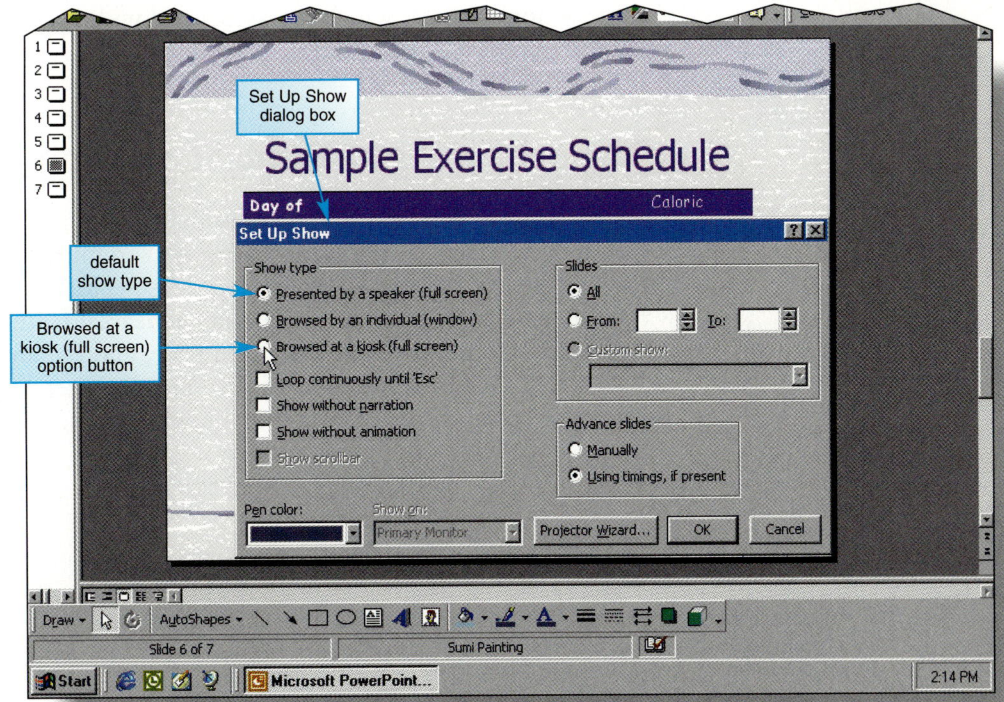

FIGURE 5-72

3 Click Browsed at a kiosk (full screen). Point to the OK button.

A check appears in the Loop continuously until 'Esc' check box, and this text is dimmed (Figure 5-73). The slides will advance automatically based on the timings you specify.

Click the OK button.

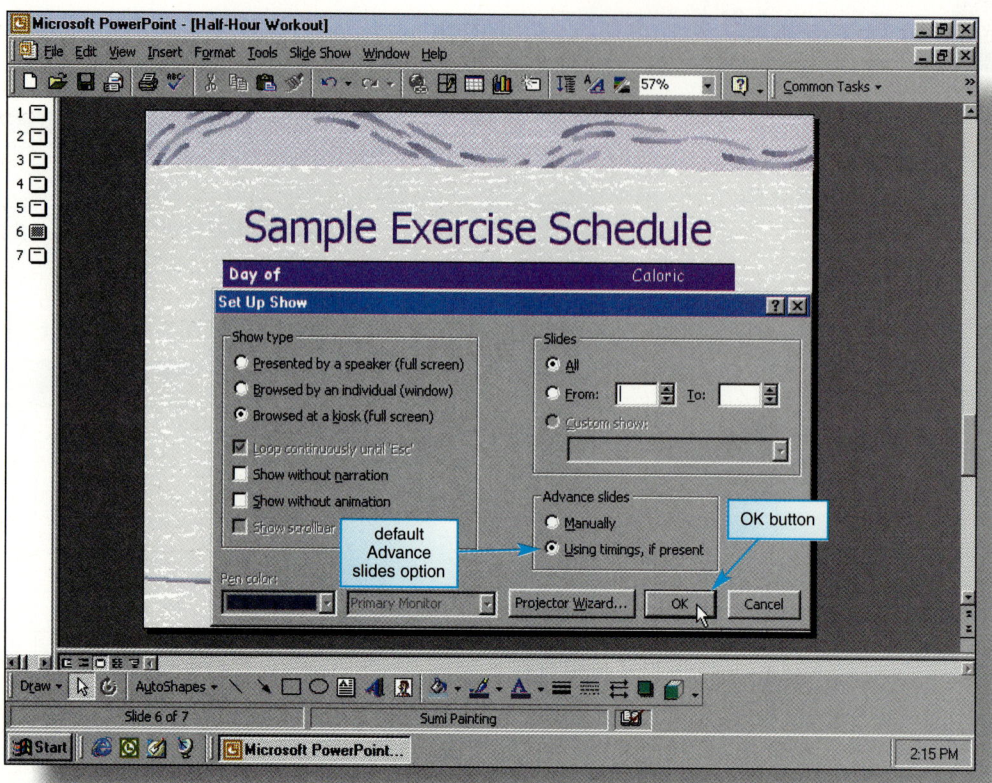

FIGURE 5-73

1. Press ALT+D, press S, press K, press ENTER

This slide show will run by itself without user intervention. You alternately could have designed the slide show to allow a user to advance through slides manually by clicking action buttons, which are associated with hyperlinks. Standard mouse clicks are ignored in both show types.

Setting Timings for the Slide Show

The slide show is designed to loop continuously at a kiosk for three minutes, so no user will move through the slides manually. You must, consequently, determine the length of time each slide will display on the screen. You can set these times in two ways. One method is to use PowerPoint's **rehearsal** feature, which allows you to advance through the slides at your own pace, and the amount of time you view each slide is recorded. The other method is to manually set each slide's display time. You will use this second technique in the following steps.

Rehearsing Presentations

More than three million people worldwide have benefited from participating in Toastmasters International, a non-profit organization established in California in 1924. Members meet frequently and practice various types of public speaking, including giving prepared and impromptu speeches, conducting meetings, and giving constructive feedback. To learn more about this organization and to find a local chapter near you, visit the PowerPoint 2000 Project 5 More About page (www.scsite.com/pp2000/more.htm) and click Rehearsal.

To Set Slide Show Timings Manually

1 Click the Slide Sorter View button. Right-click Slide 1 and then point to Slide Transition.

Slide 1 is selected (Figure 5-74).

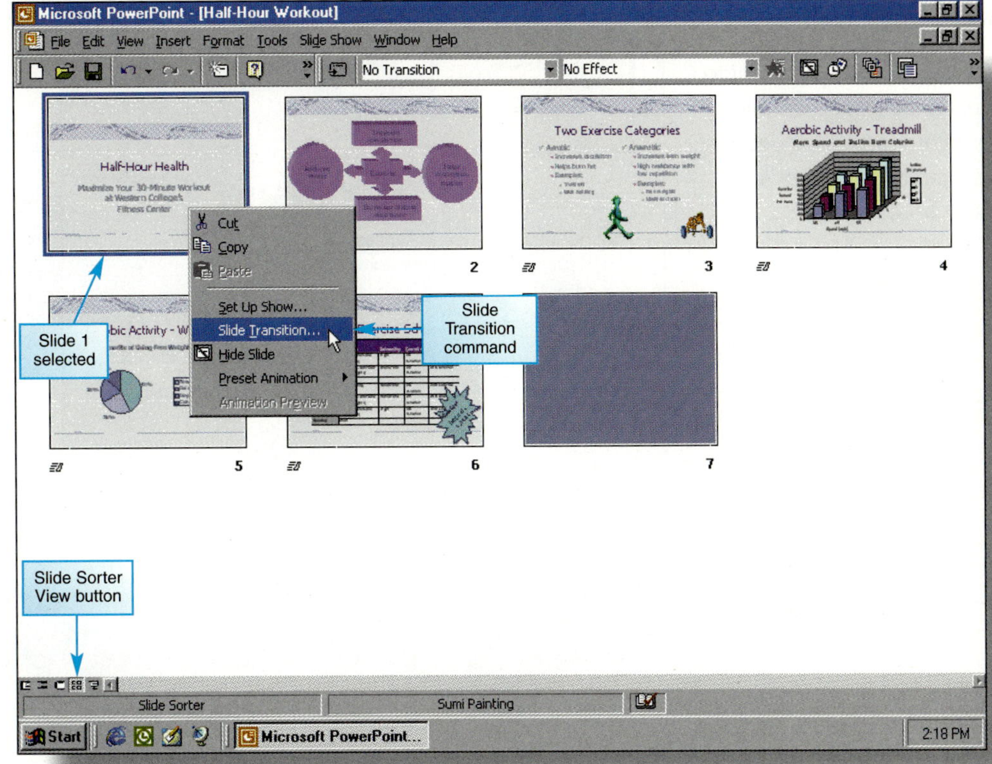

FIGURE 5-74

2 Click Slide Transition. Point to On mouse click.

The Slide Transition dialog box displays (Figure 5-75). The On mouse click Advance option is selected. A speaker generally uses this default setting to advance through the slides in a presentation.

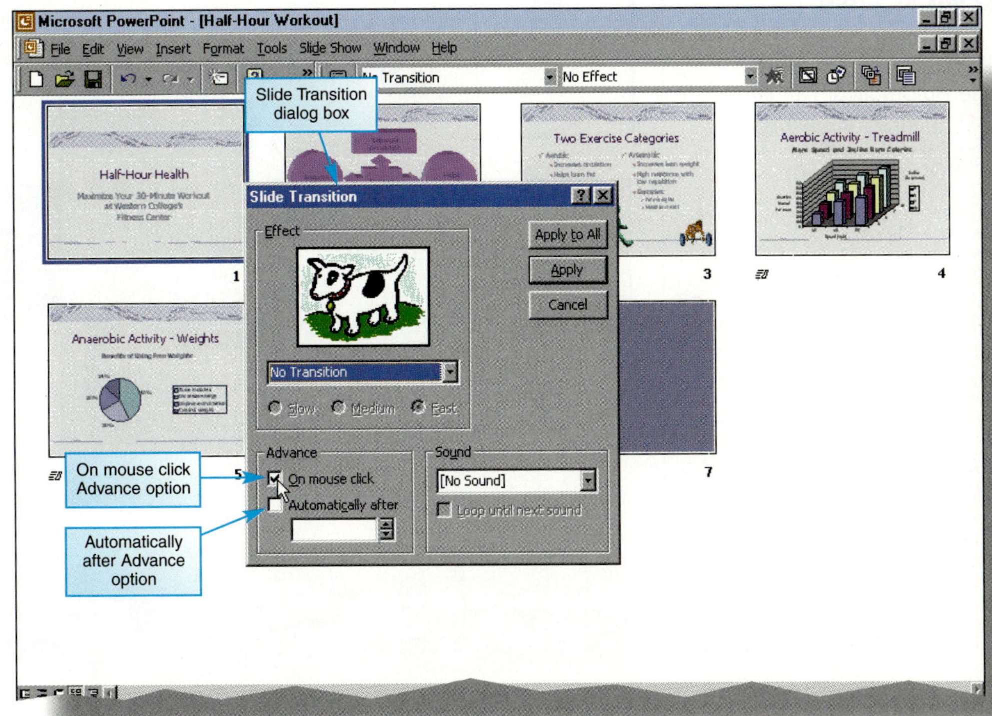

FIGURE 5-75

3 **Click On mouse click to deselect it. Point to Automatically after.**

In this slide show, you want to advance the slide automatically after it has displayed for a designated period of time (Figure 5-76).

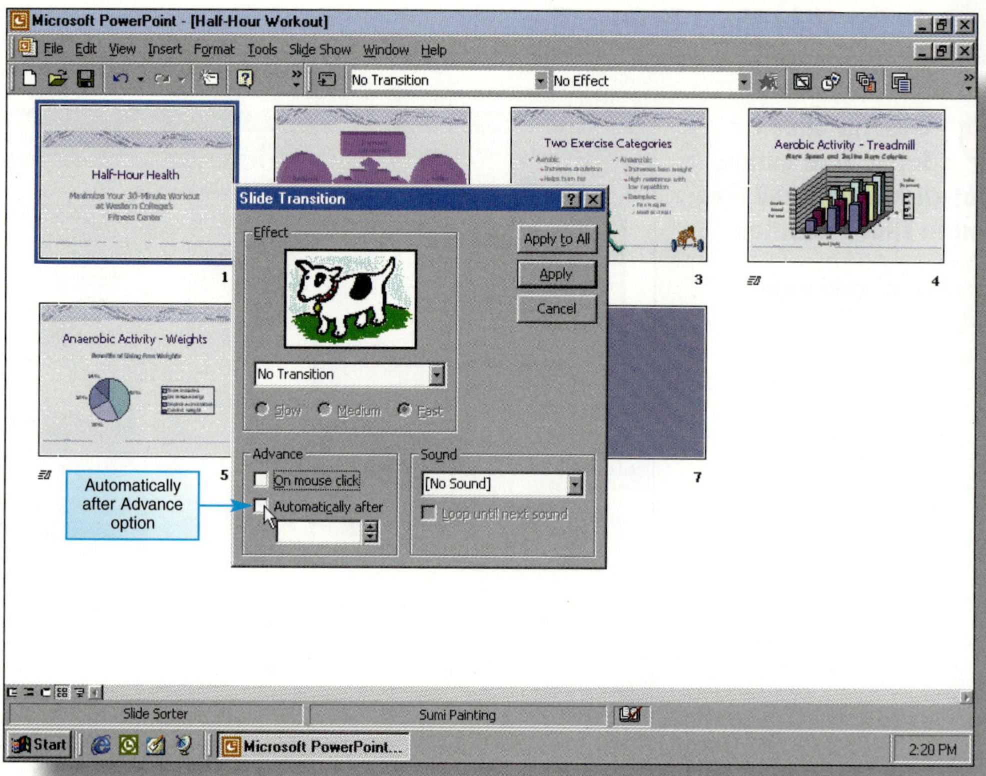

FIGURE 5-76

4 **Click Automatically after and then point to the Automatically after text box up arrow.**

You specify the length of time in the Automatically after text box that you want to slide to display (Figure 5-77).

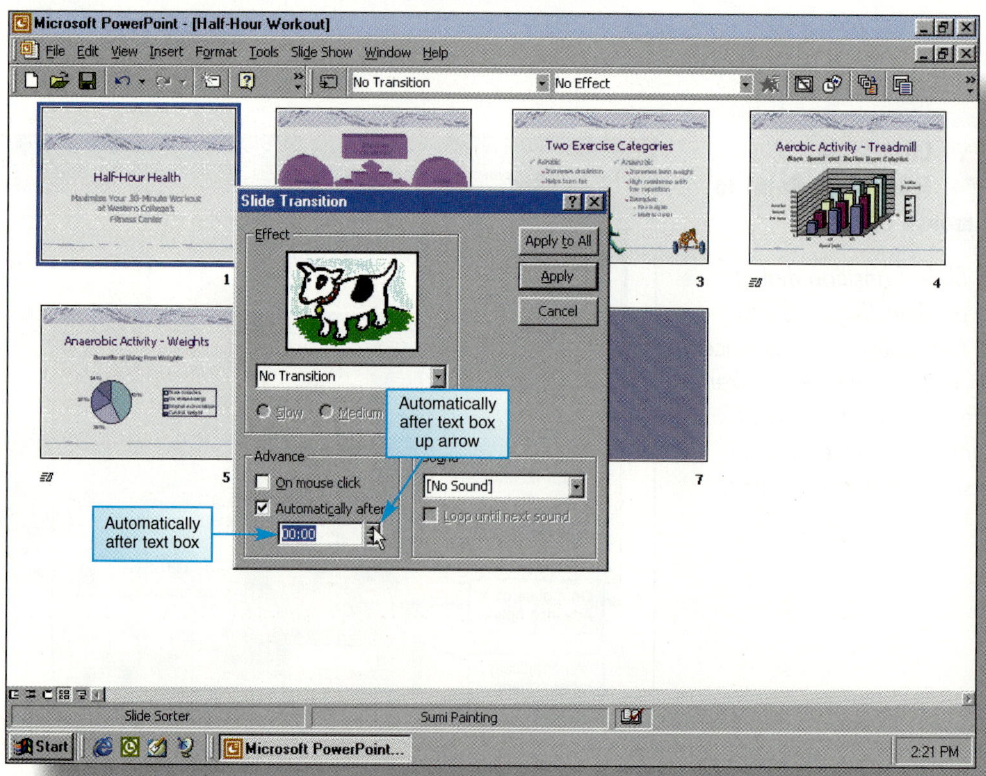

FIGURE 5-77

5 **Click the Automatically after text box up arrow 10 times. Point to the Apply button.**

The Automatically after text box displays 00:10 seconds (Figure 5-78). Another method of entering the time is to type the specific number of minutes and seconds in the text box.

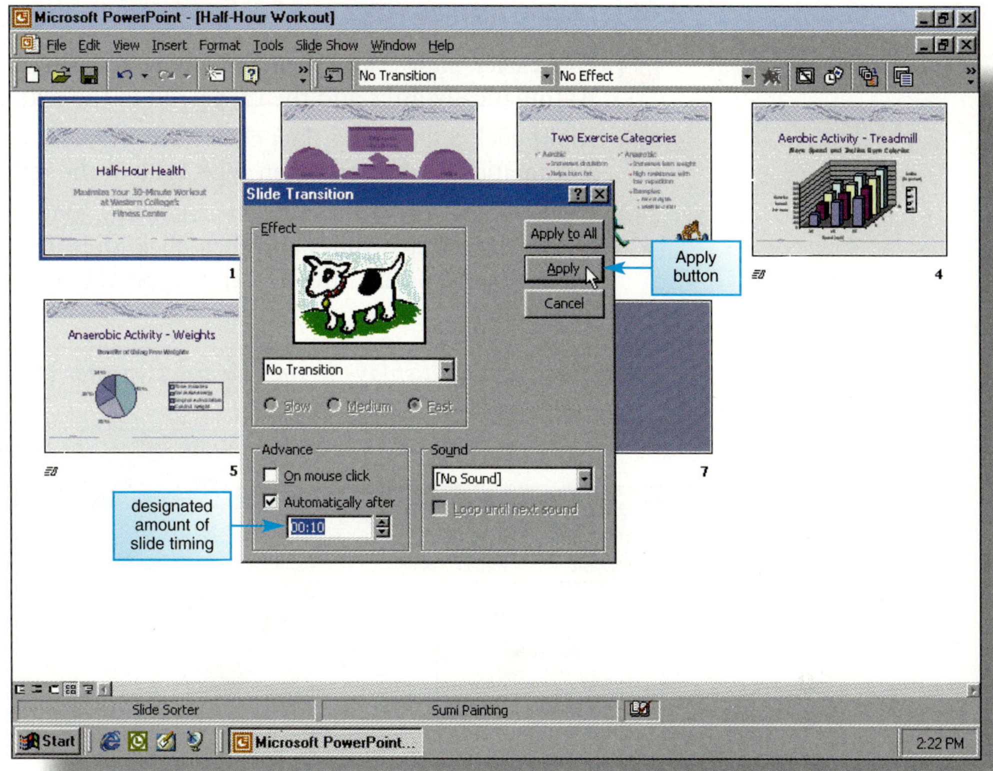

FIGURE 5-78

6 **Click the Apply button.**

The designated slide timing, :10, displays below Slide 1 (Figure 5-79).

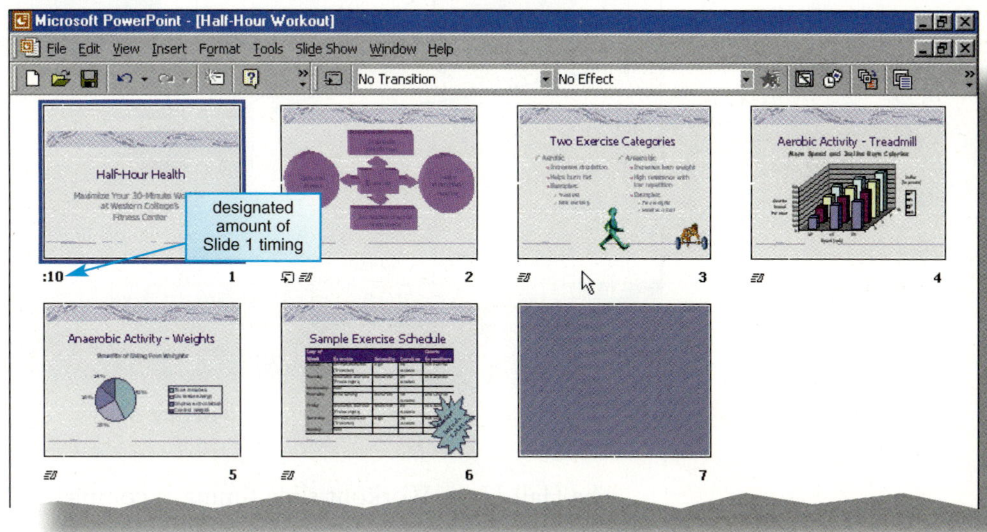

FIGURE 5-79

The timing for Slide 1 is complete. Now you need to repeat this procedure for the other slides in the Half-Hour Workout presentation. Perform the steps on the next page to set these timings.

Other Ways

1. On Slide Show menu click Slide Transition, click Automatically after, click Automatically after text box up arrow, click Apply button
2. Press ALT+D, press T, press ALT+C, press SPACEBAR, type desired time, press ENTER

TO SET SLIDE TIMINGS FOR THE REMAINING SLIDES

1. Right-click Slide 2 and then click Slide Transition. Click On mouse click. Click Automatically after and then type :30 in the text box. Click the Apply button.
2. Right-click Slide 3 and then click Slide Transition. Click On mouse click. Click Automatically after and then type 1:00 in the text box. Click the Apply button.
3. Click Slide 4, press and hold the SHIFT key, and then click Slide 7. Right-click one of the selected slides and then click Slide Transition. Click On mouse click. Click Automatically after and then type :20 in the text box. Click the Apply button.

Each slide's timing displays in the lower-left corner (Figure 5-80).

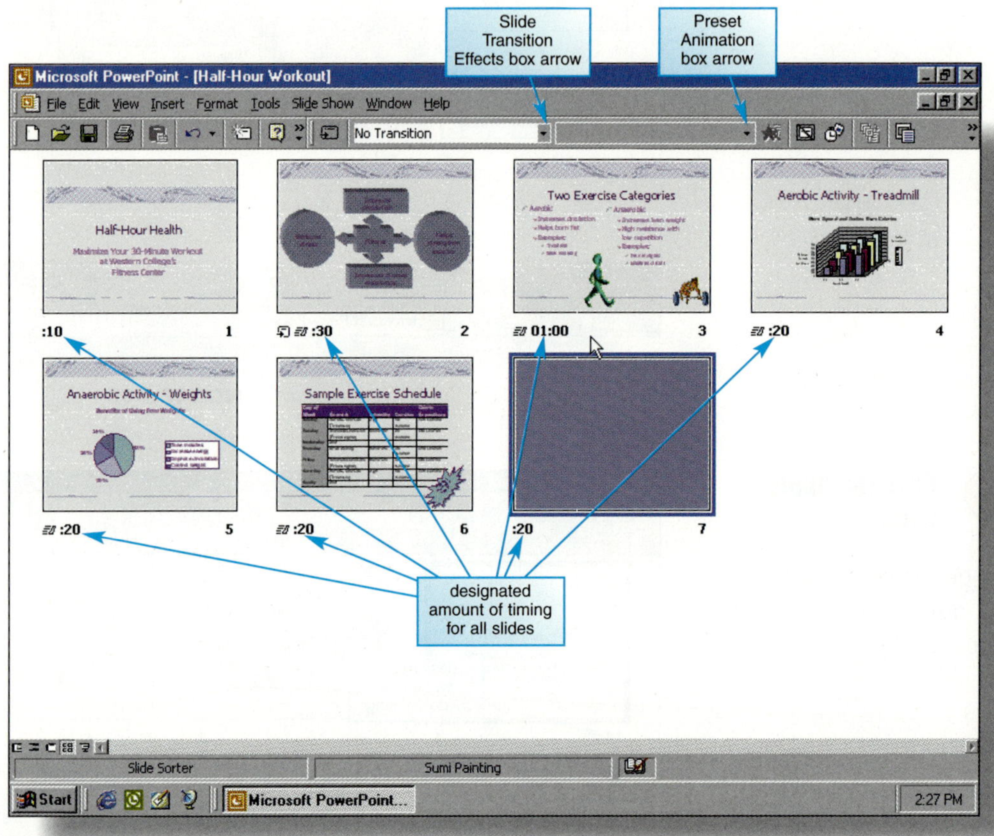

FIGURE 5-80

The Half-Hour Workout slide timing is complete. The presentation will run for three minutes at the kiosk in the Fitness Center.

Self-Running Presentations

A self-running presentation restarts when it is finished and also when it has been idle on a manually advanced slide for longer than five minutes.

Adding Slide Transition and Text Preset Animation Effects

The final step in preparing the Half-Hour Workout presentation is to add slide transition and text preset animation effects. Perform the following steps to add the slide transition and text preset animation effects.

TO ADD SLIDE TRANSITION AND TEXT PRESET ANIMATION EFFECTS

1. With Slide 7 selected in Slide Sorter View, press and hold down the SHIFT key and then click Slide 1. Release the SHIFT key.
2. Click the Slide Transition Effects box arrow. Scroll down and then click Uncover Down.
3. Click the Preset Animation box arrow. Scroll down and then click Dissolve.

The presentation displays in Slide Sorter View (Figure 5-81). Slide transition effects and preset animation effects are applied to all slides in the presentation.

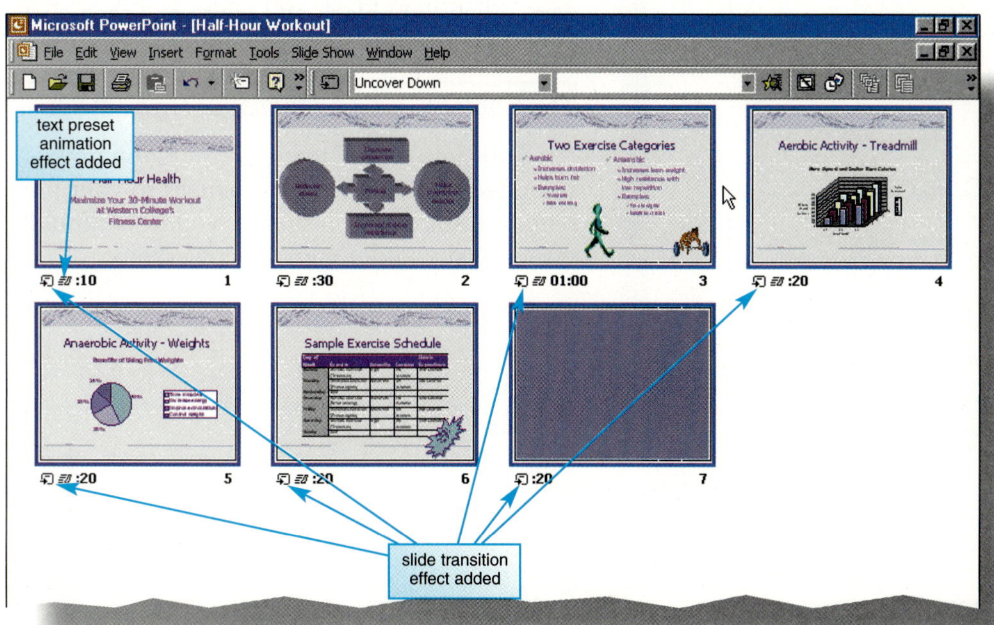

FIGURE 5-81

> **More About 2000**
>
> **Quick Reference**
>
> For a table that lists how to complete the tasks covered in this book using the mouse, menu, shortcut menu, and keyboard, see the PowerPoint Quick Reference Summary at the back of this book or visit the Office 2000 Web page (www.scsite.com/off2000/qr.htm), and then click Microsoft PowerPoint 2000.

Saving the Presentation

The presentation is complete. You now should save it again.

Starting the Self-Running Presentation

Starting a self-running slide show basically is the same as starting any other slide show. Perform the following steps to run the presentation.

TO START THE SELF-RUNNING PRESENTATION

1. Click Slide 1 and click the Slide Show button.

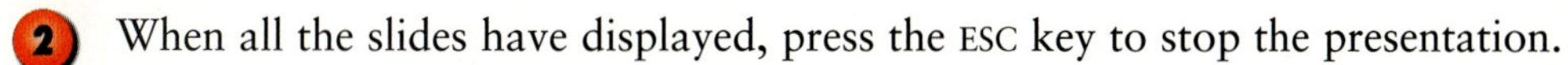

2. When all the slides have displayed, press the ESC key to stop the presentation.

The presentation will run for three minutes, and then it will loop back to the beginning and start automatically.

> **Other Ways**
>
> 1. In Slide View or Slide Sorter View, select slide to add transitions, right-click selected slide, click Slide Transition on shortcut menu, click Effect box arrow, choose desired transition, click Apply button
> 2. Select slide to add transitions, on Slide Show menu click Slide Transition, click Effect box arrow, choose desired transition, click Apply button

Printing Slides as Handouts

Perform the steps on the next page to print the presentation slides as handouts, four slides per page.

Half-Hour Health

Maximize Your 30-Minute Workout at Western College's Fitness Center

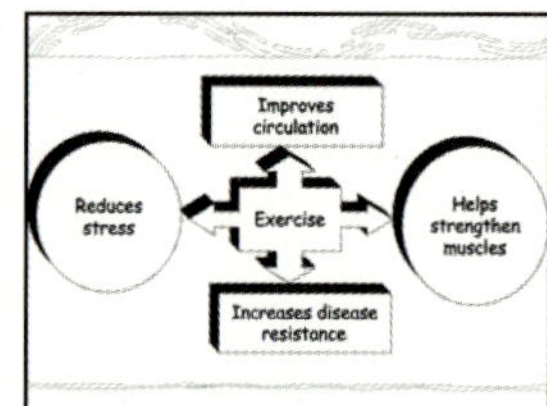

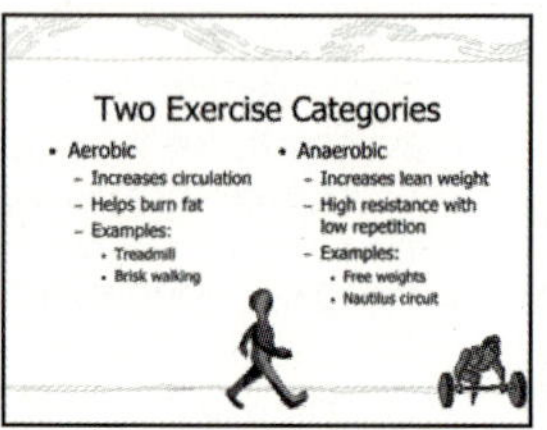

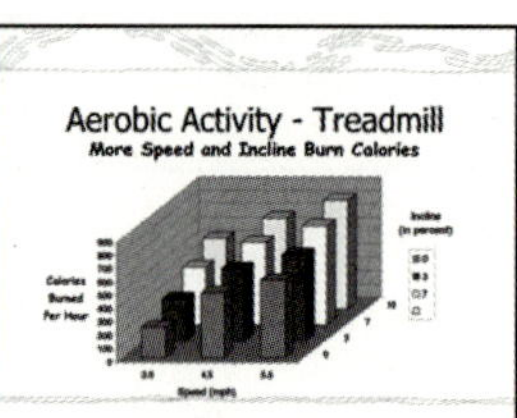

TO PRINT SLIDES AS HANDOUTS

1. Ready the printer according to the printer manufacturer's instructions.
2. Click File on the menu bar and then click Print on the File menu.
3. Click the Print what box arrow and then click Handouts in the list.
4. Click the Slides per page box arrow in the Handouts area and then click 4 in the list.
5. Click Pure black and white and then click the OK button.

The handouts print as shown in Figure 5-82.

The Half-Hour Fitness presentation now is complete. If you made any changes to your presentation since your last save, you now should save it again before quitting PowerPoint.

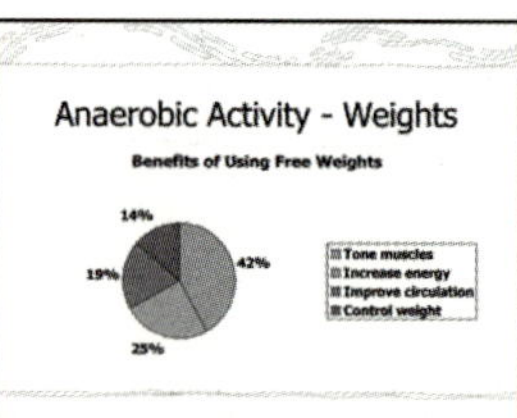

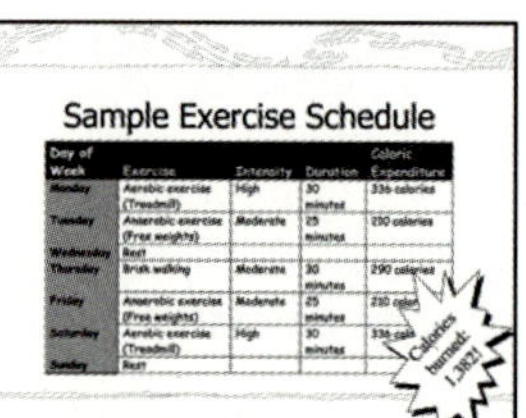

Microsoft Certification

The Microsoft Office User Specialist (MOUS) Certification program provides an opportunity for you to obtain a valuable industry credential - proof that you have the PowerPoint 2000 skills required by employers. For more information, see Appendix D or visit the Shelly Cashman Series MOUS Web page at www.scsite.com/off2000/cert.htm.

FIGURE 5-82

CASE PERSPECTIVE SUMMARY

The Half-Hour Fitness slide show should help Western College's students understand how to optimize their workouts. When they register at the Fitness Center, they can view your presentation at a kiosk and learn why exercise is important and how aerobic and anaerobic activities are beneficial. Your charts depicting use of the treadmill and free weights and your table showing how to vary the workouts explain these basic exercise principles. As director of the Fitness Center, Tiffani Olson should find your presentation beneficial for promoting the Center's holistic wellness philosophy.

Project Summary

Project 5 presented the principles of creating a self-running presentation that can run at a kiosk. You began the project by starting a new presentation and then inserting an animated slide from another presentation. Next, you embedded animated clip art, an Excel chart, a PowerPoint chart, and a Word table. You then inserted and formatted an AutoShape. Next, you created an ending slide with a purple background to separate the end of your presentation from the beginning when the slide show loops. You used custom animation effects to stagger the display of various slide objects. You then set automatic slide timings to display each slide for a designated period of time and added slide transition effects. Finally, you printed your presentation slides as handouts with four slides displaying on each page.

What You Should Know

Having completed this project, you now should be able to perform the following tasks:

- Add a Chart Title and Data Labels *(PP 5.33)*
- Add a Slide, Choose a Layout, and Add Text *(PP 5.13, PP 5.20, PP 5.26, PP 5.36)*
- Add a Shadow to an AutoShape *(PP 5.41)*
- Add Slide Transition and Text Preset Animation Effects *(PP 5.59)*
- Add Text to an AutoShape *(PP 5.42)*
- Add Text to the Right Placeholder *(PP 5.14)*
- Animate an AutoShape *(PP 5.45)*
- Change the Background Color *(PP 5.46)*
- Change the Slide Timing *(PP 5.51, 5.52)*
- Create a Self-Running Presentation *(PP 5.53)*
- Create a Title Slide in Slide View *(PP 5.7)*
- Increase the Right Object Area Placeholder Width *(PP 5.15)*
- Insert a Slide from Another Presentation *(PP 5.10)*
- Insert a Word Table *(PP 5.37)*
- Insert an AutoShape *(PP 5.40)*
- Insert an Excel Chart *(PP 5.21)*
- Insert Animated Clip Art *(PP 5.16)*
- Move Animated Clip Art Objects *(PP 5.17)*
- Omit Background Graphics and Change the Background *(PP 5.46)*
- Print Slides as Handouts *(PP 5.60)*
- Replace Sample Data in a Datasheet *(PP 5.29)*
- Rotate an AutoShape *(PP 5.44)*
- Save a Presentation *(PP 5.19)*
- Scale an Excel Chart *(PP 5.24)*
- Select a Different Chart Type *(PP 5.27)*
- Set Slide Show Timings Manually *(PP 5.55)*
- Set Slide Timings for the Remaining Slides *(PP 5.58)*
- Set the Animation Order *(PP 5.49)*
- Size the Animated Clip Art Objects *(PP 5.18)*
- Start a New Presentation *(PP 5.6)*
- Start the Self-Running Presentation *(PP 5.59)*

1 Changing the Color Scheme, Removing an Object from the Slide Master, Adding Animated Clip Art, and Inserting a Presentation

Instructions: Start PowerPoint. Open the Antivirus Basics file on your Data Disk. See the inside back cover of this book for instructions for downloading the Data Disk or see your instructor for information on accessing the files required for this book. Perform the following tasks to modify the slides to look like Figures 5-83a through 5-83f.

1. Click File on the menu bar, and then click Save As. Save the presentation with the file name, Antivirus Policy.
2. Apply the Lock And Key design template.
3. Change the slide color scheme. To make this change, click Format on the menu bar, click Slide Color Scheme, and then click the Custom tab in the Color Scheme dialog box. Next, change the Background color to red and the Title text color to dark blue. Click the Apply to All button.
4. Display Slide 2. Delete the key from the slide master by changing to slide master view, clicking the key object, and then pressing the DELETE key. Click the Slide View button.
5. On Slide 4, insert the animated question mark clip art image shown in Figure 5-83d. Scale the clip art to 285%. Drag the image under the text and center it on the slide.
6. Insert the PowerPoint file, Inoculate, after Slide 4. This file is on your Data Disk.
7. Introduce the subtitle text in the Object Area placeholder on each slide all at once grouped by 2nd level paragraphs.
8. Add a summary slide from Slides 2, 3, and 4, and reposition it after Slide 5. Change the title text to Minimizing the Virus Threat, as shown in Figure 5-83f. Insert the animated computer clip art image shown in Figure 5-83f. Scale the clip art to 400%. Drag the image to the lower-right corner of the slide.
9. Apply the Dissolve animation effect to the clip art images on Slides 4 and 6. Move each image to the top of the Animation order list, and start the animation automatically 2 seconds after the previous event.
10. Add your name and the slide number to the slide footer.
11. Apply the Split Vertical Out slide transition effect to all slides except Slide 1. Apply the Split Horizontal In preset animation effect to all text.
12. Save the Antivirus Policy file again.
13. Print the slides using the Pure black and white option. Quit PowerPoint.

Apply Your Knowledge

Project Reinforcement at www.scsite.com/off2000/reinforce.htm

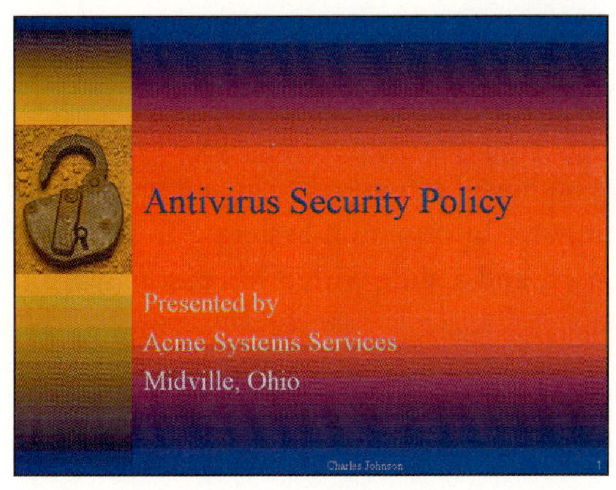

(a) Slide 1

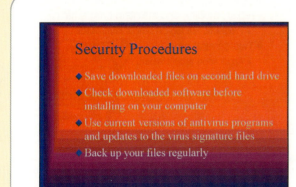

Security Rules

- Check floppy disks on standalone machine
  - Includes
    - Floppies purchased from shareware sources
    - Floppies brought from home
- Report viruses to Technical Services
- Check downloaded software

(b) Slide 2

- Save downloaded files on second hard drive
- Check downloaded software before installing on your computer
- Use current versions of antivirus programs and updates to the virus signature files
- Back up your files regularly

(c) Slide 3

Security Education

- Distinguish between actual and hoax viruses
- Determine the type of infection
- Distribute and discuss rules and procedures
  - Apply disciplinary action for violations

(d) Slide 4

(e) Slide 5

Minimizing the Virus Threat

- Security Rules
- Security Procedures
- Security Education

(f) Slide 6

FIGURE 5-83

1 Inserting Animated Clip Art, Applying Animation Effects, and Importing Word and Excel Files

Problem: In an effort to be more helpful to students, the Student Career Center (SCC) has asked to meet with various student representatives. One of the ideas adopted by the SCC is to highlight different careers every few days as part of their information kiosk. As a work-study student, you have been asked to create several of the kiosk presentations. Your first presentation is about careers in Computer Information Systems. To make the display interesting, you add clip art, a slide with a Microsoft Excel chart, and a slide with a Microsoft Word table. You create the presentation shown in Figures 5-84a through 5-84g.

(a) Slide 1

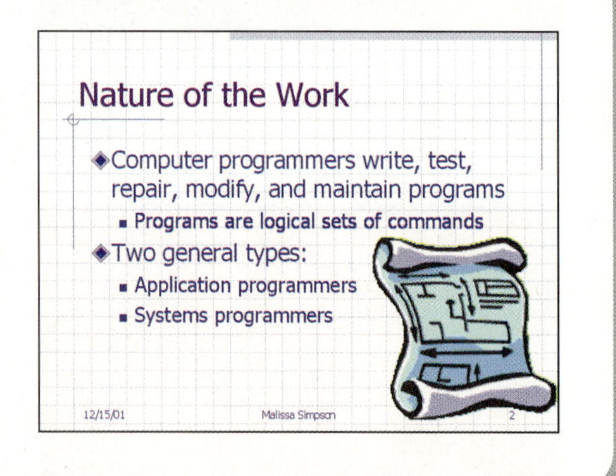

(b) Slide 2

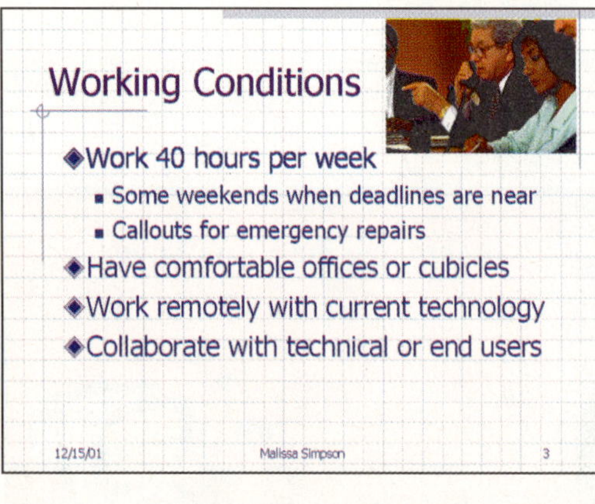

(c) Slide 3

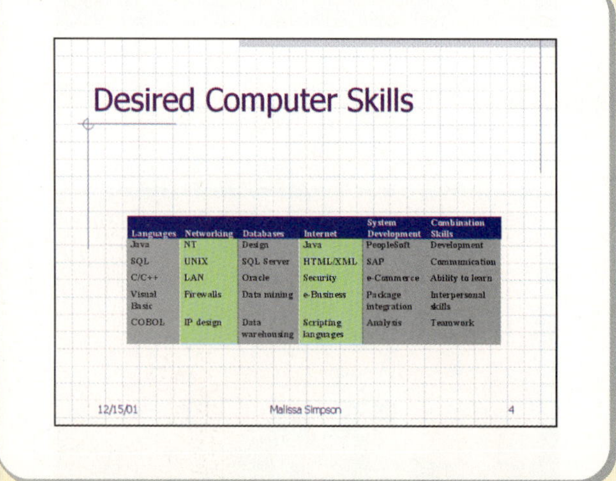

Languages	Networking	Databases	Internet	System Development	Combination Skills
Java	NT	Design	Java	PeopleSoft	Development
SQL	UNIX	SQL Server	HTML/XML	SAP	Communication
C/C++	LAN	Oracle	Security	e-Commerce	Ability to learn
Visual Basic	Firewalls	Data mining	e-Business	Package integration	Interpersonal skills
COBOL	IP design	Data warehousing	Scripting languages	Analysis	Teamwork

(d) Slide 4

FIGURE 5-84

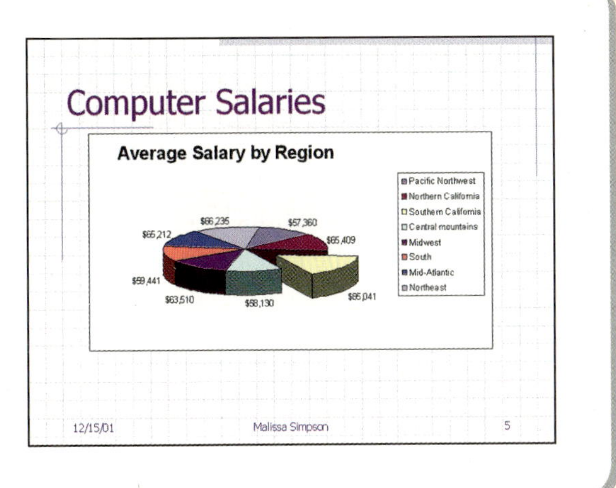

(e) Slide 5

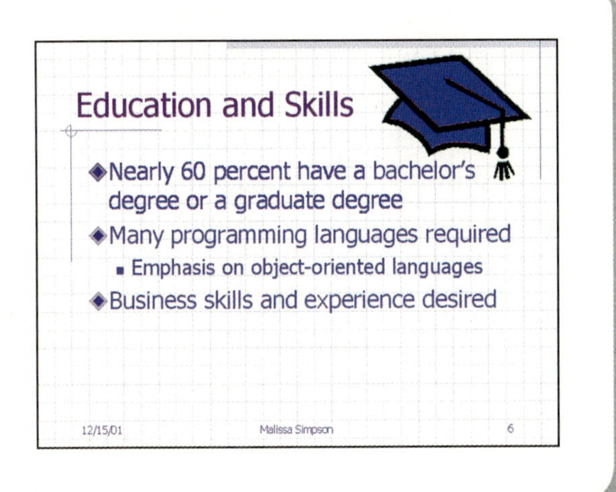

(f) Slide 6

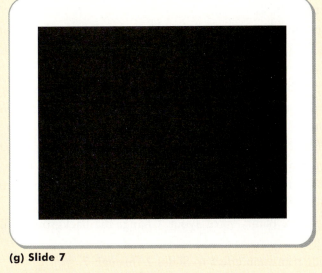

(g) Slide 7

FIGURE 5-84

Instructions: Start PowerPoint and perform the following tasks with a computer. If the designated clip art images do not display in your Microsoft Clip Gallery, see your instructor for copies of these files or substitute similar objects.

1. Open a new presentation and apply the Title Slide AutoLayout and the Blueprint design template.
2. Create the title slide shown in Figure 5-84a. Apply the Peek From Left Entry animation effect to the subtitle text.
3. Insert a new slide and apply the Bulleted List AutoLayout. Type the title text and bulleted text shown in Figure 5-84b.
4. Insert the animated clip art shown in Figure 5-84b that has the keyword, layouts. Scale the clip art to 205% and drag it to the lower-right corner of the slide.

(continued)

Inserting Animated Clip Art, Applying Animation Effects, and Importing Word and Excel Files *(continued)*

5. Apply the Fly From Bottom-Right Entry animation effect to the clip art. Start the animation automatically, 00:02 seconds after the previous event.
6. Apply the Peek From Left Entry animation effect to the Slide 2 bulleted list. Introduce this text all at once grouped by 2nd level paragraphs.
7. Insert a new slide, apply the Bulleted List AutoLayout, and create Slide 3 as shown in Figure 5-84c. Insert the animated clip art that has the keywords, business, communication. Scale the clip art to 140% and drag it to the upper-right corner of the slide.
8. Apply the Fly From Top-Right Entry animation effect to the animated clip art. Start the animation automatically, 00:02 seconds after the previous event.
9. Apply the Peek From Left Entry animation effect to the Slide 3 bulleted list. Introduce this text all at once grouped by 2nd level paragraphs.
10. Insert a new slide and apply the Object AutoLayout. Type the Slide 4 title text shown in Figure 5-84d. Insert the Employment Table file on your Data Disk. Apply the Split Vertical In Entry animation effect to this table, which is Object 2.
11. Insert a new slide and apply the Chart AutoLayout. Type the Slide 5 title text shown in Figure 5-84e. Insert the Programming Salaries file on your Data Disk. Apply the Split Vertical In Entry animation effect to this chart, which is Object 4.
12. Insert a new slide and apply the Bulleted List AutoLayout. Enter the Slide 6 text shown in Figure 5-84f. Insert the animated clip art that has the keyword, mortarboards. Scale the clip art to 145% and drag it to the upper-right corner of the slide.
13. Apply the Fly From Top-Right Entry animation effect to the animated clip art. Start the animation automatically, 00:02 seconds after the previous event.
14. Apply the Peek From Left Entry animation effect to the Slide 6 bulleted list. Introduce this text all at once grouped by 2nd level paragraphs.
15. Insert a new slide and apply the Blank AutoLayout. Change the background fill color to black. Omit the background graphics from the master.
16. Apply the Wipe Down slide transition effect to Slides 2 through 7.
17. Set the slide timings to 10 seconds for Slide 1 and 15 seconds for Slides 2 through 7.
18. Set the show type as Browsed at a kiosk.
19. Add your name, today's date, and the slide number to the slide footer.
20. Save the presentation with the file name, Programming Career. Print the slides using the Pure black and white option. Quit PowerPoint.

2 Inserting Animated Clip Art, Applying Animation Effects, Changing the Slide Background, and Creating a Chart

Problem: You are enrolled in a business seminar course called the Modern Entrepreneur. The main requirement for the course is to present a business plan on a legitimate business venture. The plan and the presentation are a "pitch" for funding, such as a small business loan. You are interested in owning and operating an Internet Service Provider (ISP), so you decide to make a presentation on launching an ISP called the New Millennium Internet Access (NMIA). To make the presentation persuasive, you add a Microsoft Excel chart showing five-year projected income. In addition, you add some clip art and change the design template background color. You create the presentation shown in Figures 5-85a through 5-85f.

(a) Slide 1

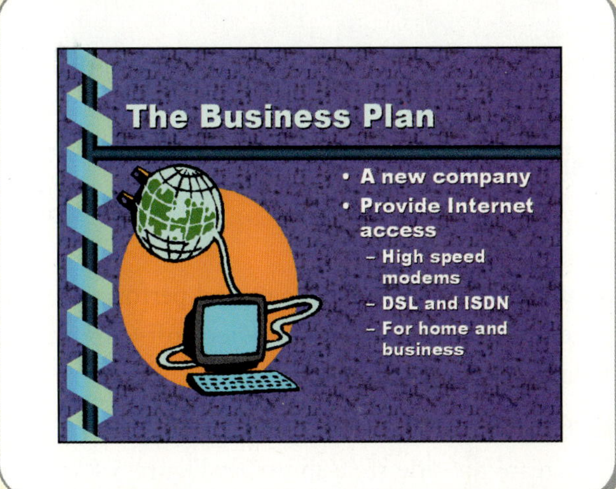

(b) Slide 2

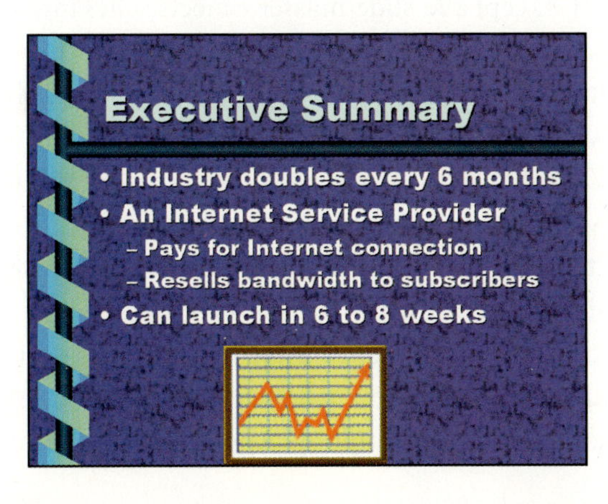

(c) Slide 3

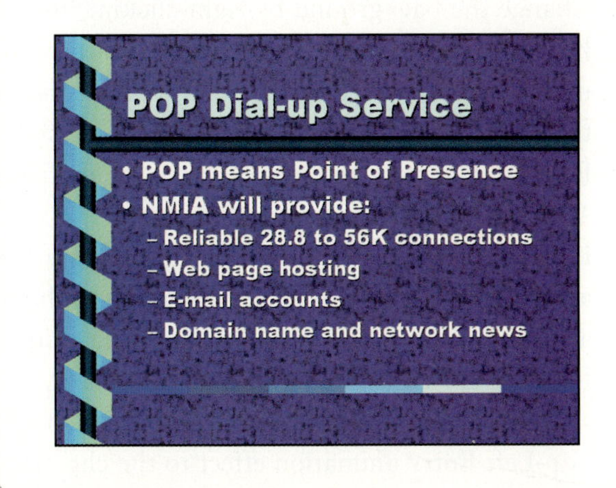

(d) Slide 4

FIGURE 5-85 *(continued)*

(continued)

Inserting Animated Clip Art, Applying Animation Effects, Changing the Slide Background, and Creating a Chart *(continued)*

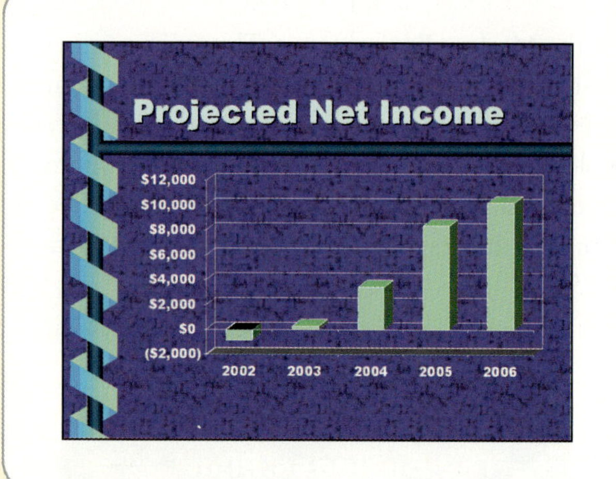

(e) Slide 5

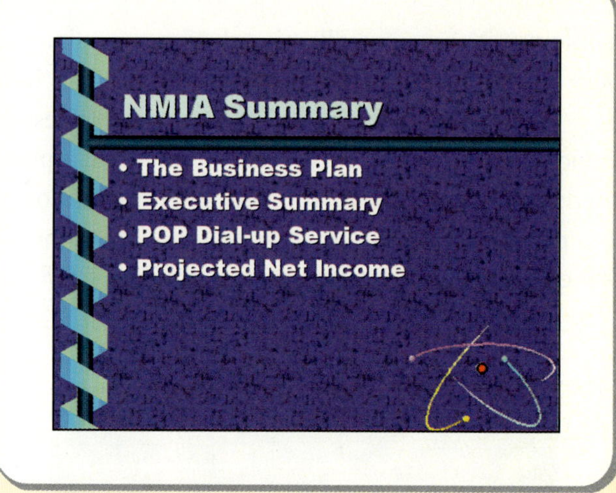

(f) Slide 6

FIGURE 5-85 *(continued)*

Instructions: Start PowerPoint and perform the following tasks with a computer. If the designated clip art images do not display in your Microsoft Clip Gallery, see your instructor for copies of these files or substitute similar objects.

1. Open a new presentation and apply the Title Slide AutoLayout and the High Voltage design template.
2. Create the title slide shown in Figure 5-85a. Use your name instead of the name Sandra Linden. Apply the Spiral animation effect to the Slide 1 subtitle text. Start the animation automatically, 00:03 seconds after the previous event.
3. Change the background by right-clicking anywhere on Slide 1 except the slide master objects, clicking Background on the shortcut menu, and then clicking the Background fill area box arrow. Click Fill Effects in the list and then click the Texture tab. Click the Purple mesh texture in row 3, column 3, and then click the OK button. To apply the change to all slides, click the Apply to All button.
4. Display the rulers and guides. Drag the vertical guide to 3.17 inches left of center and the horizontal guide 1.67 inches below center.
5. Insert the animated clip art shown in Figure 5-85a that has the keywords, technology, borders. Drag the clip art object so its upper-left corner snaps to the intersection of the guides. Apply the Fly From Left Entry animation effect to the clip art. Start the animation automatically, 00:03 seconds after the previous event.
6. Insert a new slide and apply the Clip Art & Text AutoLayout. Type the Slide 2 title text and bulleted text shown in Figure 5-85b. Insert the clip art that has the keywords, earth, technology. Apply the Fly From Top-Left Entry animation effect to the clip art, Object 3.
7. Apply the Spiral animation effect to the Slide 2 subtitle text, Text 2. Introduce this text all at once grouped by 2nd level paragraphs.

In the Lab

8. Insert a new slide and apply the Bulleted List AutoLayout. Type the Slide 3 title text and bulleted text shown in Figure 5-85c. Drag the vertical guide to 1.50 inches left of center. Insert the animated clip art that has the keywords, charts, increases. Scale it to 233% and drag it so that its upper-left corner snaps to the intersection of the guides.
9. Apply the Fly From Bottom Entry animation effect to the clip art, Picture frame 3.
10. Apply the Spiral animation effect to the Slide 3 subtitle text, Text 2. Introduce this text all at once grouped by 2nd level paragraphs.
11. Insert a new slide and apply the Bulleted List AutoLayout. Type the Slide 4 title text and bulleted list shown in Figure 5-85d.
12. Drag the vertical guide to 3.92 inches left of center and the horizontal guide to 2.67 inches below center. Insert the animated clip art shown in Figure 5-85d that has the keywords, web dividers, lines. Scale the clip art to 153%. Align the top-left corner of the clip art with the intersection of the guides.
13. Apply the Spiral animation effect to the Slide 3 subtitle text, Text 2. Introduce this text all at once grouped by 2nd level paragraphs.
14. Hide the rulers and guides.
15. Insert a new slide and apply the Chart AutoLayout. Type the Slide 5 title text shown in Figure 5-85e. Create the 3-D Column chart shown in Slide 5 by using the data in Table 5-2.

Table 5-2 Projected Net Income

YEAR	*NET INCOME*
2002	$-867
2003	$253
2004	$3,421
2005	$8,342
2006	$10,234

16. Add a summary slide from Slides 2, 3, 4, and 5, and reposition it after Slide 5. Change the title text to NMIA Summary, as shown in Figure 5-85f. Insert the animated clip art image that has the keywords, atoms, technology. Scale the clip art to 187%. Drag the image to the lower-right corner of the slide. Apply the Spiral animation effect to the Slide 6 subtitle text, Text 2.
17. Apply the Box Out slide transition effect to Slides 2 through 6.
18. Save the presentation with the file name, Business Plan. Print the slides using the Pure black and white option. Quit PowerPoint.

3 Using AutoShapes and Adding a Presentation within a Presentation

Problem: Your Aunt Julia owns the Melting Pot, which is a specialty food and kitchen utensils store. She offers numerous cooking classes with topics ranging from economy family meals to formal business dinner parties. She often is asked how to present food for buffet style dinners, so she has asked you to create a presentation on planning a buffet style dinner party. She has created an outline of the course and has assembled some graphics for you to use in the presentation.

Instructions Part 1: Start PowerPoint and perform the following tasks with a computer to create the presentation consisting of Figures 5-86a through 5-86e. If the designated clip art images do not display in your Microsoft Clip Gallery, see your instructor for copies of these files or substitute similar objects.

1. Open a new presentation and apply the Title Slide AutoLayout and the Citrus design template.
2. Create the title slide shown in Figure 5-86a. Add your name and today's date to this slide.
3. Insert a new slide and apply the Text & Clip Art slide layout. Type the Slide 2 title text and bulleted list shown in Figure 5-86b. Insert the clip art that has the keywords, meals, fried chicken.
4. Insert a new slide and apply the Object layout design. Type the Slide 3 title text shown in Figure 5-86c. Insert the Party Timetable file on your Data Disk. Apply the Split Vertical Out Entry animation effect to this table, which is Object 2. Start the animation automatically, 00:03 seconds after the previous event.
5. Insert a new slide and apply the Bulleted list slide layout. Enter the Slide 4 title text and bulleted text shown in Figure 5-86d.
6. Insert a new slide and apply the 2 Column Text slide layout. Enter the Slide 5 title text and bulleted text shown as Figure 5-86e.
7. Apply the Split Horizontal Out Entry animation effect to the Slide 1, 2, 4, and 5 subtitle text. Start the Slide 1 animation automatically.
8. Apply the Blinds Vertical Out slide transition effect to Slides 2 through 5.
9. Save the presentation with the file name, Buffet Dinner.

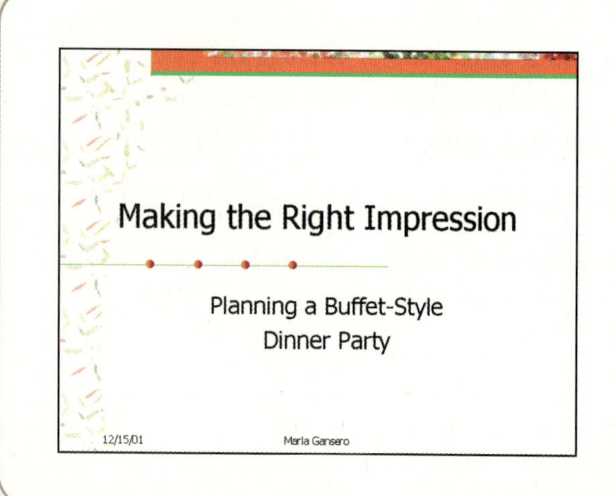

(a) Slide 1

(b) Slide 2

FIGURE 5-86

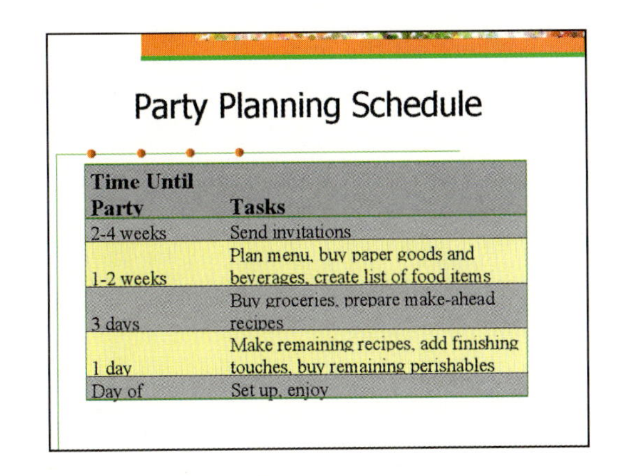

Party Planning Schedule

Time Until Party	Tasks
2-4 weeks	Send invitations
1-2 weeks	Plan menu, buy paper goods and beverages, create list of food items
3 days	Buy groceries, prepare make-ahead recipes
1 day	Make remaining recipes, add finishing touches, buy remaining perishables
Day of	Set up, enjoy

(c) Slide 3

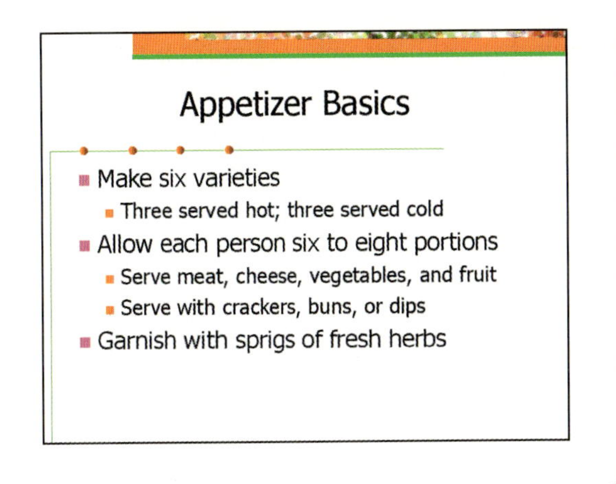

Appetizer Basics
Make six varieties
Three served hot; three served cold
Allow each person six to eight portions
Serve meat, cheese, vegetables, and fruit
Serve with crackers, buns, or dips
Garnish with sprigs of fresh herbs

(d) Slide 4

Preparation Reminders
Remember guests' special needs
Consider vegetarians and diabetics
Make familiar dishes
Make finger foods
Prepare food the previous night
Keep refrigerated or on ice
Do not use plastic plates and utensils

(e) Slide 5

(f) Slide 6

FIGURE 5-86 *(continued)*

Instructions Part 2: Perform the following tasks to create the presentation shown in Figure 5-86f and to insert this slide in the presentation created in Part 1. If the designated clip art images do not display in your Microsoft Clip Gallery, see your instructor for copies of these files or substitute similar objects.

1. Open a new presentation, apply the Blank AutoLayout, and then apply the Citrus design template.
2. Create the slide shown in Figure 5-86f.
3. Insert a bent arrow from the Auto Shapes, Block Arrows.
4. If the fill color is not already green, change the fill color to green.
5. Use the Draw, Rotate or Flip command to Flip Vertical. Rotate the arrow so it appears as shown in Figure 5-86f.
6. Insert the clip art that has the keywords dining, food, place settings.

(continued)

Using AutoShapes and Adding a Presentation within a Presentation *(continued)*

7. Select the clip art image. Ungroup the image. Click the mouse anywhere off the image.
8. Select the fork by dragging the mouse over the fork. After the sizing handles appear, click the draw button and group the image. Drag the fork to the left away from the plate.
9. Select the knife and spoon by dragging the mouse over the mouse and spoon. After the sizing handles appear, click the draw button and group the image.
10. Drag the knife and spoon next to the fork.
11. Hold the shift key down and click the fork so the fork, knife, and spoon are selected. Click the Draw button and group the two images into one.
12. Rotate the fork, knife, and spoon as one image 90 degrees to the right.
13. Insert a text box above the plate as shown in Figure 5-86f. Enter the description, 1. Plates.
14. Insert a down arrow from the Auto Shapes, Block Arrows. Change the fill color to green and place the arrow on the lower-right side of the plate, as shown in Figure 5-86f.
15. Insert the clip art dinner, food, meat, seafood, which contains a lobster, beneath the plate.
16. Insert a text box below the lobster and enter the description, 2. Main Course.
17. Insert a bent arrow from the Auto Shapes, Block Arrows. Use the Draw, Rotate or Flip command to Flip Vertical, then flip Horizontal. Rotate the arrow to so it appears as Figure 5-86f.
18. Add the remaining clip art, text box descriptions, arrows and shown in Figure 5-86f.
19. Use Table 5-3 to set the animation order and timing.
20. Save the second presentation with the file name, Buffet Table. Close this presentation.
21. Add the Buffet Table presentation slide to your Buffet Dinner presentation after Slide 5.
22. Apply the Blinds Vertical slide transition effect to Slide 6.
23. Save the Buffet Dinner presentation again. Print the slides using the Pure black and white option. Quit PowerPoint.

Table 5-3 Buffet Table Automation

ORDER AND TIMING	*START AUTOMATION*	*EFFECT*
Bent Arrow	Automatically, 1 second	Fly From Top-Right
Dinner Plate	Automatically, 1 second	Fly From Top-Right
Textbox (1. Plates)	Automatically, 1 second	Fly From Top-Right
Down Arrow	Automatically, 1 second	Fly From Top-Right
Lobster Dinner	Automatically, 5 seconds	Fly From Right
Textbox (2. Main Course)	Automatically, 1 second	Fly From Right
Bent Arrow	Automatically, 1 second	Fly From Right
Shrimp on plate	Automatically, 5 seconds	Fly From Bottom
Textbox (3. Cold Food)	Automatically, 1 second	Fly From Bottom
Left Arrow	Automatically, 1 second	Fly From Right
Salads	Automatically, 5 seconds	Fly From Left
Textbox (4. Salads)	Automatically, 1 second	Fly From Left
Bent Arrow	Automatically, 1 second	Fly From Bottom
Bread basket	Automatically, 5 seconds	Fly From Left
Textbox (5. Breads)	Automatically, 1 second	Fly From Left
Bent Arrow	Automatically, 1 second	Fly From Bottom-Left
Flatware	Automatically, 5 seconds	Fly From Top
Textbox (6. Flatware)	Automatically, 1 second	Fly From Top
Right Arrow	Automatically, 1 second	Fly From Left
Beverages	Automatically, 5 seconds	Fly From Top
Textbox (7. Beverages)	Automatically, 1 second	Fly From Top
Bent Arrow	Automatically, 1 second	Fly From Left

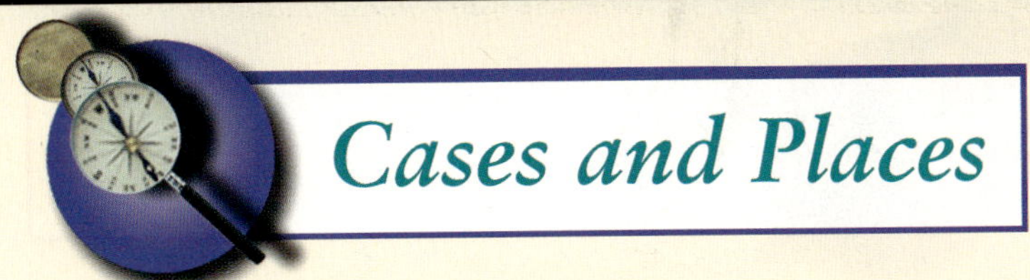

Cases and Places

The difficulty of these case studies varies:
▶ are the least difficult; ▶▶ are more difficult; and ▶▶▶ are the most difficult.

1 ▶ E-commerce is growing quickly as the number of Internet users increases. Shopping Web sites are sprouting overnight. Technology allows the average person at home to sell things over the Web. Most of the technology needed today requires Common Gateway Interfaces (CGI), Java, JavaScript, and VBScript. One technique used for tracking a shopper's visit to a Web site is to use cookies. A cookie is a mechanism used to store and retrieve data on the client's (user's) computer. In other words, it is a variable that holds data, and that data is stored on the disk in a special file. Cookie items make it easy for Web sites to keep track of user preferences because the data is stored on the user's computer, not on the Web server. Cookies set aside a small amount of disk space to save the data. The cookie then can be sent to the Web site as needed. The browser will not transfer a cookie's data to any Web site other than the one that requested it. This feature is important for security reasons. Cookies can keep track of frames, shopping cart selections, a user name for a Web site, a password for a Web site, and an account number for a Web site. Any personal data that is needed can be stored in a cookie. The only restriction is that a cookie cannot exceed 4,000 characters. Cookies cannot do certain things: they cannot read e-mail addresses, but they can save one if requested. Cookies cannot gather other sensitive data. If a server does not allow the use of CGI scripts, Web page developers can create cookies in JavaScript, VBScript, or Java. The basic logic requires these programmers to use three functions: a function that reads the cookie (if present), a function that stores the cookie, and a function that deletes the cookie. Most Web developers call these functions getCookie, setCookie, and delCookie. You have enrolled in a Web design course, and part of your coursework is to create a presentation on some aspect of Web page development. You have chosen to describe cookies. Using the techniques introduced in this project, create a short slide show explaining cookies. Include a Word Table, and modify a clip art image to display an animated object. Add the necessary slide transition effects. Submit all files on a disk to your instructor.

2 ▶ The Magnuson-Moss Warranty-Federal Trade Commission Improvement Act, better know as the Lemon Law, was enacted to give consumers rights in dealing with automobiles having persistent problems that are not rectified. The law protects any consumer of a product with a written warranty. The manufacturer must make a reasonable number of attempts to repair a defective product. After such repairs fail to correct the situation, the consumer may elect to collect a refund or ask for a replacement of the product. The Lemon Law also prohibits a warrantor from excluding or modifying warranties under the Uniform Commercial Code (UCC). The UCC or TARR BABY code, as it has been called, has been enacted in all 50 states and covers tender, acceptance, rejection, and revocation. The tender provision entitles a buyer to reject any goods that fail in any respect to conform to the contract. Acceptance covers the new car buyer who accepts the product in good faith and believes that the manufacturer will repair any problems. A new car buyer may discover defects in the car within a reasonable time to reject the vehicle. This period is inexact. Revocation protects the consumer who has used the new car for a lengthy period of time. This describes the typical lemon car, and the UCC provides that a buyer may revoke his acceptance of goods. Each state has different provisions regarding this law, so consumers must research their state's provisions. Using the techniques introduced in this project, create a short slide show describing your state's Lemon Law. Include a Word table, and modify a clip art image to display an animated object. Add the necessary slide transition effects. Submit all files on a disk to your instructor.

3 Day trading has been defined as a way to buy and sell stocks during the day based on daily price movement. Day trading has changed the traditional market that exists in a central location on the trading floor. Today's brokers and traders find each other electronically. Because of the Internet, anyone, anywhere has immediate access to the stock market. Day trading is very short-term and can involve as little as a few minutes of time. A change of a few points on 1,000 shares of a stock can translate into as much as $200 or more in a short time. These kinds of changes are attributed to growth in the market with new stocks that often increase value from 20% to 100% in one day. The goal is to be profitable, and the smart trader realizes that the opposite also can be true with massive losses in one day. Many people believe that day trading is gambling, assuming that one randomly picks stocks to "play" and does not do any research on the companies. Day trading is serious business and requires training, experience, and capital to get started. Successful day traders must have discipline and be able to learn and apply rules, strategies, and techniques. Learn some of the few simple trading strategies: have patience, do not follow the crowd, watch the stock price, don't let your emotions rule your day. Don't get greedy. Do not trade during that last hour of the day in the S&P futures market or place orders for the opening bell. If you do not like what you are holding, get out. Learn the jargon, so you will not make mistakes because you do not understand the language. Using the techniques introduced in this project, create a short slide show describing day trading principles. Include a Word table and animate two clip art objects. Add slide transition effects. Submit all files on a disk to your instructor.

4 You are a mass communication major and are enrolling in the Senior Seminar course. Your assignment is to tour a major newspaper, magazine, or book publisher to find out the process of putting together a daily newspaper, monthly magazine, or a book. You decide to visit a book publisher and to develop a slide show on how a book is made. Your show should discuss submitting a manuscript to an editor, who decides if the book is publishable. Subsequent slides should discuss the editing process, the illustrating and layout phases, and finally printing the book. One slide should use the Microsoft Draw feature to ungroup parts of a clip art object and reassemble it in the slide as animation. Enhance the presentation by modifying the slide background, placing additional clip art graphics, using text preset animation effects, and applying slide transition and animation effects to the text and the graphics. Submit all files on a disk to your instructor.

5 You have been elected president of the campus Computer Club. Your faculty advisor, who knows you are savvy about computers, suggests you do a presentation on building a computer. You decide this presentation could be a good introduction to a semester-long project, in which the club buys and assembles parts for a computer. Using the techniques introduced in this project, create a slide show describing how to build a PC. Research what components are required to build a computer and the sequence of steps used in the assembling process. List several popular places to purchase parts. Include a Word table describing CMOS settings, and modify at least two clip art images to show animated objects. Add slide transition effects. Submit all files on a disk to your instructor.

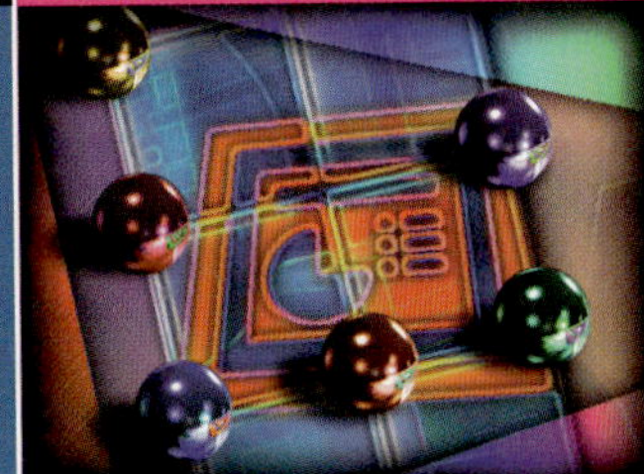

Microsoft PowerPoint 2000

Using Visual Basic for Applications (VBA) with PowerPoint

OBJECTIVES

You will have mastered the material in this project when you can:

- Create a toolbar
- Customize a toolbar by adding a button
- Use the macro recorder to create a macro
- Customize a menu by adding a command
- Open a presentation and print it by executing a macro
- Understand Visual Basic for Applications code
- Add controls, such as command buttons, option buttons, and check boxes to a form
- Assign properties to controls
- Create a form to automate data entry
- Write a procedure to automate data entry
- Create a user interface
- Use the Visual Basic Editor to enter a procedure
- Export an outline to Microsoft Word

Make a Point

Electronic Portfolios Do the Job

After taking classes for years and studying for exams for hours on end, you decide it is time to get serious and hunt for a job in your major field of study.

But where do you begin? Your college's placement center is a good start. So are two types of pages: the help wanted pages in your local paper and the Web pages on career sites.

When you peruse these ads, you will see that computer skills are in great demand. The U.S. Department of Labor predicts that soon most employees will need basic computer skills to land a job and then require additional specialized training to advance.

Many employers are seeking candidates with more than just a basic knowledge of computers; they desire individuals proficient in the latest versions of software, especially in

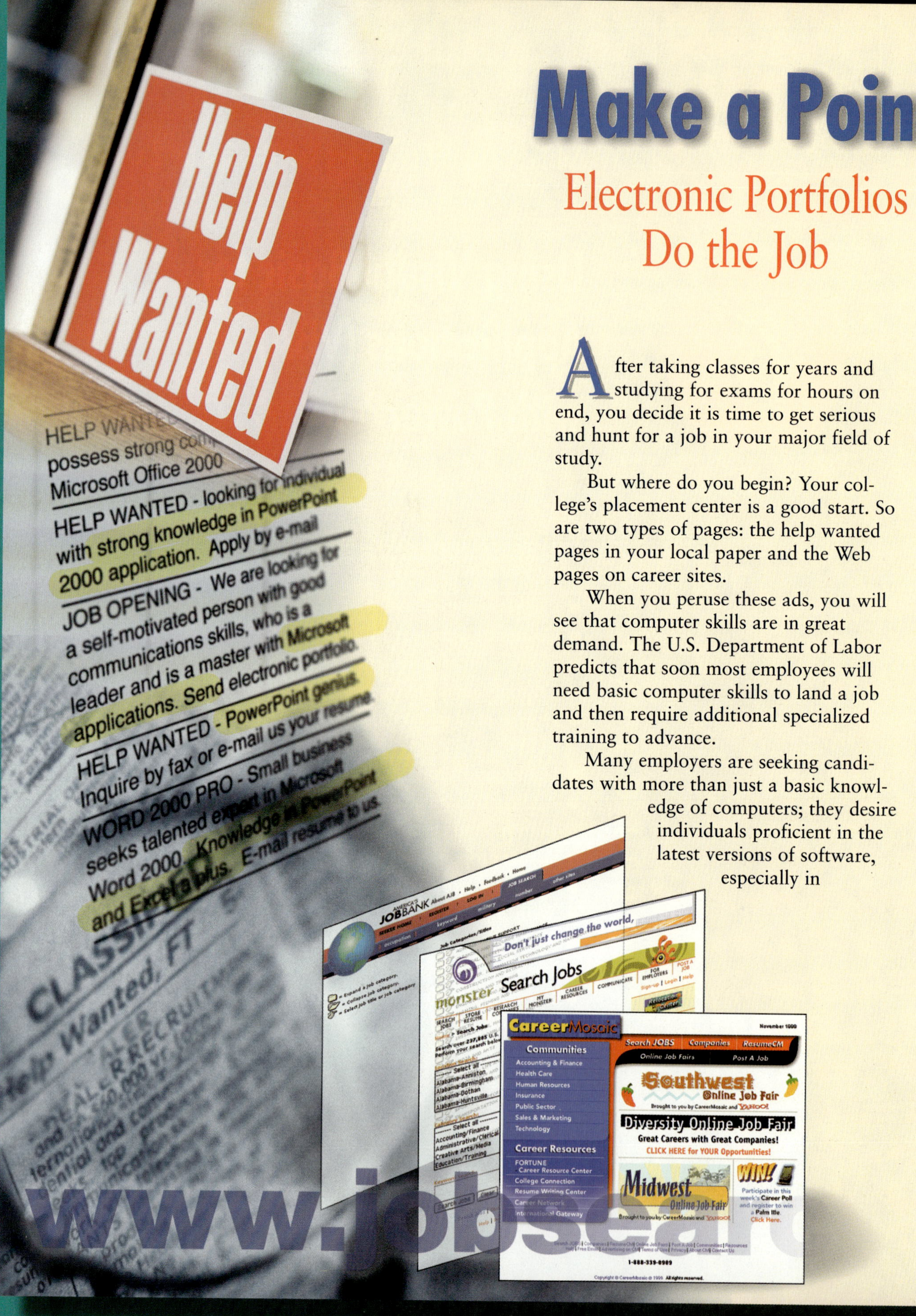

Microsoft Word, Microsoft Excel, and Microsoft PowerPoint. When you write your cover letter and resume, you need to emphasize your competency in these programs.

After you receive a call to schedule an interview, you must prepare for presenting yourself in the most persuasive manner. Career books and Web sites abound with advice on what questions to expect, what questions to ask, and what clothes to wear. In the typical 30-minute interview, you will be judged on your communications skills, leadership ability, maturity, and intelligence.

No doubt you also will be asked questions about your computer expertise. While you can list these skills on your resume and discuss them with the interviewer, nothing is more persuasive than actually demonstrating your proficiency. One of the most influential methods of showing this technological knowledge is with an electronic portfolio.

The portfolio concept is not new; artists, architects, and journalists routinely bring three-ring notebooks, scrapbooks, and folders to interviews to showcase their actual drawings and writings. But today's technology-savvy students have transformed these tangible notebooks to electronic notebooks.

Job hunters today are using Microsoft PowerPoint to display their projects, describe their experiences, and demonstrate their skills. For example, elementary education majors can import photographs taken during their student teaching experiences. Computer science majors can include flowcharts, documentation, and hypertext links to projects published to class Web pages. Music majors can import video clips of their performances. These interviewees can give interviewers copies of their presentations on a floppy disk to peruse at their convenience and to share with other employees at the worksite.

In this project, you will create an electronic portfolio for Benito Kovich, a student seeking a job in the fields of management or information systems. This presentation highlights his skills and experiences by including clip art, a photoraph, and a video clip. Benito can customize this portfolio for each interview by using Visual Basic for Applications, a programming language that extends PowerPoint's capabilities.

Recruiters state that interviewees who display eye-catching, professional looking electronic portfolios often have a definite edge over the typical interviewee. By applying the concepts you learn in this project, carefully developing your portfolio, and planning for the interview, you will be on your way to interviewing success.

Microsoft PowerPoint 2000

Using Visual Basic for Applications (VBA) with PowerPoint

CASE PERSPECTIVE

When students apply for a job and then receive an invitation to interview, they focus their efforts on presenting themselves in the best light.

Some candidates develop electronic career portfolios using PowerPoint to show on notebook computers during the interviews. Your neighbor, Benito Kovich, has asked you to help him develop a slide show for several interviews. Benito is majoring in management and minoring in information technology, and he has secured job interviews in both fields. He wants to tailor his slide show for each prospective employer.

You examine the information Benito wants to emphasize in the slide show and decide the best method for him to customize each presentation is to use a form you develop using Visual Basic for Applications. Benito's responses on the form will create a unique slide show for each interview. You also will create a toolbar and add buttons and then add a command to the File menu to simplify the related tasks he must perform: saving the presentation as a Web page, using the Pack and Go Wizard, printing a handout of his slides, and displaying the form.

Introduction

Before a computer can take an action and produce a desired result, it must have a step-by-step description of the task to be accomplished. This series of precise instructions is called a **procedure,** which also is called a **program** or **code.** The process of writing a procedure is called **computer programming.** Every PowerPoint command on a menu and button on a toolbar has a corresponding procedure that executes when you click the command or button. When the computer **executes** a procedure, it carries out the step-by-step instructions. In a Windows environment, the instructions associated with a task are executed when an **event** takes place, such as clicking a button, an option button, or a check box.

Because a command or button does not exist for every possible task, Microsoft has included a powerful programming language called **Visual Basic for Applications (VBA).** This language allows you to customize and extend PowerPoint's capabilities.

In this project, you will learn how create macros using a code generator called a **macro recorder.** A **macro** is a procedure composed of VBA code that automates multi-step tasks. By simply executing a macro, the user can perform tasks that would otherwise require many keystrokes. You also will add buttons to toolbars. You will add a command to a menu and associate it with a print macro. Finally, you will learn the basics of VBA.

The slide show you create in this project will help Benito Kovich in his job search. As he goes to each interview, he will open the BK Career Portfolio file on his notebook computer and then open a form. He will make selections on the form to indicate whether the position is in management or information systems, the company name, the type of clip art, and slide order. He then can decide to run the presentation immediately or later. VBA will create the presentation corresponding to his selections. Two possible slide shows are shown in Figures 6-1a through 6-1h.

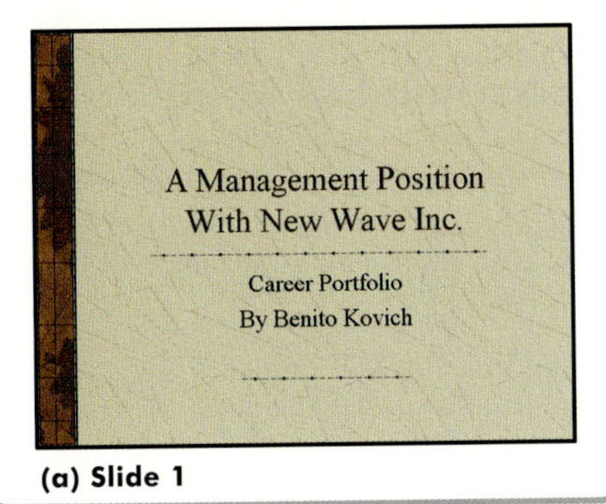

(a) Slide 1

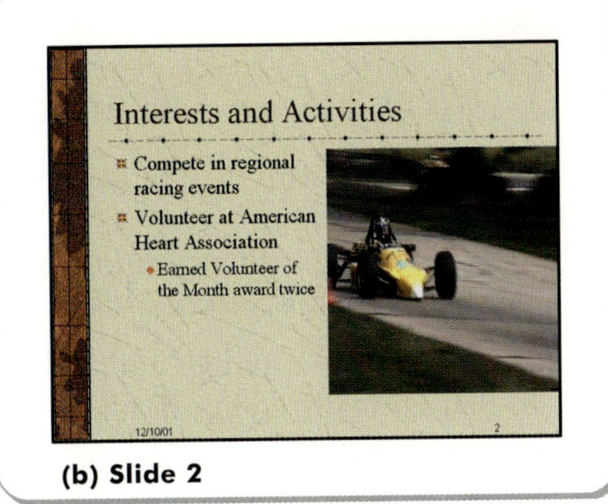

(b) Slide 2

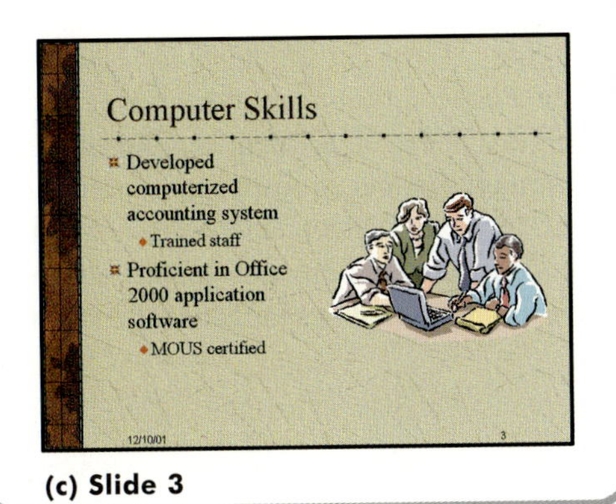

(c) Slide 3

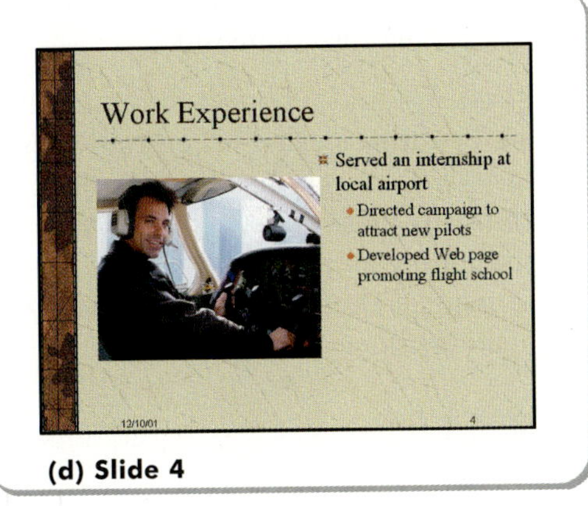

(d) Slide 4

Slide Presentation No. 1

(e) Slide 1

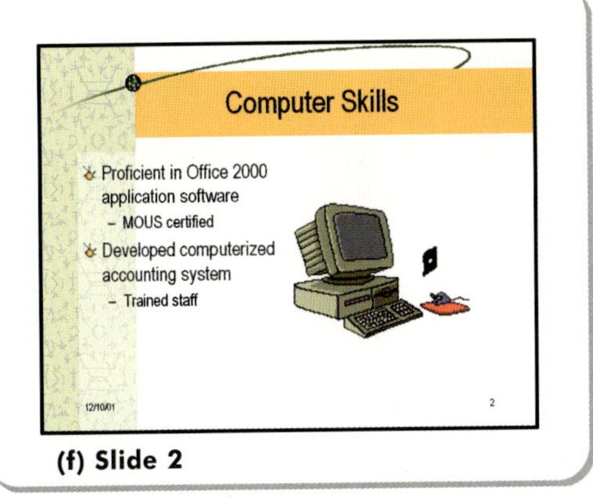

(f) Slide 2

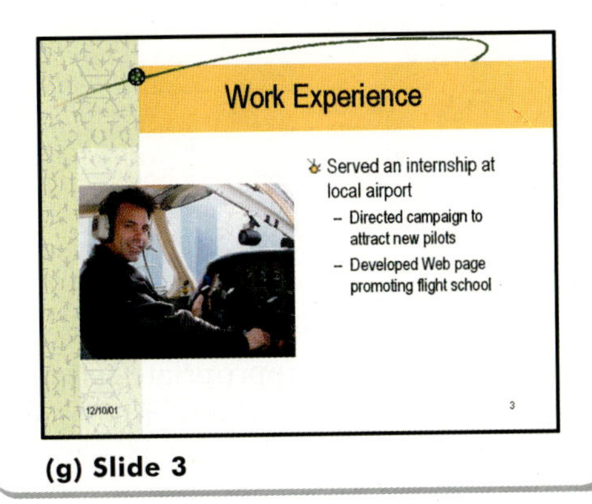

(g) Slide 3

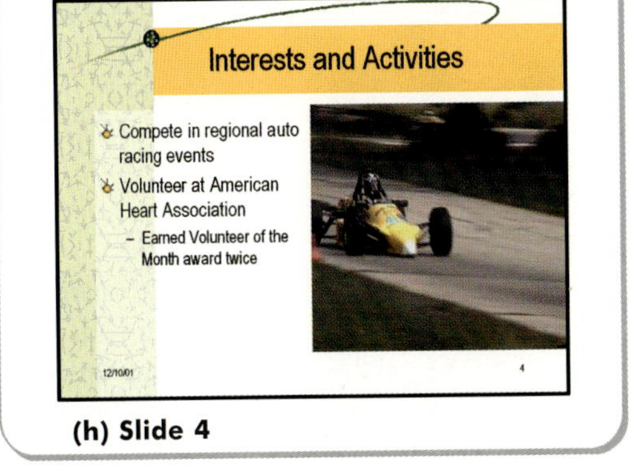

(h) Slide 4

Slide Presentation No. 2

FIGURE 6-1

Project Six — Creating an Electronic Portfolio

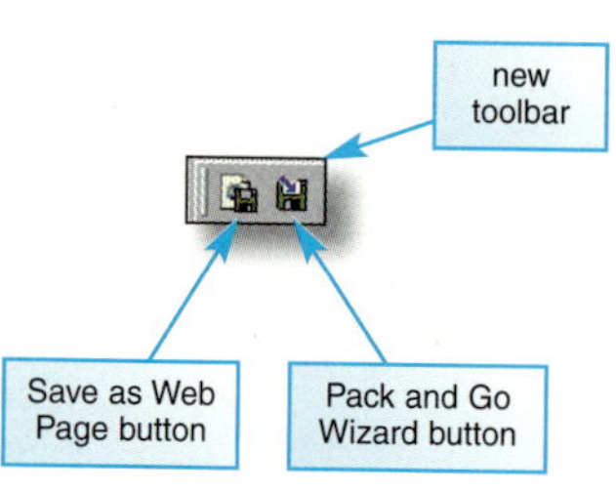

FIGURE 6-2

When you meet with Benito, you identify the following project requirements for his electronic portfolio:

Needs: The portfolio requires an easy-to-use interface. This interface will be implemented in three phases:

Phase 1 – Create a toolbar and add two buttons (Save as Web Page and Pack and Go) that normally do not display on any toolbar (Figure 6-2).

Phase 2 – Use the macro recorder to create a macro that prints handouts that display four slides per page vertically using the Pure black and white option. Assign the macro to a command on the File menu (Figure 6-3) so Benito can execute the macro by clicking the command.

Phase 3 – Add a button to the toolbar created in Phase 1 that displays a form allowing Benito to design his custom presentation (Figure 6-4). This form lets Benito select the type of position for which he is applying (management or computer), enter the company name, select clip art, change the slide order, and select whether to run the slide show immediately or later. The VBA code verifies that Benito has entered data or made a choice in each part of the form. If he has not, he is prompted to continue making choices on the form.

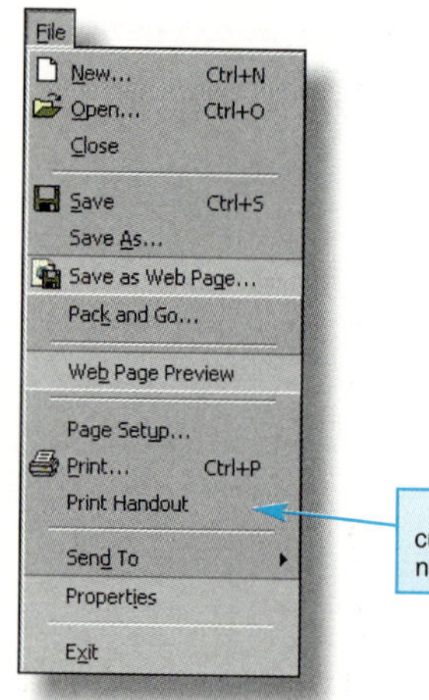

FIGURE 6-3

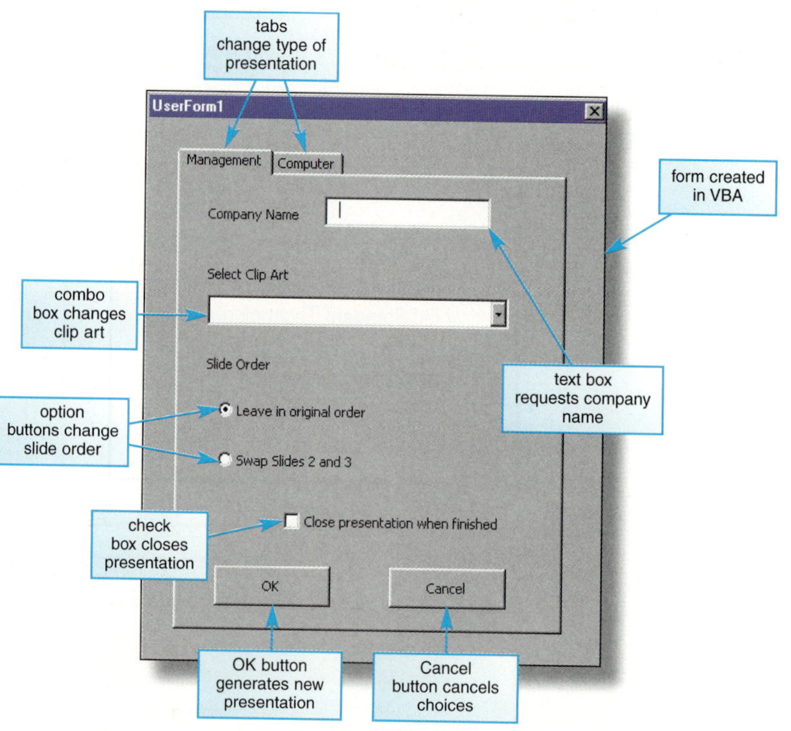

FIGURE 6-4

Source of Data: While meeting with Benito, you develop a preliminary presentation that he will complete by making appropriate selections on a form. This slide show shown in Figures 6-5a through 6-5d is available to you on the Data Disk under the file name BK Career Portfolio.

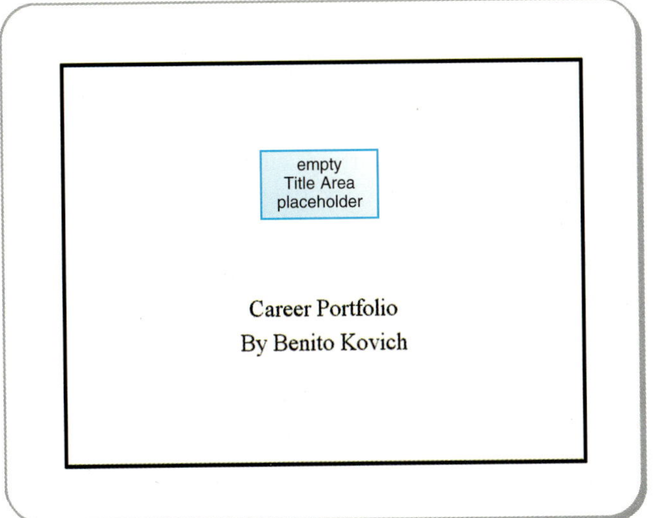

(a) Slide 1

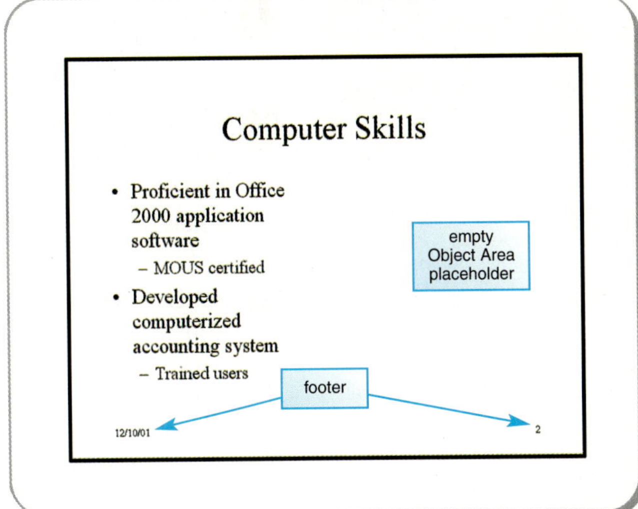

(b) Slide 2

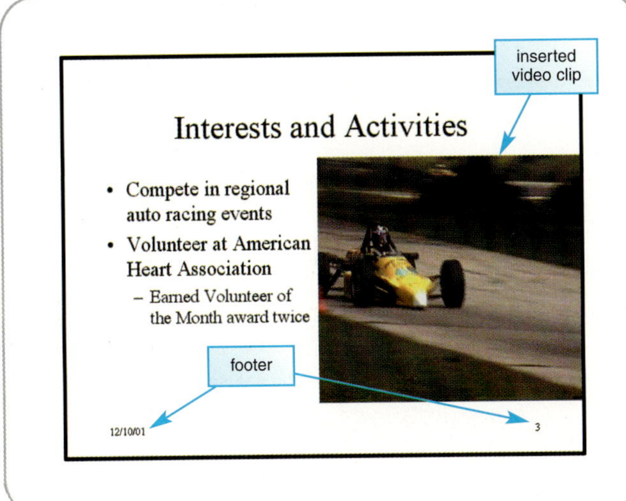

(c) Slide 3

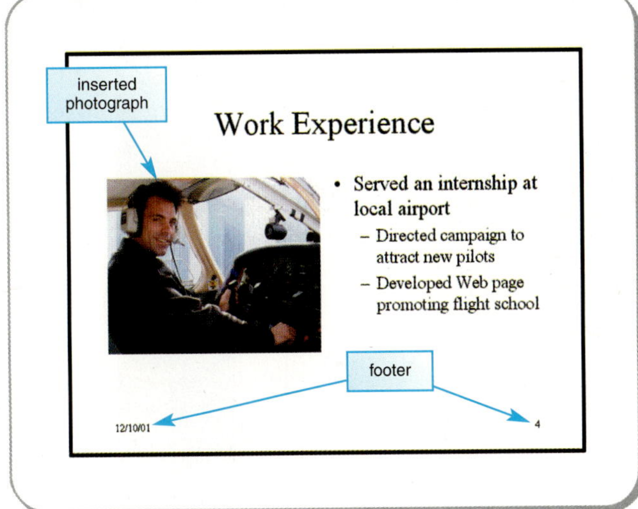

(d) Slide 4

FIGURE 6-5

Opening a Presentation and Saving it with a New File Name

To begin, start PowerPoint and open the BK Career Portfolio file on the Data Disk. Then reset the toolbars and menus so they display exactly as shown in this book. Perform the following steps.

TO OPEN A PRESENTATION AND SAVE IT WITH A NEW FILE NAME

1. Insert your Data Disk into Drive A. See the inside back cover of this book for directions for downloading the Data Disk.
2. Click the Start button on the taskbar and then click Open Office Document.
3. When the Open Office Document dialog box displays, click the Look in box arrow and then click 3½ Floppy (A:). Double-click BK Career Portfolio in the list.
4. When the BK Career Portfolio presentation displays, click View on the menu bar, click Toolbars, and then click Customize.

Electronic Portfolios

Job seekers are using electronic portfolios to emphasize their accomplishments and strengths. They are running the slide shows during interviews, mailing the files on floppy disks along with resumes, and posting the presentations on their personal home pages. Employers are impressed with the creativity and efforts these interviewees display in these presentations. To learn more about electronic portfolios, visit the PowerPoint 2000 Project 6 More About page (www.scsite.com/pp2000/more.htm) and click Portfolios.

5. When the Customize dialog box displays, click the Options tab, make sure the top three check boxes in the Personalized Menus and Toolbars area have check marks, click the Reset my usage data button, and then click the Yes button.
6. Click the Toolbars tab. Click Standard in the toolbars list, click the Reset button, and then click the OK button. Click Formatting, click the Reset button, and then click the OK button. Click Drawing, click the Reset button, and then click the OK button. Click Menu Bar, click the Reset button, and then click the OK button. Click the Close button.
7. Click File on the menu bar and then click Save As. Type `Electronic Portfolio` in the File name text box.
8. Click the Save button in the Save As dialog box.

The presentation is saved on the floppy disk in drive A with the file name, Electronic Portfolio (Figure 6-6).

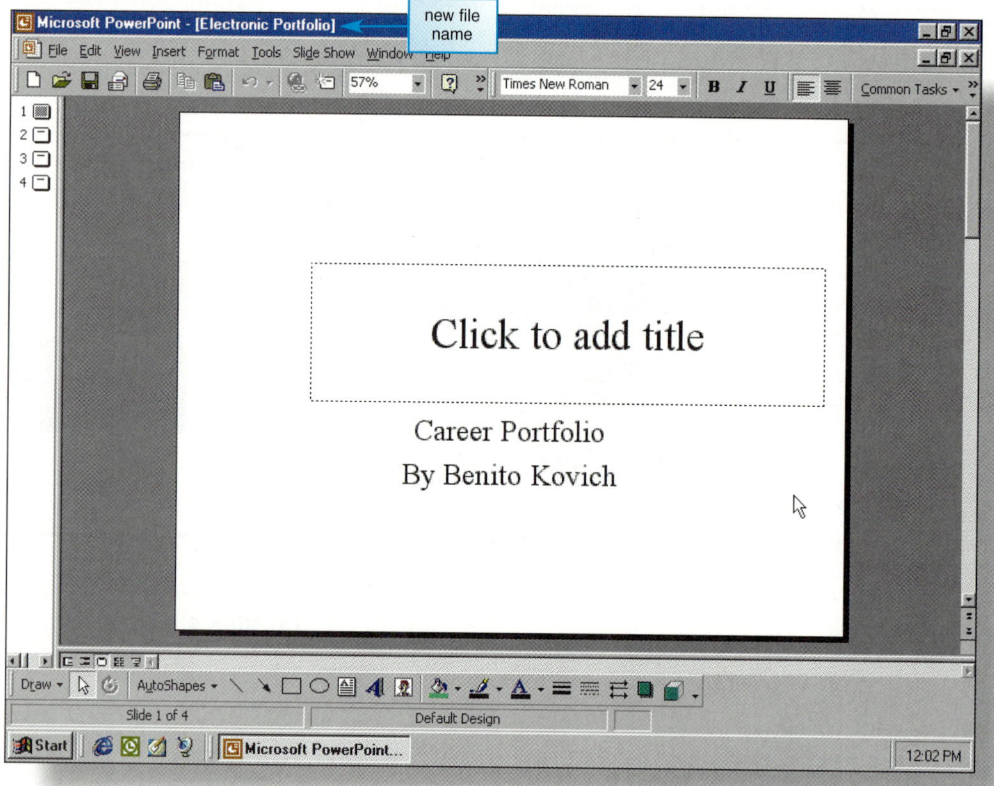

FIGURE 6-6

The Electronic Portfolio presentation is composed of four slides (Figure 6-5 on the previous page). The first is a title slide with an empty Title Area placeholder and Benito's identifying information in the Object Area placeholder. Benito will enter the company name in the Visual Basic form you will create in Phase 3 of this project, and this name will be inserted automatically in the Title Area placeholder.

Slide 2 describes Benito's computer expertise, and it uses the Text & Clip Art AutoLayout. The Object Area placeholder is empty, but it will contain one of four possible clip art files based on the selection Benito makes in the Visual Basic form. If he wants the presentation to have an information technology theme, he will select either an airplane dropping floppy diskettes or an animated computer. If he wants a management theme, he will select either clip art of people having a discussion or an animated man making a presentation.

Slide 3 highlights Benito's interests and activities. He actively competes in auto races, and you accompanied him to a local racecourse to shoot some video to insert in this presentation. In addition, Benito spends some of his spare time volunteering at the local American Heart Association. He wants to emphasize this activity and the awards he received for his efforts.

Slide 4 emphasizes Benito's work experience at the local airport. One of the most valuable experiences in his college career has been this internship, so he wants potential employers to understand his accomplishments during this full-year project. One of his activities was developing an advertising campaign to attract regional pilots to the airport to rent hangar space and buy fuel for their planes. Another achievement was developing a Web page to encourage students to take flying lessons. Benito supplied you with a photo of himself at the controls of one of the airplanes. You scanned this photo to create a digitized file that you inserted in the presentation.

Slides 2, 3, and 4 have a footer that contains the current date and the slide number. In addition, as seen in Figure 6-7, they use the Split Horizontal Out slide transition and the Split Vertical In preset animation effect. Slide 1 automatically advances in 10 seconds or when you click the mouse, and Slides 2, 3, and 4 advance 15 seconds after they display or when you click the mouse.

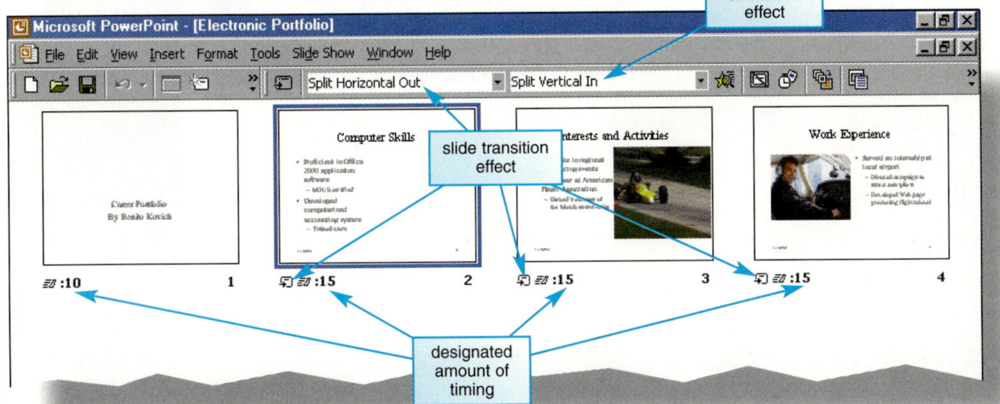

FIGURE 6-7

Voice Narration

To make your presentations even more vivid for your audiences, record narration and synchronize this sound with the slides. To record with a microphone, click Record Narration on the Slide Show menu, set the microphone level, and then choose to make the sound an embedded or a linked object. You also can rerecord narration, slide by slide, if you want to update information. When you run the slide show, the narration will automatically play with the show. To run the slide show without narration, click Set Up Show on the Slide Show menu, and then click Show without narration.

Phase 1 — Creating a Toolbar and Adding Two Buttons

The first phase of this project creates a toolbar that displays in the lower-right corner of the screen beside the Drawing toolbar. Although PowerPoint provides more than a dozen toolbars for a variety of purposes, a custom toolbar allows you to display the buttons specific to your needs.

Creating and Customizing a Toolbar

One of the buttons you will add to the custom toolbar is the Save as Web Page button. Although a user can save a file as a Web page by clicking the Save as Web Page command on the File menu, he also can click a button when he wants to make his presentation available for potential employers to view on the Internet. The second button you will add to the custom toolbar in this phase of the project will launch the Pack and Go Wizard. A user can click this button when he wants to compress his presentation files onto floppy disks. He then can transport his presentation on floppy disks to show on a computer at the interviewing site, rather than viewing

Deleting Toolbars

Once you create a toolbar, you may decide to delete it. To delete a custom toolbar, click Customize on the Tools menu and then click the Toolbars tab. Select the custom toolbar in the Toolbars box that you want to delete, and then click the Delete button. You cannot delete a built-in toolbar. If you select a built-in toolbar in the Toolbars box, the Reset button displays. When you click the Reset button, PowerPoint restores that toolbar to its default buttons, menus, and submenus.

Renaming ScreenTips

Once you have added a button to a toolbar, you can change its ScreenTip. To make this change, click Customize on the Tools menu, right-click the button, type the new name in the Name text box, and then press the ENTER key. You will see the name change when you view the ScreenTip.

it on his notebook computer. You will learn more about using the Pack and Go Wizard in the Web Feature that follows this project.

You can customize toolbars and menus by adding buttons and commands, deleting buttons and commands, and changing the function of buttons and commands. Once you add a button to a toolbar or a command to a menu, you can assign a macro to the button or command. You customize a toolbar or menu by invoking the **Customize command** on the Tools menu. The key to understanding how to customize a toolbar or menu is to recognize that when you have the Customize dialog box open, PowerPoint's toolbars and menus are in Edit mode. Edit mode allows you to modify the toolbars and menus.

Perform the following steps to create a custom toolbar and add two buttons.

To Create a Custom Toolbar and Add Two Buttons

1 Click Tools on the menu bar and then point to Customize.

The Tools menu displays (Figure 6-8).

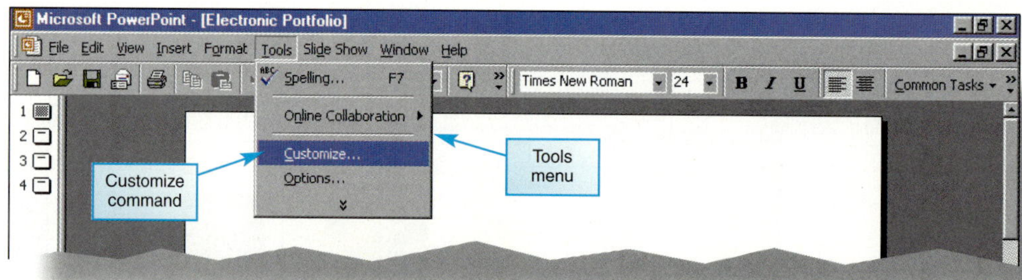

FIGURE 6-8

2 Click Customize. When the Customize dialog box displays, if necessary, click the Toolbars tab, and then point to the New button.

The Toolbars sheet in the Customize dialog displays as shown in Figure 6-9. The entire Standard and Formatting toolbars display.

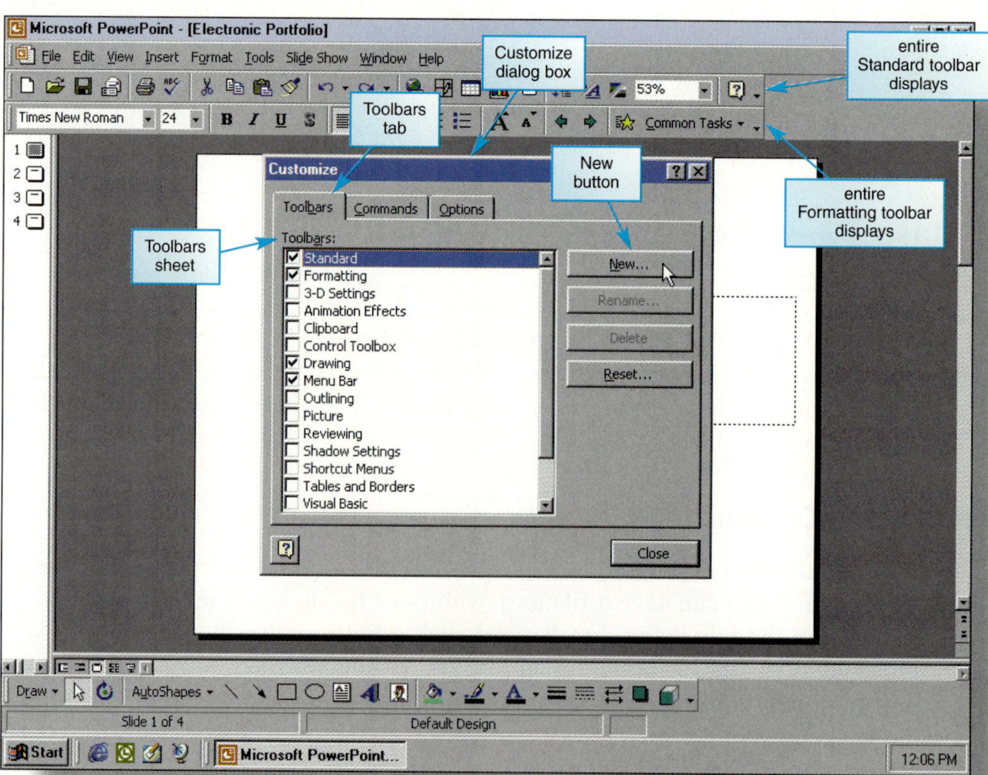

FIGURE 6-9

3 **Click the New button. When the New Toolbar dialog box displays, type** `Using Presentation` **in the Toolbar name text box and then point to the OK button (Figure 6-10).**

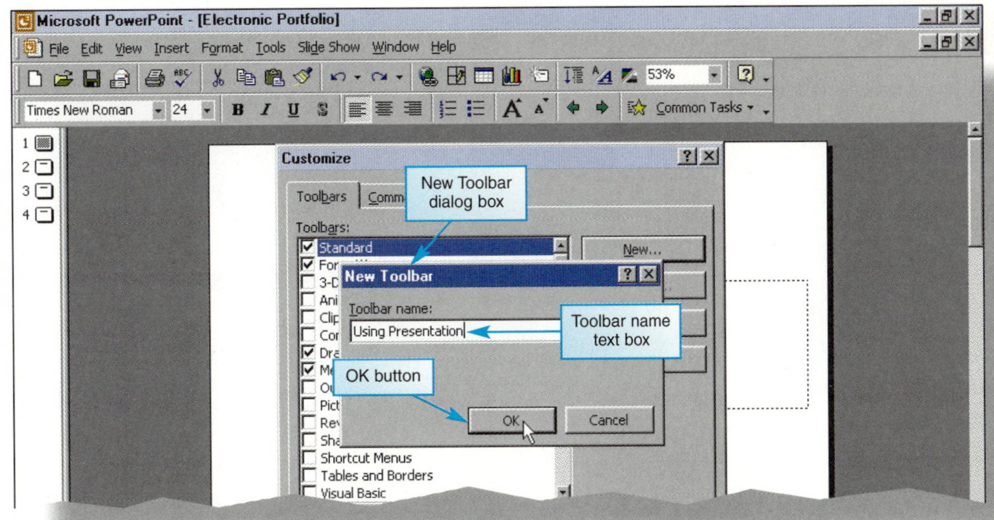

FIGURE 6-10

4 **Click the OK button. Click the toolbar and drag it to the bottom-right corner of the screen beside the Drawing toolbar.**

The Using Presentation toolbar displays in the desired location (Figure 6-11). The toolbar title does not display.

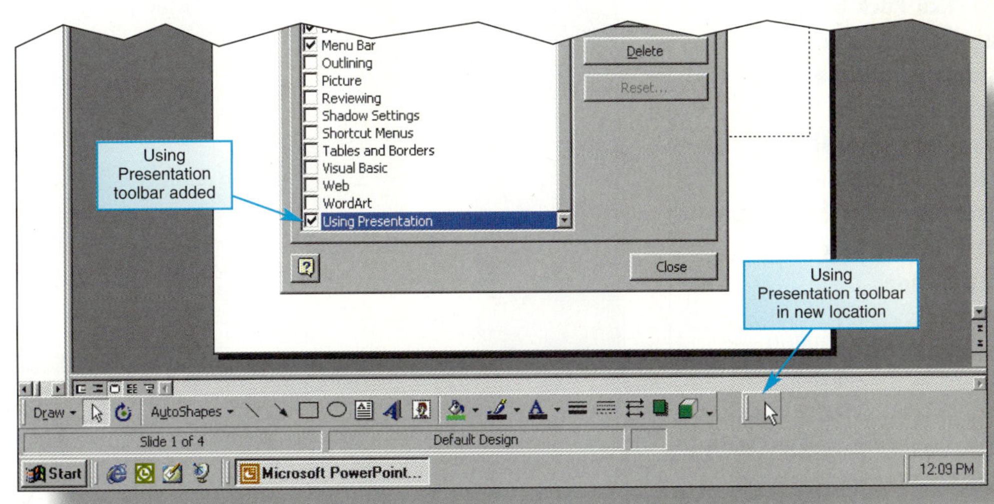

FIGURE 6-11

5 **Click the Commands tab in the Customize dialog box. Scroll down in the Commands list and then click Save as Web Page.**

You can select buttons from several categories, and each category has a variety of commands (Figure 6-12). File is the default category. Some commands have images associated with them.

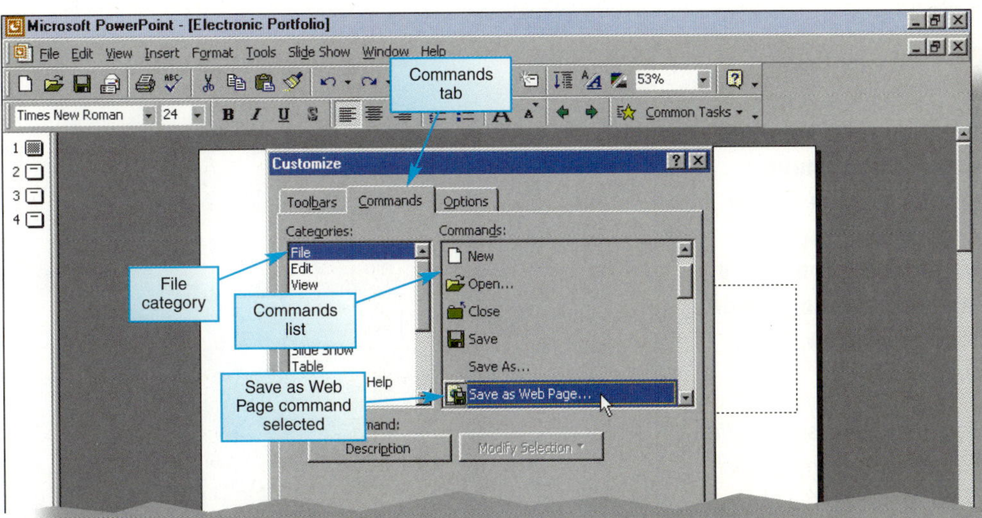

FIGURE 6-12

6 Drag the Save as Web Page command from the Commands list to the new Using Presentation toolbar.

The Save as Web Page button displays with an image on the Using Presentation toolbar (Figure 6-13). The heavy border surrounding the button indicates PowerPoint is in Edit mode.

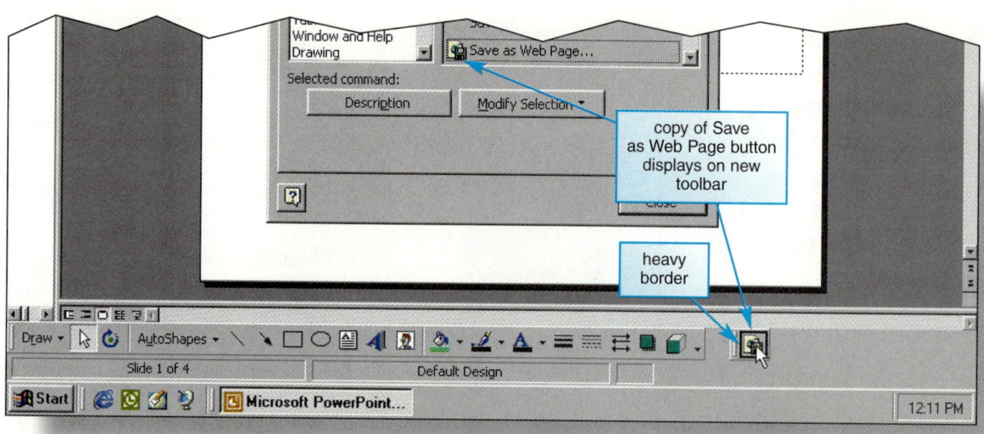

FIGURE 6-13

7 Scroll down in the Commands list and then click Pack and Go. Drag the Pack and Go command from the Commands list to the right of the Save as Web Page button on the Using Presentation toolbar. Point to the Modify Selection menu button.

The Pack and Go button displays on the Using Presentation toolbar with its name displaying on the face of the button (Figure 6-14). A heavy border surrounds the button, indicating that PowerPoint is in Edit mode.

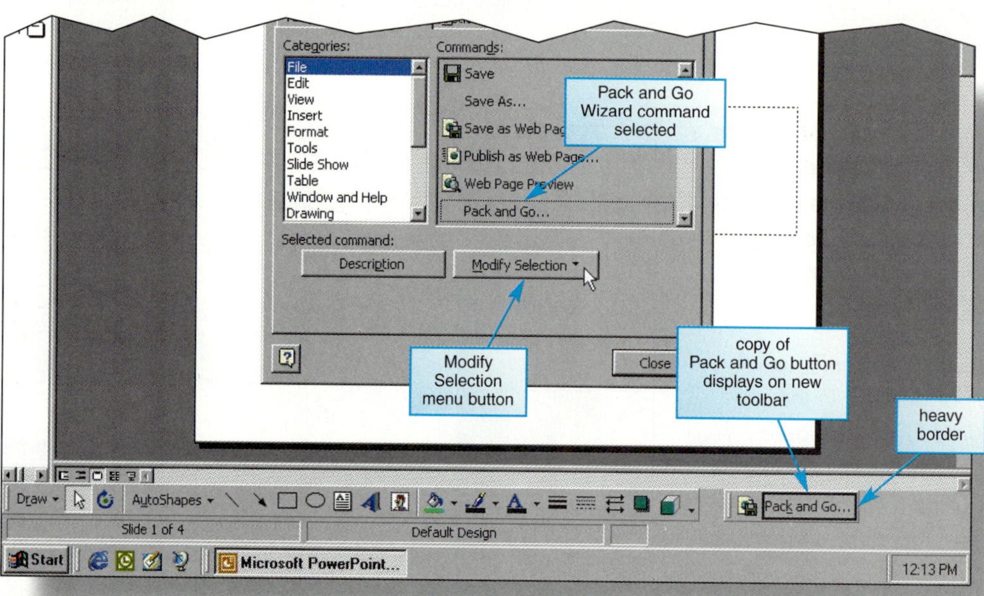

FIGURE 6-14

8 Click the Modify Selection menu button and then point to Change Button Image. When the Change Button Image palette displays, point to the button with a blue arrow pointing toward a floppy disk (row 1, column 6).

PowerPoint displays a palette of button images from which to choose (Figure 6-15).

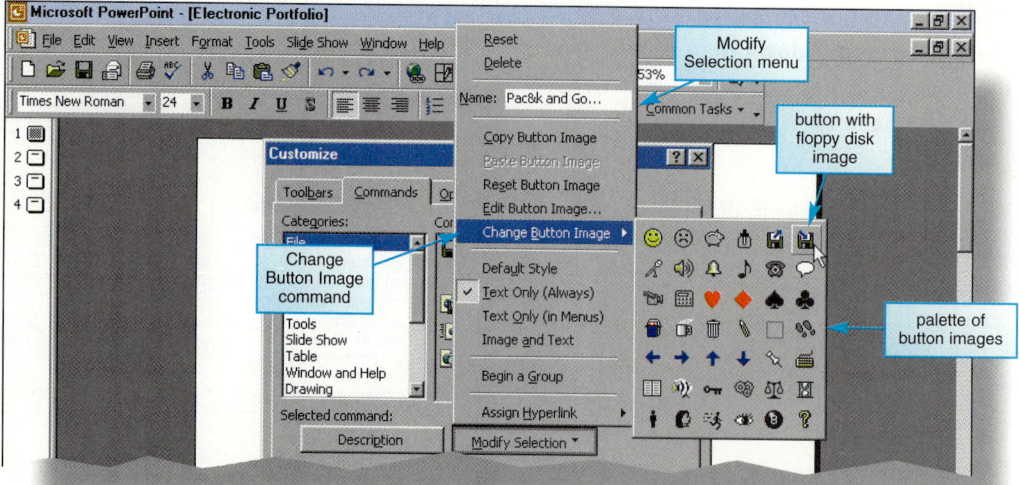

FIGURE 6-15

9 **Click the button with the floppy disk image. Point to the Modify Selection menu button.**

The Pack and Go button displays on the toolbar with the floppy disk image and the text, Pack and Go (Figure 6-16).

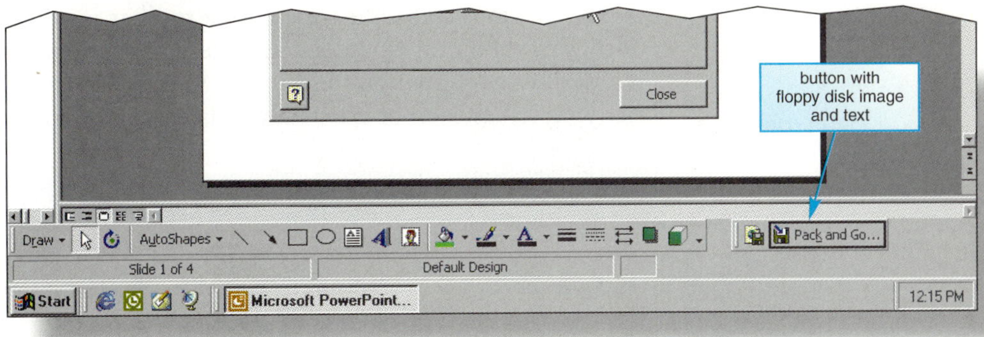

FIGURE 6-16

10 **Click the Modify Selection menu button and then point to Default Style.**

The default style includes only the image, not text (Figure 6-17).

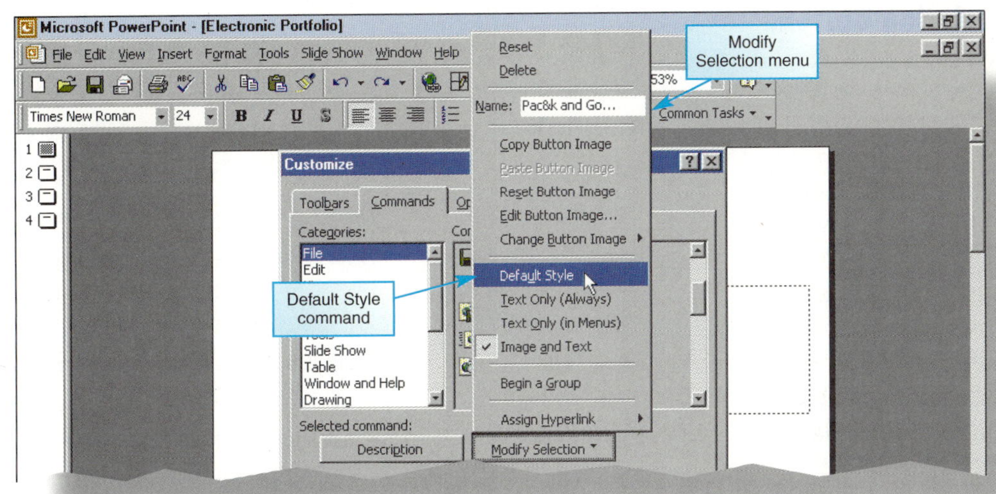

FIGURE 6-17

11 **Click Default Style. Point to the Close button.**

The Pack and Go button image displays with the floppy disk only (Figure 6-18).

12 **Click the Close button.**

PowerPoint exits Edit mode.

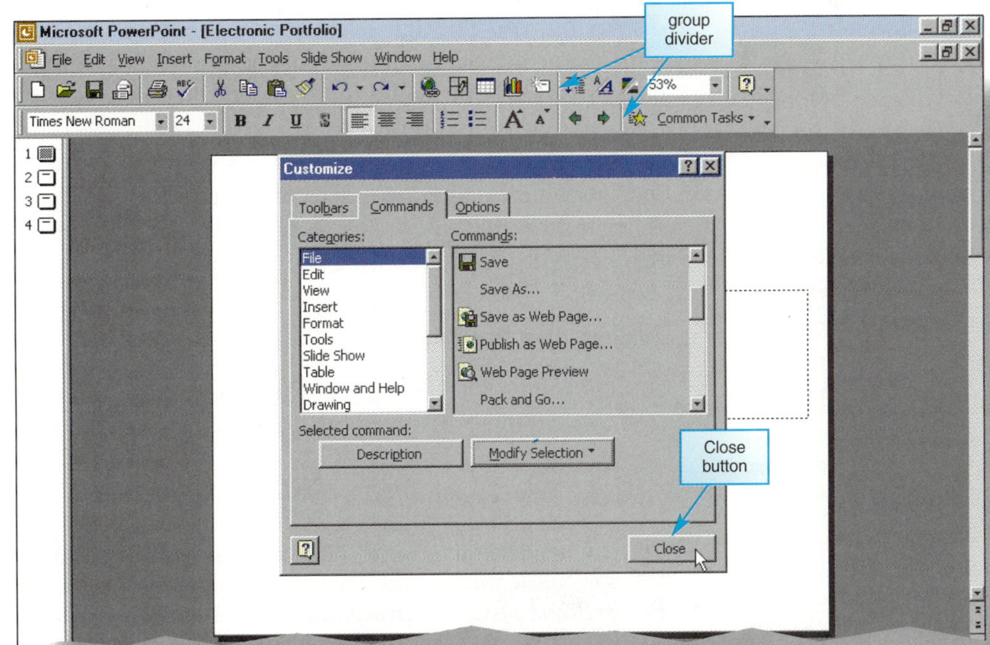

FIGURE 6-18

The previous steps illustrate how a toolbar is created easily and how buttons are added. PowerPoint includes a complete repertoire of commands for editing buttons on a toolbar as shown on the Modify Selection menu in Figure 6-17. Table 6-1 briefly describes each of the commands on this menu.

Table 6-1 Summary of Commands on the Modify Selection Menu

COMMAND	DESCRIPTION
Reset	Changes the image on the selected button to the original image and disassociates the macro with the button
Delete	Deletes the selected button
Name box	Changes the ScreenTip for a button and changes the command name for a command on a menu
Copy Button Image	Copies the button image to Office Clipboard
Paste Button Image	Pastes the button image on Office Clipboard onto selected button
Reset Button Image	Changes the button image back to the original image
Edit Button Image	Allows you to edit the button image
Change Button Image	Allows you to choose a new button image
Default Style; Text Only (Always); Text Only (in Menus); Image and Text	Allows you to choose one of the four styles to indicate how the button should display
Begin a Group	Groups buttons by drawing a vertical line (divider) on the toolbar (see the group dividing lines in Figure 6-18)
Assign Hyperlink	Assigns a hyperlink to a Web page or document
Assign Macro	Assigns a macro to the button

More About 2000

Deleting Buttons

When you delete a custom toolbar button, the button is deleted permanently. To remove a custom button and save it for later use, create a toolbar to store unused buttons, move the button to this storage toolbar, and then hide the storage toolbar. When you delete a built-in toolbar button, however, the button still is available in the Customize dialog box. Clicking the check box next to a button on the Add or Remove Buttons list does not remove the button from this list.

You can add as many buttons as you want to a toolbar. You also can change any button's function. For example, when in edit mode with the Customize dialog box displaying, you can right-click the Save button on the Standard toolbar and assign it a macro or hyperlink. The next time you click the Save button, the macro will execute or PowerPoint will launch the application associated with the hyperlink, rather than save the presentation.

You reset the toolbars to their installation default by clicking the Toolbars tab in the Customize dialog box, selecting the toolbar in the Toolbars list, and clicking the Reset button. Because it is so easy to change the buttons on a toolbar, each project in this book begins by resetting the toolbars.

Other Ways

1. Press ALT+T, press C, press ALT+B, press ALT+N, type new name, press ENTER, drag toolbar to desired location, press ALT+C, press ALT+D, press DOWN ARROW seven times, drag command to new toolbar, press DOWN ARROW three times, drag command to new toolbar, press ALT+M, press B, press RIGHT ARROW five times, press ENTER, press ALT+M, press U, press TAB key two times, press ENTER

Saving the Presentation

The changes to Phase 1 of the presentation are complete. Perform the following step to save the presentation before recording a macro in Phase 2 of this project.

TO SAVE A PRESENTATION

1. Click the Save button  on the Standard toolbar.

PowerPoint saves the presentation by saving the changes made to the presentation since the last save.

Phase 2 — Recording a Macro and Assigning It to a Menu Command

The second phase of the project creates a macro to print a handout displaying four slides per page vertically using the Pure black and white option. The default PowerPoint print setting is Slides, with one slide printing on each sheet of paper. When the Print what setting is changed to handouts, the default setting is six slides per page in a horizontal order, meaning Slides 1 and 2 display at the top of the page, and Slides 3 and 4 display below. The user can distribute a one-page handout, shown in Figure 6-19, of the four slides in the presentation printed using the Pure black and white option and displayed vertically, meaning Slides 1 and 3 display on the top, and Slides 2 and 4 display below.

The planned macro will change the output from slides to handouts and will change the slide order on the handout from horizontal to vertical. The handout will print using the Pure black and white option instead of grayscale or other default setting on your system, so all shades of gray will change to either black or white. The macro then will reset the Print dialog box to its original settings.

With the macro, a user can print a one-page handout by executing a single command, rather than performing the several steps otherwise required. He can click the Print button on the Standard toolbar and change the settings in the Print dialog box to print these handouts, or he can execute the macro to print the handout. Once the macro is created, it will be assigned to a command on the File menu.

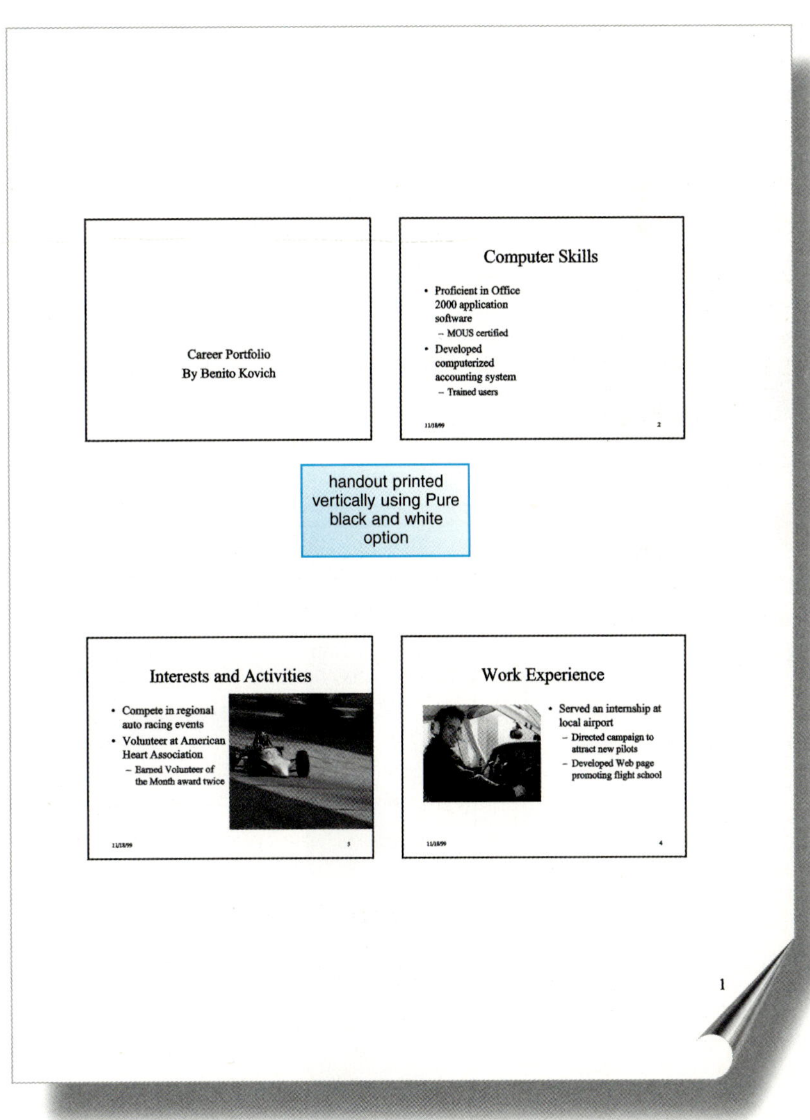

FIGURE 6-19

Recording a Macro

PowerPoint has a macro recorder that creates a macro automatically based on a series of actions you perform while it is recording. Like a tape recorder, the macro recorder records everything you do to a presentation over a period of time. The macro recorder can be turned on, during which time it records your activities, and then turned off to stop the recording. Once the macro is recorded, it can be **played back** or **executed** as often as you want.

Deleting Macros

Once you create a macro, you may decide you no longer need these steps. To delete a Macro, point to Macro on the Tools menu and then click Macros. Click the name of the macro in the Macro name box that you want to delete. Then click the Delete button.

It is easy to create a macro. All you have to do is turn on the macro recorder and carry out these steps:

1. Start the macro recorder.
2. Change the output settings from slides to handouts, the slides per page from six to four, the slide order on the handout from horizontal to vertical, and the print option from Grayscale (or default print setting on your computer) to Pure black and white.
3. Print the handout.
4. Restore the output settings from four slides per page to six, from vertical to horizontal slide order, from handouts to slides, and from Pure black and white to Grayscale (or the default print setting on your computer).
5. Stop the macro recorder.

What is impressive about the macro recorder is that you actually step through the task as you create the macro. You will see exactly what the macro will do before you use it.

When you first create the macro, you must name it. The name is used to reference the macro when you want to execute it. The name PrintHandout will be used for the macro. **Macro names** can be up to 255 characters long; they can contain numbers, letters, and underscores; they cannot contain spaces and other punctuation. Perform the following steps to record the macro.

To Record a Macro to Print Handouts in Vertical Slide Order in Pure Black and White

1 Click Tools on the menu bar, point to Macro, and then point to Record New Macro on the Macro submenu.

The Tools menu and Macro submenu display (Figure 6-20).

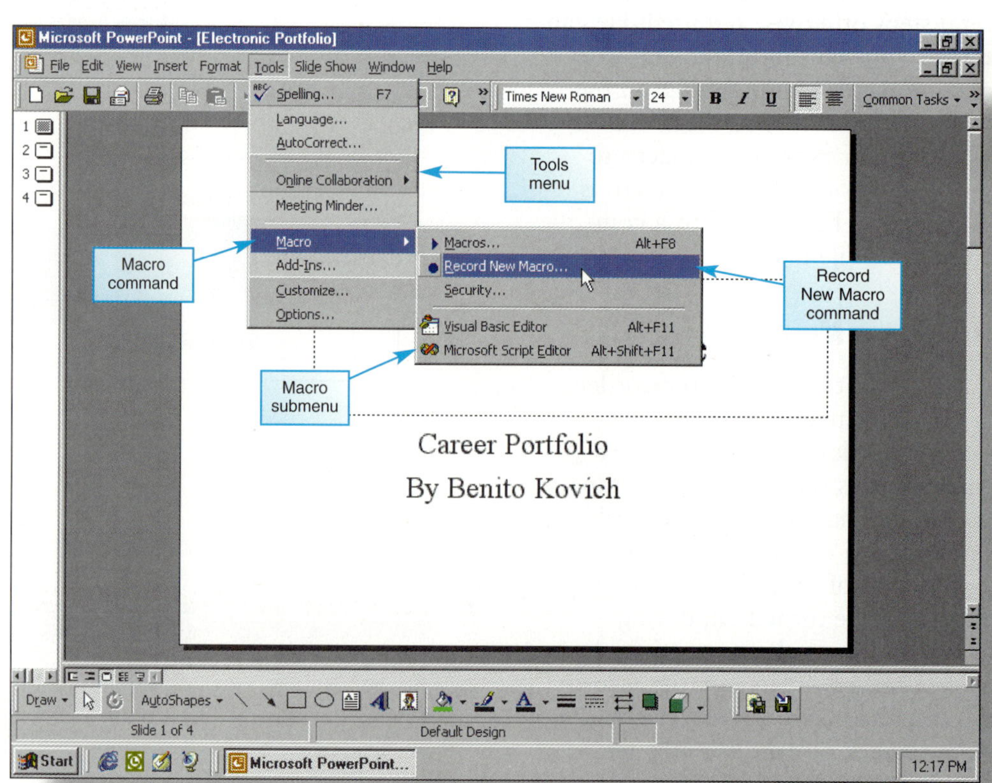

FIGURE 6-20

2 Click Record New Macro. When the Record Macro dialog box displays, type `PrintHandout` **in the Macro name text box. Type** `Macro prints pure black and white handouts in vertical slide order` **in the Description text box. Make sure the Store macro in box displays Electronic Portfolio. Point to the OK button.**

The Record Macro dialog box displays as shown in Figure 6-21.

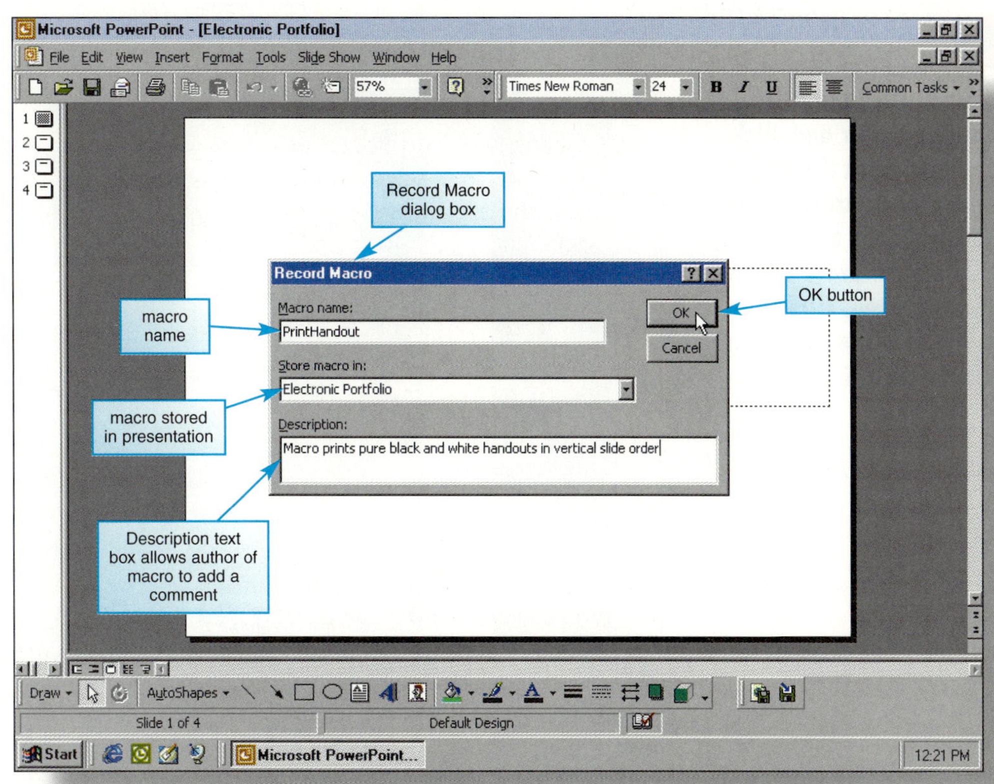

FIGURE 6-21

3 Click the OK button. Click File on the menu bar and then point to Print.

The Stop Recording toolbar and the File menu display (Figure 6-22). Any task you perform after the Stop Recording toolbar displays will be part of the macro. When you are finished recording the macro, you will click the Stop Recording button on the Stop Recording toolbar to end the recording.

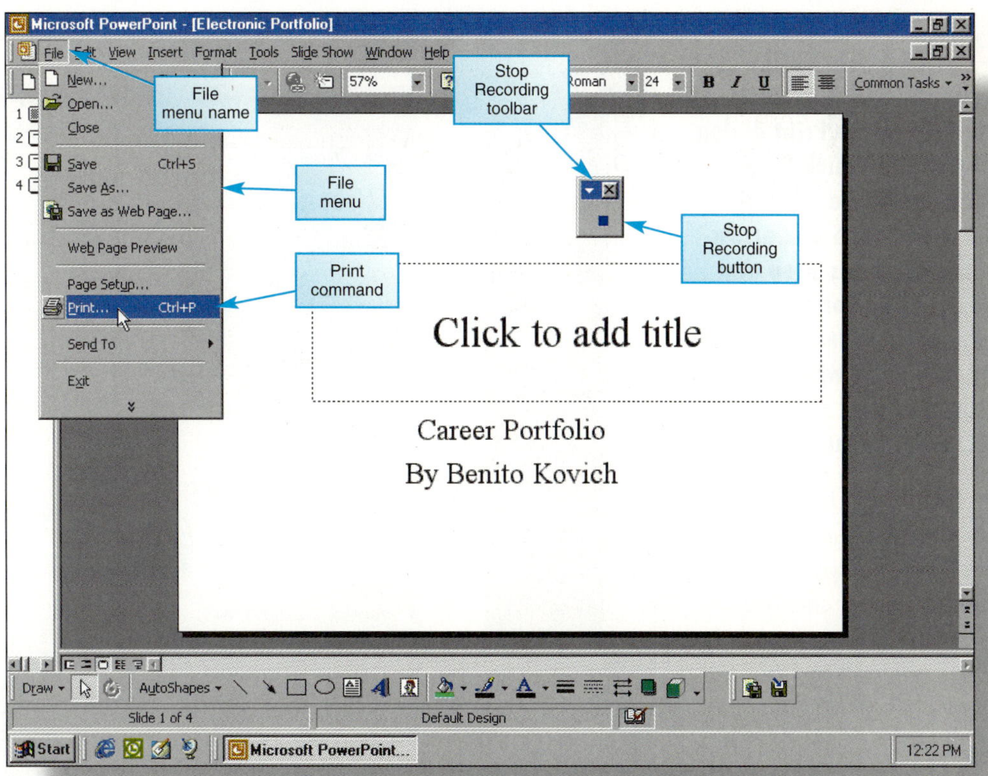

FIGURE 6-22

4 **Click Print. When the Print dialog box displays, click the Print what box arrow and click Handouts, click the Slides per page box arrow in the Handouts area and click 4, click Vertical order in the Handouts area, click Pure black and white, and then point to the OK button.**

The Print dialog box displays as shown in Figure 6-23.

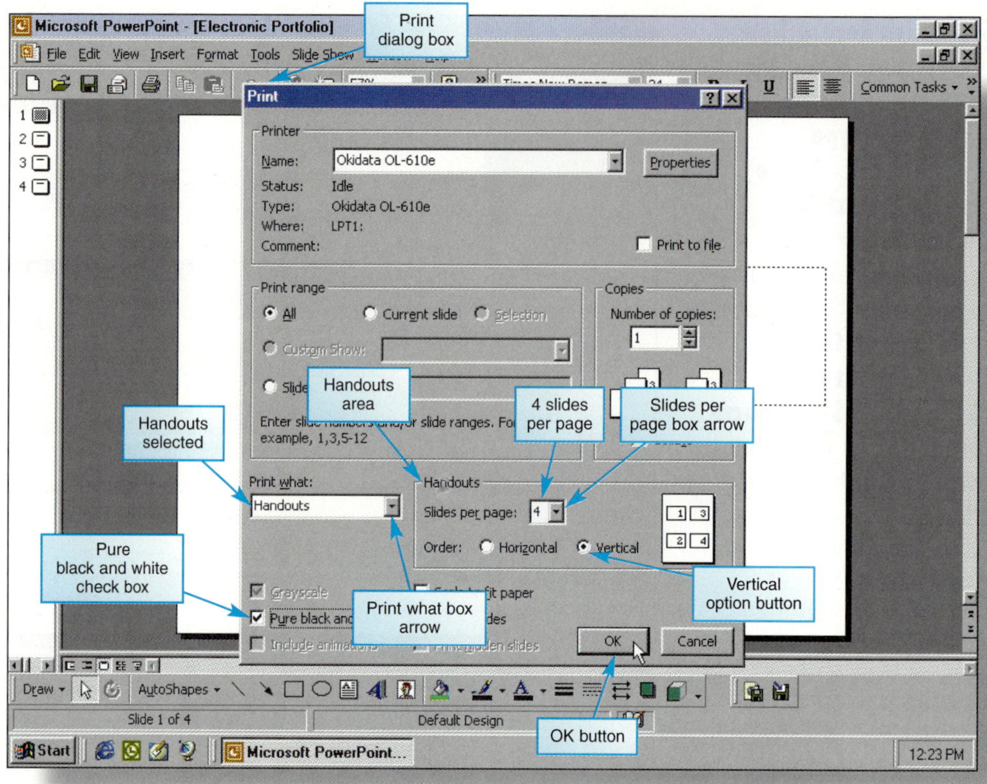

FIGURE 6-23

5 **Click the OK button. Click File on the menu bar and then click Print. When the Print dialog box displays, click Pure black and white, click the Slides per page box arrow in the Handouts area and click 6, click Horizontal order in the Handouts area, click the Print what box arrow and click Slides, and then point to the OK button.**

The Print dialog box displays as shown in Figure 6-24. The Pure black and white check box is no longer checked, restoring your computer to its default print setting. The printout resembles the handout shown in Figure 6-19 on page PP 6.15.

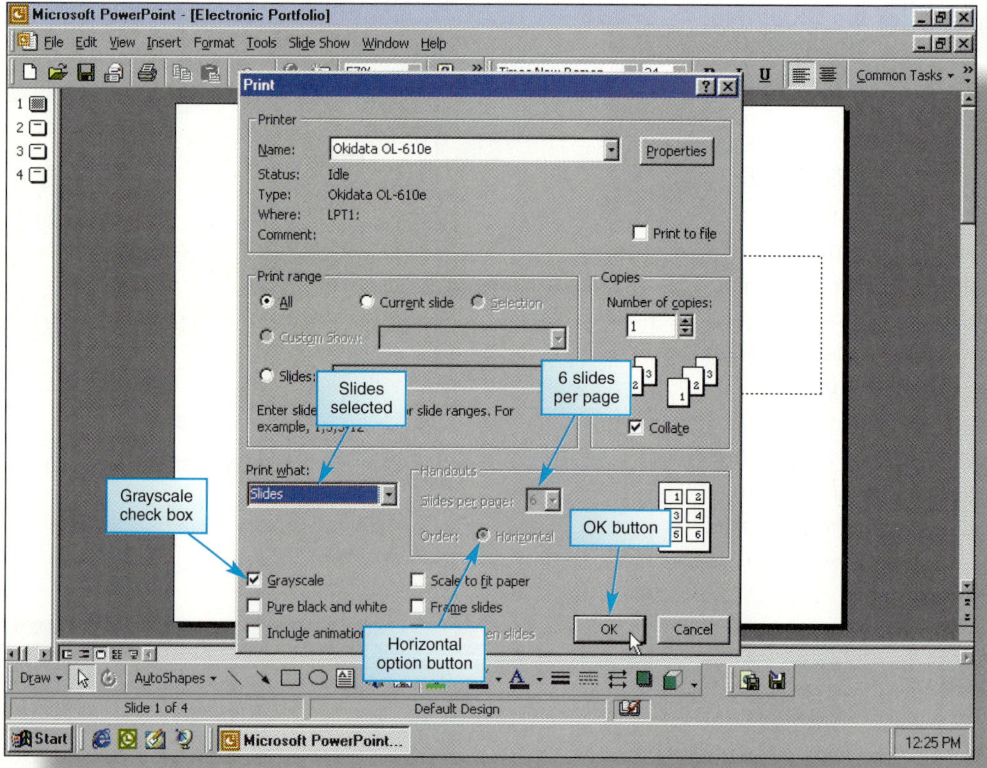

FIGURE 6-24

6 Click the OK button. Point to the Stop Recording button.

The four slides in the presentation print in the Pure black and white or your computer's default print option (Figure 6-25).

7 Click the Stop Recording button.

PowerPoint stops recording the printing activities and hides the Stop Recording toolbar.

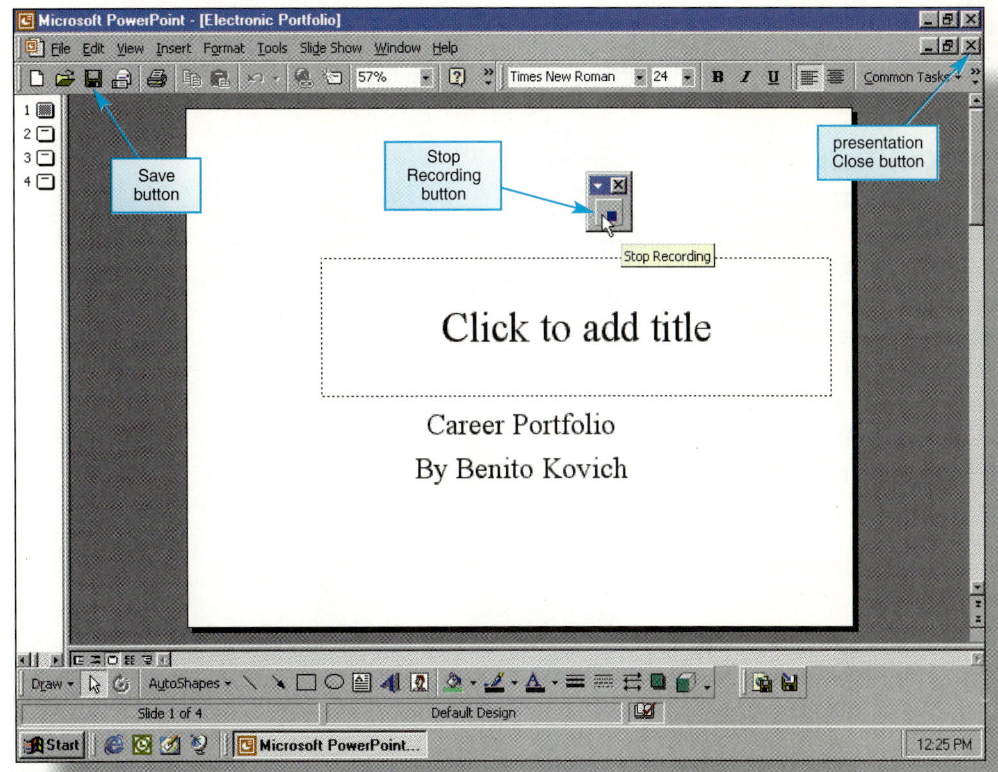

FIGURE 6-25

1. Click Record Macro button on Visual Basic toolbar
2. Press ALT+T, press M, press R

If you recorded the wrong actions, delete the macro and record it again. You delete a macro by clicking Tools on the menu bar, pointing to Macro on the Tools menu, and then clicking Macros on the Macro submenu. When the Macro dialog box displays, click the name of the macro (PrintHandout), and then click the Delete button. Then record the macro again.

Customizing a Menu

As you use PowerPoint to create presentations and print handouts, you may find yourself repeating many steps. You may find it convenient to simplify these repetitive processes by adding a button to a toolbar or a command to a menu that you can click to perform these tasks automatically. PowerPoint allows you to add commands to a button or to a menu. The steps on the next page show how to add a command to the File menu to execute the PrintHandout macro.

More About 2000

Deleting Commands

If you no longer need a command you added to a menu, you can delete this command. To perform this action, click Customize on the Tools menu, click the menu that contains the command you want to delete, and then drag the desired command off the menu.

To Add a Command to a Menu, Assign the Command to a Macro, and Invoke the Command

1 **Click Tools on the menu bar and then click Customize. When the Customize dialog box opens, if necessary, click the Commands tab. Scroll down in the Categories box and then click Macros. Click File on the menu bar to display the File menu.**

The Customize dialog box and File menu display as shown in Figure 6-26.

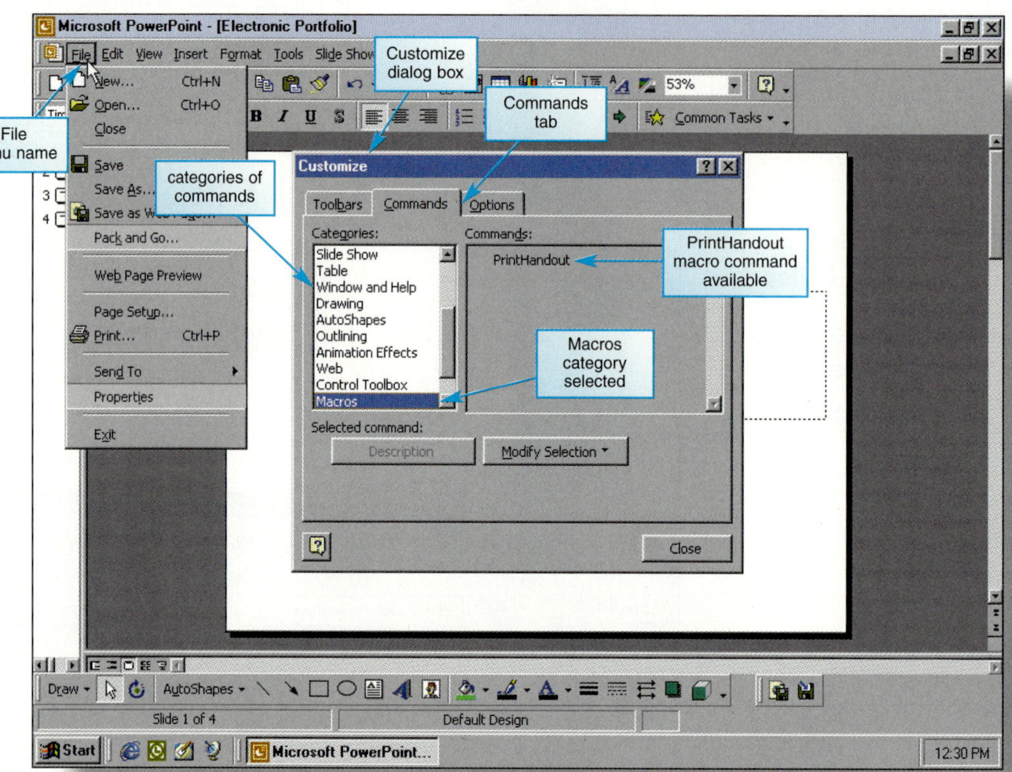

FIGURE 6-26

2 **Drag the PrintHandout entry from the Commands list in the Customize dialog box immediately below the Print command on the File menu.**

PowerPoint adds PrintHandout to the File menu (Figure 6-27). A heavy border surrounds PrintHandout on the File menu, indicating it is in the edit mode.

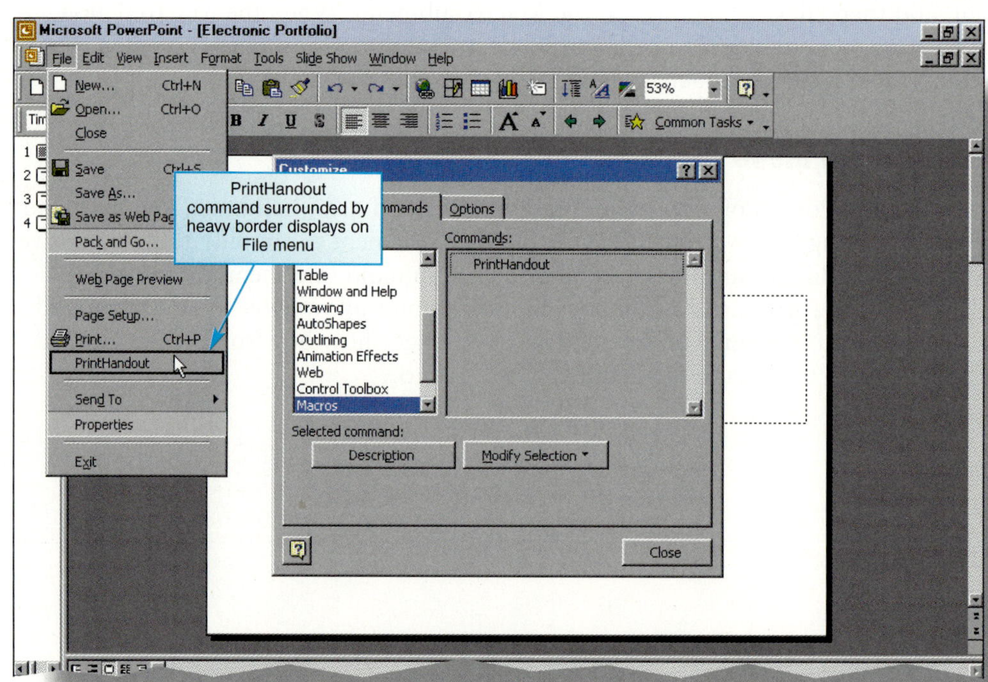

FIGURE 6-27

3 Right-click PrintHandout in the File menu and then click the Name text box on the shortcut menu. Type `Print Handout` as the new name of this command. Point to the Close button at the bottom of the Customize dialog box.

The shortcut menu displays (Figure 6-28).

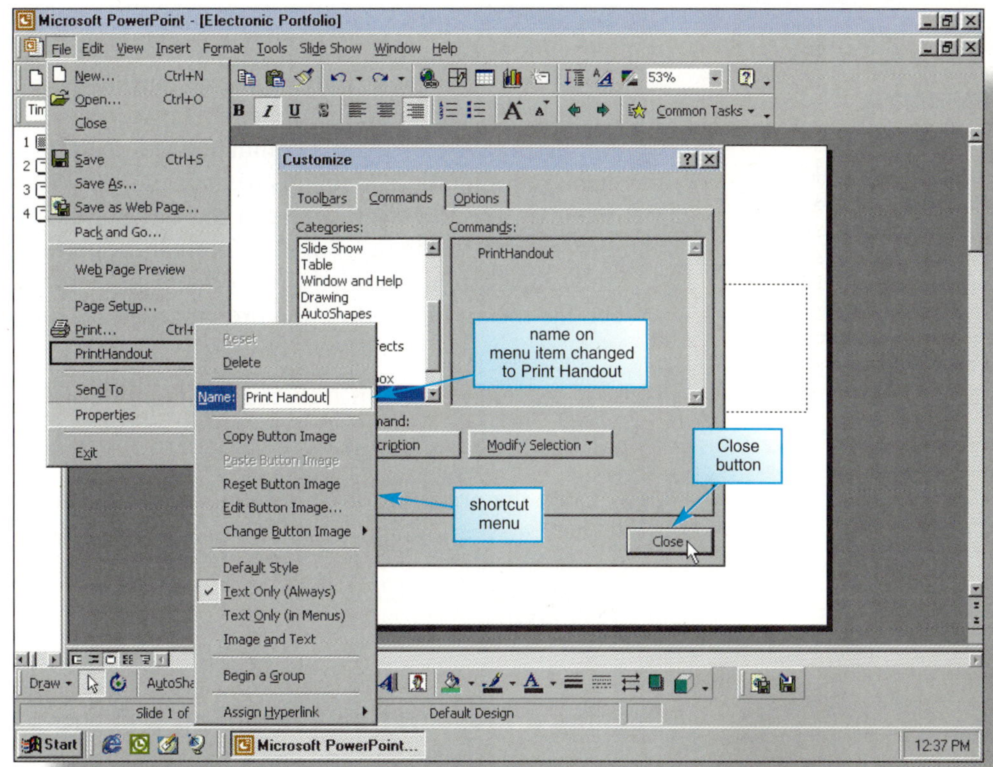

FIGURE 6-28

4 Click the Close button. Click File on the menu bar and then point to Print Handout.

PowerPoint exits the edit mode. The File menu displays with the new command, Print Handout, on the menu (Figure 6-29).

5 Click Print Handout on the File menu.

After several seconds, the handout prints as shown in Figure 6-19 on page PP 6.15. except it will be 1 3 / 2 4

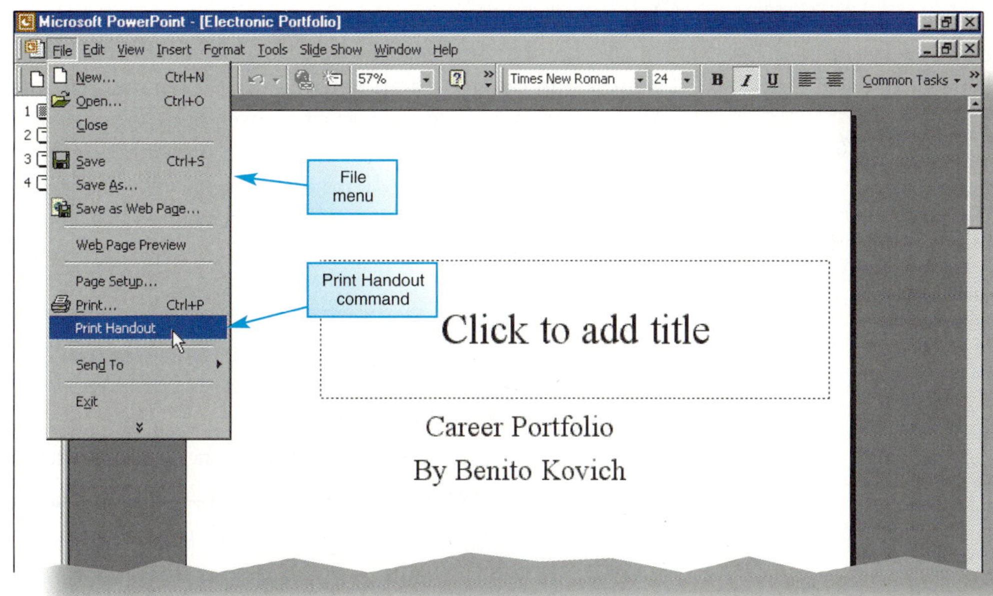

FIGURE 6-29

Other Ways

1. Right-click toolbar, click Customize on shortcut menu, click Commands tab
2. On View menu point to Toolbars, click Customize on Toolbars submenu, click Commands tab

More About

Renaming Commands

Once you have added a command to a menu, you can change its name. To rename a command, click Customize on the Tools menu, click the menu that contains the command, right-click the command, type a name in the Name text box, and then press the ENTER key.

You have the same customization capabilities with menus as you do with toolbars. All of the commands described in Table 6-1 on page PP 6.14 apply to menus as well. Any command specific to buttons pertains to editing the button on the left side of a command on a menu.

An alternative to adding a command to a menu is to add a new menu name to the menu bar and add commands to its menu. You can add a new menu name to the menu bar by selecting New Menu in the Categories list of the Customize dialog box and dragging New Menu from the Commands list to the menu bar.

Now that you have added the toolbar and macro to the presentation, you want to save the file and then close the presentation. Perform the following steps.

TO SAVE THE PRESENTATION AND CLOSE THE PRESENTATION

1. Click the Save button on the Standard toolbar.
2. Click the presentation's Close button on the right side of the menu bar to close the presentation and leave PowerPoint open.

PowerPoint saves the Electronic Portfolio presentation on drive A and then closes the presentation.

More About

Viruses

American electrical engineer Fred Cohen coined the term "virus" in 1983 to represent any program that copies itself. Since then, thousands of viruses have infected computer hardware, data files, and operating systems. To learn about the history of viruses, how the infections occur, and how to prevent viral infections, visit the PowerPoint 2000 Project 6 More About page (www.scsite.com/pp2000/more.htm) and click Virus.

Opening a Presentation Containing a Macro and Executing the Macro

A **computer virus** is a potentially damaging computer program designed to affect your computer negatively by infecting it and altering the way it works without your knowledge or permission. Currently, more than 13,000 known computer viruses exist, and an estimated six new viruses are discovered each day. The increased use of networks, the Internet, and e-mail has accelerated the spread of computer viruses.

To combat this evil, most computer users run antivirus programs that search for viruses and destroy them before they ever have a chance to infect the computer. Macros are a known carrier of viruses because people easily can add code to them. For this reason, each time you open a presentation with a macro associated with it, PowerPoint displays a Microsoft PowerPoint dialog box warning that a macro is attached and that macros can contain viruses. Table 6-2 summarizes the buttons users can use to continue the process of opening a presentation with macros.

Table 6-2 Buttons in the Microsoft PowerPoint Dialog Box When Opening a Presentation with Macros

BUTTONS	DESCRIPTION
Disable Macros	Macros are unavailable to the user
Enable Macros	Macros are available to the user to execute
More Info	Opens the Microsoft PowerPoint Help window and displays information on viruses and macros

If you are confident of the source (author) of the presentation and macros, click the Enable Macros button. If you are uncertain about the reliability of the source, then click the Disable Macros button. For more information on this topic, click the More Info button.

The following steps open the Electronic Portfolio presentation to illustrate the Microsoft PowerPoint dialog box that displays when a presentation contains a macro. The steps then show how to execute the recorded macro, PrintHandout.

To Open a Presentation with a Macro and Execute the Macro

1 With PowerPoint active, click File on the menu bar and then click Open. When the Open dialog box displays, click the Look in box arrow, and if necessary click 3½ Floppy (A:). Double-click the file name Electronic Portfolio. Point to the Enable Macros button.

PowerPoint displays the dialog box shown in Figure 6-30.

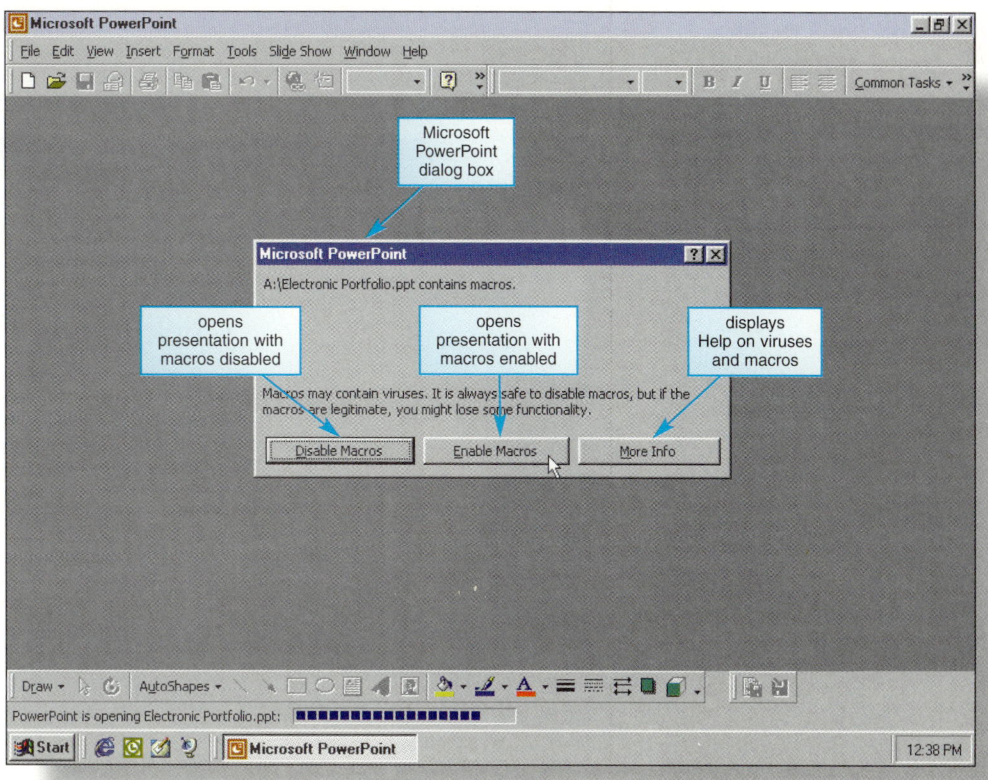

FIGURE 6-30

2 Click the Enable Macros button. When Slide 1 of the Electronic Portfolio displays, click File on the menu bar and then click Print Handout.

PowerPoint opens the Electronic Portfolio presentation, executes the macro, and then prints the handout and the four slides shown in Figures 6-5 and 6-19 on pages PP 6.7 and PP 6.15.

Other Ways

1. Click Run Macro button on Visual Basic toolbar
2. On Tools menu point to Macro, click Macros on Macro submenu, double-click macro name
3. Press ALT+F8, double-click macro name

If you are running antivirus software, you may want to turn off the security warning shown in Figure 6-30. You can turn off the security warning by clicking Tools on the menu bar, pointing to Macro, and then clicking Security on the Macro submenu. When the Security dialog box displays, click the Low button. Then the next time you open a workbook with an attached macro, PowerPoint will open the workbook immediately, rather than display the dialog box shown in Figure 6-30.

Viewing a Macro's VBA Code

As described earlier, a macro is composed of VBA code, which is created automatically by the macro recorder. You can view the VBA code through the Visual Basic Editor. The **Visual Basic Editor** is used by all Office applications to enter, modify, and view VBA code.

To View a Macro's VBA Code

1 **Click Tools on the menu bar. Point to Macro on the Tools menu and then point to Macros on the Macro submenu.**

The Tools menu and Macro submenu display (Figure 6-31).

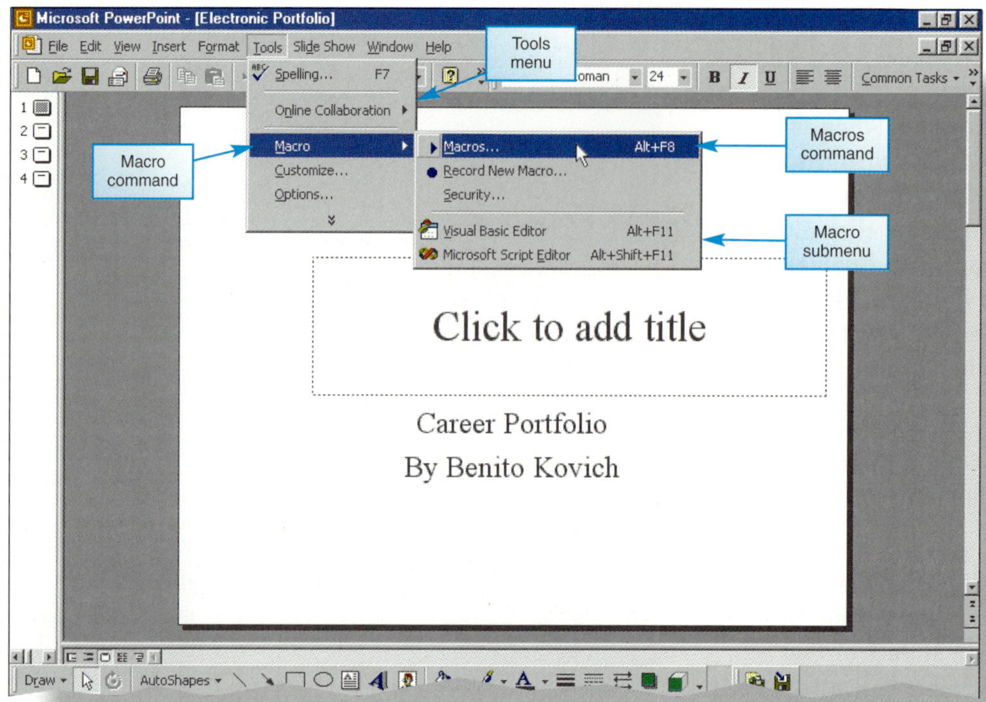

FIGURE 6-31

2 **Click Macros. When the Macro dialog box displays, if necessary click PrintHandout in the list, and then point to the Edit button.**

The Macro dialog box displays as shown in Figure 6-32.

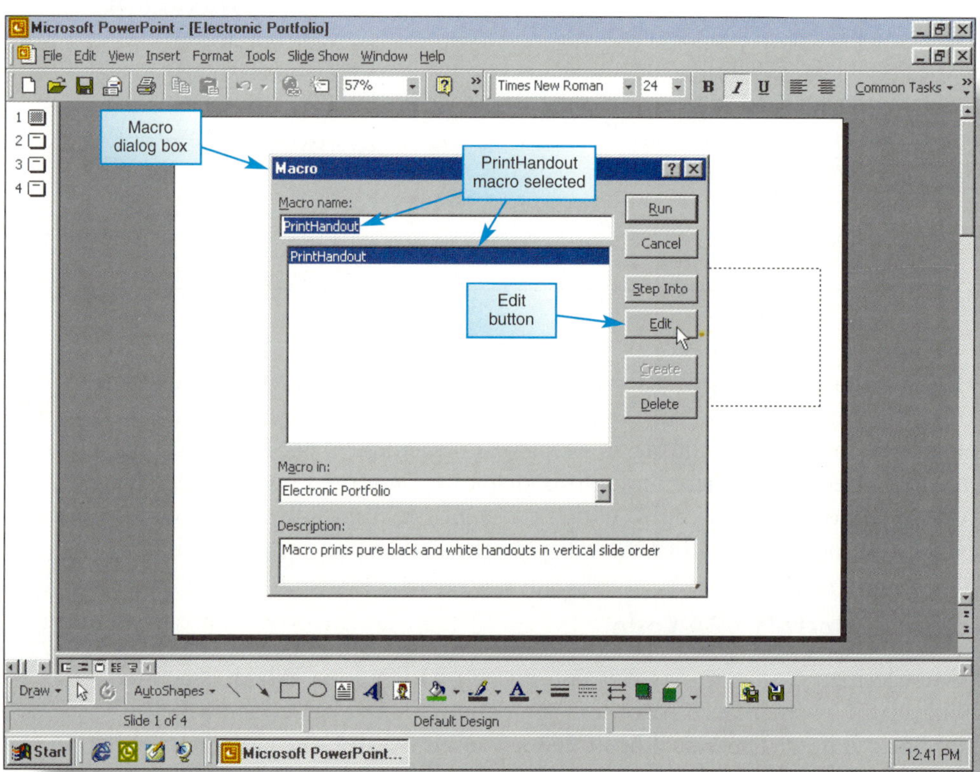

FIGURE 6-32

Click the Edit button.

The Visual Basic Editor starts and displays the VBA code in the macro PrintHandout (Figure 6-33).

4 Scroll through the VBA code. When you are finished, click the Close button on the right side of the title bar.

The Visual Basic Editor closes and Slide 1 in the Electronic Portfolio presentation displays.

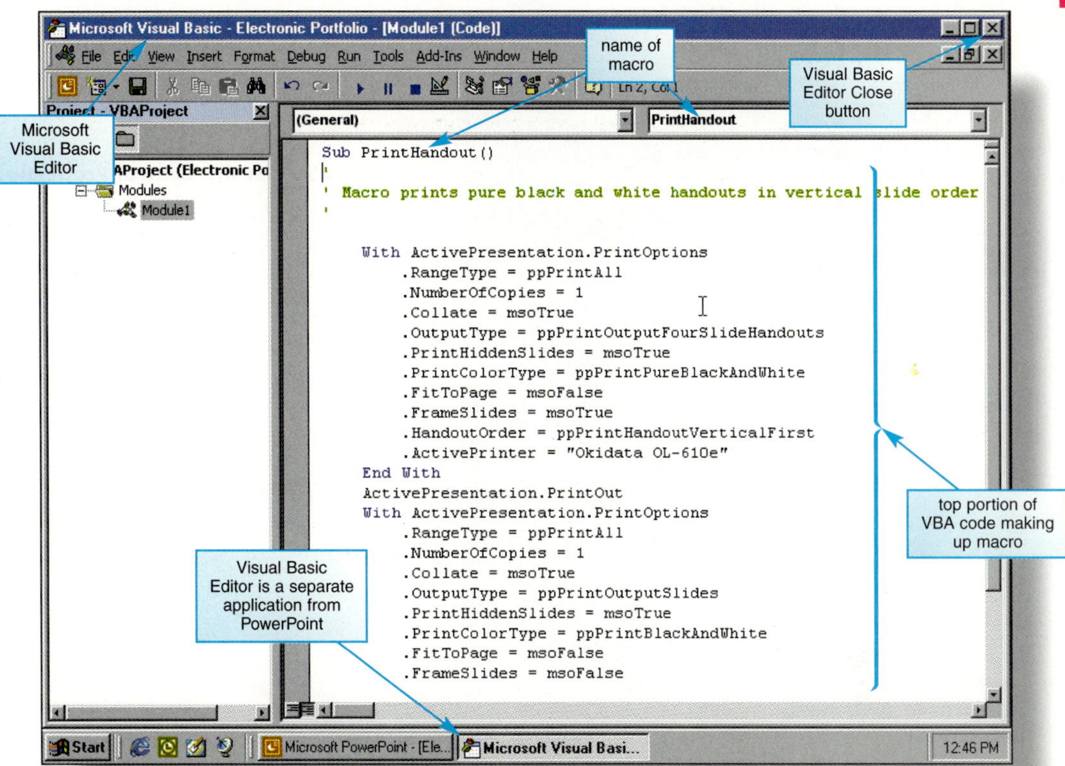

FIGURE 6-33

Other Ways

1. Click Visual Basic Editor button on Visual Basic toolbar.

This set of instructions, beginning with line 1 in Figure 6-33 and continuing sequentially to the last line, executes when you invoke the macro. By scrolling through the VBA code, you can see that the macro recorder generates a lot of instructions. In this case 32 lines of code are generated to print the handout vertically using the Pure black and white option.

Phase 3 — Creating a Form to Customize the Presentation

Now that you have added a toolbar and buttons and have recorded a macro to print handouts, you are ready to develop a form that allows the user to design custom presentations for each of his interviews. This form is called a **user interface** because it allows the user to input data, and then it displays results. This user interface and the step-by-step procedure for its implementation are called an **application**. Thus, Microsoft created the name Visual Basic for Applications (VBA) for its programming language used to customize PowerPoint and other Office 2000 programs.

Applications are built using the three-step process shown in Figure 6-34: (1) create the user interface; (2) set the control properties; and (3) write the VBA code.

More About 2000

VBA

Microsoft publishes a comprehensive book that describes how to write code using Visual Basic for Applications. Microsoft Office 2000/Visual Basic Programmer's Guide teaches readers how to customize and adapt tools for specific needs, including how to create custom commands, menus, dialog boxes, messages, and buttons, as well as how to show custom Help for all these elements. To learn more about this book, visit the PowerPoint 2000 Project 6 More About page (www.scsite.com/pp2000/more.htm) and click Microsoft Press.

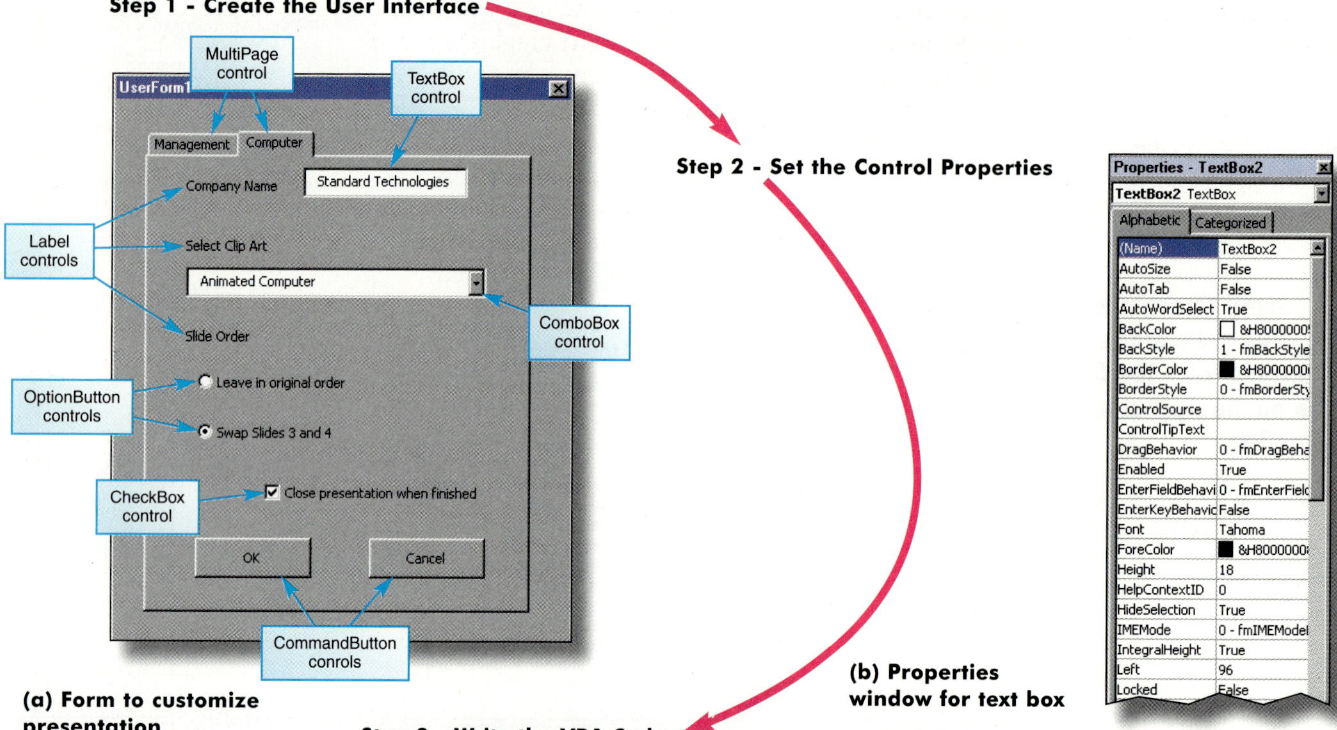

(a) Form to customize presentation

(b) Properties window for text box

Step 3 - Write the VBA Code

Microsoft Visual Basic - Electronic Portfolio - [UserForm1 (Code)]

File Edit View Insert Format Debug Run Tools Add-Ins Window Help

Ln 67, Col 15

CommandButton1 | Click

```
Private Sub CommandButton3_Click()
    ' Set the presentation to apply the template and the clip art
    Set ComputerSlides = Application.ActivePresentation
    With ComputerSlides
        .ApplyTemplate "a:\cactus.pot"
    End With
    ' Validate entries in the text box and combo box
    If TextBox2.Text = "" Then
        MsgBox "Company Name missing, add company name ", vbOK, "Computer"
        TextBox2.SetFocus
    Else
    ' Place company name in title
      CompCompanyName = TextBox2.Text
      Set CompTitleSlide = ActivePresentation.Slides(1)
      CompTitleSlide.Shapes.Title.TextFrame.TextRange.Text = "Working In Information Systems"
      'Check if clip art was chosen
      If ComboBox2.Value = "" Then
         MsgBox "Please select a clip art object from the list", vbOKOnly, "Clip art missing"
         ComboBox2.SetFocus
      Else
```

(c) VBA code associated with text box

FIGURE 6-34

Step 1 – Create the User Interface

The form shown Figure 6-34a presents the application's user interface. This interface allows the user to specify which information should be in the presentation and to cancel the procedure if required. The form contains controls and two command buttons. At the top of the form are two tabs: one for a management position, and the other for a computer-based job in the information systems field. If the user clicks the Management tab, the user will select options on a sheet pertaining to a slide show focusing on management skills. If the user clicks the Computer tab, the user will select options on another sheet regarding a computer presentation.

The first element on both sheets is a text box control, where the user will enter the name of the company where the user is interviewing. Next is the combo box containing the description of two clip art files – one animated, and one not animated. Below the clip art combo box is a Slide Order area where the user can click an option button to leave the slides in their original order or to switch the order to emphasize a specific strength. The Close presentation when finished check box allows the user to close the custom presentation after the user has completed making selections on the user form. If the user does not select this check box, the VBA procedure will assemble the custom slide show automatically and display it on his screen. The two command buttons at the bottom of the form – the OK button and the Cancel button – are standard buttons found on most forms. The OK button executes the VBA procedure; the Cancel button prevents the VBA code from executing. When the user clicks either button, the procedure hides the user form and unloads it from memory.

More About

Docking Toolbars

A toolbar becomes docked when you drag it to the edge of a program window. When you move a docked toolbar, this action may affect the location and size of other toolbars on the same row.

Creating the interface consists of sizing and locating the form and then adding each of the controls to the form and adjusting their sizes and positions. When you begin to create a user interface, you position the controls as close as you can to their final locations on the form, and then after setting the properties you finalize their positions. When you perform the following steps, therefore, do not attempt to position the controls exactly in the locations shown in Figure 6-34a.

The Standard toolbar (Figure 6-35) displays when you use VBA. Alternately, you can right-click a toolbar and then click Standard on the shortcut menu to display it.

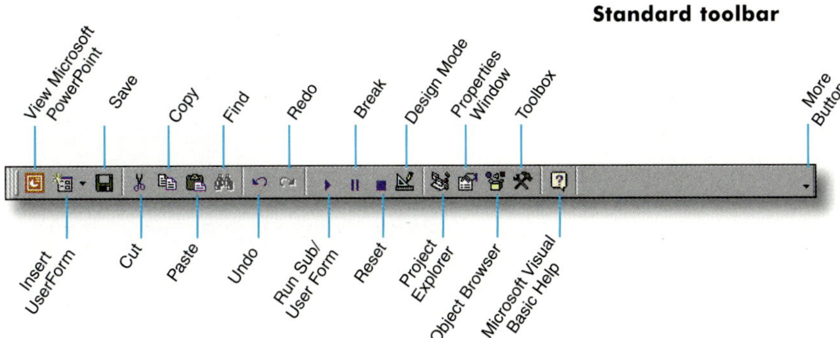

FIGURE 6-35

Opening the Visual Basic IDE and a New Form

Before you begin creating the interface, however, you need to start the **Visual Basic integrated development environment (IDE)**, which contains nine different windows and four toolbars. The windows can be **docked**, or anchored to other windows that are dockable, and the four toolbars can be docked or float in their own windows. Perform the following steps to open the Visual Basic IDE and open a new form.

To Open the Visual Basic IDE and a New Form

1 With the Electronic Portfolio still open, click Tools on the menu bar, point to Macro, and then point to Visual Basic Editor.

The Macro submenu displays (Figure 6-36).

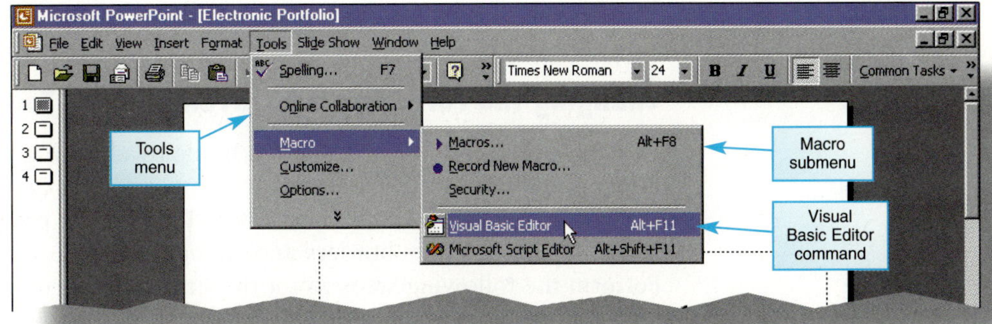

FIGURE 6-36

2 **Click Visual Basic Editor. Click Insert on the menu bar and then point to UserForm.**

The Visual Basic Editor opens and displays a Project Explorer window and a Properties window (Figure 6-37). The Insert menu displays.

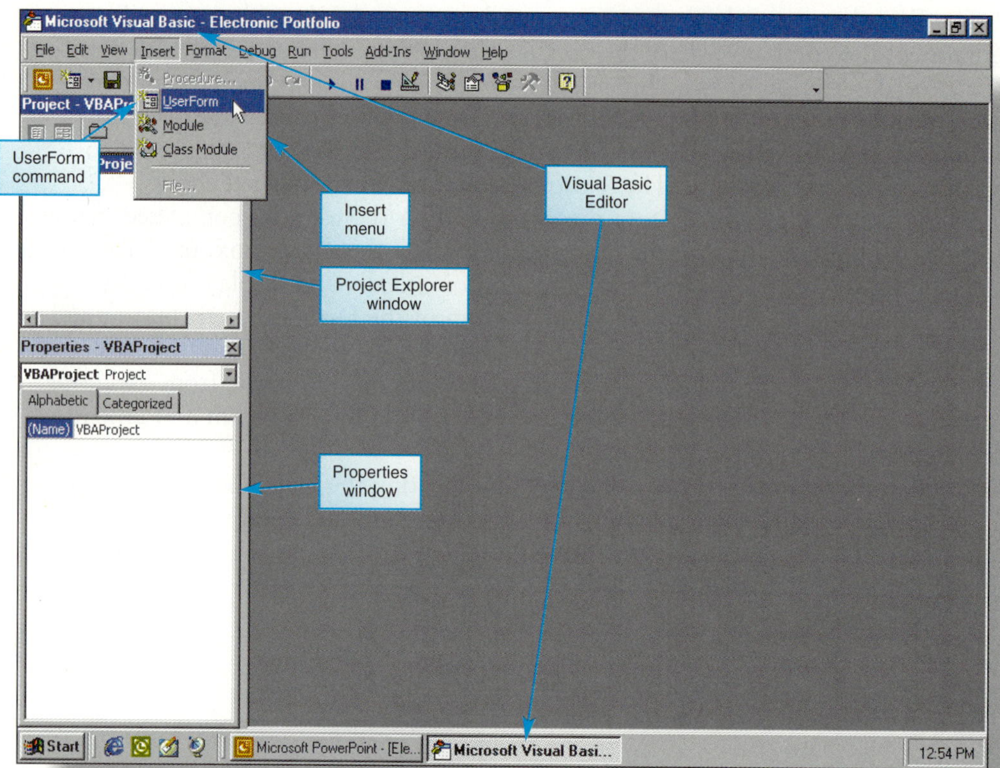

FIGURE 6-37

3 **Click UserForm.**

A new form, UserForm1, opens and the Toolbox displays (Figure 6-38). If the Toolbox does not display, click the Toolbox button.

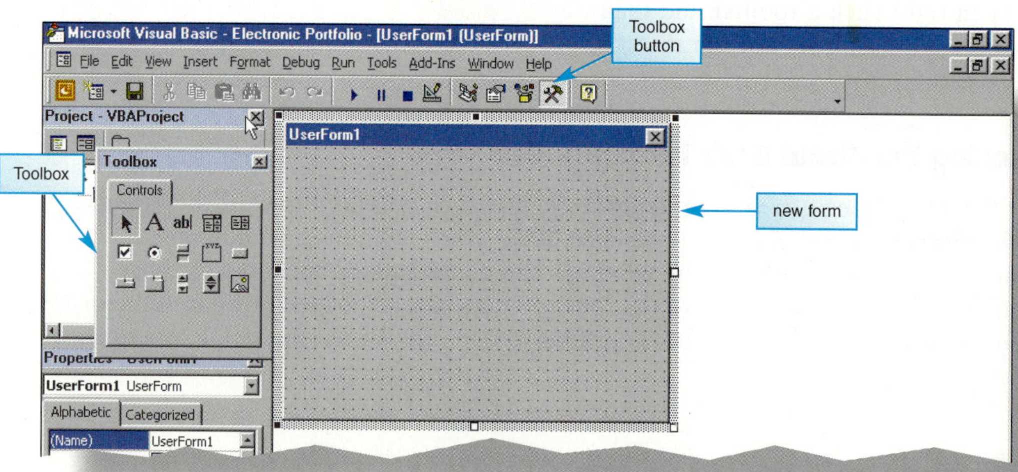

FIGURE 6-38

Changing the Form Size and Arranging the Toolbox Position

You can resize a form in design mode by changing the values of its **Height** and **Width properties** in the Properties window, and you can change a form's location on the screen by changing the values of its **Top** and **Left properties**. You also can resize a form by dragging its borders and change its location by dragging and dropping. Perform the following steps to set the size of the form by dragging its borders and set the location by dragging and dropping.

To Change the Form Size and Arrange the Toolbox Position

1 Point to the form's lower-right corner. Without releasing the mouse button, drag its corner down and to the right.

Dragging a corner of the form moves the two adjacent borders at the same time (Figure 6-39). The mouse pointer displays as a two-headed arrow.

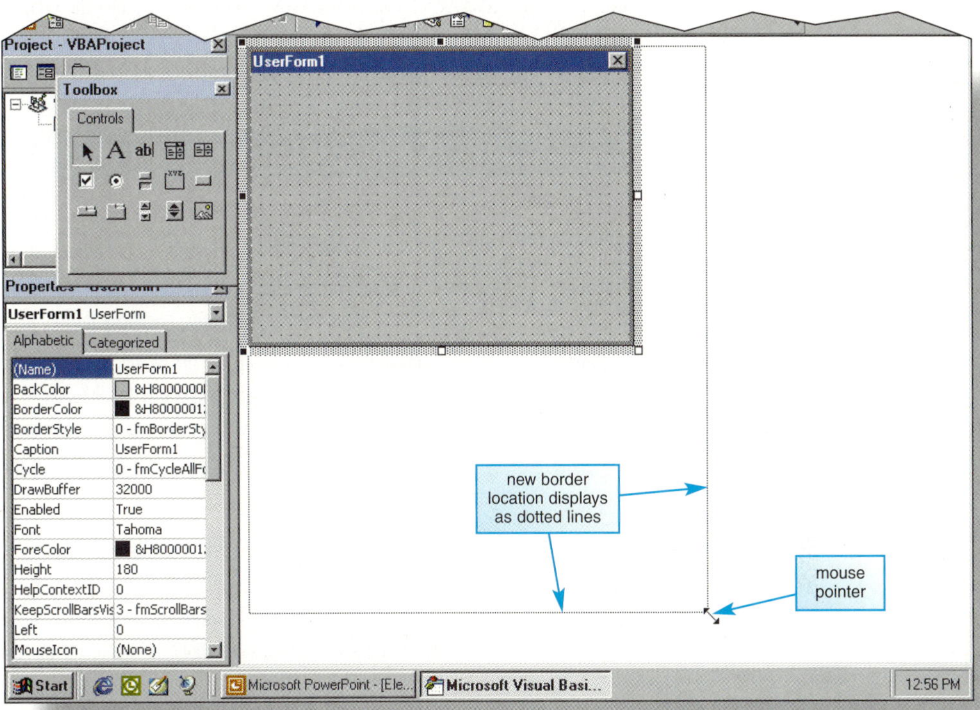

FIGURE 6-39

2 Release the mouse button. Click Toolbox title bar and drag it to the lower-right corner of the screen.

The form's size displays as shown in Figure 6-40. The Toolbox displays in the lower-right corner.

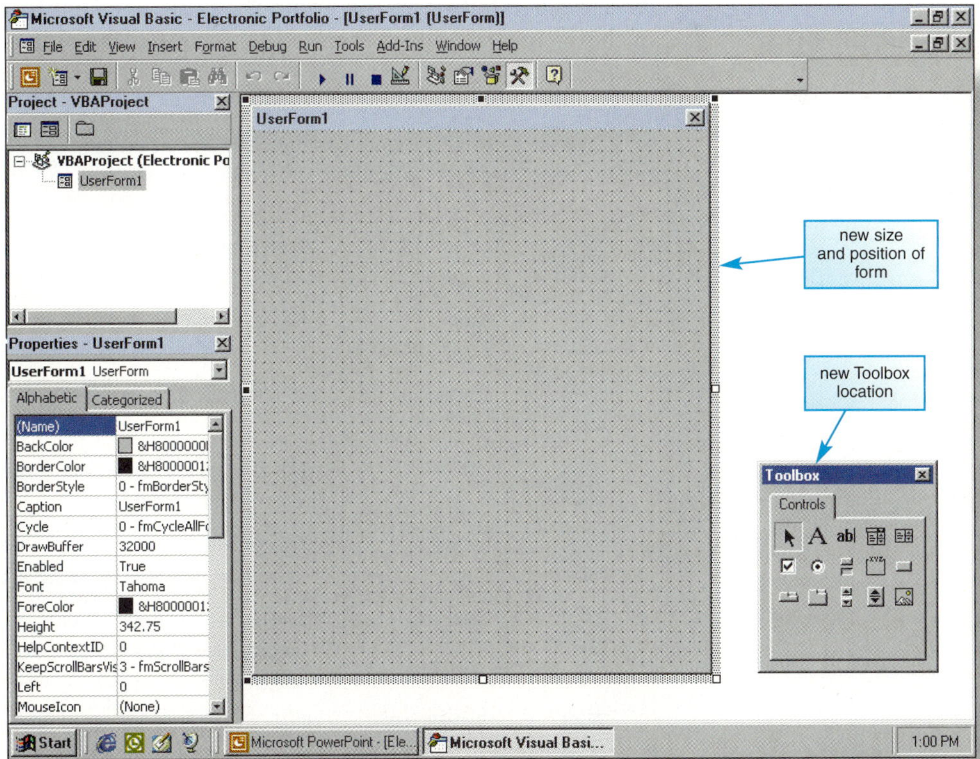

FIGURE 6-40

VBA Sites

Several Web sites collect and organize links to other sites. Some of these sites contain links to Visual Basic sites that offer information on coding, magazines, games, and tips. To view one of these sites, visit the PowerPoint 2000 Project 6 More About page (www.scsite.com/pp2000/more.htm) and click VBA Sites.

Adding Controls

Graphical images, or objects, in Windows applications include buttons, check boxes, tabs, and text boxes. In Visual Basic, these objects are called **controls**. The form will contain seven types of controls (see Figure 6-34a on page PP 6.26). These controls and their functions are described as follows.

Table 6-3 VBA Controls Used in the Form

CONTROL	DESCRIPTION
MultiPage	Creates tabbed forms.
Label	Displays text on a form. At run time, the person using the application cannot change the text on a label, such as the words, Company Name.
TextBox	Displays text on a form, but the person using the application can change its contents at run time. It frequently serves as a way for the user to supply information to the application, such as the specific name of the company where the interview is being held.
ComboBox	Presents a list of choices. When an item is selected from the list, the item displays in a highlighted color.
OptionButton	Presents a set of choices. Option buttons are placed in groups that allow the user to make only one selection within the group.
CheckBox	Turns options on or off. Clicking an empty check box places a check mark in the check box to indicate the option is selected. Clicking a selected check box removes the check mark to indicate the option is not selected.
CommandButton	Represents a button that initiates an action when clicked.

Controls are added to a form using tools in the **Toolbox**. To use a tool, you click its respective button in the Toolbox. Table 6-4 identifies the Toolbox buttons. Many of these buttons allow you to add controls that you have worked with previously in PowerPoint, such as text boxes, check boxes, and list boxes.

Table 6-4 Summary of Buttons in the Toolbox

BUTTON	NAME	FUNCTION
	Select Objects	Draws a rectangle around the controls you want to select
A	Label	Adds text that a user cannot change
ab|	TextBox	Holds text that a user can either enter or change
	ComboBox	Adds a custom edit box, list box, or combo box on a menu bar, toolbar, menu, submenu, or shortcut menu
	ListBox	Displays a list of items from which a user can choose. The list can be scrolled if it has more items than can be displayed at one time.
	CheckBox	Creates a box that a user can choose to indicate one of two choices, such as true or false, or to display multiple choices when the user can select more than one preference
	OptionButton	Displays multiple choices when a user can select only one option
	Toggle Button	Creates a button that toggles on and off

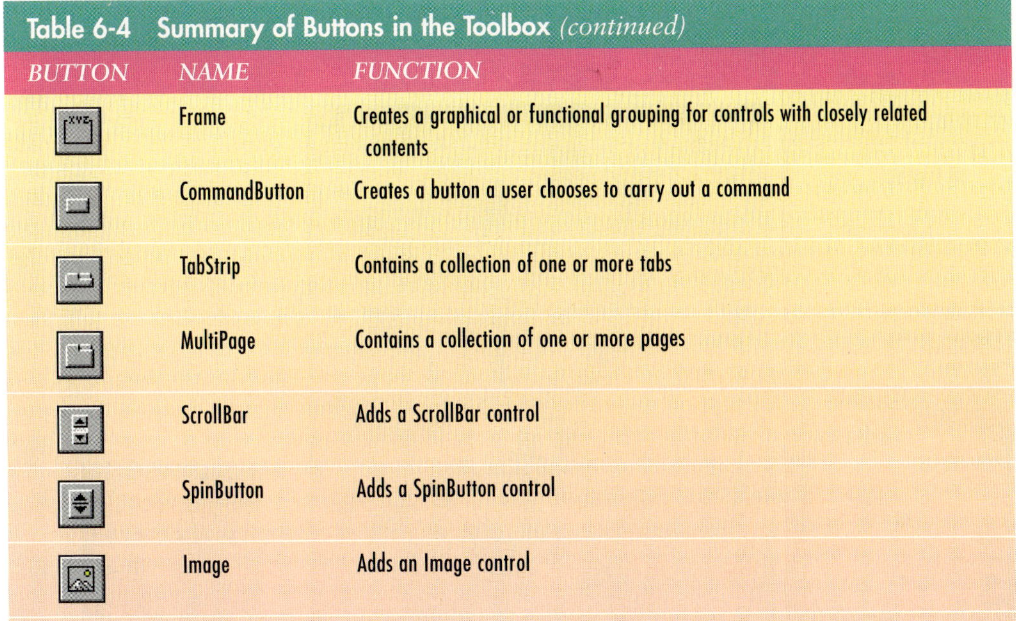

Table 6-4 Summary of Buttons in the Toolbox *(continued)*

BUTTON	NAME	FUNCTION
	Frame	Creates a graphical or functional grouping for controls with closely related contents
	CommandButton	Creates a button a user chooses to carry out a command
	TabStrip	Contains a collection of one or more tabs
	MultiPage	Contains a collection of one or more pages
	ScrollBar	Adds a ScrollBar control
	SpinButton	Adds a SpinButton control
	Image	Adds an Image control

ADDING A MULTIPAGE CONTROL The first step in building the form is to add a MultiPage control. This control will create two separate pages, or sheets, that both allow the user to input the company name, choose clip art, select the slide order, and decide whether to run the presentation immediately or later. The selections on one page are appropriate for management interviews, and those on the other page will be tailored for computer positions. Perform the following steps to add this first control.

VBA Technology

The Microsoft Visual Basic for Applications Home Page gives information geared toward independent software vendors and corporate developers. The site includes VBA news and related topics that help programmers customize their applications. To view this page, visit the PowerPoint 2000 Project 6 More About page (www.scsite.com/pp2000/more.htm) and click VBA Technology.

To Add a MultiPage Control to a Form and Increase Its Size

1 **Click the MultiPage button in the Toolbox. Position the mouse pointer in the upper-left corner of the form.**

The MultiPage button in the Toolbox is recessed, and the mouse pointer displays as a cross hair and a copy of the MultiPage button when it is on the form (Figure 6-41). The upper-left corner of the MultiPage control will be positioned in this location.

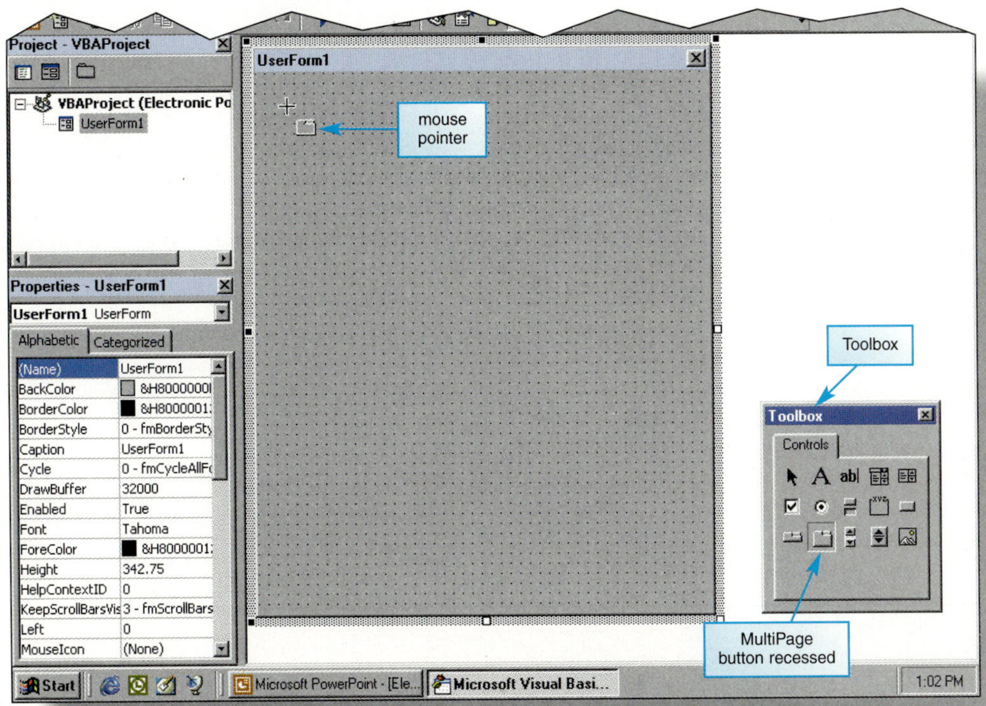

FIGURE 6-41

2 Click the mouse button. Point to the lower-right sizing handle.

The MultiPage control displays on the form with two default tabs, Page1 and Page2 (Figure 6-42). A selection rectangle and sizing handles display around the MultiPage control.

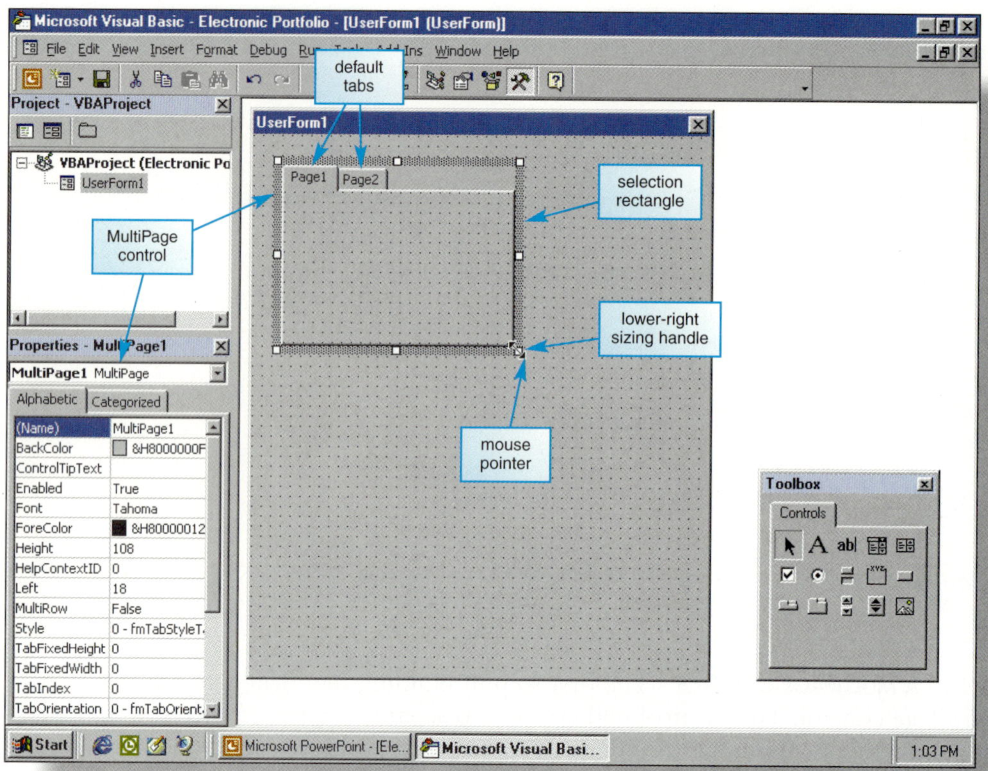

FIGURE 6-42

3 Drag the sizing handle down and to the right.

The form size increases (Figure 6-43). Additional controls now can fit on the form.

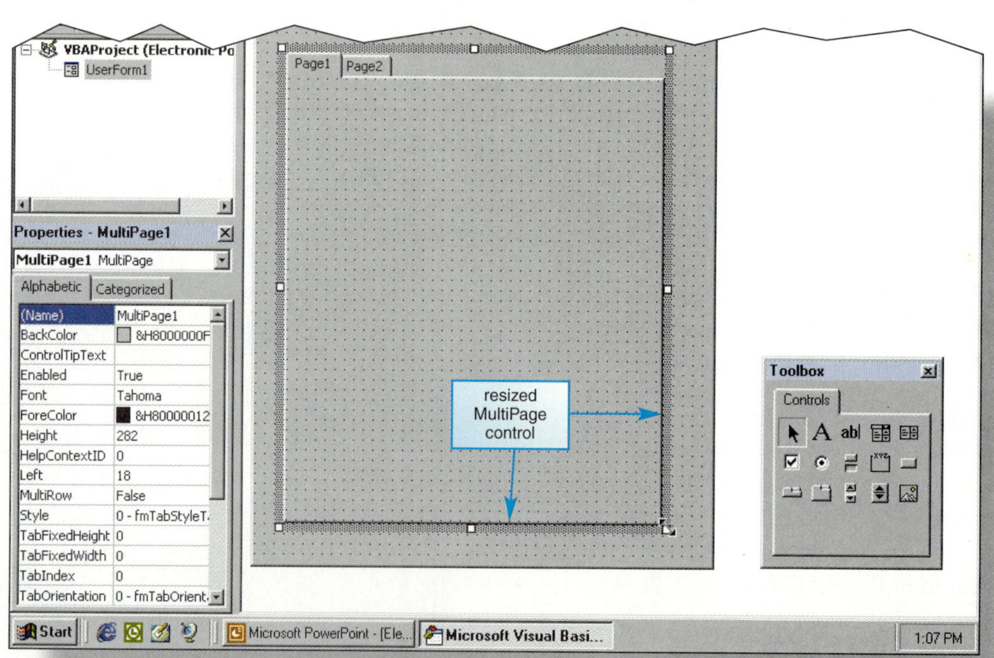

FIGURE 6-43

ADDING LABEL CONTROLS The next steps are to add the three Label controls shown in Figure 6-34a on page PP 6.26. Perform the following steps to add these controls to the form.

To Add Label Controls to a Form

1 Click the Label button in the Toolbox. Position the mouse pointer in the upper-left corner of the form.

The Label button in the Toolbox is recessed, and the mouse pointer changes to a cross hair and a copy of the Label button when it is on the form (Figure 6-44). The upper-left corner of the Label control will be positioned in this location.

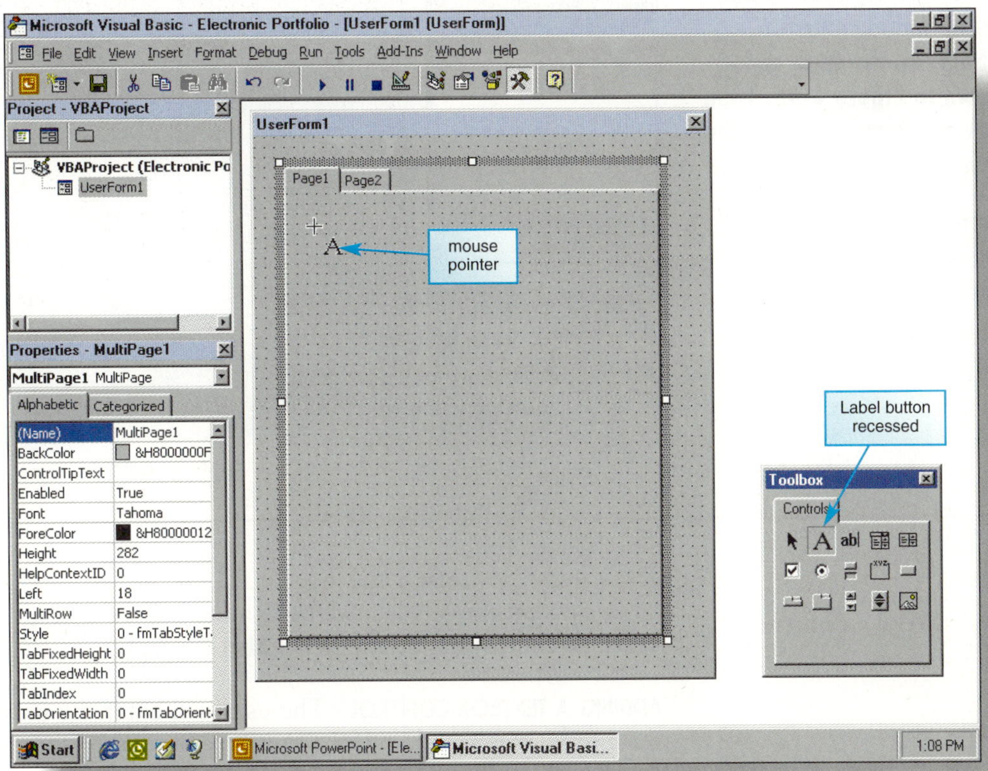

FIGURE 6-44

2 Click the mouse button.

The label displays on the form with the default caption, Label1 (Figure 6-45). The label is surrounded by a selection rectangle and sizing handles.

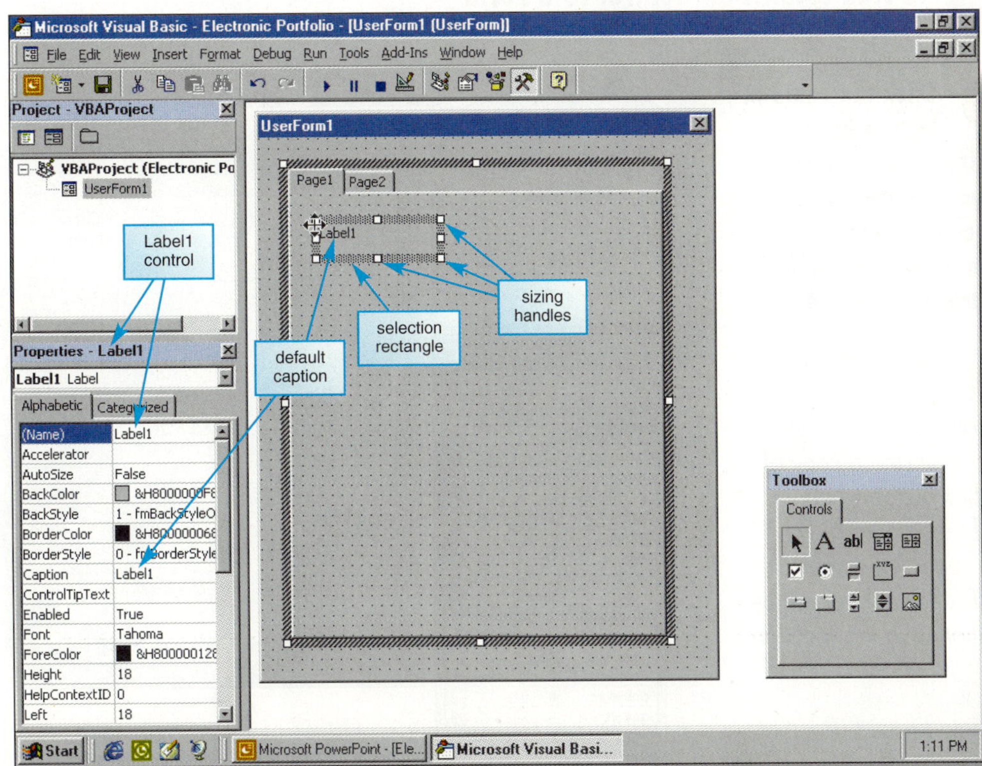

FIGURE 6-45

3 Repeat Steps 1 and 2 to draw a second Label control, Label2, and a third Label control, Label3, on the form as shown in Figure 6-46. Then click any blank area on the form.

The three Label controls display on the form (Figure 6-46).

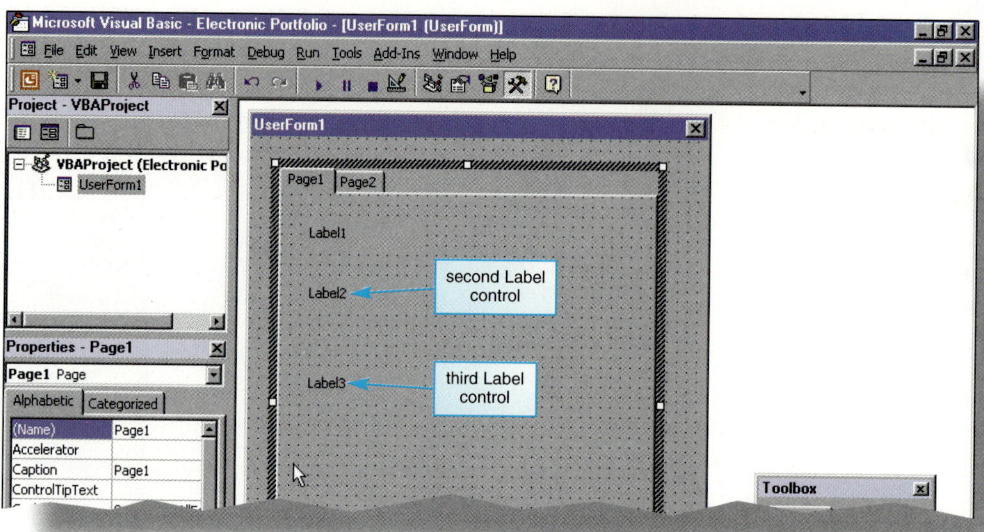

FIGURE 6-46

Now that the labels have been added to the form, the next step is to add the TextBox control beside the first Label control.

ADDING A TEXTBOX CONTROL The user will enter the name of the company where the interview is scheduled in a text box located to the right of the Label1 control. Perform the following steps to use the Toolbox to add a TextBox control to the form.

To Add a TextBox Control to a Form

1 Click the TextBox button in the Toolbox. Position the mouse pointer in the upper-right corner of the form beside the Label1 control (Figure 6-47).

The TextBox button in the Toolbox is recessed, and the mouse pointer changes to a cross hair and a copy of the TextBox button when it is on the form (Figure 6-47). The upper-left corner of the TextBox control will be positioned in this location.

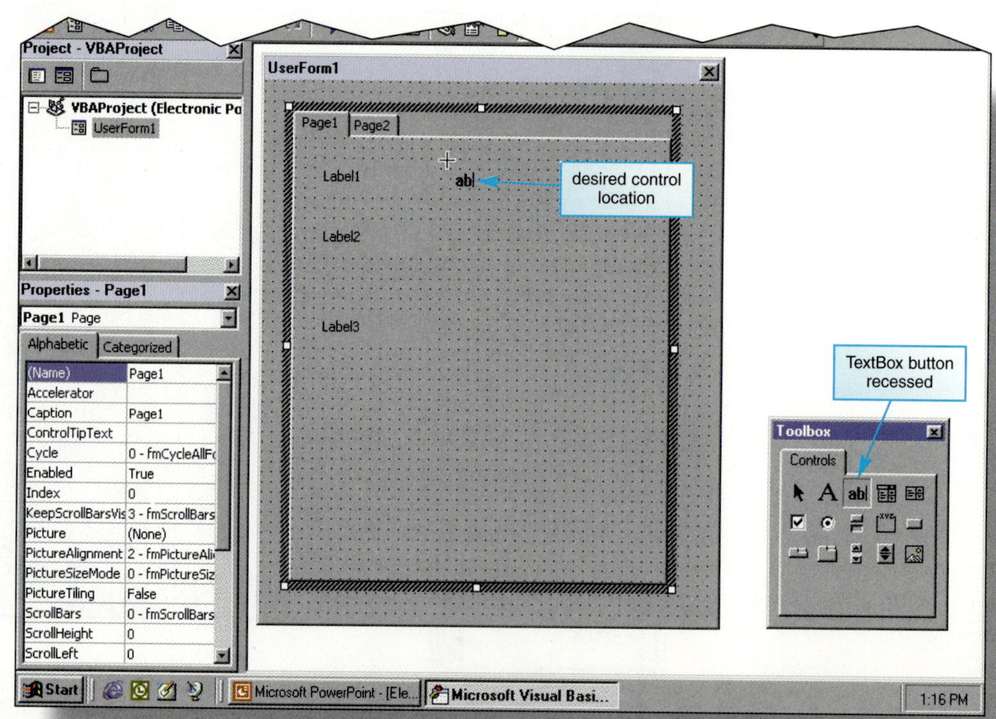

FIGURE 6-47

Click the mouse button.

The TextBox control is added to the form (Figure 6-48).

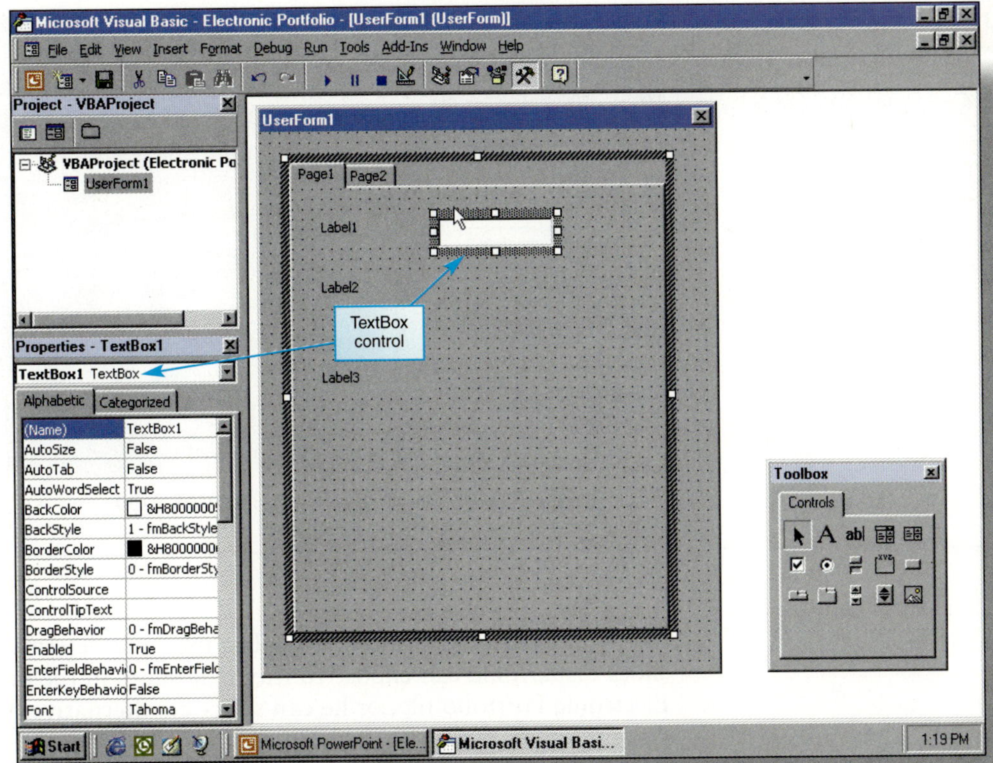

FIGURE 6-48

ADDING A COMBOBOX CONTROL The user will select one of two clip art images to insert on the second slide in the slide show. You need to add a ComboBox control to the form to display descriptions of these files. Perform the following steps to use the Toolbox to add a ComboBox control to the form.

To Add a ComboBox Control to a Form

1 Click the ComboBox button in the Toolbox. Position the mouse pointer below the Label2 control.

The ComboBox button in the Toolbox is recessed, and the mouse pointer changes to a cross hair and a copy of the ComboBox button when it is on the form (Figure 6-49). The upper-left corner of the ComboBox control will be positioned in this location.

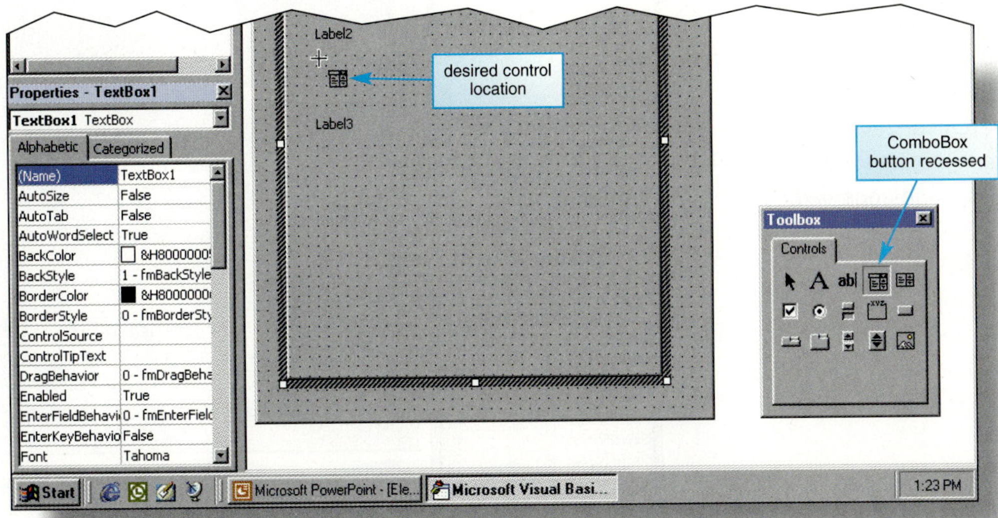

FIGURE 6-49

Click the mouse button.

The ComboBox control is added to the form (Figure 6-50).

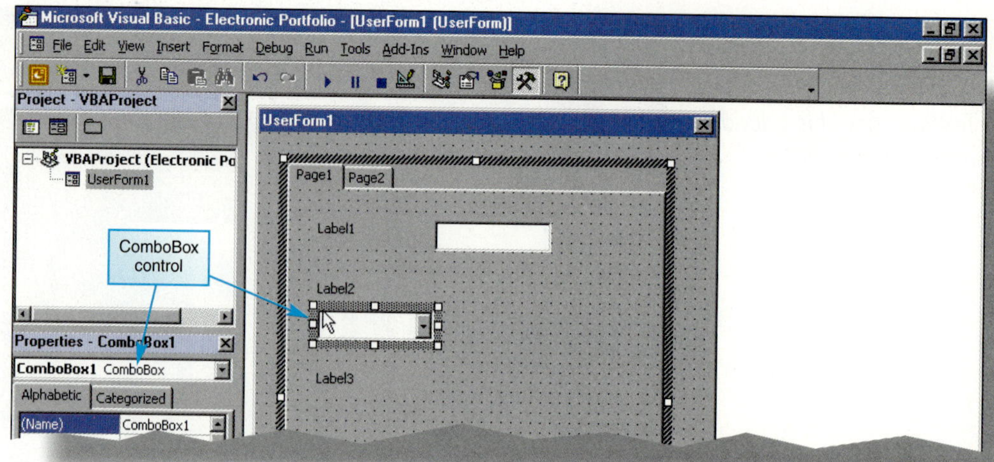

FIGURE 6-50

ADDING OPTIONBUTTON CONTROLS The user will determine the order in which the slides display. He can choose to leave the slides in the order they display in the Electronic Portfolio file, or he can select an alternative. He can opt to display the current Slide 3 display before Slide 2 in the management presentation and to display the current Slide 4 before Slide 3 in the computer presentation. He will make this selection by clicking an option button. Perform the following steps to use the Toolbox to add two OptionButton controls to the form.

To Add OptionButton Controls to a Form

1 Click the OptionButton button in the Toolbox. Position the mouse pointer below the Label3 control.

The OptionButton button in the Toolbox is recessed, and the mouse pointer changes to a cross hair and a copy of the OptionButton button when it is on the form (Figure 6-51). The upper-left corner of the OptionButton control will be positioned in this location.

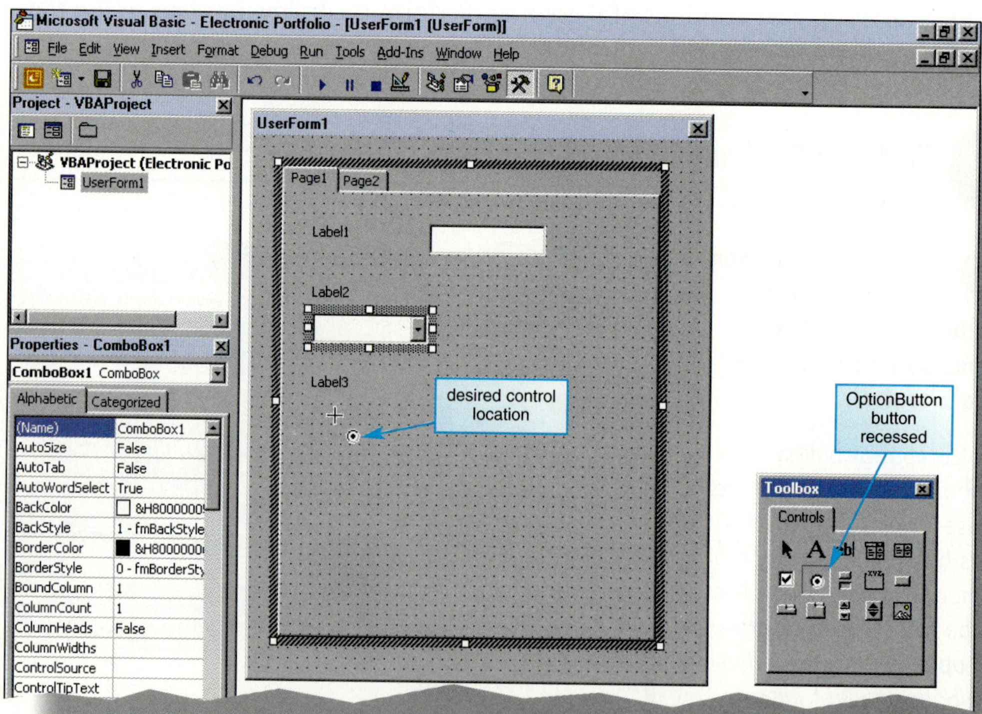

FIGURE 6-51

2 Click the mouse button.

The first Option Button control, OptionButton1, is added to the form (Figure 6-52).

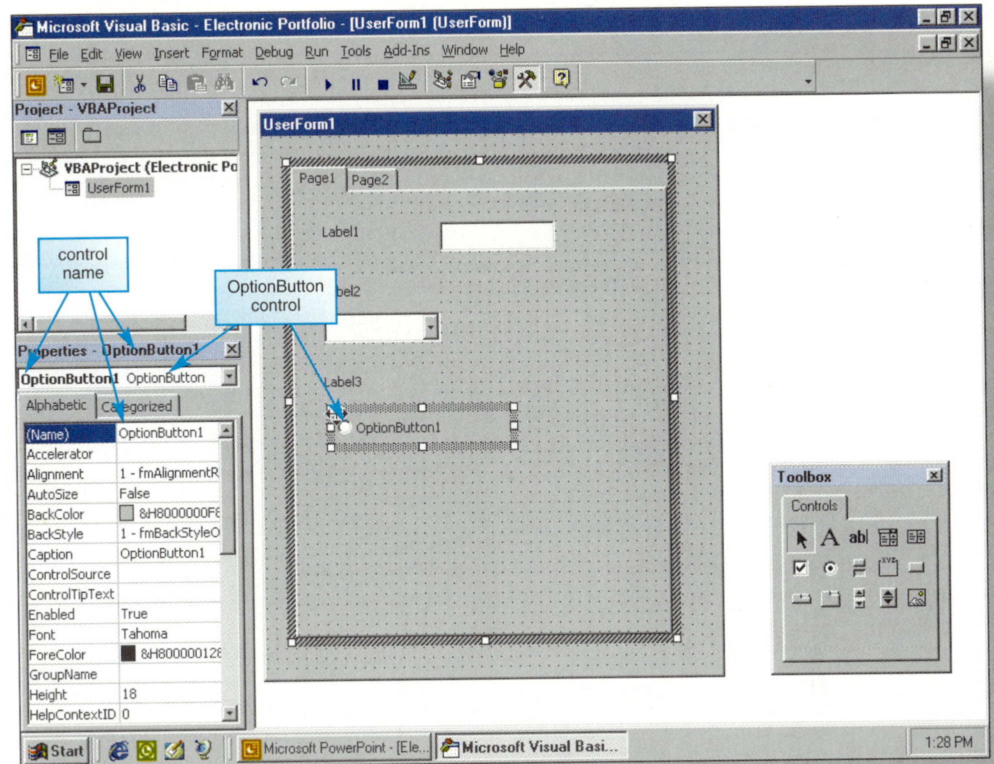

FIGURE 6-52

3 Repeat Steps 1 and 2 to add a second OptionButton control, OptionButton2, to the form below the first OptionButton control (Figure 6-53).

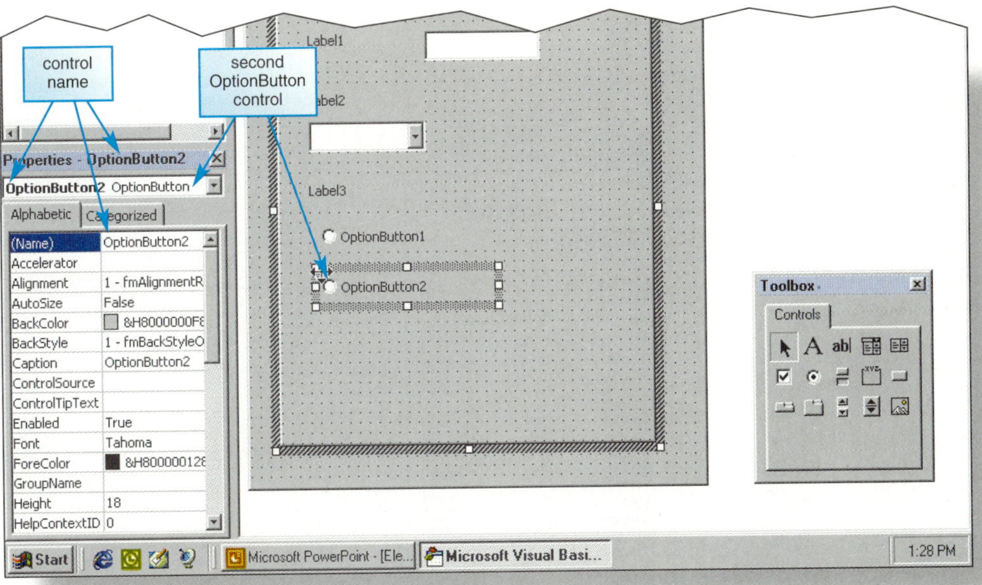

FIGURE 6-53

ADDING A CHECKBOX CONTROL The user can choose to have his slide show display immediately after he makes his selections on this form, or he can decide to save the presentation and open it later. The presentation will run immediately unless he clicks the Close presentation when finished check box. Perform the steps on the next page to use the Toolbox to add this CheckBox control to the form.

To Add a CheckBox Control to a Form

1 Click the CheckBox button in the Toolbox. Position the mouse pointer below the second OptionButton control.

The CheckBox button in the Toolbox is recessed, and the mouse pointer changes to a cross hair and a copy of the CheckBox button when it is on the form (Figure 6-54). The upper-left corner of the CheckBox control will be positioned in this location.

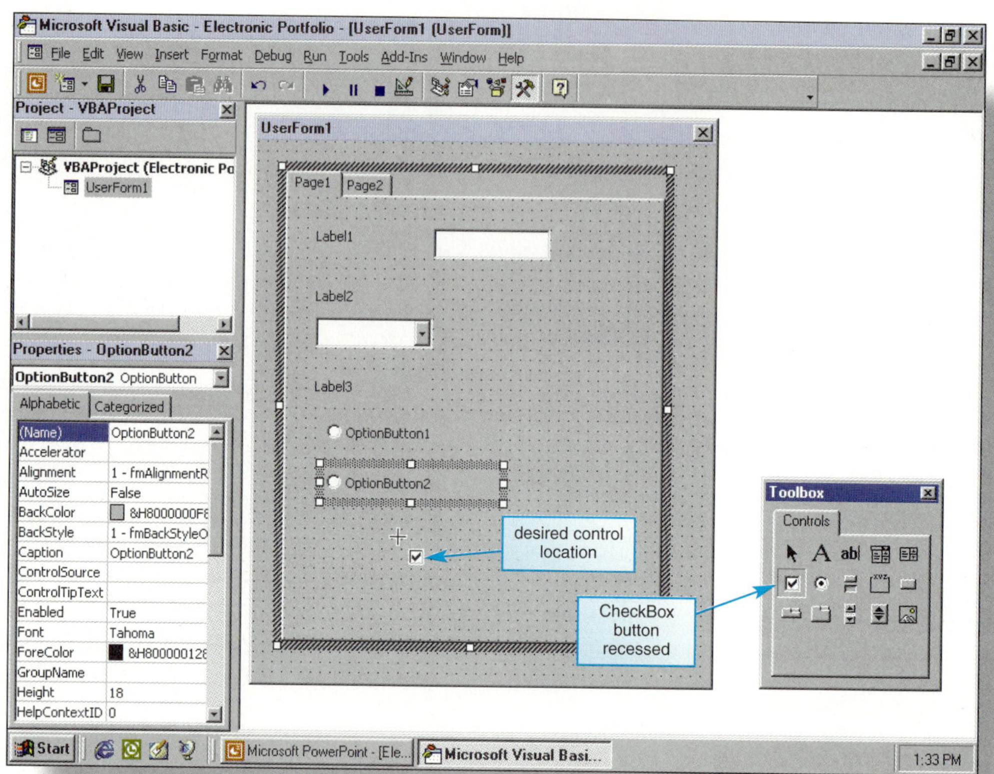

FIGURE 6-54

2 Click the mouse button.

The Check Box control, CheckBox1, is added to the form (Figure 6-55).

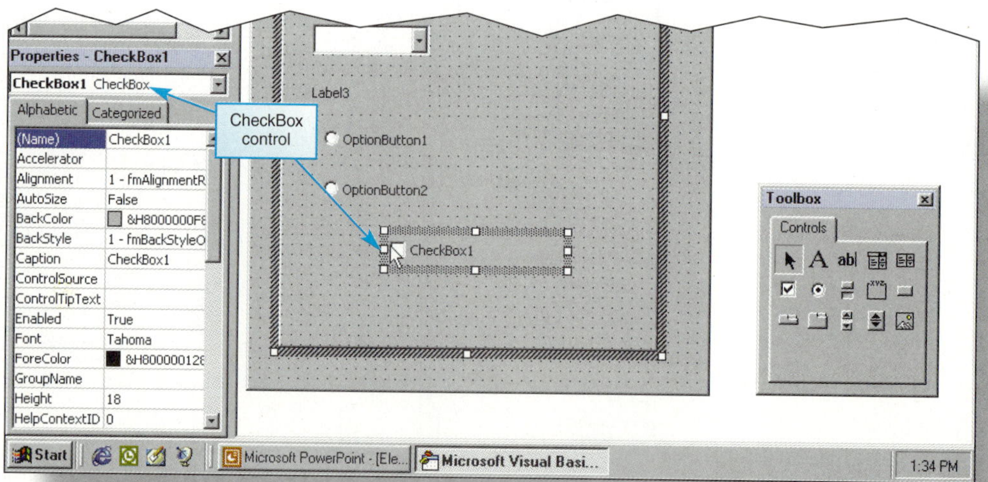

FIGURE 6-55

ADDING COMMANDBUTTON CONTROLS When the user finishes making selections on the form, then the user can click the OK button to assemble the presentation. If the user wants to exit the Visual Basic program, the user can click the Cancel button. The OK and Cancel buttons are created using CommandButton controls. Perform the following steps to add two CommandButton controls to the form.

To Add CommandButton Controls to a Form

1 Click the CommandButton button in the Toolbox. Position the mouse pointer in the lower-left corner of the form.

The CommandButton button in the Toolbox is recessed, and the mouse pointer changes to a cross hair and a copy of the CommandButton button when it is on the form (Figure 6-56). The upper-left corner of the first CommandButton control will be positioned in this location.

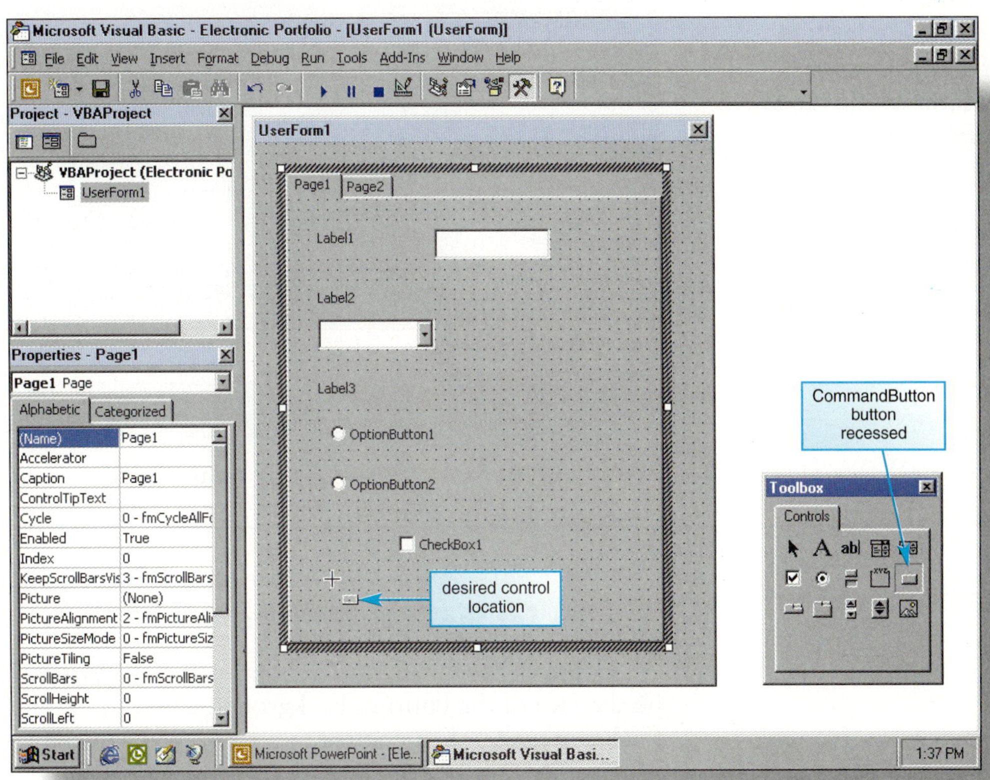

FIGURE 6-56

2 Click the mouse button.

The CommandButton1 control is added to the form (Figure 6-57).

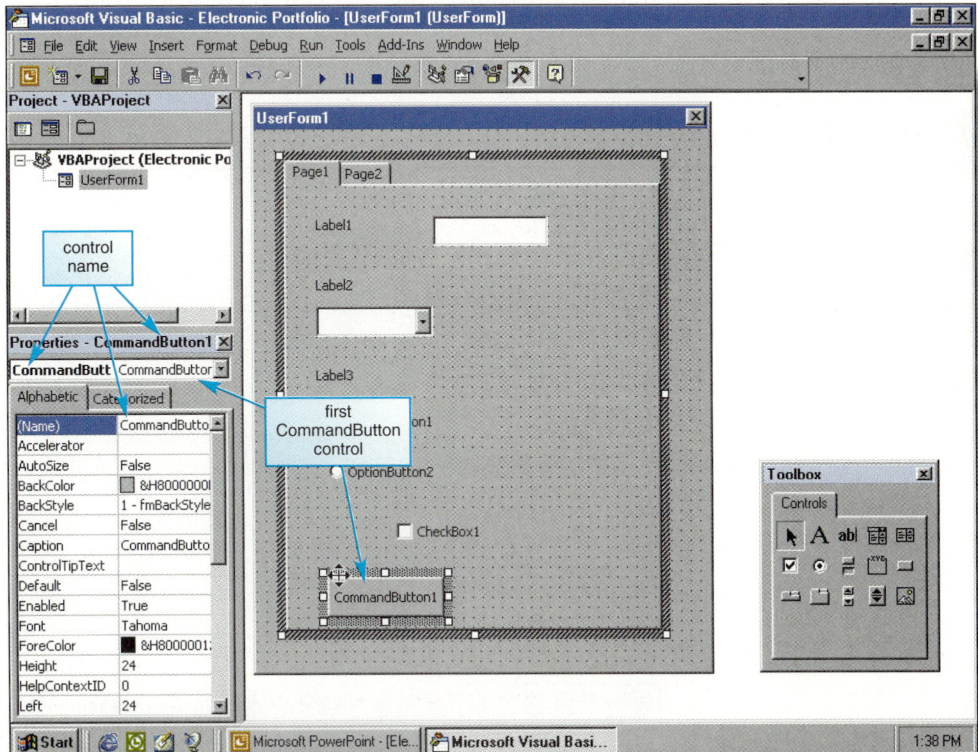

FIGURE 6-57

3 **Repeat Steps 1 and 2 to add a second CommandButton control, CommandButton2, to lower-right corner of the form beside the left CommandButton (Figure 6-58).**

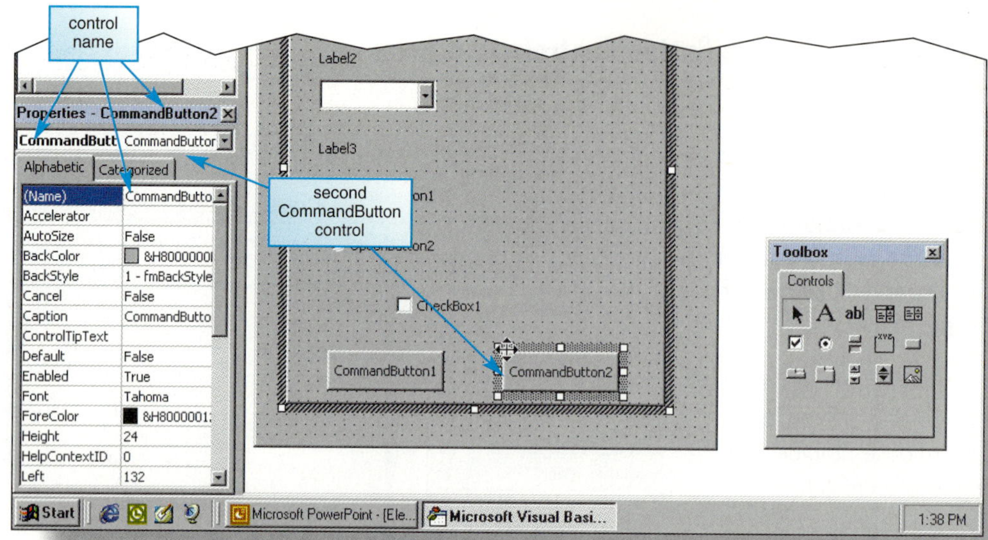

FIGURE 6-58

Step 2 – Set the Control Properties

Controls have many different **properties** (Figure 6-58), such as caption (the text on the face of the button), background color, foreground color, height, width, and font. Once you add a control to a form, you can change any of the properties to improve its appearance and modify how it works.

SETTING THE CAPTION PROPERTIES The controls on the form are not very informative because they do not state their functions. You want to provide meaningful descriptions of the choices the user can make when using the form. These descriptions are called captions. The following steps change the caption properties.

To Set the Caption Properties

1 **Click the Page1 tab. With the Page1 control selected, click Caption in the Properties window.**

The Properties window for the Page1 control displays (Figure 6-59). The default Caption property is Page1.

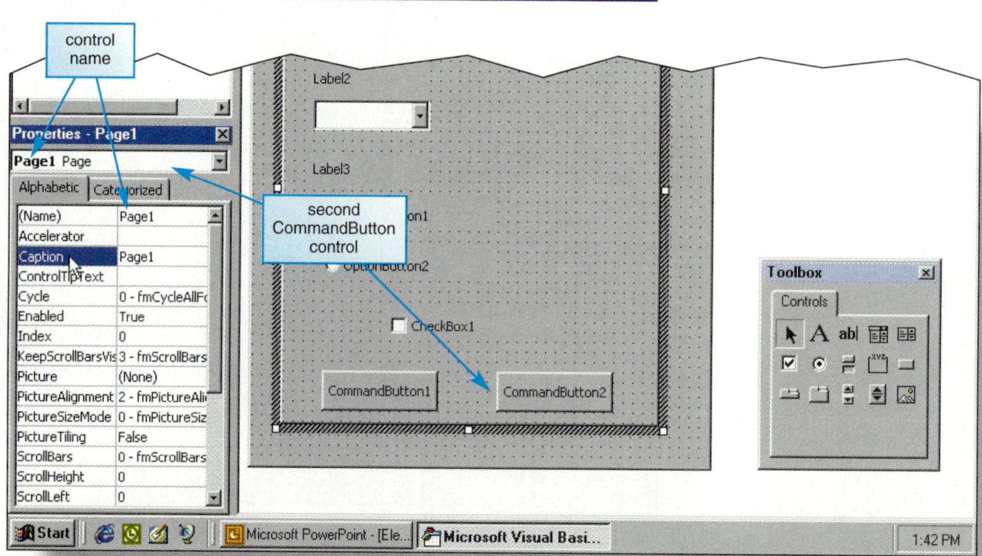

FIGURE 6-59

2 **Triple-click the current caption, Page1, to select it, type** `Management` **as the new caption, and then press the ENTER key.**

Management is the new caption for the Page1 tab (Figure 6-60). The new caption displays on the form.

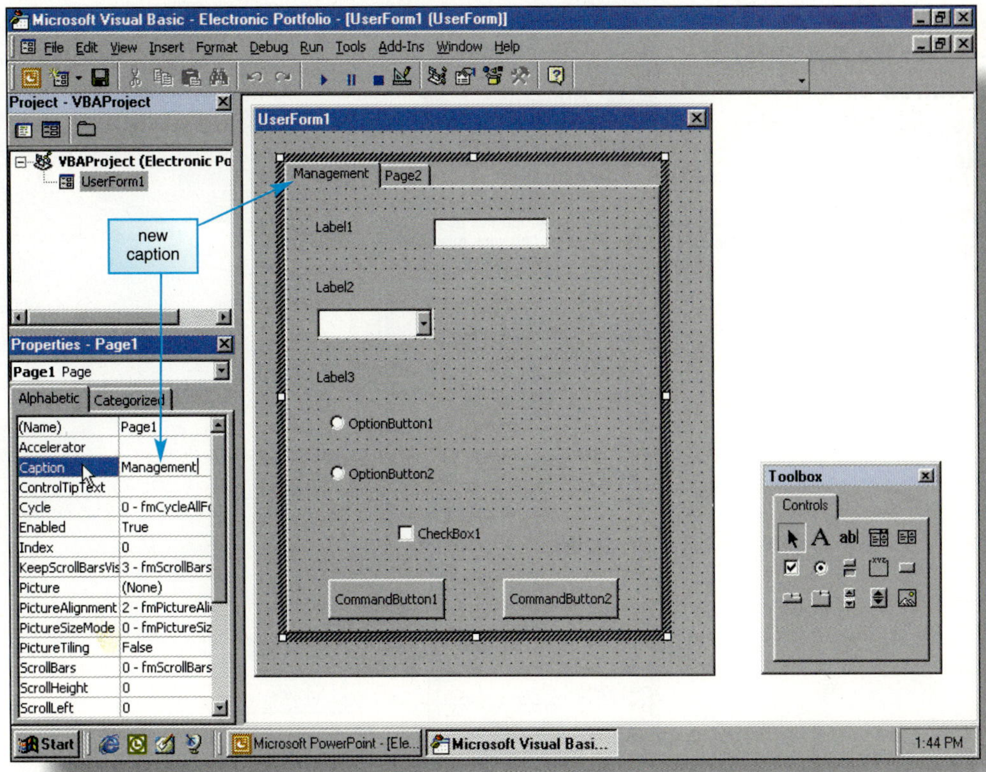

FIGURE 6-60

3 **Click the Label1 control on the form. With Caption still selected in the Properties window, triple-click the current caption, Label1, in the Properties window, type** `Company Name` **as the caption, and then press the ENTER key.**

The Properties window for the Label1 control displays (Figure 6-61). You change the default Caption property, Label1, to Company Name. The new name will display when you click another property or control.

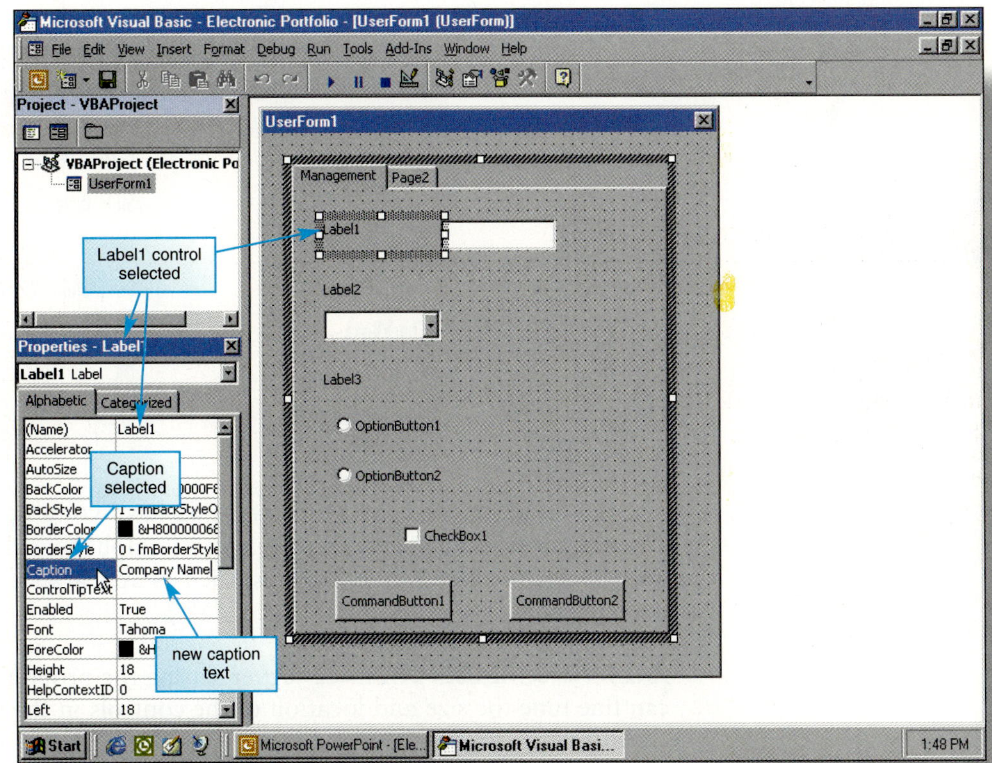

FIGURE 6-61

4 Change the captions for the remainder of the controls on the Management sheet using Table 6-5.

The captions for the Management sheet display (Figure 6-62).

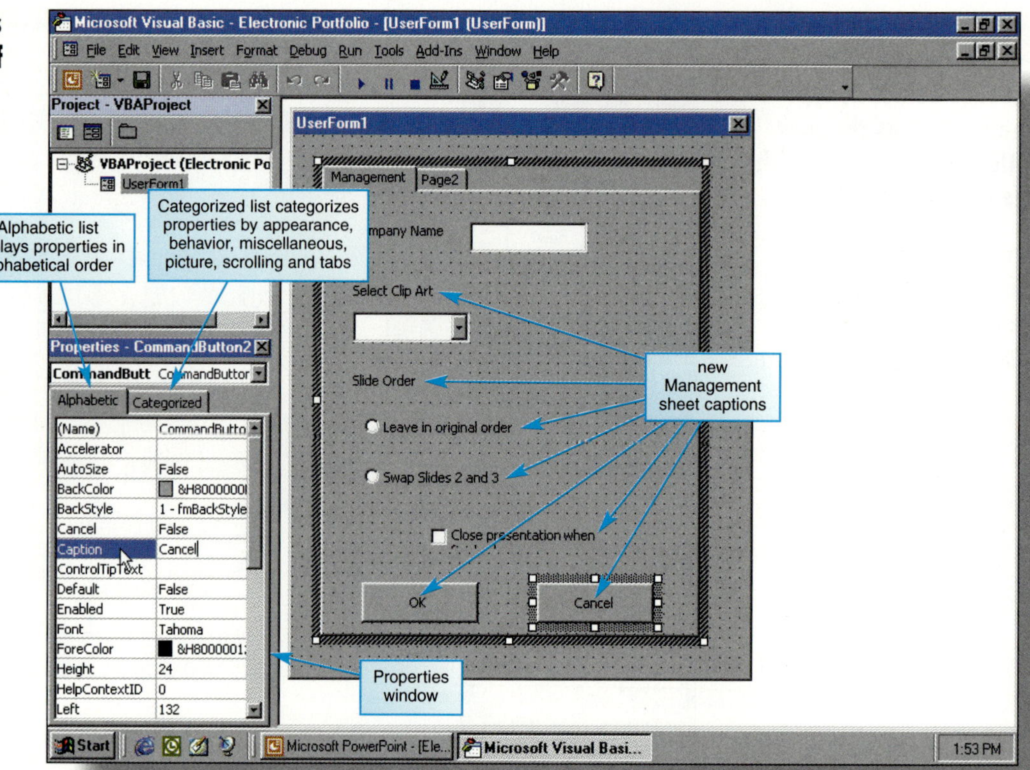

FIGURE 6-62

VBA Initiative

Microsoft Chairman and CEO Bill Gates promotes VBA as a key initiative for his company and its partners. To download and view a multimedia demonstration of his vision, visit the PowerPoint 2000 Project 6 More About page (www.scsite.com/pp2000/more.htm) and click VBA Initiative.

Table 6-5 New Management Sheet Captions

DEFAULT CAPTION	NEW CAPTION
Label2	Select Clip Art
Label3	Slide Order
OptionButton1	Leave in original order
OptionButton2	Swap Slides 2 and 3
CheckBox1	Close presentation when finished
CommandButton1	OK
CommandButton2	Cancel

The Properties window in Figure 6-62 has two tabs, Alphabetic and Categorized. The **Alphabetic list** displays the properties in alphabetical order. The **Categorized list** displays the properties in categories, such as appearance, behavior, font, and miscellaneous.

FINE TUNING THE USER INTERFACE After setting the properties for all the controls, you can fine tune the size and location of the controls in the form. You can reposition a control in the following ways:

1. Drag the control to its new location.
2. Select the control and use the arrow keys to reposition it.
3. Select the control and set the control's Top and Left properties in the Property window.

To use the third technique, you need to know the distance the control is from the top of the form and the left edge of the form in points. Recall that a point is equal to 1/72 of an inch. Thus, if the Top property of a control is 216, then the control is 3 inches (216 / 72) from the top of the form.

Controls also may require resizing. You need to increase the width of the CheckBox1 control so the caption fits on one line. You can resize a control in two ways:

1. Drag the sizing handles.
2. Select the control and set the control's Height and Width properties in the Properties window.

As with the Top and Left properties, the Height and Width properties are measured in points. Table 6-6 lists the exact points for the Top, Left, Height, and Width properties of each of the controls in the form.

The following steps resize and reposition the controls in the form using the values in Table 6-6.

Table 6-6 Exact Locations of Controls in the Form

CONTROL	TOP	LEFT	HEIGHT	WIDTH
Label1	18	18	18	57
TextBox1	12	90	18	102
Label2	54	18	18	51
ComboBox1	72	18	18	186
Label3	108	18	18	41
OptionButton1	132	24	18	103
OptionButton2	162	24	18	103
CheckBox1	198	66	18	138
CommandButton1	234	24	24	72
CommandButton2	234	132	24	72

Steps To Resize and Reposition the Controls on a Form

1 Click the Label1 control. Change its Top, Left, Height, and Width properties in the Properties window to those listed in Table 6-6.

The Label1 control Properties window displays as shown in Figure 6-63.

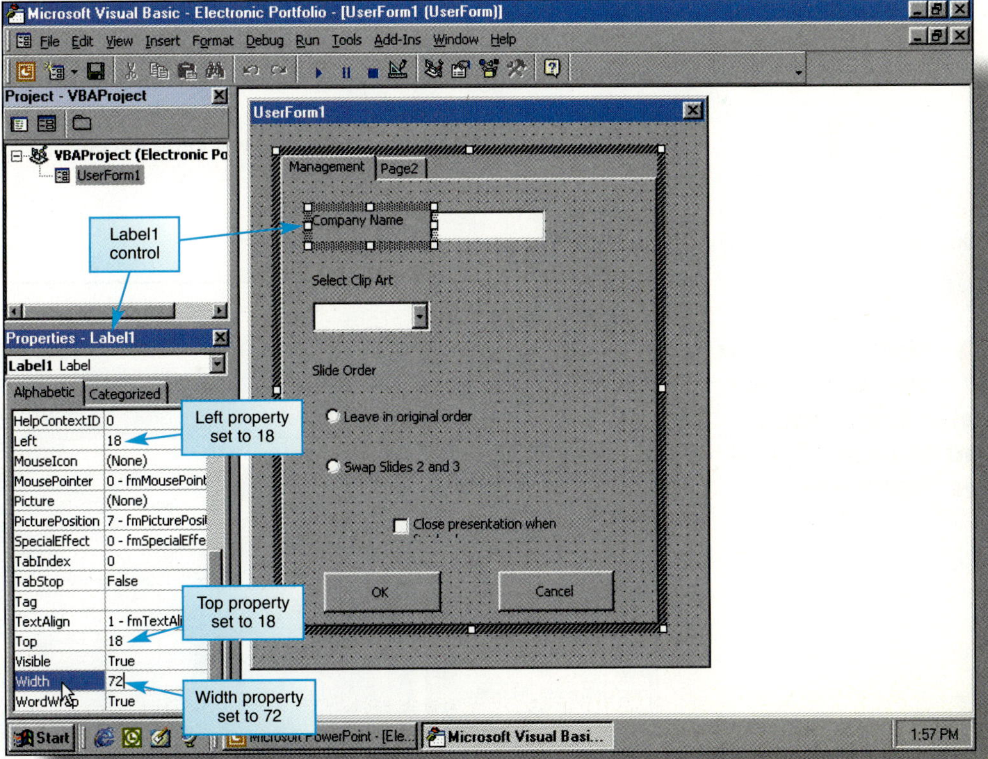

FIGURE 6-63

2 **One at a time, select the remaining controls and change their Top, Left, Height, and Width properties to those listed in Table 6-6.**

The form displays with the resized and repositioned controls (Figure 6-64).

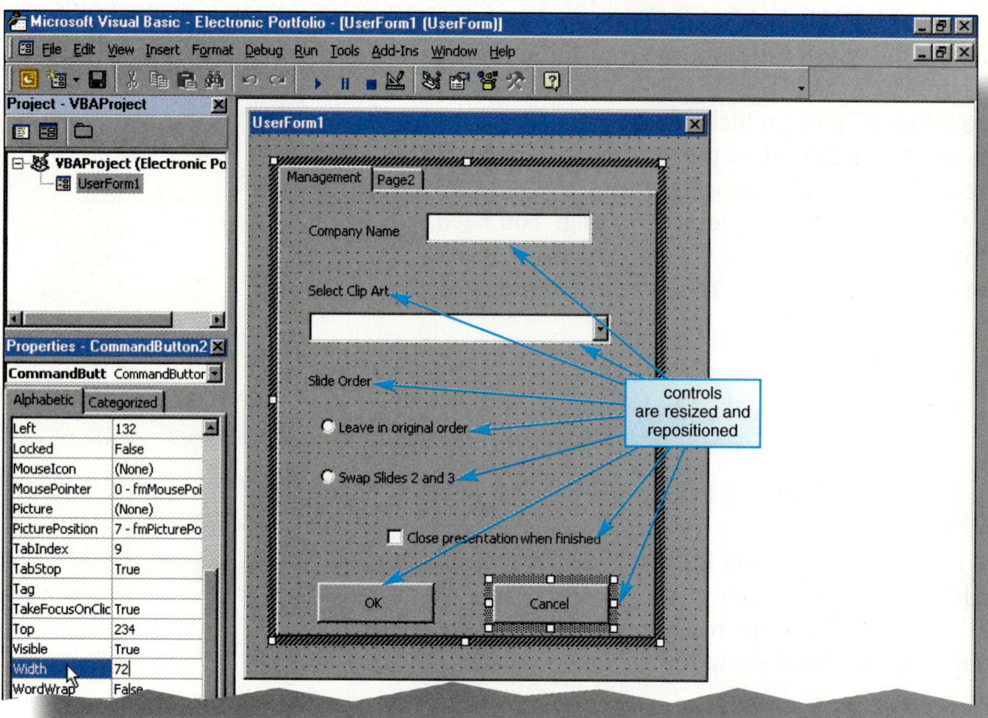

FIGURE 6-64

COPYING CONTROLS FROM ONE SHEET TO ANOTHER Now that you have added all the controls, changed their captions, and set their locations on the Page1 sheet, you want to copy these controls to the Page2 sheet. Perform the following steps to copy the controls from the Page1 sheet to the Page2 sheet.

To Copy Controls From One Sheet to Another

1 **Right-click a blank area of the Page1 sheet and then point to Select All on the shortcut menu (Figure 6-65).**

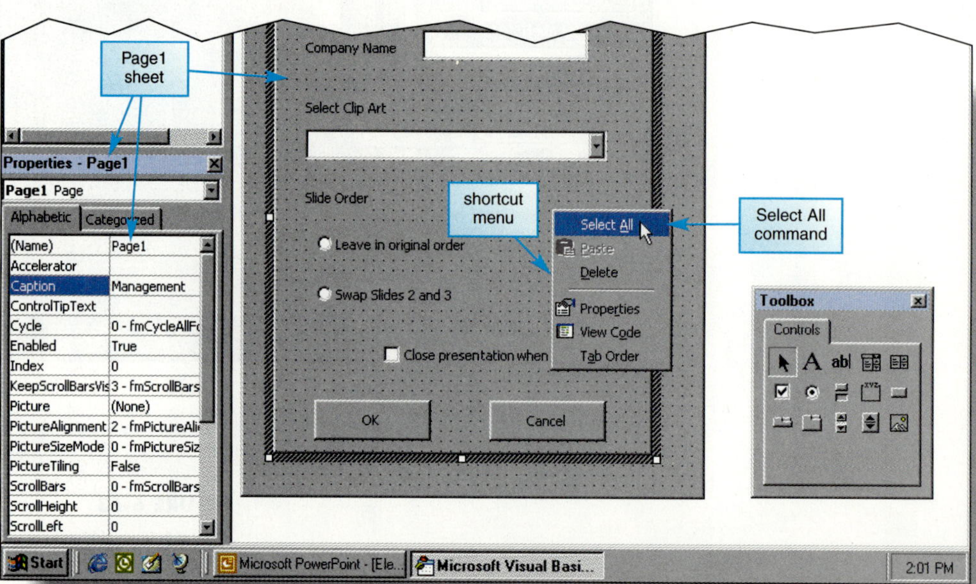

FIGURE 6-65

2 Click Select All. Point to the Copy button on the Standard toolbar.

All controls on the Page1 sheet are selected (Figure 6-66).

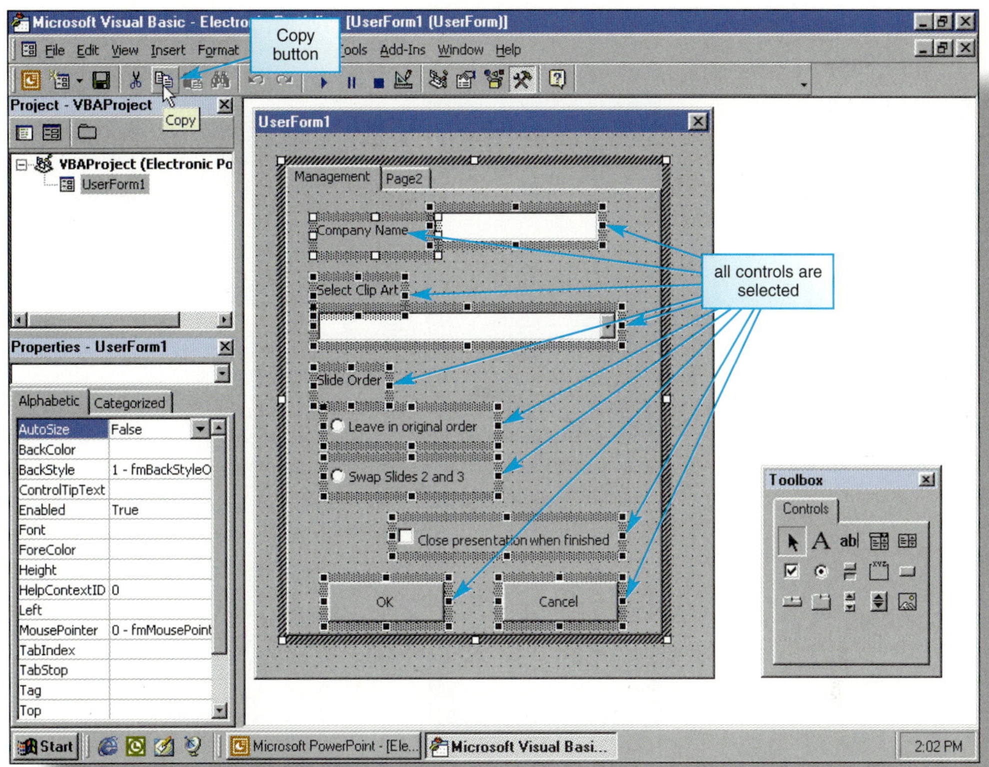

FIGURE 6-66

3 Click the Copy button. Click the Page2 tab on the form. Right-click the Page2 sheet and then point to Paste on the shortcut menu (Figure 6-67).

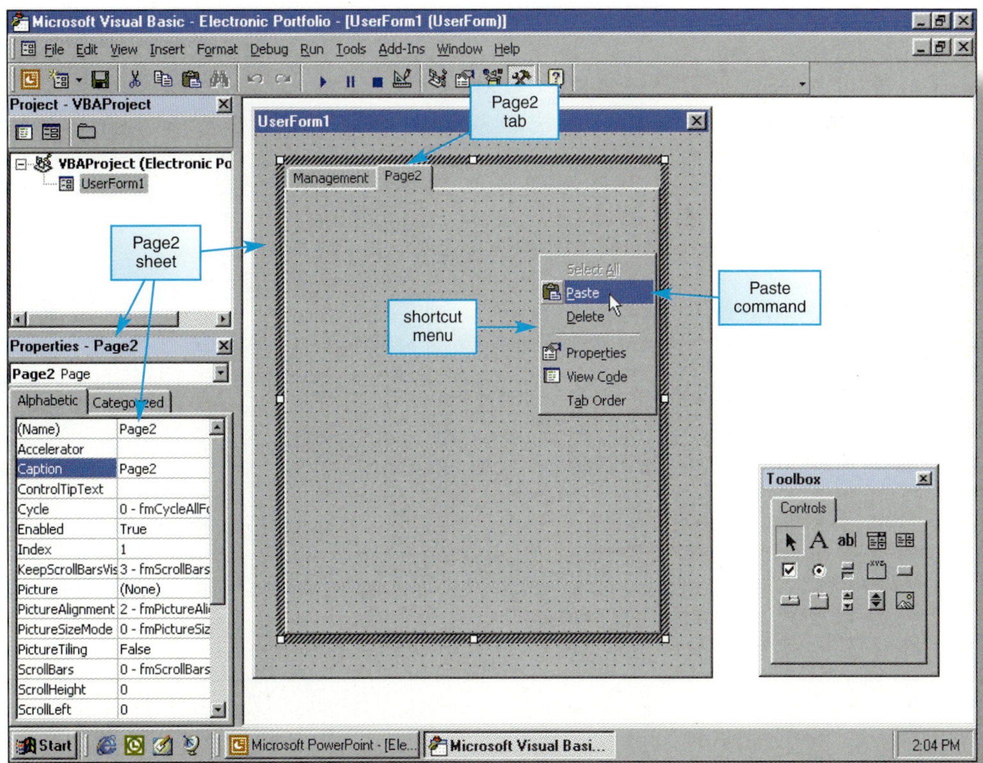

FIGURE 6-67

4 Click Paste. Point to the Page2 tab on the form.

The controls are added to the Page2 sheet (Figure 6-68).

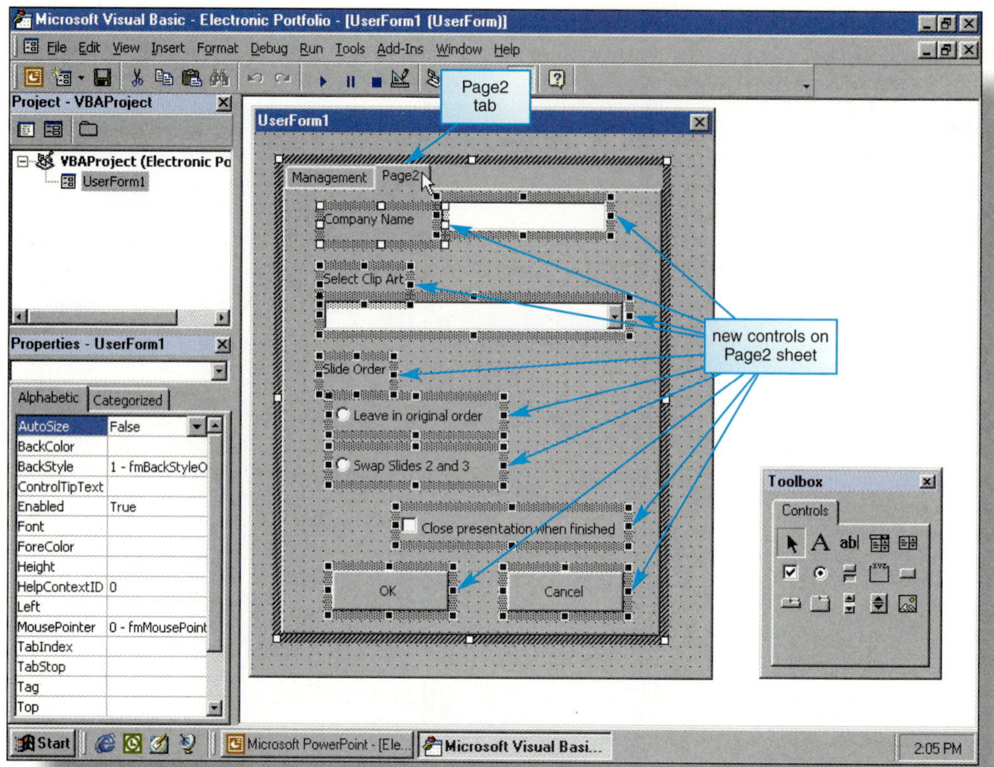

FIGURE 6-68

5 Click the Page2 tab. Click Caption in the Properties window, type `Computer` **as the new Page2 caption, and then press the ENTER key.**

The caption for the Computer sheet displays (Figure 6-69).

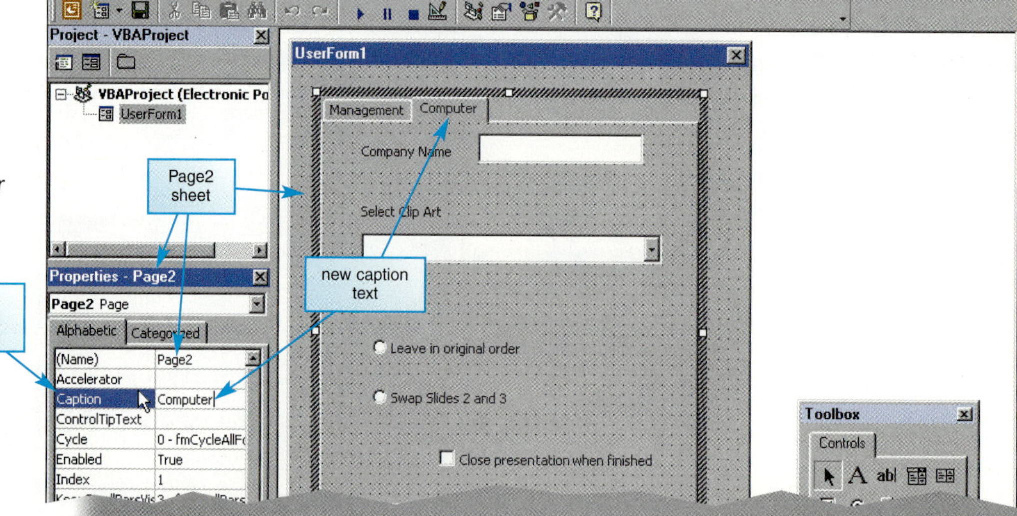

FIGURE 6-69

You want all controls on the Computer sheet are identical to those on the Management sheet except for the second option button. The user can choose to swap Slides 3 and 4 in the slide show if he is interviewing for a computer position. Perform the following steps to change the caption of the second option button on the Computer sheet, which has the control name OptionButton4.

TO CHANGE THE OPTIONBUTTON4 CAPTION

1. Click the OptionButton4 control. Click Caption in the OptionButton4 Properties window.
2. Type `Swap Slides 3 and 4` as the caption.
3. Press the ENTER key.

OptionButton4 displays on the form with the new caption (Figure 6-70).

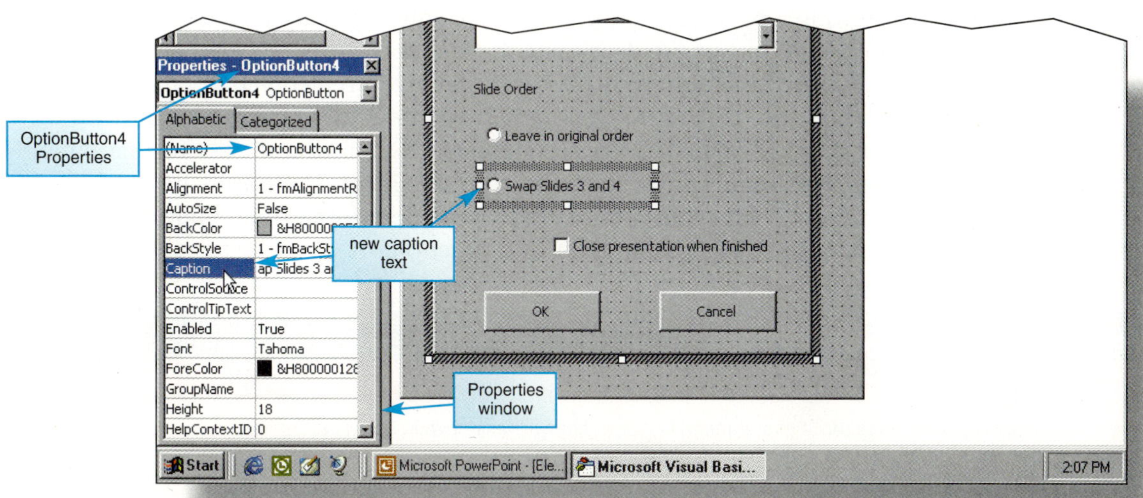

FIGURE 6-70

Saving the Form

The form is complete. Perform the following step to save your work before writing the VBA code.

TO SAVE A PRESENTATION

1. Click the Save button on the Standard toolbar.

PowerPoint saves the presentation by saving the changes made since the last save.

Step 3 – Write the VBA Code

You have created the interface and set the properties of the controls for this project. The next step is to write and then enter the procedure that will execute when you click the Create Presentation button on the Using Presentation toolbar. You will create this button near the end of this project. Clicking this button is the event that triggers execution of the procedure that assembles the custom presentation. As mentioned earlier, Visual Basic for Applications (VBA) is a powerful programming language that you can use to automate many activities described thus far in this book. The code for this project will include events and modules. A **module** is a collection of code that performs a specific task. Modules often serve as the smaller components in a program. They may, however, function independently as a macro.

The user will generate the **events** in this program by clicking buttons and boxes and by entering text in the boxes on the form. Recall that a macro consists of VBA statements associated with a menu command or button. To begin the process, you will write a module of VBA code to serve as a macro that displays a form when a user clicks the Create Presentation button.

VBA Partners

More than 100 companies using VBA are profiled in the Microsoft VBA site. They represent a variety of industries, including manufacturing, healthcare, and engineering. To learn how these companies have applied VBA, visit the PowerPoint 2000 Project 6 More About page (www.scsite.com/pp2000/more.htm) and click VBA Companies.

Editor Options

You can customize the appearance of your VBA code on the Editor Format tab sheet in the Options dialog box, accessed on the Tools menu. You can specify the foreground and background colors used for different types of text, such as Comment Text or Keyword Text.

PLANNING A PROCEDURE When you trigger the event that executes a procedure, PowerPoint steps through the Visual Basic statements one at a time, beginning at the top of the procedure. Thus, when you plan a procedure, remember that the order in which you place the statements in the procedure is important because this order determines the sequence of execution.

Once you know what you want the procedure to do, write the VBA code on paper in a format similar to Table 6-7. Then, before entering the procedure into the computer, test it by putting yourself in the position of PowerPoint and stepping through the instructions one at a time. As you do so, think about how it affects the slide show. Testing a procedure on paper before entering it is called **desk checking** and is an important part of the development process.

Adding comments before a procedure will help you remember its purpose at a later date. In Table 6-7, the first seven lines are comments. **Comments** begin with the word Rem or an apostrophe ('). These comments contain overall documentation and are placed before the procedure, above the Sub statement. Comments have no effect on the execution of a procedure; they simply provide information about the procedure, such as name, creation date, and function.

Table 6-7 Create Presentation Procedure

LINE	*VBA CODE*
1	`' Create Presentation Procedure        Author: Mary Lynn Tranita`
2	`' Date Created: 12/1/2001`
3	`' Run from: Electronic Portfolio by clicking Create Presentation button`
4	`' Function: When executed, this procedure accepts data that causes`
5	`'                           PowerPoint to build a custom presentation that adds`
6	`'                           the company name, selects clip art, and runs the slide show.`
7	`'`
8	`Sub CreatePresentationCareer()`
9	`    UserForm1.InitializeForm`
10	`    UserForm1.Show`
11	`End Sub`

A procedure begins with a **Sub statement** and ends with an **End Sub statement** (lines 8 and 11 in Table 6-7). The Sub statement begins with the name of the procedure. The parentheses following the procedure name indicate that arguments can be passed from one procedure to another. Passing arguments is beyond the scope of this project, but the parentheses still are required. The End Sub statement signifies the end of the procedure and returns PowerPoint to Ready mode.

The first executable statement in Table 6-7 is line 9, which calls the InitializeForm procedure for the form, indicated by the object name, UserForm1. Line 10 issues the command to show or display the form in the PowerPoint slide view window. Line 11 is the end of the procedure. Every procedure must conclude with an End Sub statement.

To enter a procedure, you use the Visual Basic Editor. To open the Visual Basic Editor, you can click the **View Code button** on the Project Explorer toolbar or click the Insert UserForm button arrow on the Standard toolbar and then click Module in the Insert UserForm list.

The Visual Basic Editor is a full-screen editor, which allows you to enter a procedure by typing the lines of VBA code as if you were using word processing software. At the end of a line, you press the ENTER key to move to the next line. If you make a mistake in a statement, you can use the arrow keys and the DELETE or BACKSPACE keys to correct it. You also can move the insertion point to previous lines to make corrections.

USING THE VISUAL BASIC EDITOR TO ENTER A PROCEDURE The following steps open the Visual Basic Editor and create the procedure for the Create Presentation module.

To Enter the Create Presentation Career Procedure

1 Click the Insert Module button arrow on the Standard toolbar and then point to Module.

The Insert Module list displays (Figure 6-71).

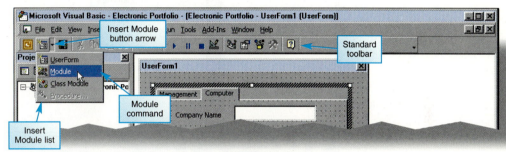

FIGURE 6-71

2 Click Module in the Insert Module list. When the Visual Basic Editor opens, type the seven comment statements (lines 1 through 7) in Table 6-7. Be certain to enter an apostrophe at the beginning of each comment line. Click the Properties window Close button.

PowerPoint starts the Visual Basic Editor and opens the Microsoft Visual Basic window (Figure 6-72). The comment lines display in green.

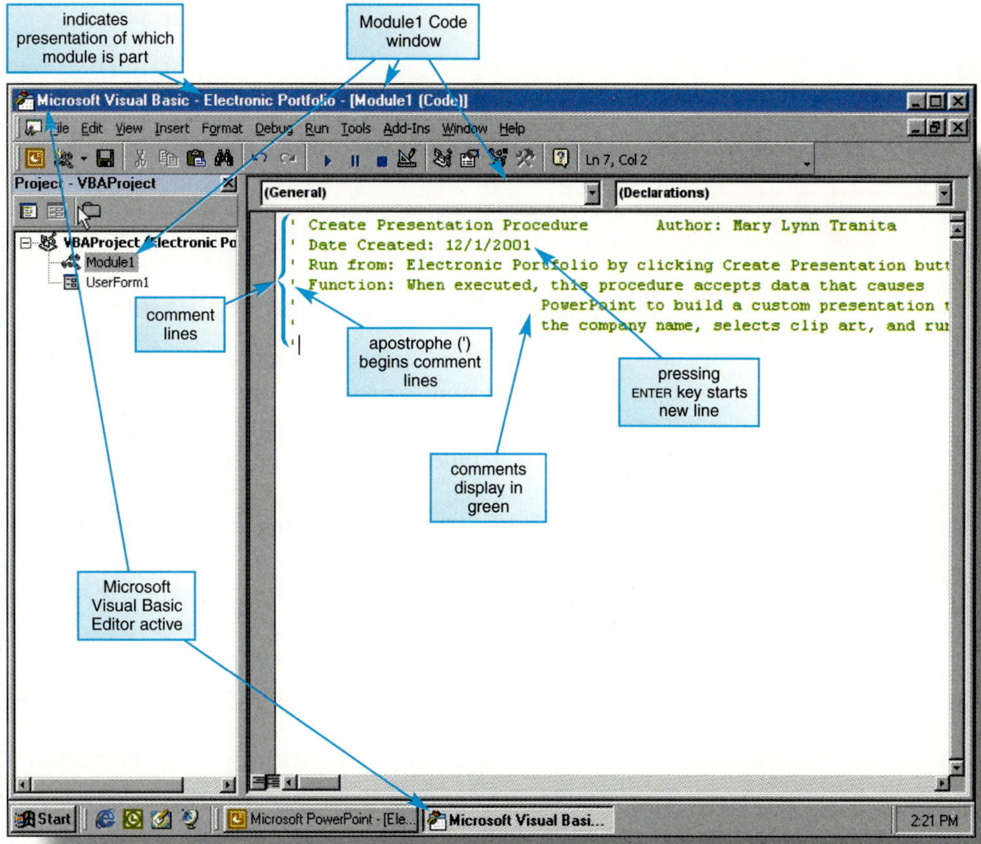

FIGURE 6-72

3 **Press the ENTER key to position the insertion point on the next line. Enter lines 8 through 10 in Table 6-7. Do not enter the End Sub statement (line 11). For clarity, indent all lines between the Sub statement and End Sub statement by three spaces. Point to the Close Window button on the right side of the menu bar.**

The Create Presentation Career procedure is complete (Figure 6-73). You do not need to enter the End Sub statement in line 11 of Table 6-7 because the Visual Basic Editor displays that line automatically.

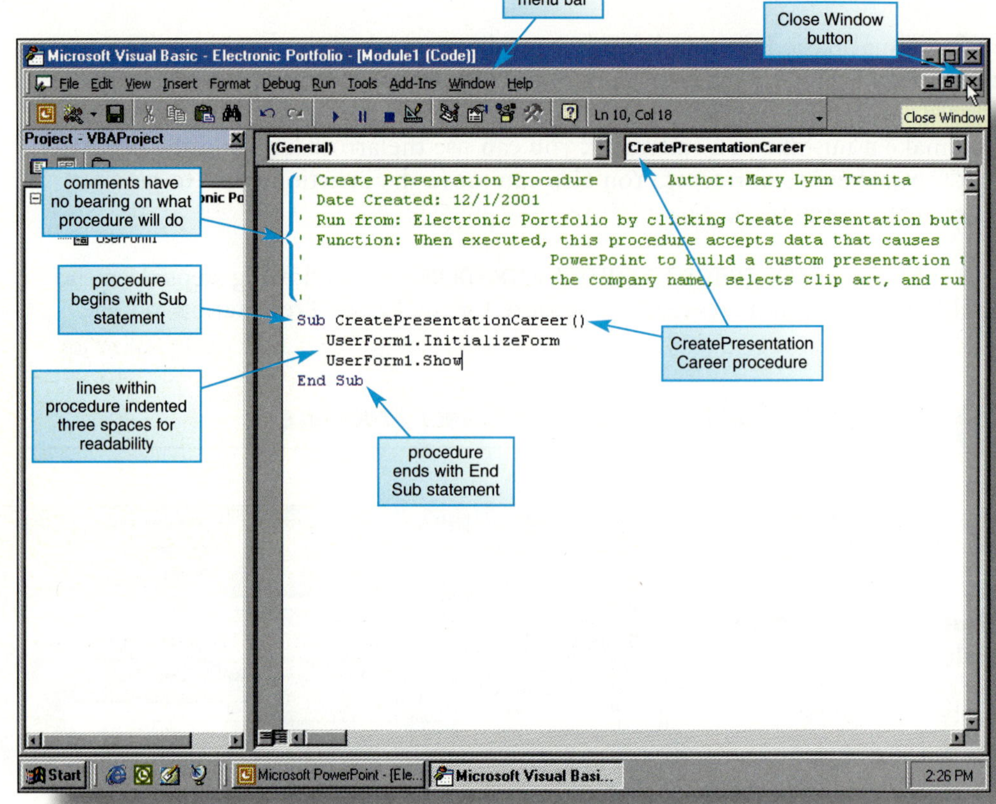

FIGURE 6-73

4 **Click the Close Window button.**

The Module1 Code window closes, and the UserForm window displays the form.

Other Ways

1. On Insert menu click Module
2. Press ALT+I, press M

More About

Variables

When variables are initialized, a numeric variable is initialized to zero, a variable-length string is initialized to a zero-length string (" "), which also is called a null string, and a fixed-length string is filled with zeros.

More About Visual Basic for Applications

Visual Basic for Applications uses many more statements than those presented here. Even this simple procedure, however, should help you understand the basic makeup of a Visual Basic statement. Lines 9 and 10 in the procedure shown in Figure 6-73 includes a period. The entry on the left side of the period tells PowerPoint which object you want to affect.

An **object** is a real-world thing. Your textbook, your car, your pets, your friends are objects. Visual Basic makes use of objects in its association with applications. This technique is described as object-oriented (OO). When it refers to programming it is called **OOP** (Object-Oriented Programming). The development of OOP provides a way to represent the world in conceptual terms that everyone understands. People relate to their everyday objects and easily can understand that these objects can have properties and behaviors.

An object is described by its properties. **Properties** are attributes that help us differentiate one object from another. For example, your car has a color, a certain body style, and a certain type of interior. These properties can be used to describe the car. The Visual Basic programming language has specific rules, or **syntax**. In Visual Basic syntax, you separate an object and its property with a period. For example, *car.color* specifies a car object and the property color. You would write the statement *car.color = "red"* to set the value of the color property to red.

An object also has certain behaviors, or methods. A **method** is a function or action you want the object to perform, or an action that will be performed on an object. You can write your own functions, or you can use the built-in methods supplied with Visual Basic. Methods associated with car, pet, and friend objects might be drive, feed, and talk, respectively. The drive method would be written as *car.drive*, just as in the statement UserForm1.Show, where UserForm1 is the object, and Show is the method.

The following example shows that you can change an object's property value during execution of a procedure. Similar statements often are used to clear the properties of controls or to set them to initial values. This process is called **initialization**. The object in this case is a text box control.

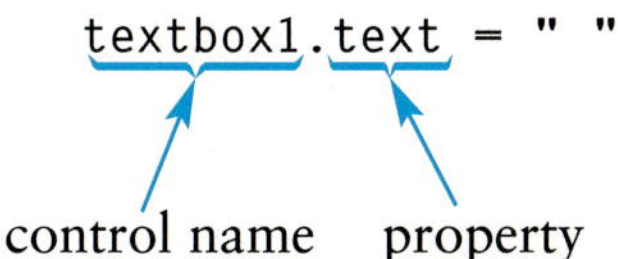

VBA Help

Microsoft offers a variety of VBA help on its Web site. Topics include understanding VBA syntax, setting References, using Object Variables, and writing efficient code. To view this site, visit the PowerPoint 2000 Project 6 More About page (www.scsite.com/pp2000/more.htm) and click VBA Help.

WRITING THE INITIALIZING VARIABLES PROCEDURE Whenever you need to work with an object's properties or methods in more than one line of code, you can use the With statement to eliminate some coding. The With statement accepts an object as a parameter and is followed by several lines of code that pertain to this object. You therefore do not need to retype the object name in these lines. Table 6-8 describes the general form of the With statement.

Table 6-8 With Statement Format

General Form:	`With object`
	`Visual Basic code`
	`End With`

Comment:	where object is any valid Visual Basic or user-defined object

Example:	`With textbox1`
	`.text = ""`
	`End With`

The next step is to write the procedure to initialize some of the control properties. Recall from Step 2 of this project how you added the controls to the form and set some of their properties. With respect to VBA, PowerPoint has two modes: design mode and run mode. In **design mode**, you can resize controls, assign properties to controls, and enter VBA code. In **run mode**, all controls are active. That is, if you click a control, it triggers the event, and PowerPoint executes the procedure associated with the control.

The initialize procedure in Table 6-9 sets some controls during run mode. If the With statement were not used in Table 6-9, then each statement would have to be preceded by the specific object name. The Initialize Form procedure ensures the text boxes are clear, adds the description of the clip art choices to the combo boxes, sets the initial values for the option buttons, and clears the check boxes.

The **With statements** in lines 3, 6, 10, 14, 18, 21, 24, and 27 provide a shortcut to some of the complicated syntax sometimes used in VBA. Lines 4 and 7 clear the text boxes. The text properties are assigned a null value. Lines 11, 12, 15, and 16 add the clip art choices to the combo boxes. The Management sheet is assigned "Meeting" and "Training" clip art choices. The Computer sheet is assigned "Parachutes" and "Animated Computer" clip art choices. Lines 18 through 23 set the Slide Order option buttons to their default values. By setting the values of Option Buttons 1 and 3 to True, the default slide order value for each sheet is Leave in Original Order. Lines 24 through 29 clear the check boxes. The check box values are set to False. Each With statement must end with an End With statement as indicated in lines 5, 8, 13, 17, 20, 23, 26, and 29. To complete the section of code for the InitializeForm procedure, an End Sub statement closes the procedure at line 30.

Table 6-9 Initialize Form Procedure

LINE	VBA CODE
1	`Sub InitializeForm()`
2	`' Clear text boxes`
3	`With textbox1`
4	`    .Text = ""`
5	`End With`
6	`With textbox2`
7	`    .Text = ""`
8	`End With`
9	`' Add items to combo box`
10	`With ComboBox1`
11	`  .AddItem "Meeting"`
12	`  .AddItem "Training"`
13	`End With`
14	`With ComboBox2`
15	`  .AddItem "Parachutes"`
16	`  .AddItem "Animated Computer"`
17	`End With`
18	`With OptionButton1`
19	`    .Value = True`
20	`End With`
21	`With OptionButton3`
22	`    .Value = True`
23	`End With`
24	`With CheckBox1`
25	`    .Value = False`
26	`End With`
27	`With CheckBox2`
28	`    .Value = False`
29	`End With`
30	`End Sub`

CommandButton Click Events

You can allow a user to press the ENTER key during run time as a substitute method for clicking a command button by changing the CommandButton control's Default property. Only one command button on a form can be the default command button. When Default is set to True for one command button, it automatically is set to False for all other command buttons on the form.

To Enter the InitializeForm Procedure

1 Click the View Code Button on the Project Explorer toolbar. Point to the Project Explorer Close button on the Project Explorer toolbar.

UserForm1 is selected in the Project Explorer window (Figure 6-74).

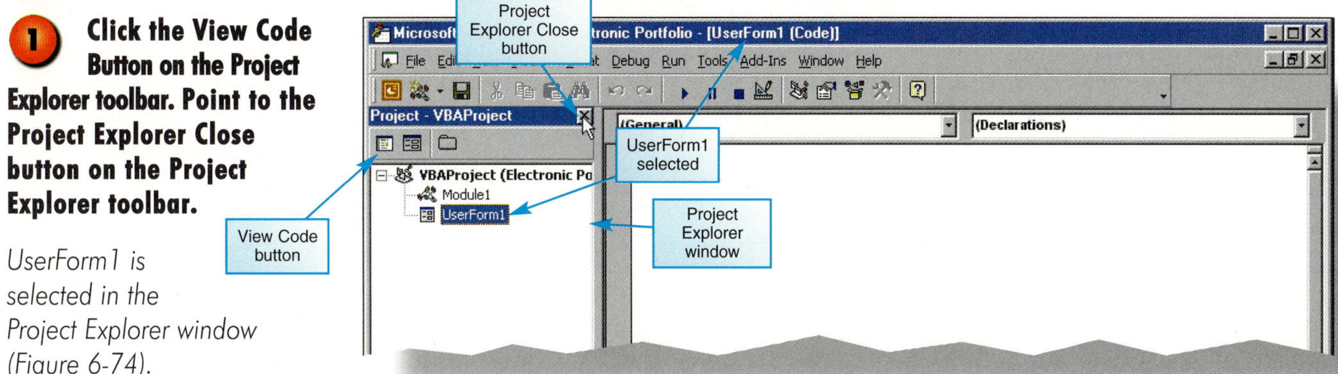

FIGURE 6-74

2 Click the Project Explorer Close button. When the UserForm1 Code window displays in its entirety, enter lines 1 through 29 of the VBA code shown in Table 6-9.

The InitializeForm procedure displays as shown in Figure 6-75. You do not need to enter line 30 in Table 6-9 because the Visual Basic Editor displays that line automatically.

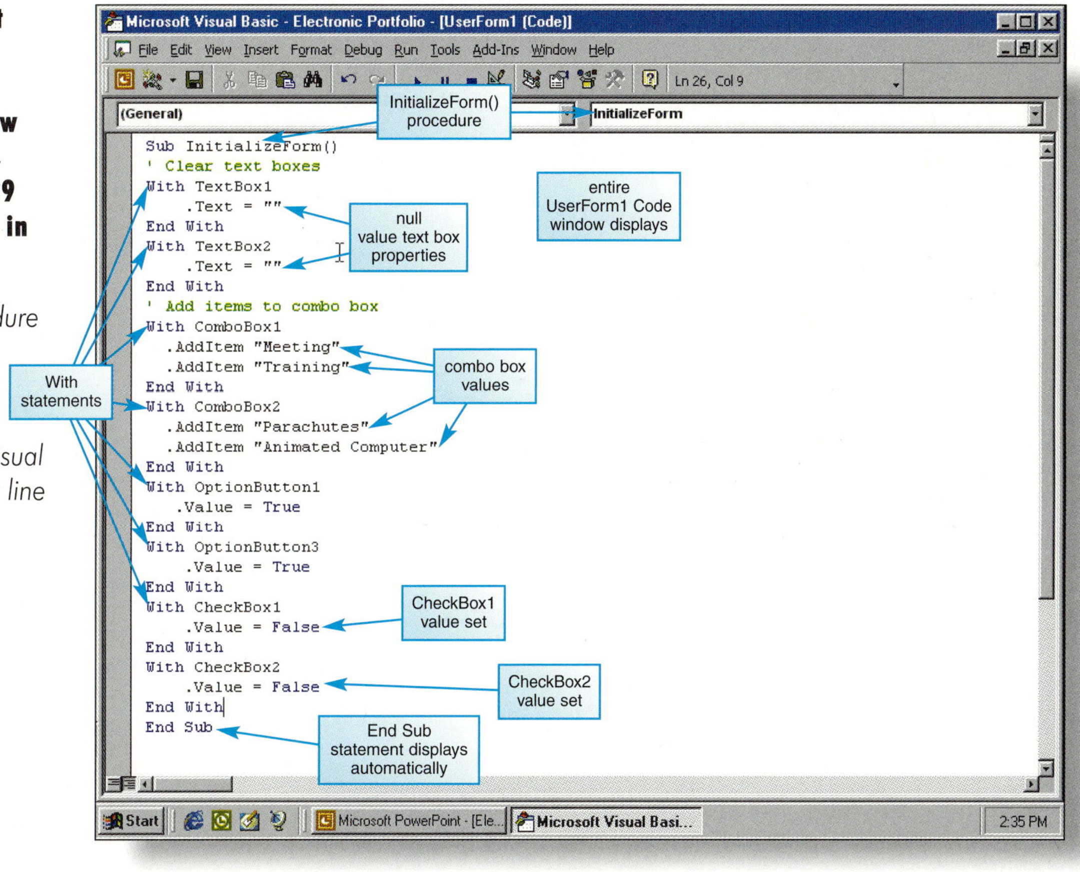

Microsoft Visual Basic - Electronic Portfolio - [UserForm1 (Code)]

```
Sub InitializeForm()
' Clear text boxes
With TextBox1
    .Text = ""
End With
With TextBox2
    .Text = ""
End With
' Add items to combo box
With ComboBox1
  .AddItem "Meeting"
  .AddItem "Training"
End With
With ComboBox2
  .AddItem "Parachutes"
  .AddItem "Animated Computer"
End With
With OptionButton1
   .Value = True
End With
With OptionButton3
    .Value = True
End With
With CheckBox1
    .Value = False
End With
With CheckBox2
    .Value = False
End With
End Sub
```

InitializeForm() procedure
entire UserForm1 Code window displays
null value text box properties
With statements
combo box values
CheckBox1 value set
CheckBox2 value set
End Sub statement displays automatically

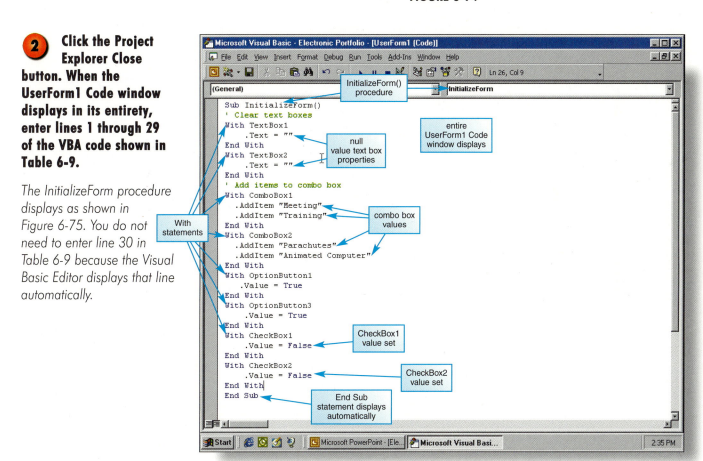

FIGURE 6-75

WRITING THE COMMANDBUTTON1 PROCEDURE The next step is to write the code for the CommandButton1 procedure shown in Table 6-10. The CommandButton1 procedure is activated when the user clicks the OK button on the form for the Management style presentation. The code for this procedure is associated with the Click event; the spaces preceding the lines are used for visual clarity.

Table 6-10 CommandButton1 Procedure

VBA CODE

```
' Set the presentation to apply the template and clip art
Set MgmtSlides = Application.ActivePresentation
With MgmtSlides
    .ApplyTemplate "a:\expedition.pot"
End With
' Validate entries in text box and combo box
If TextBox1.Text = "" Then
    MsgBox "Company Name missing, please add company name ", vbOK, "Management"
    TextBox1.SetFocus
Else
' Place company name in title
  MgmtCompanyName = textbox1.Text
  Set mgmtTitleSlide = ActivePresentation.Slides(1)
  mgmtTitleSlide.Shapes.Title.TextFrame.TextRange.Text = "A Management Position" & vbCr & "With " & MgmtCompanyName
  ' Check if clip art was chosen
  If ComboBox1.Value = "" Then
     MsgBox "Please select a clip art object from the list", vbOKOnly, "Clip art missing"
     ComboBox1.SetFocus
  Else
  ' Place selected clip art in slide
  Select Case ComboBox1.Value
     Case "Meeting"  'first
        Set MgmtClipartSlide = Application.ActivePresentation.Slides(2)
        With MgmtClipartSlide
           .Shapes.AddPicture "a:\meeting.wmf", True, True, 375, 150, 300, 350
        End With
     Case "Training"  'second
        Set MgmtClipartSlide = Application.ActivePresentation.Slides(2)
        With MgmtClipartSlide
           .Shapes.AddPicture "a:\training.gif", True, True, 375, 150, 300, 350
        End With
  End Select
  ' Check if slides should be swapped; if so, swap them
  If OptionButton2.Value = True Then
     ActivePresentation.Slides.Range(Array(3)).Cut
     ActivePresentation.Slides.Paste 2
  End If
  ' wrap up, reset combo boxes for next time,
```

Table 6-10 CommandButton1 Procedure *(continued)*

LINE VBA CODE

```
39          ' close form and run presentation
40          ResetComboxes
41          UserForm1.Hide
42          Unload UserForm1
43          ' Start slide show
44          If CheckBox1.Value = True Then
45              Set MgmtSlides = Application.ActivePresentation
46              With MgmtSlides.SlideShowSettings
47                  .RangeType = ppShowNamedSlideShow
48                  .Run
49              End With
50          End If
51         End If
52      End If
```

Line 2 sets the presentation object to MgmtSlides. Using the With statement in line 3, the assignment statement in line 4 assigns the Expedition design template file to the presentation using the ApplyTemplate method. Lines 7 through 14 verify that the Company Name text box (TextBox1) is not blank using an If-Then-Else statement (see Table 6-10). If it is blank, a message will display (line 8) notifying the user an entry must be made, and the insertion point will be placed back in the text box by the **SetFocus** method (line 9). The SetFocus method is used to set the insertion point or mouse pointer on or in a control. To set focus to a control, write the control name, a period, and the SetFocus method.

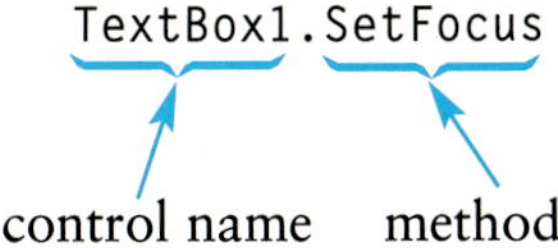

If the Company Name text box has a name entered, line 12 assigns the name (in textbox1.text) to the slide. The first slide (line 13) is designated as the title slide, and the contents of the title slide are constructed in line 14. The procedure then verifies that a clip art item has been selected from the Select Clip Art combo box (ComboBox1) in lines 16 through 18. If the ComboBox1 value is blank, a message displays notifying the user to select a clip art item (line 17) and places the focus back on the combo box (line 18). If a clip art item has been selected, the Select Case statements (see Table 6-10) in lines 22 through 33 assign the selected clip art item to the slide. Depending on the selected clip art, in the Management style presentation, lines 23 or 28 assign Slide 2 as the slide to have clip art. Lines 25 or 30 then add the picture to Slide 2 with the appropriate settings.

Color Schemes

If you develop a color scheme for one slide that you want to use on another slide, click the Slide Sorter View button on the View button bar, click the Format Painter button on the Standard toolbar, and click the slide to which you want to apply the color scheme. You also can use this technique to copy a color scheme from one presentation to another. With both presentations open, click Arrange All on the Window menu, click Arrange All, and then follow the above steps.

Next, the values of the option buttons are examined. In the Management style presentation, the user can indicate to swap Slides 2 and 3. If the Leave in original order option button has been selected, nothing happens; otherwise lines 35 and 36 swap the slides. To swap the slides, the VBA code uses the Cut and Paste technique. The last steps in the procedure (lines 40 through 52) reset the combo boxes, hide and unload the form, and examine the check box value to determine if the slide show should run immediately or later.

Line 40 calls a subroutine, which will be written later, that resets the values in the combo boxes back to blank. Line 41 hides the form with the Hide method (UserForm1.Hide). Line 42 **unloads** the form, which removes it from the desktop during run time. If CheckBox1 has been checked, the active presentation is assigned to the MgmtSlides object (line 45), the RangeType property is set to the built-in PowerPoint constant for the named slide show, and the Run method used in line 48 launches the PowerPoint presentation.

Designing Templates

You can change the predesigned formats and color schemes that are part of a design template, or you can create a new template to fit your specific needs. To design a template, open an existing presentation and make the desired changes, or click the New button on the Standard toolbar to start with a blank presentation. On the File menu click Save As, type a name for your design template in the File name text box, and then click Design Template in the Save as type box. You can save this new design template with the other design templates in the Presentation Designs folder, or you can save it in one of your own folders.

If-Then-Else Statement The If-Then-Else statement represents a two-way decision with an action specified for each of the two alternatives. The computer never executes both the true and false alternatives. It selects one or the other alternative based on the result of a test or condition. The general form of the If-Then-Else statement is shown in Table 6-11. You place the Visual Basic code to be executed if the result of the conditional test is True after the Then keyword.

Table 6-11 If-Then-Else Statement Format

General form:	`If condition Then`
	`    Visual Basic statements to execute if condition is true`
	`Else`
	`    Visual Basic statements to execute if condition is false`
	`End If`

Comment:	The condition is a statement that compares values. If the result of the comparison statement is true, Visual Basic executes the statements after the Then statement. If the result of the comparison statement is false, Visual Basic executes the statements after the Else statement.

Example:	`If textbox1.Text = "" Then`
	`    MsgBox "Company Name missing.", vbOK, "Management"`
	`    textbox1.SetFocus`
	`Else`
	`   MgmtCompanyName = textbox1.Text`
	`End If`

A **condition** is any expression that evaluates to True or False. In the example in Table 6-11, Visual Basic evaluates the condition, *TextBox1.text* = " ", by comparing the value in the text property of TextBox1 with a blank value, indicated by the empty double quotes. If the user has not entered the Company Name, the text property is blank, so the condition evaluates to True and the "Company Name missing" message displays. If the user had entered a Company Name, the value of the text property would not be blank, and the condition would evaluate to False. Visual Basic then would execute the Else statement, which assigns the entered name to the MgmtCompanyName object on the form. When writing an If statement, leave a space between the word If and the condition so Visual Basic does not interpret the If statement incorrectly. Table 6-12 shows the comparison operators and their meanings.

Table 6-12 Comparison Operators

OPERATOR	EXAMPLE	RESULTS
=	a = b	True if a equals b
<>	a <> b	True if a does not equal b
>	a > b	True if a is greater than b
<	a < b	True if a is less than b
>=	a >= b	True if a is greater than or equal to b
<=	a <= b	True if a is less than or equal to b

The If-Then-Else statements in lines 7 and 16 verify the user entered a value in the Company Name text box and selected a clip art item from the Clip Art combo box. The If-Then statements in line 34 and 44 execute code based on the values of the Slide Order option buttons and the Close presentation when finished check box.

The Select Case statements (lines 21 through 32) are used to streamline the use of multiple If-Then-Else statements. The value of the combo box is examined, and the appropriate clip art item is assigned to Slide 2. The Set statement in line 23 defines the shape object name, MgmtClipartSlide. Using the With statement described earlier, the Shapes.AddPicture property in line 25 assigns the clip art and sets the clip art dimensions. Table 6-13 describes the general form of the Select Case statement.

Table 6-13 Select Case Statement Format

General form:

```
Select Case testexpression
        Case expression1
              Visual Basic statements
        Case expression2
              Visual Basic statements
End Select
```

Comments: The Select Case statement begins the case structure. testexpression is the name of a valid Visual Basic expression or variable. If testexpression matches the expression associated with a Case clause, the Visual Basic statements following that Case clause are executed. End Select ends the Select Case structure.

Example:

```
Select Case ComboBox2.Value
        Case "Parachutes"   'first
         Set CompClipartSlide = Application.ActivePresentation.Slides(2)
         With CompClipartSlide
          .Shapes.AddPicture "a:\parachutes.wmf", True, True, 375, 150, 300, 350
         End With
        Case "Animated Computer"   'Second
         Set CompClipartSlide = Application.ActivePresentation.Slides(2)
         With CompClipartSlide
          .Shapes.AddPicture "a:\anicomp1.gif", True, True, 375, 150, 300, 300
         End With
End Select
```

The If-Then statement in line 34 checks the value of the option button. If OptionButton2 is selected, then lines 35 and 36 swap Slide 2 and Slide 3. If OptionButton1 is selected, then the original sequence of the slides is left intact. Lines 40 through 42 perform the finishing tasks. The combo boxes are reset for next time the procedure is executed, and the form is hidden and unloaded. Lines 44 through 50 contain the final If-Then statement that examines the value in the check box to see if the presentation should be run or closed upon finishing. The Set statement on line 45 assigns the active presentation to the MgmtSlides object. Recall that the With statement allows you to simplify using the current object. Consequently, the With statement on line 46 allows you to use the object name, Application.ActivePresentation, without typing this entire object name on lines 47 and 48. The RangeType property of the SlideShowSettings is set on line 47. ppShowNamed SlideShow is a built-in PowerPoint VBA constant that indicates all slides in the presentation. Finally, the slide show is run by the .Run method on line 48. The final End If statements close all the If-Then and If-Then-Else statements because every If statement needs a corresponding End If statement.

Steps To Enter the CommandButton1 Procedure

1 Click the Object box arrow at the top of the Code window, and then point to CommandButton1 in the Object list (Figure 6-76).

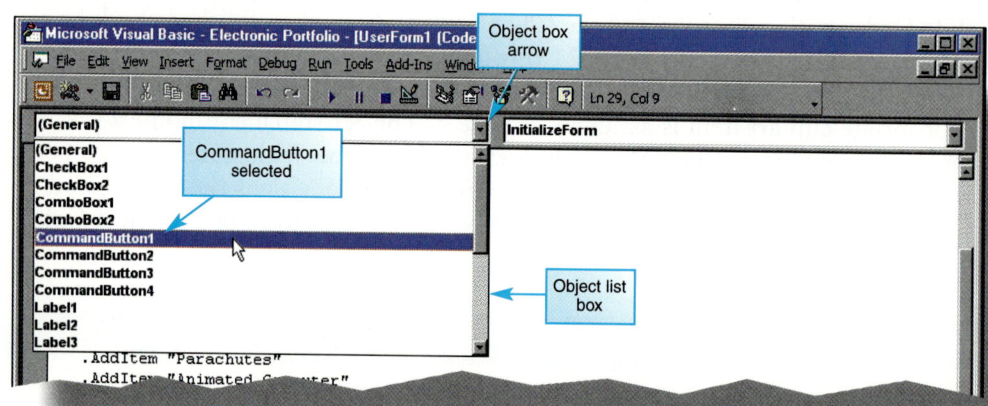

FIGURE 6-76

2 Click CommandButton1. Make sure Click is in the Procedure box.

The Visual Basic Editor displays the Sub and End Sub statements for the CommandButton1 procedure and positions the insertion point between the two statements (Figure 6-77).

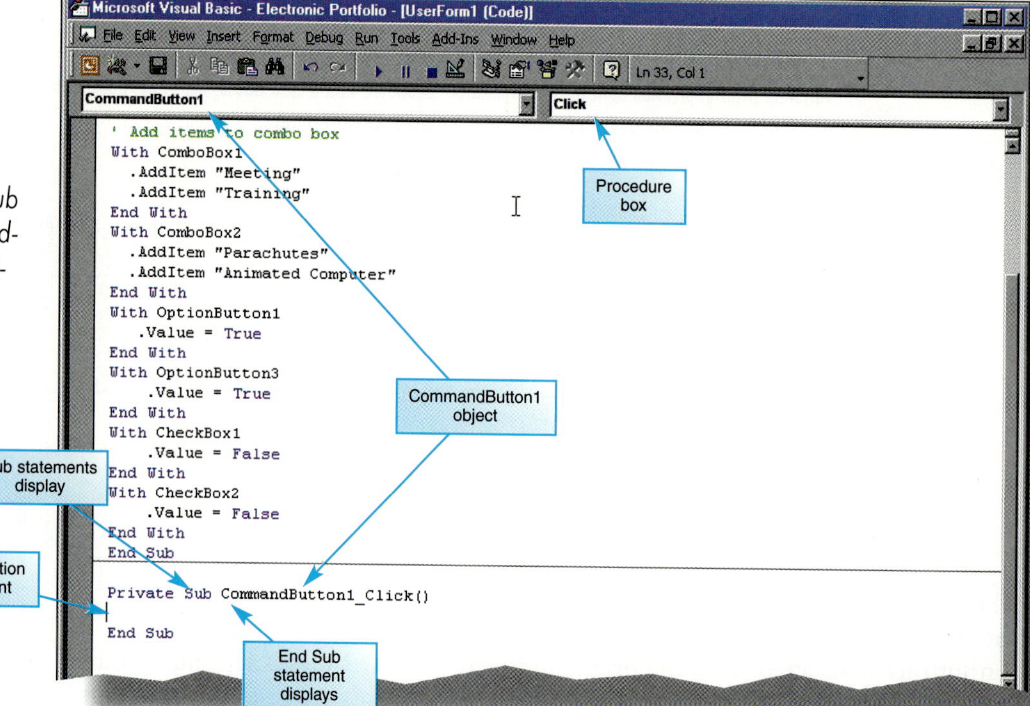

FIGURE 6-77

3 Enter the VBA code shown in lines 1 through 52 in Table 6-10.

The CommandButton1_Click() procedure displays as shown in Figure 6-78. You do not need to enter the End Sub statement in line 53 of Table 6-10 because the Visual BasicEditor displays that line automatically.

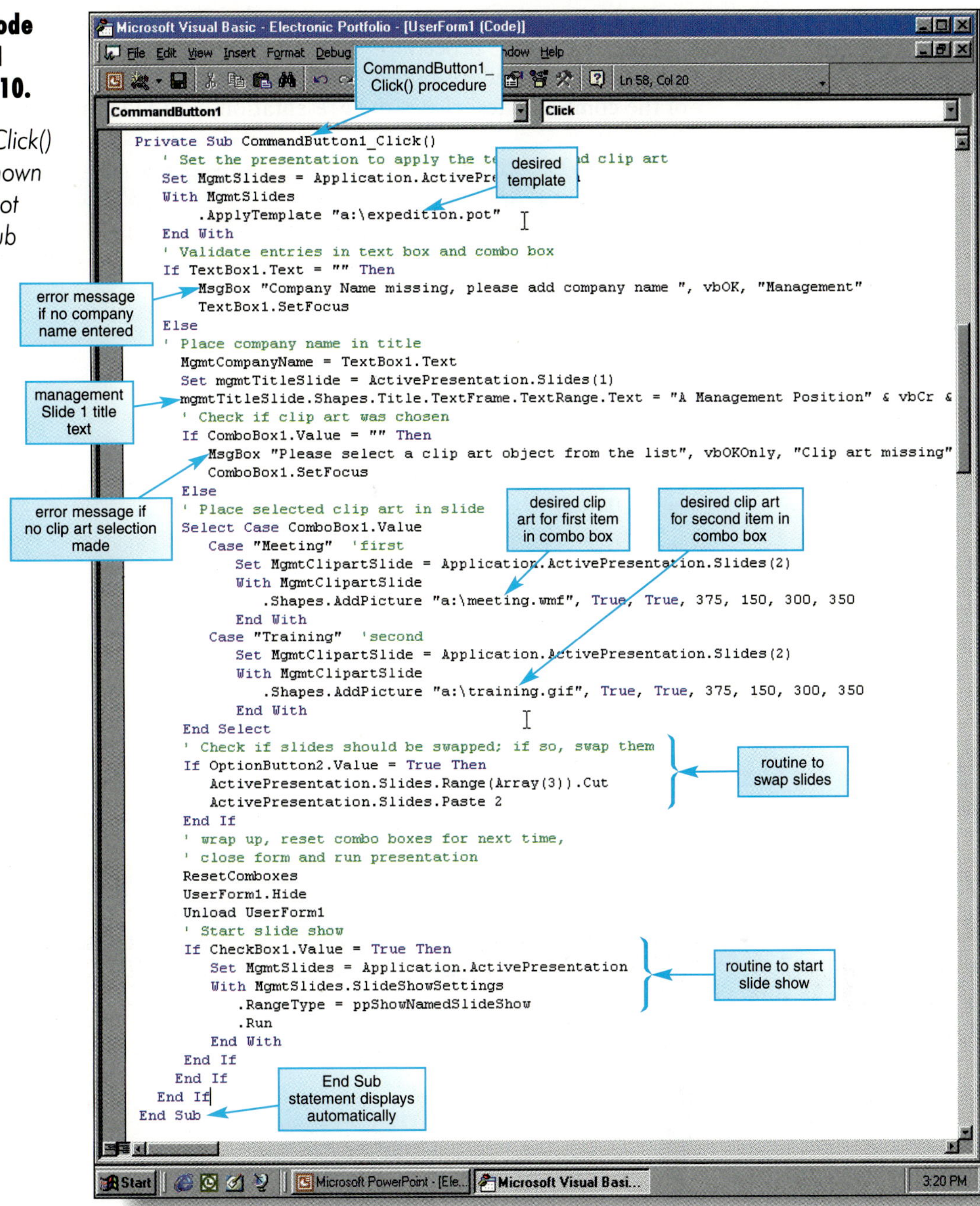

FIGURE 6-78

WRITING THE COMMANDBUTTON2 PROCEDURE The next step is to write the CommandButton2 procedure. This procedure is executed if the user clicks the Cancel button. The procedure calls a subroutine (ResetComboxes) that clears the text value of the combo boxes, closes the presentation, and hides and unloads the form.

Table 6-14 CommandButton2 Procedure

LINE	VBA CODE
1	`' Close the application presentation`
2	`' without saving`
3	`ResetComboxes`
4	`With Application.ActivePresentation`
5	`    .Close`
6	`End With`
7	`UserForm1.Hide`
8	`Unload UserForm1`

Line 3 calls the subroutine to clear the combo boxes. Lines 4 though 6 close the current active presentation. Line 7 hides the form (UserForm1), and line 8 unloads the form.

To Enter the CommandButton2 Procedure

1 Click the Object box arrow at the top of the Code window, and then click CommandButton2 in the Object list. Make sure Click is in the Procedure box.

The Visual Basic Editor displays the Sub and End Sub statements for the CommandButton2 procedure and positions the insertion point between the two statements (Figure 6-79).

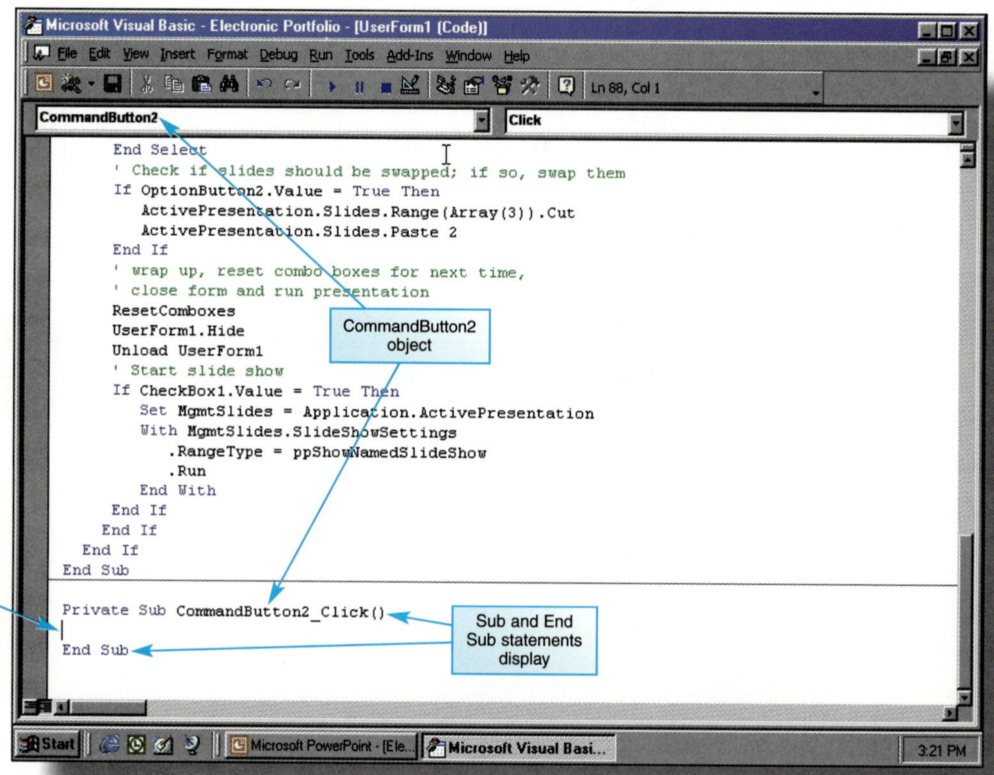

FIGURE 6-79

Enter the VBA code shown in Table 6-14.

The CommandButton2_Click() procedure displays as shown in Figure 6-80.

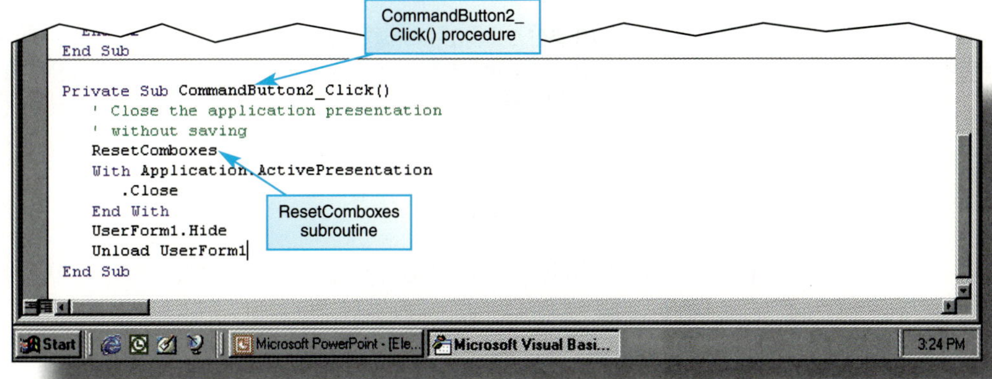

FIGURE 6-80

WRITING THE COMMANDBUTTON3 PROCEDURE The next step is to write the CommandButton3 procedure. The code for the CommandButton3 button control almost is identical to the code for the CommandButton1 control button in Table 6-10. The difference between the two procedures is that CommandButton1 sets the presentation clip art, design template, and control properties for the Management slides, while CommandButton3 sets the presentation clip art, design template, and control properties for the Computer slides.

Table 6-15 CommandButton3 Procedure

LINE VBA CODE

```
' Set the presentation to apply the template and the clip art
Set ComputerSlides = Application.ActivePresentation
With ComputerSlides
    .ApplyTemplate "a:\cactus.pot"
End With
' Validate entries in the text box and combo box
If textbox2.Text = "" Then
    MsgBox “Company Name missing, add company name ", vbOK, "Computer"
    textbox2.SetFocus
Else
' Place company name in title
  CompCompanyName = textbox2.Text
  Set CompTitleSlide = ActivePresentation.Slides(1)
  CompTitleSlide.Shapes.Title.TextFrame.TextRange.Text = "Working In Information Systems" & vbCr &
"At " & CompCompanyName
  'Check if clip art was chosen
  If ComboBox2.Value = "" Then
     MsgBox "Please select a clip art object from the list", vbOKOnly, "Clip art missing"
     ComboBox2.SetFocus
  Else
```

(continued)

Table 6-15 CommandButton3 Procedure *(continued)*

```
LINE  VBA CODE
20            ' Place selected clip art in slide
21            Select Case ComboBox2.Value
22                    Case "Parachutes"   'first
23                        Set CompClipartSlide = Application.ActivePresentation.Slides(2)
24                        With CompClipartSlide
25                            .Shapes.AddPicture "a:\parachutes.wmf", True, True, 375, 150, 300, 350
26                        End With
27                    Case "Animated Computer"   'Second
28                        Set CompClipartSlide = Application.ActivePresentation.Slides(2)
29                        With CompClipartSlide
30                            .Shapes.AddPicture "a:\anicomp1.gif", True, True, 375, 150, 300, 300
31                        End With
32            End Select
33            ' Check if slides should be swapped; if so, swap them
34            If OptionButton4.Value = True Then
35                ActivePresentation.Slides.Range(Array(4)).Cut
36                ActivePresentation.Slides.Paste 3
37            End If
38      ' wrap up, reset combo boxes for next time
39      ' close form, and run presentation
40      ResetComboxes
41      UserForm1.Hide
42      Unload UserForm1
43      ' Start slide show
44         If CheckBox2.Value = True Then
45             Set CompSlides = Application.ActivePresentation
46             With CompSlides.SlideShowSettings
47                 .RangeType = ppShowNamedSlideShow
48                 .Run
49             End With
50           End If
51        End If
52      End If
```

As indicated earlier, the code for CommandButton3 is nearly identical to the code for CommandButton1. Line 4 assigns a different template file. Although the first slide is designated as the title slide, a different title is assembled at line 14. The clip art pictures assigned to Slide 2 are different based on the Select Case statements in lines 21 through 32. In addition, lines 35 and 36 swap Slides 3 and 4, instead of Slides 2 and 3 that were changed in the CommandButton1 procedure.

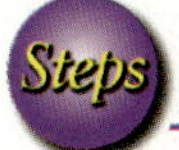

Steps To Enter the CommandButton3 Procedure

1 Click the Object box arrow at the top of the Code window, and then click CommandButton3 in the Object list. Make sure Click is in the Procedure box.

The Visual Basic Editor displays the Sub and End Sub statements for the CommandButton3 procedure and positions the insertion point between the two statements.

2 Enter the VBA code shown in Table 6-15 on the previous page.

The CommandButton3_Click() procedure displays as shown in Figure 6-81.

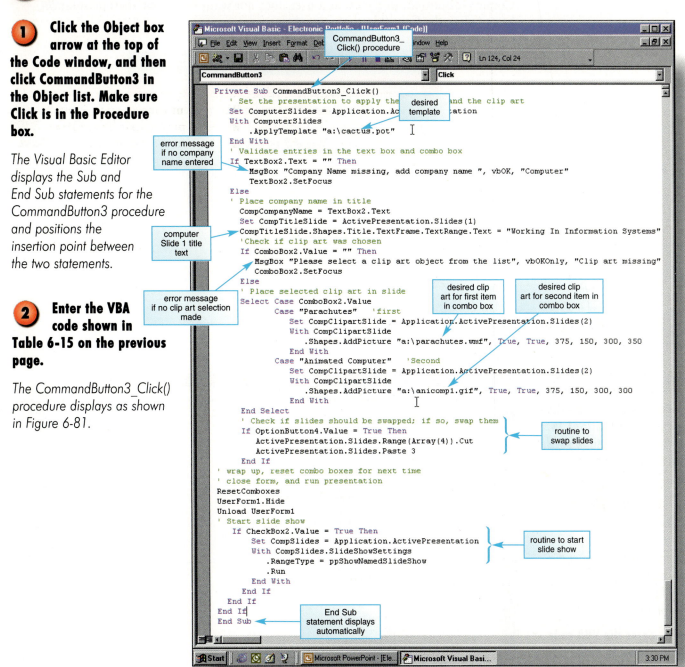

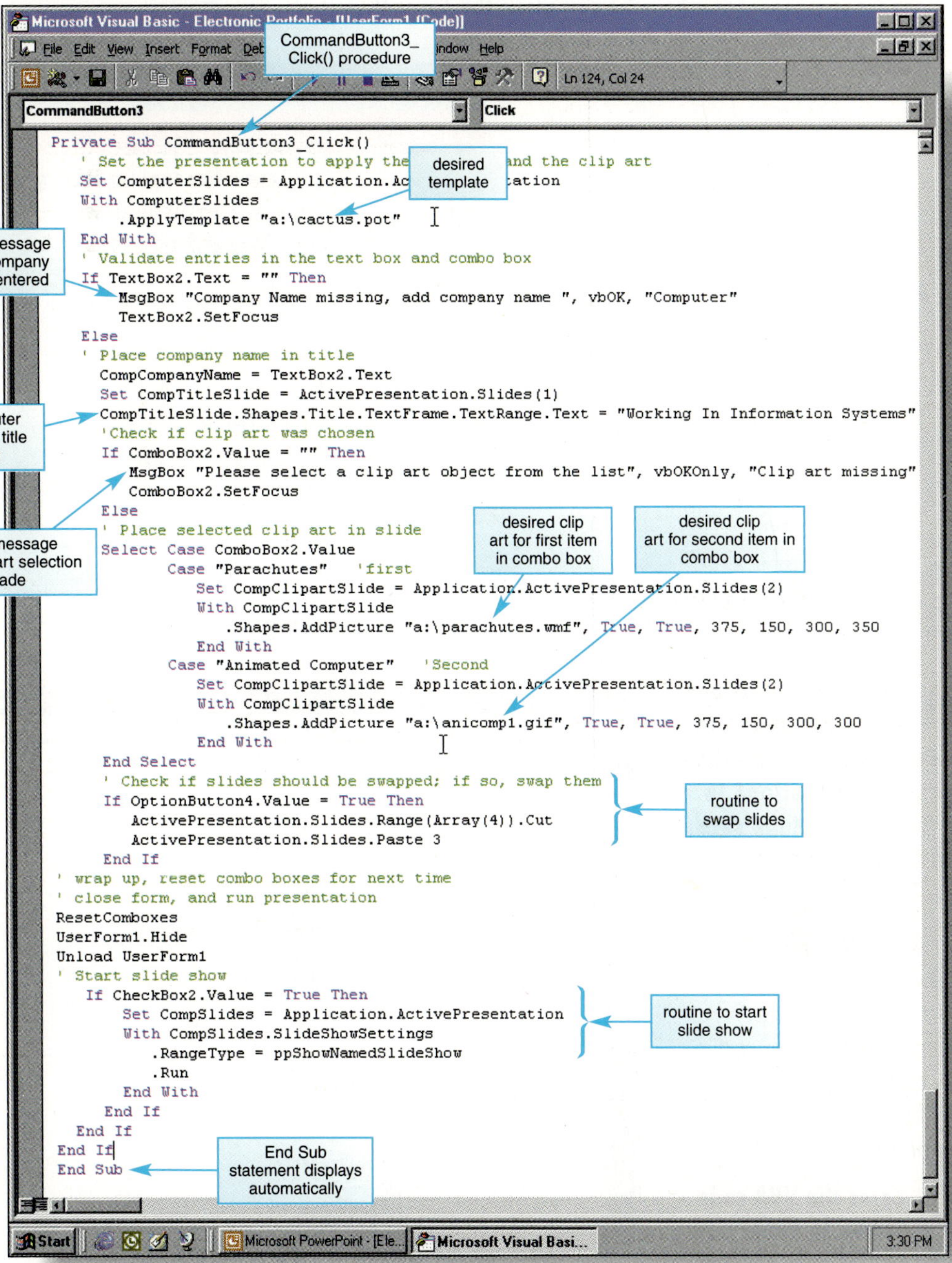

Microsoft Visual Basic - Electronic Portfolio - [UserForm1 (Code)]
File Edit View Insert Format Debug Run Tools Add-Ins Window Help
Ln 124, Col 24
CommandButton3
Click
CommandButton3_ Click() procedure
desired template
error message if no company name entered
computer Slide 1 title text
error message if no clip art selection made
desired clip art for first item in combo box
desired clip art for second item in combo box
routine to swap slides
routine to start slide show
End Sub statement displays automatically
Private Sub CommandButton3_Click()
' Set the presentation to apply the template and the clip art
Set ComputerSlides = Application.ActivePresentation
With ComputerSlides
.ApplyTemplate "a:\cactus.pot"
End With
' Validate entries in the text box and combo box
If TextBox2.Text = "" Then
MsgBox "Company Name missing, add company name ", vbOK, "Computer"
TextBox2.SetFocus
Else
' Place company name in title
CompCompanyName = TextBox2.Text
Set CompTitleSlide = ActivePresentation.Slides(1)
CompTitleSlide.Shapes.Title.TextFrame.TextRange.Text = "Working In Information Systems"
'Check if clip art was chosen
If ComboBox2.Value = "" Then
MsgBox "Please select a clip art object from the list", vbOKOnly, "Clip art missing"
ComboBox2.SetFocus
Else
' Place selected clip art in slide
Select Case ComboBox2.Value
Case "Parachutes" 'first
Set CompClipartSlide = Application.ActivePresentation.Slides(2)
With CompClipartSlide
.Shapes.AddPicture "a:\parachutes.wmf", True, True, 375, 150, 300, 350
End With
Case "Animated Computer" 'Second
Set CompClipartSlide = Application.ActivePresentation.Slides(2)
With CompClipartSlide
.Shapes.AddPicture "a:\anicomp1.gif", True, True, 375, 150, 300, 300
End With
End Select
' Check if slides should be swapped; if so, swap them
If OptionButton4.Value = True Then
ActivePresentation.Slides.Range(Array(4)).Cut
ActivePresentation.Slides.Paste 3
End If
' wrap up, reset combo boxes for next time
' close form, and run presentation
ResetComboxes
UserForm1.Hide
Unload UserForm1
' Start slide show
If CheckBox2.Value = True Then
Set CompSlides = Application.ActivePresentation
With CompSlides.SlideShowSettings
.RangeType = ppShowNamedSlideShow
.Run
End With
End If
End If
End If
End Sub
Start
Microsoft PowerPoint - [Ele...
Microsoft Visual Basi...
3:30 PM

FIGURE 6-81

WRITING THE COMMANDBUTTON4 PROCEDURE Next, the code for CommandButton4 must be written. The code for this command control is identical to the code for CommandButton2. In the event a user does not want to change the presentation, he can click the Cancel button.

Table 6-16 CommandButton4 Procedure

LINE	VBA CODE
1	' Close the application presentation
2	' without saving
3	ResetComboxes
4	With Application.ActivePresentation
5	.Close
6	End With
7	UserForm1.Hide
8	Unload UserForm1

To Enter the CommandButton4 Procedure

1 Click the Object box arrow at the top of the Code window, and then click CommandButton4 in the Object list. Make sure Click is in the Procedure box.

The Visual Basic Editor displays the Sub and End Sub statements for the CommandButton4 procedure and positions the insertion point between the two statements.

Enter the VBA code shown in Table 6-16.

The CommandButton4_Click() procedure displays as shown in Figure 6-82.

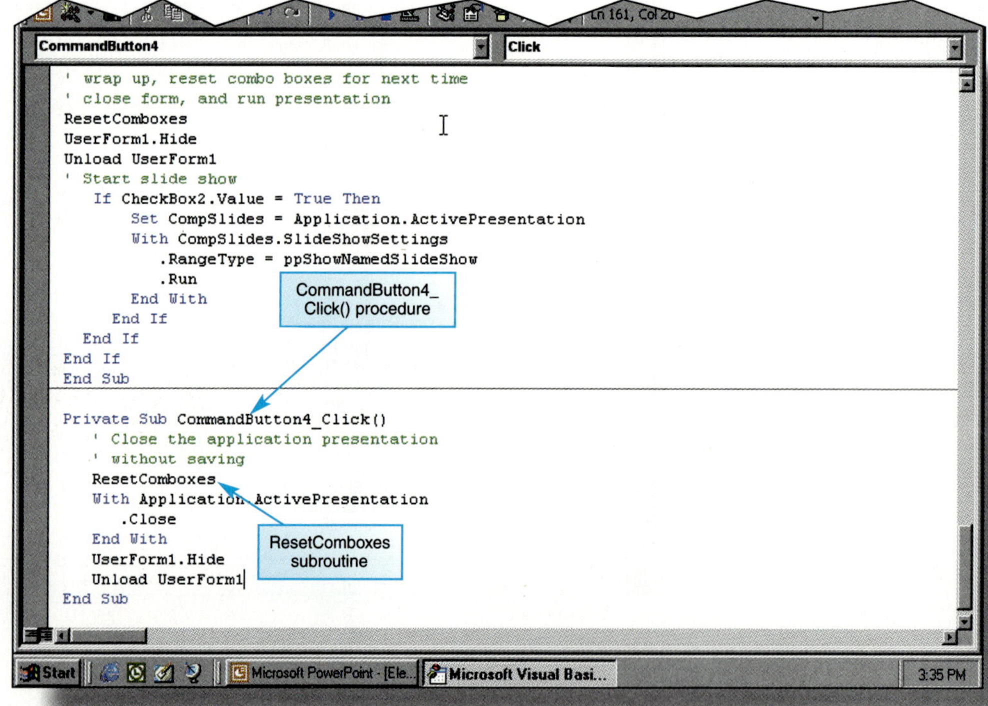

FIGURE 6-82

WRITING THE RESET COMBO BOXES PROCEDURE The final procedure that must be entered is the code that resets the combo boxes values. The Clear method is used to clear the values that were last selected.

Table 6-17 Reset Combo Boxes Procedure

LINE	VBA CODE
1	`Sub ResetComboxes()`
2	`    With ComboBox1`
3	`        .Clear`
4	`    End With`
5	`    With ComboBox2`
6	`        .Clear`
7	`    End With`

For both combo boxes, the Clear method is used in lines 3 and 6.

More About

Quick Reference

For a table that lists how to complete the tasks covered in this book using the mouse, menu, shortcut menu, and keyboard, see the PowerPoint Quick Reference Summary at the back of this book or visit the Office 2000 Web page (www.scsite.com/off2000/qr.htm), and then click Microsoft PowerPoint 2000.

To Enter the ResetComboxes Procedure

1 Click the Object box arrow at the top of the window and scroll up and click General. Make sure Declarations is in the Procedure box.

The Visual Basic Editor positions the insertion point at the top of the UserForm1 Code window (Figure 6-83).

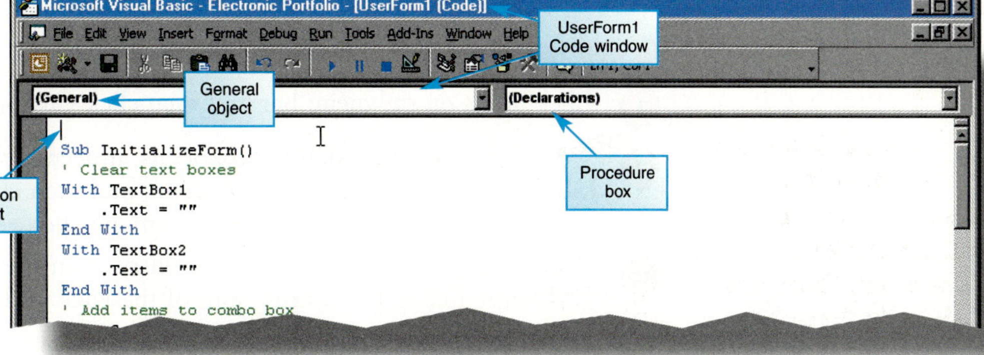

FIGURE 6-83

2 Enter the VBA code shown in lines 1 through 7 of Table 6-17.

The code for the ResetComboxes() procedure displays as shown in Figure 6-84. You do not need to enter line 8 of Table 6-17 because the Visual Basic Editor inserts that statement automatically.

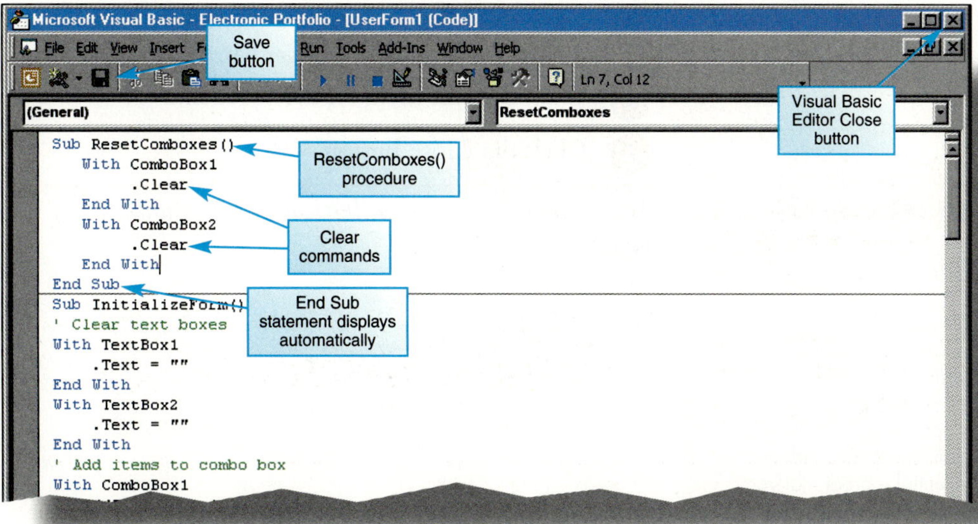

FIGURE 6-84

The VBA code is complete. The next step is to close the Visual Basic Editor and save the presentation. Before closing the Visual Basic Editor, you should verify your code by comparing it to Figures 6-72 through 6-84 on pages 6.49 through 6.65.

TO SAVE THE VISUAL BASIC CODE, CLOSE THE VISUAL BASIC EDITOR, AND SAVE THE PRESENTATION

1. Click the Save button on the Standard toolbar.
2. Click the Close button on the right side of the Visual Basic Editor title bar.
3. When the PowerPoint window displays, click the Save button on the Standard toolbar to save the presentation using the file name, Electronic Portfolio.

Adding a Button to Run the Form

The third button you will add to the custom Using Presentations toolbar is the Create Presentation button. When the user wants to create his custom presentation, he will click this button and the make his selections on the form. Perform the following steps to add this button.

TO ADD THE CREATE PRESENTATION BUTTON

1. Click Tools on the menu bar and then click Customize.
2. When the Customize dialog box opens, if necessary, click the Commands tab. Scroll down in the Categories box and then click Macros. Click CreatePresentationCareer in the Commands box.
3. Drag the CreatePresentationCareer entry from the Commands list in the Customize dialog box to the right of the Pack and Go button on the Using Presentation toolbar.
4. Click the Modify Selection menu button and then point to Change Button Image on the submenu. When the Change Button Image palette displays, click the button with a key (row 6, column 3).
5. Click the Modify Selection menu button and then click Name on the shortcut menu. Type `Create Presentation` as the new name of this button.
6. Click Default Style on the submenu.
7. Click the Close button.

The Create Presentation button displays with a key image (Figure 6-85 on the next page).

Microsoft Certification

The Microsoft Office User Specialist (MOUS) Certification program provides an opportunity for you to obtain a valuable industry credential – proof that you have the PowerPoint 2000 skills required by employers. For more information, see Appendix D or visit the Shelly Cashman Series MOUS Web page at www.scsite.com/off2000/cert.htm.

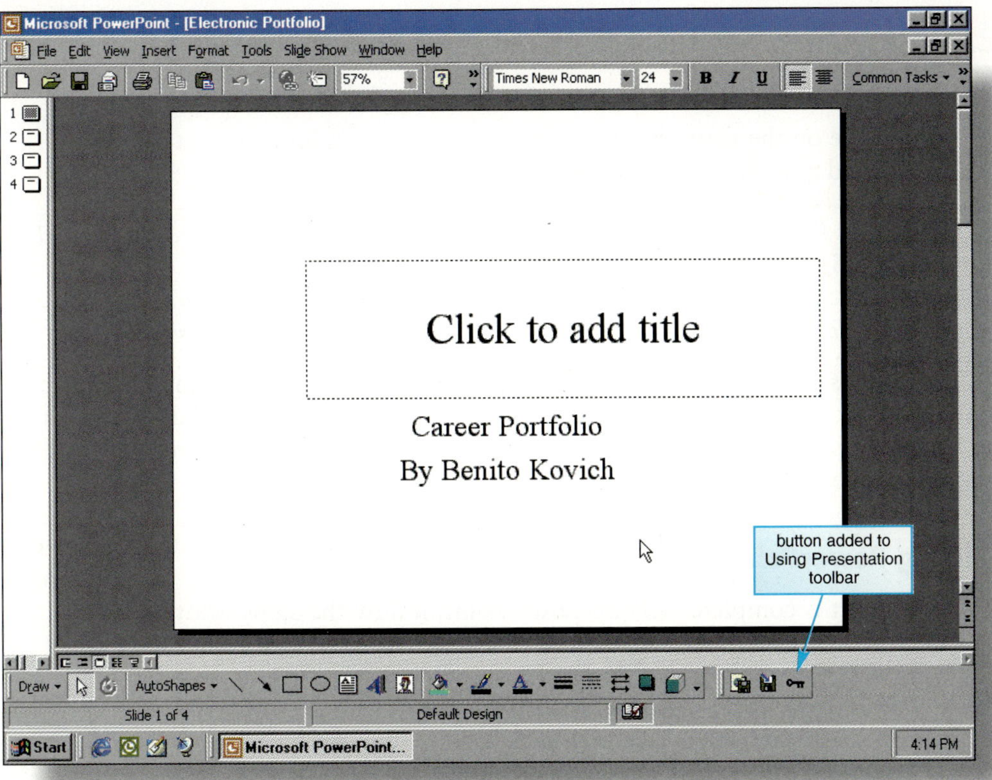

FIGURE 6-85

Saving the Presentation

The changes to the presentation are complete. Perform the following step to save the finished presentation before testing the controls.

TO SAVE A PRESENTATION

1. Click the Save button on the Standard toolbar.

PowerPoint saves the presentation by saving the changes made to the presentation since the last save.

Testing the Controls

The final step is to test the controls in the form. Use the following data: Computer interview type; Company Name: Standard Technologies; computer clip art; Swap Slides 3 and 4, and Close presentation at finish.

TO TEST THE CONTROLS IN THE FORM

1. Click the Create Presentation button on the Using Presentation toolbar.
2. When the form displays, click the Computer tab. Type `Standard Technologies` as the Company Name.
3. Click the Select Clip Art arrow and click the Animated Computer clip art.
4. Click Swap Slides 3 and 4.

5. Click Close presentation when finished.
6. Click the OK button.
7. Click File on the menu bar and then click Print Handout to print the four slides and a handout.

The Electronic Portfolio presentation will display automatically (Figures 6-1e - 6-1f on page PP 6.5). The company name, Standard Technologies, displays on Slide 1. The animated computer clip art displays on Slide 2. The slide with the pilot photographs displays as Slide 3. The slide with the race car displays as Slide 4.

If the slides do not display as indicated here, then click Tools on the menu bar, point to Macro, and then click Visual Basic Editor. Click the View Code button on the Project Explorer toolbar, and then check the controls' properties and VBA code. Save the presentation again and repeat steps 1 through 7 above.

Quitting PowerPoint

The project is complete. To quit PowerPoint, follow the steps below.

TO QUIT POWERPOINT

1. Click the Close button on the title bar.
2. If the Microsoft PowerPoint dialog box displays, click the Yes button to save changes made since the last save.

PowerPoint quits.

CASE PERSPECTIVE SUMMARY

The Electronic Portfolio slide show should assist Benito with his job search. The form you developed using Visual Basic for Applications allows him to create a unique presentation for each interview. He can add the name of the company to the title slide, choose appropriate clip art, change the slide order, and run his presentation immediately or later. In addition, the buttons on the Using Presentation toolbar you created and the new command on the File menu easily allow him to save the presentation as a Web page, to use the Pack and Go Wizard to transport this file, and to print a handout for the interviewer. Benito's extraordinary and professional custom presentation should impress interviewers and help him land the best job possible.

Project Summary

Project 6 presented the principles of customizing a presentation. In Phase 1, you learned how to create a toolbar and add two buttons, Save as a Web Page and the Pack and Go Wizard. In Phase 2, you learned how to use the macro recorder to create a macro that prints handouts displaying four slides per page and assign this macro to a command on the File menu. In Phase 3, you learned how to create a form composed of Label controls, TextBox controls, ComboBox controls, OptionButton controls, CheckBox controls, and CommandButton controls. You were introduced to Visual Basic for Applications and the concept of object-oriented programming. You worked with objects that had properties and behaviors, or methods. In this phase, you also learned how to write VBA code that included looping and decision making by writing With statements, If-Then-Else statements, and Select Case Value statements.

What You Should Know

Having completed this project, you now should be able to perform the following tasks:

- Add a CheckBox Control to a Form *(PP 6.38)*
- Add a ComboBox Control to a Form *(PP 6.35)*
- Add a Command to a Menu, Assign the Command a Macro, and Invoke the Command *(PP 6.20)*
- Add a MultiPage Control to a Form and Increase Its Size *(PP 6.31)*
- Add a TextBox Control to a Form *(PP 6.34)*
- Add CommandButton Controls to a Form *(PP 6.39)*
- Add Label Controls to a Form *(PP 6.33)*
- Add OptionButton Controls to a Form *(PP 6.36)*
- Add the Create Presentation Button *(PP 6.66)*
- Change the Form Size and Arrange the Toolbox Position *(PP 6.29)*
- Change the OptionButton4 Caption *(PP 6.47)*
- Copy Controls from One Sheet to Another *(PP 6.44)*
- Create a Custom Toolbar and Add Two Buttons *(PP 6.10)*
- Enter the CommandButton1 Procedure *(PP 6.58)*
- Enter the CommandButton2 Procedure *(PP 6.60)*
- Enter the CommandButton3 Procedure *(PP 6.63)*
- Enter the CommandButton4 Procedure *(PP 6.64)*
- Enter the Create Presentation Career Procedure *(PP 6.49)*
- Enter the InitializeForm Procedure *(PP 6.53)*
- Enter the ResetComboxes Procedure *(PP 6.65)*
- Open a Presentation and Save it with a New File Name *(PP 6.7)*
- Open a Presentation with a Macro and Execute the Macro *(PP 6.23)*
- Open the Visual Basic IDE and a New Form *(PP 6.27)*
- Quit PowerPoint *(PP 6.68)*
- Record a Macro to Print Handouts in Vertical Slide Order in Pure Black and White *(PP 6.16)*
- Resize and Reposition the Controls on a Form *(PP 6.43)*
- Save a Presentation *(PP 6.14, PP 6.22, PP 6.47)*
- Save the Visual Basic Code, Close the Visual Basic Editor, and Save the Presentation *(PP 6.66)*
- Set the Caption Properties *(PP 6.40)*
- Test the Controls in the Form *(PP 6.67)*
- View a Macro's VBA Code *(PP 6.24)*

1 Creating a Macro and Customizing a Menu and Toolbar

Instructions: Start PowerPoint and perform the following tasks.

1. Open the Snow file from your Data Disk. If you do not have a copy of the Data Disk, then see the inside back cover of this book.
2. Click File on the menu bar and then click Save As. Save the presentation with the file name, Ski Vacation.
3. Reset the toolbars to their installation settings (see Step 6 on page PP 6.8).
4. Add a footer with your name, today's date, and the slide number to all slides.
5. Use the Record New Macro command to create a macro that exports the presentation outline to Microsoft Word. Call the macro ExportWord. Change the name of the author in the Description box to your name. Make sure the Store macro in box displays Ski Vacation. Click the OK button. When the Stop Recording toolbar displays, do the following:

   (a) Click File on the menu bar and then click Save As; (b) When the Save As dialog box displays, type `Snow Outline` in the File name box; (c) Click the Save as type box arrow and click Outline/RTF in the Save as type list; (d) Be certain the Save in box location is 3½ Floppy (A:); (e) click the Save button; and (f) click the Stop Recording button on the Stop Recording toolbar.
6. Add a button to the Standard toolbar (Figure 6-86a) and a command to the File menu (Figure 6-86b) to run the macro. Use the image of a floppy disk with an arrow pointing up (row 1, column 5) and the Default Style for the button and the Export to Word command on the file menu.
7. View the ExportWord's VBA code. When the Visual Basic Editor displays the macro, click File on the menu bar, click Print, and then click the OK button. Close the Visual Basic Editor.
8. Run the macro as follows: (a) click the button you added to the Standard toolbar; (b) on the File menu, click the Export to Word command.
9. Save the Ski Vacation file again.
10. Reset the toolbars to their installation settings (see Step 6 on page PP 6.8). Hand in the macro and outline printouts to your instructor. Quit PowerPoint.

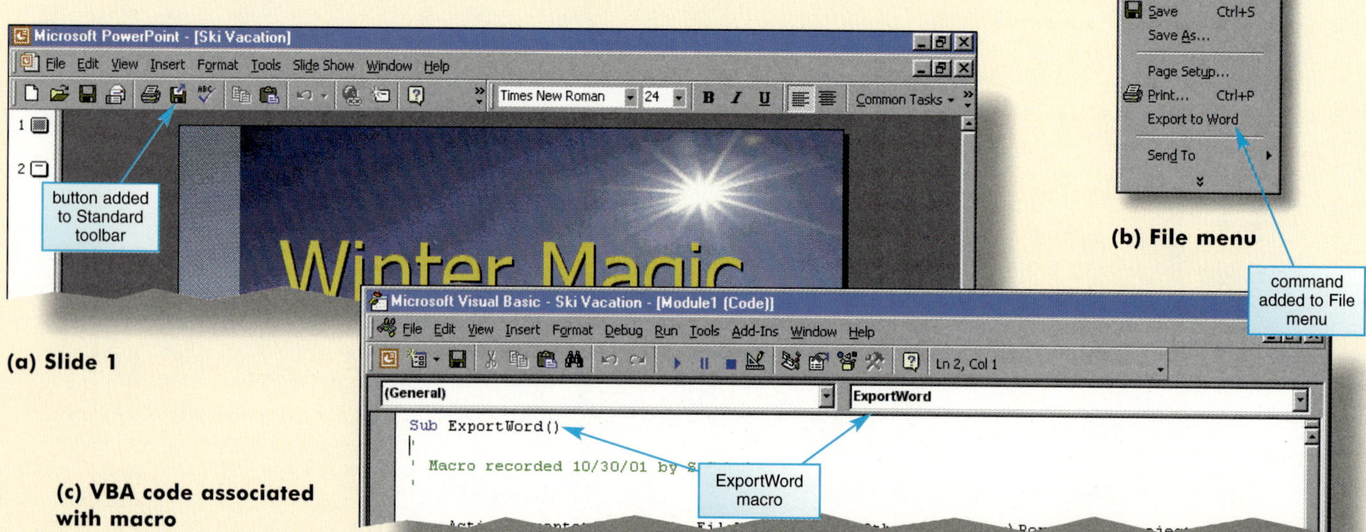

(a) Slide 1

(b) File menu

(c) VBA code associated with macro

FIGURE 6-86

1 Producing a Web Page Automatically

Problem: Your job at Z-Net is to create and post Web pages. The company owner has decided to display a Web page listing birth announcements for customers. Because the owner does not want to burden you with this task frequently, he wants you to design a process that the receptionist can use to complete this assignment. You decide to create a basic, one slide presentation. The receptionist's task will be to add the data to a basic slide (Figure 6-87a on the next page) and then save the presentation as a Web page. To streamline the process, you create a macro toolbar and place three buttons on it. The first button will run a macro that sets the background to pink for a female, the second button will set the background to blue for a male, and the third button will save the presentation as an HTML file. Figure 6-87b on the next page shows a presentation for a female.

Instructions: Start PowerPoint and perform the following tasks with a computer.

1. Open the Announce presentation on the Data Disk. If you do not have a copy of the Data Disk, then see the inside back cover of this book.
2. Reset the toolbars to their installation settings (see Step 6 on page PP 6.8).
3. Create a toolbar and name it Baby. Place the toolbar next to the Drawing toolbar.
4. Use the Record New Macro command to create a macro generates the female slide. Call the macro BabyGirl, change the name of the author in the Description box to your name, and store the macro in the Announce Update file.
5. With the Stop Recording toolbar on the screen, do the following: (a) On the Format menu, click Background, click the Background fill box arrow, click Fill Effects on the menu, click the Texture tab in the Fill Effects dialog box, double click the Pink tissue paper texture (row 3, column 2), and then click the Apply button; (b) Select the title text and change the font to Script MT (or a similar script font); and (c) Click the Stop Recording button on the Stop Recording toolbar. Click the slide anywhere except a placeholder.
6. Add a button to the Baby toolbar (Figure 6-87a) and a command to the Edit menu (Figure 6-87b and 6-87c on the next page). Assign the button and command the BabyGirl macro. Change the button image to a diamond (row 3, column 4) and use the Default Style.
7. Use the Record New Macro command to create a second macro that generates the male slide. Call the macro BabyBoy, change the name of the author in the Description box to your name, and store the macro in the Announce Update file.
8. With the Stop Recording toolbar on the screen, do the following: (a) On the Format menu, click Background, click the Background fill box arrow, click Fill Effects on the menu, double click the Blue tissue paper texture (row 3, column 1), and then click the Apply button; (b) Select the title text and change the font to Arial and the style to Bold with no Italics; and (c) Click the Stop Recording button on the Stop Recording toolbar.
9. Add a button to the Baby toolbar (Figure 6-87b) and a command to the Edit menu (Figure 6-87c). Assign the button and command the BabyBoy macro. Modify the button image to a heart (row 3, column 3) and use the Default Style.
10. Add the Save as Web Page command to the Baby toolbar. Change the button image to the Default Style.
11. Save the presentation using the file name, Announce Update.

(continued)

Producing a Web Page Automatically *(continued)*

12. Modify the slide as by replacing the XX in the title text to your last name. Enter your first name after the Announces the birth of: paragraph. Enter today's date for the date of birth. Enter the current time for the time of birth. Enter your estimated weight and length at birth.
13. If you are a male, execute the BabyBoy macro; if you are a girl, execute the BabyGirl macro.
14. Click the Save as Web Page button on your Baby toolbar. Save the file as Announce Web.
15. Save the presentation with the file name, Announce xx Baby, replacing the XX with your last name.
16. Print the presentation, print the macro code, and print the Web page. Quit PowerPoint

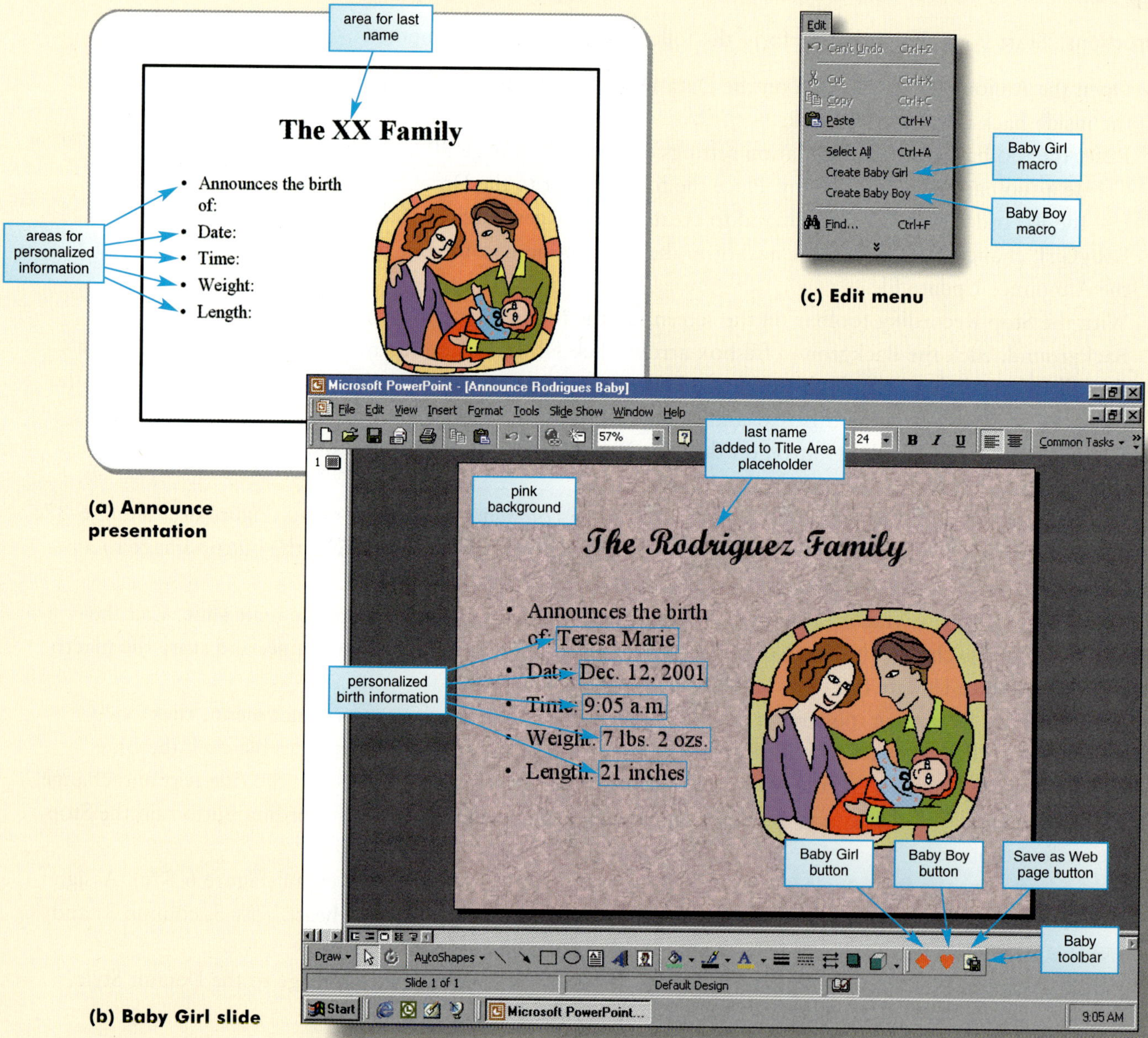

(a) Announce presentation

(c) Edit menu

(b) Baby Girl slide

FIGURE 6-87

2 Creating a Summary Slide Automatically

Problem: While talking with one of your colleagues about PowerPoint's features, you discuss how some toolbar buttons do not record as part of a macro. For example, the Insert Summary Slide button on the Slide Sorter toolbar will not record as part of a macro. Using your knowledge of how slides are treated as objects and searching through the Visual Basic help screens, you discover a method of writing a Visual Basic module that creates a new blank slide at the end of the slide sequence and reads the title text of Slides 2 through the end of the slides. By incorporating the count method and using Visual Basic For/Next statements, you can solve the problem. The completed summary slide is shown in Figure 6-88b on page PP 6.75.

Instructions: Start PowerPoint and perform the following tasks with a computer.

1. Open the Studying presentation you created in Project 1. If you did not create that presentation, see your instructor for a copy of that file.
2. Open the Visual Basic Editor and insert a new module.
3. In the General Declarations window, enter the code from the following table to declare the variables used in the module.

Table 6-18 General Declarations

VBA CODE

```
Dim mySlide As Integer
Dim SumText As String
Dim SummarySlideLines(4) As String
```

4. Start a new subroutine for a module called SummarySlide(). Type `Sub Summary_Slide()` and press the ENTER key. The End Sub statement should display automatically.
5. Enter the code in Table 6-19 to determine the total number of slides in the presentation.

Table 6-19 Determine Slide Count Procedure

VBA CODE

```
Sub SummarySlide()
Dim SlideCount as Integer
With ActivePresentation.Slides
'Determine the number of total slides
     SlideCount = .Count + 1
End With
```

6. Enter the code from Table 6-20 to collect the titles from every slide.

(continued)

Creating a Summary Slide AutomaticallyTable 6-20 Collect Titles Procedure *(continued)*

Table 6-20 Collect Titles Procedure	
LINE	*VBA CODE*
1	`For mySlide = 2 To SlideCount - 1`
2	`'Collect the titles from every slide`
3	`Set myPresentation = ActivePresentation.Slides(mySlide)`
4	`SummarySlideLines(mySlide) = myPresentation.Shapes.Title.TextFrame.TextRange.Text`
5	`Next mySlide`

7. Add the code from Table 6-21 to add a slide at the end of the presentation and insert the title for this slide.

Table 6-21 Add Summary Slide Procedure	
LINE	*VBA CODE*
1	`'Add the summary slide`
2	`Set SumSlide = ActivePresentation.Slides.Add(SlideCount, ppLayoutText).Shapes`
3	`'Insert the title for the summary slide`
4	`SumSlide.Title.TextFrame.TextRange.Text = "In Conclusion"`

8. Use the code from Table 6-22 to use a For Next loop to collect the slide titles into one long string of text. Insert a carriage return at the end of each title so the titles will display on separate lines in the slide.

Table 6-22 Collect Slide Titles Procedure	
LINE	*VBA CODE*
1	`'Collect the Slide titles into one long string of text`
2	`'inserting a carriage return at the end of each title`
3	`'so the titles will display on separate lines`
4	`For mySlide = 2 To SlideCount - 1`
5	`SumText = SumText & SummarySlideLines(mySlide) & Chr(13)`
6	`Next mySlide`

9. Insert the SumText into the Object Area placeholder using the code in Table 6-23.

Table 6-23 Insert Summary Text Procedure	
LINE	*VBA CODE*
1	`'Now insert the titles in the Text list placeholder of the slide`
2	`SumSlide.Placeholders(2).TextFrame.TextRange.Text = SumText`
3	`End Sub`

10. Add the Summary_Slide() module to the Common Tasks menu on the Formatting toolbar (Figure 6-88c).
11. Save the Visual Basic code, and then save the presentation using the file name, Studying Update.
12. Execute the Visual Basic code. Print the Visual Basic code and the slides using the Pure black and white option. Quit PowerPoint.

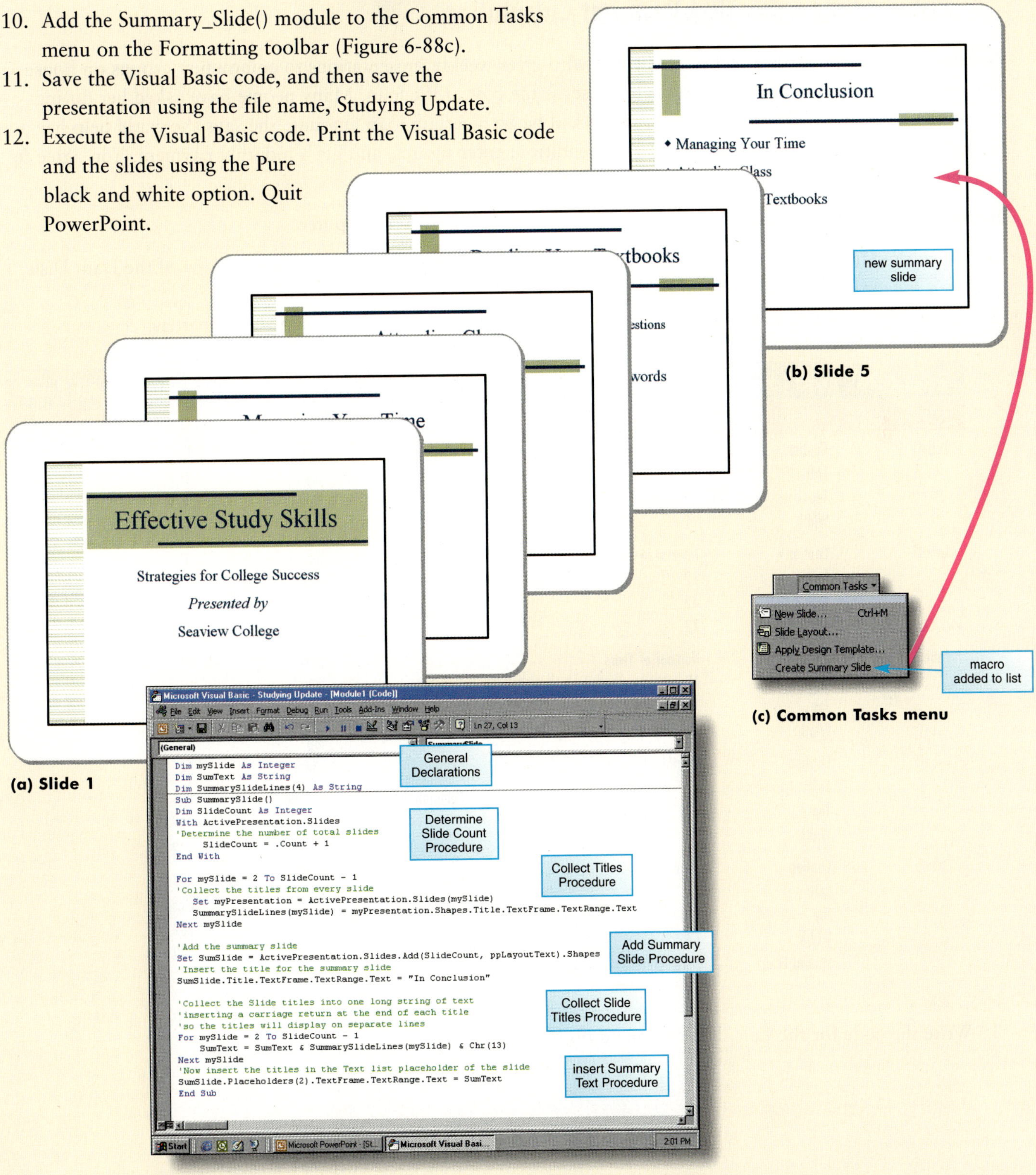

Effective Study Skills

Strategies for College Success

Presented by

Seaview College

(a) Slide 1

In Conclusion

- Managing Your Time
- Textbooks

new summary slide

(b) Slide 5

Common Tasks

New Slide... Ctrl+M

Slide Layout...

Apply Design Template...

Create Summary Slide

macro added to list

(c) Common Tasks menu

Microsoft Visual Basic - Studying Update - [Module1 (Code)]

File Edit View Insert Format Debug Run Tools Add-Ins Window Help

Ln 27, Col 13

(General)

General Declarations

```
Dim mySlide As Integer
Dim SumText As String
Dim SummarySlideLines(4) As String
```

Determine Slide Count Procedure

```
Sub SummarySlide()
Dim SlideCount As Integer
With ActivePresentation.Slides
'Determine the number of total slides
     SlideCount = .Count + 1
End With
```

Collect Titles Procedure

```
For mySlide = 2 To SlideCount - 1
'Collect the titles from every slide
   Set myPresentation = ActivePresentation.Slides(mySlide)
   SummarySlideLines(mySlide) = myPresentation.Shapes.Title.TextFrame.TextRange.Text
Next mySlide
```

Add Summary Slide Procedure

```
'Add the summary slide
Set SumSlide = ActivePresentation.Slides.Add(SlideCount, ppLayoutText).Shapes
'Insert the title for the summary slide
SumSlide.Title.TextFrame.TextRange.Text = "In Conclusion"
```

Collect Slide Titles Procedure

```
'Collect the Slide titles into one long string of text
'inserting a carriage return at the end of each title
'so the titles will display on separate lines
For mySlide = 2 To SlideCount - 1
    SumText = SumText & SummarySlideLines(mySlide) & Chr(13)
Next mySlide
```

insert Summary Text Procedure

```
'Now insert the titles in the Text list placeholder of the slide
SumSlide.Placeholders(2).TextFrame.TextRange.Text = SumText
End Sub
```

Start | Microsoft PowerPoint - [St... | Microsoft Visual Basi... | 2:01 PM

(d) Module1 VBA code

FIGURE 6-88

3 Automating a Monthly Payment Calculation

Problem: Your neighbor is a real estate broker who gives weekly presentations to community groups on house buying techniques. One of the topics she discusses is the cost of the loan. Many people have asked her during the presentations what the monthly payment would be on a certain loan amount. She says she could help her audience if she could display a form in her presentation, enter figures, and get a monthly payment. You agree to help her with this project.

Instructions: Start PowerPoint and perform the following tasks with a computer.

1. Open the Home Buying Basics presentation on the Data Disk. If you do not have a copy of the Data Disk, then see the inside back cover of this book.
2. Create the form shown in Figure 6-89a. Use the following table to set the control properties.

Table 6-24 Exact Locations of Controls in the Form

CONTROL	PROPERTY	VALUE
Label1	Caption	Loan Amount
	Left	12
	Top	12
	Width	72
Label2	Caption	Interest in Percent
	Left	12
	Top	42
	Width	72
Label3	Caption	Number of Years
	Left	12
	Top	72
	Width	72
Label4	Caption	Monthly Payment
	Left	12
	Top	102
	Width	72
Label5	Caption	Blank
	Left	96
	Top	102
	Width	72
	Special Effect	2 frmSpecialEffectSunken

Table 6-24 Exact Locations of Controls in the Form

CONTROL	PROPERTY	VALUE
TextBox1	Left	96
	Top	12
	Width	72
TextBox2	Left	96
	Top	42
	Width	72
TextBox3	Left	96
	Top	72
	Width	72
CommandButton1	Caption	Calculate
	Left	18
	Top	132
	Width	54
CommandButton2	Caption	Clear
	Left	90
	Top	132
	Width	54
CommandButton3	Caption	Close
	Left	162
	Top	132
	Width	54

3. Write the code for the Calculate command button using Table 6-25.

In the Lab

Table 6-25 Verify Values and Calculate Payment Procedure

VBA CODE

```
'Validate the text box fields
'If OK, then calculate mortgage
If TextBox1.Text = "" Then
   MsgBox "Please enter a loan amount", vbOKOnly, "Loan Amount"
   TextBox1.SetFocus
ElseIf TextBox2.Text = "" Then
   MsgBox "Please enter an interest rate", vbOKOnly, "Interest Rate"
   TextBox2.SetFocus
ElseIf TextBox3.Text = "" Then
   MsgBox "Please enter the number of years for the loan", vbOKOnly, "Years"
   TextBox3.SetFocus
Else
   Label5.Caption = FormatCurrency(Pmt(TextBox2.Text / 1200, TextBox3.Text * 12, -TextBox1.Text, 0, 0), 2)
End If
```

4. Write the code for the Clear command button using Table 6-26.

Table 6-26 Clear Procedure

VBA CODE

```
'Clear all text boxes and monthly payment
'Set insertion point in first textbox
  TextBox1.Text = ""
  TextBox1.SetFocus
  TextBox2.Text = ""
  TextBox3.Text = ""
  Label5.Caption = ""
```

5. Write the code for the Close Button Procedure using Table 6-27.

Table 6-27 Close Button Procedure

VBA CODE

```
  UserForm1.Hide
  Unload UserForm1
```

Table 6-28 Display Mortgage Form Procedure

VBA CODE

```
Sub DisplayMortForm()
    UserForm1.Show
End Sub
```

6. Insert a module, and use the code in Table 6-28 to enter the code for displaying the form.
7. Add the module to the pop-up menu for the slide show by using the Customize command on the tools menu.
8. Click the Toolbars tab and click Shortcut Menus in the Customize dialog box. Click the Commands tab and select Macros in the Categories list. Click the DisplayMortForm macro in the Commands list and drag it to the SlideShow menu on the Shortcut Menus bar.
9. Click the SlideShow menu button on the Shortcut Menus bar. When the drop down menu displays, drag the DisplayMortForm command to the Slide Show command and place it below the Go command.
10. Save the presentation as House Buying Update. Print the form and the Visual Basic code. Close the Visual Basic Editor and quit PowerPoint.

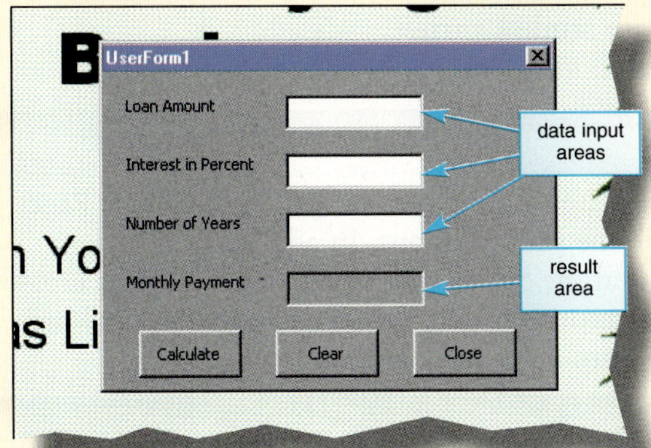

(a) Payment form

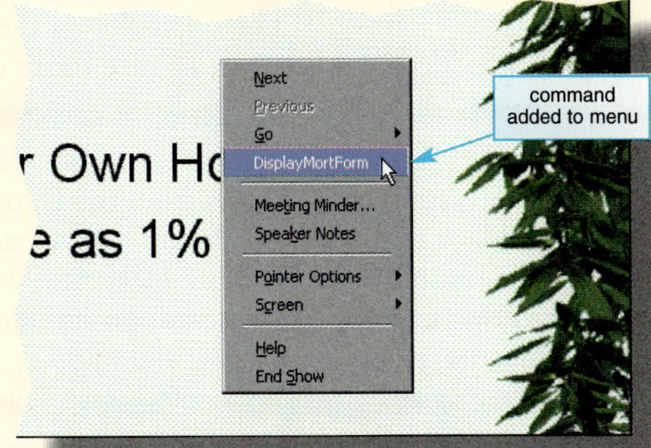

(b) Popup menu

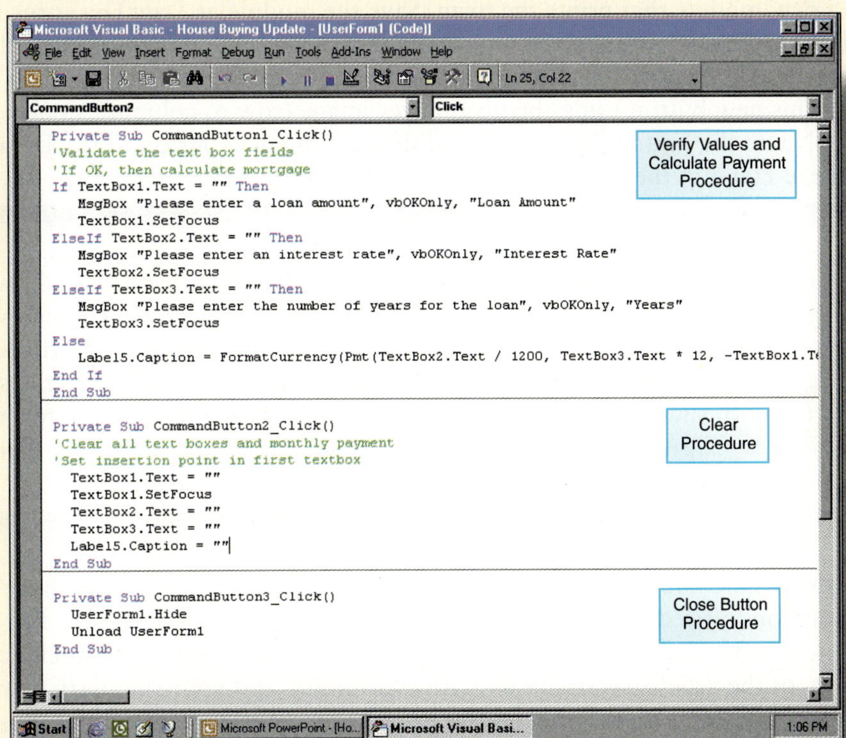


```
Private Sub CommandButton1_Click()
'Validate the text box fields
'If OK, then calculate mortgage
If TextBox1.Text = "" Then
   MsgBox "Please enter a loan amount", vbOKOnly, "Loan Amount"
   TextBox1.SetFocus
ElseIf TextBox2.Text = "" Then
   MsgBox "Please enter an interest rate", vbOKOnly, "Interest Rate"
   TextBox2.SetFocus
ElseIf TextBox3.Text = "" Then
   MsgBox "Please enter the number of years for the loan", vbOKOnly, "Years"
   TextBox3.SetFocus
Else
   Label5.Caption = FormatCurrency(Pmt(TextBox2.Text / 1200, TextBox3.Text * 12, -TextBox1.Te
End If
End Sub

Private Sub CommandButton2_Click()
'Clear all text boxes and monthly payment
'Set insertion point in first textbox
  TextBox1.Text = ""
  TextBox1.SetFocus
  TextBox2.Text = ""
  TextBox3.Text = ""
  Label5.Caption = ""
End Sub

Private Sub CommandButton3_Click()
  UserForm1.Hide
  Unload UserForm1
End Sub
```

(c) UserForm1 VBA code

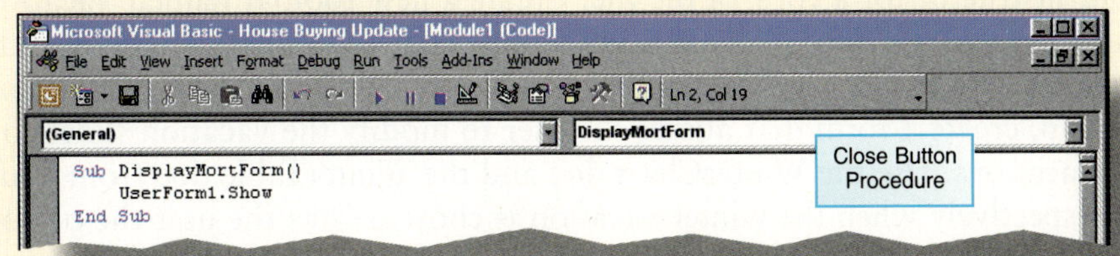


```
Sub DisplayMortForm()
    UserForm1.Show
End Sub
```

(d) Module1 VBA code

FIGURE 6-89

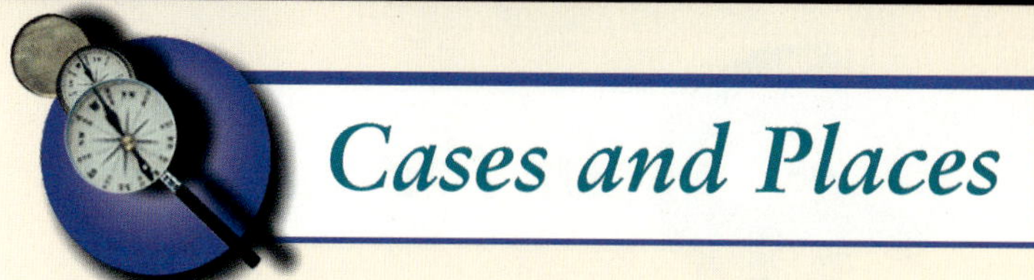

Cases and Places

The difficulty of these case studies varies:
▸ are the least difficult; ▸▸ are more difficult; and ▸▸▸ are the most difficult.

1 ▸ Open the Investing presentation from the Data Disk. Create a macro that prints the Notes Pages using the Pure black and white, Scale to fit paper, and Frame slides options. In addition, the macro should print the outline using the Pure black and white and the Scale to fit paper options. Then create another macro that exports the presentation outline to Microsoft Word. Call the macro ExportWord. Execute the macros, print the macros, and hand in the printouts to your instructor.

2 ▸▸ Open the Electronic Portfolio presentation you created in this project. You would like to share the layout of your form with various colleagues to obtain their feedback. Using the Visual Basic Editor, write a new module that prints the form. Save the module as PrintThisForm. Using the Customize command on the Tools menu, find your module in the Macro commands. Drag the PrintThisForm entry to the right of the Create Presentation button on the Using Presentation toolbar you created in the project. Modify this new button using the open pages image (row 6, column 1) on the Change Button Image palette. Name the button Print Form and then set the new button to the Default Style. Execute and print the macro. Hand in the printouts to your instructor.

3 ▸▸ Open the Home presentation from the Data Disk. Add a form that allows the user to select one of five templates from a combo box. Because slides two and four have clip art, you want the user to be able to select one of five clip art images for Slide 2 and one of five clip art images for Slide 4. The same five images may be used. Your Visual Basic code should warn the user if the same image has been selected for both slides. Write the Visual Basic module that executes this form. Name the module AddTemplates_ClipArt, and add that module to your Formatting toolbar. Print the form, the Visual Basic code, and the presentation. Hand in the printouts to your instructor.

4 ▸▸ Using Microsoft Internet Explorer, go to the Microsoft Office Developer's Web site http://msdn.microsoft.com/officedev/. Scroll down the page and enter `Visual Basic for Applications` in the Search text box. Click the Search button. Print and read three of the articles and then write a one-page summary of the articles. Hand in the article printouts and your summary to your instructor.

5 ▸▸▸ Open the Spring Break presentation you created in Project 3. If you did not complete this project, see your instructor for a copy of the file. Create a new toolbar named Vacations. Record a macro that prints handouts and notes. Place this macro on the new toolbar, and change the text of the button to an appropriate image. Next, add a button to your toolbar to execute the Pack and Go Wizard. Using Visual Basic Help, create a form that allows the user to modify the vacation slides to present either summer or winter vacations. Use the WinterChart.doc and the WinterTable.doc from your Data Disk for Slides 3 and 4 respectively when the winter vacation is chosen. Give the user the option to change templates depending on the season. Execute the print macro, and then display the form. Change the summer vacation presentation to a winter vacation presentation. Print slides, the Visual Basic code, and the form, and submit the handouts to your instructor.

Microsoft PowerPoint 2000

Distributing Presentations to Remote Audiences

CASE PERSPECTIVE

Job-hunting experts claim that searching for a full-time job is a full-time job in itself. Every day many students visit the Valley View College Placement Office to learn how to begin their job search. Jessica Cantero, the placement director, conducts several monthly seminars using a PowerPoint presentation with her talk on writing resumes.

Students attending Valley View's remote campuses have asked Jessica to deliver this speech. Jessica wants to put her PowerPoint presentation on floppy disks to take to these locations. She is not certain if PowerPoint is installed on computers where she will speak, so she needs to include the PowerPoint Viewer to ensure her slide show will run properly. Jessica has asked you to transfer her presentation and the Viewer onto floppy disks. You agree to use the Pack and Go Wizard, which optionally includes the Viewer, to compress the files.

In addition, Jessica had her network administrator transfer the Resumes With Results file to the College's Web server so she can collaborate with her cohorts about the content. Jessica wants you to develop subscriptions for the presentation to notify her when colleagues submit comments.

Introduction

PowerPoint file sizes often are much larger than those produced by other Microsoft Office programs such as Word and Excel. Presentations with embedded pictures and video, such as the one you created in Project 6, easily can grow beyond the 1.44 MB capacity of floppy disks. The large file size may present difficulties if you need to transport your presentation to show on another computer.

One solution to this file size limitation is using the **Pack and Go Wizard**. This program, which also is used in Microsoft Publisher, compresses and saves all the components of your presentation so it can be delivered on a computer other than the one on which it was created. Linked documents and multimedia files are included in this packaged file. The Wizard can embed any TrueType font that is included in Windows; however, it cannot embed other TrueType fonts that have built-in copyright restrictions.

If the destination computer does not have Microsoft PowerPoint installed, the Pack and Go Wizard can pack the **PowerPoint Viewer** along with the presentation. The Viewer is a program, PPview32.exe, that allows you to run, but not edit, a PowerPoint presentation created in PowerPoint for Windows or PowerPoint for the Macintosh. It is available on the Microsoft Office CD-ROMs and on the Microsoft Office Update Web site, http://officeupdate.microsoft.com/, which is a source for viewer updates and for additional information. You can distribute the Viewer freely and install it on computers that do not have Microsoft Office installed. It supports all features from PowerPoint 97 and PowerPoint 95; however, it does not support some PowerPoint 2000 features, such as picture bullets, automatic numbering, and animated GIF files.

Part 1: Saving the Presentation Using the Pack and Go Wizard

The resume slide show consists of five slides that provide general guidelines, specific strategies for listing education and work experience, and considerations for writing electronic resumes (Figure 1). The presentation uses clip art, slide transitions, and preset animation to add visual interest.

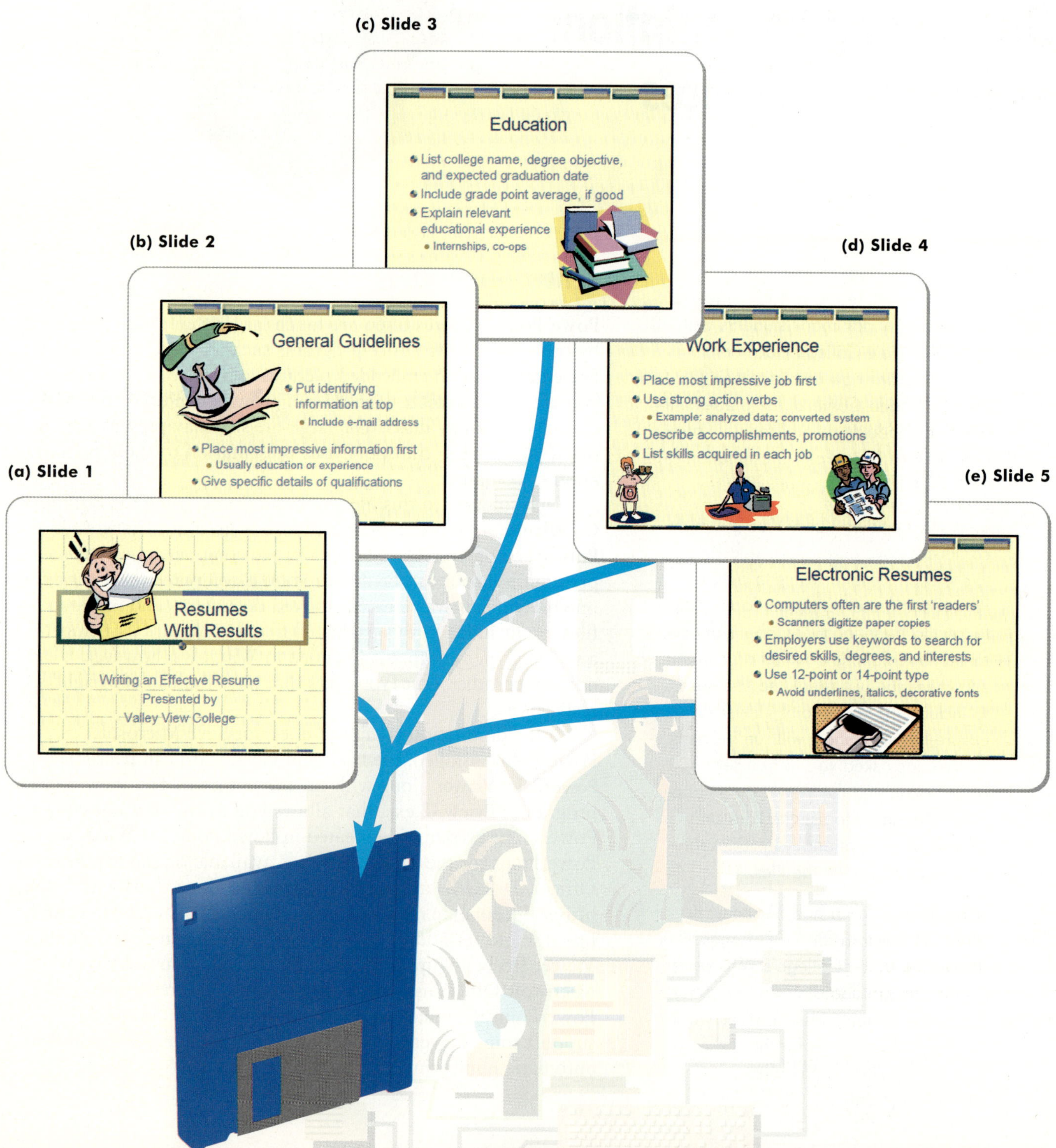

FIGURE 1

The Pack and Go Wizard will compress your presentation and package it with the PowerPoint Viewer so you can show it on another computer. As you proceed through the Wizard, PowerPoint will prompt you to select the presentation file, a destination drive, linking and embedding options, and whether to add the Viewer.

The Resumes With Results file size is 156 KB; the Pack and Go Wizard will create a compressed file with the file name pres0.ppz with a file size of 66 KB. If you add the Viewer to the package, the file increases to more than 2,700 KB, which is too large to fit onto one floppy disk. In addition, the Wizard creates another file, pngsetup.exe, which is needed to unpack, or extract, the Viewer and presentation file and copy them onto a remote computer. The pngsetup file is 55 KB. You consequently will need at least two additional floppy disks to run the Pack and Go Wizard and save the compressed files to drive A. The Wizard truncates the presentation file name to Resume~1 because it supports file names with a maximum of eight characters and cannot include spaces. Perform the following steps to use the Pack and Go Wizard and add the PowerPoint Viewer.

the Projector Wizard

When you show your presentation on another computer at a remote site, you may need to set the screen resolution according to the projection system you are using. The Projector Wizard helps you optimize viewing the slide show. To run the Projector Wizard, click Set Up Show on the Slide Show menu and follow the prompts to set up the presentation for the particular monitor or projection system you are using. If you are running Microsoft Windows 98 or 2000, you can run your slide show on one monitor and view your slides, notes, and the presentation outlines on another monitor.

To Save the Presentation Using the Pack and Go Wizard

1 Start PowerPoint and then open the Resumes With Results file on the Data Disk. Reset your toolbars as described in Appendix C. Click File on the menu bar and then point to Pack and Go.

PowerPoint opens and displays the presentation in slide view (Figure 2). The File menu displays. Depending on your computer system installation, you may be prompted to install the Pack and Go Wizard. If this message occurs, see your instructor.

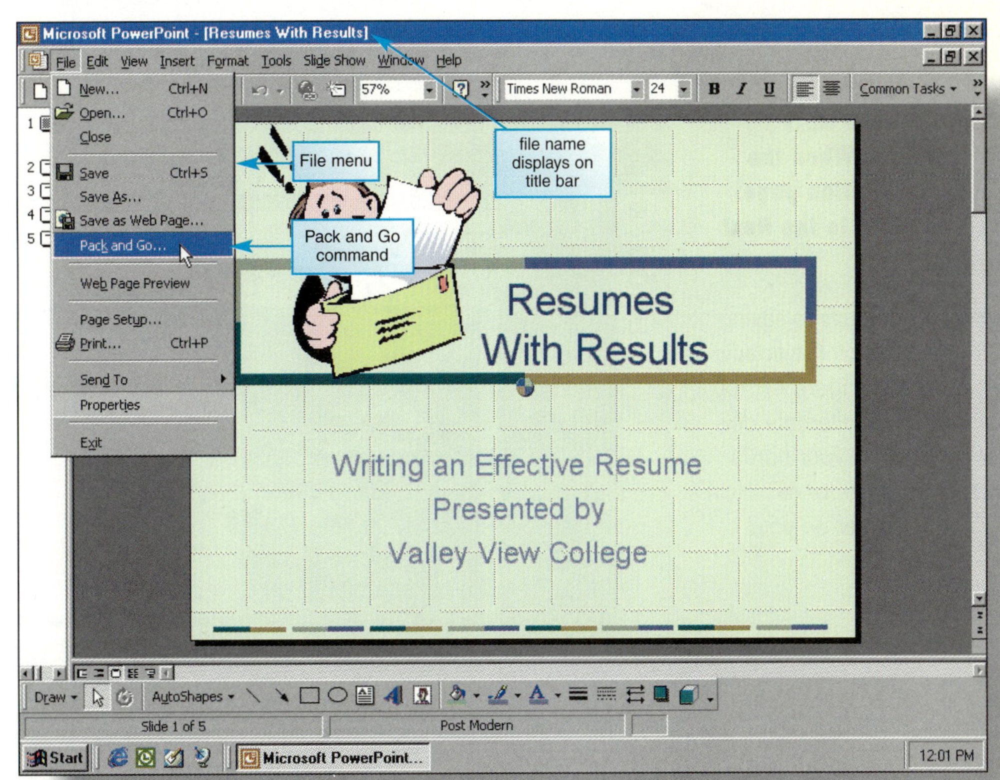

FIGURE 2

2 Click Pack and Go. When the Pack and Go Wizard dialog box displays, point to the Next button.

PowerPoint displays the Start panel, describing the function of the Pack and Go Wizard. You can click the Help button if you desire further explanations from the Office Assistant or the Cancel button to exit the Pack and Go Wizard.

3 Click the Next button. When the Pick files to pack panel displays, point to the Next button.

The Active presentation check box is selected (Figure 3). You can choose to package the Resumes With Results file with one or more other PowerPoint files. You can click the Back button to review previous panels.

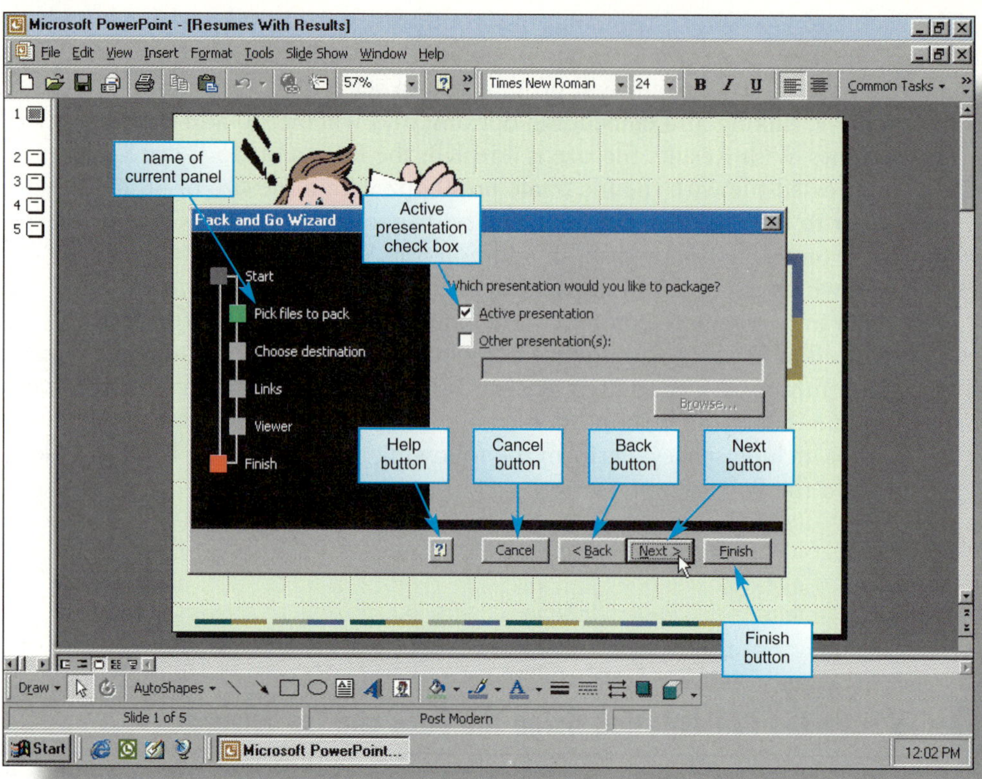

FIGURE 3

4 Click the Next button. When the Choose destination panel displays, point to the Next button.

PowerPoint defaults to saving the packed file on the floppy disk in drive A (Figure 4). You could select an alternate destination, such as your hard drive, a Zip drive, or to another computer on your network.

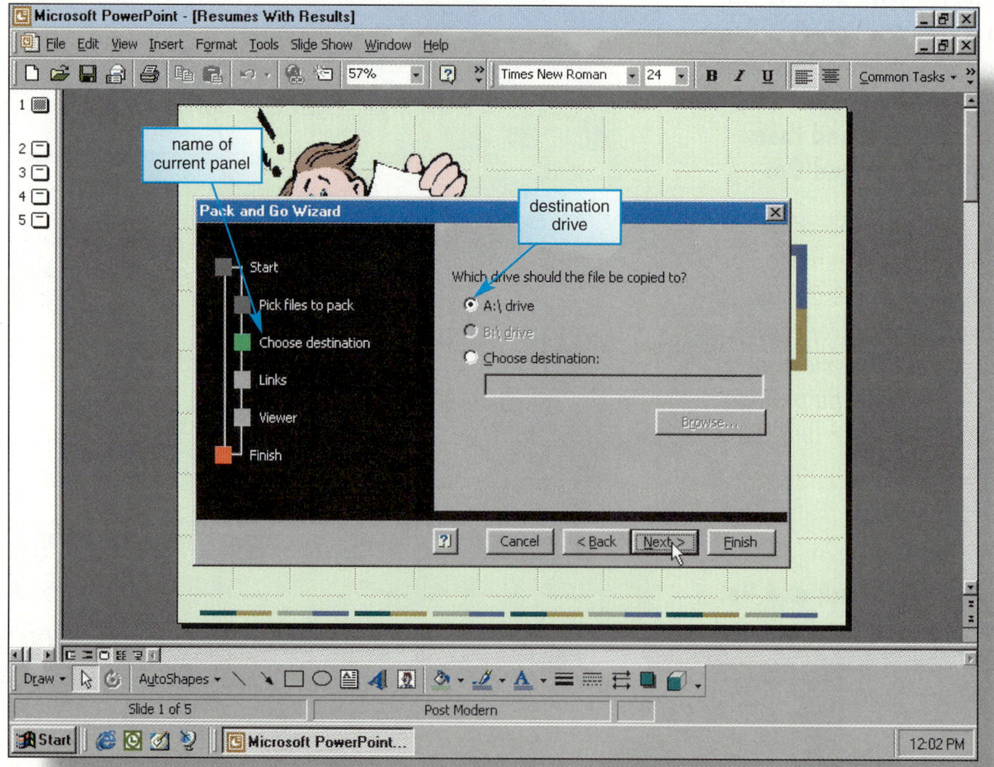

FIGURE 4

5 Click the Next button. When the Links panel displays, click Include linked files to deselect the option. Point to the Next button.

The Resumes With Results presentation does not contain any linked files, so you do not need to select this option (Figure 5). If the presentation had linked files, such as embedded Excel charts and Word tables, you would need to include these files in the package. The presentation uses the TrueType Arial font, but this standard font is found on most computers. Embedding fonts ensures the text displays correctly if the font is not installed on the destination computer.

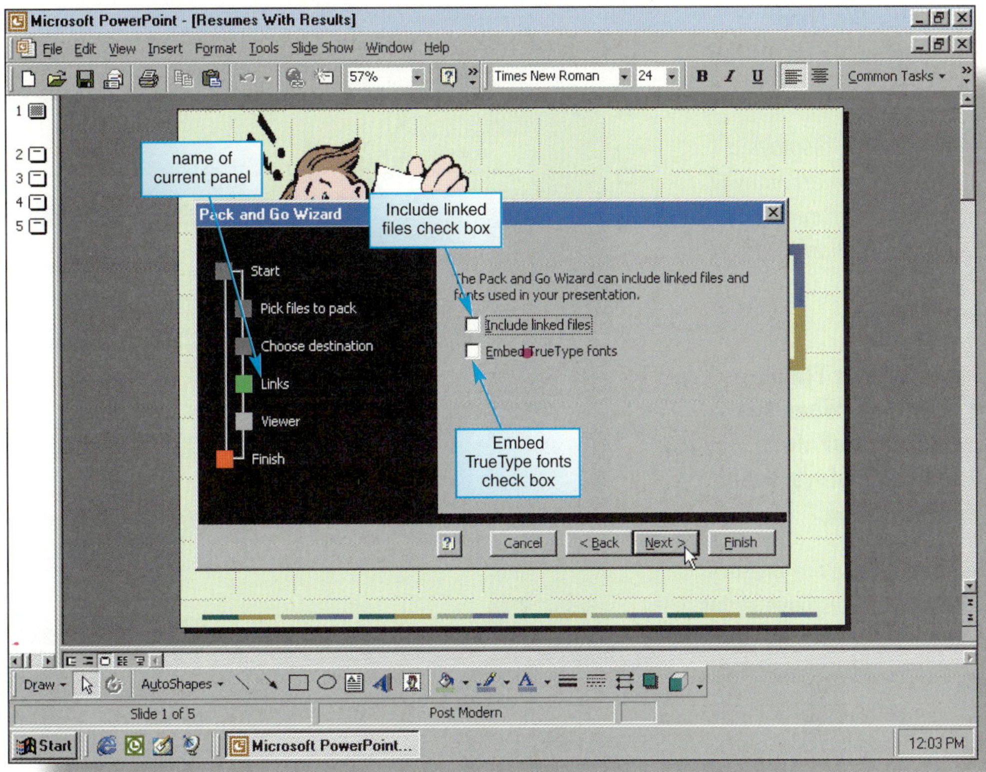

FIGURE 5

6 Click the Next button. When the Viewer panel displays, click Viewer for Windows 95 or NT. Point to the Next button.

The Viewer will run the presentation if the application is not installed (Figure 6). You want to include the PowerPoint Viewer because you are uncertain whether PowerPoint is installed on computers at the remote campuses.

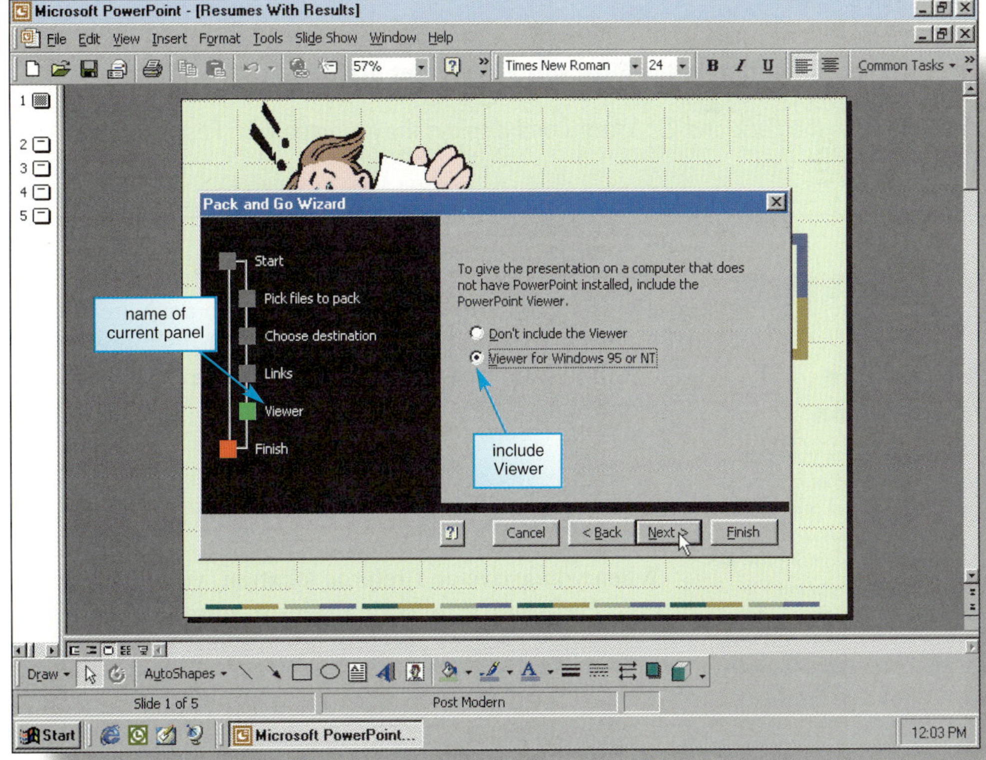

FIGURE 6

7 **Click the Next button. Point to the Finish button.**

The Finish panel displays a message that PowerPoint will compress the Resumes With Results presentation to drive A (Figure 7).

8 **Click the Finish button. When the Microsoft PowerPoint dialog box displays, point to the OK button.**

PowerPoint packs the presentation files and displays status messages of which files are being added to the package. When the packing process is completed, PowerPoint displays the message that the Pack and Go Wizard has packed the presentation successfully.

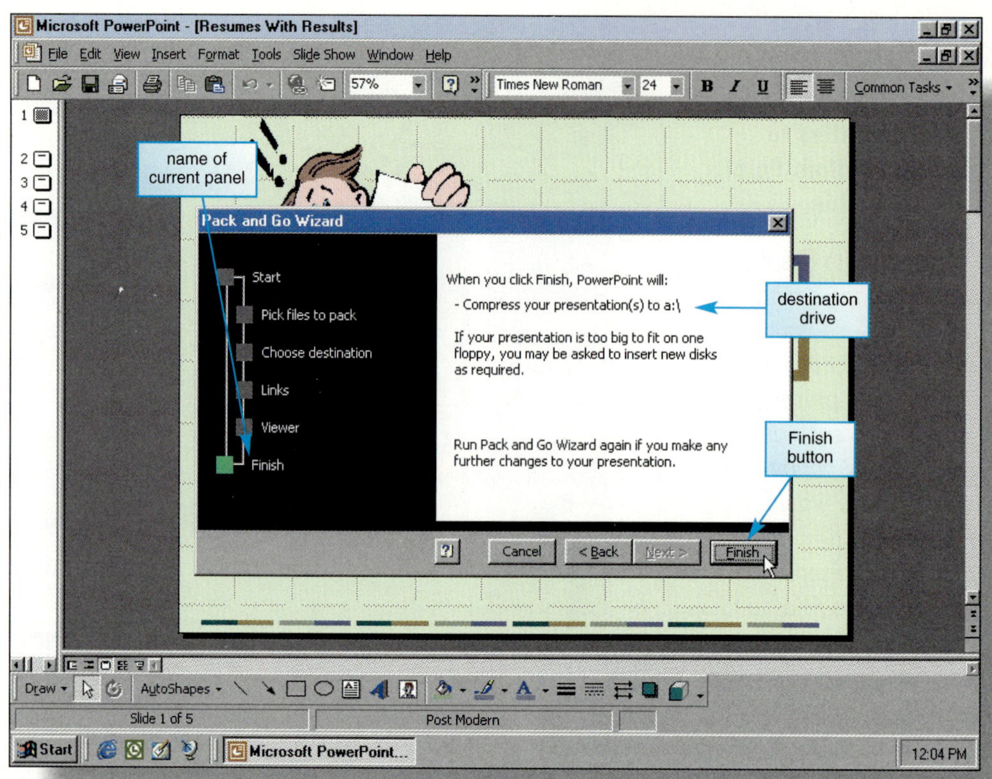

FIGURE 7

9 **Click the OK button in the Microsoft PowerPoint dialog box.**

PowerPoint closes the Pack and Go Wizard and displays the Resumes With Results presentation in slide view.

More About

Unpacking a Presentation

When you unpack your presentation on another computer, PowerPoint should prompt you to start the slide show. If you do not see this prompt browse to the folder that contains the unpacked presentation. Then double-click the Ppview32.exe file. Browse to and select the presentation, and then click Show. For more information, visit the PowerPoint 2000 Web Feature 2 More About page (www.scsite.com/pp2000/more.htm) and click Unpack.

The Pack and Go Wizard saves the package containing the presentation and Viewer as pres0.ppz on the first floppy disk, pres0.pp1 on the second disk, and pres0.pp2 on the third disk. You now are ready to transport the presentation to a remote site.

Unpacking a Presentation

When you arrive at a remote location, you will need to open the packed presentation. Perform the following steps to unpack the presentation.

TO UNPACK A PRESENTATION

1. Insert your first floppy disk of packed files in drive A. Right-click the Start button on the taskbar and then click Open on the shortcut menu.
2. Click the Up button on the Standard Buttons toolbar three times so that the My Computer window displays. Double-click 3½ Floppy (A:).
3. When the 3½ Floppy (A): window opens, double-click pngsetup.
4. When the Pack and Go Setup dialog box displays, enter `C:\RESUME` in the Destination Folder text box and then click the OK button. Click the OK button when asked to create this directory. When prompted, insert the second disk and click the OK button. Then insert the third disk when prompted and click the OK button.
5. When the Pack and Go Setup dialog box displays the message that the presentation has been installed successfully in C:\RESUME directory, click the Yes button to run the slide show now.

PowerPoint unpacks the Resumes With Results presentation and runs the slide show.

You can create a **playlist** to use with the Viewer if you have multiple presentations you want to show sequentially. To create this list, open Notepad or a new document in Microsoft Word. Next, type the file names, including the .ppt file extensions, of the desired presentations on separate lines. Save this file with the extension .lst. When you are ready to start running the presentations, start the Viewer, PPview32.exe, enter the file name of the document that contains the playlist, and then click Show.

Part 1 of this project is complete. You now should close the Resumes With Results presentation. Perform the following steps to close the presentation but leave PowerPoint running.

Playlists

Playlist (.lst) files are supported in the PowerPoint Viewer, not in the PowerPoint application. If you open a Playlist file in PowerPoint by clicking the File command and then clicking Open, PowerPoint opens the file as text within as an outline. If you want to run a series of presentations as slide shows in PowerPoint, you can use a batch file. The result is very similar to a playlist; the presentations play in order. The only difference is that you will see your desktop for a moment between presentations. The Microsoft Web site has detailed directions on how to create this batch file. For more information, visit the PowerPoint 2000 Web Feature 2 More About page (www.scsite.com/pp2000/more.htm) and click Playlist.

TO CLOSE THE PRESENTATION

1. Click File on the menu bar and then click Close on the File menu.

PowerPoint closes the Resumes With Results presentation.

1. Press ALT+F, press C

Part 2: Discussing and Subscribing to a Publication

Sending and receiving e-mail messages constitutes a major portion of the day for many students and business workers. An estimated 25 million e-mail users send 15 billion messages each year. If you want a colleague to review your PowerPoint presentation or Word document draft, you can send the document as an attachment to an e-mail message and then ask the recipient to respond with comments. Another method for soliciting comments on a document, Web folder, or discussion is a **subscription**, which automatically notifies participants by e-mail when a specified document had been modified, moved, or deleted.

The first step in beginning a subscription is to save the file on a Web server. A **Web server** is a computer that delivers requested Web pages. Your network administrator needs to **upload** your Resumes With Results file to your Web server. A file is uploaded when it is copied from a local computer to a remote computer. Before uploading the file, the network administrator has to install the **Office Server Extensions (OSE)** on the server to enable you to participate in Office's Web discussion and subscription features. The OSE are a set of technologies that provide

More About 2000

OSE

When network administrators install the Web Discussions feature they install the Office Service Extensions (OSE). These files enable subscriptions and discussions to occur. The OSE have their own Setup program and an OSE Configuration Wizard that guides installation on a Web server by configuring database, security, and e-mail server settings. For more information, visit the PowerPoint 2000 Web Feature 2 More About page (www.scsite.com/pp2000/more.htm) and click OSE.

publishing, collaboration, and searching capabilities for Office 2000 documents and Web pages. The administrator places your file in the College's **Web folder**, which is an area on a Web server where the document is stored.

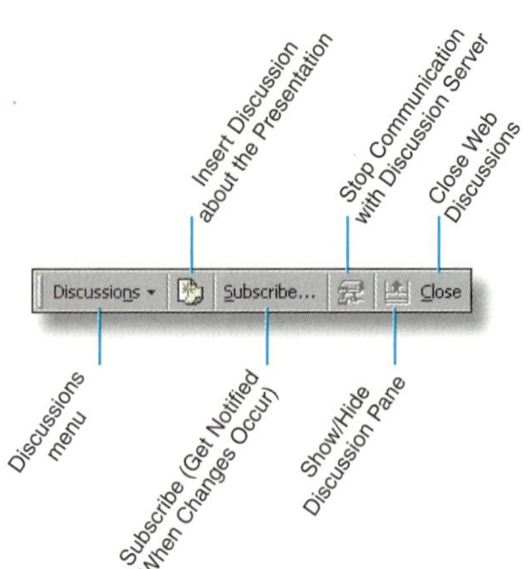

Discussions toolbar

FIGURE 8

Now you are ready to ask your colleagues to review the presentation. Each of these individuals will join a **Web discussion**, which is a new Office 2000 feature that allows users to collaborate by inserting comments on files accessible from a Web server. They will make their comments using the **Discussions toolbar** (Figure 8), which contains buttons that allow you to add, navigate through, edit, and reply to comments, to subscribe to a document, and to view or hide the Discussions window. This toolbar displays only when you start a Web discussion; it cannot be displayed from the Toolbars option in the View menu or from a shortcut menu. The participants' comments will be **threaded** so the original comments and all related replies display together. These discussion comments are stored in a database on the server, so the original Resumes With Results presentation is not altered.

You will start a discussion and then read the comments by subscribing to the Resumes With Results file at Valley View College. Ask your instructor for the location of that file on your Web server.

Opening a File in a Web Folder

To comment on a presentation, you first must **download** a copy of it from the Web server where it is stored. A file is downloaded when it is copied from a remote computer to a local computer. Perform the following steps to open the Valley View College Web folder and then download the Resumes with Results file.

Steps To Open a File in a Web Folder

1 With PowerPoint open, click File on the menu bar and then click Open on the File menu. When the Open dialog box displays, click Web Folders in the Places bar of the Open dialog box, click Valley View College in the Web Folders list, and then point to the Open button.

PowerPoint opens the Web Folders folder (Figure 9). You will need to ask your instructor to verify the location of the Resumes With Results file on your network. You also may be able to use your browser to view the list of files in a Web folder.

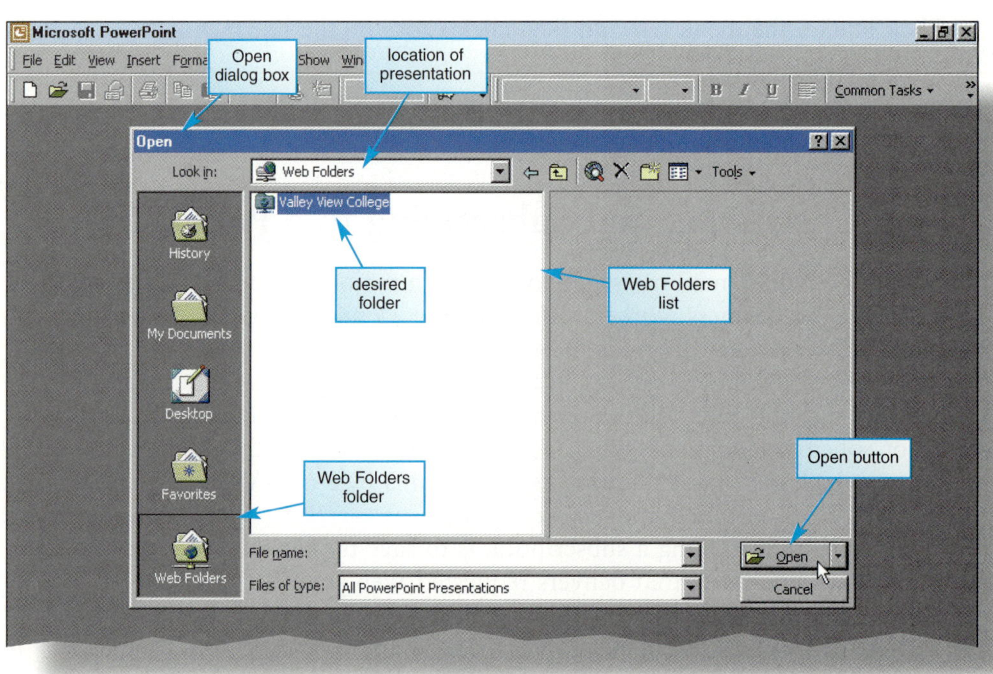

FIGURE 9

2 Click the Open button. When the Open dialog box displays again, point to the Open button.

The Valley View College folder opens and displays the one document, Resumes With Results, it contains (Figure 10). Your list of file names may vary if your network administrator has added other files to the folder.

3 Click the Open button.

As the Resumes With Results presentation downloads from the Web server to your computer, Office 2000 displays a Transferring File progress meter. Slide 1 of the presentation displays in slide view.

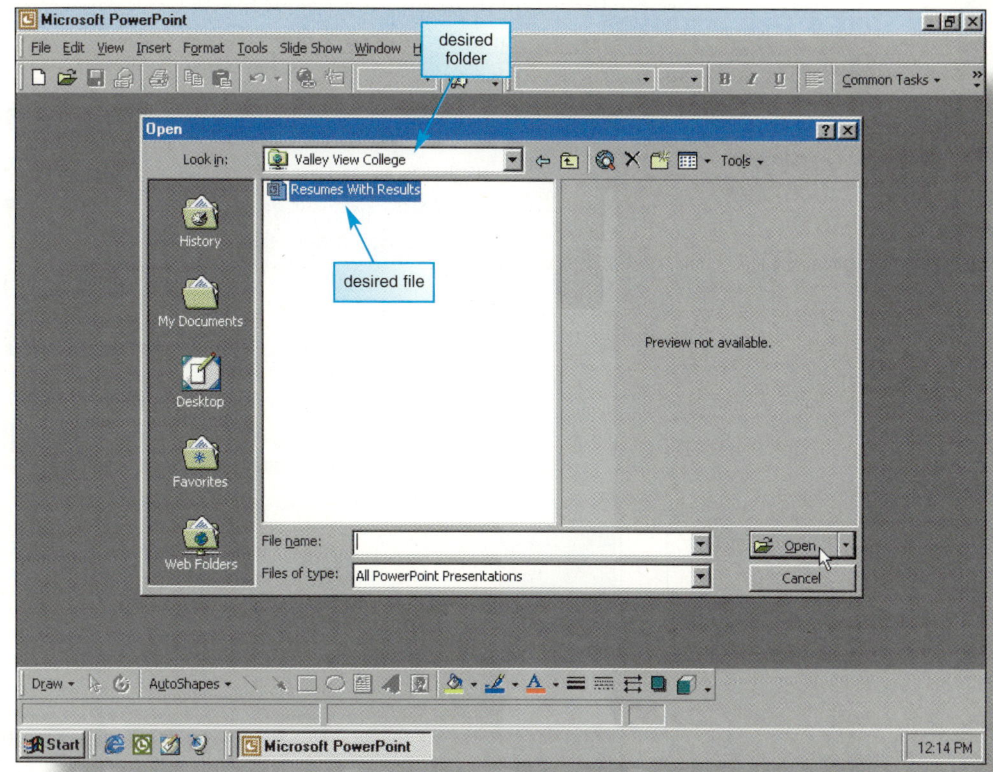

FIGURE 10

You are able to scroll through the slides in the presentation and run the slide show. Although you cannot alter the slide show, you can comment on the presentation and view comments your cohorts have made about the slides.

Starting Web Discussions

Microsoft added the Office 2000 Web discussions tool as a means of allowing Office users to view presentations and then make comments. A discussion database on the server stores the comments along with pointers to the locations where the comments belong in the document. This technology is designed to help teams work efficiently and effectively. Perform the steps on the next page to discuss the content of the presentation.

More About 2000

Newsgroup Discussions

Along with subscribing to presentations, you also can subscribe to newsgroups, which are online discussions on a wide variety of topics. When you subscribe, you can read and post comments on the topic of conversation. You can find newsgroups that interest you by searching for them through the Deja.com site. Together, newsgroups make up Usenet, a part of the Internet. For more information, visit the PowerPoint 2000 Web Feature 2 More About page (www.scsite.com/pp2000/more.htm) and click Discussions.

To Start a Web Discussion

1 **Click Tools on the Menu bar, point to Online Collaboration, and then point to Web Discussions (Figure 11).**

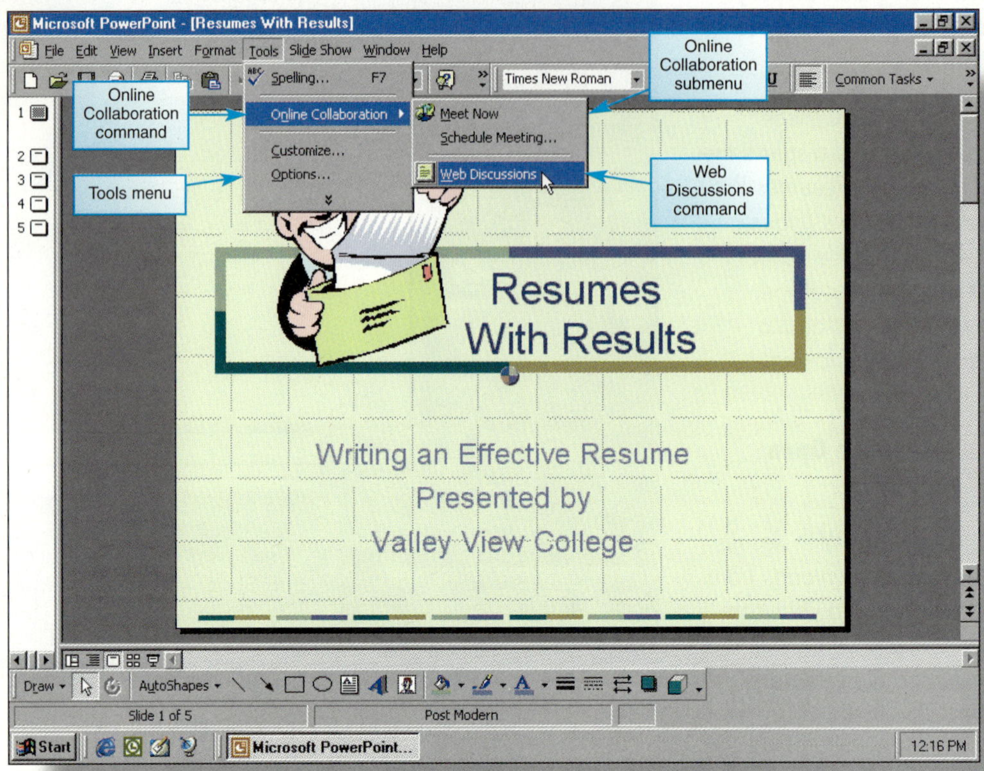

FIGURE 11

2 **Click Web Discussions. When the Discussions toolbar displays, click the Discussions menu button and then point to Discussion Options.**

The Discussions toolbar displays above the Drawing toolbar (Figure 12). Depending upon your computer's configuration, you may be prompted to enter the name of your Web discussion server in a separate dialog box.

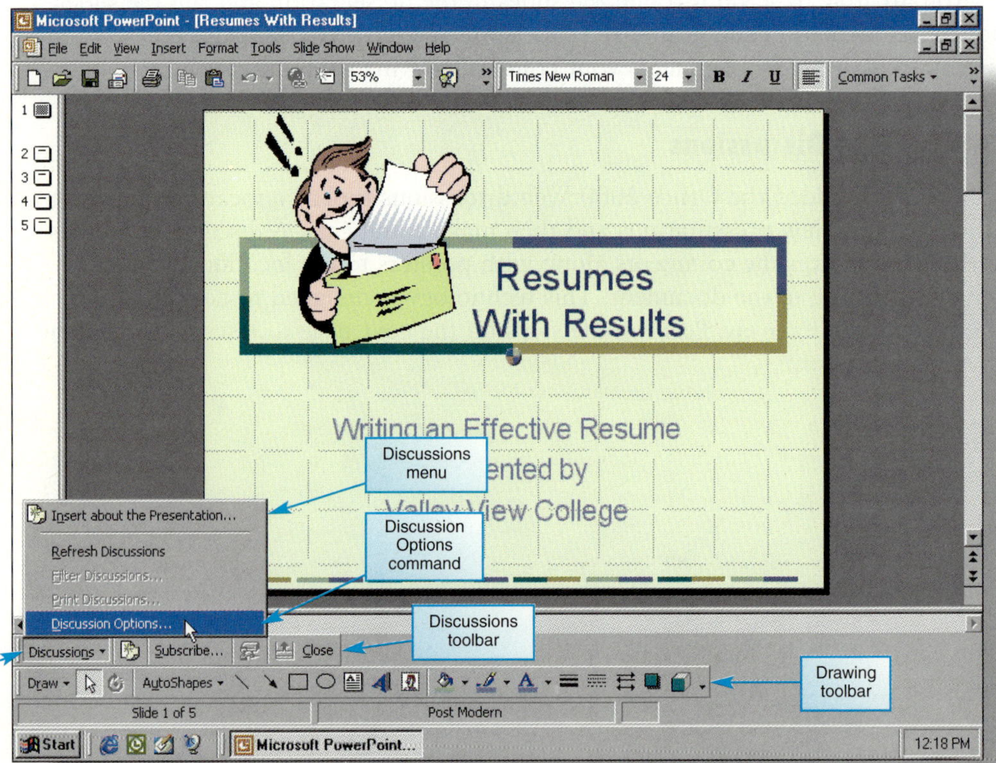

FIGURE 12

3 **Click Discussion Options. When the Discussion Options dialog box displays, point to the OK button.**

The Discussion Options dialog box allows you to select the server for the discussion group in which you are participating (Figure 13). Ask your instructor for the name of your discussion server. The selected check boxes indicate the types of information the collaborators will see in the discussion pane when they participate in the discussion.

4 **Click the OK button.**

The Discussion Options dialog box closes.

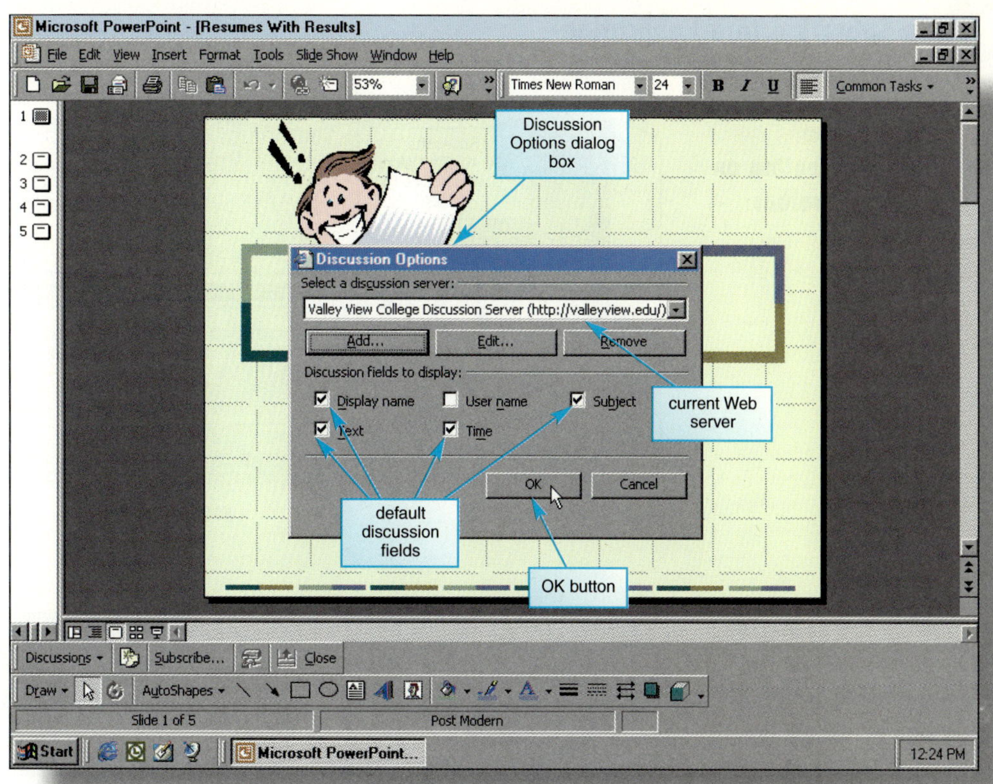

FIGURE 13

At this point, you can use the buttons on the Discussions toolbar to participate in the discussion. For example, you can initiate a discussion about the entire document, such as asking collaborators if the design template should be changed, if the title text color should be a darker shade of blue, or if the presentation needs additional content. You click the **Insert Discussion about the Presentation** button to start this type of discussion.

The **Print Discussions** command on the Discussions menu allows you to print all comments on the discussion. If participants have made many comments, you may want to use the **Filter Discussion** command, also on the Discussions menu, to view discussion items that were created by specific participants or on particular dates.

Subscribing to a Publication

Now that you have started a discussion regarding the Resumes With Results presentation, you want your colleagues to view the slide show and provide additional feedback. When they have posted a comment, you want to be aware that the comments database has been updated. Office 2000's subscription feature will notify subscribers to folders or documents via e-mail when a discussion item is inserted, edited, or deleted, when a new document is added, or when a document is modified, deleted or moved. You can choose to be notified of these changes instantly, daily, or weekly.

The steps on the next page describe how you subscribe to the Resumes With Results publication. You may ask your instructor if your network is configured so that you may alternately enter your e-mail address and participate in a discussion with your classmates.

Managing Homework Assignments Using Subscriptions

Many businesses subscribe to a publication to save time and resources. The same subscription techniques are used in education to allow students to receive and submit homework assignments and to participate in threaded discussions about documents. The Microsoft Web site offers information on how teachers are using this feature, including directions on creating a Web folder, assigning folder permissions, subscribing to a folder, instructing students how to subscribe to a folder, creating a Web discussion, submitting assignments to Web folders, and round tripping a document for editing. For more information, visit the PowerPoint 2000 Web Feature 2 More About page (www.scsite.com/pp2000/more.htm) and click Homework.

To Subscribe to a Publication

1 Point to the Subscribe button on the Discussions toolbar (Figure 14).

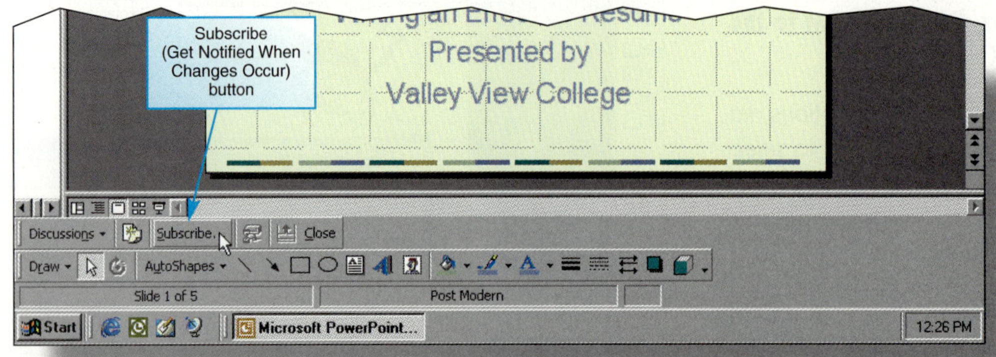

FIGURE 14

2 Click the Subscribe button. When the Document Subscription dialog box displays, type jessica_cantero@hotmail.com **in the Address text box in the Email options area. Click the Time box arrow in the Email options area and then click once a day. Point to the OK button.**

The Web address displayed in the dialog box is the location of the Resumes With Results file on the network server (Figure 15). You may select another file or folder to subscribe to. The default setting is to be notified when anything changes, but you have the options of being notified immediately or weekly whenever the document is edited, moved, or deleted.

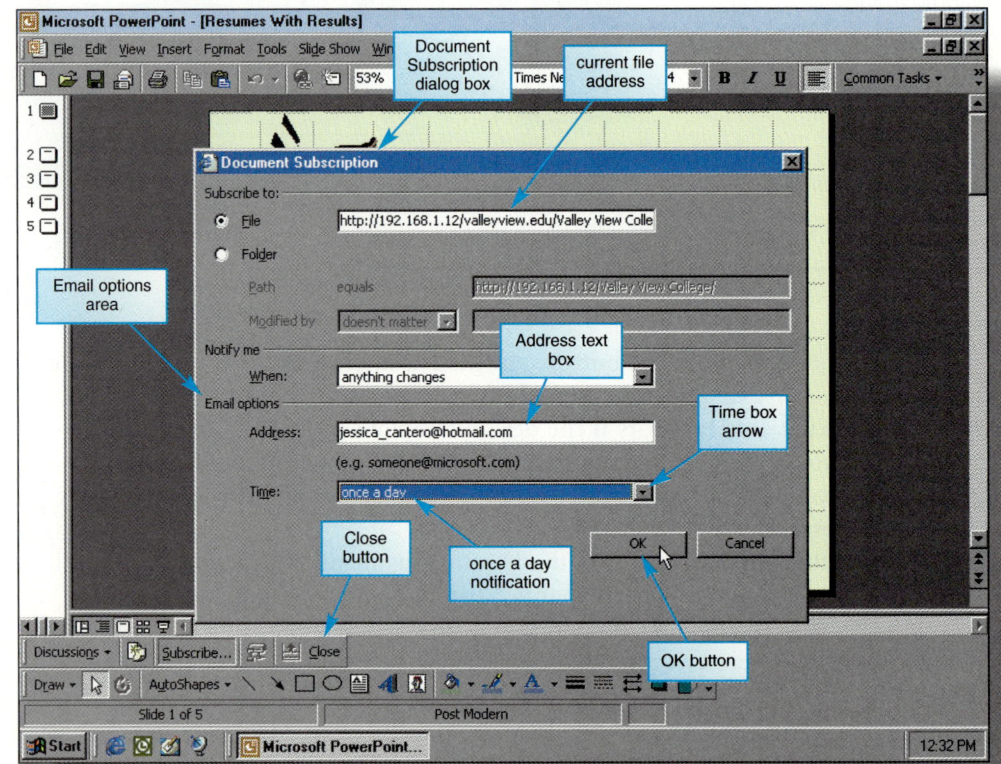

FIGURE 15

3 Click the OK button.

In a few seconds, PowerPoint notifies you that the subscription has begun.

You will receive an e-mail message daily notifying you if anyone has commented on your presentation. When you receive this message, you also have the option of unsubscribing at that time. If you choose to unsubscribe, you will click a link in the message, which will launch your default Internet browser, open a form, and permit you to confirm that you want to cancel your subscription to the presentation.

More About 2000

E-Mail

Learn e-mail terminology and techniques by surfing to the PowerPoint 2000 Web Feature 2 More About page (www.scsite.com/pp2000/more.htm) and clicking E-mail.

Ending the Discussion

When you have completed making comments and subscribing, you close the Discussions toolbar.

TO CLOSE A DISCUSSION

1. Click the Close button on Discussions toolbar.

The PowerPoint window is restored to its full size. At this point you can work on another PowerPoint presentation or quit PowerPoint.

Other Ways

1. On Tools menu point to Online Collaboration, click Web discussions

CASE PERSPECTIVE SUMMARY

Jessica Cantero can now show her Resumes With Results presentation to students attending Valley View College's satellite campuses. By using the Pack and Go Wizard, she can transport her presentation file and a copy of the PowerPoint Viewer to these sites. In addition, she can share her slide show with teachers and administrators at neighboring colleges and solicit ways to improve its content. By subscribing to this presentation, Jessica is notified daily when her colleagues submit comments.

Web Feature Summary

This Web Feature demonstrated two methods of sharing a presentation with others. In Part 1, you learned to use the Pack and Go Wizard to condense files and include the PowerPoint Viewer. In Part 2, you learned to download a file from a server, set discussion options, and subscribe to a publication so that you are notified when your associates provide comments.

What You Should Know

Having completed this Web Feature, you now should be able to perform the following tasks:

- Close a Discussion *(PPW 2.13)*
- Close a Presentation *(PPW 2.7)*
- Open a File in a Web Folder *(PPW 2.8)*
- Save a Presentation Using the Pack and Go Wizard *(PPW 2.3)*
- Start a Web Discussion *(PPW 2.10)*
- Subscribe to a Publication *(PPW 2.12)*
- Unpack a Presentation *(PPW 2.7)*

1 Saving a Presentation Using the Pack and Go Wizard

Problem: Tiffani Olson, the director of the Western College Fitness Center, wants to show the presentation you created for her in Project 5 in the cafeteria at each of the College's satellite campuses. She knows that the cafeterias are equipped with computers that have Office 2000 installed, so she would like for you to use the Pack and Go Wizard to transfer the presentation to floppy disks.

Instructions: Start PowerPoint and then perform the following steps with a computer.

1. Open the Half-Hour Workout presentation shown in Figures 5-1a through 5-1g on page PP 5.5. (If you did not complete Project 5, see your instructor for a copy of the presentation.)
2. Save the Presentation using the Pack and Go Wizard. Include the linked files, but do not embed TrueType fonts. Do not include the Viewer.
3. Hand in the floppy disks containing the presentation to your instructor. Quit PowerPoint.

2 Saving a Presentation with a Viewer Using the Pack and Go Wizard

Problem: Your friend Benito Kovich is extremely satisfied with the electronic portfolio you created for him in Project 6 using Visual Basic for Applications. He has shown the slide show successfully on several job interviews using his notebook computer. He informs you that most of the sites where he has interviewed had computers available, so in the future he would like to transport the slide show on floppy disks and install it on the companies' computers instead of taking his notebook to the interviews. You agree to help him by using the Pack and Go Wizard to transfer the presentation to floppy disks.

Instructions: Start PowerPoint and then perform the following steps with a computer.

1. Open the Electronic Portfolio presentation you created in Project 6. (If you did not complete Project 6, see your instructor for a copy of the presentation.)
2. Save the Presentation using the Pack and Go Wizard. Include the linked files, but do not embed TrueType fonts. Include the Viewer.
3. Hand in the floppy disks containing the presentation to your instructor. Quit PowerPoint.

3 Discussing and Subscribing to a Presentation

Problem: After seeing Benito Kovich's customized presentation in Project 6, you decide to create a similar presentation highlighting your academic achievements, extra-curricular activities, and employment history. You create the slide show and decide to solicit comments regarding the presentation from your professors, club advisers, former employers, and alumni. You ask your network administrator or instructor to upload this file to a folder on your school's Web server.

Instructions: Start PowerPoint and perform the following tasks with a computer.

1. Open your presentation from the folder on your school's Web server.
2. Start a Web discussion. Display the User name, Subject, Text, and Time discussion fields.
3. Subscribe to the presentation. Use your e-mail address, and request notification when a change occurs in any part of the discussion.
4. After your professional and personal associates have comented on your presentation, print their comments and hand them in to your instructor. Quit PowerPoint.

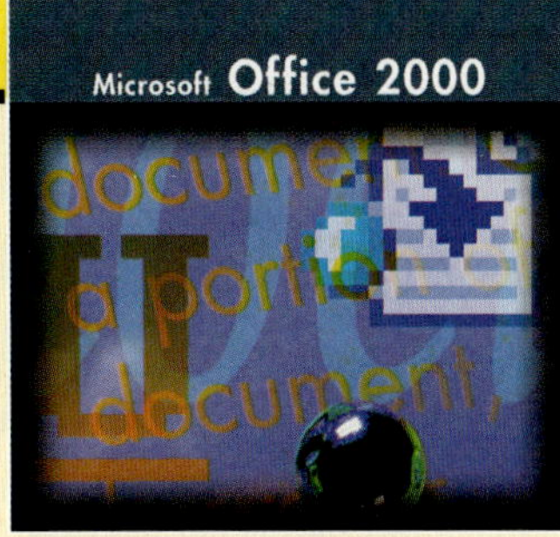

APPENDIX A

Microsoft Office 2000 Help System

Using the Microsoft Office Help System

This appendix demonstrates how you can use the Microsoft Office 2000 Help system to answer your questions. At any time while you are using one of the Microsoft Office 2000 applications, you can interact with the Help system to display information on any topic associated with the application. To illustrate the use of the Microsoft Office 2000 Help system, the Microsoft Word 2000 application will be used in this appendix. The Help systems in other Microsoft Office applications respond in a similar fashion.

The two primary forms of Help available in each Microsoft Office application are the Office Assistant and the Microsoft Help window. The one you use will depend on your preference. As shown in Figure A-1, you access either form of Help in Microsoft Word by pressing the F1 key, clicking Microsoft Word Help on the Help menu, or clicking the Microsoft Word Help button on the Standard toolbar. Word responds in one of two ways:

1. If the Office Assistant is turned on, then the Office Assistant displays with a balloon (lower-right side of Figure A-1).
2. If the Office Assistant is turned off, then the Microsoft Word Help window displays (lower-left side of Figure A-1)

Table A-1 on the next page summarizes the nine categories of Help available to you. Because of the way the Word Help system works, please review the rightmost column of Table A-1 if you have difficulties activating the desired category of Help.

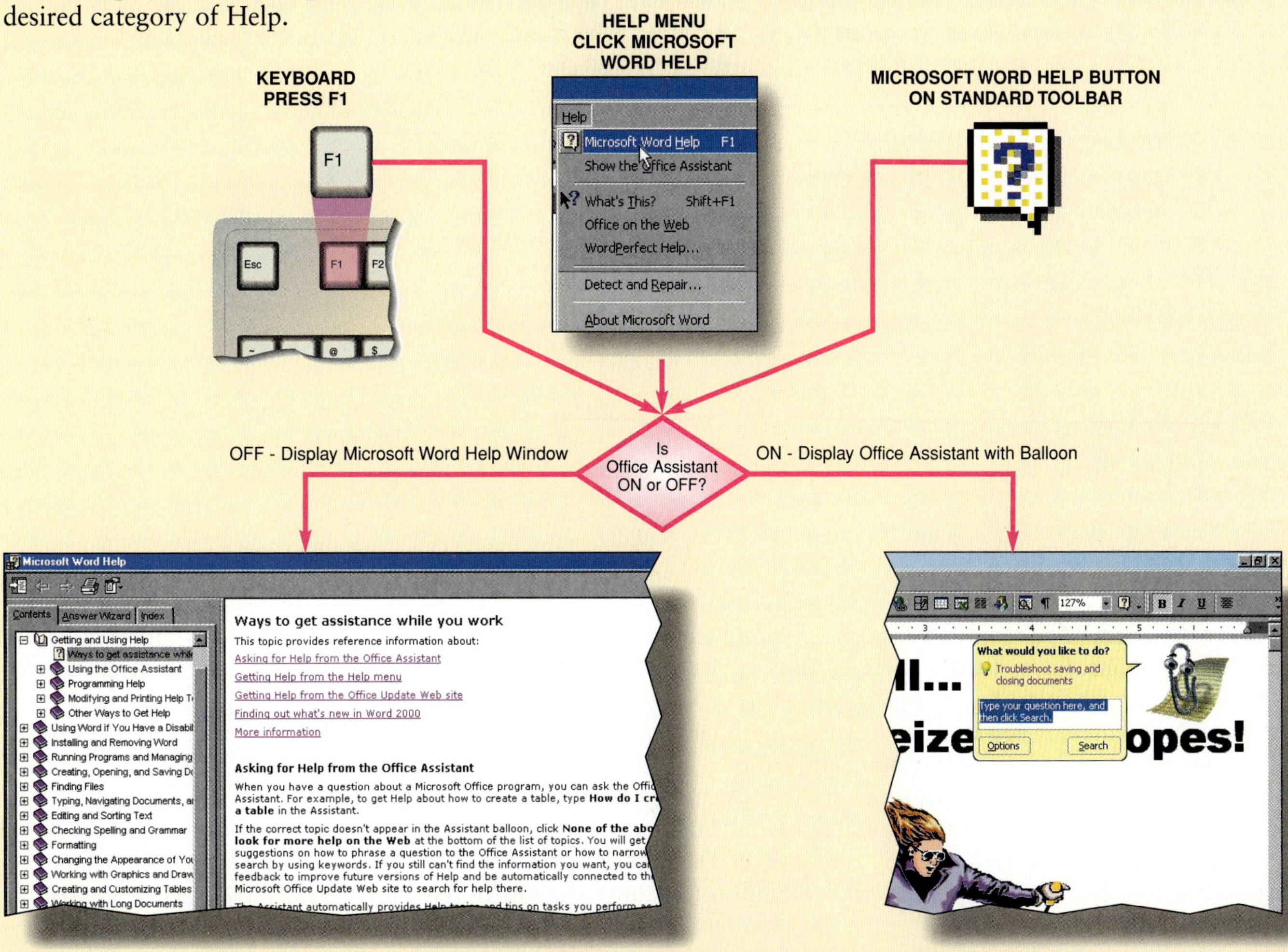

KEYBOARD PRESS F1

HELP MENU CLICK MICROSOFT WORD HELP

MICROSOFT WORD HELP BUTTON ON STANDARD TOOLBAR

OFF - Display Microsoft Word Help Window

Is Office Assistant ON or OFF?

ON - Display Office Assistant with Balloon

FIGURE A-1

Table A-1 Word Help System

TYPE	DESCRIPTION	HOW TO ACTIVATE	TURNING THE OFFICE ASSISTANT ON AND OFF
Answer Wizard	Similar to the Office Assistant in that it answers questions that you type in your own words.	Click the Microsoft Word Help button on the Standard toolbar. If necessary, maximize the Help window by double-clicking its title bar. Click the Answer Wizard tab.	If the Office Assistant displays, right-click it, click Options on the shortcut menu, click Use the Office Assistant to remove the check mark, click the OK button.
Contents sheet	Groups Help topics by general categories. Use when you know only the general category of the topic in question.	Click the Microsoft Word Help button on the Standard toolbar. If necessary, maximize the Help window by double-clicking its title bar. Click the Contents tab.	If the Office Assistant displays, right-click it, click Options, click Use the Office Assistant to remove the check mark, click the OK button.
Detect and Repair	Automatically finds and fixes errors in the application.	Click Detect and Repair on the Help menu.	
Hardware and Software Information	Shows Product ID and allows access to system information and technical support information.	Click About Microsoft Word on the Help menu and then click the appropriate button.	
Help for WordPerfect Users	Used to assist WordPerfect users who are learning Microsoft Word.	Click WordPerfect Help on the Help menu.	
Index sheet	Similar to an index in a book; use when you know exactly what you want.	Click the Microsoft Word Help button on the Standard toolbar. If necessary, maximize the Help window by double-clicking its title bar. Click the Index tab.	If the Office Assistant displays, right-click it, click Options, click Use the Office Assistant to remove the check mark, click the OK button.
Office Assistant	Answers questions that you type in your own words, offers tips, and provides Help for a variety of Word features.	Click the Microsoft Word Help button on the Standard toolbar or double-click the Office Assistant icon. Some dialog boxes also include the Microsoft Word Help button.	If the Office Assistant does not display, click Show the Office Assistant on the Help menu.
Office on the Web	Used to access technical resources and download free product enhancements on the Web.	Click Office on the Web on the Help menu.	
Question Mark button and What's This? command	Used to identify unfamiliar items on the screen.	In a dialog box, click the Question Mark button and then click an item in the dialog box. Click What's This? on the Help menu, and then click an item on the screen.	

The best way to familiarize yourself with the Word Help system is to use it. The next several pages show examples of how to use the Help system. Following the examples is a set of exercises titled Use Help that will sharpen your Word Help system skills.

The Office Assistant

The **Office Assistant** is an icon that displays in the Word window (lower-right side of Figure A-1 on page MO A.1). It has dual functions. First, it will respond with a list of topics that relate to the entry you make in the What would you like to do? text box at the bottom of the balloon. This entry can be in the form of a word, phrase, or written question. For example, if you want to learn more about saving a file, you can type, save, save a file, how do I save a file, or anything similar in the text box. The Office Assistant responds by displaying a list of topics from which you can choose. Once you choose a topic, it displays the corresponding information.

Second, the Office Assistant monitors your work and accumulates tips during a session on how you might do your work better. You can view the tips at any time. The accumulated tips display when you activate the Office Assistant balloon. Also, if at any time you see a light bulb above the Office Assistant, click it to display the most recent tip.

You may or may not want the Office Assistant to display on the screen at all times. You can hide it, and then show it at a later time. You may prefer not to use the Office Assistant at all. In this case, you use the Microsoft Word Help window (lower-left side of Figure A-1 on page MO A.1). Thus, not only do you need to know how to show and hide the Office Assistant, but you also need to know how to turn the Office Assistant on and off.

Showing and Hiding the Office Assistant

When Word is first installed, the Office Assistant displays in the Word window. You can move it to any location on the screen. You can click it to display the Office Assistant balloon, which allows you to request Help. If the Office Assistant is on the screen and you want to hide it, you click the **Hide the Office Assistant command** on the Help menu. You also can right-click the Office Assistant to display its shortcut menu and then click the **Hide command** to hide it. When the Office Assistant is hidden, then the **Show the Office Assistant command** replaces the Hide the Office Assistant command on the Help menu. Thus, you can show or hide the Office Assistant at any time.

Turning the Office Assistant On and Off

The fact that the Office Assistant is hidden, does not mean it is turned off. To turn the Office Assistant off, it must be displayed in the Word window. You right-click it to display its shortcut menu (right side of Figure A-2). Next, click Options on the shortcut menu. Invoking the **Options command** causes the Office Assistant dialog box to display (left side of Figure A-2).

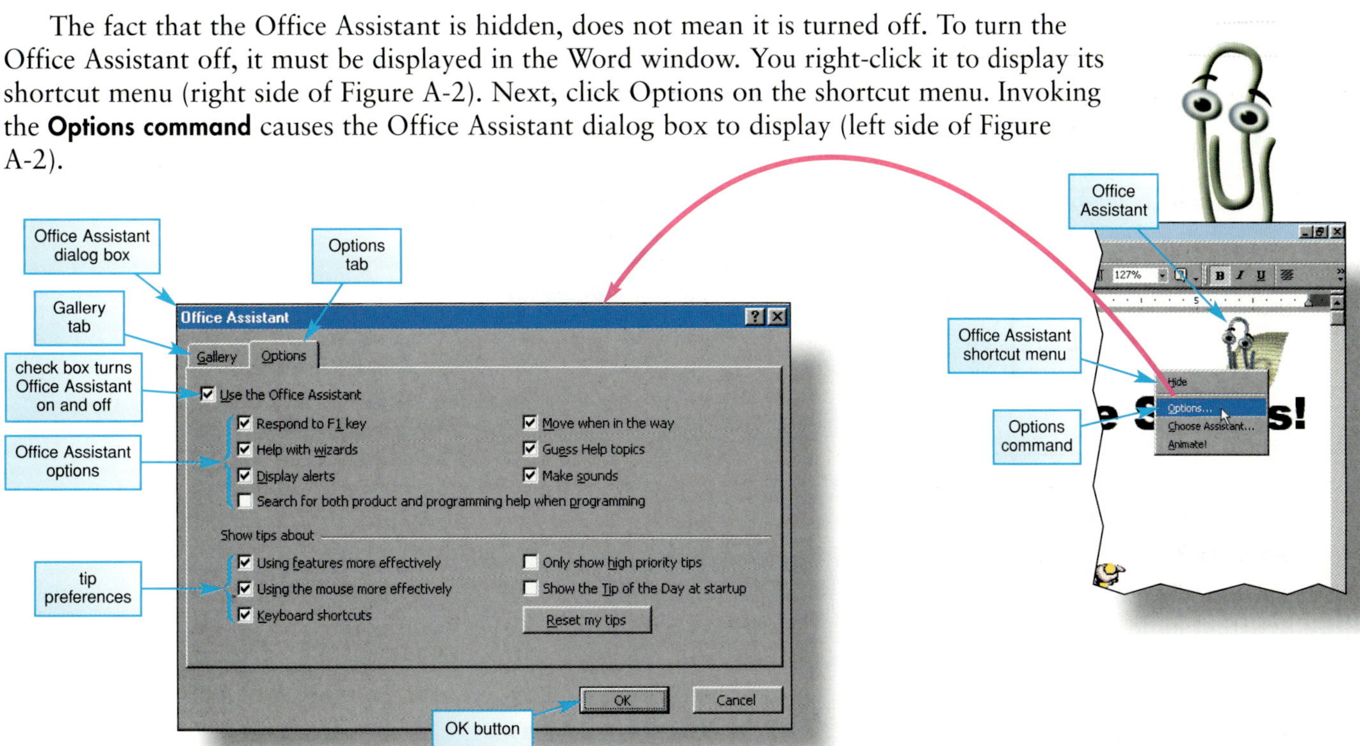

FIGURE A-2

The top check box in the Options sheet determines whether the Office Assistant is on or off. To turn the Office Assistant off, remove the check mark from the **Use the Office Assistant check box** and then click the OK button. As shown in Figure A-1 on page MO A.1, if the Office Assistant is off when you invoke Help, then the Microsoft Word Help window displays instead of the Office Assistant. To turn the Office Assistant on at a later time, click the Show the Office Assistant command on the Help menu.

Through the Options command on the Office Assistant shortcut menu, you can change the look and feel of the Office Assistant. For example, you can hide the Office Assistant, turn the Office Assistant off, change the way it works, choose a different Office Assistant icon, or view an animation of the current one. These options also are available by clicking the Options button that displays in the Office Assistant balloon (Figure A-3 on the next page).

The **Gallery sheet** (Figure A-2) in the Office Assistant dialog box allows you to change the appearance of the Office Assistant. The default is the paper clip (Clippit). You can change it to a bouncing red happy face (The Dot), a robot (F1), a professor (The Genius), the Microsoft Office logo (Office Logo), the earth (Mother Nature), a cat (Links), or a dog (Rocky).

Using the Office Assistant

As indicated earlier, the Office Assistant allows you to enter a word, phrase, or question and then responds by displaying a list of topics from which you can choose to display Help. The following steps show how to use the Office Assistant to obtain Help about online meetings.

Steps To Use the Office Assistant

1 If the Office Assistant is not turned on, click Help on the menu bar and then click Show the Office Assistant. Click the Office Assistant. When the Office Assistant balloon displays, type `what are online meetings` **in the text box. Point to the Search button.**

The Office Assistant balloon displays as shown in Figure A-3.

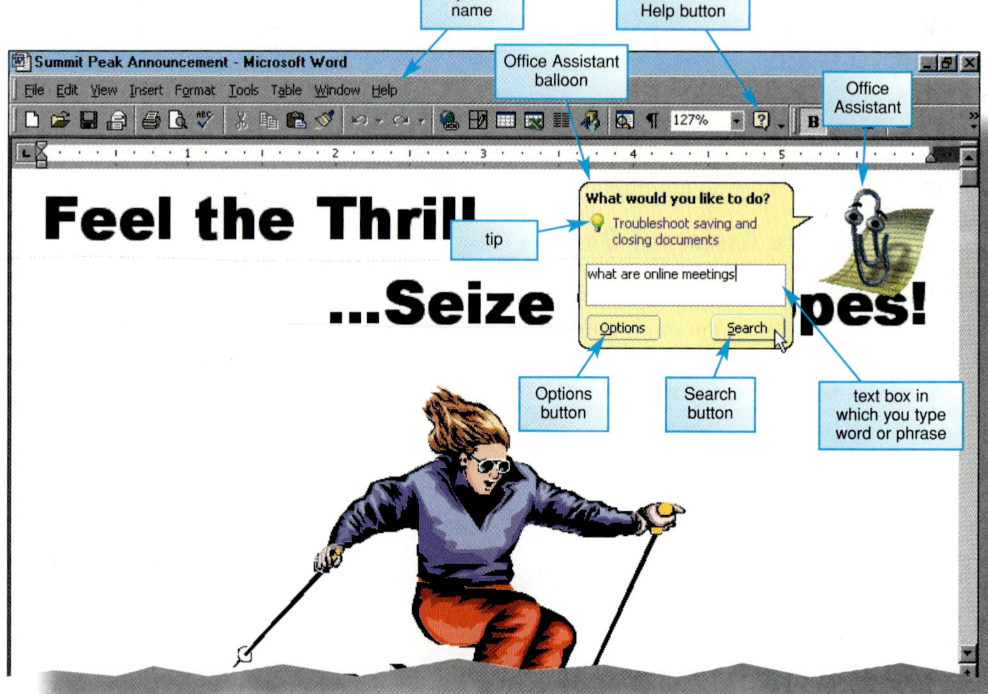

FIGURE A-3

2 Click the Search button. When the Office Assistant balloon redisplays, point to the topic, About online meetings (Figure A-4).

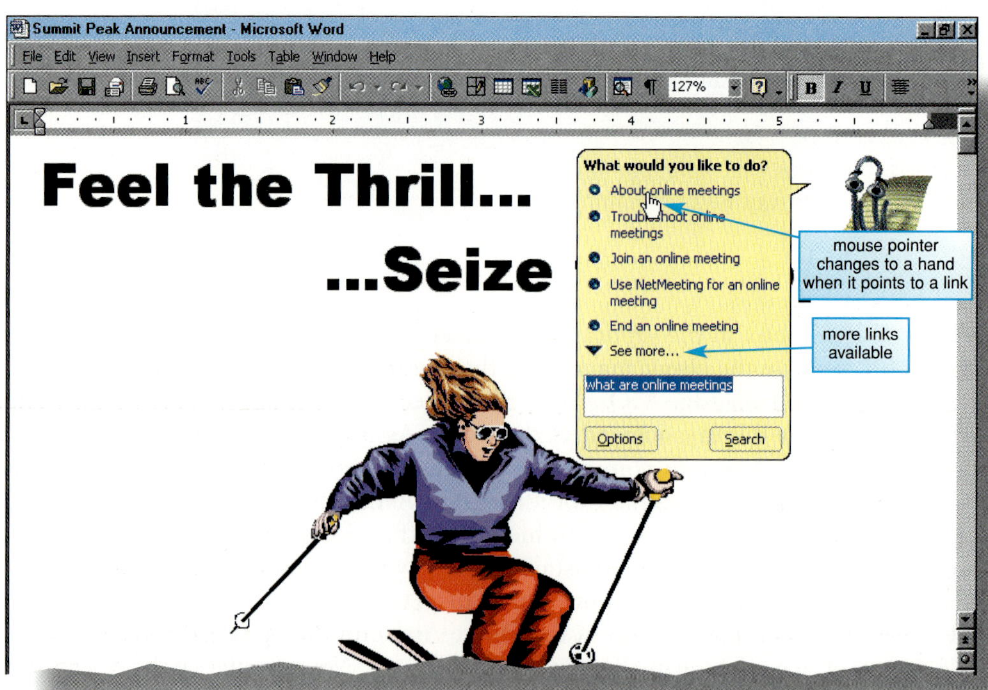

FIGURE A-4

3 **Click the topic, About online meetings. Double-click the Microsoft Word Help window title bar to maximize it. If necessary, move or hide the Office Assistant so you can view all of the text in the Microsoft Word Help window.**

The Microsoft Word Help window displays the information about online meetings (Figure A-5).

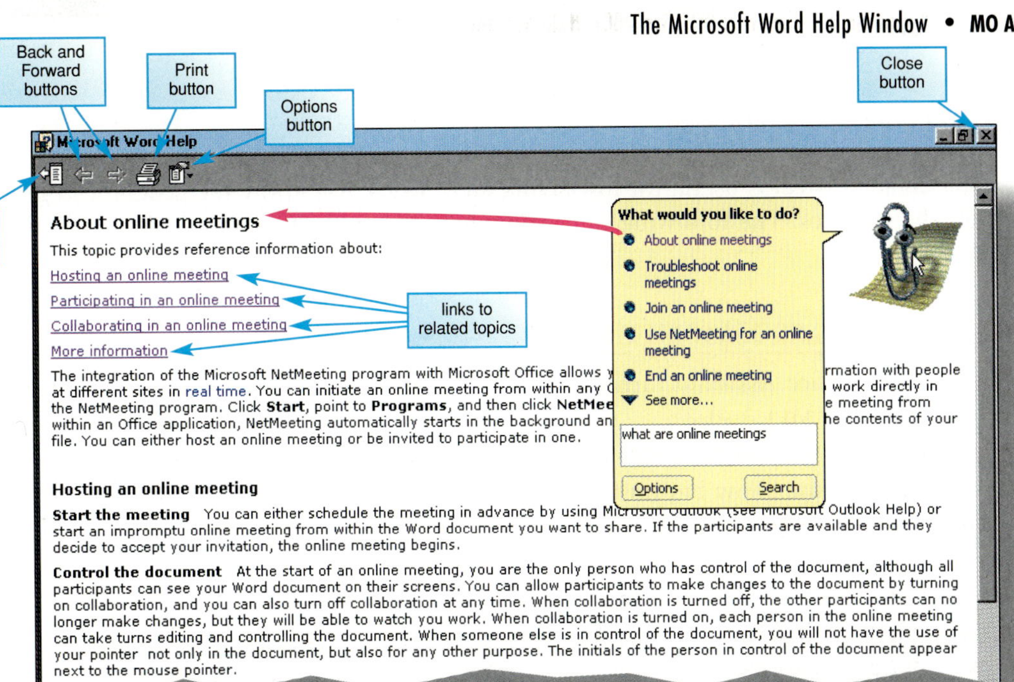

FIGURE A-5

When the Microsoft Word Help window displays, you can choose to read it or print it. To print the information, click the Print button on the Microsoft Word Help toolbar. Table A-2 lists the function of each button on the toolbar in the Microsoft Word Help window. To close the Microsoft Word Help window shown in Figure A-5, click the Close button on the title bar.

Table A-2 Microsoft Word Help Toolbar Buttons

BUTTON	NAME	FUNCTION
[icon] or [icon]	Show or Hide	Displays or hides the Contents, Answer Wizard, Index tabs
[icon]	Back	Displays the previous Help topic
[icon]	Forward	Displays the next Help topic
[icon]	Print	Prints the current Help topic
[icon]	Options	Displays a list of commands

Other Ways

1. If Office Assistant is turned on, on Help menu click Microsoft Word Help, or click Microsoft Word Help button on Standard toolbar to display Office Assistant balloon

The Microsoft Word Help Window

If the Office Assistant is turned off and you click the Microsoft Word Help button on the Standard toolbar, the **Microsoft Word Help window** displays (Figure A-6 on the next page). This window contains three tabs on the left side: Contents, Answer Wizard, and Index. Each tab displays a sheet with powerful look-up capabilities. Use the Contents sheet as you would a table of contents at the front of a book to look up Help. The Answer Wizard sheet answers your queries in the same manner as the Office Assistant. You use the Index sheet in the same manner as an index in a book.

Click the tabs to move from sheet to sheet. The five buttons on the toolbar, Show or Hide, Back, Forward, Print, and Options also are described in Table A-2.

Besides clicking the Microsoft Word Help button on the Standard toolbar, you also can click the Microsoft Word Help command on the Help menu or press the F1 key to display the Microsoft Word Help window to gain access to the three sheets. To close the Microsoft Word Help window, click the Close button in the upper-right corner on the title bar.

Using the Contents Sheet

The **Contents sheet** is useful for displaying Help when you know the general category of the topic in question, but not the specifics. The following steps show how to use the Contents sheet to obtain information about Web folders.

TO OBTAIN HELP USING THE CONTENTS SHEET

1. With the Office Assistant turned off, click the Microsoft Word Help button on the Standard toolbar (Figure A-3 on page MO A.4).
2. When the Microsoft Word Help window displays, double-click the title bar to maximize the window. If necessary, click the Show button to display the tabs.
3. Click the Contents tab.
4. Double-click the Working with Online and Internet Documents book on the left side of the window.
5. Double-click the Creating Web Pages book below the Working with Online and Internet Documents book.
6. Click the About Web Folders subtopic below the Creating Web Pages book.

Word displays Help on the subtopic, About Web Folders (Figure A-6).

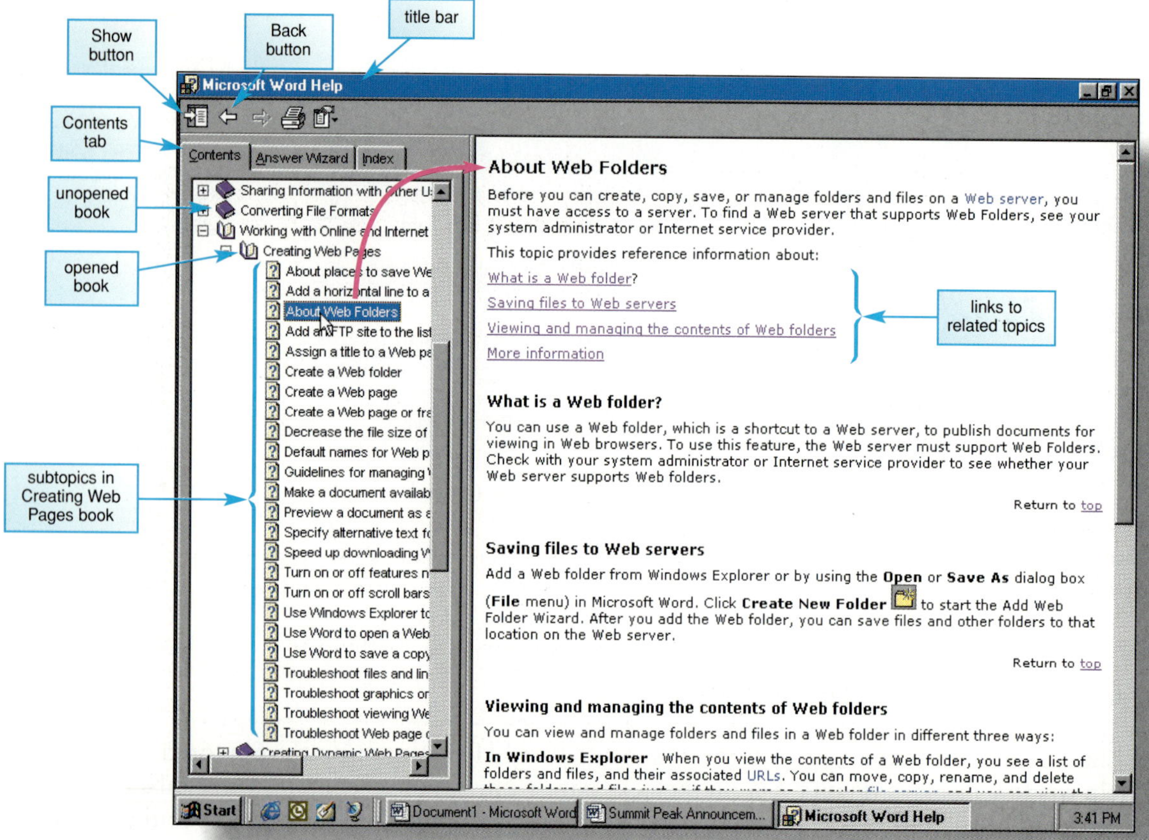

FIGURE A-6

Once the information on the subtopic displays, you can scroll through the window and read it or you can click the Print button to obtain a hard copy. If you decide to click another subtopic on the left or a link on the right, you can get back to the Help page shown in Figure A-6 by clicking the Back button as many times as necessary.

Each topic in the Contents list is preceded by a book icon or question mark icon. A **book icon** indicates subtopics are available. A **question mark icon** means information on the topic will display if you double-click the title. The book icon opens when you double-click the book (or its title) or click the plus sign (+) to the left of the book icon.

Using the Answer Wizard Sheet

The **Answer Wizard sheet** works like the Office Assistant in that you enter a word, phrase, or question and it responds with topics from which you can choose to display Help. The following steps show how to use the Answer Wizard sheet to obtain Help about discussions in a Word document.

TO OBTAIN HELP USING THE ANSWER WIZARD SHEET

1. With the Office Assistant turned off, click the Microsoft Word Help button on the Standard toolbar (Figure A-3 on page MO A.4).
2. When the Microsoft Word Help window displays, double-click the title bar to maximize the window. If necessary, click the Show button to display the tabs.
3. Click the Answer Wizard tab. Type `what are discussions` in the What would you like to do? text box on the left side of the window. Click the Search button.
4. When a list of topics displays in the Select topic to display list box, click About discussions in Word.

Word displays Help about discussions (Figure A-7).

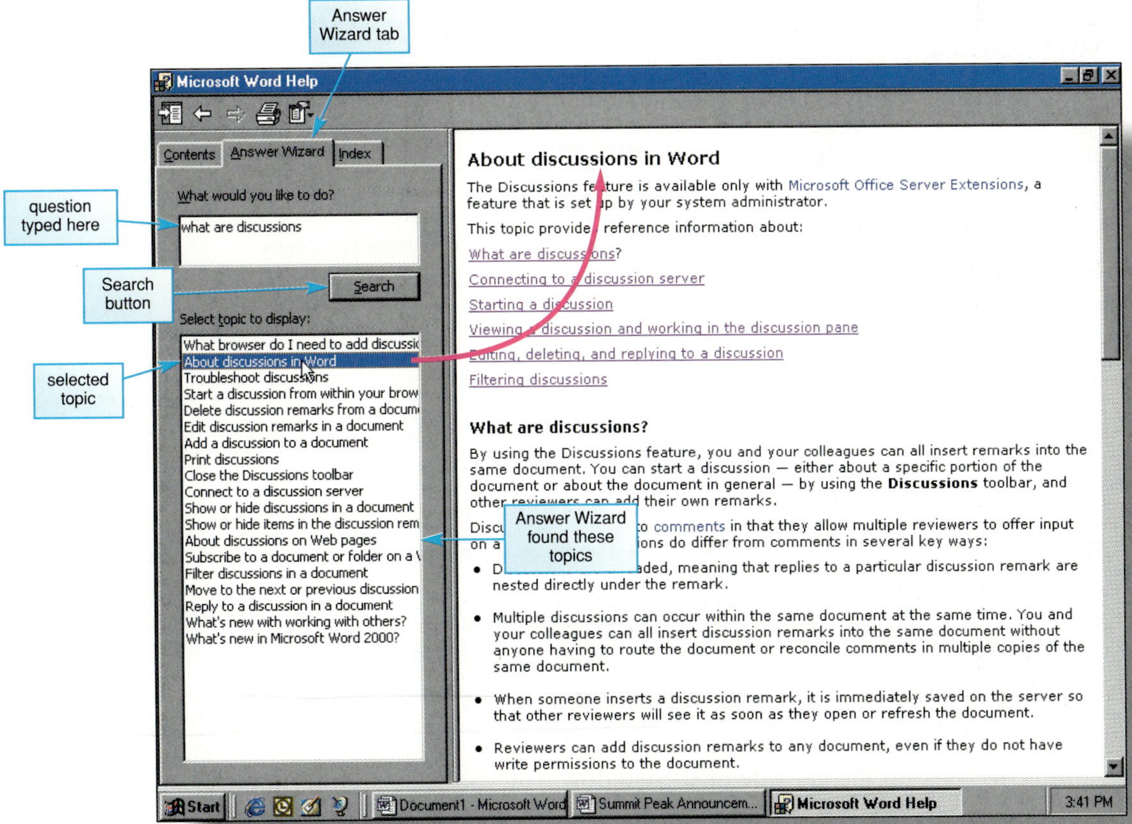

FIGURE A-7

If the topic, About discussions in Word, does not include the information you are searching for, click another topic in the list. Continue to click topics until you find the desired information.

Using the Index Sheet

The third sheet in the Microsoft Word Help window is the Index sheet. Use the **Index sheet** to display Help when you know the keyword or the first few letters of the keyword you want to look up. The following steps show how to use the Index sheet to obtain Help on understanding the readability statistics available to evaluate the reading level of a document.

TO OBTAIN HELP USING THE INDEX SHEET

1. With the Office Assistant turned off, click the Microsoft Word Help button on the Standard toolbar (Figure A-3 on page MO A.4).
2. When the Microsoft Word Help window displays, double-click the title bar to maximize the window. If necessary, click the Show button to display the tabs.
3. Click the Index tab. Type `readability` in the Type keywords text box on the left side of the window. Click the Search button.

Word highlights the first topic (Readability scores) on the left side of the window and displays information about two readability tests on the right side of the window (Figure A-8).

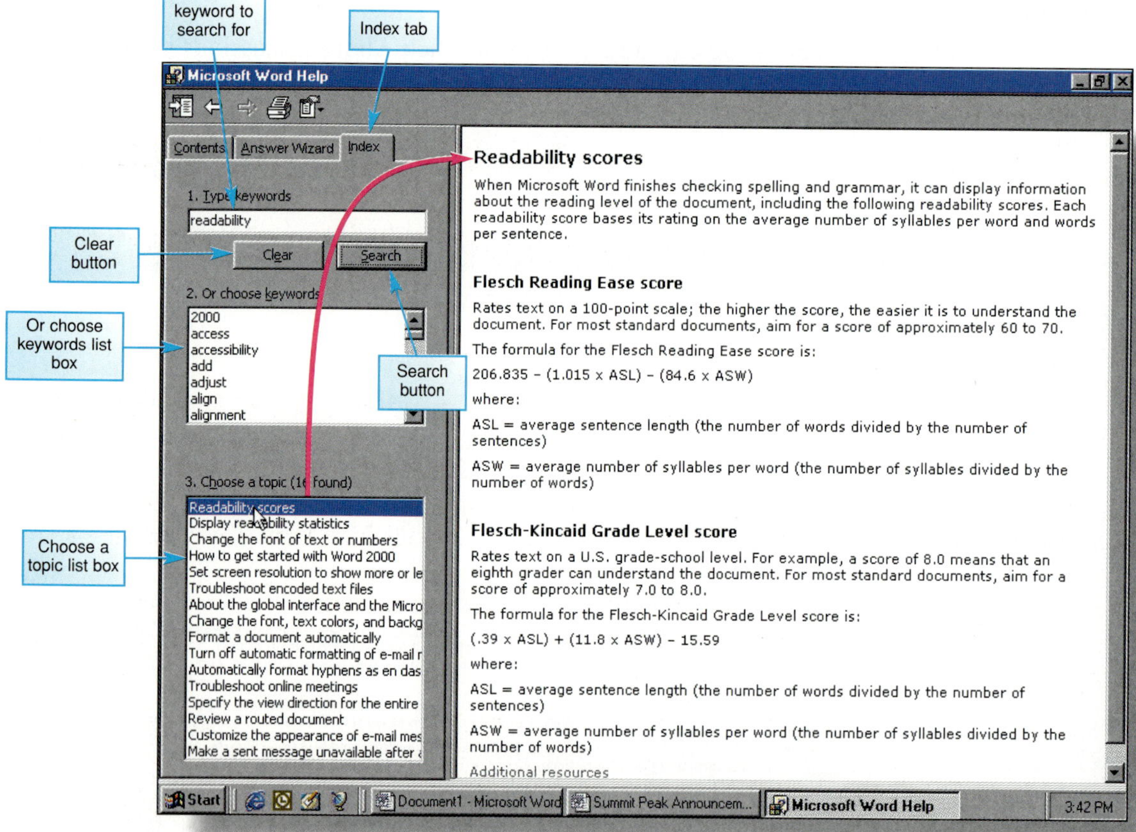

FIGURE A-8

In the Choose a topic list box on the left side of the window, you can click another topic to display additional Help.

An alternative to typing a keyword in the Type keywords text box is to scroll through the Or choose keywords list box (the middle list box on the left side of the window). When you locate the keyword you are searching for, double-click it to display Help on the topic. Also in the Or choose keywords list box, the Word Help system displays other topics that relate to the new keyword. As you begin typing a new keyword in the Type keywords text box, Word jumps to that point in the middle list box. To begin a new search, click the Clear button.

What's This? Command and Question Mark Button

Use the What's This command on the Help menu or the Question Mark button in a dialog box when you are not sure what an object on the screen is or what it does.

What's This? Command

You use the **What's This? command** on the Help menu to display a detailed ScreenTip. When you invoke this command, the mouse pointer changes to an arrow with a question mark. You then click any object on the screen, such as a button, to display the ScreenTip. For example, after you click the What's This? command on the Help menu and then click the Zoom box on the Standard toolbar, a description of the Zoom box displays (Figure A-9). You can print the ScreenTip by right-clicking it and clicking Print Topic on the shortcut menu.

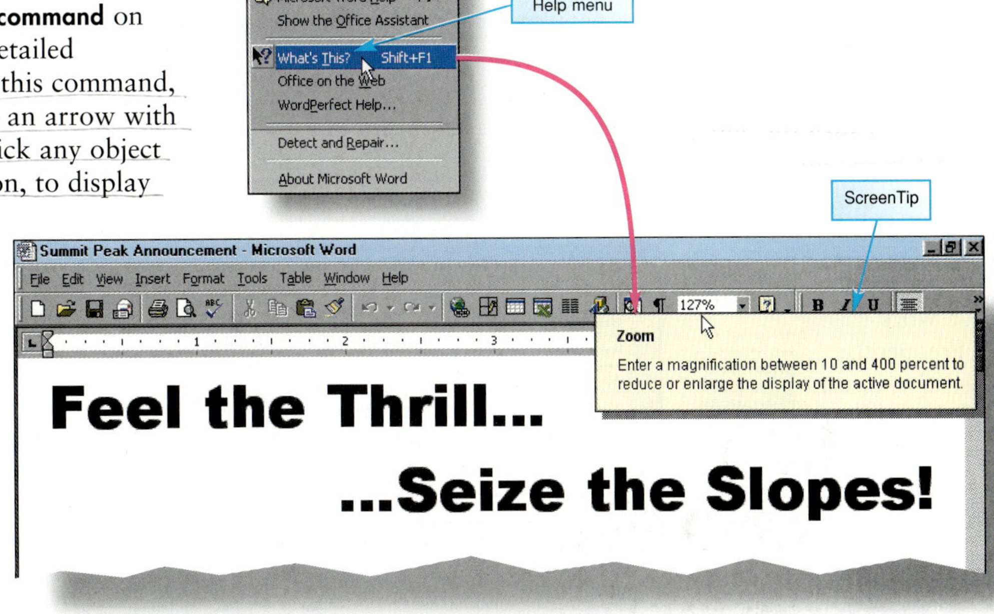

FIGURE A-9

Question Mark Button

In a response similar to the What's This? command, the **Question Mark button** displays a ScreenTip. You use the Question Mark button with dialog boxes. It is located in the upper-right corner on the title bar of dialog boxes, next to the Close button. For example, in Figure A-10, the Print dialog box displays on the screen. If you click the Question Mark button, and then click the Print to file check box, an explanation of the Print to file check box displays in a ScreenTip. You can print the ScreenTip by right-clicking it and clicking Print Topic on the shortcut menu.

If a dialog box does not include a Question Mark button, press the SHIFT+F1 keys. This combination of keys will change the mouse pointer to an arrow with a question mark. You then can click any object in the dialog box to display the ScreenTip.

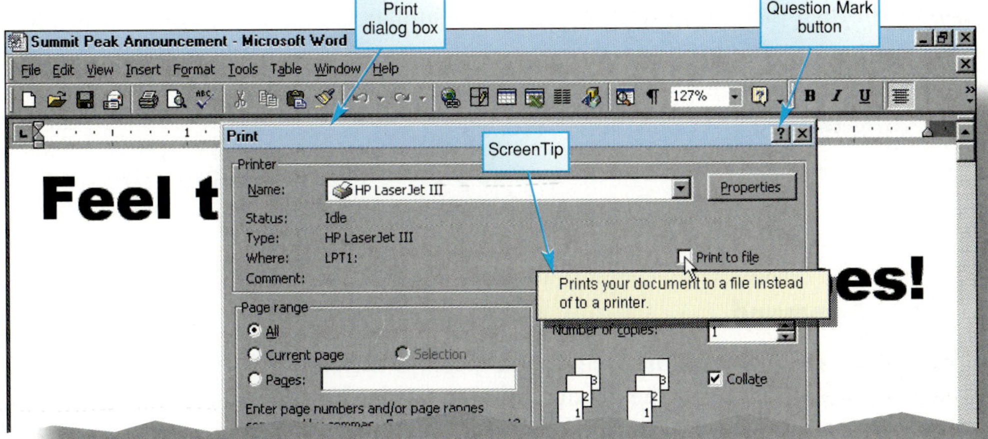

FIGURE A-10

Office on the Web Command

The **Office on the Web command** on the Help menu displays a Microsoft Web page containing up-to-date information on a variety of Office-related topics. To use this command, you must be connected to the Internet. Once the page displays, you can click the Word link on the left side of the window and then click the Assistance link (Figure A-11). The Word Assistance Web page contains several links such as Knowledge Base Articles about Word and Frequently Asked Questions about Word.

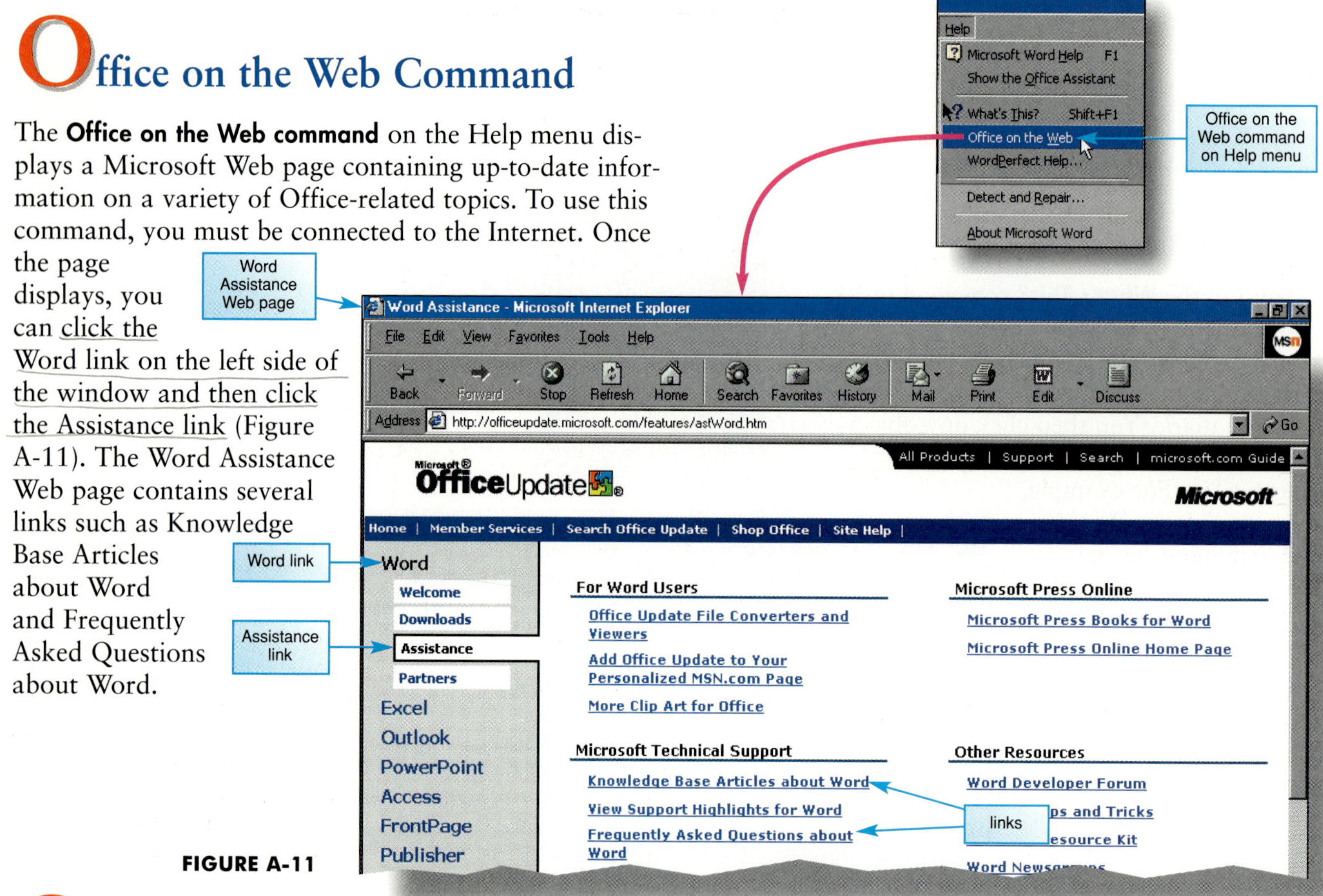

FIGURE A-11

Other Help Commands

Three additional commands available on the Help menu are WordPerfect Help, Detect and Repair, and About Microsoft Word. The WordPerfect Help command is available only if it was included as part of a Custom install of Word 2000. The Help menu of the other Office applications have similar commands that are useful when using each Office application.

WordPerfect Help Command

The **WordPerfect Help command** on the Help menu offers assistance to WordPerfect users switching to Word. When you choose this command, Word displays the Help for WordPerfect Users dialog box. The instructions in the dialog box step the user through the appropriate selections. A similar command is available in each of the other Office applications.

Detect and Repair Command

Use the **Detect and Repair command** on the Help menu if Word is not running properly or if it is generating errors. When you invoke this command, the Detect and Repair dialog box displays. Click the Start button in the dialog box to initiate the detect and repair process.

About Microsoft Word Command

The **About Microsoft Word command** on the Help menu displays the About Microsoft Word dialog box. The dialog box lists the owner of the software and the product identification. You need to know the product identification if you call Microsoft for assistance. The two buttons below the OK button are the System Info button and the Tech Support button. The **System Info button** displays system information, including hardware resources, components, software environment, and applications. The **Tech Support button** displays technical assistance information.

1 Using the Office Assistant

Instructions: Perform the following tasks using the Word Help system.

1. If the Office Assistant is turned on, click it to display the Office Assistant balloon. If the Office Assistant is not turned on, click Help on the menu bar, and click Show the Office Assistant.
2. Right-click the Office Assistant and then click Options on the shortcut menu. Click the Gallery tab in the Office Assistant dialog box and then click the Next button to view all the Office Assistants. Click the Options tab in the Office Assistant dialog box and review the different options for the Office Assistant. Click the Question Mark button and then display ScreenTips for the first two check boxes (Use the Office Assistant and Respond to F1 key). Right-click the ScreenTips to print them. Hand them in to your instructor. Close the Office Assistant dialog box.
3. Click the Office Assistant and then type `show me the keyboard shortcuts` in the What would you like to do? text box at the bottom of the balloon. Click the Search button.
4. Click Keyboard shortcuts in the Office Assistant balloon. If necessary, double-click the title bar to maximize the Microsoft Word Help window. Click the Function keys link and then click the SHIFT+Function key link to view the set of shortcut keys using the SHIFT key and function keys. Click the Print button on the Microsoft Word Help toolbar to print the list of shortcut keys. Hand in the printouts to your instructor.
5. Close all open Help windows.
6. Click the Office Assistant. If it is not turned on, click Show the Office Assistant on the Help menu. Search for the topic, what is a netmeeting. Click the Use NetMeeting for an online meeting link. When the Microsoft Word Help window displays, maximize the window and then click the the Start an impromptu online meeting with Microsoft Word link. Read and print the information. Close the Microsoft Word Help window.

2 Expanding on the Word Help System Basics

Instructions: Use the Word Help system to understand the topics better and answer the questions listed below. Answer the questions on your own paper, or hand in the printed Help information to your instructor.

1. Right-click the Office Assistant. If it is not turned on, click Show the Office Assistant on the Help menu. When the shortcut menu displays, click Options. Click Use the Office Assistant to remove the check mark, and then click the OK button.
2. Click the Microsoft Word Help button on the Standard toolbar. Maximize the Microsoft Word Help window. If the tabs are hidden on the left side, click the Show button. Click the Index tab. Type `undo` in the Type keywords text box. Click the Search button. Click Reset built-in menus and toolbars. Print the information. Click the Hide button and then the Show button. Click the four links below What do you want to do? Read and print the information for each link. Close the Microsoft Word Help window. Hand in the printouts to your instructor.
3. Press the F1 key. Maximize the Microsoft Word Help window. Click the Answer Wizard tab. Type `help` in the What would you like to do? text box, and then click the Search button. Click Ways to get assistance while you work. Read through the information that displays. Print the information. Click the first two links. Read and print the information for both.
4. Click the Contents tab. Click the plus sign (+) to the left of the Typing, Navigating Documents, and Selecting Text book. Click the plus sign (+) to the left of the Selecting Text book. One at a time, click the three topics below the Selecting Text book. Read and print each one. Close the Microsoft Word Help window. Hand in the printouts to your instructor.
5. Click Help on the menu bar and then click What's This? Click the E-mail button on the Standard toolbar. Right-click the ScreenTip to print the ScreenTip. Click Format on the menu bar and then click Paragraph. When the Paragraph dialog box displays, click the Question Mark button on the title bar. Click the Special box. Right-click the ScreenTip to print the ScreenTip. Hand in the printouts to your instructor. Close the Paragraph dialog box and the Microsoft Word window.

APPENDIX B

Publishing Office Web Pages to a Web Server

With a Microsoft Office 2000 program, such as Word, Excel, Access, or PowerPoint, you use the **Save as Web Page command** on the File menu to save the Web page to a Web server using one of two techniques: Web folders or File Transfer Protocol. A **Web folder** is an Office 2000 shortcut to a Web server. **File Transfer Protocol (FTP)** is an Internet standard that allows computers to exchange files with other computers on the Internet.

You should contact your network system administrator or technical support staff at your ISP to determine if their Web server supports Web folders, FTP, or both, and to obtain necessary permissions to access the Web server. If you decide to publish Web pages using a Web folder, you must have the Office Server Extensions (OSE) installed on your computer. OSE comes with the Standard, Professional, and Premium editions of Office 2000.

Using Web Folders to Publish Office Web Pages

If you are granted permission to create a Web folder (shortcut) on your computer, you must obtain the URL of the Web server, and a user name and possibly a password that allows you to access the Web server. You also must decide on a name for the Web folder. Table B-1 explains how to create a Web folder.

Office adds the name of the Web folder to the list of current Web folders. You can save to this folder, open files in the folder, rename the folder, or perform any operations you would to a folder on your hard disk. You can use your Office program or Windows Explorer to access this folder. Table B-2 explains how to save to a Web folder.

Using FTP to Publish Office Web Pages

When publishing a Web page using FTP, you first add the FTP location to your computer and then you can save to it. An **FTP location**, also called an **FTP site**, is a collection of files that resides on an FTP server. In this case, the FTP server is the Web server.

To add an FTP location, you must obtain the name of the FTP site, which usually is the address (URL) of the FTP server, and a user name and a password that allows you to access the FTP server. You save and open the Web pages on the Web server using the name of the FTP site. Table B-3 explains how to add an FTP site.

Office adds the name of the FTP site to the FTP locations in the Save As and Open dialog boxes. You can open and save files on this FTP location. Table B-4 explains how to save using an FTP location.

Table B-1 Creating a Web Folder
1. Click File on the menu bar and then click Save As; or click File on the menu bar and then click Open.
2. When the Save As dialog box or the Open dialog box displays, click the Web Folders shortcut on the Places Bar along the left side of the dialog box.
3. Click the Create New Folder button.
4. When the first dialog box of the Add Web Folder wizard displays, type the URL of the Web server and then click the Next button.
5. When the Enter Network Password dialog box displays, type the user name and, if necessary, the password in the respective text boxes and then click the OK button.
6. When the last dialog box of the Add Web Folder wizard displays, type the name you would like to use for the Web folder. Click the Finish button.
7. Close the Save As or the Open dialog box.

Table B-2 Saving to a Web Folder
1. Click File on the menu bar and then click Save As.
2. When the Save As dialog box displays, type the Web page file name in the File name text box. Do not press the ENTER key.
3. Click Web Folders shortcut on the Places Bar along the left side of the dialog box.
4. Double-click the Web folder name in the Save in list.
5. When the Enter Network Password dialog box displays, type the user name and password in the respective text boxes and then click the OK button.
6. Click the Save button in the Save As dialog box.

Table B-3 Adding an FTP Location
1. Click File on the menu bar and then click Save As; or click File on the menu bar and then click Open.
2. In the Save As dialog box, click the Save in box arrow and then click Add/Modify FTP Locations in the Save in list; or in the Open dialog box, click the Look in box arrow and then click Add/Modify FTP Locations in the Look in list.
3. When the Add/Modify FTP Locations dialog box displays, type the name of the FTP site in the Name of FTP site text box. If the site allows anonymous logon, click Anonymous in the Log on as area; if you have a user name for the site, click User in the Log on as area and then type the user name. Type the password in the Password text box. Click the OK button.
4. Close the Save As or the Open dialog box.

Table B-4 Saving to an FTP Location
1. Click File on the menu bar and then click Save As.
2. When the Save As dialog box displays, type the Web page file name in the File name text box. Do not press the ENTER key.
3. Click the Save in box arrow and then click FTP Locations.
4. Double-click the name of the FTP site you want to save to.
5. When the FTP Log On dialog box displays, type your user name and password and then click the OK button.
6. Click the Save button in the Save As dialog box.

APPENDIX C

Resetting the Menus and Toolbars

When you first install Microsoft Office 2000, the Standard and Formatting toolbars display on one row in some of the applications. As you use the buttons on the toolbars and commands on the menus, Office personalizes the toolbars and the menus based on their usage. Each time you start an application, the toolbars and menus display in the same settings as the last time you used the application. The following steps show how to reset the Word menus and toolbars to their installation settings.

Steps To Reset My Usage Data and Toolbar Buttons

1 Click View on the menu bar and then point to Toolbars. Point to Customize on the Toolbars submenu.

The View menu and Toolbars submenu display (Figure C-1).

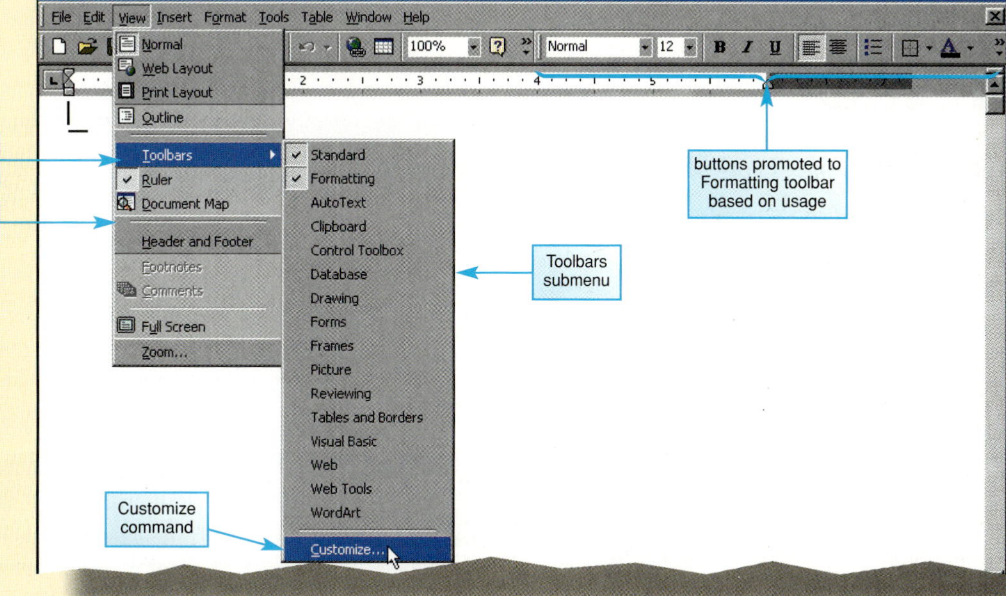

FIGURE C-1

2 Click Customize. When the Customize dialog box displays, click the Options tab. Make sure the three check boxes in the Personalized Menus and Toolbars area have check marks and then point to the Reset my usage data button.

The Customize dialog box displays as shown in Figure C-2.

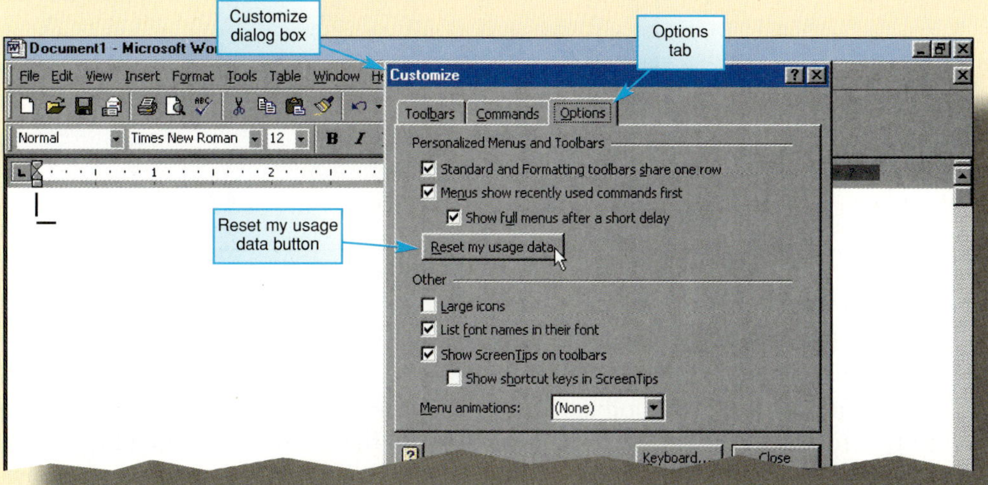

FIGURE C-2

3 **Click the Reset my usage data button. When the Microsoft Word dialog box displays explaining the function of the Reset my usage data button, click the Yes button. In the Customize dialog box, click the Toolbars tab.**

The Toolbars sheet displays (Figure C-3).

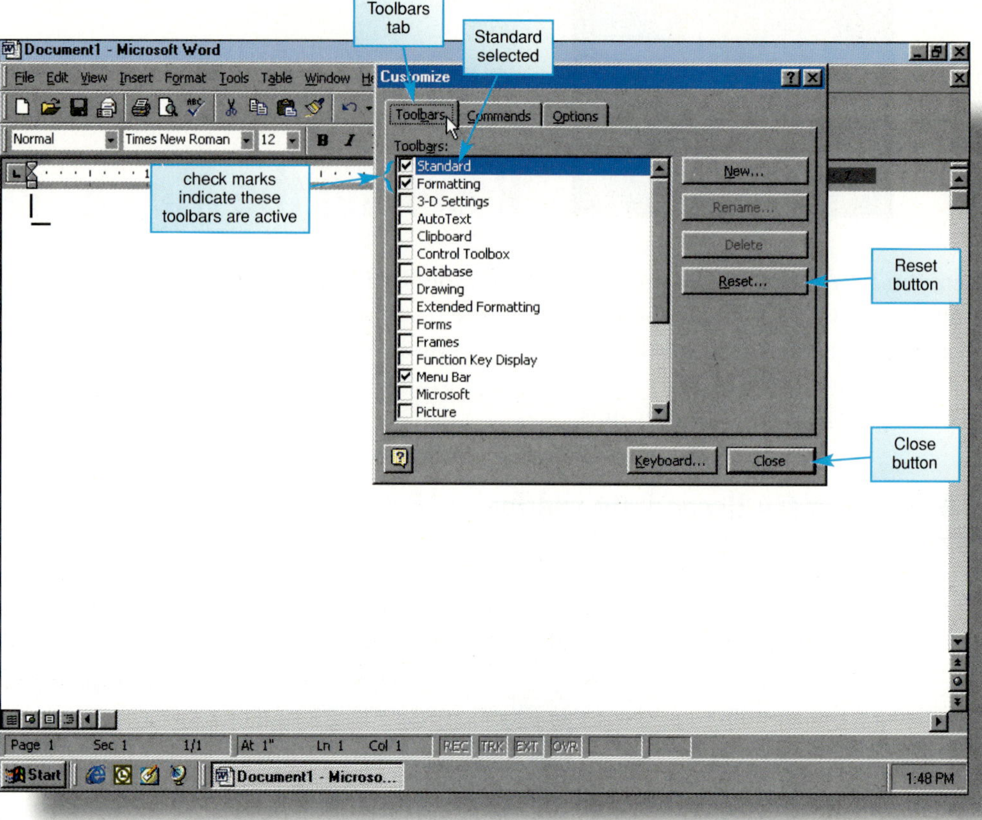

FIGURE C-3

4 **Click Standard in the Toolbars list and then click the Reset button. When the Reset Toolbar dialog box displays, click the OK button. Click Formatting in the Toolbars list and then click the Reset button. When the Reset Toolbar dialog box displays, click the OK button.**

5 **Click the Close button in the Customize dialog box.**

The toolbars display as shown in Figure C-4.

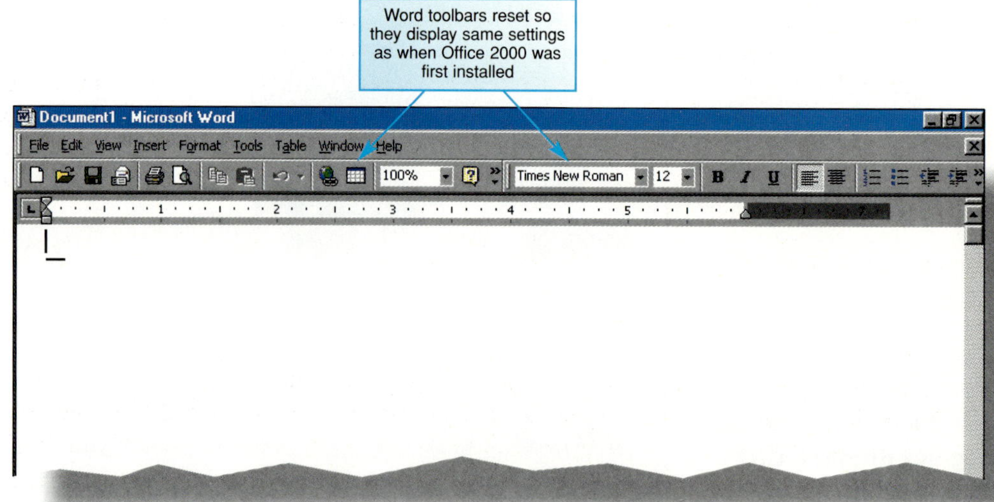

FIGURE C-4

Steps 3 and 4 display or remove any buttons that were added or deleted through the use of the Add or Remove Buttons button on the More Buttons menu.

You can turn off both the toolbars sharing a single row and the short menus by removing the check marks from the two top check boxes in the Options sheet in the Customize dialog box (Figure C-2 on the previous page). If you remove these check marks, Word will display the toolbars on two separate rows below the menu bar and will show only full menus.

APPENDIX D

Microsoft Office User Specialist Certification Program

The Microsoft Office User Specialist (MOUS) Certification Program provides a framework for measuring your proficiency with the Microsoft Office 2000 applications, such as Word 2000, Excel 2000, Access 2000, and PowerPoint 2000. Three levels of certification are available — Master, Expert, and Core. The three levels of certification are described in Table D-1.

Table D-1 Three Levels of MOUS Certification

LEVEL	DESCRIPTION	REQUIREMENTS	CREDENTIAL AWARDED
Master	Indicates that you have a comprehensive understanding of Microsoft Office 2000	Pass all FIVE of the required exams: Microsoft Word 2000 Expert Microsoft Excel 2000 Expert Microsoft PowerPoint 2000 Core Microsoft Access 2000 Core Microsoft Outlook 2000 Core	Candidates will be awarded one certificate for passing all five of the required Microsoft Office 2000 exams: Microsoft Office User Specialist: Microsoft Office 2000 Master
Expert	Indicates that you have a comprehensive understanding of the advanced features in a specific Microsoft Office 2000 application	Pass any ONE of the Expert exams: Microsoft Word 2000 Expert Microsoft Excel 2000 Expert	Candidates will be awarded one certificate for each of the Expert exams they have passed: Microsoft Office User Specialist: Microsoft Word 2000 Expert Microsoft Office User Specialist: Microsoft Excel 2000 Expert
Core	Indicates that you have a comprehensive understanding of the core features in a specific Microsoft Office 2000 application	Pass any ONE of the Core exams: Microsoft Word 2000 Core Microsoft Excel 2000 Core Microsoft PowerPoint 2000 Core Microsoft Access 2000 Core Microsoft Outlook 2000 Core	Candidates will be awarded one certificate for each of the Core exams they have passed: Microsoft Office User Specialist: Microsoft Word 2000 Microsoft Office User Specialist: Microsoft Excel 2000 Microsoft Office User Specialist: Microsoft PowerPoint 2000 Microsoft Office User Specialist: Microsoft Access 2000 Microsoft Office User Specialist: Microsoft Outlook 2000

Why Should You Get Certified?

Being a Microsoft Office User Specialist provides a valuable industry credential — proof that you have the Office 2000 applications skills required by employers. By passing one or more MOUS certification exams, you demonstrate your proficiency in a given Office application to employers. With nearly 80 million copies of Office in use around the world, Microsoft is targeting Office certification to a wide variety of companies. These companies include temporary employment agencies that want to prove the expertise of their workers, large corporations looking for a way to measure the skill set of employees, and training companies and educational institutions seeking Microsoft Office teachers with appropriate credentials.

The MOUS Exams

You pay $50 to $100 each time you take an exam, whether you pass or fail. The fee varies among testing centers. The Expert exams, which you can take up to 60 minutes to complete, consist of between 40 and 60 tasks that you perform online. The tasks require you to use the application just as you would in doing your job. The Core exams contain fewer tasks, and you will have slightly less time to complete them. The tasks you will perform differ on the two types of exams.

How Can You Prepare for the MOUS Exams?

The Shelly Cashman Series® offers several Microsoft-approved textbooks that cover the required objectives on the MOUS exams. For a listing of the textbooks, visit the Shelly Cashman Series MOUS Web page at www.scsite.com/off2000/cert.htm and click the Shelly Cashman Office Series 2000 Microsoft-Approved MOUS Textbooks link (Figure D-1). After using any of the books listed in an instructor-led course, you will be prepared to take the MOUS exam indicated.

How to Find an Authorized Testing Center

You can locate a testing center by calling 1-800-933-4493 in North America or visiting the Shelly Cashman Series MOUS Web page at www.scsite.com/off2000/cert.htm and then clicking the Locate an Authorized Testing Center Near You link (Figure D-1). At this Web page, you can look for testing centers around the world.

Shelly Cashman Series MOUS Web Page

The Shelly Cashman Series MOUS Web page (Figure D-1) has more than fifteen Web pages you can visit to obtain additional information on the MOUS Certification Program. The Web page (www.scsite.com/off2000/cert.htm) includes links to general information on certification, choosing an application for certification, preparing for the certification exam, and taking and passing the certification exam.

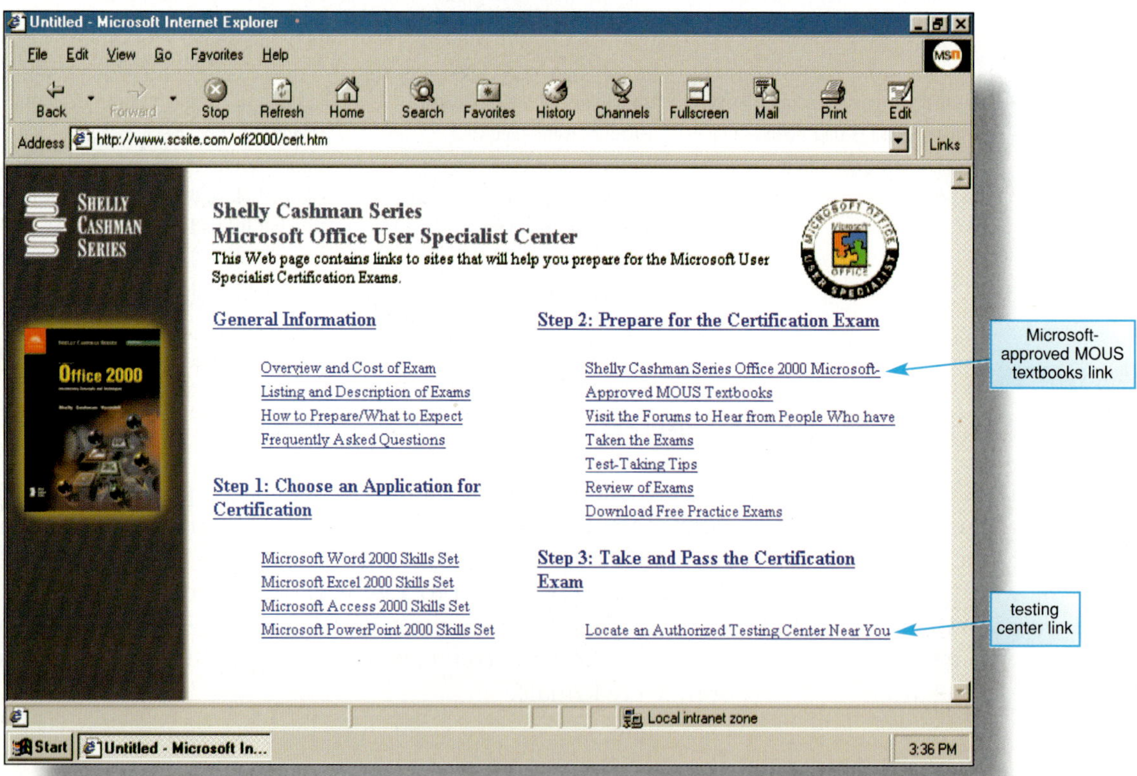

FIGURE D-1

Microsoft Office 2000 User Specialist Certification Map

The tables on the following pages list the skill sets and activities you should be familiar with if you plan to take the Microsoft Office User Specialist Certification examinations for Microsoft Word 2000, Microsoft Excel 2000, Microsoft Access 2000, or Microsoft PowerPoint 2000. Each activity is accompanied by page numbers on which the activity is illustrated in the book.

Microsoft Word 2000 User Specialist Certification Map

The Microsoft Word 2000 portion of *Microsoft Office 2000: Introductory Concepts and Techniques* (ISBN 0-7895-4635-3, 0-7895-4650-7, or 0-7895-5615-4) and *Microsoft Office 2000: Advanced Concepts and Techniques* (ISBN 0-7895-4649-3 or 0-7895-5629-4) used in combination in a two-sequence course has been approved by Microsoft as courseware for the Microsoft Office User Specialist (MOUS) program. After completing the Word 2000 projects and exercises in these two books, students will be prepared to take the Core-level Microsoft Office User Specialist Exam for Microsoft Word 2000. Table D-2 lists the skill sets, activities, and page number where the activity is discussed in the books. You should be familiar with each of the activities if you plan to take the Microsoft Word 2000 Core examination.

The Microsoft Word 2000 portion of *Microsoft Office 2000: Post Advanced Concepts and Techniques* (ISBN 0-7895-5691-X) used in combination with *Microsoft Office 2000: Introductory Concepts and Techniques* and *Microsoft Office 2000: Advanced Concepts and Techniques* in a third course has been approved by Microsoft as courseware for the Microsoft Office User Specialist (MOUS) program – Expert level. Table D-3 on the next page lists the skill sets, activities, and page number where the activity is discussed in the book for the Expert-level Microsoft Office User Specialist Exam for Microsoft Word 2000.

Table D-2 Microsoft Word 2000 MOUS Core Skill Sets, Activities, and Map

SKILL SETS	ACTIVITIES	PAGE NUMBERS
Working with text	Use the Undo, Redo, and Repeat command	WD 1.35, WD 1.36
	Apply font formats (Bold, Italic, and Underline)	WD 1.33, WD 1.39, WD 1.42
	Use the SPELLING feature	WD 1.22, WD 1.59, WD 2.50
	Use the THESAURUS feature	WD 2.48, WD 2.61
	Use the GRAMMAR feature	WD 1.22, WD 1.59, WD 2.50
	Insert page breaks	WD 2.31, WD 2.35, WD 4.21
	Highlight text in document	WDW 1.9, WD 6.61
	Insert and move text	WD 1.54, WD 2.46, WD 2.56
	Cut, Copy, Paste, and Paste Special using the Office Clipboard	WD 1.54, WD 2.45, WD 3.33, WD 3.35, WD 6.35
	Copy formats using the Format Painter	WD 6.57
	Select and change font and font size	WD 1.17, WD 1.31, WD 1.32
	Find and replace text	WD 2.43, WD 2.56
	Apply character effects (superscript, subscript, strikethrough, small caps, and outline)	WD 2.18, WD 4.16, WD 4.17
	Insert date and time	WD 6.17
	Insert symbols	WD 2.33, WD 3.37, WD 3.46
	Create and apply frequently used text with AutoCorrect	WD 2.20, WD 2.21
Working with paragraphs	Align text in paragraphs (Center, Left, Right, and Justified)	WD 1.33, WD 1.35, WD 2.17, WD 2.18, WD 6.26
	Add bullets and numbering	WD 3.50, WD 3.51, WD 4.40, WD 5.30, WD 6.63
	Set character, line, and paragraph spacing options	WD 2.9, WD 2.11, WD 2.18, WD 4.38, WD 6.42
Working with paragraphs (con't)	Apply borders and shading to paragraphs	WD 3.39, WD 4.8, WD 6.37, WD 6.45
	Use indentation options (Left, Right, First Line, and Hanging Indent)	WD 2.18, WD 2.19, WD 2.37, WD 6.43
	Use TABS command (Center, Decimal, Left, and Right)	WD 3.31, WD 3.32, WD 3.43, WD 6.49
	Create an outline style numbered list	WD 3.51, WD 5.30
	Set tabs with leaders	WD 3.31
Working with documents	Print a document	WD 1.50, WD 5.40, WD 6.47
	Use print preview	WD 3.24, WD 4.57
	Use Web Page Preview	WDW 1.11, WDW 1.14
	Navigate through a document	WD 1.25, WD 1.26, WD 1.40, WD 4.25
	Insert page numbers	WD 2.14
	Set page orientation	WD 5.24
	Set margins	WD 2.8, WD 6.7
	Use GoTo to locate specific elements in a document	WD 2.42, WD 2.43
	Create and modify page numbers	WD 2.14, WD 4.29
	Create and modify headers and footers	WD 2.12, WD 2.15, WD 4.28
	Align text vertically	WD 3.35, WD 3.36, WD 4.42
	Create and use newspaper columns	WD 6.23, WD 6.25
	Revise column structure	WD 6.30, WD 6.48, WD 6.51
	Prepare and print envelopes and labels	WD 3.58, WD 5.48, WD 5.54

(Table D-2 continued on the next page)

Table D-2 Microsoft Word 2000 MOUS Core Skill Sets, Activities, and Map

SKILL SETS	ACTIVITIES	PAGE NUMBERS
Working with documents (con't)	Apply styles	WD 2.26, WD 4.19, WD 6.33
	Create sections with formatting that differs from other sections	WD 4.21, WD 4.29, WD 6.24
	Use click & type	WD 2.13
Managing files	Use save	WD 1.26, WD 1.49
	Locate and open an existing document	WD 1.52, WD 4.23
	Use Save As (different name, location, or format)	WD 1.49, WD 3.42, WDW 1.11
	Create a folder	WD 1.49
	Create a new document using a Wizard	WD 3.7, WDW 1.5
	Save as Web Page	WDW 1.3
	Use templates to create a new document	WD 3.18, WD 5.6, WD 5.9
	Create Hyperlinks	WD 2.39, WD 2.53, WDW 1.10
Managing files (con't)	Use the Office Assistant	WD 1.55
	Send a Word document via e-mail	WD 2.54, WDI 1.7
Using tables	Create and format tables	WD 3.52, WD 3.55, WD 4.42, WD 4.49
	Add borders and shading to tables	WD 3.55, WD 4.59, WD 4.61
	Revise tables (insert and delete rows and columns, change cell formats)	WD 3.15, WD 3.62, WD 4.46, WD 4.53
	Modify table structure (merge cells, change height and width)	WD 4.47, WD 4.48, WD 4.53, WD 4.59
	Rotate text in a table	WD 4.50, WD 4.59
Working with pictures and charts	Use the Drawing toolbar	WD 4.15, WD 6.9, WD 6.40
	Insert graphics into a document (WordArt, ClipArt, Images)	WD 1.43, WD 4.12, WD 4.33, WD 4.54, WD 6.9

Table D-3 Microsoft Word 2000 MOUS Expert Skill Sets, Activities, and Map

SKILL SETS	ACTIVITIES	PAGE NUMBERS
Working with paragraphs	Apply paragraph and section shading	WD 4.10, WD 4.51, WD 6.45
	Use text flow options (Widows/Orphans options and keeping lines together)	WD 2.32, WD 7.33
	Sort lists, paragraphs, tables	WD 2.40, WD 5.45, WD 5.59
Working with documents	Create and modify page borders	WD 6.59, WD 8.48
	Format first page differently than subsequent pages	WD 4.7, WD 4.21, WD 4.28, WD 7.59, WD 9.47
	Use bookmarks	WD 7.59, WD 9.47
	Create and edit styles	WD 2.26, WD 9.17
	Create watermarks	WD 4.54, WD 6.44
	Use find and replace with formats, special characters, and non-printing elements	WD 2.45
	Balance column length (using column breaks appropriately)	WD 6.25, WD 6.51
	Create or revise footnotes and endnotes	WD 2.23, WD 2.30, WD 2.61
	Work with master documents and subdocuments	WD 7.36, WD 7.65
	Create and modify a table of contents	WD 7.57, WD 7.63, WD 7.67
	Create cross-reference	WD 7.29
	Create and modify an index	WD 7.31, WD 7.56, WD 7.63, WD 7.67
Using tables	Embed worksheets in a table	WD 7.23, WDI 2.6
	Perform calculations in a table	WD 3.62, WD 4.59
	Link Excel data as a table	WD 7.24, WDI 2.4, WDI 2.12
	Modify worksheets in a table	WD 7.22, WDI 2.12
Working with pictures and charts	Add bitmapped graphics	WD 6.53, WD 6.54, WD 9.22
	Delete and position graphics	WD 1.46, WD 5.12, WD 6.20, WD 6.46, WD 6.54
	Create and modify charts	WD 4.33, WD 4.35, WD 4.36, WD 4.37, WDI 2.6
	Import data into charts	WDI 2.8
Using mail merge	Create main document	WD 5.14, WD 5.25, WD 5.27, WD 5.29
	Create data source	WD 5.17
	Sort records to be merged	WD 5.45, WD 5.59
	Merge main document and data source	WD 5.41, WD 5.43, WD 5.59
	Generate labels	WD 5.48
	Merge a document using alternate data sources	WDI 1.4
Using advanced features	Insert a field	WD 5.34, WD 5.37, WD 8.17, WD 8.20, WD 8.28
	Create, apply, and edit macros	WD 9.26, WD 9.29, WD 9.39
	Copy, rename, and delete macros	WD 9.28, WD 9.64
	Create and modify form	WD 8.8, WD 8.15, WD 9.8
	Create and modify a form control (e.g., add an item to a drop-down list)	WD 8.17, WD 8.20, WD 8.28, WD 9.54, WD 9.57, WD 9.59
	Use advanced text alignment features with graphics	WD 5.13, WD 6.20, WD 6.28, WD 6.40, WD 6.54, WD 7.25
	Customize toolbars	WD 1.14, WD 9.30
Collaborating with workgroups	Insert comments	WD 7.10, WD 7.17
	Protect documents	WD 7.34, WD 7.42, WD 8.8, WD 8.47, WD 9.8
	Create multiple versions of a document	WD 7.15
	Track changes to a document	WD 7.13, WD 7.19
	Set default file location for workgroup templates	WD 8.56
	Round Trip documents from HTML	WDW 1.12

Microsoft Excel 2000 User Specialist Certification Map

The Microsoft Excel 2000 portion of *Microsoft Office 2000: Introductory Concepts and Techniques* (ISBN 0-7895-4635-3, 0-7895-4650-7, or 0-7895-5615-4) and *Microsoft Office 2000: Advanced Concepts and Techniques* (ISBN 0-7895-4649-3 or 0-7895-5629-4) used in combination in a two-sequence course has been approved by Microsoft as courseware for the Microsoft Office User Specialist (MOUS) program. After completing the Excel 2000 projects and exercises in these two books, students will be prepared to take the Core-level Microsoft Office User Specialist Exam for Microsoft Excel 2000. Table D-4 lists the skill sets, activities, and page number where the activity is discussed in the books. You should be familiar with each of the activities if you plan to take the Microsoft Excel 2000 Core examination.

The Microsoft Excel 2000 portion of *Microsoft Office 2000: Post Advanced Concepts and Techniques* (ISBN 0-7895-5691-X) used in combination with *Microsoft Office 2000: Introductory Concepts and Techniques* and *Microsoft Office 2000: Advanced Concepts and Techniques* in a third course has been approved by Microsoft as courseware for the Microsoft Office User Specialist (MOUS) program – Expert level. Table D-5 on the next page lists the skill sets, activities, and page number where the activity is discussed in the book for the Expert-level Microsoft Office User Specialist Exam for Microsoft Excel 2000.

Table D-4 Microsoft Excel 2000 MOUS Core Skill Sets, Activities, and Map

SKILL SETS	ACTIVITIES	PAGE NUMBERS
Working with cells	Use Undo and Redo	E 1.52, E 1.61
	Clear cell content	E 1.53
	Enter text, dates, and numbers	E 1.15, E 1.20, E 2.7, E 3.21
	Edit cell content	E 1.51, E 1.59
	Go to a specific cell	E 1.34, E 1.36
	Insert and delete selected cells	E 3.16, E 3.76
	Cut, copy, paste, paste special, and move selected cells, use the Office Clipboard	E 1.24, E 3.14, E 3.15
	Use Find and Replace	E 6.58
	Clear cell formats	E 1.53
	Work with series (AutoFill)	E 3.8-10
	Create hyperlinks	E 4.42
Working with files	Use Save	E 2.50, E 3.43
	Use Save As (different name, location, format)	E 1.41, E 3.19
	Locate and open an existing workbook	E 1.48, E 3.65
	Create a folder	E 1.44
	Use templates to create a new workbook	E 6.26
	Save a worksheet/workbook as a Web Page	EW 1.3
	Send a workbook via e-mail	E 2.62
	Use the Office Assistant	E 1.55
Formatting worksheets	Apply font styles (typeface, size, color, and styles)	E 2.28, E 2.30, E 3.36
	Apply number formats (currency, percent, dates, comma)	E 2.35, E 2.37, E 2.39, E 3.22
	Modify size of rows and columns	E 2.43, E 2.47, E 3.12
	Modify alignment of cell content	E 2.33
	Adjust the decimal place	E 2.36, E 2.39
	Use the Format Painter	E 3.10
	Apply AutoFormat	E 1.31
	Apply cell borders and shading	E 2.30, E 2.33, E 2.36
	Merge cells	E 1.33, E 2.30
	Rotate text and change indents	E 3.8
	Define, apply, and remove a style	E 6.22
Page setup and printing	Preview and print worksheets and workbooks	E 2.51, E 3.58
	Use Web Page Preview	EW 1.3
	Print a selection	E 2.54
	Change page orientation and scaling	E 2.56, E 3.58
	Set page margins and centering	E 6.49
	Insert and remove a page break	E 6.56
	Set print, and clear a print area	E 5.22
	Set up headers and footers	E 6.49
	Set print titles and options (gridlines, print quality, row and column headings)	E 6.55
Working with worksheets and workbooks	Insert and delete rows and columns	E 3.16
	Hide and unhide rows and columns	E 2.43, E 2.46
	Freeze and unfreeze rows and columns	E 3.19, E 3.32
	Change the zoom setting	E 3.59
	Move between worksheets in a workbook	E 2.61, E 3.58
	Check spelling	E 2.48, E 3.57
	Rename a worksheet	E 2.61, E 3.56
	Insert and delete worksheets	E 6.27
	Move and copy worksheets	E 6.28
	Link worksheets and consolidate data using 3-D references	E 6.61
Working with formulas and functions	Enter a range within a formula by dragging	E 2.17, E 2.20
	Enter formulas in a cell and using the formula bar	E 2.9, E 2.11, E 3.26
	Revise formulas	E 2.24
	Use references (absolute and relative)	E 3.24
	Use AutoSum	E 1.22, E 2.14, E 3.21, E 3.31, E 3.29
	Use Paste Function to insert a function	E 2.20
	Use basic functions (AVERAGE, SUM, COUNT, MIN, MAX)	E 1.22, E 2.16

(Table D-4 continued on the next page)

Table D-4 Microsoft Excel 2000 MOUS Core Skill Sets, Activities, and Map

SKILL SETS	ACTIVITIES	PAGE NUMBERS
Working with formulas and functions (con't)	Enter functions using the Formula Palette	E 2.18, E 2.20, E 3.28
	Use date functions (NOW and DATE)	E 3.21
	Use financial functions (FV and PMT)	E 4.16
	Use logical functions (IF)	E 3.27
Using charts and objects	Preview and print charts	E 2.51, E 3.58
	Use Chart Wizard to create a chart	E 1.36, E 3.45
	Modify charts	E 1.36, E 1.40, E 3.49
	Insert, move, and delete an object (picture)	E 4.42
	Create and modify lines and objects	E 6.45

Table D-5 Microsoft Excel 2000 MOUS Expert Skill Sets, Activities, and Map

SKILL SETS	ACTIVITIES	PAGE NUMBERS
Importing and exporting data	Import data from text files (insert, drag and drop)	E 9.9, E 9.13
	Import from other applications	E 9.13, E 9.18
	Import a table from an HTML file (insert, drag and drop – including HTML round tripping)	E 9.18
	Export to other applications	E 9.9
Using templates	Apply templates	E 6.26
	Edit templates	E 6.16
	Create templates	E 6.7
Using multiple workbooks	Use a workspace	E 6.62
	Link workbooks	E 6.61
Formatting numbers	Apply number formats (accounting, currency, number)	E 2.35, E 2.37, E 2.39, E 3.22
	Create custom number formats	E 6.20
	Use conditional formatting	E 2.40
Printing workbooks	Print and preview multiple worksheets	E 3.58, E 5.22
	Use Report Manager	E 8.48
Working with named ranges	Add and delete a named range	E 4.12, E 5.19
	Use a named range in a formula	E 4.14
	Use Lookup Functions (HLOOKUP or VLOOKUP)	E 5.15
Working with toolbars	Hide and display toolbars	E 1.14, E 3.37, E 3.43
	Customize a toolbar	E 7.18
	Assign a macro to a command button	E 7.18
Using macros	Record macros	E 7.11
	Run macros	E 7.15
	Edit macros	E 7.16, E 7.33
Auditing a worksheet	Work with the Auditing toolbar	E 8.10, E 8.15
	Trace errors (find and fix errors)	E 8.15
	Trace precedents (find cells referred to in a specific formula)	E 2.25
	Trace dependents (find formulas that refer to a specific cell)	E 2.25
Displaying and formatting data	Apply conditional formats	E 2.40, E 4.27
	Perform single and multi-level sorts	E 5.22, E 5.25
	Use grouping and outlines	E 5.30
	Use data forms	E 5.9
	Use subtotaling	E 5.27
	Apply data filters	E 5.35
	Extract data	E 5.43
	Query databases	E 5.32, E 5.35, E 5.40
	Use data validation	E 8.15
Using analysis tools	Use PivotTable AutoFormat	E 9.51
	Use Goal Seek	E 3.65, E 4.52, E 8.21
	Create pivot chart reports	E 9.42
	Work with Scenarios	E 8.35, E 8.48
	Use Solver	E 8.23
	Use data analysis and PivotTables	E 9.59
	Create interactive PivotTables for the Web	EW 1.1
	Add fields to a PivotTable using the Web browser	EW 2.13
Collaborating with workgroups	Create, edit, and remove a comment	E 6.47
	Apply and remove worksheet and workbook protection	E 4.49
	Change workbook properties	E 8.54
	Apply and remove file passwords	E 8.32
	Track changes (highlight, accept, and reject)	E 9.25
	Create a shared workbook	E 9.25
	Merge workbooks	E 9.61

Microsoft Access 2000 User Specialist Certification Map

The Microsoft Access 2000 portion of *Microsoft Office 2000: Introductory Concepts and Techniques* (ISBN 0-7895-4635-3, 0-7895-4650-7, or 0-7895-5615-4) and *Microsoft Office 2000: Advanced Concepts and Techniques* (ISBN 0-7895-4649-3 or 0-7895-5629-4) used in combination in a two-sequence course has been approved by Microsoft as courseware for the Microsoft Office User Specialist (MOUS) program. After completing the Access 2000 projects and exercises in these two books, students will be prepared to take the Core-level Microsoft Office User Specialist Exam for Microsoft Access 2000. Table D-6 lists the skill sets, activities, and page number where the activity is discussed in the books. You should be familiar with each of the activities if you plan to take the Microsoft Access 2000 Core examination.

The Microsoft Access 2000 portion of *Microsoft Office 2000: Post Advanced Concepts and Techniques* (ISBN 0-7895-5691-X) used in combination with *Microsoft Office 2000: Introductory Concepts and Techniques* and *Microsoft Office 2000: Advanced Concepts and Techniques* in a third course has been approved by Microsoft as courseware for the Microsoft Office User Specialist (MOUS) program – Expert level. Table D-7 on the next page lists the skill sets, activities, and page number where the activity is discussed in the book for the proposed Expert-level Microsoft Office User Specialist Exam for Microsoft Access 2000.

Table D-6 Microsoft Access 2000 MOUS Core Skill Sets, Activities, and Map

SKILL SETS	ACTIVITIES	PAGE NUMBERS
Planning and designing databases	Determine appropriate data inputs for your database	A 1.52
	Determine appropriate data outputs for your database	A 1.53
	Create table structure	A 1.15, A 1.34
	Establish table relationships	A 3.38
Working with Access	Use the Office Assistant	A 1.49
	Select an object using the Objects Bar	A 1.39, A 1.48, A 2.6
	Print database objects (tables, forms, reports, queries)	A 1.31, A 1.48, A 2.12
	Navigate through records in a table, query, or form	A 1.27, A 1.41
	Create a database (using a Wizard or in Design view)	A 1.9
Building and modifying tables	Create tables by using the Table Wizard	A 1.13
	Set primary keys	A 1.14, A 1.17
	Modify field properties	A 3.16, A 3.28
	Use multiple data types	A 1.14
	Modify tables using Design view	A 3.16
	Use the Lookup Wizard	A 6.7
	Use the Input Mask Wizard	A 6.10
Building and modifying forms	Create a form with the Form Wizard	A 4.31, A 5.21
	Use the Control Toolbox to add controls	A 4.34, A 4.37, A 4.43
	Modify format properties (font, style, font size, color, caption, etc.) of controls	A 4.36, A 4.45, A 5.42
	Use form sections (headers, footers, detail)	A 4.43, A 5.40
	Use a calculated control on a form	A 4.34
Viewing and organizing information	Use the Office Clipboard	A 6.36
	Switch between object views	A 1.42, A 3.11
	Enter records using a datasheet	A 1.21, A 1.28

Table D-6 Microsoft Access 2000 MOUS Core Skill Sets, Activities, and Map

SKILL SETS	ACTIVITIES	PAGE NUMBERS
Viewing and organizing information (con't)	Enter records using a form	A 3.8
	Delete records from a table	A 1.29, A 3.14, A 3.26
	Find a record	A 3.9
	Sort records	A 2.26, A 3.43
	Apply and remove filters (filter by form and filter by selection)	A 3.13, A 3.14
	Specify criteria in a query	A 2.17, A 2.19, A 2.21, A 2.24, A 3.26
	Display related records in a subdatasheet	A 3.42
	Create a calculated field	A 2.36
	Create and modify a multi-table select query	A 2.32, A 2.34
Defining relationships	Establish relationships	A 3.38
	Enforce referential integrity	A 3.38
Producing reports	Create a report with Report Wizard	A 1.43, A 4.9, A 4.19
	Preview and print a report	A 1.48
	Move and resize a control	A 4.27, A 6.16
	Modify format properties (font, style, font size, color, caption, etc.)	A 4.16, A 6.20
	Use the Control Toolbox to add controls	A 6.21
	Use report sections (headers, footers, detail)	A 4.14, A 4.25
	Use a calculated control in a report	A 6.20
Integrating with other applications	Import data to a new table	AI 1.3
	Save a table, query, form as a Web page	AW 1.1
	Add hyperlinks	A 5.6, A 5.18
Using Access tools	Print database relationships	A 3.41
	Backup and restore a database	A 3.6
	Compact and repair a database	A 5.48

Table D-7 Microsoft Access 2000 MOUS Expert Skill Sets, Activities, and Map

SKILL SETS	ACTIVITIES	PAGE NUMBERS
Building and modifying tables	Set validation text	A 3.31
	Define data validation criteria	A 3.28
	Modify an input mask	A 6.10, A 9.15
	Create and modify Lookup fields	A 6.7, A 7.13
	Optimize data type usage (double, long, int, byte, etc.)	A 9.12
Building and modifying forms	Create a form in Design view	A 8.35
	Insert a graphic on a form	A 8.56
	Modify control properties	A 4.16, A 5.36, A 5.37, A 5.38, A 8.14, A 8.33
	Customize form sections (headers, footers, detail)	A 4.43, A 5.40
	Modify form properties	A 4.45, A 5.33
	Use the subform control and synchronize forms	A 5.26, A 8.36
	Create a switchboard	A 6.40
Refining queries	Apply filters (filter by form and filter by selection) in a query's recordset	A 7.19
	Create a totals query	A 2.38
	Create a parameter query	A 7.20
	Specify criteria in multiple fields (AND vs. OR)	A 2.24, A 2.25
	Modify query properties (field formats, caption, input masks, etc.)	A 7.17
	Create an action query (update, delete, insert)	A 3.23, A 3.26
	Optimize queries using indexes	A 3.48, A 9.12
	Specify join properties for relationships	A 7.16
Producing reports	Insert a graphic on a report	A 7.56
	Modify report properties	A 4.15, A 7.26
	Create and modify a report in Design view	A 7.24
	Modify control properties	A 4.15, A 6.20, A 7.35
	Set section properties	A 4.15
	Use the subreport control and synchronize reports	A 7.29
Defining relationships	Establish one-to-one relationships	A 7.12
	Establish many-to-many relationships	A 7.12
	Set Cascade Update and Cascade Delete options	A 9.17
Utilizing Web capabilities	Create hyperlinks	A 5.6, A 5.18
	Use the group and sort features of data access pages	A 9.26
	Create a data access page	AW 1.3
Using Access tools	Set and modify a database password	A 9.22
	Set startup options	A 9.20
	Use Add-ins (Database Splitter, Analyzer, Link Table Manager)	A 9.8, A 9.11
	Encrypt and decrypt a database	A 9.24
	Use simple replication (copy for a mobile user)	A 9.32
	Run macros using controls	A 6.49
	Create a macro using the Macro Builder	A 6.29
	Convert a database to a previous version	A 9.7
Data integration	Export database records to Excel	AI 2.3
	Drag and drop tables and queries to Excel	AI 2.6
	Present information as a chart (MS Graph)	A 8.40
	Link to existing data	AI 1.3

Microsoft PowerPoint 2000 User Specialist Certification Map

The Microsoft PowerPoint 2000 portion of *Microsoft Office 2000: Introductory Concepts and Techniques* (ISBN 0-7895-4635-3, 0-7895-4650-7, or 0-7895-5615-4) and *Microsoft Office 2000: Advanced Concepts and Techniques* (ISBN 0-7895-4649-3 or 0-7895-5629-4) used in combination in a two-sequence course has been approved by Microsoft as courseware for the Microsoft Office User Specialist (MOUS) program. After completing the PowerPoint 2000 projects and exercises in these two books, students will be prepared to take the Core-level Microsoft Office User Specialist Exam for Microsoft PowerPoint 2000. Table D-8 lists the skill sets, activities, and page number where the activity is discussed in the books. You should be familiar with each of the activities if you plan to take the Microsoft PowerPoint 2000 Core examination.

The Microsoft PowerPoint 2000 portion of *Microsoft Office 2000: Post Advanced Concepts and Techniques* (ISBN 0-7895-5691-X) used in combination with *Microsoft Office 2000: Introductory Concepts and Techniques* and *Microsoft Office 2000: Advanced Concepts and Techniques* in a third course has been approved by Microsoft as courseware for the Microsoft Office User Specialist (MOUS) program – Expert level. Table D-9 on the next page lists the skill sets, activities, and page number where the activity is discussed in the book for the Expert-level Microsoft Office User Specialist Exam for Microsoft PowerPoint 2000.

Table D-8 Microsoft PowerPoint 2000 MOUS Core Skill Sets, Activities, and Map

SKILL SETS	ACTIVITIES	PAGE NUMBERS
Creating a presentation	Delete slides	PP 4.53
	Create a specified type of slide	PP 1.33, PP 1.40-42, PP 2.7, PP 2.11, PP 2.13, PP 2.15, PP 2.18
	Create a presentation from a template and/or a Wizard	PP 1.8, PP 2.7, PPW 1.1
	Navigate among different views (slide, outline, sorter, tri-pane)	PP 1.13, PP 2.8, PP 2.20, PP 2.21, PP 2.46
	Create a new presentation from existing slides	PP 4.6
	Copy a slide from one presentation into another	PP 3.8
	Insert headers and footers	PP 2.35
	Create a blank presentation	PP 1.10, PP 2.6, PP 3.7
	Create a presentation using the AutoContent Wizard	PP 1.8
	Send a presentation via e-mail	PP 2.55
Modifying a presentation	Change the order of slides using Slide Sorter view	PP 4.50-51
	Find and replace text	PP 1.57, PPW 1.10, PP 4.7, PP 4.24
	Change the layout for one or more slides	PP 2.22, PP 2.27-28
	Change slide layout (modify the Slide Master)	PP 1.57-63, PP 2.42, PP 3.14-18, PP 4.8
	Modify slide sequence in the outline pane	PP 2.10, PP 4.25-26, PP 4.49, PP 4.54
	Apply a design template	PP 1.18, PP 2.7, PP 3.9
Working with text	Check spelling	PP 1.54
	Change and replace text fonts (individual slide and entire presentation)	PP 1.24, PP 1.27, PP 2.47, PP 3.10
	Enter text in tri-pane view	PP 1.21, PP 1.23, PP 1.35, PP 1.37-42, PP 2.11-12 PP 2.14-19
	Import text from Word	PP 3.7-8
	Change the text alignment	PP 1.59
	Create a text box for entering text	PP 4.35, PP 4.37
	Use the Wrap text in AutoShape feature	PP 4.59
	Use the Office Clipboard	PP 3.34
	Use the Format Painter	PP 4.64
Working with text (con't)	Promote and Demote text in slide and outline panes	PP 1.37-41, PP 2.11, PP 2.14-19
Working with visual elements	Add a picture from the ClipArt Gallery	PP 2.24, PP 2.27-30, PP 3.16-18, PP 3.52, PP 4.8
	Add and group shapes using WordArt or the Drawing toolbar	PP 3.53-58, PP 4.13-21
	Apply formatting	PP 1.25, PP 1.27, PP 2.47, PP 3.14, PP 3.45-49, PP 4.34-38
	Place text inside a shape using a text box	PP 4.35
	Scale and size an object including clip art	PP 2.32, PP 3.39, PP 3.53, PP 4.21, PP 4.33
	Create tables within PowerPoint	PP 3.41-49
	Rotate and fill an object	PP 4.19-20, PP 4.34
Customizing a presentation	Add AutoNumber bullets	PP 3.18
	Add speaker notes	PPW 1.4
	Add graphical bullets	PP 3.19-21
	Add slide transitions	PP 2.38, PP 3.58, PP 4.54
	Animate text and objects	PP 2.50-51, PP 3.58, PP 4.54
Creating output	Preview presentation in black and white	PP 1.63
	Print slides in a variety of formats	PP 1.64, PP 2.51, PP 2.54
	Print audience handouts	PP 1.64, PP 2.5, PP 3.59
	Print speaker notes in a specified format	PP 3.55
Delivering a presentation	Start a slide show on any slide	PP 1.46, PP 1.48, PP 2.49
	Use on-screen navigation tools	PP 1.48, PP 2.50, PP 3.40 PP 3.41, PP 4.38, PP 4.44
	Print a slide as an overhead transparency	PP 1.67
	Use the pen during a presentation	PP 4.60
Managing files	Save changes to a presentation	PP 1.51, PP 1.65, PP 1.69, PP 2.35, PP 2.49, PP 2.57, PPW 1.4, PP 3.12, PP 4.6
	Save as a new presentation	PP 1.28, PP 2.19
	Publish a presentation to the Web	PPW 1.3
	Use Office Assistant	PP 1.67
	Insert hyperlink	PP 2.35, PP 4.27-30

Table D-9 Microsoft PowerPoint 2000 MOUS Expert Skill Sets, Activities, and Map

SKILL SETS	ACTIVITIES	PAGE NUMBERS
Creating a presentation	Automatically create a summary slide	PP 4.52-53
	Automatically create slides from a summary slide	PP 4.51
	Design a template	PP 2.11, PP 6.56
	Format presentations for the Web	PPW 1.3
Modifying a presentation	Change tab formatting	PP 5.7
	Use the Wrap text in AutoShape feature	PP 4.16, PP 5.42
	Apply a template from another presentation	PP 3.9
	Customize a color scheme	PP 4.8, PP 6.55
	Apply animation effects	PP 2.37, PP 2.46-48, PP 3.58 PP 4.54, PP 5.45, PP 5.59
	Create a custom background	PP 3.12-18, PP 4.8, PP 5.45-48
	Add animated GIFs	PPI 2.8, PP 5.16-17, PP 6.52
	Add links to slides within the presentation	PP 4.64
	Customize clip art and other objects (resize, scale, etc.)	PP 2.33, PP 3.39, PP 3.53, PP 3.54-58, PP 5.18
	Add a presentation within a presentation	PP 5.9-13
	Add an action button	PP 4.27-30
	Hide slides	PP 4.49
	Set automatic slide timings	PP 5.54-58
Working with visual elements	Add textured backgrounds	PP 4.58
	Apply diagonal borders	PP 5.33
Using data from other sources	Export an outline to Word	PP 2.51, PP 6.70
	Add a table (from Word)	PP 5.36-38
	Insert an Excel chart	PP 5.19-33
	Add sound	PP 4.27-30, PPI 2.6-8
	Add video	PPI 2.1, PP 6.9
Creating output	Save slide as a graphic	PP 5.24
	Generate meeting notes	PP 5.60
	Change output format (Page setup)	PP 2.51, PP 3.59, PP 5.19, PP 6.16-19
	Export to 35mm slides	PP 4.53
Delivering a presentation	Save presentation for use on another computer (Pack 'N Go)	PPW 1.8, PP 6.12-13, PPW 2.2-6
	Electronically incorporate meeting feedback	PP 5.50
	Use presentations on demand	PP 5.48, PP 5.52
Managing files	Save embedded fonts in presentation	PPW 2.5
	Save HTML to a specific target browser	PPW 1.6
Working with PowerPoint	Customize the toolbar	PP 2.22, PP 6.9-14, PP 6.66
	Create a toolbar	PP 6.9-11
Collaborating with workgroups	Subscribe to a presentation	PPW 2.12
	View a presentation on the Web	PPW 1.6, PPW 2.6
	Use Net Meeting to schedule a broadcast	PP 5.50
	Use NetShow to deliver a broadcast	PP 5.52
Working with charts and tables	Build a chart or graph	PP 5.25-35
	Modify charts or graphs	PP 5.29-35
	Build an organization chart	PP 3.22-40
	Modify an organization chart	PP 4.38-43
	Modify PowerPoint tables	PP 4.44-46

Index

Microsoft Office 2000 Quick Reference Summary

In the Microsoft Office 2000 applications, you can accomplish a task in a number of ways. The following five tables (one for Word, Excel, Access, PowerPoint, and Outlook) provide a quick reference to each task presented in *Microsoft Office 2000: Post Advanced Concepts and Techniques* and its companion textbooks *Microsoft Office 2000: Introductory Concepts and Techniques* and *Microsoft Office 2000: Advanced Concepts and Techniques*. Any task with a page number reference beginning with 1, 2, or 3 is from *Microsoft Office 2000: Introductory Concepts and Techniques*. Any page number reference beginning with 4, 5, or 6 is from *Microsoft Office 2000: Advanced Concepts and Techniques*. Any page number reference beginning with 7, 8, or 9 is from *Microsoft Office 2000: Post Advanced Concepts and Techniques*. You can invoke the commands listed in the MENU BAR and SHORTCUT MENU columns using either the mouse or keyboard.

Table 1 Microsoft Word 2000 Quick Reference Summary

TASK	PAGE NUMBER	MOUSE	MENU BAR	SHORTCUT MENU	KEYBOARD SHORTCUT
1.5 Line Spacing	WD 2.18		Format | Paragraph | Indents and Spacing tab	Paragraph | Indents and Spacing tab	CTRL+5
ActiveX Control, Format	WD 9.55		Format | Control	Format Control	
ActiveX Control, Insert	WD 9.54	Desired button on Control Toolbox toolbar			
ActiveX Control, Set Properties	WD 9.57	Properties button on Control Toolbox toolbar		Properties	
ActiveX Control, Write Code	WD 9.60	View Code button on Control Toolbox toolbar		View Code	
Animate Text	WD 8.45		Format | Font | Text Effects tab	Font | Text Effects tab	
AutoCorrect Entry, Create	WD 2.21		Tools | AutoCorrect | AutoCorrect tab		
AutoShape, Add	WD 7.49	AutoShapes button on Drawing toolbar			
AutoText Entry, Create	WD 3.45		Insert | AutoText | New		ALT+F3
AutoText Entry, Insert	WD 3.47		Insert | AutoText		Type entry, then F3
Blank Line Above Paragraph	WD 2.18		Format | Paragraph | Indents and Spacing tab	Paragraph | Indents and Spacing tab	CTRL+0
Bold	WD 1.33	Bold button on Formatting toolbar	Format | Font | Font tab	Font | Font tab	CTRL+B
Bookmark, Add	WD 7.59		Insert | Bookmark		
Bookmark, Go To	WD 7.60	Select Browse Object button on vertical scroll bar	Edit | Go To		CTRL+G
Border, Bottom	WD 3.39	Border button arrow on Formatting toolbar	Format | Borders and Shading | Borders tab		
Border, Outside	WD 4.8	Border button arrow on Tables and Borders toolbar	Format | Borders and Shading | Borders tab		
Border, Page	WD 6.59		Format | Borders and Shading | Page Border tab	Borders and Shading | Page Border tab	
Bulleted List	WD 3.50	Bullets button on Formatting toolbar	Format | Bullets and Numbering | Bulleted tab	Bullets and Numbering | Bulleted tab	* and then space followed by text, then ENTER
Capitalize Letters	WD 2.18		Format | Font | Font tab	Font | Font tab	CTRL+SHIFT+A

(continued)

Table 1 Microsoft Word 2000 Quick Reference Summary *(continued)*

TASK	PAGE NUMBER	MOUSE	MENU BAR	SHORTCUT MENU	KEYBOARD SHORTCUT
Caption, Add	WD 7.26		Insert | Caption		
Caption, Update Caption Number	WD 7.27			Update Field	F9
Case of Letters	WD 2.18				SHIFT+F3
Center	WD 1.35	Center button on Formatting toolbar	Format | Paragraph | Indents and Spacing tab	Paragraph | Indents and Spacing tab	CTRL+E
Center Vertically	WD 4.17		File | Page Setup | Layout tab		
Character Formatting, Remove	WD 2.18		Format | Font	Font	CTRL+Q
Character Spacing	WD 6.42		Format | Font | Character Spacing tab	Font | Character Spacing tab	
Chart, Format Axis Numbers	WD 4.35	Click axis, Increase or Decrease Decimals button on Formatting toolbar	Click axis, Format | Format Axis	Right-click axis, click Format Axis	
Chart, Move Legend	WD 4.36		Click legend, Format | Format Legend	Right-click legend, click Format Legend	
Chart Table	WD 4.33		Insert | Picture | Chart		
Clip Art, Insert	WD 1.43		Insert | Picture | Clip Art		
Clip Gallery Live	WD 4.12		Insert | Picture | Clip Art		
Close All Documents	WD 3.60		SHIFT+File | Close All		
Close Document	WD 1.54	Close button on menu bar	File | Close		CTRL+W
Color Characters	WD 3.28	Font Color button arrow on Formatting toolbar	Format | Font | Font tab	Font | Font tab	
Column Break	WD 6.31		Insert | Break		CTRL+SHIFT+ENTER
Columns	WD 6.25	Columns button on Standard toolbar	Format | Columns		
Columns, Balance	WD 6.51		Insert | Break		
Columns, Format	WD 6.25		Format | Columns		
Comment, Delete	WD 7.18	Delete Comment button on Reviewing toolbar		Right-click comment reference mark in document window, click Delete Comment	
Comment, Insert	WD 7.10	Insert Comment button on Reviewing toolbar	Insert | Comment		
Comment, Modify	WD 7.12	Double-click comment reference mark in document window	View | Comments	Right-click comment reference mark in document window, click Edit Comment	
Comment, Review	WD 7.17	Next Comment button on Reviewing toolbar			
Comment, Print	WD 7.12		File | Print | Options button		
Copy	WD 3.33	Copy button on Standard toolbar or Clipboard toolbar	Edit | Copy	Copy	CTRL+C
Count Words	WD 2.49		Tools | Word Count		
Cross-Reference, Create	WD 7.29		Insert | Cross-reference		
Current Date, Insert	WD 6.17		Insert | Date and Time		
Data Source, Add Field	WD 5.23	Manage Fields button on Database toolbar			
Data Source, Add Record	WD 5.24	Add New Record button on Database toolbar			
Data Source, Change Designation	WDI 1.4	Mail Merge Helper button on Mail Merge toolbar	Tools | Mail Merge		
Data Source, Create	WD 5.17	Mail Merge Helper button on Mail Merge toolbar	Tools | Mail Merge		

Table 1 Microsoft Word 2000 Quick Reference Summary *(continued)*

TASK	PAGE NUMBER	MOUSE	MENU BAR	SHORTCUT MENU	KEYBOARD SHORTCUT
Data Source, Delete Record	WD 5.24	Delete Record button on Database toolbar			
Delete Text	WD 1.54	Cut button on Standard toolbar	Edit | Cut	Cut	DELETE or BACKSPACE
Demote List Item	WD 3.51	Decrease Indent button on Formatting toolbar			
Distribute Columns Evenly	WD 4.48	Distribute Columns Evenly button on Tables and Borders toolbar	Table | AutoFit | Distribute Columns Evenly		
Document Map	WD 7.66	Document Map button on Standard toolbar			
Distribute Rows Evenly	WD 4.47	Distribute Rows Evenly button on Tables and Borders toolbar	Table | AutoFit | Distribute Rows Evenly		
Document Window, Open New	WD 3.27	New Blank Document button on Standard toolbar	File | New | General tab		
Double Strikethrough, Characters	WD 4.17		Format | Font | Font tab	Font | Font tab	
Double-Space Text	WD 2.9		Format | Paragraph | Indents and Spacing tab	Paragraph | Indents and Spacing tab	CTRL+2
Double-Underline	WD 2.18		Format | Font | Font tab	Font | Font tab	CTRL+SHIFT+D
Drawing Object, 3-D Effect	WD 9.24	3-D button on Drawing toolbar			
Drawing Object, Fill	WD 8.43	Fill Color button on Drawing toolbar	Format | AutoShape | Colors and Lines tab	Format AutoShape | Colors and Lines tab	
Drawing Object, Order	WD 8.42	Draw button on Drawing toolbar, Order			
Drawing Object, Rotate	WD 7.51	Draw button on Drawing toolbar, Rotate or Flip			
Drawing Object, Shadow	WD 9.24	Shadow button on Drawing toolbar			
Drawing Objects, Group	WD 7.52	Select objects, Draw button on Drawing toolbar, Group		Right-click selected object, click Grouping	
Drop Cap	WD 6.28		Format | Drop Cap		
E-mail Document	WD 2.54	E-mail button on Standard toolbar	File | Send To | Mail Recipient		
Embed Excel Worksheet	WD 7.23		Insert | Object | Create from File tab		
Embedded Object, Convert to Word Graphic	WD 7.24				CTRL+SHIFT+F9
Emboss, Characters	WD 4.17		Format | Font | Font tab	Font | Font tab	
Engrave, Characters	WD 4.17		Format | Font | Font tab	Font | Font tab	
Envelope	WD 3.58		Tools | Envelopes and Labels		
Envelopes Using Data Source	WD 5.54	Mail Merge Helper button on Mail Merge toolbar	Tools | Mail Merge		
Erase Table Lines	WD 4.45	Eraser button on Tables and Borders toolbar			
Field Codes, Display	WD 5.39		Tools | Options | View tab		ALT+F9
Field Codes, Print	WD 5.40		Tools | Options | Print tab		
Fill-in Field	WD 5.37	Insert Word Field button on Mail Merge toolbar	Insert | Field		
Find	WD 2.45	Select Browse Object button on vertical scroll bar	Edit | Find		CTRL+F

(continued)

Table 1 Microsoft Word 2000 Quick Reference Summary *(continued)*

TASK	PAGE NUMBER	MOUSE	MENU BAR	SHORTCUT MENU	KEYBOARD SHORTCUT
Find and Replace	WD 2.43	Select Browse Object on vertical scroll bar	Edit | Replace		CTRL+H
First-Line Indent	WD 2.19	Drag First Line Indent marker on ruler	Format | Paragraph | Indents and Spacing tab	Paragraph | Indents and Spacing tab	
Floating Graphic	WD 6.20	Text Wrapping button on Picture toolbar	Format | Picture | Layout tab	Format Picture | Layout tab	
Folder, Create	WD 1.49		File | Save As		
Font	WD 1.31	Font button on Formatting toolbar	Format | Font | Font tab	Font | Font tab	CTRL+SHIFT+F
Font Size	WD 1.17	Font Size box arrow on Formatting toolbar	Format | Font | Font tab	Font | Font tab	CTRL+SHIFT+P
Footnote, Create	WD 2.23		Insert | Footnote		
Footnote, Delete	WD 2.30	Delete note reference mark in document window			
Footnote, Edit	WD 2.30	Double-click note reference mark in document window	View | Footnotes		
Footnotes to Endnotes, Convert	WD 2.30		Insert | Footnote		
Form, Add Help Text	WD 8.36	Double-click form field		Right-click form field, click Properties	
Form, Change Bookmark	WD 9.47	Double-click form field		Right-click form field, click Properties	
Form, Check Box Options	WD 8.29	Double-click check box form field		Right-click form field, click Properties	
Form, Drop-Down Form Field Options	WD 8.21	Double-click drop-down form field		Right-click form field, click Properties	
Form, Insert Check Box	WD 8.28	Check Box Form Field on Forms toolbar			
Form, Insert Drop-Down Form Field	WD 8.20	Drop-Down Form Field button on Forms toolbar			
Form, Insert Table	WD 8.15	Insert Table button on Forms toolbar	Table | Insert | Table		
Form, Insert Text Form Field	WD 8.17	Text Form Field button on Forms toolbar			
Form, Protect	WD 8.47	Protect Form button on Forms toolbar	Tools | Protect Document		
Form, Remove Field Shading	WD 8.39	Form Field Shading button on Forms toolbar			
Form, Save Data Only	WD 8.52		File | Save As | Tools | General Options		
Form, Text Form Field Options	WD 8.18	Double-click text form field		Right-click form field, click Properties	
Format Painter	WD 6.57	Format Painter button on Standard toolbar			
Formatting Marks	WD 1.20	Show/Hide ¶ button on Standard toolbar	Tools | Options | View tab		CTRL+SHIFT+*
Formatting Toolbar, Display Entire	WD 1.13	Double-click move handle on Formatting toolbar			
Full Menu	WD 1.12	Double-click menu name	Click menu name, wait few seconds		
Go To	WD 2.42	Select Browse Object button on vertical scroll bar	Edit | Go To		CTRL+G
Gridlines, Show	WD 8.16		Table | Show Gridlines		
Gutter Margin	WD 7.62		File | Page Setup | Margins tab		

Table 1 Microsoft Word 2000 Quick Reference Summary *(continued)*

TASK	PAGE NUMBER	MOUSE	MENU BAR	SHORTCUT MENU	KEYBOARD SHORTCUT
Hanging Indent, Create	WD 2.37	Drag Hanging Indent marker on ruler	Format | Paragraph | Indents and Spacing tab	Paragraph | Indents and Spacing tab	CTRL+T
Hanging Indent, Remove	WD 2.18	Drag Hanging Indent marker on ruler	Format | Paragraph | Indents and Spacing tab	Paragraph | Indents and Spacing tab	CTRL+SHIFT+T
Header, Different from Previous	WD 4.28	In print layout view, double-click header area	View | Header and Footer		
Header, Display	WD 2.12	In print layout view, double-click header area	View | Header and Footer		
Headers, Alternating	WD 7.60	Page Setup button on Header and Footer toolbar	File | Page Setup | Layout tab		
Help	WD 1.55	Microsoft Word Help button on Standard toolbar	Help | Microsoft Word Help		F1
Hidden Characters	WD 4.17		Format | Font | Font tab	Font | Font tab	
Highlight Text	WD 6.61	Highlight button on Formatting toolbar			
HTML Source	WDW 1.11		View | HTML Source		
Hyperlink, Add	WDW 1.10	Insert Hyperlink button on Standard toolbar		Hyperlink	
Hyperlink, Create	WD 2.39	Insert Hyperlink button on Standard toolbar		Hyperlink	Web address then ENTER or SPACEBAR
Hyperlink, Edit	WDW 1.10	Insert Hyperlink button on Standard toolbar		Hyperlink	
IF Field	WD 5.34	Insert Word Field button on Mail Merge toolbar	Insert | Field		
Index Entry, Mark	WD 7.31		Insert | Index and Tables | Index tab		ALT+SHIFT+X
Index, Build	WD 7.56		Insert | Index and Tables | Index tab		
Index, Update	WD 7.67			Right-click selected table of contents, click Update Field	Select table of contents, F9
Insert File	WD 4.23		Insert | File		
Insert Merge Fields	WD 5.27	Insert Merge Field button on Mail Merge toolbar			
Italicize	WD 1.39	Italic button on Formatting toolbar	Format | Font | Font tab	Font | Font tab	CTRL+I
Justify	WD 6.26	Justify button on Formatting toolbar	Format | Paragraph | Indents and Spacing tab	Paragraph | Indents and Spacing tab	CTRL+J
Landscape Orientation	WD 5.24		File | Page Setup | Paper Size tab		
Last Editing Location	WD 4.25				SHIFT+F5
Leader Characters	WD 3.31		Format | Tabs		
Left-Align	WD 2.17	Align Left button on Formatting toolbar	Format | Paragraph | Indents and Spacing tab	Paragraph | Indents and Spacing tab	CTRL+L
Line Break, Enter	WD 3.22				SHIFT+ENTER
Link	WD 6.34		Edit | Paste Special		
Link Excel Data to Word Chart	WDI 2.8		Edit | Paste Link		
Link Excel Worksheet	WDI 2.4		Insert | Object | Create from File		
List Item, Demote	WD 5.32	Increase Indent button on Formatting toolbar			SHIFT+TAB
List Item, Promote	WD 5.32	Decrease Indent button on Formatting toolbar			TAB
Macro, Copy	WD 9.64	In Visual Basic Editor, Copy button on Standard toolbar, then Paste button on Standard toolbar	In Visual Basic Editor, Edit | Copy; then Edit | Paste	In Visual Basic Editor, Copy then Paste	In Visual Basic Editor, CTRL+C then CTRL+V

(continued)

Table 1 Microsoft Word 2000 Quick Reference Summary *(continued)*

TASK	PAGE NUMBER	MOUSE	MENU BAR	SHORTCUT MENU	KEYBOARD SHORTCUT
Macro, Delete	WD 9.65		Tools | Macro | Macros		
Macro, Record	WD 9.26	Double-click REC status indicator on status bar	Tools | Macro | Record New Macro		
Macro, Run	WD 9.29	Run Macro button on Standard toolbar in Visual Basic Editor	Tools | Macro | Macros		ALT+F8
Macro, Run on Exit	WD 9.52	Double-click form field		Right-click form field, click Properties	
Macro, View VBA Code	WD 9.39		Tools | Macro | Macros		ALT+F11
Mailing Label	WD 3.58		Tools | Envelopes and Labels		
Mailing Labels Using Data Source	WD 5.48	Mail Merge Helper button on Mail Merge toolbar	Tools | Mail Merge		
Main Document, Identify	WD 5.14	Mail Merge Helper button on Mail Merge toolbar	Tools | Mail Merge		
Margins	WD 2.8	In print layout view, drag margin boundary	File | Page Setup | Margins tab		
Master Document, Open	WD 7.65	Open button on Standard toolbar, then Expand Subdocuments button on Outlining toolbar			
Menus and Toolbars, Reset	WD 2.7		View | Toolbars | Customize | Options tab		
Merge Certain Records	WD 5.43	Merge button on Mail Merge toolbar			
Merge to E-mail Addresses	WDI 1.4	Merge button on Mail Merge toolbar			
Merge to Printer	WD 5.40	Merge to Printer button on Mail Merge toolbar			
Merged Data, View	WD 5.47	View Merged Data button on Mail Merge toolbar			
Move Selected Text	WD 2.46	Drag and drop	Edit | Cut; Edit | Paste		CTRL+X; CTRL+V
Nonbreaking Hyphen	WD 3.46		Insert | Symbol | Special Characters tab		CTRL+SHIFT+HYPHEN
Nonbreaking Space	WD 3.46		Insert | Symbol | Special Characters tab		CTRL+SHIFT+SPACEBAR
Normal Style, Apply	WD 4.19	Style box arrow on Formatting toolbar	Format | Style		CTRL+SHIFT+N
Note Pane, Close	WD 2.29	Close button in note pane			
Numbered List	WD 3.51	Numbering button on Formatting toolbar	Format | Bullets and Numbering | Numbered tab	Bullets and Numbering | Numbered tab	1. and then space followed by text, then ENTER
Open Document	WD 1.52	Open button on Standard toolbar	File | Open		CTRL+O
Orphan	WD 2.32		Format | Paragraph | Line and Page Breaks tab	Paragraph | Line and Page Breaks tab	
Outline Numbered List	WD 5.30		Format | Bullets and Numbering | Outline Numbered tab		
Outline, Characters	WD 4.17		Format | Font | Font tab	Font | Font tab	
Outline, Create	WD 7.37	Outline View button on horizontal scroll bar	View | Outline		
Outline, Demote Heading	WD 7.45	Demote button on Outlining toolbar			TAB
Outline, Demote Heading to Body Text	WD 7.47	Demote to Body Text button on Outlining toolbar			TAB until style is body text
Outline, Promote Heading	WD 7.45	Promote button on Outlining toolbar			SHIFT+TAB

Table 1 Microsoft Word 2000 Quick Reference Summary *(continued)*

TASK	PAGE NUMBER	MOUSE	MENU BAR	SHORTCUT MENU	KEYBOARD SHORTCUT
Outline, Show First Line of Paragraphs	WD 7.46	Show First Line Only button on Outlining toolbar			
Page Break	WD 2.35		Insert | Break		CTRL+ENTER
Page Numbers, Insert	WD 2.14	Insert Page Number button on Header and Footer toolbar	Insert | Page Numbers		
Page Numbers, Modify	WD 4.29		Insert | Page Numbers		
Paragraph Formatting, Remove	WD 2.18		Format | Paragraph	Paragraph	CTRL+SPACEBAR
Paragraphs, Keep Together	WD 7.33		Format | Paragraph	Paragraph	
Password-Protect File	WD 7.34		File | Save As | Tools | General Options		
Paste	WD 3.35	Paste button on Standard toolbar or click icon on Clipboard toolbar	Edit | Paste	Paste	CTRL+V
Picture Bullets	WD 4.40		Format | Bullets and Numbering | Bulleted tab	Bullets and Numbering | Bulleted tab	
Picture, Insert	WD 6.53		Insert | Picture | From File		
Print Document	WD 1.50	Print button on Standard toolbar	File | Print		CTRL+P
Print Preview	WD 3.24	Print Preview button on Standard toolbar	File | Print Preview		CTRL+F2
Promote List Item	WD 3.51	Increase Indent button on Formatting toolbar			
Quit Word	WD 1.51	Close button on title bar	File | Exit		ALT+F4
Rectangle, Draw	WD 8.40	Rectangle button on Drawing toolbar			
Redo Action	WD 1.35	Redo button on Standard toolbar	Edit | Redo		
Repeat Command	WD 1.36		Edit | Repeat		
Resize Graphic	WD 1.47	Drag sizing handle	Format | Picture | Size tab		
Restore Graphic	WD 1.48	Format Picture button on Picture toolbar	Format | Picture | Size tab		
Reviewer Initials, Change	WD 7.12		Tools | Options | User Information tab		
Right-Align	WD 1.33	Align Right button on Formatting toolbar	Format | Paragraph | Indents and Spacing tab	Paragraph | Indents and Spacing tab	CTRL+R
Rotate Text in Table	WD 4.50	Change Text Direction button on Tables and Borders toolbar	Format | Text Direction	Text Direction	
Ruler, Show or Hide	WD 1.11		View | Ruler		
Save as Web Page	WDW 1.3		File | Save as Web Page		
Save Document – New Name	WD 1.49		File | Save As		F12
Save Document – Same Name	WD 1.49	Save button on Standard toolbar	File | Save		CTRL+S
Save New Document	WD 1.26	Save button on Standard toolbar	File | Save		CTRL+S
Save Version	WD 7.15	Save Version button on Reviewing toolbar	File | Versions		
Section Break, Continuous	WD 6.24		Insert | Break		
Section Break, Next Page	WD 4.21		Insert | Break		

(continued)

Table 1 Microsoft Word 2000 Quick Reference Summary *(continued)*

TASK	PAGE NUMBER	MOUSE	MENU BAR	SHORTCUT MENU	KEYBOARD SHORTCUT
Security Level	WD 9.10		Tools | Macro | Security | Security Level tab		
Select Document	WD 2.46	Point to left and triple-click	Edit | Select All		CTRL+A
Select Graphic	WD 1.46	Click graphic			CTRL+SHIFT+RIGHT ARROW
Select Group of Words	WD 1.41	Drag through words			CTRL+SHIFT+RIGHT ARROW
Select Line	WD 1.37	Point to left of line and click			SHIFT+DOWN ARROW
Select Multiple Paragraphs	WD 1.30	Point to left of paragraph and drag down			CTRL+SHIFT+ DOWN ARROW
Select Paragraph	WD 2.46	Triple-click paragraph			
Select Sentence	WD 2.45	CTRL+click in sentence			CTRL+SHIFT+RIGHT ARROW
Select Table	WD 3.56	Drag through table	Table | Select | Table		ALT+5 (on numeric keypad)
Select Word	WD 1.38	Double-click word			CTRL+SHIFT+ RIGHT ARROW
Shade Graphic	WD 6.21	Format Picture button on Picture toolbar	Format | Picture | Colors and Lines tab	Format Picture | Colors and Lines tab	
Shade Paragraph	WD 6.45	Shading Color button on Tables and Borders toolbar	Format | Borders and Shading | Shading tab	Borders and Shading | Shading tab	
Shadow, on Characters	WD 4.17		Format | Font | Font tab	Font | Font tab	
Single-Space Paragraph	WD 4.31		Format | Paragraph | Indents and Spacing tab	Paragraph | Indents and Spacing tab	CTRL+1
Small Uppercase Letters	WD 2.18		Format | Font | Font tab	Font | Font tab	CTRL+SHIFT+K
Sort Data Records	WD 5.45	Merge button on Mail Merge Merge toolbar			
Sort Paragraphs	WD 2.40		Table | Sort		
Spelling Check as You Type	WD 1.22	Double-click Spelling and Grammar Status icon on status bar		Right-click flagged word, click correct word	
Spelling Check At Once	WD 2.50	Spelling and Grammar button on Standard toolbar	Tools | Spelling and Grammar	Spelling	F7
Standard Toolbar, Display Entire	WD 1.15	Double-click move handle on Standard toolbar			
Strikethrough, Characters	WD 4.17		Format | Font | Font tab	Font | Font tab	
Style, Apply	WD 6.33	Style box arrow on Formatting toolbar	Format | Style		
Style, Create	WD 9.17		Format | Style		
Style, Modify	WD 2.26		Format | Style		
Subdocument, Break Connection	WD 7.46	Remove Subdocument icon on Outlining toolbar			
Subdocument, Create	WD 7.43	Create Subdocument button on Outlining toolbar			
Subdocument, Delete	WD 7.46	Click subdocument icon, press DELETE			
Subdocument, Insert	WD 7.40	Insert Subdocument button on Outlining toolbar			
Subdocuments, Collapse	WD 7.41	Collapse Subdocuments button on Outlining toolbar			
Subdocuments, Expand	WD 7.41	Expand Subdocuments button on Outlining toolbar			
Subscript	WD 2.18		Format | Font | Font tab	Font | Font tab	CTRL+=
Superscript	WD 2.18		Format | Font | Font tab	Font | Font tab	CTRL+SHIFT+PLUS SIGN
Switch from Data Source to Main Document	WD 5.25	Mail Merge Main Document button on Database toolbar			
Switch to Open Document	WD 3.33	Program button on taskbar	Window | document name		

Table 1 Microsoft Word 2000 Quick Reference Summary *(continued)*

TASK	PAGE NUMBER	MOUSE	MENU BAR	SHORTCUT MENU	KEYBOARD SHORTCUT
Symbol, Insert	WD 3.37		Insert | Symbol		ALT+0 (on numeric keypad)
Synonym	WD 2.48		Tools | Language | Thesaurus	Synonyms | desired word	SHIFT+F7
Tab Stops, Insert	WD 3.31	Click location on ruler	Format | Tabs		
Table AutoFormat	WD 3.55	AutoFormat button on Tables and Borders toolbar	Table | Table AutoFormat		
Table of Contents, Create	WD 7.57		Insert | Index and Tables | Table of Contents tab		
Table of Contents, Update	WD 7.67			Right-click selected table of contents, click Update Field	Select table of contents, F9
Table of Figures, Create	WD 7.54		Insert | Index and Tables | Table of Figures tab		
Table, Create	WD 3.52	Insert Table button on Standard toolbar	Table | Insert | Table		
Table, Draw	WD 4.42	Tables and Borders button on Standard toolbar	Table | Draw Table		
Template	WD 5.6		File | New		
Template, Create	WD 8.9		File | New		
Text Box, Convert to a Frame	WD 7.28	Double-click text box	Format | Text Box	Format Text Box	
Text Box, Format	WD 6.41	Double-click text box	Format | Text Box	Format Text Box	
Text Box, Insert	WD 6.40	Text Box button on Drawing toolbar	Insert | Text Box		
Toolbar, Customize	WD 9.30		Tools | Customize	Customize	
Top Alignment	WD 4.22		File | Page Setup | Layout tab		
Track Changes	WD 7.13	Double-click TRK status indicator on status bar	Tools | Track Changes | Highlight Changes		
Track Changes, Stop	WD 7.14	Double-click TRK status indicator on status bar	Tools | Track Changes | Highlight Changes		
Tracked Changes, Display	WD 7.14		Tools | Track Changes | Highlight Changes	Right-click TRK status indicator on status bar, click Highlight Changes	
Tracked Changes, Print	WD 7.21		Tools | Track Changes | Highlight Changes	Right-click TRK status indicator on status bar, click Highlight Changes	
Tracked Changes, Review	WD 7.29	Click Next Change button on Reviewing toolbar		Right-click TRK status indicator on status bar, click Accept or Reject Changes	
Underline	WD 1.42	Underline button on Formatting toolbar	Format | Font | Font tab	Font | Font tab	CTRL+U
Underline Words, not Spaces	WD 2.18		Format | Font | Font tab	Font | Font tab	CTRL+SHIFT+W
Undo Command or Action	WD 1.36	Undo button on Standard toolbar	Edit | Undo		CTRL+Z
Unlink a Field	WD 5.28				CTRL+SHIFT+F9
Unprotect Document	WD 9.8	Protect Form button on Forms toolbar	Tools | Unprotect Document		
Visual Basic Editor, Close	WD 9.45	Close button on title bar	File | Close and Return to Microsoft Word		ALT+Q
Visual Basic Editor, Insert Procedure	WD 9.48	Insert UserForm button arrow on Standard toolbar	Insert | Procedure		
Vertical Rule	WD 6.37		Format | Borders and Shading | Borders tab		
Watermark	WD 4.54	In print layout view, double-click header area	View | Header and Footer		
Web Page Frame, Resize	WDW 1.9	Drag frame border	Format | Frames | Frame Properties | Frame tab		

(continued)

Table 1 Microsoft Word 2000 Quick Reference Summary *(continued)*

TASK	PAGE NUMBER	MOUSE	MENU BAR	SHORTCUT MENU	KEYBOARD SHORTCUT
Web Page, View	WDW 1.11		File | Web Page Preview		
Web Page Wizard	WDW 1.5		File | New | Web Pages tab		
Widow	WD 2.32		Format | Paragraph | Line and Page Breaks tab	Paragraph | Line and Page Breaks tab	
Wizard, Resume	WD 3.7		File | New | Other Documents tab		
WordArt Drawing Object, Format	WD 6.12	Format WordArt button on WordArt toolbar	Format | WordArt	Format WordArt	
WordArt Drawing Object, Insert	WD 6.9	Insert WordArt button on Drawing toolbar	Insert | Picture | WordArt		
WordArt Drawing Object, Shape	WD 6.14	WordArt Shape button on WordArt toolbar			
Wrap Text Around Graphic	WD 6.54	Text Wrapping button on Picture toolbar	Format | Picture | Layout tab	Format Picture | Layout tab	
Zoom Page Width	WD 1.15	Zoom box arrow on Formatting toolbar	View | Zoom		
Zoom Text Width	WD 3.17	Zoom box arrow on Formatting toolbar	View | Zoom		
Zoom Whole Page	WD 6.32	Zoom box arrow on Formatting toolbar	View | Zoom		

Table 2 Microsoft Excel 2000 Quick Reference Summary

TASK	PAGE NUMBER	MOUSE	MENU BAR	SHORTCUT MENU	KEYBOARD SHORTCUT
Advanced Filter	E 5.41		Data | Filter | Advanced Filter		ALT+D | F | A
Arrow, Add	E 6.45	Arrow button on Drawing toolbar			
AutoFilter	E 5.35		Data | Filter | AutoFilter		ALT+D | F | F
Auditing Toolbar, Display	E 8.10		Tools | Auditing | Show Auditing Toolbar		ALT+T | U | S
AutoFormat	E 1.31		Format | AutoFormat		ALT + O | A
AutoSum	E 1.22	AutoSum button on Standard toolbar	Insert | Function		ALT+=
Bold	E 1.29	Bold button on Formatting toolbar	Format | Cells | Font tab	Format Cells | Font tab	CTRL+B
Borders	E 2.30	Borders button on Formatting toolbar	Format | Cells | Border tab	Format Cells | Border tab	CTRL+1 | B
Center	E 2.33	Center button on Formatting toolbar	Format | Cells | Alignment tab	Format Cells | Alignment tab	CTRL+1 | A
Center Across Columns	E 1.33	Merge and Center button on Formatting toolbar	Format | Cells | Alignment tab	Format Cells | Alignment tab	CTRL+1 | A
Chart	E 1.37	Chart Wizard button on Standard toolbar	Insert | Chart		F11
Clear Cell	E 1.53	Drag fill handle back	Edit | Clear | All	Clear Contents	DELETE
Close All Workbooks	E 1.46		SHIFT+File | Close All		SHIFT+ALT+F | C
Close Workbook	E 1.46	Close button on menu bar or workbook Control menu icon	File | Close		CTRL+W
Color Background	E 2.30	Fill Color button on Formatting toolbar	Format | Cells | Patterns tab	Format Cells | Patterns tab	CTRL+1 | P
Column Width	E 2.44	Drag column heading boundary	Format | Column | Width tab	Column Width	ALT+O | C | W
Comma Style Format	E 2.32	Comma Style button on Formatting toolbar	Format | Cells | Number tab | Accounting	Format Cells | Number tab | Accounting	CTRL+1 | N
Command Button	E 7.27	Command Button button on Control Toolbox toolbar			
Comment	E 6.47		Insert | Comment	Insert Comment	ALT+I | M
Conditional Formatting	E 2.40		Format | Conditional Formatting		ALT+O | D
Copy and Paste	E 3.14	Copy button and Paste button on Standard toolbar	Edit | Copy; Edit | Paste	Copy to copy | Paste to paste	CTRL+C; CTRL+V
Currency Style Format	E 2.35	Percent Style button on Formatting toolbar	Format | Cells | Number tab | Currency	Format Cells | Number tab | Accounting	CTRL+1 | N
Custom Formats	E 6.20		Format | Cells | Number tab | Custom	Format Cells | Number tab | Custom	CTRL+1 | N
Cut	E 3.16	Cut button on Standard toolbar	Edit | Cut	Cut	CTRL + X
Data Form	E 5.9		Data | Form		ALT+D | O
Data Map, Add Button	E 9.36		Tools | Customize	Customize	ALT+T | C
Data Map, Change Features	E 9.40		Map | Features	Features	
Data Map, Create	E 9.37	Map button on Standard toolbar	Insert | Object | Microsoft Map		ALT+I | O
Data Map, Format	E 9. 42	In Microsoft Map Control, drag button to work area	View		ALT+V
Data Table	E 4.19		Data | Table		

(continued)

Table 2 Microsoft Excel 2000 Quick Reference Summary *(continued)*

TASK	PAGE NUMBER	MOUSE	MENU BAR	SHORTCUT MENU	KEYBOARD SHORTCUT
Data Validation, Cell	E 8.16		Data | Validation		ALT+D | L
Date	E 3.22	Paste Function button on Standard toolbar	Insert | Function		CTRL+ SEMICOLON
Decimal Place, Decrease	E 2.36	Decrease Decimal button on Formatting toolbar	Format | Cells | Number tab | Currency	Format Cells | Number tab | Currency	CTRL+1 | N
Decimal Place, Increase	E 2.36	Increase Decimal button on Formatting toolbar	Format | Cells | Number tab | Currency	Format Cells | Number tab | Currency	CTRL+1 | N
Delete Rows or Columns	E 3.18		Edit | Delete	Delete	DELETE
Draft Quality	E 6.55		File | Page Setup | Sheet tab		ALT+F | U | S
Drop Shadow	E 3.39	Shadow button on Drawing toolbar			
Embed a Clip Art Graphic	E 4.44		Insert | Picture | Clip Art		ALT+I | P | C
E-mail from Excel	E 2.63	E-mail button on Standard toolbar	File | Send To | Mail Recipient		ALT+F | D | A
File Passwords, Saving	E 8.32		File | Save As | Tools | General Options		ALT+F | A | ALT+L | G
Find	E 6.58		Edit | Find		CTRL+F
Fit to Print	E 2.56		File | Page Setup | Page tab		
Font Color	E 2.30	Font Color button on Formatting toolbar	Format | Cells | Font tab	Format Cells | Font tab	CTRL+1 | F
Font Size	E 1.30	Font Size box arrow on Formatting toolbar	Format | Cells | Font tab	Format Cells | Font tab	CTRL+1 | F
Font Type	E 2.28	Font box on Formatting toolbar	Format | Cells | Font tab	Format Cells | Patterns tab	CTRL+1 | F
Footer	E 6.49		File | Page Setup | Header/Footer tab		ALT+F | U | H
Formula Palette	E 2.18	Edit Formula box in formula bar	Insert | Function		CTRL+A after typing function name
Formulas Version	E 2.56		Tools | Options | View | Formulas		CTRL+ SINGLE LEFT QUOTATION MARK
Freeze Worksheet Titles	E 3.20		Windows | Freeze Panes		ALT+W | F
Function	E 2.20	Paste Function button on Standard toolbar	Insert | Function		SHIFT+F3
Gridlines	E 6.55		File | Page Setup | Sheet tab		ALT+F | U | S
Go To	E 1.36	Click cell	Edit | Go To		F5
Goal Seek	E 3.65		Tools | Goal Seek		ALT+T | G
Header	E 6.49		File | Page Setup | Header/Footer tab		ALT+F | U | H
Help	E 1.54	Microsoft Excel Help button on Standard toolbar	Help | Microsoft Excel Help		F1
Hide Column	E 2.46	Drag column heading boundary	Format | Column	Column Height	CTRL+0 (zero) to hide CTRL+SHIFT+) to display
Hide Row	E 2.48	Drag row heading boundary	Format | Row	Row Height	CTRL+9 to hide CTRL+SHIFT+(to display
Import Data from Access Table	E 9.14		Data | Get External Data | New Database Query		ALT+D | D | N
Import Data from Text File	E 9.9		Data | Get External Data | Import Text File		ALT+D | D | T
Import Data from Web Page	E 9.18		Data | Get External Data | New Web Query		ALT+D | D | W
In-Cell Editing	E 1.51	Double-click cell			F2
Insert Rows or Columns	E 3.16		Insert | Rows or Insert | Columns	Insert	ALT+I | R or ALT+I | C

Table 2 Microsoft Excel 2000 Quick Reference Summary *(continued)*

TASK	PAGE NUMBER	MOUSE	MENU BAR	SHORTCUT MENU	KEYBOARD SHORTCUT
Italicize	E 3.42	Italic button on Formatting toolbar	Format | Cells | Font tab	Format Cells | Font tab	CTRL+I
Link Update	E 6.63		Edit | Links		ALT+E | K
Link Worksheet to Word Document	EI 1.4		Edit | Copy; Edit | Paste Special	Copy to copy | Paste Special to paste	CTRL+C; ALT+E | S
Macro, Execute	E 7.15	Run Macro button on Visual Basic toolbar	Tools | Macro | Macros		ALT+F8
Macro, Record	E 7.11		Tools | Macro | Record New Macro		ALT+T | M | R
Macro, View Code	E 7.16		Tools | Macro | Macros | Edit		ALT+F8
Margins	E 6.49		File | Page Setup | Margins		ALT+F | U | M
Menu, Customize	E 7.22		Tools | Customize | Commands tab	Customize | Commands tab	ALT+T | C | C
Move	E 3.15	Point to border and drag	Edit | Cut; Edit | Paste		CTRL+X; CTRL+V
Name Cells	E 4.12	Click in Name box and type name	Insert | Name | Create or Insert | Name | Define		CTRL+SHIFT+F3
Name Cells, Redefine	E 5.18		Insert | Name | Define		ALT+I | N | D
New Workbook	E 1.54	New button on Standard toolbar	File | New		CTRL+N
Open Workbook	E 1.48	Open button on Standard toolbar	File | Open		CTRL+O
Outline a Range	E 4.9	Borders button on Formatting toolbar	Format | Cells | Border tab	Format Cells | Border tab	CTRL+1 | B
Outline a Worksheet	E 5.30		Data | Group and Outline		ALT+D | G | A
Page Break	E 6.56		Insert | Page Break		ALT+I | B
Percent Style Format	E 2.39	Percent Style button on Formatting toolbar	Format | Cells | Number tab | Percentage	Format Cells | Number | Percentage	CTRL+1 | N
PivotChart, Add Data to	E 9.49	Drag button from PivotTable toolbar to PivotChart			
PivotChart, Change View	E 9.54	Click interactive buttons on PivotChart			
PivotChart, Create	E 9.46		Data | PivotTable and PivotChart Report		ALT+D | P
PivotChart, Format	E 9.51	Chart Wizard button on PivotTable toolbar	Chart | Chart Type	Chart Type	ALT+C | T
PivotTable, Change View	E 9.60	Drag buttons to different locations on PivotTable			
PivotTable, Format	E 9.57	Format Report button on PivotTable toolbar	Format | AutoFormat	Format Report	ALT+O | A
PivotTable List, Add Fields	EW 2.14	Drag field from PivotTable Field List window			
PivotTable List, Add Summary Totals	EW 2.6	AutoCalc button on toolbar in browser			
PivotTable List, Change View	EW 2.10	Drag data fields to Row Field area in browser			
PivotTable List, Create	EW 2.2		File | Save as Web Page		ALT+F | G
PivotTable List, Filter	EW 2.4	Click field drop-down arrow and remove check marks			
PivotTable List, Remove Field	EW 2.12			Remove Field	
PivotTable List, Sort	EW 2.8	Sort Ascending button or Sort Descending button on toolbar in browser			
Preview Worksheet	E 2.51	Print Preview button on Standard toolbar	File | Print Preview		ALT+F | V

(continued)

Table 2 Microsoft Excel 2000 Quick Reference Summary *(continued)*

TASK	PAGE NUMBER	MOUSE	MENU BAR	SHORTCUT MENU	KEYBOARD SHORTCUT
Print Row and Column Headings	E 6.55		File | Page Setup | Sheet tab		ALT+F | U | S
Print Row and Column Titles	E 6.55		File | Page Setup | Sheet tab		ALT+F | U | S
Print Worksheet	E 2.51	Print button on Standard toolbar	File | Print		CTRL+P
Properties, Set	E 7.30	Properties button on Control Toolbox toolbar			
Protect Worksheet	E 4.49		Tools | Protection | Protect Sheet		ALT+T | P | P
Quit Excel	E 1.46	Close button on title bar	File | Exit		ALT+F4
Redo	E 1.52	Redo button on Standard toolbar	Edit | Redo		ALT+E | R
Remove Auditing Arrows	E 2.23	Remove All Arrows button on Auditing toolbar	Tools | Auditing | Remove All Arrows		ALT+T | U | A
Remove Precedent Arrows, Audit	E 8.12	Remove Precedent Arrows button on Auditing toolbar			
Remove Splits	E 3.62	Double-click split bar	Window | Split		ALT+W | S
Rename Sheet Tab	E 2.61	Double-click sheet tab		Rename	
Replace	E 6.58		Edit | Replace		CTRL+H
Rotate Text	E 3.8		Format | Cells | Alignment tab	Format Cells | Alignment tab	ALT+O | E | A
Route Workbook	E 9.27		File | Send To | Routing Recipient		ALT+F | D | R
Row Height	E 2.47	Drag row heading boundary	Format | Row	Row Height	ALT+O | R | E
Save as Web Page	EW 1.3		File | Save as Web Page		ALT+F | G
Save Workbook – New Name	E 1.41		File | Save As		ALT+F | A
Save Workbook – Same Name	E 2.50	Save button on Standard toolbar	File | Save		CTRL+S
Scenario, Add	E 8.45	Add button in Scenario Manager dialog box	Tools | Scenarios		ALT+T | E | ALT+A
Scenario, Show	E 8.47	Show button in Scenario Manager dialog box	Tools | Scenarios		ALT+T | E | ALT+S
Scenario Manager	E 8.35		Tools | Scenarios		ALT+T | E
Scenario PivotTable	E 8.52	Summary button in Scenario Manager dialog box, choose Scenario PivotTable	Tools | Scenarios		ALT+T | E | ALT+U | ALT+P
Scenario Summary	E 8.50	Summary button in Scenario Manager dialog box, choose Scenario summary	Tools | Scenarios		ALT+T | E | ALT+U | ALT+S
Select All of Worksheet	E 1.54	Select All button on worksheet			CTRL+A
Select Multiple Sheets	E 3.57	CTRL and click tab or SHIFT and click tab	Select All Sheets		
Series	E 3.8	Drag fill handle	Edit | Fill | Series		ALT+E | I | S
Shortcut Menu	E 1.51	Right-click			SHIFT+F10
Solver	E 8.23		Tools | Solver		ALT+T | V
Solver, Solve Problem	E 8.25	Solve button in Solver Parameters dialog box	Tools | Solver		ALT+T | V | ALT+S
Sort	E 5.22	Click Sort Ascending or Sort Descending button on Standard toolbar	Data | Sort		ALT+D | S
Spell Check	E 2.49	Spelling button on Standard toolbar	Tools | Spelling		F7

Table 2 Microsoft Excel 2000 Quick Reference Summary *(continued)*

TASK	PAGE NUMBER	MOUSE	MENU BAR	SHORTCUT MENU	KEYBOARD SHORTCUT
Split Window into Panes	E 3.61	Drag vertical or horizontal split box	Window | Split		ALT+W | S
Stock Quotes	E 2.58		Data | Get External Data | Run Web Query		ALT+D | D | D
Style, Add	E 6.22		Format | Style | Add button		ALT+O | S
Style, Apply	E 6.25		Format | Style		ALT+O | S
Subtotals	E 5.27		Data | Subtotals		ALT+D | B
Subtotals, Remove	E 5.31		Data | Subtotals | Remove All button		ALT+D | B | R
Switch Summary Functions	E 9.59	Field Settings button on PivotTable toolbar		Field Settings	
Text Box, Add	E 6.45	Text Box button on Drawing toolbar			
Toolbar, Customize	E 7.18		Tools | Customize | Commands tab	Customize | Commands tab	ALT+T | C | C
Toolbar, Reset	E 1.14		View | ToolBars | Customize | Toolbars tab	Customize | Toolbars tab	ALT+V | T | C | B
Toolbar, Show Entire	E 1.28	Double-click move handle			
Toolbar, Show or Hide	E 3.38		View | Toolbars	Customize	ALT+V | T
Trace Dependents	E 2.25	Trace Dependents button on Auditing toolbar		Tools | Auditing | Trace Dependents	ALT+T | U | D
Trace Precedents	E 2.25	Trace Precedents button on Auditing toolbar	Tools | Auditing | Trace Precedents		ALT+T | U | T
Track Changes, Disable	E 9.35		Tools | Track Changes | Highlight Changes | remove check mark		ALT+T | T | H
Track Changes, Enable	E 9.26		Tools | Track Changes | Highlight Changes		ALT+T | T | H
Track Changes, Review	E 9.31	Point to blue triangle	Tools | Track Changes | Accept or Reject Changes		ALT+T | T | A
Underline	E 3.42	Underline button on Formatting toolbar	Format | Cells | Font tab	Format Cells | Font tab	CTRL+U
Undo	E 1.52	Undo button on Standard toolbar	Edit | Undo		CTRL+Z
Unfreeze Worksheet Titles	E 3.32		Windows | Unfreeze Panes		ALT+W | F
Unlock Cells	E 4.49		Format | Cells | Protection tab	Format Cells | Protection tab	CTRL+1 | SHIFT+P
Unprotect Worksheet	E 4.51		Tools | Protection | Unprotect Sheet		ALT+T | P | P
Visual Basic Editor	E 7.31	View Code button on Control Toolbox toolbar	Tools | Macro | Visual Basic Editor		ALT+F11
WordArt	E 6.41	Insert WordArt button on Drawing toolbar	Insert | Picture | WordArt		ALT+I | P | W
Web Page Preview	EW 1.3		File | Web Page Preview		ALT+F | B
Workbook Properties	E 8.54		File | Properties		ALT+F | I
Zoom	E 3.59	Zoom box on Standard toolbar	View | Zoom		ALT+V | Z

Table 3 Microsoft Access 2000 Quick Reference Summary

TASK	PAGE NUMBER	MOUSE	MENU BAR	SHORTCUT MENU	KEYBOARD SHORTCUT
Add Clip Art	A 7.56	Unbound Object Frame button	Insert | Object		
Add Chart	A 8.40		Insert | Chart		
Add Combo Box	A 4.37	Combo Box button			
Add Command Button	A 8.9	Command Button button			
Add Date	A 7.39		Insert | Date and Time		
Add Field	A 3.17	Insert Rows button	Insert | Rows	Insert Rows	INSERT
Add Fields Using Field List	A 7.27	Drag field			
Add Label	A 4.43	Label button			
Add Page Number	A 7.41		Insert | Page Number		
Add Record	A 1.21, A 1.28	New Record button	Insert | New Record	New Record	
Add Rectangle	A 8.30	Rectangle button			
Add Subform	A 8.36	Subform / Subreport button			
Add Subreport	A 7.29	Subform / Subreport button			
Add Switchboard Item	A 6.44	New button			
Add Switchboard Page	A 6.43	New button			
Add Table to Query	A 2.32	Show Table button	Query | Show Table	Show Table	
Add Text Box	A 4.34	Text Box button			
Apply Filter	A 3.13	Filter by Selection or Filter by Form button	Records | Filter | Filter by Selection or Records | Filter | Filter by Form	Filter by Selection or Filter For	
Calculate Statistics	A 2.40	Totals button	View | Totals	Totals	
Change Field Properties in Query	A 7.17	Properties button	View | Properties	Properties	
Change Group of Records	A 3.23	Query Type button arrow | Update Query	Query | Update Query	Query Type | Update Query	
Change Join Properties in Query	A 7.16		View | Join Properties	Join Properties	
Change Margins	A 7.41		File | Page Setup | Margins tab		
Change Property	A 4.16	Properties button	View | Properties	Properties	
Change Referential Integrity Options	A 9.16		Relationships | Edit Relationship	Edit Relationship	
Clear Query	A 2.16		Edit | Clear Grid		
Close Database	A 1.25	Close button	File | Close		
Close Form	A 1.38	Close button	File | Close		
Close Query	A 2.14	Close button	File | Close		
Close Table	A 1.25	Close button	File | Close		
Collapse Subdatasheet	A 3.42	Expand indicator (–)			
Compact a Database	A 5.48		Tools | Database Utilities | Compact and Repair		
Convert Database to Earlier Version	A 9.7		Tools | Database Utilities | Convert Database		
Copy Object to Clipboard	A 6.36	Copy button	Edit | Copy	Copy	CTRL+C
Create Calculated Field	A 2.36			Zoom	SHIFT+F2
Create Data Access Page	AW 1.3	New Object button arrow | Page	Insert | Page		
Create Database	A 1.9	Start button | New Office Document	File | New		CTRL+N
Create Form	A 1.37, A 4.31	New Object button arrow | AutoForm	Insert | Form		

Table 3 Microsoft Access 2000 Quick Reference Summary *(continued)*

TASK	PAGE NUMBER	MOUSE	MENU BAR	SHORTCUT MENU	KEYBOARD SHORTCUT
Create Form Using Design View	A 8.35	Double-click Create Form in Design View	Insert | Form | Design View		
Create Index	A 3.48	Indexes button	View | Indexes		
Create Input Mask	A 6.10	Input Mask text box			
Create Labels	A 7.47	New Object button arrow | Report | Label Wizard	Insert | Report | Label Wizard		
Create Lookup Wizard Field	A 6.8	Text arrow | Lookup Wizard			
Create Macro	A 6.27	New Object button arrow | Macro	Insert | Macro		
Create PivotTable	A 8.47	New Object button arrow | Form | PivotTable Wizard	Insert | Form | PivotTable Wizard		
Create Query	A 2.6	New Object button arrow | Query	Insert | Query		
Create Replica	A 9.32		Tools | Replication | Create Replica		
Create Report	A 1.43	New Object button arrow | Report	Insert | Report		
Create Report Using Design View	A 7.24	Double-click Create Report in Design View	Insert | Report | Design View		
Create Snapshot	AI 2.9		File | Export	Export	
Create SQL Query	A 9.36	View button arrow | SQL View	View | SQL View	SQL View	
Create Switchboard	A 6.40		Tools | Database Utilities | Switchboard Manager		
Create Table	A 1.14	Tables object | Create table in Design view or Create table by using Wizard	Insert | Table		
Default Value	A 3.31	Default Value box			
Delete Field	A 1.19, A 3.19	Delete Rows button	Edit | Delete Rows	Delete Rows	DELETE
Delete Group of Records	A 3.26	Query Type button arrow | Delete Query	Query | Delete Query	Query Type | Delete Query	
Delete Record	A 3.14	Delete Record button	Edit | Delete Record	Delete Record	DELETE
Display Field List	A 7.24	Field List button	View | Field List		
Encrypt Database	A 9.24		Tools | Security | Encrypt/Decrypt Database		
Exclude Duplicates	A 2.29	Properties button	View | Properties | Unique Values Only	Properties | Unique Values Only	
Exclude Field from Query Results	A 2.20	Show check box			
Expand Subdatasheet	A 3.42	Expand indicator (+)			
Export Data Using Drag-and-Drop	AI 2.6	Drag object to desired application			
Export Data Using Export Command	AI 2.3		File | Export	Export	
Field Size	A 1.17, A 3.16	Field Size text box			
Field Type	A 1.16	Data Type arrow | appropriate type, appropriate letter			
Filter Query's Recordset	A 7.19	Filter by Selection or Filter by Form button	Records | Filter | Filter by Selection or Records | Filter | Filter by Form	Filter by Selection or Filter For	
Format	A 3.33	Format box			
Import Worksheet	AI 1.3		File | Get External Data | Import	Import	

(continued)

Table 3 Microsoft Access 2000 Quick Reference Summary *(continued)*

TASK	PAGE NUMBER	MOUSE	MENU BAR	SHORTCUT MENU	KEYBOARD SHORTCUT
Include All Fields in Query	A 2.15	Double-click asterisk			
Include Field in Query	A 2.10	Double-click field in field list box			
Key Field	A 1.17	Primary Key button	Edit | Primary Key	Primary Key	
Link Worksheet	AI 1.3		File | Get External Data | Link Tables	Link Tables	
Modify Switchboard Page	A 6.44, A 6.46	Edit button			
Move Control	A 4.33	Drag control		Properties | All tab | Top and Properties | All tab | Left	
Move to Design View	A 5.39	View button	View | Design View	Design View	
Move to First Record	A 1.27	First Record button			CTRL+UP ARROW
Move to Last Record	A 1.27	Last Record button			CTRL+DOWN ARROW
Move to Next Record	A 1.27	Next Record button			DOWN ARROW
Move to Previous Record	A 1.27	Previous Record button			UP ARROW
Open Database	A 1.26	Start button | Open Office Document	File | Open Database		CTRL+O
Open Form	A 3.7	Forms object | Open button		Open	Use arrow keys to move highlight to name, then press ENTER key
Open Table	A 1.21	Tables object | Open button		Open	Use arrow keys to move highlight to name, then press ENTER key
Preview Table	A 1.31	Print Preview button	File | Print Preview	Print Preview	
Print Relationships	A 3.38		File | Print Relationships		
Print Report	A 1.48	Print button	File | Print	Print	CTRL+P
Print Results of Query	A 2.12	Print button	File | Print	Print	CTRL+P
Print Table	A 1.31	Print button	File | Print	Print	CTRL+P
Quit Access	A 1.25	Close button on title bar	File | Exit		ALT+F4
Relationships (Referential Integrity)	A 3.38	Relationships button	Tools | Relationships	Relationships	
Remove Control	A 4.24	Cut button	Edit | Cut	Cut	DELETE
Remove Filter	A 3.14	Remove Filter button	Records | Remove Filter/Sort	Remove Filter/Sort	
Remove Password	A 9.25		Tools | Security | Unset Database Password		
Resize Column	A 3.21, A 5.13	Drag right boundary of field selector	Format | Column Width	Column Width	
Resize Control	A 5.29	Drag sizing handle	View | Properties | All tab | Width and View | Properties | All tab | Height	Properties | All tab | Width and Properties | All tab | Height	
Resize Row	A 5.13	Drag lower boundary of row selector	Format | Row Height	Row Height	
Resize Section	A 4.43	Drag section boundary	View | Properties | All tab | Height	Properties | All tab | Height	
Restructure Table	A 3.16	Tables object | Design button		Design View	
Return to Design View	A 2.12	View button	View | Design View		
Run Query	A 2.11	Run button	Query | Run		
Save Form	A 1.38	Save button	File | Save		CTRL+S
Save Query	A 2.42	Save button	File | Save		CTRL+S
Save Table	A 1.19	Save button	File | Save		CTRL+S
Search for Record	A 3.9	Find button	Edit | Find		CTRL+F

Table 3 Microsoft Access 2000 Quick Reference Summary *(continued)*

TASK	PAGE NUMBER	MOUSE	MENU BAR	SHORTCUT MENU	KEYBOARD SHORTCUT
Select Fields for Report	A 1.45	Add Field button or Add All Fields button			
Set Password	A 9.22		Tools | Security | Set Database Password		
Set Startup Options	A 9.20		Tools | Startup		
Sort Data in Query	A 2.26	Sort row | arrow | type of sort			
Sort Records	A 3.43	Sort Ascending or Sort Descending button	Records | Sort | Sort Ascending or Sort Descending	Sort Ascending or Sort Descending	
Specify Sorting and Grouping in Report	A 7.25	Sorting and Grouping button	View | Sorting and Grouping	Sorting and Grouping	
Switch Between Form and Datasheet Views	A 1.42, A 3.11	View button	View | Datasheet View		
Synchronize Design Master and Replica	A 9.34		Tools | Replication | Synchronize Now		
Update Hyperlink Field	A 5.18		Insert | Hyperlink	Hyperlink | Edit Hyperlink	CTRL+K
Update OLE Field	A 5.15		Insert | Object	Insert Object	
Use AND Criterion	A 2.24				Type criteria on same line
Use Documenter	A 9.13	Analyze button arrow | Documenter	Tools | Analyze | Documenter		
Use OR Criterion	A 2.25				Type criteria on separate lines
Use Performance Analyzer	A 9.11	Analyze button arrow | Analyze Performance	Tools | Analyze | Performance		
Use Table Analyzer	A 9.8	Analyze button arrow | Analyze Table	Tools | Analyze | Table		
Validation Rule	A 3.30	Validation Rule box			
Validation Text	A 3.30	Validation Text box			

Table 4 Microsoft PowerPoint 2000 Quick Reference Summary

TASK	PAGE NUMBER	MOUSE	MENU BAR	SHORTCUT MENU	KEYBOARD SHORTCUT
Action Button, Add	PP 4.27	AutoShapes button on Drawing toolbar | Action Buttons	Slide Show | Action Buttons		ALT+D | I
Action Button, Add Caption (Text Box)	PP 4.35	Text Box button on Drawing toolbar	Insert | Text Box		ALT+I | X
Action Button, Fill Color	PP 4.34	Fill Color button on Drawing toolbar	Format | AutoShape | Colors and Lines tab	Format AutoShape | Colors and Lines tab	ALT+O | O | Colors and Lines tab
Action Button, Scale	PP 4.33	Drag sizing handle	Format | AutoShape | Size tab	Format AutoShape | Size tab	ALT+O | O | Size tab
Action Button, Shadow	PP 4.35	Shadow button on Drawing toolbar			
Animate Text	PP 2.48	Custom Animation button on Animation Effects toolbar	Slide Show | Custom Animation | Effects tab	Custom Animation | Effects tab	ALT+D | M
Animation Order, Set	PP 5.49	Animation Effects button on Formatting toolbar | Custom Animation button	Slide Show | Custom Animation	Custom Animation	ALT+D | M
Apply Design Template	PP 1.18	Apply Design Template button on Standard toolbar; Apply Design Template on Common Tasks button menu on Formatting toolbar	Format | Apply Design Template	Apply Design Template	ALT+O | Y
AutoShape, Add Shadow	PP 5.41	Shadow button on Drawing toolbar			
AutoShape, Add Text	PP 5.42	Drag sizing handle	Format | AutoShape | Text Box tab | Resize AutoShape to fit text	Format AutoShape | Text Box tab | Resize AutoShape to fit text	ALT+O | O | CTRL+TAB | TAB | SPACEBAR
AutoShape, Insert	PP 5.40	AutoShapes menu button on Drawing toolbar			ALT+U
AutoShape, Rotate	PP 5.44	Free Rotate button on Drawing toolbar; Draw button on Drawing toolbar | Rotate or Flip | Free Rotate	Format | AutoShape | Size tab | Rotation text box		ALT+R | P | T; ALT+O | O | CTRL+TAB
Bullets, Remove	PP 4.48	Bullets button on Formatting toolbar	Format | Bullets and Numbering | Bulleted tab | None	Bullets and Numbering | Bulleted tab | None	ALT+O | B | SPACEBAR
Change Design Templates	PP 3.9	Double-click design template name on status bar; Apply Design Template button on Standard toolbar	Format | Apply Design Template	Apply Design Template	ALT+O | Y
Change Font	PP 3.10	Font box arrow on Formatting toolbar	Format | Font	Font	ALT+O | F
Change Font Color	PP 1.24	Font Color button arrow on Drawing toolbar | color sample	Format | Font	Font | Color	ALT+O | F | ALT+C | DOWN ARROW
Change Slide Layout	PP 2.22	Slide Layout on Common Tasks button menu on Formatting toolbar	Format | Slide Layout	Slide Layout	ALT+O | L | RIGHT ARROW
Change Slide Order	PP 4.50, PP 4.54	Drag			
Change Slide Timing	PP 5.51		Slide Show | Custom Animation	Custom Animation	ALT+D | M
Chart, Add Title and Data Labels	PP 5.33		Chart | Chart Options | Titles or Data Labels tab	Chart Options	ALT+C | O
Chart, Insert Excel	PP 5.21		Insert | Object | Create from file		ALT+I | O | ALT+F
Chart, Select Different Type	PP 5.27		Chart | Chart Type	Chart Type	ALT+C | T
Check Spelling	PP 1.55	Spelling button on Standard toolbar	Tools | Spelling		F7

Table 4 Microsoft PowerPoint 2000 Quick Reference Summary *(continued)*

TASK	PAGE NUMBER	MOUSE	MENU BAR	SHORTCUT MENU	KEYBOARD SHORTCUT
Choose a Design Template	PP 1.18	Common Tasks button on Formatting toolbar | Apply Design Template	Format | Apply Design Template	Apply Design Template	ALT+C | Y
Clip Art, Animate	PP 2.47		Slide Show | Preset Animation		ALT+D | P
Clip Art, Change Size	PP 2.33	Format Picture button on Picture toolbar | Size tab	Format | Picture | Size tab	Format Picture | Size tab	ALT+O | I | Size tab
Clip Art, Insert	PP 2.25	Insert Clip Art button on Drawing toolbar	Insert | Picture | Clip Art		ALT+I | P | C
Clip Art, Move	PP 2.32	Drag			
Clip Art, Ungroup	PP 3.54	Draw button on Drawing toolbar | Ungroup		Grouping | Ungroup	SHIFT+F10 | G | U
Connect to Microsoft Clip Gallery Live Site	PPI 1.4	Insert Clip Art button on Drawing toolbar | Clips Online button on Insert ClipArt toolbar	Insert | Picture | Clip Art | Clips Online button on Insert ClipArt toolbar		ALT+I | P | C | ALT+C
Control, Add to Form	PP 6.31	Double-click Control in Toolbox			
Create a Table	PP 3.41	Insert Table button on Standard toolbar	Insert | Table		ALT+I | B
Custom Background, Insert Picture	PP 3.16		Format | Background	Background	ALT+O | K
Decrease Font Size	PP 1.25	Decrease Font Size button on Formatting toolbar	Format | Font	Font | Size	CTRL+SHIFT+<
Delete an Object	PP 3.56	Select object | Cut button on Standard toolbar	Edit | Clear or Edit | Cut	Cut	ALT+E | A or DELETE or CTRL+X
Delete Slide	PP 4.53	Click slide icon, press DELETE	Edit | Delete Slide		ALT+E | D
Delete Text	PP 4.9	Cut button on Standard toolbar	Edit | Cut	Cut	CTRL+X
Demote a Paragraph	PP 1.34	Demote button on Formatting toolbar			TAB or ALT+SHIFT+ RIGHT ARROW
Deselect a Clip Art Object	PP 3.55	Click outside clip art object area			
Discussions, Close	PPW 2.13	Close button on Discussions toolbar	Tools | Online Collaboration | Web Discussions		ALT+T | N | W
Discussions, Start	PPW 2.10	Discussions menu button on Discussions toolbar; Discussion Options	Tools | Online Collaboration | Web Discussions | Discussions menu button | Discussion Options		ALT+T | N | W
Display Guides	PP 4.11		View | Guides	Guides	ALT+V | G
Display Rulers	PP 4.10		View | Ruler	Ruler	ALT+V | R
Edit Web Page Through Browser	PPW 1.9	Edit button on Internet Explorer Standard Buttons toolbar			
E-mail from PowerPoint	PP 2.56	E-mail button on Standard toolbar	File | Send To | Mail Recipient		ALT+F | D | A
Export Outline to Microsoft Word	PP 6.70	Save button on Standard toolbar | Save as type | Outline/RTF	File | Save As | Save as type | Outline/RTF		ALT+F | A | ALT+T
Graphical Bullets, Add	PP 3.19	Bullets button on Formatting toolbar	Format | Bullets and Numbering | Bulleted tab | Character	Bullets and Numbering | Bulleted tab | Character	ALT+O | B | ALT+H
Group Objects	PP 3.57	Drag through objects | Draw button on Drawing toolbar | Group		Grouping | Group	
Header and Footer, Add to Page	PP 2.36		View | Header and Footer | Notes and Handouts tab		ALT+V | H

(continued)

Table 4 Microsoft PowerPoint 2000 Quick Reference Summary *(continued)*

TASK	PAGE NUMBER	MOUSE	MENU BAR	SHORTCUT MENU	KEYBOARD SHORTCUT
Header and Footer, Add to Slide	PP 1.75		View | Header and Footer | Slide tab		ALT+V | H
Help	PP 1.67	Microsoft PowerPoint Help button on Standard toolbar	Help		F1
Hide Guides	PP 4.38		View | Guides	Guides	ALT+V | G
Hide Rulers	PP 4.22		View | Ruler	Ruler	ALT+V | R
Hide Slide	PP 4.49	Hide Slide button on Slide Sorter toolbar	Slide Show | Hide Slide	Hide Slide	ALT+D | H
Increase Font Size	PP 1.25	Increase Font Size button on Formatting toolbar	Format | Font	Font | Size	CTRL+SHIFT+>
Increase Placeholder Width	PP 5.15	Drag sizing handle	Format | Placeholder | Size tab | Width box arrow	Format Placeholder | Size tab | Width box arrow	ALT+O | O | RIGHT ARROW | ALT+D
Increase Zoom Percentage	PP 4.13	Zoom box arrow on Standard toolbar	View | Zoom		ALT+V | Z
Insert Slide from Another Presentation	PP 5.10		Insert | Slides from Files | Find Presentation tab | Browse | Open | Insert | Close		ALT+I | F | ALT+B | ALT+O | ALT+S | I | ESC
Italicize Text	PP 1.27	Italic button on Formatting toolbar	Format | Font | Font style	Font | Font style	CTRL+I
Macro, Create by Using Macro Recorder	PP 6.16		Tools | Macro | Record New Macro		
Macro, View VBA Code	PP 6.24		Tools | Macro | Macros | Edit		ALT+T | M | V
Menu, Customize by Adding a Command	PP 6.20	More Buttons button on Standard toolbar | Add or Remove Buttons | Customize | Commands tab	View | Toolbars | Customize | Commands tab	Customize | Commands tab	
Microsoft Organization Chart, Add Co-worker Boxes	PP 4.41	Co-worker box tool on Microsoft Organization Chart icon bar			
Microsoft Organization Chart, Add Shadow Effects	PP 3.36		Boxes | Shadow	Shadow	ALT+B | W
Microsoft Organization Chart, Add Subordinate Boxes	PP 3.27	Subordinate box tool on Microsoft Organization Chart icon bar			
Microsoft Organization Chart, Change Border Style	PP 3.37		Boxes | Border Style	Border Style	ALT+B | B
Microsoft Organization Chart, Change Style	PP 3.29		Styles		ALT+S
Microsoft Organization Chart, Copy a Branch	PP 3.31		Edit | Copy	Copy	CTRL+C
Microsoft Organization Chart, Delete a Branch	PP 4.39		Edit | Select | Branch | Edit | Clear		CTRL+B | DELETE
Microsoft Organization Chart, Open	PP 3.24		Insert | Picture | Organization Chart		ALT+I | P | O
Microsoft Organization Chart, Paste a Branch	PP 3.32		Edit | Paste Boxes	Paste Boxes	CTRL+V
Microsoft Organization Chart, Quit	PP 3.38	Close button on Microsoft Organization Chart title bar	File | Close and Return to presentation		ALT+F | C
Microsoft Organization Chart, Scale	PP 3.39	Format Object button on Picture toolbar | Size tab	Format | Object | Size tab	Format Object | Size tab	ALT+O | O | Size tab
Move a Paragraph Down	PP 2.10	Move Down button on Outlining toolbar			ALT+SHIFT+ DOWN ARROW
Move a Paragraph Up	PP 2.10	Move Up button on Outlining toolbar			ALT+SHIFT+UP ARROW

Table 4 Microsoft PowerPoint 2000 Quick Reference Summary *(continued)*

TASK	PAGE NUMBER	MOUSE	MENU BAR	SHORTCUT MENU	KEYBOARD SHORTCUT
Move Paragraph in Outline View	PP 4.25	Drag			
New Slide	PP 1.32	New Slide on Common Tasks button menu on Formatting toolbar	Insert | New Slide		CTRL+M
Next Slide	PP 1.44	Next Slide button on vertical scroll bar			PAGE DOWN
Object Area Placeholder, Increase Width	PP 3.51	Select placeholder | Drag sizing handle			
Omit Background Graphics	PP 5.46		Format | Background | Omit background graphics from master	Background | Omit background graphics from master	ALT+O | K | ALT+G
Open an Outline	PP 3.7	Open button on Standard toolbar	File | Open		CTRL+O
Open Presentation	PP 1.52	Open button on Standard toolbar	File | Open		CTRL+O
Open Presentation and Print by Executing Macro	PP 6.23	Open button on Standard toolbar | double-click file name | Enable Macros | Print | Print Handout	File | Open | double-click file name | Enable Macros | File | Print Handout		
Previous Slide	PP 1.44	Previous Slide button on scroll bar			PAGE UP
Print a Presentation	PP 1.65	Print button on Standard toolbar	File | Print		CTRL+P
Print Handouts	PP 3.59		File | Print | Print what box arrow | Handouts		CTRL+P | TAB | TAB | DOWN ARROW
Promote a Paragraph	PP 1.34	Promote button on Outlining toolbar			SHIFT+TAB or ALT+SHIFT+LEFT ARROW
Quit PowerPoint	PP 1.51	Close button on title bar or double-click Control icon on title bar	File | Exit		ALT+F4
Redo Action	PP 1.22	Redo button on Standard toolbar	Edit | Redo		CTRL+Y or ALT+E | R
Save a Presentation	PP 1.29	Save button on Standard toolbar	File | Save		CTRL+S
Save as Web Page	PPW 1.4		File | Save as Web Page | Publish button		ALT+F | G | ALT+P
Self-Running Presentation, Create	PP 5.53		Slide Show | Set Up Show | Browsed at a kiosk (full screen)		ALT+D | S | K
Set Manual Slide Show Timings	PP 5.55		Slide Show | Slide Transition | Automatically after text box up arrow | Automatically after | Apply button	Slide Transition | On mouse click | Automatically after | Apply button	ALT+D | T | ALT+C | SPACEBAR
Slide Show	PP 1.46	Slide Show button in PowerPoint window	View | Slide Show		F5 or ALT+V | W
Slide Transitions, Add	PP 2.39		Slide Show | Slide Transition		ALT+D | T
Summary Slide, Add	PP 4.52	Summary Slide button on Slide Sorter toolbar			
Table, Delete Row	PP 4.45	Select row | Cut button on Standard toolbar			
Table, Format	PP 3.47	Table button on Tables and Borders toolbar | Select Table	Format | Table	Borders and Fill	
Table, Format Cell	PP 3.45	Click cell			
Table, Insert	PP 5.37		Insert | Object | Create from file		ALT+I | O | ALT+F
Text Preset Animation Effects	PP 3.58	Slide Sorter View button in PowerPoint window	View | Slide Sorter		ALT+V | D

(continued)

Table 4 Microsoft PowerPoint 2000 Quick Reference Summary *(continued)*

TASK	PAGE NUMBER	MOUSE	MENU BAR	SHORTCUT MENU	KEYBOARD SHORTCUT
Toolbar, Create	PP 6.10	More Buttons button on Standard toolbar | Add or Remove Buttons | Customize | Toolbars tab | New button	View | Toolbars | Customize | Toolbars tab | New button	Customize | Toolbars tab | New button	
Toolbar, Customize by Adding Button	PP 6.11	More Buttons button on Standard toolbar| Add or Remove Buttons | Customize | Commands tab	View | Toolbars | Customize | Commands tab	Customize | Commands tab	
Toolbar, Show Entire	PP 1.17	Double-click move handle			
Undo Action	PP 1.22	Undo button on Standard toolbar	Edit | Undo		CTRL+Z or ALT+E | U
Visual Basic Editor, Close and Return to Microsoft PowerPoint	PP 6.66		File | Return to Microsoft PowerPoint		ALT+Q
Visual Basic Editor, Start	PP 6.27		Tools | Macro | Visual Basic Editor		ALT+F11
WordArt, Fill Color	PP 4.19	Format WordArt button on WordArt toolbar | Colors and Lines tab	Format | WordArt | Colors and Lines tab	Format WordArt | Colors and Lines tab	ALT+O | O | Colors and Lines tab
WordArt, Height and Width	PP 4.17	Format WordArt button on WordArt toolbar | Size tab	Format | WordArt | Size tab	Format WordArt | Size tab	ALT+O | O | Size tab
WordArt, Scale	PP 4.21	Format WordArt button on WordArt toolbar | Size tab	Format | WordArt | Size tab	Format WordArt | Size tab	ALT+O | O | Size tab
WordArt, Style	PP 4.14	Insert WordArt button on WordArt toolbar	Insert | Picture | WordArt		ALT+I | P | W

Table 5 Microsoft Outlook 2000 Quick Reference Summary

TASK	PAGE NUMBER	MOUSE	MENU BAR	SHORTCUT MENU	KEYBOARD SHORTCUT
Change to Day View	O 1.33	Day button	View | Day		ALT+V, press Y
Change to Month View	O 1.33	Month button	View | Month		ALT+V, press M
Change to Week View	O 1.32	Week button	View | Week		ALT+V, press K
Change to Work Week View	O 1.31	Work Week button	View | Work Week		ALT+V, press R
Create a Task	O 1.34	New button			CTRL+SHIFT+K
Create an Event	O 1.29	New button	Actions | New All Day Event	New All Day Event	ALT+A, press E
Create Contact List	O 1.40	New butonn	Actions | New Contact	New Contact	CTRL+N
Create Subfolder	O 1.11		File | New | Folder	New Folder	CTRL+SHIFT+E
Delete an Appointment	O 1.23	Delete button	Edit | Delete	Delete	CTRL+D
Delete Folder	O 1.49	Delete button	File | Folder | Delete	Delete	
Enter Appointments	O 1.14	New Appointment button	Actions | New Appointment	New Appointment	CTRL+N, ALT+A, press O
Find a Contact	O 1.42	Find button		Tools | Find	CTRL+SHIFT+F
Import/Export Folders	O 1.46		File | Import and Export		
Move an Appointment	O 1.25		Edit | Copy Edit | Paste		CTRL+C, CTRL+V
Move to Next Day	O 1.19		View | Go To | Go to Date	Go to Date	CTRL+G
Open Calendar	O 1.9		View | Go To | Calendar		
Organize Contacts	O 1.44	Organize button		Tools | Organize	
Print Calendar	O 1.35	Print button		File | Print	CTRL+P
Print Contact List	O 1.45	Print button		File | Print	CTRL+P
Recurring Appointments	O 1.17	Recurrence button on Standard toolbar in Appointment window	Actions | Recurrence	New Recurring Appointment	ALT+A, press A